DICTIONARY

OF

NATIONAL BIOGRAPHY

1971–1980

THE DICTIONARY OF NATIONAL BIOGRAPHY

1971–1980

EDITED BY

LORD BLAKE

AND

C. S. NICHOLLS

With an Index covering the years 1901–1980
in one alphabetical series

Oxford New York
OXFORD UNIVERSITY PRESS
1986

Oxford University Press, Walton Street, Oxford OX2 6DP

Oxford New York Toronto
Delhi Bombay Calcutta Madras Karachi
Petaling Jaya Singapore Hong Kong Tokyo
Nairobi Dar es Salaam Cape Town
Melbourne Auckland

and associated companies in
Beirut Berlin Ibadan Nicosia

Oxford is a trade mark of Oxford University Press

Published in the United States
by Oxford University Press, New York

British Library Cataloguing in Publication Data
The Dictionary of national biography.
1971–1980: with an index covering the years
1901–1980 in one alphabetical series.
1. Great Britain—Biography
I. Blake, Robert Blake, Baron II. Nicholls, C. S.
920'.041 CT774
ISBN 0–19–865208–9

Library of Congress Cataloging in Publication Data
Main entry under title:
The Dictionary of national biography, 1971–1980.
Includes index.
1. Great Britain—Biography—Dictionaries.
I. Blake, Robert, 1916– . II. Nicholls, C. S.
(Christine Stephanie)
DA28.D57 1986 920'.041 [B] 85–30135
ISBN 0–19–865208–9

Set by Wyvern Typesetting, Bristol
Printed in Great Britain
at the University Printing House, Oxford
by David Stanford
Printer to the University

PREFATORY NOTE

THE 748 individuals noticed in this Supplement died between 1 January 1971 and 31 December 1980.

The vast majority were—or had been—British subjects, but not all. Eamon de Valera was an American subject, yet to omit someone whose career was so deeply involved in British politics would have been to disappoint a legitimate expectation. Josep Trueta, the Catalan surgeon, spent the most important years of his life in Britain but never took up British nationality, and the same applies to the Hungarian, Tibor Szamuely, that flail of communism. Nevertheless a reader would expect them to be in. Then there is the category of those who were originally British but took up another nationality, usually American—e.g. Alfred Hitchcock and Ben Iden Payne. There are also Commonwealth politicians who were born at a time when British nationality was conferred automatically and who played a role in their own countries during and after the achievement of independence—Jomo Kenyatta and Kwame Nkrumah in Africa; Zulfikar Ali Bhutto and Krishna Menon in the sub-continent of India. Other Commonwealth figures include Borg Olivier, Archbishop Makarios, and Robert Menzies. The editors have, however, followed the decision of the previous editor in keeping down the Commonwealth numbers now that dictionaries of biography for Canada and for Australia are in the process of publication.

There is no one in the list to rival the towering figure in the 1961–70 volume of Winston Churchill whose notice was written by the previous editor; but in the military field there is Bernard Montgomery whose career is recorded by the same author, also Louis Mountbatten and Charles Portal. In the political world the most prominent figures are Anthony Eden, the only British prime minister, and—a very different character—Oswald Mosley. The two most notable entrants in music are even more of a contrast—Benjamin Britten and John Lennon. In poetry the star is W. H. Auden; in film-acting, Charlie Chaplin; on the stage, Noël Coward. Among scientists we have J. D. Bernal, P. M. S. Blackett, and Ernst Chain; in the Secret Service, Roger Hollis; in cricket, Herbert Sutcliffe and Wilfrid Rhodes; in athletics, Harold Abrahams, hero of the film *Chariots of Fire*; in the visual arts, Graham Sutherland, Oskar Kokoschka, and Barbara Hepworth; among authors, P. G. Wodehouse; and among sailors, Francis Chichester. There is also one monarch of brief reign, Edward VIII.

Certain curiosities are worth mention. The oldest man in the book is Rickard Christophers (1873–1978), who discovered the cause of blackwater fever. His biographer writes: 'Early in his career he had escaped unscathed from the yellow fever of the South American forests; then he had to face the very real threat of a white man's grave in Sierra Leone, and eventually . . . he withstood the perils of malaria and blackwater fever in the Punjab, Assam, and elsewhere in the East. The latter half of his life was spent in England, where his iron constitution continued to preserve him from the rigours of civilization.' The oldest woman in the book is Harriette Chick (1875–1977), nutritionist, who is followed closely by the novelist Berta Ruck (1878–1978). The youngest entrant is the early woodwind instrumentalist, David Munrow (1942–76), who tragically took his own life. The person with the largest number of relatives recorded in this or previous volumes is Julian Huxley, whose father, grandfather, father-in-law, and brother are all in the *DNB* as well as many other members of his family. There are two notable married couples—Agatha Christie, detective novelist, and Max Mallowan, archaeologist; and, on the stage, Cicely Courtneidge and Jack

Hulbert. Most people do not achieve fame till they have reached a certain maturity. Exceptions are Lawrence Bragg who won the Nobel prize at the age of twenty-five for his work on X-rays and crystal structure and Fay Compton the actress whose brother, Compton Mackenzie, is also in this volume. An even more remarkable figure is Daisy Ashford whose immortal work, *The Young Visiters*, was written when she was a child.

This volume adheres in most respects to the pattern adopted in the previous one with two exceptions. We have dropped the usage of recording non-photographic portraits and sculptures for every entry; many do contain such an item but the process of attaining complete uniformity wasted too much time and the advent of colour photography rendered the matter less necessary. The other departure is to publish chess games for the first time (see George Thomas and C. H. O'D. Alexander). It is customary to record certain details for every entrant—mother, father, date and place of birth and death, position in the family (e.g. third son and fourth child of . . .), details of marriage or marriages, and number of children. There can be more difficulties over this than might be expected. Some marriages which were assumed to have taken place turn out never to have occurred at all. Dates of marriages are concealed by parents whose children, or some of them, were born out of wedlock. Names are sometimes changed. There are cases of illegitimate children who do not wish their own descendants to know the truth. Forgetful parents do not register births and in certain countries registration was not required. No one knows when Jomo Kenyatta was born. It has been impossible to trace the parentage of the comedian, Sid James.

A category small in number but not unimportant consists of those who have been engaged in secret intelligence of one sort or another. They are difficult to identify except through private information because their obituary notices and entries in *Who's Who* are usually enigmatic and uninformative. Nor is it easy to find authors who both know about them and are prepared to sign an article. Happily there has been no need for any anonymous entries in this volume. If Secret Service figures of sufficient eminence deserve inclusion, so do members of the sometimes overlapping circle of enemy agents. None of the latter, as far as current public knowledge goes, expired in this period, but it is to be hoped that the names of Philby, Maclean, Blake, Blunt, and others will not be forgotten when the time comes.

The choice of both entries and authors lies with the editors. Some entrants choose themselves for inclusion, indeed most do; but there is a borderline where opinions may well differ. The editors hope that they have not omitted anyone who obviously ought to be in, but they cannot expect that the 'fringe' will be other than controversial. They recognize too that fame may surface later than the date of the publication of the volume. Gerard Manley Hopkins and Wilfrid Owen omitted from earlier volumes are famous examples, but it would be hard to blame the editors of the day.

As far as possible we have tried to choose as authors people who knew the entrant personally, though such knowledge need not be very intimate. We have tried in particular to choose those who seem not only knowledgeable but also impartial. In a few cases there are several refusals before one can find an author but these are rare and most of those invited accept on the first round. The editors have done all they can to verify facts. Any errors are their responsibility. Opinions are another matter, and the contributors must be responsible for these. The roll of authors is almost as distinguished as that of entrants; three prime ministers have contributed to this volume. With a few very rare exceptions we have avoided inviting close relations of the entrant. Whatever they thought of the person at the time there is a tendency to set up a memorial shrine.

Our greatest debt is to our contributors. Their work is a labour of little more than love—not necessarily of course love of the subject about whom they are writing—and we are most grateful to them. The list of their names that follows this note contains almost as many as the biographies in this volume.

The choice of entrants and contributors would have been a hopeless task if the editors had not been able to enlist the freely given advice of a host of specialists in the various fields of distinction. They are, almost inevitably, busy and distinguished people. We are most grateful to them, and we hope that they will forgive us for not mentioning them all by name and for not always accepting their suggestions. The editors would, however, like to mention the help they have had from the previous editor, Sir Edgar Williams, who has given them much sagacious counsel but has never obtruded his advice unasked.

The editors owe a great debt of gratitude to the Oxford University Press for its help and support, to the Bodleian Library, and to the editor of the obituaries in *The Times*, the most important material on which to base our selection. The editors' thanks go also to Mrs Joan Goodier whose secretarial help has been efficient and invaluable.

The editor would like to record the great debt this book owes to the associate editor, Dr Christine S. Nicholls, whose name appears on the title page. Her scholarly labours have been indefatigable. She has displayed a notable zeal in correcting entries (always of course resubmitted for the author's final approval), in pursuing the search for missing facts, in persuading the few dilatory contributors to send their articles before it was too late, and in the arduous task of correcting proofs.

In conclusion one historical event deserves a mention. The year 1985 was the centenary of the publication of the *DNB*. At the suggestion of the associate editor it was agreed to have a commemorative lecture on Leslie Stephen, to which all the contributors to the current volume were invited. The lecture was given at 5 p.m. on 30 January in the Sheldonian by Mr Alan Bell, librarian of Rhodes House and an expert on Stephen. The vice-chancellor presided and, thanks to the hospitality of the delegates of the Oxford University Press, a party was held afterwards in the Divinity School. Thus Oxford paid its posthumous tribute to a great Cambridge man.

BLAKE

Bodleian Library,
Clarendon Building,
Broad Street,
Oxford

1 November 1985

LIST OF CONTRIBUTORS

ABRAHAM, Sir Edward Penley:
Chain; Jephcott.
ADAM, Madge Gertrude:
Plaskett.
AINSWORTH, Geoffrey Clough:
Ramsbottom.
AITKEN, Jonathan William Patrick:
Lloyd (Selwyn-Lloyd).
ALDERSON, Brian Wouldhave:
Ardizzone; Ruck; Uttley.
ALDISS, Brian Wilson:
Carnell.
ALLEN OF ABBEYDALE, Philip Allen, Baron:
Pearson (C. H.).
ALLEY, Ronald Edgar:
Roberts (W. P.).
ALLIBONE, Thomas Edward:
Gabor; Schonland.
ARDWICK. See Beavan.
ARLOTT, (Leslie Thomas) John:
Constantine.
ARMSTRONG, Sir Robert Temple:
Radcliffe; Wilson (H. J.).
ARMSTRONG, Sir Thomas Henry Wait:
Boosey; Bullock (E.); Harris.
ATHILL, Diana:
Williams (Jean Rhys).
ATIYAH, Sir Michael Francis:
Hodge.
ATKINS, Vera May:
De Baissac; Heslop.
AUGARDE, Anthony John:
Silvester; Walcan-Bright (Geraldo).
AWDRY, Philip Neville:
Duke-Elder.
AYER, Sir Alfred Jules:
Rees.

BABINGTON SMITH, Constance:
Fielden.
BADENOCH, Sir John:
Pickering.
BAKER, John Fleetwood Baker, Baron:
Robertson (A.).
BAKER, Richard Douglas James:
Stephenson.
BARING, Sir John Francis Harcourt:
Harcourt.
BARLOW, Horace Basil:
Rushton.
BARNARD, George Alfred:
Levy (H.).
BARR, James:
Driver.
BARRAN, Sir David Haven:
Godber.
BARRINGTON, Ernest James William:
Knowles (F. G. W.).
BARTLETT, Maurice Stevenson:
Pearson (E. S.).
BATCHELOR, George Keith:
Taylor.
BEAGLEHOLE, Timothy Holmes:
Kirk.
BEAVEN, John Cowburn, Baron Ardwick:
Ewer.
BEESLEY, Patrick:
Godfrey; Winn.
BELL, Alan Scott:
Lindsay (Balniel, Wigan, Crawford, Balcarres); Plomer.
BELL, Sir Gawain Westray:
Platt (W.).
BELL, Quentin Claudian Stephen:
Grant.
BELL, Ronald Percy:
Bowen (E. J.).
BELLAMY, Joyce Margaret:
Barnes (A. J.); Postgate.
BELOFF, Max Beloff, Baron:
Wheare.
BERGEL, Franz:
Haddow.
BERLIN, Sir Isaiah:
Plamenatz.
BEST, Andrew Hall Montagu:
Curtis Brown.
BEYNON, Sir (William John) Granville:
Sutton.
BIRD, Roland:
Crowther.
BLACK, Sir Douglas Andrew Kilgour:
Platt (R.).
BLACK, Robert Denis Collison:
Hawtrey.
BLAKE, Robert Norman William Blake, Baron:
Eden (Avon); Harmsworth (Rothermere).
BLAXTER, Sir Kenneth Lyon:
Orr (Boyd Orr).
BLYTHE, Ronald:
Nash.
BOND, Brian James:
Broad (C. N. F.); Creedy.
BONINGTON, Christian John Storey:
Tilman.
BOOTH, Alan Richard:
Grubb.
BOVENIZER, Vernon Gordon Fitzell:
Bovenschen.
BOWEN, Edmund John:
Hartley (H.).

LIST OF CONTRIBUTORS

BOWNESS, Alan:
Hepworth.
BOYD-CARPENTER, John Archibald Boyd-Carpenter, Baron:
Strauss (Conesford).
BOYLE, Andrew Philip More:
De la Bedoyere.
BOYLE OF HANDSWORTH, Edward Charles Gurney Boyle, Baron:
Maudling.
BRADBEER, Joseph William:
Thomas (M.).
BRIDGE, Carl:
Casey.
BRIGGS, Asa Briggs, Baron:
Grisewood.
BRIMELOW, Thomas Brimelow, Baron:
Salt.
BROADBENT, Edward Granville:
Morgan.
BROCK, Patrick Willet:
Willis.
BROOKE, Christopher Nugent Lawrence:
Knowles (M. C., Dom David).
BROWN, David:
Hilton.
BROWN, Sir John Gilbert Newton:
Blackwell; Cumberlege.
BRUNNER, Hugo Laurence Joseph:
Ashford.
BUCKINGHAM, (Amyand) David:
Linnett.
BUCKLAND, Patrick James:
Brooke (Brookeborough).
BUCKLEY, Sir Denys Burton:
Morton (Morton of Henryton).
BURCHFIELD, Robert William:
Partridge.
BURKILL, John Charles:
Littlewood.
BURNELL, Richard Desborough:
Edwards (H. R. A.).
BURNET, John Forbes:
Willink.
BURNS, Thomas Ferrier:
Hollis (M. C.); Lunn.

CAIRD, George Bradford:
Weatherhead.
CAIRNS, Sir David Arnold Scott:
Parker (Parker of Waddington).
CALVOCORESSI, Ion Melville:
Leese.
CAMERON, (James) Malcolm:
Camps.
CAMPBELL, James:
Masterman.
CAMPBELL-KELLY, Martin:
Strachey.
CARAMAN, Philip:
Corbishley.
CAREY, John:
Coghill.
CARPENTER, Humphrey:
Tolkien.
CARR, (Albert) Raymond (Maillard):
Herbert (A. M. Y. H. M.).
CARVER, (Richard) Michael (Power) Carver, Baron:
De Guingand; Templer.
CASSELS, John William Scott:
Mordell.
CAUSEY, Andrew:
Burra.
CECIL, Lord (Edward Christian) David (Gascoyne):
Hartley (L. P.).
CHILTON, Sir (Charles) Edward:
Cochrane.
CHILVER, Sir (Amos) Henry:
Murphy.
CHILVER, Guy Edward Farquhar:
Elton (G.).
CHRISTIE, Sir George William Langham:
Ebert.
CLAPHAM, Arthur Roy:
James (W. O.).
CLARKE, Sir Cyril Astley:
Cohen (Cohen of Birkenhead); Sheppard.
CLEGG, Hugh Armstrong:
Flanders (A. D.).
CLIFFORD, Paul Rowntree:
Moberly.
CLIFTON-TAYLOR, Alec:
Constable.
COBBOLD, Cameron Fromanteel Cobbold, Baron:
Niemeyer.
COLDSTREAM, Sir George Phillips:
Simonds.
COLE, John:
Woodcock.
COLIN, Sidney:
James (S.).
COLLAR, (Arthur) Roderick:
Rawcliffe.
COLLIER, Basil:
Maltby.
COLVILLE, Sir John Rupert:
Buchan-Hepburn (Hailes).
COMLINE, Robert Semple:
Phillipson.
COOK, Alan Hugh:
Bullard (E. C.).
COOKE, Alexander Macdougall:
Penrose.
COOPER, Sir Frank:
Dean (M. J.).
COOPER, Lettice:
Bentley (P.E.).
COOPER, Martin Du Pré:
Wellesz.

COPLEY, Anthony Robert Hanchett:
Radhakrishnan; Rajagopalachari.
CORBET, Freda Kunzlen:
Hayward.
CORMEAU, (Beatrice) Yvonne:
Starr.
COTTRELL, Sir Alan Howard:
Andrade.
COWLEY, Sir John Guise:
Festing.
COWLING, Maurice John:
Butterfield.
CRAIG, David Parker:
Nyholm.
CROHAM, Douglas Albert Vivian Allen, Baron:
Edwards (R. S.).
CRUICKSHANK, Charles Greig:
Clarke (D. W.).
CUMPSTON, (Ina) Mary:
Bustamante.
CUNNINGHAM, Jeremy James:
Seago.

DACRE, Peter:
Butlin.
DAINTON, Frederick Sydney Dainton, Baron:
Norrish; Raistrick.
DALTON, (Henry) James (Martin):
Stokowski.
DALYELL, Tam:
Mackintosh.
DANIEL, Glyn Edmund:
Leakey.
DANNATT, George:
Bliss.
DAVIES, Brenda:
Reed.
DAVIN, Daniel Marcus:
Park.
DAVIS, Sir John Henry Harris:
Rank.
DAVIS, Sir William Wellclose:
Russell (G. H. E.).
DAY-LEWIS, Sean:
Day-Lewis.
DEEDES, William Francis:
Coote.
DEER, William Alexander:
Tilley.
DE L'ISLE, William Philip Sidney, Viscount:
Menzies.
DENISON, (John) Michael (Terence Wellesley):
Coward; Daubeny.
DENNISTON, Robin Alastair:
Collins; Thomson (Thomson of Fleet).
DICK, Kay:
Manning; Smith (F. M. 'S'.).
DICKSON, Sir William Forster:
Ivelaw-Chapman.
DITCHBURN, Robert William:
Tolansky.

DOBSON, Christopher Selby Austin:
Clay.
DODD, Christopher John:
Beresford.
DOLLERY, Colin Terence:
Dunlop.
DONALDSON OF KINGSBRIDGE, Frances Annesley Donaldson, Lady:
Wodehouse.
DORMAN, Sir Maurice Henry:
Olivier.
DOUGLAS-HOME, Charles Cospatrick:
Baring (Howick of Glendale); Khama.
DOUGLAS-HOME, Hon. William:
Rattigan.
DRAKE, Dorothy:
Methven.
DROMGOOLE, Nicholas Arthur:
Cranko; Haskell.
DRYDEN, Colin John:
Eyston; Hill (N. G.).
DUCKWORTH, (Walter) Eric:
Goodeve.
DURIE, Sir Alexander ('Alec') Charles:
Davies (J. E. H.).
DUTHIE, Robert Buchan:
Trueta.

EDMUND-DAVIES, (Herbert) Edmund Davies, Baron:
Morris (Morris of Borth-y-Gest).
EDWARDS, David Lawrence:
Ramsey.
EDWARDS, Harry Garner:
Fox (D. G. A.).
EGERTON, Judy:
Monnington.
ELEY, Daniel Douglas:
Rideal.
ELLIS, Sir John Rogers:
Hunter.
ELLIS, Laurence Edward:
Smith (A. L. F.).
ELTON, Sir Geoffrey Rudolph:
Neale.
ELWYN-JONES, Frederick Elwyn-Jones, Baron:
Foot; Soskice (Stow Hill).
ESHER, Lionel Gordon Baliol Brett, Baron:
Matthew; Williams-Ellis.
EVERTON, Clive:
Davis.
EZRA, Derek Ezra, Baron:
Bowman.

FARLEY, Martyn Graham:
Dowty.
FARRAR-HOCKLEY, Sir Anthony Heritage:
Galloway; Keightley.
FISHER, Patty Beatrice:
Mottram (V. H.).

FLETCHER, Hans Duncan:
Wheeler (C. T.).
FLOWER, Desmond John Newman:
Monsarrat.
FONTEYN, Dame Margot (Dame Margot Fonteyn de Arias):
Blair.
FOOT, Michael:
Owen (H. F.).
FOOT, Michael Richard Daniell:
Churchill (P. M.); Mockler-Ferryman; Nicholls; Palmer (Selborne).
FORBES, Bryan:
Evans.
FORD, Boris:
Leavis.
FORTES, Meyer:
Gluckman.
FOYLE, Christina Agnes Lilian (Mrs Ronald Batty):
Mackenzie.
FRANK, Alan Clifford:
Rawsthorne.
FRASER, Sir Hugh Charles Patrick Joseph:
Lyttelton (Chandos).
FRASER JENKINS, (Anthony) David:
Nimptsch; Richards (C. G.).
FRENCH, Philip:
Hitchcock.
FRERE, Richard Burchmore:
Williamson.
FRYER, Geoffrey:
Manton.
FULTON, John Scott Fulton, Baron:
Morris (P. R.).

GAMBACCINI, Paul:
Lennon.
GANN, Lewis Henry:
Huggins (Malvern); Whitehead.
GANT, Roland:
Scott.
GARLICK, Kenneth John:
Vaughan.
GARNHAM, (Percy) Cyril (Claude):
Christophers.
GARRETT, Stephen Denis:
Brown (W.).
GASH, Norman:
Kitson Clark.
GEOFFREY-LLOYD, Geoffrey William Lloyd, Baron:
Bullock (C. L.).
GIBSON, Quentin Howieson:
Roughton.
GIELGUD, Sir (Arthur) John:
Rutherford.
GILBERT, Michael Francis:
Sim.
GILI, John Louis:
Madariaga.
GITTINGS, Robert William Victor:
Mallaby.
GLADSTONE, Sir (Erskine) William, Bart.:
Chenevix-Trench; Corbett (Rowallan).
GLENDEVON, John Adrian Hope, Baron:
Cecil (Salisbury).
GLENDINNING, Hon. Victoria:
Bowen (E. D. C.).
GOLDMAN, Sir Samuel:
Clarke (R. W. B.).
GOLOMBEK, Harry:
Alexander; Thomas (G. A.).
GOODDEN, Robert Yorke:
Darwin.
GOODDY, William Walton:
Walshe.
GOODWIN, Trevor Walworth:
Morton (R. A.).
GORE-BOOTH, Paul Henry Gore-Booth, Baron:
Rowan.
GOULDEN, Gontran Iceton:
Bennett; Edwards (A. T.).
GRAHAM, Virginia:
Grenfell.
GRANDY, Sir John:
Humphrey.
GRAY, David:
Ryan.
GREBENIK, Eugene:
Glass.
GREEN, Peter Shaw:
Hutchinson.
GREENHAM, Peter George:
Elwes.
GRETTON, Sir Peter William:
Hughes-Hallett.
GRIFFITHS, Richard Mathias:
Mosley.
GRIGG, John Edward Poynder:
Edward VIII (Windsor).
GRIME, Geoffrey:
Glanville.
GRIMOND, Joseph Grimond, Baron:
Younger.

HALEY, Sir William John:
Astor (Astor of Hever); Reith; Stuart (C. A.).
HALSEY, Albert Henry:
Titmuss.
HAMILTON, Sir (Charles) Denis:
Thomson (Thomson of Fleet).
HAMILTON, David Ninian Hay:
Cope.
HARDING, Sir Harold John Boyer:
Wynne-Edwards.
HARKNESS, David William:
Costello; Lemass.
HARLEY, John Laker:
Blackman.
HARRIS, (David) Kenneth:
Sieff.

HARRIS OF HIGH CROSS, Ralph Harris, Baron:
McWhirter.
HART-DAVIS, Sir Rupert Charles:
Fleming.
HASLAM, Edward Brooke:
Hollinghurst.
HASSAN, Sir Joshua Abraham:
Lathbury.
HASTINGS, Max Macdonald:
Ludlow-Hewitt; Slessor.
HAWKES, (Charles Francis) Christopher:
Kendrick.
HAWKES, Jacquetta:
Wheeler (R. E. M.).
HAWTHORNE, Sir William Rede:
Ricardo.
HAYES, John Trevor:
Sutherland (G. V.).
HEARNSHAW, Leslie Spencer:
Burt.
HEATH, Edward Richard George:
Armstrong (Armstrong of Sanderstead); Chichester; Fox (U.); Wolff.
HEATON, Eric William:
Dodd; Greer.
HENDRIE, Gerald Mills:
Dart.
HENNIKER, John Patrick Edward Chandos Henniker-Major, Baron:
Hall-Patch.
HEPPLE, Bob Alexander:
Donovan.
HERRMANN, Frank:
Carter.
HERZFELD, Edgar Otto:
Bagrit.
HEUSTON, Robert Francis Vere:
Manningham-Buller (Dilhorne).
HEWETSON, Sir Reginald Hackett:
Steele.
HIBBARD, Howard:
Wittkower.
HIMSWORTH, Sir Harold Percival:
Harington.
HIRSCH, Sir Peter Bernhard:
Allen.
HOBSBAWM, Eric John Ernest:
Dobb.
HOBSON, Anthony Robert Alwyn:
Munby.
HOBSON, Sir Harold:
Darlington; Guthrie.
HODGKIN, Sir Alan Lloyd:
Adrian.
HODGKIN, Robert Allason:
Polanyi.
HODIN, Josef Paul:
Kokoschka; Leach.
HOGWOOD, Christopher Jarvis Haley:
Munrow.
HOLROYD, Michael de Courcy Fraser:
Gerhardie.
HOLTBY, Robert Tinsley:
Stopford.
HOME OF THE HIRSEL, Alexander Frederick Douglas-Home, Baron:
Stuart (Stuart of Findhorn).
HONORÉ, Antony Maurice:
Cross; Goodhart.
HOUGHTON, John Theodore:
Dobson.
HOURANI, Albert Habib:
Gibb.
HOWARD, Anthony Michell:
Crossman.
HOWARD, Michael Eliot:
Buchan; Falls.
HOWARD, Philip Nicholas Charles:
Brown (I. J. C.).
HOWARTH, Thomas Edward Brodie:
Klugmann.
HUGHES, Michael Roger:
Osborn.
HUTCHINSON, Edward Moss:
Williams (W. E.).
HUTCHISON, Sidney Charles:
Kelly; Lawrence.
HUXLEY, Hugh Esmor:
Hanson.
HYDE, Harford Montgomery:
Goddard; Herbert (Tangley); Russell (Ampthill); Travers.

INCHCAPE, Kenneth James William Mackay, Earl of:
Anderson (D. F.).
INGLIS, Brian St. John:
Campbell (Glenavy).
INGRAMS, Richard Reid:
Delmer; Morton (J. C. A. B. M.) (Beachcomber).
IRVINE, Gerard:
Driberg (Bradwell).

JACOMB, Sir Martin Wakefield:
Kindersley.
JEFFARES, Alexander Norman:
Dobrée.
JENKIN, Ian Evers Tregarthen:
Rogers.
JENKINS, Roy Harris:
Crosland.
JENNINGS, Sir Robert Yewdall:
McNair.
JOHNSON, Paley:
Adair.
JOHNSON, Paul Bede:
Hope-Wallace; Speaight.
JOHNSTON, Sir John Baines:
St. Laurent.
JOLL, James Bysse:
Adams (W.); Wiskemann.
JONES, Douglas Samuel:
Erdélyi.
JONES, Reginald Victor:
Watson-Watt.

LIST OF CONTRIBUTORS

JOSEPH, Sir Keith Sinjohn, Bart.:
D'Avigdor-Goldsmid.
JUDGE, Harry George:
Neill.
JUNOR, Sir John:
Gordon.

KATZ, Sir Bernard:
Hill (A. V.).
KAY, Harry:
Cook.
KEATING, Henry Reymond Fitzwalter:
Christie (A. M. C.); Leon (Henry Cecil); Mallowan; Montgomery (R. B.) (Edmund Crispin).
KEAY, Ronald William John:
Martin.
KEEN, Maurice Hugh:
Keir.
KEKWICK, Ralph Ambrose:
Drury.
KEMP, Peter Kemp:
Little; Syfret.
KEMP, Thomas Arthur:
Wilson (Moran).
KENDREW, Sir John Cowdery:
Bernal.
KENNEDY, (George) Michael (Sinclair):
Cardus.
KENNEDY, Paul Michael:
James (W. M.).
KENT, Sir Percy Edward ('Peter'):
Wills.
KERMODE, (John) Frank:
Richards (I. A.).
KERR, Fergus Gordon:
Mathew (A. and D. J.).
KING, Evelyn Mansfield:
Silkin.
KINGS NORTON, Harold Roxbee Cox, Baron:
Fedden.
KIRK-GREENE, Anthony Hamilton Millard:
Burns; Richards (Milverton); Wyn-Harris.
KIRKLEY, Sir (Howard) Leslie:
Schumacher.

LAMBERT, Jack Walter:
Mortimer (C. R. B.).
LARKIN, Philip Arthur:
Pym.
LASH, Nicholas Langrishe Alleyne:
Roberts (T. d'E.).
LASLETT, (Thomas) Peter (Ruffell):
Simpson.
LAW, Sir Horace Rochfort:
Denny.
LAWSON, Frederick Henry:
Cheshire.
LAWTON, Sir Frederick Horace, Lord Justice Lawton:
Stable.
LEAKE, Bernard Elgey:
George.
LEE, Sir (Henry) Desmond (Pritchard):
Pickthorn.
LEE OF ASHERIDGE, Janet Bevan, Baroness:
Levy (B. W.).
LEE OF NEWTON, Frederick Lee, Baron:
Isaacs (G. A.).
LEES-MILNE, James:
Mitford; Pope-Hennessy.
LEHMANN, John Frederick:
Connolly; Yorke (Henry Green).
LENNIE, Daphne Mair Mitchell:
Brittain; Browne (Kilmaine).
LESLIE, Anita:
Leslie.
LEVENBERG, Schneier Israel:
Stein.
LEVI, Peter Chad Tigar:
Jones (D.).
LEVY, Mervyn Montague:
Lowry.
LEWIN, (George) Ronald:
Fergusson (Ballantrae); Morton (D. J. F.).
LEWIS, John:
Lamb.
LIENHARDT, (Ronald) Godfrey:
Evans-Pritchard.
LINKS, Joseph Gluckstein:
Wheatley.
LINTOTT, Sir Henry:
Diefenbaker; Pearson (L. B.).
LLOYD OF HAMPSTEAD, Dennis Lloyd, Baron:
Chorley.
LLOYD, Peter:
Shipton.
LLOYD-JONES, (Peter) Hugh (Jefferd):
Dodds (E. R.); Page.
LOEWE, Raphael:
Abramsky; Brodie.
LOGAN, Sir Douglas William:
Parry (D. H.).
LONGFORD, Elizabeth Pakenham, Countess of:
Woodham-Smith.
LONGFORD, Francis Aungier Pakenham, Earl of:
De Valera.
LONGLAND, Sir John Laurence:
Chapman.
LOVELL, Sir (Alfred Charles) Bernard:
Blackett.
LOWRY, Robert Lynd Erskine Lowry, Baron:
MacDermott.
LUBBOCK, Roger John:
Pudney.
LUCAS, Colin Anderson:
Connell.
LUSTY, Sir Robert Frith:
Bates.

MACCARTHY, Fiona:
Gray (K. E. M.).

LIST OF CONTRIBUTORS

McCormick, Eric Hall:
Beaglehole.
McCrirrick, (Thomas) Bryce:
Ashbridge.
McCrum, Michael William:
Cary.
MacDonald, Malcolm:
Brian.
McGeoch, Sir Ian Lachlan Mackay:
Dalrymple-Hamilton.
Macindoe, David Henry:
Elliott.
Mackenzie, Ian Carville Keith:
Symonds.
McKitterick, David John:
Meynell.
Macksey, Kenneth John:
Pile.
Maclagan, Michael:
Howard (Norfolk).
McLennan, Gordon:
Gollan.
Maclure, (John) Stuart:
Newsom.
Macmillan, (Maurice) Harold:
Wyndham (Egremont and Leconfield).
McVeagh, Diana Mary:
Howes.
McWhirter, Norris Dewar:
Abrahams.
Magnus, Hilary Barrow:
Upjohn.
Mair, William Austyn:
Jones (B. M.).
Major, Kathleen:
Stenton.
Mallon, Thomas:
Blunden.
March, Norman Henry:
Coulson.
Martin, Gregory:
Davies (M.).
Martineau, Catherine Makepeace Thackeray.
Spencer.
Martin-Jenkins, Christopher Dennis Alexander:
Sutcliffe.
Masefield, Sir Peter Gordon:
Straight; Uwins.
Mason, John Frederick Arthur:
Edwards (J. G.).
Mathias, Peter:
Carus-Wilson.
Mavor, Michael Barclay:
Hahn.
Maxwell, Neville Graham:
Bhutto.
Medawar, Sir Peter Brian:
Abercrombie.
Mellanby, Kenneth:
Darling.
Meyer, Michael Leverson:
Flanders (M. H.).
Miall, (Rowland) Leonard:
Bridson.
Midwinter, Eric Clare:
Hare.
Millar, Maureen Susan:
Leitch.
Milledge, (Hylton) Judith:
Lonsdale.
Milligan, Terence Alan ('Spike'):
Sellers.
Mitchell, Donald Charles Peter:
Britten.
Moncreiffe of that Ilk, Sir (Rupert) Iain (Kay):
Innes of Learney.
Monroe, Elizabeth (Mrs Humphrey Neame):
Bullard (R. W.); Kirkbride.
Monteith, Charles Montgomery:
Morrah.
Moon, Philip Burton:
Thomson (G. P.).
Moore, Doris Langley:
Laver.
Moorhouse, Geoffrey:
Greenwood.
Morgan, David John:
Nkrumah.
Morgan, Kenneth Owen:
Griffiths; Lloyd George (Lloyd-George of Dwyfor).
Morley, Sheridan Robert:
Cooper; Thorndike.
Morphet, Richard Edward:
Carline.
Mott-Radclyffe, Sir Charles Edward:
Spears.
Muggeridge, Malcolm:
Bentley (N. C.); Knox.
Murley, Sir Reginald Sydney:
Brock.
Murray, Lionel Murray, Baron:
Feather (V. G. H.).

Neuberger, Albert:
Davidson; Dent; Williams (R. T.).
Neve, Christopher Neville:
Underwood.
Nicholas, Herbert George:
Brogan.
Nicholas, (John Keiran) Barry (Moylan):
Kahn-Freund.
Nicholls, Anthony James:
Wheeler-Bennett.
Nicholls, Christine Stephanie:
Clayton; Tovey.
Nicholson, (Edward) Max:
Hurcomb.
Nicolson, Nigel:
Nicolson.

NIMMO, Derek:
Aylmer.
NORBURY, John Frederick:
Owen (W. L.).
NORRINGTON, Sir Arthur Lionel Pugh:
Christie (J. T.).
NORRIS, Mgr David Joseph:
Heenan.
NORTHCOTT, (William) Cecil:
Somervell.

OAKSEY, John Geoffrey Tristram Lawrence, Baron Trevethin and Oaksey:
Cazalet.
OATLEY, Sir Charles William:
Smith-Rose.
O'BRIEN OF LOTHBURY, Leslie Kenneth O'Brien, Baron:
Duncan.
O'BRIEN, Terence Henry:
Hodsoll.
O'CONNOR, Neil:
Lewis; Tizard.
O'GRADY, Francis William:
Garrod.
OLIVER, William Thompson:
Andrews.
O'NEILL, Mary:
O'Brien.
OPPENHEIMER, Peter Morris:
Cohen (J. E.); Harrod.
ORR, Sir David Alexander:
Heyworth.
ORR, Louise:
Toynbee.
O'SULLIVAN, Timothy Francis:
Nabarro.
OWEN, Huw Parri:
Matthews.
OWEN, Paul Robert:
Küchemann.
OXBURY, Harold Frederick:
Knatchbull-Hugessen.

PACK, Stanley Walter Croucher:
Tovey.
PALLEY, Claire Dorothea Taylor:
Beadle; Tredgold.
PARKER, Constance Anne:
Shepard.
PARKER, John:
Henderson (Faringdon).
PARKER, Sir Peter:
Davenport.
PARR, Peter James:
Kenyon.
PATON, Alan Stewart:
Paget.
PATON, Sir (Thomas) Angus (Lyall):
Inglis.
PATON, Sir William Drummond Macdonald:
Barnes (J. M.); Brown (G. L.).
PEART-BINNS, John Stuart:
Reckitt.
PEDEN, George Cameron:
McFadyean.
PEEL, Sir John Harold:
Weir.
PEIERLS, Sir Rudolf Ernst:
Frisch.
PELCZYNSKI, Zbigniew Andrzej:
McCallum.
PENNEY, William George Penney, Baron:
Sutherland (G. B. B. M.).
PENROSE, Harold James:
Cobham.
PEPYS-WHITELEY, Derek:
Courtneidge; Hulbert; Messel.
PEROWNE, Benjamin Cubitt:
Holland-Martin.
PERRINS, Christopher Miles:
Lack.
PERRY OF WALTON, Walter Laing Macdonald Perry, Baron:
Venables.
PHILIPSON, Sir Robert James ('Robin'):
Gillies.
PHILLIPS, Sir David Chilton:
Bragg.
PIGGOTT, Leslie Sylvester:
Williams (F. C.).
PIRIE, Norman Wingate:
Bawden; Clark (F. Le G.).
PLATTS-MILLS, John Faithful Fortescue:
Bing.
POLLITT, Elizabeth:
Fields.
PORTER, Joshua Roy:
Mortimer (R. C.).
PORTERFIELD, James Stuart:
McLeod.
POUND, Reginald:
Herbert (A. P.).
POWELL, (Elizabeth) Dilys:
Balcon; Chaplin; Lejeune.
POWELL, (John) Enoch:
Law (Coleraine).
POWELL, Sir Richard Royle:
Brundrett.
POYNTON, Sir (Arthur) Hilton:
Furse.
PRESTON, Ronald Haydn:
Richardson.
PRICE, Cecil John Layton:
Davies (R.).
PRICE, William Charles:
Ellis.
PRINGLE, Alexandra Jane Reina:
Warner.
PUGH, Ralph Bernard:
Salzman.

PUGSLEY, Sir Alfred Grenvile:
Wallis.
PURSER, Philip John:
Tynan.

QUINTON, Anthony Meredith Quinton, Baron:
Broad (C. D.).

RADICE, Betty:
Rieu.
RADZINOWICZ, Sir Leon:
Mannheim.
RAWLINSON OF EWELL, Peter Anthony Grayson Rawlinson, Baron:
Tucker.
RAYCHAUDHURI, Tapan:
Menon.
RAYNE, Edward:
Hartnell.
REASON, John:
Voyce.
REILLY, Paul Reilly, Baron:
Black; Russell (S. G.).
REINHARDT, Max:
Heyer.
RICE, Noel Stephen Cracroft:
Stallard.
RICHARDS, Denis George:
Courtney; Portal.
RICHARDS, Sir (Francis) Brooks:
Humphreys.
RICHARDS, Sir James Maude:
Howell; Spence.
RICHARDS, Jeffrey Michael:
Wilcox.
RICHARDSON, Sir Charles Leslie:
Robertson (Robertson of Oakridge).
RICHARDSON, Margaret:
Maufe.
RICKETT, Sir Denis Hubert Fletcher:
Salter.
RILEY, Harold:
Wand.
ROBERTS, Sir Frank Kenyon:
Strang.
ROBERTS, John Leonard:
Lowson.
ROBERTSON, Alan:
Waddington.
ROBIN, Gordon de Quetteville:
Priestley.
ROBINSON, Frank Neville Hosband:
Kompfner.
RODGERS, William Thomas:
Donnelly.
ROLL OF IPSDEN, Eric Roll, Baron:
Bronowski; Marquand.
ROOSE-EVANS, James:
Dean (B. H.).
ROSBERG, Carl Gustaf:
Kenyatta.
ROSE, Bernard William George:
Westrup.
ROSE, Francis ('Frank') Leslie:
Ing.
ROSE, Kenneth Vivian:
Ramsay.
ROSENTHAL, Thomas Gabriel:
Ayrton; Hitchens.
ROSKILL, Sir Ashton Wentworth:
Pritt.
ROSKILL, Eustace Wentworth Roskill, Baron:
Sachs.
ROSKILL, Stephen Wentworth:
Butler; Denning; Oliver; Onslow; Parry (W. E.).
ROTHSCHILD, Nathaniel Mayer Victor Rothschild, Baron:
Primrose (Rosebery).
RUTHERFORD, Andrew:
Linklater.
RYDILL, Louis Joseph:
Sims.

SAINER, Leonard:
Clore.
ST. ALDWYN, Michael John Hicks Beach, Earl:
Dugdale (Crathorne).
ST. AUBYN, Giles Rowan:
Henry William Frederick Albert (Gloucester); William Henry Andrew Frederick (prince of Great Britain).
SANDELSON, Neville Devonshire:
Edelman.
SANDFORD, Sir Folliott Herbert:
Cunliffe-Lister (Swinton).
SATTERTHWAITE, Richard George:
Messervy.
SAVILLE, John:
Cole (M. I.); Dutt; Lawther.
SCHOFIELD, Brian Betham:
Creasy.
SELF, Peter John Otter:
Robson.
SELKIRK, George Nigel Douglas-Hamilton, Earl of:
Sackville (De La Warr).
SETH-SMITH, Michael:
Bernard (Bandon).
SHACKLETON, Edward Arthur Alexander Shackleton, Baron:
Mond (Melchett).
SHARMAN, (Frederick) Andrew:
Snow (F. S.).
SHAW, (John) James Byam:
Hendy.
SHAWE-TAYLOR, Desmond Christopher:
Teyte.
SHERFIELD, Roger Mellor Makins, Baron:
Lee.
SHILS, Edward Albert:
Johnson.

SHORE, Bernard Alexander Royle:
Tertis.
SIEPMANN, Charles Arthur:
Sieveking.
SINCLAIR, Hugh Macdonald:
Chick.
SISSONS, (Thomas) Michael (Beswick):
Peters.
SKIPWITH, Peyton:
Armfield.
SMITH, Henry Sidney:
Emery.
SMITH, Sir Thomas Broun:
Reid.
SMYTH, Denis Paul:
Hillgarth.
SOAMES, Mary Soames, Lady:
Churchill (Spencer-Churchill).
SOPER, Donald Oliver Soper, Baron:
Stocks.
SOUTHERN, Sir Richard William:
Galbraith.
SPARROW, John Hanbury Angus:
Bowra.
SPEAR, Thomas George Percival:
Williams (L. F. R.).
SPENDER, Sir Stephen Harold:
Auden.
SPURLING, John:
Farrell.
STACEY, Maurice:
Hirst.
STAMP, Gavin Mark:
Chamberlin.
STANSFIELD, Kathryn Margaret:
Sharp.
STEARN, William Thomas:
Salisbury.
STEEL, Donald MacLennan Arklay:
Smith (F.) (Bunty Stephens); Tolley.
STEPHENSON, Andrew:
Mottram (R. H.).
STEVENS, Kathleen Elizabeth:
Curtis Brown.
STOCKTON. See Macmillan.
STOKES, John Fisher:
Rosenheim.
STOYE, John Walter:
Boase.
STRAWSON, John Michael:
Gale.
STRAWSON, Sir Peter Frederick:
Ryle.
STUART, Charles Harborne:
Feiling.
STUBBLEFIELD, Sir (Cyril) James:
Bulman.
SUMMERSON, Sir John Newenham:
Erith.
SUTCLIFFE, Peter Hoyle:
Rhodes.
SUTCLIFFE, Reginald Cockcroft:
Gold.
SWANN, Michael Meredith Swann, Baron:
Gray (J.).
SWANTON, Ernest William:
Longhurst; Woolley.
SYKES, Donald Armstrong:
Micklem.

TAYLOR, Sir George:
Savill.
TENNANT, Sir Peter Frank Dalrymple:
Binney.
TETHER, Cyril Henry:
Einzig.
THOMAS OF SWYNNERTON, Hugh Swynnerton Thomas, Baron:
Szamuely.
THOMPSON, Sir Harold Warris:
Bose; Dean (W. R., 'Dixie').
THOMPSON, Sir Kenneth Pugh:
Marples.
THOMSON OF MONIFIETH, George Morgan Thomson, Baron:
Gordon Walker (Gordon-Walker).
TILNEY, Sir John Dudley Robert Tarleton:
Neave.
TINKER, Hugh Russell:
Spens.
TODD, Alexander Robertus Todd, Baron:
Robinson.
TOOLEY, Sir John:
Webster.
TRANCHELL, Peter Andrew:
Hadley.
TREVOR-ROPER, Patrick Dacre:
Fraser (Fraser of Lonsdale).
TREWIN, John Courtenay:
Compton; Ervine; Payne; Sherriff.
TREWIN, Wendy:
Albery.
TROLLOPE, Glynden Hopcyn:
Scamp.
TUCK, Patrick James Noel:
Burrows.
TUTTLE, Sir Geoffrey William:
Sorley.

UBBELOHDE, Alfred Renatus John Paul:
Newitt.
URSELL, Fritz Joseph:
Proudman.
USHERWOOD, Nicholas John:
McMillan.
VAIZEY, John Ernest Vaizey, Baron:
Snow (C. P.).
VICKERS, Hugo Ralph:
Beaton.

WAIN, John Barrington:
Grieve (Hugh MacDiarmid).

WALKER, Brian Wilson:
Jackson-Cole.
WALKER, Sheila Mosley:
Baden-Powell.
WALKER, William:
Campbell (D.).
WALLER, Ian Peter Munro:
Brayley; Sternberg (Plurenden).
WALTON, Sir John Nicholas:
Russell (W. R.).
WARDLE, (John) Irving:
Beaumont.
WARNOCK, Sir Geoffrey James:
Ross.
WARNOCK, (Helen) Mary Warnock, Baroness:
Anderson (K.).
WATERWORTH, Pamela Mabel:
Garrod.
WATSON, Colin Hugh:
Cripps; Sansom.
WAUGH, Auberon Alexander:
Woodruff.
WEBSTER, Douglas:
Warren.
WEIPERS, Sir William Lee:
Ritchie.
WELLS, Stanley William:
Nicoll.
WENDEN, Daivd John:
Elton (A. H. R.); Grierson.
WERNHAM, Richard Bruce:
Woodward.
WESTOLL, Thomas Stanley:
Watson.
WHITBY, Lionel Gordon:
Dodds (E. C.).
WHITE, Sir Dick Goldsmith:
Hollis (R. H.); Sinclair.
WHITE, Eirene Lloyd White, Baroness:
Hancock.
WHITE, Robert Edwin:
Ogg.
WHITEHORN, John Roland Malcolm:
Kipping.
WHITEMAN, Elizabeth Anne Osborn:
Clark (G. N.); Sutherland (L. S.).
WHITE-THOMSON, Ian Hugh:
Fisher.
WHITTERIDGE, David:
Guttmann.
WHITWORTH, Reginald Henry:
Baker.
WILBERFORCE, Richard Orme Wilberforce, Baron:
Cohen (L. L.).
WILES, Maurice Frank:
Lampe.
WILKINS, Malcolm Barrett:
Bennet-Clark.
WILKINSON, Sir Denys Haigh:
Chadwick; Feather (N.).
WILKINSON, Sir Peter Allix:
Gubbins.
WILLEY, Frederick Thomas:
Summerskill.
WILLEY, Gordon Randolf:
Thompson.
WILLIAMS, Anthea:
Elmhirst.
WILLIAMS, Sir Edgar Trevor:
Montgomery (Montgomery of Alamein); Veale.
WILLIAMS, (John) Kyffin:
Tunnicliffe.
WILLIAMS, Sir Robert Evan Owen:
Fildes.
WILLIAMS, Trevor Illtyd:
Hogben; Rose.
WILLIAMS-ELLIS, Amabel Williams-Ellis, Lady:
Hughes.
WILSON, Charles Henry:
Cole (G. J.).
WINDLESHAM, David James George Hennessy, Baron:
Faulkner; Isaacs (Reading and Swanborough).
WINNIFRITH, Sir (Alfred) John (Digby):
McDonnell (Antrim).
WISE, Michael John:
Rodd (Rennell of Rodd).
WITTON-DAVIES, Carlyle:
Morris (A. E.).
WOLFERS, David:
Stone.
WOLLHEIM, Richard Arthur:
Stokes.
WOOD, Donald:
Adams (G. H.).
WOODHOUSE, Hon. (Christopher) Montague:
Makarios III (Michael Mouskos).
WORSLEY, Sir Richard Edward:
Lindsell.
WRIGHT, (Eric) Peter:
Mann.
WRIGHT, (Henry) Myles:
Holford.
WRIGHT, Robert Charles:
Elliot; Evill.
WYATT, Sir Woodrow Lyle:
Harrisson.
WYKEHAM, Sir Peter:
Embry.

YARNOLD, Edward John:
D'Arcy.
YOUNG, John Zachary:
De Beer.

ZANDER, Walter:
Bentwich.
ZIEGLER, Philip Sandeman:
Mountbatten.
ZUCKERMAN, Solly Zuckerman, Baron:
Clarke (W. E. Le G.); Huxley; Thomson (A. L.).

DICTIONARY

OF

NATIONAL BIOGRAPHY

(TWENTIETH CENTURY)

PERSONS WHO DIED 1971–1980

ABERCROMBIE, MICHAEL (1912–1979), biologist, was born at Ryton, Dymock, Gloucestershire, 14 August 1912, the third son in the family of three sons and a daughter of Lascelles Abercrombie [q.v.], poet and critic, and his wife, Catherine, daughter of Owen Gwatkin, surgeon, of Grange-over-Sands. The Abercrombies were a distinguished family for, in addition to Lascelles, Michael counted among his uncles Sir L. Patrick Abercrombie [q.v.], a pioneer of town planning, Rudolph ('Rody'), physician and field naturalist, and Charles, a business man. Michael's brother David became a professor of phonetics in the University of Edinburgh.

Abercrombie attended Leeds Grammar School, proceeding as top Hastings scholar to the Queen's College, Oxford, in 1931. At Oxford he read zoology under the tuition of (Sir) Gavin de Beer [q.v.] and obtained first class honours in 1934. De Beer arranged for him to work for a period at the Strangeways Research Laboratory in Cambridge under C. H. Waddington [q.v.]. On returning to Oxford in 1935 he began to study the embryology of the domestic chicken by experimental methods under Howard (later Lord) Florey [q.v.] in the Sir William Dunn School of Pathology. He shared a room with his friend and contemporary (Sir) Peter Medawar. During this period Abercrombie took an active part in the extensive programme of research on the degeneration of peripheral nerves then in progress in the zoology laboratories under the direction of J. Z. Young, becoming a senior scholar—'taberdar'—of Queen's.

In 1938 he took a teaching appointment in the zoology department at Birmingham University, which he held concurrently with a junior fellowship. His most important enterprise at this time was to inaugurate a series of biological texts entitled *New Biology* aimed at bringing advanced biology in an intelligible form to sixth formers and first year biology students. Unfortunately the Abercrombies quarrelled with Lancelot Hogben [q.v.], the head of zoology in Birmingham, as many others had. In 1946 Abercrombie took a lecturership in the department of anatomy in University College London, working immediately under his old tutor Gavin de Beer, the head of the embryology sub-department. He was reader in embryology from 1950 to 1959.

It was here that he began the research which made his international reputation; for it was his belief (not shared by de Beer) that embryological problems could be studied in the processes of wound repair, as they might occur in adult animals. By experiments of the most simple and elegant design he revealed one of the factors at work in controlling growth—one which ensured that with the recompletion of repair growth ceased. He juxtaposed two actively growing tissue cultures which showed that when the cells migrated outwards from them they came into contact with cells from the neighbouring piece of tissue and cell movement ceased. The discovery of this phenomenon, 'contact inhibition'—much less pronounced in cancerous cells than in normal—led to his election to the Royal Society in 1958. It was the basis of his claim to become, first, titular professor of embryology at University College (1959–62) and then Jodrell professor of zoology and comparative anatomy (1962–70). In 1962 he spent eight months in the Carnegie Institute of Embryology in Washington.

Abercrombie had strongly left-wing opinions, joining the Communist Party in 1932, but in due course the humanity and sense of justice that had caused him to join the party now caused him to leave it. His last appointment (1970–9) was to succeed Dame Honor B. Fell as the head of the Strangeways Research Laboratory in Cambridge, an appointment whose administrative obligations he coped with as well as a man could who derived no pleasure whatsoever from the exercise of power. He was firm, though, and looked after the interests of his staff. At the same time he was a fellow of Clare Hall.

When the verdict of the market place brought *New Biology* to an end Abercrombie and his wife performed another public service by writing and publishing an excellent *Dictionary of Biology* (with C. J. Hickman and M. L. Johnson, 1950), a fine example of concision and clear writing. His work on contact inhibition continued and became part of the establishment of embryological understanding. He was awarded an honorary doctorate by Uppsala University and won the Ernst Bertner award for cancer research.

In 1939 he married Minnie Louie ('Jane'), daughter of Stanley Johnson, electrical engineer. They had one son. Jane Johnson was a lecturer in the zoology department at Birmingham University and became an authority on the teaching of medical students. Abercrombie died at home in Cambridge 28 May 1979.

[Sir Peter Medawar in *Biographical Memoirs of Fellows of the Royal Society*, vol. xxvi, 1980; biographical memoir by Abercrombie in Royal Society archives; personal knowledge.]

PETER MEDAWAR

ABRAHAMS, HAROLD MAURICE (1899–1978), athlete, sports administrator, and civil servant, was born at 30 Rutland Road, Bedford, 15 December 1899, the youngest in the family of two daughters and four sons of Isaac Klonimus of Vladislavovi in Russian-occupied Poland and his wife, Esther Isaacs, of Merthyr Tydfil. Klonimus (1850–1921), who proclaimed himself a Lithuanian Jew, escaped to Britain and by 1880 had changed his name to Abrahams, in recognition of his father Abraham Klonimus (born 1810).

Though Isaac Abrahams never mastered the script (and barely the speech) of his host country, he set up the Bedfordshire Loan Company in 1885 and was naturalized in 1902. In the county town in addition to money lending he dealt as a certificated pedlar in jewellery, gold, and silver plate. Despite their tempestuous marriage Esther and he raised four remarkable sons. Adolphe, the eldest, after gaining firsts at Emmanuel College, Cambridge, became a consultant physician at Westminster Hospital and was knighted in 1939. 'Solly', later Sir Sidney Solomon Abrahams, who competed for Britain at both the Olympic celebrations at Athens (1906) and Stockholm (1912), was sworn of the Privy Council after serving as chief justice of Tanganyika and Ceylon (Sri Lanka). The third son Lionel became senior partner of his firm of solicitors and was coroner for Huntingdonshire.

Harold Abrahams was sent to Bedford School, briefly to St. Paul's, and afterwards to Repton where he won the public schools' 100 yards and long-jump championships in 1918. His imagination had been fired in the summer of 1908 when he watched his brother compete in the fourth Olympic Games at the White City stadium, London. He served briefly as a second lieutenant in 1919 and then went up to Gonville and Caius College, Cambridge, to read law. If the road to popularity at university lies in never inculcating a sense of inferiority into one's contemporaries, Abrahams stood little chance of being popular. Athletically he swept all before him with three wins in the freshman's sports at Fenners and was immediately selected for the sixth Olympic Games in Antwerp. He won a unique eight victories at the 100 yards, 440 yards, and long jump in the annual Oxford versus Cambridge sports. His election to the Hawks Club was opposed due to a contribution to *The Times*, which the committee regarded as immodest. *Chariots of Fire*, a highly successful film on the life of Abrahams, stressed an anti-Semitic undertone of his time at Cambridge. Though he did not live to see the film, Abrahams, on his own testimony, would certainly have regarded such a portrayal as over-fanciful.

Before the next Olympic Games in 1924, which was to be held in the Stade de Colombes in Paris, he trained assiduously with his north-country coach Sam Mussabini, a French Arab. For nine months they worked on the theory of perfecting the start, on arm action, control of the stride pattern, and a then-unique 'drop' finish of the torso on to the tape. At the 1924 Amateur Athletic Association championship Abrahams won the 100 yards in 9.9 seconds but was still a fifth of a second outside the British record set the previous year by the great Scottish rugby and athletic hero and 440-yard champion, Eric Liddell. In Paris the twenty-three eliminating heats to bring the seventy-five starters down to twelve semi-finalists were to be staged on Sunday 6 July and Liddell, a strong Sabbatarian, felt impelled to confine himself to the 200 and 400 metres in which he took the bronze medal in the shorter event and the gold medal for 400 metres in a time which gave him the metric world record. Abrahams equalled the Olympic record in the 100 metres in the second round with 10.6 seconds and next day, despite being badly 'left' in a poor start in the semi-final, came through (again in 10.6 seconds) to beat by inches the world record holder Charles Paddock from the USA. Abrahams later said that the next three-and-three-quarter hours were the worst in his life because now he knew he could win. At 7.05 p.m. he came out with the four Americans, Paddock, Scholz, Murchison, and Bowman and the Oxford Rhodes scholar Arthur (later Lord) Porritt, from New Zealand.

Abrahams was drawn in lane four and got a perfect start. He showed fractionally ahead at half-way and dropped on to the tape two feet clear of Scholz with Porritt beating Bowman for third. His winning time of 10.52 seconds would under present rules be returned as 10.5 but was rounded up to 10.6. Abrahams thus set three Olympic record-equalling performances in the space of twenty-six hours. In Paris there were no flag-raising victory ceremonies. His gold medal, sadly later stolen, was sent to him by post. In May 1925, now a barrister, Abrahams severely injured a leg when attempting to improve on his English native long-jump record of 24 feet 2½ inches (7.38 metres), which survived for more than thirty years.

His athletic career ended, he applied his analytical mind to the bar (to which he had been called—Inner Temple—in 1924), where he practised until 1940. He also engaged in athletic administration and journalism with the *Sunday Times* (1925–67), and was a consummate radio broadcaster with the BBC for fifty years (1924–74). Against the stolid petty opposition of senior office-holders in various governing bodies, often athletes *manqués*, he managed by sheer force of personality and with very few allies to raise athletics from a minor to a major national sport. His innovative mind and drafting ability enabled him to rewrite the AAA rules of competition which themselves transformed the rules of the International Amateur Athletic Federation. He was possessed of a fresh resonant voice while his clear diction and wide vocabulary were models for any English-speaker.

He served as honorary treasurer (1948–68) and chairman (1948–75) of the British Amateur Athletic Board. In November 1976 he was elected president of the AAA. He was an unrivalled compiler of athletics statistics and was founder-president of both the world and British associations in this field. His *Oxford versus Cambridge 1827–1930* (compiled with J. Bruce-Kerr, 1931), which listed all the 7,489 blues, must have resulted in the exposure of many self-appointed ones in the bars and clubs of the world. During World War II he was with the Ministry of Economic Warfare (1939–44) and with the new Ministry of Town and Country Planning until 1963. He was secretary of the National Parks Commission (1950–63). He was appointed CBE in 1957.

In 1936 Abrahams married Sybil Marjorie, daughter of Claude Pilington Evers, assistant master at Rugby School. She was a singer and producer of light opera and died suddenly in 1963. They had an adopted daughter and an adopted son. Abrahams died 14 January 1978 at Chase Farm Hospital, Enfield.

[Private information; personal knowledge.]

NORRIS MCWHIRTER

ABRAMSKY, YEHEZKEL (1886–1976), rabbinic scholar and orthodox Jewish leader, was born in Dashkovtsy (near Most and Grodno, Lithuania) to Mordecai Zalman Abramsky, a local timber merchant, and his wife, Freydel Goldin, of Grodno, on or about 7 February 1886 (new style) as their third child and elder son. As a markedly promising talmudical student he began whilst a boy the then usual peripatetic training, at the *yeshivoth* (seminaries) of Telz, Mir, Slobodka, and particularly at Brisk under Hayyim Soloveitchik, the teacher and mentor he always venerated: and he earned his certification as a rabbi before he was eighteen.

Abramsky's ability as a jurisconsult was quickly recognized in Russia, and he was successively rabbi of Smolyan, Smolevich, and Slutzk. With the Bolshevik revolution and increasing attempts to repress traditional Jewish observance and culture, Abramsky exerted himself to encourage its continuation—for example, by surreptitious (albeit legal) arrangement for circumcisions. For the same purpose he was co-founder in 1928 of a Hebrew periodical—the last in Russia—*Yagdil Torah*, which after two issues was proscribed. The Soviet government understood well Abramsky's standing in Russian Jewry; and, partly concerned for its own reputation abroad, in 1926 and again in 1928 it refused him permission to leave and take up the rabbinate of Petah Tikvah in Palestine. Worse followed. Hoover, as president of the United States, sent an inter-faith commission to investigate religious freedom in Russia as a prerequisite to establishing closer relations with the USSR. Abramsky, when interviewed, had said nothing; his silence was construed by the authorities as defamation of the Soviet Union, and he spent months eluding arrest. He was apprehended in 1929 and the death sentence demanded, but he was condemned (without trial) to five years' hard labour in Siberia. World-wide Jewish concern elicited diplomatic intervention, and in 1931, in exchange for six communists held by Brüning's government in Germany, he was given a month to leave Russia. Two of his sons were retained as hostages, and to avoid endangering them Abramsky in 1935 declined to succeed A. I. Kook as Ashkenazic chief rabbi of Palestine. Anthony Eden (later Earl of Avon, q.v.), as foreign secretary, personally intervened to secure their release in 1937, Abramsky having come to London in 1932 as rabbi of the right-wing orthodox community (*Mahzikey Ha-dath*). He was naturalized a British subject in 1937.

The United Synagogue, whose dominance within the orthodox community is secured by act of Parliament, invited him to head its ecclesiastical court. After undertakings that there would be no lay pressure for unacceptable relaxations of the law, he accepted and discharged his duties with exemplary conscientiousness until his retirement to Jerusalem in 1951. Notably, he tightened up the standards of kosher slaughtering; and he stood firm against conversions to Judaism of dubious sincerity for matrimonial purposes.

Abramsky's clarity of exposition drew large audiences for his London discourses (delivered in Yiddish) on aspects of Jewish law: even more well attended were his twice-weekly lectures in Jerusalem *yeshivoth*, maintained until a few years before his death. As president of the Council of *Yeshivoth*, the Private Education League, and other national bodies he was no mere figure-head, and whenever he made representations to the Israeli government regarding the protection of religious interests, he was heard with unfailing respect.

His scholarly work followed traditional rabbinic methodology, ignoring external influences and parallels in, for example, Roman law. It was prodigious and fruitful. A *Memorial Volume* collects his talmudic *novellae* and *responsa*, but his major monument is the twenty-four-volume *Hazon Yehezkel*, a commentary on the *Tosefta* or 'supplementary' digest of Jewish law compiled *circa* 200 CE. Planned during World War I, its approach is quite different from Lieberman's work which paralleled it in publication. The first volume appeared in 1925, the last in 1975; Abramsky had continued work on it in Siberia, smuggling it out on cigarette-paper. In 1955 he was the first recipient of the Israel prize for literature; and he was the first commentator whose notes to the Talmud were printed alongside the classical commentaries in his own lifetime.

More significant than Abramsky's appointments and honours were his influence, his transparent saintliness, and his personal magnetism. Sir Robert Waley Cohen [q.v.], lay leader of the United Synagogue and of an upper class English background, recognized his sincerity and responded to it. And once, when an assimilated Jew, applying for a religious divorce, sneered at the 'medievalism' of Abramsky's court, he met with a dignified rebuke that elicited apology. His leadership in England partly stimulated intenser observance and wider familiarity with rabbinic sources in segments of the United Synagogue, but conversely it accentuated orthodox disregard for the analogously reinvigorated reform community. Besides his world stature in rabbinical scholarship, Abramsky was respected in Israel as the last outstanding representative of a Jewish cultural life that had for four hundred years shaped the Jewries of Russia and Poland: and the crowd (estimated at perhaps 40,000) attending his funeral made it the largest ever seen in Jerusalem, where he had died 19 September 1976.

He married in 1909 Reizel (died 1965), daughter of Israel Jonathan Jerusalimsky, head of the Jewish court at Iehumen (White Russia). They had four sons, of whom the third, Chimen, became a distinguished historian of Jewry, Eastern Europe, and Marxism, and a professor at University College, London.

[*The Times*, 20 September 1976; *Jerusalem Post* of same date; *Jewish Chronicle*, 24 September and 1 and 8 October 1976; Hebrew press tributes; *Memorial Volume* (Hebrew), ed. J. Buksbaum and A. L. Schor, Jerusalem, 1978 (portraits in most); family information.]

RAPHAEL LOEWE

ADAIR, GILBERT SMITHSON (1896–1979), physiologist and pioneer in the application of physical chemistry to biological systems, was born 21 September 1896 in Whitehaven, the elder child and only son of Harold Adair, manager of an iron ore mine in Cumberland, and his wife, Anna Mary Jackson, from Garstang. The family later moved to nearby Egremont. With his sister Lucy he was educated privately at home for several years, and encouraged by both parents, he became absorbed in the area and its natural history, particularly at the sea-shore. A room in the house was set up as a laboratory, equipped with a microscope. In his early teens Adair was sent to Bootham, the Quaker school in York. There he found life spartan, even for his simple tastes. The school recognized his talents in biology and chemistry, and he successfully took the entrance scholarship examination at King's College, Cambridge in 1914. He entered that college in 1915, obtaining a first class in part i of the natural sciences tripos in 1917.

With his rather defective eyesight Adair was not successful in his attempt to join the Friends Ambulance Unit. He entered the Food Investigation Board which had recently been set up to consider ways of preventing wastage of imported food on cargo ships—an important problem at that time as later. He returned to King's College, Cambridge, as a research student (with the R. J. Smith studentship) in 1920 and joined the Physiological Laboratory, though he retained links with the Food Investigation Board which proved to be useful. For plans were afoot for the setting up of a Refrigeration Research Station (later the Low Temperature Research Station) in Cambridge on the Downing site not far from the Physiological Laboratory. In 1922 these plans materialized and he was granted cold-room facilities which he continued to use until his death. In 1923 he was elected to a research fellowship at King's College and published several major papers during his tenure, so that in 1928 the college made him an official fellow for five years allowing him to concentrate on research. In 1931 he became an assistant director of research in the Physiological Laboratory, an appointment until 1945 when he became reader in biophysics, a post he held until his retirement in 1963, when he was made an honorary fellow of King's College. In 1939 he had been elected a fellow of the Royal Society.

After early work on the diffusion of electrolytes in gels, Adair entered on what was to be his major field, the physical chemistry of haemoglobin and its interactions with simple gases. His work between 1924 and 1930 was the first to show that haemoglobin was a well-defined material with highly specific structure, unique molecular weight, and the capability of reacting stoichiometrically and reproducibly. In particular he will be remembered for perfecting and simplifying the osmotic pressure method of measuring molecular weight which was subsequently widely used by himself and others throughout the world. By 1940 he had published some forty-five papers on the application of osmotic and membrane potential measurements to a variety of protein systems. From 1940 to 1977, although the volume of his output fell somewhat, he was in great demand from visiting scientists and Ph.D. students, to whom he was always willing to demonstrate patiently and fully his latest developments. He was an excellent teacher. Many of his later papers were written in collaboration with visitors from all parts of the world. Interestingly his last paper (with K. Imai from Japan) returned to his favourite subject, haemoglobin.

Although quiet and retiring, he made many friends. Climbing activities in the Lake District, in the Dolomites, in Colorado as well as around the university and college buildings in Cambridge in the earlier part of his life were later replaced by interest in his beautiful garden which adjoined 'Paradise', one of the better-known backwaters of the Cam. Here he and his wife spent much time, encouraging nearly all forms of wild life (ducks and rooks excluded).

In July 1931 he married Muriel Elaine, one of the three daughters of George Hardinge Robinson, a stockbroker from Southport who died when Muriel was in her early teens. Although the family had a struggle to survive, Muriel entered Girton College in 1918, obtained firsts in both parts of the natural sciences tripos, a research fellowship at Newnham, and a staff fellowship at Girton. At one stage she worked with Sir Frederick Gowland Hopkins [q.v.] but eventually she turned to proteins and collaborated with Adair in many papers from 1930 onwards. She also accompanied him on the less demanding climbing expeditions. They had no children. Muriel died on 2 January 1975; Adair on 22 June 1979, in Cambridge.

[P. Johnson and M. F. Perutz in *Biographical Memoirs of Fellows of the Royal Society*, vol. xxvii, 1981; private information; personal knowledge.] PALEY JOHNSON

ADAMS, SIR GRANTLEY HERBERT (1898–1971), prime minister of the Federation of the West Indies, was born 28 April 1898 in Bridgetown, Barbados, the second of six sons (there was also a daughter) of Fitzherbert Adams, a primary school headmaster, and his wife, Rosa Frances Turner. Education mattered in this family and Adams won a scholarship to Harrison College and then the coveted Barbados scholarship. He entered St. Catherine's Society, Oxford, in 1918, took part in undergraduate Liberal politics, played much cricket, and was president of the junior common room. He obtained third classes in classical honour moderations in 1921 and jurisprudence in 1923.

After being called to the bar (Gray's Inn) in 1923, he returned home where he built a reputation as a shrewd, forceful barrister. He was also a leader writer for the conservative *Agricultural Reporter*, but as the West Indies sank ever deeper into the depression of the 1930s, his politics became more radical as he took up the cause of the Barbadian working man. In 1934 he was elected a member of the House of Assembly for St. Joseph, surprisingly beating a white planter; he soon proved to be as adept at politics as he was at the bar. After serious riots in July 1937, the radicals sent Adams to London to press for a royal commission to examine West Indian conditions. In 1939 the Moyne commission went to the Caribbean.

This London visit had important consequences for Adams. He became friends with Labour Party members who were interested in the colonies, such as Sir R. Stafford Cripps, Arthur Creech Jones [qq.v.], and Rita Hinden; his vague but deeply felt radicalism was channelled into Fabian socialism. He also saw the need for a political party backed by a trade union. On his return he helped to found the Barbados Progressive League (1938) from which were soon to spring the Barbados Workers' Union and the Barbados Labour Party which was led by Adams.

He was appointed by the governor to the executive committee in 1942, and made leader of the House of Assembly when the Barbados Labour Party won nine seats, a bare majority, in 1946. In 1954 Adams, who had become QC (Barbados) in 1953 and who was by then a respected Caribbean statesman, became premier. Yet when Barbados became independent in 1966, Adams and his party were in opposition after a defeat by the Democratic Labour Party.

Despite his Barbadian preoccupations, Adams played his part in the wider world of cold war diplomacy in the immediate post-war years, the most successful of his life. He was in the British delegation at the first meeting of the United Nations in 1948 when he eloquently defended the British colonial record; he was appointed to the committee of experts of the International Labour Organization in 1949; he was president of the Caribbean Labour Congress and vice-chairman of the International Confederation of Free Trade Unions when these bodies were fighting against communist domination.

Even before the war Adams believed that the solution to the problems of the Caribbean colonies lay in a federation. After the war he played a leading part in the planning conferences at Montego Bay (1947) and London (1953, 1956). He became leader of the new Federal Labour Party and the first and, as it turned out, the only prime minister of the Federation of the West Indies in 1958. For various reasons Jamaica and Trinidad, the most powerful members, dropped out, leaving behind the fatally weakened rump of the small islands and Barbados. The Federation staggered on until 1962, and a frustrated and bitterly disappointed Adams returned to the parochial world of leading the opposition in Barbados. After increasing illness he resigned his seat in 1970.

Adams belonged to that generation of English-educated nationalist politicians such as Norman Manley of Jamaica and Eric Williams of Trinidad who led their countries towards independence and ensured that they followed the Westminster model afterwards. In Barbados he broke the planter domination of society, encouraged economic diversification, and laid the foundations for a welfare state.

In private life he was amiable and witty and he delighted in the post-war flowering of West Indian cricket. He married Grace Thorne from a white planter family in 1929; this was in itself a portent of social change. Their only child, Tom (born 14 September 1931), was a prime minister of Barbados in the 1970s.

Adams was appointed CMG in 1952 and knighted in 1957. In 1958 he received an honorary D.Litt. from Mount Allison. He died at Bridgetown 28 November 1971.

[F. A. Hoyos, *Grantley Adams and the Social Revolution*, 1974; *The Times*, 29 November and 3 December 1971; private information.]

DONALD WOOD

ADAMS, SIR WALTER (1906–1975), university administrator, was born 16 December 1906 at Brighton, the son of Walter Adams, a builder's clerk, and his wife, Margaret Evans. He was educated at Brighton, Hove and Sussex Grammar School and at University College, London, where he read history, being awarded the BA degree with first class honours in 1928, and where he was subsequently appointed to a lectureship in history. In 1933 he resigned in order to become general secretary of the Academic Assistance Council (later the Society for the Protection of Science and Learning), a body formed under the presidency of Lord Rutherford of Nelson [q.v.] to assist university teachers displaced on account of race, religion, or political opinion. The work gave Adams wide administrative experience as it involved the raising and administration of a fund of approximately £70,000, the establishment of local committees in nearly all British universities, and the making of contracts with government departments, national and international educational organizations, and universities all over the world, in order to help academic refugees to find posts. In this Adams was notably successful, and many refugee scholars later expressed their personal gratitude to him for his sympathy and practical help. In 1937–8 he served as secretary to a survey of the refugee question undertaken under the auspices of the Royal Institute of International Affairs and the Rockefeller Foundation.

In 1938 he was appointed secretary of the London School of Economics and after the outbreak of war had to cope with the problems of evacuating the School to Cambridge. In 1941 he was granted leave of absence to take up an appointment with the Political Intelligence Department of the Foreign Office. From 1942 to 1944 he was in America as deputy head of the British Political Warfare Mission to the United States. In 1945 he returned to London as assistant deputy director-general of the Political Intelligence Department, a post which he gave up the following year; and he devoted the rest of his career to university administration.

In 1946 Adams became the secretary of the newly formed Inter-University Council for Higher Education Overseas, and he was involved in the foundation of universities and university colleges throughout the British Commonwealth. This experience led naturally to his appointment in 1955 as principal of the newly established University College of Rhodesia and Nyasaland. This was to prove the most taxing assignment of his career, as the running of a multiracial university in Rhodesia in the 1960s became increasingly difficult, especially after the unilateral declaration of Rhodesian independence in 1965. Adams was caught between the desire to maintain the College as a multiracial institution and his belief that it was essential to maintain academic standards, even if this meant fewer black students. At the same time, he believed that the future of the College depended on remaining on good terms with the Rhodesian government. As a result he was criticized both by those who accused him of discriminating against black students and compromising with the government and by those who were against any kind of multiracial education at all.

Adams was always a man who preferred compromise to confrontation and it was unfortunate for him that, when he left Rhodesia on appointment as director of the London School of Economics in 1967, he was faced with some hostility among a section of the LSE students on account of his position in Rhodesia. This added to the student unrest characteristic of universities all over the world in 1967–9. Adams showed considerable dignity in the face of personal attacks and uninformed criticism and was also supported by the sympathy of several of the refugee scholars whom he had helped thirty years earlier and who were outraged at the suggestion that he was in any sense a 'racist'. These disturbances, which were on a very small scale compared with those in many universities in Europe and the USA, soon died down, and Adams was able to resume the task for which he was most suited of being an efficient and humane administrator, dedicated to scholarly values and academic independence.

He retired in 1974 and died suddenly 21 May 1975 while on a visit to Salisbury, Rhodesia, where he had gone to receive an honorary doctorate from the university of which he had once been head. He also had honorary degrees from Malta and Melbourne.

In 1933 Adams married Tatiana (died 1975), daughter of Alexander Makaroff, lawyer; they had three sons and one daughter. He was appointed OBE in 1945 and CMG in 1952. He was knighted in 1970. In 1935 he published in collaboration with H. W. Robinson a scholarly edition of *The Diary of Robert Hooke 1672–80*. A portrait of Adams by Robert Buhler (1974) is in the senior common room at the London School of Economics.

[*The Times*, 22 May 1975; private information; personal knowledge.] JAMES JOLL

ADRIAN, EDGAR DOUGLAS, first BARON ADRIAN (1889–1977), physiologist and Nobel prize-winner, was born in London 30 November 1889, the youngest of three sons (there were no daughters) of Alfred Douglas Adrian, civil servant, and his wife, Flora Lavinia, daughter of Charles Howard Barton. His eldest brother lived for only a few days, while the other, Harold, who showed great promise, died at the age of twenty-two. In 1903 Adrian went as a day-boy and King's scholar to Westminster School. He started in classics, but read books on science and moved to the modern side in 1906, two years before he left. He entered Trinity College, Cambridge, as a major scholar in natural sciences in 1908 and was placed in the first class in part i of the natural sciences tripos (1910) and in part ii (1911); in part i he read physics, chemistry, anatomy, physiology, and botany (most candidates took only three subjects) and in part ii he studied physiology. Adrian was also known for his skill in roof-climbing and obtained a half blue in fencing, a sport which may have been responsible for the rapid darting movement that characterized his work in the laboratory, or his method of preparing meals in the kitchen at home. While at Cambridge, he acquired a taste for hill-walking and mountaineering which remained with him all his life.

On the academic side, Adrian was most influenced by his Trinity supervisor, Keith Lucas [q.v.] a young physiologist of great distinction, who died in an aeroplane accident at Farnborough in 1916. Adrian first collaborated with Lucas and then continued on his own in a study of the nerve impulse, which won him a fellowship at Trinity College in 1913. At that time the Cambridge school of physiology was at the height of its fame, but housed deplorably. In a memoir on Lucas, Adrian has left an amusing account of the way in which Lucas, (Sir) F. G. Hopkins, A. V. Hill, (Sir) J. Barcroft, (Sir) W. M. Fletcher, (Sir) W. B. Hardy [qq.v.], G. R. Mines, and other distinguished scientists were crowded together into cellar rooms which were flooded so easily that the inhabitants had to walk about on duckboards. In addition, 'A side door led to a dark chamber in which all the frogs were kept and beyond this was the centrifuge driven by a large gas engine of obsolete design which shook the building and added the smell of warm oil and half-burnt gas to that of frog and rat.'

Some months before the war, Adrian decided to abandon research for a few years in order to complete his medical degree. He began clinical training at Addenbrooke's Hospital, Cambridge, in the summer of 1914 and started in earnest at St. Bartholomew's Hospital in July 1914. He qualified after only about a year's clinical work, which, like his part i first in five subjects, remains something of a record. After acquiring a medical degree he worked on nerve injuries and shell-shock, first at the National Hospital, Queen Square, and later at the Connaught Military Hospital in Aldershot where he remained until the end of the war, in spite of strenuous efforts to get to France. Later, Adrian wrote that he owed his interest in clinical neurology to Sir Francis Walshe [q.v.] and to Sir Adolph Abrahams. Another major influence must have been Dr L. R. Yealland of Queen Square with whom he collaborated in very successful treatment of badly shell-shocked patients. During the years that Adrian worked at Aldershot he lived at Chudleigh with a group of scientists from the Royal Aircraft Factory at Farnborough. These included F. W. Aston, F. A. Lindemann (later Viscount Cherwell), (Sir) G. I. Taylor, (Sir) W. S. Farren, (Sir) B. Melvill Jones [qq.v.], and Hermann Glauert.

In 1919 Adrian returned to Cambridge to work in the Physiological Laboratory and to Trinity College where he looked after the medical students as well as lecturing and demonstrating in the university. His teaching load was heavy but it did not seem to interfere with his research. For a time he continued with analytical electrophysiology of the kind which he had started with Lucas. These researches led to some excellent papers, but Adrian was clearly dissatisfied with this line of work as he referred later to getting bogged down in somewhat unprofitable experiments. In 1925 he started to use a valve amplifier built to the design of the American H. S. Gasser who with Erlanger was the first to record nerve impulses with a cathode ray oscilloscope and valve amplifier. The cathode ray tubes that existed in those days had such low actinic power that they would have been useless for Adrian's purposes, but he got by initially with home-made capillary electrometers, and later made good use of the excellent mechanical oscilloscope devised by his young colleague, (Sir) Bryan H. C. Matthews. With these relatively inexpensive instruments Adrian and his colleagues produced a series of outstanding papers, many of which would perhaps be even better known if the results were not so clear-cut that they now appear self-evident. The initial breakthrough was made by Adrian working on his own, perhaps with some help from Sybil Cooper, but he was joined later in 1925 by Yngve Zotterman from Sweden with whom he subsequently wrote three distinguished papers. Other important collaborations were those with Rachel Matthews on the eye, with Detlev W. Bronk on motor impulses, with Bryan Matthews on electrical waves from the sensory cortex (Berger rhythm), and much later with G. Moruzzi on the motor cortex and pyramidal tracts. The main conclusions are summarized in three short books, all written versions of lectures: *The Basis of Sensation* (1928), *The Mechanism of Nervous Action* (1932), and *The Physical Background of Perception* (1946).

Adrian's work with Zotterman (1925–6) established beyond doubt that the nerve impulse is invariant, that the intensity of sensation is conveyed by the frequency of impulses and the quality by the type of nerve fibre in action. There are subtle qualifications to this last principle but it still stands as a broad generalization. Another very important conclusion is that adaptation to a steady stimulus generally takes place peripherally and that some sense organs, like those concerned with touch, adapt rapidly whereas others like muscle spindles adapt very slowly, or not at all.

In 1927–8 Adrian and Bronk showed that there is only one kind of impulse in a motor nerve fibre as well as in a sensory one, and that the force of muscular contraction, like the intensity of sensation, is graded by varying the frequency of nerve impulses and the number of nerve fibres in action.

During the early 1930s Adrian became increasingly interested in the way in which the nervous system might generate electrical rhythms and this interest led to the well-known papers written with Matthews and Yamagiwa which consolidated the initial work of Hans Berger and helped to found the important clinical subject of electroencephalography. During World War II, Adrian somehow managed to find time to do important experimental work on vestibular receptors, the cerebellum, and the motor and sensory cortex. His last studies on the sense of smell (1937–59) rank as an important contribution to a fascinating but still largely unsolved problem.

Adrian received many honours including the Nobel prize, shared with Sir C. S. Sherrington [q.v.], in 1932, the OM in 1942, and a peerage in 1955. He was professor of physiology at Cambridge from 1937 to 1951, master of Trinity College, Cambridge, from 1951 to 1965, foreign secretary of the Royal Society (1946–50), president of the Royal Society (1950–5), chancellor of the University of Leicester (1957–71), and vice-chancellor (1957–9) and later chancellor (1968–75) of the University of Cambridge. He was president of the British Association in 1954 and of the Royal Society of Medicine in 1960–1. Adrian's tenure of all these offices is particularly remembered for the magnificent speeches that he made at important ceremonial occasions. Like Sir Francis Bacon [q.v.], he was one of the very few people of whom it could be said that when he spoke the only anxiety of the audience was that he would stop. He attended the House of Lords as regularly as his many academic commitments allowed, sitting on the cross-benches and speaking mainly on medical and scientific problems of university affairs. Adrian received honorary degrees from twenty-nine universities and was an honorary or foreign member of an even larger number of academies and scientific societies.

In 1923 Adrian married (Dame) Hester Agnes Pinsent, daughter of Hume Chancellor Pinsent, a solicitor in Birmingham, and Dame Ellen Francis Pinsent, distinguished for her work on mental health, an interest later shared by her daughter. They had three children: Mrs Ann Keynes, Mrs Jennet Campbell, and Richard Hume Adrian FRS (born 1927), who succeeded to his father's title and shared his interest in physiology.

After his wife's death in 1966, Adrian returned to Trinity College, where he lived in a beautiful set of rooms in a corner of Nevile's Court. Until failing health intervened it was his custom to entertain scholars and other undergraduates to lunch about once a week in term-time. He died in the Evelyn Nursing Home in Cambridge 4 August 1977.

Paintings of Adrian by Ruskin Spear RA (1953) can be seen in Trinity College and the Physiological Laboratory, Cambridge; another by A. R. Middleton Todd is at the Royal Society of London; and a fourth, by (Sir) Lawrence Gowing, is at the University of Leicester. There is a bronze head by F. E. McWilliam in the library of Trinity College, Cambridge.

[A. L. Hodgkin in *Biographical Memoirs of Fellows of the Royal Society*, vol. xxv, 1979.]

A. L. Hodgkin

ALBERY, Sir BRONSON JAMES (1881–1971), theatre director, was born at Greenhithe, Kent, 6 March 1881, the second in the family of three sons of James Albery [q.v.], dramatist, and his wife, Mary Moore, actress, afterwards Lady Wyndham [q.v.]. He was called after the American dramatist, Bronson Howard. His father died when he was eight and he and his two brothers were brought up by their mother, who returned to the stage when James Albery was no longer able to write. He was educated at Uppingham and Balliol College, Oxford, where he obtained a second class in modern history in 1903. He was called to the bar at the Inner Temple in 1904 but his legal career was brief (though the intricacies of theatrical contracts would never defeat him).

His first theatrical venture, with Allan Aynesworth at the Criterion in 1914, was Cyril Harcourt's comedy, *A Pair of Silk Stockings*; they put on two other plays that year. The war, in which he served in the Royal Naval Volunteer Reserve from 1917 to 1919, ended, for the time being, his connection with the theatre which he resumed in 1920 with a revival, at the Kingsway, of *The Knight of the Burning Pestle* by Francis Beaumont and John Fletcher [qq.v.]. In this production by (Sir) Nigel Playfair [q.v.] (which originated at the Birmingham Repertory Theatre) and ran for ninety-seven performances, the very young (Sir) Noel Coward [q.v.] surprisingly played the grocer's apprentice.

From his mother Bronson Albery inherited his business sense; for, although primarily a *comédienne*, it was her drive that led Sir Charles Wyndham [q.v.] to enlarge his theatrical empire—which began at the Criterion—and to build Wyndham's in 1899 and the New in 1903 (renamed the Albery in 1973). Mary Moore had played in *David Garrick* with Charles Wyndham in many revivals, so it was understandable that Bronson Albery's next choice of production should be a musical version of the play at the Queen's in 1922. He would now be of great help to his mother in the running of the three family theatres, and in 1922 (Sir) Lewis Casson and (Dame) Sybil Thorndike [q.v.] began their association with him. Sybil Thorndike's performance in *The Cenci* at a special matinée at the New convinced G. B. Shaw [q.v.] that she would be perfect for Saint Joan. With some misgivings, as it had a long cast and was, unfashionably, a costume play, in 1924 Albery agreed to do *Saint Joan* which presently broke all existing records at the theatre.

When he found the family theatres' atmosphere restricting, he was glad to help to establish the Arts Theatre Club in 1927. Nor was he obsessively commercial; when he saw the Compagnie des Quinze at the Vieux-Colombier in Paris, he decided that discerning London audiences should be given a chance to see these actors. In 1931 he brought them, in *Noë*, to the Arts and then to the Ambassador's realizing, as he told W. A. Darlington [q.v.] that 'the venture must lose'. After his mother's death in that year, he and Wyndham's son, Howard, were in joint command of the three theatres. From the Arts he transferred to the Criterion in 1932 Ronald Mackenzie's *Musical Chairs*, with (Sir) John Gielgud. This was the beginning of an association that would do much for both actor and manager. During his years at the New—in *Richard of Bordeaux*, *Hamlet*, *Romeo and Juliet*, *Noah*, and *The Seagull*—Gielgud built his unchallenged position, and Albery would be regarded as a manager of distinction and taste. Though after 1935 they no longer worked together, they remained friends; Gielgud had always found 'Bronnie' encouraging and never unduly interfering, but he was also shrewd enough to withdraw from the production of a play (by Emlyn Williams) in which Gielgud appeared and which ran a week.

During World War II while the New Theatre housed the Old Vic Company in seasons of classical acting at its best, Albery was joint administrator from 1942 to 1944 with (Sir) Tyrone Guthrie [q.v.]. Thenceforward he would be increasingly a theatre committee man, serving on such bodies as the Arts Council from 1948, the British Council drama advisory committee (1952–61), and the Society of West End Theatre Managers, of which he was president from 1941 to 1945 and 1952 to 1953. As a reader of plays his wife was of great help; perhaps through her influence he presented in 1946 the semi-autobiographical *Red Roses for Me* by Sean O'Casey [q.v.]. His manner was quiet; he gave an impression of shyness, though at the Garrick Club he was a popular member and a particularly keen bridge player. He was knighted in 1949 and was a chevalier of the Legion of Honour. His son Donald succeeded him in management.

He married in 1912 Una Gwynn (died 1981), daughter of Thomas William Rolleston, of Glasshouse, Shinrone, the Irish scholar, poet, and friend of W. B. Yeats [q.v.]. They had two sons and two daughters. Albery died in London, 21 July 1971.

[*The Times*, 22 July 1971; family papers; Wendy Trewin, *All on Stage, Charles Wyndham and the Alberys*, 1980; personal knowledge.]

Wendy Trewin

ALEXANDER, (CONEL) HUGH (O'DONEL) (1909–1974), chess master and civil servant, was born in Cork 19 April 1909, the eldest of four children and elder son of Conel William Long Alexander, professor of engineering at the University of Cork in Southern Ireland, and his wife, Hilda Barbara Bennett, of Birmingham. His younger brother became a doctor of medicine and one of his younger sisters a nun. On his father's death the family moved to Birmingham and the early years of Alexander's chess career are associated with that city. He attended King Edward's School which sent him to play in the British Boys Championship at Hastings in 1926, none of the stronger players being available. In fact he won the championship and it was not long before he was recognized as one of the future hopes of British chess.

In 1928 he went up to King's College, Cambridge, on a mathematics scholarship and signalled his arrival by winning a most brilliant game on third board in the match with Oxford University. By 1931 he was playing with great success on top board for Cambridge. He won eleven games in succession, losing only to Harry Golombek in an inter-university match that year. This meeting was the start of a firm friendship; another close friend was (Sir) P. Stuart Milner-Barry who had preceded Alexander on first board at Cambridge. These three were to be the young vanguard of British chess for the next fifteen years.

In 1932 Alexander came second in a small international tournament at Cambridge and was also second in the British Championship tournament. Leaving the university with a first class honours degree (1931) he failed to gain the star indicating special distinction and therefore also did not get a fellowship. This he rightly attributed to his spending too much time on chess. But that he was highly gifted as a mathematician was shown by the remark by Professor G. H. Hardy [q.v.] that he was the only genuine mathematician he knew who did not become one.

In 1932 Alexander went to teach mathematics at Winchester where he remained for the next six years. He continued to play chess, both nationally and internationally. During this period he met and married (in 1934) an Australian girl, Enid Constance Crichton, daughter of Ronald William Neate, sea captain. They had two sons, the elder of whom, Michael, joined the Diplomatic Service and was appointed British ambassador in Austria in 1982.

By now he was making a name for himself internationally. He played with success for England in the biennial international team tournaments, scoring the highest percentage for his side, albeit on bottom board, at Folkestone in 1933 and rising to first board at Buenos Aires in 1939. He also played regularly at the Hastings Christmas congresses and came equal second with Paul Keres ahead of some of the world's best players at Hastings in 1938. In that year too he won the British Championship.

He then left Winchester in 1938 to become head of personnel in the John Lewis Partnership in London, a change he enjoyed since, as he himself said, it was a relief to deal with adult minds. A new and vitally important change in his career came with the outbreak of war in 1939 when he joined the Government Code and Cipher School at Bletchley Park. He was given the task of breaking German naval codes, a problem exactly suited to his keen and vivid intelligence. Soon he was in charge of the whole operation and his two friends, Stuart Milner-Barry and Harry Golombek, who were also working at Bletchley, testified to the drive and skill with which he helped to win the battle of the Atlantic.

After the war Alexander was appointed OBE (1946), a somewhat insufficient recognition for the great services he had done, though subsequently he was appointed CBE (1955) and, when he eventually retired in 1970, CMG.

Meanwhile he scored a number of successes in the chess field. He was first at Hastings 1946–7 and joint first with the Soviet grand master, David Bronstein, in Hastings in 1953. There were many fine results too in the post-war chess olympiads. But gradually the demands of his profession (for most of the period from the end of the war until his retirement he was in charge of research and development at the Government Communications Headquarters at Cheltenham) lessened his participation in chess events.

When he retired from the Foreign Office he concentrated on writing about the game. He wrote some excellent books on chess and was chess correspondent of the *Sunday Times*, *Financial Times*, *Evening News*, and *Spectator*. He was about to set out for Iceland to report the Spassky–Fischer match in 1972 when he was smitten by what seemed a mortal illness. After a short respite he collapsed and died at Cheltenham 15 February 1974.

Hugh Alexander had a most vivid and attractive personality. A magnificent talker, he loved to argue but was ever ready to see his opponent's point of view. He had a razor-keen intelligence and the only chance of succeeding in an argument against him lay in placing the subject matter in fields of which he had not an expert knowledge. An amateur all his life, had it not been for World War II he might well have aspired to the World Championship title.

The following game was won by Alexander in the European zonal tournament at Hilversum in 1947. His opponent, the Hungarian grandmaster Laszlo Szabo, was one of the world's leading players at the time.

White Alexander Black L. Szabo Sicilian Defence

1 P–K4 P–QB4. 2 N–KB3 N–QB3. 3 P–Q4 PxP. 4 NxP N–B3. 5 N–QB3 P–Q3. 6 B–K2 P–

K3. 7 B–K3 Q–B2. 8 P–B4 P–QR3. 9 O–O N–QR4. 10 K–R1 B–K2. 11 Q–K1 N–B5. 12 B–B1 O–O. 13 P–QN3 N–QR4. 14 B–Q3 N–Q2. 15 B–N2 B–B3. 16 N–B3 N–B4. 17 P–K5 NxB. 18 PxN PxP. 19 PxP B–K2. 20 N–K4 Q–Q1. 21 N–B6 ch PxN. 22 Q–N3 ch K–R1. 23 PxP BxP. 24 N–K5 BxN. 25 BxB ch P–B3. 26 RxP, resigns.

[Harry Golombek, *The Encyclopedia of Chess*, 1977; Sir Stuart Milner-Barry, 'Memoir' in *The Best Games of C.H. O'D. Alexander* by Harry Golombek and W. R. Hartson, 1976; private information; personal knowledge.]

HARRY GOLOMBEK

ALLEN, NORMAN PERCY (1903–1972), metallurgist, was born in Wrexham, north Wales, 5 June 1903, the fifth of ten children, seven girls and three boys, of Sidney Edward Allen, an accountant in the borough treasurer's department at Wrexham, and his wife, Emily Eliza Davis. He was educated at Burton-upon-Trent Boys' Grammar School from 1913 to 1920. He was awarded the prestigious Linley open scholarship at Sheffield University, studied metallurgy there under Professor C. H. Desch, and graduated with a second class honours degree in 1923. After a two-year spell in the university working on low-melting-point zinc base die-casting alloys, he joined Swansea University College in 1925, to work on the porosity of copper and copper alloys. There he met Olive Gwendolen Williams, his future wife. She was a native of Swansea where her father, J. H. Williams, was a tinplate and metal merchant. In 1928 Allen joined Birmingham University as assistant lecturer, and he was married in 1929. There were two sons and one daughter of the marriage.

At Birmingham Allen studied the mechanism responsible for the porosity of commercial 'tough pitch' copper. Allen showed that this was related to the presence of hydrogen in the melt in thermodynamical equilibrium with copper oxide present, and that on solidification this would lead to the evolution of hydrogen gas or steam, forming small blowholes. On the basis of this work Allen was awarded the D.Sc. degree by Birmingham University in 1934.

In 1933 Allen joined the Mond Nickel research laboratory in Birmingham, where he remained till 1944. He was second in command to Dr L. B. Pfeil. Apart from his administrative duties for the research programme as a whole, he was involved in a major research project on the transformation characteristics of low alloy steels, in particular on the effect of alloying elements such as nickel and chromium which enabled steel to be hardened in thick sections on cooling from high temperature; this helped to economize on these strategic elements which were in short supply during the war. From 1939 he and his colleagues developed the Nimonic alloys suitable for high temperature applications in gas turbines. These alloys transformed the Whittle engine into practical reality, and even today remain the standard blading material for many aircraft and land-based gas turbine installations throughout the world. Allen made a major contribution to the speed with which these alloys became available for exploitation by engine designers.

In 1944 Allen joined the National Physical Laboratory as superintendent of the metallurgy division, and initiated a 'good mix' of programmes, ranging from the academic to the applied. While he was conversant with the whole of the work going on, he was personally involved with a number of the projects. In 1963 Allen initiated the 'superconductivity project', aimed at promoting the application of superconductors in industry.

The NPL was also very much involved in the development of materials for high temperature service. Systematic studies were carried out in the division on creep of Nimonic alloys for gas turbines, and on a variety of alloys used in power station components—for example, superheater tubes and steam pipes. These careful and objective researches were a major factor which enabled the turbine designer to increase continually the size, operating temperature, and efficiency of the turbine units.

Following the catastrophic failures of certain welded ships during the war, a long-term investigation was initiated in 1946 under Allen's leadership, to determine the effects of alloying elements on the mechanical properties of pure iron. This work contributed significantly to improved steel-making procedures in the late 1950s, and to our understanding of the complex mechanical properties.

In 1966 Allen was appointed deputy director of the NPL and until he retired at the end of 1967 was concerned with the administrative changes needed in the formation of the materials group which absorbed the metallurgy division. He received many honours, including election to the Royal Society in 1956, the Bessemer medal of the Iron and Steel Institute in 1965, and the Platinum medal of the Institute of Metals in 1967. He was president of the Institution of Metallurgists in 1961–2, was made an honorary fellow of the Institute of Metals in 1971, and was appointed CB in 1966. He had honorary doctorates from Prague (1964) and Sheffield (1966).

Allen was short and stockily built and his face was notable for the bushy eyebrows, the owlish glasses, and an ever-present smile. He was full of energy, and worked at a pace which his staff sometimes found difficult to match. He was very good at stating a case, and he appeared to enjoy an argument. He was conscientious and a very hard worker, who set high standards. He did not tolerate anything slipshod in experimental work or argument. At home he took a full interest in his family and their development. He enjoyed walking and gardening and in his later years became an enthusiastic amateur painter.

Allen died suddenly, 23 February 1972, at 10 Firlands, Weybridge, Surrey, when influenza brought on the failure of an already weakened heart.

[Sir Charles Sykes in *Biographical Memoirs of Fellows of the Royal Society*, vol. xix, 1973; *The Times*, 26 February 1972; personal knowledge.] P. B. HIRSCH

AMPTHILL, third BARON (1896–1973), naval officer and company director. [See RUSSELL, JOHN HUGO.]

ANDERSON, SIR DONALD FORSYTH (1906–1973), shipowner and chairman of the Peninsular & Oriental Steam Navigation Company (P & O), was born in London 3 September 1906, the younger son and second of the four children of (Sir) Alan Garrett Anderson [q.v.], a partner in the family shipping firm Anderson, Green & Co., managers of the Orient Line, and his wife, Muriel Ivy, daughter of G. W. Duncan, of Richmond, Surrey. He was educated at Eton and at Trinity College, Oxford, where he graduated with a third class in modern history in 1928. He joined the family firm in the same year. In 1934 he transferred to P & O, majority shareholders in Orient Line, and was appointed an assistant manager in 1936.

On the outbreak of war in September 1939 Anderson moved to the Ministry of Shipping (subsequently the Ministry of War Transport). In 1941 he joined the British Merchant Shipping Mission to the United States in Washington. He returned to P & O as a member of the board in June 1943, becoming a managing director in 1946, deputy chairman in 1950, and chairman (in succession to Sir William Currie, q.v.) in 1960. He retired from the P & O board on his sixty-fifth birthday in September 1971.

His years at P & O saw fundamental change in the company. Pre-war it was largely a passenger liner concern with a large number of free-standing and self-sufficient subsidiaries. After the dramatic losses of the years 1939–45, and the rebuilding of the late 1940s, Anderson was the main progenitor of a Group programme of tanker building decided on in 1955 which was followed, under his chairmanship, by similar programmes for bulk and oil/bulk/ore carriers, bringing existing Group subsidiaries into closer co-operation and creating new companies. The P & O Group fleet spread into almost every aspect of shipping, though Anderson was much more restrained where expansion into non-shipping business was concerned.

Co-operation with other British shipping concerns was a feature of Anderson's management. He played a leading role in the creation of Overseas Containers Ltd., a consortium of P & O, Ocean Steam Ship, Furness Withy, and British & Commonwealth. This established a radically new international cargo-handling infrastructure beyond the financial capabilities of any one line.

Anderson, to quote from his obituary notice in *The Times*, was 'probably the outstanding shipping man of his generation'. His activities beyond the confines of P & O were considerable. He was chairman of the British Shipping Federation, president of the International Shipping Federation, and joint chairman of the National Maritime Board (all 1950–62); president of the Chamber of Shipping (1953–4); president of the Institute of Shipping and Forwarding Agents (1955); president of the Institute of Marine Engineers (1956–7); chairman of the British Liner Committee (1956–8); president of the Institute of Export (1961–3); and a member of the Shipping Advisory Panel to the Minister of Transport (1962–4).

Anderson was also active in business beyond the world of shipping. He was a director of the Bank of Australasia (later Australia and New Zealand Banking Group), 1936–73; of the National Provincial Bank (later the National Westminster Bank), 1944–73; and of Times Newspapers Ltd., 1967–73.

Away from the City he carried on a family medical tradition (his grandmother was Elizabeth Garrett Anderson [q.v.], the first woman to qualify as a doctor in England) in serving as treasurer and in 1964–73 as chairman of the council of the Royal Free Hospital School of Medicine. He was also a member of the governing body of the London Graduate School of Business Studies.

But Anderson's commercial life was entirely dedicated to the P & O Company and to its development and success. He pursued that objective with single-mindedness and devotion and he combined foresight and penetrating logic with a considerable intellect. These characteristics could, at times, be both disconcerting and misunderstood by those who did not share his broad view. His achievements were formidable and his stature was internationally recognized.

Tall and patrician in appearance, Anderson was positive and strong in his approach to any problem and incisive in his decision-taking. He was rather reserved and consequently appeared somewhat aloof in manner, but he was excellent company with those whom he knew and a good after-dinner speaker with a keen wit. He was at heart a countryman, interested in all aspects of country life, particularly his sizeable farm in Gloucestershire. His principal leisure pursuit was hunting and he was a good horseman. Anyone who went to his house at Notgrove could not fail to be impressed by the close family atmosphere.

Anderson was knighted in 1954. Already an officer of the Order of Orange Nassau in 1946, he became a commendatore of the Order Al Meritio della Repubblica Italiana in 1959. He was created a deputy lieutenant for the county of Gloucester in 1969. He was also an honorary captain RNR, and honorary member of the Honourable Company of Master Mariners (1964), an elder brother of Trinity House (1965), and an honorary brother of Hull Trinity House.

In 1935 he married Margaret Elaine, daughter of Sir David Richard Llewellyn, first baronet, colliery chairman; they had four daughters. Anderson died in Oxford 20 March 1973.

A portrait by Derek Hill is in the City offices of P & O.

[P & O records; private information; personal knowledge.] INCHCAPE

ANDERSON, DAME KITTY (1903–1979), headmistress and chairman of the Girls' Public Day School Trust, was born 4 July 1903 in St. Anne's, Lancashire, the only daughter and eldest of three children of John Herbert Anderson FCA, and his wife, Lizzie Dawson. Her father moved from St. Anne's to Middlesbrough as a chartered accountant in private practice. From the High School for Girls, Saltburn-by-the-Sea, where she was head girl, Kitty Anderson went on to Royal Holloway College, London, the first girl from the school ever to win a university place. There she read history. In 1925 she went to the London Day Training College, and took a teacher's diploma. She had always wanted to teach, and indeed had announced her intention of becoming a headmistress on her first day at high school. In 1926 she took a post at a coeducational school in Hull, Craven Street Secondary School, but in 1930 she went back to Royal Holloway, as Christie scholar, to work for a Ph.D. in Elizabethan history. She received her doctorate in 1933.

Her next teaching post was at Burlington School, London, an old charitable foundation. There she very soon became second mistress. At the beginning of the war, in September 1939, she left to become headmistress of King's Norton Grammar School, Birmingham. At first the school was divided between Birmingham and Gloucestershire, half of the girls and staff being evacuated. Kitty Anderson had to divide her time between the two parts of the school. Nevertheless she was well known, as headmistress, not only for her excellent history teaching, but also for giving to the school a sense of unity and purpose. She stayed at King's Norton for five years, and then in 1944 became head of the North London Collegiate School, a direct grant girls' school, and there she stayed until her retirement.

During her twenty years at North London she became an outstanding figure in the educational world. She was a member of the Carr–Saunders committee on education for commerce from 1946 to 1949; president of the Association of Headmistresses from 1954 to 1956, and a member of the National Advisory Council for the Training and Supply of Teachers from 1953 to 1961. She was a member of the University Grants Committee (1959–61) and of the committee on higher education chaired by Lord Robbins (1961–3). In 1966 she became a member of the public schools commission, under the chairmanship of (Sir) John Newsom [q.v.]. This was a committee set up by government with an explicitly political task: 'To advise on the best way of integrating the public schools with the state system of education . . . and to create a socially mixed entry into the schools, in order to reduce the divisive influence which they now exert.' Much as Kitty Anderson enjoyed the work on this committee, travelling round with congenial colleagues to visit various schools, the terms of reference can never have pleased her. For she aimed always, as far as possible, to separate party politics from education. And when the first report was published, in 1968, she, with two colleagues, T. E. B. Howarth and John Davies [q.v.], signed a minority report. The committee as a whole, they argued, had concentrated too exclusively on the social divisiveness of public schools, taking social reform as their first priority. They had lost sight of two major educational goals: the provision of boarding education, and educational provision for the less able. The courage of refusing to sign the report was typical of Kitty Anderson, and the clearly stated grounds of her refusal equally characteristic. She was above everything interested in education, and she did not regard education as a kind of social manipulation.

When, in 1965, she retired from the North London Collegiate, of which she had been an outstanding headmistress, despite her public commitments, she became chairman of the GPDST. No more happy appointment could have been made. She now had twenty-three direct grant schools to look after. In 1965 the political threat to the direct grant system was just apparent. She was its greatest defender. She took an astonishingly well-informed interest in individual schools, and became the friend and adviser of each of their headmistresses.

Kitty Anderson was small and birdlike, full of energy, and a great talker. Words and laughter seemed to bubble out of her. But she also had the gift of instant sympathy, so that people readily confided in her. They always felt better for it. Not only was she sensible, but reassuringly firm in her beliefs. All her life she took pleasure in a wide variety of things, including clothes, and school plays and concerts. It was this enthusiasm that made her both a great teacher and a valued friend.

Kitty Anderson was appointed DBE in 1961. She became an honorary fellow of the College of Preceptors in 1966 and received an honorary LL D from Hull (1967) and a D.Univ. from York (1971). She retired from the trust, her health by now failing, in 1975. She went back to live in Yorkshire, and died in Northallerton 15 January 1979.

[*The Times*, 23 November 1979; North London Collegiate *School Magazine*; Friends of the GPDST *Newsletter*, 1979; personal knowledge.] MARY WARNOCK

ANDRADE, EDWARD NEVILLE DA COSTA (1887–1971), physicist, was born in London 27 December 1887, the second child in the family of four sons and one daughter of Henry da Costa Andrade, a solicitor, of London, and his wife, Amy Eliza Davis. In 1897 he went to St. Dunstan's College, Catford, where he was strongly encouraged by his headmaster, C. M. Stuart, who had been a research scientist. A scholarship took Andrade in 1905 to study physics under F. T. Trouton at University College, London, where he gained first class honours in physics in 1907. He stayed on to do research on the flow of solid metals under stress, a subject which remained a lifelong interest for him. His first paper, 'On the viscous flow in metals, and allied phenomena', published in the *Proceedings* of the Royal Society in 1910, was a landmark in the science of the mechanical properties of solids.

An 1851 Exhibition scholarship took Andrade in 1910 to Heidelberg, to work under Philipp Lenard and Carl Ramsauer on the electrical properties of flames. This year in Germany was a supremely happy time for him, where in the light-hearted company of Ramsauer and other friends, Andrade enjoyed the coffee-shops, inns, and weekends in the countryside, as well as very active science. He took his Ph.D. at Heidelberg in 1911, returned to England, and then in 1913 set off for Manchester to study under Ernest Rutherford (later Lord Rutherford of Nelson, q.v.). There he began to work on the measurement of the wavelength of gamma rays from radium, but the outbreak of war took him away in 1914 to become an officer (eventually a captain) in the Royal Garrison Artillery. He served in France in 1915–17 and was mentioned in dispatches. From 1917 he worked in munitions. At the end of the war he was awarded a D.Sc. of London University. On Rutherford's recommendation in 1920 Andrade became professor of physics at the Ordnance College, Woolwich (later the Military College of Science); and then in 1928 Quain professor of physics at University College, London. So began the main central period of his scientific life, when he built up and sustained for many years an outstanding research school in the physics of solids and liquids, which produced many classic papers on the growth and plastic glide of metal single crystals, on the origin of cracks in glass, and on the viscosity of liquids. In 1923 he published *The Structure of the Atom*, which ran to several editions. He was elected into the fellowship of the Royal Society in 1935 and his many students included such well-known figures as Francis Crick and Leonard Rotherham. He also had strong literary interests which brought him into contact with T. S. Eliot, W. Somerset Maugham, and Walter de la Mare [qq.v.]. He wrote and published poetry, and began a second major career as a historian of science, especially of the work of Robert Hooke [q.v.], and as a collector of historic scientific books.

Much of his time in World War II was taken up with work for the Ministry of Supply, where he became known as an 'inverted Micawber'—waiting for something to turn down—in the face of all the odd inventions that were then flooding into the Ministry for his attention. But he also found time to appear on the BBC Brains Trust, with C. E. M. Joad [q.v.] and Commander A. B. Campbell, which he greatly enjoyed. After the war he returned at first to his science at University College, but then in 1950 accepted a directorship in the Royal Institution. This was an unfortunate appointment for him and a series of bitter disputes led him to resign in 1952.

After this he returned to his researches on the flow of metals, working from 1957 as a senior research fellow at Imperial College, where he continued at full pace. Even in the weeks immediately before his death he was busy drafting a paper for the Royal Society describing his latest results. The flow of matter remained his major lifelong scientific interest and he produced some remarkable mathematical expressions which represent these processes much as Hooke's Law represents elastic deformation. The discovery of these mathematical equations of viscosity and creep must have been a great satisfaction to him, not least because Robert Hooke was the admired hero in Andrade's own memorable Wilkins lecture, given before the Royal Society in 1949.

Known as 'Percy' to many in the scientific world, Andrade was of smallish build, very neat, and always impeccably dressed in a fairly formal style. He enjoyed dinner parties, provided that the wines were excellent, and was a most witty, occasionally sharp-tongued, conversationalist.

Andrade received an honorary LL D from Edinburgh (1950) and honorary D.Scs. from Durham (1952) and Manchester (1956). He was a chevalier of the Legion of Honour. From 1943 to 1945 he was president of the Physical Society. He was the editor for physics for the fourteenth edition of the *Encyclopaedia Britannica* and from 1945 to 1952 was science correspondent of *The Times*.

In 1917 Andrade married Katherine Barbara, daughter of Thomas T. Evans, a tea merchant in Manchester. They had two sons, Trevor John, who became a group captain in the RAF, and Edward Anthony, a doctor of medicine, who died in a car accident in 1967. Andrade's first marriage broke up in 1936 and in 1938 he married (Kathleen) Mona, daughter of W. D. Martin and widow of Clennell Anstruther Wilkinson, the biographer and great friend of Andrade who had died in 1936. Andrade died in a nursing home in London 6 June 1971.

[Alan Cottrell in *Biographical Memoirs of Fellows of the Royal Society*, vol. xviii, 1972; private information; personal knowledge.]

ALAN COTTRELL

ANDREWS, SIR (WILLIAM) LINTON (1886–1972), newspaper editor, was born 27 May 1886 in Hull, Yorkshire, the youngest of the four children (three sons and one daughter) of William Andrews, author, editor, and librarian of the Royal Institution, Hull, and his wife, Jeanie Leslie Carnie (died 1892). In 1895 William Andrews married Jennie Straker (died 1902). Linton Andrews was educated at Hull Grammar School and at Christ's Hospital. He wrote leader-page articles for the press while still at school. The classical master at Christ's Hospital wanted him to take holy orders and was disappointed when he turned his back on an academic course; but he was eager to enter journalism and at sixteen joined the staff of the *Eastern Morning News* in Hull. Even so, he never lost his love of the classics.

From Hull he moved to Huddersfield and later to Sheffield, where he became a reporter on the *Sheffield Telegraph*. He contributed to other journals, including the *Globe* and the *Echo*, and by the time he was twenty he had saved enough to enable him to spend a year studying and working as a free lance in Paris. When he returned to England, it was as a leader writer on the *Sheffield Evening Mail*. Thereafter he worked in Portsmouth, Nottingham, London, and Dundee before joining up in the first week of World War I. Throughout that struggle he served with the 4th battalion of the Black Watch. While fighting on the western front he kept up a stream of articles as an unofficial war correspondent. His soldier's description of the battle of Neuve Chapelle won the attention of Lord Northcliffe [q.v.]. This led to a staff appointment on the *Daily Mail* after the war.

He spent five important years on the *Daily Mail*. Then, in 1923, he returned to his native Yorkshire to edit the *Leeds Mercury*, which had just been bought by the Yorkshire Conservative Newspaper Company, owners of the *Yorkshire Post*. In his hands the *Mercury* reflected his keen interest in affairs and in the life of the region. Almost daily he wrote a personal commentary—'It Seems to Me' by W.L.A.

Throughout the war he had kept a diary, which helped to provide material for a book, *Haunting Years* (1930), a vivid account of his experiences serving with his unit through the ordeal of the battle of the Somme and the third battle of Ypres. Two light books during his years as editor of the *Mercury* were *Wayside Pageant* (1933), in which he collaborated with A. P. Maguire, and *Yorkshire Folk* (1935), an engaging analysis of the county character. After his retirement he wrote other books, including *Problems of an Editor* (1962) and *Linton Andrews, the Autobiography of a Journalist* (1964).

In 1939 the *Leeds Mercury* was merged with the *Yorkshire Post*, which had been edited with courage and distinction for twenty years by Arthur Mann [q.v.]. To Linton Andrews fell the task of knitting together two papers that were markedly different in style and tradition. Could the combined paper satisfy two such disparate readerships? The answer came in a circulation substantially exceeding those of both papers added together.

To the *Yorkshire Post*, with its long record of independence of spirit, Andrews added his own personal touch: his lively response to news, his liking for people and for keeping in close contact with his readers, his fairness of mind and love of close, but never acrimonious, argument. He was conscious of the reputation the *Yorkshire Post* had gained as a great, influential paper of opinion, and he strove constantly to maintain this reputation. Two of the qualities that made him an outstanding editor were public spirit and tireless industry. He was utterly dedicated to the work of seeking out the truth and interpreting it to his readers. He watched Parliamentary reports jealously to ensure that they presented the arguments used by all sides.

He was assiduous also in keeping in touch with political leaders. In a tribute after his death, Lord Butler of Saffron Walden wrote of his own frequent contacts with him over the years, and added: 'I knew no editor in whom I could put greater trust than Linton Andrews'. Sir Winston Churchill described him as 'a great and justly respected editor'.

Despite the heavy preoccupations of editorship, he found time to serve many good causes, regional and national. In particular, he worked strenuously for the raising of newspaper standards and the education and welfare of journalists. He was a founder of the Guild of British Newspaper Editors, of which he became president (1952–3). He played a leading part in devising the scheme for the training of junior journalists; he was described as the 'father' of this scheme. He campaigned for the establishment of a Press Council; and, when that Council was formed, he became its first vice-chairman and later served as chairman from 1955 to 1959. Over the years he filled many other offices. He was president of the Institute of Journalists (1946), chairman of the editorial committee of the Newspaper Society (1943–50), chairman of the council of the Brontë Society (1940–70), a member of the court and council of Leeds University (1943–59), and a devoted worker for cancer research. He wrote several biographical articles for this Dictionary.

For his services to his profession and in other fields he was knighted in 1954; and, a year later, Leeds University made him an honorary LL D. In 1967 he was honoured with a D.Litt. by Emerson College, USA.

In 1915 he married Gertrude (died 1958), eldest daughter of Alexander Douglas, of Dundee, director of a timber firm, and step-daughter of James Kenyon, a grain merchant in India. There were no children of the marriage. Andrews died in Leeds 27 September 1972.

[W. L. Andrews, *Linton Andrews, the Autobiography of a Journalist*, 1964; personal knowledge.] W. T. OLIVER

ANTRIM, eighth EARL OF (1911–1977), chairman of the National Trust. [See MCDONNELL, RANDAL JOHN SOMERLED.]

ARDIZZONE, EDWARD JEFFERY IRVING (1900–1979), artist, illustrator, and author, was born 16 October 1900 at Haiphong in (then) French Indo-China. He was the eldest child of Auguste Ardizzone, a Frenchman of Italian parentage, who was an employee of the Eastern Extension Telegraph Company, married to Margaret, the daughter of Edward Alexander Irving, assistant colonial secretary at Singapore. Margaret's mother was born Christianna Margaret Kirby, and unsubstantiated family tradition traces her back to John Joshua Kirby [q.v.]. Auguste and Margaret Ardizzone had four further children, two daughters and two sons, all French by birth; Edward Ardizzone became a naturalized Englishman in 1922.

Brought to England in 1905, Ardizzone spent his childhood in East Anglia at various residences, often under the charge of his maternal grandmother. His early schooling was at East Bergholt and the junior division of Ipswich Grammar School, and in 1912, when the family moved to Wokingham, he became a boarder at Clayesmore School. This slightly unorthodox, undenominational school has been seen as an odd choice for one who was brought up, and remained, a Roman Catholic, but it was here that his growing interest in drawing and painting was encouraged. Furthermore, his housemaster, the writer and connoisseur Desmond Coke, was later to play a useful role in helping him to find commissions as a free-lance artist.

After leaving school in 1918 Ardizzone spent six months at a college of commerce and for several years he worked as a clerk. His lengthiest employment was with the Eastern Telegraph Company in London, where his father had bought a house at 130 Elgin Avenue which was to become the family home for over fifty years, figuring frequently in Ardizzone's illustrations and on the personal Christmas cards which he liked to design. During his period of clerkship he attended evening classes at the Westminster School of Art, devoting his weekends to painting, and in 1926 he gave up his job to concentrate upon a career as a professional artist. In 1929 he married Catherine Josephine Berkley, the daughter of William Cuthbert Anderson, who was chief auditor of the Great Indian Peninsular Railway. They had two sons and a daughter.

In the years up to 1939 Ardizzone worked hard as both painter and graphic artist. In a series of one-man shows, first at the Bloomsbury Gallery and then at the Leger, his very personal, domestic vision received considerable praise. Working chiefly in his favourite medium of water-colour, but also in oils and lithography (for monochrome prints), he celebrated the local life of his quarter of London: recreations in its parks and along the Regent canal, the bonhomie of its pubs and its night-life. He brought to these scenes a mixture of affection, wit, and gentle satire which places him firmly in the tradition of Thomas Rowlandson [q.v.].

His deep appreciation of the values of narrative art is reflected too in his illustrations of this period: the lengthy suite of pen-drawings for his first major commission *In a Glass Darkly* by J. Sheridan Le Fanu (1929), drawings for the *Radio Times* (which, with *Punch*, was to be a regular source of income), advertising copy for the whisky merchants Johnnie Walker, and picture books which he wrote and illustrated himself. The first of these, *Little Tim and the Brave Sea Captain* (1936), arose from stories told to his own family. It draws on memories of the harbour at Ipswich and upon his liking for ships and the sea, and in its bold integration of word and picture it stands out as one of the most significant picture-books of the age. (It was too an early example of colour offset lithography, its spacious folios being printed in the United States, where the text was hand-lettered by Grace Allen Hogarth, an editor at the Oxford University Press's New York office.)

At the start of the war in 1939 Ardizzone was serving in an anti-aircraft regiment but in 1940 he was appointed an official war artist and was attached to the British Army's GHQ at Arras. A published record of his experiences during the German invasion of France is to be found in his book *Baggage to the Enemy* (1941), just as his further work during the North African and Italian campaigns is recorded in his *Diary of a War Artist* (1974). Nearly three hundred water-colours from this time are housed at the Imperial War Museum.

After the war Ardizzone resumed his free-lance career with great energy. He regularly exhibited drawings, water-colours, and lithographs at the Leicester Gallery and at the gallery of his friend Freddy Mayor; he undertook a variety of commissions, ranging from a water-colour portrait of Sir Winston Churchill to a notable series of covers for the *Strand* magazine, and advertising brochures for Ealing Studios and Messrs Guinness; and he illustrated nearly two hundred books, winning the Library Association's Kate Greenaway medal in 1957 for *Tim All Alone* (1956). His chosen medium for these varied from the line and wash drawings which he made for his own picture-books, to pure line, as in his intensely imagined drawings for poems by Walter de la Mare [q.v.] and by his friend James Reeves, and to more elaborate processes, such as the lithographs and stencilled drawings done for the Limited Editions Club of New York.

The foundation for this prolific output was Ardizzone's complete mastery of the drawn line. Although he claimed that 'the born illustrator' should work from copies rather than from life, the existence of some fifty-three sketch-books testifies to his continuous dedication to catching with his pen the significant moments of the life around him. Out of such constant practice there grew a body of finished work that pictures with grace and with a deceptive ease the scenes and incidents of anything from mechanized war to a child's dream of toyland. Only towards the end of his life was there any slackening of his fluent control of the drawn line.

In addition to his creative work Ardizzone served as an instructor in graphic design at the Camberwell School of Art. Then, after a tour of south India for Unesco in 1952, training students in silk-screen printing, he became visiting tutor in etching and lithography at the Royal College of Art. Such variety of occupation was congenial to him, for (despite the hours devoted to his art) he loved company and was held in much affection by a wide circle of friends. He also loved good food and wine, a taste reflected in his designing of menu covers for restaurants and catalogues for wine-shippers, and in his writing and illustrating wine notes for the Royal College.

In 1960 Ardizzone retired from teaching and began to spend more time in Kent, where he bought a house at Rodmersham Green, and in 1972 he and his wife moved there permanently after selling the house in Elgin Avenue. He had a studio built in his garden and, despite declining health, he continued to work at painting and illustrating down to his death at Rodmersham, 8 November 1979.

Ardizzone was elected ARA in 1962 and RA in 1970, and he served on the hanging committee in 1969 and 1971. Among the many honours he received were CBE in 1971 and Royal Designer for Industry in 1974. Numerous self-portrait sketches and drawings are scattered through his graphic works; there is also a portrait by Henry Carr at the Imperial War Museum, and a self-portrait and a portrait drawing by Brian Robb in the possession of the family.

[E. Ardizzone, 'The Born Illustrator', *Motif*, vol. i, November 1958, and *The Young Ardizzone*, 1970; Brian Alderson, 'Edward Ardizzone, a preliminary hand-list of his illustrated books', *The Private Library*, vol. v, no. 1, spring 1972; Gabriel White, *Edward Ardizzone*, 1979; private information.]

BRIAN ALDERSON

ARMFIELD, MAXWELL ASHBY (1881–1972), artist and writer, was born at Ringwood, Hampshire, 5 October 1881, the eldest of the three children of Joseph John Armfield, a milling engineer, and his wife, Margaret Maxwell, a lineal descendant of the Earls of Nithsdale. The Armfields were a Quaker family and he was educated at the Friends' School at Sidcot and then at Leighton Park near Reading, before going to Birmingham School of Art, then under the direction of E. R. Taylor, a friend of John Ruskin and William Morris [qq.v.]. Entering immediately into the life class he was taught by Henry Payne, who introduced him to the work of Fra Angelico, and Arthur Gaskin, who fired his interest in tempera painting; his first essay in this medium was a painting based on Maeterlinck's *Aglavaine et Sélysette*. During these years he came into contact with the Pre-Raphaelite and Symbolist movements, which, together with such publications as the *Poster*, were to influence him most directly as a decorative painter and illustrator.

In September 1902 he went to Paris, where he enrolled at the Académie de la Grande Chaumière under Courtois and René Menard; he made friends with the sculptor Gaston Lachaise and with Keith Henderson, with whom he and Norman Wilkinson, a fellow student from Birmingham whose notice Armfield was later to write for this Dictionary, shared a studio. During a visit to Italy with Henderson he met Geoffrey Whitworth [q.v.], who described him thus: 'He is very quiet in manner, but at the same time has much dignity. He dresses in black velvet, with a silken orange-red bow tie which he has stencilled with patterns in gold.' At the Paris Salon in autumn 1904 he exhibited 'Faustine', a painting inspired by A. C. Swinburne [q.v.], which was purchased by M. Blanc but given to the Luxembourg.

Returning to London he embarked on the series of one-man and group exhibitions which was to mark his career. At the Rowley Galleries in 1906 he shared an exhibition with Gaston Lachaise, contributing 'A Note on the Revival of Painting in Tempera' to the catalogue, under the pseudonym E. Grant-Stuart; this was the first time he resorted to a pseudonym, though later in life, particularly in the 1940s, when he was to write extensively on eastern religions and mysticism, the subterfuge of public anonymity was to appeal to him greatly. In 1907 he shared an exhibition at The Fine Art Society with other members of the Birmingham Group, including his former teachers Henry Payne and Arthur Gaskin, as well as Joseph Southall, the leading figure of the tempera revival; the same year saw his first exhibit at the New English Art Club.

Armfield's interest in the theatre, which had been fostered by Wilkinson and Whitworth, was reinforced by his marriage on 20 January 1909 to the crippled playwright and author Constance Smedley. She was the daughter of W. T. Smedley, chartered accountant, and Annie Elizabeth Duckworth. From this point until her death on 9 March 1941, Max and Constance worked very much in tandem; *The Flower Book* (1909) was the first fruit of this collaboration, which involved not only the writing and illustrating of books but also a deep involvement with the theatre. From their first home at Minchinhampton they founded the Cotswold Players, then in London the Greenleaf Theatre, and later, in America, the course for community drama and the summer school of theatre at Berkeley, California: in all these projects they tried to revive the spirit of medieval drama as well as to create a new interest in the art of minstrelsy. Constance led him to become a Christian Scientist and to an active involvement in pacifist politics, of which his illustrations to *The Ballet of the Nations* (1915) by Vernon Lee [q.v.] were a direct result.

During these years Armfield wrote several books, most importantly *A Manual of Tempera Painting* (1930), and painting occupied only a limited amount of his time. Later he was to say that his mature style dated from the time of his wife's death; his first major painting from this period, entitled 'Red Tape and Sealing Wax' (1942), depicted a Nijinsky-like nude breaking all bonds and striding off into the unknown. At this time his belief in Christian Science was superseded by an exploration of esoteric eastern religions, and Mrs Baker Eddy's Triadic Law of Category became transformed into a new law, 'Rhythmic Vitality, Form and Colour', which was to govern his approach to painting for the remaining thirty years of his life.

The post-war years were difficult for artists working in a traditional vein. However, he lived long enough to see the revival of interest in the styles to which he had adhered; The Fine Art Society's 'Homage to Maxwell Armfield' exhibition (1970) and ninetieth-birthday exhibition of recent paintings (1971) provided a triumphant culmination to a long and creative life.

There were no children. Armfield died at Warminster, Wiltshire, 23 January 1972. Throughout his life he painted many self-portraits, one of which, dating from 1901, is in Birmingham City Art Gallery.

[Unpublished MS autobiography; Constance Smedley, *Crusaders*, 1929; *The Times*, 25 January 1972; catalogues: 'Homage to Maxwell Armfield', 1970, and 'Maxwell Armfield', 1978; personal knowledge.]

PEYTON SKIPWITH

ARMSTRONG, WILLIAM, BARON ARMSTRONG OF SANDERSTEAD (1915–1980), civil servant and banker, was born in Clapton, London, 3 March 1915, the elder son (there were no daughters) of William Armstrong, of Stirling, a colonel in the Salvation Army, and his wife, Priscilla Hopkins, also a Salvation Army officer. He was educated at Bec School, Tooting, and at Exeter College, Oxford, to which he won an open scholarship. He obtained first classes in both classical honour moderations (1936) and *literae humaniores* (1938).

Armstrong entered the Civil Service as an assistant principal at the Board of Education in 1938, becoming assistant private secretary to the president of the Board of Education in 1940. From 1943 to 1945 he was private secretary to Sir Edward (later Lord) Bridges [q.v.], secretary of the War Cabinet, after which he moved to the Treasury. During the period 1949–53 he served as principal private secretary to three successive chancellors of the Exchequer, Sir R. Stafford Cripps, Hugh Gaitskell [qq.v.], and R. A. Butler (later Lord Butler of Saffron Walden), being responsible on five different occasions for the coordination of the contributions to the budget speech and to a considerable extent for the writing of it. To work so closely with three such different personalities and in addition to accommodate himself to a change of government in 1951 undoubtedly expedited his development as a civil servant and immeasurably broadened his outlook. At the same time Westminster and Whitehall were endeavouring to adjust themselves to the economic and social changes of the post-war world, to the emergence of the first European community, that for coal and steel, and to the increased tension between the Atlantic alliance and the Soviet bloc. It was a testing but exhilarating time for Armstrong to be so close to the centres of power.

He then became under-secretary to the overseas finance division of the Treasury where for four years, from 1953 to 1957, he had to handle external financial problems, in particular those of the sterling balances, after which he moved over to the home finance division until 1958. From then until 1962 he was third secretary and Treasury officer of accounts. When the Treasury was reorganized at the end of this period, Armstrong became joint permanent secretary in charge of economic and financial policy at the early age of forty-seven. It had always been obvious that he was a high-flyer, but even this was exceptionally rapid promotion. Responsible now for both the home and overseas finance divisions of the Treasury, which had been amalgamated, he had to handle the economic problems of the recession and to implement the policy for expanding the economy pursued by Reginald Maudling [q.v.] when he became chancellor of the Exchequer in mid-1962.

The narrow defeat of the Conservative Party at the general election of 1964 and the formation of a Labour government led to the creation of the Department of Economic Affairs. This was the consequence of a widely felt dissatisfaction with the Treasury's handling of economic policy over a number of years. The tension which existed between the new department and the Treasury lasted until the department's abolition in 1969. Within a few weeks of taking office the government found itself facing a major financial crisis which was very largely a crisis of confidence. The governor of the Bank of England, Lord Cobbold, working closely with Armstrong, managed through the other central banks to mobilize the funds necessary to stabilize the situation.

In 1968 Armstrong was appointed head of the Home Civil Service and when the department at the Treasury responsible for the management of the Service was hived off to become the Civil Service Department he became its first permanent secretary. After more than twenty years' intensive activity at the Treasury during which he suffered not a little stress and strain, he was able to use his immense knowledge of Whitehall and his widespread experience of international affairs for the benefit of the Civil Service as a whole. As head of the Civil Service, the first not to be burdened with the work of secretary to the Cabinet or head of the Treasury, and permanent secretary to the Civil Service Department, he was able to devote all his skill and energies to the management of the Service he loved, and in particular to the implementation of the recommendations of the committee on the Civil Service chaired by Lord Fulton. In this wider field and freer atmosphere he blossomed and flourished.

He created the new Civil Service College, used it as a basis for greatly improved training in the Service, and introduced many innovations into methods of training. He brought about increased mobility of civil servants both between their different classes and between various departments. This was especially the case with those members with professional qualifications. He tried to spread his enthusiasm for modern methods of management and the equipment required for it throughout the Service. All this gave much encouragement to the newer and younger members of the Service as well as to those in the middle ranks. When critics complained that the Fulton committee's recommendations had not been fully carried out it had to be remembered that although he had the support of the ministers concerned he had to work against the inertia of the establishment including at times the Civil Service unions. This did not prevent him from opening up opportunities for civil servants to take part in discussions about current problems on radio and television and from participating in them himself. It was, as he saw it, an important aspect of open government.

In mid-1973 the Conservative government called together representatives of the employers and trade unions for discussions on a prices and incomes policy. Although nominally under the umbrella of the National Economic Development Council, the latter's secretariat took no part. The prime minister asked Armstrong to coordinate the work of the director-general of the Confederation of British Industry, the secretary-general of the Trades Union Congress, and the permanent secretary to the Treasury in preparation for such meetings. This task he fulfilled admirably for more than fifty meetings. He was appointed not because of any mistrust of the Treasury, as has been alleged, but so as to allow the Treasury, representing all Whitehall departments, to play an equal part with the representatives of the CBI and TUC under a chairman who could concentrate on reconciling different views. It was moreover uncharacteristically foolish of Victor (later Lord) Feather [q.v.], the general secretary of the TUC, to remark that Armstrong had become deputy prime minister, presumably because he sat next to the prime minister at conferences, something which is no more than a departmental official does for his minister. At no time did Armstrong exceed his functions as an official. He was trusted and admired by those who were present at that series of meetings. Unfortunately his health suddenly broke down early in 1974 and he was unable to take any further part in them. Later in that year he retired from the Civil Service and became a member of the board of the Midland Bank. In 1975 he was elected its chairman and on becoming chairman also of the Committee of London Clearing Bankers (1978–80) he played a major role in their collective campaign against the Labour Party's proposals for their nationalization. The chairmanship was a position he enjoyed although, or perhaps because, its circumstances were so entirely different from his own background, upbringing, and life's work.

Armstrong was unassuming, friendly, and approachable. Wise in judgement, he never attempted to force his views on those with whom he worked. Indeed his reticence made it difficult for those not closely involved with him to be certain of his personal position in the many crises with which he had to deal. He was first and foremost a public servant of the highest quality and the utmost integrity. His personal interests always came second.

Armstrong was appointed MVO (1945), CB (1957), KCB (1963), and GCB (1968). He was admitted to the Privy Council in 1973 and created a life peer in 1975. He received honorary degrees from many universities, including Oxford (1971), Sheffield (1975), City (1974), and Heriot-Watt (1975); he was an honorary fellow of Exeter College, Oxford (1963), and of the Imperial College of Science and Technology, London (1977); and he was a trustee or member of many governing bodies.

In 1942 he married Gwendoline Enid, daughter of John Bennett, company director, of Putney; they had one son and one daughter. Armstrong died suddenly in the Radcliffe Infirmary, Oxford, 12 July 1980.

[Personal knowledge.] EDWARD HEATH

ASHBRIDGE, SIR NOEL (1889–1975), engineer and broadcasting pioneer, was born 10 December 1889 in Wanstead, Essex, the fourth son and youngest child of John Ashbridge, solicitor, of Wanstead, and his wife, Sylvia Moore. He was educated at Forest School, Snaresbrook, and King's College, London, where he graduated in engineering.

Following graduation he spent a period of engineering training with Yarrow & Co., and British Thomson-Houston, before entering service with the Royal Fusiliers in 1914. In 1916 he was commissioned in the Royal Engineers and was one of the first operators of wireless equipment in the front line in France. Later in the war he transferred to instructional and research work in telecommunications.

In 1919 he joined the Marconi Company as one of the wireless development team at Writtle which in early 1922 constructed the famous 2MT (Two Emma Tock) transmitter from which the first wireless entertainment programmes were broadcast prior to the formation of the BBC at the end of the same year. Five members of this team were soon to join the BBC and assume senior engineering positions: amongst these were Peter Eckersley who became the BBC's first chief engineer in February 1923, and Ashbridge himself who joined Eckersley as assistant chief engineer in January 1926. Three years later, in 1929, he succeeded Eckersley as chief engineer.

The next few years saw a rapid expansion of the BBC's engineering activities under Ashbridge's guidance and his achievement was recognized with a knighthood in 1935. He had already, in 1934, been made a knight of the Danish Royal Order of Dannebrog for his work in advising a number of European countries on the setting up of broadcasting services.

At about this time the possibility of television broadcasting was coming to the fore and he was a member of the 1934 Selsdon committee investigating this. In 1935 Ashbridge saw and approved a demonstration of the all-electronic television system invented by (Sir) Isaac Shoenberg [q.v.] and this resulted in the following year in the establishment by the BBC of the world's first regular high-definition television service.

The 1939–45 war years brought new responsibilities for Ashbridge and the BBC engineering departments under his direction. Radio broadcasting had a vital role to play in terms of information and maintenance of public morale, both within Britain and overseas, and this had to be effected while offering the least possible opportunity for enemy aircraft to use the transmissions for navigational purposes. The television service was closed down for the duration of the war, but some planning had to be done for its future resumption and Ashbridge was a member of the 1943 committee set up for this purpose under the chairmanship of Sir Maurice (later Lord) Hankey [q.v.].

In 1943 Ashbridge was appointed deputy director-general of the BBC, while maintaining a role as chief adviser on engineering matters. With a reorganization of senior management in 1948, he relinquished the post of deputy director-general and was appointed director of technical services. In this position he supervised the very rapid and far-reaching expansion of radio and television services in the immediate post-war years. This period also saw the re-establishment and extension of international co-operation in the broadcasting field, and in 1950 Ashbridge was the BBC engineering division representative at an international meeting in Torquay which formed the start of the European Broadcasting Union.

During the war years he had been elected president of the Institution of Electrical Engineers for the 1941–2 term, and in 1948, with

(Sir) Harold Bishop, he delivered the IEE's Faraday lecture on the subject of television. He retired from the BBC in 1952 after twenty-six years' service. Following this he spent seven years on the board of the Marconi Company.

Throughout his career Ashbridge was breaking new ground, his decisions forming the basis for the pattern of broadcast engineering later adopted. As a man he was quiet, precise, and modest, tackling all problems with common sense and realism. He applied himself with the highest professional standards and demanded the same of his colleagues in the BBC engineering division.

Outside the professional sphere he was a man of broad interests, a sailor, a keen follower of cricket, and a lover of music. Nevertheless his abiding concern was with engineering matters, and the years spent in a more diffuse field as deputy director-general were not wholly to his taste. As a leader he was much liked and respected, in return showing equal respect for his staff at all levels. He was certainly intolerant of carelessness and insincerity, but was always ready with advice and encouragement when needed. The excellence of the engineering effected under his direction bears witness to his capacity for extracting the best from his colleagues.

In 1926 he married Olive Maude (died 1948), daughter of Rowland Strickland, merchant, of Erith, Kent. They had two daughters. Ashbridge died 4 June 1975 at a nursing home in Speldhurst, Kent.

[*The Times*, 6 June 1975; Edward Pawley, *BBC Engineering 1922–1972*, 1972; private information.] T. BRYCE MCCRIRRICK

ASHFORD, MARGARET MARY JULIA ('DAISY') (1881–1972), child author, was born 7 April 1881 in Petersham, Surrey, the first of the three daughters of William Henry Roxburghe Ashford, a former official of the War Office, of Petersham, and the sixth child of his wife Emma Georgina, daughter of George Walker, an industrialist of Eastwood, Nottinghamshire, and widow of Harry Langley, who had spent a year as an ensign in the 11th Hussars, by whom she had two daughters and three sons. Daisy was educated at home by a governess, by a private teacher and, for one year only, at the Priory, a convent at Hayward's Heath. By the time she went to school at the age of seventeen she had long since completed the work by which she is remembered.

At a very early age she began to tell stories, dictating them to her middle-aged parents. 'The Life of Father McSwiney' dates from 1885 when she was four, though it was not published until 1983 in *The Hangman's Daughter and Other Stories*, and reflects the ethos of a family strongly influenced by the beliefs and practices of the Roman Catholic Church. In 1889 the Ashfords moved from Petersham to Southdown House, Lewes. There Daisy dictated two romances, 'A Short Story of Love and Marriage' (1889) and 'Mr. Chapmer's Bride', which has not survived. She then embarked on the first book written in her own hand, the story of an aspirant to high society in late Victorian England. *The Young Visiters, or Mr. Salteena's Plan* combines in the most perfect form the characteristics which mark all her work: acute observation (of food and clothes as well as people), a gift for narrative, unconscious humour, and poor spelling. This was followed by a play, 'A Woman's Crime' (not extant), and two stories, 'The True History of Leslie Woodcock' (1892) and 'Where Love Lies Deepest' (1893). In the latter the darker side of life predominates, as it does in 'The Hangman's Daughter' (1894–5). This was by far her longest story and the one which in later life she considered to be 'the greatest literary achievement' of her youth. In 1896 she began a story entitled 'A Romance of the Afghan War', but only two chapters were completed. Two years later she went to school and the hope she had nourished when writing 'The Hangman's Daughter' of 'becoming an authoress' evaporated.

When she left school Daisy returned home to five years of leisure. In 1904 the family moved to Bexhill and soon afterwards she followed her sister Vera, an art student, to London, where she worked as a secretary. In 1917 her mother died and when she and her sisters were sorting out her papers they came across a box containing their childhood writings. *The Young Visiters* was soon identified as the funniest of these. In the following year Daisy lent the manuscript to her friend Margaret Mackenzie. She showed it to Frank Swinnerton, a reader and editor at the publishers Chatto & Windus. It was while working at the British legation in Berne that Daisy learned that Chatto wanted to publish her book. Sir J. M. Barrie [q.v.] was invited to commend it to the public and *The Young Visiters* appeared, with a preface by him, on 22 May 1919. Although some reviewers questioned its authenticity, most—among them A. A. Milne, (Sir) J. C. Squire [qq.v.], Holbrook Jackson, and Robert Graves—were delighted with it. And it was an immediate commercial success. The book was reprinted eighteen times in the year of publication and was accepted by an American publisher whose sales were much enhanced by the widespread though unfounded belief that Barrie himself had written the story. It was dramatized in 1920, made into a musical in 1968 and into a film (1984). The first illustrated edition, with pictures by Heather Corlass, was published in 1949, and a new edition, illustrated by Posy Simmonds, was published in 1984. The author, a shy and unworldly person, was touched but astonished by her new-found fame. She explained her feelings in the preface she wrote for *Daisy Ashford: Her Book* (1920): 'I can never feel all the nice things that have been said about "The Young Visiters", are really due to me at all, but to a Daisy Ashford of so long ago that she seems almost another person . . . the real success of the book I owe to the great kindness of Sir James Barrie in writing such a wonderful preface.' *Daisy Ashford: Her Book* contained 'A Short Story of Love and Marriage', 'The True History of Leslie Woodcock', 'Where Love Lies Deepest', 'The Hangman's Daughter', and (by Angela Ashford) 'The Jealous Governes'. The first two and last of these were published as *Love and Marriage* in 1982.

In 1920 Daisy married James Devlin (died 1956), whom she had met while working at a Catholic soldiers' club in Bexhill. They had two daughters and two sons, the elder of whom died in 1955. For some years they farmed at Framingham Pigot, near Norwich, and then for a year they ran the King's Arms Hotel, Reepham. In 1939 they settled at Hellesdon, Norwich. Daisy Ashford died 15 January 1972 in Hellesdon.

[R. M. Malcomson, *Daisy Ashford: Her Life*, 1984; Daisy Ashford's letters to and other papers belonging to Chatto & Windus Ltd; introduction to *The Hangman's Daughter and Other Stories*, 1966, by her daughter Margaret Steel, and information supplied by her and by her son Matthew Steel.] HUGO BRUNNER

ASTOR, JOHN JACOB, first BARON ASTOR OF HEVER (1886–1971), predominant owner of *The Times*, was born in New York 20 May 1886, the younger son of William Waldorf (later Viscount) Astor and his wife, Mary Dahlgren Paul, of Philadelphia. His mother died when he was eight; his father took British naturalization five years later. He was educated at Eton, for which he had an affection all his life, and for a year at New College, Oxford.

A man of great self-discipline and physical courage, he chose a military career. He left Oxford in 1906 to join the 1st Life Guards, and in 1911 he became aide-de-camp to Lord Hardinge of Penshurst [q.v.], then viceroy of India. At the outbreak of war in 1914 he went to France as a signalling officer in the Household Cavalry. At Messines in October he received his first wounds. He twice refused staff appointments. Posted at the beginning of 1918 to command the 520th Household Siege Battery, he distinguished himself by his bravery in action, and was awarded the Legion of Honour. In September 1918 he was wounded in fourteen places, his right leg having to be amputated. This ended his army career, but not his interest in the army. He retired with the rank of major, was appointed in 1927 honorary colonel of the Kent Heavy Brigade, Royal Artillery, and a year later honorary colonel of the 23rd London Regiment. His close personal interest in the Household Cavalry lasted to the end; the day in 1954 on which a squadron standard of the Life Guards was laid up in Hever church was one of the proudest of his life.

Astor's character owed much to his father, a determined man of strong views who taught his children to think before speaking, to be decisive, and never to change their minds. Because of what he considered the disesteem for the Astors in America he settled in England. He bought Cliveden, gave it to his elder son, Waldorf Astor [q.v.], in 1906, and then lived at Hever Castle in Kent, which he had acquired in 1903 and had considerably extended to make it 'a Tudor village under one roof', as indeed it looked from the battlements.

In 1916 he accepted a peerage. His elder son, who was prospering as a politician, and even more his son's wife, Nancy Astor [q.v.], were furious. To them it then seemed the eventual ruin of their political hopes. John Astor was at the front and took no part in the family quarrel. The fact that he did not join his brother in protest led to a coolness between the two branches of the family. When John Astor lost his leg in 1918, his father gave him Hever Castle, so that he should have a new interest in life. The estate, the village, and the life of Kent generally thereafter became one of his abiding affections.

On his father's death in 1919 Astor inherited the use of a great fortune. The life of a country gentleman could not satisfy his sense of duty. Modest, diffident, and sensitive though he was, he wished to play some useful part in English affairs. He entered the House of Commons in 1922 as Unionist member for Dover—he held the seat until June 1945—but as he was neither a ready speaker nor politically inclined, it was not enough. A fortunate chance, typically arising out of his character, met his need.

When Lord Northcliffe [q.v.] died in August 1922, the scramble to acquire the ownership of *The Times* alarmed the editorial staff. They favoured none of the contenders, and held a meeting among themselves. It was easily decided that what was needed was a man rich enough to see the paper through any hazard, and modest enough, having appointed an editor, to leave him and his colleagues absolutely independent. The difficulty was to find such a man. Various names were rejected. (Sir) Bruce Richmond [q.v.], editor of the *Times Literary Supplement*, then suggested Astor. Many years before, Richmond had been present at an after-dinner discussion at New College, Oxford, about the topography of one of the reaches of the Thames. When the argument had become somewhat ill-tempered, a young man, who had hitherto stayed silent, said in a weak, hesitant voice: 'Don't you think . . .'

and described the area meticulously. 'Good God, Astor, how do you know it so well?' someone asked. 'My father has a house near there.' Richmond said that when the editorial meeting seemed to have reached a dead end, memory of this episode flashed into his mind. A man who, knowing what he did, would not enter a dispute except to relieve everyone from being uncomfortable, and who could so modestly describe Cliveden, was, he was certain, the man to own *The Times*.

It was indeed in that spirit that Astor discharged his long stewardship in Printing House Square which began in December 1922 when he and John Walter the fifth [q.v.] became joint owners of *The Times* in the ratio of nine shares to one. At the outset of their relationship he handled John Walter with a firmness which Northcliffe had never achieved. He made it clear at once who was master of the board and of the management. But the four editors of the paper during his long reign could testify that he never once pressed a single view on them. On assuming control he and John Walter agreed to dismiss Wickham Steed and bring back Geoffrey Dawson [qq.v.]. Thereafter they left the policy and the contents of *The Times* and all its publications to the editors they had chosen. When Astor's friends told him that as the owner of a leading organ of opinion he had a duty to ensure that it expressed the views he thought right, he replied that the paper's staff could give much more time to the study of affairs than he could, and were far more qualified to do so.

Of course he chose editors who he was satisfied would be true to the paper's trust. It must favour no party, person, or interest, except in so far as it thought at any moment and in any controversy what they advocated was for the public good. Whatever the economic or other difficulties, *The Times* must continue to be a journal of record as well as of opinion. The financial consequences of such a course were his problem. When he eventually relinquished control he was insistent that *The Times* had not been a rich man's expensive hobby, and that averaged out over all the years of his ownership it had given him a modest rate of interest; but his staff always knew that come what may he would see the paper through. For him it was a proud and high responsibility, although he never talked in that vein.

On being offered a peerage in the 1956 New Year honours he consulted the editor on the propriety of accepting it. Traditionally men on *The Times* refused honours. It was agreed that as he had no influence on the policy of the paper, for him to become Lord Astor of Hever would raise no question about its independence. His other activities alone justified the honour. He thereafter began to transfer his share of the ownership to his eldest son, Gavin, while remaining a chief proprietor with John Walter, this office carrying the sole power to appoint and dismiss the editor. Gavin also became a chief proprietor, but John Astor did not relinquish his own post until the transfer of *The Times* to Lord Thomson of Fleet [q.v.] at the end of 1966.

While *The Times* was Astor's paramount interest, he had many others. In 1916 he married Lady Violet Mary (died 1965), the youngest daughter of the fourth Earl of Minto [q.v.], and widow of Lord Charles Mercer Nairne, younger son of the fifth Marquess of Lansdowne [q.v.]; they had three sons. It was a happy partnership. She brought Astor out of his shell. His activities widened. Weekends at Hever became occasions when statesmen and artists, soldiers and clergymen, men and women of distinction in every sphere met informally. They did not hear much from their shy host; they did come to appreciate his selflessness, common sense, and integrity. Appointments came. He was a member of the broadcasting committees of 1923 and 1935; a member of the BBC's general advisory council in 1937–9. He attended the Imperial Press Conference at Melbourne in 1925 as treasurer, and was president for many years. When the Press Council was set up in 1953 he was its first chairman, resigning in 1955 because of ill health. He was at one time and another a deputy lieutenant for Kent, a lieutenant of the City of London, a justice of the peace, honorary secretary of the King's Roll National Council, chairman of the advisory committee of St. Dunstan's, a vice-president of the British and Foreign Bible Society, chairman and president of the Old Etonian Association. His City interests included directorships of Barclays and Hambros banks, the chairmanship of the Phoenix Assurance Company (1952–8), and he had been a director of the Great Western Railway (1929–48).

It was part of his character that to all these he gave not only his name but also his assiduous interest. His chairmanship of the Middlesex Hospital took on another dimension. His hospital experiences in 1918 had given him an abiding regard for medical work, and particularly for nursing. To the Middlesex he made many gifts: £300,000 for a nurses' home completed in 1931, £400,000 for the medical school in 1955, a further £50,000 in 1957, and others never disclosed.

To a man who cherished English traditions and loved the English way of life the Finance Act of 1962 dealt a terrible blow. People domiciled in Britain henceforth must pay estate duty on assets abroad as well as on those in the United Kingdom. Aimed at rich men who had placed their wealth overseas to escape death duties, it hit also John Astor who had all his life been bringing money into England from the great Astor Trust in New York. In desperation Astor tried to resign from this Trust, the ultimate beneficiaries of which were his children. Under American law he could not do so. To leave things unchanged would have crippled the estate on his death, and have enforced the sale of *The Times* under most disadvantageous circumstances. He decided it was his duty to emigrate. On 21 September 1962 he made a frank and dignified public statement, which brought widespread sympathy, and proceeded to settle in the south of France. He never got over the hurt of this blow. Yet he did not become bitter. When he found that living in France was enriching him, he carefully calculated the difference and placed it in a trust fund to help medical education in England.

Tall, upright, crop-moustached, Astor looked a military man whatever he was doing. Few who met him casually realized that he had what he called 'a tin leg'. (He insisted on using one made by ex-servicemen and not a more luxurious kind.) He did not let his handicap end his sporting pleasures. He had been an outstanding player of ball games. He was in the Eton eleven for two years, and in 1905 won the public schools rackets championship with M. W. Bovill. In 1908 he won the army championship in singles and in the doubles with Lord Somers (whose notice he contributed to this Dictionary) and with V. Pennell the doubles in the Olympic Games. After he had lost his leg he played cricket, lawn tennis, and golf, and won the parliamentary squash rackets in 1926 and 1927. He was president of the MCC in 1937. In later life his hobby was painting. He lived sparely. He was modest and unassuming in everything he did. The iron side of his character showed in matters of principle. About these he was stern and inflexible.

He died in hospital at Cannes 19 July 1971 and was succeeded by his eldest son Gavin (born 1918). Among the many portraits of Lord Astor of Hever are those by Sargent, Birley, Orpen, Munnings, and Elwes (all in the possession of the family); and by A. K. Lawrence (Phoenix Assurance Company); and Edward I. Halliday (Middlesex Hospital).

[*The Times*, 20 July 1971; private information; personal knowledge.] WILLIAM HALEY

AUDEN, WYSTAN HUGH (1907–1973), poet, essayist, teacher, and collaborator in writing plays and libretti, was born in York 21 February 1907, the third and youngest son (there were no daughters) of Dr George Augustus Auden and his wife, Constance Rosalie Bucknell. In 1908 Dr Auden was appointed school medical officer of the city of Birmingham, to which the Auden family then moved. Dr Auden was a classicist in Greek and Latin and also had a strong interest in psychology. His wife, who had been trained as a hospital nurse, was a high Anglican, and was musical. Auden was brought up in a home where there were books on scientific subjects, English literature, and Nordic sagas. It may have been important to his own emotional development that his father was away from home (in the Royal Army Medical Corps) from 1914 to 1918. All his life the mother figure was dominant for him.

Clergymen, schoolmasters, and antiquarians were among Auden's forebears. From childhood onward he was interested in limestone landscape, superannuated mining machinery, and place names. Late in life he said that if ever there were to be a school for poets courses in geology should be obligatory. Stimulated perhaps by the Nordic sound of his surname and his Anglo-Saxon Christian name, Auden cherished the belief that he was of Icelandic origin, and made several trips to Iceland; after one of these he published, in collaboration with Louis MacNeice [q.v.], who had accompanied him, *Letters from Iceland* (1937).

He was educated first at St. Edmunds, a preparatory school at Hindhead in Surrey, where a fellow schooboy was Christopher Isherwood—who became his lifelong friend, collaborator in writing plays, and, intermittently, lover; then at Gresham's School, Holt, a self-consciously 'modern' school where the emphasis of the teaching was on science (though Gresham's was also distinguished in music and drama); and, finally, at Christ Church, Oxford. His tutor there was Nevill Coghill [q.v.], to whom, early on, he confided that it was his intention to become not just a poet but a great poet.

The decisive influence on Auden's poetry when he was at Oxford was *The Waste Land* of T. S. Eliot [q.v.]. He also derived from Eliot's early critical essays the view that the poet should be a kind of scientist of language who made, with detached objectivity, poems which were verbal artefacts rather than vehicles for expressing the poet's personality and feelings. Yet his early poems contain images of barriers, impassable frontiers, broken bridges, which seem to express his feelings of personal isolation, but in impersonal guise.

After leaving Oxford with a third class in English literature in 1928, Auden went, in August of the same year, for a year to Berlin. There he met John Layard, an ex-patient of the American psychologist and guru Homer Lane, who interested him in Homer Lane's teaching. This aimed at liberating the forces of the unconscious in the individual without applying moral censorship to whatever behaviour resulted from such release. The healing power of uninhibited love became a theme of the poetry of Auden's Berlin period.

In 1929 the allowance which his parents had given him at Oxford ceased and Auden was obliged to return to England to earn his living. For a year he did this by private tutoring in London. In 1930 he embarked on a five years' period of school-mastering; first at Larchfield Academy in Helensburgh; and then, from autumn 1932, three years at the Downs School, Colwall. Known to his pupils as Uncle Wiz, Auden's performance as a schoolmaster was later described by one of his pupils as a non-stop firework display; but through his psychological knowledge, his empathy for the very young, and his self-discipline as a writer he was a wise educator, both of the boys and his colleagues.

His first book, privately printed by Stephen Spender in an edition of about forty-five copies, was *Poems* (1928). There followed (published by Faber) *Poems* (1930), *The Orators* (1932), and numerous articles and reviews. Periodicals, pre-eminent among which were *New Verse* and the anthologies *New Signatures* and *New Country*, usually incorporating in their titles the epithet 'new', seemed to spring up in response to a new movement in poetry presumably associated with Auden. The names most often cited together with his were Cecil Day-Lewis [q.v.], Stephen Spender, and (a year or two later) Louis MacNeice.

That brilliant though obscure *tour de force*, *The Orators*—a medley of prose and verse—through wit, strangeness, surrealist effects, beautiful poetry, and uninhibited high spirits, communicated its excitement to a whole generation of Auden's young English contemporaries, often public schoolboys, who discovered in it exhilarating answers to the question posed in its first section: 'What do you think about England, this country of ours where nobody is well?'

Because of Fascism's increasing threat to individual liberty, Auden's poetry began to reflect his growing awareness that the individual was largely conditioned by the society in which he lived and that he had to defend his freedom against Fascism. In his private ideology he now added Marxism to Freudian psychoanalysis (he was later to add Christianity to both). He became involved in work and causes which were anti-Fascist. In mid-1935 he gave up schoolmastering and went to London. He joined the GPO Film Unit, where he worked with his friend the painter (Sir) William Coldstream and the producer John Grierson. In collaboration with Christopher Isherwood he wrote for the Group Theatre *The Dog Beneath the Skin* (1935) and *The Ascent of F6* (1936).

On 15 June 1935, at the instigation of Isherwood, he married Erika, daughter of Thomas Mann, who was a potential victim of Nazi persecution—and whom, before the marriage, he had never met—in order to provide her with a British passport. This particular union was never consummated.

In 1937 he visited Spain, having volunteered to drive an ambulance for the Republican side, a visit which resulted in his most politically committed poem: 'Spain' (1937). From January to July 1938 Isherwood and he travelled together to China and produced jointly *Journey to a War* (1939), a book which certainly showed that their political sympathies lay with the invaded and occupied Chinese. Its sonnet sequence about the war contains some of Auden's greatest poetry. They returned from China by way of America, a detour which changed their lives: for it was now that they decided that America was the country where they would take up residence.

The poetry Auden wrote when he was an undergraduate might be said to be well within the tradition of the modern movement; in it there were influences of James Joyce [q.v.], Gertrude Stein, and T. S. Eliot, as well as of Anglo-Saxon and Norse sagas. But the poetry he wrote during the thirties was a departure from symbolist and imagist purism. He renounced *vers libre* and the search for new forms and wrote with virtuosity in a wide variety of traditional forms. He unabashedly introduced into poetry many elements of journalism and declared that poetry, to be interesting, had to contain news. When he wrote, during his visit to Iceland, the dazzling 'Letter to Lord Byron', it was the newsy, gossipy and satiric aspects of *Don Juan* that appealed to him in Byron, not the romantic.

On 18 January 1939 Auden and Isherwood left England for New York, having every intention of taking up residence in America and becoming American citizens, though, at the time, they did not tell their friends of this decision. After the outbreak of war in September of that year they were much criticized in the English press for not returning to England. On various occasions Auden produced reasons for his leaving England, and it seems clear that the England which he had loved in his childhood and youth—an England of private values and pleasures and Edenic landscape—had in his mind ceased to exist. Moreover a result of his involvement with anti-Fascist politics and the public activities connected with them, was that he found himself regarded as leader of a movement called 'the Thirties'. This role, though flattering to him, was false to his vocation. Had he remained in England, he would have almost inevitably found himself becoming the public poetic voice of wartime England, which would have been alien to his gift.

America also meant for him Chester Kallman, a young poet whom he first met in New York in the spring of 1939 and in whom, within a matter of weeks of meeting him, he saw his destiny. In the relationship with Kallman lay his future and nothing would ever alter this. He thought of the relationship as a marriage, to which he was wholly committed. Kallman was in fact congenitally incapable of being faithful within a partnership and this brought Auden (and perhaps Kallman too) much agony.

Paradoxical as it may seem it was in America that Auden was able to reinvent the conditions necessary to his vocation, as the poet with a private voice who could 'undo the folded lie' and as teacher. After a brief spell at St. Mark's School in Massachusetts he taught undergraduate and graduate students at a whole series of universities and colleges (among them Michigan, Swarthmore, Bennington, Barnard, and Virginia). At the end of the war (April to August 1945), with the rank equivalent to major, he was one of a team of researchers into the effects of the bombing of German cities on their inhabitants (the morale division of the US Strategic Bombing Survey). He regarded New York as his home in America and would describe himself not as an American but a New Yorker. It might be said that after 1939 his true homeland was an island called Auden since he owed to New York the opportunity it offered him of being alone.

But after the end of the war he resumed, at least in part, his European life. He rented a house on the island of Ischia to which he went every spring and summer from 1949 to 1957. With the proceeds of an Italian literary prize in 1958 he bought a house in the village of Kirchstetten, near Vienna. His delight in possessing this modest home was such that on first arriving there from New York, he would sometimes stand in the garden with his eyes filled with tears of gratitude.

It is widely held, especially in England, that Auden's poetry declined after his arrival in America. Admittedly the poems written after 1938 rarely communicate the exuberance and restless vitality of some of the earlier work. In *The Double Man* (1941), *The Age of Anxiety* (1947), *The Sea and the Mirror* (1944), *Nones* (1951), and *The Shield of Achilles* (1955) the poet seems to have withdrawn into deeper levels of his consciousness, where he is much preoccupied with working out a system of religious ideas which will enclose and illuminate lived and observed experience. He now rejected utterly the idea that poetry could exercise the slightest influence on politics. Nevertheless, Auden's greatest poems are surely those of the American period, precisely because they transform into the terms of his theology and in his unique language so much of the surrounding life of our time. Moreover, several poems—notably, the title poem of *The Shield of Achilles* volume and 'In Praise of Limestone'—equal, if they do not surpass, the greatest poems of the thirties period. In America Auden also wrote highly individual and imaginative essays and lectures—themselves sometimes a kind of prose poetry—contained in *The Enchafèd Flood* (1950) (based on the 1949 Page-Barbour lecture at the University of Virginia), *The Dyer's Hand* (1962), and *Forewords and Afterwords* (1972).

Auden's collaboration with Chester Kallman in writing the libretto—*The Rake's Progress* (1951)—for Igor Stravinsky's music celebrated for him the fusion of their loves through their gifts: as did also their work together on libretti for operas by Hans Werner Henze and Nicolas Nabokov.

In 1956 Auden was elected professor of poetry at Oxford University. In his inaugural lecture, *Making, Knowing and Judging* (1956), he discussed autobiographically his experience of writing poetry. As poetry professor, Auden would go every morning to the Cadena café in Cornmarket in Oxford and make himself available for consultation and advice to whatever undergraduate poets chose to discuss their work with him. The advice he was most willing to give was about technique.

Probably his life did begin to take a downward curve in the 1960s. In October 1964 he spent six months in Berlin under an 'artists-in-residence' programme there, sponsored by the Ford Foundation. But he did not get on well with those German writers he met—who knew little about him—and he was not happy.

In the early 1970s he lobbied privately to have himself given rooms in Christ Church, his old Oxford college, on terms similar to those granted to E. M. Forster [q.v.] by King's College, Cambridge. In 1972 he was granted residence in a 'grace and favour' cottage in the grounds of Christ Church. That he ever wished for such an arrangement, and that he persisted in it when difficulties arose, are symptoms of loss of self-confidence. His isolation in his New York apartment had begun to have terrors for him. He had visions of falling dead there and his body not being discovered for a week. The return to Oxford was also an attempt to return to his origins by one whose view of his own life was perhaps cyclical. Through no-one's fault, the arrangement did not work out well. Industrialized, tourist-trodden, hooting and hustling modern Oxford did not correspond to Auden's memory of Peck Quad where, as an undergraduate, he had rooms and met his friends. The Students (fellows) of Christ Church, when they found that he was repetitive at high table and often drunk, did not extend to him the amused and admiring tolerance which he had enjoyed in New York. Auden was not in Oxford but Vienna when on 29 September 1973, after a very successful reading of his poems, he died in a hotel bedroom. He was buried in his much loved Kirchstetten on 4 October of that year.

Friends, English and American, whom Auden had known for a long time, formed a kind of constellation of smiled-at presences in his mind, an accompaniment throughout his life. That he had quarrelled with one of them—Benjamin (later Lord) Britten [q.v.]—was a source of grief to him. Despite his magnanimity and his many acts of generosity, there was a streak of inconsiderateness for others in his behaviour. This was one reason why he never found anyone to live with him. He was obsessively punctual and complained loudly if a meal, or a visitor, was five minutes late. He imposed his idiosyncrasies on others as a regime. These minor faults, which created an isolation for him, were outweighed by greater virtues. He had a sense that being a bachelor did not absolve him from family responsibility.

When he was young he was excessively funny, often in an outrageous way, and he remained greatly amusing all his life. His funniness consisted partly in his playing so uncompromisingly his own uniqueness, expressed already in his dress—the crumpled suit and the carpet slippers which he wore in later life—and even in his face, with its skin which, smooth in youth, became in age like crinkled parchment.

He was grateful for his own success and considered himself happy, though to friends it seemed that in old age he was an illustration of whatever is meant by the term 'broken-hearted'. Probably the happiest period of his life was when, a colleague among colleagues, he taught at the Downs School: as that superb poem of undiluted happiness beginning with the line 'Out on the lawn I lie in bed' would seem to testify.

Many people have found it difficult to take his religion seriously because, in irreligious company, he was inclined to 'camp it up' with references to 'Miss God' etc. But in fact theology provided the culmination of his intellectual life-explaining system; and, in the simplest way, in his benign attitude to others, his forgiveness of those who sinned against him, and the centrality of his feeling of love he was Christian and, in a quite old-fashioned sense, a Christian gentleman.

A portrait of him by (Sir) William Coldstream (1937) is in the Humanities Centre, Houston, Texas; there is a pencil drawing by Don Bachardy (1957) in the National Portrait Gallery; in private hands there are three drawings done by David Hockney (1968). There are also sketches by Maurice Field (1932–5) when he was at the Downs School, Colwall, and a page of sketches done by the Viennese artist Anton Schumich at the reading Auden gave in Vienna on the night of his death.

[Humphrey Carpenter, *W. H. Auden: a Biography*, 1981; Edward Mendelson, *Early Auden*, 1981; Stephen Spender (ed.), *W. H. Auden, a Tribute*, 1975; private information; personal knowledge.]

STEPHEN SPENDER

AVON, first EARL OF (1897–1977), statesman. [See EDEN, (ROBERT) ANTHONY.]

AYLMER, SIR FELIX EDWARD (1889–1979), actor, was born 21 February 1889 at Corsham, Wiltshire, the second child in the family of five sons (one of whom died as a child) and one daughter of Lieutenant-Colonel Thomas Edward Aylmer-Jones, Royal Engineers, and his wife, Lilian Cookworthy. He was educated at Magdalen College School and Exeter College, Oxford, where he took second classes in both mathematical moderations (1909) and physics (1911). After an undergraduate attachment to OUDS, he decided to join the stage, to his parents' displeasure.

He commenced a course of stage training under the celebrated teacher Rosina Filippi. His first professional appearance was as a two-line Italian stooge with (Sir) E. Seymour Hicks [q.v.] at the Coliseum in 1911, just after his twenty-second birthday. He then appeared in *Romeo and Juliet* at the New Theatre and in two memorable Shakespearian productions (1912) at the Savoy by Harley Granville-Barker [q.v.]. In 1913 he joined the company of (Sir) Barry Jackson [q.v.] at the Birmingham Repertory Theatre. This splendid training was interrupted by the war of 1914–18, in which Aylmer served in the Royal Naval Volunteer Reserve, hurrying back to the Birmingham stage and his wife as soon as hostilities had ceased. During the war he had married Barry Jackson's niece Cecily (died 1975), daughter of Robert Taaffe Byrne, managing director of the Leyland of Birmingham Rubber Company. They met when he played Prospero to her Miranda and on his return after the war they appeared together again as Sir Peter and Lady Teazle. They had one daughter and two sons, who both died young.

During the following years Aylmer was seen in many West End plays, including *The Doctor's Dilemma* (Kingsway, 1926) and *The Flashing Stream* (Lyric, 1938). He also appeared in plays in New York, such as *Loyalties* (Gaiety, 1922), produced by Basil Dean [q.v.], and *The Last of Mrs Cheyney* (Fulton, 1925). Some of his greatest successes were acting the parts of members of the professions of law and diplomacy. For John Drinkwater [q.v.] in 1928, he played at the Royalty a KC in the long-running comedy *Bird in Hand*. This was followed by the role of a councillor of state in *Jew Süss* (Duke of York's, 1929) and then that of a crooked solicitor in the 1934 revival at the Sadler's Wells and the Shaftesbury of *The Voysey Inheritance* by Harley Granville-Barker [q.v.]. He was also the judge in Enid Bagnold's *The Chalk Garden* (Haymarket, 1956). Diplomats which he played included the Foreign Office official in the 1954 production of *The Spider's Web* by (Dame) Agatha Christie [q.v.].

Aylmer was not fond of Shakespeare. He once confided: 'I am a bit of an anti-Shakespearian. I acknowledge his greatness, of course—but, you know, Shakespeare has done so much harm to actors. He has been responsible for so much work that is artificial and unreal that in my time he has seemed a machine for manufacturing ham actors who do not understand the psychological contents of the parts and the poetry. Everyone has to do Shakespeare if they want to make a reputation but it seems to me that they seldom do their best work in his plays. He stretches an actor's emotional range, of course—but then so do Ibsen and Strindberg.' Aylmer preferred G. B. Shaw [q.v.], whom he first met very early in his career. He played Shaw repeatedly and indeed appeared in three different parts in *St. Joan* alone.

Not one to enthuse about the rapport normally enjoyed by stage actors with a live audience, he preferred the medium of the film. He claimed that the work the film actor had to do, under the close-up of the camera's pitiless eye, called for a greater skill than anything required on stage. He appeared in a number of supporting parts in large-scale films for American directors: Plautius, a Roman converted to Christianity, in *Quo Vadis?* (1951), Isaak of York, the Jewish father of Elizabeth Taylor's Rebecca in *Ivanhoe* (1953), Merlin to Mel Ferrer's King Arthur in *Knights of the Round Table* (1953), and, in spite of his antipathy towards Shakespeare, two memorable performances in productions by Laurence (later Lord) Olivier, namely Polonius in *Hamlet* (1948) and the Archbishop in *Henry V* (1944). Television too brought him fame: he appeared with Hugh Griffith in the popular comedy series entitled *The Walrus and the Carpenter* and as Father Anselm with Derek Nimmo in *Oh Brother!* a successful series about life in a monastery.

In 1959 he published a book *Dickens Incognito*, as a result of research which had led him to some startling conclusions about that author's private life. The book created a sensation. However, the bubble burst within a week as other Dickens lovers pounced on a flaw in his argument and found gaps in his research. This upset could have humiliated a lesser man but was met by Aylmer with rueful amusement and perfect sang-froid. He was not deterred from writing a second book entitled *The Drood Case*, which was published in 1964.

He gave great service to his profession as an outstanding president of the British Actors' Equity Association from 1949 to 1969. In his official capacity, in 1963 he criticized the dirty and insanitary conditions still obtaining even in some West End theatres. He was also vice-president of the Royal Academy of Dramatic Art when the principal, John Fernald, resigned in 1965 after a disagreement on policy with the council. In 1950 Aylmer was appointed OBE for his services to the stage and in 1965 he was knighted.

Having spent some time in Germany when he was a student, Aylmer later translated a number of plays from German. One of his favourite hobbies was composing limericks, clerihews, and verse for newspaper competitions. In this he vied with his son Ian, and together they won a number of prizes. His daughter Jennifer was for several years connected with the British Theatre Museum in London. A stroke precipitated Aylmer's retirement to his country house near Cobham where he continued to live until shortly before he died, at a nursing home in Sussex, 2 September 1979.

[Personal knowledge.] DEREK NIMMO

AYRTON, MICHAEL (1921–1975), artist and writer, was born in London 20 February 1921, the only child of Gerald Gould, poet and journalist, of 3 Hamilton Terrace, London, and his wife, Barbara Ayrton, sometime chairman of the Labour Party, and whose surname Ayrton adopted on becoming a practising artist. Michael Ayrton left a co-educational private school early. He studied painting in Vienna and Paris, working briefly under Pavel Tchelitchew, and attended Heatherley's Art School and various other art schools in London.

He travelled to Spain, saw some of the siege of Barcelona during the Spanish civil war, and spent the summer of 1939 with fellow painters and friends F. John Minton [q.v.] and Michael Middleton at Les Baux in France. After the outbreak of war, Ayrton returned to London, had his first exhibition at the Zwemmer Gallery, and, with John Minton, during leave from the RAF, executed the designs for (Sir) John Gielgud's *Macbeth* staged in 1942. Ayrton was invalided out of the RAF in 1942 and shared an exhibition with Minton at the Leicester Galleries. From that time his life was marred by ill health, borne with much stoical courage, and his career as an artist developed from a precocity noted by such distinguished elders as P. Wyndham Lewis [q.v.] (for whom Ayrton acted for some time as visual amanuensis) to a versatile fruition which never brought the honours, the critical acclaim, or the financial success enjoyed by many of his contemporaries.

In this respect, in a country and society which still regards amateurism as a professional advantage, Ayrton suffered from his relentless curiosity, his considerable eclecticism, and his formidable erudition, backed by a strong physical presence which many persons of weaker intellect or personality found intimidating. In fact, his handsome head, with long, straight, swept-back hair and full beard, the powerful torso of the sculptor, and the mellifluous voice of a born teacher and conversationalist were compellingly attractive. What left him, at the height of his career, with a single honour, a doctorate from

Exeter University (1975), and no official recognition from the British 'art establishment' was the view, commonly held, that his exceptionally varied output was the sign of a jack of all trades.

For more than three decades he practised as painter, sculptor, draughtsman, engraver, portraitist, stage-designer, book illustrator, novelist, short story writer, essayist, critic, art historian, radio and television broadcaster, and cinema and television film-maker. While inevitably in an *oeuvre* so prodigious he occasionally let slip work that was not of the first rank, there was in fact none of the trades listed above of which he was not the master.

Ayrton's principal exhibitions, other than regular dealers' selling shows in Britain, Europe, the USA, and Canada, were: Wakefield City Art Gallery (and subsequently on tour) in 1949; a retrospective at the Whitechapel Art Gallery in London in 1955; the Philadelphia Museum of Art in 1963; the National Gallery of Canada (a regional tour) in 1965; Reading City Art Gallery in 1969; the Bruton Gallery, Somerset, in 1971; the University of Sussex in 1972; Portsmouth City Art Gallery (and subsequently on tour) in 1973; the University of Pennsylvania in 1973.

His most important exhibitions, however, were 'Word and Image'—a remarkably inventive show devoted to a comparison of the work of Ayrton and Wyndham Lewis showing the inter-relationship, not only of the two artists and their styles, but also of their writings as well as their visual work. This was held in 1971 at the National Book League, London. The major retrospective exhibition which Ayrton should have had in his lifetime only occurred posthumously in 1977 at the Birmingham City Museums and Art Gallery and subsequently on tour; in 1981 there was a substantial touring exhibition at the Bruton Gallery in Somerset, the National Museum of Wales, etc.

Ayrton's visual work, apart from his portraits, tended to be thematic with certain ideas and images either obsessively recorded or constantly recurring. The discovery of Greek landscape and mythology was to haunt his work till he died. (He travelled extensively in Greece and the Hellenistic world.) Daedalus and Icarus, Talos, and above all the Minotaur inspired much of his finest work, ranging from pencil sketches to huge bronzes. For a benevolently eccentric American millionaire, Armand Erpf, he created in 1968 at Arkville in New York State a gigantic maze built of brick and stone, with a seven-foot bronze Minotaur and a seven-foot bronze of Daedalus and Icarus in two central chambers.

Flight was a permanent obsession. Hector Berlioz preoccupied him for years and inspired sculptures, paintings, a memorable short story, and a remarkable BBC television programme which he devised and narrated. Mirrors fascinated him and, with their infinite variety of and capacity for reflections, dominated his later sculpture where he mingled bronze, polished metal sheet, and perspex to extraordinary effects. For the two years before his death he had been working on a major BBC television series on the multiple possibilities of mirrors and their imagery in life, art, mathematics, philosophy, and astronomy.

Ayrton's literary output was as varied as his visual work. He was a fine critic (he was art critic of the *Spectator* from 1944 to 1946) and in these fields ranged from books on *British Drawings* in 1946 and *Hogarth's Drawings* (1948) via several collections of distinguished essays, notably *Golden Sections* (1957) and *The Rudiments of Paradise* (1971), to a pioneering scholarly monograph *Giovanni Pisano, Sculptor* (1969), which had an introduction by Henry Moore.

As a poet he showed notable talent in the fragmentary *The Testament of Daedalus* (1962) (a foretaste and forerunner of his subsequent novel, *The Maze Maker*, 1967) and he published posthumously in 1977 *Archilochos*, a translation (with the assistance of Professor G. S. Kirk) of the seventh-century BC Greek poet who wrote in the Parian script. This book, containing Ayrton's last published words, was illustrated by his own characteristically spiky etchings, done in the last eighteen months of his life.

Ayrton produced one collection of short stories, *Fabrications* (1972), influenced by Borges, in the tricks they played with time, history, and memory, but entirely Ayrtonian in their dry wit, originality of imagination, and a wholly beneficent solipsism deriving not from personal vanity but from the indubitable fact that his own experiences, serendipities, and ideas were genuinely of greater creative interest to himself and others than the notions and characters of most other people, Giovanni Pisano and Hector Berlioz excepted.

His two novels, *The Maze Maker* and *The Midas Consequence* (1974) were both an integral part of Ayrton's visual life. The former, a virtuoso account of the lives of Daedalus and Icarus, dealt with mythology, Crete, the Minotaur, the excitement of flight, and, above all, the genius of the *maker*, of the artist as master craftsman. *The Midas Consequence* is an equally virtuoso performance, dealing with the joys and the pitfalls of being a prolific, omni-talented and internationally revered modern artist. The hero, Capisco, is obviously—too obviously, for the unwary—based on Picasso. He is, of course, far more than that and he is, in part at least, Michael Ayrton, but ultimately he is the paradigmatic artist and genius, enriched and pampered by society but, in the end, the property and prey of that same society.

Ayrton was a man who travelled widely throughout his life, was blessed by considerable domestic felicity, was a much loved member of the Savile Club, and had a large number of friends. In 1951 he moved, with his wife, who was a distinguished authority on English cooking, a superb hostess, and a writer herself, to Bradfields, a beautiful sixteenth-century country house in Essex, formerly the property of Sir Francis Meynell [q.v.]. Bradfields was Ayrton's principal home, social centre, and studio until his death.

Ayrton married, in 1951, Elisabeth, daughter of Douglas Walshe, writer, who had three daughters by her first marriage to Nigel Balchin, writer (1908–68). Michael and Elisabeth Ayrton had no children. He died, suddenly, of a heart attack at his London flat 17 November 1975.

[Peter Cannon-Brookes, *Michael Ayrton—an Illustrated Commentary*, 1978; T. G. Rosenthal, 'Michael Ayrton: a Memoir', *Encounter*, May 1976; private information; personal knowledge.]

T. G. ROSENTHAL

B

BADEN-POWELL, OLAVE ST. CLAIR, LADY (1889–1977), leader of the world Guide movement, was born 22 February 1889, at Stubbing Court, near Chesterfield, third child and younger daughter of Harold Soames and his wife Katherine Hill. Her father owned the Brampton Brewery Company, but retired before he was forty. Her first nineteen years were spent in ten rented country houses, including Renishaw Hall (owned by Sir George Sitwell, q.v.) and Pixton Park (belonging to the Earl of Carnarvon, q.v.). She also spent periods in London before her parents settled in Lilliput, Dorset, in 1908. She had no formal education except from a governess, and this only until the age of twelve, but her love of music, animals, and all outdoor pursuits was encouraged. She was an expert horsewoman, keen games player, and competent violinist.

In January 1912, accompanying her father to Jamaica on the *Arcadian*, she met Lieutenant-General Sir Robert Stephenson Smyth (later Lord) Baden-Powell [q.v.], the hero of Mafeking, who had founded the Boy Scout movement in 1908. He had retired from the army in 1910, aged fifty-three, to devote more time to the promotion of scouting. Olave had been born on his thirty-second birthday and he was three years younger than her father. They were married 30 October 1912, in St. Peter's Church, Parkstone. Their son, Peter (died 1962), was born on their first wedding anniversary, 1913, and their daughters, Heather and Betty, in 1915 and 1917 respectively.

Olave Baden-Powell threw all her energies into supporting her husband in his work, acting as his driver and secretary, and accompanying him to his many scouting engagements. During World War I she worked in YMCA huts for the troops in France, one provided by the Mercers Company and another sponsored by the Scouts.

Girls had been forming themselves into unofficial groups of 'Girl Scouts' and demanding recognition, although scouting had been designed only for boys. In 1910 the Girl Guides Association was formed and administered, somewhat inefficiently, by a committee in London. In 1916 Olave Baden-Powell undertook to organize guiding in Sussex and was appointed county commissioner. She travelled by bus, train, car, and bicycle to find leaders and supporters for units all over the county, and was so successful that she was made chief commissioner and asked to do the same throughout the whole of Great Britain. In every part of the country she found the right people to lead this new movement, fired them with the founder's ideals and her own enthusiasm, and left them to organize it locally, with support and advice whenever it was needed but without interference.

As guiding spread overseas, Olave Baden-Powell travelled extensively with her husband during the next twenty-five years, tirelessly seeking and encouraging the best leaders in every country they visited and charming the support of royalty, governments, and influential people wherever they went. She was made world chief guide in 1930 and created GBE in 1932. At the same time she was a devoted wife, protecting her husband from overstrain and bringing up, after her sister's death, her three nieces with her own three children in their home at Bentley, Hampshire, where she kept open house to visitors from all over the world.

Olave initiated 'friendship cruises' when chartered ships carried guiders and scouters from the United Kingdom to meet those of other countries. The first cruise in 1933 called at Holland, Poland, Lithuania, Latvia, Estonia, Finland, Sweden, and Norway, and later cruises visited Iceland, Denmark, Belgium, and the Mediterranean countries.

The uniting principles of guiding needed to be constantly ensured as the movement spread, so that all religious denominations, all races, all political persuasions, and all social classes were brought together into one association in each country. In India, the barriers between European and Indian women, between Hindus, Muslims, Parsees, and other religious divisions, were broken down. In South America, Olave induced a breakaway Catholic Scout and Guide Association to be reunited with their all-denominational national associations. In South Africa, where membership was restricted to white people while coloureds had to join a separate organization, she persuaded them that true guiding had to be an amalgamation of all women and united them into 'one country, one association' which, despite apartheid, still exists today.

After a holiday there in 1935, the Baden-Powells returned to Kenya in 1938 and, following her husband's death in 1941, Olave Baden-Powell became president of the East African Women's League and colony commissioner for the Kenya GGA. She returned to England during the war and was given a grace and favour apartment at Hampton Court Palace, from which she continued her world-wide travels, going wherever her presence would give encouragement and promote a wider knowledge of the movement. During her lifetime she travelled hundreds of thousands of miles by air alone. When at home, she entertained, wrote, broadcast, appeared on television, attended conferences and innumerable Guide functions until she developed diabetes in 1970 and was forced into semi-retirement. She died in her sleep at a nursing home near Guildford in Surrey 25 June 1977, and her ashes were buried in her husband's grave at Nyeri, Kenya.

The Girl Guides Association could not be the immense power for good that it is today, with some seven million members in more than a hundred countries all striving for the same ideals, if Olave Baden-Powell had not devoted her life to its establishment and to the advancement of friendship and understanding between women and girls of all nations. She was an instinctive leader and knew that, in a voluntary organization, a consensus of opinion, formed with mutual affection for the benefit of a common purpose, could achieve miracles whilst any hint of dictatorship would destroy it.

Of medium height, with quick movements and continually changing facial expressions, her dark brown eyes were her most noticeable feature, and her wide, ready smile was prompted by genuine amusement or pleasure. Her rather deep voice was emphatic, with clear enunciation. A brilliant raconteur and a deeply interested listener, she was always on the brink of laughter, her lively mind finding humour in the artificial or pompous as easily as in the witty or ridiculous. She was acutely sensitive to the feelings of others and therefore equally in tune with men or women, of all ages and from all walks of life. She radiated vitality and charm, with the strength of simplicity and the natural humility of the truly great.

Among the many honours she received from foreign countries were the Order of Merit (Poland) 1933; Order of White Rose (Finland) 1934; Order of Silver Phoenix (Greece) 1949; Order of Honour and Merit (Haiti) 1951; Order of Bernard O'Higgins (Chile) 1959; Order of the Sun (Peru) 1959; Order of Vasco de Balboa (Panama) 1959; Order of Cedars of Lebanon, 1960; Order of the Sacred Treasure (Japan) 1963; Order of the Grand Ducal Crown of Oaks (Luxembourg) 1965; and the Order of the Estonian Red Cross for her work in helping humanity.

[Records at Girl Guide headquarters; Olave Baden-Powell (with Mary Drewery), *Window on my Heart* (autobiography), 1973; Eileen K. Wade, *Olave Baden-Powell*, 1971; personal knowledge.]

SHEILA WALKER

BAGRIT, SIR LEON (1902–1979), industrialist, was born 13 March 1902 in Kiev, Russia, the younger son and second of three children of Manuel Bagrit, jewellery designer and jeweller, and his wife, Rachel Yousopovitch. The family left Russia when he was a small child and arrived in England from Belgium in 1914. Bagrit knew no English then but mastered it quickly and soon gained a school prize for English literature at St. Olave's School in Southwark, whose headmaster, W. G. Rushbrooke, took a close personal interest in the development of his many-sided gifts. These included music, and playing the violin in an orchestra helped him through the precarious early adult years.

After reading law at Birkbeck College, London University, Bagrit joined Messrs W. & T. Avery, manufacturers of weighing machines. He had no formal training in engineering but possessed an exceptional understanding of engineering and related matters which was vitally important to his subsequent career. In 1927 he became general manager of a competitor, Herbert & Sons.

In 1935, after leaving them, Bagrit set up his own firm, B. & P. Swift, again in the weighing machine business, in order to exploit his own technical innovations. Its abilities were soon harnessed to the war effort in aviation and other fields. In 1947 B. & P. Swift was acquired by Elliott Brothers (London) Ltd., Lewisham, an old-established and substantially larger company, which had emerged from the war without a clear view of its future. Bagrit became first joint managing director, and not long afterwards sole managing director. At this point his undoubted flair for engineering was put to its greatest test, as he resolved to base the company's future on introducing automatic control as extensively as possible. He paid many visits to the United States, where important wartime developments had taken place and many of the basic ingredients of what subsequently became known as automation systems were already available.

If automation were to be introduced successfully over the widest possible field a number of decisions of principle was vital in order to make the best use of financial and human resources. Particularly in the United States, licences were available to enable the firm's own large development effort to be concentrated elsewhere. Financial and organizational control over the multitude of facets involved in the business could only be assured by the creation of a large number of divisions or subsidiary companies under separate managements responsible for their success and controlled by a rigid system of budgets and monthly accounts, an approach which is commonplace today but which Bagrit pioneered in Britain.

The company was rapidly successful, and in 1957 a merger with other smaller companies led to the establishment of Elliott-Automation Ltd., of which Bagrit was first deputy chairman and managing director, and from 1963 onwards chairman and managing director. He expanded the group's activities into Europe and other U.K. territories. The company attracted investors in the United States and was one of the early overseas stocks to be traded there in the ADR (American Depositary Receipt) market. Bagrit's recognition in the City brought him part-time directorships, particularly—in 1963—in the early technology-oriented investment trusts,

Electronic Trust and Technology Investment Trust, which were later merged.

In 1967 Elliott-Automation, which by then employed about 24,000 people, was acquired by the English Electric Company of which Bagrit became a deputy chairman. About a year later the English Electric Company was in turn acquired by the General Electric Company, and while Bagrit remained chairman of the company, later known as GEC-Elliott Automation Ltd., until 1973, he soon retired from an active role.

What distinguished Bagrit from other successful industrialists was his early recognition of the far-reaching problems in social and other fields which automation would bring about. He was confident that they could be solved but not without active and detailed preparation. His thoughts were made public in 1964 through his Reith lectures on 'The Age of Automation' which were subsequently published as a book (1966). He had great breadth of vision and in business was more concerned with the broad sweep than with the detail, much of which he was happy to delegate to colleagues; however there is no doubt of his ability to master detail when he considered it important. This approach left him time to pursue his many other interests. He was a director of the Royal Opera House, Covent Garden, from 1962 to 1970 and the founder of the Friends of Covent Garden of which body he was chairman from 1962 to 1969. After his death Lady Bagrit created the Markova-Bagrit scholarship at the Royal Ballet School in London.

Bagrit was a notable collector in the field of visual arts. His close interest in the development of Israel centred particularly on the Haifa Technion of whose British Friends he was president from 1962 to 1975, and on the Israel Museum. Lady Bagrit established a chair in his name for computer-aided design and scientific research development at Ben-Gurion University.

Bagrit was knighted in 1962. He was a member of the Council for Scientific and Industrial Research from 1963 to 1965 and a member of the advisory council on technology from 1964 to 1969. In 1965 the Royal Society of Arts awarded him the Albert medal for his work in the application of automation to industry. He received honorary doctorates from the universities of Surrey (1966) and Reading (1968).

In 1926 he married Stella, daughter of Simon Feldman, business man, and his wife Rebecca. There were two daughters and seven grandchildren, to whom he was closely attached. Bagrit died in London 22 April 1979.

[*The Times*, 23 November 1979; interviews with Lady Bagrit; private information; personal knowledge.] E. O. HERZFELD

BAKER, SIR GEOFFREY HARDING (1912–1980), field-marshal, was born at Murree, then in India, 20 June 1912, the only son and youngest of the five children of Colonel Cecil Norris Baker, CIE, and his wife, Ella Mary Hutchinson. His father was in the Northamptonshire Regiment but bad health restricted his later career to staff appointments. He was chief paymaster in China during the Boxer rising. Baker was educated at Wellington College and the Royal Military Academy, Woolwich, where he was senior under-officer and won the sword of honour. Tall and fair-haired, he was called George the Swede by his friends: thereafter he was George.

Commissioned into the Royal Artillery in 1932 he went with the 11th Field brigade from Aldershot to Meerut in 1935. In 1937 he was given his 'jacket' in F (Sphinx) battery, Royal Horse Artillery, at Risalpur. As part of the 4th regiment RHA the battery went to Egypt on mobilization. After attending the Middle East Staff College Baker became brigade-major Royal Artillery 4th Indian division which fought against the Italians in Eritrea. He was at the battle of Keren and won the MC (1941) for his services in the field. After instructing at the Staff College he was promoted lieutenant-colonel GSO 1 at the headquarters of the Eighth Army. He was heard to criticize the failure to concentrate artillery for maximum fire effect and welcomed the change of policy at Alamein. He remained on the staff until the Sicilian campaign when he commanded the 127th Field Regiment, 51st Highland division.

Posted home in 1944 to headquarters, 21st Army Group, as brigadier general staff, he remained in this demanding post until the end of the war. After commanding the third Royal Horse Artillery at Münsterlager in the British Army of the Rhine (1950–2), he was promoted director of administrative planning in the War Office. When Field-Marshal Sir A. F. Harding (later Lord Harding of Petherton) became governor of Cyprus in 1955 he selected Baker to be chief of staff and director of operations against the dissident organization EOKA. Baker had to operate at many levels, including GHQ Middle East, and as well as working with Foreign and Colonial Office staffs oversaw subordinate district security committees which co-ordinated the work of all agencies. Baker showed flair for getting a variety of people to work together on agreed priorities and for evolving sound plans. Though complicated by the Suez operation in 1956 Baker's contribution to the pacification of Cyprus, involving twelve major army units, was considerable.

While serving as major-general, chief of staff Southern Command in 1961 Baker was selected for the new post of chief of staff contingencies (Liveoak) at Supreme Headquarters, Allied Powers, Europe (SHAPE). Liveoak was set up to deal with the four-power confrontation in Berlin, where the Russians supported, by a surprise show of force, East German measures to restrict emigration to the West. Baker's task was complex and internationally delicate, for stakes being played for over Berlin in 1961–3 were high.

Returning to the War Office in 1963 as vice-chief of the imperial general staff and lieutenant-general, Baker's tour was prolonged due to the abolition of separate Service ministries in 1964. He had a hand in evolving new staff procedures in the Ministry of Defence. After a brief respite as general officer commanding-in-chief Southern Command (1966–8) Baker was appointed chief of the general staff in 1968 when general retrenchment in defence was following the financial crisis of 1967 and garrisons overseas were being reduced. Baker proved an excellent choice. Trusted and liked, he commanded complete loyalty in the army. In the higher councils of defence he helped to heal the divisions between the Royal Navy and Royal Air Force over the carrier controversy. His sound advice was given in the best way. He was a complete master of committee procedure. Modest, always approachable and courteous to subordinates with problems, he radiated confidence through the sound and sensible advice he gave. Otherwise he let his staff get on with their work without interference.

When the army was committed in Ulster in August 1969 Baker's experience in Cyprus gave him a sure touch. His advice to politicians was sound and he guided commanders on the ground in a constructive way. His visits to Ulster did much to sustain morale and support the troops in carrying out often distasteful duties in the glare of television publicity. Baker was the first of a new type of senior officer, expert in his own field, and enjoying the respect of civil servant, diplomat, politician, and journalist alike. Always calm and capable of sound compromise, he was a man for the time, bringing the army through a period of change yet preserving the best of the past.

On retirement in March 1971 he was made field-marshal, having been master gunner, St. James's Park, since 1970 and colonel commandant Royal Artillery since 1964. He became constable of the Tower in 1975 and was a freeman of the City of London. He was a governor of Wellington and Radley Colleges. There is a portrait of him by J. Bilton at Woolwich and a stained-glass window in his memory at Sandhurst.

He was appointed OBE (1943), CBE (1946), CB (1955), CMG (1957), KCB (1964), and GCB (1968). In 1946 he married Valerie Stirling Hamilton, daughter of Major John Leonard ('Ian') Lockhart, of the Royal Hampshire Regiment; they had two sons and a daughter. Baker died 8 May 1980 at Wellington College.

[*The Times*, 10 May and 4 June 1980; Royal Artillery *Journal*, vol. cvii, no. 2, September 1980; private information; personal knowledge.]

R. H. WHITWORTH

BALCARRES, eleventh EARL OF (1900–1975), connoisseur of the arts. [See LINDSAY, DAVID ALEXANDER ROBERT.]

BALCON, SIR MICHAEL ELIAS (1896–1977), film producer, was born in Birmingham 19 May 1896, the youngest of three sons among the five children of Louis Balcon, prospector in South Africa, who later went to America before returning to England and becoming a salesman, and his wife, Laura Greenberg. He grew up in a family which he described as 'respectable but impoverished'. His Jewish father, who had connections in South Africa, was something of a wanderer, often leaving the mother to run the family, sometimes with the help of her eldest son. Michael was educated at the George Dixon Grammar School, Birmingham; he left in 1913. In 1914 he tried to join up, but was rejected because of a flaw in his left eye, and throughout the war he worked for the Dunlop Rubber Company.

When peace came he joined Victor Saville (later a well-known director and producer) in forming a modest film distribution company. Presently with a joint capital of £200 the two of them set off for London; raised financial backing from figures in the industry; imported an American star; and produced a melodrama, *Woman to Woman* (1922). It was a success, but a second venture was a failure. Not discomfited, Balcon managed to found a film company which was to become famous, Gainsborough Pictures. Also in 1924 he married a girl from Johannesburg, South Africa, Aileen Freda, daughter of Beatrice Leatherman. She was appointed MBE in 1946. The marriage lasted in happiness to the end of his life. There were two children: a son, Jonathan, and a daughter, the actress Jill Balcon, who was to marry the poet laureate, Cecil Day-Lewis [q.v.].

The first Gainsborough films were made at Islington in what was a converted power house. With the business help of Reginald Baker, his accountant and lifelong friend, Balcon bought the studios. There followed a series of silent films which included *Blighty* (1927) and two pieces with Ivor Novello [q.v.], *The Rat* (1925) and *The Lodger* (1926), which was directed by (Sir) Alfred Hitchcock [q.v.].

Balcon welcomed the advent of sound. Despite his conviction that the British screen must not be dominated by America, he was obliged for technical reasons to go to Hollywood for the production of his *Journey's End* (1930). But a year later he was in charge of production not only at Islington but also at the Gaumont-British Picture Corporation.

Years of intense activity followed. The films were not world-beaters, but they were made with a serious care for the standing of the British cinema: *The Constant Nymph* (1933); *The Good Companions* (1932) with Jessie Matthews; Conrad Veidt was brought from Germany to play in *Rome Express* (1932) and *Jew Süss* (1934); Walter Huston starred in *Rhodes of Africa* (1936). Balcon had seen the work of Alfred Hitchcock as a beginner; now he saw the blossoming of a giant talent in *The Man Who Knew Too Much* (1934) and *The Thirty-Nine Steps* (1935). And he has the credit of having backed Robert J. Flaherty's *Man of Aran* (1932).

In 1936 his work at Gaumont-British ended, and he was invited to take charge of Metro-Goldwyn-Mayer's production in Britain. The first film was *A Yank at Oxford* (1938). He disapproved of the script, and with his strong feeling about a national British cinema he was unhappy with his position. The association ended, leaving him free to pursue his true work; and, resuming his partnership with Reginald Baker, he began working, quite modestly, at Ealing Studios. By 1938 he was in charge of production. He was to make the name of Ealing internationally famous.

War was imminent: Balcon recognized the need for a documentary approach, and, joined in 1940 by the celebrated documentary director Alberto Cavalcanti, he was responsible for a series of notable war films: *The Foreman Went to France* (1941), *San Demetrio, London* (1943); *Next of Kin* (1942); and Cavalcanti's own *Went the Day Well?* (1942). After the war the serious mood continued in *The Cruel Sea* (1952), and the problems of readjustment were tackled in such films as *The Divided Heart* (1954). As early as 1945 Ealing produced a brilliant exercise in the ghostly *Dead of Night.* And Balcon was ready to explore new territory; films were made in Australia, among them *The Overlanders* (1946).

But probably the greatest achievement was in the field of comedy, *Passport to Pimlico* (1949), *Whisky Galore* (1948), *The Lavender Hill Mob* (1951), and the special triumphs of (Sir) Alec Guinness—*Kind Hearts and Coronets* (1949), *The Man in the White Suit* (1951), and *The Ladykillers* (1955). Even the Americans were won over, and in the 1950s one could see New Yorkers queueing to see Ealing comedy. And there were other notable films: *It Always Rains on Sunday* (1947), *The Blue Lamp* (1949), *Mandy* (1952), and *Scott of the Antarctic* (1948).

Balcon was knighted in 1948. Eleven years later Ealing closed. But he was still ceaselessly active. He was chairman of British Lion and of the adventurous Bryanston Company, and his name is associated with such films as *Saturday Night and Sunday Morning* (1960) and *Tom Jones* (1963). Meanwhile he became a director of Border Television. The output was huge, varied, and distinguished; truly he was among the creators of the British cinema. Quick to appreciate talent, he collected at Ealing a band of remarkable directors; the young Pen Tennyson (killed in the war), Sandy Mackendrick, Robert Hamer, Charles Frend, Harry Watt, Charles Crichton. Of a shy but sometimes explosive temperament, in private life he was a man of great charm, and his house on the Kent–Sussex borders, secluded in gardens and farmland, was a place of genial family hospitality.

Balcon was a fellow of the British Film Academy, a governor of the British Film Institute, an honorary fellow of the British Kinematograph Society, a senior fellow of the Royal College of Art, and was awarded an honorary D.Litt. from Birmingham (1967) and Sussex (1975). He died at his home at Upper Parrock, Hartfield, Sussex, 17 October 1977.

[Michael Balcon, *A Lifetime of Films*, 1969; personal knowledge.] DILYS POWELL

BALLANTRAE, first BARON (1911–1980), soldier, author, and public servant. [See FERGUSSON, BERNARD EDWARD.]

BALNIEL, LORD (1900–1975), connoisseur of the arts. [See LINDSAY, DAVID ALEXANDER ROBERT.]

BANDON, fifth EARL OF (1904–1979), air chief marshal. [See BERNARD, PERCY RONALD GARDNER.]

BARING, (CHARLES) EVELYN, first BARON HOWICK OF GLENDALE (1903–1973), colonial governor, was born 29 September 1903 in London, the third son of Evelyn Baring, first Earl of Cromer [q.v.], being the only child of his second marriage to Lady Katherine Thynne, daughter of the fourth Marquess of Bath. Lord Cromer was commissioner general of Egypt at the time the young Baring visited his father briefly in Cairo before the family finally settled in England on Cromer's retirement. Baring went to school at Winchester and in September 1921 to New College, Oxford, where he obtained a first class degree in history in 1924, and became an honorary fellow in 1960.

From his early days at Winchester, Baring never showed any doubt that his duty lay in the British imperial service. He went straight from Oxford to the Indian Civil Service in 1926. There, in the United Provinces, first at Lucknow and then at Meerut, he acquired that taste for the small patina of rural administration that continued to excite him thirty years later as a governor and commander-in-chief. His major contribution to British imperial history was to lie in Africa. But it was actually not on behalf of the imperial government, but of the Indian government, that he first came to the African continent. He was sent in 1929 to be secretary to the agent of the government of India in Durban—a relatively new appointment intended to mitigate the hardship which Natal's Indian population were suffering at the hands of the South African government. It was a problem M. K. Gandhi [q.v.] had wrestled with and inflamed only a few years previously.

On Baring's return to India, in 1932, he did a short tour in the North-West Frontier before being struck down by amoebic dysentery which finished his career in the ICS. He returned to England, dogged by the disease and its after effects. It left him a lifelong teetotaller, condemned to a regime of strict dieting, and frequent periods of exhaustion.

There was a brief intervention in the family bank, reluctantly joined by Baring. He soon found he had no great taste for City life, and turned down the offer of senior partnership in favour of joining the Sudan Development Company. His banking experience did, however, give him an insight into the world of high finance, development, and accounting which proved of benefit later in his dealings with treasuries and world banks in the colonies and at the Commonwealth Development Corporation. When war broke out in 1939 he was unfit for military service but joined the Foreign Office, in a temporary capacity, dealing mostly with Egypt. In July 1942 he was appointed governor of Southern Rhodesia at the age of thirty-eight. For him the desultory years since his departure from India were now at an end.

In Rhodesia Baring again came to grips with Africa's racial problems. Whereas before in Durban he was fighting for the Indians, in Rhodesia he found he had to contend with the attitudes of whites towards blacks, which were already hardening. As Governor, he was a constitutional monarch, with little executive power—Rhodesia already had internal self-government. But he was able to do much by example, showing that his interests lay in African administration and agriculture, which was something not expected of the governor by the vast majority of whites who regarded 'His Excellency' as *their* governor. The early experience in India had fired in him a lifelong enthusiasm for native agriculture, forestry, irrigation, land reclamation, birds, and botany, which were all available for him in profusion in the Rhodesian veld.

In 1944 he was appointed to succeed the fourth Baron Harlech [q.v.] as high commissioner to South Africa. This was a dual post combining responsibilities of an ambassador to Pretoria with those of governor of the three protectorates: Bechuanaland, Swaziland, and Basutoland. His tour encompassed the ending of the war, the last royal visit of King George VI and Queen Elizabeth, the eclipse of J. C. Smuts [q.v.] in the 1948 election and the rise of D. F. Malan [q.v.] and the Afrikaner nationalists. Nor were the territories always rural havens from high politics. The drama of the marriage of (Sir) Seretse Khama [q.v.] and the Attlee government's reaction caused difficulties for Baring, which, at the time, he felt might irretrievably damage his reputation in Africa.

He was wrong; and in 1952 was appointed governor of Kenya by (Sir) Winston Churchill. By the time he eventually arrived in Nairobi early signs of Kikuyu tribal disturbances had already blown up and one of his first acts had to be to declare a full-scale emergency.

It was in Kenya during the 1950s that Baring faced his greatest challenge. Essentially a humane man, an administrator and developer, he had to prove himself capable of defeating an armed rebellion without either losing sight of his eventual objectives—prosperity for Africans and agricultural development in Kenya—or losing the ability to achieve those goals by his association with the counter-insurgency operation. It was not always easy. His military subordinates often chafed at their constraints; settlers complained and demonstrated. Perhaps it was only Baring's humanity which enabled the rebellion first to be contained and then, through the agricultural and rehabilitation programmes, turned to Kenya's ultimate advantage.

When the rebellion was broken, in about 1956, a new middle-class African started to emerge under Baring's careful husbandry. The settlers, however, never trusted him until the end; and rightly, in the sense that his agricultural reforms introduced a fundamental change—at the European's expense—in the whole Kenyan agrarian economy. They were rushed through with a speed which would have been inconceivable except during the emergency.

When he left Kenya in 1959 it was natural that he became chairman of the Colonial Development Corporation (1960–3)—later absorbed in the Commonwealth Development Corporation (1963–72)—and of the Nature Conservancy (1962–73), managing in his retirement to continue to indulge his two passions—development and wildlife. They provided welcome breaks from the hard practical work he plunged into when managing his own Northumbrian farms. He was also president of the Liverpool School of Tropical Medicine (1967–73), chairman of the British North American Committee (1970–3), and a director of the Swan Hunter Group Ltd.

What kind of man lurked behind this rather imposing proconsular facade? Was he just a remote patrician, as his critics said? He had aristocratic good looks certainly, but also a basic shyness throughout his life, which probably originated in his youth under the eccentric gaze of a mother and very odd aristocratic aunts. After his illness, he found solace in a passion for exercise, birds, and botany. Rock climbing absorbed him and led ultimately to his unnecessary death from a modest fall in March 1973. His absorption in birds and botany led to a naturalism of phenomenal detail. After his second visit to South Africa he developed a much deeper and fundamental Christian faith, which, though very private, seemed to shine out of him to all those who knew him. Indeed during the emergency in Kenya he prayed most days in his private chapel and, when in his last month in Kenya he saved an Indian girl from drowning, semi-conscious though he was, he was heard to be praying for her life, though nearly drowning himself in the process. For his bravery he was awarded the Queen's Commendation for Brave Conduct (1959).

Baring's life in many ways appeared as a natural extention of his father's. If Cromer in Egypt, and before that in India, served as a high watermark of British imperialism, his son's career showed the best side of Britain's eventual decline from imperialist power to partner, friend, and adviser-in-development, which defines the evolving relationship with her former colonies.

In 1935 he married Lady Mary Cecil Grey, elder daughter of Charles Robert, fifth Earl Grey, whose home at Howick, Northumberland, was Baring's base through all the years of his service abroad, and then in his retirement. They had one son and two daughters. Baring was appointed KCMG in 1942, KCVO in 1947, GCMG in 1955, and KG in 1972. He had many honorary degrees. He received a hereditary barony in January 1960, and took the title Lord Howick of Glendale, in the county of Northumberland. He died 10 March 1973 and was succeeded in the barony by his son, Charles Evelyn (born 1937).

[Charles Douglas-Home, *Evelyn Baring, the Last Proconsul*, 1978.]

CHARLES DOUGLAS-HOME

BARNES, ALFRED JOHN (1887–1974), chairman of the Co-operative Party and Labour government minister, was born 17 July 1887 in the Plaistow district of London, the youngest of seven children of William Barnes, a dockland coffee-house keeper (later a docker) and his wife, Lucinda Margaret Smith. He was educated at the Star Lane boys' school, Canning Town, lost a leg at the age of eight following a fair-ground accident, and in his early teens attended the Northampton Institute and the LCC College of Art where he specialized in gold and silver design. After his apprenticeship to this trade he had his own workshop.

He became politically aware when quite a young man; and in 1908 he joined the Stratford Co-operative Society and the Independent Labour Party. Two years later he was secretary of the East London ILP Federation and he was prominent in the affairs of his trade: from 1912 to 1914 he represented the Gold and Silver Council on the LCC's education consultative committee. But it was the co-operative movement that especially appealed to him. Elected to the management committee of the Stratford Society in 1914, he became its president in 1915.

Barnes believed in the political importance of the movement within the broad spectrum of Labour, and he warmly supported the establishment of the Co-operative Party in 1917. Three years later he was elected to its national committee, and in 1922 was one of the four successful Co-operative Party candidates at the general election of that year when he became MP for East Ham South. He was made parliamentary private secretary to William Graham [q.v.], financial secretary to the Treasury in the Labour government of 1924, and became a parliamentary whip from 1925 to 1930 (in an official position as lord of the Treasury when Labour regained office in 1929).

Barnes emerged as a leading personality of the Co-operative Party, of which he was chairman from 1924 to 1945. His views were expressed in several pamphlets, the most notable being *The Political Aspect of Co-operation* (1922, revised edn. 1926) and a Fabian tract, *The Co-operator in Politics* (1923). Barnes was a vigorous proponent of the Labour Co-operative agreement, accepted by the 1927 Co-operative Congress at Cheltenham, and the compact worked well enough for the next few years. But, in the electoral débâcle of 1931, Barnes was among the many who lost their seats.

He was, however, extremely active outside Westminster in the co-operative sphere. He had played a leading role in the amalgamation of individual London societies to form the London Co-operative Society in 1920, and was its president until 1923. In 1929 the National Co-operative Publishing Society (from 1935 the Co-operative Press Ltd.), of which Barnes was the unpaid chairman, purchased *Reynolds's Illustrated News* from Lord Dalziel of Kirkcaldy [q.v.] and Barnes remained an important influence behind the paper during the next decade.

He regained his seat at East Ham South in 1935 and, like his other colleagues in the Co-operative Party, followed more or less the majority Labour Party line on domestic and international politics. An exception was the vigorous campaign launched by the editor of *Reynolds News*, Sydney Elliott, for a United Peace Alliance in 1938. This was the co-operative version of the Popular Front and Barnes backed Elliott: to be defeated by a substantial vote at the Co-operative Congress in June 1938.

Barnes remained on the back-benches of the Commons during the World War II years, but continued to be absorbed in the work of the co-operative movement: he encouraged continuous discussion on the movement's future in the post-war era; he was the prime mover behind the establishment of the Peoples' Entertainment Society; and, on the prompting of Sir R. Stafford Cripps [q.v.], Barnes formed the Anglo-Chinese Development Society.

In the government of 1945 led by C. R. (later Earl) Attlee Barnes was appointed minister of war transport (from 1946 minister of transport), a position he retained until the 1951 election. He was admitted to the Privy Council in 1945. His most important achievement was the 1947 Transport Act which established the nationalized British Transport Commission on terms which occasioned considerable criticism from Labour's left wing. He had resigned from the Co-operative Press in 1945 and when he retired from Parliament in 1955 he withdrew from national affairs.

In 1947 he had bought a bombed hotel at Walton-on-the-Naze, Essex, which he turned into flats. He subsequently went to live there, purchased the adjoining land, and organized a caravan park. He was active in local affairs as a JP and as an Independent member of the Frinton and Walton UDC. And there he stayed until his death at his home in Walton 26 November 1974.

Barnes was something of an angry young man in his early days but he was always quite untheoretical and practical life moderated his ideas and objectives. He was not a lively speaker but had considerable business ability and administrative skill. He was tolerant, good-humoured, and unpretentious and ranks with A. V. Alexander (later Earl Alexander of Hillsborough, q.v.) as among the outstanding personalities of the co-operative movement in the first half of the twentieth century.

In 1921 he married Leila Phoebe, of Pitsea, daughter of Charles Real, an engraver; there were three daughters of the marriage.

[W. H. Brown, *A Century of London Co-operation*, 1928; T. F. Carbery, *Consumers in Politics*, 1969; *The Times*, 27 November 1974; *Dictionary of Labour Biography*, vol. ii (articles on Sir John Bailey and Arthur Lockwood), ed. Joyce M. Bellamy and John Saville, 1974; *Co-operative News*, 17 December 1980; private information.]

JOYCE M. BELLAMY

BARNES, JOHN MORRISON (1913–1975), toxicologist, was born in Sheffield at midnight on 11/12 January 1913, the elder son and elder child of Alfred Edward Barnes, later professor of medicine in the University of Sheffield, and his wife, Janet ('Jessie') Morrison. Barnes's younger brother, (Harry) Jefferson Barnes (died 1979) was knighted on retirement from the Glasgow School of Art. John Barnes, after education at Repton, went to Trinity Hall, Cambridge, in 1930, was awarded a scholarship in 1932, and took first classes in both parts of the natural sciences tripos (1932 and 1933), specializing in pathology in part ii. In 1933 he entered Sheffield Medical School, gaining conjoint and Cambridge qualifications in 1936—MB, B.Chir. (Camb.), MRCS (Eng.), LRCP (Lond.).

After a residency in Sheffield, he took a house surgeonship at the Wingfield–Morris Orthopaedic Hospital in Oxford, which led to a Nuffield research fellowship in orthopaedics (1938–42). This was an important step, for it led to training under Howard W. (later Lord) Florey [q.v.] in the Sir William Dunn School of Pathology, in research on the lymphocyte, and then to work with Josep A. Trueta [q.v.] on wound drainage and arterial spasm, and to becoming honorary director of the Medical Research Council (MRC) Burns Unit at Oxford. His war service in the Royal Army Medical Corps was as a specialist pathologist in the biology section of the Chemical Warfare Defence Establishment at Porton, conducting research under the direction of (Sir) Paul Fildes and D. W. W. Henderson [qq.v.]. By 1947 he had been trained in experimental pathology, and had worked on shock, and on the toxicity of venoms, bacterial toxins, and the tannic acid used in the treatment of burns.

The Medical Research Council, during the secretaryship of Sir Edward Mellanby [q.v.], decided in 1947 to establish a Toxicology Unit to undertake research in the general field of toxicology as it applied to chemical hazards in industry and agriculture. This was in response to the increasing number of enquiries from industry about the safety or otherwise of new chemical substances. Barnes was appointed the first director. The unit was initially housed at Porton, but with the need for expansion moved in 1950 to Carshalton. At the time of his appointment, toxicology hardly existed as a discipline, but was seen as a series of routine investigations into *ad hoc* problems, which was of little scientific interest. It was Barnes's life-work to reveal its scientific potential, and to establish the value of analysing the general mechanisms by which bodily injury may be brought about as the best basis for rational decisions about control procedures. The study began with work on liver damage caused by beryllium, and on an insecticide and a weed-killer which were both widely used. It was followed by studies on DDT, tin compounds, dinitrophenol, the nitrosamines, the Senecio alkaloids, the groundnut fungal product aflatoxin, lead, dieldrin, mercury, and neuropathies and other damage due to industrial solvents. To such work was added fundamental research, usually of a biochemical type, on general mechanisms.

At the same time there was continuing service on MRC committees—those on toxicology (of which he was secretary for thirteen years), food adulterants, fungicides and insecticides, detergents, lung cancer, non-explosive anaesthetics, cancer of the tropics, and occupational health. The topics reflected the growing attention paid to toxicology both medically and politically, which owed much to Barnes's leadership in showing how to tackle extremely varied problems with scientific rigour. In turn this led to much other advisory work, especially for the World Health Organization, for which the Toxicology Unit became a reference centre.

As a man Barnes combined great steadiness of character and a dry humour with extreme modesty and a detestation of pretentiousness of any kind. He concealed his own achievements and resisted being proposed for the Royal Society. A very hard worker, he listed his recreations as 'none'. He could seem rather austere and formidable, and yet those who came to know him, or better still to work with him, found him sensitive and supportive. He had a very good eye for new talent, enjoyed bringing on younger investigators, and never took his share of appreciation for their achievements. After his death British toxicology had advanced enough to justify the formation of a British Toxicology Society, which was largely due to the initiative of his colleagues and pupils. One of their early actions, after a well-supported appeal, was to establish the John Barnes lecture in his memory. He was appointed CBE in 1962.

In 1941 Barnes married Ruth Eleanor, daughter of the Revd Edward Joseph Northcote-Green, of Oxford. There were three children: the eldest, Andrew Nicholas, trained in chemistry (D.Phil., Oxon.); the second, Stephen Edward, became a consultant paediatrician in Salisbury; and the youngest, Rachel Elizabeth, married R. E. McGavin. Barnes died 24 September 1975 in the Atkinson Morley Hospital, Wimbledon.

[Reports of the Medical Research Council from 1939–45 onwards; private information; personal knowledge.] W. D. M. PATON

BATES, HERBERT ERNEST (1905–1974), writer, was born at Rushton in Northamptonshire 16 May 1905. His maternal grandfather was a craftsman shoemaker; his father Albert Ernest Bates one of less distinction, bedevilled by the introduction of new-fangled machinery. His mother, Lucy Elizabeh Lucas, went to work at the age of ten as a 'part-timer' tying knots for a princely two shillings a week. They produced a family of two boys and a girl of which Herbert was the eldest. As he was to write later, he 'grew up in an atmosphere of intense respectability . . . My parents were never a farthing in debt; great was the pride they took, as my grandparents did, in paying their way . . . My father pursued his passion for nature and the countryside, and incidentally fostered my own.' This, indeed, was to become, next to writing, the absorption of his own life. After his death it was written 'as he wrote he gardened and as he gardened he wrote'.

From a local school Bates won a 'free place' to Kettering Grammar School where he stayed until he was just over sixteen, then achieving a third class in the Joint Oxford and Cambridge University Certificate. Such was the academic record of one destined to become regarded in his own lifetime as among the finest masters of English prose.

Known always to his friends and even to his wife and children as H. E., no other vocation than that of a writer ever occurred to him except that he would have liked to be a painter as well. Immediately upon leaving school Bates became a clerk, but very quickly turned to provincial journalism and the writing of his first novel, *The Two Sisters*, which attained publication in 1926 with its author just twenty-one. It had been rejected by nine publishers (which, even in those days, must have taken quite a while) before being submitted to Jonathan Cape [q.v.], a relatively new and lively publisher who had remarkably established his imprint within his first five years. He had wisely recruited as his chief reader and 'literary adviser' Edward Garnett, probably one of the most perceptive and distinguished 'readers' of his era. One evening, early in 1926, Garnett reported to an exasperated Cape that he had 'found another genius—a Miss Bates'.

None too pleased to find himself addressed as Miss Bates, Bates was naturally elated to be the recipient of not only the offer of a modest advance from Mr Cape (whose advances had always a tendency in that direction) but the tutelage of Garnett's brilliance which was to continue until Garnett's death in 1937. Bates was later to pay his own touching and memorable tribute in his *Edward Garnett: a Personal Portrait*, published in 1950.

For some twenty years, and for about as many books, Cape was to be Bates's publisher. His sales, claimed Cape, never earned fully the advances he paid against them.

By 1931 Cape had published two further novels and in that year, with the publication of his fourth, Bates married Marjorie Helen, the daughter of a soldier, Herbert Henry Cox. Known as Madge and well aware of the uncertainties facing aspiring young writers, she was for the rest of Bates's life to provide a background of serenity, devotion, and family warmth without which the full expression of his gifts would neither have reached any peak nor been sustained at any high level. They were to have two sons and two daughters. One son, Richard, was later to make for himself a distinguished career in television and was responsible for the translation into that medium of many of his father's most successful novels and short stories.

From the midlands Bates and his wife went immediately to Kent, walking its countryside until they came upon the village of Little Chart and 'The Granary' where Bates was to remain and write and garden for the rest of his life. With his family it was to become for him 'the still centre of the turning world', as T. S. Eliot [q.v.] had phrased it.

Times were not then easy and neither publishers nor writers faced their future with much confidence. Only a handful of authors could be regarded as financially successful and Bates was certainly not among them. His reputation was far in excess of his sales. He had already made memorable the character of Uncle Silas and was acclaimed as a brilliant new delineator of the English countryside and its people with both his novels and his short stories. Yet it required both concentration and courage to pursue undaunted his craft of writing with a young family to educate and maintain.

World War II was for Bates, as for other writers of that time, the turning point of their careers. Not only did it enlarge their horizons, it increased their sales and few were to benefit to a greater extent than Bates, for he was subseqently to become one of the most widely read writers of his time, attaining considerable prosperity and, when he felt like it, the tinsel and glitter of success. Its sometimes heady trappings were to both repel and fascinate him at the same time. It was again the unshakeable foundation provided by Madge, 'The Granary', and the interests of his growing children which maintained the deep integrity and humanity of the man and his writing.

During 1941, thanks to some clever and unprecedented inspiration, the RAF recruited Bates to the Royal Air Force as a 'short story writer'—officially a flight lieutenant to Public Relations, Air Ministry. He was granted unusual freedom of movement and access to those involved and a year later had become squadron leader and, under the pseudonym of Flying Officer X, author of *The Greatest People in the World* (1942). These stories immortalized 'the Few' who fought, mainly over the skies of Kent, the Battle of Britain. The eventual publishing success was enormous. Jonathan Cape at last had a financially rewarding H. E. Bates in his list with promising future prospects. But, possibly after the death of Garnett, there had come a certain disenchantment and, a little hardly some were to feel, his next full length novel—*Fair Stood the Wind for France* (1944)—went to the fortunate and fairly new firm of Michael Joseph who were to remain his publishers for the rest of his life.

Under the impetus of war and the sudden flowering of popular success Bates was now to write a long series of bestsellers and no less distinguished for being so. Chosen by book clubs, reissued by Penguin, translated throughout the world, made often into films, titles, which were still famous after a generation, came from him in extraordinary succession. A play, *The Day of Glory* (1945) followed *Fair Stood the Wind for France*; *The Cruise of the Breadwinner* came in 1946; *The Purple Plain* in 1947 derived from his wider travels as did *The Jacaranda Tree* in 1949. *Love for Lydia* was published in 1952. For some this seemed likely to prove the last of his best and it was not until six years later that the Larkins suddenly burst upon the scene n *The Darling Buds of May* (1958) and began an earthy series of rusticity achieving an enormous readership and for which, by many, Bates may be best remembered.

Great affluence had come to Bates and with it not only a natural enough extravagance but the always pressing need to satisfy the insatiable demands of the tax collector. There can be little doubt that there was a period of over-writing under persistent pressures. None the less Bates was a man of essential reserve, quietude, and reflection. He seemed often ill at ease when the accolade of success involved him in occasions from which, however congenial, he escaped with relief. It was only in the honesty of nature's countryside and his home in his beloved Kent that the quality of the man shone through. An early alternative ambition was to be a painter. He was always fascinated by the French Impressionists and during prosperous days acquired a valuable collection. As a writer he had an affinity with them, and as a gardener too. Bates did not create portraits in any precision of formal realism; it was more a matter of suggestion, a hint here and there, a sudden revelation, an intentional blurring of detail which leaves something to the imagination and remains thus infinitely alive. So it was with his garden, a riot of colour with its artistry never apparent.

Bates quietly exerted considerable influence on behalf of writers and their craft. Never a politician in these matters, he felt keenly about them. He enjoyed confidence in his second publishers and in the long experience of this writer there existed always a complete harmony. His literary agent was for many years Laurence Pollinger, who was indefatigable on his behalf. In 1973 Bates was appointed CBE.

Among the most enduring of his later works are likely to be his three exquisitely contrived short volumes of autobiography: *The Vanished World* (1969), *The Blossoming World* (1971), and

The World in Ripeness (1972). Each most touchingly illustrated by John Ward, and none containing an index of any kind, they most beautifully and informally portray the extraordinary world in which Bates lived his time and they identify a writer of that time whose honesty of purpose and genius of compassionate expression will clarify its mysteries for generations to come. Bates died in Canterbury Hospital 29 January 1974.

[H. E. Bates's three volumes of autobiography, as cited above; private information; personal knowledge.] ROBERT LUSTY

BAWDEN, SIR FREDERICK CHARLES (1908–1972), virologist and plant pathologist, was born 18 August 1908 in North Tawton, Devon, the younger son and youngest of the three children of George Bawden, relieving officer and registrar of births and deaths, and his wife, Ellen Balment. Later his parents became master and matron of the Okehampton Poor Law Institution (that is, the workhouse), and early observation of poverty probably helped to establish Bawden's sympathetic social outlook. The large institutional garden, mainly devoted to potatoes, and the botanical enthusiasm of the headmaster of Okehampton Grammar School may have influenced the direction of his later scientific interests. He also attended Queen Elizabeth School in Crediton. With help from a Ministry of Agriculture and Fisheries scholarship, he went to Emmanuel College, Cambridge, and studied botany, chemistry, and physiology. He obtained a first class in part i of the natural sciences tripos (1928) and the diploma in agricultural science (1930). In 1930, after working for two years under F. T. Brooks on cereal rusts, he started work at the Potato Virus Research Station (Cambridge) financed by a grant as assistant to R. N. Salaman [q.v.]. That apprenticeship led logically to his subsequent posts: virus physiologist at Rothamsted Experimental Station in 1936, head of the department of plant pathology in 1940, its deputy director in 1950, and its director in 1958.

Bawden was known primarily as a virus worker; initially because of the isolation of the first virus preparation for which reasonable claims of purity could be made, and latterly because of the four editions of *Plant Viruses and Virus Diseases* (first published 1939, fourth edn. 1964). Nevertheless, although he did no further research on fungus infections, he retained a lifelong interest in them. They occupied as much space as virus infections in his *Plant Diseases* (1948). He discussed them in several articles and condemned the tendency to segregate specialists on different infective agents into different departments or institutes. His approach to viruses was broad-minded. He published papers on their chemical, physical, and serological properties, and on their classification, multiplication, and physiological effects. He knew more chemistry than most plant pathologists, but was not bemused by the subject and readily acknowledged that much of what passed for knowledge in the 1930s about nucleic acids and proteins was baseless.

After the end of the war of 1939–45 many students from the less developed countries went to Rothamsted for training in plant pathology. Bawden welcomed them enthusiastically at first, but later he became more critical when he found that many were not given jobs in their speciality when they returned home. During frequent visits to India, the Caribbean, and some African countries he gained experience of tropical agriculture; he demonstrated to those 'on the spot' that their crops were not as healthy as they had thought and that, when a diseased state was recognized, its cause was often wrongly attributed. He had little patience with formal visits or demonstrations of elaborate equipment: he preferred to get into the field to see crops and discuss them with farmers. He served, often as chairman, on several committees concerned with tropical agriculture.

He thought of the direction of research in a similarly practical way and argued that those engaged in it, as long as they understood that the primary object of farming is to produce food, knew more about needs and possibilities than anyone else. In many articles he criticized aspects of British agricultural research policy—especially the 'customer/contractor principle' which was introduced in the 1970s. Bawden realized that, although much research is repetitive and remote, projects which are so regarded by the uninitiated may not be. He was delighted that projects which he supported in spite of criticism, such as freeing the King Edward potato clone from paracrinkle virus, and the synthesis of pyrethrin analogues, were ultimately extremely profitable. During his directorship, Rothamsted grew beyond its previous bounds in size and staff. He realized, however, that getting research applied was often harder than doing it, and in this respect he contrasted agriculture unfavourably with medicine.

Besides ensuring that his staff had adequate facilities for research, Bawden took a keen interest in the manner of its presentation. He had a sharp eye for ambiguity, prolixity, and illegitimately general statements. His suggested emendations were sometimes slightly uncouth but it was invariably wise to reconsider any phrase he had queried. In spite of a humorous, cheerful, and friendly manner, he could be as blunt as was necessary to get a point across. Apart from the routine of ensuring that there was a supply of test-plants, he made little use of assistance and insisted on doing all virus assays himself. As a rule that meant doing them out of normal working hours. To this Dictionary he contributed the notice of Tom Goodey.

He became a fellow of the Royal Society in 1949, served on many of its committees, and was treasurer from 1968 to 1972. He was knighted in 1967, had honorary degrees from Hull, Bath, Reading, and Brunel universities, and was a member of several foreign academies.

On 6 September 1934 Bawden married Marjorie Elizabeth, a childhood friend and also a botanist, the daughter of Alfred Alderman Cudmore, agricultural engineer. They had two sons. He died in Luton and Dunstable Hospital, 8 February 1972.

[N. W. Pirie in *Biographical Memoirs of Fellows of the Royal Society*, vol. xix, 1973; personal knowledge.] N. W. PIRIE

BEACHCOMBER (pseudonym), humorous journalist. [See MORTON, JOHN CAMERON ANDRIEU BINGHAM MICHAEL.]

BEADLE, SIR (THOMAS) HUGH (WILLIAM) (1905–1980), chief justice of Southern Rhodesia, was born in Salisbury 6 February 1905, the only son and eldest of three children of Arthur William Beadle OBE, later secretary to the Southern Rhodesian Treasury, and his wife, Christiana Maria Fischer. Educated at Salisbury Boys and Milton High Schools, Diocesan College, Rondebosch, and Cape Town University, Beadle, after his BA and LL B degrees, proceeded in 1928 as a Rhodes scholar to Queen's College, Oxford. He played rugby and tennis for his college, boxed for the university, flew in its air squadron and graduated with a second class BCL (1930). He later became an honorary fellow of Queen's College, although in 1968 there was an attempt to strip him of his fellowship.

After practising at the Bulawayo bar from 1930, Beadle was elected in 1939 as MP for Bulawayo North, a seat he held until 1950 for the United Party led by Godfrey Huggins (later Viscount Malvern, q.v.). After a period of military service from 1939 to 1940 as temporary captain in West Africa, Beadle's limitless energies were harnessed by Huggins, whom Beadle served from 1940 to 1946 as parliamentary private secretary, acting also as deputy judge advocate-general. Beadle was appointed minister of internal affairs and justice in 1946, the year he took silk, and was appointed OBE. In 1948 he also took on the Education and Health Ministry. In 1950 Beadle became resident high court judge in Bulawayo. He was created CMG in 1957.

Beadle was a learned, fair but also adventurous judge, restrictively interpreting the scope of the criminal law. Conservative politically, he yet rejected racialism, taking the opportunity in *Mehta v. City of Salisbury* (1961), a case involving exclusion from public swimming-baths on racial grounds, to reject South African case law, because of that country's racial policy. Africans, however, viewed Beadle more as the chairman of a tribunal which upheld the detention of nationalist politicians during the 1959 emergency.

In 1961 Beadle became chief justice of Southern Rhodesia and therefore legal adviser to the governor. Knighted in the same year, and privy councillor from 1964, Beadle presided from 1964 over Southern Rhodesian Appellate division, giving judgments generously interpreting the recently introduced Rhodesian Declaration of Rights. Particularly notable was his invalidation of an Act of the Legislative Assembly seeking to avoid the necessity of declaring a new emergency by extending the period of preventive detention. Had a Unilateral Declaration of Independence not occurred Beadle would have been remembered as a Commonwealth chief justice who upheld individual liberty.

Determined to avert UDI, Beadle incessantly initiated procedures for compromise. On UDI in 1965 he moved into the residence of the governor, Sir Humphrey Gibbs, advising him and British ministers, *inter alia*, on the crucial gubernatorial instruction that all those responsible for law and order should carry on with their normal tasks, an injunction assuring the regime of obedience by state servants and effectively giving it legitimating institutions without the embarrassment of replacing the judges. Beadle accompanied the governor to the talks held in November 1966 on HMS *Tiger*. He incurred the disapproval of Harold Wilson (later Lord Wilson of Rievaulx), who thought him 'spineless' for failing to help pressurize Ian Smith, the Rhodesian leader, into adhering to his undertaking that he would advise his Cabinet to support the *Tiger* solution.

The judges had avoided pronouncing on the regime's validity until September 1966, when two of them upheld its detention of Daniel Madzimbamuto, a nationalist politician, on grounds of necessity. On appeal, in January 1968, Beadle temporized, holding the detention invalid on a technicality, asserting that the judges still sat under the 1961 constitution, denying the regime *de jure* status, and yet simultaneously holding that the regime was a *de facto* government which the Rhodesian courts must recognize.

In February and March 1968, in litigation about Africans sentenced to death before UDI for terrorist offences on facts that would have grounded murder charges, Beadle upheld the regime's power to carry out executions on the basis that a lawful government could have taken such action. Because Ian Smith's minister of law and order had told the court that he would not observe any judgment by the Judicial Committee of the Privy Council, Beadle refused leave to appeal to the Judicial Committee and declined to stay the execution. When the Queen, acting on the Commonwealth secretary's advice, commuted the death sentences to life imprisonment, Beadle, arguing that Rhodesia was self-governing, refused to recognize her exercise of the prerogative of mercy. On Beadle's return to Government House, the governor asked him to pack his bags, and the regime began hanging Africans convicted before and after UDI. Two judges resigned, Beadle's reasoning having made it clear that the courts only sat and their decisions were only enforceable with the acquiescence of the regime.

Beadle unequivocally recognized UDI in September 1968, when he held that the Smith regime had attained *de jure* status as the lawful government of an independent state by reason of a successful revolution. He asserted it his duty to declare this the law, and to choose whether to continue in office under the 1965 UDI constitution, stating he was remaining as chief justice because the existing judges would best preserve the rights of citizens. Subsequently Beadle accepted office under Smith's 1969 constitution, which contained arrangements designed indefinitely to postpone African majority rule. After retirement in 1977, Beadle sat for three years as acting judge in trials under the special criminal procedure for serious 'terrorist' cases, carrying the death penalty.

A short, stocky man of ruddy complexion with a toothbrush moustache, Beadle had a blunt manner, looking hard at all whom he encountered. His drive and enthusiasm were overwhelming, whether at work, in charitable activities, or as a courageous hunter and fisherman. He had a warm family life and many friends.

Assessment of Beadle depends on the evaluator's predilections. 'Devious' to Harold Wilson, Vicar of Bray to British officials, 'white supremacist' to African nationalists, Beadle's own view was that he did his best for his country in a time of difficult choices. His self-confidence, optimism, and drive to get a solution led him to act as go-between, to ever new formulas for compromise, and to entanglement with the regime. Identifying his country's interests with preservation of the kind of Rhodesia he had spent his political career building, rather than with any need for transition to African majority rule, Beadle ultimately saw loyalty to the usurping regime as necessary to avoid radical political reconstruction.

In 1934 Beadle married Leonie, daughter of Cecil John Barry, farmer, of Barrydale, Cape Province; they had two daughters. His first wife died in 1953 and the following year he married Olive, daughter of Major Staley Jackson, OBE, chief Native commissioner, of Salisbury. After her death in a car accident in 1974 he married in 1976 Pleasance Johnson. Beadle died in Johannesburg 14 December 1980.

[*The Times*, 18 December 1980; L. H. Gann and M. Gelfand, *Huggins of Rhodesia*, 1964; Harold Wilson, *The Labour Government 1964–1970*, 1971; Robert Blake, *A History of Rhodesia*, 1977; private information; personal knowledge.] CLAIRE PALLEY

BEAGLEHOLE, JOHN CAWTE (1901–1971), historian, was born in Wellington, New Zealand, 13 June 1901, the second of four sons (there were no daughters) of David Ernest Beaglehole, a clerk, and his wife, Jane Butler. He grew up in a crowded quarter of the youthful city dominated, it seems worth recalling, by an eminence known as Mount Cook. Like most of his contemporaries, he enjoyed the benefits of a state education, first at Mount Cook School, then at nearby Wellington College. But the chief formative influence of his boyhood was the modest family home. Both his parents were discriminating readers and to his English-born mother he owed a lifelong interest in music. A brief apprenticeship to the book trade preceded his entry to Victoria University College, the institution to which he was happily affiliated for most of his career. He was active in student affairs, wrote poetry, edited the annual magazine, and assiduously read history. Graduating MA in 1924, he won a postgraduate scholarship for his thesis on William Hobson, first governor of New Zealand, served briefly as assistant lecturer, and left for England in 1926.

To a colonial, as he boldly proclaimed himself, London was both fulfilment and challenge. He gloried in the libraries and bookshops, he revelled in the music, and gradually he responded to the shabby elegance of Bloomsbury where he lodged. On the debit side social inequalities troubled him, he was irked by the airs of some academic superiors, and he found difficulty in choosing a subject. At last, with help from Harold J. Laski [q.v.], whom Beaglehole thought friendly enough to rank as a colonial, he joined University College to undertake research in colonial history. His thesis, completed in 1929, gained him a Ph.D., but he could not find a publisher and there seemed no prospect of employment. The only course, he reluctantly concluded, was to return home. He had been cheered by the appearance, under an American imprint, of *Captain Hobson and the New Zealand Company* (1928), a version of his MA thesis. Now he was encouraged by a commission to write a book on Pacific exploration.

For some years after his return he led an unsettled existence, moving from one temporary job to another, often in the unlikely role of Workers' Educational Association lecturer. His liberal views earned him a reputation for radicalism and lost him a university post in Auckland. More bitter still, in 1935 he failed in his bid for the chair of history at Victoria. In these adversities he had the unfailing support of his wife, Elsie Mary, daughter of Robert Arthur Holmes, a banker; they had married in 1930 and were to have three sons. And no set-back stemmed the flow of publications—poems, articles, and notably in 1934, *The Exploration of the Pacific.* This book led to his later research and, belatedly, to academic preferment: in 1936 he was appointed lecturer at Victoria University College.

Back in his native city (also the nation's capital), he was drawn into many activities and enlarged his already wide acquaintance. The casually dressed scholar, somewhat resembling E. M. Forster [q.v.], became a well-known figure not only in libraries and lecture halls but in government departments and more exalted centres of power. As a semi-official adviser on matters cultural he was in constant demand and took an active part in producing publications to mark the country's centennial. His contribution was *The Discovery of New Zealand* (1939) but of greater moment was his close association with (Sir) J. W. A. Heenan, the imaginative public servant behind the enterprise. He it was who after the war ensured state backing for Beaglehole's edition of the *Journals* of Captain James Cook [q.v.] published by the Hakluyt Society. The first volume, dedicated to Heenan's memory, appeared in 1955 and the last in 1967. A bulky appendix was *The Endeavour Journal* of Sir Joseph Banks [q.v.] (1962). When he died in his Wellington home, 10 October 1971, he was revising his biography of Cook. Edited by the historian T. H. Beaglehole, his second son, it came out in 1974. He contributed to this Dictionary the notice of Peter Fraser, New Zealand prime minister.

In his last decade Beaglehole received many honours, academic and civic, culminating in the OM conferred in 1970. He was appointed CMG in 1958 and FRSNZ in 1967. Victoria (now an independent university) appointed him to the chair of British Commonwealth history in 1963, made him an honorary Litt.D. five years later, and following his death opened in his memory the superbly situated research room, fit setting for the fine portrait by W. A. Sutton. In 1966 he received an honorary D.Litt. from Oxford. His reputation rests firmly on the Cook journals, surely one of the classic works of historical scholarship. His personal qualities included generosity, a passion for justice, and a sometimes waspish humour.

[*Landfall*, December 1971; *Turnbull Library Record*, August 1970 and October 1981; Margery Walton, *John Cawte Beaglehole: A Bibliography*, 1972; private information; personal knowledge.] E. H. McCormick

BEATON, Sir CECIL WALTER HARDY (1904–1980), photographer, artist, writer, and designer of scenery and costumes, was born at 21 Langland Gardens, Hampstead, London, 14 January 1904, the eldest in the family of two sons and two daughters of Ernest Walter Hardy Beaton, a London timber merchant, and his wife, Esther ('Etty') Sisson, of Temple Sowerby, Cumberland. After Harrow, he went up to St. John's College, Cambridge, in 1922 to read history and architecture, and though he never graduated, he took an active part in the theatrical life of the university. His first love was the theatre but his first success was in photography, a medium that had absorbed him from his earliest days. His sisters became his first models and assistants. He designed their costumes, entered them into fancy dress competitions, and photographed them. A childhood heroine was Lily Elsie (whose notice he contributed to this Dictionary). Coming down from Cambridge in 1925, he spent some unhappy months working in the Holborn office of a friend of his father's. He worked hard to escape from this and by his industry and imagination he began to establish a name as a photographer. When at the end of 1926 he suddenly found himself friends with (Sir) Osbert and (Dame) Edith Sitwell [qq.v.], and the 'Bright Young Things', he found a world thirsting for his talents. His rise to fame thereafter was nothing less than meteoric. His ingenious photographic portraits of the Sitwells led to his employment with *Vogue* as photographer, caricaturist, and illustrator, both in New York and London. In 1927 and 1930 he held one-man exhibitions at the Cooling Gallery, Bond Street, for both of which Osbert Sitwell wrote the introduction. He produced his first book, *The Book of Beauty* (1930).

In the 1930s he worked on two revues of (Sir) Charles Cochran [q.v.]—*Streamline* (1934) and *Follow the Sun* (1936)—and continued to photograph in London and New York, though as he noted 'At no stage of my photographic career could I ever have believed that photography could be my life's work'. It was in 1930 also that he rented Ashcombe, a derelict country house in the Wiltshire Downs, which he converted into an idyllic home and where he entertained friends such as Rex Whistler, Augustus John [qq.v.], and Edith Olivier. In 1937 he was chosen to photograph the wedding of the Duke of Windsor in France. Beaton's career was progressing well until a disagreement with *Vogue* brought his contract with the magazine to an abrupt end in 1938. For some years he was unable to work in America, but his career was saved by two things. First, Queen Elizabeth invited him to photograph her at Buckingham Palace, and secondly war was declared. Beaton found that he was able to make an important contribution as a war photographer. He travelled throughout England for the Ministry of Information and later journeyed to the Middle East and Far East. Any glossy magazine image his previous work may have had now disappeared and by his courage, industry, and wholly professional approach, he earned the respect of the three Services. Six books emerged from these years. One of his most famous pictures was of a bombed-out child in hospital. This photograph became the front cover of *Life* magazine in September 1940 and was said, more than any other picture, to have influenced American feeling concerning the war.

In the years that followed stage, film, ballet, and opera work gave him more opportunities. In 1945 he designed *Lady Windermere's Fan*, with an opulence of style that held an immediate appeal for post-war Britain. The following year he took the part of Cecil Graham in the American production. In 1948 he did the costumes for the films *An Ideal Husband* and *Anna Karenina*. Other noted productions on which he worked were *The School for Scandal* (1949), *Quadrille* for (Sir) Noel Coward [q.v.] (London 1952, New York 1954), *Turandot* (New York 1961 and London 1963), and *La Traviata* (New York 1966). His greatest stage success was of course the designing of costumes for *My Fair Lady* in 1956, a success he repeated when he spent a year in Hollywood in 1963 working on the film version of the play. For his costume design and art direction he won two Oscars. (He had been awarded his first Oscar for the film *Gigi* in 1958.) During this time and in fact for a period of thirty years from 1944 to 1974, he was preoccupied with the writing of his play, *The Gainsborough Girls*, staged at Brighton in 1951 and in a revised version in 1959. Unfortunately this floundered on both occasions.

Beaton also made a considerable contribution to the world of fashion. His best book is certainly his personal survey of fifty years of changing fashion, *The Glass of Fashion* (1954), and he amassed a collection of the dresses he most admired at the Victoria and Albert Museum, some of which were exhibited in 1971. He was a dedicated diarist from 1922 to 1980 and six volumes were published in his lifetime. These and his photographs combine to give a unique portrait of the age in which he lived. In 1968 his career was crowned with an important exhibition of his photographs at the National Portrait Gallery. In 1950 he was awarded the Legion of Honour. He was created CBE in 1957 and knighted in 1972. Two years later he suffered a bad stroke but gradually learned to paint, write, and photograph with his left hand. He died at his second Wiltshire home, Reddish House, Broadchalke, 18 January 1980.

Beaton was a man of immense style and sartorial elegance, forever fascinated by new ideas and attitudes. He possessed an extraordinary visual sense and an eye which in a flash took in every minor detail around him. His conversation was witty and penetrating, and while he enjoyed the company of glittering society, above all he valued and sought out talents and individuality. He suffered from the accusation that much of his work was light or trivial, but his industry alone and the wide range of his achievements makes this an unfair assessment. He was not granted much personal happiness, but relished his work, his garden, and his friends. He was unmarried.

There is a portrait of Beaton by Christian Bérard in the National Portrait Gallery.

[*The Times* and *Daily Telegraph*, 19 January 1980; Cecil Beaton, *Photobiography*, 1951; R. Buckle (ed.), *Self Portrait with Friends, the Selected Diaries of C. Beaton 1926–1974*, 1979; 6 vols. of *Diaries*, 1961, 1965, 1972, 1973, 1976, and 1978; Charles Spencer, *Cecil Beaton Stage and Film Designs*, 1975; Hugo Vickers, *Cecil Beaton*, 1985; private information; personal knowledge.] HUGO VICKERS

BEAUMONT, HUGHES GRIFFITHS (1908–1973), theatrical manager, was born 27 March 1908 in Hampstead, London, the only son of Mary Frances Morgan (née Brewer) and a Mr Beaumont with whom she departed from London to Cardiff after separating from her first husband, Morgan Morgan, barrister-at-law.

Throughout his life, 'Hugh' Beaumont preserved a passion for anonymity, and little is known of his childhood apart from an early friendship with Ivor Novello [q.v.] (a close neighbour) and his precocious appointment, at the age of sixteen, as assistant manager of the Prince of Wales Theatre, Cardiff. Still in his adolescence, he moved on to a series of other minor managerial jobs before joining the firm of Moss Empires as assistant to H. M. (Harry) Tennent, administrator of Drury Lane, with whom, in 1936, he founded the producing management of H. M. Tennent Ltd. Neither at that time, nor after Tennent's death in 1941, was anything done to publicize the name of Beaumont, but it was at his persuasion that the firm came into existence and through his gifts that it sustained its long supremacy in the West End.

Beaumont and Tennent went into business with a £10,000 float from a stockbroking member of the Cripps family. That was a reasonable sum in the days when a West End play could be presented at the average cost of £1,000. However, the partners lost much of their starting capital on a series of flops before they struck lucky with the 1937 production of Gerald Savory's *George and Margaret* which ran for 799 performances at Wyndham's. This was followed by Dodie Smith's *Dear Octopus* and other long-running shows which established Tennents as a highly profitable concern that magnetized backers like a triple-crown Derby winner.

It was during these first years that Beaumont struck up a lifelong and professionally fertile friendship with (Sir) John Gielgud. All Beaumont's early experience had been on the business side. He was, Gielgud said, 'a modern man with no pretensions to education at all and no knowledge except what he had learnt as he became successful'. Throughout his career, his main objective was to have as many productions as possible playing in London. What those productions were, however, reflected a taste acquired partly from Gielgud, with whom he broke into classical territory with a 1939 *Hamlet*, and continued with the famous wartime seasons at the Phoenix and the Haymarket, and again at the Phoenix and the Lyric, Hammersmith, during the 1950s. He also developed a love for superbly dressed, resplendently cast high comedy for which the name of Tennents became a byword.

What won Beaumont such allies as Gielgud and (Sir) Noel Coward [q.v.] in the first place was an array of personal and managerial skills which he put unreservedly at their disposal. He saw it as his mission to produce the best artists under the best possible conditions: and, having decided who the best were, he looked faithfully after their interests with an invincible blend of paternal care, oriental business acumen, and courteously absolute authority. 'The iron fist', (Sir) Tyrone Guthrie [q.v.] said of him, 'was wrapped in fifteen pastel-shaded velvet gloves.' Those who worked with him, actors and playwrights alike, had total faith in his artistic judgement. His theatre followed the West End star system, but whereas the usual practice was for a star to appear with a supporting company, stars appeared in constellations on the Tennents stage, persuaded by Beaumont to exchange solitary glory for the satisfaction of working with their equals.

Tennents never owned theatres. They had a long-standing tenancy at the Queen's and the Globe, and periodically occupied the Haymarket and theatres of the Albery group. During the war their profits were subject to the 40 per cent entertainments tax from which Beaumont sought exemption by forming a non-profit-making subsidiary—Tennent Productions—for the presentation of classical work. By the end of the war he had thus amassed a surplus of £70,000 with which, in 1946, he also took over the Lyric, Hammersmith, for classical seasons and West End try-outs by the newly created Company of Four.

The immediate post-war years marked the zenith of Tennents' prestige: a gathering of major stars and new names (including Christopher Fry and Peter Brook) mobilized in a lavish firework display exactly matching the anti-austerity mood of the time. However, there were also growing murmurs against Tennents' non-profit-making status, which reached a head with the officially 'educational' première of *A Streetcar Named Desire* (1949), at which the Arts Council withdrew its support and the Inland Revenue promptly converted the charitable surplus into unpaid tax, and put in a large demand which Beaumont unsuccessfully contested in the House of Lords.

This defeat did nothing to shake the firm's theatrical fortunes or diminish Beaumont's power (in Guthrie's words) as the man, more than any other, who could 'make or break the career of almost any worker in the British professional theatre'.

What did bring the firm into decline was the explosion of new writing that began from the Royal Court Theatre in 1956, and the growth of subsidized theatre at the expense of the commercial sector. Beaumont's West End flourished like a traditional grocery shop, selling reliable brands to regular customers. The fashions of 1956 consigned these brands to the dustbin; though Beaumont struggled to replace them with such newcomers as Robert Bolt and Peter Shaffer. Nor was there any effective way of fighting subsidized competition by a manager who lived by the ethic that the theatre should stand on its own feet.

During his twenty years of supremacy, Beaumont did more to raise the standard of the London theatre than any other manager, past or present. The new stage that overwhelmed him was one that he had done much to create. A homosexual, he had no family outside the theatre which was his business, his pleasure, and his life. He died in London 22 March 1973.

[*The Times*, 23, 28, and 29 March 1973; *Spectator*, 31 March 1973; private information.]

IRVING WARDLE

BENNET-CLARK, THOMAS ARCHIBALD (1903–1975), botanist, was born in Edinburgh 13 January 1903, the only son and youngest of four children of Thomas Bennet-Clark, JP, accountant and senior partner in the firm of R. & G. Scott, chartered accountants, of Edinburgh, and his wife, Anne Chalmers Hanna. He was educated at Marlborough (1916–20) whence he won an open entrance scholarship to Trinity College, Cambridge (1920–3). He gained first classes in both parts of the natural science tripos (1922 and 1923), specializing in botany in part ii, and the Frank Smart prize for botany (1923). Bennet-Clark's interest in botany had been kindled at an early age by his father, a keen field botanist, whom he accompanied on excursions to Ben Lawers and Norway in search of Alpine plants. As an undergraduate he developed a passionate interest in plant physiology to which he was to devote his whole career.

In 1923 he began research in plant physiology at Cambridge with F. F. Blackman [q.v.]. Two years later he became assistant at Trinity College, Dublin, to Professor H. H. Dixon, whose notice he later wrote for this Dictionary. He completed his Cambridge Ph.D. at Dublin and in 1930 he was appointed lecturer in botany at the University of Manchester. In 1936 he became the first professor of botany at the University College of Nottingham, in 1944 professor of botany at King's College, London, and finally, in 1962, professor of biology and first dean of the School of Biological Sciences, at the University of East Anglia, Norwich.

Bennet-Clark's contributions to plant physiology were in three distinct fields: the metabolism of organic acids in succulent plants, particularly members of the *Crassulaceae*; the water relations of plant cells, especially in connection with the possible existence of an active, water-uptake mechanism; and finally, the isolation, identification, and mode of action of plant growth hormones, in which he was the first (with N. P. Kefford) to use chromatography to separate naturally occurring plant growth regulating compounds.

Bennet-Clark published no more than thirty papers, but the quality and originality of his work, and its incisive and critical nature, was such that in each field it stimulated immense interest and world-wide research activity. He generated many research ideas but did not seek personal advancement, preferring to support and encourage his junior colleagues. He was an excellent university teacher, who placed more emphasis on stimulating enthusiasm and interest in his subject than on the ground covered. Possessed of an incisive, encyclopaedic mind and photographic memory, he could discuss almost any topic in experimental botany, and a good many non-experimental topics, from an informed and authoritative standpoint. He had decided ideas on the way botany should be taught—the emphasis being entirely on a rigorous experimental approach. He had little time for taxonomy or ecology which he regarded as more suitable for amateurs, though there were few more knowledgeable field botanists. His belief that plant and animal biology should be taught in an integrated manner bore fruit when he founded the School of Biological Science at the University of East Anglia.

Bennet-Clark was a gifted man of great personal charm who would do his utmost to help both colleagues and students alike. He could not stand laziness or pomposity, and did not suffer fools at all. At times he could appear unreasonable, but in reality the enormous demands made on him, together with a certain amount of traditional professorial forgetfulness, led to this misconception. Being asked to take one of his lectures might be considered an honour, until it was explained that the lecture should have begun about five minutes beforehand.

Bennet-Clark served on many national and international bodies. He founded and edited (1950–60) the *Journal of Experimental Botany*, and gave outstanding service to the Agricultural Research Council (1957–67), the Royal Society, the Society for Experimental Biology, and many other organizations. This prodigious work-load left him little time for relaxation and hobbies; the latter were principally gardening, especially scrounging and 'acquiring' plants, and carpentry, at which he was probably rather too impatient to become really skilled.

He was a man of small stature, who often wore a patched, somewhat shabby suit and a wide-brimmed trilby hat, riding a bicycle through London traffic, who was known equally well by the keepers of the Palace of Westminster and the porters of the Royal Society and of King's College as the professor who parked his bicycle in the most inappropriate places. He was an adventurous driver and many preferred public transport to a lift in his unusual cars which bore unmistakable evidence of encounters with London Transport buses. He was a quite exceptional person who was well loved and highly respected by all with whom he came in contact, regardless of their position in life.

His outstanding contributions to plant physiology were recognized by his election to a fellowship of the Royal Society (1950) and an honorary fellowship of the Royal Society of Edinburgh (1969), the award of honorary D.Sc. degrees by the university of Leicester (1968) and East Anglia (1968), and appointment as CBE (1966).

In 1926 Bennet-Clark married Elizabeth Constance, daughter of the Revd James Haythornthwaite, rector of Rathmines parish, Dublin. There were two children of the marriage, Margret Aithna, born in 1929, and Henry Chalmers, born in 1934. Bennet-Clark retired in 1967 and withdrew completely from the academic and public scene, first to his home in Essex and subsequently to a beautifully restored, mediaeval tenement flat in the Canongate, Edinburgh. After a distressing illness he died 24 November 1975 in an Edinburgh nursing home.

[*The Times*, 28 November and 4 December 1975; R. Brown in *Biographical Memoirs of Fellows of the Royal Society*, vol. xxiii, 1977; I. Manton, Obituary Notices, Royal Society of Edinburgh *Year Book*, 1977; family information; personal knowledge.]

MALCOLM B. WILKINS

BENNETT, SIR JOHN WHEELER WHEELER- (1902–1975), historian and authority on international affairs. [See WHEELER-BENNETT.]

BENNETT, SIR THOMAS PENBERTHY (1887–1980), architect and public servant, was born 14 August 1887 in London, the elder child and only son of Thomas William Bennett, clerk, and his wife, Ann Frances (previously Hodge), née Penberthy. He was educated at St. Augustine's church school, Kilburn. When his father died in 1901 he entered the drawing office of the LNWR at Euston, where he learned the elements of building. He studied architecture at evening classes of the Regent Street Polytechnic under (Sir) A. E. Richardson [q.v.] and won prizes there. He obtained a place at the Royal Academy School, where he won a year prize for sculpture. He learned to draw at Heatherley's, was a good water-colourist, and played the piano and organ well.

In 1911 Bennett left the LNWR for the architect's office of the Office (later Ministry) of Works, the chief architect saying that he could not possibly be more of a nuisance inside the office than he had been knocking at the door. He qualified ARIBA 1912, and FRIBA 1922. When war broke out in 1914 he enlisted but was called back to supervise the construction of hutting in France and Wales. There he learned the value of good site management and labour relations.

In 1919 he joined the firm of Méwès & Davis as chief assistant. He could have had a partnership there but, after eighteen months, left to set up his own practice with J. D. Hossack. At the same time he became head of the school of architecture and building at the Northern Polytechnic. He entered this field with great energy, and had become a recognized authority on technical education when in 1929 he resigned to devote more time to his practice.

During the next ten years Bennett built a mass of buildings; large scale flats and public authority housing, offices, stores and suburban shops, banks and cinemas, the Saville Theatre in Shaftesbury Avenue, and establishments for the Royal Navy. Many of these were designed with the help of Morris W. Linslade, his son Philip, and W. Bonham Galloway.

His reputation as an architect came from sound contract management and financial control rather than from innovation or refinement in design. He was not an 'architects' architect', and held the view that good architecture comes from good building backed by sound administration, and, in his case, from unbounded faith in his own judgement. His self-confidence brought many clients. His ability to assess the potential of a site, prepare alternative sketch-plans, produce carefully worked out figures of costs and likely returns, and to complete his building on time made him popular, particularly with developers. As a clear-thinking, determined, and efficient architect he was without equal.

In 1940 Lord Reith [q.v.] called him to the Ministry of Works to be controller of bricks. In 1941 he became director of works and played an important part in the construction of hospitals, airfields, ordnance factories, and naval and prisoner-of-war camps. In 1944 Lord Portal [q.v.] invited him to oversee contracts for the production of the temporary housing programme. Bennett returned to private practice at the end of the war.

In 1947 he was invited by Lewis (later Lord) Silkin [q.v.] to become chairman of Crawley New Town. He had already made a name as independent chairman of the Board of Trade boot and shoe working party (which reported in 1945), and Crawley was a new challenge which once more exercised his flair for organization. Such was his success that in 1951 Lord Dalton [q.v.], who had succeeded Silkin, asked him to be chairman of Stevenage New Town, the appointments to run concurrently. At Stevenage Bennett found irreversible planning difficulties which he was unable to resolve and he resigned in 1952.

In 1960, with Crawley almost completed, Bennett retired from public life but continued with his practice. He became consultant to the partnership in 1967. He was appointed CBE in 1942, knighted in 1946, and appointed KBE in 1954.

Of medium height and strongly built with a straight back, he walked with a measured tread. His voice was authoritative. He appeared to look neither to left nor right when speaking. A firm mouth contributed to a somewhat brusque manner. He was a keen golfer, and a proud life-president of the Highgate Golf Club. When over ninety he was still playing 'but only twice a week, apart from practice'.

In 1916 he married Mary Langdon Edis (died 1976), the portrait painter, daughter of Charles Vessey Edis, a retired clerk. Their only son, Philip Hugh Penberthy Bennett CBE, succeeded his father as senior partner in T. P. Bennett & Son in 1967, retiring in 1980. Bennett died at his home in Highgate, London, 29 January 1980.

[*The Times*, 31 January 1980; *Daily Telegraph*, 1 February 1980; *Building*, 9 February 1980; *Architect's Journal*, 6 February 1980; personal knowledge.] GONTRAN GOULDEN

BENTLEY, NICOLAS CLERIHEW (1907–1978), artist and writer, was born at Highgate, London, 14 June 1907, the youngest in the family of one daughter and two sons of Edmund Clerihew Bentley [q.v.], writer, and his wife, Violet

Alice Mary, daughter of General Neil Edmonstone Boileau, of the Bengal Staff Corps. He was educated at University College School, London, where he did not do particularly well and gave an impression outwardly of being shy and diffident. Inwardly, he was romantically inclined, and all his life cherished out-of-the-way aspirations. Thus, surveying his future, he had three ambitions—to be a fireman, a clown, and an artist. As things turned out, they were all three realized. During the blitz in the war of 1939–45 he was an intrepid fireman; after leaving school, to everyone's amazement, he managed to get a job with Ginnett's Circus when it was performing at Wembley; and he duly became a distinguished satirical artist and illustrator, having trained at Heatherley's School of Art, where Evelyn Waugh [q.v.] was a fellow-student.

As a clown, Bentley managed to design his own costume, which consisted of a top hat, a white sleeveless shirt with red dots, and enormous white gloves. The job only lasted six weeks, but in assessing Bentley's character his stint in the ring is significant. Without his knowing it, there was something of the Holy Fool in Bentley that got into his satirical drawings. Bentley also became a brilliant mimic.

After clowning, Bentley spent some months, as he put it himself, 'haunting the casting offices of film companies'. Nothing turned up except an occasional job as an extra. Then he joined the advertising department of Shell under Jack Beddington, where his colleagues were Rex Whistler [q.v.], Peter Quennell, Edward Ardizzone [q.v.], and (Sir) John Betjeman. They, together with Bentley, were responsible for producing the Shell Guides, highly regarded in their day, and later collectors' items.

Bentley quite enjoyed the three years he spent with Shell, and might well have stayed on indefinitely but for the intervention of Hilaire Belloc [q.v.], a friend and patron, urged on thereto perhaps by Bentley's godfather, G. K. Chesterton [q.v.], with whom he had an affectionate relationship. In his autobiography Bentley describes one of their meetings: 'Belloc once came to call for me at Shell. I found him waiting in the general office amid a hubbub of clerks and typists. He was sitting on a small chair quite alone, with the majesty and fierce demeanour of a mythological patriarch. He asked me in a loud and disapproving voice if this was where I worked in. I showed him where my room was—a cubicle separated by a partition from the general office. Belloc looked round the place with disgust, then said in his stentorian voice: "If you don't get out of here pretty soon, my boy, you'll be tied to the chariot wheels of commerce for the rest of your life."' It was a stern warning, and Bentley heeded it the more because Belloc had asked him to illustrate his *New Cautionary Tales*, thereby introducing him to what was to be his main occupation; by the time he died he had illustrated some sixty books (several of them written by his father and himself), all with distinction. Never expert with colour, he became a master of the thin black line.

After leaving Shell, Bentley settled down to his illustrating, and later became a director in a new publishing house set up by André Deutsch. Diana Athill, a colleague there, praised his 'judgement, good sense, integrity and *presence*', and especially his skill at coping with staff differences by being 'always calm and sensible and shrewd and funny'. For a time in the 1960s Bentley also drew a regular cartoon for the *Daily Mail*, but the work exhausted him. He much preferred to write thrillers and he was also a good editor (at Nelson's). He contributed to this Dictionary the notices of C. B. Bairnsfather and Barnett Freedman.

In 1934, after five years of courtship, he married Barbara Hastings, daughter of Sir Patrick Gardiner Hastings [q.v.], a successful and much sought after barrister who became attorney-general in Ramsay MacDonald's first Labour government. She bore him one child, a daughter; their marriage had its ups and downs, but was never finally disrupted.

Bentley was fascinated by his father-in-law, and gives a full and perceptive account of him in his autobiography. Of the three men who had most influenced him, he writes, Hastings was the foremost, the other two being Jack Beddington of Shell, and Stephen (later Lord) Taylor, under whom he worked in the home intelligence department of the Ministry of Information in World War II. The choice of these three, rather than fellow-artists or writers, might seem surprising, but less so if account is taken of how, despite his quiet exterior and gentle manner, he had a strong ambitious urge, a desire to make some startling mark in the world. Richard Ingrams, a close friend, and editor of *Private Eye*, in which Bentley's drawings regularly appeared, described him as 'a quiet and dapper man with an almost cranky concern for symmetry and order in small things'. This was so (indeed he removed the 'h' from his first forename to make his signature symmetrical), but all the same inside him there was another tempestuous man struggling to get out. The conflict between his two selves was never resolved, which perhaps accounts for a certain melancholy underlying his amiable temperament and also apparent in his drawings.

Towards the end of his life Bentley moved out of London, and settled down in a converted village school in Somerset. Though becoming elderly, he retained his youthful appearance—slim and shy and friendly. Bentley died in a Somerset hospital 14 August 1978. Social historians of the middle decades of the twentieth century will find Bentley's drawings invaluable, conveying, as they do, quietly and accurately the times in which he lived and the people with whom he associated.

[Nicolas Bentley, *A Version of the Truth*, 1960; private information; personal knowledge.]

MALCOLM MUGGERIDGE

BENTLEY, PHYLLIS ELEANOR (1894–1977), novelist, was born 19 November 1894 in Halifax, the fourth child and only daughter of Joseph Edwin Bentley, master dyer and finisher, of 8 Heath Villas, Halifax, and his wife, Eleanor, daughter of Thomas Kettlewell, representative of a cloth-manufacturing firm in Huddersfield. She was educated at the Princess Mary High School for Girls, Halifax, and at Cheltenham Ladies College, where she obtained a first class London University pass degree.

Phyllis Bentley had a romantic devotion to the west riding of Yorkshire; born into the heart of the textile trade it was her ambition from her school days to describe the region in fiction. But her novels were never narrowly provincial. She saw her own district as a microcosm of the world and in her novels expressed her strong belief that only by understanding could its troubles be cured. It took her some time to master the technique of her craft. Her first novel, *Environment*, was published in 1922. Ten years and seven novels later she achieved her great success with *Inheritance* (1932), a chronicle of the Oldroyd family and their mill from the time of the Luddites to the closing of the mill in 1930. The sequels *The Rise of Henry Morcar* (1946), *A Man of His Time* (1966), and *Ring in the New* (1969) carried the chronicle of the Oldroyds up to 1968. The whole series became a television serial. These and all Phyllis Bentley's succeeding novels were published by Victor Gollancz, in an association happy and profitable to author and publisher.

She produced an enormous quantity of work, an especially remarkable feat since she looked after her widowed mother who lived to be ninety. There were twenty-eight novels, three volumes of short stories, several historical children's books, an autobiography '*O Dreams O Destinations*' (1962), a short biography *The Brontes* (1947), *The Brontes and their World* (1969), and detective stories for American magazines. She also contributed many reviews and articles to various journals, for years writing a fortnightly column of fiction reviews in the *Yorkshire Post*, one of which she was engaged on a few days before her death.

Brought up Conservative and Church of England, in her teens Phyllis Bentley became moderate Labour and atheist, but she never joined any political party, believing that novelists should avoid affiliations that might constrict their judgement. A practical woman of sound common sense, she neglected no honourable step that might advance her career. If she had not been a writer she might have restored the fortunes of a mill. She did not care much for ordinary social life which to her was a waste of time. Her intimacies were few and deep; she was a stimulating companion, a loyal and affectionate friend. She vigorously supported any local activities connected with the arts, particularly with the amateur theatre; she was an effective speaker, thorough in preparing her material as in everything that she did. She always enjoyed committee work: 'Committees are an article of faith with me, the basis of democracy.' Her novel *Quorum* (1950) dealt with one meeting of a committee, and with the secret preoccupations that helped to sway the members' votes. In *Crescendo* (1958) she expressed her deep sense of personal responsibility: one bit of carelessness nearly brought disaster on several people who were finally only saved by a responsible action.

An austere upbringing had made pleasure, and especially anything that bordered on extravagance, suspect to her. This wore off as she saw more of the world outside her home, but not entirely. She liked the theatre, which was her greatest treat on her visits to London; she loved walking in the Yorkshire dales and holidays by the sea, especially in the Isle of Man, the scene of her childhood holidays. Although she enjoyed her American lecture tours, PEN congresses in Europe, and occasional visits to Italy or France, foreign travel on the whole meant very little to her. With growing success she came to enjoy buying good clothes. Probably because she was obliged to wear spectacles from very early days she thought herself plain. Yet she had a beautiful fine skin and abundant hair, reddish in youth but later pure white, and the vivacity and kindness of her manner made her an attractive figure. She would chatter freely and gaily in congenial company. She was unmarried.

Phyllis Bentley's main purpose in life was so all-absorbing that she had only marginal attention to spare for anything else. It was really of herself that she wrote in her novel *Noble in Reason* (1955) when the chief character was summing up his life: 'I will try to see, to understand. I hope that my last conscious moments will be occupied by the attempt rationally to comprehend, lovingly to compassionate human destiny.' She was awarded an honorary D.Litt. by Leeds University in 1949, became FRSL in 1958, and was appointed OBE in 1970. She died in Halifax 27 June 1977.

[*The Times*, 29 June 1977; Marie Hartley's talk at the memorial service in Halifax; Phyllis Bentley, '*O Dreams, O Destinations*' (autobiography), 1962; private information; personal knowledge.]

LETTICE COOPER

BENTWICH, NORMAN DE MATTOS (1883–1971), exponent of Jewish ideals, was born in London 28 February 1883, the elder son and second of eleven children of Herbert Bentwich and his wife Susannah, daughter of Joseph Solomon, leather merchant, and sister of Solomon J. Solomon [q.v.], painter. His father, a solicitor, was an active member of the Anglo-Jewish community who brought up his family in the fervent belief that Israel had a continuing religious mission to fulfil, whilst his mother stressed the universal values of music and art. He attended St. Paul's School whence he went as major scholar to Trinity College, Cambridge. He read classics, winning the Yorke essay prize twice, and rabbinics under Solomon Schechter. He obtained first classes in both parts of the classical tripos (1903 and 1905). In 1905 he took up law with the Whewell scholarship and was called to the bar by Lincoln's Inn in 1908.

In 1912 he entered the Egyptian Ministry of Justice as inspector of native courts. In 1915 he joined the British Army in Egypt (Camel Transport Corps) and took part in the conquest of Jerusalem, which earned him the rank of lieutenant-colonel, an MC, and appointment as OBE (1918).

In 1918 Bentwich became legal secretary to the British military administration in Palestine and after the establishment of the mandatory government in 1922 he became the country's first attorney-general. In Zionist politics he was moderate, working for Arab–Jewish understanding and a bi-national state. But with the conflict between the two nations steadily intensifying, the government was bound to find a Jewish attorney-general a political embarrassment, however reconciling his personal views might be. He was recalled in 1929 to work in the Colonial Office, was offered promotion in the service outside Palestine, and, when he declined, was retired in 1931.

In 1932 he was appointed professor of international relations at the Hebrew University of Jerusalem. His inaugural lecture, 'Jerusalem, City of Peace', was interrupted by students who opposed his pacifying approach and had to be continued under police protection. The terms of the chair provided that the holder would lecture during only one of the two terms of the year and otherwise be free to work in the field of international relations where he wished. He made full use of these opportunities. Thus, when the Nazi persecutions began, he became one of the foremost fighters for the rescue of the oppressed. He travelled to all countries, pleading with governments and investigating possible places of refuge. He became director both of the League of Nations high commission for refugees from Germany (1933–5) and of the Council for German Jewry.

During World War II Bentwich served in the Ministry of Information, and for a time in the Air Ministry. He lectured for the government, especially in the United States. In 1943 he went to the Middle East and to Ethiopia where he advised the emperor on the treaties to be concluded with Great Britain. During the following years he was engaged, as chairman of the Anglo–Abyssinian Society, in furthering Ethiopia's claim for the recovery of Eritrea, and attended the Paris conference of 1946 as a member of the Ethiopian delegation. In addition he took up the cause of the Falashas, an Ethiopian tribe who consider themselves Jews, but are not recognized as such by Israel and most Jewish communities.

He was chairman of the National Peace Council (1944–6) and in the post-war period had a major part in securing restitution and compensation for the victims of Nazi persecutions.

In 1951, having reached the statutory age, he retired as professor at the Hebrew University, and was elected a member and vice-chairman of its board of governors. Work for the university now became his main concern. Since its foundation the Hebrew University had been to him the symbol of Jewish renaissance and of all the causes he served probably this was nearest to his heart. He was president of the London north-western reform synagogue from 1958 until his death.

He was the author of nearly thirty books ranging from Judaeo–Greek civilization to international law, refugees, and the rebirth of Israel. He was awarded honorary doctorates from the universities of Aberdeen (1942), Melbourne (1938), and Jerusalem (1956). He was always ready to help others, indefatigable in the causes he had taken up, and deeply committed to what he considered right. He sometimes wondered whether his life had perhaps lacked a certain 'one-pointedness' and had been too much divided between different worlds. But however this may be, all divisions were overcome and reconciled by his gentle personality and his spirit of service.

In 1915 he married Helen Caroline (died 1972), daughter of Arthur Ellis Franklin, banker and company director. She became chairman of the London County Council (1956–7) and was appointed CBE in 1965. There were no children. Bentwich died in London 8 April 1971 and according to his wish was buried in Jerusalem on Mount Scopus.

[Norman Bentwich, *My Seventy-Seven Years*, 1962; *The Times*, 10 April 1971; private information; personal knowledge.]

WALTER ZANDER

BERESFORD, JACK (1899–1977), sculler and oarsman, was born Jack Beresford Wiszniewski at 36 St. Mary's Grove, Chiswick, London, 1 January 1899, the elder son and eldest of the three children of Julius Beresford Wiszniewski, a furniture manufacturer who was brought to England by his governess from Poland at the age of twelve, and his wife, Ethel Mary Wood. He was educated at Bedford School, served with the Artists' Rifles in 1917, was commissioned in the Liverpool Scottish Regiment, and was wounded in northern France in 1918. He then entered his father's business, working at the furniture factory Beresford & Hicks, of Curtain Road, London EC2.

Beresford had an outstanding record as an amateur sculler and as an oarsman with Thames Rowing Club. He was champion sculler of Great Britain from 1920 to 1926 and won the Diamond Sculls at Henley Royal Regatta four times during that period. He made his mark internationally by winning the silver medal at the Olympic Games in Antwerp in 1920, losing the sculling final by one second to an Irish bricklayer from Philadelphia called Jack Kelly. The two men, who in later years became friends, encapsulated the controversy of the day concerning the amateur status of sportsmen. Before competing in the Olympics, Kelly's entry at Henley was refused by the regatta stewards possibly because, as a manual worker, he was considered to be a professional. Beresford, however, epitomized the idea of an amateur oarsman prevalent at the time. He was sporting, displayed club loyalty, dressed for dinner, was wealthy enough, and behaved like a gentleman. Off the water he was an ambassador for a certain way of life. A colleague remembers him as never wearing a waistcoat or an overcoat, no matter what the temperature.

From the beginning of his rowing career he displayed the tactical brilliance of a winner, assessing his opponent's capabilities and pacing his training, and usually his racing, to do just enough to beat them, although he was clearly possessed by the killer instinct which motivates a winner and a breaker of records. He won the Philadelphia Gold Cup for the world amateur title in 1924 and 1925. After 1920 he won four more medals in the next four Olympic Games. He took the single sculling title in 1924 in Paris, was second in the British eight at Amsterdam in 1928, first in the British four at Los Angeles in 1932, and at the age of thirty-seven won the Double Sculls, with L. F. ('Dick') Southwood, at Berlin in 1936, ahead of the German crew. This was Beresford's finest moment. At that point the Double Sculls was the only title in the regatta to be lost by the Germans, under the watchful eye of their chancellor, Adolf Hitler, who was presenting the medals. It was, Beresford said later, 'the sweetest race I ever rowed in'. The tactics which the Englishmen adopted of revealing some of their cards in the heat but by no means their whole hand justified the Germans' nickname for Beresford, 'The Old Fox'. His record of five medals, three of them golds, in five consecutive Games is unsurpassed.

But this was not the end of his competitive career. He crowned his outstanding record at Henley of two wins in the Grand, two in the Goblets, one in the Stewards', and four in the Diamonds by coming out of retirement with Southwood for a new event in 1939, the invitation Double Sculls. Their famous victory in Berlin had inspired the stewards to introduce this class of boat, and Beresford and Southwood won the final in a dead-heat with the Italians G. Scherli and E. Broschi. All four were awarded medals.

Beresford always competed for Thames RC, following the distinguished rowing record of his father, but he lived at Shiplake, near Henley on Thames, and was often seen out sculling there on Leander waters. He devoted considerable efforts to coaching and sports administration, leading the British Olympic team in 1936 and managing rowing teams on tour in South America and at the British Empire and Commonwealth Games and the Olympic Games. He was awarded the gold medal of the international rowing federation (FISA) in 1947, and the Olympic diploma of merit in 1949 after helping to organize the Games in London and Henley on Thames in 1948. He was elected a Henley steward in 1946 and was on the committee of management for many years. He was connected with the National Playing Fields Association, the British Field Sports Society, the British Olympic Association, the Greater London and South-East Sports Council, and the Amateur Rowing Association. Unlike his father he did not shine as a coach. He was a keen swimmer and beagler with the Farley Hill Beagles and played the umpire in the film musical *Half a Sixpence*. He was rowing correspondent of *The Field* from 1966 to 1971.

Beresford was a member of the court of the Furniture Makers' Guild and a liveryman of the Painters' and Stainers' Company. He was made a freeman of the City of London in 1952 and was appointed CBE in 1960.

Beresford was courteous both to colleagues and younger oarsmen. When over seventy he competed in the 4½-mile Head of the River race for scullers. He was shaken in his last years by a tragic incident at the National Schools Regatta at Pangbourne in 1969, when he dived into the Thames from his umpire's launch to rescue a boy who had caught a crab and been swept out of his boat during a race. Beresford, an expert swimmer, reached him under the surface but had to struggle with the boy's desperate attempts to cling to him, and the boy was drowned. It was a courageous and lone act for an elderly man and an eternal blow to him that he was unable to master the victim's plight and the tricky Thames currents. The incident troubled him for the rest of his life. He died at his home, Highlands House, Shiplake, 3 December 1977.

In 1940 Beresford married Mary Elizabeth, daughter of Robert Craske Leaning, medical doctor. They had one son and one daughter. This marriage was dissolved and in 1958 he married Stroma Jean Margaret, daughter of the Revd Andrew Morrison; they had two daughters.

[Private information; personal knowledge.]

CHRISTOPHER DODD

BERNAL, (JOHN) DESMOND (1901–1971), physicist, was born 10 May 1901 at Nenagh, county Tipperary, Ireland, the eldest in the family of three sons and two daughters (one of whom died very young) of Samuel George Bernal, farmer, of Limerick, and his wife, Elizabeth, elder daughter of the Revd William Miller, Presbyterian clergyman, of San José, California. He was educated at Stonyhurst and Bedford School, and in 1919 went up to Cambridge as a scholar of Emmanuel College. He took part i of the mathematics tripos (second class, 1920) and both parts of the natural sciences tripos, obtaining a first class in part i in 1922 and a second class (first division) in part ii (physics) in 1923.

He had an extraordinarily wide knowledge of many branches of science, and of many fields outside science; if anyone in this century deserved the name polymath, it was he. Even as an undergraduate he was given the nickname Sage which stuck to him for the rest of his life. Not only did he know a great deal about many things, but he was creative in many fields. He had an infectious delight in new ideas, whether his own or another's; the question of credit did not arise, for all that mattered was that the idea was exciting and that it had to be pursued. Other people's results gave him as much pleasure as his own. He had an immensely stimulating influence on scientists of his own and younger generations, which was far beyond, and possibly more important than, his own personal contributions. He played a major role in the development of modern crystallography and he was one of the founding fathers of molecular biology.

During his undergraduate period at Cambridge two events had a major influence on him. The first was his study of the theory of crystal symmetry, which so impressed Arthur Hutchinson [q.v.] that he recommended Bernal to Sir William Bragg [q.v.] for a place at the Royal Institution. The other event was his enthusiastic acceptance of Marxist philosophy, which led to him becoming a member of the Communist Party.

He went to the Royal Institution in 1923, shortly after Bragg became director of the Davy–Faraday laboratory. Besides many crystallographic activities, he became interested in the structures of biological molecules, as a result of discussions with W. T. Astbury [q.v.], and this became his principal scientific interest.

In 1927 he returned to Cambridge as lecturer (later assistant director of research) in structural crystallography. During his ten years there he developed several interests that continued as major preoccupations throughout his career.

The first (1931) was the study of the crystal structures of the sex hormones and other sterols. By simple methods he was able to show that the structures proposed by the chemists were wrong, and to correct these. It was one of the first major successes of crystallography in the field of complex organic molecules.

The second (1932) was the structure of water. Originally in collaboration with (Sir) R. H. Fowler [q.v.], Bernal made fundamental contributions to the understanding of this throughout his career, using remarkably simple model-building techniques.

The third (1934) was the structure of protein crystals. He was the first to discover how to obtain sharp X-ray patterns from them and pioneered their study with Dorothy Crowfoot (later Hodgkin), Isadore Fankuchen, and M. F. Perutz, thus opening up an important field of molecular biology.

The fourth (1936) was tobacco mosaic virus (TMV). Nothing was then known about the structures of viruses. With Fankuchen Bernal showed that TMV is rod-shaped and that another virus, bushy stunt, is polyhedral. After the war of 1939–45 these studies were continued in Birkbeck under Bernal's direction by Rosalind Franklin, Aaron Klug, and others. Thus he opened the door to another fascinating example of geometrical order in biological systems.

The other major scientific interest was the origin of life, which began to fascinate him as a result of conversations with J. B. S. Haldane [q.v.] and A. I. Oparin. His book *The Origin of Life* (1967) was an outcome of this interest.

During this period he also began his lifelong interests in the social relations and history of science. In 1939 he published *The Social Functions of Science.* Today almost everything in the book seems obvious; in its time it had an immense influence. Also in this field were *Science in History* (1954) and *The Extension of Man, a History of Physics before 1900* (published posthumously in 1972).

In 1938 Bernal went to Birkbeck College, London, and was based there for the rest of his career, first as professor of physics and, from 1963 to 1968, of crystallography.

Less than two years later the war began. Before this, Bernal had been a member of the Cambridge Scientists' Anti-war Group. As such he so much impressed Sir John Anderson (later Viscount Waverley, q.v.), then minister of home security, that when war came he was called to the research and experimental department of that ministry, and he and Solly (later Lord) Zuckerman became the dominant figures there. In 1941 he went to Bomber Command and then to Combined Operations, where he and Zuckerman were personal advisers to Lord Louis Mountbatten (later Earl Mountbatten of Burma, q.v.), who wrote an account of Bernal's wartime activities (included in Dorothy Hodgkin's biographical memoir for the Royal Society—see reference below). He was involved at Combined Operations with the ambitious but abortive 'Habakkuk' project for huge floating artificial icebergs to act as aircraft carriers, and in South-East Asia with bomb tests and other matters. His major contribution later was in the scientific planning for the invasion of Europe.

After the war he returned to Birkbeck. He hoped his laboratory there would become what he called an 'Institute for the Study of Things'—a place where all the varied subjects that interested him could be studied. But in those later years, although the laboratory did undertake many major projects—protein structure, virus structure, electron optics, computing, and cement—it never quite developed as he had hoped, because it was always short of funds.

The reasons for this were largely political. In the atmosphere of the cold war Bernal's extreme left-wing views were unpopular. He was a founder member (later president, 1958–65) of the World Peace Council; he was also active in founding the World Federation of Scientific Workers. He frequently visited the Soviet Union and knew Khrushchev well personally. He was a strong supporter of the Russian agriculturalist Lysenko, who was responsible during the period of his political power for the effective destruction of Soviet genetics. It soon became clear that scientifically Lysenko was a fraud; unlike J. B. S. Haldane who resigned from the Communist Party largely over this issue, Bernal maintained his support of Lysenko. This caused much pain to his scientific colleagues.

He became fellow (1937) and Royal medallist (1945) of the Royal Society; he was awarded the medal of freedom with palms of the United States (1945) and the Lenin prize for peace (1953). He was foreign member of the academies of science of seven countries. He was honorary fellow of Emmanuel College, Cambridge (1965), and fellow of Birkbeck College (1969), and received many other honours.

In 1922 he married (Agnes) Eileen, daughter of Dr William Carr Sprague. They had two sons: Michael, who became reader in numerical analysis at Imperial College, London, and Egan, farmer. He also had by Margaret Gardiner a son, Martin, who became a fellow of King's College, Cambridge, and later associate professor of government at Cornell; and by Margot Heinemann a daughter, (Susanna) Jane, doctor of medicine.

After a severe stroke in 1963 he became increasingly incapacitated but he maintained his mental alertness until his death in London 15 September 1971.

[Dorothy M. C. Hodgkin in *Biographical Memoirs of Fellows of the Royal Society*, vol. xxvi, 1980; Maurice Goldsmith, *Sage, a Life of J. D. Bernal*, 1980; personal knowledge.]

JOHN C. KENDREW

BERNARD, PERCY RONALD GARDNER, fifth EARL OF BANDON (1904–1979), air chief marshal, was born some twenty minutes before his twin brother at Gillingham, Kent, 30 August 1904, the eldest of the three children (the last of whom was a daughter) of Ronald Percy Hamilton Bernard, great-grandson of the second Earl of Bandon and a captain in the Rifle Brigade, and his wife, Lettice Mina, daughter of Captain Gerald Cecil Stewart Paget, son of Lord Alfred Paget, fifth son of the first Marquess of Anglesey [q.v.]. Percy Bernard, invariably known as 'Paddy', lived during his childhood on the Theobald's Park estate in Hertfordshire where his parents had been loaned a house by the eccentric Lady Meux. In the summer of 1914 he and his twin brother were sent to St. Aubyn's Preparatory School at Rottingdean, and four years later both boys entered 'Orange' dormitory at Wellington College where the elder was incorrectly referred to as Bernard minor throughout his school-days. Although he showed promise as an athlete and rugger player he never excelled academically and it was only after spending the summer of 1922 at a Norfolk crammer that he passed the entrance examinations to the Royal Air Force College at Cranwell.

In May 1924 he became the fifth Earl of Bandon on the death of his grandfather's cousin. The peerage being Irish did not carry with it a seat in the House of Lords. His inheritance was the estate of Castle Bernard in county Cork, but the castle had been burnt down by the Sinn Fein in 1920 and the fourth Earl had deliberately made little financial provision for his successor. The saving grace was the £123,000 compensation paid by the governor for the destruction of the castle. From the viewpoint of the Royal Air Force the fact that Cadet Bernard was now the Earl of Bandon had immediate significance and future value. The army and navy had counted men of title amongst their serving officers for generations, but it was unprecedented for a twenty-year-old peer of the realm to be making his career in the RAF which was still struggling to retain its independence as the third Service.

During the next two decades Bandon served as an instructor at Sealand, near Birkenhead; was posted to Egypt for five halcyon years where he became adjutant of No. 216 Squadron and gained renown as the pilot of the first Vickers Victoria to fly non-stop from Khartoum to Cairo; commanded No. 82 Squadron at the outbreak of World War II; was appointed to the DSO (1940); and in 1941 became station commander at West Raynham. The next year he was posted to AHQ India before joining headquarters, South-East Asia Command. At the end of the Burma campaign, already mentioned three times in dispatches he was honoured by the Americans who awarded him the USAAF Distinguished Flying Cross for 'leadership and command' and the Bronze Star medal.

On his return to England he became commandant of the Royal Observer Corps and revitalized their morale which was low since wartime incentive had departed and their future was uncertain. He was air officer commanding No. 2 Group of the British Air Forces of Occupation, Germany, in 1950–1 and subsequently, as AOC No. 11 Group had the responsibility for organizing the coronation fly-past over Buckingham Palace and the coronation review of the RAF at Odiham in 1953. After serving as assistant chief of air staff (training), he was appointed C-in-C 2nd Allied Tactical Air Force in Germany, and in March 1957 was officially reprimanded by the secretary of state for air, George Ward (later Viscount Ward of Witley), for giving information to foreign pressmen that tactical atomic weapons would soon be stored in Europe. As C-in-C Far East Air Force from 1957 to 1960 he received a 'rocket' telegram from Earl Mountbatten of Burma [q.v.] in August 1959 after he had shrewdly realized the strategic importance to the RAF of the Indian Ocean island of Gan and virtually 'commandeered' it. His final posting was as commander Allied Air Fores, Central Europe, 1961–3. He was promoted to air chief marshal in July 1959, and placed on the retired list in February 1964. He was created CB (1945), CVO (1953), KBE (1957), and GBE (1961).

Throughout his distinguished career Bandon retained the *élan* of the pioneering days of the Royal Air Force which was always his first love. He possessed moral courage to a high degree and had the gift of conveying to those around him, irrespective of rank, a sense of loyalty. Affectionately known as 'The Abandoned Earl', in his later years he epitomized the man that young airmen hoped a senior RAF officer would be. His qualities of leadership were acknowledged to be outstanding, but equally his schoolboy humour, his practical jokes, and his crude language allied to his non-conformist attitude were frequently resented, particularly by those who found it difficult to recognize his true ability.

In 1933 he married (Maybel) Elizabeth, second daughter of Raymond William Playfair, banker, of Nairobi, Kenya. Two daughters were born before the marriage was dissolved in 1946. In that year he married Mrs Lois White, daughter of Francis Russell, banker, of Victoria, Australia.

He always found pleasure in fishing, particularly in the river Bandon where salmon abounded, and in shooting, especially in the bogs where snipe and woodcock were to be found in the vicinity of Castle Bernard. He was also an enthusiastic gardener with considerable knowledge of rhododendrons. He died 8 February 1979 at the Bon Secours Hospital in Cork, after a short illness. As there was no male heir the earldom became extinct.

A portrait in oils (*c.* 1969) of Bandon in the uniform of an air chief marshal and the robes of a peer of the realm hangs in the dining hall at the Royal Air Force College, Cranwell.

[*The Times*, 23 November 1979; private information.] MICHAEL SETH-SMITH

BHUTTO, ZULFIKAR ALI (1928–1979), prime minister of Pakistan, was born 5 January 1928 at Larkana, the third of three sons and one of five children of Sir Shahnawaz Khan Bhutto, landlord and politician in Sind; and the only son born to Sir Shahnawaz and his second wife, Khurshid, who was of a Hindu family and converted to Islam on her marriage. The Bhuttos were a long-established and powerful Sindi family, and Sir Shahnawaz was active in the politics of British India.

Bhutto's education began at the Larkana mosque and continued at high schools in Karachi and Bombay, whence he went in 1947 to study political science first at the University of Southern California and then at the Berkeley campus of the University of California. He graduated with honours in 1950 and went on to Oxford, reading jurisprudence at Christ Church, and being called to the bar by Lincoln's Inn in 1953. Bhutto's six years in the West gave him a wide educational background and left him at one level of personality thoroughly westernized, but did not weaken his links with his own culture; and on his return to Pakistan in 1953 he moved easily not only into Karachi social life but also into the feudal ways of rural and small-town Sind. He practised law, but moved steadily towards politics. The president of Pakistan, Iskander Mirza, a friend of the Bhuttos, favoured the young Sindi lawyer, appointing him in 1957 a member of Pakistan's UN delegation and the following year leader of the delegation to the Geneva law of the sea conference. When, in 1958, Mirza abrogated the constitution and took power himself he brought Bhutto, then only thirty, into his cabinet and Ayub Khan, the army commander-in-chief, kept him on when he ousted Mirza and made himself president.

Bhutto enjoyed, in addition to intelligence, diligence, and administrative ability, charm and tact, and he moved quickly into the inner group of Ayub's confidants. His successive portfolios grew in importance, and in 1963 he was made foreign minister. Already by then he had demonstrated a flair for diplomacy and for international politics, and began to influence the foreign policy of Pakistan even before he was formally entrusted with it—Pakistan's approach to China about a border settlement, although begun when Bhutto was at the commerce ministry, owed much to his urgings and it could later be recognized as the first step in a radical change of the country's international posture, away from dependence upon the USA and towards non-alignment, that Bhutto was to direct as foreign minister.

But Pakistan's relations with India overshadowed all other aspects of foreign policy. Ayub's attempts in the first years of his presidency to reach an understanding with India that would resolve the Kashmir dispute on terms acceptable to Pakistan had failed, and as foreign minister Bhutto began to argue that both honesty and policy pointed to pursuing by other means the objective which diplomacy had failed to reach. His idea was to jolt the Indian government by dispatching armed infiltrators into Kashmir to set off an uprising, which might be supported openly by Pakistani forces and could lead to effective UN intervention. But the result was a classic instance of unintended escalation, culminating in September 1965 in war with India. The cease-fire, accepted by Ayub despite Bhutto's protests after only three weeks, was to mark the beginning of Ayub's decline and fall—and, it seemed at first, of Bhutto's too. The failure of Pakistan's attempt to shake Kashmir loose from India was sealed and formalized under Soviet auspices at the Tashkent conference in 1966 with Bhutto again opposing what he saw as diplomatic surrender. Bhutto offered his resignation; but the Tashkent settlement was unpopular in Pakistan and Ayub kept him on for a few months, dropping him from the cabinet only when public dissatisfaction on that score had died down. By that time Ayub's government was coming under increasing pressure and demands were made for the re-establishment of democracy in the parliamentary form which Ayub had abolished. Bhutto found himself a natural candidate for the leadership of that movement in West Pakistan, a position which was confirmed when Ayub had him imprisoned for a few months in 1968–9; and, for the first time, he began to develop and articulate a political ideology.

Bhutto found in himself a flair for populist leadership, linking an ability to play upon the passions of a crowd with skill in tailoring political platforms to fit the contradictory demands of different supporting groups, together with the ruthlessness such leadership required. From that experience emerged the Pakistan People's Party (PPP), a grouping which was first anti-Ayub, second—and essentially—pro-Bhutto, and third progressive in its platform and in its rhetoric. Bhutto's organizational gifts now found a new arena, and by the time of the elections that, in 1970, followed the fall of Ayub, the PPP had built up majority support in the west wing. But in the eastern part of Pakistan the victory of Sheikh Mujibur Rahman's Awami League had been overwhelming. As Ayub had done, Bhutto identified the Awami League's programme as secessionist, and by ordering the PPP to boycott the constituent assembly that might have found a way to compromise, he played a significant role in bringing about the very outcome of which the threat had prompted him to boycott the assembly—the disintegration of Pakistan. With the secession of the east wing of the country achieved in 1971 Bhutto was left to tower, almost unchallenged, in the reduced political arena of the remainder of Pakistan.

The collapse of the Pakistan army after Indian intervention in East Pakistan practically necessitated the resignation of the military government that had taken over from Ayub two years before. Bhutto, who had been serving as a minister in the final months of united Pakistan, was the only possible civilian who could assume the presidency and, after making a passionate defence of his country's cause at the UN, he returned to Pakistan on 20 December 1971 to be sworn in immediately as president. Bhutto speedily restored his country's internal stability and returned it to a respected position internationally. Furthermore, he began to implement progressive PPP undertakings. He introduced drastic land reforms and moved to broaden and improve the educational and health services. Nationalizing some key industries, he instituted basic wages with bonuses and pensions for industrial workers—moves whose impact quickly faded, even before Bhutto's fall, but which nevertheless seeded in the popular consciousness the knowledge that government could be used directly to benefit the poor, and were thus likely to have long-term effects on Pakistan's political development. By 1973 a new constitution had been promulgated, under which Bhutto became prime minister.

Internationally, Bhutto's first tasks were to turn the cease-fire with India into peace and normalize relations with what had now become Bangladesh. At an Islamic conference he convened in Lahore in 1974, which confirmed the warm relations Bhutto had developed for Pakistan with the Arab countries, he was able to greet Sheikh Mujib, now president of Bangladesh, whose release from a Pakistani gaol had been one of Bhutto's early acts as president.

But there was another side to Bhutto's exercise of power, and it was to destroy him. Vindictiveness raised to the level of vendetta, an intolerance of criticism and readiness to employ brutal physical coercion against those he counted his enemies, an openness to the flattery of sycophants: contrary to the friendly side of Bhutto, those negative, almost feudal, attributes meant that with time the political opposition to him became infused with intense personal hostility. Meanwhile he had shifted the political base of the PPP, bringing into its fold the powerful landed interests of Sind and Punjab whose social aims were contrary to those which the PPP's platform proclaimed. By March 1977, when general elections were held under the new constitution, a powerful undercurrent of dissatisfaction was running in the country, and the diverse opposition parties formed a single organization, the Pakistan National Alliance. Bhutto and his party survived the electoral challenge of that coalition: the PPP won a clear victory—but not, to the opposition, a convincing one. Charging that the results were rigged, the opposition took their campaign to the streets. The PPP's popularity in the cities had waned, the compromises and concessions Bhutto now offered were taken by his opponents as signs of weakness, and he had to rely on troops to contain the urban mob turbulence the opposition continued to whip up. Bhutto, always aware of the danger of revived political ambitions among the generals, had attempted to prevent further intervention by dismissing the former commanders and promoting his own placemen. But, finding the civilian order once more dependent upon the military, the army seized power again in July 1977, dismissing the government and planning—the generals said—new elections. Then Bhutto was arrested on a charge of murder, accused of having given orders for the assassination of a political opponent. During the ensuing trials the military authorities issued white papers in effect adding political charges of corruption and malfeasance to that of murder. Bhutto was convicted and sentenced to death in March 1978, and the following February the Pakistan supreme court, on appeal, confirmed by four to three the verdict and sentence. Internal protests on Bhutto's behalf were crushed by the army, international pleas ignored, and Bhutto was hanged on 4 April 1979 in Rawalpindi gaol.

Bhutto was married to a cousin when he was thirteen, but had no children from that marriage, in which, though it was not dissolved, the couple spent almost no time together. In 1951 he married Nusrat Sabunchi, of Iranian descent, and they had three sons and two daughters. After Bhutto's execution—or judicial assassination, as he described it when under sentence—leadership of the PPP devolved to his widow and daughter Benazir, who, thereby incurring the animosity of the military regime, spent long periods in detention in the years after his death.

[Salman Taseer, *Bhutto: A Political Biography*, 1979; personal knowledge.]

NEVILLE MAXWELL

BING, GEOFFREY HENRY CECIL (1909–1977), barrister and politician, was born 24 July 1909 at Craigavad near Belfast, the only son and elder child of Geoffrey Bing, headmaster of Rockport School and Orange Lodge supporter, of Rockport, Craigavad, county Down, and his wife, Irene Hare Duke. He was educated at Tonbridge School and Lincoln College, Oxford, where he obtained a second class in modern history in 1931. He was Jane Eliza Procter visiting fellow at Princeton University in 1932–3. He was called to the bar at the Inner Temple (1934), at Gibraltar (1937), the Gold Coast (1950), and Nigeria (1954).

His early experience in Ulster gave him a hatred of discrimination and a willingness to defend human rights wherever they were threatened. He became a sort of joyful revolutionary, hurled himself into every scene where his interests were engaged, and always emerged with a good story however sombre his report. In the mid-1930s he helped to give early strength to the Haldane Society and the National Council for Civil Liberties, founded by Ronald Kidd in 1934. He entered several prisons in Fascist countries in search of the 'disappeared' and joined the International Brigade in Spain as a journalist, barely escaping at Bilbao.

His first wife helped Claud Cockburn to edit the left-wing paper *The Week*. Bing found himself very much at home in these surroundings and some of his own foreign exploits were aimed at investigating or enlarging an embryo story. He became one of the first anti-Nazis of the 1930s. As a result, when he was called up in the Royal Signals in 1941 he had no prospect save the most menial in a large home establishment. A serious political battle had to be fought in his favour before he was given any chance of worthwhile employment. He then entered an Officer Cadet Training Unit, from which he passed out top. In 1943 he did experimental work with parachutes in the GSO2 Airborne Forces Development Centre. One of the experiments undertaken marred his face for many years. In 1943 he was a signals officer in North Africa and, in 1944, accompanied the British liberation forces in western Europe with the rank of major. He was wounded and mentioned in dispatches.

In 1945 Bing was elected Labour MP for Hornchurch, a seat he held until 1955. He was at once appointed as an unpaid junior whip. It was generally accepted that this was a mistake for another man of a similar name, who was as much to the right of the party and so acceptable to Ernest Bevin [q.v.], as Bing was to the left. The appointment lasted for nine months and then was ended without comment. Bing was a committed supporter of communist China. He specialized in Northern Ireland, the brewers' monopoly, and parliamentary procedure. His was almost the sole voice in the years after the war calling for help for the Ulster minority. He became adept at the parliamentary devices whereby any issue can be raised, perhaps late at night, which no deputy Speaker can reject. Indeed, when Labour was in opposition he was called upon by colleagues to guide them through the intricacies of this procedure.

At the bar (he took silk in 1950) Bing built up a small practice in West Africa where he met Dr Kwame Nkrumah, leader of the main party in the Gold Coast. In 1955 the programme for independence was already arranged and Nkrumah urgently needed a legal and constitutional adviser. Bing, having lost his parliamentary seat, got the job in 1956. In 1957 he was appointed attorney-general in Ghana (previously the Gold Coast) and was thus involved in many of the territory's problems. The British government seemed obsessed with the idea that all colonial civil servants would withdraw; Bing had to dissuade them. He also had to order Emil Savundra out of the country for fraud at a time when his true character was not known. When a *Daily Telegraph* journalist was arrested Bing announced, on behalf of the Ghanaian government, that he may have any counsel he might choose; when Christopher Shawcross QC arrived, Bing, on the orders of Krobo Edusie, the minister of the interior, announced that he was excluded, an act which made it impossible for him ever again to get work at the English bar. It is arguable that he should have resigned as attorney-general rather than act on Edusie's order.

Bing ceased to be attorney-general in 1961, whereupon he became Nkrumah's adviser. Emancipation of the African colonies was new and the one-party African state was unforeseen. Bing and Nkrumah thought that a liberated colony must try to establish an independent economy, an effort which seemed to require one-party dictatorship whether benign or evil. When Nkrumah was ousted by a *coup d'état* in February 1966 Bing was arrested and ill-treated. He had done no wrong and after some months was sent home. He had been appointed CMG in 1960.

In 1940 Bing married Christian Frances, the former wife of Edward Archibald Fraser Harding, and daughter of Sir Ralph Barrett Macnaghten Blois, ninth baronet, of Cockfield Hall, Yoxford, Suffolk. They had two sons. The marriage was dissolved in 1955 and in 1956 Bing married Eileen Mary, daughter of Frederick Cullen, alderman and parliamentary agent for Hornchurch. They had one adopted son. Bing died in London 24 April 1977.

[Geoffrey Bing, *Reap the Whirlwind*, 1968, and *John Bull's Other Ireland*, 1950; family information; personal knowledge.]

JOHN PLATTS-MILLS

BINNEY, SIR (FREDERICK) GEORGE (1900–1972), explorer, business man, and blockade runner, was born 23 September 1900 at Great Bookham, Surrey, the second of two sons of the Revd Maximilian Frederick Breffit Binney, vicar of Richmond, Surrey, and his first wife, Emily Blinkhorn, who died when her son was born. There were two more sons of a second marriage. He won a scholarship from Summer Fields, Oxford, to Eton and later to Merton College, Oxford. He obtained a third class in English in 1923.

While at Oxford, at a chance meeting with (Sir) Julian Huxley [q.v.] in Blackwells, he was asked as editor of *Isis* to back an expedition to Spitsbergen and to become its organizer and secretary. This was the Oxford University Spitsbergen Expedition of 1921. In 1923 he organized and led the Merton College Arctic Expedition and in 1924 the Oxford University Arctic Expedition. The first to use a seaplane for arctic surveys, he recorded his experiences in his book *With Seaplane and Sledge in the Arctic* (1925). His achievements were recognized by the Back award of the Royal Geographical Society, the gold medal 'de la roquette' of the Geographical Society of Paris, and in 1957 by the Founder's gold medal of the RGS.

Binney joined the Hudson's Bay Company in 1926, spending the winters in England recruiting young apprentices and the summers planting them on trading stations in the Canadian Arctic. A *Times* leader on his *The Eskimo Book of Knowledge* (1931), the first book other than the Bible to be made available to the Eskimos in their own language, made his chairman offer him promotion to the company's headquarters in Winnipeg, but he refused and joined the United Steel Companies Ltd. the next day. He was appointed to build up a central export department and became the company's export director, distinguishing himself by his remarkable success as an unconventional negotiator. He remained with United Steel till it was nationalized, travelling the world on their behalf, from Europe to North and South America, Russia, Iran, India, and the Far East.

Having narrowly missed service in World War I he was determined to play a part in World War II. In December 1939 he was sent by Iron and Steel Control (Ministry of Supply) as their Scandinavian representative to Sweden to negotiate the purchase and shipment of special steels, machine tools, and ball-bearings which were vital for the British armament industries. The German invasion of Denmark and Norway on 9 April 1940 cut Sweden off from the West, whereupon Binney decided to run the gauntlet of the Skagerrak blockade.

He defeated opposition to his plan at home and in Sweden, was given diplomatic status as assistant commercial attaché at the British legation, and recruited British, Norwegian, and Swedish crews for five Norwegian merchantmen. Operation Rubble, as it was called, sailed from Bro Fjord north of Göteborg on 23 January 1941 with Binney as commodore. It got through to Kirkwall in the Orkneys with 25,000 tons of vital war supplies and five ships for the Allied merchant fleets. Binney refused an important appointment in Washington and returned to Sweden to run Operation Performance in March 1942 with ten ships. Only two got through with 5,000 tons of cargo, two returned to Sweden, and the rest were sunk or scuttled.

Binney was expelled from Sweden as *persona non grata* for smuggling scuttling charges and arms on board his ships but reappeared as commander RNVR in 1943 in charge of Operation Bridford. This consisted of a flotilla of five motor-coasters (of which two were lost) which delivered 347½ tons of valuable cargo while another 88 tons were airlifted. Having been invalided out after a heart attack Binney still involved himself in yet another operation—Moonshine—which delivered arms to the Danish Resistance. He was knighted in 1941 and appointed to the DSO in 1944 for these remarkable exploits. His unique contribution to the war effort was to help meet the shortfall of ball-bearings when there were too few coming from British factories and insufficient imports from the USA and Canada.

After demobilization in 1945 Binney returned to United Steel, leaving them once only, for a brief foray for the government as leader of the UK trade and industrial mission to Ghana in 1959.

This jovial buccaneer with his puckish sense of humour, his stocky physique, ruddy complexion, and keen blue eyes was a man of discriminating taste in books, antiques, and the good things of life. His homes were perfect settings for his treasures and his restoration of Horham Hall was typical of his taste. He was an obstinate individualist with scant respect for authority, a man of impeccable integrity, and meticulous in his attention to detail. Cyril Alington [q.v.], his headmaster at Eton, called him 'the ingenious and ingenuous Binney': this he always remained.

Binney was married first, in 1946, to Evelyn Mary, widow of Flight-Lieutenant A. P. F. Fane, RAFVR, and elder daughter of Thomas G. Marriott, of Putney Hill, London. This marriage was dissolved in 1955 and in the same year Binney married Sonia, widow of Lieutenant-Colonel Francis Crofton Simms, MC, and daughter of Paymaster Rear-Admiral Sir William Marcus Charles Beresford Whyte. He adopted her son Marcus. He died 27 September 1972 at his home Domaine des Vaux, Haut de la Vallée, St. Lawrence, Jersey, Channel Islands.

[Family and private papers; Public Record Office; Ralph Barker, *The Blockade Busters*, 1976; personal knowledge.] PETER TENNANT

BLACK, SIR MISHA (1910–1977), architect and industrial designer, was born 16 October 1910 in Baku, Russia, the second of the three sons (there was also a daughter) of Lionel Tcherny, merchant, and his wife, Sonia Markovna, who brought him at the age of eighteen months to London where he lived all his life except for a short spell studying art in Paris after attending the Dame Alice Owen School, Islington. Lionel Tcherny changed his name to Black in 1911/12 and his son Moisei became Misha.

In spite of so modest an education Black ended his life as a professor emeritus of the Royal College of Art (from 1975), a trustee of the British Museum (from 1968), an honorary Doctor of Technology of Bradford University, and an internationally recognized authority on the teaching and practice of industrial design. He arrived at these distinctions by a circuitous route, for industrial design was an unknown, untaught subject when he was born. He had to work his way towards his final goal through what he called 'stomach fillers' such as book-plates, book jackets, posters and, more important for his future career, exhibition stands. He conducted these youthful free-lance activities from an attic overlooking Seven Dials, but in 1934 he joined Milner and Thomas Gray and others in the Industrial Design Partnership. It was through his work on commercial display stands that he eventually became a leader in the field of exhibition design working as co-ordinating architect for the 1938 MARS (Modern Architectural Research Society) exhibition and as interior designer for the British Pavilion at the 1939 New York World's Fair.

From 1940 to 1945 he was principal exhibition architect to the Ministry of Information, but his real chance came in 1951 at the Festival of Britain South Bank exhibition, of which he was co-ordinating architect and co-architect of the popular Regatta restaurant. Thereafter he was endlessly busy as architect, designer, or consultant, having formed in 1946, at the instigation of Marcus Brumwell and (Sir) Herbert Read [q.v.], his lifelong partnership with Milner Gray, CBE, RDI, which they cleverly called Design

Research Unit (DRU), thereby winning national and international standing as the leading design consultancy in Britain. Although the DRU practice ranged across the whole spectrum of design, Black's own leanings were towards blending art with technics and bridging the gap between industrial and engineering design, particularly in the field of public transport. This led him to consultancies with British Rail, London Transport, the Orient Line, BOAC, Beagle Aircraft, and finally the Hong Kong Rapid Transport System.

In 1933 he had, again with Milner Gray, been a founder member of the British Society of Industrial Artists and in 1954–6 was its president, an experience which together with his many foreign friendships led him to become a prime mover in the establishment of the International Council of Societies of Industrial Design (ICSID), the first meeting of which was held in London in 1957 and of which Black was president from 1959 to 1961.

It was in 1959 too that he acquired another string to his bow and one that brought him almost more acclaim world-wide than had his widespread professional practice, for it was in that year that he was appointed professor of industrial design at the Royal College of Art, a chair he held until his retirement in 1975. Although he never himself went to a university, his arrival at the Royal College of Art soon gave academic authority to the profession he had adopted and he became in great demand as a writer and lecturer. His mastery of language was a joy to witness, developing as it did from early pretentiousness to such clarity of thought and expression as to leave audiences eating out of his hand. No one could sum up a debate or seminar or conference more precisely or punctiliously, thereby sending everyone home comforted that some wisdom had transpired. It was indeed for his wisdom that he was picked for membership of all manner of organizations such as the Council of Industrial Design (1955–64), the Design and Industries Association, the National Advisory Council on Art Education (1959–72), the advisory council to the Science Museum (from 1966), the Faculty of Royal Designers for Industry, of which he was master in 1973–4, the British Association for the Advancement of Science, and even the National Union of Students which offered him honorary membership in 1967. He was appointed OBE in 1946 (he was naturalized in 1950, whereupon the OBE was reissued) and knighted in 1972. He became RDI in 1957.

He was married twice—first in 1935 to Helen Lillian, daughter of Frank Foster Evans, engineer, by whom he had one son and one daughter (this marriage was dissolved in 1952); and secondly in 1955 to Edna Joan, daughter of George Septimus Fairbrother, engineer, by whom he had one son. He died in London 11 August 1977.

[Private information; personal knowledge.]

PAUL REILLY

BLACKETT, PATRICK MAYNARD STUART, BARON BLACKETT (1897–1974), physicist and political and military strategist, was born 18 November 1897 at Kensington, London, the only son and the second of the three children of Arthur Stuart Blackett, stockbroker, of London, and his wife, Caroline Frances, daughter of Major Charles Maynard, RA. He was educated at a preparatory school in Guildford and in his thirteenth year entered Osborne Naval College, from which he moved to Dartmouth. In World War I he saw action in the battles of the Falkland Islands and Jutland. He was promoted lieutenant in May 1918.

In January 1919 the Admiralty sent the officers whose training had been interrupted in 1914 to Cambridge for a course of general duties. The Cavendish Laboratory made a great impression on Blackett and he decided to leave the navy to study mathematics and physics. He entered Magdalene College, Cambridge, and in May 1919 obtained a second class in part i of the mathematics tripos. Two years later he achieved a first in part ii of the natural sciences (physics) tripos. He then obtained a fellowship at Magdalene, and became a research student in the Cavendish. Sir Ernest Rutherford (later Lord Rutherford of Nelson, q.v.) had already discovered that by firing fast α-particles into nitrogen, the nucleus of the nitrogen atom could be disintegrated, and he asked Blackett to use the cloud chamber (expansion chamber) to obtain visible tracks of this disintegration. By 1924 Blackett had taken 23,000 photographs showing 415,000 tracks of ionized particles. Eight of these were forked, giving the visible evidence for the disintegration of the nitrogen atom into an isotope of oxygen and a proton. A year earlier he had become a fellow of King's College, Cambridge, a position he held until 1933. He spent the academic year 1924–5 in Germany at Göttingen working with James Frank on atomic spectra.

In 1932, in collaboration with G. P. S. Occhialini, Blackett devised a system of geiger counters so that photographs were taken only when a cosmic ray particle traversed the chamber. In 700 automatic expansions there were 500 tracks of high energy cosmic ray particles. Fourteen tracks gave evidence for the existence of the positive electron (positron), but C. D. Anderson in America was able to claim priority for this discovery.

In the autumn of 1933 Blackett moved to London as professor of physics at Birkbeck College and four years later he succeeded (Sir) W. L.

Bragg [q.v.] as the Langworthy professor of physics in the Victoria University of Manchester, where he created a major international research laboratory.

Blackett was already involved in military affairs when war broke out in September 1939. Since 1935 he had served on the committee, under the chairmanship of Sir H. T. Tizard [q.v.], to advise on the defence of the country against air attack. By deciding to press for the development of radar this committee transformed the air defence of the country. In the early stages of the war Blackett divided his time between various committees and the Royal Aircraft Establishment, Farnborough. There he made a major contribution to the design of the Mark 14 bomb-sight which removed the need for a level bombing run before release.

In August 1940 Blackett became scientific adviser to Lieutenant-General Sir F. A. Pile [q.v.], the C-in-C of Anti-Aircraft Command, and thereby began his remarkable development of operational research. He revolutionized the operational techniques of Anti-Aircraft Command and of Coastal Command (1941–2). In January 1942 he transferred to the Admiralty as chief adviser on operational research (subsequently director of naval operational research) where he exerted a major influence on the techniques used in the war against the U-boats. His association with atomic policy began shortly after the discovery of nuclear fission. In 1940 he was a member of the 'Maud' committee. Blackett dissented from the conclusion of this committee that Britain could produce an atomic bomb by 1943 at a cost of £5 million and he recommended that the project should be discussed with the Americans. In August 1945 he was appointed to the advisory committee on atomic energy. His views diverged from the majority opinion and the publicity which he gave to his attitude in *Military and Political Consequences of Atomic Energy* (1948) led to his exclusion from government advisory circles for more than a decade.

Blackett relinquished his Admiralty post in the summer of 1945 and was then able to concentrate on the restoration and expansion of the physics department in Manchester. He stimulated the development of the research work on cosmic rays and encouraged the adaptation of wartime techniques by (Sir) A. C. B. Lovell that eventually led to the creation of the radio observatory at Jodrell Bank. In 1946 he became interested in problems of geomagnetism and suggested that magnetic fields, such as that of the Earth, were a fundamental property of rotating matter. He proceeded to develop a magnetometer of great precision and sensitivity in order to make a laboratory test of this theory. In 1952 he described this in a paper for the Royal Society which revealed his extraordinary technical skills and his greatness as an experimentalist. Blackett's theory was not correct but the new magnetometer was admirably suited for the measurements of the magnetic properties of rocks back to the 500 million years for which fossil dating was possible. The impact of this work in supporting the theory of continental drift came after Blackett's move to London where he succeeded Sir G. P. Thomson [q.v.] at Imperial College in 1953, having been pro-vice-chancellor at Manchester from 1950 to 1952.

Blackett played a major part in the post-war expansion of the universities as a member of the committee headed by Sir J. A. N. Barlow [q.v.]. He stimulated the development of science and technology by his advocacy on many other committees, including the National Research and Development Corporation (1949–64). He was a member of the council of the Department of Scientific and Industrial Research, and chairman of the research grants committee (1956–60), and of the European Organization for Nuclear Research (1954–8).

The post-war nadir of Blackett's political fortunes changed when Harold Wilson (later Lord Wilson of Rievaulx) succeeded to the leadership of the Labour Party in 1963, and the Blackett–Wilson relationship became of cardinal importance to British science and technology. Since 1950 he had been the senior member of a group whose aim was to evolve a scientific and technological policy for the country. The development of the ideas of the Blackett group led to the creation of the Ministry of Technology after the Labour victory in the general election of October 1964. Initially Blackett wielded great power as deputy chairman and scientific adviser to the Ministry and it was at his insistence that the support of the computer industry was made a priority. His ties with the Ministry gradually loosened, especially after his election as president of the Royal Society in 1965—for a five-year period which he regarded as the climax of his whole career.

Blackett's internationalism found its greatest expression in his deep sympathy for India. There, in 1947, he met Jawaharlal Nehru [q.v.] who sought his advice on the research and development needs of the armed forces. For the next twenty years he became a frequent visitor as adviser on military and civil science. These visits deepened his concern for the underprivileged and the poor and his conviction that the problem could be solved by the application of science and technology.

Blackett was one of the great scientists of the twentieth century whose significance extended far beyond the laboratory into military affairs and politics. He was appointed a Companion of Honour in 1965, and to the Order of Merit in 1967, and was otherwise richly endowed with many distinctions. He was awarded the Nobel prize for physics in 1948, elected FRS in 1933, and awarded the Royal medal of the Royal Society in 1940 and the Copley medal in 1956. In 1946 he received the American medal for merit. He held twenty honorary degrees and was an honorary member of academic or other institutions in eleven countries, including the Soviet Union and China. In 1969 he was created a life peer.

Blackett was a dominant and immensely powerful personality but his public image veiled a sensitive and humane spirit. He enjoyed sailing and walking but otherwise had few recreations. Nature endowed him with outstanding physical and intellectual gifts which he used abundantly for the benefit of science and mankind. In March 1924 he married Costanza, daughter of Eugenio Bayon. She survived him together with a daughter Giovanna (born 1926) and a son Nicolas Maynard (born 1928).

[Bernard Lovell in *Biographical Memoirs of Fellows of the Royal Society*, vol. xxi, 1975 (and separate publication 1976); private information; personal knowledge.] BERNARD LOVELL

BLACKMAN, GEOFFREY EMETT (1903–1980), ecologist, plant physiologist, and agriculturist, was born 17 April 1903 in Kensington, London, the elder son in the family of three children of Professor V. H. Blackman [q.v.], plant physiologist, then an assistant in the British Museum (Natural History) and afterwards head of the department of biology at Imperial College, and his wife, Edith Delta, daughter of Joseph and Rebecca Ann Emett of Mangotsfield, Gloucestershire. Blackman was educated at King's College School, Wimbledon, and at St. John's College, Cambridge, where he obtained a second class in both parts of the natural sciences tripos (1924 and 1926). He was a good rugby player, a half blue for rifle shooting, president of the Dance Club, and a jazz fan. His interest in biology started when he was a boy, and throughout life he was a generalist, keeping up his interest in field botany as well as in laboratory and field experimentation. At Cambridge he also became interested in the applications of mathematical statistics to biological problems, first through the influence of G. E. Briggs, and later during a short period at Rothamsted Experimental Station under (Sir) Ronald Fisher [q.v.] in 1926.

From 1927 to 1935 Blackman worked at the Imperial Chemical Industries agricultural research station at Jealott's Hill under Sir Frederick Keeble [q.v.]; there he founded the botany section of which he became head. He studied, in particular, the competition between plants, and in this context designed experiments to test the effects of fertilizers and poisonous substances on the interaction of species. The treatments were carefully replicated and capable of exact statistical appraisal. In the course of his work at ICI Blackman laid the foundations of the study of selective herbicides, which was to become an important agricultural pursuit during and after the war and one to which he made fundamental and outstanding contributions. During this time he also developed the hobby of gardening in which he became a great expert, sometime scientific editor of the *Gardeners' Chronicle*, and well known for his gardens on acid soil, and became passionately fond of winter sports and of mountains, making regular visits to the Alps until he was over seventy.

From 1935 to 1945 he was lecturer in ecology at Imperial College, London. He was one of the first to analyse statistically the results of ecological experiments done in natural habitats. His work with A. J. Rutter on the autecology of the bluebell and on the dispersion, whether random or not, of plants in natural habitats was essentially pioneering in its methods of analysis. They also applied the techniques of plant growth-analysis, then being used at Cambridge and Rothamsted, to work in natural vegetation. These methods were later to become an important tool in Blackman's studies of the growth of crop-plants alone and in association.

When war broke out Blackman was a prime mover in the establishment and work of the biology war committee, of which he became secretary (1942–6). He also supervised research under the aegis of the Agricultural Research Council on many agricultural problems, including the possible use of selective herbicides, and the introduction of new crops such as oilseed rape, maize, and flax. In 1945 he was elected to the Sibthorpian chair of rural economy in Oxford and to a fellowship at St. John's College, Oxford. He completely altered the outlook on agriculture of his department and of the university. His wartime research teams joined him to form the unit of agronomy, and both teaching and research in agriculture became scientific and forward-looking. In the next fifteen years there were great changes; the establishment of the university field station; the formation of one of the first plant physiology laboratories using isotopic tracers, and the expansion of work on hormone physiology and selective herbicides. From the department, the Weed Research Organization, Letcombe laboratory, and other smaller units originated.

Blackman took a full part in college and university activities, and was approachable and helpful to undergraduates and research students alike. He remained scientifically active even after his retirement in 1970, travelling to Hong Kong and Vancouver as visiting professor, and serving as adviser to various bodies, including the Rubber Research Institute, and as chairman of the section on production and processes in the International Biological Programme. In 1970 he was invited to join a committee set up by the United States National Academy of Sciences for Congress to report on the use and effects of herbicides for military purposes. He took a very active part, in spite of his age, in the surveys and experiments on defoliants undertaken in Vietnam and elsewhere. He was satisfied that an objective assessment of the extent and consequences of the military use of herbicides was made, but disappointed that a more detailed investigation could not be done.

Blackman was elected to the Royal Society in 1959 and served on its council and as vice-president (1967–8). He was elected to the Royal Swedish Academy of Agriculture (1963), to an honorary fellowship of Imperial College (1968), and as honorary councillor of the Superior Scientific Circle of Spain (1968). The annual Blackman lecture is given in Oxford in his honour.

In 1931 he married Audrey Babette Seligman, well known for her ceramic statuettes, with whom he shared many of his interests, including the collection of British water-colour paintings. She was the daughter of Richard Seligman, president of the Institute of Metals. They had no children. Blackman died near Abingdon 8 February 1980 after a short illness.

[J. L. Harley in *Biographical Memoirs of Fellows of the Royal Society*, vol. xxvii, 1981; private information; personal knowledge.]

J. L. Harley

BLACKWELL, RICHARD (1918–1980), bookseller and publisher, was born 5 January 1918, at 1 Frenchay Road, Oxford, the eldest in the family of two sons and three daughters of (Sir) Basil Henry Blackwell, bookseller, whose father had founded the bookselling business of Blackwell's in Oxford on 1 January 1879, and his wife, Marion Christine, daughter of John Soans, schoolmaster, of Ramsgate. He was educated at the Dragon School in Oxford. He won a scholarship to Winchester College, and from there a scholarship to New College, Oxford, where in 1938 he achieved a first class in classical honour moderations. However, the war cut short his academic career, and he did not return later, but was content with a wartime MA (1944).

His six-and-a-half years of war service was spent in the Royal Navy, as lieutenant (S) RNVR. He saw action and hardship on the Russian convoy route and also in the Mediterranean where in 1944 he was awarded the DSC. In 1946 he joined his father in the family business.

At the time Blackwell's enjoyed a high and enviable reputation as one of the best retail booksellers in the English-speaking world, but the actual size of the business in financial terms was by no means great. It was Richard Blackwell's lifework to build a large, complex, and successful international business on this base. He achieved this by foreseeing the spread of English as the main international language, the post-war growth of higher education throughout the world, and the establishment of many new universities and libraries, and thus the opportunities for export.

He travelled widely and took every opportunity for development. He nurtured many small and not so small subsidiary and associated companies in the book trade. The most significant of these was perhaps Blackwell Scientific Publications Limited. In 1964 he formed, with the Oxford University Press as a joint partner, a chain of university bookshops. When the Richard Abel library supply business in the United States failed, he developed Blackwell North America Inc. to take over the business. His aim was to develop a world-wide service supplying English periodicals and books to academic and specialist libraries and customers.

In all such enterprises he always ensured the ultimate control by the Blackwell family. It was not only a question of seeing his inheritance multiply, it was also his intention that the family business should remain wholly independent and private.

During the years of growth, Richard had been supported by his family, above all his father, his younger brother, Julian, and latterly, and much to his happiness, his two sons, Miles and Nigel, all actively involved in the management of the business. In the early days the wisdom and guidance of his father was an essential feature in his success, but he steadily took over the main burden of responsibility, becoming managing director in 1956 and chairman in 1969. In 1976 he became chairman of Basil Blackwell Publisher Limited, the publishing business originally established by his father as Blackwell & Mott.

Although motivated by the determination that Blackwell's should be supreme, Richard Blackwell was conscious of the responsibility to his fellow booksellers that such a leadership entailed. In 1962 he worked hard for the defence of the net book agreement and played an arduous part in the case itself before the Restrictive Trade Practices Court, as described in detail in the work, *Books are Different*, edited by R. E. Barker and G. R. Davies (1966). For two years (1966–8) he was president of the Booksellers' Association.

As a person he was quiet and modest and somewhat difficult to get to know. He always said that he had had an easy wicket and he was generous in his praise of his colleagues and staff. His style of management was quiet but persistent. He allowed his chosen managers a considerable degree of autonomy and freedom, both for action and speech. He had a stoic character, never displaying personal problems even during his illness.

His relaxations were few, and these—mainly fishing and shooting—were mostly taken with his travels on business. At Winchester he had rowed for the school for two years winning the Public Schools fours both years, the second time as captain, and he rowed for several years for the New College first eight. Later in life, he enjoyed his membership of Leander Club and sailing his cruising yacht off the south coast.

In 1971 he was awarded an honorary D.Litt. at York University, Ontario, and in 1978 he was elected a fellow of St. Cross College, Oxford.

In 1942 he married Marguerite, the daughter of Major Lionel Brook Holliday OBE, industrialist and landowner, of Copgrove Hall, Yorkshire. They had two sons. He died at his home, Tubney House, Oxford, 26 February 1980.

[A. L. F. Norrington, *Blackwell's 1879–1979*, 1983; personal knowledge.] JOHN BROWN

BLAIR, DAVID (1932–1976), ballet dancer, was born David Butterfield 27 July 1932, at Halifax, Yorkshire, the elder child and only son of John Butterfield and his wife, Zette Carolyne Elizabeth Whiteley, both of Halifax where David Blair received his primary education at Trinity School. As a child David Blair attended local dancing classes and was selected by the Royal Academy of Dancing for extra coaching under its scholarship scheme in the Yorkshire region, which led, when he was fourteen, to the Royal Ballet School, London. Only a year later, in 1947, he joined the Sadler's Wells Theatre Ballet and progressed so quickly that at sixteen he was dancing the exacting *Casse Noisette pas de deux* and in 1950 he was made a principal dancer.

From the start his exceptional virtuosity, enhanced by good looks and a most engaging stage presence, endeared him to the public and critics alike in a variety of roles. His first lead in a new choreography came when Michael Somes cast him for his *Summer Interlude*; and a few months later Balanchine chose him for *Trumpet Concerto* at Sadler's Wells Theatre. But it was John Cranko [q.v.] who worked most closely with Blair for several years developing his talents over a wide range and creating for him, in 1951, the unforgettable Captain Belaye in *Pineapple Poll* to the music of Sir W. S. Gilbert and Sir Arthur Sullivan [qq.v.]. Blair's portrayal of the dashingly handsome but ludicrously vain captain was a masterpiece of comedy which, combined with his brilliant dancing, helped to establish the ballet as one of the favourite British classics.

In 1953 Blair transferred to the 'parent' company, Sadler's Wells Ballet (later the Royal Ballet) at the Royal Opera House, Covent Garden. The change to a larger company and larger theatre was timely for his artistic development in the classical repertoire for which his slightly mischievous boyish charm and exuberance were almost a disadvantage—although of course making him the ideal Franz in *Coppélia*.

He soon mastered the noble style and partnered with great distinction all the Royal Ballet ballerinas including Svetlana Beriosova, Violetta Elvin, Annette Page, Rowena Jackson, Anya Linden, (Dame) Margot Fonteyn, and especially Nadia Nerina with whom he had an exceptionally successful partnership.

Blair's repertoire with the Royal Ballet included *Le Tricorne* (1953), *Swan Lake* and *Sleeping Beauty* (1955), *Cinderella* (1956), *Giselle* and *Prince of the Pagodas* (1957), *Petrushka* (1959), and much more. In 1960 (Sir) Frederick Ashton choreographed one of his greatest works, *La Fille mal Gardée*, for Nadia Nerina and David Blair who shared a triumphant success. Blair danced superbly the role of Colas, the country youth, giving him an irresistible air of amiable cheekiness. Another triumph was his Mercutio in Kenneth MacMillan's *Romeo and Juliet*. In 1961, on Michael Somes's retirement, David Blair succeeded him as principal dancer of the Royal Ballet.

Blair had a delightfully fresh enthusiasm for dance even when encountering the ups and downs from which no one is immune—the road is always bumpier at the top than on the way up. But it would be hard to find a man more straightforward, staunch, without malice or guile, warm-hearted, and lovable. He spoke his mind in the forthright manner of a true Yorkshireman and he was also very human—he had a soft shell for criticism.

While still on the top as a dancer, he branched out into production with the complete versions of *Swan Lake* (1965) and *Sleeping Beauty* (1966) for the Atlanta Civic Ballet. For American Ballet Theatre he produced *Swan Lake* (1967) and *Giselle* (1968). He was also the producer of the Hong Kong Ballet's *Giselle* and a filmed version of *Giselle* starring Carla Fracci and Erik Bruhn (1969).

In the history of British ballet David Blair stands in the forefront of today's accomplished male dancers. He set a standard of virtuoso dancing in the 1950s that inspired and influenced the following generation. In addition he gave much time and effort, mainly through his involvement with the Royal Academy of Dancing (he was a member of its executive committee from 1971), to the teaching of students and the resettlement of retiring professionals. His was a life devoted to dance and fellow dancers. For services to ballet he was appointed CBE in 1964. In 1973 his farewell to the stage at the Royal Opera House was an overwhelming personal triumph.

He was about to take up directorship of the Norwegian Ballet in Oslo when, on 1 April 1976, he died suddenly of a heart attack at his home in London.

David Blair married in 1957 ballerina Maryon Lane who was born Patricia Mills, the daughter of an Irish doctor in Melmouth, Zululand. Twin daughters, Diana and Catherine Blair, were born in 1960, and Diana, following her parents' profession, became a member of the Hamburg Ballet.

[*The Times*, 2 April 1976; *Dancing Times*, May 1976; *Concise Oxford Dictionary of Ballet*, 1977; private information; personal knowledge.]

MARGOT FONTEYN

BLISS, SIR ARTHUR EDWARD DRUMMOND (1891–1975), composer and Master of the Queen's Music, was born in Barnes, London, 2 August 1891, the eldest of the three sons (there were no daughters) of Francis Edward Bliss, an American business man resident in England, and his second wife, Agnes Kennard, daughter of James Davis, a minister of religion, of Great Yarmouth. There was also a son of a previous marriage. Arthur Bliss, whose mother died when he was four, was educated at Rugby and went in 1910, with a classical exhibition, to Pembroke College, Cambridge. There his mentors in music were the strict disciplinarian Charles Wood and the internationally minded Edward Dent [qq.v.]. He took his BA and Mus.Bac. in 1913 and was then at the Royal College of Music for some months where he received constructive advice from Ralph Vaughan Williams and Gustav Holst [qq.v.]. Shortly after the declaration of war on 4 August 1914 he enlisted and was on active service with the Royal Fusiliers and, later, with the Grenadier Guards; he was twice wounded, gassed, and mentioned in dispatches.

On his release from the army in 1919 he embarked upon a period of experimentation in unusual instrumental ensembles with, generally, a vocal line as an integral part, as in *Madam Noy*, *Rhapsody*, and *Rout* of 1918–20. Bliss began a lasting association with the world of the theatre by writing, in 1921, imaginative incidental music for Viola Tree's production of *The Tempest* at the Aldwych. He possessed an abiding interest in painting, particularly that of his contemporaries, and one of his earliest large orchestral pieces, the balletic *Mêlée Fantasque* (1921), written in memory of the stage designer, Claud Lovat Fraser [q.v.], evokes something of his fascination with colour, movement, and changing patterns. The scrupulous attention which Bliss paid to the scoring of the heraldic *A Colour Symphony* (1922) had a lasting effect upon the orchestration of subsequent works. So, too, did the setting of a sequence of texts, by way of the *Pastoral* and the *Serenade* (1928 and 1929), upon one of his most powerful and individual compositions, *Morning Heroes* (1930). This symphony, which skilfully brings together a spoken part, chorus, and orchestra, was written in memory of his brother, Kennard, 'and all other comrades killed in battle' and through it he exorcized the lasting horror of his war experiences.

Bliss had paid his first visit to America, to Santa Barbara, California, in 1923, where he lived for two years. He and Gertrude ('Trudy') Hoffmann, a daughter of Ralph Hoffmann, an American, director of the Natural History Museum at Santa Barbara, were married there in 1925 and immediately took up residence in London. They had two daughters.

Between 1927 and 1933 Bliss wrote three important chamber music works, the Oboe Quintet, the Clarinet Quintet, and the Viola Sonata, for (Sir) Eugene Goossens [q.v.], Frederick Thurston, and Lionel Tertis [q.v.] respectively. Again for particular soloists he wrote the Piano Sonata (1952) for Noel Mewton-Wood, the Violin Concerto (1955) for Alfredo Campoli, and the Cello Concerto (1970) for Rostropovich. It was with Solomon in mind as soloist that he wrote the Piano Concerto of 1939.

The composer, his wife, and their two young daughters were in America for the first performance of the Piano Concerto at the New York World Fair in 1939. He remained there as visiting professor (from 1940) at the University of California, Berkeley, and wrote two significant works, the *Seven American Poems* and the First String Quartet. Unhappy at not helping the war effort, he returned to England to join the BBC Overseas Music Service where, in 1941, he framed a far-reaching memorandum, his 'music policy statement', a motivating factor in the eventual creation of the Third Programme. He was BBC director of music from 1942 to 1944.

Bliss wrote music for six films commencing with that for *Things to Come* (released in 1936, produced by (Sir) Alexander Korda, with a script by H. G. Wells, qq.v.), four ballets of which the first, *Checkmate* (1937), is the most widely known, and two operas, *The Olympians* (libretto by J. B. Priestley) produced at Covent Garden in 1949, and, for television, *Tobias and the Angel* (1960) to a libretto by Christopher Hassall [q.v.]. He delighted in working in new mediums and was adept in providing Fanfares, of which he wrote over thirty, each singularly apposite to the occasion celebrated.

In *Music for Strings* (1935) Bliss explored to the full the nuances obtainable from the string orchestra and achieved one of his tautest and most lyrical compositions. The Second String Quartet of 1950 he considered to be his best chamber-music work and he felt a particular affection towards his two large compositions of 1955, the Violin Concerto and the *Meditations on a Theme of John Blow*. There is a deep sense of awe underlying these orchestral variations and this same spirituality is found in the five cantatas written between 1961 and 1974. The first of these, *The Beatitudes*, was in fulfilment of an invitation to contribute a work for the opening in 1962 of the new Coventry Cathedral and the last, which he did not live to hear, was the *Shield of Faith*, written for the quincentenary in 1975 of St. George's chapel, Windsor. *The Golden Cantata*, written in 1963 to poems provided by Kathleen Raine, celebrated the giving of the first degree in music by Cambridge University in 1464, and is an essay in music of the act of musical composition. His last big orchestral score, *Metamorphic Variations* of 1972, embodies the dramatic, lyrical, and meditative qualities inherent in so much of Bliss's music.

Bliss wrote over a hundred and fifty compositions of which at least fifty are major works. Through his exceptional ability to turn from the needful isolation of the creative artist to the pressures imposed upon the committee man and administrator, to both of which roles he brought an appraising and incisive mind, he became one of the outstanding musical personalities of the twentieth century.

A dedicated Master of the Queen's Music (from 1953), he nevertheless accepted time-absorbing appointments in the service of music and of fellow musicians in this country and abroad; he was an early and active member of the International Society for Contemporary Music and was chairman of the music committee of the British Council from 1946 to 1950. In 1956 he led a group of British musicians to perform in Russia and, invited by Shostakovich, was in Moscow again in 1958 as a member of the jury for the Tchaikovsky competition for pianists. In 1964 he conducted at a number of centres in Australia, and in Japan. Throughout his life Bliss was a talented and sensitive conductor and gave authoritative interpretations of his own music in the concert hall and in the recording studio. He worked steadfastly for the Performing Right Society, as a director from 1947 and as president from 1954. In his memory an annual postgraduate scholarship in composition at the Royal College of Music was inaugurated in 1982 by this society.

Bliss's marriage was a happy one. He and his wife enjoyed many deeply shared interests and he entered closely into the pursuits, joys, and sorrows of his children and grandchildren. He never lost his enthusiasm for the game of chess; he was a brilliant conversationalist with a playful and pungent humour.

Bliss was knighted in 1950 and appointed KCVO in 1969 and CH in 1971. He received many further honours amongst which were honorary degrees from London, Cambridge, Edinburgh, Bristol, Glasgow, and Lancaster. He was honorary freeman of the Worshipful Company of Musicians (1954) and gold medallist of the Royal Philharmonic Society (1963). In 1953 he was made an honorary fellow of his Cambridge College, Pembroke.

Bliss died at his London home 27 March 1975.

[Arthur Bliss, *As I Remember* (autobiography to 1966), 1970; Bliss papers in Cambridge University Library and in the Imperial War Museum; George Dannatt, a critical appreciation of the life and works in *Arthur Bliss: Catalogue of the Complete Works*, ed. Lewis Foreman, 1979; private information; personal knowledge.]

GEORGE DANNATT

BLUNDEN, EDMUND CHARLES (1896–1974), poet, teacher, critic, and biographer, was born in London 1 November 1896, the first of the nine children (five sons, four daughters) of Charles Edmund Blunden and his wife, Georgina, daughter of Henry Tyler, secretary to Sir Ralph Verney, of London. Both parents were schoolteachers. Blunden spent most of his early years in the village of Yalding in Kent. He was educated at Cleave's Grammar School and Christ's Hospital, whose 'Blues' of a century before, including Coleridge, Lamb, and Leigh Hunt, settled into his imagination and came to be the subjects of the graceful and sensitive criticism and biography he would write. Blunden's first poems, like Shelley's, were printed at Horsham, in 1914. In *Pastorals* (1916) he announced: 'I sing of the rivers and hamlets and woodlands of Sussex and Kent, Such as I know them . . .' The natural world and man's life in it continued to be the foremost subject of his poetry for the next five decades.

Another would be the war of 1914–18 and its echoes. Commissioned in 1915, Blunden fought in France and Belgium with the Royal Sussex Regiment and was awarded the MC in 1916. In *Undertones of War* (1928), a prose memoir to which a series of poems was appended, he quietly memorialized the wounds suffered by man and countryside, seeking 'that coincidence of nature without and nature within . . .'

After the war Blunden briefly claimed his scholarship to the Queen's College, Oxford, but poetry and literary journalism (for the *Athenaeum*) soon claimed all of his time. The poems in *The Waggoner* (1920) and *The Shepherd* (1922, the winner of the Hawthornden prize) were justly acclaimed for their vigorous language and for the authentic bond apparent between poet and nature. During the twenties Blunden journeyed far from Europe. A voyage to South America resulted in *The Bonadventure* (1922), and in 1924 Blunden accepted an invitation to be professor of English literature at Tokyo Imperial University. His generosity with his time and attention made him enormously popular with his Japanese students, but in three busy years he continued to produce the verses for *English Poems* (1925) and *Undertones of War*.

He returned to England in 1927. He began to work on the *Nation* (which had merged with the *Athenaeum*) and to contribute to the *Times Literary Supplement*. Some of his literary essays were published in 1931 as *Votive Tablets*. The title was appropriate to the attitude of celebration which ruled Blunden's criticism. His first biography, *Leigh Hunt*, appeared in 1930. Works of criticism from this period included *On the Poems of Henry Vaughan* (1927) and *Nature in English Literature* (1929). New collections of poems also continued to appear: *Retreat* (1928), *Near and Far* (1929), *Poems 1914–30* (1930).

Blunden spent the 1930s as a fellow and tutor of Merton College, Oxford (1931–43). His students included the critic Northrop Frye and the poet Keith Douglas. As in Japan, his unassuming ways, combined with his extraordinary feeling for the English literary tradition, made him a quietly inspiring teacher and presence. Poems from this period were collected in: *Halfway House* (1932), *Choice or Chance* (1934), *An Elegy, and Other Poems* (1937), and *Poems 1930–1940* (1940). Sketches and essays included *The Face of England* (1932) and *The Mind's Eye* (1934); and he continued to turn to the Romantic era for subjects of criticism and biography: *Charles Lamb and his Contemporaries* (1933; the Clark lectures given at Trinity College, Cambridge, 1932) and *Keats's Publisher: A Memoir of John Taylor* (1936).

Profoundly distressed by the outbreak of World War II, Blunden served as an instructor in the Oxford University Senior Training Corps, but left teaching at the University to write for the *Times Literary Supplement*. His poems from the war years are found in *Shells by a Stream* (1944); biographies of Thomas Hardy and Shelley appeared in 1942 and 1946; and *Cricket Country*, about the sport he loved and played for half a century, came in 1944.

After the war Blunden embarked upon a short but outstanding career as a diplomat. Returning to Japan thirty years after his first residence there, he served with the UK liaison mission in Tokyo from 1947 to 1950, giving hundreds of lectures on English literature and culture. His enormous efforts earned him honorary membership in the Japan Academy (1950) and the Order of the Rising Sun, third class (1963). His influence on two generations of Japanese scholars of English literature is still felt.

The fifties and sixties brought numerous honours. Blunden was appointed CBE in 1951 and made a C.Lit. (1962) by the Royal Society of Literature. The Queen's gold medal for poetry came to him in 1956, and he received an honorary Litt.D. from both Leeds and Leicester. Financial security for his growing family was a continuing concern, however, and, after a brief return to literary journalism in England early in the fifties, Blunden accepted a professorship at the University of Hong Kong in 1953. He remained there for the next decade, earning the same reputation for tireless generosity he had won in Japan. In the post-war years *After the Bombing* (1949), *Poems of Many Years* (1957), and *A Hong Kong House, Poems 1951–1961* (1962) joined the long line of volumes celebrating nature, warning against war, and meditating upon man's experience of time, love, and God. Many of his Japanese lectures were published, and he continued his many editorial labours on behalf of 'wayside' English poets. Those labours had begun decades before with work on John Clare's unpublished poetry that resulted in the twentieth century's rediscovery of the great peasant poet of the Romantic age. To this Dictionary Blunden contributed the notices of Sir John Squire, Gordon Bottomley, and R. M. B. Nichols.

Blunden retired to Long Melford in Suffolk in 1964. His last collection of verse, *Eleven Poems*, appeared in 1965. In the following year he was elected professor of poetry at Oxford, occupying until 1968 the chair once held by Matthew Arnold.

Like his friend Siegfried Sassoon [q.v.], Blunden remained largely unimpressed by the modernist revolution in poetic style. He chose to be the skilled and devoted user of forms inherited from the eighteenth century and the Romantic age. The reputation of his poems on nature and war is secure, but less highly regarded than they should be are his many philosophical verses, which show a receptivity to religious and human love, and a quiet defiance of the powers of time and death. In 'Report on Experience' he wrote:

> Say what you will, our God sees how they run.
> These disillusions are His curious proving
> That He loves humanity and will go on loving;
> Over there are faith, life, virtue in the sun.

Blunden's eyes were extremely expressive, and their play against his craggy face and birdlike nose gave him a look of kindly but shrewd percipience. His humour, gentleness, and generosity inspired the protectiveness and loyalty of countless friends and students. But just as he knew and insisted that Charles Lamb had been a more complicated personality than the endlessly sweet-natured figure of legend, so too was Blunden. He was both more nervous and more courageous than people often realized. Decades of overwork in pursuit of a living, and a long battle against asthma, tested and strained a steeliness that was usually unapparent on the surface.

Blunden's first two marriages, in 1918 to Mary Daines, who bore him a son and two daughters (one of whom died in infancy), and in 1933 to Sylva Norman, the novelist, ended in divorce. In 1945 he married Claire Margaret, daughter of John Whitfield Elford Poynting, of Manchester, a retired Indian civil servant. She bore him four daughters, taught with him in Hong Kong, and devotedly cared for him during his last years of poor health. Blunden died at Hall Mill, Long Melford, 20 January 1974.

[Alec Hardie, *Edmund Blunden*, 1958; *The Times*, 21 January 1974; E. Blunden, extract from 'Report on Experience', from *Poems 1914–30* (Cobden-Sanderson), 1930; private information.] THOMAS MALLON

BOASE, THOMAS SHERRER ROSS (1898–1974), historian and teacher, was born in Dundee 31 August 1898, the only son and elder child of Charles Millet Boase, the manager and part owner of a bleaching mill at Claverhouse outside Dundee, and his wife, Anne Malcolm, daughter of Thomas Sherrer Ross, a merchant of the same city. Books abounded in his home and he read widely from an early age. Moving from a local preparatory school to Rugby in 1912, he long believed himself at a disadvantage because he was so bad at ball games. However, he became head of his house, and won a prize essay contest on the subject of Lorenzo de' Medici and then an exhibition to enter Magdalen College, Oxford. From 1917 to 1919 he was with the Oxford and Buckinghamshire Light Infantry and for the last year of the war fought on the front between St. Quentin and Cambrai. He was awarded the MC. His Oxford education had already begun, the cadet battalion which he joined on leaving Rugby being housed in Wadham College. At this time he first met F. F. ('Sligger') Urquhart of Balliol, whose style and standards were to influence him profoundly. He returned in 1919 to read modern history at Magdalen, took a second class degree in 1921, and was elected to a fellowship at Hertford College in 1922.

Boase rapidly became an effective teacher. He lectured both on medieval and modern themes, a breadth of view reflected thirty years later in his equal concern for medieval and Victorian art. An interest in Italy developed into his first book, *Boniface VIII* (1933), and a study of *St. Francis of Assisi* (1936). He was at the same time immersed in Oxford activities academic and social. As treasurer of the Oxford University Dramatic Society he made the acquaintance of the finest theatrical talent of the day; for the rest of his life he delighted to take pupils to the theatre, and patronized drama. He also turned his attention to the visual arts. The 1930 exhibition of Italian art at the Royal Academy deeply impressed him, and he learnt much from his friendship with Kenneth (later Lord) Clark and Lord Balniel (later Earl of Crawford and Balcarres, q.v.), who helped to mount the exhibition. Beside his frequent visits to Urquhart's chalet in the French Alps, constant travel in western Europe and the Near East was meanwhile making him an experienced viewer of pictures, monuments, and buildings.

In 1936 these interests brought him to the attention of those who were involved with the problems of the Courtauld Institute, founded in 1932 for the study of art history. Following the resignation of W. G. Constable [q.v.] as director the committee of management selected Boase for the post in 1937 (he also held the London University chair in the history of art from 1937 to 1947), although he seemed to some art historians, critics, and students an amateur not properly qualified to succeed Constable. In taking up this challenge Boase enjoyed one advantage. Maintaining old friendships in Berlin and Frankfurt, participating in the Council of World Churches with its concern for events in Germany under Hitler, he was the better prepared to collaborate with scholars who had moved with the Warburg library and institute to London, and to learn from them. The Courtauld discovered that, although he did not satisfy everybody, the new director was able to give it an improved syllabus and greater stability. The two foundations were brought closer together; the first of his own numerous contributions to the *Journal of the Warburg and Courtauld Institutes*, on 'The Arts in the Latin Kingdom of Jerusalem', appeared in 1939. Later Boase contributed the notice of Samuel Courtauld to this Dictionary.

Immediately on the outbreak of war Boase went to the Government Code and Cipher School at Bletchley, and from there to Cairo where he worked for the RAF for nearly two years. From the end of 1943 he was once again based in Cairo, in charge of British Council activities in the Middle East. He travelled widely, made many friends both Arab and Jewish, enriched his old passion for the history of the Crusades, and in 1945 returned to the Courtauld 'with resilience a little dulled for the taking up of a former life' (MS memoir). Aided principally by Anthony Blunt he contributed to the revival and expansion of art-historical studies in post-war London, but in 1947 accepted the presidency of his old college, Magdalen. It was quickly evident there that the new president's deft style of management, combined with a splendid talent for getting to know large numbers of undergraduates, would leave its mark. He remained vigorously in control for a dozen years, until tenure of the vice-chancellorship of the university (1958–60) and less robust health led to a phase of diminished activity. He retired in 1968.

All this time Boase gave equal attention to his work for the arts. His main undertaking was the *Oxford History of English Art*, as general editor and author of two out of eleven volumes. *English Art*

1100–1216 (1953) and *English Art 1800–1870* (1959) offer sturdy summaries of modern knowledge; in the first illuminated manuscripts, and in the second minor rather than major artists, were the topics on which he wrote most effectively. Meanwhile he contributed many articles to books of reference, and generous introductions to work by other scholars. He served as trustee or adviser for the National Gallery (1947–53), the British Museum (1950–69), the Victoria and Albert Museum (1947–70), the Shakespeare Memorial Theatre, the Gulbenkian Foundation, and other institutions. He received several honorary degrees (including the Oxford DCL, 1960), and was a fellow of the British Academy (1961).

Boase died at his home in Wimbledon 14 April 1974, having completed his contribution for a history of the Cilician kingdom of Armenia (published 1978) and a study of Vasari (published 1979). He was always energetic, a bachelor who organized his time with great precision and worked rapidly. He was an excellent speaker; collected good pictures; and disliked extravagance. Brought up in the Scottish Episcopalian Church he remained a firm Christian, a great supporter of his college choir and chapel. His portrait by Anthony Devas, emphasizing a characteristic gesture of his hands, hangs in the hall of Magdalen.

[*The Times*, 15 and 20 April 1974; an autobiographical memoir in typescript, written in 1972–3; Cyril Bailey, *Francis Fortescue Urquhart*, 1936; *Burlington Magazine*, vol. lxxi, 1937, pp. 107–8, 188–9, 237–8, and vol. cxvii, 1975, p. 809; private information; personal knowledge.] JOHN STOYE

BOOSEY, LESLIE ARTHUR (1887–1979), music publisher, was born in Bromley, Kent, 26 July 1887, the eldest of five children (three sons and two daughters) of Arthur Boosey, music publisher, and his wife, Lucy Ashton. After some years at Malvern College he chose, instead of going to a university, to work for a time in the music publishing house of Durand in Paris, before joining the family business, a conservative and rather old-fashioned one largely associated at that time with the Boosey Ballad Concerts in the Albert Hall.

Long before 1914 Boosey had been a keen territorial officer, and throughout the war he served in France with the 22nd London Regiment. Captured, as a major, in the March offensive of 1918, he was put up against a wall to be shot for refusing to give information to the enemy: at the last moment, however, the German officer changed his mind: 'All right', he said, 'you can go back; you're a gentleman.' Boosey was recommended for appointment to the DSO, but the recommendation miscarried—the first but not the last occasion on which deserved recognition, sponsored by responsible people, was not forthcoming.

When he got back to the publishing business in 1920 Boosey had to adapt himself to conditions very different from those of 1914. Recording and radio transmission had created new problems and possibilities, and Boosey met the challenge by establishing firm friendships with many leading composers. A merger with the firm of Hawkes, completed in 1930, led to important developments in the manufacture of musical instruments and increased publishing activity, especially in the American market. The culmination of this vigorous expansion came with the acquisition in 1947 of the Koussevitsky catalogue, which added the names of Prokofiev, Rachmaninov, and Stravinsky to a list that already included those of Strauss, Bartok, Copland, and Britten. By this time the firm of Boosey & Hawkes, in its own field, was one of the most influential in the world.

Leslie Boosey was an adventurous and shrewd publisher, but he was also a very scrupulous one. His weakness, if weakness it was, lay in his readiness to trust everybody and to believe that people would not do to him the things he would never do to them: he lived to learn that this was over-optimistic. In the later years of his publishing career he began to find himself involved in circumstances that were distasteful; and in 1963, after some years of increasing discomfort, he severed his connection with the firm whose prosperity he had done so much to create and sustain.

Boosey retained until the end of his life a great influence in the Performing Right Society, which he had joined in 1926, and whose chairman he became in 1929. This office he held with distinction until 1954, when he gave up the post to Sir Arthur Bliss [q.v.]. During his period of office he attended all the great international conferences, where he was respected by publishers, authors, and composers alike. In 1976 he was awarded the International Society's gold medal: he was also a chevalier of the Legion of Honour and was honoured by the Royal Philharmonic Society of London, with which he was closely associated during most of his life.

Boosey should be remembered, if for nothing else, for the fact that in 1944, by his personal initiative, he saved the Royal Opera House from becoming a Mecca dance-hall. He had learnt that a lease was about to be signed which would produce that very result, and he acted quickly. With his partner Ralph Hawkes, having been to Washington to gain the support of Lord Keynes [q.v.], he secured the lease for the firm of Boosey & Hawkes and the Covent Garden Opera Company. It was an achievement of great importance at the time and for the future.

A casual observer, meeting Leslie Boosey, might have taken him for a typically urbane and conventional business man: it would have been a mistake, for beneath the polished surface there lay a different reality. Experience in the trenches, which included the death of a loved brother and many friends, had led him to examine and reject most of the comfortable beliefs learnt at home and at school, and to search for more dependable convictions. His mind was naturally sceptical and critical: he read widely in philosophy, theology, history, and science, and wrote a great deal, though not for publication: he was always ready to submit his views to criticism and discussion. And these studies, continued until the onset of his last illness, were undertaken not as an intellectual pastime, but in order to discover a way of life. That he was successful in this endeavour is suggested by the fact that he was able to accept without bitterness the realization that a long and helpful career had passed without public recognition—a source of surprise and regret to those who knew his work. His gaiety, his lively mind, and his amused observation of the world and its ways, made him a sought-after companion in the Savile Club and elsewhere. To those fortunate enough to know him better he was a great deal more than that.

In 1921 he married Ethel Torfrida, daughter of Frank Marchant, paper maker; they had three sons and a daughter. He died at his home in Hampshire 5 September 1979.

[Personal knowledge.] THOMAS ARMSTRONG

BORG OLIVIER, GIORGIO (GEORGE) (1911–1980), prime minister of Malta. [See OLIVIER.]

BOSE, SATYENDRANATH (1894–1974), physicist, was born 1 January 1894 in Calcutta, the only son and eldest of the seven children of Surendranath Bose, an accountant who worked for the East Indian Railways and later founded a small chemical and pharmaceutical company, and his wife, Amodini Devi, who had little education but much domestic ability in bringing up a large family.

Bose attended the local elementary school in Calcutta until he moved to the Hindu School in 1907. He was much interested in science, in which he was encouraged by the headmaster and mathematics teacher. In 1909 he entered Presidency College, Calcutta, and was awarded science degrees in 1913 (B.Sc.) and 1915 (M.Sc.) with top place in various branches of mathematics. Since the existing regulations denied Indians entry to the administrative government service, he continued to study physics, in spite of the lack of appropriate textbooks and literature. Hardly anything was known in India at that time about the newer developments of quantum theory in Germany and other European countries just after the turn of the century. Moreover, there were no satisfactory laboratories or equipment for research. At that point there was established at Calcutta a University College of Science for postgraduate studies and research which obtained some recent European books and published research on new aspects of physics. In 1917 Bose and Meghnad Saha [q.v.] became lecturers there.

Bose developed a special interest in statistical mechanics, and was much stimulated by J. Willard Gibbs's book, published by Yale University Press in 1902, from which he learnt more about phase space and Boltzmann statistics. Then, following the analysis of data from the solar eclipse of 1919 by (Sir) A. S. Eddington [q.v.], Bose's attention was also directed to relativity and Einstein's recent papers about it. With the author's permission, he translated for circulation in India Einstein's 1916 paper on the general theory of relativity.

In 1921 Bose went to Dacca University as a reader in physics. He had now studied Planck's book on the theory of heat radiation, and became interested in Planck's radiation formula, the expression which gives the distribution of energy in the radiation from a black body. This had been one of the starting points of the quantum theory. Neither Planck nor Einstein had been satisfied with their attempts to derive this formula by classical methods. The basic assumptions of the quantum theory were not reconcilable with the laws of classical electrodynamics.

In this context, Bose made his single great contribution. He derived the Planck formula in a logical manner using the principles of Boltzmann statistics. He did not assume the classical electrodynamics, but relied on phase space arguments, treating the radiation as an ideal photon gas, each photon having energy $E=h\nu$ and momentum $h\nu/c$. The distribution of radiation at temperature T was deduced by finding the distribution in phase space that maximizes the entropy of the system. When the same treatment is used to find the equilibrium distribution for a dilute system of non-interacting atoms, one of the results is the ideal gas law. But a photon gas differs from the more usual ideal gas in that the particles must be treated relativistically, photons are mass-less, and the number is not conserved. Most important, the photons must be regarded as indistinguishable. All arrangements of a given number of phase points within an elementary phase cell of volume h^3 are to be regarded as identical arrangements, whereas in classical physics they would be distinct. Thus the numbers of permutations of phase points for systems of distinguishable and non-distinguishable particles differ considerably and result in very different equilibrium distributions. For a photo-gas the result leads to Planck's radiation formula.

Bose's derivation of the Planck formula made a short paper of about four pages, but it had far-reaching consequences. It was incomparably more significant than any of his other scientific publications. Yet he was isolated in India, and needed others to advise him or discuss his work with him. He revered Einstein, although they had never met, and in June 1924 sent him his paper, asking that Einstein should examine it and if he thought it suitable get it translated into German and published in the *Zeitschrift für Physik*.

Einstein was greatly impressed by the work, and got it translated and published within two months. He had not foreseen the statistical basis of Planck's radiation formula, and noticed an important point, that Bose had not introduced the wave/particle duality which had been indicated by recent experimental work in Europe.

Bose longed to meet European scientists, and in 1924 applied to Dacca University for a leave of absence of two years to study abroad. After seeing Einstein's reply to Bose, expressing high appreciation of the latter's achievement, the university granted him leave and made adequate financial provision for his family during this period. He first went to Paris, in 1924, where he met Langevin, Madame Curie, and the de Broglies, and among many other things learned something about spectroscopy and crystallography. In October 1925 he went to Berlin and met Einstein, who had made many advances during the previous twelve months, partly arising from Bose's ideas, but was now mainly interested in a unified field theory. Through Einstein, Bose was delighted to meet many of the distinguished scientists in Berlin at that time. He heard talks by Max Born and others about the new quantum mechanics.

Bose returned to Dacca in 1926 and was appointed a professor of physics in 1927. In 1946 he became the Khaira professor of physics at Calcutta University. He retired in 1956, became the vice-chancellor of Viswa-Bharati University, Santiniketan, and in 1958 accepted the honorific appointment of national professor (*Padma Vibhushan*).

Throughout his life, Bose tried to improve education, science, and culture in India, and to encourage the use of better technology for the people's welfare. He was proud of his Bengali origins and hoped for Indian independence. He was president of the physics section of the Indian Science Congress (1939), general president of the 31st session of the Indian Science Congress, Delhi (1944), and president of the National Institute of Science of India (later the National Academy of Sciences) in 1949. In 1958 he was elected a fellow of the Royal Society of London.

It is rare, indeed, for any scientist living in an environment or milieu which could not really teach, or help him, to make an important contribution like that of Bose, and send it to a leading world scientist whom he had never met asking for an assessment of its value. Bose's name is now established by the terms Bose–Einstein statistics, which are used in the interpretation of numerous physical phenomena, and bosons (particles obeying Bose–Einstein statistics).

In 1915 Bose married Ushabala, daughter of Dr Jogendra Nath Ghosh. They had two sons and five daughters. Bose died in Calcutta 4 February 1974.

[Jagdish Mehra in *Biographical Memoirs of Fellows of the Royal Society*, vol. xxi, 1975; W. A. Blanpied, 'Bose—Co-Founder of Quantum Statistics', *American Journal of Physics*, vol. xl, p. 1212, 1972.] H. W. THOMPSON

BOVENSCHEN, SIR FREDERICK CARL (1884–1977), civil servant, was born 26 March 1884 in Forest Hill, London, he and his older sister being the only children of Carl Bovenschen, silk merchant, of Forest Hill, and his wife, Catherine Hoare. As a scholar of the King's School, Canterbury, his record in work and games was outstanding. He got an open classical scholarship to Corpus Christi College, Oxford, and obtained first classes in both classical honour moderations (1905) and *literae humaniores* (1907).

Both fitting and fortunate in 1908 was his initial appointment to the Civil Service as assistant private secretary to R. B. (later Viscount) Haldane [q.v.], secretary of state for war, whose timely reforms gave the army the strong and elastic structure that stood up to such stern tests in 1914. Four years in Haldane's office gave Bovenschen incomparable opportunities to grasp facts and principles fundamental to military organization. His next three years (1912–15) as private secretary to Sir Charles Harris, whose expertise in the scrutiny of army votes was famous, gave him parallel experience of finance in peace and war. That experience benefited the government of India in 1931 when he served on their army retrenchment committee. In 1921 he became assistant secretary at the War Office.

Bovenschen had two conspicuous traits: persistent integrity of purpose; painstaking mastery of detail. These dominated his working life for half a century. They were subtly suggested by the strokes of his round, deliberate handwriting and by an occasional quizzical glance above half-moons of gold-rimmed spectacles. They combined towards securing value for money—sometimes, in the eyes of his military colleagues, with unjustifiable severity—over varied sections of army expenditure, when, for a decade from 1932, he was successively director of army contracts; of finance (1936); and deputy under-secretary of state for war (1936–42). They combined more conspicuously, and with more unconditional appreciation, towards building from inevitably ill-assorted pieces a strong framework for the administration of occupied enemy territory through military government and civil affairs staffs set up under Anglo-American co-operation. The completion of this huge, unprecedented task in Europe owed more to Bovenschen than to anyone. From 1942 to 1945, as joint permanent under-secretary of state for war, he chaired the main committees concerned, reconciling conflicting interests of Whitehall departments and within the armed services, sometimes forcing awkward decisions affecting supplies, enlisting American co-operation, twice by visits to Washington, and above all, applying, with the continuity essential in exasperatingly confused conditions, intellectual objectivity and powers of persuasion. It is widely accepted that shortcomings in military government, especially in the Control Commission for Germany, resulted not from the organization agreed on Bovenschen's committees but primarily from mistakes in staffing.

Retirement from the Civil Service in 1945 restricted the scope more than the quality of his work. Its benefits to Westminster Hospital and Kent County and Hythe Borough Councils covered the years until 1960 during which his broadly based if at times over-rigid financial judgement was applied on their governing bodies or main committees and in less formal discussions in which, as throughout his public life, he never became heated, endearing himself to a new assortment of colleagues by a characteristic combination of charm and shrewdness.

He was a dedicated and good-humoured golfer. On four or five of his favourite Kent courses his small, compact figure would, according to an admirer, 'lead the field like a light infantryman at a good 140 paces to the minute'. He had also enjoyed a slower pace—walking in the Queen's coronation procession in his robes as a baron of the Cinque Ports (1953).

Among the pleasures of his eighties were a return to reading classical Greek and practical interests in education on managing committees of two schools for young children in Hythe or as a long-established governor of the King's School, Canterbury. And there were richer rewards in the happiness of his home life. He married in 1919 Mabel Alice, only daughter of Sir A. H. D. Acland [q.v.], thirteenth baronet. She had studied painting under Walter Sickert [q.v.]. Her gentle, artistic temperament complemented her husband's punctilious devotion to duty. He seemed lost when she died in 1975. A solace in the last year of his life was the return of their only child and her husband from South Africa to settle in Hythe, where Bovenschen died 9 November 1977.

Bovenschen was appointed chevalier of the Legion of Honour (1920), CB (1927), KBE (1938), and KCB (1943).

[Private information; personal knowledge.]

V. G. F. Bovenizer

BOWEN, EDMUND JOHN (1898–1980), chemist, was born in Worcester, 29 April 1898, the eldest in the family of two sons and two daughters of Edmund Riley Bowen, headmaster of St. John's Elementary School for Boys, Worcester, and his wife Lilias, daughter of Thomas Kamester, carpenter, of Clewer, Windsor. He was educated at his father's school and at the Royal Grammar School, Worcester, from which he won the Brackenbury science scholarship at Balliol College, Oxford, at the age of sixteen years seven months. He went into residence in October 1915 and, apart from war service, was to spend the rest of his life in Oxford. Towards the end of 1916 he trained as a gunner officer and in April 1917 was posted to France with the Royal Garrison Artillery.

'Ted' Bowen's scientific gifts were fostered by his father's wide interests in natural history and collecting and by the sound teaching in chemistry at the Royal Grammar School. After demobilization he returned to Oxford in January 1919 and took first class honours in chemistry in 1920 after only five terms of study. Of the twenty-nine people who had entered Balliol with him in 1915 only thirteen had survived the war. He was one of several highly gifted scientists whose abilities were recognized by his tutor, (Sir) H. B. Hartley (whose notice he later wrote for this Dictionary), and he was also much stimulated by his contemporary at Balliol, (Sir) C. N. Hinshelwood [q.v.]. Immediately after graduation he was appointed a demonstrator in the Balliol and Trinity laboratories. This was followed by a lectureship (1921) and a fellowship (1922) at University College which he held until his retirement in 1965, when he was made an honorary fellow. He overlapped with eight masters of the college, a record which few can equal. From 1938 onwards he also held the post of university lecturer and later Aldrichian praelector. As junior proctor in 1935–6 he served on numerous university committees and he was subsequently an elected member of the general board of faculties and a curator of the University Chest. However, his main contributions to university administration were related to special interests of his own, notably in connection with the University Museum, the Museum of the History of Science, and the University Observatory.

Bowen's scientific work lay almost entirely in the field of photochemistry and the related phenomenon of fluorescence. His pioneer work in the period 1923–35 provided some of the earliest experimental confirmation of the fundamental laws of photochemistry which had long been implicit in the theoretical work of Einstein. His early equipment was extremely primitive by modern standards, being largely home-made from components such as tin cans, sealing wax, and scent bottles, but it worked. Although Bowen always welcomed any opportunity of making things with his own hands, he made extensive use in his later work on fluorescence of the electronic and optical devices which became available from 1945 onwards. One of the notable results of this later work was the demonstration that energy could be transferred from one molecule to another over distances much greater than a molecular diameter. During World War II he was a member of the Oxford research team working on respirator problems for the Ministry of Supply.

Although certainly no mathematician, he took a keen interest in the developments in quantum theory, which were of basic importance for his experimental work, and he had a remarkable gift for explaining abstruse theories by means of simple diagrams and models. This was put to good use in his book *The Chemical Aspects of Light* (1941) and in stimulating discussion with pupils and colleagues. He was widely read in many branches of science outside chemistry, and from his schoolboy days onwards he was an avid collector of fossils and antiquities, which he gave away freely to museums and experts. One ammonite from Dorset, where he had a holiday house, was named *Perisphinctes boweni* after him. He was keenly interested in the history of science, and published several articles on the early history of the Royal Society and of science in Oxford. To this Dictionary he contributed the notice of D. L. Chapman.

Bowen was elected FRS in 1935, and subsequently served on council (1943–5) and was awarded the Davy medal (1963). He also became vice-president of the Chemical Society and of the Faraday Society and was Liversidge lecturer of the Chemical Society in 1966.

Bowen was a truly inventive scientist, not interested in the accumulation of detail, but with a deep urge to pursue fundamental truths. His enthusiasm and kindness to others are acknowledged by all who knew him. He changed remarkably little in youthful appearance over fifty years or so, and even less in boyish character.

In 1924 Bowen married Edith, eldest daughter of Joseph and Margaret Moule, farmers, of Hartlebury, Worcestershire. Their marriage was very happy, and both their children, Margaret Lilias (born 1927) and Humphry John (born 1929) had distinguished university careers, though only Humphry followed his father into science. Bowen died at his home in Oxford 19 November 1980 following a heart attack.

[*The Times*, 22 November 1980; R. P. Bell in *Biographical Memoirs of Fellows of the Royal Society*, vol. xxvii, 1981; private information; personal knowledge.] R. P. Bell

BOWEN, ELIZABETH DOROTHEA COLE (1899–1973), writer, was born 7 June 1899 in Dublin, the only child of Henry Charles Cole Bowen, barrister, of Bowen's Court, Kildorrery, county Cork, and his wife, Florence Isabella Pomeroy, third of the ten children of Henry Fitz-George Colley, of Mount Temple, Dublin. She was educated at Harpenden Hall School, Hertfordshire, and Downe House, Kent.

She spent the summers of early childhood at Bowen's Court—the house completed by her ancestor, Henry Bowen, in 1775. The first Bowen to settle in county Cork had come over from Wales with Cromwell's army. Elizabeth Bowen set down the history of her family and of the house in *Bowen's Court* (1942). Winters were spent in the pre-World War I Dublin nostalgically evoked by her in *Seven Winters* (1942). When she was seven her father suffered a severe nervous breakdown; she and her mother, on his doctors' advice, moved to England. Her lifelong stammer dated from this family upheaval. They lived happily enough in rented holiday houses on the Kent coast, an area for which she retained a lasting affection, until when she was thirteen her mother died of cancer, in Hythe: she never fully recovered from this loss, which is reflected in the sense of displacement experienced by many of the child characters in her fiction. After her mother's death, 'Bitha', as she was known in the family, was brought up by what she called 'a committee of aunts'. The holidays of her adolescence and young womanhood were spent with her father—now recovered and remarried, to Mary Gwynn—at Bowen's Court, a period of her life on which she later drew for her novel *The Last September* (1929), in which the house 'Danielstown' is based on Bowen's Court.

In 1923 she married Alan Charles Cameron, an educationist, then assistant secretary for education for Northamptonshire. Born in 1893, he had seen action on the Somme and in Italy, and had been awarded the MC. Her first book, the collection of short stories entitled *Encounters*, was published in the year that she married, and her first novel, *The Hotel*, in 1927. In 1925 Alan Cameron was appointed secretary for education for the city of Oxford, and they moved to the house called Waldencote in Old Headington. In Oxford she made important friendships with the Tweedsmuirs (John, q.v., and Susan Buchan), Lord David Cecil, Sir Isaiah Berlin, Sir Maurice Bowra and his circle, and had a considerable personal success. In 1935, the year she published *The House in Paris*, her husband's work—now with the central council of the BBC's schools broadcasting service—brought them to London. In London, at 2 Clarence Terrace, Regent's Park, she established herself as a hospitable and frequent party-giver. The dinner guests, like the afternoon callers, were her own friends from the artistic and literary worlds—including Bloomsbury, and with a constant leaven of Colley cousins from Ireland—rather than her husband's. But the marriage was an affectionate and stable one, although childless, and in spite of her greater fame and her close friendships with, at different times, Humphry House [q.v.], Goronwy Rees, Sean O'Faolain and, lastingly, the Canadian diplomat Charles Ritchie.

The best-known novels of her London period, in which she makes Regent's Park her own literary territory, are *The Death of the Heart* (1938) and *The Heat of the Day* (1949), a war novel that was her greatest commercial success both in Britain and in the United States. She remained in London throughout World War II, working as an ARP warden and returning to Ireland from time to time chiefly to provide reports for the Ministry of Information on the Irish political climate. Some of her finest short stories, many of them touching on the supernatural, are set in blitz-torn London. After the war she was one of the two women members of the royal commission on capital punishment.

In 1930, on the death of her father, she had inherited Bowen's Court, where she entertained English, Irish, and American friends during holiday periods. After the war she and her husband made Bowen's Court their permanent home; and there, in 1952, Alan Cameron died. She had the support of close friends in Ireland—notably at this time Edward Sackville-West (Lord Sackville, q.v.), who had settled nearby at Clogheen—but she was unable to keep up the big old house on her own in spite of successful lecture tours for the British Council and in the United States, periods as writer-in-residence at American universities, and a great deal of journalism. In 1959, in New York, she was unwell and under stress; on her return, she sold up the property in some haste. The new owner, being interested only in the land and the timber, demolished the house at once.

She returned to live in England—first in Oxford, and then in a small modern house in Hythe. She returned regularly to Ireland, generally staying with Lady Ursula Vernon at Kinsale: she wrote the narrative for a pageant on Kinsale's history, performed there in 1965.

She was a large-boned, handsome woman, classically Anglo-Irish, caught between two worlds; Churchillian in her politics, staunchly Anglican in her religion, conventional in her social attitudes and demeanour. In Headington, she had enjoyed belonging to the Women's Institute. Yet she was also thoroughly Celtic in her imaginative range, her basic secretiveness, and her sense of the spirit of place. She had a love of talk, a talent for intimacy, and a hankering after the bizarre and the vulgar: she described herself as 'farouche'. She enjoyed intense friendships with country neighbours of no social pretension in Ireland just as she did with literati in London and New York, but she kept her relationships in separate compartments. She never lost her stammer and was always a little shy and self-concealing, preferring to be introduced as 'Mrs Cameron'.

She published twenty-seven books in her lifetime, which include travel (notably *A Time in Rome*, 1960), criticism, reminiscence, and history, but it is for her novels and short stories that she will be remembered. She was adept at tracing in her fictions what she called 'the cracks in the surface of life'—the displacements, shocks, and shifts of feeling that take place beneath a controlled, conventional exterior. Sometimes her style is excessively convoluted and 'Jamesian'; sometimes it is subtly precise, taking sensitive perception to a point further than anyone except her friend Virginia Woolf [q.v.]. During and after the war, the class structure and codes of accepted behaviour on which her themes largely depended were eroded, and her preoccupations seemed to lose some of their significance. She charted the disintegration of the world she had known in the wartime short story 'The Disinherited'. *A World of Love* (1955) was the last novel she wrote in her old-established mode; in her final two novels, *The Little Girls* (1964) and *Eva Trout* (1969), which won the James Tait Black memorial prize, she was breaking new ground, but had neither the time nor the strength left to her to consolidate new approaches and techniques.

She was appointed CBE in 1948 and C.Lit. in 1965. She was a member of the Irish Academy of Letters and received honorary D.Litts. from Trinity College, Dublin (1949), and Oxford (1956). In 1972 lung cancer was diagnosed—she was a heavy smoker—and she died in University College Hospital, London, 22 February 1973. She is buried beside her father and husband in Farahy churchyard, which adjoins the Bowen's Court demesne.

[Victoria Glendinning, *Elizabeth Bowen: Portrait of a Writer*, 1977.]

VICTORIA GLENDINNING

BOWMAN, SIR JAMES, first baronet, of Killingworth, county Northumberland (1898–1978), vice-president of the National Union of Mineworkers and chairman of the National Coal Board, was born at Great Corby, near Carlisle, Cumberland, 8 March 1898, the fifth of the seven children of Robert James Bowman, blacksmith, and his wife, Mary Murray. On leaving school, Bowman was presented with a watch inscribed 'for being never late and never absent'. At the age of fifteen he started work at Ashington Colliery. In the war of 1914–18 he served in the Royal Marines. On returning to Ashington 'Big Pit', where he was a coal filler, he showed an active interest in trade unionism and within a few years became a prominent local leader.

His years of active lodge membership gave him a keen understanding of the working miner and fostered his gift for exposition and advocacy. He gained respect for his moderate views combined with a certain toughness. In 1935 he was elected general secretary of the Northumberland Miners' Association. He reached national level within the union in 1936 when he was elected to the executive committee of the Mineworkers' Federation of Great Britain (MFGB). In 1939 he was elected vice-president of the MFGB and he was re-elected, unopposed, until his resignation in 1949. He also travelled widely overseas as a British representative on the Mineworkers' International Executive Committee.

Throughout the 1940s Bowman shared power within the MFGB with (Sir) William Lawther [q.v.], president, and Arthur Horner [q.v.], general secretary. He played a major part in merging the Federation, with its deep historical and traditional roots in the district unions, into the National Union of Mineworkers and he spoke on this subject at the special conference of the MFGB to deal with the reorganization, held at Nottingham in August 1944.

In the period immediately after World War II he was invited by Sir Stafford Cripps [q.v.] to advise on the reorganization of the German trade unions. In 1946 he was elected to the general council of the TUC and was appointed to serve on its international, economic, education, disputes, and organization committees. In 1947–9 he was a member of the royal commission on the press and in May 1949 became a member of the committee on broadcasting chaired by Lord Beveridge [q.v.]. In January 1950, having resigned his former posts, he was appointed chairman of the Northern Division (Northumberland and Cumberland) of the NCB, at the instigation of Hugh Gaitskell [q.v.], then minister of fuel and power. Bowman had no doubts about the move; he believed passionately in nationalization, which he saw as the means to a more efficiently managed industry which would bring increased prosperity and security to those employed within it.

In 1955 Bowman was appointed deputy chairman of the NCB and in 1956, on the death of his predecessor, Sir Hubert Houldsworth [q.v.], he was appointed chairman. He inherited a revised organization, following the acceptance by the Board of the report of a committee chaired by Alexander (later Lord) Fleck [q.v.], which had recommended a strengthening of functional departments and of the central authority of the Board. As chairman he dealt mostly with general matters of policy and left supervision of the Board's day to day business to the deputy chairman, (Sir) Joseph Latham. An exception was Bowman's use of his trade union connections to maintain good industrial relations. He supported the introduction of new techniques such as method study and did much to secure increased mechanization of production methods. This was undoubtedly his most valuable and enduring legacy to the industry.

In 1957 the Board faced a crisis as, with increased use of oil, the market for coal declined rapidly. Over the next three years 124 pits were closed and the number of industrial employees was reduced from 710,000 to 583,000. Although opencast production was almost halved, undistributed coal stocks rose to 36 million tons. It was a tribute to Bowman's skill and his understanding of the mining community that, despite criticism, these policies were effected without opposing industrial action. Meanwhile the pace of mechanization was maintained, with output per manshift reaching what was up till then a record.

There is evidence that Bowman considered, during this period of his chairmanship, that the prospects were bleak and that he had little power to improve things for the mining industry, which had been his whole life. The principal reason for his wish to retire on the expiry of his term of office in 1961 was, however, ill health. He and his wife returned to Newcastle, which they had always regarded as home, upon his retirement. He was succeeded, as chairman of the NCB, by Alfred Robens (later Lord Robens of Woldingham). After retirement he continued to take a keen interest in the affairs of the coal industry and attended, as a special guest, a number of the annual meetings of the National Union of Mineworkers.

Bowman was a powerfully built man of medium height, whose confident physical presence, recalling his early career as a miner, was allied to an ease of manner which enabled him to deal with equal success with trade unionists, mining engineers, civil servants, and politicians. He possessed an outgoing personality which was demonstrated in his strength as a public speaker, whether delivering a prepared set-piece or an impromptu tribute, and in his skill as a raconteur, where he was helped by an accent which retained attractive traces of his Cumbrian origin and Northumbrian upbringing.

Bowman was made a JP in 1935. He was appointed CBE in 1952 and knighted in 1957. In January 1961 he was created a baronet. In October 1958 he was awarded an honorary DCL of Durham University.

In 1923 he married Jean, daughter of Henry Brooks, a miner, of Ashington, Northumberland. They had one son, George (born 1923), who succeeded to the baronetcy, and one daughter. Bowman died 25 September 1978, at his home in Killingworth, Northumberland.

[*The Times*, 6, 10, and 12 October 1978; private information; personal knowledge.]

DEREK EZRA

BOWRA, SIR (CECIL) MAURICE (1898–1971), scholar and warden of Wadham College, Oxford, was born 8 April 1898 at Kiukiang on the Yangtze, where his father, Cecil Arthur Verner Bowra, was a commissioner in the Chinese Customs Service. Maurice was the second son of his parents, and had two younger sisters. In 1903 his father was granted an extended period of leave, and brought his family home, to spend two years in Kent. In 1905 his parents returned to China, leaving the two boys to be looked after by their paternal grandmother and her second husband, a Church of England clergyman named George Mackie, who inspired in Maurice, as he records in his memoirs, 'a lasting trust and affection'. In 1910, after a prolonged visit to China, where his father was stationed at Mukden, he and his brother Edward were brought home by their parents and placed at Cheltenham College. Maurice was bored by Cheltenham and did not like the school; but he became a college prefect and head of his house, and in 1916 won the top scholarship to New College, Oxford. Being too young for the army, he joined his parents in Peking, where his father was chief secretary of the Customs Service, returning in the summer of 1916. On his way home he paid an extended visit to Petrograd, of which he gives a fascinating account in his *Memories*. That visit sowed the seed of an interest in Russia which flowered later in his studies of the Russian language and Russian literature. After spending the Michaelmas term in a depleted Oxford, early in 1917 Bowra joined the Royal Field Artillery, in which he was commissioned, and in September went to France, where he took part in the later stages of the third battle of Ypres.

The war made an ineffaceable impression on Bowra: 'the memory of the carnage and the filth', he says in his *Memories*, 'has never left me. Yet,' he declares, 'the war did me a lot of good. It greatly extended my horizon, reduced my conceit, and formed in me a love for the comradeship that comes from living with other people and sharing their interests and their work. All this I owe not to the army but to the war.'

Going up to New College (which made him an honorary fellow in 1946) in 1919, he read classics. His college tutors were H. W. B. Joseph [q.v.] and A. H. Smith, but the strongest influence upon him was G. Gilbert A. Murray [q.v.], regius professor of Greek, to whom he was sent, with two other undergraduates from New College, for Greek composition. He duly took first classes in both classical honour moderations (1920) and *literae humaniores* (1922) and in 1922 was elected, with the support of Murray and A. S. Owen, classical fellow and tutor of Keble, to a tutorial fellowship at Wadham.

Wadham was Bowra's home (he was unmarried), and the centre of his interests and affections, for the rest of his life. He became, in due course, dean and senior tutor, serving as proctor in 1930–1, and in 1938, at the early age of forty, he was elected warden. He was vice-chancellor in 1951–4, and served the university, during the last forty years of his life, on the hebdomadal council, the University Chest, and the general board, besides being a delegate of the University Press, and professor of poetry 1946–51.

Bowra, though he spent his whole life in Oxford, had many contacts with the world of learning and literature on both sides of the Atlantic, especially in Germany, where he spent most of his sabbatical year in 1932, travelling with his friend Adrian Bishop. It was on this trip that he had his legendary meeting with Hitler, at which he is said to have replied to the Führer's 'Heil, Hitler!' with 'Heil, Bowra!'—a story which, he says in his *Memories*, 'brought me nothing but credit, but it was not true'. In January 1936 the regius professorship of Greek fell vacant on the retirement of Gilbert Murray. Bowra was certainly on the short list of possible successors to the post, and he did not conceal his disappointment when E. R. Dodds [q.v.] was selected; but he was consoled by being elected to the headship of his college. In the meantime, he spent a term lecturing at Harvard, where he stayed in Lowell House. While he was at Harvard, he was offered the professorship of Greek at three universities in the United States: at Harvard itself, at Columbia, and at Princeton. Much to the relief of his Oxford friends, he declined these offers. He made many friends in America, especially at Harvard, to which he returned in 1948–9 as Charles Eliot Norton professor, to deliver a course of lectures which formed the substance of his *The Romantic Imagination* (1950), and again in 1963 to receive an honorary degree.

Bowra did not allow his official and administrative duties in the university to interrupt his literary and classical pursuits. Besides articles in classical journals, he published some thirty books. They fall into two categories: textual or expository studies in Greek scholarship, and critical essays on classical or contemporary literature. His first book, published by the Nonesuch Press in 1928, was a translation, composed in collaboration with his Wadham colleague H. T. Wade-Gery, of Pindar's Pythian

Odes; this was followed by *Tradition and Design in the Iliad* (1930); *Ancient Greek Literature*, in the Home University Library (1933), *Pindari Carmina*, in the Oxford Classical Texts (1935); and *Greek Lyric Poetry* (1936), of which he produced a revised edition in 1961. In 1943 appeared his first excursion into a wider field of literary criticism, *The Heritage of Symbolism*, a study of post-Symbolist poetry. During the next twenty years Bowra explored the field of literary criticism in directions indicated by such titles as the following: *From Virgil to Milton* (1945); *The Creative Experiment* (1949); *The Romantic Imagination* (1950); *Inspiration and Poetry* (1955); *Poetry and Politics, 1900–1960* (1966). These covered the whole range of European (and Russian) literature; but he did not abandon the field of classical scholarship: *Sophoclean Tragedy* (1944), *Heroic Poetry* (1952), *Problems in Greek Poetry* (1954), *The Greek Experience* (1957), and the posthumously published *Periclean Athens* (1971) and *Homer* (1971)—all these attest his continuing devotion to classical Greek culture and literature.

Bowra was a unique personality, a living legend in the Oxford of his day. Whether as tutor, as dean, or as warden, he won the admiration and affection of colleagues and pupils alike. He was a formidable figure, short, squat, clean-shaven, with an incisive voice, and a sense of humour the expression of which was not restrained by conventional inhibitions: he was the best company in the world. He was—without any political affiliation or interest—a liberal and a libertarian, 'the leader' (in Lord Annan's words) 'of the movement against the *funeste* and soft-spoken philistine conformity', and uninhibited in his criticism, and ridicule, of those he disapproved of. His autobiographical *Memories 1898–1939*, published in 1966, gives a full account of his life down to the outbreak of World War II, and conveys a vivid impression of the man himself.

A more diversified portrait is presented by *Maurice Bowra, a Celebration* (1974), in which seventeen of Bowra's friends paid tribute to his gifts and recorded the impressions made upon them by his personality. The contributors include figures as diverse and as distinguished as Sir Isaiah Berlin (who delivered the memorial address in the University Church on 17 July 1971), Cyril Connolly [q.v.], Sir John Betjeman, Anthony Powell, Sir Osbert Lancaster, Anthony (later Lord) Quinton, Sir R. E. Mortimer Wheeler [q.v.], and Hugh Lloyd-Jones, regius professor of Greek at Oxford, the editor of the volume, whose memoir was published in the *Proceedings* of the British Academy, of which Bowra was president from 1958 to 1962. The most extended piece in the collection is that of Lord Annan, which gives a superb full-length portrait of its subject, quoting from his letters, and giving specimens of his unpublished verse.

Bowra became FBA in 1938. He was knighted in 1951 and appointed CH in 1971. He had many honorary degrees; Oxford University conferred upon him an honorary DCL on his retirement in 1970 from the wardenship, his tenure of which had been prolonged for two years by a special resolution of the fellows, who made him an honorary fellow in 1970 and invited him also to reside in the college after retirement—a privilege which he enjoyed only for some eighteen months: he died there 4 July 1971.

[C. M. Bowra, *Memories 1898–1939*, 1966; Hugh Lloyd-Jones (ed.), *Maurice Bowra, a Celebration*, 1974; Hugh Lloyd-Jones in *Proceedings* of the British Academy, vol. lviii, 1972; personal knowledge.] JOHN SPARROW

BOYD ORR, BARON (1880–1971), nutritional physiologist and Nobel peace prize-winner. [See ORR, JOHN BOYD.]

BRADWELL, BARON (1905–1976), journalist and politician. [See DRIBERG, THOMAS EDWARD NEIL.]

BRAGG, SIR (WILLIAM) LAWRENCE (1890–1971), physicist and Nobel prize-winner, was born 31 March 1890 in Adelaide, Australia, the elder son (the younger was killed in 1915) and eldest of three children of (Sir) William Henry Bragg [q.v.], physicist, and his wife Gwendoline, the daughter of Sir Charles Todd [q.v.], the government astronomer of South Australia. Bragg was educated at Queen's preparatory school and at St. Peter's College, Adelaide, the leading Church of England school in South Australia. Always ahead of his age group, Bragg left school at fifteen to enter Adelaide University where he read mathematics, with subsidiary courses in physics and chemistry, in his father's department. He graduated with first class honours in mathematics in 1908. Most of Bragg's tuition was from his father—he had a desk in his father's office—and he was drawn into detailed discussion of his father's developing research work on the nature of X-rays. In 1909 Bragg's family moved to England, where his father had been appointed professor of physics at Leeds University, and Bragg entered Trinity College, Cambridge. He read part i of the mathematical tripos (first class, 1910) and part ii of the natural sciences tripos (physics), graduating in 1912 with first class honours.

In the summer of 1912 von Laue and colleagues in Munich discovered the diffraction of X-rays by crystals and, in the autumn of that year, Bragg showed, first, that the phenomenon can be simply understood in terms of the reflection of X-ray waves by planes of atoms in the crystals (according to Bragg's law) and, secondly, that the observed effects are capable of revealing the detailed arrangements of the atoms in the crystals. In this single piece of work, Bragg opened the way to the detailed study of the wave nature of X-rays and, at the same time, began the X-ray analysis of crystal structures that has since revealed the arrangement of the atoms in all kinds of substances from the chemical elements to viruses. Both of these new opportunities for research were quickly exploited. Bragg's demonstration of X-ray reflection from mica led immediately to his father's development of the X-ray spectrometer and the discovery that each element emits a characteristic X-ray spectrum of definite wavelengths, which led in turn to the discovery of the atomic numbers of the elements by H. G. J. Moseley [q.v.]. At the same time, Bragg quickly determined the atomic arrangements in sodium and potassium chloride in a study that has been described as 'the great breakthrough to actual crystal-structure determination and to the absolute measurement of X-ray wavelengths'.

The X-ray spectrometer provided a more powerful method of analysing crystal structures than von Laue photographs and Bragg worked in Leeds during the summer of 1913, using the instrument to analyse a number of mineral structures while his father concentrated mainly on spectroscopic studies of the X-rays. Together they determined the structure of diamond. For this work, interrupted by the outbreak of war in 1914, Bragg was awarded the Nobel prize for physics jointly with his father in 1915. Aged twenty-five at the time, he is still the youngest ever Nobel prize-winner.

Bragg served throughout World War I, first in the Leicestershire Royal Horse Artillery and then, from August 1915, as officer in charge of sound ranging, a method of locating enemy guns from the sound of their firing. He was awarded the MC (1918), appointed OBE (1918), mentioned in dispatches three times, and rose to the rank of major.

In 1919 Bragg was appointed Langworthy professor of physics at Manchester in succession to Sir E. Rutherford (later Lord Rutherford of Nelson, q.v.). There he created the leading school of crystallography, to some degree in competition with his father who established another school at the Royal Institution. They seem to have agreed that Bragg should study metals and minerals, and crystal-physics more generally, while his father concentrated on organic structures. Bragg's achievements in Manchester included the introduction of the idea of atomic radii; experimental verification of the theory of X-ray diffraction from perfect and imperfect crystals; the derivation of experimental atomic scattering factors for sodium and potassium that stimulated theoretical work by D. R. Hartree [q.v.]; the development of methods for analysing increasingly complex structures, including especially the Fourier method of calculating the electron-density distribution in a crystal; the demonstration that X-ray analysis is properly regarded as a branch of optics; and the development, with E. J. Williams, of the theory of order–disorder changes. In structural studies Bragg's main achievement was the analysis of a wide range of silicate mineral structures that led to a detailed understanding of silicate chemistry, but he also promoted the study of metals and alloys by A. J. Bradley and others that underlies modern solid-state physics.

Bragg became director of the National Physical Laboratory in November 1937 but he occupied the post less than a year, being appointed Cavendish professor of physics at Cambridge in March 1938 in succession to Rutherford who had died the previous October. Thus he followed Rutherford in a major chair for the second time, much to the disappointment of nuclear physicists, who had hoped to see one of their number continue Rutherford's work in Cambridge. In the event nuclear physics remained the largest single activity in the Cavendish Laboratory but Bragg concentrated mainly on promoting the development of other new lines of research. Even in his first year, which was taken up increasingly with preparations for war, he made further advances in X-ray optics, strengthened the study of metals in the crystallographic laboratory, and enthusiastically supported the crystallographic studies of proteins by M. F. Perutz, which had been started under the influence of J. D. Bernal [q.v.] and were to be Bragg's chief research interest for the rest of his career.

Bragg played no part in the war research that was conducted in the Cavendish but he acted as consultant to the Sound Ranging Section in the army (the method was still useful and was employed, furthermore, in plotting the trajectories of the V2 rockets) and to the Admiralty on underwater detection by the use of sound waves (Asdic or sonar). He also served on committees set up by the Ministry of Supply to keep its scientific activities under review and as a member of the advisory council of the Department of Scientific and Industrial Research. For six months in 1941 Bragg was scientific liaison officer in Ottawa, Canada, and in 1943 he visited Sweden to re-establish contacts with Swedish scientists.

From 1939 to 1943 Bragg was president of the Institute of Physics. While working hard to maintain the activities of the institute and foster discussion about the needs of the post-war world, he was mainly responsible for the creation of the X-ray analysis group to promote X-ray research in both universities and industry. At the end of the war this led to the formation of the International

Union of Crystallography, of which he was the first president.

After the war Bragg reorganized the Cavendish Laboratory, giving each research section as much autonomy as possible. The principal activities included nuclear physics; low-temperature physics; radio physics, which embraced radio astronomy, in which Bragg took a particular interest as a further example of physical optics; and the crystallography and metal physics which were his chief concern. The interest in protein crystallography had been maintained during the war and, in 1947, Bragg persuaded the Medical Research Council to set up a research unit on the molecular structure of biological systems at the Cavendish Laboratory. This was the origin of the MRC laboratory of molecular biology: the original grant of £2,550 per annum supported M. F. Perutz and (Sir) J. C. Kendrew with two assistants.

Bragg left Cambridge in January 1954 to become resident Fullerian professor and director of the Davy–Faraday laboratory at the Royal Institution in London. There he maintained the traditional activities but he also involved industry more closely through corporate memberships; began an intensive programme of lectures for school children; gave popular science lectures on television; and built up a research team that collaborated with Kendrew and Perutz in the first successful studies of protein structures (myoglobin and haemoglobin) and was the first, in 1965, to determine the structure of an enzyme (lysozyme). By the time of his retirement in 1966 he had made the Royal Institution again a leading centre of scientific research and a focus for the popular exposition of science to a wider audience than ever before.

In 1921 Bragg married Alice Grace Jenny, the daughter of Albert Hopkinson, a Manchester physician who became, in retirement, a demonstrator in anatomy at Cambridge, and his wife, Olga Cunliffe Owen. They had two sons, one of whom became vice-chancellor of Brunel University, and two daughters.

Bragg had a stocky build, a somewhat military appearance resembling his father, and a diffident manner. He was not self-confident in public affairs and he found committees and personal relations generally difficult to handle. He was essentially a private man, who delighted in reading, painting, gardening, bird-watching, sailing, and domestic activities with his adored wife and family. But he wrote quickly and vividly, his public lectures were models of popular exposition, he had a profound grasp of classical physics, and he brought about a major scientific revolution. Through his development and promotion of X-ray crystallography in three major scientific appointments, Bragg transformed our understanding of the natural world: modern mineralogy, metallurgy, chemistry, and molecular biology were largely created by his discoveries.

Bragg's achievements were recognized by the award of many honours including, in addition to the Nobel prize (1915), a Royal medal (1946) and the Copley medal (1966) of the Royal Society. He had become FRS in 1921. He had honorary degrees from eleven universities, including Cambridge. He was knighted in 1941 and appointed CH in 1967. He died in hospital near his home at Waldringfield, Suffolk, 1 July 1971.

[Sir David Phillips in *Biographical Memoirs of Fellows of the Royal Society*, vol. xxv, 1979; personal knowledge.] D. C. PHILLIPS

BRAYLEY, (JOHN) DESMOND, BARON BRAYLEY (1917–1977), business man and junior government minister, was born at Pontypridd, mid-Glamorgan, 29 January 1917, the only son of Frederick Brayley, a café owner, and his wife, Jennie Bassett. He was educated at Pontypridd Grammar School which he left at the age of seventeen to join the regular army in the Royal Artillery and then as a physical training instructor. During the war of 1939–45 he served in the Parachute Regiment with distinction in the African desert campaigns, being awarded the MC for gallantry in 1942, and then in Crete and Sicily where he received a mention in dispatches.

In 1946 he joined the Phoenix Glass Company of Bristol and became managing director in the 1950s. In the process he became a wealthy man and was noted in Bristol for his free spending habits and interest in horse racing. In 1961 he became chairman, and a major shareholder, of the Canning Town Glass Works, a bottle manufacturing firm in London which he was instrumental in developing. He had been a lifelong member of the Labour Party and did not allow success and wealth to affect his loyalty to it or to blur his early memories of poverty in Wales. He was a generous benefactor to the party and donated 60,000 shares in Canning Town Glass Works to its funds. When the Labour government was defeated in 1970 Harold Wilson (later Lord Wilson of Rievaulx) recommended him for a knighthood in his resignation honours list, citing his services to the Bristol Labour Party.

Brayley was, however, little known in the party and there was much adverse comment when Wilson made him a life peer in 1973. This was intensified when he was appointed parliamentary under-secretary for defence (army) in March 1974. A few months later rumours began to circulate about his business affairs before becoming a minister. On taking office he had sold his shares in Canning Town Glass Works for £1 million but on 7 September he was named at a shareholders meeting as owing the company £16,515 for expenses which had been queried by the auditors.

Although Brayley claimed ignorance of this, concern over allegations affecting a minister's business interests led the president of the Board of Trade to order on 15 September an inquiry under the Companies Act, and Brayley simultaneously resigned from the government. Coming in the midst of the general election campaign these events were embarrassing enough for the Labour Party but the more so when Brayley's close association with Harold Wilson, and his gift of shares to the party, became known.

Wilson first met Brayley through Lord Wigg, a close political ally and paymaster-general in his 1964 government. Wigg, a former regular soldier, shared Brayley's devotion to the army and his interest in horse racing, while self-made, flamboyant, and wealthy entrepreneurs always seemed to appeal strongly to Wilson. Several received titles from him, some of whom, like Brayley, also became involved in highly controversial financial dealings which suggested a lack of judgement of character on Wilson's part.

After Brayley's resignation there were further allegations about misuse of the company's funds and in July 1976 he was arrested on five charges of fraud which he strongly denied. He died suddenly 16 March 1977, at Cardiff Royal Infirmary, and the case was closed without the truth ever being known. His will published on 10 June 1979 showed an estate of nil net value; his assets of £87,091 were far exceeded by his liabilities in spite of the share sale.

It was a tragic end to the career of a man of great talents and, his friends always insisted, of high honour whose death, they believed, had been accelerated by the shame of a scandal not of his wilful doing. Nor had he been prepared for the glare of publicity surrounding his ministerial appointment before even the storm broke over his business life.

He had always been noted for his work for charities, particularly those helping the mentally handicapped and those in his native Pontypridd, but not until after his death did the full extent of his personal generosity become known through tributes published in *The Times*. The controller of the Royal Artillery Benevolent Fund wrote of his 'boundless generosity' to the regiment and the chairman of the Middlesex sessions, Ewen Montagu, paid tribute to his unfailing readiness to meet anonymously appeals for financial help for prisoners and their families in distress or to assist their rehabilitation on release.

In 1961 Brayley became a freeman of the City of London. In 1970 he was appointed an honorary colonel commandant of the Royal Artillery and in the same year became a deputy lieutenant for Greater London. He was also a JP for Middlesex (1968). He had been a noted sportsman and athlete, and had been an army championship boxer. He held his own private pilot's licence.

In 1945 he married Queenie Elizabeth Selma, daughter of Horace Bee, estate agent; they had two daughters. The marriage was dissolved in 1960.

[*The Times*, 17 and 19 March 1977.]

IAN WALLER

BRIAN, (WILLIAM) HAVERGAL (1876–1972), composer, was born in Dresden, Staffordshire, 29 January 1876, the eldest survivor of the seven sons (four of whom died in infancy) and one daughter of Benjamin Brian, a potter's turner, and his wife, Martha, daughter of James Watson. He was educated at the local infants' school and at St. James's School, Longton, which had a strong musical tradition. His formal education ceased at the age of twelve: he had already shown musical talent, both as a chorister and on violin, cello, and piano—and while trying a variety of trades (carpenter's apprentice, railway office boy, clerk and buyer for a timber firm) he essayed to become a professional musician. He trained with a reactionary but thorough local music teacher, Theophilus Hemmings, and began to gain some reputation as a fine church organist (it was at this time that he assumed the name Havergal, probably after the hymn composer W. H. Havergal, q.v.). At the 1896 Staffordshire Triennial Festival he heard Beethoven's Ninth Symphony and the première of a contemporary English work, *King Olaf*, by (Sir) Edward Elgar [q.v.]—and, fortified by encouragement from Elgar, he resolved to become a composer.

The years 1906–12 saw Brian resident in Stoke-on-Trent and recognized as a promising figure among British composers of the younger generation, with his choral compositions becoming staple fare as test-pieces in competitions and his early cantatas and orchestral works produced to critical acclaim at various festivals. He was also active as a critic; consorted with leading musicians—Elgar, Frederick Delius, (Sir) Thomas Beecham, Ernest Newman, (Sir) Henry Wood, and especially (Sir) Granville Bantock [qq.v.], who became a close and lifelong friend—and was supported by the patronage of the pottery magnate Herbert Minton Robinson. This palmy period was shattered by the break-up of his first marriage in 1913, and for the next fourteen years Brian struggled to make ends meet in London, Birmingham, and Sussex, producing hack-work and occasional journalism. On the outbreak of war he joined the Honourable Artillery Company as a private, but was invalided out in 1915 (having not served abroad) and worked first in the audit office of the Canadian Forces Contingent, listing the effects of men killed in action, and later as a clerk in munitions for Vickers Ltd. in Birmingham. After the war he was a music copyist for various publishers. The price of this hectic and unsettled life was professional obscurity: his early music dropped out of the repertoire, even though in the meantime he had developed considerably, composing two works of extraordinary brilliance—the satirical anti-war opera *The Tigers* (1917–19) and the huge First Symphony, *The Gothic* (1919–27), for gigantic choral and orchestral forces.

Brian moved back to London in 1927, and his position stabilized when he became assistant editor of the journal *Musical Opinion*, a post he held until 1939. In these years, as well as producing copious and acute journalism, he continued to write a series of large-scale symphonies (Nos. 2–5), but hardly any of his post-1912 music was performed: he was virtually a forgotten composer. During World War II he was awarded a Civil List pension and worked as a clerk for the Ministry of Supply, remaining in the Civil Service until retirement in 1948. From that latter date—possibly partly as a result of the publication of a short biography by Reginald Nettel, *Ordeal by Music: the Strange Experience of Havergal Brian* (1945)—began an extraordinary Indian summer of creativity which produced a vast body of music including four operas and twenty-seven more symphonies (twenty-one of these after the age of eighty). Largely due to the efforts of the composer and producer Robert Simpson, Brian's works began to be broadcast by the BBC, beginning with his Eighth Symphony in 1954, and there was a revival of interest in his music—gradual at first but much accelerated by a performance of *The Gothic* at the Royal Albert Hall in 1966 to mark the composer's ninetieth birthday. The army of performers included 500 singers, 50 brass, 16 percussionists, and 30 woodwind players.

In 1958 he moved from Harrow (where he had spent the previous twenty years) to Shoreham-by-Sea, Sussex. Manchester University conferred on him the honorary degree of Doctor of Music in 1967; the following year he moved into a council flat on Shoreham beach and composed his last works there. In July 1972 he received the accolade of composer of the year from the Composers' Guild of Great Britain.

Physically a small man, of impassive and unassuming mien, his conversation richly flavoured by the Potteries accent he never lost, Brian dedicated his life to music with the utmost tenacity of a sardonic, idiosyncratic, and deeply original mind. His knowledge of past and contemporary music was more encyclopaedic than that of practically any of his contemporaries, and he was deeply stirred by nature, by Gothic architecture, and Romantic literature—he taught himself German, French, and Italian. Despite his humble origins and lack of worldly success he did not regard himself as socially or artistically disadvantaged, and the early termination of his formal education left him free to follow his own interests to the furthest degree.

Though in his early years he wrote many songs and part-songs, as well as some instrumental music, after the age of fifty he concentrated almost exclusively on music-drama and works for large orchestra. Several of these pieces remain unperformed, and his largest—a cantata-setting of Shelley's *Prometheus Unbound* (1937–44)—is lost, a fate which has overtaken several earlier scores. His music developed from the stylistic basis of the late Romantics (Berlioz, Wagner, Elgar, and Strauss), but a pronounced streak of scepticism led him to question the heroic assumptions of these masters and to counterbalance their harmonic opulence with a muscular, 'objective' polyphony inspired by the example of Bach and Handel [q.v.], searching development of motivic cells, and ironic juxtapositions of highly contrasted and mutually subversive kinds of music. While his works are generally 'tonal', therefore, their argument is elliptical, rejecting carefully formalized solutions in favour of open-ended procedures that continually undercut the listener's expectations. It is not comfortable (though it can be inspiring) music to listen to; it is also extremely difficult to play without extensive rehearsal, and few of his symphonies have yet been performed to a standard sufficiently high to project their substance with the force it deserves. Nevertheless the 'Brian revival' proved no temporary phenomenon; a gradual realization grew that he was one of the most important British composers of the century.

Brian was twice married. In 1899 he married Isabel Alice, daughter of George Dalton Priestley, painter and decorator; they had four sons (one died in infancy) and a daughter. After his first wife had died he married in 1933 Hilda Mary (died 1980), daughter of Creswell Hayward, decorator of china and other pottery; previously they had had three daughters and two sons. His youngest child, a daughter, predeceased him by seven months. He died 28 November 1972 at Southlands Hospital, Shoreham, as a result of complications following a fall outside his home.

[Kenneth Eastaugh, *Havergal Brian: the Making of a Composer*, 1976; Reginald Nettel, *Havergal Brian and his Music*, 1976; Malcolm MacDonald, *The Symphonies of Havergal Brian*—3 vols., 1974, 1978, and 1983; personal knowledge.] MALCOLM MACDONALD

BRIDSON, (DOUGLAS) GEOFFREY (1910–1980), writer and man of radio, was born 21 August 1910 in Stockport, the only child of John Douglas Bridson, a Manx shipping manager, of Stockport, and his wife, Marion Barlow. His parents soon moved to Lytham St. Annes, where he attended King Edward VII's School, matriculating brilliantly at an early age.

In 1927 he and his mother went back to Manchester, already, as he later described it, 'the waning capital of a grimly autonomous Northern republic'. He soon relieved a routine office job by contributing both verse and criticism to local and national publications. Bridson's poems of social protest, written during the depression while he was still under twenty-one, caught the eye of Ezra Pound, the American poet. They also brought him to the notice of E. A. F. ('Archie') Harding, the talented BBC programme director in Manchester whose Marxist views had caused Sir John (later Lord) Reith [q.v.] to remove him from being a features producer in London.

Bridson began to contribute programmes for Harding and found they shared a crusading passion for the radio feature as an organ of social change. In 1935 he abandoned free-lancing and joined the BBC staff. An early Bridson programme, and the BBC's first verse feature, was *The March of the '45* (1936), an account of the Jacobite rising. It was repeated nine times, and heard by an estimated audience of 100 million around the world. His radio output was prolific: in twenty-five years over 800 documentaries, plays, and feature programmes carried the imprint of D. G. Bridson. Four hundred had recorded repeats. Some, such as *Aaron's Field* and *Steel*, became microphone classics. In 1934 he had married Vera, the fabric designer daughter of Harry Richardson, a bookseller. Twins, a boy and a girl, were born to them in 1936, but the marriage did not survive the war.

From 1939 to 1945 broadcasts to America about the British war effort occupied most of Bridson's time. In 1943 he crossed the Atlantic for the first time, and rapidly made friends with folk singers such as Burl Ives and Alan Lomax, as well as Josh White and other Black musicians leading the struggle for Negro integration. Much later he was to produce (with Langston Hughes) *The Negro in America* (1964), a series of nineteen separate shows broadcast in the Third Programme, which vividly recalled the disturbing developments of a dramatic decade.

After VE-Day Bridson travelled the world widely for the BBC. Growing up before the cautious days of pre-recorded radio, he approached the developing technology of his profession with zest. He was the first British producer to exploit the use of magnetic tape recording, with equipment captured from the Germans in Norway.

Bridson's limited experience in television was less successful but he was the natural choice for BBC television to send as its adviser—and indeed watch-dog—for the American documentary series *The Valiant Years* based on Sir Winston Churchill's memoirs. The BBC had taken an option on the American series, but was profoundly depressed by the quality of the first scripts and considered cutting its losses. Bridson helped reshape the programmes into an acceptable and moreover popular series. This assignment, due to last six months, in fact kept Bridson in New York for a year. It followed immediately upon his second marriage, on 9 April 1960, to Joyce Thirlaway Rowe, the BBC's first radio publicity officer. She was the daughter of Claude Harold Rowe, an antiques dealer in London who was a direct descendant of Nicholas Rowe [q.v.], poet laureate. Her good nature tolerated the separation with equanimity. Geoffrey and Joyce Bridson's Highgate home became a convivial meeting place for poets, actors, and writers. Bridson was a short, neat man with red hair and an imperial beard; a courteous host and a witty raconteur. He loved books and collected them with discrimination. He had a well-stocked cellar and a well-stocked mind.

Much of Bridson's most distinguished writing was for the Third Programme. Its transformation into Radio 3 made him unhappy, as did the eventual winding up of the once outstanding Features Department, of which he had become the assistant head. His autobiography *Prospero and Ariel* (1971) reflected this malaise. It is a disappointing book, because it eschews samples of his creative writing for radio and contains irritating and untypical inaccuracies. Other publications by Bridson include *Aaron's Field* (1943); *The Christmas Child*, a collection of poems for reading aloud (1950); *The Quest of Gilgamesh* (1972); and *The Filibuster, a Study of the Political Ideas of Wyndham Lewis* (1972).

After Bridson retired from the BBC in 1969 he adapted and dramatized French and English novels, which continued to be broadcast in the domestic and external services of the BBC long after he died in hospital in Hampstead 19 October 1980. In the memories of his contemporaries, many of Bridson's distinguished contributions to a largely ephemeral art similarly survived him.

[*Daily Telegraph*, 22 October 1980 and 11 August 1981; *The Times*, 21 and 24 October 1980; Wynford Vaughan-Thomas, funeral address, 24 October 1980; *They Did It First*, Radio 4 feature, 26 October 1981; Francis Watson, 'D. G. Bridson 1910–1980', in the Society of Authors' *Broadcasting Bulletin*, May 1981; D. G. Bridson, *Prospero and Ariel* (autobiography), 1971; personal knowledge.]

LEONARD MIALL

BRIGHT, GERALD WALCAN-, ('GERALDO') (1904–1974), dance-band leader and musician. [See WALCAN-BRIGHT.]

BRITTAIN, SIR HENRY ERNEST (HARRY) (1873–1974), journalist and MP, was born at Ranmoor, near Sheffield, 24 December 1873, the second and eldest surviving child of five children of William Henry Brittain, master cutler and one-time mayor of Sheffield, and his wife, Frances Mellor. From Repton he went up to read law at Worcester College, Oxford, in 1892 and there spent four extremely happy years, captaining the college tennis six and soccer team and obtaining a third class degree in jurisprudence in 1896. He was called to the bar, Inner Temple, in 1897 but practised for only one week, and then became secretary to (Sir) C. Arthur Pearson [q.v.], owner of the *Evening Standard*. A visit to America on behalf of this paper started his lifelong connection with that country and led to the formation of the Pilgrims' Society of which he became co-founder and honorary secretary. Intense activity in Britain on behalf of the Tariff Reform League, which the *Standard* was supporting, further widened his contacts, especially amongst the leading figures in the retail trade, and in 1907 he undertook the first of many overseas trips as a representative of the Board of Trade. By 1909 he had proposed, found backing for, and organized the first Imperial Press Conference (later the Commonwealth Press Union). By 1914 he had visited most countries in the world and made numerous influential friends. On the declaration of war he was sent to the United States to clarify Britain's war aims and, once they were in the war, conducted American journalists over the battlefields and formed a London club for American officers. In 1918 he was created KBE for public services.

In 1918 he became Conservative member for the new seat of Acton and joined the boards of various business enterprises. During the following eleven years, amongst numerous other activities, he saw the Brittain bird protection law passed, served on the executive committee of the Empire Parliamentary Association, helped to raise money for the founding of Overseas House, accompanied the Prince of Wales on a tour of the US arranged by the Pilgrims' Society, received an honorary LLD from McGill University, served as chairman of the press hospitality scheme for the Wembley exhibition and as chairman of publicity for the British Travel Association which had been formed at his suggestion, and (in 1924) was appointed CMG.

In the 1929 general election he lost his parliamentary seat, a great personal blow to his vanity. He behaved badly, rounding on his supporters for not having worked hard enough to get him re-elected, and was not asked to stand again. He continued with his various interests, civil aviation, ballooning, tourism, broadcasting (he was disappointed not to have been made chairman of the BBC), film-making, journalism, and as chairman of the Regent's Park Open Theatre. When the Oxford Society was founded in 1932 his contacts and his particular affection for Oxford made him the obvious person to organize publicity and support amongst Commonwealth newsmen. His gift for instant friendships was counterbalanced by intense egotism, impatience, and ruthlessness, which less than endeared him to others. On the outbreak of war his hopes of some Anglo-American post were disappointed, undoubtedly for this reason, and his official activities virtually came to an end.

Harry Brittain's gregarious nature, physical stamina, and zest for publicity were well suited to the journalistic and political worlds in which he found himself. His two great achievements (the Commonwealth Press Union and the co-founding of the Pilgrims' Society) were over by the time he was thirty-six, with his Bird Protection Bill eleven years later, but his energies continued little diminished into old age. Athletic in youth, he could still swim a daily quarter-mile at ninety, and made a ten-minutes' after-dinner speech, without notes, at the age of 100. His lifelong habit of wearing a carnation buttonhole was celebrated, to his delight, with a new strain named after him in 1937. The United States and Oxford (especially Worcester College) remained in the forefront of his interest and affections. He made two happy marriages: the first, in 1905, to Alida Luisa, daughter of Sir Robert Harvey, who worked in the South American nitrate trade. A distinguished amateur harpist, also involved in journalism and politics, she was appointed DBE in 1929. There were two children: Robert Edmund Godefroy (Group Captain, founder of the Royal Air Force Flying Club) and Alida Gwendolen Rosemary (Mrs J. K. Harvie). Dame Alida died in 1943. In 1961 he married Muriel Leslie, daughter of H. Leslie Dixon. Brittain died in London in his 101st year, 9 July 1974.

[H. E. Brittain, *Pilgrims and Pioneers, an Autobiography*, 1945, and *Happy Pilgrimage, Autobiography*, 1949; Alida Harvie, *Those Glittering Years*, 1980; private information; personal knowledge.]

D. M. LENNIE

BRITTEN, (EDWARD) BENJAMIN, BARON BRITTEN (1913–1976), composer, was born in Lowestoft 22 November 1913, the youngest of four children (two sons and two daughters) of Robert Victor Britten (1878–1934), dental surgeon, and his wife, Edith Rhoda, daughter of Henry William Hockey (1874–1937), King's messenger at the Home Office, London. Hockey was also an active amateur singer and pianist and the secretary of the Lowestoft Choral Society. Benjamin Britten much admired his father but his mother was the dominant influence on his early years. His musical gifts declared themselves astonishingly early, his first attempts at composition dating from *c.* 1919. His mother gave him his first music lessons and a local piano teacher, Ethel Astle, succeeded her in 1921. His family were his first patrons and performers, many of his juvenilia being written for their use.

In 1923 Britten entered South Lodge Preparatory School, Lowestoft, and began viola lessons with Audrey Alston. His prodigious talent for music—he passed Grade VIII of the Associated Board piano examination at the age of twelve—did not affect his conventional school success: he was academically bright, was an excellent and enthusiastic sportsman, and became head boy in 1927. Although these years were largely happy, his leaving prep. school was shadowed by the fuss caused by an essay in which he argued against hunting, thus revealing his budding pacifist and humanist convictions. The choice of Gresham's School, Holt—at the height of its reputation as a 'progressive' public school—reflected his parents' desire to find an environment that would accommodate his views and neither stifle nor disparage his musical gifts. Whatever its merits, Gresham's was not altogether a happy experience: the music teaching and activities—his diaries make frequent caustic references to performances by his teachers—fell far below his expectations and standards.

Two juvenile works, *Quatre Chansons Françaises* for voice and orchestra (1928) and *Quartettino* (1930), disclose a creative precocity which will stand comparison with Mendelssohn's or Mozart's. That Britten's gift was so technically advanced by this time was due largely to the teaching of the composer Frank Bridge [q.v.] whom he had first met in 1927. From Bridge he acquired the integrity of his technique, his professionalism, and his awareness of the 'new' music in Europe. Bridge was a viola player and a pacifist—reasons for an immediate sympathy between master and pupil—and Britten regarded him as his 'musical conscience' throughout his creative life. In 1930 Britten won an open scholarship to the Royal College of Music, London. At Bridge's insistence he studied with another composer, John Ireland [q.v.], while continuing at the college his piano lessons with Arthur Benjamin (1893–1960), having previously studied the piano, for about a year, with Harold Samuel (1879–1937). Britten was an industrious, conscientious, and ambitious student, twice winning the Ernest Farrar composition prize (1931 and 1933) and funds (though not the award) from the Mendelssohn scholarship, but it was his life outside the college—London's music, cinemas, and theatres—that gave him the enlarged horizons that influenced his development.

John Grierson [q.v.], the innovative head of the GPO Film Unit, employed Britten—on the recommendation of the college—to write some film music and he soon became in effect the unit's resident composer and music editor. He found himself in sympathy with the leftish social and political preoccupations of the unit and significantly assisted in the development of the documentary film, incidentally developing his own gifts as a dramatic composer. In 1935 he began his collaboration with W. H. Auden [q.v.], then working for the unit as script-writer and occasional director, on two of the most memorable of British documentary films, *Coal Face* (1935) and *Night Mail* (1936). Auden's influence was profound: the apostle incarnate of bohemianism blew away any vestiges of provinciality still clinging to Britten and it was probably about this time that he began to acknowledge and accept his homosexual nature. His work in films led to his writing music for the theatre (principally for Rupert Doone's Group Theatre) and radio. He had achieved his ambition to enter on full-time employment as a composer without any transitional period whatever. Key works from this period include *A Boy was Born* (chorus, 1933); *Phantasy* (oboe and string trio, 1933); and *Variations on a Theme of Frank Bridge* (string orchestra, 1937). *Our Hunting Fathers* (voice and orchestra, 1936), with a text devised by Auden, is notable for its technical virtuosity and for its reflection of the poet's and composer's impassioned reaction to the threat of European Fascism. Exhilarating optimism was equally of Britten's nature and the 'Bridge' variations brought him further international recognition at the Salzburg Festival of 1937 (earlier successes had been at International Society for Contemporary Music festivals in 1934 (Florence) and 1936 (Barcelona)).

Despite the signs of a career of high promise and achievement, Britten, with the singer (Sir) Peter Pears (born 1910), left England for the USA in May 1939. Various factors influenced this decision: the worsening political situation; the persuasive examples of Auden and Christopher Isherwood (born 1904), who had already emigrated; loosening family ties (his father had died in 1934, his mother in 1937); discouraging reviews of his music in the English press; and the growth of his friendship with Pears. The two men made their life together from 1937 onwards, an exemplary personal relationship that developed into one of the most distinguished and celebrated voice and piano duos of the twentieth century. They travelled first to Canada and then to New York. For two and three-quarter years they lived in the USA, mainly on Long Island, at Amityville, where they shared the family home and life of Dr and Mrs William Mayer, moving briefly (in 1940) to the Brooklyn house of which Auden was proxy landlord and spending the summer of 1941 at Escondido, California. When World War II began they were advised officially not to attempt to return to England, and it was not until March 1942 that they made the Atlantic crossing from Halifax, Nova Scotia, to Liverpool. Their return was the result of anxiety at wartime separation from friends and relatives and a profound sense, on Britten's part, of deracination. What finally fired his resolve to quit the USA was the chance reading of an article by E. M. Forster [q.v.] on the Suffolk poet, George Crabbe [q.v.], which sowed the seed of the opera *Peter Grimes*. While in the USA Britten composed or completed a number of works in the larger instrumental forms, among them the Violin Concerto (1939), *Sinfonia da Requiem* (1940), and String Quartet No. 1 (1941), the first cycle of songs, the *Seven Sonnets of Michelangelo* (1940), composed especially for Pears, and the operetta *Paul Bunyan* (libretto by Auden), his first full-length stage work—a failure on its first performance in New York in 1941 and withdrawn by the composer until 1976.

On their return to England Britten and Pears registered as conscientious objectors. Britten was granted exemption from military service on the condition that he and Pears gave concerts for CEMA (Council for the Encouragement of Music and the Arts). The principal work to emerge from the wartime years was *Peter Grimes*, which affirmed the composer's Suffolk roots and his preoccupation with the English language, already revealed in the *Hymn to St. Cecilia* for chorus (1942, words by Auden), *A Ceremony of Carols* for treble voices and harp (1942), and *Serenade* for tenor, horn, and strings (1943). One may note the oddity of the première, at Sadler's Wells Theatre on 7 June 1945, of so bleak and pessimistic a work coinciding with the Allies' triumph in Europe, an irony compounded by the opera's unprecedented public success. *Grimes* was a watershed in Britten's life. Its success established his international reputation and was the brilliant first step in the creation of a national tradition of opera. He composed no fewer than nine further operas—among them *Billy Budd* (1951), *Gloriana* (for the coronation of Queen Elizabeth II in 1953), *The Turn of the Screw* (1954), *A Midsummer Night's Dream* (1960), and *Death in Venice* (1973)—three church parables, and three theatrical works for children.

From 1947 Britten lived in the small coastal town of Aldeburgh, Suffolk, and established a special relationship with the community of which he saw himself to be part. His prowess as a pianist of exceptional gifts was almost exclusively devoted to accompanying Pears in song recitals. As a conductor he was known as a 'musicians' conductor', orchestral players admiring his insight and unfussy technique. His opera conducting was the result of an invitation from John Christie [q.v.] to reopen the post-war Glyndebourne season with a new opera. In 1946 Ernest Ansermet conducted Britten's *The Rape of Lucretia* at Glyndebourne, but in 1947 Britten conducted his *Albert Herring* there himself. Earlier that year he and a group of colleagues had formed the English Opera Group, dedicated to the commissioning of chamber operas from Britten's contemporaries, the first performances of which invariably took place at the annual Aldeburgh Festival; and from 1947, with only occasional exceptions, all Britten's musico-theatrical works were written for and first performed by the Group. The Aldeburgh Festival, which he, Peter Pears, and Eric Crozier founded in 1948, was in its twenty-ninth year when Britten died. Such was his prestige that many of the best performing artists of his time were drawn to Aldeburgh each June. Composing; directing and inspiring the English Opera Group and Aldeburgh Festival; partnering Pears; recording and occasionally conducting: this was the agenda that kept Britten preternaturally busy for most of his life. There were frequent trips overseas, of which two require special mention: a concert tour of the German concentration camps with Yehudi Menuhin in August 1945; and the round-the-world journey with Pears in the winter of 1955–6. His encounter with oriental music, in Japan and Bali, had profound consequences for his technical development from *Curlew River* (1964) onwards. The pattern of his life was determined by his composing; the only interruptions were due to occasional bouts of ill health and the building (1967) and rebuilding (after the 1969 fire) of the Maltings Concert Hall at Snape.

Britten composed prodigiously in almost every genre: songs and song cycles (of which he was an acknowledged master); chamber music (e.g. four string quartets); orchestral music (e.g. the Sinfonietta (chamber orchestra, 1932), at the beginning of his professional career, and the Symphony for Cello and Orchestra (1963), written at the height of his mature powers, both showing the scale, conviction, and vigour of his instrumental thinking); and diverse works for chorus and orchestra. One of the largest of these was *War Requiem* (1961), which gave fullest expression to his long-standing pacifist and anti-militarist beliefs and caught the imagination of a whole generation. *Owen Wingrave* (opera for television, 1970) used a mass medium to put across the same message. For his music for children and young people he developed quite specific musical techniques—different in kind from a mere simplification of his established musical usage—and his masterpiece in this area was undoubtedly *Noye's Fludde* (1957). Britten regarded himself as a communicator, a role which, at least in part, was responsible for his unshakeable attachment to the principle of tonality, although that principle underwent continual scrutiny, modification, and revision. He was open always to almost every aesthetic and technical influence and incorporated what he found useful or stimulating into his own eclectic but highly individual musical language.

Despite the assurance of public acclaim of a scale and global spread that had been enjoyed by no other British composer, Britten remained inwardly uncertain of his achievements. This insecurity was undoubtedly responsible for the unquestioning support he exacted of his friends and collaborators, and led in later years to an intellectual climate which did not much favour debate or dissonance, in contrast with the challenges and engagements of the pre-war period. He was a truly modest, gentle, courteous, and generous man; but he could be ruthless when it came to professional standards or the achieving of a creative ambition, when he would absolutely not be thwarted. He was ready to sacrifice himself and others if the musical task demanded it.

In 1973, while completing his last opera, *Death in Venice*, he was dogged by increasing ill health; and in May he underwent open heart surgery for the replacement of a defective valve. The operation was not wholly successful and he suffered a slight stroke during it. He showed great courage and fortitude during his last years and continued to compose, often at a very high level of inspiration. He was unsentimental about death, a convinced humanist rather than a man of religious belief, and on 4 December 1976 he died calmly at Aldeburgh, with his lifelong companion, Peter Pears, by him.

He was created CH in 1953; was admitted to the Order of Merit in 1965; and in 1976 was created Baron Britten, of Aldeburgh in the county of Suffolk, the first time a life peerage had been bestowed on a British composer. He received honorary doctorates from Cambridge (1959), Oxford (1963), and nine other British universities, and was an honorary fellow or member of many colleges and institutions. Among his many prizes and awards were the Coolidge medal (1941), the Hanseatic Goethe prize (1961), the first Aspen award (1964), the Wihuri-Sibelius prize (1965), the Ravel prize (1974), and the Mozart medal (1976). His executors were approached with a request for his burial in Westminster Abbey but he had declared a preference for the graveyard of Aldeburgh parish church, where he was laid to rest on 7 December 1976. A thanksgiving service took place at Westminster Abbey on 10 March 1977. The abbey was packed, fitting tribute to the foremost British composer of his time.

[D. Mitchell and J. Evans (eds.), *Benjamin Britten (1913–1976): Pictures from a Life*, a pictorial biography, 1978; D. Mitchell, *Britten and Auden in the Thirties: The Year 1936* (T. S. Eliot memorial lectures for 1979), 1981; B. Britten, *On Receiving the First Aspen Award*, 1964; Peter A. Evans, *The Music of Benjamin Britten*, 1979; Michael Kennedy, *Britten*, 1981; private information; personal knowledge.]

DONALD MITCHELL

BROAD, SIR CHARLES NOEL FRANK (1882–1976), lieutenant-general, was born at Lahore 29 December 1882, the only child of Major Charles Herbert Broad, 5th Fusiliers, and his wife, Ann Paul. He was educated at Wellington and Pembroke College, Cambridge, but did not take a degree. After serving in the South African war as a private in the militia he was commissioned into the Royal Artillery in 1905. He went to the Staff College, Camberley, in 1914 and eventually went to France as a brigade-major in the late summer of 1915. In the Somme campaign of 1916 he was chief staff officer (as a major) to General (Sir) H. C. C. Uniacke, an outstanding gunner, who was major-general Royal Artillery in the Fifth Army. He was appointed to the DSO in 1917, and received the croix de guerre and Legion of Honour.

Broad's proven ability was recognized by his appointment as artillery instructor at the Staff College in 1919 where his students included four future chiefs of the imperial general staff. Four years later he transferred to the newly established Royal Tank Corps and during the next decade made his chief contribution to the profession as an exponent of mechanization and armoured warfare. Broad's talents were at once recognized by his appointment as commandant of the Tank Gunnery School at Lulworth, and in 1925 he succeeded another brilliant newcomer to the Corps, George Mackintosh Lindsay [q.v.], as chief instructor at the Tank Corps Central School. Here he contributed to the first tactical manual for armoured forces and developed the Medium tank, equipped with anti-tank gun and machine-guns and designed to fire on the move.

During the years 1927–31, which witnessed the climax of British experiments with mechanized forces, Broad served in the staff duties section of the general staff at the War Office responsible for organizing for war. In 1929 he drafted what was to become a famous manual—*Mechanised and Armoured Formations*—popularly known in the army as the 'Purple Primer' from the colour of its covers. Though progressive in tone, Broad's manual skilfully avoided the extremism and polemics which characterized much of the literature on mechanization. He stressed the superiority of armoured forces over infantry in power, mobility, and endurance; moreover he made what was then a revolutionary suggestion that armoured forces might keep up advances of thirty to fifty miles a day for nearly a week—a feat which was achieved by Germany's Panzer divisions in the early campaigns of World War II. General Heinz Guderian later acknowledged Broad's influence on his thinking, though it should be noted that the infantry component of the Panzer divisions was much stronger than Broad had recommended.

In 1931 Broad, now a brigadier, was given a wonderful opportunity to try out his ideas as commander of the experimental 1st brigade RTC. According to the expert on tank warfare, (Sir) Basil Liddell Hart [q.v.], those trials on Salisbury Plain were 'the most influential tactical experiments in the British Army since Sir John Moore's training of the Light Brigade at Shorncliffe Camp' during the Napoleonic wars. Broad demonstrated that his units, composed of medium and light tanks, could play a more adventurous role than close co-operation with slow-moving infantry. He proved that tank formations could be controlled while manoeuvring over difficult terrain by a combination of flags and radio telephony. These trials lent support to the proposition that only mechanized armoured forces could be manoeuvred under the intense fire to be expected on the modern battlefield. Unfortunately Broad's 'five year plan' for the creation of four permanent armoured brigades was shelved as a consequence of the financial crisis and the resignation of the Labour government in 1931. The momentum generated by Broad and his colleagues such as Lindsay, Sir F. A. Pile and (Sir) P. C. S. Hobart [qq.v.] was lost and six years elapsed before mechanization began in earnest in 1937.

This proved to be Broad's last direct connection with mechanization though he remained deeply interested in the subject for the rest of his life. He became major-general in 1936. In 1937 he made an excellent impression on the new secretary of state for war, I. L. (later Lord) Hore-Belisha [q.v.], but was given only the dead-end job of major-general in charge of administration at Aldershot. Since the main duty there was to organize the annual tattoo this was a scandalous waste of expertise. Whether there was an actual conspiracy at the War Office against Broad and the other tank pioneers is uncertain; but there was evidently a feeling in the military hierarchy that they should not be conspicuously rewarded in competition with sound but conservative officers of equivalent rank. Broad had not helped his prospects by a contretemps with the chief of the imperial general staff Viscount Gort [q.v.] (see B. H. Liddell Hart, *Memoirs*, 1965, vol. ii, p. 35).

On the outbreak of war in 1939 Broad was promoted to the Aldershot Command, and the following year he was made lieutenant-general and GOC-in-C Eastern Army India where he worked hard to modernize the Indian Army under the threat of a Japanese invasion. He was appointed CB in 1938 and KCB in 1941 and retired the following year on reaching retirement age, though he continued to be colonel commandant of the RTC until 1948.

Slight of stature and generally mild of manner, Broad occasionally showed impatience with slower-minded senior officers. Several of his peers rated him an outstanding officer but one also mentioned his occasional want of tact. Perhaps it was this flaw which caused his estrangement from Gort over a trivial misunderstanding. Broad was sometimes depressed by the lack of funds for new equipment and realistic training, and also felt that the army was bedevilled by cliques. In later years he was apt to reproach himself for lacking the crusading zeal of a Joan of Arc, but it is hard to see that he could have made more of his brief opportunities in comparatively junior positions. Indeed his reputation is assured as a shrewd and balanced theoretician of armoured warfare in the years when Britain led the world in its tank manuals and field exercises.

Broad married first in 1915 Lillian Mary, daughter of Edwin Mackintosh, who worked in shipping; they had one daughter. She died in 1942 and two years later he married Diana Myrtle, younger daughter of Colonel Philip Robert Bald, of Barton Lodge, Cerne Abbas; they had three sons (one deceased) and one daughter. Broad died at Beaminster, Dorset, 23 March 1976. A portrait by Jeffrey Courtney, depicting Broad as a brigadier in 1931, was unveiled at the Royal Tank Corps headquarters in London in 1979.

[B. H. Liddell Hart, *Memoirs*, 2 vols., 1965; K. Macksey, *The Tank Pioneers*, 1981; private information.] BRIAN BOND

BROAD, CHARLIE DUNBAR (1887–1971), philosopher, was born at Harlesden, Middlesex, 30 December 1887, the only child of Charles Stephen Broad, wine merchant, of an old family of Bristol builders, and of his wife, Emily Gomme. Broad was brought up in quietly comfortable circumstances and in an environment of elderly relatives, of varying degrees of eccentricity, relieved by a modest family trust from the need to work. He was at Dulwich College from 1900 to 1906 when A. H. Gilkes was headmaster. Moved from the 'engineering side' to the 'science side' of the school, he won a science scholarship to Trinity College, Cambridge, and went up there in 1906. At that time, he says of himself, he adhered to a 'smug and thin rationalism' under the influence of the writings of H. G. Wells [q.v.] and other advanced thinkers of the age. An interest in philosophy had been awoken at school by reading Schopenhauer. In 1908 he got a first in part i of the natural sciences tripos but, doubting his chances of doing first class work in science, turned to philosophy.

That decision was justified in 1910 by his achievement of first class honours, with special distinction in 'moral science'. His main teachers were J. M. E. McTaggart, whose notice he later wrote for this Dictionary, and the logician W. E. Johnson [q.v.]. He also had some contact with Bertrand Russell [q.v.], the philosopher to whom technically he was closest, sharing Russell's conviction that science is very substantially inconsistent with common sense and more worthy of belief than common sense, and with G. E. Moore [q.v.]. It was the early and largely shared doctrines of these two major philosophers that Broad was to elaborate and to defend, despite Laodicean protestations, throughout his career.

In 1911 he was elected a fellow of Trinity on the basis of a dissertation that was published in an improved form in 1914 as *Perception, Physics, and Reality*. From 1911 to 1920 Broad was at St. Andrews University, first as assistant to G. F. Stout [q.v.], then as lecturer at the Dundee part of the university. During the war he gave some time to work at a neighbouring munitions factory. In 1920 he succeeded C. Lloyd Morgan [q.v.] as professor at Bristol, returning to Trinity in 1923 to succeed McTaggart in his teaching post there. For the rest of his life he continued to live in Trinity, for most of the time in rooms once inhabited by Newton, from 1933 until his retirement in 1953 as Knightbridge professor of moral philosophy (in succession to W. R. Sorley, q.v.) and from 1953 to his death.

As a philosopher, Broad, as he was the first to admit, had little in the way of new ideas to contribute to philosophy. If anything, indeed, he was inclined to exaggerate both his uncreativeness and the rapidity with which he lost any real interest in the subject. In fact, he was a creditable specimen of what Locke claimed to be, namely an 'under-labourer' for whom it is 'ambition enough to be employed . . . in clearing the ground a little and removing some of the rubbish'. In a long series of books on a wide range of philosophical topics he explored the interests and doctrines of Russell with much greater care and thoroughness than Russell and those of Moore without Moore's repetition and exasperating slowness.

The Lockean account of perceptual knowledge, as a rather precarious inference from private 'sensa' to public objects endowed with only a few of the qualities commonly ascribed to them, developed at length in his dissertation, reappears as part of a general account of the philosophy of science, taking account of recent developments in science, in *Scientific Thought* (1923) and as part of a comprehensive philosophy of mind in his Tarner lectures *The Mind and its Place in Nature* (1925). Here for the first time appears a discussion of the psychical research to which he was to devote much of his energy. In 1927 he brought out the second and less abstract volume of his teacher McTaggart's *The Nature of Existence*, still in draft at its author's death. In 1934 *Five Types of Ethical Theory* gave careful, sometimes idiosyncratic accounts of some major moral philosophers. Broad's main work in the 1930s was his *Examination of McTaggart's Philosophy* (vol. i, 1933, vol. ii, 1938), the largest and most impressive of his works, giving enormously fair, even if ultimately negative, consideration to what was for him an ideal example of the kind of speculative philosophy that he believed to be possible in principle over and above the analytic or critical philosophy orthodox in his time.

Later works were essay collections—*Ethics and the History of Philosophy* (1952) and *Religion, Philosophy and Psychical Research* (1953), his *Lectures on Psychical Research* (1962), and posthumously published lecture series on Leibniz and Kant. Broad had several honorary degrees, including both a Litt.D. and Sc.D. from Cambridge, and was elected FBA in 1926.

Broad was a conspicuous example of the traditional bachelor don of his epoch. Boyhood interests in railways and the Nordic world persisted into later life, particularly the latter. In 1946 at the age of fifty-nine he made his first trip out of Britain to Scandinavia and found the young men of Sweden a source of profound delight from that time forward. In World War II he served as junior bursar of his college and acquitted himself well. He did not visit America until the academic year following his retirement, 1953–4, when he lectured at Michigan and the University of California at Los Angeles. He was a conscientious supervisor of his pupils but a dull lecturer, dictating matter already written out. He claimed to have lost all interest in philosophy by the time he became professor in 1933, but that is belied by the amplitude and seriousness of the work he continued to produce at least until the end of the 1930s. The sour retrospection more probably reflects his resentment at the fashionable obsession with Ludwig Wittgenstein [q.v.], who returned to Cambridge in 1929 and soon stole any fire Broad may have had.

In appearance Broad was short, a little stocky, and bald from an early age. In later life he resembled nothing so much as a very senior warrant officer in the Royal Army Service Corps, with his rigidly set face and darting, suspicious eyes. He died in his rooms in Trinity College, Cambridge, 11 March 1971.

[C. D. Broad, 'Autobiography' in *The Philosophy of C. D. Broad*, ed. P. A. Schilpp, 1959; Karl Britton in *Proceedings* of the British Academy, vol. lxiv, 1978.]

ANTHONY QUINTON

BROCK, RUSSELL CLAUDE, BARON BROCK (1903–1980), surgeon, was born 24 October 1903 at 840 Old Kent Road, London, the second of six sons and fourth of eight children of Herbert Brock, a master photographer, and his wife, Elvina, daughter of James Carman, of Hinderclay, Walsham-le-Willows, Suffolk. He was educated at Haselridge Road School, Clapham, and at Christ's Hospital, Horsham. An accident in the school laboratory, resulting in severe burns to his face and hands, may well have inspired his interest in medicine and he entered Guy's Hospital medical school in 1921 with an arts scholarship. After an outstanding undergraduate career he qualified LRCP (Lond.) and MRCS (Eng.) in 1926, and graduated MB, BS (Lond.) with honours and distinction in medicine, surgery, and anatomy in 1927.

Following resident appointmens at Guy's he was appointed as demonstrator in anatomy and in pathology and passed the final FRCS (Eng.) in 1929. Elected to a Rockefeller travelling fellowship in 1929–30, he worked in the surgical department of Evarts Graham at St. Louis, Missouri, and there developed a lifelong interest in thoracic surgery. On returning to Guy's he became surgical registrar and tutor in 1932 and was appointed research fellow of the Association of Surgeons of Great Britain and Ireland. He won the Jacksonian prize of the Royal College of Surgeons of England in 1935 and was elected a Hunterian professor in 1938.

His more senior posts began with appointment as consultant thoracic surgeon to the London County Council, 1935–46, and surgeon to the Ministry of Pensions at Roehampton Hospital, 1936–45. In 1936 he was appointed surgeon to Guy's and the Brompton hospitals, each of which he served faithfully, diligently, and with great distinction until 1968. During the war of 1939–45 he was also thoracic surgeon and regional adviser in thoracic surgery to the Emergency Medical Service in the Guy's region. Following the war his surgical appointments were confined to Guy's and the Brompton during a period when cardiac surgery, and especially operations on the open heart, were developing apace. He played a major part in pioneering the surgical relief of mitral stenosis and of other valvular lesions of the heart. His introduction of the technique of direct correction of pulmonary artery stenosis was certainly inspired by exchange professorships between himself and Dr Alfred Blalock of Johns Hopkins Hospital, Baltimore. Thereafter Brock, when not the initiator, was ever to the fore of new developments in this fast-expanding field of surgery. Inevitably this came to overshadow some of his earlier contributions to lung surgery which had emanated from his own classical publication on the anatomy of the bronchial tree in 1946.

Brock was an outstanding diagnostician, the equal in clinical acumen to the best of his physician colleagues. He was as conscientious in the training of undergraduates as he was meticulous in the care of his patients. He gave great service to the Royal College of Surgeons of England, serving on its council from 1949 to 1967 and being an active member or chairman of many of its standing committees. He was vice-president 1956–8 and president 1963–6. He gave the Bradshaw lecture in 1957 and the Hunterian oration in 1961. He was knighted in 1954 and elevated to a life peerage in 1965. On retirement from his hospital appointments in 1968 he continued in private practice for a while and became director of a newly formed department of surgical sciences at the Royal College of Surgeons which had been set up during his presidency. For a variety of sound reasons the college subsequently had to alter the character of this department and this caused him much upset and disappointment.

Brock's medical awards and honours were numerous. He was president of the Thoracic Society of Great Britain and Ireland in 1952; and of the Society of Cardiovascular and Thoracic Surgeons of Great Britain and Ireland, and also of the Medical Society of London in 1958. An elected fellow of the Royal College of Physicians of London in 1965, he had become an honorary fellow of the American College of Surgeons, 1949; the Brazilian College, 1952; the Australasian College, 1958; the Royal College of Surgeons in Ireland, 1965; and the Royal College of Physicians and Surgeons of Canada and the Royal College of Surgeons of Edinburgh, 1966. He was honorary fellow or member of a number of surgical societies abroad, as well as the recipient of many foreign and domestic prizes and gold medals. He received the highly prestigious international Gairdner award, 1960–1, and was appointed Lister medallist and orator, 1967. He also received honorary degrees from the universities of Hamburg (1962), Leeds (1965), Cambridge (1968), and Guelph and Munich (1972).

Having been appointed assistant editor of the Guy's Hospital reports before his election to the senior staff, he was editor 1939–60. Thenceforward he contributed a stream of important papers on cardiac and thoracic surgery to medical and surgical journals and textbooks. He was the author of several important books: *The Anatomy of the Bronchial Tree* (1946), *Lung Abscess* (1952), *The Life and Work of Astley Cooper* (1952), and *The Anatomy of Congenital Pulmonary Stenosis* (1957).

Brock could be a difficult person to get to know and to some he seemed excessively fussy and meticulous. But he was a man of total dedication and enormous integrity who gave unswerving support to his juniors and trainees once they had shown themselves prepared to live up to his own very high standards. His students were taught with firmness and courtesy, and he was quick to seize upon and to criticize loose thinking and careless use of either the spoken or written word.

He was basically a shy man who could often seem brusque; but he was a kindly and thoughtful person when not under pressure. Tension during operations was sometimes high and, unlike many surgeons, he did not find it easy to relax in the operation theatre. Outside his professional work he had considerable knowledge of old furniture and prints, and of the history of London Bridge and its environs, and was an eager student of medical history. Less well known was his dedication to the complementary interests of private medicine and the NHS, for he served on the governing body of Private Patients Plan and was chairman (1967–77) before becoming its president. He was responsible for the discovery and restoration of an eighteenth-century operation theatre on the Guy's site which was formerly in the old St. Thomas hospital.

Brock was married in 1927 to Germaine Louise, daughter of Léon Jacques Ladavèze, of Paris, a gentleman of independent means. They had three daughters, the eldest of whom died in 1977. After his wife's death in 1978, he married in 1979 Chrissie Palmer Jones, who had been his personal secretary for many years. She was the daughter of John Alfred Jones, secretary to a colliery. Brock died in Guy's Hospital 3 September 1980. A portrait by Carlos Sancha hangs in the Royal College of Surgeons at Lincoln's Inn Fields, and there is a copy at Guy's.

[Records of the Royal College of Surgeons; *The Times*, 5 and 12 September 1980; *British Medical Journal*, 20 September 1980; *Lancet*, 13 September 1980; information from family and surgical colleagues; personal knowledge.]

REGINALD MURLEY

BRODIE, SIR ISRAEL (1895–1979), chief rabbi of the United Hebrew congregations of the British Commonwealth, was born at Newcastle upon Tyne 10 May 1895 as the second son and second of the five children (one daughter; a son died in infancy) of Aaron Uri Brodie (originally Braude or Broide), a sales representative who had immigrated from Kovno, and his wife, Sheina Maggid, whose surname derived from her father's occupation as a popular preacher in Lithuania (Tsemach Isaac, 'the Tsemach maggid'). His schooling at Rutherford College, Newcastle upon Tyne, was supplemented by Jewish instruction, and in 1912 he entered University College, London, and simultaneously Jews' College to prepare for a career in the Jewish ministry. A first class BA (1915) in Hebrew, Arabic, and Syriac qualified him for research, and he proceeded to Balliol College, Oxford, in 1916 to work for a B.Litt. (completed in 1921) on the origins of Karaism (medieval Jewish sectaries). He served from 1917 to 1919 as a chaplain on the western front. He returned to Balliol in 1919–20. Formal rabbinical training followed, with ordination in 1923 and practical experience in congregational and youth work in the East End of London under the guidance of J. F. Stern. He was in these years also much influenced by the impressive Jewish club leadership of (Sir) Basil Henriques [q.v.] and by Herbert Loewe at Oxford, who involved him in Jewish adult education and introduced him to the study circle of Claude Montefiore [q.v.].

In 1923 Brodie went to Melbourne, Australia, to succeed Joseph Abrahams as rabbi and to take charge of the Jewish ecclesiastical court of Victoria. He was the first minister to visit all the continent's Jewish communities, thereby contributing to a Jewish federal cohesion. He returned to Balliol in 1937 as an advanced student. In 1939 he joined the staff of Jews' College, as tutor and lecturer in homiletics—an appropriate assignment since he was an impressive speaker. But World War II took him back to chaplaincy work in France, and he was amongst the last to be evacuated from Dunkirk (*Jewish Chronicle*, 2 July 1948, p. 13). Service in the Middle East with the Royal Air Force prepared him to succeed as senior Jewish chaplain in 1944. He returned to Jews' College, briefly, as its principal in 1946, and in that year he married Fanny Levine, whom he had known years before as a teacher in Jewish classes: her father, Jacob Levine, was a Hebrew teacher. There were no children. The same year saw the death of Chief Rabbi J. H. Hertz [q.v.], to whom Brodie was an obviously eligible successor, and he was appointed to the office in 1948: in 1965 he became the first incumbent to retire. Distinctions followed: the presidency of Jews' College, a fellowship (1950) of University College, London, an honorary DCL from Durham University and DD from Yeshiva University, New York, and in 1969 appointment as KBE. *Essays Presented . . . on . . . his Seventieth Birthday* (ed. H. J. Zimmels *et al.*) appeared in 1967.

Brodie's courteous manner contrasted with the masterful personality of Hertz, whose public statements had sometimes embarrassed lay leadership. An attempt was made to impose on Brodie a consultative committee; but, while declaring willingness to consult, he made it clear that he would make his own decisions on all matters. The availability of air travel meant that his tenure would be very different from that of Hertz, and his achievements are best compartmentalized geographically.

Australian experience familiarized him with the situation of Jewish outposts, their educational problems and risks of erosion. He visited the antipodes, and also quite frequently South Africa, even after it left the Commonwealth, and he tried to attract ministerial trainees to Jews' College. In 1957, as a contribution towards reconstruction of the pitiful remnants of European Jewry, Brodie convened what became a standing conference of European rabbis, the limitations of which were, however, implicit in its restriction to orthodox representatives, whose following by then constituted minorities within the European Jewish pattern; and the sort of topics that it was prepared to discuss were largely matters of detail.

Brodie had always been a Zionist. He visited Israel frequently, and once declared his willingness to subordinate his halakhic (i.e. jurisprudential) responsibilities to a central authority in Jerusalem should one ever emerge, although he must have known that this was unlikely. He supported not only the secular Hebrew University of Jerusalem, but also the creation of the religiously articulated Bar Ilan University, where a chair was named in his honour. At home he worked hard to advance Jewish education. He secured purpose-built premises for Jews' College, he supported the movement to create Jewish day-schools, and concerned himself with the reorganization of part-time Jewish education, whilst ruling that children whose mothers were not Jewish by birth or orthodox conversion must be excluded from synagogue classes. He fought a rearguard action, in the face of enthusiasm for all things Israeli, against the introduction in the Ashkenazic synagogues under his jurisdiction of the Israeli (broadly Sephardic) pronunciation of Hebrew. The emergence of the state of Israel stimulated significant reversion towards traditionalism and greater use of Hebrew in prayer amongst the progressive, i.e. non-orthodox congregations; but because of the movement's self-determination in matters involving Jewish status, Brodie maintained an aloofness from it no less distant, if less fulminating, than his predecessor's.

The greatest crisis of Brodie's incumbency made national headlines of a domestic Jewish issue. Rabbi Louis Jacobs, a lecturer at Jews' College and an impressive preacher, had in popular writings acknowledged the view that if reason is considered God-given, issues of biblical fundamentalism, criticism, and modern science should not nowadays be evaded in the pulpit and be restricted to muted discussion by mature Jewish minds only. Jacobs was passed over for the principalship of Jews' College; and in 1963 his former congregation purported to re-engage him as minister, despite Brodie's withholding his requisite approval. The attempt was blocked as unconstitutional. Brodie, sensitive to views of rabbis on his own ecclesiastical court whose education had been entirely talmudic, and concerned at what was regarded as an implicit threat to the authority for Jewish observance, found himself driven into making a statement about intellectualism and authentic Jewish tradition that upset some Jewish intellectuals (including rabbis).

His main scholarly work was the publication (1962–7) of the *Etz Hayyim* of Jacob of London, a thirteenth-century compendium of Jewish liturgy, ceremonial, and law. A select bibliography of his works appears in *Essays Presented. . . .*

Brodie's tenure of the chief rabbinate, itself otherwise unremarkable, reflects changed conditions: the wane of Anglo-Jewish, as of British influence, and the rise of Israel as the renewed centre of gravity for post-Hitlerian Jewry. The chief rabbinate, safeguarded by act of Parliament, represented the hub of a nineteenth-century Anglo-Jewish solidarity that no longer corresponded to the statistical facts of Jewish observance and intermarriage, but it nevertheless remains entrenched by Anglo-Jewish conservatism. Within its framework, any attempt to transcend separatisms (save where Israel's security, and fund-raising for Israel were concerned) would have required a character capable of riding out any storm, which Brodie did not possess. As a gentleman, a representative figure of dignity in bearing, as a well-liked chaplain to the forces, and by his devotion to what he considered his duty, he handed on intact to his successor an office of potential leadership, and retained the broad loyalty of some English-born Jews who might otherwise have lapsed. Brodie died in London 13 February 1979.

[A. S. Super in the *Jewish Monthly*, ii, 3, 1948, pp. 134–40; *Jewish Chronicle*, 16 February 1979, p. 23; J. M. Shaftesley in *Essays* (see above), pp. xi–xxxix (both with portraits); personal knowledge.]

RAPHAEL LOEWE

BROGAN, SIR DENIS WILLIAM (1900–1974), historian and student of politics, was born 11 August 1900 in Glasgow, the eldest of the four sons of the second marriage of Denis Brogan, a master tailor, and his wife, Elizabeth Toner. His father, a native of Donegal, had briefly lived in the USA and Brogan grew up in a home responsive to the politics both of Ireland and America. Educated at Rutherglen Academy, Glasgow University (MA, 1923), and Balliol College, Oxford, where he obtained a first class in history in 1925, he was guided towards the USA by Samuel Eliot Morison, then visiting Harmsworth professor at Oxford. A year at Harvard on a Rockefeller research fellowship established the study of the American past and the American present as the ruling passion of his life.

Returning from the USA, after a brief period on the staff of *The Times*, he was appointed in 1928 as lecturer in history at University College, London, and in 1930 as lecturer in politics at the London School of Economics. The literary product of these years was his deservedly best known book, *The American Political System* (1933). Appearing at a turning point both in American national development and in British awareness of the United States, its freshness, pungency, wit, and zest rediscovered America for a generation of British readers and profoundly influenced the perception of American politics in both academic and non-academic circles. The book's emphasis was on the actualities of the political process, made vivid by personal observation, a brilliant if teasing allusiveness, and an astonishing breadth of reading both in contemporary and historical literature. *An Introduction to American Politics* (1954) had the same qualities; it was indeed a comprehensively revised and rewritten version.

In 1934 Brogan left London for Oxford, as fellow and tutor at Corpus Christi College. There he expanded his academic interests to take in the study of France, with a brio, a range, and an intimacy analogous to his study of the USA. The impressive first-fruit of this was *The Development of Modern France, 1870–1939* (1940; revised edition, *1870–1959*, 1967), over twice the length of *The American Political System*, and packed with detail. Here for the first time, in English or French, the complex phenomena of modern French politics, at home and abroad, were reduced to a comprehensible narrative that does justice to economic and social factors but keeps the individual, from peasant to president, at the heart of the story. The tone is affectionate, but free of illusion, vivacious and sharp-edged. A later study, *The French Nation from Napoleon to Pétain, 1814–1940* (1957), is marked on a smaller scale by the same characteristics.

To fit a figure like Brogan into the machine of World War II was never easy. He began in the Foreign Research and Press Service, moved briefly to the American Division of the Ministry of Information, was then for a short time with the Political Warfare Executive, but finally found his niche with the overseas services of the BBC. Perhaps one should rather say 'niches' because Brogan's exuberant energies overflowed from the European Service to the North American Service; in each capacity his role was that of an intelligence officer, providing background information and policy guidance from his diverse and capacious store of contemporary and historical knowledge. Thrown off, almost, in the midst of these taxing labours was *The English People: Impressions and Observations* (1943), characteristically precise, yet wide-ranging and shrewd, an essay in presenting the distinctive features of the English way of life by 'a foreigner of a kind'. *The American Problem* (1944) was a series of loosely linked essays on the evolution of modern America, which discharges an analogous function from west to east.

In the spring of 1939 Brogan had been elected to the professorship of political science at Cambridge and to a fellowship at Peterhouse and to this he returned at the war's end. His approach to his chair was that of a liberal, a pragmatist, and a historically-minded student of institutions. Sceptical of systems, suspicious alike of sociological and philosophical abstractions, he warned in his inaugural lecture, *The Study of Politics* (1946), against imposing on his subject 'a degree of abstractness or bogus neutrality that it cannot stand'. His lectures, delivered with a minimum of notes, regrettably do not survive, but some of the fruits of his approach can be gathered from *The Price of Revolution* (1951), a characteristically sceptical analysis in terms not so much of revolutionary professions or doctrines but of the discrepancy between cost and benefit, expectations and performance, moral claims and concrete results.

For a historian and an Americanist it was regrettable that Brogan produced no study of the American past on a scale comparable to *The Development of Modern France.* His *Abraham Lincoln* (1935, revised 1974, posthumously) is a miniature, albeit a classic one. *The Era of Franklin D. Roosevelt* (1950, published in Britain as *Roosevelt and the New Deal*, 1952) is a useful, balanced, compact treatment curiously lacking in its author's individual touch. *American Aspects* (1964), which reprints a number of historical and political articles, including the classic 'The Illusion of American Omnipotence', has far more of Brogan's range and historical penetration about it. The fact is, however, that the student who would gather all that Brogan has to offer would have to glean the pages, particularly the review pages, of a host of journals, but in particular the *Times Literary Supplement*, where his fecund genius, particularly in his later years, found a more natural outlet. Very far from being 'mere' journalism, these occasional writings were as remarkable for their concentration and wit as for their diversity and volume. To this Dictionary he contributed the notices of Gilbert Harding and Sir W. H. Lewis.

Brogan retired from his chair in 1968 and died in Cambridge 5 January 1974. In addition to many honorary doctorates from France and the United States, he was an honorary LL D of Glasgow (1946) and an honorary D.Litt. of Oxford (1969). He was an honorary fellow of Peterhouse and Corpus Christi and became a fellow of the British Academy in 1955. He was knighted in 1963. He was married in 1931 to Olwen Phillis Frances, an archaeologist, daughter of William Kendall, medical practitioner. There were three sons and a daughter of the marriage.

[H. G. Nicholas in *Proceedings* of the British Academy, vol. lxii, 1976; private information; personal knowledge.] H. G. Nicholas

BRONOWSKI, JACOB (1908–1974), mathematician, poet, and humanist, was born in Lodz, Poland, 18 January 1908, the eldest of three children and elder son of Abram Bronowski, the owner of a haberdashery firm which traded between Poland and London, and his wife, Celia Flatto. He lived with his parents in Germany during World War I and went with them to England in 1920.

Bronowski was educated at the Central Foundation School, London, and then at Jesus College, Cambridge. He obtained a first class in part i of the mathematical tripos (1928) and was a wrangler in part ii (1930). He stayed at Cambridge to continue mathematical research, mainly in algebraic geometry and topology, receiving his doctorate in 1933, the year in which he became a naturalized British subject. Later he became interested in statistics and the mathematical aspects of biology, but already while at Cambridge his interests had extended not only into other sciences but also into literature and philosophy. He was particularly interested in the nature of poetry, which he practised himself, stimulated by friendship with Laura Riding and Robert Graves with whom he spent some time on the island of Majorca.

In 1934 he became lecturer, then senior lecturer at the University College of Hull, where he stayed until war work claimed him in 1942. He took a great interest in various progressive movements, particularly during the Spanish civil war, when he wrote some of his best poetry. His writings also reflected the threatening cloud of Nazism that was hanging over Europe.

His most important work during the war was to develop operational research methods, a field in which he was a pioneer and which he applied particularly fruitfully in the bombing survey (1945) when he was scientific deputy to the British Chiefs of Staff Mission to Japan. He wrote a masterly report on the *Effects of the Atomic Bombs at Hiroshima and Nagasaki*. Later he had the opportunity to apply similar methods to government research into industrial problems, particularly when, from 1950, he became director of the Coal Research Establishment of the National Coal Board. He played a central part in the development of smokeless fuel and from 1959 to 1964, as director-general of process development, he was wholly responsible for this aspect of the Board's work. He also spent some time in 1948 on loan to Unesco in Paris and as Carnegie visiting professor at the Massachusetts Institute of Technology in 1953.

No matter what his activity, Bronowski always transcended the confines of his own speciality. His early interest in the humanities not only never left him, but as his experience of the world grew, so did his constant search for a comprehensive view of man in all his multifarious aspects and activities. In 1939, in his first major book, *The Poet's Defence*, he had wrestled with the relation between the truth of science and that of poetry, a subject which was to reappear frequently, for example in his classic study *William Blake, a Man Without a Mask* (1944), followed by *William Blake and the Age of Revolution* (published USA 1965, Britain 1972). In 1953, while at MIT, he broadened the enquiry in his later published lectures on *Science and Human Values* (1961), from which the great debate on the 'two cultures' sprang—one in which Bronowski never accepted the idea of a separation between the scientific and the humanistic aspirations of man. Many other works on this theme followed.

Bronowski became an accomplished broadcaster in the 1950s and 1960s, acquiring great popularity in the 'Brains Trust'. In his broadcasts he showed—and developed—a quite exceptional talent for exposition in popular form of most complicated scientific and philosophical issues and for bridging the gaps which existed between different disciplines. In 1964 he became senior fellow at the Salk Institute for Biological Studies in La Jolla, California, and in 1970 director of the Council for Biology in Human Affairs. Between July 1971 and December 1972 he filmed a thirteen-part television series for the BBC, *The Ascent of Man* (published in book form in 1973), which spread his fame as a thinker and expositor far and wide.

Among many academic and other honours, Bronowski became, in 1967, an honorary fellow of Jesus College, Cambridge, and, in 1960, foreign honorary member of the American Academy of Arts and Sciences.

He married in 1941 Rita, daughter of Benjamin Coblentz, furrier. She was a talented sculptor (under the professional name of Rita Colin), and they had four daughters, the eldest of whom, Lisa Jardine, became a fellow of Jesus College. Bronowski died, from a heart attack, 22 August 1974, at East Hampton, Long Island, New York.

[*The Times*, 23 August and 11 September 1974; *New York Times*, 23 August 1974; *New York Herald Tribune*, 24 August 1974; private information; personal knowledge.] ERIC ROLL

BROOKE, BASIL STANLAKE, fifth baronet, and first VISCOUNT BROOKEBOROUGH (1888–1973), politician, was born 9 June 1888 at Colebrooke Park, county Fermanagh, Ireland, the eldest of the five children (three sons and two daughters) of (Sir) Arthur Douglas Brooke, fourth baronet, of Colebrooke, and his wife, Gertrude Isabella, only daughter of Stanlake Batson, of Horseheath, Cambridgeshire. He was educated at Winchester and the Royal Military College, Sandhurst, succeeded his father as fifth baronet on 27 November 1907, and served with distinction during World War I as a captain in the 10th Hussars, being awarded the MC (1916) and croix de guerre with palm.

As befitted a descendant of a Protestant Anglo-Irish family who had occupied lands in the border areas of Ulster since the late sixteenth and mid-seventeenth centuries, Brooke spent most of his life as a country gentleman and Unionist politician in Northern Ireland. A lazy man of limited ability and considerable charm, he so much preferred country pursuits, especially fishing, to the work of government that one colleague remarked that 'Those who met him imagined that he was relaxing away from his desk. What they didn't realize was that there was no desk.' As a politician, his distinguishing characteristics were a certain indolence and a commitment to traditional unionism—the British connection, the partition of Ireland, and Unionist ascendancy in Northern Ireland. He was one of the founders of the Ulster Special Constabulary in the troubled years 1920–2. He was appointed CBE in 1921. He sat in Stormont for over forty years, as senator, 1921–2, and MP for the Lisnaskea division of Fermanagh, 1929–68; and he occupied high office for thirty years. He was assistant parliamentary secretary, the Ministry of Finance, and assistant whip, 1929–33, and, as minister of agriculture, 1933–41, he became known for his anti-Catholic speeches and absences from Belfast, being content to leave affairs in the hands of his civil servants. Nevertheless, their energy in modernizing Northern Ireland agriculture in the 1930s established Brooke's reputation as an effective minister, thus paving the way for his appointment as minister of commerce and production, in 1941–5, and, following a Unionist Party revolt, as prime minister in 1943 with a threefold programme: to maintain the constitution; to maximize Northern Ireland's flagging war effort; and to prepare for post-war problems. From 1933 he had been PC, Northern Ireland.

During Brooke's long premiership, thanks mainly to changes in Britain, Northern Ireland's economy became more diversified and its standard of living improved so dramatically as to reinforce its separation from the Irish Republic and enable it to survive a prolonged but ill organized campaign of violence by the Irish Republican Army, 1956–62. Despite being created viscount in 1952 for his services to Northern Ireland and the United Kingdom, Brooke never became a national leader. He remained a Unionist Party boss and helped perpetuate the long-standing and ultimately fatal sectarian divide in Northern Ireland politics by failing to recognize the changes taking place in Catholic social and political attitudes after World War II and by refusing to support those liberal Unionists who sought accommodation with Catholics. For him Catholics remained beyond the pale, because of their religion and commitment to Irish nationalism: 'There is no use blinking the fact that political differences in Northern Ireland closely follow religious differences. It may not be impossible, but it is certainly not easy for any person to discard the political conceptions, the influence and impressions acquired from religious and educational instruction by those whose aims are openly declared to be an all-Ireland republic.'

He resigned as prime minister in 1963, ostensibly because of ill health but largely because of criticism in the Unionist Party of his failure to combat rising unemployment and stop the drift of Unionist voters in Belfast to the Northern Ireland Labour Party. He retained his seat in parliament until 1968, was created KG in 1965, and developed commercial interests as chairman of Carreras (Northern Ireland), a director of Devenish Trade and president of the Northern Ireland Institute of Directors. He was honorary LL D of Queen's University, Belfast.

In 1919 he married Cynthia Mary, second daughter and co-heir of Captain Charles Warden Sergison, of Cuckfield Park, Sussex; they had three sons. The eldest and youngest were killed in action during World War II but the second son, John Warden, also a soldier, survived the war and later entered Northern Ireland politics. Cynthia Brooke served in World War II as senior commandant of the Auxiliary Territorial Service and was created DBE in 1959. She died in 1970 and in the following year Brooke married Sarah Eileen Bell, daughter of Henry Healey, of Belfast, and widow of Cecil Armstrong Calvert, FRCS, director of neurosurgery, Royal Victoria Hospital, Belfast. Brookeborough died at home at Colebrooke 18 August 1973 and was succeeded by his only surviving son from his first marriage.

[P. Bew, P. Gibbon, and H. Patterson, *The State in Northern Ireland 1921–72: Political Forces and Social Classes*, 1979; P. Buckland, *A History of Northern Ireland*, 1981; T. O'Neill, *The Autobiography of Terence O'Neill*, 1972.]

P. J. BUCKLAND

BROOKEBOROUGH, first VISCOUNT (1888–1973), politician. [See BROOKE, BASIL STANLAKE.]

BROWN, SIR (GEORGE) LINDOR (1903–1971), physiologist, was born in Liverpool 9 February 1903, the only son and younger child of George William Arthur Brown, schoolmaster in Warrington, and his wife, Helen Wharram, of Yorkshire. He went first to his father's school and then to the Boteler Grammar School in Warrington. At eighteen he won a scholarship to the

University of Manchester, following his sister Kathleen, and read medicine rather than chemistry as he had originally intended. He did well in pre-clinical studies, and his physiology teachers, A. V. Hill [q.v.], H. S. Raper, and B. A. McSwiney influenced him towards a research career. Before his clinical studies, encouraged by McSwiney, he took an honours B.Sc. in physiology (1924), and then, after winning the Platt physiological scholarship, spent a further year doing research in McSwiney's laboratory, earning an M.Sc. (1925). He qualified in medicine in 1928 (MB, Ch.B. Manch.), winning the Bradley prize and medal for operative surgery.

McSwiney had moved in 1926 to the physiology chair in Leeds, and in 1928 Brown joined him there as lecturer in physiology, to work for some years on the nervous control of the motility of gastric muscle. In 1932 he took advantage of six months' leave to work in the laboratory of Sir C. S. Sherrington [q.v.] at Oxford, collaborating with J. C. Eccles in an electrophysiological analysis of vagal action on the heart. On return to Leeds he began his own first fully independent research on ganglionic transmission, with kindred methods.

Brown, in giving papers to the Physiological Society, had attracted the attention of Sir Henry H. Dale [q.v.], who offered him a job at the National Institute for Medical Research in Hampstead. Brown took up the appointment in March 1934, joining (Sir) John H. Gaddum [q.v.] and W. S. Feldberg in Dale's laboratory. There followed 'anni mirabiles', during which the cholinergic theory of chemical transmission was established: namely that excitation is transmitted from a motor nerve to its target structure not by electric currents but by the release of a chemical transmitter, acetylcholine. The character of that transmission was important, not only for general physiology, but also because if the link were chemical, it would be susceptible to chemical manipulation for therapeutic purposes (as has proved to be the case). Brown brought to the group electrophysiological methods, a beautiful experimental technique, and an insight into the physiology of excitable tissues that was vital at the time. With this work he became increasingly significant in the Physiological Society; he joined its editorial board in 1940 and was its honorary secretary from 1941 to 1949.

With the advent of World War II, the Institute turned to new activities. Brown first engaged in research on motion sickness, body armour, and tank design. Then in 1942 the royal naval personnel research committee was set up jointly by the Medical Research Council and the chief executive. An underwater subcommittee was the first to be formed, in which Brown brought together scientists (including such as J. B. S. Haldane, q.v.) and naval officers involved with diving and submarine operations, in an exceptionally fruitful co-operation. He had a flair for removing barriers, and commanded the confidence of his naval colleagues to a remarkable degree. The Hampstead physiology laboratory, now under Brown's direction, turned to the study of underwater breathing, the effects of excess of oxygen or carbon dioxide in man (using themselves and colleagues as subjects), and the design of diving apparatus. Other committees, on clothing, gunnery, habitability, and visual problems, followed. Brown remained secretary of the RNPRC until 1949, and was then its chairman for nearly another twenty years.

With the end of the war the laboratory returned to its previous work, but Brown was now a prominent figure. He was elected FRS in 1946 and appointed CBE in 1947. In 1949 he accepted the Jodrell chair of physiology at University College, London. He was happy and successful there, much strengthening both the physiology department and that of biophysics under (Sir) Bernard Katz, and developing with J. S. Gillespie important work on adrenergic transmission. Although he gave up the secretaryship of the RNPRC and of the Physiological Society with the move, he was now carrying many outside activities. A sudden gastric haemorrhage in 1952 made him shed some of these. But new demands appeared, and having served on various Royal Society committees, he became its biological secretary from 1955 to 1963.

In 1960, after advising the electors to the Waynflete chair of physiology in Oxford, he was himself offered, and accepted, the post. He became a fellow of Magdalen. Three years later he was a member of hebdomadal council, and he also became a member of the Franks commission of inquiry into the working of Oxford University. In 1967 he was elected principal of Hertford College. He resigned his chair, but continued with his research group in the pharmacology department. He inaugurated the college's major appeal, negotiated two senior research fellowships, and dealt with the student restiveness with a light touch.

Brown was knighted in 1957 and made FRCP in 1958. At various times he served on the Medical Research Council, the Council for Scientific and Industrial Research, and the governing body of the Lister Institute, latterly as chairman. He was president of the Institute of Information Scientists and of the International Union of Physiological Sciences. He was Feldberg prize lecturer in 1961 and Royal Society Croonian lecturer in 1964. He held honorary doctorates at St. Andrews (1958), the University of Brazil (1958), Liège (1959), Leicester (1968), and Monash (1969), was a member of the Danish and Brazilian Academies of Science, and an officer of the Order of the Southern Cross of

Brazil (1959). The Physiological Society, which had made him an honorary member in 1970, established the G. L. Brown lecture in his memory.

Brown had a friendly, invigorating, light-hearted but determined personality. He was an excellent judge of talent and character, a stimulating and supportive head of department, devoted to laboratory work despite all his outside activities, and best and happiest in the company of the young. His recreations included workshop practice, making woodcuts and engravings, playing the flute, and writing topical ballades.

In 1930 he married Jane Rosamond (died 1975), daughter of Charles Herbert Lees, FRS, professor of physics in the University of London, and vice-principal of Queen Mary College. They had met five years earlier in clinical school. There were four children: Helen (Mrs Aly Uygur), who graduated in medicine; Christopher, an engineer; Stephen, an airline pilot; and Humphrey, a biomedical engineer. Early in 1970 Brown was immobilized by a stroke, and made a good recovery, but he was struck by biliary obstruction in December. The primary tumour was rapidly operated on, but subsequently renal failure set in and he died in the Radcliffe Infirmary, Oxford, 22 February 1971.

[F. C. MacIntosh and W. D. M. Paton in *Biographical Memoirs of Fellows of the Royal Society*, vol. xx, 1974; personal knowledge.]

W. D. M. PATON

BROWN, IVOR JOHN CARNEGIE (1891–1974), journalist, author, theatre critic, and wordsmith, was born 25 April 1891 in Penang, Malaya, the younger of two sons of Dr William Carnegie Brown, of Aberdeen, and his first wife, Jean Carnegie. His father, a graduate of Aberdeen University and an expert in tropical diseases, had a practice in the Federated Malay States.

Ivor Brown was sent to England to be educated at Suffolk Hall preparatory school and then Cheltenham College. After a year's private tuition by a crammer, he headed the Balliol scholarship list, and took a double first in classical honour moderations (1911) and *literae humaniores* (1913). He passed sixth into the Civil Service, and was sent to the Home Office. His career lasted two days, still something of a Whitehall record. For his first job he was instructed to minute an application by Staffordshire policemen for an increased provision of water-closets. He wrote his comments and walked out, to earn his living as a free lance by writing about more interesting matters.

During the war he was a conscientious objector, and hotly engaged in progressive politics. He lectured for the Oxford tutorial classes committee; published two ephemeral books of political theory and three novels; and wrote iconoclastic articles for the *New Age*. His versatile, profuse, and very fast pen fitted him exceptionally for journalism—so in 1919 he joined the London office of the *Manchester Guardian*. There he wrote everything from editorials to colour pieces about sport; but particularly he wrote about the theatre, which became the master passion of his life. He was dramatic critic for the *Saturday Review* from 1923 to 1930.

In 1916 he married Irene Gladys, the elder daughter of Bertha (Posener) and Carl Hentschel, a photo-engraver who made blocks for Fleet Street newspapers. She was a professional actress who became a successful director of plays. Her knowledge of the far side of the footlights enriched her husband's criticism. There were no children of the marriage.

In 1926 Brown was appointed Shute lecturer on the art of the theatre at Liverpool University. In 1929 he became theatre critic of the *Observer*, and for the next thirty years, through a period of change, experiment, and brilliance on the London stage, he was the most influential and perceptive voice in British dramatic criticism. In 1939 he was made professor of drama to the Royal Society of Literature. When the Council for the Encouragement of Music and the Arts (CEMA, later to become the Arts Council) was set up during World War II, Ivor Brown was the obvious choice for its director of drama (1940–2).

When J. L. Garvin [q.v.] retired from the editorship of the *Observer* in 1942, Brown was appointed to the post. He carried on as chief dramatic critic, and managed also to make time to write regular leading and feature articles, and, when the muse struck, elegant satiric verses. As editor Brown led the *Observer* with a light and liberal hand through the difficult wartime shortages of staff and newsprint. He put news on the front page; introduced new blood; broadened the paper's interests and changed its typography; and made it exceptionally well written.

But writing was the element in which he lived; so in 1948 he resigned to have less administrative work and more time for writing. He continued as dramatic critic until 1954, and carried on writing as naturally as breathing for the rest of his life.

Brown published more than seventy-five books, including novels, essays, biography, autobiography, criticism, coffee-table books, and even a light and not very good play. He was among the most prolific and versatile writers of his generation. As well as using the English language expertly, he was one of those logophiles, like F. G. and H. W. Fowler [q.v.] and Eric Partridge [q.v.], thrown up regularly by the English, who are fascinated by the language itself. He became famous for his word books, agreeable rambles around correct usage and philology, enlivened by literary allusion, quotation, wit, and personal anecdote. He wrote thirteen in all, collecting words as other men collect porcelain. In the first, *A Word in Your Ear* (1942), he was observing how gargantuan journalese was ruining such good old words as 'epic', 'odyssey', and 'tragedy'. In *A Charm of Names* (1972) he explored the history of Christian or given names from Abigail to Zuleika, not forgetting Ivor. He was the most good-humoured of prescriptivists, but incorrigibly convinced that there exists such a thing as correct English, and that it is to be preferred to the other kind. To this Dictionary he contributed the notices of James Agate, Lena Ashwell, Robert Donat, Sir Harry Lauder, and Sir George Robey.

Shakespeare was another lifelong enthusiasm. Brown wrote a number of books about him full of amateur common sense and expert theatrical and linguistic wisdom. He was a very professional master of the English language and literature, happiest when writing, which he did very fast, chewing the end of his handkerchief on the rare occasions when he was stuck for a word cr an idea. He was a big, burly, shy man, with Aberdonian *gravitas*, who could suddenly spark with a flash of frivolity or frolic.

He was chairman of the British Drama League from 1954 to 1965, a fellow of the Royal Society of Literature, and an honorary LLD of St. Andrews and Aberdeen universities (1950). After the war he lectured much in Denmark, which conferred on him a knighthood of the Order of Dannebrog. In 1957 he was appointed CBE. He died in London 22 April 1974.

[*The Times*, 23 April 1974; J. B. Priestley in *Observer*, 28 April 1974; Ivor Brown, *The Way of My World*, 1954.] PHILIP HOWARD

BROWN, SPENCER CURTIS (1906–1980), literary agent. [See CURTIS BROWN, SPENCER.]

BROWN, WILLIAM (1888–1975), mycologist and plant pathologist, was born 17 February 1888 at Middlebie, Dumfriesshire, the second son and child of Gavin Brown, small farmer and agricultural engineer, and his wife, Margaret Broatch. In 1900 William Brown went to the Annan Academy as a day-scholar and left in 1904 with a bursary for Edinburgh University, after getting a leaving certificate in mathematics, English, Latin, French, and German. In 1908 he took his MA degree, with first class honours in mathematics, qualifying also in physics and other sciences. For his first two years he had continued to study Latin (first prize and medal); for the rest of his life Brown was to continue reading both Greek and Roman authors in their native texts. He spent two more years at Edinburgh as a postgraduate student, qualifying in 1910 for a B.Sc. in advanced botany and zoology; in these six years he was awarded fourteen medals.

After two years as a temporary lecturer in plant physiology in the Edinburgh botany department, Brown moved in 1912, with a two-year scholarship from Edinburgh, to the botany department of the Imperial College of Science and Technology (University of London), to become a research student under V. H. Blackman [q.v.], and was awarded the London D.Sc. in 1916. In 1923 he was appointed assistant professor on the college staff, and in 1928 was made professor of plant pathology in the University of London, the first such post to be established in Britain. In 1921 Brown had married Lucy Doris Allen (died 1966), a graduate of London University (Bedford College) with first class honours in botany; she was the daughter of a shipping agent and her mother was from a family of London clock makers. They had a son and three daughters, one of whom, Lucy, achieved academic distinction as a teacher in the London School of Economics.

Brown's experimental work on the physiology of fungal growth in culture and of infection of plant tissues was published in a series of eighteen papers (1915–28) and is regarded as the outstanding pioneering achievement in these twin subjects. He showed that soft-rot of plant tissues is mediated by fungal secretion of pectinase enzymes and, secondly, that fungal infectivity is enhanced by nutrients diffusing through the thin cuticle of flower petals and young leaves. His studies of growth of *Fusarium* species in culture revealed serious flaws in the taxonomic disposition of species in this genus, which was later revised accordingly. From his paper in the *Annals of Botany* of 1922, on combinations of gas and cold storage for control of fungal rots of apple fruits, Brown concluded that the effect of such fungistatic factors was greatest when the fungal energy of growth was least. This was Brown's major generalization and led to the later concept of fungal inoculum potential for colonization of plant tissues, both living and dead. The quality of Brown's researches was due to an analytical mind well versed in the physical sciences; his rapid output of data reflects his unusually good co-ordination of movement, also shown by his prowess in tennis, golf, and billiards. He was elected FRS in 1938.

As a supervisor Brown was regarded with affection as well as respect by his many research students, who included a number from overseas, and especially from India, which he later visited. They soon found that Brown, though conventional in dress and behaviour, was anything but so in his approach to research. Similarly in his lectures to undergraduates he disdained any tricks of oratory but his lucid exposition, enlivened by flashes of dry humour, compelled close attention. These qualities are revealed by his lecture on 'Spontaneous Generation', published in the Royal College of Science *Journal* in 1952.

In 1938 Brown became head of the botany department and continued thus until his retirement in 1953. He was beset by many problems during the period of post-war reconstruction but left his department in good order for his successor. After retirement his chief outdoor interest was in the raising of unfamiliar species of plant in his large garden, in which he continued to labour until well into his eighties. He died in Manchester 18 January 1975.

[Information from Dr Lucy M. Brown (daughter); S. D. Garrett in *Biographical Memoirs of Fellows of the Royal Society*, vol. xxi, 1975; personal knowledge.] S. D. GARRETT

BROWNE, JOHN FRANCIS ARCHIBALD, baronet, of Nova Scotia, and sixth BARON KILMAINE (1902–1978), trust administrator, was born in Dublin 22 September 1902, the eldest of three children and elder son of John Edward Deane Browne, fifth Baron Kilmaine (an Irish representative peer) and his wife, Lady Aline Kennedy, daughter of Archibald, third Marquess of Ailsa. The family lived at Gaulston in county Mayo until 1925 when their last estates were sold and they moved to Kent. John Browne was educated at Winchester (where he won the English speech prize, was captain of the school shooting eight, and represented Ireland at rifle shooting) and at Magdalen College, Oxford. He passed moderations in modern history in 1922 and obtained third class honours in philosophy, politics, and economics in 1925. He then spent four years (1925–9) with British Xylonite before moving to University College, Southampton (as it then was) as administrative secretary in 1930.

In 1933 the Oxford Society had been in existence for a year and was looking for a full-time professional secretary. John Browne was appointed and threw himself with characteristic energy and enthusiasm into the task of not only establishing the society as a world-wide organization but of allaying the suspicions of the colleges which in those days felt that a university society might subvert the loyalty of their old members. He launched the magazine *Oxford* and set up branches throughout the English-speaking world. In 1937 he organized the Society's assistance to the university's appeal for the extension to the Bodleian Library and for the improvement of facilities for scientific research. By 1939 he was proposing to raise an endowment fund for the society when war came and he joined the Royal Army Service Corps. He served from 1940 to 1945, rose to the rank of lieutenant-colonel, served on the staff, and was twice mentioned in dispatches.

In 1945 he succeeded Thomas Jones [q.v.] as secretary of the Pilgrim Trust. He remained there for twenty-two years, during which time the scope of its benefactions widened enormously. His predecessor's interest had been mainly towards social welfare; Kilmaine (he succeeded to the title in 1946) directed the attention of the trustees towards a wider field of art, learning, and the preservation of the national heritage. He was active in persuading G. F. Fisher (later Lord Fisher of Lambeth, q.v.), the archbishop of Canterbury, to set up the Historic Churches' Preservation Trust, which the Pilgrim Trust then supported by annual block grants. He secured help for the 'little houses' scheme of the National Trust for Scotland, and his support for the conservation of vernacular housing round the old quay at Harwich was rewarded by his appointment as high steward of the borough (1966–76). He ensured the systematic listing and rescue of medieval wall paintings and was equally active in the preservation of medieval glass, arranging for the glaziers' workshops at York Minster to be converted into a national centre for its repair and preservation. He obtained charitable status for the workshops as the York Glaziers' Trust. He was one of the first to recognize and support the claims of industrial archaeology.

In 1953 Kilmaine, by then the recognized doyen of trust administrators, also took on the secretaryship of the newly-founded Dulverton Trust, which he retained until 1966. Meanwhile, in 1949, he had become chairman of the Oxford Society, to which he devoted much time and energy. When in 1957 several colleges approached the Pilgrim Trust for help with the restoration of their buildings, sadly neglected during the war years, John Kilmaine immediately saw not only the advantage of uniting them in a general appeal but also the necessity for a preliminary assessment of the total amount to be raised. Thus arose the highly successful Oxford Historic Buildings Appeal. His services to the nation were acknowledged by his appointment as CBE in 1956, and his services to Oxford by an honorary DCL in 1973, the year he retired from his chairmanship of the Oxford Society.

Kilmaine was a distinctive figure, tall, fair, formal in speech and manner. His capacity for work, attention to detail, unerring eye for accuracy, and clarity in summing up a problem were formidable. He could be tactless, and was not above an occasional, somewhat malicious amusement in cutting people down to size. Conscious of his heritage and background, he understandably regretted that events had deprived him of a seat in the Lords. If he expected deference, he also extended it to others, with a somewhat old-fashioned respect for position, though his warm sympathy with and interest in all he met (and perhaps his Irish upbringing) caused this to fall short of snobbery. His very happy marriage, in 1930, to Wilhelmina Phyllis, daughter of Scott Arnott, solicitor, of Brasted in Kent, produced two daughters and a son. Kilmaine died at Brasted 26 July 1978. He was succeeded by his son, John David Henry Browne (born 1948).

[Private information; personal knowledge.]
D. M. LENNIE

BRUNDRETT, SIR FREDERICK (1894–1974), scientist and public servant, was born 25 November 1894, the eldest in the family of seven sons and three daughters of Walter Brundrett, general secretary and accountant with the Ebbw Vale Steel, Iron, and Coal Company, of Hinxhill, Kent, and his wife, Ada, daughter of James Richardson, of Chorlton cum Hardy. He was educated at Rossall and at Sidney Sussex College, Cambridge. He obtained a first class in part i of the mathematical tripos (1914) and was a wrangler in part ii (1916). He then served in the Royal Naval Volunteer Reserve, joining the wireless branch in 1916. After demobilization in 1919 he joined the scientific staff of the Admiralty and was appointed to the Royal Naval Signal School. He remained there until 1937, when he was transferred to the headquarters of the Royal Naval Scientific Service in London and promoted to principal scientific officer. He became a superintending scientist in 1939, assistant director of scientific research in 1940, deputy director in 1942, and in 1946 succeeded Sir Charles Wright as chief of the Royal Naval Scientific Service. In 1950 he was appointed deputy scientific adviser to the minister of defence, serving first under Sir H. T. Tizard and then under Sir J. D. Cockcroft [qq.v.], whom he succeeded in 1954 as scientific adviser and chairman of the Defence Research Policy Committee.

During his service in the RNVR he became engaged in research work on underwater communications with submarines. At the Signal School he played a leading part in the development of short-wave radio. He would not, however, have claimed to have made a great contribution to fundamental scientific knowledge; and he once described himself as the worst circuit engineer who ever joined the Royal Naval Scientific Service. His great strength lay in his ability to apply scientific principles to the practical development of new types of equipment. He also showed a great talent for administrative work in the field of science and it was this that enabled him to play such an effective role, first as chief of the Royal Naval Scientific Service and later during his time at the Ministry of Defence.

Before he became scientific adviser himself, he had taken an increasing share of the work-load, especially after Tizard's retirement, when Cockcroft combined the position of scientific adviser with that of head of the Atomic Energy Research Establishment. He was thus well prepared and established when he himself succeeded in 1954.

In those days, before the absorption of the separate Service departments and the Ministry of Supply into the Ministry of Defence, the scientific adviser's function lay in the co-ordination of policy towards scientific research and the development of new equipment for the armed forces. Brundett fulfilled this with great skill. He won the confidence not only of successive ministers, but also of successive members of the Chiefs of Staff Committee, who came to rely more and more upon his practical approach and valued his advice on problems ranging well beyond the strictly scientific. Much of the co-ordinating work was done in the Defence Research Policy Committee or in specially appointed working groups. Brundrett, being a shrewd judge of people, proved a masterly chairman. He felt his way unerringly through complex arguments and was able through persistence and persuasion to come up at the critical moment with an acceptable solution to the most controversial problem.

After his retirement from the Ministry of Defence in 1959, he undertook many other tasks in the public service. He was a Civil Service commissioner for seven years (1960–7); chairman of the Air Traffic Control Board; and chairman of the naval aircraft research committee of the Aeronautical Research Council (1960–6).

In appearance he was small and spare, with bright blue eyes and the air of an inquisitive bird. His approach was direct, his personality warm and outgoing, his interests wide; and despite the controversies in which he inevitably became involved, he made no enemies. Throughout his life he was keenly interested in agriculture, and he was himself a very successful farmer. He was chairman of the council of the Red and White Friesian Cattle Society, and an authority on the management of contagious abortion in cattle. He became president of the Agricultural Co-operative Association and devoted much energy to the development of co-operative marketing for poultry and eggs. He was an enthusiastic and skilful player of ball games, excelling particularly in hockey, where he was captain of the Hampshire County and Civil Service teams. He also played cricket for the Civil Service, and was an eminent stamp collector.

In 1954 Brundrett became an honorary fellow of Sidney Sussex College. He was appointed CB in 1946, KBE in 1950, and KCB in 1956. He received an honorary D.Sc. from Manchester in 1956.

In 1920 he married Enid, daughter of George Richard James, schoolmaster, of Chesterton, Cambridgeshire. Their only child, a son, was killed in Italy in 1944.

[*The Times*, 6 August 1974; personal knowledge.] RICHARD POWELL

BUCHAN, ALASTAIR FRANCIS (1918–1976), writer on strategic and international affairs, was born at 76 Portland Place, London, 9 September 1918, the third son and the fourth and youngest child of John Buchan, first Baron Tweedsmuir [q.v.], and his wife, Susan Charlotte, daughter of Captain Norman de l'Aigle Grosvenor, third son of the first Lord Ebury [q.v.]. He was educated at Eton and at Christ Church, Oxford, where he took second class honours in modern history in 1939. After spending a short while at the University of Virginia, he was commissioned in the Canadian Army in 1939 (his father being at that time governor-general of the Dominion) and saw active service at Dieppe in 1942 and, as a major, in north-west Europe in 1944–5.

After demobilization Buchan turned to journalism. He served as assistant editor of *The Economist* from 1948 until 1951, when he went to Washington as correspondent for the *Observer*. There he remained until 1955, observing at close quarters the political turmoil resulting from the Korean war and the witch-hunts initiated by Senator McCarthy. It was then that he laid the foundations of his expertise in the major problems of defence and nuclear armament that were of increasing concern to decision makers at this period in Washington and elsewhere; and his writing on this topic gained him the respect of senior officials and political figures, as well as his fellow-journalists, in both the United States and Europe.

In 1955 Buchan returned to London and continued to work for the *Observer* as its diplomatic and defence correspondent. He was there able to pursue a private interest in the life and work of the founder of *The Economist*, Walter Bagehot [q.v.], which led to the publication in 1959 of an excellent brief study, *The Spare Chancellor*. But his main interest lay in the increasingly complex and controversial field of defence and nuclear deterrence, and he accepted with alacrity the invitation to become the first director of the newly formed Institute for Strategic Studies in 1958.

The object which the founders of the Institute had in mind was to make generally available information on defence questions in order to educate public opinion in a debate that was at that time engendering more heat than light. An essential element in this programme was to persuade responsible officials to release more information and share their concerns with a wider public. A difficult path had therefore to be trod in order to retain the confidence both of Whitehall and of Fleet Street, and in this Buchan succeeded brilliantly. Further, his contacts in the United States enabled him to enlist the interest of such seminal strategic thinkers in that country as Bernard Brodie, Albert Wohlstetter, Thomas Schelling, and Henry Kissinger. European thinkers such as Raymond Aron in France and Helmut Schmidt in Germany were also drawn in. As a result the International Institute for Strategic Studies (as it later became) developed from a simple information centre into the principal forum of strategic debate in the western world, where officials, journalists, academics, and military men met and freely exchanged ideas. To these ideas Buchan himself made a continuing contribution with his books and articles; but his real talents were entrepreneurial, the capacity to draw ideas out of others. The increasing intelligence and moderation with which such questions as nuclear deterrence, nuclear proliferation, and arms control were publicly discussed in the 1960s in all western countries owed a very great deal to Buchan's influence.

Buchan retired from the directorship of the Institute in 1969 to take up an appointment as commandant of the Imperial Defence College: the first non-official civilian ever to hold the post. Under his leadership the syllabus was broadened and the membership extended; its changed role being expressed in a new title: the Royal College of Defence Studies. In 1972, at the conclusion of his tour of duty, he became Montague Burton professor of international relations at Oxford, and began to develop a serious graduate school of international politics in that university. He had time barely to lay the foundations, however, when he died suddenly in his sleep 3 February 1976, in his home at Brill, near Oxford. A readership in international relations was established in his memory by Oxford University in 1980.

Although Eton and Christ Church had equipped Buchan with the agreeable worldliness of an upper-class Englishman, he was fundamentally a Scot, with formidable powers of work and a granite-hard integrity which impressed people even more than did his intellectual ability and the literary fluency he inherited from his father. He was appointed MBE in 1944 and CBE in 1968. In 1973 he gave the Reith lectures, with the theme 'Change without War'. A portrait painted by David Poole in 1969, the property of his family, hangs in the Council Room of the International Institute for Strategic Studies.

He married in 1942 Hope Gordon, daughter of David Gordon Gilmour, of Ottawa, Canada, lumberman. They had two sons and a daughter.

[Personal knowledge.] MICHAEL HOWARD

BUCHAN-HEPBURN, PATRICK GEORGE THOMAS, BARON HAILES (1901–1974), politician and governor-general of the Federation of the West Indies, was born 2 April 1901 at Smeaton Hepburn, East Lothian, the third son (there was also a daughter) of Sir Archibald Buchan-Hepburn, fourth baronet, a barrister, and his wife, Edith Agnes, daughter of Edward Kent Karslake, KC. He was educated at Harrow (1915–19) and Trinity College, Cambridge, which he left without a degree.

Buchan-Hepburn was a painter of more than amateur skill who, from his youth, was much attracted to the arts. He was equally interested in politics and in 1926 became honorary attaché at the British embassy in Constantinople at an early stage of the Kemalist regime. After two years of diplomatic experience, he returned to England in 1927, and, though not established as a civil servant, was appointed personal private secretary to the chancellor of the Exchequer, (Sir) Winston Churchill. His work with Churchill fed his political ambition. In the general election of 1929 he unsuccessfully contested the seat of Wolverhampton East as the Conservative candidate, but in the following year he was elected a member of the London County Council for North Kensington. In the landslide general election of 1931 he became Conservative MP for the East Toxteth division of Liverpool, a seat he held until in 1950 he switched to Beckenham.

On entering the House of Commons in 1931 he was invited to be parliamentary private secretary to Oliver Stanley [q.v.], then under-secretary of state in the Home Office. He remained with Stanley in the same capacity when he moved through the ministries of Transport, Labour, and Education to become president of the Board of Trade in 1937. Buchan-Hepburn thus acquired knowledge and experience of no less than five important government departments.

In 1939 he resigned his appointment with Stanley on being invited to be an assistant government whip and, shortly thereafter, a junior lord of the Treasury. He retired from that office to serve with the 11th (City of London Yeomanry) Light Anti-Aircraft Regiment of the Royal Artillery and was brigade major from 1940 to 1943.

In 1944 he was reappointed a junior lord of the Treasury, and when in July 1945 the Conservative government lost office, he became deputy Opposition chief whip. In 1948 he was promoted to chief Conservative whip, and on the return of his party to power in October 1951, he retained that office in the new government, becoming parliamentary secretary to the Treasury and a privy councillor.

As chief whip, both in Government and in Opposition, he was faultlessly efficient and entirely trusted by the prime minister, Churchill. He was also respected for his administrative competence by members of the Cabinet, though his occasional petulance did not always endear him to the back-benchers. He was loyal to Churchill personally, and devoted to him, but he was anxious for him to retire in favour of Anthony Eden (later the Earl of Avon, q.v.) at least two years before he actually did so, and from 1953 onward he made strenuous though unavailing efforts to that end.

In 1955, under Sir Anthony Eden, he became minister of works with a seat in the Cabinet. It was an office for which his architectural good taste and love of the arts made him eminently suitable, but in 1957, when Harold Macmillan (later Earl of Stockton) succeeded Eden in January, Buchan-Hepburn retired. He was created a peer, reviving a family title to become Baron Hailes. The first Lord Hailes, also called Patrick Hepburn, had been ennobled in 1452 and was the ancestor of the notorious Earl of Bothwell, husband of Mary, Queen of Scots [qq.v.].

Shortly afterwards Macmillan offered him the challenging assignment of governor-general of the newly created Federation of the West Indies. The British empire was about to be dissolved. In the process the experiment was made of uniting the larger British colonies in the Caribbean, several of which were clamouring for self-government, in one federation, even though the islands were separated by wide expanses of ocean. Lord and Lady Hailes established themselves at Government House, Port of Spain, the capital of Trinidad. Hailes worked hard to make the Federation acceptable to all concerned, and he won the confidence as well as the personal esteem of the political leaders in the different islands. However, it became clear that the concept, imaginative though it was, with the prospect of ultimately uniting all the British Caribbean islands in one closely knit independent Federation, could not be translated into lasting reality, for the conflicting claims and ambitions of Trinidad and Jamaica were irreconcilable.

So in 1962 the Federation was dissolved and the governor-general returned home, being appointed CH in recognition of his efforts to make a success of the endeavour. He had been appointed GBE in 1957. In 1963 he became chairman of the Historic Buildings Council for England, a task which he undertook with energy, making full use of the talents which were natural to him and the profound knowledge he had acquired over the years.

Hailes was intelligent, quick on the uptake, practical in handling awkward problems, articulate, and invariably painstaking. He was also tall and strikingly good-looking, with fair wavy hair, large grey eyes, and an engaging smile. At the same time he was vain, basically unsure of himself, and sensitive to criticism, whether direct or implied. Nor can patience be listed among his qualities, though he was consistently conscientious. A calm, serene discussion might suddenly, and often bewilderingly, end in storm and anger.

In 1945 Buchan-Hepburn married Diana Mary (died 1980), daughter of Brigadier-General the Hon. Charles Lambton and widow of Major William Hedworth Williamson. There were no children and the barony became extinct when Hailes died in London 5 November 1974.

[Personal knowledge.] J. R. COLVILLE

BULLARD, SIR EDWARD CRISP (1907–1980), geophysicist, was born 21 September 1907, the only son and eldest of four children, of whom the last were twins, of Edward John Bullard of the well-known Norwich brewing family, and his wife, Eleanor Howes, daughter of Sir Frank Crisp, first baronet, solicitor and vice-president of the Linnean Society. Bullard was educated at Repton and at Clare College, Cambridge, where he obtained first class honours in both parts of the natural sciences tripos (1928 and 1929), specializing in physics in part ii. He then spent two years at Cambridge as a research student in the Cavendish Laboratory before being appointed, in 1931, to the newly created post of demonstrator in the fledgling department of geodesy and geophysics. He gained his Ph.D. in 1932. He was Smithson research fellow of the Royal Society from 1936 to 1943 but upon the outbreak of war in 1939 joined HMS *Vernon*, the naval mine station, as an experimental officer.

Bullard's achievements from 1931 to 1939 were outstanding. The first two years that he spent in the Cavendish Laboratory were given to a joint study with (Sir) Harrie Massey of the scattering of slow electrons by gases in which the specifically relativistic effects predicted by the new equation of P. A. M. Dirac were established experimentally, but on moving to the department of geodesy and geophysics he turned his attention to new and improved methods for measurements in geophysics. He first developed a method in which the periods of freely swinging pendulums used in the comparative measurements of gravity were related through broadcast time signals, so that variations of gravity in a distant country could be measured from comparisons between pendulums in that country and others in Cambridge. Bullard undertook a survey in East Africa but then moved on to the systematic study of methods used for seismic surveys, applying his improvements in an investigation of the palaeozoic floor below East Anglia. Following that, he made measurements of the flow of heat out of the Earth in boreholes in South Africa. His most significant work before the war was undoubtedly his successful attempt to make seismic studies at sea, for, sailing from Channel ports in two Brixham trawlers, he initiated one of the most informative and influential fields of geophysics of the last half century, the geophysical study of the ocean floor.

At *Vernon*, Bullard was responsible for much of the very hazardous initial investigation of magnetic mines swept ashore by chance in the Thames estuary. He subsequently moved on to the demagnetizing of ships. The later part of the war he spent in operational research in the Admiralty, becoming assistant director of naval operational research from 1944 to 1945. He returned to Cambridge as reader in experimental geophysics in 1945, having been elected a fellow of Clare College in 1943, but in 1948 he moved to the University of Toronto as professor of physics until in 1950 he accepted appointment as director of the National Physical Laboratory at Teddington. He gained his Sc.D. in 1948. He returned to Cambridge as a senior research fellow of Gonville and Caius College in 1956, and subsequently received appointments as assistant director of research (1956–60) and reader in geophysics (1960–4) before being elected the first professor of geophysics (1964–74). He was a fellow of Churchill College from 1960 and held a professorship at the University of California at San Diego from 1963. After his retirement from his Cambridge chair in 1974, Bullard spent much of his time at La Jolla.

At Cambridge after the war Bullard took up again many of the investigations that he began before 1939 and especially marine geophysics, with seismic gravity and magnetic studies, so that, along with Woods Hole in the USA the small department at Cambridge became one of the two or three leading groups in that extremely important work. His investigations of the magnetic field of the Earth led him on to the theory of the self-sustaining dynamo as the source of the field and, partly as a result of the large calculations that were involved, he developed a keen interest in the applications of electronic computers including, subsequently, the recording and management of marine geophysical data at a time when such uses were novel. He maintained these interests at Toronto and at the National Physical Laboratory and after his return to Cambridge he both applied and encouraged others to apply the widest range of physical and mathematical studies to the investigation of the Earth, so that almost all subsequent methods of observation, except for those associated with spacecraft, can be seen to have arisen from his imagination and inspiration. Throughout his career he concentrated on the problems of the oceans and, while later ideas of plate tectonics came from others at Cambridge, his work provided the ground in which they could develop.

Bullard was called upon by many people and organizations for help and advice. He was a member of a number of government advisory committees in the United Kingdom and in the USA, and he was a director of his family brewery until it was sold and also of IBM (UK).

Bullard's scientific work was marked by inspired simplicity that always went to the heart of a problem. He was also very quick to see the point of anything he was being told, and then often advised his informant how to do better. He was at times forgetful or oblivious, but with that there went informality, enjoyment of the absurd, and a complete freedom from pomposity. He was very sociable and witty, but these traits covered also a deep seriousness about science and scholarship and the academic life, exemplified perhaps in his support for the retention of Latin as a qualification for entrance to Cambridge and also his interest in the history of science and in old books, of which he was a notable collector. He was a great innovator in geophysics and an inspiring supervisor and director; the geophysics department at Cambridge still bears his stamp as do many of the distinguished geophysicists who worked there in his time.

Bullard was elected to the Royal Society in 1941 and received many other honours; he was a foreign member of the American Academy of Arts and Sciences (1954), of the US National Academy of Sciences (1959), and of the American Philosophical Society (1969). He was awarded the Hughes medal of the Royal Society (1953), the Chree medal of the Physical Society (1956), the Day medal of the Geological Society of America (1959), the gold medal of the Royal Astronomical Society (1965), the Agassiz medal of the US National Academy of Science (1965), the Wollaston medal of the Geological Society of London (1967), the Vetlesen prize (1968), the Bowie medal (1975) and the Ewing medal (1978)—both of the American Geophysical Union—and the Royal medal of the Royal Society (1975). He was knighted in 1953.

Bullard married first, in 1931, Margaret Ellen, daughter of Frederick Bevan Thomas; they had four daughters, the middle two of whom were twins. This marriage was dissolved and in 1974 he married Mrs Ursula Curnow, daughter of Dr E. J. Cooke, of Christchurch, New Zealand. There are portraits at the National Physical Laboratory and in Churchill College. Bullard died 3 April 1980 in La Jolla, California.

[*Quarterly Journal of the Royal Astronomical Society*, vol. xxi, 1980, pp. 483–6; *The Times*, 5 April 1980; personal knowledge.] A. H. Cook

BULLARD, Sir READER WILLIAM (1885–1976), diplomat, was born at Walthamstow 5 December 1885, the younger child and only son of Charles Bullard, a dock labourer, and his wife, Mary Westlake. Later his father became a wharf foreman earning forty-two shillings per week, then enough to provide his small family with a roof, victuals, and reading matter. The son became a voracious reader, and at ten won an Essex county scholarship to the Drapers' School at Walthamstow. From here, with the help of evening classes, he hoisted himself up what he himself later called 'the rickety educational ladder' of the nineties to a pupil-teachership. He was good at languages, and, spotting by chance a crammer's prospectus for the Levant Consular Service, worked through a correspondence course at two dead and three living ones. He passed the relevant examination in 1906, and went for two years to Queens' College, Cambridge, to study Arabic, Turkish, and Persian under Professor E. G. Browne [q.v.].

His first post was Istanbul. Here he arrived in 1908 as a student interpreter, to catch a glimpse of the last stage of Abdul Hamid's gilded autocracy; most of his time was spent ciphering, filing, and badgering Turkish departments for their debts to British suppliers. He served as acting consul at Trebizond and Erzerum, and in the summer of 1914 was sent by horse, raft, and steamer to do the same at Basra for six months. Caught there by the war, he stayed in the Middle East for six years, rubbing shoulders first with the Indian Expeditionary Force and later with its chief political officer, Sir Percy Cox [q.v.]. He twice accompanied the latter to Persia. By May 1920 he was military governor of Baghdad.

Returning to England and settling in Oxford for what he hoped would be a long spell of leave, he was seized on by friends made in Iraq for the new Colonial Office department under (Sir) Winston Churchill, which was attempting to settle the ex-Ottoman lands. Among his colleagues were (Sir) Hubert Young, T. E. Lawrence [qq.v.], and others intent on fulfilling promises to the Hashemite amirs. They installed Faisal as king of Iraq, and Abdullah as amir of Jordan, and at least by Lawrence's standards, had paid a debt of honour and emerged 'with clean hands'.

Bullard preferred Foreign Services duties, and returned to these in 1923 as consul at Jedda. He led a limited social life, enlivened only by efforts to stop the Hashemite kings from cheating the pilgrims. He witnessed most of the prolonged siege of the port by Ibn Saud, but in 1925, leaving the Hashemite king, Ali, vacillating to the last, left for the consulate at Athens, where he became consul in 1926. From there he was moved to Addis Ababa (1929–30) and the Soviet Union (1930–4) where he watched first in Moscow and then in Leningrad the huge discrepancy between the Soviet picture of affairs and the realities of public and domestic life. In 1934 he was moved to the pleasanter atmosphere of Morocco.

His stay there was cut short by promotion into the Foreign Service proper. He returned to Jedda as minister in 1936, was appointed KCMG to match the rank of his predecessor, and whenever he met King Ibn Saud, enjoyed the royal appetite for discussion of world events. He never forgot the roar of laughter with which the king greeted his description of Harry St. John Philby [q.v.]—'Everyone's out of step but my Johnnie'. He crossed Arabia to watch the American search for oil, and to fix the frontiers between the Saudi kingdom and the British-protected amirates on the coast; the resultant map meant little to Ibn Saud. Before leaving, he entertained the Earl of Athlone [q.v.], the brother of Queen Mary, and his wife, Princess Alice. He had done well enough to be thought fit for a higher post, and in December 1939 was moved to Tehran, first as minister and from 1943 as ambassador to Persia.

His new work was not easy. Persia was thick with German spies. Reza Shah, at the height of his megalomaniac power, was a believer in German might. Not until Russia came into the war did he abdicate in favour of his young son, and leave for South Africa. Thereafter Bullard's chief concern was regulation of the supply line to Russia, chiefly by lorry; feeding the population (which varied by several million depending on whether the count was for lorry driving or for sugar rationing) was rendered almost impossible by Russian intrigue over supplies from the northern area that they occupied, and that held the bulk of the country's produce.

In December 1943 Churchill, Roosevelt, and Stalin arrived in Tehran for the second of their wartime conferences. To Bullard fell the task of organizing Churchill's entertainment of his colleagues; a plaque lettered in silver on the wall of the British embassy commemorates the dinner that he ran on Churchill's behalf. At the end of the war, though invited to accept another post, he preferred to retire.

His retirement was as busy as his diplomatic life. He was for five years director of the Institute of Commonwealth Studies, Oxford (1951–6); he wrote for Hutchinson's University Library *Britain and the Middle East* (1951), which is a model of brevity; he edited the third volume (1958) of the Chatham House *Middle Eastern Survey*; he chaired both the Libyan currency commission and the British delegation to the abortive conference on Buraimi oasis. He also took some part in local government affairs, and did much lecturing in Britain and the United States. In 1961 he published his readable autobiography—*The Camels Must Go.* He contributed the notice of Sir Hubert Young to this Dictionary.

But it is for his personality that he is chiefly remembered. He was a humble man. Short and stocky, with a craggy face and deep set eyes, he gave an immediate impression of rock-like solidarity, firmly held principles, and unyielding rectitude. His sense of fun was acute, and he was always ready to share his experiences and purvey his wisdom to students and colleagues, doing so from a mind stored with imaginative parallels, apt quotations, and forthright recollection.

He was appointed CIE (1916) for his services in Iraq, CMG (1933), and KCMG on appointment to Jedda in 1936. His KCB (1944), recommended by Churchill for his services during the Tehran conference, he always regarded as somewhat lightly earned. He was an honorary fellow of Queens' College, Cambridge, the School of Oriental and African Studies, London, and Lincoln College, Oxford.

He married in 1921 at Bamburgh, Northumberland, Miriam (died 1973), daughter of Arthur Lionel Smith [q.v.], master of Balliol College, Oxford; they had four sons and a daughter. On his appointment to Russia, she and he realized that if these were to be educated as they wished, a house of their own in Oxford was a necessity. Only in Addis Ababa were they all together for any length of time. The choice was vindicated. One son became a fellow of All Souls, and another captained the university at rugby. To Bullard's delight, both of these followed him into the Foreign Service.

As a well-loved grandfather, he survived his wife by three years, dying in his son's house at West Hendred, Wantage, 24 May 1976. He stands out as the only diplomat of his era who reached the top from a primary school start.

[Sir Reader Bullard, *The Camels Must Go* (autobiography), 1961; personal knowledge.]

ELIZABETH MONROE

BULLER, REGINALD EDWARD MANNINGHAM-, VISCOUNT DILHORNE (1905–1980), lord chancellor. [See MANNINGHAM-BULLER.]

BULLOCK, SIR CHRISTOPHER LLEWELLYN (1891–1972), public servant, scholar, and business man, was born 10 November 1891 at Whiston, Northamptonshire, the second child and second son in the family of seven children (one of whom died at birth) of the (Revd) Llewellyn Christopher Watson Bullock, later rector of Great and Little Wigborough, Essex, and his wife, Cecil Augusta Margaret Isabella, daughter of Edmund Robert Spearman, CMG, a Leeds business man, and granddaughter of the fifth Earl of Orkney. He was educated at Rugby, where his father was a master, becoming captain of the Running Eight and gaining a classical scholarship to Trinity College, Cambridge, where he had a truly remarkable career. He won not only the Abbott and Porson university scholarships in classics, the Members' Latin essay prize, and the Browne medals for Latin ode (twice) and Greek epigram, but also the Charles Oldham Shakespeare scholarship and the Whewell scholarship in international law. He was placed in the first division of the first class of the classical tripos in 1913 and was offered a fellowship at Trinity.

It was, however, to the public service that Bullock turned. After taking first place in the open competition for the Home and Indian Civil Services in 1914, he chose India. But World War I intervened before he took up his appointment and he volunteered for service with the Rifle Brigade. He was seriously wounded at Ypres in 1915 and mentioned in dispatches; later, seconded to the Royal Flying Corps, he gained his wings first as an observer and then as a pilot. Becoming unfit for flying in 1917, he was appointed to the air staff and, in 1919, became principal private secretary to (Sir) Winston Churchill, the secretary of state for air. From 1923 to 1930 he served successive secretaries of state in the same capacity and, in 1931, at the exceptionally early age of thirty-nine, was promoted directly to permanent secretary of the Air Ministry and member of the Air Council.

It was at the Air Ministry that Bullock's best work was done. In 1919 the government had decided to establish a permanent independent Royal Air Force and Sir H. M. (later Lord) Trenchard [q.v.] was given the task of creating and building up the new service. Bullock became his right-hand-man on the civilian side and Trenchard, when he retired in 1929, recorded his gratitude for Bullock's great contribution during what he called 'the hardest years that I think any Department could pass through'. For there were forces in Whitehall, particularly in the other Service departments and in the Treasury, that were hostile to the young Royal Air Force and its very survival as a separate service was at times in doubt. Later, the rising menace of Nazism changed all this and the expansion of the RAF became a concern of first importance. Bullock's part in this was crucial. Against the pacific temper and financial stringency of the times, he strove—no one more—to awaken public and Parliament to the need for strengthening the RAF to meet the dangers ahead, his powerful intellect and superb administrative skills harnessed unstintingly to the task and himself drafting nearly all important air staff papers for the Cabinet. It was during these critical years that decisions were taken in the Air Ministry that were vital to Britain's air defence capability when war finally came. In the opinion of Lord Hankey [q.v.], secretary of the Cabinet and of the Committee of Imperial Defence, of all the civil servants he had known, Bullock had made by far the greatest creative contribution to the defence effort.

Bullock also made a major contribution during the 1920s and 30s to the development of civil aviation, in particular to the pioneering Empire air mail scheme.

Bullock had a strong, at times combative, personality and, once embarked upon a course in which he believed, was not easily turned aside. Inevitably, this made him enemies during his years at the Air Ministry, notably in the Treasury. This was no doubt a factor in his summary dismissal in 1936. This followed a report by a board of inquiry, appointed by the prime minister, to investigate allegations that Bullock had misused his official position by writing to the chairman of Imperial Airways (with which the Air Ministry was still in negotiation over the Empire air mail scheme) regarding the possibility that, if at some future date he were to retire prematurely from the Civil Service, he (Bullock) might become a government director, and ultimately chairman, of the company. Though, as a result of the inquiry, the prime minister (Stanley Baldwin) approved dismissal, he later wrote that, had he known the whole story, he would never have done so. Its injustice was implicitly recognized during World War II, when Bullock was invited (but felt unable because of commitments to vital war work) to resume a permanent secretary's appointment in the Civil Service. But public acknowledgement of the wrongness of the decision (and tribute to his immense contribution to the RAF and the nation) was not paid until after his death, when his memorial service was attended by a representative of the prime minister, members of the Air Force Board, and the permanent under-secretary of the Ministry of Defence.

After 1936 Bullock developed a range of business interests, becoming a director of a number of well-known companies and remained active in business until his late seventies. He married in 1917 Barbara May, daughter of Henry Lupton, of Leeds and Torquay, and had two sons, both of whom have had successful careers in the public service.

Bullock was appointed OBE in 1919, CBE in 1926, CB in 1929, and KCB in 1932. He died in London 16 May 1972.

[Private information; personal knowledge.]

GEOFFREY-LLOYD

BULLOCK, Sir ERNEST (1890–1979), organist, composer, and teacher, was born in Wigan 15 September 1890, the youngest child of Thomas Bullock and his wife, Eliza Stout. He had one sister, the eldest of the family, and four brothers, and both his parents died while he was still at school. As a small boy he joined the choir at Wigan parish church, an event that proved decisive in his career by bringing him into the care of (Sir) E. C. Bairstow [q.v.], then organist at Wigan. Bairstow recognized the boy's talent and his difficult circumstances, and took him as an articled pupil, providing general education at Wigan Grammar School. When Bairstow moved to Leeds in 1906 he took the pupil with him into his own home, and assumed responsibility for an apprenticeship that was severe but enlightened. Bullock was later to write the notice of Bairstow for this Dictionary.

Appointed in 1912 to be assistant to (Sir) S. H. Nicholson [q.v.] at Manchester, Bullock soon became known as a promising composer of church music, chamber music, and songs, and it seemed that his future lay in the field of composition. In 1914 he obtained his D.Mus. (Durham). But the war upset all his plans, and it was not until 1919, after four years of arduous and distinguished service in France, as a captain and adjutant in the King's Own Yorkshire Light Infantry, that he was able to return to music.

A few months as organist at St. Michael's College, Tenbury, prepared him for an important spell from 1919 to 1928 as organist at Exeter Cathedral, where, with determination that was considered at times ruthless, he put new life into the music of the cathedral, the diocese, and the whole area.

Promoted to Westminster Abbey in 1928 Bullock brought similar reforming energy into a reorganization of the daily choral offices and many special occasions, the most spectacular of which was the coronation of 1937, whose music was said to be the finest ever heard in Westminster Abbey. Bullock's own fanfares, composed for the ceremony, were greatly admired, and are still in use.

His life was soon to be disrupted for a second time by war. After the bombing in 1940, in which his house, with all his property and papers, was destroyed, the Abbey music establishment had to be dispersed, and Bullock's career seemed to be in ruins. In fact it was not so much ruined as wrenched violently into a new direction when in 1941 he was appointed to be principal of the Royal Scottish Academy of Music and Drama, a post at that time involving also the professorship of music in the University of Glasgow.

Here, as in earlier years at Exeter, his task was one of reconstruction and development. Wartime difficulties had been severe and had not been lessened by animosities among leading local musicians: it was therefore something of a triumph for an Englishman, and an uncompromising one, to solve many problems and revive many loyalties by an example of generous musicianship and personal integrity. In eleven years Bullock made a significant contribution to Scottish music.

It was with this varied experience that Bullock returned to London in January 1953 to follow Sir George Dyson [q.v.] as director of the Royal College of Music, where little surprise was felt when he proved to be an able administrator and a director as enterprising as financial conditions allowed. What had not been so confidently foreseen was the skill that he showed in dealing with temperamental students and even more temperamental professors. His own musical influence, moreover, was more far-reaching than was immediately recognized, his classes in improvisation, in particular, being considered by many discerning students as among the finest experiences that the curriculum offered.

Although circumstances did not allow him to devote a major part of his time to composition Bullock produced throughout his career a steady stream of music for church and secular use, some of which was widely performed.

Before 1914 his style, derived from Sir C. H. H. Parry and Sir C. V. Stanford [qq.v.], had been a warmly romantic one; but after the war, influenced by the new fashion for austerity, modal harmony, and homespun diatonic melodies, it became more reticent but not less basically emotional. In his music, as in his life, Bullock was disciplined, fastidious, and somewhat austere. His friends could rely on absolute loyalty and generosity but realized that there was no welcome for anything frivolous, pretentious, or effusive.

Bullock was appointed CVO in 1937 and knighted in 1951. In 1955 he was given an honorary LL D at Glasgow University. He was also honorary RAM and president of the Royal College of Organists (1951–2). After retirement from the Royal College in 1960 he settled in Long Crendon, Buckinghamshire, where he died 23 May 1979. His widow, a devoted companion for sixty years, survived him by only a few months. He had married in 1919 Margery, daughter of George Hope Newborn, solicitor, of Epworth, Lincolnshire. They had two sons and a daughter.

There is a portrait in the Royal College of Music.

[Personal knowledge.] THOMAS ARMSTRONG

BULMAN, OLIVER MEREDITH BOONE (1902–1974), geologist, was born 20 May 1902 at Wandsworth, the second of three children and younger son of Henry Herbert Bulman RBA, artist, and his wife, Beatrice Elizabeth Boone, daughter of W. A. Boone ARCA, of Canterbury and Ramsgate, art master of King's School, Canterbury. Of the three Bulman children, only Oliver inherited the graphic ability which he was to use so effectively when making, with his left hand, the hundreds of drawings and diagrams illustrating his scientific papers, books, and lectures; some people even collected his 'doodles' after committee meetings.

He went to Battersea Grammar School in 1910, but an operation for a malignant cyst in his left femur kept him at home for a year when he was twelve years old. Wishing to study geology, which his school could not provide, he became an evening—and later a day—student at Chelsea Polytechnic as a pupil of A. J. Maslen. He gained the London University geology scholarship in 1920 and in 1921 he proceeded to Imperial College where he studied geology under the aegis of W. W. Watts, A. Morley Davies, and others;

his instructors in zoology were E. W. MacBride, and Lancelot Hogben [q.v.]; he also attended vertebrate palaeontology lectures by D. M. S. Watson [q.v.] at University College London. In 1923 he took a first class B.Sc. in geology with zoology as the subsidiary subject and also the ARCS.

Awarded a Beit scientific research fellowship, he proceeded to a Ph.D. degree jointly with (Sir) C. J. Stubblefield with a thesis entitled 'The Shineton Shales of the Wrekin district, Shropshire'. This led him to receive an 1851 senior studentship. He spent the first year of its tenure (1925–6) at Imperial College where among his fellow research students was W. F. Whittard [q.v.] with whom he wrote a paper on Permian Branchiosaurid amphibia. For the remaining two years of the studentship, he moved to Sidney Sussex College, Cambridge, to study dendroid graptolites under the supervision of Gertrude Lilian Elles at the Sedgwick Museum. As well as Whittard (1902–66), his fellow research students included L. R. Wager [q.v.] and Maurice Black who died three months before him.

Bulman's researches were faciliated by following a technique devised by Gerhard Holm of using hydrochloric or hydrofluoric acid to dissolve the rock matrix from the graptolite and also by making serial sections by grinding as did W. J. Sollas [q.v.] for *Palaeospondylus*. Bulman produced two parts of the Palaeontographical Society's monograph on *British Dendroid Graptolites* (1927 and 1928) which, with several subsidiary papers, earned him a Cambridge Ph.D. degree (1926). Bulman was awarded the Imperial College Huxley memorial medal when he returned there in 1928, as a demonstrator in the zoology department. He moved in 1929 to a similar post in the geology department; then in 1931 he became a demonstrator in geology at Cambridge.

Whereas previously he had been elucidating the structure of dendroid graptolites, he turned to true graptolites when E. A. Sensiö of Stockholm placed with him for description a series of South American graptolites, isolated from their matrices by G. Holm. Assisted by Holm's skilfully retouched photographs, Bulman produced a spectacular paper published in the *Arkiv för Zoologie*. This paper was followed by a seven-part study of Scandinavian graptolites, also published in the *Arkiv*. Bulman provided new information concerning the early growth stages of graptolite taxa which had a bearing on the interpretation of the evolution of particular groups. Appreciation of his views was helped by the wax enlargements made from serial sections of the fossils. He contributed the article on Graptolithina to the *Handbuch der Paläozoologie* (ed. O. H. Schindewolf, 1938) but perhaps his most influential publication was the second edition (1970) of his *Graptolithina* volume (in part with R. B. Rickards) of the *Treatise on Invertebrate Paleontology* (ed. C. Teichert).

After W. B. R. King [q.v.] became Woodwardian professor at Cambridge in 1943, Bulman was made reader in palaeozoology (1944). When King retired in 1955 Bulman succeeded to his post and occupied the chair until he resigned in 1966, when he became emeritus professor. He retained editorship of the *Geological Magazine*, which he took up in 1934, until 1972. With W. G. Fearnsides [q.v.] he was author of the sixpenny Penguin *Geology in the Service of Man* (1944, third edn. 1961).

Elected FRS in 1940, he served on the Royal Society's council in 1952–4 and as a trustee of the British Museum (Natural History) from 1963 to 1970. He became successively president of the geology section of the British Association (1959), the Palaeontological Association (1960–2), the Geological Society (1962–4), and the Palaeontographical Society (1971–4). He was a fellow of Sidney Sussex College (1944) and of Imperial College (1961). He received the Lyell medal of the Geological Society (1953) and an honorary Dr.Phil. of Oslo University (1965). He was Sc.D. of Cambridge University and an honorary member of the Geological Society of Stockholm and of the Palaeontological Society of India. A volume of twenty essays on graptolites, by his students and friends, designed to form a Festschrift, but destined to be a memorial tribute to him, was published by the Palaeontological Association (1974) to which body he had given an inaugural address in 1958.

Bulman was six feet tall but sparsely built. Though he could strongly voice dislike of some, he was kindly and generous, and a staunch friend of others; he had a ready wit and was especially keen to help the careers of his students. He was a lucid and inspiring teacher.

In 1938 Bulman married Marguerite, the elder daughter of William George Fearnsides FRS [q.v.], professor of geology at Sheffield University, and his wife, Beatrix, daughter of Professor William Whitehead Watts FRS. They had a son and three daughters. Bulman died at his home in Cambridge 18 February 1974.

[*The Times*, 20 February 1974; *Annual Report* of the Geological Society of London, 1974; R. B. Rickards and D. E. Jackson, *Special Papers in Palaeontology*, no. 13, 1974, pp. 1–17; Sir James Stubblefield in *Biographical Memoirs of Fellows of the Royal Society*, vol. xxi, 1975; personal knowledge.] JAMES STUBBLEFIELD

BURNS, SIR ALAN CUTHBERT MAXWELL (1887–1980), colonial governor, was born 9 November 1887, at Basseterre, St. Kitts, the fourth son and fifth child of James Burns, treasurer of the presidency of St. Christopher-

Nevis and member of the executive council of the Leeward Islands, and his wife, Agnes Zulma Delisle. He was educated at St. Edmund's College, Ware. One of his brothers, Cecil Delisle, was an academic; another, Robert Edward Burns, like their father and grandfather, was in the Colonial Service; and a third, Emil, was a leading British communist. In 1905 he was appointed to the Treasury and Customs Department of St. Kitts. His appointment in 1909 as clerk to the magistrate of Basseterre was followed by that of deputy coroner and JP for St. Kitts, magistrate on Anguilla, and in 1912 clerk and provincial secretary to the administrator of Dominica.

In 1912 he became supervisor of customs in Nigeria, and served in Koko and Lagos. No sooner had he earned promotion to the secretariat cadre than he enlisted in the West African Regiment. He saw service in the Cameroons campaign, became adjutant of the Nigeria Land Contingent, and took part in the Egba expedition of 1918. As private secretary to Sir Frederick (later Lord) Lugard and then to Sir Hugh Clifford [qq.v.], Burns (like the latter, a Roman Catholic) confirmed his reputation as a highly efficient staff officer, and he was soon mounting the promotional secretariat ladder for Colonial Service high-climbers. A period as colonial secretary of the Bahamas from 1924 to 1929, during which he acted as governor, was followed by his return to Nigeria, for further grooming for high office, as deputy chief secretary. In 1934, Burns, still under fifty, was given his first governorship, that of British Honduras.

In 1940 he was seconded to the Colonial Office on special duty in the rank of assistant under-secretary, as part of the wartime experiment of bringing a serving governor into Whitehall. He became governor of the Gold Coast in 1941, and acted as governor of Nigeria for five months in 1942. At his initiative, and to his unending pride, in 1942 he persuaded a reluctant Colonial Office to admit Africans on to the executive council of the governor of the Gold Coast, and to sanction the appointment of Africans as district commissioners there. He also inspired the constitutional advances of 1946, which provided for an unofficial majority in the Gold Coast legislative council. The fact that the Watson commission enquiring into the Accra riots of 1948 stigmatized the Burns constitution as outmoded at birth perhaps reflects more on the Gold Coast's capacity for political pioneering than on Burns's foresight. His last year in Accra was, for him, marred by the so-called 'juju murder' appeal and the decision in London prompted Burns's resignation. In 1945 his name was put forward by the Colonial Office for the governorship of the new Malayan Union, but the colonial secretary's nomination was not accepted by Downing Street. From 1947 until his retirement in 1956 Burns, following the proconsular footsteps of his old master Lugard after World War I, became Britain's representative on the trusteeship council of the UN. At the age of seventy-two he accepted the chairmanship of an enquiry into land resources and population problems in Fiji.

Burns was a typical example of a scholar-administrator. A scrupulous and hard-working official, he also delved into African history, so that his well-travelled career was marked by a number of authoritative books. His first contained an index to the laws of the Leeward Islands. In 1917 he began a comprehensive annual review, the *Nigeria Handbook*; he also initiated the *Nigeria Civil Service List*. His *History of Nigeria*, first published in 1929, had reached its eighth revised edition by the time of his death. After his retirement he published four books: *Colour Prejudice* (1948), originally written when he was governor of British Honduras, *History of the British West Indies* (1954), *Colonial Civil Servant* (1949), and *In Defence of Colonies* (1957), a riposte to the positive anti-colonialism of the UN which he had found so disillusioning. On completion of his Fiji mission, he published a volume on that country in the Corona series (1963), and in his nineties he contributed to the BBC series of reminiscences: 'Tales from the Dark Continent'.

Burns's recreations were cricket, writing, ornithology (he maintained an aviary in Christiansborg Castle), and bridge (at one time in the 1920s he was bridge correspondent of the *Daily Telegraph* and wrote a book on the game). He served as a purposeful president of the Hakluyt Society, chairman of the Royal Commonwealth Society library committee, and as a council member of the Zoological Society. He had an assertive humanity and an ever-ready humour. Invariably he wore a dark suit. Sparing with words, he was never short on kindness or courtesy. In character and the stout expression of his opinions he was a big man, straight dealing, and impatient of cant.

Burns was appointed CMG in 1927, KCMG in 1936, and GCMG in 1946. He was made a Knight of St. John of Jerusalem in 1942.

In 1914 he married Kathleen ('Kate') Fitzpatrick, daughter of Robert Allman Hardtman, sugar planter, of Antigua. She died in 1970. There were two daughters of the marriage. He died 29 September 1980 at the Westminster Hospital, London.

[*The Times*, 1 October 1980; Sir Alan Burns, *Colonial Civil Servant* (autobiography), 1949; *Colonial Office List*; A. H. M. Kirk-Greene (ed.), *Biographical Dictionary of the British Colonial Governor*, 1980; D. H. Simpson, Royal

Commonwealth Society *Library Notes*, 239/1980; *West Africa*, 20 October 1980; tape-recorded interview, 14 September 1967, Oxford Colonial Records Project; private information; personal knowledge.]

A. H. M. KIRK-GREENE

BURRA, EDWARD JOHN (1905–1976), painter, was born in South Kensington, London, 29 March 1905, (he had an elder brother who died young and a younger sister), the son of Henry Curteis Burra of Rye, Sussex, a barrister by profession who sat as a JP and was at one time chairman of East Sussex County Council, and his wife, Ermentrude Ann, daughter of J. S. O. Robertson-Luxford of Salehurst, Sussex.

Burra went to Northaw Place preparatory school, Potters Bar, but had to be withdrawn on account of ill health. He suffered all his life from anaemia. He was at Chelsea Polytechnic school of art 1921–3 and the Royal College of Art 1923–5. In his early paintings of figures in landscapes he used bright colours decoratively, in a manner recalling the designs of Bakst and others for the Russian Ballet and also contemporary book illustration.

From 1926 Burra made regular trips to Paris, visiting night-clubs and music-halls as well as the art galleries. As an artist he was attracted to the seamier side of life, finding his subjects in the sailors' bars and clubs in the Mediterranean ports of Marseilles and Toulon. He had a keen eye for human eccentricities and an excellent visual memory which enabled him to capture without elaborate sketching scenes, poses, and styles of dress which he would recreate, subtly satirized, in the studio. Though aware of the tradition of French urban realism from Toulouse-Lautrec to Fernand Léger, Burra's linearity and obsessive detail mark his Englishness. In 1931 he met in Rye the American poet Conrad Aiken who shared his attraction to low-life subjects, and in 1933–4 Burra made the first of at least four visits to America (others were in 1937, 1948, and 1955), spending part of the time in Harlem where he observed Negro life with a mixture of amused curiosity and detachment.

From the beginning Burra worked chiefly in water-colour, but made a small number of oil paintings between 1927 and 1931, and a few collages, reminiscent of the work of the Berlin Dadaists, in 1929–30. Also in the early years he made numerous ink drawings of figure groups unrelated to paintings, a practice he later discontinued. His paintings, especially from the mid-thirties, were often unusually large for the water-colour medium, and frequently consist of more than one sheet of paper joined together. Burra liked to work on a flat table-top, drawing the design in lightly in pencil and completing the picture section by section in a manner that recalls the Pre-Raphaelites.

Burra had his first one-man shows at the Leicester Galleries in 1929 and 1932. Encouraged by Paul Nash [q.v.], a friend and neighbour at Rye, he joined in 1933 the avant-garde Unit One, the only artists' group he was ever a member of. In 1936 he showed both at the International Surrealist Exhibition in London and in 'Fantastic Art, Dada, Surrealism' at the Museum of Modern Art, New York. Though influenced by a number of painters in the Surrealist circle—Georgio de Chirico, Max Ernst, and Salvador Dali, in particular—Burra was not in the truest sense a Surrealist. The more conservative side of his temperament shared with P. Wyndham Lewis [q.v.], whom he admired, a notion of realism founded on rigorous outline drawing wich ran counter to the more anarchic aspects of Surrealism.

The Spanish civil war and World War II stimulated important changes in Burra's art: while a strong fantasy element persisted, Burra became less the wry, uncommitted observer, his designs became stronger and clearer, and his imagination responded to the violence with images of brutish soldiers, weird, hooded skeletons, and predatory monsters in bird-like masks. Burra showed these pictures at the Redfern Gallery in 1942, in his first exhibition for a decade. He was beginning to receive more recognition, with five pictures entering the Tate Gallery's collection between 1939 and 1942, and the publication in 1945 of a monograph in the Penguin Modern Painters series with an introduction by (Sir) John Rothenstein. Later he was fortunate in developing a particularly happy relationship with the Lefevre Gallery where he showed more or less biennially from 1952. The public and critical response to the exhibitions, though generally favourable was modest, and it was not until the retrospective exhibition at the Tate in 1973 that his work began to be widely appreciated. He was appointed CBE in 1971.

Latterly Burra turned increasingly to landscape for his subjects, liking especially lonely places such as the west of Ireland, the Yorkshire moors, north Wales, and the Lake District. In immediate appearance his pictures were calmer than before, but he continued none the less to imbue his landscapes, and even arrangements of flowers and other still-life subjects, with a menacing aspect. Parallel with his other work Burra was involved in designing for the theatre. Starting with sets and costume for (Sir) Frederick Ashton's production in 1931 of the ballet *Rio Grande*, Burra worked between then and the late 1950s on six ballets, an opera, and a musical play.

Except when he was at art school Burra lived in or near Rye all his life. He has been called a recluse, but this is not true. Though a private man and not one for casual acquaintances, he had long-standing and valued friendships, several of them dating from his art school days. The range of his activities was circumscribed by his poor health. He loved travel and discovering new places, and he read widely, if not systematically, in literature and poetry, in French and Spanish as well as English. He made regular visits to London for the art exhibitions and, above all, the cinema.

Burra was unmarried. He died in hospital at Hastings 22 October 1976. There was a posthumous exhibition of his work at the Hayward Gallery in 1985.

[John Rothenstein, *Edward Burra* (Penguin Modern Painters), 1945, and *Edward Burra* (Tate Gallery publications), 1973; William Chappell (ed.), *Edward Burra. A Painter Remembered by his Friends*, 1982, and *Well Dearie! The Letters of Edward Burra*, 1985; Andrew Causey, *Edward Burra Complete Catalogue*, 1985.] ANDREW CAUSEY

BURROWS, SIR FREDERICK JOHN (1887–1973), president of the National Union of Railwaymen and last governor of Bengal, was born 3 July 1887 at Bollow, Westbury on Severn, Gloucestershire, the fifth of five sons and youngest of eleven children of John Burrows, general labourer, and his wife, Ellen Abell.

Burrows was the only trade-union leader to become head of an Indian province. With only three short breaks involving war service from 1914 to 1918, the presidency of the NUR from 1942 to 1944, and membership of the Ceylon constitutional commission in 1944, Burrows was always a working railwayman until his appointment as governor of Bengal in August 1945. Educated at Walmore Hill School, he became a goods checker for the Great Western Railway at the wayside halt of Backney before war service took him into the Grenadier Guards in 1914. He became company sergeant-major and won the meritorious service medal, returning to the railway at Grange Court in 1919 and moving thence to Ross in the early 1920s. For sixteen years he served as secretary of the Ross branch of the NUR. He was elected to the national executive in 1938, and finally to the presidency in 1942.

Although Burrows became a member of the executive of the Labour Party in 1942 he was not a national figure in the Labour movement. Politically he stood on the right of the party, though the viceroy of India, Viscount (later Earl) Wavell [q.v.], probably exaggerated when he described him in 1945 as 'a complete conservative in his ideas'. Burrows was to leave the party in 1959 over the issue of steel nationalization, thereafter describing himself as an independent. His tact, moderation, and patient pragmatism in pay negotiations as a wartime trade-union leader commended themselves to (Sir) Winston Churchill, who selected him in 1944 as one of the Labour members of the commission for the revision of the Ceylon constitution chaired by Lord Soulbury. Attlee records in his memoirs that Burrows's impressive performance both on this commission and subsequently on the Colonial Advisory Board in early 1945 won 'the highest appreciation on all sides'.

When the Bengal governorship fell vacant after the Labour election victory in 1945, Attlee recommended this 'former parcels clerk' with some warmth for the most crucial of the Indian governorships. Burrows's appointment aroused some misgivings. The outgoing governor, R. G. (later Lord) Casey [q.v.], told Wavell that Burrows would be 'all at sea' in Bengal and in the hands of his officials for the first six months. After his first meeting with Burrows the viceroy, however, expressed optimism. Wavell described him in various passages of his journal as 'an attractive person, steady, sensible, straight, with a slow West Country speech . . . solid, imperturbable and quietly humorous' and as a 'really sterling character, the best type of Englishman we breed'. Such qualities were to be severely tested in the situation confronting the government of Bengal on Burrows's arrival in February 1946. As governor he had to defuse communist agitation and resolve a series of industrial strikes; but his main task was to pacify mounting communal friction between Muslims and Hindus. The small numbers and low morale of the Calcutta police, and the diminishing confidence and authority of both Indian army units and the civil administration in the last two years of British rule meant that the instruments for achieving a peaceful transition of power were deteriorating as communal disturbances increased.

Burrows's problems were compounded by his difficulties in dealing with the Muslim-dominated government of Bengal elected in 1946. The Bengal cabinet led by H. S. Suhrawardy promoted locally the national strategies of agitation devised by the Muslim League of M. A. Jinnah [q.v.]. These were directed partly against the Hindu community. The ensuing communal upheavals in Calcutta and at Noakhali led to considerable loss of life, though Burrows's prompt and intelligent disposition of police and military units helped to contain the further spread of disorder. It is in part Burrows's achievement that, while in the Punjab disorders continued to escalate, in 1947 up to the transfer of power Bengal remained calm.

On his return to England Burrows served as chairman of the Agricultural Land Commission from 1948 until 1963 and as a director of Lloyds Bank from 1950 to 1958. These appointments did not hinder his growing involvement in county and local affairs. He became high sheriff of Herefordshire in 1955, and chairman of the Wye

River Authority in 1965; and he served as deputy lieutenant for the county from 1950 until his death in 1973. He was appointed GCIE in 1945 and GCSI in 1947.

In 1912 Burrows married Dora Beatrice (died 1968), daughter of G. Hutchings, a railway guard, of Hereford. Lady Burrows was awarded the Kaiser-i-Hind gold medal in 1947. They had one son and one daughter. Burrows died at Ross on Wye, Herefordshire, 20 April 1973.

[Obituaries from *The Times*, 24 April 1973, and *Ross Gazette*; Nicholas Mansergh and Penderel Moon (eds.), *The Transfer of Power*, vols. vi–ix, 1976–80; Penderel Moon (ed.), *Wavell: the Viceroy's Journal*, 1973; information from the family.] PATRICK J. N. TUCK

BURT, SIR CYRIL LODOWIC (1883–1971), psychologist, was born in Westminster 3 March 1883, the elder child of Cyril Cecil Barrow Burt (born 1857) and his wife, Martha Evans, of Monmouth. At the time of his son's birth Burt senior was a medical student at the Westminster Hospital. He qualified MRCS in 1887 and LRCP in 1890, and in 1893 moved to a country practice at Snitterfield in Warwickshire, which remained the family home for thirty years. There was one other child of the marriage, Marion Burt (1891–1978), who became a school medical officer.

Burt received a classical education at King's School, Warwick, Christ's Hospital (then located in the City of London) and Jesus College, Oxford, where he won a scholarship. He had, however, early become interested in psychology largely as a result of contact with (Sir) Francis Galton [q.v.], to members of whose family living in Warwickshire Dr Burt was general physician. Burt's interest was confirmed when he attended the Oxford lectures of William McDougall [q.v.], as an optional part of his 'Greats' curriculum. Having obtained second classes in both classical honour moderations (1904) and *literae humaniores* (1906), it was at McDougall's instigation that in 1907 Burt participated in the anthropometric survey of the British people sponsored by the British Association for the Advancement of Science. His task was to check some of the ideas on the existence and nature of general intelligence recently propounded by Charles Spearman [q.v.]. This project set the pattern for the whole of Burt's career. From the publication of his first article in 1909 to his death in 1971 the central topic of Burt's interest was intelligence, its distribution in the population, and its determination largely, as Galton had maintained, by hereditary influences. In 1907 Burt was awarded the John Locke scholarship in mental philosophy by the University of Oxford, and this enabled him to spend the summer of 1908 at the University of Würzburg and study under the distinguished German psychologist, Oswald Külpe.

Burt's first post was at the University of Liverpool, where he remained for five years (1908–13) as lecturer in psychology attached to the department of physiology headed by (Sir) Charles Sherrington [q.v.]. While in Liverpool he continued his researches into intelligence, and lectured in psychology to medical, science, and education students.

In 1913 Burt was appointed psychologist, part-time, to the London County Council. This was a new post, and the first of its kind in Great Britain. Burt remained with the LCC from 1913 to 1932, combining his council duties with several other part-time posts: assistant in the Cambridge psychological laboratory (1912–13), in the Ministry of Munitions, at the National Institute of Industrial Psychology (where he headed the vocational guidance department from 1922 to 1924), and finally at the London Day Training College, where he was part-time professor of educational psychology from 1924 to 1932. Burt's main task as LCC psychologist was to identify and assess pupils who required special educational treatment, either by reason of mental subnormality or behavioural maladjustment, and to assist in the selection of gifted pupils for secondary education. This work of Burt's was of a highly important pioneering nature, and laid the foundations of educational psychology and child guidance in England and Wales. The material he collected during these years formed the basis of his classic works, *The Distribution and Relations of Educational Abilities* (1917), *Mental and Scholastic Tests* (1921), *The Young Delinquent* (1925), and *The Backward Child* (1937).

In 1932 Burt was appointed to the chair of psychology at University College, London, in succession to Charles Spearman. He held this post until his retirement in 1950, five years of his tenure of the chair being spent at Aberystwyth as a result of wartime evacuation. Almost immediately after moving to University College Burt married Joyce Muriel, daughter of a deceased commercial traveller, P. F. Woods. Joyce Woods had been one of his students at the London Day Training College after graduating in English and history from King's College, London. The marriage took place at the registry office at Upton-upon-Severn on 9 April 1932. Joyce Woods was twenty-three years of age at the time; Burt was then forty-nine. This disparity of ages was probably one reason for the final breakdown of the marriage in 1950. Joyce Burt decided to take up medicine in the 1930s, and qualified in 1943. Eventually she became a distinguished gynaecologist and FRCOG (1960). There were no children of the marriage.

While at University College Burt turned his interests to theoretical and methodological questions, chief among which was factor analysis, a statistical technique for extracting a small number of basic dimensions, or factors, from a large population of variable measurements. His views which differed in certain respects from those of his predecessor, Spearman, were set out definitively in *The Factors of the Mind* (1940) and later in the pages of the *British Journal of Statistical Psychology*, of which he was joint editor. This work, together with advisory work, both civil and military, in which Burt became increasingly involved following his University College appointment, brought Burt much renown and various distinctions. He was awarded honorary degrees at Aberdeen and Reading; was knighted in 1946; was elected to a fellowship of the British Academy in 1950; and in the same year was made an honorary fellow of Jesus College, Oxford.

Burt lived for twenty-one years in retirement, keeping extremely busy, writing articles, reviewing books and manuscripts, examining, editing the statistical journal, and until 1960 giving occasional lectures. Most of his publications during this period were of a theoretical nature—on consciousness, values, psychical research, factor analysis, and, in particular, the multifactorial theory of inheritance. These final years were, however, a period of considerable tension and difficulty. Burt's marriage had broken down; his health was problematical (in 1941 he had developed Ménière's disease); he had lost many of his personal papers and research records in the wartime bombing of University College; his relations with former colleagues became more and more strained; and his views on the inheritance of intelligence were becoming increasingly unpopular and under attack. After his death several striking anomalies were discovered, particularly in his work on inheritance, and an examination of his diaries and other material confirmed beyond reasonable doubt that some of his data on inheritance and on the decline of educational standards were, as alleged by his critics, fabricated. His reputation, therefore, suffered a catastrophic decline not long after his death, which occurred in London 10 October 1971.

Nevertheless Burt's great contributions to psychology, particularly in the field of education in the 1920s and 1930s, deserve to be recognized. He was one of the pioneers, and was largely responsible for the establishment of educational psychology on a sound basis in this country. He was a man of great ability and learning; well versed in philosophy; with a wide knowledge of the sciences; and he became a self-taught mathematician of considerable competence. To those who sought his help he was kind and unstintingly generous. There was, however, a certain deviousness in his make-up, an inability to accept opposition or rebuffs, and an almost pathological intellectual ambition. In the last resort he chose to cheat rather than to see his opponents triumph. His downfall in later life was a tragedy, but it should not be allowed to eclipse his genuine contributions to the early development of applied psychology.

[L. S. Hearnshaw, *Cyril Burt: Psychologist*, 1979; Burt's remaining correspondence, diaries, and other papers in the Archives Department of the University of Liverpool; personal knowledge.] L. S. Hearnshaw

BUSTAMANTE, Sir (WILLIAM) ALEXANDER (1884–1977), first prime minister of Jamaica, was born William Alexander Clarke 24 February 1884 at Blenheim, Hanover, Jamaica, the elder son and second of the five children of Robert Constantine Clarke, an Irishman planter, of Hanover, and his second wife, Mary Wilson, a Jamaican. In later life he shrouded his upbringing in legend.

He attended elementary school. In 1904 he was a store clerk, and went to Belmont, St. Catherine, to train as an overseer. In 1905 he left for Cuba, where a tramway company employed him. They transferred him as inspector to Panama, where he courted Mildred Edith Blanck, the widow of an English engineer, who had two sons. In 1910 they married at Kingston, Jamaica. Bustamante thus had two stepsons, but no children of his own. He worked for the tramway company in Panama certainly until 1919, and reportedly joined the Cuban special police in 1919 or 1920. In 1932 he went to New York as Alejandro Bustamanti, a Spanish gentleman, apparently becoming a hospital attendant. He claimed he made his fortune on the New York Stock Exchange, but once said he left New York to avoid having to establish his legal status to the US immigration authorities.

He opened a money-lending office in Kingston, Jamaica, in 1934. His secretary was Gladys Maud Longbridge JP, daughter of Frank Longbridge; he married her in 1962. He wrote anti-government letters to the press, sympathizing with the underprivileged. In 1937 he became treasurer of the Jamaica Workers and Tradesmen's Union.

By May 1938 he was undisputed labour leader. He was arrested on 24 May on a sedition charge, which was later withdrawn. He was a key figure in the development between 1938 and 1943 of two rival trade-union blocs and two political parties supported by trade-union wings. He registered the Bustamante Industrial Trade Union in 1939, installing himself as life president-general. After a waterfront address he was interned on 8 September 1940, but released on 8 February 1942. The hierarchy of the People's National Party of Norman Manley looked after the BITU, but on release Bustamante repudiated them. He left the PNP to form the Jamaica Labour Party in 1943. To avoid disqualification from nomination as a candidate under a name not legally his own, he became William Alexander Bustamante by deed poll. His party won the 1944 elections, and he became leader of government business and minister of communications, 1945–53.

In 1947 he was elected mayor of Kingston. The JLP won the 1949 elections with a reduced majority. In 1951 its constitution stated the goals as self-government, British Caribbean federation, and dominion status within the Commonwealth. Bustamante, however, never supported federation strongly. He became chief minister and minister of local government in 1953, but after his party's defeat in 1955, led the opposition. He was president of the West Indies Democratic Labour Party from 1958 to 1960, but resigned to campaign for Jamaica's withdrawal from the federation. His opposition led to the 1961 referendum which decided on secession. The JLP won the 1962 elections. With independence in 1962 he became the first prime minister, keeping responsibility for external affairs and defence. He was appointed to the Privy Council in 1964. He retired in 1967, at the age of eighty-three.

Bustamante was a Roman Catholic with deep respect for the church's guidance. He was tall, striking, flamboyant, vigorous, and courageous. His recreations were farming, swimming, motoring, and, in youth, horse-breaking. He was a spell-binding, clowning demagogue with great authority over the masses. He was economically and politically conservative, and led a conservative labour-based party. He opposed socialism and upheld the traditional values of Jamaican society. In 1962 he told the House: 'I am for the West. I am against communism.'

He had deep compassion for the working classes and strove to improve their economic lot. He said: 'I belong to no class. I belong to all classes. But I plead for the poor of the poor, for I come from the gutter of poverty and I once knew what hunger was and what nakedness was.' He shared working-class affection for the British monarchy.

Bustamante was knighted in 1955, appointed GBE in 1967, and became a National Hero (Jamaica) in 1969. He was an honorary Doctor of Laws of Fairfield University, USA (1963) and of the University of the West Indies (1966). He held the National Order of Cedars, Lebanon; the Distinguished Order of the Brilliant Star with Special Grand Cordon, Republic of China; the Grand Gold Cross, Order Gran Heraldica de Cristobal Colon, Dominican Republic; and the Gran Cordon, Order of Liberatador, Venezuela.

Bustamante died at his residence in Irish Town, Jamaica, 6 August 1977.

[G. E. Eaton, *Alexander Bustamante and Modern Jamaica*, Kingston Publishers Ltd., 1975; R. M. Nettleford (ed.), *Norman Washington Manley and the New Jamaica*, Longman Caribbean, 1971; *Personalities Caribbean*, 6th edn., 1977–8, Personalities Ltd. Jamaica.]

I. M. Cumpston

BUTLER, Sir JAMES RAMSAY MONTAGU (1889–1975), historian, was born in the master's lodge, Trinity College, Cambridge, 20 July 1889. Both his grandfather and his father Henry Montagu Butler [q.v.] had been headmaster of Harrow School, and in 1886 the latter was appointed master of Trinity College. His first wife had died three years earlier, and in 1888 he married secondly a twenty-one-year-old former Girton student who had recently graduated in top place in classics, Agnata Ramsay, daughter of Sir James Henry Ramsay, tenth baronet, of Bamff, Perthshire. 'Jim' Butler, as he was always known to his friends and in his family, was the eldest of the three sons born of the second marriage. Of the first marriage there were two sons and three daughters.

At the age of thirteen Butler moved from St. Faith's Preparatory School, Cambridge, to Harrow School with an entrance scholarship and quickly showed great ability and brilliant promise. Four years later he became head of the school. In 1905 Butler took the Trinity College examination and was awarded a scholarship; but he did not matriculate until October 1907. As an undergraduate his great ability was further confirmed by the award of a long succession of university scholarships and prizes for Latin and Greek verse and prose, culminating in the Chancellor's classical medal (1911). In 1910 he was elected president of the Union, and he crowned his successes by gaining first class honours in part i of the classical tripos (1909) and in part ii of the history tripos (1910). In 1913 his college elected him into a prize fellowship, and the thesis which he submitted for the competition was published as *The Passing of the Great Reform Bill* (1914, reprinted 1964).

On the outbreak of war in 1914 Butler joined the Scottish Horse, a Yeomanry regiment with which he served in the Gallipoli campaign of 1915 and in Egypt. In 1916 he joined the Directorate of Military Operations in the War Office, and then served on the General Staff in France. He was twice mentioned in dispatches and in 1919 was appointed OBE (military division) 'for services in connection with operations in France'.

On demobilization Butler returned to Trinity College and was appointed one of the tutors to Prince Albert (later King George VI) and Prince Henry (later Duke of Gloucester) when they came to Cambridge for a year. This duty led him to be appointed MVO (4th class) in 1920.

In 1922 Butler was nominated for one of the two parliamentary seats then allocated to the ancient universities and was elected as an Independent. He played a prominent part in the debates leading to the passing of the Oxford and Cambridge Universities Act in July 1922, whereby commissions were set up with powers, for a limited period, to amend the universities' and colleges' statutes and ordinances. This ultimately led to the admission of women to full membership of Cambridge University. In the general election of December 1923, fought on the issue of tariff reform, Butler stood again as an Independent Liberal; but he was narrowly defeated by his cousin, Sir G. G. G. Butler [q.v.], on the second ballot under the transferable vote system then in force.

Soon after his father's death in 1918 Butler moved from the Lodge to the set of rooms at the top of the spiral staircase at the north-west corner of the Great Court, with lovely views over The Backs. There almost for the rest of his life he delighted to entertain his friends, especially to small luncheon and dinner parties. Though a teetotaller himself he was always a generous and delightful host. In 1925 he published a memoir of his father's thirty-one years as master of Trinity College, which remained a valuable social history of the politics and mores of Cambridge in that period. He was appointed a tutor by his college in 1928, and in the following year a university lecturer in history. In 1931 Trinity appointed him senior tutor, a responsible post which he held with success for seven years.

In World War II Butler served in the Army Intelligence Corps, and from 1942 at the Civil Affairs and Military Government central organization. His work for France was recognized by his appointment as chevalier of the Legion of Honour.

In 1947 Butler was appointed regius professor of modern history in succession to (Sir) G. N. Clark [q.v.], and he held that chair until 1954. In his inaugural lecture, delivered on 26 January 1949, he argued that 'History has a strong claim to rank as one staple of a liberal education' and outlined the plans for the military histories (*The Present Need for History*, 1949). Meanwhile in 1946 C. R. (later Earl) Attlee as prime minister had announced the government's intentions on the latter subject, and that Butler had been appointed chief military historian and editor of the whole series. It finally comprised forty-one volumes on grand strategy, the principal campaigns, and civil affairs and military government after the end of hostilities. Butler himself wrote the two grand strategy volumes covering September 1939 to August 1942 (vol. ii, 1957, and vol. iii, part ii, 1964). For his work on this project he was knighted in 1958.

In February 1955 Butler was elected vice-master of his college, an arduous and responsible post which he held with distinction for five years. On resigning the regius chair in 1954 the university promptly elected him an emeritus professor of modern history. Having thus shed some of his responsibilities he accepted a request that he should write the authorized biography of Philip Kerr, eleventh Marquess of Lothian [q.v.], a wartime ambassador in Washington (*Lord Lothian*, 1960). To this Dictionary he contributed the notice of G. M. Trevelyan.

In his very full life Butler's chief recreations were rock climbing and long walks in wild country—on the Continent as well as in the British Isles. He never married, and his college and university always stood first in his interests and affections. He made a generous benefaction to Trinity College in his lifetime and another under his will. As a young man he left the Anglican Church of his father and adopted the doctrines of Christian Science, to which he adhered strictly to the end of his life. When in 1975 he apparently suffered an accident and was obviously in great pain it was only with difficulty that he was persuaded to enter a nursing home—for a rest and not for treatment. He died there 1 March, and on 10 May 1975 a large congregation in the college chapel was bidden to recall 'the rare beauty of his character' and 'the gentle humorous charm of his manner'. No one who knew him would challenge that encomium.

[Harrow School records; Trinity College and Cambridge University archives; private information; personal knowledge.]

STEPHEN W. ROSKILL

BUTLIN, SIR WILLIAM HEYGATE EDMUND COLBORNE (1899–1980), holiday camp founder, was born 29 September 1899 in Cape Town, South Africa, the elder child (the younger son died as a child) of William Butlin, who ran a cycle business and whose father and grandfather were west country clergymen, and his wife, Bertha Hill, daughter of a baker in Coaley near Stroud, Gloucestershire, who used to sell his own gingerbread at local fairs. The marriage was not successful, and with her two children Bertha Butlin returned to England and travelled the fairgrounds selling gingerbread. His parents divorced and his mother married a Bristol gas fitter, Charlie Rowbotham. Around 1910 the family emigrated to Toronto, Canada.

Butlin left school at twelve (in all, he had no more than five years' education at ten schools) and after a couple of jobs he joined the Canadian Army at fifteen, becoming one of the youngest soldiers to serve in France during World War I. Demobbed and back in Canada, he could not settle and returned to England in 1921, working his passage on a cattle boat, to join his mother's relatives, who were fairground people.

His uncles gave him a hoop-la stall with which he toured the west country fairs. With new ideas 'Billy' Butlin quickly became a major travelling showman, constantly introducing new fairground attractions like the Figure Eight, the Wall of Death, and the Dodgems, which he brought to Britain in 1928. In the mid-twenties, with the advent of the motor car and the charabanc, he followed the crowds to the seaside and set up a small amusement park at Skegness. By the mid-thirties he had nine coastal amusement parks and also ran the Christmas fairs at London's Olympia, Glasgow's Kelvin Hall, and Edinburgh's Waverley Hall.

Through the years, however, he had had a dream born in the early twenties when he spent a short, rain-drenched holiday and saw how miserable families were who had been turned out of their boarding houses. Remembering the happy summer camps he had known in Canada, he decided to build something similar in Britain but with more indoor facilities to cater for the British weather.

It took him fifteen years to amass the capital needed, but on a snowy Easter Saturday in 1936, after trials, tribulations, and near bankruptcy he opened the first Butlin camp on the site of a former sugar-beet field just outside Skegness.

It was an immediate success. In 1937 Butlin's became a public company and a year later he opened a second camp at Clacton. But World War II interrupted his ambitious plans. His coastal amusement parks were closed and Skegness was taken over by the Royal Navy (it became HMS *Royal Arthur*) and the Germans claimed to have sunk it) and Clacton by the army. Filey camp which he had already started building was completed for the RAF, and he also built two more camps for the navy, at Pwllheli (HMS *Glendower*) and Ayr (HMS *Scotia*). He had an option to buy these three camps back at the war's end for three-fifths of the building costs.

Lord Beaverbook [q.v.] at the Ministry of Supply then appointed Butlin director of hostels. His brief was to improve the living conditions of some 50,000 'conscripted' women factory workers who were leaving the hostels in droves. Butlin stopped the exodus by making various attractive changes, and for this work he was appointed MBE (1944).

His next and final wartime job was honorary adviser to Field-Marshal B. L. Montgomery (later Viscount Montgomery of Alamein, q.v.) and his 21st Army Group, on the provision of leave centres in Europe after the Allied invasion. As a result, he set up nine social centres known as '21 Clubs' in Belgium and Germany where servicemen could meet carefully vetted girls.

This done, Butlin threw his immense energy into reopening his camps. The first to be handed back by the Services was Filey, but the others soon followed. He took up the option to buy back Filey, Pwllheli, and Ayr and so by 1946 he had five camps ready to cater for the huge demand from a holiday-starved population. A gamble taken in the darkest days of the war now paid off handsomely.

In the post-war years the camps boomed and four more were added. Butlin camps became a national institution with their famous redcoats, many of whom went on to become show-business stars. The camps' regimented 'Wakey, Wakey' and 'never-a-dull-moment' was loved by millions and sneered at by others. But undoubtedly Butlin gave countless people cheap and happy holidays. His secret, he always said, was to give people what *he* liked, and because he was an ordinary person he gave ordinary people what *they* liked. He also had the knack of doing the right thing at the right time, for the start of his camps coincided with the introduction of holidays-with-pay. Butlin announced: 'A week's holiday for a week's wage.' The weekly average in the late 1930s was £3 10s. (£3.50).

But at the height of his success Butlin suffered his first set-back. In 1948 he set up a company to launch an ambitious project in the Bahamas to cater for American tourists, with an up-market Vacation Village on the small island of Grand Bahama. The venture foundered and the company went into liquidation. Butlin himself lost £250,000. This failure led to a clash with the big City shareholders, but Butlin finally won the day.

By the 1960s the Butlin empire was catering for up to a million people a year. In 1972, after fighting off a take-over bid, the company was sold to the Rank Organization for £43 million.

Meanwhile, in 1968, for tax reasons (he estimated he and his companies had paid some £50 million in taxes over the years) Butlin handed over the running of the company to his son Robert and retired to Jersey. Here he promptly began a new career, building a holiday village and buying two hotels, but he also devoted more time to gardening, which he loved, his 1,200 budgerigars, his immensely successful dabblings in the stock-market, and his widespread work for charity. Butlin gave away at least £5 million to various charities, mainly to help underprivileged children, his main interests being the Variety Club of Great Britain and the Grand Order of Water Rats.

A shortish, stocky man who wore nondescript suits and a trilby which he often lost, Butlin was the antithesis of his public image. On the surface he was a brash super-showman and publicist, an opportunist who could be ruthless in business. Yet beneath this tough exterior lay a genuinely shy and modest man. He was knighted in 1964.

Butlin was married three times. In 1927 he married Dorothy, daughter of John Cheriton, fish and chip shop proprietor, of Tiverton; they had a daughter who died in 1972. She died in 1958 and in 1959 he married her sister, Norah Faith (died 1976); they had a son and two daughters, one of whom died in 1976. This marriage was dissolved in 1975 and in 1976 he married Sheila, daughter of Walter Devine, a multiple grocer of Liverpool; they had a son and daughter. He died 12 June 1980 at Blair Adam house, his Jersey home, and is buried in St. John's cemetery, Jersey, in a site he chose himself.

[Billy Butlin and Peter Dacre, *The Billy Butlin Story*, 1982; personal knowledge.]

PETER DACRE

BUTTERFIELD, SIR HERBERT (1900–1979), historian, was born at Oxenhope, Yorkshire, 7 October 1900, the eldest of three children (two sons and one daughter) of Albert Butterfield and his wife, Ada Mary Buckland, a member of the Plymouth Brethren who came from Leominster. Albert Butterfield had left school at the age of ten because of his own father's premature death, and had been unable to fulfil an ambition of proceeding to the Methodist ministry. The elder Butterfield was employed first as a clerk and then as chief clerk in a Keighley wool firm whose chairman gave both father and son a good deal of literary and intellectual encouragement. Butterfield himself was educated at the Trade and Grammar School, Keighley, and entered Peterhouse as a history scholar in 1919 when Sir A. W. Ward [q.v.] was master, and H. W. V. Temperley [q.v.] and P. C. Vellacott were the college's history fellows. He took first classes in both parts of the historical tripos (1921 and 1922), won a number of university prizes, and in 1923 was elected to a Peterhouse fellowship which he retained continuously, except during his mastership, until his death in 1979. He was a devoted servant of the college, and from 1955 to 1968 was a well-liked and conservative master. From 1959 to 1961 he was vice-chancellor of the University of Cambridge.

As a fellow of Peterhouse Butterfield examined in the college entrance examination and taught in supervision for six hours a week for about twenty weeks of the year for twenty years before taking up the university chair of modern history in 1944. By this time he had been in charge of history teaching in Peterhouse for five years and had been lecturing and examining in the history faculty for nearly fifteen. He was a successful editor of the *Cambridge Historical Journal* (1938–52) and had written books and articles about *The Historical Novel* (1924), *The Peace Tactics of Napoleon* (1929), *The Whig Interpretation of History* (1931), 'History and the Marxian Method' (in *Scrutiny*, 1933), *Napoleon* (1939), *The Statecraft of Machiavelli* (1940), and *The Englishman and his History* (1944).

Until 1936 Butterfield was a lay preacher in Methodist churches in Cambridge and the surrounding villages. His preaching did not at this time leave a direct mark on his historical writing. This on the contrary embodied the historical relativism with which he approached all intellectual systems when teaching his Peterhouse pupils and with which in public he treated the intellectual positions that *The Whig Interpretation of History* identified as contemporary obstacles to historical understanding—the humanistic whiggism and elevated liberalism endemic in the generation before his own. In the 1940s Christianity began to impregnate these mainly negative ideas, turning them in the process into the positive doctrine that Butterfield elaborated first in *The Englishman and his History* which, as an avowedly 'Whig' book, appeared to reverse many of his earlier positions, connected Christianity with freedom, and provided one of the earliest intellectual consecrations of the deliverance which the English had experienced between 1940 and 1942.

The Englishman and his History led out in three directions—towards the history of historiography, towards the reconstruction of English history, and towards systematic consideration of Christianity. The first reached its culmination in *Man on his Past* (1955) and *George III and the Historians* (1957). In relation to the second Butterfield produced *George III, Lord North and the People* (1949) which, though it had merits that were unrelated to the demand for reconstruction, left the impression that the reconstruction Butterfield was demanding was so extensive that he did not have the equipment to achieve it. *George III, Lord North and the People*, moreover, was the last serious statement that he made about the history of England. He did not write his projected life of Charles James Fox [q.v.]. Even if *George III and the Historians* showed him at his best, using the historiography of the subject in order to contextualize Sir L. B. Namier [q.v.], it was only in the third of these directions that he was as productive as he would have wished to be.

In his first five years as professor of modern history Butterfield wrote *The Origins of Modern Science* and *Christianity and History* which, like *George III, Lord North and the People*, were published in the same month in 1949, and were closely connected with one another. *The Origins of Modern Science* described 'modern science' as sustaining a 'new civilization' superseding that of the middle ages, while *Christianity and History* discussed the relationship which should subsist between this new civilization and Christianity. *Christianity and History*—the most influential of

Butterfield's works—was translated into many languages and became the occasion for the establishment of the Wiles lectures at Queen's University, Belfast. It was followed by similar discussions in *History and Human Relations* (1951), *Christianity in European History* (1951), *Christianity, Diplomacy and War* (1953), and *International Conflict in the Twentieth Century* (1960), where political implications were extracted from Christian principles, and the Christian tradition was said to have accumulated around it the various forms of worldly wisdom which condensed the experience of centuries and 'came to stand as part of our European heritage'.

Butterfield's writings after 1944 were the work of a liberal or dissenting mind congratulating itself and its fellow dissenters that Christianity was no longer an established religion, while arguing also that diplomacy and power politics could be understood in Christian terms and justified according to Christian categories. In the writings that were published between 1944 and 1953, there was a balance between the positive doctrine and the attempt to educate liberals and dissenters in the broadest English sense. But at the same time that *Christianity, Diplomacy and War* was being written in response to the atomic bomb, Butterfield was overtaken by the arrival of the hydrogen bomb, and a doctrine which was realistically conservative in relation to power politics and international diplomacy became an emotionally taut commitment to a form of nuclear renunciation and 'Christian international science' involving capitulation to the dissent that Butterfield had been educating. 'The revolutionary character of the present world situation does not call for the kind of Christianity which in a settled world associates itself with the defence of the existing order. It calls for the other kind of Christianity, the insurgent type, which goes back to first principles and measures the present order of things against these.' (*International Conflict in the Twentieth Century*, 1960, p. 119).

Butterfield was below middle height and in the most active periods of his life was sparely built. Until he became master of Peterhouse, he dressed carelessly. When young he had a Shelleyesque beauty of feature combined with a great deal of hair, a refined Yorkshire accent, and an attractively modest decisiveness of manner. In 1929 he married Edith Joyce ('Pamela') Crawshaw, the daughter of the Revd James E. Crawshaw, a methodist minister; they had three sons, of whom one died young, one became a schoolmaster, and one a lecturer at University College, Dublin, where Butterfield had been external examiner and made many friends, and from which he became a member of the Eire government's O'Dalaigh commission on higher education.

Butterfield was an enthusiastic pianist. He was a teetotaller and, until his seventies, a continuous smoker. From the middle 1950s onwards he was much in demand as a lecturer, travelled widely in America and the rest of the English-speaking world, and was the recipient of thirteen honorary degrees, including an honorary Litt.D. from Cambridge in 1974. In 1965–7 he delivered a course of Gifford lectures at Glasgow University. He served a term as president of the Historical Association (1955–8) and in 1965 was elected to a fellowship of the British Academy. He was appointed regius professor of modern history at Cambridge in 1963 and was knighted in 1968. For the last twenty years of his life he took pleasure in the British Committee for International Politics of which he was the founder-chairman.

In religion Butterfield was a lifelong Methodist who in his fifties also became an unconfirmed Anglican communicant. Politically he began as an Asquithian Liberal and ended by admiring (Sir) Winston Churchill, Harold Wilson (later Lord Wilson of Rievaulx), and Enoch Powell. Academically he had reservations about the 'historical profession', official history, and all claims to have achieved definitive understandings of the past.

In 1968 Butterfield retired early from the mastership of Peterhouse in order to write. For the rest of his life he lived at 26 High Street, Sawston, Cambridge, where he died 20 July 1979. He had an Anglican funeral service which was followed by a Methodist cremation, and his ashes were later buried in Peterhouse chapel. His papers were placed in Cambridge University Library.

[Maurice Cowling in *Proceedings* of the British Academy, vol. lxv, 1979; G. R. Elton, 'Herbert Butterfield and the Study of History', *Historical Journal*, vol. xxvii, 1984, No. 3, pp. 729–743; personal knowledge.]

MAURICE COWLING

C

CAMPBELL, SIR DAVID (1889–1978), president of the General Medical Council, was born at Patna, Ayrshire, 6 May 1889, the son of Agnes Smith Campbell, a seamstress. He was educated, by scholarships throughout, at Ayr Academy and at Glasgow University where he graduated B.Sc. and MA with honours in 1911 and MB, Ch.B. with honours in 1916, the most distinguished graduate of his year. He served as captain and then acting major in the Royal Army Medical Corps from 1916 to 1919 and in France in 1918 was awarded the MC as an immediate decoration in the field. On demobilization he returned to Glasgow as assistant to the renowned Professor Ralph Stockman in materia medica and therapeutics and in 1921 became Pollok lecturer in materia medica and pharmacology. In 1924 he took his MD with honours with a thesis on rheumatoid arthritis, winning the coveted Bellahouston gold medal. He spent 1925–6 as Rockefeller medical fellow at Johns Hopkins University, and in 1928 published *A Handbook of Therapeutics*, a great advance in its time on most preceding textbooks in the subject. During this period he was physician to outpatients (1920–9) and later assistant physician (1929–30) to the Western Infirmary, Glasgow.

The phase of major public achievement in Campbell's career opened with his appointment to the regius chair of materia medica in Aberdeen in 1930. Within two years he was dean of the faculty, a post he held for twenty-seven years, until his retirement in 1959. He found the Aberdeen school in an early stage of outward-looking reform, and accelerated the process immensely. His shrewdness, pawky humour, tight mental discipline, nice judicial sense, and firmness with opposition made him a formidable chairman and administrator. Several major and beneficial appointments were largely to his credit, notably those of (Sir) James Learmonth [q.v.] in surgery, (Sir) Dugald Baird in obstetrics, and John Stirling Young in pathology. He put his influence behind the creation of an imaginative medical complex on the spacious heights of Foresterhill, to include the clinical and related departments of the university, and soon to become the envy of many other medical schools. At the same time he ran an efficient department and was a conscientious and approachable teacher: his lecture notes, meticulously written out as they were meant to be read, with nicely judged classical allusion and quotation, bear witness to a medical scholarliness regrettably all but dead. His lectures on tea, tobacco, and alcohol are particularly remembered.

In 1936 Campbell joined the General Medical Council as representative of Aberdeen University and in 1949 became its president, serving also as chairman of its disciplinary committee. The challenges he met here on a larger scale were similar to those he had faced earlier in Aberdeen, and the same qualities again served him well. Those post-war years were a time of radical and potentially stressful change for medical education and practice, and a more volatile personality than Campbell's might have served these causes less well than he did. He resigned from the Council in 1961.

Campbell was knighted in 1953. He received the honorary degree of LL D from the universities of Glasgow, Liverpool, Dublin, and Aberdeen and of DCL from Durham. He was a fellow of the Royal Society of Edinburgh and of the Royal Colleges of Physicians of London and of Glasgow.

In his long retirement Campbell was a kenspeckle figure often seen on the Aberdeen golf links and occasionally in the medical school. He excelled in golf and also in billiards: he is believed in Aberdeen to have been billiards champion of the Athenaeum. For many years he organized, with the flair and efficiency once devoted to more serious things, an annual golf competition for which he was the handicapper, later presenting the Ashley Mackintosh cup to the winners at the annual dinner of the Aberdeen Medico-Chirurgical Society: year by year the company waited affectionately for the well-known references in his presentation speech, not only to the competition but to settled convictions of Campbell himself—rabbits and tigers in handicapping, and the best of all arrangements being a committee of one, with powers.

In 1921 Campbell married Margaret, daughter of Alexander Lyle, head teacher at Kerse near Grangemouth. He often said that this was by far the best thing he had ever done. There were no children.

Campbell died at his home in Milltimber, Aberdeen, 30 May 1978. A fine portrait by Alberto Morrocco hangs in the council chamber of the General Medical Council.

[Private information; personal knowledge.]

WILLIAM WALKER

CAMPBELL, PATRICK GORDON, third BARON GLENAVY (1913–1980), journalist, was born in Dublin 6 June 1913, the elder son and eldest of three children of Charles Henry Gordon Campbell, second Baron Glenavy, later governor of the Bank of Ireland, and his wife, Beatrice Moss, daughter of William Elvery, business man, of Rothbury, Foxrock, county Dublin, and a grandson of 'the old lord' as he was known in the family, lord chancellor of Ireland under the Union, later to become chairman of the Irish Free State Senate after the treaty of 1921. As both father and grandfather were supporters of the pro-treaty party, they were marked for IRA reprisals during 'the troubles'; at the age of nine, on Christmas eve, Patrick Campbell was roused at gunpoint with his family, and herded out on to the lawn, there to watch while their home was burned down, fearing for their lives.

Campbell was already tall and gangling (his knees knocked together so hard, he was to recall, that they were severely bruised); he developed a sometimes paralysing stammer; and his time at preparatory schools in Ireland, at Rossall, and briefly at Pembroke College, Oxford, was undistinguished. When he went down without taking a degree his father did his best to launch him in business, without success. As a last resort he sent him with an introduction to Robert Maire Smyllie, the Falstaffian but shrewd editor of the *Irish Times*. Smyllie tested him out by sending him to do a piece on a visit to the Dublin zoo; it appeared unchanged the following day; and after a spell learning to type and failing to learn shorthand, Patrick Campbell was launched on his successful career.

Smyllie pursued a policy of sending his more promising recruits on a round of jobs: Campbell was briefly a feature writer, a leader writer, literary editor, film critic, and parliamentary sketch writer, his mordant humour at the expense of some members of the Dail establishing his reputation with readers, but giving his father reason to worry. 'I began to feel', Campbell recalled in his *My Life and Easy Times* (1967), 'that Dublin was getting too small'; and he left for Fleet Street to work for Lord Beaverbrook [q.v.], who had known and admired his grandfather. He failed to make an impression; and when war broke out in 1939, he returned to Ireland where, as Smyllie declined to take him back, he joined the Irish Marine Service, in which he stayed until, in 1944, Smyllie relented, and offered him the job of writing 'An Irishman's Diary', a column which he had to produce five days a week.

It was an instant success and by 1947 he felt sufficiently confident to return to Fleet Street to do a weekly column for the *Sunday Dispatch*. It proved to be very popular, as did the monthly article he wrote for the magazine *Lilliput*. 'He could toss up a trifle of experience and keep it in the air with great dexterity for minutes', *The Times* obituarist was to recall, 'before letting it spin away into fantasy.' His ability attracted the attention of the Rank Organization, then at the height of its film-production era, and he was employed as an 'additional dialogue writer' for Pinewood Studios. He also made his mark as hilarious company in gatherings such as the Thursday Club, whose president was the Duke of Edinburgh, which met once a week for a protracted and noisy lunch.

Agreeable though the life was, it did Campbell's writing no good; it became, as he admitted, mechanical. One by one he lost his regular jobs, the *Dispatch* column, the *Lilliput* retainer, the Pinewood salary. But after a shaky spell, a series of entertaining recollections of past episodes in his life for the *Spectator* led to his being offered a column in the *Sunday Times*; and when E. G. ('Ned') Sherrin suggested he should become one of the resident talkers in BBC television's *Not so Much a Programme, More a Way of Life*, he decided to risk trying out his stammer on a mass audience.

It worked. Some stammers invite laughter *at*: Campbell's won laughter *with*, as he used it to point up jokes—or, often, to make ordinary statements sound as if they were jokes. Later he was to win more kudos in the *Call My Bluff* series, a protracted battle between his side and Frank Muir's. Gratifying though it was for him to receive tributes, as he often did, for giving the stammer a new image, he always insisted that he would willingly have got rid of it if he could, even if it provided him with an income greater than he had ever earned with his typewriter.

It also helped to sell his books, of which fifteen were published, chiefly for the Christmas market, in the space of twenty-three years. Most of them were collections of his articles; the exceptions being his autobiography—which was also a moving tribute to his father, for whom he had a feeling almost approaching veneration—and *How to Become a Scratch Golfer* (1963), a light-hearted look back over one of the two recreations he listed in *Who's Who* (the other being, simply, 'pleasure'). As a golfer he had in fact been quite close to international standard, on one occasion surviving four rounds of the Irish Open Amateur Championship, defeating a leading Walker Cup contender in the process.

Campbell married first, in 1941, Sylvia, daughter of Captain Kenneth Willoughby-Lee MC, of Muizenberg, South Africa. They had no children. After a divorce in 1947, he married in the same year Cherry Margaret, daughter of Major George Lowson Monro, of the Indian Army; they had a daughter. This marriage was dissolved in 1966 and he married in the same year Vivienne, previously wife of Charles Orme, and daughter of Charles Knight MC. He had worked with her for years on film and television scripts, and it was she who—as he explained in an introduction—'produced' his autobiography, by 'causing me to look at the realities in my life, and to write them down as honestly as I could'. After their marriage they went to live in the South of France, where they remained—except when television and other commitments brought him back to England—until he died in London 9

November 1980. He was succeeded in the barony by his brother Michael Mussen (born 1924).

He had succeeded his father as Lord Glenavy in 1963; but as he retained 'Patrick Campbell' for his articles, books, and broadcasts, it was by that name he continued to be known. Thanks to his stammer, his height, and his imposing appearance—he had something of the look of a Roman emperor about him—he was almost too well known for his own comfort; he could not walk down a London street without people stopping to stare, nudge each other, and make remarks or imitate his television manner. He deserved his reputation not only as a performer but as, at his best, a very funny writer and—what is unusual—an equally funny raconteur in person.

[*The Times*, 11 November 1980; Patrick Campbell, *My Life and Easy Times*, 1967; personal knowledge.] BRIAN INGLIS

CAMPS, FRANCIS EDWARD (1905–1972), expert in forensic medicine, was born 28 June 1905 at Teddington, the eldest of the three sons (there were no daughters) of Percy William Leopold Camps FRCS, and his wife, Alice, daughter of Joseph Redfern, of Matlock. He was educated at Marlborough College, Guy's Hospital, the School of Tropical Medicine at Liverpool, and Neuchâtel University, Switzerland. He qualified MRCS, LRCP (1928), MB, BS (Lond. 1930), MD (1933), DTM&H (Liverp. 1931), FRCPath. (1964), and FRCP (1968).

After qualifying in medicine in 1928 Camps practised firstly as a house physician at Guy's Hospital and then as a junior partner in general practice in rural Essex, before becoming a pathologist at the Chelmsford and Essex Hospital, specializing in bacteriology and epidemiology.

It was not, however, until after World War II that he turned to forensic medicine as a full-time career. He started lecturing at the London Hospital Medical College in 1945, being appointed lecturer in 1953, reader in 1954, and professor in 1963, and becoming emeritus professor in 1970 on his retirement.

Apart from lecturing to undergraduates and postgraduates at the London Hospital, he lectured in forensic medicine at the Royal Free Hospital Medical School and the University College Hospital Medical School. At various times he was an examiner at most of the principal universities in the United Kingdom, playing a big part in persuading the Worshipful Society of Apothecaries to set up the diploma in medical jurisprudence. He was consultant pathologist to the Emergency Medical Service during the war, a holder of a travelling fellowship of the Kellogg Foundation, and honorary consultant in forensic medicine to the army from 1964 until 1970, an appointment he particularly valued.

He was tireless in his enthusiasm and advocacy for his subject and he served on many committees, the most notable perhaps being the British Medical Association special committee on the recognition of intoxication in the relation of alcohol to road accidents in 1951, the coroners' rules committee of the Home Office in 1953, the mortuaries' committee of the Ministry of Housing and Local Government in 1955, and the Home Office scientific advisory council. He was one of the original founders of the British Association in Forensic Medicine in 1950, and was its president in 1958–60. His was the inspiration and moving force behind the formation of the British Academy of Forensic Sciences in 1959 and his was the guiding hand as its first secretary-general from then until October 1971, except during 1963, when he served with distinction as its president. At the time of his death he was president of the Society for the Study of Addiction and vice-president of the Foundation for the Study of Infant Deaths.

Francis Camps, a man of strong views, many of which were contrary to those of his colleagues, was blessed with exceptional stamina and could accomplish a prodigious amount of work. He hardly ever refused a case or an invitation to speak. His bibliography was formidable and many of his textbooks are landmarks in forensic medicine. To this Dictionary he contributed the notice of Sir Sydney Smith. He travelled widely visiting medico-legal centres and attending congresses and meetings, to which he almost always contributed. He had only just returned from the Sudan shortly before his final admission to the hospital in which he had trained as a pathologist.

Of the large number of important cases in which he was involved, perhaps the best known were the Setty, the Christie, and the Emmett Dunne cases. He was also most interested in Jack the Ripper. As a person he was impressive, though essentially modest, radiating vitality with great personal charm, urging himself and others on—'God bless, we must get on'—never tiring, always enthusiastic. Socially, he was a delightful host or guest, having a rich vein of humour in his make-up. A perpetual cigarette between his lips, he was a loyal, devoted friend and stimulating colleague and teacher.

By a first marriage Camps had a son and two daughters. In 1942 he married Mary Ross Mackenzie, MD, daughter of Dr James Ross Mackenzie, MD, DA, FFARCS, lecturer in anaesthesia at Aberdeen. They had a son and a daughter. After her death in 1970, Camps married Dr Anne Elizabeth Robinson, Ph.D., FRIC, in 1972. Camps died at the Chelmsford and Essex Hospital 8 July 1972.

[*Lancet*, 15 July 1972; *British Medical Journal*, 22 July 1972; *London Hospital Gazette*, October 1972; *Medicine, Science and the Law*, October 1972; private information; personal knowledge.] J. M. CAMERON

CARDUS, SIR (JOHN FREDERICK) NEVILLE (1889–1975), writer and critic, was born possibly 2 April 1889 at 2 Summer Place, Rusholme, Manchester, the home of his maternal grandparents. His maternal grandfather was a retired policeman. His unmarried mother, Ada Cardus, died in 1954, and on his marriage certificate he gave the name of his father (whom he never knew) as the late Frederick Cardus, Civil Service clerk. In his *Autobiography* (1947) Cardus disclosed that his real father was 'one of the first violins in an orchestra' who vanished from his mother's life almost as soon as he casually entered it. His mother and his aunt he described as having joined 'the oldest of professions'. Even Cardus's year of birth is uncertain. Although he gave it in *Who's Who* as 2 April 1889, on his marriage certificate of 17 June 1921 he gave his age then as thirty-one. Cardus was equally evasive about his childhood and education at a board school, but Summer Place in Rusholme was not the slum that his book implies. He educated himself by reading and had various menial jobs. His first connection with journalism was in a printer's works, where he had to boil the type in a pan to clean it after it was removed from the page-formes. Later he sold chocolates in the Manchester theatre where the repertory company of Annie Horniman [q.v.] later performed. There his lifelong relish of the music hall began. In 1901 he first entered Lancashire's county cricket ground at Old Trafford, where he saw A. C. MacLaren [q.v.] hit a boundary before rain stopped play. But it was enough to start another passion; thereafter he went there often and watched the cricketers of the 'Golden Age'.

In 1904 Cardus was a clerk in a marine insurance agency, where his employers were indulgent towards his frequent absences in the reference library or at Old Trafford. He began to read the music criticism of Ernest Newman [q.v.] and the dramatic criticism, in the *Manchester Guardian*, of C. E. Montague, James Agate [qq.v.], and Allan Monkhouse, and he also began to write in imitation of them. This was Manchester's cultural heyday, when Hans Richter and Adolf Brodsky guided its musical life. Cardus went to the Free Trade Hall on the night of 3 December 1908 when the First Symphony of Sir Edward Elgar [q.v.] had its first performance, and he educated himself in opera during the regular visits of the touring companies.

In 1912 he became assistant cricket coach at Shrewsbury School, where the headmaster was Cyril Alington [q.v.]. Cardus acted as his secretary from 1914. He volunteered for the army but was rejected because of his short sight. Returning to Manchester in 1916, Cardus was for three months Manchester music critic of the Socialist newspaper *Daily Citizen*. Unemployed and unfit for the army, he wrote to C. P. Scott [q.v.], editor of the *Manchester Guardian*, seeking any kind of work on the paper. Scott took him on as a secretary, then decided he did not need one. But three months later, in 1917, he appointed Cardus to the reporting staff at 30 shillings (£1.50) a week. Soon the initials 'N.C.' appeared at the end of music-hall notices, but he made his real mark on the paper in the summer of 1919, after an illness, when the kindly news editor sent him to recuperate by reporting the opening of Lancashire's first post-war cricket season. Soon he was writing about cricket not merely as a reporter, but as an essayist, an observer of character. His prose was allusive, studded with poetical quotations and musical analogies. A game had not been written about in this way before. He adopted the pseudonym 'Cricketer', and before long was one of the *Guardian*'s chief attractions to readers. Other writers on cricket have displayed more strategic knowledge of the game; none has captured its spirit and atmosphere as perceptively and humorously. He created a Dickensian gallery of characters, as he admitted, and the characters themselves played up to him. In 1922 Grant Richards published Cardus's *A Cricketer's Book*. There followed *Days in the Sun* (1924), *The Summer Game* (1929), *Good Days* (1934), and *Australian Summer* (1937).

In spite of cricket, Cardus still hankered after the arts. His interest in music being known to Scott, in 1920 he became assistant to the paper's chief critic, Samuel Langford, succeeding him in 1927. Unlike some critics, Cardus did not isolate himself from the artists upon whom he passed judgement, for he enjoyed their company as much as their performances. Thus he became the friend of Sir Thomas Beecham, Kathleen Ferrier, Sir John Barbirolli [qq.v.], Artur Schnabel, and Claudio Arrau. In his writings on music, as on cricket, Cardus was more interested in aesthetics than technicalities, in emotional rather than intellectual response. Newman described him as a 'sensitized plate', and he did not demur. Cardus inherited Langford's championship of the music of Gustav Mahler. His essay on Mahler in *Ten Composers* (1945, revised as *A Composers' Eleven*, 1958), made as many converts to the music as Bruno Walter's 1936 recording of *Das Lied von der Erde*. It is Cardus at his best, whereas his analytical study of the first five symphonies (*Gustav Mahler: his Mind and his Music*, 1965) was not a success and was significantly not followed by a planned second volume.

In January 1940 Cardus arrived in Australia where he wrote on music for the *Sydney Morning Herald* and gave many broadcasts. He returned to Britain in June 1947, writing on cricket for the *Sunday Times* while expecting to succeed the long-lived Newman as music critic. In 1951 he returned to the *Manchester Guardian* as its chief London music critic and occasional cricket contributor. He continued in this role to the end of his life although he felt increasingly out of sympathy with the paper after it loosened its Manchester ties. Even if he now visited his native city ever more rarely, his spiritual home remained Scott's *Guardian* in Cross Street. He was happiest in his late years holding court behind the Warner Stand at Lord's—he was a wonderful raconteur—or in the Garrick Club. He returned to Australia for brief visits in 1948, 1949, and 1954. After he had reached his mid-seventies, many honours came to him—the CBE in 1964, a knighthood in 1967, Austria's decoration of honour (1st class) for science and art in 1970, and honorary membership of the Royal Manchester College of Music (1968)—his sole Manchester honour—and of the Royal Academy of Music in 1972. But he valued highest the presidency of Lancashire County Cricket Club in 1970–1, seventy years after he had seen MacLaren's drive for four. His last book of essays, *Full Score*, was published in 1970.

In 1921 Cardus married Edith Honorine Watton (died 1968), a schoolmistress, daughter of John Thomas Sissons King, schoolmaster; there were no children. Edith was active with one of Manchester's most enterprising amateur stage companies, the Unnamed Society. Cardus died in London 28 February 1975.

[Neville Cardus, *Autobiography*, 1947, and *Second Innings*, 1950; Robin Daniels, *Conversations with Cardus*, 1976; Christopher Brookes, *His Own Man* (biography), 1985; *Daily Telegraph*, *Guardian*, and *The Times*, 1 March 1975; private information; personal knowledge.]

MICHAEL KENNEDY

CARLINE, RICHARD COTTON (1896–1980), painter and writer, was born in Oxford 9 February 1896, the youngest of the five children (four sons and one daughter) of George Francis Carline, painter (1855–1920), and his wife Anne, in later life also a painter, daughter of John Smith, of Buckhurst Hill. As a painter Carline also followed earlier family generations, as well as his brother Sydney (1888–1929) and only sister Hilda (1889–1950). After attending the Dragon and St. Edward's schools, Oxford, he studied art from 1913 under Percyval Tudor-Hart at his schools first in Paris and then in Hampstead, being influenced by Tudor-Hart's theories of colour and tonal value.

In 1916 he joined the Middlesex Regiment before serving as an officer in the Royal Flying Corps, first in wireless and then in experiments in camouflage and aids to identification of enemy targets from the air. In 1918 he and Sydney were appointed official war artists, Richard recording the war from the air on the western front and then (in 1919) both brothers depicting the aerial warfare in British zones in the Middle East. Their work constitutes the most comprehensive group of paintings from the air in the Imperial War Museum.

Carline studied at the Slade School of Art in 1921–4. In 1916 his parents had moved to Hampstead. With all three artist children living there their home became what Gilbert Spencer [q.v.] described as 'a focal centre', combining hospitality with endless discussion on art and its theory. The participation in this circle of Henry Lamb, I. Charles Ginner, Mark Gertler, and John Nash [qq.v.] indicates its principal characteristics—always Carline's: the clear but careful representation of familiar motifs, freshly seen. For a few years from as early as 1914 he achieved an unusually simple and direct realism of striking psychological concentration. Elected to the London Group in 1920, he exhibited with it till the 1970s. His work was consistently admired by (Sir) Stanley Spencer [q.v.], whose importance in Carline's circle was consolidated by his marriage to Hilda Carline in 1925. In 1930 a series of often vertiginous paintings of masts and rigging was the last in which, during seventeen years, Carline's work had been marked by an unusual clarity and feeling for light. Thereafter his painting was less exceptional and less continuous. Remaining a strong colourist and more interested in content than in style, he developed a controlled sensuousness of paint owing something to Gauguin and Fauvism.

The change in Carline's art coincided approximately with the premature deaths of his remaining brothers (he had taught under Sydney's mastership at the Ruskin Drawing School, Oxford, in 1924–9), with the impact of the break-up of the Spencers' marriage, with intensification in the climate of discussion to include socio-political as well as aesthetic concerns, and with an expansion in Carline's own horizons. His art was influenced by the community-orientated figurative painting he saw in four pre-war visits to the USA, and he became a strong advocate of public mural painting in Britain. In the USA he also admired schemes to improve the place of artists in society and the work of artists' own organizations.

Carline's principal achievement during his last five decades was to generate contacts and creative interaction within local, national, and international communities and across boundaries of style, genre, and culture. He was motivated by strong beliefs in peace, friendship, and freedom. Tirelessly active, he was a natural organizer, finding it difficult to say no (a trait related to his instinct always to seek what was positive in the art of others rather than to criticize it). Organizations of which he was at various times chairman included the Artists' International Association (including its important refugee and regional committees); the International Artists' Association (co-founder, 1952; chairman of the UK national committee from 1959; honorary president, 1968–80), an affiliated organization of Unesco, for which as its first art counsellor he organized its first post-war international art exhibition in Paris; and the Hampstead Artists' Council (co-founder). A member of the Britain/China Friendship Association, he selected and accompanied to China historical exhibitions of British Historical art and water-colours in 1957 and 1963.

Opposed to exclusiveness in selection, Carline felt that exhibitions and organizations should be broadly based and that child, naïve, and ethnic art were as worthy of serious consideration as western fine art. Through books and exhibitions he advanced appreciation of African art and of the picture postcard, and in his work at home and overseas under Cambridge University as an adviser on art education and examiner, he contributed significantly to the establishment of more liberal criteria for conducting art examinations and judging excellence in children's art. His *Draw They Must* (1968) is a history of four centuries of art teaching in general education in Britain and of its modern extension overseas.

From 1939 to 1945 Carline did important technical and liaison work on camouflage, writing the Ministry of Aircraft Production's official report on industrial and aircraft camouflage. In 1950 Carline married Nancy, painter and daughter of Douglas Stanley Higgins, business man; they had a son and a daughter. They continued the tradition of broad-ranging hospitality of Carline's parents. In his last decade Carline was instrumental in the creation of several exhibitions on the art of his family circle and in twentieth-century Hampstead. His *Stanley Spencer at War* (1978) is a key account of his brother-in-law as man and artist up to 1932.

Carline's general attitude was consistently open and progressive. He preferred art of pronounced directness, a quality seen in the clarity of his own early work and in his manner of expression as writer and speaker. A certain combination of idealism with outspokenness may account for his remaining somewhat outside the establishment of his day, despite the unfailing courtesy of his approach. In the last years of his life appreciation of his early achievement as a painter increased notably. He is represented in the Tate Gallery, the Ashmolean Museum, and other public collections. He died in Hampstead 18 November 1980. A memorial retrospective was held at the Camden Arts Centre, London, June–July 1983.

[*The Times*, 25 November 1980; exhibition catalogues; private information; personal knowledge.] RICHARD MORPHET

CARNELL, EDWARD JOHN (1912–1972), pioneer of British science fiction, editor, and literary agent, was born 8 April 1912 in Plumstead, the only child of William John Carnell, a charge hand who worked at the Royal Arsenal in Woolwich, and his wife, Louisa Woollett.

'Ted', as he was always known, became a printer, but joined the army at the outbreak of war in 1939, was promoted to sergeant, and served as a gunner in Combined Operations, when he was involved in more than one beach-head invasion. He was already devoted to the more peaceful microcosm of science fiction, and loved to tell the tale of how, patrolling the Mediterranean in a corvette, he had boarded a deserted ship; on the captain's desk lay a gold watch and a copy of *Astounding Science Fiction*. He took the latter.

He attended Britain's first science fiction convention in 1937, together with other devotees who were later to succeed as writers, including Arthur C. Clarke and Eric Frank Russell. His administrative abilities soon came to the fore. He was made treasurer of a newly formed Science Fiction Association, and edited the journal of the British Inter-planetary Society. After the war, with backing from dedicated followers, Carnell published *New Worlds*, Britain's most successful and long-lived science fiction magazine (200 issues between 1946 and 1970). As *New Worlds* achieved regular publication, Carnell added a sister magazine, *Science Fantasy* (eighty-one issues between 1950 and 1966). Later Carnell added a third magazine, the American-originated *Science Fiction Adventures*, which, through his intervention, survived when the parent magazine died, to yield twenty-seven issues between 1958 and 1963.

These magazines were crucial to the development of British science fiction; they allowed native writers to find their own audience, instead of having to adopt an American idiom for the New York market. Writers who took advantage of this, and supported Carnell, included Arthur Sellings, J. G. Ballard, Brian Aldiss, and Michael Moorcock—the last taking over the editorship of *New Worlds* in 1964, when Carnell's health, and his publishers, were failing. Under Moorcock, *New Worlds* became as much a crusade as a magazine, while Carnell went on to lead a quieter life as editor of a regular series of anthologies, *New Writings in S-F*, which provided a forum for the generation of authors which included

Christopher Priest and Charles Partington. Twenty-one numbers were published between 1964 and Carnell's death in 1972, whereupon H. Kenneth Bulmer—another British stalwart—took over the editorship.

Carnell also edited many anthologies: *No Place Like Earth* (1952), *Gateway to Tomorrow* (1954), *Gateway to the Stars* (1955), *The Best from New Worlds Science Fiction* (1955), *Lambda I and Other Stories* (reprinted 1964), *Weird Shadows from Beyond* (1965), and *Best from New Writings in S-F 1–4* (1971).

Carnell was always steady, reliable, and honest, and thoroughly understood science fiction. As his magazines and his writers succeeded, he was practically forced to become a literary agent in order to market the fiction he had summoned into being. He knew none of the techniques, but learnt fast, representing such writers, in whole or in part, as John Christopher, Theodore Sturgeon, Damon Knight, Frederik Pohl, Samuel Delaney, Harry Harrison, and the British authors already mentioned. He never failed to be surprised when he managed to sell a book to a regular publisher such as Faber & Faber, or to get £30 from the Spanish. Then his high, nervous chuckle would come into play—not always echoed by the more ambitious of his authors.

The science fiction world provided Carnell with his few recreations. He was chairman of the first world convention to be held outside the United States (London, 1957). He was one of the four founders of the respected International Fantasy Award in 1951, which immediately recognized the merits of such works as George Stewart's *Earth Abides* (1949) and the trilogy by J. R. R. Tolkien [q.v.]. Very little science fiction appeared in hardcover before the 1950s. Carnell helped promote hardcovers, becoming a founder and member, with Kingsley Amis and Dr George Porter, of the selection board of the Science Fiction Book Club, on which he served for many years. He was English linkman for the Trieste Science Fiction Film Festivals (1961 onwards), the first such international events. Throughout all this activity, Carnell remained a Plumstead man, modest and pleasant, a good friend to his friends and authors. Indisputably, he did far more for British science fiction on the administrative side than anyone else. His was an example of the way in which devotees valiantly supported the literature no one but they seemed to love; his pleasant nature and fondness for 'loony' jokes left their imprint on British science fiction.

In 1939 Carnell married Irene Truth, daughter of William Henry Read Cloke, a caterer. They had a son and a daughter. Carnell died at St. Nicholas Hospital, Plumstead, 23 March 1972.

[*Index to SF Anthologies and Collections*, ed. William Contento, Boston, 1978; private information; personal knowledge.]

BRIAN ALDISS

CARTER, JOHN WAYNFLETE (1905–1975), bibliographer and bookman, was born at Eton 10 May 1905, the eldest in the family of two sons and two daughters of the Revd Thomas Buchanan Carter and his wife, Margaret Teresa Stone. On both sides of the family there were long-standing links with Eton College and King's College, Cambridge, and Carter won scholarships to both. He had a distinguished school career, both academically and as an athlete, and he took first classes in both parts of the Cambridge classical tripos (1926 and 1927). His family's slender means encouraged him to support himself from an early age and imbued him with a fixity of purpose whch did not often reveal itself to others. Eton and Cambridge fostered in Carter the three things that dominated his life: a love of books, the pursuit of elegance, and an inclination to concentrate only on what he found congenial.

In 1927, immediately after leaving Cambridge, he joined the London branch of the New York publishing house, Charles Scribner, and helped to create an antiquarian bookselling side of the business which attained a considerable reputation among book collectors on both sides of the Atlantic. Aided by his bibliographical scholarship and enquiring mind, Carter quickly developed a propensity to see changing patterns in collecting and he eventually became Scribner's London managing director. In 1936 he married Ernestine Marie, daughter of Siegfried Fantl, a member of the Cotton Exchange in Savannah, Georgia; she had worked for the Museum of Modern Art in New York and subsequently became a well-known fashion writer and associate editor of the *Sunday Times*. She was appointed OBE in 1964.

During the war Carter joined the Ministry of Information, first the censorship division, and in 1944 he was seconded to the British Information Services in New York. He returned to Scribner's in London after the war, but in 1953 finally left on being invited to become personal assistant to Sir Roger Makins (later Lord Sherfield), who had just been appointed British ambassador to the United States. This post made the fullest use of Carter's singularly wide-ranging contacts in the USA, his unusually sensitive understanding of the American mind, and his organizational skills. For his services during this period he was appointed CBE in 1956.

In 1955, after some initial hesitation, he became Sotheby's representative in America and an associate of the firm. It was the moment when wartime controls on the export of sterling and the import of goods to the UK had been relaxed, and for the ensuing decade Carter, or 'Jake' as he was known to his friends, campaigned brilliantly to bring major American properties to the London auction room. Here was scope for his remarkable memory for people who mattered, his knowledge of rare books and the book trade, his forensic skills, and a strong commercial flair. He played an important role in the sensational expansion of Sotheby's during this period and in its acquisition in 1964 of New York's leading auction house, Parke–Bernet. After 1964 he continued to work for Sotheby's book department in London until shortly before his death.

But Carter's fame rests principally on his writings. His name will always be linked with that of (Henry) Graham Pollard. Together they undertook the investigative research which led to the unmasking of the master forger of supposedly rare editions, Thomas James Wise [q.v.], at a time when the latter was at the peak of his bibliographic career. Carter and Pollard's daring exposure of Wise's malfeasances in the innocuously titled *An Enquiry into the Nature of Certain Nineteenth Century Pamphlets* was a pioneering study in bibliographic detection which made full use of the microscopic study of type and the chemical analysis of paper, and caused a sensation when it was published in 1934. In 1947 Carter was appointed Sandars reader in bibliography at Cambridge and the resulting *Taste and Technique in Book-collecting* (1948), based on these lectures, well reflects the wit and elegance of style he brought to all his writings, the consequence of much drafting and repolishing, penned, incidentally, in a striking humanistic hand. His *ABC for Book Collectors* (1st edn. 1952, 6th edn. 1980), which was frequently reprinted, made him known to a much wider audience and gave him an opportunity to challenge some of the well-worn shibboleths of bookish connoisseurship.

After many years on the council of the Bibliographical Society he became its president in 1968–9, and was posthumously awarded its gold medal in 1976. He was a member of the editorial board of the *Book Collector* and for many years the organizer of the bibliographical pages of the *Times Literary Supplement.* He helped to mount many notable exhibitions, the most important of which was 'Printing and the Mind of Man' in 1963. Particularly in his younger days he contributed lively journalism pseudonymously to various USA papers. He became a fellow of Eton in 1967 and did much work on behalf of the College Library. He continued all his life with a strong interest in A. E. Housman [q.v.] and Catullus which had begun at Eton, and formed major collections of their work.

Above all Carter enjoyed meeting people: he was loved and revered among an enormous circle of friends on both sides of the Atlantic, and in America particularly this erudite, stylish old Etonian of haughty mien and impeccable manners, with his slim figure, immaculately cut suits, his monocle (which he always referred to as his eyeglass), his pipe, and his irreverent wit, personified the typical Englishman. Together with his friends A. N. L. Munby and Michael Sadleir [qq.v.] he formed a unique triumvirate of bibliographical scholars that changed the course of book collecting in the English-speaking world.

Carter died in London 18 March 1975.

[Private information; personal knowledge.]

FRANK HERRMANN

CARUS-WILSON, ELEANORA MARY (1897–1977), English medieval economic historian, was born in Montreal 27 December 1897, the only daughter and younger child of Charles Ashley Carus-Wilson, then professor of civil engineering at McGill University, Montreal, and his wife, Mary Louisa Georgina, daughter of Colonel Martin Petrie [q.v.], who had been one of the earliest women students at University College, London. Apart from her early transatlantic years, Eleanora Carus-Wilson was quintessentially English, in both her personal and scholarly style. Her life and work were accomplished in symbiosis with Westfield College, London. Her maternal grandfather had been a foundation trustee of the college. Its benefactor and foundress, Miss Dudin Brown, had been introduced to its future principal by her mother, who was subsequently a lecturer in English on the staff for five years in the 1880s and then active in the administration. Eleanora went to Westfield herself in 1918 after St. Paul's Girls' School, graduating BA in 1921, and returned after some years as a schoolteacher, taking her MA with distinction in 1926 and being appointed a part-time lecturer at Westfield in 1930–1. Her first edited book in 1932 was a history of the college. She was Leverhulme research fellow there in 1936–8. Then, when a senior academic, once again she became increasingly identified with Westfield—as a governor after 1965 and as president of the Westfield College Association from 1974. She was due to take the chair at the governing body on the day she died.

Apart from her years as a temporary civil servant in the Ministry of Food during World War II, her own life, as that of her parents, was encompassed by scholarly pursuits, always centred on London. Eileen Power [q.v.] became her main mentor when she became a member of her seminar in the 1930s. The research bridgeheads made under Eileen Power's direction proved to be the territories which Eleanora Carus-Wilson consolidated with magisterial authority during the remainder of her life and eventually the mantle of Eileen Power fell upon her own shoulders when she herself had become a leading medievalist: as lecturer (after 1945) at the London School of Economics, then reader (1948), and as professor of economic history at London University from 1953 to her retirement in 1965.

English medieval trade was her first and last major field—with the study of the urban centres which cradled it, the organizations which sustained it, and the principal industry which provided its base. 'The Overseas Trade of Bristol' and 'The Iceland Trade' appeared in a volume edited by Eileen Power and M. M. Postan in 1933, consolidated by a substantial volume of documents edited for the Bristol Record Society in 1937. This aspect of her work culminated in 1963 with the authoritative volume, written jointly with her own pupil Olive Coleman, on *England's Export Trade 1275–1547* (1963)—a meticulous and comprehensive critical assessment of the surviving customs accounts. Concern with the quantitative record of medieval trade (involving formidable difficulties of interpreting refractory documents) matched equally meticulous investigations into its commercial structures (notably the Merchant Venturer organizations in London and Bristol) and into the connections between trade, industry, and urban development more widely—in particular for Bristol and Exeter. Integral with this was the study of the cloth industry itself, notably in the major chapter in the *Cambridge Economic History of Europe* (volume ii, 1952). Her most renowned article, which raised some controversy over its wider interpretation, was provocatively entitled 'An Industrial Revolution of the Thirteenth Century' (*Economic History Review*, vol. xi, 1941) and was an equally meticulous documentation of the introduction and diffusion of the fulling mill.

With such a steady consolidation of scholarship in a major, defined field her intellectual authority became widely recognized: as associate member of the Royal Academy of Belgium (1961); fellow of the British Academy (1963); trustee of the Cassel Educational Trust (1963); Ford's lecturer in English history at Oxford University (1964–5); president of the Economic History Society (1966–9); president of the Society of Medieval Archaeology (1966–9); Hon.LL D of Smith College (1968); honorary fellow of LSE (1969). In all this the person matched the scholarship. Eleanora Carus-Wilson knew her own measure and her own mind. She kept things very much under control. She was precise, clear-cut, self-assured, always restrained and polite. But her eyes could slightly narrow behind her glasses and remarks dulcet in tone, softly-spoken in the reticent, even prim, style of a very English lady, could mask a devastating content. She had a personal and intellectual authority about her which women academics in England—particularly, perhaps, distinguished women academics of her own generation—possessed in unrivalled measure.

Not having married, her days filled with activities over a wide spectrum of academic and cultural affairs right to the end of her life. She listed 'music and mountains' as her recreations, which signalled long-standing membership of the Bach Choir and annual active holidays with friends in Switzerland. Even in her scholarship there was vivid personal awareness; usually hidden but allowed to escape in some of her less formal pieces. 'The Significance of the Secular Sculpture in the Lane Chapel, Cullompton', for example, is a charming account of medieval cloth-making equipment, with teazel frames and shears being wielded by angels in the vaulting (and John Lane's merchant's mark prominent upon the frames). Its splendid precision of observation and detail establishes a lively dialogue between present and past, between her own awareness and the living history of which she wrote and to which she had dedicated her life.

Eleanora Carus-Wilson died at St. Charles Hospital, Ladbroke Grove, London, 1 February 1977.

[Marjorie Chibnall in *Proceedings* of the British Academy, vol. lxviii, 1982; personal knowledge.] PETER MATHIAS

CARY, SIR (ARTHUR LUCIUS) MICHAEL (1917–1976), civil servant, the eldest of four sons (there were no daughters) of (Arthur) Joyce (Lunel) Cary [q.v.], author, and his wife, Gertrude Margaret Ogilvie, was born at Harrow 3 April 1917. A scholar of Eton College, where he won the King's prize for German, and of Trinity College, Oxford, where he obtained first classes in classical honour moderations and *literae humaniores* (1937 and 1939), Cary quickly made his mark. Entering the Air Ministry in 1939 as an assistant principal, he served as assistant private secretary to the chief of the air staff until in 1940 he joined the Royal Naval Volunteer Reserve. Radar officer in the aircraft carrier *Illustrious* in 1942–3, he later became fleet radar officer until his transfer in 1944 to work on operational design at the Directorate of Radio Equipment. Thus early did he show something of his considerable practical bent.

After the war he returned as principal in 1945 to the Air Ministry where he became private secretary to the secretary of state for air. From then until his death he spent most of his career in the Service ministries and Ministry of Defence. From the start he was thought likely to go far, and by 1951 he had become an assistant secretary and was appointed head of Air Staff Secretariat in 1955. Transferred in July of that year to the old Ministry of Defence, he spent two happy and successful years from 1956 to 1958 as counsellor to the United Kingdom delegation to NATO in

Paris. Meeting able representatives from many countries gave his linguistic skill and his outgoing personality full play.

From 1961 to 1964 he served the governments of Harold Macmillan (later the Earl of Stockton) and Sir Alec Douglas-Home (later Lord Home of the Hirsel) as deputy secretary of the Cabinet with such success that in February 1964 he was appointed the last secretary of the Admiralty. There followed four difficult years for him in which as second permanent secretary for the navy he had to turn the old Admiralty into the new Navy Department of the combined Ministry of Defence, a hard task made the harder for an ex-Air Ministry man by the rivalry between the navy and the air force. During this time, too, he had to deal with the problems caused by the government's unpopular decision to phase out the aircraft carriers. Despite this and the first onset of ill health, he backed his minister, Christopher Mayhew, with panache and firmness.

In 1968 he was promoted to the permanent secretaryship of the Ministry of Public Buildings and Works, and later, in 1970, when the ministry was absorbed into the Department of the Environment, he became secretary of housing and construction in that Department. It was during 1968 to 1970 that he vigorously introduced the controversial reform proposed by Lord Fulton, by which the parallel hierarchies of professional architects and administrators were replaced by the structure of open posts and line management. His sternest architectural critics could not but admire his powerful advocacy of these changes, and the profession as a whole was most grateful for his support for their proposals on the fee scale for private architects which have so benefited the profession since then.

When in 1971 the Procurement Executive was established at the Ministry of Defence he returned there as its permanent secretary and a year later in October 1972 became its chief executive, doing much during its formative period to ensure its successful and permanent integration into the Ministry.

His last two years (1974–6) as permanent under-secretary of state at the Ministry of Defence were largely spent on the Labour government's first and most thorough defence review and their subsequent strenuous efforts to reduce the cost of defence expenditure. He was able to suggest economies that did minimal damage to the country's defence capability and to the morale of his staff. His work was much helped by his good relationships with not only the defence industries but also all those involved in the international aspects of defence.

Great personal charm and powers of imagination, a natural warmth, vitality, and friendliness, brilliant and fluent conversation, and a wide range of interests were his most striking characteristics. Considered by some the golden boy of post-war Whitehall, he perhaps never quite lived up to his early promise, partly because his mind was so quick to seize the main points of major policy issues that he did not spend enough time on mastering the detail. Nevertheless he achieved much: he had a good political instinct and considerable diplomatic skill, and although not a great administrator, he was firm when necessary and was well liked by those who worked alongside and under him.

He gained a half blue in lacrosse and was a keen sailor, but his main recreational interest in later life was making and selling clavichords and harpsichords.

He was appointed CB in 1964, KCB in 1965, and GCB in 1976; in 1967 he was elected a fellow of Eton as masters' representative, in 1971 commodore of the Civil Service Sailing Association, in 1972 president of the Institution of General Technician Engineers, and in 1973 an honorary fellow of his old college, Trinity, and a fellow of the Royal College of Art.

Married first in 1942 to Betty Yingcheng, daughter of Sao-Ke Alfred Sze, a retired Chinese diplomat, he divorced her in 1946 and in the same year married Isabel Margaret, daughter of Charles Duff Leslie, mining engineer; they had four sons and one daughter. He died at Oxford 6 March 1976.

[RIBA *Journal*, 1976, 83, p. 218; *The Times*, 9 March 1976; private information; personal knowledge.] MICHAEL MCCRUM

CASEY, RICHARD GARDINER, BARON CASEY (1890–1976), Australian politician, diplomat, and imperial proconsul, was born 29 August 1890 in Brisbane, Queensland, the elder son (there were no daughters) of Richard Gardiner Casey, a pastoralist with mining interests, of Brisbane, and his wife, Evelyn Jane, younger daughter of George Harris, merchant, of Brisbane. He was educated at Melbourne Church of England Grammar School, Melbourne University, and Cambridge University, where he graduated with a second class in mechanical sciences in 1913. Casey returned to Australia via the United States and had barely begun an engineering career when he joined the Australian Imperial Force in October 1914. He served in Egypt, Gallipoli, and France, rising to the rank of general staff officer. He was appointed to the DSO (1918) and awarded the MC (1917).

The war over, he returned to Australia and assumed several of his late father's mining directorships. However, he craved travel and public service, and on 1 October 1924 the Australian prime minister, S. M. Bruce (later Viscount Bruce of Melbourne, q.v.), appointed him Australia's first liaison officer attached to the

Cabinet Secretariat in Whitehall. Casey's task was to keep Bruce *au courant* with day-to-day imperial problems, and occasionally to act for the Australian government in relations with the City.

In 1931 Casey entered the Australian Federal Parliament as member for Corio (Victoria) in the United Australia Party interest. His rise was rapid—assistant treasurer 1933–5, treasurer 1935–9. Casey's financial management was orthodox, though he had a social conscience which in 1938 led to Australia's first National Health Insurance Bill. Unfortunately (Sir) R. G. Menzies [q.v.] chose the issue to split the Cabinet in a challenge to the leadership of the prime minister, Joseph Lyons [q.v.], and the Bill was shelved. In April 1939 Lyons died, and Casey, Lyons's favourite for successor, chose to stand aside for Bruce. It was a bad miscalculation: Bruce reneged, Casey's rival Menzies assumed the mantle, and Casey lost the Treasury.

Menzies appointed Casey minister for supply and development to organize the economy for the impending war. In October 1939 Casey visited London for supply talks and to help decide Australian military commitment to Europe. With Casey out of the country, Menzies won over the Country Party, who still had wanted Casey as prime minister. Consequently Casey resigned his seat to become Australia's first minister to the United States in March 1940.

In Washington Casey worked hard, usually in harness with the British ambassador, to bring the Americans into the war against Hitler and to secure a guarantee of aid against potential Japanese attacks on British possessions in the Pacific. Both objectives were achieved by late 1941.

Casey's work impressed (Sir) Winston Churchill, who, in early 1942, appointed him British minister resident in the Middle East with a seat in the War Cabinet. Among his most ticklish jobs was negotiating the replacing of Sir Claude Auchinleck as commander by Alexander and Montgomery [qq.v.] in August 1942. After El Alamein, Casey concentrated upon civil administration. He employed characteristically simple and direct methods. Cabinet was persuaded to 'mop up' inflation in the Middle East, including Iran, by buying up £22¼ million of local currencies with gold, 1943–5. Wheat shortages were solved by massive procurement campaigns. A Lebanese political crisis was averted when a Casey bluff induced the French to release the local Cabinet from jail.

So successful was Casey's trouble-shooting that, in early 1944, Churchill made him governor of Bengal to secure the base for the drive by Mountbatten [q.v.] against the Japanese in Burma. Here too his new broom was effective. He reorganized the embattled administration, inoculated virtually the whole population (54 of 65 million) against smallpox, and set about a gigantic food procurement programme to offset the likelihood of another famine of 1943 proportions when over a million had died. Casey's methods impressed the government of India, which gave him an extra £10 million subvention in his first year, but upset local politicians, and in his last year in Bengal he ruled by decree. In March 1946 he returned to Australia.

It took Casey three years to re-enter Australian politics and the ministry. From 1951 to 1960, as minister for external affairs, he encouraged closer relations with Asia and the United States via the Colombo plan and ANZUS and SEATO pacts. A notable achievement was the Antarctic treaty (1959) which secured the continent for peaceful scientific research. In 1956 he privately opposed the use of force over Suez; an issue which lost him a ballot for the deputy leadership of the Liberal Party of Australia. He retired in 1960 and was created a life peer, Baron Casey, of Berwick and the City of Westminster. From 1965 to 1969 he was governor-general of Australia. He died of pneumonia in Melbourne 17 June 1976.

Casey married Ethel Marian Sumner ('Maie'), daughter of Major-General Sir Charles Snodgrass Ryan, surgeon, of Melbourne, on 24 June 1926. He was survived by his wife who died in 1983, daughter, and son. His pleasant, direct manner and capacity for work made him an outstanding diplomat and administrator, though he lacked the mental agility and political sense necessary to achieve the Australian prime ministership to which he aspired.

Casey was admitted to the Privy Council (1939), appointed CH (1944) and GCMG (1965), and created KG (1969).

[Casey Papers, National Library of Australia; T. B. Millar (ed.), *Australian Foreign Minister: The Diaries of R. G. Casey, 1951–60*, 1972; W. J. Hudson and J. North (eds.), *My Dear P.M.: R. G. Casey's Letters to S. M. Bruce, 1924–1929*, 1980; Ethel Marion S. Casey, *Tides and Eddies*, 1966; R. G. Casey, *An Australian in India*, 1947, *Double or Quit*, 1949, *Friends and Neighbours*, 1954, *Personal Experience: 1939–1946*, 1962, and *Australian Father and Son*, 1966; private information.] CARL BRIDGE

CAZALET, PETER VICTOR FERDINAND (1907–1973), trainer of racehorses, was born 15 January 1907 at Fairlawne, near Tonbridge in Kent, the fourth and youngest child and third son of William Marshal Cazalet, of Fairlawne, and his wife, Maud Lucia Heron, daughter of Sir John Robert Heron-Maxwell, seventh baronet, of Springkell, Dumfriesshire. The Cazalets were a Basque family who came to England as Huguenot refugees. Peter Cazalet was educated at Eton, where he developed as an excellent all-round player of ball games and made a century in the cricket match against Harrow at Lords, and at Christ Church, Oxford, where he obtained a third class in chemistry in 1930, a cricket blue, and half blues for rackets, real tennis, and squash.

It was during his three years at Christ Church that the young man, who, as a child, used to hide whenever a pony was produced, suddenly took to riding. Determined, fearless, and superbly co-ordinated, he soon became a proficient amateur rider over fences and hurdles. After a brief unproductive flirtation with industrial chemistry, he spent two years improving his jockeyship and learning stable management with the successful Berkshire trainer 'Sonny' Hall.

In 1932 Peter Cazalet inherited Fairlawne, a large William and Mary house, his eldest brother having been killed in World War I and the second brother wishing to live elsewhere. He began to build up his own small string of jumpers with H. E. (Harry) Whiteman holding the trainer's licence. It was then, in the early thirties, that Anthony Mildmay (later Lord Mildmay of Flete, q.v.), who had been in Cazalet's house at Eton, asked whether he could come and ride out in the mornings on his way to work in the City. Thus was born a friendship and sporting partnership which flourished until Mildmay's untimely death by drowning in 1950. Its saddest and best known moment, at least before the war, was when Mildmay's reins came unbuckled in the 1936 Grand National, allowing his horse Davy Jones, who had a clear lead and looked a certain winner, to run off the course before the last fence. Cazalet rode in that and four other Nationals but a bad fall in 1939 compelled him to give up riding and take out his own trainer's licence.

He spent the war, first in the Royal Artillery (1939–40) and then, with Mildmay as one of his platoon commanders, as a Welsh Guards company commander in the Guards Armoured division. But the moment peace came the two friends returned to Fairlawne, determined to create a training stable run on the best possible lines and, above all, to win the Grand National, preferably with Mildmay in the saddle.

That goal they were never to achieve—thwarted a second time when Mildmay finished a close third on Cromwell in 1948, having ridden blind over the last two fences with his head forced down on his chest by an attack of cramp which, almost certainly, was to cause his death two years later. But 'M'Lord', as a devoted racing public knew him, was leading amateur in each of the post-war seasons leading up to his death and did National Hunt racing a great service by communicating his enthusiasm to Queen Elizabeth and persuading her and her daughter, then Princess Elizabeth, to have a horse in training with Peter Cazalet. The partnership horse, Monaveen, won for the first time in 1949 but when Princess Elizabeth became Queen she decided to concentrate on flat racing. So it was in the Queen Mother's blue and buff colours that Dick Francis went out from the Cazalet stable to ride Devon Loch in the 1956 Grand National. Fifty yards from the winning post, with victory in his grasp, Devon Loch collapsed. That bitter disappointment did not diminish the Queen Mother's support for National Hunt racing and, of the 1,100 winners Cazalet trained at Fairlawne, more than 250 carried her colours. They were ridden by several great stable jockeys including Bryan Marshall, Dick Francis, Bill Rees, Arthur Freeman and, perhaps the most stylish of all, David Mould.

Three times leading trainer, Cazalet sent out what was then a record total of eighty-two winners in 1964–5. Fairlawne was run on old-fashioned lines but, though a strict disciplinarian with a merciless eye for detail, its master was also scrupulously fair. A high proportion of his stable-lads stayed with him throughout their working lives and were both glad and proud to do so. They and the horses alike were always beautifully turned out and, even if some later trainers with 'all weather' gallops at their disposal might reckon the Fairlawne facilities barely adequate, the Cazalet horses were always as fit as horses can be made.

Himself rather shy and uninterested in what he considered pointless chit-chat, Cazalet was, by normal standards, a somewhat aloof figure on the racecourse. But, once formed, his friendships were very seldom broken and those lucky enough to enjoy them knew how often a highly developed sense of humour warmed and brightened his attitude to life.

In 1932 he married Leonora, daughter of Leonard Rowley and step-daughter of (Sir) Pelham Grenville Wodehouse [q.v.], author; they had a son and daughter. The son, Edward, particularly delighted his father by becoming a first-rate amateur rider; having forsaken the turf for the bar, he later became a QC. Cazalet's first wife died in 1944 while undergoing a minor operation and in 1949 he married Zara Sophie Kathleen Mary, daughter of Sir Harry Stapleton Mainwaring, fifth baronet, and former wife of Major (Alexander) Ronald George Strutt, later fourth Baron Belper, by whom she had one son. They had three sons, one of whom died in 1956. Cazalet died at Fairlawne 29 May 1973.

Each January, weather permitting, the Anthony Mildmay Peter Cazalet Memorial Steeplechase is run over 3m. 5f. at Sandown. When it was first run, called simply the Mildmay Memorial, Cazalet won it with Cromwell, Mildmay's favourite horse, ridden by Bryan Marshall. Cazalet also contributed the notice of Mildmay to this Dictionary.

[Private information; personal knowledge.]

JOHN OAKSEY

CECIL, HENRY (pseudonym), author and county court judge. [See LEON, HENRY CECIL.]

CECIL, ROBERT ARTHUR JAMES GASCOYNE-, fifth MARQUESS OF SALISBURY (1893–1972), politician, was born 27 August 1893 at Hatfield House, the elder son and second of the four children of Lord James Edward Hubert Gascoyne-Cecil [q.v.], who became the fourth Marquess of Salisbury in 1903. Educated at Eton and at Christ Church, Oxford, as Viscount Cranborne, he did not cmplete his degree because of service in World War I in the Grenadier Guards; he was awarded the croix de guerre. After the war he worked in the City for some years and entered politics in the 1929 general election, when he held South Dorset for the Conservatives.

In 1934 he was appointed parliamentary private secretary to Anthony Eden (later the Earl of Avon) who was lord privy seal and minister without portfolio in the 'national' government. His first ministerial appointment was that of under-secretary of state for foreign affairs when Eden succeeded Sir Samuel Hoare [q.v.] as foreign secretary in 1935. He worked in complete harmony with his chief and, when Eden resigned in February 1938 in protest against the appeasement of Mussolini, he resigned also. His resignation speech greatly annoyed the prime minister, Neville Chamberlain. After the Munich agreement in October 1938 Cranborne again expressed his unhappiness when he referred in the Commons to Czechoslovakia as 'a country thrown to the wolves'.

When Chamberlain resigned in May 1940 (Sir) Winston Churchill brought Cranborne back into office as paymaster-general and then into the Cabinet in October as secretary of state for the dominions. In January 1941 he was raised to the Lords as Baron Cecil of Essendon so that he could deal with foreign affairs in that House. In February 1942 he was appointed secretary of state for the colonies and leader of the House of Lords. He returned to the Dominions Office in September 1943, having declined an invitation to succeed Lord Linlithgow [q.v.] as viceroy of India. Linlithgow had hoped he would accept once it had been decided that Eden could not be spared, as he thought highly of Cranborne's abilities.

The victory of the Labour Party in the general election of 1945 marked the start of what were probably Cranborne's most effective years, as leader of the Opposition in the Lords. His first major challenge came with the Parliament Bill of 1947. The bill was a direct attack upon the delaying powers of the Lords; Salisbury, as he became on the death of his father in April 1947, fought it with all the formidable debating qualities at his command. After noting the tributes paid by the government to the Opposition in the Lords for passing bill after bill without obstruction, he referred to this bill as 'a bomb in a battle of flowers'. He rounded on the government's doctrine that any government had the right to interpret the views of the people even when these were not accurately known, calling it 'the doctrine of a blank cheque with a vengeance'.

In the same speech Salisbury made a strong plea for the reform of the House of Lords on the grounds that it was still true to say that parties of the right were in too great a majority. He pointed out that in 1888 his grandfather had introduced bills to create life peers and to eliminate peers who did not attend their duties, bills which were defeated not in the Lords but in the Commons. He remained an ardent champion of reform.

The government postponed the bill so that all-party talks on reform could be held. The talks began in February 1948 and embraced the composition of the Lords as well as their powers. Although the Conservatives were prepared to recommend that a permanent majority should not be assured for any one political party and that heredity should not alone constitute a qualification for admission, the talks foundered on the question of powers.

Salisbury had done his best in the cause of reform and he could now resume his attack upon the Parliament Bill in the House. The Lords defeated it in three successive sessions and it was passed against their will in December 1949.

Meanwhile Salisbury tackled the Iron and Steel Nationalization Bill. His tactics were to delay the coming into operation of the Act until 1 October 1950, after the general election, in order to give the electorate a chance of giving a considered opinion on the proposals. The tactics were effective in so far as the government, admitting that they had to face the realities of a situation which they were powerless to alter, tabled an amendment which had the effect that the bill, although it would be on the statute book immediately, could not be implemented in full unless the government were returned to power. The Opposition in both Houses accepted this compromise. Salisbury protested against the accusation by Herbert Morrison (later Lord Morrison of Lambeth, q.v.) of 'intolerable interference' by the Lords and claimed that the government's decision was a complete justification for the existence of a second chamber.

With the return of the Conservatives to office in 1951 Salisbury was appointed lord privy seal and again leader of the House of Lords. In March 1952 he became secretary of state for Commonwealth relations and then, in November, lord president of the council. He carried the sword of state at the coronation of Queen Elizabeth II.

At about this time he was deputed by Churchill to address the Conservative back-benchers on the subject of independent television. He argued, on behalf of the Cabinet, against its introduction but the Parliamentary Party were strongly in favour of it as a safeguard against monopoly broadcasting and did not welcome his words, especially when he deployed the double-edged weapon of the theory of the mandate—a theory which had always attracted him.

Salisbury supported Eden loyally through the Suez crisis in 1956. His advice was sought by the Crown when a successor to the fallen prime minister had to be found; he was in no doubt, after consultation with his Cabinet colleagues, that Harold Macmillan (later the Earl of Stockton) was their choice. In Macmillan's government he was again appointed lord president of the Council and leader of the House of Lords. It is probable that he was never really happy in the new administration (he was very different in temperament from the prime minister) and by March 1957 he had clearly had enough when he suddenly resigned over the release from detention of Archbishop Makarios [q.v.]. There was a banner headline in an evening paper 'Salisbury: the Storm Breaks', but there was no storm of any kind, although there was distress in the constituency parties, where his influence had always been strongest. It was a sad ending to a distinguished career.

From then on Salisbury concentrated upon strong and often strident criticism of the government's African policies. Macmillan's 'wind of change' did not impress him and he lashed out at what he believed was the over-hasty emancipation of the African colonies. Accusing Iain Macleod [q.v.], the colonial secretary, of deceiving the white settlers in Kenya, he indulged in language that conspicuously lacked the dignified tone which he had always adopted so effectively in the past, and described him as 'too clever by half'. It was a savage attack and it certainly harmed the colonial secretary. Salisbury followed it up by resigning his presidency of the Hertfordshire Constituency Conservative Association.

As the crisis in Rhodesia gathered momentum, he attacked the policies of both government and opposition. When the Rhodesians made their unilateral declaration of independence he would not support it, admitting that it was unconstitutional. At the same time he compared their action with that of the American colonists at the time of the war of independence, quoting Burke's words: 'It is not what a lawyer tells me I may do; but what humanity, reason and justice tell me I ought to do.' He did not live to see the creation of Zimbabwe.

Bitterly though he felt about events in Africa, and bitterly though he spoke about them in public, at no time did the charm and courtesy of 'Bobbety', as his friends knew him, desert him in private. On a day's shooting or at a dinner party he was still a delightful companion. He was a man who loved his country, his church, and his family, and who had served without fear.

Salisbury was appointed privy councillor in 1940 and created KG in 1946. He was chancellor of Liverpool University from 1951 to 1971 and had honorary degrees from Toronto (1949), Birmingham (1950), Oxford (1951), St. Andrews (1953), Manchester (1954), Cambridge (1954), London (1955), and Exeter (1956). He was a fellow of Eton College from 1951 to 1966 and, because of his work for science while lord president of the Council, was elected FRS in 1957.

In 1915 he married Elizabeth Vere (died 1982), daughter of Lord Richard Frederick Cavendish. They had three sons, the second of whom died in 1934 and the third in 1944. The eldest son, Robert Edward Peter Cecil (born 1916), succeeded as marquess when his father died at Hatfield 23 February 1972.

[Lord Todd in *Biographical Memoirs of Fellows of the Royal Society*, vol. xix, 1973; personal knowledge.] GLENDEVON

CHADWICK, SIR JAMES (1891–1974), nuclear physicist, was born in Bollington, Cheshire, 20 October 1891, the eldest of three sons (there was also a daughter who died early) of John Joseph Chadwick, cotton spinner, farm worker, and laundryman, and his wife, Anne Mary Knowles. After primary school he attended Manchester Municipal Secondary School from which, at sixteen, he won a scholarship to Manchester University. He intended to read mathematics but was accidentally enrolled into physics and graduated with first class honours in 1911. He was awarded an 1851 senior research scholarship and went to the Reichsanstalt in Berlin where, in 1914, he made his first important discovery: that the β-particles emitted in radioactive decay show a continuous spectrum up to some limit. Chadwick continued to work at the Reichsanstalt after war was declared, until he was interned at Ruhleben where, he records, he 'really began to grow up'. Internment damaged his health; subsequently he always suffered from gastric problems about which he often grumbled.

In 1918 he returned to Manchester where he worked with Sir Ernest Rutherford (later Lord Rutherford of Nelson, q.v.) on the disintegration of the nucleus by α-particles. In 1919 Rutherford moved to the Cavendish chair in Cambridge and took Chadwick with him. Gonville and Caius College gave Chadwick a Wollaston studentship and then, in 1921, a research fellowship.

Chadwick acted as Rutherford's scientific and administrative assistant; he did little teaching except as Rutherford's deputy. His personal research included (1925) the absolute measurement of nuclear charge by α-particle scattering. His great discovery came in 1932 when he showed that radiations produced in the bombardment of beryllium by α-particles gave rise to recoil nuclei in hydrogen and other light elements consistent with the hypothesis that they were an electrically neutral particle, the neutron, of mass approximately equal to that of the proton. This revolutionized the understanding of nuclear structure and led to the atomic bomb and the nuclear reactor; the Nobel prize followed in 1935.

Unlike Rutherford, Chadwick favoured the construction of large nuclear accelerators. In 1935 he accepted the Lyon Jones chair of physics at Liverpool University and encouraged a programme of accelerator construction that continued for thirty years.

Chadwick considered that he inexcusably missed several important discoveries: the positron, artificial radioactivity, and fission. In 1939 he was consulted on the feasibility of a fission-based atomic bomb, and, following the classic paper of Bohr and Wheeler, he corrected his initially negative response. He urged complete co-operation with the United States; after the Quebec agreement of August 1943 he was appointed technical adviser and head of the British Mission in Washington, where he played a key role in the Anglo-American collaboration that, in 1945, produced the ^{235}U and ^{239}Pu bombs.

Chadwick returned, tired and strained, to Liverpool in 1946. His subsequent involvement in international affairs, through the UN, was disillusioning. He remained active in nuclear energy and nuclear weapons work in Britain and served on the board of the Atomic Energy Authority until he was seventy.

Chadwick returned to Cambridge in 1948 to become master of Gonville and Caius College—a move which surprised his friends. He immersed himself in college life and was active in national and international nuclear affairs but he had almost no contact with physics in Cambridge and was almost never seen inside the Cavendish Laboratory, the diversified development of which after the appointment of Sir W. L. Bragg [q.v.] as Cavendish professor in 1938 being one with which he had little sympathy. College life at a time of changing priorities and values brought strains and divisions within the fellowship that Chadwick was unable to resolve: he resigned in 1958 and retired to north Wales; in 1969 he returned to Cambridge.

Chadwick was knighted in 1945 and appointed CH in 1970. He was elected FRS in 1927; he received the Hughes medal in 1932 and the Copley medal in 1950 but had little involvement in Royal Society affairs. He received honorary degrees from the universities of Reading, Dublin, Leeds, Oxford, Birmingham, Exeter, McGill, Liverpool, and Edinburgh, was an honorary member of numerous foreign academies, and received many awards including the US medal for merit and the Mackenzie Davidson, Trasenter, Melchett, Faraday, Franklin, and Guthrie medals.

Chadwick was of an austere mien with a dry, wry, sometimes acerbic humour; he was given to long, disturbing, silences; his judgements were uncompromising but beneath them there was concern, humanity, and compassion. His own commitment to institutions and colleagues inspired lasting loyalty.

In 1925 Chadwick married Aileen Maud, daughter of H. Stewart-Brown, of Liverpool; there followed twin daughters.

[Sir Harrie Massey and N. Feather in *Biographical Memoirs of Fellows of the Royal Society*, vol. xx, 1976; personal knowledge.]

DENYS WILKINSON

CHAIN, SIR ERNST BORIS (1906–1979), biochemist and Nobel prize-winner, was born 19 June 1906 in Berlin, the only son of the two children of Dr Michael Chain, chemist and industrialist, and his wife, Margarete Eisner. He was educated in Berlin at the Luisengymnasium and the Friedrich–Wilhelm University from which he graduated in chemistry and physiology in 1930. He then obtained a Dr.Phil. for research in the chemical department of the Institute of Pathology at the Charité Hospital.

Chain's father was of Russian origin and his mother was related to Kurt Eisner, the socialist who became prime minister of Bavaria in 1918 and was then assassinated. Both his parents were Jewish. With no future and his life in jeopardy in Hitler's Reich he emigrated to England in 1933. After a few months at University College Hospital, London, he obtained a place in the department of biochemistry at Cambridge and worked under Sir Frederick Gowland Hopkins [q.v.] for a Ph.D.

The election of Howard (later Lord) Florey [q.v.] to the chair of pathology at Oxford in 1935 set the scene for Chain's subsequent life. Florey believed that experimental pathology would benefit from the collaboration of pathologists with chemists and offered him a position in the Sir William Dunn School of Pathology. In 1936 he became university lecturer and demonstrator in chemical pathology. At Florey's suggestion he began to study the mode of action of a bacteriolytic enzyme, lysozyme, discovered in 1920 by (Sir) Alexander Fleming [q.v.], and this led him to read accounts of many other observations of the production by micro-organisms of anti-microbial substances. During discussions with Florey about the future direction of their research and its financial support he suggested in 1938 that they should jointly investigate some of these substances. Both Florey and Chain emphasized that their decision to do this was motivated by scientific interest and not by the belief that it would lead to substances of clinical value, but fortunately penicillin, found by Fleming in 1928, was one of three substances initially chosen for study. Fleming had first believed that penicillin might be useful as an antiseptic for application to infected wounds, but he was quickly disheartened by its instability and did not envisage the possibility that it would cure generalized bacterial infections. Thus for more than ten years after its discovery penicillin aroused little medical interest.

Although Chain was confident that problems associated with the instability of penicillin could be easily overcome, little progress with its purification was made until N. G. Heatley suggested that it could be transferred from an organic solvent to a neutral aqueous solution. In the spring of 1940 Florey, urged by Chain to begin his intended biological experiments, showed that preparations of penicillin that were no more than 1 per cent pure would protect mice from infections with streptococci and staphylococci when introduced into the blood stream. This dramatic result entirely changed the outlook and high priority was given to the production in the laboratory, by a group of people, of enough penicillin for a small clinical trial. With the success of this trial, limited though it was by lack of material and that only about 3 per cent pure, penicillin became a substance of major medical importance and one which was likely to be of value in surgery during World War II.

During this time Chain and (Sir) Edward P. Abraham showed that the resistance of some bacteria to penicillin was due to the ability of these organisms to produce a penicillin-inactivating enzyme, penicillinase. They then began to purify penicillin and early in 1943 joined with Sir Robert Robinson [q.v.], Wilson Baker, and others in the Dyson Perrins Laboratory to study its chemistry. Chain became a strong supporter of a β-lactam structure for penicillin, which was proposed in the Sir William Dunn School of Pathology in October 1943 but remained controversial until Dorothy Hodgkin and Barbara Low established it two years later by X-ray crystallography. During these war years Chain played an active part in a major Anglo-American enterprise whose goal was the production of penicillin by chemical synthesis. But although this collaborative effort threw interesting light on the chemistry of penicillin it failed in its final aim; in the event it was an astonishing increase in the yield of penicillin obtainable by fermentation of *Penicillium chrysogenum* that enabled the substance to be produced on a large scale.

Chain was a stimulus to Florey and for some years their relationship was amicable, but it deteriorated when Chain began to complain that he was receiving too little credit for his contribution to the penicillin story and to believe that his failure to realize his large ambitions in England was due to his alien origin. In 1948 he left Oxford for Rome to become director of an international research centre for chemical microbiology at the Instituto Superiore de Sanità. Before leaving he married in 1948 Dr Ann Ethel Beloff, daughter of Simon Beloff, general export merchant, of London NW3, who was herself a biochemist, and they subsequently collaborated in studies of the mode of action of insulin. They had a son and then a son and daughter who were twins. Their married life was most contented.

In Rome Chain faced no financial problems and set up a pilot plant for antibiotic production. He became a consultant to the Beecham Group Ltd. and suggested that it should explore further the potentialities of penicillin. Two members of this company, G. N. Rolinson and F. R. Batchelor, were seconded to his laboratory in 1956 to become acquainted with penicillin fermentation. During their visit they made observations that led after their return to England to the isolation of the nucleus of the penicillin molecule and to the chemical synthesis from this nucleus of a series of new and clinically valuable penicillins.

In the 1950s Chain became anxious about the future of the Instituto Superiore di Sanità after its influential director-general, Domenico Marotta, had retired. In 1961 he accepted the chair of biochemistry at Imperial College, London, although he retained his position in Rome until 1964. His requirements were expensive and the return to England involved him in plans for a new department with a fermentation plant and the raising of relatively large sums of money to construct and maintain it. Although a grant of £350,000 from the Wolfson Foundation was supplemented by substantial sums from research councils and the University Grants Committee the financial base for his operations was not entirely secure.

At Imperial College he worked with different colleagues on a variety of topics, ranging from a phytotoxin to an inducer of interferon production and the mode of action of insulin. But, as the time for his retirement in 1973 approached, he became deeply absorbed in an unsuccessful attempt to ensure that his successor would be in a field closely related to his own and would not be a molecular biologist. Two chairs were finally advertised, but neither was filled to his liking.

Chain's role in the initiation of the work on penicillin in Oxford was his major contribution to medicine. He shared a Nobel prize with Fleming and Florey in 1945 and was elected to the fellowship of the Royal Society in 1949. He became an honorary fellow of the Royal College of Physicians in 1965 and was knighted in 1969. His many honours from other countries included the Paul Ehrlich centenary prize in 1954, the Order of the Rising Sun, second degree, from Japan in 1976, and the Grand Decoration of Honour in Gold of the Federal Republic of Austria in 1973. In 1976 he became foreign member of the Academy of Sciences of the USSR.

He held strong views on science policy; he emphasized the value of collaboration between academic and industrial institutions and had connections with many pharmaceutical companies, among which those with Astra in Sweden and with Beecham were the most important; and his various activities involved him in world-wide travel.

Chain was a highly gifted and voluble man with some physical resemblance to Albert Einstein. He was able to converse fluently in German, French, Russian, and Italian, as well as in English. As a young man he had been faced with a choice between science and music for a career. Music remained a major interest in his life and he played the piano with distinction. He was socially engaging. But his tenacity and emotional involvement when fighting for policies that commanded little support could irritate others and brought turmoil into his life. In 1971 he built a house at Mulranny in county Mayo and died there 12 August 1979.

[Sir Edward Abraham in *Biographical Memoirs of Fellows of the Royal Society*, vol. xxix, 1983; Ronald Clark, *The Life of Ernst Chain*, 1985; personal knowledge.] E. P. Abraham

CHAMBERLIN, PETER HUGH GIRARD (1919–1978), architect and planner, was born in London 31 March 1919. His mother, Eleanor Penelope, née Chamberlin, died soon after he was born and he was brought up by great-aunts. He was educated at Bedford School and at Pembroke College, Oxford, where he read politics, philosophy, and economics from 1938 to 1940, when he left. Chamberlin's entry into architecture was fortuitous. During World War II he first, as a conscientious objector, worked on the land in Wales and then served in Civil Defence in London. To occupy his spare time he was enrolled as a part-time student at the School of Architecture in Kingston, Surrey, where he was living, by his wife, the daughter of William Raper Bingham, a civil servant; they had married in 1940. Having qualified as an architect in 1948, Chamberlin taught at the Kingston School and became the deputy head of staff. The head was Eric Brown, with whom Chamberlin first entered into partnership. Together they designed the Seaside section at the Festival of Britain of 1951.

The Kingston School was also responsible for the architectural partnership with which Chamberlin was principally associated. In 1951 another lecturer, Geoffry Powell (born 1920), won the competition for the Golden Lane housing estate just north of the City of London. To handle this rather daunting commission for a young architect, Powell invited Chamberlin and a third Kingston colleague, Christof Bon (born 1921), to join him in the work and in 1952 the partnership of Chamberlin, Powell & Bon was founded. The firm established a reputation with the completion of two small and utilitarian buildings: the Cooper Taber seed warehouse at Witham, Essex, of 1955 and the Bousfield School, South Kensington, London, of 1956. Both combined a straightforward and expressive use of a steel frame with good brickwork in rectilinear forms. In these and subsequent jobs the firm established itself as one of the leading practices in the emerging post-war generation of British architects wholly committed to the ideals of Modernism in architecture and strongly influenced by Le Corbusier.

While some of their contemporaries concentrated on public housing, Chamberlin, Powell & Bon were principally concerned with new university buildings, a type which comprised a conspicuous element in British architecture at the time. This was work in which Chamberlin's leadership and ability to organize and control detail became very important. He prepared a development plan for the University of Leeds and the firm designed a number of buildings there in the 1960s and 1970s, including laboratory and lecture blocks, halls of residence, and libraries. The most notable university commission was for New Hall, Cambridge, begun in 1962. Here, to give the college's new buildings a distinct character, the firm's earlier austere manner was made richer by historical allusions and by extravagant use of space, culminating in the strange mosque-like dome over the hall.

The monumentality and Romanticism evident at New Hall is even more conspicuous in the Barbican in the City of London, the massive scheme of comprehensive redevelopment which is the firm's principal achievement and in which the particular influence of Chamberlin's talents, both as a designer and as an organizer, is most evident. The first of several plans for the badly bombed area was published in 1955, but work on the residential blocks and towers did not commence until 1963 and the Arts Centre was not begun until 1971 and only completed four years after Chamberlin's death. The Barbican project was so dogged by difficulties and delays that by the time it was eventually finished it represented, in its failings as well as in its triumphs, one of the last monuments to the idealism of the 1950s.

In contrast to the adjacent Golden Lane estate designed by the firm, the Barbican is much heavier and more monumental; the pick-hammered dark granite aggregate of the concrete and the great brick arches of the podia have a sublime character, reminiscent of Piranesi or the work of the Victorian engineers. This manner reflects the personal intervention of Chamberlin, who, as well as following the planning ideas of Le Corbusier, came to admire the Swiss master's late, more expressionistic works such as the Unité d'Habitation in Marseilles. As a result, the three towers at the Barbican are possibly the most carefully modelled and successful tall buildings in British architecture of the period.

The buildings designed by Chamberlin, Powell & Bon received several awards and medals from the RIBA. Chamberlin himself was awarded the RIBA's distinction in town planning in 1963; he had become an associate of the Institute in 1948 and a fellow in 1959. He was appointed CBE in 1974 and elected an associate of the Royal Academy in 1975. Always called 'Joe', he was a large and gentle man much loved by his friends, but he was also compulsively energetic and determined, if not inflexible, when it came to an important architectural point, over which he could exhaust himself. He drove large black cars, loved the theatre, and was addicted to the cinema; it is recorded that he saw *Singing in the Rain* over thirty times. He and his wife were enthusiastic travellers and it was at the temple at Abu Simbel that he was first taken ill before dying, suddenly, 23 May 1978, while gardening on the island in the Thames at Sonning where he had made one of his several homes.

[*The Times*, 26 May 1978; *RIBA Journal*, August 1978; personal knowledge.]

GAVIN STAMP

CHANDOS, first VISCOUNT (1893–1972), colonial secretary and business man. (See LYTTELTON, OLIVER.)

CHAPLIN, SIR CHARLES SPENCER (1889–1977), film actor and director, was born 15 April 1889 in East Street, Walworth, London, the son of Charles Chaplin, variety comedian, and his wife, Hannah ('Lily Harley'), daughter of Charles Hill, cobbler, of county Cork. The birth appears not to have been registered. His father drank and the parents separated a year after Charles was born; however the mother was successful enough as a vaudeville singer to support herself and her two sons (the elder, Sydney, was the result of an early affair which had taken her to South Africa). But her voice failed, engagements dwindled, and the family was reduced to the workhouse. Mental instability followed, and Chaplin has described how as a child, with his brother at sea in the navy, he struggled alone in London to keep alive, employed as newsboy, printer's boy, doctor's boy, and, for a brief disastrous adventure, glass-blower. He had for a time been a member of a team of clog-dancers, the Eight Lancashire Lads; he continued to dream of the stage, and when Sydney, released from the navy, was back in London and able to help him he found employment in the theatre, first in a short-lived play called *Jim*, then as the page-boy in *Sherlock Holmes*, which with H. A. Saintsbury in the title-role toured for three years. Music hall followed; he joined Sydney in the Fred Karno Company. He quickly learned the vaudeville technique which was to serve him so well. Soon he was in America, touring with the second Karno company. In 1913 he received an invitation from Keystone, a company producing short comic films. Doubtful of his future in the world of the cinema, he hesitated, but the offer of $150 per week persuaded him, and at the end of the year he was in Hollywood, working for Mack Sennett.

The story of his beginnings in the cinema is familiar. There was an inauspicious start: then Sennett told him to go and pick out a costume and make-up of his own choice. He selected baggy trousers, outsize shoes, a tight jacket, a hat too small, a moustache, and a cane. With the outfit the idea of the character grew in his mind. There was, of course, no script; he knew only, he was to say, that Mabel Normand (she was a star of silent comedy) was involved with her husband and a lover. He was not allowed to develop the character he had created. The old hands could not accept what they saw as his stage technique. Used to inventing his own comic business, he chafed.

In May 1914 he was allowed to write and direct a one-reel piece. His creative career had begun; and for the next four years, first with Keystone, then with other companies—Essanay, Mutual, First National—he made the series of short silent comedies which were to establish him as the darling of the public. The figure in the baggy pants became the universal Tramp. The titles are indicative: *The New Janitor* (1914), *The Rink* (1916), *The Floorwalker* (1916). Chaplin appeared as various characters; he was the fireman, the roller-skater, the boxer, the pawnbroker, the immigrant, and the patient in the sanatorium. In the earlier pieces he was the scallywag capable of snatching the coin from the blind man's wallet. But the character softened and absorbed sentiment. Pathos was added to laughter.

By the end of 1918 he was extending not only in emotional scope but in length. His ironic joke about the miseries of trench warfare, *Shoulder*

Arms (1918), ran for three reels, and in 1920 there came the first of his feature films, *The Kid*, a story with fully developed action. It was followed in 1923 by the four-reel *The Pilgrim*, and Chaplin, now his own master, took a rest. There was a much fêted visit to London, Paris, and Berlin; then he embarked on an experiment in a mood alien from the works which had made him world-famous. Himself appearing for no more than a few moments, and with Edna Purviance from his short comedies cast as the heroine, he directed *A Woman of Paris* (1923), a melodramatic story of a country girl frustrated in love who becomes a notorious Paris beauty; Adolphe Menjou played the insouciant seducer. The playing had a restraint far ahead of the period. But without the expected Chaplin comedy the film was a failure. Withdrawn, it remained a mere title in film history books until the 1980s, when it was revived to a critical acclaim greater than it deserved. Its chief interest is still historical. Fortunately Chaplin returned to the path of his true genius. In 1925 he made *The Gold Rush* with its enchanting visual jokes such as the hand-dance and the meal off a shoe. In 1928 *The Circus* followed.

In 1931 there was *City Lights*, perhaps the culmination of Chaplin's career. In Europe again, he was hailed by the great and the humble; he was admired by G. Bernard Shaw [q.v.] and royalty received him. Police had to restrain crowds gathered to see him. Nevertheless times were changing in the cinema for the screen had found its voice; now Chaplin was faced with the challenge of the 'talkies'. He compromised: *City Lights* had sound, but it was not a 'talkie'; in one hilarious moment he mimicked the hiccups of a man who has swallowed a toy whistle but he did not speak. Five years later he was still compromising; in *Modern Times* (1936) Chaplin contented himself with a nonsense song. And he was committing himself to political opinions; the film, ridiculing the mechanization of factory work; was taken as a defence of unions and the labour movement. Political unpopularity (Chaplin was openly pro-Russian) in the United States was followed by moral attack when he was involved in a painful paternity case. His Hitler satire, *The Great Dictator* (1940), failed to win back his popular esteem. He was losing the sureness of his touch in mingling comedy and sentiment—for example, the fervour of his final speech in *The Great Dictator* seemed hollow. The American public turned against its favourite—who had never renounced his British citizenship.

Chaplin was shedding the Tramp character. In *The Great Dictator*, with Chaplin attempting the role of a political leader, the figure of a barber shared the narrative with a satirized Hitler figure. Seven years later, in *Monsieur Verdoux* (1947), he completely abandoned his famous early character; now he was playing a multiple murderer who, comparing his handful of deaths with the massive exterminations of war, becomes the advocate of pacifism. It was a brilliant film; but it was a failure with the public. Chaplin was to make one more film in America, *Limelight* (1952), a sentimental tale of an old music-hall star and the young dancer he befriends. Chaplin's name carried it through, but Buster Keaton, playing a minor role, outshone him. When he left the United States for the European première the American government banned his re-entry and he took up residence in Switzerland. His two last films were made in Britain: *The King in New York* (1957), an attempt, only momentarily successful, to revive his old comedy style, and *A Countess from Hong Kong* (1966), a romantic comedy in which he directed Sophia Loren and Marlon Brando but himself made only brief appearances.

Chaplin was the supreme example of the artist in one sphere of entertainment who was able not only to transfer to a much larger field the talents he had acquired but also to transform the development of the second sphere. Beginning in the British music hall, given a chance in the American cinema, he had insisted that he had something to contribute: insisted against opposition, for his physical comedy—the falls, the run suddenly halted by the limits of the stage—was at first pure vaudeville. But nature had endowed him with a genius for invention. Creator as well as performer, he observed the oddities of human behaviour and enshrined them in a superb gallery of fictions. To the character he had invented in his first days in Hollywood he added social and political satire—and emotional range. He was the born novelist who wrote in visual absurdities. Enormously gifted, he composed music for his films and wrote autobiographical books which stand the test of time. The miseries of his childhood, combined with the triumph of his maturity, gave him the confidence to attack the society which had fostered him, and inevitably he was attacked as a result. His latest work was flawed by sentimentality; and like many comedians he sometimes stretched his gifts beyond their proper limits. But his invention was boundless; and in *Monsieur Verdoux* he showed that his genius went far beyond physical comedy. His finest films were illuminated by passages of a visual brilliance which have never been surpassed. It is possible to argue that his best work is to be found in the short pieces which preceded his feature-length successes: in *Easy Street* (1917), for example, or in the miraculous details of *The Pawnshop* (1916). But however one assesses his genius, he must be recognized as one of the creators of the art of the cinema.

In social encounters Chaplin was an easy and inspiring companion, eager to lavish on chance acquaintance his gifts as raconteur and mimic. In

1962 he received honorary D.Litts. from Oxford and Durham universities and in 1971 he became a commander of the French Legion of Honour. In 1973 he was received back into the American film establishment and given a special Oscar. He was appointed KBE in 1975.

He was married four times: in 1918 to Mildred Harris (died 1944); in 1924 to Lolita McMurry ('Lita Grey'); in 1936 to Marion Levy ('Paulette Goddard'). These three marriages, which were stormy and racked with scandal, ended in divorce (in 1920, 1927, and 1942). Of the first there was a son who lived three days, of the second two sons, and of the third no children. Finally in 1943 he married the daughter of the playwright Eugene O'Neill, Oona, with whom he lived happily for the rest of his life. They had three sons and five daughters, one of whom, Geraldine Chaplin, achieved considerable success as a film actress. Chaplin died 25 December 1977 at his home, Vaud, Vevey, Switzerland. There is a statue by John Doubleday (1981) in Leicester Square.

[Theodore Huff, *Charlie Chaplin*, 1952; Charles Chaplin, *My Autobiography*, 1964, and *My Life in Pictures*, 1974; David Robinson, *Chaplin, his Life and Art*, 1985.] DILYS POWELL

CHAPMAN, FREDERICK SPENCER (1907–1971), explorer, mountaineer, jungle warfare expert, and author, was born 10 May 1907, at Kensington, London, the younger son and younger child of Frank Spencer Chapman, solicitor, of Oakwood Court, Kensington, and his wife, Winifred Ormond, who died within a month of the birth. She was the daughter of William Ormond, solicitor. Frank Spencer Chapman's business failed and he left for Canada to become a farmer when his younger son was two, leaving his boys in the care of the Revd Ernest Dewick, an elderly clergyman, and his wife, Sophie. The boys lived with them near Carlisle and later at Lindale, where Frederick began to develop a lifelong interest in the creatures and plants of wild countryside. A young ordinand in the house took him up Helvellyn at the age of eight. When the Dewicks retired the Chapman boys went to live with the Revd Sam Taylor, vicar of Flookburgh in Cartmel, and his wife Ella, both of whom were a stalwart support during Frederick's subsequent turbulent career. Their father wrote to them regularly but in 1914 enlisted in the Canadian Mounted Rifles and was killed during the Somme battle in September 1916.

In 1921 Chapman went to Sedbergh School, where he began to display his endurance and passion for exploration. He won a Kitchener scholarship to St. John's College, Cambridge, and obtained third classes in both English part i (1928) and history part ii (1929). At Cambridge he met Geoffrey Winthrop Young [q.v.], the Alpine mountaineer who held open house for young climbers and others. Chapman learned rock climbing on the walls and roofs of colleges and was taken to the Alps by Lawrence Wager [q.v.] and (Sir) Jack Longland. He became acquainted with young explorers, pre-eminently H. G. ('Gino') Watkins [q.v.] who invited him to join him on an expedition to Greenland.

The British Arctic Air Route Expedition (1930–1), which surveyed air routes with two Tiger Moths, gave Chapman an opportunity to display his toughness, particularly in the cleverly navigated rescue of Augustine Courtauld (whose notice he was later to write for this Dictionary) from the completely snowed-up meteorological station on the 10,000 ft. Greenland ice-cap. Of all his expeditions, it was the one to which he contributed most. Chapman's *Northern Lights* (1932) vividly recalls the enchantment and rigours of exploring, sledging, and keeping alive in the Arctic. In 1932–3 Watkins led another party to continue the Arctic air survey but was drowned when seal hunting in a kayak in the first few weeks. On his return Chapman, who had been one of the party, wrote *Watkins' Last Expedition* (1934), which is full of fascinating vignettes of Eskimo life and the party's success in living, like them, off the creatures of sea and land.

Chapman then turned to teaching, accepting a post at Aysgarth preparatory school. He found the change from his Greenland adventures difficult, although his reputation as an explorer was an asset in dealing with small boys, whom he took into the wilder country near the school and inspired with some of his own passion for natural history. Meanwhile, and for most of the rest of his life, he was in demand as an admirable lecturer on his Arctic and other adventures. Remarkable as these were, they lost nothing in the telling.

But the mountains still called, and after two years he left Aysgarth in 1935 to join Marco Pallis's Himalayan expedition. This was perhaps not exactly right for him: he did not share Pallis's passion for Tibetan culture, and had hoped to be chosen for an Everest expedition, for which his mountaineering experience was too slight. He was however invited to join a government mission to Lhasa, capital of Tibet, which he thought a more exciting prospect than running a prep school. But this too proved not quite what he wanted. He found the Tibetans less approachable than his beloved Eskimos. In 1937 however, when his time at Lhasa came to an end, he mounted an expedition with one English companion and only three Sherpas to Chomolhari, a striking and challenging 24,000-ft. mountain on the southern borders of Tibet. His account of its ascent, with only one novice Sherpa porter, was doubted by some experienced mountaineers, but a later analysis in the *Alpine Journal* gave him the credit for having succeeded against the odds and in wretched weather. Two books record this stage of his career: *Lhasa, the Holy City* (1938) and *Helvellyn to Himalaya* (1940), both reasonably successful but not reaching the standard of his earlier Greenland books.

After Chomolhari, still uncertain whether a life of expeditions or of schoolmastering was to give him what he wanted, Chapman was introduced to Kurt Hahn [q.v.], headmaster of Gordonstoun School, who in 1938 appointed him a housemaster. Gordonstoun and Hahn's educational beliefs suited Chapman well, and helped to shape ideas which he was to put into practice later in Germany and South Africa. But he had completed only four terms there when war came, and as a Territorial officer with the Seaforth Highlanders he joined up at once. He was soon given appropriate work, helping to train a mountain division and the first of the Commandos in Scotland. He was then transferred to Australia.

Chapman was posted to Singapore in September 1941, and when the first Japanese landings in Malaya came two months later he was sent to Kuala Lumpur 'expressly to organize and lead reconnaissance and operational parties behind the enemy lines'. He did this for nearly three years. He himself felt that he had missed the 'real war', and yet his record of endurance and resourcefulness and his ability to escape from the Japanese who had put a price on his head is almost unmatched in the history of World War II. When taken out by submarine in 1945 he returned to Colombo a justified hero. His story came later in the best of all his books, *The Jungle is Neutral* (1948), which was an enormous success. Chapman had also earned a DSO (1944) and bar (1946).

In 1946 Chapman married Faith Mary, daughter of Major George Harrison Townson. They were to have three sons. He spent a year as first organizing secretary of the Outward Bound Trust. In 1948 he was appointed to build up a new boarding school, for the British Forces Education Service, the King Alfred School at Plön in West Germany. He had a free hand to appoint staff and develop the school as he wished. He made a success of the post but resigned in 1952 to caravan across Africa with his wife and three small boys. The book which resulted, *Lightest Africa* (1955), was not a success.

From 1956 to 1962 Chapman was headmaster of the Anglican foundation of St. Andrew's College, Grahamstown, South Africa. He was not really happy there and resigned when South Africa became a republic in 1961. From 1962 to 1966 he was warden of the Pestalozzi Children's Village at Sedlescombe, but this was another job that did not suit him. He was rescued by an old friend of Special Operations Executive days, Professor Vernon Mallinson, of Reading University, who in 1966 offered him the wardenship of Wantage Hall, one of the university halls of residence. There he was contented and made a useful mark. Yet he became worried about his impending retirement and his health. He began to doubt what his life, with all its adventures and heroism and sheer indestructibility, amounted to. Despite his remarkable record, all his life he aspired towards greater fame than he felt he had actually achieved. He shot himself in his office in Reading 8 August 1971.

Among his awards were the Arctic medal (1931), Gill memorial medal (RGS, 1941), Mungo Park medal (RSGS, 1948), *Sunday Times* special award and gold medal (1949), and Lawrence of Arabia memorial medal (RCAS, 1950).

[Ralph Barker, *One Man's Jungle* (biography), 1975; *The Times*, 10 August 1971; private information; personal knowledge.]

JACK LONGLAND

CHAPMAN, SIR RONALD IVELAW- (1899–1978), air chief marshal. [See IVELAW-CHAPMAN.]

CHENEVIX-TRENCH, ANTHONY (1919–1979), headmaster of Bradfield, Eton, and Fettes, was born at Kasauli in the Punjab 10 May 1919, the youngest of the four sons (there were no daughters) of Charles Godfrey Chenevix-Trench, CIE, revenue commissioner in the Indian Civil Service, and his wife, Margaret May, daughter of John Holmes Blakesley, engineer, of The Avenue, Kew Gardens. The Trench family had been a Huguenot one settled in Ireland. Having spent his early years in India Anthony attended Highfield School at Liphook whence he won a scholarship to Shrewsbury. His schooldays were happy and successful and he entered Christ Church, Oxford, as a scholar in 1937, gaining a first class in classical honour moderations (1939) before the outbreak of World War II.

He joined the Royal Artillery and was seconded to the 4th Mountain Battery, Frontier Force, Indian Artillery. He was captured during the Japanese advance in Malaya in 1942 and remained a prisoner of war for three and a half years in Malaysia, working on the Thailand–Burma railway. His undaunted personal qualities enabled him and helped others to survive the ordeal. During his captivity he translated all the English poetry he knew into Latin and Greek, and before returning home—his name already something of a legend—collected many of his men and personally saw them back to India. Back at Oxford in 1946 he was runner-up in the Craven and Ireland scholarships and obtained a first class in *literae humaniores* (1947), with alpha marks in every paper.

He was offered three Oxford fellowships but chose to return to Shrewsbury School in 1948 to take the sixth-form classics. He left to become tutor in classics at Christ Church in 1951, but agreed to return to Shrewsbury the following year when an unexpected vacancy left the housemastership of the School House open. It was not, however, long before he was offered a headmastership, which he took up at Bradfield College in 1955. He was a member of the Robbins committee on higher education (1961) and became headmaster of Eton College in January 1964. He left Eton in 1970 and became headmaster of Fettes College in 1971.

Trench's success was due to a combination of intellectual gifts, personality, and a deep understanding of boys. He was, first and foremost, an outstanding schoolmaster. His interest lay in the education of the young as individuals, his compassion for those in difficulty heightened by his experience as a prisoner of war. His quality as a notable headmaster depended more on his leadership of staff and pupils by personal example than on any deliberate policy of innovation.

At Bradfield he inherited a somewhat divided staff with a modest academic record, but he soon drew them together and motivated them and their pupils towards a new period of progress and success. His shortcomings as an administrator were detected, but his reputation led to his appointment at Eton with the dual role of modernizing the curriculum and getting to know more of his staff and pupils than had been possible for his predecessors. In both roles his headmastership was remarkably successful. He revolutionized the sixth form work of the school, bringing it into the mainstream of GCE A-level studies and achieving unprecedented success in open scholarships at Oxford and Cambridge. At the same time he contrived to get to know a great number of pupils and to earn their affection and respect. Small of stature and full of humour, he was entirely lacking in arrogance and pomposity and was a witty conversationalist and raconteur.

Trench had been well aware from the outset that his methods were better suited to a small school than a very large one, and it was with difficulty that he was persuaded to migrate from Bradfield to Eton. His flexible and pragmatic approach helped him to face with a high degree of success the notorious problems of school discipline in the 1960s, but his habit of improvisation caused some criticism at Eton. The unstinted devotion of his time to individuals exhausted him physically and the effects of his wartime deprivation began to take their toll. He left after six years and was obliged to take a long rest before embarking on his third headmastership.

His achievement at Fettes was as remarkable as at Bradfield and Eton and received even more contemporary approbation. He found the college with some 420 boys and fifteen girls; and left it with 490 boys, forty girls, and a new junior school. During his tenure its financial position and scholarship endowments were greatly improved, but above all he transformed its rather rigid and hierarchical disciplinary system into a more liberal one based on trust and common sense. He became FRSE in 1978. His health became a matter of growing concern and he died in Edinburgh 21 June 1979, just before his planned retirement. Never happier than when out of doors, especially enjoying rough shooting and ornithology, he had hoped to return to Norfolk where his parents had retired.

Trench married in 1953 Elizabeth Chalmers, eldest daughter of Captain (Sir) Stewart Dykes Spicer (later third baronet), RN, who ably supported him in his three headmasterships and enabled him to keep open house for all comers. They had twin daughters and two sons.

[School archives; personal knowledge.]

WILLIAM GLADSTONE

CHESHIRE, GEOFFREY CHEVALIER (1886–1978), academic lawyer, was born at Hartford, Cheshire, 27 June 1886, the second son of Walter Christopher Cheshire, solicitor and registrar of Northwich County Court, Cheshire, and his wife, Claira Hatt Cook. He was educated at Denstone College and Merton College, Oxford. He obtained first class honours in jurisprudence in 1908 and a second class in the BCL degree in 1910. From 1909 to 1911 he lectured at the University College of Wales, Aberystwyth. In 1911 he was called to the bar by Lincoln's Inn and returned to Merton as assistant lecturer in law; and in 1912 he was elected to a fellowship at Exeter College.

In 1914 he obtained a commission in the Cheshire Regiment, but on transfer to the Royal Flying Corps in 1916 he was assigned to the Kite–Balloon Section, which involved him, for a few months, in sitting in a basket a thousand feet above the British lines and spotting German targets for the gunners.

After the war he returned to his teaching at Exeter College, where from 1919 to 1933 he also acted as bursar. As law tutor he regularly had about thirty pupils, for whom he covered the whole range of the law examinations. As a lecturer he always drew large audiences, speaking in a clear gentle voice and with lucidity and directness. During that period he produced, in 1925, his *The Modern Law of Real Property*, in which he prepared readers for the coming into force of the seven statutes which cleaned up and greatly modified property law. In the book he traced the shifting policies underlying the law and the techniques employed in achieving them, and enunciated the law in its new more perspicuous and rational form. The book enjoyed an immediate and lasting success. In 1927 he undertook, with four colleagues, the task of reorganizing, for a nineteenth edition, *Stephen's Commentaries of the Laws of England* (4 vols., 1928). His main personal contribution was an attempt to display the law of property as a single whole, instead of merely describing successively the separate laws of real and personal property. Unfortunately his synthesis, though it received a welcome from academic reviewers, was shipwrecked on the conservatism of the teachers, and can now be consulted only in libraries or in second-hand copies.

In 1922 Cheshire added to his other offices that of All Souls lecturer in private international law and, in 1935, two years after relinquishing the position for that of All Souls reader in English law, he brought out the results of his work under the title *Private International Law*. That part of English law is the perfect antithesis to real property law, for it is still fluid and in course of development. Hence it offered the freest scope to the mere jurist; and Cheshire, like Saul among the Prophets, entered a territory quite different from that to which he had been accustomed. This highly original book also was 'born a classic'.

In 1944 he was elected Vinerian professor of English law. In 1945, in collaboration with his former pupil C. H. S. Fifoot, he published *The Law of Contract* with a companion *Cases on the Law of Contract* (1946). *Cheshire and Fifoot* was the first entirely new book on the subject to appear for many years. In spite of the critical temper pervading it, it has held the field and is a stand-by not only of teachers and students but of the bench and bar.

Cheshire retired prematurely from the chair in 1949, but continued for many years to lecture to bar students. He was also employed as a member of several committees concerned with law reform. He served as a JP and presided over a juvenile court.

In retirement he became deeply involved in his son Leonard's scheme for the support of terminal patients and was mainly responsible for drawing up the memorandum of association and articles of the Leonard Cheshire Homes Foundation. In consequence, in 1950, he abandoned his Berkshire home and moved to the old laundry cottage in the grounds of the Cheshire Home in Hampshire.

He was tall, spare, and of athletic build. From the time when he represented Merton at soccer and tennis he played games actively and to the end he kept himself fit. He was very practical: he built his Berkshire house with the aid of an architect and a clerk of works but without a contractor. He was handy with machinery and drove his ageing car to an advanced age, in fact until the accident that caused his death. He was genial and had many friends of all ages. His dry wit made him excellent company, though he did not relish large groups or great occasions.

He was, beyond doubt, the most eminent English academic lawyer of his generation, excelling as a lecturer, college tutor, and systematic writer. In his three books he introduced a new stage in the development of important branches of English law by raising their literary treatment to a higher level and subjecting them to reasoned criticism. The books have been described as intermediate between treatises and manuals. They are not exhaustive: they do not deal with every judicial decision or legislative provision relevant to the subject. But they do not merely state rules and general principles: they also allow scope for historical explanation, criticism, and, above all, the discovery and development of logical strands of doctrine. These qualities not only commend them to teachers and students but lead both bench and bar to look to them for help in basing argument on principle.

One of the secrets of Cheshire's success as a writer was that he did not find law easy. He wrestled with a problem in his own mind and then worked out the best way to convey the conclusion he had arrived at, subjecting it also to the reactions of his audiences and pupils. 'Cheshire', said Lord Edmund-Davies, 'contrived to be both clear and stylish, he transformed the *look* of a page, he lightened the drudgery of learning.' Moreover, in the many editions of his books, for which he retained responsibility to an advanced age, he was always ready to change his mind when convinced of the arguments of others. He was indeed the least opinionated of legal writers.

In 1945 he was elected FBA and an honorary bencher of Lincoln's Inn. He became an honorary fellow of both Merton and Exeter colleges; and he received the honorary degree of LLD from London, Manchester, and Jadavpur universities.

He married in 1915 Primrose (died 1962), the younger daughter of Colonel Thomas Adam Anderson Barstow, of the Seaforth Highlanders. They had two sons, Group-Captain Leonard Cheshire, VC, DSO, and Christopher, head of Shell in Spain. In 1963 he married Dame Mary Kathleen Lloyd, DBE, who had been director of the Women's Royal Naval Service from 1950 to 1954. She was the daughter of Aloysius Joseph Lloyd, master draper, of Channonrock, Hayling Island. She died in 1972. Cheshire himself died 27 October 1978 in Portsmouth General Hospital, ten days after a car accident.

[*The Times*, 30 October 1978; F. H. Lawson in *Proceedings* of the British Academy, vol. lxv, 1979; private information; personal knowledge.] F. H. Lawson

CHICHESTER, Sir FRANCIS CHARLES (1901–1972), airman, sailor, and navigator, was born 17 September 1901 at Shirwell, the younger son (there were later two daughters) of the Revd Charles Chichester, vicar of Shirwell, Devon, seventh son of the eighth baronet, and his wife, Emily Annie, daughter of Samuel Page, of Chitt's Hill, Wood Green, London. He was educated at the infants' school in Barnstaple, at preparatory schools in Ellerslie and Bournemouth, and at Marlborough. He spent an unhappy childhood, left Marlborough at the age of seventeen, and emigrated in December 1919 to New Zealand with only ten sovereigns in his pocket. There he tried a variety of jobs, until as a land agent and property developer he was able to earn a substantial income and to accumulate some capital. In 1923 he married Muriel Eileen, daughter of M. L. Blakiston; they had two sons, the first stillborn, the second, George, who died in 1967. The marriage broke up within three years and in 1929 his first wife died. George was brought up by his New Zealand grandparents until Chichester's second marriage.

Chichester became the hero of the British people and achieved world fame when at the age of sixty-five he sailed solo around the world between August 1966 and May 1967, 29,600 miles in 226 days sailing time. Nearly forty years earlier he had established himself as a record-breaking pilot in small aircraft and his feats as a navigator became well known. Indeed navigation is the link between his exploits in both spheres. He would not have claimed to be either a natural pilot or a natural sailor and it is in the technique of navigation that he made his immediate contribution to the development of aviation and later demonstrated his capabilities at sea.

Together with his partner in the estate agency, Geoffrey Goodwin, he formed an aviation company, and learnt to fly at a New Zealand air force station. Returning after ten years' absence to England he took further flying lessons at Brooklands, bought a plane, a Gipsy I Moth, gained his A licence, made a preliminary tour of Europe, and then in 1929 set off for Australia. After nineteen days' solo flight and a variety of incidents, including twice damaging the plane, he landed at Sydney, New South Wales, to an uproarious welcome from thousands of people, being only the second pilot successfully to accomplish this hazardous operation.

Back in New Zealand Chichester determined to be the first to fly solo from east to west across the Tasman Sea. This necessitated landing on two small islands, roughly equally spaced across the ocean, to refuel. To do so demanded absolutely accurate navigation. His method was to aim off the mark and having reached the selected point, checked by a sun sight, to turn and sweep along the position line until he could see his target. He used a sextant, five-figure logarithmic tables, and a scribbling pad strapped to his knee, all in the very cramped space of a small cockpit. Having fitted floats to his Gipsy I Moth to enable him to land on the island lagoons, he made accurate landfalls at Norfolk Island, where he encountered engine trouble on take off, and Lord Howe Island, where his plane sank and had to be rebuilt, before reaching Jarvis Bay, south of Sydney. By his resourcefulness, skill, and determination he had triumphed. Continuing by stages what he now envisaged as a round-the-world tour later in 1929 he crashed in Japan after hitting telephone wires at Katsuura, seriously injuring himself and writing off his plane. Back in England he married in 1937 Sheila Mary, daughter of Gerald Craven, of Belle Eau Park, Nottinghamshire, the son of Thomas Craven, of Kirklington Hall, Nottinghamshire; they had one son, Giles. After a year in New Zealand together they returned to live permanently in England and Chichester took up a post as a navigation specialist with a firm of instrument makers.

Frustrated during the first years of World War II by the failure of the RAF to make use of his navigational experience, he was eventually appointed navigation officer at the Empire Flying School (1943–5). After the war he established his own publishing firm for maps and guides. He then took up ocean racing, first as a navigator and later, in 1958, with his own boat Gipsy Moth II. In 1958–9 he suffered from lung cancer but recovered and in 1960 with Gipsy Moth III he won the first single-handed transatlantic race. In the same race two years later he knocked nearly seven days off his previous record but came second. Gipsy Moth IV was built to circumnavigate the globe which he successfully accomplished with one stop at Sydney. What had been denied him in the air he had been granted at sea. He failed in his subsequent attempt in Gipsy Moth V to sail four thousand miles in twenty days, from Guinea Bissau across the Atlantic to San Juan del Norte in Nicaragua, but his time of twenty-two days established another record. The fourth single-handed transatlantic race in 1972 proved to be his last. Frail when he started, he became ill and returned to Plymouth. He died there shortly afterwards 26 August 1972.

Chichester was appointed CBE in 1964 and KBE in 1967, when he reached Sydney half way through his single-handed voyage round the world. The Queen dubbed him with Sir Francis Drake's sword at Greenwich after his return. He received many other honours and awards. He recorded his exploits both in the air and at sea in a number of books, but his personality and his philosophy can best be summed up in his own answer to a question after his tumultuous welcome at Plymouth. Why did he do it? 'Because', he replied, 'it intensifies life.'

[Francis Chichester, *The Lonely Sea and the Sky*, 1964; Anita Leslie, *Francis Chichester*, 1975; personal knowledge.] EDWARD HEATH

CHICK, DAME HARRIETTE (1875–1977), nutritionist, was born at 5 Newman Street, London, 6 January 1875, the fifth child and third daughter of the eleven children (four boys and seven girls) of Samuel Chick, a prosperous lace merchant and property owner, and his wife, Emma Hooley, the daughter of a grocer and corn merchant, of Macclesfield in Cheshire. Her parents, who were both Methodists, brought up their large family strictly with family prayers twice daily and a ban on such worldly pleasures as theatres and dancing. They sent their daughters to Notting Hill High School, which provided an excellent education (including science) for girls. Consequently five of them became university graduates in botany, physics and chemistry, English, and medicine.

Harriette Chick graduated B.Sc. from University College, London, and turned her attention to bacteriology, obtaining her London D.Sc. in 1904 partly by a study of green algae in polluted waters. With an 1851 Exhibition she worked in the Hygiene Institutes of Vienna and Munich under Professor Max Gruber, a pioneer in bacteriology, and in Liverpool under (Sir) Rubert Boyce [q.v.]. (Sir) Charles Sherrington [q.v.], professor of physiology in Liverpool, suggested she should apply for the Jenner memorial research studentship at the Lister Institute of Preventive Medicine near Chelsea Bridge, of which (Sir) Charles Martin (whose notice Harriette Chick later wrote for this Dictionary) had become director in 1903. Her application was vigorously opposed by two members of the staff who implored the director not to appoint a woman, but she joined the Institute in 1905. The following year she started to investigate the process of disinfection by chemicals and heat. The standard test for disinfectants was that introduced by Samuel Rideal and J. T. Ainslie Walker in 1903, but was unrealistic as it was carried out in distilled water. The Chick–Martin test, which replaced it, added organic matter (3 per cent dried human faeces). This led Chick and Martin to carry out pioneer work on the nature of proteins, demonstrating that heat coagulation was an orderly process governed by established chemical laws. Three important papers in 1908, two with Martin, occupied 117 pages of vol. viii of the *Journal of Hygiene*.

In 1915, following the outbreak of war, Harriette Chick went to Elstree to assist the urgent task of testing and bottling tetanus antitoxin for the army. She soon returned to Chelsea to supervise the preparation of agglutinating sera for the diagnosis of typhoid, paratyphoid, and dysentery, then prevalent in Allied troops in Flanders and the Middle East. Later with colleagues she studied the distribution and stability in foods of the antiscorbutic vitamin. She became a fellow of University College, London, in 1918. From 1918 to 1945 she was secretary of the accessory food factors committee, making a particular contribution to *The Present State of Knowledge Concerning Accessory Food Factors (Vitamins)*, the first of a series of monographs published between 1919 and 1932. From 1934 to 1937 she was secretary of the League of Nations health section committee on the physiological bases of nutrition.

In the spring of 1919 information reached Britain that nutritional deficiencies were rife in eastern Europe. The accessory food factors committee sent Harriette Chick and Elsie Dalyell from the Lister Institute to investigate the deficiencies in Vienna; a few months later Margaret Hume joined them. They found scurvy, rickets, and xerophthalmia were prevalent in infants and young children, and osteomalacia in the elderly. Working with the staff of the Universitäts Kinderklinik, the team confirmed both Huldschinsky's discovery that ultraviolet light healed rickets and the healing property of cod-liver oil. These were important contributions to public health.

Back at the Lister Institute in 1922 Harriette Chick returned to the study of proteins, this time of their nutritional value. This led to the purification of diets for rats and so to B-vitamins, at a time when little was known about them. She became interested in pellagra and the relation of maize to this disease, and gave a series of lectures on it in the USA in 1932. When World War II started, the Lister division of nutrition, which she directed, moved from Chelsea to Martin's house in Cambridge. She continued to work on the nutritive value for rats of bread, flour, and potatoes. After retirement in 1945 she kept in contact with the Lister Institute as a member of its governing body, attending the annual general meeting in June 1975.

She was a founder member of the Nutrition Society in 1941 and was elected an honorary member in 1949. From 1956 to 1959 she was president despite being over eighty years of age. In 1974 the British Nutrition Foundation awarded her its annual prize, for which she prepared a lecture on her work in Vienna; shortly before her 100th birthday she gave a lively introduction, leaving the remainder to be read by Dr A. M. Copping. She remained mentally and physically active until her death in Cambridge 9 July 1977 at the age of 102 years. For her work in nutrition she was appointed CBE in 1932 and DBE in 1949. She was awarded an honorary D.Sc. by Manchester University in 1933.

Harriette Chick was short in stature, neat in dress, lively, and interested in conversation until her sudden death. She was unmarried. There is no painting, but a photograph taken at her desk in her 100th year is in the possession of the British Nutrition Foundation.

[Information from her niece Dr Katharine Tansley (Mrs Lythgoe) and her nephew Dr Peter Blackman; Margaret Tomlinson (niece), *Three Generations in the Honiton Lace Trade*, 1983; Harriette Chick, Margaret Hume, and Marjorie Macfarlane, *War on Disease, a History of the Lister Institute*, 1971; personal knowledge.] H. M. SINCLAIR

CHORLEY, ROBERT SAMUEL THEODORE, first BARON CHORLEY (1895–1978), lawyer and conservationist, was born 29 May 1895 at Kendal, Westmorland, the eldest of three sons (there were no daughters) of Richard Fisher Chorley, a solicitor, and his wife, Annie Elizabeth, daughter of Samuel Frost, farmer, of Hardingstone, Northampton. After attending Kendal School Chorley proceeded to Queen's College, Oxford, obtaining a BA in 1916. During World War I he served in the Foreign Office, the Ministry of Labour, and the Cheshire Regiment.

In 1920 he was called to the bar (Inner Temple). Although he did some practice, mainly in the commercial field, he soon turned to law teaching and became tutor and lecturer at the Law Society School of Law. His expertise in banking and commercial law, on which he wrote several books, led to his appointment to the Sir Ernest Cassel chair of commercial and industrial law at the London School of Economics, which he held from 1930 until 1946. During World War II Chorley joined the Home Office and Ministry of Home Security (1940–1) and was appointed a deputy regional commissioner for Civil Defence (1942–4). In 1944 he became chairman of Westmorland quarter-sessions, a post he held until 1968.

The end of the war marked a significant stage in Chorley's career. He unsuccessfully contested the Northwich division as a Labour candidate in 1945. Afterwards he was created a peer in the same year and made lord-in-waiting, an office he held from 1946 to 1950. In that capacity and as chief spokesman for the government in the House of Lords on a number of subjects he played a full part in securing the passage of the huge legislative programme of the Labour government and as a result in 1946 he found it necessary to resign his chair. He was active as a member of government and other committees.

Chorley was a man in the broad tradition of Victorian radicalism and shared fully in the belief in a progressive society to be brought about by universal education and a strong legislative programme. He envisaged a complete change of attitude towards the legal system. For him the human and social problems underlying the morass of technical law were the matters of real concern. He thus became persuaded that what was lacking in Britain was a legal journal of contemporary outlook encompassing the whole problem of law reform in its social and humane context. He was fond of saying that his most important achievement was the foundation and successful development of the *Modern Law Review*, of which he became the first general editor in 1937, and whose editorship he continued until 1971. This publication played a crucial role in the outlook of successive generations of lawyers who learned from its pages to appreciate that law was no arid field whose interest was confined to a narrow 'closed-shop' of professionals, but something of immense concern to every citizen in the land, and that the law's development called for a legal profession imbued with the sense of a social task.

For Chorley compassion was a sentiment not simply to be indulged in but something which must be manifested in practical action. Thus it was the reform of the penal system which seized his imagination, and into which his long service at quarter-sessions gave him a deep insight. It was therefore most fitting that in 1961 he was made a QC by the lord chancellor, Viscount (later the Earl of) Kilmuir [q.v.], who so far departed from the general practice by offering silk to Chorley without previous application. Chorley was vice-president of the Howard League for Penal Reform from 1948, chairman of the Institute for the Study and Treatment of Delinquency (1950–6, president 1956–76), and president of the Haldane Society (1957–72) and of the National Council for the Abolition of the Death Penalty (1945–8).

Above all Chorley had a deep attachment to and lifelong concern for the English countryside. As a native of Kendal he had a profound love for the Lake District and became involved in all the major battles to resist encroachments on that hallowed territory. Chorley served as president of the Fell Rock Climbing Club of the English Lake District (1935–7), as vice-chairman of the National Trust, and as honorary secretary for the Council for the Preservation of Rural England (1935–67).

Those who only knew Chorley in his later years, when he presented a bent figure peering behind thick glasses, had some difficulty in envisaging him as a mighty man in the world of mountaineering, but in his younger years he was recognized as a leading mountaineer, and later became president of the British Mountaineering Council (1950–3) as well as a vice-president of the Alpine Club (1956–8). With all these accomplishments there was a warmth and geniality to his personality. Despite the difficulties he encountered in recognizing people visually, he had a wonderful and unfailing memory for all his innumerable circle of friends and acquaintances, and not least his students, especially those from overseas. In 1970 he became an honorary fellow of LSE.

In 1925 Chorley married Katharine Campbell, the daughter of Edward Hopkinson, MP, D.Sc., of Alderley Edge, Cheshire. They had two sons and one daughter. Chorley died in hospital in London 27 January 1978 and was succeeded in the barony by his elder son, Roger Richard Edward (born 1930).

[*The Times*, 28 January and 9 February 1978; *Modern Law Review*, vol. xli, 1978, 121–3; private information; personal knowledge.]

LLOYD OF HAMPSTEAD

CHRISTIE, DAME AGATHA MARY CLARISSA (1890–1976), detective novelist and playwright, was born 15 September 1890 at Torquay, the third and youngest child and second daughter of Frederick Alvah Miller, of independent means, formerly of New York, and his wife, Clarissa ('Clara') Margaret Boehmer. She had no schooling at all, not even a governess. But, once having frustrated her mother's current belief that no child should read until the age of eight, she devoured books voraciously, as well as conducting in her mind an endless school story with a vivid and varied cast. She began to write, too. At eleven there was a poem in a local paper ('When first the electric tram did run'). But the notion of being a writer as such, she says in *An Autobiography* (1977), never entered her head.

Her talents were seen to lie in the direction of music. At sixteen she went to Paris and studied both singing and the piano, hoping for a concert career only to learn that her temperament was too reticent for public performance. Her happy, quiet life in Torquay—it was to be reflected in the values that underlay all her books—was plunged into a more dramatic tempo when, rejecting a suitor with whom she had an unannounced engagement, she fell in love with a young officer, Archibald Christie (died 1962), just about to join the Royal Flying Corps. She married him, at two days' notice, in 1914 during his first leave after war had broken out, and then returned to the Voluntary Aid Detachment nursing she had taken up and the dispensary work that followed.

It was during lulls in the dispensary that she began a detective story. Seeking some point of originality for a sleuth in the Sherlock Holmes tradition she thought of the Belgian refugees in Torquay and Hercule Poirot, retired Belgian policeman evacuated to England, was born, though it was not until 1920 and six unsuccessful trips to publishers that he saw the light of day in *The Mysterious Affair at Styles*, a book that shows little indeed of the prentice hand. Once embarked on a writing career, however, books followed in regular succession until in 1926 she produced *The Murder of Roger Ackroyd* which by its daring reversal of the understood conventions of the genre created a considerable sensation.

It was a sensation that in the same year was echoed in her own life. Her husband, now Colonel Christie, had fallen in love with a friend's secretary, Nancy Neele, and at the same time following the death of her much loved mother she undertook the clearing up of the old family home. The strain was too much. Leaving no explanation, she made her way from Surrey to a Harrogate hotel where she registered under Miss Neele's name. The disappearance of a figure associated with crime and a highly popular form of writing caused an immense furore, and when after nine days she was recognized the newspaper brouhaha left her always suspicious of publicity. She divorced Colonel Christie in 1928. There was one child of the marriage, a daughter.

It was as the result of a visit during an impromptu holiday to the archaeological site at Ur then being excavated by (Sir) C. Leonard Woolley [q.v.], whose wife was a passionate admirer of *The Murder of Roger Ackroyd*, that she met (Sir) Max Mallowan [q.v.]. They were married in 1930 and for the remainder of her life, except for his period of service in the war of 1939–45, she was closely associated with his work, learning to photograph, clean, and register the hundreds of small finds of a dig, to run a camp and pay the many workmen. She accompanied her husband on his expeditions, and a handful of her novels reflect the archaeological life, notably *Death Comes As the End* (1945), ingeniously set in Ancient Egypt, as well as a slim factual account enlivened with humour, *Come Tell Me How You Live* (1946).

But archaeology did not prevent her producing a book a year, sometimes more, and her best work is to be found in the twenty-five novels she wrote up to the end of the war of 1939–45 with two 'last books' written in the war years and consigned to her solicitor's safe to appear, *coronat finis opus*, as *Curtain: Hercule Poirot's Last Case* in 1975 and as *Sleeping Murder* in 1976, which contained the final appearance of Miss Marple, her equally popular sleuth brought from short stories to the novel in *Murder at the Vicarage* (1930), whose intuition replaced the logicality of Poirot's 'little grey cells'.

These books show her two great gifts, ingenuity of puzzle and unhesitating narrative. The ingenuity is to be found both in basic plot and in beautifully skilful minor misdirection. That basic conjuring trick may be exemplified in the idea for *Evil Under the Sun* (1941) in which a character is presented to the reader as the archetypal misused wife only to be revealed finally as co-conspirator with her supposedly arrogantly straying husband. The minor misdirections—

there are scores of them—may be typified as either verbal sleight of hand ('I did all that was necessary', neutrally says the character who has in fact been arranging his alibi) or visual trickery (seeping blood that is nail polish with a real wound self-inflicted later).

The narrative skill is always unobtrusive. It consists primarily in a shunning of all irrelevance, even of the fine phrase, that is almost heroic, coupled with a fine sense of timing (perhaps deriving from her musicality). To these two positive factors must be added, in accounting for the enormous success of the books, some more negative ones. Characters are seldom portrayed in any depth or much described, so that readers as far apart as Nicaragua and Bengal can each see them through their own experience. Nor did she often leave the territory she knew best, upper middle-class English life, limiting but safe. Physical description of all kinds is minimal and as much as possible of the story is told through dialogue, easy everyday talk.

These virtues, and these avoidances of the pitfalls awaiting the ambitious, account too for her success as a playwright, artistic in *Witness for the Prosecution* (1953), financial in *The Mousetrap* (1952). Two other aspects of her work should be mentioned, the six romantic novels she wrote as Mary Westmacott, uneven but personally revealing, and the volume of religious stories for children, *Star over Bethlehem* (1965), which speaks a little of the spiritual commitment that sustained her until her death, wheeled in her invalid-chair from the luncheon table by her husband at their Oxfordshire home, Winterbrook House, Wallingford, 12 January 1976.

So popular did her books become that totalling her sales defied all the efforts of her publishers and literary agent. She was translated into 103 languages. Her film rights were sold for record sums. Her play *The Mousetrap* achieved a run on the London stage exceeding a quarter of a century and far outpacing any other. She was honoured with the CBE in 1956 and appointed DBE in 1971. She was a D. Litt. of the University of Exeter.

[Agatha Christie, *First Lady of Crime* (ed. H. R. F. Keating), 1977, and *An Autobiography*, 1977; Janet Morgan, *Agatha Christie*, 1984.]

H. R. F. KEATING

CHRISTIE, JOHN TRAILL (1899–1980), headmaster and college principal, was born at Chipping Ongar 19 October 1899, the fourth son (there were no daughters) of Charles Henry Fehler Christie, DL, JP, stockbroker, and his wife, Margaret Eleanor, daughter of the Revd Charles Samuel Palmer, canon of Hereford. He was educated at Winchester and (after a brief period in the Coldstream Guards, in which he was a second lieutenant in 1918) at Trinity College, Oxford, where he obtained firsts in classical honour moderations (1920) and *literae humaniores* (1922). His vocation had become clear before he took finals, and in that same year he accepted an invitation from W. W. Vaughan [q.v.] to teach classics to the upper bench at Rugby. 'I enjoy teaching more and more,' he wrote, 'I wouldn't be a don.' But he very soon became known as a fine teacher and scholar and in 1928 was persuaded to go back to Oxford as fellow and tutor in classics at Magdalen.

In 1932 he was appointed headmaster of Repton, and in 1937 he succeeded H. Costley-White as headmaster of Westminster. Two years later the life of the school was violently disturbed by the war. The government, and everyone else, was convinced that London would be bombed, and in 1938 plans were already being made for schools to be evacuated from the danger area. When the code signal 'Pied Piper' was sent out by the government, Christie led his staff and boys down to Sussex, where Lancing and Hurstpierpoint contrived to accommodate them. Nine months later, when a German invasion of the Channel coast was expected, they had to move again. Christie eventually settled his flock in makeshift quarters in and near Bromyard, and there they stayed till the end of the war. To keep the school in good heart and true to its educational ideals demanded unusual powers of leadership, and the headmaster was never at less than full stretch. The return to London in 1945 brought fresh problems, for the school buildings had been severely damaged and in part destroyed in the air raids. In 1946, worn out at last by his unceasing labours, Christie went down with a severe illness and was out of action for some months. He spent three more strenuous years at Westminster, but in 1950 he welcomed the opportunity to return to Oxford as principal of Jesus, succeeding his old friend Sir Frederick Ogilvie [q.v.].

It was not the Oxford he had known twenty years earlier. He watched ruefully the encroachment of administration on the time that surely belonged by rights to study and teaching. But he was a dutiful man, and only a recurrence of ill health stopped him from offering to shoulder the burden of the vice-chancellorship when his turn came in 1960. He retired in 1967.

Christie's advice in educational matters was widely sought. He went to India with the commission on secondary education appointed by the Indian Ministry of Education (1952–3) and himself wrote the report, and in 1956 he undertook for the British Council an inspection of schools throughout South America to report on the suitability of the teachers sent out by the Council. He served on the governing bodies of Rugby, Haileybury, Glenalmond, and Brecon and was the first governor of the Dragon School at

Oxford. To this Dictionary he contributed the notice of Cyril Bailey.

He was an entertaining speaker and an impressive preacher, but he was, above all, a teacher. He excelled in poetry, especially, perhaps, Sophocles and Shakespeare, but he enjoyed all literature, grave and gay. He was a lifelong admirer and champion of Sir Walter Scott and was president of the Walter Scott Society in 1953. Messrs Collins engaged him to write the introductions to a new edition of the Waverley novels launched by them in 1955, but only three volumes were published.

Christie was a tall spare man with a normally serious, almost stern expression which was shaken easily into deep laughter. He was strong and active as a young man, something of a rock climber, and a redoubtable walker. He welcomed a companion but was happy to walk *solus*. It was not everyone that could keep up with him.

He married in 1933 Lucie Catherine, only daughter of Thomas Philip Le Fanu, CB, commissioner of public works in Ireland, and a nephew of the Irish novelist J. S. Le Fanu [q.v.]. There were two daughters of the marriage. Christie died 8 September 1980 at Sudbury. He is buried in the parish churchyard of Great Henny, Suffolk, where he and his wife had bought a country cottage many years earlier.

There are portraits at Jesus College (of which he was elected an honorary fellow in 1967) by Peter Greenham, at Westminster by Allan Gwynne-Jones, and at Repton by Edward Halliday.

[Private information; personal knowledge.]

A. L. P. NORRINGTON

CHRISTOPHERS, SIR (SAMUEL) RICKARD (1873–1978), protozoologist and expert in tropical medicine, was born 27 November 1873 in Liverpool, the elder son and eldest of three children of Samuel Hunt Christophers, of Cornish extraction and head statistician of the Mersey Docks and Harbour Board, and his wife, daughter of William Rickard, a mining expert in Redruth, Cornwall. Christophers was educated at the Liverpool Institute and entered University College, Liverpool, as a medical student at the age of sixteen where he became strongly influenced by (Sir) C. S. Sherrington [q.v.]. He qualified as MB, Ch.B. in 1896.

He was then appointed a medical officer on a steamer of the Booth Line bound for the upper reaches of the Amazon; he was probably inspired by the recently published *Huit Cents Lieues sur l'Amazone* of Jules Verne (1881); this experience gave him a taste for the tropics which he never lost. On his return to England he was appointed a member of the joint malaria commission of the Royal Society and Colonial Office from 1898 to 1902. His senior colleague was J. W. W. Stephens and together they investigated malaria in the inhabitants of Central and West Africa and later in India; they recommended measures for the control of the disease and, over fifty years later, Christophers formulated a definitive policy based on a lifetime's experience.

He joined the Indian Medical Service (IMS) in 1902 and remained in the research branch for the next thirty years; this included service in Mesopotamia during World War I. In the IMS he was appointed in turn director of the following research establishments: King Institute in Madras (1904), Central Malaria Bureau (1910), Central Research Institute of Kasauli (1920–32), and kala-azar commission (1924–5). India in those years was the Mecca of malariologists, and Christophers was the star figure in the constellation which included John A. Sinton, S. P. James, (Sir) Gordon Covell, H. E. Shortt (his favourite companion), and their Indian fellow officers, M. K. Afridi and Jaswant Singh. The joint production by Christophers, Sinton, and Covell of successive editions of *How to do a Malarial Survey* (first edn. 1928), despite the simplicity of its title, was based on profound knowledge and became the Bible of malariologists of the era.

Christophers left India with the rank of brevet colonel in 1932 and on his return to England he was made professor of malaria studies at the University of London, in the London School of Hygiene and Tropical Medicine. In collaboration with J. D. Fulton, he worked on the biochemistry of the respiratory metabolism of *Plasmodium knowlesi*, a lethal parasite of rhesus monkeys, and on *Trypanosoma rhodesiense*, the cause of human sleeping sickness. In 1938, at the age of sixty-five, he left London and was given accommodation in the department of zoology in Cambridge. Here he reverted to entomology, probably his favourite subject, and in 1960 appeared his magnum opus *Aedes aegypti (L): the Yellow Fever Mosquito*. An earlier landmark was the issue in 1933 of the fourth volume (*Family Culicidae, Tribe Anophelini*) of *The Fauna of British India*. At the age of ninety he finally retired and spent his remaining years at Broadstone in Dorset.

Christophers's life was devoted to research. His first studies on the effects of malaria on the inhabitants of the tropics had revealed the paradox that the greater the density of the infection, the less was its severity as a disease, and he showed that this was due to the operation of acquired and racial immunity. He unveiled the cause of the dreaded blackwater fever by demonstrating its relationship to the irregular consumption of quinine by patients chronically afflicted with malignant tertian malaria. He made notable contributions to the taxonomy of malaria and other parasites. He was greatly interested in the transmission of leishmaniasis (kala-azar), which he suspected was due to the bite of infected sandflies, and was delighted when his friend H. E. Shortt confirmed the truth of this assumption. He worked for some years on the developmental stages of *Babesia canis* (which causes a fatal disease in dogs) in ticks, and tentatively described sexual stages and zygotes; his theory had to wait almost eighty years for confirmation by electron microscopy. To this Dictionary he contributed the notices of Sir David Bruce and Sir Ronald Ross.

Christophers treated scientific visitors of all ages as equals, and with typical humility. He was shy and modest, imperturbable, patient, and kind. He was quiet but cheerful, and loved the open-air life of the tropics. In this way, he survived until he was 104, the record age of any fellow of the Royal Society. Early in his career he had escaped unscathed from the yellow fever of the South American forests; then he had to face the very real threat of a white man's grave in Sierra Leone, and eventually, by means of simple prophylaxis, he withstood the perils of malaria and blackwater fever in the Punjab, Assam, and elsewhere in the East. The latter half of his life was spent in England, where his iron constitution continued to preserve him from the rigours of civilization.

His centenary was celebrated by the Royal Society of Tropical Medicine and Hygiene of which he had been president (1939–43) and the Royal Entomological Society of London; while a year before his death, a symposium of the 'Birth of Medical Entomology' was dedicated to him. In the course of his life he accumulated many honours: he was honorary physician to King George V from 1927 to 1930, and in 1931 received a knighthood; he was appointed CIE in 1915 and OBE in 1918; he was elected FRS in 1926 and an honorary fellow of Downing College, Cambridge, in 1942. In addition to medals and prizes from British societies he was given honorary foreign membership of societies in the United States of America, Brazil, India, France, and Holland.

In 1902 Christophers married Elise Emma (died 1963), daughter of Fitzroy Frederick Colin Sherman, a coffee planter in the Nilgiri Hills, India, and his wife, Elise Blacas, daughter of the Duc de Blacas, a French admiral. They had a son and a daughter. Christophers died 19 February 1978 at Broadstone, Dorset.

[H. E. Shortt and P. C. C. Garnham in *Biographical Memoirs of Fellows of the Royal Society*, vol. xxv, 1979; family information; personal knowledge.] CYRIL GARNHAM

CHURCHILL, CLEMENTINE OGILVY SPENCER-, BARONESS SPENCER-CHURCHILL (1885–1977), was born in London 1 April 1885, the second of the four children (three daughters, one son) of Colonel (Sir) Henry Montague Hozier, and his wife Lady Henrietta Blanche Ogilvy, eldest daughter of the tenth Earl of Airlie. Following a distinguished military career, her father was secretary to Lloyd's of London from 1874 to 1906.

Clementine Hozier's childhood and adolescent years were not easy: her parents separated for ever in 1891 when she was nearly six, and after the break-up of her parents' marriage her mother was financially very badly off, and she and her children led a peripatetic existence between rented houses and furnished rooms, mainly in England, but they also lived in Dieppe and Paris for short periods. Clementine was educated mainly at home, but she attended Berkhamsted High School for Girls from 1901 to 1904. Because of her mother's straitened finances and social situation, Clementine made her appearance on the London social scene under the auspices of a benevolent relation. She soon became known for her great beauty, charm, and intelligence, and was much in demand.

Clementine Hozier first met (Sir) Winston Churchill in 1904, at a ball in London. He was the elder son of Lord Randolph Churchill [q.v.] and of the beautiful Jennie Jerome of New York City. He had recently left the Conservative Party to join the Liberals. Their first meeting was brief, and they did not meet again until the spring of 1908, when, after a short courtship and engagement, they married at St. Margaret's, Westminster, on 12 September 1908. Churchill was nearly thirty-four and a Cabinet minister, his wife was twenty-three.

It was a love match which was to endure undimmed for fifty-seven years. There were five children of the marriage: four girls and one boy. A daughter, Marigold, died in infancy. From the earliest days of their marriage Clementine threw herself into her husband's political life with enthusiasm: she had espoused not only Winston Churchill but his cause, and these early years of her marriage when the Liberal government was in the full spate of its radical reforming programme, made a strong imprint upon her: she was to look back upon them as the happiest of her life. She then and later took a lively and active interest in her husband's constituency, participating to the full in the hurly-burly of elections. Throughout their married life they wrote to each other even if they were separated for only a few days. Their letters breathe spontaneity and affection; Clementine's to Churchill show the degree to which she was interested and involved in his political life; and his to her demonstrate the confidence he reposed in her discretion and judgement. But while she supported her husband loyally, from time to time she was to hold different views from him on various issues. Moreover, fiercely protective of his political reputation, she did not always approve or like some of his friends, sometimes showing better judgement than him on both issues and personalities. Clementine Churchill was outwardly friendly and confident, and her tact and charm were always great assets, but throughout her life she remained indifferent to the blandishments of purely social life. She was basically a shy woman, giving her trust and friendship slowly.

During World War I Clementine Churchill shared to the full the anguish and near despair felt by her husband after the débâcle of the Dardanelles expedition, as a result of which he eventually resigned from the government and went out to serve as a soldier at the front. Their letters to each other during that period (November 1915 to March 1916) are among the most moving and politically interesting of their long correspondence. Clementine Churchill worked energetically organizing canteens for munition workers, and in 1918 she was appointed CBE.

In 1922 Winston Churchill bought Chartwell, near Westerham in Kent, which was to be their home for forty years, and the place where he loved best to be. But for his wife it was never the source of pleasure and ploys it was for him: during the twenties and thirties they were in a fragile financial position, and she found Chartwell an expensive incubus. When Churchill rejoined the Conservative Party in 1924 after some years of increasing disenchantment with the now divided Liberals, his wife also transferred her allegiance, but although she continued to work loyally for her husband in his constituency, she remained at heart a somewhat old-fashioned and radical Liberal, and able to maintain at times robustly independent views.

Between the wars her domestic and political life largely consumed her energies. The priorities in her life had emerged early: her husband came first; thereafter their children, friends, and her own interests and pleasures competed for what was left of heart and energy. She was a devoted, conscientious mother, but, especially with the elder children, she delegated not only their care but also the sharing of their company and pleasures to others, which in retrospect she was to regret. She had great vitality and she loved sports and games: riding and hunting featured briefly in her early married life; she played tennis to tournament standards; when she was over fifty she learned to ski. She also loved travelling, while Churchill preferred to paint, usually in the South of France. During the thirties therefore from time to time she pursued her own pleasure and enjoyed some long and interesting voyages to the East and West Indies.

With the outbreak of World War II, Winston Churchill joined the government as first lord of the Admiralty and his wife threw herself once more into war work. But her own personal role assumed a special importance when Churchill became prime minister and leader of the coalition government (1940–5). In addition to her care for him and the official obligations of a prime minister's wife, she accompanied her husband on many of his tours of inspection and visits to bombed cities. From 1939 she was a member and faithful attender of the house committee of the Fulmer Chase Maternity Hospital for Wives of Officers. In 1940 and at other times during the war she visited air-raid shelters in the London area, reporting directly to the prime minister on the conditions many thousands of Londoners were enduring; through her efforts improvements resulted. From 1941 to 1947 Clementine Churchill was president of the YWCA Wartime Fund, taking a particular and active interest in their hostels for service women. (After the war she continued her work for the YWCA and was chairman of its national hostels committee from 1949 to 1952.) In 1941 she embarked upon what was to become the most consuming work she was to undertake, when she was appointed chairman of the Red Cross Aid to Russia Fund. In all, the Fund ('Mrs Churchill's Fund', as it became popularly known) raised a total of some £7½ million. In March 1945, at the invitation of the Russian Red Cross, Clementine Churchill visited Russia to inspect many of the institutions equipped or otherwise assisted by her Fund; she travelled widely in the Soviet Union, and was received by Stalin. She was awarded the Order of the Red Banner of Labour. At home, in recognition of her work for the Russian Fund and her other signal services, she was appointed GBE in the victory honours list.

The war years had taken their toll of her health and stamina, and, both in and out of office, Churchill's life continued to make many demands on her; but after his final resignation in 1955 she was able to lead a less arduous life. She now had a special position in the public eye, and enjoyed the many marks of affection and esteem which were accorded her. But these latter years were overshadowed by the deaths in 1963 of Diana, their eldest daughter, and in 1968 of Randolph, their only son. As Churchill's vitality ebbed, life closed in too for her, for she never liked to be away from him for long. He died 24 January 1965 in his ninety-first year.

In 1966 Clementine Churchill was created the Baroness Spencer-Churchill, of Chartwell; she was much gratified by this, and was only prevented from taking a regular part in parliamentary life by her increasing deafness. Outstandingly lovely as a young woman, her beauty lasted on into old age. All her life she maintained high personal standards and disciplines: both in public and private she always presented an elegant and soignée appearance. She kept a lively interest in public as well as family affairs, and despite bouts of illness she led a pleasant life in her last years, surrounded by love, care, and esteem. In 1945 Clementine Churchill was given the freedom of Wanstead and Woodford, her husband's constituency. In 1946 she was awarded two honorary degrees: an LL D by Glasgow University, and a DCL by Oxford University. In 1975 she was awarded an honorary LL D by Bristol University, of which her husband had been chancellor for more than thirty years.

Clementine Spencer-Churchill died suddenly and peacefully 12 December 1977 at her home in London, in her ninety-second year. Her memorial service was held in Westminster Abbey.

[Mary Soames (daughter), *Clementine Churchill*, 1979; personal knowledge.]

MARY SOAMES

CHURCHILL, PETER MORLAND (1909–1972), secret agent, was born in Amsterdam 14 January 1909, the eldest of four children (three sons and a daughter) of William Algernon Churchill, British consul there, who ten years later was consul-general in Milan, and his wife, Violet Myers. He was educated at Malvern, in Switzerland, and at Caius College, Cambridge, where he got a pass degree and a half blue for ice hockey, a game he several times played for England. He was British pro-consul in Oran in 1933–4.

In the autumn of 1940 he was commissioned into the intelligence corps, and served with the independent French section of the Special Operations Executive (SOE); he became a captain in May 1942. He distinguished himself that spring in the tricky and dangerous task of ferrying other agents ashore on to the Mediterranean coast of France from submarines or small boats at night. He had been to France himself in January 1942, to carry messages and to find out who 'Carte' was. 'Carte' turned out to be André Girard, a painter at Antibes who claimed to control a secret army over 200,000 strong. On 27/28 August Churchill was parachuted into France to establish liaison with this army. In his new role he was almost entirely ineffective, save that he organized the reception on the Riviera of several more parties of agents. 'Carte's' army turned out to be merely notional and soon after the German occupation of France on 11 November 1942 Girard's followers dispersed. Churchill retired to St. Jorioz, a small resort near Annecy in Savoy, with his wireless operator Adolph Rabinovitch and his courier Odette Marie Celine Sansom, wife of Roy Sansom (by whom she had three daughters) and daughter of Gaston Brailly. He returned to England by light aircraft for further orders on 23/24 March 1943. There he was told that Odette Sansom was engaged in dangerous talks with a supposed German colonel, and ordered to avoid her when he returned. However, she received him when he was parachuted back on 14/15 April, and on the following night her German acquaintance—Sergeant H. Bleicher of the Abwehr—arrested him and her, finding him fast asleep.

With more skill than truth, he passed her off as his wife and himself as a cousin of the British prime minister. He survived two years' severe imprisonment, partly in Fresnes, partly in German concentration camps. After the war he was appointed to the DSO (1946) and awarded a French croix de guerre and Legion of Honour. He married Odette Sansom in 1947, and in her wake became something of a newspaper hero; she divorced him in 1955. He married secondly in 1956 Irene Mary ('Jane'), daughter of William E. Hoyle, sometime manager of the SPCK bookshop in Exeter: she survived him. He had no children.

He wrote three light-hearted books, cited below, on his wartime adventures; a novel, *By Moonlight* (1958), on the Glières Maquis which he had helped to arm; and a short travel guide, *All About the French Riviera* (1960), concerning the area where he spent his closing years, as an estate agent. He lived at Le Rouret, a dozen miles west of Cannes, and died of cancer in Cannes 1 May 1972.

[Peter Churchill, *Of Their Own Choice*, 1952, *Duel of Wits*, 1953, and *The Spirit in the Cage*, 1954; M. R. D. Foot, *SOE in France*, second impression, 1968; private information.]

M. R. D. FOOT

CLARK, FREDERICK LE GROS (1892–1977), expert in social and industrial problems, was born 3 September 1892 in Chislet, Kent, the eldest in the family of three sons and one daughter of the Revd (Edward) Travers Clark, of Washfield, Tiverton, and his wife, Ethel May, daughter of Edward Clapton, physician. Both grandfathers were on the staff of St. Thomas's Hospital, one brother, (Sir) Wilfrid Le Gros Clark [q.v.], was professor of anatomy in Oxford and London, and the other brother, when chief secretary to the government of Sarawak, was killed by the Japanese. His sister worked for the Red Cross. From Blundell's School he went to Balliol College, Oxford, in 1911 and graduated with a second class in classical honour moderations in 1913. On the outbreak of war in 1914 he joined the Middlesex Regiment as a private: by the end of the war he was a lieutenant in the 3rd Hampshire Regiment. On the last day of the war, as a result of an accident, he lost his right hand and eye. His left eye was so seriously damaged that he gradually became completely blind.

By 1941 Clark had published two novels and seventy short stories; some of these were collected in *The Adventures of the Little Pig* (1937).

But he never thought of writing as his profession. Because of his interest in the psychology of blindness, and of his wish to help others to cope with it, he wrote some articles in the *St. Dunstan's Review* on his own experience and on how he organized his work and thoughts. His later thoughts on these matters were collected in *Blinded in War* (1969). He wrote clearly and concisely, typing the first draft himself hastily and then rewriting extensively. He makes the point, which is equally valid for sighted writers, that when the person reading the material hesitates, there is something wrong with a sentence. He had a remarkable memory and trained it assiduously. He was proud of what independence he could manage. On coming into a house which he had already visited once or twice, he would ask if there had been any rearrangement: on being reassured, he would demonstrate his spatial memory by moving confidently and unguided. He enjoyed walking on country roads, when traffic was sparse during the war of 1939–45, guided only by his companion's voice.

By 1930 Clark had found his vocation as an integrator of knowledge and experience on problems connected with welfare and nutrition. After two visits to the USSR he wrote (with L. N. Brinton) *Men, Medicine and Food in the USSR* (1936). He was the prime mover in starting the 'Committee against Malnutrition' which called attention to the extent of malnutrition in Britain in the 1930s. In this work he had active encouragement from Sir Frederick Gowland Hopkins and Sir John (later Lord) Boyd Orr [qq. v.]. He was secretary of the Children's Nutrition Council and edited the *Nutrition Bulletin* of the National Council for Health Education.

In *Feeding the Human Family* (1947) he gave a brief history of nutritional research, commented on the conflict between the commercial interest of food producers and our nutritional requirements, described the discussions which preceded the establishment of the Food and Agriculture Organization (FAO), and discussed themes such as soil erosion which only later had general recognition. In *Four Thousand Million Mouths* (edited with N. W. Pirie, 1951) a group of scientists argued that, by full application of existing knowledge, enough food for such a population could be produced. He was, briefly, a consultant to FAO on school feeding; earlier he had had a grant from the Leverhulme Trust for similar studies.

Aided by grants from the Nuffield Foundation, he started a prolonged study of the part played by tradition and preconceptions, rather than incapacity, in fixing the age of retirement. Among other publications on this subject were: *Ageing in Industry* (with A. C. Dunne, 1955), *Growing Old in a Mechanized World* (1960), and *Women, Work and Age* (1962). Much of his work was given limited circulation in Nuffield Foundation reports. The general conclusion was that most workers accepted retirement at sixty-five unwillingly, largely because they feared that it would lead to physical and mental deterioration.

Publications in braille covered little of the literature he consulted. He therefore needed co-operation from sighted people who understood what they were asked to read. This help was willingly given by his many friends because of his friendly personality and shrewd and amusing comments. Politically he was to the left: a member of the Association of Scientific Workers and a committee member of Science for Peace. Those who knew him through science called him 'Bill'—a nickname bestowed in the war of 1914–18 because of a fancied resemblance to the cartoon character 'Old Bill'. To those who knew him through St. Dunstan's he was 'Clarkie'.

Clark took his Oxford MA in 1944 and was given an honorary D.Sc. by Bristol University in 1972.

In 1921 he married Ida Searle and, after her death, he married in 1952 Winifred Collier. There were no children. Clark died in Cambridge 22 September 1977 soon after becoming partly paralysed.

[*The Times*, 30 September 1977; private information; personal knowledge.] N. W. Pirie

CLARK, Sir GEORGE NORMAN (1890–1979), historian, was born in Halifax, Yorkshire, 27 February 1890, the second son in the family of three sons and two daughters of James Walker Clark, CBE, JP, draper, a leading citizen of Halifax and successful business man, and his wife, Mary, daughter of Alderman S. T. Midgley, JP, of Halifax. His family was a cultured one with strong intellectual interests: his elder brother became professor of German at Glasgow University, and his sister, Barbara Callow, a leading expert on nutrition; his mother's sister had married the Dutch philologist, A. J. Barnouw.

Clark was educated at Bootham School, York, and later at Manchester Grammar School, to prepare him for Cambridge. It was to Oxford, however, that he was destined to go. In 1908 he was elected to a Brackenbury scholarship at Balliol, and placed in the first class in *literae humaniores* in 1911, and in modern history in 1912. Election to a prize fellowship at All Souls in 1912 enabled him to spend some time abroad perfecting his languages. A former member of the university Officers' Training Corps, which he joined after carefully rejecting pacifist views, he was commissioned when war broke out in the 1st battalion of the Post Office Rifles, wounded twice, and taken prisoner in May 1916, at Vimy ridge. His years of captivity were profitably spent, learning languages, reading widely, and working on Netherlands history when on parole in The Hague with his aunt and uncle by marriage.

On his return to England he was elected, in 1919, a fellow of Oriel College, Oxford. In the same year he married Barbara, sister of a Balliol friend killed in the war; they had a son and a daughter. His appointment as editor of the *English Historical Review* in 1920 recognized one of his outstanding skills; he was to resume this role, after resignation in 1926, from 1938 to 1939. He took a renewed interest in the Oxford Fabian Society of which, before the war, he had been a member with G. D. H. Cole [q.v.]; he spoke at Labour meetings about the general strike in 1926, and was invited to stand as Labour candidate for Oxford. In his radical sympathies he was joined by his wife, who had worked actively for the Women's Trade Union League. In 1927 he became a university lecturer in modern history and was proctor in 1929–30. His steadily growing reputation as a historian led to his election in 1931 to the newly-established Chichele professorship of economic history, tenable at All Souls, where he remained until, after the Munich crisis, he joined those working at Chatham House, where his specialized knowledge of the Low Countries could be profitably used. He returned to full-time academic life, however, in 1943, becoming regius professor of modern history at Cambridge, and a fellow of Trinity.

Clark's previous experience made him an excellent choice for the editorship of the Oxford History of England, an ambitious and largely successful project. He wrote the first volume to be published, *The Later Stuarts, 1660–1714* (1934), a work of remarkable scholarship, and continued to edit the series down to the last volume published in 1965. He later undertook to edit the New Cambridge Modern History, for the most part following the original scheme devised by Lord Acton [q.v.], but also arranging for chapters on areas and subjects which had no place in the earlier work. He was also editor of the Home University Library of Modern Knowledge. He was for some time a delegate of the Clarendon Press.

Clark returned to Oxford in 1947 upon election as provost of Oriel, and soon became immersed again in university business. Outside Oxford he was also busy, as a trustee of the British Museum (1949–60), a member of the University Grants Committee (1951–8), and from 1954 to 1958 as president of the British Academy, of which he had been a fellow since 1936. A knighthood in 1953 marked recognition of his many services to learning and public life. His retirement in 1957 gave him more time for scholarship. He was delighted in 1960 to be invited to write *A History of the Royal College of Physicians* (2 vols., 1964 and 1966) and his election as honorary FRCP (1966) gave him particular pleasure. He contributed a large number of notices to this Dictionary and remained a dedicated and disciplined worker until just before his death.

As a historian Clark was workmanlike and lucid; his judgements were carefully balanced and judiciously set out, and he tried above all to be fair. He was not interested in flights of fancy; he preferred to stick closely to the evidence and, in the main, the questions he posed were down-to-earth rather than speculative, though in conversation how deeply he thought about problems of all kinds was obvious. He could combine clear narrative with crisp comment to excellent effect. The finest of his books, *The Seventeenth Century* (1929; revised edn., 1947), displays another of his strengths, his capacity for comparative history, based on careful analysis and a sensitive awareness of cultural similarities and differences. This remarkable survey broke new ground, and nothing similar to it, or its equal in learning, was to appear for a quarter of a century. Clark's writings on Anglo-Dutch relations also remain valuable. The esteem in which he was held as a scholar is witnessed by the number of invitations to deliver special lectures he received, and his many honorary degrees, including D.Litt. from Oxford (1947) and Cambridge (1961). He had honorary fellowships at Balliol and Oriel (both 1957) and was re-elected to an All Souls fellowship in 1961.

Clark always retained some of the characteristics of the reserved north-countryman. He had many friends, enjoyed social life, and was an excellent and witty conversationalist, but could appear somewhat aloof with mere acquaintances. Known as 'James' or 'Jas' to his intimates, he was 'G.N.' to historians everywhere. Of medium height and sturdily built, he might well have been mistaken for one of his yeoman-farmer ancestors from the east riding, or even for a Dutch business man (some erroneously believed that he was partly Dutch). Starting life as a Nonconformist, he became a member of the Church of England in 1936. But like others of his generation, he owed much all his life to the intellectual vigour and sturdy independence of his dissenting family background.

He died in the Radcliffe Infirmary, Oxford, 6 February 1979.

[Geoffrey Parker in *Proceedings* of the British Academy, vol. lxvi, 1980; papers left by G. N. Clark in the care of the British Academy and in the Bodleian Library, Oxford; information from the family.] ANNE WHITEMAN

CLARK, GEORGE SIDNEY ROBERTS KITSON (1900–1975), historian. [See KITSON CLARK.]

CLARK, THOMAS ARCHIBALD BENNET- (1903–1975), botanist. [See BENNET-CLARK.]

CLARK, SIR WILFRID EDWARD LE GROS (1895–1971), anatomist, was born in Hemel Hempstead 5 June 1895, the youngest of three sons and third of the four children of the Revd (Edward) Travers Clark, of Washfield, Tiverton, and his wife, Ethel May, daughter of Edward Clapton, physician. A notice of his brother, Frederick, appears above. His second brother, Cyril, was killed by the Japanese in Borneo in July 1945. After the death of his mother when he was eight years old he became a delicate child, developing a bad stammer which he overcame in later life with the help of psychoanalysis. He attended Blundell's School in Tiverton, and in 1912 entered the Medical School of St. Thomas's Hospital, on whose consultant staff both his grandfathers had served with distinction. His paternal grandfather (Frederick Le Gros Clark) had also been president of the Royal College of Surgeons. Qualifying MRCS, LRCP in 1916, Le Gros Clark immediately joined the RAMC, serving in France from the beginning of 1918. He was demobilized in 1919 and, having passed the FRCS examination, was appointed a year later principal medical officer in Sarawak, a post which he filled for three years. In addition to discharging his medical duties, he was able to cultivate a deep-seated interest in natural history. He got on well with the natives, and because of his success in treating yaws, was made a fellow member of the Sea Dyaks, whose tattoo marks he bore on his shoulders.

In 1924 he left Borneo to become head of the department of anatomy at St. Bartholomew's Hospital Medical School, first as university reader and from 1927 to 1929 as professor. In 1930 he succeeded to the chair of anatomy at St. Thomas's Hospital Medical School. Four years later he was appointed Dr Lee's professor of anatomy in Oxford, a post he occupied until his retirement in 1962.

Le Gros Clark's scientific work reflected the main interests of the anatomical profession during the inter-war years, and in particular the problem of man's relationship to other members of the order of primates. In Borneo he had collected specimens of the spectral tarsier (*Tarsius*) and the tree-shrew (*Tupaia* and *Ptilocercus*), two creatures whose evolutionary affinities were at the time much disputed. His specimens of *Tarsius* were studied anatomically by H. H. Woollard, and today it is generally accepted that this creature represents a surviving group of the primitive mammals of the Eocene period from which all other primates evolved. Le Gros Clark made a corresponding study of the tree-shrew, which he also regarded as a primitive primate. His investigations of the structure of its brain marked the beginning of a long series of valuable studies of the central nervous pathways of the visual and other senses.

In 1934 Le Gros Clark published his first book on the subject of man's evolution, *Early Forerunners of Man*, essentially a compilation of existing knowledge of the anatomy of living and fossil primates. After a visit to South Africa in 1946 he became persuaded that the Australopithecines, the ape-like fossils which had been unearthed in that country during the 1920s and 1930s, were in the direct line of man's descent. After his death, many more primate fossils came to light in Africa and Asia, and it became clear that the evidence which had been available to him had not justified the firm opinions about the Australopithecines which he had expounded in some six short books, as well as in a popular British Museum handbook *History of the Primates* (1949). An element of speculation will always colour the subject, but the prevailing view today is that the Australopithecines were not direct ancestors of man.

Le Gros Clark played a part in the exposure of the Piltdown forgery, to which his attention was drawn by J. S. Weiner, and, with Weiner and K. P. Oakley, published the results of this inquiry in the *Bulletin of the British Museum (Natural History)* (1953). He also wrote numerous papers for scientific journals, two general books on the structure and tissues of the body, and an autobiographical memoir, *Chant of Pleasant Exploration* (1968). He was elected FRS in 1935, knighted in 1955, received several honorary degrees, and was an honorary member of foreign academies. In 1950 he was president of the International Anatomical Congress, in 1952–3 of the Anatomical Society, and in 1961 of the British Association for the Advancement of Science. He became an honorary fellow of Hertford College, Oxford, in 1962. To this Dictionary he contributed the articles on F. W. Jones and Sir Arthur Keith.

In 1923 Le Gros Clark married Freda Constance, daughter of Frederick Giddey, shipping agent; they had two daughters. She died in 1963, and in 1964 he married Violet, widow of Dr Leonard Foster Browne, psychiatrist, and daughter of the Revd Richard Bott, vicar of Newlands, Keswick.

Le Gros Clark died 28 June 1971, while staying with friends in Burton Bradstock in Dorset.

[Information lodged by Le Gros Clark at the Royal Society; Wilfrid Le Gros Clark, *Chant of Pleasant Exploration*, 1968 (autobiography); S. Zuckerman in *Biographical Memoirs of Fellows of the Royal Society*, vol. xix, 1973; personal knowledge.]

S. ZUCKERMAN

CLARKE, DUDLEY WRANGEL (1899–1974), soldier, was born in Johannesburg 27 April 1899, the elder son and eldest of four children of (Sir) Ernest Michael Clarke, business man, of Oxted, Surrey, and his wife, Madeline Sidonia Louisa, daughter of Edward Bennett Gardiner, general manager of the Standard Bank of South Africa and later of Carse Grange, Errol. He was educated at Charterhouse from 1912 to 1915; and in May 1916 entered the Royal Military Academy, Woolwich. In November 1916 he was commissioned second lieutenant in the Royal Field Artillery and went as conducting officer to France. On his return to England he joined the Royal Flying Corps and in October 1917 was posted to the School of Military Aeronautics, Reading, where he flew DH6s and Avro monoplanes. From April 1918 he served with the RFC in Egypt, returning to Britain in January 1919. He was promoted lieutenant (aeroplanes) in July 1919, but two months later transferred back to the RFA.

In November 1919 he was posted to Mesopotamia. While on leave in 1922 he went on the grand tour, and when war between Britain and Turkey threatened reported to the British commander in Constantinople, who employed him on special missions. In 1924 (again on leave) he spent two months as *Morning Post* correspondent covering the Riff rebellion in Morocco. In 1926 he became adjutant to the Territorial Army and in 1927 adjutant to the 98th Surrey and Sussex Yeomanry. He joined the Transjordan Force in 1930. He qualified for the Staff College, Camberley, at his fourth attempt thanks to the 1932 Middle East Command course for Staff College candidates where (in his words) 'the whole thing became plain and simple' as a result of instruction by B. L. Montgomery (later Viscount Montgomery of Alamein, q.v.). In 1932 he was captain in 18th battery, 3rd Field brigade. He attended the Staff College in 1933–4, visiting Germany and Italy, the college exercise having been changed from the Far East to a European war in alliance with France. He was posted at his own request to Aden in 1935 and served in Palestine in 1936–8. Promoted major in 1938, in the following year he became a deputy assistant military secretary in the War Office and lieutenant-colonel.

In *Seven Assignments* (1948) he described his early tasks in World War II, the principal being: reconnoitring a route from Mombasa to reinforce Egypt, lest the Mediterranean be closed; two assignments to Norway in April 1940; visiting a neutral country to ensure its continued neutrality; and, most important, the creation of the commandos. On 4 June 1940 the prime minister approved a scheme for small raiding forces put forward by Clarke which his experience of guerrilla warfare in Palestine well qualified him to implement. He recruited volunteers mainly from the 'independent companies' which had served in Norway under (Sir) Colin Gubbins [q.v.]; and a mere three weeks after their formation 200 commandos raided the coast between Boulogne and Berck. Clarke accompanied them but was ordered not to go ashore.

In the late summer of 1940 he was posted to the staff of Sir A. P. (later Earl) Wavell [q.v.] in the Middle East where he set up 'A' Force, the deception organization. It played a vital part in Allied victories in spite of the fact that large-scale deception was a new element in strategy and that Clarke's plans were at first hindered by Wavell's insistence on absolute secrecy. To his colleagues he was a meticulous professional endowed with great energy, and above all with the imagination needed to see into the minds of the enemy intelligence staffs and to induce them to advise their high command to do what best suited the Allies. The misleading clues he scattered round the Mediterranean theatre led the enemy to overestimate Allied strength there by nearly a quarter of a million men and tied down troops which otherwise might have been used to resist the Allied invasion of Normandy. He thus blazed a trail successfully followed by the sister organizations of Colonel John Bevan in London and Lieutenant-Colonel R. Peter Fleming [q.v.] in the Far East. Like them he suffered the fate of men engaged in secret work whose contribution is unnoticed except by a few 'in the know', themselves precluded by their vow of secrecy from paying tribute even long after the event; and he resisted the temptation to commit to paper his secret wartime experiences for financial gain. Earl Alexander of Tunis [q.v.] believed that he had done as much to win the war as any other single officer, a view which would certainly be substantiated were the official history of 'A' Force ever to be published.

Clarke, promoted colonel in 1942 and brigadier in 1943, retired from the army in 1947. From 1948 to 1952 he was head of public opinion research in the Conservative Central Office; and was for a time a director of Securicor Ltd. He was appointed OBE in 1942, CBE in 1943, and CB in 1945, and he was awarded the US Legion of Merit. He died in London 7 May 1974. He was unmarried.

[*The Times*, 9 and 14 May 1974; Dudley Clarke, *Seven Assignments*, 1948, and 'A Quarter of my Century' (unpublished memoirs); David Mure, *Master of Deception* (biography), 1980; Air and Naval Historical Branches, Ministry of Defence; private information.]

CHARLES CRUICKSHANK

CLARKE, SIR RICHARD WILLIAM BARNES (1910–1975), journalist and civil servant, was born in Heanor, Derbyshire, 13

August 1910, the only son of William Thomas Clarke, chemistry master of the Grammar School in Heanor, and his wife, Helen Barnes, also a schoolteacher. He had an elder sister. Clarke, known throughout his life to his family and friends as 'Otto', was educated at Christ's Hospital and Clare College, Cambridge, where he read mathematics and was posted sixth wrangler in 1931, finally switching to economics in his fourth year and receiving a second class in part ii of the economics tripos in 1932. Then at the nadir of the depression came the arduous search for a job. A brief spell (1932–3) with the British Electrical and Allied Manufacturers' Association was followed by six years at the *Financial News*, later amalgamated with the *Financial Times*, where his most lasting achievement was to devise the Ordinary Share Index, still as the FT Index the principal measure of its kind. On the outbreak of war in 1939 he moved successively through the Ministries of Information, Economic Warfare, and Supply and Production, and spent a vital year (1942–3) in Washington in the Combined Production and Resources Board.

Clarke's main career as a civil servant can be said to have begun when in 1945 he joined the Treasury where he remained for the next twenty-one years.

During this time two periods stand out as those in which his contribution was outstanding and of lasting importance. The first was between 1946 and 1952 when he chaired the official programmes committee, the group saddled with the task of wrestling with the management of what became and remained for many years Britain's central economic problem, the chronic tendency to deficit of the United Kingdom's balance of payments. As chairman of the programmes committee he dominated a large group of senior and sophisticated officials drawn from all government departments in the preparation for ministers of a unique series of reports. No one who was a member of that body will forget his methods of working, his ability to draft papers while presiding as chairman, his fluency and command of facts and figures. His work on the planning of both the United Kingdom and the whole European response to the Marshall Plan, which constituted the key to the salvation of Western Europe after the war, was unequalled. The second of these two periods was the eight years from 1958 to his departure from the Treasury in 1966 when in a number of jobs, culminating in 1962 as second permanent secretary in charge of the Public Sector Group, he, more or less single-handed, succeeded in securing the adoption of an entirely new approach to control and management of public expenditure known as PESC, an acronymn for the public expenditure survey committee, the inter-departmental instrument employed for administering the new system. It was Clarke who formulated the central ideas contained in the 1961 report of the committee of enquiry into Treasury control of public expenditure chaired by Lord Plowden, which he largely drafted. This advocated taking a view of the public sector as a whole, embracing central government, local government, and the public corporations, and the need to look at its progress over time against a background of the development of the national economy—seemingly simple ideas but new and indeed revolutionary in their implications. The control system which he advocated and pioneered must be regarded as the principal monument by which Clarke will be remembered. From 1966 to 1970 he was permanent secretary in the Ministry of Technology.

Clarke always took the architectonic rather than the piecemeal approach to his responsibilities. Thus, he regarded the new Ministry of Technology, of which he became permanent secretary in 1966 (having been for a short while previously permanent secretary in the Ministry of Aviation), and which expanded greatly in size and scope while he was its official head, as a model for the group of super-departments which he saw as the principal instruments of executive government in future. This prediction has been only partially fulfilled. Some have survived but others, including the Ministry of Technology itself, have disintegrated, their component parts absorbed elsewhere. It could be that Clarke underestimated the difficulties, political, administrative, and indeed human, of holding together such vast conglomerates.

Clarke was a man of many parts. He was a first-class chess player and a leading figure in the higher management of British chess. Physically commanding, intellectually pre-eminent, a strong character of decided and passionately held views, he was ruthless in argument and impatient with those who did not share his own convictions and approach to the matter in hand. Clarke's exceptional numeracy also led him to a low opinion of colleagues whose mental arithmetic did not go beyond their twelve-times table. His own writings, particularly in reports to ministers, were interspersed with figures, always relevant, employed to devastating effect in conjunction with a staccato style, the sentences coming at the reader like a succession of pistol shots.

Clarke was appointed OBE in 1944, CB in 1951, and KCB in 1964. Following his retirement from the Civil Service in 1971, he accepted directorships in a number of large companies both in industry and finance, where all testified to his deep concern, his detailed knowledge and understanding, and his qualities of judgement.

Not surprisingly for one of his literary talents Clarke's published work was extensive. He wrote numerous articles in learned journals; his more substantial works included *The Socialisation of Iron and Steel* (1936) under the pseudonym Ingot, *The Economic Effort of War* (1940), *The Management of the Public Sector of the National Economy* (the Stamp memorial lecture, 1964), *New Trends in Government* (1971), and *Public Expenditure, Management and Control* (1978), a posthumous work meticulously edited by his friend and colleague Sir Alexander Cairncross, which provided fascinating insights into the deeper recesses of the governmental machine.

Clarke was twice married. In 1938 he married Joan Edith Barrington Simeon in the United States. The marriage was dissolved in 1945 and in 1950 he married Brenda Pile, daughter of W. J. Skinner of Frosterley, Bishop Auckland. She had represented the Ministry of Transport in the heroic days of the programmes committee and the marriage was outstandingly happy. They had three sons. Clarke died in University College Hospital, London, 21 June 1975.

[Private information; personal knowledge.]

SAMUEL GOLDMAN

CLAY, SIR CHARLES TRAVIS (1885–1978), editor of medieval charters and House of Lords librarian, was born 30 July 1885 at Rastrick House, near Halifax, Yorkshire, the younger son (there were no daughters) of John William Clay, historian and genealogist, and his wife Alice, daughter of Colonel Henry Pilleau, Army Medical Corps and artist, who descended from the family of Pezé Pilleau, the Huguenot silversmith. He was educated at Harrow and Balliol College, Oxford, where he won a mathematical scholarship in 1904. He gained only a second class in mathematical moderations in 1905, but was allowed to keep his scholarship and read history. In this subject he was guided mainly by H. W. C. Davis and A. L. Smith [qq.v.]. The former coached Clay in the special subject he had chosen—medieval land tenure—and gave him the interest in charter material which he later developed with distinction. He obtained a first class in modern history in 1908.

In March 1909 Clay became assistant private secretary to the Earl (later Marquess) of Crewe [q.v.], then colonial secretary, and stayed with him after Lord Crewe became secretary of state for India and leader of the House of Lords. In the summer of 1914 he was appointed assistant librarian to the House of Lords. But less than a year later he was commissioned in the Royal Devon Yeomanry and went to France, where he was twice mentioned in dispatches. He attained the rank of major. His elder brother was killed in 1918.

In 1922 Clay was appointed librarian to the House and began a distinguished tenure of office lasting thirty-four years, until he retired in 1956. He possessed the ideal temperament and intellect for this post. His remarkably accurate memory and his immense knowledge of literature and history—invariably imparted to peers with great courtesy—were highly valued by the House. He was recognized as an authority on peerage history and was frequently consulted when peerage cases came before the House. While librarian he compiled five articles for volumes viii and x of *The Complete Peerage* of which he was a trustee for many years. In 1952 he was appointed a member of the reviewing committee on the export of works of art, on which he served for thirteen years. Clay's wide knowledge of art, in particular Italian painting, was valued by that committee.

But it is as one of the most distinguished editors of medieval charters England has produced that Clay will be remembered. His work on medieval documents had begun in October 1908 when H. W. C. Davis gave him advice on collecting material from the Public Record Office for a volume of *Placita coram rege* or *de banco* (published 1911) for the Yorkshire Archaeological Society (of which he was to be a member for seventy years and president from 1953 to 1956). He drew constant inspiration from his father J. W. Clay (died 1918) who is remembered as the editor of the *Visitation of Yorkshire* by Sir William Dugdale [q.v.]. In 1922 Clay was invited to continue a series of *Yorkshire Deeds* and during the next eighteen years edited five volumes calendaring and annotating deeds to the death of Elizabeth I. In 1932 he was invited by the Yorkshire Archaeological Society to continue the series of *Early Yorkshire Charters* (*EYC*) begun by William Farrer [q.v.]. In Clay's first two volumes, on the honour of Richmond, his precision in the dating of the charters immediately set a new standard of editing, only surpassed by Clay himself in volume viii (1950) covering the honour of Warenne, which prompted Sir Frank Stenton [q.v.] to write that it was 'for the moment the last number in the finest series of Charters now appearing anywhere in the world'. Clay's *EYC*, in ten volumes published between 1935 and 1965, is regarded as a masterpiece and in Sir Richard Southern's opinion is a work of 'all but impeccable scholarship'. A bibliography of his works and an appreciation of Clay by Professor Christopher Brooke accompanied his last published work, *Notes on the Family of Clere*, a privately printed volume presented to the author on his ninetieth birthday in 1975.

Clay had a mind of crystal clarity which he retained to the end of his life. Although somewhat reserved in manner, he was a delightful and stimulating friend to anyone who shared his interests, and he took particular pleasure in helping younger historians. The range of his interests can be gauged by the many societies to which he belonged. He was a fellow of the

Society of Antiquaries for sixty-five years and vice-president in 1934–8; and honorary vice-president of the Royal Historical Society. He was a member of the Huguenot Society and the Harleian Society, for both of which he edited a volume. Membership of the Roxburghe Club, to which he presented a fine facsimile of a thirteenth-century York psalter, gave him pleasure for thirty-seven years. His chief outdoor interest was cricket, his record of attendance at the Eton and Harrow match at Lord's being probably unique.

Clay received an honorary doctorate from Leeds University in 1943. He was appointed CB in 1944 and knighted in 1957. In 1950 he was elected a fellow of the British Academy.

He married in 1913 Violet (died 1972), second daughter of William Snowdon Robson, Lord Robson [q.v.], lord of appeal. They had three daughters, of whom the eldest, Rachel Maxwell-Hyslop, became a noted archaeologist. Clay died at Oxford 31 January 1978.

[Christopher Brooke in *Proceedings* of the British Academy, vol. lxiv, 1978; *The Times*, 2 and 7 February 1978; private information; personal knowledge.]

CHRISTOPHER S. A. DOBSON

CLAYTON, PHILIP THOMAS BYARD (1885–1972), founder of the Toc H movement, was born 12 December 1885 at Maryborough, Queensland, Australia, the third son and sixth and youngest child of Reginald Byard Buchanan Clayton, manager of a sugar plantation, and his wife, who was also his first cousin, Isobel Byard Sheppard. In 1886 the family returned to England and Reginald Clayton started an agency in the City for the export and import of goods to and from Australia. Philip Clayton was educated at St. Paul's School and, as Squire scholar, at Exeter College, Oxford. He obtained a third class in classical honour moderations in 1907 and a first in theology in 1909. He then went to live in the deanery of Westminster and read with the dean, J. Armitage Robinson [q.v.]. In 1910 he was made deacon and in 1911 was ordained in Guildford Cathedral by E. S. Talbot [q.v.], bishop of Winchester.

Clayton began his clerical career in 1910 in the parish of St. Mary, Portsea, where Cyril Garbett [q.v.], later archbishop of York, was vicar. Volunteering as an army chaplain when war broke out, he worked in hospitals in France. The senior chaplain of the 6th division, Neville Talbot (son of the bishop of Winchester and later bishop of Pretoria), was looking for someone to establish a rest-house for the troops in the bottle-neck on the way to and from the Ypres salient. He interested his friend Clayton in the idea and together they found an empty mansion at Poperinghe and transformed it into Talbot House, named thus in memory of Neville Talbot's brother, who had been killed in action a few months previously. Thousands of men used the house, which had a canteen, recreation and writing room, library, chaplain's room, and chapel, and which became known as TH, or Toc H in morse signallers' language. Clayton, always known as 'Tubby', used it as a base for visiting men in the front line. He was given a roving commission with the 14th East Ham heavy battery in 1916. Tirelessly energetic, his magnetic personality became known and loved by thousands behind and in the front line. He was awarded the MC in 1917.

Returning to England after the war, he established an ordination school at the former Knutsford prison, from which 435 priests were eventually ordained, and where he himself was chaplain and tutor. He also established a Talbot House in London in 1920 and began the Toc H movement which had forty branches by 1922, the year in which it became an association incorporated by royal charter. The premises of the movement were fellowship, service, fair-mindedness, and the kingdom of God.

To collect funds Clayton went on a Canadian tour in 1921. In 1923 the archbishop of Canterbury, Randall Davidson (later Lord Davidson of Lambeth, q.v.), gave All Hallows by the Tower as a living to Clayton to redeem as the spiritual centre of Toc H. It became Toc H's guild church, and Clayton remained its vicar until 1963. A lamp, which became the movement's symbol, was lit by the Prince of Wales in the Albert Hall in 1923. From that year onwards Clayton embarked on world tours for fund-raising. The movement prospered and eventually numbered a thousand branches in Britain, hundreds overseas, and a Women's Association of similar strength. Clayton was appointed CH in 1933.

In 1934 Clayton undertook a strenuous tour of the Rhodesias and South Africa which led to a nervous breakdown. He recovered during a year spent in India at Belgaum with his brother, (Sir) Hugh Clayton. For a few months in 1935 he was chaplain on *Codrington* and then *Beagle*, stationed at Malta. Early in 1936 he returned to England and to work at All Hallows and the Tower Hill Improvement Trust, which he had launched ten years before.

In the early years of World War II Clayton was with the Royal Navy in the Orkneys, establishing Toc H clubs around Scapa Flow. In 1940 All Hallows was destroyed by a bomb and Clayton was given the chaplaincy of the Anglo-Saxon tanker fleet, which took him to various parts of America. In 1943 he sailed to Gibraltar in a small naval craft and thence went on a tour of Karachi, Abadan, Tehran, Basra, Baghdad, and Haifa, returning to Gibraltar late in 1944. The next year discussions began on reviving All Hallows;

Clayton was active in raising funds, undertaking an exhausting tour of Canada and the USA, which resulted in the Americans sending the Winant volunteers to help rebuild the church, which was rededicated in 1957. From 1958 onwards he was connected with the voyages of (Sir) Francis Chichester [q.v.], three of whose yachts he personally blessed.

A man of enormous sympathy and courage, never sparing himself, convinced that his work was God-ordained, Clayton was unaware of time or his own appearance. He was frequently late for appointments, causing much distress and anxiety to his ADCs and to those who awaited his arrival. He was an imaginative and original speaker with a retentive memory and a sense of humour which made him excellent company. His voice had a deep growling resonance and his eyes were mischievous. His way with people of all ages and circumstances was renowned, but he was rarely at ease with women. Despite his thousands of admirers and disciples he was a deeply lonely man with very few close friends. His constant companion was his dog.

Clayton received the degree of DD (Lambeth) in 1954. He died at his home on Tower Hill 15 December 1972. He was unmarried.

[Tresham Lever, *Clayton of Toc H*, 1971; Melville Harcourt, *Tubby Clayton, a Personal Saga*, 1953.] C. S. Nicholls

CLORE, Sir CHARLES (1904–1979), financier and industrialist, was born in London 24 December 1904, the youngest but one child in the family of five sons and two daughters of Israel Clore and his wife, Yetta Abrahams. His father was an immigrant who had arrived in Liverpool from Russia some years earlier, and had moved to London where he established himself as a textile merchant in the East End. After education at a local elementary school, Charles Clore spent some time in his father's business where he acquired some experience in textiles, shops, stores, and property.

At the age of twenty he went to South Africa and lived with a cousin who was engaged in fruit farming on a large scale. There he acquired some experience in agriculture and also met people interested in the film industry. On his return to England he bought the South African rights to a film of a world championship fight, which he took to South Africa and resold at a profit. He returned to England in 1927 and became interested in the entertainment business, buying a derelict skating rink in Cricklewood which he turned into a successful concern within a few years. This led him to engage in property and other transactions, some of which he was forced to abandon through lack of available finance.

His interest in property and entertainment led him in 1930 to buy at auction for £700 the lease of the Prince of Wales Theatre which had about seven years to run. Finding it impossible to obtain a profitable rent for the theatre he found some associates to run it and thus entered the field of theatre management. He subsequently bought the freehold of the theatre which was rebuilt, the finance being raised by the flotation of his company which later (after two intermediate mergers) became part of the portfolio of Land Securities Investment Trust Limited.

He maintained his contacts with South Africa, in 1938 making a substantial investment in a South African gold mining company which he held for several years and which subsequently proved most profitable. During the war years he was engaged in building premises, mainly for the government. Later he continued these activities by putting together sites for office buildings to be let to the government. These formed part of his property investment company.

He became involved in the City, his first venture being the purchase of a coach works which was floated as a public company. He also became involved in stores by purchasing both the bankrupt Richard Shops chain which he expanded and a department store in Reading which he later sold at a substantial profit.

In 1951 he ventured into the engineering industry and bought Furness Shipbuilding Company for about £3 million. This he reorganized to become extremely profitable until the shipbuilding slump came. The yard was maintained making losses for some years and it was subsequently sold to Swan Hunter. In 1952 he bought a knitting machinery business which, with further similar acquisitions, was merged into the Bentley Engineering Group, a successful concern until the slump in the late 1970s. After a take-over battle with Lord Fraser of Allander [q.v.] he acquired control of the Scottish Motor Traction Company, adding to it the businesses in England and thus creating a substantial automobile business.

His major acquisition was J. Sears (Tru-Form) Boot Company Limited in 1953 which then owned the Tru-Form and Freeman Hardy & Willis footwear manufacturing and retailing businesses. This was expanded materially by the acquisition of the well-known businesses of Dolcis, Manfield, Saxone, and Lilley & Skinner, which were all combined into the British Shoe Corporation, forming the largest footwear business in the United Kingdom.

The group of businesses which Clore then controlled was merged into a holding company, Sears Holdings Limited, which expanded, mainly in retail, first by the acquisition of the jewellery group, Mappin & Webb, to which Garrards, the crown jewellers, were added, and then by the purchase of the Selfridge/Lewis's store group in 1965. In these business acquisitions

Clore's preoccupation was to expand and increase profitability and employment. He rarely sold anything, it being his philosophy that an asset was worth as much to him as anyone would wish to pay for it.

His personal activities consisted in the main in agriculture. He acquired two large estates, one near Hungerford and the other at Hereford, which he spent a great deal of time and money improving. He also became interested in horse-racing and breeding and owned Valoris, the winner of the Oaks in 1966—his only classic success, although he won a number of other important races. Although self-taught he acquired a valuable collection of paintings and *objets d'art* and enjoyed seeking for and living with them. He established a charitable foundation with a value substantially in excess of £10 million and gave generously to a large number of charities, in particular to London University, University College Hospital, the Zoological Gardens, and a number of Jewish causes. Clore was knighted in 1971.

He married Francine Rachel, daughter of Henri Jules Halphen, a company director, of Paris, in 1943. They had a son and a daughter. The marriage was dissolved in 1957. Clore died in the London Clinic 26 July 1979.

[Personal knowledge.] LEONARD SAINER

COBHAM, SIR ALAN JOHN (1894–1973), aviator, was born 6 May 1894 at Camberwell, London, the only child to survive of Frederick Cobham, tailor, and his wife, Elizabeth Burrows. He attended a local council school and Wilson's Grammar School and started work in a clothes' store. He became a pupil farmhand in 1912. He was a warehouse employee when World War I was declared. Promptly enlisting, he served as an Artillery NCO veterinary assistant in France until 1917, before managing to transfer to the Royal Flying Corps where he was eventually commissioned as a flying instructor.

Although of lively temperament and boundless energy, his only marketable asset, when demobilized in January 1919 at the age of twenty-four, was his piloting skill. But after obtaining the requisite civil flying licence through the recommendation of his commanding officer, he found prospects were negligible in the post-war depression, and was lucky to find a job as a 'joy-riding' pilot during which he carried 5,000 passengers until the company over-extended and became bankrupt. Down to his last £3 he became a photographic pilot with Airco Ltd., owned by Holt Thomas who was helping (Sir) Geoffrey de Havilland [q.v.] to form De Havilland Aircraft Ltd. which Cobham joined in 1920 as a taxi-pilot. He built up a ten-man team ready to 'fly anywhere anytime' using ex-war DH9s. The business thrived, thanks to his great capacity for hard work and organization, and Cobham established himself as a public figure in 1921 by making a hitherto unimaginable 5,000 mile air tour of Europe in which seventeen cities were visited in three weeks amid mystery and publicity caused by his American passenger withholding his name. Other trail-blazing flights followed, extending from Europe to North Africa. In 1924 he flew to Rangoon and back in the newly introduced DH50 taxi-plane carrying Britain's director of civil aviation, Sir W. Sefton Brancker [q.v.]. Then with the same machine he went to the Cape of Good Hope and back in 1925–6 and also to Australia and back in 1926. That brought independence, and registration of Alan Cobham Aviation Ltd. In the following year he used a big twin-engined Short Singapore flying boat on behalf of Imperial Airways to make the first encirclement of Africa, and in 1931 he similarly surveyed the Nile route to the Belgian Congo using a triple-engined Short Valetta twin-float seaplane.

By then he had become the self-appointed vigorous professional propagandist for British aviation, and in 1929, backed by C. C. (later Viscount) Wakefield [q.v.], had undertaken a Municipal Aerodrome Campaign using a DH61 *Youth of Britain* for demonstrations at many key cities during which 10,000 children were given educational flights. From that he developed the idea of a great 'barnstorming' business, in 1932–3 under the title of National Aviation Day Ltd. and as National Aviation Displays Ltd. in 1934–6, during which 1,250 payment admission displays were given by a skilled aircraft circus and 900,000 passengers carried.

Meanwhile Cobham's ambition to set a new Australian record by refuelling in flight created a unique line of development. Initial experiments in 1933 were a failure, but nothing defeated Cobham for long, and in 1934 he was able to demonstrate to Air Marshal Sir Hugh (later Lord) Dowding [q.v.] a Handley Page tanker feeding 120 gallons of fuel to an Airspeed Courier. An official development contract followed, leading to the establishment of Flight Refuelling Ltd. at Ford, Sussex, where several penurious years of experimentation produced a method of rocket-line ejection for the hose-coupling which was successfully applied in 1939 to an Empire flying boat enabling 2.7 tons of fuel to be added after take-off at maximum weight and thus give transatlantic range. With the advent of World War II official interest waned and Cobham devoted attention to such matters as thermal de-icing and methods of towing fighters by long-range bombers. After long advocacy he induced both the USAF and RAF late in the war to experiment with flight refuelling to give the range for raids on Japan.

Interest in refuelling airliners revived in 1947–8 when success was achieved with British South American Airways' flights to Bermuda, but the advent of the fast, long-range DH Comet stopped further Air Ministry support. Prospects for Cobham's business dropped to a low ebb until a new association with the USA brought contracts totalling over $7,500,000 to supply refuelling equipment for B29s and B50s. By then he had moved to Tarrant Rushton, Dorset, where a still more effective system was developed by which the receiver aircraft flew a self-locking probe into a cone-funnel on the tanker's hose. That led to formation of an American company in 1951, after which all US fighters and bombers were equipped with this system. The RAF followed suit to more limited extent.

Cobham was awarded the Britannia Trophy for 1923 as the first British pilot to cross the Channel in an ultra-light plane; he also won the King's Cup race in 1924. For his London–Rangoon flight he gained the Britannia Trophy for 1925, and for his London–Cape Town flight of 1925–6 was awarded the AFC (1926). In 1926 he received the Royal Aero Club gold medal, Simms gold medal, Aviation gold medal of the Institute of Transport, again won the Britannia Trophy, and was honoured with the KBE for his Australian flight. In the following year he was made an honorary fellow of the Royal Aeronautical Society. He was a founder member of the Guild of Air Pilots and Air Navigators of which he became master in 1964–5.

Since his early background emphasized the desirability of a good start in life, he not only initiated his company's training school but endowed a scholarship at Southampton University. At Wimborne he provided a garden city factory for his employees and a river park for the community. He was chairman of the Bournemouth Symphony Orchestra (1956–67) and raised £25,000 to secure its future.

He was author of *Skyways* (1925), *My Flight to the Cape and Back* (1926), *Australia and Back* (1926), *Twenty Thousand Miles in a Flying Boat* (1930), many articles, and an autobiography. He also featured in a number of films on his travels and activities.

He married in 1922 the actress Gladys Marie Lloyd (died 1961), daughter of William Lloyd, of Bristol. They had two sons. On retirement he resided at Tortola, British Virgin Islands, where he died 21 October 1973.

[Sir Alan John Cobham, *A Time to Fly* (autobiography, ed. by C. Derrick), 1978; public and private information; personal knowledge.]

H. J. Penrose

COCHRANE, Sir RALPH ALEXANDER (1895–1977), air chief marshal, was born 24 February 1895 at Crawford Priory, Springfield, Fife, the second youngest son in the family of four boys (one of whom died in childhood) and four girls (two of whom did not survive) of Thomas Horatio Arthur Ernest Cochrane (from 1919 the first Baron Cochrane of Cults), MP, and his wife, Lady Gertrude Julia Georgina Boyle, OBE, the elder daughter of the sixth Earl of Glasgow. He went to school at Ardvreck, Crieff, then to Osborne and Dartmouth. He entered the Royal Navy in 1912. He volunteered for the airship branch and was accepted as a flight sub-lieutenant in March 1915. He was commissioned in the RAF in April 1918 and awarded the AFC in 1919.

Cochrane was posted to the Middle East Command in 1921 for experimental duties with No. 70 Squadron, and after qualifying as an aircraft pilot at No. 4 Flying Training School he moved on to No. 45 Squadron as a flight commander under (Sir) Arthur Harris. He was mentioned in dispatches for operations in Kurdistan in 1924. He returned to Britain and in the next three years gained further valuable experience, performing administrative duties at the Boys' Wing at Cranwell, attending the RAF Staff College at Andover, and then becoming a squadron leader staff officer with the Essex Bombing Area headquarters. He returned to the Middle East in 1928 for air staff duties at the Aden headquarters, but was soon given command to No. 8 Squadron.

Returning to Britain in November 1929 Cochrane was appointed as an instructor at the RAF Staff College. After two years he moved to the Air Ministry to become assistant to C. F. A. Portal (later Viscount Portal of Hungerford, q.v.) in the plans division of the air staff. After two years in the Air Ministry, Cochrane moved on to a higher commanders' course at the School of Army Co-operation, followed by a course at the Imperial Defence College in 1935. After that he served briefly on the air staff at Inland Area and Training Command headquarters. In 1936 he was specially selected to advise the New Zealand government on air defence and he remained there to become the first chief of the air staff of Royal New Zealand Air Force. During his stay there he was promoted to group captain.

Cochrane returned to Britain in the summer of 1939 to become the deputy director of intelligence but was soon transferred to take over command of RAF Station Abingdon in Bomber Command in December 1939. He was also air ADC to the King in 1939–40. In 1940 he became senior air staff officer at No. 6 Group, and on being promoted to air commodore became air officer commanding No. 7 Group. In spite of the opportunities these appointments gave him for developing his talents in bombing and advanced training techniques there were demands for his gifts elsewhere.

In his new post of director of flying training Cochrane was to have great scope for a strenuous application of all the qualities he was known to possess. He returned to the now expanding Bomber Command as an air vice-marshal in September 1942 in command of No. 3 Group, but Sir Arthur Harris (by then C-in-C Bomber Command) had him appointed as AOC No. 5 Group in February 1943. No. 5 Group with its long-range Lancasters had become the formation primarily responsible for the development of the technique of precision bombing by night, and it was in this appointment that Cochrane had his greatest opportunities as a wartime commander. Under his efficient and determined leadership the Group was entrusted with many of the most spectacular missions of the bomber offensive, such as the breaching of the Möhne and Eder dams (October 1943) and the sinking of the *Tirpitz*. 'He certainly played a major part in organising and training the "Dambusters" ', wrote Sir Arthur Harris, 'and it was because of my absolute reliance on his efficiency and organising ability that I entrusted him with ... [their] raising and training and direction.'

In February 1945 Cochrane was appointed AOC-in-C Transport Command, when there was the shift of the Allies' concentration from Europe to the Far East theatre, involving a vast air-trooping programme. The RAF was then asked to assist in repatriating the tens of thousands of prisoners of war, and Transport Command rapidly took on the major share of this vast migration. In a period of some twenty-one months Transport Command completed more passenger miles than had British civil aviation in the preceding twenty-one years, carrying some 500,000 troops and 200,000 tons of equipment. However, Transport Command's work had dwindled considerably by the time Cochrane left his headquarters in September 1947, although a vast amount of information and experience had been acquired.

Cochrane's next appointment took him to Flying Training Command as commander-in-chief (1947). He experienced another testing period as he saw the Command through post-war recession and the reshaping of flying training units.

When the post of chief of the air staff became vacant on the retirement of Lord Tedder [q.v.], in 1950, Cochrane was seriously considered as his successor. There is little doubt that he would have been chosen had there not been another outstanding candidate for this appointment, Air Chief Marshal Sir John Slessor [q.v.], who had played a key part in the war as a strategic and air force planner, a fact that tipped the scale in Slessor's favour. Cochrane, promoted air chief marshal, became Slessor's vice-chief of air staff. Having been appointed as air ADC to the King in 1945 he became ADC to the Queen in 1952. After his retirement from the RAF in 1952 he held a number of posts in industry.

Cochrane was appointed CBE (1939), CB (1943), KBE (1945), KCB (1948), and GBE (1950). He was twice mentioned in dispatches in World War II. He won the RUSI gold medal essay in 1935 and the Edward Busk memorial prize of the Royal Aeronautical Society (of which he became a fellow) in 1948, and he gained the Institute of Transport's triennial award of merit in 1958.

In 1930 he married Hilda Frances Holme (died 1982), third daughter of Frances Holme Wiggin, a tea-planter in Ceylon. They had two sons and one daughter. Cochrane died 17 December 1977 at Burford, Oxfordshire. There is a portrait in oils by Henry Lamb in the Scottish United Services Museum, Edinburgh.

[*Times* and *Daily Telegraph*, 19 and 20 December 1977; information from RAF senior officers; Air Historical Branch (MOD); private information; personal knowledge.]

EDWARD CHILTON

COGHILL, NEVILL HENRY KENDAL AYLMER (1899–1980), translator of Chaucer, was born 19 April 1899 at Castle Townshend, Skibbereen, county Cork, the second of the three sons (the youngest child was a daughter) of Sir Egerton Bushe Coghill, fifth baronet, a noted amateur landscape painter, of Glen Barrahane, Castle Townshend, and his wife, (Elizabeth) Hildegarde (Augusta), the younger daughter of Colonel (Thomas) Henry Somerville, and sister of Edith Anna Oenone Somerville [q.v.], the writer. He was educated at Bilton Grange and Haileybury, and served as second lieutenant in the trench mortar division of the Royal Artillery in Salonika and Bulgaria during the last few months of the war of 1914–18. In 1919 he went up as a scholar to Exeter College, Oxford, to read history, being placed in the second class in 1922. He then spent part of a recent legacy on an additional year at Oxford reading English under the tuition of F. P. Wilson [q.v.], later Merton professor, and gaining a first class in 1923. After a short period of teaching at the Royal Naval College, Dartmouth, he was elected a research fellow of Exeter in 1924, and became an official fellow and librarian in 1925.

In 1927 he married Elspeth Nora, daughter of Richard James Harley, a medical practitioner, of Inchture, Perthshire. There was one daughter, and the marriage was dissolved in 1933.

A sympathetic tutor, Coghill numbered W. H. Auden [q.v.] among his pupils, and his interest in medieval literature was reflected in *The Pardon of Piers Plowman* (Sir Israel Gollancz memorial lecture, British Academy, 1945) and *The Poet Chaucer*, 1949 (second edition, 1967). But in these years he also began to develop his talents as a dramatic producer and as a translator of Middle English verse, activities which were to make him widely known. His dramatic productions began with *Samson Agonistes* in Exeter College garden in 1930, and he went on to produce many plays and some operas for OUDS, the Oxford University Opera Club, and various college societies, mostly in the open air. These spectacles, which became something of a legend at Oxford, included *Troilus and Cressida*, 1937, *The Winter's Tale*, 1946, and *Hamlet*, 1940 (on an apron stage). *The Masque of Hope*, which he organized and wrote with Glynne Wickham, was presented at University College, Oxford, to the then HRH Princess Elizabeth in 1948. *The Tempest*, 1949, in Worcester College gardens, was remembered for one of Coghill's most magical effects: Ariel appeared to run across the surface of the lake (supported, in fact, by a gangway hidden just beneath water-level).

Coghill's translations from Middle English began as a series of broadcasts for BBC radio of selections from *The Canterbury Tales* (first series, 1946–7; second series, 1949). His complete translation of the *Tales* (Penguin Classics, 1951) was extremely popular, creating for the first time since the Middle Ages a nation-wide audience for Chaucer. In 1947 he broadcast translations from Langland's *Piers Plowman* (published as *Visions from Piers Plowman*, 1949) and from Chaucer's *Troilus and Criseyde* (which was published in Coghill's modern English version by Penguin in 1971). On the retirement of F. P. Wilson from the Merton chair of English literature in 1957, Coghill was elected his successor—much to his surprise, according to Lord David Cecil. In 1959 he gave the Clark lectures, published as *Shakespeare's Professional Skills* (1964).

He remained an inspiration to generations of undergraduates in Oxford theatre, and directed, in the year of his retirement, 1966, Richard Burton (an ex-pupil) and Elizabeth Taylor in *Dr Faustus* at the Oxford Playhouse. The film of *Dr Faustus*, with almost the same cast, was shot in Rome the following year, with Coghill and Burton co-directing. This was followed, in 1968, by his highly successful musical stage version (with Martin Starkie) of the *Canterbury Tales*, which ran for five years at the Phoenix Theatre, London, and was also shown for a period on Broadway, and toured Europe and Australia.

Coghill was elected a fellow of the Royal Society of Literature in 1950, and had honorary doctorates from Williams College, Massachusetts (1966) and St. Andrews, Scotland (1971). He died in a nursing home in Cheltenham, 6 November 1980.

Brought up in the old-world atmosphere of the south of Ireland, where sailing, fishing, hunting, shooting, and the painting of pictures provided gentlemanly pleasures, Coghill had the easy grace of the consummate amateur. A tall, handsome figure with rather leonine features, he was known in Oxford for the charm and vivacity of his conversation and the fineness of his taste.

[*The Times*, 10 November 1980; Lord David Cecil in *Postmaster* (Merton College magazine), 1981; information from Coghill's sister.] JOHN CAREY

COHEN, HENRY, BARON COHEN OF BIRKENHEAD (1900–1977), physician, was born in Birkenhead 21 February 1900, the youngest of the five children (three boys and one girl) of Isaac Cohen, a draper and a considerable Jewish scholar, of Liverpool, and his wife, Dora Mendelson, the dominant personality in the family. Her son was devoted to her to the end of her long life. Both parents were of Russian origin, and the family was very poor. Cohen was educated at the church school of St. John, from which he won a scholarship to Birkenhead Institute. There he captained the rugby XV and the cricket XI, was champion gymnast, and gained some experience in theatricals. From the Institute he won a scholarship to Oxford but on grounds of expense transferred it to Liverpool.

His original intention had been to study medicine in order to become a criminal lawyer, but as his work continued he realized that medicine alone had enough to offer him. He graduated MB, Ch.B. in 1922 with first class honours and a distinction in every subject in the curriculum, and obtained his MD with special merit in 1924. In the same year he was appointed assistant physician to the Liverpool Royal Infirmary, where he remained on the staff until his retirement forty-one years later.

To obtain such a post within two years of qualifying showed exceptional brilliance, and in 1934 Cohen was appointed to the chair of medicine at Liverpool University. This, as usual in those days, was a part-time position, enabling him to follow up the results of his teaching by keeping a contact with the practitioners in the area who asked him for a second opinion. However there was an administrative problem which he never really solved. The four general teaching hospitals considered themselves autonomous units, and even when they were nominally incorporated into the United Liverpool Hospitals in 1936 there was little love lost between them. Welding a teaching and research unit together under such circumstances presented insuperable difficulties to a young man of whom many people were jealous. It was perhaps this background in his early years which determined Cohen's individualistic approach to his career.

From the time when he was appointed to the chair to the end of the war he rose to eminence in the conventional way. He was elected FRCP in 1934 (MRCP, 1926) and later became an examiner to the college and a member of council in 1943–6. He was all this time increasingly in demand as an orator. One of his outstanding accomplishments was his ability to speak in public, and his lectures and orations were brilliant performances, showing originality, breadth of vision, erudition, and wit. Towards the end of a long series of named lectures came the Harveian oration at the Royal College of Physicians in 1970, 'On the Motion of Blood in the Veins'.

Of the same standard as his great clinical ability and his oratory was his grasp of administration, particularly his chairmanship of committees, and it was this capacity which was to be of special use after the introduction of the National Health Service, when he became one of the principal outside expert and voluntary advisers to the Ministry of Health. He was the first vice-chairman of the Central Health Services Council when it was formed in 1949, and became chairman in 1957. His great contribution was that he brought to the Ministry the professional knowledge of the active clinician so that the administration was kept closely in touch with the outside medical world.

In 1952 he was seriously ill with a coronary thrombosis. Unlike most doctors, he strictly adhered to the medical advice he was given, and on recovery gave up his vast private practice and dedicated himself to the national work of the organization and advancement of British medicine. He presided over countless committees and was a household name to general practitioners, who had good reason to bless the Cohen categories as they struggled with the drugs to be used in the NHS. One of his most important scientific contributions arose by virtue of his chairmanship of the committee dealing with the organization of poliomyelitis vaccination in this country. He also played a large part in the preparation of the reports on the medical care of epileptics and on staphylococcal infections in hospital, to mention just two among many.

He was proud of his Jewish heritage, although more concerned with its ethical, cultural, and historical aspects than with religious detail. However, throughout his public life if there was anything to be done in the Jewish fashion he did it; for example, when he entered the House of Lords he took the oath on the Old Testament and with his head covered. His contributions to Jewish causes and charities were very considerable.

Outside medicine his first love was the theatre and he took a very active part in the running of the Liverpool Playhouse. He personally helped to select the plays, and as he was a shrewd business man the Liverpool Repertory Company was one of the few in the country to make money. His favourite theatre story was that when a small boy he had taken the part of the first watchman in *Much Ado About Nothing*, and it had been reported in the local press that 'the first watchman had two lines to speak and both were inaudible'. His later distinction as an orator showed that the words of the theatre critic had not fallen on stony ground.

His other great love was the collection of old silver, and when he was president of the Liverpool Medical Institution in 1954 his inaugural lecture on the subject delighted his medical and lay audience. As he said, it satisfied the intellect as well as the aesthetic senses as a leisure occupation.

He obtained numerous prizes, medals, and honorary fellowships, and honorary degrees at Oxford, Cambridge, London, Liverpool, Manchester, Hull, Dublin, and Sussex. He was chancellor of Hull University from 1970. He was knighted in 1949 and elected president of the BMA in 1951 and of the Royal Society of Medicine in 1964. In 1956 he accepted a barony.

Cohen died unexpectedly after a short illness 7 August 1977, at Bath. He was unmarried and the barony became extinct. There is a portrait of him by Harold Knight in the Liverpool Medical Institution.

[*The Times*, 9 August 1977; personal knowledge.] CYRIL A. CLARKE

COHEN, SIR JOHN EDWARD (JACK) (1898–1979), grocer and creator of Tesco stores, was born in the City of London 6 October 1898, the fifth of six children and the second of three sons of Avroam Kohen, an immigrant Polish-Jewish tailor, and his first wife, Sime Zamremba. He was originally named Jacob Edward. He was educated at Rutland Street LCC elementary school until the age of fourteen, after which he joined his father as an apprentice tailor. His mother died in 1915, and his father remarried soon afterwards. Tensions between stepmother and children encouraged 'Jack' to volunteer in 1917 at the age of eighteen for the Royal Flying Corps, where his tailoring skills were in demand for the making of balloon and aircraft canvas. He served in France, Egypt, and Palestine, narrowly escaping death in December 1917, when his troop carrier was sunk by a mine outside Alexandria. Demobilized early on account of a malarial infection which he had contracted, he returned to London in March 1919. As he was unwilling to resume tailoring and unable to obtain an office job in the City, he used his £30 demobilization gratuity to buy surplus NAAFI foodstuffs and established a stall in a street market in Hackney. Within a short time he was trading in a different market in the London area on each day of the week.

In 1924 he married Sarah ('Cissie'), daughter of Benjamin Fox, master tailor and immigrant

Russian Jew; they had two daughters. His wife encouraged his business endeavours, and Cohen extended his interests to wholesaling. Street trading remained, however, his main activity in the 1920s. One of his most successful lines was tea. He established the brand name 'Tesco' by joining the first two letters of his surname to the initials of the T. E. Stockwell, of Messrs Torring & Stockwell of Mincing Lane, his tea suppliers. Around 1930 he changed his given name by deed poll to John Edward in response to a plea from his bank manager at Mare Street, Hackney, whose staff could not distinguish the several Jacob Cohens among their customers.

The rapid expansion of London's suburbs in the house-building boom of the 1930s brought new retailing opportunities. The first two Tesco shops were opened at Becontree and Burnt Oak in 1931. Cohen's formula was to seek maximum turnover through low profit margins and prices. By 1939 there were 100 Tesco grocery shops in London and the Home Counties. During World War II, which precluded further shop development, Cohen acquired Goldhanger Fruit Farms in Essex and set up a fruit canning business, besides marketing their produce in Tesco shops. After the war, and a visit to the United States in 1947, Cohen became a pioneer in Britain of American-style retailing, based on self-service and payment at turnstile exits in place of traditional over-the-counter service. The new pattern made rapid strides, once the last elements of wartime consumer rationing were abolished in 1953. By 1959 the Tesco group comprised 185 stores, of which 140 were self-service, and net profits had increased from £78,000 in 1952 to almost £1 million.

Cohen had a colostomy operation in 1958, but returned promptly to resume his direction of the company. Take-overs and mergers brought faster growth in the 1960s. By 1968, when Tesco had acquired the Victor Value chain, it owned a total of 834 self-service shops, including many supermarkets, making it the fourth largest chain in the United Kingdom (after the Co-op, Fine Fare, and Allied Suppliers). Its net profits were nearly £6.7 million on a turnover of £240 million. By his trading policies during this period Cohen also played a major role in the campaign against resale price maintenance (RPM), the system whereby manufacturers of many products controlled the prices at which distributors sold them to the public. Tesco followed Fine Fare and other supermarket chains in introducing trading stamps, agreeing a deal in October 1963 with the Green Shield Trading Stamp Co. The use of stamps was widely seen as a roundabout way of cutting prices, and its opponents, who included both suppliers (such as the Distillers Company and Imperial Tobacco) and retailers (who formed the Distributive Trades Alliance under the leadership of Lord Sainsbury), took action to prevent the use of stamps in connection with items subject to RPM. The issue was settled with the help of government legislation: the Resale Prices Act was passed in 1964 and implemented gradually over the rest of the decade, eliminating RPM on all goods except books and pharmaceuticals.

Cohen was knighted in 1969. He relinquished the chairmanship of Tesco later that year, but remained active in the company's affairs until his death in the Harley Street Clinic, London, 24 March 1979. He was a freemason and a member of the Worshipful Company of Carmen, of which he served as master in 1976–7. His distinctive features—broad nose and mouth, high cheekbones, and prominent ears—made him easily recognizable in public. He was an outgoing, restless, sociable man, deeply attached to his family and valuing the accomplishment of a task rather than its material rewards.

[Maurice Corina, *Pile it High, Sell it Cheap: The Authorised Biography of Sir J. Cohen, Founder of Tesco*, 1971; private information.]

PETER M. OPPENHEIMER

COHEN, LIONEL LEONARD, BARON COHEN (1888–1973), lord of appeal in ordinary, was born 1 March 1888 in London, the only child of (Sir) Leonard Lionel Cohen KCVO, banker, and his wife, Eliza Henrietta, daughter of Sigismund Schloss, of Bowden, Cheshire. His paternal grandfather sat as MP for Paddington jointly with Lord Randolph Churchill [q.v.].

Lionel Cohen was educated at Eton and New College, Oxford, where he obtained a first class in history (1909) and in law (1910). He was called to the bar by the Inner Temple in 1913 but later joined Lincoln's Inn of which he became a bencher in 1934 and treasurer in 1954. During the 1914–18 war he served with the 13th Princess Louise's Kensington battalion of the London Regiment, was wounded in France, and on recovery held a staff appointment. On demobilization he joined the chambers of Alfred Topham, a leading practitioner in company law, and acquired a big practice in this field. He took silk in 1929. He became recognized in commercial circles as the leading expert in his subject. In court he was a sound and successful advocate whose integrity and industry always gained him an attentive hearing, though he lacked the forensic brilliance of some of his contemporaries. In chambers, and on paper, his advice, shrewd, practical, and authoritative, and his excellent judgement put him in the first rank.

After a period of service in the Ministry of Economic Warfare (1939–43) he was appointed a judge of the Chancery division and knighted in 1943 and was quickly promoted to the Court of Appeal in 1946 and to the House of Lords as a life peer in 1951. He was a popular judge, courteous and sensible and a good colleague. Though, as at the bar, he was perhaps outshone by some of his more flamboyant contemporaries, his judgements appeal for their balance, conciseness, and avoidance of dogmatism and rhetoric.

His contribution to the law would certainly have been more ample but for his diversion on so many occasions to the wide field of public affairs: there his performance was remarkable. As chairman of the company law amendment committee he was largely responsible for the contents of the Companies Act of 1948, the first major reconstruction since 1908. In 1946 he was a member, together with Lord Greene [q.v.], of the tribunal established to assess compensation for the assets vested in the National Coal Board on nationalization. In this demanding task, involving very large sums of money, his industry and acumen were invaluable. From 1946 to 1956 he was chairman of the royal commission on awards to inventors for the use of their inventions during the 1939–45 war—these included radar and the jet engine. In 1951 he was made chairman of another royal commission, that on taxation of profits and income, but retired from this on appointment as a lord of appeal. His most conspicuous and somewhat controversial assignment was as one of the 'three wise men' (the other two were Sir Harold Howitt and Sir Dennis Robertson, qq.v.) whom Harold Macmillan (later the Earl of Stockton) appointed in 1957, in effect to devise an incomes policy. This Council of Prices, Productivity, and Incomes produced three reports which aroused a great deal of interest after which Cohen resigned in 1959. In 1960 he retired as a lord of appeal in ordinary, but continued to sit in the House of Lords on invitation. His last case was *Phipps v. Boardman* (1967 2AC 46), where, his four colleagues being equally divided, it fell to him, much to his anxiety, to give the casting decision.

Another area to which Cohen gave a great deal of time and devotion was that of Jewish culture and charity. He had been brought up in the Orthodox tradition, and came to take the Reformed and Liberal positions. He was not a Zionist but interested himself in many Jewish causes. He was president for seven years of the Jewish Board of Guardians: he did much for the Hebrew University of Jerusalem as chairman of its English Friends, and a Lionel Cohen Foundation was created there in his honour. He served as vice-president of the Jewish Board of Deputies from 1934 to 1939. To this Dictionary he contributed the notice of Lord Warrington of Clyffe.

His personality at once inspired confidence. For a lawyer his appearance was unusual. He had a remarkably shaped cranium, warm brown eyes which conveyed essential kindliness; a moustache and a wide smile; and a rather husky voice which produced quick and effective utterance. He was totally lacking in arrogance and pomposity, but expressed his views with confidence and firmness. He had an effective penetrating mind without any claim to be considered 'intellectual'. He was a man of many friends, gregarious and clubbable. He was an excellent golfer, handicap 3 at his best: a member of nine golf clubs. He won the Bar Tournament twice—once at the age of sixty—and achieved the crowning glory of captaincy of the Royal and Ancient. He was a brilliant card player—of bridge, bézique, and piquet—and a member of White's, St. James's, and the Garrick Club, the epitome of a successful and popular barrister.

His other appointments included fellowship of Eton College, 1950–60, honorary fellowship of New College, 1946, membership of the council of St. Mary's Hospital Medical School, of which he was president in 1961–6, and chairmanship of the college committee, University College, London, 1953–63. He was a prominent Freemason. He died on 9 May 1973.

He married in 1918 Adelaide (died 1961), daughter of Sir Isidore Spielmann CMG, director of art exhibitions; they had two sons and a daughter.

[Private and family information: personal knowledge.] RICHARD WILBERFORCE

COLE, CECIL JACKSON- (1901–1979), business man and charity founder. [See JACKSON-COLE.]

COLE, GEORGE JAMES, BARON COLE (1906–1979), chairman of Unilever, was born in Singapore 3 February 1906, the second of the three children and only son of James Francis Cole, who was on the staff of the Eastern Telegraph Company, and his wife, Alice Edith Wheeler. He was educated first at the Raffles Institution, Singapore. Later he went to England and attended Herne Bay College, Kent, until he was seventeen. Thereafter his education was in what his later employer, the first Viscount Leverhulme [q.v.], once called 'the University of Hard Knocks': here he matriculated with distinction. In 1923 he joined the Niger Company, recently acquired in a dramatic but expensive stroke by Lord Leverhulme. In 1926 he made his first visit to Africa. Joined with Leverhulme's other extensive interests in African commerce, and in 1929 with the African and Eastern Trading Company under the name of the United Africa Company, Cole's employers represented a powerful influence in African affairs. Keying his natural abilities into theirs he rose steadily, soon to be charged with the responsibility for provisions buying and, later, transport.

When war broke out in 1939 he returned from Nigeria to London to manage all the United

Africa Company's affairs in British West Africa. Two years later he was seconded to the staff of Lord Swinton [q.v.], British resident minister in West Africa. He was, *inter alia*, responsible for handling materials through these territories for the Allied campaign in North Africa. When the war ended, he was appointed to the board of the United Africa Company, becoming joint managing director from 1952 to 1955 and simultaneously chairman of Palm Line Ltd. From 1948 he was elected to the board of the parent company, from 1929 renamed 'Unilever' after its amalgamation with the Dutch Margarine-Unie. He thus found himself at the top of two linked giant companies, one in Africa, the other in Europe, jointly one of the world's largest trading complexes increasingly described in popular jargon as a 'multinational'. His appointment to the British and Dutch boards of Unilever was primarily as the expert on African and overseas trade, but his talents were increasingly employed in the affairs of Unilever world-wide, and in 1956 he was appointed vice-chairman of (British) Unilever Ltd. When its redoubtable chairman, Lord Heyworth [q.v.], retired in 1960, after a long reign of eighteen years, George Cole succeeded him: a formidable task, for under Heyworth and his Dutch colleague, Rykens, Unilever had itself made giant steps in Europe, India, Africa, and North and South America.

Once again he rose to his new responsibilities. He strengthened not only the organizational basis of his firm to meet the growing competitive challenge of the sixties but also the personal ties with his Dutch colleagues. By nature he was warm, friendly, and wholly without affectation or pomposity. He infused these personal characteristics into his business relationships. His philosophy of business was basically simple but applied with shrewd business acumen. He understood 'business' to mean 'profitable trade'. (He gleefully adopted the title 'the African Trader' invented for him by a waggish colleague.) He fully accepted the current need to adopt scientific and technological methods for managing industry: always provided they did not obscure the fundamental end and purpose of profitable trade. Thus he stoutly defended Unilever's advertising budget against the Monopolies Commission which criticized it as excessive. In international affairs he believed that trade was a better means of bringing welfare to the third world than 'aid' loosely administered. One black Monday morning he strode into a meeting in Unilever House waving a copy of a Sunday newspaper colour supplement in which (Cole alleged) some well-meaning exponent of the higher journalism had praised the freedom given to Unilever scientists at the Port Sunlight laboratories to follow their own pursuits as and when they pleased with (in Cole's opinion) too little regard for the purposes for which they had been hired. 'Is it correct', he asked, 'that such indiscipline exists? If so, why? What is being done about it? If not, which of us has allowed or encouraged this rubbish to be printed and published?'

Such mercurial flashes of temperament were characteristic. They did nothing to blunt his warm relations with his colleagues and staff. They knew him as a generous and inspiring business leader whose secret was his belief in mutual confidence between man and man.

Physically he was generously built, with strong features, a fresh complexion, and bright eyes that smiled readily. He occasionally betrayed an attractive diffidence, perhaps deriving from a consciousness that his formal education had ended early in life. His widened responsibilities never dimmed his affection and understanding for Africa and its peoples.

He was created a life peer in 1965. In 1970 he retired from Unilever but emerged six months later at the invitation of the government to be chairman of Rolls-Royce when its future in the aero-space industry was jeopardized by its losses on the Tri-star engine. To appoint a trader to bring order to the engineers in their own industry was a brave stroke but Cole accepted the challenge. He met it with his customary brisk efficiency and was rewarded with the GBE (1973). He was a commander of the Order of Orange Nassau (1963) and a member of the governing bodies of a large number of societies concerned with Dutch, African, South American, and international affairs; a trustee of the Leverhulme Trust (1970–5); and a director of Shell Transport & Trading (1971–5).

He married in 1940 Ruth (died 1978), daughter of Edward Stanley Harpham. They had a son and a daughter. He died in London 29 November 1979.

[Charles Wilson, *The History of Unilever*, vol. iii. 1968, and combined index; private information; personal knowledge.]

CHARLES WILSON

COLE, DAME MARGARET ISABEL (1893–1980), socialist writer and Labour Party activist, was born 6 May 1893 in Cambridge, the eldest in the family of two daughters and four sons of John Percival Postgate [q.v.], Latin scholar, a fellow of Trinity College, Cambridge, and later professor of Latin at the University of Liverpool, and his wife, Edith, daughter of T. B. Allen, tea merchant. Her mother had been a pupil at the North London Collegiate School and then attended Girton College, Cambridge. For most of her life Margaret was closest to her brother Raymond Postgate [q.v.], himself an active socialist, son-in-law to George Lansbury [q.v.], and the begetter of the *Good Food Guide* in the years after World War II. Early in their lives the Postgate children were introduced to Latin by the direct method, and Margaret went on to read classics at Girton. Her schooling was first private, and then at the age of fourteen she was sent to Roedean, which she hated. But Girton was different: it represented freedom, and it was intellectually exciting. She worked very hard, took full measure of the academic joys Cambridge had to offer, fell easily out of religious belief and just as easily into socialism: 'the non-dogmatic, idealistic English socialism of the early twentieth century'. H. G. Wells [q.v.] had the greatest influence upon her, as indeed, upon so many of her generation. She obtained her first in 1914—it was expected—and left Cambridge just before the outbreak of war to take up a position as junior classics mistress at St. Paul's Girls' School in London.

The school was congenial, she enjoyed teaching and some of her colleagues, but her life changed drastically in the spring of 1916 when her brother Raymond was imprisoned as a conscientious objector. It greatly affected her, and within a few months she was deeply and passionately involved in 'the Movement'. She began working spare time for the Fabian (later Labour) Research Department, the secretary of which was Robin Page Arnot and whose leading intellectuals were G. D. H. Cole [q.v.] and William Mellor. By New Year 1917 she had resigned from St. Paul's—the high mistress enquired whether she had made proper provision for her old age—and became a member of the permanent staff of the Research Department, taking over as acting secretary when Page Arnot himself was arrested and imprisoned. She married G. D. H. Cole (died 1959) in 1918, and from this time her life and work was intimately bound up with work for the Labour movement. Her partnership with Douglas Cole was one of the outstanding intellectual marriages of the radical left in the twentieth century, and it ended only with his death forty years later. At the time of their marriage the Coles were Guild Socialists, but with the rapid decline of the movement in the early twenties they both became active in adult education, and were largely responsible for the establishment of the Tutors' Association. In 1925 Douglas Cole was appointed university reader in economics at Oxford, and the family moved there in the autumn. Margaret Cole hated Oxford: it was a male-dominated world and both to residents and friends she adopted the role of disconsolate exile; and from 1929 they maintained a house in London.

The thirties were years of intense intellectual and political activity. She joined with her husband and friends in establishing the Society for Socialist Inquiry and Propaganda in 1930, and the New Fabian Research Bureau in the year following; and it was in this decade that she began to publish on nearly as extensive a scale as her husband. They had already begun their collaboration on detective novels—they published twenty-nine between 1923 and 1942—and they now wrote two massive introductions to the problems of their times: *The Intelligent Man's Review of Europe Today* (1933) and *A Guide to Modern Politics* (1934). Their *The Condition of Britain* appeared in 1937. Of her own individual writings the volume in the *Fact* series, *The New Economic Revolution* (1937) and the book on *Marriage Past and Present* (1938) are among the most interesting. The latter is a very good example of her general approach to social questions: cool, rational, and sensible. The extreme feminist position she rejected, but her socialist insistence upon women's rights was expressed in clear and intelligible analysis. Her historical writing became more important after World War II. She published a well-used text in 1948, *Makers of the Labour Movement*, but it was her work on Beatrice Webb [q.v.], and especially her edition of the *Diaries* (1952, 1956) that were important to the world of scholarship. In 1961 she published a history of the Fabian Society, which added much to the original volume by Edward Pease [q.v.], and in 1971 *The Life of G. D. H. Cole*, which in many ways should be read as an extension of her own autobiography, *Growing Up Into Revolution* (1949). She contributed to this Dictionary the notices of Pease, J. F. Horrabin, and J. S. Middleton.

Her politics were always on the left of the labour movement. In the thirties she was a dedicated supporter of Republican Spain; she worked consistently against appeasement, and supported the Popular Front. In the post-war years she moderated her politics somewhat, but was never on the right of the Labour Party; her distaste for the Conservative Party always remained vigorous. Towards the end of World War II she became a member of the LCC education committee and was later an alderman. She was always deeply interested in children and young people and between 1951 and 1960 she was chairman of the further education committee, at which she worked enormously hard and successfully. Her semi-autobiography *Servant of the County* (1956) is an excellent introduction to the work of an activist in local government.

Margaret Cole liked people and was continuously interested in them; and she needed them. As a young woman she had been extremely shy which was offset on many an occasion by a notable fierceness: she was the original Valentine Wannop in *The Fifth Queen*, a trilogy by Ford Madox Ford [q.v.]; and to the end of her days she could be waspish as well as devastatingly frank. But she was generous and sympathetic and a humanist; much respected by many, and loved by her friends; a woman of great intellectual liveliness, an entertaining companion, well-read and a serious scholar. She never became cynical and she believed, to the end, in the common people. She had three children, two daughters and a son, and she was appointed OBE in 1965 and DBE in 1970. In 1977 she became an honorary fellow of LSE. She remained intellectually active to within a year of her death in a nursing home at Goring on Thames 7 May 1980, the day after her eighty-seventh birthday.

[*The Times* and *Guardian*, 8 May 1980; Betty D. Vernon, *Margaret Cole 1893–1980*, 1986; personal knowledge.] JOHN SAVILLE

COLERAINE, first BARON (1901–1980), politician. [See LAW, RICHARD KIDSTON.]

COLLINS, SIR WILLIAM ALEXANDER ROY (1900–1976), publisher, was born in Glasgow 23 May 1900, the eldest of three sons and four children of William Alexander Collins, CBE, of Glasgow, and his wife, Grace, daughter of William Brander, stockbroker. His family had for four consecutive generations headed the firm of William Collins, Sons & Co. Ltd., leading Scottish publishers of books, stationery, bibles, classics, and diaries. He was educated at Harrow and Magdalen College, Oxford, where he distinguished himself more as a sportsman than a *littérateur*. He obtained a third class in modern history in 1922 and entered the family firm in the mid-1920s.

During the years before World War II 'Billy' Collins and his cousin Hope—who managed the Glasgow end of the business—gradually took over from his father and his redoubtable uncle Sir Godfrey. His interests were less in printing, stationery, and the consolidated fortunes of a solidly based Scottish manufacturer and more in the more tempting and glamorous world of London publishing. At that time the scene was dominated by Macmillan, Heinemann, and Hodder & Stoughton, with important new and more literary lists being built by Hamish Hamilton, Jonathan Cape [q.v.], and Michael Joseph, and with (Sir) Allen Lane [q.v.] poised to launch his revolutionary Penguins. Collins's list then relied heavily on bibles, classics, and cheap children's books, though in (Dame) Rose Macaulay [q.v.] and Rosamond Lehmann it included two outstanding quality novelists on which it proved possible to build a more literary list.

Through the 1940s and 1950s Collins attracted a variety of successful and important authors to his firm—Thomas Armstrong, Nigel Balchin, James Barke, Marguerite Steen, Norman Collins, Howard Spring [q.v.], and George Blake amongst them. In this enterprise he was helped notably by four people: Sydney Goldsack, an archetypal high-pressure salesman who could build impressive sales results out of the most improbable projects but who retained a sensitive and loyal relationship within the firm and the trade; Ronald Politzer, by common consent the greatest book promoter of his generation; F. T. Smith, the inventor and sustainer of the Crime Club all through its heyday; and above all Collins's wife. It was she who in the early 1950s was the inspiration behind the move into religious publishing—and the pre-eminent builder of the Fontana religious list. By acquiring Geoffrey Bles, the Collinses were able to publish cheap paperback editions of the works of C. S. Lewis [q.v.] and J. B. Phillips and on this foundation a truly remarkable list of good popular and wide-ranging theology came to be associated with that name. Along with Bles came the Harvill Press. The fruitful relationship that developed between the Collinses and the two redoubtable ladies—Manya Harari [q.v.] and Marjorie Villiers, who *were* the Harvill Press, resulted in the publication in the British market of Boris Pasternak's *Dr Zhivago* and eventually the work of Alexander Solzhenitsyn himself.

But if Collins's wife led him enthusiastically towards religious books and world literature it was as a result of his own enthusiasms and intuitions that three other major developments were successfully accomplished. Perhaps the most important was the launching of Fontana paperbacks into a market hitherto dominated by Penguin and Pan: by withholding titles by best-selling authors like Peter Cheyney, (Dame) Agatha Christie [q.v.], and Hammond Innes from Pan, Collins was able to launch his own Fontana with a magnificent flying start. It remained a market leader for several types of paperback and proved consistently profitable and successful.

Less spectacular, and against a background of considerable scepticism both within the firm and outside, he bought Hatchards bookshop when the fortunes of that excellent Piccadilly establishment were at a low ebb, and by sheer impatient enthusiasm rejuvenated and restored it.

Perhaps his most significant achievement in the long run was the harnessing of his love of natural history and sport, of travel and wildlife, via the New Naturalist series which he created with James Fisher [q.v.], naturalist and general editor, to the publication of a whole string of successful non-fiction bestsellers ranging from Joy Adamson's account of her life and friendship with Elsa the lioness in a Kenyan nature reserve to David Attenborough's highly admired television tie-in *Life on Earth*.

While developing books to fulfil his own enthusiasms he did not neglect the building of the all-important Collins fiction list. A notable feature of this was the lasting mutual loyalty between author and publisher, exemplified by the fact that all Hammond Innes's adventure stories have come from the same house, which at one time supported the struggling young writer with a guaranteed income. The list was in the main solidly commercial and the accent was on selling. Collins himself set the tone. He knew what the leading booksellers throughout the world had ordered, when they should reorder, when they were overstocked. He and his wife visited Commonwealth booksellers regularly and became welcome friends as well as suppliers of best-selling books of all kinds. Branch managers and UK representatives were often harried unmercifully if they seemed to fail to appreciate the full saleability of each season's offerings but the enthusiasm was so infectious, and usually so well justified that lapses were few. They also visited the United States regularly, returning with numerous new manuscripts, notably James Jones's *From Here to Eternity*.

The secret of Collins's great success as a publisher lay in three outstanding qualities. Of his contagious enthusiasm mention has already been made. Equally important was his obsessive attention to detail. Grand designs and global strategies had no place in his thinking. 'Publishing is detail . . . isn't it?' he would insist. Thirdly, he drove himself and his colleagues hard. Opening the office post started his day, and a rush to St. Pancras to catch the late train to Market Harborough on Fridays completed the working week. Weekends were vigorously occupied in farming, hunting, gardening, and above all reading manuscripts.

These strengths were offset, his critics maintained, by a lack of purely intellectual or cultural concern, by a tendency to see other people's swans as geese, and by an apparent insensitivity to others' feelings which a privileged upbringing and a driving ambition would account for. His manner was abrupt, his temperament impatient, but his was a kind heart. Through his fifties, sixties, and early seventies his publishing interests and drive never varied. A constant attender at the Frankfurt Book Fair, he died twenty-four hours after his return from one such occasion in 1974. Those accompanying him on the plane home noted he seemed a little tired but full of enthusiasm for what he had sold and those he had met. He was appointed CBE in 1966 and knighted in 1970. In 1973 he was awarded an honorary LL D at the University of Strathclyde.

In 1924 he married Priscilla Marian, daughter of Samuel Janson Lloyd, of Pipewell Hall, Kettering, chairman and managing director of Lloyds Ironstone Co., Corby, Northamptonshire. They had two sons, the elder of whom succeeded his father as chairman and the younger of whom became managing director of the publishing division, and two daughters, one of whom died of gunshot wounds in South America, and the other of whom became a production controller in the family firm and married Peter Lewis, of the John Lewis Partnership. Collins died at his home in Kent 21 September 1976.

[Private information; personal knowledge.]

R. A. DENNISTON

COMPTON, FAY (1894–1978), actress, was born in West Kensington, London, 18 September 1894, the fifth and youngest child and third daughter of Edward Compton (Mackenzie), actor and manager, and his wife, the actress Virginia Bateman, daughter of Hezekiah Linthicum Bateman [q.v.], of Baltimore. Fay was a stage name; she was christened Virginia Lilian Emmiline. Her elder brother was (Sir) E. Montague Compton Mackenzie [q.v.], the author.

Educated at Leatherhead Court School, Surrey, and in Paris, Fay Compton's professional début was at the Apollo Theatre in August 1911, acting and singing with the Follies, a troupe created by Harry Gabriel Pélissier [q.v.], who had a rare talent for revue. Before the programme opened, and after a seven-week engagement, Fay Compton was married to Pélissier. The marriage lasted only two years, for Pélissier died in the early autumn of 1913, aged thirty-nine, leaving an infant son.

Almost at once his young widow got the small part of a German girl in a comedy called *Who's the Lady?* at the Garrick Theatre and she went on to appear in various musical comedies, one of them (in December 1914) in New York. From the first this red-haired beauty was an assured professional; no actress of her time was more versatile. She earned an early reputation by performing in the works of Sir J. M. Barrie [q.v.]; but she went on to every type of play, from Shakespeare to romantic drama, high and light comedy, farce, and even as principal boy in pantomime.

She had a small part in the revival at the Savoy by H. B. Irving of *The Professor's Love Story* (1916). She acted the title-role in Barrie's *Peter Pan* at Christmas 1917. In April 1920, at the Haymarket, which would always be her favourite theatre, she experienced her first real triumph when she played Mary Rose in Barrie's fantasy of the girl who vanishes on a Hebridean island and returns after many years as a ghost. Fay Compton acted the ghost scenes with an enchanted stillness. Now recognized as a leading lady, presently she had a long and improbably contrasted sequence of West End parts, among them the runaway wife in *The Circle* by W. Somerset Maugham [q.v.] (March 1921), Phoebe Throssel in *Quality Street* by Barrie (August 1921), and two characters in the complex and long-running *Secrets* (1922), in which she had to alter her age several times.

During 1923 she moved to the declining Ruritanian drama, as Princess Flavia in a Haymarket revival of *The Prisoner of Zenda*. She was happy as Lady Babbie in Barrie's *The Little Minister* (revived at the Queen's in November 1923); less so as Yasmin in *Hassan* by James Elroy Flecker [q.v.], directed by Basil Dean [q.v.] at His Majesty's where she succeeded Cathleen Nesbitt in the spring of 1924. In February 1925 she had her first major classical opportunity: to appear at the Haymarket as Ophelia to the American John Barrymore's Hamlet, a performance of which the critic James Agate [q.v.] wrote: 'She was fragrant, wistful, and had a child's importunacy unmatched in my time.'

In spite of the number of her later parts (more than eighty in several genres) Fay Compton never quite recaptured her early brilliance. At the Haymarket (1925) she had the voice and technique for the Lady in the felicitous dialogue of a comedy set in a Regency inn, *The Man With a Load of Mischief* by Ashley Dukes [q.v.]. In April 1926 she was aptly cast as the girl in a man's world in *This Woman Business* by Benn Levy [q.v.]. With a generous professionalism that seldom failed, she employed in very many plays her stage sense, her emotional powers, and her swift comedy. Twice more she was Ophelia, to Henry Ainley [q.v.] at the Haymarket (1931), and to (Sir) John Gielgud in the final performances (1939) at the Lyceum, and afterwards in Elsinore, Denmark. She was often in Shakespeare, notably several times at the Old Vic where she appeared as Regan (1940) in the Gielgud *King Lear* which was guided by Harley Granville-Barker [q.v.]. She also appeared in such long-running West End plays as *Autumn Crocus* (1931), *Call it a Day* (1935), *Blithe Spirit* (1941), *No Medals* (1944), and *Bonaventure* (1949). Her last Barrie role was the Comtesse in *What Every Woman Knows* (Old Vic, 1960). She acted small parts at the opening of the Chichester Festival (1962) and the Yvonne Arnaud Theatre, Guildford (1965), and she was much applauded for her Aunt Ann in the television serial of *The Forsyte Saga* (1967). In 1975 she was appointed CBE.

Fay Compton's second husband, the actor Lauri de Frece, died in 1921 when he was only forty-one, and in 1922 she was married to Leon Quartermaine (died 1967), with whom she had acted in *Quality Street*. Her third marriage was dissolved in 1942, and in that year she married Ralph Champion Shotter (Ralph Michael, the actor); this marriage was dissolved in 1946. There were no children of these last three marriages.

It was only towards Fay Compton's last decade that a strenuous life told on her and her memory wavered. She will be remembered most as Barrie's Mary Rose, from her youth, and over nearly fifteen years, in various productions, as the supreme Ophelia of her time. Fay Compton died at Hove 12 December 1978.

[Fay Compton, *Rosemary: Some Remembrances*, 1926; James Agate, *The Contemporary Theatre*, 1925; personal knowledge.] J. C. TREWIN

CONESFORD, first BARON (1892–1974), lawyer and politician. [See STRAUSS, HENRY GEORGE.]

CONNELL, AMYAS DOUGLAS (1901–1980), architect, was born at Eltham, Taranaki, New Zealand, 23 June 1901, the second child of six (five sons and one daughter) of Nigel Douglas Connell, a photographic artist, and his wife, Gertrude Matilda Weber. He was educated at Stratford Boys High School, Taranaki, and New Plymouth Boys High School, and was later articled to Stanley Ferne, architect in Wellington, for three years. In 1923 he and Basil Ward worked their way to England in SS *Karamarin*, as stokers 'before the mast'. On arrival in England he continued his studies at the Bartlett school of architecture, University College, London. He won the Rome scholarship in architecture for 1926. In 1928, after travelling extensively in Europe, he set up in practice as an architect in London, being joined in 1930 by Basil Ward (who had married his sister two years previously), and later, in 1933, by Colin Lucas, to form the partnership Connell, Ward & Lucas.

As a Rome scholar, with all the arduous training which that implies, Connell was a talented designer in the classical tradition, and a superb draughtsman. It was therefore not a little surprising that his first major architectural work proved to be an outstanding example of the modern movement—a complete breakaway from classicism. In fact it was soon to become well known as the earliest true example of the modern movement in England—a house called 'High and Over' in Amersham, Buckinghamshire, designed and built for Professor Bernard Ashmole in 1929. In 1976 it was listed by the Department of the Environment as a building of historic interest.

Later, when Basil Ward joined Connell, they developed a much more unorthodox design system using reinforced concrete in shell-type monolithic structures, in place of traditional masonry. A very interesting house at Grayswood, Haslemere, was designed and built along these lines for Sir Arthur Lowes-Dickinson, and also some smaller houses, including a controversial group of speculative houses at Ruislip, Middlesex. Colin Lucas, who had been experimenting with similar methods of reinforced concrete design, joined them in 1933, and from then until the time of the Munich crisis immediately preceding World War II, their work continued to develop along these lines, culminating in a house in Frognal, Hampstead, for

Geoffrey Walford, which met with considerable opposition, both from the London County Council planning committee and the estate surveyors. Walford took the case to the High Court and won, and the house was built, virtually as designed. It has recently been listed as a building of architectural and historic interest.

Connell, who was always quite obviously, although unassumingly, the leader of the partnership, was admired, particularly among students of the 1970s and 1980s, for his courage and determination in pursuing the cause of modern architecture. Practically all the buildings which came from this partnership met with opposition of one kind or another, from local councils, planning authorities, and estate surveyors. Many of these buildings achieved a world-wide reputation. It was largely through Connell's dedication to the cause of modern architecture, and his renegade approach to the stylists of the older schools, that the modern movement developed as it did in Britain. Connell became ARIBA in 1937 and FRIBA in 1964.

The war interrupted the work of the partnership, which was dissolved in 1939, and after a brief period with the Ministry of Works, Connell settled in East Africa and worked at Tanga. He was then offered a job in Nairobi by H. Thornley Dyer, an opening which led to a completely different phase of his architectural career. He remained in Nairobi, and established a practice to which he gave the name 'Triad'. Among his Nairobi buildings were the Aga Khan Hospital and the Crown law offices. It was not until 1977 that he returned permanently to England whereupon he continued to take an active interest in the firm of his own making. He eventually handed over the practice to his eldest son.

Connell was a man of striking appearance. He hid a warm and affectionate smile under the pointed beard he always wore, and he showed great kindness to others. But he would never tolerate falseness or untruthfulness in architecture, and he considered most contemporary work to be at fault in this respect—not only that designed in the neo-classical tradition, but also many 'modern' buildings. Creative and energetic to the end, he died peacefully in London, 19 April 1980. It is characteristic of his abounding energy, and his dedication to architecture, that he continued to work full-time in the firm he had established, up to a few days before he died.

In 1928 Connell married Maud Elizabeth, daughter of Harry Hargroves, business man; they had two sons and one daughter. He was later divorced, and in 1960 married Margret Hendricks; they had one daughter.

[Personal knowledge.] COLIN LUCAS

CONNOLLY, CYRIL VERNON (1903–1974), author, literary editor, and journalist, was born in Coventry 10 September 1903, the only son of Major Matthew Connolly, a conchologist, of Bath, and his wife, Muriel Vernon, who was Irish. He went up to Eton as a King's scholar, and then in 1922 to Balliol College, Oxford, where he was Brackenbury scholar. He obtained a third class in modern history in 1925. His schooling imbued him with a love of the classical authors, which never left him, and made a powerful imprint on his prose style, in its clarity, balance, and pungent concision of judgement. Connolly was a complex character, a wit, a nostalgic hedonist, a gourmet, and the most entertaining of companions and conversationalists when he was in the mood, but inspiring something akin to terror when the company (or the food) was not congenial to him. He hated all that was philistine or pompously conventional, and was quick in his appreciation of every development that was fresh and original in art as well as literature. He was especially devoted to French literature, both ancient and modern, his taste ranging from La Fontaine to Marcel Proust. He was the coiner of many *bon mots* which have passed into general usage, the best known of which is his remark that 'imprisoned in every fat man a thin one is wildly signalling to be let out'.

After going down from Oxford, Connolly became for a time the secretary of the rich, fastidious Anglo-American man of letters, Logan Pearsall Smith [q.v.], who allowed him great liberty to develop himself as a writer, while reinforcing his repugnance for the cliché and whatever was woolly and imprecise in prose expression. The great freshness, wit, and conversational ease of Connolly's fully matured prose style owes not a little, one cannot help thinking, to the standards of this early mentor.

Connolly proclaimed that he had a passion for travel, and wrote in *Who's Who* that his recreation was 'travel'; but he had none of the zeal that distinguished some of his contemporaries for exploring remote and little known places where the amenities of civilization were few. He preferred those areas where comfort and good food were available, and characteristically his first book was his short novel about the South of France, *The Rock Pool* (1936). It has spice and charm, and still has its admirers; but it showed, not least one fancies to its author, that he was not born to be a novelist. His next book, *Enemies of Promise* (1938), revealed his true gifts as witty commentator on the contemporary literary scene and analyst of the dangers that lie in wait for the literary aspirant. Not a few of the more sweeping generalizations have dated, but though some of the enemies have inevitably changed their aspect they are still there. The second section of the book, 'A Georgian Boyhood', a candid account of his years at Eton, remains one of the best sustained pieces of writing he ever produced. During the war he prepared a book of aphorisms of his own and observations on the aphorisms of his favourite authors, such as Chamfort. *The Unquiet Grave* (1944, revised edn. 1945) was published under the *nom de plume* of Palinurus, a disguise which deceived nobody and was probably not intended to. It was deeply steeped in nostalgia for the lost pleasures of peacetime, and has the distinction of being the least warlike of all the books produced during that cataclysmic conflict. It revealed for the first time his deep love of the delicate exotic creatures of the lemur family: many of the most touching and haunting passages in the book are devoted to them.

Connolly tempted providence by asserting in the opening paragraph of *The Unquiet Grave* that 'the true function of a writer is to produce a masterpiece and that no other task is of any consequence'. Though *The Unquiet Grave* abounds in felicities of writing and observation that could not have come from any other pen, it is difficult to see it, disjointed in structure and relying as it does so heavily on quotations from his most admired authors, as the masterpiece he longed to achieve. His most enduring monument will almost certainly be his editorship of the literary magazine *Horizon*, which he founded with Peter Watson and (Sir) Stephen Spender in 1939 and edited until 1950. In the first number he announced uncompromisingly 'our standards are aesthetic ones, politics are in abeyance'. He remained true to this ideal throughout the magazine's life, though not without difficulty, as it had its narrow-spirited enemies in the war bureaucracy, who did not consider it sufficiently uplifting to morale, but rather a waste of scarce paper. Connolly was not to be deflected, with the result that *Horizon* was one of the greatest morale-boosters of the war among intellectuals and artists, and came to be a symbol for them of what we were truly fighting to defend. The enormous variety and excellence of its most outstanding contributions in poetry, short fiction, and criticism were superbly illustrated by the selective anthology he published in 1953, *The Golden Horizon*. Connolly had his prejudices and his moods, which were clearly apparent in his editorial comments, and though he showed signs of wearying of his task towards the end, the magnitude of his achievement cannot be denied.

Early on in his career he began writing reviews and articles for the weekly press; he was literary editor of the *Observer* between 1942 and 1943, and during the last phase of his life he became a leading book reviewer for the *Sunday Times*. He collected these reviews, together with longer articles written for other English and American periodicals, into four volumes: *The Condemned Playground* (1945), *Ideas and Places* (1953), *Previous Convictions* (1963), and *The Evening Colonnade* (1973). In the first of these volumes, he confessed in a typically self-revealing fashion: 'Like most critics I drifted into the profession through a lack of moral stamina: I wanted to be a poet, and to revive the epic; I wanted to write a novel about Archaic Greece—but my epic and my novel fell so short of the standards which my reading had set me that I despaired of them, and, despairing, slipped into the interim habit of writing short-term articles about books.' Nevertheless his reviews were always readable, well informed and beautifully written, and characterized by an individual personal note that made one look out for them with pleasure from week to week, though when he was writing about a book that bored him the lowering of the critical tension was immediately apparent. He had a curiously persistent passion for making lists, the chief example of which is his *catalogue raisonné* of 'one hundred key books from 1880 to 1950', which he called *The Modern Movement* (1965). He was rewarded by a great exhibition of first editions of all the books he had chosen by the University of Texas, in a way the apotheosis of his career as a critic, arbiter of taste, and bibliophile.

Connolly was a chevalier of the Legion of Honour, became FRSL, and was appointed both CBE and C.Lit. in 1972.

In 1930 he married Frances Jean Bakewell, of Baltimore. This marriage ended in divorce and he married, secondly, Barbara Skelton. There were no children of either marriage. After the dissolution of the second marriage he married in 1959 Deirdre, formerly the wife of Jonathan Craven, of the 9th Lancers, and daughter of Major (Patrick William) Dennis Craig, MBE, son of the first Viscount Craigavon [q.v.], first prime minister of Northern Ireland. They had a son and a daughter. Connolly died in London 26 November 1974.

[Stephen Spender, *Cyril Connolly*, 1978 (reprinted from *Times Literary Supplement*, 6 December 1974); *The Times*, 27 and 30 November and 3 December 1974; David Pryce-Jones, *Cyril Connolly, Journal and Memoir*, 1983; personal knowledge.]

JOHN LEHMANN

CONSTABLE, WILLIAM GEORGE (1887–1976), art historian, was born at Derby 27 October 1887, the elder child and only son of William George Samuel Constable and his wife, Remeliah Isabella Webb. John Constable [q.v.] belonged to the same family although the relationship, never precisely established, was not very close; but the fact that he possessed a fairly exact facsimile of the painter's prominent and somewhat bird-like nose was frequently commented upon.

He went to Derby School, of which his father was headmaster, and thence to St. John's College, Cambridge, where he was the MacMahon law student and Whewell scholar of the university. He obtained a first class in part ii of the economics tripos in 1910. From Cambridge he went to London and, joining the Inner Temple, read for the bar, to which he was called in 1914. But the direction of his career was entirely changed after a horrific experience which befell him in 1916. He had enlisted in the Sherwood Foresters and had risen after two years to the rank of major. Then one day a heavy shell exploded in a trench a few feet away and he was literally buried alive. His life was saved by the energy and devotion of his batman, who succeeded in digging him out. The aftermath of this experience was always to remain with him physically.

It was during his long convalescence that he decided to give up law and to look to the arts for a living. He enrolled as a student at the Slade School and came under the influence of Henry Tonks and Philip Wilson Steer [qq.v.], with whom in due course, as he described in 'Some Notes for an Obituary' (*Apollo*, January 1963), he used to share a weekly supper, the fourth member of the party being George Moore. He became a competent but never a very interesting painter, as he himself recognized, so in 1922 he turned to guide-lecturing at the Wallace Collection, and soon afterwards to art criticism for the *New Statesman* and the *Saturday Review*.

Late in 1923 he moved to the National Gallery, where he was to remain for eight years, the last two as assistant director. Had he stayed on, there was every prospect of his succeeding (Sir) Augustus Daniel as director; but in 1931 he was persuaded to become the first director of the newly formed Courtauld Institute of Art in the University of London, which opened in the following year. Here Constable achieved a most notable success. No British university had, until then, offered a degree course in the history of art. To him, therefore, fell the great responsibility of framing the initial course of study. At the time, because of its total exclusion from school and university curricula, the history of art was a subject on which even the most highly educated people in Britain were almost unbelievably ignorant. Constable therefore sought to provide a course which ranged widely over the whole field of art history. He enlisted the help of distinguished scholars not only from England but also from the Continent, including a number of refugee scholars from Nazi Germany.

Unhappily, difficulties arose with the governing body, who were more concerned with the maintenance of numbers than of the highest academic standards. On this issue Constable was not prepared to compromise, and early in 1937, to the consternation of his friends and many of the students, he resigned.

From 1935 to 1937 he was Slade professor of fine arts at Cambridge in succession to Roger Fry [q.v.]; he was now offered the curatorship of painting at the Museum of Fine Arts at Boston. Thus in March 1938 the Constables set sail for 'the other Cambridge', in Massachusetts. Although he never renounced his British citizenship, it was to remain their home for the rest of his life. In 1926 he had married Olivia, daughter of Arthur Carson Roberts, of Chelsea, legal adviser to the Ministry of Health, and their two children, John and Giles, were both to rise to eminence in the USA.

Constable held the curatorship of paintings at Boston until October 1957: almost twenty years. He rehung the main galleries, made some notable acquisitions, and was responsible for many important exhibitions.

He was an excellent administrator, but it is for his work as a writer and thinker that he is now chiefly remembered. He wrote two major books. *Richard Wilson*, which appeared in 1953, has remained the standard work on this painter. *The Times* obituarist described it as 'one of the best and most comprehensive works ever written about an English artist'. *Canaletto*, published in two volumes in 1962, is the leading book on this artist. Constable was always an indefatigable traveller, and in 1937, after he had left the Courtauld Institute, a Leverhulme fellowship enabled him to spend some months in Venice, vital for this work. He took the trouble to see personally almost all the 500 paintings and 300 drawings described, in addition to sketch-books, engravings, and etchings. *The Painter's Workshop* (1954) is a useful handbook for laymen on the technical processes of painting and on problems of conservation. Other books include *John Flaxman* (1927), *Art History and Connoisseurship* (1938), and *Art Collecting in the United States* (1964). He also compiled or edited, with punctilious accuracy, a long series of exhibition and other catalogues.

In his personal relations 'W.G.', as he was universally known, even to his wife, was unfailingly kind, generous, and approachable. Yet at heart he was a shy and very private man, not easy to know, for all his outward geniality and friendliness.

He received many honours. They included fellowships of the Society of Antiquaries and of the American Academy of Arts and Sciences, an honorary fellowship of St. John's College, Cambridge (1956), honorary doctorates of the universities of Durham, Nottingham, and New Brunswick, chevalier of the Legion of Honour, and commendatore of the Crown of Italy. He died at Cambridge, Massachusetts, 3 February 1976.

[Memoir by Gardner Cox for the records of the Saturday Club of Boston, Mass., 1982; family information; personal knowledge.]

ALEC CLIFTON-TAYLOR

CONSTANTINE, LEARIE NICHOLAS, BARON CONSTANTINE (1901–1971), cricketer, barrister, political figure, and the first Black peer, was born at Diego Martin, near Port of Spain, Trinidad, 21 September 1901, the eldest in the family of three sons and one daughter of Lebrun Constantine and his wife, Anaise, daughter of Ali Pascall, escaped slave. Lebrun Constantine, a cocoa plantation foreman, toured England with the West Indian cricket teams of 1900—when he scored the first century made for a West Indian side in England—and 1906. Learie was brought up as a cricketer, trained in family play in which his father insisted on the importance of fielding—often a weakness in early West Indian cricket. That was influential in making his son, eventually, by general consent, the finest fieldsman in the history of the game. He was, too, a spectacular all-round cricketer as a fast bowler and attacking batsman: from time to time a match-winner, even in test matches, though not a consistent performer at that level.

His major impact on the world outside games, in elevating and defending the standing of coloured people in Britain, was a subsequent development. Although his father was the grandson, and his mother the daughter, of slaves, and he was sensitive on the subject, he was not politically aware nor active until relatively late in his life.

He was educated in Port of Spain, at St. Ann's Government School and later at St. Ann's Roman Catholic School until he was fifteen, but he showed no enthusiasm for studies. He then worked in a solicitor's office and, although he became adept at typing, he was preoccupied with cricket. In 1923, after only three first-class matches, he was chosen for the West Indian team to tour England. He had no great success but won respect for his fielding; he perceived that his only hope of material success lay in cricket.

Returning home he devoted himself to the practice which won him a place in the West Indian party of 1928 for their first test tour of England. He achieved little in the test matches but was outstanding against the counties and made himself a considerable public reputation by a remarkable performance in a single match, West Indies versus Middlesex at Lord's. The county scored 352 for 6 declared; and West Indies were saved from following on only by Constantine's 86 (made in an hour), their solitary score of over 30. As Middlesex appeared to pull clear in their second innings, Constantine took 6 wickets for 11 (7 for 57 altogether) leaving West Indies 259 to win. At 121 for 5 they seemed to be losing, when Constantine scored a most spectacular 133 in an hour to turn the game and win it for West Indies by 3 wickets. That performance, its attendant publicity, and its demonstration of his quality as a match-winner brought him the offer of a contract as a professional with Nelson in the Lancashire League. He accepted and, supported by his wife through some early setbacks—many of the people of Nelson had never seen a coloured man before—he shaped a career there. He wanted part-time work which would enable him to study law: England was the only place, and cricket his only means, of doing both. His success as a cricketer was beyond doubt. Virtually the perfect league professional, he played a major part in Nelson's unparalleled success in winning the Lancashire League eight times during his ten seasons there and breaking the attendance record of every ground in the competition. He became a public hero in the town, and in 1963 he was awarded the freedom of the borough of Nelson.

In 1929, playing as a guest of West Indian cricketers in New York, he was advertised: 'Come and see L. N. Constantine, the fastest bowler in the world. Incomparable as a fieldsman, a harder hitter than G. L. Jessop.' On the following day, however, he was asked, because of his colour, to move out of his seat to another part of a Roman Catholic church. That left a deep and lifelong impression on him and affected his attitude to America.

League cricket and his studies meant that he never returned to domestic cricket in the West Indies. In his whole career he played in only 117 first-class matches; 194 innings for 4,451 runs at an average of 24.32, and 424 wickets at 20.60. The statistics of his eighteen test matches are not impressive: 641 runs at 19.42, 58 wickets at 30.10. Figures, however, do not do justice to the quality of his cricket. Certainly he turned two test matches and reshaped another. In 1929–30 at Georgetown his bowling—4 for 35 and 5 for 87—by far the best figures on either side, won West Indies their first test match. At Port of Spain in 1934–5 his all-round performance levelled the series which West Indies eventually took by two to one; he bowled Leyland to win the match with only one ball remaining. In his last test, at the Oval, in 1939, he effectively gave West Indies a first innings lead.

That was the end of his first-class cricket. Throughout his career his fielding was outstanding. Superbly equipped, quick in reaction, agile, long-armed, perfectly balanced, as a young man his speed over ground and ability to pick up on the run and throw with power and accuracy made him a great cover-point or deep field. As he grew older his still rapid responses, fearlessness, concentration, absolute fitness, and, above all, his prehensile catching, made him equally great close to the wicket. Although he played for Windhill from 1946 to 1948, his major cricket ended, happily, in 1945 with the match between the Dominions and England to celebrate the end of the war, when the other Dominions players—all white-skinned—elected him as their captain. In a handsome batting partnership and by shrewd captaincy he played a prominent part in winning a close-run match.

There lies his cricketing fame; but it ended before he made his most important contribution to the history of his time. His lifelong friend, C. L. R. James, had said that Constantine 'revolted against the revolting contrast between his first-class status as a cricketer and his third-class status as a man'. He did not, however, involve himself in colour issues until after 1940. He had found friends and respect in Nelson; and he stayed in England during World War II, when he became a Ministry of Labour welfare officer with particular responsibility for West Indian workers. In 1944 he fought and won a historic court case on the issue of colour prejudice against the Imperial Court Hotel in London for 'failing to receive and lodge' him.

Urged on by his wife, he had studied doggedly since his arrival in Nelson and, in 1954, he was called to the bar by the Middle Temple. Returning to Trinidad in 1954 he was made chairman of the People's National Movement: in the first democratic elections there, he became an MP and was appointed minister of works in 1956. Soon, however, he went back to London as high commissioner for Trinidad and Tobago from 1962 to 1964. Appointed MBE in 1945, knighted in 1962, honorary master of the bench in 1963, life peer in 1969, he had now become a considerable figure in British life; and, most significantly, in the eyes of the coloured peoples—especially the West Indians—in Britain. His position as the most prominent member of the British coloured community was widely recognized: he was appointed a governor of the BBC; was elected rector of St. Andrews, which gave him an honorary LL D in 1968; was president of the League of Coloured Peoples; and became a significant member of the Race Relations Board and of the Sports Council. A gentle person, a contented family man, a devout Roman Catholic, a compassionate radical, and an unflinching defender of coloured rights, Contantine loved England. Although he had been warned that a lung condition threatened his life if he did not live in a warmer climate, such as that of the West Indies, he remained in Britain, and he died in London 1 July 1971. His wife survived him by only two months. Trinidad posthumously awarded him its highest honour, the Trinity Cross. His only child, a daughter, Gloria, brought up in Nelson, became a school teacher in Trinidad. He had married in 1927 Norma Agatha, daughter of Faustin Cox, a chemist, from Port of Spain.

Most of the books credited to him were about cricket and were written with assistance, notably that of C. L. R. James; among them are *Cricket and I* (1933), *Cricket in the Sun* (1946), *Cricketers' Carnival* (1948), and *Cricketer's Cricket* (1949). The exception was *Colour Bar* (1954).

[*Wisden Cricketers' Almanack*; Gerald Howat, *Learie Constantine*, 1975; personal knowledge.]

JOHN ARLOTT

COOK, SIR JAMES WILFRED (1900–1975), chemist and vice-chancellor, was born in South Kensington, 10 December 1900, the younger son (there was also a daughter) of Charles William Cook, coachman to a private family, of Hitchin, and his wife, Frances, daughter of Aaron Wall, of Kimbolton, Herefordshire. Cook himself commented that though neither parent had much education his intelligent mother had a marked influence upon him. He attended Sloane School, Chelsea, and entered University College London in 1917, where he became Tuffnell scholar and gained second class honours at the end of his second year. He was still only eighteen and by the age of twenty-five London had awarded him his M.Sc. (1921), Ph.D. (1923), and D.Sc. (1925).

Such dedication was the hallmark of Cook's career. His first appointment (1920–8) was as lecturer at the Sir John Cass Technical Institute, where he worked with Dr E. de Barry Barnett, publishing some thirty papers on anthracene derivatives. Collaboration with Sir Ernest Kennaway [q.v.] led to Cook's appointment at the Research Institute of the Royal Cancer Hospital in 1929. Over the next ten years 'he made his outstanding contribution to cancer research, first demonstrating the carcinogenicity of polycyclic benzenoid hydrocarbons and then isolating from coal tar its main carcinogenic component, which he showed to be the pentacyclic hydrocarbon, 3:4-benzpyrene. This work ... showed for the first time that cancer could be induced by minute quantities of a pure chemical compound' (H. N. Rydon). Recognition quickly followed. London University appointed him reader in pathological chemistry (1932) and professor of chemistry (1935). He was awarded, with Kennaway, the prize of the International Union Against Cancer (1936) and elected a fellow of the Royal Society in 1938.

A second phase of Cook's career began in 1939 on his appointment to the regius chair of chemistry in Glasgow, which he held until 1954. Teaching in a large department and a host of other duties, including the presidency of the Royal Institute of Chemistry (1949–51) and membership of the University Grants Committee (1950–4), did not diminish his research output. Work continued on polycyclic aromatic hydrocarbons, whilst his research on colchicine, an alkaloid with the important biological property of arresting division in plant and animal cells and consequently capable of inhibiting tumour growth, established its later accepted formula and led to new work on the tropolones.

In 1954 Cook was appointed principal of the University College of the South West, a critical time in the fortunes of the college which had been seeking university status for some thirty years and teetering on the brink for the last five. Preliminaries were soon completed, the University of Exeter received its charter in 1955, and Cook became its first vice-chancellor. Much expansion of British universities preceded the Robbins report of 1963, reflecting the tide of goodwill flowing in their direction in the late 1950s. Given such support expansion was easy enough but it was Cook's task both to establish the academic standards of his new university and to plan the development of its buildings. Under Cook Exeter soon began to be recognized in students' eyes as one of the most attractive universities in the country. Exeter did not expand so spectacularly as some new universities but what was done was well done and its future assured.

Cook had long been concerned with higher education in developing countries and on his retirement from Exeter in 1966 he accepted the vice-chancellorship of the federal University of East Africa, consisting of the colleges at Kampala, Nairobi, and Dar es Salaam. It was not an easy time for an Englishman to head a federal university with the 'wind of change' making it likely that Kenya, Uganda, and Tanzania would insist on their own independent universities. Cook appreciated what had to be done and won the respect of all parties. Soon after he left in 1970 all three colleges were established as national universities.

On his return Cook renewed his association with the New University of Ulster where he had been chairman of its academic planning board and now became chairman of its academic advisory committee.

Cook's contributions as scientist and administrator were widely recognized, by his knighthood in 1963, by honorary degrees from the universities of Dublin (1948), Rennes (1960), Nigeria (1961), Exeter (1967), and Ulster (1970), and his many research prizes, including the Davy medal of the Royal Society in 1954.

Many of his contemporaries mention his reserve and his dry sense of humour, contributing to an appearance of strength and some aloofness. Those who knew him well, and especially in later life, found him more relaxed and entertaining. In 1930 he married Elsie Winifred Griffiths. They had three sons. She died in 1966, just before Cook retired from Exeter. In 1967 he married Vera Elizabeth Ford, a biologist, whom he had first met when she was recorder of Section X of the British Association and Cook was president-elect of the section. She was the daughter of William John Ford, surveyor in the Customs and Excise, London. Cook died at Exeter 21 October 1975.

[J. M. Robertson in *Biographical Memoirs of Fellows of the Royal Society*, vol. xxii, 1976; H. N. Rydon in *University of Exeter Gazette*, vol. lxxx, 1976; private information; personal knowledge.]

HARRY KAY

COOPER, DAME GLADYS CONSTANCE (1888–1971), actress and theatre manager, was born at Lewisham 18 December 1888, the eldest of the three children (all daughters) of Charles William Frederick Cooper, journalist and editor of *Epicure*, founded by himself, and of his second wife, Mabel, daughter of Captain Edward Barnett of the Scots Greys. She was educated first at home by a French governess, then briefly at school in Fulham and from the age of seven began regular photographic modelling for the studio of Downey's in Ebury Street.

In the autumn of 1905 she was taken by a schoolfriend to an open audition at the Vaudeville Theatre and somewhat to her own surprise was offered the title role in a tour of *Bluebell in Fairyland* by (Sir) E. Seymour Hicks [q.v.], which opened at Colchester on her seventeenth birthday. Within another year she had joined George Edwardes's company at the Gaiety, signing a contract for £3 (rising to £5) a week to play as cast, primarily small singing and dancing roles in such musicals as *The Girls of Gottenberg* (1907), *Havana* (1908), and *Our Miss Gibbs* (1909).

Gladys Cooper was not however the kind of Gaiety girl taken to Romano's by wealthy young men about town; her ambition was to be a serious actress, though all thoughts of a career were interrupted when one night she was seen on stage by Herbert John Buckmaster, a twenty-six-year-old Boer war soldier then working for Ladbroke's. Within days he had arranged an introduction to her, and they were married on 12 December 1908 much to the disapproval of her parents who felt that at nineteen she was still too young to leave home.

For a year or so after the marriage she continued to work at the Gaiety but then came the birth (in July 1910) of Joan, the first of her two children by Buckmaster, and when she returned to the stage after that it was at last to the straight theatre; she began to get small roles in comedy at the Royalty Theatre and then joined Sir George Alexander [q.v.] for a revival of *The Importance of Being Earnest* (1911) at the St. James's. Her first real break came in 1912 with a small but showy last-act role in *Milestones* by E. Arnold Bennett [q.v.] and Edward Knoblock, which ran for eighteen months during which time she would also take on many other roles at other theatres in other plays provided they finished early enough in the evening to allow her to get back to the Royalty for her entrance in *Milestones*. When that run ended she went into *Diplomacy* (1913) at Wyndham's which lasted another year, throughout which she played for the first time with the man who was to become the most constant and beloved of her stage partners, (Sir) Gerald du Maurier [q.v.]. By now she was earning £40 a week, and the strain was beginning to show on her marriage to a man still only earning about half that from Ladbroke's; then however came World War I. 'Buck' joined the cavalry and went to France with the Royal Horse Guards, while his wife spent the Christmas of 1914 also at the front, though with a concert party organized by Seymour Hicks. By now she was carrying her second child John (born June 1915).

It was in the following year, 1916, that she first began to act at the theatre she was later to manage, the Playhouse on the corner of the Embankment and Northumberland Avenue by Charing Cross, a building that was for the next fifteen years to become her professional home. By 1917 she had joined Frank Curzon in its management, thereby becoming the only woman other than Lilian Baylis [q.v.] at the Vic to run a London theatre before World War II, and the plays that she presented, acted in, and sometimes unofficially directed there were to include four W. Somerset Maugham [q.v.] premières (*Home and Beauty, The Letter, The Sacred Flame*, and *The Painted Veil*) as well as revivals of *My Lady's Dress, The Second Mrs Tanqueray*, and *Magda*.

Herbert Buckmaster returned from the war in 1918 to find that the chorus girl he had married a decade earlier had now become a professional actress and theatre manager, neither of them attributes he was looking for in a wife. Accordingly and amicably they were divorced in 1921; he was to marry twice more and make an eventual home at Buck's Club which he had founded in Clifford Street and where fifty years after their divorce she would still frequently be found at parties given by him to celebrate yet another first night. They were always to be the best of friends.

Gladys Cooper spent the 1920s bringing up her two children and running the Playhouse; in 1928 came a second marriage (to Sir Neville Arthur Pearson, second baronet); by him she had her third and last child Sally, but it was to be a short-lived marriage (dissolved in 1937) and by the early 1930s there was little to keep her in England. Changing theatrical tastes brought an end to her years of success at the Playhouse; Maugham had ceased to write plays, and despite her discovery of such interesting new works as *The Rats of Norway* (which gave Laurence (later Lord) Olivier one of his early stage successes in 1933) and a West End success in *The Shining Hour* (1934) Gladys Cooper began to feel that she had lost touch with London theatre-goers. The bright young things for whom she had worked so hard and successfully in the 1920s were no longer thronging the stalls, and she herself had by now fallen in love with the actor Philip Merivale who was to become her third and last husband and whose already successful career on Broadway encouraged Gladys to try her luck there too.

Hers was always a cut-and-run philosophy, and by the middle 1930s the London where she had once been a definitive *Peter Pan*, where she had run her own theatre and brought up her elder children, was a place of the past. America was where she would now live and despite a catastrophic Broadway start in which she played (unsuccessfully) both Desdemona and Lady Macbeth opposite Merivale (whom she married in Chicago in April 1937) it was indeed America that was to become her home for the second half of her long life.

She returned to London in 1938 for another brief and unsuccessful Shakespeare season (this in the Open Air Theatre, Regent's Park) and a West End run in *Dodsworth*, by now always appearing in partnership with Merivale. They returned to New York for Dodie Smith's *Spring Meeting* (1938) on Broadway and then, in the autumn of 1939, came an offer from (Sir) Alfred Hitchcock [q.v.]. He was making his first-ever Hollywood film, *Rebecca* (1940), and wanted Gladys Cooper for the small role of Laurence Olivier's sister; she went out to California for three weeks and stayed thirty years.

She fell immediately and totally in love with the sun, the sea, and the surroundings of California; though she was never there to get the leading roles that an actress of her stage distinction might have expected, she went under contract to MGM and played in a total of thirty films between 1940 and 1967, of which the most distinguished were *Now Voyager* (for which she got an Oscar nomination in 1943), *Separate Tables* (1958), and *My Fair Lady* (1964). Though Philip Merivale died in California in 1946, Gladys Cooper was to live on there alone, making a home for herself and those of her many relatives and friends seeking however temporarily a place in the Californian sun.

But during the 1950s and 60s she also began with increasing frequency to return to the London stage, first in *Relative Values* (1951) by (Sir) Noël Coward [q.v.] and then in such later successes as *The Chalk Garden* (1955) and the revival of Maugham's *The Sacred Flame* (1967). She bought a house on the regatta stretch of the Thames at Henley and, as the old English colony in California began to disappear, spent more and more of her time back home again amid children, grandchildren, and great-grandchildren. In 1967 she was appointed DBE, a year later she celebrated her eightieth birthday, and 17 November 1971, having just played in another revival of *The Chalk Garden*, she died at home in Henley only a month away from the start of her eighty-fourth year.

She left one son (John Buckmaster, himself for some time an actor), two daughters both of whom married actors (Joan married Robert Morley in 1940; Sally married Robert Hardy in 1961), five grandchildren, two great-grandchildren, just over £34,000, and the unforgettable memories of one of the most remarkable and resilient actresses of her generation.

[Sheridan Morley, *Gladys Cooper*, 1980; Gladys Cooper, *Gladys Cooper*, 1931; Sewell Stokes, *Without Veils*, 1953; personal knowledge.] SHERIDAN MORLEY

COOTE, SIR COLIN REITH (1893–1979), newspaper editor, was born 19 October 1893 at Fenstanton in Huntingdonshire, the eldest of three sons, one of whom died in infancy, (there were no daughters) of Howard Browning Coote, landlord, coal merchant, and later lord lieutenant of Huntingdonshire, and his wife, Jean Reith, daughter of Alexander Reith Gray, of Aberdeen. A French–Swiss governess gave Colin Coote from childhood a love for France and its language. He was educated at Rugby and Balliol College, Oxford, where he obtained a second class in *literae humaniores* in 1914.

Soon after he had taken his degree the European war broke out, and he obtained an immediate commission in the 4th battalion of the Gloucestershire Regiment. Transferred to the Italian front, he was promoted captain and won a DSO (1918)—rare for an officer below field rank. He was gassed and three times wounded. In 1917 Neil Primrose, Liberal MP for the Isle of Ely, was killed in action. Coote was given leave to contest the by-election as a Liberal candidate. Having won it, he returned to the front. A year later, demobilized, he was re-elected as a Coalition Liberal (and the youngest member in the Commons) in the 'coupon' election of 1918. His four years in Parliament, during which he shared a house with his lifelong friend Walter Elliot [q.v.], became a useful experience, but journalism was beckoning. His free-lance writing was noticed. Already bilingual in French, Coote had added mastery of Italian during his war service. Though he was without formal experience as a journalist, he caught the eye of G. Geoffrey Dawson [q.v.]. When he lost his seat in 1922, he was appointed Rome correspondent of *The Times*.

Four years in Rome gave Coote an insight into the city which persuaded him to write two books—*Italian Town and Country Life* (1925) and *In and About Rome* (1926). It was also the time of the rise to power of the efficient young Mussolini. The distaste implanted in Coote's liberal mind for that stamp of regime was decisively to shape his judgements a decade later at the time of Munich. By nature a commentator rather than a news-gatherer, he made his mark in Rome by his interpretation of these events. In 1926 *The Times* called him back to the House of Commons, this time to write the newspaper's sketch of parliamentary proceedings. That helped to develop his intimacy with politics. It also enhanced his facility for writing clean English as fast as a pen could travel. Coote wrote his copy and his innumerable private letters in a minute but beautifully legible handwriting with few pauses or corrections, successive lines sloping from the left margin. In 1929 he became a *Times* leader writer, mainly on political affairs but sharing responsibility for a range of other subjects at home and abroad. As the 1930s and the rise of the dictators marched on, difficulties arose for him over his newspaper's editorial policy. *The Times* endorsed the so-called appeasement policy of Neville Chamberlain and Viscount (later the Earl of) Halifax [qq.v.]. Coote's detestation of Fascism and National Socialism was absolute. He did not resign, but withdrew from foreign leader writing, increasingly confining himself to home topics. At odds with his friend, Walter Elliot, he came to detest Chamberlain and to abhor Munich. When war came, his knowledge of military matters served his newspaper well enough for a time; but an invitation in 1942 to join the *Daily Telegraph* was a welcome signal.

He joined as a leader writer. Now forty-nine with twenty years of varied experience, an immense range of public friendships, and a grasp of national and international politics, he was an acquisition. Three years later he was appointed deputy to Arthur E. Watson [q.v.], who had been editor since 1924. When Watson retired in 1950, Coote was invited by Viscount Camrose [q.v.] to succeed him. Though more of a writing editor than Watson had been, he had the qualities to lead a staff of journalists and to keep a national newspaper on course. Tall, good-looking, urbane, he could when he chose bring great charm to bear. In a more Olympian mood, he could make someone he thought guilty of a folly feel very small indeed. After his retirement in 1964 he described one essential duty of an editor in these terms: 'to keep his paper independent of all outside influences, British or Foreign, commercial or political'. Another duty, he thought, was 'to maintain the English language'. In both these respects he lived up to his precepts. His term as editor, 1950–64, coincided with the Conservative regimes of 1951–64. Yet his wide political sympathies led him to observe more than once that among all the political leaders he had known (and he claimed the friendships of ten prime ministers) he liked best Churchill and Hugh Gaitskell [qq.v.]. His editorship also fell into the period of Great Britain's dalliance with

Europe. Like many of his generation who had spent youthful years in the first European war, Coote was an ardent European as well as an active protagonist for Anglo-French accord. Under his influence the *Daily Telegraph* was a strong advocate for joining the European common market.

On main issues his basic political principles and moral values were founded on rock. On particulars and intermediate values he always liked to seek the views of his staff experts, and if they were soundly presented would always accept them. Lord Camrose would occasionally tease Coote about his old Liberal blood, but in so far as this was ever reflected in the editorial columns of the *Daily Telegraph* it did the newspaper no harm whatever. Coote's relations with Lord Camrose and, after 1954, with W. M. Berry (later Lord Hartwell) were amicable. The greatest quality which an editor can possess, Coote wrote after retiring, is luck. During his time as editor a rapid rise in the standards of life of the average citizen was reflected in the fortunes of the newspaper with which he was associated. Between 1950 and 1964 the circulation of the *Daily Telegraph* rose from 971,000 to 1,319,000.

Coote believed in and practised the civilizing qualities of a balanced life. He was an enthusiastic golfer, with low handicap, an authority on good wine and food. At dinner parties given by Coote and his wife in their Hampstead home, guests were feasted. One of the things which made him good company was his readiness with the right sort of remark for all occasions. One illustration of this occurred in a London street when Coote, after dodging a bus, landed on all fours on a traffic island. Picking himself up and shaking off the dust, he came face to face with Sir William Haley. 'Good morning', said Coote coolly. 'How appropriate to find the editor of *The Times* in the middle of the road.' His humour, never broad, was frequently astringent.

Apart from his two books on Italy, he put together a volume called *Maxims and Reflections of Winston S. Churchill* (1947) and wrote *A Companion of Honour, the Story of W. Elliot* (1965). He wrote for this Dictionary the articles on Walter Elliot, Viscount Milner, and W. S. Morrison (Dunrossil).

He was three times married. In 1916 he married Marguerite Doris, daughter of Colonel William Henry Wellstead, of the Royal Engineers, of Tranby Lodge, Hessle, east Yorkshire; they had two daughters. This marriage was dissolved and in 1925 he married Denise, daughter of Emile Dethoor, of Doulieu, France; they had no children. She died in 1945 and in 1946 he married Amalie, daughter of Samuel Lewkowitz, business man, of Amsterdam. They adopted Amalie's nephew who became a correspondent for the *Daily Telegraph* and was killed in a flying accident a few months after Coote died at his London home 8 June 1979.

[E. F. L. (Lord) Burnham, *Peterborough Court, the Story of the Daily Telegraph*, 1955; Gavin Astor (ed.), *Fleet Street*, 1966; Colin Coote, *Editorial, the Memoirs of Colin R. Coote*, 1965; *Daily Telegraph*, 9 June 1979; private information; personal knowledge.] WILLIAM DEEDES

COPE, SIR (VINCENT) ZACHARY (1881–1974), surgeon and medical historian, was born in Kingston upon Hull 14 February 1881, the youngest of ten children (of whom three died in early childhood) of Thomas John Gilbert Cope, a minister of the United Methodist Church in Brougham Street, and his wife, Celia Ann Truscott, daughter of a dairy farmer and general dealer in St. Austell. His education was entirely in London and he passed from Westminster City School, where he was head boy, to London University, graduating BA in 1899 and passing with a scholarship to St. Mary's Hospital Medical School, where his teachers included Augustus Waller and (Sir) Almroth Wright [q.v.]. He graduated MB, BS in 1905 with distinction in surgery and forensic medicine, and proceeded to train in surgery at St. Mary's Hospital. He was appointed consultant surgeon at St. Mary's in 1911 and became a popular clinical teacher. In 1912 he also became surgeon to the Bolingbroke Hospital, where he remained until his retirement in 1946.

During World War I he served from 1916 to 1918 as a surgeon with the rank of captain in Mesopotamia, in a campaign notable for the problems of ill health in the forces, including the death from cholera of the commander Sir F. S. Maude [q.v.]. He was mentioned in dispatches in 1918. During this time he made the useful observations which were the basis of his first book *Surgical Aspects of Dysentery* (1920). In the following year he published *The Early Diagnosis of the Acute Abdomen* and this sound text, with its assumption of urgency in dealing with these conditions, met the needs of the advances in abdominal surgery at the time. Cope supervised all fourteen editions of this work in the next fifty years, and the fourteenth edition, published in 1972 when the author was ninety years old, was distinguished by being shorter than the first. The text had an international reputation and was translated into five languages, among them Greek in an unauthorized version.

In 1941 Cope was appointed sector officer of No. 6 sector of the Emergency Health Service and in the post-war years was a successful chairman of a number of influential inquiries and committees, notably as part of the hospital survey, and that dealing with national registration of the professions auxiliary to medicine. These reports were published between 1949 and 1952, during which time he also edited two substantial volumes of the official medical *History of the Second World War*, those on medicine and pathology (1952) and on surgery (1953). For these public services he was knighted in 1953.

His retirement years were numerous and much occupied by the writing of medical history, which often added to knowledge of familiar persons and events. He combined a readable style with an awareness of the importance of social history. He published two histories of his own medical school at St. Mary's Hospital (1954 and 1955), an account of the Royal College of Surgeons of England (1959), two historical reviews of abdominal surgery, and two collections of essays. In addition he compiled biographies of Sir Henry Thompson, Bt. (1951), William Cheselden (1953), Florence Nightingale (1958), Sir John Tomes (1961), and Almroth Wright (1966). In his earlier years he gave numerous lectures, notably the Arris and Gale lecture (1922) of the Royal College of Surgeons of England, and he was the College's Hunterian professor on four occasions (1916, 1920, 1925, and 1927). Though he may have preferred executive roles to high office, he was nevertheless vice-president of both the British Medical Association and the Royal College of Surgeons of England, honorary librarian of the Royal Society of Medicine, and president of the Medical Society of London. His contributions to medical history were marked by an honorary fellowship of the Worshipful Society of Apothecaries, and he was a director of Pitmans, the medical publishers.

Cope was short in stature, and stood on a small platform to reach to a conventional level while operating. In his professional life his assumption was to avoid controversy or intrigue. He was fond of composing light verse, both as a *memoria technica* in surgical teaching, and to mark personal events and public occasions. He was an early enthusiast for the use of the motor car and owned one from 1916 onwards.

He was twice married, first in 1909 to Agnes Dora (died 1922), daughter of James Newth, a glazier's diamond manufacturer, of Ruislip; they had no children. In 1923 he married Alice May (died 1944), daughter of Charles John Watts, engineer, of King's Lynn; they had one daughter. Cope died in Oxford 28 December 1974.

[*British Medical Journal*, 11 January 1975; *Lancet*, 11 January 1975; *Medical History*, vol. xix, 1975, p. 307; unpublished autobiography by V. Z. Cope, in the possession of his daughter; private information.]

David Hamilton

CORBETT, THOMAS GODFREY POLSON, second Baron Rowallan (1895–1977), chief scout of the British Commonwealth and Empire, was born in Chelsea 19 December 1895, the second of three children and elder son of Archibald Cameron Corbett and his wife, Alice Mary, (died 1902), daughter of John Polson of Castle Levan, Gourock, director of the firm Brown & Polson. His father, a Scottish business man and landowner, for many years a Liberal MP and a notable benefactor of the city of Glasgow, was created Lord Rowallan in 1911. He was educated at Eton and joined the Ayrshire Yeomanry at the age of eighteen, serving in Gallipoli, Egypt, and Palestine in World War I. After the second battle of Gaza he transferred to the Grenadier Guards, and suffered a severe leg wound on the western front. He was awarded the MC, but was invalided out of the army. His brother was killed in action.

In 1918 he married Gwyn Mervyn (died 1971), eldest daughter of Joseph Bowman Grimond, of St. Andrews, Fife, a Conservative MP from a Dundee jute family. They had five sons (one of whom was killed in action in 1944) and a daughter. On leaving the army he devoted himself to the family estate in Ayrshire and became a successful breeder of pedigree dairy cattle. He campaigned for the eradication of tuberculosis in cattle and was instrumental in the promotion of a government scheme for improvement. In 1929 he became president of the Ayrshire Herd Book and later was president of the Royal Highland Agricultural Society. In 1936 he led a committee involved in the improvement of livestock in the Scottish islands and crofting areas. His interest in cattle was lifelong and in 1963 he played an active part in the campaign to eliminate brucellosis.

The family firm of Brown & Polson also engaged his attention and he became in due course its chairman. He inherited the title of Baron Rowallan on his father's death in 1933. He devoted much time to public service, including the Boy Scouts, and interested himself in hospitals and in the problem of juvenile employment. He also maintained close links with the Territorial Army and in 1939 he was called upon to raise and train a new battalion of the Royal Scots Fusiliers. Led by Rowallan, the battalion went to France in April 1940, and saw fierce action before being evacuated in June. In spite of the inevitable problems arising from a shortage of experienced officers and NCOs, the battalion left the French coast better equipped than it had arrived, having collected arms and ammunition abandoned by others.

Thereafter Rowallan's leg wound confined him to home service. He commanded a Young Soldiers battalion where his training methods gained notable success with many of the toughest and least disciplined youngsters. Later, at a pre-OCTU training centre, he showed that many borderline or failed candidates could be brought up to the standard required in officers, and there is no doubt that the methods which he, with others, devised in wartime had immense influence on the training of young people in the post-war era, especially in the Outward Bound schools, the Duke of Edinburgh's award scheme, the Boy Scouts, and the cadet forces of the armed services.

He retired from the army in 1944 with the rank of lieutenant-colonel, and was appointed chief scout of the British Commonwealth in 1945 after the early death of Lord Somers [q.v.]. He had become district commissioner for north-west Ayrshire in 1922 and from 1944 was Scottish headquarters commissioner for leader training. As chief scout he devoted himself to reforging the international links broken by the war and to recovery and consolidation at home following the loss of many young leaders. He built on Lord Somers's 'post-war commission', introducing Air Scouts and replacing Rovers by Senior Scouts. He travelled widely throughout the Commonwealth, being of an apparently iron constitution although his leg wound necessitated a walking-stick. Tall, well-built, and always wearing the kilt, he had a fine presence and he was a resourceful and effective speaker to large audiences of boys, never consulting a note and making good use of anecdote to illustrate the value of scout training. He was, however, more at home in the company of adult leaders than of boys, and he sometimes gave vent to intolerance to youngsters who did not achieve the standard he expected. He had great personal charm and a hearty laugh, though not perhaps a great sense of humour. He took endless trouble to write long letters of thanks and appreciation to all and sundry in his mostly illegible handwriting.

Rowallan remained chief scout until 1959, having seen the movement grow throughout the world and, in the United Kingdom, achieve a membership of nearly 600,000. He was governor of Tasmania from 1959 to 1963. He was appointed KBE in 1951 and KT in 1957, and received honorary degrees from three universities: McGill (1948), Glasgow (1952), and Birmingham (1957).

Rowallan died in the Nuffield Nursing Home, Glasgow, 30 November 1977. He was succeeded in the barony by his eldest son, Arthur Cameron Corbett (born 1919).

[*Rowallan, Autobiography*, 1976; Scout Association archives; personal knowledge.]

WILLIAM GLADSTONE

CORBISHLEY, THOMAS (1903–1976), Jesuit priest and writer, was born at Preston 30 May 1903, the second of four sons and second of five children of William Corbishley, master painter and decorator, of Preston, Lancashire, and his wife, Catherine Bamford. He was educated at Preston Catholic College. From this Jesuit secondary school he entered the novitiate of the Society of Jesus at Roehampton on 7 September 1919. After studying scholastic philosophy at St. Mary's Hall, Stonyhurst, Lancashire, he went up to Campion Hall, Oxford, in 1926 to read classics. He took a first both in honour moderations (1928) and in *literae humaniores* (1930), an uncommon achievement for one who had not studied Greek at school. On leaving Oxford he joined the teaching staff of Stonyhurst College for three years before beginning his course of theology in 1933 at Heythrop College, then at Chipping Norton.

By the time of his ordination in September 1936 he had amassed an extensive knowledge of the New Testament which later informed his spiritual conferences, sermons, and counselling. In the area of doctrine he made a special study of the genuineness of Christ's human knowledge.

It was at this time that Corbishley made his only important contributions to classical scholarship; an essay on the date of the Syrian governorship of M. Titus in the *Journal of Roman Studies* (1934) and another on the census of Quirinius in the *Journal of Theological Studies* (1935). These two essays contained crucial implications for the chronology of the life of Jesus.

Corbishley's early years as a priest were occupied mainly with the academic preparation of Jesuit students for their strictly professional studies. At the outbreak of war in 1939 he became actively engaged in the 'Sword of the Spirit', an inter-church activity, jointly sponsored by Archbishop William Temple and Cardinal Arthur Hinsley [qq.v.], which anticipated the ecumenical movement launched by the second Vatican Council. It was not unexpected that ecumenism should become the principal preoccupation of his last twenty years.

In 1945 Corbishley was appointed master of Campion Hall in succession to Martin D'Arcy [q.v.], who had transferred the private Hall from a building in St. Giles leased from St. John's College to a hall in Brewer St. which is the only contribution by Sir Edwin Lutyens [q.v.] to the architecture of Oxford. In 1958 Corbishley left the university to become superior of the Jesuit church of Farm Street in Mayfair. On the expiration of his term of office in 1966 he remained on the staff at Farm Street until his death.

Corbishley acknowledged that the greatest single influence in his life had been the personality and writings of his fellow Jesuit, C. C. Martindale, who in the inter-war period had revolutionized hagiography by showing that true sanctity could exist along with hereditary and human weaknesses. Like Martindale, whose notice he wrote for this Dictionary, Corbishley deserted purely academic studies and spread his interest widely, as the titles of his better known books witness: *Roman Catholicism* (1950), *Religion is Reasonable*, a collection of mainly Oxford conferences (1960), *The Spirituality of Teilhard de Chardin* (1971), and *One Body, One Spirit* (1973), which was chosen as the archbishop of Canterbury's Lenten book. A versatile popular theologian, he believed that he had something to contribute to the moral and theological discussions of his day.

Both at Oxford and in London he devoted himself to many Christian causes such as the needs of Polish and Hungarian exiles, the Oxford University joint action committee against racial intolerance, the Council for Christians and Jews, and Oxfam to which he gave valuable guidance when it was establishing its policy of granting money for family planning programmes. But he is best known for his work in the ecumenical movement. While seeking closer understanding between the churches he came in for much criticism from ultra-conservative Roman Catholics. An enthusiastic pioneer, he sometimes stretched traditional discipline to breaking point in his eagerness to hold out a hand of friendship to fellow Christians of all denominations. Unassuming and tolerant, he was well fitted to represent his church in ecumenical discussions.

Corbishley died in London 11 March 1976. On the following 17 May his life and work was commemorated at the service of evensong in Westminster Abbey. In his address on this occasion the Revd Alan Booth spoke of Corbishley as 'one of the truly distinguished minds of our day who chose deliberately to occupy himself in the chores of faithful, very practical little efforts to heal the great wounds of mankind'.

[*The Times*, 12 March 1976, with photograph; personal knowledge.] PHILIP CARAMAN

COSTELLO, JOHN ALOYSIUS (1891–1976), prime minister of the Republic of Ireland, was born in Dublin 20 June 1891, the second of the three children (he had an elder brother and a younger sister) of John Costello, Land Registry clerk, of Rathdown Road, North Circular Road, Dublin, and his wife, Rose Callaghan. Educated at the Christian Brothers' O'Connell Schools, Dublin, and University College, Dublin, where he graduated in modern languages and law in 1911, he was called to the bar (King's Inns) in 1914, after winning the King's Inns Victoria prize in 1913. Making his career in the law he was called to the Inner Bar in 1925 and became a bencher of the Honourable Society of King's Inns in 1926. Closely associated with Hugh Kennedy, principal architect of the constitution of the Irish Free State and first attorney-general, Costello served as assistant law officer, provisional government, 1922, and assistant to the attorney-general 1922–6, replacing Kennedy as attorney-general in the latter year, and serving in that capacity until the fall of the government of W. T. Cosgrave [q.v.] in February 1932.

During these years, when rapid change was occurring in the British Commonwealth, the young Irish Free State did much to make dominion status synonymous with full sovereignty and at the League of Nations and more especially in the Commonwealth conferences of 1926 and 1930, and at the 1929 conference on the operation of dominion legislation, which hammered out the terms of the Statute of Westminster, 1931, Costello played a significant role. Part of a team, he prepared the briefs for his political colleagues to present, and to Costello, as to Desmond FitzGerald, Kevin O'Higgins [q.v.], and Patrick McGilligan, successive ministers for external affairs, much credit belongs. It was in these years too that much of Costello's reputation was secured: enduring friendships were forged, and the respect of political opponents won.

After the advent of Eamon de Valera [q.v.] as head of government in 1932, Costello sought to enter Dáil Eireann and did so successfully in the snap general election of January 1933, as a member for Dublin County. Representing Dublin Townships in 1937, he was returned there also in 1938, was unsuccessful in 1943, but swiftly returned in 1944, remaining in the Dáil until his retirement in 1969, his constituency changing in 1948 to Dublin South East.

Costello was not leader of Fine Gael, the largest opposition party, when the February 1948 elections brought the possibility of an end to sixteen years of rule by de Valera's dominant Fianna Fáil party. The man who filled that post, General Richard Mulcahy [q.v.], was unacceptable to some of the potential members of a new coalition, however, and after deliberation Costello was approached to lead an alternative government. Much against his own inclination he agreed to serve and for the next three years the qualities which commended him—his patience, integrity, no-nonsense directness, his loyalty, courage, and humanity—kept together an uneasy association of parties and individuals. That he succeeded surprised many, but there is no doubt that in surviving for so long he not only brought a renewed conviction to the Irish people that alternative government was possible, but he demonstrated the practicality of what had become a growing personal conviction. Tired of opposition for opposition's sake, tired too of what he felt was one-man rule dressed up as party government, he had increasingly felt the need for greater consensus in the making of constructive national policy. Inter-party government from 1948 to 1951 provided a working model, and one which he was to lead again from 1954 to 1957.

During his first period as taoiseach commendable progress was made, after the war and post-war years of stagnation, in the fields of housing and health, agriculture and social welfare, but two major landmarks stand out. The first was the Republic of Ireland Act which changed the title of the state to meet nationalist aspiration and so, it was hoped, to take the gun out of politics. The Act, announced amidst controversy in September 1948 and operative from Easter Monday 1949, removed independent Ireland from the Commonwealth and probably reinforced Northern Irish unionist determination to remain within the United Kingdom. The second, even more controversial and also strengthening Ulster unionism, was the attempt of the minister of health to make maternity welfare provision through a generous Mother-and-Child Bill in 1950. The Bill brought an open conflict with the Roman Catholic hierarchy which led to the resignation of the minister of health in April 1951 (Costello himself took the portfolio) and soon to the break-up of this first attempt of coalition government, in May.

After acting as leader of the opposition from 1951 to 1954, Costello once more became taoiseach after the May 1954 elections. With experience of office behind him and with a more compact inter-party grouping, he nevertheless chose to continue his quiet form of leadership. He saw to the development of greater economic expertise in the service of the state, and to the provision of welfare services more in keeping with the expansionist western world of the 1950s. Inflation and a resurgence of militant nationalist activity placed too great a strain on the coalition by 1957, however, and Fianna Fáil returned to power after the elections of March of that year.

On leaving office Costello once more built up a successful legal practice, retiring to the backbenches in 1959 when Richard Mulcahy resigned the leadership of Fine Gael to James Dillon. During his last decade in the Dáil he helped to modernize further his party along social democratic lines.

Made a member of the Royal Irish Academy in 1948, and a freeman of the City of Dublin in 1975, and awarded the Grand Cross of the Pian Order, 1962, Costello received honorary LL Ds from Montreal, Ottawa, and Fordham, 1948; and the Catholic University of Washington, St. John's University (New York) and Iona College, New Rochelle (New York), 1956. A portrait in oils (1948) by Leo Whelan hangs in the King's Inns, Dublin; a pencil drawing by Sean O'Sullivan (1949) is in Dáil Eireann.

To the end of his life Costello remained untouched by either public office or acclaim. Modest, accessible, helpful, he retained the tolerance and thoughtfulness that had always characterized him. His contributions to the consolidation of the infant state, to its continued enjoyment of parliamentary democracy, and to a more humane and progressive society will not be underrated by future historians. That he made his mark at all in these fields will have been his own reward.

On 31 July 1919 he married Ida Mary (died 1956), daughter of David O'Malley, MD, of Glenamaddy, county Galway; they had three sons and two daughters. His son Declan also became attorney-general (1973–7) and subsequently a judge of the High Court (from 1977). Costello died in Dublin 5 January 1976.

[*Irish Times*, 6 January 1976; *Ireland To-day*, 30 January 1976; personal knowledge.]

D. W. HARKNESS

COULSON, CHARLES ALFRED (1910–1974), theoretical chemist, was born at Dudley 13 December 1910, one of twin sons (there were no other children) of Alfred Coulson, who became principal of Dudley Technical College and later HM inspector of technical colleges in south-west England, and his wife, Annie Sincere, headmistress of Tipton School and daughter of the inventor Charles Lamb Hancock. Alfred Coulson acted as superintendent of the local Methodist Sunday school, and although Charles's mother was originally an Anglican, both he and his brother were brought up as Methodists. His whole outlook, in fact, was coloured by his immensely strong Christian faith; he became an accredited local preacher and subsequently vice-president of the Methodist Conference (1959–60). His brother, John Metcalfe, became professor of chemical engineering at the University of Newcastle upon Tyne.

Coulson was awarded a scholarship to Clifton College in 1923, and in 1928 gained an entrance scholarship in mathematics to Trinity College, Cambridge. During these years he was a good cricketer and an excellent chess player. He was elected to a college senior scholarship. In the mathematical tripos he obtained a first class in part i (1929) and was a wrangler in part ii (1931). He then took part ii of the natural sciences tripos in which he also obtained a first (1932). He was later elected to a research scholarship; his first supervisor in research was (Sir) R. H. Fowler [q.v.], who greatly influenced his attitude and outlook. Later Coulson worked with (Sir) J. E. Lennard-Jones [q.v.] and was directed by him into molecular orbital theory, which played a dominant role in his subsequent researches.

At Cambridge Coulson became a leader of a group of Methodists which included graduates, undergraduates, and other students. The group included Eileen Florence Burrett, who was training as a specialist in the teaching of small children, and she and Coulson were married in 1938, just before he left Cambridge. She was the daughter of William Alfred Burrett, house furnisher in Leeds. They had two sons and two daughters.

In 1934 Coulson was elected to a prize fellowship at Trinity for four years. He obtained his Ph.D. in 1936. In 1938 he became senior lecturer in mathematics at University College, Dundee. During World War II he was a conscientious objector. In 1945 Coulson moved to the Physical Chemistry Laboratory in Oxford on an ICI fellowship, and was appointed a lecturer in mathematics at University College. From there he was invited by Professor (Sir) J. T. Randall to apply for the newly established chair of theoretical physics at King's College, London, which he took up in October 1947. In 1952 he moved to the Rouse Ball chair of mathematics at Oxford and a professorial fellowship at Wadham College. He spent much energy organizing the new Mathematical Institute at Oxford, which was completed in 1963. In 1972 he became Oxford's first professor of theoretical chemistry, although he was already beginning to suffer the effects of his final illness. There is now an established chair in Oxford in that subject, bearing his name. He founded a summer school of theoretical chemistry which was outstandingly successful.

Coulson was very productive in his research. The Royal Society, to which he was elected a fellow in 1950, recorded in his obituary over 400 publications in scientific journals. His early book, *Waves* (1941), went into several editions. The work which he did with W. E. Duncanson, on electronic structure of molecules in momentum space, was pioneering, and their papers continued to have great influence. Coulson himself rightly thought his most important work was that on bond-order related to bond-length. He also carried out significant research on hydrogen bonding, and was influential in promoting the description of solids as the limiting case of large molecules—a theory which later gave rise to the field of low-dimensional solids. In his foreword to the book *Orbital Theories of Molecules and Solids* (ed. by N. H. March, 1974), dedicated to Coulson by his friends and colleagues, H. C. Longuet-Higgins describes the personal consequences of their association: 'Above all I was impressed by the simplicity of Coulson's thinking and by his determination to make things so clear that even a novice could grasp the essential ideas.' The professional consequences were a series of brilliantly influential papers by Coulson and Longuet-Higgins in the *Proceedings* of the Royal Society. The clarity and simplicity of Coulson's thinking is nowhere better exemplified than in his best-selling book, *Valence* (1952).

Coulson was an outstanding scientist and expositor and also a man of unusually wide interests. In 1962–8 he was a member of the central committee of the World Council of Churches and in 1965–71 he was chairman of Oxfam. His religious publications and television appearances made him well known to the public. He enjoyed a happy family life, and, together with his wife, opened his home to his students on many occasions. This greatly enriched the relationships which he formed with them. He was tall and imposing, and occasionally a little unconventional in his attire. He could work almost anywhere and on his travels he would concentrate on writing letters and lecture notes.

He had twelve honorary degrees, including a Cambridge Sc.D. (1971) and he was an honorary fellow or member of several British and foreign learned societies. His many medals included the Royal Society Davy medal (1970) and the Faraday (1968) and Tilden (1969) medals of the Chemical Society. Coulson died at home in Oxford 7 January 1974.

[S. L. Altmann and E. J. Bowen in *Biographical Memoirs of Fellows of the Royal Society*, vol. xx, 1974; personal knowledge.] N. H. March

COURTNEIDGE, Dame (ESMERALDA) CICELY (1893–1980), actress, was born 1 April 1893 in Sydney, Australia, the second of the three children and elder daughter of Robert Courtneidge, of Edinburgh, who became an actor, and subsequently theatre manager in London and the provinces, and his wife, Rosaline May Adams, who had three sisters on the stage, one of whom was Ada Reeve, well known in her day as principal boy in the Drury Lane pantomimes. Cicely Courtneidge had early aspirations towards a stage career, and her first appearance (with one line to speak) was as Peasblossom in her father's production of *A Midsummer Night's Dream.* She was aged eight.

At the age of fifteen, after two years' schooling in Switzerland, she returned to England more determined than ever to be 'a great actress', and in this ambition she was encouraged by her father; but neither father nor daughter as yet realized her true *métier* in the theatre—that of a comedienne. Until the outbreak of war in 1914 she was destined to play *ingenue* roles in her father's productions, and at any rate was accomplished enough to be allowed (at her urgent request) to succeed Phyllis Dare in a leading part in her father's immensely successful musical comedy *The Arcadians*, at the Shaftesbury Theatre in London.

At the same theatre, in September 1913, she played the part of Lady Betty Biddulph (a typical example of musical comedy nomenclature of that time) in *The Pearl Girl*, and it was then that she first met and played opposite her future husband, Jack Hulbert [q.v.], a young graduate aged twenty-one, just down from Cambridge. In June 1914 they again played opposite each other in an adaptation (mainly contrived by Hulbert) from a German comic opera, whose English version was entitled *The Cinema Star.* It ran successfully at the Shaftesbury Theatre until the outbreak of war, when its Germanic origin deterred London audiences, and the play was withdrawn prematurely.

There followed for Cicely Courtneidge a depressing period of frustration, involving fruitless applications to theatre agents for engagements. The agents were not only discouraging as to her future in the theatre but inclined to attribute her rather frail reputation as a musical comedy *ingenue* to the influence of her father.

None the less, encouraged by her husband—they had married in 1916—who wrote daily letters to her from the army camp where he was stationed, and by her father, who had belatedly realized where her talent in the theatre could be put to the best advantage, in her own words she 'took to the halls'. 'Make them cry—and then make them laugh' was the substance of the advice given by her husband, and she did so for the remainder of her long stage career.

Then began a hard life for her, from 'fit-ups' and 'one-night stands' to occasional engagements in the provincial towns which in those days almost invariably contained a Victorian or Edwardian music hall, with twice, or even thrice, nightly shows. Helped by her father, she commissioned popular lyric writers to provide her with songs and words. These included 'the Knut in the RAF', the first, and one of the most successful, of her many male impersonations in uniform. There was about her a buoyancy and gaiety, an indefinable zest, that held the attention. With her tuneful voice, forceful humour, and vital personality, no one knew better how to get the right song across to an audience. By the end of the war in 1918 she had firmly established herself as music-hall artiste, both in the provinces and in London.

Although after the armistice she continued to perform in music halls, her prevailing desire was to rejoin her husband in the stage partnership which had proved promising in the immediate pre-war period. But both now realized that light-hearted humour and burlesque, in revue and musical comedy, should be the dominant theme in their stage careers, although until the end Cicely Courtneidge retained a broader style—a foothold in the music hall of an earlier day.

In September 1921 Cicely Courtneidge appeared in a revue with her husband at the Royalty Theatre, but it was not until 1923 that they established their triumphant partnership and joint management, which resulted in a series of uninterrupted successes throughout eight years, in which both partners had 'star' parts. Each was produced and stage-managed by Hulbert. These 'milestones in their joint career' (as they were called by Hulbert) were: *Little Revue Starts at Nine o'Clock* (Little Theatre, 1923); *By-the-Way* (Apollo and Gaiety Theatres, 1925–6); *Lido Lady* (Gaiety, 1926–7); *Clowns in Clover* (Adelphi Theatre, 1927–9); *The House that Jack Built* (Adelphi Theatre, 1929–30); and *Folly to Be Wise* (Piccadilly, 1931).

In 1931 there occurred a set-back to the partnership which came as a surprise to both partners. The business side of their theatrical ventures had been entirely entrusted to a financier, through whose speculations the partnership became heavily in debt and the business went into liquidation. Hulbert at once accepted responsibility for the debts and undertook to repay all creditors, an undertaking he was able to fulfil by abandoning his stage career and devoting the next eight years to acting in films, a period which happened to coincide with a boom in the British film industry engendered by the coming of sound to the cinema.

Cicely Courtneidge co-starred in two of the succession of films in which her husband appeared. In Noel Gay's *Soldiers of the King* she sang one of the most popular songs of her career, 'There's Something about a Soldier'; and in *Jack's the Boy* she shared with her husband a memorable sequence acted in Madame Tussaud's, with its climax in the chamber of horrors.

It was not until November 1938 that she reappeared with her husband in London in *Under Your Hat*, a spy story (with music and burlesque) by Arthur Macrae, which they both regarded as the happiest engagement of their joint stage career. It ran at the Palace Theatre until 1940, with a short interruption at the beginning of the war. During 1941 Cicely Courtneidge gave a nightly three-hour entertainment in aid of the Services at home and abroad, and at the end of each performance, she appealed on the stage and from the auditorium for contributions from the audience, a personal request that was never in vain. Later in the war she formed a small company and took it at her own expense to Gibraltar, Malta, North Africa, and Italy, playing nightly to hospitals and to the Services.

Returning to London after the war, in November 1945 she played the star part in Arthur Macrae's *Under the Counter*, produced by her husband at the Phoenix Theatre, making fun of wartime shortages, and the measures (legal and illegal) taken by the public to overcome them. This topical sally at recent restrictions had a run for two years in London, but when the show was produced (by Hulbert) in New York it was taken off after three weeks: the American audience did not comprehend the allusions to distresses they had not themselves endured. The set-back, however, was followed by a successful tour of the piece in Australia and New Zealand.

A few lean years followed, but Cicely Courtneidge made a great West End success, which proved to be the climax of her career, in *Gay's the Word* (Saville, February 1951) in a part written and songs composed for her by Ivor

Novello [q.v.], a personal triumph marred during the early part of its long run by the sudden death of Novello.

In 1967 at the Haymarket Theatre she gave a sensitive and endearing performance as Dora Randolph (originally played by (Dame) Marie Tempest, q.v.) in a revival of Dodie Smith's *Dear Octopus*, in which Hulbert played as convincingly the part of Dora's husband. The revival ran for nearly a year. As late as 1971, the year in which Cicely Courtneidge celebrated her seventieth year on the stage, she played a leading part in a farce entitled *Move Over Mrs Markham*, which ran for eighteen months in London.

Further evidence of her versatility was given in her final film, *The L-shaped Room*, in which she played, movingly and memorably, the part of an elderly spinster, a lodger in a squalid London flat, involuntarily involved in the intrigues of others, and spending her lonely days in arranging Christmas cards for sending to friends who had forgotten her.

Cicely Courtneidge was appointed CBE in 1951 and advanced to DBE in 1972. She died in Putney 26 April 1980, being survived by her only child, a daughter.

[Cicely Courtneidge, *Cicely*, 1953; Jack Hulbert, *The Little Woman's Always Right*, 1975; personal knowledge.]

D. Pepys-Whiteley

COURTNEY, Sir CHRISTOPHER LLOYD (1890–1976), air chief marshal, was born at Hampstead, London, 27 June 1890, the fourth son and youngest of the seven children of William Leonard Courtney [q.v.], of Oxford and London, author and editor, and his wife, Cornelia Blanche, daughter of Commander Lionel Place, RN. Courtney spent two years at Bradfield College, but left at fourteen on his mother's wishes to compete for a naval cadetship. He secured entry to HMS *Britannia* in 1905, and after some years' service in warships qualified as lieutenant in 1911.

By then Courtney had already developed wider interests. Having seen aeronautical displays he applied in 1910 for flying training. He got this at length in 1912, at Eastchurch, and quickly qualified as a pilot (Royal Aero Club Certificate No. 328). Four months later he was a flight commander at Yarmouth and by the outbreak of war a squadron commander in the newly constituted Royal Naval Air Service.

After recruiting No. 4 (later 204) Squadron on the Isle of Grain Courtney was given command of all the air units at Dover. Command at Eastchurch with his squadron then followed, and thus he built up No. 4 Wing. It then joined other RNAS units in the Dunkirk area where he commanded it from May 1916 to November 1917. Its work in reconnaissance, supporting naval attacks on the Belgian coast and intercepting Zeppelins, quickly brought him recognition. He was mentioned in dispatches in May 1917 and in November of that year was appointed to the Legion of Honour (chevalier) and the DSO.

On the formation of the RAF Courtney opted to join the new Service and was soon director of air equipment in the new Air Ministry. Early in November 1918 he was promoted acting brigadier-general and sent out to form and command a new brigade—the 11th—in the Independent Force RAF, which was then bombing Germany from Lorraine. The armistice supervened; Sir H. M. (later Viscount) Trenchard [q.v.], the Force commander, returned home and Courtney succeeded him. He was still only twenty-eight.

Such rapid promotion, with appointment as CBE in 1919, marked Courtney out for the highest positions. Nevertheless, he had to revert to wing commander when he received his permanent RAF commission. During the next twenty years he filled with quiet distinction a large variety of posts. In 1920–3 he commanded No. 2 (Indian) Wing at Ambala, subsequently graduating from the Staff College at Quetta and moving on to be an instructor at the RAF Staff College, Andover (1925–8). In 1931 (having been promoted air commodore in January) he successfully organized operations against rebel forces in southern Kurdistan, and was appointed CB (1932) for his work. He remained in Iraq as chief staff officer until 1933, then returned home to a succession of posts in the Air Ministry, culminating in that of deputy chief of the air staff (1935–6). In the years immediately before World War II he was air officer commanding British Forces in Iraq (1937–8), had talks with General Milch of the German Air Ministry in Germany (1937), represented the RAF in the investigation by Lord Chatfield [q.v.] into the defences of India (1938–9), and, with increasing emphasis on reserves, commanded No. 16 (Reserve) Group (1938) and finally the new RAF Reserve Command (March 1939). These further services were acknowledged by appointment as KCB (1939).

Courtney was now being considered for the topmost posts in the Service. He had narrowly missed becoming chief of the air staff in 1937, when C. L. N. (later Lord) Newall [q.v.] was preferred; but he was still young enough to succeed Newall. Meanwhile, in July 1938, he was notified that he was to succeed Sir Hugh (later Lord) Dowding [q.v.] at Fighter Command on 1 September 1939. Intensified war preparations then caused Dowding to be retained at Fighter Command longer than planned, but in June 1939 Courtney (now an air marshal) was again told that he would be succeeding him—this time on 31 March 1940. But he never did. The outbreak of war brought Dowding further short extensions of command; and in 1939 Courtney was injured in an aircraft accident during bad weather. One of his kneecaps was badly fractured—his leg was still in plaster when he accompanied the mission of Lord Riverdale [q.v.] to Canada three months later—and there was a permanent loss of mobility.

The major post that Courtney finally got, in January 1940, was that of air member for supply and organization. This gave him a seat on the Air Council and put him in charge of a vast department responsible not only for Service organization but also for the provision of virtually every item required except (after May 1940) aircraft. And from 1942 onwards his huge responsibilities were greatly increased by the arrival of the American air forces, for whom he provided airfields (over a hundred of them), station buildings, and the like. Within the department there were directorates-general for organization, for equipment, for works, and for servicing and maintenance and beneath these there were scores of directorates and deputy directorates: in the *Air Force List* of April 1945 the names of the principal officers in works alone occupy twenty-five printed pages.

Over this huge realm Courtney presided with impeccable efficiency throughout the rest of the war. He won golden tributes from the Americans, and in general provided a magnificent service for the RAF. His final honours included promotion to air chief marshal (temporary from January 1943 and confirmed in June) and appointment as GBE (1945) and as commander in the US Legion of Merit (1946).

After his retirement in November 1945 Courtney developed business interests and also gave much time to charitable activities like the Victory Club and the Star and Garter Home. He derived much pleasure from his honorary membership of the Vintners' Company and was its master in 1964–5.

Courtney married in 1926 Constance ('Micky') May Rayson, daughter of George Edward Greensill, an accountant. He had no children, but there was a step-daughter from his wife's first marriage. In appearance Courtney was tall, distinguished, and very dark—so dark as to acquire as a cadet the nickname 'Black' Courtney, which stuck to him for the rest of his career. Among his characteristics were his intelligence, his powers of administration, his capacity for work, his modest demeanour, and his natural courtesy. He was greatly liked as well as admired. He died in London 22 October 1976, two years after his wife.

There is a portrait by Cowan Dobson in the Vintners' Company hall, and a collection of photographs in the records section of the RAF Museum.

[Air Historical Branch, Ministry of Defence (interviews between Courtney and E. B. Haslam); Courtney papers in RAF Museum; private information; personal knowledge.]

Denis Richards

COWARD, Sir NOËL PEIRCE (1899–1973), actor, playwright, composer, lyricist, producer, author, occasional poet, and Sunday painter, was born 16 December 1899 at Teddington, Middlesex, the second in the family of three sons (the eldest of whom died at the age of six) of Arthur Sabin Coward (described as a clerk, but whose passion was music) and his wife Violet Agnes, daughter of Henry Gordon Veitch, a captain in the Royal Navy. His grandfather was James Coward [q.v.], organist and chorister. Both parental backgrounds had a strong influence on the boy and the man. His mother was also musical—the parents met as members of the local church choir—and was an ardent and knowledgeable theatre-goer. Coward was soon to be a chorister himself, but was frustrated by the absence of applause after his solos. His birthday treats were invariably visits to the theatre; and by the time he was 'rushing towards puberty' he could play accurately by ear numbers from the show he had seen that day. His formal education was sporadic, not helped by a quick temper—he left one school after biting the headmistress in the arm; and though he attended the Chapel Royal choir school at Clapham in 1909, he failed surprisingly, but perhaps providentially, to be accepted for the choir. The start of his professional career was less than a year away—27 January 1911—playing Prince Mussel in *The Goldfish* as one of a 'Star Cast of Wonder Children'. (Indeed, they included Michael MacLiammóir, and (Dame) Ninette de Valois.) His success led to a number of engagements with (Sir) Charles Hawtrey [q.v.], from whom he learned much about playing comedy, and—quite as important—gained an insight into the anatomy of writing plays. In 1913 he appeared as an angel in *Hannele* by Hauptmann with the fifteen-year-old Gertrude Lawrence [q.v.]. (And so began a very special personal and professional relationship which lasted until her death in 1952.) Christmas 1913 saw a dream realized when he played Slightly in *Peter Pan* with Pauline Chase.

Throughout 1914–15 there was little work and some anxiety about his health. However the period was not uneventful. Worldly-wise for his years, his sophistication was purely theatrical; but in June 1915 an invitation to visit a Mrs Astley Cooper at Hambleton Hall gave Coward a first exciting view of that undiscovered country of high society, in which he would become increasingly at home, as welcome as he was at ease, and from which, both as writer and actor, he was to develop an important element of his comedy. Also from this period comes that distinctive mark of self-awareness—a new and durable signature, described by Sir John Betjeman at the Coward memorial service: 'Noël with two dots over the "e", and the firm decided downward stroke of the "l".' At Christmas 1915 he at last worked again, in *Where the Rainbow Ends*; followed by a tour in the thankless part of Charley in *Charley's Aunt* (1916). After a two-week run in *Light Blues*, singing and dancing with the newly-wed Jack Hulbert and (Dame) Cicely Courtneidge [qq.v.], he had his first solo number in *The Happy Family* (1916), of which one critic wrote: 'He combined the grace of a Russian dancer with the manner of an English schoolboy'. In 1916 he wrote the lyrics and music of his first song; by 1917 he had written three plays. The best of them, *The Rat Trap* (produced in 1924), was described as 'lousy in construction' by American impresario Gilbert Miller. Dialogue is not enough, was Miller's message. Coward took it to heart. Miller was enthusiastic about his acting however, and engaged him for the juvenile lead in a star-studded production of *The Saving Grace* (1917). Before that he appeared in his first film, *Hearts of the World*, directed by the legendary D. W. Griffith.

In the spring of 1918 began a frustrating nine-month 'engagement' in the army. Though at home with the rigorous discipline of the theatre, and already recognizing the no less demanding self-discipline required of the writer, Coward found that the military equivalent actually made him ill. (Would it have been the same, one wonders, if his call-up had been to the navy?) Although personally little affected by 'the war to end war' Coward shared the hectic relief of his contemporaries that it was over; and was soon considered by press and public as typical of the Bright Young Things, and also paradoxically, of the cynically disillusioned minority as well. The epithet 'brittle' was first applied to him now; it was to haunt him and his reputation to the grave and beyond.

Through his friendship with the tragically short-lived Meggie Albanesi he came to know Lorn Macnaughtan, who as Lorn Loraine became his secretary and 'one of the principal mainstays' of his life until her death forty-six years later. (It was she who first called him 'master'—as a joke.) In 1920 he first appeared in London in a play of his own *I'll Leave It to You*, which, despite good notices, closed in five weeks. Undaunted, he went abroad for the first time, visiting Paris, and going on to Alassio to Mrs Astley Cooper, where he met another lifelong member of his inner circle—Gladys Calthrop, who was to design sets and costumes for a host of his plays. A rapid escape abroad, when his contribution to a production was over (whatever its fate), became hereafter part of the pattern of his life. 'Like a window opening in my head', he called it.

In *The Young Idea* (1922) Coward shamelessly borrowed his brother and sister from the twins in *You Never Can Tell* by George Bernard Shaw [q.v.]. Shaw was not offended, but wrote Coward a most constructive letter, including the advice 'never to see or read my plays. Unless you can get clear away from me you will begin as a back number, and be hopelessly out of it when you are forty'. (In 1941, when Coward had unwittingly breached the currency regulations and received much bad publicity, Shaw was his doughty champion, reminding him that there was no guilt without intention, and telling him to plead 'not guilty' despite his lawyers' advice. He did; and received a minimal fine.) He was composer and part-author of *London Calling* (1923), a revue starring himself and Gertrude Lawrence. As with *The Young Idea* the majority of critics preferred his writing to his performances. The rest would only accept him as a performer in the works of others—a contradiction only explicable by the hostility of both factions to versatility. (Meanwhile in 1921 he had paid his first exciting but impoverished visit to New York, meeting Alfred Lunt—Lynn Fontanne he already knew from London; and also Laurette Taylor and family, whose absent-minded hospitality and parlour games gave him the idea for *Hay Fever*.)

In November 1924 *The Vortex*—his play about drug addiction—put Coward triumphantly and controversially on the map, winning the allegiance of the beau monde led by the Mountbattens; confirming the worst fears of the stuffier elements of society. During its seven-month run—the longest he would ever permit himself—his output included *On With the Dance* (1925), a revue for (Sir) C. B. Cochran [q.v.], an association which lasted for nine years (to see its Manchester opening Coward left *The Vortex* briefly to his understudy—(Sir) John Gielgud); *Fallen Angels* (1925) with Tallulah Bankhead—another *succès de scandale;* and *Hay Fever* (1925) with (Dame) Marie Tempest [q.v.], which ran for a year. In September 1925 *The Vortex* took New York by storm, and Coward bought his first Rolls-Royce. *Easy Virtue* (1925) was written and produced while he was there. There were two consequences of this astonishing burst of successful activity, neither surprising. In 1926 he suffered a severe breakdown; and he yielded to the temptation to allow the production of three plays from his bottom drawer. All were failures—the most notorious being *Sirocco* (1927), which starred his great friend Ivor Novello [q.v.]. It was the only time they worked together.

Thanks to Cochran, Coward soon bounced back, with his most successful revue *This Year of Grace* (1928). *Bitter Sweet* (1929) followed—its most famous number 'I'll see you again' being composed in a taxi in a New York traffic jam. Even a Far Eastern holiday was productive. Alone in Shanghai, he had a mental picture of 'Gertie' in a white Molyneux dress in the South of France. Four hours later *Private Lives* had been mapped out; the actual writing took four days. It opened in London in 1930—Laurence (later Lord) Olivier playing a minor role—and was sold out for its three-month season, as it was in New York. Arnold Bennett [q.v.] called Coward 'the Congreve of our day'. 'Thin' and 'brittle' replied the critics. *Cavalcade* (1931) was his most ambitious production, suggested to his ever fertile mind by a photograph of a troop-ship leaving for the Boer war. It gave him the opportunity to proclaim in a brilliant mixture of pageantry and understatement his intense patriotism, coupled with a warning that 'this country of ours which we love so much' was losing its way. His enemies found it obscene that the author of *The Vortex* should treat such a subject. The nation and the English-speaking world responded differently. *Design for Living* (1932) was written in South America to redeem a promise made to the Lunts. It was so successful that he broke his three-month rule and played five in New York, using the mornings to write his first volume of autobiography *Present Indicative* (1937). From a Caribbean cruise with the navy he emerged with the libretto of *Conversation Piece* (1934), his last collaboration with Cochran. 1935 saw the writing of the nine playlets, some with music, which were presented in three programmes as *To-night at 8.30* (1936). *Operette* (1938) broke this long run of success, despite the hit number 'The Stately Homes of England'. Coward spent the summer of 1939 writing *Present Laughter* and *This Happy Breed*, but their production was postponed until 1942 by the outbreak of war, and by Coward's prearranged war job in Paris. This and a proposed intelligence assignment in America came to nothing, due in part, he believed, to the hostility of Lord Beaverbrook [q.v.]. Angry and frustrated, he turned with relief to his own field. The results included his longest running comedy *Blithe Spirit* (1941); his finest film script *In Which We Serve* (1942) about the sinking of Mountbatten's destroyer *Kelly*; and one of his most enduring songs 'London Pride'.

Cole Lesley, who died in 1980, writer of the best biography of Coward, came to work for him in 1936; Graham Payn joined the resident 'family' in 1947, completing with Joyce Carey, Lorn Loraine, and Gladys Calthrop the inner circle, which apart from Lorn Loraine's death in 1967, remained unchanged until his own. But if the domestic background was serene, Coward for the next twenty years was to endure much professional disappointment and disparagement. Between 1946 and 1964 six musicals and two plays fell short of Coward's highest hopes; fortunately *Relative Values* (1951), *Quadrille* (1952), *South Sea Bubble* and *Nude With Violin* (1956), though not his own favourites, were box-office successes.

In 1948, after a disastrous New York revival of *To-night At 8.30*, Coward took Graham Payn, who had starred in it with Gertrude Lawrence, to Jamaica. He fell in love with the island, built a house by the sea called Blue Harbour, and later, on the hill above ('piling Pelléas on Mélisande' he called it) a small retreat—Firefly Hill (where he died, and is buried.) Also in 1948 he performed *Present Laughter* (*Joyeux Chagrins* in French) in Paris—a remarkable achievement, which failed dismally. His French was too good, they said, and the humour did not translate.

In 1951 he accepted an engagement which led to lifelong financial security. He appeared singing his own songs in cabaret at London's Café de Paris. Three more sell-out seasons followed; and then one in 1955 at Las Vegas, at 35,000 dollars a week for four weeks. From this in turn came highly lucrative American television and film engagements; and the difficult decision to emigrate, first to Bermuda and later to Switzerland, to mitigate the depredations of the Inland Revenue, and because, intending to perform less in future, 'I might as well do it for double the appreciation and ten times the lolly'. In any case, as Sir Winston Churchill told him, 'An Englishman has an inalienable right to live wherever he chooses'.

In 1953 he had a great success as King Magnus in Shaw's *The Apple Cart*; in 1960 his only novel *Pomp and Circumstance* was predictably more successful in America than Britain.

In 1964 an invitation by Sir Laurence Olivier to direct Dame Edith Evans [q.v.] in *Hay Fever* for the National Theatre marked the beginning of the last sunlit years of Coward's career, demonstrating once again that the British only feel comfortable with talent or genius when their possessors are 'over the hill'. Coward decided to risk his new reputation as 'demonstrably the greatest living English playwright' (Ronald Bryden) by appearing one last time in the West End. The result was *A Song at Twilight* and a double bill *Come Into the Garden, Maud*, and *Shadows of the Evening* (1966). Though seriously weakened by the onset of arterio-sclerosis, and by amoebic dysentery caught in the Seychelles, and for the only time in his life suffering the indignity of occasionally drying up, the season was a triumphant sell-out. There was only one bad notice. 'Good', he said reading it, 'I thought I might be slipping.' Professionally that was the final curtain. What followed was a trip round the world with Cole Lesley and Graham Payn; the seventieth birthday celebrations, culminating in an emotional midnight tribute by his fellow professionals; his long delayed and much deserved knighthood (1970); in America a special Tony award (1970)—his first—for services to the theatre; an honorary D.Litt. from Sussex University (1972); peaceful days in Switzerland and Jamaica with his friends, and finally, without warning, the end in Jamaica 26 March 1973.

How to assess him? His staccato speech, developed, it is said, to penetrate his mother's deafness, became the instrument of both his comedy and of his conversation. A hostile journalist once asked him for what he would be remembered after his death. 'Charm', he replied. T. E. Lawrence [q.v.] called him 'a hasty kind of genius'. In 1930 W. Somerset Maugham [q.v.] predicted that he would be responsible for the manner in which plays would be written for thirty years. He said himself that it was only natural that 'my writing should be appreciated casually, because my personality, performance, music and legend get in the way'. Of his homosexuality Dame Rebecca West, a close and clear-sighted friend, wrote: 'There was impeccable dignity in his sexual life, which was reticent but untainted by pretence.'

A quintessential professional himself, he could be a scathing and witty critic of the second-rate; but he was outstandingly generous in his praise, never standing on dignity because of his position. He had the capacity to inspire great devotion. Gertrude Lawrence's last letter to him ended: 'It's always you I want to please more than *anyone*'—a sentiment that would be widely echoed among those who knew him.

There are portraits of him by Edward Seago in the Garrick Club and the Phoenix Theatre and by Clemence Dane in the National Portrait Gallery. In 1984 a black memorial stone, with the words 'A talent to amuse', was unveiled in Westminster Abbey.

[*Noël Coward Autobiography*, 1986 (ed. Sheridan Morley); Cole Lesley, *The Life of Noël Coward*, 1976; Charles Castle, *Noël*, 1972; Sheridan Morley, *A Talent to Amuse*, 1969; *Who's Who in the Theatre* (15th edn.) for a comprehensive list of his writings and performances; personal knowledge.]

MICHAEL DENISON

CRANKO, JOHN CYRIL (1927–1973), ballet dancer, choreographer, and director of the Stuttgart Ballet, was born 15 August 1927 in Rustenburg about sixty miles from Johannesburg, South Africa, the only child of Herbert Cranko, a lawyer who later went on to practice in Johannesburg itself, and his wife, (Hilda) Grace, daughter of Thomas Hinds, farmer at Magaliesberg, Transvaal, of English ancestry. She had a daughter from a previous marriage. The father's family were of Dutch ancestry, their name originally having been Krankoor. John Cranko spent his childhood in Johannesburg. After attending the coeducational Highlands North State High School and studying ballet privately with Marjorie Sturman, at the age of seventeen he joined the University of Cape Town Ballet School in 1944 and went to London to attend the Sadler's Wells Ballet School in 1946. Largely for ideological reasons, he never worked in South Africa again.

In 1947 he danced with the Sadler's Wells Ballet and was encouraged to choreograph by (Dame) Ninette de Valois. In 1951 he achieved popular success with *Pineapple Poll*, a cheerful retelling of a Sir W. S. Gilbert [q.v.] absurdity with more than a hint of *HMS Pinafore*, to a medley of tunes by Sir Arthur Sullivan [q.v.], and this willingness to refashion material well within his audience's theatre-going experience became a characteristic of his later work. Whereas the Diaghilev Company seemed almost embarrassed at the success of their pot-boiling *Boutique Fantasque* (1919), that kind of success was far more representative of Cranko's achievements. It was a crucial difference. His *Beauty and the Beast* (1949) remade in dance Jean Cocteau's more successful film. His *Harlequin in April* (1951), and the well-known *Lady and the Fool* (1954), both used *commedia dell'arte* themes. In 1957 with *Prince of the Pagodas*, and in 1961 with *Antigone* he attempted a level of creativity he could not sustain. His intimate revue *Cranks* in 1955 had been very successful, enlarging the dance content of the popular but overworked genre of intimate revue, but his attempt to repeat the formula in 1960 with *New Cranks* was unsuccessful, as was his involvement in a musical *Keep Your Hair On* (1958).

A scandal in his private life (a prosecution for homosexuality) as well as these artistic set-backs led him to change direction and become director of the Opera Ballet in Stuttgart in 1961, where Nicholas Beriosoff as previous director had already begun to raise standards. Cranko made the company a popular success, the focus for a general renaissance of ballet in Germany, and choreographed a series of works for them, achieving an increasing reputation until his tragically early death in 1973.

His artistic set-backs from 1957 to 1960 were a watershed in his career. The Stuttgart Ballet audience had little experience of ballet, particularly of British ballet, and in the pressure for new works, itself a symptom of an unsophisticated public, Cranko inclined to opt for the easy way out artistically, to borrow other people's ideas and achievements, which a more knowledgeable audience might have been less willing to accept. His Neapolitan dance in his *Swan Lake* (1963), for example, came as close to being a crib of the Neapolitan of Sir Frederick Ashton as possible without being a straight copy, and these borrowings were too often apparent in Cranko's work. He tended also not to worry about an occasional clumsiness in the pressure to complete work and get it on stage, rather than revise and refine, particularly as he increasingly became aware that his Stuttgart audiences were easily pleased. He was most acclaimed for his 'story' ballets, making much use of effects from legitimate theatre, showing a shrewd sense of what worked in theatrical terms, and using broad effects with skill. In *Swan Lake* his prince was finally engulfed in a watery grave, appearing and disappearing in the waves in fine Romantic style, and his *Romeo and Juliet* (1962) showed a sensitive understanding of how to arrange dance transitions from scene to scene. His best works for Stuttgart depended on other people's achievements, *Romeo and Juliet, Swan Lake, Onegin* (1965), *Taming of the Shrew* (1969), and *Carmen* (1971).

Stuttgart, as an industrial centre, lacked the activity in all the arts which stretched Cranko's capacity and imagination in London, and his Stuttgart company tended to exist as an artistic enclave. This made for a family atmosphere and Cranko, who was extrovert and emotionally insecure, came to depend very much on his dancers as a substitute family. He increasingly relied on his principals and his ballet *Initials RBME* (1972) was created for and by them—Richard Cragun, Birgit Keil, Marcia Haydée, and Egon Madsen. The long-term effects of this gifted quartet dancing most of the leading roles may not have been altogether healthy for the company's development as a whole. Cranko, impulsive and idealistic, had great charm, and in his curtain speeches achieved an impressive personal relationship with his German audience.

The Stuttgart ballet company's achievements were based on a long-term and sensible plan worked out by Cranko. He encouraged choreographers, including John Neumeier and Jiri Kylián, to develop within the company, and also encouraged Kenneth MacMillan to work there as well. MacMillan's major work, *The Song of the Earth* (1965), originally turned down at Covent Garden, was performed by the Stuttgart company. Cranko also developed a ballet school to serve the company. His company and his narrative ballets won considerable praise and popular success, at the Edinburgh Festival in 1963, in South America in 1967, in New York at the Lincoln Center, on tour in America in 1969 and 1973, and at Covent Garden just after his death.

While returning to Stuttgart by plane from Philadelphia with his company after a successful tour, on 26 June 1973 Cranko succumbed to a vomiting fit brought on by a sleeping drug, and choked to death. He was unmarried.

[Horst Kögler and others, *John Cranko und das Stuttgarter Ballett*, 1969; John Percival, *Theatre in my Blood* (biography of Cranko), 1983; personal knowledge.] NICHOLAS DROMGOOLE

CRATHORNE, first BARON (1897–1977), minister of agriculture and fisheries. [See DUGDALE, SIR WILLIAM LIONEL.]

CRAWFORD, twenty-eighth EARL OF (1900–1975), connoisseur of the arts. [See LINDSAY, DAVID ALEXANDER ROBERT.]

CREASY, SIR GEORGE ELVEY (1895–1972), admiral of the fleet, was born 13 October 1895 at Badulla, Ceylon, the second of the three sons (there were no daughters) of Leonard Creasy, a civil engineer, the son of the judge, historian, and author Sir Edward Shepherd Creasy [q.v.], and his wife, (Ellen) Maud, the eldest daughter of Sir George Job Elvey [q.v.], organist of St. George's chapel, Windsor. George's elder brother, Robert, was killed in France in 1918; his younger brother, (Sir) Gerald, became governor and commander-in-chief respectively of the Gold Coast (1947–9) and of Malta (1949–54).

George Creasy joined the Royal Naval College, Osborne, in September 1908. On completion of his naval training in May 1913, he was promoted midshipman and joined the battleship *Conqueror* in the second battle squadron. On promotion to sub-lieutenant in September 1915, he was appointed to the destroyer *Lively* in the ninth flotilla of the Harwich Force under Commodore (Sir) Reginald Tyrwhitt [q.v.]. Later he transferred successively to the *Milne, Recruit*, and *Nonsuch*. On 15 December 1916 he was promoted to lieutenant and when the war ended in November 1918 he joined the *Vernon*, the torpedo school ship, to undergo the long (T) course. He spent the next ten years in various appointments requiring his specialized knowledge. In 1924 whilst serving on the staff of the *Vernon*, he met and married Monica Frances (died 1975), daughter of Wilfred Ullathorne, business man, of Melbourne, Australia. They had a daughter who died in 1934 at the age of nine and a son.

On 30 June 1930 Creasy was promoted to commander. There followed two years on the staff of the tactical school and a further two years as staff officer (operations) on the staff of the commander-in-chief, Mediterranean Fleet. In July 1934 he joined the cruiser *Sussex* as her executive officer and second-in-command. In December 1935 he was promoted to captain and joined the Admiralty plans division as an assistant director. Two years later, in June 1938, he returned to sea in the *Grenville*, in command of the first destroyer flotilla in the Mediterranean Fleet. Soon after the outbreak of World War II in September 1939 the Admiralty concentrated all available destroyers in home waters where they were needed for a great variety of duties. Whilst so employed the *Grenville* was mined and lost. She was replaced by the *Codrington* and it was in this ship that on the invasion of Holland in May 1940 Creasy rescued Princess Juliana and her family. For the skill and initiative he displayed during this and subsequent operations for the evacuation of the British Army from Dunkirk on 11 July 1940, he was appointed to the DSO.

For a short time thereafter he served as personal assistant to the first sea lord, Admiral Sir Dudley Pound [q.v.], before taking up the important post of director of anti-submarine warfare at the Admiralty in September 1940. Creasy, ably assisted by (Sir) C. R. N. Winn, played an important part in countering the moves made by Admiral Dönitz, head of the U-boat section of the Germany navy. After just over two years in this post he returned to sea in command of the *Duke of York*, flagship of the commander-in-chief, Home Fleet. His tenure of this important command was however, cut short by his early promotion to rear-admiral on 8 July 1943. Admiral Sir Bertram Ramsay (whose notice Creasy later wrote for this Dictionary), who had been entrusted with the conduct of the naval side of the re-entry into Europe, immediately applied for Creasy as his chief of staff and it was on the latter's shoulders that the task of drafting the detailed orders for the movement of some 5,000 ships was to fall. The success of the landings was mainly due to the careful planning which preceded them.

His next appointment was that of flag officer (submarines). War experience had persuaded the Admiralty of the need for more British and Allied submarines in the Far East. Rear-Admiral (Sir) C. B. Barry, his predecessor, had fallen sick and Creasy's first task was to implement this policy. He arrived back on 26 March 1945. With the surrender of Germany on 7 May 1945 followed by that of Japan three months later, he then had to concern himself with the disposal of the enemy submarines as they arrived in British ports.

His next appointment was that of flag officer (air) in the Far East which he assumed on 8 March 1947. Nine months later, on 4 January 1948 he was promoted to vice-admiral. Soon afterwards he rejoined the Admiralty as fifth sea lord and deputy chief of the naval staff. On 30 November 1949 he became vice-chief of the naval staff, a post he was to occupy for almost two years. Meanwhile, on 15 January 1951 he was advanced to admiral and a year later, on 3 January 1952, he hoisted his flag in the *Vanguard* as commander-in-chief, Home Fleet. On 22 September 1954 he took up his last appointment, that of commander-in-chief, Portsmouth, and on 22 April 1955 he was promoted to admiral of the fleet.

Creasy was appointed MVO (1934), CBE (1943), CB (1944), KCB (1949), and GCB (1953). He was commander of the US Legion of Merit, of the Dutch Order of Orange Nassau, and of the Polish Order of Polonia Restituta.

In 1957 he and his wife settled in the Old House, Great Horkesley in Essex, where he spent the last sixteen years of his life. He took a great interest in local affairs and especially in the Essex branch of the Royal British Legion of which from 1958 to 1969 he was the president. He was an avid reader, kept himself up to date with world affairs, and made many friends among the local populace. A keen fisherman and a good shot, he pursued these activities until his health began to fail in the mid-1960s. He died at his home in Great Horkesley 31 October 1972 and was buried in the churchyard at Little Horkesley.

[Personal knowledge.] B. B. SCHOFIELD

CREEDY, SIR HERBERT JAMES (1878–1973), civil servant, was born 3 May 1878 in London, the elder son (there were no daughters) of Robert Henry Creedy, head of the trustee department of the National and Provincial Bank, and his wife, Eliza Horn. He was educated at Merchant Taylor's School and won a scholarship to St. John's College, Oxford, where he took a double first in classical honour moderations (1898) and *literae humaniores* (1900). He was a senior scholar of the college from 1901 to 1905 but decided that an academic career would be too sheltered.

He joined the War Office as clerk of the higher division in 1901 and was seconded for special duty in South Africa in 1903. In the same year he became private secretary to Sir Edward Ware [q.v.], then permanent under-secretary of state for war, and five years later he was promoted to take charge of the War Office central management branch. In 1913 he became private secretary to the secretary of state and thus began his long service to seven war ministers including Asquith, Kitchener, and Winston Churchill [qq.v.].

In 1920 he succeeded the ailing Sir Reginald Brade as secretary of the War Office, becoming also a member and secretary of the Army Council, and four years later he became the sole permanent under-secretary of state for war, a post which he held until his retirement in 1939. Thus for thirty-six years (1903–39) Creedy was never far removed from the central controls of the War Office; indeed his was a longer continuous association with one department than even the justly celebrated service of Sir Maurice (later Lord) Hankey [q.v.] with the secretariat of the Committee of Imperial Defence and the Cabinet.

Creedy's period as PUS covered the drastic

run-down of the army in the 1920s and its hectic rearmament in the 1930s so there were numerous occasions for quarrels with the generals and Treasury officials. Creedy's method was to avoid confrontations by patient diplomacy behind the scenes. In private he might hint that some of the generals, markedly less intelligent and well-educated than himself, needed delicate handling and tutoring in the mysteries of War Office procedures, but he achieved this without a trace of condescension. He seems to have been universally liked and respected by the soldiers who worked with him, more than one recalling that his successor, Sir P. J. Grigg [q.v.], was more acerbic and also more forceful and dynamic.

Though fascinated by his work, Creedy felt strongly that it should not dominate his whole life. He cultivated a wide circle of friends from many professions, travelled a good deal, and kept up his classical studies. Inevitably he had strong personal opinions about some public issues; he is known for example to have opposed the creation of a Ministry of Defence, and he disliked the RAF's strategic bombing policy; but he hated intrigues and was a man of monumental discretion. Characteristically he did not preserve letters or documents and wrote no memoirs.

Creedy continued to enjoy robust health and to pursue an active life for many years after his retirement. During World War II he was a member, and in 1943–5 chairman, of the Security Executive. Among many other activities he was a governor of Wellington College (1939–53), a commissioner of the Royal Hospital, Chelsea (1945–57), and a trustee of the Imperial War Museum (1942–59). He was admired and much consulted as doyen by later generations of public servants and men of affairs. He eventually retired to Oxford where he had many friends, particularly at his old college which had made him an honorary fellow in 1931. Creedy was appointed MVO (1911), CVO (1917), KCVO (1923), CB (1915), KCB (1919), and GCB (1933).

In appearance Creedy was short and plump with an almost globular head and small, well-cut features. A model of urbanity, he could nevertheless inspire awe with his quickness of mind and uncanny ability to detect the tiniest error in what he read or heard. His skill in mastering files, seizing on the main points, settling acrimonious disputes in a conciliatory manner, and hitting upon the right phrase in minutes and reports became legendary.

He married in 1904 Mabel Constance (died 1958), daughter of Samuel James Lowry, of Grove Park, Kent, who worked in the City; they had one daughter. Creedy died in the Civil Service Home at Horsham 3 April 1973.

[*The Times*, 5 April 1973; private information.]

Brian Bond

CRIPPS, Dame ISOBEL (1891–1979), was born at Denham, Buckinghamshire, 25 January 1891, the second daughter and youngest of three children of Commander Harold William Swithinbank, landowner, of Denham Court, and his wife, Amy, daughter of James Crossley Eno, of Dulwich, founder of the firm of that name which manufactured a well-known brand of fruit salts. She was educated privately and at Heathfield, near Ascot.

She met Stafford Cripps in 1910. Her father was standing in the Conservative interest at Wycombe, and Stafford was supporting his father's candidature with his customary zeal. He was the fifth child and fourth son of Charles Alfred Cripps [q.v.], later first Baron Parmoor. The father, who came from a traditionally Conservative family, was a distinguished lawyer who later served as lord president of the Council under Ramsay MacDonald. Among his helpers was Isobel Swithinbank. C. A. Cripps was elected but his success did not see the end of his son's acquaintanceship with Miss Swithinbank. They corresponded; Isobel visited the Cripps home at Parmoor and stayed in the family's London house. The following year both were members of a family party which went to the winter sports in Switzerland and they soon became engaged. Cripps had earlier shown great promise as a scientist and had attracted the attention of Sir William Ramsay [q.v.], the experimentalist chemist, but, as he wished to marry, he turned from science to the bar for which he had already begun to read.

The young couple—he was twenty-two and she twenty—were married at Denham parish church on 12 July 1911. It was in every sense a marriage of true minds, a close and sympathetic partnership. Both held firm Christian beliefs. Throughout his sometimes stormy political career—he was for a time expelled from the Labour Party—Isobel remained his unswerving supporter. Above all she was the protector of his always indifferent health. After his death she came in for much praise for the care she bestowed on him but it would be a mistake to regard her as solely an admirable wife and mother. She was a woman of commanding presence. She was tolerant and she listened but she went her own way. She was not a political animal and she did not entertain much when Cripps was in office, though they gave occasional small dinner parties. When Cripps was ambassador in the Russian capital during World War II she spent a year with him in conditions that were restrictive and socially far from rewarding.

Her true bent was for helping others. More than one political contemporary of her husband later recalled her shrewd kindness. She was, for example, a source of much comfort to the first wife of Herbert Morrison (later Lord Morrison of Lambeth, q.v.) whose life was not always easy. But she was not narrow in her friendships, bore no malice to her husband's political enemies, and had friends in all political parties.

During World War II she was president of the British United Aid to China Fund. She was an able and active leader and in June 1946 was appointed GBE for her public services. Later that year she undertook an extensive and arduous tour of China where she was the guest of General Chiang Kai-shek and Madame Chiang. At Nanking she pointed out that the fund did not confer its benefits on Nationalist China alone. During her tour she was invited by Mao Tse-tung to visit Yenan. This she did and was welcomed on her arrival by Madame Mao. The word arduous in connection with her trip is rightly used for the journey, one of 30,000 miles which included travel by air, sea, road, rail, and truck. Most of the great cities of China were visited and to see co-operative work in rural areas the Gansu desert was crossed by lorry. Her interest in China did not wane and she was to hold the chairmanship of the Sino-British Fellowship Trust for some years.

Throughout life her aim, simple and never proclaimed, was to do good in the world. After her husband's death she kept up with many of those friends at home and abroad in whose lives Stafford Cripps had shown interest. She also developed an interest in affairs in Ghana after the marriage of her daughter Peggy to Joe Appiah, lawyer and politician. In 1962 she visited him in Accra at a time when he was being held under a preventive detention order.

Though not witty she laughed easily and was never dull. It has sometimes been said that Isobel and Stafford Cripps were vegetarians and food cranks. This was untrue. For reasons of health Cripps was compelled to be a vegetarian and abstainer. Isobel followed his lead but at her table guests were given the usual kinds of hospitality and, except in times of national shortages, drinks of all sorts were available. To the last she thought in Christian terms and acted in accordance with Christian standards.

In addition to her GBE she was given the Special Grand Cordon of the Order of the Brilliant Star of China, first class. In 1946 she was given the award of the National Committee of India in celebration of International Women's Year.

Of her marriage to Stafford Cripps there was a son, Sir John Cripps, who was for many years editor of the *Countryman*, and three daughters. She died 11 April 1979 in Minchinhampton, Gloucestershire.

[Private information.] COLIN WATSON

CRISPIN, EDMUND (pseudonym), detective novelist. [See MONTGOMERY, ROBERT BRUCE.]

CROSLAND, (CHARLES) ANTHONY (RAVEN) (1918–1977), politician and writer, was born 29 August 1918 at St. Leonard-on-Sea, Sussex, the only son and the second of three children of Joseph Beardsel Crosland, CB, under-secretary, War Office, and his wife, Jessie Raven, lecturer in Old French at Westfield College, University of London. He was educated at Highgate School and, as a classical scholar, at Trinity College, Oxford, where he obtained a second class in classical honour moderations in 1939. His university years were interrupted by World War II, in which he served from 1940 to 1945. He was commissioned in the Royal Welch Fusiliers in 1941, transferred to the Parachute Regiment in 1942, and subsequently served in North Africa, Italy, France, and Austria. His most notable military exploit was to land by parachute on the casino at Cannes, during Operation Anvil in the summer of 1944.

At Oxford he had a notable career, both academically and as an undergraduate politician. He lost interest in classics and turned to philosophy, politics, and economics (primarily economics). After his return to the university in 1946, he secured a first class in PPE in 1946 and was elected a lecturer and later a fellow in economics at Trinity. He held this position from 1947 to 1950, and in 1966 became an honorary fellow. Before the war he was an active and orthodoxly Marxist member of the Labour Club. In the early months of the war, however, he found himself increasingly out of sympathy with its fellow-travelling and neutralist line, and in May 1940 he joined with others to lead the successful breakaway of the Democratic Socialist Club, which was much closer to the national Labour Party position. He was elected treasurer of the Union Society, but was defeated for the presidency. Six years later, however, on his return from the army, he redressed this set-back and secured the higher office.

Crosland was an imposing undergraduate, apparently self-confident, irreverent, and even glamorous, with striking good looks, intellectual assurance, a long camel-hair overcoat and a rakish red sports car. Later, as a young don, he with one or two contemporaries formed something of a cult group, of which the distinguishing characteristic was the unusual combination of hard intellectual endeavour and undisciplined, even rather riotous, relaxation. Crosland was, and remained, a puritan (his family were Plymouth Brethren) shot through with strains of self-indulgence.

In 1950, at the age of thirty-one, he was first elected an MP, for the constituency of South Gloucestershire, which he was able to win for the

Labour Party and hold for the next five years because it contained a good deal of Bristol suburb as well as south Cotswold countryside. He gave up his Oxford fellowship a few months later, and never returned to professional academic life, although he remained very much an intellectual in politics. In the House of Commons he had a considerable, although not perhaps a remarkable, success. He was an economic specialist, and a close friend and assistant of Hugh Gaitskell [q.v.], who for most of that period was shadow chancellor of the Exchequer. In 1952 Crosland married Hilary Anne Sarson, of Newbury, the daughter of Henry Sarson, a member of the vinegar family, but the marriage was short-lived and was finally dissolved in 1957.

Before the 1955 general election the boundaries of South Gloucestershire were redrawn in a way unfavourable to Labour, and Crosland decided to seek another seat. This was a mistaken move, for the one which he found, Southampton, Test, produced a larger Conservative majority than the one he had left. He was not, however, greatly disconcerted by his exclusion from Parliament, for although devoted to politics in a broader sense, he regarded the trappings and life of the House of Commons with some indifference.

He had other things to do. In 1953 he had already published his first book, *Britain's Economic Problem*. This was a lucid but fairly conventional analysis of the country's post-war trading difficulties. By 1955 he was already well into a much more original and substantial work, which he completed in the next year and published in the autumn of 1956. *The Future of Socialism* was well received at the time, but only gradually, over the next decade or so, achieved its position as the most important theoretical treatise to be written from the moderate left of British politics in the twenty-five post-war years. It assumed the triumph of Keynesianism, and with it a future of broadening abundance and the withering of the Marxist class struggle. It disputed the importance of nationalization and challenged the bureaucratic socialism of the Fabian tradition of Sidney and Beatrice Webb [qq.v.]: 'Total abstinence and a good filing system are not now the right sign-posts to the socialist Utopia; or at least, if they are, some of us will fall by the wayside.' It was at once libertarian and strongly egalitarian. It saw no conflict which could not be resolved by the flowing tide of continuing economic growth. It was in the mainstream of the optimism, many would now say the complacency, of the English liberal tradition. It influenced a generation.

Political theory having been disposed of with imagination, even if not total prescience, Crosland showed his practical sense by devoting the next two years to acting as secretary (under Gaitskell's chairmanship) to the independent committee of inquiry into the Co-operative Movement and writing a good report. Then he re-entered the House of Commons in 1959 as member for Grimsby, the constituency which he represented for the remaining seventeen and a half years of his life. He was quickly involved in all the Labour Party disputes which followed that lost election, urging Gaitskell on in the argument over 'clause four' (the nationalization clause in the Party's constitution), supporting him against unilateral disarmament, sharply disagreeing with him over his reticence towards Macmillan's initiative for British entry to the European community. Even apart from the European issue, however, he was in no way a client of his leader. He had too strong a personality and too critical a judgement for that. In some ways Gaitskell sought him more than he sought Gaitskell, and he was less thrown by Gaitskell's early death in 1963 than were some others in the circle. In the election to the leadership which followed he supported James Callaghan, who ran a bad third, rather than George Brown (later Lord George-Brown) who was the candidate of the majority of the 'Gaitskellites'.

In 1964 Crosland married again and also entered government for the first time. His second marriage was to Mrs Susan Barnes Catling, daughter of Mark Watson, of Baltimore, Maryland, who subsequently (under the name of Susan Barnes) became a prolific writer of skill and perception; unlike the first marriage, it was a great and continuing success and brought Crosland two step-daughters. His initial government post was minister of state in the newly-created Department of Economic Affairs, but after only three months he filled an unexpectedly early Cabinet vacancy and became secretary of state for education and science. He was admitted to the Privy Council in 1965.

The combination of these events, some close observers felt, produced a considerable change in Crosland's personality. He had a happier and more rounded life, and became more benign. He also became more of a party politician, more stirred by ambition, less the uninhibited and fearless commentator. He was a successful departmental minister, a master of various subjects, but occasionally lacking in decisiveness, always believing that a decision had so carefully and logically to be thought through that he sometimes missed the moment at which to make it. His popular impact was also limited, and, surprising though this may seem in retrospect, he was frequently confused in the public mind with Richard Crossman [q.v.].

He stayed at education for two and a half years and then became president of the Board of Trade in 1967, hoping that this would lead on to the Exchequer. When the vacancy in the chancellorship occurred a few months later and this did not follow, he was deeply disappointed. His relations with Harold Wilson (later Lord Wilson of Rievaulx) were not close, and in the autumn of 1969 there was some doubt about his survival in the government. But he was too able a man to lose and for the last few months of that government occupied a co-ordinating role over unmerged departments as secretary of state for local government and regional planning.

There followed nearly four years in opposition. He worked hard as a party spokesman, published another book, *Socialism Now*, in 1974 (which, like its 1962 predecessor, *The Conservative Enemy*, was a collection of political essays, but more circumscribed in scope by his housing and local government responsibilities) but surprised and disappointed many of his friends by failing to vote with sixty-eight Labour MPs in favour of Britain's entry to the European community in the decisive division of October 1971; he did not vote against, but abstained. This probably accounted for his poor result in the deputy leadership election of 1972.

In the 1974 Wilson government he was secretary of state for the environment, essentially the same job but with a different name, tighter control over his subordinate ministers, and a more senior position at the Cabinet table than he had occupied in 1969. His experience as an upper middle rank departmental minister was unrivalled. The great offices of state continued to elude him. He responded by being increasingly effective in his department, and by exercising more authority in the Cabinet than in the previous government, while moving consciously away from the right and towards the centre of the party. In March 1976, when Harold Wilson resigned as prime minister, Crosland was determined to contest the succession. He ran fifth of five candidates, securing only seventeen votes. Yet the contest did not damage him. He succeeded to the Foreign Office in the new Callaghan administration with an unimpaired authority, and had he lived might well have been a stronger rival to Michael Foot in 1980 than Denis Healey proved to be.

He was foreign secretary for only ten months. Although he had always tried to think and write in an internationalist context, his experience was insular. He was unacquainted with the intricacies of foreign or defence policy. He was impatient of many of the nuances of the game. He knew foreign sociologists rather than foreign statesmen. Yet, after a hesitant start, he impressed most of his officials and his foreign colleagues by his authority, his wit, and his intellect. His personality, if not his fame, was a match for that of his principle confrère, Henry Kissinger. He was no longer the glamorous *enfant terrible* of his Oxford days, or even the adventurous thinker of *The Future of Socialism*. He was not old, but he had become a little tired in body, heavy and hooded-eyed, yet mordant of phrase, contemptuous of pomposity, and capable of a still dazzling charm.

He was pleased to be foreign secretary, but he still wanted, as ten years before, to be chancellor of the Exchequer, and devoted some of his overtaxed and waning energy to preparing for that job which he was never to hold. This was a last but typical manifestation of the paradox of Anthony Crosland. His intellect was one of the strongest in post-war British politics, and he fortified it by exceptional powers of application. But it was weakened by some uncontrolled demon of discontent, which marred his satisfaction in his own particular roles of excellence. He died at Oxford 19 February 1977, in office and at the age of fifty-eight, six days after a massive cerebral haemorrhage.

[Susan Crosland, *Tony Crosland*, 1982; personal knowledge.] ROY JENKINS

CROSS, SIR (ALFRED) RUPERT (NEALE) (1912–1980), academic lawyer, was born at Chelsea 15 June 1912, the second son and younger child of Arthur George Cross, quantity surveyor, of Hastings, and his wife, Mary Elizabeth Dalton. His elder brother became Baron Cross of Chelsea, lord of appeal in ordinary. He was one year old when he was operated on for cancer of the eyes and he became totally blind. His mother, however, inculcated in him a sturdy independence. His school, the Worcester College for the Blind, reinforced this. He rowed for the school at Henley in 1927 and took up chess. He became proficient enough to captain Oxford University Chess Club and to come fourth in the British Chess Championship in 1935. He was disappointed to obtain only a second class in history (1933) at Worcester College, Oxford, but redeemed this by a first in jurisprudence in 1935. He soon acquired a deep love and knowledge of the law. With the help of G. S. A. Wheatcroft he became articled to a firm of solicitors and, before admission, married in 1937 (Aline) Heather Chadwick, herself a solicitor and the daughter of a solicitor, Robert Agar Chadwick, who practised in Leeds. Without her staunch and loving support his later success would have been unthinkable. They had no children.

In 1939 Cross was admitted a solicitor and during World War II he practised in London, mainly in family law. After the war he turned his mind to law teaching. In 1945 he became a full-time lecturer at the Law Society School of Law. He had a talent for lecturing, in which he combined great lucidity with a keen sense of the limitations of his audience. In 1946 he began to help with the law teaching at Magdalen College,

Oxford. He became an excellent tutor, and was a fellow of the college from 1948 to 1964. Though forthright and outspoken, he had a sensitive feeling for the needs of his pupils, several of whom attained high office, and possessed an impressive mastery of many branches of law which was aided by an almost infallible memory. With the help of his wife, his secretaries, and books in braille he read widely and soon began to publish. An elementary but popular *An Introduction to Criminal Law*, written with P. Asterley Jones in 1948, made him known to a wide circle of lawyers; but it was *Evidence*, published in 1958, that established his reputation in Britain and the Commonwealth as one of the leading academic lawyers of the day. It was the first time that the subject had been treated scientifically in England. Based on a wide range of sources, legislative, judicial and literary, domestic and foreign, it expounded the law of evidence with virtually perfect precision. Though it attracted hardly any reviews it was immediately recognized by judges, practitioners, and law teachers as an indispensable guide to the pitfalls of the subject. What had been a confused jumble of doctrines, statutes, and decisions became an academic discipline.

Though evidence was thenceforth Cross's main speciality he had wide interests. Jurisprudence attracted him, and he wrote books on *Precedent in English Law* (1961) and *Statutory Interpretation* (1976). These married an exact knowledge of the authorities to wide reading in legal philosophy. In later life his thoughts turned more and more to penology. His inaugural lecture *Paradoxes in Prison Sentences* (1965) is a plea to those who profess criminal law to widen their horizons. He wrote a successful book on *The English Sentencing System* (1971). For his Hamlyn lectures (1971) he chose as a topic *Punishment, Prison and the Public*. He called himself merely an 'armchair penologist' but he devoted himself to bodies such as the criminal law revision committee, in whose deliberations his provocative advice, conceived in a Benthamite spirit, and backed by an unrivalled mastery of detail, often carried great weight.

His status was recognized by his election to the Vinerian chair of English law at Oxford University in 1964. In this he owed something to the self-effacement of his colleague J. H. C. Morris, who had himself a strong claim to the chair. Cross held this, the most ancient and prestigious of English law chairs, for fifteen years with great distinction. He shirked none of the chores of college and university life, such as examining. Indeed he could establish a rapport with a student at a viva voce examination more quickly than most sighted people. He enjoyed life immensely, though he would remark ironically that it was bearable only as long as he knew where the next bottle of champagne was coming from. With his zest for wine, food, gossip, chess, and long walks one could easily overlook his regular routine and steady output. He had a wide circle of friends many of whom claimed him as in a special sense their own. He was invited abroad to Australia, Africa, and America and was honoured by the Middle Temple, who made him an honorary bencher (1972), and by the award of a knighthood (1973). He was a doctor of his own university (DCL, 1958) and an honorary LLD of Edinburgh (1973) and Leeds (1975). He was elected FBA in 1967. In 1973, however, his cancer returned in a painful form and, though he faced and in the end dominated the pain, he was conscious that his career was drawing to a close. Yet he remained buoyant and, the day before he died, was still planning a book on Sir James Fitzjames Stephen [q.v.] and taking pleasure in the news of a volume of essays (*Crime, Proof and Punishment*, 1981) which his friends were preparing in his honour. He died at Oxford 12 September 1980.

Cross was unusual among English academic lawyers in the degree to which he spoke the language of judges and practitioners without sacrificing scholarly rigour or theoretical insight. But it was as a blind man that his achievement was most striking. To his undaunted spirit blindness was not a barrier, nor even a handicap, but just a nuisance to be overcome. He refused to submit to it, and by his courage rose to the summt of his chosen profession.

[Tony Honoré (ed.), *Crime, Proof and Punishment*, 1981, p. xxi; personal knowledge.]

TONY HONORÉ

CROSSMAN, RICHARD HOWARD STAFFORD (1907–1974), journalist, diarist, and politician, was born 15 December 1907 in Bayswater, London, the third of six children (three boys and three girls) of (Sir) (Charles) Stafford Crossman, of Buckhurst Hill House, Essex, and his wife, Helen Elizabeth, daughter of David Howard, DL. His father, appointed to the bench in 1934, was an industrious Chancery barrister of strictly conservative disposition; there was little rapport between the cautious parent and his ultimately rebellious middle son. There was never any doubt, however, that more than any of the other five children Crossman inherited his father's intellectual ability and academic bent: at the age of twelve, like his father he won a scholarship to Winchester. His school career, which ended with his becoming prefect of hall and winning a scholarship to New College, Oxford, was conventionally successful but his father's hope that his son would follow him into the law did not survive Crossman's own declaration that, if so, he would want to be 'a famous criminal advocate'—an aspiration that caused his father, as a bencher of Lincoln's Inn, such pain that he readily accepted his son's alternative ambition to become a don.

Having again followed in his father's footsteps by taking first classes in both classical honour moderations (1928) and *literae humaniores* (1930), Crossman was duly offered a fellowship by his own college in 1930. To ease the transition from junior to senior common room, a condition was that he should first spend a year abroad. Crossman elected to go to Germany and, given the rise of Hitler at the time, it turned out to be a fateful choice. Though he had hitherto taken little interest in politics, his year in Germany awakened a political appetite in Crossman that was to remain unabated for the rest of his life. He also met in Berlin a twice-married German Jewess, Erika Simon (née Landsberg), who in 1931 became his first wife.

Back in Oxford Crossman soon made his mark, lecturing to crowded houses in the Examination Schools and acquiring renown as a brilliant tutor with a special gift for the toughest sort of dialectic. His technique of teaching is probably best preserved in the books he wrote at the time—*Plato Today* (1937), *Socrates* (1938), and *Government and the Governed* (1939). By the time the latter two were published he had already left the university—though he retained his links with the city through his leadership from 1936 to 1940 of the Labour group on the Oxford City Council, to which he had first been elected in 1934.

The occasion of Crossman's departure from New College lay in a development in his private life. In 1937 he was married for the second time—on this occasion to the divorced wife (Inezita Hilda Baker, née Davis, who died in 1952) of one of his own colleagues in the New College senior common room. But the cause of his wanting to get away from Oxford had deeper roots than this personal difficulty. By the mid 1930s he had become an active participant in Labour politics, nationally as well as locally; along with Hugh (later Lord) Dalton [q.v.] and a few others he was a lonely champion of British rearmament in the Labour Party. In 1937 he unsuccessfully fought a by-election in Labour's interest at West Birmingham and a year later was adopted as the party's prospective candidate for the then single seat of Coventry.

In the ordinary course of events, Crossman could have expected to enter the House of Commons in 1940 at the latest. But the outbreak of war, and the extension of the 1935 Parliament, meant he had to wait another five years. He initially used the waiting time in Workers' Educational Association lecturing and political journalism (becoming an assistant editor of the *New Statesman* in 1938)—but in 1940 he was drafted into the Ministry of Economic Warfare by Hugh Dalton to organize the British propaganda effort against Hitler's Germany. Of the official view of his performance in this role one piece of contemporary evidence survives in the Public Record Office. It is the final character assessment written on him in 1945 by Sir Robert Bruce Lockhart [q.v.], his immediate superior, who said that he lacked team spirit and defied regulations but his energy and agility of mind made a notable contribution to political warfare. 'I have no hesitation in saying that his virtues greatly outweigh his faults. In other words, if he doesn't win a prize for good conduct, he certainly deserves a commendation for distinguished service.' During 1944–5 Crossman was assistant chief of the Psychological Warfare Division, SHAEF.

The antithesis noted by Lockhart was to run right through Crossman's career and, no doubt, does something to explain why he languished for nineteen years on the back-benches before being appointed to any ministerial office. Elected Labour MP for Coventry East in 1945, a seat which he held until 1974, he was offered no front-bench post throughout the six years of the Attlee government. The nearest he ever came to official favour was when he was nominated by Ernest Bevin [q.v.], then foreign secretary, to serve in 1946 as a member of the joint Anglo-American Palestine commission. The report, providing for further Jewish immigration into Palestine to an upper limit of 100,000 European refugees, was however far from welcome to Bevin who blamed Crossman for it, even aiming his famous 'stab in the back' reference at the following year's Labour Party conference directly at him.

Denied any regular chance to display his gifts within the House of Commons, Crossman turned to the party conference, being elected to the party's national executive committee in 1952 and staying on it for the next fifteen years. A founder member of the original Bevanite rebellion of 1951, he remained a formidable and influential lieutenant to Aneurin Bevan [q.v.] until the latter's resignation from the shadow cabinet in 1954 when he, virtually alone among the Bevanites, defended the right of Harold Wilson (later Lord Wilson of Rievaulx) to take Bevan's place at the shadow cabinet table. Although his attitude made him very unpopular with his left-wing colleagues, it proved a shrewd investment for the future—providing, indeed, the foundation for his subsequent close association with Harold Wilson whose campaign for the leadership, following the death of Hugh Gaitskell [q.v.] in January 1963, he effectively managed.

With Gaitskell, Crossman's relationship, though personally cordial enough (they had been at Winchester and New College together), had tended to be politically bumpy. Only with Wilson's election to the leadership in February 1963 did Crossman at last become an integral part of the Labour leadership team. In 1964 he made an important contribution to constitutional debate by his controversial introduction to a new edition of Bagehot's *The English Constitution*. Appointed to the front-bench as opposition spokesman on higher education and science, he had confidently expected to be made secretary of state for education and science when Harold Wilson formed his first government in October 1964. Instead, as a result of a last-minute switch, he was sent to the Ministry of Housing and Local Government, where he proved a strong, if turbulent, head. His effectiveness at the dispatch box persuaded the prime minister in August 1966 to promote him to lord president of the Council and leader of the House of Commons—a post in which he started promisingly, originating the Commons departmental select committees, but finished somewhat frustratedly, even having to watch from the sidelines as his own pet scheme for the reform of the House of Lords foundered in face of a parliamentary filibuster by Labour and Conservative back-benchers alike. Crossman's last two years as a Cabinet minister (from November 1968 to June 1970) were spent at the newly created mammoth Department of Health and Social Security, where he worked hard and conscientiously to weld together two former disparate ministries, though perhaps without conspicuous success. He also had to endure the ultimate disappointment of seeing his national superannuation plan (a subject to which he had given his sporadic attention from 1957 onwards) fail to come into law as a result of Harold Wilson's defeat in the election of 18 June 1970.

For most politicians leaving Cabinet office at the age of sixty-two, their careers are effectively over. If it was not so in the case of Crossman, this had little to do with the post he immediately took up—that of being editor of the *New Statesman*, a reversion that had been privately promised to him, regardless of the election result, the previous October. It was a job that Crossman had always hankered after—at one stage, in 1955, even at the price of giving up his parliamentary career. But the reservations registered at that time by the paper's editor, Kingsley Martin [q.v.], proved in the event to be fully vindicated. True, in 1955, when he left the paper's staff to become a twice-weekly political columnist for the *Daily Mirror*, he was only forty-eight and might still have had the capacity to subordinate his own personality to that of the paper; but by 1970 it was much too late. The gap in age, celebrity, and sheer intellectual fire-power between Crossman and the rest of his staff proved too great to bridge: the following twenty-one months, until his somewhat brutal dismissal by the *New Statesman*'s board in March 1972, were to prove unhappy ones both for him and the paper.

The circumstances of Crossman's departure hurt him deeply—but, ironically, they gave him the opportunity for the triumphant coda to his career. From his days on the opposition back-benches in the early 1950s to his years in the Cabinet between 1964 and 1970, he had regularly kept a full political diary recording not only his own daily activities but also his reflections on the entire British political process. Leisure and the relaxed setting at his Oxfordshire farm inherited via his father-in-law (following his third and very happy marriage in 1954 to Anne Patricia, daughter of Alexander Patrick McDougall, farmer), enabled him to prepare the diaries for publication. Having already undergone a major operation at the beginning of 1972, he knew that time was not on his side—but before his death in 1974 he had the satisfaction of handling the first page proofs of what eventually was to be a three-volume work, *The Diaries of a Cabinet Minister* (1975, 1976, and 1977), subsequently to be followed by an additional volume, *The Backbench Diaries of Richard Crossman* (1981). The publication of the first volume of the *Diaries* was preceded by a great legal battle: the Labour attorney-general of the day vainly sought an injunction before the lord chief justice to prohibit their distribution in book form, even after they had been successfully serialized in the *Sunday Times* for nine consecutive weeks.

Crossman did not live to see this battle but he would have been highly gratified at the result. Although frequently criticized for inconsistency, one principle to him was as constant as the northern star: he never wavered in his belief that democracy must mean that people were entitled to know just how the decisions were reached that were taken in their name. In the earliest of all his books, *Plato Today*, published when he was only twenty-nine, he had made his subject wonder out loud whether parliamentary democracy was not in essence 'a sham, a gaily-painted hoarding behind which are kept hidden the government and the machinery of the state'. That was a paradox that he continued to tussle with until the day he died—and, with his well-known iconoclasm, he would have delighted in the fact that, through his *Diaries*, his own doubts were passed on to a succeeding generation. He died at his home at Prescote Manor 5 April 1974, being survived by his wife and a son and a daughter. There were no children of his previous marriages. Crossman was appointed OBE in 1945 and sworn of the Privy Council in 1964.

[R. H. S. Crossman, 'My Father', *Sunday Telegraph*, 16 December 1962; Susan Barnes, 'The Man Who Thinks Out Loud', *Sunday Times*, 29 November 1970; Kingsley Martin, private memorandum, 1955; James Fenton, 'Mr Crossman's Dogsbody', *New Review*,

November 1976; BBC 2 'Reputations' script, 'Richard Crossman: Chronicler of the Cabinet', *Listener*, 5 April 1979; Janet Morgan, editor's introduction, *The Backbench Diaries of Richard Crossman*, 1981; private information.]

ANTHONY HOWARD

CROWTHER, GEOFFREY, BARON CROWTHER (1907–1972), economist, journalist, and business man, was born 13 May 1907 at Headingley, the eldest son of Charles Crowther, scientist and university teacher, of 6 Broomfield Road, Headingley, and his wife, Hilda Louise Reed. He was educated first at Leeds Grammar School and later at Oundle, where he won a scholarship to read modern languages at Clare College, Cambridge (of which he was to become an honorary fellow in April 1958). In his third year, however, he switched to economics, became president of the Union in 1928, and gained a double first. He was awarded a Commonwealth Fund fellowship and pursued further studies at Yale and Columbia universities in 1929–31. These years marked the beginning of his lifelong attachment to American affairs and people. During his stay in the United States he met Margaret, daughter of E. H. Worth of Claymont, Delaware; they were married in 1932; they had two sons and four daughters, one of whom died. On the recommendation of J. M. (later Lord) Keynes [q.v.] Crowther became economic adviser on banking to the Irish government; his report on Irish banking, written at the age of twenty-five, was the first of many distinguished public documents to come from his pen.

In 1932, on a further recommendation by Keynes to Walter (later Lord) Layton [q.v.], then editor, he joined the staff of *The Economist*; he became its editor in 1938, putting his first issue of the paper to press on the night of Munich. He held the editorship until March 1956, for a period longer than that of any of his important predecessors, including Walter Bagehot [q.v.] himself, saying (though few believed him) that he was then 'written out'. Crowther shared many of Bagehot's qualities. His writing was succinct, uncomplicated, sparing of polysyllables, and always brightened by wit. He composed in a neat small hand and with seemingly effortless facility pellucid leading articles on questions of great inherent complication and his envious colleagues on the paper tried as best they could to model their own style on his uncluttered prose. He thus inspired, though he never sought to impose, a quality of writing in *The Economist* which rapidly attracted readers so that the circulation multiplied during his editorship from 10,000 to 55,000. As the paper grew in influence and resources, he attracted spirited people to join it and he was one of the first newspaper editors to appoint distinguished women to his staff. Crowther's concern for Anglo-American relations led him to introduce into the paper late in the war an American survey, which was intended to inform non-American readers about American affairs but which quickly became required reading for thousands of Americans, from presidents downwards. *The Economist* was indeed Crowther's monument and under his editorship it became one of the most influential and most widely quoted papers in the world.

Crowther's editorship continued during the war of 1939–45, but he was also heavily engaged in the Ministry of Supply in 1940–1, in the Ministry of Information 1941–2, and became deputy head of the joint war production staff, Ministry of Production (1942–3). He continued as active editor until March 1956 and in 1957 was knighted for his services to journalism. But business was beginning to attract him soon after the war. He succeeded Lord Layton as chairman of The Economist Newspaper Ltd. and remained in the chair until his death. For some time Crowther was deputy chairman of Commercial Union Assurance and he was an important member of the team (including Commercial Union interests) that created the successful Trafalgar House property group, of which he later became chairman. Unfortunately it cannot be said that Crowther's achievements in business matched his outstanding successes at *The Economist*. He had the capacity for the highest responsibilities in national and international business but his moral judgement was sorely tried in a number of companies of rather less importance. Crowther was impelled to leave Trafalgar House when it entered into the hotel business, with which he himself had been associated since 1944 as a director of Trust Houses. He created the British Printing Corporation by a merger of Hazell Sun, which he had joined in 1957, and Purnell, only to discover many things amiss on the Purnell side. Eighteen months later, in the summer of 1965, he had a bitter fight to remove the Purnell chairman from the board. Crowther had become chairman of Trust Houses in 1960 and worked hard to improve and expand its interests before the agreed merger with Forte Holdings in 1970. He then became head of the biggest hotel group in the country, but his hold on the chair of Trust Houses Forte in the ensuing year became increasingly precarious because of differences about policy and between personalities. His last despairing act was to support an offer by Allied Breweries to take over the company, but this was comfortably defeated and he and most of his ex-Trust Houses colleagues resigned. Undoubtedly these bitter boardroom quarrels were a primary factor in his sudden death, 5 February 1972, at Heathrow Airport, just as he had returned from Australia.

Crowther never sought high public office but his public service, particularly in education, was of the highest importance. He was chairman, 1956–60, of the Central Advisory Council for Education which in 1959 recommended the raising of the school-leaving age to sixteen in what became known as the 'Crowther Report'. Between 1968 and 1971 he was chairman of the committee on consumer credit which sought to modernize the law and practice of this phenomenally expanding business. Among the many governing bodies on which he sat, he was perhaps proudest of becoming chancellor of the Open University in 1969. In that year he became chairman of the commission on the constitution (as well befitted Bagehot's successor), on which he was working when he died. He was created a life peer in June 1968. Seven honorary degrees were conferred upon him by English and American universities. He wrote in his early career several books on economic subjects of which the most widely read was *An Outline of Money*, published in 1941. Crowther was of stocky build with small hands and a dominating head well fitted to house his varied talents as economist, journalist, businessman, educationist, and reformer working from what he would always call 'the extreme centre'.

[Private information; personal knowledge.]

ROLAND BIRD

CUMBERLEGE, GEOFFREY FENWICK JOCELYN (1891–1979), publisher, was born 18 April 1891 at Walsted Place, Lindfield, Sussex, the third son and youngest of five children of Henry Mordaunt Cumberlege, landowner, and his wife, Blanche Pacquita Genevra Fenwick. He was educated at Charterhouse and Worcester College, Oxford.

On graduating from Oxford (BA, 1913) he was commissioned in the Oxford and Buckinghamshire Light Infantry and he served with great distinction throughout World War I, in France (1915–18) and Italy (1918–19). He was promoted substantive captain in October 1917. He received the MC and was appointed to the DSO. He was mentioned in dispatches three times and was awarded the croce di guerra.

On demobilization in 1919 he joined the Oxford University Press under (Sir) Humphrey Milford [q.v.] and was immediately dispatched, with minimum training in publishing, to succeed E. V. Rieu [q.v.] as manager of the Indian branch of the Press in Bombay. In 1927 he was recalled from India and appointed president of Oxford University Press Inc. in New York, where he remained until 1934 when he returned to England as Milford's principal assistant in the London business of the Press. In 1945 Cumberlege was appointed publisher to the University of Oxford and from then until his final retirement in 1956, all books published by the London business of the Press bore his name in the imprint. It was then the practice to distinguish in this way the scholarly publications of the Clarendon Press in Oxford from all others.

It was Cumberlege's fate throughout his career to have to deal with exceptional circumstances and conditions of unusual difficulty. In India he found a very small business which had barely survived the war. His predecessor was ill and had to leave for England immediately. London was remote and communication slow so that effectively he was entirely his own master. His task was to publish textbooks for Indian primary and secondary schools, which could afford only the lowest possible prices. However, he worked enormously long hours, established suitable offices in Bombay and branch offices in Calcutta and Madras, and left a branch which continued to thrive.

Arriving in New York, by then happily married, he found a disorganized business losing money and then had to return it to profitability in the very adverse conditions of the depression. He set about this task by cutting everyone's salary, including of course his own, and he also saved overheads by temporarily amalgamating the office with Longmans. Most significantly he embarked on a very successful and enterprising publishing programme. He initiated a distinguished list of American children's books, which were also successful in England, and, among many other long-lasting books, he published a translation of *The Odyssey of Homer* (1932) by T. E. Shaw (T. E. Lawrence, q.v.) and *The Growth of the American Republic* by S. E. Morison and H. S. Commager (1930).

Leaving a reorganized American branch well set for its subsequent successful development, and many American friends, he returned to four years of peaceful publishing and administration as Milford's principal assistant and potential successor. It was at this time that he published Arthur Upham Pope's monumental *A Survey of Persian Art* (1938) but then war came in 1939 and he had to organize the complete evacuation of the London business to Oxford. At the end of World War II he faced the daunting task of re-establishing the Press in London, rebuilding the staff, reorganizing the Canadian and Australian branches for which as publisher he was responsible, and laying the foundations of the great post-war expansion of the Press outside Oxford. He encouraged the development of books for the teaching of English as a second language which led subsequently to the establishment of profitable branches in Africa and Asia. He changed the children's book list radically to an altogether higher degree of acceptability.

Perhaps his most significant publishing achievement was the organization and production, jointly with the Cambridge University Press, of the New English Bible. This gave him great pleasure as he was a loyal Anglican churchman. He played his part in the book trade as a member of the council of the Publishers Association but he refused to become president, because he had too little time remaining.

Cumberlege had been a distinguished soldier and to all these critical problems of his publishing career he brought the military virtues of leadership, quick decision, and positive action, but these were cloaked and modified by great charm of manner. He entirely disregarded his own interests and he inspired lasting loyalty, much helped by his extraordinary powers of mimicry, in his staff, his authors, and his friends, by whom he was universally known as 'Jock'. He had patrician qualities and was an amateur in the eighteenth-century definition of the word. Never an intellectual by academic standards, his instinctive publishing judgement was sound in the difficult field that lies between works of academic rigour and the popular trade book. For this Dictionary he wrote the article on E. J. ('Jim') Corbett, destroyer of man-eating tigers.

In appearance he was tall and thin with aquiline features and very expressive hands. Among his private interests was the collection of early English water-colours and he was a keen gardener.

He was awarded an honorary DCL by Durham University in 1953 and elected an honorary fellow of Worcester College, Oxford (1952).

In 1927 he married Vera Gladys, daughter of Major Sir Alexander Doran Gibbons, seventh baronet, landowner, of Stanwell Place, Middlesex. They had one daughter and three sons. He died at his home Idlehurst, Birch Grove, Horsted Keynes, 29 July 1979.

[*Bookseller*, 11 August 1979; personal knowledge.] JOHN BROWN

CUNLIFFE-LISTER, PHILIP, first EARL OF SWINTON (1884–1972), politician, was born 1 May 1884 at East Ayton near Scarborough, the third son of Yarburgh George Lloyd-Greame, later of Sewerby House, Yorkshire, and his wife, Dora Letitia, daughter of James Thomas O'Brien, the bishop of Ossory. Philip Lloyd-Greame assumed the name of Cunliffe-Lister in 1924.

Lloyd-Greame was at school at Winchester and read law at University College, Oxford, of which he subsequently became an honorary fellow (1959). He obtained a second class in jurisprudence in 1905. He was called to the bar (Inner Temple) in 1908 and specialized in mining law. In 1912 he married Mary Constance ('Mollie') (died 1974), daughter of the Revd Charles Ingram William Boynton, of Barmston, Yorkshire, and granddaughter of Samuel Cunliffe Lister, first Baron Masham [q.v.]. Lloyd-Greame was later adopted as Conservative candidate for Buckrose, and though he never sat for a Yorkshire constituency, he maintained strong political links with Yorkshire throughout his life.

Lloyd-Greame was commissioned in 1914, won the MC on the Somme and served as brigade-major before being invalided from France in November 1916. Subsequently he served on the staff of Auckland (later Lord) Geddes [q.v.], the director of recruiting at the War Office, and, when Geddes was appointed minister of National Service in 1917, Lloyd-Greame was offered and accepted a senior post in that department. As chairman of an important inter-departmental committee on manpower priorities, he caught the eye of Lloyd George, Bonar Law, and Smuts.

In 1918 Lloyd-Greame was elected as Conservative member for Hendon, which he held until he left the Commons in 1935. He became parliamentary secretary to the Board of Trade in 1920 and secretary of the Department of Overseas Trade in 1921. In the latter capacity he attended the Genoa conference, where he worked closely with Lloyd George, and he was joint leader of the UK delegation to the Hague conference. When the coalition broke up in 1922, Lloyd-Greame followed Bonar Law and was appointed to his Cabinet as president of the Board of Trade at the age of thirty-eight. It was an office he was to hold, apart from two short periods in opposition, until 1931.

During this period, which was marked by persistent unrest in the coal industry and the general strike of 1926, and by growing unemployment, the protection or safeguarding of British industry became a leading political issue, together with the possibility of developing a meaningful system of empire preference. Lloyd-Greame's approach was essentially pragmatic, but, under Stanley Baldwin, he worked in increasingly close collaboration with Neville Chamberlain, who was later to acknowledge that, in office and in opposition, he had done more than anyone else to secure the adoption of the general tariff in 1932. But Cunliffe-Lister, as he became in 1924, when his wife inherited the Masham estate of several thousand acres near Ripon, was also active in sponsoring the first Films Act, in the reform of company law, and in measures to increase safety at sea; and it was he who suggested the creation of the Empire Marketing Board.

When Ramsay MacDonald formed his national government in August 1931, Cunliffe-Lister was one of the four Conservatives included in his Cabinet, again as president of the Board of Trade; and when changes were made in November of that year, the possibility of his becoming foreign secretary was canvassed. In the event he went to the Colonial Office, where he immediately set in hand the first comprehensive survey of the economic position of the colonies. This was to bear fruit at the Ottawa economic conference of 1932, when imperial preference became empire-wide with the dominions entering into reciprocal arrangements with a number of colonies. This was a period of tension in the mandated territories of Iraq and Palestine, in Cyprus, and in East Africa, all of which Cunliffe-Lister visited by air. It also saw the implementation of major changes in recruitment to a unified Colonial Service; and, in the opinion of many who served in the Colonial Office and the Colonial Service, Cunliffe-Lister was the outstanding colonial secretary between the wars.

In June 1935, Baldwin succeeded MacDonald as prime minister and, convinced as he now was that German rearmament had become a major threat to world peace, he moved Cunliffe-Lister to the Air Ministry. Cunliffe-Lister had already become chairman of a new air defence research committee, which brought together ministers, serving officers, and scientists, notably (Sir) Henry Tizard and (Sir) Robert Watson Watt [qq.v.], and of a sub-committee of the Cabinet specifically charged to recommend what should be done to implement the pledges which the government had given on 'parity' in the air. The first of these committees, on which Churchill later agreed to serve in a personal capacity, sponsored the development of radar with the highest priority. The second made recommendations which involved a considerable acceleration of the air force programme and a major increase in production (measures which included for the first time the placing of orders for certain types while still under development); and on 22 July 1935 Cunliffe-Lister was able to put to the House of Commons a revised expansion scheme, known as Scheme C.

The government's policy of rearming was endorsed at the general election of 1935, but when the new government was formed, Cunliffe-Lister opted to go to the House of Lords as Viscount Swinton. His reason was no doubt a desire to concentrate all his powers on what he regarded, then and subsequently, as the most exacting task of his career, without the distractions of a constituency or the House of Commons. But it was, as he later recognized, a serious error of judgement in that he failed to realize, or chose to disregard, the controversial issues which would inevitably arise in implementing and presenting a major rearmament programme which had not been launched until after the initiative had begun to pass to the Germans, which coincided with revolutionary changes in the design and construction of aircraft, and which, throughout his tenure of office, was in large measure controlled by economic and political factors. Similar considerations applied in the field of civil aviation where the British performance notably lacked panache and was attracting many critics from the back-benches.

Nevertheless, the years 1935 to 1938, during which Swinton worked in close association with Lord Weir [q.v.] and with a number of exceptionally gifted air force officers, were years of major achievement, during which many of the decisions which bore fruit in the Battle of Britain and subsequently were taken and implemented.

The respective responsibilities of the Air Ministry and the Admiralty for 'naval aviation' were redefined by the Inskip award of July 1937, which, though at the time it gave no satisfaction to either party, has effectively remained in force ever since; and despite doubts and opposition on political grounds the Cabinet was persuaded in November 1936 to approve the construction of an aerodrome at Gibraltar, which was to prove of the greatest strategic importance.

No doubt during these years of high pressure there were mistakes and omissions: no doubt too some arguments and claims were advanced which were not justified in the result, just as there were technical advances for which credit could not be claimed publicly at the time. Certainly there was friction with Lord Nuffield [q.v.] over the shadow factory scheme, with Churchill and F. A. Lindemann (later Viscount Cherwell, q.v.) on air defence, and indeed with the aircraft industry which had to be persuaded by the prime minister in December 1937 to appoint an independent chairman, (Sir) Charles Bruce-Gardner, in whom the government felt confidence. During the winter of 1937–8 there was growing criticism, in the House of Commons and in the press, coupled with demands for the presence of the secretary of state in the Commons, which were given added weight by the highly critical report of the committee on civil aviation chaired by Lord Cadman [q.v.]. On several occasions Swinton offered his resignation, and though in April 1938, after the German invasion of Austria, the Cabinet at last abandoned the policy that there must be no interference with normal production to meet civilian and export requirements, and approved an expansion scheme (Scheme L) designed to secure the maximum production of aircraft during the following two years, this decision came too late to satisfy the critics and, after a stormy debate on 12 May, Chamberlain decided that a change should be made. Swinton resigned, and it was to be many years before the full measure of his achievement could be assessed.

Soon after the outbreak of war, Swinton became chairman of the United Kingdom Commercial Corporation, established to act as the commercial arm of the Ministry of Economic

Warfare and to pre-empt the purchase of materials, initially in south-eastern Europe and subsequently throughout the Middle East. In May 1940, at the time of Dunkirk, when invasion appeared imminent and when experience on the Continent underlined the risks of parachute landings and fifth column activities, Churchill appointed him in addition to be chairman of a new Security Executive with wide responsibilities under the lord privy seal for the co-ordination of security measures and the elimination of what he described as over-laps and under-laps. Two years later, in June 1942, Swinton left the Security Executive to become resident minister in West Africa, which, as a result of Allied set-backs in the Mediterranean and the Far East, had become of increasing importance for its bases, its sea and air communications, and its raw materials; it was shortly to assume a new dimension in connection with the launching of the North African campaign. Swinton, with his wide experience and driving force, had special, if not unique, qualifications for all three appointments, and though information on the Security Executive is still restricted, there is ample evidence that he performed outstanding services of a highly individual character in each of them. For example, when he left the Security Executive, the lord privy seal, Sir John Anderson (later Viscount Waverley, q.v.), wrote that he knew of no-one who could have achieved comparable results, and in West Africa he proved, in the words of one governor, 'a travelling dynamo', who 'split the atom of West African governmental complacency and released the energy latent therein'.

By the summer of 1944 the success of the North African campaign had relieved pressure in West Africa; and both in London and Washington increased attention was already being given to post-war development. It was clear that the reintroduction and control of civil aviation would present special problems, which might lead to a major divergence of views between the United States, which had the funds and the aircraft capacity, and the British Commonwealth, which had constructed and was operating many strategically placed airfields. Swinton had earlier declined the chairmanship of the BOAC, but in October 1944 he was summoned by telegram to return to London to become minister of civil aviation and to lead the United Kingdom delegation to the conference which President Roosevelt had convened to meet in Chicago in November 1944. It soon appeared that there was indeed a major difference of view between the United States, which had the support of the South American countries, Holland and Canada, and the United Kingdom, which had the backing of the rest of the Commonwealth and a number of other countries. Moreover, differences in objective were accentuated by personal incompatibilities between Swinton and Adolf Berle, who led the American delegation. In consequence little was achieved, but the blood-letting of Chicago did pave the way for the Bermuda agreement of 1946. By contrast the Swinton plan for the post-war organization of British civil aviation, which was adopted by the Cabinet in January 1945, and published as a white paper, was scrapped in favour of nationalization after the general election and the return of a Labour government in July.

The ensuing six years, during which Swinton was a member of the shadow Cabinet and chairman of a number of committees at the Conservative Central Office, saw the publication of his reminiscences with the title *I Remember* in 1948, and the creation of the Conservative College at Swinton. On Churchill's return to office in 1951, Swinton became chancellor of the Duchy of Lancaster, minister of materials, and deputy leader of the House of Lords (with responsibility for co-ordinating government information services) and in 1952 he returned to the Cabinet as secretary of state for Commonwealth relations. In this capacity he paid an extensive visit to New Zealand, Australia, India, Pakistan, and Ceylon, and he greatly enjoyed renewing contacts with statesmen of the old Commonwealth. He was less happy in his dealings with Jawarharlal Nehru [q.v.], and he did not emerge wholly unscathed from the discussions on Central African Federation. His last state paper discussed the future of the Commonwealth with particular reference to the claims of Ghana to full membership.

To the regret of Churchill, Harold Macmillan (later the Earl of Stockton), and R. A. Butler (later Lord Butler of Saffron Walden) Swinton was not included in the 1955 Cabinet of Sir Anthony Eden (later the Earl of Avon), and he retired from public office with the high honour of an earldom. Swinton remained active in the House of Lords and in particular served as chairman of the select committee on the powers of the House of Lords in regard to attendance. In 1966, in collaboration with James D. Margach, he published *Sixty Years of Power*; and until his death he remained high in the confidence of senior members of the Conservative Party.

Despite the length of his political career and his considerable achievements in a succession of Cabinet posts, Swinton never captured the imagination of the House of Commons or the country; and it is almost certain that by 1935 he had satisfied himself that he would not achieve the highest posts. Recognition of his achievement at the Air Ministry was slow in coming, and none of the appointments he held in World War II attracted wide public notice. Looking back in 1948, he wrote 'though I have held tenaciously some truths which are to me the foundations of my political belief, the attraction has lain in getting things done'; and some at least of his contemporaries regarded him basically as an administrator undertaking public duties as they came his way, rather than as a politician to whom the administrative tasks of office were incidental. This, however, is to ignore both Swinton's compulsive interest in what, following F. S. Oliver [q.v.], he called the 'endless adventure' of politics and government, and the considerable influence which he exercised in all the Cabinets in which he served, and subsequently in the House of Lords. Swinton never ceased to preach the virtues of an acquisitive mind, and it was this, with his powers of leadership, the encouragement he gave wherever he detected promise, his ability to draft and present, and his capacity for achieving his objectives, which impressed and attracted the vast majority of those at all levels who served under him as well as many people outside politics and the Services, whose views and advice he sought throughout his career to an extent which showed him to be in advance of his time. With his virtues went considerable astringency of speech and manner. He did not suffer fools gladly, nor prigs. Nor was he prepared to humour individuals, however eminent, who sought to rock the boat or to change its direction when he had embarked on a policy which he was convinced was right; this surely is the clue to his relations with Nuffield, with the Churchill-Lindemann partnership, with back-bench critics and editors, and to an increasing extent with Chamberlain, over the scale and priorities of rearmament and indeed, years later, to the gladiatorial contest with Berle at Chicago.

He was fortunate in having a wife who not only brought him a home and great wealth, but whose courage and strong personality, matching his own, were an abiding source of strength in the political disaster of 1938 and the subsequent tragic loss of both their sons. The elder, John, born in 1913, died of wounds received in North Africa in 1943, and the younger, Philip, born in 1918, who won the DSO while serving as a meteorological reconnaissance pilot, died in 1956. Swinton was succeeded in the earldom by his grandson David Yarburgh (born 1937), whose wife had, to Swinton's delight, received, in 1970, a life peerage as Lady Masham of Ilton.

Swinton was appointed KBE in 1920, was sworn of the Privy Council in 1922, and was appointed GBE in 1929 and CH in 1943. He was also a *grand officier* of the Order of Leopold of Belgium (1963). He was honorary air commodore of 608 Squadron, Royal Auxiliary Air Force, and a deputy lieutenant of the north riding; and he received the honorary degree of LLD of Liverpool in 1951. There are at Masham portraits by Sir Oswald Birley and Sir James Gunn.

[Viscount Swinton, *I Remember*, 1948, and *Sixty years of Power*, 1966; J. A. Cross, *Lord Swinton*, 1982; Swinton papers at Churchill College, Cambridge; personal knowledge.]

FOLLIOTT SANDFORD

CURTIS BROWN, SPENCER (1906–1980), literary agent, was born in London 20 January 1906, the younger son and youngest of three children of Albert Curtis Brown, who founded a literary agency, and his wife, Caroline. He was educated at Harrow School, and at Magdalene College, Cambridge, where he was an exhibitioner. He obtained a second class (second division) in part i of the history tripos in 1926 and a third in part ii of the English tripos (1927).

In 1927 Spencer Curtis Brown went down from Cambridge and joined the firm which still bears his father's name to run the play department. In 1928 he married Jean, daughter of the Revd William Watson DD, a Presbyterian minister; they had one daughter. By that time the Curtis Brown agency was well abreast of its rivals, J. B. Pinker and A. P. Watt. Michael Joseph, who was manager of the agency, went on in 1935 to found his own publishing house. He was succeeded as manager by Spencer Curtis Brown in 1936.

The occasional news sheet of Curtis Brown Ltd. of 1930 gives an indication of the business in which Spencer Curtis Brown found himself as a young man. The agency's New York branch had already been set up at 130 W. 42nd Street, and there was also a branch in Leipzig. The magazine department was thriving under the direction of Nancy Pearn; the agency was selling English language rights on behalf of Continental publishers—the sale of *Emil und der Detektiv* by Erich Kästner was reported; short stories were being sold to Continental publishers at a loss, but such sales were winning authors a new audience; Curtis Brown was acting for thirty-one American publishers on their British rights and for a further sixteen on their European rights; volume translation rights were at last making a profit for the agency; first novels had been placed with British publishers for Nancy Mitford [q.v.], R. C. Hutchinson, and (Dame) Daphne du Maurier; and non-fiction titles placed for Ivor Brown, G. D. H. Cole, Sir J. R. Shane Leslie, D. B. Wyndham Lewis, (Sir) Herbert E. Read, (Dame) Edith Sitwell [qq.v.], Ethel Mannin, and Major F. Yeats-Brown; 'Reproduction of Mr Milne's world-famous Winnie the Pooh and other characters has been arranged for in various forms . . . ; Arrangements have been made for a series of twelve monthly articles to be written for a group of newspapers by the Rt. Hon. Winston Churchill . . . ; In the last six months we [and this was Spencer Curtis Brown's department] have made play deals . . . for (inter alia) Noël Coward, John Galsworthy, Maurice Maeterlinck, A. A. Milne, R. C. Sherriff . . . We have even made a contract for performances of "Journey's End" in the Dutch East Indies!'

These may not be Spencer Curtis Brown's words, but they express the climate of the agency in which he worked.

Then came a major reverse, not without bitterness. Nancy Pearn, Lawrence Pollinger, and David Higham left Curtis Brown to set up their own agency, D. H. Lawrence and Dorothy L. Sayers [qq.v.] going with them. Shortly afterwards World War II broke out, severing at once the agency's links with Europe, and causing Curtis Brown to sell the New York branch to Alan Collins, while maintaining a reciprocal trading relationship. During the war, after a short spell in the British army, Spencer Curtis Brown worked from 1941 to 1943 for the Polish forces in exile as personal adviser to General Sikorski. He then joined the Intelligence Corps (Special Services).

In 1945 he assisted in reorganizing the book trade in liberated countries and became chairman of Curtis Brown. The agency's American book department was never more active and successful, helping to establish the reputation of writers such as John Steinbeck, William Faulkner, and Norman Mailer in Britain and the Commonwealth. Spencer Curtis Brown was acting for C. P. (later Lord) Snow [q.v.], (Sir) Angus Wilson, Lawrence Durrell, Gerald Durrell, Kingsley Amis, Alan (later Lord) Bullock, (Sir) J. H. Plumb, and (Sir) Isaiah Berlin. All remained with Curtis Brown except for Amis and Plumb. He quarrelled with C. P. Snow, but the relationship continued none the less. Colin Wilson was turned away on the evidence of *The Outsider* (1956). His colleagues included Peter Janson-Smith who left Curtis Brown to set up on his own, Ronald Barker who became secretary to the Publishers Association (1958–76), and two celebrated theatre personalities, Kitty Black and John Barber. Curtis Brown had an ambition to set up a branch in Australia—during the appropriate test match year. He used to discuss this with his friend and client Richard Gordon (Dr Gordon Ostlere), with whom he shared a fondness for cricket, but it was left to his colleague and successor Graham Watson to fulfil this particular dream.

Shortly before his retirement, Spencer Curtis Brown and Alan Collins quarrelled, and the link with Curtis Brown New York was severed. After a brief flirtation with the William Morris agency, he founded a new American office, John Cushman Associates New York. He retired in 1968, having sold Curtis Brown to Industrial Finance Investments Ltd. To the end of his life he maintained a personal and professional interest in the works of certain of his authors. He was, with the widow, the executor of A. A. Milne [q.v.]. He was literary executor to W. Somerset Maugham [q.v.]. He held the same position for Elizabeth Bowen [q.v.], and wrote the biographical introduction to her *Pictures and Conversations* (1975). He remained life president of Curtis Brown. An undated memorandum, addressed to his staff, contains the following words of wisdom: 'You have many authors, but each author has only one agent'.

A memorandum dated 2 March 1962, probably addressed to a visiting American agent who had no knowledge of the London publishing scene, gives a series of hard-hitting sketches of the major British publishers of the day. Of Allen & Unwin, Curtis Brown writes: 'Practically all decisions have to be taken by Stanley Unwin [Sir Stanley Unwin, q.v.]. He is absolutely sweet and, to my mind, very easy to deal with. He will probably try to ask for all translation rights, but will not insist. He has a reputation for being stingy, but this is quite untrue . . . They can keep a book in print and on sale longer than almost any publisher, and can sell copies in more obscure parts of the world better than almost anyone else.' Of Wren Howard of Jonathan Cape: 'He is not only a tough bargainer, but will waste endless time haggling about trivialities. He will do this with good humour, and does not appear to resent one's own irritation.' Of Sir William Collins [q.v.]: 'Billy Collins does practically everything himself but, being so busy, is a tremendous procrastinator and it is hard to get an answer out of him. He finds it hard to believe that disagreement is not caused either by malice or sin.'

In a period of great personalities in the publishing world, Curtis Brown was a larger-than-life figure. He was a complex man, capable of inspiring great affection and great animosity. Clever, shrewd, with a sardonic sense of humour, he was interested in people. His *Who's Who* entry listed his hobby as 'listening to other people'. He had a genuine dislike of display and snobbery. Frequently his companion at Lord's was ex-Sergeant Garrard who packed the parcels in the office. With his ability to recognize quality in literature of all kinds, and his relish for the tussle of negotiation, he encouraged and stimulated his staff to give of their best. He could be charming, particularly to women. Irascible, he did not easily forgive those whom he felt had let him down. Tall, leonine in appearance, he preferred casual to formal dress. Although a Londoner for most of his life, he had a deep attachment to Monks Hall, his seventeenth-century house in Suffolk, and it was there that he spent his retirement.

Curtis Brown died in London 16 January 1980. He was reading a book at the time.

[Office memoranda; James G. Hepburn, *The Author's Empty Purse and the Rise of the Literary Agent*, 1968; private information.]

ANDREW BEST
ELIZABETH STEVENS

D

DALRYMPLE-HAMILTON, Sir FREDERICK HEW GEORGE (1890–1974), admiral, was born in London 27 March 1890, the younger son and youngest of three children (the middle child, a daughter, died two months after he was born) of Colonel the Hon. North de Coigny Dalrymple, Scots Guards, second son of the tenth Earl of Stair, and sometime ADC to the Duke of Connaught. His mother was Marcia Kathleen Anne, daughter of the Hon. Sir Adolphus Frederick Octavius Liddell. The name Hamilton was added in 1896, when Colonel Dalrymple inherited the house and property of Bargany in Ayrshire. King George V, who as Prince George had stood sponsor to the future admiral, nominated him for a cadetship in the Royal Navy, which he entered in 1905. An early appointment on completion of training was to HM Yacht *Victoria and Albert* as sub-lieutenant. In August 1914 he joined the cruiser *Cumberland*, seeing action in charge of armed boats in the Cameroon river. Thereafter he served throughout the war in destroyers, gaining command in 1917.

Between the wars Dalrymple-Hamilton served in the battle cruiser *Renown* with the Prince of Wales embarked for his visit to the emperor of Japan in 1922; again in the *Victoria and Albert*; in the plans division of the naval staff; in the cruiser *Effingham* on the East Indies station; and as commander of the Royal Naval Barracks, Devonport. Promoted captain in 1931, he commanded the fourth destroyer flotilla in the Mediterranean and was then selected to command the Royal Naval College, Dartmouth, which he joined early in 1937. It was an ideal choice. Considerate, but always firm, though with a light touch, he inspired great devotion in the staff and created a good atmosphere, exemplifying to the cadets personal qualities of the highest order. A visit by King George VI and Queen Elizabeth to the college in July 1939 was, despite the portents, a particularly happy occasion for Dalrymple-Hamilton as he had known them both since their childhood.

In November 1939 Dalrymple-Hamilton took command of the battleship *Rodney*, where his close interest in his officers and men, and his fine ship handling, won him universal liking and respect. The crucial test came in May 1941, during the *Bismarck* chase. The *Rodney* found herself operating independently to cover the possible courses of the still formidable German battleship towards the French coast. Ignoring contradictory instructions in a confused situation and using his own judgement Dalrymple-Hamilton skilfully brought his ship to the support of the *King George V* in the final gun action which sank the *Bismarck*. For this he was appointed CB (1941). Promotion to rear-admiral followed quickly, and appointment as admiral commanding Iceland Command. Here his care for the hard-pressed escort crews, and his excellent relations with the Americans, newly allied, ensured the most effective use of this vital base. In 1942 he became naval secretary to the first lord.

Early in 1944 he was given command of the tenth cruiser squadron, promoted to vice-admiral, and made second-in-command of the Home Fleet. In tactical command of north Russian convoy operations, with his cruisers in the bombardment force at the Normandy landings, and in sweeping the Bay of Biscay clear of German surface warships, he was conspicuously successful. An important innovation was his use of an escort carrier as flagship in a convoy support force, so that he could make the best use of his aircraft. In January 1945 he was created KCB and appointed vice-admiral, Malta, where for a time he was acting governor. In 1946 he became flag officer Scotland and Northern Ireland and in January 1948 was promoted admiral.

In the following September he went to Washington DC as admiral, British Joint Services Mission, where he served until his retirement in 1950. In this, as in all his previous shore appointments including Iceland, Dalrymple-Hamilton was most ably supported, despite her almost total blindness, by his wife Gwendolen, whom he married in September 1918. She was the third daughter of Sir Cuthbert Edgar Peek, second baronet, of Rousden, Devon, and his wife, the Hon. Augusta Louisa Brodrick, daughter of the eighth Viscount Midleton. She died in November 1974. They had two daughters and a son, Captain North Edward Frederick Dalrymple-Hamilton, of the Royal Navy, CVO, MBE, DSC, DL, of Bargany.

Dalrymple-Hamilton was an elder of Inch parish church, lieutenant in the Royal Company of Archers, HM Body Guard for Scotland, deputy lieutenant for Wigtownshire, and a member of many public and charitable bodies. He died 26 December 1974 in Ayr.

[*The Times*, 30 December 1974; Stephen W. Roskill, *The War at Sea*, 4 vols., 1954–61; private information; personal knowledge.]

Ian McGeoch

D'ARCY, MARTIN CYRIL (1888–1976), Jesuit provincial, was born 15 June 1888 near Bath, the youngest of four sons, two of whom died in childhood, of Martin Valentine D'Arcy, a barrister on the Northern circuit, and his wife, Madoline Mary Keegan. He was educated at

Stonyhurst, and in 1906 followed his brother Edmund Conyers-D'Arcy into the Jesuit noviciate at Roehampton. His career at first took the normal course of two years of noviceship, followed by a year of juniorate devoted largely to the classics, and three years of philosophical studies in the scholastic tradition at St. Mary's Hall, a Jesuit seminary situated beside his old school. His early promise led his superiors to send him in 1912 to read classics at Pope's Hall, the Jesuit private hall of Oxford University. He had to be content with a second class in moderations in 1914, a set-back which made him all the more determined to gain a first in *literae humaniores*, as he duly did in 1916. He also won a series of university prizes; the Charles Oldham prize in 1915, the John Locke scholarship in 1918, and the Green moral philosophy prize in 1923.

On leaving Oxford, D'Arcy returned to Stonyhurst as a master, and later as assistant prefect of studies. His teaching methods were unconventional and stimulating. One pupil was encouraged to read Pierre Rousselot, a 'progressive' French theologian killed at the front in 1915, as well as James Joyce [q.v.] and the still relatively unknown Gerard Manley Hopkins.

In 1919 he began the four-year course of theology of a Jesuit ordinand. The first year he spent with his exiled French *confrères* at Hastings (where Pierre Teilhard de Chardin had studied a few years before); there he deepened his interest in modern French philosophy and theology. The remaining three years were passed at St. Beuno's College, north Wales (where Hopkins had written some of his best poetry), and he was ordained priest there in 1921. In 1923 he returned to Stonyhurst for a further year of teaching before going to Tullamore in Ireland for his tertianship, the third year of probation which concludes a Jesuit's long training.

In 1925 his superiors directed him to doctoral work in philosophy with a view to his teaching the subject to Jesuit students. The first year of these studies he spent in the normal way at the Gregorian University, Rome, the second in the headquarters of the English Jesuits at Farm Street (Mount Street) in London. At some point in this period he is said to have protested to the superior general of his order, Wladimir Ledochowski, at the suspicions of unorthodoxy entertained concerning Rousselot's writings. With remarkable wisdom the general offered D'Arcy the choice of some less constricting work than teaching in a seminary. D'Arcy's chosen scene was Oxford.

Accordingly he returned to Campion Hall (as Pope's Hall had now become) in 1927, and began lecturing and tutoring in philosophy in the university. The impact he made both at Oxford and more widely over the next twelve years was dramatic. He became the foremost English apologist for Roman Catholicism, and received into that church a stream of distinguished converts, of whom the most articulate was Evelyn Waugh [q.v.]. (Father Rothschild in *Vile Bodies* is said to have been modelled partly on D'Arcy.) Indeed, Muriel Spark in an early novel described becoming a Roman Catholic as 'doing a D'Arcy'. From his fellow Jesuit Cyril Martindale [q.v.] he inherited a prominent position in Christian broadcasting.

A succession of books flowed from him, notable among them being *The Nature of Belief* (1931), in which he developed the ideas of Cardinal Newman's *An Essay in Aid of a Grammar of Assent* (1870), *The Pain of this World and the Providence of God* (1935), and *The Mind and Heart of Love* (1945), his favourite among his own works. He wrote in what was, even for his own generation, a rhetorical and decorated style. His writing was always allusive, and, at least in his later years, his reflections on life tended to take the form of books about books. Of his preaching it has been said that 'he would argue that the essence of a good sermon was "magic", that it did not matter, if the emotions were memorably stirred, whether or not anybody could subsequently remember what the preacher had actually been saying.' Part of the secret of his own magic lay in his very striking and much painted features; a portrait of him by Augustus John [q.v.] is a well known example of that artist's work.

In 1933 he became master of Campion Hall. His predecessor had already begun to make plans for a new building. D'Arcy conceived the vision of a hall worthy of a historic order in a great university. He was advised to approach Sir Edwin Lutyens [q.v.], who agreed to undertake the task. When the building was completed D'Arcy set about adorning it with a collection of works of sacred art (the famous *objects D'Arcy*), always insisting that the vestments and chalices, however precious, should remain in liturgical use.

Complementary with this ideal of a Jesuit contribution to English Christian humanism was an attachment to an English Catholic past, hazily and romantically conceived, and an addiction to the English Catholic gentry. He took immense pleasure in an eleven foot long genealogical table, scripted in 1617 and illuminated with numerous coats of arms and two coronets, which allegedly traced his family back to the Norman conquest.

The 1930s were the golden age of D'Arcy and his Hall. His young Jesuits won a succession of firsts and university prizes. His guest nights acquired a reputation for brilliant conversation.

In 1935 he paid the first of many visits to the United States to preach in New York and to receive an honorary LLD at Georgetown University. This was the first of several American honours, including the Aquinas-Spellman medal of the Catholic Philosophical Association of

America (1967). Over the years he lectured at Georgetown, Fordham, Boston College, and Notre Dame. He continued his visits even during the war, at the request of the Ministry of Information. December 1942 saw him under the same auspices in Spain and Portugal. In 1956 he was elected a fellow of the Royal Society of Literature, and in 1960 an honorary member of the American Academy of Arts and Sciences.

In 1945 he left Oxford to become provincial of the English Jesuit province. He formed imaginative plans for influencing the life of a country newly restored to peace, though his term of office is sometimes best remembered for his proclivity towards purchasing old houses with Catholic associations. Unfortunately he neglected to achieve results by personal contact, and in particular failed to explain what he was about to the general in Rome. In February 1950 he was relieved of his post, about a year and a half before the normal time. His own province expressed its confidence by electing him its representative at a congregation in Rome, but he took his dismissal hard. He was in his sixty-second year.

The last twenty-six years of his life were something of a protracted dark night. He was out of sympathy with post-war Oxford and England; he saw no merit in the type of analytical philosophy then in the ascendancy; the changes in the liturgy and theology of his church left him with a sense of betrayal. The United States, to which he returned nearly every year, came to be the place where he found his ideals most appreciated and felt most at home. Death, when it came to him in London 20 November 1976, was not unwelcome.

[*The Times*, 22 November 1976; *Tablet*, 27 November 1976; *Letters and Notices*, November 1977; Jesuit records; private information; personal knowledge.] E. J. YARNOLD

DARLING, SIR FRANK FRASER (1903–1979), ecologist, was born 23 June 1903 at 3 Soresby Street, Chesterfield, Devon, the son of Harriet Ellse Cowley Darling. On his birth certificate his forenames were given as Frank Moss and no father's name was entered. On his third marriage certificate Darling claimed that his father was Frank Moss, captain in the South African army. He attended the Midland Agricultural College, and in 1924 joined the staff of the Buckinghamshire County Council, where he remained for three years. In 1928 he became a research student in the Institute of Animal Genetics in the University of Edinburgh. In 1930 he was appointed chief officer of the Imperial Bureau of Animal Genetics under Professor F. A. E. Crew. Notwithstanding his excellent relations with Crew, this was an office job which he did not enjoy. He hankered after the freedom of the wild countryside, and made several unsuccessful applications to work on reindeer in the Arctic and on elephants in tropical Africa.

In 1933 he was successful in obtaining a Leverhulme research fellowship to work on red deer. For the next twenty years, precariously supported by further grants from the Carnegie and Rockefeller foundations, and by his writing, he lived in the wildest parts of Scotland, both on the mainland and the islands. He produced several books such as *A Herd of Red Deer* (1937) and *A Naturalist on Rona* (1939), which vividly described his observations and experience. His *Bird Flocks and the Breeding Cycle* (1938) was more strictly scientific, and was not so successful as his more descriptive works. At this time Fraser Darling was widely read and admired by naturalists, but his publications were too 'popular' to obtain the approval of the scientific establishment.

At the instigation of Thomas Johnston [q.v.], who was one of his admirers, he was director of the West Highland Survey from 1944 to 1950. He hoped that the government would implement his proposals, which would have done much to improve the life of the highlanders and islanders, while at the same time preserving the wild countryside for posterity. His findings were published under the title *West Highland Survey* in 1955 and he was deeply disappointed when no such action was taken.

In 1953, at the age of fifty, he returned to academic life as senior lecturer in ecology at Edinburgh University, a post he held until 1958, when there was an unhappy parting. He was invited by the Nature Conservancy to advise them on red deer research, and had the satisfaction of seeing this started on the island of Rhum, the very place where he had hoped to work in 1933 but had been refused permission by the landowner. However, Fraser Darling felt rather out of the academic stream in Britain, whereas his work was widely admired in the United States. In 1959 he accepted an invitation from Dr Fairfield Osborn to become vice-president of the World Conservation Foundation in Washington DC. He held this post until 1972, during which time he travelled widely throughout the world and published several accounts of his investigations. These include *Alaska: an Ecological Reconnaissance* (with A. S. Leopold, 1953), *Wild Life in an African Territory* (1960), and *The Nature of a National Park* (1968).

After he moved to America, British scientists started to appreciate Fraser Darling, particularly for his contribution to the ecology of wildlife conservation. Therefore there was considerable approval of his appointment in 1969 as Reith lecturer by the BBC. His lectures, and the subsequent publication *Wilderness and Plenty* (1970), made a considerable impact on a community that had just discovered the meaning of the word 'conservation'.

From then on Fraser Darling enjoyed much greater recognition in his own country. He was knighted in 1970, and was invited to be one of the first members (1970–3) of the royal commission on environmental pollution. He was much in demand as a speaker, particularly by student bodies. It is somewhat ironical that one who was so physically vigorous and apparently unaffected by extremely rigorous conditions during his years in the highlands and islands should have been prevented by ill health during his later years in preaching the gospels to admiring audiences which would have ignored his advice twenty years earlier. He was a fellow of the Royal Society of Edinburgh and had honorary degrees from Glasgow, Heriot-Watt, the New University of Ulster, and Williams College, Massachusetts.

He was married three times. In 1925, when with the Buckinghamshire County Council, he married Marian Fraser. They had one son. This marriage was dissolved, and he married the ornithologist Averil Morley in 1948. They had two sons and a daughter. She died of cancer in 1957 and in 1960 he married a children's nurse, Christina Macinnes Brotchie, daughter of Alexander Brotchie, joiner. Fraser Darling died 22 October 1979 in Forres, Morayshire.

[Vance Martin and Mary Inglis (eds.), *Wilderness, the Way Ahead*, 1984; *The Times*, 19 November 1979; personal knowledge.]

KENNETH MELLANBY

DARLINGTON, WILLIAM AUBREY CECIL, (1890–1979), drama critic and author, was born at Taunton 20 February 1890, the only son and eldest of four children of Thomas Darlington, a notable scholar who became an inspector of schools for Wales, and his wife, Annie Edith Bainbridge. Darlington was educated at Shrewsbury and at St. John's College, Cambridge, where he obtained a second class in the classical tripos (1912) and a third in the medieval and modern languages tripos (1913). He was devoted to cricket and rowed in his college boat. He was commissioned in the 7th battalion of the Northumberland Fusiliers in 1915, and served in the trenches (being wounded at Arras) during World War I, at the end of which he was a captain. He enjoyed himself even in such conditions, and in 1916 he began sending humorous sketches to *Punch* from the trenches. He was editor for a brief period of *The World* and wrote a successful novel, *Alf's Button* (1925), which was equally successfully dramatized. He followed these up with other Alf stories, and a burlesque of *The Streets of London* (1932) by Dion Boucicault [q.v.]. He also wrote an autobiography with the expressive title, *I Do What I Like* (1947). But his life-work was his drama criticism for the *Daily Telegraph*.

This covered a forty-eight year period, from 1920 to 1968, and a series of theatrical developments unparalleled in the career of any other metropolitan critic. Darlington came into professional London criticism with the last plays of John Galsworthy [q.v.]; he followed the philosophical plays of J. B. Priestley during the 1930s, the poetic drama of Christopher Fry and T. S. Eliot [q.v.] after World War II, and the theatrical revolution brought about by John Osborne and the Royal Court dramatists after the production of *Look Back in Anger* in 1956. He retired in 1968 after the opening night of *Hair*, which was the first play to introduce nudity to the public stage, and was the first public production after the abolition of censorship. Many people thought it symbolic that Darlington and the authority over the theatre of the lord chamberlain should leave the stage simultaneously.

Darlington's preference was always for the well-made, well-bred type of drama. But he was by no means intolerant. Greatly as the young lions of the kitchen sink drama affronted his convictions, Darlington did his best to be fair to them. He regarded them with the benevolent air of a genial uncle giving the benefit of the doubt to a group of nephews and nieces who had suddenly become unruly. Curiously and dramatically, it was only on the very last night of his professional career that his attitude of friendliness to the young (whom he lived to see grow to middle age) became acerbic. The first night of *Hair* was the only dramatic event to disturb the peaceful, even flow of Darlington's forty years of gentle activity. *Hair* was presented by young people who were briefly known as Flower Children. Members of the revolutionary youth of the 1968 movement which began in the Latin Quarter of Paris, they believed in brotherly love in a boisterous way, and at the end of the performance, just as Darlington was hurrying from the theatre to catch his last date-line, several of them leaped from the stage and together embraced Mrs Darlington, who was frightened and called out to a colleague for help. Thus a disillusioned Darlington finished his professional career.

Darlington had a streak of hardness which sometimes showed itself in his behaviour to his subordinates, but he was a well-loved figure, and influential in his low-keyed, lucid, middle-of-the-road reviews. His long life was distinguished by his eminence in his profession: his delight in it: and the happiness of his disposition and his marriage. He was appointed CBE in 1967, and he was unique in his profession in that, whenever a colleague received any honour, he never failed, even up to his ninetieth year, to send his congratulations. His generosity of mind was shown also in his criticisms, which exactly hit the taste of the large majority of middle-class theatre-goers. Yet beneath the smooth surface of his work there was a stern moral and social conviction, which sometimes revealed itself in a sudden flash of ruthless condemnation. Of a fellow critic with whom he regularly played golf he once remarked, 'He was a very wicked man'; and he meant it. Darlington wrote several contributions for the DNB.

In 1918 he married Marjorie (died 1973), daughter of Sydney Sheppard; they had two daughters, one of whom predeceased Darlington. He died 24 May 1979 at Seaford, Sussex.

[*Daily Telegraph*, 25 and 28 May 1979; *The Times*, 23 November 1979; personal knowledge.] HAROLD HOBSON

DART, (ROBERT) THURSTON (1921–1971), musicologist and harpsichordist, was born at Surbiton, Surrey, 3 September 1921, the only child of Henry Thurston Dart, metal merchant's clerk, and his wife, Elizabeth Martha Orf. He was educated at Hampton Grammar School and was a chorister at the Chapel Royal, Hampton Court, subsequently studying at the Royal College of Music in 1938–9 and then at University College, Exeter, where he read mathematics and took the London external degree of BA in 1942. He became ARCM in the same year. He served in the RAF from 1942 to 1945, using his mathematics training within the field of operational research. He was mentioned in dispatches. A minor hand injury caused him some concern but fortunately did not affect his subsequent performing career. His ex-service gratuity enabled him to study in Brussels in 1945–6 with Charles van den Borren. Returning to England he established himself quickly as a harpsichordist and as one knowledgeable in early music, English particularly, and in early musical instruments. In 1947 he was appointed assistant lecturer in the Cambridge music faculty and in 1952 university lecturer in music.

Dart had a prodigious capacity for work. From 1947 to 1955 he was editor of the *Galpin Society Journal*, the society having been founded the previous year by Dart and others to commemorate and continue the work of Canon Francis Galpin (1858–1945) on early musical instruments. From 1948 onwards he became a regular broadcaster for the BBC's new Third Programme, equally at home speaking or performing. He was secretary to the editorial board of the series Musica Britannica (1950–64) and remained a vigorous member of its committee until his death, seeing thirty-three volumes through the press, a number of which were edited by young scholars he himself had trained.

Dart was a fellow of Jesus College, Cambridge, from 1953 to 1964, visiting lecturer at Harvard University in 1954, and recipient of the Cobbett prize in 1957. His book *The Interpretation of Music* appeared in 1954, incorporating many of his discoveries and hypotheses relating to early music. It was from around 1950 that he began his long association with the firm of L'Oiseau-Lyre, Monaco, both as editor of music publications and as performer on L'Oiseau-Lyre recordings. He became a lifelong friend of the proprietor, Mrs Louise Hanson Dyer, and her husband; their patronage was undoubtedly influential in furthering his career.

From 1955 to 1959 Dart was artistic director of the newly-formed Philomusica of London (formerly the Boyd Neel Orchestra). With Granville Jones and then Neville Marriner as concert masters, he directed numerous performances and recordings from the harpsichord (and latterly as conductor). The recordings were based on editions he had prepared from autographs and other prime sources and in some cases tested certain hypotheses; they thus remain a valuable testament to Dart's scholarship and musicianship. He made about ninety recordings in all of solo, chamber, and orchestral music.

In addition Dart undertook the editing of a large amount of music and the re-editing of the monumental series on English madrigalists and the works of William Byrd (first prepared by E. H. Fellowes, q.v.). Yet his work as university lecturer and teacher was by no means neglected. His lectures were memorable for their meticulous preparation, excellent delivery, and stimulating content; and his influence as a teacher was perhaps his most considerable contribution, a whole generation of students (for whom Dart and Cambridge were virtually synonymous) being affected by him, not a few becoming in turn influential in the field of English music.

In 1962 he became professor of music at Cambridge and, as ever, brought fresh thinking to bear upon old problems and conventions. He found it virtually impossible to change established customs however and resigned the chair in 1964 to take up the challenge of establishing a new faculty of music at King's College, London, which he did most successfully as King Edward professor of music, a post he held until his death.

Dart was a complete musician, an instinctive performer (he played harpsichord, clavichord, viols, recorder, other woodwinds, and sang) and one whose intellect and imagination were unusually matched. Indeed, despite his reputation as solo performer his most outstanding performances were probably those in which he played harpsichord or organ continuo (often directing the ensemble at the same time), for it was in such performances that his perfect sense of rhythm, his self-discipline, his scholarly approach, and at the same time his creative flair for musical improvisation, were most fully matched and realized.

As a scholar Dart was concerned chiefly with English music of the sixteenth to eighteenth centuries, but also with aspects of French music of the period and, especially, Handel and J. S. Bach. (He was engaged in recording a particularly controversial account of Bach's *Brandenburg Concertos* at the time of his final hospitalization resulting from the cancer of which he died.) He had a wide and practical knowledge of earlier musical notations, western and non-western, and wrote on the subject in the fifth edition of *Grove's Dictionary of Music and Musicians* (1954). He also had an unusual knowledge of music-printing past and present. However, he by no means confined himself to early music. He often played Chopin for private relaxation, he commissioned a harpsichord concerto from Roberto Gerhard, and his music syllabus at London paid due attention to the nineteenth and twentieth centuries, and to electronic and non-western music.

In person 'Bob' Dart was large and somewhat formidable. He did not suffer fools gladly, particularly as demands on his time increased. His hobby-horses were not always securely stabled. However, to those who had worked with him and knew him well he was brilliant and amusing (with a delightful sense of the absurd) and generous in spirit and deed. He had a large library of books and scores and possessed many early instruments, most of which he gave away. He collected paintings and enjoyed the good things of life.

Dart was unmarried. He died in London 6 March 1971.

[I. D. Bent, '(Robert) Thurston Dart', *The New Grove Dictionary of Music and Musicians*, ed. Stanley Sadie, vol. v, 1980; *The Times*, 8, 12, and 24 March 1971; S. Jeans, *Galpin Society Journal*, vol. xxiv, 1971; N. Marriner, *Gramophone*, vol. xlix, 1971; A. Percival, *Musical Times*, vol. cxxii, 1971, and in *Source Materials and the Interpretation of Music: a Memorial Volume to Thurston Dart*, ed. I. D. Bent, 1981; private information; personal knowledge.] GERALD HENDRIE

DARWIN, SIR ROBERT VERE (ROBIN) (1910–1974), landscape and portrait painter, was born in Chelsea 7 May 1910, the second of three children and only son of Bernard Richard Meirion Darwin [q.v.], golf correspondent, and his wife, Elinor Mary, daughter of William Thomas Monsell, herself a painter and sculptor of distinction. He was thus great-grandson of Charles Darwin [q.v.], the author of *The Origin of Species* and a descendant of Erasmus Darwin [q.v.]. He was educated at Eton College and went on to study painting at the Slade School of Art in 1929. He began his professional career as art master at Watford Grammar School and in 1933, at the age of only twenty-three, was appointed to Eton College in the same capacity. There he quickly proved himself an inspiring teacher and within a year had turned the Drawing Schools from a scene of discrete activity in drawing from the cast and painting in water-colour into a vital centre of the College's daily life.

Soon after the outbreak of war in 1939 he went to the camouflage directorate of the Ministry of Home Security at Leamington Spa (of which he became secretary) having lately taken a characteristically bold gamble in throwing up his job at Eton so as to live in a small grand manor house in Gloucestershire, with which he had fallen in love, and to concentrate on painting. Towards the end of the war he moved to the Ministry of Town and Country Planning and in 1945 was appointed education officer in the newly formed Council of Industrial Design, where his important contribution was a report on the training of industrial designers in which he examined in particular the proper role of the Royal College of Art, commenting that the appointment of the next principal would be of pivotal importance to the future of the college.

In 1946 Darwin was appointed director of the King Edward VII School of Art in Newcastle upon Tyne and professor of fine art at Durham University, but in 1948 he returned to London to take up the principalship of the Royal College of Art—the very appointment whose vital importance his own report foreshadowed. All his previous experience now fell into place and combined with his huge energy and gusto to fit him perfectly to plot a new course for the college in full knowledge of what to aim for and how to achieve it. To that end he widened the range of disciplines taught to match the industries the college ought to serve, developed academic and administrative systems that would win respect for the place and its products among those most sceptical of the art student's value in an industrial society, and attracted many of the leading practitioners of the day to organize and staff the various schools.

Within fifteen years of his appointment the Royal College of Art, which had rather lost direction in its wartime exile from London, had become by general consent the foremost institution of its kind in the world and its influence spread through the whole edifice of art education in Britain. Its academic stature was recognized by the grant of a university charter in 1967, when Darwin became its first rector and vice-provost, retiring in 1971 to devote himself to his friends, to painting and travel and the affairs of the Royal Academy.

His painting was an expression of the exuberance of his own nature and his love of paint marked him as the heir of John Constable [q.v.], Courbet, and Derain. His realism was decisive and he attacked his subject with generosity which showed his instinctive largeness of vision. He painted many fine and sympathetic portraits, among them a small gallery of his colleagues at the Royal College of Art (where hangs also his own very characteristic portrait by Ruskin Spear RA) but it is his landscapes that particularly reveal his sense of breadth and personal feeling for place. His originality was never better expressed than in his water-colours, where his remarkable skill combined strength, tenderness, and spontaneity. He exhibited regularly at the Redfern and Leicester Galleries, at Agnews, and at the Royal Academy, and his pictures were bought by the Contemporary Art Society, public galleries, and many private collectors. He was elected ARA in 1966 and RA in 1972.

As a young man he seemed a slight and apparently vulnerable figure, an impression which he adjusted by the menacing black moustache and heavy spectacles which he retained when maturity had built up his frame and bearing into a being of formidable weight and proportions. His character was full of contradictions. He was a man of outward gravity and inner gaiety; he made working for him seem of the greatest importance but also the greatest fun, and yet on the very rare occasions when his judgement was at fault in making an appointment he could hardly forgive the victim of his own mistake. He could be fierce and domineering, but behind the imperious manner was a shy man who did not easily establish personal relationships. He made enemies among those who did not understand the gentle character he concealed behind the stern facade, yet he was a warm and constant friend to very many and a marvellous travelling companion.

At the end of his life he was president of the Royal West of England Academy and served during his reign at the Royal College of Art on virtually all the councils and committees which modelled Britain's system of art education and encouraged excellence in art and design, as also on the advisory councils of the Science and Victoria and Albert Museums and the governing body of the Imperial College of Science and Technology. He was elected honorary fellow of the Society of Industrial Artists and Designers (1950), fellow of University College, London (1962), senior fellow and honorary Doctor of the Royal College of Art (1971), and honorary D.Litt. of Newcastle (1964) and Birmingham (1966). In 1962 he was awarded the bicentenary medal of the Royal Society of Arts. He was appointed CBE in 1954 and knighted in 1964.

He married first, in 1931, (Margaret) Yvonne, daughter of Herbert James Darby, solicitor; this marriage was dissolved in 1949. He married secondly in 1962, Ginette, formerly wife of Lt.-Col. Kenneth Morton Channer Evans, OBE, and daughter of Captain Francis W. Hewitt and his wife Adriana née Pelliccioni, who had married in 1941 (Arnold) John Hugh Smith, of Hambro's Bank and treasurer of the National Art Collections Fund. There were no children of either marriage. He died in Chelsea 30 January 1974.

[*The Times*, 1 February 1974; information from Roger de Grey RA, Richard Guyatt CBE, and Colin Hayes RA; personal knowledge.] ROBERT YORKE GOODDEN

DAUBENY, SIR PETER LAUDERDALE (1921–1975), theatrical impresario, was born 16 April 1921 in Wiesbaden, Germany, the youngest of the three children and only son of Lieutenant-Colonel Cyril James Brooke Daubeny, a regular soldier, and his wife, Margaret Duncan. On retirement Cyril Daubeny served as military attaché to the Low Countries and Scandinavia, from a base in Brussels. Neither he nor his wife had any special interest in the theatre, but they provided a cosmopolitan background to their son's early years and he was fluent in French when he went to boarding school (Selwyn House, Broadstairs) in 1930. There, in his own words, he was 'hopelessly unsporting, a small stage-struck bookworm'. Marlborough followed, and by now his obsession with the theatre was complete.

Daubeny's life-work was to be built on a foundation of wide-ranging, but discriminating, practical—and largely requited—hero-worship. His first idol was (Sir) Hugh Walpole [q.v.], who did not disappoint. Daubeny, aged thirteen or so, having read all his novels, invited him to lunch at the Ritz. Walpole moved the rendezvous to his own house. 'It was one of the most important events of my life', Daubeny says in his autobiography; the boy was listened to and spoken to without condescension. (Sir) Alec Guinness and Walpole recommended the London Theatre Studio, run by Michel Saint-Denis and George Devine [q.v.], as the only worthwhile drama school; he enrolled but hated it, finding it 'more suitable for psychiatric therapists than drama students'. In 1937 Walpole again came to the rescue with an introduction to William Armstrong [q.v.], distinguished director of the well-known Liverpool Repertory Company. His first part was a monkey; this was followed by the trauma of going on (for Alan Webb) at a day's notice at the age of eighteen as an elegant man of the world in a suit that did not fit and a 'dickey' which 'popped out with rude assertiveness' whenever he approached the heroine.

In 1940 he joined the Coldstream Guards, and after training in Syria and a visit to the tomb of a crusader ancestor, Sir Philip d'Aubigni, in the church of the Holy Sepulchre in Jerusalem, he took part in the battle for Tunisia, and the Salerno landing, where he lost his left arm. He was invalided out of the army in 1943.

While convalescing in Tripoli he confessed to a sympathetic (Sir) Noël Coward [q.v.] his determination to become a theatrical manager. His qualifications were 'a brazen confidence, an unquenchable enthusiasm, an ardent desire to learn everything and . . . an army of carefully cultivated contacts and some genuine friends'. For money he had formed a syndicate with a few fellow officers.

In the thirty years of his managerial career he put on 200 productions in London without a penny of Arts Council support. In the first phase (1945–51) successes were few. They included *But for the Grace of God* (1946), which he had to dragoon Frederick Lonsdale [q.v.] into completing; *We Proudly Present* (1947), written for him by Ivor Novello [q.v.], and in which he gave his only post-war performance in a part based on himself; and *The Late Edwina Black* (1949), which ran for a year. Meanwhile in May 1948 he had married Mary ('Molly') Vyvyan, daughter of Vyvyan Kempster, of Durban, Natal, a business man and farmer. They had one son and one daughter.

Ironically, it was through a resounding flop—*The Gay Invalid* (1951), from Molière's *Le Malade Imaginaire* (starring A. E. Matthews, q.v., and Elisabeth Bergner, with choreographer Walter Gore responsible for the mime) that Daubeny discovered a passion for the dance. Between 1951 and 1955, starting with the Spanish dancers Antonio and Rosario, he presented companies from France, India, America, Yugoslavia, and Russia, and at least six other ensembles from Spain. In 1955 Edwige Feuillère's *La Dame aux Camélias* signalled the return of drama, and thereafter the range of Daubeny's offerings expanded. He presented drama from Russia, China, East Germany, Sweden, and Italy; dance from Africa, Hungary, and Poland; opera from Austria—together with return visits of previous favourites. This unique achievement (to which his wife made an incalculable contribution as supporter, confidante, and diplomatic hostess) turned him into 'the most discerning and knowledgeable connoisseur of the theatre arts' (Ronald Bryden). It was also the exciting overture to the eleven World Theatre Seasons at the Aldwych.

In the first season Daubeny presented the Comédie Française; Schiller-Theater; Peppino de Filippo's Italian Theatre; Abbey Theatre, Dublin; Polish Contemporary Theatre; Greek Art Theatre; and Moscow Art Theatre. The playwrights included Molière, Feydeau, Goethe, Sean O'Casey [q.v.], Aristophanes, Gogol, and Chekhov. And so the World Theatre Seasons went on, from 1964 to 1975, for two or three months every year, bar one. The choice, the organization, the negotiations, the languages, the travelling, the temperaments (artistic and governmental), and the triumphs and disasters—all rested ultimately on the shoulders of one man. He was a man moreover fighting ill health from 1965 and mortally sick from 1973.

He wrote two volumes of autobiography, *Stage by Stage* (1952) and *My World of Theatre* (1971). The latter contains an eloquent foreword and afterword by Ronald Bryden who makes a strong case for the influence of Daubeny's imports not only on his audiences but also on Laurence (later Lord) Olivier, (Sir) Peter Hall, Peter Brook, and Trevor Nunn when they were creating the National Theatre and Royal Shakespeare Company, and on the ensemble playing which is a feature of both companies. Daubeny was made a consultant director of the RSC.

His honours include OBE, 1961; CBE, 1967; Legion of Honour (officer 1957, chevalier 1971); Gold Cross of the Royal Order of King George I of the Hellenes, 1965; Gold Medal of Czechoslovakia, 1967; Order of Merit of the Italian Republic, 1966; and Ordre des Lettres et des Arts (France), 1974. He was knighted in 1973. He died in London 6 August 1975.

[Peter Daubeny, *Stage by Stage*, 1952, and *My World of Theatre*, 1971 (autobiographies); *Who's Who in the Theatre*, 15th edn., 1972; private information; personal knowledge.]

MICHAEL DENISON

DAVENPORT, ERNEST HAROLD ('NICHOLAS') (1893–1979), economist, business man, and writer, was born 12 August 1893 at Ashby de la Zouche, the youngest in the family of three sons and one daughter of Thomas William Davenport, a brewer and High Anglican lay preacher of Ashby de la Zouche, who died when E. H. Davenport was twelve, and his wife, Florence Lowe. He was educated at Cheltenham College where he proved an outstanding scholar and athlete—an all-rounder from the start; then at Queen's College, Oxford, where he obtained a first class honours degree in modern history (1915) and won the Lothian historical prize (1914).

Barred for medical reasons from military service he worked in the War Office and Ministry of Supply: his experience of government, and of wasteful expenditure, was reflected in his second book, *Parliament and the Taxpayer* (1918); he had already written *The False Decretals* in 1916. After the war he was called to the bar (Inner Temple, 1919) and uncertainly he contemplated a conventional career of law and politics, even canvassing the mining village where his father had his mission. But instead he entered the City: his earliest venture, with a British-American oil company, was an abrupt failure but crucially instructive. These were struggling times, financially and domestically. He had married Winifred, the daughter of Ernest Wood, business man. The marriage was shadowed by the collapse of her health. She died in 1946. They had one child, a son, Antony, born in 1922.

Meanwhile, somewhat in desperation he turned to journalism and there found his destiny. His success was instant. His first articles, on the politics of the oil business, were given centre-page prominence in *The Times*—and his long and influential career as a writer had begun. He became oil correspondent for the *Guardian* in 1920, and from 1930 to 1953 City columnist for the *New Statesman and Nation*; during these years he contributed to the *Economist* and wrote leaders for the *Investors' Chronicle* (as 'Candidus'). By now he had begun to use the name 'Nicholas'. Then for twenty-five years he wrote the City column for the *Spectator*; he survived nine editors and was asking for more space than usual in the week's issue of his death. The consistent quality of his commentaries was a matchless achievement in economic journalism. Under weekly pressure for almost six decades, his flow of ideas and elegant prose lost neither wit nor boldness, neither originality nor radicalism.

His writings were rooted in the reality of his own City career. A broker in the 1920s, he was appointed in 1931 to the board of the National Mutual Life Assurance Society, of which J. M. (later Lord) Keynes [q.v.] was chairman; he became its deputy chairman from 1960 to 1969. His own business ventures ranged beyond institutional commitments, and included the funding of films with Gabriel Pascal in the first (1938) *Pygmalion* of G. B. Shaw [q.v.]. Later he worked with Sir Alexander Korda [q.v.]. He served on the short-lived National Investing Council, 1946–7, and briefly on the National Film Finance Council, founded by Harold Wilson (later Lord Wilson of Rievaulx) in 1947. At the time of his death he was still a consultant of the internationally respected stockbrokers, L. Messell & Company. So, despite the awkward independence of his views he enjoyed a lifetime of diverse City affairs and sustained a remarkably wide circle of relationships.

Among these his work and association with John Maynard Keynes were decisive. His own interpretation of Keynes became central to the purpose of all his writing. It was Keynes who encouraged him to write *The Oil Trusts and Anglo-American Relations* in 1923 (with S. R. Cooke), and to join the *Nation* where he worked with other socially-minded economists and mixed actively with the leading Fabians of the Labour Party. But above all it was the Keynesian challenge to the established ideas of the City that inspired Davenport's radicalism: the sheer humanity and gaiety of Keynes chimed with Davenport's own spirit. He became dedicated to making a mixed economy work harmoniously.

Not that he was ever a tidy 'party-liner'. He was certainly close to the Fabian leadership of the Labour Party in the 1930s and 40s; but at the same time he was also a friend of R. J. G. (later Lord) Boothby and close to (Sir) Winston Churchill and the non-appeasers. He never ceased his mental fight with both sides of 'the Split Society'. In 1932 he was one of the founders of the XYZ Club to advise the Labour Party on economic and financial matters, but he despaired of the Labour Party's indifference to wealth-creation. He described its post-war government as the Second Puritan Revolution, and Labour's 1964–70 period as the Socialist Miscarriage. Equally, he belaboured the Conservative Party for its alienation of the working-class: 'economics without psychology' was meaningless, in his judgement, and it would end in explosion.

His strategies for the reconstruction of capitalist society were developed in two books: *Vested Interests or Common Pool?* (1942) and in 1964 the more elegant and cogent diagnosis, *The Split Society*. This latter work showed a disenchantment with revolutionary Marxism of the left; its flexibility repudiated his earlier, wartime, optimism about planning—such as the proposal for a National Investment Board. He argued that it must be possible to reconcile the imperatives of vigorous private enterprise with the inevitable commitment in any advanced industrial society to a degree of public enterprise.

He never succeeded in persuading any government with his particular strategies: the theme, however, of unity through a wider spread of shares in results and of shared commitment has continued to grow in influence. And his contribution to the build-up of that momentum was unique.

Davenport's individuality found a special focus in his happiness at his Oxfordshire home, Hinton Manor, a superb Tudor house, which in the seventeenth century had belonged to Henry Marten [q.v.], republican and regicide, but no Leveller, with whose free spirit Davenport felt a lively affinity. He married secondly in 1946 the actress and painter Olga Edwardes who had taken the lead in his one venture into theatre, his play *And So to Wed*, written that year. She was the daughter of J. M. Solomon, distinguished architect in South Africa, and stepdaughter of Hugh Edwardes, architect and portrait painter, also of South Africa, and the widow of Anthony Baerlein, who had been killed in action in 1942. His sheer joy in their life at Hinton shines through his *Memoirs of a City Radical* (1974), and in his last work, about the house itself, *The Honour of St. Valery: the Story of an English Manor House* (1978).

He was appointed CBE in 1977 and died at Hinton Manor 26 May 1979.

[Nicholas Davenport, *Memoirs of a City Radical*, 1974; *Spectator*, 2 and 9 June 1979; personal knowledge.] PETER PARKER

DAVIDSON, (JAMES) NORMAN (1911–1972), biochemist, was born 5 March 1911 in Edinburgh, the only child of James Davidson, FRSE, who then occupied the position of treasurer of the Carnegie Trust of Scotland, and his wife, Wilhelmina Ibberson, the sixth of seven children of the Revd James Foote, minister of Bath Street Congregational church in Dunfermline. Norman Davidson was educated at George Watson's Boys College, Edinburgh, where he became dux gold medallist and George Watson memorial prizeman. He then entered Edinburgh University where, on the advice of Sir James C. Irvine [q.v.] he combined the study of chemistry and medicine. Davidson graduated MB, Ch.B. with honours in 1937, having obtained a first class honours degree in chemistry in 1934. Davidson never had any clinical (pre-registration) appointment which was then not required for registration within the General Medical Council.

On the completion of his medical course and on the advice of George Barger [q.v.], Davidson joined the laboratory of Otto Warburg in Berlin-Dahlem. On his return from Germany Davidson was appointed in 1938 lecturer in biochemistry in the University of St. Andrews, and then lecturer in the University of Aberdeen in 1940. He gained his MD in 1939 and D.Sc. in 1945. In the latter year he went to London and accepted an appointment as a member of staff of the Medical Research Council: a year later in April 1946 he was appointed to the chair of biochemistry at St. Thomas's Hospital Medical School. In 1947 he was offered the Gardiner chair of physiological chemistry at Glasgow. Davidson had an intense loyalty to Scotland and he therefore felt compelled to accept the Glasgow post. He spent the rest of his life in Glasgow.

Davidson's early work was concerned with the metabolism of fructose, the purification and mode of action of uricase, and the intestinal absorption of monosaccharides, but his most important contribution to biochemistry was in the field of nucleic acids. At the time when Davidson started his work in this field it was known that there were two types of nucleic acid: deoxyribonucleic acid (DNA), which was generally but wrongly assumed to be found exclusively in animal tissues, and ribonucleic acid (RNA), which was considered to be characteristic for plant tissues. By applying quantitative and improved methods for the measurement and isolation of the two types of nucleic acid from a great variety of biological material, Davidson and Charity Waymouth showed that this belief was incorrect. They demonstrated that both types of nucleic acid occur in almost all types of living matter. Davidson's work displayed considerable chemical rigour. His isolation and full chemical characterization of ribonucleic acid from mammalian liver was an important milestone in the development of modern nucleic acid research. He demonstrated with the aid of isotopic traces the fact that DNA was metabolically relatively stable, but that RNA turned over at an appreciable rate. He also showed that the nucleolus contained RNA and that cytoplasmic RNA was heterogeneous. In addition, Davidson carried out important and pioneering work in applying quantitative chemical methods for investigating changes which occur in cells grown in tissue culture. Davidson's book, *The Biochemistry of the Nucleic Acids* (1950), became a classic and was translated into many languages. He was also joint editor of the annual publication *Progress in Nucleic Acid Research.*

Davidson created one of the largest departments of biochemistry in the United Kingdom, and he was a powerful member of the court and senate of his University. He played an important part in the foundation of the International Union of Biochemistry and he was one of the two secretaries of the Royal Society of Edinburgh, becoming its vice-president in 1955–8 and president in 1958–9 and 1964–7. He became a fellow of the Royal Society in 1960 and was appointed CBE in 1967.

Davidson had two outstanding loyalties: one was to biochemistry and the other to Scotland. He had a somewhat austere personality, which was largely due to intense shyness. He was an active member of the Church of Scotland and fully accepted Christian ethics. He had a very happy married life. He met his wife, Morag McLeod, when they were students together in Edinburgh. She was the third daughter of a family of seven children of Alexander Mathers McLeod, a lawyer in Edinburgh, whose family had lived for generations on the Waternish peninsula in Skye. They married in 1938 and had two daughters who followed their parents into medicine and biochemistry: the elder, Rona, became professor of dermatology in the University of Glasgow; and the younger, Ailsa, became senior lecturer in the department of biochemistry at Glasgow. Davidson died 11 September 1972 at Bearsden, Glasgow.

[Albert Neuberger in *Biographical Memoirs of Fellows of the Royal Society*, vol. xix, 1973; private information; personal knowledge.] ALBERT NEUBERGER

DAVIES, JOHN EMERSON HARDING, (1916–1979), industrialist and government minister, was born at Blackheath, 8 January 1916, the younger son (there were no daughters) of Arnold Thomas Davies and his wife, Edith

Minnie Malchus Harding. His father was European partner of an international firm of chartered accountants and the family lived for many years in Paris where Davies was greatly influenced towards European and business affairs. He went to Windlesham House Preparatory School and St. Edward's School, Oxford.

Before war broke out in 1939 Davies had become the youngest qualified chartered accountant in Britain. In later years he was the only chartered accountant MP. After war service, in which he became a lieutenant-colonel in the Royal Army Service Corps, joined the Combined Operations Experimental Establishment, and was appointed MBE (1946), Davies joined the Anglo-Iranian Oil Co. (later to become British Petroleum) as an executive trainee in the marketing department. An international career took him to Stockholm, Paris, the United States, and finally to Shell Mex and BP Ltd. in London as vice-chairman and managing director, 1961–5. Here Davies greatly enjoyed the political responsibilities of his work with Whitehall.

The seeds of his later political career were sown just now, nourished by membership of the FBI which was about to be reconstituted as the CBI, and where a successor to Sir Norman Kipping [q.v.] was required. Davies's lively mind, highly articulate persuasive powers, great courtesy, and sense of humour provided formidable qualifications for the post of director-general of the new 'bosses'' trade union which he assumed in 1965.

The administration of Harold Wilson (later Lord Wilson of Rievaulx), elected in 1964, brought the CBI leaders into continuous involvement and opposition. In their often acrimonious debates it was frequently a matter, said Davies, of 'winning the argument and losing the battle'. After four years he became convinced that the best way for him to help steer industry and the economy was to become a Conservative MP. He resigned to seek a seat in Parliament but it was to be a frustrating experience for such a talented newcomer to the hustings. Twice he failed to be selected but finally at Knutsford he gained a sweeping majority in the election of June 1970. The absence of such a household name from a junior post in the new administration formed by Edward Heath evoked some comment but this was quickly overtaken by distress at the untimely death of Iain MacLeod [q.v.] and surprise at Davies's appointment, after forty days as a backbencher, as minister of technology (July–October 1970) and later secretary of state for trade and industry and president of the Board of Trade (1970–2). He was sworn of the Privy Council in 1970.

The arrival in the Cabinet of a business man who was seen by the opposition to be a spokesman of management posed problems for Davies in the House of Commons and he must have yearned for the comfortable responses to the probing questions directed at him by parliamentarians in his oil industry days. He spent the last two years of the Heath government as chancellor of the Duchy of Lancaster (1972–4).

In opposition in 1976, under the leadership of Margaret Thatcher, he became shadow foreign secretary and immediately was able to direct his linguistic skills, his international experience, and his attachment to Europe to advantage, and to his personal satisfaction. His earlier life in Paris which he often referred to as 'my love affair with France' enabled him to know and understand the French. He spoke German, Swedish, Spanish, and Italian which reflected his musical ear and the great joy music gave him. Despite his frustrating parliamentary career he was never disappointed with his achievements and was always prepared to 'change his hat' to develop the potential he was sure he possessed.

In 1978 he was taken seriously ill at the 1978 Conservative Party conference and resigned from Parliament in November of that year. Three weeks after receiving a life peerage he died 4 July 1979 at St. Thomas's Hospital. In anticipation of taking a seat in the House of Lords he changed his name by deed poll to Harding-Davies. But letters patent had not been completed so the intended title became null and void. Later by royal warrant the style and precedence passed to his wife whom he had married on 8 January 1943. She was Vera Georgina, only child of George William Bates, a Northampton business man. They had one son and one daughter.

Davies had Welsh, Scottish, and Armenian blood. Of short and sturdy stature, he possessed direct and vigorous characteristics which probably denied him a wide circle of close friends. Nevertheless, he was in great demand for membership of many academic, public, and institutional bodies. Although hard work often forced him to play strong and dominant roles he was essentially a family man, of a retiring nature at heart. He held honorary degrees from Essex (1967) and Loughborough (1972).

[Private information; personal knowledge.]

Alec Durie

DAVIES, Sir MARTIN (1908–1975), director of the National Gallery, was born in Cheyne Walk, London, 22 March 1908, the younger son and younger child of Ernest Woodbine Davies, CBE, who worked in the Stock Exchange and later as chief inspector of aliens at the Home Office, and his wife, Elizabeth Eleanor, daughter of the Revd Isaac Taylor. Having attended Rugby School, he went up to King's College, Cambridge, in 1926. He obtained a third class in mathematics part i in 1927 and first classes in both parts i and ii of the modern languages tripos in 1928 and 1930. He joined the National Gallery staff as an attaché in October 1930 and became part of that institution's permanent establishment on 1 January 1932, as assistant keeper.

Davies was early to play a significant part in developing a new critical approach to the study of the collection. In an issue of the *Burlington Magazine* of 1937, he announced the National Gallery's new objective: 'A proposed re-edition of the National Gallery catalogues to embody a scholarship more ample and more up-to-date (which) has forced the staff to consider many difficult problems'. The complex results of such research were to be expressed by developing the catalogue entry, which Davies was to make into a discipline in itself. Of almost equal importance—and perhaps his first interest—were Davies's critical biographies of artists and their *oeuvres*. He was always to be dismissive of inherited wisdom and the speculative theory.

His early concern with the Netherlandish school was interrupted from 1938 to 1941 by the task of finding a safe refuge where the collection could be housed to escape the bombardment of London. But as a result of his industry and dedication, he had by the war's end prepared catalogues of the Netherlandish, French, and British schools of painting; these were published in 1945 and 1946. In 1951 there followed his acclaimed catalogue of *The Earlier Italian Schools*. He was to be responsible for revised editions of all these catalogues. In 1970 was published his contribution to *Les Primitifs Flamands Corpus de la Peinture des Anciens Pays Bas*, vol. iii (The National Gallery, London), which updated his study of the Gallery's Netherlandish holdings.

Davies was made deputy keeper in 1947 and keeper in 1960; in 1968 he was appointed director, which post he held for five years. He followed the policies of his predecessor, Sir Philip Hendy [q.v.]; the remodelling of the display rooms and the programme of cleaning and restoration of paintings in the collection were both continued. He was to develop the educational services provided by the Gallery; and in addition he was confronted by the inherited project of the building of a northern extension, which was to be opened to the public some three months after his death.

As director he was to insist on the Gallery's role in Great Britain as the prime public purchaser of masterpieces. The policy was put to the test in 1971, when he had mounted the first public appeal made by the National Gallery itself, for the outstanding amount of money required to purchase Titian's 'Death of Actæon'. The appeal was a success. Other notable acquisitions—of works by Duccio, G. B. Tiepolo, Rubens, Rogier van der Weyden, and Henri Rousseau—were made during his directorship. In 1972 was published his monograph on Rogier van der Weyden, in which he displayed many of his idiosyncracies both as scholar and connoisseur.

Davies was a civil servant in the old mould—a precise, fastidious, and unobtrusive administrator. He never married, and his social life—at least in later years—centred on the Reform Club. Otherwise, his life and career were bound up with the institution he had joined as a young man. Indeed, the National Gallery and its staff were to be the chief beneficiary of his will. His unfailing courtesy, disdain for publicity (and those who sought it), and his retiring demeanour concealed a sharp view of human affairs that could be expressed with a marked, if oblique, wit.

Davies was elected a fellow of the British Academy in 1966, and in 1968 received an honorary D.Litt. from Exeter University. He was appointed CBE in 1965 and knighted in 1972. He died in a London hospital 7 March 1975.

[*Sir Martin Davies* (with a bibliography), published by the trustees of the National Gallery, 1975; annual report of the council of King's College, Cambridge, November 1975; Michael Levey, 'Sir Martin Davies', *Burlington Magazine*, vol. cxvii, 1975; Ellis Waterhouse in *Proceedings* of the British Academy, vol. lxi, 1975; personal knowledge.]

GREGORY MARTIN

DAVIES, RHYS (1901–1978), novelist and short story writer, was born Rees Vivian Davies 9 November 1901 at 6 Clydach Road, Blaenclydach, Tonypandy, the second of three sons and the fourth of the six children of Thomas Rees Davies, grocer, of Blaenclydach, and his wife, Sarah Ann Lewis, a teacher, of Maerdy, mid Glamorgan. He attended Porth County School from 1913 to 1916, but found more important food for his imaginative development at the local Miners' Institute library, where he read translations of *Candide*, *Madame Bovary*, and Émile Zola's *Drink*. When he went to live in London in 1918, he closely observed his colleagues in offices and shops and, in his own significant phrase, 'stripped them as social beings'. Eventually his mind turned back to the Welsh valleys he had left, and he tells us in his autobiography, *Print of a Hare's Foot* (1969), that he set about 'ridding Anglo-Welsh writing of flannel and bringing some needed flesh tints to it'. From childhood he associated the fresh flannel shirt put on before chapel services with the pressures and torments of strict nonconformity. Caradoc Evans had done something to relieve them but his stories lacked humanity. The time had come to give the flesh ease and bring out its bloom.

Rhys Davies met Charles Lahr, owner of the Progressive Bookshop, and in 1927 three of

Davies's 'carnal stories' appeared in the *New Coterie*, a quarterly handled by Lahr. In the same year *The Song of Songs and Other Stories* (with a portrait of Davies by William Roberts as frontispiece), another tale, *Aaron*, and his first novel, *The Withered Root*, were published. The novel contains three memorable characters (Reuben, his mother, and Morgans) and shows intensity of feeling in its account of a young collier's leading a revival in Wales, but the last three chapters, intended to show the triumph of flesh over spirit, are less credible.

Davies now became a professional writer and, with an advance from an American publisher, spent some months of 1928–9 in Paris and Nice. His autobiography includes a description of a visit to D. H. Lawrence [q.v.] at Bandol that is acute, and Lawrence's letters reveal that he appreciated the Welshman's good nature and trusted him. When Davies returned to London he carried with him the complete typescript of Lawrence's proscribed poems *Pansies* and evaded a customs seizure.

He applied himself to writing and, by 1939, produced a further ten volumes of stories and six more novels, three of them chronicling over eighty years the impact of industrialization on a Welsh mining valley. Between 1939 and 1941 he worked as a civilian at the War Office, but managed to bring out *Tomorrow to Fresh Woods* (1941), an affectionate evocation of growing up in the coalfield. *The Black Venus* (1944) is set in rural Wales and gives us Olwen Powell's spiritedly comic defence of 'bundling', the old practice of courting on a bed. Rhys Davies's delight in unconventional people is evident in *The Dark Daughters* with May, whose theatrical temperament prepares us for Guy Aspen, the musical-comedy idol, and his mother, in the *The Painted King* (1954). Three other novels were printed by 1960. Davies was also prolific in short stories, and five new collections of his appeared between 1942 and 1967. The last of them took as its title *The Chosen One* (1967), from the tale printed in the *New Yorker* which won the Edgar award for the best short story published in the United States in 1966.

Two further novels were published: *Nobody Answered the Bell* (1971), an account of a lesbian relationship, and *Honeysuckle Girl* (1975), a study of the mind and actions of a heroin addict.

Davies was a friendly, generous man, who loved London and the theatre. He enjoyed 'cultivating ruined characters', a claim which shows that the question put by Sybil in his last novel came from his heart: 'Why can't people accept without resentment that a woman or a man need not conform?' His wry sense of humour made for tolerance, though he is not too kind towards himself. The title of his detached autobiography suggests that he was too quick to seek solitude and would leave little trace behind him, but some of his novels and many of his stories will preserve his name as a writer who could command many moods and a fine exactness of expression.

He died 21 August 1978 at University College Hospital, London. He had already chosen a dozen of his best stories for republication, and they appeared as *The Best of Rhys Davies* (1979). He was unmarried.

[Rhys Davies, *Print of a Hare's Foot* (autobiography), 1969; R. L. Mégroz, *Rhys Davies, a Critical Sketch*, 1932; A. Huxley (ed.), *The Letters of D. H. Lawrence*, 1932; David Rees, *Rhys Davies*, Cardiff, 1975; private information.]

CECIL PRICE

D'AVIGDOR-GOLDSMID, SIR HENRY JOSEPH, second baronet (1909–1976), politician and bullion broker, was born at Somerhill, Kent, 10 June 1909, the elder son (there were no daughters) of (Sir) Osmond Elim d'Avigdor-Goldsmid, first baronet (created 1934) and his wife, Alice, daughter of Joseph Landau, of Warsaw. Osmond d'Avigdor had assumed by royal licence the name and arms of Goldsmid on succeeding to the Goldsmid settled estates in 1896. 'Harry', as he was always called, united both in blood as well as name the vitality, attitudes, and temperaments of two Jewish banking dynasties—the Goldsmids, established and respected in London since the late eighteenth century, and the d'Avigdors, brilliant sensitive sophisticates from Nice.

He had himself an almost Renaissance range and depth of abilities—intellectual, artistic, political, social, soldierly, and financial: a commanding personality and appearance; wit, bravery, patriotism, a sense of public and Jewish service, and a capacity for friendship and family life. He was capable of swift changes of mood: he could be impatient, he could not tolerate fools, he was easily bored. Despite all his talents things did not come easily to him: he was introspective, self-doubting, and drove himself by sustained self-discipline.

He was educated at Harrow and at Balliol College, Oxford. He obtained second class honours in philosophy, politics, and economics in 1931. In Oxford he met a number of gifted contemporaries in the literary world, forming friendships that lasted for the rest of his life. On leaving Balliol he went into the family firm of Mocatta and Goldsmid, bullion brokers. In business his honesty, shrewdness, prudence, and judgement of people brought him success. He was also to be an able manager of the large family estates which he inherited. In 1940 his father died and he succeeded to the title.

In the same year he married Rosemary Margaret, former wife of Sir Peter James Cunliffe Horlick, third baronet, and daughter of Lt.-Col. Charles Rice Iltyd Nicholl. He was already serving in the Royal Armoured Corps (the Royal West Kent Regiment) having got himself transferred from staff duties. Overcoming a strong sense of fear he led a reconnaissance unit during the campaign in north-west Europe with courage and resourcefulness, and was wounded. He won the MC (1945) and two mentions in dispatches, and was appointed to the DSO (1945). He ended the war with the rank of major.

Between 1945 and 1955 he worked as a bullion broker with Mocatta & Goldsmid, and served in local government in Kent, rising to be leader of the Conservatives on the county council.

Entering politics as Conservative member for Walsall in 1955, he became devoted to and beloved by his constituents, to whom he was endlessly patient and helpful. In the House of Commons he was rapidly accepted as a financial authority and rose to the chairmanship of important all-party committees, including the select committee on public expenditure. On two occasions, by short, moderate, rational speeches, he effectively demolished efforts to outlaw the Jewish ritual method of slaughter. He was parliamentary private secretary (1955–6) to Duncan Sandys (later Lord Duncan-Sandys) when minister of housing. He was no orator, but was widely liked and respected. Why he never became a minister is a mystery. Perhaps he was too successful to be invited to junior office; perhaps his uncompromising and fearless opinions and his contempt for mediocrity made him seem too mature for team work. He resigned his seat at the 1974 election.

In parallel with his business and his political lives he was active in public service—JP (1949), high sheriff of Kent (1953), deputy lieutenant (1949). He inherited from his father a strong sense of Jewish community service. For twenty-five years he was president of the Jewish Colonization Association, set up and endowed by Baron de Hirsch in 1892 to spend its revenue to establish and train Russian Jews as farmers in South America. Judging that, had Israel then existed, it would have been there that the baron would have wished to establish Jewish farming communities, d'Avigdor-Goldsmid, over time, redeployed the main efforts of the JCA from the Americas to Israel. His was a notable, strong, and effective presidency. He was also chairman of the Anglo-Israel Chamber of Commerce and chairman of both Bank Leumi (UK) and of the Anglo-Israel Bank. He accepted the caretaker chairmanship of Pergamon Press which he worked effectively to re-establish from 1969 to 1971 in close co-operation with Robert Maxwell, the ousted former chairman who rejoined the board as a non-executive director and eventually re-assumed his old post.

At his fine inherited home at Somerhill in Kent d'Avigdor-Goldsmid established a warm and strong family and social life with his wife and their two daughters. It was there that he increased his family collection of paintings and books, wrote his contributions to the *Times Literary Supplement* and other book reviews, entertained a wide circle of friends, built up a stable, and made himself a bold rider to hounds. But it was there also that the zest for life left him when his beloved elder daughter Sarah died in a sailing accident at sea in 1963. Though he forced himself to carry on his activities, and though his sparkle and wit sometimes returned, he never recovered.

He was a man of rich and varied gifts; high principle; public spirit; a proud independence of character and judgement; and a brilliant intellect—with a keen eye for the ridiculous. Despite all his achievements his potential was never fully realized. In 1974 he became an honorary freeman of Walsall. He died in Eaton Mansions, London, 11 December 1976 and was succeeded in the baronetcy by his brother, Major-General James Arthur d'Avigdor-Goldsmid (born 1912).

[*The Times*, 13, 14, and 15 December 1976; private information; personal knowledge.]

KEITH JOSEPH

DAVIS, JOSEPH (1901–1978), billiards and snooker player, was born 15 April 1901 at Whitwell, Derbyshire, the eldest in the family of three sons and three daughters of Fred Davis and his wife, Ann-Eliza Clark. While he was still at elementary school at Newbold, he spent virtually every spare moment in the billiard room of his father's public house, the Queen's Hotel in Whittington Moor, another Derbyshire village, developing the skill which was to enable him to win the World Professional Billiards Championship four times and hold the World Professional Snooker title continuously from 1927 until he relinquished it in 1946. The youngest child of this family, Fred junior, is the only other player to have held the world title at both games though, unlike Joe, he never did so simultaneously.

Davis was only thirteen when he won the Chesterfield and District Amateur Billiards Championship. He practised assiduously at the home of his coach, Ernest Rudge, who also staged exhibitions in the area featuring leading exponents whom his protégé might thus study at first hand. He managed various billiard halls in which his family or Rudge had an interest and after very few professional engagements won the Midland Professional Billiards Championship in 1922 and also the (later defunct) Second

Division Championship, which gave him right of entry to the World Championship.

He was well beaten by Tom Newman as happened again when, much more experienced, he next entered in 1926, but after losing narrowly to Newman in 1927 he beat him by a small margin to win the title in 1928. After retaining the title in 1929, 1930, and 1932, he was beaten in 1933 and 1934 by the Australian Walter Lindrum [q.v.], the only player in the history of the game whom either statistics or informed opinion rated above him.

No other sport has been so thoroughly conquered by its leading practitioners as billiards was in the late twenties and early thirties by Lindrum, Davis, Newman, and the New Zealander, Clark McConachy. Their very mastery killed billiards as a public spectacle.

Among the scoring feats of this era which now seem more appropriate to the realms of fantasy, Davis himself was prouder of the break of 1,247 with which, having occupied the non-striker's chair for two and a half sessions, he immediately responded to Lindrum's world record of 4,137 than of such efforts as 2,501 in the championship against Newman, 2,002 under a new baulk line rule designed to limit the potency of nursery cannons, and 1,784 under an even more stringent baulk line rule.

From his days managing billiard halls round Chesterfield, however, he knew that snooker was increasingly becoming the people's game. The establishment was slow to appreciate snooker's possibilities but Davis and a Birmingham equipment trader, Bill Camkin, prevailed on the then governing body, the Billiards Association and Control Council, to sanction a professional snooker championship in the 1926–7 season. Davis, who won the title with ease, pocketed £6 10s. 0d. for his trouble.

Davis was an innovator in that, in the time he could spare from billiards, he evolved the positional and break building shots, sequences, and techniques which are taken for granted nowadays but which were then far in advance of the rudimentary assets of his rivals.

In January 1928 he made the first public snooker century break, exactly 100, of the 687 he made in public before his retirement in 1964. He retained the world title annually with little apparent difficulty until his younger brother Fred extended him to 17–14 in the 1939 semi-final and 37–35 in the 1940 final. By this time snooker had become the premier billiard table game. The World Professional Billiards Championship had lapsed and the UK Professional Billiards Championship, won annually by Davis from 1934 until 1939, did not attract a level of public interest commensurate to the skill displayed. By 1938 he had gradually increased the record snooker break to 138.

During the war he raised over £125,000 for war charities and appeared on various variety stages including the London Palladium with a trick shot performance involving the use of a large tilting mirror. In 1946 Davis won the last of his fifteen world professional snooker titles. His skill and personality had brought snooker to its first peak of popularity but his decision to retire from world championship play while continuing to compete in other tournaments devalued the game's premier event and contributed to a decline which reached its nadir in the suspension of the championship from 1957 until 1964. As the best player (even when he was not officially champion), the chairman of the players' body, the partner with the biggest say in who played at Leicester Square Hall, then the showcase of professional snooker, Davis virtually ran the game. He also wrote several books on the techniques of playing. Outside the world championship, professional tournaments were conducted on a handicap basis with Davis inevitably the back marker. Victory confirmed his superiority, defeat did not threaten his pre-eminence. In his entire career he lost only four matches on level terms, all of them to his brother Fred.

In 1951 and 1954 he made century breaks in three consecutive frames and in 1955, having just made a break of 146, he achieved his dearly held ambition of a break of 147, the first time a player had potted fifteen reds, fifteen blacks, and all the colours in one break in record conditions. He was appointed OBE in 1963 shortly before his retirement.

In 1921 he married Florence Stevenson; they had a son and a daughter. This marriage was dissolved in 1931 and in 1945 he married the singer June Malo, daughter of William Warrent Triggs, a consultant engineer and patent agent. Davis died 10 July 1978 at Grayshott.

[Joe Davis, *The Breaks Came My Way*, 1976; Clive Everton, *The Story of Billiards and Snooker*, 1979; private information; personal knowledge.] CLIVE EVERTON

DAY-LEWIS, CECIL (1904–1972), poet laureate and detective novelist, was born 27 April 1904 at Ballintubbert, Queen's county (now county Laois), Ireland, the only child of the Revd Frank Cecil Day-Lewis, Church of Ireland curate, and his wife, Kathleen Blake, daughter of William Alfred Squires, civil servant. His mother died when he was four and he was brought up in London by his father and his selfless aunt Agnes Olive ('Knos') Squires. Educated at Wilkie's preparatory school, London, and Sherborne, he entered Wadham College, Oxford, in 1923 with a classics exhibition. He began writing verse as a schoolboy and, sure of his poetic vocation, he chose mainly literary friends and acquaintances at Oxford. During his third year there he met the undergraduate W. H. Auden [q.v.], the major influence on his early work. Their collaboration continued through 1927–8 when Day-Lewis held a teaching post at Summer Fields preparatory school in Oxford. Together they edited *Oxford Poetry 1927*. Day-Lewis obtained a second class in classical honour moderations in 1925 and a third in *literae humaniores* in 1927.

After his two early slim volumes of verse, more or less 'Georgian' in style, *Beechen Vigil* (1925) and *Country Comets* (1928). Day-Lewis became more rigorous with *Transitional Poem* (1929). This sequence was the first public manifestation of what was to become known as the Auden Gang or, as their unsympathetic contemporary Roy Campbell [q.v.] satirically put it, the MacSpaunday (Louis MacNeice, Stephen Spender, W. H. Auden, C. Day-Lewis) beast. Though this poetic movement was really little more than a convenient pigeon-hole for critics its supposed members were contemporaries subject to the weather of the times and responding to it with a similar leftish stance. Day-Lewis in particular remained spellbound by Auden's work. Though private themes often provided a framework they were used to question the social order and brimmed with Audenesque images and metaphors drawn from natural science. His sequences from *From Feathers to Iron* (1931) and *The Magnetic Mountain* (1933) to *A Time to Dance* (1935) and *Noah and the Waters* (1936) were exuberant, eclectic, and voguish enough to make him fashionable but delayed the finding of his true voice as a lyric poet of nature and private emotion. At the same time he provided a critical manifesto for the young poets of his generation, *A Hope for Poetry* (1934), claiming Gerard Manley Hopkins, Wilfred Owen, and T. S. Eliot [q.v.] as their immediate ancestors.

He had married in 1928 when he took his second teaching post at Larchfield School, Helensburgh, near Glasgow. His wife was (Constance) Mary, daughter of one of his former Sherborne form-masters, Henry Robinson King. Two years later he moved to Cheltenham Junior School in Gloucestershire. By 1934 he had two sons as well as a wife to support and it was primarily to make money that he became the detective novelist Nicholas Blake. His *A Question of Proof* (1935), set at a prep. school mixing aspects of those he had taught at, proved to be the first of twenty Blake novels mostly featuring the detective Nigel Strangeways. Its success was a factor in encouraging him to retire from teaching to become a full-time writer and political activist, in December 1935. He joined the Communist Party three months later and there followed two intense years when he wrote three straight novels, two detective novels, weekly book reviews, and many polemical pamphlets and essays. He was in demand as a speaker and lecturer and in the organization of the tiny Gloucestershire branch of the party. By early 1938 he had decided he must make a choice between 'being an amateurish political worker or trying to make myself a better poet'. Poetry won.

In order to break with political and public life he moved with his family to a secluded thatched cottage on an upper slope of Castle Hill above Musbury, a straggling east Devon village, in August 1938. It was a move crucial to his poetic development. In *Overtures to Death* (1938) the verse concerned with the possibilities of heroic action had been overshadowed by that where the political militant retired to wait for the inevitable disaster of war. As Auden sailed for the United States, Day-Lewis found his new and true home close to the Dorset border, and Thomas Hardy [q.v.] country. With his translation of Virgil's *Georgics* (1940) and his own verse collections *Word Over All* (1943) and *Poems 1943–1947* (1948) he achieved his full stature as a poet. The Hardy influence now predominated. He could parody his idol as in 'Singing Children: Luca della Robbia', part of the 'Florence: Works of Art' section of *An Italian Visit* (1953). He could make pastiche as in 'Birthday Poem for Thomas Hardy' in the 1948 collection. More importantly he was able to absorb and transmute the influence into a voice unmistakably his own. His poetry in this period reflected his private concerns, his responses to war, his Devon neighbours and their landscape, his divided emotional life.

After a hilarious period in command of Musbury's Home Guard platoon he went to London in the spring of 1941 to become an editor in the Ministry of Information's publications division. In 1946, soon after his release from the ministry, he became senior reader for the publishers Chatto and Windus, an association that lasted until the end of his life. Increasingly through this decade there was a conflict between the private Devon poet nourished by the countryside and the public London literary figure, the conscientious committee man.

This conflict was echoed in his emotional life. In 1939–41 he took part in a volcanic love affair with the wife of a neighbouring Musbury farmer, dwelt on in several poems and the final somewhat autobiographical Nicholas Blake story *The Private Wound* (1968). They had a son. From 1941 he began a more complete relationship with the novelist Rosamond Lehmann, commuting for the rest of the decade between her and his family at Musbury. She inspired some good poems, she broadened his personality, and she encouraged him to travel abroad and to take on such tasks as the 1946 Clark lectures at Cambridge. Such a divided life was a great strain on all concerned. At the end of 1949 he fell in love again, this time with the twenty-four-year-old actress Jill Angela

Henriette Balcon, daughter of Sir Michael Balcon [q.v.], film producer. The following year he left both Mary and Rosamond for a second marriage with Jill, which took place after the dissolution of his first marriage in 1951. There were two sons (one of whom was to write his father's biography) of the first marriage, and a daughter and a son of the second.

In the last two decades of his life he looked wistfully back towards Dorset, the county of his school-days as well as Hardy, and to his Irish roots. But he settled against becoming the rural regional poet that he might have been and opted permanently for London and the literary life. With every passing year the profile of his public honours and responsibilities moved upwards and the one indicating critical esteem curved in the opposite direction. In 1951, the year in which his translation of Virgil's *Aeneid* commissioned by the BBC was broadcast as part of the Festival of Britain, he was elected Oxford professor of poetry. His five-year term opened a period when he became more preoccupied with public poetry reading, mainly in partnership with his second wife, prestigious lectureships, and his public-spirited work for organizations like the Apollo Society, the Royal Society of Literature (he received its C.Lit. in 1965), and the Arts Council. His taste for public honours was most gratified in 1968 when he was chosen to succeed John Masefield [q.v.] as poet laureate, the first Irish-born holder of that office since Nahum Tate (1652–1715) [q.v.]. He also received honorary degrees from Exeter (1965), Trinity College, Dublin, (1968), and Hull (1970). In 1968 he became an honorary fellow of Wadham College and was elected to the Irish Academy of Letters.

Though no longer fashionable and much diverted by this public activity, his work as a publisher, and the raising of a second family, he continued to regard the writing of poetry as the point of his life. His final volumes of verse, *Pegasus* (1957), *The Gate* (1962), *The Room* (1965), and *The Whispering Roots* (1970), were received with woundingly faint praise by reviewers. They nevertheless contain some of Day-Lewis's best poems and display a mature mastery of craftsmanship and a fluency of technique that delighted his discriminating band of admirers. His themes ranged from the public and prosaic to those private explorations of love and living that put him firmly in the poetic family of Hardy, Edward Thomas [q.v.], and Robert Frost. His health declined after 1969 and he died 22 May 1972 at Lemmons, Hadley Wood, Hertfordshire, the home of the novelists Elizabeth Jane Howard and Kingsley Amis. Appropriately he is buried at Stinsford in Dorset only a few feet from Hardy's grave and less than thirty miles from the Devon border country where he found his voice.

Day-Lewis was a man of considerable generosity, charm, and elegance who laughed easily and was as stylish in his movements as in his dress. In his younger days he had a light lyric tenor voice very effective in the Irish songs of Tom Moore he learned at his aunt's knee, and good enough to be heard several times on BBC radio. If he loved women and was always vulnerable to them he was also good at making and keeping friends of both sexes. He was a tireless advocate of English literature in general and poetry in particular and unsparing in his encouragement of younger writers in whom he found any glimmer of talent.

A 1946 portrait of Day-Lewis by Lawrence Gowing was commissioned by Rosamond Lehmann and is the property of Sean and Nicholas Day-Lewis.

[C. Day-Lewis, *The Buried Day* (autobiography), 1960; Sean Day-Lewis, *C. Day-Lewis: An English Literary Life*, 1980; personal knowledge.]

SEAN DAY-LEWIS

DEAN, BASIL HERBERT (1888–1978), theatrical producer, was born 27 September 1888 in Croydon, south London, the second son and second of the four children of Harding Hewar Dean, cigarette manufacturer, of Sanderstead, near Croydon, and his wife, Elizabeth Mary Winton. He was educated at Whitgift Grammar School, Croydon. After leaving school he spent two years in the Stock Exchange and then joined the repertory company at Manchester run by Miss A. E. F. Horniman [q.v.]. After four years' training as an actor and playwright, in 1911 he directed an experimental theatre season in Liverpool. That year he became the first director of the Liverpool Repertory Theatre (later the Playhouse). In 1913 he became assistant stage director at His Majesty's, London.

On the outbreak of World War I in 1914 Dean joined the Cheshire Regiment. By 1917 he had risen to the rank of captain and the directorship of the entertainment branch of the Navy and Army Canteen Board (later the NAAFI), with control of fifteen theatres and ten touring companies. After the war he began operations in London as managing director of a syndicate—Reandean. With his partner, Alec Lionel Rea, he leased St. Martin's Theatre. Under Reandean a series of notable productions was staged including plays by John Galsworthy, W. Somerset Maugham, Sir James Barrie, and Clemence Dane [qq.v.]. Dean had two particular successes: *The Constant Nymph* (1926) by Margaret Kennedy [q.v.], and *Hassan* (1923), by James Elroy Flecker [q.v.], both of which Dean dramatized with the authors. For the latter, a spectacular oriental drama, he commissioned the music from Frederick Delius [q.v.], the choreography from Léonide Massine, and the costumes from

George Harris. The cast was also illustrious and the production lavish.

Dean was a perfectionist and, because he never learned to suffer fools gladly, he made many enemies. He was meticulous about detail and had a high respect for his technical staff, the importance of whose contribution to a production he always generously acknowledged. He was less loved by actors because of his dictatorial methods as a director. He was a pioneer in the use of stage lighting, importing new equipment from Germany and the United States, as well as devising equipment of his own.

In 1924 he was employed as joint managing director of Drury Lane Theatre in an attempt to revitalize it. In the press he spoke of making Drury Lane a site for a permanent national theatre, but his remarks were greeted with derision, and the idea of a state subsidy for theatre ignored. Dean, however, was one of the first advocates of a national theatre and for a permanent ensemble of actors as outlined by Harley Granville-Barker [q.v.]. 'There is always better work accomplished', he said in an interview in 1958, 'when it is possible to have corporate effort and a corporate spirit. It is like a football team, the closer and longer you are together, the more goals will be scored.'

Dean's estrangement from Alec Rea led to the break up of Reandean in 1929. In that year he became first chairman and joint managing director of Associated Talking Pictures, which he had founded (this later became Ealing Studios). During the 1930s Dean's career fluctuated between film and theatre: (Dame) Gracie Fields [q.v.] always felt indebted to him that he had made her into 'a real film star'. His first love remained theatre and in the late 1930s Ealing Studios, feeling that the theatre was claiming too much of his time, forced his resignation. J. B. Priestley at once offered him a lifeline by inviting him to go into management in order to produce mainly Priestley plays, of which three were done: *When We Are Married* (1938), *Johnson over Jordan* (1939), and *An Inspector Calls* (1946).

At the approach of World War II Dean wrote pamphlets outlining what could be done by the entertainments industry to sustain national morale not only among the armed services but also among factory workers and the civilian population. When war broke out he became director of entertainments for the Navy, Army, and Air Force Institutes and put forward the name ENSA (Entertainments National Service Association). During six and a half years more than 80 per cent of the entertainments industry gave it service in 2,500,000 performances of plays, revues, and concerts before 3,000,000 people in the Services and industry. Richard Llewellyn, Dean's assistant at the time, described him as a 'monolith, a kindly—sometimes—tyrant, a bully.... But his was the influence, the hand on the wheel, that never faltered.'

After the war Dean directed a Priestley play for the Old Vic Company in the West End, organized the first British Repertory Theatre Festival in 1948, and directed revivals of *Hassan* and other plays in various countries. He also wrote a good deal, including an official history of ENSA and two volumes of autobiography. He contributed to this Dictionary the notice of L. L. Henson.

Dean was thrice married. In 1914 he married Esther, daughter of Albert Henry Van Gruisen, of Oxton, Cheshire; they had three sons. This marriage was dissolved in 1925, the year in which he married Lady Mercy Greville (the actress Nancie Parsons), daughter of Francis Richard Charles Guy Greville, fifth Earl of Warwick, MP; they had one daughter. This marriage was dissolved in 1933 and in 1934 Dean married Victoria, daughter of Matthew Garfield Hopper, of Dunston on Tyne. This marriage was dissolved in 1948. Dean died at his home in Gloucester Place, London, 22 April 1978.

[Basil Dean, *Seven Ages, an Autobiography 1888–1927*, 1970, *Mind's Eye, an Autobiography 1927–1972*, 1973, and *The Theatre at War* (the official history of ENSA), 1956; Richard Fawkes, *Fighting for a Laugh: Entertaining the British and American Armed Forces, 1939–1946*; *The Times*, 24 April 1978; personal knowledge.] JAMES ROOSE-EVANS

DEAN, SIR MAURICE JOSEPH (1906–1978), civil servant, was born in London 16 September 1906, the youngest in the family of two daughters and two sons of William Joseph Dean, a schoolmaster, of Purley, Surrey, and his wife, Eleanor Maurais. Dean went to St. Olave's Grammar School, Southwark, from 1918 to 1925 and then won an open exhibition to Trinity College, Cambridge. He gained firsts in both parts of the mathematical tripos (1926 and 1928), was senior scholar and a wrangler, and was awarded the Mayhew prize (in applied mathematics) and the Walker prize. He was president of Trinity Mathematical Society, 1927–8. His brother, W. R. Dean, later became Goldsmid professor of mathematics at University College, London.

Having won first place in the Home Civil Service examination, Dean joined the Air Ministry in October 1929. In 1934 he became private secretary to the chief of the air staff, Sir Edward Ellington [q.v.], and subsequently to his successor, Cyril (later Lord) Newall. In January 1937 he moved to the air staff secretariat of which he became head in 1940 and later in June 1943 the assistant under-secretary of state.

This was a long, friendly and fruitful association covering the scientifically exciting and acutely demanding tasks which produced the

Royal Air Force of the early days of the war. Dean made many lasting friendships as a result of working closely with those RAF officers who were to lead the RAF throughout the war, particularly C. F. A. Portal (later Viscount Portal of Hungerford, q.v.) and (Sir) Arthur Harris. This sense of having worked with great men never left him. It extended to the scientists who harnessed their inventions to aerial warfare. His mathematical education, intellectual stature, sympathy, and understanding enabled him to develop an abiding but not uncritical love for the RAF and a belief in the relevance and efficacy of air power. This is reflected in his book *The Royal Air Force and Two World Wars* (1979) which he completed just before he died. To this Dictionary he contributed the notices of Sir A. G. R. Garrod, Lord Newall, and Sir W. J. Worboys.

In 1946 Dean followed his old chief, Sir Arthur Street [q.v.], to the Control Commission for Germany and Austria and the German section of the Foreign Office. He spent roughly a year in each as a deputy secretary. He moved to the Ministry of Defence in 1948, had a brief spell in the Treasury as a third secretary in 1952 where he was head of the overseas co-ordination section, and moved on from there at the end of the year as a second secretary to the Board of trade. From 1955 to 1963 he was permanent under-secretary of state in the Air Ministry. Nothing could have pleased him more.

It was during this period that the Royal Air Force was assuming its role as the provider of the British nuclear deterrent through the creation of the V Bomber force; there was the ill-fated Suez campaign, strong inter-Service arguments about the defence of a dwindling Empire and the respective roles of naval and air power, including not least the contribution that land-based aircraft could make at sea and in transport; together with arguments about the organization of the Ministry of Defence and the future of the Service ministries and the Ministry of Supply. In these, and other issues, Dean played a major part. It was he, for example, who arranged for a number of eminent scientists to come together to advise the Air Ministry about strategic policy and weapons. He stood strongly for the maximum use of air power in general and for the retention of Coastal Command by the Royal Air Force. He argued for the transfer of the supply function from the Ministry of Supply to the Air Ministry. He disagreed with, and was much saddened by, the moves towards the unification of the Service departments and their eventual integration into the Ministry of Defence, not least because he believed the result would be a large, cumbersome organization lacking in imagination and motivation.

This view and this prospective reorganization took Dean in 1963 away from defence for the remainder of his career. He was appointed an additional second secretary in the Treasury before becoming joint permanent secretary (April–October 1964) of the Ministry of Education. There the main tasks were to co-ordinate the work arising from Lord Robbins's report on higher education and from the report of the committee of inquiry into the organization of civil science. From 1957 to 1960 he was also a member of the Cambridge University Appointments Board and subsequently of the Cambridge University Women's Appointment Board. In October 1964 he was asked to become permanent secretary of the Ministry of Technology where he remained until he retired from the Civil Service at the end of June 1966.

Following his retirement he became a director of the British Printing Corporation, and was a visiting professor at the University of Strathclyde, which awarded him an honorary LLD (1970). He was a member of the 1972 review committee at the University of Birmingham and of the council of Bedford College, London.

Dean had outstanding intellectual abilities, a great capacity for meticulous analysis, an enquiring and innovating mind, and absolute integrity. Although there was a certain shyness about him and he carried a strong sense of authority, he was an outgoing man of much humour. He could express himself pungently and directly on occasion but rarely so as to give offence since his sense of humour was so well developed and his motives never in question. He had the rare gift of combining intellectual enthusiasm for solving problems with an abiding and positive interest in people. Indeed he sought to bring the right person to the right problem. He made a point of encouraging the young especially to extend their horizons and seek the future. He was above all a man of great personal kindness who enjoyed a particularly wide circle of friends. He had many outside interests, including music and golf; and he was no mean cabinet maker.

Dean was appointed CB in 1946, KCMG in 1949, and KCB in 1957.

In 1943 Dean married Anne Emalie, daughter of William Farquhar Gibson, building contractor, of Cardiff. They had a daughter and a son. Dean died at his home in Wimbledon 7 April 1978.

[Personal knowledge.] FRANK COOPER

DEAN, WILLIAM RALPH ('DIXIE') (1907–1980), footballer, was born 22 January 1907 in Birkenhead, the only son of William Dean, formerly an engine-driver on the Great Western Railway, who had transferred to the Wirral Railway so as to be near his girlfriend, at the time in domestic service at Birkenhead, whom he married. William Dean had four older sisters and one sister younger than himself.

From the age of five to fourteen he was at the Laird Street School, Birkenhead. At the age of eleven, however, he voluntarily joined also the Albert Industrial School—for delinquents—where he could play, occasionally, in a higher standard of football, and sometimes after doing an early milk round he played two football matches on the same day. He also joined the Boys' Brigade Club where there were facilities for athletics, tennis, and for golf, at which by the age of fifteen his handicap was 2, and later scratch. He also liked baseball, and much later in 1936 was a member of an England baseball team which played in London against a representative American team. He played football for the Birkenhead Schoolboys team at the age of twelve.

At fourteen he left school and became an apprentice at the Wirral Railway engine shop; he played football for their team in the West Cheshire League. It was always his ambition to play for the Everton Football Club in the Football League Division I. He first attracted the attention of Tranmere Rovers FC, who signed him on during the season 1923–4, when he played two matches for them. In the next season, 1924–5, he played 27 games for Tranmere in Football League Division III and one FA Cup tie and scored 28 goals, a remarkable feat for a lad of seventeen. Late in the season, to his great delight and after declining offers from other clubs, he was transferred to Everton FC, for which he played seven games in the season 1924–5. The transfer fee was £3,000.

Thirteen exciting years for Everton FC then followed, in which 'Bill' Dean (as he preferred to be called) played a major part. In the season 1925–6 he played 40 League and Cup matches and scored 33 goals. He had already become a local hero, called 'Dixie' apparently because of his black hair. There was consternation when in June 1926 he suffered a serious motor-cycle accident in which he sustained a fractured skull and other injuries. The general feeling was that he would never play again, certainly not to head the ball with his outstanding skill. However, he made a remarkable recovery. In the season 1926–7, he played in 31 League and Cup matches and scored 24 goals, and in addition he scored 12 goals in representative games and Internationals (in which he played for England). The following season, 1927–8, was to be his greatest. In 39 League games he scored 60 goals, as well as 3 goals in two FA Cup games. He also scored 37 goals in 15 International and representative games, which made a total of 100 in all first class matches. At the match against Arsenal there were 60,000 people to watch him score his sixtieth goal, and Everton won the championship. Dean was still only twenty-one years old.

During the next five seasons, he continued to score many goals—26, 23, 39, 45, and 24 in League matches and a total of 190 in all games. Injuries then began to limit his scope. In season 1929–30 he played in only 29 matches, scoring 26 goals, and his absence may have been one reason why his club was relegated to Division II. In 1930–1, however, they came back strongly to win promotion back to Division I, Dean scoring 39 goals in 37 matches. In 1931–2 he scored 45 goals in 38 League matches, and in 1933 he scored five goals in helping Everton to win the FA Cup.

During the following four seasons he was again frequently injured and his goal tally suffered. After playing many games in the reserve team in 1937–8 he was transferred in March 1938 to Notts County FC in Division III. The Merseyside Football public was surprised and shocked by this. Dean had scored 349 goals in 399 League games for Everton, and also 28 goals in 33 FA Cup ties. He had been captain for several seasons, and many felt that the manner of his departure had been ungracious. More than twenty years later, (Sir) John Moores gave him a job as a security officer and arranged a testimonial match in his honour.

Dean played a few games for Notts County, but broke a bone in his foot, and in January 1939 the club allowed him to leave. In the Football League, FA Cup, and other first class matches he had scored 473 goals in 505 games. In the League his average per match was 0.87, and in all 0.94. He had won 16 International caps, and scored three goals in a match 37 times. For a few months in 1939 he joined Sligo Rovers in Ireland, scoring 11 goals in 11 matches and helping them to the Irish Cup Final.

At the outbreak of war Dean joined the King's (Liverpool) Regiment and later the Royal Tank Regiment. After the war he became licensee of The Dublin Packet in Chester. In 1961 he returned to Liverpool and retired.

In 1931 Dean married Ethel, daughter of William Fossard, who worked in an insurance company. They had three sons and a daughter. Dean's wife died in 1974 and he himself had much ill health, having a leg amputated in 1976.

'Bill' Dean had strength of character, modesty, and principles of honour and sportsmanship. In his football he was always scrupulously fair. He was a remarkable header of the ball, jumping high above others and directing it well. He died 1 March 1980, perhaps as he would have wished, watching the match between Everton and their local rivals Liverpool FC at Goodison Park.

[Nick Walsh, *Dixie Dean*, 1977; Tony Pawson, *The Goalscorers. From Bloomer to Keegan*, 1978; *The Times*, 3 March 1980.] H. W. THOMPSON

DE BAISSAC, CLAUDE MARC BOUCHERVILLE (1907–1974), liaison officer with the French Resistance, was born 28 February 1907 at Curepipe, Mauritius, the younger son and youngest of three children of Marie Louis Marc de Boucherville Baissac and his wife, Marie Louise Jeannette Dupont. His father was a British subject of French origin and represented the Sun Insurance Company, of London. De Baissac attended school in Mauritius until he was sent as a boarder to the Lycée Henri IV in Paris where he finished his studies. He was physically strong, nearly six feet tall with brown hair and blue eyes, with an attractive personality, courage, resourcefulness, and a great zest for life.

Due to a change in family circumstances his father sent him to direct Mica Mine exploration in southern Madagascar in 1931, and he was the only European for miles around. In 1933 he returned to Paris and became publicity director for a film company. In 1937 he was appointed commercial director of Cie. Simmons, a light metal company. He left Paris in early 1940, crossing the Pyrenees on foot, and headed for the British consulate in Barcelona. He was arrested by the Spanish in Barcelona, and imprisoned for seven months. After his release he reached Gibraltar from where he was shipped to Glasgow.

He joined Special Operations Executive (SOE) in March 1942 and was dropped 'blind' on 30 July near Nîmes with Henri Peulevé [q.v.] as his wireless-telegraphy (W/T) operator and assistant. Although both landed badly, Peulevé breaking a leg and de Baissac spraining an ankle, they reached their safe house in Cannes. When his ankle had recovered, de Baissac proceeded to Bordeaux in accordance with his brief to train and lead a network of Frenchmen willing to resist enemy occupation. His chief contact was Grandclément, son of Admiral Grandclément, in charge of Region B of the OCM (Organisation Civile et Militaire), a grouping of men, mainly with a military or naval background, who were spread across occupied France. Region B extended from the Pyrenees to the Charente and was centred on Bordeaux, which was extremely important as a submarine base and port for the Far Eastern blockade-runners. De Baissac established contacts in the docks, and sent back vitally important information on the movement of ships and submarines, for which he was appointed to the DSO.

On 24 September 1942 de Baissac's sister Lise Villameur was dropped near Poitiers to establish another circuit and organize safe houses. On 1 November de Baissac received his new W/T operator Major Roger Landes MC. In December Charles Hayes arrived as arms instructor and Mary Herbert as courier. De Baissac was flown back to London on 13 March 1943 to report; he returned to France on 14 April. In May a second W/T operator, Marcel Defence, was sent to assist Landes in order to allow the latter to take a more active part in the organization, which had rapidly expanded to about 20,000 men under paramilitary training. In 134 parachute operations supplies had been received on ten different grounds. Sabotage attacks were made on aerodromes and railway lines, notably at Dax, Facture, Bayonne, La Réole, and against the transformer station at Belin. The last of these operations stopped traffic between Bordeaux and the Spanish frontier for about three weeks at a time when the Germans were pressing Franco to co-operate.

Trouble started in July with the arrest of Grandclément's wife and there were fears for the safety of the whole circuit. De Baissac was recalled to London on 15 August. The circuit remained active during the rest of the war under Landes's direction. It engaged in intensive sabotage shortly before D-day, attacking all the enemy communication targets at the time of the landings.

De Baissac's next mission was to Normandy, in preparation for a possible Allied landing. He was dropped near Chartres with his W/T operator on 10 February 1944. He once again built up small groups, mainly in the Orne and Calvados, which he armed and trained for sabotage action designed to demoralize the Germans and delay their movements after the landings. He received his sister Lise as courier, four more agents and W/T operators, and a group of SAS. He set up two sub-circuits to concentrate on intelligence work of value to Allied army commanders, and himself crossed back and forth through enemy lines. When overrun by the Americans in mid-August, he was flown out to London and promptly briefed for a further mission, which was cancelled in view of the pace of the Allied advance.

For his achievements in Normandy de Baissac received a bar to his DSO. The French gave him the croix de guerre with palm and made him a chevalier of the Legion of Honour.

In May 1945 de Baissac left SOE and joined General Koenig's staff at Châlons-sur-Marne as liaison officer to the Allied command. From November 1946 until he relinquished his commission in May 1947 he served with the Control Commission in Wuppertal.

He returned to mining and mineral interests in Africa and was later director of the Compagnie de Dépôt de Pétrolier in West Africa.

On 11 November 1944 in London, de Baissac married his former courier Mary Katherine, daughter of Brigadier-General Edmund Arthur Herbert, CMG, MVO, DL, JP: they had one daughter. The marriage was dissolved in 1959–60 and on 9 November 1964 at the British consulate in Yaoundé, Cameroons, de Baissac married Colette Françoise, daughter of Marcel Frédéric Avril, a commercial director. They retired to Aix-en Provence where de Baissac died 22 December 1974.

[SOE adviser; M. R. D. Foot, *SOE in France*, 1966; private information; personal knowledge.] VERA M. ATKINS

DE BEER, SIR GAVIN RYLANDS (1899–1972), zoologist and historian, was born 1 November 1899 at Malden, Surrey, the only son and elder child of Herbert Chaplin de Beer, journalist, and his wife, Mabel. Herbert was the son of Arnold de Beer and Irene Chaplin and his wife was the daughter of John Rylands and Anne Chaplin (sister of Irene).

He was educated by a tutor and governesses and then from 1909 to 1912 at the École Pascal in Paris, where his father was then working as correspondent of the Exchange Telegraph Company. He later went to Harrow from which he won a leaving scholarship and in 1917 he went with a demyship to Magdalen College, Oxford. After one term he became a second lieutenant in the Grenadier Guards and was posted to France but saw no fighting and served in the Army Education Scheme in the army of occupation.

Returning to Oxford in 1919 he took first class honours in zoology in 1921. He taught in the zoology department at Oxford until 1938, as demonstrator and Jenkinson memorial lecturer in embryology (from 1926). He also became a prize fellow of Merton College (1923) and sub-warden.

In 1938 he became reader, and in 1945 professor, in embryology at University College London until 1950. During World War II he served on the general staff, dealing with military intelligence and propaganda, and later in SHAEF as lieutenant-colonel in charge of psychological warfare in the field. He was stationed at the headquarters of Sir B. L. Montgomery (later Viscount Montgomery of Alamein, q.v.), and was concerned after the Normandy landing with supervising amplifier and leaflet units. From 1950 to 1960 he was director of the British Museum (Natural History) and in 1958 president of the 15th International Congress of Zoology. After retirement in 1960 he became director and later editorial consultant of the publishing firm of Thomas Nelson & Sons. He lived at Bex in Switzerland from 1965 to 1971.

De Beer was essentially an international scholar, both as a scientist and a humanist. As a boy he visited many countries and spoke and read fluently French, German, and Italian. From childhood he read widely and had a large memory. His major scientific work was on the structure of the skull. His treatise *The Development of the Vertebrate Skull* (1937) contains many anatomical facts but hardly mentions function, and reveals no new principles of morphology. He was interested in the early experiments on the development of embryos and his books on *Growth* (1924) and *An Introduction to Experimental Embryology* (1926) were successful pioneer summaries, made possible by his knowledge and capacity for orderly presentation. His most influential scientific writing was his analysis of the relationship between development of the embryo and evolutionary change. In his book *Embryology and Evolution* (1930) he demolished the widely held idea that the embryo recapitulates the history of its ancestors.

De Beer's interest in evolution was given full play when as director of the British Museum he organized the exhibits on evolution in the main hall and the publication of an authoritative *Atlas of Evolution* (1964), which was translated into German, Dutch, and Spanish. He was an expert on the life and works of Charles Darwin [q.v.] and devised a card index from which he could tell what Darwin was studying at any time. This led to an edition of *Darwin's Notebooks on the Transmutation of Species* (1960) and *Charles Darwin* (1963). To this Dictionary he contributed the notice of E. S. Goodrich.

De Beer was interested in humanism and wrote about the lives and ideas of individuals as different as Gibbon, Voltaire, Byron, Shelley, and Madame de Staël. His *Jean-Jacques Rousseau and his World* (1972) was published after his death. From childhood he was fascinated by Switzerland, its country, people, and place in history and in the world. He wrote many books and papers on tourism, climbing, and the history in that country, including *Alps and Elephants: Hannibal's March* (1955).

De Beer was of small stature but assertive character. With his pleasure in using his knowledge of languages and of historical matters he was a vivacious and interesting companion.

He was elected to fellowship of the Royal Society in 1940 and from 1946 to 1949 was president of the Linnean Society. He was a chevalier of the Legion of Honour and held honorary doctorates at the universities of Bordeaux, Lausanne, and Cambridge, and received the Darwin medal of the Royal Society (1958) and also the gold medal of the Linnean Society (1958). He was knighted in 1954 and was FSA.

In 1925 he married Cicely Glyn, daughter of the Revd Sir Hubert James Medlycott, sixth baronet, and Julia Ann Glyn. They had no children. De Beer died at Alfriston, Sussex, 21 June 1972.

[E. J. W. Barrington in *Biographical Memoirs of Fellows of the Royal Society*, vol. xix, 1973; personal knowledge.] J. Z. YOUNG

DE GUINGAND, SIR FRANCIS WILFRED (1900–1979), major-general, was born 28 February 1900 at Acton in Middlesex, the second of the four children and eldest of the three sons of Francis Julius de Guingand, a manufacturer of briar-root pipes, and his wife, Mary Monica Priestman. Educated at Ampleforth and the Royal Military College, Sandhurst, he was commissioned into the West Yorkshire Regiment (The Prince of Wales' Own) in December 1919. Two years later his regiment was serving in the 17th Infantry brigade at Cork in southern Ireland. The brigade-major was Captain (Brevet-Major) Bernard Montgomery (later Field Marshal Viscount Montgomery of Alamein, q.v.). It was as chief of staff to him, when he commanded the Eighth Army and 21st Army Group in World War II, that de Guingand became prominent.

Their paths crossed again when 'Freddie', as de Guingand was universally known, was at his regimental depot at York in 1922. Montgomery, on the staff of the 49th Territorial division, lived in the same officers' mess, and they struck up a friendship. Their paths then diverged; de Guingand, bored with regimental soldiering in England and keen to increase his income—he had expensive tastes: gambling, card-playing, and racing, as well as shooting and fishing—volunteered in 1926 to serve with the King's African Rifles in what was then Nyasaland, now Malawi. He stayed there for five years, acquiring a lifelong affection for Africa.

In 1932 he returned to his regiment as adjutant of its 1st battalion in Egypt, where Montgomery was commanding the 1st battalion of the Royal Warwickshire Regiment. On an important exercise Montgomery was made to act as brigade-commander, with de Guingand as his brigade-major. It was the first of several occasions on which, later in life, de Guingand was to claim that his cooler judgement saved Montgomery from the consequences of his own impetuousness. Montgomery was certainly impressed with his ability, and persuaded him to attempt the Staff College examination, rather than return to Nyasaland. De Guingand had left it late; but, in 1934, when he was in India, pressure from Montgomery obtained a nomination for him to the Staff College at Camberley. On graduation in 1936 he was appointed brigade-major to the Small Arms School at Netheravon, and was still there in June 1939 when he was posted as military assistant to the secretary of state for war, Leslie (later Lord) Hore-Belisha [q.v.]. This appointment gave him an insight both into the conduct of military affairs at the highest level and into its political aspects. His judgement in these matters was to prove sounder than Montgomery's.

When Hore-Belisha was dismissed in January 1940, de Guingand, at his own request, left also, being posted as an instructor, now in the rank of lieutenant-colonel, to the newly formed Middle East Staff College at Haifa, moving on from there at the end of the year to become the army member of the joint planning staff in Cairo. He became highly critical of his C-in-C, accusing Sir A. P. (later Earl) Wavell [q.v.] of taking an over optimistic view of the prospects of British intervention in Greece in May 1941.

He therefore welcomed Wavell's supersession by Sir Claude Auchinleck, whom he warmly admired. The admiration was mutual, Auchinleck appointing him as the director of military intelligence in February 1942, and subsequently, when he had taken direct command of the Eighth Army from General (Sir) Neil Ritchie and halted Rommel on the Alamein line in July of that year, as brigadier general staff at Eighth Army headquarters. De Guingand felt that his experience had qualified him for neither of these appointments. But his clarity and speed of mind, his sense of the possible, his ability to analyse a problem and draw together the different characters at work on it, made him the perfect staff officer.

It was therefore a fortunate chance which brought de Guingand at 7.30 a.m. on 13 August 1942 to the point near Alexandria where the road from Cairo joined the coastal road which led to El Alamein and eventually Tunis. There he met the newly arrived Montgomery. De Guingand expressed his disquiet at the general malaise of the Eighth Army. This was music to Monty's ears, and the dramatic results have been fully recorded. Montgomery announced that de Guingand was to be accepted as his chief of staff with full authority over all branches, logistic as well as operational. It was therefore something of a shock to be warned by his master a few days later that he had asked the War Office to replace him by Brigadier (Sir) Frank Simpson, his principal staff officer in a succession of his commands. Fortunately for both de Guingand and Montgomery, Sir Alan Brooke (later Viscount Alanbrooke, q.v.) refused; 'Freddie' stayed with 'Monty' until the war's end.

But then the intimate relationship, which had been established and which lasted until VE-Day, began to fall apart on the issue of where the credit lay for the decisions on which Montgomery's claim to fame rested. De Guingand never ceased to express the highest admiration for Montgomery, while acknowledging that he had defects of judgement and character which led him into error from time to time. In later years de Guingand claimed credit for the important change of plan in the later stages of the Battle of El Alamein, which led to the final breakthrough: for the change of plan at Mareth to switch the main effort far out to the left and for devising, with (Sir) Harry Broadhurst, the exceptional air support for it: for recognizing that the initial plans for the invasion both of Sicily and Normandy were unsound, and recommending the changes on which Montgomery insisted: all of these decisions Montgomery made much of as being his own. While fully supporting Montgomery against the criticisms levelled at him by Sir Arthur (later Lord) Tedder [q.v.] and others over the Normandy campaign, he never concealed his disagreement with his chief in the protracted argument with Eisenhower over the subsequent strategy and the need for an overall land force commander. De Guingand admitted failing to see the importance of an early clearance of the Scheldt estuary in order to open Antwerp as the Allies' main supply port, but took no responsibility for Arnhem, as he was away sick at the time.

Sickness, in the form of stomach trouble, which long after the war was diagnosed as due to a gallstone, removed de Guingand from the scene at several crucial periods, the first being after El Alamein. If the doctors then had had their way, his period as chief of staff to Montgomery would have been short; but Montgomery overruled them, and de Guingand used the opportunity to marry (in 1942) Arlie Roebuck Stewart, the beautiful Australian widow of a brother officer, Major H. D. Stewart, and daughter of Charles Woodhead, director of companies, of Brisbane. There was one daughter of the marriage, which was dissolved in 1957.

The disagreement between Montgomery and Eisenhower festered throughout the last winter of the war, and came to a head as a result of the former's tactless briefing of the press during the Ardennes campaign. His remarks were taken as an insult to the American generals, Bradley and Patton, and Eisenhower had drafted a signal to General Marshall protesting that he could stand it no longer. Fortunately his chief of staff, Bedell Smith, was on excellent terms with de Guingand who, in very hazardous weather, flew to see Eisenhower and flew back to persuade Montgomery to dispatch an apologetic signal. Eisenhower tore up his draft. De Guingand believed that he had saved his master from dismissal, and resented Montgomery's pretence in his memoirs that he had himself taken the initiative to send de Guingand to see Eisenhower.

He never forgave his chief for that and three other actions. The first was the brusque refusal to let de Guingand be present at the formal surrender of the Germans on Lüneburg Heath: the second, the failure to give him any part in the victory parade; and the final blow, the abandonment of his pledge to make de Guingand vice-chief of the imperial general staff, when he became the chief. The last blow was especially hard, not only because Simpson received the post, but because it was delivered in an offhand manner, and de Guingand, against medical advice and his own wishes, had taken up the post of director of military intelligence at the War Office in 1945 to prepare himself for it. He never knew that it was Alanbrooke who had insisted that Montgomery could not import his favourites from 21st Army Group into all the important posts in the War Office. He became major-general and left the army in 1946.

This bitter blow was almost certainly a blessing in disguise, since it forced him to turn his hand to business, at which, through the influence of friends and his own natural ability, he was successful, gaining an income which allowed him to indulge in his favourite activities, as bon viveur, gambler, and sportsman. His first venture was in Southern Rhodesia at the end of 1946 and he moved later to Johannesburg, becoming deputy chairman of Tube Investments Ltd. He left in 1960 to join the tobacco firm of Rothmans, as chairman of their subsidiary group in Britain. His first book, *Operation Victory*, published in 1947, was one of the first authoritative accounts of the war and ran into seven editions in hardback and three impressions in paperback. His other publications, *African Assignment* (1953), *Generals at War* (1964), and *From Brass Hat to Bowler Hat* (1979), were not of the same standard.

In addition to his clear and agile mind and his grasp of detail, one of his principal gifts was his ability to bring people of different views and interests together. He himself had an open mind and by nature was inclined to welcome strangers. All who worked with him regarded him with admiration and affection in equal proportions. He was the perfect foil to Montgomery. His imaginative and widely ranging mind, fertile with ideas, was subjected to his master's passion for simplification and concentration on one fundamental issue. He was to Montgomery what Berthier was to Napoleon, and perhaps more.

He was appointed OBE in 1942, CBE in 1943, KBE in 1944; CB in 1943, and to the DSO in 1942. He died in Cannes 29 June 1979.

[*The Times*, 19 November 1979; private information; personal knowledge.]

MICHAEL CARVER

DE LA BEDOYERE, COUNT MICHAEL ANTHONY MAURICE HUCHET (1900–1973), author, editor, and journalist, was born 16 May 1900 in St. Servan, Brittany, France, the only child of Vicomte Yvon Huchet de la Bedoyere and his wife, Sybil Emily, daughter of Anthony Wilson Thorold, bishop of Rochester and then bishop of Winchester [q.v.], and sister of Algar Thorold, biographer and journalist. The de la Bedoyeres were an old Breton family of whom the Vicomte was the first to gain acceptance in London, in the 1890s. Michael de la Bedoyere came under the influence of the Jesuits early, first at a school in Jersey, and then at Stonyhurst, where, being exceptionally gifted, he enjoyed the intellectual stimulus of work.

A creature of routine, at school he avoided organized sports; so far as he dared, he accepted them passively. Like quicksilver in tackling demanding problems, he gave such promise that soon the Jesuits were earmarking him as a likely candidate for the Society. He made few friendships; only once did he display a flash of indignation by taking part in a protest march against the school authorities during World War I. Having made his point, there was no come-back.

His decision to enter the Society, as a novice, seemed ill advised. In his nineteenth year and still unformed, he was possibly under the influence of over-zealous spiritual directors. After the rigorous training of noviciate, he enjoyed his Oxford interlude at Campion Hall, obtaining first class honours in 1928 in the newly-founded school of philosophy, politics, and economics. He was the only man in his year who took his finals in hospital, after recovering from peritonitis. Then he slowly realized that he was not only wasting his time but could no longer believe in Catholicism. The long crisis left him both bewildered and uncertain. He wandered through Europe and scarcely knew where to turn. It was a temporary lapse. His relatives advised him to wait and rest and gradually pull himself together. One person above all who imparted strength, love, and a new reason for living was Catherine Thorold, his cousin, then living in Florence. Eventually they became engaged and in 1930 they married. She was the daughter of Algar Labouchere Thorold.

Because of his grounding as a scholastic and philosopher, in 1930 he was invited to lecture in the University of Minnesota. His wife accompanied him, although neither of them wished to settle down in America. They returned in 1931 when their first child was expected. De la Bedoyere was helped to break into active journalism by his father-in-law, Algar Thorold, the editor of the *Dublin Review*, and the biographer and former kinsman of Henry Labouchere [q.v.] of *Truth*. Thorold made room for him in the advisory role of assistant editor. By now his first two books, both biographies, had appeared; *Lafayette* (1933) and *George Washington* (1935) were somewhat affected by his recent American experience and his Anglo-French inspiration.

Then came a touch of providence when the proprietor of the *Catholic Herald*, Charles Diamond, advertised for a young Catholic, possessing some journalistic experience and flair, who would learn the business and might eventually take over the paper on Diamond's death. De la Bedoyere responded at once and got the job. In 1934 the paper's circulation was meagre, its outlook was narrow, and its Irish influence still predominated. With the support of new members of his small staff, de la Bedoyere transformed the *Catholic Herald* in both content and readability. In five years circulation tripled for the paper became at once lively and radical, yet intellectual. At the height of the war its circulation had slowly risen to nearly six figures. De la Bedoyere had been influenced by his uncle, Algar Thorold, once a devoted disciple of Baron von Hügel. It was said of the new editor that he was 'ecumenical long before his time'. He also used forceful language, which was hardly designed for a weekly previously as traditional as this. There were strong critics of the paper, notably among the clergy. A number of bishops and priests tended to be hurt, even scandalized, by some of his articles and cavalier opinions, which were often controversial and disrespectful. Thus de la Bedoyere created difficulties for himself by being occasionally 'banned', for the *Catholic Herald* in the 1940s and 1950s still depended on church door sales. He retired as its editor in 1962.

De la Bedoyere also wrote numerous books. Apart from the essay he wrote in Edward Eyre's *European Civilization* (vol. v, 1936), he produced in the earlier part of World War II *Christian Crisis* (1940), *Christianity in the Market Place* (1943), and *No Dreamers Weak* (1944). The combination of writing and editing made his thoughts flow. Being independent-minded, he attacked political critics, including MPs and some members of (Sir) Winston Churchill's wartime government. He was never at a loss for pithy answers, particularly when false morality and dubious values were involved. He was the first, for example, to point out the destructive and totally disproportionate effects of area bombing; he was equally forthright in questioning the proposal for unconditional surrender by the Allies, as well as the betrayal of Poland by the Soviet Union at the end of the war.

He finally decided to retire after twenty-eight years as editor without too much regret. By then he had completed most of the serious work that he wanted to do. His best books, in both Britain and America, belonged to the closing period of his work. They included *Catherine, Saint of Siena* (1947), *Francis, a Biography of the Saint of Assisi* (1962), and *The Meddlesome Friar, the Story of the Conflict between Savonarola and Alexander VI* (1958); and studies of von Hügel (1951) and Fenelon's correspondence with Madame Guyon, entitled *The Archbishop and the Lady* (1956). He also wrote memoirs of Cardinal Griffin (1955) and Canon Cardijn (1958).

Great credit was due to him for his exceptional work as an editor, for he had, despite the claims of his worst critics, the power of seeing things in perspective. In 1962 he founded and edited (until 1968) *Search Newsletter*, a monthly, which won respect and had a sympathetic response. In a sense the second Vatican Council of the mid-1960s cut ground from under his feet, even before his premature retirement. He both contributed to and edited *Objections to Roman Catholicism* (1964), which attracted much attention and reflected the unchanged spirit of questioning authority which he had long embodied.

His first wife died in 1959 and in 1961 he married Charlotte, daughter of Julian Halbik, merchant. He had four sons and one daughter by his first marriage and two sons by his second. He died 13 July 1973 at The Priory, Roehampton Lane, London SW15.

[Private information; personal knowledge.]

ANDREW BOYLE

DE LA WARR, ninth EARL (1900–1976), government minister. [See SACKVILLE, HERBRAND EDWARD DUNDONALD BRASSEY.]

DELMER, (DENIS) SEFTON (1904–1979), journalist, was born in Berlin 24 May 1904, the only son and elder child of Professor Frederick Sefton Delmer and his wife, Mabel Hook. His father was an Australian lecturer in English at Berlin University and author of a standard textbook for German schools, *English Literature from Beowulf to Bernard Shaw* (1913). His mother was also Australian. 'Tom' Delmer was brought up to speak German and as late as 1939 still spoke English with a slight accent. At the outbreak of World War I his father was interned, and Delmer had the highly unusual experience of going to school in Berlin as an enemy alien. But he was not subjected to much persecution, and on the whole enjoyed himself. Professor Delmer was released in May 1917 and given permission to go to England. Delmer was then sent to St. Paul's School, Hammersmith, and from there won a scholarship to Lincoln College, Oxford, where he obtained a second class in German in 1927.

After the war his father returned to Germany and by 1927 was earning a living as a 'stringer' for a number of English newspapers in Berlin. It was here in that year while helping his father out that Delmer first caught the eye of Lord Beaverbrook [q.v.] who gave him a job on the *Daily Express*. Within a year he was back in Berlin as head of the paper's new bureau. He was only twenty-four and was destined to remain in Lord Beaverbrook's employment for another thirty years—something of a record.

Delmer, like many young Englishmen, threw himself into the social life of the Weimar republic, reporting with relish the stories of political scandal and corruption. He later laid great stress on the number of charlatans of one kind or another who at that time flourished in Germany and how when he first attended a Nazi meeting in Berlin in 1929 and heard Hitler exhorting his audience not to eat foreign fruit such as oranges, he dismissed him as yet another crackpot. Later however he became friendly with Ernst Rohm and as a result was the first British reporter to interview Hitler at his Brown House headquarters in Munich. Eventually he became so familiar with the Nazis that the Foreign Office suspected him of being a German agent. In 1932 he travelled in Hitler's aeroplane during his election campaign and the following year secured his most famous scoop when he walked through the burning Reichstag at Hitler's side. (He used to remark ruefully that when he phoned his story through to the *Daily Express*, the sub-editor was only interested in the details of the fire.) Delmer was later criticized in some quarters for his close Nazi contacts, but he regarded it as all part of a reporter's job. Besides which there is no doubt that he enjoyed himself immensely. In 1933 he was sent to Paris for a year as *Daily Express* correspondent, and in 1936 to Spain to report the civil war. He spent two years in Spain and at the outbreak of the war was in Poland and subsequently in Paris.

In September 1940 Delmer, who had been engaged to broadcast on the German Service of the BBC, was recruited by Special Operations Executive to organize what were known as 'Black Propaganda' broadcasts to Germany. The object was to sabotage the German war effort by spreading rumours and false reports. Delmer could not have had a job better suited to his background and talents. He began in May 1941 by inventing 'Der Chef', a right-wing German patriot opposed to the Nazis broadcasting to members of his secret organization apparently from within Germany. This was followed by several other RUs (research units) which ranged from bona fide Roman Catholic propaganda to astrology. Following the construction of the new 500 kw transmitter ('Aspidistra') at Crowborough in 1942 Delmer launched his most successful project, a pseudo-German forces programme 'Soldatensender Calais', a 'grey' station as opposed to 'black' which relied on its snappy presentation and especially its popular music to attract listeners among the German forces, even though many of them would know or suspect it to be an enemy wavelength. Though it was never possible precisely to estimate the effect of these various propaganda exercises, post-war research suggests that they did, in fact, contribute a great deal to the undermining of enemy morale. For his war work, Delmer was appointed OBE in 1946.

At the end of the war, after a short spell in Germany working for the Control Commission, Delmer rejoined the *Daily Express* as chief foreign affairs reporter. He covered virtually every major foreign news story until his departure from the paper in 1959, becoming an almost legendary Fleet Street figure, famous for his knack of being in the right place at the right time. In 1956 he was the only British reporter in Poland at the time of the Poznan riots. The same year he was expelled from Egypt after he described President Nasser as a 'frightened Pharaoh'. Two months later he marched with Hungarian rebels in Budapest and secured an exclusive interview with Colonel Pal Maleter, leader of the insurgents who was later executed by the Russians. Germany, however, remained his chief interest and he was always quick to point out any sign of Nazi resurgence.

Delmer's eventual departure from the *Daily Express* was blamed by colleagues on his increasingly extravagant expenses claims, which were by then very much part of the legend. 'I can only think clearly in a five-star hotel', he once said. He liked to have a suite at his disposal and lavish hospitality laid on to entertain his guests. In 1959 Lord Beaverbrook dismissed him and he retired to his idyllic farmhouse in Suffolk where he wrote two volumes of autobiography which contain a great deal of valuable historical material, though he never managed to shed his reporter's style. In 1963–4 he returned to Germany and spent a year as editorial adviser to *Der Spiegel.* He also published *The Counterfeit Spy* (1973), an account of the successful attempt to deceive the Germans about Allied invasion plans as well as a short historical survey *Weimar Germany* (1972).

In later life Delmer was a huge Falstaffian figure of benign and monk-like appearance. It was hard to picture him as a sleuth or to imagine that in his youth he had been famous for his Byronic good looks. Unlike many of his Fleet Street colleagues he was essentially a humble man who inspired deep affection and loyalty from a wide variety of people. Some fellow journalists saw him as a guru or prophet. He liked to clown, but his strength as a reporter lay in his shrewdness and his down-to-earth approach.

He married in 1935 Isabel, daughter of Captain Philip Llewellyn Nicholas, master mariner. She was a model for the sculptor (Sir) Jacob Epstein [q.v.]. Delmer claimed that he had determined to marry her after first seeing a bust of her in an exhibition. The marriage was dissolved in 1946 and Isabel Delmer subsequently married Alan Rawsthorne [q.v.]. In 1948 Delmer married Zoë Ursula ('Peggy'), daughter of Thomas Stubley Black, printer. They had one son and one daughter. Delmer died 4 September 1979 at his home at Lamarsh, Suffolk, after many years of ill health.

[Sefton Delmer, *Trail Sinister*, 1961, and *Black Boomerang*, 1962 (autobiographies); Ellic Rowe, *The Black Game*, 1982; personal knowledge.] RICHARD INGRAMS

DE MADARIAGA, SALVADOR (1886–1978), writer, professor, and diplomat. [See MADARIAGA.]

DENNING, SIR NORMAN EGBERT (1904–1979), admiral, was born at Whitchurch, Hampshire, 19 November 1904, the youngest in the family of one daughter and five sons of Charles Denning (1859–1941), a draper, and his wife, Clara Thompson. Two of the sons died during World War I and Denning's other two brothers became Lieutenant-General Sir Reginald Denning and Lord Denning, master of the Rolls.

Norman Denning, who was always known as 'Ned', joined the navy from Andover Grammar School as a special entry cadet in 1921. As indifferent eyesight prevented him becoming an executive officer he joined the paymaster (later supply and secretariat) branch—in which he quickly showed outstanding ability being several times appointed secretary to senior executive officers. As a paymaster lieutenant-commander he was appointed to the Admiralty's intelligence division in 1937 and quickly realized its unreadiness for the war with Germany which was plainly approaching. He therefore studied the records of World War I, and especially the accomplishments of the cryptographic office known as Room 40 OB. He appreciated the fundamental weakness which lay in the separation of the work of that office from the operational conduct of the war at sea—which produced disastrous results, notably on the night following the Battle of Jutland (31 May–1 June 1916), and so began to plan and organize an operational intelligence centre (OIC) in which the two functions would be totally integrated. Encouraged by Rear-Admirals J. H. Godfrey [q.v.] and J. A. G. Troup, the directors of naval intelligence of the period, he soon got the principles on which the new centre was to work accepted; but on the outbreak of war the staff allocated to it was tiny. Admiral Godfrey used the author Charles Morgan [q.v.] to recruit suitable outsiders and gradually built up a brilliant team which manned and operated the OIC throughout the war. From 1941 it was situated deep underground in the heavily reinforced concrete citadel built on the west side of the main Admiralty building.

In the OIC large-scale plots were maintained showing the course and position of all Allied warships and of every mercantile convoy or independently routed merchant ship, and the positions and probable movements of all enemy units derived from every form of intelligence but especially from the decrypts produced by the Government Code and Cipher School (GCCS), the name by which the cryptographic and cryptanalytical centre at Bletchley Park was known. This became increasingly important after the German machine cipher known as Enigma had been broken in 1941. The OIC thus became the brain centre for the conduct of the war at sea, and in it the responsible officers, and (Sir) Winston Churchill when first lord, could see at a glance the position (or presumed position) of the forces of both sides.

At first Denning was in charge of all the OIC's work including the U-boat plot and tracking room, but after Captain (Sir) C. R. N. Winn RNVR had taken over that responsibility he devoted his whole energies to the surface ship plot on which the movements of enemy warships and disguised raiders were recorded. From those two plots, which were manned continuously, the operational authorities were able to initiate the measures necessary to improve the safety of Allied shipping and, if possible, direct forces to intercept the enemy. Denning thus became the chief adviser to the first lord and first sea lord on the conduct of that aspect of the conflict. He also acted as the link between the OIC and other sections of the Naval Intelligence Division, with the Ministry of Economic Warfare (MEW), the army, Fighter and Bomber Commands of the RAF, the Secret Intelligence Service (SIS), and the Special Operations Executive (SOE).

He was promoted paymaster-commander in 1941 and paymaster-captain in 1951; but it was not until the establishment of the general list for officers at the beginning of 1956 that the invidious distinction between the executive and non-executive branches was abolished. Denning then dropped his paymaster title and in 1958 became a rear-admiral on the general list—a position which his abilities had always merited.

After the war Denning's first appointment was as director of administrative planning in the Admiralty, but in 1956 he moved to the Royal Naval College, Greenwich, as its director. Two years later he became deputy chief of naval personnel and in 1959 director of manpower in the Admiralty. Earl Mountbatten of Burma [q.v.] has told how he selected Denning to be director of naval intelligence—the first non-executive officer to be appointed to that important post. He held it in 1960–4 very successfully, and it was again Mountbatten's confidence in him and appreciation of his abilities which brought him to the top of the tree as deputy chief of defence staff (intelligence) from 1964 to 1965.

Denning was appointed OBE in 1945, CB in 1961, and KBE in 1963. After his retirement in 1967 he became secretary of the services, press, and broadcasting committee (known as the 'D notice committee'), in which capacity his wide experience of security problems and his tactful handling of the press proved invaluable.

In 1933 he married Iris, daughter of Captain Richard James Curtis, master mariner, of Singapore; they had two sons, one of whom died in 1977, and a daughter. He died at Micheldever, Hampshire, 27 December 1979.

[R. H. Hinsley and others, *British Intelligence in the Second World War*, HMSO, 3 vols., 1979–83; Patrick Beesly, *Very Special Intelligence*, 1979, and *Very Special Admiral. The Life of Admiral J. G. Godfrey*, 1980; Donald McLachlan, *Room 39*, 1968; Stephen W. Roskill, *The War at Sea 1939–1945*, 4 vols., 1954–61; Lord Denning, *The Family Story*, 1981; *The Times*, 28 December 1979; personal knowledge.] STEPHEN W. ROSKILL

DENNY, SIR MICHAEL MAYNARD (1896–1972) admiral, was born at the vicarage in Kempley, Gloucestershire, 3 October 1896, the seventh son and thirteenth and youngest child of (Canon) Edward Denny, MA, vicar of Kempley, and his wife, Alona Mary Chesshyre. Entering the Royal Naval College, Osborne, in 1909 and then Dartmouth he was appointed midshipman in the *Neptune* prior to the outbreak of World War I and later to the *Royal Sovereign* in which ships he served throughout the war.

After specializing in gunnery in 1920 and gaining the Egerton memorial prize for the top student of his year he did the advanced 'G' course and alternated his service from lieutenant to commander between experimental work and 'G' in the *Emperor of India* (which under his tutelage demolished two battle practice targets and won the C-in-C's prize) and the *Nelson*. Promoted to commander in 1930, he was experimental commander and then fleet gunnery officer, Mediterranean Fleet, and was made captain in 1936 after being second-in-command of the *Shropshire*. Denny served in the naval ordnance department until 1940 during a time of hectic rearmament when his capacity for work and for mastering technical detail played a dominant part in design and in encouraging industry to provide the capacity needed.

The end of the 'phoney' war found him in the thick of the landings and then the evacuation around Trondheim from which he was the last to leave. He was sent to Dover as chief staff officer to organize the evacuation from Dunkirk and was created CB (1940), awarded the Norwegian Order of St. Olaf (1st class), and mentioned in dispatches for gallantry and distinguished service in these operations.

Denny commanded two ships in the war, the cruiser *Kenya* and the aircraft carrier *Victorious*, and was chief of staff Home Fleet during much of the time that convoys were being fought through to Russia.

Kenya escorted Arctic and Mediterranean convoys, and operated against German raiders and in raids on the Norwegian coast. *Victorious*, which he joined at the end of 1943, took part in raids against the *Tirpitz* and against Japanese-held islands in the East Indies, and then joined the Pacific Fleet. His skilful handling avoided damage from the kamikaze attacks. He was appointed to the DSO and promoted to rear-admiral in July 1945.

Then followed a new role for Denny in the department of the chief of naval personnel. Here his amazing grasp of detail and his ability to sustain long hours of work seven days a week needing only three or four hours sleep a night proved what was needed for the rapid but orderly demobilization of the fleet which was accomplished without organizational breakdown.

After commanding the small ship flotillas in the Mediterranean for sixteen months, Denny returned to the Admiralty as third sea lord and controller of the navy for the years 1949–53, having been promoted to vice-admiral in 1948. As the board member responsible for *matériel* and weapons, he introduced the Daring class destroyers and Ton class minesweepers and did much to rationalize the naval shipbuilding capacity swollen by the needs of war. His hours of work remained long and his need for sleep seemed to diminish. He was appointed KCB in 1950 and promoted to admiral in 1952.

Denny's last naval appointment was to the Home Fleet and to the command of the NATO Eastern Atlantic area from 1954 to 1956. He was appointed GCB in 1954. In 1956 he was made chairman of the British Joint Services Mission in Washington and British representative on the NATO military committee. He held this double post for three years and impressed his colleagues as much by his complete grasp of military affairs as by his stamina for work and recreation.

He was placed on the retired list in July 1959. He became chairman of Cammell Laird, shipbuilders and engineers, on retirement but resigned after six years as his health was deteriorating. From then his health and memory got steadily worse and in 1970 he had to enter a hospital from which he did not emerge. He died at Gloucester 7 April 1972.

In 1923 Denny married Sarah Annie Esmé, daughter of Colonel Loftus Welman, of the Royal Irish Rifles. There were no children of the marriage and his wife predeceased him in 1971. His application to his work seldom allowed his wife to take part in his life. His only hobby was to form a collection of dolls. He sailed service boats occasionally and as a lieutenant led a rugger side well, but later showed no special bent for sport. He showed no interest in religion. He was shy and reserved with his colleagues and unnecessarily feared for his knowledge and efficiency. And with it he maintained an energetic social life ashore wherever he went. The rapid decline of his mental powers was a sad end to a brilliant career.

[Private information; personal knowledge.]

HORACE R. LAW

DENT, CHARLES ENRIQUE (1911–1976), physician and biochemist, was born in Burgos, Spain, 25 August 1911, the second son and youngest of the three children of Dr Frankland Dent, chemist and analyst, who worked in the Rio Tinto Mining Company, and his wife, Carmen Colsa de Mira y Perceval, daughter of Colsa de Mira, who held judicial office. Dent's paternal grandfather was a Church of England parson, but his father became a Roman Catholic on his marriage and all the children were brought up in the Catholic faith. In 1912 the family went to Singapore, but returned to England on the outbreak of war in 1914. Dent received his early education first at Bedford School and later at Wimbledon College, a Jesuit foundation. After leaving school in 1927 he worked first as a bank clerk, then as a laboratory technician, and took evening classes at Regent Street Polytechnic. In 1930 he passed the intermediate B.Sc. examination and entered Imperial College as a student in chemistry. He graduated in 1930 with first class honours and proceeded immediately to a Ph.D., which he obtained in June 1934, whereupon he obtained employment as a chemist in the dyestuffs division of Imperial Chemical Industries in Manchester. In 1937 Dent decided to study medicine and entered University College, London, as a medical student. After passing his second MB examination he transferred to the medical school.

His clinical studies were interrupted several times by the war. Dent had been in the Territorial Army since 1929, had become involved in intelligence work, and was an expert on secret writing. He went to France with the British Expeditionary Force in 1939, and participated in the retreat to Dunkirk. For his work as a dispatch rider he was mentioned in dispatches (*London Gazette*, 20 December 1940). Later he spent two years in Bermuda and was promoted to captain in the Intelligence Corps. He finally completed his medical course in 1944 and became the last house officer of the distinguished physician Sir Thomas Lewis [q.v.]. In the same year he became MRCP and was appointed assistant to the medical unit of University College Hospital Medical School under (Sir) Harold Himsworth.

In 1945 Dent was a member of the medical team involved in the investigation and treatment of survivors of the Belsen camp. The rest of his professional career was spent at University College Hospital Medical School, London; he was appointed reader in medicine in 1951, and professor of human metabolism in 1956.

Dent's early scientific work, carried out with (Sir) R. P. Linstead [q.v.], was on phthalocyanines. In 1946 he applied the newly discovered method of paper chromatography to an investigation of the metabolism of amino acids in man. He studied the pattern of amino acid excretion in the urine, and applied these methods to an investigation of metabolic disorders such as hypophosphatasia and cystinuria. He established that the latter was not an error of metabolism *per se*, but was caused by a malfunction of a transport mechanism. Dent's later work was more oriented towards clinical medicine and he became an outstanding expert on diseases affecting the metabolism of calcium, phosphorus, and magnesium, as well as the pathology of bone. He also worked extensively on the pathology of vitamin D metabolism.

Dent had unusually high standards of personal behaviour, largely based on his complete loyalty to the Roman Catholic Church, and he did not believe that there was any conflict between science and religion. He was always very keen on games, particularly rugby football. Later he took up cross-country running, and was a very competent player of squash rackets. Another favourite hobby was wine-making from his own vines.

Dent was made FRCP in 1954, elected FRS in 1962, gave the Humphry Davy Rolleston lecture in 1962, received the Gairdner Foundation award in 1965, and was made honorary MD of Louvain in 1966, and of Uppsala in 1974. He was appointed CBE in 1976.

In 1944 Dent married Margaret Ruth, daughter of the Revd William Samuel Coad, a residentiary canon of Chester Cathedral. They had met while working in intelligence in Bermuda. They had six children, five daughters and one son, of whom two took up medicine. Dent died from leukaemia in London 19 September 1976, eleven days before his retirement date.

[Albert Neuberger in *Biographical Memoirs of Fellows of the Royal Society*, vol. xxiv, 1978; private information; personal knowledge.]

ALBERT NEUBERGER

DE VALERA, EAMON (1882–1975), prime minister and later president of the Republic of Ireland, was born in New York 14 October 1882, the only child of a Spanish father, Vivion Juan de Valera, artist, and an Irish mother, Catherine (Kate), daughter of Patrick Coll, a farm labourer of county Limerick. His father died when he was two. His mother took him home to Ireland in 1885 before returning to America. He was brought up on the small farm of his mother's brother Patrick Coll. He obtained his education the hard way. He went to the village school at Bruree, a more advanced school in Charleville, to which he frequently had to walk seven miles a day, and thence as a lay boarder at the age of sixteen to Blackrock College in Dublin. Two years later he secured a place at University College, Blackrock. By the age of twenty he had acquired the passion for mathematics which remained with him to the end of his days. At twenty-one he obtained a teaching appointment at Rockwell College near Cashel. In 1904 he gained a pass degree in mathematical science in the Royal University of Ireland. Later he became a professor of mathematics in the training college of Our Lady of Mercy, Carysfort, Blackrock.

He came to acquire a lifelong interest in the Irish language of which he knew little as a boy. Among his teachers was a young woman about four years older than himself, Sinéad Flanagan, who had already won a gold medal in a major competition. She was the daughter of Laurence Flanagan, of Carbery, county Kildare. Their marriage on 8 January 1910 in St. Paul's Church, Arran Quay, Dublin, was to prove the happiest of partnerships. Mrs de Valera was a woman of strong personality and literary gifts, but she dedicated herself to her husband and their seven children (five sons, one of whom was killed in a riding accident in 1936 at the age of twenty, and two daughters).

In 1913 a Home Rule Bill had been passed through the British House of Commons, but overwhelmingly rejected by the Lords. It could not become law until summer 1914. The Ulster Protestants set up a provisional government and organized full-scale military resistance. De Valera was crucially affected by these developments. In November 1913 a public meeting was held in Dublin to found a volunteer force in the South in reply to the Ulstermen. De Valera attended, joined the Volunteers, and committed himself irrevocably to a share in the armed conflict which he thought was inevitable.

He became a wholehearted and efficient Volunteer. He was in no way concerned with the decisions which led to the 1916 rising, but in that traumatic week his military performance was impressive. He expected the death sentence but he was not among the first to be court-martialled, and his sentence was commuted to life imprisonment. He was saved by the delay and a change in government policy, not, as is sometimes said, because of his American birth. After the executions it was natural that he should be looked on as the senior commander. In various British prisons he exhibited a marked gift for leadership. Along with other prisoners he was released by a general amnesty in June 1917. Soon after his release he won a memorable by-election in East Clare on a policy of complete and absolute independence for an Irish Republic. At a convention on 25 October 1917, in the Mansion House, Dublin, he was elected as president of Sinn Fein. By now he was becoming a thorn in the British side. In May 1918 he was rearrested and imprisoned in Lincoln Gaol, from which he made a sensational escape in February 1919. By this time a republic had been declared in Ireland and an alternative and 'illegal' system of government established. De Valera, the newly elected president, remained in hiding till he set off for the United States in June 1919. He did not return to Ireland until

December 1920, by which time the guerrilla war of independence was reaching a climax. One purpose of his visit, that of raising funds, was achieved most successfully; the wider propagandist purpose, less obviously. But at least the Irish case was placed fairly and squarely before the American people, and identified henceforward with that of other struggling nations, India and Egypt among them.

Back in Ireland at the end of 1920, de Valera was once again in hiding. During the first half of 1921 the British government fluctuated between a policy of stepping up coercion and putting out fresh feelers. On 23 June King George V, opening the new Stormont parliament, set up under the 'Partition Act' of 1920, made a historic plea for reconciliation. The next step was to hand de Valera a letter which invited him to a conference in London with Lloyd George and Sir James Craig (later Viscount Craigavon, q.v.), prime minister of Northern Ireland. De Valera could on no account accept a parity between his position and that of Craig. But the latter in any case refused. A truce was negotiated. De Valera went to London and had several meetings with Lloyd George. There was no meeting of minds personally or politically. De Valera reaffirmed the Irish demand for a republic Lloyd George offered dominion status, an immense advance compared with the Act of 1920, or the Home Rule Bill of 1912, but hedged round with significant qualifications.

The Irish Cabinet found the Lloyd George terms quite unacceptable. De Valera now worked out the notion of external association, of which much would be heard later and which to the end of his life probably expressed his own conception of the best Anglo-Irish relationship. Ireland would not be a dominion or a member of the Commonwealth, but a friendly country externally associated with the latter. After prolonged correspondence five Irish delegates came to London in October 1921. Two months of intense negotiations followed. A treaty was signed in the small hours of 6 December 1921. The Irish Free State would be established as a dominion, and thus after 750 years the British occupation of twenty-six counties would be ended.

De Valera had not gone to London for these negotiations—a decision which was to have fateful consequences. To the end of his life he was anxious to defend his decision at considerable length. But in essence he had believed at the time that he would be able to exercise a stronger influence if he stayed in reserve. In the event he misjudged his control over the delegates, especially Arthur Griffith and Michael Collins [qq.v.]. At the crunch, under threats of 'immediate and terrible war' they signed the treaty without referring back to him. A nominally republican delegation agreed to an arrangement in which a republic could have no place. In the light of his declared convictions, de Valera had little option but to repudiate the document. The Dáil however supported the treaty by 64 votes to 57. He was supplanted as president and became an unofficial leader of the opposition. Many republicans prepared to resist the treaty in arms. A civil war followed inexorably. De Valera was bitterly attacked by the treaty party in Ireland and by almost everyone of influence in England for causing the civil war. It is fairest to conclude that once he had repudiated the treaty there was nothing which he could do to avert the tragedy. The republicans were totally defeated. De Valera who had been on the run made a spectacular reappearance at Clare in the general election of 1923. He was not released until nearly a year later (July 1924). His fortunes seemed to be at a nadir, his career quite possibly at an end.

But he had never ceased to plan a political resurrection for the republican cause. In 1926 he launched a new party, Fianna Fáil. Initially their elected deputies declined to take their seats in the Dáil because of the required oath of allegiance to the British Crown. But in 1927 de Valera made a much derided volte-face, doing the right thing it must seem now, but showing far less consistency than usual. On 12 August 1927 the Fianna Fáil deputies took their seats in the Dáil. In the general election of 1932 they increased their seats from 57 to 72. This did not give them an overall majority but an arrangement with the Labour Party enabled de Valera to form a government. At the age of fifty, after an interval of ten years, he was once again the official leader of the Irish people.

The pre-war years, 1932–9, were disfigured by the economic dispute with Britain which ended in a kind of draw with the agreement of 1938. De Valera and his eventual successor, Sean Lemass [q.v.], made a virtue of necessity and introduced measures of self-sufficiency which were in any case in line with Fianna Fáil and Sinn Fein thinking. On the constitutional front de Valera's largest personal achievement was the new constitution of 1937. In social policy it gave expression to Catholic social teaching. The special position of the Catholic Church in Ireland was emphasized, but Protestant and Jewish Churches were explicitly mentioned. Protestants at the time were pleased, but many years later the special position accorded to the Catholic Church came to seem sectarian and the clause in question was repealed.

The name of the state was changed from Irish Free State to Eire. The Anglo-Irish side of the constitutional revolution has been well summed up by Professor P. N. S. Mansergh—'Taken together, the External Relations Act and the new Constitution destroyed the dominion settlement of 1921. Relations with Britain and the Commonwealth had been taken out of the Constitution, where Mr de Valera felt that they had no place, and had become matters of external policy for the Government of the day. This was the most significant development in the whole period' (1926–39). (N. Mansergh, 'The Implications of Eire's Relationship with the British Commonwealth of Nations', *International Affairs*, January 1948.) After the agreement of 1938, and six years of neutrality in the war, it was manifest to all that total independence for the twenty-six counties had been secured. Under the agreement of 1938, de Valera secured what he had hardly hoped for, the return of 'the ports'—that is to say the renunciation by Britain of the naval and air facilities in certain Irish ports enjoyed under the treaty. De Valera and Neville Chamberlain, the British prime minister, struck up a remarkably cordial relationship. If war had not come so soon, an effective defence arrangement might have led to a united Ireland. In retrospect, de Valera dwelt occasionally on this 'might have been'.

In the event, war came all too rapidly. De Valera instantly proclaimed neutrality. The British representative in Dublin, Sir John Maffey (later Lord Rugby, q.v.) privately advised the British Cabinet that no government could exist in Ireland that 'departed from the principle of neutrality'. In various secondary ways de Valera made his neutrality highly benevolent to the Allies; it will always remain a matter of dispute as to how far the Allied cause was damaged by the non-availability of the ports. At the beginning of the war Churchill showed an interest in recovering the facilities by force. Sir John Maffey, who maintained throughout the war an excellent relationship with de Valera, played a notable part in defeating any such initiative. At different times during the war the Germans, the British, and the French brought extreme pressure to bear, but de Valera maintained his iron nerve throughout six desperately anxious years. Perhaps the most successful address he ever delivered was a radio reply to Churchill at the end of the war. Churchill had boasted of the restraint and poise which the British government had shown in not laying violent hands on Ireland. De Valera's speech was moderate and conciliatory, but contained the telling question 'could he [Mr Churchill] not find in his heart the generosity to acknowledge that there is a small nation . . . that could never be got to accept defeat and has never surrendered her soul?' Never had he spoken so clearly for the nation and never had the nation been so proud of him. Churchill privately conceded that de Valera had the better of the exchanges.

After the war, the independence of the twenty-six counties was not in dispute. But, although large numbers of southern Irishmen had served often with distinction in the British forces, this could not weigh against Britain's conviction that her foothold in the North had been essential to survival and victory. Partition was thus more firmly entrenched than ever. In the general election of 1948 de Valera was not surprised to be defeated by a rather strange combination of Fine Gael, traditionally more pro-British than Fianna Fáil and Clann na Poblachta, a new radical republican party, under the charismatic Sean MacBride. The new government proceeded to sever the last link with the Commonwealth by repealing the External Relations Act which de Valera had sedulously preserved. De Valera acquiesced but he did not pretend that he would have proceeded along these lines. The change was announced in the clumsiest way possible. The British responded by strengthening their guarantee to Northern Ireland.

De Valera was returned to power in 1951, but was out of office from 1954 to 1957. In the latter year, aged seventy-five, he came back with the first overall majority since the wartime election of 1944, but by 1959 he recognized that the time had come to hand over to a younger generation and to repair as president to 'The Park' where he served for fourteen years, a model of mellow dignity. One great regret in old age was his failure to make any headway with the ending of partition. From 1920 onwards he had insisted that 'Ulster must not be coerced', that force, in other words, must be renounced, in seeking to achieve Irish unity. It sometimes seemed that the distinctiveness of the Northern Unionist culture never fully came home to him. They were all Irishmen and equally dear accordingly. He persisted in the belief that the Gaelic Ireland which he had tried so hard, though with limited success, to establish in the twenty-six counties, would itself be instrumental in promoting Irish unity. Not many today would share that opinion. On the other hand, the modern notion that a united Ireland should be of a federal rather than a unitary character was completely in line with his later thinking.

In international affairs, one speculates wistfully about what he could have achieved if he had been at the head of a great state instead of a small nation. He was by chance president of the council of the League of Nations in 1932, the same year that he became head of the Irish government. He made a profound impression on that occasion. His opportunities of exercising widespread international influence were afterwards limited, but in his dealings, usually at a disadvantage with world leaders, he proved himself fully their equal. Churchill who at one time had no good word to say of him came to recognize at the end his pre-eminent quality.

Eamon de Valera was six feet one inch in height and looked even taller by reason of his upright carriage. His athletic frame was that of a man who had once played in a Munster trial at rugby football. His features were strongly developed, his eyes were dark and deep set behind the spectacles he had worn since he was a youth. He never lost his passion for mathematics. For many years before his death he was virtually blind. For most of his life he was involved in bitter controversy, but no one ever denied the dignity and courtesy of his bearing. His religious devoutness would be hard to parallel among statesmen. Once installed in the president's residence he visited the oratory five times a day. He had long been a daily communicant. But he was no Catholic bigot. It was Daniel O'Connell [q.v.] who said 'I take my religion from Rome, but my politics from Ireland'. It was a phrase de Valera himself might have coined. In the civil war of 1922–3 the Irish bishops condemned the side that he was nominally leading. At the end of his life he was at pains to point out to more than one visitor that he had *not* been excommunicated. He had taken the matter up with the pope of the day a few years after the civil war and found that the pope agreed with him. He was asked 'what would you have thought if the pope had disagreed with you?' He replied with his familiar dead-pan humour 'I should have considered that His Holiness was misinformed.' One of his chaplains, later a bishop, is on record as saying of him: 'He would have made a good Protestant.'

Though he was a man of subtle mind and complex personality, he stood through life for simple conceptions: religion, the family, democracy, law and order, fair dealing between nations, justice for the oppressed. In all these respects, he left an indelible mark on the state which he did so much to create and foster.

He died in Dublin 29 August 1975 at the age of ninety-two. His personality had dominated the Irish scene for nearly sixty years. No Irishman in this century, or indeed any other, has achieved so prolonged an eminence in his lifetime.

[The Earl of Longford and Thomas P. O'Neill, *Eamon de Valera*, 1970; private information; personal knowledge.]

FRANK LONGFORD

DIEFENBAKER, JOHN GEORGE (1895–1979), prime minister of Canada, was born 18 September 1895 at Neustadt in Grey County, Ontario, the elder son (there were no daughters) of William Thomas Diefenbaker, schoolteacher and, later, government official, and his wife, Mary Florence, daughter of John Bannerman. He was a 'fourth generation' Canadian on both sides: his father's grandparents had emigrated to Canada from Germany, his mother's from Scotland. In 1903 the family moved to the prairies, settling first in the country and then in Saskatoon. He was educated at the Saskatoon Collegiate Institute and the University of Saskatchewan, where he graduated in political science in 1915. In 1916 he volunteered for military service and went to France as a subaltern with the 196th battalion. He was invalided home in 1917. He resumed his studies, obtained a law degree, and was called to the Saskatchewan bar in 1919. As a lawyer, he was successful from the beginning: he acquired a reputation as a defence counsel in criminal cases, securing some sensational acquittals. He developed a large practice in civil law as well.

His real passion was, however, politics, and political success eluded him for many years. He stood unsuccessfully as a Conservative in two federal elections before he was elected to the House of Commons in 1940. The Liberals were in power, and he spent sixteen frustrating years on the opposition back-benches. He stood for the leadership of the Conservative Party in 1942 and in 1948, without success; he was recognized as an effective parliamentary performer, but he was not liked by the party establishment, based in the business circles of Toronto, who dubbed him a 'prairie populist'. He was indeed by temperament a radical and an enemy of privilege. He was at last elected leader in 1956, with support from the parliamentary party and the Western delegates.

In the following year Louis St. Laurent [q.v.], the Liberal prime minister, called a general election. The Liberals, after twenty-two years in office, were not popular, Diefenbaker put forward a progressive manifesto in a barnstorming campaign, and the Conservatives emerged as the largest party in the House, though short of an absolute majority. St. Laurent resigned and in June 1957 Diefenbaker formed the first Conservative administration since 1935.

The new government began well, with a vigorous programme of legislation, and Diefenbaker made his mark as a colourful character on the political scene. In 1958 he called another election, which he won with the largest majority in Canadian history: 208 seats out of 265. The Liberals, now under the leadership of L. B. Pearson [q.v.], were reduced to forty-nine seats. But the majority was too large to be healthy. Factions soon developed within the government ranks as difficult problems arose; unemployment was rising in the late 1950s and there were sharp divisions over economic problems; there was an undignified public quarrel with the governor of the Bank of Canada. Diefenbaker, one of whose favourite slogans was 'One Canada', had no sympathy for the aspirations of French-speaking Canadians for a separate identity, at a time when that problem was coming to the fore in politics, and he could not hold the large support he had won in Quebec in the landslide of 1958. In foreign affairs he antagonized both of Canada's traditional friends: Britain over trade and European policy and the United States by indecision over defence. In the election of 1962 (conducted during an exchange crisis) the Conservatives lost ninety-two seats and their overall majority. Then acute differences over defence policy split the Cabinet and led to defeat in Parliament in February 1963. In the resulting election, the Liberals came back as the largest party, but Diefenbaker's powerful personal campaign denied them a clear majority; and in 1965, when the Liberals called another election, Diefenbaker, despite dissension within his own party, held them to a minority by his masterly campaigning.

Pearson formed a new administration in April 1963, and Diefenbaker was leader of the opposition for the next four years. His view of opposition was destructive; it was said of him that he 'went for the jugular'. He harried the Liberal government mercilessly; his methods were often effective, but did not raise the tone of the House of Commons. Finally dissatisfaction within the Conservative Party came to a head, and resulted in a leadership convention in 1967, in which he unwisely stood and was ignominiously defeated. He retained his parliamentary seat until his death.

Diefenbaker's most significant impact on Canadian history may be seen in the effect of his election campaigns of 1957 and 1958 in reshaping the pattern of federal politics. He brought the fresh wind of the prairies into the Conservative Party, long dominated by the urban tycoons, and made it the party of reform, forcing the Liberals to follow in the same direction. The startling reversal of the Conservatives' fortunes in four years was due less to their policies than to their lack of the experience required for government and party management and to their internal feuds. Diefenbaker was intensely ambitious for power; but he did not know how to handle it when he secured it. Nevertheless, for ten years, through the sheer force of his personality he held a dominating position in Canadian politics.

He was a tall man, with expressive rugged features and a strong, harsh voice. He was at his best a superb platform speaker, responding instinctively to the mood of his audience, switching in a moment from high idealism to savage mockery; he made great play with the accusing finger and the penetrating eye. In private, he could be very amusing company, a good story-teller and mimic. He was a lifelong Baptist and teetotaller.

He was married twice: in 1929 to Edna May Brower, a schoolteacher in Saskatoon, who died in 1951, and in 1953 to Olive Evangeline Palmer, daughter of the Revd D. B. Freeman; she was also a schoolteacher and died in 1976. There were no children of either marriage.

He was appointed CH in 1976, and held numerous honorary degrees. He was admitted to both the Canadian and British Privy Councils in 1957. He died in Ottawa 16 August 1979.

[*The Times*, 16 November 1979; J. G. Diefenbaker, *One Canada* (memoirs), 3 vols., 1976–8; Peter Stursberg, *Diefenbaker*, 2 vols., 1975, 1976; private information; personal knowledge.]

H. LINTOTT

DILHORNE, first VISCOUNT (1905–1980), lord chancellor. [See MANNINGHAM-BULLER, REGINALD EDWARD.]

DOBB, MAURICE HERBERT (1900–1976), economist, was born in London 24 July 1900, the only child of Walter Herbert Dobb, merchant, and his wife Elsie Annie Moir. He was educated at Charterhouse, and went up to Pembroke College, Cambridge (where other Dobbs had been before him) in 1919 as an exhibitioner, saved from military service by the armistice of 1918. There he switched from history to economics, then a somewhat unusual choice of subject, gained a double first (1921 and 1922), and, after two years of research under Edwin Cannan [q.v.] at the London School of Economics from which he acquired a London Ph.D., returned to Cambridge as a university lecturer in 1924. There, apart from visiting lectureships and professorships, he remained for the rest of his life. He became a reader in economics in 1959.

In 1923 Dobb married Phyllis, daughter of Carleton Grant, artist. This marriage ended in divorce and he married in 1931 Barbara Marian Nixon, stage-manager and author, daughter of Christopher Nixon, a Gloucestershire merchant, whose acquaintance he had made some time after she had come up to Newnham as an undergraduate in 1926. Her professional activities in London (during the war as an air-raid warden and instructor) prevented them from setting up a permanent joint domestic establishment until 1951, when they moved to the village of Fulbourn. There were no children.

The somewhat unusual pattern of his earlier marital life suggests that his career was less conventional and tranquil than might be supposed from this outline. Dobb had become a socialist through opposition to World War I, before leaving school. He joined the small band of Cambridge socialists as soon as he went up and, in 1922, the Communist Party. Neither body was then used to such notably well-dressed recruits of such impeccably bourgeois comportment. He remained quietly loyal to his cause and party for the remainder of his life, pursuing a course, at times rather lonely, as a communist academic. From the 1930s on he was increasingly recognized, in Britain and outside, as an exceptionally distinguished Marxian economist, and indeed the founder of this field of academic study in this country. He published much, especially during the last fifteen years of his life. While his learned output contains relatively little that does not repay rereading, his reputation as a scholar is likely to rest above all on the closely argued *Political Economy and Capitalism* (1937) and the modestly titled *Studies in the Development of Capitalism* (1946), which form a landmark in the Marxist, and indeed the wider, historiography of European economic development, and on his association with his close friend Piero Sraffa in the monumental edition of the *Works of David Ricardo* (11 vols., 1951–73) which bears his name as well as Sraffa's. It recalls both his erudition in the history of economic thought and a collaboration whose roots may go back to a common visit to the USSR in 1930.

The relations between even so gentlemanly and quiet a revolutionary and the conventional academic world were far from easy. Nor were they smoothed by the dangers apprehended from a Communist presence in a university which might educate royalty, or by a divorce which some in the Cambridge of those days found difficult to distinguish from other varieties of subversive behaviour. Pembroke withdrew its undergraduates and dining rights, and though he taught there from 1926 it was not until 1948 that Dobb obtained a college fellowship at Trinity. He himself, isolated in Cambridge, found political encouragement in the 1920s in work for the (London) Labour Research Department and the National Council of Labour Colleges, of whose journal *Plebs* he was, for some years, the *de facto* editor. After 1930 Marxism became less uncommon, and Dobb increasingly made his mark as a writer and an unofficial as well as official teacher of students. After a renewed period of relative isolation in the 1950s, his intellectual merits and achievements finally won the wider recognition they undoubtedly deserved.

Dobb received honorary doctorates from the universities of Prague (1964) and Leicester (1972) and, upon his retirement, a Festschrift from a distinguished international company of pupils and colleagues (*Socialism, Capitalism and Economic Growth*, edited by C. H. Feinstein, Cambridge University Press, 1967). To his considerable satisfaction, he was elected a fellow of the British Academy in 1971. He received his distinctions with his habitual, unjustified but perfectly genuine, diffidence.

Dobb's life was that of the scholar and teacher rather than the political activist, though he took the duties of his party membership seriously. R. P. Dutt [q.v.] almost certainly had him in mind when he complained, at one moment, about certain 'incurably professorial' communist intellectuals. His lifetime of devotion to his cause—which was by no means always uncritical—never had the slightest effect on the natural courtesy which once led a visiting foreigner to say that he had always heard about English gentlemen, but had never met any until he encountered Maurice Dobb. A slight touch of unconventionality in his *toilette* and domestic arrangements, which was not discouraged by his marriage to Barbara Nixon, did not disturb this impression. As a teacher, he took endless trouble. As a friend, he was uneffusively loyal. Perhaps he is best remembered, rosy-faced and ageing well—he had been a very handsome young man—in the many settings of the Cambridge which finally accepted him as one of its own.

He died at Cambridge 17 August 1976 and was survived by his wife.

[*The Times*, 19 August 1976; E. J. Hobsbawm, 'Maurice Dobb' in C. Feinstein (ed.), *Socialism, Capitalism and Economic Growth*, 1967; Ronald L. Meek in *Proceedings* of the British Academy, vol. lxiii, 1977; 'Maurice Dobb, Random Biographical Notes', *Cambridge Journal of Economics*, vol. ii, 1978; material from the Dobb papers, by courtesy of Mrs B. Nixon Dobb and Mr B. Pollitt; personal knowledge.] ERIC HOBSBAWM

DOBRÉE, BONAMY (1891–1974), professor of English literature at Leeds, was born in London 2 February 1891, the only son in the family of three children of Bonamy Dobrée and his wife, Violet Chase. The Dobrées were a well-known Guernsey family, originally armament manufacturers; both Dobrée's father and grandfather were bankers. He was educated at Haileybury and at the Royal Military Academy, Woolwich; and was commissioned in the Royal Field Artillery in 1910. He resigned, as a subaltern, in 1913 and in November of that year married the artist and poet Valentine Gladys May Pechell (died 1974), daughter of Sir (Augustus) Alexander Brooke-Pechell, seventh baronet, a colonel in the RAMC. The young married couple toured France in a horse-drawn caravan until April 1914, then stayed in Florence until the outbreak of war when Dobrée rejoined the army, serving with the Royal Horse Artillery and Royal Field Artillery in France, Egypt, and Palestine. He was twice mentioned in dispatches and attained the rank of major. After the war he went to Christ's College, Cambridge (1920–1), and was captain of the university fencing team.

From 1921 to 1925 the Dobrées lived mainly at Larrau, a village in the Pyrenees. Here he wrote *Restoration Comedy* (1924), *Essays in Biography* (1925), and edited Congreve's *Comedies* (1925). His editions of Vanbrugh's plays (1928) and of Congreve's *The Mourning Bride, Poems and Miscellanies* (1928) were followed by *Restoration Tragedy 1660–1720* (1929). In 1925–6 Dobrée was a lecturer at East London College (London University); from 1926 to 1929 he was professor of English at the Egyptian University, Cairo.

From 1929 to 1935 the Dobrées lived at Meadham Priory, Harleston, Norfolk; their daughter Georgina was born in 1930. This was a period of intense literary activity. In addition to being a drama critic and contributing essays on many diverse topics to various journals, Dobrée wrote several books; he also compiled the *London Book of English Verse* (1931) with his friend (Sir) Herbert Read [q.v.], edited the *Letters* of Philip Dormer Stanhope, Earl of Chesterfield (6 vols., 1932), and collected his earlier biographical conversations in *As Their Friends Saw Them* (1933).

The Dobrées moved to Earls Colne, Essex, in 1936; in that year he was appointed to the chair of English literature at the University of Leeds, a post he held until his retirement in 1955. He rejoined his regiment in 1939, worked in the War Office, and was appointed officer commanding the Leeds University Senior Training Corps with the rank of lieutenant-colonel; he resumed his university post in 1945. Dobrée lectured widely, in France, Canada, and the United States as well as in the United Kingdom; gave the Clark lectures (1952–3); and was Lord Northcliffe memorial lecturer (1963). He was Gresham professor in rhetoric at the City University, London (1955–61).

Dobrée's distinction was recognized by his appointment as OBE (1929), and honorary degrees from Dijon (1960) and Kent at Canterbury (1968), where the library has a Dobrée collection. There is a Dobrée Hall at the University of Leeds, a tribute not only to his work in the department of English literature (handsomely described by Richard Hoggart in *Of Books and Humankind*, essays and poems presented to Dobrée in 1964) but also in the university, where he promoted a department of fine art and where he persuaded his friend Peter Gregory to establish the pioneering Gregory fellowships in poetry, painting, sculpture, and music. Dobrée's broad humanity informed his teaching of literature; he brought to Leeds a connoisseur's attitude to the arts. Also the author of a play, a novel, and much poetry, his scholarship and criticism had an inspiring effect upon his colleagues and pupils. His own publications continued, with essays, editions, and such stimulating books as *Alexander Pope* (1951) and *Rudyard Kipling* (1965) reflecting an impressive intellectual energy. In 1949 he and Herbert Read completed *The London Book of English Verse*; in 1959 his volume in the *Oxford History of English Literature* (of which he was co-editor with F. P. Wilson, q.v.] showed his liking for the liveliness of early eighteenth-century literature.

Like Swift he enjoyed the bagatelle; and like him he enjoyed it in good company. His many friends included T. S. Eliot, Leonard and Virginia Woolf, Wyndham Lewis [qq.v.], and Henry Moore. Dobrée's appreciation of literature was wide; he was a man of letters who wore his learning lightly. Witty, yet profoundly serious, he disliked solemnity in others. His military training had given him a briskness that enabled him to execute his business, whether teaching, writing, or administering, with prompt efficiency. This left him time for the civilities of life, for innumerable kindnesses, and for the hospitality he and his wife always dispensed so generously. He conveyed his enjoyment of the creative arts convincingly, was patron as well as critic. He died at his home in Blackheath 3 September 1974.

[G. Wilson Knight, 'Emeritus Professor Bonamy Dobrée, OBE', *University of Leeds Review*, 1955; Margaret Britton, 'A Selected List of the published writings of Bonamy Dobrée', *Of Books and Humankind*, ed. John Butt, 1964; private information; personal knowledge.]

A. N. JEFFARES

DOBSON, GORDON MILLER BOURNE (1889–1976), physicist and meteorologist, was born at Knott End, Windermere, 25 February 1889, the youngest child in the family of two sons and two daughters of Thomas Dobson, a general practitioner in Windermere, and his wife, Marianne Bourne. He was educated at Sedbergh School and Gonville and Caius College, Cambridge. He obtained a first class in part i of the natural sciences tripos in 1910.

From an early age Dobson showed an interest in practical things. When a young boy he set up a field telephone between the house and the stable, and at school spent much of his spare time in the physics laboratory. While an undergraduate he devised a simple apparatus he set up at his father's boathouse, for recording the seiches on Windermere. The results were published in *Nature* in 1911.

As a result of the *Nature* article Dobson came to the notice of (Sir) W. Napier Shaw [q.v.], director of the Meteorological Office, who offered him a post at Kew Observatory under Charles Chree. In 1913 Dobson was appointed meteorological adviser to the newly formed Military Flying School on Salisbury Plain where he carried out, using pilot balloons, the first measurements of the variation of wind with height.

During the war of 1914–18, Dobson was director of the experimental department at the Royal Aircraft Establishment, Farnborough. He worked closely with, among others, F. A. Lindemann (later Viscount Cherwell, q.v.). After the war Lindemann moved to Oxford as Dr Lee's professor of experimental philosophy. Dobson followed him in 1920, taking up an appointment at the Clarendon Laboratory as university lecturer in meteorology. He immediately began to work with Lindemann on the subject of meteors. Lindemann concentrated on the theory of the burn up of meteors in the upper atmosphere; Dobson analysed the observations. In 1922 they published in the *Proceedings* of the Royal Society a paper clearly demonstrating the presence of a warm layer at a height of about 50 km in contrast to the expected result of a steady fall of temperature with height throughout the atmosphere. Dobson obtained an Oxford D.Sc. in 1924.

Realizing that the source of heating for the warm layer was likely to be the absorption of ultraviolet radiation by ozone, Dobson embarked on the study of atmospheric ozone, a subject which he pursued with unrelenting vigour for the rest of his life. Ozone measurements were made by means of ultraviolet solar spectroscopy. In building his spectrograph, a task which he carried out personally in the laboratory of his home on Boar's Hill near Oxford, Dobson showed a great deal of ingenuity and practical skill. For the measurement of the photographic plates he built the first photoelectric microphotometer using a potassium photocell, the current from which was measured by a Lindemann-Keeley electrometer, both photocell and electrometer being made in the Clarendon Laboratory. These new techniques for photographic photometry developed by Dobson, I. O. Griffith, and D. N. Harrison were described in a small monograph published by the Clarendon Press in 1926.

During 1925 and 1926 five spectrographs were built and deployed at various locations in Europe, the photographic plates being returned to Oxford for measurement. More extensive measurements of atmospheric ozone were organized during 1928 and 1929 by redistributing the instruments to locations widely scattered over the world including one as far afield as Christchurch, New Zealand. By the end of 1929 the main features of the variations of ozone with synoptic conditions with latitude and season had been established. The year 1927 saw recognition of Dobson's work by his election to a new university readership in meteorology, to a fellowship at Merton College, and to fellowship of the Royal Society.

Dobson continued with instrument development. The inconvenience of the photographic technique led him to design and build a photoelectric spectrophotometer which enabled the relative intensity at two wavelengths and hence the ozone amount to be measured directly. The first instrument, which was remarkably advanced for its day, was completed in 1927 or 1928. It became the standard instrument for measuring atmospheric ozone and its basic design was little changed for many decades. For the International Geophysical Year in 1956, 144 were distributed throughout the world, the organization and much of the calibration of the instruments still being carried out from Dobson's home in Oxford.

In the 1930s Dobson became concerned with the study of atmospheric pollution. From 1934 to 1950 he served as chairman of the atmospheric pollution committee of the Department of Scientific and Industrial Research. Under his guidance reliable methods were developed for the measurement of smoke, deposited matter, and sulphur dioxide.

During World War II Dobson became involved with the Meteorological Office in the forecasting of conditions under which aircraft form condensation trails. This led him to a further piece of ingenious instrument design, the Dobson–Brewer hygrometer for measuring the very low humidities found in the stratosphere. The first water vapour measurements in the stratosphere together with a summary of the ozone work were described in the Bakerian lecture of the Royal Society which Dobson gave in 1945. To explain the results from these measurements together with the seasonal and latitudinal variations of ozone, a simple arrangement of the mean motions of air in the stratosphere was proposed which became known as the Dobson–Brewer circulation. In 1942 Dobson was awarded the Royal Society Rumford medal and in 1945 Oxford University conferred on him the title of professor. In 1947–9 he was president of the Royal Meteorological Society. In 1951 he was appointed CBE. He retired from his readership in 1950 and from his demonstratorship in 1956.

In 1914 Dobson married Winifred Duncome Rimer, the sister of one of his friends at Sedbergh School. She was the daughter of Henry Rimer, solicitor. There were three children of the marriage, a daughter and two sons. His wife died in 1952 and in 1954 he married Olive Mary Bacon who survived him. She was the daughter of Ernest Arthur Bacon, assistant registrar for the diocese of Oxford. In 1937 he moved his home and private laboratory to Shotover Hill on the east side of Oxford where ten acres of ground allowed him to pursue his interests in farming, especially in fruit growing. He was a keenly religious man, being a churchwarden at St. Aldate's church, Oxford, for many years.

Throughout his retirement years Dobson continued with work on ozone, helping considerably with its international organization through the International Ozone Commission. Observations were made from Shotover Hill on all possible occasions, the last being made on 30 January 1976, the day before he had the stroke from which he died 10 March 1976 at Thames Bank Nursing Home, Goring-on-Thames.

[J. T. Houghton and C. D. Walshaw in *Biographical Memoirs of Fellows of the Royal Society*, vol. xxiii, 1977; private information; personal knowledge.] J. T. Houghton

DODD, CHARLES HAROLD (1884–1973), biblical scholar, was born 7 April 1884 at Wrexham, Wales, the eldest of a family of four sons of Charles Dodd, headmaster of Brookside School, and his wife, Sarah, daughter of Edward Parsonage, of Wrexham. The family's love of learning and its deep involvement in the life of the local Independent chapel were strong formative influences on Dodd as a boy, although it was on his own initiative that he learnt Welsh. He was educated in Wrexham (of which in 1963 he was to become an honorary freeman), first at his father's school and then at Grove Park Secondary School. In 1902 he went up to University College, Oxford, with an open scholarship in classics and achieved a first both in honour moderations (1904) and in *literae humaniores* (1906). Later his college was to make him an honorary fellow (1950).

In 1907 he was elected a senior demy of Magdalen College, Oxford, and started research in early Christian epigraphy, but in less than a year he put his academic future at risk by entering Mansfield College, Oxford, to be trained for the ministry of the Congregational church. After being ordained in 1912, he served for three years as the minister of Brook Street church, Warwick, before being recalled to Oxford to succeed James Moffatt [q.v.] at Mansfield College, as Yates lecturer (subsequently professor) in New Testament Greek and exegesis. This appointment in 1915 launched him on a life of scholarship so free of major crises that his bibliography is virtually his biography.

The years 1915–30 were Dodd's great Oxford period, during which the first of his twenty books were published (*The Meaning of Paul for Today*, 1920, *The Authority of the Bible*, 1928) and many of the themes of his later writings adumbrated. As Grinfield lecturer on the Septuagint (1927–31), he developed that consuming interest in the background of early Christianity and that meticulous handling of language which characterized all his work. Two papers in this period (1923 and 1927) contained the germ of his most influential contribution to the interpretation of the New Testament. His revolutionary affirmation that the kingdom of God is a present reality in the ministry of Jesus came to be known as 'realized eschatology' and won wide acceptance, more popularly through his *The Parables of the Kingdom* (1935). Aberdeen University crowned this phase of Dodd's career with its honorary DD, the first of no less than eleven honorary degrees: from Oxford (DD and D.Litt.), Cambridge, London, Manchester, Glasgow, Wales, Harvard, Oslo, and Strasburg. Curiously, the British Academy failed to make him a fellow until 1946.

In 1930 Dodd moved to Manchester to succeed A. S. Peake [q.v.] in the Rylands chair of biblical criticism and exegesis and his new professorial duties gave him more time for his own books. These included the classic 'Moffatt Commentary' on *The Epistle of Paul to the Romans* (1932), *The Bible and the Greeks* (1935), and *The Apostolic Preaching and its Developments* (1936), a little masterpiece culled in haste from his Manchester lectures, which for the first time demonstrated an oral tradition behind the New Testament epistles.

In 1935 Dodd succeeded F. C. Burkitt [q.v.] as the Norris-Hulse professor of divinity in Cambridge and so became the first non-Anglican since the Restoration to hold a chair of divinity at either of the ancient universities. In 1936 he was elected a fellow (and in 1949 an honorary fellow) of Jesus College and immensely enjoyed the company at high table. During his fourteen years in Cambridge Dodd turned his attention to the enigmatic character of the fourth gospel, although the magisterial scale of his investigations delayed the publication of the results until after his retirement. In *The Interpretation of the Fourth Gospel* (1953) he analysed the evangelist's relationship to his complex cultural milieu and in *Historical Tradition in the Fourth Gospel* (1963) he argued that the evangelist was independent of the other gospels and had access to unique historical material about the ministry of Jesus. The implications of this second work, perhaps the greatest of his writings, have yet to be fully explored.

Dodd was always too enthusiastic a teacher and churchman to accept the view (especially prevalent in Cambridge) that popular lectures and broadcast talks were beneath the dignity of a scholar and, since he nearly always wrote his lectures and published almost everything he wrote, a large number of small books (rarely equalled for their clarity) extended his influence far beyond the universities. It was this rapport with the wider public, as well as his formidable learning, which led to the most sustained enterprise of his whole career. No sooner had he retired from his Cambridge chair in 1949 than he was appointed the general director of *The New English Bible*. Those who considered this undertaking a misguided dissipation of Dodd's time and energy were quite mistaken. To observe him at work with the translation panels over a period of twenty years was to know beyond a doubt that it engaged all his gifts and fulfilled all his deepest aspirations. In 1961, the year of publication of the New Testament, he was created CH, and in Westminster Abbey on 16 March 1970, less than a month from his eighty-sixth birthday and only four years before his own memorial service there, he had the immense satisfaction of presenting the completed translation to the Queen Mother and the representatives of the sponsoring churches.

In the same year he published *The Founder of Christianity* (1970). This last book summed up his lifelong conviction that the quest of the historic Jesus lies at the core of New Testament scholarship.

Dodd was a tiny man (once the cox of his college boat), neat in dress, rapid in speech, and physically immensely energetic. Despite his strict Puritan upbringing, he was tolerant and catholic in his sympathies and a leading figure in the ecumenical movement. In 1925 he married Phyllis Mary, (died 1963), the widow of John Elliott Terry and the daughter of George Stockings, of Norwich. They had two children, a son, Mark, who was to become controller of the external services of the BBC, and a daughter, Rachel, who married E. W. Heaton, later dean of Christ Church, Oxford. In his youth he had enjoyed organizing camps for boys and in his later years he took great pleasure in the company of his seven grandsons and two granddaughters. He spent his years of retirement in Oxford and died 22 September 1973 in a nursing home at Goring-on-Thames.

[F. W. Dillistone, *C. H. Dodd*, 1977; George B. Caird in *Proceedings* of the British Academy, vol. lx, 1974; R. W. Graham, *Charles Harold Dodd 1884–1973. A Bibliography of his Published Writings* (Lexington Theological Seminary Library Occasional Studies, 1974); personal knowledge.] E. W. HEATON

DODDS, SIR (EDWARD) CHARLES, first baronet (1899–1973), medical scientist and professor of biochemistry in the University of London, was born 13 October 1899 at Liverpool, the only child of Ralph Edward Dodds, shop inspector, of West Derby, Liverpool, and his wife Jane, daughter of Charles Pack, business man, of London. He was educated at Harrow County School for Boys, and entered the Middlesex Hospital Medical School in 1916.

At the Middlesex Dodds very quickly showed his abilities as a scientist. He won the class prize for chemistry in his first year and, soon after returning to the Medical School following a period of military service that ended after he had a bout of pneumonia, he became a demonstrator in chemistry to Dr A. M. Kellas; this helped him to meet the costs of his medical education, and he obtained further income by coaching students. In 1919, after achieving distinction in the second MB examination, he became assistant in physiology to Professor Swale Vincent, and in 1920 he succeeded (Sir) E. L. Kennaway [q.v.], the first assistant in chemical pathology to the Middlesex Hospital. Dodds was appointed lecturer in biochemistry in 1921, the year in which he qualified MRCS, LRCP. The following year he graduated MB, BS with honours. He had been an exemplary student, and had already proved his abilities as an excellent teacher, especially of the emerging subject of biochemistry. This was, however, only the end of the beginning of an outstanding career.

His early researches were concerned principally with gastric and upper intestinal secretions, and their relationship to changes in alveolar carbon dioxide tensions. However, from 1923 onwards, Dodds became increasingly involved in endocrinological research, where his early interests included improving the methods then available for the purification of insulin, and studies that sought to identify the 'female sex hormone'. He graduated Ph.D. in 1924 and MD in 1926.

In 1925 Samuel Augustine Courtauld was persuaded by A. E. (later Lord) Webb-Johnson [q.v.], dean of the Medical School, to endow the Courtauld chair of biochemistry for Dodds and, at the age of twenty-five, he became the youngest professor in the university. Courtauld also financed the building of an Institute of Biochemistry for the Middlesex, and in 1927 Dodds became the first director of the 'Courtauld', which was officially opened in 1928. He continued to hold both these posts until he retired in 1965.

For some, such early and meteoric promotion would have been counter-productive. Not so with Dodds. Because of his standing as one of the country's leading clinical biochemists he was called upon in 1928, by Lord Dawson of Penn [q.v.], to undertake some investigations required during the illness of King George V; for this he was appointed MVO the following year. However, his greatest claim to fame derived from his work on the synthetic oestrogens; this began in 1932 and led to the discovery of diethylstilboestrol in 1938. In carrying out this research Dodds demonstrated one of his greatest strengths—the ability to recognize and to attract to the Courtauld highly talented research workers, of whom Wilfrid Lawson deserves special mention for the part he played in the synthesis of the artificial oestrogens.

Diethylstilboestrol had the great advantage of being active by mouth. It proved valuable for the control of menopausal symptoms, but its major therapeutic application was in the control of metastastic carcinoma of the prostate. It was also used in veterinary practice, for caponizing, and for the tenderizing of meat. In recognition of this work, Dodds was elected FRSE in 1941 and FRS the following year. He had become FRCP in 1933.

Professionally, Dodds's pre-eminence and scholarship were recognized in many ways. At various times he held office as chairman of the Biochemical Society, chairman of the section of biological chemistry of the International Union of Pure and Applied Chemistry, master of the Worshipful Society of the Apothecaries of London, and Harveian librarian of the Royal College of Physicians of London. He became FRIC in 1968. He was knighted in 1954 and created baronet in 1964. He was awarded numerous prizes and medals and was invited to deliver many named lectures. He received honorary degrees from the universities of Birmingham, Bologna, Cambridge, Chicago, Glasgow, and Melbourne, and honorary fellowships from several colleges world-wide. However, the recognition that undoubtedly gave him most pleasure was his election as president of the Royal College of Physicians of London, the first time this distinction had been accorded to a laboratory-based physician; he held the post from 1962 to 1966. His portrait, by Raymond Piper, hangs in the College.

Dodds served on many important committees, including Research Council committees, the National Research Development Corporation, the Food Standards committee, the scientific advisory committee of the British Empire Cancer Campaign, and the council of the Royal Society. He was chief consultant to the Beecham Group, and was to a large extent responsible for the development of facilities that enabled it later to produce and market successfully several semi-synthetic penicillins.

Despite the weight of his many responsibilities, Dodds maintained several other interests that made up for his lack of recreations. As a young man he had greatly enjoyed motor racing, and for some years drove as an amateur at Brooklands. Thereafter he retained his love of Bentleys, latterly chauffeur-driven because (he said) he always speeded if he drove himself. Dodds liked to entertain, and his taste in the selection of food and wine was of the highest order. For twenty-three years he was custodian of the cellar of the Society of Apothecaries.

Throughout his professional career Dodds was constantly supported by his wife, whom he had known from early childhood as his parents moved to Darlington when he was young. He married in 1923 Constance Elizabeth (died 1969), only daughter of John Thomas Jordan, business man, of Darlington. They had only one son, Ralph Jordan (born 1928), who succeeded to the baronetcy when his father died, at his home in Sussex Square, Paddington, London, 16 December 1973.

[F. Dickens in *Biographical Memoirs of Fellows of the Royal Society*, vol. xxi, 1975; B. W. Windeyer in *Munk's Roll*, vol. vi; *The Times*, 18 and 28 December 1973; private information.]

GORDON WHITBY

DODDS, ERIC ROBERTSON (1893–1979), classical scholar, was born 26 July 1893 at Banbridge, county Down, the only child of Robert Dodds, the headmaster of Banbridge Academy, a small grammar school, and his wife, Anne Fleming Allen. He lost his father at the age of seven, and after that his mother supported him and herself by teaching; she was a conscientious but possessive and unsympathetic parent, and Dodds's childhood was by no means altogether happy. At St. Andrew's College, Dublin, and later at Campbell College, Belfast, Dodds obtained a good grounding in ancient and modern literature and held his own among the boys; but at the latter place he came into conflict with a pompous headmaster and was expelled for 'gross, studied and sustained insolence'.

In 1912 he won a scholarship to University College, Oxford. Coming from a different country and holding radical opinions, he did not find life in Oxford entirely easy; but he discovered some congenial persons, including Aldous Huxley, T. S. Eliot [qq.v.], and T. W. Earp, and he was successful in his studies. He had a good tutor in A. B. Poynton, and found inspiration in the teaching of G. Gilbert A. Murray [q.v.]; in 1913 he won the Craven scholarship and in 1914 obtained a first class in classical moderations and the Ireland scholarship. After the outbreak of war he worked for a time as a medical orderly in a hospital in Serbia, but returned to take his final examinations. His support of the Irish Easter rebellion of 1916 led to his being asked to leave Oxford, but he was able to sit for *literae humaniores* and obtained a first class in 1917.

For a time Dodds taught in a school in Dublin, where he met W. B. Yeats, AE, E. S. Lennox Robinson [qq.v.], and Stephen McKenna, whose journal and letters he edited in 1936. But in 1919 he was appointed lecturer in classics at the University College of Reading (later Reading University) and studied neoplatonism, then an unfashionable subject, with the enthusiasm of a believer; later after the belief had left him the interest would remain. In 1923–4 he published two useful volumes of *Select Passages Illustrative of Neoplatonism* (texts and translations). In 1923 he married the intelligent and cultivated Annie Edwards Powell (died 1973), who was lecturer in English in the same university. She was the daughter of the Revd Canon Astell Drayner Powell and the sister of the Right Revd G. E. Powell.

In 1924 Dodds was appointed professor of Greek in the University of Birmingham, where he occupied a delightful house and was at the centre of a congenial circle, including W. H. Auden and Louis MacNeice [qq.v.], whom he appointed to a lectureship in his department, and whose *Collected Poems* he later edited (1966). He published further important studies of neoplatonism, which culminated in his admirable edition of *The Elements of Theology of Proclus* (1933), the most useful summary of neoplatonic metaphysics surviving from antiquity: he also brought out important and original articles about Euripides. Some of the *Thirty-two Poems* which he published in 1929 have found places in various anthologies.

In 1936 Dodds was appointed to succeed Gilbert Murray in the regius chair of Greek at Oxford. The appointment seemed surprising, and was by no means generally welcomed; there was more than one strong candidate in the Oxford faculty, and Dodds's rumoured support of Socialism and Irish nationalism did not make him popular. A more outgoing character might have overcome more rapidly the difficulties which Dodds had to face; but he did not quickly get on terms with new acquaintances, and for a long time greatly regretted Birmingham. But his lectures, delivered in a deep and impressive voice and combining scholarly exactitude with literary sensitivity, were from the first greatly appreciated by their audiences.

In 1939 Dodds volunteered for war service. In 1941 he joined the Foreign Office Research Department and in 1942–3 was in China on a cultural mission; in 1945 he visited the United States, and when the war was over went to Germany to help in the rehabilitation of the educational system. In 1944 he published a memorable edition of Euripides' *Bacchae*, with introduction and commentary. Technical matters are dealt with with the highest competence; but an even more notable feature of the book is the imaginative sympathy with which the Dionysiac religion and its antagonists are treated.

In 1949 Dodds travelled to Berkeley, California, to give the Sather lectures, which resulted in the publication two years later of *The Greeks and the Irrational*. Interest in the problems with which the book dealt was hardly new, neither was the application of modern anthropology and psychology to their solution; but Dodds went about his task with deep learning and with solid judgement, handling early Greek religion with a sympathetic understanding seldom attained by nineteenth-century rationalists. It may be argued that his account of the 'enlightenment' of the fifth century and the reaction against it is somewhat conditioned by an unconscious identification of the ancient with the modern 'enlightenment'; and one may doubt whether Dodds's cautiously expressed hope will be fulfilled—a hope that in future psychology may save us from that 'fear of freedom' which he found chiefly responsible for the decline of Greek rationalism. But the book is written with great literary skill, and uses consummate learning to throw light on problems of central importance not only for the past but also for the present and the future. For many years it has exercised great influence.

After the war Dodds and his wife began to feel far more at ease in Oxford; younger members of the faculty held him in high esteem, and gradually the great value of his work was coming to be appreciated.

In 1959 Dodds brought out a text of Plato's *Gorgias* with commentary, excellent both from the technical and the interpretative point of view; and in 1964 he published *Pagan and Christian in an Age of Anxiety*, a book consisting of three Wiles lectures delivered at the Queen's University, Belfast. In these he deals with the beliefs of Christians and pagans between the accession of Marcus Aurelius and the conversion of Constantine, and well brings out the distressing resemblances between the superstitions entertained by both. In 1973 he included six old and four new articles in a collection called *The Ancient Concept of Progress*; and in 1977 appeared *Missing Persons*, an admirable autobiography which was awarded the Duff Cooper memorial prize.

Like his teacher and predecessor Gilbert Murray, Dodds was actively interested in the work of the Society for Psychical Research, serving on its council from 1927 and being president from 1961 to 1963. He found the evidence for telepathy convincing, but was never persuaded by the alleged evidence for survival after death.

Dodds was never easy to get to know well; his moods varied, like those of many sufferers from asthma, and at times he withdrew into himself. His complicated character seemed to combine various Irish strains, emanating from both south and north, and sometimes one and sometimes another seemed to be uppermost. But those who could penetrate his defences found him a good friend and an agreeable companion. His talk, like his writing, showed much wit and humour; he read widely and ranged over many topics; and though his early radicalism became milder, he showed deep understanding of the rebellious young, even when their kind of rebellion differed from his own. In the inaugural lecture which he gave at Oxford in 1936, with the title *Humanism and Technique in Greek Studies*, Dodds suggested that the time had come when we should devote less energy to textual studies and more to general interpretation. He himself excelled in both, and made a contribution to the understanding of Greek thought which is likely to find a permanent place in the history of scholarship.

Dodds was a corresponding member of the Academia Sinica, the Bavarian Academy, the American Academy of Arts and Sciences, and the French Institut; he held honorary degrees from Manchester, Dublin, Edinburgh, Birmingham, and Belfast. He became a fellow of the British Academy in 1942, and received its Kenyon medal in 1971. In 1960 he became an honorary fellow of University College, Oxford and in 1962 an honorary Student of Christ Church.

After retiring in 1960 he went on living in his house in Old Marston, in which Cromwell is believed to have received the surrender of the city, keeping in touch with friends and colleagues until his death at home 8 April 1979.

[E. R. Dodds, *Missing Persons*, 1971; D. A. Russell in *Proceedings* of the British Academy, vol. lxv, 1979; H. Lloyd-Jones, *Gnomon*, vol. lii, 1980, pp. 78–83; personal knowledge.]
HUGH LLOYD-JONES

DONNELLY, DESMOND LOUIS (1920–1974), MP and writer, was born 16 October 1920 at Gohaingaon in the Sibsagar district of Assam, the only son and elder child of Louis James Donnelly, a tea-planter, and his wife, (Florence) Aimée Tucker. He was educated in Gloucestershire and at Bembridge School, Isle of Wight. At the age of nineteen he joined the RAF and served in it, with the rank of flight lieutenant, until 1946. In the same year he became editor of *Town and Country Planning*, and from 1948 to 1950 was director of the Town and Country Planning Association at a time when post-war reconstruction put such matters in the forefront of public affairs.

But Donnelly had already taken steps towards a political career by fighting Evesham as a Common Wealth candidate in the general election of 1945 and being adopted as Labour candidate for county Down the following year. However, his real opportunity was to come in 1950 when at Pembroke he defeated the long-established member, Gwilym Lloyd-George (later Viscount Tenby, q.v.) by 129 votes in a straight fight.

During his early years in Parliament he was associated with the Bevanite wing of the Labour Party but broke dramatically with the Left in a speech on German rearmament delivered at the Labour Party conference at Scarborough in 1954. He had always seen himself as a patriot and he now began to take a vigorous part in controversies on international matters, showing a particular interest in Soviet affairs and the cold war. He became a supporter of Britain's membership of the European Community and a strong opponent of unilateral nuclear disarmament. He also became something of a transatlantic figure and his major book *Struggle for the World* (1965) was, perhaps, more suited to an American than a British readership. He also wrote regularly for newspapers and was a political columnist for the *Daily Herald* (1960–3) and chief political correspondent of the *News of the World* (1968–70).

Donnelly became an ally of Hugh Gaitskell [q.v.] from his election as leader of the Labour Party in 1955. Although not within the inner circle of Gaitskell's friends, it is probable that he would have received ministerial office had Gaitskell lived. But there was no chance that Harold Wilson (later Lord Wilson of Rievaulx) would find a place for him when he formed his government in 1964.

Donnelly did not delay long in making his views known from the back-benches in a House where Labour's majority was soon reduced to two. Together with Woodrow Wyatt, he succeeded in postponing the government's plans for the nationalization of the steel industry.

He then moved quickly into an even more independent position where general criticism of the Labour government became the rule. Despite the arrival of Roy Jenkins at the Exchequer and a more hopeful mood amongst his old friends, he resigned the whip in January 1968 and was later expelled from the Labour Party. In due course, he launched his own Democratic Party but at the 1970 general election he was beaten into third place in Pembroke, getting a little over 20 per cent of the vote. Within a year, he was on the move again, startling his erstwhile allies by joining the Conservative Party and explaining that this had been his ultimate destiny since the death of Gaitskell. He threw himself into Conservative activities and made a strong bid for the safe seat of Hove. He was to be disappointed. The 1974 general election was the first he had failed to contest since he came of age. Lonely and increasingly isolated, he took his own life in a hotel room at West Drayton, Middlesex, 4 April 1974.

Donnelly was an enjoyable companion, thoroughly sybaritic with an engaging touch of vulgarity. Apart from writing, travelling, and his parliamentary work, he found time for business contacts and activities. In his progress across the political spectrum, he mirrored others of his generation and he was prescient in his analysis of the shortcomings of the Labour Party. In an earlier age, less attached to party, his individual style might have won him a more enduring political role.

In 1947 Donnelly married Rosemary, daughter of (William) John Taggart, medical doctor, of Belfast; they had a twin son and daughter and a second daughter.

[*The Times*, 5 April 1974; private information; personal knowledge.] WILLIAM RODGERS

DONOVAN, TERENCE NORBERT, BARON DONOVAN (1898–1971), lord of appeal in ordinary, was born 13 June 1898 in Walthamstow, Essex, the second son in the family of five children of Timothy Cornelius Donovan, Liberal political agent and private tutor, and his wife, Laura, daughter of James McSheedy, of Cardiff. After Brockley Grammar School, he enlisted at the age of eighteen, being commissioned in the Bedfordshire Regiment. He was at the front in France and Belgium in 1917 and 1918, and was later a rear gunner in the Royal Air Force, as a lieutenant. Upon demobilization, he won first place in an open examination for higher posts in the Civil Service and entered the revenue department in 1920. In his spare time he studied for the bar and was called by the Middle Temple in 1924. Lacking the financial resources and connections to support the early years of practice, he waited until 1932 before resigning his appointment to begin, in chambers at 3 Temple Gardens, what soon developed into a substantial practice in revenue cases. He took silk in 1945.

It was the war and the unemployment which followed it that sparked his active involvement in the Labour Party, the Fabian Society, and the League of Nations Union. In the 1945 general election he was the successful Labour Party candidate for the East Leicester constituency, and in February 1950 he was returned for North East Leicester. He was a good constituency MP, particularly concerned with slum clearance in Leicester, but apart from his work as chairman of the Parliamentary Labour Party's legal and judicial group, he made relatively little impression as a back-bencher.

His real ambitions were in the legal world. His reticence about expressing those ambitions led to some surprise when he resigned his seat in July 1950 to accept appointment as a judge in the King's Bench division. The foundation had been laid in his work, from 1946, as a JP for Hampshire, chairman of the Winchester county bench, and deputy chairman of the appeals committee of Hampshire quarter-sessions. He was knighted upon his appointment to the High Court and remained there until 1960 when he was promoted to the Court of Appeal and admitted to the Privy Council. In 1963 he was appointed a lord of appeal in ordinary. Surprisingly for one whose practice had been almost exclusively at the revenue bar, he was a conscientious and effective trial judge, being selected by the lord chief justice, Lord Parker of Waddington [q.v.] to sit on the highly publicized and arduous trial in 1958 of several members of the Brighton police force, including the chief constable, on charges of conspiracy to obstruct the course of justice. As an appeal judge he made no significant contribution to the development of the law, but his judicial colleagues valued his expertise in tax cases, his prodigious memory, and his ability, manifest in his judgements, to express himself accurately and tersely. He was a supporter of a new activist tendency in judicial lawmaking, led by Lord Reid [q.v.]. In Donovan's words, 'the common law is moulded by the judges, and it is still their province to adapt it from time to time, so as to make it serve the interests of those it binds'. He usually had a good feeling for the policy of legislation. This was evident in his judgement in the Court of Appeal in the seminal trade union case of *Rookes v. Barnard* (1962) when he took the view that if a threat to strike in breach of contract constituted unlawful means for the purposes of the tort of conspiracy, a point that no one had thought of before that case, the immunities conferred upon strikers by the Trade Disputes Act of 1906 would be 'largely illusory' and this would encourage lightning strikes without warning. Although the House of Lords subsequently disagreed with his view, it was restored by the amending Trade Disputes Act of 1965.

Despite his lack of experience in industrial relations, the sympathy displayed in that case towards the traditional values of collective bargaining, as well as his political background, made him an acceptable choice as chairman of the important royal commission on trade unions and employers' associations (1965–8). He had previously shown his abilities as a law reformer on the Denning committee on divorce procedure (1946), the Lewis committee on court martial procedure (1946–8), and as chairman of the criminal appeals committee (1964). He drove the royal commission on a very light rein, leaving organization and the programme of research to others. He presided graciously and wittily when evidence was heard, but did not question witnesses closely. At the internal meetings he was still less forceful, allowing his colleagues to debate and develop the themes of the report. He drafted the introduction and chapter xiv (Changes in the Law), but left the rest to a drafting committee without the slightest intervention. When the work was done he appended his own addendum and other supplementary notes and reservations. This was a style different in most respects from other contemporary judicial chairmen of industrial relations inquiries such as Lord Devlin and Lord Pearson [q.v.].

His views were, however, decisive on one central issue. Six commissioners proposed that collective agreements should be made legally enforceable, while the remaining six argued that this would be inconsistent with the main argument of the report. Donovan knew that there was strong support for enforcement in the Labour Cabinet. Yet after careful thought, for the reasons set out in his addendum, he came to the view that there was no case for legislative enforcement of collective agreements, contrary to the will of the parties. He continued to voice these views in the subsequent debates on the Labour government's *In Place of Strife* (1969), and the Conservative government's Industrial Relations Bill (1971). He joined with a majority of the commissioners in proposing that immunity from actions in tort for inducing breaches of contract should be confined to registered trade unions and this was reflected in the Industrial Relations Act of 1971. He saw the differences between Labour and Conservatives as ones of means not ends, but was critical of the 1971 Bill for not doing enough to win worker co-operation.

He opposed the permanent intrusion of the High Court in this field. He regarded the essential difference between the report and the Bill as being the priority the report gave to causes not symptoms, in particular the reform of procedures and the formalization of plant bargaining, but he recognized that the Bill reflected some of the commission's thinking, such as the creation of the commission for industrial relations and the extension of the jurisdiction of industrial tribunals, the right for employees not to be unfairly dismissed, and the procedures to deal with disputes over trade union recognition.

Donovan was created a life peer in 1964. In 1970 he became treasurer of the Middle Temple, a strenuous task for a man who had for some years been in ill health. He died of heart failure in London 12 December 1971.

He married on 13 April 1925 Marjorie Florence, daughter of Leah and Charles Murray, a chemist of Winchester. They had two sons and a daughter.

There is a portrait of Donovan at the Middle Temple.

[*The Times*, 13 December 1971; private information.] B. A. Hepple

DOWTY, Sir GEORGE HERBERT (1901–1975), aeronautical engineer, inventor, and industrialist, was born 27 April 1901 at Pershore, Worcestershire, the son of William Dowty, a druggist and chemist in Pershore, and his wife, Laura Masters. He was the elder of twin boys by half an hour and the seventh son in the family. The twin boys were educated in a small private school in Pershore until 1913, when they both entered the Worcester Royal Grammar School, which they were obliged to leave at the age of fourteen because their older brothers had been conscripted into the army and they had to help in running the various family businesses. At the age of twelve George Dowty lost his right eye during some experiments with photographic materials, when a bottle of magnesium powder exploded.

Dowty spent a year in the family business, but his early interest in engineering and applicational science led him to join Heenan & Froude as a workshop boy entry. His first job, pressure testing, using a hydraulic hand pump, of the cast iron cylinder for aero-engines introduced him to hydraulics, which were later to be so important to him. Realizing his need for a special engineering education he began what became a lifetime of study and joined evening classes at the local Victoria Institute, paying his own fees. At the same time he took postal courses on the internal combustion engine. This interest in engineering was soon noticed by a benevolent foreman who encouraged Dowty to move through a variety of departments in order to widen his experience and knowledge. He finally joined the drawing office, the centre of decision-making for engineering products and an excellent training ground for a future engineering designer.

In July 1918 Dowty answered an advertisement in *Flight* and obtained a new job as a draughtsman with the British Aerial Transport Company in London. The company's chief designer was Bobby Noordvyn, a Dutchman and a pioneer of aircraft design in Britain and later in Canada. Dowty, eager to learn, worked on undercarriages and, in Noordvyn's creative environment, accelerated his career rapidly and perhaps impatiently.

After a brief post-war flirtation with several non-aircraft companies (for example, he designed moulds for gold balls at Dunlop in 1920) he joined the A. V. Roe Company at Southampton. There he specialized in undercarriages, in the design office. Here his further hydraulics reading was useful. He knew the formulae for determining the resistance of oil through an orifice (vital for calculating the energy absorption of an aircraft undercarriage). By the age of twenty-one he had designed landing gear for the first Ciera Autogyro and for the Avro Aldershot.

In 1924 Dowty left A. V. Roe to join the Gloucestershire Aircraft Company (later the Gloster Aircraft Co.). By this time he had read a number of papers on undercarriage design to the Institution of Aeronautical Engineers, and was already working at home on several ideas that he was later to patent. He also wrote articles for the technical press to supplement his income and examined the application of his hydraulics theory to other fields—for example, in his 'Balanced and Servo Control Surfaces' (Tech. Memo. No. 563, 1926). This was a principle so advanced that it was not to be developed for nearly thirty years. In 1927 he took out a patent for a wheel incorporating oil shock absorbers, steel springs, and brakes operating on the wheel rims. In 1931 he set up his own one-man company while still employed at Gloster Aircraft—the Aircraft Components Company, which was designed to answer a need to provide main aircraft design companies with specialist accessories and equipment. It advertised many of George Dowty's designs and patents, at first to no avail. But June 1931 saw a change of fortune when he received his first order from Kawasaki in Japan, to fit Dowty internally-sprung undercarriage wheels to their Type 92 aircraft. Dowty left Gloster Aircraft the same month, borrowed against a life assurance, and established single-handed the first foundations of a vast international engineering enterprise. With one order, no factory, but subcontract manufacture and the help in only the evening of two friends, Dowty designed, ordered, and assembled two of his wheels and within nine weeks shipped them to Japan, being paid on shipment.

Dowty recruited his first two employees in November 1931. A major breakthrough occurred in 1934 when Dowty offered to HP, Holland, a pair of oleostruts of new design for the Gloster Gauntlet aircraft. This gave him his first large production order and was followed by a similar order for the Gladiator. Company growth was now possible. The company went public in 1936, Dowty holding only a small percentage of the equity. During World War II Dowty's inventive and creative engineer's mind was fully unleashed. Twenty-eight different aircraft were fitted with Dowty equipment, which included 12,900 sets for the Hurricane, over 90,000 other undercarriage units, and over a million hydraulic units. Plants were set up throughout Britain and in Canada and the USA.

After World War II Dowty applied his new approaches to hydraulics to wider fields—motorcycle forks, hydraulic pit props, industrial pumps, and hydraulic control systems. In 1954 a group holding company was formed with the Canadian operation generating 50 per cent of the total turnover. Rotal Propellor Ltd. were acquired in 1959, Boulton Paul in 1954, and Meco of Worcester in 1964.

From 1935 Arle Court in Cheltenham was both the company's headquarters and Dowty's home. He walked along the corridor to his office until three years before he died, when he took up semi-retirement on the Isle of Man.

Dowty was active in the Royal Aeronautical Society, being elected its president for 1952–3. The society made him an honorary fellow and awarded him the gold medal in 1955. He was also president of the Society of British Aircraft Constructors in 1960–1. He was knighted in 1956 and received honorary doctorates from Bath University (1966) and Cranfield Institute of Technology (1972). In 1971 he was master of the Worshipful Company of Coach Makers and Coach Harness Makers. He was an honorary freeman of Cheltenham (1955) and Tewkesbury (1964).

Keenly interested in cricket, Dowty put the Worcestershire County Cricket Club on to a sound financial basis during his term as its president (1962–6). He played tennis and golf well and captained England against Scotland at curling. Chess and snooker were other interests and he was very much involved in the community and social activities in the area around Tewkesbury and Pershore.

In 1948 he married Marguerite Anne Gowans, daughter of M. J. H. Lockie, of Newmarket, Ontario, Canada. They had a son and a daughter. Dowty died 7 December 1975 at his home in the Isle of Man.

[*The Times* and *Daily Telegraph* 9 December 1975; Flight Directory of British Aviation; memorial lecture by Sir Robert Hunt for the Royal Aeronautical Society, 9 April 1981; personal knowledge.]

M. G. Farley

DRIBERG, THOMAS EDWARD NEIL, Baron Bradwell (1905–1976), journalist and politician, was born at Crowborough, Sussex, 22 May 1905, the youngest of the three sons of John James Street Driberg, of the Indian Civil Service, and his wife, Amy Mary Irving Bell, of Lockerbie, Dumfriesshire.

His father, who had been born in 1842, died when he was fourteen. As his brothers were already adult when he was born, the formative influence on his childhood was his majestic, clinging, and not totally lovable mother, under whose tutelage he grew up in lonely and genteel penury at Crowborough, a town which came to symbolize all he found most death-dealing in British bourgeois life. His inevitable adolescent rebellion took the twin forms of riotous Anglo-Catholicism and the delights of homosexual seduction, which he discovered, somewhat prematurely, at the age of twelve, playing then, as always, the active role. At the age of fifteen to these he added the third of his lifelong ruling passions by joining the Communist Party.

In 1918 he went to Lancing College on a scholarship. Although hopeless at games and a natural rebel, he was a success at school, rising to be deputy head boy. Unfortunately one of his sexual adventures came to the notice of authority. He left under the traditional cloud, took private tuition, and won the third scholarship in classics at Christ Church, Oxford, in 1924. He never sat for his finals, since he went down in the summer of 1927, under another cloud which had little to do with his undistinguished performance in classical honour moderations. During this time however, he rapidly identified himself with the aesthetes, whose upper-class and bohemian lifestyle stood for all that Crowborough was not. He joined the editorial board of *Cherwell*, then at the height of its *réclame*, and wrote poetry which was commended by (Dame) Edith Sitwell [q.v.]. At the same time he was an active member of the Communist Party. During the general strike he volunteered for work at the party's headquarters; he spent one vacation as a cub-reporter on the communist *Sunday Worker*; in another he earned a few pounds as a pavement artist operating in Russell Square.

Down from Oxford, gifted with good looks, literary ability, smart friends, and no money, and determined under no circumstances to live at Crowborough, he found employment, satisfying to his *nostalgie de la boue*, in a Soho café, which doubled up as a brothel whose speciality was fat girls. From this he was rescued by (Dame) Edith

Sitwell [q.v.]. Appalled by his descriptions of the life, she gave him an introduction to (Sir) Beverley Baxter, then managing director of the *Daily Express*; he, in his turn, in 1928 found him a niche in the organization as assistant to the gossip columnist 'Dragoman'. Here he attracted the attention of Lord Beaverbook [q.v.] who suppressed the Dragoman column, and gave Driberg the freedom of a column of his own, 'These Names Make News', under the signature of William Hickey, the name of a gossipy eighteenth-century diarist. Here he widened the content of the column from the trivia of the merely rich and fashionable to cover the *haute bohème* of his friends, with sympathetic mention of contemporary experiment in the arts and increasingly explicit left-wing criticism of the establishment. Although the column was designedly written in the jerky style derived from *Time*, it was nevertheless meticulously literate, to the despair of sub-editors, but with the result that the Hickey column maintained a literary standard unsurpassed since then.

With Beaverbrook he maintained a permanent love–hate relationship, later made explicit in his *Beaverbrook: A Study in Power and Frustration* (1956). There were violent rows; but Beaverbrook allowed him political latitude; gave him considerable sums of money; and once when he was faced with a criminal charge (on which he was acquitted) paid the legal expenses, and contrived that no mention of the case should appear in the press. In 1943, however, he was dismissed after a disagreement with Arthur Christiansen [q.v.], the editor. He then transferred his column to *Reynolds News*, and later wrote regularly for the *People* and the *New Statesman*. But it was in the *Daily Mail* he pulled off in 1956 the scoop of his career; an interview in Moscow with Guy Burgess. He also made frequent appearances on radio and television.

By this time he was in Parliament. In 1942 he stood at the Maldon by-election as an Independent. This was made possible by the fact that he had, the year before, been summarily dismissed from the Communist Party because the party caucus discovered that he was an agent of MI5, to which he had been recruited in the late 1930s. He was returned by an overwhelming majority in what had become his home constituency; for in 1938 he had bought Bradwell Lodge, a fine Regency house in the district. This remained his chief home until 1971; and here he entertained generously, with fine disregard for the class or moral repute of his guests.

At the 1945 election he retained the seat—but this time as an official Labour candidate—and represented the constituency for the next ten years. From 1949 he was annually elected to the national executive, rising to chairman in 1957–8. Despite this eminence, he lost the seat in 1958; but next year he won in Barking, which he represented until his retirement in 1974.

An outstanding back-bencher, with a high reputation as a constituency MP, the hero of the young left and the way-out (for he was always on the side of the young and championed the socially least acceptable causes), he was too maverick to be trusted by the party establishment with whom he had several brushes, notably when he was severely censured in 1950 for gross neglect of parliamentary duties by taking three months off to be a war correspondent in Korea. Moreover, as rumour of his sexual *mores* had become widespread, it is not surprising that he never attained Cabinet rank. Possibly in the hope that his chances of promotion might be increased by the semblance of respectability conferred by matrimony, he married, on 30 June 1951, Mrs Ena Mary Binfield, daughter of Myer Lyttleton, with the full panache of pontifical high mass at St. Mary's, Bourne Street. Despite the valiant attempts of his wife to keep the marriage afloat, it collapsed almost from the beginning. Though never formally separated they lived increasingly independent lives. Mrs Driberg—she refused the title from socialist principle—died in 1977.

Retiring from the Commons in 1974 Driberg was created a life peer in the following year under the title of Baron Bradwell, of Bradwell-juxta-Mare. Although he enjoyed the dignity, he played only a minimal part in the Lords in the nine months that remained to him. He was unused to the conventions of the upper chamber; he was in poor health, and preoccupied with writing his memoirs, an unfinished version of which was published posthumously in 1977 under the title *Ruling Passions*. On 12 August 1976 he had a heart attack in a taxi, and died in St. Mary's Hospital, Paddington. A funeral requiem was sung at St. Matthew's, Westminster (in whose clergy house he had lived for three of his last years). His body was interred in Bradwell church and within sight of the house which he loved possibly more than any other object in his life.

His personality was more than life-size, both better and worse than most men's. He showed a paradoxical mixture of extreme left-wing convictions and upper-class social attitudes. He was a convinced monarchist; permissive in morals and pedantic in etiquette; a liturgist; a gourmet; a collector of old books; and a patron of the avant-garde in painting and drama; a terrific tease. He was lovable and exasperating. He had hundreds of friends and none to whom he opened his inmost heart. He was voracious for experience and invariably disappointed by it; arrogant, and yet with a deep self-hatred which induced him to leave dispositions that at his memorial service, in place of the conventional panegyric, a friend should preach an 'anti-panegyric' exposing and excoriating his vices.

[Tom Driberg, *Ruling Passions*, 1977; private information; personal knowledge.]

GERARD IRVINE

DRIVER, SIR GODFREY ROLLES (1892–1975), Hebraist and Semitist, was born in Christ Church, Oxford, 20 August 1892, the eldest in the family of three sons and two daughters of Samuel Rolles Driver [q.v.], regius professor of Hebrew and canon of Christ Church, and his wife, Mabel, daughter of Edmund Burr, of Burgh, Norfolk. Classics formed the centre of his education at Winchester and New College, Oxford, but he was then already developing his knowledge of Hebrew, gained from his father. He obtained a second class in classical honour moderations in 1913. War service during 1915–19 took Driver to the Balkans, France, and the Near East. He gained an MC and was mentioned in dispatches.

In 1919 he became a fellow of Magdalen College, and remained one throughout his life until on his retirement in 1962 he became an honorary fellow. His tutorship was in classics, but his interest in Semitic languages quickly became dominant. 1925 saw the publication of books from three different regions of the Semitic spectrum: a grammar of colloquial Arabic, basically prepared during the war, a translation from Syriac of the theological treatise *The Bazaar of Heracleides* (jointly with L. Hodgson), and a volume of Akkadian letters. In 1927 Oxford appointed Driver lecturer (and in 1928 reader) in comparative Semitic philology. The thirties saw his academic distinction even further enhanced: he held the Grinfield lectureship on the Septuagint (1935–9), was deputy professor of Hebrew in 1934 during a vacancy (not being in holy orders, he was not eligible for the chair which his father had held), and published (with Sir John Miles) *The Assyrian Laws* (1935) and his seminal *Problems of the Hebrew Verbal System* (1936), following up a subject to which his father also had made a notable contribution. He was an editor of the *Journal of Theological Studies* (1933–40); its pages formed one of the main outlets for the stream of detailed philological notes in which he was a master. His distinction was recognized by the award of the title of professor of Semitic philology in 1938 and by election as a fellow of the British Academy in 1939. He was president of the Society for the Study of the Old Testament in 1937 and long continued a devoted member. The distractions of war did not prevent him from delivering the Schweich lectures of the British Academy in 1944, published in 1948 as *Semitic Writing* (revised edition, 1976). To this Dictionary he contributed the notices of G. B. Gray, Sir Arthur Cowley, and S. H. Langdon.

The post-war years saw Driver at the height of his influence, an internationally renowned scholar whose methods and results were widely discussed. Major publications included editions of Babylonian laws, of Aramaic documents, and of Ugaritic mythological texts. His historical judgements on the Dead Sea scrolls, on the other hand, were not widely accepted. In Oxford he took a leading part in the inauguration and direction of the Oriental Institute, and led a campaign to separate the regius professorship of Hebrew from a Christ Church canonry; this change was effected in 1959–60. Particularly important to Driver was his large collection of lexical materials, and along with it his work on the Old Testament of the New English Bible; the translation (published in 1970) incorporated numerous ideas from his notes.

Further honours came his way: the Burkitt medal in 1953, and honorary fellowships and doctorates from a variety of institutions including Oxford itself (1970). He was appointed CBE in 1958 and knighted in 1968. Two volumes were published in his honour: the *Journal of Semitic Studies*, vol. vii, 2 (1962) and *Hebrew and Semitic Studies* (ed. D. W. Thomas and W. D. McHardy, 1963); the latter contains a select bibliography of Driver's works up to 1962, supplemented by J. A. Emerton in *Vetus Testamentum*, vol. xxx (1980), pp. 185–91.

Driver's scholarship had two main aspects: the editing of new-found texts, and the use of comparative philology to solve problems of the Hebrew Bible. The critical study which his father had done so much to make accepted in England was of less interest to the son, though he continued broadly to accept its findings. He believed that the meanings of many biblical words had been lost and could be restored through Arabic and other cognate evidence; Driver was fertile in imagination in the pursuit of this method, and may of his cherished results were enshrined in the New English Bible. On other linguistic problems, such as the Semitic verb systems, his work left a lasting mark. He was, however, hardly a systematic thinker, and sometimes failed to discern the consequences to which his approach, if pressed too hard, might lead: in fact many interpretations of the New English Bible were idiosyncratic and failed to carry conviction.

As a teacher Driver was enthusiastic and exciting, and much beloved by his pupils. He had an acute sense of fun, sometimes bordering on frivolity. He had a profound *pietas* towards his father and a deep devotion to his school and college. He was one of the great personalities of Hebrew and Semitic scholarship in his time. Yet he had his own ways and style, and was comparatively untouched by the waves of new ideas that began to agitate biblical study from the mid-century on.

In 1924 he married Madeleine Mary, daughter of John Goulding, accountant, of east Yorkshire.

They had three daughters. After a heart attack in 1967 Driver suffered poor health, and he died in Oxford 22 April 1975.

[J. A. Emerton in *Proceedings* of the British Academy, vol. lxiii, 1977; private information; personal knowledge.] JAMES BARR

DRURY, SIR ALAN NIGEL (1889–1980), experimental pathologist, was born in Hackney, London, 3 November 1889, the youngest of five children, the eldest of whom was a girl, of Henry George Drury MVO, superintendent of the Great Eastern Railway, and his wife, Elizabeth Rose Seear. Alan Drury's great-great-grandfather, John, born in the early 1700s, was a surgeon to the East India Company.

In 1902 Drury entered Merchant Taylors' School, which was then a day school in Charterhouse Square, London, at a time when it was developing a good scientific side; his interest in biology was stimulated also by an elder brother-in-law William Stokes, secretary of the Quekett Microscopical Club. He entered Gonville and Caius College, Cambridge, as an ordinary student in 1909 and at the end of his first year was awarded a scholarship. He obtained first classes in both parts of the natural sciences tripos (1910 and 1913). In 1913 he was awarded the Schuldam Plate prize and the Shuttleworth studentship. He started research under (Sir) W. B. Hardy [q.v.] at whose suggestion he went to work at the Marine Biological Research Station, Plymouth. In 1914 he was awarded the George Henry Lewes studentship and reawarded the Shuttleworth studentship, both of which were held over for the duration of the war of 1914–18. Late in 1918 he entered St. Thomas's Hospital and, as he had already done some clinical work at Addenbrooke's Hospital, Cambridge, soon took his final medical examinations. He qualified MRCS, LRCP, and MB, BS (Cambridge) in January 1916.

He then joined the Royal Army Medical Corps and was posted to Mount Vernon Hospital, Hampstead, for the study and treatment of 'disordered action of the heart' which caused invalidism in young soldiers. There he met (Sir) Thomas Lewis [q.v.]. After only a few months he was drafted to India and attached to the Secunderabad pathological laboratory. In 1918 he was promoted major and appointed to the 9th divisional headquarters staff at Bangalore at DADMS (sanitary) having the care of 50,000 troops in relation to epidemic disease and a large clinico-pathological laboratory to direct.

Drury returned briefly in 1919 (the year in which he gained his MD) to the pathology department in Cambridge and then, in 1920, supported by the Medical Research Council, joined Thomas Lewis at University College Hospital, London, in developing the basic electrocardiological procedures for the experimental and clinical study of auricular fibrillation and flutter. This fruitful and intensive collaboration ended abruptly in 1926 when Drury developed a tuberculous lung lesion. After a year's recuperation in 1927 he rejoined the Cambridge pathology department under H. R. Dean, where with H. W. (later Lord) Florey [q.v.] he organized the new part ii of the tripos course in pathology. He continued experimental cardiological research in animals with A. Szent-Gyorgi, examining the effects of nucleic acid derivatives. In 1934 he was appointed Huddersfield lecturer in pathology and a fellow of Trinity Hall.

Discussions initiated by (Dame) Janet Vaughan with the Medical Research Council in 1939, led to the establishment of four blood transfusion centres in the London region to facilitate the treatment of air-raid casualties. Drury came to London to administer these for the Medical Research Council and became chairman of the associated MRC blood transfusion research committee which had an outstanding impact in solving biomedical and logistical problems of blood transfusion practice. Later a draft scheme drawn up by Drury and (Sir) Philip Panton led to similar centres, administered by the Emergency Medical Service and covering the whole country, being established in provincial towns. Drury was instrumental in obtaining finance and expediting the construction at Cambridge of large-scale plant for freeze-drying human plasma essential for the treatment of war casualties.

In 1943 Drury succeeded Sir J. C. G. Ledingham [q.v.] as director of the Lister Institute, while still continuing his MRC work. Departments of the Institute were widely dispersed because of war conditions and he immediately began its successful reintegration. By incorporating some MRC units he established it after the war as a national centre for research on blood transfusion problems and for the provision of blood products for clinical use. After a period of poor health Drury resigned in 1952 and went to live in Cambridge.

At that time I. de Burgh Daly, who was establishing the new Agricultural Research Council Institute of Animal Physiology at Babraham, Cambridge, invited Drury to develop its department of experimental pathology. The department's overall pattern of research was defined by the choice he made of scientists to join him. These included E. J. H. Ford, A. E. Pierce, and D. C. Hardwick. With Elizabeth Tucker he examined various characteristics of erythrocyte behaviour in sheep and new-born lambs especially in relation to natural and immune haemolysins and the formation and persistence of foetal haemoglobin. He retired from Babraham in 1960 but continued an interest in research in the department of pathology at Cambridge. Although he contributed notably by his own research his greatest contribution came from his profound impact on the scientific development of blood transfusion. He was a quiet man with an ironic sense of hmour and had wide cultural interests. He was especially kind and unobtrusively helpful to young people at the outset of their careers.

He was elected FRS (1937) and was a council member (1940–1 and 1955–6) and vice-president (1955–6). He was appointed CBE (1944), knighted (1950), and admitted FRCP (1951). He was a member of the Agricultural Research Council (1947–51) and of the Medical Research Council (1944–8), and he was chairman of many MRC committees. He was secretary of the Beit memorial fellowships for medical research (1944–52) and honorary secretary of the Physiological Society (1938–43).

Drury married in 1916 Daphne Marguerite (died 1975), elder daughter of H. A. Brownsword, a lace manufacturer, of Nottingham. They had a daughter and a son. Drury died at Letchworth, Hertfordshire, 2 August 1980.

[R. A. Kekwick in *Biographical Memoirs of Fellows of the Royal Society*, vol. xxvii, 1981; private information; personal knowledge.]

R. A. Kekwick

DUGDALE, WILLIAM LIONEL, first baronet, and first Baron Crathorne (1897–1977), minister of agriculture and fisheries, was born at Bucklands Hotel, Brooke St., London, 20 July 1897, the only son (he had one sister) of James Lionel Dugdale, of Crathorne, Yorkshire, an army captain, and his wife, Maud Violet, daughter of George William Plukenett Woodroffe, of the Royal Horse Guards. He was educated at Eton and the Royal Military College, Sandhurst. In 1916 he joined the Royal Scots Greys and served in France and Belgium. After the war he was captain (1923), and later adjutant (1927) in the Yorkshire Hussars (Alexandra, Princess of Wales's Own) Yeomanry (TA).

His parliamentary career began when he was elected Conservative MP for the Richmond division of the North Riding of Yorkshire in 1929. He retained this seat until 1959. In 1931 he became parliamentary private secretary to Sir Philip Cunliffe-Lister (later Earl of Swinton, q.v.), president of the Board of Trade in the national government, and he continued as his PPS when he became colonial secretary and secretary of state for air. In 1935 Stanley Baldwin (later Earl Baldwin of Bewdley), the prime minister, selected Dugdale to be his own PPS.

He was therefore deeply involved from the first moment that the prime minister took cognizance of the relationship between the King and Mrs Simpson and was totally in the prime minister's confidence, in fact long before the members of the Cabinet became aware of what Baldwin was doing. He was in attendance on the prime minister on almost every occasion when he saw either the King or other members of the royal family and later on when the Cabinet colleagues were consulted. He was also present at the final dinner at Fort Belvedere before the King abdicated. He gave Baldwin much moral support and helped him to deal with an immensely difficult task so that the matter could be concluded with as little disturbance as possible to the country as a whole, and with the minimum amount of damage to the monarchy.

From 1937 to 1940 Dugdale was a junior lord of the Treasury, and then was on active service in Egypt with the Yorkshire Hussars. In February 1941 he returned to England and became deputy chief government whip. He left that office in 1942 to become chairman of the Conservative Party Organization (he had been vice-chairman in 1941–2), but he became ill and resigned in October 1944. He received a baronetcy in the New Year honours in 1945.

During the Labour government after 1945 Dugdale was opposition spokesman on agriculture, a position for which his landowning interests in Yorkshire well-fitted him. He was therefore an obvious choice as minister of agriculture in (Sir) Winston Churchill's government in 1951. At the same time he was admitted to the Privy Council, and in September 1953 he was made a member of the Cabinet.

He inherited, like most other ministers, a vast amount of wartime regulations which the Labour government had done little to remove and this was largely the cause of the mishandling of the Crichel Down affair. The Air Ministry had taken over some land in Dorset for use as a bombing range and had later passed it on to the Ministry of Agriculture. The original owners wished to repurchase the land, but the Crown Land commissioners instead found another tenant without informing the owners. This action aroused the anger of farmers and MPs, who demanded a public inquiry. Dugdale resisted this, without avail, and the inquiry's report severely criticized various civil servants who, it was said, had deliberately deceived the minister. Dugdale was a man of very high principles who firmly believed that if a Ministry made a mistake, the minister, as ultimately responsible, should resign. This he did, although many of his colleagues tried to dissuade him as he bore no personal responsibility. The ending of Dugdale's political career in this way forced ministers and senior civil servants to think seriously about the reduction or elimination of the vast powers they had acquired during the war.

One of his passions in life was racing and as a young officer in the Royal Scots Greys he occasionally rode on the flat and in point-to-points and over fences. He had often watched his father's horses working on Middleham Moor, where his own horses were subsequently trained. In 1951 he owned a good horse, Socrates, which was beaten, although favourite, in the Cambridgeshire; it subsequently won the Zetland and Manchester Cups. His contribution to racing administration was unobtrusive but extremely effective, stemming from his friendly, unassuming nature and his integrity. In 1959–60, when the issue of a levy on horse-racing was an extremely controversial subject, it was he who played a key role in the departmental committee which resolved the matter. Subsequently he served as one of the first Jockey Club representatives on the Horserace Betting Levy Board from 1964 to 1973.

Deeply interested in European affairs, in 1958 he became a member of the Council of Europe. He also joined the NATO parliamentarians conference, of which he became president in 1962–3. He did a great deal of work through both organizations to interest British MPs in the vital importance of European countries and the USA working together to guarantee peace. When he retired from Parliament in 1959 Dugdale was created first Baron Crathorne. He was chairman of the north of England advisory committee for civil aviation from 1964 to 1972, and chairman of the political honours scrutiny committee from 1961.

In 1936 he married Nancy (died 1969), formerly wife of Sylvester Govett Gates and daughter of Sir Charles Tennant [q.v.], merchant and art patron. They had two sons, of whom the elder, Charles James (born 1939), succeeded his father in the barony when he died at home at Crathorne Hall, Yarm, Cleveland, 26 March 1977.

[Family papers; private information; personal knowledge.] St. Aldwyn

DUKE-ELDER, Sir (WILLIAM) STEWART (1898–1978), ophthalmologist, was born 22 April 1898 in Dundee, the second of three sons of the Revd Neil Stewart Elder, of Tealing, a minister of the United Free Church of Scotland, and his wife, Isabella, daughter of the Revd John Duke, minister of the same Church at Campsie, Stirlingshire.

After attending the Morgan Academy, Dundee, where he achieved gold medals in English, Greek, biology, and religious knowledge, he entered St. Andrews University as a foundation scholar in 1915. In July 1919 he graduated MA with first class honours in natural science and in the same year became B.Sc. with special distinction in physiology. He completed his medical course at the Royal Infirmary, Dundee, and the Royal Infirmary, Edinburgh, in 1923 graduating MB, B.Chir. The following year he became a fellow of the Royal College of Surgeons of England. In 1925 he was also awarded a gold medal for his MD thesis at St. Andrews and the gold medal of the British Association, in addition to a London D.Sc. and Ph.D. Whilst at St. Andrews he found time to become president of the Students' Union, representing it at council in 1921–2, at which time Sir James M. Barrie [q.v.] was lord rector. Demonstrator in physiology at St. Andrews in 1918–19, university scholar in 1919, he then demonstrated anatomy at University College, Dundee, in 1920–1.

After graduation he decided to go to London. After a number of junior appointments at St. George's Hospital he was appointed honorary consulting surgeon both there and at Moorfields Eye Hospital, London, at the age of twenty-seven. His great interest at this time was the physiology of the eye. He was encouraged and directed by Professor E. H. Starling [q.v.]. He had been using the name Duke-Elder and confirmed this by deed poll in January 1928, shortly before his marriage.

In 1932 Duke-Elder operated on the prime minister, J. Ramsay MacDonald, for glaucoma and the following year received a knighthood. During World War II he was consultant ophthalmic surgeon to the army, achieving the rank of brigadier in the RAMC.

Duke-Elder made four important contributions to ophthalmology and of these his many writings on ophthalmology are pre-eminent. In 1927 appeared his *Recent Advances in Ophthalmology* and the following year his *The Practice of Refraction.* These remained in print and are now (1986) in their seventh and ninth editions revised respectively by P. D. Trevor-Roper, 1975, and D. Abrams, 1978. Four years later appeared the first of the seven volumes of *Text-Book of Ophthalmology* (1932–54). This work, every word of which was written out in longhand, is known throughout the world as the ophthalmologists' bible. Almost as soon as the final volume was published Duke-Elder felt that the work needed updating, so he embarked on his fifteen-volume *System of Ophthalmology* (1958–76). The first of these volumes was entirely his own work, and although for subsequent volumes he enlisted the collaboration of his colleagues, his superb command of English and his lucidity of thought were still dominant. These books represent a distillation of the world's ophthalmic literature and are respected as the definitive work on all aspects of the subject. It is said that it is virtually impossible to write a paper in an ophthalmological journal without including Duke-Elder's name amongst the references. To this Dictionary he contributed the notice of Sir John Parsons.

His second achievement was the creation of the Institute of Ophthalmology in London. This was a research institute, in the founding of which he played a leading role, closely associated with Moorfields Eye Hospital, and came about following the amalgamation in 1947 of the three major London eye hospitals (the Central London, the Royal London, and Moorfields). It officially opened in 1948 with Duke-Elder as director of research, a post he held until 1965. It was largely for his research at the institute that Duke-Elder was elected in 1960 to a fellowship of the Royal Society, a distinction rarely awarded to a clinician no matter how distinguished.

His third major contribution was the inauguration in 1945 of the faculty of ophthalmologists at the Royal College of Surgeons. It was to become the single authoritative body for the profession of ophthalmology. Duke-Elder was its first president and served for four years.

His fourth interest was the Hospital of St. John in Jerusalem. He became hospitaller in 1954 in succession to Lord Webb-Johnson [q.v.] and as a result of his enthusiasm and hard work a new eighty-bed hospital was opened in 1960. Later he became bailiff grand cross of the Order of St. John.

Duke-Elder was surgeon oculist to the royal family for twenty-nine years—to Edward VIII, George VI, and Elizabeth II. None of his predecessors had held this appointment for so long a period. He was appointed KCVO in 1946 and GCVO in 1958.

Despite his world-wide reputation Duke-Elder never lost his interest in and concern for young ophthalmologists, who were often referred to as Duke-Elderberries. He was a man of charm and wit, had a delightful Scottish sense of humour, was always accessible to his juniors, and was never stinting in praise and encouragement where due. At the same time if he felt that criticism was needed, it would be offered in a spirit of friendly helpfulness.

He received medals from sixteen universities, held nine honorary doctorates, six honorary fellowships, and was an honorary member of twenty-eight national ophthalmological societies. He received the Howe medal of the USA in 1946, the Donders medal of Holland in 1947, the Doyne medal of the Oxford Ophthalmological Congress in 1948, and the Gullstrand medal of Sweden in 1952. He was life president of the International Council of Ophthalmology and in 1954 was presented with a Gonin medal, the highest award in international ophthalmology.

In 1928 he married Phyllis Mary, daughter of William Edgar, manufacturer of gas fires and geysers, of Ealing. She was herself an ophthalmologist and played a very active part in the production of the seven volumes of *Text-Book of Ophthalmology*. They had no children. Duke-Elder died 27 March 1978 at his home in St. John's Wood, London.

[*The Times*, 3 April 1978; T. K. Lyle, Sir Stephen Miller, and N. H. Ashton in *Biographical Memoirs of Fellows of the Royal Society*, vol. xxvi, 1980; personal knowledge.]

PHILIP AWDRY

DUNCAN, SIR JOHN NORMAN VALETTE (VAL) (1913–1975), industrialist, was born in Pinner, Middlesex, 18 July 1913, the only son and eldest of the four children of Norman Duncan MC, barrister, of Wardes, Otham, Kent, and his wife, Gladys Marguerite Dauvergne Valette. Duncan was educated at Harrow and at Brasenose College, Oxford, where he read law, in which he obtained a third class in 1936. In June 1938 he was called to the bar in Gray's Inn but never practised.

Instead that autumn he became a transport trainee with the Southern Railway. At the time this may not have seemed to be a very inspiring start in life but in the event it proved to be a well-chosen springboard for his subsequent career. Within a year World War II had begun and Duncan found himself commissioned in the Royal Engineers as a railway transport officer. Here he first displayed the gifts for large-scale administration and organization which came to such brilliant fulfilment when the war was over. Duncan served on the staffs of Generals Alexander (later Earl Alexander of Tunis, q.v.), Montgomery (later Viscount Montgomery of Alamein, q.v.), and Eisenhower, seeing service in France before Dunkirk and during 1944–5 when he was a member of the team which planned the Normandy invasion and the subsequent European campaign. For war services Duncan was twice mentioned in dispatches and was appointed OBE in 1944. He was also made a commander of the Order of Orange Nassau, and twice received the US Legion of Merit medal.

When the war ended Duncan held the rank of colonel (acting brigadier) and he decided not to return immediately to civilian life. In 1946 he joined the Control Office for Germany and Austria working immediately under Sir R. M. C. Turner, under-secretary, and Sir Arthur Street [q.v.], deputy head of the Control Office. Both of these men influenced Duncan's subsequent career, Turner decisively so. He was an experienced merchant banker and industrialist who recommended Duncan to gain top-flight industrial experience. His advice did not go unheeded. Street left the Control Office to become deputy chairman of the National Coal Board and in 1947 Duncan joined him there as assistant director of marketing.

Duncan stayed with the NCB little more than a year, however, because Turner, who by that time was acting as a stopgap managing director of the Rio Tinto Company, persuaded him to come in as commercial manager, with the intention that he should eventually take over as chief executive; which he did in January 1951. Rio Tinto was then at the lowest ebb in its long history. Duncan's task was to extricate the company from the stranglehold of the Spanish authorities and to revitalize an ailing and dispirited enterprise. This he most brilliantly accomplished within the next ten years, his crowning achievement being the merger with Consolidated Zinc in July 1962 to form the Rio Tinto Zinc Corporation (RTZ) of which Duncan became managing director and, in 1964, chairman.

Duncan now presided over a highly diversified mining group with profitable operations in many countries, most notably in Australia and Canada. By the early 1970s the established international importance and success of RTZ had brought social problems. Overseas mining companies extracting national resources came under increasing local criticism. Duncan responded to these problems with skill and a ready understanding of nationalistic sensitivities.

Duncan was a rather short, fair-haired, good-looking man of some girth in later life. He was tirelessly energetic, alert, and lively. His notably blue eyes were, it has been said, the beacons of an eager boyish spirit and yet of a deeply enquiring mind. He was a convinced Christian Scientist ever since his father's life had been saved by faith when the doctors had despaired of it. He played the violin well and enjoyed golf, swimming, tennis, croquet, and gardening. His gift for friendship was remarkable, as many can testify, particularly those who enjoyed his happy hospitality at his farmhouse above Soller in Majorca.

Duncan was knighted in June 1968. He was deputy lord lieutenant of Kent, a governor of Harrow School, an honorary fellow of Brasenose College, Oxford (1974), chairman of the Mermaid Theatre Trust, and a governor of the National Institute of Economic and Social Research. He was a non-executive director of the Bank of England and a director of British Petroleum. In 1968–9 he chaired the committee to review overseas representation which produced a somewhat provocative report urging a more commercially oriented and informed diplomatic service.

In November 1950 Duncan married Lorna Frances (died 1963), daughter of Robert Eyre Archer Houblon, gentleman, of British Columbia, Canada. There were no children. Duncan died 19 December 1975 in Beaumont House, Beaumont Street, St. Marylebone, London, very shortly after returning from one of his many long and punishing visits abroad for RTZ.

[Rio Tinto Zinc records; private information; personal knowledge.] O'BRIEN OF LOTHBURY

DUNLOP, SIR DERRICK MELVILLE (1902–1980), physician, was born in Edinburgh 3 April 1902, the only son and younger child of George Henry Melville Dunlop, MD, FRCP, a physician in Edinburgh, and his wife, Margaret Boog Scott. He was educated at the Edinburgh Academy, Brasenose College, Oxford (where he obtained a third class in natural science—physiology—in 1923), and Edinburgh University where he graduated MB, Ch.B. in 1926, MD in 1927, MRCP in 1929, and FRCP (Edin.) in 1932. He spent a short time as a morning-suited, top-hatted, general practitioner in London but hated it and returned to the University of Edinburgh to pursue an academic career as a lecturer in therapeutics and assistant in the tuberculosis department. He was a superb teacher and students flocked to hear him even before he was appointed to the chair of therapeutics and a consultant physician at the Royal Infirmary in 1936. The chemical revolution in therapeutics had scarcely begun at that time and his role was that of a polished interpreter of existing knowledge through his lectures and writing. He collaborated closely with (Sir) L. Stanley P. Davidson and they were editors (with (Sir) John W. McNee) of the well-known *Textbook of Medical Treatment* (1939).

Dunlop was a keen territorial soldier and he always claimed that it was only septicaemia caused by the bite of a ferret on his estate at Bavelaw Castle that prevented him from being posted to Singapore and being imprisoned by the Japanese. After the war he resumed his teaching and clinical work in Edinburgh and increased his already high reputation. In 1948 he became FRCP (Lond.) and was elected FRSE. In the same year he became chairman of the British Pharmacopoeia Commission, a post he held until 1958. He was in great demand as a lecturer and in 1951 travelled widely in the antipodes as Sims British Commonwealth travelling professor. He delivered the Lumleian lecture of the Royal College of Physicians of London in 1954 on 'Complications of Diabetes'. He was knighted in 1960 and appointed physician to the Queen in Scotland in 1961.

He was an elegant figure with a remarkable presence, a fine resonant voice, and impeccable delivery. His lectures and after-dinner speeches were masterpieces of timing and gesture. They appeared to be quite spontaneous but it was said he rehearsed them before a full-length mirror at his home at Bavelaw Castle. His Harveian oration at the tricentenary dinner at the College of Physicians in 1957 was the most memorable address in the history of the Edinburgh college.

In 1962, at the age of sixty, he retired from his chair at Edinburgh University, but his greatest contributions were yet to come. The thalidomide disaster had led to great public concern about drug safety and the lack of official procedures for reviewing safety before drugs were marketed. In 1964, in the aftermath of this tragedy, he was asked to set up the Committee on Safety of Drugs. He proceeded with remarkable speed, tact, and sagacity and quickly assembled a talented academic committee supported by a small but able band of professional officers and civil servants from the Department of Health. His powers of persuasion enabled him to convince the pharmaceutical industry to collaborate fully with the 'Dunlop committee' although, at that time, it had no statutory powers. Under his chairmanship the committee set up the voluntary system of drug adverse reaction reporting by doctors on 'yellow cards' which were pre-addressed and stamped fold-over yellow post-cards on which doctors could record brief details of suspected drug toxicity. This system, and a similar system in Sweden, were the most successful adverse reaction reporting systems in the world, and led to the detection of a number of important toxic effects of drugs. A notable success was the demonstration of a relationship between oestrogen dose in the combined oral contraceptive pill and the risk of thrombosis and embolism in blood vessels. In 1969, when the Committee on Safety of Drugs acquired statutory powers and became the Committee on Safety of Medicines under the wing of the Medicines Commission Dunlop became a first chairman of the commission, a post he held until 1971. He continued his contacts with the pharmaceutical industry and was for a time a director of Winthrop Laboratories.

He received a great many honours including the fellowship of the American College of Physicians, honorary fellowships from Brasenose College, Oxford (1968), and the Royal College of Physicians of Edinburgh (1972), and honorary doctorates from Birmingham (1967), Bradford (1970), Edinburgh (1967), and the National University of Ireland (1968). Despite his formidable reputation and imposing exterior he remained a kindly and liberal-minded man who did much to help younger members of the medical profession. He had fire in his belly, but he used his power with discrimination and tact.

He married on 17 March 1936 Marjorie, eldest daughter of Henry Edward Richardson, writer to the Signet, of Broadshaw, Harburn, West Lothian. They had a son and a daughter. Dunlop died in Edinburgh 19 June 1980. The Winthrop Foundation created an annual travelling fellowship in clinical pharmacology and therapeutics as a memorial to him.

[Private information; personal knowledge.]

COLIN T. DOLLERY

DUTT, (RAJANI) PALME (1896–1974), British communist leader, was born at Cambridge 19 June 1896, the younger son (there was also a daughter) of Upendra Krishna Dutt, a Bengali, who had come to study medicine in England, became a surgeon, and settled in Cambridge. Dutt's mother, Anna, was Swedish, Palme being the family name which he subsequently added; and the family home in Cambridge was inevitably the meeting place for visiting Indian nationalist leaders. Dutt was educated at the Perse School, Cambridge, and he won a scholarship to Balliol College, Oxford, where he took up residence in the autumn of 1914. In 1916 he took a first class in classical honour moderations and in the following year he was sent down for a speech to a private meeting of a students' society giving a Marxist analysis of the war and of the approaching Bolshevik revolution, and was imprisoned as a conscientious objector on socialist grounds. He returned to Oxford in 1918 to take the final school of *literae humaniores* and obtained an outstanding first. After a very short period in teaching he joined the Labour Research Department in March 1919—G. D. H. Cole [q.v.] was honorary secretary—and worked first on home affairs and then in September 1919 became responsible for a new international section. He remained with the Department until he began publishing *Labour Monthly* in July 1921.

Dutt had become a foundation member of the Communist Party in 1920 although still a member of the 'left-wing committee' of the Independent Labour Party. His *Labour Monthly*, for which he wrote the 'Notes of the Month' for over fifty years, was to become essential reading for working-class militants in the inter-war years; and it probably did more to inculcate an anti-imperialist Marxism than any other journal of the period. Dutt's own anti-colonial interests were, not surprisingly, centred upon India. Although only a young man his outstanding intellectual qualities were quickly recognized and his place in the leadership of the British Communist Party was important from the middle twenties. In 1922 he was one of a three-man commission on the 'Bolshevization' of the British Communist Party; and although he spent some of the middle years of the twenties outside Britain, for health reasons, he was always in close touch with British politics. In particular he developed a close relationship with Harry Pollitt [q.v.] with whom he was intimately involved in the bitter struggles within the British Communist Party concerning the application to Britain of the 'class against class' tactic. The sixth world congress of the Comintern in 1928 elaborated its 'social-fascist' analysis and Dutt, Pollitt, and R. Page Arnot were in the minority of those who supported the new line. When the Comintern imposed its will upon the British Communist Party, Pollitt became general secretary and Dutt a member of the Politburo; and for the next three decades these two dominated the CPGB. The only partial break in the partnership was in the autumn of 1939 when Pollitt could not accept the Comintern's change of policy that the war was an imperialist war; and Dutt took over the position of general secretary until the Nazi invasion of Russia in 1941, when the Comintern's policy was again reversed. Dutt's own position followed the new line and his *Britain in the World Front* (1942) reflected the new, unswerving support for the alliance against Germany. In 1945 Dutt stood, unsuccessfully, as the Communist candidate in Sparkbrook, Birmingham, and in 1950 for Woolwich East. For the next decade and a half until his retirement in 1965 Dutt was vice-chairman of the British CP; and during the most serious crisis in the history of the CP—that which followed the revelations in the secret speech of Khrushchev at the twentieth congress of the Russian Communist Party in 1956—Dutt was the most unyielding defender of the Stalinist position.

Palme Dutt's political ideas and allegiances were formed by the Bolshevik revolution of 1917, and further developed within the Comintern under Stalin. Dutt became the outstanding interpreter in the English-speaking countries of Stalinism. He was also the foremost writer in English of anti-colonialism and anti-imperialism of an orthodox Marxist, i.e. Stalinist, position. His first important study, *Modern India*, published in Bombay in 1926 and the next year in England, led to a major debate within the Comintern. Dutt had argued that despite distortions due to imperialist control, India and other Asiatic countries were undergoing rapid industrial development. This became known as the theory of 'decolonialization' and was vigorously attacked by the Russian-controlled Comintern secretariat. After being severely criticized by Comintern speakers, there was no further occasion—in public that is—when Dutt revealed any disagreement with the policies and tactics of the International Communist movement that derived from Moscow.

His general political influence in Britain and the countries of the British empire before World War II was considerable. It was especially important in India and upon the Indian Left well beyond the communist groups. He knew for instance Jawaharlal Nehru [q.v.] well from the later 1920s.

In addition to his 'Notes of the Month'—each a substantial essay on current political issues—Dutt wrote a number of books and many pamphlets. *Fascism and Social Revolution* (1934), *India Today* (1940), and *The Crisis of Britain and the British Empire* (1953) were among his most important writings. His work, immensely erudite, logically argued, and often offering subtle and interesting insights, suffered from two serious disabilities, and these became more evident as he got older. The first was his unswerving devotion to the political strategy and tactics of the Comintern, and to the end of his days Dutt remained a Stalinist; and the second was the absence of any serious and sustained critique of his work within the British Communist Party. His theoretical writing, notably after World War II, became increasingly inadequate and unsubstantial. With his immense intellectual gifts Dutt remains an individual exemplar of the tragedy of Stalinism in its impact on the international working-class movement. In 1962 he became an honorary doctor of history at Moscow University, and in 1970 he received the Lenin centenary medal.

In 1922 he married Salme (died 1964), daughter of Ernst Murrik, of Karkski, Estonia. She had come to Britain as a representative of the Communist International in 1920. There were no children of the marriage. Palme Dutt died in London 20 December 1974.

[*The Times*, 21 December 1974; *Labour Monthly*, February–June 1975; *Labour Research*, February 1975; personal knowledge.]

JOHN SAVILLE

E

EBERT, (ANTON) CHARLES (1887–1980), actor and opera director, was born 20 February 1887 in Berlin, the eldest child of Count Potulicky, a Prussian government official in Berlin, who was Polish, and his wife, Mary Collins, who was Irish. He was legally adopted by Wilhelm and Maria Ebert of Berlin. Customarily known as 'Carl', Ebert was educated at Friedrich Werder'sche Oberrealschule, Berlin, and then at Max Reinhardt's School of Dramatic Art, Berlin. After a short spell as a clerk in a private bank to help to support his foster-parents he embarked on an acting career. He was accepted, even as a student, by Max Reinhardt for a number of important roles in productions at the Deutsches Theater, Berlin, which was under Reinhardt's direction. He then joined the Frankfurt-am-Main Drama Theatre and in the seven years up to 1922 played most of the major roles in that theatre. He joined the Berlin State Drama Theatre in 1922 and continued his career as one of Germany's leading actors until 1927.

In 1919 he had founded the Frankfurt Drama College and in 1925 he became director of the Berlin Academy of Music and Drama with the title of professor. In 1927 he became the first actor to be appointed Generalintendant of the Hessische Landestheater in Darmstadt where until 1931 he had the opportunity of practising his ideas on modernizing attitudes and methods in opera production. In 1931 he was appointed to the post of Intendant of the Staedtische Oper, Berlin.

When the Nazis took power in Germany Ebert decided, despite the offer of an enhanced position in the Berlin theatre, to build a new career abroad. He settled with his family in Switzerland. His first major assignment was as director of the opening production of the first 'Maggio Musicale' in Florence (1933). Subsequently he directed in the major opera houses of the world, including La Scala, Metropolitan Opera, Vienna State Opera, Teatro Colon Buenos Aires, and at the Salzburg Festival, among others.

In 1934 he was invited by John Christie [q.v.] and his wife Audrey to join with them and Fritz Busch to help to launch the Glyndebourne Opera. He accepted the appointment as Glyndebourne's artistic director, a position he held until 1959. During this period he directed almost every production mounted by Glyndebourne both in the festivals there and in the first Edinburgh Festivals of 1947 to 1955. His productions initially concentrated on the operas of Mozart, but soon embraced a wide variety of repertory extending from the British premier of Verdi's *Macbeth* and of Stravinsky's *The Rake's Progress* (the world première of which he had in 1952 directed in Venice) through the works of Strauss, Rossini, Debussy, Gluck, and Donizetti. His collaboration with Busch immediately gave Glyndebourne the hallmark of artistic excellence which established its reputation as a Festival of international importance. His subsequent work with a variety of conductors, in particular Vittorio Gui in the 1950s, maintained Glyndebourne's position at the forefront of operatic enterprise. Perhaps his greatest contribution to British opera was to establish it as a Gesamtkunst—an artistic synthesis—of music and theatre, giving dramatic credibility in the production of opera in a way that had been previously absent. Glyndebourne's artistic foundations and its policy of operation were to a major extent established by Ebert and Busch and the weight of their contribution has played a vital part in Glyndebourne's early years and as a heritage for its continued success since Ebert's final production there in 1962.

During World War II Ebert 'fathered' Turkish opera and drama, having from 1936 advised Kemal Ataturk on the establishment of the Turkish national opera and theatre companies and helped to establish music and drama academies there.

In 1948 he created the opera department of the University of Southern California, Los Angeles, the success of which resulted in the establishment of a new professional company, the Guild Opera Company of Los Angeles. At this time he obtained American citizenship. In 1954 he accepted an invitation to resume his pre-war position at the Staedtische Oper (later renamed the Deutsche Oper), Berlin. In 1961 he supervised the rebuilding and directed the opening production of the new opera house in Berlin.

Among Ebert's honours were: honorary doctorate of music, Edinburgh University (1954); honorary doctorate of fine arts, University of Southern California (1955); the Ernst Reuter plaque of the City of Berlin (1957); a knighthood of the Dannebrog Order of Denmark (1959); Grosses Verdienstkreuz mit Stern, Germany (1959); Grosse Ehrenzeichen for services to Mozart, Austria (1959); honorary CBE (1960); and grande medaille d'argent de la ville de Paris (1961).

He was a man of majestic appearance, powerfully built with in later years a mane of white hair. He was a man of considerable resolve, displaying on occasions a fiery temperament, but more often than not exercising a considerable amount of persuasive charm.

In 1912 Ebert married Lucie Karoline Friederike, daughter of Oskar Splisgarth, electrical engineer. They had one daughter, who became a prominent German actress and died in

1946, and one son, Peter, theatre producer and administrator, who was awarded an honorary D.Mus. of St. Andrews in 1979. This marriage was dissolved in 1923 and in 1924 he married Gertrude Eck (died 1979). Of the second marriage there were two daughters and one son. Ebert died in Santa Monica, California, 14 May 1980.

[*The Times*, 16, 22, and 28 May 1980; personal knowledge.] GEORGE CHRISTIE

EDELMAN, (ISRAEL) MAURICE (1911–1975), politician and novelist, was born 2 March 1911 at Cardiff, the third of five children (two sons and three daughters, one of whom died in infancy) of Joshua Edelman and his wife, Esther Solomon, who had emigrated from eastern Europe in the wake of pogroms at the turn of the century. His father, a photographer, was an early socialist and member of the local Labour Party. His indigent background was a spur to Maurice Edelman. He secured an exhibition from Cardiff High School to Trinity College, Cambridge, and also gained a state scholarship, a rare achievement in Wales at that time. He obtained a first class in part i of the modern and medieval languages tripos in 1930 and a second class (division I) in part ii in 1932. Later in life he was an accomplished linguist, fluent in French, Italian, German, and Russian.

Going down in a year of economic slump, Edelman sought employment in London and for a time gave French lessons. The following year he met and married Mathilda ('Tilli'), daughter of Harry Yager, a timber merchant and manufacturer. Edelman was endowed with singular good looks, natural charm, and a mellifluous voice, and his marriage provided him with a secure anchorage. It proved a happy marriage and his wife played a notable part in his subsequent career. There were two daughters.

For some years Edelman worked in his father-in-law's business. This took him to Russia and he perfected his command of Russian. In 1938 he wrote a critical study of Soviet law called *GPU Justice* and in 1942 in contrast he wrote as a Penguin Special *How Russia Prepared*, a starry-eyed eulogy of Soviet achievements. His interest in wartime production and the cost-plus system of payments led him to write *Production for Victory, not Profit!*, published by the Left Book Club (Gollancz, 1941). He now became a war correspondent for *Picture Post* in North Africa, Italy, and, after D-Day, France. Edelman was a gifted journalist and his articles were graphic and politically intelligent. De Gaulle was his wartime hero and throughout his life he was a leading francophile. He was made an officer of the Legion of Honour in 1960. Towards the end of the war his Penguin Special *France: the Birth of the Fourth Republic* (1944) received much acclaim.

At the general election in 1945 Edelman, who had been almost fortuitously selected as a candidate, was elected Labour MP for Coventry West. From 1950 until 1974 he represented Coventry North. He seemed an obvious candidate for office and few then would have believed that he would remain a back-bencher for the next thirty years. Edelman was independent-minded and not afraid to say unpopular things but he lacked *gravitas* and he was an ineffective parliamentary performer. Like many other versatile Westminster figures he was seen as a talented and colourful personality whose politics and relationships tended to be superficial. Nevertheless, he played an active role on the Council of Europe and was chairman of the Socialist Group in the Western European Union from 1968 to 1970. His fluency in French made him a well-known figure in continental politics and he held numerous Anglo-French Parliamentary Group positions. He was a staunch Jew and, as president of the Anglo-Jewish Association, he made strong protests about Russia's treatment of the Jews.

Edelman had little interest in money, and even politics were secondary to his dream of artistic achievement. The thwarted politician revealed a rare versatility in the arts. He loved to write, paint, play the balalaika, and sing melodiously. His writing covered a wide spectrum from the serious political works which grew from his experience as a war correspondent to articles, plays, biographies, and novels mainly on political themes and many of them bestsellers. *Who Goes Home* (1953), his first novel, was widely read and, like other later novels, was published in several languages. *A Call on Kuprin* (1959), set in Moscow, showed a prophetic sense of the perils for MPs abroad trapped in compromising situations. He will be best remembered for his last two novels which were authentic portrayals of Disraeli, with whom Edelman felt a special affinity. *Disraeli in Love* (1972) and *Disraeli Rising* (1975) have a lasting quality. His deep research and understanding of the man and his period was apparent to leading historians. In 1972 Edelman, imbued with the Disraelian tradition, leased a wing of Hughenden Manor, Disraeli's country house in Buckinghamshire, from the National Trust.

Although lacking a confident political identity, Edelman was an elegant man of great charm and conversational wit. While he did not fulfil his potential in the political arena, his imaginative writings which often turned on the dichotomy of the public and private faces of those in politics, represented a distinct contribution to the post-war period. He died suddenly of an embolism 14 December 1975, at the Brompton Hospital, west London, on his return from a parliamentary visit to India.

[*The Times*, 15 December 1975; R. H. S. Crossman, *The Diaries of a Cabinet Minister*, 3 vols., 1975–7; tapes of radio interviews; parliamentary colleagues and private information; personal knowledge.]

NEVILLE SANDELSON

EDEN, (ROBERT) ANTHONY, first EARL OF AVON (1897–1977), statesman, was born at Windlestone Hall near Bishop Auckland in County Durham 12 June 1897, the third of the four sons and fourth of the five children of Sir William Eden, seventh baronet of the first creation and fifth of the second, who owned an estate of some 800 acres. Eden's mother was Sybil Frances, daughter of Sir William Grey (1818–1878) [q.v.], great-niece of the prime minister, the second Earl Grey, and a distant cousin of Edward, Viscount Grey of Fallodon [q.v.]. Her grandmother was Danish, descended from a family, one of whose forebears had been a general in the Thirty Years' War. The Eden baronetcy of the first creation dated back to 1672 and two of the sons of the third baronet were given peerages which still exist, Auckland and Henley. Eden was thus closely connected on both sides with the traditional landed governing class. Sir William Eden was an irascible eccentric given to furious outbursts of uncontrolled temper which terrified his children. A description of him is given in *The Tribulations of a Baronet* (1933), by Eden's brother Timothy. Of his mother Eden enigmatically wrote in his autobiography *Another World 1897–1917* (1976): 'I think my mother preferred the simpler relationship which existed between donor and recipient to the more complicated one between mother and child.'

He went to Sandroyd School in Surrey at the age of nine and to Eton four years later, making little impression on either. He remembered his school-days with no pleasure. He spent much of his holidays in France and Germany and spoke fluent French—perhaps the only twentieth-century prime minister to do so, apart from Harold Macmillan (later the Earl of Stockton). He was still at Eton when World War I began. His second brother was interned in Germany at once, and within three months his eldest brother, John, was killed. His father died in February 1915. Greatest tragedy of all—his younger brother Nicholas to whom he was devoted, a midshipman of only sixteen, was killed at the Battle of Jutland in the summer of 1916. Meanwhile Eden had joined the King's Royal Rifle Corps in September 1915. His connection with the Rifle Brigade was something which he never forgot. He became adjutant of his battalion in 1917 and was awarded the MC that year for rescuing his sergeant under fire. In 1918 at the age of twenty he was made brigade-major, the youngest in the British Army.

Demobilized with the substantive rank of captain in 1919 he decided to complete his education at Christ Church, Oxford. He read Persian and Arabic, with a view to a career in the Diplomatic Service, and obtained first class honours in 1922. He took no interest in the politics of the Oxford Union, though he was persuaded by one of the local Conservative agents to speak from time to time in Oxfordshire villages. His principal hobby was art. He and Lord David Cecil founded the short-lived Uffizi Society. Sir William Eden, in between bouts of rage, had been a discerning collector of the modern pictures of his time. His son was to find in the same pursuit a welcome distraction from the strains of public life. On leaving Oxford he felt too impatient to face the slow course of promotion in the Diplomatic Service. He saw a quicker route to the top via politics. He stood as Conservative candidate in the general election of November 1922 for the unwinnable seat of Spennymoor in County Durham but in 1923 he was adopted for the safe constituency of Warwick and Leamington. In the election of that December he was opposed by an orthodox Liberal and a highly unorthodox Labour candidate, Frances, Countess of Warwick [q.v.], former mistress of King Edward VII and mother-in-law of Eden's sister. Eden won easily and retained his seat through eight subsequent elections till his retirement from politics. In the same year he married Beatrice Helen (died 1957), daughter of Sir Gervase Beckett, created a baronet in 1921, banker and chairman of the *Yorkshire Post*, a staunch Conservative organ which gave helpful publicity to Eden's early speeches and writings.

Eden's maiden speech on 9 February 1924 seems surprisingly aggressive, given his later reputation for diplomacy. It was a vigorous defence of air-deterrence sprinkled with gibes against the pacifism of some of the Labour government's supporters. Eden specialized in defence and overseas policy but after the Conservative victory of October 1924 he became parliamentary private secretary (unpaid) to Godfrey Locker Lampson, a junior minister in the Home Office. In 1925 he obtained leave of absence for five months to go on a tour of the Empire partly financed by the *Yorkshire Post* for which he wrote articles converted into an unmemorable book, *Places in the Sun* (1926), with a foreword by Stanley Baldwin (later Earl Baldwin of Bewdley) for whom he had a genuine admiration. In *Facing the Dictators* (1962) he wrote 'No British statesman in this century has done so much to kill class hatred.' In July 1926 Eden was made parliamentary private secretary to the foreign secretary, Sir Austen Chamberlain [q.v.]. This was an important step in his career.

In 1929 Labour won the election. Eden survived in his constituency, though winning on a minority vote for the first and last time. In opposition he constituted part of a small 'ginger group' which held weekly dinners and included Oliver Stanley, William Ormsby-Gore (later Lord Harlech), Walter Elliot, and W. S. Morrison (later Viscount Dunrossil) [qq.v.]. They were left of centre and supporters of Baldwin whose position seemed precarious. The events of late August 1931 which resulted in Ramsay MacDonald forming a coalition government gave Eden an opening. The foreign secretary was a Liberal, Rufus Isaacs, first Marquess of Reading [q.v.], and Eden became his parliamentary under-secretary; he was thus the sole official voice of the Foreign Office in the House of Commons. The situation lasted only two months but enhanced his political stature. A general election in October produced a landslide victory for the national government. In the reconstructed Cabinet Sir John (later Viscount) Simon [q.v.] was foreign secretary. He liked Eden who reciprocated at first but later found his chief less congenial. Eden's position was decisively enhanced by his role in the abortive world disarmament conference of 1932–4 where he had to speak at length.

At the end of 1933 he was made lord privy seal, though not in the Cabinet and with the same Foreign Office duties as before. In February 1934 he represented the Foreign Office on a visit to Paris, Berlin, and Rome, trying to 'sell' the government's new memorandum on disarmament. He met Hitler and Hindenburg in Berlin, and Mussolini in Rome. Hitler made a favourable impression on him. At a meeting in Berlin a year later they discovered that in 1918 they had been opposite each other on the western front. The French ambassador who overheard the conversation said to Eden: 'And you missed him? You should have been shot'. Mussolini too impressed Eden. There seems no truth in the story that they took against each other from the start. The negotiations, however, came to nothing and the disarmament conference expired in April. Later that year Eden won diplomatic laurels as rapporteur for the League council after the assassination in Marseilles of King Alexander of Yugoslavia and the French foreign minister Barthou. He gained further prestige by skilful handling of the Saar plebiscite. Early in 1935 he visited Moscow. He was the first British minister to be received there since the revolution. He was not deceived by Stalin 'whose courtesy', he writes, 'in no way hid from us an implacable ruthlessness'.

When in June 1935 Baldwin succeeded MacDonald Eden entered the Cabinet as minister without portfolio for League of Nations affairs. The new foreign secretary was Sir Samuel Hoare (later Viscount Templewood, q.v.). Eden had misgivings about this arrangement, only accepting on the understanding that it would be temporary. His relations with Hoare proved, however, to be friendly, and their differences over policy have been much exaggerated. The question of the day was the action to be taken by the League of Nations against Mussolini's contemplated invasion of Abyssinia. Eden was in favour of a compromise, like Hoare and the rest of the Cabinet. But, also like Hoare, he believed that sanctions, or the threat of them, could be a serious deterrent to Mussolini, if France co-operated. It was soon clear that France, under Pierre Laval, would not. The difficulty was that the peace ballot and the Conservative programme in the general election held on 14 November made a deal with an obvious aggressor very difficult. Eden was not an ardent 'sanctionist'. He regarded Hoare's famous speech on 11 September to the League Assembly as going too far, but the Italian invasion early in October convinced him that the League should apply sanctions including oil, in order to encourage Mussolini to negotiate.

The plan which Hoare put to Laval on his ill-fated visit to Paris with Sir Robert (later Lord) Vansittart [q.v.] on 7 and 8 December 1935 gave away more of Abyssinia to Mussolini than Eden expected—but not much more. Neither he nor his colleagues appreciated that compromise with Italy would be regarded as surrender to an aggressor and cause a furore in Britain. Hoare who had never seriously exceeded his brief was forced to resign. Eden was in Geneva during the crisis. Baldwin summoned him on his return and asked him whom he would like to see as foreign secretary. He dismissed the name suggested and then said: 'It looks as if it will have to be you'. In this somewhat unflattering way Eden was appointed on 22 December to an office that he was destined to hold, though not continuously, for longer than anyone else in the twentieth century, apart from Edward Grey.

At thirty-eight he was the youngest foreign secretary since Lord Granville [q.v.]. He was also the best looking since Palmerston. Slim, debonair, well dressed, wearing the hat named after him, and talking with the clipped yet languid accents of the Eton and Christ Church of his day, he might have stepped out of a play by (Sir) Noël Coward [q.v.]. He seemed more like a man of fashion than a serious public figure. The appearance was deceptive. Eden was a tireless worker, and he drove his secretaries and assistants hard. Behind an urbane manner he was both tough, and sensitive. He stood up for his rights in no uncertain fashion, putting Sir N. F. Warren Fisher [q.v.] in his place when that formidable head of the Civil Service claimed that ambassadorial appointments had to be submitted through him for approval by the prime minister. Eden replied that the foreign secretary might consult the prime minister but that he recommended appointments to the King on his own responsibility. His parliamentary under-secretary was Robert Cecil, Viscount Cranborne, later fifth Marquess of Salisbury [q.v.] who had much influence on him at this time and whose judgement he greatly respected.

Eden's first tenure of the Foreign Office lasted little over two years. The features of it were the triumph of Mussolini in Abyssinia, the reoccupation of the demilitarized Rhineland by Hitler, the outbreak of the Spanish civil war, and a growing crisis in the Far East. There was little Eden could do about Abyssinia without French co-operation. When he pressed for oil sanctions in February 1936, Flandin, the new French foreign minister, asked him on 3 March what Britain's reaction would be if Italy withdrew from Locarno and the Germans moved into the demilitarized zone. Eden could not answer, and four days later this was what Hitler did. In fact Eden had no intention of upholding every clause of the Versailles settlement. He was in favour of conciliating Germany. The problem was to placate France while securing a deal with Hitler that would stabilize Europe and protect British interests. In these matters Eden was fully supported by Baldwin and the Cabinet. The fact remained that both dictators had won their immediate aims. On 10 June Neville Chamberlain, without consulting Eden, referred to continuance of sanctions as 'the very midsummer of madness', and they were dropped a few weeks later.

In mid-July 1936 civil war broke out in Spain. Eden was convinced that neutrality was the only safe course and that it was vital to limit intervention by other European powers. He succeeded in keeping Italian interference within bounds and in preserving the British naval position in the Mediterranean. He effectively scotched the Italian threat to Spain's territorial integrity. But the price was the loss of any chance to reconstruct the Stresa Front (Britain, France, and Italy) and thus put a curb on German expansionism. The emerging threat of simultaneous hostilities with Germany, Italy, and Japan worried others more than Eden himself who seems at this time to have been curiously optimistic about the state of Britain's defence. The creation of the Rome–Berlin axis in November 1936, followed closely by the anti-Comintern pact between Germany and Japan, emphasized this danger which became even greater when Italy joined the pact a year later. Eden did, however, achieve two notable diplomatic successes which had their effect in World War II—the Montreux convention with Turkey on 20 July and the Anglo-Egyptian treaty on 26 August. He put relations between Britain and those two countries on a friendly footing that was to be of much importance during the next decade.

On 28 May 1937 Neville Chamberlain succeeded Baldwin as prime minister. Eden had got his way on most matters under Baldwin, but, ironically, he welcomed the more active successor whose positive views were in the end to drive him into resignation. Their differences were more over method than content. Both were against the policy advocated, though not always consistently, by (Sir) Winston Churchill—collective security involving continental commitments which had little chance of acceptance by Parliament at that time. Eden, unlike Churchill who now saw Hitler as a real threat, regarded Mussolini with greater dislike. But Chamberlain and Eden believed in 'appeasement' of the dictators in the sense, as Eden points out, of the Oxford Dictionary's first definition—'to bring to peace, settle strife etc.' Where they differed was on emphasis, conditions, and timing. The precise course of their increasing divergence is impossible to chart. In retrospect Eden made much of a private message sent by Chamberlain to Mussolini without consultation on 27 July but he did not complain at the time. The first major quarrel was over the visit to Germany of the first Earl of Halifax [q.v.] in November 1937. Chamberlain's idea was to use the opportunity of an invitation to Halifax from Goering to an international sporting exhibition for informal talks with Hitler. Eden at first agreed but changed his mind after learning that the talks were to be in Berchtesgaden, not Berlin—which made it look as if Halifax was 'running after' Hitler. He was suffering from influenza but hastened to see Chamberlain and protest both about the visit and the delay in rearmament which worried him far more than it had a year earlier. He became so excited that Chamberlain urged him to 'go back to bed and take an aspirin'. The visit took place without notable result. No immediate breach occurred and the two men were agreed on getting rid of Vansittart whose voluble anti-Germanism had become a liability. He was replaced by Sir Alexander Cadogan [q.v.] early in 1938.

Two episodes brought their differences to a head. On 13 January 1938 while Eden was on holiday in the South of France Chamberlain without consulting him politely rejected a secret proposal from Roosevelt to summon the diplomatic corps in Washington and launch an international peace plan. Apprised by Cadogan Eden returned two days later, justifiably furious at being bypassed, the more so since the deadline for reply was not till 17 January. He sent off a telegram reversing Chamberlain's message. When they met he threatened resignation and Chamberlain gave way. Roosevelt, however, for reasons still obscure, dropped the proposal.

The second episode was the final straw. Chamberlain wished to concede *de jure* recognition of Italy's annexation of Abyssinia and to open formal diplomatic conversations with the Italian government on Spain. Eden was not in principle against *de jure* recognition but he was irritated by his knowledge that Chamberlain was conducting personal diplomacy behind his back through Austen Chamberlain's widow who was living in Rome. He was convinced that conversations should not be opened until Mussolini gave a tangible sign of good faith by beginning to withdraw his 'volunteers' from Spain. This time Chamberlain refused to compromise and Eden resigned on 20 February after protracted efforts by the prime minister and the Cabinet to persuade him to remain. Cranborne and J. P. L. Thomas (later Viscount Cilcennin, q.v.), his parliamentary private secretary, resigned with him. Halifax was appointed the new foreign secretary.

No resignation since that of Lord Randolph Churchill [q.v.] has been the subject of greater controversy. Did Eden expect to bring down the government? Was he in a state of nervous exhaustion? What were the real differences of policy? His detractors played them down, alleging vanity and wounded *amour propre*. There was also talk about poor health, but it had no substance. Eden was certainly sensitive about his position. He was under pressure from Cranborne, Thomas, and others to stand up for his office and some of his friends believed that his departure would break up the government. But there was a genuine divergence between him and Chamberlain about conversations with Mussolini though it concerned tactics not strategy. It would be wrong to categorize him as in any sense a Churchillian at this time. For example his speech in the Munich debate was far more conciliatory than Churchill's and although the so-called 'Eden Group' of some twenty MPs, like Churchill's friends, abstained in the division, there was no liaison between them. Later events should not be allowed to disguise the fact that Eden and Churchill were rivals for the succession to Chamberlain if events obliged the latter to retire.

When war broke out on 3 September 1939 Chamberlain dealt a blow to Eden's chances by appointing Churchill to the small War Cabinet as first lord of the Admiralty and offering Eden the Dominions Office without a seat in the Cabinet. Eden accepted patriotically but unhappily. Both Churchill and Halifax were now ahead of him. Even when Churchill succeeded Chamberlain in May 1940 Eden still remained outside the War Cabinet, though he was given the more important office of war secretary and Churchill told him that 'the succession must be mine' declaring that he did not intend to linger like Lloyd George after the war ended. Eden was closely involved in all the major decisions arising from the fall of France. He was most reluctant to release the French prime minister from his pledge not to conclude a separate peace. He was almost certainly right, but he did not get his way. However, he successfully resisted Churchill's wish to remove Sir John Dill and Sir Archibald (later Earl) Wavell [qq.v.] from their respective posts of CIGS and C-in-C Middle East. In October Eden went out to Cairo. He was opposed to the diversion of troops to meet Mussolini's attack on Greece, deeming Egypt to be the vital place. On this he was overruled by Churchill who, however, offered him, rather surprisingly, the Middle East Command which he firmly declined. The post that he really wanted became vacant with Halifax's departure to Washington as ambassador. On 23 December Eden was appointed foreign secretary for the second time and was to retain the post till the Labour victory of 1945. He now at last entered the War Cabinet.

Early in 1941 he reversed his previous attitude towards Greece and pressed for sending more troops and supplies. He feared a deal between the Greeks and the Axis powers which might prevent Yugoslavia and Turkey coming out on the side of Britain—a prospect which he regarded with excessive optimism. On 12 February Churchill and the Defence Committee sent him with Dill on a new mission first to Cairo and then on 22 February to Athens. Eden promised to send reinforcements and thought he had the agreement of the Greek commander, General Papagos, to withdraw from Salonika to the so-called Aliakmon line. But when he returned on 2 March, having been to Cairo and Ankara, he found to his dismay that no troops had been withdrawn. Churchill, now thoroughly alarmed, gave him a free hand to call the whole thing off. Eden's military advisers, however, wanted to go ahead and so did Eden. The Greek expedition proved to be a major disaster for which Eden must bear his share of responsibility.

Hitler attacked Russia on 22 June 1941. Eden strongly supported Churchill's decision to announce, without Cabinet authority, an offer of full working partnership. He also agreed with Churchill's policy of doing nothing to improve the worsening relations between America and Japan. They hoped that it would lead to American involvement in Europe, as indeed it did, though the result was due to luck rather than good judgement—Hitler's unnecessary and still incomprehensible declaration of war on America immediately after Pearl Harbour. On 7 December, the very day of that calamity, Eden set out for Moscow to negotiate with Stalin. The Russian dictator sought recognition of his 1941 frontiers. Eden went dangerously near to promising this. There was a Cabinet revolt after he returned, and, if Molotov had not accepted a much more anodyne treaty under American pressure, Eden could have been in major trouble.

Eden's relationship with Churchill was not as harmonious as their memoirs, written in each other's lifetime, suggest. Eden remained optimistic about Russia far longer than Churchill and was much keener on opening a 'second front'. If Oliver Harvey (later Lord Harvey of Tasburgh, q.v.), his Foreign Office private secretary, is correct he seriously contemplated as early as February 1942 taking steps to remove the prime minister, and began by pressing for a separate minister of defence. Churchill riposted by making Clement Attlee deputy prime minister and Sir Stafford Cripps [q.v.] leader of the House. Eden did not pursue the matter, and on 16 June Churchill on the verge of sailing to Washington left a letter with the King's private secretary advising that Eden should be his successor if anything happened to him. Eden took no part in the attacks launched against Churchill after the fall of Tobruk five days later, and Cripps, the other principal critic, found himself out on a limb. On 22 November Eden himself became leader of the House, retaining the Foreign Office—an almost impossible burden until eased in 1944 by the flying bombs which kept MPs out of London. Another source of dispute with Churchill was the question of 'recognizing' General de Gaulle's FCNL (French Committee of National Liberation). Eden correctly saw that this could be the only rallying point for Free France. Roosevelt, however, detested de Gaulle, and Churchill, indiffferent on the merits of the case, was determined to support the president. Matters came to a head in July 1943 when Eden tried to persuade the Cabinet to make a unilateral announcement of recognition. Churchill forced Eden to climb down but in the end events obliged Roosevelt to give way.

Shortly before this episode Churchill had invited Eden to become viceroy of India. He was sorely tempted but he consulted Baldwin with whom he had always had friendly relations, and the old man advised him against it on the ground that 'if he went to India he would never come back to be PM'. Except for Casablanca from which foreign ministers were excluded he accompanied Churchill on all the major summit conferences with Roosevelt in 1943–4—the first Quebec conference in August, the first Cairo conference in November, Tehran (with Stalin as well) at the end of the month, the second Cairo conference in December, and the second Quebec conference in September 1944 where Eden violently objected to the 'Morgenthau plan' supported by Roosevelt for the 'pastoralization' of Germany. He was entirely in the right and had a public row with Churchill. Luckily Roosevelt dropped the plan soon afterwards. Churchill and Eden then went to Moscow in October where the famous 'percentage agreement' was initialled by Chuchill and Stalin, dividing the Balkan states into spheres of interest, Greece being ninety per cent British and American.

Earlier that year Eden was involved in decisions for which he has been fiercely attacked in books based on Foreign Office papers first made available in the 1970s. These concerned the problem of Russians wearing German uniforms who had fallen into British hands. The Soviet government insisted on repatriation. It was well known that this meant either execution or a slower death in Siberia. Since many of them had joined the German Army in order to escape murder or torture and others were not even Soviet citizens the propriety of agreeing seems highly questionable now. The principal reason for repatriation was a desire to meet Stalin's wishes in a matter to which Britain attached no great significance but which he evidently regarded as so important that refusal might have endangered the alliance and damaged the chances of a deal over the Balkans. Legally, moreover, Stalin was in the right. It was a fearful price to pay for averting a hypothetical threat, though Eden's biographer, David Carlton, may be correct in writing (*Anthony Eden*, 1981, p. 242): 'Yet, if as seems likely, the alternative was the loss of Greece into the Soviet orbit, the decision may possibly have constituted the lesser of two evils'. Whatever the truth of this, the policy was that of the War Cabinet. It was not a personal decision by Eden.

Greece was to be the only Balkan country salvaged from communism. The initiative came from Churchill who on this point was not going to give way to Roosevelt, but Eden was involved too, visiting Athens soon after the German withdrawal in the face of British occupation in October 1944, and again with Churchill that Christmas. He played an important part in persuading Churchill to agree to a regency rather than an immediate restoration of the monarchy—a decision which was undoubtedly correct in the circumstances.

Eden accompanied Churchill on that last great summit conference—Yalta in late January 1945. Proceedings were dominated by Stalin and Roosevelt. Neither Churchill nor Eden could make much difference to the new Russian empire taking shape in eastern Europe. Poland in particular, the *casus belli*, was abandoned to her fate. Eden felt bitterly about it but there was nothing he or any British statesman could do. The war was now drawing to an end. Eden was tired. On 12 April Roosevelt died. Eden represented Britain at the funeral and stayed on in America for the San Francisco conference which laid the foundations of the United Nations Organization. He did not return till 17 May, thus missing the VE-day celebrations in London. Replying to his congratulatory telegram Churchill said: 'Throughout you have been my mainstay'. The coalition had broken up and on 23 May Churchill formed a caretaker government, Eden retaining the same post. An election was scheduled for 5 July.

At this juncture Eden became seriously ill with a duodenal ulcer. Apart from a broadcast at the end of June he played no part in the campaign. The result, owing to the delay necessitated by a postal vote for the forces, was not announced till 26 July. The month of June was made even more miserable for Eden by the news that his elder son and elder child, Simon, a pilot officer, was missing in Burma. With much courage Eden accompanied Churchill to the conference at Potsdam on 15 July. Two days later he wrote in his diary: 'Depressed, and cannot help an unworthy hope that we may lose, or rather have lost this election.' On 20 July Simon's death was confirmed—the last and most poignant of Eden's many wartime bereavements. On 26 July back in London Eden had his 'unworthy hope' fulfilled. The Conservatives, heavily defeated, were out for the next six years. After their last Cabinet meeting Churchill said to Eden: 'Thirty years of my life have been passed in this room. I shall never sit in it again'. The prophecy depended, however, on the prophet.

The end of the war left Eden physically and emotionally exhausted. His illness and bereavement go far to explain the inconspicuous part that he played at first on the opposition benches. Nor were these set-backs the only sources of his unhappiness. For some time past he and his wife had been drifting apart. When they made a visit to America late in 1946 she remained behind in New York and did not return with him. Divorce even for the 'innocent party' would have been a grave handicap before the war, but times had changed. Eden did not suffer politically: he was to be the first divorced person to become prime minister.

Eden adopted during most of his time in opposition a bipartisan approach to foreign policy. He admired Ernest Bevin [q.v.] and felt it his duty to support him against the vociferous Labour pro-Soviet lobby. This meant a certain caution about attacks on Russian policy, since they might be counter-productive. Eden did not welcome Churchill's celebrated 'Iron Curtain' speech at Fulton, Missouri, in March 1946, and maintained a studied silence. Much intrigue against Churchill's continuance as leader—he was over seventy—ensued. But Eden, however impatient he may have felt for the succession, did not participate, and it came to nothing. On the home front Eden was relatively quiescent. He made an important speech at the Conservative conference of 1946 about 'a nation-wide property-owning democracy'—a feature, as he saw it, of American society, which deserved attention in socialist Britain. He was to make it the keynote of his electoral appeal in 1955. But he did not take any great interest in the detailed domestic programmes designed to show that the Conservatives had a 'constructive' alternative. He warmly welcomed, as did Bevin, the Marshall Plan for economic aid to Europe. In the election of February 1950 Eden held his seat comfortably and the Conservatives were only defeated by the narrowest of margins.

Churchill showed no signs of retiring. Eden had to reconcile himself to a further period as second-in-command but there was now a prospect of returning to office. His attitude became less bipartisan. Although he strongly supported Bevin on the Korean war, he criticized Labour's hostility to the Schuman plan, a move towards the pooling of the French and German coal and steel industries. He disapproved too of Labour's policy towards Egypt. His divergence became more marked when Bevin was succeeded by Herbert Morrison (later Lord Morrison of Lambeth, q.v.) whom he disliked and who had once described him as 'worth his weight in gold as a shop-walker in one of the West End stores'. When the Iranian oil crisis flared up in April 1951 he accused Morrison of feebleness in the face of Mussadeq's policy of nationalizing the British oil installations in Abadan. His speeches on most topics at this time were vigorous assertions of the greatness of Great Britain.

The election of October 1951 gave the Conservatives a parliamentary majority of seventeen. Eden became foreign secretary for the third time, Churchill at the age of seventy-seven still showing no sign of bowing out. Eden was fifty-four and the indisputable crown prince, but would the king ever abdicate? He was at first leader of the House as well as foreign secretary but in May 1952 the offices were separated. In foreign policy he possessed what the Earl of Kilmuir [q.v.] called 'a silencing authority' in the Cabinet room. He did not always get his way with the prime minister but their differences were settled in private. Outside Europe there were four problem areas—Korea, Iran, Egypt, and Indo-China. In Europe there was the minor but tiresome matter of Trieste and the much more important question of reconciling France to German rearmament. In all these matters Eden recognized that Britain had to take second place to America, eight times as rich and far better armed. If the American view was clear it prevailed, but there were questions on which American opinion was hesitant, and in these the Foreign Secretary could influence events.

To Eden Britain was a balancing force between the American continent, Europe, and the Commonwealth. The Americans regarded their continent as their monopoly, the Commonwealth as an anachronism, and Britain as just another European power. They feared a world-wide challenge from communism. Eden did not regard this as the only issue. He was concerned with traditional British interests. He wanted to leave the Far East to America and avoid trouble with China which might involve the loss of Hong Kong. The Middle East on the other hand he regarded as 'British'. Withdrawal from Egypt threatened the route through the Suez canal. Capitulation to Mussadeq would endanger British investments all over the world. In his memoirs Eden tends to personalize these differences in terms of his relations with Dulles whom he disliked. In reality they were as acute during the first fifteen months of his tenure when Acheson was secretary of state. They stemmed not from personalities but divergent national interests.

In fact the accession of Dulles was an advantage in Iran, for he agreed, as Acheson would not have, to the British proposal of a coup in conjunction with the CIA to overthrow Mussadeq. This came off successfully in August 1953 and solved the Iranian problem for the time being. In Egypt Eden had to deal with King Farouk's abrogation of the 1936 treaty in October 1951—an issue of which he had made much during the election. There was disorder in Cairo and Ismailia and several deaths after British punitive action. He refused Acheson's proposal to recognize Farouk as King of the Sudan. The King was deposed in July 1952 by a military coup and after a short interval Colonel Nasser became the effective ruler. The American government applied strong pressure for a deal. Eden agreed in 1954 to the evacuation of the Suez base with the right to return in an emergency. Some Conservative MPs led by Captain Waterhouse and known as the 'Suez Group' bitterly opposed the withdrawal. Privately Churchill was indignant too. Eden made a major contribution in negotiating an armistice and exchange of prisoners with North Korea in 1953, and in 1954 he was able to restrain Dulles from armed intervention in support of the tottering cause of France in her long-drawn-out war with the Vietminh in Indo-China.

Eden's most durable achievements were in Europe. In 1954 the French Assembly voted down the European Defence Community which involved unacceptably close integration of forces at too low a level. Eden's suggestion of an alternative form of alliance, together with his promise at just the right psychological moment to station British divisions in Europe, saved NATO from ruin, and the arrangement has lasted ever since. He was also prominent in healing two other sores, the Trieste question where Yugoslavia and Italy had been bickering for years, and the Austrian peace treaty which had been held up ever since 1945 by Soviet intransigence but was signed just after he became prime minister.

Meanwhile an important change took place in his private life. His marriage had been dissolved in 1950 and in August 1952 he married (Anne) Clarissa, daughter of Major John Strange Spencer-Churchill and the prime minister's niece. She was thirty-two and he was fifty-five, but, despite the gap in years, it was a most happy marriage which brought stability into his somewhat restless life. Within a year, however, he had a serious set-back. He had been suffering much pain and one attack of jaundice when gallstones were diagnosed. In April 1953 he had two operations in England which failed, and had to have a third in Boston in May which was relatively successful. But he was out of action till October, and at the end of June Churchill who had taken over the Foreign Office had a stroke. He made a remarkable recovery but he was never the same again. If Eden had been well he might have resigned, but he argued that it was his duty to remain. Otherwise R. A. Butler (later Lord Butler of Saffron Walden) would have become prime minister and Eden would be deprived of the succession. In the event he stayed on for another eighteen months.

Eden became prime minister on 6 April 1955. He made few changes in the Cabinet. Lord Swinton [q.v.] retired with an earldom. Macmillan went to the Foreign Office. Eden would have preferred Salisbury but considered it unwise to appoint a peer. His immediate problem was the timing of the next general election. He could have postponed it till October 1956, but the economy was booming, unemployment was negligible, and, largely thanks to Eden's own efforts, the international scene was tranquil. A tax-reducing budget was announced and he resolved to go to the country as soon as possible. His decision was vindicated. The election held on 26 May increased the Conservative majority over all other parties from seventeen to sixty. The result owed something to Eden's own conduct of the campaign. Repeating his theme of a 'property-owning democracy'; he was the first prime minister to make effective use of television, addressing his audience alone, face to face and without a script.

The government, however, soon ran into trouble. There were strikes by London busmen and dockworkers during the weeks before the election. These may have damaged Labour, but a strike by ASLEF which was only ended by an inflationary settlement damaged the economy. The trade figures deteriorated and the 'give away' spring budget came to look like an electoral bribe. An autumn budget increasing purchase tax on various goods had to be introduced on 26 October. R. A. Butler, the chancellor of the Exchequer, was clearly an exhausted man and Eden decided to move him to the leadership of the House, replacing him at the Exchequer by

Macmillan. The Foreign Office went to J. Selwyn B. Lloyd (later Lord Selwyn-Lloyd, q.v.) who carried lighter political guns and was less likely to disagree with the prime minister. Shortly after this there was a reshuffle in the Labour Party. Attlee retired and Hugh Gaitskell [q.v.] was elected in his place. Eden did not welcome the change and his relations with the new leader were never as cordial as with the old. Gaitskell's accession seemed to give a mild boost to Labour who had a nine per cent swing in their favour at a by-election at Torquay. Personal criticism of the prime minister, already expressed with much malevolence by Churchill's son Randolph in the *Evening Standard*, began to spread to other Conservative organs. Eden, highly sensitive to an adverse press, took the unprecedented step of publicly denying that he intended to retire, and he referred in a speech in Bradford on 14 January 1956 to 'cantankerous' London newspapers. The impression was left that he was not quite as calm and cool as he had hitherto appeared.

Foreign affairs dominated Eden's premiership. There was a summit conference on the subject of Germany at Geneva in July 1955, but nothing came of it apart from a promise by the two Russian leaders, Khrushchev and Bulganin, to visit England in the spring of 1956. The major problem which faced Eden was the Middle East whose oil supplies were crucial for Europe. The Egyptian dictator had been in no way appeased by Britain's withdrawal and he continued to pour out pan-Arab propaganda against the pro-British regimes in the area, particularly Iraq and Jordan. Nasser was not pro-Soviet but he was ready to play the Russian card against Britain and America. The politics of the Middle East became more and more like a personal duel between Eden and Nasser. They only met once—at the Cairo embassy in February 1955 while Eden was still foreign secretary. Nasser claimed that Eden behaved 'like a prince dealing with vagabonds'. No doubt it was an exaggeration but Eden may have shown annoyance at Egyptian refusal to join the proposed Baghdad Pact between Iraq and Turkey, to which he intended to adhere and hoped to be supported by Pakistan, Iran, and the USA.

This was an error of judgement. Eden had not consulted Washington. What Dulles had been encouraging in a somewhat dilatory way was an Anglo-American alliance with the three non-Arab states on Russia's southern frontier. To include Iraq was quite another matter; it seemed an attempt to divide the Arab world and was bound to enrage both the Egyptians and the Saudis. Although Pakistan and Iraq did in the end join, Dulles would only send 'observers' to Baghdad. Eden felt he had been deceived. The episode contributed to their mutual mistrust.

In September 1955 Nasser announced a huge arms deal with Czechoslovakia which was obviously acting as a cat's paw for Russia. On paper it would change the whole balance of power in the Middle East, and the potential infiltration at once raised another question—that of the Aswan high dam. The purpose of this long-planned project was to improve the irrigation of the Nile and alleviate the poverty of the fellahin. Eden was anxious that it should be constructed by a western consortium rather than by Russian engineers. This meant some degree of western financial support. In December the American and British governments together with the International Bank made an offer of a loan of $400 million towards the cost. Nasser did not immediately accept, and the matter rested for several months.

Meanwhile Eden had been involved along with Macmillan in a vexatious problem of security. Guy Burgess and Donald Maclean, the two Soviet spies in the Foreign Office who had fled the country in 1951, were widely believed to be in Moscow, but no hard evidence emerged until 1955 when a Soviet defector published his memoirs. The government in September published a white paper on proposed ways of tightening up security. It was generally regarded as feeble, and Colonel Marcus Lipton, a Labour MP, took advantage of parliamentary privilege to name Harold ('Kim') Philby as the 'third man' who had enabled the spies to escape. He was right but there was no clear evidence, only strong suspicion. Eden and Macmillan, the latter with unnecessary emphasis, had to deny Philby's guilt. There was much press criticism of an alleged cover-up by 'the establishment', but Eden won general applause with a declaration in the debate on 7 November that he would never head a government which eroded the principle that a man is innocent until proved guilty.

Early in December Eden made an attempt to bring Jordan into the Baghdad Pact. It misfired. Riots inspired from Egypt brought down the government, and King Hussain's personal position was threatened. Jordanian refusal became inevitable; Eden ran into further trouble in the new year, this time at home. Macmillan was anxious to adopt deflationary measures, among others to abolish subsidies on bread and milk. Eden was reluctant in view of his election pledges. The chancellor threatened resignation. Eden agreed to a compromise which, Macmillan later claimed, 'gave me four-fifths of my demands'. On 1 March 1956 came another blow from the Middle East. King Hussain dismissed General (Sir) John Bagot Glubb, commander of the Arab Legion and the symbol of British influence in Amman. Eden's first instinct was to break off relations. On second thoughts he decided that Nasser was the culprit. His speech in the House dispirited a sour Conservative Party which scented appeasement. He was, however, able to dispel this impression to some extent soon afterwards by firm action in Cyprus. The movement for Enosis, i.e. union with Greece, had been gathering momentum under its leader Archbishop Makarios [q.v.]. There was a terrorist wing, EOKA, which did not hesitate to use violence. Britain could not acquiesce in Enosis if only because of the Turkish minority on the island, and efforts to produce an agreement between Greece and Turkey predictably failed. There seemed some evidence that Makarios was involved in EOKA's activities, and Eden decided to deport him to the Seychelles. This action rallied his supporters.

For the next few weeks Eden had slightly plainer sailing. The promised visit from the Soviet leaders took place. It did no particular good, but also no particular harm. One curious episode occurred. With the authority of MI6, but certainly without Eden's, a frogman, Commander ('Buster') Crabb engaged in underwater examination of the naval vessels which had escorted the Russian leader to Portsmouth. He was spotted and was never seen alive again. The Russians made a strong protest. Eden was furious. The director of MI6, Sir John Sinclair [q.v.], was on the verge of retirement; otherwise he would have been dismissed. In his place Eden appointed Sir Dick White, head of MI5. The two organizations detested each other. It was a crushing rebuff.

By now there was increasing concern, political and economic, about the still unaccepted loan for the Aswan dam. Dulles and Lloyd decided to 'let it wither on the vine'. Nasser, aware of their decision, resolved to press the matter in order to have a public excuse for something he had long planned anyway—the nationalization of the Suez Canal Company. On 19 July Dulles without consulting London called off the loan, after a series of importunate demands from Cairo. A week later in a flamboyant speech in Alexandria Nasser announced his take-over of the Canal Company. Eden received the news in 10 Downing Street while he was entertaining the young King of Iraq and his prime minister, Nasser's *bête noire* Nuri es-Said, to dinner. It could scarcely have come at a more painful moment.

Nasser's action was generally regarded as a breach of international law. Whether it justified the use of force was less clear, but from the outset Eden and Guy Mollet, the French prime minister, claimed that, if other methods failed, military action would be warranted in order to re-establish international control over a waterway so essential at that time to the interests of western Europe. The two prime ministers made no bones in private and in confidential communications with Washington that they hoped not only to 'internationalize' the canal but to 'topple' Nasser. Preparations were at once put in train for a joint Anglo-French amphibious operation based on Malta. It could not be ready till 8 September. Meanwhile the strongest pressure was to be applied. Eden's line received general support in Parliament and the country. Hugh Gaitskell [q.v.] spoke equally strongly against Nasser but, contrary to later legend, he made it clear, albeit in small rather than big print, that he could not endorse military action except with the agreement of the UN, and he repeated the point in several private letters of warning to Eden. This was broadly the American view too. For Washington the canal was not of vital importance. Eisenhower and Dulles had no use for Nasser, but they did not regard his action as sufficiently outrageous to produce the sympathy in the non-communist world needed by Britain and France for successful military intervention. If Nasser interfered with the operation of the canal it would be a different matter, but in fact shipping passed through without hindrance till the balloon went up on 29 October.

Apprehensive of a British resort to arms Dulles hastened to London on 31 July to argue for diplomatic pressure. He and Eden who for the time being had no choice announced on 2 August the summoning of a conference of the principal maritime powers. This met from 16 to 23 August. A five-man committee headed by the Australian prime minister, (Sir) Robert Menzies [q.v.], was deputed to persuade Nasser to put the canal under an international board. It got nowhere. Eden now wished to refer the matter to the Security Council. Dulles was opposed, and came up with the idea of the Suez Canal Users' Association (SCUA). Eden agreed with much misgiving to announce this to Parliament on 12 September. It was most unpopular. The plan, which involved the user nations asserting their rights under the 1888 convention by hiring their own pilots and collecting their own dues, was deliberately ambiguous about force. The SCUA conference met from 19 to 22 September. Next day, contrary to Dulles's wishes, Eden and Mollet referred the dispute to the Security Council to be considered on 5 October. Meanwhile in a press conference on 2 October Dulles gave an interview on SCUA. This was claimed by some of Eden's intimates to have been the last straw. He observed that some people had said that the teeth had been pulled out of the plan, 'but I know of no teeth: there were no teeth in it as far as I am aware'. Eden was outraged. He knew that any UN resolution on this matter was sure to be vetoed by Russia, as indeed occurred on 13 October. The expedition could not be kept indefinitely on ice, and the end of the diplomatic road had been reached—at a very awkward moment, the week of the annual Conservative Party conference.

The fog of historical obscurity now begins to thicken. Of the British Cabinet ministers who have written their accounts only Selwyn Lloyd pierces the gloom to some degree; the full truth will probably never emerge. It is known that on 14 October two French emissaries, General Challe and Albert Gazier, put to Eden the idea perhaps not entirely new to him of making use of the Israelis who were contemplating a pre-emptive strike against the Jordanian and Egyptian frontier bases. If they could be persuaded to avoid Jordan, concentrate on Egypt, and threaten the Suez canal, Britain and France could intervene ostensibly to separate the combatants and ensure the free passage of shipping. With any luck Nasser would fall and the canal would be recovered in the process. On 16 October Eden and Lloyd conferred with Mollet and Pineau in Paris; no officials were allowed to attend. On 22 October Selwyn Lloyd and, two days later, (Sir) Patrick Dean of the Foreign Office had meetings of the utmost secrecy at a villa in Sèvres with French and Israeli representatives. A document was signed which has never been published, though the gist of it is known from Israeli sources. The attack would be launched on 29 October before the American presidential election. Although Israel had no need to threaten the canal, she would do so if Britain guaranteed to 'take out' the Egyptian air force, and she promised not to attack Jordan. Britain and France would launch an ultimatum calling for both sides to cease fire and withdraw ten miles from the canal and for Egypt to agree to temporary occupation of the canal by Anglo-French forces. On 25 October the Cabinet with varying degrees of knowledge and enthusiasm endorsed the plan. These arrangements were highly secret. Only a very few in the Foreign Office knew about them. No ambassadors were informed, and American enquiries were fobbed off with what can only be described as a series of lies.

On 27 October Israel mobilized and invaded Egypt two days later. On 30 October Eden announced the ultimatum which Egypt predictably refused to accept. The Anglo-French force had already set out from Malta, while on 31 October RAF planes based on Cyprus effectively eliminated the Egyptian air force. On 5 November a parachute descent at dawn was made on Port Said, and twenty-four hours later the main force landed. It met little resistance and the troops were soon twenty miles along the causeway of the canal. Meanwhile there was continuous uproar in Parliament. The pretence that the Israeli invasion had created an unexpected emergency deceived few people, but most Conservatives were all for a hit at Nasser anyway, though there were some dissidents. Two junior ministers, Anthony Nutting and Sir Edward Boyle (later Lord Boyle of Handsworth), resigned. Eden never forgave Nutting who had been minister of state at the Foreign Office. The Cabinet, though increasingly worried, remained united. Gaitskell, who had only been told of the ultimatum a quarter of an hour before its announcement, did all he could to persuade the Conservative doubters to bring down the government, but his appeal was probably counterproductive. Britain had little support in the Commonwealth or United Nations. At Lake Success the Americans did all they could to halt the action; Britain and France twice had to use their vetoes. On 6 November Egypt and Israel both accepted the call for a cease-fire. Eden ordered the troops on the canal to halt at midnight.

He has been as much criticized for stopping as starting the Suez operation. His reasons are still not clear. He could have ridden out the trouble in the UN and he did not take seriously vague Russian threats about rockets. His government was in no danger of falling. Public opinion polls were on his side. But Eisenhower who probably learned about 'collusion' at an early stage was very angry. He may have made threats that have not been revealed. There was a run on the pound and Macmillan, hitherto strong for action, went abruptly into reverse. Moreover what Selwyn Lloyd revealingly calls in his book the 'ostensible' purpose of the operation had been achieved; the combatants had been separated, hostilities had ceased. Eisenhower now took a very strong line against Britain and France. He refused Eden's requests for a personal interview. No Anglo-French troops were to participate in the Emergency Force (UNEF) set up by a UN resolution, nor were they allowed to take any part in clearing the canal which was now full of sunken block-ships.

Eden's health had been poor throughout the crisis. On 5 October he had collapsed with a temperature of 106 degrees—the first onset of the periodic fevers resulting from his bile duct troubles, which were to plague the rest of his life. He recovered in a few days but he was in constant need of drugs, and suffered sleepless nights because of the time gap between London and Washington. On 21 November he announced that on medical advice he was flying to Jamaica to recuperate, staying at the house of Ian Fleming [q.v.]. He left Butler in charge. He returned on 14 December and his speeches by no means rallied his demoralized party. On 9 January 1957 he resigned on medical advice, and was succeeded by Harold Macmillan. It is untrue, though often alleged, that the Queen did not consult him about his successor. He never revealed his choice, nor was it necessarily decisive, but there is good evidence that he did not recommend Butler.

It is unlucky that the Suez débâcle will always

be the episode most clearly associated with Eden's name. The decision was, as Henry Kissinger said, 'misconceived', but in the same assessment Kissinger also pointed out that, if acts of international brigandage are not resisted the world becomes one of anarchy, and he is highly critical of the attitude of Washington. It might have been better to take military action as soon as the inevitable Russian veto was applied, thus avoiding any involvement with Israel. American pressure would probably have compelled withdrawal but the charges of duplicity and hypocrisy could not have been made. Eden's real error, however, was not 'collusion' nor an anachronistic overestimation of British strength. He was well aware that Britain and France were not superpowers. Where he erred was in failing to appreciate that Eisenhower and Dulles really meant what they said about their objection to force. They perhaps erred in not spelling out what America would do, if Britain and France decided to 'go it alone'. Perhaps they did not believe it would happen. What has been published of the exchanges between Washington and London reads like a dialogue of the deaf.

Eden lived, despite indifferent health, for another twenty years. He at first entertained some hope of a return to politics but realism broke through and he took his seat as the Earl of Avon on 26 July 1961. He spoke from time to time in the Lords and wrote occasional articles on foreign affairs, but he had little influence on events. In 1960 he published the first of three volumes of memoirs *Full Circle* which chronologically covers the last part of the period and leaves the key questions about Suez unanswered. Neither then nor later did he comment upon 'collusion'. It might have been better to write the volumes in the proper sequence but Eden was under strong pressure from *The Times* which had paid a large sum for the serial rights. *Facing the Dictators* (1962) and *The Reckoning* (1965) are, however, major contributions which every historian of the period is bound to consult. His last publication, *Another World 1897–1917*, appeared in 1976 shortly before his death. It is a beautifully written nostalgic memoir of his youth. He was taken seriously ill in the winter of 1976 while staying in Florida as a guest of Averell Harriman. Early in the new year it became clear that he could not live much longer. With the prime minister's assent he was flown back to England in an RAF plane. He died at his home, Alvediston in Wiltshire, 14 January 1977. His wife who had done so much to ease his life in retirement survived him. He was succeeded in the earldom by his son, Nicholas (born 1930), who died in 1985.

Eden was sworn of the Privy Council in 1934 and was made KG in 1954. He was awarded honorary degrees by thirteen universities (including Oxford and Cambridge), and elected honorary Student of Christ Church, Oxford, in 1941. He was chancellor of Birmingham University 1945–73. He was made an honorary bencher of the Middle Temple in 1952, and an honorary member of the Salters' Company in 1946 and of the Fishmongers' in 1955. He became an elder brother of Trinity House in 1953 and honorary FRIBA in 1955. He was a trustee of the National Gallery 1935–49. He was honorary colonel Queen's Westminsters KRRC 1952–60 and of the Queen's Royal Rifles 1960–2. He was honorary air commodore of No. 500 (County Kent) Squadron RAF 1943–57. He was president of the Royal Shakespeare Theatre 1958–66.

[Eden's own writings mentioned in the text; Winston Churchill, *The Second World War*, 6 volumes, 1948–54; Harold Macmillan, *Memoirs*, 6 volumes, 1966–73; Anthony Nutting, *No End of a Lesson*, 1967; Selwyn Lloyd, *Suez 1956*, 1978; David Carlton, *Anthony Eden, a Biography*, 1981—somewhat impersonal and unsympathetic but an essential work; private information; personal knowledge.]

BLAKE

EDWARD VIII (1894–1972), King of Great Britain, Ireland, and the British Dominions beyond the seas, Emperor of India—the only British sovereign to relinquish the crown voluntarily—was born at White Lodge, Richmond Park, 23 June 1894, the eldest of the family of five sons and one daughter of the then Duke and Duchess of York. With the death of Queen Victoria in 1901 his parents became Prince and Princess of Wales, and in 1910, when Edward VII died, King George V and Queen Mary. As their eldest son Prince Edward was from birth in the direct line of succession, and of the seven names (Edward Albert Christian George Andrew Patrick David) given to him at his baptism four were those of British patron saints. In the family he was always known as David.

Though in most respects pampered by Fate, he was unlucky in the inability of his parents to communicate easily with their children, who consequently suffered from a lack of human warmth and encouragement in early life. Their father, though kind-hearted, was a martinet in his treatment of them, and their mother was deficient in the normal maternal instincts. Nor did the man chosen to be their principal tutor, Henry Peter Hansell, make up for what their parents failed to give, since he too was a rather aloof and limited character.

Edward was an intelligent child, endowed with curiosity and a powerful memory. Though it is unlikely that he would ever have developed as a scholar, his mental gifts deserved imaginative teaching. As it was, he grew up with a poor grounding of knowledge, no taste at all for any books worth the name, and unable even to spell properly. Only as a linguist were his attainments equal to his position, since he learnt French and German in childhood, and later acquired a fluent command of Spanish.

Other valuable qualities belonged to him naturally. Despite his small stature he had exceptional good looks, which never lost their boyish appeal. He had boundless energy and zest, and was full of courage. Above all, he had a spontaneous charm of manner which drew people to him and put them at their ease. His personality would have been remarkable even if he had not been royal; allied to his princely status it was irresistible.

In 1907 he was sent to Osborne, and two years later to Dartmouth. While he was there his father became King, and he himself heir apparent to the throne. On his sixteenth birthday he was created Prince of Wales, and on 13 July 1911 became the first English holder of the title to be formally invested at Caernarvon castle. The ceremony was stage-managed by the constable of the castle, David Lloyd George (later Earl Lloyd-George of Dwyfor) who personally taught him a few words of Welsh to utter when he was presented to the crowd at Queen Eleanor's gate.

The following year he went into residence at Magdalen College, Oxford, but there was little to show for his brief university career. During vacations he paid two visits to Germany and one to Scandinavia. In 1914 he was anyway due to leave Oxford at the end of the academic year, to begin a period of service in the army; but in the event he did so as Britain was entering the most terrible war in her history.

Commissioned in the Grenadier Guards, he asked only to be allowed to fight alongside his contemporaries, but was told that this would not be possible, because of the danger that he might be captured and used as a hostage. Soon, however, he managed to get himself posted to the staff of the British Expeditionary Force's commander in France, and thereafter spent most of the war abroad, attached to various headquarters but essentially serving as a visitor of troops and general morale-raiser. He lived frugally and, though provided with a Daimler, preferred to travel around on a green army bicycle, covering hundreds of miles. His desire always was to be at the scene of action, and he had a narrow escape when visiting front-line positions before the battle of Loos.

Given his enforced role as a non-combatant he could hardly have done more to share the ordeal of other young men of his generation. Yet he was mortified that he could not share it more fully, and genuinely embarrassed when he was awarded the MC. The humility of his attitude enhanced the value of the work he did, which was never forgotten by the countless ordinary soldiers to whom he brought understanding and cheer.

His war service was a crucially formative episode in his own life, vastly broadening his range of human experience and showing how good he was at establishing contact with his fellow-men, whatever their backgrounds. As well as meeting people of all classes from the United Kingdom, he also got to know Allied troops, including Americans, and a variety of British subjects from overseas. While visiting the Middle East in the spring of 1916 he met Australians and New Zealanders evacuated from Gallipoli. At the time of the armistice in 1918 he was with the Canadian Corps in France, and after the armistice was attached to the Australian Corps in Belgium.

Thus he was unconsciously introduced to the next and most fruitful phase of his career, which began with his visits to Newfoundland, Canada, and the United States in the summer and autumn of 1919. Lloyd George, now prime minister, was convinced that 'the appearance of the popular Prince of Wales in far corners of the Empire might do more ... than half a dozen solemn Imperial Conferences'. So it proved. The Canadian tour was a triumphal success, in Quebec no less than in the English-speaking provinces. Wherever he went the response was overwhelming. In Alberta he bought a ranch for himself—an admirable gesture, though a source of trouble to him later.

His first visit to the United States was equally successful, though briefer and far less extensive. In Washington, he called on the stricken President Wilson, and in New York was given a ticker-tape welcome as he drove to the City Hall to receive the freedom. Yet it was not such important occasions that lingered most persistently in his mind after his return to England, but rather the song 'A Pretty Girl is like a Melody', which he had heard at the Ziegfeld Follies. His endless whistling of this 'damned tune' caused annoyance to his father, and shows that American culture had made an immediate conquest.

In 1920 he visited New Zealand and Australia, travelling there in the battleship *Renown*, by way of the Panama canal, Hawaii, and Fiji. Again, he carried all before him. In 1921–2 he toured India, where nationalists had been disappointed by the modest scope of the Montagu–Chelmsford reforms, and where the Amritsar massacre was still a recent memory. Despite the unfavourable circumstances, he made an excellent impression on such Indians as he was allowed to meet, many of whom were quoted by a British observer as saying: 'If only all you Europeans were like him!' In many places large and friendly crowds turned out to greet him, defying the Congress boycott of his visit.

The same voyage took him to Nepal, Burma, Malaya, Hong Kong, Japan, the Philippines, Borneo, Ceylon, and Egypt. On his return to London after eight months' absence there was a banquet in his honour at Guildhall, at which his health was eloquently proposed by Lloyd George—the last official act of his premiership.

This intensive travelling during the early post-war years was not a flash in the pan, but set the pattern for his subsequent way of life as Prince of Wales. In all but three years until his accession he spent long periods outside Britain. Hardly any part of the Empire, however small or remote, failed to receive at least one visit from him, and he was also welcomed in many foreign countries. Particularly noteworthy were his South American tours in 1925 and 1931, which inspired the greatest enthusiasm in a region traditionally important to Britain, though much neglected by British public figures. (A by-product of the second tour was the Ibero-American Institute of Great Britain, founded under his auspices, which led in turn to the creation of the British Council in 1935.)

At home, too, he was very busy and mobile, giving special attention to ex-servicemen and young people. In a period of mass unemployment and widespread social deprivation there might be little he could do to help the victims, but at least he went out of his way to talk to them, and it was obvious that they had his sympathy.

For all his exertions in the public interest, his life was by no means all work. While touring overseas, no less than in Britain, he would always devote a lot of his time to games and sport, and at the end of the most arduous day he was usually eager to dance into the small hours. His daylight recreations could be dangerous—after repeated spills and fractures he was prevailed upon to give up steeplechasing, only to take to flying instead—but in the long run his late nights were more harmful to him. A tendency to unpunctuality and moodiness was certainly made worse by lack of sleep.

As he moved from youth to middle age the strain of his life began to tell upon a nature that was nervous as well as physically robust; and at the same time, inevitably, he was becoming rather spoilt by the universal adulation to which he was exposed. Above all he seemed increasingly solitary, and without any firm base to his existence.

From 1919 he had his own London establishment at York House, St. James's Palace, and in 1929 he obtained from his father the 'grace and favour' use of Fort Belvedere, a small architectural folly near Windsor (originally built for the Duke of Cumberland in the 1750s, but improved by Sir Jeffry Wyatville, q.v., in the reign of George IV). 'The Fort' became his favourite residence, where he could entertain a few friends at weekends, and in whose garden he invested much of his own—and his guests'—hard labour. But something vital was missing, as no one knew better than himself.

While his brothers were acquiring wives, the world's most eligible bachelor remained single. His natural craving for domesticity was satisfied only by a succession of affairs with married women. For many years he was very closely attached to Mrs (Freda) Dudley Ward, and his love for her was not fundamentally affected by passing affairs with Lady (Thelma) Furness and others. But through Lady Furness he became acquainted with her friend and fellow-American, Mrs Simpson (died 1986), and within a few years acquaintance had turned into the supreme passion of his life.

Wallis Simpson, daughter of Teakle Wallis Warfield who died when she was a few months old, came from Baltimore, Maryland, where she was brought up as a rather impoverished member of a family with pride of ancestry on both sides. When her first marriage (to Lieutenant Earl Winfield Spencer, of the US Navy, who became an alcoholic) ended in divorce, she married an Anglo-American, Ernest Simpson (who had a shipping business in England), with whom she lived comfortably in London. For a time they were together friends of the Prince, but when it became apparent that he wanted nothing less than to make Wallis his wife, Simpson resigned himself to divorce.

Her attraction, so far as it can be defined, owed much to her vivacity and wit, her sophisticated taste, and her ability to make a house feel like a home. She and the Prince shared a mid-Atlantic outlook—he being a child of Old-World privilege excited by American informality, she an east coast American with a hankering for the Old World and its gracious living. They met, as it were, half-way.

When George V died, on 20 January 1936, Edward came to the throne in the strong hope that he would be able to make Wallis Queen. This may, indeed, have been his principal motive for accepting a charge which he had often said, privately, he would rather be spared. Impatient of ritual and routine, he knew that his temperament would be less well suited to the role of King than to that of Prince of Wales.

There was, indeed, much that needed changing in the royal set-up, and it is possible that Edward VIII might have had some success as a reforming monarch if he had reigned for a fair number of years, with his mind on the job. No judgement can confidently be made either way on the strength of his brief reign, during which he was largely distracted by his anxiety about Wallis and their future. As it was, he merely gave offence to old courtiers and retainers by relatively trifling changes, and caused misgivings in official quarters by his casual attitude to state papers.

The public, however, neither knew nor cared about such matters, and he was a popular King. There was a shock when, in July, a loaded revolver was thrown in front of his horse on Constitution Hill, and relief that he had come to no harm. Later in the year he was cheered lustily in the Mall by the Jarrow hunger marchers at the end of their pilgrimage.

Meanwhile the so-called 'King's matter' was unfolding in a way destined to bring his reign to a swift close. It was only in Britain that his intimacy with Mrs Simpson was a secret. When, during the summer, she accompanied him on a cruise in the Adriatic and eastern Mediterranean, in the private yacht *Nahlin*, full reports appeared in the foreign press, more especially in the United States, with the correct conclusions either stated or implied. The British press remained silent from a sense of loyalty, but it could not be long before the story would break at home. At the end of October the Simpsons' divorce suit was due to come up, and this might well arouse speculation even though it was to be heard in a provincial court.

On 20 October, therefore, the prime minister, Stanley Baldwin (later Earl Baldwin of Bewdley), saw the King by request and raised with him for the first time the question of his relations with Mrs Simpson. At this meeting Baldwin tried to enlist the King's co-operation in persuading her to withdraw her divorce petition, but to no avail. The King would not co-operate, and at the end of the month a decree *nisi* was duly granted.

An interlude followed during which (on 3 November) the King opened Parliament—driving there in a closed car rather than in the traditional open carriage—and inspected the fleet at Portsmouth. But on 16 November there was another meeting with Baldwin, at which the King stated his determination to marry Mrs Simpson, despite the prime minister's advice that the marriage would not receive the country's approval. On 18–19 November he visited the distressed areas of south Wales, where he made the much-quoted remark about the unemployed: 'Something must be done to find them work.' His hearers little knew how soon he would be unemployed himself.

On 25 November he saw Baldwin again, having meanwhile been persuaded by Esmond Harmsworth (later Viscount Rothermere, q.v.) to suggest that he might marry Mrs Simpson morganatically. This was a disastrous error, since it could be said to carry the admission that she was unfit to be Queen.

It is probable, though unprovable, that majority opinion in Britain and throughout the Empire would have been against the idea of Mrs Simpson as Queen, though whether most people would have maintained their opposition, knowing that the price would be to lose Edward as King, is more doubtful. Ecclesiastical anathemas counted for much less, even then, than those who pronounced them liked to believe, and objections to Mrs Simpson on social grounds were likely to be much stronger in privileged circles than among the people at large. But the idea of a morganatic marriage would almost certainly have been less generally acceptable.

In any case it would have required legislation, and this the government was not prepared to introduce. Moreover, the leader of the opposition, Clement (later Earl) Attlee, told Baldwin that Labour would not approve of Mrs Simpson as Queen, or of a morganatic marriage; and similar, though rather less clear-cut, views were expressed by the dominion prime ministers. When, therefore, the facts were at last given to the British public on 3 December, the crisis was virtually over. If the King had no option but to renounce either Mrs Simpson or the throne, the only possible outcome—granted the man he was—was abdication.

He would have liked to make a broadcast, taking his subjects into his confidence, before reaching a final decision; but when Baldwin told him that this would be unconstitutional and divisive, he at once abandoned the idea. Even (Sir) Winston Churchill's plea that he should stand and fight went unheeded. On 10 December he signed an instrument of abdication, and the following day ceased to be King when he gave his assent to the necessary Bill. That evening he delivered his farewell broadcast from Windsor Castle, containing the celebrated words: 'I have found it impossible to carry the heavy burden of responsibility, and to discharge my duties as King as I would wish to do, without the help and support of the woman I love.'

Later the same night he crossed to France, and the rest of his life was spent in almost permanent exile. It was some months before Mrs Simpson's divorce became absolute, but in June 1937 she and Edward were married, at a chateau in Touraine, by a Church of England parson acting without authority from his bishop. No member of the royal family came to the wedding, which was attended only by a few old freinds, including Walter Monckton (later Viscount Monckton of Brenchley, q.v.), the attorney-general to the Duchy of Cornwall, and a busy go-between during the abdication crisis, and Major E. D. ('Fruity') Metcalfe, who was best man. There were no children of the marriage.

The new King, George VI (formerly Duke of York), had some of the qualities of his father, George V, but hardly any of his elder brother's—a fact of which he was painfully conscious. From the moment of his accession he seems to have been haunted by the fear that the ex-King would overshadow him, and this fear was undoubtedly shared by his wife and other members of his entourage. It was felt to be essential that the ex-King should be kept out of England, out of the limelight, out of popular favour; and self-righteousness came to the aid of self-interest, in the form of a myth that the Prince's abdication and marriage had brought disgrace upon the British monarchy.

Though it is unlikely that George VI was familiar with *The Apple Cart* by G. B. Shaw [q.v.], he was nevertheless immediately alive to the theoretical danger that his brother might, unless made a royal duke, be tempted to stand for the House of Commons, in the manner of Shaw's King Magnus. The first act of his reign was, therefore, to confer upon Edward the title of Duke of Windsor. But under letters patent issued the following year the title Royal Highness was restricted to him, and expressly denied to his wife and descendants, if any. This studied insult to the Duchess cannot have been solely due to uncertainty about the duration of the marriage, since it was maintained by George VI and his successor throughout the thirty-five years that the Windsors were man and wife (and into the Duchess's widowhood).

As a result relations between the Duke and his family were poisoned, and further bitterness was caused by an indecent wrangle over money. No provision was made for the Duke in the Civil List, but the King eventually agreed that he should receive a net £21,000 a year, which was mainly interest of the sale of Sandringham and Balmoral to royal trustees, at a valuation which favoured the King rather than the Duke. An attempt to make the agreement conditional upon the Duke's willingness to stay abroad at the King's pleasure was only with difficulty resisted. (In addition to the income thus assured, the Duke had capital deriving from Duchy of Cornwall revenue unspent while he was Prince of Wales.)

Between their marriage and World War II the Windsors lived in France, but in October 1937 they paid an ill-advised visit to Germany as guests of the Nazi government. The Duke's declared reason for going was to see how unemployment had been tackled and to study labour relations, but of course the Nazis made the most of the visit for propaganda purposes, as he should have foreseen. At a meeting with Hitler the Duke gave no indication (according to the interpreter) of any sympathy with Nazi ideology, and there is, indeed, virtually no evidence that he had any such sympathy. But he had considerable affection for the German people, with whom he had many links, and above all he had the feeling—overwhelmingly prevalent at the time—that another war would be an unimaginable calamity.

When war came, however, he at once offered to return to Britain without conditions, and at first was offered a choice of two jobs, one of which, that of assistant regional commissioner in Wales, would have enabled him to stay in Britain. But when he accepted it, no doubt unexpectedly, it was promptly withdrawn, and he was then obliged to take the other job, that of liaison officer with the French army (which involved a drop in rank from field-marshal to major-general). He did it well, among other things sending home a remarkably prescient report of French weakness on the Ardennes front. But when France fell in the summer of 1940 he and the Duchess had to escape as best they might.

They made their own way to Madrid, whence the Duke was able to communicate with the British government, now headed by his old friend Winston Churchill. His requests for suitable employment at home, and the barest recognition for the Duchess (not that she should have royal status, but merely that his family should receive her) were turned down, even Churchill having in the circumstances neither time nor inclination to champion the Duke's cause against Buckingham Palace. He then reluctantly accepted the governorship of the Bahamas, and on 1 August sailed from Lisbon, as agreed, despite an elaborate plot engineered by Ribbentrop to keep him in Europe. Though at this time he undoubtedly believed that there would have to be a negotiated peace, he did not despair of his country and had no desire to be a German puppet.

In the Bahamas the Windsors were on the whole a conspicuous success, in a post which was both difficult and unpleasant. The Duke stood up to the 'Bay Street boys' (as the local white oligarchy was called), achieved some economic improvement in the neglected outer islands, and dealt effectively with a serious outbreak of rioting for which he was in no way to blame. In December 1940 he had the first of about a dozen wartime meetings with Franklin D. Roosevelt, at the president's invitation, and the two men got on particularly well. The authorities in London tried very hard to prevent the meeting, and in general did not at all favour visits by the Windsors to the United States, though a few were grudgingly permitted. The Duke's immense popularity there was regarded at home as invidious and embarrassing, rather than as a major potential asset to Britain.

In May 1945 the Windsors left the Bahamas and returned to Europe, no better alternative having been offered to the Duke than the governorship of Bermuda. The rest of his life was spent chiefly in France, where he was treated as an honoured guest. Partly to repair his finances—which had suffered from mismanagement, and more especially from a costly and futile attempt to strike oil on his Canadian ranch—he turned to authorship. With the help of 'ghosts' he wrote his memoirs, which were serialized in *Life* magazine and then published in book form as *A King's Story* (1951). This became a world bestseller, and was later turned into a film. He also published two much slighter books—*Family Album* (1960) and *The Crown and the People 1902–1953* (1953)—and two more were written, though unpublished at the time of his death.

Because of the continued ostracism of the Duchess, his post-war visits to Britain were brief and rare. On 28 May 1972 he died at his house in the Bois de Boulogne, from throat cancer. His body was then flown back to England and lay in state for three days in St. George's chapel, Windsor, while 57,000 people came—many over long distances—to pay their respects. On 5 June there was a funeral service in the chapel, and afterwards the Duke was buried in the royal mausoleum at Frogmore. The Duchess was present as the Queen's guest.

Though King for less than a year, Edward VIII will rank as an important figure in the history of the British monarchy. During the dangerous and volatile period which followed World War I, when republicanism was sweeping the world, he and his father succeeded, in their very different ways, in giving new strength to an old tradition. Neither could have succeeded so well without the other, and the contrast between them was of great value to the monarchy.

Edward will also be remembered as a character out of the ordinary. His faults were substantial, and aggravated by the circumstances of his life. His mind, inadequately trained, was incapable of deep reflection and prone to erratic judgement. He could on occasion be selfish, mean, inconsiderate, ungrateful, or even callous. Yet his virtues more than compensated for his faults. He was a brave man, morally as well as physically, and his nature was basically affectionate. He had a marvellous gift for conversing easily with people, and for making charming, unpompous speeches off the cuff. There was about him the indefinable aura known as star quality.

In a sense he was a harbinger of the Americanization of Europe. Superficially, his values were more those of the New World than of the Old. Playing the bagpipes wearing a white kilt or golfing in plus-eights, he seemed more like a Hollywood representation of a Scottish laird or English gentleman than like the genuine article. His anyway slightly Cockney accent became overlaid with American intonations (in his farewell broadcast he referred to the *Dook* of York), and he also acquired a number of American habits long before he was married to an American.

Yet at heart he was more a creature of the Old World than he appeared to be, or probably realized himself. What a Labour MP, Josiah (later Lord) Wedgwood [q.v.], said at the time of the abdication—that he had given up his royalty to remain a man—was only a half-truth. Though he had, indeed, given up his kingship, he never ceased to be royal. Had it been otherwise, there would have been no problem about the duchess's status. All the same, he surely deserves honour for the chivalrousness of his decision to abdicate, no less than for the perfect constitutional propriety with which it was carried out; and above all for his pioneering work as Prince of Wales.

There are many portraits of Edward, representing almost every phase of his life. Only a selection can be mentioned here. A caricature appeared in *Vanity Fair* on 21 June 1911 (the original is in the National Portrait Gallery). The first full-length portrait in oil was painted by Sir A. S. Cope in 1912, the year after Edward's investiture as Prince of Wales. It is in the Royal Collection, which also contains, from the same period, a sketch (head only) by Sir John Lavery. A charcoal drawing by J. S. Sargent (c. 1918) belonged to the Duchess of Windsor. In 1919 H. L. Oakley painted a full-length profile, and in c. 1920 R. G. Eves a half-length portrait in uniform. Both of these are in the National Portrait Gallery. A full-length portrait in golfing dress (1928), by Sir William Orpen, hangs in the Royal and Ancient Golf Club, St. Andrews; and a full-length portrait in Welsh Guards uniform (1936) done by W. R. Sickert from photographs, in the Beaverbrook Art Gallery, Fredericton, NB, Canada. A full-length portrait in Garter robes by Sir James Gunn (c. 1954) was in the Duchess of Windsor's possession, as were a number of portraits by the French artist A. Drian. Apart from paintings and drawings, there is a bronze statuette by Charles S. Jagger (1922) in the National Museum of Wales at Cardiff, and a marble bust by Charles Hartwell (c. 1920–4) belonging to the Corporation of London.

[Hector Bolitho, *Edward VIII*, 1937; Compton Mackenzie, *The Windsor Tapestry*, 1938; Duke of Windsor, *A King's Story*, 1951; Duchess of Windsor, *The Heart Has Its Reasons*, 1956; John W. Wheeler-Bennett, *King George VI*, 1958; Frances Donaldson, *Edward VIII*, 1974; Michael Bloch, *The Duke of Windsor's War*, 1982, and *Operation Willi*, 1984; private information.]

JOHN GRIGG

EDWARDS, (ARTHUR) TRYSTAN (1884–1973), architect and town planner, was born 10 November 1884 at Merthyr Tydfil, the son of Dr William Edwards, an inspector of schools and later chief inspector of the Central Welsh School Board, and his wife, Johanna Emilie Phillipine Steinthal. He was educated at Clifton and Hertford College, Oxford, where he took a first class in mathematical honours moderations (1905) and a third in *literae humaniores* (1907). Interested in the visual arts, and particularly in architecture, he was articled to (Sir) Reginald Blomfield [q.v.] in 1907. In 1911 he joined the department of civic design at Liverpool University run by S. D. Adshead [q.v.]. In 1915 he volunteered as a 'hostilities only' rating in the Royal Navy, and served four years. He liked the service so much that he spent twelve peacetime years as an RNVR rating, and considered his naval experiences one of the major cultural influences in his life. After his war service he published a book of reminiscences *Three Rows of Tape* (1929), revised as *Spoilt Child of the British Navy*, 1972).

Edwards qualified ARIBA, with distinction in town planning, in 1919, in which year, while still in bluejackets' uniform he joined the housing department of the Ministry of Health. He remained in the department, then led by (Sir) Raymond Unwin [q.v.], for six years. For several months he and Unwin ran the government's housing policy almost on their own. In 1925 Edwards left the ministry to concentrate on what was to be his life's work: the containing of urban sprawl by the formation of new towns strategically placed about the country.

He became FRIBA in 1933. Edwards wrote a series of articles for the *Builder* which were brought together as *A Hundred New Towns for Britain* (1933), a book much ahead of its time, which was not recognized as having the importance it deserved, although he pressed his case with enormous energy, and formed the Hundred New Towns Association. In this book Edwards proposed more houses to the acre than were generally thought to be acceptable, and when in 1945 the Chadwick trustees gave him a grant for research into the densities of houses in large towns, his report *Modern Terraced Houses* (1946) was much criticized for once more favouring higher densities. In the event Edwards was proved right and his critics wrong.

At first he made little impression on the various commissions and committees then concerned with industrial population, land utilization, and new towns, although he gave evidence before all of them. Gradually, however, they began to be influenced by his thought, and both the reports of the committees chaired by Sir Augustus (later Lord) Uthwatt [q.v.] (1941) and Sir Leslie Scott [q.v.] (1941–2) show the effect of his constant campaigning. Lord Greenwood of Rossendale, realizing the greatness of Edwards's contribution, wrote of him as being 'appallingly under-recognized'.

Although he wrote many pamphlets, articles, and books on town planning Edwards also had other interests. Among his books were: *The Things Which are Seen; a Revaluation of the Visual Arts* (1921), *Good and Bad Manners in Architecture* (1924), *Style and Composition in Architecture* (1925), and (with Cyril Farey) *Architectural Drawing, Perspective and Rendering* (1931). In 1953 Edwards published *A New Map of the World*, which contained his 'homalographic' projection. This was an attempt to solve the problem of projecting a sphere on to a flat surface, and to correct the comparative areas of continents. He revised it as *The Science of Cartography* (1972) and hoped to see it accepted for use in all schools. He also proposed a scheme for the realignment of national frontiers in order to give all nations an outlet to the sea. Another of his unrealized projects, which he called 'Trojan's tunnel', was a fully insulated overground tunnel which would pass over Christ Church meadow and act as a bypass for Oxford. He also produced a plan for the extension of the Palace of Westminster across Bridge Street.

Having retired to Merthyr Tydfil he continued to write well into old age. He produced *Merthyr, Rhondda and 'the Valleys'* (1958), *Towards Tomorrow's Architecture, the Triple Approach* (1968), and *Second-best Boy: the Autobiography of a Non-speaker* (1970).

A little round man with a gnomish and mercurial Welsh temperament, Edwards had a speech impediment, which, accompanied by a disconcerting winking of one eye, reduced the impact of his platform appearances. Nevertheless his Celtic enthusiasm was irresistible. He made up for his faltering speech by the intensity and forcefulness of his writing.

In March 1947 Edwards, then sixty-two, married Margaret Meredyth (died 1967), daughter of Canon Frederick Charles Smith, of Hailsham, Sussex. He died at St. Tydfil's Hospital, Merthyr Tydfil, 30 January 1973.

[*The Times*, 31 January and 3 and 14 February 1973; *Building*, 9 February 1973; A. Trystan Edwards, *Second-best Boy: the Autobiography of a Non-speaker*, 1970; personal knowledge.]

GONTRAN GOULDEN

EDWARDS, HUGH ROBERT ARTHUR (1906–1972), oarsman, was born at Westcote Barton, Oxfordshire, 17 November 1906, the fifth (fourth son) of six children of the Revd Robert Stephen Edwards, rector of Westcote Barton, and his wife, Annie van Mottman. He was educated at Westminster School and Christ Church, Oxford.

Edwards was commissioned in the RAF in 1929. He was awarded the AFC in 1943 in recognition of his feat of airmanship in bringing home a badly damaged Hampden from one of the thousand bomber raids on Cologne, and the DFC in 1944. Whilst commanding a squadron of Liberators on convoy escort duty he suffered the loss of three engines but successfully brought his aircraft down in the sea off the Cornish coast and escaped by sculling his rubber dinghy into the shipping lanes. His outstanding achievement, for which he was officially commended, was his command of No. 53 Squadron which he took over when his brother Cecil was killed. He retired from the RAF in 1956 with the rank of group captain.

Edwards was well known as a racing pilot flying his own aircraft, and was placed second in the King's Cup air race in 1933. His elder brother Cecil had won the race four years earlier.

It was however as an oarsman, and later as a rowing coach, that Edwards, who was known affectionately and almost universally as 'Jumbo', is likely to be longest remembered. After rowing for Westminster School he gained his blue as a freshman at Oxford in 1926, but collapsed half way along Chiswick Eyot. It was said at the time that he had outgrown his strength. In the following year, rowing for London Rowing Club, he reached the final of the Grand Challenge Cup at Henley Regatta. He won the Grand in 1930, and in 1931 achieved his most remarkable Henley success, never since repeated, winning three finals in the same day.

In 1930 Edwards rowed for England and won a gold medal in the Empire Games in Hamilton, Canada. But the crowning achievement of his rowing career came in the Olympic Games in Los Angeles in 1932. Selected to represent Great Britain in the coxless pairs, with his Christ Church partner Lewis Clive, Edwards was called on during the Olympic Regatta to take the place of a sick member of the Thames Rowing Club coxless four, and went on to win two gold medals for rowing in the same day.

Edwards coached Oxford nineteen times between 1949 and 1972, with five wins in this era when Cambridge were generally dominant. However he undoubtedly sowed the seeds which led to Oxford's resurgence in the 1970s. He also coached Britain's Olympic eight, provided by Oxford, in 1960, and was the first national coach to the unsuccessful Nautilus scheme in 1964.

As a teacher of rowing Edwards had few equals; he placed a strong emphasis on the orthodox traditions of Dr Edmond Warre [q.v.]. But it was as a technical innovator that he was most widely known, and aroused most controversy. Many of the technical innovations of modern rowing stemmed from Edwards, most notably perhaps the development of long oars and 'spade' blades, Edwards being among the first to appreciate that increasing boat speeds called for more severe gearing. He also pioneered 'interval training'—the practice of conditioning a crew by setting them to row a large number of repetitive short periods at full pressure, rather than longer set distances. He also introduced the use of ergometers to measure and develop physical strength, and strain gauges, accelerometers, and trace recorders to calculate work output throughout the stroke cycle.

Since Edwards was second to none in knowledge and expertise one may wonder why his success rate was not greater. The answer perhaps lies in one flaw in his methodology. He tended to ignore one cardinal rule in experimentation—the need to hold fast to a fixed datum point. By experimenting with longer oars, wider blades, and unfamiliar training schedules, all at the same time, he vitiated logical assessment of the results. Others, following on, reaped the harvest which he had so lavishly sown.

Edwards married in 1934 Michael Lydia Williams, daughter of Major John Williams, Royal Fusiliers. They had two sons, David, who rowed for Oxford in 1958–9, and John, a distinguished agronomist (died 1983).

Edwards, who included sailing among his many interests, took part in the first Round Britain race in 1966. After his retirement he spent much time in teaching sailing and navigation. He collapsed on board his yacht at Hamble, and died in a Southampton hospital 21 December 1972.

[*The Times*, 23 December 1972; private information; personal knowledge.]

RICHARD BURNELL

EDWARDS, SIR (JOHN) GORONWY (1891–1976), historian, was born 14 May 1891 in Salford, Lancashire, the only child of John William Edwards, railway signalman, the descendant of Welsh farmers in the Vale of Clwyd, and his wife, Emma Pickering, the daughter of an English miner. The family moved back to Flintshire in 1893; the son spoke and read Welsh before he did English. He attended Halkyn National School and then Holywell County School. Edwards was a Welsh foundation scholar in modern history of Jesus College, Oxford, from 1909 and gained first class honours in history in 1913—a year late because of illness. He did research at Manchester University from 1913 to 1915, when he enlisted in the Royal Welsh Fusiliers. Of his war service in France as an officer in their Pioneer battalion he did not easily speak. He was demobilized with the rank of captain, and had first shown his administrative capacity during a period as adjutant.

In 1919 Edwards was elected a fellow of Jesus and tutor in modern history. As a tutor he was incisive, humorous, and helpful, ranging with ease from Claudius to Charles II (he had been *proxime accessit* in the Stanhope essay prize competition on 'Danby' in 1913). He allowed no pretentiousness: to an undergraduate foolish enough to use the word 'transcendental' in a political thought essay he urged 'Oh no, not that. We leave that to the philosophers'. Edwards's pupils did consistently well in prize competitions and their final examination, and his help to them continued long afterwards. His university lectures, especially those on Stubbs's *Select Charters* and their unpublished sequel on fourteenth-century constitutional history were renowned;

judicious, perhaps almost too measured, but supremely clear, especially when arguing a case, they set many problems for examiners. As tutor, lecturer (officially so from 1928 to 1936 and in 1947–8), or writer, he always left a message. His three heroes were his tutor C. T. Atkinson of Exeter College, T. F. Tout [q.v.], who supervised his research at Manchester, and 'the great Reginald Lane Poole' [q.v.], former editor of the *English Historical Review*. As joint editor of the *Review* from 1938 to 1959 Edwards more than sustained its high reputation: his comments to would-be contributors were terse but constructive. His diligent and conscientious discharge of these and other duties undoubtedly limited his own historical work, considerable though that was.

Edwards held various offices in his college in turn; but its highest prize was denied him, as was the Oxford regius chair of modern history. In 1948 came the inevitable summons elsewhere, to the directorship of the Institute of Historical Research and a concomitant professorship of history in the University of London. The director's obligations to the Institute's students (whose numbers expanded vastly) and to the learned world at large were many, but all were successfully and meticulously discharged; among them was the editorship of the Institute's *Bulletin*.

Edwards's writings dominated the study of two subjects, medieval Wales and the medieval English Parliament. As a Welshman who made his career in England he saw a supreme contrast between the multiple kingship of Wales (taken over by the Normans in the *marchia Walliae*) and the strong single kingship of England; this in the thirteenth century created an omnicompetent *parliamentum* which was one root of th omnicompetence of the Commons by whom that *parliamentum* was afforced. He imparted his message mainly in numerous articles and in the introductions to his editions of texts vital for Anglo-Welsh history. His technical skill and robust common sense were equally evident in his examination of the *plena potestas* formula in the published early parliamentary writs of summons (*Essays presented to H. E. Salter*, 1934) and in his investigation of the record evidence for 'Edward I's Castle-Building in Wales' (*Proceedings* of the British Academy, vol. xxxii, 1946). To this Dictionary he contributed the notice of Sir John Lloyd.

Edwards was of medium height and broad in build; his round cheerful face was notable for his searching eyes. His academic activities, his alertness, geniality, and sense of humour, and his exertions at golf gave little idea of the rheumatism which long troubled him. (Other interests were photography and music.) He became to many generations of Jesus men, whether historians or not, and especially perhaps to the ex-warriors of two wars, increasingly the personification of the college, of which he was made an honorary fellow in 1949; his high regard for the standing of his college made English members as fervent as Welsh in their affection for its special characteristics. He served the principality, and Flintshire in particular, long and loyally; especially on the Royal Commission on Historical Monuments of Wales and Monmouthshire and on the Ancient Monuments Board for Wales; he was proud of being Welsh, but for Welsh nationalism he had no time. He edited leading periodicals, and presided over the Institute of Historical Research, both with distinction, at a time of special importance for historical studies. He was a shrewd, lucid, exact, and original scholar, a lively personality, and a most fair-minded man.

Edwards had been made FBA in 1943, and was given honorary doctorates by four universities and an Oxford D.Litt. in 1960. He was Ford's lecturer at Oxford in 1960–1, the subject of his lectures being 'The Second Century of the English Parliament' (printed in 1979). He also gave the Rhys (1944), Raleigh (1956), David Murray (1955), and Creighton (1957) lectures. He was elected FSA in 1959 and was knighted on his retirement from the Institute in 1960. From 1961 to 1964 he was president of the Royal Historical Society. He remained active until three months before his death.

His marriage in 1925 to Gwladys (died 1982), daughter of the Revd William Williams (also of Halkyn), was supremely happy, and their hospitality was inexhaustible. They had no children. Edwards died in Queen Mary's Hospital, Roehampton, 20 June 1976.

There is a photograph at the Institute, and a pencil drawing by B. Fleetwood Walker at Jesus College.

[*The Times*, 21 June 1976; *Archaeologia Cambrensis*, vol. cxxv, 1977, pp. 174–7; *Bulletin of the Institute of Historical Research*, vol. xlix, 1976, pp. 155–8; *English Historical Review*, vol. xci, 1976, pp. 721–2; J. S. Roskell in *Proceedings* of the British Academy, vol. lxiv, 1978, pp. 359–96; *Welsh History Review*, vol. viii, 1977, pp. 466–74; private information; personal knowledge.] J. F. A. MASON

EDWARDS, SIR ROBERT MEREDYDD WYNNE- (1897–1974), civil engineer. [See WYNNE-EDWARDS.]

EDWARDS, SIR RONALD STANLEY (1910–1976), accountant, university teacher, and industrialist, was born in New Southgate, London, 1 May 1910, the elder child and elder son (another son had previously died in childhood) of Charles Edwards, a gas engineer employed by the Romford Gas Company, and his wife, Alice Osborne. He was educated at Southgate County School, leaving immediately after matriculation at the age of sixteen. He continued to educate himself by painstaking evening study.

His first jobs were as office boy for the Romford Gas Company and as junior clerk in a firm of accountants. He qualified as a certified accountant in 1930 and began to study for a B.Com. degree by correspondence. The originality of his work and the excellence of his eventual degree induced the London School of Economics to offer him a teaching post in business administration in 1935. Thereafter the academic world remained his spiritual home, he wrote several books and articles, and he retained a permanent interest in the training and development of young active minds. He gained his London D.Sc. (Econ.).

World War II drew him into executive work in the Ministry of Aircraft Production, dealing in turn with factory repair, direction of labour, and preparations for post-war industrial reconstruction. These experiences both developed his self-confidence and created a continuing interest in manufacturing industry, especially in its technology.

He returned to the London School of Economics as reader in commerce in 1946, becoming professor in 1949. His postgraduate seminars in industrial administration, with discussions initiated by the heads of large organizations, soon achieved wide renown and were to continue for over twenty years, first at LSE and then, after a break, at the London Business School.

After his wartime experience Edwards readily accepted tasks connected with industrial enterprise and innovation. He became chairman of the British Clock and Watch Manufacturers Association (1946–59), and a member of the Privy Council committee for scientific and industrial research (1949–54). Membership of the Herbert committee on electricity supply (1954–5) led to his becoming deputy chairman (1957–61) of the Electricity Council which resulted from its recommendations. As his involvement with this council increased he abandoned teaching apart from his seminars. His chairmanship of the Electricity Council (1962–8) was the central and in many respects most important period of his working life.

Edwards's major contribution to the electricity industry was to apply economic principles and to gain acceptance for profitability as a prerequisite for both effective motivation of staff and better service to customers. He emphasized the need for tighter financial control, for pricing related to marginal cost, and for improved industrial relations. At the same time he remained keenly interested in all aspects of the British economy, devoting nearly every lunch-time to discussion with some leading figure. Other activities multiplied. In addition to non-executive directorships, he was a member of the University Grants Committee (1955–64) and of the National Economic Development Council (1964–8), president of the Market Research Association (1965–9), and a governor of the London Business School, of the Administrative Staff College at Henley, and of the London School of Economics. He was appointed KBE in 1963.

Edwards's chairmanship of the committee of inquiry into the civil air transport industry (1967–9) exemplified his general style and his diligence. He would always begin with a critical review of facts and make a committee argue through to hypotheses thoroughly tested in discussion. He could sum up complicated matters in terms readily understandable to laymen and attached great importance to the written word. He insisted that this committee's proposals were realistic and cogently presented; devoting every evening for several weeks to that end so as to make it probable that the major recommendations would be accepted by government. They were. Edwards became a founder member of the board of British Airways from 1971.

In 1968 he became chairman of the Beecham Group, a position he held until 1975. He always had a strong belief in the virtues of competition and enjoyed working in an internationally competitive industry, although the immediacy of decision-making which was sometimes required was not entirely to his taste. Death was to cut short his subsequent chairmanship of British Leyland (from 1975).

Edwards hid a very warm and generous personality behind what on first acquaintance seemed somewhat professorial mannerisms. His calm authority inspired real affection. He was devoted to his family. He loved the sea and went sailing on most of the week-ends he spared from work. He was passionately keen on music, opera, and ballet, and he enjoyed painting and sculpture, encouraging the work of younger artists. Despite the immense range of his mental activity he was modest and endearing and very aptly described as a 'builder of bridges between men's minds'.

Edwards was awarded honorary doctorates from Edinburgh (1966), Strathclyde (1973), Bath (1966), and Warwick (1973). He was also an honorary fellow of LSE (1975).

In 1936 Edwards married Myrtle Violet, daughter of John Alfred Poplar, of the Royal Navy. They had two daughters. He died in London 18 January 1976.

[Private information, including unpublished autobiographical material; personal knowledge.] CROHAM

EGREMONT, first BARON, and sixth BARON LECONFIELD (1920–1972), civil servant and author. [See WYNDHAM, JOHN EDWARD REGINALD.]

EINZIG, PAUL (1897–1973), journalist and author, was born in Brasov, Transylvania, then a province of the Austro-Hungarian Empire, the son of Bernard Einzig, a forwarding agent, and his wife, Giselle Weisz. He was educated at the Oriental Academy of Budapest and, while still a student, turned his hand to financial journalism with some success. An 'irresistible urge to be at the centre of things', as he described it, took him to London in 1919. His specialist knowledge of Hungary's post-war communist experiment enabled him to get articles accepted by such reputed journals as the *Economist* and the *Economic Journal* almost immediately. But his initial success did not last and for a time he supplemented his earnings from journalism by working as a clerk.

Subsequently, having come to the conclusion that a degree in economics would greatly assist his progress and that it could be obtained more easily in France, he moved to Paris in 1921 and two years later was granted his degree of Doctor of Political and Economic Science. Having acted as Paris correspondent for the *Financial News* of London while studying for his doctorate he was able to persuade the paper to make him its foreign editor on his return to London in 1923.

The foundations for what was to be a highly successful writing career were thereby laid. Initially the emphasis was on journalism and more particularly financial journalism. The Lombard Street column he began to contribute to the paper in 1926 became a major feature of the financial writing scene. This was not only because of the extent and depth of its coverage; it was also because of Einzig's determination to use it for promoting what he considered good causes 'from behind the scenes'—a notable example being its role in the 1939 Czech gold scandal.

On the outbreak of war in 1939, Einzig was appointed political correspondent, though he went on writing his Lombard Street column to deal with matters relating to banking and finance. When the *Financial News* was merged with the *Financial Times* in 1945 he turned down the suggestion that he should return to City affairs, it having been made clear that there would be no scope for 'campaigning' in the new setting. He stayed on as lobby correspondent until ill health forced him to accept premature retirement in 1956, his main journalistic activity thereafter being a weekly column in the *Commercial and Financial Chronicle* of New York.

The book written in 1921 as the thesis for his Paris degree apart, Einzig's first venture into authorship came in 1929 when he incorporated into a small book all available published material on gold movements—then a crucial aspect of the international financial scene—and persuaded Macmillan to publish it. Its success encouraged him to follow it up with a book on the emergent Bank for International Settlements in 1930 and a further two—*The Fight for Financial Supremacy* and *The World Economic Crisis*—in the ensuing twelve months.

Altogether Einzig wrote over fifty books, mostly published by Macmillan though his relationship with the firm became somewhat less cordial after his book *Appeasement: Before, During and After the War* (1941) caused it to be involved with him in a libel action in the early 1940s. His output, bearing in mind that it was largely concerned with matters demanding specialist knowledge, was prodigious. The books fall into two main categories—one dealing with topical issues and relying heavily on material that had already appeared in his daily articles, the other comprising works of a technical character resulting from in-depth study of their subjects. Einzig enjoyed most writing books of the first type, maintaining that his temperament was not that of a textbook writer.

The extent of his output and his tendency to exaggerate when he thought this would help to advance a cause he was prosecuting resulted in his acquiring a reputation for superficiality. He himself, never afraid to engage in self-criticism, admitted in his autobiography that some of his books had deservedly faded into oblivion. Yet it must be said that they nearly all served a useful purpose, that they were almost invariably at least moderately financially successful, and that a number of them—notably *Primitive Money* (1949) and *Dynamic Theory of Forward Exchange* (1961) were scholarly enough to have become acknowledged works of reference.

In his autobiography, written in 1960, Einzig takes a sober view of the value of his achievements. What cannot be disputed is that he was one of the principal architects of the great advance seen in economic and financial writing since World War I.

Naturalized in 1929, he had deep affection for his adopted country and greatly admired its institutions, most of all the City. He married in 1931 Eileen Ruth, daughter of Joseph Telford Quick, stockbroker, of St. Mawes, Cornwall. They had a son and a daughter. Einzig died in a London hospital 8 May 1973.

[Paul Einzig, *In the Centre of Things* (autobiography), 1960; private information; personal knowledge.] C. GORDON TETHER

ELDER, SIR (WILLIAM) STEWART DUKE- (1898–1978), ophthalmologist. [See DUKE-ELDER.]

ELLIOT, SIR WILLIAM (1896–1971), air chief marshal, was born 3 June 1896 at Forgan, Fife, the elder son of Gilbert John Elliot, schoolteacher, of Chetwynd, Shropshire, and his wife, Bessie Clark Davidson. He was educated in Switzerland, and at Tonbridge School (1910–1914).

The strict influence of his father led to an early development of Elliot's alert intelligence, and to his joining the army just before the outbreak of World War I. At the age of eighteen he was in France with the Army Service Corps, and active service led to an early interest in flying and his repeated applications for transfer to the Royal Flying Corps, all of which were ignored until the summer of 1917 when he was finally seconded to the RFC. Sent to Egypt for training as a pilot, he joined No. 142 Squadron in March 1918, serving in the Palestine brigade and winning a DFC. At the end of the war Elliot volunteered for service in south Russia with the Allied forces which were supporting the White Russians in their clash with the Bolsheviks. He joined No. 47 Squadron and was involved in a great deal of operational flying until he suffered a severe fracture of his elbow and then caught typhus, which led to his being invalided back to England. His success in his flying, which included the destruction in the air of six enemy aircraft, brought him a bar to his DFC.

Granted a permanent commission in the Royal Air Force in 1919, Elliot spent the whole of the next ten years on flying and staff duties at home and abroad, including two years as air staff liaison officer with the French in Syria. During 1932 he was a student at the RAF Staff College, after which he was given command of No. 501 Squadron. This was followed by two years on the higher commanders course at the School of Army Co-operation. Early in 1937 he was appointed, with promotion to wing commander, assistant secretary (air) to the Committee of Imperial Defence, and during the next four years he became highly respected for his exceptional ability as a staff officer. But with the outbreak of war Elliot wanted active service, and he became particularly interested in the new radar-controlled night fighting. By this time a group captain, he was given command early in 1941 of RAF station Middle Wallop, from which rapid strides were being made proving the worth of the radar night fighters. He did so well there that only four months later he became air commodore in charge of night operations of Fighter Command. In January 1942 he was appointed CBE.

Appointed director of plans at the Air Ministry in February 1942, Elliot served there for two years. He then became air officer commanding Gibraltar, was appointed CB (1944), and was promoted to air vice-marshal. A few months later in 1944 he became the first air officer commanding the venturesome Balkan Air Force. He returned to England in March 1945 with appointment as assistant chief executive of the Ministry of Aircraft Production. In June 1946 he returned to the Air Ministry to be assistant chief of the air staff (policy). Earlier in the year he had been appointed KBE. In November 1947, with promotion to air marshal, he became air officer commanding-in-chief, Fighter Command. This was to be his last operational command, and during the eighteen months that he spent in it he again left the imprint of his own individual style. For two years during 1949 to 1951 Elliot was chief staff officer to the minister of defence and deputy secretary (military) to the Cabinet. His work then led to the minister, Emanuel (later Lord) Shinwell, describing him after his death as 'a man of remarkable intelligence, whose diplomatic skill and possession of singular charm would have made him an ideal Foreign Secretary'. On 1 January 1950 he was appointed air ADC to King George VI, with reappointment in February 1952 as air ADC to Queen Elizabeth. Well known to the royal family, he received in the coronation honours list in 1953 the rare distinction of being appointed GCVO.

In the spring of 1951, with promotion to air chief marshal, Elliot's broadness of vision led to his being appointed chairman of the British joint services mission in Washington and British representative on the standing group of the military committee of NATO. He had already been made by the Americans a commander of their Legion of Merit; and in the summer of 1951 he was created KCB. Of particular importance to him in serving in the United States was the further development of his great liking for the Americans and their way of life. In return, they liked and trusted him, and he became one of the most popular British senior officers who served in the United States. While there he had a recurrence of heart trouble, but he was able to continue with his work in Washington until the spring of 1954 when he retired from the RAF. It was felt by some that but for ill health he could have become chief of the air staff.

The wide range of Elliot's experience led to his being elected late in 1954 to the office of chairman of the council of the Royal Institute of International Affairs, and over the next four years his work, which gave him great pleasure, was again of unique value. He had always been a voracious reader, and he was a prolific correspondent, and he maintained these interests during the rest of his life, interspersed with visits to the United States and, unhappily, spells in hospital. On 27 June 1971 he died in the RAF hospital at Wroughton.

In 1931 Elliot married (Elizabeth) Rosemary (died February 1971), daughter of Sir John Robert Chancellor, soldier and administrator [q.v.]. They had two sons (one of whom died in 1938) and a daughter.

A portrait of Elliot painted by Catherine Mann is in the possession of the family.

[Information provided by the Air Historical Branch (RAF); *The Times*, 28 and 30 June and 9 July 1971; private information; personal knowledge.] ROBERT WRIGHT

ELLIOTT, SIR CLAUDE AURELIUS (1888–1973), head master and provost of Eton College, was born 27 July 1888 in India, the only child of Sir Charles Alfred Elliott [q.v.], lieutenant governor of Bengal, who later resided at Fernwood, Wimbledon Park, SW, and his second wife, Alice Louisa, daughter of Thomas Gaussen of Hauteville, Guernsey, and widow of T. J. Murray of the Bengal Civil Service. Sir Charles also had three sons and one daughter of a previous marriage. From Stoke Park, the notorious preparatory school, Claude Elliott was elected a King's scholar of Eton in the 1902 election, on the strength of his history paper. His school career as a colleger was undistinguished, although he made many friends, and he left Eton a year earlier than he need have, to go up to Trinity College, Cambridge; here his promise as a historian burgeoned, and he got a first class in both parts of the history tripos, constitutional history being his forte. BA in 1909, he became a fellow of Jesus College, Cambridge, in 1910, and in 1914, tutor.

At an early age he developed an inherited love of mountaineering which he practised in Britain, Switzerland, and France, but his ambition to tackle the Caucasus and the Himalayas was thwarted by a fall in the Lake District in 1912 which broke his kneecap and damaged his hand. These injuries did not prevent later expeditions, but they precluded active service in World War I. After service in a Red Cross unit in Flanders in 1915, he spent the rest of the war at the Admiralty and was appointed OBE in 1920 for his services. After the war he returned to Jesus College, where his administrative skill and vigorous sense of purpose were invaluable, as they were also to the university financial board, the general board, and the council of senate.

In 1933 C. A. Alington [q.v.] retired from the headmastership of Eton, and Elliott was appointed to succeed him. Among the candidates he had been the darkest horse; and although the world at large may have been surprised at his selection, there was no doubt in the minds of those who knew him that he had the capacity for this formidable task. He was the first head master of Eton who was not in holy orders; and neither his preaching in chapel nor his teaching in school were as impressive as those of his charismatic predecessor. But he proved himself a headmaster of the highest quality; he was admired and respected by the governing body for his sound judgement and his administrative skill, by his staff for his honesty and steadfastness of purpose, and by boys for his imposing presence, his dry almost earthy humour, his firmness in disciplinary matters, and his simple manliness; his very glance bespoke straight dealing. As an educationist he was no reformer; Alington had made several changes in the curriculum and Elliott was content to make the system work efficiently; he believed that his most important task as head master lay in the choice of masters; and in this, he showed himself a sound judge of character.

After six years in office came World War II. Despite pressure in some quarters, he stubbornly refused even to contemplate the removal of the school to a safer place; and, man of action that he was, he rallied his staff to cope with all the problems of a school in wartime, while ensuring that school life continued as normally as possible; two bombs which fell on the school in 1940 only hardened his rocklike resolve; he was never happier than when climbing over the roof-tops at night to look for incendiaries. To have kept Eton going throughout the war was his greatest achievement.

In 1949, after sixteen arduous years as head master, he was appointed provost, and for the next fifteen years he guided Eton's affairs with an experienced hand; a successful appeal was launched; a vast rebuilding and modernization programme was begun; and he was responsible for the replacement of the shattered glass in the chapel windows with the brilliant designs of Evie Hone [q.v.] and John Piper. As provost, he did more for the fabric of the school than any of his predecessors for five centuries.

Throughout his life he retained his passion for mountaineering. He knew all the famous climbers of his time; his own skill was universally recognized in his forty visits to the Alps, and countless other expeditions in Wales, the Lake District, and Skye; but for his injury, he must have taken part in the Everest expeditions of 1921–4. President of the Alpine Club in 1950–2, he showed the shrewdness of his judgement and his courage in the choice of John (later Lord) Hunt, rather than of Eric Shipton [q.v.], to lead the successful 1953 Everest expedition.

His appearance was impressive; of well over medium height he carried himself with dignity, and he had the strong physique of the mountaineer and oarsman (he was a member of Leander).

In 1913 he married Gillian (died 1966), daughter of Frederick Turner Bloxam, chief Chancery registrar. Their only child, Nicholas Elliott, worked in intelligence during and after World War II and subsequently in business. He was awarded the US Legion of Merit for his services to the Office of Strategic Services during the war and was knighted in 1958.

After his retirement from Eton in 1964, he lived in Buttermere in sight of his beloved mountains, until, active till the end, he died at his home there 21 November 1973.

[*The Times*, 24 November and 10 December 1973; private information; personal knowledge.] D. H. MACINDOE

ELLIS, SIR (BERTRAM) CLOUGH WILLIAMS- (1883–1978), architect. [See WILLIAMS-ELLIS.]

ELLIS, SIR CHARLES DRUMMOND (1895–1980), physicist, was born in Hampstead, London, 11 August 1895, the son of Abraham Charles Ellis, a general manager of the Metro Railway, London, and his wife, Isabelle Flockhart Casswell. He first went to Peterborough Lodge Preparatory School in Hampstead and from there won a scholarship to Harrow, where from 1909 to 1913 he had a happy and successful time. He excelled in athletics and was victor ludorum in 1912 and 1913. He passed third in order of merit into the Royal Military Academy, Woolwich, which he entered on 3 September 1913 as a cadet in preparation for his chosen army career in the Royal Engineers. In July 1914 he passed out first of his class. That summer he went on holiday with a party to Germany where he was trapped by a sudden internment order at the outbreak of World War I.

At the Ruhleben internment camp near Spandau he met (Sir) James Chadwick [q.v.]. Chadwick excited Ellis's interest in physics and they embarked on many scientific projects together. The German officials were very sympathetic to their activities and they were allowed to purchase chemicals and to have contacts with German scientists like Nernst, Rubens, Planck, and Meitner. Another significant meeting was with Paula Warzcewska, a librarian in the nearby town and daughter of Paul Warzcewski, a Polish shipbuilder. Her first marriage, to H. S. Hatfield, an inventor physicist who had also been interned in Ruhleben, subsequently brought her to England as a British citizen. After her divorce she married Ellis in 1925 and, as the colourful 'Polly' Ellis, lived happily with him until her sudden death in 1966. There were no children, although a daughter from the first marriage was adopted.

After release from internment Ellis entered Trinity College, Cambridge. In 1919 he gained a first class in part i of the mathematical tripos and in 1920 a first in part ii of the natural sciences tripos (physics). The award of a college scholarship enabled him to start his career of research at the Cavendish Laboratory and in 1921 he was elected to a fellowship at Trinity and appointed assistant lecturer in natural science. In that year he published in the *Proceedings* of the Royal Society a paper under the title 'Magnetic spectrum of the β-rays excited by γ-rays, a forerunner of the many papers in the following fifteen years which made him the leading authority in this field and fully justified his inclusion as joint author of the classic work *Radiations from Radioactive Substances* (1930) by Sir E. Rutherford (later Lord Rutherford of Nelson, q.v.), Chadwick, and Ellis. While Rutherford and Chadwick concentrated mainly on α-radioactivity Ellis concerned himself with the photoelectric effect of γ-rays on various metal targets. He refined the photographic techniques used in this work not only for measuring the energy of the photoelectrons but also for determining the relative intensities of the different energy groups. Using the photoelectron equation E (atom) = hν − E (photoelectron) he was able to establish the existence of energy levels in the nucleus and to obtain the main features of the level distribution for radioactive nuclei both natural and artificial. His observations and discussion of the nature of continuous regions of β-ray spectra were major contributions to the discovery of the neutrino with its zero rest mass. He was elected FRS in 1929.

In 1936 Ellis left the Cavendish to take up the Wheatstone chair of physics at King's College, London. However, before he could establish new lines of research all scientific effort was diverted into preparing for the imminent war. When, in 1939, the physics department at King's was moved to Bristol he was granted leave of absence for war work. From an early stage Ellis recognized and advocated the feasibility of producing a nuclear device, and in 1940 he became a member of the 'Maud' committee. In 1943 he became scientific adviser to the Army Council. In this office he collected a group of outstanding colleagues who contributed to the solution of a wide variety of operational research problems. He was knighted in 1946 for his work during the war. When the National Coal Board was established in the same year he was a natural choice for the member responsible for the setting up of a viable and productive scientific service for the industry. For nine years until the reorganization of the NCB in 1955 he was responsible for initiating many valuable activities in its research and development. He encouraged liaison with university research groups and became president of the British Coal Utilization Research Association. In order to facilitate the reorganization of the NCB in 1955 its members offered their resignations. Unfortunately Ellis was not reappointed to the reconstituted board, largely because of the objection to 'technicians' on boards by H. S. Morrison (later Lord Morrison of Lambeth, q.v.).

Ellis continued to find many outlets for his active mind, and in 1955 became scientific adviser to the board of the British American Tobacco Company. He also greatly encouraged dialogue between industry and the medical profession.

In 1955 the chairman of the Gas Council, Sir Harold Templar-Smith, secured his services as part-time scientific adviser. Ellis took his responsibilities very seriously and brought system and logic to bear upon the Council's research activities. Great technological changes revolutionized the gas industry in Ellis's time but his insistence on high standards in staff and research made a vital contribution to the success of the industry. He retired from this appointment in 1966 and from British American Tobacco in 1972. He died in a nursing home in Cookham 10 January 1980 after a short illness.

[Sir Kenneth Hutchison, J. A. Gray, and Sir Harrie Massey in *Biographical Memoirs of Fellows of the Royal Society*, vol. xxvii, 1981.]

W. C. PRICE

ELMHIRST, LEONARD KNIGHT (1893–1974), co-founder of the Dartington Hall Trust, was born 6 June 1893 at Laxton, Yorkshire, the second of eight sons and nine children of the Revd William Heaton Elmhirst, clerk in holy orders, of Laxton, subsequently owner of the Elmhirst estate, Worsbrough Dale, Yorkshire, and his wife, Mary, second daughter of the Revd William Knight, clerk in holy orders, of Hemsworth, Yorkshire. He was educated at Repton School; at Trinity College, Cambridge, where he obtained third classes in both parts of the historical tripos (1914 and 1915); and, from 1919 to 1921, at New York State College of Agriculture, Cornell University (where he obtained a B.Sc. in agriculture in 1921).

Countryman by upbringing, philanthropist and internationalist by conviction, and friend to all sorts and conditions of men, Elmhirst was committed to improving the quality of life in rural communities. In World War I YMCA work took him to India where he learned of that country's rural problems. From 1921 to 1925 he worked with Rabindranath Tagore [q.v.], the Indian educationist, poet, and social reformer. Elmhirst was the first director of the Institute of Rural Reconstruction at Santiniketan, Bengal. In 1925 he married Dorothy Payne, daughter of William Collins Whitney, lawyer, politician, and millionaire business man, of New York. She had been married previously to Willard Dickerman Straight (died 1918), American diplomat and financier, and had two young sons and a daughter by that marriage—Whitney, a notice of whom appears in this volume, Beatrice, and Michael. The Elmhirsts had one son and one daughter.

In 1925 the Elmhirsts bought the Dartington estate near Totnes, Devon. They started a progressive school, restored the medieval buildings, and did much new building. Forestry was conducted as both commercial venture and research undertaking, as was farming in association with the estate's laboratory and agricultural economics research department. In 1943 Elmhirst helped establish privately the Dartington Cattle Breeding Centre. There were experiments with small enterprises: orchards, cider, sawmilling, woodworking, and poultry. The building department, with its quarries, became Staverton Builders. Joinery, textile mill, and craft shops also lasted. Alongside regeneration of a depressed rural economy went the provision of welfare benefits for employees. There were opportunities for all for further education and enjoyment of the arts, of which the Elmhirsts were eclectic patrons. They also created Dartington's fine gardens. While remaining fully involved, they relinquished personal ownership and control of the enterprise in 1931–2 to the Dartington Hall Trust, a charitable trust of which Elmhirst was chairman until 1972.

As active outside as inside Dartington, and an inveterate traveller, Elmhirst was a founder member of the international conference of agricultural economists in 1930, its first president until 1958, and founder president until his death. Elmhirst's World War II contribution arose from his international connections and agricultural interests. He was a member of a Board of Trade mission to the USA. At the US Department of Agriculture's invitation he toured the USA for discussions on wartime agriculture. He was a member of an agricultural mission from the Ministry of War Transport to advise the Middle East Supply Centre. In 1944 and 1945 he was agricultural adviser to the governor of famine-stricken Bengal. He visited India regularly from 1949 to 1961 as honorary consultant on land use to the Damodar Valley Corporation and member of the council of Visva-Bharati University, Santiniketan. In 1954 and 1955 he served on the Indian government's committee on higher education in rural areas.

At home, Elmhirst and his wife supported the research organization Political and Economic Planning from its inception in 1931; Elmhirst was chairman from 1939 to 1953. From 1950 to 1960 they supported the Withymead Clinic, Exeter, which helped people under psychological stress. Elmhirst was on the National Parks committee from 1945 to 1947 and a development commissioner from 1949 to 1965 . He was president of the Agricultural Economics Society from 1949 to 1950. He served on the committee on the provincial agricultural economics service from 1954 to 1969. Close to his heart was his championship of private forestry. He was president of the Royal Forestry Society from 1946 to 1948 and an architect of the dedication scheme introduced in the Forestry Acts of 1947 and 1951. A favourite occupation was working in the Dartington woodlands. He was involved in local affairs as Devon county councillor, Dartington parish councillor, governor and manager of schools in Totnes and Dartington, and member of the council of first the University College of the South West and then Exeter University.

Elmhirst's indefatigable and unostentatious service, which went with unfailing optimism and zest for life, was recognized by honorary degrees: D.Pol.Sci. Freiburg, 1953; D.Litt. Visva-Bharati, 1960; DCL Durham, 1962; DCL Oxford, 1970; and DCL Exeter, 1972.

Elmhirst appeared unmistakably an English country gentleman, well groomed and dressed with unobtrusive good taste, with an erect although not an imposing figure, a trim moustache, and an eagle eye for detail. His manner combined impeccable courtesy with lively and sympathetic interest in people and places.

Widowed in 1968, in 1972 Elmhirst married Susanna Isaacs, daughter of Hubert Foss, music publisher. Elmhirst died 16 April 1974 in Beverly Hills, California.

[Dartington Hall Records Office; Victor Bonham-Carter, *Dartington Hall 1925–56, a Report*, and *The Enterprise of Dartington Hall, First Supplement 1956–65* (these two reports, written for the trustees, are kept at Dartington Hall); Michael Young, *The Elmhirsts of Dartington*, 1982; private information.]

ANTHEA WILLIAMS

ELTON, SIR ARTHUR HALLAM RICE, tenth baronet (1906–1973), documentary film producer, was born in London 10 February 1906, the elder son (there were no daughters) of Sir Ambrose Elton, ninth baronet, barrister, of Clevedon, and his wife, Dorothy Wynne, daughter of Arthur Robert Wiggin, of Oddington estate, Ceylon. He was educated at Marlborough. From there, together with (Sir) John Betjeman, he would cycle to Swindon to haunt the Great Western Railway yards and buy the first items in his collection of books on locomotives and industrial machinery. At Jesus College, Cambridge, he took third classes in the English tripos (1926) and part ii of the moral sciences tripos (1927), and acquired his other major passion the cinema, as a film critic for *Granta*.

In 1927 he became a script-writer for Gainsborough Pictures Limited, working in London and Germany. Four years later he was recruited by John Grierson [q.v.] for the Empire Marketing Board film unit, joining the group of enthusiasts who created the British documentary film movement. He was associated with many of their outstanding achievements, as an assistant director for the coal-mining sequences of Robert J. Flaherty's *Industrial Britain* (1931), as director of films including *Shadow on the Mountain*, dealing with the study of grassland in the Welsh Hills, and *Housing Problems*, and after 1935 as a producer organizing the work of others for the GPO, the Gas Council, and the Ministry of Labour, who financed the revolutionary (both socially and cinematically) work of the group. Elton moved easily from his privileged landowning and Cambridge background into the factories and slums of the depression. He pioneered the use of direct film interviews on location and won the confidence of working men and women. He carried his passion for machinery into the cinema in films such as *Aero Engine* (1933) that portrayed technology and industrial processes as vividly as other documentaries portrayed social conditions. In 1938 Grierson, Elton, and Basil Wright formed Film Centre Limited to offer a consultative and managerial service for the producers and sponsors of documentary films.

During the war the government became responsible for most non-fictional film making. The Ministry of Information asked Elton to become a supervisor of films in April 1940. He soon brought order into a confusion of competing interests and personalities. He inspired the work of creative directors and writers, while retaining the confidence of the civil servants, who feared that the irresponsibility of film-makers might evade their budgetary controls. A steady stream of impressive propaganda films appeared from Elton's studios. In 1946 he was sent as film adviser to the Danish government and subsequently (1947) to the British Control Commission in Germany.

In 1947 he returned to Film Centre Limited and became adviser to the Shell Petroleum Company for a number of years before being appointed production head of Shell Films in 1957. He made for Shell an outstanding group of short films on the history, achievement, and world-wide impact of British technology. Elton, together with Edgar Anstey at British Transport Films and for a few years Paul Rotha at the BBC, kept alive the spirit of the British documentary movement. Elton sent Shell cameramen to Egypt, India, Iraq, and Venezuela. He combined his enthusiasm for art and technology in works such as *The Flintknappers*, *The Chairbodgers*, *How an Aeroplane Flies*, or *Prospecting for Oil*. Future generations of historians will be grateful for his work in recording, as only moving pictures can, aspects of mid-twentieth century British life and industry, with a combination of poetry and scientific insight that was essentially Elton. He will also be remembered for recognizing the importance of film as historical evidence in his address 'The Film as Source Material for History' in 1955 (Aslib *Proceedings*, vol. vii, No. 4, 1955). Elton was a tireless advocate of the need to preserve film as carefully as literary source materials.

But cinema was only one of his interests. After inheriting the family title and estates when his father died in 1951 he devoted himself to local affairs at Clevedon, Somerset, returning to roots markedly different from his life in industry. He restored Clevedon Court, dating from 1320 and occupied by Eltons from 1709, and handed the house over to the National Trust in 1960. As chairman of the Clevedon Printing Company, he helped to run the *North Somerset Mercury*. The technical skill that he had devoted to the house was next dedicated to the project to rebuild Clevedon pier, an outstanding Victorian iron structure that collapsed in 1970. It is unlikely that any other small community has contained architectural features as different as Clevedon Court and the pier, together with a local squire with the knowledge and energy to care for both.

Elton was a lifelong collector of industrial art, artefacts, and literature. Edgar Anstey said that 'a constant theme in his life was a love of order' and he reduced to order his unique collection of pictures, prints, books, and objects recording British industrial development. After his death the collection, valued at over £250,000, was passed to the Ironbridge Museum in Shropshire. Elton had sponsored exhibitions in industrial art and archaeology before they became fashionable in the 1970s. In 1968 he revised and reissued his friend Francis Klingender's *Art and the Industrial Revolution* first published in 1947. Elton was the outstanding builder of bridges between 'the two cultures' of the arts and the sciences.

Elton's appearance was as impressive as his personality. He stood well over six feet tall with a broad frame, usually dressed informally even in the City, and surmounted by blonde hair and beard. He carried himself like a Viking, and made a strong impression even before he began to pour out his enthusiasms. The powerful exterior concealed a basic shyness: he did not make friends easily and could sometimes appear obstinate and over-bearing when he tried to overcome this reserve. He would rather wound a susceptibility than lose a cause. But he was unfailingly kind and generous to those he trusted. Elton was a remarkably gifted man, who believed that his good fortune in being born with these talents in a comfortable home carried with it an obligation to serve his fellow men. He was a pioneer whose work in non-fictional film, in 'the aesthetics of technology', and in film and history, was developed extensively in the decade after his death.

In 1948 he married Margaret Ann, daughter of Dr Olafur Bjornson MD, FRCS, professor of obstetrics at the University of Manitoba. They had two daughters and a son, Charles Abraham Grierson (born 1953), who succeeded to the baronetcy when Elton died in Bristol 1 January 1973. Portraits of Elton by J. M. Heaton, Sir Cedric Morris, and Eve Disher hang in Clevedon Court.

[Private information] D. J. Wenden

ELTON, GODFREY, first Baron Elton (1892–1973), historian, was born at Sherington rectory, Newport Pagnell, 29 March 1892, the elder son and eldest of the three children of Edward Fiennes Elton, of Burleigh Court, Gloucestershire, and Ovington Park, Hampshire, and his wife, Violet Hylda, daughter of the Revd Carteret John Halford Fletcher, rector of Carfax Church, Oxford. He was educated at Rugby and at Balliol College, Oxford, which he entered with a classical scholarship in 1911. He obtained a first class in classical honour moderations in 1913 and then turned from classics to history. But although his tutors thought extremely highly of him, he never took his finals, for in September 1914 he was commissioned in the 4th Hampshire Regiment and saw service in Mesopotamia. During the siege of Kut-el-Amara he was wounded, and was then taken into captivity in Turkey when Kut surrendered in April 1916. His interest in history was maintained so far as conditions allowed, and soon after the war ended Queen's College, Oxford, elected him in 1919 to a fellowship and praelectorship in modern history.

He was dean of the college from 1921 to 1923 and tutor from 1927 to 1934. With his wife, he was exceptionally generous in entertaining colleagues and undergraduates. As a tutor he was painstaking and interesting, though his only strictly historical publication was *The Revolutionary Idea in France, 1789–1878* (1923), which went to many impressions. He was devoted to his college, but it cannot be said that in college and university affairs his attitude changed much as the years went on. He believed strongly not only in customs but in rules: the dean of Queen's in the 1930s remembers being urged by Elton to conduct a close investigation into the reasons why a young lady, in a gown, had been seen descending an undergraduate staircase at 11 a.m. Yet his career was paradoxical. Soon after the war he had joined the Labour Party, and he was their (unsuccessful) candidate for Thornbury, Gloucestershire, in 1924 and 1929. He looked back, as did many of those demobilized in 1918, to pre-war social and economic conditions which he found distasteful; he greatly disliked militarism; and he was dissatisfied with the efforts of the Allies to prevent war recurring. Whether he ever absorbed deeply the principles or details of Labour policy is doubtful, and when the government broke up in 1931 he followed Ramsay MacDonald into the National Labour Party. He was a strong admirer of the prime minister, whose son Malcolm had been his pupil at Queen's, and in 1939 he published the first volume of his biography. He wrote the notice of MacDonald for this Dictionary, as well as that of Philip Guedalla. In 1934 Elton was made a peer.

(Sir) L. B. Namier [q.v.] commented that 'whereas in the 18th century the tutors of peers were made Under-Secretaries, in the 20th the tutors of Under-Secretaries are made peers'. But if this was intended as a criticism of Elton, it was quite unfair. By 1935, it is true, he had lost much interest in the questions which excited most people at that time, but he spoke often and ably in the Lords on such subjects as the environment, agriculture, broadcasting, and ecclesiastical affairs (he was a devout Anglican). He also served on a wide range of governmental and semi-public committees. He wrote several books, including novels and, in 1938, an autobiographical volume, *Among Others*.

In 1939 he gave up his teaching fellowship at Queen's and became a supernumerary fellow. To his younger colleagues in recent years he had undeniably seemed to be a reactionary. But they were pleased when they could agree with his advice, which could often be helpful; and when they disagreed they were never apprehensive that either discourtesy of unpleasantness would result. He was a man without malice.

In later years he served above all as secretary to the Rhodes Trust (1939–59), but he continued much other work on committees. His academic life was perhaps disappointing in the light of his early promise. But he was a man of energy and wide interests, and in these later years he performed widely and well.

In 1921 he married Dedi (died 1977), daughter of Gustav Hartmann of Oslo, Norway. They had two daughters and a son, Rodney (born 1930), who succeeded to the barony when his father died in Sutton Bonington, Leicestershire, 18 April 1973.

[Lord Elton, *Among Others*, 1938; *The Times*, 19 April 1973.] G. E. F. CHILVER

ELWES, SIMON EDMUND VINCENT PAUL (1902–1975), portrait painter, was born 29 June 1902 at Hothorpe Hall, Northamptonshire, the sixth and youngest son (two daughters were born later) of Gervase Henry Elwes [q.v.], the singer, a famous Gerontius, and his wife, Lady Winefride Mary Elizabeth, fourth daughter of Rudolph William Basil Feilding, eighth Earl of Denbigh. The boy went to Catholic schools—Lady Cross School, Seaford, and The Oratory, Edgbaston. In 1918, at the age of sixteen, he entered the Slade School, when Henry Tonks and Philip Wilson Steer [qq.v.] taught there, and soldiers of the great war, such as Gilbert and (Sir) Stanley Spencer, A. R. Middleton Todd [qq.v.] and Allan Gwynne-Jones were taking up their studies again. Courteous, handsome, and a devout Catholic, Elwes might have come out of Brideshead.

Elwes spent eight years in Paris after leaving the Slade, first at the École de l'Écluse and then at the Académie des Beaux Arts, and also he visited the galleries of Germany, Holland, and Italy. He came back to England in 1926 and next year showed a portrait at the Royal Academy of Lady Lettice Lygon. She was the first of his many noble sitters, who included the Duke and Duchess of York (later King George VI and Queen Elizabeth), the Princess Royal, Prince George and Princess Marina, Queen Mary, Prince Henry, Duke of Gloucester, Princess Margaret, and Queen Elizabeth II. His portraits hung in the summer exhibition of the Royal Academy every year. In 1929 he was created a Knight of Malta and in 1933 was elected a member of the Royal Society of Portrait Painters.

He joined the Welsh Guards at the outbreak of World War II, to be transferred later to the 10th Royal Hussars in Egypt. After fighting in the battles of Benghazi, Mersa Matruh, and 'Knightsbridge', he was made an official war artist. In Cairo he painted King Farouk and Queen Farida, in South Africa the King and Queen of the Hellenes as well as J. C. Smuts [q.v.], and in India the viceroy Wavell [q.v.], the Maharaja of Patiala, Lord Louis Mountbatten (later Earl Mountbatten of Burma, q.v.), and Indian Army soldiers who had won the VC. The journeys, the heat, and the astonishing activity must all have helped to bring about the stroke he suffered when he came back to England after the Japanese surrender. He spent two years in hospital. He was never to use his right hand for painting again, but as soon as he could stand, taught himself to paint with his left. Till then, his portraits owed much to Sir William Orpen [q.v.], not only the light reflected on the side of the face, the folds of the curtain radiating from the sitter's waist, the chair which brought the hands high up in the composition, but also the fluent and continuous surface of paint.

There is not much in the way of manual skill that a painter needs; but he wants to be able to control the direction of his brush. In default of that precision of movement, Elwes now broke his surface with separate touches, which, instead of weakening his pictures, gave them a new vivacity. He surmounted his disability enough to become president of the Guild of Catholic Artists, vice-president of the Royal Society of Portrait Painters from 1953, an associate of the Royal Academy in 1956, and a full RA in 1967.

To read through a list of his sitters is like turning over the pages not only of *Who's Who* but of Debrett and the *Almanach de Gotha*. No other painter since Philip de Lázló [q.v.] has painted such eminences, not even Frank Salisbury [q.v.]. Like de Lázló and Salisbury, Elwes was sustained by a craft which ensured that his portraits went ahead as he intended; they owed their virtue to their confidence. Elwes endowed his subjects with a good nature and a joy of life which, enhanced by brilliant colour, were the expression of his own character and appearance. He had none of the guilt which seems to afflict some portrait painters, either from talent unfulfilled or taxes unpaid.

Nothing could be stronger than the contrast at a council meeting of the Royal Academy between Elwes and the rest of the members, teachers to a man. Handsome, fresh of complexion, finely dressed, with a scarlet flower in his buttonhole, he enriched the proceedings with his smile, no less than with his air of being a visitor from a world more carefree and elegant than the one in which deficits and disappointments were certain to be discussed. When he used the old ballroom in Burlington House to paint a portrait, a beautiful girl brought him his brushes and set up his paintbox, for that was his own exhilarating way of making light of his useless right arm and dragging leg. It was natural that he should have been at ease painting Cardinal Hinsley [q.v.], richly robed in a red cassock, yet benign, and Sir Thomas Beecham [q.v.] in a white dressing gown, and mischievous. It is not to be wondered at that his paintings of roses, peonies, and lilies are not in the least like the hedgerow flowers of his contemporary Allan Gwynne-Jones, but blithe and sumptuous. His DNB notice of Frederick Lonsdale, the playwright, is equally light-hearted.

In the last months of his life, he had to be pushed about in a chair, hardly able to speak, no longer spotless in his dress; but his face, thinner and paler, had a look of the greatest nobility—wistful, unearthly; not old. He could have been the embodiment of the dying Gerontius. He died 6 August 1975, in Sussex.

In 1926 Elwes married Gloria Elinor, daughter of James Rennell Rodd, first Baron Rennell [q.v.], diplomat and scholar. They had four sons, one of whom died in infancy, and one of whom, Dominic, died in the same year as his father. Elwes's wife died two months after Simon.

[Family information; personal knowledge.]

PETER GREENHAM

EMBRY, SIR BASIL EDWARD (1902–1977), air chief marshal, was born in Longford, Gloucestershire, 28 February 1902, the youngest of the three children and second son of the Revd James Embry, an Anglican clergyman, and his wife, Florence Ada Troughton. In conversation he always claimed to be Irish, though only his paternal grandfather is traceable to Ireland.

His early years were uneventful, and he attended Bromsgrove School without scholastic distinction but showing athletic prowess coupled with a precocious longing, from his tenth year onwards, to fly aeroplanes. The main part of his schooling coincided with World War I, and when it ended he thought that his chance of flying was gone. However, in spite of strong opposition from his parents, who wanted him to go to Cambridge, he managed to join the Royal Air Force as a short service officer, and was commissioned on 29 March 1921.

After flying training he joined No. 4 Bomber Squadron, but found the immediately post-war home service scene too tame for his taste, and applied for service in Iraq. This was the first of his many initiatives to 'march towards the sound of the guns'. In Iraq he was able to pioneer the airmail route across the desert and join in the development of new techniques of 'air control', devised by Sir H. M. (later Lord) Trenchard [q.v.], to keep the peace in the Kurdish border districts. This, and his work with the first air ambulance service, won him an AFC in 1926, and the award of a permanent commission. In 1927 he returned to England and qualified as a flying instructor, commanded a training flight, and specialized in the development of instrument flying. He remained an instructor until he took the RAF Staff College course in 1933.

For Embry this was more than enough of training and home service, so he applied for a posting to India. He arrived in 1934, and after suffering staff and training appointments was promoted to squadron leader in 1936 and given his first command, No. 20 Squadron at Peshawar. This was far more to his taste, and in the hazardous flying on the North-West Frontier, during the various campaigns of 1937 and 1938, he was appointed to the DSO (1938), and established a lifelong reputation for courage and leadership.

He was therefore discontented to find himself, at the outbreak of war in 1939, in the directorate of operations in Whitehall. It took him eight days to get out, to the command of No. 107 Day Bomber Squadron, and to the opportunity to continue to apply his principles of leadership in operational practice. The air service's greatest morale problem had always been the confinement of commanders to the ground, due usually to their age and lack of flying practice, so that while their men endured the greatest dangers of any combatant they themselves were safer than many civilians. It might be deplorable, but it was accepted. Embry would have none of this. His own Blenheim was riddled with bullets on his first sortie over Germany, but he continued to lead the squadron on missions of great danger, bringing home a damaged aircraft fifteen times and even flying in the air-gunner's position, the better to understand his problems. It would be hard to exaggerate the affection he inspired in the members of his squadron. His extreme personal recklessness made them feel protective to him.

His luck could not last. On the day he was promoted and posted from his squadron he was wounded and shot down over France. Captured and marched towards a prison he passed a sign-post labelled 'Embry', and taking this as a portent he slipped away from the column and hid in a French farm. He was recaptured and escaped again by belabouring his guards with an iron bar, finally arriving safely in Gibraltar.

Back in England he was promoted to group captain, and commanded a night fighter wing and a fighter sector. During this period at home he was received into the Roman Catholic faith. He was sent to North Africa in 1941, at the request of Sir A. W. (later Lord) Tedder [q.v.] to advise on tactics. He then had two staff appointments in England, until in May 1943 he was given command of No. 2 Bomber Group, with the rank of air vice-marshal. His task was to prepare this tactical group for the Overlord invasion, and thereafter to support the Allied armies in Europe. In these operations he continued to use his individual style of personal leadership, flying with his crews and carrying forged identity documents, for fear of execution if captured. He was awarded the DFC (1945) for these operations, a most unusual decoration for a man of his rank. In 1945 he was awarded a third bar to his DSO, appointed CB and KBE, and received a number of foreign honours, thus making him one of the most highly decorated officers in the three fighting services.

But the end of the war brought him to Whitehall again as assistant chief of air staff (training). Although he liked training he hated Whitehall; yet through this appointment he was able to supervise the complete overhaul of RAF training that followed the war. In April 1949 he was promoted air marshal and made commander-in-chief Fighter Command, and though there was now nobody to fight he used all his explosive energy to bring the Command to a new peak of efficiency. In 1953 he was appointed KCB, and, in December, air chief marshal. In July 1953 he was posted to France as commander of Allied Air Forces Central Europe, in the new NATO organization. This ponderous multinational organization was little suited to his qualities. Though buttressed by his great reputation he spoke little French, distrusted politicians, suspected diplomats, and was unenthusiastic about foreigners generally. It was not the best use of an outstanding fighting leader, and this miscasting contributed to his early retirement in September 1956, at the age of fifty-four, when he was appointed GCB.

He had long planned to take his whole family to start life anew in New Zealand, and he now put this scheme into practice, though shortly after arriving he moved on to Western Australia. There he bought a tract of bush and worked, helped by his wife and eldest children, to create a farming estate out of the wild. As the years went by the Embry family, now naturalized Australians, gradually conquered all obstacles. Embry built a house with his own hands, and by 1972 he was president of the Farmers Union of Western Australia and founder and first chairman of the Rural Traders Co-operative. He was made first chairman of the world-wide RAF Escaping Society, a freeman of the City of London and of the Cinque Port of Dover, and a liveryman of the Worshipful Company of Glass-sellers. He died at Boyup Brook, Western Australia, 7 December 1977. He bequeathed to the Royal Air Force an example of personal leadership which became an enduring tradition of the service.

Embry was a small spare man, wiry and strong, Celtic in colouring with extremely piercing blue eyes under fierce eyebrows. He had a puckish face, by no means handsome, which could express a wide variety of emotions from demoniac rage to delight, laughter, and goodwill, often within a few seconds. He had a trick of speaking to people from such close range, and with so fixed a blue glare, that even those whom he meant only to please were disconcerted. Though not particularly witty, he had a strong sense of fun, and a great capacity to inspire and charm most people, coupled with a talent to dismay and antagonize some others.

Embry married in 1928 (Margaret Mildred Norfolk) Hope, daughter of Captain Charles Sinclair Elliott, RN, and had three sons and one daughter. There is a portrait by Eric Kennington in the possession of the family, and another by the same artist is held by the Ministry of Defence.

[B. E. Embry, *Mission Completed*, 1956; private information; personal knowledge.]

PETER WYKEHAM

EMERY, (WALTER) BRYAN (1903–71), Egyptologist, was born 2 July 1903 at Liverpool, the second son of Walter Thomas Emery, principal of the Technical College at Liverpool, and his wife, Beatrice Mary Benbow, also of Liverpool. He was educated at St. Francis Xavier's College, Liverpool, and early became fascinated with Egyptology, which, after a brief apprenticeship to a firm of marine engineers, he studied from 1921 to 1923 under T. E. Peet [q.v.] at the Institute of Archaeology of Liverpool University. In 1923–4 he worked on the Egypt Exploration Society's excavations at El-ʿAmarna under F. G. Newton and F. L. Griffith [q.v.]. In 1924 he was appointed by (Sir) Robert Mond [q.v.] to direct the Liverpool expedition to clear and restore the tomb of the vizier Ramose and other New Kingdom nobles' tombs in the

Theban necropolis. While accomplishing this, Emery saw the tomb of Tutankhamun during excavation, and discovered the burial place of the Buchis bulls at Armant, which he helped the Egypt Exploration Society to excavate in 1927–8.

In summer 1928 Emery married Mary ('Molly'), daughter of James Joseph Cowhey, head postmaster of Liverpool, returning with his bride to Thebes. They had no children. Emery was then appointed by the Egyptian Government Antiquities Service to direct the Second Archaeological Survey of Nubia. From 1929 to 1934 the Emerys and their assistants traversed the southern part of Egyptian Nubia by boat and on foot, excavating each site discovered. At Ballana near the Sudanese frontier Emery discovered and excavated rich royal burial mounds (fourth to sixth century AD), the treasure from which now graces the Cairo Museum. *The Excavations and Survey between Wadi es-Sebua and Adindan*, with L. P. Kirwan (Cairo, 1935), *The Royal Tombs of Ballana and Qustul*, with L. P. Kirwan (2 vols., Cairo, 1938), and *Nubian Treasure* (London, 1948) resulted.

From 1935 Emery excavated at Saqqara for the Egyptian government, uncovering a series of rich tombs of the First to Third Dynasties illuminating the beginnings of Egyptian history. He enlisted in 1939, and was employed at the headquarters of the British troops in Egypt with the Long Range Desert Patrol, later serving with the Eighth Army. He was mentioned in despatches in 1942 and appointed MBE (military) in 1943. He ended the war as director of military intelligence in Egypt as a lieutenant-colonel. In 1945–6 he returned to Saqqara, but, owing to financial difficulties, accepted a post in the British embassy at Cairo, where he rose to the rank of first secretary (1950–1).

In 1951 he was elected to the Edwards chair of Egyptology at University College, London. He returned to Saqqara as field director of the Egypt Exploration Society in 1952, and completed excavation of the First Dynasty tombs in 1956 (*Great Tombs of the First Dynasty*, vol. 1, Cairo, 1949; vol. 2, London 1954; vol. 3, London, 1958). After the Suez crisis of 1956 Emery led the Egypt Exploration Society to the Sudan to excavate the magnificent Middle Kingdom brick fortress town of Buhen, built c. 1970 BC. His work there was published posthumously in *The Fortress of Buhen* (2 vols., London, 1974–9). Emery advised both the Egyptian and the Sudanese Antiquities Services throughout the Unesco campaign to save the monuments of Nubia (1959–64); he arranged for the temple of Buhen to be moved to Khartoum, organized the Third Archaeological Survey of Egyptian Nubia, and excavated the cemeteries of Qasr Ibrim, a Meroïtic city which later became a fortress of the medieval Nubians.

In 1964 he returned to Saqqara, where he discovered the sacred animal necropolis of Memphis, comprising the catacombs of mummified cows, baboons, ibises, and falcons. The associated temple site yielded rich hoards of bronze figurines and temple furniture, and valuable documents of the sixth to first centuries BC in Egyptian, Aramaic, Greek, and Carian. Late in 1967 Emery underwent major lung surgery, but returned immediately to Saqqara to make further spectacular discoveries. He retired as professor in 1970. He died in Cairo 11 March 1971, after collapsing on the excavations at Saqqara, and was buried in the British cemetery in Cairo. His Saqqara work is being published posthumously by the Egypt Exploration Society.

Emery's direct approach and knowledge of terrain were the basis of his flare for finding major sites. His outstanding contributions were undoubtedly his magnificent architectural reconstructions of ancient buildings. He loved Egypt, the Sudan, and their peoples, and his infectious enthusiasm and absolute integrity led them to love and respect him. His versatility and attractive personality earned him friends everywhere, whom he regaled with his delightful stories of archaeology and archaeologists. His academic distinction was recognized by many awards, of which the principal were: honorary MA (Liverpool University, 1939), D.Lit. (London University, 1959), FBA (1959), and CBE (1969).

[Adolf Klasens in *Proceedings* of the British Academy, vol. lviii, 1972; personal knowledge.]

H. S. Smith

ERDÉLYI, ARTHUR (1908–1977), mathematician, was born Arthur Diamant 2 October 1908 in Budapest, the eldest of the five children (three sons and two daughters) of Ignác József Ármin Diamant and his wife Frederike ('Frieda') Roth. After his father's death his mother married Paul Erdélyi, who subsequently adopted Arthur. His secondary school education was at Madách Imre Fögimnázium in Budapest (1918–26). He started his university education in 1926, studying electrical engineering in the Deutsche Technische Hochschule at Brno, Czechoslovakia. He passed the first examination with distinction in 1928 but left, without completing the course, for employment as a mathematician. He acquired the degree of Dr. rer. nat. (Doctor rerum naturalium) from the German University of Prague in 1938 having submitted a collection of his published papers in lieu of a thesis. He was awarded his doctorate at the last degree ceremony before the university was taken over by the Nazis.

To escape the Nazi persecution of Jews he emigrated to Britain and arrived at Edinburgh in February 1939. At first he was supported by a research grant from the university and financial aid from the Academic Assistance Council (later the Society for the Protection of Science and Learning Limited). This state of affairs continued, despite the award of the degree of D.Sc. by Edinburgh in 1940, until 1941 when he was appointed assistant lecturer. He was promoted to a lectureship in 1942. At this time he was also a consultant to the Admiralty and, with others, was responsible for the proposal to create a National Mathematical Laboratory which eventually became part of the National Physical Laboratory. He became a naturalized British citizen in 1947 and was promoted to a senior lectureship in 1948, having been elected a fellow of the Royal Society of Edinburgh in 1945. Two of his brothers and one sister died in a concentration camp during the war.

In 1949 he was appointed as full professor by California Institute of Technology, one of his duties being the direction of the Bateman project, the task of editing the mass of notes left by Harry Bateman on his death in 1946. With the assistance of W. Magnus, F. Oberhettinger, and F. G. Tricomi three volumes of *Higher Transcendental Functions* and two volumes of *Tables of Integral Transforms* were ready by 1951. Erdélyi carried out the mammoth job of seeing the five volumes through the press while fulfilling a normal teaching load at the Institute, supervising two research students, and looking after his wife who had contracted tuberculosis. These books have been used and referred to by so many scientists that their impact on science is immeasurable and the scientific community is indebted to Erdélyi for his devotion to this project. He was elected a foreign member of the Academy of Sciences of Torino in 1953.

He returned to Edinburgh as head of department and professor of mathematics in 1964 at considerable personal sacrifice because he felt that his 'alma mater' (as he regarded it) needed his help. Here, as a talented violinist and violist, he participated in chamber music and, as a keen walker, explored the Scottish Highlands awakening a deep interest in geology (and a passion for deserts when he was abroad).

He contributed nearly 200 papers to learned journals and his quality was recognized by election as FRS in 1975. In 1977 he had the rare distinction of being awarded the Gunning Victoria Jubilee prize of the Royal Society of Edinburgh. He was also president of the Edinburgh Mathematical Society (1971–2). A special issue of *Applicable Analysis* and the *Proceedings* of the 1978 Dundee conference on differential equations were dedicated to him. He was a superb expositor and lecturer, who received ovations at international colloquia. One reason for this was his mastery of special functions, for he unveiled the beauty of the underlying patterns with typical elegance. Another area in which he was a major figure was asymptotics; his systematic exploitation of asymptotic scale and Volterra singular integral equations provided a general theory for differential equations and subsequently for the asymptotic evaluation of integrals. Later he was involved in laying the foundations of matched asymptotic expansions. Another field for which he forged the fundamental tools was that of fractional integration—the Erdélyi–Kober operations, leading to many applications in integral and partial differential equations, are now basic. Erdélyi's innovation and exposition initiated a considerable amount of modern research.

As a head of department he was a gentleman, displaying courtesy and faultless manners to all. Level-headed and tolerant he was always in command and his natural authority was immediately recognizable. His dress was dapper, with spotless white shirts and bow tie. His cheerful disposition was unaffected by ill health in later years. He remarked, on appearing in the department not long after major surgery, 'My doctor forbade me to teach; he did not forbid me to learn.'

He married, on 4 November 1942, Eva, daughter of Frederic Neuburg, of Litoměrice, Czechslovakia, and Helene (née Feitis), second cousin of Max Perutz. They had no children, but there was a stepson who came to know Erdélyi well when he was a teenager. Erdélyi died suddenly 12 December 1977 in Edinburgh.

[D. S. Jones in *Biographical Memoirs of Fellows of the Royal Society*, vol. xxv, 1979.] D. S. JONES

ERITH, RAYMOND CHARLES (1904–1973), architect, was born 7 August 1904 at 50 Filey Avenue, Upper Clapton, East London, the second child and eldest of three sons in the family of five children of Henry Charles Erith, mechanical engineer, and his wife, Florence May Laubenberg. In the year after his birth the Eriths moved from Clapton to Sutton, Surrey, where Raymond was brought up. At four, he contracted tuberculosis and this led to twelve years of intermittent illness (he only attended school for two terms), leaving him permanently lame in his left leg. During these long periods of enforced idleness, Erith discovered an interest in drawing, to which his father's work gave a technical twist, leading him to architecture. At fifteen he received an honourable mention in a competition for model houses, conducted by the *Daily Express*. In 1921 his mother took him and his two sisters to Italy. Later that year he entered the Architectural Association school of architecture.

The AA school was then in a phase of enthusiastic reaction to influences from abroad, especially those of the more avant-garde kind. These had no appeal for Erith who, nevertheless, enjoyed the course and won several awards, including the Henry Florence travelling studentship (1924). To obtain the practical office experience requisite for professional qualification he served for a period in the office of P. Morley Horder [q.v.]. He was elected ARIBA in 1927.

In 1928, on the strength of a modest legacy from his grandfather, Erith opened an office of his own in Westminster but moved in the following year to Warwick Street, forming a partnership with Bertram Hume which was to last till 1939. In 1934 he married Pamela Dorothy, younger daughter of Arthur Spencer Jackson, solicitor; they were to have four daughters. Two years later Jackson became a client, commissioning him to build a house in the main street of Dedham, Essex. In the design of this house, the Great House, Erith adopted the idiom of the most refined and reserved domestic architecture of *circa* 1800, thus defining the route he was to follow, with variations, for the remainder of his career. He adopted the same style when in 1939, on the recommendation of the president of RIBA, H. S. Goodhart-Rendel [q.v.], he was appointed to design lodges at the approach to the Royal Lodge, Windsor Great Park, for King George VI. Unluckily these were damaged by a bomb soon after completion and the design was altered in the course of reconstruction by another hand.

With the outbreak of war the practice was wound up and in 1940 Erith bought a farm with 150 acres of arable land at Little Bromley, Essex. He farmed successfully till 1945, enjoying the life; but in 1946 architecture reclaimed him and he opened an office in Ipswich. He became FRIBA the same year. Now forty-two, he found himself with few opportunities measuring up to his abilities. He possessed no flair whatever for self-advertisement but in 1949 started, to please himself and perhaps others, to send drawings to the Royal Academy exhibitions. These combined his idiosyncratic quality as a designer with draughtsmanly execution of exceptional beauty. To some they seemed the work of a brilliantly eccentric deviationist but they deeply impressed those who were sceptical about the universal validity of the modern manner. The first worthwhile commission to come his way was a terrace of three houses in Aubrey Walk, Kensington (for the Misses Alexander, 1949). In 1955 he was invited to design new lodgings for the provost of the Queen's College, Oxford. This, though not a large work, is notable for an ingeniously simple plan and for the subtle handling of rustication on the front towards Queen's Lane. It was followed immediately by a commission for a new library at Lady Margaret Hall, Oxford. This was to run parallel with a block by Sir Reginald Blomfield [q.v.] so as to form a new quadrangle which would be closed by another new block, the Wolfson residential building. Erith designed both, the library being completed in 1961 and the Wolfson building, providing a new entrance to the college, in 1966.

In 1958 Erith received the most exacting commission of his career, the reconstruction of Nos. 10 and 11 Downing Street and the rebuilding of No. 12. The rationalization of this intricate complex of Georgian buildings, involving the preservation of historic rooms, was a task to which he was ideally suited. The progress of the work, however, was bedevilled by disputes in the building trade and extravagant delays, causing him great anxiety and distress before its ultimate completion in 1963.

Erith's later work included the Pediment, Aynho, Northamptonshire (for Miss Elizabeth Watt, 1956–7); the Folly, Gatley Park, Herefordshire (for Mrs Victor Willis, 1961–4), a fortress-like tower on an elliptical plan; the rebuilding of Jack Straw's Castle, the famous Hampstead tavern (for Charrington and Co., 1963–4), where he adapted an eighteenth-century weather-boarded vernacular to a modern function; Wivenhoe New Park (for Mr Charles Gooch, 1962–4), a study in Palladian villa design; King's Walden Bury (for Sir Thomas Pilkington, Bt., 1969–71), where Palladianism is combined with evocations of Queen Anne; and the common-room building at Gray's Inn (1971–2).

Erith was unique among the architects of his generation for his resistance to the influence of 'functionalism' and his consistent adherence to what he conceived to be the true nature of architecture. This he believed to have been at the heart of a tradition which had disintegrated in the middle of the nineteenth century, and from whose ruins it could be retrieved. He admired Sir John Soane [q.v.] and sometimes, but rarely, imitated him. Later influences in his work include Italian mannerism, Swedish neo-classicism (the original as well as the revived varieties), and the vernacular of the Essex countryside, for which he had a deep affection. His unpublished writings show a rooted conviction that it is the purpose of architecture not merely to serve practical purposes efficiently but to bring positive delight and spiritual comfort to mankind.

From 1958 Erith conducted his practice from Dedham but took an active part in professional affairs, notably in architectural education. He was elected ARA in 1959 and RA in 1964. From 1960 to 1973 he served on the Royal Fine Art Commission. He was a shy man, of singular modesty and charm, marked but not embittered by physical suffering, happy at his drawing-board, in his married life, and with his daughters. He died in the London Hospital 30 November 1973.

[Lucy Archer, *Raymond Erith: Architect*, 1985.]

JOHN SUMMERSON

ERVINE, (JOHN) ST. JOHN (GREER) (1883–1971), author and drama critic, was born 28 December 1883 in Belfast, the son of William Ervine, schoolmaster, and his wife, Sarah Jane Park (née Greer). Of deeply based Ulster stock, he had a boyish enthusiasm for the stage, bred when he saw (Sir) Frank Benson [q.v.] in Shakespeare at the Belfast Theatre Royal. He crossed to London as an insurance clerk, but this did not last: he was obsessed by writing in general, and the theatre in particular, and through life, with Ervine an obsession had to take its course.

His first play, an uncompromising one-act piece, *The Magnanimous Lover*, about Protestant complacency in Ulster, was written in 1907. It did not reach the Abbey, Dublin, until 1912, but he was known by then for the Ulster realism of *Mixed Marriage* (in four acts) about young people in the power of the religiously fanatical old: this was at the Abbey in 1911. Probably his most durable play, *Jane Clegg*, in which (Dame) Sybil Thorndike [q.v.] acted (1913) at the Gaiety, Manchester, had an English setting: here a woman, aching for independence, who has suffered much from her wastrel husband, refuses to forgive him again. Ervine wasted no time in manoeuvring: he generated a direct theatrical force that served him in the tragic gloom of *John Ferguson* (Abbey, 1915) from a mortgaged farm in county Down. His plots were melodramatic in outline, but they could fire the theatre. At this time he was an ardent Fabian, a founder member of the Fabian 'Nursery'.

Though contentious always, he managed the Abbey for a short period (1915), but management was no place for an individualist. He had to be writing, whether for the stage or in such a novel as *Mrs Martin's Man* (1914), one of seven during his career and at their most veracious when dealing with his own Ulster. Joining the army as a trooper in the Household battalion during 1916, he was wounded in France (May 1918) as a lieutenant in the Royal Dublin Fusiliers and lost a leg; a disaster that he never allowed to affect his later life.

From 1919, after a spell in London as drama critic of the *Daily Citizen* and other papers, he went to the *Observer* where his blunt, good-humoured candour appealed to the editor, J. L. Garvin [q.v.], if not always to the people of the 'commercial' theatre Ervine criticized. In the 1930s, when a formidably successful playwright, he would usually confine himself to writing a discursive arts feature, 'At the Play', but not necessarily on that subject. As Ivor Brown [q.v.] put it, Ervine saw the theatre as 'a piece of life, an aspect of the National Being'. He was appointed dramatic critic to the BBC in 1932.

By the early 1920s two of his plays, *John Ferguson*, which established the fame of the Theatre Guild of New York, and *Jane Clegg* had had uncommon success in the main cities of the United States. In London he continued to write, with invention and relish, plays (much gentler than of old), novels, and monographs, though nothing really got home to the English public until a cheerfully artificial Haymarket light comedy, *The First Mrs Fraser*, entirely remote from his Ulster world. With the benefit of (Dame) Marie Tempest and Henry Ainley [qq.v.], it ran for more than a year from 1929 and Ervine thoroughly appreciated his fortune. He would have two other long runs before World War II, the lightweight *Anthony and Anna* (1935) which did not have a London hearing until, ironically, *The First Mrs Fraser* had established him as a viable West End dramatist; and the deeper *Robert's Wife* (1937), fortified by the technique of (Dame) Edith Evans [q.v.] and Owen Nares.

His critical candour, dogmatism rarely smoothed by tact, made enemies, but his friends were many and loyal. Fair-haired, pink-cheeked, and a headstrong talker, he was in the words of Frank Swinnerton, who knew him well, observant, genial, and bland, 'but in the very moment of geniality . . . he keeps his head and fails to allow his judgment to nod'. He realized exactly what he wanted. When he was addressing a literary conference in the ebb of his career, he began with the plain statement, 'I shall speak for two hours, and anyone who wants to go had better consider it now.'

After World War II, as a veteran of the theatre, his final plays, such as *Private Enterprise* (1947), were unremarkable. He settled in his Devon retreat near Seaton to write vast biographical studies of people who had excited him. He had published shorter works in the past, studies of Lord Carson [q.v.] and—notable for its balance—of Charles Stewart Parnell [q.v.], but now he applied himself to a detailed examination, in two volumes, of 'General' William Booth [q.v.] of the Salvation Army, *God's Soldier* (1934); important to the social historian, it would have been more effective at half its length. He followed this by *Craigavon—Ulsterman* (1949), and his valuable *Bernard Shaw: His Life, Work and Friends* (1956) which was as wise and searching a portrait of G. B. Shaw [q.v.], a friend for many years, as there had been. Another work, *Oscar Wilde: a Present Time Appraisal* (1951) was unfortunate: Ervine had no sympathy for Wilde, and the book proved to be a long speech for the prosecution. To this Dictionary he contributed the notices of Sir Gerald du Maurier, Dame Margaret (Madge) Kendal, R. J. McNeill, Sir Arthur Pinero, G. B. Shaw, and Dame Marie Tempest.

From 1933 to 1936 he was professor of dramatic literature of the Royal Society of Literature, of which he was a fellow. He was president of the League of British Dramatists in 1937 and became a member of the Irish Academy. He received an honorary LL D from St. Andrews in 1934 and D.Litt. from Queen's University, Belfast, in 1945.

In 1911 he married Lenora Mary (died 1965), daughter of George William Davis, bookseller, of Birmingham; they had no children. Their life together was very happy, latterly in a beautiful east Devon house, overlooking the hills and the sea. She predeceased him and his health declined. Spending his last years in nursing homes, he died 24 January 1971 at Fitzhall, Iping, Sussex.

[*The Times*, 25 January and 1 February 1971; Frank Swinnerton, *Swinnerton: an Autobiography*, 1937; Ivor Brown, *The Way of My World*, 1954; Allardyce Nicoll, *English Drama: 1900–1930*, 1973; personal knowledge.]

J. C. TREWIN

EVANS, DAME EDITH MARY (1888–1976), actress, was born 8 February 1888 in Ebury Square, London, daughter of Edward Evans, a minor civil servant, and his wife, Caroline Ellen—a son born in 1886 died at the age of four. She was educated at St. Michael's Church of England School, Pimlico, until in 1903, at the age of fifteen, she was indentured as a milliner to a Mr Blackaller in the Buckingham Palace Road.

Her first appearance on the stage, as an amateur, was with Miss Massey's Streatham Shakespeare Players in the role of Viola in *Twelfth Night* in October 1910. In 1912 she was discovered by the noted producer William Poel [q.v.], and made her first professional appearance for Poel at the Cambridge University Examination Hall in August of that year, playing the role of Gautami in an obscure sixth-century Hindu classic, *Sakuntala.* Her talents were then noted by novelist George Moore [q.v.] who became her passionate mentor and was responsible for her being engaged at the Royalty Theatre, Dean Street, in February 1914 on a year's contract at a salary of two pounds ten shillings a week. Previous to this she had created considerable attention by her performance as Cressida in *Troilus and Cressida* directed by Poel for the Elizabethan Stage Society in the King's Hall, Covent Garden, and subsequently at Stratford-upon-Avon. Thus her extraordinary career spanned sixty-six years and she performed without a break until a few months before her death—her final public appearance being a BBC radio programme before an invited audience in August 1976. From the outset she was a leading player ('God was very good to me', she once remarked, 'he never let me go on tour') and was dedicated to the truth, saying that 'I don't think there is anything extraordinary about me except this passion for the truth', and indeed it is difficult to call to mind any other leading actress of this century who had such single-minded application towards her profession. She played over 150 different roles in the course of her long career and created six of the characters of George Bernard Shaw [q.v.], namely the Serpent, the Oracle, the She-Ancient and the Ghost of the Serpent in *Back to Methuselah* (1923); Orinthia in *The Apple Cart* (1929); and Epifania in *The Millionairess* (1940). She gave what many consider to be definitive performances as Millamant in *The Way of The World* (1924), Rosalind in *As You Like It* (1926 and 1936), the Nurse in *Romeo and Juliet* (1932, 1934, and 1961) and, most notably, as Lady Bracknell in *The Importance of Being Earnest* (1939). Indeed she became so identified with Lady Bracknell in the public eye that she grew to hate the role.

She commenced her film career in a silent film called *A Welsh Singer*, made for Henry Edwards at Walton-on-Thames studios in 1915, but then concentrated on stage roles until Emlyn Williams directed her in his own film *The Last Days on Dolwyn* in 1948, the same year as she appeared in Thorold Dickinson's widely admired *The Queen of Spades*. Although she recreated two of her most famous stage roles for the cinema—Lady Bracknell and Mrs St. Maugham from Enid Bagnold's *The Chalk Garden*—they are but pale versions of the originals and she herself was not proud of them. Perhaps her most rounded screen performance was as Mrs Ross in *The Whisperers* (1966), for which she received the Golden Bear for best actress at the Berlin Film Festival, the British Academy award, the New York Film Critics award, and was nominated for an American Oscar and other international prizes. Her last screen performance (in which she sang and danced) was in *The Slipper and The Rose* (1975), when she was eighty-seven.

Her most widely admired asset was her voice, a highly individual instrument, often imitated but never surpassed. She often professed herself unaware of the extraordinary effect it had on her audiences, but she set great store by clear diction and in her later years was openly critical of the slovenly standards of speech prevalent in the theatre. Belonging as she did to the old school, she imposed severe disciplines on herself and, although she liked to be in complete control of her audiences, always kept them at a distance, becoming over the course of the years a remote and finally very lonely figure. She had a love for and natural feeling for poetry; her taste was catholic and when she felt unable to undertake the task of learning any new roles, she embarked upon a highly successful one-man show of poetry readings (1973) and indeed her last appearance on any West End stage took place during a revival of this entertainment on 5 October 1974.

She was the complete actress, dedicated, always professional, sublimating all other aspects of her life in the service of the theatre. A prime mover and lifelong supporter of British Actors' Equity, though not actively political, she was honoured by being appointed DBE in the New Year's list of 1946. She also received four degrees *honoris causa* from the universities of London (1950), Cambridge (1951), Oxford (1954), and Hull (1968). Walter Sickert [q.v.] painted her, Shaw flirted with her, playwrights queued to write for her, but she remained curiously untouched by fame and whenever she was not active in the theatre or the film studios, retired to her Elizabethan manor house in Kent, there to tend her garden, read, 'recharge my batteries', and watch football on television.

She was a Christian Scientist, a devout woman, a woman who frequently did good by stealth, and when she died she left the bulk of her considerable estate for the benefit of the Actors' Charitable Trust. James Agate [q.v.] wrote of her 'there has never been a more versatile actress' and indeed she had a way of acting that was unique in the annals of our theatre and must place her amongst the immortals. She said of herself 'I can't imagine going on when there are no more expectations' but she fulfilled those expectations to the very end of her days and died in harness. 'Marking ages', she said, 'is a sign of deterioration. Age has nothing to do with me.'

In 1925 Edith Evans married George ('Guy') Booth, whom she had known since she was sixteen. The marriage was childless and Booth died in 1935. Edith Evans died at her home in Kilndown, Kent, 14 October 1976.

[Bryan Forbes, *Ned's Girl*, 1977; J. C. Trewin, *Edith Evans*, 1954; Jean Batters, *Edith Evans*, 1977; personal knowledge.] BRYAN FORBES

EVANS-PRITCHARD, SIR EDWARD EVAN (1902–1973), social anthropologist, was born 21 September 1902 at Crowbridge, Sussex, the younger of two sons, the only children of the Revd Thomas John Evans-Pritchard, a Welsh-speaking Church of England clergyman from Caernarvon, and his wife, Dorothea, daughter of John Edwards, of Liverpool. 'Evans' came into the name from his maternal grandmother, daughter of Eyre Dixon Evans JP, merchant of Liverpool. He was educated at Winchester College (1916–21) and Exeter College, Oxford (1921–4), where he took a second class in modern history.

Though Evans-Pritchard never lost the values and sentiments of his upbringing, there was a non-conforming side to him, attracted to the unconventional, the Bohemian, even the raffish. When at Oxford he was a member of the privileged artistic coterie, the Hypocrites Club, and is described at that time by a fellow member, Anthony Powell, the novelist, as 'Evans-Pritchard the anthropologist, grave, withdrawn, somewhat exotic of dress'. In middle and later life, his conviviality, and sometimes mischievous humour, often concealed that deeper reclusiveness, while in dress he became notably careless, though formal enough for formal occasions.

At Exeter College, with anthropologist R. R. Marett [q.v.] as a fellow and later rector, Evans-Pritchard read works on primitive cultures by Sir Edward B. Tylor and Sir James G. Frazer [qq.v.]. The immense variety of the forms of social life they described, with all that remained to be discovered, caught his imagination; and—Celt as he was—people who held to their own customs and beliefs, in the face of powerful foreign interference, had his sympathy. In their direction he saw a future that would satisfy both his appetite for adventure and his intellectual curiosity. So it was that he chose an anthropological career, for which he was well endowed by physical stamina, self-reliance, sociability, and a subtle understanding of human relationships.

Since no teacher in Oxford then had experience of anthropological field-research, in 1923 he moved to the London School of Economics, where C. G. Seligman [q.v.] and B. Malinowski were gathering around them young anthropologists with aspirations similar to his own. Malinowski (though Evans-Pritchard came to dislike him personally and sometimes to depreciate his work) set an outstanding example of thorough field-research conducted through the native language. Seligman, who, with his wife B. Z. Seligman, had earlier made surveys in the (then Anglo-Egyptian) Sudan, arranged with the Sudan government for him to undertake more intensive research there. He chose eventually to study the Azande of the southern Sudan among whom he lived on and off between 1926 and 1930. With characteristic industry, in 1927 he gained the Ph.D. of the University of London for a preliminary thesis on them.

His first book, *Witchcraft, Oracles and Magic among the Azande* (1937), a brilliant analysis of Zande mystical belief and practices, implicitly raised general questions of the relationship between faith and reasoning, impressing not only the anthropologists but philosophers (for example, R. G. Collingwood and Michael Polanyi, qq.v.) and social historians (for example, Keith Thomas). In this book Evans-Pritchard already shows two characteristics of his own style of social anthropology; the development of general ideas through detailed ethnography rather than by abstract argument, and unusual insight into the intellectual and moral coherence of apparently disparate social phenomena. As in his other writings, sociological analysis never deprives the reader of a living and sympathetic impression of the people themselves. In later life, he regretted that, in their formalism, some of his successors in the subject were losing this touch, and making of the study of man what the scholastics had made of the study of God.

Between 1930 and 1940 he was a wandering scholar, with part-time lectureships in London and Oxford, and three years (1932–4) as professor of sociology at King Fuad I University in Cairo, where he began to learn Arabic. His field-research continued the while, mostly in the southern Sudan. In 1930 he started twelve months' difficult and interrupted work among the warlike, pastoral Nuer tribes of the Upper Nile swamps, where he arrived shortly after a government punitive expedition; but though, as he wrote, he 'entered [the Nuers'] cattle-camps not only as a stranger but as an enemy', he respected their recalcitrance and eventually gained their confidence. The research produced many articles and three books: *The Nuer, a Description of the Modes of Livelihood and Political Institutions of a Nilotic People* (1940); *Kinship and Marriage among the Nuer* (1951); and *Nuer Religion* (1956). The first provided a model for much subsequent anthropological analysis of political institutions, showing as it did the structural principles of political order among peoples without any centralized authority. *African Political Systems* (1940), a symposium which he co-edited with his friend Meyer Fortes, extended that discussion.

Nuer Religion (unusually, for a social anthropologist, written from an explicitly theistic viewpoint) again brought him readers among psychologists, theologians, and philosophers, and he was wryly pleased that the meaning of Nuer expressions should add to British philosophical speculations. Evans-Pritchard had become a Roman Catholic in 1944 and, though he was not, as some were led to suppose, a zealous convert, he advocated religious faith, for him an answer to his own inveterate scepticism. This religious stance, and his dismissive attitude to claims then being made for social anthropology as 'a natural science of society', raised controversy, and some polemic, among professional colleagues.

In 1939 Evans-Pritchard married Ioma Gladys, daughter of George Heaton-Nicholls, later South African high commissioner in London; they had three sons and two daughters. He was commissioned in the Sudan Defence Force in 1940, and for some time returned to the Sudan-Ethiopian border to fight against the Italians alongside irregular troops of the Anuak, whom he knew from his brief researches there in 1935 (published as *The Political System of the Anuak of the Anglo-Egyptian Sudan* in 1940). Later he spent some time among the Alawites in Syria, and ended the war as a political officer of the British administration among the Bedouin of Cyrenaica. His book *The Sanusi of Cyrenaica* (1949) shows the effect, on an acute anthropological observer, of close personal involvement in practical affairs. But though he never wished, as he wrote later, 'to become just, I almost said, an intellectual', and had many friends outside intellectual circles, he remained by temperament a scholar and in some measure a contemplative.

He was appointed reader in social anthropology in Cambridge in 1945, and professor of social anthropology in Oxford in 1946. There he built up a large and lively postgraduate school at the Institute of Social Anthropology. His energies, diverted from field-research, were then directed towards promoting and consolidating the position of his subject within the academic world and beyond it, as, for example, in his course of lectures for the BBC, published as *Social Anthropology* (1951). He was president of the Royal Anthropological Institute (1949–51), a founder and first life president of the Association of Social Anthropologists of the British Commonwealth, FBA (1956), foreign honorary member of the American Academy of Arts and Sciences (1958), and honorary fellow of the School of Oriental and African Studies (1963). Among other distinctions were honorary doctorates of the universities of Chicago (1967), Bristol (1969), and Manchester (1969) (in company there with the sculptor Henry Moore, and Lord Sieff, q.v., who became a friend). He was knighted in 1971 and became a chevalier of the Legion of Honour in 1972.

Meanwhile he continued to teach and to write prolifically (his bibliography has nearly 400 entries), co-edited the *Oxford Library of African Literature*, promoted the translation of French anthropological classics, and gave numerous foundation lectures. He retired in 1970 and died suddenly 11 September 1973 at his home in Oxford, The Ark, Jack Straw's Lane, where he had continued to bring up his family after his wife's early death in 1959. He never got over that loss, which is commemorated by a junior fellowship in her name at her Oxford college, St. Anne's.

Evans-Pritchard's international academic reputation, wide range of friendships, and sharp intelligence, at once pragmatic and intuitive, gave him a central position in his profession, and on his retirement he could not relinquish it. Even in his last few years, when intermittent illness, deafness, and a sometimes factitious, or nostalgic, conservatism, might have reduced his circle of friends or admirers, they remained with him, whether in All Souls College, or gathered regardless of age or status in his favourite Oxford pubs. Disarming though he was, he could make enemies; nevertheless, the many Festschriften and dedications in his honour affectionately acknowledge the debt so many owed to his example, encouragement, and personal generosity.

In ease of manner, literary and artistic taste, and love of the wild and the natural world, Evans-Pritchard preferred to remain in some ways an Edwardian country gentleman; but he had a free, inventive imagination uniquely his own, which undermined—and from within—the bastions of Edwardian prejudice alienating 'modern' from 'primitive' man.

[Personal knowledge.] R. G. LIENHARDT

EVILL, SIR DOUGLAS CLAUDE STRATHERN (1892–1971), air chief marshal, was born 8 October 1892 at Broken Hill, New South Wales, Australia, the only child of Frederick Claude Evill, general practitioner, of Barnet, Hertfordshire, and his wife, Sybella Strathern Murray, of Kingsclere, Hampshire. A first cousin of Air Chief Marshal Sir Arthur Longmore [q.v.], Evill always thought of him more as a brother.

Educated privately in Hertfordshire and from 1905 as a cadet at the Royal Naval Colleges at Osborne and Dartmouth, he excelled as a student. Despite his slight build, he was also good at all games, and from the beginning he was recognized as a natural leader. He was commissioned in May 1913, and while on leave in the summer of that year he stayed at Upavon with Longmore who was there as one of the naval instructors at the Central Flying School. Already more a thinker than merely a man of action, Evill took Longmore's advice and learned to fly at a civil school at Hendon. On 13 June 1913 he received the recognized aviator's certificate, but he failed in his repeated requests over the course of the next year for transfer to the Royal Naval Air Service, and at the time of the outbreak of World War I he was serving in destroyers. In December 1914, however, he was finally transferred to the RNAS.

Evill spent most of the war on operational flying in France, and in 1916 he was awarded the DSC. In 1919 he was granted a permanent commission in the Royal Air Force and awarded the AFC. Over the next four years he commanded early flying-boat bases, and attended the course at the Army Staff College; and in 1923 he went to Iraq to command No. 70 Squadron. Returning to England in 1925 he became, with promotion to wing commander, an instructor at the RAF Staff College. Four years later he was appointed assistant commandant of the RAF College, Cranwell, of which the commandant during part of his time there was Arthur Longmore. In 1932, with promotion to group captain, he was appointed assistant commandant of the RAF Staff College, and a year later he attended the course at the Imperial Defence College.

In 1934 Evill became deputy director of war organization at the Air Ministry. This led, after promotion to air commodore earlier in the year, to his being appointed in September 1936 senior air staff officer of Bomber Command. Two years later he became, with promotion to air vice-marshal, the air officer in charge of administration of the Command. In January 1937 he was a member of the important mission to Germany that was led by Air Vice-Marshal (Sir) Christopher Courtney [q.v.] on a tour of inspection of the new *Luftwaffe*. Just before the outbreak of World War II Evill was briefly the British air deputy on the staff of the Supreme War Council at the time when the views held by the French conflicted seriously with those of the RAF. In February 1940 he was appointed senior air staff officer of the ill-fated British Air Forces in France.

Immediately after the evacuation from France, and with appointment as CB (1940), Evill was appointed senior air staff officer to Air Chief Marshal Sir Hugh (later Lord) Dowding [q.v.], the air officer commanding-in-chief, Fighter Command. He served in this vitally important post during the whole of the Battle of Britain, the blitz, and the offensive fighter operations of 1941. In commenting on Evill's work—which was unique in operational command appointments—Dowding later stated: 'I could not have had a sounder or more reliable man supporting me. He was always there, always on the job, and always so pleasant in that quiet way of his.' As Dowding's right-hand man, Evill was all too well aware of the arguments that developed over fighter tactics towards the end of the Battle of Britain. He took it upon his shoulders as his duty to shield Dowding from the details of what he considered was unnecessary wrangling within the Command; and he was strongly critical of the intervention by the Air Ministry in what he described as a 'stupid controversy'. He was always of the opinion that the treatment that was accorded Dowding was 'deplorable'. Towards the end of his time at Fighter Command Evill suffered a grievous blow when one of his sons, only eighteen years of age, was killed while serving as a pilot in Bomber Command.

Early in 1942 Evill became, with promotion to air marshal, head of the RAF delegation in Washington, where he served until March 1943 when he returned, after being created KCB, to the United Kingdom on appointment as vice-chief of the air staff and additional member of the Air Council. He continued in this post for the remaining years of the war, becoming an air chief marshal with elevation to GBE in January 1946. A year later he retired from the RAF. He had by then received from the Americans the Legion of Merit (commander), from the French promotion to commandeur of the Legion of Honour which he had first received in 1917, from the Poles the

Order of Polonia Restituta, and from the Czechs the Order of the White Lion.

During the early years of his retirement Evill was active as honorary air commodore of No. 3617 (County of Hampshire) Fighter Control Unit, and as a member of the council of the King Edward VII's Hospital for Officers. For two years between 1947 and 1949 he was director-general of the English Speaking Union. But in later years he became afflicted with severe arthritis. He died at his home in Winchester 22 March 1971. At the memorial service for Evill, Air Chief Marshal Sir Donald Hardman concluded his address with the apt and touching comment: 'He was a very perfect gentle knight.' He was also a markedly devout man with, throughout his life, a pronounced sense of duty that led him to the placing of Service interests first, even before those of his family, in the ordering of that life.

In October 1920 Evill married Henrietta Hortense (died 1980), daughter of Sir Alexander Drake Kleinwort, Bt. They had three sons and two daughters.

There is a portrait of Evill painted by Thomas Dugdale in the Imperial War Museum.

[Information provided by the Air Historical Branch (RAF); *The Times*, 24 March 1971; private information; personal knowledge.]

ROBERT WRIGHT

EWER, WILLIAM NORMAN (1885–1977), journalist, was born at Hornsey 22 October 1885, the only son of William Thomas Ewer, silk merchant, and his wife, Julia Stone. Scholarships took Ewer to Merchant Taylors' and Trinity College, Cambridge, where in 1907 he took a middle first in the mathematical tripos—he was classed as fifteenth wrangler out of thirty-one. He won the Members' English prize in 1908 and in the same year took a first in part ii of the history tripos.

His eye was on the Civil Service but he became secretary to the future Liberal MP for West Ham, Baron M. A. de Forest, who used his Austrian title in Britain by royal licence, yet was a radical. Thus Ewer met George Lansbury [q.v.], MP for the adjoining constituency. In 1912 Lansbury became one of the founders of the *Daily Herald* and recruited Ewer as one of 'Lansbury's Lambs', a brilliant flock that included G. D. H. Cole, (Sir) Francis Meynell, Harold Laski [qq.v.], Gerald Gould, and William Mellor. The paper had no central policy; yet it was usually opposed to the official policy of the Labour movement, preached syndicalism, backed every strike, encouraged the suffragettes in their law-breaking militancy, and rejoiced over the two Russian revolutions.

In 1914 the *Herald* was reduced to a weekly for the duration of the war and in 1916 Ewer, a political conscientious objector (like several of his colleagues) was drafted to Cliveden to tend the pigs of W. W. (later Viscount) Astor [q.v.]. In 1919, when the *Herald* resumed daily publication, Ewer became foreign editor and went to the Paris peace conference. For the next thirty years he was to attend every great international conference. He was a bitter critic of the Versailles treaty; he exposed more than once the inadequacies of the blue book which described events in the days leading up to the war; and he told the Foreign Office on the day of its publication that the Zinoviev letter was a forgery.

When the *Herald* was taken over by the Trades Union Congress and the Labour Party in 1922 it lost much of its gaiety, *élan*, and incompetence. Most of the lambs wandered away but Ewer stayed on, although he was a member of the Communist Party and was to remain so until 1929. In that year he wrote an article for the communist *Labour Monthly*, an intellectual review of which he was joint founder. Ewer suggested that Anglo-Russian problems were not wholly ideological but derived also from the two countries' old rivalries as Asiatic powers. Next month, the editor, R. Palme Dutt [q.v.], who had been away, denounced Ewer's piece as being 'in glaring contradiction to the line of the *Labour Monthly* and of the revolutionary working class'. The political bureau also repudiated the article and Ewer was expelled from the party. He was to become eventually the holder of orthodox Labour views and a resolute anti-communist.

To generations of journalists Ewer was known as 'Trilby', a nickname given to him in youth because, like the heroine of George du Maurier [q.v.], he liked to go barefoot. Ewer is remembered for a laconic quatrain, famous throughout the English-speaking world. In the 1920s a guest at the Savage Club asked Benno Moisewitsch if there was any anti-Semitism in the club. 'Only among the Jews', the Jewish pianist answered and Ewer spontaneously murmured: 'How odd/Of God/To choose/The Jews'. *The Oxford Dictionary of Quotations* also gives the lines ending each stanza of his 'Five Souls' (1917), often recited at pacifist meetings: 'I gave my life for freedom—this I know:/For those who bade me fight had told me so.'

In his late seventies, as the doyen of diplomatic correspondents, Ewer remained an upright, sturdy figure, distinguished by his white head, sceptical, penetrating eye, and a well-modulated bass voice. His pieces for the *Herald* were models of clarity and concision and the BBC Overseas Service gave him frequent opportunities of expressing himself at adequate length. It was to the amiable Trilby that young journalists would turn to interpret for them the contrived circumlocutions of Foreign Office spokesmen and they found it hard to believe that this urbane and companionable man had once belonged to the far and fiery Left. When he was appointed CBE in 1959 stories were retold of the way he had rebuked Mussolini for an anti-British remark and silenced even Vishinsky at a Moscow press conference.

Ewer retired, aged seventy-nine, in 1964, as the *Herald* was transformed into the *Sun*. That same year he lost his wife Monica, whom he had married in 1912. She was daughter of William Marcus Thompson [q.v.], who had edited the radical *Reynolds's Newspaper*. She was to write fifty romantic novels and countless articles. They had one son, Denis William Ewer, who became professor of zoology at the University of Ghana and a fellow of the Royal Society of South Africa. Ewer died 25 January 1977 at Great Missenden.

[Information from William Forrest, Alan Wykes, and D. W. Ewer; *The Times*, 31 January and 7 February 1977; *Daily Herald* and *Daily Worker* clippings; Communist Party library and archive; George Lansbury, *The Miracle of Fleet Street*, 1925; Raymond Postgate, *The Life of George Lansbury*, 1951; Francis Williams, *Dangerous Estate*, 1957; personal knowledge.]

ARDWICK

EYSTON, GEORGE EDWARD THOMAS (1897–1979), racing motorist, was born at Bampton, Oxfordshire, 28 June 1897, the elder son and elder child of Edward Robert Joseph Eyston, gentleman, and his wife, Annie Maude Earle. He was educated at Stonyhurst and Trinity College, Cambridge, a process interrupted by the war of 1914–18. Commissioned as second lieutenant in the 3rd battalion, Dorset Regiment, he was transferred to the Royal Artillery where his mathematical and engineering skills could be put to better use.

He served in France throughout the war. He was wounded at the battle of Arras, became a staff captain, won the MC, and was twice mentioned in dispatches. After the armistice he resumed his engineering studies at Cambridge which he combined with an interest in rowing, being captain of the Trinity Boat Club and spare man to the Cambridge crew of 1919 which won the international eights in Paris.

In 1921 he returned to France to study the language and it was while holidaying with a French family near Le Mans that he was to discover his true *métier*: cars and speed. The American ace Ralph de Palma was testing a French Ballot racing car and Eyston decided that this was something he had to try.

Returning to England he bought a second-hand Sunbeam grand prix car and in 1922 stripped down and reconditioned a four-and-a-half litre Vauxhall to get experience of racing machinery. Although he was gaining practical engineering knowledge it was a meeting with Lionel Martin that really set Eyston on the road to racing and record-breaking success. Martin suggested that he should drive an Aston Martin at the 1923 Brooklands Whitsun meeting. 'The Captain', as he was generally known, won two races and was placed second in two others.

Eyston drove many marques of racing car including Bugatti in which he won the 1926 Boulogne Grand Prix, Monza Alfa Romeo, Maserati in sports car races, Bentley, and Riley. But the name of Eyston became linked with MG because of the number of races won and records set with those cars, from the early 1930s onwards. Eyston first achieved fame with his Magic Midget when he exceeded 100 miles per hour with a 750-cc car.

He then announced his intention of driving the 750-cc Midget for an hour at over 100 m.p.h. at the Monthlhéry circuit near Paris. At this period Eyston was spending half as much time in France on speed attempts as he was to spend later in America, and was known as 'Le Recordbreaker'.

He achieved the 750-cc 100 miles in the hour record but on the last lap of Monthlhéry the engine blew up and the car caught fire. With his clothing in flames Eyston had to jump for his life and was severely burnt. Undeterred, he started work from his hospital bed on an improved midget to achieve 120 m.p.h. with a 750-cc car. As a by-product, Eyston invented flameproof racing overalls and then, defying doctor's orders, left his bed to break the 120 m.p.h. record.

After having taken so many class records for long and short distances, Eyston realized that world records were also within his grasp and in 1932 he decided to attach the world hour record using the unlikely Panhard et Levassor 8-litre sleeve valve car. Heavy, old, and difficult to handle, this was by no means the ideal vehicle for the purpose but after a tyre burst Eyston succeeded in averaging 130.73 m.p.h. for the hour.

The thin tyres of the day were a major hazard in prolonged high-speed running and even Eyston's engineering skill could not overcome the danger. After the record was beaten at the Avus track in Berlin, he took it back in 1934 again with the old Panhard which he persuaded to run for an hour at 133.21 m.p.h. Many other records were achieved by Eyston in a great variety of marques including Riley, Hotchkiss, Delage, and diesel-engined cars which he designed and built himself. In fact he held more records than any driver before or since. A first-class engineer and designer as well as a thoughtful racing driver who achieved results by attention to detailed preparation, Eyston invented the Powerplus supercharger and a rudimentary disc brake. A steward of the Royal Automobile Club he was also for many years on the RAC technical and engineering committee.

Apart from the Magic Midget, the Eyston car which captured the public imagination was

Speed of the Wind which had a V12 Rolls-Royce Kestrel aero-engine. Extremely advanced for the 1930s the car had automatic transmission, front-wheel drive, and independent suspension. In July 1936 Eyston drove it 162 miles in an hour to take the world hour record.

Success with Speed of the Wind led to the design, again in collaboration with Ernest Eldridge, of Thunderbolt to attack the world land-speed record. A monster vehicle with two Rolls aero-engines and a total capacity of 56 litres, it had four front wheels and twin rear tyres. At his first attempt Eyston set a new record in 1937 at 312 m.p.h. His old friend and rival John Cobb [q.v.] then took the record, but Eyston beat him at 345.5 m.p.h. in 1938 and raised the speed later the same year to 357.5 m.p.h. Sadly neither Speed of the Wind nor Thunderbolt survived for honourable retirement in a motor museum. Both were destroyed, Speed of the Wind by a flying bomb in Eyston's Kilburn workshop and Thunderbolt in a fire during a visit to Australia and New Zealand. However, one of his engines is in the Science Museum in South Kensington.

During World War II Eyston was a regional controller for the Ministry of Production. After the war he became a director of Castrol but, feeling himself not fully qualified, he returned to Cambridge in 1950 to read geology. He also still took part in world and American sports car speed and distance records at Utah for both Austin-Healey and MG.

A well-built, quiet, bespectacled man, Eyston liked nothing better than to relax during delays in record-breaking attempts with a trout rod by a mountain stream. A devout Roman Catholic and descendant of Sir Thomas More, he was a member of the board of governors of the Oxford and Cambridge University chaplaincy and a papal chamberlain. In 1937 he was awarded the Segrave Trophy. The following year he became a chevalier of the French Legion of Honour. In 1948 he was appointed OBE. Modest to a fault, he sought records for his country rather than for himself. He never received the knighthood that many felt was his due.

In 1924 he married Olga Mary, the daughter of Edward Eyre, a banker with W. R. Grace & Co., of New York and London. They had two daughters. His diary still filled with engagements, Eyston died 11 June 1979 in a railway carriage between Winchester and London.

[George Eyston, *Flat Out*, 1933; George Eyston and Barre Lyndon, *Motor Racing and Record Breaking*, 1935; George Eyston and W. F. Bradley, *Speed on Salt*, 1936; private information.]

COLIN DRYDEN

F

FALLS, CYRIL BENTHAM (1888–1971), military historian and journalist, was born in Dublin 2 March 1888, the elder son in the family of three children of (Sir) Charles Fausset Falls, who represented Fermanagh and Tyrone at Westminster in 1924–9, and his wife, Clare, daughter of William Bentham, JP, of county Dublin. He was educated in England at Bradfield College and London University, in Ireland at Portora Royal School, Enniskillen, and on the Continent; but he remained a loyal Ulsterman throughout his life.

In 1914 he joined the 11th battalion of the Royal Inniskilling Fusiliers which formed part of the 36th (Ulster) division—a remarkable formation which had grown out of the paramilitary Ulster Volunteer Force raised by Sir Edward (later Lord) Carson [q.v.] to defend Ulster against home rule. Falls went to France with his battalion in 1915 and served on the western front for the remainder of the war; at regimental duty, on the staff of the 36th and later the 62nd divisions, and finally as liaison officer with the French, with the rank of captain; being twice mentioned in dispatches and twice cited for the croix de guerre. At the conclusion of the war he was employed to write the history of the 36th division, work which brought him into contact with the team writing the official history of the war for the historical section of the Committee of Imperial Defence. He joined that team in 1923 and remained with it until 1939, writing the official volumes on the Egyptian and Palestine campaigns (1928), on the Macedonian campaign (1933), and one volume on the campaign on the western front in 1917 (1940). A fluent and prolific writer and one deeply versed in English and French literature, he also published numerous articles and reviews which made his name familiar to the reading public at large. In 1939 he was the natural choice to succeed Captain (Sir) B. H. Liddell Hart [q.v.] as the military correspondent of *The Times*, a task he fulfilled throughout the war and until 1953 with great distinction. Falls's deep knowledge of military matters, his good contacts with senior military figures, and his balanced judgement made his comments on the course of the war widely appreciated by both military and civil readers.

After the war Falls was elected to the Chichele chair of the history of war in Oxford (which brought with it a fellowship of All Souls), a post he held from 1946 to 1953 and which enabled him, while lecturing on military history in general, to focus his researches on his first love and to write two works on Irish military history, *Elizabeth's Irish Wars* (1950) and *Mountjoy: Elizabethan General* (1955). After his retirement he continued to produce a stream of books of which perhaps the most notable was his *The First World War* (1960); while at the same time writing a weekly commentary on political affairs for the *Illustrated London News*.

Falls was a small, neat man who cultivated an elegant Edwardian moustache and took justifiable pride in his immaculate appearance. A somewhat dry manner concealed a wide range of historical and literary interests, and a deep humanity which found expression in all that he wrote. He attached great importance to conveying the realities of war as they were experienced by the men fighting it, and his *The History of the 36th (Ulster) Division* (1922) contains some of the finest descriptions of conditions on the western front to be found anywhere in the literature of the war. But he had no time for those historians who concentrated on the horrors of war to the exclusion of all else, and his critical study *War Books* (1930) set the anti-war literature in a balanced historical context. He never claimed to be making any major contribution to strategic thought, but he did much to improve the general understanding of the nature and problems of war in an age of rapid technological transition; and his historical works are notable for their solid knowledge, their good sense, and the distinction of their prose. He contributed several articles to this Dictionary.

He married, in 1915, Elizabeth, daughter of George Heath, farmer; they had two daughters. He was appointed CBE in 1967. Falls died at Walton on Thames 23 April 1971. A portrait photograph is in the possession of All Souls College, Oxford.

[*The Times*, 24 April 1971; private information; personal knowledge.] MICHAEL HOWARD

FARINGDON, second BARON (1902–1977), Labour politician. [See HENDERSON, (ALEXANDER) GAVIN.]

FARRELL, JAMES GORDON (1935–1979), novelist, was born 23 January 1935 at Liverpool, the second of the three sons (there were no daughters) of William Francis Farrell, accountant, of Liverpool, and his wife, (Prudence) Josephine, eldest daughter of Robert Gordon Russell, timber merchant, of Portlaoise, Ireland. He was educated at Rossall School and Brasenose College, Oxford, where he graduated BA with a third class in modern languages (French and Spanish) in 1960. At school he had been a distinguished games player as well as a notable contributor to the school magazine and it was after playing a game of rugby for Brasenose that he was suddenly taken ill with polio. He used the experience of being in an iron lung as the basis for his second novel, *The Lung* (1965). Only those who knew him well would have noticed that he was partly paralysed in one arm, though his hair turned prematurely white and he liked to suggest that the illness transformed him from a conventional public school 'hearty' into a writer.

After leaving Oxford Farrell spent a rather lonely and unhappy period teaching in Toulouse, where he wrote his first novel, *A Man from Elsewhere* (1963). In 1965 he went to the United States on a Harkness fellowship and his third novel, the last with a contemporary setting, was published in 1967 (*A Girl in the Head*). The American visit had little obvious effect on his writing, though it was on an island off New England that he first saw the ruined hotel which, transferred to Ireland, he used as the setting for *Troubles* (1970), winner of the Geoffrey Faber memorial prize of that year. *Troubles* was his first novel with an historical setting—Southern Ireland in 1919–21—which was also a family setting. His parents were Anglo-Irish and he had been brought up in Dublin. *The Siege of Krishnapur* (1973), which won the Booker prize that year, was based on the siege of Lucknow in the Indian mutiny and *The Singapore Grip* (1978) on the fall of Singapore in World War II. The family connections here were that his parents had married in India and lived there for some years before his birth and that his father had worked in Singapore before meeting his mother.

The common denominator in all his novels after the first was an ironic manner—which in the later books certainly owed something to Thomas Mann, though Stendhal, Malcolm Lowry, and Richard Hughes [q.v.] were earlier influences—and a rich vein of inventive fantasy. The disasters that befall Farrell's characters are ludicrous as well as horrific, comic as well as epic. Observed in long-shot his historical events have a grim dignity, but once he closes with the characters, absurdity tends to prevail. These middle-class imperialists at bay may deserve, because they are essentially innocent, to survive, or at least to be pitied for their experiences, but they also deserve, because they are arrogant, foolish, selfish, and greedy, to suffer and be laughed at. Yet the humour is seldom savage, probably because the events are seen mainly through the eyes of sympathetic, well-intentioned narrators (their doyen is the major in *Troubles* and *Singapore*), whose optimism buoys up the reader if not always the other characters.

The charm of Farrell's narrators came directly from himself. He had many friends and enjoyed being entertained by them or, after he had moved from a single room in Notting Hill to a tiny flat near Knightsbridge (he was unmarried), entertaining them in return. He taught himself to cook and spent part of his Booker prize on buying fine wines at auction, but his outstanding attribute as either host or guest was his self-deprecating, mock-gloomy manner of telling anecdotes. His social life, however, was strictly subordinate to his work as a novelist. He did almost no reviewing and was extremely hard-up until the last year of his life. When, finally, with the accumulating success of *Krishnapur* and *Singapore* and the advance on a new novel, provisionally called *The Hill Station* (published in its unfinished state in 1981), he had some money to spare, he spent it on a cottage beside Bantry Bay in Ireland. Four months after moving there he was drowned on 12 August 1979 while fishing from a rock. He left behind a sense of literary as well as personal loss, for remarkable as his novels are—certainly among the best of his generation—they promise more. His modesty about his own books was not an affectation but a measure of what he still hoped and intended to achieve.

[Private information; personal knowledge.]

JOHN SPURLING

FAULKNER, (ARTHUR) BRIAN (DEANE), BARON FAULKNER OF DOWNPATRICK (1921–1977), prime minister of Northern Ireland, was born at Helen's Bay, county Down, 18 February 1921, the elder son of a successful Belfast business man, James Alexander Faulkner, OBE, and his wife, Nora Lilian Deane. Although an Ulster Presbyterian, Faulkner like the sons of other professional families was educated partly in the south, attending the Anglican College of St. Columba at Rathfarnham, county Dublin, from 1935 to 1939. After he had spent one term at the Queen's University of Belfast World War II broke out and the eighteen-year-old Faulkner was needed to help manage the family shirt-making business, the Belfast Collar Company. He was appointed a director in 1941 and remained closely involved with its affairs until he resigned on becoming minister of commerce in 1963.

Faulkner joined the Orange Order in 1946, the first member of his family to do so. Then, while still active in business, he began to take an interest in politics as chairman of the newly formed Young Unionists. He entered the Parliament of Northern Ireland in 1949 as MP for East Down, a constituency which he represented without break until the Parliament at Stormont was prorogued by legislative act of the UK Parliament in 1972. A young man of energy and ambition could expect to make his way rapidly in the Unionist-dominated politics of the period, and by 1956 Faulkner had obtained ministerial office as government chief whip and parliamentary secretary to the Ministry of Finance. From then on his ascent was steady: in 1959 he became minister of home affairs and a privy councillor

(Northern Ireland), followed by six years between 1963 and 1969 as minister of commerce. Both at commerce, where he worked hard to attract overseas investment to the province, and later as minister of development from 1969 to 1971, where his responsibilities included housing, planning, new towns, local government, roads, and transport, Faulkner's keen interest in modernizing the economic structure of the province and increasing the opportunities for employment showed itself to good effect. The reshaping of local government in particular owed much to his persistence. While the economy of Northern Ireland was improving the political situation was deteriorating. Communal violence mounted, particularly on the streets of Belfast and Londonderry, and in August 1969 at the request of the government of Northern Ireland the home secretary, James Callaghan, authorized British troops to be brought in to aid the civil power. Although one of the most senior and experienced ministers, Faulkner was not at the centre of events in 1969, largely due to the animosity between him and the prime minister, Terence O'Neill. The clash arose from differences of character and personality as well as the handling of issues. O'Neill regarded Faulkner as ambitious and untrustworthy, while Faulkner questioned O'Neill's judgement and considered that his inclinations were leading in the direction of a closer association with the south than would prove acceptable to a majority of Protestant opinion in the north. Even when O'Neill finally lost the support of his party and resigned in April 1969 it was to James Chichester-Clark (later Lord Moyola), the minister of agriculture, that the Unionist Party turned rather than to Faulkner.

It was not until March 1971 that his chance finally came. In an atmosphere of mounting crisis Chichester-Clark stood down. In the hour of its greatest need the Unionist Party appointed Faulkner as its leader. His twelve months as prime minister saw sectarian violence reach its height. The near dormant IRA had revived and split into Official and Provisional wings which vied with each other in their claims to act as the self-appointed protectors of a beleaguered Catholic minority. Protestants were outraged at the apparent inability of the security forces to provide protection. With intimidation becoming widespread the demand for the reintroduction of internment without trial could no longer be resisted. Acting with the prior knowledge and consent of the British Cabinet, Faulkner authorized the arrest and detention of 337 men in the early hours of 9 August 1971. As he later recognized, he miscalculated the effect of internment on public opinion, both within Ulster and more widely in Britain, the Republic of Ireland, and the United States. In Northern Ireland itself, internment consolidated all sections of the Catholic community against him. Ironically, it was after the British government and Parliament had assumed the responsibility for the direct rule of Northern Ireland in March 1972 that Faulkner's evident political skill matured into statesmanship and he made his most constructive contribution towards the establishment of a new political order.

That the experiment of power-sharing failed could not be laid at Faulkner's door. Indeed had it not been for his negotiating ability at a lengthy series of talks held at Stormont Castle, Darlington, and Sunningdale, it is questionable whether the all-Party Northern Ireland Executive, and the directly elected Assembly to which it was answerable, would ever have come into existence. Yet in the process of reaching agreement between the parties, and in accepting the practical necessity for the new constitutional arrangements to be underwritten by the Republic of Ireland as well as by the UK government (the 'Irish Dimension'), his own position in the Unionist Party was fatally undermined. Only days after taking up office as chief executive on 1 January 1974 he resigned as leader of the Unionist Party following the rejection of the proposed Council of Ireland by the Unionist Party's 600-strong council. Since eighteen of the elected Unionist members of the Assembly continued to give him their support, as did the other two parties represented on the Executive, Faulkner still had a majority in the Assembly. But outside Stormont, Protestant opposition to the concept of sharing power, allied to acute apprehension over the proposed Council of Ireland, was gathering strength. On 16 May the Ulster Workers Council called a general strike and two weeks later the power-sharing Executive, the brightest hope for a more politically stable future, collapsed when Faulkner and his colleagues resigned on 30 May. There was no question of another administration being formed; it was clear to everyone that with Faulkner's fall the Assembly and the whole 1973–4 experiment was at an end.

The Constitutional Convention, an initiative of the Labour government which had inherited responsibility at Westminster following the British general election in February 1974, was no more successful when it met in 1975. In the elections to the Convention Faulkner's supporters, now organized as a separate Unionist Party of Northern Ireland, were decimated, securing only five seats out of a total of seventy-eight. Disillusioned about the past and deeply pessimistic as to the future, Faulkner announced his retirement from politics in 1976. The following year in the New Year honours he was created a life peer taking the title Baron Faulkner of Downpatrick. On 3 March 1977, a week after taking his seat in the House of Lords, Faulkner was killed in a hunting accident at Saintfield, county Down. He was fifty-six years old.

Brian Faulkner was a short man, neat in appearance and in his habits, and an energetic one. He went upstairs two at a time. His style was always brisk, sometimes veering towards the aggressive. A politician to his fingertips he was essentially a political manager, a doer rather than a talker. In this he was helped by being a lifelong teetotaller, like his strong-willed father before him, a habit which enabled him to avoid spending long hours with glass in hand in political dialogue. His misfortune was that when he finally achieved the one office to which he so patently aspired, that of prime minister of Northern Ireland, it was too late for him to have any real scope to exercise his skill in public administration, his flair for presentation, and his shrewdness in judging the public mood.

For all his ability Faulkner was never personally popular, either with his Unionist colleagues or with the public. Throughout his career, as he ruefully acknowledged in his memoirs, he had to face accusations of being overly ambitious and devious. In private life he kept to himself and his family in county Down. Horses and fox-hunting meant much to him. He was an expert horseman and bred his own pack of hounds; even during the worst of the troubles he continued to find his main relaxation in riding to hounds. He married in 1951 Lucy Barbara Ethel, only daughter of William John Forsythe, JP; they had two sons and a daughter. In 1978 his widow became BBC national governor for Northern Ireland. A portrait of Faulkner by the Ulster artist Raymond Piper, a gift from his former political colleagues, hangs in their home at Seaforde, county Down.

[Brian Faulkner, *Memoirs of a Statesman*, ed. John Houston, 1978; David Bleakley, *Faulkner: Conflict and Consent in Irish Politics*, 1974; *Sunday Times*, 6 March 1977; private information; personal knowledge.]

WINDLESHAM

FEATHER, NORMAN (1904–1978), nuclear physicist and pedagogue, was born in the schoolhouse at Pecket Well, Yorkshire, 16 November 1904, the eldest of the family of two sons and one daughter of Samson Feather, later headmaster of Holme primary school on Spalding moor, and his wife, Lucy Clayton, a teacher at the same school, which Feather himself attended. Siblings of both parents were also teachers, and Feather wrote, 'Teaching was in my blood'. A county minor scholarship took him to Bridlington Grammar School where he was influenced towards physics by a former pupil of Sir J. J. Thomson [q.v.], later master of Trinity College, Cambridge, where Feather went, supported by state, county, and college scholarships, in 1923. He obtained a first class in part i of the natural sciences tripos in 1925. In his finals year he spent much time on speculative research and gained only a second class in his part ii (1926) but in the same year he took a first in the London external B.Sc. and remained proud of this. He enjoyed examinations.

Feather began research in the Cavendish Laboratory in 1926 with (Sir) James Chadwick [q.v.] studying the ionizing tracks and the nuclear interactions of α-particles. A Trinity prize fellowship came in 1929. After a year at Johns Hopkins University in Baltimore Feather brought back some powerful radioactive sources which provided the α-particles that Chadwick used in 1932 to generate neutrons through their bombardment of beryllium. Feather confirmed Chadwick's discovery by observing the recoil of nitrogen under the impact of the neutrons and the disruption of the nitrogen nucleus with emission of a proton: the first neutron-induced disintegration. Study of the deuteron's photo-disintegration in 1937 provided an accurate value for the neutron's mass.

Feather submitted for his Ph.D. in 1930 and became a university demonstrator in 1933; in 1935 he accompanied Chadwick to Liverpool with the Leverhulme fellowship and lectureship. A university lectureship and a Trinity fellowship brought him back to Cambridge in 1936 where he began extensive studies of β-particles and nuclear isomerism.

During the war of 1939–45 Feather stayed in Cambridge as acting head of the Cavendish Laboratory and in general charge of the work there on nuclear fission. In 1940, with Egon Bretscher, he wrote a paper saying that the capture of slow neutrons by ^{238}U should result in the β-decay of the resultant ^{239}U to ^{239}Np, thence by further β-decay to ^{239}Pu which should fission more readily than ^{235}U so that this route to the atomic bomb would be more efficient than the difficult separation of ^{235}U from ^{238}U. The British nuclear effort was largely transferred to the United States and Canada in 1943, but Feather remained in charge in Cambridge, spending a few months in Montreal in 1944.

Feather went to Edinburgh as professor of natural philosophy in October 1945 and fostered teaching and research there at a time when both were at a low ebb. His own research remained in nuclear physics, chiefly in β-spectroscopy, nuclear masses, and stability rules.

Around 1960 Feather's interests moved towards pedagogical writing: *An Introduction to the Physics of Mass, Length and Time* (1959); *An Introduction to the Physics of Vibration and Waves* (1961); *Electricity and Matter: an Introductory Survey* (1968); *Matter and Motion* (1970). These works are personal, idiosyncratic, rich in historical sense, and written in a precise, unambiguous, yet convoluted style as though the unravelling of the sentence were held to be an improving exercise in its own right. He had earlier written two research texts: *An Introduction to Nuclear Physics* (1936) and *Nuclear Stability Rules* (1952) in a similarly personal style. Later he returned to research and published some twenty papers, chiefly on ternary fission and related matters, before and after his retirement in 1975, including three in the year of his death; for him life was inseparable from scholarship and research. To this Dictionary he contributed the notices of F. W. Aston and Richard Whiddington.

Norman Feather was an extremely proper person in behaviour, appearance, and dress; as strict in his moral principles as in his use of language, exemplified by his preaching in Trinity College chapel; a man of total integrity and commitment and of the greatest punctiliousness; reserved and yet humorous, kindly, helpful, and friendly. It was difficult to penetrate beyond his surface manner, yet one felt the essential humanity within.

Feather was elected FRS in 1945 and FRSE in 1946, became honorary LL D of the University of Edinburgh in 1975, and was awarded the Mackdougall Brisbane prize of the Royal Society of Edinburgh in 1970.

In June 1932 Feather married (Kathleen) Grace, daughter of Andrew Francis Burke, school teacher. The Feathers had a son and twin daughters. Feather died 14 August 1978 at the Christie Hospital, Manchester.

[W. Cochran and S. Devons in *Biographical Memoirs of Fellows of the Royal Society*, vol. xxvii, 1981; personal knowledge.]

DENYS WILKINSON

FEATHER, VICTOR GRAYSON HARDIE, BARON FEATHER (1908–1976), general secretary of the Trades Union Congress (TUC), was born 10 April 1908 in Bradford, the second of the three sons and four children of Harry Feather, a french polisher of Bradford, and his wife, Edith Mabel Bean, domestic servant.

Through almost the whole of his life Feather was active in trade unionism. When at fifteen his formal education was brought to an abrupt end by the necessity to take a job on the death of his father at the age of forty-two, he went to work in a grocery shop of the Co-operative Society in Bradford. At first he gave his spare time to the Independent Labour Party, learning the skills of public speaking at its open air meetings and of writing in the columns of its weekly paper. By 1931 his allegiance was to the Labour Party, where it was to remain, and his activities were increasingly in the distributive workers' trade union, in which he became branch chairman and divisional council member.

In 1937 Sir Walter (later Lord) Citrine, then TUC general secretary, selected him to fill the advertised post of assistant in the Organization Department of the TUC and there he developed his talents for administration and organization enthusiastically and resourcefully, while gaining his first major experience abroad by aiding the much divided Greek trade union movement towards unification. The TUC's governing body, the general council, in 1947 chose him to be assistant secretary, a newly created post. He enhanced his reputation as a trade union spokesman by an arduous programme of speaking engagements all over the country and lecture tours in the USA and South-east Asia. He helped settle a railway strike in Japan, had his first books published (*Trade Unions, True or False?*, 1951, and *How Do the Communists Work?*, 1953, both expressions of his antipathy to communist attempts to control trade unions) and took part in an official inquiry into the nation's information services overseas.

Promotion to the assistant general secretaryship of the TUC came in 1960 and his third book, *The Essence of Trade Unionism*, in 1963. He encouraged and guided amalgamations of unions, notably in shipbuilding, served on the royal commission on local government (1968–9), organized the celebration of the TUC's centenary in 1968, helped an official inquiry into the pay of postmen, continued in his untiring round of nation-wide platform appearances expounding TUC policy, presented the TUC's evidence to the royal commission on reform of the trade unions and employers' organizations, and still made time for his interests in the arts, abandoning his own painting to lend practical help to young artists.

In the absence in hospital of the TUC general secretary, George Woodcock [q.v.], he presented the general council's policy on major issues to the annual assembly of the Trades Union Congress in 1966. His success in this paved the way to his appointment as acting general secretary in 1969 when Woodcock resigned (to become chairman of the newly formed commission on industrial relations) and later in the year he was confirmed in the secretaryship by election at the annual Congress.

Meanwhile, he had led the TUC team in arduous negotiations with the Labour government of Harold Wilson (later Lord Wilson of Rievaulx), the outcome of which was the withdrawal of plans for anti-strike legislation in return for a TUC pledge to intervene in an unprecedented way in inter-union and unofficial industrial disputes. Feather showed prodigious energy and resourcefulness in keeping that pledge, making full use of his knowledge of trade unionism and its personalities.

At the same time he built a new reputation—as a broadcaster. As his television appearances became more frequent a national audience became appreciative of his earnestness and enthusiasm, and of the vigour of his argument supplemented by good humour and wit.

He needed these qualities when Edward Heath's Conservative administration, formed in 1970, secured the passing of the Industrial Relations Act despite the massive campaign against it initiated by the TUC and organized by Feather. The TUC then set out, under Feather's leadership, to make the Act inoperative without an unconstitutional challenge to the right of the government to legislate. The Act's main provisions—on the registration of unions, legally binding contracts, the closed shop, and compulsory ballots on strikes—were made ineffective by a policy of non-co-operation with which all but a few of the TUC unions, most of them small, complied.

Within the TUC itself Feather gave great encouragement to a process designed to give the trade union movement greater cohesion in policies and practices by fostering the formation of industrial committees, in which national representatives of unions in important groups of industries came together to agree on a common approach to their problems.

Feather's term of indefatigable activity as general secretary ended in September 1973 under the TUC's age-limit and he moved into an equally active retirement, serving for a year as the first president of the European Trade Union Confederation he had helped to found. He was made a life peer in January 1974 (having been appointed CBE in 1961), joined the Arts Council and the council of the Open University, became a governor of the BBC and vice-chairman of the British Waterways Board, and gave voluntary service to many other bodies. Three universities conferred doctorates on him: Bradford (1970), Manchester (1974), and the Open University (1974).

In 1930, he married Alice Helena Ferneyhough Ellison, and they had a daughter and a son. Feather died in London 28 July 1976.

[*The Times*, 29 July and 6 August 1976; TUC Annual Reports; Eric Silver, *Victor Feather, TUC*, 1973.] LIONEL MURRAY

FEDDEN, SIR (ALFRED HUBERT) ROY (1885–1973), engineer, was born in Bristol 6 June 1885, the youngest of three sons (there were no daughters) of Henry Fedden, sugar merchant of that city, of St. Mary's, Stoke Bishop, and his wife, Mary Elizabeth, daughter of the Revd Samuel Romilly Hall, also of Bristol. Fedden was educated at Clifton and the Merchant Venturers' Technical College in Bristol. In 1907 he went into the drawing office of the well-known automobile firm of Brazil Straker, and when only twenty-four years old he became their works manager and chief engineer. In 1914 he became the company's technical director.

His interest in motor cars, which in those early days he not only built but raced, never left him, but World War I changed the course of his engineering career. His factory turned to the manufacture of Rolls-Royce and Renault aircraft engines and during the rest of his life as a professional engineer, aircraft engines were his dominant interest.

In 1920 he joined the Bristol Aeroplane Company, where he stayed for twenty-two years as chief engineer of the aero-engine division which he had created, and which, under his leadership, produced one of the most remarkable series of machines in engineering history, the radial piston engines Mercury, Jupiter, Pegasus, Perseus, Taurus, Hercules, and Centaurus. These powered RAF aeroplanes such as the Bulldog, the Gladiator, the Wellesley, and the Wellington, as well as the HP 42 and the Empire Flying Boat of Imperial Airways. They were built under licence all over the world. In their development Fedden screwed more and more out of the radial configuration, making the vital move from the poppet-valve to the slide valve, and carrying the design to a degree of refinement which made it difficult to believe that, when he left the Bristol company in 1942 after a disagreement with the management, there was any more to be got from it. Moreover, by then the writing was on the wall for the aircraft piston engine, radial or otherwise: the gas turbine, in the development of which Fedden had played no part, had arrived, and it seems probable that there was no more fitting moment for him to end his work at Bristol. His achievement there was of the first magnitude, not only in technology but in determination and leadership, and his fame was world-wide.

From 1942 to 1945 Fedden was special adviser to the minister of aircraft production, Sir R. Stafford Cripps [q.v.], and was sent with a powerful team to North America to seek technology which might help the war effort. It was while studying American technical education that an idea first came to him which had consequences of major importance. As a result of Fedden's persuasion, Cripps set up an inter-departmental committee, under Fedden's chairmanship, to study the higher educational needs of the British aircraft industry. In October 1944 this produced what became known as the Fedden report. It recommended the creation of a postgraduate college of aeronautics, which came into being at Cranfield in 1946, with Fedden on the board of governors until 1969.

The college developed first as a major aviation establishment. In the late 1950s a policy of diversification began, leading to a strong and broadly based advanced engineering faculty, to a management school which has become one of the leading schools of its kind, and, in 1969, to the grant of a royal charter: the college became the Cranfield Institute of Technology, the only wholly postgraduate, post-experience, university in the country. Fedden was concerned with Cranfield from its first day to the end of his life. He supported it, he worked for it, he criticized it, he loved it. It is the embodiment of his vision.

After the war Fedden held a number of consultancies, notably as aeronautical adviser to NATO, 1951–2, followed by an association with the Dowty Group (1953–60).

He was an exacting man to work for. He demanded only the best and expected lesser mortals to possess the same physical and mental resources as himself. His views were convictions, firmly held and invariant. He was tireless in pursuing the ends he believed in. Whatever he did, he did with tremendous zest, whether at work or at play—and he did sometimes play. In his middle years he was an enthusiastic yachtsman, and he was a fisherman all his life.

Fedden was appointed MBE in 1920, was knighted in 1942, and was president of the Royal Aeronautical Society in 1938–40 and 1944–5. He received honorary doctorates from Bristol (1934) and from Cranfield, and was honoured by the aeronautical institutions of the USA and Germany as well as those of his own country.

In 1948 he married Norah Lilian, the third daughter of Edgar Crew of Clifton, and formerly wife of Air Chief Marshal Sir Arthur Sheridan Barratt. There were no children. Fedden died 21 November 1973 in his house, Buckland Old Mill, on the Usk at Bwlch.

There is a bronze portrait bust by Patricia Kahn in the library at Cranfield, and a portrait at the Royal Aeronautical Society.

[William T. Gunston, *By Jupiter! The Life of Sir Roy Fedden*, 1978; personal knowledge.]

KINGS NORTON

FEILING, SIR KEITH GRAHAME (1884–1977), historian, was born 7 September 1884 at Elms House, Leatherhead, the elder son (there were no daughters) of Ernest Feiling, stockbroker, and his wife, Joan Barbara Hawkins who was a sister of the novelist Anthony Hope (Sir Anthony Hope Hawkins, q.v.) and a first cousin of Kenneth Grahame [q.v.]. He was educated at Marlborough and Balliol College, Oxford. Starting in 1903 his undergraduate career was one of mounting success culminating in 1906 with a brilliant first class in modern history and a prize fellowship at All Souls College.

These successes pointed him towards an academic career. In 1907 he was appointed lecturer in history at the University of Toronto. In October 1909 he returned to Oxford as lecturer and tutor in modern history at Christ Church with the expectation of a Studentship (i.e. fellowship). In June 1911, his fellowship at All Souls having determined, he was duly elected a Student of Christ Church—a position he was to retain for the next thirty-five years. In December 1912 he married Caroline (died 1978), daughter of Dearman Janson, gentleman, to whom he was devoted for the rest of his life. (They were to have a family of two daughters and a son.) At that time marriage still required a Studentship to be vacated and reappointment to be sought. In Feiling's case reappointment was granted immediately, though not before a small minority of the governing body had voted to postpone it for a year. As a tutor before 1914 Feiling shared with his senior colleague, Arthur Hassall, the care of between thirty and thirty-six pupils. This was more than two tutors could properly sustain even in the somewhat relaxed atmosphere of pre-war Christ Church and at the end of 1913 a third tutor was appointed, (Sir) J. C. Masterman [q.v.]. Feiling wished to apply more positive tutorial methods than had hitherto obtained; Hassall dissented, telling Masterman that undergraduates should be encouraged to depend on themselves and deploring Feiling's 'rather too kind' approach. The war postponed the resolution of this difference.

In December 1914 Feiling was commissioned in the Black Watch. In 1916 he was posted to India, served for a year with his battalion, and then, in 1917, became secretary to the Central Recruiting Board of India. He held this post until early in 1919, being appointed OBE for his services in 1918. He was back at Christ Church for the summer term of 1919 and immediately threw himself into his teaching. Hassall, now in sight of retirement, yielded to his enthusiasm which Masterman shared. Together these two gave a new impetus to the Christ Church history school which, many years later, Masterman generously described as 'the creation of Keith Feiling'. For his part Feiling paid tribute to Masterman's 'system and staff work'. Both were right. Their complementary talents and sympathetic co-operation explain their outstanding success. Between 1921 and 1936, while Feiling was an active tutor, Christ Church historians won thirty-one first classes although it was no part of his teaching to emphasize the importance of the class list. For the first three years after his return Feiling taught some twenty pupils a term. At the same time he examined in the final schools, 1920–2, and served on the faculty board acting as its chairman in 1924–5.

Naturally this burden of teaching and administration interfered with his research; the appointment of a fourth history tutor in 1922 to teach the medieval period provided some easement and for one term that year he was allowed to halve his teaching—but at his own expense. These indulgences enabled him to complete his first big book, *A History of the Tory Party 1640–1714*, which was published in 1924. Three terms of sabbatical leave in 1927–8 led to his *British Foreign Policy 1660–1672*, which appeared in 1930, and in the same year he brought out his *Sketches in 19th Century Biography*, a collection of essays originally written for *The Times* and the *Times Literary Supplement*. These works earned him the degree of D.Litt. in 1932. His research interests were now moving towards the eighteenth century. When in 1931–2 he was appointed Ford's lecturer in English history—he had been a university lecturer since 1928—he took as his subject the 'Tories in Opposition and in Power 1714–1806' and these lectures were the foundation of his book *The Second Tory Party 1714–1832*, published in 1938. He also planned at this time to draw together his wide knowledge in a narrative *History of England*. This great project took twenty years to complete in spite of his giving up all undergraduate teaching in 1936 when Christ Church elected him to a research Studentship. He allowed himself to be diverted between 1932 and 1936 by helping (Sir) Winston Churchill first with his life of Marlborough and then with the first volume of his *History of the English-speaking Peoples*. Then when the war came he nobly returned to a period of teaching and examining between 1940 and 1943. Finally, at the particular request of the Chamberlain family, he turned aside to write *The Life of Neville Chamberlain*. Only when this was published in 1946 was he free to turn back to his projected *History*.

The year 1946 also saw his election to the Chichele chair of modern history which he held until his retirement in 1950 when his *History of England* finally appeared. His short tenure of his chair, to which he had been seen as the natural heir for many years, was the unfortunate result of his predecessor's longevity. In retirement his distinction was acknowledged at home and abroad by his election to an honorary studentship at Christ Church in 1952, by his knighthood in 1958, and by his becoming an honorary member of the Massachusetts Historical Society in 1958. Meanwhile he had continued to work on his life of *Warren Hastings*, first planned in 1946, which was awarded the James Tait Black memorial prize on its appearance in 1954. His last book, a charming collection of biographical essays entitled *In Christ Church Hall*, was published in 1960. He lived in retirement first in London, then in Norfolk, and for his last years in Gloucestershire. When well into his eighties he endured major abdominal surgery which he overcame with characteristic courage. He died in a nursing home in Putney 16 September 1977.

Neat and thoughtful in appearance, kindly and courteous in manner with a slight stammer which reinforced his charm, Keith Feiling has rightly been described as a cultured, well-informed, and liberal-minded man. The dedications of his books indicate his loyalties—to his wife, to his pupils, and to his friend and colleague in caring for those pupils, J. C. Masterman. He was exceptionally perceptive in his judgement of young scholars and in sustaining in their early days those who would later make their mark. As a writer his style was allusive, sometimes congested, but particularly in his essays and his *History* he wrote in a way that was clear, stimulating and, on occasions, moving. As a historian he was, as G. M. Trevelyan [q.v.] wrote of him, 'more interested in religious, political and constitutional issues than in the social and economic'. His outlook was that of a romantic Tory and a patriot. He was English to the core. Although he had founded the Oxford University Conservative Association in 1924 and was accepted as the leading historian of the Tory Party he was not politically partisan. He drew a distinction between Toryism and Conservatism, identifying more with the first than the second. Above all he was optimistic closing his inaugural lecture in 1947 with Robert E. Lee's moving words 'it is history that teaches us to hope'.

[*The Times*, 19 September 1977; *English Historical Review*, 1925; J. C. Masterman, *On the Chariot Wheel: an Autobiography*, 1975; Lord David Cecil, foreword to *Essays in British History* (ed. H. R. Trevor-Roper), 1964; H. R. Trevor-Roper, address in Christ Church Cathedral, 22 October 1977 (privately printed 1977); Christ Church archives; private information.]

CHARLES STUART

FERGUSSON, BERNARD EDWARD, first BARON BALLANTRAE (1911–1980), soldier, author, and public servant, was born in London 6 May 1911, the third son in the family of four sons and a daughter of (General) Sir Charles Fergusson, seventh baronet, of Kilkerran [q.v.], and his wife, Lady Alice Mary Boyle, second daughter of the seventh Earl of Glasgow. Educated at Eton and the Royal Military College, Sandhurst, in 1931 he was commissioned into the Black Watch: during a life of many loyalties and varied achievement, perhaps nothing gave him greater satisfaction than his appointment (1969–76) as colonel the Black Watch (Royal Highland Regiment). In 1935 he became aide-de-camp to the regiment's most distinguished representative, Major-General (later Field-Marshal Earl) Wavell [q.v.], whom he later served as staff officer in North

Africa and India and recalled in *Wavell: Portrait of a Soldier* (1961). He wrote the notice of Wavell for this Dictionary, as he did those of Thomas Inskip, Viscount Caldecote, and Sir Arthur Wauchope. He also published, in 1950, *The Black Watch and the King's Enemies*.

But Fergusson was never the typical regimental soldier. Though 'a bonny fechter', he was ardently unorthodox. Apart from a brief spell with his battalion outside Tobruk, preceded by service in Palestine (1937) and an instructorship at Sandhurst, he was selected for wartime duties of the most diverse character. In 1941 he was staff officer to General Sir James Marshall-Cornwall during his mission of liaison with the Turkish Army. For a while in 1942 he was GSO 1 Joint Plans, India. In 1945–6 he was director of Combined Operations (Military) and from 1946 to 1947 assistant inspector-general, Palestine Police. But it is for the part he played under Orde Wingate [q.v.] in operations behind the Japanese lines in Burma that he will be chiefly remembered.

Fergusson joined Wingate's embryonic Chindit group in October 1942 and trained with it for the first long-range penetration experiment (as it was assessed by the C-in-C, Wavell). Early in 1943 a number of independent columns, one under Fergusson's command, made their way by foot into Japanese territory, crossing both the Chindwin and the Irrawaddy. After much suffering and severe losses the remnants withdrew, having proved the viability of some of Wingate's techniques, particularly air supply, but achieved little beyond a boost to British morale. From Fergusson's column of 318 only 95 returned.

Nevertheless, when a special force of six brigades was assembled under Wingate for operations in 1944, Fergusson accepted command of the 16th brigade and with it a formidable commitment. Whereas other brigades in Operation Thursday were to be flown into the heart of Burma, Fergusson's task was to march southwards from General Stilwell's territory around Ledo on the Chinese border, over mountain ranges 8,500 ft. high and through some of the heaviest rainfall in the world. With extraordinary tenacity and ingenuity the brigade reached the edge of its objective, the airfields at Indaw in central Burma. But now, largely due to Wingate's unpredictable orders and counter-orders, everything fell apart. After a futile assault at Indaw 16th brigade was soon flown out to India: its sacrificial efforts were denied their due reward. Strongly though Fergusson always defended Wingate's military virtues, he was too clear-sighted to join the band of his unqualified hero-worshippers. The ghosts of those who had died unnecessarily kept him company. He described his experiences in *Beyond the Chindwin* (1945) and *The Wild Green Earth* (1946).

There is an extensive analysis of Wingate in Fergusson's engaging autobiography, *The Trumpet in the Hall* (1970), which also describes frankly another near-disaster. Post-war Palestine was a maelstrom: these were the days of the Hagana, the Stern Gang, and the Irgun Zwai Leumi. To further his counter-terrorist role within the police Fergusson recruited a small group of officers whose wartime experiences fitted the situation: including Roy Farran who, before he was twenty-three, had won two DSOs and three MCs. A young Jew mysteriously disappeared and Farran, accused of his murder, bolted. There was international uproar and Fergusson's neck was on the block. After anxious months he survived the courts martial and other enquiries, but he knew that his professional career had been within a hair's breadth of ruin. Instead, he was put in command of the 1st battalion, the Black Watch, in Germany. A period as colonel (Intelligence) at SHAPE in Paris, a brief appointment as director of psychological warfare during the Suez venture of 1956, and command of the 29th Infantry brigade at Dover completed an idiosyncratic record. Brigadier was perhaps his peacetime 'ceiling'.

After he had hung up his 'trumpet in the hall' Fergusson sailed calmer waters. Like his father, he was an outstanding governor-general of New Zealand (1962–7), where both his grandfathers had been governor. Since childhood, indeed, he had loved and known New Zealand intimately as the braes of Ayrshire. As lord high commissioner to the general assembly of the Church of Scotland he was equally at home: relishing ritual and ceremony, he was also a Christian of sure and tranquil faith. Chairman of the British Council from 1972 to 1976, he interpreted his responsibilities as global, travelling assiduously and revelling in his scope. A productive writer, he lived during his last years largely by his pen, excelling (like Wavell) in the tricky art of light verse.

Except for those moved by envy, or who mistook brio for froth, Fergusson's charm was irresistible. He and W. J. (later Viscount) Slim [q.v.] were the only 'limeys' accepted by the acidulous Stilwell. Bumptious, perhaps, in his youth—and with a proper ambition—he still lacked all the unattractive trimmings of the 'Scotsman on the make' of Sir James Barrie [q.v.]. As a friend he was sword-true. The New Zealanders—the Maori in particular—showed at his death that time and distance had not diminished their affection. He was the hero-figure John Buchan [q.v.] always just failed to capture in his novels, and he lived to the last on the principle of 'homo sum: humani nil a me alienum puto' . . . except the enemies of the realm.

Ballantrae died in London 28 November

1980, from a cancer whose earlier onset he had mastered with a cool, indifferent fortitude which, like his faith, enabled him also to absorb the tragic loss of his wife who, during a gale on their estate in 1979, was killed in a car accident as she sat beside him. He had married in 1950 Laura Margaret, younger daughter of Lieutenant-Colonel Arthur Morton Grenfell, DSO. They had one son.

Ballantrae was appointed OBE (1950), to the DSO (1943), GCMG (1962), and GCVO (1963). He was created KT (1974) and a life peer (1972). He was made honorary DCL of Canterbury (1965), D.Univ. of Waikato (1967), honorary LLD of Strathclyde (1971) and Dundee (1973), and honorary D.Litt. of St. Andrews (1974), of which university he became chancellor in 1973.

A portrait by Ruskin Spear is in the Black Watch headquarters and museum in Balhousie Castle, Perth. A presentation portrait of Ballantrae as governor-general is now in the possession of the New Zealand government.

[Bernard Fergusson, *The Trumpet in the Hall*, 1970; personal knowledge.] RONALD LEWIN

FERRYMAN, ERIC EDWARD MOCKLER- (1896–1978), soldier. [See MOCKLER-FERRYMAN.]

FESTING, SIR FRANCIS WOGAN (1902–1976), chief of the imperial general staff, was born in Dublin 28 August 1902, the only child of Brigadier-General Francis Leycester Festing, of Chalford, Gloucestershire, and his wife, Charlotte Katharine Grindall Festing, a second cousin. He was educated at Winchester where he displayed an independence of mind which continued throughout his career.

After leaving the Royal Military College at Sandhurst in 1921 'Frankie' Festing was commissioned in the Rifle Brigade. Thirteen years later he went to the Staff College at Camberley, where he became an instructor in 1938. It was clear to the students taught by him that he was a man who took a broad view, and who was not interested in unnecessary details—a man who would make his name as a commander rather than a staff officer.

On the outbreak of war in 1939 he was appointed to the command of the 2nd battalion of the East Lancashire Regiment. After serving in France and Norway during the difficult early battles when the Allies were confronted by far better-equipped Germans, he was given command of a brigade which made the assault landing in Madagascar in 1942, where he earned a reputation for leadership and indifference to danger. He was appointed to the DSO (1942) for his part in this operation.

In 1942 he was promoted major-general commanding the 36th division, which he led in the Arakan campaign in 1944. Later that year his division took over from the Chindits and fought their way through very difficult country to capture Maymyo, help clear Mandalay, and then advance to Rangoon. During all these operations he led his men from the front, even to the extent of taking over command of the leading unit when their commanding officer had been killed. During his service in the Far East he became a keen collector of rare Japanese swords, an interest which lasted the rest of his life.

In August 1945 he was appointed general officer commanding land forces Hong Kong. Early in 1946 he was posted to the War Office as director of weapons and development—an office job which did not suit his talent as an active commander of men. In 1949 he was again in Hong Kong, as commander of all British forces, but his appointment was cut short by illness and he was sent back to Britain as president of the Regular Commissions Board. In 1952, after a short spell in SHAPE, he became GOC British troops in Egypt. In 1954 he was appointed GOC Eastern Command in England with headquarters in Hounslow, a job which again did not suit his active military mind—and in 1956 he returned to the Far East as commander-in-chief Far East land forces, with the rank of general.

In 1958 he succeeded Field-Marshal Sir Gerald Templer [q.v.] as chief of the imperial general staff. His main task was to put into effect the measures laid down in the defence white paper of the previous year, one of which was to reduce the size of the army to 165,000 men. He insisted that the number of men proposed was not adequate to meet Great Britain's military commitments and largely due to his influence it was increased to 180,000. Festing did not like being confined to an office dealing with politics and politicians and those responsible for briefing him had a difficult time.

In 1960 Festing was promoted to the rank of field-marshal, and in 1961 he retired from the army. He went to live in his family home in his beloved Northumberland, taking with him his collection of Japanese swords, which by then had become one of the most well-known private collections in the world.

Festing was at his best and happiest as an inspiring commander. The details of office work, the confines of Whitehall, the conventions of dressing in the correct uniform, and the restrictions of being precisely on time for his appointments were not to his taste. Soldiering was to him training and leading men. Beneath his bluff and cheerful outlook on life lay a strong religious belief. He had been converted to the Roman Catholic faith as a schoolboy and it had a great effect on his character, which was an unusual combination of religious humility and personal confidence. Festing was appointed CBE (1945), CB (1946), KBE (1952), KCB (1956), and GCB (1957). He received an honorary DCL from the University of Newcastle (1964).

In 1937 Festing married Mary Cecilia, daughter of Cuthbert David Giffard Riddell, of Swinburne Castle, Northumberland. They had four sons. Festing died 3 August 1976 at his home Birks, Tarset, Hexham, Northumberland.

[*The Times*, 5 August 1976; personal knowledge.] JOHN COWLEY

FIELDEN, SIR EDWARD HEDLEY (1903–1976), air vice-marshal, was born at Bracknell, Berkshire, 4 December 1903, the elder son (there were no daughters) of Edward Fielden, a surgeon, and his wife, Maud Jennie Armstrong. At Malvern College, where he joined the Officers' Training Corps, he was a keen motor cyclist and took part in several London–Exeter runs. At twenty-one he obtained a short-service commission in the RAF.

His ability as a pilot and his perfectionism in all things mechanical were soon recognized and in 1926 he was posted to the meteorological flight at Duxford. There he showed himself to be 'keen, very quick, full of commonsense and reliable . . . an excellent officer in every way'.

In 1929, when the five years of his commission were up, he was awarded the AFC, and was transferred to the reserve of officers as a flight lieutenant. He was then appointed private pilot to the Rt. Hon. Frederick Guest and shortly after this the air-minded Prince of Wales, who had just acquired a Gipsy Moth biplane—the first of a long line of royal aircraft—chose him as his personal pilot. In the 1932 King's Cup race Fielden flew a Comper Swift racing monoplane entered by the Prince of Wales and narrowly missed first place.

In 1933 came his appointment as chief air pilot and extra equerry, and in 1936 it was Fielden who flew the Prince, as Edward VIII, from Sandringham to London on the day of his accession. A few months later a radical innovation in the Royal Household was announced: the King's Flight had been established, with Fielden as its captain. When George VI came to the throne he maintained the King's Flight under Fielden's captaincy.

Fielden had remained in the reserve (he was promoted wing commander in 1936, when he was also appointed MVO) but early in the war he returned to active service in the RAF and in 1942 he formed and took command of No. 161 Squadron, which was to undertake many hazardous sorties in support of the resistance movements in Europe. He himself carried out and then directed many of these flights, and in 1943 he was awarded the DFC. He continued with this highly secret work until the end of 1944, having become commanding officer of RAF Tempsford. Early in 1945 he was appointed commander of the base at Woodhall Spa with the rank of air commodore, and then became deputy senior air staff officer at Transport Command headquarters. Before he left the RAF in 1946 he was appointed CB, and he was also decorated by the French.

Soon after this the King's Flight was reformed at Benson and expanded as a unit of Transport Command. Fielden was again its captain. His devoted services to the Royal Family had already been acknowledged by his promotion to CVO in 1943, and in 1952, on the accession of Queen Elizabeth, when his unit became the Queen's Flight, he was created KCVO.

In 1962 he relinquished his appointment as captain of the Queen's Flight, but at the same time he was appointed senior air equerry and promoted air vice-marshal. He was promoted GCVO in 1968 and retired as senior air equerry in 1969.

Throughout his forty years of service as a member of the Royal Household his supreme aim had been to assure safe and timely air travel for the royal family. He had always avoided the limelight, and this preference for being quietly in the background accounted for his nickname 'Mouse'. With his neat, spare frame and bright, vital air, Fielden was very much a traditionalist—in style, clothes, choice of friends, choice of words. By temperament an autocrat, stubborn and obstinate, he was nevertheless unassuming in manner, always courteous and often witty and amusing. His endearing charm along with his zest and sense of fun and his contagious enthusiasm enabled him to get on with everyone and he was loved and respected by young and old alike, not least by the members of the royal family.

Fielden relished outdoor life: he was an excellent shot and in his later years a keen fisherman. His wife shared in his enthusiasm for outdoor sport. In 1940 he had married Mary Angela Ramsden Jodrell, daughter of Lt.-Col. Henry Ramsden Jodrell, CMG, of Taxal, Cheshire. They had one son and one daughter. Their son was killed in a tragic motor-racing accident at Silverstone in 1963. After Fielden's retirement he and his wife moved from their Berkshire farm to the Scottish borders and he died in Edinburgh 8 November 1976.

[Ministry of Defence, Air Historical Branch; *The Times*, 9 November 1976; private information.] CONSTANCE BABINGTON SMITH

FIELDS, DAME GRACIE (1898–1979), music-hall artiste and film star, was born Grace Stansfield in Rochdale, Lancashire, 9 January 1898, the eldest of four children (three daughters and a son) of Fred Stansfield, engineer, and his wife,

Sarah Jane Bamford. Her education, at Rochdale Parish School, was disrupted by her mother's attempts to put her on the stage, and ceased when she was thirteen. It was at this time that she changed her name to Gracie Fields.

Her stage career began with singing competitions, brief appearances at local music halls, and membership of various juvenile troupes, but in 1913, when she was fifteen, she became a member of a touring music-hall company, and began a full-time career as a singer and *comédienne.* In 1916, Archie Pitt, another member of the company, broke away to form a company to perform his own revues, and invited Gracie Fields to be his leading lady. She toured with Pitt for eight years, acquiring a tremendous depth of experience in all aspects of music-hall and revue work. She was naturally versatile, and Pitt worked hard to exploit her many talents—dancing, singing, mimicry, acting, improvisation—and to reinforce in her that dedication to her work and to the show which her mother had instilled in her at an early age. Archie Pitt exercised an almost complete control over Gracie's life, and in 1923 they married—an arrangement of convenience on both sides. Pitt (a stage name) was the son of Morris Selinger. There were no children of the marriage.

In 1924 Pitt's company, which had been touring continuously since 1916, was invited to stage its current revue, 'Mr Tower of London' in the West End. This was the company's first exposure to the London critics, and the production was widely acclaimed. Gracie Fields found that she had become a star, literally overnight.

Her fame spread rapidly—she became known to millions as 'Our Gracie'—and soon she was in demand everywhere. As well as starring in Pitt's revues, she also performed in cabaret after each nightly show, and made records during the day. Pitt guided her career and used her vast earnings to create a lifestyle of luxury and display which Gracie Fields, always a simple Lancashire girl at heart, neither desired nor enjoyed. Their marriage, which had never been a close one, deteriorated further, but although by 1931 separation was imminent, the professional partnership flourished, and Pitt seized the opportunity to launch Gracie Fields into the most recent development in popular entertainment—film-making.

In this new venture Gracie Fields was instantly successful with the film *Sally in our Alley* (which included the famous song). The plots of the early films were weak, and the direction poor, but in spite of this the public flocked to see them. In 1935 Monty Banks (Mario Bianchi), an Italian director, was brought in, the quality of the films improved, and in 1938 Gracie Fields began to make films in Hollywood, with a contract which made her the best paid film star in the world.

In 1939 Gracie Fields underwent major surgery for cancer, and it is a measure of her popularity at this time that prayers were said for her in the churches, and newspapers and radio carried daily bulletins. She made a complete recovery, but the outbreak of war a few months later led to an event in her life which overnight changed public adulation into almost universal condemnation.

In 1938 Gracie had agreed to marry Monty Banks, and in 1940 she followed him into voluntary exile in America (Banks's Italian nationality meant that he ran the risk of internment if he remained in Britain) and, after a divorce from Archie Pitt in 1940 (the year in which he died) they were married there the same year. The popular press immediately accused Gracie Fields of deserting Britain in its moment of need, and of taking her wealth with her. Although the accusations were unfounded, her reputation was tainted for many years: her dedicated work for ENSA throughout the war did little to redeem her in the eyes of the British public.

After the war, Gracie Fields settled at her home in Capri. She was gradually taken back into the favour of the British, and she returned home periodically to record and give concerts. In 1950 Monty Banks died, and in 1952 she married Boris Alperovici (died 1983), a Bessarabian radio engineer living in Capri. With him she at last found real contentment and she led a peaceful life in Capri. She had no children.

Gracie Fields's career cannot be fully appreciated without recognizing that her roots lay in the music hall, where she received her training and formulated her act. When the music halls died, and she progressed to films, records, and variety work, it was the grounding in the music hall which gave her the strength and the ability to project herself, which was the key to her success. The great talent which she undoubtedly had, combined with her excellent training and her dedication to her work meant that, whatever the medium, she could win her audience and allow them to share a memorable experience.

On stage she was exceptionally versatile, her only prop a headscarf, held in her hand during romantic or sentimental songs, but tied over her head for the comic Lancashire songs which had made her famous. Even her voice changed according to the song—her lovely, clear singing voice became in the comic songs coarse and raucous. Her hold over her audience was so great that she could move in a moment from a comic to a religious song, and change laughter into tears. Only Gracie Fields could offer 'The Lord's Prayer' and 'Ave Maria' alongside 'The Biggest Aspidistra' and, 'Walter, Walter, lead me to the Altar'.

In her personal life, Gracie Fields never allowed her success to affect her. She remained open, affectionate, home-loving, generous with both time and money, and with a deep religious faith. She gave thousands of pounds to charity and in 1935 endowed and maintained the Gracie Fields Orphanage at Peacehaven, Sussex. She was also very humble—and touchingly unsure of herself when meeting other stars, almost unable to believe their respect for her.

Gracie Fields was appointed CBE in 1938 and DBE in 1979. In 1937 she received the freedom of Rochdale. She made over 500 records and fifteen films and she appeared in eleven Royal Variety performances. Her portrait, by Sir James Gunn, hangs in Rochdale Art Gallery.

She died in Capri 27 September 1979.

[Gracie Fields, *Sing As We Go* (autobiography), 1960; private information; personal knowledge.] ELIZABETH POLLITT

FILDES, SIR PAUL GORDON (1882–1971), microbiologist, was born in Kensington, London, 10 February 1882, the third of six children and second of four sons of Sir (Samuel) Luke Fildes KCVO, RA [q.v.], painter, and his wife Fanny, daughter of William Woods, of Warrington. He was educated at Winchester (1895–1900) and at Trinity College, Cambridge, where, perhaps because of recurrent illness, he gained only a third class in part i of the natural sciences tripos (1904). In 1904 he entered the London Hospital Medical College, where he soon found that his interests inclined towards pathology; in his fourth student year he started helping William Bulloch [q.v.], the professor of pathology, and soon after graduating MB, B.Ch. in 1909 was appointed as assistant to Bulloch, a post that he held, interrupted only by the war years, until 1933.

Fildes assisted Bulloch in an extensive review of haemophilia, but his main interest soon switched to syphilis, and in collaboration with James McIntosh he conducted a clinical trial of Salvarsan (606), the arsenical chemotherapeutic agent recently discovered by Paul Erhlich. To conduct the trial was a considerable achievement, since many of the clinicians thought it unethical. With McIntosh, Fildes worked on the standardization of the diagnostic test for syphilis, the Wassermann reaction, and he also demonstrated the need to use water free from bacterial pyrogens for injection of the Salvarsan.

Early in the war of 1914–18 he and McIntosh invented the method still used for cultivating strictly anaerobic bacteria in a glass jar (the 'McIntosh and Fildes jar') from which all oxygen could be removed by the use of a palladium asbestos catalyst. For most of the war years Fildes worked at the Royal Naval Hospital at Haslar, first as a civilian and from 1917 as surgeon lieutenant-commander, RNVR; he studied alleged dysentery in men returning from Gallipoli and meningococcal meningitis.

In 1919 Fildes returned to the London Hospital, still as assistant pathologist, and took up the study of the bacterium *Haemophilus influenzae*, then thought to be the cause of the influenza that had raged through the world in 1918–19. For the cultivation of the bacterium, Fildes used a peptic digest of sheep blood (still known as 'Fildes digest'). His conclusion on the relevance of *Haemophilus influenzae* to epidemic influenza was mistaken but it was his interest in this microbe that led him into the field in which he made his most important contributions to microbiology, namely bacterial nutrition and metabolism. He devised chemically defined culture media for various pathogenic bacteria, and in doing so recognized that different species had needs for particular growth factors. He also showed that the bacilli of tetanus were able to grow and produce their toxin only in wounds in which the oxidation-reduction potential was reduced, either by the presence of soil or, in the experimental animal, calcium salts.

In 1934, on Fildes' suggestion, the Medical Research Council established a unit for bacterial chemistry to be housed in the Middlesex Hospital Medical School, where McIntosh was now the professor of pathology. In this unit Fildes gathered a group of microbiologists who, with Marjory Stephenson [q.v.] at Cambridge, laid the foundations of the science of chemical microbiology.

Early in the war of 1939–45, Fildes became concerned about the possibility of bacterial warfare, and saw the need for experimental work to assess its potential and to devise protective measures. With characteristic bluntness, he persuaded the Medical Research Council, reluctant to become associated with such work, to second him to the Chemical Warfare Experimental Station at Porton Down; there he remained as a civilian in a military establishment for the rest of the war. He was joined by several members of his unit and by D. W. W. Henderson [q.v.]; together they laid the foundations of what became, after the war, a major centre for research into the pathogenesis of microbial disease and the mechanisms of airborne infection. Fildes continued as an active adviser, and later father figure, to the Microbiological Research Establishment for many years.

The MRC chemical bacteriology unit was reconstituted in 1946, at the Lister Institute, but Fildes retired from it in 1949; he did not, however, give up laboratory work but moved to the laboratory at Oxford run by H. W. (later Lord) Florey [q.v.], where for the next fifteen years he studied the factors that enable bacterial viruses—bacteriophages—to be adsorbed to bacterial cells. Even when, in 1964 at the age of eighty-two, he returned to London, he started research into his family, especially his great-grandmother, Mary Fildes, who had been president of the Female Radical Reformers of Manchester.

Fildes was appointed OBE (1919) for his work in the war of 1914–18, elected FRS in 1934, and knighted in 1946. He received an honorary Sc.D. from Cambridge (1948) and Reading (1959) and was awarded the Royal medal of the Royal Society in 1953 and the Copley medal in 1963.

In 1920, with three colleagues, Fildes founded the independent *British Journal of Experimental Pathology*, which he edited for many years. The *Journal* was converted into a limited company in 1939, with Fildes as its president until 1966.

Fildes gave the outward appearance of uncompromising reserve: he had a remarkably expressionless face and a slow deliberate voice, even when angry; but behind the mask was a great sense of humour and capacity for companionship. He was held in great respect by his colleagues and was assiduous in ensuring that their work was fully acknowledged. Fildes never married; he was a very skilful cabinet maker, a keen philatelist, and an excellent photographer, and he enjoyed a wide range of cultural and artistic activities.

Fildes died in London 5 February 1971.

[G. P. Gladstone, B. C. J. G. Knight, and G. S. Wilson in *Biographical Memoirs of Fellows of the Royal Society*, vol. xix, 1973; *The Times*, 6 February 1971; private information, personal knowledge.] R. E. O. WILLIAMS

FISHER, GEOFFREY FRANCIS, BARON FISHER OF LAMBETH (1887–1972), archbishop of Canterbury, was born 5 May 1887, the youngest of the ten children (of whom three girls and four boys survived) of the Revd Henry Fisher and his wife, Katherine Richmond. His father was curate and then rector of Higham-on-the-Hill in the county of Leicester for forty years. His grandfather and great-grandfather had been rectors of the parish for similar periods of time, and this long country parson background may well have accounted for Geoffrey's own love of the countryside. He was educated at Marlborough which he entered as a foundation scholar in 1900. During his years there he came under the influence of the headmaster, (Sir) Frank Fletcher [q.v.], a talented teacher who encouraged his pupils to think for themselves. Fisher did well at school in games and in work. He became senior prefect, a position in which he showed the qualities of courage and firmness which were much in evidence all through his life.

From Marlborough he went to Exeter College, Oxford, on a scholarship in 1906. He became president of the junior common room, captain of boats, and was given his colours for rugby. He attended chapel services regularly and shared in many of the activities connected with them. Of Fisher's deep Christian convictions there seems to have been no doubt at this or indeed at any time in his life. He gained first classes in classical honour moderations (1908), *literae humaniores* (1910), and theology (1911).

After Oxford he was offered a teaching post at Marlborough by Frank Fletcher. He remained there for three years during which time he was ordained. He went to Wells Theological College in the long vacation of 1911, was ordained deacon in 1912, and priest in 1913. The following year he was encouraged to apply for the headmastership of Repton, vacant through the resignation of William Temple [q.v.], who later became archbishop of Canterbury. He was elected and took up the appointment in June 1914 at the age of twenty-seven. This was a difficult time for any headmaster as it was within weeks of the outbreak of World War I. One problem which Fisher faced immediately was that a number of masters and senior boys had left to join the forces. A fresh timetable had to be drawn up, and this was done very effectively by the new headmaster. Another problem was that of discipline, which had become somewhat lax under the otherwise remarkable headmastership of William Temple. The problem proved to be short-lived, for Fisher was a born disciplinarian who achieved his ends by acting quickly, firmly, and when necessary with severity.

In 1917 Fisher married Rosamond Chevallier, daughter of the Revd Arthur Francis Emilius Forman, a former master at Repton, and granddaughter of S. A. Pears [q.v.], a former headmaster of the school. She was the ninth of fourteen children, and her marriage to Fisher marked the beginning of a happy, loving, and close-knit family life. There were six sons of the marriage, each of whom achieved distinction in his particular sphere.

Fisher's years as headmaster were successful both from the administrative and pastoral points of view, but he felt that after eighteen years he had been there long enough. He would gladly have moved to a parish in the country, but there were other plans for him. When he was offered the bishopric of Chester, he accepted and was consecrated in York Minster on 21 September 1932. The new bishop succeeded the greatly loved Luke Paget, and their difference in churchmanship proved to be no obstacle to the affection and regard each had for the other. Fisher set about his new work energetically and with a kind of all-embracing good humour. He was from all accounts very popular with clergy and laity alike, though he could be on occasions somewhat dictatorial. Among his chief qualities were his sense of humour, his imperturbability, his resilience, and his astonishing physical stamina. Short and sturdy in build, he seemed to exude energy and strength. For example, he always drove himself to institutions in the diocese, and when the service was over he joined in the festivities in the parish hall with the greatest enthusiasm. He loved meeting people, and it was the informal friendliness of his approach which won their respect and affection wherever he went both at home and abroad. His appointment as bishop of Chester brought him into close contact for the first time with convocation and the church assembly. He enjoyed taking the chair at meetings and was an admirable chairman though, as he said himself, he was apt to talk too much. His predecessor when once asked how he survived the ordeal of taking the chair at meetings of the assembly for the inside of a week three times a year humorously replied 'By prolonged bouts of deliberate inattention'. Fisher was never inattentive. His first big task in the diocese was an Industrial Christian Fellowship Mission. This involved him speaking in the evenings in the slums of Birkenhead. He accepted the unaccustomed task with that genuine humility of spirit which was reflected in so many of his activities. The seven years at Chester were happy ones for both the Fishers. As mother of six growing boys Rosamond Fisher had plenty to do at home but also took her full share in the life of the diocese, becoming president of the Diocesan Mothers' Union and later its central president.

In 1939 Fisher was called upon to succeed Arthur Foley Winnington-Ingram [q.v.], who had been bishop of London since 1901. He had no wish to leave Chester, but London provided a fresh challenge which he faced with cheerfulness and confidence. There seemed little cause for either for World War II had broken out by the time of Fisher's enthronement in November 1939. Mass evacuation was causing immense problems, and in September 1940 the nightly bombing of London began. The diocese itself had its own problems, chiefly those of church order and ecclesiastical discipline, and because of the war there was also a shortage of clergy, disorganization of parish life, and destruction on a vast scale of churches and other buildings. Yet in the words of Bertram Simpson, suffragan bishop of Kensington and afterward bishop of Southwark, Fisher 'left London a much more orderly diocese than he found it'. One of his major contributions was the setting up of the metropolitan area reconstruction committee which included all the churches, the Salvation Army, the Quakers, and the Jews, and which dealt directly with the Ministry of Works. He was also chairman of the churches' main war damage committee, which gave invaluable help to the war damage commission. Another important development which began in Fisher's time was the amalgamation of Queen Anne's Bounty with the ecclesiastical commission to form the Church Commissioners for England. A further concern of Fisher's was his association with the Sword of the Spirit movement founded in August 1940 by Cardinal Hinsley [q.v.], archbishop of Westminster. He became chairman of a joint committee, the aim of which was to promote co-operation between the Roman Catholic and other churches.

In 1944 an event occurred which profoundly affected Fisher's future. William Temple died suddenly and unexpectedly. Fisher knew that his was one of the names that had been mentioned as a possible successor, and he was aware of Temple's hope that he would succeed him. The prospect did not alarm him unduly; he was not easily frightened, but he had no wish to leave London or the people he had learned to love. After some delay, however, the choice was made, and on 2 January 1945 his appointment was announced. Shortly afterwards in a BBC broadcast Henry Montgomery-Campbell, later bishop of London, laid special stress on the new archbishop's pastoral gifts. He predicted that Fisher would still remain at heart the true pastor he had always shown himself to be. And so it was. But he had many other gifts. He was a born organizer; he revelled in administrative details, and it came as no surprise that one of the first tasks to which he set his mind was the revision of the canon law of the church. Unrevised since 1604 there was much clarifying and modernizing to be done. Fisher approached this monumental task with enthusiasm. He once described it as 'the most absorbing and all-embracing' topic of his life.

The archbishop was also deeply involved in the political and social issues of the day. He had important and often controversial things to say on matters as various as the Suez crisis, the law in relation to homosexuality, marriage, discipline, lotteries, and premium bonds (to which he was strongly opposed), and the Wolfenden committee report which dealt with such moral problems as the practice of human artificial insemination.

One of the greatest national events in the years of his archiepiscopate was the coronation of Queen Elizabeth II in Westminster Abbey on 2 June 1953. Fisher was at his best on such an occasion. He conducted the ceremony with dignity and with an almost fatherly concern for the welfare of the young Queen. He succeeded in creating a person-to-person relationship with the monarch which was obvious to those who were present at the service. This was equally true of his relationship with other members of the royal family. He once said on this topic, 'I who am no courtier by nature at all found myself at ease with them.' They were equally at ease with him. It was the same, though the circumstances were very different, in his relationship with successive prime ministers, Sir Winston Churchill, Harold Macmillan (later the Earl of Stockton), Anthony Eden (later the Earl of Avon), Clement (later

Earl) Attlee, and other members of the government. He preferred the direct personal approach to people, though he was never afraid to express his views in public debate. So it was with the press, with whom his relations were reputed to be bad. He was quite prepared to criticise the press in public if he thought it was abusing its freedom, but he normally got on very well with individual reporters.

Fisher's relations with the other churches and their leaders were always cordial. He was one of the presidents of the World Council of Churches (1946–54). His own initiative in drawing together the Church of England and the Free Churches will always be associated with the sermon he preached in Cambridge on 3 November 1946. During the course of it he pleaded for a free and unfettered exchange of life in worship and sacrament between the churches; he suggested that as a step towards full communion the Free Churches should 'take episcopacy into their own system'. In a notable passage towards the end he posed the crucial question, 'Cannot we grow to full communion with each other before we start to write a constitution?' The response was immediate. Discussions took place between the Church of England and the Free Churches over the next five years, and in 1958 the Methodist Church declared its 'readiness to proceed to a further stage in the promotion of intercommunion with the Church of England' subject to being given certain assurances. Although the conversations ended in breakdown in 1963, Fisher continued to show a lively interest in this as in all schemes for reunion.

Fisher's archiepiscopate will, however, be remembered chiefly for the number of journeys which he took to various parts of the Anglican communion and beyond. He was by far the most widely travelled archbishop of Canterbury in Anglican history, as, with the advent of the television camera, he was far the best known by sight. Between 1946 and 1960 he visited the United States and Canada several times, and in 1950 he and his wife went to New Zealand and Australia. In 1951 he visited West Africa; in 1955 Central Africa; in 1959 India, Japan, Korea; in 1960 Nigeria for its independence day celebrations, and East Africa. The visits to West, Central, and East Africa had as their chief purpose the inauguration of new provinces. All the new provinces of the Anglican communion which came into existence after World War II, and in addition the jurisdiction of the archbishopric in Jerusalem and the East Asian episcopal conference belong to his archiepiscopate. As Edward Carpenter wrote in his *Cantuar* (1971), 'Wisely, he appreciated the need to divest himself of authority for the African and Asian areas of the Communion, and it is probably here that historians will see his most enduring work.' In 1960, at the age of seventy-three, Fisher embarked on his final journey. In his own words, 'The actual idea came to me all in one flash. I was in my study . . . thinking about one thing and another, and suddenly there came, as a single inspiration, Jerusalem, Istanbul, Rome.'

The grand climax of the tour was the visit to Pope John XXIII. It was the first time an archbishop of Canterbury had visited the Holy See since Thomas Arundel [q.v.] made his journey in 1397. 'We talked', wrote Fisher, 'as two happy people, who had seen a good deal of the world and of life, and of the Churches.' In speaking o the Pope he said: 'We are each now running on parallel courses; we are looking forward, until, in God's good time, our two courses approximate and meet.' After a moment's hesitation the Pope replied: 'You are right.' The courtesy call, which was all Fisher claimed it to have been, was nevertheless a historic occasion, a significant breakthrough, and a triumphant conclusion to the tour. Fisher arrived back in England on 3 December, and on 17 January 1961 the announcement of his resignation came from Downing Street. He was appointed to a life peerage at the same time. He had been sworn of the Privy Council in 1939 and appointed GCVO in 1953. After a number of moves the Fishers went to live in Trent rectory near Sherborne in Dorset. Acting as assistant curate, Fisher ministered on Sundays in Trent and neighbouring churches with obvious content until his death in hospital in Sherborne 15 September 1972. He was buried in the churchyard at Trent.

Fisher received honorary degrees from Cambridge, Princeton, Pennsylvania, and Colombia (all 1946), London (1948), Manchester (1950), Edinburgh (1953), Yale (1954), British Columbia (1954), Northwestern University Evanston (1954), Gen. Theol. Sem. New York (1957), Trinity College Dublin (1961), and Assumption University of Windsor, Ontario (1962). He was prelate of the Order of St. John of Jerusalem (1946–67). He was awarded the Royal Victorian chain (1949) and became a freeman of the cities of London and Canterbury (1952) and of Croydon (1961).

The official portrait (1953) by Middleton Todd is in Lambeth Palace.

[W. E. Purcell, *Fisher of Lambeth*, 1969; Edward Carpenter, *Cantuar*, 1971; personal knowledge.] IAN H. WHITE-THOMSON

FITZALAN-HOWARD, BERNARD MARMADUKE, DUKE OF NORFOLK (1908–1975), Earl Marshal and Hereditary Marshal of England. [See HOWARD.]

FLANDERS, ALLAN DAVID (1910–1973), authority on industrial relations, was born 27 July

1910 in London, the only child of Frederick William Flanders, shop manager, and his wife, Emily Louisa Shaw. Unusually for that time, he passed school certificate at a central school and was transferred to the Latymer School, Hammersmith, a grammar school where he began to work for a university scholarship. However, a growing interest in politics brought him to the tiny British section of a small German organization, the Internationaler Sozialistischer Kampfbund, which emphasized the ethical basis of its socialism, and he spent two years at the latter's residential college near Kassel, the Walkemühle. When Hitler's rise to power appeared inevitable, he was sent back to England to help the British group keep the ISK's teaching alive.

The group survived and grew, to merge into Socialist Union in 1950. It established and sustained a journal, *Socialist Vanguard*, which later became *Socialist Commentary*. Meanwhile Flanders worked at a range of jobs from colliery labourer to door-to-door salesman, ending up as a draughtsman in Sheffield and an active trade unionist. In 1943 he was appointed a research assistant in the economic department of the TUC and shared in the preparation of the TUC's *Interim Report on Post-War Reconstruction* (1944) which provided the blueprint for the domestic policies of the 1945 Labour Government. In 1946 his knowledge of German and the German labour movement led to his appointment as head of the political branch of the British Control Commission in Germany. Next came a Whitney Foundation fellowship to study unions in the United States; and in 1949 he was appointed to the newly established post of senior lecturer in industrial relations at Oxford. He lacked formal academic qualifications, but with his varied experience and mastery of the Socratic method acquired at the Walkemühle he was well prepared for the post.

Thereafter he remained the leading figure in the Socialist Union until it was dissolved in 1959, and chairman of the editorial board of *Socialist Commentary*, which became the leading exponent of Social Democratic ideas within the Labour Party. But after his appointment at Oxford the chief claims on his time and energies were the development of industrial relations as an academic subject, and the formulation of policies for the reform of British industrial relations.

He began with an introductory text, *Trade Unions* (1952), which has been periodically reprinted ever since. Later he set about a general theory of trade unionism, approaching it through an inquiry into union growth. Although this ultimately led to a major research project at Warwick University, at the time he found the task greater than he had expected, and in 1960 turned with relief to a case study of the first famous plant productivity agreement which appeared as *The Fawley Productivity Agreements* (1964). It provided the keys to both theory and reform. Theoretically Fawley showed that in plant industrial relations, as Flanders had already found in union growth, the structure of collective bargaining was the main explanatory factor; and that, in Britain, the structure of collective bargaining was largely determined by management. The lesson for reform was that, for management control of production to be effective, collective bargaining must be acknowledged to include the organization of work as well as pay and conditions of employment, especially at plant level. If ever there was an 'Oxford school of industrial relations', as critics of Flanders and his colleagues asserted, he was its theorist and these were its tenets. The essays in which he developed his ideas were collected together in *Management and Unions* (1970). His work was acknowledged by election to a fellowship at Nuffield College in 1964 and a visiting professorship at Manchester University in 1969. He was appointed CBE in 1971.

Opportunity to apply what he had learned came in 1965 when he became industrial relations adviser to the National Board for Prices and Incomes, in whose reports productivity bargaining figured prominently; and when he was appointed in 1969 to the Commission on Industrial Relations whose creation owed much to his influential evidence to the royal commission on trade unions and employers' associations (1965–8), chaired by Lord Donovan. At the CIR Flanders was especially responsible for the early investigations into plant industrial relations. It seemed that he might play a major part in the reconstruction of British industrial relations. However, in the summer of 1970 he contracted a severe paraplegic disease, and in any case he would not have wished to continue at the CIR once the Conservative Industrial Relations Act became law. In 1971 he recovered sufficiently to take up a readership in industrial relations at Warwick University, but the improvement was temporary, and he died at Edinburgh 29 September 1973, being survived by his wife.

In 1951 he married Annemarie Klara Laura, daughter of Walter Tracinski, a general practitioner. She was formerly a Labour Court judge in Berlin; they had no children.

[*The Times*, 2 October 1973; private information; personal knowledge.] HUGH CLEGG

FLANDERS, MICHAEL HENRY (1922–1975), actor, lyricist, and dramatic author, was the eldest of three children and the only son of Peter Henry Flanders and his wife, Rosa Laura ('Laurie') O'Beirne. He was born in Hampstead, London, 1 March 1922. His father had followed various occupations, including that of cinema manager; his mother was a professional musician. Flanders was educated at Westminster School, where he was one of a remarkable theatrical quartet—himself, Donald Swann, Peter Ustinov, and Peter Brook—but to anyone who remarked that the school performances must have been something to see, he explained that drama had been somewhat frowned upon apart from the annual Latin play, so that apart from Swann, the only accomplished Latinist among them, the rest had been little more than spear-carriers. In 1940 he went to Christ Church, Oxford, to read history. There he both acted and directed for the OUDS and the Experimental Theatre Club, playing among other roles Brabantio in *Othello*, Pirandello's Henry IV, in which he achieved a notable success, and Shawcross in *The Ascent of F6*. He also wrote witty drama criticisms for *Cherwell* and made his first professional appearance on the stage, in October 1941, at the Oxford Playhouse as Valentine in *You Never Can Tell*. A lean and long-striding six feet three, a fine oarsman and quarter-miler, he was by far the outstanding actor of his generation. With his height, athleticism, thin, handsome face, deep intelligence, and splendid voice, he was formidably equipped.

He left Oxford to join the RNVR, and in 1943 contracted poliomyelitis, which condemned him to spend the rest of his life in a wheelchair. His application to return to Christ Church to continue his studies was refused, something which he had difficulty in forgiving, and for the best part of a decade he was a sad figure, arranging small musical evenings at his parents' home with other amateur instrumentalists, including Gerard Hoffnung. Occasionally he took small parts in radio plays. None of his friends was prepared for the extraordinary career he was to carve out for himself after the age of thirty.

In 1951 the impresario Laurier Lister commissioned him to write songs and lyrics for a revue, *Penny Plain*. These were acclaimed, as were his contributions to Lister's subsequent revue, *Airs on a Shoestring*, in 1953. The same year he wrote the libretti for two operas, *Three's Company* and *A Christmas Story*; then, in 1954, he translated, with Kitty Black, Stravinsky's *The Soldier's Tale* for the Edinburgh Festival. In 1956 he collaborated with Donald Swann, who had written much of the music for the two previous Lister revues, in a third, *Fresh Airs*. They then decided to write a show between them which they would perform together, mainly comprising songs they had written which nobody had wanted to sing. The result was *At the Drop of a Hat*, which opened on 31 December 1956 for a fortnight's run at a small fringe theatre, the New Lindsey in Kensington. It was the first time either of them had appeared professionally on stage apart from Flanders's Valentine at Oxford. *At the Drop of a Hat* was so enthusiastically received that it transferred immediately to the Fortune Theatre, where it ran for no less than 759 performances. In October 1959 they took it to Broadway, where it was equally successful, and they toured it widely through the United States and Canada during 1960–1. The combination of Flanders's genial yet caustic lyrics and Swann's witty and tuneful music, and the contrast between Flanders's robust exuberance and the prim appearance of Swann, exerted a seemingly universal appeal.

In 1962 Flanders appeared at the Aldwych Theatre, still of course in his wheelchair, as the story-teller in the Royal Shakespeare Company's production of Brecht's *The Caucasian Chalk Circle*. He and Swann toured the United Kingdom and Eire in 1962–3 with *At the Drop of a Hat*; then in October 1963 they appeared at the Haymarket Theatre, London, in *At the Drop of Another Hat*, which proved as successful as its predecessor. They toured a combined version of the two 'Hat' programmes through Australia, New Zealand, and Hong Kong, then reopened *At the Drop of Another Hat* at the Globe Theatre, London. In 1968 Flanders appeared at the Queen Elizabeth Hall, London, as the narrator in *The Soldier's Tale*, and in 1970 at the Mayfair Theatre in a revue, *Ten Years Hard*. In 1969 he wrote the libretto for a cantata by Joseph Horowitz, *Captain Noah and his Floating Zoo*, which proved almost as popular as the 'Hat' shows. He was often seen on television, on the concert platform in such works as *Façade* and *Peter and the Wolf*, and especially enjoyed working on radio, in feature, documentary, and music programmes. He also appeared in several films, notably *The Raging Moon* (1970).

Flanders was one of the most popular stage personalities of his time, both with audiences and with his fellow professionals. Like the great music-hall comics, he had the rare talent of making every member of an audience feel that he was addressing him or her personally, and with his fine speaking voice he was a master of the aside. He was one of the few great lyric writers that the theatre has known, arguably the best since Sir W. S. Gilbert [q.v.]. His disability caused him much pain and sleeplessness, which he bore with fortitude and humour; far from exploiting it, he sought to persuade audiences to forget it, though outside the theatre he was tireless in championing the cause of disabled people. He developed unexpected skills from his chair: gardening (for which he invented ingenious implements, such as an apple corer wired on to a long stick for weeding), bar billiards, table tennis, and certain kinds of cooking. He was the warmest and wittiest of companions. He was appointed OBE in 1964.

In 1959 he married Claudia, the daughter of the journalist Claud Cockburn and stepdaughter of Robert Gorham Davis, professor of English at

Columbia University, New York. There were two daughters of the marriage, which was very happy. On 15 April 1975 he died suddenly of a cerebral haemorrhage while on holiday at Betws-y-Coed in Wales. His ashes were scattered in the grounds of Chiswick House, London, where he had loved to sit on fine afternoons.

[*Who's Who in the Theatre*; private information; personal knowledge.] MICHAEL MEYER

FLEMING, (ROBERT) PETER (1907–1971), writer and traveller, was born 31 May 1907 at 27 Green Street, Park Lane, London, the eldest of the four sons of Valentine Fleming, later Conservative member of Parliament for South Oxfordshire, and his wife, Evelyn Beatrice Ste. Croix, daughter of George Alfred Ste. Croix Rose, JP, of the Red House, Sonning, Berkshire. His grandfather Robert Fleming, starting penniless in Dundee, had come to London and made a fortune in the City.

Peter's childhood was clouded by a mysterious and incapacitating illness, which left him without sense of taste or smell, but he recovered in time to be an outstanding success at Eton. Although outdistanced in athletics by his younger brother Ian [q.v.] he became a member of Pop, editor of the school magazine, and finally captain of the Oppidans. Most of his lifelong friends were made at Eton. At Christ Church, Oxford, he was equally successful—as president of the OUDS, a member of the Bullingdon Club, and editor of *Isis*. He obtained first class honours in English in 1929.

Valentine Fleming had been killed in action in 1917 and Peter's family decided that he, the senior male heir, should carry on the flourishing family business, but a few months' apprenticeship in the New York office convinced him that his life's work lay elsewhere. After a shooting expedition on the slopes of a volcano in Guatemala he came home, and in the spring of 1931 joined, as assistant literary editor, the staff of the *Spectator*, with which he was to be associated for most of his life. Some months later he got leave to attend a conference of the Institute of Pacific Relations, and so obtained his first experience of Russia, the Trans-Siberian railway, and especially China, where he was always to feel at home.

In April 1932 he answered an advertisement in the agony column of *The Times*, which led him to take part in a crack-brained and amateurish expedition to the hinterland of Brazil, ostensibly to look for Colonel P. H. Fawcett, a missing explorer. Fleming persuaded *The Times* to appoint him their unpaid special correspondent. This mixture of farce, excitement, discomfort, and danger achieved nothing except to provide him with the subject-matter for his first book, *Brazilian Adventure*, published in August 1933. In it he blew sky-high the excessive reverence and solemnity with which travel books had hitherto been treated, mocking the dangers and himself with infectious humour. People could not believe that a story of true adventure could be so funny, and the book had immense success at home and in America.

In June 1933 he set out on his second journey to China, again as special correspondent of *The Times*, to report on the war against Communists and bandits. After reaching Mukden in Manchuria and taking part in a sortie against bandits, he travelled south, achieving an interview with Chiang Kai-Shek, the commander-in-chief of the Nationalist forces, penetrating into Communist-held territory, and finally returning home via Japan and the United States.

Again the excursion furnished him with the material for a bestseller, *One's Company*, published in August 1934. 'One reads Fleming,' wrote Vita Sackville-West [q.v.], 'for literary delight and for the pleasure of meeting an Elizabethan spirit allied to a modern mind.'

At the end of August he once again set off for the Far East with a far-ranging commission from *The Times*. After a brief shooting trip with friends in the Caucasus he travelled on to Harbin in Manchuria, where he by chance met the Swiss traveller Ella (Kini) Maillart. It transpired that they both wanted to walk and ride from China to India, and though they both preferred to travel alone, they agreed to join forces. This epic journey of some 3,500 miles on foot or ponies, through the forbidden province of Sinkiang, with many dangers, hardships, and hold-ups, took them seven months, from February to September 1935. This, the most arduous of Fleming's long journeys, he chronicled in fourteen long articles in *The Times* and later in his book *News from Tartary* (1936).

In December 1935 he married the actress Celia Johnson. She was the daughter of John Robert Johnson, MRCS, LRCP. Their son Nichol was born in 1939, their daughters Kate and Lucy in 1946 and 1947.

In 1936 Fleming joined the staff of *The Times*, having declined the offer of J. L. Garvin [q.v.] of the editorship of the *Observer*. The editor of *The Times*, Geoffrey Dawson [q.v.], was anxious that Fleming should eventually succeed him, but Fleming's interest in politics was minimal, and the idea was gradually dropped.

In March 1938, taking Celia with him, he made his fourth journey to China, to report on the Sino-Japanese war and on the completion of the Burma Road, the only remaining access to China from the west.

On the outbreak of war in September 1939 Fleming immediately joined the Grenadier Guards, on whose Special Reserve he had served for many years. In March 1940 during a week of German measles he wrote a short and very amusing fantasy of Hitler landing accidentally in England by parachute, with uproarious consequences. *The Flying Visit* was published in July, and when, less than a year later, Rudolf Hess arrived in Scotland by air, Fleming's joke began to look like prophecy.

His one desire now was to see active service with his regiment, but for almost the whole war he was seconded to various intelligence and other jobs all over the world—first in Norway with (Sir) Adrian Carton de Wiart [q.v.], then training a post-invasion force of guerrillas in Kent, then in Cairo with Sir A. P. (later Earl) Wavell [q.v.], then in Greece, from which he was lucky to escape alive. Next he ran a street-fighting course in London until Wavell, now commander-in-chief in the south-west Pacific, summoned him to India and appointed him head of Deception. From 1942 to 1945 he shuttled between Delhi and the Chinese capital at Chungking, besides making an unauthorized and almost disastrous glider flight into Burma with the Chindits under Orde Wingate [q.v.]. After the Japanese surrender in 1945 he returned to civilian life as a full colonel having been appointed OBE.

Now, with his desire to travel satisfied, he settled down to the life of a literary squire at Merrimoles, the house he had built just before the war, near his grandparents' old home at Nettlebed in Oxfordshire, and in the middle of a 2,000-acre estate which his uncle had given him. People had always imagined he was wealthy, but owing to muddled wills he never in fact had any money of his own except an allowance from his mother, until his books and journalism began to provide him with an adequate income.

He continued to write amusing fourth leaders for *The Times*, and for many years contributed a column signed 'Strix' to the *Spectator*. Then he found a new role as an extremely competent amateur historian. *Invasion 1940*, a clever analysis of Hitler's plans for the conquest of Britain and our counter-measures, published in 1957, was a great success on both sides of the Atlantic and earned him more than any of his other books. There followed *The Siege at Peking* (1959), an account of the Boxer rebellion in 1900; *Bayonets to Lhasa* (1961) on the 1903–4 expedition of (Sir) Francis Younghusband [q.v.]; and *The Fate of Admiral Kolchak* (1963), concerning the White Russian commander in Siberia. At the time of his death he was engaged on the official history of strategic deception in World War II, which, but for several years of official obstruction, he would have had time to complete.

Apart from these major works, his essays from the *Spectator* and elsewhere were published in five volumes: *Variety* (1933), *My Aunt's Rhinoceros* (1956), *With the Guards to Mexico!* (1957), *The Gower Street Poltergeist* (1958), and *Goodbye to the Bombay Bowler* (1961).

Fleming was slim, medium-tall, black-haired, very good-looking and attractive. He habitually smoked a pipe. Shooting, at which he excelled, was the passion of his life, and he was at his happiest on long solitary patrols of his own acres with a gun and one of his beloved dogs. On every available day he walked or rode for miles. Every autumn he went to Scotland for a shooting holiday.

His persistent shyness with strangers was sometimes mistaken for arrogance: he was at his ease with contemporaries and old friends; those who served under him in peace and war would do anything for him; and he had a special relationship with men of his father's age—Carton de Wiart, Wavell, Geoffrey Dawson—to whom perhaps this dashing young man brought memories of their own youth. He was a man of courage and imagination, a faithful and generous friend. His literary style was compounded of clarity, a large vocabulary, and his own brand of incongruous and often self-deprecatory humour.

He died at Black Mount, Argyllshire, 18 August 1971, in exactly the way he would have chosen—a glorious summer's day, a grouse shoot on his beloved Scottish moors, a right-and-left, an instantaneous heart attack. He is buried at Nettlebed. A portrait in oils by John Ward and two pencil drawings by Augustus John are owned by his family.

[Duff Hart-Davis, *Peter Fleming: a Biography*, 1974; Fleming's own writings; personal knowledge.] RUPERT HART-DAVIS

FOOT, SIR DINGLE MACKINTOSH (1905–1978), politician and lawyer, was born at Plymouth 24 August 1905, the eldest of the five sons (there were also two daughters) of Isaac Foot [q.v.] and his wife, Eva Mackintosh. His father, a solicitor, was MP for the Bodmin division of Cornwall and in 1931–2 parliamentary secretary for mines. Dingle Foot wrote of him: 'He was always very proud of the fact that he came from working class origins and indeed we were always reminded of it.' The family were brought up as west country Methodists—and in politics. Whenever his father returned at the week-end every parliamentary speech—by Lloyd George, Asquith, or Churchill—would be fully described and every scene in the Commons would be re-enacted. Dingle Foot commented: 'We were therefore left with the impression that the House of Commons is the greatest theatre in the world and that all the principal dramas of public life are enacted on its floor. This happens to be true.' Three of Dingle Foot's brothers became parliamentarians: Hugh, who became Lord Caradon, and as Sir Hugh Foot was the last governor of Cyprus; Michael, who became leader of the Labour Party; and John, who received a life peerage in 1967.

Dingle Foot was educated at Bembridge School, Isle of Wight, and Balliol College, Oxford, where he obtained a second class in modern history in 1927. He became involved in politics early. He was president of the University Liberal Club in 1927 and of the Oxford Union in 1928. In 1929 he stood unsuccessfully as Liberal candidate for Tiverton but in 1931 he was returned as Liberal member for Dundee, which he represented until 1945.

He was called to the bar at Gray's Inn in 1930 and joined the Western circuit. Throughout his career his qualities as a lawyer and as a politician blended together. What inspired him in both fields was his passion for justice. The two causes which appealed to him most were civil liberties and equal rights for all men under the law. Racial and colour prejudice were to him not so much detestable as incomprehensible. His Commonwealth practice was unequalled in its breadth. He appeared as counsel in the courts of Kenya, Uganda, Tanganyika, and Nyasaland. He was admitted to practice as counsel in India, Ceylon, the Gold Coast, Nigeria, Northern and Southern Rhodesia, Sierra Leone, Malaya, and Bahrain. As Lord Diplock said in paying tribute to him in the Privy Council, he was 'an ambassador of the common law throughout the Commonwealth'. Among those he defended were Kwame Nkrumah [q.v.], later president of Ghana, Hastings Banda, later president of Malawi, and Jomo Kenyatta [q.v.], later president of Kenya, the Kabaka of Buganda, and Sheikh Muhammed Abdullah, former chief minister of Kashmir.

Although Foot was happier addressing a court than speaking in the House, his independence, wit, and resolution made him respected in the Commons; (Sir) Winston Churchill appointed him in 1940 as parliamentary secretary to the Ministry of Economic Warfare for which he went on important missions to Washington and Switzerland in furtherance of the blockade. In 1945 he was a member of the British delegation to the San Francisco conference which framed the United Nations charter. After his defeat in the 1945 general election, he went back to the bar and took silk in 1954. He became a bencher of Gray's Inn in 1952 and treasurer in 1968.

In July 1956 Dingle Foot, alienated by what he believed was 'a general drift to the Right in the Liberal Party', joined the Labour Party. On the death of Richard Stokes MP he was adopted as Labour candidate for the 1957 Ipswich by-election which he won. He represented it until his defeat by thirteen votes in 1970. When Labour won the election in 1964 he was appointed solicitor-general and knighted. He took an active part in the legislative programme of the administration of Harold Wilson (later Lord Wilson of Rievaulx), particularly in its measures for law reform. He also appeared in a varied range of civil and criminal cases on behalf of the Crown. He resigned from his office in 1967, was made privy councillor, and returned to the back benches of the House of Commons. He again resumed practice at the bar. One of his cases was his defence in 1969 of Bernadette Devlin (later McAliskey), then MP for mid-Ulster, at Londonderry. Following his life's pattern, he went to appear in a case in Hong Kong, and died there 18 June 1978.

Foot was a writer and broadcaster of distinction and wit. His book, *British Political Crises* (1976), drew on his great store of political experience and knowledge. Chairman of the Observer Trust from 1953 to 1955, he was an honorary LL D of Dundee University (1974) and commander of the Order of the Cedars, Lebanon (1969).

He married in 1933 Dorothy Mary, daughter of Rowley Elliston, at one time recorder of Great Yarmouth. They had no children. It was a happy marriage and his wife was his constant support and companion.

[Private information; personal knowledge.]

ELWYN-JONES

FOX, DOUGLAS GERARD ARTHUR (1893–1978), schoolmaster and musician, was born 12 July 1893 at Putney, the only son and elder child of Gerard Elsey Fox, an engineer, and his wife and first cousin, Edith Makinson Spencer. His mother, a good pianist, began to teach him the piano when he was four and already showing signs of unusual musical talent. Gerard Fox became manager of the firm's branch in Bristol, whereupon his son entered the preparatory department of Clifton College, where Arthur Peppin was already making his name as director of music. The boy caused some consternation in the sight-reading tests by experiencing no difficulty with any of the pieces put before him. Peppin sent him for tuition to R. O. Beachcroft, a fine teacher and a pianist of distinction.

In 1907 Fox went up to the senior school and became the first holder of Clifton's newly-founded music scholarship (value £24 per annum). In March 1910 he left Clifton, having won an open organ scholarship to the Royal College of Music. There he was taught by Sir Walter Parratt [q.v.] (organ), Herbert Sharpe (piano), S. P. Waddington and later Charles Wood [q.v.] (harmony and counterpoint), and Sir C. V. Stanford [q.v.] (orchestral rehearsals). In 1911 he became ARCO in January, winning the Sawyer prize, and FRCO in July. In 1912 he entered Keble College, Oxford, with the organ scholarship.

At Oxford Fox came to know (Sir) Hugh Allen [q.v.], later Heather professor of music, and Henry Ley [q.v.], organist of Christ Church and later precentor of Eton. Fox had joined the university Officers' Training Corps in May 1914 but when war broke out the warden of Keble turned down his application for leave to apply for a commission with the explanation: 'Your duties here are so necessary for the College life.' Later he was able to join the 4th Gloucestershire Regiment. He served in France in 1916, was sent home with trench fever, and returned to the front in 1917.

On 4 September 1917 he wrote with his left hand to Arthur Peppin: 'I was wounded on the 27th August and on the 28th they took my arm (right) off just above the elbow. Apparently they consulted very carefully before doing it, but it seems to have been hopelessly shattered, and they thought I probably should not have lived if they had left it.' The letter is devoid of regret, bitterness, self-pity, or despair. Sir C. H. H. Parry [q.v.] wrote a few days later to Peppin: 'I don't think anything that happened in this atrocious war has so impressed me with the very malignity of cruelty as the utter destruction of that dear boy's splendid gifts.' Stanford wrote to Fox's father: 'I am sure his art will come out somehow.' When Hugh Allen, then organist of New College, heard the news he played evensong in the chapel using only his left hand and the pedals. This sort of encouragement was a major factor in helping Fox adjust to his handicap. In January 1918 Allen invited him to become president of the Oxford University Musical Club for the summer term and he returned to Oxford, immersing himself in its musical life. In that term he was offered and accepted the post of director of music at Bradfield College. This was a major turning-point in his life.

Fox was director of music at Bradfield from 1918 to 1930, when he moved to the same position at Clifton College. In both posts he made an outstanding contribution to musical education. He was recognized as one of the finest teachers of his day, setting the highest standards for his pupils, and reaching them constantly himself in spite of his physical handicap. He built up a sizeable repertoire for organ and piano recitals which he gave in all parts of the country and for the BBC, and he gave especially memorable performances of the Ravel Concerto for the Left Hand. He produced a steady stream of successful candidates for scholarships at the universities and colleges of music, but perhaps his greatest achievement was to infect with his enthusiasm that larger number of boys who were not themselves performers on any instrument and whose interest was latent. His remarkable qualities were widely recognized; he was president of the Music Masters Association (1931) and of the Incorporated Society of Musicians (1958).

Retiring from Clifton in 1957, he became organist of Great St. Mary's Church, Cambridge, where he remained until 1963, making a valuable contribution to the musical life of both the city and the university. He was appointed OBE in 1958, and Bristol University conferred on him an honorary D.Mus. in 1966. His doctorate of music at Edinburgh University in 1938 was by examination (he had become B.Mus. at Oxford in 1920). He was made a fellow of the Royal College of Music in 1973 and he was also honorary RAM.

Fox died 23 September 1978 at 28 Pembroke Road, Bristol, where he had lived for some years with his devoted sister Winifred, who survived him by three years. He was unmarried. In his address at the crowded memorial service held in Clifton College chapel on 25 November, Sir Thomas Armstrong, who had succeeded Fox as organ scholar of Keble in 1916 and later became principal of the Royal Academy of Music, said: 'Douglas stands, in a way, for the whole of that doomed generation, for all the men killed and maimed on the Somme, in the Salient, and on many fronts—the men whose hardships and joys, whose sufferings and sacrifices, he shared. We speak of them as heroes: but heroism manifests itself in different ways: sometimes it is a matter of a moment's instinctive decision: sometimes of patient endurance, without the excitement of battle, perhaps for a lifetime: sometimes, it is a question of facing death, more often of facing life. Douglas's heroism was of the latter kind, begun in a moment of tragedy, continued in the daily problems of professional life, and ended in the recognition, freely accorded him, of a task well done.'

[Winifred Fox, *Douglas Fox, a Chronicle*, 1976 (privately printed for the Royal College of Music); *The Times*, 28 September 1978; memorial service address, Clifton College, 25 November 1978; personal knowledge.]

H. G. Edwards

FOX, UFFA (1898–1972), naval designer and boat builder, was born 15 January 1898 at East Cowes in the Isle of Wight, the only son and second of the three children (another son and daughter died in childhood) of Arthur Walder Fox, a skilled carpenter engaged on the construction of Osborne House, and his wife, Lucy Cobbold, a housekeeper to Queen Victoria in one of the annexes to Osborne House. He was educated at the nearby village school of Whippingham until the age of fourteen when he became a boatbuilding apprentice at Cowes with S. E. Saunders, builder of fast motor boats, hydroplanes, and flying boats. He studied naval architecture and mathematics at evening school. As a youth his interests were those of the countryside and the sea, particularly Sea Scouting. His favourite sport was cricket and as a chorister at St. James's church he developed a love of music which lasted throughout his life. In World War I he served in the Royal Naval Air Service for nearly two years.

After the war Fox had a variety of jobs, sailed twice to the United States, and started work on his own as a boat builder. In 1925 he married Alma Philips whose father ran the Old East Medina Mill on the Isle of Wight. She divorced him in 1939 and he married Laura Louisa, Mrs Enoch, a widow from Bembridge, Isle of Wight, who divorced him in 1945. In 1956 he married Yvonne, daughter of Edouard Bernard, of Paris, the widow of a French industrialist, who survived him. There were no children by any of the marriages.

Fox's first major successes as a designer were in the fourteen-foot racing dinghy class. He concentrated on trying to produce a fast planing boat. Ariel, his first design, won every race in her class in Cowes Week in 1925. Rodicut, his second design, although not yet carrying out his intention, was second in the race for the Prince of Wales Cup in 1927. In 1928 Avenger, the initiator of the planing dinghies, captured fifty-two firsts, two seconds, and three thirds out of fifty-seven starts. With the deep V-shaped hull for the first third of her length Fox introduced a new feature into such boats which greatly increased their speed. This was widely copied and made him world famous. All these triumphs were greatly assisted by the fact that he was himself a first class helmsman. He used his experience with these dinghies in designing the canoe in which he won both the American Championship for paddling and sailing and the New York International Canoe Championship in 1933. It was the first occasion on which the latter trophy had left the United States of America since fifteen presentations in 1866.

In World War II Fox's main contribution to the war effort was the design and construction of the first parachuted airborne lifeboat which proved to be of great value in air–sea rescue work. Much of his time was taken up with organizing the Local Defence Volunteers, later to become the Home Guard, of which he was a lieutenant in the Isle of Wight. When peace was restored Fox returned to designing dinghies. His twelve-foot Firefly won the Royal Yachting Association Design Competition and was selected as a class for the 1948 Olympics. He then turned his attention to the creation of a planing keel-boat. The result was the Flying Fifteen—fifteen feet on the water-line, twenty feet overall with a draught of two feet six inches—a successful boat with which he achieved all his ambitions. It became well known not only to the sailing fraternity but also with the general public. The town of Cowes presented *Cowslip*, a Flying Fifteen, to Prince Philip, Duke of Edinburgh, who sailed her with Fox, as later did Prince Charles, and she and the class were soon established as popular favourites.

In 1968 he designed the twenty-two-foot Atlantic Row Boat *Britannia* in which John Fairfax rowed across the Atlantic and *Britannia II* in which he crossed the Pacific in 1970, with both drawing on his wartime experience with the airborne lifeboat. Throughout his life he produced many one-off designs for individual clients, wrote a considerable number of articles, and published some ten books on maritime matters, including his reminiscences in two volumes, *Joys of Life* (1966) and *More Joys of Living* (1972). He was appointed RDI in 1955 and CBE in 1959.

Uffa Fox will be widely remembered as a naval architect—membership of the Royal Institution of Naval Architects was conferred on him in 1952, thus crowning the achievements of a boy denied the full formal education for this profession—but among his friends, who included members of the royal family, and those who lived in the Isle of Wight he will be recalled as 'a character', one whose traits were often attractive but sometimes lacking in taste. At home he was always hospitable—he loved good food and wine, the latter sometimes a little too much so—and was invariably amusing. His ebullient nature displayed itself both in a jovial heartiness and in an explosive temper which at times he found difficult to control. At dinner parties he would launch into a singsong which included his rendering of various sea shanties, some not well known, a number of which he recorded. He was free with wise advice to fellow sailors and showed innumerable kindnesses to those less robust than himself. Yet his attitude to others who dared to question his views or his actions, the well-known and unpleasant complications of his domestic life, his handling of his precarious and unpredictable financial affairs, and his abrasive attitude towards those in authority and those who were in his employment lost him some of the admiration and affection which his inventiveness, skill, determination, and honesty deserved. He died 26 October 1972 at Alvechurch, Worcestershire.

[Uffa Fox, *Joys of Life*, 1966, and *More Joys of Living*, 1972; personal knowledge.]

EDWARD HEATH

FRASER, (WILLIAM JOCELYN) IAN, BARON FRASER OF LONSDALE (1897–1974), supporter of blind welfare, was born in Eastbourne 30 August 1897, the elder son (his brother died in infancy) and eldest of three children of William Percy Fraser, of Johannesburg, a prospector and financier, who had been one of the original Rand pioneers, and his wife, Ethel Maude, daughter of Joscelyn Percy Cooke, of Escourt, Natal.

His early enthusiasm was for 'soldiering'. He joined the Cadet Corps at Marlborough College at the age of fourteen, became the youngest cadet to gain 'certificate A', passed on to Sandhurst in 1915, and enlisted in the King's Shropshire Light Infantry. After two months of fighting on the Somme in 1916, and one month short of his nineteenth birthday, he was wounded by a German sniper whom he was attempting to dislodge from behind an iron loophole plate. The bullet traversed both eyes without damaging the lids or rendering him unconscious. On his retirement from the army in 1917 he was promoted captain. While in hospital in London he was contacted by St. Dunstan's, a hostel and traiing centre for blinded servicemen founded and run by Sir (Cyril) Arthur Pearson [q.v.], who was also blind. In September 1916 Fraser went to stay in one of its annexes, 21 Portland Place, where Pearson himself lived. He also met Pearson's assistant, whom he later married.

As assistant and, from 1921, successor to Pearson as chairman of St. Dunstan's, Fraser devoted his life to blind welfare. He mastered technical devices and soon set about his chosen task of easing the existence of the blind, by improving the braille system then in use, and, after long experiments with recording devices, by instigating the 'talking book' project.

He was a commanding figure, tall and handsome, and a forceful speaker, with a prodigious memory. He entered the London County Council in 1922 and served for three years as a Conservative member for North St. Pancras. He was elected to Parliament in 1924, for the same constituency, which he represented until 1929 and from 1931 to 1936, when he resigned. From 1940 to 1950 he was the member for Lonsdale, Lancaster, and from 1950 to 1958 for Morecambe and Lonsdale, Lancaster. During the whole of this period he was the ex-servicemen's champion in and out of Parliament, fighting tirelessly for their pensions to be increased. A founder-member of the Royal British Legion, he was for eleven years its national president (1947–58). He also served for thirty years on the council of the Royal National Institute for the Blind, whose vice-president he became, and for two terms (1936–9 and 1941–6) as a governor of the BBC. He qualified as a barrister (Inner Temple, 1932) and became director and chairman of many companies (including his own family business in South Africa); but always his major concern was for the blinded ex-servicemen of St. Dunstan's, thinking up schemes for its development and extension, which culminated in the opening of their renovated home at Ovingdean, later known as Sir Ian Fraser House.

He had a great zest for life, was impatient with bureaucratic delays (although endlessly patient with his blind protégés), and he was something of a showman, which indeed helped to advertise the projects near to his heart. His hobbies included fishing, riding, and bridge, and (as he readily admitted) arguing; indeed he was proud of his Scottish descent, and especially of a turbulent ancestor, Simon Fraser, twelfth Baron Lovat [q.v.], who was hung, drawn, and quartered for his part in the 1745 Jacobite rebellion. He published an autobiography *Whereas I was Blind* in 1942 and *My Story of St. Dunstan's* in 1961.

Fraser was appointed CBE in 1922 and CH in 1953. In 1934 he was knighted and in 1958 he became a life peer. He also held several foreign awards.

On 23 July 1918 he married Irene Gladys (died 1978), the daughter of George Frederick Mace, of Chipping Norton, Oxfordshire. She was appointed CBE for her work for the blind. They had one daughter. Fraser died in a London hospital 19 December 1974.

[*The Times*, 21 December 1974; Ian Fraser, *Whereas I was Blind*, 1942, and *My Story of St. Dunstan's*, 1961.] PATRICK TREVOR-ROPER

FRASER DARLING, SIR FRANK (1903–1979), ecologist. [See DARLING.]

FREUND, SIR OTTO KAHN- (1900–1979), academic lawyer. [See KAHN-FREUND.]

FRISCH, OTTO ROBERT (1904–1979), physicist, was born in Vienna 1 October 1904, the only son of Justinian Frisch, a printer with a considerable talent for painting, and his wife, Auguste Meitner, a gifted musician who started on a career as a concert pianist but gave it up on marriage. Her sister was the famous physicist Lise Meitner, who exerted a considerable influence on her nephew.

Frisch inherited some of the talents of both his parents. Like his mother, he was very musical, with the gift of absolute pitch, and became a pianist of near-professional standard. He liked to sketch, and his 'doodles' at meetings included portraits or caricatures of his colleagues.

There is some confusion about his first name. At home he was always called Otto Robert, as if the names were hyphenated; he later called himself Robert, until at Los Alamos there were too many Roberts and he was persuaded to become Otto. On returning to England he tried to revert to Robert, but his name appeared as Otto on many articles, and on his book of reminiscences.

As a boy, and later in the Piaristen Gymnasium, he showed considerable talent and fascination for mathematics, but on entering the University of Vienna he decided to study physics, since a career in mathematics seemed to him too dry. He qualified for his Dr.Phil. (1926) with a thesis under Karl Przibram on the effect of electrons on salts.

After an interlude in a small industrial laboratory, and three years at the Physikalisch–Technische Reichsanstalt in Berlin, the state physical laboratory, he moved to Hamburg to work under Otto Stern, who was awarded the Nobel prize for his work on molecular beams. Here Frisch made his first important contributions to physics. In collaboration with Stern he was able to show the diffraction of atoms by crystal surfaces and, particularly, to measure the magnetic moment of the proton, which came out as substantially larger than simple theory predicted.

When Hitler came to power in Germany Frisch moved to London, and spent the year 1933–4 in the laboratory of P. M. S. Blackett [q.v.] at Birkbeck College, where he developed some refinements in cloud chamber technique, and later turned to the new subject of artificial radioactivity. Here, as later, his enjoyment in designing and making apparatus was evident. This period was followed by five years in Niels Bohr's institute in Copenhagen, where he settled down happily, continuing his work in nuclear physics and specializing in neutron physics.

At Christmas 1938 he was visiting Lise Meitner, then in Stockholm, when she received news of the experiments by Otto Hahn and Strassman in Berlin, which showed that barium was one of the products of the collision of a neutron with a uranium nucleus. Hahn knew this meant the nucleus had been split in two, but this seemed very implausible physically. Frisch and Meitner gave the explanation in terms of the excessive electric charge of the nucleus, and estimated the energy released in the process, for which Frisch proposed the term 'fission'. On his return to Copenhagen he set up an experiment to look for the fission fragments, and in a few days had discovered them.

Denmark seemed uncomfortably close to Nazi Germany; in the summer of 1939 Frisch went to Birmingham for an exploratory visit but was prevented from returning to Copenhagen by the outbreak of war. He continued thinking about fission, and in March 1940 he and (Sir) Rudolf Peierls wrote what has become known as the 'Frisch–Peierls memorandum'. This pointed out that a chain reaction was possible in separated uranium-235 (^{235}U), that the critical mass would be reasonably small, and that such a chain reaction would release an appreciable part of the available fission energy, causing a powerful explosion. The memorandum specified many of the consequences of such an explosion. This was the start of the atomic energy project in Britain. In 1940 Frisch went to Liverpool to work with (Sir) James Chadwick [q.v.] on the nuclear problems involved, and in 1943, having been naturalized in record speed, went to Los Alamos with other members of the British team to join in the American work.

In 1946 he returned to England to become head of the nuclear physics division of the Atomic Energy Research Establishment at Harwell, and in 1947 he accepted the Jacksonian professorship of natural philosophy in Cambridge, and in 1948 a fellowship of Trinity College. At Cambridge he continued in research, mostly in nuclear physics, and taught both undergraduates and research students. His lectures managed to make abstruse problems transparent, and his training of graduates conveyed to them some of his pleasure in making things work. He retired from his chair in 1972. He became a great popularizer and wrote four books and numerous articles. He also became the chairman of a firm (Laserscan) formed to exploit his invention of an instrument to analyse photographs of particle tracks.

In 1951 he married Ursula ('Ulla'), daughter of Dr Karl Blau, a civil servant, of Vienna. They had a daughter and a son, who became a physicist. Frisch was appointed OBE in 1946 and elected FRS in 1948. He died in Cambridge 22 September 1979.

[O. R. Frisch, *What Little I Remember*, 1979; R. Peierls in *Biographical Memoirs of Fellows of the Royal Society*, vol. xxvii, 1981; personal knowledge.] RUDOLF PEIERLS

FURSE, SIR RALPH DOLIGNON (1887–1973), civil servant in the Colonial Office, was born in London 29 September 1887, the only child of John Henry Monsell Furse, a sculptor, of Halsdon, Dolton, Devon, and his wife, Ethel, daughter of the Revd John William Dolignon, rector of Cockley Cley, Norfolk. (His mother died of scarlet fever ten days after his birth.) He went to Eton in 1901 and left in 1906. He was one of the earliest history specialists, but his main subject was classics. He was elected to the Eton Society in 1906. In later years he was a generous benefactor to Eton College library.

He matriculated at Balliol in 1907 and graduated in 1909 with third class honours in *literae humaniores*, was secretary of the Chatham Society, and was a member of the college rugby XV and cricket XI. While still at Balliol he joined King Edward's Horse (1908) and would have chosen an army career had it not been for incipient deafness. In 1909 he was placed on the Special Reserve. He joined the Colonial Office in 1910 as assistant private secretary (appointments) to the secretary of state, Lewis (later Viscount) Harcourt [q.v.].

From 1914 to 1919 he was on active service in France and Italy, being wounded in 1917, twice mentioned in dispatches, and appointed to the

DSO in 1918 with bar in 1919. Demobilized with the rank of major he rejoined the Colonial Office in 1919 as assistant private secretary (appointments) to successive secretaries of state till 1930 (Lord Passfield, q.v.), when as a result of a major office reorganization (see below) he became in 1931 director of recruitment, Colonial Service; which post he held till his retirement in 1948. After retirement he served as adviser on training courses for the Colonial Service till 1950. He was appointed CMG in 1935 and KCMG in 1941. In 1949 he was made an honorary DCL, Oxford. In 1962 he published *Aucuparius: Recollections of a Recruiting Officer*.

When Furse joined the Colonial Office there was no unified Colonial Service (except the West African medical staff): appointments were made to the individual colonial governments. Soon after World War I, however, it became increasingly clear that this system could not be relied upon to provide a career service, particularly in smaller territories. In 1927 a governors' conference recommended the empire-wide unification of the various functional branches of the Colonial Service. Moreover, in 1929 (largely on Furse's own recommendation) a committee was set up under the chairmanship of Sir (N. F.) Warren Fisher [q.v.], permanent secretary to the Treasury, to review the whole system of appointments to, and the structure of, the public services in the colonies. The committee upheld 'selection' by the appointments staff as against 'competitive examination' since selection had worked well despite theoretical objections. In 1930, therefore, Passfield introduced a new system of unified services and created a comprehensive Colonial Service personnel division in which Furse, who had himself played a prominent part in bringing about these reforms, became director of recruitment, a new post designed to cope with a greatly increased number and variety of appointments.

In 1943 Furse submitted a detailed scheme for training and refresher courses for the post-war Colonial Service. His scheme, warmly endorsed by a committee under the Duke of Devonshire (parliamentary under-secretary of state) was introduced in 1946. Though always known as the 'Devonshire Courses' they were in fact entirely Furse's brainchild.

Although Furse's main responsibility was the recruitment and training of the Colonial Service (later 'H.M. Overseas Civil Service'—HMOCS) he was also greatly interested in agriculture and veterinary and forestry work, especially the last. He regularly attended the empire forestry conferences, was a member of the committee on colonial agricultural and veterinary services (1925–8, chaired by Lord Lovat, q.v.), a member of a committee on forest officers' training (1930), and a governor of the Imperial Forestry Institute at Oxford.

Throughout his career Furse travelled widely —in his early days much more than was usual— and won universal affection and respect both from the Service and outside. He was an unusually shrewd judge of character, in selecting members for the Service and in choosing his own staff. He had a kindly charm of manner, with an ever fertile imagination and a forthright personality which enabled him to carry through reforms often in advance of contemporary thinking. His increasing deafness was a handicap in later years, though at times he was able to turn this to good account during 'sticky' meetings. The fact that, as colonies advanced later to independence, so many members of HMOCS were able to adapt themselves smoothly to their changed role and retain the confidence of the new governments is itself a striking testimony to the wisdom and skill of the aucuparius (i.e. birdcatcher) who had originally netted birds of such high quality.

Furse married in 1914 Margaret Cecilia ('Celia'), daughter of (Sir) Henry Newbolt [q.v.]. He had two sons and two daughters. He died at Exeter 1 October 1973.

[*The Times*, 5 October 1973; information from Eton and Balliol; Ralph Furse, *Aucuparius: Recollections of a Recruiting Officer*, 1962; private information; personal knowledge.]

HILTON POYNTON

G

GABOR, DENNIS (1900–1979), electrical engineer, physicist, humanist, Nobel prizewinner, and inventor, was born 5 June 1900 in Hungary as Gábor Dénes. His Jewish forebears emigrated from Russia and from Spain in the eighteenth century; his father Bertalan Günsberg, born at Eger in Hungary in 1867, changed his name to Gábor in 1899, the year he married an actress, Adrienne Kálman, then aged twenty, the daughter of a watch maker. Both were very talented; he, an engineer, became director of the Hungarian General Coalmines. Dénes and his two younger brothers (there were no sisters) grew up multilingualists, well developed in music and the arts; though Dennis did not sing professionally, he had a good voice and could sing parts of most operas in their original language and knew the great paintings of the world from illustrated books at home. He was a voracious reader, almost too good at school, but his fidgetiness was due to impatience with the low average standard in class; at sixteen he knew optics up to degree standard.

He took the university entrance examination but was called up for military service in 1918 and was sent to the north Italian front; here he learned Italian and developed a love for Italy which remained all his life and finally drew him there for retirement.

On demobilization he entered the technical university of Budapest to study mechanical engineering but after two years he was called up for further military service so left Hungary and entered the Technisches Hochschule at Charlottenburg to study electrical engineering. After graduating in 1924 he chose, for his Dr.Ing., the study of electrical transients on transmission lines, building one of the first high-voltage oscillographs incorporating two important inventions, an iron-clad focusing solenoid and a circuit which tripped the oscillograph only when the transient arrived.

He left the Hochschule just as the properties of short solenoids to focus electron beams were revealed mathematically and thus missed the opportunity of building the world's first electron microscope; this was constructed by two others using his old oscillograph. Instead, he spent five years in the Siemens Company researching on lamps, and then returned to Hungary in 1933 to work on his plasma discharge patents. He went to England in April 1934 to work in the British–Thomson–Houston Company at Rugby. Here he met, in musical circles, Marjorie Louise, the eldest daughter of Joseph Thomas Kennard Butler, a railway engineer employed by the London, Midland & Scottish Railway Company; they were married in 1936. Gabor anglicized his name (he was naturalized in 1946).

His work in BTH from 1937 to 1948 covered four phases; properties of electron beams in lamps, in television tubes, and in electron microscopes; speech compression so that cables could carry more speech channels; a complex system for three-dimensional image projection for cinemas; and a scheme for detecting heat from the exhaust of an aeroplane.

In 1947 he invented holography, a system by which the resolving power of the electron microscope might be increased: two electron beams, one passing through the specimen, the other bypassing it, interfered with each other and the combined pattern—which he called a hologram—was recorded on a photographic plate; when this was illuminated with a beam of light a greatly magnified image of the specimen was produced. It was a brilliant concept but was never applied successfully to electron microscopy and the invention was dropped.

From 1949 to 1958 as reader in electronics, Imperial College, London, he conceived the flat television tube and with many students produced a working model by 1958. That year he was made professor and in his inaugural lecture spoke of the advances in technology creating a society 'in which only a minority need work to keep the great majority in idle luxury, a nightmare of a leisured world for which we are socially and psychologically unprepared' and pleaded for inspired humanists to take the lead: he expanded his views in the very successful book *Inventing the Future* (1963). This described a future 'which preserves the value of civilisation and yet is in harmony with man's nature'. It was translated into many languages and should have been read by all politicians faced with coping with the galloping future of technology.

With the invention of the laser in 1961 holography leaped ahead finding powerful applications in almost all the sciences; thousands of papers were written and Gabor's inventive mind produced many valuable patents. On retirement in 1967 he joined CBS Laboratories, Stamford, Connecticut, working on holography in America part of the year and writing in the summer in his Italian home, where he produced *The Mature Society* (1972). It was the brilliant flowering of holography which turned attention to the inventor. He received many honours, among them FRS (1956); D.Sc. (London 1964); CBE (1970); honorary D.Sc. (Southampton 1970, Delft 1971, Surrey 1972, Bridgeport Engineering College 1972, City 1972, and Columbia, New York, 1975); honorary LL D (London 1973); and the Nobel prize for physics in 1971. He was invited to lecture all over the world.

He joined the Club of Rome in 1968 and wrote *Beyond the Age of Waste* (1978). His huge output of printed lectures reveals a penetrating intellect of great power. The Gabors are remembered for their extremely happy home life, generous hospitality, and stimulating company. Gabor died 9 February 1979 in a nursing home close to South Kensington in London. He had no children.

[T. E. Allibone in *Biographical Memoirs of Fellows of the Royal Society*, vol. xxvi, 1980; family information; personal knowledge.]

T. E. Allibone

GALBRAITH, VIVIAN HUNTER (1889–1976), historian, was born 15 December 1889 in Sheffield where his father, David, who came from Belfast, was secretary at Hadfields. His mother was Eliza Davidson McIntosh. He was the youngest of a family of four sons and a daughter. His family moved first to London, where he was educated at Highgate School from 1902 to 1906, and then to Manchester. He went to the university in 1907 and attended the lectures of T. F. Tout [q.v.] whose warm support, destined to be lifelong, was a turning point in his career. Galbraith's other teachers were James Tait and (Sir) F. M. Powicke [qq.v.], with whom he also retained a lifelong friendship. He was later to write the notices of both Tout and Tait for this Dictionary. In 1910 he obtained a first class in modern history at Manchester University and gained a Brackenbury scholarship to Balliol College, Oxford. He did his first piece of serious research for the Stanhope prize which he won in 1911 with an essay on the chronicles of St. Albans. He received, however, a severe academic set-back by getting a third class in *literae humaniores* in 1913—a subject to which he was wholly unsuited. It was a bitter blow which set back his prospect of an academic career for many years despite another first class in modern history which he obtained in 1914.

Tout immediately persuaded Manchester University to make him the Langton research fellow for three years, and he plunged with enthusiasm into the records of the abbey of Bury St. Edmunds in the British Museum. War took him by surprise. So far as he thought about it during its early months, he was against it; but not to the point of declining to 'join up', which he did in January 1915. He served as a company commander in the Queen's Regiment with impetuous courage in Palestine in 1917 and France in 1918.

He returned to academic life in January 1919, first as a temporary lecturer at Manchester and then with a renewed Langton research fellowship which allowed him to live in London and pursue his former research. In January 1921 he joined the Public Record Office as an assistant keeper, and this position determined the shape of his later historical development by giving him daily access to the records of English medieval government. Meanwhile, he began his first important piece of editorial work, an edition of the Anonimalle chronicle of St. Mary's, York, which appeared in 1927. In June 1921 he married a fellow medievalist, whom he had met at Manchester, Georgina Rosalie, daughter of Lyster Cole-Baker, MD.

In 1928 he returned to Oxford to succeed R. L. Poole [q.v.] as reader in diplomatic; he was also elected a tutorial fellow of Balliol. Thus began the golden years of his life. His effervescent vitality, and his intimate knowledge of documents, gave his pupils the feeling that this was the real thing in historical scholarship. His bold judgements on historical issues and his uninhibited comments on contemporary masters of the subject brought a breath of freedom to the most timorous pupils. In the intervals of teaching, lecturing, talking, and golfing he continued his work on chronicles and charters, including the important edition of the St. Albans Chronicle 1406–20 in 1937. In 1934 he published his readable and stimulating *Introduction to the Use of Public Records*. In 1937 he became professor of history at Edinburgh; in 1939 he was elected a fellow of the British Academy; and in 1940 he was Ford's lecturer at Oxford. In 1944 he succeeded A. F. Pollard [q.v.] as director of the Institute of Historical Research, and in January 1948 Sir Maurice Powicke as regius professor at Oxford.

He brought to all these posts the same unflagging zest. The main themes of his historical interests never changed, though he extended his range in two ways. First he undertook a fundamental reappraisal of the purpose of Domesday Book. Next he initiated a series of critically edited texts and translations of medieval sources. His detailed study of Domesday Book had its origin in the discovery of a late twelfth century annotated copy of the Herefordshire portion of the survey in a manuscript in the Balliol library. From this, he was led to challenge the accepted orthodoxy about the purpose and method of compilation of the great survey which had been formulated by J. H. Round [q.v.]. Galbraith's views were expressed in a series of works from 1942 to 1974 culminating in *Domesday Book: its Place in Administrative History*. The series of medieval texts arose from discussions with H. P. Morrison, the managing director of the Edinburgh publishing firm of Nelson, and it developed into one of the most successful attempts to make original sources of medieval history widely available to students. Apart from the notices of Tait and Tout, he also wrote those of B. H. Sumner, M. V. Clarke, and Sir H. C. M. Lyte for this Dictionary. He retired in 1957 and died in Oxford 25 November 1976. He was an honorary fellow of Balliol (1957) and Oriel (1958) and he received many honorary doctorates.

Galbraith was the last important representative of the modern history school at Oxford in the period when it concentrated on the continuous institutional and constitutional development of England from the early Middle Ages. His talk and presence suggested his power as a teacher. His early white hairs and stooping gait would have suggested premature old age if they had not been contradicted by a general appearance of intense vitality. Next to the study of medieval charters, golf was the activity which gave him most pleasure. His features were mobile and striking, and his outspoken judgements were without malice. His family life was exceptionally harmonious and hospitable, and he found a deep satisfaction in his son and two daughters. His appearance is best preserved in photographs of which two good examples can be found in the volume, *Facsimiles of English Royal Writs to A.D. 1100*, presented to him on his retirement in 1957, and in the *Proceedings* of the British Academy, 1978. There is also a drawing of him by Gilbert Spencer in Balliol and a bust in the Modern History Faculty Library in Oxford.

[R. W. Southern in *Proceedings* of the British Academy, vol. lxiv, 1978; personal letters and papers in the Manchester University Library (T. F. Tout and James Tait papers) and in the Bodleian Library (Galbraith papers); private information; personal knowledge.]

R. W. SOUTHERN

GALE, SIR HUMFREY MYDDELTON (1890–1971), lieutenant-general, was born 4 October 1890 in London, the elder son and eldest of the five children of Ernest Sewell Gale, architect, of Liphook, and his wife, Charlotte Sarah, daughter of Eugene Goddard, surgeon. He was educated at St. Paul's School, and from 1908 to 1910 studied at the Architectural School, Westminster. During this time he served with the Artists Rifles, a Territorial Army regiment, and then decided to try for the Indian Army and applied for Sandhurst. He was successful and became a cadet there in September 1910.

He did not pass out high enough to join the Indian Army, and instead was gazetted second-lieutenant in the Army Service Corps in September 1911. There followed peacetime soldiering at Woolwich and Aldershot where he improved his horsemanship and learned something about supply and transport. During World War I he served in France both at regimental duty and as a staff captain. He was awarded the MC and was twice mentioned in dispatches. In 1917 he married Winifred (died 1936), second daughter of William Cross, farmer. They enjoyed a very happy marriage and had two daughters.

Between the wars Gale served at regimental duty and on the staff both at home and in Egypt. In 1934 he became an instructor at the Staff College, Camberley, where he also hunted with the drag, and while on holiday enjoyed fishing and painting. In 1937 Gale became a staff colonel in the War Office, and then soon after World War II started, he was appointed brigadier, DAQMG III Corps which went to France in 1940. During the withdrawal to Dunkirk Gale was responsible for all administrative arrangements for 70,000 men. By his energetic leadership and practical improvisation Gale was able to keep the supply system working and morale high. He was appointed CBE (1940) for his service.

Back in Britain Gale became major-general administration, Scotland, and in 1941 was in charge of administration for all home forces. Here his cheerfulness, experience, and planning ability did much to prepare for the forthcoming offensives which the joint Anglo-American forces were soon to undertake. In 1942 he was appointed chief administrative officer to General Eisenhower for the north-west African operation, and it was as Eisenhower's principal administrative expert that Gale made his great contribution to Allied victory. In 1942 Gale was also appointed CB. Apart from successfully organizing support for the huge and complex Operation Torch, Gale's gift for running a happy, efficient Allied team was invaluable. After the successful conclusion of the North African campaign, Gale was appointed CVO (1943) and awarded the US Legion of Merit. Eisenhower then appointed him deputy chief of staff (administration) for the invasions of Sicily and Italy, both of which depended on the smooth assembly and movement of troops and stores at a time when the shortage of shipping was critical. In August 1943 Gale was created KBE.

In January 1944 he left Allied Force HQ, Algiers, to accompany General Eisenhower to Britain for the intended invasion of Normandy. Never before in the history of warfare had there been such an administrative problem of landing and distributing supplies to support the invading forces and then move on from the beachheads. Gale's responsibilities were to advise the supreme commander on all administrative matters and to ensure that operational plans were viable. He co-ordinated resources between army groups and generally oversaw all supply, military and civil. Until the very end of the war in Europe, Gale continued to be Eisenhower's administrative right-hand man.

With the war over he was awarded the US Distinguished Service Medal, and in July 1945 supervised distribution of resources between the Allied armies. In September he was appointed European director for UNRRA, where he stayed until July 1947, when he retired from the army to hold further positions with the Anglo-Iran Oil Company. From 1954 to 1964 he was the chairman of the Basildon New Town Development Corporation. It was Harold Macmillan who persuaded him to do this job and who described Gale as one of the most efficient officers he had ever known. Gale was also colonel commandant of the RASC from 1944 to 1954 and of the Army Catering Corps from 1946 to 1958. He received foreign awards from France, Panama, and Morocco.

In 1945 he married Minnie Grace (died 1970), daughter of Count Gregorini-Bingham, of Bologna, and widow of Prince Charles Louis de Beauvau-Craon. They made their home in La Tour de Peilz, Vaud, Switzerland, where Gale died 8 April 1971. It is not only as a superbly successful administrative soldier that Gale will be remembered, but as a man devoted to his family, deeply religious, a talented linguist, sportsman, and artist, a fine leader and a sure friend.

[*The Times* and *Daily Telegraph*, 10 April 1971; W. H. D. Ritchie, *Lieutenant General Sir Humfrey M. Gale KBE CB CVO MC*, supplement to the *Waggoner* (Journal of the Royal Corps of Transport), March 1982; personal knowledge.] JOHN STRAWSON

GALLOWAY, SIR ALEXANDER (1895–1977), lieutenant-general, was born at Minto Manse, Hawick, Scotland, 3 November 1895, the second son and youngest of the four children of the Revd Alexander Galloway, then minister of Minto, and his wife, Margaret Rankin Smith. Educated at King William's College, Isle of Man, he was at a peak of schoolboy success academically and at games, about to go up to Cambridge, when the war broke out in 1914. Volunteering immediately, he was commissioned on the basis of his service in the school Officers' Training Corps into the Cameronians (Scottish Rifles) but first saw active service with 4th King's Own Scottish Borderers at Gallipoli, where he earned a high reputation for bravery. Among the last to leave the peninsula, he then took part in the campaigns in Egypt and Palestine before being posted to the western front. There he was awarded the MC in 1918.

He became a regular officer in 1917 and when the war ended was one of the many experienced junior officers serving long years without promotion. After service abroad, Galloway's quick brain, energy, and regimental reputation earned him entry to the Staff College at Camberley. He was then thirty-three, noted by his contemporaries as a man of hot temper, a generous friend, and a deadly fast bowler. Almost ten years later he returned to Camberley to instruct before commanding 1st Cameronians, an appointment cut short by promotion to command the Staff College at Haifa in February 1940.

When the war in the Western Desert began in earnest, Galloway was picked as brigadier, general staff—chief staff officer—to Sir H. M. (later Lord) Wilson [q.v.]. He made an important contribution to the desert victory of 1940 and equally to the evacuation from Greece in 1941. Back in Egypt, he became chief staff officer to the newly forming Eighth Army under Lieutenant-General Sir Alan Cunningham, whose task it was to destroy the combined German–Italian army. Operation Crusader began to this end in November 1941 with high success but the German command then reversed the situation. Exhausted and ill, Cunningham decided to break off the battle and withdraw. With extraordinary resolve, Galloway decided to withhold the order, convinced that such a move would be disastrous. He told the commander-in-chief, Sir Claude Auchinleck, that they must fight on though very weak in armour. His advice was taken and proved sound. A British success resulted. Galloway, having risked removal and perhaps disciplinary action, was promoted and sent to the United States to select equipment for the Eighth Army. However, the incident brought him to the attention of General Sir Alan Brooke (later Viscount Alanbrooke, q.v.). At the time Brooke needed a major-general for the exacting post of director of staff duties and ordered Galloway to London, much to his vexation, for he was commanding a division in battle.

At last, in 1944, Galloway was sent to 1st Armoured division in the Mediterranean; but it remained in reserve during the campaign through the Italian mountains. He took temporary command of 4th Indian division at Cassino before being recalled to the staff, this time at the wish of Field-Marshal Sir B. L. Montgomery (later Viscount Montgomery of Alamein, q.v.). Thus he was in north-west Europe at the end of the war when he was promoted and, paradoxically, given a series of commands: XXX Corps, the army in Malaya, and in 1947 as high commissioner and commander-in-chief British forces in Austria.

As he arrived, the Soviet Union was seeking to establish Austrian communists as police and local government authorities in the western occupation zones. The skill of Galloway and his United States colleague in preventing this earned the praise of the foreign secretary, Ernest Bevin [q.v.]. When Galloway left Austria in 1949 the struggle to institute an independent democratic state was largely won.

Galloway was now penalized by age from holding another appointment in an army over-full of senior officers. By mischance, his talents as a dynamic and courageous leader had been sacrificed to his reputation as a staff officer. He retired in 1950 but remained active in several commercial activities until 1965.

He was appointed CBE and to the DSO in 1941. Created CB in 1946 and KBE in 1949, he was twice mentioned in dispatches, besides being awarded the 1st class military cross of both Greece and Czechoslovakia, the Orders of Merit and the White Lion of Czechoslovakia, and the Order of Orange-Nassau of the Netherlands.

He married in 1920 Dorothy Hadden, daughter of Frank Hadden White, stockbroker, of Norham, Northumberland. They had three sons, one of whom died in 1955. Galloway died 27 January 1977 at Norham.

[Army and public records; family and private sources.] ANTHONY FARRAR-HOCKLEY

GARROD, LAWRENCE PAUL (1895–1979), clinical bacteriologist, was born 7 December 1895 at 71 Mountview Road, Stroud Green, Hornsey, Middlesex, the younger son (there were no daughters) of Cubbitt Garrod, draper, of Exeter, and his wife, Gertrude Dwelley Davey. He was descended from a Suffolk farming family that over the years produced a number of distinguished physicians, including Sir Alfred Baring Garrod, Alfred Henry Garrod, and Sir Archibald Edward Garrod [qq.v.]. His brother died in childhood and he was brought up as an only child. He was educated at Sidcot School which he left in 1913 to spend several months in Germany, founding his grasp of the language, before going up to King's College, Cambridge, in 1914. He entered St. Bartholomew's Hospital as a clinical student in 1916 but interrupted his studies to serve as a surgeon sub-lieutenant, Royal Naval Volunteer Reserve, in 1917–18.

Returning to Bart's after the war, he completed his clinical studies with distinction, winning the senior prize, the Brackenbury scholarship in medicine, in 1919. He graduated BA from Cambridge in 1918, MRCS (Eng.) and LRCP (Lond.) in 1920, and MA, MB, and B.Chir. in 1921. He worked in clinical medicine for five years, passing the MRCP in 1923, before his interests turned decisively to bacteriology. His MD thesis on the use of inhibitors in selective culture media was written in 1932 (he gained the degree in 1938) before the momentous discovery of prontosil in 1935 opened the era of effective antimicrobial chemotherapy. This was the subject with which Garrod quickly became identified and on which, during almost fifty years of prodigious advances, he was the premier British authority. He spent almost the whole of his professional life at Bart's, becoming senior demonstrator of pathology in 1925, reader in bacteriology in 1934, and professor of bacteriology in 1937. He was elected FRCP in 1936. After his retirement in 1961, when he became emeritus professor, he held the part-time post of honorary consultant in chemotherapy at the Royal Postgraduate Medical School.

Early in his career Garrod's investigations centred on antiseptics, about which comparatively little was then known. He elucidated their action and efficacy and developed a new test which was rapidly adopted as a British Standard Method. During the war Bart's was evacuated to Hill End Hospital and there he conducted important work on hospital cross-infection, particularly with streptococci, in the large plastic surgery and burns unit. However, it is for his work on antibiotics that he is best remembered.

When the therapeutic properties of penicillin were first recognized, St. Bartholomew's was one of the first four hospitals outside Oxford to pioneer its study. It was a time of unusual effort, reward, and excitement, as patients recovered from previously incurable infections. Garrod was a member of the original penicillin clinical trials committee of the Medical Research Council. He later became chairman of the MRC antibiotics clinical trials committee, and served on several expert committees on antimicrobial chemotherapy of the World Health Organization and Department of Health and Social Security. From 1965 to 1970 he was chairman of the antibiotics panel of the Committee on Medical Aspects of Food Policy.

Garrod was a skilful writer and his output was prodigious. In addition to his books with various co-authors—five editions of *Recent Advances in Pathology* (first edn. 1932), two editions of *Hospital Infection* (first edn. 1960), and five editions of *Antibiotic and Chemotherapy* (first edn. 1963)—he wrote some 200 scientific papers and over 600 unsigned editorials for the *British Medical Journal*. His pungent comments, wit, and style were instantly recognizable. From 1951 to 1957 he was editor of the *British Journal of Experimental Pathology*. To this Dictionary he contributed the notice of M. H. Gordon.

Until his first retirement in 1961 Garrod was bacteriologist to St. Bartholomew's Hospital from 1934, bacteriologist of the City of London from 1936, and consultant in antibiotics to the army from 1948. He was president of the pathology section of the Royal Society of Medicine in 1954–6 and president of the Institute of Medical Laboratory Technology from 1949 to 1953. He also served as vice-president of the British Medical Association.

In 1922 Garrod married Marjorie, daughter of Bedford Pierce, MD, FRCP, medical superintendent of the Retreat at York. Their daughter spent the war years working in his department and of their three sons, two followed him to Bart's and went into general practice and the third became a meteorologist. Warm and generous to those who knew him well, his tall figure presented a forbidding aspect to the world at large and his ability to deliver devastating dismissals may have had something to do with the paucity of conventional honours he received. Some acclaimed his worth: he was a Lister fellow of the Royal College of Physicians of Edinburgh, an honorary alumnus of the University of Louvain, an honorary LL D of the University of Glasgow (1965), and an honorary fellow of the Royal College of Pathologists (1979). He died 11 September 1979 at the Royal Berkshire Hospital, Reading.

[*British Medical Journal*, 22 September 1979; *Nature*, 14 February 1980; private information; personal knowledge.] FRANCIS O'GRADY
PAMELA M. WATERWORTH

GEORGE, FRANCES LOUISE LLOYD, COUNTESS LLOYD-GEORGE OF DWYFOR (1888–1972), political secretary. [See LLOYD GEORGE.]

GEORGE, THOMAS NEVILLE (1904–1980), geologist, was born 13 May 1904 in Swansea, the only son and elder child of (Thomas) Rupert George (1873–1933), a schoolmaster originally from Port Eynon, Gower, and his wife, Elizabeth Evans (1875–1937), a schoolmistress, of Swansea. His paternal grandfather was also a schoolmaster and no doubt this background influenced his lifelong interest and dedication to education.

George was educated at Morriston Boys' Elementary School, and from 1914 to 1919 Swansea Municipal Secondary (Dynevor) School in which in his last year he suddenly discovered science because a chemistry master encouraged him to investigate the rusting of iron. In 1919–20 he attended Swansea Grammar School. At the age of sixteen he entered the University College of Swansea with a senior scholarship as one of its first students. In 1924 he was the first student to obtain in Swansea a first class honours B.Sc. (Wales) in geology, having been diverted from chemistry by (Sir) A. E. Trueman [q.v.]. He published two research papers while an undergraduate.

As a student he was called 'TN', a name by which he was generally known for the rest of his life. He stayed on at Swansea and obtained his M.Sc. (1926) under Trueman. He then went to St. John's College, Cambridge, where he studied spiriferid brachiopods under Henry Woods [q.v.], obtaining his Ph.D. in 1928. That year he returned to Swansea as a demonstrator in geology.

He remained in Swansea until 1930 when he was appointed to the Geological Survey of Great Britain and set to work mapping the English Midlands. During his short stay of only three years he was asked to write the first editions of the British Regional Geology handbooks of *North Wales* (1935) with Bernard Smith and *South Wales* (1937) with J. Pringle. These proved to be enormously popular and he subsequently undertook several revisions over four decades. In 1933, at the age of only twenty-nine, he was appointed to the chair of geology and geography at University College, Swansea, which had been vacated by Trueman.

In 1946 Trueman resigned from the chair of geology at Glasgow University and in 1947 George succeeded him. There he remained until his retirement in 1974. He ruled his department in every detail, and not the smallest expenditure could be incurred without his permission. He determined the syllabus and content of lectures; his students loved him. He retired after initiating plans for a new building for the department.

George was an excellent lecturer, full of pedagogical eloquence and euphonic felicitous phrases. His lectures, especially to first year students, were, like Trueman's, very popular both in the university and abroad. He possessed a high reputation as an examiner and acted for almost half the geology departments in Britain at one time or another and for many abroad. He was particularly fearsome as an examiner of student mapping.

George published forty-two articles while in Swansea and about a hundred during his time in Glasgow. Most were single-authored. His more important contributions were in synthesizing British landscape evolution, and Carboniferous stratigraphy and palaeontology.

George carried a very heavy load of committee work both within and without the university. Adult education was a lifelong interest. He loved debate, and had a puckish sense of humour and a brisk manner. He was rather ascetic, being an abstainer from alcohol and smoking, and he rarely took lunch. He enjoyed the piano. He worked very hard and consistently right up to his death. Even after partial paralysis in 1977 he continued to teach and write from a wheelchair.

He received many honours: the Lyell medal of the Geological Society of London (1963); the Clough medal of the Edinburgh Geological Society (1973); the Neill prize of the Royal Society of Edinburgh (1978); the medal of Charles University, Prague; the Kelvin prize of the Royal Philosophical Society (1975); an honorary D.-ès. Sc. of Rennes (1956); and an honorary LL D of Wales (1970). He was a corresponding member of the Geological Society of Belgium. He was president of, among others, the Association of University Teachers (1959–60), the Geological Society of London (1968–70), and the Palaeontological Association (1962–4). He received the D.Sc. (Wales), the Sc.D. (Cambridge), and was elected FRS (1963).

In 1932 he married Sarah Hannah Davies, MA, Ph.D., teacher and university lecturer, who always used her maiden name. Her father was Joseph Davies, a writer and draper, and her mother was Florence Annie Roberts, a schoolmistress. There were no children. George died 18 June 1980 at Glasgow.

[*The Times*, 25 June 1980; B. E. Leake in 1982 *Year Book* of the Royal Society, Edinburgh, for 1981; T. R. Owen in *Proceedings* of the Geological Association, vol. xcii, 1981, B. E. Leake and W. J. French in the Geological Society, London, *List of Fellows*, 1983.] B. E. LEAKE

GERALDO (pseudonym), dance-band leader and musician. [See WALCAN-BRIGHT, GERALD.]

GERHARDIE, WILLIAM ALEXANDER (1895–1977), novelist and critic, was born at St. Petersburg in Russia 21 November 1895, the fifth of six children (one son died in childhood) of Charles Alfred Gerhardi, a British industrialist settled in Russia, and his wife, Clara, daughter of John Wadsworth.

William Gerhardi, their youngest son, was educated at the St. Annen Schule and Reformierte Schule, St. Petersburg. In his late teens he was sent to London to train for a commercial career, either in banking or by way of marrying a rich bride. These plans, and his own dreams of taking by storm the London theatre with a melodrama called 'The Haunting Roubles', were interrupted by World War I in which, as a trooper, he joined the Royal Scots Greys. To improve his English he had been studying Oscar Wilde [q.v.], arriving at the cavalry barracks in York with an elegant cane, languid expression, and longish hair under a bowler hat. Applying for a commission he was posted (1916–18) to the staff of the British embassy in Petrograd and, having provided himself with an enormous sword bought second-hand in the Charing Cross Road, was greeted as an old campaigner. From here he viewed through a monocle several stages of the Russian revolution which was to ruin his father who, escaping in a barrel to Bolton in Lancashire, owed his life to being identified as the famous British socialist Keir Hardie [q.v.]. In 1918 Gerhardi was attached to the Scots Guards and sent on the British military mission in Siberia, being demobilized two years later, retaining the rank of captain and with an OBE, the Order of St. Stanislav of Imperial Russia, and the Czechoslovak war cross.

Gerhardi then travelled round the world and went up to Worcester College, Oxford, where he obtained a BA (shortened course, in Russian, 1922) and wrote a book on Anton Chekhov (1923) and his first novel *Futility* (1922), which was sponsored in Britain by Katherine Mansfield [q.v.], who found a publisher for it, and in America by Edith Wharton, who wrote an introduction. The critical acclaim he gained with this novel on Russian themes increased after the publication of his next novel, *The Polyglots* (1925), which remained the most celebrated of all his books and was described by Anthony Powell as 'a classic'.

Over the following fifteen years Gerhardi was prolific. Among his best fiction were a collection of short stories *Pretty Creatures* (1927), *Pending Heaven* (1930)—a novel based on his friendship with the writer Hugh Kingsmill—*Resurrection* (1934)—a complex and ambitious semi-autobiographical book that uses an occult experience as an illustration of future life—and *Of Mortal Love* (1936)—a novel charting the progress of love erotic into love imaginative which C. P. (later Lord) Snow [q.v.] called 'one of the most wonderful books of a generation'.

Up to the early 1930s Gerhardi had travelled widely over Europe, India, and America. In 1931, at the age of thirty-five, he published his autobiography *Memoirs of a Polyglot* and moved into a flat in Rossetti House, behind Broadcasting House in London, where he lived for the rest of his life. His last book published in his lifetime was *The Romanovs* (1940), a massive and unorthodox study of the Russian dynasty. In World War II he joined the European division of the BBC, being transferred in 1942 to the Central Productions Unit for which he wrote scripts for use by overseas services. The following year he pioneered the successful 'English by Radio', of which he was the first editor and where he continued working until 1945 when, the programme becoming more elementary, Gerhardi resigned in order to concentrate more fully on his literary work.

During the 1920s Gerhardi had been one of the most talked about literary figures of his day. H. G. Wells [q.v.] roared his praises: Arnold Bennett [q.v.] called him a genius: Evelyn Waugh [q.v.] acknowledged having learnt 'a great deal of my trade from your novels'. He was taken up by Lord Beaverbrook [q.v.], who makes several bows in his work as 'Lord Ottercove' and whom he attempted to repay with a written invitation to collaborate on a musical comedy. His novels in the 1930s which, Graham Greene wrote, 'fulfil all the fine promise of his earlier books and showed him to be a poet as well as a wit', indicate that his chief literary influence had passed from Chekhov to Proust: from the comic agonies of procrastination to the imaginative power of time regained. It was perhaps as a symbol of this preoccupation with the past that he reverted to an ancestral spelling of his name by adding an 'e' to Gerhardi. This name appears for the first time on the title pages of the second Collected Edition (in ten volumes) of his work issued from 1970 to 1974.

Over the last thirty-seven years of his life he lived in increasing obscurity, a hermit in the West End of London, his only link with the world outside an endless telephone line and the remembrance of things past. Though his entry in *Who's Who* lengthened fantastically over these years and, in 1975, he was made a fellow of the Royal Society of Literature, Gerhardie published no new book—merely broadcasting a little, writing a few essays (of which the most interesting is 'My Literary Credo' appearing at the beginning of the 1947 edition of *Futility*), and experimenting with various unpromising plays with promising titles (*English Measles*, *The Private Life of a Public Nuisance*, etc.) He was rumoured to have long been at work on another novel, a tetralogy entitled 'This Present Breath', the two concluding chapters of which, Gerhardie-style, had been published in Neville Braybrooke's *The Wind and the Rain* (1962). But after he died in London, 15 July 1977, though he had left an astonishingly elaborate card index for a work of fiction, no consecutive narrative was uncovered and, it was concluded, there was no novel. Instead an original work of non-fiction in several drafts was found, a biography of the age 1890–1940 called *God's Fifth Column*, which plotted the view of men of action versus men of imagination over this period. This was edited for publication by Michael Holroyd and Robert Skidelsky and published posthumously (1981).

There is a portrait bust of Gerhardie in his mid-thirties by Bianca, Princess of Loewenstein (privately owned).

[William Gerhardi, *Memoirs of a Polyglot*, 1931; BBC written archives; private information; personal knowledge.] MICHAEL HOLROYD

GIBB, SIR HAMILTON ALEXANDER ROSSKEEN (1895–1971), Arabic scholar, was born 2 January 1895 at Alexandria, Egypt, the third of the three sons and youngest of the four children of Alexander Crawford Gibb, manager of the Aboukir Dairy Company of Aboukir, Alexandria, and his wife, Jane Anne Gardner. His father died when he was two and his mother remained in Alexandria as a teacher, but he himself was sent back to Scotland for his education at the age of five. He studied at the Royal High School, Edinburgh, from 1904 to 1912, and then at Edinburgh University; his studies there were interrupted by World War I, during which he saw service in France and Italy in the Royal Field Artillery, but he was awarded a 'war privilege' MA. After the war he studied Arabic at the School of Oriental Studies of London University, and obtained his MA in 1922. In the same year he married Helen Jessie (Ella), daughter of John Stark, OBE; they had two children, a son and a daughter.

From 1921 to 1937 he taught Arabic at the School of Oriental Studies, as lecturer, then reader (from 1929), and finally professor (from 1930) in succession to his teacher Sir T. W. Arnold, whose notice he later wrote for this Dictionary. (He also wrote the notices of Sir Muhammad Iqbal, S. E. Lane-Poole, and R. A. Nicholson.) In these years his remarkable gifts as a teacher revealed themselves; more than anyone else, he formed the minds of those who were to be the teachers and scholars of the next generation. In this period also he made his reputation in the world of scholarship: he visited Egypt and other countries frequently, became one of the editors of the international *Encyclopaedia of Islam*, and wrote a number of books and articles which showed a wide range of knowledge, depth and originality of thought, and mastery of an elegant and precise style. They included an introductory book on *Arabic Literature* (1926), a translation of selections from the travels of Ibn Battuta (1929), another translation of an Arabic chronicle of the period of the Crusades (1932), a series of articles on contemporary Arabic literature, perhaps the first serious treatment of the subject by a western scholar, and some short but penetrating articles on Islamic political theory. These works reveal two of his abiding and dominant concerns: to make the history of the Arabs available to scholars in other fields, and to understand and explain what was for him the central thread of that history, the continuous development of the *umma*, the community formed by the preaching of the prophet Muhammad, accepting the Koran as the revelation of God, articulating the deposit of faith into systems of thought and practice, protecting them against the self-interest of the holders of worldly power and the vagaries of human self-will, and transmitting them from generation to generation.

In 1937 he became Laudian professor of Arabic at Oxford in succession to D. S. Margoliouth [q.v.] and was elected to a fellowship at St. John's College. He remained in Oxford for eighteen years. They were years in which the teaching of Arabic and cognate subjects expanded, as students returned from World War II with knowledge of the Middle East, and others from the United States and the Middle East itself were attracted to Oxford by Gibb's growing fame. As a result of the 1947 report of a committee set up by the Treasury and chaired by the Earl of Scarbrough [q.v.], Oxford was given special funds to develop the teaching of Middle Eastern subjects, and the administration of the scheme was mainly in Gibb's hands. He found time, however, to continue with his own thought and writing. Together with Harold Bowen he produced *Islamic Society and the West* (volume I part i 1950, part ii 1957); a survey of Ottoman society in the late eighteenth century, before the full impact of European expansion was felt, it was intended as an introduction to a larger study of that impact. It carried further his thought on one of his central themes, the complex relationship between government and society, and between the holders of power and the men of learning who were the leaders and spokesmen of the *umma*. The same theme was developed in a number of works on Islam as a religious system, in particular *Mohammedanism* (1949), a masterpiece of simple but subtle exposition, which was to remain for more than a generation the first book put into the hands of most students of the subject in English-speaking countries, and *Modern Trends in Islam* (1947), a penetrating analysis of the problems of the Muslim community in the modern world, with its balance and continuity threatened by external forces and by modernizing regimes and thinkers prepared to cast aside much of its heritage. It was this sense of a civilization under threat which led him also in this period to write and lecture occasionally (although more rarely as time went on) about the political problems of the day.

In 1955 Gibb left Oxford to become James Richard Jewett professor of Arabic at Harvard University and also 'university professor', a rare title given to a few scholars 'working on the frontiers of knowledge, and in such a way as to cross the conventional boundaries of the specialities'. He became director of Harvard's Center for Middle Eastern Studies, and this opened for him, at the age of sixty, a new field of activity which called out all his energy and enthusiasm; he became one of the leaders of the movement which led American universities in this period to set up 'centers' of regional studies, bringing together teachers, researchers, and students in different disciplines to study the culture and society of a region of the world. Teaching, administration, and academic statesmanship left him less time for research, but he was able to take up again some of his earlier interests in history and literature, and in particular to undertake a complete translation of the travels of Ibn Battuta; his vast knowledge of Arabic and sensitive feeling for the nuances of literary style made him a remarkably good translator. (He had also supervised the translation of V. V. Barthold's *Turkestan down to the Mongol Invasion* for the E. J. W. Gibb memorial series.) In this period, as throughout his career, teaching was central to his life, and once more he trained not only scholars for the next generation but officials for a government facing new responsibilities in the world. Once more, too, what they remembered of him was not only his great learning and skill in exposition, but the special flavour of his personality. Those who knew him well became aware, behind his mild and restrained manner and appearance, of an intellectual authority, a willingness to question received ideas, an imagination ranging among distant peoples, times and places, and a warmth of sympathy and affection: a warmth which, as a younger colleague was to write, 'came from the secure feeling of loyalty, perhaps the strongest of his qualities'.

In 1964, shortly before his planned retirement, he had a severe stroke, and soon afterwards returned to Oxford. His powers of speech and movement were impaired, and he had to lead a quiet life, but he was able to keep in touch with a wide circle of friends and colleagues and continue working on a reduced scale. His wife died in 1969, and in 1971 he moved to a cottage at Cherington, a village north of Oxford. He died in hospital at the neighbouring town of Shipston-on-Stour 22 October 1971.

By the time of his death he had accumulated many distinctions. He was an honorary fellow of St. John's College, Oxford (1955), a fellow of the British Academy (1944) and the Danish Academy, and a member of, among other bodies, the American Philosophical Society, the American Academy of Arts and Sciences, the Academy of the Arabic Language in Cairo, and the Institut d'Égypte. He was awarded honorary doctorates by Edinburgh, Harvard, and Algiers universities. He was knighted in 1954, and also held French and Dutch honours.

[Obituaries in *Bulletin of the School of Oriental and African Studies*, vol. xxxc, 1972, pp. 338–45 (A. K. S. Lambton), *Journal of the American Oriental Society*, vol. xciii, 1973, pp. 429–31 (G. Makdisi), and *Proceedings* of the British Academy, vol. lviii, 1972, pp. 493–523, with photograph (A. Hourani); G. Levi Della Vida, 'Letter of dedication', G. Makdisi, 'Biographical notice' and S. J. Shaw, 'Bibliography of Hamilton A. R. Gibb', all in G. Makdisi (ed.), *Arabic and Islamic Studies in Honor of Hamilton A. R. Gibb*, 1965; private information; personal knowledge.] ALBERT HOURANI

GILLIES, SIR WILLIAM GEORGE (1898–1973), painter and art teacher, was born at Haddington in the county of East Lothian, Scotland, 21 September 1898, the second of the three children and only son of John Gillies, tailor and tobacconist of Haddington, and his wife Emma, fourth daughter of William Smith, hotelier and carrier, of Kirriemuir, Angus. He was educated at the local primary school, progressing in due course to Knox Academy where he took his school leaving certificate in 1916, winning the Dux medal. From the outset he had a natural artistic talent and inborn love of nature and through the interest and friendship of his uncle William Ryle Smith, art master of Grove Academy, R. A. Dakars, editor of the *Haddington Courier* and an accomplished painter, and Alexander Wright, a local watchmaker, he was introduced to the Scottish 'Impressionists' and the rich and paintable landscape of the Lothians. From this moment was established a lifelong habit of 'working among his own folk and in the land of his fathers'. Between him and his environment there was to be established a bond of sympathy and affection of the most profound importance to his art.

He entered the Edinburgh College of Art in 1916, was called up for National Service with the Scottish Rifles in 1917, and, although appearing to have no conscious scruples about war, he hated the experience which he looked upon as 'two years of wasted time'. In 1919 he resumed his studies and at this time his father died. He became a close friend of William McTaggart (grandson of the Scottish 'Impressionist' William McTaggart, q.v.) and D. M. Sutherland, under whose stimulus he developed an interest in the modern movement and the technique of using broken colour.

After graduation in 1922 he stayed for a post-graduate year at the College, and then, from the summer of 1923, he spent a year on a scholarship working in the studio of André Lhote in Paris. This proved to be a salutary and disappointing experience for he recoiled from Lhote's system of rigid pedagogic methodology. After a brief visit to Florence and Venice he moved back to Edinburgh where he became an active member of the 1922 Group, which he had helped to form, where to be young and serious were the only qualifications necessary. The Group, though short-lived (its last exhibition was in 1928), became a force of some importance in the history of Scottish art. In 1925 Gillies became the art master at Inverness Academy but the following year he returned to Edinburgh as a part-time assistant in the School of Drawing and Painting. In 1928 he and his mother and sisters moved into Edinburgh. He was unmarried.

In 1932, when only thirty-three years old, Gillies was elected a member of the Society of Eight. Founded in 1912, this was a forward-looking body of painters with a distinguished record and reputation and included among its members Sir James Guthrie, Sir John Lavery [qq.v.], and F. C. B. Cadell. At this time Gillies shared a studio with William McTaggart who brought to Edinburgh for the first time an exhibition of the work of Eduard Munch. To Gillies who was then freeing himself from the influence of Lhote, this event made everything that he had seen previously seem tame. He had not before experienced so much contained and compressed emotion and there followed a series of powerful, rough-hewn paintings, both still life and landscape, which today are unique. After his death many were found off their stretchers flattened under linoleum and carpets, providing an important record of this period.

In 1939, after the tragic death of his sister Emma three years earlier, an event from which he never fully recovered, he moved with his mother and other sister to the village of Temple in Midlothian, where he was to spend the rest of his life and where drawing the landscape was to become a major preoccupation. To accomplish this a powerful motor cycle was persuaded to take him to almost inaccessible vantage points. He was forty years old and firmly established as the leading figure in contemporary Scottish painting. In 1946 he succeeded David Alison as head of the Edinburgh School of Drawing and Painting. In his hands the School burgeoned and became widely known. From 1961 to 1966 he was principal of the College of Art, Edinburgh.

After his retirement from the college and the death of both his mother in her hundredth year and his sister, he lived alone in Temple concentrating on his painting and his garden. He made no fuss about being a painter; it followed inevitably his love of life and passion for the visual world. In appearance he was slight of build but tough, and his features, which were finely drawn, never lost the appearance of youth. He was rather like a bird and his sharp blue eyes twinkled with knowing alertness. He was very thrifty. As a teacher he was like an elf in a knee-length smock scurrying from studio to studio inspiring, enlightening, and always encouraging; frizzled hair awry and the minuscule remnant of a cigarette miraculously held under a frail moustache. He was also a severe critic who gave few compliments.

As with all his generation he inherited the legacy of Impressionism, Cubism, and Fauvism. For a decade after his visit to Paris his course was uneven, a struggle between the romantic and the intellectual. From 1926 his work centred more on Cubism, and there were some fine still lifes from this period. From 1932 there followed an obsession with Expressionism but just before World War II he relaxed and recalled his earlier awareness of Vuillard and Bonnard. During the 1940s he found his own style which he continued to refine and in 1970 the Scottish Arts Council mounted a large retrospective exhibition demonstrating without doubt a powerful, original, and sensitive mind. Portraits, still lifes, and landscapes were the evidence of his complete psychological fulfilment—evidence, moreover, of an outstanding mastery of drawing, unparalleled skill in the handling of water-colour, and great versatility in the use of oil paint. For one so deeply involved in academic activity his output was enormous.

Although his work is in many public and private collections throughout the world he made little effort to promote himself. He was quite without conceit except perhaps for his skill in preparing varieties of home-made wine. He enjoyed his association with the Scottish Gallery in Edinburgh, the Stone Gallery in Newcastle upon Tyne, and the Loomshop Gallery in Fife. But for him the greatest pleasure came from visitors to his studio who came to look and perhaps acquire, and none more than Dr Robert Lillie who over the years acquired the most representative collection of his work.

In 1940 Gillies was elected an associate of the Royal Scottish Academy, as something of an 'enfant terrible'. In 1947 he became a full member and there followed in 1950 membership of the Royal Scottish Society of Painters in Watercolour, whose presidency he held in 1963. He became associate of the Royal Academy (1964), honorary D.Litt of the University of Edinburgh (1966), and fellow of the Educational Institute of Scotland (1966). He was appointed CBE in 1957, knighted in 1970, and elected RA in 1971.

He died suddenly at his home in Temple on Palm Sunday, 15 April 1973, leaving with two small exceptions all his property to the Royal Scottish Academy.

[T. Elder Dickson, *W. G. Gillies* (Modern Scottish Painters Two), 1974; personal knowledge.] Robin Philipson

GLANVILLE, Sir WILLIAM HENRY (1900–1976), civil engineer, was born 1 February 1900, the only son and second of three children of William Glanville, a London builder, and his wife, Amelia Venning. He was educated at Kilburn Grammar School and East London (Queen Mary) College of the University of London, and graduated in 1922 with first class honours in civil engineering. In 1925 he gained his Ph.D. and in 1930 his D.Sc.

All Glanville's working life was spent in the scientific civil service, the greater part in the Department of Scientific and Industrial Research, which he entered in 1922 as an engineering assistant at the newly formed Building Research Station, first located at Acton and later, in 1925, at Garston near Watford. Here he headed the engineering section until his transfer in 1936 to the Road Research Laboratory near West Drayton as deputy director; three years later he became director, a post he held until he retired in 1965.

Glanville was outstanding both as a scientist and as a director. His chief personal contribution in research was his early work at the Building Research Station on the properties of reinforced concrete, the most important results of which were embodied in a three-part paper entitled 'Studies in Reinforced Concrete' published in 1930. With a further paper published in 1939, these researches formed the basis for a code of practice for the design of reinforced concrete structures.

Glanville's qualities as a director were shown not only in his direction of and involvement in research, but in his vision of the ways in which the work of the laboratory might be extended. In 1939 he immediately turned over the laboratory to war work, with such success that it soon became one of the foremost centres of 'back-room' research. Electronic methods were applied to record the blast pressures from bombs and other munitions in air and water and earth movements from buried bombs. Models were extensively employed to investigate not only explosion phenomena, but also the attack of concrete by projectiles and shaped charges. The most spectacular of these model investigations was that which determined the position and charges for the successful attacks on the Möhne and Eder dams. The expertise of the laboratory in road-making materials and in soils helped in the rapid construction of forward airfields and in the design of plastic armour for merchant ships. Studies of soil sampled from operational areas made important contributions to the invasion of Europe.

After the war ended Glanville decided to widen the scope of the laboratory to include traffic and safety; and following a visit to America to study work there, the traffic and safety division was set up in 1947. A further expansion took place in 1955 when the colonial section, later the tropical section, came into being to carry out research specifically concerned with the problems of developing countries. These developments led to many advances and innovations: in safety, for example, concerning vehicle inspection, anti-locking brakes, tyres and road surfaces, and vehicle stability; while in traffic research, relationships were found between the speed and the flow of traffic, and new ideas on road networks and the design of towns emerged.

There were also advances in materials research in the use of concrete, tar, and bituminous materials, together with studies of individual soils, for the construction of roads. Road aggregates were also classified in terms of their engineering properties. The laboratory acquired an international reputation in road research, a large part of which can be attributed to the vision and ability of its director. He retired in 1965.

Glanville was a large man of commanding presence, who expressed his views clearly and firmly, and he therefore seemed rather unapproachable, at least to his junior staff. However, he won respect for his intelligence and judgement, for his intellectual honesty, and for his loyalty to his staff.

His main interest was always in his work, and after he retired he continued to work as a consultant, both in private practice in Britain and internationally for the International Road Federation.

He took a particular interest in the activities of the Institution of Civil Engineers and became president in 1950–1. He was awarded its Ewing gold medal in 1962, and the gold medal of the Institution of Structural Engineers, of which he was a fellow, in 1961. In 1965 he received the Viva shield and the gold medal of the Worshipful Company of Carmen. He was an honorary member of the Institution of Municipal Engineers, and of Highway Engineers, of the Royal Engineers, and of the Concrete Society. He was an almoner and governor of Christ's Hospital and a fellow and governor of Queen Mary College, University of London. He was elected FRS in 1958, appointed CBE in 1944, CB in 1953, and knighted in 1960. He was a devoted family man, having married Millicent Patience, daughter of Eli John Carr, railway official. They had one son, who was also a civil engineer, and one daughter. Glanville died at Northwood 30 June 1976.

[Lord Baker in *Biographical Memoirs of Fellows of the Royal Society*, vol. xxiii, 1977; personal knowledge.] G. GRIME

GLASS, DAVID VICTOR (1911–1978), sociologist and demographer, was born in the East End of London 2 January 1911, the elder child of Philip Glass, a journeyman tailor who was the son of immigrants from eastern Europe, and his wife, Dinah Rosenberg. He was educated at a public elementary school and Raine's Grammar School. In 1928 he entered the London School of Economics as an undergraduate, specializing in economic and social geography.

On graduating in 1931, Glass was appointed research assistant to Sir William (later Lord) Beveridge [q.v.], the director of LSE. The development of his thinking was greatly influenced by his association with Lancelot Hogben [q.v.], who was professor of social biology at LSE, and his collaborators. From them he acquired an interest in the relationship between social and biological problems and a conviction, which was to last throughout his life, of the importance of quantitative research in the social sciences. Hogben encouraged him to work on population problems and his work turned increasingly in that direction. When in 1936 the population investigation committee was founded under the chairmanship of (Sir) A. M. Carr-Saunders [q.v.], Glass was appointed its first research secretary. For the next five years of his life Glass was engaged in full-time demographic research and rapidly established a reputation as one of the most promising young scholars in that field. His work was concerned with demographic trends and policies in European countries and culminated in the publication, early in 1940, of his doctoral thesis *Population, Policies and Movements in Europe*, which has remained the standard work on this subject.

During the war, Glass entered government service and worked as deputy director of the British Petroleum Mission in Washington and for the Ministry of Supply in London. He returned to academic life in 1945, when he became reader in demography at LSE. He was promoted to a chair of sociology in 1948 and became Martin White professor in 1961.

Between 1944 and 1949 Glass's work was actively associated with that of the royal commission on population. Though not himself a member of the commission, he served on its statistics committee and its biological and medical committee and directed the family census of 1946 on its behalf. He could thus exercise considerable influence on the commission's thinking and conclusions. In the family census he pioneered the use of the method, which has been widely adopted since, of cohort analysis for the study of fertility. But his interests extended beyond demography. As research secretary of the population investigation committee, he stimulated and encouraged a number of social research projects, the most important of which were the first nationwide enquiry, carried out by Dr Lewis Faning, into the prevalence of contraceptive practice, the repeat survey on the intelligence of Scottish schoolchildren conducted by Dr J. Maxwell, which established that apprehensions of a decline in national intelligence which had been voiced by a number of scholars were unfounded, and the National Survey of Health and Development of Children, directed by Dr J. W. B. Douglas, in which extensive information was collected on environmental and other factors related to the development of a group of children born in March 1946, who were interviewed at different periods of their lives. Although the actual direction of this work was left to others, Glass took a close interest in it and served on steering committees; many of his ideas were incorporated in the surveys. He also became the UK delegate to the newly founded Population Commission of the United Nations and helped shape the policies and work of that body.

Another of Glass's major interests was in the study of social mobility. Very little factual information about the extent of social mobility in Britain was available at the time of Glass's appointment to his chair and he set about to remedy this. He organized a number of enquiries and his study *Social Mobility in Britain*, published in 1954, not only provided new facts and insights into the subject, but pioneered methods which became standard. During his last twenty years, Glass continued working on these topics, but also became increasingly interested in historical demography, a subject to which he made important contributions. To this Dictionary he contributed the notice of R. R. Kuczynski.

His scientific work brought him many academic honours. He was elected FBA in 1964 and achieved the rare distinction for a social scientist of election to the Royal Society in 1971. He was a foreign associate of the United States

National Academy of Sciences and received honorary degrees from a number of universities. His demographic colleagues honoured him by electing him to the presidency of the International Union for the Scientific Study of Population.

Glass's work was within the tradition of British empirical social research. His early association with workers in the biological sciences resulted in an approach to social problems which had more in common with that of the experimental scientist than of the social philosopher. His emphasis on the need for quantitative information in the discussion of social problems, and his suspicions of generalization were not universally shared by his fellow sociologists at the time and led him to stand somewhat apart from the profession. None the less, his influence was considerable, not only in Britain but also in the less developed countries, and particularly in India, a country to which he became greatly attached and which he visited regularly during the later years of his life.

Glass was a keen bibliophile and amassed an outstanding collection of books and pamphlets on the subject of population. He was no mere collector, however, but was familiar with the contents of all items of his library. As one of his colleagues remarked of him: 'He seemed incapable of forgetting anything that he had ever read.'

In 1942 Glass married Ruth Durant, daughter of Eli and Lilly Lazarus, and herself a sociologist of repute. They had a son and a daughter. Glass died in London 23 September 1978.

[W. D. Borrie in *Proceedings* of the British Academy, vol. lxviii, 1982; personal knowledge.] E. Grebenik

GLENAVY, third Baron (1913–1980), journalist. [See Campbell, Patrick Gordon.]

GLOUCESTER, Duke of (1900–1974). [See Henry William Frederick Albert.]

GLUCKMAN, (HERMAN) MAX (1911–1975), social anthropologist, was born in Johannesburg 26 January 1911, the second child in the family of three sons and one daughter of Emmanuel Gluckmann, a lawyer of strong liberal views, and his wife, Kate Cohen, who was a leading personality in the Zionist movement. Proud of their Russian-Jewish background, the family, except for Max, emigrated to Israel after the establishment of the state. From King Edward VII School, Johannesburg, Gluckman went up to the University of the Witwatersrand in 1928. He intended specializing in law, but attendance at Mrs Winifred Hoernlé's lectures diverted him to social anthropology. A first class honours degree, combined with an excellent athletic and sporting record and prominence in extra-curricular student activities—he was a powerfully built six-footer gifted with boundless energy and holding strong principles all his life—gained him the Transvaal Rhodes scholarship for 1934, which took him to Exeter College, Oxford. He was there drawn into the new 'functionalist' movement in British social anthropology. But most important for his career was the friendship which developed with (Sir) E. E. Evans-Pritchard [q.v.]. Awarded his D. Phil. in 1936, he returned to South Africa for two years of field research in Zululand. Three papers (1940, 1942) that resulted are significant as presenting the germs of later key ideas. Thus enriched by his first field study of a changing African society, he returned to Oxford in 1938. Influenced by A. R. Radcliffe-Brown, newly appointed to the Oxford chair, Evans-Pritchard, Meyer Fortes, and B. Malinowski, he established the framework of theory that guided all his research thereafter.

In September 1939 Gluckman was appointed to the staff of the Rhodes-Livingstone Institute in Northern Rhodesia at the insistence of the director, Godfrey Wilson, in the teeth of some settler and official anti-Semitic and anti-liberal opposition. Prevented from enlisting in the armed forces and after daunting initial obstructions Gluckman embarked on the field-work in the Barotse kingdom that became the ethnographic foundation of all his later researches. When Wilson resigned in 1941, Gluckman became temporary director and then director in 1942. At once he began to implement single-handedly the research, advisory, and educational programmes that later made the institute famous. He expanded, himself largely producing, the institute's publications, developed collaboration with government departments, drew officials and other residents into its activities, and, above all, ensured the goodwill and support of government and industry. In 1945, with the war over, and with funds from the Colonial Development and Welfare Fund, he recruited and trained a group of research officers, most of whom subsequently attained professorial rank in Britain or abroad. A series of outstanding monographs on both tribal and industrialized communities resulted from this programme.

In 1947, concluding that he had demonstrated the importance of locally based social research for both practical and academic purposes, Gluckman accepted a lectureship at Oxford. Two years later he moved to Manchester to the chair specially established for him and remained there (after 1971 as Nuffield research professor) until his death. Gluckman continued for fifteen years to work with the Rhodes-Livingstone institute, notably by providing facilities for the staff to write up their field research in his department. He assumed British nationality in 1950.

Indefatigable, outspoken, and passionately

committed to the advancement of sociological science, Gluckman created a centre of vigorous and innovative research and teaching which quickly gained international recognition. Defining social anthropology as a comparative science of social systems and institutions, he promoted research in contexts ranging from factory floor and rural village organization in Britain to both tribal and modern urban communities abroad, notably in Israel. His celebrated research seminar was frequented not only by his students and staff but by eminent fellow-professors of philosophy, politics, and economics (such as his friend and collaborator Ely Devons, q.v.) and by the distinguished visiting scholars, mostly from abroad, whom he brought to Manchester with the help of the Simon Trust. Many later publications bear the stamp of this seminar's influence. Throughout he also served on various university and national bodies concerned with the social sciences, and participated in non-academic activities that brought him into contact with the Manchester public. In 1960, while on a visit to the Australian National University, ignorant political intervention barred him from New Guinea, much to the later embarrassment of the responsible ministry. In 1965 the newly independent Zambian government invited him over and it was partly dismay over changes in tribal life he then observed that led him to concentrate on Israel thereafter.

Gluckman's impressive scholarly output ranges over all aspects of social anthropology. Often frankly personal in developing an argument, he sought always to elicit general principles from a close examination of empirical data. His semi-popular books—*Custom and Conflict in Africa* (1955) and *Politics, Law and Ritual in Tribal Society* (1965)—indicate well where his chief interests lay. Maintaining that tribal society is invariably built up on a balance of criss-crossing ties (e.g. kinship) and cleavages (e.g. political allegiance) between individuals and groups, he argued that conflict, inducing either social change or redressive response, is intrinsic to it, and this became the cornerstone of the research theory of the 'Manchester School'. However, Gluckman's main claim to fame rests on his masterly researches in legal anthropology and comparative jurisprudence, which revitalized these studies. In *The Judicial Process among the Barotse* (1955, 1967) Gluckman demonstrated his method of analysing directly observed court cases and showed that 'tribal' judges follow procedures and apply standards (e.g. of 'the reasonable man') wholly comparable to those of western judges. *The Ideas in Barotse Jurisprudence* (1965, 1972) reconsiders these findings with impressive and felicitous learning in the widest context of historical and theoretical jurisprudence, shows how tribal law is dominated by the law of persons and status, and emphasizes the idea of debt as against right, in conformity with theories of power and responsibility in social organization. Other jurisprudential issues were dealt with in publications elsewhere.

A meticulous scholar, Gluckman gave careful editorial attention to his own and his students' publications. Spontaneous, sociable, and self-assured, Gluckman attracted a following wherever he went. An unswervingly loyal friend, colleague, and teacher, he gave generously of his time and support. Ever ready to answer—or advance—criticism without acrimony, he was punctilious in his tributes to his predecessors and his acknowledgements of his contemporaries. Strenuous country walks, golf, and cricket, and attending Manchester United football games with his sons, gave outlet to his abundant physical vitality.

Gluckman was elected FBA in 1968 and foreign honorary member of the American Academy of Arts and Sciences in 1970. An honorary D. Soc. Sci. of the Free University of Brussels (1965), he held visiting lectureships at some dozen universities abroad and was Lady Davis visiting scholar at the Hebrew University, Jerusalem, at the time of his death. Among many other awards and honours he particularly prized his appointment to give the Storrs lectures in jurisprudence at Yale (1963) and the Radcliffe-Brown lecture at the British Academy in 1974. He contributed notably to the work of the International African Institute as a member of council (1956–65), consultative director (1966–74), and vice-chairman (1974), and likewise to the development of the Association of Social Anthropologists of the British Commonwealth as honorary secretary (1951–7) and chairman (1962–6). Among a number of academic and non-academic public positions held by him, his membership of the social studies sub-committee of the University Grants Committee (1966–70) and of the advisory committee to Her Majesty's Sports Council (1974) which gave him special pleasure, deserve particular mention.

In 1939 Gluckman married Mary, the only child of Guiseppe Brignoli, an attorney. A gifted linguist, she worked regularly with Gluckman both in the field and in his later researches, and helped to make their home a centre of genial hospitality. They had three sons. Gluckman died in Jerusalem 13 April 1975.

[*The Times*, 21 April 1975; Raymond Firth in *Proceedings* of the British Academy, vol. lxi, 1975; M. J. Aronoff, *Freedom and Constraint*, 1976; private information; personal knowledge.]

M. Fortes

GODBER, FREDERICK, first Baron Godber (1888–1976), international industrialist, was born in London 6 November 1888, the third son and youngest of the five children of Edward Godber, engineer, of Camberwell, and his wife, Marion Louise Peach. He attended the local school and left at the age of fifteen when he joined the Asiatic (later Shell) Petroleum Company in March 1904, as an office boy.

In 1906–7 he was fortunate to be a member of the small secretarial group under G. S. Engle while the long and complex negotiations were under way for the merger in 1907 of Shell Transport and Trading Company and Royal Dutch Petroleum. From 1912 to 1919 he was head of the newly-formed American department looking after the rapidly growing involvement in the western hemisphere. From 1919 to 1929 he spent ten years in the USA, being appointed president of Rhoxana Petroleum in St. Louis in 1922. In this position he was intimately involved in the detailed negotiations which resulted in the acquisition of the Union Oil Corporation of Delaware and the creation of Shell Union Corporation, the predecessor of Shell Oil and the foundation of Shell's fortunes in the USA.

He was recalled to London in 1929 to become a managing director of the Royal Dutch/Shell Group in one of its principal operating companies. From then until the outbreak of war he travelled widely to visit all parts of Shell's steadily expanding empire throughout the world.

During World War II Godber was chairman of the overseas supply committee of the Petroleum Board. This committee, composed of senior executives of international oil companies, coordinated supplies of petroleum from all sources to all war fronts and also dealt with home country needs. Godber's wide contacts in both Britain and the USA, together with his capacity for getting on with people, enabled him to weld it into a very effective instrument. For this and other war work he was knighted in 1942.

After the war he succeeded in 1946 to the chairmanship of the Shell Transport and Trading Company, following the retirement of the second Viscount Bearsted. While this relieved him of detailed day-to-day involvement in company activities, he turned himself wholeheartedly into raising money for relief work in Holland, as chairman of the Help Holland Fund. For this and other services to Anglo-Dutch relations he was created in 1947 a grand officer of the Order of Orange Nassau. In 1946 he also became chairman of Shell Petroleum Company Ltd. In the post-war years he played an important part in reconstructing the Group's affairs, expanding its activities, and modifying them to cope with the new nationalism in large producing countries. In consequence of this very varied career from beginning to end he acquired a remarkable insight into the circumstances in which 'the Group' was formed, and played a considerable part in bringing it from a merger between two small, relatively unknown companies, mainly engaged in producing and selling oil in the Far East, into a world-wide corporation. He retired from both chairmanships in 1961, having served the Shell Group for fifty-seven years. From 1953 to 1968 he was chairman of the Commonwealth Development Finance Corporation.

To all the tasks he faced he brought to bear a formidable battery of intelligence, appetite for work, prodigious memory, and perhaps especially, talent for dealing with people. Even those with whom he locked horns in carving a place for Shell in the USA gave him their admiration and indeed affection because of his integrity and honesty. He had a tall, erect figure, a kindly smile, an invariably courteous manner to all, no matter how lowly their position, and an unassailable rectitude which never became either pompous or priggish.

He was raised to the peerage as Baron Godber in 1956. He was also an honorary bencher of the Middle Temple (1954), Cadman medallist (1957), a trustee of Churchill College, Cambridge (1958), an honorary liveryman of the Leathersellers' Company (1962), and an honorary fellow of the Institute of Petroleum (1965).

He married in 1914 Violet Ethel Beatrice, daughter of George Lovesy, chartered accountant, of Cheltenham. They had two daughters. Godber died at his home in Mayfield, east Sussex, 10 April 1976 and the barony became extinct. A portrait of him by Sir James Gunn, RA, hangs in Shell Centre.

[Private information.] David Barran

GODDARD, RAYNER, Baron Goddard (1877–1971), lord chief justice of England, was born 10 April 1877 in Notting Hill, London, the second of the three sons and third of the five children of Charles Goddard, solicitor, of London, and his wife, Janet Gertrude, daughter of John Jobson, an ironmaster, of Derby. Called after his paternal grandmother, whose maiden name was Rayner, he was educated at Marlborough College, where he excelled as an athlete, becoming victor ludorum and also captain of the rifle corps, and at Trinity College, Oxford, where he obtained a second class in jurisprudence (1898), besides winning the 100 yards in the university sports in 10.6 seconds and getting a full blue in athletics.

His father's influence had early stimulated his interest in the law, and was largely responsible for his determination to become a barrister. While he was still up at Oxford, he became a student at the Inner Temple where he was called to the bar in 1899. Because of his family connection with Wiltshire, it was inevitable that he should join the Western circuit and enter chambers in the Temple whose members practised on that circuit. The chambers he chose were those of

(Sir) A. Clavell Salter [q.v.], whose pupil he became and whom he was later wont to refer to as his 'father in the law'. He stayed on in Salter's chambers when he had completed his pupillage and immediately joined the Western circuit where he got his first brief, at Salisbury assizes. It was to prosecute a man for breaking into a brewery. His client was acquitted which he jocularly used to recall was 'a grave miscarriage of justice'. His forthright manner of conducting his cases soon secured him plenty of work from local solicitors and at the same time he began to build up a London practice.

A hard and extremely conscientious worker, he invariably went to chambers on Saturday mornings. On one such morning he was consulted by a well-known firm of City solicitors acting for the Midland Bank, in the absence of the firm's regular counsel, and Goddard's opinion so impressed the instructing solicitor that he was briefed in the case which followed. This led to his becoming a foremost practitioner in banking and other commercial cases. At the same time he did not lose touch with the Western circuit, becoming successively recorder of Poole (in 1917), of Bath (in 1925), and of Plymouth (in 1928). For a time during World War I he was a temporary civil servant in the capacity of legal adviser in the Board of Trade. He resumed practice immediately after the war and in 1923 took silk, continuing as a KC to specialize in commercial cases.

Politically Goddard was a staunch Conservative. But his only appearance as a parliamentary candidate was unfortunate for him and ended disastrously. Shortly before the general election of 1929, the sitting member for the safe Conservative constituency of South Kensington, Sir William Davison, later Lord Broughshane, had been divorced. A hastily formed emergency committee of the constituency party opposed Davison's candidature on account of the divorce and invited Goddard to contest the seat as an Independent Conservative. He agreed, and was surprised when the Liberals also put up a candidate. In the result Goddard came bottom of the poll with only 6,000 votes against the triumphant Conservative's 28,000. The Independent's ill-timed intervention earned him the soubriquet of 'purity Goddard', although he was neither prudish nor sanctimonious in the least.

In the same year he was elected a bencher of his Inn and was clearly marked out for professional promotion. This came in 1932, when he was appointed a judge of the King's Bench division. The appointment carried with it the traditional knighthood, and when Goddard went to Buckingham Palace to receive the accolade from King George V, they discussed the recent increase in crimes of violence and the monarch remarked that he hoped the new judge would not hesitate to sentence violent criminals to flogging, advice which Goddard invariably took when he considered it appropriate. From the outset he proved himself a strong judge, dominating his court and giving short shrift to dilatory counsel and evasive witnesses, although he normally behaved with studied courtesy on the bench. His judgements, usually delivered extempore, were characterized by robust common sense rather than abstruse legal learning. His perception was acute and he was quick, sometimes too quick, in making up his mind. On the other hand, he was always ready to admit that he had been wrong and made amends accordingly.

Among the murder trials at which he presided as a puisne judge was that of a nurse, Dorothea Waddingham, in Nottingham in 1936 for the murder of a patient in a nursing home. The jury found Nurse Waddingham guilty and she was sentenced to death, which sentence was subsequently carried out. 'I see no reason why a woman convicted of murder should not hang', Goddard subsequently told the royal commission on capital punishment. In 1938 he became an appellate judge on the enlargement of the Court of Appeal, at the same time being sworn a member of the Privy Council, and six years later he was further promoted to the House of Lords as lord of appeal in ordinary taking the title of Lord Goddard, of Aldbourne, the Wiltshire village where his forebears had lived. Thus, at the age of sixty-seven, this might have seemed the climax to a successful career. But events were to turn out otherwise.

Early in 1946, the lord chief justice, Viscount Caldecote [q.v.], who was in poor health, intimated to C. R. (later Earl) Attlee, the Labour prime minister, that he wished to retire. It had long been customary for the attorney-general of the day to have the reversion of the lord chief justiceship whenever it fell vacant. However, the Labour government had been in office for such a short time that the attorney-general, Sir Hartley (later Lord) Shawcross, as he then was, did not consider it proper for him to succeed to the office, although he was consulted on the appointment and in any event he thought it should no longer be a political one. Thus the choice fell on Goddard following Caldecote's resignation and he was appointed lord chief justice of England 17 January 1946. It was traditional for a new chief to be offered an hereditary peerage, and as a law lord Goddard was only a life peer. But when the offer was made, he declined it on the ground that he had no son to inherit. Thus he established another precedent in addition to being the first non-political holder of his new office.

Goddard envisaged himself in that office for three years. In fact he held it for twelve, and during this period he was responsible for a wide variety of administrative changes and improvements in its discharge. First, he cleared the backlog of cases and delays which had built up during the time of his predecessor. Then he suggested fixed dates for trials, an innovation which was adopted and proved most successful. He was also largely responsible for the establishment of the crown courts in Manchester and Liverpool which did much to speed up the administration of criminal justice in those areas. It was also mainly due to him that the Court of Criminal Appeal was empowered to order a new trial. Although he tried a large number of civil causes, such as the unsuccessful libel action brought in 1946 by Professor Harold Laski [q.v.], chairman of the Labour Party national executive, against a number of newspapers and their editors for having allegedly stated that he advocated 'revolution by violence', it was in relation to the criminal law that Goddard was most conspicuous and also most controversial.

Among the murder cases which he tried was that of Thomas Ley, a former minister of justice in New South Wales, the so-called 'chalk pit murder', in 1947, the accused being found guilty but insane. In 1949 he sent Sylvester Bolam, editor of the *Daily Mirror*, to prison for three months for contempt of court and fined the newspaper's proprietors £10,000, the contempt consisting of the advance publication of facts calculated to prejudice the trial of the acid-bath murderer John George Haigh. A year later Goddard sentenced the atom bomb spy Klaus Fuchs to the maximum of fourteen years under the Official Secrets Acts. However, the trial which created the most public controversy was that of Christopher Craig, aged sixteen, and Derek Bentley, aged nineteen, who were convicted of murdering a policeman who had been shot dead in a Croydon warehouse in 1953 while trying to arrest them for burglary. The anomaly in this case was that Craig, who fired the fatal shot, could not be executed because of his age, while Bentley could be as an accomplice, although he was actually under arrest when the policeman was killed. In finding Bentley guilty, the jury added a recommendation to mercy, but the judge had no alternative but to sentence him to death. Goddard, whose conduct of the trial was impeccable, thought that in the circumstances Bentley was bound to be reprieved. But the home secretary Sir David Maxwell Fyfe (later Earl of Kilmuir, q.v.) refused to intervene and Bentley was hanged.

Goddard was a strong supporter of both corporal and capital punishment and he sincerely deplored the abolition of the former in 1948 and that of the latter in 1967. In the event Parliament, though not necessarily popular opinion, disagreed with him. Yet he was neither cruel nor vindictive, as evidenced by the fact that he and his colleagues in the Court of Criminal Appeal frequently set aside sentences of imprisonment and substituted probation orders. His clerk had recalled occasions when he bought boots for ragged young burglars and gave other prisoners money to help them make a fresh start.

Slightly below medium height, Goddard was an impressive figure, particularly on the bench, with his massive head, firm mouth, strong chin, and rugged features; if his manner was sometimes gruff, he was essentially friendly, free from any trace of pomposity and conceit. He was also a humble man and would usually travel from his home in Chelsea to the law courts by bus. His domestic life was happy with a wife and daughters whom he adored. Nor did he ever feel disposed to remarry after his wife's relatively early death. He was excellent company and had a fund of anecdotes, which he would retail over the port at dinners in the inns of court and the Western circuit, some of which were a trifle bawdy and shocked some of his more strait-laced colleagues.

Failing eyesight and hearing caused his resignation from his judicial office in 1958, by which date he was an octogenarian, although he was to live for another thirteen years. It was usual for a retiring lord chief justice to be raised a step in the peerage, but this was not possible in Goddard's case since his peerage was a life one in which no promotion was possible. Instead he was created GCB (1958). He was later recalled for a short time to sit in the Court of Appeal, and he continued to attend the House of Lords, both in its legal and its legislative capacity, the last occasion being in May 1965 when he spoke against the Earl of Arran's private member's Bill to make homosexual acts between consenting adults in private no longer a criminal offence. 'He was listened to with great attention and affection', his colleague Viscount Dilhorne [q.v.] recalled, 'although—perhaps alas!—his views did not receive the support of the majority.'

At the time of his ninetieth birthday in 1967 three of the inns of court gave dinners in his honour—his own inn, the Inner Temple; the Middle Temple, of which he had also been elected a bencher; and Gray's Inn. In addition numerous academic honours were conferred on him. Trinity, his old Oxford college, made him an honorary fellow (1940), and he received honorary degrees from the universities of Oxford (1947), Cambridge (1954), Sheffield (1955), Montreal (1945), New York (1945), and the College of William and Mary, Virginia (1954). He died in his flat in Queen Elizabeth Building, Temple, 29 May 1971. At his personal request his remains were cremated and there was no memorial service.

In 1906 he married Mary Linda ('Mollie'), daughter of the banker Sir Felix Otto Schuster [q.v.]; they had three daughters, the second of whom married (Sir) Eric Sachs [q.v.]. Lady Goddard died in 1928.

In the Inner Temple there is a portrait by Sir James Gunn of Goddard in his robes as lord chief justice. There is a similar portrait by the same artist in Trinity College, Oxford.

[*The Times*, 31 May 1971; Eric Grimshaw and Glyn Jones, *Lord Goddard*, 1958; Arthur Smith, *Lord Goddard*, 1959; Fenton Bresler, *Lord Goddard*, 1977; personal knowledge.]

H. MONTGOMERY HYDE

GODFREY, JOHN HENRY (1888–1971), admiral, was born in Handsworth, Birmingham, 10 July 1888, the third son and youngest of the four children of Godfrey Henry Godfrey, company secretary of Mapplebecks & Wilkes, and his wife, Kathleen Castley. He was educated at King Edward's Grammar School and entered *Britannia* in 1903. He was promoted lieutenant in 1909 and specialized in navigation. He served in the destroyer *Welland* (1909), the Yangtse gunboat *Bramble* (1910–12), the light cruiser *Blanche* (1913), and on the outbreak of war joined the old cruiser *Charybdis*, the flagship of Rosslyn Wemyss (later Lord Wester Wemyss, q.v.).

Godfrey followed Wemyss to the Mediterranean in the armoured cruiser *Euryalus* and took part in the entire Gallipoli campaign. Promoted lieutenant-commander (1916), he became assistant to Commodore (Sir) Rudolf Burmester, chief of staff first to Wemyss and then to Vice-Admiral (Sir) Somerset Gough-Calthorpe [q.v.] under whom Godfrey served in the Mediterranean and Black Sea (1917–19) and from whom he earned high praise as an exceptional staff officer. He was mentioned in dispatches and awarded the Legion of Honour (chevalier) and the Order of the Nile.

After promotion to commander and appointment as war staff officer in the Home Fleet (*Queen Elizabeth*, 1920), Godfrey served in plans division (1921–3), and on the directing staff of the Staff College, Greenwich. He was appointed second-in-command of the cruiser *Diomede* on the New Zealand Station (1925–8). Promoted captain (1928), he was deputy director, Staff College (1929–31) and commanded the cruiser *Suffolk* on the China Station (1931–3), returning as deputy director, plans division (1933–6). His very successful command of the battle cruiser *Repulse* in the Mediterranean (1936–8) brought the early award of the CB and appointment to the key post of director of naval intelligence with immediate promotion to rear-admiral (February 1939).

Godfrey tackled the task of repairing years of neglect of the intelligence division with great energy and foresight, but not all the weaknesses had been overcome when the war suddenly spread to Norway. However, the situation was very different when Godfrey was relieved in December 1942. The division had been expanded tenfold by the recruitment of many talented civilians, the operational intelligence centre (OIC) had become the nerve centre of the war at sea, the analysis and distribution of information derived from the code-breakers at Bletchley Park perfected, a simple system of grading intelligence introduced, the Inter-Service Topographical department successfully created at Oxford, the joint intelligence committee firmly established, and the principle of the indivisibility of intelligence widely accepted. For these and other vital developments Godfrey had been either entirely or primarily responsible. Weaknesses in British naval ciphers, not fully realized at the time, did remain but for this the blame in fact lay elsewhere.

Godfrey's insistence that intelligence must adopt a critical, sceptical, and scientific approach and present its findings without fear or favour had led to early clashes with (Sir) Winston Churchill and, by mid-1942, his uncompromising and at times abrasive attitude had aroused the hostility of his colleagues on the joint intelligence committee who appealed to the chiefs of staff for his removal. The first sea lord, Admiral Sir Dudley Pound [q.v.], although he had only recently extended Godfrey's appointment and approved his exceptional promotion to vice-admiral on the active list (September 1942), informed him that he would be relieved as soon as a successor could be found, a decision considered by many, including the historian Stephen Roskill, to have been both ill-judged and unjust.

Godfrey was nevertheless appointed flag officer commanding Royal Indian Navy (February 1943). The RIN, a tiny force in 1939, had been expanded enormously but without, unfortunately, sufficient attention being paid to recruitment and training or the establishment of a proper naval staff or infrastructure. Godfrey tackled these pressing problems with his accustomed incisiveness and success so that the RIN was able to play a gallant and valuable part in the war in the Far East. He had been placed on the retired list and promoted admiral (September 1945) but continued to serve in his old rank until March 1946. The sudden ending of the war, the need to reduce the navy to a peacetime size, and the political ferment in India unfortunately resulted, as it did in other Services there, in an outbreak of mass disobedience, in fact mutiny. Godfrey, with Field-Marshal Sir Claude Auchinleck's backing, treated it as such and succeeded in restoring discipline within a few days, a remarkable achievement. This endeared him neither to the British government nor to extreme nationalist opinion in India. He returned to England and after leave finally retired in September 1946.

For the next fifteen years he devoted himself to voluntary work as chairman of the Chelsea

Group of hospitals in the newly formed National Health Service and as the driving force in the creation of the now renowned Cheyne Centre for spastic children.

Godfrey was the only officer of his rank to receive no official recognition whatsoever for his immense services to the Allied cause during the war, a palpable injustice. He had been, under very different conditions, just as great an intelligence chief as Sir W. R. ('Blinker') Hall [q.v.]. An intellectual and highly cultured man, liberal minded and forward looking, capable of many acts of personal kindness, he was nevertheless reserved and sensitive. He did not suffer fools gladly and although greatly admired by all his staff some found his unwavering blue eyes and formidable mien daunting. Like Admiral Sir H. W. Richmond [q.v.] before him, under the immense strains of war he sometimes offended important colleagues and superiors. Earl Mountbatten of Burma [q.v.] considered that but for this weakness he might have reached the very top of his profession.

In 1921 he married (Bertha) Margaret, daughter of Donald Hope, managing director of Henry Hope & Sons Ltd., window-frame manufacturers, of Birmingham; they had three daughters. Margaret Godfrey was a tower of strength to her husband in their home life, in ISTD, and in India, where she was head of the Indian WVS. He died 29 August 1971 at Eastbourne.

[The Naval Memoirs of Admiral J. H. Godfrey (typescript), 1964–8; Patrick Beesly, *Very Special Admiral. The Life of Admiral J. H. Godfrey, CB*, 1980; Donald McLachlan, *Room 39*, 1968; Ewen Montagu, *Beyond Top Secret U*, 1977; *The Times*, 31 August 1971.]

PATRICK BEESLY

GOLD, ERNEST (1881–1976), meteorologist, was born 24 July 1881 at Berkswell, near Coventry, the third of four sons and fourth of eight children of John Gold, tenant farmer, and his wife, Ellen Peckett, of Barnsley, Yorkshire. He was educated at Coleshill Grammar School and Mason's College, Birmingham, the forerunner of that city's university. In 1900 he entered St. John's College, Cambridge, to become third wrangler (bracketed) in the mathematical tripos (1903) and to take a second class in part ii of the natural sciences tripos (1904). After a short spell in the Meteorological Office he returned to Cambridge in 1906 as a fellow of his college and (from 1907) first Schuster reader in meteorology until, in 1910, he took up an appointment in the Meteorological Office and began his lifelong career.

Gold's quality in research was established early. A 1908 paper was a timely comparison of the measured wind in the free atmosphere with its theoretical value and in 1909 a treatment of radiation exchange provided an explanation of the existence of the stratosphere, then something of a mystery. By these papers and related work Gold established a leading position in the science, which was recognized by his election as a fellow of the Royal Society in 1918. He continued with a steady output of useful writings although his official duties soon became demanding. When World War I came Gold accepted a commission in 1915 as captain with the Royal Engineers and moved to France with a very small company from which nucleus, with no precedent to guide him, he gradually created a military meteorological service. In due course he was providing advice including weather forecasts for ballistics, for gas warfare, and, with ever-growing importance, for the new aviation. Eventually, as lieutenant-colonel, he controlled over 200 personnel, being appointed to the DSO in 1916 and OBE (military) in 1919. He was known as Colonel Gold for the next twenty years.

Gold returned to his civilian post after the war and in 1919 when the International Meteorological Organization was reactivated he was elected president of the Commission for Synoptic Weather Information, an onerous position he retained for twenty-eight years. He presided at its meetings in nine different countries and attended numerous other international gatherings, becoming well known throughout the meteorological world for his tenacity in controversy.

With the approach of World War II the Meteorological Office again called upon Gold, this time to organize a comprehensive military service mostly of uniformed personnel in the RAF, but with the civilian office in control. When hostilities spread to all parts of the world the British meteorological service eventually reached a strength of some 6,000 with Gold in all but name its general-in-command. To this dictionary he contributed the notice of L. F. Richardson.

Gold was appointed CB in 1942 and received the American medal of freedom with silver palms in 1946. Before his retirement in 1947 he was influential in planning the totally reorganized and much expanded peacetime Meteorological Office, then under Sir Nelson Johnson [q.v.], in which scientific research was accorded a substantial role for the first time. Gold was slow in speech, deliberate in thought, given to long silences, and not always an easy superior to work with. He rarely conceded a point in argument but was conscientious and loyal.

Gold attended many meetings of the Royal Society and spoke there in his ninetieth year. He was a prominent fellow of the Royal Meteorological Society, Symons gold medallist in 1926, president 1934–5, and honorary member from 1958. In 1958 the International Meteorological Organization awarded him its medal and prize and the following year honorary membership was conferred by the American Meteorological Society.

Marriage came early, in 1907 while he was still in Cambridge, to Catherine ('Kitty') Lockerbie (died 1973), daughter of John and Mary Harlow, of Edinburgh. John Harlow was a tailor. They had met through the Cambridge Nonconformist Union; their religious belief was a permanent bond for more than sixty years. Mary Gold, their only child, cared for her father in his latter years. From 1910 their home was in the newly developed Hampstead Garden Suburb where Gold and his wife were active in local affairs. Apart from his broad intellectual interests Gold had his garden, which won him prizes locally, his golf and his bridge, and the graces of entertaining, particularly his many friends from abroad. He died 30 January 1976 at home, 8 Hurst Close, London NW11.

[R. C. Sutcliffe and A. C. Best in *Biographical Memoirs of Fellows of the Royal Society*, vol. xxiii, 1977; family papers; personal knowledge.]

REGINALD C. SUTCLIFFE

GOLDSMID, SIR HENRY JOSEPH D'AVIGDOR-, second baronet (1909–1976), politician and bullion broker. [See D'AVIGDOR-GOLDSMID.]

GOLLAN, JOHN (1911–1977), general secretary of the Communist Party of Great Britain, was born in Edinburgh 2 April 1911, the third of eight children of Duncan Gollan, sign-writer and house-painter, and his wife, Mary Dunn. He was educated at James Clark School, Edinburgh, which he left before he was fourteen. His parents were socialists, and he became involved in political activity at an early age, selling strike bulletins produced by the Edinburgh Council of Action during the 1926 general strike. In the following year he joined the Young Communist League and the Communist Party. In July 1931 he was arrested for selling socialist papers to soldiers outside their barracks. After a trial in which he conducted his own defence he was sentenced to six months' solitary confinement.

He moved to London in 1932 to become editor of the Young Communist League's paper, *Challenge*, and in 1935 was elected general secretary of the League. During the 1930s a very wide range of youth organizations, political, religious, social, and trade-union, joined together in activity against Fascism, and in particular in support of republican Spain, and John Gollan was one of the principal figures in the movement. He was also much concerned with the problems of young people in Britain, and in 1937 his book *Youth in British Industry* was published by the Left Book Club. It made a detailed examination of the wages and conditions of young workers and the inadequacy of their training and educational facilities, and helped to bring about improvements.

In 1939 he became secretary of the Communist Party's north-east district committee, and in 1941 took over as secretary of the party's Scottish committee. In 1948 he wrote a comprehensive economic and social study of Scotland entitled *Scottish Prospect*. The ideas it put forward were important factors in the development of the movement for Scottish devolution and a Scottish assembly.

From 1947 to 1949 he worked in London as assistant general secretary of the party, and between 1949 and 1954 he was assistant editor of the *Daily Worker*. He then became national organizer of the party, and in 1956, when Harry Pollitt [q.v.] retired from the post, was elected general secretary.

Gollan was involved from the outset in the elaboration of the party's programme *The British Road to Socialism*, which in 1950 broke new ground in the development of a revolutionary strategy for Britain. It replaced the previous strategy of insurrection and soviets, and argued that socialism could be achieved without a civil war, and through the transformation of Parliament by a combination of parliamentary and extra-parliamentary struggle.

Subsequent editions further developed these ideas, and Gollan took an active part in the preparation of all of them, including the 1978 edition. During these years he wrote a further book, *The British Political System* (1954), and a number of pamphlets, including *Democracy and Class Struggle* (1964) and *The Case for Socialism in the '60s* (1966). Two chapters of the book on which he was working when he died were published posthumously under the title *Reformism and Revolution* (1978).

He was a firm upholder of the internationalist traditions of the British Communist party, helping in the organization of solidarity campaigns with the colonial peoples and with opponents of Fascism. He took part in delegations to many countries, including two to Vietnam during the course of the war there. From his early years he was a firm supporter of the Soviet Union, and continued to hold that the 1917 October revolution was the greatest event in human history. His attitude was not, however, uncritical, and in 1976 he published in *Marxism Today* a lengthy article entitled *Socialist Democracy—Some Problems*, which was written on the request of the party's executive committee. It dealt with the crimes and distortion of the Stalin period in the Soviet Union as well as with that country's great achievements, criticized the current treatment of dissidents there, and made suggestions for the development of socialist democracy.

Gollan was an exceptionally lucid speaker and a formidable debater. He disliked demagogy, and held his audience by his capacity to build up a logical case and support it by thoroughly researched facts. Though small in physique and frail in appearance he was engaged in arduous political campaigning throughout his life, and his favourite relaxation from such activity was climbing in the mountains of his native Scotland.

He met his wife, Elsie, daughter of Charles William Medland, a civil servant, when she was also working in the anti-Fascist and progressive movement in the 1930s, and after they married in 1939 she played an active part in the communist movement with him. Gollan died in London 5 September 1977. His wife and a son and daughter survived him.

[Personal knowledge.] GORDON MCLENNAN

GOODEVE, SIR CHARLES FREDERICK (1904–1980), industrial scientist, was born 21 February 1904 in Neepawa, Canada, the third of five children and eldest of three sons of Frederick William Goodeve, an Anglican clergyman, and his wife, Emma Hand. His father gave to him the sense of duty and moral commitment that governed his life, and his mother gave him her redoubtable energy. He was educated at Kelvin High School, Winnipeg, and in 1919 entered Manitoba University. In 1925 he passed his B.Sc. examination with honours in chemistry and physics. During the third year Goodeve joined the Royal Canadian Naval Volunteer Reserve as a midshipman and took every opportunity to go to sea. His contact with senior officers developed his social poise.

In 1927 he was awarded an 1851 Exhibition scholarship at University College London, where he joined Professor F. G. Donnan [q.v.] who had good connections with industry. Goodeve used them to enable his future wife, Jane Irene Wallace, to work for a Ph.D. under his supervision. They were married in 1932. Her father was the Revd James Muir Wallace, of Winnipeg, a minister of the Presbyterian Church of Canada. Their two sons were born in 1936 and 1944.

In 1928 Goodeve became an assistant lecturer, in 1930 lecturer in physical chemistry, and in 1937 reader at University College. Goodeve's major researches between 1927 (when he obtained his M.Sc.) and 1939 (he received his D.Sc. in 1936) were in the absorption spectroscopy of rather unstable molecules, photochemistry, the fading of paints and their oxidation, the oxides of chlorine and sulphur, colloid chemistry, and vision in the ultraviolet and extreme red. This research led to his election as a fellow of the Royal Society in 1940. Despite this active research he continued in the RNVR. In 1936 he was promoted to lieutenant-commander and appointed to HMS *Vernon* in 1939.

Goodeve's wartime work has been ably described by Gerald Pawle in *The Secret War* (1956) and Goodeve's first, and possibly his major, triumph was the conquest of the magnetic mine, first by the double L sweep method, which enhanced the magnetic field in the sea to a sufficient extent to detonate the mines, and then by the method of degaussing, which induced a reverse polarity magnetic field within the ships so that the residual field above the mine was not sufficient to detonate it.

In 1940–2 Goodeve was attached to the new department of miscellaneous weapon development, which was concerned with anti-aircraft weapons and devices. Its two most important inventions were plastic armour and the hedgehog anti-submarine weapon.

For this work Goodeve was appointed OBE in 1941 and in 1942 he became assistant and subsequently deputy controller, research and development, Admiralty. He set up the Royal Naval Scientific Service, was knighted in 1946, and was awarded the US medal of freedom with silver palm.

In 1945 he became the director of the new British Iron and Steel Research Association. The greatest achievements of BISRA during its twenty-one years of independent existence before absorption into the British Steel Corporation were undoubtedly the development of sinter as a feedstock for blast furnaces, the continuous casting of steel, automatic gauge control of sheet rolling mills, and the pioneering of the controlled rolled, low carbon, high strength, low alloy steels later used extensively in oil and gas pipelines.

Goodeve actively promoted organizational efficiency through the development of operational research. BISRA had the world's first operational research department. Goodeve founded the Operational Research Club, started the first journal, the *Operational Research Quarterly*, transformed the club into a society in 1954, fathered a first international meeting in 1957, set up the International Federation of Operational Research Societies and, finally, set up within the Tavistock Institute of Human Relationships the Institute for Operational Research. To this Dictionary he contributed the notice of Sir Frank E. Smith.

Goodeve was awarded many honours and distinctions. For example, he was president of the Iron and Steel Institute in 1961–2, the Faraday Society in 1950–2, and the chemistry section of the British Association in 1956; a vice-president of the Royal Society from 1968 to 1970 and of the Parliamentary and Scientific Committee from 1950 to 1962; and a director of three industrial companies. He received honorary doctorates from the universities of Manitoba (1946), Sheffield (1956), Birmingham (1962), Newcastle (1970), and Salford (1974).

The Goodeves pursued an active social life. Their ballroom dancing was of exhibition standard and their skating, if not as good, was equally enthusiastic. During Goodeve's last years he was stricken with Parkinson's disease, which undermined his strength and led to the fall that killed him. Throughout his illness he never lost his sense of humour. He died 7 April 1980 in the Royal Free Hospital, Hampstead.

[Gerald Pawle, *The Secret War*, 1956; F. D. Richardson in *Biographical Memoirs of Fellows of the Royal Society*, vol. xxvii, 1981; family information; personal knowledge.]

ERIC DUCKWORTH

GOODHART, ARTHUR LEHMAN (1891–1978), academic lawyer and Anglophile, was born 1 March 1891 in New York City, the younger son and youngest of three children of Philip Julius Goodhart, a well-known New York stockbroker, and his wife, Harriet Lehman, a strong-minded woman, the elder sister of Herbert Lehman, governor of New York (1932–42) and senator (1948–56), and of Irving Lehman, chief judge of the New York Court of Appeals. On both sides of the family he came of wealthy Jewish stock and his intelligence, generosity, and sense of humour were in the family tradition. He was educated at Hotchkiss School and Yale University, where he graduated with distinction and was popular enough to be elected to a hitherto gentile fraternity. In 1912 he left for Trinity College, Cambridge, and, being advised against having J. Maynard (later Lord) Keynes [q.v.] as a tutor, chose to read law rather than economics. He took part ii of the law tripos after a year, and continued his legal studies under Professor H. D. Hazeltine until the outbreak of war.

This was the beginning of a deep attachment to Britain, in which he spent nearly all his working life, though he retained his American citizenship and, unlike many Anglophiles, never became Anglicized. He offered to join the British forces in 1914 but was rejected. He took a position as a lawyer in New York until the United States joined the war, whereupon he returned as a member of the American forces. He was counsel to the American mission to Poland in 1919 and his concern for Jews in Poland is recorded in *Poland and the Minority Races* (1920), an account of his experiences with the mission. He was called to the bar by the Inner Temple in 1919.

Prompted by his director of studies, H. A. Hollond, he decided after the war to teach law in Cambridge and became a fellow of Corpus Christi College. He filled a gap in the faculty teaching arrangements by lecturing in jurisprudence, though his main interest was in the common law. Indeed, he took jurisprudence to be mainly concerned with the general principles that underlie the common law and found the clue to these in the analysis of decided cases. The chair of jurisprudence at Oxford, long dominated by historical scholarship, fell vacant in 1931 and Goodhart, though only thirty-nine, was invited to fill it. Though never much interested in theory, he was popular both as a lecturer and writer. A steady stream of notes and articles, written in a clear and amusing style, came from his pen. His New York contacts added a transatlantic perspective to his common-sense views and, while cultivating the friendship of judges, he criticized their decisions with a freedom which at that time was more American than English. Devoted as he was to the common law, he saw the need to modernize it.

From this point of view he had three main platforms. At Cambridge he had been instrumental in founding and active in editing the *Cambridge Law Journal* (1921–5). He proved himself so adept at showing contributors how better to express their thoughts that it was no surprise when in 1926, at the behest of Sir Frederick Pollock [q.v.], himself editor of the *Law Quarterly Review* for thirty-five years, Goodhart took on the editorship of that prestigious journal. It was from the editorial chair that he made his main contribution to legal scholarship. Composing thirty or forty unsigned notes a year, besides dozens of articles, he established an unrivalled position as a critic, friendly but formidable, of the decisions of English judges.

He was also able to advance the cause of law reform. Invited by Viscount Sankey [q.v.] to join the Law Revision Committee, he used his membership of this and other *ad hoc* bodies to promote improvements in various branches of the law, for example in the rights of visitors to premises to claim compensation for injury. His pragmatism appealed to his practising colleagues and he did not talk above their heads. He led them to accept that some academic lawyers at least could make a contribution to their concerns. His views were strong and simple, sometimes over-simple. He believed passionately, for example, that a negligent wrongdoer should not be made to pay for unforeseeable harm. In this and other instances his views were presented with such courtesy, clarity, and force that they often prevailed with the courts and with reform committees, at least in part. But, more than any particular view he held, his presence and continued influence over a long period created bonds between practitioners, judges, and academic lawyers which had not previously existed.

Goodhart published a number of short books and collections of essays, of which *Essays in Jurisprudence and the Common Law* (1931) is the best known. But it was his case-notes, concise and going straight to the heart of a matter that had, rightly, the greatest impact. To this Dictionary he contributed the notices of C. S. Kenny and Lord Asquith of Bishopstone.

In 1951 Goodhart gave up the chair of jurisprudence but remained at University College, Oxford, as a successful and popular master (1951–63). He endowed the college more handsomely than anyone else since the foundation and, with his wife, created a harmonious and hospitable atmosphere. In 1924 he had married Cecily Agnes Mackay (died 1985), daughter of Eric M. Carter, a chartered accountant practising in Birmingham. They had three sons. Many honours came his way. Twenty universities in the English-speaking world awarded him honorary degrees. He took silk in 1943 and was elected FBA in 1952. He also became an honorary fellow of Trinity College, Cambridge. From 1940 to 1951 he was, though a foreigner, chairman of the Southern Price Regulations Committee at Reading. Lincoln's Inn made him an honorary bencher in 1938, an honour which he prized. For Goodhart delighted in the company of lawyers and in the discussion of law, politics, and public affairs. Good company and an excellent raconteur he remained at heart deeply serious. He was especially devoted to the cause of Anglo-American understanding. He kept alive a sense that English lawyers had much to learn from American experience at a time when they were disinclined to look across the Atlantic. Conversely, he worked tirelessly to put Britain's case to his American friends and to the wider American public. This was above all true during World War II. At that time, among many efforts to promote mutual understanding, he made two successful lecture tours of the United States. For his services in this respect he was, greatly to his pleasure, made an honorary KBE in 1948.

To other causes he was only slightly less devoted. Himself a noted jay-walker, he was for many years president of the Pedestrians' Association, a small pressure group on whose behalf he wrote many letters to *The Times*. As a member of the royal commission on the police he wrote a powerful memorandum of dissent in which he advocated the reorganization of the police as a national force. In his last years he became absorbed in attempts to defend President Nixon's conduct over Watergate and the Israeli claims to the West Bank. He still displayed in these unpromising causes the independence and force of character that earlier had enabled him so successfully to build bridges between academic and practising lawyers and between the interests of Britain and America, and to win such high regard as master of University College. He remained active and sociable, indeed, into old age. It was not until his eighty-eighth year that he suffered a stroke and, on 10 November 1978, died in London. There is a portrait by A. R. Middleton Todd in the hall of University College, Oxford.

[*The Times*, 11 November 1978; Lord Diplock and others in *Law Quarterly Review*, vol. xci, 457–88; personal knowledge.] TONY HONORÉ

GORDON, JOHN RUTHERFORD (1890–1974), newspaper editor, was born in Dundee 8 December 1890, the elder son and eldest of three children of Joseph Gordon, wine merchant, and his wife, Margaret Rutherford. He was educated at Morgan Academy, Dundee, and left school at the age of fourteen to start work on the Dundee *Advertiser* at 4*s*. 6*d*. a week. His diligence and flair as a junior reporter (one of his innovations was to take carrier pigeons to football matches to ensure the quicker receipt of the results in the office) and later as sub-editor were the first indication of a good newspaperman in the making.

By the age of nineteen he was in charge of the Perthshire and Dundee editions of the *People's Journal*, sister newspaper of the *Advertiser*, and was being paid 25*s*. a week, a sum less than that paid to older men doing less responsible work. Gordon, who throughout his life had a shrewd assessment of his own worth, felt that he was being exploited. On 28 June 1910 he wrote a stern letter signed 'John R. Gordon' to his superior J. Leng Sturrock, pointing out that his duties were such that Monday evening was the only evening in the week in which he was free before midnight, and that for such prolonged efforts his remuneration was inadequate. He wrote: 'At present I receive 25/- per week—10/- less than the next lowest paid sub-editor. I do not expect or ask for an increase of this amount but five shillings would, I think, be fair compensation for the lengthy hours.' But displaying the caution which was also one of his characteristics he added a postscript: 'If 5/- is too much, 2/6d will do.' He was paid 2*s*. 6*d*.

In 1911 he left Dundee for London where he worked in the London offices of first the *Advertiser* and then the *Glasgow Herald*. After World War I broke out he served in France as a Rifleman signaller in the Rifle Brigade and the King's Royal Rifle corps. At the end of the war he joined the London *Evening News* where he became chief sub-editor in 1922. His inspired handling and assessment of news brought him to the notice of other Fleet Street newspapers and in 1924 he accepted a similar post on the *Daily Express*, then edited by (Sir) A. Beverley Baxter. Although his success was again immediate, after a time he once more felt that he was being inadequately rewarded financially and one night when Baxter, who was a great theatre-goer and bon viveur, returned dinner-jacketed from his evening meal to cast an eye over the first edition Gordon raised the subject with him. According to Gordon, Baxter, immediately and generously conceding his chief sub-editor's worth, told him that his salary would be raised by £10 a week.

Unhappily, the editor forgot to inform the accounts department of his good deed and during the next three months when the increase had still not been implemented Gordon neither reminded the editor nor complained. At the end of that period he simply resigned and announced his intention of going back to the *Evening News*.

Meanwhile Lord Beaverbrook [q.v.] had recognized Gordon's talent. 'Beaverbrook', said Baxter, 'was the first to sense the burning flame within the granite exterior.' In 1928 Beaverbrook appointed Gordon editor of the *Sunday Express*, a post which he held jointly for the next three years with James Douglas who had been in the chair since 1920. The *Sunday Express* was then in deep trouble with a circulation of only 450,000. In his twenty-four years of editorship Gordon was to turn the ailing newspaper into one of the most successful and profitable in the world with a circulation in excess of 3,200,000.

His innovations were many. He introduced both the first crossword puzzle and the first 'What the Stars foretell' column to be published in a British newspaper. The latter happened after Gordon had commissioned an astrologer, R. H. Naylor, to cast a horoscope on the birth of Princess Margaret as he 'was seeking something different to write about her'. The result was so spectacularly successful and popular that it remained a feature. It also led to the appearance in the dock at Mansion House of both Gordon and Naylor. They were charged with being rogues and vagabonds and telling fortunes. The charges were dismissed on the grounds that the statements made were so vague that they did not come within the terms of the Vagrancy Act. Gordon did not always see eye to eye with his astrologer. When he read Naylor's forecast that Russia would not be invaded by Germany, he told him to think again, but Naylor was adamant that he was right. In the next issue of the *Sunday Express* Naylor said one thing and Gordon the other. Russia was invaded. Gordon had proved himself a better forecaster than his astrologer.

Gordon's belief was that above all other things news sold a newspaper. Right to the end of his active editorship he personally was responsible for the choice and display of every page one story. He ensured that the newspaper both commented and entertained. The cartoonist Carl Giles was one of his greatest captures and it was under his direction that the humorist Nathaniel Gubbins became a household name. Salacity was the one ingredient in many popular newspapers which neither he nor Beaverbrook would tolerate. It was an essential part of his philosophy that the *Sunday Express* should be a 'newspaper fit for all the family to read'. Indeed the market at which he was aiming his newspaper was the family man who either has a car in his garage or means to have one'—in other words, the young man on the way up.

In World War II Gordon emerged as a writer and commentator of considerable force. Although all his life he was contemptuous of politicians of all parties he had an extraordinary capacity to sense what the man in the street was thinking and to put these inarticulate thoughts forcefully into words. During the war *Sunday Express* readers read his critical comments on the conduct of the war especially during the dark days of 1941 and 1942 with a respect which was only second to that which they accorded (Sir) Winston Churchill.

Gordon was never an intimate of Beaverbrook's in the way that Viscount Castlerosse (later sixth Earl of Kenmare), his chief columnist, was. Unlike other Beaverbrook employees such as Michael Foot, Frank Owen [q.v.], and Peter Howard, he was not a frequent guest at Beaverbrook's dinner table. Proprietor and editor eyed each other warily. Each recognized the quality of the other and Beaverbrook certainly understood the importance of John Gordon to the *Sunday Express*.

When Gordon reached the age of sixty-two Beaverbrook wanted a younger man in charge of the newspaper. He suggested that Gordon should be editor-in-chief, a title which sounded grand but was empty in terms of power. Although Gordon accepted the post he realized he was being 'pushed upstairs' and as a consolation Beaverbrook suggested that Gordon might like to write a column. Gordon accepted the challenge in a way which Beaverbrook had not anticipated and went on as columnist to greater public renown than he had known before. His current events column was sharp, incisive, abrasive, and doffed its cap to nobody, from the royal family downwards. In that job (although often racked with pain and having had to suffer the amputation of a leg) he continued until his death which occurred at Croydon 9 December 1974, one day after his eighty-fourth birthday.

In 1915 Gordon married Evelyn Hinton (died 1967). In 1972 he married Margaret, former wife of Cedric Blundell-Ince, and daughter of Alexander Guthrie, linotype operator. She was a former personal assistant to Lord Beaverbrook. Gordon contributed the notice of R. D. Blumenfeld to this Dictionary.

[Private information; personal knowledge.]

JOHN JUNOR

GORDON WALKER, PATRICK CHRESTIEN, BARON GORDON-WALKER (1907–1980), politician, don, author, and broadcaster, was born 7 April 1907 at Worthing, the elder son and child of Alan Lachlan Gordon Walker, a Scottish judge of the supreme court of Lahore in the Indian Civil Service, and his wife, Dora Marguerite Chrestien.

He was educated at Wellington College after spending his early years in the Punjab and won a scholarship to Christ Church, Oxford, where he narrowly missed first class honours in history in 1928. A thesis on the national debt, for which he obtained a B.Litt., earned him election in 1931 as a Student and history tutor at Christ Church. A formative year at this period at German universities left a lasting impression on his life and work. He became a fluent German speaker, acquired a passionate philosophical detestation of totalitarianism in both its Nazi and communist forms, and made deep and lasting friendships with German social democrats. His father was an early Fabian and he inherited from him both a strong sense of social justice and of responsibility for the welfare of those who were part of Britain's colonial empire. His first unsuccessful parliamentary election was in 1935 for the Oxford City seat, where he increased the Labour vote. In the famous Oxford by-election of 1938, he stood down in favour of the master of Balliol, A. D. Lindsay (later Lord Lindsay of Birker, q.v.), who stood as an Independent Progressive. Gordon Walker, however, his deep convictions about democratic socialism already firmly established, was unattracted by the fashionable left-of-centre Popular Front politics of the time with its strong pro-communist undertones.

When war came his facility with the German language and his intimate contacts with German social democrats became valuable assets in the BBC's broadcasting offensive into Europe. In 1944 he accompanied the invading troops and was amongst the first British broadcasters to take possession in 1944 of Radio Luxemburg which became the Allies' main radio station on mainland Europe and where he remained for a time as chief editor. He returned from that work to be director of the German service at the BBC, and in October 1945, shortly after the Labour victory in the general election of that year, he was elected to Parliament in a by-election in the Birmingham constituency of Smethwick.

It was a political future full of promise. He came from the same high-minded upper middle-class background of professional service as the prime minister, C. R. (later Earl) Attlee. His active political work at Oxford and during the war had made him a respected member of that group of democratic socialists who included Hugh Gaitskell (whose notice he later wrote for this Dictionary) and Douglas Jay, and were to be joined shortly by men like Roy Jenkins and Anthony Crosland [q.v.]. His advancement was speedy. In 1946 he became parliamentary private secretary to Herbert Morrison (later Lord Morrison of Lambeth, q.v.), who was both deputy prime minister and manager of the Labour Party in Parliament and in the country. In 1947 he first earned ministerial office as under-secretary of state to the Commonwealth Relations Office. Because of subsequent events, Gordon Walker's contribution to the peaceful transformation of Empire into Commonwealth has never been given proper credit. At a time when Burma had already opted to leave the Commonwealth, and it looked as if India's determination to become a republic might make its break with the Commonwealth inevitable, Gordon Walker was sent to the sub-continent as the personal representative of the prime minister. He successfully conducted the delicate negotiations which enabled India to remain as a republic within the Commonwealth, and in doing so completely won the trust of Jawaharlal Nehru [q.v.]. When Labour narrowly retained power in the general election of 1950, Gordon Walker was promoted to the Cabinet at the age of forty-three, as secretary of state for Commonwealth relations. At the same time he was admitted to the Privy Council. In retrospect this must be seen as the most successful point in his political career, five years after entering Parliament, and thirty years before his death.

In that short-lived Labour Cabinet, two events took place in the field of Commonwealth relations in Africa which were subsequently to obscure the immense contribution Gordon Walker made to the creation of the modern Commonwealth. He handled the events with his usual painstaking integrity and with his total commitment to the creation of a multi-racial Commonwealth, but the pace of change in Africa, which no one foresaw at that time, was subsequently to expose him to criticism. The first incident was the government's decision in Bechuanaland to refuse recognition as head of the dominant Bamangwato tribe to (Sir) Seretse Khama [q.v.] who had married an Englishwoman, Ruth Williams. In the circumstances of the time this was vigorously and even stubbornly defended by Gordon Walker as being in the best interests of the welfare of the tribe. The second issue which disturbed his prospects within his own party was the controversy over the degree of his identification with the plans for setting up a Central African Federation in the face of the hostility of the black African leadership in Nyasaland and Northern and Southern Rhodesia. The Federation blueprint was being discussed at the Victoria Falls conference in October 1951 when he had to return to the United Kingdom for the general election which sent his party into opposition and left the new Conservative government to establish and later dismantle the ill-fated Federation.

During the thirteen years of opposition (1951–64) he remained one of the Labour Party's principal spokesmen on international affairs. He travelled the Commonwealth widely and in addition, as a keen European, played an active role in the consultative assembly of the Council of Europe.

On the home front he continued his vigorous ideological commitment to the social democratic, anti-communist wing of the Labour Party. Although one of nature's dons, and an intellectual in politics, Gordon Walker had not a particle of intellectual snobbery. It was characteristic of him that he chose to play an active part in political education through unfashionable National Council of Labour Colleges which provided correspondence courses for rank-and-file trade unionists. He was one of Hugh Gaitskell's most loyal lieutenants in the campaigns for the modernization of the party's constitution and against unilateral disarmament. On Gaitskell's death, he declined to become a candidate for the leadership and Harold Wilson (later Lord Wilson of Rievaulx) in 1963 appointed him shadow foreign secretary. As the prospect of serving in a second Labour Cabinet approached he was at the height of his powers and enjoyed a general respect as a man of high principle and mature judgement, insulated from intrigue, not driven by personal ambition. In the shadow cabinet, he and Wilson alone had the experience and authority of having served in the Attlee Cabinet. But the prospect of prolonged high office was to be tragically unfulfilled.

In the general election of October 1964 he was defeated in his Smethwick seat by 1,774 votes—the only member of the shadow cabinet to suffer this humiliation. As the Labour spokesman who had directed the opposition campaign against the Conservative Immigration Act he fell victim to the extreme racist feeling which ran strongly in that area of Birmingham. It was a sad irony that the same integrity which had compelled Gordon Walker to suffer stoically the false charges of appeasing white feeling over the Seretse Khama and Central African affairs should thirteen years later make it impossible for him to trim in the face of white racism in Britain. The feeling amongst ministers and officials alike who served under him during his brief but extraordinary tenure of the Foreign Office was that Gordon Walker would have gone on to be a distinguished holder of the foreign secretary's post. But further electoral disaster awaited him in January 1965 in the London East End constituency of Leyton where the sitting member, the Revd Reginald Sorensen, had been persuaded to vacate the seat with its 7,926 majority and accept a life peerage. Whether the voters resented losing a locally well-loved figure to suit the convenience of Whitehall and Westminster, or whether Gordon Walker lacked the popular flair to deal with such a by-election under the spotlight of the world's press, the Labour majority was turned into defeat by 205 votes. He refused to desert the constituency and in the next general election in 1966 he was returned comfortably by over 8,000 votes, but in the meantime he had to go into the wilderness. He became chairman of the Book Development Council and adviser to the Initial Teaching Alphabet. He acted for the government as a roving ambassador and undertook a sensitive fact-finding mission in South-East Asia to advise the government on its approach to the Vietnam conflict. On his return in 1965 he prophetically reported that this was a war 'in which there could be neither victory nor defeat, and which must in the end be settled by negotiations in which there is some compromise'.

After his return to Parliament in 1966 he rejoined the Cabinet, first as minister without portfolio and then from 1967 to 1968 as secretary of state for education and science. But he was never able to resume his former high place in the counsels of his party. He was created CH in 1968 and in 1974 became a life peer. From the House of Lords he continued his interest in international affairs and in 1975–6 was one of the British members of the European Parliament.

Gordon Walker may well be considered the unluckiest and most ill-starred of his generation of political leaders. He would undoubtedly have made a wise and courageous foreign secretary. In the sense that parliamentary politics are as important a test of character as of ability he will be remembered as having personal qualities rare in public life. In the face of heartbreaking disappointment that might well have crippled his spirit, he remained totally without self-pity or bitterness. He had a quiet depth of conviction and a magnanimity of spirit that set an example of dignity in the face of adversity. He was greatly supported by his wife Audrey Muriel Rudolf, whom he married in 1934 and who herself had been born in Jamaica and reflected his imaginative sympathy for the ideal of a multi-racial Commonwealth of nations. They had twin sons and three daughters. Gordon Walker died in London 2 December 1980.

[*The Times*, 3 December 1980; personal knowledge.] THOMSON OF MONIFIETH

GRANT, DUNCAN JAMES CORROWR (1885–1978), painter, was born at Rothiemurchus, Inverness, 21 January 1885, the only child of Major Bartle Grant and his wife, Ethel McNeil. His early years were spent in Burma where his father's regiment was stationed; he returned to England in 1893. At Hillbrow preparatory school he met the young Rupert Brooke [q.v.] and received lessons from an art teacher who interested him in Japanese prints. From 1899 he was at St. Paul's School, but a more important educational experience was provided by the relations with whom he stayed during his parents' absence abroad. Jane Maria Grant had married (Sir) Richard Strachey [q.v.]

and the younger members of her numerous family—Lytton [q.v.], Margery, and James—were particularly valuable in providing a lively, intelligent, and very cultured milieu.

Even more important was the advent of the French painter Simon Bussy, who had been a pupil of Gustave Moreau and who later married Dorothy Strachey. From infancy Grant had prayed nightly that God would make him as good a painter as Sir Edward Burne-Jones [q.v.]; the demand persisted although the form of it changed. His bent was such that Lady Strachey prevailed upon his parents to let him abandon the army and study at the Westminster School of Art. In 1902 and 1903 he was able to visit Italy: he copied Masaccio in Florence and was impressed, permanently, by the Piero della Francesca frescoes in Arezzo. A legacy of £100 allowed him to spend a year (1906–7) in Paris where he studied under Jacques-Emile Blanche at La Palette; he spoke with enthusiasm of the teaching in that establishment. It was then, so it appears, that he met Picasso and on a later visit (1909) Matisse.

But from about 1907 he was increasingly in London where he soon had many friends, notably J. M. (later Lord) Keynes, Virginia Stephen (later Woolf), and, of greater professional importance, Clive and Vanessa Bell and Roger Fry [qq.v.]. Although aware of the innovations which were so evident in Paris, Grant's work remains sober in form and restrained in colour until about 1910; of this early phase the last and perhaps the finest example is 'Lemon Gatherers' (1910, Tate Gallery), where the influence of Cézanne is less apparent than that of Piero della Francesca. After 1910 Grant became recognized as one of the most gifted proponents in this country of 'modernism'; the development is very rapid, culminating in 'Kinetic Abstract' (Tate Gallery), in which totally abstract forms were set upon a scroll designed to move to a musical accompaniment.

In 1913–14 Grant's aesthetic partnership with Fry and the Bells was given a new form by an emotional attachment to Vanessa Bell; hitherto his passions had been engaged almost always by members of his own sex and, although this essential component of his sexual nature never ceased to affect him strongly, his union with Vanessa Bell and his friendship with her husband played a determining role in the conduct of his life. It was Vanessa Bell who sustained and assisted him in his resolution not to fight in the war of 1914–18, finding him non-combatant work and bringing him to Charleston, the Sussex home in which he was to spend most of the rest of his life. In 1918 she bore him a daughter, Angelica, who married David Garnett. Despite many emotional peripeties Grant's relationship with Vanessa Bell endured to the end; it was a working partnership, the two artists painting side by side, often in the same studio, admiring but also criticizing each other's efforts.

In 1913 Roger Fry had invited Grant to join him as a decorator in the Omega Workshops at a fee of ten shillings a week, which for him at that time was affluence. His nervous and highly personal brushwork, his witty and lyrical invention made him an outstanding ornamentist and, when Omega came to an end in 1919, he continued to seek decorative commissions. In the years immediately following the war his work lost something of its gay decorative quality and he returned to sombre colours and a very careful examination of volumes; there was no return to the abstraction of earlier years. Nevertheless his palette did slowly regain richness and brilliance; by the end of the twenties he had completed a number of decorations, was a good deal imitated by his juniors, and was at the zenith of his popularity. In 1935 he and Vanessa Bell were commissioned to execute decorations for the new Cunard liner *Queen Mary*, but, despite the fact that he was beginning to be regarded as an establishment figure, his painting still had the power to shock and his large murals were rejected by the company. In 1941 he received his most important commission (again with Vanessa Bell): the decoration of the interior of the church at Upper Berwick in Sussex. The main part of this work was completed in 1943. In 1941 he was made RDI for his work on printed textiles.

After the peace of 1945 Grant became aware that he had gone out of fashion; his reputation had evaporated and he could no longer sell except at very low prices. In 1961 Vanessa Bell died and he was left to live alone, forgotten by all save a few friends. In this situation he did not repine but continued to work, it seems not unhappily. But in his last decade he was rediscovered by some younger artists and critics and again could enjoy some of the fame that had once been his. He continued to paint until a few days before his death.

Grant is assured of his place in British art history as an innovator of very great talent, as an accomplished decorator, and as a painter of large though unequal achievement. It is probable that he will be valued for his landscapes and his still lifes, for a few of his portraits, and for the *Queen Mary* decorations. As a man he was distinguished by great personal beauty and an uncommon sweetness of character; no one who met him could fail to be impressed by his gentle dignity, and his faintly ironical vivacity. His enthusiastic generosity as a critic of other artists' work derived from a firm conviction that, of all human activities, painting is the best. He died at The Stables, Aldermaston, 8 May 1978.

[Memoirs and biographies of the period;

Michael Holroyd, *Lytton Strachey*, 2 vols., 1967, 1968; Paul Roche, *With Duncan Grant in Southern Turkey*, 1982; Angelica Garnett, 'Duncan Grant, Works on Paper', Anthony d'Offay *Catalogue*, 1981; personal knowledge.]

QUENTIN BELL

GRAY, SIR JAMES (1891–1975), zoologist, was born in Wood Green, London, 14 October 1891, the only son and younger child of James Gray, a Scottish accountant from Coatbridge, and later chairman and managing director of the Electrical Construction Company in London, and his wife, Jessie Taylor. Gray's mother was also Scottish. Gray was educated at Merchant Taylors' School, and at King's College, Cambridge, where he was a foundation scholar. He obtained first classes in both parts of the natural sciences tripos (1911 and 1913). He did further study in Naples and was elected to a King's fellowship in 1914, but almost immediately joined the Queen's Royal West Surrey Regiment, where he served with distinction in France and Palestine, being awarded the MC (1918), and the croix de guerre avec palme, the latter presented to him in the field by Marshal Ferdinand Foch. He attained the rank of captain.

He returned to Cambridge in 1919, resumed his fellowship at King's, and soon took on a number of college posts. But in 1924 he was made a university demonstrator, and in 1926 a university lecturer. At this stage he gave up his college commitments and turned to the department of zoology and research. In 1929 he was made a fellow of the Royal Society, and in 1931 he became reader in experimental zoology. Though he was not to be made professor of zoology until the retirement, in 1937, of Professor J. Stanley Gardiner, it was in large measure Gray who provided the impetus, and raised the money to build the splendid new department of zoology, completed in 1934. He reigned over it with immense authority for twenty-two years. He was also Fullerian professor of physiology at the Royal Institution in 1943–7.

Gray was an impressive teacher, with, despite his austere manner, an occasional impish sense of humour, and many generations of students recall his classes with admiration, tinged perhaps with awe. But his greatest contribution was without doubt his research and still more its influence on others. When Gray was a young man, zoology was mostly a descriptive science, heavily influenced by Charles R. Darwin [q.v.] and the theory of evolution, and only just beginning to spread out into genetics. Significantly, one of his teachers at Cambridge was Leonard Doncaster, a cytologist and embryologist, with whom he wrote his first paper in 1911. It had an experimental approach, and Gray's classic book, *A Text-book of Experimental Cytology*, published in 1931, stemmed without doubt from this early collaboration. It established a wholly new branch of biology, and it is difficult now to appreciate what a revolutionary first step this was.

Perhaps more significant than Gray's own research, however, was the influence he had on others, an influence that became more profound when he was appointed head of what was to become a very large department. In the 1930s and for a time after the war it was pre-eminent in Britain, and indeed in Europe. At one point no less than nine members of his staff were fellows of the Royal Society, and many of his pupils gained distinction in Cambridge and elsewhere.

Curiously, however, and well before even he could have realized the full impact that his work on experimental cytology was to have, he switched completely his line of research. From the early 1930s, and for the rest of his active career, he worked on animal locomotion, believing, rightly, that new techniques and ideas were needed before a study of the cell could be much further advanced.

His work on animal locomotion was meticulous and scholarly, but it did not have, and perhaps in its very nature could not have had, a seminal quality. One of his junior colleagues, working in the field of experimental cytology, recalls Gray asking to be told 'when my work becomes boring', and it has to be said that his later work was never as significant as his earlier research. To this Dictionary he contributed the notice of G. P. Bidder.

Gray's activities extended far beyond his department. He was for many years editor of the leading *Journal of Experimental Biology*, his control of it, in the words of one observer, being 'that of a wise and beneficent autocrat'. And amongst many other things he was chairman of the advisory committee on fishery research (1945–65), president of the Marine Biological Association (1945–55), and president of the British Association (1959). He received honorary degrees from Aberdeen, Edinburgh, Durham, Manchester, and Wales. He was appointed CBE in 1946 and was knighted in 1954.

Gray was tall and distinguished in appearance. In manner, as a close friend has put it, he was 'reserved and quite shy, a formidable fighter for things he wanted, austere, kind-hearted and hospitable, with a lot of personal things to say but with great difficulty in doing so'.

In 1921 he married Norah Christine, daughter of Ernest Carter King, director of the Cannon Brewery in Hampstead. They had two adopted children, a son and a daughter. Gray died in Cambridge 14 December 1975. There is a bust of him by Sir Jacob Epstein in the department of zoology.

[H. W. Lissmann in *Biographical Memoirs of Fellows of the Royal Society*, vol. xxiv, 1978; Sir Alister Hardy—obituary in *Journal of the Marine Biological Association*, vol. lvi, 1976; obituary in *Annual Report* of King's College, Cambridge, 1976; private information; personal knowledge.] MICHAEL SWANN

GRAY, (KATHLEEN) EILEEN (MORAY) (1879–1976), designer and architect, was born 9 August 1879 at Brownswood, the family estate in Enniscorthy, county Wexford. She was the third of three daughters and youngest of five children of James Maclaren Smith, an amateur painter, and Eveleen, daughter of Jeremiah Londsdale Pounden, of Brownswood, and his wife Lady Jane, sister of the fourteenth Earl of Moray. In 1895 Eileen Gray's mother inherited the title Baroness Gray, and two years later her father changed his name to Smith-Gray, by royal licence. From then on the children took the surname Gray.

Her background of aristocratic ease, compounded by a rather pleasantly erratic upbringing, makes her later professional achievement all the more remarkable. She seems to have had little formal education and spent most of her childhood with her mother, either at Brownswood or in London, where her mother used to winter. She occasionally travelled in Europe with her father, on his long artistic sojourns in Switzerland and Italy, and it may have been his love of painting which encouraged her to enrol at the Slade School in 1898.

During this early period in London Eileen Gray first learnt the rarified technique of lacquer making; first in the workshop of D. Charles in Dean Street, Soho, and later on in Paris, where, working mainly with Sugawara, the great Japanese craftsman, she began to develop the designs for lacquered furnishings which became the basis of her growing reputation.

From her student days she showed a great affinity for Paris, visiting there often, and in 1902 decided to live and work there permanently. Five years later she moved into the flat at 21 rue Bonaparte which was to be her base until her death. By 1913, the year in which she first showed examples of her work in the 'Salon de la Société des Artistes Decorateurs', she had many useful contacts in the world of art and fashion: with Paul Poiret, for example, and with Jacques Doucet, the couturier and collector, who was to buy several important works from her.

Through this period of consolidation Eileen Gray was also designing some highly original abstract rugs and carpets which were handmade in her studio in the rue Visconti, run by an English colleague, Evelyn Wyld. In 1922 Eileen Gray opened a furniture gallery—Jean Désert—in the rue du Faubourg St. Honoré, but she does not seem to have really had her heart in it, probably because by the middle 1920s her career was undergoing a quite fundamental change.

Her work was developing from that of decorator, albeit decorator of rare vision and talent, to that of architect of international modernism. This new outlook was encouraged by her contacts among the avant-garde Dutch architects, especially Wils and Oud, who had admired her work in the Salon des Artistes Decorateurs in 1922. Two years later a whole issue of the Dutch review *Wendingen* was devoted to Eileen Gray. This special issue had an introduction written by Jean Badovici, Romanian architect and influential critic. It was Badovici, the editor of *L'Architecture Vivante*, who was most responsible for her enlargement of ambition. They were close friends and they worked together over many years.

Eileen Gray and Jean Badovici collaborated on 'E-1027', otherwise known as 'Maison en Bord de Mer', the house at Roquebrune in the South of France which is generally held to be one of the classic modern buildings of its period. Le Corbusier, a friend of Badovici's, painted a large mural in the living-room, and it was, ironically, from the rocks below the house that he took his last, and fatal, swim. Between 1932 and 1934 Eileen Gray designed and built a second house nearby at Castellar, named 'Tempe a Pailla', a building of similarly innovative quality and perfectionist detail. This house was later acquired by Graham Sutherland [q.v.].

Eileen Gray, although an architect and a designer of acclaimed originality, suffered a long lapse of reputation after these two buildings. She continued working. Le Corbusier invited her to show her large-scale scheme for a vacation centre in his pavilion at the 1937 Paris International Exposition. But for many years—a period of decline exacerbated by the hardships of the war years in France, during which she was interned—few of her projects saw fruition.

In 1968 the architectural historian Joseph Rykwert wrote an article in *Domus*, pointing out how odd it was that no one had paid homage to Eileen Gray for thirty years. From then on the forces of reparation were, some might say, almost super-active. In 1971 a retrospective of her work was organized in London at the RIBA Heinz Gallery and was followed by larger exhibitions at the Victoria and Albert Museum and the Museum of Modern Art, New York. In 1972, at the age of ninety-three, she was appointed a Royal Designer for Industry. Prices in the salerooms for her original pieces, especially the lacquer work of her early period, rose spectacularly. New editions of her modernist furniture of the 1920s and early 1930s were put into production in the 1970s.

Eileen Gray was not so much a theoretic

innovator, not perhaps even a major design influence, but she was a practitioner with a unique breadth of vision, encompassing both luxuriance and purism, a designer of consummate judgement and finesse. In appearance she was as stylish and as *soignée* as one of her own interiors. In conversation she had a quiet wit, showed an endless curiosity, and was always avid for the stimulus of new experience. Her character, however, had its areas of elusiveness. She never married. She died in Paris 30 October 1976.

There are examples of Eileen Gray's furniture in the collections of the Victoria and Albert Museum and the Musée des Arts Decoratifs, Paris; and drawings and models in the collection of RIBA in London.

[*The Times*, 3 November 1976; Joseph Rykwert, 'Eileen Gray: pioneer of design', *Architectural Review*, December 1972; Stewart Johnson, *Eileen Gray: Designer 1879–1976*, 1979; private information.]

FIONA MACCARTHY

GREAME, PHILIP LLOYD-, first EARL OF SWINTON (1884–1972), politician. [See CUNLIFFE-LISTER.]

GREEN, HENRY (pseudonym), writer. [See YORKE, HENRY VINCENT.]

GREENWOOD, WALTER (1903–1974), novelist and playwright, was born 17 December 1903 in Salford, Lancashire, the elder child and only son of Tom Greenwood, master hairdresser, and his wife, Elizabeth Matilda Walter. He was educated locally at the Langworthy Road Council School until he was thirteen, having worked as a pawnbroker's clerk outside school hours for the previous twelve months. His father had died even earlier and the family experience was typical of many in the area at the time, long stretches of unemployment alternating with brief periods of ill-paid and usually manual work. By the age of thirty Greenwood had been a clerk, a stable boy, a packing-case maker, a sign-writer, a driver, a warehouseman, and a salesman, and he had never earned more than thirty-five shillings a week. He had also started to record his impressions of working class life in south Lancashire, drawing on what he himself knew of subsistence in the slums and the emotional escape from them in books and music, as well as physical release in cheap day excursions to the Pennine hills and the Peak District. These were the materials he used in his first and best known work, *Love on the Dole*, which was published in 1933.

Its strength as a novel lies not in its descriptions or its narrative, but in the honesty with which it tells its story of urban poverty and in the richness and accuracy of its dialogue. It is occasionally comic, it ends in tragedy, and it is essentially an account of courage in desperately universal circumstances. Though written in prose it can be seen as successor to the idiomatic plays of W. S. Houghton [q.v.] and Harold Brighouse, dramatists of the Manchester school a generation earlier, and to the verse of Samuel Laycock which came half a century before: and *Love on the Dole* was itself redrafted for the stage by its author in collaboration with Ronald Gow in 1934, subsequently filmed (1941), and eventually resurrected as a musical in 1970. But it became a landmark in its original form because it vividly told recognizable truths when the country was suffering them in the slump.

Greenwood produced nine other novels and a book of short stories, and among them *Only Mugs Work* (1938) was also turned into a play. As he mastered the techniques of drama, he looked more and more to the stage for his successes, and *My Son My Son* (1935), *The Cure For Love* (1951), and *Saturday Night at the Crown* (1953) were highly applauded for their vigour, their humour, and their characterization, while always remaining within a strictly conventional view of the theatre. Film scripts, too, appeared from 1935, when Greenwood wrote *No Limit* for the comedian George Formby [q.v.], and during the war he wrote the screen-play for a documentary about the merchant navy. He found yet another outlet for his talents in the growth of television, producing many scripts for the BBC, notably the serial *The Secret Kingdom* in 1960. Much more adaptable than most writers of his period, he was fundamentally a story-teller of primitive gifts which were never in danger of being obscured by literary finesse. His most disappointing work was his autobiography *There Was a Time* (1967), which betrayed his uneasiness with writing outside his chosen forms.

Greenwood remained throughout his life a man of the people from whom he came, affable and guarded, someone who had achieved respectability but still bore the marks of the battering he received in his early years. In 1971 he was made an honorary D.Litt. by Salford University. He never married, and he died 10 or 11 September 1974 (he was found on the 11th) after heart failure at his home in Douglas, Isle of Man, where he had lived for many years.

[*The Times*, 16 September 1974; *Who's Who in the Theatre*; Walter Greenwood, *There Was a Time* (autobiography), 1967; personal knowledge.]

GEOFFREY MOORHOUSE

GREER, WILLIAM DERRICK LINDSAY (1902–1972), bishop of Manchester, was born 28 February 1902 at St. Matthew's rectory, Belfast, the younger son and second of the four children of the Revd Richard Ussher Greer, of Rhone Hill, county Tyrone, and his wife, Elizabeth Lindsay Greer (his second cousin), daughter of Frederick Greer, RN, of Tullylagan, county Tyrone.

Greer's home background in Ulster gave him a lively awareness of the interaction of religion and politics, the needs of the socially deprived, and the virtue of tolerance. He was educated first at Campbell College, Belfast, and from 1915 to 1920 at St. Columba's College, Rathfarnham, Dublin, where his deep love of literature was first kindled. In 1920 he won a scholarship to Trinity College, Dublin, and in 1924 graduated a senior moderator in mental and moral philosophy.

Although Greer was deeply involved in the Student Christian Movement at Trinity College, his decision to offer himself for ordination was not made until after he had joined the Northern Ireland Civil Service, in which from 1925 to 1929 he served as assistant principal in the Ministry of Home Affairs.

In 1929, after spending three terms training for the ministry of the Church of England at Westcott House, Cambridge, he was ordained to a curacy at St. Luke the Evangelist, Newcastle upon Tyne, where, contrary to the established convention, he succeeded his vicar three years later. In 1935 he left Tyneside for London to become the general secretary of the Student Christian Movement. Although he was temperamentally more at home in the university world than in parish life, five of his nine years in this influential and congenial office were made exceptionally difficult by wartime conditions. The letters he wrote to students on active service were much appreciated and have been compared to those written in Germany by Dietrich Bonhoeffer. The ecumenical character of the Student Christian Movement entirely accorded with his own convictions. He was involved in the formation of the World Council of Churches and spoke out explicitly for the reunion of the Anglican and Methodist churches.

In 1944 Greer was appointed to the principalship of his old theological college, Westcott House, with the formidable task of following Canon B. K. Cunningham, whose eccentric and endearing personality had dominated the college since its foundation in 1919. His knowledge of the world, his quiet sagacity and keen sense of the incongruous were just the qualities needed for dealing with the problems of ex-servicemen returning to begin their training for the ministry. His devotion to the comprehensiveness of the Church of England and to the decent order enshrined in the Book of Common Prayer inspired confidence that the distinctive tradition of Westcott House was secure for many years to come.

In 1947, however, to the surprise and dismay of many of his friends, Greer was taken from Cambridge to become bishop of Manchester. He was consecrated in York Minster on 29 September. The diocese presented him with almost insuperable post-war problems, especially those of repairing bomb damage and finding clergy to serve in its 372 parishes. Despite these burdens, he promoted ambitious programmes of adult education and threw his energies into his chairmanship of the BBC's central religious advisory committee. His principal aim was always to integrate the life of the church with the life of society at large and he was singularly successful in establishing close relations with the Manchester business community. He himself was an enthusiastic president of the Manchester and Salford Savings Bank. At the same time, he pursued his lifelong concern for the underprivileged. He played a leading part in founding (in 1963) William House at Withington, a hostel for discharged prisoners, and (in 1971) St. Ann's Hospice in Cheadle for terminal cancer patients. It was well known that the bishop held firm convictions on disarmament and, despite his extreme caution, he publicly advocated the unilateral renunciation by Britain of atomic weapons.

In the early 1960s Greer's health began to fail and only a strong sense of duty enabled him to persevere until his retirement in April 1970. Twenty-three years in so conservative and demanding a diocese was far too long for anybody and especially so for a man of his shy intelligence.

Although his personal distinction was recognized by honorary doctorates from Trinity College, Dublin (1947), and the universities of Edinburgh (1951) and Manchester (1971), Greer was not (like some bishops of his generation) a frustrated academic. He wrote only one book and that was the biography of an Irish friend who died when still a curate: *John Bainbridge Gregg* (1931). On his retirement, he sought seclusion in his rural retreat at Woodland, near Coniston, but, unhappily, he was already too ill to enjoy his favourite pastimes of walking and gardening. He died there 30 October 1972.

In 1946 Greer married Marigold Hilda Katharine, daughter of the Revd Edgar Stogdon, vicar of Harrow-on-the-Hill. They had one son, Richard Edgar, and two daughters, Elizabeth Louise and (Martha) Lindsay Dundas.

[*The Times*, 1 November 1972; private information; personal knowledge.] E. W. Heaton

GRENFELL, JOYCE IRENE (1910–1979), actress and broadcaster, was born in London 10 February 1910, the elder child and only daughter of Paul Phipps, an architect and a fellow of RIBA, and his wife, Nora Langhorne, from Virginia, USA, who was the sister of Nancy (later Viscountess) Astor [q.v.], the first woman to sit in the House of Commons. Educated at Francis Holland School, London, and the Christian Science school Clear View in South Norwood, and then 'finished' in Paris, stage-struck Joyce Phipps, in the intervals of going to debutante dances, attended classes at the Royal Academy of Dramatic Art, but shortly abandoned her histrionic dreams to become the wife of Reginald Pascoe Grenfell, chartered accountant. They married in 1929, Joyce then being nineteen, and remained happily so until her death, fifty years later. They had no children.

Meeting J. L. Garvin [q.v.], editor of the *Observer*, and conveying to him in all innocence, and with no ulterior motive, her interest in and affection for the radio, she found herself, much to her surprise, the radio critic on that paper, writing a weekly column from 1936 to 1939 when, also unsuspecting of the outcome, she met Herbert Farjeon, theatre critic of the *Tatler* and author of a current revue, *Nine Sharp*. At a party given by Stephen Potter, with whom she was later, in 1943, to broadcast the popular 'How' programmes (and whose notice she subsequently wrote for this Dictionary), Joyce was persuaded to entertain the company with a rendering of a talk she had heard at a Women's Institute meeting. It was called 'Useful and Acceptable Gifts', and was the foundation stone upon which her stage career was built. For Farjeon was so amused by it that he invited her, absolute amateur though she was, to give this talk in his coming revue, *The Little Revue*, which was to open in March 1939. Feeling she had nothing to lose, and being of a fearless disposition, Joyce accepted.

Thus began Joyce Grenfell's long and successful career as an entertainer. Not only did she write a large number of monologues, many of which, notably the 'Nursery School' series, became classics, but lyrics as well, the music for which was, for the most part, composed by Richard Addinsell. Her monologue characters, ranging through every stratum of society, catching the tones and manners of, among others, a chairman of a north country ladies' choral society, a wife of an Oxbridge university vice-chancellor, a foreign visitor at a cocktail party, a country cottager, an American mother, and a cockney girl friend, were masterpieces of observation. Along with her songs, sung in a small but pretty and perfectly tuned voice, they provided evenings of rare entertainment.

She had an instantaneous success. There were two more Farjeon revues, *Diversion* and *Light and Shade*, and then, during World War II, she went on two long tours abroad for the Entertainments National Service Association, visiting hospitals and isolated units in fourteen countries. She was appointed OBE in 1946.

In 1945 she appeared in the revue *Sigh No More* by (Sir) Noël Coward [q.v.], in 1947 *Tuppence Coloured*, and in 1951 *Penny Plain*. She also took part in a radio discussion programme, 'We Beg to Differ', in 1949, and over the years appeared in a variety of films: *Genevieve*, *The Happiest Days of Your Life*, *The Million Pound Note*, *The Yellow Rolls-Royce*, to name the better known; and the St. Trinian's series in which her interpretation of a much badgered games mistress brought her increased fame.

But it was in 1954 that she reached the height of her profession, for in that year she had her own show, *Joyce Grenfell Requests the Pleasure*, which led eventually to her handling a two-hour programme solo (like her well-known friend Ruth Draper) and touring the world with it. Her tours abroad were numerous and glorious. Canada, the USA, Australia, New Zealand, Hong Kong, Switzerland, (not South Africa), all saw her many times, and so of course did every part of Britain, her dearest local triumph being a short season at that most stylish of London theatres, the Haymarket. After nearly forty years of entertaining a grateful public composed of all classes, age groups, and nationalities, she retired from the stage in 1973, her final performance of songs and monologues being given before the Queen and her guests at the Waterloo dinner in Windsor Castle.

She continued to appear on television, making a particularly pleasing contribution to the musical quiz programme 'Face the Music' and giving a memorable TV interview to Michael Parkinson in September 1976.

Through the years Joyce Grenfell was committed to projects unconnected with show business. In 1957 she became president of the Society of Women Writers and Journalists; from 1960 to 1962 she served on the committee concerned with the 'future of the broadcasting services in the UK', chaired by Sir W. H. (later Lord) Pilkington; in 1972 she was appointed a member of the council of the Winston Churchill Memorial Fellowship Trust, the grants from which enable students to go overseas to study their special subjects.

A lifelong Christian Scientist she was deeply interested in metaphysics, and on a number of occasions spoke in the 'dialogues' initiated by the Revd Joseph McCulloch from the two pulpits in St. Mary-le-Bow church in London. She also spoke in Truro Cathedral and Westminster Abbey (in which latter church she was given, in 1980, the rare honour of a memorial service). She lectured on 'communication', about which she was naturally very experienced, to all sorts of groups, in universities, colleges, and technical institutes, being made an honorary fellow of the Lucy Cavendish College, Cambridge, and the Manchester Polytechnic, and often contributed to the BBC morning programme 'Thought for the Day'.

During her partial retirement from public life she wrote her autobiography in two volumes, *Joyce Grenfell Requests the Pleasure*, a bestseller published in 1976, and *In Pleasant Places*, published in 1979.

Joyce Grenfell's total enjoyment of life was the keynote to her character. She had a genuine love of goodness and sought it in all things, in music, literature, nature, and above all people. Her talent was unique in that although she caricatured her subjects and pin-pointed their idiosyncracies, there was never a hint of censure. Although she became a true professional she retained one attractive element of the amateur, in that she seemed to be doing it all for fun; and her manifest zest for living coupled with her artistry, kind-heartedness, and sense of humour had a cherishing effect upon her audiences. They loved her. On the stage, television, and radio she had a huge following and at her death, in London 30 November 1979, she had become in the nature of an institution. As the critic Clive James wrote in an obituary: 'Beyond those favoured hundreds who knew her in person are the thousands and the millions who could tell just from the look of her that she had a unique spirit.' She was to have been appointed DBE in the 1980 New Year honours list.

[Joyce Grenfell, *Joyce Grenfell Requests the Pleasure*, 1976, and *In Pleasant Places*, 1979; Reggie Grenfell and Richard Garnett (eds.), *Joyce*, 1980; personal knowledge.]

VIRGINIA GRAHAM

GRIERSON, JOHN (1898–1972), founder of the British documentary film movement, was born 26 April 1898 at Deanston, Kilmadock, Scotland, the fourth of eight children and the elder son of the local headmaster Robert Morrison Grierson, whose forebears were lighthouse keepers, and of his wife Jane Anthony, a teacher, the daughter of a shoemaker in Stewarton. Educated at Stirling High School he worked for two years in a munitions factory before serving from 1917 to 1919 in the Royal Naval Volunteer Reserve as a telegraphist on naval minesweepers. This confirmed the love of the sea that permeated the rest of his life and work.

In 1923 he graduated MA, with second class honours in philosophy, from the University of Glasgow, which he had entered in 1919. Grierson was interested in student politics, but although he adopted the radical views of his mother, an early suffragette, and of the Clydeside Independent Labour Party, he was never a party political figure. After a year as assistant registrar to Armstrong College, Newcastle upon Tyne, he won a Rockefeller fellowship to study American politics and newspapers. At the University of Chicago Dr Charles Merriam encouraged him to turn his attention to the social significance of the cinema. Travels throughout America, including a visit to Hollywood, encounters with Robert Flaherty, Walter Lippmann, and (Sir) Charles Chaplin [q.v.], and the Soviet film *Battleship Potemkin*, prompted his first writings on motion pictures. Over the next forty years he produced some of the best commentaries on film by an active film-maker.

In London in 1927 he persuaded (Sir) Stephen Tallents [q.v.], secretary of the newly-formed Empire Marketing Board, to employ him as assistant film officer and to allocate £2,500 for the first Grierson documentary film, *Drifters* (1929). Imaginative photography and cutting created something very different from the conventional British cinema of the time. But surprisingly Grierson followed up its success, not by making more films himself, but by building up a group of young directors under his leadership. 'Documentary films', a term he introduced to describe the artistic presentation of factual film material as propaganda, were made for the EMB by a team that included Basil Wright, Paul Rotha, (Sir) Arthur Elton [q.v.], Stuart Legg, and Edgar Anstey. When the EMB was dissolved in 1933 Tallents, an imaginative patron, became public relations officer for the General Post Office and took Grierson with him. Here they contrived to make left-of-centre films for a public corporation controlled by the right-of-centre national government. More outstanding young men such as W. H. Auden, Benjamin (later Lord) Britten [qq.v.], (Sir) William Coldstream, Humphrey Jennings, and Harry Watt were recruited by Grierson. The films he produced included *Industrial Britain* (1933), *The Song of Ceylon* (1934–5), *Coal Face* (1935), and *Night Mail* (1936); their quality has sometimes been overrated but they were important since they showed working people, and their homes and problems, on film for almost the first time in Britain and brought creative artists into the cinema industry. Grierson raised the standards and prestige of his team by employing two outstanding foreign directors, Robert Flaherty, a Canadian, and Alberto Cavalcanti, a Brazilian, although he did not find it easy to work with these talented and experienced men.

In 1937 Grierson sought independence from the GPO and established an advisory service, the Film Centre. He wrote reports on sponsored film for the Canadian, Australian, and New Zealand governments and in 1939 was invited to head the National Film Board of Canada. Here he created his lasting monument, a large organization that made many memorable films and was able to survive his departure in 1945. For the next twelve years Grierson moved restively from one position to another, inspiring and agitating, but never able to satisfy either his own ambition or the hopes of his sponsors, the International Film Associates of

New York (1945), Unesco (1946–8), the British Central Office of Information (1948–50), or Group 3 established by the National Film Finance Corporation to make British feature films (1950–5). Finally he found a more stable base in the new medium, television, producing a regular programme *This Wonderful World* for the Scottish Television Company with the backing of Roy Thomson (later Lord Thomson of Fleet, q.v.), who took Tallents's place as an understanding patron. He also travelled to film festivals and conferences throughout the world as lecturer and adjudicator, enjoying his role as a provocative elder statesman. After a grave illness in 1968 he became a part-time professor of mass communication at McGill University until he died at Bath 19 February 1972.

Grierson exuded energy and ideas from his short frame and piercing eyes. On an early visit to a film studio he unsettled Gloria Swanson who exclaimed: 'There is a man here whose eyes are hurting me. Throw him out.' Many film-makers, civil servants, and journalists were also unsettled by Grierson, but those whom he respected, and who respected and accepted his determination to lead, drew from him the inspiration for their own work and the support that made it possible. He was a teacher rather than an artist, who recognized the creative talents of others, but 'insisted that in sponsored film work the price to be paid for the privilege of aesthetic experiment was the discipline of public service'.

He was appointed CBE in 1961 and awarded honorary degrees by Glasgow (1948) and Heriot-Watt (1969) universities. In 1930 he married Margaret (died 1982), daughter of W. J. Taylor, of Dorset. They had no children.

[*The Times*, 21 and 28 February and 4 March 1972; Forsyth Hardy, *John Grierson*, 1979, and *Grierson on Documentary*, 1946 (new editions 1966 and 1979); Rachel Low, *History of the British Film 1929–39*, 1979; Paul Rotha, *Documentary Diary*, 1973; Elizabeth Sussex, *The Rise and Fall of British Documentary*, 1975; private information.] D. J. WENDEN

GRIEVE, CHRISTOPHER MURRAY (1892–1978), poet and prose writer, who used the pseudonym HUGH MACDIARMID, was born 11 August 1892, at Langholm in Dumfriesshire, Scotland, the elder son (there were no daughters) of James Grieve, postman, and his wife, Elizabeth, daughter of Andrew Graham, farm-hand, of Waterbeck. He was educated at Langholm Academy, and his first published poem appeared in the *Eskdale and Liddesdale Advertiser* while he was in his teens. During a spell as a pupil-teacher in Edinburgh, he joined the Edinburgh branches of the Independent Labour Party and the Fabian Society. After working on various newspapers in Scotland and south Wales, he joined the army in July 1915, rising through the ranks to become a sergeant. In 1916 he was posted to the RAMC in Salonika from where he sent home poems to be read and judged by one of his previous schoolmasters; he contracted malaria and in 1918 he was invalided home. In June 1918 he married Margaret Cunningham Thompson Skinner (Peggy) (died 1962), a one-time colleague on the *Fife Herald*. They were to have a son and a daughter.

The end of the war found him in an Indian hospital in Marseilles, from which he was demobilized in July 1919. His first book, *Annals of the Five Senses* (1923), largely consisted of poems written in Salonika. After the war Grieve worked as a journalist, largely on the *Montrose Review*, and became widely known as the editor of three successive anthologies of current Scottish poetry called *Northern Numbers* (1920, 1921, and 1922).

From 1920 onwards a movement was started towards the revival of Scots as a literary medium. At first Grieve resisted this, believing it to be a 'backwater', but he finally started to experiment with it, assuming the pen-name of Hugh MacDiarmid. He employed a literary Scots based largely on the speech of his native countryside, but also using and reviving words from the Scots poets and prose writers of the past. In this medium he wrote the beautiful short lyrics of *Sangschaw* (1925) and *Penny Wheep* (1926), but his most notable use of it is in his long poem *A Drunk Man Looks at the Thistle* (1926). His method is best described in his own words: 'a long poem . . . split up into several sections, but the forms within the sections range from ballad measure to *vers libre*. The matter includes satire, amphigouri, lyrics, parodies of Mr. T. S. Eliot and other poets, and translations from the Russian, French and German. The whole poem is in braid Scots, . . . and it has been expressly designed to show that braid Scots can be effectively applied to all manner of subjects and measures' (1925). Hand in hand with this interest in Scots went his involvement with Scottish nationalist politics. When the National Party of Scotland was formed in 1927–8, Grieve was very active in encouraging it, and he became a founder member in 1928, but was expelled in 1933. He was a Labour member of the Montrose Town Council and a JP. He moved to Liverpool and London, becoming in 1928 editor of the short-lived radio journal *Vox*.

In 1932 his first marriage ended in divorce, and in 1934 he married a Cornishwoman, Valda Trevlyn Rowlands, who had borne him a son two years previously. After a brief spell in East Lothian, in 1933 they moved to Whalsay, a small remote island in the Shetlands, where they lived until Grieve was called up for war work, first in a factory, and later in the merchant navy. Grieve joined the Communist Party of Great Britain in

1934, but four years later was expelled for 'national deviation'. The long poems written during this period, which include two 'Hymns to Lenin' (1931 and 1935), are composed in a mixture of Scots and English, but during the later part of his life his poems are largely written in English. He continued his political involvement, standing as an Independent Scottish Nationalist candidate for Kelvingrove in 1945. In *Who's Who* he listed his recreation as 'Anglophobia'. In 1957 he rejoined the Communist Party and was the communist candidate for Kinross in 1964. In 1950 he visited Russia with members of the Scottish–USSR Friendship Society, and in the same year was awarded a Civil List pension; he went to China in 1956 as a member of the delegation of the British–Chinese Friendship Society. During this time he moved to the cottage in Biggar, Lanarkshire, where he lived until his death.

In 1957 an honorary LL D was conferred upon him by the University of Edinburgh, and in the following year he was presented with the Andrew Fletcher Saltoun medal for 'service to Scotland'. He was also honorary RSA. As part of the Robert Burns bicentenary celebrations in 1959 he visited Czechoslovakia, Romania, Bulgaria, and Hungary. In 1976 he was elected president of the Poetry Society of Great Britain. His most sustained work in prose is *Lucky Poet: A Self-study in Literature and Political Ideas, Being the Autobiography of Hugh MacDiarmid (Christopher Murray Grieve)* (1943); this also includes a 'Third Hymn to Lenin'. Of his overall contribution to Scots literature, he has characteristically written; 'My job, as I see it, has never been to lay a tit's egg, but to erupt like a volcano, emitting not only flame but a lot of rubbish.' He died in hospital in Edinburgh 9 September 1978.

[Gordon Wright, *MacDiarmid, an Illustrated Biography*, 1977; Kenneth Butley, *Hugh MacDiarmid (C. M. Grieve)*, 1964; Hugh MacDiarmid, *Lucky Poet*, 1943, and *The Company I've Kept*, 1966 (autobiographies); Alan Bold (ed.), *The Letters of Hugh MacDiarmid*, 1984; *The Times*, 11 September 1978.] JOHN WAIN

GRIFFITHS, JAMES (1890–1975), trade unionist and politician, was born in Betws, Ammanford, Carmarthenshire, 19 September 1890. He was the youngest of ten children (six sons, two of whom died at birth, and four daughters) of William Griffiths, a blacksmith, and his wife, Margaret Morris, the daughter of a handloom weaver. He attended Betws board school and at the age of thirteen went to work in the local anthracite coal pit. The Amman valley in Griffiths's youth was a notable centre of Welsh culture. Griffiths himself spoke no English until he was five, while his older brother, David Rhys ('Amanwy'), was to become a well-known bard. The area, however, was also stirred by powerful religious and political currents. The young Griffiths was much influenced by the religious revival of 1904–5, and by the teachings of R. J. Campbell's 'new theology' as expounded by a local Congregationalist minister, John 'Gwili' Jenkins. Visits by James Keir Hardie [q.v.] and other socialists also had a powerful impact and in 1908 Griffiths became a founder-member and secretary of the Independent Labour Party branch newly launched at Ammanford. He played a lively part in ILP election campaigns in East Carmarthenshire in 1910 and 1912, and campaigned strongly against Britain's involvement in world war after 1914. He was also active in the 'workers' forums' organized at the 'White House' in Ammanford, and in 1916 became secretary of the Ammanford Trades and Labour Council.

A notable watershed in his life came in 1919–21 when he was a student at the Central Labour College in London. Here, his instruction was strongly Marxist in tone. However, Griffiths's own Welsh Congregationalist background, then as later, always lent his socialism an ethical, fraternal quality. He rebelled against class-war dogma. In the twenties and early thirties, he rapidly rose to prominence in the South Wales Miners' Federation. He became a miners' agent in the anthracite district (Ammanford No. 1) in 1925. However, he did not take up his duties until early 1926, which spared him direct involvement in the violent anthracite strike in the Ammanford area in mid-1925. But he was, inevitably, implicated in the general strike in 1926, and the continuing suffering of the Welsh mining community. He rose to become vice-president of the South Wales Miners in 1932, and in 1934, at the relatively young age of forty-four, their president. Here, he faced a difficult task, for membership of the Federation had fallen sharply since 1926. Only 76,000 of the 126,000 miners still at work in south Wales were members of the union. Griffiths immediately launched a successful campaign to build up the membership, and also negotiated a rise in the miners' subsistence wage, the first such rise for ten years. Moreover, he handled with calm statesmanship the crisis of the 'stay-down' strikes at Nine Mile Point colliery, Monmouthshire. As a result, the 'Spencer' company union was totally destroyed in south Wales, and the miners prevailed.

Griffiths, however, always had a passion for politics. In 1922–5 he had been agent for the Labour Party in the Llanelli constituency. In 1936 he was elected MP for Llanelli and resigned his presidency of the South Wales Miners. His majority was over 16,000 and he held the seat easily thereafter; in 1945 his majority was to be more than 34,000. He soon became prominent in Commons' debates, especially on social questions, and also took a keen interest in foreign affairs. A cogent speech on tuberculosis in Wales on 22 March 1939 was published as a separate pamphlet. In February 1943 he moved Labour's motion urging the Churchill government to accept the proposals of the report by Sir William (later Lord) Beveridge [q.v.], *Social Insurance and Allied Services*. He also played a leading part on the Welsh advisory committee on post-war reconstruction. It was regarded as inevitable that he would receive office in a future Labour government, and it was appropriate that C. R. (later Earl) Attlee should appoint him minister of national insurance after the 1945 general election.

At his new department, along with his fellow Welshman, Aneurin Bevan [q.v.], the new minister of health and housing, Griffiths became a foremost architect of the Welfare State. He passed two highly important measures. The 1946 National Insurance Act followed the Beveridge scheme in creating a comprehensive system of social security, including unemployment and sickness benefit, retirement pensions, and benefits for maternity and widows. In 1948, in another significant measure, Griffiths passed the Industrial Injuries Act, in which he drew upon his own experience as a working miner. He was also prominent on the Labour Party national executive (on which he had served since 1939) and acted as chairman of the Labour Party in 1948–9. Here, he played a leading part in shaping Labour's policy for the next election, especially in trying to secure the public ownership of industrial assurance companies. In the end, the resistance of Herbert Morrison (later Lord Morrison of Lambeth, q.v.) ensured that Griffiths and Bevan had to accept the more modest scheme of 'mutualization' of industrial assurance, which fell by the wayside after 1950.

When Labour returned to office in February 1950, with a much reduced majority, Griffiths became secretary of state for the colonies, a new area of interest for him, but one that brought him rare personal satisfaction. During the nineteen months he served here, he travelled widely and took pleasure in the twelve new constitutions adopted in emerging colonial countries, including Nigeria and Singapore. He also pursued the military campaigns against insurgents in Malaya with much success. More controversial was the advocacy by Griffiths and Patrick (later Lord) Gordon-Walker [q.v.], the Commonwealth relations secretary, of a Central African Federation embracing Northern and Southern Rhodesia and Nyasaland. Griffiths felt there were political and economic advantages to such a federation, but at the Victoria Falls conference in September 1951 he encountered the full force of African opposition. Thereafter, he campaigned strongly against the Federation being pushed through. He might have risen higher still in the government, since in March 1951 he was seriously considered for the Foreign Office on the retirement of his fellow trade-unionist, Ernest Bevin [q.v.]. Hugh (later Lord) Dalton [q.v.] and Bevin himself both favoured him, but Morrison was preferred.

Like the Labour Party, Griffiths left office in October 1951, and remained in opposition until October 1964. In the early fifties he was a notable reconciler between the Labour right and the Bevanites. His popularity was shown in the 1952 party conference when he was the only non-Bevanite elected to the constituency section of the national executive. Dalton canvassed him as a possible successor to Attlee in early 1952. In 1956, he was elected deputy leader under Hugh Gaitskell [q.v.], defeating Bevan 141–111. He remained deputy leader through the Suez crisis, giving way to Bevan in October 1959. On the other hand, Griffiths's place on the Labour right was not in doubt. His relations with Bevan were always somewhat cool. In 1952, he became a founder-member of the new Socialist Union associated with the moderate journal, *Socialist Commentary*, and attempted to deflect Labour away from a commitment to further nationalization. In 1963, on Gaitskell's death, he backed George Brown (later Lord George-Brown) for the party leadership in preference to Harold Wilson (later Lord Wilson of Rievaulx).

Throughout his career, Griffiths had always been closely identified with his native Wales, and with trying to reconcile socialism with Welsh national identity. Before and during the war of 1939–45, he had campaigned for a Welsh secretaryship of state. The adoption in Labour's 1959 election manifesto of a pledge to create a Welsh Office owed much to Griffiths's influence on Gaitskell, and when Labour returned to power in October 1964, Griffiths, although seventy-four years old, was appointed by Wilson to become the first Welsh secretary of state. Here he launched the new office with some success, acquiring new executive as well as purely administrative responsibilities, until he gave way to Cledwyn Hughes in April 1966. One disappointment, however, was that his scheme for a new town in mid-Wales failed to be adopted by the government. After 1966 he remained politically active, and published a volume of memoirs, *Pages from Memory*, in 1969. He retained his seat at Llanelli until 1970 to prevent Plaid Cymru striving to emulate their electoral success in neighbouring Carmarthen. In his latter years, Griffiths urged his countrymen to support devolution and an elected council for Wales. He was also strongly in favour of Britain's joining the European community and wrote frequently to the press on this and other subjects.

Griffiths embodied the nonconformist ethos so powerful in the making of the Labour Party.

R. H. Tawney [q.v.] was his ideological inspiration. His emotional Welsh oratory was sometimes thought to be unduly sentimental, but his passions arose directly from his background, from the comradeship of pit and village from which he sprang. The sentiment was always allied to tactical shrewdness and much executive ability, which made him a highly successful minister under Attlee. He was personally always warm and approachable, not least to the young, and to those he met in Africa and Asia from 1950 onwards. His interests included Welsh literature and rugby football. He was a most amusing raconteur with a fund of stories about south Wales. He symbolized the rise of Labour in modern Britain, as a moral crusade with strongly Christian overtones, and was a major figure in public life for over thirty years.

In 1918 Griffiths married Winnie Rutley, of Overton, Hampshire; later he delighted to recall that his first letter to his bride-to-be had begun 'Dear Comrade'. Their marriage was exceptionally happy, and they had two sons and two daughters. Griffiths became a privy councillor in 1945, received an honorary LL D from the University of Wales in 1946, and was appointed CH in 1966. He was also a governor of the BBC. He died at Teddington 7 August 1975. There is a bust of him in Ammanford Public Library and in Parc Howard, Llanelli.

[James Griffiths papers in National Library of Wales, Aberystwyth, and Coleg Harlech; Hugh Dalton papers in the London School of Economics; Labour Party archives; Winnie Griffiths, *One Woman's Story*, 1979 (privately printed); James Griffiths, *Coal*, 1942, and *Pages from Memory*, 1969; James Callaghan and J. Beverley Smith, *James Griffiths and his Times*, 1978; *Western Mail* and *The Times*, 8 August 1975; private information; personal knowledge.]

KENNETH O. MORGAN

GRISEWOOD, FREDERICK HENRY (1888–1972), broadcaster, was born 11 April 1888 at Daylesford, then in Worcestershire, the elder son and eldest of the three children of the Revd Arthur George Grisewood, rector of Daylesford, and his wife, Lilian Lockwood. He was educated at Radley and Magdalen College, Oxford (where he gained a pass degree in Greek and Latin moderations in 1908), before studying singing in London, Paris, and Munich. He sang bass solo part in the first performance in England of I. G. Henschel's *Requiem* in 1913. Later he was to give singing lessons to, among others, Robert (later Lord) Boothby and John Cyril Maude. His career was transformed, however, first as a result of war service with the Oxford and Buckinghamshire Light Infantry—he was invalided out in 1918—and second by the development of broadcasting. It was not until 1923 that he recovered from his war disabilities, and it was not until 1929, when he had already broadcast on a number of occasions as a singer, that he joined the staff of the still young British Broadcasting Corporation. 'Freddie', as he was always known, was to continue his association with it until the eve of his death, becoming what *The Times* called in his obituary notice 'a well-loved broadcaster'. Grisewood was one of the BBC's best-known personalities, and in 1959 he published *My Story of the BBC*, a popular book on its history. It was interspersed with pictures, many of himself at the microphone.

Grisewood applied for a job in the BBC without being interviewed by Sir John (later Lord) Reith [q.v.], whom he subsequently came greatly to admire. He began his work as an announcer (a versatile occupation at a time when within the BBC there was an unusual blend of formality and improvisation) at Savoy Hill. It was the unexpected, he wrote later, that made life worth living, and there was much that was unexpected even in *Children's Hour* in which he was expected to take part. His voice was well known to a growing listening public by the time that he ceased to be an announcer in 1937. Indeed, before then he had taken part in 1931 (as the narrator) in Leslie Bailey's first *Scrapbook*. From announcing Grisewood moved into outside broadcasting, making a new reputation with *The World Goes By* and savouring an entirely new experience when he was one of the commentators at George VI's coronation. He was technically a free lance, though a very professional one, as he was to be again from 1945 after working full-time during World War II, first as an announcer in the Overseas Service and then as the regular speaker in *The Kitchen Front*, a programme originally devised by the Ministry of Food. His voice became as well known at this time as those of J. B. Priestley and Charles Hill (later Lord Hill of Luton), and like theirs his was distinctive, beautifully modulated, and full of warmth. He also revealed during these war years a sense of humour and an unfailing courtesy which were to be among the main marks of his broadcasting after 1945. The ability to make people laugh, he maintained, was a priceless asset.

Although his sports commentaries were much appreciated and revealed a knowledge and love of sport which he had demonstrated at Radley and Oxford, it was through his role as question-master, an occupation brought into existence during the war, that Grisewood excelled. The programme series which is most remembered is *Any Questions*, which was devised in Bristol and first broadcast from Winchester in September 1949. The wartime *Brains Trust* was one of its begetters, but very soon it established an identity of its own. Grisewood was the perfect chairman, keeping politicians, including the most awkward, in their place, prompting and at the same time cosseting artists, writers, and academics, and always making the newcomer feel at home. The programme series was to move after his death out of the West Region and into other parts of the country, but under Grisewood's deeply appreciated chairmanship there was a strong rapport between chairman and local west country audiences. He was crippled by arthritis in his last years and walked with a stick, but he always seemed cheerful and in the most difficult circumstances even-tempered. Indeed, as he explained in his autobiography, his optimism was profound: 'Good is always coming, though few have at all times the simplicity and courage to believe it.' He was appointed OBE in 1959.

In 1915 Grisewood married at Writtle (a village which was to play a major role in the early history of broadcasting) Gladys Elizabeth ('Betty'), the eldest daughter of William Thomas Roffey, a City merchant, of Chelmsford, Essex; they had one daughter. The marriage was dissolved and in 1941 he married Aileen Croft, sister of one of England's most successful women tennis players and daughter of Edgar Clarkson Scriven, merchantman, of Leeds. Grisewood died 15 November 1972 in a nursing home in Grayshott, Hampshire.

[*The Times*, 16, 20, and 22 November 1972; *Ariel*, 24 November 1972; Frederick Grisewood, *The World Goes By* (autobiography), 1952; personal knowledge.] ASA BRIGGS

GRUBB, SIR KENNETH GEORGE (1900–1980), churchman, explorer, missionary, and public servant, was born 9 September 1900 in Oxton, Nottinghamshire, the youngest in the family of three sons and one daughter of the rector of the village, the Revd Harry Percy Grubb, and his wife, Margaret Adelaide Crichton-Stuart. His father was an Irishman of evangelical leanings and his mother counted Henry Labouchere [q.v.], who defended 'free thought' against Gladstone, as a great-uncle. He won a foundation scholarship to Marlborough College but towards the end of World War I absconded to join the Royal Navy by misrepresenting his age. His failure to enter upon a university education when peace came remained for him a source of lifelong dissatisfaction.

He was moved instead to a clear religious commitment at this time and enlisted with the Worldwide Evangelization Crusade to study the Indian dialects of the Amazon basin, where the Crusade intended to start work. His five years of lonely exploration of the upper Amazon revealed his capacity to make contact with suspicious indigenous tribes, and to master 200 dialects—his linguistic survey being published in 1927. Then shaking himself free of a too narrow and fractious employer, he joined the Survey Application Trust and devoted ten more years to the production of a series of surveys of the missionary situation in all of Latin America from the Rio Grande to Cape Horn—models of factual analyses allied to shrewd judgement—followed by further surveys in other parts of the world.

As the war with Hitler loomed, Grubb was recruited to the group planning the proposed Ministry of Information and subsequently appointed head of section for Latin America. In 1941 he was promoted on merit to be overseas controller of publicity, covering the whole world except the USA, a position that brought him into touch with the highest level of debate on foreign policy and war aims, and made him familiar with Civil Service procedures and the ways of the Foreign Office. When the end of the war was in sight, Archbishop William Temple [q.v.] and others perceived the contribution a layman of such experience could make in the ecumenical enterprise of rebuilding and renewal facing the church world-wide.

He became president of the Church Missionary Society in 1944 and for quarter of a century guided the strategy of its operations across the world through the period of decolonization and the emergence of indigenous and independent churches in Asia and Africa. At the same time he was recruited as a participant in a new ecumenical experiment in post-war peace making, under the initial chairmanship of John Foster Dulles, later to be named the Commission of the Churches on International Affairs, jointly sponsored by the World Council of Churches and the International Missionary Council. For the first twenty-three years of its life Grubb chaired this commission, composed of laymen prominent in foreign affairs and churchmen of every church except the Roman Catholic, which brought a new level of professionalism to its task, and a wider international representation to bear than ever before. His enigmatic and formal manner was matched by an intuitive sensitivity and a relentless practicality that gave the commission a unique style in ecclesiastical circles, and a weighty authority. Meanwhile, maintaining his business interests, he organized in 1946 the Hispanic Council and the Luzo Brazilian Council in response to the needs of Anglo-Latin American business groups in Britain. He was a distinguished member of the Royal Institute of International Affairs, and was a founder-member and first chairman of council of the Institute for Strategic Studies.

He edited successive editions of the *World Christian Handbook* for twenty years, and among his own writings were *Amazon and Andes* (1930), *Parables from South America* (1932), and his autobiography which was published in 1971 by Hodder & Stoughton under the title *Crypts of Power*. He was appointed CMG in 1942 for his services in the Ministry of Information and was advanced to KCMG in 1970 'for services to the Church of England'. He had been knighted in 1953.

Grubb was a man of lonely and melancholy disposition, apparently remote except to a small circle of intimate friends to whom he revealed unexpected affection and merriment. A linguist, he was an exacting artist in the use of words, a master of English literature, a skilful committee chairman, a demanding employer, and an unwavering friend to the strangely varied circle of his closest associates. To them he also disclosed the depth of his central religious devotion, as well as the burden he bore as a lifelong sufferer from petit mal.

He married in 1926 Eileen Sylvia, daughter of Alfred Knight, assayer of metals; they had two sons. She accompanied him on one of his long journeys into the interior of Brazil, but died in childbirth in Almada, Portugal, in 1932. In 1935 he married Nancy Mary, daughter of Charles Ernest Arundel, a company secretary; they had a son and a daughter. Grubb died at Salisbury 3 June 1980.

[Sir Kenneth Grubb, *Crypts of Power*, 1971; private information; personal knowledge.]

ALAN R. BOOTH

GUBBINS, SIR COLIN MCVEAN (1896–1976), major-general and leader of Special Operations Executive, was born in Tokyo 2 July 1896, the younger son and third-born in the family of two sons and three daughters of John Harington Gubbins, who was oriental secretary at the British legation, and his wife, Helen Brodie, daughter of Colin Alexander McVean, JP, of Mull. Educated at Cheltenham College and at the Royal Military Academy, Woolwich, he was commissioned in 1914 into the Royal Field Artillery.

In the war of 1914–18 he served as a battery officer on the western front, was wounded, and was awarded the MC. In 1919 he joined the staff of W. E. (later Lord) Ironside [q.v.] in north Russia. It was the Bolshevik revolution no less than his subsequent experience in Ireland in 1920–2 that stimulated his lifelong interest in irregular warfare. After special employment on signals intelligence at GHQ India, he graduated at the Staff College at Quetta in 1928, and was appointed GSO 3 in the Russian section of the War Office in 1931. Promoted to brevet major, in 1935 he joined MT 1, the policy-making branch of the military training directorate. In October 1938, in the aftermath of the Munich agreement, he was sent to the Sudetenland as a military member of the international commission—an experience which left him with a lasting sympathy for the Czechs. Promoted to brevet lieutenant-colonel, he joined G(R)—later known as MI(R)—in April 1939. In this obscure branch of the War Office he prepared training manuals on irregular warfare, translations of which were later to be dropped in thousands over occupied Europe; he also made a rapid visit to Warsaw to exchange views on sabotage and subversion with the Polish general staff.

On mobilization in August 1939 Gubbins was appointed chief of staff to the military mission to Poland, led by (Sir) Adrian Carton de Wiart [q.v.]. Among the first to report on the effectiveness of the German Panzer tactics, Gubbins had no illusions about the Polish capacity to resist. Yet the campaign left him with an enduring sense of obligation to the Poles, whose chivalrous and romantic nature was somewhat akin to his own.

In October 1939, having returned to England, he was sent to Paris as head of a military mission to the Czech and Polish forces under French command. The mission was viewed with suspicion by the French since its main purpose was to keep the War Office in touch with the burgeoning Czech and Polish Resistance movements. Gubbins was recalled from France in March 1940 to raise the 'independent companies'—forerunners of the commandos—which he later commanded in Norway. Although criticized in some quarters for having asked too much of untried troops, he showed himself to be a bold and resourceful commander, and was appointed to the DSO (1940). Back in England, he was charged by GHQ Home Forces with forming a civilian force to operate behind the German lines if Britain were invaded. Stout-hearted but utterly inexperienced, these so-called auxiliary units could not have survived for long; but their secret recruitment, training, and equipment in the summer of 1940 was a remarkable feat of improvisation and personal leadership.

In November 1940 Gubbins became acting brigadier and, at the request of E. H. J. N. (later Lord) Dalton [q.v.], was seconded to the Special Operations Executive (SOE) which had recently been established 'to co-ordinate all action by way of sabotage and subversion against the enemy overseas'. Besides maintaining his connections with the Poles and Czechs, he was initially given three tasks for which he was admirably qualified: to set up training facilities, to devise operating procedures acceptable to the Admiralty and Air Ministry, and to establish close working relations with the joint planning staff. Inevitably he bore the brunt of the suspicion and disfavour which SOE provoked in Whitehall—partly because of the nature of its operations and partly because of the excessive secrecy which surrounded them. However, Gubbins had no doubt it was his duty to identify with SOE notwithstanding all the risk of misrepresentation of his motives that this entailed.

Despite frustrations and disappointments—and there were many, due mainly to the shortage of aircraft—he persevered with his task of training organizers and dispatching them to the field. The first liaison flight to Poland took place in February 1941, and during 1942 and 1943 European Resistance movements patronized by SOE scored a number of notable successes, including the raid on the heavy water installation in Norway which aborted Hitler's efforts to produce an atom bomb.

At this stage Gubbins had no direct responsibility for SOE's subsidiary headquarters in Cairo whose activities in Yugoslavia and Greece had for some time been raising awkward issues of foreign policy. However, in September 1943 these issues came to a head; Sir Charles Hambro [q.v.] resigned; and Gubbins, now a major-general, became executive head of SOE. He immediately faced a concerted attack on SOE's autonomy, mounted by the Foreign Office, GHQ Middle East, and the joint intelligence committee (JIC). As always he had the steadfast support of his minister, the third Earl of Selborne [q.v.], but it was not until a meeting on 30 September, presided over by the prime minister, that a *modus operandi* was agreed. Nevertheless Gubbins's position remained precarious and in January 1944 there was a further attempt to dismantle SOE. This followed the disclosure that SOE's operations in Holland had been penetrated by the Germans—for which Gubbins characteristically took the blame. Undaunted he set about co-ordinating the activities of the various Resistance movements, now supported world-wide by SOE, with the operational requirements of individual commanders-in-chief. Although control was decentralized wherever possible, harnessing the force of Resistance to the conventional war effort proved a delicate and controversial task—as often political as military—involving consultation at the highest level with the Foreign Office and the chiefs of staff; as well as with representatives of the patriot organizations, the governments-in-exile, and other allied agencies—in particular the United States Office of Strategic Services (OSS). In the event the effectiveness of organized resistance exceeded Whitehall's expectations. In north-west Europe, where SOE's activities remained under Gubbins's personal control, General Eisenhower later estimated that the contribution of the French Resistance alone had been worth six divisions.

When SOE was wound up in 1946 the War Office could offer Gubbins no suitable employment, and on retirement from the army he became managing director of a large firm of carpet and textile manufacturers. However, he kept in touch with the leading personalities in many of the countries he had helped to liberate; invited by Prince Bernhard of the Netherlands he joined the Bilderberg group; and he was an enthusiastic supporter of the Special Forces Club of which he was a co-founder. A keen shot and fisherman, he spent his last years at his home in the Hebrides. He was appointed CMG in 1944, advanced to KCMG in 1946, and appointed deputy lieutenant of the Islands Area of the Western Isles in 1976. He held fourteen foreign decorations.

Gubbins had a creative spirit that made him a natural leader of the young; and he delegated generously to those he trusted, both men and women. Above all, he was a dedicated professional soldier. With his quick brain, the imagination and energy necessary to transform ideas into action, and his force of will, he might have held high command in the field had his abilities not been confined to special operations. As it was, he left his mark on the history of almost every country which suffered enemy occupation in the war of 1939–45.

In 1919 Gubbins married Norah Creina, daughter of Surgeon-Commander Philip Somerville Warren RN, of Cork; the marriage was dissolved in 1944. In 1950 he married secondly Anna Elise, widow of Lieutenant R. T. Tradin, Royal Norwegian Air Force, and daughter of Hans Didrik Jensen, of Tromsö, Norway. He had two sons by his first marriage, the elder of whom was killed at Anzio in 1944. Gubbins died at Stornoway in the Hebrides 11 February 1976.

There is a portrait by Susan Beadle in the possession of the family.

[*The Times* 12, 17, and 19 February 1976; private information; personal knowledge.]

PETER WILKINSON

GUTHRIE, SIR (WILLIAM) TYRONE (1900–1971), director and theatre designer, was born 2 July 1900 at Tunbridge Wells, the elder child and only son of Thomas Clement Guthrie, doctor and surgeon, and his wife, Norah Power. He had much theatrical blood in his veins, since his mother was the granddaughter of Tyrone Power [q.v.], the first of a long line of popular actors, of whom Tyrone Power, the film actor, was Guthrie's cousin. He was educated at Wellington, and won a history scholarship at St. John's College, Oxford. He early showed that independence of spirit which later enabled him to transform the shape of theatre in Britain, Canada, and America by telling the authorities of St. John's that if he won a scholarship he did not need the money, which he hoped would be given to a poorer man. It was not until he had done this that he told his father of the magnanimous gesture he had made on his behalf.

He went up to Oxford at the time of the armistice in a state of high exhilaration. He declared that 'certainly we are living in the most marvellous times since the Reformation—if not since Christ. . . . For the young . . . it's an opportunity such as the world has never known before'. His Scots–Irish blood roused greater fires in him than were kindled by the gracious propriety of Tunbridge Wells. Immediately he left Oxford he plunged into the society of those as yet unknown, but who were, with him, to become famous. He joined the company of J. B. Fagan [q.v.] at the Playhouse, Oxford, which in the early 1920s had in it such young players as (Sir) John Gielgud, Richard Goolden, and (Dame) Flora Robson. He was to see Flora Robson frequently in subsequent years, and proposed to her, but the proposal came to nothing because they could not agree whether to have children. Guthrie was further dashed by his great height and comparatively small head, and so gave up acting.

After working in radio in Belfast and then with the BBC, and at one or two other indeterminate occupations, he at last found his vocation by directing *The Anatomist* by James Bridie [q.v.] at the Westminster Theatre (1931), with Henry Ainley [q.v.] as Dr Knox and Flora Robson as the unfortunate prostitute, Mary Paterson, a part which she considered the finest performance she ever gave. Guthrie immediately recognized that he had a great gift, aided by his commanding height, his gentle voice, and inflexible determination, for controlling actors, and two years later Lilian Baylis [q.v.] appointed him as director of plays at the Old Vic and Sadler's Wells.

His years at the Old Vic were a period of ambition, achievement, and frustration. He raised the standard of productions, but angered Lilian Baylis by bringing in outside stars like Charles Laughton (whom she resented as too expensive), Flora Robson, and Athene Seyler. After Lilian Baylis's death in 1937 Guthrie was appointed administrator. When war came he was much criticized for evacuating the Old Vic to Burnley. He developed his conviction that the director was a more important element in a production than the actor, but when the Old Vic came back to London in 1944, reaching tremendous success in a temporary West End home at the New (later Albery) Theatre, Guthrie was overshadowed by the performances of Laurence (later Lord) Olivier, (Sir) Ralph Richardson, and (Dame) Sybil Thorndike [q.v.], who had now joined the company. He felt rebuffed when knighthoods were conferred on Richardson and Olivier in 1947, and he himself was passed over. He ended the war very depressed, quite different from his mood of 1918, and resigned from the Old Vic. He travelled restlessly, and produced a fine *Oedipus Rex* for the Habimah company in Tel Aviv.

The turning point in his life came in 1948, when he directed an adaptation of Sir David Lindsay's *Ane Satyre of the Three Estaits* in the Assembly Hall of the Church of Scotland at the second Edinburgh Festival. Guthrie had long felt dissatisfied with the separation of audience and players by the conventional proscenium arch, and the thrust stage of the austere Assembly Hall, with the audience on three sides of it, enabled him to bring about a sense of participation between players and audience which became the keynote of the work by which he was to change the nature and shape of theatre in the western world. Here he came into his kingdom, of which he felt he had been hitherto deprived. He suddenly saw the kind of theatre he wanted—a theatre of processions and banners and ritual, a theatre that was in itself a Festival, an Event, a Celebration, in which the actor played an important but essentially subordinate part in the pageantry and splendour of the director's conception of the play, which he insisted was essentially subjective and need not conform with the author's. Inspired by this revelation, he established the Stratford Ontario Festival in 1952, in the second largest theatrical tent in the western hemisphere, and in 1963 a theatre in Minneapolis based on the principles worked out at Edinburgh. Guthrie's theories have influenced the building of nearly all new theatres, and are particularly apparent in England in the construction of the Chichester Festival Theatre (1962) and the Olivier (1976). It was thus, rather than by individual productions, that Guthrie justified his conviction of 1918 that a new world was opening to those that could seize it.

Guthrie received many honours. He was knighted in 1961 and was chancellor of Queen's University, Belfast (1963–70). He was an honorary fellow of St. John's College, Oxford (1964). He received honorary degrees from Queen's University, Trinity College, Dublin, (1964), St. Andrews (1956), Franklyn and Marshall university (Pennsylvania), Western Ontario (1954), Ripon College (Wisconsin), and Citadel Military College, Charleston.

In 1931 he married Judith, daughter of Gordon Bretherton, solicitor, and Nellie Lacheur, and, as he himself said, lived happily ever after. She died in 1972. There were no children of the marriage. Guthrie died 15 May 1971 at his family estate in Newbliss, county Monaghan, Eire.

[*The Times*, 17 May 1971; James Forsyth, *Tyrone Guthrie*, 1976; Tyrone Guthrie, *A Life in the Theatre*, 1960; personal knowledge.]

HAROLD HOBSON

GUTTMANN, SIR LUDWIG (1899–1980), neurosurgeon, was born 3 July 1899 in Tost, Upper Silesia, then in Poland, the only son among the four children of Bernhard Guttmann, an innkeeper and distiller, and his wife, Dorothea, daughter of Marcus Weissenburg, a farmer. He was educated in Konigshütte, a coal-mining town which had the first accident hospital in the world, where he worked as a medical orderly in 1917–18. He started medical studies in Breslau and continued in Würzburg and Freiburg, where he experienced the anti-Semitism of a nationalistic student corps. He passed his final examination (MD, Freiburg) in 1924 and, rather by chance, obtained a post with Professor Otfrid Foerster in Breslau. Foerster, a neurologist and self-taught neurosurgeon, was an exacting master, and Guttmann worked eighteen hours a day for the next four years.

In 1928 Guttmann went to Hamburg to run a neurosurgical service in a municipal psychiatric hospital with 3,000 beds. Here he gained valuable experience, before returning to Breslau in 1929 as Foerster's first assistant and in 1930 as *Privatdozent*. Foerster was passionately interested in the pathophysiology of nervous disease and the influence of his teaching and writing can clearly be seen in Guttmann's investigations and in his *Spinal Cord Injuries* (1973, 2nd edn. 1976). Unfortunately Foerster's neurosurgical technique was not good, and in this respect he and his pupils did not commend themselves to British neurosurgeons.

In 1933 the National Socialists came to power, and at once forced all Jewish doctors to leave Aryan hospitals. Guttmann became neurologist and neurosurgeon to the Jewish Hospital in Breslau and in 1937 was elected its medical director. He wrote that he was neither 'mishandled' nor insulted personally. He witnessed the burning of the books of non-Aryan authors at the university in 1934, and the burning of the synagogue on 9 November 1938—the Kristallnacht—when he admitted to hospital any male person who presented himself. Next morning he had to justify to the Gestapo sixty-four admissions. By improvised diagnoses most patients were saved, but a few, and some doctors, were taken to concentration camps.

In 1938 Guttmann was allowed to visit England, where he made contact with the Society for the Protection of Science and Learning and was invited to Oxford. He emigrated from Germany with his wife and children in March 1939. The family was helped by A. D. Lindsay (later Lord Lindsay of Birker, q.v.), the master of Balliol, and by the fellows, and Guttmann started work in the department of surgery under (Sir) Hugh Cairns [q.v.]. He carried out sweating tests on patients to delimit the area of cutaneous loss from nerve injuries and taught orthopaedic surgeons the diagnosis and treatment of nerve injuries. He also took part in animal experimental work on nerve injuries in Oxford. He was frustrated by the lack of responsible clinical work, and in 1943 accepted an offer from Brigadier George Riddoch to start a centre for paraplegics in the hutted hospital of the Emergency Medical Service at Stoke Mandeville. At this time paraplegics were regarded as hopeless cases who died within two years as there was no effective treatment.

The new centre opened on 1 March 1944. The only hope came from Dr D. Munro of Boston, who had started turning patients every two hours day and night to allow bedsores to heal, and had had some success in the treatment of urinary infections. Guttmann began with these measures and improved on them. He showed that all antiseptics retarded the healing of bedsores, which were finally mastered by excision of necrotic tissues, skin grafting, and the training of patients in constant vigilance. Penicillin and later streptomycin made the control of infections and especially urinary infections possible, and the disturbing condition of autonomic dysreflexia, in which the blood pressure might rise 100 mmHg. if the bladder pressure rose, was elucidated and brought under control. Patients were encouraged to sit up, to walk with calipers, and after 1947 to take part in sports such as wheelchair basketball, archery, and table tennis. Sheltered workshops were a great success and were encouraged by the Ministry of Labour. During his retirement Guttmann greatly expanded the facilities for sport and wrote a *Textbook of Sport for the Disabled* (1976).

Medical staff from many countries came to Stoke Mandeville for training, and there are now centres named after Guttmann in Spain, West Germany, and Israel. His influence also spread through the journal *Paraplegia* and the International Society for Paraplegia which he founded. The Stoke Mandeville Games and the Olympic Games for the Paralysed, which he started, have been successful and inspiring events. He was loved by his patients and his staff, but his conviction of the rightness of his decisions made him a difficult colleague on committees. His work totally changed the outlook for paraplegics, and many other disabilities are likely to be influenced by his programme of continuous personal care from the acute injury to discharge from hospital and long after.

Guttmann was naturalized in 1945. He was appointed OBE in 1950, CBE in 1960, and was knighted in 1966. He became FRCS in 1961, FRCP in 1962 (MRCP, 1947), FRS and honorary FRCP(C) in 1976, and was given honorary degrees by Durham (1961), Trinity College, Dublin (1969), and Liverpool (1971). He held many foreign honours. In 1971 the Sports Stadium was opened by the Queen. In 1927 he married Else, daughter of Solomon Samuel, furniture dealer, of Mulhouse. In 1972 she received a severe head injury in a road accident which left her unconscious for the last twenty-one months of her life. They had a son, Dennis, who became a consultant physician, and a daughter. Guttmann died at Aylesbury 18 March 1980.

[*Paraplegia*, May 1979, vol. xvii, issue in honour of Guttmann's eightieth birthday; D. Whitteridge in *Biographical Memoirs of Fellows of the Royal Society*, vol. xxix, 1983; private information; personal knowledge.]

D. WHITTERIDGE

H

HADDOW, Sir ALEXANDER (1907–1976), experimental pathologist (oncology), was born at Leven, Scotland, 18 January 1907, the elder son and elder child of William Haddow, from Newarthill, Glasgow, originally a miner and himself the son of a miner, and his wife, Margaret Docherty, of Wick, the daughter of a hawker (later a coachman to landed gentry). He was brought up in Broxburn, West Lothian, where his father became the landlord of a hostelry. His parents were dissimilar in temperament, the father a strict disciplinarian, and the mother, by contrast, gentle and sensitive. Both boys were early encouraged to read books, to visit the theatre, and to enjoy music. Haddow was educated at Broxburn High School and then at Broxburn Academy, where he won the Dux gold medal. During his youth he was of an introvert nature.

In 1917 Haddow fell seriously ill with scarlet fever, and the following year suffered an attack of inflammation of a perforated appendix. On both occasions he was treated by the family doctor, Alexander Scott, who made a deep impression on the boy, with the result that he decided to make a career in medicine. Scott was intensely concerned with the effect on public health of the local shale mines, which were causing cancers of the skin and scrotum through their vapours and distillation products. As early as 1918 Haddow had resolved on his vocation, and his father had promised to support him financially at Edinburgh University. In 1922 a double tragedy struck the family: Haddow's twelve-year-old brother, Willie, was killed in a street accident and his mother, unable to survive her loss, died later in the same year. Haddow, despite his shyness, weathered the blow, and began his medical studies in 1924.

Haddow graduated MB, Ch.B. in 1929 and was appointed assistant lecturer in the bacteriological department, under Professor T. J. Mackie. He was supported by a studentship until he became a full lecturer in 1932. He became Ph.D. and MD in 1937 and D.Sc. in 1938. His professional career spanned three main periods, the first from 1930 to 1936 at Edinburgh University medical school, where he laid the grounds for his outstanding contributions in the field of cancer research. The second period, from 1936 to 1946, was spent at the research institute of the Royal Cancer Hospital, London, later to become the Institute of Cancer Research and the Royal Marsden Hospital. Here Haddow worked under (Sir) Ernest L. Kennaway and with (Sir) James W. Cook [qq.v.] and W. V. Mayneord, among others. In 1946 he was appointed successor to Kennaway as director of the Chester Beatty Research Institute, Fulham Road, which had been endowed by the mining millionaire Sir (Alfred) Chester Beatty [q.v.]. There Haddow guided and inspired a growing and changing team, retiring in 1969. In conjunction with his directorship he was appointed professor of experimental pathology in the University of London.

In 1929, when Haddow wrote an essay on 'neoplasm', very little was known about cancer. However, by 1969, when he resigned his laboratory work, lectures, and mentorship to many collaborators at the Chester Beatty Research Institute and Pollards Wood Research Station, Buckinghamshire, he had succeeded in clarifying many of the puzzles of carcinogenesis and the inhibition of malignancy. Together with Sidney Farber and Charles B. Huggins, he was one of the founders of carcinochemotherapy.

Between 1933 and 1969 Haddow published about a hundred articles. He was the first to discover the carcinolytic effects of the carcinogenic polycyclic hydrocarbons (identified by Kennaway's team at the Royal Hospital), mainly 3:4-benzopyrene, in contrast to noncarcinogenic compounds. From 1946 he extended this study to derivatives of cholic acids and steroids and to other polycyclic systems, such as oestrogenic substances. The experimental activities of carbamic esters and alkylating agents, i.e. crosslinking bi-functional haloalkylaryl amines and sulphonic acids, encouraged him and his clinical colleagues to use these compounds as novel carcinotherapeutic agents. They included chlorambucil and melphalan, which were used against specific cancers, and Myleran, effective against chronic myelogenous leukaemia.

As chemotherapy came to be practised worldwide in the fight against certain cancers, Haddow received many awards and honours. He became FRS (1958), FRSE, and honorary FRCP (1968). From 1962 to 1966 he was president of the International Union against Cancer. At the end of his active life diabetic blindness put an end to his experiments and sketching, but he replaced them with music and singing. To the last he kept his polymath mind, still lecturing and spreading his ideas about malignant growth and its demands. He was also interested in sociopolitical problems, such as disarmament. He was president of the Medical Association for the Prevention of War and deputy chairman of the Association for World Government. His last energies were devoted to the dictating of his memoirs.

In 1932 Haddow married a medical practitioner, Lucia Lindsay Crosbie Black (died 1968); she was the daughter of Captain George Black of

Castle Douglas, Scotland. In 1969 he married Feo Standing (née Garner). He had one son, William George (born 1934), and two stepchildren.

Haddow died 21 January 1976 at the General Hospital, Amersham, Buckinghamshire.

[F. Bergel in *Biographical Memoirs of Fellows of the Royal Society*, vol. xxiii, 1977; A. Haddow, unpublished biographical notes; information from Lady Haddow and library of the Institute of Cancer Research, London; personal knowledge.] F. BERGEL

HADLEY, PATRICK ARTHUR SHELDON (1899–1973), music composer and teacher, was born in Cambridge 5 March 1899, the younger son (there were no daughters) of William Sheldon Hadley, fellow and later master of Pembroke College, Cambridge, a distinguished classical scholar, and Edith Jane, daughter of the Revd Robert Foster, chaplain of the Royal Hibernian Military School, Dublin. After attending the King's College School, Cambridge, he was educated from 1912 to 1917 at Winchester College. His elder brother was killed in action in World War I. In 1918 he joined the Royal Field Artillery, and was commissioned second lieutenant. Within a few weeks of going into action on the western front he was wounded, losing one leg above the knee. A prosthetic limb acquired, he drove, bicycled, swam, played tennis, and walked, especially in western Ireland which he deemed a spiritual home, wore the leg back to front to amuse friends, gave tuition with it standing at his side, chuckling 'mind my leg' as pupils arrived, and often kept up the sock on it with a drawing pin.

In 1919 he resumed his education with three years at Pembroke College, Cambridge, gaining a Mus.B. in 1922. His MA followed in 1925, and he was to achieve Mus.D. in 1938.

From 1922 to 1925 he studied at the Royal College of Music in London, where he gained his FRCM and won the Sullivan prize for composition. He was a composition-pupil of Ralph Vaughan Williams [q.v.] and R. O. Morris. He took conducting with (Sir) Adrian Boult. He shared Vaughan Williams's enthusiasm for folk-song, but his creative genius absorbed this unscathed. He often incorporated a folk-song unaltered in his works, but in the symphonic ballad *The Trees so High* (1931) he used a single Somerset tune to make a fully fledged four-movement choral symphony well-wrought in its own right. In 1925 Hadley was appointed to the staff of the RCM. He made the acquaintance of Frederick Delius [q.v.] whose music greatly influenced him (and whose notice he later contributed to this Dictionary), and kept company with many such as Henry Balfour Gardiner, (Sir) Arnold Bax, Constant Lambert, Ernest Moeran, Alan Rawsthorne, Peter Warlock [qq.v.], Herbert Howells, and (Sir) William Walton.

In 1938 he was elected to a fellowship at Gonville and Caius College, Cambridge, and took on lecturing duties in the university music faculty. He became an official university lecturer in 1945 and professor of music in 1946, whereupon the office of precentor of Caius was created for him. By the time of his arrival in Cambridge he had to his credit nine major compositions which had received important public performances. As a fellow of Caius he took his share of committee work and served on the college council. His musical province comprised the direction of Caian music students, the stimulation of secular music-making, and the supervision of music for chapel services. In 1938 the choir included trebles, but on the outbreak of war in 1939 these were discontinued, and during the next twenty-four years Hadley built up and maintained a remarkable male-voice tradition with both chapel choir and secular chorus. A high standard was achieved and the chorus was sizeable because it was fun to be in. For the chorus, Hadley was an indefatigable arranger of exceptional adroitness.

His own major compositions at Cambridge included music for the Greek play committee's 1939 *Antigone* (Sophocles) and 1953 *Agamemnon* (Aeschylus), and by 1962 numbered twelve. From 1941 to 1945 he conducted the Cambridge University Musical Society's chorus and orchestra. Despite this he was able to produce his most substantial work, *The Hills*, another choral symphony (1946). A love duet and a wedding feast are the central themes between rhapsodic meditations on the unseen influences of nature upon human life.

A meticulous composer, the creative process was for him a laborious effort. Economy, practicality, and precision were hallmarks of his fastidious artistry. But he knew just where to unbend lyrically and emotionally, to place colour and effect, and his vocal lines 'sang' with natural beauty.

He was a trustee of the Cambridge Arts Theatre throughout his professorship, and under him the new Cambridge music tripos emerged, the music faculty quadrupled, and processes were set afoot to acquire a new music school building. He was a co-founder of the King's Lynn Festival and of the Noise Abatement Society.

He was an unusually hospitable and accessible don. Generations of undergraduates knew him affectionately as 'Paddy' and regularly visited his rooms for his amusing company.

In 1962 he retired prematurely to pursue his folk-song collection, but the onset of throat cancer prevented him from completing the task. He died at his home in Heacham near King's Lynn,

Norfolk, 17 December 1973. He was unmarried.

[Nigel Fortune, 'Patrick Hadley', *The New Grove Dictionary of Music and Musicians*, ed. Stanley Sadie, vol. viii, 1980; W. Todds, *Patrick Hadley: a Memoir*, 1974; personal knowledge.] PETER TRANCHELL

HAHN, KURT MATTHIAS ROBERT MARTIN (1886–1974), headmaster and citizen of humanity, was born in Berlin 5 June 1886, the second of the four sons (there were no daughters) of Oskar Hahn, a business man in steel works, and his wife, Charlotte Landau, whose family was Polish. Hahn was educated at the Wilhelmsgymnasium in Berlin. After suffering severe sunstroke in 1904, which caused him discomfort for the rest of his life, he spent two years at Christ Church, Oxford, and from 1906 to 1910 studied at the universities of Berlin, Heidelberg, Freiburg, and Göttingen. He then returned to Oxford until 1914 (although he did not sit for a degree there, or at any of the universities he attended), moving to Moray in the north of Scotland for the summer vacations. By now Hahn had formed his outlines for a school, based on long thought when lying in a darkened room in 1904, on the progressive school Abbotsholme, Herman Lietz (the founder of the progressive education movement in Germany), his reading of Plato, the products of English public schools, and the sea and the mountains of Moray.

In 1914 the outbreak of World War I scored but strengthened this plan. It is an extraordinary fact that in this first war the Jewish Hahn worked in the German Foreign Office and later in the Supreme Command as a lector of British newspapers, yet in Scotland in 1938, just before World War II, he became a British citizen, during it he saved many seamen's lives through the thinking that went into the founding of the first Outward Bound School at Aberdovey in Wales in 1941, and at its end he was baptised into the Church of England.

After World War I Hahn became secretary to Prince Max von Baden, the last imperial chancellor of Germany, and in 1919 he attended the conference of Versailles; already Hahn was an outward-looking man who knew that political vigilance and education together had to find a moral alternative to war.

In 1920, with Prince Max, Hahn founded Salem, a co-educational boarding school by Lake Constance. Hahn wanted to reverse what he saw as decays in self-discipline, enterprise, fitness, in the skill and use of craftsmanship, and in compassion. Only by developing strength of every sort—but most of all strength of character—could the young become responsible citizens of mankind. When in 1932 some Nazis kicked a communist to death and Hitler sent a telegram of support to them, Hahn wrote to all old pupils of Salem telling them that they had to choose between Salem and the Nazis. In 1933 he was imprisoned by Hitler. He was released in the same year partially by the intervention of Ramsay MacDonald, and emigrated to Britain.

He founded Gordonstoun in Moray in 1934. Many distinctive features of Salem were continued at Gordonstoun: the emphasis on producing the whole person; projects in pursuit of *grandes passions*; the involvement of the school in the local community, latterly at Gordonstoun by means of highly professional rescue services (Hahn's favourite story was that of the Good Samaritan. He was once told that the Good Samaritan had needed no training in rescue work. 'Ah', Hahn replied, 'but if only the Priest and the Levite had received it!'); the election of colour bearers (good citizens rather than games-players; Hahn loved hockey and tennis but was glad to dethrone games); physical fitness and the trust involved in the training plan, in which boys were asked to give a plain and private yes or no to factual questions; scaled fees so that the rich and the poor paid according to their means; and the stretching of oneself in the face of the mountains and the sea. Hahn took on all sorts of pupils—the brilliant and the difficult, the swift and the weak. With a high moral seriousness he believed in the dignity of achievement in any field, that one's disability could become one's opportunity and that there was more in everyone than they thought. Yet he had a prodigious memory for personal and family details and with a twinkle could comment 'this cheese goes straight to the soul' or that 'human nature is very prevalent'.

Despite his imprisonment, apparent exile, and occasional poor health, Hahn's ideas flourished: he was a headmaster and much more. The Outward Bound Trust was formed in 1945 and became a world-wide movement; though Hahn retired as the headmaster of Gordonstoun in 1953 the Moray badge became the County badge and was launched as the Duke of Edinburgh's Award Scheme in 1956; in 1949 he instigated the Greek Gordonstoun at Anavryta; 1962 saw the opening at St. Donat's castle in Wales of the first United World College (sixth-form boarding schools for children of the free world), of which there are now six; Hahn was the impetus behind the Trevelyan scholarships at Oxford and Cambridge and in 1964 he was midwife to yet another birth—that of the medical commission on accident prevention.

In 1964 Hahn was appointed CBE. He received honorary doctorates from the universities of Edinburgh (1953), Göttingen (1956), Tübingen (1961), and Berlin (1966). In 1962 he was awarded the Freiherr-vom-Stein prize for pioneering work in education.

Hahn, who was unmarried, spent most of the last part of his life in Hermannsberg, near Salem, where he died 14 December 1974. In the otherwise ornate graveyard of Stefansfeld Hahn's grave is marked by a piece of plain marble.

[Henry Lloyd Brereton, *Gordonstoun, Ancient Estate and Modern School*, 1968; D. A. Byatt (ed.), *Kurt Hahn 1886–1974, an Appreciation of his Life and Work*, 1976; *The Times* and *Guardian*, 16 December 1974; personal papers; private information.]

MICHAEL MAVOR

HAILES, BARON (1901–1974), politician and governor-general of the Federation of the West Indies. [See BUCHAN-HEPBURN, PATRICK GEORGE THOMAS.]

HALL-PATCH, SIR EDMUND LEO (1896–1975), civil servant, was born in Chelsea 4 March 1896, the youngest of the three sons (there were no daughters) of William Hall-Patch (earlier known as Hall) and his Irish wife, Honora Riley. His father, who became—with his children—a convert to Roman Catholicism, had started life in the Royal Navy and, after a period as major-domo at the legation in Brussels, was then a verger at the Brompton Oratory. Edmund never married and his family was important to him. When his second brother, an engineer rear-admiral, was killed in 1945, he assumed the guardianship of his children and, after his father's death, did much for his widowed stepmother.

As a child he was delicate and was sent to a religious house in the South of France. Both these experiences—France and a Roman Catholic education—strongly influenced his life. In France he became bilingual and he always felt quite as much at ease in France and in Europe as he did in England, while the only home he ever owned and to which, but for financial and legal difficulties, he would later in life have emigrated was in the South of France. And wherever in the world he worked he was always close to the Catholic hierarchy.

After a spell at school in England he returned at sixteen to Paris to train as a professional musician. He got a union card—later to be of great value to him—but soon decided he was not good enough. By 1914 he was studying French at the Sorbonne; he joined up, was commissioned in the Royal Artillery, won the croix de guerre with palms, was gassed, medically downgraded, and ended the war as a captain and railway transport officer near Paris.

In 1919 he was earning his living in the band of a Paris cabaret when he met (Sir) Frederick Leith-Ross [q.v.] of the Treasury who, with his family, became a lifelong friend and patron. Leith-Ross found him a job first with the Supreme Allied Economic Council and then in 1920 with the Reparations Commission. There he prospered and from 1925 to 1929 was head of its finance section. When this came to an end he went to Siam as financial adviser to the government. He greatly enjoyed it, learned the language, and steeped himself in the life of the country. But it was not an easy assignment for so scrupulous a man—and in 1932, unable to approve the Siamese government's financial policies and at loggerheads with the Bank of England whose expectations he regarded as unrealistic, he resigned.

There were few jobs in the depression. He tried America, living in a smart hotel and playing the saxophone at night. Back in London he was a successful if intrepid and often injured riding instructor. By 1933, however, he was back on course, as financial adviser to a British group in Turkey and in 1934 in Romania as British member of a League of Nations commission of economic experts. All this was prelude. In 1935 Leith-Ross invited him to join the Treasury as an assistant secretary, to accompany him on a mission to China, and then to stay on from June 1936 as financial adviser to the British embassy. He was a great success there and in Japan, which was soon added to his bailiwick. In 1938 he was appointed CMG and in 1940 became the government's financial commissioner throughout the Far East.

By 1941 war had closed in and he returned to the Treasury to keep an eye on the Far East and be involved in negotiations, on such matters as Lend-Lease, with the United States. In 1944 he was promoted to assistant under-secretary and transferred to the Foreign Office to direct and lay enduring foundations for its growing economic work. In 1946 he was promoted to deputy under-secretary and in the following year knighted as a KCMG. As the principal economic adviser to Ernest Bevin [q.v.] he played a central and demanding role in the British response to the Marshall Plan. In 1948 he was promoted again—this time to become ambassador and leader of the British delegation to the nascent Organization for European Economic Co-operation (OEEC). For the next four years he was chairman of its executive committee, working and travelling prodigiously, popular with his colleagues—American and European—and seen by them, and perhaps by himself, as the champion of closer British ties with Europe. In 1951 he was appointed GCMG. But by then the job was done; by 1952 Marshall aid was over and in Britain the initial attraction and impetus of the European ideal had faded. Hall-Patch handed over to his deputy, and went, a little sadly but still as ambassador, to be the British executive director of the International Monetary Fund and the International Bank for Reconstruction and Development in Washington. In 1954 he retired from the public service, and joined Leith-Ross on the board of the Standard Bank of South Africa, succeeding him as chairman from 1957 to 1962. The wind of change was blowing in Africa and under Hall-Patch the Bank prepared itself to ride the storm and made a start on the sweeping changes which were mainly carried through by his successor and friend, Sir F. Cyril Hawker. By 1962 his health was declining and he retired. In the years that followed he retained financial interests in Britain and the USA, wrote occasional articles, was on the board of Lambert International in New York, and travelled often to America and France.

His career was as surprising as it was successful. He had a brilliant, but rather tortuous and pessimistic mind, perhaps more French than English. He was a very private person and cultivated an air of myth and mystery; even to his family he tended to appear and disappear like a magician. Stories abounded—seldom confirmed, but few were finally denied; stories of sorrows and romances, of the anonymous authorship of a daring French novel, or of popular music for film or review, of unusual friends—Chou En Lai and Syngman Rhee, Yvonne Printemps and Sacha Guitry. His dress—slightly theatrical and antique, with stocks and stick-pins—, an unscrutable air behind thick spectacles, and a tendency to break suddenly into French, all added to the enigma.

A cheerful and charming companion, his friends were many and various; he was always kind and ready to help—and a special delight to children. He enjoyed his material pleasures and everything French—food and wine, his music, and the rewards of his success. But he never felt quite at home in Whitehall and this diminished his influence and effectiveness. Perhaps exaggeratedly, he felt he had experienced life and taken its buffets at the grass roots and always saw himself as an outsider looking into the establishment, impelled by an austere conscience to warn his more sheltered and unwary colleagues against facile optimism or complacency. Bevin valued him and was amused by his Cassandra role. 'Morning 'all-Patch', he would say as he saw Hall-Patch lowering ominously in the corridor 'and what's the snags to-day?' When he had heard, he felt forearmed against the worst.

What, perhaps, was most surprising was that with his sceptical and traditional cast of mind, Hall-Patch often seemed a pioneer and even a rebel involved in great changes. His most lasting achievements were the pioneering and strengthening of the economic side of the Foreign Office and the handling of all the European developments arising from the Marshall Plan, with Britain very much in the lead. He was often a fervent, and some even thought an intemperate, advocate of attenuating Britain's diminished position in the world by closer involvement in Europe rather than by the more traditional and fashionable alternatives of closer Commonwealth ties and a special relationship with the USA. In this he was ahead of his time—and if he was disappointed that his views did not prevail, he accepted this loyally and played, with real distinction, a constructive and significant part in developments of great moment for the future of his country.

He died in a nursing home at Ascot 1 June 1975.

[Private information; personal knowledge.]

HENNIKER

HALLETT, JOHN HUGHES- (1901–1972), vice-admiral. [See HUGHES-HALLETT.]

HAMILTON, SIR FREDERICK HEW GEORGE DALRYMPLE- (1890–1974), admiral. [See DALRYMPLE-HAMILTON.]

HANCOCK, DAME FLORENCE MAY (1893–1974), president of the Trades Union Congress, was born at Chippenham, Wiltshire, 25 February 1893, daughter of Jacob Hancock, woollen textile weaver, and his second wife, Mary Pepler, née Harding, who had herself been previously married. In all, there were fourteen children, of whom Florence was the eldest of the third union, with one sister and two brothers younger than herself. She left Chippenham Elementary School at the age of twelve to work in a local café. Two years later she moved to the local condensed milk factory. Before her eighteenth birthday she lost both parents and had to care for her two younger brothers and their sister. An intention to accomplish this, while working a fifty-five hour week for a wage of 8*s*. 9*d*., no doubt sharpened her resolve to help organize the strike in her factory in 1913. In that year she joined the Workers' Union and became in turn a collector, shop steward, and branch secretary. In 1917 she was appointed a full-time organizer in Wiltshire, later moving to Gloucester. When in 1929, at the instigation of Ernest Bevin [q.v.], her union was merged with the Transport and General Workers' Union, she became the woman officer for Area 3 based in Bristol. In 1942 she was promoted to London as chief woman officer of the Transport and General Workers' Union, a position she held until her retirement in 1958.

Meanwhile, in 1935, Florence Hancock had been elected as one of the two women members of the general council of the Trades Union Congress. In 1947–8 she was the second woman to preside over the TUC (following Dame Anne Loughlin, who held office in 1943). She remained a member of the general council until 1958.

Although she joined the Independent Labour Party in 1915 and later regularly attended Labour Party gatherings, Florence Hancock remained firmly on the industrial side of the trade-union movement and had no personal parliamentary ambitions. But she acquired an immense experience of industrial organization and of the statutory and administrative framework within which it operated. From the age of twenty-four, as a full-time trade-union officer, she was in demand as a member of courts of referees and of trade boards, dealing especially with women's work, not least in engineering, important in World War I, but also in more traditional spheres. She was particularly concerned to improve the depressed lot of women outworkers, and of workers in laundries and the catering trades.

In 1936 she became a member of the National Advisory Council for Juvenile Employment and campaigned against dead-end jobs for youngsters, turned off as soon as they could claim an adult wage. She was concerned, too, with the trade-union aspects of work done in prisons. In 1945 Ernest Bevin, then minister of labour, asked her to join with Violet Markham [q.v.] in a report on women in domestic service. Bevin had earlier ensured that she was appointed trade-union adviser to the wartime south-west regional commissioner and a member of major committees on national service and wartime productivity. In 1953 she joined the committee chaired by Lord Piercy [q.v.] in its review of provision for the disabled and in 1955, the committee on administrative tribunals chaired by Sir Oliver (later Lord) Franks. She was a governor of the BBC, 1956–62, and a director of the *Daily Herald*, 1955–7, and of Remploy, 1958–66.

Florence Hancock was brought up in a strongly radical atmosphere. From the age of eight she would read *Reynolds's Newspaper* to her father each Sunday and she never forgot being taken to hear his hero, David Lloyd George, at his radical best. Years later at a function in Chippenham, she reminded the company that her mother, too, had been a redoubtable political heckler and active in the local Co-operative Society. But it was the radicalism of nonconformity, not Marxism, and in 1951 she became a patron of Christian Action. She believed in orderly progress and expressed contempt for those who failed to give fair work for fair pay.

Her experience and loyalty appealed to Arthur Deakin [q.v.], successor to Bevin as general secretary of the TGWU, who supported her many international missions, most importantly as a regular British TUC representative at the International Labour Organization. She was appointed OBE in 1942, CBE in 1947, and DBE in 1951.

She was well-built, always neat in dress and trim, though her tailored suit and blouse or discreet frock marked a solid provincialism which she never abandoned. Her voice was soft and west country, her smile friendly, her reading never more than middle-brow. Her hobbies of needlework, crochet, and cooking were domestic, but it was not until late in life that she had a home of her own. Work had solaced the loss of a brother and a sweetheart in World War I. On 3 September 1964 she married John Donovan CBE, the son of John Donovan, stevedore. He was a widower with six grown-up children, who had been her colleague in the TGWU for many years and who subsequently became an executive member of the docks and inland waterways executive of the British Transport Commission. They had both retired to Bristol, where he died 13 November 1971, aged seventy-nine. She herself died while visiting her sister's home in Chippenham 14 April 1974.

[Information from the libraries of the Trades Union Congress, the Transport and General Workers' Union, and the Labour Party; Wiltshire County Council libraries and museums service; family and private sources; personal knowledge.] EIRENE WHITE

HANSON, (EMMELINE) JEAN (1919–1973), biophysicist and zoologist, was born in Newhall, Derbyshire, 14 November 1919, the only child of Thomas Hanson and his wife, Emma Jane Badger, daughter of the superintendent of police for Derbyshire. Both her parents were schoolteachers, but her father died only a few months after her birth, and she was brought up entirely by her mother, who became headmistress of a primary school. Mrs Hanson was a woman of considerable character and wide interests, and her daughter Jean developed the same sturdy common sense, and love of music and the arts. Jean Hanson was educated at the High School for Girls, Burton-upon-Trent (1930–8), where her interests in biology were first stimulated. Scholarships enabled her to attend Bedford College, London, and she graduated in 1941 with first class honours in zoology. As a research student she began a very substantial body of work on the vascular system of annelids. However, this was interrupted by the evacuation of Bedford College to Cambridge during the war, where she worked on the histogenesis of the mammalian epidermis in tissue culture, at the Strangeways laboratory, and her Ph.D. thesis was not finally submitted until 1951. She was a demonstrator in zoology at Bedford College from 1944 to 1948.

In the meantime, one of the major developments which influenced the nature of her scientific work took place. In 1947 the Medical Research Council, on the urgings of (Sir) John Randall (of magnetron fame), established a Biophysics Research Unit at King's College, London. The purpose of this unit was to apply the powerful new physical methods that were becoming available to problems in biology, especially to structural problems. It was in this unit that Rosalind Franklin and Maurice Wilkins obtained the X-ray diffraction evidence which contributed substantially to the discovery of the double-helical structure of DNA. Jean Hanson joined the unit as a founder-member and was responsible for building up the biological side of the laboratory. Then, starting in 1948, her interests in muscle began to develop and she initiated the use of isolated myofibrils, prepared from glycerol-extracted rabbit skeletal muscle, which could be caused to contract in physiological salt solutions. These were one of the first examples of the many 'model' systems subsequently used in molecular and cell biology to study the structural and biochemical properties of assemblies of molecules under realistic but controllable conditions. Jean Hanson's experience as a microscopist enabled her to realize that myofibrils provided ideal experimental material for examination in the phase contrast light microscope, which was just coming into use at that time. She made a number of important initial observations, but soon recognized that to understand the underlying structural changes responsible for contraction she would also have to make use of the electron microscope, an instrument of much greater resolving power, which has subsequently revolutionized biology and which was then coming into general use in the United States.

She therefore went in 1953–4 to the biology department of the Massachusetts Institute of Technology, which under Professor Francis O. Schmitt had already become a centre for research into biological fine structure, and it was there that she carried out, jointly with H. E. Huxley, the experiments which established the structural basis of the sliding filament mechanism of muscular contraction, a theory which has dominated muscle research since that time. Huxley had also gone to MIT to learn electron microscopy and apply it to muscle structure, and their collaboration enabled them to discover the overlapping arrays of actin and myosin filaments which are responsible for the characteristic appearance of striated muscle and which slide past each other by an active process during contraction. They suggested that the sliding force might be produced by moving myosin crossbridges.

Jean Hanson returned to the Biophysics Research Unit in 1954 and continued her studies of muscle structure by light and electron microscopy. She joined forces with a physiologist, Dr Jack Lowy, and was able to demonstrate unequivocally the existence of the double filament system and the sliding filament mechanism in a wide variety of muscle types, including several 'smooth' muscles from invertebrates.

Her work then turned increasingly towards molecular aspects of the contraction mechanism, and together with Lowy she achieved another considerable success in using electron microscopy to elucidate the internal structure of the actin filaments in muscle and the location of the regulatory protein tropomyosin. Her scientific contributions were by now widely appreciated and she received the title of professor of biology in the University of London in 1966 and was elected a fellow of the Royal Society in 1967.

She also assembled around her a small but talented group of investigators, who profited greatly from her ability to see how to approach important problems in a direct and fruitful way, from her boundless energy and enthusiasm, and from her unusual capacity for genuine and unstinting delight in other peoples scientific successes. Her abilities as an administrator and teacher who earned the friendship and gratitude of the students for whom she was responsible were exemplified in her major contributions to the success of the School of Biological Sciences at King's College, London; and her qualities of common sense, understanding, and tenacity earned her several offers of important non-scientific office in the academic world. However, she decided to continue with her scientific work for some more years and in 1970 became director of a Muscle Biophysics Unit at King's College, London. Tragically, her life was cut short in 1973 when she contracted a rare brain infection and died within a few hours, at her home in London, 10 August 1973.

Jean Hanson was unmarried and lived alone, but her interests in music and the arts, as well as science, brought her a wide circle of appreciative friends. Her outstanding qualities in research lay in her ability to pick the right experiment, her immense capacity for hard work, and her enjoyment of a good scientific discovery for its own sake.

[Sir John Randall in *Biographical Memoirs of Fellows of the Royal Society*, vol. xxi, 1975; personal knowledge.] H. E. HUXLEY

HARCOURT, WILLIAM EDWARD, second VISCOUNT HARCOURT (1908–1979), merchant banker, was born at 14 Berkeley Square, London, 5 October 1908, the youngest of the four children and only son of Lewis Harcourt, first Viscount Harcourt [q.v.], politician, and his wife, Mary Ethel, only daughter of Walter Hayes Burns, of New York and North Mymms Park, Hatfield. 'Bill' Harcourt, as he was always to be known, was brought up at his parents' house, Nuneham Park near Oxford, and was educated at West Downs, Eton, and Christ Church, Oxford, where he obtained a third class in jurisprudence in 1930. He succeeded his father in 1922 while still at Eton.

Through his mother, who was a granddaughter of J. S. Morgan the American banker, Harcourt had an entrée to the City and in 1931 joined Morgan Grenfell & Co. Ltd. in which J. P. Morgan & Co., of New York, held approximately a one-third interest. After working in the firm's London office and for a short period with J. P. Morgan and Morgan Stanley & Co. in New York, he was in 1938 made a managing director. Up to the outbreak of war in 1939 he participated in the wide-ranging activities of the firm and gained steadily in experience and judgement.

In 1939 he joined the 63rd (Oxford Yeomanry) Anti-Tank Regiment, Royal Artillery, and served with it and on the staff throughout World War II, ending in Italy with the rank of captain and being appointed MBE and OBE in 1943 and 1945 respectively.

He married in 1931 Maud Elizabeth ('Betty'), only daughter of Francis Egerton Grosvenor, fourth Baron Ebury. After the marriage they lived at Nuneham Park. They had three daughters. This marriage was dissolved in 1942 and in January 1946 he married Elizabeth Sonia ('Betty'), widow of Lionel Cyril Gibbs and daughter of Sir Harold Edward Snagge, a director of Barclays Bank.

Nuneham Park had been taken over by the army during the war and Harcourt, with his three daughters of his first marriage and two stepsons from his second marriage, made his home with his second wife at first in the agent's house at Nuneham Courtenay and in London at 23 Culross Street. It was soon clear that in the post-war world there was no real chance of their moving back into a house the size of Nuneham which was eventually sold to Oxford University. They moved to the other family property at Stanton Harcourt which had been let for many years and stood in the centre of the village, facing into a large informal garden covering several acres enclosed by walls. The garden was completely overgrown and for the next few years their main preoccupation, apart from Harcourt's work as a managing director of Morgan Grenfell & Co., was the alteration and extension of the house at Stanton Harcourt and the reclamation and creation of what was to become an enchanting garden. The house was always full of people at weekends, when hard work in the garden was a notable feature of the entertainment afforded to the guests. Harcourt was never happier than when surrounded by the debris and clutter of reclaiming his garden or bespattered with mud from cleaning out his ponds.

In 1954 Harcourt was invited to go to Washington to become economic minister in the British embassy and head of the UK Treasury delegation in the USA, which in turn made him UK executive director of the International Bank for Reconstruction and Development and of the International Monetary Fund. With his American connections, both by blood and through banking, and his wife's own experience of war work also in Washington, the three years they spent there were a happy and busy time. He was appointed KCMG in 1957.

When he returned to England and took up his work with Morgan Grenfell again, he was appointed a member of the Radcliffe committee on the working of the monetary system (1957–9). He also became chairman of the Legal & General Assurance Society on the board of which he had sat since 1958. He served on the Plowden committee on overseas representational services (1962–4) and from 1965 as chairman of the governors of the Museum of London. His name was certainly canvassed as a possible governor of the Bank of England when Lord Cobbold retired in 1961.

His interests in and around Oxford expanded in line with his City interests and he came in time to be chairman of the Oxford Preservation Trust, chairman of the Rhodes trustees, an honorary fellow of St. Antony's College, and vice-lord lieutenant of Oxfordshire. In 1978 was made an honorary DCL of Oxford University, something which gave him enormous pleasure. In the same year he was made an honorary D.Litt. of City University.

Harcourt was intensely proud of his family and the part it had played in English history since Norman days, as he was too of anything with which he was connected and particularly of Morgan Grenfell, its customers and business. If his loyalty to a company he was advising on occasion led him into conflict with the newly evolving regulatory bodies in the City, it was a fault on the right side and one understood and forgiven by those who knew him well. He was chairman of Morgan Grenfell from 1968 to 1973. Son of a colonial secretary and grandson of a chancellor of the Exchequer though he was, he was never tempted to become involved in politics himself.

Very much a family man, Harcourt suffered a cruel blow in the death of his second wife in 1959 and another when his youngest daughter, Virginia, was drowned in Nigeria in 1972. He died in London 3 January 1979 and the viscountcy became extinct.

[Private information; personal knowledge.]

John Baring

HARE, (JOHN) ROBERTSON (1891–1979), actor, was born in London 17 December 1891 at 26 Cloudesley St., Islington, the family home, the younger child and only son of Frank Homer Hare, an accountant, and his wife, Louisa Mary

Robertson. He was educated at Margate College and was then coached for the stage by Lewis Cairns James.

His first professional stage appearance was in 1911 when he played the Duke of Gallminster in *The Bear Leaders* in a provincial production. The following year he made his London début as one of the crowd in the Covent Garden production of *Oedipus Rex*, and in 1913 he had his first part in a metropolitan production, as Kaufman in *The Scarlet Band* at the Comedy Theatre. He then toured the provinces for a number of years, notably in the title role of *Grumpy*, which thereafter remained his favourite part. It commanded considerable success on tour during the early years of the war of 1914–18, after which Hare served for the last two years of the war with the army in France.

1922 was the crucial year of his career. He played James Chesterman in *Tons of Money* at the Shaftesbury Theatre under the joint management of Tom Walls and Leslie Henson [qq.v.]. In February 1924 he transferred, with the same management, to the Aldwych, where he opened as William Smith in *It Pays to Advertise*. This inaugurated the era of the famous Aldwych farces, and, for over ten years, the outrageous comedies of Ben Travers [q.v.] offered their contribution to the madcap climate of the twenties and early thirties in London. Chief among Hare's parts were the Revd Cathcart Sloley-Jones in *A Cuckoo in the Nest* (1925), Harold Twine in *Rookery Nook* (1926), Hook in *Thark* (1927), and Ernest Ramsbotham in *A Cup of Kindness* (1929). In all, he featured in twelve consecutive farces at the Aldwych between 1924 and 1933. The pattern of his career was by then firmly established. Apart from an occasional appearance in revue—*Fine Fettle*, for instance, in 1959—or in 'period' farce in 1963, as Erronius in *A Funny Thing Happened on the Way to the Forum*, he was fairly strictly type-cast as the nervy and fussy innocent, continually trapped in awkward situations. Between 1933 and 1960 he created such a character in over twenty more farces, several of them at the Strand Theatre. Herbert Holly (*Aren't Men Beasts!*, 1936), Humphrey Proudfoot (*One Wild Oat*, 1948), and, very successfully, Willoughby Pink (*Banana Ridge*, 1938) are perhaps his best-remembered roles from this period. During the sixties his extraordinarily active stage appearances began to diminish as he rested on his well-earned laurels, although he toured in *Arsenic and Old Lace*—a rare example of his playing in a comedy already well-tried—and, after opening in the play at the Lyric in 1968, he visited South Africa as Dr Simmons in *Oh, Clarence!* in 1970, when he was almost eighty years old.

His cinema work was of early vintage. In 1929 Herbert Wilcox [q.v.], production chief of British and Dominion Studios at Elstree, began the straightforward and uncomplicated filming of several of the Aldwych farces, and Hare also made a few film appearances in the post-war years. *Thark* (1932) is usually regarded as the pleasantest cinematic translation of a Travers comedy. Hare wrote, not too successfully, a couple of plays, and then, late in life, turned energetically to television. He will be most easily recalled by the seventies generation, who would scarcely have recognized him as a stage performer, for his playing of the archdeacon in *All Gas and Gaiters*, a creditable comedy series with a clerical orientation, starring Derek Nimmo as Noote, a young and naïve clergyman.

Robertson Hare created a cosily familiar style and was identified completely with, in effect, one part, that of the prissy little man, constantly in a state of unease and agitation, invariably sucked into some maelstrom of domestic upset and dislocation, unfailingly compromised and often trouserless. The bald dome, with brows furrowing anxiously beneath it; the spectacles, emphasizing the shock and bewilderment with which he responded to his travails; the jerky, staccato movements as his distress grew—these made him a highly recognizable stage figure. In concert with the worldly-wise Tom Walls and the affable Ralph Lynn and, later, in alliance, on stage or screen with the likes of Gordon Harker or Alfred Drayton, he became perhaps the premier exponent of English farce, particularly in the between-wars period. Above all, there was the somewhat archdeaconal, tremulous, and vacillating (although, from an audience stance, always clearly intelligible) voice. Rarely has a comic actor become so intimately associated with one word. Robertson Hare, faced with disaster, was wont to warble the five syllables of 'Oh, calamity' in a characteristic kind of plainchant. It is fitting that many should remember and identify him thus, and that 'Oh, calamity' should have passed into popular usage. His autobiography *Yours Indubitably* was published in 1957. He was appointed OBE in 1979, just before he died.

In 1915 Hare married Irene Mewton, who predeceased him in 1969. They had one daughter. He died in London 25 January 1979.

[*The Times*, 16 November 1979; *Who's Who in the Theatre*; personal knowledge.]

ERIC MIDWINTER

HARINGTON, SIR CHARLES ROBERT (1897–1972), biochemist and director of the National Institute for Medical Research, was born 1 August 1897 at Llanerfyl, north Wales, the elder son (there were no daughters) of the Revd Charles Harington, younger son of Sir Richard Harington, of Ridlington, eleventh baronet, and his wife, Audrey Emma, daughter of the Revd Robert Burges Bayly, vicar of Hampton

Bishop. Harington grew up in a rural clerical household against a background of service in the church, the law, and less often, the armed forces. His younger brother died at the age of twenty.

In 1906 he went to a preparatory school at Malvern Wells. The next year, however, he had the misfortune to develop tuberculosis of the hip, which left him with a permanent severe limp, and for the following six and a half years he was immobilized at home. Despite this, he succeeded in winning a scholarship to Malvern College whence, in 1916, he won an exhibition to Magdalene College, Cambridge (of which he became an honorary fellow in 1944). There, in 1919, he took a first class in part i of the natural sciences tripos. Having developed an interest in the chemical aspects of pharmacology, in 1920 he went to the department of medical chemistry in Edinburgh run by Professor George Barger, whose notice Harington later wrote for this Dictionary (as he did that of Harold King), and subsequently to that of therapeutics under Professor J. C. Meakins, where he acquired a Ph.D. in 1922. Here he met his future wife. On Barger's strong recommendation Harington was then appointed lecturer in charge of the new department of chemical pathology at University College Hospital Medical School in London. He arrived there in 1923, after a year at the Rockefeller Institute in New York, launched himself into research on the internal secretions of the thyroid gland, and only four years later had succeeded in establishing the chemical constitution of the prototype, thyroxine, and effecting its synthesis. For this he was elected FRS in 1931 and promoted professor (he had become reader in 1928). He was editor of the *Biochemical Journal* from 1930 to 1942.

Harington's research now expanded rapidly so that by the end of the decade he had a succession of achievements to his credit which put him in the first rank of biochemists. It was not this, however, that accounted for his growing reputation in wider circles, but the range of his understanding in the biomedical field. Thus, in his *The Thyroid Gland: its Chemistry and Physiology* (1933), he covered not only the gland's chemistry but also its physiology, pathology, and the clinical features of its disorders. In 1938 he was appointed a member of the Medical Research Council (and in 1941–5 of the Agricultural Research Council) and in 1942, despite his lack of medical qualifications, he was chosen to succeed Sir Henry Dale [q.v.] as director of the National Institute for Medical Research.

Both professionally and temperamentally Harington was well suited to direct a major multidisciplinary research institute. Because of his wide knowledge of biomedical subjects he was capable of appraising its activities both individually and collectively. He saw, of course, that he himself could not usefully exercise any direct control over work in its individual departments. But he equally saw that, without overall direction, such an institute could easily become a collection of self-centred interests. To counteract this tendency would, he recognized, be his overriding responsibility. Accordingly, he paid close attention to the balance of effort within the Institute and its continuing relevance to developments in biomedical knowledge and the fields in which these found practical expression. On this basis he formed his decisions or recommendations to the Medical Research Council, on the recruitment of staff, the initiation or expansion of particular lines of work, and the contraction or closing down of others. The fact that, throughout his tenure of office, the Institute continued to fulfil a central need in Britain's provision for biomedical research is an indication of his prevision in these respects.

When Harington first took over he had thought that it would be possible to combine, as his predecessor had done, the post of director with that of head of one of its divisions, in his case biochemistry. Soon after he arrived, however, he had to implement the deferred move of the Institute to much larger premises and a corresponding expansion of its programme and staff, and he realized that such a combination was no longer possible. Being the man he was, he had no doubt where his duty lay. He must abandon further hopes of personal scientific distinction and henceforth devote himself to forwarding the work of others. Despite his reserve, this was sensed by those with whom he had to work and, even when unwelcome decisions had to be taken, they responded to his leadership accordingly.

Harington retired under the age limit in 1962. To the pleasure of all at the Medical Research Council's headquarters, however, he agreed to act as consultant adviser to the secretary on non-clinical matters. This he did for five years with his customary objectivity and insight. Thereafter his health declined.

In 1923 he married Dr Jessie McCririe, younger daughter of the Revd James Craig, minister of Kirkpatrick Durham, Dalbeattie; they had a son and two daughters. His wife, his son, and one of his daughters were medically qualified. Harington died 4 February 1972 at Mill Hill, London.

In 1944 he gave the Croonian lecture and won the Royal medal of the Royal Society. In 1951 he was elected FRSE and in 1959 honorary FRSM. Harington was knighted in 1948 and appointed KBE in 1962. In 1963 he was elected honorary FRCP, one of the two first non-medical men (the other was Sir Austin Bradford Hill) to be accorded this honour. He was awarded honorary doctorates by Paris (1945), Cambridge (1949), and London (1962). But perhaps the most significant recognition he received came in the many public and private tributes paid to him after his death, for in them the word that regularly recurred was 'integrity'.

[Harold Himsworth and Rosalind Pitt-Rivers in *Biographical Memoirs of Fellows of the Royal Society*, vol. xviii, 1972; personal knowledge.]

HAROLD HIMSWORTH

HARMSWORTH, ESMOND CECIL, second VISCOUNT ROTHERMERE (1898–1978), newspaper proprietor, was born in London 29 May 1898, the third and youngest son (there were no daughters) of Harold Sidney Harmsworth, first Viscount Rothermere [q.v.], and his wife, Mary Lilian, daughter of George Wade Share, of Forest Hill. The first viscount, younger brother of Lord Northcliffe [q.v.], was the financial genius behind the rise of the Harmsworth press. Educated at Chatham House (Ramsgate) and Eton, Esmond Harmsworth was commissioned into the Royal Marine Artillery in 1917. Both his elder brothers were killed in the war and he became heir to his father's peerage and newspaper properties which after the death in 1922 of Northcliffe included, under the umbrella of 'the Associated Newspapers Group', the *Daily Mail* and many other papers. In 1919 he accompanied David Lloyd George as his aide-de-camp at the Paris peace conference. In the same year on 15 November he won a by-election in the Isle of Thanet as a Conservative 'anti-waste' candidate. He was 'the baby of the House'. His political career was not helped by an over-zealous father who in 1922 told Andrew Bonar Law that he would withdraw his newspapers' support unless Esmond was given Cabinet office—a threat which the prime minister disregarded. He was also handicapped because of his father's eccentric right-wing views for which he was sometimes regarded as a mouthpiece; in fact his own attitude was Conservative but far more liberal.

In 1929 he abandoned Parliament and concentrated on his business interests. In 1932 he became chairman of Associated Newspapers. He created a chain of provincial papers and under his regime the flagging fortunes of the *Daily Mail* revived in the 1930s and 1940s. In 1934 he was elected, surprisingly young, to succeed Lord Riddell [q.v.] as chairman of the Newspaper Proprietors Association (NPA)—a post he retained till 1961. He was an able and tactful negotiator, praised widely for his dealings over the allocation of newsprint in the war and with the printing unions after it. He was chairman of the Newsprint Supply Company 1940–59.

From his youth he moved easily in the social world—the slightly raffish post-war society patronized by the Prince of Wales and censured by King George V and Stanley Baldwin (later Earl Baldwin of Bewdley). He was tall (6ft. 4in.), slim, fair-haired, blue-eyed, and very handsome with great charm of manner. Women fell for him 'like ninepins'. He was an excellent player of tennis both 'lawn' and 'real'. He preserved his looks and athletic skill long into old age. He was a friend of the Prince and Mrs Simpson and in the autumn of 1936 played an important part in keeping the press silent for so long about their friendship. It was he who suggested to Baldwin that the abdication crisis might be solved by a morganatic marriage. This required legislation. Baldwin had little love for the Harmsworth family but he felt obliged to consult the Cabinet and the dominion governments. There was no support for the proposal.

In 1940 he succeeded his father. From then onwards he and Lord Beaverbrook [q.v.] were, till the latter's death, the two leading, though friendly, rival owners of the British mass-circulation press. He greatly strengthened Associated Newspapers by diversification into television—though he sold out too soon—property, and North Sea oil exploration. He also had wide interests in the Canadian paper-making industry. He was the first chancellor of the Memorial University of Newfoundland from 1952 to 1961. In 1952 he took over the ailing *Daily Sketch* from Lord Kemsley [q.v.] and in 1960 reached the high point of his Fleet Street career when the *News Chronicle* and the *Star*, despite their Liberal affiliations, felt obliged to accept amalgamation with the *Daily Mail* and its companion, the *Evening News*. Rothermere was a strong supporter of press freedom and was much concerned with the journalists who worked under him. It was sad that in 1970 the decline of Fleet Street obliged him to accept economies and redundancies which were not well handled and aroused bitter protest. The following year he retired in favour of his son, Vere.

Though an unwavering Conservative he never engaged in the direct intervention in his papers, publicly disclaimed but privately practised by Beaverbrook in his. Like his father he was more concerned with finance than journalism. He had many interests—farming, racing, and history in which he was widely read. He had something of a scholar's disposition and at times something of the indecisiveness which can go with it. He was a connoisseur of books and art. In 1946 he bought Daylesford near Chipping Norton, the former seat of Warren Hastings [q.v.]. He filled it with Hastings memorabilia. The house was sold and its contents dispersed in 1977 shortly before he died. He also owned the Crown lease of a part of St. James's Palace—Warwick House—given by his father as a birthday present in 1923. The generous and courteous hospitality extended in both houses was famous.

He was married three times; first in 1920 to

Margaret Hunam, daughter of William Redhead, of Carville Hall, Brentford; they had a son and two daughters. The marriage ended in divorce in 1938. He married secondly in 1945 Ann Geraldine Mary, widow of Shane Edward Robert O'Neill, third Baron O'Neill, and daughter of the Hon. Guy Lawrence Charteris. He divorced her in 1952, and she married in the same year the author, Ian Fleming [q.v.]. His third marriage was in 1966 to Mrs Mary Ohrstrom, of Dallas, Texas, daughter of Kenneth Murchison; they had one son. Rothermere died in London 12 July 1978 and was succeeded in the viscountcy by his elder son, Vere Harold Esmond (born 1925).

[Obituaries in the *Daily Mail* and *The Times*, 13 July 1978; Frances Donaldson, *Edward VIII*, 1974; A. J. P. Taylor, *Beaverbrook*, 1978; private information; personal knowledge.]

BLAKE

HARRIS, SIR PERCY WYN- (1903–1979), colonial governor. [See WYN-HARRIS.]

HARRIS, SIR WILLIAM HENRY (1883–1973), organist, choral conductor, and composer, was born in London 28 March 1883, the eldest in the family of two boys and one girl of William Henry Harris, of Fulham, post office official and for many years honorary organist of Brixton Prison, and his wife, Alice Mary Clapp. Harris showed such promise as a choirboy in Holy Trinity church, Tulse Hill, that a number of local people assembled the means for him to be articled, at the age of fourteen, to Herbert Morris, organist of St. David's Cathedral. Harris was happy there, and in a long life never lost his love of the Pembrokeshire coastline.

At sixteen, already a fellow of the Royal College of Organists, Harris won an open scholarship at the Royal College of Music, and became a pupil of Sir Walter Parratt, Charles Wood, and (Sir H.) Walford Davies [qq.v.], whose assistant he was for a time at the Temple church, and whose style influenced Harris strongly. From 1911 till 1919 Harris was assistant organist at Lichfield Cathedral, and a teacher, greatly inspired by (Sir) Granville Bantock [q.v.], at the Birmingham and Midland Institute. He also served in the Artists' Rifles during World War I. In 1919, in an appointment that occasioned some surprise, he was chosen to follow (Sir) Hugh Allen [q.v.] as organist of New College, Oxford, where he remained until 1928.

Harris's early years in Oxford were not easy ones. Having taken his D.Mus. under old regulations that required no residence and conferred no real membership of the university, he could not become a member of the senior common room in his college, or take an effective part in university life. He therefore took a time-consuming arts degree, to the detriment of various musical projects. In addition, he had to follow a man of unusual power and personality, who found it difficult to relax his grip on any of the many aspects of Oxford music that he had controlled. Harris finally solved the problem by locking the practice-room door when the weekly full-rehearsal was being held. It was a turning point, marking a growth in his self-confidence, and coinciding with a general recognition in Oxford that here was a musician in his own way as good as his predecessor, and perhaps better.

From 1926 to 1933 Harris conducted the Oxford Bach Choir in succession to Allen. But he was a fastidious musician, better suited to a small professional choir than a large amateur one. With the university Opera Club, in whose formation he was active, he was more at home. Opera had been almost a passion with him ever since as a young man he had helped to prepare Marie Brema for her Wagnerian roles. He conducted memorable performances in the 1925 production, by (Sir) Jack Westrup [q.v.], of Monteverdi's *Orfeo*. Harris directed the Balliol concerts from 1925 to 1933.

In 1928, after the death of Noel Ponsonby, Harris became organist of Christ Church, whose cathedral status and choral eucharists were more congenial to him than the cool ascetic evensongs of New College chapel: but his time there was short, for in 1933 he was appointed to succeed C. Hylton Stewart at St. George's chapel, Windsor, where he worked until his retirement in 1961.

It was here that he spent what were probably the happiest years of his life, concentrating on the chapel services and producing a steady stream of music for the choir. The atmosphere was less tense than that of Oxford, the society of the cloisters was congenial, he found himself able to cope successfully with great ceremonial occasions, and derived satisfaction from involvement in the attempt to provide some musical education for the two young princesses. In 1946–8 Harris was also president of the Royal College of Organists and in 1956–61 director of musical studies at the Royal School of Church Music.

As an organist Harris represented the purest style of English organ-playing. H. J. White [q.v.], dean of Christ Church, who regarded himself as a connoisseur of organ-playing, preferred Harris's playing to that of the much admired Henry Ley [q.v.]. 'When Ley plays', he said, 'it's like Liszt extemporizing on the piano: when Harris plays it's like Bach playing his own fugues.'

In the restricted field in which he chose to work Harris was an imaginative and skilful composer, having a fine sense of what is possible with a small choir, singing *a cappella* or with organ accompaniment. His style, derived from that of S. S. Wesley and Sir C. H. H. Parry [qq.v.], was more adventurous than theirs in harmonic resource and the use of choral colour, and was influenced by a discerning choice of literary texts for setting. A number of his motets and anthems passed into the repertory of cathedral choirs and choral groups in many parts of the world, and are highly valued. His largest choral work, a setting of *The Hound of Heaven* (1919), is still awaiting revival.

As a teacher in Oxford and at the Royal College of Music (he was professor of organ and harmony at the RCM, 1921–53) Harris was too self-effacing to be really effective. Organ lessons would start with the declaration that he had nothing to give to a pupil who could already play the Mozart Fantasia. Gross errors in a harmony exercise might be treated as interesting evidence of originality. But there was no such atmosphere of vagueness or indecision when he was playing the music that he loved, or extemporizing with an unexpectedly romantic warmth of feeling. Everything, then, was direct and authoritative. He was a kind and affectionate friend, somewhat elusive in personality, more expansive in the right company, but perhaps only fully himself when composing or making music in congenial circumstances.

Harris was married in 1913 to Kathleen Doris (died 1968), youngest daughter of James Perrins Carter, JP, a merchant, of Redland, Bristol. There were two daughters of the marriage. Harris died at Petersfield 6 September 1973.

Harris was appointed CVO in 1942 and KCVO in 1954. He was also honorary RAM.

[Private information; personal knowledge.]

THOMAS ARMSTRONG

HARRISSON, THOMAS HARNETT (TOM) (1911–1976), traveller, explorer, and scholar, was born in the Argentine 26 September 1911, the elder son (there were no daughters) of Brigadier-General Geoffrey Harnett Harrisson, CMG, DSO, and his wife, Dolly, daughter of William Eagle Cole, a well-known naturalist. His father, after retiring from the army, held senior posts in the Argentine railways, becoming general manager, Entrerios and Argentine North Eastern Railways.

Tom Harrisson's childhood was spent partly at school in England and partly holidaying in the Argentine where he travelled widely in the family private railroad car, acquiring a taste for ornithology which he developed at Harrow, writing while at school his first book, *Birds of the Harrow District* (1931). Bird-watching led him to watching the other boys at Harrow, keeping a card index recording their characteristics, a habit which developed later into Mass-Observation. Such detachment made bearable his time at Harrow, a school he disliked intensely. His organization of boys on unusual school holidays prompted an article in *The Times* which led to an invitation to join the Oxford University expedition to the Arctic in 1930. This gave him grounding in scientific methods of study in the field. On his return he went up to Pembroke College, Cambridge, where he lasted an unsatisfactory four terms, finding Cambridge even less congenial than Harrow. Consequently he spent much of his time in Oxford, the atmosphere of which he preferred. In 1932 he went with the Oxford University expedition to Borneo and behaved with great discourtesy to the authorities in Sarawak, particularly to the officials at the museum at Kuching which, after World War II, he was to turn into one of the most remarkable museums in the world.

Despite the wild living of his team (drink and women were to be shared), he described twelve kinds of birds previously unknown to science and stimulated the other members of the expedition into getting useful new information about plant and animal life. For Harrisson the most important part of the expedition was the realization of his affinity with the local inhabitants not yet changed by contact with western civilization. Harrisson was usually but not always polite to and appreciative of primitive people, keeping most of his deliberate rudeness and unreasonable criticisms for Europeans and his friends. Native communities suited him and it was not just affectation which prompted him to perambulate Oxford in bare feet and red toenails selling his *Letter to Oxford* which he wrote in 1933, publishing it himself under the imprint of the Hate Press. Soon he was on another Oxford University expedition, this time to the New Hebrides where he was entranced by cannibals with whom he identified even to eating human meat, of which 'the taste is like that of tender pork, rather sweet'.

Harrisson now began to study, as he put it, 'the cannibals of Britain'. With Charles Madge he founded Mass-Observation and collected enthusiastic observers throughout the country to write detailed daily reports of their own customs and activities as well as of those they encountered. The first study was of what ordinary people were doing, thinking, and saying on the day King George VI was crowned in 1937.

Harrisson established himself in an unfurnished back street house in an alley in Bolton, which he renamed Worktown. His subjects were the factory workers and their families whose living style he adopted, feeling that if an observer is observed the observation is invalid. With his genuine leadership qualities he persuaded writers, artists, undergraduates, and others that what he was doing was not only entertaining but worthwhile and thus acquired considerable unpaid organizational help. In 1939 the validity of Mass-Observation's reports was so well accepted that the Ministry of Information employed it for detailed studies on civilian morale during World War II. These have become important historical documents, particularly about the blitz.

In 1942 Harrisson joined the King's Royal Rifle Corps. In 1944 he joined the Special Operations Executive to lead an expedition behind the Japanese lines in Borneo and was dropped there by parachute in February 1945 with his team. The friends he had made during the 1932 Oxford University Expedition were delighted to see him and Harrisson well deserved the DSO (1946) which he earned. Mopping up the Japanese continued after the official ending of the war as many of them did not know that their country had surrendered.

Harrisson returned to England in the autumn of 1946 but found the post-war British scene unattractive. He could not repair the damage done to his first marriage and he realized that the original techniques of Mass-Observation would not survive in an age where computers and questions were taking the place of detached observation. He discarded the idea of entering politics because the Liberal Party, which was the only one acceptable to him, showed no likelihood of winning him an influential position. Consequently he accepted the job of running the museum in Kuching in Sarawak whence he returned in 1947 as a person of considerable importance in the life of Sarawak. Intending to stay for two years he stayed for nearly twenty, not only giving the museum a world-wide importance but also making significant archaeological discoveries including that of human habitation in caves as far back as 40,000 BC. Characteristically he had an original approach to the layout and labelling of the museum with such notices as, 'How old are these carvings? We think they date back to about 950 AD. What do you feel?'

During and after the Sarawak Museum period Harrisson continued his interest in the habits of birds, animals, and their conservation, trying to protect threatened species such as turtles and orang-utans. Leaving Sarawak in 1966 after handing over to a dayak he had trained for the job, he became a visiting professor at Cornell University (1967–8). He wrote many books and articles, and, with Hugh Gibb, won the grand prix at Cannes for the film *Birds' Nest Soup*. When he died he was still writing, researching, fighting numerous causes, barging rumbustiously into the lives of any whose services he needed.

Harrisson received the Speleological Society award, USA, in 1960, the Founder's medal of the Royal Geographical Society in 1962, and a medal of the Royal Society of Arts in 1964. He was appointed OBE in 1959. Wherever he went and whatever he did his enthusiasm and determination never to assume anything was as it appeared, or was believed to be, but to examine it thoroughly *de novo*, made a tremendous impact.

Tom Harrisson was married first in 1941 to Mrs Betha Clayton (died 1961), a wealthy divorcée who provided a comfortable base for him in Ladbroke Grove. She was the daughter of Thomas Pellatt, headmaster of Durnford Preparatory School, Dorset. They had one son and were finally divorced in 1954. Harrisson married secondly, in 1956, Dr Barbara, daughter of Dr Gerhart Güttler, of Berlin, Nikolassee, and Bad Tolz. She was herself an expert in similar fields to Harrisson and gave him much support. After this marriage ended in 1970 he married in 1971 Baronne Christine Forani who held the croix de guerre and was a Belgian sculptor and industrialist. She was the widow of Professor N. Bonncompagnie, of Brussels. While on holiday Harrisson and his wife died 18 January 1976 in a touring bus road accident near Bangkok in Siam.

[*The Times*, 21, 23, 26, and 30 January 1976; *Spectator*, 31 January 1976; Timothy Green, *The Adventurers*, 1970; Tom Harrison Mass-Observation archives, University of Sussex; *Journal of the Malaysian Branch of the Royal Asiatic Society*; private information; personal knowledge.] WOODROW WYATT

HARROD, SIR (HENRY) ROY (FORBES) (1900–1978), economist, was born in London 13 February 1900, the only child of Henry Dawes Harrod, a solicitor and a member of the London Metals Exchange, and his wife, Frances Marie Desirée, who was one of the eleven children of John Forbes-Robertson, art critic and journalist, and the younger sister of (Sir) Johnston Forbes-Robertson [q.v.], the actor. Frances Harrod, aided by her literary and artistic gifts and her maternal determination, exercised an immense influence on her son, overshadowing that of her husband, whose later years were darkened by his bankruptcy (after misinvesting his remaining capital in a copper mine in Anglesey, he was 'hammered' on the Metals Exchange in 1907 and remained an undischarged bankrupt until 1917, the year before his death).

Roy Harrod won a scholarship to St. Paul's (from its preparatory school, Colet Court), but stayed there only two years. His mother insisted that he move to Westminster, which he duly entered as a King's scholar at the second attempt in 1913. Five years later he won a history scholarship to New College, Oxford. After a period from September 1918 in the Royal Garrison Artillery, he went to Oxford and obtained a first in *literae humaniores* in 1921 despite a discordant relationship with his philosophy tutor, H. W. B. Joseph [q.v.]; and another first in modern history only twelve months later. He was elected by Christ Church, Oxford, to a lectureship in 1922, and in 1924 to a Studentship (i.e. fellowship) in modern history and economics, which he held for forty-three years until his retirement in 1967, combining it for the final fifteen years with the Nuffield readership in international economics. He was a fellow of Nuffield College, Oxford, from 1938 to 1947 and 1954 to 1958. From 1945 to 1961 he was joint editor of the *Economic Journal*.

Apart from some study of British currency, banking, and public finance in the context of the Oxford modern history school, Harrod's immersion in economics began after his election to Christ Church. His principal mentors in the subject were J. M. (later Lord) Keynes [q.v.] and colleagues (with whom, at King's College, Cambridge, he spent the autumn of 1922 as part of two terms' leave before embarking on his tutorial responsibilities at Christ Church) and F. Y. Edgeworth [q.v.], Drummond professor of political economy at Oxford. His own principal contributions to economics, dating mostly from the 1930s, covered three main areas of theory: the firm; aggregate demand; and economic growth and fluctuations.

Under the first head, Harrod was one of the originators of the marginal revenue curve; clarified the relation between short-period and long-period cost curves; and helped to develop the theory of pricing and output decisions of imperfectly competitive producers, i.e. those which are in some degree 'price-making'. His papers on these topics were reprinted in *Economic Essays* (2nd edn., 1972). As regards aggregate demand, Harrod's *International Economics* (1933, 4th edn., 1957) and *The Trade Cycle* (1936) pioneered the application of the 1931 'multiplier' concept of R. F. (later Lord) Kahn to an economy engaging in foreign trade. Harrod showed how an increase in exports would, in the presence of under-utilized resources and inflexible prices, expand total output and employment up to the point at which imports had risen to match the new level of exports. Keynes's use of the multiplier mechanism in *The General Theory of Employment, Interest and Money* (1936) followed Kahn in concentrating on the closed economy, where it was investment and savings rather than exports and imports that were brought into balance through changes in income.

The investment/savings relationship was also of central importance in Harrod's path-breaking formulation of a one-sector growth model—'An Essay in Dynamic Theory' (*Economic Journal*, 1939) later incorporated in *Towards a Dynamic Economics* (1948, 2nd revised edn., 1973)—in which he sought to analyse the macro-economic properties of a long-run expansion path. In the so-called 'Harrod–Domar' model (the Russian-American economist Evsey Domar having produced in 1946 a model similar in important respects to Harrod's) the odds were overwhelmingly against the attainment of steady-state growth. This finding initiated a spate of theoretical literature on macro-economic growth models in the 1950s and 60s.

Harrod's own economic writings after World War II concentrated mainly on questions of policy, especially British economic management (*Are These Hardships Necessary?*, 1947, *Topical Comment: Essays in Dynamic Economics Applied*, 1961, *Towards a New Economic Policy*, 1967) and international monetary issues (*The Dollar*, 1953, and *Reforming the World's Money*, 1965). Following the Keynesian revolution and the post-war development of 'growth economics', Harrod became a persistent and somewhat extreme advocate of fiscal and monetary expansion, arguing that an economy must be run under strong demand pressure if it was to realize its full growth potential; and that inflation and balance-of-payments deficits should be curbed not through general restraints on demand but through direct intervention—namely, incomes policy in the case of inflation and export subsidies and import restrictions in the case of payment deficits. Internationally, Harrod favoured a rise in the official price of gold to enhance the volume of international reserves. His insistence on expansionary policies at all points owed something to his belief that, even in the post-Keynesian era, it was easier to maintain economic activity at a high level than it would be to restore it after another slump.

Besides his economic writings, Harrod made noteworthy contributions to biography and to philosophy. His official *Life of John Maynard Keynes* (1951), though criticized for undue obtrusion of its author's personality in the selection and presentation of material, was a compelling and magisterial account of Keynes's career and achievements. *The Prof* (1959), his memoir on F. A. Lindemann, Viscount Cherwell [q.v.], was a slighter work, more in the nature of an extended essay, recalling the author's own disappointingly short period of service in (Sir) Winston Churchill's 'S branch' in the early part of World War II, as well as painting a sympathetic portrait of the aloof and controversial figure of Cherwell.

In philosophy, Harrod's most ambitious venture, and one to which among all his work he himself attached particular importance, was *Foundations of Inductive Logic* (1956). This attempted—unsuccessfully, in the opinion of professional philosophers—to refute Hume by providing a strictly logical justification for induction, i.e. for assuming that, 'because the sun has risen every day so far, it will do so again tomorrow'. But his most influential philosophical work was a paper in *Mind* (1936) entitled 'Utilitarianism Revised', which sought to defend the utilitarian approach against certain criticisms by elaborating the doctrine. Harrod argued, first, that morality is concerned with means rather than ends, i.e. with the promotion of whatever ultimate goals are sought by the greatest number of people; and, secondly, that utilitarian principles call for adherence to universal rules of conduct (rather than case-by-case decisions) in matters (e.g. promise-keeping) where repetition and predictability are themselves socially beneficial.

Harrod combined originality of mind with breadth of interest and immense power of assimilation and concentration with a fluent and sometimes picturesque writing style. Although not averse to lecturing or orating (including political campaigning, to which he gave considerable energy through much of the inter-war period) he preferred to write (including memoranda and letters to his colleagues on college or university business, characteristically marked 'Immediate' on the envelope). He was of lean physique and above-average height; even in later years, when he had a stoop, his manner retained an Olympian element. He was irresistibly discursive with pupils, to whom he conveyed a sense of contact with great minds and grand decisions, and unfailingly courteous to all.

He was made FBA in 1947 and knighted in 1969. He received honorary degrees from the universities of Aberdeen, Glasgow, Warwick, Pennsylvania, Poitiers, and Stockholm. In 1962–4 he was president of the Royal Economic Society. He was an honorary Student of Christ Church (1967) and an honorary fellow of Nuffield College (1958) and New College (1975).

In 1938 he married Wilhelmine Margaret Eve ('Billa'), daughter of Captain Francis Joseph Cresswell, of the Norfolk Regiment, and Lady Strickland, DBE, of Old Hall, Snettisham, Norfolk. They had two sons. He died at the family home in Holt, Norfolk, 8 March 1978.

[Henry Phelps-Brown, 'Sir Roy Harrod: A Biographical Memoir', *Economic Journal*, 1980; private information; personal knowledge.] PETER M. OPPENHEIMER

HARTLEY, SIR HAROLD BREWER (1878–1972), physical chemist, was born 3 September 1878 in London, the only son of Harold Thomas Hartley, a mineral water manufacturer and later a partner in the publishing firm of Emmot, Hartley & Co., of Fleet Street, and his wife, Katie, daughter of Francis Brewer. After three years schooling at Dulwich College, in 1897 he entered Balliol College, Oxford, on a Brackenbury scholarship. In 1900 he graduated with first class honours in natural science (chemistry and mineralogy), and in 1901 was appointed tutorial fellow of Balliol in the place of his tutor, Sir John Conroy, who had just died.

Besides the usual tutorial and lecturing duties he had the responsibility of teaching in the Balliol–Trinity laboratory which the two colleges had jointly set up twenty years earlier. In 1904 it was arranged that the laboratory should develop for the university course in the then novel subject of physical chemistry, and this later achieved a notable reputation.

At the outbreak of the 1914–18 war he joined the 7th Leicestershire Regiment, but early in 1915, when German gas attacks began, he contrived to be sent to France as chemical adviser to the Third Army. He became a lieutenant-colonel and assistant director of Gas Services at GHQ, was thrice mentioned in dispatches, won an MC (1916), and was appointed OBE. Rising to the rank of brigadier-general in 1918 and created CBE (1919), he was given charge of the Chemical Warfare Department at the Ministry of Munitions, not being released until the early summer of 1919. He never lost his interest in chemical defence, and late in life he exchanged notes with Fritz Haber's son on the 1914–18 operations of gas warfare. He had met Haber, who organized the German use of gas, soon after the war and was amused to find that, whereas he had risen to be brigadier-general, his enemy opposite number had not been elevated above a captaincy.

He returned to Oxford keen to start up work in physical chemistry, and was fortunate in having as pupils a succession of able young Balliol scholars. Most notable was (Sir) Cyril Hinshelwood [q.v.], later to receive a Nobel prize and to become president of the Royal Society.

In the 1920s Hartley realized what poor opportunities to become knowledgeable in physical chemistry had been available to science masters and mistresses in schools. For several years therefore he organized summer schools at Balliol College with lectures and laboratory work on the subject. These were a great success and did much to raise teaching standards throughout the country.

Hartley's way of conducting undergraduate tutorials was not what might have been anticipated by one straight from school. No formal instruction was given; he expected his students to instruct him. Tutorial hours were often unusual; during his breakfast time before he had to catch a London train or very late in the evening on his return. He directed his students towards the history of chemistry in its growth to a rational subject and laid stress on the need for technique and precision in measurements. This appealed to him more than speculative theories. Mathematical treatments of any complexity were a closed subject, and he relied much on his more able pupils for an introduction to the rapid post-war developments. In spite of this handicap his powers of judgement on broader aspects and his ability to concentrate on essential issues prevented him from falling behind in the 1920–30 period.

In research he returned to an earlier interest in the electrical conductivity of solutions. The subject then appeared to many as one already supplied with enough useful data, but the situation was transformed in 1923 by the publication of the Debye–Hückel theory. Realizing that a study of non-aqueous solutions afforded the best test, Hartley began a systematic series of conductivity measurements of salts dissolved in alcohols and other organic solvents. This body of work made a substantial contribution towards the understanding of ionic solutions, for which Hartley was in 1926 elected a fellow of the Royal Society.

Immediately after the 1914–18 war Hartley was dispatched as leader of a team to investigate the chemical side of German wartime activities. What he saw made a lasting impression; not merely the sheer magnitude of industry as viewed by an academic but also the high scientific qualifications of its leaders and its support by the government. The team's report recommending positive action for British industry had its effect, and Hartley became a member of the Chemical Warfare Board, in which he played a prominent part up to 1950. The development of chemical industry now seemed to him to be of vital importance to the country; in 1922 he joined the Society of Chemical Engineers and the board of the Gas Light and Coke Company, on which he served until 1945, being deputy governor during the 1939–45 war. The efficient use of fuels occupied his mind, and in 1929 he joined the Fuel Research Board of the Department of Scientific and Industrial Research, acting as chairman from 1932 to 1947.

In 1930 Hartley was finding his interests in securing improvements in the nation's use of science more congenial than those afforded by his academic prospects. With much heart-searching he came to the decision to resign from his tutorial fellowship and to accept a full-time post of vice-president and director of research of the railway system which had been reorganized as LMS.

In 1934 he was appointed chairman of the newly formed Railway Air Services and this led to chairmanship of British European Airways (1946–7) and the British Overseas Airways Corporation (1947–9) and a lifelong interest in air travel. Removed to his regret from these posts by the then minister he became the first chairman of the Electricity Supply Council (1949–52), continuing (later as deputy chairman) until 1954. Again he collected distinguished scientists on to the Council, and later, as consultant to the Central Electricity Generating Board, he was active in helping with its research problems.

Hartley never tired of urging the upgrading of British chemical engineering. In 1951–2 and 1954–5 he was an active president of the Institution of Chemical Engineers and was awarded its Osborne–Reynolds medal (1954). The Society of Instrument Technology elected him president from 1957 to 1961 and a Hartley medal and lecture were introduced. The firm of constructors John Brown appointed him adviser (1954–61), and enabled him to develop his views of the importance of replacing batch chemical and biochemical processes by continuous plant, and of the need for high-level studies of methods of precise control. During the period 1935–50 Hartley was chairman of a number of World Power conferences and associated meetings and organizations.

Hartley had a long connection with the Goldsmiths' Company. He received the freedom in 1929 and was admitted to the livery, thereafter serving the Company in a number of ways and becoming prime warden in 1941–2. Through his influence the Company provided powerful support for historical research in science and the preservation of instruments and records. He had always been attracted by the problems facing nineteenth-century chemists and had great admiration for such leading figures as Michael Faraday, Joseph Priestley, Sir Humphry Davy, John Dalton [qq.v.], J. J. Berzelius, and A. L. Lavoisier, whose work he described in various publications. He was a very active editor of *Notes and Records of the Royal Society* from 1952 to 1970.

As a judge of character Hartley was quick to distinguish the efficient from the inefficient, but he went further and divided people into those who were helpful and those who either opposed or disregarded his views. He never argued with opponents, but faced them with a blank blandness, though in private he could sum them up very frankly. His numerous chairmanships were very efficiently conducted; he came fully briefed on all necessary matters and with very clear ideas on what he considered the right course to adopt. It needed unusual strength and persistence among members of a meeting to prevent agreement on the proposals he would put forward. He was skilful at cutting short arguments which did not seem to be going his way. Those who agreed admired his abilities, but others sometimes thought they had been treated with a degree of intolerance. He was knighted in 1928 and created KCVO in 1944, GCVO in 1957, and CH in 1967.

His activities persisted undiminished almost up to his death 9 September 1972 at the age of ninety-four. To this Dictionary he contributed several notices. For the last thirty years of his life he suffered increasing arthritic trouble in the legs, first needing sticks, then a wheeled chair, until he was finally confined to a bedroom in a London nursing home. This he treated as an office for carrying on his ceaseless interests, writing and interviewing with an energy and clarity which astonished his colleagues. It was there that he died.

Hartley followed his father's admiration of Japanese art. He appreciated objects of neatness, symmetry, and colour. As a young man minerals and crystals excited his attention, and he enjoyed demonstrating the brilliant colours of thin crystals in polarized light, skilfully using a projection microscope with a heating stage. His increasingly busy later life did not allow much time for these interests.

In 1906 he married Gertrude Mary Forster, daughter of Arthur Lionel Smith [q.v.], later master of Balliol. She died in 1970. Their family was a son, Air Marshal Sir Christopher Hartley, and a daughter.

[A. G. Ogston in *Biographical Memoirs of Fellows of the Royal Society*, vol. xix, 1973; private information; personal knowledge.]

E. J. BOWEN

HARTLEY, LESLIE POLES (1895–1972), novelist and critic, was born 30 December 1895 at Whittlesea, the only son of Harry Bark Hartley, solicitor of Peterborough and later director of a brickworks, and his wife, Mary Elizabeth Thompson. Hartley was brought up at the family house, Fletton Tower, Peterborough. He was educated at Harrow and Balliol College, Oxford, where he was elected to an exhibition in history in 1915. His Oxford career was interrupted when he enlisted in April 1916. He became a second lieutenant in the Norfolk Regiment and was invalided out of the army in September 1918. He returned to Balliol in April 1919 and gained a second class in modern history in 1921.

It was during this period at Oxford that his literary and social gifts first fully displayed themselves. Some characteristic stories were printed in the *Oxford Outlook*, of which he was an editor; and, in the brilliant phase of undergraduate social life which followed World War I, he was a leading figure in its most agreeable circles. Outside Oxford, he became a welcome guest of Lady Ottoline Morrell [q.v.] at Garsington Manor and of Margot, Countess of Oxford and Asquith, whose notice he later wrote for this Dictionary. Through them he first made acquaintance with the literary and social worlds of London. A man of independent means, he spent the next eighteen years partly in England and partly in Venice. He also became a regular and successful reviewer, mainly of fiction, and notably in the *Saturday Review* and the *Sketch*. As a creative writer, he fared less happily. He published two volumes of short stories, *Night Fears* (1924) and *The Killing Bottle* (1932), and a short *nouvelle*, *Simonetta Perkins* (1925); but these, though politely received, made no great impression. In consequence, Hartley grew disappointed and his creative impulse inhibited. During the war of 1939–45, which he spent living in retirement in Wiltshire and Dorset, this inhibition disappeared and he wrote most of the trilogy of novels, *The Shrimp and the Anemone* (1944), *The Sixth Heaven* (1946), and *Eustace and Hilda* (1947), which were to be his most sustained achievement.

For the next twenty-three years of his life, he poured forth a steady stream of books; twelve novels and four volumes of short stories as well as a collection of critical studies including the Clark lectures on Nathaniel Hawthorne, delivered at Cambridge in 1964. Hartley's later life was divided between Bath, where he bought a house in 1946, and London.

As a writer Hartley was unequal; his later books especially—though always marked by an individual flavour and sense of style—were sometimes disfigured by melodrama and improbability. Moreover his peculiar imaginative power only showed its full strength in his best-known works; the 'Eustace and Hilda' trilogy and *The Go-Between* (1953), which was made into a film. These are among the most original and distinguished of twentieth-century English novels; conveying, in a graceful and subtle prose, a vision of reality which combines a penetrating and accurate observation of social and psychological fact enlivened by the play of a delicate humour, with an intense and mysterious poetry—now dark with unearthly terror, now lit up with glimpses of spiritual beauty—and made poignant by an exquisite quality of feeling, pensive, ironical, tender. His best short stories exhibit, in a concentrated form, the same characteristics.

Hartley's social gifts made him well known not only as an author but also as a personality. Quiet and unobtrusive in appearance and manner, his generous and sympathetic disposition and the charm of his conversation—intimate, humorous, and fanciful—made him many close friends including such distinguished artistic and social figures as Osbert and Edith Sitwell, Elizabeth Bowen, L. H. Myers, Henry Lamb, Lady Cynthia Asquith [qq.v], and Ethel Sands.

He was appointed CBE in 1956 for his services to literature and in 1972 the Royal Society of Literature made him a Companion of Literature. For many years he was a member of the management committee of the Society of Authors and was president of the English section of the PEN Club.

Hartley was unmarried. He died in London 13 December 1972. There are portraits by Henry Lamb RA and Derek Hill.

[Private information; personal knowledge.]

DAVID CECIL

HARTNELL, SIR NORMAN BISHOP (1901–1979), dress designer, was born at Hassocks, Sussex, the only son and younger child of Henry Bishop Hartnell, hotelier, and his wife, Emily Polly. He had three half-sisters. He was educated at Mill Hill and, from 1921, Magdalene College, Cambridge, which he left after two years. Whilst at Cambridge Hartnell was first able to indulge his passion for the theatre. He joined the Footlights dramatic club where he not only acted but designed the costumes and the sets. His designs were so good that they were commented on in the *Evening Standard* by one of the leading journalists of the day who said that Norman Hartnell was likely to become Britain's outstanding dress designer.

Such appreciation prompted Hartnell, on leaving Cambridge, to seek a job in the fashion business in London and after a few trials and tribulations he and his sister, with some financial help from their father, opened in 1923 a couture establishment at 10 Bruton Street. The business survived and prospered. Apart from society ladies his clients increasingly included many of the leading actresses of the day such as Gertrude Lawrence [q.v.], Mistinguett, Evelyn Laye, and Alice Delysia. He also designed dresses for many of the shows produced by (Sir) Charles Cochran [q.v.], the André Charlot [q.v.] reviews, and the plays of (Sir) Noël Coward [q.v.].

Hartnell's reputation for creating beautiful clothes steadily increased and in 1935 he was requested by Lady Alice Montagu-Douglas-Scott to produce her wedding gown for her marriage to the Duke of Gloucester [q.v.]. He was also asked to produce the dresses for the bridesmaids amongst whom were the Princesses Elizabeth and Margaret. The wedding dress was a great success and shortly afterwards he was asked to produce some designs for the Duchess of York (the future Queen Elizabeth the Queen Mother).

However, the pre-war highlight of Hartnell's career came in 1938 when he was asked to design the clothes for the Queen's state visit to Paris. The court was in mourning and it was at his suggestion that all the clothes, which became the subject of world-wide admiration, were in white. For his services to fashion the French government made him an officier d'Académie (1939). In 1940 he received his first royal warrant of appointment to the Queen.

The war period brought about two developments in Hartnell's career. First he started to design 'utility' dresses for the mass market, and then in 1944 he became a founder member of the Incorporated Society of London Fashion Designers, a couture body which was formed to deal with government departments. He became its second chairman with his period of office lasting from 1947 to 1956.

The year 1947 was excellent for Hartnell. He was asked to design the wedding dress for Princess Elizabeth together with the dresses for her bridesmaids, the maid of honour being Princess Margaret. In the same year he received the American Neiman-Marcus award given annually for an outstanding contribution to world fashion.

In 1953 Hartnell produced the coronation robe for Queen Elizabeth II. This again proved to be a resounding success and he was appointed MVO. He then designed wardrobes for the Queen's royal tours to Australasia and other parts of the Commonwealth and for state visits to the capital cities of Europe. He increasingly became known as 'the royal dressmaker'. He was a much loved man with great personal charm who made a major contribution to enhancing the prestige of British fashion.

In 1977, the year of the Queen's silver jubilee, Hartnell was appointed KCVO, the first knighthood conferred for services to fashion. Shortly afterwards his health began to deteriorate and he died at King Edward VII Hospital, Windsor, 8 June 1979. He was unmarried.

[Norman Hartnell, *Silver and Gold* (autobiography), 1955; personal knowledge.]

EDWARD RAYNE

HASKELL, ARNOLD LIONEL DAVID (1903–1980), balletomane, was born 19 July 1903 in London, the only child of Jacob Silas Haskell, banker, of Queen's Gate, London, and his wife, Emmy Mesritz. He was educated at Westminster School, and Trinity Hall, Cambridge, where he studied law, obtaining a second class (second division) in part i (1924). He left without finishing his degree and, after a brief and unsuccessful attempt at business, became a reader for William Heinemann Ltd. from 1927 to 1932. He was a joint founder of the Camargo Society in 1930, in 1933–4 worked as an administrative assistant to Colonel de Basil's Russian Ballet on their American tour, and in 1934 published a widely successful book, *Balletomania*, adding that word to the language. From 1935 to 1938 he was dance critic to the *Daily Telegraph* and again worked with the Russian Ballet on their Australian tour of 1938–9. During the war he assisted Air Raid Precautions and gave lecture tours for the forces and industry. In 1946 he was asked by (Dame) Ninette de Valois to become director of the new Royal Ballet School, which became his main activity from 1946 to 1965.

Slight and small in build, Haskell had considerable charm and force of personality. He fell in love with ballet early in life, and as a result of childhood friendship with (Dame) Alicia Markova, had an immediate entrée to the dazzling world of the Diaghilev Ballet when Markova joined that company in 1925. His enthusiasm and attractive personality quickly gained friends among dancers and choreographers, and his wide interests as an avowed dilettante, particularly in sculpture and painting, but also literature and music, gave him the necessary intellectual background to make the most of the Diaghilev Company, then reaching the height of its influence as the élitist avant-garde of Parisian culture.

Yet Haskell's real strength was as a popularizer, and in a stream of books and articles on ballet, all well written and compulsively readable, he helped to spread enthusiasm for ballet from a small if influential upper-class Opera House audience, to the average middle-class theatre-going public. During the 1930s de Basil's Russian Ballet, gathering popular success on the coat-tails of Diaghilev's status and largely depending on past achievement, captured Haskell's allegiance more than the struggling British Ballet, but by 1946 what was to become the Royal Ballet was firmly established, and, as director of its school for the first two crucial decades, Haskell established as an educator a style and an ambience that influenced succeeding generations of dancers. His urbane, civilized, and tolerant approach helped to counterbalance the fiercely competitive pressures inevitable in a specialized school where pupils were very much aware that only a few precious places would be available at the end of each year in the dance company itself.

Appropriately for a ballet critic Haskell was fascinated by sculpture, vigorously defending (Sir) Jacob Epstein [q.v.] in *The Sculptor Speaks* (1931). After visiting Australia with the Russian Ballet in 1938 he wrote three books on Australia, *Waltzing Matilda* (1940), *Australia* (1941), and *The Australians* (1943). To this Dictionary he contributed the notice of Harold Turner. He also wrote two books of autobiography, *In His True Centre* (1951) and *Balletomane at Large* (1972), but his major achievement rests on over twenty books on the art of ballet. Closely in touch with dancers and choreographers, his judgement widened and assisted by his lifelong enthusiasms in so many arts, he approached new work with an open mind, was sympathetic to current trends, and had a rare gift for defending, explaining, and clarifying for his readers what ballet was attempting to achieve. His careful analysis invariably spotted what was wrong as well as what was right, and as a critic his kind but firm integrity shone through everything he wrote. The development of British ballet was fortunate to have such a persuasive and influential publicist to espouse its cause in its vital early years, and the subsequent popularity of the art owes something to Haskell's efforts as well as to the dancers, choreographers, composers, and designers he wrote about so attractively.

In 1927 he married Vera (died 1968), daughter of Mark Saitzoff, a Russian émigré industrialist; they had two sons, one of whom, Francis, became professor of art at Oxford University, and one daughter. In 1970 he married Vivienne Diana, third daughter of Arthur Tristman Marks, mining engineer, and sister of Alicia Markova. Haskell died at his home in Bath 15 November 1980.

He became a chevalier of the Legion of Honour (1950), was appointed CBE (1954), was awarded an honorary D.Litt. by Bath (1974), became FRSL (1977), and won the Queen Elizabeth Coronation award of the Royal Academy of Dancing (1979).

[Arnold Haskell, *In His True Centre*, 1951, and *Balletomane at Large*, 1972 (autobiographies); private information; personal knowledge.]

NICHOLAS DROMGOOLE

HAWTREY, SIR RALPH GEORGE (1879–1975), Treasury economist, was born 22 November 1879 at Langley, near Slough, the first son and third and last child of George Procter Hawtrey, headmaster of St. Michael's preparatory school, Slough, and his first wife, Eda Strahan. He was educated at Eton and Trinity College, Cambridge, where he read mathematics and graduated as nineteenth wrangler in 1901. At Cambridge he was elected to the Apostles and was deeply influenced by the philosophy of G. E. Moore [q.v.]. Many of his Cambridge friends later formed part of the Bloomsbury Group and it was through his continued association with Bloomsbury that Hawtrey met (Hortense) Emilia Sophie d'Aranyi (died 1953), the concert pianist, whom he married in 1915; they had no children. She was the daughter of Taksony d'Aranyi de Hunyadvar, chief of police of Budapest, and the sister of Jelly d'Aranyi and Adila Fachiri [qq.v.].

Hawtrey entered the Home Civil Service in 1903, and after one year in the Admiralty, moved to the Treasury. He was appointed its director of financial enquiries in 1919, and remained at the Treasury until 1947. In 1928–9 he was given leave of absence to take up a visiting professorship of economics at Harvard University, and from 1947 until 1952 he was Price professor of international economics at the Royal Institute of International Affairs, London.

Although Hawtrey spent his working life as an economic adviser at the Treasury and learnt his monetary economics largely from experience there, outside office hours he wrote and published more contributions to monetary theory than most of his academic contemporaries. The system of analysis which he developed continuously in them was based on one central idea—'inflation; the cyclical alternations of activity and depression; financial crises, disturbances of the balance of payments and rates of exchange—all these were to be traced to changes in the wealth-value or purchasing power of the monetary unit' (*Currency and Credit*, 4th edn., 1950). Hawtrey laid particular emphasis on the influence of Bank rate changes on traders' stock holdings and this was the main source of difference between him and his friend and contemporary J. M. (later Lord) Keynes [q.v.] in whose theories long-term investment played a greater part. Throughout the twenties and thirties Hawtrey was a constructive critic of Keynes and their debates were a major formative influence in the development of monetary theory.

The advice on policy which Hawtrey gave at the Treasury also developed consistently from his view that maintaining constancy in the wealth-value of the monetary unit must be the primary objective. In 1919 he therefore supported the policy of a return to the gold standard, but in the form of a gold exchange standard with international agreements on uncovered paper issues and credit control. An opportunity to have something like this plan put into effect offered when an international economic conference was convened at Genoa in 1922 and Hawtrey as one of the British delegates secured the incorporation of his proposals into the resolutions adopted by the conference. These were never put into effect and when it became clear in 1925 that the return to gold involved continued deflation Hawtrey became a persistent critic of British monetary policy. Nevertheless he did not favour the policy of reducing unemployment through public works advocated by Keynes and the Liberals in 1929 and had some responsibility for the white paper (Cmd. 3331) which set out the famous 'Treasury view' of its inefficacy.

Since the 1930s witnessed a decline in the use of interest rate changes in monetary policy it is not surprising that Hawtrey's influence on policy also declined in these years. After World War II Hawtrey's doctrines made him critical of the Bretton Woods proposals and in later years he constantly argued that the 1949 devaluation of sterling had been a policy error comparable in magnitude to the 1925 return to gold and was the root cause of Britain's later inflationary problems. Gentle in character and courteous in debate, Hawtrey was nevertheless a tenacious advocate of his ideas, whether or not they were fashionable. The post-war success of Keynesian theories led to some under-estimation of the value of Hawtrey's contribution to macro-economics but later its importance was again recognized.

Hawtrey was a prolific writer. Among his books were *Good and Bad Trade* (1913), *Currency and Credit* (1919), *The Economic Problem* (1926), *The Gold Standard in Theory and Practice* (1927), *The Art of Central Banking* (1932), *Capital and Employment* (1937), *Economic Destiny* (1944), and *Incomes and Money* (1967). To this Dictionary he contributed the notice of Lord Bradbury, who had influenced him considerably at the Treasury.

Hawtrey was elected a fellow of the British Academy in 1935, received the honorary degree of D.Sc. (Econ.) from London University in 1939, was president of the Royal Economic Society in 1946–8, and became an honorary fellow of Trinity College, Cambridge, in 1959. He was appointed CB in 1941 and knighted in 1956. He died at Kensington, London, 21 March 1975.

[*The Times*, 22 March 1975; *International Encyclopedia of the Social Sciences*, vol. vi, 1968, pp. 328–30; R. D. Collison Black in *Proceedings* of the British Academy, vol. lxiii, 1977; Hawtrey Papers, Churchill College, Cambridge; private information.]

R. D. Collison Black

HAYWARD, Sir ISAAC JAMES (1884–1976), trade union general secretary and leader of the London County Council (1947–65), was born 17 November 1884 at Blaenavon, Monmouthshire, the second of five sons in the family of seven children of Thomas Hayward, engine-fitter, and his wife, Mary Elizabeth French. He went to the local elementary school, leaving at the age of twelve. His subsequent education was at night school.

For three years he worked in the nearby pits, after which he entered engineering. Early becoming involved in union work, in a voluntary capacity, he became a full-time official of the National Union of Enginemen, Firemen, Mechanics, and Electrical Workers, the general secretaryship of which he attained in 1938. In his later years he would proudly refer to the union card he had held continuously from the age of sixteen—and still held at his death. In World War I, in the interest of industrial harmony there began a new partnership between government and unions. Hayward played his part in this new union role, the work bringing him frequently to London, to which he and his family moved in 1924. Here his service in various committees brought him in contact with Herbert Morrison (later Lord Morrison of Lambeth, q.v.), who was anxious at that time to supplement his small team—then in opposition at County Hall—with qualities he felt to be essential. Rating Hayward's union experience and balanced judgement very highly, Morrison encouraged him to seek election to the London County Council. From the time Hayward became a member (Rotherhithe 1928–37; Deptford 1937–55) Morrison availed himself fully of the qualities he had discerned, deferring to a large extent to Hayward's advice on union affairs.

With Labour's resounding victory at the polls in London, the way was open to a project dear to Hayward's heart—the humanization of the Poor Law, a responsibility that had passed in 1929 from the boards of guardians to the county councils. He became chairman of the council's public assistance committee (1934–7), in which capacity he steered through the many reforms calculated to ease the existing harshness. In particular, he initiated a more generous and flexible set of scales to be applied to outdoor relief, which became a nation-wide model. And again, he set in motion the replacement of the large barrack-like institutions (or workhouses) by the small type of home that has become the norm.

For Hayward there were to follow years of service as chairman of important council committees, as its representative on outside bodies, and as expert adviser on others. He became a part-time member of the board of British European Airways on its formation in 1946 and also chairman of the consultative council of the London Electricity Board (1948–60). In 1947, while he was chairman of the London County Council education committee (1945–7), the development plan required under the 1944 Education Act came down decisively in favour of a comprehensive school system which, in due course, spread nation-wide. For Hayward this was the fulfilment of a dream: 'Why should not the crossing sweeper have a university degree?' He was himself in 1952 awarded the honorary degree of LL D by the University of London, on whose court he served from 1947, drawing closer the ties between university and council.

When in 1947 he began his record period of leadership of the council, he was sixty-three and steeped in the traditions of a council honoured for its integrity. Ever young in mind, as sturdy in body, he was to devote his whole being to the council's service, transporting its beneficent operations to spheres hitherto undreamed of. Such was his power of imagination and his strength of purpose that he could embark on the much acclaimed South Bank venture—the Royal Festival Concert Hall, Elizabeth and Purcell Halls, and Hayward Gallery (named after him)—partly on land reclaimed from the Thames. He played a major part too, in the birth of the National Theatre, for when doubt ruled the day, he offered a grant from the council of £1 million, from which stemmed the ultimate decision to proceed. As with the South Bank, vision, determination, and a clear view of the way forward led to the realization of the Crystal Palace Sports Centre, for which he had carefully assessed the nation's need. He was to be disappointed in his plan for an exhibition centre there, which was abandoned for reasons of finance.

In the field of the arts, Hayward broke new ground, initiating the role of the public authority as 'benefactor', to some extent in place of the private 'patron' of earlier times. Grants to opera, orchestral music, ballet, sculpture, and painting came to the rescue of the then languishing artistic world. Hayward threw himself with vigour into the affairs of the International Union of Local Authorities, of whose British section he became chairman.

Mild mannered, almost diffident, Hayward revealed a firmness of purpose that commanded the greatest respect from colleagues and political opponents. His knighthood (1959) was a mark of this esteem, as were the freedoms of the boroughs of Bermondsey and Deptford bestowed upon him in 1955 and 1961 respectively, and his honorary FRIBA (1970). His recreations—literature and music, chess and bowls—contributed to the making of the 'full man'.

Hayward married in 1913 Alice Mayers, daughter of a master builder. She died in 1944 and in 1951 he married Violet Cleveland. There were four sons of the first marriage, of whom the eldest was killed in action in 1944.

[Greater London Council documents; private information; personal knowledge.]

FREDA CORBET

HEENAN, JOHN CARMEL (1905–1975), cardinal, eighth archbishop of Westminster, was born in Ilford, Essex, 26 January 1905, the youngest in the family of three sons and one daughter of James Carmel Heenan, a civil servant at the Patent Office, and his wife, Anne Pilkington. John Heenan's parents were Irish and he was brought up in an atmosphere of fervent Catholicism. He early showed a desire for the priesthood and was especially encouraged in this vocation by his mother and his parish priest at Ilford.

He was educated at St. Ignatius' College, Stamford Hill, London, and began his studies for the priesthood at St. Cuthbert's College, Ushaw, Durham. From there he was awarded a bursary at the Venerable English College, Rome, in 1924. While there he obtained doctorates in philosophy and theology. He was ordained priest in 1930 and, after completing his studies in Rome, was appointed assistant priest at the church of SS. Mary and Ethelburga, Barking, in the diocese of Brentwood in 1931.

As a young priest, in 1936 Heenan visited the Soviet Union, disguised as a lecturer in psychology, in order to study conditions there. He had been encouraged in this venture by his old rector at the English College, Arthur Hinsley [q.v.]. On his return to England, Heenan was able to give a first-hand account of life in Russia to the cardinal and to the public.

He was appointed parish priest of St. Stephen's, Manor Park, in 1937. During the next few years he became known as a public speaker at Catholic functions and also wrote a series of popular books explaining the Catholic faith. As a result of this work he was recommended to the BBC and during the early years of the war of 1939–45 he became a popular broadcaster. Heenan spent the whole of the war years with his parishioners at Manor Park.

In 1947 Heenan was asked by the Catholic bishops to become the superior of the re-established Catholic Missionary Society, a group of diocesan priests from England and Wales who were to give missions to Catholics and non-Catholics all over the country. After four years of this work, he was appointed bishop of Leeds in 1951. He showed himself extremely hard-working but admitted later that he was too impulsive and made many mistakes. During his time at Leeds, Heenan became an accomplished television speaker and the best-known Catholic bishop in the country.

In 1957 Heenan was translated to Liverpool as its eighth archbishop and metropolitan of the northern province. There his most notable achievement was the building of the Roman Catholic cathedral. Plans for the cathedral had been made about thirty years before, but by 1957 the cost had become prohibitive. Heenan decided that a more contemporary and necessarily cheaper design was needed and, by the time he left Liverpool, the new cathedral, designed by (Sir) Frederick Gibberd, was well on the way to completion.

On the death of Cardinal Godfrey in 1963 Heenan became the eighth archbishop of Westminster. Until 1966 most of his time was spent in attendance at the second Vatican Council. Even before the announcement of the Council, he had been appointed to the newly established Secretariat for Christian Unity. He was by no means the first Roman Catholic ecumenist in this country, but his appointment and his energy began for the first time to make an immediate impression on ordinary Catholics.

He was created cardinal in 1965. As leader of the English and Welsh bishops at the Council, Heenan was particularly active in the preparation of the Council's declaration on non-Christian religions and the decree on ecumenism. His work at the Council was particularly acceptable to the Jewish community in Britain, especially as he had already ensured, in the face of the Roman Curia's disapproval, the re-entry of Catholics into the Council of Christians and Jews in this country.

As archbishop of Westminster and president of the bishops' conference of England and Wales, Heenan had to put into practice the decrees of the Council. He managed to keep the Catholic church in England and Wales on an even keel in all the upheavals that followed the Council. This country was neither intellectually nor psychologically ready for all the changes, but the fact that Catholics remained a fairly cohesive body was largely the result of his handling of the situation.

Heenan had boundless energy and was almost a compulsive worker. He was regarded by most people as an expert politician and he certainly had the ability to say the right thing at the right time. He had great charm and seemed able to persuade whoever he was addressing that he was the most important person to the cardinal at the time. However, he also had great simplicity. His life was based on his simple belief in the goodness of God. While he accepted the changes that came from the second Vatican Council, he remained at heart a traditional Catholic. He realized that many of the changes brought about by the Council were good but he missed the certainty Catholics once had and hoped that they would soon settle down once more to a united church. He never reconciled himself to the number of priests leaving the priesthood—he could not understand how a priest could give up his vocation. He had had his greatest happiness in being a priest and looked on his time at Manor Park as the highlight of his life.

Heenan's last years were darkened by ill health. He had already decided to resign before his last illness. He died in Westminster Hospital 7 November and was buried beside the fourteenth station of the cross in Westminster Cathedral.

[Cardinal Heenan, *Not the Whole Truth*, 1973, and *A Crown of Thorns*, 1974 (autobiography); *A Tribute to Cardinal Heenan*, Catholic Information Services, 1976; personal knowledge.]

DAVID NORRIS

HENDERSON, (ALEXANDER) GAVIN, second BARON FARINGDON (1902–1977), Labour politician, was born 20 March 1902, the eldest in the family of three sons and one daughter of Lt.-Col. Harold Greenwood Henderson (1875–1922), of Buscot Park, Berkshire, and Lady Violet Charlotte Dalzell, daughter of the fourteenth Earl of Carnwath. He succeeded his grandfather (the first Baron Faringdon, 1850–1934), a railway magnate, who had been a Unionist MP. He was educated at Eton; McGill University, Montreal; and Christ Church, Oxford, where he obtained a fourth class in modern history in 1924. He also obtained a diploma of the International Exhibition (Brussels, 1935).

In the early 1920s Henderson was a somewhat notorious member of 'The Bright Young Things'. By 1934 he had become keenly interested in public affairs and joined the Labour Party; he helped Christopher (later Viscount) Addison [q.v.] when he was elected in a by-election that year for Swindon, which included Faringdon. Meanwhile, having inherited Buscot, he restored this pleasant eighteenth-century house internally and externally, demolishing the Victorian wing his grandfather had added for his large family. He later made arrangements for the house to pass to the National Trust. An enthusiastic Georgian, he did much to advance the growing appreciation of Georgian architecture.

A strong supporter of the Spanish Republican cause, he not only flew its flag whenever appropriate, but helped to find homes for Basque child refugees. Also a strong pacifist, he reconciled his conscience when World War II came by joining the fire service and giving sterling service during the blitz in London, Bristol, and other large cities. In his fire brigade uniform with Faringdon, the name of his local branch, written across his chest, he frequently attended the House of Lords and Fabian committees when in London. He was a member of a parliamentary goodwill mission to the USSR in January–February 1945, which toured around in one of the Tsar's old trains. The party of eight MPs and two peers was served by members of the Soviet Foreign Office and British embassy. Thomas (later Lord) Brimelow, later head of the Diplomatic Service, was its secretary. Faringdon upset the Russians by making clear his disapproval of many of (Sir) Winston Churchill's pre-war policies. They told the leader of the British delegation, Walter Elliot [q.v.] that he had a dangerous Trotskyite in his ranks. However, in due course Faringdon's idiosyncrasies were accepted. He had brought his fire brigade uniform with him and spoke with authority about fire-fighting in the blitz. As a result he was asked officially to inspect the fire brigades of Moscow, Leningrad, and other cities, which he did in great style.

Faringdon became an active Fabian, being an elected or co-opted member of the executive committee (1942–66), its vice-chairman in 1959–60, chairman in 1960–1, and vice-president in 1970–7. He was particularly interested in colonial and international affairs and became chairman of the Fabian Colonial Bureau (1952–8). For many years he acted as host at Buscot to many Fabian specialist groups, including that under R. H. S. Crossman [q.v.], which produced the latest Fabian Essays. The last important conference held there was in 1970 after the fall of the Labour government. Faringdon also played an active part in London government, being a London county councillor in 1958–61 and alderman in 1961–5. After the creation of the Greater London Council he became a member of its historic buildings committee.

Other political activities included the treasurership of the National Council for Civil Liberties (1940–5) and membership of the Colonial Economic and Development Council (1948–51). Faringdon also had a keen interest in housing problems, being appointed chairman of a committee to consider the appearance of local authority housing estates for the National Buildings Record (1942) and serving on the Central Housing Advisory Committee (1946).

He had a lively interest in the arts, being a trustee for the Wallace Collection in 1946–53 and 1966–73, and president of the Theatres Advisory Council (1946). He was a member of the Historic Buildings Council in 1964–73, and president of the Friends of City Churches (1943). He was a keen garden designer. Among other activities, Faringdon was a Lords member of the Parliamentary Labour Party's executive in 1957–60 and served on the executive committee of the Fire Service Association (1960–9) of which he became chairman. In 1936 he became a fellow of the Royal Society of Arts.

In 1927 he married Honor Chedworth Philipps, third daughter of Lord Kylsant, director of the Southern Railway Company. The marriage was annulled in 1931; there were no children. He died at 28 Brompton Square, London, 29 January 1977.

[Personal knowledge.] JOHN PARKER

HENDY, SIR PHILIP ANSTISS (1900–1980), director of the National Gallery, was born at Carlisle 27 September 1900, only son of Frederick James Roberts Hendy, director of the Department of Education, Oxford University (1919–28), and his wife, Caroline Isabelle, daughter of A. W. Potts, first headmaster of Fettes College. He was elected a King's scholar of Westminster in 1914, and a Westminster exhibitioner of Christ Church, Oxford, in 1919. In 1923, after obtaining his BA degree with a third class in modern history (MA, 1937), he became assistant to the keeper and lecturer at the Wallace Collection, London, where he began work on a new edition of the catalogue. It was on the strength of his draft entries for this, shown by the keeper, S. J. Camp, to one of the trustees of the Isabella Stewart Gardner Museum, Boston, that Hendy was invited to catalogue the Gardner paintings; he was financed by the trustees to live in Italy for three years, preparing the catalogue, which was published in 1931.

With a growing reputation in Boston, Hendy was appointed in 1930 curator of paintings in the Museum of Fine Arts. Among his acquisitions he indulged his own taste for Impressionist and Post-Impressionist art, buying at prices which later seemed extremely advantageous; but this was not the taste of his trustees at the time. There was a quarrel, and Hendy resigned.

A year after his return to England he accepted in 1934 the directorship of the Leeds City Art Gallery. The wartime evacuation of that gallery to Temple Newsam House nearby gave Hendy scope for his undoubted talents, in rearranging the pictures in a fine eighteenth-century setting; and from 1936 until 1946 he combined his work for Leeds with the Slade professorship at Oxford. It was his success at Leeds and Temple Newsam that led to his appointment in 1946 to succeed Sir Kenneth (later Lord) Clark as director of the National Gallery. He held that post for twenty-one years; and he was knighted in 1950. He was president of the International Council of Museums 1959–65; and after retirement in 1967 he spent three years (1968–71) as adviser to the Israel Museum in Jerusalem. In 1975 he suffered a severe stroke, and spent his last years in sad physical condition, devotedly cared for by his wife Cicely, at Great Haseley near Oxford.

At the National Gallery Hendy's first task was to undertake the rehabilitation of the pictures returned from air-conditioned storage in Wales during the war to the damaging atmosphere of London. His exhibition of pictures cleaned by the restorer, Helmut Ruhemann, occasioned criticism, much of it unjustified; letters to the press had alleged that Rubens' 'Chapeau de Paille' and Rembrandt's 'Woman Bathing' were spoilt. But Hendy rode the storm. He was naturally contentious and uncompromising, and his relationship with some of his trustees and senior staff was often turbulent; but he had loyal friends also, among his trustees and chairman—Henry Moore, Sir J. Alan N. Barlow [q.v.], Lord Robbins, and Sir John Witt—and many would regard his achievement as considerable, as director in a difficult period.

His writings on art are graced with original observations and ideas, even if sometimes marred by immature prejudices (his criticism of the Pre-Raphaelites, for instance, was intemperate). His publications included a general essay on Spanish art (1946), monographs on Giovanni Bellini (1945), Masaccio (1957), and Piero della Francesca (1968), and a small book on Matthew Smith (1944). His best achievement, probably, remains the Gardner catalogue, completed when he was less than thirty years old (republished 1974); his descriptions and appreciations of individual pictures there are more interesting than those of most modern catalogues. He belonged to a generation of museum officials who were still, strictly speaking, amateurs: interested in art, but self-taught in art history; in some cases perhaps even the better for that. An appointment such as Hendy's to the Wallace Collection in 1923, straight from Oxford with such limited experience, would probably be impossible today, now that art history is taught in many of our universities and a new class of professionals has grown up. In spite of the disadvantage, Hendy acquitted himself with remarkable success.

He was handsome in a slightly exotic way, dark, tall, and thin; and he had undeniable charm of manner. He married twice: first, in 1925, Kythé, eldest daughter of Francis Ogilvy, a member of the London Stock Exchange; they had a daughter and a son; secondly Cicely, widow of (Charles) Christopher Martin, and daughter of Captain Thomas Lewis Prichard, of the Royal Welch Fusiliers. No portrait of him, drawn or painted, seems to be known. He died in Oxford 6 September 1980.

[*The Times*, 8 September 1980; *Burlington Magazine*, vol. cxxiii, January 1981, p. 33; private information; personal knowledge.]

JAMES BYAM SHAW

HENNESSY, (RICHARD) JAMES (ARTHUR) POPE- (1916–1974), writer. [See POPE-HENNESSY.]

HENRY WILLIAM FREDERICK ALBERT, PRINCE OF YORK, and later DUKE OF GLOUCESTER (1900–1974), was born at York Cottage, Sandringham, 31 March 1900, the fourth of six children and third of five sons of Prince George, Duke of York (later King George V) and Princess (Victoria) Mary ('May') of Teck [qq.v.]. The Prince's oppressive upbringing, in which disparagement played a more prominent role than affection, inspired him with feelings of inadequacy. In 1910, the year his father became King, Prince Henry was sent to St. Peter's Court, a preparatory school at Broadstairs. Three years later he passed into Eton where his housemaster, S. G. Lubbock, found him cheerful and unassuming but lacking in self-confidence. In 1918 he entered Sandhurst and was commissioned the following summer. His formal education ended with a year's course at Trinity College, Cambridge (1919–20).

Prince Henry, an outstanding horseman and shot, was attracted by the life of a cavalry officer. His inclinations and talents were those of a country gentleman, and he felt completely at home in the 10th Royal Hussars to which he was posted in 1921. Nothing irritated him more than to discover that as a King's son he was repeatedly prevented from joining his regiment overseas on active duty.

In 1928 Prince Henry was created Duke of Gloucester and began undertaking official engagements, such as his mission to Japan in 1929 to confer the Garter on the Emperor Hirohito, to Abyssinia in 1930 to attend the coronation of Haile Selassie, and to Australia and New Zealand in 1934–5.

In 1935 the Duke of Gloucester married Alice Christabel, the third daughter of John Charles Montagu-Douglas-Scott, seventh Duke of Buccleuch. The wedding took place in the chapel of Buckingham Palace on 6 November. The Gloucesters moved into York House, and in 1938 bought Barnwell Manor, Northamptonshire. They had two sons: Prince William, born in 1941 (see below), and Prince Richard, born in 1944. There were no daughters. The Duke's family life was supremely happy, and Princess Alice gave him the support and confidence he had hitherto lacked.

The death of George V and the abdication of Edward VIII in 1936 left the Duke third in line to the throne. Moreover, until Princess Elizabeth came of age in 1944, he was also regent designate. Under these circumstances he was reluctantly obliged to abandon peacetime soldiering.

Soon after the outbreak of war in 1939 the Duke was appointed chief liaison officer between the British and French armies in Europe. In May 1940 he was slightly wounded after his staff car was dive-bombed. In 1941 he was appointed second-in-command of the 20th Armoured brigade. During the war he visited troops throughout the United Kingdom, North Africa, the Middle East, and as far afield as India and Ceylon.

Early in 1945 the Duke succeeded the first Earl of Gowrie [q.v.] as governor-general of Australia, where he wielded greater powers than those of the King in Britain. The country was ravaged by strikes, and several members of the new Labour government proved eager to advertise their disenchantment with royalty. To make matters worse, Prince Henry was infectiously shy and lacked the winning charm and fluent small-talk of his eldest brother (the Duke of Windsor, q.v.). Nevertheless, he won the hearts of many Australians by his forthright simplicity, his informed interest in farming, and his willingness to visit scattered communities in the remotest parts of their continent. During his two years of office he travelled over seventy-five thousand miles. In 1947 he was summoned back to England to act as senior counsellor of state, while the King, Queen, and two Princesses visited South Africa.

The accession of Elizabeth II in 1952 did nothing to diminish her uncle's duties, nor to shorten the list of institutions to which he gave considerably more than his name: prominent among which were those concerned with hospitals, youth, and farming. In 1953 the Duke represented the Queen at the inauguration of King Faisal II at Baghdad, and of King Hussain in Amman, and in 1957 he conferred independence within the Commonwealth upon the Malayan Federation. The following year he revisited Ethiopia where he was cordially entertained by the Emperor. He returned to Africa in 1959 to represent the Queen at the proclamation of Nigeria's independence.

Early in 1965, while returning to Barnwell from Sir Winston Churchill's funeral, the Duke overturned the Rolls-Royce he was driving. He was not seriously injured in the accident, but his health gradually deteriorated from then onwards. Later that year, he revisited Australia to mark the fiftieth anniversary of Anzac Day, and in 1966 he returned to Malaysia. His strength, however, was failing, and in 1968 he was rendered helpless by two severe stokes. Princess Alice nursed him solicitously, struggling the while to fulfil his public engagements. The Duke died at Barnwell Manor 10 June 1974 and was buried at Frogmore. He was succeeded in the dukedom by his younger son, Prince Richard Alexander Walter George (born 26 August 1944).

During his career Prince Henry acquired a dazzling array of orders. To list but a few, in 1921 he became a Knight of the Garter, in 1933 a Knight of the Thistle, in 1934 a Knight of St. Patrick, and in 1942 Great Master and Knight Grand Cross of the Order of the Bath. He was sworn of the Privy Council in 1925, and received a host of foreign decorations, ranging from the Ethiopian Order of the Seal of Solomon (1930), to the Order of Mohamed Ali (1948). Prince Henry served in virtually every rank of the army, from lieutenant (1919) to field-marshal (1955). The regiments of which he was colonel-in-chief included the 10th Royal Hussars, the Gloucestershire Regiment, the Gordon Highlanders, and the Scots Guards.

Prince Henry's volatile temper, crisp invective, and penetrating stare could be momentarily terrifying, but his wrath was short-lived and soon dispelled by his shrill, staccato laugh. Probably he would have preferred the life of a country gentleman to that of a public figure, but he was sustained in his royal role by the peremptory sense of duty instilled in him by his parents.

WILLIAM HENRY ANDREW FREDERICK (1941–1972), prince of Great Britain, the elder son and elder child of Prince Henry (see above) and Princess Alice of Gloucester, was born 18 December 1941 in Lady Carnarvon's Home, Barnet, a Hertfordshire nursing home. His schooling began in 1950 at Wellesley House, Broadstairs. Four years later he passed high into Eton, where he proved gregarious, enterprising, and intelligent. Prince William's student days were spent at Magdalene College, Cambridge (1960–3), where he obtained a third class in part i and a second class (2nd division) in part ii of the historical tripos. With his parents' full approval, he shared the unsheltered life of his fellow undergraduates. Indeed, the unprecedented freedom with which he chose his companions, male and female, was seen as a challenging novelty. In 1963–4 he spent a postgraduate year at Stanford, California.

The Prince was a born explorer and in the summer vacation of 1963 made a film for the BBC of a twelve thousand mile safari in Africa. Those who accompanied him on such journeys praised his resource, humour, integrity, and courage. He never wearied of travel, partly because of the opportunities it gave him to fly, drive, climb, ski, shoot, and skin-dive. But he was no mere playboy.

Suspecting that the army might treat him as a 'mascot', Prince William sought a career elsewhere. Possibly the deepest need of his nature was to achieve greatness and not have it thrust upon him. In 1965 he joined the Commonwealth Relations Office as third secretary on the staff of the British high commission at Lagos, from which vantage point he witnessed the Nigerian civil war. Three years later he was transferred to the British embassy in Tokyo as second (commercial) secretary. During his tour of duty he vigorously promoted Anglo-Japanese trade, travelled all over the country, and helped restore friendly relations with the imperial family. His charm, good looks, and informality won Britain many friends.

Prince William returned to England in 1970 to undertake some of his father's public duties. In that year he represented the Queen at the celebrations marking Tonga's independence, and in 1971 at the state funeral of President Tubman of Liberia. The Prince was killed in a flying accident at Halfpenny Green, Staffordshire, 28 August 1972, while competing in an air race.

Prince William was something of a nonconformist, torn between the demands of his inheritance and his love of independence. In struggling to resolve this conflict he pioneered a new style of royalty. He was unmarried.

[Noble Frankland, *Prince Henry, Duke of Gloucester*, 1980; Princess Alice, Duchess of Gloucester, *Memoirs*, 1983; Giles St. Aubyn (ed.), *William of Gloucester*, 1977; personal knowledge.] GILES ST. AUBYN

HEPBURN, PATRICK GEORGE THOMAS BUCHAN-, BARON HAILES (1901–1974), politician. [See BUCHAN-HEPBURN.]

HEPWORTH, DAME (JOCELYN) BARBARA (1903–1975), sculptor, was born 10 January 1903 at Wakefield, Yorkshire, the eldest in the family of three daughters and one son of Herbert Raikes Hepworth CBE, civil engineer to the west riding of Yorkshire, and his wife, Gertrude Allison Johnson. She was educated at Wakefield Girls' High School. She entered the Leeds School of Art in September 1919, and a year later moved to the Royal College of Art in London to study sculpture. A fellow student in the sculpture departments at both Leeds and London was Henry Moore, who remained a friend and colleague for the whole of her working life.

Winning a scholarship for a year's study abroad, she left for Italy in 1924. She remained until 1926, marrying John Rattenbury Skeaping (died 1980), a fellow sculptor, in 1925 and living in Florence and Rome. Skeaping's father was Kenneth Mathieson, painter, of Woodford, Essex. They had one child, Paul, born in 1929, who was killed serving in the RAF in Malaya in 1953. In Italy she learned how to carve stone—not part of a regular sculptor's training at the time, and considered the work of a stonemason.

In 1928 she moved to 7 The Mall Studios, Parkhill Road, Hampstead, and had her first one-man exhibition at the Beaux Arts Gallery in London, showing stone carvings of figures and animals. Slowly, however, the forms in her work became more and more simplified, and by 1934 she was making totally abstract sculpture. This development was greatly furthered by her association with the painter Ben Nicholson, who became her second husband. Her marriage to John Skeaping was dissolved in 1933. Visits to Paris had put them in contact with an international avant-garde, in particular Brancusi, Picasso, Braque, and Mondrian. They were both members of the Paris-based group, Abstraction-Creation, from 1933, and in England of the Seven and Five Society, and of Unit One. By the mid-1930s Barbara Hepworth's studio in Parkhill Road had become the centre of the abstract art movement in Great Britain, as Nicholson, Henry Moore, the writer and art critic (Sir) Herbert Read [q.v.], the Dutch painter Mondrian, and the Russian constructivist artist Naum Gabo were all living nearby.

In 1938 Barbara Hepworth was married to Ben Nicholson (died 1982), son of Sir William Newzam Nicholson [q.v.], artist. In August 1939, with war in Europe imminent, they and their five-year-old triplet children (a son and two daughters) and the boy Paul left London for St. Ives in Cornwall, at the invitation of the painter and critic, Adrian Stokes [q.v.]. This small Cornish fishing port and tourist centre, long a magnet for artists, was to become Hepworth's home for the rest of her life. During the war years she was able to make little sculpture (and much that had been done in London in the 1930s was abandoned and lost) but when she began working again in 1944 the influence of the Cornish landscape immediately made itself felt. Her sculpture was no longer austerely abstract, but now contained references to landscape forms, and to the patterns of nature. The movement of tides, pebble and rock formations, and the Cornish moorland landscape all enriched her work. The ancient standing stones of west Cornwall provided an analogy for her own sculpture which became increasingly a paradigm for the figure in a landscape, and an expression in abstract terms of man's relationship to his fellows, and to the world in which he lives. The inherent classicism of all Hepworth's work comes to the fore: her art always aspires to a timeless, universal concept of abstract beauty.

Though her marriage to Ben Nicholson was dissolved in 1951, he remained in St. Ives until 1958, and the mutually beneficial influence of painter and sculptor on each other's work persisted. They regained their international reputation after the hiatus of the war of 1939–45.

Barbara Hepworth had important retrospective exhibitions at the Venice Biennale in 1950, at the Whitechapel Art Gallery in 1954 and 1962, at the Sao Paolo Bienal, Brazil, in 1959 (where she was awarded the grand prix), and at the Tate Gallery in 1968. She exhibited her sculpture regularly in London and New York, and was shown throughout Europe and the United States, in Japan and Australia. The most important of her sculpture commissions was 'Single Form', outside the United Nations building in New York. It was unveiled in 1964 as a memorial to Dag Hammarskjöld, who was a personal friend. She made drawings, paintings, and lithographs, and designed the sets and costumes for the first performance in 1955 of (Sir) Michael Tippett's opera *The Midsummer Marriage*.

Barbara Hepworth won public recognition in the last years of her life, when she was widely regarded as the world's greatest woman sculptor. In her obituary the *Guardian* described her as 'probably the most significant woman artist in the history of art to this day'. No militant feminist herself, she asked simply to be treated as a sculptor, irrespective of sex.

She was appointed CBE in 1958 and DBE in 1965. Honorary degrees were awarded to her by the universities of Birmingham (1960), Leeds (1961), Exeter (1966), Oxford (1968), London (1970), and Manchester (1971), and by the Royal College of Art in London (1964), where she was also senior fellow (1970). She was made a bard of Cornwall in 1968, and in 1973 an honorary member of the American Academy of Arts and Letters. She served as a trustee of the Tate Gallery from 1965 until 1972.

Barbara Hepworth was small and intense in appearance, deeply reserved in character, and totally dedicated to her art. It was always a measure of surprise that such a frail woman could undertake such demanding physical work, but she had great toughness and integrity. She remained proud of her Yorkshire origins, though devoted to St. Ives and the west Cornish landscape which provided her with enduring inspiration.

Barbara Hepworth died in a fire in her studio in St. Ives 20 May 1975, after suffering serious illness for some time. As she herself had hoped, Trewyn studio, where she had lived from 1949, was presented to the nation by her executors in 1980, together with a representative collection of her work. It is now an outstation of the Tate Gallery, which also has a very considerable Hepworth collection. Her work is represented in more than a hundred public collections throughout the world, with particularly fine work in the Leeds and Wakefield City Art Galleries, in the Scottish National Gallery of Modern Art, and in the Rijksmuseum Kröller-Müller at Otterloo in Holland.

[Herbert Read, *Barbara Hepworth*, 1952; J. P. Hodin, *Barbara Hepworth*, 1961; Alan Bowness, *The Complete Sculpture of Barbara Hepworth 1960–69*, 1971; Barbara Hepworth, *A Pictorial Autobiography*, 1970, 2nd edn. 1978; Margaret Gardiner, *Barbara Hepworth*, 1982; personal knowledge.] ALAN BOWNESS

HERBERT, SIR ALAN PATRICK (1890–1971), author and wit, was born 24 September 1890, the eldest of the three sons of Patrick Herbert Herbert, of Ashtead Lodge, Ashtead, Surrey, an Irishman, who was a civil servant at the India Office, and his wife, Beatrice Eugénie, daughter of Sir Charles Jasper Selwyn [q.v.], a lord justice of appeal. Alan's mother died when he was eight.

Herbert was educated at Winchester College and New College, Oxford. At Winchester he developed aptitudes that gained him the King's medal for English speech and the King's medal for English verse. While he was at Winchester he published the first of his many later volumes of light verse, a genre that became one of the several main strands in his versatile writing career. He went up to New College in 1910. In the same year he became a free-lance contributor to *Punch*. He came down from New College in 1914 with first class honours in jurisprudence. Career considerations went into abeyance at the outbreak of war in August 1914. Herbert enlisted as an ordinary seaman in the Royal Naval Volunteer Reserve.

In December 1914 he married Gwendolen Harriet, daughter of Harry Quilter [q.v.], artist and newspaper art critic. The composer Roger Quilter [q.v.] was his nephew. Herbert was commissioned as a sub-lieutenant RNVR early in 1915 and was on active service with the Royal Naval Division at Gallipoli and in France. He was wounded on the western front in 1917 and invalided home. During his convalescence he wrote *The Secret Battle*, its theme cowardice in war. Published in 1919, a year of general war weariness, it attracted little attention until with the approach of the 1939–45 war it was reissued as a classic of its kind. *The Secret Battle* had the reverberating after-effect of bringing about an improvement in court martial procedure.

Herbert was called to the bar (Inner Temple) in 1918 but he did not practise. After two years in the chambers of Sir Leslie Scott [q.v.] he joined the staff of *Punch* in 1924. From that time the initials A.P.H. were as familiar to readers as the front cover cartoon of 'Mr Punch', whose profile oddly prefigured A.P.H.'s in his last decade. For him as a literary entertainer *Punch* was both stage and platform. The crusading spirit that animated much of his life and work first found expression in those pages. In them were foreshadowed social and political causes that he subsequently championed in Parliament and elsewhere. His long running 'Misleading Cases' series of articles (published as a book in 1927) that amusingly and pungently satirized the law and its anomalies and brought him celebrity in legal circles throughout the English-speaking world was a sustained and compulsive argument for the sovereignty of common sense.

Until his forties Herbert's was mainly a metropolitan reputation, resting on his *Punch* connection, his *Riverside Nights* (1926) revue at the Lyric Theatre, Hammersmith, his sequence of operettas that followed it there, *La Vie Parisienne* (1929), *Tantivy Towers* (1931), *Derby Day* (1932), enhancing the gaiety of London life in the twenties and early thirties, and the frequent appearance of his name in the correspondence columns of *The Times*, where his letters were often the talk of the West End clubs. His novel about the canal people, *The Water Gipsies* (1930) brought him a new public, *Holy Deadlock* (1934) possibly a more discriminating one. The latter fictionally exposed crudities of the English divorce laws and was later credited with helping to create a more favourable attitude to reform.

Herbert became a figure of the wider public scene when he stood as an Independent candidate at the general election of 1935 and was elected junior burgess of Oxford University. Within a year his Matrimonial Causes Act, 1936, reached the Statute Book, a remarkable achievement for a private member who was also a newcomer to Parliament.

In September 1939 he joined the River Emergency Service which operated on the Thames as part of the London defences. When the Service was merged in the Royal Naval Auxiliary Patrol he was given the rank of petty officer RN and the right to fly the white ensign on his converted canal boat, *Water Gipsy*. He gave an account of his wartime years on the Thames in *A.P.H., his Life and Times* (1970). In June 1940 he went ashore to do battle in the House of Commons with the chancellor of the Exchequer, who was proposing to subject books to purchase tax. His speech was a philippic of outraged sensibility. The chancellor exempted books from tax three weeks later. Herbert received a knighthood in (Sir) Winston Churchill's resignation honours list of 1945. The abolition of the university franchise in 1950 deprived him of his place in Parliament after fifteen years: 'an independent Member *par excellence*' (*The Times*, 12 November 1971). His book, *Independent Member* (1950) was a convincing reaffirmation of the worth of the private member in a parliamentary democracy.

After the war Herbert deployed his talent to amuse in a number of spectacular musical plays for the West End stage, of which the conspicuous success was *Bless the Bride* (1950). The bright lights did not distract him from the serious business of campaigning for a passenger traffic service on the Thames, against the entertainments tax, for a public lending right for authors, against a spelling reform bill, for a betting tax, against bureaucratic and business jargon, for a Thames barrage.

Herbert was a trustee of the National Maritime Museum, president of the London Corinthian Sailing Club, president of the Inland Waterways Association, president of the Society of Authors, vice-president of the Performing Rights Society. He was appointed CH in 1970. Queen's University, Kingston, Ontario, made him an honorary Doctor of Laws, 1957, Oxford University a DCL, 1958.

Herbert was tall, loose-limbed, and little concerned with his appearance in terms of fashion or style. He suffered from a nervous reflex of the head and neck when talking. He died 11 November 1971 at 12 Hammersmith Terrace, London W6, his home and working base for the previous fifty-four years. He was survived by his wife, three daughters, and son. His death was marked by speeches of condolence in the House of Representatives, Washington, USA.

[Reginald Pound, *A. P. Herbert, a Biography*, 1976; personal knowledge.]

REGINALD POUND

HERBERT, AUBERON MARK YVO HENRY MOLYNEUX (1922–1974), Catholic gentleman and champion of oppressed nations, born in Egham 25 April 1922, was the only son of Aubrey Nigel Henry Molyneux Herbert MP, of Pixton Park, Dulverton, second son of the fourth Earl of Carnarvon [q.v.], and his wife, Mary Gertrude Vesey, only child of the fourth Viscount de Vesci. He had three sisters, one of whom married Evelyn Waugh [q.v.]. From his father, who died shortly after his birth, he inherited an interest in national causes. His militant Catholicism came from his mother, a strong character converted by Hilaire Belloc [q.v.].

An unorthodox pupil at Ampleforth (1934–40), his career at Balliol (1940–2) was academically undistinguished. Already at Oxford his mannered charm and the variety—indeed eccentricity—of his intellectual interests brought him a circle of friends that was to extend from Taiwan to Alberta. It included (Sir) Roy Harrod [q.v.], whose intercession helped to save him from disciplinary disaster at Balliol.

On leaving Oxford, he was rejected for service not only in the British Army but also by the Free French and Dutch forces. Undeterred, he applied and was accepted as a private by the Polish Army in the 14th Jazlowiecki Lancers; transferred to the 1st Polish Armoured Division, he became the only British-born officer in the Polish Army. He fought through the Normandy campaign of 1944 and was awarded the Polish Order of Merit with swords. In 1944, when on a personal mission from (Sir) Winston Churchill to the Polish Armoured Division, he was arrested by Canadian Military Police in a Ghent bar; his striking appearance, an absence of identity papers combined with an abundance of money, and fluency in both Polish and English led his captors to suspect him as a spy, beating him up so severely that his face remained scarred.

Poland and its fate became Herbert's passionate concern: a Catholic country had been allowed to slip under a monstrous tyranny by what he regarded as a cowardly betrayal by the West at Yalta. He devoted his energy to the organization of the Polish Resettlement Organization and to the Anglo-Polish Society. Individual acts of kindness gave the 'London Poles' the sense that they were not without friends in their darkest hours of isolation and despair. He was awarded the civil decoration Polonia Restituta by the exile government.

Herbert saw in what he was to call in a letter to *The Times* (30 August 1957) the 'ethnic revolution' a hope for the oppressed in the Soviet Union. He became vice-president of the Anglo-Ukrainian Society, visiting Ukrainians in Canada and returning with renewed enthusiasm. He was founder president of the Anglo-Byelorussian Society, his championship of that nation deepened by its attachment to an age-old liturgy untouched by reforming hands that destroyed his own Latin mass.

Herbert's devotion to these causes derived from a sense that it was the duty of his class, in return for the advantages it received, to support unfashionable causes, however remote their chance of success, simply because few others cared. Pixton, his large house near Dulverton, where he kept up the open house tradition of his Acland forebears, was a refuge for exiles: Anatoli Kuznetzov, the Chinese pianist Fou Tsong, and indeed for anyone in trouble. He also inherited property at Portofino where he enjoyed and entered into the feuds of local politics with the gusto of an English *grand seigneur*.

His efforts to follow his father into British politics were a predictable failure. He stood as a National Liberal candidate in two post-war elections; the electors of Aberavon and Sunderland revelled in his vivid oratory in a hopeless contest. His great disappointment was that the Conservative Party never gave him a safe seat in the west country. The mastery of tongues, which was his special gift, and his awkward sympathies for the oppressed, appeared to respectable Conservatives disqualifications for public office and proof of some incurable eccentricity—an impression heightened by his unreliability in mundane matters.

After a painful legal action to recover a large sum of money which the carelessness of a London bank and his own incapacity for business had allowed a Polish 'friend' to appropriate by forging cheques, his health suffered and he retired to Pixton, finding in the local life in which he had always taken an active interest and the care of his estate some compensation for the disappointment of his larger ambitions. Without his Catholic faith and his family he would have been rudderless. Like his brother-in-law, Evelyn Waugh, he despaired at the reforms of the second Vatican Council, particularly the abandonment of the Latin mass.

He never married. He died suddenly at Pixton 21 July 1974.

[John Jolliffe (ed.), *Auberon Herbert*, 1976; private information.] RAYMOND CARR

HERBERT, EDWIN SAVORY, BARON TANGLEY (1899–1973), solicitor, company director, and public servant, was born 29 June 1899 in Egham, Surrey, the eldest child of Henry William Herbert, chemist, and his wife, Harriett Lizzie Elmes. He was one of a closely knit family of five children (four boys and one girl), brought up in a Methodist household under the kindly but strict influence of his God-fearing parents. This influence had a lasting effect on his character throughout his life. It was initially reflected in the fact that after finishing his schooling at Queen's College, Taunton, in 1916, he was articled as a solicitor's clerk to George Macdonald, son of the Revd F. W. Macdonald, president of the Methodist conference.

In 1917 he joined the RNVR as a signalman, serving at sea, and after two years in the navy he returned home to complete his articles of clerkship. A London University law scholar, he studied in the Law Society's School of Law and he gained first class honours in the LL B examination in 1919, qualifying as a solicitor in the following year. From 1921 to 1924 he practised alone in Egham, after which he became a partner in the well-known City firm Sydney Morse, in which he eventually rose to be senior partner, having proved himself a practitioner of exceptional ability. For nearly thirty years after 1935 he was a member of the Law Society Council and in 1956 he was elected the Society's president. In 1967 he was the moving spirit in the foundation of the Solicitors' European Group of the Law Society with the object of promoting better understanding in the profession throughout the Continent. He served as the Group's first president which he remained until his death when the Group numbered close on 20,000 members.

Herbert also served on many government departmental and inter-departental committees, beginning on the outbreak of war in 1939 with the aliens tribunal and the regional price regulation committee, of which later he was chairman. In 1940 he was appointed director-general of the Postal and Telegraph censorship department at a time when it was barely emerging from its early teething troubles. Within eighteen months Herbert's energy and organizing powers had converted it into a highly efficient machine, spreading a world-wide net over both enemy and neutral mails and other means of communication, particularly at the imperial censorship stations in Bermuda and Vancouver. Convinced that the United States would eventually be forced into the conflict, he fostered and trained a shadow organization there, with the assistance of his censorship colleague Charles des Graz, director of the western area, to ensure that an integrated operation could immediately start up in the US on similar lines when required. As soon as he heard the news of Pearl Harbour, with characteristic personal courage Herbert had himself flown across the Atlantic in a bomber so as to be at hand to offer the American director-designate of censorship in Washington his advice and encouragement. From that moment until the end of the war the two departments functioned as one in a remarkable display of co-operation and harmony. For his wartime services Herbert was knighted in 1943. He was subsequently awarded the US Medal for Merit and the Norwegian King Haakon's Liberty Cross.

After the war, while he remained a partner in his law firm, Herbert acquired a wide range of commercial interests in concerns where his expertise proved of great value. In 1946 he became chairman of the oil company Ultramar, and was likewise chairman, deputy chairman, or director of the Industrial and General Trust, the Trustees Corporation, Imperial and Continental Gas, Yorkshire Insurance, Rediffusion, and other companies. In addition he served on the inter-departmental committees on matrimonial causes and on leaseholds in 1947 and 1948 respectively. He chaired the departmental committees on intermediaries (1949), and on the inquiry into the electricity supply industry (1954). In 1956 he was promoted KBE. A year later he was appointed chairman of the royal commission on local government in Greater London, which reported in 1960. For his work in this connection he was created a life peer in 1963, taking the title Baron Tangley, of Blackheath, Surrey. Another royal commission on which he sat at this period was that on reform of the trade unions and employers' associations, 1965–8. In 1970 he became president of the court of arbitration of the International Chamber of Commerce.

In the House of Lords Tangley sat on the cross-benches where he proved a lucid and persuasive speaker, although he usually confined himself to subjects of which he possessed expert knowledge such as local government, the legal profession, law and order, and law reform, including the measure to abolish the death penalty for murder which he supported.

Tangley was a modest man of great determination and energy, with an unlimited capacity for hard work. His recreations were sailing and mountaineering; he was an enthusiastic climber in his younger days, being honorary secretary (1935–40) of the Alpine Club, of which he later became president from 1953 to 1955. In the same year he chaired the Everest committee when the world's highest peak was scaled for the first time. He had previously been chairman of the finance committee of the Commonwealth Trans-Antarctic Expedition led by (Sir) Vivian Fuchs. He held honorary LL Ds from Montreal (1956) and Leeds (1960). In 1969 he became an honorary fellow of Darwin College, Cambridge, and an honorary LL D of the university.

Herbert married in 1932 Gwendolen Hilda, daughter of Thomas Langley Judd CBE, an accountant, of London. They had one son and three daughters. He died at St. George's Hospital, London, 5 June 1973.

There is a portrait of Tangley by William Narraway in the Law Society's premises and another by the same artist is in the possession of the family.

[*The Times*, 7, 11, and 14 June 1973; H. Montgomery Hyde, *Secret Intelligence Agent*, 1982; private information; personal knowledge.] H. MONTGOMERY HYDE

HESLOP, RICHARD HENRY (1907–1973), liaison officer with the French Resistance, best known by his code name 'Xavier', was born 22 January 1907 at Cierp, Haute Garonne, the only son and younger child of William Heslop, horse trainer, and his wife, Vera Molesworth Muspratt. He was educated at Shrewsbury where he distinguished himself as a sportsman, being good at golf, tennis, boxing, and swimming, and keen on all team games. He played football for his school and later with the Corinthian Casuals. Between leaving school and 1939 he had two years in Siam, followed by two years first in Spain, then Portugal, before returning to England during the depression and finding a job as secretary to a golf club in Devon.

At the outbreak of war he joined a unit of the Devonshire Regiment but as he spoke several languages he was transferred to the Field Security Police, later known as the Field Security Corps. Whilst stationed at Freetown, West Africa, he was selected for officer training and sent to Dunbar. There he was seen by an officer who instructed him to report to Room 055A, the War Office, which was in fact the interviewing room for the Special Operations Executive (SOE).

It was obvious to the recruiting officer that he was the right type of man. Richard Heslop became Raymond Hamilton and started a six-month training. He passed out with the assessment: 'Has the great qualities of fearlessness, discipline, diplomacy and leadership. Le chef idéal.' In July 1942 he was landed by felucca near Cannes and received by Peter Churchill [q.v.]. He made his way to Limoges where he was arrested and interrogated and, after passing through various prisons, he finished up in a camp near Lyons. In November 1942, as the Germans entered the unoccupied zone, the French commandant enabled British prisoners to escape. Heslop contacted Peter Churchill who informed London. He was told to join a group at Angers and await a Lysander pick-up. There he took charge of five dropping operations before being flown out on 23 June 1943.

This abortive mission proved that Heslop could withstand severe interrogation, solitary confinement, and physical hardship. He had also gained experience of working in France. He was chosen as the man to co-ordinate the scattered Resistance groups in the Ain, Isère, Savoie, and Haute Savoie as the representative of the Allied high command and, in preparation for this mission, was sent on specialist courses in sabotage and air operations. He was flown out by Hudson on 21 September 1943 accompanied by 'Cantinier', a member of the Free French section under General de Gaulle, to survey the area and make a report. They flew back on 16 October and returned to the field on 18 October with Heslop placed in charge of a British/French/American mission.

Now began a period of intense activity. The Maquis were in the high mountains, scattered over approximately 700 square miles, and very inaccessible. Morale was at a low ebb and the various groups lacked cohesion and leadership. Heslop formed separate Maquis supported by groups of 'armée secrète'—men living in the villages who supplied food and blankets, acted as couriers, and searched out dropping zones. In November the first supply drops took place and morale improved at the sight of arms and explosives. By January 1944 Heslop had 3,500 armed and trained men under his orders. He toured the camps ceaselessly to inspect, question, praise, and organize actions against targets.

The chief operation brought the ball-bearing factory at Annecy to a standstill for two-and-a-half months, after which it operated at only about 10 per cent capacity. The railways were constantly under attack. Over 160 locomotives, three turntables, two signal boxes, and numerous railway lines, bridges, and tunnels were sabotaged. Raids took place on German stores for food and clothing and German convoys were harassed. In April 1944 continuous attacks on German troop movements began. Four troop trains, one oil-tanker train, and three trains conveying war *matériel* were derailed. German convoys and patrols were ambushed. The Germans counter-attacked and their losses whilst fighting in the mountains were estimated at 500 killed and 700 wounded. Guerrilla activities pinned down a large number of enemy troops. A British surgeon, flown out to deal with Maquis casualties, set up a hospital which was kept very busy in the summer of 1944, by which time the number of men under arms had grown to over 5,000.

By the spring of 1944 small pockets of the countryside were under Maquis control. Supplies had come in forty-eight dropping operations and at dawn on 25 June Flying Fortresses, in a 'daylight' operation, delivered 420 containers. There was a similar operation on 1 August when 468 containers came floating down. 'Xavier's Express' ran Dakotas and Hudsons in and out of an airstrip with impudent ease. A plane carrying heavy machine-guns and mortars, too weighty to be dropped by parachute, landed on a plateau and was hidden for twenty-four hours before taking off again under cover of darkness the following night.

After D-day the Germans were determined to secure a safe escape route for their units stationed in the South of France. The battle against the Maquis, which lasted seventeen days, dislodged some of the camps, but did not achieve its objective. The Americans then landed in the south and were assisted by the Maquis. By mid-September the whole of the area had been liberated by the Allies. Heslop returned to England on 24 September 1944, his mission accomplished.

He had the mesmeric quality of a quietly strong man who could be trusted and whose leadership none would wish to question. He was outposted from SOE in May 1945 in the rank of lieutenant-colonel. He was appointed to the DSO for 'a record of success beyond all praise'. He was also awarded the croix de guerre with bronze palm in July 1944 and was later made a chevalier of the Legion of Honour. He received the American medal of freedom with bronze palm.

Heslop then joined the Colonial Service, spending two years as a district officer in Tanganyika, followed by two years in Malaya where his experience of underground warfare was most valuable in conducting jungle battles against Chinese infiltrators. Later he had a period in the British Cameroons and then went to settle in Kent. He wrote an account of his wartime missions—*Xavier* (1970).

In 1947 Heslop married Joan Violet Clack, daughter of a London Transport official; they had two daughters and two sons. He died in Canterbury 22 January 1973. His ashes were interred in a monument on the Plateau d'Echallon, in the foothills of the Alps in the Ain, erected in the memory of the Allied airmen who had flown so many dangerous missions with supplies for the French Resistance.

[Richard Heslop, *Xavier*, 1970; Geoffrey E. Parker, *The Black Scalpel*, 1968; SOE adviser; George Reid Millar, *Horned Pigeon*, 1946; family and private information; personal knowledge.] VERA M. ATKINS

HEWITT, SIR EDGAR RAINEY LUDLOW- (1886–1973), air chief marshal. [See LUDLOW-HEWITT.]

HEYER, GEORGETTE (1902–1974), novelist, was born 16 August 1902 at Wimbledon, the eldest of three children and the only daughter of George Heyer, MA, MBE, teacher at King's College School, Wimbledon, and his wife, Sylvia, daughter of John Watkins, Thames tugboat owner, of Blackheath. She was educated at various schools in Paris and London, and at the age of seventeen she started telling the story of what was to be her first historical novel, *The Black Moth* (1921), to one of her younger brothers, who at that time was recovering from a serious illness. Her father encouraged her to seek publication, and within the next eight years she wrote *The Great Roxhythe* (1922), *Powder and Patch* (1923), and *These Old Shades* (1926), the latter two, like *The Black Moth*, set in the Georgian period. A fifth book, which she later suppressed, was *Simon the Coldheart* (1925), set in the England of Henry IV.

In August 1925 she married George Ronald Rougier (died 1976), a mining engineer, son of Charles Joseph Rougier and Jean Cookston of York. During the next few years she followed her husband on prospecting expeditions to Tanganyika, where she wrote her next Georgian novel, *The Masqueraders* (1928), and Macedonia. In the early 1930s they finally settled in England, and Ronald Rougier, with his wife's encouragement, began to read for the bar, at the Inner Temple—he was called in 1939, eventually becoming a QC in 1959. In 1932 their only child, a son, was born, who in due course also read for the bar and also became a QC.

Between the 1930s and 1950s Georgette Heyer wrote a number of modern detective novels, based on plots and legal situations suggested to her by her husband, among which *Death in the Stocks* (1935) proved particularly popular at the time. However, it is upon her historical novels that her reputation rests, and although over the years she used the Restoration (*The Great Roxhythe*), the Elizabethan period (*Beauvallet*, 1929), and the Norman Conquest (*The Conqueror*, 1931), as background for occasional novels, as her writing developed she turned increasingly to the Regency period. Here her deep and meticulous research into the social customs, the manners and mannerisms of polite society, and the minutiae of everyday life and speech of the time allowed her to develop into one of those rare novelists who are able to create a totally convincing world of their own. Nor did she confine herself entirely to comedies of manners. What to many readers are her two finest novels, *An Infamous Army* (1937) and *The Spanish Bride* (1940), are superb accounts respectively of the Battle of Waterloo and the last stages of the Peninsular War, where in each case a romantic plot is skilfully intertwined with a masterly account of the military history.

Georgette Heyer always vehemently denied that she herself was a romantic; her heroines are always young women of good sense and humour, able to remain level-headed through the vicissitudes that beset them. Perhaps the most memorable characteristic of the Regency novels, however, is their sparkling wit and pace, and it is this verve and the sound common sense and knowledge of human nature that lie beneath it that distinguish her books from those of her many imitators.

In her latter years Georgette Heyer's interest turned once again to the medieval world, and she did a good deal of detailed research for a trilogy on the life of John, Duke of Bedford, brother of Henry V. The stringencies of the British tax system, which required payments for past successes, forced her to lay this work aside at intervals to write other bestselling Regency romances, and at her death her work on the Duke of Bedford remained unfinished. She had, however, almost completed the first volume, *My Lord John*, and this was eventually prepared for publication by her husband, appearing in September 1975.

A professional to her fingertips, Georgette Heyer's manuscripts were always delivered on time in immaculate condition, and it was a foolhardy publisher's editor who dared question her use of the vocabulary of the period she was describing, particularly the Regency period. Finding much about the modern world distasteful, she had a lively impatience with intrusive journalists and admirers, and although her family and friends and her letters bear witness to a person of great warmth, humour, loyalty, and affection, she regarded her private life as very much her own. She confined herself to a small, select circle of friends whom she trusted, and this may have made her appear to the outside world a little aloof and detached. She had a great sense of fun, and was thrilled when after the Queen had asked her to one of her informal lunches, she was told that Her Majesty had bought a number of her latest books to give away for Christmas, and had commented that she seemed to be a formidable person. 'Me formidable?' said Georgette Heyer, completely astounded.

Her readership was enormous—her readers were among all ages and both sexes and included professional historians. She also had odd fans like the engineering tycoon who arrived on a West Indian island in his private jet airliner, and half an hour later both he and his wife were comfortably seated with a dozen Georgette Heyer novels each. He explained that the sun, the sea, and a Georgette Heyer book was his idea of a perfect holiday, though he had read them many times before.

Georgette Heyer gave pleasure to many millions of people, and her fans have remained undiminished since her death, in Guy's Hospital, 4 July 1974.

[Jane Aiken Hodge, *The Private World of Georgette Heyer*, 1984; private information; personal knowledge.] MAX REINHARDT

HEYWORTH, GEOFFREY, first BARON HEYWORTH (1894–1974), industrialist, was born 18 October 1894 at Oxton near Birkenhead, the third of four sons (the second son had a twin sister) of Thomas Blackwell Heyworth, a Liverpool business man, and his wife, Florence, daughter of Thomas Francis Myers, of Bolton, Lancashire. Geoffrey Heyworth's father died when he was quite young. In order to provide for her family his mother took charge of a boarding-house at the Dollar Academy, Clackmannanshire, and the Heyworth boys were educated at that school.

In September 1912 Geoffrey Heyworth joined Lever Brothers Limited at Port Sunlight, starting as a clerk at a wage of fifteen shillings a week. After a short while in the accounts department he was sent abroad to work for Lever Brothers' Canadian subsidiary. Canada had a great influence on Heyworth's life. Not only did he get his business grounding in that vast territory, but he served with the 48th Highlanders in the Canadian Army from 1915 to 1918 (receiving a leg wound which troubled him for the rest of his life) and later found his wife there.

In Canada Heyworth was at first concerned with sales and distribution. He experienced the business methods of the efficient and highly competitive American industry over the border. For the rest of his career he kept closely in touch with American business developments, firmly believing that a healthy operation in the United States was essential to Unilever's strength in the rest of the world.

In 1924 Heyworth returned to London, first to look after Lever Brothers' export trade and later to head the UK soap company based at Port Sunlight. In 1931 he became a director of Lever Brothers and Unilever Limited and was at once entrusted with the task of reorganizing the Lever soap interests in the British market. The first Viscount Leverhulme [q.v.] had acquired many of his competitors' businesses in building up the home soap trade. This left a disparate collection of companies still competing amongst themselves and jealous of their individual identities. The job of rationalizing this group of independent companies was a delicate one. Regional strengths had to be maintained, order instilled, and managers appraised and appointed in accordance with business needs. Heyworth's programme of reorganization was a pioneering move for those times and a model for the future.

Heyworth clearly made his mark on the board and when (Sir) F. D'Arcy Cooper [q.v.], who had succeeded Lord Leverhulme as chairman of Lever Brothers in 1925, died in 1941, Heyworth—though only forty-seven—was the natural successor. He was chairman from 1942 to 1960. During the war years his job was essentially to keep supplies flowing but as soon as the war was over he faced the massive task of rebuilding the business at home and abroad.

By then the 1930 merger between Lever Brothers and the Dutch Margarine Union had become fully effective. In the reconstruction of Unilever, the group was fortunate in having had at its head a talented team—Geoffrey Heyworth with his extensive business experience and capacity for logical analysis, and, from the Dutch side, Paul Rykens, an internationalist of wide vision. Together they assembled and trained the senior staff (many recently returned from the forces) to restore the strength of the Unilever companies. In the post-war period the family dominance in great industrial companies was giving way to the age of the employee manager. Heyworth established an international reputation as an expert in the field of professional management. This included not only technical and production skills but also accounting, distribution, marketing, and personnel management. His speeches dealing with these topics at the Unilever annual general meetings became management textbooks.

He realized that industry would have to work closely with the universities to ensure a better flow of graduates to its ranks. This interest in management education involved him in the establishment of the Administrative Staff College at Henley and he became the first chairman of its court of governors. His advice on industrial matters was widely sought. His public duties were numerous. He sat on the royal commission on the taxation of profits and income (1951–5), and the company law amendment committee of the Board of Trade in 1943. He was a part-time member of the Coal Board from 1950 to 1953 and of the board of London Passenger Transport from 1942 to 1947.

In the years after the war as Unilever grew rapidly to become one of the largest companies in the world, his clarity of thought informed all the major decisions. He kept personal contact with the subsidiary companies at home and abroad. He had boundless energy, despite the pain he suffered from arthritis which made him increasingly dependent on his walking sticks. He did not spare himself on his visits to overseas units, ascending the steepest steps in the factory and bearing the heat of the day in the local bazaar.

Despite a shy manner he was always approachable. There was no pomposity or self-importance in him and he could talk easily with men and women of all ranks. He had a real interest in people which was reflected in the attention he gave to management development. He created challenging opportunities for young managers but had little patience with any who shirked the demands of the job. He was not naturally a gifted speaker. He spoke haltingly and frequently left his sentences incomplete. But because of his lively imagination and his profound knowledge he always communicated clearly.

Heyworth realized earlier than most other industrialists that business could not stand aside from the far-reaching changes taking place in society around it. New relationships had to be formed with government, and new links with the educators. A better understanding of the consumer was also required. He helped to enhance the standing of the National Council of Social Service and was its president from 1961 to 1970. As chairman of the Leverhulme Trust, which had been founded under the will of the first Viscount Leverhulme for purposes of education and research, he encouraged support for the social sciences.

He was a member of the University Grants Committee from 1954 to 1958. A special interest was Nuffield College and in 1947 he became a visiting fellow. He remained on the governing body of Nuffield well after his retirement from Unilever and in 1961 was elected to an honorary fellowship. He had honorary LL Ds from St. Andrews (1950), Manchester (1950), London (1962), Bristol (1966), Sussex (1966), and Southampton (1970); an honorary DCL from Oxford (1957); and an honorary D.Litt. from Warwick (1967). He received a knighthood in 1948 and was created first Baron Heyworth in 1955. He was appointed Grand Officer in the Order of Orange Nassau by the Queen of the Netherlands in 1947.

In 1924 he married Lois (died 1983), daughter of Stevenson Dunlop, of Woodstock, Ontario, Canada. They had no children and the barony became extinct when Heyworth died at his home in Sussex Square, London, 15 June 1974. His portrait by Maurice Codner hangs in the boardroom of Unilever House, Blackfriars, London.

[*The Times*, 17 June 1974; Charles Wilson, *History of Unilever*, 2 vols., 1954; A. M. Knox, *Coming Clean*, 1976; private information; personal knowledge.] DAVID ORR

HILL, ARCHIBALD VIVIAN (1886–1977), physiologist and Nobel prize-winner, was born 26 September 1886 at Bristol, the only son and elder child of Jonathan Hill, timber merchant of Bristol, and his wife, Ada Priscilla, daughter of Alfred Jones Rumney, wool merchant. The father left his family when his son was three. A. V. Hill was educated at Blundell's School, in Devonshire, obtaining a foundation scholarship in 1901 and specializing in mathematics under J. M. Thornton. In 1905 he won a scholarship to Trinity College, Cambridge, and in 1907 finished as third wrangler in the Cambridge mathematical tripos, but then decided—under the influence of (Sir) W. M. Fletcher and (Sir) F. G. Hopkins [qq.v.]—to turn to physiology. In 1909 Hill took a first in part ii of the natural sciences tripos and started his life's work as a research worker in the Cambridge physiological laboratory under the direction of J. N. Langley [q.v.]. He had obtained a George Henry Lewes studentship and in 1910 was elected a research fellow of Trinity College, a position he held until 1916, when he accepted a fellowship at King's, Cambridge (1916–22).

During the years preceding World War I Hill's activities were of two kinds: his first published papers were concerned mainly with a theoretical and quantitative analysis of experimental results obtained by himself and by his senior colleagues in the Cambridge laboratory. They included an analysis of drug action in muscle tissue, of the reaction between oxygen and haemoglobin, and of the effects of electric stimuli on nerves. Although in his later years Hill regarded these as juvenile efforts of little importance, they did in fact contain the first mathematical formulation of drug kinetics later generally known as the Michaelis-Menten or Langmuir equation, and also introduced the concept of 'co-operativity' in complex chemical reactions, signified by a quantity which is still widely referred to as the 'Hill coefficient'.

From 1910 onwards Hill's main efforts were devoted to measurments of heat production and energy exchanges in nerve and muscle. He soon established himself as the international leader in this field and attracted pupils from many countries. He excelled in designing new thermoelectric methods for his experiments, using them to carry out very precise measurements of physical changes which are associated with muscular contraction and impulse conduction in nerves, and in the mathematical treatment of the results. By applying physico-chemical concepts to biological events, and by his continuous emphasis on accurate quantitative measurement, Hill greatly promoted a branch of physiology known as 'biophysics'; together with his famous forerunner Hermann Helmholtz in Germany, Hill is regarded as one of the founding fathers of this science.

On the outbreak of war in August 1914 Hill joined the army, and his physiological research was interrupted until demobilization in March 1919. He entered the Cambridgeshire Regiment as a regimental captain, but was soon transferred to other duties. He was asked to form and direct an anti-aircraft experimental section, in the munitions inventions department. Hill assembled a distinguished group of scientists, including (Sir) R. H. Fowler and E. A. Milne [qq.v.], who engaged in what was later called operational research. Hill was promoted to the rank of brevet major; in 1918 he was appointed OBE. The work of his anti-aircraft section was later incorporated in important textbooks (for example, *Textbook of Anti-aircraft Gunnery*, 2 vols., 1924 and 1925).

In 1918 Hill was elected FRS and in 1919 returned to his researches on muscle in the Cambridge laboratory, analysing the various phases of heat production during muscular contraction, and their relation to the development of muscle force and to the chemical changes associated with the active phase of contraction and the period of recovery thereafter.

In 1920 Hill left Cambridge to take the chair of physiology at Manchester University, reorganizing a large teaching department and at the same time greatly intensifying his research on muscular movement, working with human beings as well as with isolated frog muscles. Hill's measurements of the various phases of heat production during muscle activity and recovery paralleled biochemical studies carried out at the same time by the German physiologist Otto Meyerhof and led to the concept that the initial phase of activity and the development of muscle force did not require oxygen, but was accompanied by anaerobic breakdown of carbohydrate to lactic acid; the subsequent phase of chemical recovery and restoration, however, did depend on oxygen consumption and on the oxidative removal of a small portion of the lactic acid molecules. The impact of this work, through Hill's exploitation of an ingenious biophysical technique and the convergence of his results with those of an outstanding German biochemist, was very great; it threw new light on an important biological process, that is the production of mechanical work by a cycle of chemical reactions in a living muscle cell, and it led to early recognition, by the award in 1923 of a Nobel prize to Hill and Meyerhof (the prize was dated 1922).

In 1923 Hill succeeded E. H. Starling [q.v.] in the chair of physiology at University College London. Three years later he transferred from this post to the Foulerton research professorship of the Royal Society, a post he held at UCL until his retirement in December 1951. Although he formally relinquished his appointment at the age of sixty-five, he continued to be active as an experimenter until 1966. There are many important scientific achievements which could be listed during this period, among them the discovery and measurement of the heat production associated with the nerve impulse, the improved analysis of heat development which accompanies active shortening in muscle, the application of thermo-electric methods to the measurement of vapour pressure in minute fluid volumes, the analysis of physical and chemical changes associated with nerve excitation, and the formulation of electric excitation laws. Hill was also the author of several important books, some on his special scientific subjects (for example, *Adventures in Biophysics*, 1931; *Chemical Wave Transmission in Nerve*, 1932; and *Trails and Trials in Physiology*, 1965), and others on more general subjects (for example, *The Ethical Dilemma of Science*, 1960). To this Dictionary he contributed the notice of Sir W. B. Hardy.

Hill combined his intensive personal research work in the laboratory with a remarkable life given to public service. He gave many years of service to the British Physiological Society as editor of their journal and as foreign secretary, and to the International Union of Physiology. He served as biological secretary of the Royal Society from 1935 to 1945, and as foreign secretary in 1945–6. He was also secretary-general of the International Council of Scientific Unions in 1952–6. During World War II he was an Independent MP for Cambridge University (1940–5), went on important missions to the United States, and in 1943–4 visited India to advise the Indian government on post-war reconstruction and furnished a very influential report, dealing especially with the subject of medical education. Before the war, in 1935, Hill joined P. M. S. (later Lord) Blackett and Sir H. T. Tizard [qq.v.] on the committee which was responsible for the initiation of radar and for the early development of an effective air warning system. But one of Hill's most important contributions was his upright defence of colleagues who had been persecuted and driven out by the Hitler regime. He was one of the protagonists in the formation of the Academic Assistance Council (later the Society for the Protection of Science and Learning), and both before 1939 and later, as an MP, was always ready to intervene and help his fellow scientists in distress. For this he earned the gratitude and admiration of countless colleagues all over the world. He was always ready to help and encourage younger colleagues and imparted to them his sense of fairness and his unrelentingly self-critical attitude.

In 1913 Hill married Margaret Neville (died 1970), daughter of Dr (John) Neville Keynes, registrary in the University of Cambridge and lecturer in moral science, and sister of John Maynard (later Lord) Keynes [q.v.], the economist, and (Sir) Geoffrey Keynes the surgeon and author. Margaret Hill was very active in social welfare work, especially in organizing sheltered housing for old people during and after World War II. The Hills had four children. Polly became an authority on African rural economy, David a physiologist and professor of biophysics (FRS, 1972), Janet who married Professor John Humphrey, immunologist (FRS, 1963) qualified in medicine and practised as a psychiatrist, and Maurice (died 1966) became a geophysicist and an authority on exploration of the ocean floor (FRS, 1962). Hill died 3 June 1977 in Cambridge.

[Sir Bernard Katz in *Biographical Memoirs of Fellows of the Royal Society*, vol. xxiv, 1978; personal knowledge.] BERNARD KATZ

HILL, (NORMAN) GRAHAM (1929–1975), racing motorist, was born at Hampstead 15 February 1929, the elder son and elder child of Norman Herbert Devereux Hill, stockbroker, of Belsize Park, and his wife, Constance Mary Philp. He was educated at a technical college in Hendon, where he and the property millionaire Harry Hyams were picked out as the two boys least likely to succeed. Undeterred, Hill left at sixteen for a five-year apprenticeship with Smiths, the instrument makers.

In the early 1950s rowing was his main sporting interest and he would later carry the London Rowing Club's dark blue and white colours round the world on his racing helmet. He served in the Royal Navy in 1950–2. Hill was launched on his unique motor racing career by pure chance. With no idea in 1953 what he was going to do with his life, his eye was caught by a magazine offer of laps in a racing car at the Brands Hatch circuit for five shillings (25 pence) a time. The most important pound he ever spent enabled him to have four laps and a chance meeting with A. Colin B. Chapman, who was starting the Lotus Car Company at Hornsey. Hill became a mechanic there for £1 a day.

In 1957 he was taken on as a driver and the following year Lotus and Hill entered their first Formula 1 Grand Prix at Monaco. Disappointed with two unsuccessful years, Hill told Chapman he was joining BRM for the 1960 season. He had a little more success with the Bourne team, scoring seven points in two seasons. But 1962 was the first of his momentous years and was mainly spent duelling with James ('Jim') Clark [q.v.], a rising star with the Lotus–Climax team which Hill had left. Hill won his first Grand Prix in Holland with the BRM P57 and was also first in Germany and Italy. As Clark had won the Belgian, British, and American races everything depended on that in South Africa. Hill won and became world champion, the first British driver to do so in an all-British car.

For the next three years he had to be content with being runner-up: to Jim Clark in 1963; to John Surtees (Ferrari) in 1964, by one point; and to Clark again in 1965. The 1966 Formula 1 season caught most teams, apart from Brabham, unprepared for the change from 1½-litre to 3-litre engines. BRM was no exception and, for a former world champion, Hill had a mediocre year with seventeen championship points. This included a win at Indianapolis, later to be an element in his triple crown. It was a controversial race, beginning with a sixteen-car crash in the opening seconds, but eventually Hill was confirmed as the winner, the first 'rookie' (raw recruit to the event) in forty years.

Tired of waiting for the fast but erratic H-16 BRM engine to achieve its potential, Hill rejoined Lotus for the 1967 Grand Prix season as equal No. 1 driver with Jim Clark. It was a wise move because this was the year of the Lotus 49, the first car to use the Ford–Cosworth DFV V-8 engine that was to win 155 *grandes épreuves* by 1984. Hill led for the first ten laps of the Dutch Grand Prix but his race ended when the timing gear failed on the brand new engine. Clark went on to win but Denis Hulme took the title that year with his Brabham–Repco. The 1968 season tested Hill's strength of character to the full following the death of Jim Clark during a Formula 2 race at Hockenheim in April. By the last race in Mexico, Hill, Stewart (Matra–Ford), or Hulme (McLaren–Ford) could have become the champion. Both his rivals had mechanical misfortunes; Hill won the race and became world champion for the second time.

He won his last Grand Prix in 1969, inevitably at Monaco. Hill's luck ran out that autumn in the American Grand Prix at Watkins Glen. A crash, caused by a puncture, shattered his legs so badly that surgeons feared he would never walk again without a stick. Despite intense pain, Hill finished in sixth place the following January in the South African race, driving a Rob Walker Lotus–Ford 49c. His many admirers throughout the world felt that he had made his point and should now retire, a veteran of forty.

He scored seven points that season and although driving Brabham–Fords in 1971 and 1972, Shadow–Fords in 1973, and Lola–Fords in 1974 and 1975 before forming his own Embassy Hill team, his Grand Prix racing career was in sad decline. But in 1972 he shared the winning Matra–Simca MS670 with Henri Pescarolo at Le Mans. Hill's tenth attempt at the twenty-four hour endurance classic made him the only driver to achieve the triple crown of the

Formula 1 world championship, Indianapolis, and Le Mans. He retired as a driver in 1975, the most experienced in Grand Prix history, having competed in 176 races, of which he won fourteen, was second fifteen times, and took thirteen pole positions. He then embarked on a second career as a team manager and elder statesman of motor racing.

Every inch the popular conception of the racing driver, with an engaging buccaneering manner, Hill was at ease in any walk of life and a superb ambassador for motor racing. As the Prince of Wales wrote in the foreword to *Graham*, his zest for life was 'intoxicating and with it went a memorable sense of humour'. He was appointed OBE in 1968 and made a freeman of the City of London in 1974. An accomplished after-dinner speaker, he was given the Guild of Professional Toastmasters' award in 1971.

He married in 1955 Bette Pauline, daughter of Bertie Shubrook, a compositor's assistant on *The Times*. They had two daughters and a son. He was killed with other members of his team 29 November 1975 in a flying accident at Arkley, Hertfordshire, when returning to Elstree from testing in France. He was a highly experienced pilot and the cause of the crash was not established. In his memory £112,000 was raised for the National Orthopaedic Hospital at Stanmore, Middlesex, where he was treated in 1969.

[Graham Hill (with Neil Ewart), *Graham*, 1976, and *Life at the Limit*, 1969; Bette Hill, *The Other Side of the Hill*, 1978; private information; personal knowledge.] COLIN DRYDEN

HILLGARTH, ALAN HUGH (1899–1978), intelligence officer and captain in the Royal Navy, was born 7 June 1899 at 121 Harley Street, London, the second son and third of five children of Willmott Henderson Hillgarth Evans, a general surgeon with a special interest in dermatology, and his wife, Ann Frances, also a doctor, the daughter of the Revd George Piercy, of Canton, China. Alan assumed the surname of Hillgarth by deed poll in 1928. Alan Hillgarth's father imbued his children with a respect for tradition, as was evident in his third son's choice of career. When Alan entered the navy in 1911 he was the representative of the eighth generation of his family to become naval officers. However, his own tastes for travel and adventure were expressed in a preference for the career of ordinary naval officer over that of naval surgeon, which had been the customary familial role in the senior service. Having entered Osborne naval college in 1907, at the age of eight, he proceeded to Dartmouth naval college in 1913, but his education was interrupted the following year with the outbreak of war. He soon saw active service as a midshipman, particularly in the Dardanelles where he was seriously wounded when still only sixteen years old. However, he recovered and was sent to King's College, Cambridge, at the end of the war, to make good his formal education. There he consolidated his interest in international affairs, cultivated his love for English literature, and developed his mastery of foreign languages, including German. He was promoted to the rank of lieutenant in 1919, returned to active service, and pursued his naval career with distinction until his retirement on 15 December 1927, with the rank of lieutenant-commander.

By then Hillgarth had already embarked upon a second career as a writer of adventure novels. He was an author who understood that the best research for his literary genre was personal experience. Thus, a prospecting trip to Bolivia in 1928 yielded not gold but literary treasure—*The Black Mountain* (1933), his fifth and penultimate novel, which was favourably reviewed by Graham Greene and translated into Spanish. In 1929 Hillgarth married Mary Sidney Katharine Almina, third daughter of Herbert Coulstoun Gardner, Baron Burghclere, and former wife of Geoffrey Hope Hope-Morley, later Baron Hollenden, by whom she had two daughters; they had one son, who became professor of history at the University of Toronto. They lived on the island of Majorca where Hillgarth was appointed British vice-consul at Palma in 1932. He was therefore strategically located at the outbreak of the Spanish civil war in 1936.

Throughout that conflict he was busily engaged in humanitarian work, a disinterested labour which culminated, in February 1939, in his arranging the peaceful surrender of Republican-held Minorca. Hillgarth's civil wartime role in Majorca not only earned him promotion to consul and appointment as OBE in 1937, but also won the admiration of Captain (later Admiral) J. H. Godfrey [q.v.], whose ship, the *Repulse*, was able to visit Barcelona in 1938, free from fear of Fascist air attack, thanks to Hillgarth's influence with the Francoist camp. When Franco won the civil war in 1939 Godfrey, then director of naval intelligence, secured the appointment of Hillgarth, who was fluent in Spanish, as naval attaché in Madrid (with promotion to the rank of commander, and in 1940, captain) where his many contacts with the new regime could be exploited in the British interest.

Godfrey never regretted his choice, coming to regard Hillgarth as a 'super-attaché' in view of the latter's varied and valuable services to the British cause in Spain during World War II. These included the deterrence of the Francoist authorities from all but desultory collaboration in the Nazi logistical effort to refuel and resupply their U-boats in Spanish ports. The vigilant team of agents which Hillgarth organized throughout the Spanish ports limited incidents of submarine reprovisioning to twenty-three or twenty-four.

However, the naval attaché also moderated British policy towards Spain. Hillgarth, and under his influence Britain's wartime ambassador to Spain, Sir Samuel Hoare (later Viscount Templewood, q.v.), succeeded in dissuading London from applying so rigorous an economic blockade of Franco's Spain as to push that country into the war, at the very time, 1940–1, that the odds were already so heavily stacked against British survival. Again, Hillgarth's role in alerting the British government to the dangers of precipitate, preventive military action against Iberian territory was crucial in averting an unnecessary provocation of hostilities with Franco, at this most delicate juncture in the war. (Sir) Winston Churchill was ready to listen to Hillgarth's counsels of prudence on Spain because he knew the attaché personally, had real affection for him, and regarded him as a 'very good' man, 'equipped with a profound knowledge of Spanish affairs'. The very forthrightness of Hillgarth's advice impressed Churchill, as may be seen in this prime ministerial assessment: 'Captain Hillgarth of whom I think very highly . . . is an extremely independent person.'

With such powerful support it was no wonder that Hillgarth was afforded an unusual authority over, and autonomy within, the sphere of British intelligence operations in Spain. Much to the professional envy of MI6's Kim Philby, Hillgarth was granted substantial funds to maintain his own network of information and influence in Franco's Spain. However, his clandestine activities were not confined to espionage. He won London's approval for a large-scale effort to bribe the ten leading Spanish generals (half in cash down and half in a blocked account in Argentina) to exert themselves in favour of upholding their country's non-belligerency. Using the good offices of the financier, Juan March, Hillgarth was able to disburse large sums among members of the Spanish military to secure Spain's neutrality. The scale and significance of this affair may be deduced from the fact that the British were trying, in the autumn of 1941, to free from US government control ten million dollars which had been paid to Spaniards 'for a consideration', an effort being made at Churchill's prompting: 'We must not lose them now after all we have spent—and gained. Vital strategic issues depend on Spain keeping out or resisting [German invasion].'

By 1943 the battle for Spanish neutrality was won. In 1943 Hillgarth was transferred to Asia to become chief of intelligence, Eastern Fleet. The following year he was appointed chief of British naval intelligence, Eastern Theatre. In these positions he developed an intelligence organization whose high-grade product, particularly that emanating from the cryptanalytical establishment, HMS *Anderson*, materially aided the Allied war effort at sea against Japan and eased US naval resentment at the belated participation of a British Pacific fleet in that struggle.

In 1943 Hillgarth was appointed CMG. His first marriage having been dissolved in 1946, in 1947 he married Jean Mary (died 1975), daughter of Frank Cobb, who owned and ran a silverware manufacturing firm in Sheffield; they had two sons and a daughter. He retired to an estate in Tipperary, Ireland, where he devoted much time to his passion for forestry. He walked several miles a day, inspecting his trees. He also joined the Rio Tinto Company and acted as Juan March's representative in the UK. Of medium height, he had dark brown hair and eyes, with pronouncedly bushy eyebrows. He had a slight figure, which gave the impression of immense energy, and he was always well dressed. Later in life, he became a Roman Catholic. Despite his literary inclinations, he refrained from writing memoirs, believing that an intelligence operative has a lifelong responsibility under the Official Secrets Act. Consequently many of his secrets died with him, 28 February 1978, at his home in Ballinderry, Tipperary.

[Papers of the Prime Minister's Office and the War Cabinet, Public Record Office; Templewood Papers, University Library, Cambridge; Winston S. Churchill, *The Second World War*, vol. ii, 1949, and vol. iii, 1950; Patrick Beesly, *Very Special Admiral: The Life of Admiral J. H. Godfrey, CB*, 1980; Martin Gilbert, *Finest Hour: Winston S. Churchill, 1939–1941*, 1983; Donald McLachlan, *Room 39: Naval Intelligence in Action, 1939–45*, 1968; Kim Philby, *My Silent War*, 1968; Nigel West, *MI 6: British Secret Intelligence Service Operations, 1909–45*, 1983; private information.] DENIS SMYTH

HILTON, ROGER (1911–1975), painter, was born at Northwood, Middlesex, 23 March 1911, the second son and second child in the family of three sons and a daughter of Oscar Hildesheim MD, a general medical practitioner, a cousin of the founder of the Warburg Institute, and his wife, Louisa Holdsworth Sampson, who before her marriage had trained as a painter at the Slade School of Fine Art. Because of anti-German feeling during World War I, the family name of Hildesheim was changed to Hilton in 1916. He was educated at Bishop's Stortford College and then at the Slade (1929–31 and 1935–6), where he was awarded the Orpen prize in 1930 and the Slade scholarship, which was not taken up, in 1931.

Between 1931 and 1939, he spent a total of about two and a half years in Paris, partly attending the Académie Ranson, where Roger Bissière taught. Hilton had his first one-man exhibition at the Bloomsbury Gallery, London, in 1936. He joined the army in December 1939, transferring to the newly-formed commandos in August 1940. He took part in the Dieppe raid in 1942 and was taken prisoner of war. He taught art at Bryanston School in 1947–8.

It was not until he was more than forty years old that Hilton became prominent as a painter. He was one of the tiny band of British artists inspired by E. J. Victor Pasmore's conversion to abstract painting in 1947–8. Hilton's first abstract was executed in 1950. His paintings of 1950–2, in which forms are located in shallow pictorial space, reflected Paris abstraction of the time. In 1953, after meeting the Dutch artist Constant in London and visiting Amsterdam and Paris with him, Hilton simplified his painting, limiting his palette to the primaries, black and white, and a few earth colours, applying them in a few ragged shaped areas; some works suggest landscape or the human female figure but some are among the most uncompromisingly abstract paintings of their time executed in Britain. In works of 1953–4 the forms appear to move out into the real space in front of the picture plane, not into illusory pictorial space behind. This could have led to making three-dimensional constructions, but this possibility was rejected by Hilton, who was committed to painting on a flat surface.

From 1955 Hilton's paintings show a return to using shallow pictorial space. He made visits to St. Ives in Cornwall from 1956 onwards and from that year there are increased suggestions of rocks, boats, beaches, and bodies floating in water in his pictures. An allusive abstraction (neither completely abstract nor representational) characterizes much of his work. In 1961, however, he surprised many of his admirers and perhaps dismayed not a few when he painted the first of a few large-scale female nudes which were overtly figurative. In 1965 Hilton and his family moved from London to St. Just in west Cornwall where he lived for the rest of his life. When confined to bed through ill health for more than two years before his death, he was only able to paint in gouache; his themes included abstracts, animals wild and domestic as well as imaginary, boats, carts, and the female nude, executed in colours which seem to have become brighter as death approached.

Making art involves taking risks and that is something Hilton was always doing. A courageous painter whose work was frequently well ahead of the taste of even the informed public, often he was not fully appreciated at the time. Hilton thought deeply about painting; acutely perceptive and outspoken about art and people, he was often discomfiting company, particularly when inflamed by alcohol, when he often became verbally aggressive, though he had a deep streak of tenderness. Like his art, he could be both abrasive and life-enhancing. Hilton was a painter and draughtsman of authority and a subtle colourist, almost unable to make marks on paper not charged with energy, used to produce images of great vitality, many with suggestions of the sensual and sexual, some both erotic and absurd. Hilton's paintings hint at some of the essential qualities of life: slightly messy, awkward, unpredictable, comic, and transient.

Hilton was appointed CBE in 1968. He won the first prize at the John Moores Exhibition at Liverpool in 1963 and represented Britain at the Venice Biennale in 1964 when he was awarded the Unesco prize. He exhibited at Gimpel Fils, London, between 1952 and 1956 and at Waddington Galleries, London, from 1960. Hilton's work is represented in the Tate Gallery collection and about twenty other public collections in Britain, as well as the Stedelijk Museum, Amsterdam, the Gulbenkian Foundation, Lisbon, the National Gallery, Ottawa, and the Museum des 20 Jahrhunderts, Vienna.

In 1947 Hilton married the violinist Ruth Catherine David, daughter of the Revd James Frederick Paul David, teacher of classics at a public school. They had a son and a daughter. This marriage ended in divorce and in 1965 he married the painter Rosemary Julia Phipps, daughter of Robert Charles Phipps, a master baker: they had two sons. Hilton died at St. Just 23 February 1975.

[*Roger Hilton: Night Letters and Selected Drawings*, selected by Rosemary Hilton, introduction by Michael Canney, Newlyn 1980; private information; personal knowledge.]

DAVID BROWN

HIRST, SIR EDMUND LANGLEY (1898–1975), chemist, was born 21 July 1898 in Preston, Lancashire, the elder son (there were no daughters) of the Revd Sim Hirst, a Baptist minister, and his wife, Elizabeth, daughter of Joseph Langley, flour merchant and baker, of Liverpool. Owing to the frequent ministries of his father, Edmund Hirst had a mixed schooling. He attended kindergarten school in Burnley, had lessons privately, and studied at schools in Burnley, Ipswich, and finally St. Andrews where he spent four happy years at Madras College finishing in 1914 as head boy. He gained a £40 bursary and a Carnegie scholarship to the University of St. Andrews.

In 1917 he was called up for military service and then seconded back to the university for the urgent study of mustard gas. In 1918 he joined the Special Brigade of the Royal Engineers and saw service in northern France. He returned in 1919 to study classics, mathematics, and chemistry and graduated in that year with honours in chemistry, gaining medals for Greek, mathematics, and chemistry. He was awarded a Carnegie research scholarship and studied carbohydrate chemistry under (Sir) W. N. Haworth [q.v.]. He graduated Ph.D. in 1921. In 1923 he secured a lectureship in chemistry at Manchester University and a year later rejoined Haworth who was now at Armstrong College at Newcastle upon Tyne. Thus began a partnership which lasted for over twelve years and which was spoken of as the 'golden age of carbohydrate chemistry'.

In 1925 Haworth moved to the Mason chair of chemistry at Birmingham University and in 1927 appointed Hirst as a lecturer and his assistant director of research. Despite a heavy teaching load, Hirst assisted Haworth in the direction of a talented team of research students which unravelled the molecular structures of simple sugars and complex polysaccharides, and whose work culminated in determining the structure and synthesis of vitamin C.

He obtained his D.Sc. (Birmingham) in 1929 and his readership and fellowship of the Royal Society in 1934. In 1936 he was appointed to the Alfred Capper Pass chair of organic chemistry in Bristol University and began researches on starch, plant gums, and mucilages. However during 1939–44 Hirst was heavily involved in the Bristol laboratories' research on explosives. He served on numerous committees and travelled widely to inspect ordnance factories for the Ministry of Supply. He also served as Home Office senior gas adviser for the South West Region.

In 1944 he was appointed to the Samuel Hall chair of organic chemistry at Manchester University. Here he built up a strong research group, planned new laboratories, and served as the able chairman of the research section of the working party set up by Sir R. Stafford Cripps [q.v.] to report on the cotton industry. He also became a member of the research committee of the Shirley Institute. In 1947 he was invited to occupy the newly established Forbes chair of organic chemistry of the University of Edinburgh. Here with a large group of staff and students he spent twenty-one happy years devoting himself to work of benefit to the country and particularly to Scottish agriculture and higher education. His research work was devoted to carbohydrate chemistry. His early work established the ring structures of monosaccharides and laid the foundations of his later work on vitamin C and complex polysaccharides. These embraced starch, cellulose, glycogen, hemicelluloses, plant and tree gum exudates, grass and plant mucilages, and seaweed polysaccharides. With his colleagues and students he published about 300 papers which made him known world-wide.

His work was recognized by the award of a Coronation medal in 1953, appointment as CBE in 1957, and a knighthood in 1964. He received honorary doctorates from the universities of Aberdeen, Birmingham, St. Andrews, and Trinity College Dublin, and the fellowship of Herriot-Watt College. For the Royal Society he served twice on the council and on various committees and was awarded the Davy medal (1948) and the Bakerian lectureship (1959). He was president of the Chemical Society (1956–8), gave the Tilden, Hugo Muller, Pedler, and C. S. Hudson lectures, and was awarded the Longstaff medal in 1957. He held important positions in the Royal Society of Edinburgh (to which he was elected in 1948), becoming president (1959–64), giving the Bruce Preller lecture in 1951, and winning the Gunning Victoria Jubilee prize in 1965. He was an honorary member of the Royal Irish Academy (1967) and an honorary fellow of the Royal Scottish Society of Arts (1964). He was a member of the scientific advisory council of the Ministry of Supply and was chairman of the chemistry research board of the Department of Scientific and Industrial Research (1950–5).

In 1925 he married Beda Winifred Phoebe, daughter of Frank Ramsay, solicitor, of Glasgow. This marriage was dissolved in 1948 and in 1949 he married Kathleen ('Kay') Jennie, daughter of Charles Lyall Harrison, headmaster. She was an inspector of schools. This marriage was an ideally happy one. There were no children of either marriage. Hirst's hobbies were hill climbing and studies of railways of which he had an encyclopaedic knowledge. He was of distinguished appearance and of quiet and humorous disposition. He died in Edinburgh 29 October 1975.

[M. Stacey and Elizabeth Percival in *Biographical Memoirs of Fellows of the Royal Society*, vol. xxii, 1976; personal knowledge.]

MAURICE STACEY

HITCHCOCK, SIR ALFRED JOSEPH (1899–1980), film director, was born 13 August 1899 in Leytonstone, London, the second son and youngest of the three children of William Hitchcock, a greengrocer and poulterer, and his wife, Emma Jane Whelan. He was educated at various Catholic boarding schools in London, and always spoke of his childhood as lonely and protected. But the memory of the period he most often quoted as having shaped his attitude towards authority, fear, and guilt, was being sent by his father at the age of five with a note addressed to the superintendent of the local police station, where he was locked in a cell for ten minutes and then released with the words, 'That is what we do to naughty boys'.

His father died when Hitchcock was fourteen and he left St. Ignatius's College, a Jesuit institution in Stamford Hill, to study at the School for Engineering and Navigation, and then became a draughtsman and advertising designer with a cable company. After some free-lance work designing silent-movie titles, he obtained a full-time job at Islington Studios in 1920, and under its American owners, Famous Players–Lasky, and their British successors, Gainsborough Pictures, he gained a knowledge of all aspects of the business before the producer (Sir) Michael Balcon [q.v.] gave him the opportunity to direct his first picture, the extravagant melodrama *The Pleasure Garden*, in 1925.

The following year Hitchcock drew on his fascination with the classic English murders to make a movie about a man suspected of being Jack the Ripper, *The Lodger*, which was his first thriller and the first time he 'signed' a film by making a brief personal appearance. In 1929 he directed the first British talking film, *Blackmail*, another thriller. With its plot of a police officer in love with an accidental murderess, its innovative use of sound, and a finely staged climactic chase in the British Museum, *Blackmail* had all the characteristics of his mature work.

Although he directed adaptations of *The Manxman* (1928) by (Sir) T. H. Hall Caine [q.v.], *Juno and the Paycock* (1930) by Sean O'Casey [q.v.], and *The Skin Game* (1931) by John Galsworthy [q.v.], Hitchcock soon came to specialize in thrillers, and after the success of *The Man Who Knew Too Much* (1934), only one film—a version of the Broadway comedy *Mr and Mrs Smith* (1941)—took him away from his chosen *métier*. Starting in the late 1920s, he cultivated the acquaintance of journalists and cinephiles, becoming one of the most articulate and frequently quoted exponents of his craft and winning the title 'master of suspense'. His pictures were meticulously planned before they went into production and he often said that the real interest lay in the preparation, the actual shooting being a necessary chore. The performers, however eminent their reputations, were there simply to realize his and his screenwriters' conception. This is what he meant when he said: 'Actors should be treated like cattle.'

Through such films as *The Thirty-Nine Steps* (1935), *Sabotage* (1936), and *The Lady Vanishes* (1938), the comedy-thriller many consider the finest achievement of his English period, Hitchcock became the most successful and highly regarded director in Britain. But he was increasingly attracted by the greater technical facilities, larger budgets, and more substantial international fame that working in America would bring him. Equally the apparent classlessness of American society afforded opportunities for social acceptance denied him in the hide-bound Britain of that time. So in 1939, after completing a film of (Dame) Daphne du Maurier's *Jamaica Inn*, he left for Hollywood where his first assignment for his new employer, David O. Selznick, was to adapt Daphne du Maurier's *Rebecca* (1940). It won an Academy award for the best film of the year.

Except for three brief sojourns in Britain—first making as a patriotic gesture two short films in French in 1944 for distribution by the Ministry of Information in newly liberated France, next directing *Under Capricorn* (1949) and *Stage Fright* (1950), then later his penultimate picture *Frenzy* (1971)—Hitchcock remained in Hollywood. A number of his early American films, however, had English settings, and most of his Hollywood productions featured British actors in key roles. He remained deeply attached to his native country and did not take out American citizenship papers until 1955.

During the 1940s and 1950s, Hitchcock developed a fascination for solving technical problems. His wartime melodrama *Lifeboat* (1943) is confined to the inside of a lifeboat after an American merchant ship has been torpedoed by a German U-boat. His version of Patrick Hamilton's play *Rope* (1948) is shot in a series of ten-minute takes so that the whole picture appears seamless and unedited. In 1954 he filmed another play, *Dial M for Murder*, using the three-dimensional camera, and in the same year he restricted the point of view of *Rear Window* to what a temporarily crippled photographer could see from the window of his New York apartment.

In the decade between his psychological thriller *Strangers on a Train* (1951) and his influential horror film *Psycho* (1960), Hitchcock produced within the perimeters of his chosen genre an extraordinarily varied range of work. It included *I Confess* (1952), the story of a Canadian priest prevented by the confidences of the confessional from clearing his name of a murder charge; *The Wrong Man* (1957), the reconstruction of a true story of a New York musician falsely accused of robbery; and *North by Northwest* (1959), an immaculate comedy-thriller that recaptured the light touch of his pre-war British films.

In this period his reputation advanced on two quite different fronts. In 1955 he began a ten-year association with television through his series of tales of mystery, crime, and the occult, *Alfred Hitchcock Presents* (1955–61) and *The Alfred Hitchcock Hour* (1961–5), some editions of which he directed, and all of which he introduced in his gentle, even London accent, and with his own brand of deadpan, often rather macabre, humour. This regular exposure on television, added to those eagerly awaited glimpses of him in the feature films, helped make his short portly figure (his weight varied between fourteen and twenty stones) and chubby face immediately recognizable and beloved by film-goers the world over. He became the only director in the history of the cinema to be instantly recognizable to the general public.

On another front, Hitchcock became the idol of the young French critics of the monthly journal *Cahiers du Cinéma* who were later to become the directors of the *nouvelle vague*. They regarded him as not merely a master film-maker with a unique ability to manipulate audiences, but also a profound psychologist, social observer, and Catholic moralist. A full-length study by Claude Chabrol and Eric Rohmer in the 'Classique du Cinéma' series (1957) was the foundation-stone for what by the end of Hitchcock's life was to be a substantial body of scholarship.

The English-speaking world at first resisted these larger claims that were being made for a man thought of largely as a skilled entertainer. But as film studies grew on the campuses of America, Hitchcock was accorded a similar status in his adopted and native countries. Honorary doctorates came his way, he received the Irving G. Thalberg memorial award (1972) from the American Film Academy, the Life Achievement award from the American Film Institute (1979), and finally in the 1980 New Year's honours list a KBE.

After *The Birds* (1963), the story of a mysterious avian attack on a small Californian community that initiated a cycle of ecological horror films, there was something of a decline in Hitchcock's work. His old-fashioned psychological melodrama *Marnie* (1964) was a throwback to the Freudian thrillers of the 1940s he had inspired with *Spellbound* (1945); his cold-war espionage pictures, *Torn Curtain* (1966) and *Topaz* (1969), and his film about a psychopathic murderer in London, *Frenzy* (1971), seemed dated, the products of a man not really living in the contemporary world. Then in 1976, working with a cast of mostly young American actors in the sprightly *Family Plot*, he showed himself once more the unchallenged master of the comedy-thriller, his set pieces as ingenious as ever, the Hitchcock touch as deft and definite. He was still discussing projects and planning a new film when he died in Los Angeles 29 April 1980.

In 1926 Hitchcock married Alma Reville (died 1982), the daughter of an employee of Twickenham Film Studio and herself a script girl and assistant editor. She collaborated on the screenplays of many of her husband's films. This man who took a gleeful delight in terrifying audiences with movies that were often violent, sadistic, and erotic in character (he often spoke of taking filmgoers for an emotional roller-coaster ride), lived a happy, quiet domestic life of impeccable rectitude. When not busy filming, he devoted much of his spare time to indulging a gourmet's taste for good food and wine. The Hitchcocks had one child, a daughter Patricia, born in 1928, who trained as an actor at RADA in London and appeared in three of her father's films.

[John Russell Taylor, *Hitch*, 1978; *The Times*, 30 October 1980; private information.]

PHILIP FRENCH

HITCHENS, (SYDNEY) IVON (1893–1979), painter, was born 3 March 1893 at 35 Kensington Square, London, the only child of Alfred Hitchens, painter, and his wife, Ethel Margaret Seth-Smith. He was educated at Bedales. After leaving Bedales he became severely ill and went on a long, recuperative voyage to New Zealand, travelling via Ceylon and Australia, in 1909–10. He began his formal art education at the St. John's Wood Art School in 1911, while living with his parents in London. From 1912 to 1916 and 1918 to 1919 he studied at the Royal Academy Schools where his teachers included Sir William Orpen [q.v.].

Between 1919 and 1940 he had a studio at 169 Adelaide Road, London, and in 1940, driven out by wartime bombs, he moved with his wife and infant son to a caravan in Sussex. Greenleaves, Lavington Common, near Petworth, which began as a caravan and a small studio, gradually grew with Hitchens's growing success to become, with numerous additions, a delightful, sprawling, one-storey, spacious home with the caravan as a modest guest house. The house and its extensive wilderness-like grounds with massive rhododendrons and a small lake, complete with wooden boat, totally secluded (by a virtually concealed drive) from the outside world, enabled the artist to live like a recluse when he so chose. Visitors came by invitation only and could not find the house without careful directions from its owner. Yet, while he lived *like* a recluse, he and his wife were in fact selectively gregarious and both generous and hospitable. Greenleaves was both protection and inspiration for the gently ruthless pursuit of his painting. It kept outsiders at bay and it provided, with its vast, wild garden, endless raw material for landscapes, his flower pieces, and, via the caravan, a temporary home for the occasional models he used for his figure paintings.

The move to Greenleaves was the watershed of his life and career, forming the base for nearly four decades of entirely individualistic and largely unfashionable activity. But before the move, Hitchens had been very much part of the mainstream of the modern movement in Britain. In 1921 he had exhibited at the second Seven and Five show and, in 1922, was elected a member of the Seven and Five Society, one of the most influential of British twentieth-century groups of modern artists, including as it did David Jones, (Dame) Barbara Hepworth, Frances Hodgkins [qq.v.], Henry Moore, Ben and Winifred Nicholson, John Piper, and Christopher Wood.

In 1925, aged thirty-two, he had his first one-man exhibition at the Mayor Gallery. His second followed at Tooth's in 1928 and his reputation burgeoned both at home and abroad (he exhibited at the 1937 and 1938 Pittsburgh international exhibitions) until the outbreak of war in 1939 began the restriction of his reputation to the United Kingdom.

Hitchens's art before 1939 was heterogeneous and to a considerable extent influenced, particularly in his landscapes, by Cézanne as in 'Curved Barn' (1922). In his experiments with abstraction he was inevitably influenced by Ben Nicholson as in 'Control' (1935) or the superb 'Coronation' (1937) which was bought by the Chantrey Bequest for the Tate Gallery. Yet, significantly, by 1934, he took part in an exhibition at the Zwemmer Gallery entitled 'Objective Abstractions' which represented a move away from the Seven and Five and teamed him with, among others, Victor Pasmore, Rodrigo Moynihan, and Ceri Richards [q.v.].

After 1940, he moved to the Leicester Galleries and showed regularly there until 1960 when the Waddington Galleries became his dealer and ensured for him a quiet and highly organized prosperity. In the 1940s, having found his true home in Sussex, Hitchens also found his mature style and developed the paintings for which he is principally known, the subtle, quasi-abstract landscapes, invariably 'cinemascope' in shape, in a restricted number of sizes and always meticulously framed, under his own supervision, in considerable depth. Although abstract in appearance and often divided into three carefully, almost architecturally organized sections, these paintings are in fact supremely sophisticated landscapes inspired by the Sussex downlands in general or his own estate in particular. They are often analogous to musical compositions, reflecting his wife's early career as a pianist and his own abiding passion for music which was often on the gramophone while he painted. Hitchens was a sumptuous colourist and these landscapes are among the glories of English painting in the second half of the twentieth century.

Hitchens was also a figure painter of much distinction and his nudes are probably second in quality and appeal in England in this century only to those of Sir Matthew Smith [q.v.]. Hitchens excelled in the difficult and now rare art of mural painting and his huge (5 metres high by 25 metres wide) mural for the English Folk Song and Dance Society at Cecil Sharp House in Regent's Park is, apart from its great size, a major work of the intellect and the visual imagination.

Hitchens exhibited at the 1956 Venice Biennale, was appointed CBE in 1958, and received a major Arts Council retrospective exhibition at the Tate Gallery in 1963 and a Royal Academy retrospective in 1979. For his friends and serious admirers, he was a remarkably lucid, discursive, and critically gifted correspondent. To those who knew him well he was a man of paradox. A prolific artist who worked rapidly, yet frequently modified and improved canvases for up to ten years before considering them finished. A frail figure wearing multiple layers of warm clothing even in summer, yet a hardy and ceaseless worker into his eighties. A ruthlessly dedicated artist for whom the act of painting came before everything else, yet a man of great human warmth, much grace, both internal and external, and of a genuinely gentle disposition and true sweetness of spirit. In both his art and his life he was quintessentially English and of true distinction.

He married, in 1935, Mary Cranford, daughter of the Revd Matthew Francis Coates, of Hove. Their only son, John, born in 1940, himself became a successful painter. Hitchens died at Greenleaves 29 August 1979.

[Patrick Heron, *Ivon Hitchens*, 1955 (Penguin Modern Painters series); *Ivon Hitchens*, ed. by Alan Bowness with an introductory essay by T. G. Rosenthal, 1973; private information; personal knowledge.] T. G. ROSENTHAL

HODGE, SIR WILLIAM VALLANCE DOUGLAS (1903–1975), mathematician, was born in Edinburgh 17 June 1903, the younger son and second of three children of Archibald James Hodge, a searcher of records in the property market, and his wife, Janet, daughter of William Vallance, proprietor of an Edinburgh confectionary business. He was educated at George Watson's School, Edinburgh (1909–20), proceeding on a mathematical bursary to Edinburgh University where he graduated with first class honours in mathematics in 1923. With a van Dunlop scholarship from Edinburgh and an exhibition from St. John's College, he then went to Cambridge and took part ii of the mathematical tripos, as a wrangler with distinction, in 1925. He spent a further year in Cambridge supported by a Ferguson scholarship.

In 1926 Hodge went to Bristol as an assistant lecturer. With a helpful head of department in Professor H. R. Hasse and a stimulating and learned colleague in Peter Fraser the next few years were very profitable. By 1930 Hodge had taken the first steps in the direction which would rapidly establish his international reputation. Thus in November 1930 he was elected to a research fellowship at St. John's College, Cambridge, and shortly afterwards, in 1931, he was awarded an 1851 Exhibition studentship. Supported in this way he was able to take up an invitation from Solomon Lefschetz, the foremost geometer and topologist of the age, to spend a year at Princeton University. Hodge was already a firm follower of Lefschetz's mathematics and his stay at Princeton, under the influence of Lefschetz's dominant personality, propelled him further along his already chosen path. In addition, while in America, Hodge spent a couple of months at Johns Hopkins University where Oscar Zariski was the leading light in algebraic geometry.

Hodge returned to Cambridge in 1932 and in the next few years was rapidly appointed to a university lectureship (1933) and fellowship (1935) at Pembroke College. In 1936, by a stroke of good fortune, H. F. Baker (whose notice Hodge later wrote for this Dictionary) retired from the Lowndean chair of astronomy and geometry and Hodge, although only thirty-two, was elected as his successor.

Hodge's major achievement in mathematics was his development of the theory of harmonic integrals. This work, for which he was awarded the Adams prize (1937), was published in definitive form in 1941. It was described by Hermann Weyl as 'one of the great landmarks in the history of science in the present century'. Essentially Hodge's work extended to higher dimensions the basic relation between the topology and analysis of algebraic functions of one variable which had been established in the nineteenth century. The passage of time has merely served to justify Weyl's assessment, and the theory of harmonic integrals has continued to occupy a central place in mathematics.

During the war the shortage of staff in Cambridge led to Hodge taking on the additional post of steward (or bursar) of Pembroke. This further involvement in college affairs no doubt played its part in his eventual appointment in 1958 as master of the college, a post he held until his simultaneous retirement from the Lowndean chair in 1970.

On the national scene Hodge was, for several decades, one of the dominating mathematical figures. He was one of the founders of the British Mathematical Colloquium and was chairman of the International Congress of Mathematicians in Edinburgh in 1958. He also played an important part in the International Mathematical Union, helping to revive it after the war.

Elected FRS in 1938 he was the Royal Society's physical secretary from 1957 to 1965 and was involved in the move from Burlington House to Carlton House Terrace. He was awarded the Royal medal of the Royal Society in 1957 and the Copley medal in 1974. He was knighted in 1959.

Hodge's standing in mathematics is indicated by the many honours he received. He held honorary degrees from the universities of Bristol (1957), Edinburgh (1958), Leicester (1959), Sheffield (1960), Exeter (1961), Wales (1961), and Liverpool (1961). He was an honorary member of several foreign academies including the USA National Academy of Sciences, and was an honorary fellow of both St. John's (1964) and Pembroke (1970).

Despite his high offices and honours Hodge was modest and unassuming. Genial in manner and temperament, endowed with sturdy Scots common sense, he got on well with colleagues and students. He was also one of those who thrive on hard work and responsibility. In 1929 Hodge had married Kathleen Anne, daughter of Robert Stevenson Cameron, publishing manager of the Edinburgh branch of the Oxford University Press. They had a son and a daughter. Hodge died 7 July 1975 in Cambridge.

[M. F. Atiyah in *Biographical Memoirs of Fellows of the Royal Society*, vol. xxii, 1976; personal knowledge.]
M. F. Atiyah

HODSOLL, Sir (ERIC) JOHN (1894–1971), civil servant, was born in Marylebone, London, 11 October 1894, the only child of Commander John French Hodsoll, RNR, and his wife, Wilhelmina Ann White. He was educated at Christ's Hospital (1904–11). He then hoped to take up engineering and went to the Great Western Railway's works at Swindon to train. On the outbreak of World War I he joined the Royal Naval Air Service.

With the rank of temporary sub-lieutenant he first served at Calshot in the Solent. In June 1918 he became squadron commander in command of the seaplane base at Alexandria. He transferred to the Royal Air Force when it was formed in April 1918 and a month later was mentioned in dispatches. After the end of the war (having been mentioned in dispatches on two further occasions) he was given a permanent commission as captain in the RAF. Promotion to the rank of squadron leader and three years at the Air Ministry (1919–22) were followed by a year's course at the Staff College, Camberley (1923–4).

In 1925 he was again posted overseas, to the imperial secretariat at Delhi, New Delhi, and Simla. After his return home in 1929 he was made assistant secretary (air) to the Committee of Imperial Defence, whose secretary, Sir Maurice (later Lord) Hankey [q.v.], chose him to act as one of Britain's two secretaries at the London naval conference in 1930. Two years later, when Hankey was attending the Lausanne conference, he left Hodsoll as one of two British secretaries acting in his place. By then air attack on Britain was regarded as more likely and the government's planning of Air Raid Precautions (the precursor of Civil Defence) took on more urgency. Hodsoll was appointed secretary of the ARP (policy) and ARP (official) committees. In 1934 he was put in charge of a newly-formed ARP department in the Home Office. In May 1935, now on the RAF retired list, he was appointed assistant under-secretary, thus becoming senior to some Home Office officials. Inevitably this caused friction for it was almost unknown to appoint, without open competition, an outsider with no previous experience of a department.

Hodsoll's function was to make ARP widely known. In July 1935 the department issued to all local authorities (and sold to the public for twopence) a 'first circular' or statement on Civil Defence asking local authorities and private employers to co-operate with Whitehall in creating machinery for this purpose and suggesting the public volunteer for part-time duties in their home districts, for example as air-raid wardens or members of rescue squads. Hodsoll's RAF background enabled him fully to comprehend the threat the Germans presented and the probable scale, intensity, and effects of bombing. With 'a hide like a rhinoceros' and determined to achieve his aims he tirelessly toured Britain and lectured in an effort to convince local officials, industry, and the public of the need for effective co-operation. In 1938, the year of 'Munich', more was done at the centre aimed, in the home secretary's words to Parliament, at 'greatly strengthening' ARP organization. In that year Hodsoll was appointed to another new post, inspector-general of ARP Services, in which he remained until the end of the war. After the Allied landings in North Africa in 1943 he went to Allied headquarters in Algiers to help French authorities to plan Civil Defence.

In the first half of 1945 British Civil Defence services were 'stood down' by a progressive release of members. However, the dropping of an atomic bomb on Hiroshima in August opened the possibility of the spread of atomic warfare. A full review of Civil Defence was necessary and Hodsoll, who had been confined to the oversight of a small training organization, was now appointed director-general of Civil Defence training, a post he held until his retirement from the Civil Service in 1954. He then became chief Civil Defence adviser to NATO (then based in Paris), in charge of 'civil emergency' planning. He retired in 1961.

Hodsoll was appointed CB in 1934 and knighted in 1944. In his last years he was awarded the first gold medal of the (British) Institute of Civil Defence, and similar honours in Denmark, the USA, and India, and honorary chieftainship of the Scancee tribe of Alberta, Canada.

In 1919 he married Winifred Joyce, daughter of Colonel Morton Tomlin, OBE, DL. She died in 1935, and in 1937 he married her sister Elizabeth Morton. By his first wife he had one daughter, and by his second twin daughters. He died 14 March 1971 at Tarrant Rushton, Blandford Forum, Dorset.

[*The Times*, 17 March 1971; Stephen W. Roskill, *Hankey, Man of Secrets*, vols. ii and iii, 1972 and 1974; private information.]

TERENCE H. O'BRIEN

HOGBEN, LANCELOT THOMAS (1895–1975), biologist, was born in Southsea, Portsmouth, 9 December 1895, the eldest of three surviving sons of Thomas Hogben: he had three elder sisters (an elder brother died in infancy). His father, son of a thatcher, was a drysalter who devoted himself to fundamentalist Methodist preaching. His mother, Margaret Alice Prescott, also a Methodist, was the daughter of a successful building contractor in Stoke Newington who retired to Southsea. There he made over part of his house so that Hogben could give himself wholly to the redemption of souls. When her father died, the family returned to Stoke Newington in 1906. It was assumed that Lancelot, too, would enter the mission field, but he began to doubt the literal truth of the Bible as he read avidly in the Stoke Newington public library. Such doubts did not destroy his belief in the basic tenets of Christianity. At Cambridge, he joined the Quakers; ultimately he professed scientific humanism.

At the age of ten Hogben was sent to Middlesex County Secondary School, where he developed a keen interest in biology. In 1912 he won a major entrance scholarship to Trinity College, Cambridge. There he took a first in part i of the natural sciences tripos, his subjects being botany, zoology, and physiology: in his fourth term, he took an external B.Sc. in London University. His political sympathies led him to join the Fabians.

At Cambridge, and even at school Hogben displayed a complexity and irrationality of character that makes it difficult to evaluate his true worth: on his own admission his brilliance was combined with 'a sheer genius for making enemies'. The relative contribution of nature and nurture to the make-up of the individual is debatable but it is clear that Hogben had an inborn awkwardness of character that would have been a handicap to him whatever his profession. This was aggravated by the extreme narrowness of his upbringing and, as he conceived it, the patronizing attitude of his contemporaries at Cambridge. To these disadvantages must be added a third: he suffered from an over-active thyroid.

His career began inauspiciously, with the outbreak of war in 1914. He volunteered for noncombatant service of a kind which would have exempted him from conscription for military service: characteristically, he chose not to continue but to declare himself a conscientious objector, for which he was imprisoned for three months.

He then made a precarious living from journalism until appointed lecturer in zoology at Birkbeck College, London, in 1917. In the same year he married Enid, daughter of the Revd James Charles, a Welsh Congregational minister. She was a graduate in economics of Liverpool University and shared his socialist views. By this marriage he had two sons and two daughters. In 1919 Hogben moved to the Royal College of Science, where he had facilities for experimental work, and did some original research on chromosome cytology; he also worked to improve his mathematics. At twenty-seven he had already had two academic appointments and he subsequently held eight others, as well as an appointment (1944–6) as acting director of medical statistics at the War Office.

Hogben moved to Edinburgh in 1922, as deputy to F. A. E. Crew, director of the Institute of Animal Genetics, continuing research on colour changes and metamorphosis in amphibians. In 1925 he moved again, to take up an appointment as assistant professor of medical zoology in McGill University, Montreal. In his two years there he published important papers on the blood of invertebrates. In 1927 he became professor of zoology in the University of Capetown. There, in addition to radically revising the teaching curriculum, he investigated the endocrine physiology of *Xenopus*, a local frog: this led to the Hogben pregnancy test. In many ways this was a rewarding appointment, but his antipathy to apartheid drove him to leave. In 1930, at the instigation of Harold Laski [q.v.], he was appointed to the new research professorship of social biology at the London School of Economics. The political ambience was to his taste and he could pursue his research on amphibians at a nearby laboratory. He also turned his mind increasingly to the racial aspects of eugenics. In 1936 election to fellowship of the Royal Society set the seal on his reputation: typically, he believed that enemies had prevented his earlier election.

In 1933, during a period of convalescence, he wrote the immensely successful *Mathematics for the Million*: this has sold half a million copies since publication in 1936 and it has been translated into many foreign languages. This he followed, in 1938, with the scarcely less successful *Science for the Citizen*, which he rated higher, written while commuting between London and a weekend retreat in Devon.

In 1937 Hogben was back in Scotland as regius professor of natural history in Aberdeen, where he developed a lasting interest in comparative linguistics. Believing in the need for an international language, he compiled an 8,000-word dictionary of his 'Interglossa', but this was never published. Again, his outspokenness and informality did not endear him to senior colleagues; in 1941 he moved to Birmingham University, first as Mason professor of zoology and later (1947) as professor of medical statistics, a new chair created with him in mind. There he did research on temperature control in invertebrates and the sense organs of *Drosophila*.

In 1942 he bowed to necessity, and underwent an operation for thyroidectomy: a second was necessary in 1951. At this time he sought to revive a breaking marriage by buying a cottage at Glyn Ceiriog in Wales as a retreat, but it made no appeal to Enid, who finally left him in 1953. By this time he had formed an attachment to a local headmistress, (Sarah) Jane Roberts, a widow seven years his junior, daughter of John Evans, quarryman, and in 1957, after an agreed divorce in the same year, they married. After retiring in 1961, Glyn Ceiriog became their home—broken by a brief spell (1963–5) as vice-chancellor of the newly founded University of Guyana. The health of both deteriorated from this point: Jane died in 1974 and he himself in the local hospital on 22 August 1975. In 1963 he received two honorary degrees—D.Sc. (Wales) and LL D (Birmingham).

[*The Times*, 23 and 27 August and 1 September 1975; G. P. Wells in *Biographical Memoirs of Fellows of the Royal Society*, vol. xxiv, 1978.]

TREVOR I. WILLIAMS

HOLFORD, WILLIAM GRAHAM, BARON HOLFORD (1907–1975), architect, was born in the Berea district of Johannesburg 22 March 1907, the elder child and elder son of William George Holford (1866–1927), a mining engineer in South Africa, and his wife, Katherine Maud Palmer (1875–1966), who came from Port Elizabeth. The Holfords came originally from Lancashire. Holford's grandfather, the Revd William Holford (1831–1911) had gone to South Africa as a missionary. His mother's grandfather and great-grandfather had been post-captains in the Royal Navy.

Holford's later school education was at Diocesan College (Bishops), Rondebosch, near Capetown, a leading South African public school, where he did not greatly distinguish himself. Things changed when he arrived, in October 1925, at the Liverpool University School of Architecture, then the best known in Britain. He was an outstanding student in a distinguished year, and was an all-rounder who fitted in several games, singing, acting (at which he could have excelled), editing the student magazine, and writing weekly letters home which sometimes ran to forty pages. Although not very tall Holford was very strong, though in Britain (but not in South Africa) he suffered a lot in summer from hay fever and asthma.

In 1930 Holford graduated B.Arch. with first class honours and in the same year he won the Rome scholarship in architecture, then the chief prize available to young British and Commonwealth architects. He spent three years in Italy, learning to speak Italian fluently, and there met his future wife, also a Rome scholar (in mural painting). She was Marjorie, daughter of John Bunyan Smedley Brooks (of the Brooks perambulator family), of Icklesham, Sussex, and his wife Caroline. She later turned to portrait painting and, apart from those of her husband, her best known portrait is of Sir Charles Reilly, whose notice Holford wrote for this Dictionary. There were no children of the marriage.

In 1933 Holford was appointed a senior lecturer in the Liverpool School of Architecture, against strong competition. This achievement was outclassed in 1936 by his appointment as third Lever professor of civic design when (Sir) L. Patrick Abercrombie, whose notice Holford later wrote for this Dictionary, transferred to London. His knowledge of town planning was then small.

In 1937 Holford was appointed planning consultant to the government industrial estate at Team Valley near Newcastle upon Tyne. There he met (Sir) Hugh Beaver [q.v.] of Alexander Gibb & Partners. Beaver—together with (Sir) Ian Richmond [q.v.] and W. S. Morrison (later Viscount Dunrossil, q.v.)—had great influence on Holford's outlook and methods of work. Holford seemed to have no national or political views and worked in Italy and travelled in Germany untroubled by Fascism or Nazism. Yet in the late 1930s he and his wife had a German refugee architect to live with them.

During the war of 1939 to 1945 Holford guided teams of architects in the building of ordnance factories and their hostels and was principal adviser (1943–7) to the new Ministry of Town and Country Planning. In 1948 he moved, as professor of town planning, to University College, London. By then he had begun the building up of the firm later called Holford Associates. In guiding his practice Holford's only failings were an inability to refuse work and a tendency to charge too little. His partners were in some dismay until they coaxed him into leaving money matters to them.

Holford's greatest gifts were those shown in committee. He could see at once the key points in agenda or supporting papers, and remember them in due order. He would then put forward lucidly, with charm and wit, suggestions that appealed to fellow members. If need be, his powers as an actor were also used. As a result of these talents he was offered many commissions: the City of London plan, work for Eton, King's College Cambridge, City companies, five universities, Canberra, the surroundings of St. Paul's, and Piccadilly Circus, and much in Scotland.

Holford was an excellent draughtsman but cannot be called a great architect, which he himself admitted. His years in Italy had given him a deep affection for Renaissance buildings, with their balanced compositions and deep modelling of facades. He had returned to Britain to find that 'Modernism' at its very bleakest was worshipped by the brightest architects of his own age. Holford had appeared to join in, but a study of what he himself designed when he could please himself (for example, Barclays Bank at Maidstone) discloses his love of patterns. He had little feeling for building materials, but good taste in colour, textiles, furniture, and pictures. When he relaxed, Holford was full of fun and spread gaiety to all with him. He also spent much time in helping younger men and women towards their first job or first big job. He was most loyal to those who had worked with him, even when, particularly when, they did not deserve it.

Holford was president of the (Royal) Town Planning Institute (1953–4) and the Royal Institute of British Architects (1960–2), and received the gold medals of both institutions (1961 and 1963). He became ARA (1961), RA (1968), and eventually treasurer (from 1970) of the Royal Academy. He was a member (1943–69) of the Royal Fine Art Commission and (from 1953) of the Historic Buildings Council, a member of the Central Electricity Generating Board, and a trustee of the British Museum (and of the Soane). He received honorary degrees from four universities and gave the Romanes lectures at Oxford in 1969. He was knighted in 1953 and became a life peer in 1965.

In 1972, when oppressed by the serious illness of his wife, Holford surprised most friends, and three professions, by accepting appointment as director of the Leverhulme Trust. To this he devoted most of his declining energies. In 1975 he was told he had not long to live and he died in St. Thomas's Hospital, London, 17 October of that year. His wife died in 1980.

[Personal knowledge.] MYLES WRIGHT

HOLLAND-MARTIN, SIR DOUGLAS ERIC (DERIC) (1906–1977), admiral, was born in London 10 April 1906, the fourth of six sons (there were no daughters) of Robert Martin Holland, banker and later a director and chairman of the Southern Railway, and his wife, Eleanor Mary, daughter of George Edward Bromley-Martin, of Ham Court, Upton on Severn. From the early 1920s their home was Overbury Court, Tewkesbury. The family name was changed to Holland-Martin in 1923. He entered the Royal Naval College, Osborne, in 1920 and was promoted midshipman and went to sea in 1924. From then until 1939 he held a series of increasingly responsible junior appointments in which he showed great promise and that he had in abundance all the qualities required of an officer. He was an outstanding all-round games player, playing cricket for the navy between 1928 and 1933.

At the outbreak of war he was executive officer of the *Tartar*, based at Scapa Flow. When his captain was taken ill in October his superiors had sufficient confidence in his ability to appoint him in command, and he commanded her in North Sea operations until January 1940. Later that month he was awarded one of the earliest DSCs of the war. He was promoted to commander in 1940. Subsequently during the war he commanded *Holderness* off the east coast and in the Channel, *Nubian* in the Mediterranean, and *Faulknor* in home waters as part of an international flotilla. These arduous commands were interspersed with short spells ashore, when he distinguished himself as a staff officer.

It was in *Nubian* that he enhanced his reputation as a dashing and effective destroyer captain. In December 1942 she joined Force K in Malta to interrupt supplies to Rommel and was constantly in action for the next six months. Holland-Martin was appointed to the DSO (1943) for his skilful leadership and enterprise during this period. *Nubian* then participated in the capture of the central Mediterranean islands and the landings on Sicily and at Salerno. The latter landings won Holland-Martin a bar to his DSC. He left *Nubian* in December 1943.

Promoted to captain in 1946, he distinguished himself in a series of important posts—as naval attaché in Argentina, Paraguay, and Uruguay 1947–9; captain D4 in the *Agincourt* 1949–50; director of plans in the Admiralty 1952–3; and in command of the *Eagle* 1954.

Promoted to rear-admiral in July 1955 he was flag officer flotillas, Mediterranean, for the next eighteen months, during which he trained and commanded the assault forces in the landings of the Royal Marine Commandos at Port Said in November 1956. He commanded a British contribution of over 100 ships to this force, probably the last flag officer to command such a large number of British ships.

In May 1957 he was appointed deputy chief of naval personnel (officers). Five months later he was promoted to be second sea lord with the acting rank of vice-admiral and assumed responsibility for the whole of the Royal Navy's personnel at the time of great change. He was the youngest and most junior second sea lord in the history of this post and his distinguished service was rewarded by promotion to vice-admiral and his appointment as CB in January 1958. In January 1960 he was appointed flag officer air (home) and promoted to KCB. In 1961 he became admiral and took up the appointment of commander-in-chief, Mediterranean, and commander-in-chief, allied forces Mediterranean, a post he held with great distinction at a time of stress when the government was imposing reductions on the British forces there and running down the Malta base. In 1964 he was promoted to GCB. Finally in April 1964 he became commandant of the Imperial Defence College.

In 1962 he was a strong contender to relieve Admiral Sir Caspar John as first sea lord, but his outspoken support for a strategy which emphasized the importance of the Mediterranean at a time when oil was just being discovered in North Africa, and the British bases in Malta, Cyprus, and Gibraltar were being run down led him to clash with his political and Service masters at home. In addition he had a well voiced belief that the United Kingdom could not afford to continue with an independent nuclear deterrent, and he had seen the abandonment of the Blue Streak project as an excellent opportunity for the United Kingdom to bow out of this commitment instead of adopting the Polaris submarine programme. Once the latter had been accepted he was a strong advocate of funding any strategic nuclear deterrent force outside the normal defence budget in order that conventional forces of the Service carrying out this function should not suffer, for he foresaw that funding the strategic nuclear submarine force could seriously affect the size of the conventional fleet. His outspoken support for these views probably ensured that he did not become first sea lord in the summer of 1963.

On his retirement in 1966 his services were in great demand. He was a trustee of the Imperial War Museum and its vice-president and chairman (1967–77). He was chairman of the Severn region of the National Trust (1967–77) and of the governors of Malvern School (1967–76). In 1968 he was appointed chairman of the committee of enquiry into trawler safety after three trawlers had been lost with all hands in gales. His speedy and thorough enquiry gained the confidence of the industry. As a result he joined the White Fish Authority and the Herring Industry Board in 1969. In 1973–6 he was vice-admiral of the United Kingdom and lieutenant of the Admiralty.

In 1951 Holland-Martin married Rosamund Mary Hornby, OBE (1948), daughter of Charles Henry St. John Hornby, of Dorchester, Dorset, printer and director of W. H. Smith; they had one son and one daughter. It was a most happy marriage and his stable family life contributed to the success of his career. Holland-Martin died 6 January 1977 at his home, Bell's Castle, Kemerton, Tewkesbury.

[*The Times*, 10 January 1977; private papers; personal knowledge.] B. C. Perowne

HOLLINGHURST, Sir LESLIE NORMAN (1895–1971), air chief marshal, was born at Muswell Hill 2 January 1895, the younger son and second of three children of Charles Herbert Hollinghurst, master lithographer, of Brentwood, and his wife, Teresa Petty. His brother Charles Stanley Hollinghurst MC DSM served in the Royal Air Force in World War I. His sister Phyllis served in the WRAF in 1918.

He was educated at schools in Essex. Hollinghurst, riding his own motor cycle, enlisted in the Royal Engineers at the outbreak of war in 1914. He saw service in Gallipoli and was wounded at Salonika. He was commissioned to the 3rd battalion Middlesex Regiment in April 1916 and seconded to the Royal Flying Corps later that year. He learned to fly in Egypt. After a course at the Central Flying School he was posted to No. 87 Squadron in France. To his proven courage and toughness Hollinghurst now added above-average flying skills and was awarded the DFC in October 1918.

He was given a permanent commission in the Royal Air Force in 1919 and served in India for three years with No. 5 (Army Co-operation) Squadron. He saw action in Waziristan. He became adjutant of the Boys' Wing at the RAF Cadet College, Cranwell, and then attended the RAF Staff College course (1925). His next interesting assignment was in China at the headquarters (RAF) of the Shanghai Defence Force (1927). He was back in India in 1929 and commanded No. 20 Squadron with distinction (1933–4), having been appointed OBE (1932) and mentioned in dispatches. His reputation was growing and he was clearly destined for high rank. He had a special interest in the athletic and sporting prowess of the airmen under his command.

On return to Britain he became a member of the directing staff of the Royal Air Force Staff College (1935–7). In 1938 he took the course at the Imperial Defence College. From there he joined the staff of the air member for supply and organization at the Air Ministry in 1939. He was promoted group captain the same year. In his posting as director of organization (1940) he revealed a remarkable administrative talent. He became air commodore in 1941 and acting air vice-marshal in 1942 (he attained substantive rank in 1946). In 1943 after his arduous staff duties as RAF director-general of organization (1941–3) he was given command of No. 9 Group.

In November 1943 he was chosen by Air Marshal Sir Trafford Leigh Mallory [q.v.] to command a new formation—No. 38 Group. This was to provide the aircraft, gliders, and crews to airlift British airborne forces. Hollinghurst grappled brilliantly with the intricate problems of acquiring aircraft and experienced crews and of providing the necessary realistic training required for the D-Day landings in June 1944. He learned to co-operate closely with the British parachute forces, especially those under his friend General (Sir) Richard Gale, and with the United States airborne forces. When the long-awaited invasion of Europe took place, the first pathfinder aircraft which left Harwell at 23.03 hours on 5 June 1944 carried Air Vice-Marshal L. N. Hollinghurst as a passenger.

His Group made a major contribution to Operation Market, the Arnhem landings, and Hollinghurst was awarded the American Distinguished Flying Cross for exercising command and control of his troop carrier fleet from a crew position in a Stirling aircraft on the initial glider lift of that operation.

In 1944 he was appointed air officer commanding, Base Air Forces, South-East Asia, and returned home to become air member for supply and organization (1945–8). In the chaotic post-war period his abilities were needed, and were evident. After a spell as inspector-general of the RAF (1948–9) he became air member for personnel in 1949 until he retired in 1952. He was promoted air chief marshal in 1950. He was appointed CB (1942), CBE (1944), KBE (1945), KCB (1948), and GBE (1952). His great abilities and diligence were still sought and he chaired two major investigations (1953–61) to produce reports on command and administration in the RAF and on technical matters such as pressure refuelling installations.

Hollinghurst remained a bachelor, dedicated to the Service. He was a member of the Royal Air Force Club and of the East India and Sports Club, popular at both with his particular group of friends. His vast range of experience gave him an air of authority and command. His opinions were carefully formed and firmly expressed but he was a man of good humour, fond of company. In his retirement he continued an early association with the Boy Scout movement in Essex. He died in London 8 June 1971.

There is a portrait of Hollinghurst by his father in the possession of the family. A collection of his personal photographs is in the RAF Museum, Hendon.

[Air Historical Branch (RAF); RAF Museum archives; *The Times*, 9, 12, and 15 June 1971; private information.] E. B. Haslam

HOLLIS, (MAURICE) CHRISTOPHER (1902—1977), author, schoolmaster, and politician, was born at Axbridge in Somerset 29 March 1902, the second of four sons (there were no daughters) of George Arthur Hollis, later bishop suffragan of Taunton, and his wife, Mary Margaret, the daughter of Charles Marcus Church, canon of Wells, a grand-niece of R. W. Church [q.v.], dean of St. Paul's, the friend of Gladstone and Newman [qq.v.]. A notice of his brother Roger appears below.

He went to Eton as a scholar in September 1914 and then to Balliol College, Oxford (1920), where he won a Brackenbury scholarship. He was elected president of the Oxford Union Debating Society in 1923 and subsequently toured the USA, New Zealand, and Australia as a member of the Union team. He obtained a third class in *literae humaniores* in 1924. From 1925 to

1935 he taught history at Stonyhurst College. In 1929 he married Margaret Madeleine, daughter of the Revd (William) Richard (Cambridge) King, of Cholderton Rectory, Salisbury. They had three sons and one daughter. In 1935 he became a visiting professor of Notre Dame University, Indiana, having attracted attention by his writings on monetary theory. He was engaged on economic research there from 1935 to 1939. With the outbreak of World War II he returned to England and served with the RAF as an intelligence officer throughout the war.

From 1945 to 1955 he was Conservative MP for the Devizes division of Wiltshire. In Parliament he showed independence, for example, in his abolitionist views on capital punishment, which was not the received doctrine of the Conservative Party. He was popular on both sides of the House and when he left he became an observant and able reporter of its happenings for *Punch*, where he became a member of the Table. When he resigned his seat in Parliament he retired to his beloved Somerset, passionately interested in the future of the Somerset Cricket Club and all that concerned the county. At home in Mells he devoted himself to authorship and occasional journalism as well as having a somewhat tenuous relationship with the publishing firm which carried his name, Hollis & Carter, a subsidiary company of the publishers Burns & Oates. He averaged a book a year on a wide variety of historical and political subjects.

His wide-ranging mind had led him throughout his working life to embark on such diverse subjects as Lenin and the origins of Soviet Communism, St. Ignatius Loyola and the foundation of the Jesuits, Erasmus, Thomas More, Dryden, Dr Johnson, monetary reform and foreign policy, as well as some works of fiction. His intuitive approach and clarity of expression was marred by a somewhat slapdash style in this great output of some thirty books. They were all honest endeavours and he could not be accused of special pleading. To this Dictionary he contributed the notices of W. J. Brown and R. A. Knox.

Hollis recounted his life in two autobiographical works: *Along the Road to Frome* (1958) and *The Seven Ages* (1974). He can hardly be said to have pursued the seven ages of the Shakespearian sequence himself because he seemed to live simultaneously in all of them: he had a youthful zest and sense of fun in his old age, whereas he was rather doctrinaire, precocious, and opinionated in his youth.

Undoubtedly the turning point in his life was his conversion to the Roman Catholic Church as an undergraduate in 1924. Through his close friend, Douglas Woodruff, he had, as he put it himself, fallen 'a victim to the theories of the "Chesterbelloc", to Belloc's theses of the Catholic Church as Europe's creative force and of the coming of the Servile State, to Chesterton's . . . rhetorical verse and the vision of the Distributist society'. It was a dramatic step from a deeply respected Anglican background. He never regretted it, but, in the words of T. S. Eliot [q.v.], he came to see it as 'the right deed for the wrong reason'. He described himself later as an Anglican parson *manqué* and in his later years attached much more importance to the spiritual bond between Christians than to denominational divisions.

Hollis had a warmth of heart and a range of sympathy rare in men of fixed ideas and passionate convictions. He loved life and in his autobiographical writings he showed this by his constant delight in anecdotes, describing the small details of friendly occasions. He was a family man above all but also had a genius for friendship with all sorts of people, often with those his junior by many years.

In religion, beginning with a convert's overzealous ecclesiastical outlook, he ended with a benign view of the varieties of religious experience, totally convinced of his own position but equally aware of the rights of other to have opinions, some of which he would certainly have challenged in his youth.

He was a man who loved life but was always conscious of its transient quality. He had no worldly ambitions or acquisitive instincts. An impatient mind and an abrasive manner disguised a character that was essentially humble, diffident, and affectionate. His characteristic loud laugh certainly did not bespeak an empty mind but a confidence in the goodness of creation. His last book, *Oxford in the Twenties*, with the sub-title *Recollections of Five Friends*, was published a year before his death. The friends were (Sir) Maurice Bowra, Leslie (later Lord) Hore-Belisha, Evelyn Waugh [qq.v.], R. C. Robertson-Glasgow, and Sir Harold Acton, and many others were mentioned in the pages of the book. It showed his appreciation of widely different characters and, unwittingly, their esteem and affection for him. In the preface to his first autobiography he says that he has 'no sort of record of achievement to recount to the world'. This is an understatement. His achievement was considerable and may be summed up in the words of his beloved Hilaire Belloc [q.v.]:

> From quiet homes and first beginning,
> Out to the undiscovered ends,
> There's nothing worth the wear of winning,
> But laughter and the love of friends.

Christopher Hollis died suddenly as he was watching television in his home in Mells, 5 May 1977.

[Christopher Hollis, *Along the Road to Frome*, 1958, and *The Seven Ages*, 1974; Hilaire Belloc, extract from 'Dedicatory Ode' from *Sonnets and Verse* (Duckworth), 1954; personal knowledge.] T. F. BURNS

HOLLIS, SIR ROGER HENRY (1905–1973), head of MI5, was born at Wells, Somerset, 2 December 1905, the third of the four sons (there were no daughters) of George Arthur Hollis, vice-principal of Wells Theological College and later bishop suffragan of Taunton, and his wife, Mary Margaret, the daughter of Charles Marcus Church, canon of Wells, a grand-niece of R. W. Church [q.v.], dean of St. Paul's. His elder brother, M. Christopher Hollis [q.v.], one-time Conservative MP for Devizes, has described the early years of his family life in his autobiography, *The Seven Ages* (1974, p. 4): 'I grew up not merely as a clergyman's son, but in a cleric-inhabited society—in a sort of Trollopean world.'

Roger Hollis was educated at Leeds Grammar School, Clifton College, and Worcester College, Oxford. At school he was a promising scholar who went up to Oxford with a classical exhibition. But at Oxford he read English and in the view of his contemporaries seemed to prefer a happy social life to an academic one. In the memoirs of Evelyn Waugh [q.v.] he appears as 'a good bottle man' and in Sir Harold Acton's as an agreeable friend. Because of this easy-going approach and for no more dramatic reason, he went down four terms before he was due to take his finals.

After barely a year's work in the DCO branch of Barclays Bank he left England to become a journalist on a Hong Kong newspaper. This too proved a brief assignment and in April 1928 he transferred to the British American Tobacco Co. in whose service he remained for the following eight years of his residence in China. His work enabled him to travel widely in a country torn by the almost continuous conflict of Chinese warlords and Japanese invaders. His family possess an unusually complete collection of his letters home—dry and witty accounts of life in China, free of the travel romanticism then so much in vogue. A further insight into his Chinese experiences comes from the lecture he gave to the Royal Central Asian Society in October 1937 (see the society's *Journal*, vol. xxv, January 1938). Entitled 'The Conflict in China', it shows a considerable grasp of a complex situation. The nine formative years in China were terminated by an attack of tuberculosis which led to him being invalided out of the BAT and returned to England in 1936, and a further brief spell with the Ardath Tobacco Co., an associate of the BAT. On 10 July of the following year he was married in Wells Cathedral to Evelyn Esmé, daughter of George Champeny Swayne, of Burnham-on-Sea, Somerset, solicitor in Glastonbury. Their one child, Adrian Swayne Hollis, became a fellow and tutor in classics at Keble College, Oxford, and a chess player of international reputation.

Hollis began his new career in the security service in 1938. It was to last twenty-seven years and to constitute his most absorbing interest. By qualities of mind and character he was in several ways well adapted to it. He was a hard and conscientious worker, level-headed, fair-minded, and always calm. He began as a student of international communism, a field in which he was to become an acknowledged authority in the service. During the war, when the bulk of the service's talents and resources were committed to German, Italian, and Japanese counter-intelligence, he managed with small resources to ensure that the dangers of Russian-directed communism were not neglected. Consequently when the war was over and the security service turned to face the problems of the cold war, he had already become one of its key figures. In 1953 he was appointed deputy director-general and three years later, when his predecessor was unexpectedly transferred to other work, he inherited the top position.

It was a post which he was to hold with quiet efficiency for the next nine turbulent years. For the whole of that time the cold war was at its height and especially manifest in the field of Soviet espionage. Spy case followed spy case at the Old Bailey: Anthony Wraight, W. J. Vassall, George Blake, Harry Houghton, Ethel Gee, Gordon Lonsdale, and the Krogers became notorious figures, while in a different context the case of John Profumo caused great political consternation. Parallel with these events new sources of information became available to the security service from Russian and satellite defectors arriving in the West. These depicted the KGB in vast and threatening terms but were difficult to assess and only rarely provided sure and certain guidance. In the light of these events and circumstances the governments of the day felt the need to allay public and parliamentary concern over national security standards, and during his nine-year tenure of office as director-general Hollis had to face on behalf of his service three major official inquiries which both he and the service survived with considerable credit. Lord Denning, in the course of his memoirs later serialized in *The Times*, commented on the confidence he felt in Hollis during the inquiry for which he was responsible.

By the time he retired in 1965 Hollis had become a respected figure in Whitehall. He was similarly respected inside his own service (and others within the intelligence community), though he did not enjoy easy personal relations with its ordinary members who tended to find him reserved and aloof. Outside these two fields he was hardly known at all, which was exactly how he would have wished things to be and how they would have remained but for the misfortune that clouded the last years of his life.

On his retirement he moved first to a house in Wells which he occupied only until 1967. In 1968 his first marriage was dissolved and he married, secondly, Edith Valentine Hammond, his former secretary, the daughter of Ernest Gower Hammond, of Stratford-upon-Avon. They moved to a new home in the village of Catcott in Somerset. Here Hollis was able to indulge his formidable skills as a golfer and to undertake some modest jobs in local government. He was then suddenly asked to visit his old service where he learned that, as a result of information tending to imply a high-level penetration of the service, he had among others become a subject of investigation. He was asked to submit himself to interrogation and agreed. Members of a service in the front line of attack by the KGB can appreciate the need for secret enquiries of this kind at whatever rank they may apply. Unfortunately some of the facts became public because of internal leaks and in 1981 *Their Trade is Treachery*, by Chapman Pincher, was published. This book's picture of the Hollis investigation implied that the former director-general of the security service had probably been a Russian spy throughout his career in the service. Not unnaturally it provoked such an outcry in press and Parliament that Margaret Thatcher, the prime minister, had to intervene. On 25 March 1981 she informed the House of Commons that the outcome of the last Hollis investigation (by Lord Trend, secretary of the Cabinet from 1963 to 1973) had been the clearance of his name and reputation. The great public interest in the matter was a severe ordeal for Hollis's family and a sad aftermath to the career of a man who had worked so hard and responsibly at his job. Hollis died at Catcott 26 October 1973.

He was appointed OBE (1946), CB (1956), was knighted (1960), and was created KBE (1966).

[Private information; personal knowledge.]

DICK WHITE

HOPE-WALLACE, PHILIP ADRIAN (1911–1979), music and theatre critic, was born in London 6 November 1911, the only son (there were two elder sisters) of Charles Nugent Hope-Wallace MBE, charity commissioner, and his wife, Mabel, daughter of Colonel Allan Chaplin, Madras Army, of Dorking. He grew up a tall boy but with a weak constitution, and after schooling at Charterhouse he was sent to a sanatorium in Germany and then to lodge with a Protestant pastor in Normandy. By the time he went up to Balliol College, Oxford, to read modern languages he had already acquired a thorough grasp of French and German and a lifelong passion for Racine and Goethe. He graduated with a third class honours degree (1933) at the worst point of the great depression and for a while found it impossible to obtain congenial employment, or indeed any at all. He worked briefly and disastrously (1933–4) for the International Broadcasting Co. in France, at Fécamp radio station, and then (1935–6) as press officer for the Gas Light & Coke Co. In later life he claimed he had hawked appliances as a door-to-door salesman.

In 1935 he got his first chance as a critic, covering song recitals for *The Times*. By the time war came he had established himself as a sensitive and exceptionally knowledgeable judge of theatre and music (especially opera), being sent to Zurich in 1938 for the world première of Paul Hindemith's *Mathis der Maler* and to Frankfurt for the drama festival. Ill health prevented active war service, and he spent six years in the Air Ministry press office. With peace he became, and remained to his death, one of the most prolific and influential arts critics in the West, first with the *Daily Telegraph* (1945–6) and with *Time and Tide* (1945–9), and then for a quarter-century (1946–71) on the arts staff of the *Guardian*. He was for many years the paper's chief drama critic, though for the last decade of his life he concentrated almost exclusively on opera. He was also a mainstay of the *Gramophone*, a member of the editorial board of *Opera*, and a frequent contributor to the *Listener*, the *New Statesman*, and other journals. For thirty-five years he broadcast with great success, especially on such key programmes as *The Critics* and *Music Magazine*. In 1958 he was president of the Critics' Circle, and in 1975 he was appointed CBE for services to the arts.

Hope-Wallace was the least assertive of men but he had an imperturbable confidence in his own artistic judgement and so remained serenely impervious to fashion. As a young critic he championed Handel and Verdi, then little regarded, and he always admired uncerebral but theatrical masters like Gounod, Massenet, and Bizet. In the theatre he appreciated a good Shavian argument but anything which smacked of dogma, ideology, or 'message' filled him with dismay; from the mid-sixties he quite lost sympathy with most contemporary playwrights. He was concerned, above all, with what actually happened on stage, and was perhaps the last great British critic to regard assessment of the performance as his chief function. He did not see the critic as a privileged high priest but as spokesman for the theatre-goers. 'The best critic', he wrote, 'will be the epitome of the best part of any given audience, its head, heart and soul.' Hence, though mandarin in mind, he was democratic at heart, and in spirit always close to the ordinary London theatre and opera patron. Loving skilled performance, he enjoyed Chinese acrobats, Kabuki players, or the Royal Tournament almost as much as great actors and singers. He admitted he was easily moved to tears: by Emlyn Williams reading the death of Paul Dombey, for instance, or by Irina's line 'They are gone away' from *The Three Sisters*.

Hope-Wallace's sense of theatrical occasion, his intuitive sympathy with performers, his vast experience and wonderful memory made him the outstanding judge, in his generation, of dramatic celebrities, especially women. He wrote with superb precision of such fine actresses as (Dame) Edith Evans [q.v.], Edwige Feuillère, (Dame) Peggy Ashcroft, and (Dame) Sybil Thorndike [q.v.]. But his greatest enthusiasm was for the diva: 'I love a soprano', he wrote, 'a loud soprano, even a lame one'. He treasured the personalities, follies, triumphs, and misadventures of the prima donna, and much of his best writing revolved around stars like Elisabeth Schwarzkopf, Birgit Nillson, Kirsten Flagstad, Maria Callas, and (Dame) Joan Sutherland.

He was close to Bloomsbury in its silver age, but he was essentially a journalist rather than a literary man. His only books were *A Key to Opera* (written in collaboration with Frank Howes, q.v.), published in 1939, and *A Picture History of Opera* (1959), though a selection of his notices and essays, *Words and Music*, was published posthumously in 1981. He gently rejected the entreaties of his friends to write an autobiography. For him, immediacy of impression was everything: many of his best notices were dictated straight to the copy-takers from a call-box. He worshipped words but drew no hard distinction between their written and spoken form. Indeed his real genius lay in conversation. For many years some of the best talk in London could be heard at his favourite table at El Vino's in Fleet Street. His noble head, his mellifluous voice, his thesaurus of anecdotes and the shafts of wit, sharp but never cruel, which he played on the personalities of the day, attracted a gifted circle of writers, editors, lawyers, and public men, over which he presided with grace, generosity, and a quiet but unmistakable moral authority. To his younger admirers, who were legion, he epitomized the best characteristics of the pre-war generation: breadth of culture, fine breeding, flawless manners, and delightful urbanity. At the age of sixty-seven a visit to a health farm led to a fall and a broken hip, providing him with his last, ironic joke; he never left Guildford hospital and died there 3 September 1979. With his death, his circle broke up, and it contained, alas, no Boswell. He was unmarried.

[Private information; personal knowledge.]

PAUL JOHNSON

HOWARD, BERNARD MARMADUKE FITZALAN-, sixteenth DUKE OF NORFOLK (1908–1975), Earl Marshal and Hereditary Marshal of England, was born at Arundel Castle 30 May 1908, the only son (there were also three daughters) of Henry FitzAlan-Howard, fifteenth Duke of Norfolk [q.v.], by his second wife, Gwendolen Mary Constable-Maxwell, daughter of Marmaduke Francis, eleventh Baron Herries, and heiress of that Scottish title. He succeeded to the title in 1917, his half-brother from a previous marriage having died in 1902. He was educated privately and at the Oratory School, Birmingham; although accepted by Christ Church, he was unable to pass responsions, the university examination.

The young duke, whose duties as Earl Marshal were performed until 1929 by his uncle, Viscount FitzAlan of Derwent [q.v.], was commissioned into the 4th (Territorial) battalion of the Royal Sussex Regiment early in 1928, but at the end of that year transferred to the Royal Horse Guards, with whom he was not happy. He returned gladly to the Sussex Regiment in 1934, rising to the rank of major and serving in France and at Dunkirk in 1940. He succeeded his mother as thirteenth Baron Herries in 1945. His interests were emphatically those of a countryman; he loved hunting, shooting, racing, and cricket and in 1936 became master of the Holderness hunt. He was admitted to the Privy Council in 1936. In 1938 he sold Norfolk House on the corner of St. James's Square.

His apprenticeship in official duties came with the funeral of King George V (1936), followed by the coronation of King George VI, initially planned for Edward VIII. He rapidly demonstrated that he had inherited his father's capacity for solemn ritual and that he would stand no nonsense from anybody in ensuring the precise and punctual performance of majestic ceremonial. Later in 1937 he was appointed a Knight of the Garter, at an unusually early age. His experience was put to good use in 1953 at the coronation of Queen Elizabeth II which the Duke managed with magisterial authority and expertise. On this occasion he coped skilfully with the introduction into Westminster Abbey of television, to which he was initially opposed. His hereditary position also made him responsible for the College of Arms and its officers in whom he took a consistent interest and with whose aid he regulated two other great state occasions, the (long prepared) funeral of Sir Winston Churchill in 1965 and the investiture of the Prince of Wales at Caernarfon in 1969, where the size of the budget and the weather both gave grounds for apprehension.

The Duke was a lifelong devotee of the turf and made his mark both as an administrator and as an owner and breeder of horses. He became a member of the Jockey Club in 1933 and served as steward 1966–8; in addition he was vice-chairman of the Turf Board (1965–8), where he took a traditionalist attitude to the problems of modern racing. Nothing gave him greater pleasure than his position as the Queen's representative at Ascot (1945–72); the victory of Ragstone, trained and bred at Arundel, in the Ascot Gold Cup of 1974 was a fine climax to his career. Another sporting enthusiasm was cricket. Not only did he welcome visiting teams with an opening game in the Park at Arundel, but he took a team to tour the West Indies in 1956–7, playing occasionally himself; then in 1962–3 he acted as manager of the English team to Australia, bringing his bluff common sense to bear on the problems of the tour. It was an unusual role for the senior duke of England.

In Sussex he played his proper part. He was mayor of Arundel in 1935–6 and lord lieutenant of the county from 1949 to 1974, as well as sitting on the county council. From 1941 to 1945 he served as parliamentary secretary to the Ministry of Agriculture in the coalition government, putting his robust knowledge of farming to the public good, but his heart was not in politics. In parallel with these official duties went his position as a spokesman for the Catholic laity of England. As a chairman he was terse and efficient; in general his attitude was conservative and he did not welcome the alterations in language and ritual of the second Vatican Council. In 1970 he participated in the canonization of the Forty Martyrs, who included his ancestor St. Philip Howard (1557–1595, q.v.), and was received by Pope Paul VI. His local experience also led him to be a powerful and ardent advocate of the Territorial Army; in 1956–9 he was chairman of the Territorial Army Council.

The Duke of Norfolk was happier in the countryside than in the metropolis; but his potent sense of duty drove him to undertake a broad variety of tasks, some hereditary, some of obligation but also many of inclination. His often unmoving face concealed a considerable sense of humour and power of anecdote. In his old-fashioned way he was a grandee by birth, a countryman by inclination, and a good man who did his duty.

He married in 1937 Lavinia Mary, only daughter of Algernon Henry Strutt, third Baron Belper; they had four daughters, the eldest of whom succeeded to the Scottish barony of Herries. He was appointed GCVO (1946), GBE (1968), and received the Royal Victorian Chain (1953). He died at Arundel Park House, which he had himself built in the grounds of Arundel Castle, 31 January 1975. He was succeeded in the dukedom by his cousin, Miles Francis Stapleton FitzAlan-Howard (born 1915), Baron Beaumont and Howard of Glossop.

[*The Times*, 1 February 1975; private information; personal knowledge.]

MICHAEL MACLAGAN

HOWELL, WILLIAM GOUGH (1922–1974), architect, was born in London 5 February 1922, the younger child and only son of Charles Gough Howell, a barrister of Welsh descent who first practised on the Western circuit but in 1926 joined the Colonial Legal Service, serving in Kenya, Fiji, Malaya, and finally Singapore where he became attorney-general. He was taken prisoner by the Japanese when Singapore fell and died in a prison camp in Formosa. In 1915 he had married Sidney Gretchen Innes-Noad, an Australian.

William Howell, at school at Marlborough, was visiting his family in Singapore at the outbreak of World War II and was unable to get back to England until Christmas 1939. After one more term at Marlborough he joined the Royal Air Force, serving first at the radar establishment at Stanmore and then in the Middle East as a navigator in night fighters. He was awarded the DFC in 1943. After the war he embarked on a career in architecture, which he studied first at Cambridge (where he was at Caius College) and then at the Architectural Association school in London. He qualified in 1952 having joined the architect's department of the London County Council. This was a time when the architectural profession, especially the younger members who had entered it during the euphoric post-war years that saw the creation of the Welfare State, was deeply concerned with integrating building programmes with social needs, an aim in which the LCC took the lead, most notably in schools and housing. Howell was one of the group of young architects responsible for the LCC's Roehampton estate, one of its most admired and forward-looking post-war housing projects. His experience at the LCC coloured Howell's later approach to architecture and to its proper role in the community.

In 1956 Howell left the LCC to practise architecture privately and to teach at the Regent Street Polytechnic, London. In 1959 he and three other architects who had been his colleagues at the LCC set up the partnership of Howell, Killick, Partridge & Amis. They entered the competition for Churchill College, Cambridge, held in that year, and theirs was one of four designs chosen for the final stage. They were not the eventual winners but their participation brought them a number of commissions for university buildings. These included buildings at Oxford, for St. Anne's and St. Antony's colleges, and at Cambridge for Downing and Darwin colleges and the University Centre; also buildings at Birmingham and Reading universities. The work at Cambridge was Howell's particular concern. Its style was uncompromisingly modern, characterized by a vigorous use of precast concrete, but he showed sensitivity about the relation of new buildings to old in his sympathetic addition of a new combination room to Downing College, completed in 1970. Others of the firm's projects in which Howell played the leading part were a group of unusual houses for visiting mathematicians at Warwick University and an arts centre for Christ's Hospital, Horsham.

In 1973 Howell was appointed to the chair of architecture at Cambridge, where he became a fellow of Caius, but he had had only a little over a year to establish himself there when he died. He had shown promise of becoming a highly successful professor and a useful influence on Cambridge architecture. His personal qualities were well suited to this position. He had a relaxed and sociable nature, strong convictions, and the ability to express them persuasively. His stocky figure, bushy moustache, and genial personality were familiar on many architectural occasions, for he gave much to the profession besides his buildings and his teaching. He was active at the periodical conferences of CIAM (*Congrès Internationaux d'Architecture Moderne*), notably those at Aix-en-Provence in 1953 and Dubrovnik in 1955. He served on the council of RIBA and was vice-president in 1965–7. He was elected ARA in 1974.

Outside architecture his interests and pursuits were characteristically various: rugby football; horsemanship; the history of World War I. His collection of objects connected with the last was the source of a book, *Popular Arts of the First World War*, published in 1972, which he compiled in collaboration with Barbara Jones. Another interest in his last years was his family's weekend home near Savernake Forest, originally a Victorian Methodist chapel, which he converted with zest and wit.

On 10 August 1951 Howell married Gillian Margaret, daughter of Edward Vipan Sarson, an army colonel who spent most of his service in India. She and Howell were fellow students at the AA school of architecture and colleagues at the LCC. They had three sons and one daughter. On 29 November 1974 Howell was killed in a motor-car accident near Leighton Buzzard, Bedfordshire, at the age of fifty-two.

[Private information; personal knowledge.]

J. M. Richards

HOWES, FRANK STEWART (1891–1974), music critic of *The Times* and author, was born at Oxford 2 April 1891, the elder child and only son of George Howes, a grocer and confectioner of Oxford, and his wife, Grace Phipps. He was educated in his home town, at the Oxford High School, then at St. John's College (1910–14) where he obtained third classes in both classical honour moderations and *literae humaniores*, rowed for his college, and sang in the chorus for the performances of *Fidelio* and *Der Freischütz* conducted by (Sir) Hugh Allen [q.v.]. He became a schoolmaster, served a brief prison sentence as a conscientious objector, then went to the Royal College of Music (1920–2) as a member of the criticism class run by H. C. Colles [q.v.]. In 1925 he joined Colles on *The Times*, succeeding to the principal post on Colles's sudden death in 1943.

His first book, *The Borderland of Music and Psychology* (1926) and his editing of what became the *Journal of the English Folk Dance and Song Society* (1927–45) soon indicated the cast of his mind, in which speculation was rooted in the soil of his native country. His *A Key to Opera* (with P. Hope-Wallace, q.v., 1939) revealed another enthusiasm, and in his *Full Orchestra* (1942) his experience as a lecturer together with his lively, lucid prose, produced a popular success.

He lectured at the RCM from 1938 to 1970, during the war coming up from his family retreat, a mill near Standlake, where the river Windrush flows into the Thames. When he took over *The Times* in 1943, readers were jaded, and both newsprint and music were in short supply. With vigour and assurance he directed the post-war expansion. He approved the anonymity then in force—though his own views and style were recognizable enough—as an aid to objective, responsible criticism without personal display. He insisted on a wide coverage, so that the paper reported débuts and amateur events as well as major national occasions. He refused to look at scores in advance and liked writing on the night, believing that the pressure made for immediacy, and also allowed no opportunity for outside influence. He retained the weekly music article, valuing the chance it gave him to expand on a remote or a topical point, and was once delighted to be complimented simply on the range of his subjects.

He threw his considerable weight behind such causes as opera in English (he himself had no modern languages), the building of the Festival Hall, and the founding of *Musica Britannica* while he was president of the Royal Musical Association (1948–58). His authority and urbane common sense made him much in demand on committees: he was chairman of the Musicians' Benevolent Fund (1938–56), and of the English Folk Dance and Song Society (1932–46), and also served the Arts Council, the British Council, the BBC, the British Institute of Recorded Sound, and Music in Hospitals. He gave the Cramb lectures at Glasgow University in 1947, and the first Crees lectures (1950) for the RCM. He was created CBE in 1954; he was an honorary fellow of the RCM, an honorary RAM, and an honorary freeman of the Worshipful Company of Musicians.

In spite of his many commitments, his early *William Byrd* (1928) was followed by valuable and substantial studies of *The Music of Ralph Vaughan Williams* (1954) and *The Music of William Walton* (2 vols., 1942, 1943, revised 1965). Though his approach was on the whole analytical, he was always concerned to uncover the thoughts behind the sounds, to relate music and ethics, to consider symbolism and aesthetics. These ideas he set out in *Man, Mind and Music* (1948). His wide sympathies extended notably to Lord Britten [q.v.], but less to Stravinsky and hardly at all to Schönberg and his school; but his strong intellect and professional curiosity enabled him to write stimulatingly about music he disliked, and only occasionally could he be provoked to bluntness. His probity and good humour were respected even by those who might disagree with his taste.

He retired from *The Times* in 1960, and out of his study with its continuous murmur of the mill-race came an account of *The Cheltenham Festival* (1965) while he was its chairman, and a jubilee record of *Oxford Concerts* (1969). But the major works, summarizing his life's interest, were *The English Musical Renaissance* (1966), a synthesis of a period he had largely lived through, and *Folk Music of Britain—and Beyond* (1969). He contributed many notices to this Dictionary.

Howes was a deeply emotional but self-reliant man, to whom music was one of the humanities. He was a trenchant speaker who enjoyed great occasions; but was as happy among his family and close friends on his river bank. There in the end he suffered cancer, and he died in hospital at Oxford 28 September 1974.

Howes married Barbara Mildred, daughter of John Tidd Pratt, a solicitor, in 1929, and had one son and three daughters.

[Private information; personal knowledge.]

DIANA MCVEAGH

HOWICK OF GLENDALE, first BARON (1903–1973), colonial governor. [See BARING, (CHARLES) EVELYN.]

HUGESSEN, SIR HUGHE MONTGOMERY KNATCHBULL- (1886–1971), diplomat. [See KNATCHBULL-HUGESSEN.]

HUGGINS, GODFREY MARTIN, first VISCOUNT MALVERN (1883–1971), Rhodesian statesman, was born 6 July 1883 at Bexley, Kent, the eldest son and second in the family of four sons and three daughters of Godfrey Huggins, a member of the London Stock Exchange and the son of a brewer, and his wife, Emily Blest, daughter of a Woolwich innkeeper. Huggins was educated at Brunswick House, Hove, a preparatory school, at Sutherland House, Folkestone, and at Malvern College. Held back at school through a troublesome ear disease, he subsequently studied at St. Thomas's Hospital, London, and qualified as a physician (MRCS and LRCP, 1906), and subsequently as a surgeon (FRCS, 1908). Huggins received postgraduate appointments as house surgeon at St. Thomas's and later as medical superintendent at the Hospital for Sick Children at Great Ormond Street, London. He would have liked to take up a career in academic medicine, but he needed a well-paying job, partly in order to help his ageing father. He was attracted to Rhodesia by the romance of empire that still hung over the distant colony, and in 1911 accepted an offer to join a medical partnership in Salisbury.

On the outbreak of World War I, Huggins decided that he must do his patriotic duty, and he joined the Royal Army Medical Corps in England as a surgeon. He saw service in Great Britain, Malta, and France, and was demobilized at the end of 1917. His wartime experiences led him to publish his first and only book *Amputation Stumps: Their Care and After-Treatment* (1918). On his return to Rhodesia he resumed his medical practice, and in 1921 began to specialize as a consultant surgeon, becoming one of Rhodesia's leading medical men. In the same year, he married Blanche Elizabeth, daughter of James Slatter, a physician, of Pietermaritzburg, and step-daughter of Major Thomas Power, a retired officer from the South African Constabulary, later a Salisbury accountant. There were two sons of this long and happy marriage.

At the end of 1922 the regime of the British South Africa Company, in power since 1890, was drawing to a close. In 1922 Southern Rhodesia embarked on a referendum to decide whether the country should join the Union of South Africa, a course favoured by most well-to-do whites, or embark on an autonomous existence as a 'self-governing colony', an option supported mainly by the white lower middle class and working class. Huggins at first inclined toward the Union, but when the referendum brought victory in 1922 to the Responsible Government Association of Sir Charles Coghlan [q.v.], Huggins decided to support the new administration. In 1924 he was elected to the Southern Rhodesian Legislative Assembly for the Salisbury North constituency, a middle-class seat, and served as a back-bencher in the governing Rhodesia Party. The new government turned out to be more conservative than both its supporters and opponents had anticipated. The world slump hit Rhodesia severely, and in 1931 Huggins left his party in protest against economy measures designed to cut Civil Service salaries. In 1932 the opposition Reform Party elected Huggins to be their leader, and in 1933 he took office as prime minister. A year later the majority of the Reform Party and the Rhodesia Party joined to form the United Party which was returned with an overwhelming majority during the elections of 1934. Huggins received the 'doctor's mandate' he had requested, and his party remained in office for nearly three decades.

The new government's first concern was to deal with the consequences of the slump; the state intervened to assist the farming industry through bodies like the Cold Storage Commission (set up in 1937 to promote the export of beef under government auspices). In addition, the government introduced an Education Act which provided for the compulsory school attendance of European children up to the age of fifteen. As regards African affairs, Huggins at the time believed in a modified system of racial segregation, known as the 'two pyramids' policy; his approach involved giving restricted powers of local self-government to African health and educational services in the reserves. Huggins's line in this and other respects much resembled that of J. C. Smuts [q.v.] in South Africa, a statesman whom Huggins much admired. At the same time, Huggins pushed for closer union with Northern Rhodesia (later Zambia) and Nyasaland (later Malawi), without, however, making much progress in his design for a British Central African state ruled from Salisbury rather than London.

When World War II broke out, Huggins unreservedly supported the British cause. Militarily, the Southern Rhodesian war effort was co-ordinated with South Africa's. (In 1942, the so-called 'Libertas' resolution demarcated the Zambezi as the boundary between the East and South African Commands.) Economically, Southern Rhodesia, with its growing secondary industries, itself began to exert considerable influence on the two northern territories, and in 1944 the Central African Council was set up to co-ordinate a variety of services between Salisbury, Lusaka, and Zomba. A British patriot to the core, Huggins never had any doubts that the war must be won at all costs; otherwise the colony might just as well 'be wound up'. Given its limited resources, Southern Rhodesia's war effort—made under Huggins's stewardship—was remarkable. White Rhodesians, unlike South Africans, were subject to conscription; a total of 8,448 European men and 1,479 European women served in the armed forces. This was about 15 per cent of the European population, of whom no less than 2,665 earned commissions in Rhodesian or British forces and 693 lost their lives. In addition 262 coloureds and 14,302 Africans put on khaki; 136 of them died. At the same time, Rhodesia took steps to develop its secondary industries through a combination of private enterprise and state support. In 1942 an Iron and Steel Commission came into being; a year later the country's first spinning mills opened their doors at Gatooma. In 1944 the government set up an Industrial Development Commission to give further support to manufacturing. Despite the vast effort involved, the colony under the stewardship of Max Danziger, Huggins's minister of finance from 1942 to 1946, succeeded in largely paying for the war out of current income. In addition, Southern Rhodesia indirectly assisted the British war effort by providing improved transport facilities for the strategically vital copper mines of Northern Rhodesia, by manufacturing war materials on a small scale, and by increasing its farming potential. The British government recognized Huggins's services to the imperial cause by appointing him KCMG (1941) and CH (1944), and admitting him to the Privy Council (1947).

Under the impact of war, Huggins began to modify his views on African policy. Having started in politics as an advocate of segregation, he became convinced, for both administrative and economic reasons, that segregation would have to be changed, and that the two lines of 'parallel development' would ultimately have to meet. As industrialization proceeded and as farming methods grew more complex, the Europeans would have to accept the permanence of the Africans' stake in the cities. The whites would have to come to terms with the growth of a skilled African working class, and a substantial African lower middle and middle class. Education for Africans would have to improve. Euro-African co-operation should be incorporated in a form of partnership in which the Africans would be entitled to a minority holding. The new approach was symbolized by the appointment in 1946 of (Sir) Edgar Whitehead [q.v.] to the key position of minister of finance.

Huggins's approach met with strong opposition from the right-wing opposition, known as the Liberals, as well as from the conservative wing within the United Party. The conservatives, supported mainly by the smaller white farmers and the skilled white workers, would have liked to maintain the social status quo at home and to obtain dominion status for Southern Rhodesia in the international sphere. Their opponents, on the other hand, looked both to the imperial connection and to a form of closer union with the northern territories which would supply the growing Southern Rhodesian secondary industries with a larger market than that available in the 'midget dominion'; the new British Central African state would have a balanced economy that could rely on manufactures, mining wealth, and agriculture; the new state would also be more credit-worthy on the international capital market than three smaller and separate colonies. The cause of closer association also had an international dimension. In 1948 Smuts, Huggins's mentor, fell from office in South Africa where his place was taken by D. F. Malan [q.v.], a militant Afrikaner nationalist. In addition, white Rhodesians of Huggins's persuasion looked with dismay on the development of African nationalism in West Africa. A British Central African state would form an imperial bastion, going neither to one extreme nor to the other, and assuring the future of what Huggins regarded as a policy of enlightened moderation in Africa.

Huggins failed to obtain his original object, an amalgamation of Northern and Southern Rhodesia into a quasi-dominion. After lengthy negotiations, he did attain a compromise solution that united the three British Central African states in the Federation of Rhodesia and Nyasaland, a somewhat ill-defined association that left extensive powers (including African policy) with the constituent states. In 1953 Huggins became prime minister of the Federation of Rhodesia and Nyasaland, leaving Whitehead in charge of Southern Rhodesia. For a time, the Central African economies experienced a boom; secondary industries expanded. The federal government initiated the construction of the great Kariba dam, entailing the construction of one of the world's major hydro-electric undertakings. In 1956 Huggins, a septuagenarian, resigned, having held the prime minister's office for nearly a quarter of a century. He had several honorary doctorates: DCL, Oxford, 1951; LL D, Witwatersrand, 1953; LL D, London, 1955; DCL, Rhodes, 1957. He was raised to the peerage as first Viscount Malvern, of Rhodesia and of Bexley in the county of Kent (1955); Huggins's choice of title characteristically gave recognition to first his old public school, then his adopted country, and finally his English birthplace.

Malvern's career ended at the right time. When he left office, the traditional partnership between London and Salisbury still continued. Decolonization in British Africa was only just about to begin with Ghana's independence in 1957. In Central Africa, the forces of African nationalism had not as yet become mobilized. The Federation was still swept forward on a tide of economic prosperity. Within seven years of his resignation, Malvern's world was shattered. The Federation was dissolved in 1963; two years later, in 1965, Malvern's own white Rhodesian countrymen broke away from thir British allegiance. When Malvern died 8 May 1971 on his farmstead 'The Craig' near Salisbury, he was all but forgotten. He was succeeded as Viscount Malvern by his elder son, John Godrey (born 1922).

Malvern was a remarkable man—tough, forceful, with a robust sense of humour that did not leave him even at the time of his approaching death. He never questioned the assumptions on which he had been raised. He felt sure that the natural leaders of society would normally, though not inevitably, be derived from the ranks of those 'who had fagged at [a public] school and been flogged at school'. No cataclysm could shake his calm cultural self-assurance. To Malvern, World War I was not a searing emotional experience of the kind that disillusioned so many British intellectuals of his generation. The war was but a sad necessity and, as far as he was concerned, 'a gigantic refresher course in surgery'. Malvern's instinctive British patriotism was free of xenophobia whether directed against Germans, Jews, Russians, or Afrikaners. He was likewise free from crude racial prejudices against Africans. As a medical man, he became convinced that there were no essential differences between the various human races, and that the Nazis and their admirers deserved only contempt. However, Malvern did not know many Africans. His knowledge of black people essentially derived from the mental images that he had formed on contacts with servants, labourers, and also with those poverty-stricken African patients whom he used to treat gratis in the old spirit of *noblesse oblige*.

[Robert Blake, *A History of Rhodesia*, 1977; L. H. Gann, *A History of Southern Rhodesia: Early Days to 1934*, 1965; L. H. Gann and M. Gelfand, *Huggins of Rhodesia: The Man and His Country*, 1964; L. H. Gann and Thomas H. Henriksen, *The Struggle for Zimbabwe*, 1981; M. Gelfand and J. Ritchken (eds.), 'The Rt. Hon. Godfrey Martin Huggins: First Viscount Malvern of Rhodesia and Bexley: His Life and Work', *Central African Journal of Medicine*, 1971; Claire Palley, *The Constitutional History and Law of Southern Rhodesia, 1888–1965*, 1966; personal knowledge.] L. H. GANN

HUGHES, RICHARD ARTHUR WARREN (1900–1976), novelist, playwright, and poet, was born in Weybridge 19 April 1900, the second son and third child of Arthur Hughes (died 1905), who worked in the Public Record Office, and his wife, Louisa Grace, daughter of Ernest Warren. Both his brother and sister had died by the time he was two years old. He was educated at Charterhouse and at Oriel College, Oxford, where he got fourth classes in classical moderations (1920) and English (1922).

Hughes's first book of poems, *Gipsy-night, and Other Poems* (1922), was well received, but his first sustained work, *A High Wind in Jamaica* (1929), proved a bestseller that was praised by both the most influential critics of the time and his fellow novelists. Outwardly a 'rattling good yarn' with a background of storms and tropical jungles, of Victorian children captured by ineffectual pirates, it was at once seen as a work of art of singular freshness and as an original contribution to child study. 'The strangeness is never exaggerated. . . .' 'The descriptions are exact as well as beautiful. . . .' What made the descriptions of jungle and of a tropical climate such a *tour de force* was the fact that Hughes had never been to Jamaica but had derived the material indirectly from his mother who, as a little girl, had spent some two years there. A play, *The Sisters' Tragedy* (1922), was praised by G. Bernard Shaw [q.v.], while *Danger* (1924), written for sound radio and produced by (Sir) Nigel Playfair [q.v.] for the BBC, was the first play written for this new and untried medium. The action takes place underground in the echoing, total darkness of a mining disaster.

After leaving Oxford Hughes travelled on the Continent and then went to live in Laugharne in Wales. In 1932 he married the landscape painter Frances, daughter of Gardner Bazley. They were to have two sons and three daughters. He had travelled widely, and at that point they set up house at the Old Hall at Stiffkey, Norfolk, and eventually settled in Wales.

A first novel's instant success notoriously constitutes a problem for a young and dedicated writer, and Hughes, though he contemplated the idea of a biography, did not immediately begin another full-scale book. But in 1938, with *In Hazard*, he again showed his capacity for entering into other people's memories and consciousness, but this time into that of the whole crew of a modern steamer, a crew in an extremity of danger. The ship, *Archimedes*, and the hurricane in which she was caught, had real and recent originals. From this reality Hughes wove an impressive and compelling pattern. 'Patternating' reality was what, years earlier (1921), he had set down as the artist's task in what he called his 'Credo'. The artist, he said, whether using words, music, or paint, was not to be an imitator but should create and communicate by initiating or revealing a pattern in his material—reality. His first two books show the faithful and diligent following of these principles by an admirable craftsman, a craftsman moreover who, believing that the world is odder than is generally supposed, is prepared to challenge and startle his public into paying attention. Both books and the radio play were widely translated.

In 1961 appeared *The Fox in the Attic*, which he called 'a historical novel of our own time'. It was intended as the first part of a whole to be called 'Human Predicament'. Of this, a second part, *The Wooden Shepherdess*, appeared in 1973. Rich, far-reaching, and deeply researched, the work is notable for his convincing portrait of Hitler, whose character is followed from its early nervous manifestations as it gradually changed as Hitler dominated Germany. He is also shown as 'Uncle 'Dolph', a chilling reminder of what can lie behind a smile.

In between Hughes's four major compositions, he wrote children's books and short stories and, as Gresham professor of rhetoric at Gresham College, delivered a notable series of lectures on Lady Murasaki's *The Tale of Genji*. Of these no complete records seem to have survived. In them he reaffirmed much that he had said in his young man's 'Credo', about the necessity of the arts for adequate human communication. Poetic influences were John Skelton [q.v.], a collection of whose poems he edited in 1924, and his friend Robert Graves. His favourite pursuits were adventurous travelling (particularly in Morocco and Greece) and sailing his small cabin cuiser, *Tern*. During World War II Hughes worked at the Admiralty and, with J. D. Scott, was the author of the volume *The Administration of War Production* (1955) in the Official History of the War. For his war services he was appointed OBE in 1946. He was also FRSL and in 1956 received an honorary D.Litt. from the University of Wales.

He very much valued his Welsh descent, and mainly lived in Wales, in later life becoming an active churchman. Tall and athletic as a young man, and even in the twenties wearing a neat beard, he could then, suitably, have been painted by El Greco, but was painted by Augustus John. In later and middle years he was impressive in a Merlin-like way, and in conversation, as in his books, liked to ambush and surprise. He died at his home near Talsarnau, north Wales, 28 April 1976.

[*The Times*, 30 April 1976; unpublished 'Credo' (1921); Peter Thomas, *Richard Hughes*, 1973; private information; personal knowledge.] AMABEL WILLIAMS-ELLIS

HUGHES-HALLETT, JOHN (1901–1972), vice-admiral, was born in Ealing 1 December 1901, the second of three sons (there were no daughters) of Colonel (James) Wyndham Hughes-Hallett, Indian Staff Corps, by his second marriage to Clementine Mary Loch. There were also two sons and a daughter by the first marriage. Educated at Bedford School and the Royal Naval Colleges at Osborne and Dartmouth, and for a year after World War I at Gonville and Caius College, Cambridge, he saw war service in the battle cruiser *Lion* in 1918. As a lieutenant he entered the torpedo branch, gaining the Ogilvie prize for his year. The branch was responsible for torpedoes, mines, and the electrical installations of ships, and his ingenuity was to bring him numerous expressions of their lordships' appreciation for his inventions.

As torpedo officer of the carrier *Courageous* in 1933–5 'Jock' Hughes-Hallett helped to design a night deck-landing system and produced plans for a gliding torpedo which was to be dropped from aircraft. The latter was ahead of its time and the Admiralty rejected it. He then learned to fly. The most interesting feature of his next job, which was at the Admiralty in 1935–7 as a commander, was to act as the secretary to the Anglo-German naval conference of June 1935.

At the start of the war of 1939–45 he was executive officer of the cruiser *Devonshire* which took part in the Norwegian campaign, after which he was mentioned in dispatches. On promotion to captain in June 1940, he was sent to the local defence division of the naval staff which was responsible for preparations against invasion. Here his energy and ingenuity were invaluable and he produced many ideas for defending the ports and beaches. He also found time to give useful service as chairman of a low-cover radar committee, which planned the use of this new invention. He was again mentioned in dispatches in March 1941, an unusual honour for an officer based ashore.

In December 1941, mainly at the request of Lord Louis Mountbatten (later Earl Mountbatten of Burma, q.v.), he was made naval adviser to combined operations where he was extremely successful in helping to build up the organization. He assisted in the planning of the St. Nazaire raid and was the naval commander of the Dieppe raid in August 1942, when his landing-craft carried out their task with skill. Losses were heavy and, although many lessons for the future were learnt, the raid was a failure. Hughes-Hallett would have preferred not to land on the main beach, but he was overruled by his military colleagues. He was appointed to the DSO (1942). As commander, Force J, he played an outstanding role in developing the techniques of amphibious warfare. Based mainly on the Isle of Wight, the force became very large: as a junior captain, serving in the rank of commodore, first class, Hughes-Hallett was in charge of 15,000 service personnel. He was lent for three months in the summer of 1942 to the organization preparing for the invasion of France, and was responsible for the initial naval plan for Operation Overlord in 1944. It is generally acknowledged that he played the major role in conceiving the idea of the artificial harbours off the beaches and he used to recount that he thought of sinking old ships to form a breakwater when at morning service in Westminster Abbey.

As it was deemed necessary for his career for him to go to sea he was appointed to command the cruiser *Jamaica*, thus missing the invasion. The ship took part in the battle off the North Cape when the *Scharnhorst* was sunk in December 1943, and Hughes-Hallett was mentioned in dispatches. As captain he demanded a high standard of efficiency and was ruthless in obtaining it; he was respected rather than loved. In September 1945 he was appointed CB for his services to amphibious warfare and in the *Jamaica*. After the war he commanded the torpedo school at HMS *Vernon* where he made far-reaching changes to adapt to new techniques. He was then for a year captain of the carrier *Illustrious*, a post in which his pilot's licence was of assistance. Promoted to rear-admiral in June 1950, he was appointed vice-controller of the navy, where his technical flair was useful. His last job in the navy was as commander, heavy squadron, Home Fleet (1952–3), during which time he was made a vice-admiral.

A man of high ideals, he came to the conclusion that he wanted to serve his country in politics and he resigned in September 1954, finding a safe Conservative seat at a by-election at Croydon East, which became Croydon North-East in 1955. He found politics puzzling and was irritated by the delays and compromises necessary in a democratic institution. As a backbencher he served on the public accounts committee and on the select committee on the estimates, and between 1958 and 1960 he was a British representative to the consultative assembly of the Council of Europe at Strasburg and also to the assembly of the Western European Union in Paris. Here his experience of defence matters proved useful. After the Suez débâcle of 1956 he did much to promote a permanent United Nations peace force, but without success.

In April 1961 he was promoted to the post of third parliamentary secretary at the Ministry of Transport, with responsibility for shipping and shipbuilding. He introduced some far-reaching measures, some of which were considered 'interventionist' by many of his colleagues. His minister, A. E. (later Lord) Marples [q.v.], and he formed a strong team. He was well liked in politics, having become less abrupt and more approachable, and he was known for a pungent wit. He was conscientious in looking after his constituents. The reasons for his leaving politics in 1964 are difficult to discern. Perhaps he was disappointed in his progress. He chose a bad moment to retire as pensions for MPs were introduced shortly afterwards.

He was a consultant director to the British Shipping Council (1964–9) and he acquired several honorary tasks, among them membership of the Council of Advanced Motorists. An ardent and fast car driver, he also used a bicycle all his life. He was unmarried. His last years were clouded by a fear of penury, caused mainly by a dispute with the Admiralty over the size of his pension about which he had been misinformed before he retired. He died at Slindon, Sussex, 5 April 1972.

[Private information; personal knowledge.]

PETER GRETTON

HULBERT, JOHN NORMAN (JACK) (1892–1978), actor, producer, and theatre manager, was born in Ely 24 April 1892, the elder son (there were no daughters) of Henry Harper Hulbert, MRCS, LRCP, and his wife, Lilian Mary Hinchliff. He was educated at Westminster School, and Gonville and Caius College, Cambridge. He decided as a schoolboy to earn his living as an actor, and this early decision was actively encouraged by his father's enthusiasm for the theatre. Later, indeed, Dr Hulbert was to forsake the medical profession and give up his practice in order to lecture on voice production to stage aspirants. Meanwhile, father and son would regularly visit the London theatres, seated usually in the gallery on a Saturday night, and earnestly discuss the acting techniques and personalities (as projected on the stage) of the players. (Sir) Charles Hawtrey and (Sir) Gerald du Maurier [qq.v.] were their particular favourites.

Although at the end he managed to scramble into a degree during his three years at Cambridge (he used to refer to them as the best years in his life) Jack Hulbert spent his days and nights on any university or local theatre stage that was offered—except when he was rowing. In his last year he was secretary of the Caius boat club, and on one memorable afternoon was tried as bow in the university boat. For the Amateur Dramatic Club and the Marlowe Society he played as many diverse parts as were offered—from Anthony Absolute to Sir Toby Belch. In his second year, at the local theatre in a privately sponsored production, he acted the title-part, which was played in London by Charles Hawtrey, in the comedy *Jack Straw* by W. Somerset Maugham [q.v.]. In his last term, for 'The Footlights' revue of May week 1913, he wrote most of the sketches, produced, and played the leading part, achieving a personal success which led, in the following week, to a special matinée at the Queen's Theatre in London. It was Hulbert's father who had arranged this venture, and among the London theatre managers invited was Robert Courtneidge. Courtneidge at once engaged Hulbert on a three-year contract, and to go into immediate rehearsal to play opposite his twenty-year old daughter, Cicely, at the Shaftesbury Theatre. And so began a sixty-five year partnership perhaps unique in theatrical annals. Hulbert married (Esmeralda) Cicely Courtneidge [q.v.] in 1916. He served in the army from 1917 to 1919.

The stage careers of Hulbert and his wife are so interlinked that they have been treated together in the notice of Cicely Courtneidge. It is unnecessary to outline them again except to refer to the years between 1931 and 1938 when Hulbert exclusively devoted himself to acting for the cinema.

One of his earliest films, made at the old Gaumont–British studios, and directed by Victor Saville, was an English translation from the German, renamed *Sunshine Susie*, with the German actress Renate Muller in love with Owen Nares, the manager of a Viennese bank, of which Hulbert was the hall porter. With the director's delighted approval, Hulbert played this apparently incongruous role in his musical comedy manner of breezy good humour, in amusing contrast to the delicate 'legitimate' technique of Nares, an actor whom Hulbert greatly admired. The film, in spite of its German origin, was refreshingly and unmistakably English, and proved an immediate success, first in London and then throughout the country.

There followed for Hulbert a succession of films in which he starred. These films were in a sense the culmination of his stage career in the musical comedy world of the 1920s and 1930s, to which he really belonged. Their titles, which were typical of his stage and screen personality, are significant: *Jack's the Boy* (1932), *Jack Ahoy* (1934), *Bull-Dog Jack* (1935), and *Jack-of-all-Trades* (1936). Tall, fair, and angular, Hulbert had a chin which protruded with an amiable resolution. His dancing may have lacked the technical and rhythmic precision of a Fred Astaire or Jack Buchanan [q.v.] but it had a quality of impromptu ease in its variations.

As a producer of plays, and particularly of musical comedies, Hulbert was not only ingenious and competent but had the gift of getting into his shows a vitality and movement on the part of his choruses which could only have been obtained by a perfectionist—as indeed he was, in everything that concerned him in the theatre as actor, producer, trainer of choruses, and author. He had the reputation in the profession, and particularly among the choruses he trained, of being a genial slave-driver, but the discipline he called for and inspired was mitigated by his understanding, good humour, and the certain knowledge that he never spared himself.

Hulbert was a man of many interests and hobbies, among them farming. He owned and worked a farm for many years at Essendon, in Hertfordshire, and (in his own words) escaped there whenever he reasonably could. Among his interests was geology. Samuel Pepys was one of his historical heroes, and during Hulbert's not infrequent visits to Cambridge when on tour he usually found time to include a visit to the Pepys Library in Magdalene College.

Jack Hulbert died at home in London 25 March 1978, being survived by his wife and their only child, a daughter.

[*Daily Telegraph*, 27 March 1978; *The Times*, 4 April 1978; Cicely Courtneidge, *Cicely*, 1953; Jack Hulbert, *The Little Woman's Always Right* (autobiography), 1975; personal knowledge.]

D. Pepys-Whiteley

HUMPHREY, Sir ANDREW HENRY (1921–1977), marshal of the Royal Air Force, was born in Edinburgh 10 January 1921, the second of the three sons (there were no daughters) of John Humphrey, CBE, of Karachi, an exchange broker, and his wife, Agnes Florence, daughter of Colonel John Beatson-Bell, judge advocate-general in India. He was educated at Belhaven Preparatory School, Dunbar, and Bradfield. In 1939 he entered the RAF College, Cranwell, from which he graduated in April 1940.

Posted to No. 266 (Spitfire) Squadron Humphrey flew on active operations in the Battle of Britain; after a transfer to night-fighter work he was awarded the DFC in 1941. There followed operational experience on Hurricane fighter bombers with No. 175 Squadron prior to transfer to the Middle East as a rocket attack instructor. In 1943 he was awarded the AFC, to which were to be added bars in 1945 and 1955.

After service in India there came staff work at home at HQ No. 106 Group and survey work in Africa with No. 82 Squadron after which he was appointed OBE in 1951. During a tour as instructor at the RAF Flying College, Manby, Humphrey established in 1953 a new record for the Cape Town to London flight flying the twin jet Canberra bomber Aries IV. In 1954 he flew the same aircraft on the first RAF jet flight to the North Pole.

Following a course at the RAF Staff College, Bracknell, he was posted to the Air Ministry, becoming deputy director of operational requirements in 1957, with particular responsibility for the introduction of the Lightning supersonic single-seater fighter. His flair for technical detail and wide flying experience enabled him to make a major impact on operational efficiency and flight safety standards. For this work he was appointed CB (1959); it was an exceptional recognition for a group captain.

After commanding the large RAF station at Akrotiri, Cyprus, from 1959 to 1961, Humphrey attended the Imperial Defence College in 1962, being promoted air commodore that year. He was subsequently posted to the Ministry of Defence, serving from 1962 to 1965 in senior air planning appointments.

Humphrey's potential as a 'high flier' was by this time well recognized by his seniors; promotion to air vice-marshal in 1965 and selection for appointment as air officer commanding Middle East, with his headquarters at Aden, reflected their confidence. This tour was not easy; as the last AOC Humphrey was intimately concerned with the highly complex withdrawal plan for all British forces; he did well.

He returned to the MOD as air member for personnel in 1968 and was advanced to KCB in June that year, the acting rank of air marshal being confirmed in January 1969. There followed a tour as commander-in-chief Strike Command, during which he was promoted air chief marshal and created GCB (1974); he was air ADC to the Queen in 1974–6.

Early belief in Humphrey's destiny reached ultimate fulfilment when he became firstly chief of the air staff in April 1974 and then, after promotion to marshal of the Royal Air Force in August 1976, chief of the defence staff in October that year.

Humphrey loved flying and had a personal pride in his flying skill and a deep knowledge of the art. From the earliest days his colleagues and peers came to recognize the emerging human attributes which Humphrey had in abundance. Ability to listen, modesty, consideration for others, sensitivity, warmth, love of sport, infectious humour—all these facets developed in him with the years and none were diminished as responsibilities increased. He had a capacity for dispassionate and unbiased analysis and he thought that the inter-service approach was vital. Greatly concerned at the ever increasing build-up of Soviet Forces he spoke and wrote fearlessly and frequently about this.

In March 1952 Humphrey married Agnes Stevenson Wright, a former flight officer in the WRAF and younger daughter of James Wright, architect, of Stirling, Scotland. Agnes Humphrey endeared herself to all by her constant and painstaking care for the needs of Service personnel and their families. There were no children. Humphrey died 24 January 1977 at Princess Mary's RAF Hospital, Halton.

There are two portraits of Humphrey: one by Mara McGregor in College Hall, Cranwell, and the other, by John Hughes-Hallett, in the officers' mess of HQ Strike Command, High Wycombe.

[Air Historical Branch, Royal Air Force; *The Times*, 25 January and 1 February 1977; personal knowledge.] JOHN GRANDY

HUMPHREYS, LESLIE ALEXANDER FRANCIS LONGMORE (1904–1976), organizer of clandestine communications to and from German-occupied western Europe for the Special Operations Executive (SOE), was born in Budapest, 4 July 1904, the younger child and only son of Richard John Edward Humphreys and his wife, Elizabeth Agnes Lyons. His father, a musician who went first to Austria-Hungary in 1894, taught English in Budapest and subsequently became commercial secretary at The Hague, Budapest, and Bucharest. From Cardinal Vaughan School Humphreys went to Stonyhurst. Too young to fight in the war of 1914–18, he was old enough to become an ardent patriot in his teens and never lost this fierce emotion, nor the deep faith acquired as a 'Jesuit child'. After a year at the Faculté des Lettres in Dijon he went up to Magdalene College, Cambridge, and gained a third class in modern languages in 1925 and a lower second in part ii of the history tripos in 1926. Virtually trilingual, he could add to French and German a fair fluency in Romanian.

For six years between periods of business work in London, Humphreys was at the British legation in Bucharest as assistant to his father and attaché to the controller for the League of Nations of an international loan to Romania, a Frenchman. Early in 1939 he joined SOE's predecessor, Section D of the British secret service, and before the outbreak of war made two operational trips to Holland and one to Poland. He was sent to Paris in September with the rank of major, as liaison with the French Fifth Bureau, planning sabotage lines from Paris and later a sabotage network inside falling France. He was evacuated on 20 June 1940 by warship from the Gironde amid tumult. On the formation of SOE in July he became head of its F Section, charged with organizing subversion in France. Humphreys was preoccupied with one principle—communications are the essential basis of all clandestine work, but he was miscast as executant of (Sir) Winston Churchill's directive to E. H. J. N. (later Lord) Dalton [q.v.] 'to set Europe ablaze'. In December he was moved over to work on clandestine communications (DF Section), a task better suited to his temperament and abilities. He visited Lisbon twice during the winter of 1940–1 to investigate reported lines for passing letters, parcels, and people into France: he decided to construct links of his own. He gradually designed a blueprint of a system that would serve SOE through western Europe for secret travel and secret supply. His first agent, a Maltese schoolteacher, was put ashore near Perpignan in April 1941 and established working contacts with smugglers operating across the Pyrenees. In May he sent the Chilean actress wife of a French Jew, Victor Gerson ('Vic'), on reconnaissance to Vichy. Gerson followed and in the course of six separate clandestine visits built SOE's biggest and best escape line. Many of those he recruited were also Jews, more at risk than Gentiles, but determinedly anti-Nazi and used to keeping themselves to themselves. Other helpers included a Swiss Social Democrat and a Norwegian Quaker ship-broker in Marseilles. Jacques Mitterand, brother of the future president of France, became his chief lieutenant in Paris.

Humphreys, a strong administrator who harped on secrecy, kept his people inconspicuous and this was the main reason for his DF Section's run of successes. The effectiveness of his security precautions was demonstrated when the Abwehr in 1943 penetrated the 'Vic' line: none of the eleven arrested sub-agents provided the Germans with exploitable information and the line continued to function unchecked.

DF's methods were sometimes unorthodox. In launching the extremely effective 'Var' escape line which carried seventy people (including François Mitterand) across the beaches of the north Breton coast in the winter and spring of 1943–4, the section's seaborne projects officer dextrously bypassed the proper SOE channels and made his arrangements direct with the naval section of the Secret Intelligence Service (SIS or MI6). At a time when relations between the two organizations were less than cordial, this tendency to 'play the SIS card within SOE' did not go down well with some of Humphreys's SOE superiors, though there was obviously much less clash of professional interest between DF and SIS than in the case of the other SOE country sections. The results achieved were remarkable: several hundred passengers were carried without loss and the carrier's casualty rate of 2 per cent was by far the lowest of SOE's French sections. Humphreys attained the rank of lieutenant-colonel and was appointed OBE (1945).

After the war Humphreys returned to the business world, but in 1950 he accepted an opportunity to serve again under the Foreign Office. His postings took him to Frankfurt, Pusan (South Korea), Vienna, and, finally, London. In 1964 he retired and joined the staff of the Stonyhurst preparatory school. He was, as always, punctilious about his duties. Each day began with mass and he walked the corridors telling his beads. But his piety did nothing to obscure his habitually jocular, virile approach. Behind the penetrating gaze and powerful jaw he remained pessimistic and thorough, 'with no illusions about man's inevitable progress towards the realms of light or any nonsense about natural innocence'. The boys loved him.

Even after his second retirement in 1973 to Bexhill, he continued to teach until the heart attack that caused his death there 19 December 1976. He was unmarried and his sister kept house for him both at Stonyhurst and Bexhill.

[M. R. D. Foot, *SOE in France*, first impression, 1966; obituary by the Revd C. K. Macadam in *Stonyhurst Magazine*, summer 1977, vol. xl, No. 463; *The Times*, 29 January 1977; Roger Huguen, *Par les Nuits les Plus Longues*, 4th edn., 1978; Foreign and Commonwealth Office records; private information; personal knowledge.] BROOKS RICHARDS

HUNTER, DONALD (1898–1978), physician and authority on occupational medicine, was born 11 February 1898 at Forest Gate, London E7, the second of the five sons (there were no daughters) of George Hunter, Post Office executive engineer, of East Ham, and his wife, Maria-Louisa Edwards. He was brought up in the East End of London. After school at Forest Gate he became a student at the London Hospital in 1915, but spent a year at sea serving as a probationary surgeon lieutenant before qualifying MB, BS (Lond.) in 1920. He gained his MD (Lond.) in 1922 and MRCP (Lond.) in 1923. He went to

Harvard as a research fellow in 1926, working with Aub who was studying lead poisoning. In 1927 he was elected assistant physician to the London Hospital, which he served till retirement in 1963. He became FRCP in 1929.

In 1943 he was appointed director of the Medical Research Council's department for research in industrial medicine, which he established at the London and ran until it was closed on his retirement, after which he taught for a period at the Middlesex Hospital, then became research fellow in the occupational health department at Guy's Hospital, until finally returning to an office at the London where he worked until shortly before his death.

Hunter is rightly considered the father of occupational medicine in Britain. He was the first editor, in 1944, of the *British Journal of Industrial Medicine*, later to become one of the world's leading journals on the subject, which he advanced also through many important lectures, including the Goulstonian (1930), Croonian (1942), and Ernestine Henry (1949), and the Harveian oration (1957) of the Royal College of Physicians. He was Sims Commonwealth travelling professor in 1955 and in the same year published his major work, *The Diseases of Occupations*, the comprehensive classic textbook on the subject, which reached its seventh edition not long before his death.

Hunter himself made a great contribution to the knowledge of occupational medicine through his own research into industrial toxicology, particularly the clinical investigation of poisoning by lead, mercury, and organic mercury compounds. Even greater was the impact of his lucid and fascinating record of the immense amount of information he gleaned throughout the world on the way men work, on the diseases to which they thus become vulnerable, and on how these can be prevented. Greater still was the influence of the man himself on the attitudes of those with whom he came into personal contact as a teacher and examiner. Despite his commitment to research, he never ceased to be a practising doctor, and had the supreme gift of being able to kindle in others his own joy in medicine and to fire them with his unceasing curiosity. He built up, as a teaching instrument, a remarkable museum at the London Hospital.

In the hospital as Hunter went from ward to ward, head forward, white coat-tails flying, his feet attempting to keep pace with his words, the faces of the students and young doctors streaming after him were always alight with excitement. At the bedside, even the student being berated by Hunter would enjoy what he would never forget, 'You are standing on holy ground where Hughlings Jackson stood', and Hunter would twist his stethoscope tight round the student's neck, 'And you tell me you don't know where this patient lives or what he does at work.' He was also well known as an examiner and a medical traveller, being an enthusiastic member of the Medical Pilgrims' Travelling Club.

Hunter was appointed CBE in 1957 and was awarded an honorary D.Sc. by the University of Durham in 1960. He is commemorated by the Donald Hunter memorial lecture of the Faculty of Occupational Medicine.

In 1925 Hunter married Dr Mathilde ('Thilo') Eglantine Freda Bugnion, the daughter of the Revd Gustave Adolphe Bugnion, a Swiss pastor in Lausanne. Of their two sons and two daughters, one daughter, Elizabeth, became a consultant in psychiatry at St. George's Hospital, and one son, Peter, a consultant in endocrinology at Shrewsbury Royal Infirmary.

Hunter died in Norwood and District Hospital, south London, 12 December 1978.

[*The Times*, 19 November 1979; *Daily Telegraph*, 15 December 1978; personal knowledge.] JOHN ELLIS

HURCOMB, CYRIL WILLIAM, BARON HURCOMB (1883–1975), civil servant, was born in Oxford 18 February 1883, the eldest of three children of William Hurcomb, bookseller, and his wife, Sarah Ann Castle. He was educated at Oxford High School and, as a scholar, at St. John's College, Oxford, where he obtained a first in classical moderations in 1903 and a second in *literae humaniores* in 1905. He entered the Civil Service in the Post Office in 1906, and was briefly outposted before being assigned to the secretary's office; after five years he became private secretary to the postmaster-general, and was thus marked out for promotion. He was strongly influenced in this period by Sir Matthew Nathan and Herbert (later Viscount) Samuel [qq.v.].

After the outbreak of World War I Hurcomb was transferred to the Admiralty and then, in 1916, to the newly formed Ministry of Shipping. There he became deputy director and, later, director, of commercial services, working closely with a group of men who were to play important parts in shaping his future career, such as his Oxford contemporary J. A. (later Lord) Salter [q.v.]. His work was operational rather than conventionally administrative, and he showed an aptitude for managerial duties which characterized all his later posts. It was here also that he acquired an ease and skill for working with and winning the confidence of colleagues drawn from business, the professions, and other walks of life. The international aspects of the work appealed to him, and he developed a remarkable capacity for forming relations of close trust with a wide variety of foreigners, especially Europeans. The challenges presented to him by wartime shipping problems determined the rest of his career.

His work at Shipping had brought him to the notice of Sir Eric Geddes [q.v.] who in 1919 persuaded him to join the new Ministry of Transport which Geddes headed. His main task there was to negotiate the regrouping of the railway companies in 1921. He was appointed permanent secretary of the Ministry of Transport in 1927, at the early age of forty-four. He had then to face an immediate challenge from the Treasury, which proposed to abolish his Ministry as a measure of economy. Making full use of the impact at that time of the motor vehicle on society, Hurcomb fought a skilful and patient holding action. In 1929 the tables were turned with the arrival, as minister in the new Labour government, of the able and energetic Herbert Morrison (later Lord Morrison of Lambeth, q.v.), with whom he quickly established a close personal friendship. Jointly they piloted the pioneering legislation to establish the London (Passenger) Transport Board, which amalgamated a large number of separate concerns. Simultaneously they pushed through Parliament the Road Traffic Act of 1930, which introduced tests for drivers, compulsory third party insurance, licensing of road passenger services, a Highway Code, and a speed limit for built-up areas. Further legislation in the 1930s led to trouble with the Home Office which objected to the growing burden placed upon the police by some of these measures. The result was an increased number of negotiations which Hurcomb found wearying.

In 1937 therefore he was glad to take the opportunity of transferring to the Electricity Commission, where, as chairman from 1938, he was at one remove from politics. Although he retained this post for ten years, from 1939 his time was to be pre-empted for most of them by war and post-war responsibilities as director-general of the Ministry of Shipping (later War Transport), where he was able to apply the principles which he had learnt in World War I. In this he was greatly helped by the renewed collaboration of Salter, now in Parliament, who as a junior minister in the department provided strong intellectual support. The necessity of deploying the British-controlled and United States merchant fleets as if they were one, made it imperative to establish close relations of trust with the shipping authorities in Washington, and this task was excellently performed from April 1941 by Salter, whose intimate understanding of Hurcomb's thoughts and style enabled him to act as head of the British Merchant Shipping Mission in full harmony with London. One of Hurcomb's main concerns was to block outside interference, and this he achieved with entire success, even in face of determined attempts at encroachment by F. A. Lindemann (later Viscount Cherwell, q.v.).

The post-war Attlee administration embarked on a major programme of nationalization under Herbert Morrison, who turned naturally to Hurcomb to bring into operation the British Transport Commission, of which he served as chairman from 1947 to 1953. Partly owing to a reversal of policy by the succeeding Conservative government this was probably the least successful of his official assignments, and certainly the least enduring. Although his robust health continued he was less ready to tackle trouble than in his earlier years. Having become keenly interested in the growing movement for conservation of nature he was not unwilling to relinquish his thankless task at the Commission under the post-war Churchill government, and at the age of seventy to move elsewhere.

He had already taken a first step in April 1947 by becoming chairman of the committee of bird sanctuaries in the Royal Parks, and he took great pains to produce an authoritative annual report, and to ensure that the bailiff and each of his officers was fully advised of anything relevant to bird protection. In 1953 he joined the official Nature Conservancy, serving as chairman of its committee for England and in 1961–2 as chairman of its council. From 1954 to 1960 he was vice-president of the International Union for the Conservation of Nature and Natural Resources, and his disarming intervention with a vintage House of Lords speech at a moment of crisis helped to avert a threatened split in the Union at its meeting in Poland in 1960. He was president of the Society for the Promotion of Nature Reserves in 1950–61, of the Field Studies Council from 1957, and of the Royal Society for the Protection of Birds in 1961–6. He was also active in several other naturalist and conservation bodies. Apart from his lifelong devotion to fishing, and his renewal in later life of an early interest in bird-watching, he was deeply read in the classics and in English literature and was fond of serious conversation. His tolerance and sense of humour were shown by his choice as supporters for his coat of arms of 'a heron proper gorged' on either side, upholding a branch of willow on which sat a kingfisher with wings elevated, with the motto 'Quoad potero perferam'.

Hurcomb's pallid complexion and worn appearance belied his toughness and stamina, just as his austere mien disguised his receptiveness as a listener and his great consideration for others. These, combined with his clarity of mind and tenacity of purpose, made him an outstanding negotiator. His manner was never ingratiating, but his arguments were fair and persuasive, winning respect if not always affection. Without being an expert on any subject he learned enough of a number to be taken seriously by experts, and to complement their expertise with his own wisdom.

He was appointed CBE in 1918, CB in 1922, KBE in 1929, KCB in 1938, GCB in 1946, and was created first Baron Hurcomb in 1950. He also had many foreign decorations. In 1938 St. John's College, Oxford, made him an honorary fellow. In 1911 he married Dorothy Ethel (died 1947), daughter of Alfred Brooke, solicitor. They had two daughters. The title became extinct upon Hurcomb's death at Horsham 7 August 1975.

[MS autobiographical notes by C.W.H. in possession of the family; private information; personal knowledge.] MAX NICHOLSON

HUTCHINSON, JOHN (1884–1972), botanist and writer, was born at Wark on Tyne, Northumberland, 7 April 1884, the second in the family of four sons and three daughters of Michael Hutchinson, head gardener at nearby Blindburn Hall, and his wife, Annie Willey. He was educated at the village school, although later he attended evening classes at Rutherford College, Newcastle, and, even later, at Chelsea and Regent Street polytechnics in London.

On leaving school in 1900 he first worked under his father as a garden boy and a year later, to gain further experience, moved to Callerton Hall, near Ponteland, and then to Axwell Park, Blaydon on Tyne, where he took the opportunity of attending evening classes in botany at Rutherford College. His abilities as an artist had been noted and encouraged in childhood and he continued to practice drawing and water-colour painting.

In April 1904 Hutchinson moved south to the Royal Botanic Gardens, Kew, and worked in the arboretum as a gardener. His abilities caught the attention of his superiors and after about a year he was offered a post in the herbarium as a preparer. Between 1907 and 1916 he was appointed assistant, first for India and then Africa. In 1917 he joined the permanent staff taking charge of the African section, a responsibility he retained until, in 1936, he became keeper of the museums at Kew, a post he held until he retired in April 1948. However, he continued to work daily in the herbarium right up to and including the Saturday on which he died.

Work on the African flora dominated his earlier years and his first major contributions were to the *Flora of Tropical Africa* (1912, 1915) and the *Flora Capensis* (1915). In 1923 he commenced work on a *Flora of West Tropical Africa* which, with the assistance of J. M. Dalziel, he completed in 1937. This Flora set a new pattern of conciseness for such works.

In another direction Hutchinson contributed greatly to knowledge of the horticulturally important genus *Rhododendron*, on which he wrote large parts of several major works. He was much honoured by the Royal Horticultural Society who in 1945 awarded him their Victoria medal of honour.

However, the work and publications for which he is most noted are those on the classification of flowering plants. Although that set out in his *The Families of Flowering Plants* (2 vols., 1926 and 1934; second edn. 1959, third edn. 1973) has not been generally followed, these works, together with his *Evolution and Phylogeny of Flowering Plants* (1969)—each fully illustrated by his own line-drawings—have provided a powerful stimulus to others, while his keys and descriptions have been widely used.

In 1949, at the age of fifty-six, he commenced working on a project of a lifetime: a major revision of all genera and families of flowering plants. The first volume of *The Genera of Flowering Plants* was published in 1964, the second three years later, and at the time of his death he was working hard on the third (of a projected seven volumes).

Hutchinson's record of publications is incomplete, however, without mention of his popular books. In 1945 Penguin published his *Common Wild Flowers* which sold 250,000 copies in the first year. This was followed by *More Common Wild Flowers* (1948) and *Uncommon Wild Flowers* (1950) which, together, were revised and expanded into the two-volume *British Wild Flowers* (1955), in all of which the text was complemented by his own illustrations. With Ronald Melville he also wrote *The Story of Plants and their Uses to Man* (1948).

Hutchinson travelled widely, collecting plants and making observations. His journeys in southern Africa in particular are noteworthy, especially that in 1930, accompanied by his friend General J. C. Smuts [q.v.], to Lake Tanganyika, experiences described in his *A Botanist in Southern Africa* (1946).

In 1934 the University of St. Andrews conferred on him an honorary LL D. The Linnean Society, of which he had become a fellow in 1918, presented him with their Darwin–Wallace centenary medal (1958) and their highest award, the Linnean gold medal (1965). In 1947 he was elected FRS and in 1972 appointed OBE. He was very proud of his humble origins and wrote an unpublished autobiography, 'From Potting Shed to F.R.S.', a copy of which is deposited in the library at Kew.

In 1910 he married Lilian Florence, daughter of James Firman Cook, decorator, of Richmond, Surrey. They had two sons and three daughters. He died at home at Kew 2 September 1972, his wife dying a week later.

[J. P. M. Brennan and C. Pope in *Kew Bulletin* vol. xxix, 1974; C. E. Hubbard in *Biographical Memoirs of Fellows of the Royal Society*, vol. xxi, 1975; private information; personal knowledge.] P. S. GREEN

HUXLEY, Sir JULIAN SORELL (1887–1975), zoologist, philosopher, and public servant, was born in London 22 June 1887, the eldest of the three sons and four children of Leonard Huxley [q.v.], second son of the Victorian scientist and evolutionist T. H. Huxley [q.v.], assistant master at Charterhouse and subsequently editor of the *Cornhill Magazine*, and his first wife, Julia Frances, daughter of Thomas Arnold [q.v.], son of Thomas Arnold [q.v.], headmaster of Rugby School, and of Julia, the daughter of William Sorell, governor of Tasmania. One of Julian's brothers died in 1914 and the other was the writer Aldous Huxley [q.v.]. His mother's sister was Mrs Humphry Ward, the novelist [q.v.].

In his last year at Eton, to which he had gone as a King's scholar, Julian Huxley won the school's poetry, Shakespeare, and biology prizes. In 1906 he went up to Oxford as Brackenbury scholar at Balliol. In 1908 he won the Newdigate prize for poetry, the theme of his poem being Holyrood. In 1909 he gained a first class honours degree in natural science (zoology), and a scholarship which allowed him to work for a year in the celebrated marine biological laboratory that had been founded in Naples by Dr Dohrn. After Naples Huxley returned to Oxford where he spent two years as lecturer in zoology at Balliol (1910–22). He then moved to a chair of biology in the newly-created Rice Institute in Texas, where he remained from late 1913 to 1916. 'As one of the most sensible things' he ever did, so Huxley wrote, he induced the American geneticist, Hermann Muller, who was then working in Columbia University, to join him as his assistant. Muller carried on with his genetical experiments on the effects of radiation on the germ plasm, for which he was later awarded the Nobel prize. It was mainly out of this association that Huxley gained his appreciation of the importance of genetics as a discipline basic to an understanding of the processes of selection and evolution.

In November 1916 Huxley returned to England, and in the spring of 1917 he enlisted in the Army Service Corps, the Intelligence Unit into which he was then commissioned being posted to Italy in October of that year. In 1919 he returned to Oxford as a fellow of New College and as senior demonstrator in zoology. In 1925 he was appointed professor of zoology at King's College, London, a post from which he resigned in 1927 in order to devote his time to writing and research. From 1927 to 1931 he held the office of Fullerian professor of physiology at the Royal Institution.

Huxley was endowed with great energy and a keen and constructive interest in a wide field of scientific and social problems. He was a pioneer in the scientific field-study of animal behaviour, and remained an ardent ornithologist throughout his life. His paper on the courtship of the great crested grebe, published in 1914, introduced the concept of the ritualization of behaviour. His work on the effect of genetic changes on the time relations of developmental processes in the water flea, *Gammarus*, was outstanding in its time. He studied the hormonal reactions of invertebrates, and was among the first to demonstrate the importance of thyroid hormone in the metamorphosis of axolotls into salamanders. He turned his attention to the differential growth of the parts of the body, and in 1932 published a book, *Problems of Relative Growth*, which, too, was a turning-point in the study of the subject.

Like his grandfather before him, Huxley achieved a special place among exponents of the theory of evolution. In 1940 he edited an important work called *The New Systematics*, to which he contributed an outstanding chapter in which he described the impact on animal classification of the newer discoveries that were being made in genetics. His *Evolution, the Modern Synthesis*, first published in 1942 (third edn. 1974), brought together the fruits of a wide range of naturalistic, genetical, and mathematical studies. In shorter books published in 1952 and 1953, he elaborated an idea, first developed in his *Modern Synthesis*, that because of his mastery of the environment of the world, man had become 'the *de facto* agent for further evolution on this planet', and alone possessed any further potentiality for significant evolutionary progress.

With his concern about man's dominant and responsible influence as a selective force in the world, Huxley turned his attention to demographic studies. He had become deeply conscious of the social dangers which the unrestrained growth of human population would bring. Much of his knowledge about conditions in underdeveloped countries came from travel. *Africa View*, published in 1931, was based on a visit paid to East Africa in 1929 to advise on native education. Huxley later became a member (1933–8) of the general committee for *An African Survey* by Lord Hailey [q.v.] (1938), and also a member of the 1944 commission set up to study the problem of higher education in West Africa. Because of his experience and powerful interest in these questions, as well as his concern with public education, he was approached by the British government and persuaded to become the secretary-general of the preparatory commission for Unesco. When this international organization was set up in 1946 he was appointed its first director-general for a period which proved immensely exciting and creative. His awareness of the need to conquer world-wide illiteracy, coupled with his skill as a general writer on scientific matters, provided just those qualities necessary to launch a project as grand as Unesco. But, as Huxley himself recognized, he did not have the temperament to be an administrator.

The years from 1935 to 1942, when he had served as the full-time secretary of the Zoological Society of London (in succession to Sir Peter Chalmers Mitchell, q.v.), had been a taxing period, and none of his previous experience had prepared him for the many administrative frustrations by which any director-general would have been beset in a fledgling international organization whose development was constrained by complex political pressures.

Huxley was one of the most influential popularizers of science of his age. In 1929 he was co-author with H. G. Wells [q.v.] and his son G. P. Wells of a monumental work entitled *The Science of Life*. He became a national figure in the war years of 1939–45 as a member of the BBC Brains Trust. His concern with public education was always paralleled by a determination to do what he could to promote the movement to conserve the world's disappearing wild fauna. He played a powerful part in the organization of wild-life conservation in all parts of the world, but particularly in East Africa. In 1948, while at Unesco, he was a leading figure in the setting up of the International Union for the Conservation of Nature, and later, in 1961 of the World Wild Life Fund. In his earlier days, he also helped launch the Society for Experimental Biology, as well as the organization Political and Economic Planning. He served a term as president of the Association of Scientific Workers.

In the preface to his autobiography, *Memories* (2 vols., 1970 and 1973), Huxley referred to his 'many-sided professional career', adding that he was inwardly timid, but that he liked getting his own way, that 'looking back, I seem to have been possessed by a demon, driving me into every sort of activity, and impatient to finish anything I had begun: an impatience which, I fear, may have pressed annoyingly those of my colleagues who preferred a more systematic approach. I have been accused of dissipating my energies in too many directions, yet it was assuredly this diversity of interests which made me what I am . . .' What he was was a man who contributed greatly to the culture of his age, one who at the same time found that his 'enjoyment of nature and natural beauty, coupled with a sense of poetic wonder' provided a refuge for his intellectual restlessness.

Huxley was the author of numerous books and scientific monographs. He was knighted in 1958, having been elected a fellow of the Royal Society in 1938. He was awarded the Royal Society's Darwin medal in 1956, and was the recipient of many honorary degrees and awards from British and foreign universities and societies. In 1974 he became the first recipient of the Frink gold medal for British zoologists.

In 1919 he married (Marie) Juliette, daughter of Alphonse Baillot, solicitor, of Neuchâtel, Switzerland. They had two sons, Francis, an anthropologist, and Anthony, a botanist. His wife was a constant support to him, seeing him through his many episodes of depression. Huxley died 14 February 1975 at his home in Hampstead, London.

[Julian Huxley, *Memories*, 2 vols., 1970 and 1973; J. R. Baker in *Biographical Memoirs of Fellows of the Royal Society*, vol. xxii, 1976; W. H. Thorpe in *Ibis*, vol. cxvii, 1975; *The Times*, 17 February 1975; family information; personal knowledge.]

S. ZUCKERMAN

I

ING, (HARRY) RAYMOND (1899–1974), reader in chemical pharmacology at Oxford, was born at Alford, Lincolnshire, 31 July 1899, one of the three sons of Arthur Frank William Ing, a solicitor's clerk originally of Herefordshire stock, and his wife, Anne Garrard. At the age of twelve he won a scholarship to Oxford High School. In 1917 he entered New College, Oxford, with an exhibition. Resuming his studies after interruption during World War I when he served in the postal censorship department, he attained first class honours in chemistry in 1921, and went on to do a D.Phil. under W. H. Perkin, Jr. [q.v.], in the meantime also teaching chemistry at Wadham College.

He would have preferred to continue this combination of research and instruction but no college fellowship was available at the time, so in 1926 he moved instead to Owens College, Manchester, to work as a Ramsay memorial fellow with (Sir) Robert Robinson [q.v.], and then as a chemist with the Manchester committee on cancer. He was not altogether happy there, but it was the latter work which probably confirmed his interest in chemical structure in relation to biological activity. It also led to a post at University College London as lecturer (1929) and then reader (1937), in pharmacological chemistry: the first chemist ever to hold such an appointment in a university department of pharmacology in Great Britain. Here he was content and considered his time in the college as 'a flowering period, full of intellectual excitement and warm friendships'. His friends included the physical chemist F. G. Donnan [q.v.], physiologists and anatomists like (Sir) C. A. Lovatt Evans, A. V. Hill [qq.v.], and Elliott Smith, and others in the medical school, while his early schooling in the arts undoubtedly attracted him also to close association with many members of that faculty.

In 1938 his professor (Sir) J. H. Gaddum [q.v.], obtained for him a fellowship at the Rockefeller Institute in New York to work with the outstanding organic chemist Max Bergmann. World War II, however, took him back to England in 1939 and to the renewal of his career at Oxford, which was his real spiritual home, first in a chemical research group, then by invitation in 1945 to join Professor J. H. Burn at the department of pharmacology where he stayed until the end of his working days (1966).

Ing's early postgraduate essays in organic chemistry were set in the classical mode on the determination of the molecular structure of substances from natural sources, which was then still in its earliest days. With the aid of modern spectrometry many of these problems could often have been solved in as many days as it took years in Perkin's time. Nevertheless, in Ing's time, they required considerable ingenuity and experimental skill. The methods were essentially degradative but were increasingly being complemented by new methods of synthesis, including substitution into aromatic molecules. Ing moved on to the latter with Robinson who had recently developed a concept in which the position of entry of new substituents into benzene derivatives, for example, was governed by the particular distribution of the electronic charges in the conjugated ring system. Ing was also helping to break new ground in his next task in Manchester working with a medical collaborator for the first time, on mule-spinners' cancer. They were able to show which fractions of the petroleum oils used in the cotton industry were the more carcinogenic (in mice) and to relate this for the first time to the degree of unsaturation or aromaticity in the hydrocarbon chains.

The years at Oxford saw Ing applying these early ideas to more general concepts of biological activity, and in so doing helping to pioneer the conversion of the growing band of university pharmacologists in the country towards a philosophy of their own, away from that of a 'physiologist in disguise'. For example, the researches led by the physiologist Sir Henry H. Dale [q.v.] had recently revealed much of the properties and structures of neurohumoral and neuromuscular transmitter compounds such as acetylcholine and the catecholamines, but the notion of specific affinity for effector cells, i.e. the existence of receptors, had not yet generally been conceded. Ing, however, accepted their possible existence albeit with caution, and amongst other things developed the notion of molecules closely related to the agonists which by preferential attachment at receptor sites could exhibit antagonist properties. Indeed, most of his experimental work and theoretical writing over the years that followed were devoted to the elaboration and rationalization of structure-action relationships particularly in terms of physical and chemical properties. In doing so, he laid the foundation of many of the principles that are practised in modern drug discovery.

The importance of his work was recognized in 1951 by his election to the Royal Society, but throughout he remained a modest and lovable person. His main dislike was abuse of the English language, something he shared with his wife. In 1941 he married Catherine Mills Francis (died 1983), daughter of Bertie Mills, professional musician, and Sarah Francis. She taught English literature at Lady Margaret Hall and St. Hilda's College, Oxford. They had no children. Ing died 23 September 1974 at Oxford.

[H. O. Schild and F. L. Rose in *Biographical Memoirs of Fellows of the Royal Society*, vol. xxii, 1976; personal knowledge.] FRANK L. ROSE

INGLIS, SIR CLAUDE CAVENDISH (1883–1974), civil engineer in the field of irrigation and hydraulic research, was born in Dublin 3 March 1883, the sixth and youngest son (there was subsequently a daughter) of Sir Malcolm John Inglis, JP, deputy lieutenant of the county of Dublin, and his wife, Caroline Johnston. He was educated at St. Helen's School, Dublin, Shrewsbury School, England, and at Trinity College, Dublin, under Professor John Joly [q.v.]. He obtained his BA and BAI (Bachelor of Engineering, 1905).

He was appointed to the India Service of Engineers in 1906 and served first in Sind. In 1911 he was promoted to the Bombay Deccan as executive engineer, Godaveri canals, to introduce northern Indian methods of irrigation. In 1913 Inglis moved to Poona irrigation district in charge of the Nira canals, where he carried out research into waterlogging at an experimental station at Baramati. His success in drainage later involved him in a survey of half a million acres in the Bombay Deccan to improve conditions. Against opposition from farmers, he persuaded the government to control the type of irrigated crops most suitable for the nature of the soils and also demonstrated the benefits of using sewage mixed with canal water. In 1928 Inglis advised on the large Sukkur barrage in Sind and on five major points the design was changed on his recommendations.

Hydraulic research was then transferred to Khadakwasla downstream of a dam near Poona where clear water and climatic conditions enabled large models to be used in the open. This Poona station was probably the first to use mobile beds, and after much lobbying by Inglis on behalf of Bombay, it was selected in 1937 as the central station for the whole of India with Inglis as its first director. Basic studies were carried out in river meanders, scour, and sediment control as well as special investigations on barrages, bank protection, river training, and canal intakes. Inglis was in charge for eight years, playing a major part in all the work of the station until his retirement in 1945. He was succeeded by D. V. Joglekar, who had served with him for twenty-one years.

As an independent consulting engineer in England, Inglis continued to advise on river problems in India, Burma, and Persia. In 1947 he was back in harness as director of research for the UK Hydraulic Research Board formed by the government to solve the urgent problems of river training, harbours, and coastal erosion. Inglis had to fight hard for a site for hydraulic research near to London. By 1955, when the first stage of construction had been completed at Wallingford in Berkshire, British hydraulic engineers were able greatly to benefit from the results of the model work on many schemes at home and overseas.

In the words later of his successor as director, Fergus Allen, Inglis 'with a judicious blend of pugnacity and charm' ensured that the establishment would be of sufficient size, sophistication, and international standing. He retired in March 1958, aged seventy-five, but continued, despite failing eyesight, to work as a consultant with a lively interest in new developments.

Inglis was appointed CIE in 1936, knighted in 1945, elected FRS in 1953, and awarded the James Alfred Ewing gold medal by the Institution of Civil Engineers in 1958. He became honorary MAI in 1952.

His main contributions to engineering were in irrigation canals and river training. He pioneered the use of large models with mobile sand beds, but his recommendations in river training depended more on his personal judgement than the model results. In the words of his great friend, Gerald Lacey, 'We might almost say that he studied river psychology . . . He asked himself the question "What would I do if I were the river?" and almost invariably got the answer right.'

Inglis enjoyed music, playing the cello and piano, and was a keen golfer. He married in 1912 Vera Margaret St. John (died 1972), daughter of John Redmond Blood, JP, of Malahide, county Dublin, brewer, company director, and commissioner for Irish Lights. She had a subtle sense of humour and at times exerted a good modifying influence on her husband. They had one son, Brian St. John Inglis, writer and broadcaster. Inglis died, shortly after a second operation for cataract, 29 August 1974, at Henfield, Sussex.

[A. Rylands Thomas and Sir Angus Paton in *Biographical Memoirs of Fellows of the Royal Society*, vol. xxi, 1975.] ANGUS PATON

INNES OF LEARNEY, SIR THOMAS (1893–1971), Lord Lyon King of Arms, was born in Aberdeen 26 August 1893, the only son and elder child of Lieutenant-Colonel Francis Newell Innes of Learney, Royal Horse Artillery, and his wife, Margaret Anne, daughter of Archer Irvine-Fortescue, twelfth of Kingcausie, Kincardineshire. His ancient family descended through the Innes baronets of Innermarkie from Berowald the Fleming, granted the barony of Innes in 1160. He himself held the old territorial baronies of Learney, Kinnairdy, and Yeochrie, was superior of the town of Torphins, and restored Kinnairdy castle, home of his ancestors, the thanes of Aberchirder.

Educated at Edinburgh Academy and University, in 1922 he 'passed advocate' to the Scots bar, where he practised for many years. His main interests were heraldic, and in 1926 he became

Carrick Pursuivant, soon establishing himself as a leading heraldic and peerage counsel. His principal case was perhaps Maclean of Ardgour, where he acted successfully for the heiress, who held the principal inheritance, against her cousin the heir male. This stimulated his later preference for the descent of both name and arms to immediate heirs female rather than remoter heirs male; though some heraldists felt that constant female line changes of name when the male line still existed were not to be encouraged when no 'principal inheritance' except the arms was involved.

His authoritative work, *Scots Heraldry* (1934), with its later revised edition (1956), as also his books on clans and tartans, played an important part in the remarkable development of public interest in heraldry, genealogy, and clans that gathered momentum under his leadership. More new coats of arms were recorded in Lyon Register during his time than during the whole previous three centuries put together.

He learnt the practical administration of Lyon Office and Court as interim Lyon Clerk in 1929 and again in 1939–40. Promoted Albany Herald in 1935, ten years later he became Lord Lyon King of Arms, being appointed KCVO in 1946. He was also secretary to the Order of the Thistle from 1945 to 1969 and was FSA (Scotland).

As Lord Lyon, he felt himself custodian of the spirit of Caledonia allegorically embodied in the sovereign. He stage-managed the renewal of historic Scottish pageantry under Queen Elizabeth II, who paid more official visits to Scotland than any other sovereign since 1603. His most important tasks were the ceremonial for the St. Giles service after the coronation, at which the honours of Scotland appeared for only the second time since the union; the state visits of the Kings of Norway and Sweden (the first ever by foreign sovereigns); the opening of the General Assembly twice by the Queen in person (she was the first sovereign since James VI to do this); and the Silver Jubilee. In 1967 the Queen recognized his wise guidance by promoting him GCVO, an honour not bestowed on other modern Kings of Arms.

Learney distinguished carefully between his office as Lord Lyon, the judge, and his ministerial capacity as King of Arms. He had a natural modesty and sought no reward beyond his meagre official salary. His erudition and panoptical view of Scottish genealogical history enabled him to lay down a body of heraldic law by a series of considered judgements, though he sometimes tended to carry law to a logical conclusion that startled narrower historical specialists and occasionally misused Gaelic expressions. Lyon sought to unite in goodwill Scotsmen world-wide and above all to maintain the extended family or clan. The Standing Council of Scottish Chiefs was founded at his suggestion; he controlled claimants to chiefship, whose only unimpeachable right at law is to the undifferenced arms of their name; and he encouraged clan societies since the clan spirit cuts across social barriers, removing snobbery from heraldry and allowing all to share the traditions of their name.

Perhaps the last laird to speak naturally in the aristocratic but homely Doric, Sir 'Tam' combined common sense with humour, was completely without pretension, and utterly unselfconscious: in his bar days it is said he even appeared in wig and gown over tartan bicycling-breeches, and once secured the acquittal of an accused criminal by assuring the jury: 'My client must be innocent. He tells me so himself.' He was probably the greatest Lyon since the seventeenth century. He was also a member of, and held office in, many Scottish learned societies.

Learney retired in 1969, becoming Marchmont Herald, and died at Edinburgh 16 October 1971. A Knight of St. John of Jerusalem and Archer of the Queen's Body Guard for Scotland, he was honorary LL D of St. Andrews (1956). He was married in 1928 to Lady Lucy Buchan, daughter of Norman Macleod, eighteenth Earl of Caithness; they had three sons and a daughter. In 1981 the youngest son, Malcolm Innes of Edingight, also became the Lord Lyon.

[Personal knowledge.]

IAIN MONCREIFFE OF THAT ILK

ISAACS, GEORGE ALFRED (1883–1979), Labour politician, was born 28 May 1883 in Finsbury, London, the eldest of the nine children of Alfred Isaacs, a printer, and his wife, Flora Beasley. He was educated at the Wesleyan Elementary School at Hoxton, London. He then entered the printing trade as a reader's boy, becoming a machine room assistant. He unsuccessfully contested the North Southwark constituency in 1918 and Gravesend in 1922. He was mayor of Southwark from 1919 to 1921. He first entered Parliament as Labour member for Gravesend in 1923–4 and sat for North Southwark in 1929–31 and from 1939 to 1950.

From 1950 to his retirement in 1959 he represented the Southwark division. His parliamentary apprenticeship included periods as parliamentary private secretary to the secretaries of state for the colonies (1924), the dominions (1929–31), and to the first lord of the Admiralty (1942–5).

The duplication of a parliamentary career with that of a trade union official was quite common in those days and Isaacs, whose family had for three generations been connected with the printing industry, became in 1909 general secretary of the National Society of Operative Printers and Assistants, a position he retained for some forty years. When challenged to explain the many restrictive practices in the industry, he would explain that they were forced upon him by the 'press barons' who were determined to keep less wealthy competitors out of contention.

Isaacs published *The Story of the Newspaper Printing Press* (1931). In 1945 Isaacs became chairman of the Trades Union Congress General Council, and during his year of office was appointed minister of labour and national service by C. R. (later Earl) Attlee. Because of this appointment he was unable to preside at that year's Trades Union Congress, and afterwards lamented the fact that he was never presented with the bell which is customarily given to the Congress chairman.

He presided at the world conference of trade unions which took place in London in 1945. He became minister of labour and national service as the ministry's vital wartime activities under Ernest Bevin [q.v.] were coming to an end. During the war with Germany, the ministry had posted some three million men to the forces, directed nearly one million men to the Home Guard, and a quarter of a million to part-time Civil Defence. On the industrial front it became necessary for the department to put into operation long-term plans for the use of the whole of the nation's labour force.

Isaac's part, for which he has not been given sufficient credit, in unwinding this huge operation, with hardly a pocket of unemployment showing in any part of the country, and with every effort being made to place men and women in the type of work which would be of most benefit to themselves and the nation, was quite outstanding. There was some understandable impatience at the delay to which some of the men and women who had been away from their homes for long periods were subjected but to have dumped huge numbers on to a labour market which was unable to absorb them would have produced industrial chaos. Demobilization of the forces commenced in June 1945. Releases were based either on age and length of service or on special qualifications for urgent work of national importance. By the end of 1947 nearly five million men and women had been released and absorbed into industry. Isaacs gradually relaxed such wartime orders as the essential work orders, the control of engagement order, and the registration for employment order. Priorities in the supply of labour through employment exchanges were adjusted to the new situation and changes were made in the conditions for receiving financial assistance on transfer to work away from home as a means of inducing workers to remain in, or transfer to, work of national importance. He also widened the facilities for industrial training for skilled occupations.

In his appreciation of the future role of his ministry in the greatly changed industrial conditions into which the nation had moved, Isaacs was on less firm ground. His objective was to recreate the ministry of pre-war days with the administration of the Conciliation Act of 1896 and the Industrial Courts Act of 1919 as the centre of its activities, and with the minimum of government intervention in the processes of collective bargaining. The settlement of wages and conditions of employment must be left to the joint negotiating machinery established by agreement between employers and workers' organizations, and only when requested for assistance by the parties to an industrial dispute would the ministry render assistance of the type laid down in the two main Acts. The leisurely application of this policy was in marked contrast to the activities of other government departments.

The Board of Trade under Harold Wilson (later Lord Wilson of Rievaulx) was creating a network of regional boards on which both sides of industry were represented along with government representatives, in an effort to plan industrial development, and Sir R. Stafford Cripps [q.v.] as chancellor of the exchequer was holding regular discussions with the TUC with a view to gaining their agreement to a form of incomes policy. As the pattern of active government participation through these departments became stronger, the position of the Ministry of Labour as the appropriate ministry on industrial matters declined. Distribution of industry policy, which played an ever-increasing role in job creation, was under the control of the Board of Trade and Isaacs's non-intervention principles resulted in his ministry becoming irrelevant to the main industrial strategy of the government. The subjects discussed at the national joint advisory council, which consisted of the leading organizations of employers and trade unions and was chaired by the minister of labour, became of rather secondary importance as the vital matters under the control of the Treasury and the Board of Trade conditioned both sides of industry in their negotiations with government.

In January 1951 George Isaacs left the Ministry of Labour and became minister of pensions, a position in which he was able to exercise to the full his warm and sympathetic nature. He remained there until in October 1951 the Attlee government fell. Isaacs stayed in the Commons, where he was a popular figure with members in all parts of the House, until the general election of 1959, when he retired from public life. In 1905 Isaacs married Flora, daughter of Richard Beasley, of Whipps Cross, Essex. They had one daughter, and also adopted a nephew whose parents had died. Isaacs died in a nursing home in Surrey 26 April 1979.

[*The Times*, 19 November 1979.]

LEE OF NEWTON

ISAACS, STELLA, MARCHIONESS OF READING and BARONESS SWANBOROUGH (1894–1971), chairman and founder, Women's Royal Voluntary Service, originally known as the Women's Voluntary Service for Civil Defence (WVS), was born in Constantinople 6 January 1894. Her father, Charles Charnaud, was of Huguenot descent, and was director of the tobacco monopoly of the Ottoman Empire. In 1893 Charnaud married as his second wife Milbah Johnson, daughter of a Lincolnshire family, and Stella was their eldest child and Charnaud's third daughter. Due to a spinal ailment in her youth she never went to school but read and studied at the family home at Moda on the Asian side of the Bosphorus. By 1914 Stella Charnaud, whose health was still regarded as delicate, was in London training as a secretary and it was in that capacity that she went to India in 1925 to assist Lady Reading, the wife of the viceroy, Rufus Isaacs, Earl (later Marquess) of Reading [q.v.]. Later she worked as private secretary to the Marquess of Reading, both at the headquarters of Imperial Chemical Industries of which he was president, and at his London home in Curzon Street. In 1930 his wife died and the following year Reading married Stella Charnaud on whom he had come increasingly to depend. They had no children.

For most young women the transition from private secretary to marchioness, wife of the foreign secretary (August–October 1931), and former viceroy, as well as marriage to a man nearly twice her age, would have been formidable. Yet Stella adapted quickly and easily, her natural dignity and authority, combined with her support of her husband, earning her widespread acceptance in her new role.

During the remaining years of Reading's life his wife devoted herself almost exclusively to him, although in 1932 she took on the chairmanship of the Personal Service League, a voluntary society concerned with the welfare of the needy. After a period of shock and disorientation following her husband's death in 1935 she stood out as a considerable figure in her own right: forceful, practical, and determined, finding various outlets for her abundant energy and idealism. In 1938 the Dowager Marchioness of Reading was sent for by the home secretary, Sir Samuel Hoare (later Viscount Templewood, q.v.), and invited to form a service of women, to be attached to local authorities throughout the country and giving their services on a voluntary basis, in order to prepare for the dislocation that would inevitably be caused to the civil population if war was to come. The plan was far-sighted, ambitious, and timely. The detailed structure was proposed by Stella Reading herself. Not for the first or the last time in her career, once her interest had been aroused and she had concluded there was a need, she lost no time in setting about finding ways of meeting it. Thus she was much more than simply the head of what was to become one of the largest and most remarkable of all voluntary organizations, mobilizing the resources of over a million women by 1942, but was genuinely its founder and continuing inspiration.

Lady Reading served as the unchallenged leader of the WVS throughout World War II and after. It became her life's work. From the start it was a service organized on original lines. Its founder had seen enough of well-intended charitable and philanthropic ventures to have developed a strong dislike of committees, bureaucracy, and fund-raising. The WVS had a minimum of committees, titles, and ranks, and efforts were made to enrol women from the widest possible social base. It was a uniformed service, directly funded by government and local authorities, and one that soon became established as a vital and highly valued part of the war effort. Conformity was never encouraged. Lady Reading retained absolute power and authority in her own hands, yet she was convinced that the strength of voluntary service lay in the character of each volunteer. She saw to it that individual initiative counted for more than regimentation, even in the matter of the strikingly different angles at which WVS hats were worn. Churchill was disapproving, but Stella Reading was unrepentant.

The wartime work of the WVS, particularly notable in the evacuation of many thousands of children from London and other cities, the caring for refugees and the victims of enemy bombing, and the provision of a wide variety of welfare services for the armed forces, as well as in a multitude of other useful ways, largely ended in 1945. By then the WVS was a national institution and Lady Reading met a heartening response when she called on her members to keep it in being. The needs of the British people in the immediate post-war era of shortages of food, fuel, and housing were different. But the opportunity the WVS afforded women to render practical service to the communities of which they were a part remained unchanged.

Although the WRVS (the accolade 'Royal' was bestowed in 1966) was at the centre of her life, Lady Reading had many other interests. For over thirty years, from 1936 to 1968, she was vice-chairman of the Imperial Relations Trust and from 1946 to 1951 she served as a governor of the BBC and was its vice-chairman from 1947 to 1951. Later she demonstrated once again her ability to keep up with the changing social problems of the day by seeking to improve the condition of Commonwealth immigrants to Britain and also of ex-prisoners. For the Home Office she chaired the advisory council on Commonwealth immigration and a working party on the place of voluntary service in after-care of prisoners. She was appointed DBE in 1941 and GBE in 1944. As Baroness Swanborough she was the first woman life peer to take her seat in the House of Lords in 1958. The universities of Reading (1947) and Leeds (1969) conferred honorary doctorates upon her, as did Yale (1958) and Smith College (1956) in the United States and Manitoba University in Canada (1960).

In character and appearance Stella Reading was a large woman with a deep voice and an evidently powerful personality. Although she never occupied herself with party politics she maintained an extensive network of political and official contacts which she used resolutely to achieve her objects. While she could be fierce and demanding at times her charm and innate sense of modesty, as well as the laudable purposes of the causes which she championed, made her universally respected, and often loved. Throughout her long public career she was capable of acts of great personal kindness and consideration, while her qualities of leadership were underpinned by a consistent generosity of mind and sense of forward vision. She died, active to the last as chairman of the WRVS, at her London home 22 May 1971. A service commemorating her life and work was held at Westminster Abbey. A portrait by Sir James Gunn hangs in the headquarters of the WRVS in London.

[*The Times*, 24 May 1971; *Stella Reading: Some Recollections by her Friends*, 1979; private information.] WINDLESHAM

IVELAW-CHAPMAN, SIR RONALD (1899–1978), air chief marshal, was born in Georgetown, British Guiana, 17 January 1899, the youngest of three children and only son of Joseph Ivelaw-Chapman, a successful merchant, and his wife, Shirley Farley. In the early 1900s the family returned to England and set up house in Cheltenham and St. Ives, Cornwall. His education at Cheltenham College, for which he had a lifelong affection, did much to mould his character and set the standards which distinguished his life. He volunteered for active service in the war at the age of eighteen and the challenge of the air and a mechanical bent made the Royal Flying Corps his choice. He was commissioned as a pilot in September 1917.

He served in France in No. 10 Squadron engaged on artillery observation, was awarded the DFC (1918) and appointed flight commander with the rank of captain. By the armistice he had acquired a reputation as a competent pilot and a responsible clear-thinking young officer. After the war he received a permanent commission in the Royal Air Force and immediately sought further service overseas. In 1920 he was posted to No. 60 Squadron in India where he took part in operations on the North-West Frontier and other early activities of the air force in India including the first Indian air mail service. Home from India in 1922 with an enhanced reputation for intelligence and skill as a pilot he was posted to the RAF experimental establishment at Marlesham Heath where he flew and tested some seventy-eight different types of aircraft. There followed a tour with No. 99 Squadron after which he went abroad again to No. 70 Squadron in Iraq where he was continuously engaged on air support operations. In December 1928 he went to India with a flight of Vickers Victoria aircraft of his squadron to take part in the Kabul evacuation, the first major airlift in history. For his part in this difficult and hazardous operation, which included a remarkable forced landing in the mountains, he was awarded the AFC (1930).

Various staff and squadron postings followed and at the start of the World War II he was station commander at Linton upon Ouse with the rank of group captain. From 1941 to 1943 he served on the policy and planning staff at the Air Ministry working on the planning of the bomber offensive and the invasion of Europe. It was his knowledge of certain aspects of these plans that caused alarm in high places when he was shot down over France during his tour in 1944 as a Bomber Command base commander at Elsham Wolds. He was not a man to command such a unit without flying on at least one mission and he set out on an operation flight as an extra crew member in a Lancaster. The aircraft was hit and he parachuted into occupied France, a situation which led (Sir) Winston Churchill to issue personal orders for his immediate recovery. He was later captured but the secrets remained safe because of his intellectual agility under interrogation. He became a prisoner of war and was liberated by advancing American forces in 1945.

In 1945–6, having been promoted air vice-marshal, he commanded No. 38 Group at Upavon. He held posts at the Air Ministry and on the directing staff of the Imperial Defence College between 1947 and 1949. He then returned to India as C-in-C of the Indian Air Force on loan to the government of India where he was considered the driving force behind the Indian Air Force as an effective organization. During this appointment he formed a close friendship with Jawaharlal Nehru [q.v.], although the two men often disagreed on matters of policy. In 1952 he was appointed air officer commanding-in-chief, Home Command. He returned to the Air Ministry again in 1952 as deputy chief of the air staff and in 1953 became vice chief of the air staff and a member of the Air Council, and air chief marshal.

After his retirement he had many active interests. He was president of the Cheltonian Society and on the council of the College for many years.

He was a trustee of the *Observer*. He was chairman of the RAF Escaping Society, devoting much time to raising funds for the support of the organization which risked so much to rescue him and others, and he was concerned with the RAF Association and the Overseas League. He was a pillar of strength to the village of Nether Wallop and its church. He was co-author with Anne Baker of *Wings over Kabul*, 1976.

Ivelaw-Chapman was a kind, Christian man devoted to his Service and invariably loyal to his commanders, his juniors, and his friends. It was totally in character that he should appear at the Nuremberg war crimes trial to speak in defence of his German camp commandant. He was an excellent pilot and a remarkably clear-headed planner, with a high reputation both in and outside the Royal Air Force.

Ivelaw-Chapman was appointed CBE (1943), CB (1949), KBE (1951), KCB (1953), and GCB in 1957, the year in which he retired.

In 1930 he married (Grace Elizabeth) Margaret, daughter of Charles William Shortt, fellow of the Chartered Institute of Secretaries, of Beckenham; they had a daughter and a son. Ivelaw-Chapman died at his home in Nether Wallop 28 April 1978.

[Private information; personal knowledge.]

WILLIAM DICKSON

J

JACKSON-COLE, CECIL (1901–1979), business man and charity founder, was born 1 November 1901 at 27 Knox Road, Forest Gate, London, the elder child and only son (there was another son by a subsequent marriage) of Albert Edward Cole, a dealer in new and second-hand furniture, and his wife (who was also his cousin), Nellie Catherine Jackson. Baptized Albert Cecil Cole he changed his name by deed poll on 11 December 1927 to Cecil Jackson-Cole, in memory of his mother who died that year. His boyhood, which was difficult, was spent primarily at 44 Whitehall Road, Grays Thurrock, Essex, but as his father moved house fairly frequently he lived also at various times in Barking, Walthamstow, Stratford, Walworth, Deptford, and Holborn. His father died in 1934.

Jackson-Cole attended several council schools, averaging only nine months in any one. He started full-time work at the age of thirteen, as an office boy at the Tooley Street branch of George & John Nickson, importers and general provision merchants. He left Nicksons in 1919 to become owner and manager of Andrews Furnishers, Highbury Corner, Islington. Andrews later had branches in Hammersmith, The Angel, and Oxford. In 1928 he enrolled as an external student for one year at Balliol College, Oxford, studying economics under G. D. H. Cole [q.v.]. In 1930 a kidney complaint kept him bedridden for almost three years. Later in life he was to suffer from indigestion.

Jackson-Cole first became involved in charitable work through the Soldiers and Sailors Home, Watford. A pacifist, he was attracted towards the Quakers who had the same beliefs. In May 1942 a group of concerned Oxford Quakers gathered in their meeting house in Oxford to consider how to further opposition to the blockade of Greece, where thousands were dying of starvation. Encouraged by Jackson-Cole and Canon Richard Milford, a broadly based public meeting was convened in Oxford the following October. It included not only the Quakers, but also representatives from the other main churches, the university, and local business men. The Oxford Committee for Famine Relief (subsequently Oxfam) was formed with Jackson-Cole as first honorary secretary. He became the business brain and dynamic driving force behind this relief and development agency. In 1948 arose the question of whether Oxfam should terminate its activities because Europe was felt to be on the road to recovery. The committee decided unanimously against this and Jackson-Cole spearheaded the growth and expansion of the charity. For five years he virtually ran it himself. As a member of Oxfam's council of management he retained his interest and involvement until 1979, serving as secretary emeritus in later years. His vision led to the setting up of autonomous Oxfams in Canada, Quebec, the USA, and Belgium.

In 1945 Jackson-Cole created a business, Andrews & Partners, the staff for which were recruited from young men and women of Christian conviction or public-spirited ideals. His philosophy was that business men and women were essential to the development of charities. He was willing that some of his senior staffs' time should be given to charitable works. By this means he set up a number of charitable trusts and charities, the first of which was the Phyllis Trust, named after his first wife. Its objectives were broadly to give practical expression to the Christian injunctions. There followed the Voluntary and Christian Service Trust and the Christian Initiative Trust. To all these trusts he gifted some of the equity shares of his businesses. VCS set up Help the Aged in 1961 and Help the Aged established the Help the Aged Housing Association in 1968. This later became independent as the Anchor Housing Association. VCS likewise set up Action in Distress in 1973, later known as Action Aid.

A successful entrepreneur, Jackson-Cole aimed to introduce business methods to fund raising and charitable work and in this he was immensely successful. He believed, too, in seeking out new constituencies for charitable giving and increasingly saw charitable work on a global scale—both for giving and spending. He was a man of great integrity, believing passionately in doing good for its own sake. This allowed him space to work anonymously and with relative peace of mind. He refused the civic and national honours he was offered. His creative energy was paralleled by unpredictability, quick temper, and a single-mindedness of purpose, buttressed by an almost childlike enthusiasm for the cause in hand. He was endowed with vitality and energy. He woke mid-morning but would work through to the small hours, often seven days a week. He valued friends greatly and had little time for hobbies and recreations, other than walking. Although he was brought up an Anglican, he was ecumenical in outlook. A strong believer in divine healing, he was also convinced he had contact after their death with both his mother and first wife. It was his religious motivation which gave rise to his world-wide concern for the plight of the poor and under-privileged, both at home and overseas.

In 1937 Jackson-Cole married his cousin Phyllis Emily (died 1956), daughter of Sidney and Florence Cole. He married secondly in 1973

Mary Theodora ('Theo') Handley, a teacher and college lecturer and a lifelong friend, daughter of the Revd Thomas Handley of Keighley, Yorkshire. There were no children of either marriage. Jackson-Cole died 9 August 1979 at Burrswood, Groombridge, near Tunbridge Wells.

[Linette Martin, *Cecil Jackson-Cole*, 1983; private information; personal knowledge.]

BRIAN W. WALKER

JAMES, SIDNEY (died 1976), comedian. Sidney James, as he was known professionally though this may not have been his original name, was born in South Africa, probably in Johannesburg, the son of Jewish music hall artistes. He was born on 6 or 8 May; the year of birth is variously reported as 1913 or 1915. On his death certificate the date of birth is given as 6 May 1913. He made his first stage appearance at the age of ten, as part of the family soft-shoe dancing act. As a young man, however, his inclination was towards more adventurous pursuits, and he earned a living variously as stevedore, coal heaver, diamond digger and polisher, professional ballroom dancer, and skating instructor. His love of sports led him to the boxing ring, where he acquired that somewhat battered appearance which was to serve him so well when later he was to choose comedy acting as his career.

At the outbreak of World War II he joined the Witwatersrand Rifles, served in an entertainments unit, and rose to the rank of lieutenant in an anti-tank regiment which saw action in the Middle East. With peace came a renewed interest in the theatre, and after a spell with the Gwen Ffrangcon-Davies Company in South Africa, he invested his army gratuity in a ticket to England, and arrived in London, more or less penniless, on Christmas Day, 1946.

It took him very little time to establish himself as a useful small part actor, much in demand for his portrayal of slightly sinister cockneys, and, with his authentic-sounding American accent, in parts which culminated, in 1951, in a memorable performance as one of the two inept gangsters who sang 'Brush Up Your Shakespeare' in Cole Porter's *Kiss Me Kate*. In particular, the still-burgeoning British film industry made good and frequent use of his services. In 1947 he appeared in *It Always Rains on Sunday* and in 1951, in a more prominent role, in Ealing Studios' justly celebrated film, *The Lavender Hill Mob*.

By 1952, with *The Titfield Thunderbolt*, again for Ealing Studios, Sid James's work had begun to veer more and more towards comedy, and this trend was triumphantly confirmed when, in 1954, he joined the cast of the BBC radio show, 'Hancock's Half-Hour'. Cast in the role of friend and accomplice, his down-to-earth realism was always in conflict with the boundless optimism of Tony Hancock [q.v.], his wry commentary deflating the latter's grandiose schemes for social advancement, all of which inevitably ended in disaster. It was a perfect partnership, and it provided some of the finest moments in British comedy. The shows, both on radio and television, were enormously successful; the radio version ran from 1954 to 1959, over a hundred episodes; the television show (1956–61) for more than sixty.

Throughout the Hancock period James had continued to appear in films: in 1955 *Joe Macbeth*, *The Deep Blue Sea*, and *A Kid for Two Farthings*; in 1956 *Trapeze*. And in 1960 he was to appear in *Carry on Constable*, his first in what was to be an almost endless series of 'Carry On' films (by 1974 he had appeared in eighteen), in which his portrayal of such outlandish characters as the Rumpo Kid, Sir Sidney Ruff-Diamond, Bill Boosey, and Gladstone Screwer, were to earn him the reputation of possessing 'the dirtiest laugh in show business'.

His TV work continued, but now, since the dissolution of the Hancock partnership, as a star in his own right; first, in a BBC series, *Taxi*; then, moving over to ITV, in *East End, West End*; and in 1966 in *George and the Dragon*, in which he co-starred with Peggy Mount. Nor did he desert the theatre. In 1965 he appeared opposite (Dame) Margaret Rutherford [q.v.] in the London production of *The Solid Gold Cadillac*.

He was indeed a compulsive worker, and in 1967 he suffered a heart attack, which, while slowing him down a bit, seemed scarcely to worry him. He continued to work as hard as ever. The 'Carry On' films appeared biannually, and he achieved his most enduring success in television as the harassed paterfamilias in *Bless This House*, a series which ran from 1971 until 1975.

In 1973, and again in 1975, he toured Australia and New Zealand in a stage farce called *The Mating Game*. In 1974 he was at the Victoria Palace in London in a stage version of his popular films, called *Carry on London*. In 1976 he toured Britain in *The Mating Game*, and it was on 26 April, opening night at the Empire Theatre in Sunderland, that he collapsed on the stage and was rushed to hospital, where he died.

Sid James was twice married; first to the dancer Meg Williams, by whom he had a daughter; and secondly to the actress Valerie Ashton, by whom he had a son and a daughter.

[*The Times*, 28 April 1976; Thames Television records; personal knowledge.] SID COLIN

JAMES, SIR WILLIAM MILBOURNE (1881–1973), admiral and naval writer, was born 22 December 1881 near Farnborough, the younger son and second of the four children of Major William Christopher James, Scots Greys, and his wife, Effie, daughter of the painter Sir John

Everett Millais [q.v.], of Kensington. W. C. James was the only son of Lord Justice Sir William Milbourne James [q.v.]. The most notable portrait of William James was done when he was four, sitting for his maternal grandfather; Millais' painting found its way, via the *Illustrated London News*, to Pears Soap, which used it as its famous 'Bubbles' advertisement. This nickname remained with James for life.

After Trinity College, Glenalmond, he entered the *Britannia* naval college at Dartmouth in 1895. His progress in the service was smooth and by 1913 he was a commander and the executive officer of the new battle cruiser *Queen Mary*, whose captain was the formidable (Sir) W. R. ('Blinker') Hall [q.v.]. Although best known for their work at naval intelligence, the years of these two officers aboard the *Queen Mary* were also a most creative period, preparing the crew for war and making the vessel the first in the Royal Navy to possess a chapel, cinematograph, bookstall, and laundry. In March 1916 James became flag commander to Vice-Admiral (Sir) F. C. D. Sturdee [q.v.] on the *Benbow*, thereby missing the fate of the *Queen Mary*'s crew at Jutland two months later. By the following year he had been promoted captain and appointed to the Naval Intelligence Division, at the request of Hall, who was by then its director. Despite his preference for a post afloat, James clearly enjoyed his work at the NID, whose vital cryptographic service he later described in his book *The Eyes of the Navy: A Biographical Study of Sir R. Hall* (1955). It was during the war that James began his writings, pseudonymously, as a naval poet.

James's career in the inter-war years confirmed his early potential as a staff officer. After a tour on the China station he was appointed deputy director of the Royal Naval Staff College at Greenwich in 1923 and its director in 1925. During that period he expanded his staff lectures upon the naval side of the war of American independence into the book *The British Navy in Adversity* (1926), which was for many years the standard work. Another brief spell abroad, in the Mediterranean, was followed in 1928 by his appointment as naval assistant to the first sea lord and his promotion to rear-admiral. In late 1928 he was chief of staff to the Atlantic Fleet and, from 1930, to the Mediterranean Fleet, both under A. E. M. (later Lord) Chatfield [q.v.].

In 1932 the plum job of commander of the battle cruiser squadron came James's way, and he was promoted vice-admiral in 1933. From 1935 to 1938 he was deputy chief of naval staff and centrally involved in Admiralty policy during the critical 'appeasement' years, being made a full admiral in 1938. After a brief rest, he occupied the important post of commander-in-chief, Portsmouth, between 1939 and 1942, being made a freeman of that city upon his retirement. Appropriately enough, he succeeded (Sir) Roger (later Lord) Keyes [q.v.] as MP (Unionist) for Portsmouth North in 1943, which he combined with his new post as chief of naval information.

James was not a natural Commons man, although showing interest in educational as well as naval issues there, and he willingly retired before the 1945 election. He was now, moreover, devoting much more time to talks and writing. *Blue Water and Green Fields*, pieces on World War I, was published in 1939, and a biography *Admiral Sir William Fisher* in 1943. His job as chief of naval information involved constant writing, part of which formed the basis for *The British Navies in the Second World War*, published in 1946—the same year as *The Portsmouth Letters*. Biographies of Nelson (1948), St. Vincent (1950), and Admiral Sir Henry Oliver (1956) were published in later years, as was a study of the unhappy relationship between John Ruskin [q.v.] and James's maternal grandmother, Effie Gray. His two most important books in these years were his autobiography, *The Sky Was Always Blue* (1951), and his book upon Hall. He contributed several notices to this Dictionary. Appointed Lees-Knowles lecturer at Cambridge (1947) and naval editor of Chambers Encyclopedia, the ever-lively James was a source of much information to younger naval historians, as well as being active in youth education and rural matters.

James was appointed CB (1919), KCB (1936), and GCB (1944). In 1915 he married Dorothy ('Robin') (died 1971), the youngest daughter of (Admiral Sir) Alexander Duff [q.v.]; they had one son and one daughter, who died when she was nineteen. James's son predeceased him. He himself died 17 August 1973 at Hindhead, Surrey.

[*The Times*, 20 August 1973; William James, *The Sky Was Always Blue* (autobiography), 1951; private information.] PAUL KENNEDY

JAMES, WILLIAM OWEN (1900–1978), plant physiologist, was born 21 May 1900 at Tottenham, London N17, the elder son (there were no daughters) of William Benjamin James, primary school headmaster, of Tottenham, and his wife Agnes Ursula Collins. He was at Tottenham Grammar School from 1910 until 1916, when he joined the flourishing family firm of accountants in Birmingham. He did not enjoy the work and the first of a series of tubercular attacks forced him to leave in 1918. In 1919 he was able to attend courses in botany at University College, Reading, and the lectures of Professor Walter Stiles [q.v.] gave him a special interest in plant physiology. In 1923 he gained first class honours in the London external B.Sc. examination and secured a training grant for research in Cambridge under Dr. F. F. Blackman [q.v.]. He took his Cambridge Ph.D. in 1927, the publication of his results in 1928 revealing his high quality as a research worker. Meanwhile he had joined the research team of V. H. Blackman [q.v.] at the Imperial College of Science, working largely at Rothamsted where the team had field-plots.

In 1927 James accepted an invitation from (Sir) A. G. Tansley [q.v.], newly appointed professor of botany at Oxford, to join his small staff as a demonstrator. The department's buildings, close to Magdalen bridge, were quite inadequate for teaching and research in experimental botany, and funds were scanty. James acted with characteristic determination and resourcefulness. He, his technician, and some research students with their own hands converted an old lecture room into a reasonably spacious and well-equipped research laboratory. From the start his imaginatively prepared lectures and practical classes greatly impressed able students. Many sought to work for a research degree under his supervision, and he was soon also attracting graduates from other universities. In 1946 he became reader in botany.

In April 1928 James married a fellow botanist at Reading, Gladys Macphail, daughter of Ernest William Redfern, of Leeds, and his wife, Charlotte Elizabeth, née Lowe, and they found a comfortable house in Islip, quite close to Oxford. Their two daughters were born in 1930 and 1932. Despite his frail physique and the inescapable concern over his health James was quite active in the pleasant Islip garden and played his part in village life. He became, too, a member of the senior common room of Oriel College, where he dined fairly regularly. His health remained good until the late 1930s when he had a further serious tubercular attack and spent some time in a sanatorium, but he recovered after eighteen months or so.

Tansley retired in 1937 and was succeeded by T. G. B. Osborn, who had soon to face the disruptive consequences of the war of 1939–45. With the help of his wife and numbers of undergraduate and research students James explored the feasibility and wartime value of the home-cultivation of certain medicinal plants and the collection by members of the public of medically useful material of wild plants such as foxglove. The success of his efforts led to national recognition of the 'Oxford Medicinal Plants Scheme' and later to departmental research on the biosynthesis of plant alkaloids.

Osborn's untiring pressure for better departmental accommodation was rewarded in 1951 by the move to a well-designed new building close to related departments, and James much welcomed the improved facilities. He was now widely known and respected. He had been an editor of the *New Phytologist* since 1931, was elected FRS in 1952, and he accepted in 1959 an invitation to the chair of botany at Imperial College. A stream of publications, all written in a notably clear and simple yet elegant style, reported his numerous contributions to his subject. By the mid-1930s plant respiration had become a major interest, and his high reputation as a research scientist and expositor rests largely on his achievements in this field. To this Dictionary he contributed the notice of Sir F. W. Keeble.

In his new post in London he sought primarily to broaden the scope of the teaching and research, in particular by an increased emphasis on intracellular and ultrastructural studies. He retired in 1967, and was made emeritus professor. In 1969 he was elected an honorary fellow of Imperial College. Towards the end of 1977 he and his wife decided, because of his failing health, to join their two daughters in New Zealand, setting up house in Wellington. He died peacefully in his sleep, after a stroke, 15 September 1978, in Wellington.

Many will remember James for his distinction as a person. Although frail-looking he carried himself with almost military erectness, and his sharp features and piercing blue eyes warned that he was not to be trifled with. His whole aspect, his habitual reserve, and his pungency of expression suggested a somewhat formidable personality. Yet his students and colleagues were well aware of another side to his nature, and to his close friends he revealed a basic warmth and kindliness.

[A. R. Clapham and J. L. Harley in *Biographical Memoirs of Fellows of the Royal Society*, vol. xxv, 1979; personal knowledge.] A. R. Clapham

JEPHCOTT, Sir HARRY, first baronet (1891–1978), pharmaceutical chemist and industrialist, was born 15 January 1891 at Redditch, Worcestershire, the youngest of the five children and of the three sons of John Josiah Jephcott, train driver and former miner, and his wife, Helen, daughter of Charles Matthews, of Coundon, Warwickshire. He was educated at King Edward's Grammar School, Camp Hill, Birmingham, and was then apprenticed to a pharmacist. In 1912 he entered the Customs and Excise and in 1914 was seconded to the department of the government chemist. He studied at West Ham Technical College and in 1915 obtained a B.Sc. degree with first class honours in chemistry from London University. This was followed by an M.Sc. (1918) and a fellowship of the Royal Institute of Chemistry (1920).

In 1919 Jephcott was offered a position in Joseph Nathan, an Anglo-New Zealand company which marketed dried milk under the trade name Glaxo. This was a turning point in his life: from then on he could exercise the energy, business acumen, and vision that enabled him to become the architect of a major pharmaceutical company.

After visiting Australia and New Zealand he went in 1923 to the International Dairy Congress in Washington DC and learned about the extraction of the antirachitic vitamin D from fish liver oil. An outcome of this visit for the Nathan Company was a licence to fortify milk powder with vitamin D and later a British licence to use a process patented at the University of Wisconsin for increasing the vitamin D content of foods by irradiation.

One consequence of Jephcott's grasp of the potential commercial value of these developments was the marketing by Glaxo of a vitamin concentrate in 1924. Another was his appreciation of the important role of patents in the pharmaceutical industry, which led him to read for the bar and be called to the Middle Temple in 1925. His unusual abilities were recognized by the Nathans. He was made the general manager of the Glaxo department in 1925, a director of the parent company in 1929, the managing director of Glaxo Laboratories in 1935, and managing director of the parent company in 1939.

By the 1940s Jephcott was convinced that Glaxo's future lay in the science-based production of therapeutic substances. In 1944 Glaxo Laboratories built factories for penicillin production by deep fermentation and licensing agreements were negotiated with two American companies, Merck and Squibb. In 1948 vitamin B12, the anti-pernicious anaemia factor, was isolated in the company's laboratories. When the National Research Development Corporation asked British pharmaceutical companies in 1955 for co-operation in the development of cephalosporin antibiotics only Glaxo showed serious interest. After a period of uncertainty, in which Sir Howard (later Lord) Florey [q.v.] offered encouragement by saying 'don't lose your nerve, Jephcott' Glaxo's persistence was rewarded.

Glaxo absorbed the parent company in 1947. Jephcott retired as a managing director in 1956 but became a non-executive chairman of the Glaxo group and later its honorary life president. He continued to travel widely to explore overseas markets. Sensing that many British companies were too small for effective competition he initiated negotiations which led Glaxo to acquire a controlling interest in several related concerns.

His qualities were much in demand in other spheres. During the war he was adviser on manufactured foods to the Ministry of Food and chairman of the Therapeutic Research Corporation. From 1948 to 1969 he was chairman of the council of the school of pharmacy at London University. He became a director of Metal Box, chairman and later president of the Association of British Chemical Manufacturers (1947–55), chairman of a government committee on synthetic detergents (1953–5), a member of the Advisory Council on Scientific Policy (1953–6), chairman of the Council for Scientific and Industrial Research (1956–61), and a governor of the London School of Economics (1952–68). He was president of the Royal Institute of Chemistry from 1953 to 1955.

He was knighted in 1946 and created a baronet in 1962. He received an honorary D.Sc. from Birmingham University in 1956 and the Pharmaceutical Society's Charter gold medal in 1970.

Jephcott was a man of great energy whose insight and enthusiasm were largely responsible for providing Glaxo with the scientific base on which its prosperity depended. Firm and shrewd in commercial transactions, he was also generous and humane. He endowed several charities. He owned land in south Devon and gave thirty-five acres of the coastline to the National Trust.

In April 1919 he married at Hampstead Doris (died 1985), daughter of Henry Gregory, a builder, of Swiss Cottage, London, and herself a pharmaceutical chemist of distinction. There were two sons of the marriage. He died 29 May 1978 at Northwick Park Hospital, Harrow, near to his home at Pinner in Middlesex where he had lived for fifty years. He was succeeded in the baronetcy by his elder son, (John) Anthony (born 1924).

[Sir Frank Hartley, 'Sir Harry Jephcott', *Pharmaceutical Journal*, 3 June 1978; R. P. Davenport-Hines in *Dictionary of Business Biography*, vol. iii, 1985.] E. P. Abraham

JOHNSON, HARRY GORDON (1923–1977), economist, was born 26 May 1923 in Toronto, Canada, the elder son of Henry Herbert Johnson, newspaperman and later secretary of the Liberal Party of Ontario, and his wife, Frances Lily Muat, lecturer in child psychology at the Institute of Child Study of the University of Toronto. He was educated at University of Toronto Schools and at the University of Toronto, from which he graduated in political economy in 1943.

After teaching for a year at St. Francis Xavier University in Antigonish (Nova Scotia), Canada, he joined the Canadian armed forces. Being demobilized in the United Kingdom he became an affiliated student of Jesus College, Cambridge, where he took another bachelor's degree with first class honours in the economics tripos. He then returned to Toronto where he took the degree of MA and taught for a year; in 1947 he enrolled as a graduate student in economics at Harvard where he quickly made a mark on a generation of remarkable young economists. He completed the requirements for the doctorate in three terms and then, on the invitation of (Sir) Dennis Robertson [q.v.], returned to Cambridge to take up a post in the faculty of economics as an assistant lecturer. He soon became a lecturer (1950) and was also elected to a fellowship at King's College, Cambridge, then at the height of the fame to which it had been raised by J. M. Keynes and A. C. Pigou [qq.v.]. He remained in Cambridge until 1956 when he was appointed to a professorship of economic theory at the University of Manchester. In 1959 he accepted a professorship of economics at the University of Chicago. In 1966 he joined to his chair at Chicago a professorship at the London School of Economics, which he held until 1974; he spent a quarter of each year in London and half in Chicago. He had a severe stroke in the autumn of 1973, but, despite physical incapacity, from which he never fully recovered, he did not reduce the extraordinary amount of work which he undertook. When he returned to Chicago in 1974 to devote all his energy to teaching and research, he became the Charles F. Grey distinguished service professor of economics. In 1976 he became professor of international economics at the École des Hautes Études Internationales of the University of Geneva while continuing to perform his regular duties at Chicago.

Johnson was regarded by his fellow economists as one of the major figures in the history of their science. His work covered a wide range of problems, which was unusual at a time when economics had become divided into many fields, each with a large body of literature; he covered all these subjects with a mastery of both the classical literature of the eighteenth and nineteenth centuries and the most abstruse, refined, and narrow articles in many contemporary journals. To breadth and erudition he added an unyielding rigour and precision of thought. He wrote nineteen books and edited and contributed to twenty-four more. Among his books were: *Essays in Monetary Economics* (1967); *Aspects of the Theory of Tariffs* (1971); *Macroeconomics and Monetary Theory* (1972); *The Theory of Income Distribution* (1973) and *On Economics and Society* (1975). He also wrote over four hundred papers. Although he worked incessantly and with exceptional speed, his intellectual powers were always maintained at the highest pitch. He wrote clearly in long sentences which traced the ramifications of his thought into many implications, without losing sight of his main argument. His main fields of work were the theory of international trade and monetary theory, tariffs, the theory of economic growth, income distribution, the economics of scientific research, and the history of economic thought. From 1960 to 1966 he was editor of the *Journal of Political Economy* which, as a result of his discriminating and demanding judgement and his helpfulness towards authors, became the leading economic journal. He was also the founder and co-editor of the *Journal of International Economics*.

Johnson was a fellow of the British Academy (1969), the Econometric Society (1972), and the Royal Society of Canada (1976), and a member of the American Academy of Arts and Sciences. In 1976 he was named an officer of the Order of Canada. He was awarded an honorary D.Sc. by Manchester (1972) and an honorary D.Litt. by Sheffield (1969); he also was an honorary LL D of St. Francis Xavier, Windsor, Queen's, Carleton, and Western Ontario universities in Canada. As a member of the Council on Science Policy of the United Kingdom he made a valiant effort to promote the economic analysis of fundamental scientific research. He was invited to serve as visiting professor at universities and to speak at conferences all over the world. He travelled eagerly, even after his severe illness, to and throughout the six continents, and made a profound impression by the acuity of his analysis of important problems of theory and policy and by his quick grasp and generosity in discussion with economists of all countries, of all generations, and of all degrees of eminence. He was revered by his students for whom he always found time despite his continuous production of books and papers, his determination to master all the literature of the entire field of economics, and his travels.

He was always ready to discuss economic problems with other economists, to listen courteously and to respond pointedly, succinctly and yet elaborately. He attempted to raise the intellectual level of the profession of economics and to make it more rigorous, better founded, and more critical of political demagogy and narrow nationalism. Physically he gave the impression of intense and disciplined intellectual and physical energy which shone through his dark brown eyes and which was kept under control by his continuous carving of wooden statuettes, of which he made thousands in many different artistic styles. He carved at seminars and in his rooms, throughout the most concentrated discussions of intricate economic problems.

He married in 1948 Elizabeth Scott, daughter of Harold Victor Serson, civil engineer. She was one of the editors of the collected writings of Keynes. They had one son and one daughter. He died in Geneva 9 May 1977.

[James Tobin in *Proceedings* of the British Academy, vol. xxxiii, 1977; 'Harry G. Johnson 1923–1977', *University of Chicago Record*, 1978, pp. 156–61; Grant Reuber and Anthony Scott, 'Harry Gordon Johnson, 1923–1977', *Canadian Journal of Economics*, 1977, pp. 670–7; personal knowledge.] EDWARD SHILS

JONES, SIR (BENNETT) MELVILL (1887–1975), professor of aeronautical engineering, was born in Rock Ferry, Birkenhead, 28 January 1887, the elder son and eldest of three children of

Benedict Jones, of Birkenhead, a Liverpool barrister, and his wife, Henrietta Cornelia Melvill, of South Africa, widow of George William Bennett, who had three other children by her earlier marriage. From Birkenhead School he entered Emmanuel College, Cambridge, in 1906 as an exhibitioner, becoming a scholar one year later and graduating with first class honours in the mechanical sciences tripos in 1909. After gaining some workshop experience he worked for two years in the newly formed aeronautical department at the National Physical Laboratory and for one year in industry on airship design. On the outbreak of war in 1914 he went to the Royal Aircraft Factory at Farnborough, where he worked on problems of aerial gunnery and the development of instruments to assist flying in clouds. In 1916 he moved to the Air Armament Experimental Station at Orford Ness where he continued his work on gunnery and qualified as a pilot. In 1918 he served in France for about six weeks in No. 48 Squadron of the Royal Flying Corps and the RAF as a rear-gunner of a Bristol fighter. He was awarded the AFC (1918) and attained the rank of lieutenant-colonel.

Early in 1919 he returned to Cambridge as a fellow of Emmanuel College, but only a few months later the Francis Mond professorship of aeronautical engineering was established at Cambridge and he was appointed to it, retaining the post until his retirement in 1952. The Air Ministry had agreed to provide aeroplanes and flying facilities, which gave Jones the opportunity to develop a very successful school of aeronautical research, using aeroplanes in flight as the major research tool. The research team was always small, usually about four people, and with characteristic modesty Jones made it clear that the members of the team were expected to work with him and not for him. After a few years working on aerial surveying he turned his attention to a detailed study of the processes occurring when an aeroplane stalls. This led to a major advance in understanding and helped to reduce accidents. His later work, from 1926 onward, was all concerned with the drag of an aircraft and ways of reducing it. In a particularly important paper in 1929 he introduced the concept of the ideal streamline aeroplane whose drag would be very much less than that of the aeroplanes then flying. This gave designers for the first time an ideal at which to aim and led to a rapid evolution of the clean monoplane with retractable undercarriage. During the 1930s the research by Jones and his small team was aimed at understanding and eventually reducing the drag experienced even by an aeroplane of good streamline form and this work was of great value in laying a foundation for later research elsewhere on reduction of drag.

Shortly before the start of World War II the Air Ministry asked Jones to return to his work on aerial gunnery. He worked energetically in this field for four years, laying the foundations for the development of the gyro gunsight, and in 1943 moved to the Ministry of Aircraft Production and became chairman of the Aeronautical Research Committee (later Council) until 1946. On his return to Cambridge after the war he took up again his flight research on reduction of drag. After his retirement in 1952 he worked for a number of years as a part-time consultant at the Royal Aircraft Establishment.

Jones was of stocky build, a strong swimmer and an enthusiastic rock climber. Known as Bones to his friends, he was an excellent teacher and one of the kindest and friendliest of men. He was described by a former colleague, Sir William Farren [q.v.], as 'a man of unsurpassed charm and simplicity'. He was appointed CBE in 1938, elected FRS in 1939, and knighted in 1942. In 1947 he was awarded the medal of freedom by the president of the USA for his work in World War II on aerial gunnery and in the same year he received the gold medal of the Royal Aeronautical Society, of which he became an honorary fellow (1951).

He married in 1916 Dorothy Laxton (died 1955), daughter of Frederick Charles Jotham, a Kidderminster wine merchant. They had one daughter and two sons, one of whom was killed in action in August 1941. The younger son, Geoffrey, was elected FRS and appointed director of the aviation medical research unit at McGill University. Jones died in north Devon, 31 October 1975. There is a portrait by Allan Gwynne-Jones in the engineering department of Cambridge University.

[Sir Arnold Hall and Sir Morien Morgan in *Biographical Memoirs of Fellows of the Royal Society*, vol. xxiii, 1977; *The Times*, 6 November 1975; A. V. Stephens in *Emmanuel College Magazine*, 1976; personal knowledge.]

W. A. Mair

JONES, DAVID (1895–1974), painter, poet, and essayist, was born 1 November 1895 in Brockley, Kent, the younger son and youngest of three children of James Jones, printer, from Holywell, Flintshire, and his wife, Alice Ann, former governess, daughter of Ebenezer Bradshaw, a mast and block maker of Rotherhithe, Surrey. His father's father was a master plasterer from Ysceifiog, his mother's mother Italian. His father worked on the *Flintshire Observer* until 1883 and knew some Welsh songs; David learnt what Welsh he knew later. He was baptized Walter, which name he discarded. His earliest animal drawings, some of which survive, date from 1902 or 1903. From 1910 to 1914 he attended Camberwell School of Art under A. S. Hartrick (who had known Van Gogh and Gauguin) and others.

After trying to join the Artists' Rifles and some new Welsh cavalry, he enlisted in the Welch Fusiliers, 2 January 1915, serving as a private soldier until December 1918, in a London unit of Lloyd George's 'Welsh army'. He was wounded in the leg on the night of 11 July 1916 in the attack on Mametz Wood on the Somme. He returned to action in October but by chance avoided the Passchendaele offensive. He left France with severe trench fever in February 1918. On demobilization he wished at first to rejoin, but accepted a grant and some parental help to work (1919–21) at Westminster School of Art. He already spoke at that time of Post-Impressionist theory fitting in with Catholic sacramental theology, and in 1921 became a Roman Catholic and went to work under A. Eric R. Gill [q.v.], then at Ditchling in Sussex, and from August 1924 at Capel-y-ffin in the Black Mountains near the Welsh border. Jones was brought up at home on Bunyan and Milton, but with strong touches of inherited Catholic feelings; he had been deeply moved by a mass just behind the front line glimpsed through a barn wall. He had liked the businesslike atmosphere. His first job was to paint the lettering of the war memorial at New College, Oxford.

In 1924 he got engaged to Gill's daughter, Petra. His close friend René Hague was in love with her sister, Joan, and married her, but Jones had little money and no prospects; Petra broke off the engagement in 1927 to marry someone else, and Jones never did marry, though he was not homosexual and had *amitiés amoureuses*, mostly conducted on the telephone as he grew older. He visited the Gills at Pigotts in Buckinghamshire often until 1933, but he was too devoted to his work and usually too poor not to live alone. His closest friends loved him intensely; they included Tom Burns, Harman Grisewood, Douglas Cleverdon, Jim Ede, Father M. C. D'Arcy [q.v.], and Helen Sutherland, his greatest patron. He spent time in the twenties on Caldey Island, in Bristol, at Brockley with his parents, in Berkshire with Robert Gibbings of the Golden Cockerel Press, and in France. In 1928 Ben Nicholson had him elected to the Seven and Five Society, where he exhibited with Henry Moore, Christopher Wood, (Dame) Barbara Hepworth [q.v.] and John Piper. The same year he began *In Parenthesis* (1937), which has its climax at Mametz in World War I. This book won the 1938 Hawthornden prize.

The delicacy and freshness of his colours, and the purity and power of his forms as a painter, let alone the strength and grace of his engraving work and his occasional wooden sculpture, would be enough to win him a high place among the artists of his generation and in a tradition that goes back to William Blake [q.v.], whose nature and genius with many differences David Jones recalls. His work as a poet, in *In Parenthesis*, *The Anathemata* (1952), and *The Sleeping Lord* (1974), was almost more impressive, and in the lettering and the texts of his 'inscriptions', words painted on paper, he devised a new and moving art. In his severest engravings he was warm, in painting of solemn beauty lyrical and humorous. His visions of nature were as fresh as Ysceifiog, his poetry as thrilling and abundant as the Thames at Rotherhithe. He greatly admired the Cornish fisherman painter, Alfred Wallis.

His intellectual insights were profound and complex. They were based on a restless and never-ending meditation of the art of painting, of theology for which he had a brilliant flair, of the nature of technology, of heroic legends, prehistoric archaeology, and the history of the British Isles. He admired James Joyce, T. S. Eliot, Baron Friedrich Von Hügel [qq.v.], Christopher Dawson, and Père de la Taille; at least for a few years in the late thirties he flirted heavily with Oswald Spengler's *Decline of the West* and unseriously with Adolf Hitler's *Mein Kampf*, although he was innocent of the faintest trace of fascism; he simply loved mankind, and hated what everyone hates about modern times. In London in the blitz he wrote a lot of poetry, painted some of his finest mythical paintings, and began his great 'inscriptions'. His 'Aphrodite in Aulis' (1941) is the goddess and lover of dying soldiers both German and English. His work was grossly interrupted by eye trouble from 1930 onwards, by a severe breakdown in 1932 with chronic insomnia, and then by a worse attack in 1947. He bore all this with an uncomplaining goodness he seemed to have learnt in the trenches.

In 1934 Jones was taken to Cairo and Jerusalem by Tom Burns. It was there he conceived the equivalence of British and Roman soldiers, and of his central statement, *The Anathemata*. In the later thirties he lived mostly at Sidmouth. After the 1947 breakdown he lived in fine rooms on the hill at Harrow, later in a little hotel in the town, and in the end in Calvary Nursing Home, Harrow, where he was looked after by the nuns. Among the new friends of his last years were Nancy Sandars, archaeologist, and Philip Lowry, silversmith.

Jones had a boyish gaiety and a charmingly wide smile. His conversation was full of humour and inventive parody; his sympathy and the range of his interest were extraordinarily wide. The fulcrum of his morality was the decency of the infantrymen of 1914. Under stress he would drop his shopping, lose his papers, or find himself smoking two cigarettes, one in each hand. His notes became long writings, and his letters, annotated in several colours, tumbled effortlessly from sheet to sheet and subject to subject like the dialogues of Plato. He concentrated on a friend, on a subject of conversation, on a detail of any kind, historical or technical or visual or intellectual, with uncommon intensity. His eyes twinkled and glittered deeply.

His first retrospective exhibition at the National Museum of Wales and the Tate Gallery was in 1954–5, his second (posthumously) in 1981. He was appointed CBE in 1955 and CH in 1974. He won many prizes and awards, and received an honorary D.Litt. from the University of Wales in 1960. He died at the Calvary Nursing Home, Harrow, 28 October 1974, after some years of increasing illness.

[René Hague (ed.), *Dai Greatcoat, a Self-Portrait of David Jones in his Letters*, 1980; Paul Hills in Tate Gallery catalogue, 1981; David Jones, *The Roman Quarry*, with foreword by Harman Grisewood and notes by René Hague, 1981; Colin Hughes, *David Jones, The Man who was in the Field*, 1979; private information.]

PETER LEVI

K

KAHN-FREUND, SIR OTTO (1900–1979), academic lawyer, was born in Frankfurt am Main 17 November 1900, the only child of Richard Kahn-Freund, a merchant, and his wife, Carrie Freund. He grew up in a cultured Jewish household and though in religious matters he was agnostic, he himself said that the most important fact in his life had been the awareness of being a Jew. To this he attributed the passion for justice and the concern for the disadvantaged which lay at the root both of his interest in labour law and of his socialist convictions.

He studied principally at the University of Frankfurt, where he was powerfully influenced by Hugo Sinzheimer, who first interested him in labour law. In 1929 he entered the judiciary as a judge of the Berlin Labour Court. When the Nazis came to power he was already known for a small book criticizing the ideology behind the decisions of the Supreme Labour Court, and he was soon in collision with the Party. He refused to uphold the dismissal of employees of the radio service who were alleged to be communists and to have tried to sabotage Hitler's first broadcast. The result was his own dismissal and departure to England. There he became a student at the London School of Economics, which for the next thirty years was the focus of his life and which was ideally suited to one of his temperament and views. Appointed an assistant lecturer in 1936, he became a professor in 1951. He was also called to the bar by the Middle Temple in 1936 and was for a time in chambers with Patrick (later Lord) Devlin. He was naturalized in 1940.

Kahn-Freund was an outstandingly exciting lecturer, with a command of English which any native speaker might envy. The lecture was indeed his favourite medium and his most brilliant work originated in that form. He played an important part in the establishment of labour law as an independent area of legal study in England, and in his later years he was unquestionably its leading authority. He also enjoyed a great reputation on the Continent and in the United States (he was for many years a visiting lecturer at the Yale Law School). In 1965 he was appointed to the royal commission on the reform of the trade unions and employers' associations. His hand can be seen in the legal sections of its report.

Though labour law was his dominant concern, he was remarkable for the range of his interests. He was a respected authority on the conflict of laws, being one of the editors of the sixth to ninth editions of *Dicey*. And he was an enthusiastic promoter of the study of family law; there, as in labour law, he constantly emphasized the need to see legal rules in terms of their social and human consequences. He was also a passionate advocate of the European ideal and vigorously advanced the study of Community law.

In 1964 he was persuaded to move to the chair of comparative law at Oxford and a fellowship at Brasenose College. The comparative approach was a natural concomitant of his broad interests, but he brought to the subject also a capacity for striking generalization. For anyone less youthful in spirit and less appreciative of new experiences the transition from the LSE to Oxford at the age of sixty-three might have been difficult, and indeed he was genially impatient of the constraints on rapid change imposed by the collegiate and tutorial systems, but he rapidly became at home and during his seven years (his tenure of the chair was, exceptionally, extended) he was influential in the establishment in the syllabus not only of comparative law, but also family law, labour law, and European Community law. A naturally sociable man, he also enjoyed the friendly diversity of senior common room life.

After his retirement he continued to lecture and to write and he held visiting professorships at Paris and Cambridge. He became FBA in 1965 and an honorary bencher of the Middle Temple in 1969; he was given silk in 1972 and was knighted for his services to labour law in 1976. He held many honorary doctorates.

Kahn-Freund married in 1931 Elisabeth, daughter of Friedrich Klaiss, mechanic. She shared his political convictions and his interests. They had an adopted daughter. He died at Haslemere 16 August 1979.

Lists of his publications are found in his *Selected Writings* (1978) and in F. Gamillscheg *et al.*, *In Memoriam Sir Otto Kahn-Freund* (Munich, 1980).

[*The Times*, 16 November 1979; *Modern Law Review*, 1979; *The Brazen Nose*, 1979; Lord Wedderburn in *Proceedings* of the British Academy, vol. lxviii, 1982; private information; personal knowledge.]

J. K. BARRY M. NICHOLAS

KEIGHTLEY, SIR CHARLES FREDERIC (1901–1974), general, was born at Anerley, near Croydon, 24 June 1901, the only surviving child of the Revd Charles Albert Keightley, then vicar of Anerley, and his wife, Kathleen Ross. He just missed service in World War I. Due to his ability, he was accelerated in promotion from the outset of World War II, successfully commanding a division, corps, and army without having commanded a squadron or regiment.

Educated at Marlborough and the Royal Military College, Sandhurst, he was commissioned into the 5th Dragoon Guards in 1921, a tall, well-built young man with a direct yet friendly manner and a strong sense of humour.

The regiment was then serving in the Middle East, where it was uneasily amalgamated with the 6th Inniskilling Dragoons. Difficult days there were mitigated by removal to India and, later, operations on the North-West Frontier. When the 5th Inniskilling Dragoon Guards returned to York in 1929, Lieutenant Keightley had made a name for himself as 'an exceptionally capable officer who has excelled in a range of duties'. He had also excelled in polo, playing on occasion for the army in India.

At York, the regiment was in danger of becoming a drafting unit for overseas requirements. It fell to a dynamic commanding officer with Keightley as his adjutant to preserve regimental identity and expertise, activity in which Keightley again enhanced his reputation. He passed competitively into the Staff College at Camberley for the 1934–5 course, unaware that his regimental service had ended.

Passing out with high marks in 1935, he became staff officer to the director-general, Territorial Army (1936), then brigade-major to the cavalry in Cairo (1937–8) before returning to instruct at Camberley in 1938. At short notice, early in 1940, he was detached to be assistant adjutant and quartermaster-general (principal administrative staff officer) of 1st Armoured division in France and Belgium. Among many critical problems he dealt with in the ensuing defence and withdrawal operations was the replacement of armoured vehicles in units, developing and implementing an embryo scheme which was adopted subsequently for the army as a whole. His work came to the notice of General Alan Brooke (later Viscount Alanbrooke, q.v.) who drew him out of the administrative staff stream first to a brigade command and later in 1941 to direct, as a major-general, all Royal Armoured Corps training in the United Kingdom. When a force was formed to land in French North Africa, Keightley was chosen to command the 6th Armoured division within it. He was then forty-one.

During the fleeting opportunities of late 1942 and the trials of 1943, he demonstrated sound judgement in tactics and in the nurturing and driving of his command. By the time of the Allied advance in Italy in the latter part of the year, his standing was such that he was moved to command 78th Infantry division when the opportunity for armoured warfare had diminished. He quickly won the support of this famous battle-worthy formation, taking them through the Cassino operations in the following year, when he was promoted to command V Corps. He continued no less successfully at this level, notably in the Argenta gap operations leading to the final collapse of the German forces in Italy.

With the end of the war and rapid demobilization, there were too many temporary lieutenant-generals for a shrinking army. Some retired, some reverted, but Keightley retained his rank, becoming director-general of military training in 1946 and military secretary in 1948. Then Lt.-Gen. Sir Brian Horrocks fell ill and Keightley was sent to replace him, embarking on a series of commands-in-chief overseas for a span of almost ten years: the British Army of the Rhine 1948–51, the Far East land forces 1951–3, and the Middle East land forces 1953–7.

In the latter he was prolonged due to the Suez crisis, in which he found himself in the worst of positions as the responsible army commander; with a shifting political concept, inter-allied plans of which he had no knowledge until a late stage, a protracted delay in mounting operations because of logistic factors, and the absence of a unified commander. From this misconceived venture Keightley emerges with credit. He coped readily with order and counter-order, insisting that any landing must be properly supported and maintained. In the political aftermath of the operations, his departure at last from the Middle East in 1957 was falsely rumoured in London to be due to mismanagement. The story took no root in the army and was dissipated by his appointment as governor and commander-in-chief, Gibraltar, a post from which he finally retired in 1962 after more than forty years of service. He had become a general in 1951.

Keightley persistently regretted that circumstances prevented him from commanding his regiment and was proud to own that his ideas of soldiering were shaped principally by it, from which came his belief that every man, however junior, must be expected and encouraged to think for himself whether alone or part of a team. Yet, though a cavalryman to the core, he acquired a remarkable insight into—not simply a knowledge of—the infantry art, the potential and the burdens of the infantry soldier—an important factor in his success as a commander.

His honours and appointments were many. Admitted to the DSO (1944) and the American Legion of Merit (1942), appointed OBE (1941), CB (1943), KBE (1945), KCB (1950), he was advanced to GCB in 1953 and GBE in 1957 and made a grand officer of the Legion of Honour in 1958. From 1953 to 1956 he was ADC general to the Queen. He was colonel of his regiment for ten years (1947–57) and colonel commandant of the Royal Armoured Corps (Cavalry Wing) (1958–68).

In 1932 he married Joan Lydia, daughter of Brigadier-General George Nowell Thomas Smyth-Osbourne, of Ash, Iddesleigh, north Devon; they had two sons. Keightley died 17 June 1974 at Salisbury General Infirmary.

[Army and regimental records; information from the family; personal knowledge.]
ANTHONY FARRAR-HOCKLEY

KEIR, SIR DAVID LINDSAY (1895–1973), university teacher and administrator, was born 22 May 1895 at Bellingham, Northumberland, the eldest in the family of two sons and three daughters of the Revd William Keir, Presbyterian minister, of Aberuthven, Perthshire, and his wife, Elizabeth Craig. The family moved from Bellingham to Newcastle, to Birkenhead, and later to Glasgow, where David attended Glasgow Academy. In 1913 he won a bursary to Glasgow University. War intervened in his second year: he was commissioned in 1915 in the King's Own Scottish Borderers, rising ultimately to the rank of captain. He was wounded on the Somme, and again at Arras: he also served in Ireland, and this laid the foundations of a long affection for that country.

After the war, Keir entered New College, Oxford, and in 1921 he obtained an outstanding first in history. University College immediately elected him to a fellowship. There he served as dean (1925–35) and later as estates bursar (1933–9): from 1931 to 1939 he was also university lecturer in English constitutional history. These Oxford years were productive: in 1928 he published with F. H. Lawson *Cases in Constitutional Law* and in 1938 *The Constitutional History of Modern Britain*. The latter book bears witness to his special talents as a legal historian: clear and thorough, with a humane sense of perspectives in legal history and a meticulous mastery of detail.

In 1939 Keir was appointed to the vice-chancellorship of Queen's University, Belfast. He was particularly well fitted for this post: Oxford had given him a sound training in academic administration, and his Scottish upbringing and his knowledge of Ireland gave him a sympathetic understanding of the problems of Ulster and of Ulstermen. Liked and trusted, he became widely involved in the life of the province: from 1942 to 1949 he was chairman of the Northern Ireland Regional Hospitals Board, and his appointment to the Northern Ireland Planning Advisory Board made him contacts in government that were supremely useful to his university. He was instrumental in securing that in 1945 the Northern Ireland government invited the University Grants Committee to visit Queen's, and the results of that visitation ensured funding comparable with that of other British universities. This paved the way for post-war expansion, and the years 1945 to 1949 saw a successful appeal and a new building programme, a substantial increase in staff, and a steady growth in student numbers. In 1949, when Keir resigned the vice-chancellorship to become master of Balliol College, Oxford, Queen's University had been set on the path toward a newly substantial role in post-war Ulster. His stewardship had earned him a knighthood in 1946.

The debates preceding Keir's election at Balliol had been protracted and at times bitter, and he found there a fellowship whose members were able, outspoken, undocile, and who disagreed easily on college policy. They were not a comfortable body to lead, and besides, Keir was not much in sympathy with some developments in Oxford in the 1950s and 60s, such as the rapid growth of graduate studies and the looming prospect of coeducation. Where he was most successful was in reaffirming links between Balliol and her old members, and in maintaining her position as a cosmopolitan institution, admitting a high proportion of students from overseas. His chairmanship of the advisory committee on overseas colleges of arts, science and technology (1954–64), and his membership of numerous committees on higher education overseas gave him influence here, as it gave him also a role in shaping the future of academic institutions in Africa and Asia in the post-colonial era. He also maintained his interest in medical affairs, and from 1950 to 1958 was chairman of the United Oxford Hospitals Trust. The greatest triumph of his Balliol years was, however, the launching of the college's septcentenary appeal, which raised more than a million pounds, and freed Balliol from the constraints of the comparative indigence that had dogged her history from the foundation to his time. Keir retired in 1965.

In politics Keir was a liberal conservative, in religion a sincere Christian, in his ways methodical and very careful. He did not relish the cut and thrust of controversy, and made his mark by the weight of mature and benign influence rather than by dramatic initiatives. Outwardly dignified and decorous, he had a generous spirit and a sense of fun, which, alas, invariably left him when speaking in public. He had a real love of the countryside, of cricket, football and boating, and of the 'old ways'.

He married in 1930 Anna Clunie, daughter of Robert John Dale, shipping underwriter, of Montreal; they had a son and a daughter. His very happy marriage and his wife's great charm were pit-props of his successful career. Keir died at his home at Boar's Hill, Oxford, 2 October 1973.

Keir had many honorary degrees including a DCL from Oxford (1960), was an honorary fellow of University, Balliol, and New Colleges, and was honorary FRIBA (1948).

[*University College Record*, 1974; Russell Meiggs, 'Sir David Lindsay Keir', *Balliol College Record*, 1974; private information; personal knowledge.]
MAURICE KEEN

KELLY, SIR GERALD FESTUS (1879–1972), portrait painter, was born in Paddington, London, 9 April 1879, the youngest of three children and only son of the Revd Frederic Festus Kelly who was then a curate in Paddington but, in the following year, became vicar of St. Giles, Camberwell, where he served for thirty-five years and Gerald spent his boyhood. The mother was Blanche, daughter of Robert Bradford of Farningham in Kent but, like her husband, of Irish descent. Gerald, a sickly child, was on his own admission rather spoiled but, encouraged by his father, he developed a love of watching cricket and, through being taken to Dulwich College Picture Gallery, an interest in pictures which led to his trying his hand with water-colours. His schooling at Eton was ended abruptly through illness and a winter's convalescence in South Africa. He then, in 1897, entered Trinity Hall, Cambridge, where he read much poetry and took a poll degree.

Although without any formal training in art, Kelly had decided by this time to become a painter and, with this in mind, moved to Paris in 1901 whence, helped by the art dealer Paul Durand-Ruel, he visited Monet, Degas, Rodin, and Cézanne, among others, and made friends with Walter Sickert, J. S. Sargent, and, in particular, W. Somerset Maugham [qq.v.]. Fired by this background, his own experiments enabled him to develop meticulous craftsmanship with great attention to detail, as is shown by his immense care in painting hands, following an overheard criticism. He became, in 1904, a member of the Salon d'Automne and his work soon gained for him the patronage of (Sir) Hugh Lane [q.v.] and, in 1908, election as an associate of the Royal Hibernian Academy. Then, having been deserted by his dancer girl-friend, he spent a year in Burma, thrilled by its colour and life-style.

Kelly settled down in London, at his parents' house in Gloucester Place, in 1909 although, thereafter, he made many study visits to Spain. In World War I he joined the intelligence department of the Admiralty. By 1920, when he married a young model from a working-class family, namely Lilian (although he always called her Jane), the fifth daughter among Simon Ryan's eight children, he was becoming well established as a portrait painter. Donning his boiler suit, he worked hard each day not only at his easel but, as a connoisseur of wines, in preparing them for the frequent and lively dinner parties at the house. The couple had no children.

This busy period, during which he was elected as associate of the Royal Academy in 1922 and RA in 1930, culminated in his being commissioned, in 1938, to paint the state portraits of King George VI and Queen Elizabeth which, following the outbreak of World War II, he worked on at Windsor Castle until 1945 when they were at last finished, exhibited at the Academy, and Kelly was knighted. In the same year he undertook to be honorary surveyor of Dulwich College Picture Gallery and soon he was in the forefront of a major argument on what he, and many others, considered to be too drastic cleaning of paintings in the National Gallery. He was a member of the Royal Fine Art Commission from 1938 to 1943.

At seventy years of age, in December 1949, Kelly was elected president of the Royal Academy and devoted most of his time to its loan exhibitions, not only persuading owners to lend works but becoming the star of related television programmes. Five years later he had to retire under the Academy's age limit and in 1955 was appointed KCVO. He remained active for a considerable time longer but, after an unsuccessful eye operation in his ninetieth year, he had to give up painting. Among his honours were RHA (1914), Hon. RSA (1950), Hon. FRIBA (1950), and Hon. LL D (Cambridge and Trinity College Dublin, 1950).

Undoubtedly Kelly was a charmer, both in speech and in his letters, and of indomitable spirit, but he was often petulant and tactless. Hardly five feet six inches in height, he darted in thought and action at most things but with the contradictory exception of being completely methodical and painstaking at his easel. His output of portraits and many landscape studies was considerable. Among his best early works are pictures of his father, entitled 'The Vicar in his Study' (1912), and of W. Somerset Maugham, called 'The Jester' (1911), which many years later was purchased through the Chantrey Bequest and placed in the Tate Gallery. He never tired of painting his wife and perhaps the finest portrait of her is 'Jane XXX' (1930), deposited in the Royal Academy as his diploma work. Among his other sitters were 'Hugh Walpole' (1925), 'Dr. M. R. James' (1937), 'Sir Malcolm Sargent' (1948), and 'Dr. Ralph Vaughan Williams' (1953) and he painted many versions of beautiful Asian dancing girls. He contributed to this Dictionary the notice of Sir Alfred Munnings.

He died at his home in Gloucester Place, London, 5 January 1972.

[Derek Hudson, *For Love of Painting: The Life of Sir Gerald Kelly*, 1975; Royal Academy records and *Catalogue* of Sir Gerald Kelly exhibition, 1957; personal knowledge.]

S. C. HUTCHISON

KENDRICK, SIR THOMAS DOWNING (1895–1979), director and principal librarian of the British Museum, was born at Birmingham 1 April 1895, the eldest child of Thomas Henry Kendrick and his wife, Frances Downing; he was educated at Charterhouse and entered Oriel

College, Oxford, with a scholarship in 1913. After one year in residence Kendrick left Oriel to serve during the war of 1914–18 in the Warwickshire Regiment. While fighting in France, as a captain, he was severely wounded in a hand and a leg, but this did not deter him, later on, from pursuing his favourite hobbies, fly-fishing and (after his retirement) gardening. He returned to Oriel College in 1919 and read anthropology, receiving a diploma with distinction in 1921. Under the influence of Robert Marett [q.v.] he studied the prehistoric archaeology of the Channel Islands, publishing in 1928 *The Archaeology of the Channel Islands I, Bailiwick of Guernsey*; *Jersey* was completed by Jacquetta Hawkes, 1939.

In 1922 he joined the department of British and medieval antiquities at the British Museum as an assistant under Ormonde Dalton [q.v.]. He became an assistant keeper in 1928 and keeper in 1938; in 1950 he was appointed director and principal librarian, a post which he held until retirement in 1959. He was created KCB in 1951.

He introduced a number of modern techniques, including the bright polishing of silver, into the department's exhibition range. This provided opportunities for many of his interests, above all those in Anglo-Saxon art, by enhancing the beauty of jewellery and metalwork. Because of wartime conditions the Sutton Hoo treasure could not be shown as soon as it was excavated in 1939, but Kendrick was responsible, after the war, for attractively displaying all the best of it. Throughout, in the British Museum, he combined a readiness for practical innovations with preserving the museum's superlative usefulness to scholars and the general public alike. His enlivening it thus, without flashiness, reflected the humanity and humour in his character, lightening his lean blond countenance stiffened by a harder disposition underneath.

Kendrick had infectious enthusiasm, shown in his many lectures and articles, and in his books. *The Axe Age* (1925) and *The Druids* (1927, reprinted 1966) were followed by *A History of the Vikings* (1930, reprinted 1968), *Anglo-Saxon Art to AD 900* (1938, reprinted 1972), and *Late Saxon and Viking Art* (1949, reprinted 1974). He also published *Archaeology in England and Wales, 1914–1931* (in collaboration with C. F. C. Hawkes, 1932), and edited the seven volumes of *The County Archaeologies*.

He had interests beyond prehistory and Anglo-Saxon times; he came to be deeply attracted by medieval legend and history, both in Britain and abroad. These he made the subject of his *British Antiquity* (1950, reprinted 1970); and in his retirement he published, after *The Lisbon Earthquake* (1956), *St. James in Spain* (1960), *Mary of Agreda, the Life and Legend of a Spanish Nun* (1967), and a novel, *Great Love for Icarus* (1962).

Kendrick was a fellow of the British Academy (1941) and of the Society of Antiquaries, of which society he was secretary from 1940 to 1950. He was made an honorary fellow of his Oxford college, Oriel, and an honorary FRIBA; he had German and Swedish academic distinctions, and honorary degrees from Dublin, Durham, and Oxford.

In 1922 he married Ellen Martha (Helen), daughter of Louis Holland Kiek, a merchant banker; she died in 1955, and he married in 1957 Katharine Elizabeth Wrigley (died 1980); by his first marriage he had a daughter. In his very last years he lost his sight, and he died at Dorchester 2 November 1979.

[*The Times*, 23 November 1979; private information; personal knowledge.]

C. F. C. Hawkes

KENYATTA, JOMO (1890s–1978), African nationalist and first president of Kenya, was born at the advent of British colonial rule in East Africa in the 1890s (the exact date of birth is unknown) to Muigai, a Kikuyu farmer, and his wife Wambiu, at Ngenda, in the north-eastern part of the Kiambu district. He spent his early childhood in traditional Kikuyu peasant homesteads. Early an orphan, he was called Kamau wa Ngengi; he lived with his father's brother, Ngengi, and then his grandfather, Kongo wa Magana, a tribal medicine-man.

In November 1909 Kenyatta became one of the earliest boarders at the newly founded Scottish mission at Thogota (near Nairobi). At the end of his formative years he was baptized Johnstone Kamau in 1914, but he had retained his traditional ties to his people by being initiated into his tribal age-grade (Mubengi) in 1913. After completing his primary education, the young Kenyatta held a number of jobs in Nairobi and the surrounding area during the next fourteen years, of which the most important was with the Nairobi Water Department in the 1920s. He married his first wife, Grace Wahu, in 1919; this union produced a son and a daughter. (His daughter, Margaret Wambui, was mayor of Nairobi from 1969 to 1976.)

Now known as Johnstone Kenyatta, he embarked in 1928 on his political career as general secretary of the aspiring Kikuyu Central Association (KCA) as well as the first editor of the Kikuyu vernacular monthly, *Muigwithania*, 'The Unifier'. In 1929–30 he spent some eighteen months primarily in Britain, representing the KCA, presenting its grievances and promoting its aims. During this period he made his first trip to the Soviet Union; he also visited Germany, France, and Holland.

In 1931 Kenyatta returned to Britain with Parmenas Mockerie on behalf of the KCA to give evidence before the joint parliamentary commission on closer union in East Africa, but they were not asked to testify. This time Kenyatta remained for fifteen years, during which he matured into a confident and commanding leader. He wrote articles and letters to the press, attended the Quaker College of Woodbrook, Selly Oak (1932), and gave evidence to the Carter land commission prior to its departure for Kenya. In 1932–3 he made a second visit to the Soviet Union and then later travelled to various European countries.

In London Kenyatta associated with a number of Pan-Africanists, including George Padmore, T. R. Makonnen, and C. L. R. James, who championed Ethiopia's plight in its struggle against conquest by Italy, and in 1937 founded the International Africa Service Bureau to advance the ideas of Pan-Africanism and self-determination. A student of Malinowski's at the London School of Economics, Kenyatta published a study of Kikuyu customs and practices in 1938. Entitled *Facing Mount Kenya*, it remains an important anthropological document of the Kikuyu people. By now he had dropped 'Johnstone' in favour of 'Jomo'. The banning of the KCA in 1940 and the exile of its main leaders to the northern part of the country cut Kenyatta's channels of communication with Kenya. He spent part of World War II in Sussex farming and lecturing to British troops about Africa. He was married in 1942 to Edna Grace Clarke—his second wife—and in 1943 their son, Peter Magana, was born. Before answering a call to return to Kenya, he took part in the sixth Pan-African Congress (1946) in Manchester.

In 1946 Kenyatta returned to Kenya, leaving his wife behind (she only visited Kenya at independence), and he became president of the Kenya African Union (KAU) in 1947, articulating a concept of Kenyan nationalism, although the organizational base of the movement was largely among the Kikuyu. The immediate post-war period was one of an expanding conflict between Africans, especially Kikuyu, and Europeans. The KAU sought increased and elected representation in the Legislative Council and a resolution of major African land grievances. As the politics of moderation gave way increasingly to violence in the early 1950s, Kenyatta was accused of leading a secret movement known as 'Mau Mau'. A state of emergency was declared on 20 October 1952, and Kenyatta, along with several colleagues in the Kenya African Union, was arrested and charged with heading 'Mau Mau'. He was unjustly convicted of this charge on 8 April 1953. The evidence on which he was convicted was later proven to be false, and he spent the next seven years in prison and two additional years under restriction in the northern desert part of Kenya.

While Kenyatta was detained there developed a new nationalism, far more national in character and organization, which embraced leaders and followers from many ethnic groups. However, the colonial government refused to permit a national African organization to exist, and by 1958 Kenyatta again had become the symbol of Kenyan nationalism and unity. In early 1960 Britain made a critical decision to allow Kenya to become an African-governed state, and the first general election took place in February 1961 with Kenyatta as the *de facto* leader of the dominant Kenya African National Union (KANU).

The British colonial government continued to regard Kenyatta as a 'leader into darkness and death', but it finally had to release him from restriction in August 1961. He assumed the presidency of KANU in October 1961, entered Parliament in January 1962 as leader of the opposition, and led KANU to the London constitutional conference, February–March 1962. In April 1962 he joined the transitional coalition government as minister of state for constitutional affairs and economic planning, and in June 1963 KANU won the internal self-government election with Kenyatta becoming prime minister. On 12 December 1963 Kenya became independent with Kenyatta as prime minister, and a year later the Republic of Kenya was established and Kenyatta became president.

Kenyatta ruled Kenya for fourteen years, during which he faced no serious challenges. He was a moderately conservative 'presidential monarch' who elevated the presidency to a far more powerful institution than anticipated in the independence constitution of 1963. Though parliament was clearly not supreme, it none the less remained a vital forum for political debate and the expression of public attitudes. An Africanized provincial administration 'modelled' on that of the colonial period became the president's direct personal link with the people and the critical channel of rule. The spirit of his administration from the beginning was one of conciliation and unity which did much to heal the inter-racial wounds of the 'Mau Mau' emergency of the 1950s. A grass-roots democracy persisted within the framework of a *de facto* one-party state. There was genuine competition in the elections of representatives to the national parliament, and many members and ministers suffered electoral defeats. But Kenyatta himself was above the electoral struggle.

Kenyatta did not radically alter Kenya's economy after independence, although major efforts were made to expand and Africanize important sectors. To some, Kenyatta's favouring of private enterprise and foreign investment resulted in a neo-colonial economy of marked inequalities in wealth and opportunity; to others that strategy accelerated the comparatively high rate of economic growth Kenya enjoyed during his presidency. His greatest contribution was building the foundations for a Kenyan state and establishing the authority of the national government.

Pan-Africanism to Kenyatta was primarily the ending of colonial rule. He was a founding member of the Organization of African Unity (OAU), but he did not play a prominent role in continental politics. In 1964 he sought to bring about a reconciliation between rival Congolese leaders, and again in 1975 he endeavoured to negotiate a compact between Angola's competing leaders and groups. Both efforts, however, ended in failure. The East African Community also collapsed during his regime (1977) but it is doubtful that Kenyatta was seriously concerned. A strong and orderly Kenya was his major goal, not regional unification.

As a political leader Kenyatta was a commanding figure, able to capture the loyalty of the African masses while dominating would-be rivals. He refused to pick a successor, but his passing led to a succession in which the constitution's provisions were observed, rather than the struggle for power which was widely expected. His death at Mombasa, 22 August 1978, was noted throughout the world, attesting to his stature as a leading African nationalist and statesman.

Kenyatta married Grace, daughter of Senior Chief Koinange, soon after returning to Kenya in 1946. She died in childbirth. In 1951, he married for the final time the daughter of Chief Muhoho, Ngina. They had two sons and three daughters.

In July 1974 Kenyatta became life president of KANU. His other honours included an honorary fellowship of the London School of Economics; a knighthood of St. John, 1972; the Order of the Golden Ark of the World Wildlife Fund, 1974; and honorary LL Ds of the University of East Africa (1965) and Manchester University (1966).

[Jeremy Murray-Brown, *Kenyatta*, New York, 1973; Jomo Kenyatta, *Suffering Without Bitterness: The Founding of the Kenya Nation*, Nairobi, 1968; Carl G. Rosberg and John Nottingham, *The Myth of 'Mau Mau': Nationalism in Kenya*, 1966; F. D. Corfield, *Historical Survey of the Origins and Growth of Mau Mau* (Cmnd. 1030), 1960; personal knowledge.]

CARL G. ROSBERG

KENYON, DAME KATHLEEN MARY (1906–1978), archaeologist, was born 5 January 1906 in London, the elder daughter (there were no sons) of (Sir) Frederic George Kenyon [q.v.], of Pradoe, Shropshire, and London, director and principal librarian of the British Museum, and his wife, Amy, daughter of Rowland Hunt, of Boreatton Park, Shropshire. She was educated at St. Paul's Girls' School, where she became head girl, and at Somerville College, Oxford, where she read modern history, obtaining a third class degree in 1928. She also took an active interest in sport, gaining a hockey blue, and in the University Archaeological Society, of which she was the first woman to be elected president. Shortly after leaving Oxford she joined (in 1929) the British Association's expedition to Zimbabwe (Southern Rhodesia), as photographer and assistant to the director, Gertrude Caton-Thompson. In the following year she became a member of the large team excavating the Roman city of Verulamium (St. Albans) under (Sir) Mortimer Wheeler [q.v.] and his wife. She was one of the Wheelers' ablest pupils.

She participated from 1931 to 1934 in J. W. Crowfoot's expedition to Samaria and was, almost single-handedly, responsible for introducing British methods into the region. In 1939 she published a short paper in the *Palestine Exploration Quarterly* on her theory of excavation, which, however, appearing as it did on the eve of the war, had little impact, and it was not until two decades later, with her work at Jericho, that what has come to be known as the 'Wheeler–Kenyon method' began to have a real influence in Near Eastern archaeology. She also wrote considerable parts of the final report on the Samaria excavations.

Her experience in Palestine had not alienated her from British archaeology, and in the late 1930s she was actively digging Iron Age and Roman sites in Leicester and Shropshire. Her friendship with Wheeler and her obvious organizational abilities led to her being involved with him in the founding in 1937 of the University of London Institute of Archaeology, of which she was secretary (1935–48) and acting director (1942–6); and the fact that this fledgling institution survived these troubled times was very largely due to her. The war kept her busy in other ways also, notably with the British Red Cross Society, the youth department of which she directed from 1942 until 1945.

The end of the war enabled her to return to field-work, and the next few years saw her active at sites in London, Herefordshire, and Leicester again. She was appointed lecturer in Palestinian archaeology at the Institute of Archaeology (1948–62). The political situation did not permit her to work in this area immediately, and she had to be content with excavating on the Phoenician and Roman site of Sabratha, in Tripolitania (now Libya) from 1948 until 1951, when she became honorary director of the reconstructed British School of Archaeology in Jerusalem. In 1952 she embarked on what was to be the greatest achievement of her career, the excavation of the mound of Jericho, in the Jordan valley. In *Archaeology in the Holy Land* (1960) she largely rewrote the history of ancient civilization in Palestine. In

1961 she began excavating in Jerusalem and by 1967, when the work ended, much information had been added to the understanding of its ancient topography.

She was not altogether a popular figure especially with those of her peers who did not know her well and saw her only as an autocrat, unable to delegate responsibility. She had a very forceful character and a determination which at times verged on the obstinate. Yet she was never ruthless, and much of her self-sufficiency and of the brusque manner which went with it stemmed from an inherent shyness. Once this was overcome, she was revealed as a kind and warm person, particularly concerned for young people (and animals), who was greatly loved by all who worked really closely with her. Her directness of approach and simplicity of manner were reflected also in her scholarship, which has been seriously underestimated by her critics. She was certainly not a great scholar in the conventional sense, and paradoxically her archaeological interpretations were often marked by a lack of that attention to detail and of precision for which her field-work was so famed. She often seemed unaware of the work of other researchers, and her arguments were sometimes too simplistic to be convincing. Yet she could also display brilliant flashes of intuition in her writings, and she was responsible for a number of new interpretations in books and articles of the archaeology of both Palestine and of Iron Age and Roman Britain which have since become generally accepted.

The final season at Jerusalem in 1967 marked the end of her career as an excavator. In 1962 she had left the Institute of Archaeology to become principal of St. Hugh's College, Oxford, where, until her retirement in 1973, she was an energetic administrator, responsible notably for the ambitious programme of expansion on which the college had embarked. She continued to maintain a close control over the affairs of the British School of Archaeology in Jerusalem, as chairman of the governing body from 1966 until her death, and regularly visited the Near East, while she was also actively involved in the negotiations which eventually, shortly after her death, led to the foundation in Amman, Jordan, of the new British Institute for History and Archaeology. Her years of retirement, which she spent at Erbistock, near Wrexham in north Wales, were spent mainly upon the preparation of the materials from her excavations at Jericho and Jerusalem for publication, and it was upon this task that she was engaged when she died at Erbistock 24 August 1978. She was unmarried.

She was appointed CBE (1954) and DBE (1973), and elected FBA (1955) and FSA. She had several honorary doctorates and was an honorary fellow of Somerville (1960) and St. Hugh's (1973).

[*The Times*, 25 August 1978; personal knowledge.] PETER J. PARR

KHAMA, SIR SERETSE (1921–1980), first president of Botswana, was born 1 July 1921 in Serowe, Botswana, the son of Sekgoma, himself son of the Great Khama who ruled the Bamangwato people of Bechuanaland for more than fifty years. At the turn of the century Sekgoma had been sent into exile for twenty-three years because he chose a wife—Tebogo, mother of Seretse Khama—of whom the Great Khama disapproved. Sekgoma died in 1925, when Seretse was only four years old, and a struggle for power ensued within the Bamangwato leading to the recall from college of Tshekedi Khama [q.v.], another of the Great Khama's sons, to be acting chief of the tribe. Tshekedi decided to bring up Seretse as his own son, and thereafter administered his territory under British overall control, with great energy and efficiency.

Seretse was educated in South Africa and Britain. He took a degree in history at Fort Hare University and was then sent to Balliol College, Oxford, with the intention to read for the bar at the Inner Temple and return to take over the chieftainship of the tribe from his uncle and foster father in December 1948.

He then risked his future by marrying in 1948 an English girl, Ruth, daughter of Captain George Williams, a retired army officer, without waiting for the customary permission from Tshekedi and the tribe. Tshekedi reacted forcefully. He saw that a mixed marriage such as Seretse's not only flouted the tribal procedures, but, in doing so, created a potentially divisive element within Bechuanaland at a time when its future was under threat from South African plans to absorb the High Commission territories. He attempted to forbid Seretse's marriage and have him recalled to Africa. The dispute between foster father and son became the stuff of headlines. Although Tshekedi maintained his opposition, the Bamangwato tribe eventually came to see the issue as a choice between the two Khamas for the future leadership of the tribe and chose the younger man, in spite of his white wife. The British government and High Commission staff in Pretoria were deeply divided but maintained the ban on Seretse because it was finally concluded that—whatever happened within the tribe—the preservation of British authority within Bechuanaland and the stability of future relations with South Africa over the sensitive issue of the High Commission territories could not be guaranteed in the event of the leader of the Bamangwato having a white wife. The Labour government in Britain therefore exiled Seretse Khama and his family in spite of the overwhelmingly favourable verdict for him of a tribal gathering at Serowe on 24 June 1949.

Seretse's exile lasted until September 1956 when the British government announced that he was being allowed to return home having renounced all claim to the Bamangwato chieftainship for himself and his offspring. In 1961 he became a member of the protectorate's executive council. Subsequently in 1962 he founded the moderate multiracial Democratic Party and it won a landslide victory in Bechuanaland's first election in 1965, when Seretse became the country's first prime minister. From this position he negotiated independence, renaming Bechuanaland Botswana, and becoming the country's first president.

His first term of office as president was for three years but his mandate was then renewed on every occasion until his death. The vulnerability of Bechuanaland, which had so influenced the British government's handling of the crisis of Seretse Khama's marriage, was still an important factor affecting the position of the new republic of Botswana. Botswana had a long common frontier with South Africa and another one with Southern Rhodesia, by then in a state of rebellion. A small population, an agrarian economy, and extreme poverty made it impossible for him to indulge in diplomatic heroics over sanctions. But gradually, through patient administration, and moderate policies, he achieved for Botswana not just an economic self-confidence, but a role in the developing black alliance of southern Africa which brought its weight to bear on the ultimate nature of settlement in Southern Rhodesia and established Botswana as a country which could maintain its integrity in black councils, without provoking South African hostility. These achievements no doubt came easier to a man who possessed a natural dignity and modesty and went about his business with patience and tolerance.

By his marriage to Ruth Williams, who outlived him, he had three sons and a daughter. His own disclaimer of rights of succession to the chieftainship was set aside by the tribe, which stated that his descendants were equally eligible for the chieftainshp.

He was appointed OBE in 1963 and KBE in 1966, and became an honorary fellow of Balliol in 1969. He was chancellor of the University of Botswana, Lesotho, and Swaziland, 1967–70. He held honorary degrees from several universities. He died at Gaborone, Botswana, 13 July 1980.

[*The Times*, 14 and 16 July 1980.]

CHARLES DOUGLAS-HOME

KILMAINE, sixth BARON (1902–1978), trust administrator. [See BROWNE, JOHN FRANCIS ARCHIBALD.]

KINDERSLEY, HUGH KENYON MOLESWORTH, second BARON KINDERSLEY (1899–1976), banker and soldier, was born at Egerton Terrace, London SW, 7 May 1899, the second son and second child in the family of four sons and two daughters of (Sir) Robert Molesworth Kindersley, later first Baron Kindersley [q.v.], banker, and his wife, Gladys Margaret, daughter of Major-General James Pattle Beadle, of the Royal Engineers. He was educated at Eton, and served in World War I in the Scots Guards (1917–19), winning the MC in 1918. His elder brother was killed in action in 1917. After the war he joined Lazard Brothers & Co. Ltd., the merchant bankers. His father had been appointed to the London branch of Lazard, Paris, in 1906, and with Robert (later Lord) Brand [q.v.] and Emil Pusch as his partners the firm expanded rapidly. In 1919 with the introduction of capital from the Pearson (Cowdray) family the branch became an independent limited liability company.

Kindersley was given a thorough grounding in what was really still a family business, working for various periods in the Paris and New York offices, as well as in Canada and elsewhere in Europe.

He was appointed a managing director of Lazards in 1927, (chairman in 1953–64) and thenceforth became an increasingly distinguished figure in the City of London. He joined the court of the Royal Exchange Assurance in 1928, becoming governor in 1955. He was one of the team appointed to sort out the chaos left by the crash of the Kruger & Toll Swedish match empire. In 1939 as war became inevitable his sense of duty was such that he left his important business appointments in the City and rejoined the army.

By 1942 he was in command of the 3rd battalion of the Scots Guards, part of the Guards Armoured division. In 1943 he was appointed to command the 6th Air Landing brigade in the 6th Airborne division. He held the rank of temporary brigadier when he landed in Normandy on the first night of the Allied invasion in 1944. Within a few days he was seriously wounded while assisting Lord Lovat who himself had been severely injured. Not long afterwards it became clear that the injury to Kindersley's leg was permanent and he had to retire from the army. He was an outstanding soldier, with evident qualities of leadership, requiring loyalty and courage from those he commanded and displaying these attributes to the full himself. He was appointed MBE in 1941 and CBE in 1945.

His eminence in the City came not so much from creative financial ability but from qualities such as leadership, integrity, loyalty to his colleagues, and willingness to accept responsibility for the acts, especially mistakes, of his subordinates. He belonged to a generation in which important positions of leadership in business came where these qualities were combined with family connections. He succeeded his father to the peerage in 1954.

Later he was thrown into the limelight by the Bank rate tribunal. This was established in late 1957 to ascertain whether anyone who knew of the decision to raise the Bank rate from 5 per cent to 7 per cent in September of that year had profited from that knowledge by selling fixed-interest securities before the decision was announced. Kindersley was a central figure in the inquiry, for not only was he a director of the Bank of England (1947–67), and in that capacity had learned of the decision to raise the Bank rate three days before the actual event, but he was chairman of Lazard Brothers & Co., and governor of the Royal Exchange Assurance, both of which firms had sold gilt-edged securities during the three-day period. Kindersley was closely examined to ascertain whether his inside information had influenced the selling decisions of those firms. But it was found that the sales had been in the ordinary course of business and had been initiated by others.

Kindersley was completely exonerated. There was no doubt that he had not used his inside knowledge for his own benefit, nor had he communicated it to the firms with which he was associated so that they could sell their gilt-edged securities in advance of the event. However, the case was something of a milestone because thereafter it was clear that honesty alone in financial affairs was not enough. It established that those in high positions which involved conflicting interests must, to escape criticism, so conduct themselves that there could be no possibility or even suspicion of wrongful use of inside information. This change would have occurred in any event, but the Bank rate tribunal and Kindersley's part in it highlighted the issue with stark clarity.

He was chairman of Rolls-Royce Ltd. from 1957 to 1968. During this time Rolls Royce committed itself to the development and manufacture of the RB211 aero-engine, a commitment which was a commercial failure and the cause of the downfall of the company and the appointment of a receiver in 1971. The engine involved three major technological developments, which did not go as planned, with resulting delays and increased costs. Although he shared in the collective responsibility of the board for the commitment, the blame for the failure was directed elsewhere and indeed had Kindersley remained in the chair, he might have been able to negotiate assistance from the government which would have ensured the survival of the firm.

His sense of duty and his wartime experiences led him to significant charity work, particularly fund-raising in the medical field, and he became an honorary FRCS in 1959. He was chairman of the review body on doctors' and dentists' remuneration from 1962 to 1970 and chairman and president of the Arthritis and Rheumatism Council until 1970. He was high sheriff of the county of London in 1951.

In 1921 he married Nancy Farnsworth (died 1977), daughter of Dr Geoffrey Boyd, ear, nose, and throat specialist, of Toronto. They had a son and two daughters. Kindersley died at his home, Ramhurst Manor, near Tonbridge, Kent, 6 October 1976 and was succeeded in the title by his son, Robert Hugh Molesworth (born 1929).

[Personal knowledge.] MARTIN JACOMB

KIPPING, SIR NORMAN VICTOR (1901–1979), industrial statesman, was born at 40 Allerton Road, Stoke Newington, 11 May 1901, the younger son and second of three children of Percival Philip Kipping, electrical engineer and owner of the Universal Telephone Company, and his wife, Rose Eleanor Allam. Educated at University College School and Birkbeck College, London University (he did not take a degree), he joined the General Post Office in 1920 as a junior engineer. Over the next twenty years he worked his way up the electrical engineering industry, finally becoming works manager of Standard Telephones & Cables in charge of a staff of 10,000.

In May 1942 he was called into the Ministry of Production and put in charge of its regional organization, which he set up and led; and at the end of the war he was appointed under-secretary in the Board of Trade. For these services he was knighted in 1946. His wartime knowledge of industry stood him in good stead when appointed director-general of the Federation of British Industries in the same year, and there too he created a structure of regional councils for consultations and representation with member companies across the land. For the next nineteen years he led the FBI until it became a major voice for industry.

An early initiative was the setting up in 1948 (with the Trades Union Congress and the British Employers' Confederation) of the Anglo-American Council on Productivity. Consisting of leading industrialists and trade unionists on both sides of the Atlantic and financed by Marshall Aid, the AACP set out to raise productivity standards in British industry by drawing on American experiences; and to this end some sixty-six teams made study visits to the USA and reported back to their industries. Kipping served as joint secretary both of the AACP and of the British Productivity Council which succeeded it in 1952.

A great believer in joint endeavour between unions and management to national ends he was a leading founder-member in 1949 of the Dollar Exports Board (later Council) and from 1960 of the Western Hemisphere Export Council and the Export Council for Europe; and, with government, of the tripartite National Production Advisory Council, the precursor of the National Economic Development Council. In this work he won the confidence and respect of ministers and civil servants under successive governments and of successive general secretaries of the TUC, who became personal friends.

A major strand in his FBI career was the promotion of British trade; and in a series of British trade exhibitions overseas he developed a flair for showmanship coupled with a meticulous attention to organizational detail. After successful exhibitions in Copenhagen and Baghdad, he persuaded the FBI to set up in 1953 for such enterprises British Overseas Fairs Ltd., which he led. Successful fairs were mounted each year, successively in Copenhagen, Damascus, Helsinki, Brussels, Lisbon, New York, Moscow, Stockholm, Sydney, Barcelona, Tokyo, and Oslo—in all of which Kipping and his wife played a leading role with grace and zest.

No linguist, he was nevertheless a convinced internationalist. He revived in post-war Europe an annual gathering of his counterparts around the Continent and their wives, which made him many devoted friends. He was also diligent in the Council of European Industrial Federations; and became a convinced supporter first of the European Free Trade Area and later of the European Economic Community.

Outside Europe he regularly quartered the globe on behalf of British industry, promoting investment as well as trade; and led, for example, a major trade mission to Nigeria (1961) and a voyage of rediscovery to Japan in the same year. India became a special love: he visited it often and invented what the Indians affectionately dubbed 'Kipping Aid', whereby vital supplies were financed by UK aid for British companies producing there, to the mutual benefit of them and of the Indian economy.

After doubling the membership of the FBI during his term, perhaps the achievement of which he was most proud was his role as co-author of the merger which in 1965 brought into being the Confederation of British Industry. That done, he retired happy and spent his still unflagging energies as a director of Joseph Lucas and of Pilkingtons; president of the Anglo-Finnish Society; chairman of the governing council of University College School; and vice-chairman of the Fulton committee on the civil service (1966–8), to name only a few. In 1966 he was appointed GCMG, having been created KBE in 1962. He also held honours from Denmark, Finland, Italy, and Sweden. He was an honorary fellow of the British Institute of Management and an honorary D.Sc. of Loughborough (1966). To this Dictionary he contributed the notices of Sir Hugh Beaver, Sir Richard Costain, and Sir John Woods.

A big man, in physique and personality, he was also genial and kindly to friends and colleagues; and, though no intellectual, a shrewd judge of people, ideas, and the issues that mattered. He married in June 1928 Eileen, daughter of Thomas Rose, produce company secretary, and had two sons and a daughter to whom with his grandchildren he was deeply devoted. From his often arduous day he would return to his home in Barnet (where he was also a JP) for solace and for what the family knew as father's SLITS (something light in the study). Kipping once said to this writer: 'You can find many who will push a rock up a hill, and a few who will push it across the top: but if you find one who will push it down the other side, you have found a winner.' He was such a one. Kipping died in his Barnet home 29 June 1979.

[Sir Norman Kipping, *Summing Up* (memoirs), 1972, and *The Suez Contractors*, 1969; *Daily Telegraph*, 30 June 1979; *The Times*, 23 November 1979; private information; personal knowledge.] JOHN WHITEHORN

KIRK, NORMAN ERIC (1923–1974), leader of the New Zealand Labour Party and prime minister, was born at Waimate, a small South Canterbury farming centre, 6 January 1923, the elder son of Norman Kirk and his wife, Vera Janet Jury. His father, a cabinet maker by trade, found little work in Waimate; the family moved to Christchurch, but as the effects of depression deepened, Norman's childhood experience was of a father often unemployed. He attended the Linwood Avenue primary school, leaving at twelve in 1935, the year in which New Zealand elected its first Labour government. A number of short-lived jobs followed: assistant to a roof painter, apprentice in a welding firm; then, at sixteen, a move away from home to the North Island and a job with the railways at Frankton. While working in Auckland as a ferry engineer Kirk married, in 1943, Ruth, daughter of George Frederick Miller, who worked in the post office at Paeroa. The same year he joined the Labour Party. There followed five lean years as an engineer boilerman in a dairy factory at Katikati near Tauranga. Then in 1949 the growing family—three sons and a daughter, and a second daughter yet to arrive—returned to the South Island, to Kaiapoi just out of Christchurch where the Jurys had lived. Having built his own house Kirk turned to politics. He revived the moribund local branch of the Labour Party and in 1953, at thirty, was elected mayor of Kaiapoi. An effective administrator, he was re-elected but resigned in 1957 to enter Parliament in the marginal seat of Lyttelton which he held until 1969 when he won the Sydenham seat with a record majority.

In 1963 Kirk was elected vice-president of the Labour Party; twelve months later he became its president. In 1965 he became leader of the Parliamentary Labour Party, the youngest leader in the party's history. He was re-elected leader in 1968. Kirk's impatience for power, stemming in part from his conviction that he was destined to die young, found a response in the party's pre-occupation with finding a leader who could convince the voters of Labour's relevance to New Zealand in the second half of the twentieth century. With little sympathy for theoretical or doctrinaire lines of action, Kirk was a practical man, a politician largely motivated by his own experience. That experience, paradoxically, was more characteristic of the Labour leadership of an earlier generation than of Kirk's contemporaries. His remarkable rise to leadership in the party was not, at first, matched by a comparable impact on the country. The party was defeated at the general election of 1966 and again, more narrowly, in 1969. Kirk knew he would almost certainly be given only one more chance. This vulnerability strengthened his feeling of being a loner, his distrust of his colleagues, his authoritarian streak. It also led to a change of style; obesity was tempered to a commanding presence, television revealed a quietly persuasive manner. Moreover, at a time when the United States was disengaging in South-East Asia and British entry to the European common market was imminent, Kirk's call for greater New Zealand self-reliance, for independence of judgement and action, carried conviction. In December 1972, to the surprise of many but not Kirk himself, he led the Labour Party to a sweeping victory. He was then admitted to the Privy Council.

In his short period of office Kirk proved to be a vigorous prime minister and an innovative foreign minister ready to probe accepted assumptions about the nature of international political relations and especially New Zealand's place within them. New Zealand foreign policy reflected Kirk's firm adherence to moral principles in foreign relations. Its successful implementation, he believed, rested on understanding and acceptance by the New Zealand public. In 1973 he unequivocally called on the New Zealand Rugby Union to 'postpone' the tour by an all-white South African side for the sake of the country's wider interests. In the case of French nuclear testing in the Pacific he sought to mobilize opinion more widely both by sending a New Zealand naval vessel into the Mururoa testing zone and subsequently by taking New Zealand's case against testing to the International Court of Justice. Both intellectual conviction and warm humanity strengthened a particular concern with the problems of the neighbouring Pacific and Asian areas where he sought to encourage regional co-operation and the more effective use of increased New Zealand aid. He established close personal relations with such third world leaders as Julius Nyerere of Tanzania and Sheikh Mujibur Rahman of Bangladesh and in particular with the leaders of Commonwealth countries with whom he developed a strong rapport at the Commonwealth heads of government meeting in Ottawa in 1973.

Kirk's broad humanitarian philosophy, his striking intellect, his strong sense of New Zealand identity, came together brilliantly in his conduct of foreign policy. His government was notably less successful in its domestic policies. Kirk himself was conservative on many social questions, his practical experience often an inadequate basis for grappling with problems of social and economic change. In his last year of office ill health exacerbated his aggressive determination to have his own way and stretched the loyalty of colleagues, while Kirk himself was increasingly less able to provide effective leadership. A minor operation in April 1974 led to a series of complications. Kirk resisted proper treatment and with obstinate courage struggled to carry on. On 31 August, three days after finally agreeing to enter hospital in Wellington, he died of heart failure.

In his brief twenty-one months as prime minister Norman Kirk captured the imagination and the affection of many New Zealanders. In intellect as in physical stature he was a big man. He was also a complex man. Possessed of tremendous drive for self-improvement, of a capacity to listen, to reflect, and to judge that was unmatched in prime ministers since Peter Fraser [q.v.], New Zealand's wartime leader, he could also be prickly, petty minded, and prejudiced. To his Labour colleagues he bequeathed the example but not the secret of success.

[Margaret Hayward, *Diary of the Kirk Years*, Wellington, 1981; private information.]

T. H. BEAGLEHOLE

KIRKBRIDE, SIR ALEC SEATH (1897–1978), diplomat, was born 28 August 1897 at Mansfield, Nottinghamshire, the elder son of Joseph Kirkbride, lithographer, and his wife, Isabel Bradley. In 1906 his father moved to a post in the Egyptian state customs service. Though a Protestant, he sent his two sons to a Jesuit college where the teaching was in French, and where they learnt fluent Arabic from schoolfellows.

In January 1916 Kirkbride enlisted in the Royal Engineers. After six months spent recruiting local personnel for the Egyptian Labour Corps, he was posted to Beersheba, and instructed to prospect the possibility of a motorable track from there to Tafileh on the escarpment across the Jordan. He proved this impossible, but during the job met T. E. Lawrence [q.v.] in a snowstorm on the heights. Lawrence later offered him a post in the Arab army of regulars, chiefly Iraqi, that gave him his first contact with educated Arab nationalists. With them he took part in the successful destruction of the railways round Deraa, and, with Nuri, watched the British cavalry streaming north towards Damascus. 'They could have done it without us', said Nuri. But not so cheaply in human life, reflected Kirkbride. As one of the first Englishmen into Damascus, he helped Lawrence to clear the streets of marauders and clean up the shambles in the Turkish hospital. This won him the MC.

When Faisal was banished by the French from Syria, Transjordan became a vacant lot, and Kirkbride was chosen as one of the six Arabic-speaking British officers temporarily to administer it. He ran what he called 'the National Government of Moab' from Kerak until the Amir Abdullah arrived from the Hejaz bent on avenging his brother and taking Syria. Kirkbride sent him north to Amman, whence he met the British colonial secretary, (Sir) Winston Churchill, in Jerusalem, and was confirmed as amir of Transjordan; he remained so until it became a kingdom in 1946.

Kirkbride was posted to Jerusalem in 1922, where he served the Palestine government first as junior assistant secretary and from 1926 as assistant secretary. In 1927, to his pleasure, he returned to Amman as assistant British resident. He had always liked Abdullah, with his realism and his sense of humour. In 1930 the local pastime of tribal raiding was checked by the appointment of (Sir) J. B. Glubb to raise a police force from among the nomadic tribes, whose dislike for their semi-settled brothers was proverbial. Meantime Kirkbride, with French colleagues, demarcated the Syria-Transjordan boundary.

This smooth existence was interrupted when, on 26 September 1937, his friend L. Y. Andrews was murdered by Arabs at Nazareth. Instructed to replace him at once as commissioner for Galilee, Kirkbride was transported into a district seething with rebellion. But he was a good listener, and aware since his schooldays of the processes of Arab and Jewish thought. By a calm practice of calling steadily on both communities, he earned much goodwill and left in 1939 as a popular figure.

He returned to Transjordan to take up the post for which he is best remembered—that of chief British representative; he became its first British minister when it was transformed into a kingdom in 1946. Keeping Arab spirits up in the first two years of the war was difficult, but for Transjordanians the turning point was the failure of the Rashid Ali rebellion in Iraq, in which a small contingent of the Arab Legion played a distinguished part. No longer did Kirkbride need to drive around looking cheerful.

Contingents of the Legion, commanded by British officers, did guard duty in Palestine until the end of the mandate. When in September 1947 the British announced their intention of giving up the mandate, few but King Abdullah believed them. Abdullah met a Jewish representative to discuss the future, while Kirkbride, seeing no reason to risk his life by driving into the chaos in Jerusalem to visit the high commissioner, gave up the practice. He was appalled at the Arab failure to assess Jewish strength, and, when war finally broke out on the British departure, was unsurprised that only the Arab Legion distinguished itself in the fighting. In December 1948 King Abdullah, to the fury of the rest of the Arab League, annexed the parts of Palestine that the Legion had held.

In July 1951, to Kirkbride's deep distress while he was on leave in England, King Abdullah was murdered in Jerusalem. Kirkbride attended his funeral, but did not think that he would be happy with the heir, Talal, and asked the Foreign Office for another Arab post. He was offered the headship of the diplomatic mission about to be accredited to Libya, and became its first British minister. He got on well with King Idris. When, soon after his arrival, a pro-Egyptian faction was obstreperous, the prime minister asked for help from British troops. Kirkbride replied that an independent country must do its own policing. A year later (1953) he was able to negotiate an Anglo-Libyan treaty that was to maintain British bases there for nearly twenty years. He became ambassador in 1954 and retired the same year.

Kirkbride, who was six feet four inches in height, could never have passed for an Arab. Though taciturn with fellow countrymen, he was successful with most people on account of his solid common sense and his belief in telling the truth, however unpleasant. For these virtues he was appointed to the OBE in 1932, the CMG in 1942, a knighthood in 1946, the KCMG in 1949, and the CVO when Queen Elizabeth visited Libya in 1954.

On retirement, he became a director of the British Bank of the Middle East (1956–72), and wrote three books of memoirs. His recreations were amateur archaeology, coin collecting, and shooting at weekends, usually alone. He married in 1921 Edith Florence, daughter of William James, of North Finchley, who bore him three sons; she died in 1966. In 1967 he married Ethel Mary James, his former wife's niece, who nursed him through the long illness of which he died at Worthing 22 November 1978.

[Sir Alec Kirkbride, *A Crackle of Thorns*, 1956, *An Awakening*, 1972, and *From the Wings*,

1976; private information; personal knowledge.] ELIZABETH MONROE

KITSON CLARK, GEORGE SIDNEY ROBERTS (1900–1975), historian, was born in Leeds 14 June 1900, the younger son and second of the three children of Edwin Kitson Clark, of Leeds, lieutenant-colonel of the Territorial Army and mechanical engineer, the son of E. C. Clark, regius professor of civil law at Cambridge. His mother was Georgina, a painter, the daughter of George Parker Bidder QC, lawyer, and granddaughter of G. P. Bidder [q.v.], engineer, who was exhibited in his youth as a 'calculating' phenomenon. He was educated at Shrewsbury School. Brought up in a cultured and spacious home at Meanwoodside, he was not happy at school where he appeared awkward, untidy, and ineffective at games. He entered Trinity College, Cambridge, as an exhibitioner in 1919. There he found the environment in which he could blossom. With his genial and hospitable nature, he entered with zest into college activities. In part i of the historical tripos he obtained a lower second and in part ii he was placed in the second division of the first class (1921). He became a research fellow of his college in 1922, college lecturer in 1928, university lecturer in 1929, college tutor in 1933, and in 1954 university reader in English constitutional history.

As a tutor, teaching and administration absorbed most of his time and energy. He liked young people, both children and undergraduates, and won their affectionate respect. To the end he retained a certain boyishness himself. Burly, courageous and outspoken, he became one of the notable characters of the university. As fellow of his college and member of the history faculty, he was both active and innovatory. Though generally conservative in his views, he had a flexible and imaginative mind. He played a prominent part in the enlargement of the tripos syllabus to include American and imperial history. In his last two decades he was an outstanding supervisor of research students and made Cambridge a centre for research in English nineteenth-century history. He helped to establish New Hall, the third women's college at Cambridge. He founded the university's Educational Film Council.

He never married and with the deterioration in his father's health and finances between the wars, he took on large and continuing responsibilities towards the rest of the family. After World War II, when college and family pressures eased, his life widened. Underneath his bluff exterior there was a sensitive temperament, easily hurt and sometimes momentarily petulant. Though disappointed not to become vice-master of his college or Cambridge professor of modern history, he remained singularly free from professional envy. He had strong feelings, which he found difficult to suppress, and could offend unwittingly; he himself forgave easily. At heart he was a humble man. A devout Anglican, he revealed something of his deeper beliefs in two books, *The English Inheritance* (1950) and *The Kingdom of Free Men* (1957).

His first and longest book (but not his best, nor the one he most enjoyed writing) was *Peel and the Conservative Party: A Study in Party Politics 1832–41* (1929, 2nd edn. 1964); this was a development of his fellowship dissertation. Apart from a brief life of *Peel* (1936), he produced nothing more for twenty years and never again a major piece of research. As late as 1952 he was contemplating a companion volume on 'Peel and the Corn Laws' and a study of mid-Victorian society which would fill the gap in Elie Halévy's classic *Histoire du Peuple Anglais au XIXe Siècle*. All that came of the first were three memorable articles on the social background. In place of the second came the books which constitute his main historical achievement: *The Making of Victorian England* (1962), *An Expanding Society, Britain 1830–1900* (1967), and *Churchmen and the Condition of England 1832–1885* (1973). Significantly all were based on series of lectures. He had found his medium and with it an attractive style, half-way between essay and conversation. The fruit of capacious reading and much reflection, his books were designed to redirect and illuminate, to stimulate rather than satisfy. A Kitson Clark school of historians would have been foreign to his mentality but generations of students at Cambridge and many contemporary historians were influenced by his outlook and grateful for his friendship.

He was Ford's lecturer at Oxford (1959–60), Maurice lecturer at King's College, London (1960), Birkbeck lecturer at Cambridge (1967), and visiting lecturer at the universities of Pennsylvania (1953–4) and Melbourne (1964). Besides his Cambridge Litt.D., which he took in 1954, he received honorary degrees from Durham (1960), East Anglia (1970), Glasgow (1971), and Leeds (1973); and in 1975 he was elected foreign honorary member of the American Academy of Arts and Sciences. He died at Trinity College 8 December 1975.

[*The Times*, 11 December 1975; *Trinity College Review*, Lent 1963; *Cambridge Review*, 30 January 1976; *American Historical Review*, October 1976; private information; personal knowledge.] NORMAN GASH

KLUGMANN, NORMAN JOHN ('JAMES') (1912–1977), a leading member of the Communist Party of Great Britain, was born in Hampstead 27 February 1912, the third son and fourth child of Samuel Klugmann, a wealthy Jewish rope and twine merchant, and his wife,

Anna Rosenheim. He entered Gresham's School, Holt, in 1926, leaving in 1931 with a modern languages scholarship to Trinity College, Cambridge. A contemporary schoolfellow was the future defector Donald Maclean. At Cambridge Klugmann gained a first in French and an upper second in German in part i of the tripos (1932) and a first in part ii (1934). He was researching during the academic year 1934–5, but was already deeply immersed in what was to become his lifelong work for the Communist Party. He was to prove one of the most effective and durable activists of the Cambridge far left, then at its zenith. Prominent among a slightly older generation of his comrades were David Haden-Guest, Anthony Blunt, and Maurice Cornforth, who married Klugmann's sister Kitty. Outstanding undergraduate contemporaries included Maclean, Guy Burgess, and the spectacular John Cornford, killed in Spain in 1936. Cornford, a tireless zealot, and Klugmann, amiable, assiduous, and gently persuasive, worked outwards from the growing communist cell in Trinity to expand successfully the Cambridge Socialist Society and similar student groups in other universities, ensuring that, in the Popular Front mode of the day, they were all Marxist dominated.

Klugmann's outstanding linguistic ability and missionary zeal soon impelled him to work for the party abroad. From 1935 to 1939 he was secretary of the World Student Association against War and Fascism in Paris, visiting the Balkans, the Middle East, India, and China, where he led a student delegation to meet Mao Tse-tung. Conscripted into the Royal Army Service Corps, he transferred to the Intelligence Corps and by 1942 was a corporal clerk in the Cairo headquarters of the Special Operations Executive. Within a year he was commissioned and by the spring of 1943 was promoted captain. His pre-war knowledge of Yugoslavia and of its youthful anti-Fascists enabled him to make a widely praised contribution to the briefing and organization of SOE agents. During his wartime career in Cairo, which culminated in his promotion to the rank of major, he was much respected and liked for his intelligence and warm, good-humoured manner.

Between April 1945 and July 1946 Klugmann worked with the UNRRA mission to Yugoslavia. Returning then to England, he lived in Clapham, at times almost submerged physically in his vast library of communist texts. He was head of the party's education department from 1950 to 1960, and a member of its executive committee from 1952 and later of its political committee, until compelled to resign in 1963 owing to chronic asthma. At the inception of the monthly *Marxism Today* in 1957 he became assistant editor to John Gollan [q.v.], succeeding in 1963 to the editorship, which he retained till 1977.

An undeviating adherence to party orthodoxy contrasted oddly with Klugmann's general reputation for civilized enlightenment. Thus, in his *From Trotsky to Tito* (1951) he roundly condemned the Yugoslav leaders, once his heroes, observing that 'their treachery had been long and carefully concealed'. Commenting on Stalin's death in *Labour Monthly* (April 1953), he described him as 'the world's greatest working class leader' and as 'the man of peace, of international fraternity'. He worked for many years on his *History of the Communist Party of Great Britain*. Volume i, dealing with the early years 1920–4, was published in 1968; volume ii, covering 1925 and the general strike, in 1969. He was also prominent in the activity known as Christian–Marxist dialogue. In 1968 he collaborated in *What Kind of a Revolution?* with the Anglican priest Paul Oestreicher, who in that work described Marxists as part of the latent church. In the same year Klugmann edited *Dialogue of Christianity and Marxism*, essays originally published in *Marxism Today*. Without deviating an inch from his Marxist orthodoxy, he managed to convey in this area of his work for the party a general impression of bridge-building benevolence. A revealing aspect of his mind and character is to be found in *A Reader's Guide to the Study of Marxism*, an undated pamphlet, in which his advice to tutors and leaders of discussion groups is a model exposition of how to teach cogently and attractively and goes a long way to explain the affection and respect he commanded among the young faithful of the party.

He died of a heart attack in Stockwell Hospital 14 September 1977. He was unmarried.

[*The Times*, 26 September 1977; *Morning Star*, 16 September 1977; Andrew Boyle, *The Climate of Treason*, 1979.] T. E. B. HOWARTH

KNATCHBULL-HUGESSEN, SIR HUGHE MONTGOMERY (1886–1971), diplomat, was born in London 26 March 1886, the fourth son of the Revd Reginald Bridges Knatchbull-Hugessen, rector of Mersham, Kent, and his second wife, Rachel Mary, daughter of Admiral Sir Alexander Leslie Montgomery; his grandfather, Edward Knatchbull [q.v.] had been paymaster-general in 1834–5 and 1841–5. The history of the Knatchbull family is recounted in Sir Hughe's *Kentish Family* (1960).

After education at Eton and Balliol College, Oxford, where he obtained a third class in modern history in 1907, Knatchbull-Hugessen entered the Foreign Office in 1908. In 1912 he married Mary (died 1978) daughter of Colonel (later Brigadier-General Sir) Robert Gordon-Gilmour; they had one son and two daughters. During the war of 1914–18 he worked in the Contraband Department, and, in 1919, was a member of the British delegation to the peace conference. After the war it became possible for Foreign Office staff to serve abroad, and in November 1919, Knatchbull-Hugessen went to The Hague as secretary to the legation. He served for four years in this post under Sir Ronald Graham [q.v.], and then, for a year, worked under Lord Crewe [q.v.] as head of chancery in Paris. In 1926 he became counsellor of embassy in Brussels, and stayed there until 1930 when he was appointed minister to the three Baltic States, Estonia, Latvia, and Lithuania. He expected to remain in Europe, but, in 1934, was surprised to be asked to go to Tehran as minister; he embarked upon his new work with some anxiety, but, when he was again transferred in 1936, he looked back on his time in Persia (Iran) as one of the most interesting and pleasant periods of his life. He was on leave in London when he was offered the post of ambassador in China, in succession to Sir Alexander Cadogan [q.v.] who was returning to London to become permanent under-secretary of the Foreign Office. In 1920 he had been gazetted CMG, and now, in 1936, he was promoted KCMG.

It is clear from Knatchbull-Hugessen's autobiography, *Diplomat in Peace and War* (1949), that, by the time he set out for China, he was thoroughly enjoying diplomatic life; he liked the protocol and ceremony, and the variation of scene that attended each new move; through his skill at sketching, he was able to capture some of the more interesting sights in the course of his travels. He also found pleasure in the companionship and loyalty of his staff.

During the two years Knatchbull-Hugessen spent in China, that country was in turmoil. Chiang Kai-shek and the Kuomintang government had succeeded in driving the Communists into the north-west, but the efforts of the generalissimo to assert his authority throughout China were threatened by unco-operative warlords and by the Japanese. At the ambassador's first meeting with Chiang Kai-shek in Nanking it appeared that some accommodation could be reached with the Japanese. However, in August 1937, the shooting of two Japanese officers in Shanghai led to open war. Knatchbull-Hugessen regarded it as his duty to visit the British community in Shanghai, and set out by car from Nanking with his financial adviser and military attaché. The Union Jacks on the windscreen were insufficient protection, however; a Japanese aeroplane fired on the party and the ambassador was severely wounded.

Although disappointing to Knatchbull-Hugessen, it was essential to his recovery that he should have long leave in England, and because of the situation in China, his post there had to be filled without delay. After a year recuperating from his wound, he was posted as ambassador to Turkey. The war of 1939–45 had already broken out when he arrived in Ankara. In the autumn of 1939 Turkey signed a tripartite treaty with Britain and France, and throughout the next five years Knatchbull-Hugessen's task was to counter the efforts of Franz von Papen, the German ambassador, to thwart any closer understanding between Turkey and the Allies. During 1941 and 1942, when the war seemed to be going in Hitler's favour, the Turks concentrated on keeping the peace with both sides. As the war progressed, they seemed to be as suspicious of Russian ambitions as of those of the Germans. Although early in 1943 (Sir) Winston Churchill visited Turkey and conferred with President Inönü about Turkey taking an active part in the war, the Turks maintained their cautious neutrality until February 1945 when they declared war on Germany. It seems unlikely that Knatchbull-Hugessen, in spite of his cordial relations with the Turkish leaders, was able to make any marked impression upon their policy. He himself expressed the view that Turkey was so unprepared for war in the years between 1939 and 1944 that it was better that she should remain a friendly neutral.

After a period of some ten years in the Middle East and China, in his final posting abroad he returned to Europe. Brussels had been relieved by British and American troops when he arrived there in September 1944 as ambassador in Belgium and minister in Luxemburg, but V1s were still falling nearby. During the next three years he witnessed the gradual recovery of Belgium from the effects of the German occupation; he thoroughly enjoyed the enthusiasm aroused by Churchill's visit to Brussels in 1945. In 1947 he retired.

Knatchbull-Hugessen's years of retirement were clouded by his anxiety to clear his name of the imputation that, while he was ambassador in Ankara, his failure to observe strict security measures had provided Franz von Papen with information regarding the plans for the Allied invasion of Europe. In consequence of a brief lapse of essential precautions to ensure the secrecy of important documents, the ambassador's Albanian valet was able to obtain a duplicate key to a box in which highly confidential papers were kept. The man had been vetted by the normal security procedure, but he seized his opportunity to make easy money, and was able from November 1943 to February 1944 to sell to the German embassy in Ankara films of documents to which he should not have been able to gain access. After the war sensational accounts appeared of the activities of this spy, to whom the Germans had given the code name 'Cicero', and, for years, Knatchbull-Hugessen was preoccupied with his concern to put the record straight. The information passed to the Germans included accounts of the Moscow, Cairo, and

Tehran conferences, and may have included a reference to 'Overlord'. Von Papen may have deduced that this related to the D-Day landings, but it is certain that the British ambassador had no information regarding the details of the Allied plans and that no knowledge of those plans could have been revealed to the Germans through 'Cicero'. Nevertheless, a successful diplomatic career was marred by this unfortunate misadventure.

Towards the end of his life Knatchbull-Hugessen was crippled as a result of the injury he had suffered in China. He died at his home near Canterbury 21 March 1971.

[Sir Hughe Knatchbull-Hugessen, *Diplomat in Peace and War*, 1949; family papers; private information.] H. F. Oxbury

KNOWLES, Dom David (1896–1974), monk and monastic historian. [See Knowles, Michael Clive.]

KNOWLES, Sir FRANCIS GERALD WILLIAM, sixth baronet (1915–1974), biologist, was born 9 March 1915 at Ottawa, the only child of Sir Francis Howe Seymour Knowles, fifth baronet, prehistorian and sometime physical anthropologist to the Geological Survey of Canada, and his wife, Kathleen Constance Averina, daughter of William Lennon, county inspector, Royal Irish Constabulary. He was educated in England, at Radley and at Oriel College, Oxford, graduating BA in 1936 (second class) in the honour school of zoology, MA and D.Phil. in 1939, and D.Sc. in 1963. He was elected FRS in 1966. Awarded the Oxford University Naples scholarship, he visited the Stazione Zoologica in 1937–8 and began investigating the role of hormones in the regulation of colour change in lampreys and crustaceans.

When his scholarship ended he joined the staff of Marlborough College in 1938 and stayed there for twenty years as senior biology master. During this period he published several biological texts, including *Man and Other Living Things* (1945) and *Biology and Man* (1950), and also continued his researches on crustacean colour change, working during school holidays at marine biological laboratories with support from the Royal Society and the Nuffield Foundation. These activities gave his pupils an exceptional degree of excitement and stimulus that could have been found in few other schools at that time. He succeeded his father as baronet in 1953.

Meanwhile he had become aware of the new perspectives that had been opened in comparative endocrinology through the discovery of neurosecretion: the process by which certain nerve cells secrete hormones into the blood stream. He was quick to exploit this concept, making skilful use of a variety of new techniques, including electron microscopy, which captured and always retained his special interest. Impressive presentation of his elegant results, delivered at international gatherings with calculated panache, brought him a distinguished reputation that led to his appointment in 1958 as lecturer, with special responsibility for electron microscopy, in the department of anatomy at Birmingham University. Quickly establishing himself as a dynamic biologist, satisfied with nothing less than perfection in technique, he expanded his researches to include the study of neurosecretory pathways in the brain and pituitary gland of the dogfish and, later, of the rhesus monkey. He was promoted reader in 1963 and professor of comparative endocrinology in 1967, in which year, however, he moved to the University of London as professor of anatomy at King's College.

Here he soon abandoned primate research and turned once again to fish, despite the obvious difficulties of working on these animals from a London base. He took a full share in administration, serving with distinction as dean, and, at national level, becoming chairman of the biological sciences committee of the Science Research Council and a member of its science board. The sixth international symposium on neurosecretion was held in London in September 1973, and he took particular pleasure in organizing it, for this was the twentieth anniversary of the first of these symposia, where, as a schoolmaster, he had presented the results of his pioneering crustacean studies. Within a year, however, his career came to a premature end before his studies of neurosecretory pathways in vertebrates could come to full fruition.

His approach to research was essentially that of a classical electron microscopist, who preferred to work on his own or with single collaborators at home or at a distance, rather than to develop a team. But he took pleasure in wide-ranging discussions, free of disciplinary constraints, and enjoyed provoking reactions to the sometimes unorthodox views which flowed from his fertile and speculative mind with the touch of flamboyance that was a marked feature of his character. This element came to the fore in 1955 with his purchase of Avebury Manor in Wiltshire, an Elizabethan residence which he planned to develop into a family home. Its repair, and the purchase of suitable furnishings, became an absorbing love, and an outlet for his unerringly elegant taste. Set against this background, remote from academic biology, he appeared to one of his colleagues as 'a fascinating man who would really have been more at home in the eighteenth century'. To another he gave proof that 'one could be both a distinguished scholar and a warm vibrant person'.

In 1948 he married Ruth Jessie, daughter of the Revd Arthur Brooke-Smith and widow of Pilot Officer Richard Guy Hulse of the RAF. They had one son, Charles Frances (born 1951) who succeeded as seventh baronet, and three daughters, one of whom was the son's twin. There was also a stepdaughter. Knowles died in London 13 July 1974.

[E. J. W. Barrington in *Biographical Memoirs of Fellows of the Royal Society*, vol. xxi, 1975; private information; personal knowledge.]

E. J. W. BARRINGTON

KNOWLES, MICHAEL CLIVE, DOM DAVID (1896–1974), monk and monastic historian, was born at Studley in Warwickshire 29 September 1896, the only surviving child of Herbert Henry (Harry) Knowles and his wife, Caroline Morgan. His father was partner in a firm which made needles and pins, whose modest prosperity enabled him to send his son to school at Downside (1910–14). On 4 October 1914 he was received into the monastic community at Downside, and was a Benedictine monk for the remainder of his life, although he lived apart from his community from 1939. At Downside he early came under the influence of the abbot, E. J. A. Butler (Dom Cuthbert, whose notice he later wrote for this Dictionary), monastic reformer and scholar, and also met the elderly layman Edmund Bishop [q.v.], one of the most distinguished medievalists of his generation. Knowles made his simple profession in 1915 and took solemn vows in 1918; he was ordained subdeacon in 1920, deacon in 1921, and priest on 9 July 1922. Meanwhile he had spent three years at Christ's College, Cambridge (1919–22): he took a first in both parts of the classical tripos, with a distinction in philosophy in part ii; he also received a college scholarship in 1920, and the Skeat prize for English literature. His love of reading and exceptional memory gave him a rich store of literature, English, Latin, and Greek, on which he frequently drew in the writings and conversation of his later years.

For some years he taught classics at Downside; but otherwise the main preoccupation of the 1920s was with theology and the religious life. In 1922–3 he completed his study of theology at the great Benedictine house of Sant' Anselmo in Rome. In the late 1920s he began to show a deepening anxiety about what he believed to be the tension between the life of prayer and worship and the outward-looking, teaching function of the community, brought to a head in 1933. With a group of the younger monks he formed the idea of setting up a new community; when the plan was finally rejected at Rome in 1934, all but Knowles submitted, and most of the group remained at Downside. Knowles never accepted this verdict. In 1933 he had been moved to Ealing Priory, still unreconciled, and in 1939 he left his community, to live apart for the rest of his life; although a formal reconciliation was arranged in 1952, by which he was 'exclaustrated', that is, had permission to live outside the monastery. From 1939 until his death he was cared for by a devout Swedish doctor, a convert to the Catholic Church, Dr Elizabeth Kornerup. He lived first in London; later he divided his time between London and Cambridge, and after his retirement in 1963, between Wimbledon and Linch (Sussex).

Long before 1939 he had begun his life as a scholar. In 1926 he published *The American Civil War*, a remarkable essay in historical literature. Serious history began in 1929 when he started work on *The Monastic Order in England*, which was published by the Cambridge University Press in 1940. He was already known to other scholars from his articles in the *Downside Review* and some personal contact, but *The Monastic Order* immediately established his reputation as a medieval historian. In 1941 he proceeded Litt.D. at Cambridge; in 1944 he was elected to a teaching fellowship at Peterhouse (he remained a fellow until 1963); in 1947 he succeeded his friend Z. N. Brooke, whose notice he wrote for this Dictionary, as professor of medieval history; in 1954 Sir Winston Churchill appointed him to the regius chair of modern history, from which he retired in 1963. He was a fellow of the Royal Historical Society, and president 1956–60; fellow of the Society of Antiquaries; and fellow of the British Academy (1947). In later years he was honorary fellow of Christ's and Peterhouse, and received honorary doctorates from eight universities, including his own.

During the years he taught in Cambridge he had a deep influence on many students who were inspired by his lectures and supervisions, and won an international reputation as one of the world's most eminent medievalists. *The Monastic Order in England . . . 940–1216* (1940, 2nd edn. 1963) and *The Religious Orders in England* (3 vols., 1948–59) comprise a great set piece of historical writing, celebrated alike for its scale and learning, and as a model of English prose. *The Monastic Order* has been widely reckoned his most inspired book; the last volume, *The Religious Orders*, iii, on the dissolution of the monasteries, was perhaps his literary masterpiece. He wrote many other books on medieval ecclesiastical history, the Becket controversy, mysticism, and related themes; and his published lectures showed the range of his learning and culture. He also contributed the notice of C. W. Previté-Orton to this Dictionary.

Austere yet richly gifted; conservative in theology yet abundantly charitable; reserved yet warm and deep in his affections; deeply serious yet capable of gaiety, wit, and a delicious vein of humour: to his friends and pupils and to many of his acquaintances he was one of the remarkable personalities of the British academic world of his day. His breach with Downside brought out a strength of purpose, as some thought a fierce obstinacy, which was hidden from many who knew him, and revealed some of the complexity of his nature. His closest friends recalled his fondness for walking and rambling, and the quality of his conversation; very characteristic was the tenacity of his memory for books read long ago (and even for long departed steam engines), and the remarkable harmony in which these memories lived with an ordered, strict, regime of spiritual life. To a wider public he will be especially remembered as one of the greatest of Benedictine historians, a worthy successor of the Maurists, whom he so much admired. He died in Sussex 21 November 1974.

[Adrian Morey, *David Knowles, a Memoir*, 1979; for his autobiography (MS) see C. N. L. Brooke in *Proceedings* of the British Academy, vol. lxi, 1975; A. Stacpoole, 'The Making of a Monastic Historian', *Ampleforth Journal*, vol. lxxx, 1975; Knowles, 'Academic History', *History*, vol. xlvii, 1962; W. A. Pantin, 'Curriculum Vitae', in *The Historian of Character and Other Essays*, 1963; personal knowledge.]

C. N. L. Brooke

KNOX, EDMUND GEORGE VALPY (1881–1971), writer and editor of *Punch*, was born in Oxford 10 May 1881, the second child and eldest son in the family of two daughters and four sons of Edmund Arbuthnott Knox [q.v.], a fellow of Merton College, Oxford, and later bishop of Manchester, and his wife, Ellen Penelope (died 1891), daughter of Thomas Valpy French [q.v.], later bishop of Lahore. He won a scholarship to Rugby, and then in 1900 went up to Oxford to study classics, to his father's old college, Corpus Christi, with every expectation that he would likewise distinguish himself there as a scholar; as it turned out, he obtained a second class in classical honour moderations in 1902 and went down without taking *literae humaniores*, having acquired a reputation as a wit and promoter of bizarre jokes. Like his brothers, he was temperamentally a don, but unlike them never became one.

All the four brothers were in their different ways remarkable. There was Dillwyn (or 'Dilly'), a classical scholar, mathematician, and fellow of King's College, Cambridge, who in both the 1914–18 and the 1939–45 wars distinguished himself as a cryptographer, and during the latter participated in the great Ultra feat; Wilfred [q.v.], an Anglican priest, an authority on the Apostle Paul, and a saint and mystic; and Ronald [q.v.], who became a Roman Catholic and a monsignor, and enchanted especially undergraduates with his wit and parodies.

Edmund Knox decided to be a writer, and, after spending a year teaching at North Manchester Preparatory School, when he began dispatching manuscripts they flew like homing pigeons in through the window of the *Punch* office in Bouverie Street and on to the desk of Sir Owen Seaman who edited *Punch* from 1906 to 1932, and whose notice Knox was later to write for this Dictionary. Knox started contributing soon after he came down from Oxford, using the pseudonym of 'Evoe', defined in the dictionary as 'a cry of rejoicing uttered by the followers of the wine-god'. As an appellation this would have suited him well enough, but it seems more likely that his purpose in choosing to be Evoe rather than just using his initials was a very understandable wish to ensure his not being confused with E. V. Lucas, also a *Punch* contributor, whose notice Knox later wrote for this Dictionary. For Evoe, Seaman was what Charles Lamb called an imperfect sympathy; in a letter quoted by his daughter Penelope Fitzgerald in her book *The Knox Brothers* (1977), he writes that Seaman 'had indeed a strong sense of vocation, and I remember his saying sadly of somebody or other "he is the kind of man who doesn't take his humour seriously" '. Even so, Evoe managed to keep on sufficiently good terms with Seaman to work regularly for *Punch*, deputizing in the office during holiday periods or when someone was away ill.

After war was declared in 1914 Knox joined the Territorials, and by Christmas was a second lieutenant in the Lincolnshire Regiment. He was first sent to Ireland, and then in 1917 to France. In September he was wounded in the third battle of Ypres. After being demobilized in April 1919 he worked for eighteen months at the Ministry of Labour in order to support his wife and small children.

In 1920 he joined the Table—the *Punch* weekly confabulation to decide the subject of the main political cartoon, originally called the Big Cut—and the regular staff in 1921, following Seaman in the editorial chair eleven years later. R. G. G. Price, in his *A History of Punch* (1957), writes that, with the Knox propensity to donnishness, Evoe saw *Punch* as a college and the members of the Table as fellows, but that though his editorship was marred by a certain temperamental neglect of detail and wild swoops of invention, under his auspices the magazine 'printed some of the best work that had ever appeared in *Punch*', adding, in true *Punch* style, 'as well as some of the worst'. Knox also wrote several books, and to this Dictionary, in addition to the notices of Lucas and Seaman, he contributed those of E. T. Reed, Sir Bernard Partridge, Leonard Raven-Hill, and A. A. Milne. In 1943 he was made an honorary

MA of Oxford, and in 1951 he gave the Leslie Stephen lecture at Cambridge.

Knox was twice married, first in 1912 to Christina Frances (died 1935), daughter of Edward Lee Hicks [q.v.], bishop of Lincoln; they had one son and one daughter. In 1937 he married, secondly, Mary Eleanor Jessy, daughter of Ernest Howard Shepard [q.v.], a *Punch* artist and A. A. Milne's illustrator. Both marriages were happy; in the second, of which there were no children, there was a considerable disparity in age, giving rise to badinage at *Punch* gatherings when Ernest Shepard called his son-in-law to order.

To match the two Christian zealots, Ronnie and Wilfred Knox, Evoe and Dilly were agnostics, but this did not seriously divide the brothers. Towards the end of his life Evoe drifted back into the church, and could be seen on most Sunday mornings as one of the sidesmen getting in the collection at a Hampstead church near where he lived. Though the eldest, he was the last of the four brothers to die. He was a hard man to get to know, an enigmatic person altogether. The touch of sadness in his face in repose, in his attitudes and expositions, in his jokes even, was congenital, not acquired. He died at his Hampstead home 2 January 1971.

[Penelope Fitzgerald, *The Knox Brothers*, 1977; personal knowledge.]

MALCOLM MUGGERIDGE

KOKOSCHKA, OSKAR (1886–1980), painter, graphic artist, and author, was born 1 March 1886 in Pöchlarn, Austria, the second in the family of three sons and one daughter of Gustav Kokoschka, jeweller and goldsmith from Prague, and his wife (Maria) Romana, daughter of Ignaz Loidl, forester, of Lower Austria. His elder brother died when Oskar was five. In 1904 he matriculated at the non-classical secondary school in Vienna's XVIIIth district and in 1905 began his art studies as a scholarship student at the School of Arts and Crafts in Vienna where he stayed until 1909.

In 1907 Kokoschka received his first commissions from the Wiener Werkstätte (Vienna Workshop) and produced work which included fans, coloured postcards, posters, and ex libris designs. In 1908 he met the modern architect Adolf Loos who became his patron and introduced him to literary personalities such as Karl Kraus and Peter Altenberg. His early portraits, referred to as X-ray images, exposed the inner man and made him famous. In 1908 Kokoschka wrote *Die träumenden Knaben* (*The Dreaming Youths*) which, inspired by William Morris [q.v.], he illustrated and printed himself. He also wrote the first expressionist play, *Mörder, Hoffnung der Frauen* (*Murderer, Hope of Woman*), the performance of which in 1909 provoked a scandal. Other titles of his were *Hiob* (*Job*, 1911) and *Der Gefesselte Kolumbus* (*The Fettered Columbus*, 1913). In 1910 Kokoschka was sent by Loos to Switzerland to paint a portrait of the biologist Auguste Forel. In the same year he became a member of the editorial staff of Herwarth Walden's *Sturm*, the Berlin avant-garde review. After his return to Vienna, in 1911, he became an assistant teacher at the School of Arts and Crafts but public opinion was against him and he had to resign.

In 1912 Kokoschka met Alma Mahler, the widow of the composer, the *femme fatale* of his life. On the outbreak of World War I in 1914 he left her to volunteer as an officer cadet. Severely wounded on the eastern front he convalesced in Vienna, Dresden, and Stockholm. The painful break with Alma Mahler prompted important works such as 'The Tempest' (oil) and the lithographs inspired by the Bach Cantata (opus 60) (both 1914). Previously he had illustrated Karl Kraus's *Die chinesische Mauer* (*The Chinese Wall*, 1913) and had executed some highly expressionist paintings with typical distortions, a strong colour scheme, and powerful brushwork.

In 1919 Kokoschka was appointed professor at the Dresden Art Academy but in 1923 gave up this post to regain his independence. In the crescendo of work produced during this time, in addition to the now famous oil paintings, Kokoschka also created lithographic cycles such as 'The Concert', a series of large portrait drawings, and sizeable water-colours. In 1924 he visited Paris and in 1925 he started his many travels, to the Riviera, Spain, Portugal, England, Holland, Switzerland, and France. In 1928 he went to North Africa; in 1929 to Ireland and Scotland, Egypt, Istanbul, and Jerusalem; in 1930 to Algiers and Italy. After these journeys Kokoschka came to be considered as the foremost portrait and landscape painter of Europe. This period ended in his feeling an increasing uneasiness connected with the political developments which led to World War II.

In 1934, after a short visit to Budapest, Kokoschka went to Prague where he met his future wife, Dr Olda Palkovska, a doctor of jurisprudence at Prague University, daughter of Dr Bretislav Karel Palkovsky, lawyer and politician in Prague. Here he painted the portrait of the president of Czechoslovakia, T. G. Masaryk, and many views of the beautiful city. In 1937 all Kokoschka's paintings in German museums were confiscated and declared as degenerate. After the Munich agreement in 1938 Kokoschka fled with Olda Palkovska to London where they were married on 15 May 1941. They had no children. Kokoschka remained in London until 1953; in 1947 he acquired British citizenship. It was in England that he painted several political pictures, wrote pamphlets, and fought for human rights and humanist ideas. The deep impressions of the elemental power of nature made upon him when he visited Switzerland in 1947 resulted in a series of grand Alpine landscapes. In 1948 Kokoschka was in Venice as guest exhibitor at the Venice Biennale, and also visited Florence, Rome, and Boston. The previous pattern of his life and work was repeated. He created a great number of portraits, landscapes, graphic works, and drawings, and he undertook many journeys. A large number of exhibitions took place between 1950 and 1980 in Germany, Austria, London, Madrid, Athens, Yugoslavia, the USA, and Japan.

In 1953 Kokoschka built himself a house and studio in Villeneuve near Montreux where he lived until he died. In the same year he also began teaching at the Summer Academy in Salzburg ('The School of Seeing'), a task which he continued until 1963.

The first monumental work Kokoschka painted in London before leaving England for Switzerland was 'The Prometheus Saga', a three-part ceiling painting for Count Antoine von Seilern's London house. This was followed in 1954 by 'Thermopylae', upon which Kokoschka worked for two years and which was acquired by the University of Hamburg. These two works can be seen as a prologue to his large, mostly lithographic, *oeuvre* on Greek themes ('The Apulian Journey', 'Homage to Hellas', and illustrations for Homer's *Odyssey*, Aristophanes' *The Frogs*, and Euripides' *The Trojan Women*). The execution of these works, together with many journeys to Greece and to the whole area of Hellenistic tradition around the Mediterranean, filled the two decades of Kokoschka's life from 1961 onwards.

Kokoschka's first designs for the theatre were created in 1955, for *The Magic Flute* at the Salzburg Festival. They were followed in 1960 and 1962 by designs for the Burgtheater in Vienna and in 1963 for Verdi's *Ballo in Maschera* in Florence. In 1964 he created stage and costume designs for Geneva.

During his long working life Kokoschka drew and painted many prominent personalities of his time, amongst them Karl Kraus, Altenberg, Walden, Loos, Pau Casals, Ezra Pound, Dame Agatha Christie [q.v.], Konrad Adenauer, and the Duke and Duchess of Hamilton. His activities as a writer were prolific. Four volumes of *Schriften* were published in Hamburg, 1973–6. In 1971 the artist wrote an autobiography, *Mein Leben*, which was published in English in 1974 as *My Life*.

In 1951 Kokoschka was honoured with the Lichtwark prize in Hamburg and in 1956 with the Pour le Mérite Order of West Germany. In 1959 he was appointed CBE and received the Rome prize; in 1960 he shared the Erasmus prize of the Netherlands with Marc Chagall; and in 1963 he was honoured with the American Academy award. In 1963 he also received an honorary D.Litt. at Oxford University. In 1970 he became an honorary academician of the Royal Academy.

Kokoschka was a man of middle size with a strongly built physique, and with blue eyes in a sculptural face; he combined great fascination and charming social manners with an indomitable fighting spirit where questions of creative art and the crisis of humanism were concerned. He died in Montreux 22 February 1980.

[J. P. Hodin, *Kokoschka*, 1966; Oscar Kokoschka, *My Life*, 1974; Frank Whitford, *Oskar Kokoschka*, 1986; private information; personal knowledge.] J. P. Hodin

KOMPFNER, RUDOLF (1909–1977), engineer and scientist, was born in Vienna 16 May 1909, the only son and elder child of Bernhard Kömpfner, accountant, and his wife, Paula Grotte, of Vienna. In 1931 he graduated from the Technische Hochschule zu Wien with a diploma in engineering (architecture). This was a difficult time for Jews in Austria and, in 1934, helped by Roy Franey, his cousin's English husband, Kompfner came to London. He joined Franey's building firm as managing director (1936–41) and a house that he designed is described in H. M. Wright (ed.), *Small Houses, £500–£2,500* (Architectural Press, London, 1937).

Kompfner spent his evenings reading about physics in the Patent Office library, keeping a series of notebooks which he maintained until his death. These notebooks (later acquired by Stanford University) soon contained original concepts, and his first patent (BP 476311), a television camera tube, was accepted in 1937. In June 1940 he was interned as an enemy alien on the Isle of Man, where he shared quarters with a mathematician, Wolfgang Fuchs, with whom he discussed physics. Before his internment he had sent a paper on magnetrons to the *Wireless Engineer*, whose editor, Hugh Pocock, showed it to the Admiralty. This brought Kompfner's abilities to the attention of (Sir) Frederick Brundrett [q.v.], who sent him to the physics department at Birmingham University when he was released in December 1940. There, within two years, he invented the travelling-wave tube (see his *The Invention of the Traveling-Wave Tube*, San Francisco Press, California, May 1964), the first of a family of devices, many developed by Kompfner and his associates, which are still (1980s) used in radar and space communications.

In 1944 Kompfner was transferred to the Clarendon Laboratory, Oxford, where he remained until 1951, obtaining a D.Phil. in physics that year. He became a British subject on 19 March 1947, and was appointed a principal scientific officer in the Admiralty, attached to the

Services Electronics Research Laboratories under R. W. Sutton. The years at Oxford (where he was a member of Queen's College) were not particularly fruitful in inventions, although they saw the genesis of the backward-wave oscillator. However, the Clarendon was a lively centre of low-temperature and microwave physics and Kompfner's interests rapidly broadened while he was there, while from D. K. C. MacDonald he gained an understanding of noise and fluctuations that influenced his later thinking.

In December 1951, at J. R. Pierce's invitation, Kompfner joined the Bell Laboratories as associate director, communication science (systems) research. He became a US citizen in 1957. This period was the culmination of his career. While he concentrated on microwave tubes he was stimulated by collaboration with Pierce and H. T. Friis, and as his research group grew, his interests widened still further. His talent as a director of scientific and engineering enterprises was outstanding. He was influential in the programmes for the maser amplifier, super-conducting magnets, lasers, and optical communications. When Pierce interested him in communication satellites Kompfner's team designed the first of these, Echo, launched in 1960, and its successor, Telstar. Later, in 1963, two scientists that he had recruited, A. A. Penzias and R. W. Wilson, discovered the three degree cosmic radio noise for which they received the Nobel prize in 1978. Kompfner became director of the new Crawford Hill Laboratory, where much of the technology of optical communication was developed.

After retiring from Bell in July 1973, he divided his time between Stanford as research professor of applied physics and Oxford as a research professor of engineering science and fellow of All Souls College, working there on acoustical and optical microscopes. He skied and swam, read widely, and was devoted to music. A spirited conversationalist, he was above all generous and warm-hearted. These qualities caused him to be surrounded by devoted friends and, allied with his originality, made him a fine director of research. His stimulating, but gentle, guidance had an abiding influence on his younger colleagues, many of whom subsequently achieved eminence. He was a member of the National Academy of Engineering (1966) and the National Academy of Sciences (1968) of Washington and his other principal honours included the Duddell medal of the Physical Society (1955); the Stuart Ballantine medal of the Franklin Institute (1960); the David Sarnoff award (1960) and medal of honour (1973) of the Institute of Electrical and Electronics Engineers; the John Scott award from the City of Philadelphia (1974); the Silvanus Thompson medal of the Rontgen Society (1974), and the President's national medal of science (1974). He also received honorary doctorates from Oxford (1969) and Vienna (1965).

In 1939 Kompfner married Peggy, the daughter of John Mason, a musician. They had a son and a daughter. Kompfner died at Stanford, California, 3 December 1977.

[J. R. Pierce, Kompfner memorial lecture, *International Journal of Electronics*, vol. xlviii, 1980; private information; personal knowledge.] F. N. H. Robinson

KÜCHEMANN, DIETRICH (1911–1976), aerodynamicist, was born in Göttingen, Germany, 11 September 1911, the eldest of three children and only son of Rudolf Küchemann, schoolmaster, and his wife, Martha Egener. Between 1921 and 1930 he attended the Oberrealschule, Göttingen, at which his father taught and from which, in 1933, his father was to be dismissed for his refusal to subscribe to National Socialist doctrine: the culmination of a long and determined opposition, shared, but more circumspectly displayed, by his son Dietrich. He entered the faculty of mathematics and physics in the University of Göttingen in 1930, and eventually studied for his doctorate in theoretical aerodynamics under Ludwig Prandtl, who later described Küchemann as the best research student of his generation.

On the successful completion of his dissertation in 1936, he joined the Aerodynamische Versuchsanstalt, Göttingen, where, after some early work on bird flight, he began, in 1940, his monumental study of the aerodynamics of aircraft propulsion. It was a subject upon which he concentrated during the remainder of World War II, and he initiated a collaboration with Dr Johanna Weber that continued for the rest of their working lives. Their treatment, systematic, comprehensive, and refreshingly original, was subsequently described in their book *Aerodynamics of Propulsion* (1953). He volunteered for the army and was called up for short periods of training in the Luftnachrichtentruppe (Signals) in 1938 and 1939, but he saw no real active service during the war.

Küchemann left Göttingen in September 1946 for the Royal Aircraft Establishment, Farnborough, on a temporary basis, to be joined soon afterwards by Dr Weber and then, in 1948, by his family. In that year he indicated his willingness to become a naturalized British subject, and was given a permanent appointment in 1951 (he was naturalized in 1953). Thereafter, his ascent through the hierarchy of the Scientific Civil Service was singularly rapid: senior principal scientific officer on individual merit 1954, deputy chief scientific officer 1957, chief scientific officer and head of the aerodynamics department

1966. He held the latter post until his nominal retirement in 1971, but remained in the department as an individual research scientist until his death. Throughout, whether officially charged with administrative responsibilities or not, he maintained a continuous flow of original publications over a wide range of aerodynamic problems, embodying, as a central and developing theme, concepts of aerodynamic design, bold, elegant, revolutionary, which were to lead to the slender wing characteristic of the 'Concorde' aeroplane. Those concepts were summed up in his last work, *The Aerodynamic Design of Aircraft* (1978).

That the success of his Civil Service career was accompanied by none of the envy such achievement could generate was due, partly, to the incontrovertible evidence of his brilliance and originality, but mainly to the character of the man himself. Whilst resolute in the pursuit of his scientific ideas and the challenge they presented to aerodynamic convention, in his relations with colleagues, junior or senior, he was invariably gentle, courteous, modest, inclined to dwell upon problems that perplexed him in preference to those he had successfully solved; and at all times prepared to listen with genuine sympathy to their difficulties, eager whenever possible to offer help and encouragement.

His warmth and sensitivity were at their most apparent in his response to music. A gifted cellist, his standard of playing was high enough to have led him at one time to consider a professional career as a musician. As it was, he performed in many orchestras and, to his special delight, quartets, both in Germany and in England, once remarking that such activity provided him with the feeling, at its most intense, of belonging to a community: a feeling not narrowly experienced, since in science he was a dedicated internationalist and played an influential part in fostering research collaboration in aerodynamics among the nations of Europe.

Küchemann was elected a fellow of the Royal Society in 1963. He was appointed CBE (1964) and awarded the silver medal (1962) and the gold medal (1969), of the Royal Aeronautical Society, and, in the same year, the Enoch Thulin medal of the Swedish Society for Aeronautics and Astronautics. He received the Prandtl ring of the Deutsche Gesellschaft für Luft- und Raumfahrt (1970), and was granted honorary doctorates by the Cranfield Institute of Technology (1973), the Technical University of Berlin (1975), and the University of Bristol (1975). From 1972 he was visiting professor in the department of aeronautics, Imperial College, London.

In 1936 Küchemann married Helga Janet, daughter of Surgeon-Admiral Viktor Praefcke of the German Navy; they had a son and two daughters. Küchemann died in Farnham, Surrey, 23 February 1976.

[P. R. Owen and E. C. Maskell in *Biographical Memoirs of Fellows of the Royal Society*, vol. xxvi, 1980; R. W. Slaney, Royal Aircraft Establishment Library Bibliography 357, 1976; private information; personal knowledge.]

PAUL OWEN

L

LACK, DAVID LAMBERT (1910–1973), ornithologist, was born 16 July 1910 in London, the eldest in the family of three sons and one daughter of Harry Lambert Lack MD, FRCS, ear, nose, and throat surgeon, of London, and his wife, Kathleen, an actress, daughter of Lt.-Col. McNeil Rind, of the Indian Army. He was educated at Gresham's School, Holt, Norfolk, and Magdalene College, Cambridge, where he read zoology and found it very dull, for at that time there was almost no interest in field studies. He obtained a second class in both parts of the natural sciences tripos (1931 and 1933).

His first paper—a study of nightjars—was completed while he was still at school and although his contributions influenced a wide range of people including taxonomists, ethologists, ecologists, and evolutionists, virtually all his works were on birds. After leaving Cambridge he became a schoolmaster at Dartington Hall from 1933 to 1940—there being no jobs for ornithologists. While there, partly initially to interest the children, he started to put colour-rings on the local robins. From this emerged his *The Life of the Robin* (1943), one of the pioneer monographs on a bird population.

Encouraged by (Sir) Julian Huxley [q.v.]—at that time one of the very few professional zoologists with an enthusiasm for field studies—he went to visit R. E. Moreau in Tanganyika in 1934 and to the USA in 1935 where he met, among other people, Ernst Mayr; both these became lifelong friends and important academic associates. In 1938–9 he spent a year in the Galapagos studying Darwin's finches. From this emerged his *Darwin's Finches* (1947, reprinted 1983).

By the time he returned to England war had broken out. He joined the Army Operational Research Group (1940–5) and was engaged to work on radar research and became one of the first people to realize that the masses of small, slow moving objects on the radar screens were migrating birds. In the late 1950s he used radar to make important contributions to the study of migration.

In 1945 Lack became director of the Edward Grey Institute of Field Ornithology at Oxford, a post which he held until his death. He built the Institute into a small unit of international standing. Amongst the things he initiated was an annual student conference in bird biology. He was a fellow of Trinity College from 1963. Lack started another study of robins, but as a result of visits to Holland (which were largely responsible for persuading Niko Tinbergen to move to Oxford) was so impressed by H. N. Kluijver's studies of the great tit that he changed species. The great tit, a hole-nesting bird which readily accepts nesting-boxes and is therefore easy to monitor during the breeding season, became a major study species of the Institute. As a result of both this and the Dutch studies, it became one of the bird 'classics'. Shortly after this, Lack also started work on swifts.

In 1954 he produced *The Natural Regulation of Animal Numbers*, a book which covered a wide range of animal groups. This had more impact than his other books and made him a leading figure in the arguments about population regulation. Since Lack strongly believed that an understanding of natural selection played an important part in ecology he became involved in another long-running debate—the importance of group selection in comparison with individual selection.

Lack was so devoted to his family and his work that he tended to steer clear of committees; they interfered with the things which he felt important in life. He was also a devout Christian and wrote *Evolutionary Theory and Christian Belief* (1957). He was interested in music and an avid reader.

He was awarded his Sc.D. in 1948 and elected a fellow of the Royal Society in 1951, largely, as he put it, on his achievements as an amateur. His main honours included the Godman–Salvin medal of the British Ornithologists' Union (1958), presidency of the International Ornithological Congress (1966), and, probably the one that pleased him most, the Darwin medal of the Royal Society (1972).

In 1949 he married Elizabeth Theodora Twemlow, second child of John ('Jack') Silva, director of a factory manufacturing starch. They had three sons and a daughter. Lack died in Oxford 12 March 1973.

[W. H. Thorpe in *Biographical Memoirs of Fellows of the Royal Society*, vol. xx, 1974; D. Lack, 'My Life as an Amateur Ornithologist', *Ibis*, vol. cxv, pp. 421–31.] C. M. PERRINS

LAMB, LYNTON HAROLD (1907–1977), painter, illustrator, and book designer, was born in Hyderabad 15 April 1907, the second son of a Methodist minister, the Revd Frederick Lamb, and his wife, (Charlotte) Annie Brown. Lamb was a firm believer in the faith and in due course married Barbara ('Biddy') Grace, daughter of the Revd John Henry Morgan. He was educated at Kingswood School, Bath, and at the Central School of Arts and Crafts, London, where he studied painting under Bernard Meninsky and engraving under Noel Rooke and later with R. J. Beedham. A. S. Hartrick introduced him to lithography and gave him a lasting affection for the work of the French *Intimistes*, Vuillard and Bonnard.

In 1930 Lynton Lamb was invited to join the Oxford University Press at Amen House, to design bindings for prayer books and bibles. To this end he returned to the Central School to study bookbinding under Douglas Cockerell [q.v.], a skill that he brought back into play when he designed the Commemorative Bible for St. Giles Cathedral in 1948 and the Coronation Bible in 1953. At the Press, he developed an interest in typography and produced many book covers and wrappers.

The war interrupted Lamb's career as a painter and designer. In 1940 he was commissioned into the Royal Engineers as a staff officer (Camouflage). He was in congenial company, for among others, (Sir) William Coldstream, Oliver Messel, Blair Hughes-Stanton, Brian Robb, and the writer of this piece were fellow officers. He found the war both a tempering and a widening experience.

In 1946 Lamb returned to Amen House and, with the appointment of Geoffrey Cumberlege as publisher to the University, he found a sympathetic employer. One of their happiest collaborations was in the production of the Oxford Illustrated Trollopes, which Lamb designed with a simple and attractive format. For this series he illustrated *Can you Forgive Her?* His tentative drawings illuminated Trollope's political scene, yet he was not a particularly strong draughtsman. His resolve never to do any preliminary pencil work and his belief that 'groping for the form' was an essential part of the drawing found little sympathy from his friend Edward Ardizzone [q.v.]. In contrast to his pen drawings, the wood engravings he did in the 1930s, particularly for an unpublished edition of *Religio Medici* and *Urne Buriall*, were most assured and accomplished pieces of work. Lamb illustrated over sixty books. His book jackets, mainly executed in the decade after the war for the World's Classics, were among his most successful graphic designs, working as he did with the most economical means to achieve his effects.

As a painter Lamb's aims were modest. He was a member of the London Group and in 1951 was one of the fifty artists invited by the Arts Council to contribute a painting for the Festival of Britain Exhibition. Over the years he had a number of shows, his first at the Storran Gallery in 1936, the last at the Radlett Gallery in the year before he died. In 1950 Lamb became head of lithography at the Slade School, an appointment that gave him much satisfaction. He was a good teacher and gave further evidence of this when, from 1956 to 1970, he lectured to the Painting School at the Royal College of Art. His subject was 'Methods and Materials of Painting'.

Lamb was president of the Society of Industrial Artists and Designers (1951–3); he served on the Art Panel of the Arts Council (1951–4), on the Council of Industrial Design (1952–5), and on the Graphic Panel for the National Council for Diplomas in Art and Design (1962), visiting numerous art schools as an external examiner. He became FSIA in 1948, FRSA in 1953, and RDI in 1975.

As a man, Lamb was charming, elegant in his dress, a most witty speaker, and as happy in the Reform Club as he was on the village cricket field. In his profession he was a jack of all trades and master of several. He also wrote with clarity and urbanity. In 1974 he suffered a series of strokes which left him partially paralysed. Wonderfully supported by his wife Biddy, he continued to see his friends and to write, with considerable difficulty, the most amusing letters. The Lambs had two sons, James who became a publisher and Andrew who owned a typesetting firm. Lamb died at Sandon 4 September 1977.

Lamb's publications included *The Purpose of Painting* (1936), *County Town* (1950), *Preparation for Painting* (1954), *Cat's Tales* (1959), *Drawing for Illustration* (1962), *Death of a Dissenter* (1969), *Worse than Death* (1971), *Picture Frame* (1972), and *Man in a Mist* (1974). He also wrote articles for *Graphis* (1950), *Studio* (1951), *Signature* (1947 and 1951), and *Penrose Annual* (1956).

[John Lewis, articles on Lynton Lamb in *Alphabet & Image*, 1947, and *Graphic Design*, 1954; private information; personal knowledge.] JOHN LEWIS

LAMPE, GEOFFREY WILLIAM HUGO (1912–1980), theologian, was born at Southbourne 13 August 1912, the only child of Bruno Hugo Lampe, musician, originally from Alsace, and his wife, Laura Mary Burton. From Blundell's School he won a scholarship to Exeter College, Oxford, where he achieved first class honours in *literae humaniores* in 1935 and in theology in 1936. After training at Queen's College, Birmingham, he was ordained deacon in 1937 to serve as curate of Okehampton. Following ordination to the priesthood in 1938 he became assistant master and assistant chaplain of King's School, Canterbury (1938–41). For the last four years of the war he gave distinguished service as a chaplain to the Forces, which led in 1945 to the award of the MC for bravery under fire.

The remainder of his career was spent in the work of theological teaching and research in three English universities: chaplain and fellow of St. John's College, Oxford, until 1953; Edward Cadbury professor of theology in the University of Birmingham, 1953–9; Ely professor of divinity at Cambridge, 1959–70, and regius professor there from 1970 until his retirement in 1979. He was a fellow of Gonville and Caius College from 1960. Academic honours were soon forthcoming: BD and DD from Oxford (1953), honorary DD from Edinburgh (1959), and FBA (1963). His three major publications reflect the range of his scholarly interests. *A Patristic Greek Lexicon*, an indispensable tool for all patristic scholars, on which work had started before he was born, was finally completed under his editorship and with substantial contributions from his own pen, appearing in five volumes between 1961 and 1968. But his interest was not primarily philological. *The Seal of the Spirit* (1951) is a detailed historical and doctrinal study of Christian initiation in the early church, a subject prompted not only by purely historical but also by contemporary pastoral concerns, arising out of his experience as an army chaplain. And in his Bampton lectures (1975–6), *God as Spirit* (1977), he once again drew on his extensive patristic learning to illuminate an even more central issue of contemporary debate, the Christian doctrine of God.

His scholarship, though detailed and precise, was never narrowly conceived. He was both a historian of doctrine and a theologian in the liberal tradition. He was not afraid to ask challenging and radical questions about traditional beliefs. At times, as with his broadcast Easter sermon in 1965, these gave rise to public controversy. But such questioning was always undertaken with the positive goal of making faith more real and more accessible in the world of today. The breadth of his interests was reflected in the wide range of ways in which he contributed to the life of the universities in which he worked, and of the wider church. For his last three years in Birmingham, for example, he was vice-principal of the university and at Cambridge he held office as chairman of the board of extra-mural studies. For many years he served as a proctor in convocation and as a member of the general synod of the Church of England. There his scholarship, his personal friendliness, and his evident concern for the furtherance of Christian faith in the ordinary life of the church ensured that he was always listened to with great attention and respect, even when he was advocating causes which were unacceptable to the majority of members. He was a passionate advocate of the ordination of women to the historic ministry of the church, and of increasing ecumenical co-operation between the churches. He was also the leading figure for many years in a series of Anglo-Scandinavian conferences, an activity recognized not only by an honorary D.Teol. of the University of Lund in 1965 but also by his appointment as a commander of the Northern Star by the King of Sweden in 1978.

Lampe was a product of the old 'liberal evangelical' tradition in the Church of England, but was always a man of wide and catholic sympathies. He was a large man physically and the largeness of his physique matched the largeness of vision with which he approached the issues alike of scholarship and of life. He had a great gift for friendship, was a splendid raconteur, and could be the life and soul of a party. He never gave evidence of being anxious or in a hurry, however many the engagements or great the load of work that he had undertaken. His calmness and courage were never more unostentatiously but conspicuously displayed than in the way he faced critical illness in 1976 and 1978. In spite of that illness and the treatment it necessitated, the last years of his life were lived with undiminished zest and generosity until his death at Cambridge 5 August 1980.

In 1938 he married Elizabeth Enid, daughter of Arthur Griffith Roberts, a civil engineer. They had a son and a daughter.

[C. D. F. Moule in *Proceedings* of the British Academy, vol. lxvii, 1981; *Theology*, September 1977; *The Times*, 7 August 1980; C. D. F. Moule (ed.), *G. W. H. Lampe, Christian, Scholar, Churchman—a Memoir by Friends*, 1982; personal knowledge.] MAURICE WILES

LATHBURY, SIR GERALD WILLIAM (1906–1978), general, was born in Murree, India, 14 July 1906, the only child (a daughter born previously had died very young) of Colonel Henry Oscar Lathbury and his wife, Katherine Fanny Cobbett, granddaughter of William Cobbett [q.v.]. He was educated at Wellington College and the Royal Military College, Sandhurst (1924–5). He was commissioned 2 February 1926 and gazetted to the Oxfordshire and Buckinghamshire Light Infantry stationed in Germany. He was seconded to the Gold Coast Regiment from 1928 to 1933. He rejoined his own regiment at Bordon and went to the Staff College, Camberley, in 1937–8.

After World War II broke out Lathbury served in France, being appointed MBE in 1940. He then became GSO 2 at the Staff College and GSO 1 at the War Office. He was given command of the 3rd Parachute battalion and soon selected to command the 3rd Parachute brigade and then the 1st Parachute brigade in North Africa, Sicily, and Italy where he was appointed to the DSO (1943). He commanded the 1st Parachute brigade in the Arnhem operation in 1944.

After attending the Imperial Defence College in 1948 he commanded the 16th Airborne division (TA) as major-general that year. He was appointed CB in 1950. He became commandant of the Staff College in 1951, vice-adjutant-general in 1954, and commander-in-chief East Africa in 1955. This was at the height of the operations in Kenya to defeat the Mau Mau rebellion and on reaching Nairobi Lathbury pursued his task with enthusiasm. It was made easier by his genuine liking for Africans and his pleasure in the spectacular Kenya countryside—he was an ardent naturalist, conservationist, and bird-watcher. Moreover, he was able to establish friendly relations with the white settlers at an awkward time for them, given the policies of the British government during Britain's withdrawal from empire. He brought the operations to a successful conclusion and was appointed KCB (1956) for his work. Back home he was promoted lieutenant-general, becoming director-general of military training in 1957. He was appointed GOC-in-C Eastern Command in 1960 and promoted general. In 1961 he became quarter-master-general to the forces, a post he held until 1965 when he retired from the army.

Lathbury was governor of Gibraltar from August 1965 until April 1969. This covered a period when conditions there were becoming more difficult almost daily. Frontier restrictions were being intensified; Spanish propaganda was at its height; adverse resolutions were being passed in the United Nations; abortive and unpopular talks were held with the Spanish government; there was, until 1967, a virtual pay freeze. The people, firm and unyielding before these pressures, were nonetheless indignant, confused, and anxious. Throughout all these difficulties Gibraltar's stately, elegant soldier–governor radiated a serene imperturbability. This quality was in his nature, but it exactly met the need of the moment, as it helped to counter the people's anxiety and responded to and reinforced their resolve.

There were silver linings in those years as well; the fast-growing evidence of British political and moral support; the start of the development programmes; the gradual consolidation of popular feeling and pride in the community; the triumph of the referendum; the new constitution, with its guarantees that the people would remain with Britain as long as this was their wish. In these matters, too, Lathbury remained apparently unmoved, but he deeply shared the Gibraltarians' satisfactions as well as their trials and disappointments and worked hard to promote and further their interests.

Lathbury was colonel commandant of 1st Royal Green Jackets and the Parachute Regiment from 1961 to 1965, and was much involved in planning the amalgamation of the former with the King's Royal Rifle Corps and the Rifle Brigade to form the Royal Green Jackets in 1966. He was also colonel of the West India Regiment in 1959 and of the Jamaica Regiment from 1962 to 1968. He was ADC general to the Queen from 1962 to 1965 and was appointed GCB in 1962.

In 1942 he married Jean Gordon, daughter of Lieutenant-Colonel Edward Gordon Thin, of Aston Somerville Hall, Broadway, Worcestershire; they had two daughters. This marriage was dissolved in 1972 and he married in the same year Mairi Zoë, widow of Patrick Somerset Gibbs and daughter of Patrick Mitchell, rubber planter in Malaya, and stepdaughter of Arthur Macmillan, the brother of Harold Macmillan (later the Earl of Stockton). He died 16 May 1978 at his home in Mortimer, Berkshire. The funeral was held at Mortimer parish church, the bearers appropriately being found from the Royal Green Jackets and the Parachute Regiment.

[Royal Green Jacket *Chronicle*; personal knowledge.] JOSHUA HASSAN

LAVER, JAMES (1899–1975), fashion expert, novelist, dramatist, broadcaster, and museum keeper, was born in Liverpool 14 March 1899, the second child and only son of Arthur James Laver, maritime printer and stationer, and his wife, Florence Mary Barker. The family were strict Congregationalists. He was educated at the Liverpool Institute and New College, Oxford, his college fees and the expenses of many English and foreign travels being subsidized by a rich shipping magnate, Lawrence D. Holt who, as a governor of the Institute, had taken note of the youth's talents and application. His war service as a second lieutenant caused his residence at New College to be deferred until 1919, but by 1921 he had taken his BA degree, gaining a second class in modern history, and by 1922 had added a B.Litt. in theology, for a thesis on John Wesley [q.v.]. In 1921 he won the Newdigate prize with a poem on Cervantes, and began moving in literary, instead of 'hearty', circles, becoming a regular contributor to *Isis* with a retaining fee. Holt paid for him to have an extra year as a student and was rewarded by seeing his protégé do well. In the long vacation he climbed mountains in Switzerland, travelled in Germany, and developed his keen visual faculties at every opportunity.

Having to earn his living, he entered a competitive examination for the Victoria and Albert Museum, and was one of three successful candidates. In August 1922 he was allotted to the department of engraving, illustration, design, and painting, of which he was ultimately the keeper (1938–59). While he was mastering all he could learn of these arts and techniques, and also of miniatures, Old Master drawings, posters, etchings, fashion plates, and playing cards, all of which came under the one comprehensive heading, he used his leisure to write contributions to magazines, and much light verse. What he described as 'my first real piece of luck as a literary man' was the publication of a verse narrative, an open pastiche of Alexander Pope [q.v.] called *A Stitch in Time* (1927). Being in exactly the right key for the period, it sold rapidly, and he was soon in demand at the fashionable parties for which the decade was notable.

No social activities, however, were allowed to interfere with his voluntary classes for the Working Men's College at Camden Town. At first he ran an English literature course but after two years—about 1926–with the aid of Percy Horton [q.v.], he reorganized the art class, which until then had never had living models and had been based chiefly on copying from casts of the antique.

Although his puritan upbringing had prevented his going to a theatre until he was adult, he now became an enthusiast. This may partly have been due to his having in his charge a vast accumulation of theatre material (he produced a book on theatre design with George Sheringham in 1927), but it was enhanced by his attachment to a lovable and gifted Irish actress, (Bridget) Veronica Turleigh, daughter of Martin Turley, of the Royal Irish Constabulary. He married her in 1928; they had a son and a daughter.

The couple spent their first years in a flat in Piccadilly where their theatrical friends formed a habit of 'dropping in for drinks after the show'. This was agreeable but it also involved late hours and hospitality beyond their means. Laver engaged in any literary work for which he could receive payment—dramatic criticism, book reviews, and translations of plays, all done after a full day at the museum.

It was after moving to Chelsea that he found time to write *Nymph Errant* (1932), a novel about the adventures of a girl on her way back to her finishing school. Not only was this a bestseller, but in 1933 it was turned into a musical by the leading impresario, (Sir) C. B. Cochran [q.v.], with songs by Cole Porter and Gertrude Lawrence [q.v.] as leading lady. Its success was immense and the film rights were competed for. Laver confessed to having been made 'a little dizzy' by this heady experience, but the reality of income tax on royalties more than ten times his museum salary brought him down to earth. He continued to write fiction and to do theatrical and film work on a less ambitious scale, but renounced the transient idea of living by his pen.

He wrote a book on J. A. McN. Whistler [q.v.] (1930), James Tissot (1936), French nineteenth-century painting (1937), and several on costume for museum publication. His interest in costume had grown out of his need to know the details of dress in order to date pictures. He became so associated with the subject that he was frequently mistaken for the keeper of the museum's collections, which were actually in the department of textiles. He formed a real philosophy of costume, expounded in *Taste and Fashion* (1937), an important work on which he elaborated in several later books. Not all his theories were unquestionable (for example, the idea that the feminine waistline is raised or lowered in times of war or civil strife can only be upheld by very selective glimpses of the mode), but he brought a much more knowledgeable eye to his study of the sources and cycles of fashion than most of his predecessors in this field, and he had an entertaining yet not flippant style which suited a topic so often dealt with too heavily or too lightly.

The outbreak of war in 1939 engendered many problems in connection with dispersing the treasures of the museum to places of safety. By now he was a very senior official, and he urged that almost the greatest treasures of all were the catalogues. 'To replace a hundred years of cataloguing', he said, 'would take a hundred years.'

During the closure of the museum he was transferred for a brief period to the Treasury, but it was soon decided that so good a public speaker would be put to better use promoting the National Savings Campaign. He addressed innumerable speeches to munition workers, miners, shipbuilders, labourers constructing airfields, often eating and sleeping under the most gruelling conditions: but he had the knack of holding the attention of tired or even reluctant audiences.

Somehow during those troubled days, he managed to study the prophecies of Nostradamus, about whom he brought out a book in 1942. He had long been interested in the occult, and this work, received with scepticism by some, brought him letters from believers in the supernatural all over the world. He disliked spiritualism and was unimpressed by the seances he attended, but as to magic, black or otherwise, he thought there was 'something in it'.

On returning to the museum after the war, he resumed his writing on costume and allied subjects, and also did a full-scale biography of J. K. Huysmans, *The First Decadent* (1954). He became well known for his part in radio programmes, especially 'The Brains Trust' and 'The Critics', and was probably the first to demonstrate through television the workings of fashion, using genuine costumes. He was also a frequent and valued contributor to this Dictionary.

He retired from the museum in 1959 and later moved to Blackheath. His personality was equable and adaptable to an uncommon degree. He was learned without being pedantic, and convivial without becoming intemperate, a quietly genial man, very easy and obliging to work with, and so free from pretension that many thought his scholarship superficial, which was far from the case, although it may be that he spread his talents too widely. He is likely to be remembered for his analysis of fashion trends and his books on art and artists.

He was appointed CBE in 1951, and was also FRSA, FRSL, and honorary RE. An honorary doctorate was conferred on him by Manchester.

His wife died in 1971 as the result of an accident, which saddened his last years, though his two children and numerous friends gave him all the comfort they could. His own death took place in a fire at his Blackheath home 3 June 1975.

[James Laver, *Museum Piece* (autobiography), 1963; private information; personal knowledge.] DORIS LANGLEY MOORE

LAW, RICHARD KIDSTON, first BARON COLERAINE (1901–1980), politician, was born 27 February 1901 at Helensburgh, Dunbartonshire, the second son in the family of four sons and two daughters of Andrew Bonar Law, Conservative prime minister from October 1922 to May 1923, and his wife, Annie Pitcairn, daughter of Harrington Robley, of Glasgow. She died in 1909. While Bonar Law was a Canadian by birth, the son of an Ulster Presbyterian minister in humble circumstances and reared in Scotland by well-to-do relatives (Richard's second name, Kidston, was the surname of one of them), Richard was brought up in affluence and received an English education at Shrewsbury school and St. John's College, Oxford, where he received a third class in modern history in 1923. He was never distinctively Scottish, Canadian, or Ulster.

After experience as a journalist on the *Express* and the *Morning Post* and in the United States, he entered Parliament as the Unionist member for Hull South-West at the landslide election of 1931 and sat there until the reverse landslide of 1945. He had married in 1929 an American Mary Virginia, daughter of Abram Fox Nellis, of Rochester, New York, to whom he remained conspicuously devoted down to her final years of infirmity which ended in her death in 1978. They had two sons.

In the large Conservative majorities of the 1931 and 1935 parliaments, he attracted attention less by any striking speeches or actions than as the son of a respected former party leader. His most remembered contribution was his speech in June 1933, relating that, but for sickness, he believed his father would have broken up the new Conservative administration rather than accept the harsh terms agreed in January 1923 for repayment of the American war debt. Luckily escaping office—he was among those who opposed 'appeasement' and did not vote to approve the Munich agreement—Law was included in (Sir) Winston Churchill's 1940 war coalition and served successively as financial secretary to the War Office 1940–1, parliamentary under-secretary of state at the Foreign Office 1941–3, and minister of state at the Foreign Office, with cabinet rank, 1943–5. In 1943 he was admitted to the Privy Council. In his last office he was principally concerned with inter-allied arrangements for food, raw materials, and post-war relief.

When Churchill scraped the ministerial barrel to form a 'caretaker government' after the coalition was dissolved in May 1945, Law became minister of education; but after six weeks he lost both office and seat, though returning in the spate of contrived by-elections to the opposition front bench as member for South Kensington before 1945 was out. He showed little taste or talent for the work of opposition, and his disastrous performance in debating the National Health Service Bill against Aneurin Bevan [q.v.] may well have been the deciding factor in excluding him from Churchill's government in October 1951. By then he had already, to his credit, migrated back to Hull, winning there Haltemprice, a new seat formed by redistribution; but the back-benches in government were no more congenial than the front-bench in opposition, and in 1954 he took his peerage and went to the Lords. The title, Coleraine, alluded to the county Londonderry origins of his grandfather.

Law was now on the list of 'the great and the good' from whom the chairmen and members of respectable public bodies are recruited. He was chairman of the National Youth Employment Council (1955–62), the central transport consultative committee (1955–8), the British Sailors' Society, the Marshall scholarship commission (1956–65), the standing advisory committee on the pay of the higher Civil Service (1957–61), and the Royal Postgraduate Medical School of London (1958–71), of which he became a fellow in 1972; and these occupied him along with numerous business directorships, including the chairmanship of Horlicks. He received an honorary LL D from New Brunswick University in 1951.

Meanwhile, something else had been happening: he had found the detachment to think his politics through and discovered in the process first that he was a Conservative and second, more significantly, that he was a Tory. Coleraine concluded an article contributed to *The Times* in mid-1974 with the words: 'Probably it is time that we began to think about the unthinkable.' That was what he did himself during his thirty years out of political office. The beginning and the end of the process were marked by two polemic works. These were *Return from Utopia* (1950), published as Attlee's Labour government was nearing its close, and *For Conservatives Only* (1970), published at the corresponding stage of that of Harold Wilson (later Lord Wilson of Rievaulx) and on the eve of the accession to office of Edward Heath, an event which Coleraine deeply mistrusted. It was through these two books that a political generation which had never known him in office or in the House of Commons found him influential in formulating its own changing perceptions.

Somewhat to their surprise, readers discovered that Coleraine commanded a remarkably pure and perspicuous English prose. Two sentences which strike the keynote of the respective books are fair specimens of the style. 'I know of no cure for living, and society is a living thing, bound to the trials and pains of life. A perfect society is no more to be realised than a perfect human being, and the search for Utopia has always ended in disillusionment' (1950). 'The dangerous and demeaning delusion that man can properly be regarded as raw material for the sociologist to mould as he thinks fit has implications as absurd as they are terrifying. No one can say what will be the effect of the most carefully considered system of education upon a child. How then can it be possible to predict with any assurance at all the consequences of this kind of social engineering upon that infinitely more complex and baffling organism, human society?' (1970).

Right at the end, in the presence of bereavement and infirmity, Coleraine made the last discovery; he was not only a Conservative and not only a Tory; he was also, and therefore, an Anglican. In his last two or three years Coleraine became a regular communicant and valued member of the congregation of the Thames-side parish church of Battersea. It was there that his friends took leave of him when he died in London 15 November 1980. His elder son, (James) Martin (Bonar) Law, born in 1931, succeeded him in the barony.

[*The Times*, 17 November 1980; personal knowledge.] J. Enoch Powell

LAWRENCE, ALFRED KINGSLEY (1893–1975), portrait and figure painter, was born 4 October 1893 at Southover, Lewes, in Sussex, the son of Herbert Lawrence, solicitor and at that time clerk to the clerk of the peace, and his wife, Fanny Beatrice, daughter of John Williams, solicitor, of Lewes. 'A.K.' (as he became known to his friends) seldom spoke of his youth but it seems that he had a brother (who died in his early teens as the result of an accident), that the father died when they were still boys, and that the mother was then remarried to a 'Mr Giffin', by whom she had two more sons.

His art training began at Armstrong College, Newcastle upon Tyne, where he met his future wife, Margaret Crawford Younger (daughter of Robert Younger of that city, gentleman, and his wife Catherine), whom he married in 1915. It was, however, interrupted by service in the Northumberland Fusiliers throughout World War I and, on demobilization, he continued his studentship at the Royal College of Art in London, whence he won a travelling scholarship in 1922 and the prix de Rome in 1923. The consequent period of study in Italy greatly influenced his aims and he became devoted to the works of Piero della Francesca, particularly the mural paintings at Arezzo. Thereafter he was for ever attempting to achieve in his own compositions the simple structure of form, the clarity of colour, and the statuesque quality of the figures which he so much admired in the masterpieces of the quattrocento.

His first opportunity to emulate such works came immediately when, in 1924, he painted 'The Altruists' for the basilica in the international exhibition at Wembley, quickly followed by 'Building Pons Aelii' for the Laing Art Gallery, Newcastle, and, in 1926, 'Queen Elizabeth Commissions Sir Walter Raleigh to Discover Unknown Lands, AD 1584', one of the cycle of mural paintings in St. Stephen's Hall at the Houses of Parliament. He was then asked to carry out, in the early 1930s, a group of large paintings, including 'The Committee of the Treasury' (1928) for the new Bank of England and, subsequently, 'Queen Elizabeth Visits her Armies at Tilbury, AD 1588' which was installed in the County Hall at Chelmsford in 1939. There were no opportunities for such work throughout World War II and, except for 'The Resurrection', an altar-piece for the church of St. James, Beckenham, in 1954, thereafter no further commissions of comparable nature seemed to come his way. He still, however, retained his interests in the British School at Rome, being a member of its faculty of painting from 1926 to 1950, and in the encouragement of mural painting, having been a founder member of the Incorporated Edwin Austin Abbey memorial scholarships and serving on the council from 1926 to 1953.

He had been elected an associate of the Royal Academy, where he exhibited regularly from 1929, in 1930 and RA in 1938, and a member of the Royal Society of Portrait Painters in 1947. His easel paintings included various classical subjects, particularly depictions of the female nude, such as Venus, Leda, and Persephone (e.g. his diploma work deposited in the Royal Academy), as well as theatrical themes, such as scenes from *Romeo and Juliet* and 'Miss Vivien Leigh as Cleopatra' (1952), and presentation portraits such as 'Mrs Eveline M. Lowe, Chairman of the London County Council' (1941) and 'Sir Robert Robinson, President of the Royal Society' (1950). Many portraits by him, particularly in the latter part of his career, were in pencil, pastel, charcoal, or pen and wash, as for example 'Sir Malcolm Sargent' (1954), 'The Countess of Dundee' (1961), and most members of the royal family.

Lawrence had a great interest in the theatre and, had he turned professional actor instead of painter, he might well have been equally successful, especially in heroic roles. He was a tall, dignified man with a resounding voice, a stalwart in debate, forthright in his adherence to traditions, and rather grand in his renderings of Shakespeare. He was, however, prone to be too lengthy both in speech and in his frequent letters, self-typed and with innumerable amendments and insertions. Just as he hated anything unfinished or ephemeral, so was he a stickler for the correct use of words. He affirmed that all art was abstract and therefore considered that word's modern connotation in regard to painting to be a nonsense. He was also strongly against the use of photography as an aid or substitution for good draughtsmanship.

His wife died in 1960 and, apart from their daughter, Margaret, and son, Julius, who settled in New Zealand, Lawrence seemed to be rather a solitary figure in his last years. He still continued with his art but withdrew himself from aesthetic arguments. He died suddenly, from a heart attack, at his home in Holland Park Road, London, 5 April 1975.

[*Daily Telegraph*, 7 April 1975; *The Times*, 9 and 11 April 1975; Royal Academy records; personal knowledge.] S. C. Hutchison

LAWTHER, Sir WILLIAM (1889–1976), miners' leader, was born 20 May 1889 at Choppington, Northumberland, the eldest son of Edward Lawther, a coal miner of Choppington, and his wife, Catherine Phillips. It was a family of radical traditions: a grandfather had been an active Chartist, and Edward became politically sympathetic to the Independent Labour Party. 'Will' Lawther began to work in the mines soon after he was twelve, and in 1907 the family—there were fifteen children of whom eleven survived—moved to the new colliery of Chopwell in County Durham. The village was already developing a militant tradition—it was known later as 'Little Moscow'—and Will Lawther became a political and industrial activist from his late teens.

He continued his education at night school, read widely in socialist literature—*Merrie England* (1893) by R. P. G. Blatchford [q.v.] was especially influential—and the Durham Miners' Association sent him to study at the Central Labour College in London from September 1911 for nearly two years. When he returned to Durham he joined Ebenezer Edwards [q.v.] in establishing Plebs League classes, and in 1914 helped found the Socialist Sunday School in Chopwell, known locally as the 'anarchist school'. During World War I Lawther adopted a strong anti-militarist position and was one of a small number who refused to subscribe to the Red Cross. In these years he began to occupy official positions in the union hierarchy and attended his first TUC in 1918. In the aftermath of the war he consolidated his reputation as a left-wing militant, although by this time he had shed his earlier version of anarchist syndicalism and had become very active within the Labour Party: probably through the influence of Peter Lee. By 1923 he was a member of the national executive, upon which he served until 1926. From 1925 to 1929 he was on the Durham County Council. During the 1926 general strike he was a leading figure in his own region, and spent two months in jail on charges of intimidation and interference with food distribution.

Lawther stood unsuccessfully on three occasions (1922, 1923, and 1924) as parliamentary candidate for South Shields before he was elected for Barnard Castle in 1929. He proved an effective back-bencher with an abrasive speaking manner but lost his seat in the Labour débâcle of 1931. For the next eighteen months he was unemployed, but came back into union affairs when he was appointed an agent for the Durham miners in 1933, moving to the full-time treasurer's position in December of the same year. From then on he was always a full-time official. He was elected vice-president of the Mineworkers' Federation of Great Britain in 1934, president in 1939, and when the National Union of Mineworkers replaced the Federation, Lawther became its first president, retiring under the age-limit rule when he was sixty-five. He had been on the general council of the TUC since 1935.

Throughout the 1930s Lawther had remained on the left of the Labour movement. He was pro-Soviet, a supporter of the communist-led hunger marches, vigorous in defence of republican Spain—his brother Clifford was killed in February 1937 while serving with the International Brigade—, and a trenchant critic of the policy of appeasement. Within the Labour Party he advocated both the United Front, and the Popular Front of Sir R. Stafford Cripps [q.v.], and only the threat of expulsion made him withdraw his support from the latter. As late as 1943, on behalf of the MFGB, he moved an amendment at the Labour Party conference, in favour of accepting the affiliation of the Communist Party. But the later war years was a period of marked change in Lawther's political views and with the Labour victory in the summer of 1945 he emerged as one of the triumvirate who dominated the TUC and who used the large votes of their respective unions to defeat the Left. Together with Arthur Deakin [q.v.] of the Transport Workers and Tom Williamson of the Municipal Workers, Lawther played a major part in first containing the Communist Party and their allies in the TUC, and then the Bevanites within the Labour Party. In these post-war years Lawther became as paranoid about the Left as Deakin; and it was the consistent use of their block votes that kept the Right–Centre in political control of both the TUC and the Labour Party. Not all members of the Lawther family were sympathetic with his shift to the political Right.

Lawther was knighted in 1949 and had also been awarded the decoration of chevalier of the Legion of Honour. He retired in 1954 and went to live in Whitley Bay where he was a magistrate. His wife Lottie (the daughter of Joseph Laws, a coal miner), whom he had married in 1915, was active in his support during the whole of his career. The marriage was childless. Lottie died in 1962 and Lawther, in hospital at Newcastle upon Tyne 1 February 1976. He left an estate valued at £11,921.

[Correspondence, press cuttings, and other papers, County Archives Department, Newcastle upon Tyne; *Dictionary of Labour Biography* Collection, Hull University, *Bulletin* of the Society for the Study of Labour History, No. 19, autumn 1969, pp. 14–21; North-East Group/Labour History, *Bulletin* 10, October 1976, pp. 27–33; *The Times*, 3 February 1976; private information.] JOHN SAVILLE

LEACH, BERNARD HOWELL (1887–1979), potter, was born in Hong Kong 5 January 1887, the only child of Andrew John Leach, a barrister, and his wife, Eleanor Sharpe, who died in childbirth. His maternal grandparents took the baby to Japan. In 1890 he returned to Hong Kong where his father remarried. The second wife, Jessy Sharpe, was a cousin of his first wife. In 1894 Leach moved with his parents to Singapore where his father was appointed British colonial judge. In 1897, at the age of ten, he was sent to England to attend the Beaumont Jesuit College near Windsor where he remained for six years.

In 1903, showing a definite creative talent, Leach entered the Slade School of Art to study drawing under Henry Tonks [q.v.]. In 1904 his father died and Leach, realizing that he had no chance of pursuing his artistic studies, prepared himself in Manchester between 1905 and 1908 to enter the Hong Kong and Shanghai Bank. A new opportunity for continuing his art studies offered itself, and in 1908 he entered the London School of Art to be taught the technique of etching by (Sir) Frank Brangwyn [q.v.]. With the aim of practising and teaching this unknown art in Japan, Leach, who had been affected by Lafcadio Hearn's writings, travelled there in 1909, going first to Nagasaki, then to Tokyo, where he built a house and exhibited his etchings.

It was there that in the same year he married his cousin, Edith Muriel, daughter of Dr William Evans Hoyle, director of the National Museum of Wales, Cardiff; they had two sons and three daughters. At the beginning of his career he was an etcher but not a potter. In 1910 he experimented for the first time with a Raku kiln belonging to Kozan Horokawa. The year 1911 proved to be decisive. At a tea-party organized by the Shirakaba Society of young artists, the guests were each asked to throw a pot. It was then that Leach decided to become a potter. A friendship with the poet and painter Kenkichi Tomimoto and with Soetsu Yanagi, later the director of the Museum of Folk Art in Tokyo, anchored him firmly in his new ambition. Ogata Kenzan VI, with whom Leach studied, built him a kiln in his workshop in Abiko. Leach persuaded Tomimoto to work with Kenzan. Both received certificates from the master, making Leach the VIIth in the Kenzan tradition. His enthusiasm for pottery influenced even Hamada who finally became the greatest modern potter in Japan, as Leach himself was proclaimed to be the greatest potter of his age in the West.

In 1915 Leach moved to Peking where he was visited by Yanagi who persuaded him to return to Japan. There Leach rebuilt Kenzan's kiln. In 1919 his workshop, containing all his notes on clays and glazes, shapes and colours, burned down. Fortunately other potters came to his rescue. In 1918 Leach and Yanagi visited Korea, where, as in Japan, the great tradition of pottery, initiated in China and reaching its climax in the Sung and T'ang periods, had been revived.

In 1914 appeared Leach's *A Review, 1909–1914*, which contained poems, prose pieces, and illustrations of etchings, drawings, and pots. This was the start of a long series of books in which Leach propounded his personal philosophy, his aesthetic, moral, and religious concepts. Through the influence of his friend, the American painter Mark Tobey, whom he met in Dartington Hall, he became interested in the Bahá'í faith (1932) and, in 1940, he declared himself a believer in Bahá'u'lláh, the Persian prophet's creed. *A Potter's Outlook* was published in 1928, *A Potter's Book* in 1940. The latter, containing detailed descriptions of his methods and materials, is Leach's best known work. *A Potter's Portfolio* followed in 1951, *A Potter in Japan* in 1960, and *A Potter's Work*, with an introduction by J. P. Hodin, in 1967. *The Unknown Craftsman* (1972) interpreted for the West the aesthetics of Japan. *Drawings, Verse and Belief* appeared in 1973, *Hamada* in 1976, and *The Potter's Challenge* (ed. by D. Outerbridge), a new edition of *A Potter's Portfolio*, in 1976. The philosophical volume *Beyond East and West* (1978) was his last book. Both *Hamada* and *Beyond East and West* were dictated on to tapes because in 1974 Leach suffered an attack of glaucoma which blinded his right eye. The deterioration in his other eye made it impossible for him to continue his work as a potter. His last pot-making year was 1973.

In 1920 Leach had returned to England accompanied by Shoji Hamada and established a pottery in St. Ives, building the first oriental climbing kiln in Europe. In 1923 Hamada went back to Japan. Their lifelong friendship ended only with Hamada's death in 1978. The first of Leach's students, Michael Cardew, who became an outstanding potter himself, joined the pottery in 1923. More than a hundred pupils were to work there.

During his long creative life Leach held many one-man exhibitions both in England and Japan. There were extended lecture and demonstration tours and travelling exhibitions in the USA, Australia, New Zealand, and South America (1966). Altogether Leach visited Japan fourteen times.

In 1936, after his divorce from his first wife, Leach married Laurie, daughter of Horace John Cookes; she was then secretary of the St. Ives pottery. They separated a few years later. In Japan he met Janet, daughter of Charles Walter Darnell. She was a young potter from Texas whom he married after his return to England in 1955. She gradually took over the management of the St. Ives pottery, allowing Leach to spend all his time creating his individual pots. These were signed with the emblem of the St. Ives pottery and his personal initials, B.L. At the height of its activity the pottery produced some 22,000 pieces of standard domestic ware; Raku soft ware was dominant in the beginning and later stone ware, some porcelain, and salt glaze ware were produced.

Bernard Leach was a person of great integrity both as a creative artist and as a teacher. He had profound influence on his pupils, and charisma. The renewer of the contemporary craft of pottery, his high standards were based on a sound tradition with its roots in China, Japan, and Korea, combined with an appreciation of the heritage of old English pottery, particularly slip ware, of which he produced a large amount until 1937. Two fundamental ideas dominated his working life: hand production by studio potters against a background of industrialism, and the bridging of the cultural gap between East and West (Tao and Zen—European humanism and depth psychology) in an attempt to create a wholeness of human spiritual achievement. He stood for the honest and personal involvement of the potter with his philosophical and religious overtones; this was a social service to the community, which was not to be dominated by purely economic (mass production) and rationalistic considerations. Two films have been produced about his work and thought: *A Potter's World* (BBC, 1960) and an NHK (Japan) television film (1974).

Leach received many honours including the Binns medal of the American Ceramic Society (1940) and an honorary D.Litt. from Exeter University (1961). In 1962 he was appointed CBE, in 1966 he received in Japan the Order of the Sacred Treasure, second class (Kusimito Zuihôshô), in 1968 he was made a freeman of St. Ives, and in 1970 he accepted the World Crafts Council honour. In 1973 he became a CH and in 1974 won the Japanese Foundation cultural award. He died in St. Ives 6 May 1979.

[Bernard Leach, *Beyond East and West* (autobiography), 1978; personal knowledge.]

J. P. Hodin

LEAKEY, LOUIS SEYMOUR BAZETT (1903–1972), archaeologist, anthropologist, and human palaeontologist, was born 7 August 1903 at Kabete, Kenya, the third of the four children of Canon Harry Leakey and his wife, Mary Bazett, one of the thirteen children of Colonel Bazett who had retired to Reading after serving in the Indian Army. Both his parents were missionaries with the Church Missionary Society working among the Kikuyu west of Nairobi in the Kenyan highlands.

The outbreak of war in 1914 prevented him from going to school in England. The first sixteen years of his life were spent at Kabete: taught by a governess and later by his father, he freely associated with Kikuyu boys and through them was to learn and love Africa. One Kikuyu chief described him as 'the black man with a white face . . . we regard him as one of ourselves'. He sometimes regarded himself as more a Kikuyu than a European: and called the first volume of his autobiography *White African* (1937). From these early days there dated his overmastering passion for everything to do with Africa—its people, their past, their future, and their environment—which was to last all his life.

In 1919 he went to school at Weymouth College and then to St. John's College, Cambridge, where he first read for the modern language tripos (getting a first in the two languages he offered, namely French and Kikuyu). In his third year he read the archaeology and anthropology tripos, gaining a first in 1926. His interests in these subjects were fostered and encouraged by A. C. Haddon [q.v.] and M. C. Burkitt. He was a keen member of the St. John's rugby club but had a leg accident which resulted in later life in a femur operation which left him lame until his death. In 1923 he was concussed and told to take a year off: this enabled him to become a member of the British Museum East African Expedition to Tanganyika in 924 to collect dinosaur fossils.

Between 1926 and 1935 he himself led four expeditions to East Africa which established the sequence of early cultures in Kenya and northern Tanzania: these important discoveries about the prehistory of East Africa and his discovery of early hominids were published in *The Stone Age Cultures of Kenya Colony* (1931), *The Stone Age Races of Kenya* (1935), and *Stone Age Africa* (1936). He took his Ph.D. in 1930 and was elected a research fellow for six years in his old college of which in 1966 he became an honorary fellow.

During his six years as a don at St. John's College he revealed himself as an enthusiastic and inspiring teacher. He learnt how to knap flint, having developed his techniques from the account by Llewellynn Jewitt [q.v.] of the methods used by the nineteenth-century flint forger, Edward Simpson, and from watching the knappers at work in Brandon.

His work in the fields of archaeology, human palaeontology, and anthropology did not prevent his taking a wide interest in Kenya and its politics. He was a great lover of animals, domestic and wild, was a trustee of the National Parks of Kenya and of the Kenya Wild Life Society, and became vice-president of the East Africa Kennel Club. His long association with and knowledge of the Kikuyu made him particularly well equipped to understand Kenyan problems as can be seen from his *White African* (1937) and his *Kenya: Contrasts and Problems* (1936). He wrote a book of 700,000 words, with the co-operation of the tribal elders, on the Kikuyu but could not find a publisher during his lifetime. After his death this work, which was based on research financed by the Rhodes trustees during 1937–9, is at long last being published.

At the outbreak of war in 1939 he was in charge of a special branch of the Criminal Investigation Department in Nairobi and continued as a handwriting expert to the department until 1951.

When the war ended Leakey was only too happy to get back to his archaeological and palaeontological researches: he was made curator of the Coryndon Memorial Museum at Nairobi in 1945 and held this post until 1961. His work was conducted under the aegis of this museum and later by the National Centre of Prehistory and Palaeontology in Nairobi, as well as with the support of many learned research foundations of which the National Geographical Society of Washington gradually became the most important. He founded the Pan-African Congress on Prehistory of which he was general secretary from 1947 to 1951, and president from 1955 to 1959.

Before he went on leave to England in 1950 Leakey had heard rumours of a secret society among the Kikuyu calling itself Mau Mau. He warned the Kenya government of the possible dangers but his warnings were not heeded for some while. He wrote in 1952 *Mau Mau and the Kikuyu* and two years later *Defeating Mau Mau* (1954). Reviewing the first book in the *Times Literary Supplement* (26 December 1952), a reviewer wrote: 'It is not too much to say that if this book had been written thirty years ago and policy shaped accordingly by administrators and settlers, the present discontents in Kenya might never have arisen.' In that year a state of emergency was declared in Kenya and Jomo Kenyatta [q.v.] and five others were charged with running Mau Mau. At their trial the court interpreter was Leakey.

In 1942 Leakey and his wife, Mary, discovered the Acheulian site of Olorgesailie in the Rift Valley. After the war Leakey continued his work on the Miocene deposits of western Kenya and produced, among other discoveries, the almost complete skull of *Proconsul africanus*, the earliest ape yet found.

But the work that will for ever be associated with Leakey is that at Olduvai. In their first season, 1959, Mary Leakey found the skull of *Australopithecus (Zinjanthropus) boisei* and next year their son Jonathan discovered the first remains of *Homo habilis*, a hominid dated by the potassium–argon method to 1.7 million years. Also in the same year the Leakeys discovered the skull of one of the makers of the Acheulian culture at Olduvai to which he gave the name *Homo erectus*. These remarkable researches are still being published in a series of books entitled *Olduvai Gorge*. After Leakey's death his work has been continued by his wife Mary and his son Richard who, just before his father's death, was able to show him the remains of a human being found on the shores of Lake Rudolf below a tufa dated to 2.6 million years.

Leakey revolutionized palaeolithic archaeology which had hitherto been largely thought of in terms of Europe. He began and promoted the study of early Africa and turned prehistory into world prehistory. His discoveries of early hominids are as important as his discovery of the early African cultural sequence. Charles Darwin [q.v.] had speculated that Africa might have been the continent where man emerged and the first hominids would be found. Leakey found them in Africa and what he, his wife, and family have done and are doing for our knowledge of early man will always be regarded as one of the great archaeological and human palaeontological achievements of the twentieth century. No one other than Leakey has hitherto, as a single person, contributed more to the discovery of early man and his culture.

His interests were as wide as his energy and enthusiasm. He became fascinated with the problem of primate behaviour and organized research in this new field: Jane Goodall was one of his first pupils and he encouraged her and her work at all times.

He was a person of untiring energy and devotion to his researches, and his enthusiasm and excitement were unbounded. He was a human volcano and erupted frequently to the dismay of his friends and enemies. He would express his views violently and often be intolerant of criticism: but he loved controversy among unbiased equals. It has often been said that his enthusiasm and sharply expressed convictions carried him to extremes. But although ill-disposed to what he thought were ill-informed opposing views, he realized that in the many fields in which he operated it was necessary to be a more than competent archaeologist, human palaeontologist, anatomist, zoologist, and geologist—and hardly anyone could, in this century, pretend to be an expert in all of these. It was easy for experts in one of these fields to denigrate his work. Many of his early discoveries were controversial but his persistence, faith, and increasingly scientific presentation of his work were completely justified.

After his death the Kenya authorities established a museum and research institute now called the Louis Leakey Memorial Institute for African Prehistory. In California a Leakey Foundation was established to promote his work. Honours were very properly showered on him—honorary doctorates in Oxford (1953), California (1963), East Africa (1965), and Guelph (1969), the fellowship of the British Academy (1958), and medals and awards from societies all over the world—including the Royal medal of the Royal Geographical Society of London in 1964 (which he much valued) and the Hubbard medal of the National Geographic Society, Washington (1962).

When flying to London in the autumn of 1972 he suffered a fatal heart attack on 1 October. He is buried by the side of his parents in Kenya looking over the Rift Valley where he had lived and worked for so long. As a young student and research worker in Cambridge he determined to devote his life to finding out the past of Africa. He succeeded beyond all reasonable expectation.

He was married first to Henrietta Wilfrida, daughter of Henry Avern, of Reigate: this was in 1928. There were a son and a daughter of this marriage, which ended in divorce in 1936 when he married Mary Douglas, daughter of Erskine E. Nicol, artist. She had been working with him for some while. There were three sons of this second marriage, and one daughter who died when only a few weeks old. One son, Richard, was to follow in his father's footsteps and himself become a distinguished archaeologist and palaeontologist.

[L. S. B. Leakey, *White African*, 1937, and *By the Evidence: Memoirs, 1932–1951*, 1974; Sonia Cole, *Leakey's Luck: the Life of Louis Seymour Bazett Leakey, 1903–1973*, 1975; Mary Leakey, *Disclosing the Past* (autobiography), 1985; J. Desmond Clark in *Proceedings* of the British Academy, vol. lix, 1973; private information; personal knowledge.]

GLYN DANIEL

LEAVIS, FRANK RAYMOND (1895–1978), literary critic, editor, teacher, and educationist, was born 14 July 1895 in Cambridge, the second child of three and elder son of Harry Leavis, who sold pianos and musical instruments, and his wife, Kate Sarah Moore. Except for the years of his service in World War I, Leavis lived in Cambridge throughout his life. His boyhood home was affectionate and cultivated, with much music and with readings from Shakespeare and Dickens. Educated at the Perse School, he gained a history scholarship to Emmanual College, switching to the English tripos for his part ii in which he obtained a first class in 1921. Between school and university, however, lay the horrifying 'great hiatus' (as he later described it) of his years on the western front, serving with the Friends' Ambulance Unit as a stretcher-bearer; and this experience permanently impaired his digestion and left him with insomnia. It was partly in order to exhaust himself into sleep that he took up long-distance running; he continued to run till he was an old man and his academic career was to reveal a good deal of the wiry, relentless tenacity of the long-distance runner.

As an undergraduate, and later while researching for his doctorate (which he received in 1924) into the relationship of journalism to literature, he was a good deal influenced by I. A. Richards [q.v.] and Mansfield Forbes. The latter, more than anyone else, had brought 'Cambridge English' into being and Leavis retained the strongest admiration for him. In 1927 he was appointed a probationary faculty lecturer in English; he was already known for having stimulated students to take an interest in writers like James Joyce, T. S. Eliot, and D. H. Lawrence [qq.v.], none of them acceptable at that time in academic circles. His first major book, *New Bearings in English Poetry* (1932), was to be a similar revaluation of poetry in the modern world, in which he argued that G. M. Hopkins, W. B. Yeats [q.v.], Eliot, and Ezra Pound were the most significant and creative writers. Reflecting on this period forty years later, he remarked that 'We didn't need Nietzsche to tell us to live dangerously; there is no other way of living', and in 1931 both his probationary lectureship and his fellowship at Emmanuel were terminated. However, he declined to leave Cambridge, and the offer of the new directorship of studies in English at Downing College (1932) provided him with a modest livelihood. He was not appointed to a lectureship in the English faculty until 1936 (when he was over forty) and then only part-time; not until 1954 was he invited to join the English faculty board, and only in 1959, at the age of sixty-four, was he appointed reader. He was to retain for the rest of his life, even when success and wide recognition had come to him, including appointment as CH in 1978, an embittered sense of having been the victim of 'obloquy, slander and worldly disadvantage'. Undoubtedly this sharpened his formidable wit and led him into uncompromising animosities, although with students and friends he was a gentle person of great courtesy, humour, and charm.

In 1929 Leavis married Queenie Dorothy Roth (1906–1981). She was the daughter of Morris Roth, master draper and hosier, and his wife, Jenny Davis. Educated at the Latymer School, she went as Carlisle scholar to Girton College, Cambridge, and took first class honours in the English tripos in 1928. An outstanding research student, she was now working for her Ph.D. (1932) on the theme that was to be published in the same year as *Fiction and the Reading Public.* This 'socio-literary study', in Leavis's own words, was 'a wholly original kind of research . . . into the old working-class culture of which the processes of civilization were eliminating the traces', and it extended historically, and with great verve, the central theme of Leavis's *Mass Civilization and Minority Culture* (1930). In that year Queenie Leavis became the first woman to be awarded the Amy Mary Preston Reid scholarship by the university. In 1933, they and Denys Thompson, a schoolmaster, wrote *Culture and Environment* and this early critique of mass culture, which offered itself as an 'education against the environment', had a seminal influence on teachers and students. This concern with what Leavis later castigated as 'the hubris of a technologico-positivist or Benthamite enlightenment', allied to his own profound anti-reductionism, made him a strong anti-Marxist. He made this the theme of such noted forays as his calculatedly destructive dismissal of C. P. (later Lord) Snow [q.v.] in his Richmond lecture of 1962, and of the many closely and trenchantly argued essays which he gathered together in *For Continuity* (1933) and in *Nor Shall My Sword* (972), with its revealing sub-title 'Pluralism, Compassion and Social Hope'. But he also pursued this theme in much of his specifically literary criticism, having coined the concept that it is 'the great novelists [who] give us our social history'; thus his first essay on Dickens, in 1948, was on *Hard Times*, that bitter denunciation of an inhuman utilitarianism, to be followed by the full-scale study, *Dickens the Novelist* (1970), which he and his wife wrote jointly and which was the peak of their work as literary critics. And the same preoccupation formed a major strand in his studies of George Eliot [q.v.] (1945 and 1946) and of D. H. Lawrence (1930, 1955, 1976), who became for Leavis the major, life-enhancing writer of this century.

Leavis's twenty or so books were nearly all created out of essays originally written for *Scrutiny*. It was this quarterly, which he and his wife helped to launch in 1932 and which they kept in being for twenty-one years, which eventually established their reputation. It was an achievement of singular timeliness and total devotion. It provided a constant, even an unremitting, incentive to write; and it became, in Leavis's mind, a vitalizing 'centre' of standards, of literary studies and discussions. *Scrutiny* gained a considerable reputation for its critical rigour; for its detailed textual 'revaluations' of a very wide range of writers and themes; for its pioneering analyses of 'novels as dramatic poems', particularly Leavis's essays on George Eliot, Henry James, and Joseph Conrad [qq.v.] which made up the major part of his influential book, *The Great Tradition* (1948); and for its comparable articles on music, education, mass society, and the cultural establishment. It has been said that *Scrutiny* educated a generation of future teachers of English teachers. But finally in 1953 the Leavises gave up the struggle. It had become impossible to keep together a team of regular contributors, and above all Queenie Leavis, who had carried the sub-editorial burden, had been fighting for very many years a battle against cancer. Her many articles, especially the series, 'A Critical Theory of Jane Austen's Writings' (1941–2), and her penetrating and high-spirited reviewing had been a distinctive feature of *Scrutiny*. The total run of *Scrutiny* was republished in 1963 by the Cambridge University Press. If *Scrutiny* had been one source of education, the Downing English school was a second. Until his retirement in 1962, Downing was the centre of Leavis's teaching. He was a compelling and devoted teacher: genial, often racy, attentive to individual students, possessing an immediate command of a vast body of literature in many languages, and with a marvellous sensitivity for the distinctive movement and texture of a passage of poetry or prose. And his reading of poetry, in his oddly nasal, high-pitched voice, was a triumph of sincerity and meaning. He dedicated *Revaluation* (1936), the book in which he established the non-Spenserian–Miltonic–Tennysonian 'tradition and development in English poetry' as he saw it, to 'those with whom I have discussed literature as a "teacher": if I have learned anything about the methods of profitable discussion, I have learned it in collaboration with them'.

In 1962, at the age of sixty-seven, Leavis retired from his university readership and was appointed to honorary fellowship at Downing, which however he resigned in 1964 because he felt the college was turning its back on the English policies he had established. This rupture preoccupied him emotionally till the end of his life. However, he continued teaching for many more years. In 1964 he was Chichele lecturer at Oxford; in 1965 he became visiting (later honorary visiting) professor at the University of York; in 1968 he and his wife made their first lecturing visit to the USA, out of which came *Lectures in America* (1969). In 1967 he delivered the Clark lectures at Cambridge on the theme *English Literature in our Time and the University* (published in 1969) in which he took up the major preoccupation of an earlier book, *Education and the University* (1943): the university's task is to be 'a focus of humane consciousness, a centre where . . . intelligence, bringing to bear a mature sense of values, should apply itself to the problems of civilization': this was to be achieved pre-eminently through an English school which 'trains, in a way no other discipline can, intelligence and sensibility together'. For Leavis, to read seriously is to discriminate, and in the last resort such judgements, closely linked to the words on the page, are liable to be moral judgements. It was in these exacting terms that he understood and practised the discipline of literary criticism. Finally, in 1969 he was visiting professor at the University of Wales, and in 1970 Churchill visiting professor at Bristol University.

Leavis's lectures during these years, if often still laced with polemic, were intricately argued. His style remained sinewy, urgent, authoritative, as he grappled with the central concepts that had formed the burden of his life's thinking: 'life is growth and growth change' and 'the nature of livingness in human life is manifest in language, [which] embodies values, constatations, distinctions, promptings, recognitions of potentiality'. The titles of his last books, during what proved an astonishingly productive decade, testified to his indestructible sense of urgency and hope: *Nor Shall My Sword* (1972), *The Living Principle* (1975), and *Thought, Words and Creativity* (1976).

Leavis died in Cambridge 14 April 1978. Now a familiar and influential figure, he had been awarded honorary doctorates at Leeds, York, Queen's University (Belfast), Delhi, and Aberdeen. Yet he would probably not have found it easy to accept the tributes and the expressions of admiration that quickly proliferated in obituaries, articles, and books. *The Times* (18 April 1978) best summed up the man in words at once judicious and intimate: 'A certain Spartan frugality and fine intensity of living marked him with a mixture of vitality and asceticism . . . above all the flame-like nimbleness of his speech and glance compelled attention. . . . His influence extended far beyond the boundaries of the subjects to which he confined himself.'

In her remaining years, Queenie Leavis lectured widely and edited and wrote with energy on the Brontës, George Eliot, and Herman Melville. Her last lecture, for the Cheltenham Festival of 1980, was on 'The Englishness of the English Novel', and it was of a remarkable scope and sympathy. She died in Cambridge 17 March 1981, being survived by their two sons and a daughter. F. R. and Q. D. Leavis dedicated their book *Dickens the Novelist* to each other, as proof 'of forty years and more of . . . devotion to the fostering of that true respect for creative writing, creative minds and . . . the English tradition, without which literary criticism can have no validity and no life'.

[D. F. McKenzie and M.-P. Allum, *F. R. Leavis: A Check-List 1924–1964*, 1966; William Baker, 'F. R. Leavis, 1965–1979, and Q. D. Leavis, 1922–1979: A Bibliography of writings By and About Them', in *Bulletin of Bibliography*, vol. 37, iv, 1980; *The Times*, 18 April 1978; Ronald Hayman, *Leavis*, 1976; William Walsh, *F. R. Leavis*, 1980; Denys Thompson (ed.), *The Leavises*, 1984; private information; personal knowledge.] BORIS FORD

LECONFIELD, sixth BARON, and first BARON EGREMONT (1920–1972), civil servant and author. [See WYNDHAM, JOHN EDWARD REGINALD.]

LEE, SIR FRANK GODBOULD (1903–1971), civil servant and master of Corpus Christi College, Cambridge, was born at Colchester, Essex, 26 August 1903, the eldest of three children and the only son of Joseph Godbould Lee and his wife, Florence Brown. Both parents were schoolteachers, and they soon moved to Brentwood where Frank won a scholarship to Brentwood School and from there in 1921 another to Downing College, Cambridge. He read English in part i of the tripos (1923) and history in part ii (1924) and took a first class in both. He then passed into the Indian Civil Service, but, under parental pressure, returned to teach at Brentwood for a year. In 1926 he took the Civil Service examination again and entered the Colonial Office. He spent two years as district officer in Nyasaland and visited Cyprus and Bechuanaland. He became a principal in 1934. On 25 September 1937 he married Kathleen Mary, the daughter of Walter Harris, a chartered accountant in Hull, and in the following year he went to the Imperial Defence College.

In January 1940 he moved to the Supply side of the Treasury, where he dealt with the Service departments and the Ministry of Supply. He became head of the division in 1943, but in 1944 he went to Washington as deputy head of the Treasury delegation under R. H. (later Lord) Brand [q.v.]. There he became closely associated with Lord Keynes [q.v.] in negotiations over the end of Lend-Lease and the British loan agreement. He got on well with Keynes and was able to deal with him on equal terms. A racy account by him of the Lend-Lease negotiations appears in chapter 19 of the *Essays on John Maynard Keynes*, edited by Milo Keynes (1975). In 1946 he returned to London as deputy secretary of the Ministry of Supply but in 1948 he went back to Washington as a minister at the embassy. He returned to London in 1949 as permanent secretary of the Ministry of Food. In 1951 he became secretary to the Board of Trade, and in 1960 he returned to the Treasury as joint permanent secretary in charge of financial and economic policy. In 1962 he had a heart attack, and left the service. He was appointed CMG in 1946, KCB in 1950, GCMG in 1959, and a privy councillor in 1962.

Frank Lee was an outstanding civil servant. Apart from an insatiable capacity for work, he was lucid and persuasive in argument, and had good personal relations with his staff, his colleagues in other departments, and his ministers, who were generally disposed to take his advice. His understanding of Americans and their ways was profound; in return Americans admired and liked him, as did his Commonwealth colleagues, and this was a great help in his negotiations. His weakness as an administrator was a temperamental inability to delegate; he often drove himself too hard and his staff too lightly. Nevertheless he was a success at the Board of Trade, and perhaps this was the apogee of his official career. He showed great promise at the Treasury but his reign there was short. As a committed advocate of European integration he did, however, play an influential part in the reappraisal of British policy towards Europe in 1960–2.

In 1962 he was elected master of Corpus Christi College, Cambridge, and threw himself into the life of the college and the university. He became chairman of the Press Syndicate, of the faculty board of engineering, and, as deputy to the vice-chancellor, of the University Appointments Board. He was also a member of the financial board of the university, and treasurer of the University Rugby Club. He was a governor of the Leys School, and vice-chairman of the board of Addenbrooke's Hospital, where he initiated a project for a sports and social centre for young doctors and nurses from the hospital which was completed after his death and named the Frank Lee Recreation Centre.

Outside Cambridge he was a member of the council of the University of East Anglia, a governor of the London School of Economics, and a director of Bowaters. He was an honorary fellow of Downing and received an honorary LL D of London University. He carried on all these varied activities with undiminished zest in spite of three further heart attacks and three strokes. He died in Cambridge 18 April 1971.

He was a short, stocky man with a florid face, sharp pointed nose, and black, often crew-cut, hair. Energetic and forceful, he attacked the business in hand like a keen terrier attacking a large rat. He found enjoyment in work of all kinds and it was never a burden to him. He was full of humour, gregarious, and a lover of good food, good wine, and good company. He had a well-stocked and retentive mind and a fund of quotations and good stories. He was an avid reader of poetry, especially contemporary work. A good footballer in his youth, he played cricket whenever he could, and became a baseball fan. He wrote very little, and did not approve of public servants publishing their memoirs. But his Stamp memorial lecture of 1958, *The Board of Trade* (University of London, Athlone Press), reveals much of his quality of mind and his approach to life. It was characteristic of him to decline a peerage, and to prefer appointment as a privy councillor. Before moving to Cambridge, the Lees lived a happy family and social life for twenty years at Much Hadham with their three daughters, all of whom followed their grandparents into the teaching profession.

[*The Times*, 29 April 1971; private information; personal knowledge.] SHERFIELD

LEESE, SIR OLIVER WILLIAM HARGREAVES, third baronet (1894–1978), lieutenant-general, was born in London 27 October 1894, the eldest in the family of three sons and one daughter of Sir William Hargreaves Leese, second baronet, of Send Holme, Send, Surrey, and senior partner of Freshfields, solicitors, and his wife, Violet Mary, daughter of Albert George Sandeman, of Presdales, Hertfordshire. Educated at Ludgrove and Eton, where he excelled at cricket and football, he was commissioned into the Coldstream Guards in August 1914. During World War I he was wounded three times, the third nearly fatally in October 1916, was appointed to the DSO (1916), and was twice mentioned in dispatches.

From 1920 to 1922 Leese was adjutant of the 3rd battalion, Coldstream Guards. He then (1922–5) became adjutant of the OTC at Eton. He studied at the Staff College, Camberley, in 1927–8. After various posts he became general staff officer, 2nd grade, at the War Office in 1935, and in the following year took command of the 1st battalion, Coldstream Guards. He succeeded his father as baronet in 1937. In 1938 he went to India as chief instructor at the Staff College, Quetta.

Recalled home in 1940, he held five posts that year, including that of deputy chief of the general staff of the British expeditionary force until the evacuation of France. He helped prepare the outline plan for the Dunkirk evacuation. He was promoted major-general in 1941. He then formed the Guards Armoured division, training it with great thoroughness and enthusiasm. In September 1942, with the rank of temporary lieutenant-general, he was sent for by General B. L. Montgomery (later Viscount Montgomery of Alamein, q.v.) to command XXX Corps, Eighth Army, before the battle of Alamein, his task being to break through the German minefields so that the armour could fan out. With Australian, New Zealand, South African, and

Indian divisions under his command Leese made a vital contribution to victory, causing Montgomery to inform Sir Alan Brooke (later Viscount Alanbrooke, q.v.) that 'the best soldier out here is Oliver Leese—first class'. The relationship between Montgomery and Leese is important. Montgomery regarded him as a great friend and Leese considered his superior the finest general in the field since the Duke of Marlborough [q.v.]. Leese was a perfect foil to Montgomery, being intensely loyal though not a yes-man, and thoroughly disliking publicity.

After a refit, Leese's Corps led the advance to Tripoli and Mareth. In March 1943 Sir H. R. L. C. Alexander (later Earl Alexander of Tunis, q.v.) asked Montgomery to release Leese so that he could command the First Army. Montgomery refused, although he could have spared him ten days later, after the battle of Mareth, and this might have made a great difference to Leese's career. As it was, Alexander then took control himself. In July 1943, with Canadian troops under his command, Leese landed in Sicily and penetrated along the eastern side of the island. He then took XXX Corps back to England.

At the end of December 1943 Leese was appointed to succeed Montgomery as general officer commanding Eighth Army 'before Monty could return and prevent his departure', as (Sir) Frank Simpson put it. In March 1944, the American Fifth Army having failed to capture Cassino, Alexander ordered Leese to take the Eighth Army across the Apennines, a task he completed in utter secrecy, in order to capture the monastery position. Partly thanks to the Polish Corps (led by General Anders), which respected Leese more than any other British commander, the battle was won in May. When on reaching the 'Gothic Line' the Eighth Army was held up, Leese again moved with complete surprise eastwards to the Adriatic, and breached its defences.

In October 1944 Leese became C-in-C Allied Land Forces, South-East Asia, with his headquarters in Calcutta. He was directed to establish the Fourteenth Army, under General W. J. (later Viscount) Slim [q.v.], in central Burma by the end of 1945 but, partly due to his drive, Burma was recaptured by June. There then occurred a setback in Leese's military career. He started planning the invasion of Singapore for September 1945. Slim was tired and requested three months' leave in England. As Leese required a commander in India, with combined operations experience, to plan the landings, he suggested to Lord Louis Mountbatten (later Earl Mountbatten of Burma, q.v.), supreme allied commander, South-East Asia, that Slim should command the Twelfth Army in Burma to mop up, and a new invasion commander be appointed. Mountbatten instructed Leese to sound out Slim, who agreed at first, and then retracted, preferring retirement and implying that Leese had sacked him. Mountbatten then dismissed Leese for exceeding instructions. Leese never disclosed his version but in his diaries Alanbrooke wrote that after reprimanding Leese, who took it in manly fashion, never blaming anyone else, he still had a 'feeling that, although he may have been at fault, he had a raw deal at the hands of Mountbatten'. Leese next became GOC-in-C Eastern Command. He retired from the army in 1946.

Leese then turned to horticulture, becoming expert on mushrooms, cacti, and bonzai trees. He wrote three books on cacti, accumulated a collection at Worfield Gardens, Shropshire, and travelled extensively collecting specimens, being known affectionately as Cactus Pete. He won many gold medals at the Chelsea Show and was often found by his stand producing, from memory, Latin names of exhibits (just as he had given lectures on military strategy without notes). He was elected to the Royal Horticultural Society floral committee.

As national president of the British Legion (1962–70) he changed its image, increasing a declining membership by 50,000, and always contacting local branches on his travels abroad. President of the Combined Cadet Force Association (1950–71) he encouraged close relations between the services and schools with cadet units. He ran the Alamein reunion, and was chairman of the Old Etonian Association, a director of Securicor, lieutenant of the Tower of London, and colonel of the Shropshire Yeomanry. Cricket was a great love, as was fly fishing. President of Warwickshire County Cricket Club (1959–75) and of the Shropshire CCC, he was prominent in their administration. He was elected president of MCC (1965–6) and accompanied their tour of Australia.

A tall, strong man, informal, unorthodox in dress, with the manner (which masked an astute mind) of a 'Wodehouse' character, he possessed a sense of humour and schoolboy fun but was sometimes impatient and intolerant and had an explosive, petulant temper. His refusal to get immersed in paper work (although he never took an important decision without the most detailed examination) gave him more time to see his troops, waving to those he passed, as they did to him, or appearing unexpectedly on a gun site. He regarded as important the distribution of 'comforts' to them. He surrounded himself with predominantly young officers whom he sent on important missions with complete confidence, having instilled in them his determination 'to achieve'. He offered warm hospitality in his Eighth Army mess, among whose visitors were King George VI (who knighted Leese in the field at Arezzo), (Sir) Winston Churchill, and J. C.

Smuts [qq.v.]. A prolific letter writer (once sending at least 150 postcards from Australia), he kept up with a variety of friends. His will-power overcame a leg amputation when he was seventy-nine. His determination 'never to look back' was an important part of his character.

Leese was appointed CBE (1940), CB (1942), and KCB (1943). In 1944 he was awarded the Virtuti Militari, the highest Polish military honour. He also won the croix de guerre and was a commander of the Legion of Honour and of the American Legion of Merit.

In 1933 Leese married Margaret Alice (died 1964), daughter of Cuthbert Leicester-Warren, of Tabley House, Knutsford, country gentleman; they had no children. Leese died 22 January 1978 at his home in Cefn Coch, near Llanrhaedr, Wales. He was succeeded in the baronetcy by his brother, Alexander William (1909–1982). In 1982 the baronetcy became extinct.

[Unpublished memoirs and letters of Oliver Leese; *The Memoirs of Field-Marshal Montgomery*, 1958; Nigel Hamilton, *Monty*, 1981; David Fraser, *Alanbrooke*, 1982; private information; personal knowledge.]

ION M. CALVOCORESSI

LE GROS CLARK, FREDERICK (1892–1977), expert in social and industrial problems. [See CLARK.]

LE GROS CLARK, SIR WILFRID EDWARD (1895–1971), anatomist. [See CLARK.]

LEITCH, CHARLOTTE CECILIA PITCAIRN (CECIL) (1891–1977), golfer, was born at Silloth, Cumberland, 13 April 1891, sixth of the seven children and fourth of the five daughters of Dr John Leitch, medical practitioner and botanist, formerly of Monimail, Fife, and his wife Catherine Edith, second daughter of the Revd Francis Redford. She was educated privately and at Carlisle Girls' High School.

Completely self-taught on the windswept links of Silloth-on-Solway, all the sisters were championship golfers, Cecil, Edith (Guedalla), and May (Millar) being English internationals.

Cecil Leitch herself made a dramatic début as a seventeen-year-old in the 1908 British Ladies' Championship at St. Andrews when, although she lost in the semi-final, her decisive and powerful game was immediately hailed as setting a new standard for women's golf. A strong but graceful figure, already with a commanding presence, employing an unorthodox flat swing and palm grip to produce shots of exceptional length and accuracy, she was soon established among the leaders. Her first appearance for England however was not until 1910 when the residential qualification was specially reduced from twenty to eighteen years. In the same year, receiving half a stroke over 72 holes, she defeated the leading amateur Harold Hilton in the first challenge match to test the disparity between men and women players, a result as much publicized on the suffragette platform as in golfing circles. In 1912 she won the French championship, and by 1914, when at Hunstanton she took her first British Open as well as the French and English titles, she was recognized as the foremost woman player of the day and one of the game's greatest personalities.

After the war she retained all her championships, winning the British on its resumption in 1920 at Newcastle, county Down, and in 1921 at Turnberry. Her dominance was undisputed until a shock defeat by Joyce Wethered (later Lady Heathcoat-Amory) in the 1920 English final. Thereafter, apart from a year when an arm injury kept Cecil Leitch out of action, their duels were front-page news, arousing an enthusiasm unmatched by any successor. The historic final of the 1925 British Open at Troon before a crowd of thousands, when she succumbed to Joyce Wethered at the thirty-seventh hole, was regarded by Cecil Leitch as her greatest match. She regained the title at her final attempt in 1926 at Harlech, thus winning it in each of the four home countries, and retired from competition in 1928, her record including victory in the French championship five times, the English twice and the Canadian once. She represented England in thirty-three matches, losing only three, and was an honorary member of twenty-five clubs and five associations. In 1967 she was elected to the American Golf Hall of Fame.

Before journalism was ruled as violating the amateur status Cecil Leitch contributed regular articles to newspapers and magazines on all aspects of the game, and published three books, *Golf for Girls* (1911), *Golf* (1922), and *Golf Simplified* (1924). She served for some years on the council of the Ladies' Golf Union, with a term as chairman, until disagreement with its new form of constitution in 1928 caused her resignation. Now living in the south of England, she turned her energies to business, firstly to the antiques world and later as a working director of the Cinema House group, which was concerned largely with introducing the first foreign films to Britain. At the same time she allied herself with the ideals of the infant National Playing Fields Association, on whose executive and finance committees she was to serve devotedly for nearly fifty years. Always an excellent speaker, she made numerous appeals and also organized fund-raising tournaments, receiving the President's certificate for her services in 1963 (she became a vice-president in 1967). Her equally long spell with the Kent Playing Fields Association saw the institution of her popular Five Club competitions. She was also on the executive of the Central Council of Physical Recreation and the publicity council of the YWCA. She was an active member of the Embroiderers' Guild. The Women Golfers' Museum was her proudest achievement; on the founding committee in 1938 and subsequently chairman until her death, she was responsible for building up a remarkable collection of *memorabilia* and books. She established it as the only museum of its kind accessible to the public.

Conscientious and thorough with a keen mind and firm opinions but not lacking in humour, she was often critical but never unfair, and her generosity and concern for others were sincere. Equally ready to support the Veterans or counsel young players, she fiercely defended amateurism in golf. In 1976 she revisited Silloth as lady president to present the British Amateur Trophy. She was on the platform the following year at the European Professional Ladies' final. A month later, 16 September 1977, she died at her London home. She was unmarried.

[Donald Steel and Peter Ryde (eds.), *The Shell International Encyclopaedia of Golf*, 1975; Enid Wilson, *A Gallery of Women Golfers*, 1961; private information; personal knowledge.]

M. S. MILLAR

LEJEUNE, CAROLINE ALICE (1897–1973), film critic, was born 27 March 1897 at Didsbury, Manchester, the youngest in the family of five daughters and three sons of Adam Edward Lejeune and his wife, Jane Louisa, daughter of Alexander MacLaren, a Nonconformist minister. Adam Lejeune belonged to a Huguenot family who had settled in Germany; as a young man he had come from Frankfurt to England to learn the cotton trade. Caroline never knew her father, who died in Switzerland before she was two years old; but presumably he left his widow comfortably well off, for the children were brought up without anxiety in a large house with servants and a nanny.

Caroline Lejeune was educated at Withington Girls' School. But there were more potent influences, for C. P. Scott [q.v.], editor of the *Manchester Guardian*, was a close friend of her mother and a regular visitor to the Lejeune household; he was to be the patron and supporter of the career of the youngest child. She was expected to go to Oxford and she passed responsions, then the entrance examination to the university. But she took a dislike to the place and, electing instead to work from home, after taking a secretarial course and working as a secretary she enrolled in the English school of Manchester University; she left with a first class degree (1921). She was already writing for the *Manchester Guardian* while she was still a student. Those were the days of the Beecham Opera Company at Manchester and of D'Oyly Carte seasons; delightedly she became a reviewer. But she was sensitive also to the younger arts of the period and at the age of twenty-four she took a decision—she would be a film critic.

It was a bold and courageous step. In 1921 there were no regular film critics in England, and certainly no women film critics; the cinema was not yet taken seriously. A suggestion came from C. P. Scott: such work, he said, would have to be done from London. A graduate scholarship from Manchester University paved the way. She would read at the British Museum, write a thesis, and obtain a Ph.D. With her mother, a significant force in her career who would settle near her wherever she went, Caroline Lejeune moved south. By the beginning of 1922 she had a film column of her own in the *Manchester Guardian*, signed C.A.L. Three years later she married (Edward) Roffe Thompson, a journalist and later editor of *John Bull*. He was the son of Edward Thompson, musician. However she never changed her professional name and it was as C. A. Lejeune that she was to be known.

Presently the couple settled, with her mother living close by, in Pinner. In 1928 a son, their only child, was born; and in the same year Caroline Lejeune moved, with the blessing of C. P. Scott, from the *Manchester Guardian* to the *Observer*. She wrote for the paper for over thirty years, making its film criticism well known.

A pioneer, she was already writing about television before World War II; but it is on her recognition of the achievements of cinema that her distinction rests. She came to the post at a crucial time. The screen was still silent when she began; the years of invention and development and experiment were to come. She was there to see the coming of sound and the victory of colour. She was not herself a friend of revolution; on the contrary she was a non-political writer. But she never shrank from the new or the unfamiliar. She was among the few who welcomed the advent of the 'talkies'; she saw *The Battleship Potemkin* in Berlin long before it reached England and was quick to hail the startling film with enthusiasm. She also saw the cinema from the other side of the screen. At Pinner she lived within reach of the Pinewood and Denham studios, which were being built between the wars. Her house was hospitable to the great figures of the British cinema; (Sir) Alexander Korda, (Sir) Alfred Hitchcock, and (Sir) Michael Balcon [qq.v.] were her friends. In her way she was an educator; she noted the absurdities of a popular medium and she recorded wittily but without malice. Her clear, lively, literate style persuaded a whole generation to look with attention at the creative genius of the screen.

After her retirement in 1960 she never went to the cinema. She received an honorary D.Litt.

from Durham University in 1961. In the same year she completed a novel, *Three Score and Ten*, left unfinished by Angela Thirkell [q.v.]; her autobiography, *Thank You For Having Me*, appeared in 1964. There had been an early study, *Cinema* (1931), and a lively collection of her reviews, *Chestnuts In Her Lap* (1947). She was a home-keeping figure; she never went to Hollywood, never attended the Continental festivals so much frequented by later critics. Her final years were spent in the quiet of her home and the garden which she loved. Her husband and her son, Anthony Lejeune, survived her, the former for only six months.

[C. A. Lejeune, *Thank You For Having Me* (autobiography), 1964; personal knowledge.]

DILYS POWELL

LEMASS, SEAN FRANCIS (1899–1971), prime minister of the Irish Republic, was born in Ballybrack, county Dublin, 15 July 1899, the second son and second child of John Timothy Lemass, hatter, of Dublin, and his wife, Frances Phelan; their family eventually numbered five boys and four girls. Educated at the Christian Brothers' O'Connell Schools, Dublin, and Ross's College, he joined the Irish Volunteers before his sixteenth birthday, took part in the 1916 rising, was released because of his youth, but soon returned to active duty and was elected lieutenant in 1917. Active against the British forces, he was imprisoned in December 1920 but released one year later, after which he adopted an anti-treaty stance and fought against the Free State forces. He escaped after the surrender of the Four Courts garrison, but was captured and imprisoned again from December 1922 until October 1923. It was typical of the man that he put his confinement to good use, studying history and economics and, so far as the latter is concerned, laying the basis of a lifelong interest.

In November 1924, after an unsuccessful contest for Dublin South City earlier in the year, he was elected to Dáil Eireann for that constituency but abstained from sitting, with the rest of his Sinn Fein colleagues. He was returned for this seat until 1948, and for Dublin South Central from then until 1969. He was made 'defence minister' in the clandestine government of Eamon de Valera [q.v.] in 1924, but, with his leader, broke with Sinn Fein to form the Fianna Fáil Party in 1926, becoming honorary secretary at its first convention that November, and its director of elections the following year. On the party's decision to enter the Dáil in 1927, Lemass became shadow minister for industry and commerce and on 9 March 1932, when de Valera formed his first government, minister, the youngest in the Cabinet. With a short break between September 1939 and August 1941 he was to hold the industry and commerce portfolio until 1948, and again between 1951 and 1954, and from March 1957 to June 1959. He was also minister for supplies from September 1939 to June 1945 and deputy prime minister during his other periods of office from 1945, becoming premier from June 1959 until November 1966.

Already the architect of his party's economic policy before assuming office in 1932, Lemass responded to the ideology of Arthur Griffith [q.v.] and the circumstances of the depression to implement a policy of protection. The 'economic war' with Britain, part of a wider constitutional and financial dispute which lasted from mid-1932 until April 1938, gave an added incentive to the drive for self-sufficiency and protection while at the same time providing a nationalist focus which helped to divert the political consequences of some notable failures. Protection was undoubtedly needed and Lemass was able to boost industrial employment from 111,000 to 166,000 during these years, but agriculture declined painfully, it proved impossible to find alternatives to the British market, or for British imports, and the attempt at self-sufficiency was bought at the price of expensive goods and the creation of vested interests not all of which were beneficial to the state. Even so, Lemass emerged with credit: his Condition of Employment Act, 1936, was something of a worker's charter (which also helped to win him acclaim as president of the International Labour Office congress in Geneva in 1937); his Control of Manufacturers Acts brought majority shareholding into Irish hands; while his other initiatives included the successful establishment of state boards to exploit turf production, air transport, and tourism.

During World War II Lemass created a national transport service by amalgamating bus companies and reorganizing the rail services, but his main preoccupation was to ensure adequate supplies of the necessities of life and his success in this was recognized when he became deputy premier in 1945. In 1946 he established a Labour Court to improve industrial relations but the next decade of austerity and governmental change saw little achievement associated with his name. By 1957, however, external conditions and internal planning had begun to argue for change, and once more Lemass seized the opportunity. In partnership with T. K. Whitaker, the leading economic planner in the Civil Service, a 'First Economic Programme' was adopted, from 1958, and vitality and dynamic expansion at last replaced stagnation in the Irish economy. As prime minister from 1959 to 1966 Lemass successfully reversed most of the policies which different circumstances had dictated in the thirties; his bid to join the EEC in 1961, though thwarted, epitomized an urge for integration not isolation, while his recipe for expansion now was free trade, not protection. Here was contrast, but not contradiction. New times required new approaches and Lemass judged the moment correctly, to achieve something of an economic miracle for his country. In one other sphere too he broke new ground, journeying to Belfast to take tea with T. M. O'Neill (later Lord O'Neill of the Maine), prime minister of Northern Ireland, in January 1965, a recognition of the northern administration and a gesture of friendship and co-operation, but also of commitment in his view to an eventual Irish unity based on agreement and harmony of interests.

Before his retirement in 1966 Lemass had carried through a reorganization of government introducing a Department of Transport and Power, had created a National Industrial and Economic Council, had initiated a vast capital programme which stimulated wide expansion, and had bequeathed his successor, Jack Lynch, a formidable electoral machine. He continued to sit in the Dáil until 1969, but devoted much energy to numerous directorships until his death.

Amongst the awards and honorary degrees conferred upon him were the Grand Cross of the Order of Gregory the Great, 1948; the Grand Cross of the Pian Order, 1962; the Grand Cross of the Order of Merit of the Federal Republic of Germany, 1962; and the Greek Grand Cross of the Order of St. Dennis of Zante, 1967. He had honorary LL Ds from Iona College, New Rochelle (New York), 1953, the University of Villanova (Philadelphia), 1963, and the University of Dublin, 1965; and an honorary D.Econ.Sc., National University of Ireland, 1954. Portraits were executed by Sean O'Sullivan (privately owned) and by Leo Whelan and there is also a bronze by Seamus Murphy (also in private ownership). Always well dressed, Sean Lemass was a keen pipe smoker and his portraits reveal a broad-shouldered and burly figure with dark hair brushed back, his face distinguished by a strong mouth and clipped moustache and brown, humorous eyes. His few relaxations included golf, fishing, and the occasional race meeting.

Longer in office than any other minister, and throughout at the heart of Ireland's economic life, Lemass was a decisive man, always prepared to risk a mistake rather than do nothing. A pragmatist, he had a tenacity of purpose allied to a quick understanding, a strong will and intellect, but also a readiness to listen and accept reasoned argument. Shy, he could be ruthless and brusque as a young man, and he remained demanding as a political boss. He liked to get things done. It was his contribution to ensure that many things were done for his country's good, and done with integrity.

On 25 August 1924 he married Kathleen (died 1985), daughter of Mr Hughes, a carpet buyer for Arnotts, a Dublin store. They had three daughters, the eldest of whom married C. J. Haughey, a future Irish prime minister, and one son, Noel (died 1976), who followed his father into Dáil Eireann. Lemass died in Dublin 11 May 1971.

[*Bulletin of the Department of Foreign Affairs*, No. 837, 18 June 1971; *Irish Times*, 12 May 1971; J. Lee, 'Sean Lemass' in J. Lee (ed.), *Ireland since 1945*, 1979; personal knowledge.]

D. W. HARKNESS

LENNON, JOHN WINSTON (1940–1980), musician and composer of popular music, was born in Liverpool 9 October 1940, the only child of Alfred Lennon, a ship's steward, and his wife, Julia Stanley. The father was away when his son was born; the mother's sister, Mary, was present and named him John. Aunt 'Mimi' and her husband George Smith raised the boy at their house. Lennon attended Dovedale Primary and Quarry Bank High School. His academic work deteriorated as he cultivated a fondness for practical jokes, and he failed all his O levels by one grade. In 1957 he entered the Liverpool College of Art, but he obtained no degree.

That year a mutual friend brought (James) Paul McCartney to see Lennon's skiffle group the Quarrymen. One week later Lennon invited McCartney to join. He accepted, and in a few months brought his younger friend George Harrison into the group. In the four years that followed the act changed its name and its membership. In 1960 they became the Beatles and in August 1962 Ringo Starr became their drummer. None of the four could either read or write music.

It was while appearing in clubs in Hamburg from 1960 to 1962 and in the Cavern, Liverpool, in 1961–2 that the Beatles received invaluable experience. They played for hours, mastering a rock and roll repertoire while Lennon and McCartney wrote new songs. Lennon's controlled hysteria on the Isley Brothers' 'Twist and Shout' was an exciting example of rock and roll singing.

On 6 June 1962, the Beatles successfully auditioned for George Martin, the Parlophone label manager, and on 5 October they released their first single, 'Love Me Do', which was produced by Martin. It slowly climbed to number seventeen in the charts.

In 1963 the phenomenon known as Beatlemania swept Britain. 'She Loves You' was the first single to exceed sales of one and a half million in the United Kingdom. Hysterical crowds greeted the group's every appearance. In 1964 the fever spread to the United States, where six of their records reached the top of the charts in the first year. In one week in April, the Beatles held the top five positions in the national hit parade, an achievement never equalled.

Throughout the 1960s the Beatles were the leading recording act in the world.

It is difficult to distinguish between the contributions of the individual Beatles at the beginning of their popularity. Lennon and McCartney were writing their songs together, and as a performing unit it was as John, Paul, George, *and* Ringo that they captivated the world as the 'Fab Four'. The Beatles were the first major pop group to write, sing, and play their own material; subsequent rock stars would be expected to do the same. The unprecedented demand for their long-playing discs put rock music on albums, which were previously predominantly the territory of film sound-track or stage cast recordings.

The considerable foreign exchange the Beatles brought to Britain was a factor in their investiture as MBEs on 26 October 1965. On 26 November 1969 Lennon, who was passionately involved in left-wing and utopian politics, returned his MBE to the Queen as a protest against Britain's role in Biafra, Britain's support for American involvement in Vietnam, and the slipping sales of his Plastic Ono Band single 'Cold Turkey'. The other Beatles happily kept their decorations. The rebel of Dovedale Primary School never became an establishment figure, unlike Paul McCartney, who seemed to thrive on success and mass acceptance. After 1966 Lennon embraced transcendental meditation, drugs, and mystical religion.

The Beatles translated their success to other forms with a series of popular films and Lennon's two best-selling collections of stories and drawings, *John Lennon in his own Write* (1964) and *A Spaniard in the Works* (1965). It was around the time the latter work was published that Lennon and McCartney began to write songs individually. 'Help', 'In My Life', and 'Strawberry Fields Forever' were particularly outstanding Lennon pieces. In 1965 the Beatles released *Sergeant Pepper's Lonely Hearts Club Band*, which was considered the finest rock music album.

Lennon's association with the Japanese avant-garde artist Yoko Ono led him to lose interest in the Beatles, and by the time the group split in 1970 (the partnership was finally wound up in the High Court in 1971) Lennon had already made several 'solo' recordings. These almost inevitably included contributions from or were partly inspired by Yoko Ono. In 1971 Lennon composed 'Imagine', which became his best-known song. During the 1970s Lennon's relationship with Yoko Ono went through a rocky period, partly due to his use of drugs. He had difficulties with the United States Immigration Service which wanted to deny him permission to live there because of a British conviction for drug offences, but in 1972 the permission was granted.

Lennon's post-Beatle work was uneven but punctuated by heights of artistic achievement. His 1970 set *Plastic Ono Band* contains gripping examples of how emotional suffering can be conveyed musically. The single 'Cold Turkey' accurately recalls the agony associated with heroin withdrawal. 'Woman', from *Double Fantasy*, his 1980 collaboration with Yoko Ono, generates the warmth the artist himself was enjoying in his domestic life. For five years he had kept house and cared for his young son while Yoko Ono managed the business side of the marriage, buying property.

In 1962 Lennon married Cynthia, daughter of Charles Edwin Powell, commercial traveller. They had one son, (John Charles) Julian. This marriage ended in divorce in 1968 and on 20 March 1969 Lennon married Yoko, daughter of Eisuke Ono, of the Yokohama specie bank, Tokyo. They had one son, Sean Ono. Lennon was shot dead outside his New York City apartment 9 December 1980. The gunman made him a martyr in fans' eyes, proving that the words of 'All You Need Is Love' and 'Give Peace a Chance', which in moments of cynicism seemed trite, had meaning. At the time of his death Lennon's fortune was estimated at £100 million.

[Philip Norman, *Shout! The True Story of the Beatles*, 1981; *Sunday Times*, *John Lennon The Life and the Legend*, 1980; personal knowledge.]

PAUL GAMBACCINI

LEON, HENRY CECIL (1902–1976), author under the name of HENRY CECIL and county court judge, was born 19 September 1902 at Norwood Green, Middlesex, the youngest of the three sons (there were no daughters) of Joseph Abraham Leon, analytical chemist, and his wife, Esther Phoebe Defries. He achieved most fame with light novels set in the world of the law, a handful of them extremely successful in other media. But he also had a legal career which, but for a personal tragedy, was likely to have taken him high and he wrote half a dozen books on legal matters to which he brought shrewdness of judgement and the same sense of fun that marks out his fiction.

He was educated at St. Paul's School, of which he was a foundation scholar, and, at the age of eighteen, his eldest brother, destined for the law, having been killed in action in the war of 1914–18, he joined Gray's Inn (where he ended his days in a book-lined flat up many flights of wooden stairs) and was admitted as an exhibitioner to King's College, Cambridge. He obtained second classes in classics part i in 1921 and law part ii in 1923. Called to the bar in 1923, by the exercise of the four qualities he was later to cite as necessary for success in his engaging book of advice, *Brief to Counsel* (1958), namely quickness of understanding, patience in listening, integrity, and the capacity for hard work, he acquired a considerable practice.

It enabled him as early as 1930, together with his surviving brother, to present his parents, whose means had always been modest, with their first car and someone to drive it, an early example of a notorious generosity. Success also enabled him, in 1935, to marry Lettice Mabel, daughter of Henry David Apperly, of Chalfont St. Peter, whom he later characterized in his discursively anecdotal autobiography *Just Within the Law* (1975) as 'the most skilful dentist for whom I have ever opened my mouth'. In 1939, having from a sense of duty joined the Army Officers Emergency Reserve, he was called to the 1/5 battalion of the Queen's Royal Regiment, in which he gained the MC (1942) at the Battle of Alamein for, in the words of his commanding officer, 'sheer refusal to be intimidated by every kind of enemy projectile' while taking weapons through a minefield gap. It is typical of his fundamental modesty that the award goes unmentioned in his autobiography.

He had not long resumed his bar career when his wife was stricken by cancer. He at once applied for a county court judgeship in order to spend as much time as possible with her in the country. She died in 1950. In 1954 he married Barbara Jeanne Ovenden, daughter of Thomas Blackmore, farmer, of Weston-super-Mare. It was a marriage, he later said, as happy as his first. Neither had issue, but there was a stepson in the second marriage.

To restore his income (county court judges then received only £2,000 a year) he began writing. First a collection of stories, *Full Circle* (1948), based on diverting tales told to his fellow soldiers on board ship, and then a succession of twenty-four novels, of which *Brothers in Law* (1955), made into a play then a film, brought him most success. They are written much as their author talked, amusingly, with ingenuity and shrewd illustrative anecdote but ballasted with common sense and an uncompromising belief in goodness. Yet they are never 'goody-goody': Cecil's sense of mischief, noted of himself in an article 'I Haven't Changed Since I Was Eight', is too pervasive for that.

He served as a county court judge at Brentford and Uxbridge from 1949 to 1953 and at Willesden from 1953 to 1967, a term marked by compassion and reform. He instituted an unofficial welfare officer system to help litigants after trial, and, thanks largely to his instigation, debtors faced with prison were obligatorily informed of their rights. Such imprisonment was at once cut by half. His conduct on the bench, he said of himself, was marked by frequent intervention, occasionally from his sense of mischief, at other times from his passion for properly conducted justice. This latter prevented him admitting in undefended divorce cases less than strict proof and eventually at his request the lord chancellor relieved him of divorce work.

His latter days, bow-tied as ever, were much enjoyed. Some six months before his death giving the Saintsbury oration—he was a most clubbable person—he quoted with high approval Charles Lamb [q.v.] on retirement: 'I walk about, not to and from.' But he also served—as chairman of the British Copyright Council (from 1973) and of the Society of Authors and in lecturing and talking to students and others. He died in Brighton 21 May 1976.

In sum, it can be said of him, an aim he offered to a correspondent he feared would be soured by a legal reverse, that he led a 'happy, sensible and useful life'.

[Cecil's own writings; private information; personal knowledge.] H. R. F. KEATING

LESLIE, SIR JOHN RANDOLPH ('SHANE'), third baronet, of Glaslough, county Monaghan (1885–1971), man of letters, was born 24 September 1885 at Stratford House in London, the eldest of the four sons of Sir John Leslie, second baronet, and his wife, Léonie Blanche, youngest daughter of Leonard Jerome of New York. His boyhood was spent in Ireland. He was educated at Eton College and at King's College, Cambridge, where he obtained a second class in part i of the classical tripos in 1907. At Cambridge he became a Roman Catholic and an Irish nationalist, persuasions which deeply affronted the Anglo-Irish Protestant ascendancy into which he had been born. He began to use the Irish form of his name—Shane.

Having changed his religion and renounced the Irish estates entailed on him, in the winter of 1907 Leslie travelled to Russia and stayed with Leo Tolstoy at Yasnaya Polyana. One day as they walked through the snow-covered village discussing pacifism, Tolstoy said to him: 'They must choose between me and the bayonets'. Leslie would later write: 'That choice was made after his death. He did not write or speak as an idle dreamer.'

Leslie was a first cousin of (Sir) Winston Churchill, his mother Léonie being a sister of Lady Randolph Churchill. Churchill, who was in favour of home rule, showed interest in Leslie's political views and introduced him to John Redmond [q.v.], leader of the Irish Nationalists in the House of Commons. Inspired by Redmond, Shane agreed to stand for Londonderry as a Nationalist in the 1910 election. He did not win the seat and departed for America where he worked with Bourke Cockran, the Irish orator, who was a friend of Churchill's. Both Cockran and Leslie were seeking to lessen the dislike of the American Irish for England. While in America Leslie met and married in 1912

Marjorie (died 1951), youngest daughter of Henry Clay Ide, judge of the Vermont Supreme Court and recently governor-general of the Philippines. Marjorie was a sister of Mrs Bourke Cockran and the wedding took place in the Cockrans' Long Island home. As well as working politically Leslie began to produce books of verse. In the war of 1914–18 his brother Norman, a captain in the Rifle Brigade, was killed and Leslie, attached to a British Ambulance Corps, was on his way to the Dardanelles when he became ill and was placed in a military hospital in Malta. Here he wrote his first major book, *The End of a Chapter*, which described the civilization he now saw perishing. Published in 1916, it made his name.

During 1916 and 1917 Leslie worked in Washington with the British ambassador, Sir Cecil Spring-Rice [q.v.], who was trying to soften Irish American hostility to Britain and convince the United States of the urgency of declaring war against Germany. Leslie published a magazine entitled *Ireland* and strove with Spring-Rice to establish understanding between Westminster and Washington. Perhaps the bravest thing that Leslie ever did—certainly the most perspicacious—was to implore the British politicians not to execute the leaders of the 1916 Easter rising in Dublin. His arguments went unheeded. Sixteen outstanding Irishmen were shot, rendering friendship between the two peoples more difficult than ever. After the war, and indeed to the end of his life, Leslie tried to build bridges of friendship across the Irish religious divides. With passion he believed that both peoples could live amicably, tolerating each other's contrasting opinions in a United Ireland. He died before his view could be proved wrong.

During the twenties and thirties Leslie wrote *Henry Edward Manning, his Life and Labours* (1921), *Mark Sykes: his Life and Letters* (1923), *The Skull of Swift* (1928), *Mrs. Fitzherbert* (1928), and *Studies in Sublime Failure* (1932). And from his pen also came three novels: *Doomsland* (1923), about his Ulster boyhood; *The Oppidan* (1922), a discerning book about Eton College; and *The Cantab* (1926), describing the adventures of a Cambridge undergraduate. He also wrote in verse *Jutland, a Fragment of Epic* (1930) and, being a classical scholar, he produced *The Greek Anthology* (1929). His *American Wonderland* (1936) and the autobiographical *The Film of Memory* (1938) appeared shortly before World War II. From 1940 to 1945 Leslie served in the Home Guard at the London headquarters of General Sir Hubert Gough [q.v.]. There on his camp-bed he wrote *The Irish Tangle for English Readers* (1946) about the increasing bitterness engendered around his Monaghan home. He succeeded to the baronetcy in 1944. His last book, *Long Shadows*, published in 1966 when he was over eighty, presented a final memoir. Small books of verse were interspersed throughout his other work and many anthologies include his poems. For this Dictionary he wrote the notices of W. P. Ward, Mark Sykes, Michael Logue, and Alfred Noyes.

Leslie had fine conversational powers and wit. To the end of his days he could galvanize the most erudite audience with his lectures or entrance the young with reminiscence. The well-turned phrases of his writings were outmatched by the speed of his repartee. Keenly interested in reafforestation he led a campaign for more general planting and was well known in the organization 'Men of the Trees'. After the death of his first wife he married Iris, daughter of C. M. Laing. Leslie died at his home in Hove 14 August 1971, leaving two sons and a daughter. His elder son, John Norman Ide (born 1916), succeeded to the baronetcy.

At Castle Leslie in county Monaghan there is a bust of Leslie by Clare Sheridan and a portrait by John Eves. In the Monaghan Museum is a portrait by Frederick White.

[Private information; personal knowledge.]

ANITA LESLIE

LEVY, BENN WOLFE (1900–1973), playwright and director, was born in London 7 March 1900, the younger child and only son of Octave George Levy, a prosperous wool broker, of Hyde Park Gate, and his wife, Nannie Joseph. He was educated at Repton, was a cadet in the RAF in 1918, and in 1919 went to University College, Oxford, which he left without a degree. He entered publishing in 1923, becoming managing director of Jarrolds. At this stage he spelt his name Benn Wolf Levy.

Levy developed an interest in the theatre, having a comedy he had written, *This Woman Business*, produced at the Haymarket in 1925, with Fay Compton [q.v.] and Leon Quartermaine in the cast. It was then produced in New York in 1926. Between 1928 and 1939 he had several plays produced in London and New York, among them *A Man With Red Hair* (1928), an adaptation of a novel by (Sir) Hugh Walpole [q.v.], *Mud and Treacle* (1928), *Mrs Moonlight* (London 1928, New York 1930), *Art and Mrs Bottle* (London 1929, New York 1931), *The Devil Passes* (London 1930, New York 1932), *Topaze* (an adaptation of a play by Marcel Pagnol, London and New York 1930), and *Evergreen* (with music by Richard Rodgers, London 1930). He both wrote and directed *Springtime for Henry* (New York 1931, London 1932) and (with John van Druten as co-author) *Hollywood Holiday* (London 1931, Pasadena 1936). In 1937 he directed in New York his adaptation of *Madame Bovary*.

These plays varied in quality, although *Topaze* was a Broadway hit and *Springtime for Henry* toured America for years. With the coming of sound he was in demand as a writer of dialogue for films and worked on *Blackmail* (1929), the first talking film directed by (Sir) Alfred Hitchcock [q.v.]. He also worked on films for a while in pre-Hitler Germany.

In 1933 he married the actress Constance Cummings, the daughter of Dallas Vernon Halverstadt, American lawyer. She was one of Hollywood's most glamorous young film stars but was persuaded to make her home in London. In 1934 he directed her on her first stage appearance in London. He directed her again in New York in his adaptation of *Madame Bovary* and in London during World War II in the American comedy *Skylark*.

When war broke out in 1939 Levy joined the Royal Navy as an able-bodied seaman, became a sub-lieutenant, and then was drafted into the intelligence service. In 1944 he was appointed MBE, having been wounded in the Adriatic. He decided to stand for Parliament in the general election of 1945 and won the new constituency of Eton and Slough for Labour with a majority of 2,424. He represented the constituency for five years, becoming a close friend of Aneurin Bevan [q.v.] and his wife Jennie Lee (later Baroness Lee of Asheridge), who frequently visited his house in Chelsea, a work of Walter Gropius. Levy had very good taste, filling his house with works of art which he bought from young artists. He also helped many Hollywood 'refugees', excluded from American films during the McCarthy purges.

In 1950 Levy declined to seek re-election and returned to the theatre. He had directed his play *Clutterbuck* in London in 1946 (it had a New York run in 1949), with his wife in the cast, and it had run for 366 performances. He also directed her in his *Return to Tyassi* in 1950, which would have been more successful had he agreed to suggestions to rewrite parts of it. He directed none of his later plays, among which were *The Great Healer* (London 1954), *The Rape of the Belt*, a comedy on the ninth labour of Hercules (London 1957, New York 1960), *The Tumbler*, directed by Laurence (later Lord) Olivier, (New York 1960), and *Public and Confidential* (Malvern and London 1966).

From 1953 to 1961 Levy served as a member of the executive committee of the Arts Council, and in 1946–7 and again from 1947 to 1952 was chairman of the executive committee of the League of Dramatists. He wrote for the *New Statesman* and *Tribune* and played an active part in the Council for Civil Liberties and the Fabian Society. He was also an active campaigner for unilateral nuclear disarmament, publishing *Britain and the Bomb, the Fallacy of Nuclear Defence* in 1959. To the end of his life he continued to be interested in the major public issues of the time, although, after recovering from a serious heart attack, in 1960 he made his home mainly at Cote House Farm, Aston, Oxfordshire, where he supervised personally his 600-acre farm and in time established a well-known breed of Friesian cattle.

Levy died in Oxford 7 December 1973, being survived by his wife and their son and daughter.

[*The Times*, 8 December 1973; private information; personal knowledge.] JENNIE LEE

LEVY, HYMAN (1889–1975), mathematician, philosopher, and political activist, was born 28 February (not, as registered, 7 March) 1889, in Edinburgh, the second of four sons and third of eight children of Marcus Levy, picture dealer, of Edinburgh, and his wife, Minna Cohen. He was educated at George Heriot's School and the university of Edinburgh. With first class honours in mathematics and physics from Edinburgh (1911) he won a Ferguson scholarship, an 1851 Exhibition, and a Carnegie research fellowship which enabled him to work under Hilbert and Runge in Göttingen.

Escaping from Germany at the outbreak of World War I, he worked for a time with A. E. H. Love [q.v.] at Oxford and then, from 1916 to 1920, in the aerodynamics division of the National Physical Laboratory. With W. L. Cowley he published *Aeronautics in Theory and Experiment* (1918), perhaps the earliest text covering, at advanced level, the whole theory of aeroplane design and operation. In 1920 he joined the Royal College of Science as assistant professor, being promoted full professor in 1923. He became head of the mathematics department in 1946 and initiated the transformation of a department whose student numbers had rarely reached two figures into the large department it later became. From 1946 to 1952 he was dean of the Royal College of Science. He reached retirement age in 1954 and was designated professor emeritus, but he continued as acting head until 1955.

From aeronautics Levy's research interests developed into numerical analysis, numerical solution of differential equations, the calculus of finite differences, and statistics. He published books on these topics long before their importance, later taken for granted, was recognized in Britain.

Strongly influenced by the poverty and degradation he saw around him in childhood, Levy devoted his life to the idea that science should be used to provide the basis of a full life for all humanity. His mathematics was a refuge to which he could resort for renewal of his energies. Active in the Labour Party in the early 1920s he persuaded it to set up a science advisory committee of which he was chairman from 1924 to 1930. In a series of books and broadcast discussions with such as (Sir) Julian Huxley [q.v.] he brought hope to many during the world depression, though he qualified Huxley's optimism with his assessment of the forces that had to be overcome if the full potential of science were to be achieved.

Influenced by a personal encounter with N. I. Bukharin in 1931, Levy became, for the next quarter of a century, one of the Communist Party's best-known publicists. But on a party delegation to Moscow in 1956 he had the specific task of investigating reports of persecution of Jews. His findings appalled him, as did a personal encounter with M. A. Suslov. Rejecting suggestions that he should resign from the party he continued to denounce these injustices, demanding to know how much the British communist leadership had known of what was taking place. He was expelled from the party in 1958.

Levy's materialist philosophy first received explicit expression in *The Universe of Science* (1932). Arguing that we perceive the changing material universe through a 'web of thought and action', Levy introduced the term 'isolate' to describe those sub-systems of experience which are studied by science. Their imperfect reproducibility accounts for the limited validity of scientific laws, while the preference for simplicity in these laws, stressed by H. Jeffreys, results from our search for isolates having this simple character. Though labelled Marxist his philosophical work shows a strongly independent character.

He was elected a fellow of the Royal Society of Edinburgh in 1916. Elected to the council of the London Mathematical Society, 1929–33, he served as vice-president in 1931–2.

With the soft Scottish accent that he retained throughout his life, Levy's warmth, human kindness, and ready wit won him many friends and much respect amongst those who strongly disagreed with his politics. In 1918 his marriage to Marion Aitken, devout Presbyterian daughter of David Fraser, headmaster of a school at Selkirk, caused a rift with his orthodox Jewish family. There were two sons and a daughter of the lifelong marriage. Levy died in Wimbledon 27 February, 1975.

[Imperial College archives; information from widow and family; personal knowledge.]

GEORGE A. BARNARD

LEWIS, SIR AUBREY JULIAN (1900–1975), psychiatrist, was born in Adelaide, Australia, 8 November 1900, the only son of George Solomon Lewis, a watchmaker, and his wife Rachel Isaacs, a teacher in the synagogue Sabbath School. He was educated in Adelaide at the Christian Brothers' College from 1911 to 1917. He early showed himself to be a master of language and a precocious scholar, earning many commendations at both school and university for his literary achievements. He left school with qualifications in Greek, Latin, French, German, English literature, history, and mathematics, many with credit, as well as in physics and chemistry. He also received private tutoring in biology. This education was supplemented by hours of reading in the Adelaide public library.

In 1923 he graduated MB, B.Ch. from Adelaide University's medical school, remaining as resident medical officer and medical and later surgical registrar until 1926. Between 1923 and 1926 he carried out jointly an anthropological study of Australian aborigines, investigating their physical measurements, their implements, their songs, their vocabulary, and their dreams, and reading a paper on the need for such research to the Royal Society of South Australia. In 1926 he was awarded a Rockefeller medical research travelling fellowship intended for training in psychological medicine and nervous diseases. For the next two years he worked in the Phipps clinic, Johns Hopkins; in Boston Psychopathic Hospital; with Adolf Meyer in Baltimore; at the National Hospital, Queen Square, London; at the University Clinic, Heidelberg; and at the Charité in Berlin with Karl Bonhoeffer. On returning to Australia he was offered no suitable employment and returned to London where he joined the staff of the Maudsley in 1929. He also became a member of the Royal College of Physicians (1928), once more demonstrating his linguistic ability by passing all four language examinations. In 1931 he took his MD from Adelaide and in 1938 became FRCP.

Lewis was soon recognized as a leading intellect in his field and in 1936 became clinical director at the Maudsley Hospital. When the hospital was evacuated to Mill Hill during the war he gave academic guidance to its staff. He became at this time consultant in psychological medicine to the British Post Graduate Medical School and later civilian consultant in psychiatry to the RAF (1945–67). During the war the Maudsley Hospital achieved an international reputation, largely because of his influence, and in 1946 he was offered the chair of psychiatry there. Two years later the Medical Research Council set up the Occupational Psychiatry Research Unit (later the Social Psychiatry Unit), appointing him honorary director. During this period his publications reflected an interest first in melancholia (1934) and then in neurosis among the unemployed (1935) and in soldiers (1942). Later he developed his views on health as a social concept.

In the post-war years, Lewis accomplished two important aims: he transformed psychiatry from a clinically oriented study to a respected academic discipline and he established a group of research workers in psychiatry and associated disciplines which became a model for similar hospital groups in other parts of the world. These two achievements alone would justify his recognition as an outstanding leader in his field. Even so, during this period he found time to be the Manson lecturer to the British Institute of Philosophy, 1949; Maudsley lecturer, RMPA, 1951; Bradshaw lecturer, RCP, 1957; Galton lecturer, Eugenics Society, 1958; Hobhouse lecturer, UCL, 1960; Bertram Roberts lecturer, Yale, 1960; Maurice Bloch lecturer, 1962; Harveian orator, RCP, 1963; Linacre lecturer, Cambridge, 1967; and Mapother lecturer, Institute of Psychiatry, 1969. He became a member of the American Philosophical Society, 1961; Hon. F.R.C.Psych., 1972; Hon. D.Sc. Belfast, 1966; and Hon. LL D Toronto, 1966. Lewis was knighted in 1959. Among his many publications his chapter on 'Social Psychiatry' in *Lectures on the Scientific Basis of Medicine* (vol. vi, 1957, ed. by Francis R. Fraser) and his 'Health as a Social Concept' in the *British Journal of Sociology* (1953) are important and definitive. His entry on 'Psychiatry' in *Price's Textbook of Medicine* (1941) is an outstanding statement of his views. He retired in 1966.

In 1934 Lewis married Hilda Stoessiger, MD, FRCP (died 1966), a psychiatrist and expert on adoption, the daughter of Alexander Goodwin Stoessiger, wholesale importer, and Emily Louisa North. There were four children of the marriage, two girls and two boys. Apart from his considerable contribution to psychiatry and its history, Lewis had a lively interest in general history and biography. His occasionally austere public image concealed a genial, even roguish, sense of humur. All his activities, public and private, were informed with his quick, perceptive, and penetrating intellect. He wrote well and with a lightness of touch. To this Dictionary he contributed the article on Sir C. H. Bond. He died 21 January 1975 at Charing Cross Hospital, London.

[*The Times*, 22 January 1975; Michael Shepherd, Adolf Meyer lecture, 1976; private information; personal knowledge.]

NEIL O'CONNOR

LEWIS, CECIL DAY- (1904–1972), poet laureate and detective novelist. [See DAY-LEWIS.]

LINDSAY, DAVID ALEXANDER ROBERT, LORD BALNIEL, BARON WIGAN, twenty-eighth EARL OF CRAWFORD, and eleventh EARL OF BALCARRES (1900–1975), connoisseur of the arts, was born 20 November 1900 at 49 Moray Place, Edinburgh, the son of David Alexander Edward Lindsay, Lord Balcarres (later twenty-seventh Earl of Crawford, q.v.) and his wife, Constance Lilian, daughter of Sir Henry Carstairs Pelly, third baronet, MP. He was the elder son, and eldest of six children, the heir both to an ancient Scottish house and to a long line of learned collectors in which the twenty-fifth earl [q.v.] was especially prominent. Hereditary taste is most uncommon, but Crawford, brought up amidst the treasures of the family homes at Haigh Hall, Wigan, 7 Audley Square, and Balcarres, Fife, was a worthy upholder of the learning and sensitivity that had marked his family for several generations. Administrative skill and personal charm enabled him throughout his life to place his knowledge unreservedly at the service of the arts in Great Britain.

He was educated at Eton (where he gained much from the informal encouragement of A. S. F. Gow, who became a lifelong friend), and, from 1919, at Magdalen College, Oxford, where he obtained a second class in French in 1922. A period as honorary attaché at the British Embassy in Rome gave him opportunities for developing his knowledge of Italian Renaissance painting; he remained a dedicated and well-informed traveller in Italy. In 1930 he shared in the active organization of the Burlington House exhibition of Italian art, 1200–1900, with Kenneth (later Lord) Clark, and was joint editor of the enormous commemorative catalogue (1931).

As Lord Balniel, he had entered the House of Commons as Conservative member for the Lonsdale Division of Lancashire in 1924, and sat until he succeeded to the earldom in 1940, whereupon he sat in the House of Lords as Baron Wigan. Although he enjoyed life in the Commons, his main contribution to public life lay elsewhere. In October 1935 he was appointed to the board of trustees of the National Gallery, and (with short intermissions) remained a trustee until June 1960. He served as chairman in 1938–9 and 1946–8, his first tenure being particularly important in defusing unpleasant tensions between the director and his staff, and in making preparations for the evacuation of the collections from Trafalgar Square at the outbreak of war.

The National Gallery was but the first of an astonishing range of demanding trusteeships concerned with the national heritage. He served on the board of the British Museum from 1940 to 1973; as chairman of the Royal Fine Art Commission from 1943 to 1957, of the National Library of Scotland from 1944 to 1974, and of the National Trust from 1945 to 1965. He was chairman of the National Art-Collections Fund from 1945 until 1970, when he became its president; he joined the board of the National Gallery of Scotland in 1947, serving as chairman 1952–72; and he was a Pilgrim trustee from 1949.

His prolonged tenures of these and other appointments made him uniquely influential, and he applied himself energetically to each with wide-ranging knowledge, unobtrusive forcefulness, and a charm of manner that communicated itself to junior officials as well as to the senior directing staff. He was unsparing of himself, conducted a vast correspondence in a minute and idiosyncratic hand, and travelled constantly from Fife (Haigh was given up in favour of Balcarres after the war) to meetings in London, or on National Trust business throughout England and Wales. Perhaps his most celebrated effort was on behalf of the National Art-Collections Fund (of which his father had been a founder), when in 1962 he personally supervised the special appeal to secure for the National Gallery the Leonardo da Vinci cartoon of the Virgin and St. Anne, to be sold by the Royal Academy; £800,000 was asked, and Crawford's energetic, but personally exhausting, efforts succeeded in raising the essential £450,000 in four months, the balance being found by the government.

Constant voluntary work took its toll of his health, but even in his last years he vigorously opposed the Labour government's wealth tax proposals which threatened the existence of the great private collections of Britain. His opposition was the reverse of self-interested, but he had seen the great Crawford family holdings much reduced by death duties, and he cherished the more keenly the still marvellous collections that remained.

He was deeply versed in the history of the family and its possessions, and in the reduced public activity of his last years he gave urgent and learned encouragement to several younger scholars working on his family papers. Nicolas Barker's *Bibliotheca Lindesiana* (Crawford's own presentation volume to the Roxburghe Club, issued in 1977) was the principal result of this activity; Crawford was working on the typescript at the time of his death at Balcarres, 13 December 1975. He was buried at the family chapel there.

Crawford was created GBE in 1951, and KT in 1955. He received many honours, academic and artistic, including the Oxford DCL (1951) and the Cambridge LL D (1955). He was rector of St. Andrews University in 1952–5. He became an honorary fellow of Magdalen in 1975.

In 1925 he married Mary Katharine, daughter of Lord Richard Frederick Cavendish, of Holker Hall, Cartmel, who survived him with their three sons. He was succeeded in his peerages by his eldest son Robert Alexander, Lord Balniel, PC (born 1927); his younger sons also continued the family interest in the fine arts, Patrick (died 1986) as a senior director of Christie's, Thomas as a specialist restorer of paintings.

[*The Times*, 16, 24, and 29 December 1975; *Burlington Magazine*, April 1976; Kenneth (Lord) Clark, *Another Part of the Wood*, 1974; private information; personal knowledge.]

ALAN BELL

LINDSELL, SIR WILFRID GORDON (1884–1973), lieutenant-general, was born at Portsmouth, Hampshire, 29 September 1884, the younger son and second child in the family of two sons and three daughters of Colonel Robert Frederick Lindsell, CB, of the Gloucester Regiment, from Holme, Biggleswade, and his wife, Kathleen, daughter of Richard Eaton, advocate, of Mitchelstown, Southern Ireland. Educated at Birkenhead School, Victoria College in Jersey, and the Royal Military Academy, Woolwich, Lindsell showed from an early age an unusual capacity for wrestling problems through to a logical conclusion which was to stand him in good stead later in his chosen career. He was commissioned into the Royal Garrison Artillery in 1903.

After Gunnery School at Shoeburyness Lindsell went to Malta in the Garrison Regiment. There his administrative talents were noted by Major-General Sir Harry Barron who on appointment as governor-general of Tasmania in 1909 took Lindsell with him as ADC. Four years later when Barron became governor of Western Australia, Lindsell accompanied him in the same capacity.

In 1914 Lindsell returned to England and became ADC to the general officer commanding 7th division, with whom he went to France with the British Expeditionary Force. A succession of wartime regimental and staff appointments followed, notably with VIII Corps and the French Cavalry Corps. The armistice found Lindsell as a major, having been awarded the MC (1916) and the croix de guerre (1918), and having been appointed to the DSO (1918) and OBE (1919), in addition to having four mentions in dispatches. In 1916 he married Marjorie Ellis (OBE, 1946), daughter of Admiral Swinton Colthurst Holland, of Langley House, Chichester; they had a son, who died in infancy, and two daughters.

Lindsell was selected to attend the first post-war staff course at Camberley. He was then appointed to the adjutant-general's staff at the War Office (1920–1) and later became instructor at the School of Military Administration (1921–3). Here he began to realize his true *métier* and produced the first edition of *Military Organization and Administration* (1923) which was to prove a fund of knowledge for successive generations of officers in passing their promotion examinations and studying for the Staff College. By 1944, when the twenty-sixth edition had gone out of print, this work had become a standard military publication and when rewritten was renamed *Lindsell's Military Organization and Administration* (1948).

Lindsell was instructor at the Staff College, Camberley, from 1925 to 1928, becoming brevet lieutenant-colonel in 1927. During his service in the War Office (1930–3) he became colonel (1931) and attended one of the early courses at the newly established Institute of Defence Studies. A brigadier in 1937, he was appointed major-general in charge of administration in Southern Command in 1938.

On the outbreak of World War II, as temporary lieutenant-general he was appointed quarter-master-general of the British Expeditionary Force. After being evacuated from Dunkirk he returned to England to help reconstruct the British Army. Establishing his headquarters at Kneller Hall he set about his task with vigour. After a year's work he was selected by H. D. R. (later Viscount) Margesson [q.v.], the secretary of state for war, for secondment to the Ministry of Supply under Sir Andrew Duncan and Lord Beaverbrook [qq.v.]. His post was that of senior military adviser for the re-equipment of the army. He performed his task with such marked success that less than a year afterwards Britain had thirteen fully trained and equipped divisions in readiness to defend the country against a German invasion. In 1942 Lindsell was appointed lieutenant-general in charge of administration in the Middle East, as one of General Montgomery's (later Viscount Montgomery of Alamein, q.v.) team to revitalize the Eighth Army.

Following the successful desert campaign Lindsell was selected in 1943 to be principal administration officer to the Fourteenth Army in India in preparation for the attack against the Japanese in Burma led by General W. J. (later Viscount) Slim [q.v.]. In 1945 'Tommy', as he was affectionately known, returned to England for attachment to the Board of Trade to co-ordinate the clearing of factories used for wartime storage, so that peacetime production could commence.

He finally retired from the active list in December 1945, after which he lived at The Haymersh, Britford, Salisbury, Wiltshire. He was governor and commandant of the Church Lads' Brigade (1948–54) and also a church commissioner (1948–59). From 1946 to 1955 he was chairman of the board of Ely Breweries (later Watney Mann) and was active in the affairs of the Royal Artillery Institution for whose journal he wrote a series of articles on his wartime experiences entitled 'Reminiscences on Four Fronts'.

The death of his first wife in 1957 marked a gradual withdrawal from public life. In 1958 he married secondly, Evelyn Nairn, daughter of Gamaliel Henry Butler, of Hobart, Tasmania, formerly premier of Tasmania. In 1970 he moved to 159 Queen's Gate, London, where he died 2 May 1973. His wife returned to her native Tasmania where she died in 1982.

Lindsell was appointed KBE (1940), CB (1942), KCB (1943), and GBE (1946). World War II also brought him the US Legion of Merit (degree of commander) and three mentions in dispatches. He was made an honorary LL D by Aberdeen University.

[Royal Artillery *Journal*, vol. c, No. 2, 1973; Royal Artillery Institution library; information from relatives.] RICHARD WORSLEY

LINKLATER, ERIC ROBERT RUSSELL (1899–1974), novelist and man of letters, was born 8 March 1899 at Penarth, Glamorganshire, the only son and elder child of Robert Baikie Linklater, master mariner, of Dounby, Orkney, and his wife, Mary Elizabeth, daughter of James Young, master mariner. Though herself no Scot, Elizabeth Linklater was passionately Scottish in her loyalties. She insisted on maintaining a holiday house in Orkney, where the Linklaters had lived for many generations, and once it became possible she transferred the family home from Cardiff to Aberdeen. Eric Linklater attended Aberdeen Grammar School from 1913 to 1916.

In 1914 he enlisted in a Territorial battalion of the Gordon Highlanders, but when war broke out he was rejected for service because of his eyesight. In 1917, however, by which time his father had died in Ceylon after an engagement with a German U-boat, he contrived to get himself accepted by the army and then posted to France. He served with the Black Watch in late 1917 and early 1918, until wounded in the course of the German spring offensive. The war was for him a deep emotional experience, as he records in *Fanfare for a Tin Hat* (1970): it ranks with Orkney life as a major influence on his character and outlook in later years.

From 1918 to 1925 he was a student at Aberdeen University, first, unsuccessfully, in medicine, on which he had begun in 1916, and then in arts. A well-known figure in the small university community, he graduated MA in 1925, with first class honours in English, being awarded the Seafield medal, the Minto memorial prize, and the Senatus prize in English. He spent the years 1925–7 in Bombay, as an assistant editor of the *Times of India*. There followed a year in Aberdeen (1927–8) as assistant to the professor of English, and two years (1928–30) in the USA as a Commonwealth fellow, based first at Cornell and then at Berkeley.

It was at this time that he committed himself to the career as novelist on which he had already made a tentative beginning. His reputation was effectively established by his third novel, *Juan in America* (1931), a richly comic, picaresque extravaganza based on his observations in the USA. His fertile, inventive talent issued in a varied series of highly entertaining works of fiction, while he also tried his hand, less successfully, at history and drama. In 1933 he stood as Scottish Nationalist candidate in a parliamentary by-election in East Fife. In the same year he married

Marjorie, daughter of Ian MacIntyre, writer to the Signet, of Edinburgh. After a period in Italy, the couple settled at Dounby in Orkney. Their family consisted of two daughters and two sons.

In 1939–41 Linklater commanded the Orkney Fortress Company, Royal Engineers. Posted thereafter to the directorate of public relations in the War Office, he wrote pamphlets on several aspects of the army at war, and also, in his personal capacity, a number of conversation pieces on war aims. He served in Italy in 1944–5; and *Private Angelo* (1946), with its comic gusto and compassion, is the product of his deep affection for both Italy and the Eighth Army.

In 1945 he was elected rector of Aberdeen University, which awarded him an honorary LL D in 1946. In 1947 the Linklaters left Orkney, where conditions had changed greatly during the war, for Pitcalzean House in Easter Ross. Here they lived till 1972 when, faced with industrial developments in the locality, they moved to Aberdeenshire. In 1951 he published a semi-official history of *The Campaign in Italy*, and visited Korea with the temporary rank of lieutenant-colonel. In 1954 he was appointed CBE; from 1968 to 1973 he was deputy lieutenant of Ross and Cromarty; and in 1971 he was elected a fellow of the Royal Society of Edinburgh. His novels of this later period are well written and ingenious, but lack the zest of their predecessors; and finding himself less in rapport with the public, he turned more to history as time went on. To this Dictionary he contributed the notice of O. H. Mavor (James Bridie).

He was notable for his craftsmanship, his sense of style, his love of wit, and his zest for life, all of which are apparent in his autobiographies. As a novelist he excels mainly in providing civilized entertainment for intelligent middle-brow readers. Although he travelled widely (to India and China in 1935–6, for example, and to Australasia in 1951), his roots were deep in Scottish rural life: he loved fishing, walking, and boating, and once described himself as 'an old peasant with a pen', though his life-style was in fact more that of a country gentleman. His manner tended to the brusque and military. In appearance, his most striking features were a high domed forehead, prematurely bald head with a deeply indented skull due to his war wound, rimless spectacles, and a moustache. He died in St. John's Nursing Home, Aberdeen, 7 November 1974. Excellent portraits of himself and his wife, by their friend Stanley Cursiter, RSA, are in the keeping of Aberdeen University.

[Eric Linklater, *The Man on My Back*, 1941, *A Year of Space*, 1953, and *Fanfare for a Tin Hat*, 1970 (autobiographies); Michael Parnell, *Eric Linklater*, 1984; Aberdeen University records; private information.] ANDREW RUTHERFORD

LINNETT, JOHN WILFRID (1913–1975), chemist, was born 3 August 1913 at Coventry, the only child of Alfred Thirlby Linnett, works accountant in the Rover Company, of Birmingham and Coventry, and his wife, Ethel Mary, typist, daughter of William Ward, ribbon weaver, of Coventry. He was educated at King Henry VIII School, Coventry (1919–31), whence he won the Sir Thomas White scholarship to St. John's College, Oxford. He graduated in 1935 with first class honours in chemistry. He spent two further years in Oxford, doing research on spectroscopy and photochemistry of metal alkyls under (Sir) Harold W. Thompson, and was awarded a D.Phil. in 1938.

In 1937–8 he was a Henry fellow at Harvard University where he worked under G. B. Kistiakowsky and E. Bright Wilson on infra-red and Raman spectroscopy and on the quantum theory of molecular vibrations. In September 1938 he returned to Oxford where he was to remain for twenty-seven years. He held a junior research fellowship at Balliol College from 1939 to 1945 and was engaged on wartime research in Oxford. In 1944 he was appointed university demonstrator (having previously been departmental demonstrator) in the inorganic chemistry laboratory and in 1945 was elected official fellow and praelector in chemistry at Queen's College, Oxford. He was dean of Queen's in 1945–8. In 1948 and in 1950 Linnett visited the University of Wisconsin where he worked with Professor J. O. Hirschfelder. In 1960 he made his first of several visits to the University of California in Berkeley.

Linnett's research in Oxford was concentrated on molecular force fields, on the measurement and interpretation of burning velocities in gases, on recombination of atoms at surfaces, and on theories of chemical bonding. His undergraduate textbook *Wave Mechanics and Valency* (1960) was widely read. He was elected a fellow of the Royal Society in 1955 in recognition of his distinguished work 'on molecular structure and on the physical chemistry of combustion and flame propagation'. Oxford University appointed him to a readership in 1962, and in 1964 he was made a JP.

In 1965 he was elected to succeed R. G. W. Norrish [q.v.] as professor of physical chemistry in Cambridge, and to a professorial fellowship at Emmanuel College. The Cambridge department of physical chemistry enjoyed a fine reputation in gas-phase chemical kinetics and in photochemistry. Linnett preserved and fostered this strength and introduced research on surface chemistry. His own investigations were mainly devoted to quantum chemistry and to the development of simple and practical models of chemical bonds.

In 1970 he was elected master of Sidney Sussex College, and after only three years in that office he became vice-chancellor of the University of Cambridge. This was an especially difficult time for vice-chancellors because of student unrest, and Cambridge was not immune from this challenge. Linnett served the university with high distinction as vice-chancellor, his qualities as scholar, teacher, and man winning him the respect and affection of all sections of the university. He was concerned that the growth of the university had strained internal communications, so he strove to keep people informed. He played a vital part in discussions with David Robinson which led to a remarkable benefaction for the foundation of Robinson College.

During the period he was vice-chancellor there was growing parliamentary and public criticism of the universities and there was a fear that this could lead to more government control than had so far been considered compatible with academic freedom. Linnett believed that there was a need to inform the public about the role of universities and in 1975 he produced a survey of 'useful' research in progress in Cambridge.

Linnett consistently displayed those qualities which a university looks for in its head: a thorough knowledge of the business; an ability to see the issues which matter most; wisdom and judgement in guiding debates; and dignity and assurance on public occasions. Despite the heavy demands on him from his department, college, and university, he found time for individuals and gave them his full, courteous, and good-humoured attention.

Linnett was president of the Faraday Society (1971–3). He received an honorary D.Sc. from Warwick University (1973) and the Coventry award of merit (1966). He was an honorary fellow of St. John's College, Oxford (1968), and a fellow of the New York Academy of Sciences (1965).

On 20 December 1947 he married Rae Ellen Fanny, daughter of Lawrence John Libgott, a schoolmaster, of Birmingham. They had a son and a daughter. On 7 November 1975 Linnett died suddenly of a cerebral haemorrhage at his club, the Athenaeum. A posthumous portrait by W. E. Narraway hangs in the hall of Sidney Sussex College.

[A. D. Buckingham in *Biographical Memoirs of Fellows of the Royal Society*, vol. xxiii, 1977; private information; personal knowledge.]

DAVID BUCKINGHAM

LISTER, PHILIP CUNLIFFE-, first EARL OF SWINTON (1884–1972), politician. [See CUNLIFFE-LISTER.]

LITTLE, SIR CHARLES JAMES COLEBROOKE (1882–1973), admiral, was born at Shanghai 14 June 1882, the son of Louis Stromeyer Little, FRCS, surgeon. He joined HMS *Britannia* in 1897 and after service in battleships as midshipman and sub-lieutenant volunteered for the infant submarine branch in 1903. At the outbreak of war in 1914 he commanded the *Arrogant* and the submarine flotilla attached to the Dover Patrol, and in 1915 was selected as assistant to the commodore (submarines) at the headquarters at Gosport. He took over command of the *Fearless* and the submarines attached to the Grand Fleet in 1916, the flotilla consisting of the new steam-driven K-class submarines designed to operate tactically with the Grand Fleet in battle. He remained in this appointment until the end of the war, being promoted captain in 1917 and appointed CB (civil). Immediately after the war he commanded the cruiser *Cleopatra* in the abortive Baltic operations against the Russian communists, for which service he was appointed CB (military, 1919).

In 1920 Little went to the Admiralty as director of the trade division of the naval staff and, while holding that appointment, was a member of the British delegation to the Washington naval conference of 1921 on the limitation of naval armaments. He was captain of the fleet in the Mediterranean in 1922 and returned home in 1924 to become senior staff officer of the Royal Naval War College. He commanded the *Iron Duke* in 1926–7 and was then selected as director of the Royal Naval Staff College at Greenwich. On promotion to rear-admiral in 1930 he was appointed in command of the second battle squadron of the Home Fleet and as second-in-command of the fleet. In 1931 he returned to his first naval love as rear-admiral (submarines), responsible for the well-being and efficiency of the entire submarine branch.

His wide experience, both afloat and at the Admiralty, had already marked Little for high command and in 1932 he joined the Board of Admiralty as deputy chief of the naval staff, remaining in the appointment for the three years which saw the beginning of naval rearmament and the conclusion of the Anglo-German naval treaty, in both of which he played a considerable part. He was promoted vice-admiral in 1933 and appointed KCB in 1935. The following year he became commander-in-chief of the China station, an appointment which corresponded in time with the Japanese attack on China. Little found himself responsible for the protection of British nationals in China, particularly at Shanghai which was the centre of much of the fighting, an anxious and strenuous duty in particularly difficult circumstances which he performed with skill and complete success. His promotion to admiral came in 1937 while he was still in China.

He returned to the Admiralty in 1938 as

second sea lord, responsible for the personnel of the navy. There were few by then who thought that war with Germany could be averted and within a few weeks of taking up his appointment Little found himself responsible for the mobilization of the fleet ordered as a result of the crisis which preceded the Munich conference. Although the result of the conference averted the immediate danger of war, this mobilization provided invaluable experience for that of eleven months later when war against Germany was declared. Again the responsibility for the smooth running of the machine fell entirely on Little and that full mobilization was achieved with speed and precision was due largely to his administrative skill. The next two years saw the huge expansion of personnel which the war demanded, again the responsibility of the second sea lord.

In 1941 he was appointed to Washington as head of the British Admiralty delegation and it was during his tenure of that appointment that the United States entered the war. As head of the delegation, Little was the British Admiralty's representative on the joint chiefs of staff committee in Washington, a task calling for diplomacy and fortitude in his dealings with Admiral Ernest King, the American chief of naval operations and a noted Anglophobe. On his relief in 1942 by Admiral Sir Andrew Cunningham (later Viscount Cunningham of Hyndhope, q.v.) he was appointed GBE.

He returned from Washington to become commander-in-chief at Portsmouth, an appointment he held until the end of the war in 1945. In May 1943 he was ordered to act as the naval commander-in-chief designate for the invasion of Europe during the absence of Admiral Sir Bertram Ramsay [q.v.] who had originally been selected for the post, and as such became deeply involved with the operational planning for the forthcoming assault. This appointment lapsed on Ramsay's return after the successful invasion of Sicily and Italy, though Little still had many duties directly linked with the invasion, being responsible for the provision of training areas and the organization of exercises for the vast armada collected for the operation as well as for accommodation for all the crews and the supply of stores, ammunition, and fuel.

At the end of the war Little was placed on the retired list after forty-eight years of continuous service and was advanced to GCB (1945). He held the bronze medal of the Royal Humane Society for life-saving and among many foreign orders he was made a grand officer of the Legion of Honour (France) and commander of the Legion of Merit (USA) and was awarded the Grand Cross of the Order of Orange-Nassau (Holland) and the Order of St. Olaf (Norway). During his retirement he was president of the British Legion (Southern Area) and a vice-president of the Navy Records Society and the Royal United Services Institution.

Little was twice married, first to Rothes Beatrix, daughter of Colonel Sir Charles Leslie, seventh baronet; they had one daughter. His wife died in 1939 and in 1940 he married his cousin Mary Elizabeth ('Bessy'), daughter of Ernest Muirhead Little, FRCS. Little died 20 June 1973 at his home in Sussex.

[Admiralty records; *The Times*, 22 June 1973; private information; personal knowledge.]

P. K. KEMP

LITTLEWOOD, JOHN EDENSOR (1885–1977), mathematician, was born at Rochester 9 June 1885, the eldest of three sons (there were no daughters) of Edward Thornton Littlewood and his wife, Sylvia Maud Ackland. E. T. Littlewood, the son of W. E. Littlewood [q.v.], was the first headmaster of a school at Wynberg, near Cape Town, taking his family there in 1892. To secure the best education for John he sent him in 1899 to St. Paul's School in London, where the top mathematical form was taught by F. S. Macaulay. Littlewood entered Trinity College, Cambridge, as a scholar in 1903 and was senior wrangler in 1905. In part ii of the mathematical tripos (1906) Littlewood was placed in class I, division 1.

He then started research on problems suggested by his director of studies E. W. Barnes [q.v.], later bishop of Birmingham, of which one, the Riemann hypothesis, is still open. In *A Mathematician's Miscellany* (1953) he recalled that 'this heroic suggestion was not without result—rather luckily I struck oil at once, and there was a consolation prize'. From 1907 to 1910 he was at Manchester as Richardson lecturer (a special lectureship with a stipend of £250 instead of the usual £120 or £150). In 1908 he won a Smith's prize and was elected a fellow of Trinity, returning there in 1910 to succeed A. N. Whitehead [q.v.] as college lecturer.

In 1910 he proved the difficult Abel–Tauber theorem and soon began his thirty-five-year collaboration with G. H. Hardy [q.v.], a partnership in pure mathematics without parallel which established a school of analysis in Britain second to none in the world. Among the topics in which Hardy and Littlewood made fundamental and far-reaching advances were inequalities, summability of series, Abelian and Tauberian theorems, Fourier series, diophantine approximation, and the analytic theory of numbers and the zeta function of Riemann. Hardy was in Oxford from 1920 to 1931, when he returned to Cambridge as Sadleirian professor. The collaboration was nearly always by letter even when both were living in Trinity. A careful analysis of manuscripts of Hardy, Littlewood, and others, shedding light on their methods of work, has recently been made by M. L. Cartwright in

Bulletin of the London Mathematical Society, vols. xiii (1981), xiv (1982), and xvii (1985).

From 1914 to 1918 Littlewood held a commission in the Royal Garrison Artillery. From December 1915 he was freed from regimental duties and was employed in improving methods currently used in the ballistic office—for example, to calculate trajectories of anti-aircraft missiles. In the war of 1939–45 the service departments sent him problems encountered in operational research.

From 1920 to 1928 Littlewood was Cayley lecturer in the University of Cambridge. From 1928 to 1950 he occupied the newly founded Rouse Ball chair of mathematics. Under the pre-1926 statutes of Trinity, he was a fellow for life with rights to rooms in college and dinner in hall.

Littlewood distilled the essence of his lectures into two highly individual books, *The Theory of Real Functions* (1926) and *Lectures on the Theory of Functions* (1944). He initiated into research and encouraged a succession of young graduates, many of whom achieved fame. Apart from his joint papers with Hardy he wrote many independently. He also collaborated with R. E. A. C. Paley (on Fourier series and power series), with A. C. Offord (on zeros of power series with random coefficients) and with (Dame) M. L. Cartwright (on non-linear differential equations). Littlewood and Paley enunciated in 1931 ten *Theorems on Fourier Series and Power Series*, of which proofs would follow later. Paley died in an avalanche in 1933, aged twenty-six. It took Littlewood until 1937 to complete the details of the proofs. The authors showed a sure instinct that this work would develop further. In the 1960s, in connection with probability theory, the elegant concept of bounded mean oscillation was exploited by a number of mathematicians, among whom E. M. Stein was prominent. The work with Cartwright on differential equations involved topological structures of extreme complexity.

Littlewood had a well ordered routine of work and recreation. He was adept in avoiding administrative commitments and he did not go to congresses of mathematicians. He had muscular strength, balance, and agility which made for enjoyment in rock-climbing and skiing. Living in college during term he would on most days walk several miles in the country. A mathematical idea would come to his mind, and he would be able to follow it up without paper and pencil. He had an intense interest in classical music—particularly Bach, Beethoven, and Mozart—and, as an adult, taught himself to play the piano. Vacations were spent by the sea or among mountains. For many years he shared houses in the Isle of Wight or in Cornwall.

In retirement Littlewood visited the USA several times. He wrote papers and some *jeux d'esprit*, notably 'The Mathematician's Art of Work' (*Rockefeller University Review*, 1967). He was publishing original work at the age of eighty-five, and he resided in college until August 1977, when he had a fall. He moved to the local Evelyn Nursing Home, where he died suddenly 6 September 1977. He was unmarried.

Littlewood was elected FRS in 1916 and received the Royal (1929), Sylvester (1943), and Copley (1958) medals. The London Mathematical Society awarded him in 1938 the De Morgan medal and in 1960 the senior Berwick prize for two papers on celestial mechanics. He was a foreign member of the Swedish (1948), Danish (1948), and Dutch (1950) academies, and a corresponding member of the Göttingen (1925) and Paris (1957) academies. He had honorary degrees from Liverpool (D.Sc. 1928), St. Andrews (LL D, 1936), and Cambridge (Sc.D., 1965).

[J. C. Burkill in *Biographical Memoirs of Fellows of the Royal Society*, vol. xxvi, 1978; *The Times*, 8 September 1977; private information; personal knowledge.] J. C. Burkill

LLOYD, JOHN SELWYN BROOKE, Baron Selwyn-Lloyd (1904–1978), Speaker of the House of Commons and politician, was born 28 July 1904 in West Kirby, Wirral, the third of four children and only son of John Wesley Lloyd MRCS, LRCP, a dentist in Hoylake and a leading member of the local Methodist church, and his wife, Mary Rachel Warhurst. He was educated at Fettes College, Edinburgh, and Magdalene College, Cambridge, where he was president of the Union in 1927. He obtained a second class in both classics part i (1925) and history part ii (1926) and a third class in law part ii (1927). His Nonconformist background and a family connection with the Lloyd Georges of Criccieth at first drew him towards the Liberal Party and in the 1929 election he stood unsuccessfully as the Liberal parliamentary candidate for Macclesfield. Some months later the economic crisis persuaded him of the need for a protective tariff and he became a Conservative for the rest of his political career.

Selwyn Lloyd was called to the bar, as a member of Gray's Inn, in 1930 and steadily built up a general common law practice on the Northern circuit. He took an active part in local government affairs in Cheshire, serving on the Hoylake Urban District Council for ten years. His diligence and competence were rewarded when he became chairman of the council at the early age of thirty-two.

In 1939 Selwyn Lloyd enlisted in the Royal Horse Artillery as a private and was commissioned as a second lieutenant at the outbreak of war. By 1942 he had been promoted to lieutenant-colonel on the general staff. He was posted to the headquarters of the Second Army on its formation in May 1943 to head the assault on Europe.

His industrious dispatch of military paperwork, combined with intense loyalty to sometimes difficult commanders, made him a successful staff officer. He was promoted to brigadier in 1944. In 1943 he was appointed OBE, in 1945 CBE, and he was twice mentioned in dispatches.

In the 1945 general election Selwyn Lloyd's good war record helped him to win a comfortable majority when he was elected MP for Wirral, where he had been adopted as Conservative candidate in 1939. In his maiden speech, and throughout his thirty-five years of service as an MP, he often spoke of his pride at representing the area in which he was born and bred.

During his first years in Parliament, Selwyn Lloyd concentrated more on his legal practice than his political career. He remained busy in the Northern circuit, taking silk in 1947. He was recorder of Wigan from 1948 to 1951. But as the Conservative Party sharpened its attacks in Parliament on the record of the Labour government, Selwyn Lloyd emerged as one of the most promising and hard-working of the 1945 intake of opposition back-benchers. In 1949 he was selected as one of the three parliamentary members of the Beveridge committee set up to inquire into the organization of the BBC. When the committee's findings were published in January 1951, Selwyn Lloyd submitted a minority report of his own opposing the retention of a BBC monopoly of broadcasting and advocating a competitive television system with power to draw revenue from advertising. His view was later put into practice by the Conservative government.

In 1951 Selwyn Lloyd married his secretary Elizabeth ('Bay'), daughter of Roland Marshall, solicitor, of West Kirby, Cheshire. They had one daughter. The marriage was dissolved in 1957.

In 1951, when the Conservative government returned to power, Selwyn Lloyd became minister of state at the Foreign Office. Under the tutelage of the foreign secretary, Anthony Eden (later the Earl of Avon), Selwyn Lloyd overcame his own doubts about his inexperience and enjoyed considerable success. He led the United Kingdom delegation to the sixth, seventh, eighth, and ninth sessions of the General Assembly of the United Nations, and made several notable speeches there. In the Middle East he was instrumental in guiding the Sudan to independence, and in negotiating the terms of the agreement for the withdrawal of British troops from Egypt. During 1954, when Eden was away for long periods on overseas visits and with bouts of ill health, much of the day-to-day conduct of foreign policy was in Selwyn Lloyd's hands. This brought him into close contact with Sir Winston Churchill, who gave him praise and eventual promotion to the post of minister of supply in October 1954. Six months later, when Eden became prime minister, Selwyn Lloyd entered the Cabinet as minister of defence and in December 1955 he was made foreign secretary. Although this last appointment was partly due to the friction that had developed between Eden and the outgoing foreign secretary, Harold Macmillan (later the Earl of Stockton), nevertheless Selwyn Lloyd's rise owed much to his own impressive performances in Cabinet committees as a strong departmental minister as well as to his good, if somewhat subservient, relationship with the prime minister.

As foreign secretary, Selwyn Lloyd's immediate priority was to mobilize international public opinion against the Egyptian leader, Colonel Nasser, and to seek support for international control of the Suez canal. Nasser, whom Selwyn Lloyd regarded as 'a potential Hitler who must somehow be checked if British influence is not to be eliminated from the Middle East and all our friends destroyed', had nationalized the Suez Canal Company on 26 July 1956. In August Selwyn Lloyd organized and chaired a conference in London attended by twenty-two countries who were the principal users of the canal. Eighteen of them agreed on a resolution asserting six principles for international control, recognizing Egypt's sovereign rights, guaranteeing her a fair return for the use of the canal, and proposing the negotiation of a new convention for canal usage. Unfortunately the high hopes encouraged by the almost unanimous support for the conference resolutions were short lived for it emerged that Selwyn Lloyd and the entire British Cabinet had seriously misjudged the degree of American support for their policy. The conference had dispatched a mission, led by Sir Robert Menzies [q.v.], to Cairo, which was undermined by President Eisenhower unexpectedly saying at a press conference that the United States would only support a peaceful solution. As the threat of force was one of the few good cards which Menzies held, Eisenhower's statement made the mission futile and Nasser promptly rejected the proposals of the eighteen nations.

Selwyn Lloyd regarded the collapse of the Menzies mission as the initial major tragedy in what proved to be an uncoordinated and divided response by the West to the seizure of the canal. Further strains in the alliance occurred when John Foster Dulles, the US secretary of state, thwarted the initial British attempt to refer the crisis to the UN Security Council by insisting that his own plan for a Suez Canal Users Association (SCUA) was tried first. After this plan proved abortive, a series of subsequent American statements and actions showed only too clearly to Nasser that the allies were in disarray.

During this period of the crisis, Selwyn Lloyd

had profound political and personal misgivings about the search for the next steps in policy-making. He had doubts about toppling Nasser and feared having to prop up a pro-western regime in Cairo. He privately believed that the judgements and temperaments of both Eden and Dulles were being affected by the onset of their respective illnesses, while he saw Eisenhower as being excessively preoccupied with the domestic considerations of the November 1956 presidential election. Although on at least one occasion he offered his resignation to the prime minister and Cabinet, when it was refused he continued to work in vain at the United Nations towards greater agreement for an international policy on the operation of the canal.

Meanwhile the lack of American support had prompted the French government to move towards a secret plan for military collusion with Israel. Selwyn Lloyd, who was at the United Nations in New York until 15 October still struggling to obtain a Security Council resolution on the canal, was entirely ignorant of this Franco–Israeli plan. On 16 October he and Eden went to Paris for talks with the French ministers Pineau and Mollet. Their discussions resulted in Britain's acceptance of Operation Musketeer, which envisaged Anglo–French intervention to halt an Israeli thrust if this occurred. However this conditional acceptance was apparently inadequate in the view of Pineau, so on 22 October Selwyn Lloyd again flew to France for secret talks with French and Israeli leaders at Sevres. This has subsequently led to the allegation that he was implicated in the Franco–Israeli agreement for military collusion which had been made some weeks earlier. The charge is unfair. Selwyn Lloyd neither knew of the collusion before Sevres, nor approved of it at the meeting. Indeed throughout the talks at Sevres he made it clear that a pre-arranged Israeli–French–British agreement to attack Egypt was impossible because of the risks to the lives and property of British subjects in Arab countries.

The Israeli invasion began on 26 October 1956. During the ten days following Selwyn Lloyd was stretched to the limits of his physical and political endurance by the hectic pace of the crisis. In Parliament he made statements, answered questions, and spoke in debates almost every day including Saturday. He was in constant touch, often throughout the night, with Britain's delegation to the United Nations and other diplomatic missions overseas. He was intensively involved in the planning of the military operation and attended all Cabinet meetings. He was required to make platform speeches in the country and to give a ministerial broadcast. An additional burden which he had to bear was the fundamental policy disagreement of his minister of state at the Foreign Office, (Sir) H. Anthony Nutting, who resigned on 2 November. Selwyn Lloyd, who regarded Nutting as a friend and protégé, was shaken by this resignation which he felt to be a personal and political stab in the back.

By the time British troops parachuted into the canal zone on Monday 5 November Selwyn Lloyd was a tired and disappointed minister. His disappointment deepened when, despite a successful military operation which secured the first twenty-three miles of the canal in as many hours, the Cabinet felt it had to order a cease-fire on 6 November.

With hindsight Selwyn Lloyd came to believe that he should have argued more forcefully in Cabinet for delaying the cease-fire until Britain had taken the whole canal. But at the time he bowed to the chancellor of the Exchequer's advice that an American-induced sterling crisis would be the consequence of continuing the fighting.

Although the aftermath of Suez brought about the resignation of Eden, it had no adverse effect on the career of Selwyn Lloyd. Credited with having carried out the Cabinet's policy loyally and conscientiously, he retained the post of foreign secretary for the next three-and-a-half years in Macmillan's government. As the new prime minister enjoyed playing a dominant role in foreign affairs, Selwyn Lloyd was at times somewhat overshadowed at the Foreign Office. Nevertheless he soon built up a good working partnership with Macmillan. Their immediate priority in the post-Suez period was the reaffirmation of Anglo–American relations and this was largely achieved in March 1957 at the Bermuda conference where they had long discussions with Eisenhower and Dulles. In 1959 Selwyn Lloyd and Macmillan made a ten-day visit to the Soviet Union where they had talks with Khrushchev and other Soviet leaders which improved Anglo–Soviet relations. Later that year Selwyn Lloyd opened the first set of negotiations for Britain's entry into the European Economic Community.

In July 1960 Selwyn Lloyd became chancellor of the Exchequer. His economic policy was cautious and orthodox, dedicated to curbing the now familiar inflationary pressures of rising wage demands and soaring government expenditure. To achieve these objectives he introduced an unpopular but effective freeze on wages known as the 'pay pause' which he followed with a more flexible incomes policy that allowed increases of up to 2.5 per cent. This became known as 'the guiding light' and was partially successful, although it led to further political unpopularity because of its allegedly unfair effects on some public sector employees, notably nurses and teachers. Selwyn Lloyd's major innovation at the Treasury was the setting up of the National Economic Development Council, nicknamed 'Neddy', a discussion forum for representatives of the employers, the trade unions, and the government.

By the spring of 1962 Selwyn Lloyd's strategy of restraint was causing the Conservative party some public relations difficulties, particularly in local and by-elections. On Friday 13 July he was abruptly dismissed from the government, the senior casualty of a surprise ministerial reshuffle, known as 'the night of the long knives', in which a third of the Cabinet was removed. Although remaining characteristically loyal in public to the prime minister throughout the controversy that followed this upheaval, Selwyn Lloyd was deeply hurt by the manner and timing of his departure. He felt that Macmillan had betrayed both a personal friendship and a political alliance by sacrificing his chancellor just as their jointly-planned economic policy of counter-inflationary wage restraint was ready to be relaxed. He believed that his career was over and in the twilight of approaching retirement he began writing memoirs and accepting honours. In July 1962 he was created CH. In 1963 he became deputy lord lieutenant of Chester and an honorary fellow of Magdalene College. He also had honorary degrees from Sheffield, Liverpool, Oxford, and Cambridge.

After his dismissal Selwyn Lloyd carried out a nation-wide inquiry into Conservative Party organization and published a report in June 1963 which contained a number of important recommendations on matters such as candidate selection, subscriptions, and the role of agents. It was to influence party administration for the next two decades.

In October 1963 a combination of political misfortune and personal ill health caused Macmillan's resignation as prime minister. To the surprise of many, though not of Selwyn Lloyd who played an influential role in guiding the succession, the new Conservative leader was his close friend the Earl of Home (afterwards Sir Alec Douglas Home and later Lord Home of the Hirsel). Amidst widespread approval from party loyalists, Selwyn Lloyd was brought back into the government as leader of the House of Commons. His tenure of this office for the next eleven months was perhaps the happiest period of his entire political career. His natural gift for conciliation and his readiness (not easy in an election year) to eschew political partisanship in the wider interests of the House of Commons as a whole, gave him a degree of parliamentary popularity he had never previously enjoyed. The good personal relationships he built up at this time among MPs of all parties were the foundation of his successful Speakership in later years.

After the Conservative government was defeated in the general election of 1964, Selwyn Lloyd remained a member of the shadow cabinet. When Edward Heath became leader of the opposition in 1965 Selwyn Lloyd was appointed the Conservative Party's principal front bench spokesman on Commonwealth affairs. In this capacity he visited New Zealand and Australia in 1965 and Rhodesia in 1966 shortly after Ian Smith's unilateral declaration of independence. He remained on the front bench for three months after the 1966 general election, until resigning from the shadow cabinet at his own request.

During the next five years Selwyn Lloyd was active in the world of business and accepted several company directorships. But he did not neglect politics, remaining an indefatigable speaker and fund raiser for the Conservative Party, particularly in the north-west of England. Although rarely participating in parliamentary debates, he was always a diligent House of Commons man, happily serving on the estimates, privileges, procedure, and services committees.

In 1971 Selwyn Lloyd was elected Speaker of the House of Commons. His election was vigorously opposed by some fifty MPs who held the view that a Speaker who had served for so long as a Cabinet minister might not be sufficiently zealous in protecting the rights of backbenchers. Once installed as Speaker, Selwyn Lloyd soon calmed these fears. He amended the practice of giving automatic priority to privy councillors in catching the Speaker's eye and took great pains to ensure that minority parties and viewpoints were heard. However, he faced some criticism from those who believed he was too lenient with vociferous and at times badly behaved parliamentary exhibitionists.

After skilfully guiding the House through twenty-one difficult months of minority government, Selwyn Lloyd retired as Speaker in 1976, and was created a life peer. Gardening, charitable fund raising, and authorship were the main activities of his retirement. In 1976 he published *Mr. Speaker Sir*, a personal account of that office, and followed this with *Suez 1956*, a memoir of the crisis which was posthumously published in 1978. He died at Preston Crowmarsh, Oxfordshire, 17 May 1978.

Selwyn Lloyd's career surprised some of his contemporaries. Shy to the point of awkwardness in manner, and reticent in conversation, he lacked many of the extrovert gifts of the natural politician. Although a good Whitehall administrator and an effective platform speaker when using a prepared text, his parliamentary debating skills were limited, and his public persona was stamped with caution rather than charisma. Yet he was the embodiment of the dictum of the fifth Earl of Rosebery [q.v.] that in political life it is the 'character breathing through the sentences that counts'. He was the confidant whose discretion could always be trusted; the lieutenant whose loyalty was unshakeable; the political ally whose reliability never faltered. This inherent goodness of character was supported by an ability to make shrewd political judgements and by an immense capacity for application which he developed as a compensation for his lonely personal life.

[J. S. B. Selwyn Lloyd, *Mr. Speaker Sir*, 1976, and *Suez 1956*, 1978; Nigel Fisher, *Harold Macmillan*, 1982; Earl of Kilmuir, *Political Adventure*, 1964; personal knowledge.]

JONATHAN AITKEN

LLOYD GEORGE, FRANCES LOUISE, COUNTESS LLOYD-GEORGE OF DWYFOR (1888–1972), political secretary, was born in London 7 October 1888, the eldest in the family of three daughters and one son of John Stevenson, descended from Lanarkshire farmers of sternly religious outlook, and his wife, Louise Augustine Armanino, the daughter of a Genoese who had lived in the Latin Quarter of Paris and married a French woman. Puritan and Bohemian strains thus mingled in Frances Stevenson. Her father was secretary to a firm of French import agents, and he sent Frances to Clapham High School. Her friends there included Mair Lloyd George, the eldest daughter of her future husband, destined to die tragically young. She went on to study classics at Royal Holloway College, London, and to take up a post at a girls' boarding school in Wimbledon. At this time, she was an ardent supporter of the suffragette movement.

The turning-point in her life came in July 1911 when she was invited to act as private tutor in French and music to Megan [q.v.], the younger daughter of David Lloyd George (later Earl Lloyd-George of Dwyfor), then chancellor of the Exchequer. The impact that Lloyd George at once made upon her was dramatic. She felt 'a magnetism which made my heart leap and swept aside my judgment, producing an excitement which seemed to permeate my entire being'. Soon she and Lloyd George were becoming intimately friendly; he gave her a copy of a biography of Charles Stewart Parnell [q.v.] by his mistress, Kitty O'Shea. When he became embroiled in the crisis of the Marconi shares affair, she realized that she could not part from him. She accepted his frank proposal that she should stay on with him as personal secretary 'on his own terms', even though it conflicted with her Victorian upbringing. Her relationship as secretary-mistress scandalized both her parents; inevitably, it led to prolonged tension with Lloyd George's wife, Margaret, who usually preferred to remain in north Wales. Nevertheless, despite private pressures and public scandal, Frances Stevenson remained the person closest to Lloyd George from the time of their 'real marriage' (in her own words) on 21 February 1913 until his death in 1945.

When war began in 1914, Frances Stevenson was now installed as Lloyd George's personal secretary, jointly with J. T. Davies. She worked closely with Lloyd George when he moved to the new Ministry of Munitions in May 1915, and then to the War Office in July 1916. When he became prime minister in December 1916, she became his joint principal private secretary, the only woman to hold that post, although she never formally joined the permanent Civil Service. She travelled with Lloyd George to Italy in the autumn of 1917 after the disaster of Caporetto; she helped marshal Lloyd George's case when he was attacked by General Sir Frederick Maurice [q.v.] in May 1918 for withholding reinforcements from the western front; at the Paris peace conference in 1919, she worked with the British delegation there, sharing a hotel room with Lloyd George's daughter, Megan. Throughout the trials of Lloyd George's peacetime premiership in 1918–22, she was his faithful confidante; indeed, their affection steadily deepened. In 1921 they arranged to purchase sixty acres, at Churt, Surrey, on which they built a house named 'Bron-y-de'. Later, Frances Stevenson built for herself a small house, 'Avalon', on land adjacent to Lloyd George's estate. At Churt they shared many common interests, including the development of the farm and experiments in horticulture.

But Frances Stevenson's life continued to be geared to Lloyd George's public career. She declined the suggestion made by Sir (N. F.) Warren Fisher [q.v.] when Bonar Law became prime minister that she should stay on in the Civil Service. Instead, she now headed Lloyd George's personal secretariat from 1922 onwards, years which saw his leadership of a reunited Liberal Party after 1924, and his final bids for power in 1929 and 1935. After the creation of the 'national' government in 1931 she was deeply involved in the research and writing of his *War Memoirs* (6 vols., 1933–6). She accompanied Lloyd George on holiday to Morocco in 1935–6, while having to accept his continuing formal relationship with Dame Margaret. After the outbreak of World War II Lloyd George's dependence on her increased, especially after Margaret's death in 1941. On 23 October 1943, at Guildford Registry Office, she became Lloyd George's second wife; she had had a daughter, Jennifer, born in October 1929. She returned with her husband to Wales and lived briefly at Criccieth, during which time he became Earl Lloyd-George of Dwyfor in January 1945. But on 26 March 1945 Lloyd-George died in the presence of his wife. The aftermath was a bitter one, with quarrels with Lloyd George's four surviving children, disputes over a memorial fund and the small museum set up at Llanystumdwy, arguments over Lloyd George's statue in the House of Commons. She soon left Wales and lived quietly at Churt with her sister, Muriel, for the rest of her life. She had sold her private papers to the Beaverbrook Foundation, but published an attractive and generous work of reminiscence, *The Years that are Past*, in 1967. A. J. P. Taylor edited and published her diary, covering the period from 1914 to 1944, in 1971, a year before the Dowager Countess Lloyd-George's death at her home, Farm Cottage, Churt, 5 December 1972. She had been appointed CBE in 1918.

Frances Stevenson's long association with Lloyd George openly flouted current moral conventions. In fact, her relationship with him fulfilled a vital need for them both. Just as his first wife kept him in touch with his Welsh roots, Frances, with her charm, intelligence, and social poise, was at ease in the world of high politics. She was always sympathetic and responsive to male and female company. She was an immensely capable person, with shrewd political judgement, and deeply loyal to Lloyd George. They had their occasional quarrels, notably over Frances's affair with Colonel T. F. Tweed, one of Lloyd George's political organizers. But the relationship remained unshaken to the end. Her life, and the records she has left, are testimony to a unique political partnership.

There is a portrait of her, in the possession of her daughter, by Peter Rasmussen.

[Frances Stevenson, *The Years that are Past*, 1967; A. J. P. Taylor (ed.), *Lloyd George: a Diary by Frances Stevenson*, 1971; A. J. P. Taylor (ed.), *My Darling Pussy*, 1975; Kenneth O. Morgan (ed.), *Lloyd George, Family Letters, 1885–1936*, 1973; Colin Cross (ed.), *A. J. Sylvester: Life with Lloyd George*, 1975; Lloyd George Papers, House of Lords Record Office; *The Times*, 7 December 1972.]

KENNETH O. MORGAN

LLOYD-GREAME, PHILIP, first EARL OF SWINTON (1884–1972), politician. [See CUNLIFFE-LISTER.]

LONGHURST, HENRY CARPENTER (1909–1979), golf journalist, author, and television broadcaster, was born 18 March 1909 at Bromham, Bedfordshire, the only child of (William) Henry Longhurst, the owner of a large furnishing business in Bedford, and his wife, Constance Smith. From St. Cyprians, Eastbourne, Longhurst won a classical scholarship to Charterhouse, whence he proceeded to Clare College, Cambridge. He obtained third classes in both parts (1929 and 1930) of the economics tripos. Winning a golf blue as a freshman, he played four years in the university match, being captain in his last and leading his side to victory. He was a very good golfer, a little short of the top rank, winner of the German amateur (1936), runner-up in the French (1937) and also the Swiss (1938), and an essential part of the Old Carthusian team which used so regularly to win the Halford–Hewitt Cup at Deal.

When therefore he soon settled into golf journalism he did so with the advantage of knowing not only the personalities involved but also, from first-hand, the difficulties as well as the delights, the troughs as well as the peaks, of this most subtle of games. It was Bernard Darwin [q.v.] who, in *The Times* and *Country Life*, had made the writing of golf a literary exercise with a following among many who never handled a club. Where Darwin led the way, Longhurst followed. Neither made the mistake of treating the game too seriously, nor of confusing ordinary mortals over-much by the use of technicalities.

When Longhurst first took up his pen in the early 1930s Darwin was the uncrowned king of responsible games-writers, the model towards which others vainly aspired. Longhurst wisely took his own line, quickly becoming adept at the shorter essay. He acknowledged in later life his debt to (Sir) P. G. Wodehouse [q.v.], who taught him, he said, that 'to write well you did not have to write on a serious subject', and also that 'good writing flows'. It was important not only to have the right words but to put them in the right order. Though most of Longhurst's work was done on the spot and against time—he left his untopical pieces to the last minute—he never wrote an ugly sentence.

Success in his chosen profession came to him very quickly. His first (unpaid) efforts in a small periodical, *Tee Topics*, in 1931 led to an offer in 1932 from the *Sunday Times*, which had not previously employed a golf correspondent. Neither had the *Tatler*, the next to sign him on. Then the *Evening Standard* reporting job became vacant. These last appointments ended with the war in 1939, but his association with the *Sunday Times* extended over forty-five years. Longhurst's five-minute pieces, on the back page, always on a given point and usually containing a quotable anecdote, were required early-morning reading in the golf world and beyond, and he was proud of having written more than a thousand of them without missing a Sunday.

He had a keen ear for an amusing story, and in his travels round all the continents, taking in more than four hundred club-houses, picked up an unending store of them. At Turnberry over breakfast he discovered Lord Brabazon of Tara [q.v.] poring over what turned out to be a chess match, played with a friend by correspondence. It was midsummer and his lordship said he had lost a bishop in February and had been in difficulties ever since. When next they met Brabazon confided, said Longhurst, ' "I was mated last week". We agreed that he might add to his many other distinctions that of being the only peer to have been mated by post.'

Longhurst began the war with the Home Guard (as they became), spent the bulk of it as an anti-aircraft gunner officer, and the last two years (1943–5), having fought a by-election, as the Conservative member for Acton. He emerged with an undying devotion to (Sir) Winston Churchill, duly lost his seat at the 1945 general election, and was soon adding to his writing activities the pioneering of golf presentation on BBC television. It is scarcely too much to say that Longhurst 'made' golf on TV. He conveyed with an enviable economy of words, to handicap players and non-golfers, the emotions of the man in the eye of the camera. So often a word or a phrase conveyed everything, his dry laconic comments interspersed by brilliant flashes of silence. His technique caught on in the United States where the viewers had been fed on far too much talk and too many superlatives.

Indispensable to the BBC, he also became an institution in America, and was specially proud in 1973 of winning the Walter Hagen award 'for furtherance of golfing ties between Great Britain and America'. He had been appointed CBE a year earlier. At the autumn meeting of the Royal and Ancient Golf Club in 1977 came the honour which he prized most of all. Amid the warmest possible acclaim (and, like his hero, Bobby Jones, before him) he was made an honorary life member. Not a few who were then present at St. Andrews will have contrasted the master of his crafts, serene and benevolent, with the somewhat prickly, outspoken undergraduate who had made his first mark on the golfing scene all but fifty years before. He also wrote twelve light-hearted books, including an autobiography.

He married in 1938 Claudine Marie Berthé, daughter of Horace Evelyn Sier, senior partner of the accountants Viney, Price and Goodyear and chairman of Burroughs Wellcome, pharmacists. They had two children, Oliver William Henry, killed in a motor accident aged thirty-one, and Susan Jane, widowed when thirty. There were six grandchildren. Longhurst died 21 July 1978 at Clayton Windmills, Hassocks, Sussex.

[Henry Longhurst, *My Life and Soft Times* (autobiography), 1971; M. Wilson and K. Bowden (eds.), *The Best of Henry Longhurst*, 1979; personal knowledge.] E. W. SWANTON

LONSDALE, DAME KATHLEEN (1903–1971), crystallographer, convinced Quaker, and pacifist, was born 28 January 1903 at Newbridge, Southern Ireland, youngest of the ten children (four girls and six boys) of Harry Frederick Yardley, postmaster, and of his wife Jessie, daughter of Archibald John Hanbury Cameron, commercial traveller, of Islington.

In 1914 she won a county minor scholarship to the Ilford County High School for Girls, and in 1919 was awarded a county major scholarship, and the Royal Geographical Society's medal for the highest marks in the geography and physical geography papers. She was admitted to Bedford College at sixteen to study mathematics, but changed to physics at the end of her first year—a decision she never regretted. She was secretary of the Music Society, coxed the college eight, headed the university list in the honours B.Sc. examination (1922) with the highest marks in ten years, and was invited by Sir W. H. Bragg [q.v.] to join his research team, first at University College London, and then at the Royal Institution. Her first major contribution to crystallography, W. T. Astbury [q.v.] and Yardley's 'Tables for the Determination of Space Groups', appeared in the Royal Society *Philosophical Transactions* in 1924, and space-group theory remained a lifelong interest.

For two years after her marriage in 1927 to a fellow student at University College, Thomas Jackson Lonsdale, son of James Jackson Lonsdale who was senior science master at the Sloane School in Chelsea, she worked in the University of Leeds on what she herself considered to be the most fundamental of her own researches: the proof, by analysing the structures of crystals of hexamethylbenzene and hexachlorobenzene given to her by the young professor of chemistry, (Sir) C. K. Ingold [q.v.], that the carbon atoms in the benzene nucleus are coplanar and hexagonally arranged, with an interatomic spacing nearly the same as that in graphite.

When she returned to the Royal Institution in 1931 as Bragg's research assistant (he had managed to find money so that she could hire a home help while her children were young) there was no X-ray equipment to spare, so she accepted the offer of a big electromagnet and spent the next ten years making measurements of diamagnetic anisotropy. In the course of this work she was able to provide experimental verification of the postulated delocalization of electrons and the existence of molecular orbitals—results of considerable importance to theoreticians. For this and later work she was awarded the Davy medal of the Royal Society in 1957.

In 1938 a colleague at the Royal Institution, Dr I. E. Knaggs, asked Kathleen Lonsdale to measure the magnetic anisotropy of benzil, and showed her some Laue photographs exhibiting beautiful diffuse patterns in addition to the expected sharp spots. Thus began her interest in both static and dynamic disorder in crystals, for although the diffuse reflections observed for many substances were found to be temperature-sensitive, some peculiar extra reflections first observed for diamond by Sir C. V. Raman [q.v.] and P. Nilakantan were not. She made detailed studies of both phenomena and for these and other researches became in 1945 one of the first two women elected to the fellowship of the Royal Society, an honour which gave her particular pleasure. She was a vice-president at the time of the Society's tercentenary celebrations.

Working in the room of Michael Faraday [q.v.] at the Royal Institution, she read his notebooks and absorbed his approach to experimentation, and enjoyed tackling new problems from first principles; typically, she was able to show that the lattice parameters of individual diamonds could be measured with an accuracy of 1 in 70,000 from divergent-beam photographs, using an ordinary ruler.

Returning to University College London in 1946 in the newly created post of reader in crystallography in Professor C. K. Ingold's department, she became a professor of chemistry in 1949. She gave university extension lectures which she subsequently wrote up as a book, *Crystals and X-rays* (1948), developed an undergraduate practical course in crystallography which was copied in many other institutions, taught part of the new intercollegiate M.Sc. in crystallography developed by J. D. Bernal [q.v.] at Birkbeck College, and built up a research school of her own. The main impetus for its development came from her own earlier work in crystal dynamics, and it eventually came to include short-range order in solid solutions, order–disorder transitions and structural aspects of photo-reactions in the organic solid state, as well as diamagnetism.

In 1946 she also became general editor of the *International Tables for X-Ray Crystallography*, and the enormous amount of work which this involved curtailed her own research activities, but she found time to work on synthetic diamonds (hexagonal diamond found in meteorites is now called lonsdaleite) and to begin work on methonium compounds and endemic bladder stones because she wanted to make some contribution to medical research, although she had no background knowledge in this area. The stone work prospered, and she continued with it after she had retired in 1968, actually spending the last few weeks of her life trying to complete a book on the subject rather than one on thermal expansion which was also in preparation.

Outside the laboratory, her life was equally busy and demanding. Coming from different religious backgrounds and exercised by the proper moral framework within which to educate their three young children (two daughters and a son), she and her husband eventually became Quakers by convincement in 1935, and she began to have a public as well as a private life in 1943 when she was imprisoned because as a Quaker she refused to pay a £2 fine imposed on her for declining on conscientious grounds to register for Civil Defence, although she was quite willing to do voluntary work. This turned out to be one of her most formative experiences, which not only helped to broaden her outlook, but also gave her both motivation and opportunity in later life to work for penal reform. Thereafter her scientific activities and her social and religious concerns became closely interwoven, and she seldom undertook a journey for one purpose without also managing to further the other.

She liked to remind audiences that she had been born in the year in which the Wright brothers first flew an aeroplane, and she lived long enough to see moon landings appear almost commonplace. The problems attendant on such spectacular progress in science and technology were among her most constant preoccupations, because she felt very strongly that scientists had a special responsibility to ensure that science as a whole is rightly used. She implemented her concern for the right use of science in many ways, finding time to prepare several broadcasts, lectures, and articles intended for non-specialist audiences, including a Penguin Special *Is Peace Possible?* (1957). She was president of the British section of the Women's International League for Peace and Freedom, vice-president of the Atomic Scientists Association, and general secretary (1959–64) and president of the Physics Section (1967) before becoming the first woman president of the British Association in 1968. She also travelled widely in the service of the Society of Friends, and gave the Swarthmore lecture, *Removing the Causes of War*, in 1953.

She was vice-president of the International Union of Crystallography (1960–6), and president in 1966 at its Moscow congress, having first visited the Soviet Union as a member of a Quaker delegation in 1951 and edited their report (*Quakers Visit Russia*, 1952).

She was appointed DBE in 1956, and received honorary degrees from the universities of Wales, Leicester, Manchester, Lancaster, Oxford, Bath, Leeds, and Dundee. Her laboratory still forms part of the Kathleen Lonsdale Building at University College London. There is a pastel portrait by Juliet Pannett at University College London. She died in University College Hospital 1 April 1971.

[*The Times*, 2 April 1971; H. J. Milledge in *Acta Crystallographica*, vol. xxxi A, 1975; D. M. C. Hodgkin in *Biographical Memoirs of Fellows of the Royal Society*, vol. xxi, 1975; P. P. Ewald (ed.), *Fifty years of X-Ray Diffraction*, 1963; private papers; personal knowledge.]

H. J. MILLEDGE

LOWRY, LAURENCE STEPHEN (1887–1976), painter, was born 1 November 1887 at 8 Barrett Street, Stretford, Manchester, the only child of Robert Stephen McAll Lowry, an estate agent's clerk, and his wife, Elizabeth, daughter of William Hobson, a member of a Manchester firm of hatters. She was an accomplished pianist and a teacher of music. He was educated at the Victoria Park School which he began attending in 1895. When he was fifteen there were heated family arguments about what he should do. Since childhood he had been interested only in drawing, and wanted to continue. This distressed his mother who considered it a useless pursuit. The outcome was a compromise. In 1904 he began work with a Manchester firm of accountants, and in 1905 started to attend evening classes at the Manchester Municipal College of Art. His teacher, Adolphe Valette, a Frenchman, was an exponent of the Impressionist style. He exerted a profound and lasting influence upon the young artist.

In 1910 he became rent collector and clerk with the Pall Mall Property Co. in Manchester, and was to remain in their employ until his retirement on full pension in 1952, having risen to the rank of chief cashier. The fact that for more than fifty years the artist had been regularly employed in a 'nine to five' job was the most closely guarded secret of his life, for the good reason that he had a horror of being thought of as an 'amateur'. Not until after his death was this information made public. The fact provides a vital clue to the nature of his art and the evolution of his vision and style.

After ten years as a student at Manchester the artist began attending evening classes at the Salford School of Art where he was to remain for a further five years. It was about this time that he 'discovered' the industrial scene (1915–16). 'One day he missed a train from Pendlebury, and as he left the station he saw the Acme Spinning Company's mill . . . he experienced an earthly equivalent of some transcendental revelation' (Sir John Rothenstein, *Modern English Painters*, vol. ii, 1976).

Over the years ahead many of his finest pictures—'Daisy Nook', 1946 (private collection), 'The Cripples', 1949 (Salford Art Gallery), 'The Pond', 1950 (Tate Gallery)—were painted by artificial light usually between the hours of 10 p.m. and 2 a.m. This might account for the fact that the artist always omitted shadows. When the author once asked him why this was he replied: 'Because shadows would mess up the composition.' Working at night, away from the subject, and substantially from imagination, would have released him from the need to include shadows as a matter of fact, and omit them for the sake of the clarity of his compositions. Although he frequently made factual drawings on location, his major industrial paintings were what he called 'my composite landscapes'. Here is the key to his main achievement as a painter: the representation of the industrial scene not simply as fact but as a poetic vision cleansed of its impurities and composed with a majestic and classical grandeur. In these composite visions, teeming with his own intensely personal images of people and buildings, he would rearrange the elements of mills, smoking stacks, and actual architectural features as he wished. One of these, the Stockport viaduct, always haunted his imagination and appears out of context in many of his paintings (for example, 'The Pond').

A bachelor, the artist lived at home and, after his father's death in 1932, devotedly nursed his ailing mother until her death in 1939 when he was fifty-two.

In 1930 Manchester City Art Gallery purchased his picture 'An Accident' (1926). It was the first of the artist's works to be bought by a public gallery. In 1934 he was elected to the Royal Society of British Artists. But the major event of his life was the chance discovery of his work by the art dealer A. J. McNeil Reid of the Lefevre Gallery, London, who in 1938 noticed some of the artist's paintings on the premises of James Bourlet & Sons, picture framers. Reid instantly recognized the importance of his work and in 1939 gave the artist his first one-man exhibition. In 1948 he moved to the bleak house at Mottram in Longdendale, Cheshire, where he was to live until his death. He was awarded an honorary MA (1945) and LL D (1961) by Manchester University. He was elected ARA in 1955 and RA in 1962. In 1965 he received the freedom of the City of Salford, and in 1967 the GPO issued a stamp reproducing one of his industrial scenes. In 1975 the universities of Salford and Liverpool conferred upon the artist the degree of D.Litt. Among the honours he refused as a knighthood proposed in 1967 by Harold Wilson (later Lord Wilson of Rievaulx).

As a man Lowry was an eccentric in the grand tradition. Tall in build he cared nothing for appearances and in the 1970s frequently wore the mackintosh and cap in which he had painted his celebrated self-portrait of 1925 (Salford Art Gallery). In the tiny front room of his house were a number of clocks all of which told different times. When once asked why this was he replied: 'Because I don't want to know the *real* time.' He collected Pre-Raphaelite drawings and paintings and at his death possessed a notable group of female portraits by D. G. Rossetti [q.v.]. His recreation was listening to music, especially Donizetti and Bellini.

The main collection of his work—over 150 drawings and paintings—is owned by the City Art Gallery, Salford. There are portraits of the artist by Mervyn Levy (pencil, 1961, in the Herbert Art Gallery, Coventry) and Olwyn Bowey (oil, 1963–4, in the Tate Gallery). There is a bronze bust (1967) by Leo Solomon in the Royal Academy of Arts. Lowry died 23 February 1976 at Woods Hospital, Glossop, following an attack of pneumonia, and was buried in Southern Cemetery, Manchester.

[Shelley Rohde, *A Private View of L. S. Lowry*, 1979; Tilly Marshall, *Life with Lowry*, 1981; Allen Andrews, *The Life of L. S. Lowry*, 1977; personal knowledge.] MERVYN LEVY

LOWSON, SIR DENYS COLQUHOUN FLOWERDEW, first baronet, of Westlaws, (1906–1975), financier, was born 22 January 1906 at Stratford-upon-Avon, the youngest of three children and younger son of James Gray Flowerdew Lowson, paper merchant of Aberdeen, and his wife, Adelaide Louisa, daughter of Colonel Courtenay Harvey Saltren Scott, of the Indian Army and Dublin. He was educated at Winchester and at Christ Church, Oxford, where he obtained a third class in modern history (1927) and a fourth in jurisprudence (1928). He was called to the bar (Inner Temple) in 1930.

Denys Lowson (he was registered at birth as Denis but always used the other spelling) inherited the remarkable talents of a father who had graduated in physics *summa cum laude* from Heidelberg University. After a period of working in a German bank and then in stockbroking with the London firm of Quilter, followed by a spell at the merchant banking house Dawnay Day, he set up in business on his own just before he reached the age of thirty.

Within five years he had achieved the first of two ambitions: to dominate the unit trust movement. He bought out the unit trust management interests of his former employer, Dawnay Day, and during the 1940s gained control of the National Group of Unit Trusts. The second ambition he realized within ten years by becoming lord mayor of London at the unusually early age of forty-four in 1950–1 (Festival of Britain year).

The two ambitions reflect two important traits in Lowson's character: a desire to control considerable financial funds as if their management conferred the benefits of ownership, and a love of pomp and ceremony. His mayoralty was notable for his extensive travel overseas—remarkable in the austere atmosphere of post-war Britain—where he was fêted with great display, and the considerable sums he spent on photographs of himself.

For all his considerable abilities, Lowson remained throughout his career a controversial figure in the City of London. Through the funds he managed in unit trusts he gained control of a number of investment companies and made that control secure by interlocking shareholdings: each of ten trusts would hold 5 per cent of the eleventh. This system was further exploited in two ways. Certain of the investment companies would be almost entirely owned by their fellow members of the network to the point where only a handful of shares remained with outside investors and so were freely traded on the Stock Exchange. It thus became easy to manipulate share prices to an artificially high level which then would be reflected in the balance sheets of the network members. The investment companies and unit trusts were also used to build up controlling shareholdings in a series of commercial and industrial companies. The operation was cloaked throughout by the use of nominees—individuals as well as companies—in whose names the shareholdings were registered.

By this means Lowson controlled a financial empire worth about £200 million at its zenith in 1972. His interests ranged from railways in Canada and South America (his obsession with railways expressed itself in model railways running throughout each of his homes); merchant trading in the Far East; cattle and sheep farms in Australia, restaurants in the West End of London, gold mines, rubber plantations, and a diversity of other activities.

A man of great personal generosity, Lowson gave freely of his time to charities and good works. He was a church commissioner for England (1948) and a member of the ruling body of several hospitals and the St. John Ambulance Brigade; held office in five of the City of London livery companies and guilds; served as grand warden of the United Grand Lodge of England; took part in local government in London; and became a life governor of Dundee University. He collected and rejoiced in a string of minor foreign honours. He was also one of Britain's leading philatelists. He was created a baronet in 1951.

His intellectual gifts included a phenomenal memory—he could recall instantly and accurately intricate details of transactions several years old—and an ability to analyse a business situation. He was impatient with those of lesser abilities and became so autocratic that men of ability and strong personality refused to work with him. The fellow directors of his companies were described in a government-commissioned report into his activities as having rubber-stamped his decisions. He abused the power this gave him, using the network system of company control to provide himself with such appurtenances as cars, country homes, shoots, and fishing rights.

This reached its climax late in Lowson's career when, failing in health, he surreptitiously bought the management company of the National Group of Unit Trusts at a price which valued it at less than half a million pounds and six months later sold it for about £6½ million. He was exposed and disgraced.

After government-appointed inspectors had investigated the affair he was served with an indictment summons but died 10 September

1975 in London, a few weeks before the case against him was due to be heard.

In 1936 he married Ann Patricia, daughter of (James) Ian Macpherson, first Baron Strathcarron [q.v.], politician. They had two daughters and a son, Ian Patrick (born 1944), who succeeded his father in the baronetcy.

[*The Times*, 11 September 1975.]

JOHN ROBERTS

LUDLOW-HEWITT, SIR EDGAR RAINEY (1886–1973), air chief marshal, was born at Eckington, Worcester, 9 June 1886, the second son and second of five children of Thomas Arthur Ludlow-Hewitt, of Clancoole, county Cork, and later vicar of Minety, Wiltshire, and his wife, Edith Annie, daughter of Alfred Ricketts Hudson, of Wick House, Worcestershire. Educated at Radley and Sandhurst, he was commissioned into the Royal Irish Rifles in 1905. He learnt to fly at Upavon a few weeks before the outbreak of World War I, and in August 1914 became a probationary member of the infant Royal Flying Corps. Early in 1915 he was posted to No. 1 Squadron in France, and gained a reputation as an exceptionally able and courageous pilot. He won an MC (1916), was six times mentioned in dispatches, and was rapidly promoted to command No. 3 Squadron. In February 1916 he was promoted wing commander, taking over III Corps Wing at Bertangles. He became a chevalier of the Legion of Honour in 1917, and was appointed to the DSO the following year. By the end of the war, a brigadier at thirty-one, he was marked by Sir H. M. (later Viscount) Trenchard [q.v.] as one of the outstanding brains of the newly created Royal Air Force.

Between the wars, Ludlow—as he was always known—served as commandant of the RAF Staff College, Andover (1926–30), air officer commanding in Iraq (1930–32), director of operations and intelligence, Air Ministry (1933–5), and AOC in India (1935–7). An austere, sombre figure, his intelligence and devotion to duty were widely recognized, but his lack of humour and teetotal dedication to Christian Science did not encourage good fellowship. The tall, lanky figure of Ludlow-Hewitt striding across the tarmac of an airfield was respected, but loved only by those who knew him well. 'Most knowledgeable; very sound on paper; probably more detailed knowledge of service matters than anyone in the RAF', Air Chief Marshal Sir Hugh Pughe Lloyd wrote of him in his diary. 'As a commander a hopeless bungler and fuddler; unable to make up his mind and will change it five times in as many minutes; easily flustered.'

This may be a little ungenerous. But as a commander on the eve of war, Ludlow-Hewitt became the victim of his own intelligence. In 1937 he was recalled from India to become AOC Bomber Command and he became air chief marshal. Since 1918, like almost every senior RAF officer of the period, he had shared that mystical faith in the power of a bomber offensive to win wars held by Viscount Trenchard [q.v.]. Yet in his new post he was quickly forced to terms with the fact that no hard thinking had ever been done about how the bombers were to find their targets; how they were to aim their bombs; how the bombs were to destroy large structures; above all, perhaps, how a credible offensive was to be mounted with the very small force at Bomber Command's disposal. From 1936 onwards, Fighter Command profited greatly from the attention of politicians and scientists—above all Sir Henry Tizard [q.v.]—who addressed themselves determinedly to the problems of creating a workable air defence system for Britain. Perhaps principally because so many politicians and civilians found the concept of a bomber offensive repugnant, no parallel outside stimulus was applied to Bomber Command. Ludlow-Hewitt pressed the Air Ministry in vain for the creation of a Bombing Development Unit. He met Tizard for the first time only in July 1939.

It was Ludlow-Hewitt's thankless task to identify frankly and accurately, on the very edge of the war, the grave shortcomings of his Command. His relentless minutes to the Air Ministry exposed him to the charge of pessimism, even defeatism, yet they were perfectly confirmed by battle experience. He wrote reporting that air-gunners possessed no confidence in their ability to use their equipment. After a generation in which the theory of the 'self-defending bomber formation' had been at the heart of RAF policy, he declared his conviction that fighter escorts would be essential in war. He stated a few weeks before the opening of hostilities that if his force were ordered to undertake an all-out offensive against Germany, the medium bombers—the Blenheims—would be destroyed in three and a half weeks, the heavies—Hampdens, Whitleys, and Wellingtons—would be eliminated in seven and a half weeks. The air staff reluctantly accepted the view that the government had anyway reached for political reasons, that the RAF should not embark on an immediate strategic offensive. In September 1939 Bomber Command began the war with a programme of leaflet-dropping which confirmed Ludlow-Hewitt's worst fears about his command's aircraft navigation, and also carried out operations against the German fleet at sea and in support of the British Expeditionary Force in France. When the first disastrous operations of No. 3 Group's Wellingtons against the German fleet caused heavy casualties, Ludlow-Hewitt flew personally to visit the squadrons, and astonished his men by his own sensitivity to the losses. He was too passionately humanitarian to maintain the confidence of others, and too realistic about the shortcomings of his own force. An officer was needed of less sensitivity and more positive faith in his Command's powers, however ill-founded. In April 1940, before the war began in earnest, Ludlow-Hewitt was removed to become inspector-general of the RAF, a post in which he served with great insight and dedication until 1945. Sir C. F. A. Portal (later Viscount Portal of Hungerford, q.v.) replaced him at Bomber Command.

Ludlow-Hewitt was appointed CMG (1919), CB (1928), KCB (1933), GBE (1943), and GCB (1946). From 1943 to 1945 he was principal air ADC to the King. In 1945 he became chairman of the board of the new College of Aeronautics, a position he held until 1953. One of the founding fathers of the RAF, an exceptionally thoughtful service officer, he lacked the steel for high command in war.

He married in 1923 Albinia Mary (died 1972), daughter of Major Edward Henry Evans-Lombe, of Marlington Hall, Norwich, and widow of Francis William Talbot Clerke and of Captain Anthony Henry Evelyn Ashley, both of the Coldstream Guards. There were no children of the marriage. Ludlow-Hewitt died at Queen Alexandra's RAF Hospital, Wiltshire, 15 August 1973.

[RAF Museum; C. Webster and N. Frankland, *The Strategic Air Offensive against Germany*, 4 vols., 1961; Max Hastings, *Bomber Command*, 1979; private information.]

MAX HASTINGS

LUNN, SIR ARNOLD HENRY MOORE (1888–1974), ski pioneer and Christian controversialist, was born in Madras 18 April 1888, the eldest in the family of three sons (the second of whom was Hugh Kingsmill) and one daughter of (Sir) Henry Simpson Lunn [q.v.], medical missionary and travel agent, and his wife Ethel, eldest daughter of Canon Thomas Moore, rector of Middleton, county Cork, and headmaster of Middleton College. He was educated at Harrow and Balliol College, Oxford. He failed to take a degree but founded two clubs: the Oxford University Mountaineering Club and the Alpine Ski Club. He also became secretary of the Union and edited *The Isis*. In 1915 he went to France with a Quaker ambulance unit, and, having returned home and been medically rejected for military service, went to work at Mürren on behalf of British and French internees.

In 1910 Sir Henry Lunn had opened up Mürren for winter sports and the Swiss hamlet was transformed into one of the most favoured resorts in Europe. It was here that Arnold Lunn invented the modern slalom in 1922 and gained, against great opposition, the international and Olympic recognition of both downhill and slalom racing. In 1931 he organized in Mürren the first world championships in these events; he arranged another in 1935. He introduced these races into the 1936 Olympic Games.

When barely twenty, he was exploring the high Alps and crossed the Bernese Oberland on skis from end to end. He also made the first ski ascent of the Dom, the highest mountain entirely in Switzerland. In 1909 he suffered a serious fall when making a solo descent from the east ridge of Cyfrwy in Wales. His right leg was shattered and shortened permanently by three inches. He suffered constant pain from this accident for the rest of his life but never complained. His disability did not prevent him from making the first ski ascent of the Eiger in 1924.

Actively engaged in skiing and mountaineering as he was from his early years, he marked these also with a succession of books on various aspects of the subject, twenty-three in all, as well as editing the *British Ski Year Book* from 1919 to 1971. The physical and mental effort involved in so many alpine activities would exhaust the capabilities of most men, who would also be content with the wide recognition accorded for such achievements. Lunn, however, also made a reputation in quite a different field, that of religious controversy. Of his sixty-three published books sixteen were in the field of Christian apologetics, or what he preferred to call advocacy. They began with *Roman Converts* (1924) before he himself became one in 1933 (he had been brought up a Methodist) and continued with epistolary arguments with Ronald Knox [q.v.] (*Difficulties*, 1932), with C. E. M. Joad [q.v.] (*Is Christianity True?*, 1933), with J. B. S. Haldane [q.v.] (*Science and the Supernatural*, 1935), and with G. G. Coulton [q.v.] (*Is the Catholic Church Anti-Social?*, 1946). Six books of somewhat repetitive memoirs published in this period and later also dwelt largely on his religious views. He contributed to this Dictionary the notices of Lord Conway of Allington, F. S. Smythe, and G. W. Young.

During World War II Lunn was a press correspondent in the Balkans, Chile, and Peru. In June 1941 he was attached to the Ministry of Information.

The liberalism which he inherited from his father had inspired in him a passionate opposition to Hitlerism and he went on many government-sponsored lecture tours to the USA and elsewhere during the war. He also denounced communism which he saw as the ultimate enemy of his faith. The Spanish civil war was to him a communist rehearsal of a world-wide attack on Christian civilization, a threat both to the arts which he loved and the spiritual way of life which he followed with dogged devotion and exemplary moral courage.

His achievements in the two totally different areas of skiing and Christian apologetics might suggest a dual or split personality, but Lunn was very much himself and the same person on the ski slopes and on the uplands of religious speculation and argument. Although he liked to think of himself as a rationalist in matters of religion, he had an almost mystical apprehension of eternal beauty as he contemplated his beloved mountains. Conversely, the zest and dexterity of his endless religious discussions had their counterpart in the expertise of all his alpine enterprises. He kept these disparate interests together with the help of a multitude of friends in both camps. High-spirited and gregarious, he was also unworldly and absent-minded to a degree. Those who would accuse him of egotism and even arrogance in his writings might also recognize a certain selflessness and humility in his way of life.

He was very happy and well-cared-for in his two marriages. He married first in 1913 Lady Mabel (died 1959), daughter of Revd the Hon. John Stafford Northcote, and sister of the third Earl of Iddesleigh; they had two sons and one daughter. The elder son, Peter, was captain of the British ski team at the 1936 Olympics. In 1961 he married Phyllis, elder daughter of Oliver Needham Holt-Needham, who farmed his own land in Gloucestershire.

Lunn was knighted in 1952 for his services to British skiing and Anglo-Swiss relations and was a recipient of many civic and academic awards in Switzerland, France, and Spain. He is commemorated by the annual Arnold Lunn memorial lecture held under the auspices of the Ski Club of Great Britain and the Alpine Ski Club.

Lunn died in London 2 June 1974.

[Arnold Lunn's own writings; private information; personal knowledge.] T. F. Burns

LYTTELTON, OLIVER, first Viscount Chandos (1893–1972), colonial secretary and business man, was born 15 March 1893, the only son (another died in infancy) and elder child of Alfred Lyttelton [q.v.], later colonial secretary under Balfour, and his wife, (Dame) Edith ('Didi') Sophy, daughter of Archibald Balfour. She was a friend of G. B. Shaw [q.v.] and a pioneer of the National Theatre. He was educated at Eton where his uncle, Edward Lyttelton [q.v.], was headmaster, and at Trinity College, Cambridge, where he spent two years studying classics and playing golf (he was a blue). As soon as war was declared Lyttelton volunteered for service and in December 1914 he became a subaltern in the Grenadier Guards. He was appointed to the DSO (1916), won the MC, and was thrice mentioned in dispatches. He was wounded in April 1918, when he was brigade-major in the 4th Guards brigade.

When he was demobilized he joined the merchant bankers, Brown, Shipley & Co., as a clerk at £180 per annum. He stayed less than a year and then joined the British Metal Corporation, in which he became a manager and later managing director. Given his abilities and a flair for judging odds already manifest at Cambridge, the advancement of his career and fortune was rapid. British control both of the non-ferrous markets and of world tin and copper production were greatly strengthened. On the outbreak of war in 1939 Lyttelton was made controller of non-ferrous metals and by astute if unconventional dealings saved the nation vital copper supplies and much money.

With the reorganization of the war's direction under (Sir) Winston Churchill in October 1940 Lyttelton was made president of the Board of Trade and, with other ministerial parliamentary outsiders, found a seat in the House of Commons as MP for Aldershot (1940–54). As president, assisted by a young civil servant—Harold Wilson (later Lord Wilson of Rievaulx)—he introduced a clothes rationing system which was both practical and popular. In June 1941 Lyttelton joined the War Cabinet as minister of state in Cairo. He reorganized supply and was responsible for peace negotiations with the Vichy proconsuls in Syria and Lebanon from which perhaps foolishly de Gaulle was excluded. Good relations were established with the still friendly Shah of Persia and with the Hashemites. More controversial were the methods he used to force King Farouk to dismiss a palace government and install Nahas Pasha as prime minister. But, for wartime purposes, the move was a success.

In March 1942 he was recalled to the new Ministry of Production. The creation and exercise of this department was key to the war effort and to the avoidance of any repetition of the rows of 1916. As Britain moved from the defensive towards the preparation of offensives in new theatres, supply problems grew. Parts of the Admiralty and Supply departments had to be recoordinated, direction of the aircraft industry reorganized, and a reassessment made of manpower priorities. After Pearl Harbour, Lyttelton was responsible for initiating with the USA the effective Combined Production and Resources Board which saved waste duplication and shipping.

After the Tory defeat of 1945, Lyttelton was an opposition financial spokesman. He returned to the City as chairman of a major company, Associated Electrical Industries (AEI). He found peacetime politics uncongenial and was preparing to leave Parliament. But when in 1951 Churchill offered him the Colonial Office, a post held by his father, he accepted with alacrity and obtained a leave of absence from AEI. His colonial theme was simple: effective government and the orderly, gradual, but necessary progress towards self-government within the Commonwealth. He saw clearly that dominion over palm and pine could no longer be enforced permanently. Except with the Central African Federation, of which he was a stalwart advocate, these policies were largely successful in spite of a Labour Party which after 1951 abandoned any bipartisan approach to colonial affairs, although in Malaysia and colonial investment, their relicts were little short of chaotic. In Uganda he had to deal with the threat of secession by the Kabaka of Buganda and sided reluctantly but probably rightly with the governor, Sir Andrew Cohen [q.v.], on the Kabaka's temporary exile.

His greatest successes were in Malaya, Kenya, and Nigeria in dealing with two rebellions and the collapse of a constitution. In Malaya, the Chinese communist incursion from the safety of the Kraa Isthmus, beginning in 1951, posed a vast array of racial, military, administrative, and political problems to a vital and wealthy area of British interest. For his complex programme of military and administrative action and political advance, he was fortunate to find as proconsul Field-Marshal Sir Gerald Templer [q.v.]. In Kenya the Mau Mau rebellion in 1952 was even more complex in its racial, tribal, and all-African implications. Its atrocities were more hideous and its black and white politics even more sensitive. Again Lyttelton was fortunate in finding Sir Evelyn Baring (later Lord Howick of Glendale, q.v.) to carry out his policies not just to enforce order but to see that justice went unimpaired. Again successful military action went hand in hand with political reform. It was perhaps to Nigeria in his reform of the constitution, and in remedying the state of a federation falling into the disarray of its four constituent parts, that Lyttelton gave his most sparkling intellectual performance. In 1953 and at the Lagos constitutional conference of 1954 he won the confidence of such sophisticated and articulate critics as Chief Awolowo and Dr Azikiwe. At both conferences he dominated, and showed flattery and laughter to be the artillery of negotiation. The Kenyan and Malayan crises had been surmounted and in July 1954 Churchill allowed him to resign to return to industry, as chairman of AEI until his retirement in 1963. He followed an energetic expansion policy and the capital employed by the company rose from £58 million to £150 million.

For a man who only spent fourteen years of his life in politics, Lyttelton's achievements were considerable, but he always regarded himself as a limited politician. In spite of his popularity, he was innately a shy man. Had he joined Parliament earlier, the essential spark or ambition of a great political career might have been fired by the very thing he despised, the rancour of party politics.

Lyttelton was admitted to the Privy Council in 1940, and was created first Viscount Chandos in 1954 and KG in 1970. He was responsible for establishing the Institute of Directors, of which he was president, 1954–63. He was a trustee of colleges in Oxford and Cambridge and of the National Gallery. He took special pride as fund-raiser and first chairman (1962–71) of the National Theatre to whose cause his mother had been so devoted. In 1962 he published his *Memoirs* and in 1968 *From Peace to War, a Study in Contrast: 1857–1918*. To this Dictionary he contributed the notice of Viscount Crookshank. He was a fair shot and an excellent golfer, a mimic with a great fund of stories, witty, well read, and civilized, and perhaps the last of the great amateurs in English politics.

In 1920 he married Lady Moira Godolphin (died 1952), daughter of George Godolphin Osborne, tenth Duke of Leeds. They had three sons (one of whom was killed in action in Italy in 1944) and one daughter. Chandos died in London 21 January 1972 and was succeeded as viscount by his elder son Antony Alfred (1920–80).

[Colonial Office records; *The Memoirs of Lord Chandos*, 1962; personal knowledge.]

HUGH FRASER

M

McCALLUM, RONALD BUCHANAN (1898–1973), historian and master of Pembroke College, Oxford, was born 28 August 1898 at Paisley, Renfrewshire, the last of four sons of Andrew Fisher McCallum, master dyer, of Paisley, and his wife, Catherine Buchanan Gibson. He was educated at Paisley Grammar School and Trinity College, Glenalmond. He did two years' service in the Labour Corps of the British Expeditionary Force in France (1917–19) and then read modern history at Worcester College, Oxford, obtaining first class honours in 1922. After a year in Princeton and another as a history lecturer at Glasgow University, in 1925 McCallum was elected to a fellowship and tutorship in history at Pembroke College, Oxford; among his colleagues there were R. G. Collingwood and J. R. R. Tolkien [qq.v.]. After holding several college offices McCallum was elected master of Pembroke in 1955, becoming the first non-clerical head of the college since Queen Anne's annexation of the mastership to a canonry of Gloucester Cathedral.

McCallum was quintessentially an Oxford don whose centre of life was the college and university. He tutored several generations of undergraduates in British and foreign history and political institutions, and conducted an important university seminar on British parliamentary procedure; some of its participants became prominent political leaders in Britain and the United States. He was senior proctor (1942–3) and pro-vice-chancellor (1961) of the university and university member of the City Council (1958–67), and played a part in the creation of Nuffield College. He was senior treasurer of the Union and edited and contributed regularly to the *Oxford Magazine*. His vignettes of Oxford, published under a pseudonym, give an amusing picture of university life.

The twelve years of McCallum's mastership saw a marked transformation of Pembroke. The number of tutorial fellows increased and began to include natural scientists. The quality of undergraduates and their academic performance improved. A new quadrangle was created in 1962 by converting and incorporating a row of historic houses between Pembroke Street and Beef Lane. McCallum was an ideal master for this expansionary period in the college's history. He combined traditional beliefs in the virtues of Oxford education with the recognition of a need to bring the college into the post-1944 Butler Education Act era. His sense of fairness and toleration of views with which he disagreed were valuable qualities in a governing body that became increasingly large and diverse.

Steeped in the tradition of Scottish Presbyterianism and Liberalism at home, McCallum was a lifelong Liberal himself and a prominent member of the Unservile State Group. His political background nurtured his academic interests. His first published work was a life of Asquith (1936) and one of the last was *The Liberal Party from Earl Grey to Asquith* (1963). He contributed a chapter on Liberalism to *Law and Opinion in England in the Twentieth Century* (1959, ed. by Morris Ginsberg, q.v.) and published, with an introduction, the political writings of John Stuart Mill (1946) in Blackwell's series of political texts, which he edited jointly with C. H. Wilson. In his most controversial work, *Public Opinion and the Last Peace* (1944), which analysed British attitudes to the treaty of Versailles, McCallum sought to correct what he considered to be serious distortions in the accounts of J. M. Keynes [q.v.] and other writers. With *The British General Election of 1945* (1947), written with Alison Readman, McCallum inaugurated the well-known series of Nuffield election surveys. Although the work gave currency to 'psephology' (a word McCallum coined as a name for the academic study of elections) it eschewed any sociological approach; like the rest of his books it was a fine example of traditional historical scholarship. McCallum's special gift as a historian was for the analysis of political opinions. He was also a very gifted letter writer and conducted with friends, colleagues, and former pupils (such as Senator J. W. Fulbright) an extensive correspondence, which is remarkable for its attractive style and graphic quality. He loved serious conversation and had an unusually good memory. His portly figure dominated any gathering he attended.

In 1967 McCallum resigned the mastership, shortly before retirement, in order to become principal of St. Catharine's, Cumberland Lodge, Windsor Great Park, a position which he held till 1971. He was an honorary fellow of Pembroke (1968) and Worcester (1961) colleges and honorary LL D of Dundee University (1967), the latter in recognition of his advice on the new university's constitution and development.

McCallum was married twice: first, in 1932, to Ischar Gertrude (died 1944), of Wallasey, Cheshire, daughter of Frederick Bradley, schoolmaster; secondly, in 1950, to Evelyn Margaret, daughter of (Sir) Douglas Veale [q.v.], registrar of Oxford University. There were two daughters of the first marriage, and two sons and a daughter of the second. McCallum died 18 May 1973 at Letcombe Regis, Oxfordshire (formerly Berkshire). A portrait of him by John Ward is in Pembroke College hall.

[*The Times*, 21 May 1973; Pembroke College *Record*, 1974; the first R. B. McCallum memorial lecture, by J. W. Fulbright, 24 October 1975; private information; personal knowledge.] Z. A. Pelczynski

MacDERMOTT, JOHN CLARKE, Baron MacDermott (1896–1979), lord chief justice, Northern Ireland, was born in Belfast 12 April 1896, the third surviving son and sixth of seven children of Revd John MacDermott DD, minister of Belmont and moderator of the Presbyterian Church in Ireland, and his wife, Lydia Allen, daughter of Robert Wilson, solicitor, of Strabane. Educated at Campbell College, Belfast, and awarded a scholarship at Queen's University (1914), before reading law there he served in the Machine Gun battalion (51st Highland division) in France, winning the MC (1918). In 1921 he graduated LL B (with a first class and the Dunbar Barton prize). He was Victoria prizeman and exhibitioner at King's Inns, Dublin, and, with first class honours in his bar final, was called to the bar in both Dublin and Belfast.

Endowed with ability, learning, and industry, MacDermott's progress was sure. His sense of relevance, courteous but firm approach, pleasant and clear voice, and impressive appearance, constituted a formidable armoury. His height was 6 feet 4 inches, his face handsome and strong and his turn-out impeccable (albeit without a hint of pride or affectation). He lectured in jurisprudence at Queen's University 1931–5 while conducting a busy practice. Taking silk in 1936, he was immediately as busy as ever.

In 1938 he entered the Parliament of Northern Ireland as a Unionist member for Queen's University but joined the army, as a major RA, in 1939. After Dunkirk he was released at government request to be minister of public security (in which post he showed resolution and also an organizing genius typical of the man but unusual in his profession) and became a privy councillor (NI) in 1941. Appointed attorney-general in 1941 and a High Court judge in 1944, his judicial quality was soon apparent. In 1947 he became a privy councillor, a life peer, and the first lord of appeal appointed from Northern Ireland. Frequently in the minority, many of his dissenting speeches exemplify the quality of his legal thinking.

With his roots still in Belfast he was happy to accept appointment as lord chief justice of Northern Ireland (1951–71) when a vacancy arose on the death of Sir James Andrews, whose notice MacDermott later wrote for this Dictionary. He still sat occasionally in London and on retirement often sat as an additional judge, devoting himself largely to wardship, an interest fostered by his love of family and curiosity about human nature.

As a judge MacDermott was inspired by a deep sense of right and wrong, which was based on Christian standards. Knowing every branch of the law, he was its master, not just its servant. His eye for the merits and his sense of justice, while not causing him to spurn the law (which he loved and respected), helped him to reach the goal by way of the law and not in spite of it.

Although he inspired affection, he could be and often was severe. To those who did not know him, and to some who did, he was not only formidable but frightening, an impression not lessened by his dominating presence. Some felt that, appointing himself the agent of retribution, he adopted as his text the words 'Whom the Lord loveth he correcteth'. One should rather think of him as saying 'Train up a child the way he should go, and when he is old, he will not depart from it'. Slackness he could not tolerate. Not to do your best was a fault; not to do your best and be paid for it was a crime. But, while censorious of minor failings, he was generous, compassionate, and understanding when the trouble was real.

Strong in his views, he could be magnanimous in argument. The enjoyment of conversation which he experienced and imparted was obvious and infectious. Fond of travel, he would render a fascinating account of his latest expedition, which showed his ability to assimilate facts and ideas. He was a practical expert, as befitted an old machine-gunner, knew about cameras and car engines, and was a first class woodworker.

MacDermott's courage was shown when, over eighty, he offered in 1977 to redeliver at the Ulster College a lecture interrupted by a bomb meant for him which had severely wounded him. In 1957 he chose as his subject for the Hamlyn lectures 'Protection from Power' and therein merged two favourite themes: the importance of the rule of law and the rights and personality of the individual.

He maintained with enthusiasm the connection with Gray's Inn, which had elected him an honorary bencher in 1947; he was also an honorary bencher of King's Inns and an honorary LL D of Queen's University (1951), Edinburgh (1958), and Cambridge (1968). He was chairman of the committee on road and rail transport in Northern Ireland (1939), the National Arbitration Tribunal (NI) (1944–6), the commission on the Isle of Man constitution (1958), and the Northern Ireland branches of the Multiple Sclerosis Society and the Cancer Research Centre. He was Northern Ireland president of the Boys' Brigade, a governor of Campbell College (1934–59), and pro-chancellor of Queen's University (1951–69).

In 1926 he married Louise Palmer, daughter of Revd John Corry Johnston DD, another moderator of the General Assembly; they had two sons (one a High Court judge in Northern

Ireland since 1973 and one a Presbyterian minister) and two daughters. MacDermott died at home in Belfast 13 July 1979. There is a portrait in the Bar Library, Belfast, and a photograph in the Judges' Assembly Room.

[J. C. MacDermott, *An Enriching Life* (unfinished autobiography, privately published, 1980); private information; personal knowledge.] LOWRY

MACDIARMID, HUGH (pseudonym), poet and prose writer. [See GRIEVE, CHRISTOPHER MURRAY.]

McDONNELL, RANDAL JOHN SOMERLED, eighth EARL OF ANTRIM (1911–1977), chairman of the National Trust, was born in Kensington 22 May 1911, the second of four children and elder son of Randall Mark Kerr McDonnell, then Viscount Dunluce and, from 1918, seventh Earl of Antrim, and his wife, Margaret Isabel, daughter of John Gilbert Talbot PC, MP for Oxford University. He was educated at Eton (1924–9) and Christ Church, Oxford, where he studied modern history. He left without a degree.

In 1932, the year he succeeded his father in the earldom, he was appointed honorary attaché in Tehran but resigned the following year to take up a post as clerk in the House of Lords. He resigned his clerkship in 1934 to pursue his plans for developing his Glenarm estate in county Antrim, particularly its farming which was his lifelong interest. He started many local enterprises to create employment—hotels, coalmines, and fisheries. In the same year he became an Antrim JP and DL.

When war broke out in 1939 he joined the Royal Naval Volunteer Reserve and commanded a motor torpedo boat until swept by Lord Louis Mountbatten (later Earl Mountbatten of Burma, q.v.) into a series of staff appointments. On taking command of the Ulster division in 1954 (a post he held until 1957) he was promoted captain.

In 1948 he was appointed chairman of the National Trust's committee for Northern Ireland. In 1965 he became chairman of the National Trust, on whose evolution and development he was to make a greater impact than any previous chairman. His mettle was soon tested. In 1967 a group of members requisitioned an extraordinary general meeting. It was long and disorderly and a number of accusations were made. The Trust had until then enjoyed an immaculate reputation. Now, though the meeting, and a later poll of all members, decisively rejected the critics, the Trust received bad publicity. Antrim's great contribution at this crucial stage was to see that only by making changes in the Trust's constitution and organization could its reputation be restored. To recommend what should be done an advisory committee was set up, consisting of three members of the Trust's council, with Sir Henry (later Lord) Benson, an eminent chartered accountant, as chairman. Benson recommended greater control over the Trust's policy by its members, greater access to its historic houses, and big changes in organization. Not all these ideas were palatable to Antrim's more traditional colleagues. All had to be steered through them, the council, the annual general meeting, and, since the Trust's constitution was embodied in a private Act of Parliament, through Parliament.

Antrim put all his energy (and charm) into this task of persuasion and the longer work of implementing the changes. He knew that the great increase in the number of properties accepted—many more were in prospect—made it essential for regional committees to take over much of the management from head office committees. He set regionalization in progress, simultaneously improving head office liaison and introducing effective control of the ever-increasing budget. He made the staff changes needed, some of them painful.

In 1977 his health was failing and he announced his wish to retire. By then regionalization was virtually completed and the new constitution was working. Rapport with members had been greatly improved especially by setting up seventy-four new local 'centres'; only eleven had existed in 1965. Fifty further historic houses had been accepted and 50,000 acres added to the 400,000 in hand. Enterprise Neptune, the appeal he had promoted to save the coastline, had extended the protected coast from 187 to 380 miles. A membership drive, at one time thought indecent, had brought numbers up from 150,000 to 600,000. New sources of revenue, including shops at historic houses, enabled an annual expenditure of £11 million to be financed. The reputation of the Trust was as high as ever.

Antrim would never have claimed that the restoration and modernization of the National Trust was his doing. However, those who worked with him knew that, without his leadership and drive, these objectives would not have been secured. The Trust was his paramount interest and he led others to give it the same devotion, masking his fervour behind great natural charm and an irrepressible sense of humour.

He worked not only for buildings and landscape. In 1959 he became chairman of the new Ulster Television station, where many potential explosions were defused by his wisdom, wit, and good humour. From 1966 he was chairman of the St. Peter's group of hospitals in London. No figurehead, he visited constantly and was known by all the staff. He promoted actively the group's urological and nephrological research. In 1972–4 he was a member of the Sports Council.

Antrim was appointed KBE in 1970. In 1972 he became honorary FRIBA and received a D.Litt. from the New University of Ulster.

In 1934 he married Angela Christina (died 1984), daughter of Sir Mark Sykes, sixth baronet [q.v.], traveller, soldier, and politician. They had three sons, the second of whom died at a day old, and a daughter. Antrim died at his Chelsea home 26 September 1977 and was succeeded in the earldom by his elder son, Alexander Randal Mark, Viscount Dunluce (born 1935), keeper of conservation at the Tate Gallery.

[*The Times*, 27 July 1977; National Trust records; personal knowledge.]

JOHN WINNIFRITH

MCFADYEAN, SIR ANDREW (1887–1974), Treasury official, international diplomat, business man, and Liberal politician, publicist, and philosopher, was born at Leith 23 April 1887, the eldest of the three sons (there were also two daughters) of (Sir) John McFadyean, professor of anatomy in the Royal (Dick) Veterinary College, Edinburgh (and later principal of the Royal Veterinary College, London), and his wife, Mara Eleanor, daughter of Thomas Walley. He was educated at University College School, London, and University College, Oxford, where he took a second class in classical honour moderations (1907) and a first in *literae humaniores* (1909).

He entered the Treasury in 1910, and between 1913 and 1917 was private secretary to six financial secretaries, including Charles Masterman, Edwin Montagu, and Stanley Baldwin [qq.v.], and for a time doubled as private secretary to Sir John (later Lord) Bradbury [q.v.], the joint permanent secretary. In 1917, at a time when Britain was becoming increasingly dependent on American credit, McFadyean accompanied Sir S. Hardman Lever, whose notice he later wrote for this Dictionary, on an important financial mission to the United States, and from 1917 to 1919 served under J. M. (later Lord) Keynes [q.v.] in the Treasury division dealing with external finance. For the final four months of the peace conference McFadyean was Treasury representative in Paris.

In 1920 he was seconded for service with the Reparation Commission, which had been set up in Paris to decide the extent of Germany's obligations. For two years he served as secretary to the British delegation, before succeeding Sir Arthur Salter [q.v.] as general secretary of the commission. McFadyean agreed with Keynes's *The Economic Consequences of the Peace* (1919), and in 1924 played an important role in reducing Germany's obligations when he was secretary of the principal committee of experts, which drew up what became known as the Dawes plan. Hyperinflation had shown the need for rehabilitation of Germany's finances, and for some means by which reparations could be paid without upsetting exchange rates. Under the Dawes plan payments were rescheduled, and were to be met from new taxes to be imposed as Germany's economy recovered. The mark was stabilized, on gold, restoring confidence, so that an international loan could be raised, covering the first year's instalment. Finally reparations were to be held in a fund which was not to be converted into other currencies if that would cause depreciation of the Reichsmark. McFadyean himself held that the men chiefly responsible for the Dawes plan were Sir Josiah (later Lord) Stamp [q.v.] and the American Owen D. Young, but Stamp's letters to his wife at the time made plain he and McFadyean worked closely and harmoniously at all stages of drafting.

McFadyean was appointed one of four Allied controllers to supervise payments under the plan, being based in Berlin as commissioner for controlled revenues. He was knighted in 1925. In 1929 the Young plan, with which McFadyean had no direct part, aimed at final settlement of reparations. As McFadyean pointed out prophetically, falling prices in a world depression meant the real burden on Germany under the Young plan was likely to be heavier, and not lighter, than her obligations under the Dawes plan, which were adjustable to such a change. He himself returned from Berlin in 1930 before there was any clear sign of default.

After eleven years abroad, McFadyean decided against a return to the Treasury, and embarked on a career in the City, where his reputation for uncompromising probity made him a valuable member of a number of boards of directors, particularly of refugee firms from Germany. He was chairman of S. G. Warburg and Co. Ltd., from its foundation (as the New Trading Co. Ltd.) in 1934 until 1952, and a director until 1967, by which time it had become a leading merchant bank.

He also turned to politics, becoming the Liberal Party's joint treasurer, 1936–48; president, 1949–50; and vice-president, 1950–60. He stood as a candidate in the 1945 and 1950 general elections (for the City of London and for Finchley respectively), and, far from being discouraged by defeat, he was one of a small core who helped sustain the party in its darkest days. He described himself as an 'Asquithian' and a 'Whig', and his pamphlet *The Liberal Case* (1950) was a statement of classical Liberalism, tinged with wry realism: 'Those who in the last thirty years have worked for the restoration of the Liberal Party can be suspected of no worldly hope', he observed. He was an advocate of proportional representation, and a supporter of the Scottish covenant.

He was a member of the council of the Royal Institute of International Affairs 1933–67, and its president in 1970, and from 1944 was chairman of the Institute of Pacific Relations committee. As a publicist of European unity on Liberal principles he translated two works of R. N. Coudenhove-Kalergi, *The Totalitarian State Against Man* (1938), arguing against the Hegelian conception of the state, and *Europe Must Unite* (1940), calling for a European Commonwealth, based on a European ideal transcending, without weakening, national patriotisms. After the war McFadyean helped found the Liberal International, of which he was vice-president 1954–67, and he was a tireless advocate of the common market.

He believed tariffs, and monopolist practices and restrictive practices in industry, were destroying Britain's competitiveness, and he was president of the Free Trade Union 1948–59. Nevertheless, he was no dogmatic advocate of *laissez-faire*. As a member of the court of the British North Borneo Chartered Company, and of the international rubber regulation committee, he knew how producers of primary products might suffer from overproduction. In *The History of Rubber Regulation, 1934–1943* (1944), which he edited, he noted how demand might be a good deal more elastic than supply, and that the alternative to regulation had been the 'slow and cruel play of market forces'.

Other causes with which he was associated included assistance to persecuted Jewry, and also to 'enemy aliens' unjustly interned during the war.

McFadyean was tall and muscular, with a long, Scottish face, and a quizzical expression. He was a passionate devotee of opera and theatre.

In 1913 he married Dorothea Emily, daughter of Charles Keane Chute, an actor; they had one son and three daughters. McFadyean died in London 2 October 1974. There is a portrait by Joseph Oppenheim in London.

[John Harry Jones, *Josiah Stamp, Public Servant*, 1964; Sir Andrew McFadyean, *Reparation Reviewed*, 1930, and *Recollected in Tranquillity*, 1964; *The Times*, 3 October 1974; private papers and information.] G. C. PEDEN

MACKENZIE, SIR (EDWARD MONTAGUE) COMPTON (1883–1972), writer, was born 17 January 1883 at West Hartlepool, the eldest in the family of two sons and three daughters of Edward Compton (Mackenzie), the founder and actor manager of the Compton Comedy Company, and his wife, Virginia, daughter of Hezekiah Linthicum Bateman [q.v.], of Baltimore. Edward Compton was the son of Henry Compton [q.v.], the actor, whose real name was Charles Mackenzie. One of Compton Mackenzie's sisters was Fay Compton [q.v.], the actress. He was educated at St. Paul's School and at Magdalen College, Oxford, which he chose for its beauty. He obtained second class honours in modern history in 1904.

'Monty', as his friends called him, was an imaginative child. He had almost total recall and remembered seeing a field of rabbits when he was a year old and being spoken to by the Empress of Austria when he was two. Belonging to a Bohemian family, he travelled the country, meeting artists and writers. He was always at ease with people, not knowing the meaning of shyness. His mother knew Karl Marx and Taglioni, and he himself met (Sir) Edmund Gosse, James Elroy Flecker [qq.v.], and Buffalo Bill, and was on friendly terms with Henry James, (Dame) Ellen Terry [qq.v.], Reggie Turner, and Axel Munthe, whom he called one of the world's great liars, only surpassed by Ford Madox Ford [q.v.] and Cosmo Hamilton.

He could have achieved fame as an actor, but books were his love and inspiration. To Logan Pearsall Smith [q.v.] he owed his determination to become a writer, to Frederick Marryat's *The Children of the New Forest* (1947) his espousal of the Jacobite cause, and to Johann Wyss's *The Swiss Family Robinson* (1920) his love of islands. Most of all, Stendhal's *La Chartreuse de Parme* (1939) gave him the assurance that life was worth writing about, as well as living.

Mackenzie's first book, a volume of poems, was published in 1907. His first novel appeared in 1911, *Carnival* in 1912, and then his most successful book *Sinister Street*, considered very outspoken in 1913, influenced a whole generation of young people.

Having been a second lieutenant in the 1st Hertfordshire Regiment in 1900–01, Mackenzie became a lieutenant in the Royal Marines in 1915. He served with the Royal Naval Division on the Dardanelles expedition of 1915 and was invalided in September. In 1916 he became military control officer in Athens and the following year was appointed director of the Aegean Intelligence Service at Syra. His work in the Secret Service in World War I led to his writing *Gallipoli Memories* (1929), *Athenian Memories* (1931), and *Greek Memories* (1932—withdrawn, reissued 1940), for which he stood trial in the Old Bailey, charged with an offence against the Official Secrets Act.

He went to stay on the island of Capri where he found material for *Vestal Fire* (1927) and *Extraordinary Women* (1928), in which practically every character was a portrait of one of that curious coterie—G. Norman Douglas, W. Somerset Maugham, D. H. Lawrence [qq.v.], and Romaine Brooks. From 1931 to 1935 he was literary critic of the *Daily Mail* and from 1931 to 1934 rector of Glasgow University. From 1923 to 1961 he was editor of the *Gramophone*.

Mackenzie stayed on the island of Barra during World War II, and his sojourn produced the delightful *Whisky Galore* (1947). By what the islanders regarded as a benign act of providence, the *Politician*, loaded with thousands of cases of whisky, struck a rock off Ericksay and the resulting bonanza to the islanders was just the subject for Mackenzie. The book was made into a very successful film (1948). Besides a great many novels, Mackenzie wrote some enchanting children's books and an autobiography in ten volumes.

He was a romantic and attractive figure with blue eyes and a poet's brow. A charming kindly man, he appeared ageless. He was very sensitive to beauty, loving flowers such as the wild sweet peas in Capri, the purple clematis at Folkestone, and the meadow of lilies at Grindelwald. He had a passion for islands—Capri, Herm, Jethou, Barra—and chose to live on them to escape the tyranny of time. He adored cats and was life president of the Siamese Cat Club. He was also president of the Wexford Festival from 1951, of the Croquet Association (1954–66), of the Songwriters' Guild from 1956, of the Poetry Society (1961–4), and of the Dickens Fellowship (1939–46).

Although always the professional, living in harmony and keeping faith with his publishers and editors, he never saved money and his life moved from one financial crisis to another. He had an endearing habit, when worried by something particularly severe, to restore his spirits by ordering a new suit or indulging in a charming extravagance. He had great courage, both moral and physical, for throughout his life he was seldom without pain from sciatica. He stood by the unfortunates: he supported Norman Douglas, when threatened with deportation, and P. G. Wodehouse [q.v.], when vilified for his broadcasts to America during World War II, and he gave evidence of character for Rupert Croft-Cooke on a homosexual charge. He so arranged it that he always managed to live his life the way he wanted to live it with the people he wanted to live it with, and in the places where he wanted to be. As a result, he enjoyed his life enormously.

He was appointed OBE in 1919 and knighted in 1952. He was C.Lit. (1968), FRSL, honorary RSA, and honorary LL D of Glasgow and St. Francis Xavier University.

He married first, in 1905, Faith (died 1960), daughter of the Revd Edward Daniel Stone, of Abingdon, previously a master at Eton. They had no children. In 1962 he married Christina, elder daughter of Malcolm MacSween, of Tarbert, Harris. She died the following year and in 1965 he married her younger sister, Lilian (Lily). Mackenzie died in Edinburgh 30 November 1972.

[Compton Mackenzie, *My Life and Times*, 10 vols., 1963–71; personal knowledge.]

CHRISTINA FOYLE

MACKINTOSH, JOHN PITCAIRN (1929–1978), politician and professor of politics, was born in Simla 24 August 1929, the elder of two brothers. He spent his first eleven years in British India where his mother, Mary Victoria Pitcairn, taught at a Teacher Training College. Her husband, Colin M. Mackintosh, had gone to India to sell cotton piece goods; then he represented McCallum's Perfection Whiskey, finally transferring to insurance work. Later, John Mackintosh used to recall how one of his earliest childhood memories was the image of demonstrators lying round the lorries carrying Lancashire piece goods, so that they could not move. The campaign of M. K. Gandhi [q.v.] to protect Indian home industry was, perhaps, Mackintosh's introduction to his lifelong concern with overseas issues, and the problems of the third world.

At the beginning of World War II the Mackintosh family returned to Edinburgh, sending the boys to Melville College. Mackintosh was to speak with affection of individual teachers, and of unhappy times at the school. He progressed to Edinburgh University, where he achieved a first class honours degree in history (1950), and then to Balliol College, Oxford, to read PPE, in which he achieved a second class in 1952.

At Oxford certain lifelong scars were inflicted. Whereas Scottish undergraduates, straight from school or National Service, tended to enjoy Oxbridge, those already having a degree from a Scottish university often returned disenchanted. Mackintosh held that Balliol men were very arrogant: 'I resented them very much. They said that a first class honours degree at a Scottish University meant that one was probably fit to come up to Oxford as an undergraduate.' This early encounter with the English establishment possibly sowed the seed of lifelong scepticism about mandarin-level civil servants, and caused his concern with Scottish devolution and an assembly in Edinburgh. The Oxford experience might also partially account for Mackintosh giving vent to witty irreverence towards so many of the products of Oxbridge, something that was to disadvantage him in later life when his political preferment was being contemplated. His malicious tongue was more wounding than perhaps he realized, and therefore sour jokes at his expense were well received both among his university colleagues and MPs. For example, the story went the rounds that Harold Wilson (later Lord Wilson of Rievaulx), in 1967, commented to the long-serving secretary of state for Scotland: 'You had better keep an eye on that man Mackintosh, Willie. He wants your job.' 'No, Harold', came Ross's reply, 'He wants yours!'

This rather-too-obvious and impatient ambition, dangerously allied with an incapacity to suffer fools gladly, may have been developed by an American influence, fostered during postgraduate work at Princeton, where he was Sir John Dill memorial fellow in 1952–3. Brash, Mackintosh was not. Insensitive, as to how he could grate on other less gifted men, he certainly was.

His first job was that of a junior lecturer in history at Glasgow University (1953–4), followed by seven years as lecturer at Edinburgh University between 1954 and 1961. His many pupils testify to the brilliance of his lecturing and his capacity to inspire undergraduates. He was entertaining and articulate to the point of being envied by his colleagues, and he displayed a genuine concern for his students. In 1957 he married one of his history students, Janette, daughter of J. D. Robertson; they had a daughter and a son. Having unsuccessfully contested the Pentlands division of Edinburgh as Labour candidate in the 1959 general election, in 1960 a parliamentary career seemed open to Mackintosh when he had the all-powerful backing of the general secretary of the Scottish Trades Union Congress, George Middleton, in a by-election for the Paisley seat. At the last moment, Mackintosh declined to go forward and departed to take up a professorial post at the University of Ibadan in Nigeria. It was in this period that he was to publish his book *The British Cabinet* (1962), which, in the eyes of Richard Crossman [q.v.], who reviewed the volume of this still obscure academic, initiated the concept of prime ministerial government and placed Mackintosh in the same league as Walter Bagehot [q.v.]. It was indeed a seminal thesis. The irony is that, had Mackintosh gone to Parliament as MP for Paisley in 1960, he could hardly have been denied a post in the 1964 Labour government, leading to a Cabinet position before the end of the first Wilson administration in 1970. He would then doubtless have written about the myth and the reality of Cabinet government, in the light of experience.

In 1963 he returned to be senior lecturer in politics at Glasgow University, and, to the dismay of his friends, his marriage to Janette Robertson, willing hostess to a generation of undergraduates, was dissolved. In that year he married Catherine Margaret Una Maclean, a lecturer in social medicine, the daughter of the Revd C. Maclean, of Scarp, Harris; they had a son and a daughter.

In 1965–6 he was professor of politics at the University of Strathclyde, working on *The Devolution of Power: Local Democracy, Regionalism and Nationalism*, which was to be published in 1968. This was the intellectual furniture of much of the Scottish devolution campaigns of the 1970s—though Mackintosh himself, shortly before his death, was scathing about the opportunism and unworkability of the proposals embodied in the Labour government's Scotland Bill. With some justice, he supposed that any prime minister, really concerned to allow devolution, other than for reasons of sheer short-term political expediency, would have given him the post of minister of state in the Cabinet Office, responsible for the devolution proposals.

Mackintosh was elected Labour MP for Berwick and East Lothian in 1966. The fact that so talented a man, who was arguably, alongside Brian Walden, the most compellingly persuasive parliamentary orator of his generation, never achieved ministerial office, requires some explanation. One clue is to be found in his maiden speech, a dazzling performance, which lingers in the memory of all who heard it. His tribute to his defeated opponent, Sir William Anstruther-Gray, former deputy chairman of ways and means and chairman of the 1922 Committee, was one of the handsomest ever heard: 'It is perhaps not well known to hon. Members that Sir William was one of the men who returned from the Front in May, 1940, and persuaded 32 of his back bench colleagues to go into the Lobby against their own Government—against the leadership of Neville Chamberlain—thus helping to bring down that Government. On that occasion he was a true patriot. Like my predecessor, I hope to represent efficiently the constituency which has elected me. I shall work hard on its behalf' (*Hansard*, 9 May 1966, col. 77).

This he did, prodigiously, with a six-month interregnum in 1974, when he was defeated in February and returned the same October. At the memorial meeting in the House of Commons, Gerald O'Brien, the full-time agent of the Berwick and East Lothian Constituency Labour Party, moved an ultra-sophisticated audience by claiming that the Lammermuir hills wept when Mackintosh died; and, on the way to his funeral, little groups of constituents from the farming areas could be observed all along the route of the cortege paying their last respects to a politician who had come to be loved by those for whom he worked. In dealing with constituents' problems Mackintosh was patient, caring, and charming, a different person from he who, in London, chastised the Wilsons and the Callaghans with his acerbic wit. Moreover, the very point which Mackintosh selected in Anstruther-Gray's career for favourable mention was, with hindsight, to be a trailer for his own rebellions, too numerous to chronicle. Among the more remembered must be that hectic night in November 1976, when Mackintosh and Walden abstained on the Docks Bill, which was consequently lost, to the consternation of the hierarchy of Labour ministers.

Mackintosh's interest in constitutional and procedural questions was put to immediate use when he entered Parliament by his appointment to the select committees for the oversight of government, and he served on experimental committees on agriculture (1967–8) and Scottish affairs (1968–70), forerunners of the departmentally related committee system introduced in 1979. Never was there a more spectacular, intellectual, verbal clash of arms, than when Mackintosh bearded Richard Crossman, then leader of the House, on the proposal to terminate the activities of the embryo agriculture committee. After a Wagnerian battle Mackintosh lost, but won the war of select committees. He delighted in arguing questions of parliamentary reform with his colleagues and the clerks of the House, and was generous with his time in exposition of the practicalities of parliamentary government to those outside. He gave valuable help to the Commonwealth Parliamentary Association, and to the Hansard Society, of which he was chairman fom 1974 until his death. To this Dictionary he contributed the notice of Lord Morrison of Lambeth.

No picture of Mackintosh can be complete without an attempt to convey his demonic energy—apparent whether playing with his children, step-children, or the children of others, or pouring out polished, provocative articles for *The Times*, the *Scotsman*, the *Political Quarterly*, and a host of other newspapers and journals, or fascinating Königswinter conferences, or electrifying the special conference of the Labour Party, a largely hostile audience, when speaking in the Central Hall, Westminster, on EEC entry, from an unusual and even physically hazardous position, in the front row of the gallery, leaning over a balcony. There was also the extraordinary courage and self-discipline which he exercised during the last year of his life, when he knew he was fatally ill, but kept the knowledge to himself, seeking no pity, and working with frenetic effort. He died in the Western General Hospital, Edinburgh, 30 July 1978.

[Personal knowledge.] TAM DALYELL

McLEOD, (JAMES) WALTER (1887–1978), bacteriologist, was born 2 January 1887 at Dumbarton, near Glasgow, the second of three sons (there were no daughters) of John McLeod, a successful Scottish architect, and his wife, Lilias Symington, daughter of James McClymont, a gentleman farmer of Borgue House, Kirkcudbrightshire.

After early schooling in Switzerland, where his mother had moved after the death of his father, McLeod was educated at Mill Hill School, London, where (Sir) John McClure was headmaster. He did well there, and in 1903 at the age of sixteen he became a medical student at the University of Glasgow, where he graduated MB, Ch.B., with commendation, in 1908. He was an enthusiastic sportsman, playing rugby and cricket and also gaining a blue for athletics. He held two house appointments in Glasgow, and after a trip to India as a ship's surgeon, he was made a Coates scholar in 1909, and a Carnegie scholar in 1910–11 in the department of pathology, Glasgow, under (Sir) Robert Muir [q.v.]. Here he studied streptococcal haemolysins under Carl H. Browning. In 1912 McLeod moved to London to become assistant lecturer in pathology at Charing Cross Medical School, where he continued his work on streptococci and also studied spirochaetes.

When war broke out in 1914 he joined the Royal Army Medical Corps as a temporary lieutenant, and later became captain in charge of the eighth mobile laboratory. He was mentioned in dispatches four times and was appointed military OBE (1919). During his military service he worked on trench fever, trench nephritis, bacillary dysentery, and influenza. In 1919 he became the first lecturer in bacteriology in the department of pathology in Leeds, under Professor Matthew J. Stewart, and in 1922 he became the first Brotherton professor of bacteriology at Leeds. He remained in Leeds until he retired with the title of professor emeritus in 1952.

During the 1920s McLeod worked primarily on bacterial metabolism, but an outbreak of diphtheria in Leeds directed his attention to the diagnostic problems of this disease, and it is for his work on defining its different forms that he is best known as a microbiologist. He described different colonial forms of diphtheria bacilli and defined new media that were capable of distinguishing pathogenic from less pathogenic organisms. When sulphonamides became available he studied their action on bacteria, and later he was involved in early studies on penicillin.

Following his retirement and his wife's death, McLeod returned to laboratory work with support from the Scottish Hospital Endowments Research Trust (1954–63), initially in the department of surgery in Edinburgh, then at Edenhall Hospital, Musselburgh. In 1963 he joined the central microbiological laboratory at the Western General Hospital, Edinburgh, supported by the Royal Society and the Medical Research Council (1963–73). During this period much of his work was on urinary tract infections with special reference to prostatectomy and paraplegia, and on staphylococcal toxins. It was not until his eighty-seventh year that failing health obliged him to give up laboratory work.

In 1928 McLeod was made a corresponding member of the Société de Biologie, Paris, and in 1933 he was elected FRS. He became an honorary member of the Scottish Society for Experimental Medicine and a fellow of the Royal

Society of Edinburgh in 1957. He became an honorary member of the Pathological Society of Great Britain and Ireland in 1961, and an honorary fellow of the Royal College of Pathologists in 1970. He was president of the Society for General Microbiology in 1949–52. He received honorary degrees from the universities of Dublin (Sc.D.) in 1946 and Glasgow (LL D) in 1961.

The bronze head by Sir Jacob Epstein made on McLeod's retirement from the University of Leeds conveys something of his character. He was a large man, a teetotaller, something of a puritan, with a deep Christian faith. He was an effective elder of the Presbyterian Church and an active Boys' Brigade officer for half a century. He combined this with a great sense of fun and capacity for enjoyment.

In June 1914 McLeod married Jane Christina ('Jean'), an MA of Glasgow University, daughter of Thomas Garvie, a Scot who was a director of the Zyrardow textile factory in Poland. There were two sons and five daughters of this marriage. One son died as a result of an accident at the age of four; other members of the family all had successful professional careers and between them, to his great pleasure, gave him twenty grandchildren. Jane McLeod died in 1953, shortly after the couple left Leeds and retired to a cottage at Longformacus in the Lammermuir Hills. McLeod moved to Edinburgh and in 1956 he married Joyce Anita Shannon, MB, Ch.B. (St. Andrews University), daughter of Edgar Frederick Shannon, office equipment manufacturer, and his wife, Anita Lily (née Frost). McLeod died in the Royal Victoria Hospital, Edinburgh, 11 March 1978.

[Sir Graham Wilson and K. S. Zinnemann in *Biographical Memoirs of Fellows of the Royal Society*, vol. xxv, 1979; obituary notice by K. I. Johnstone in *Journal of General Microbiology*, vol. cix, 1978, information from Sir Gordon Cox and Dr Joyce Anita McLeod; personal knowledge.] J. S. PORTERFIELD

McMILLAN, WILLIAM (1887–1977), sculptor, was born at Aberdeen 31 August 1887, the son of William McMillan, master engraver and printer, of 37 Powis Place, Aberdeen, and his wife, Jane Knight. He was trained professionally as a sculptor first at the city's art school, Gray's School of Art, and then went on to complete his studies at the Royal College of Art (1908–12). His early career in London was interrupted almost immediately by World War I in which he saw active service in France as an officer with the 5th Oxfordshire and Buckinghamshire Light Infantry.

Even before the war was over he had begun to establish himself professionally, exhibiting for the first time at the Royal Academy Summer Exhibition in 1917, and continuing to do so thereafter, with only one exception, every year until 1971. Commissions to design the Great War medal and the Victory medal confirmed a reputation which by 1925 had grown sufficiently rapidly for him to be elected an associate of the Royal Academy at the precocious age of thirty-eight; he subsequently became RA in 1933. In 1929 he was appointed master of the sculpture school in the Royal Academy Schools, a position he held until 1940.

He had the reputation of a good teacher, relaxed and with a gift for quietly explaining a point. He did not expect or demand followers nor did he attack those with whom he disagreed. He had in short a sense of the world which was of considerable importance in a time of revolutionary change in British sculpture, when the impact of European avant-garde ideas began to be felt in Britain through the work of Henry Moore, (Dame) Barbara Hepworth [q.v.], and others.

From 1940 until 1966, when he finally gave up the Chelsea studio in Glebe Place, which he had used for most of his life, he became involved in a whole series of important public sculptures, among them 'King George VI' (1955) in Carlton Gardens, 'Sir Walter Raleigh' (1959) in Whitehall, 'Alcock and Brown' (1966) at London Airport, and the bronze group of 'Nereid and Triton with Dolphins' (1948) for the Beatty memorial fountain in Trafalgar Square.

As a sculptor he is notable for working on an exceptionally wide range of subjects from war memorials to medals, statues of royalty and generals to works for garden and architectural decoration. All are distinguished by his feeling for the particular material used and a strong sense of design and outline, but, in historical retrospect, it will probably be the imaginative and decorative pieces in native British stones and woods dating from the 1920s and early 1930s that will come to be seen as his most original and significant contribution to twentieth-century British sculpture. Such attitudes to materials are now so widely accepted that it is hard to imagine the impact in their day of works like 'Statuette' (1927), carved in green slate, or the 'Birth of Venus', in Portland stone (1931, Tate Gallery) in the Royal Academy. As with all his best sculpture, they have a classical purity of line and poetic quality that places them among the more distinctive sculptural achievements of the time. McMillan was by nature a conservative however, and this, combined with his technical skills, drew him increasingly into the field of public sculpture. The subtle pressure and demands inherent in such work led to a much blander style that is rather more anonymous in character and somewhat dull.

McMillan was an elusive and very private person, fond of a daily routine that took him to the Chelsea Arts Club for lunch and a game of billiards. He was a tall and extremely handsome man, the quizzical expression the chief outward sign of a very dry and very good Scottish sense of humour that led him in younger days to be involved in organizing the Chelsea Arts Ball.

He was elected an associate member of the Royal Society of British Sculptors in 1928 and a full member in 1932. He was appointed CVO in 1956. He was also made a freeman of Aberdeen, and the university there conferred upon him an honorary doctorate of law.

In 1916 he married Dorothy (died 1964), daughter of Maurice Charles Williams, an architect, of Carlisle. There were no children. He died 25 September 1977 in hospital at Richmond on Thames shortly after his ninetieth birthday, a few days after an assault and robbery in the street had left him badly injured.

[*The Times*, 28 September 1977; William Scott RA; private information; personal knowledge.]

NICHOLAS USHERWOOD

MCNAIR, ARNOLD DUNCAN, first BARON MCNAIR (1885–1975), university teacher and administrator, legal scholar, and judge, was born 4 March 1885 at Court Lane, Dulwich, the eldest child in the family of four sons and one daughter of John McNair, of Paisley, a member of Lloyd's, and his wife, Jeannie, daughter of John Ballantyne, of Paisley. He was educated at Aldenham School and at Gonville and Caius College, Cambridge. He was senior in both parts of the law tripos, proceeding BA, LL B in 1909, LL M in 1913, MA in 1919, and LL D in 1925.

After graduating he practised as a solicitor in the City of London before returning to Cambridge to become a fellow of his college in 1912 and eventually senior tutor. He was called to the bar of Gray's Inn in 1917. After a short spell as reader in the University of London (1926–7) he returned to Cambridge. He considered his work as a don to be the most important of his roles; and he greatly influenced and inspired many generations of pupils, his interest in them continuing long after they had gone down.

Easily approachable, he received everyone with the same grave and gentle courtesy. A small man but neatly built, he had a ready smile when sharing some gently amusing quality of whatever he was discussing. He had a light voice, lacking edge, yet clear, because even in conversation his speech was measured. He was a charming and persuasive speaker (he had been president of the Cambridge Union in 1909) and a superb lecturer. He would delineate a problem; and after a pause, as though for further reflection, lean over the lectern, eyes wide with discovery, finger raised, to indicate the correct solution in a phrase. Though sceptical about the importance of boards and committees he had great influence on them.

His first interest was the common law and for many years he lectured on contract. But he early developed a special interest in international law, though he always urged that international lawyers should first make themselves good private-law lawyers. His constant endeavour was to distinguish and develop what he liked to call 'hard law', solving specific problems.

His many writings covered a wide field of both international law and English law. Besides important articles (see *Lord McNair; Selected Papers and Bibliography*, ed. Clive Parry, 1974) they included: *Legal Effects of War*, mainly a study of English law (1920, 2nd edn. 1944; 3rd and 4th edn. with A. D. Watts, 1948, 1966); the pioneer work on *The Law of the Air* (1932, 2nd edn. with M. R. E. Kerr and R. A. MacCrindle, 1953); *Roman Law and Common Law* (with W. W. Buckland, q.v., 1936); *The Law of Treaties* (1938); the three volumes of *International Law Opinions* (1956), a collection, with commentary, of opinions of law officers of the Crown culled from papers in the Public Record Office; *The Law of Treaties* (a new, major treatise, 1961). He also edited the important fourth edition (1926–8) of *International Law* by L. F. L. Oppenheim [q.v.]. To this Dictionary he contributed the article on H. C. Gutteridge.

In 1935 he succeeded to the Whewell chair in international law at Cambridge, but only two years later left to be vice-chancellor of Liverpool University. He served on many government committees and commissions. He returned to Cambridge in 1945 to be professor of comparative law; but was elected a judge of the International Court of Justice in The Hague in 1946, and was its president from 1952 to 1955.

McNair was a very good judge: a task to which his scrupulous scholarship and shrewd, cautious, practical sense were ideally suited. His opinions showed his characteristic clarity, good sense, and independence. After his retirement from the Hague Court he became the first president of the European Court of Human Rights at Strasburg from 1959 to 1965. He was also president of an Argentine–Chilean Court of Arbitration to determine a disputed Andes boundary; his award (HMSO, 24 November 1966), delivered when he was eighty-one, showed his shrewdness and effectively disposed of the matter.

McNair was gazetted CBE in 1918, knighted in 1943, and became first baron in 1955. He took silk in 1945. He had honorary doctorates from Oxford, Birmingham, Brussels, Glasgow, Liverpool, Reading, and Salonika. He was made master of the bench of Gray's Inn in 1936 and was its treasurer in 1947. He was president of the Institut de Droit International in 1949–50, and later president d'honneur. He became FBA in 1939.

McNair married in 1912 Marjorie (died

1971), daughter of Sir Clement Meacher Bailhache [q.v.], judge; they had a son and three daughters. He died at home in Cambridge 22 May 1975. He was succeeded in the barony by his son, (Clement) John (born 1915).

There are portraits by Phyllis Dobbs at Gonville and Caius College, Cambridge, and at the International Court of Justice.

[*The Times*, 24 May 1975; *British Year Book of International Law*, vol. xlvii; 'Lord McNair memorial lecture', International Law Association, 1976; personal knowledge.]

R. Y. JENNINGS

MCWHIRTER, (ALAN) ROSS (1925–1975), editor and litigant, was born in Winchmore Hill, north London, 12 August 1925, the third and youngest son and younger twin son (there were no daughters) of William Allan McWhirter, national newspaper editor, and his wife, Margaret ('Bunty') Moffat Williamson. Ross was educated with his brothers at Marlborough College. After volunteering for the Royal Navy at seventeen, he became a midshipman in the Royal Naval Volunteer Reserve in 1944 and served two arduous years in minesweeping. In January 1947 he returned to Trinity College, Oxford (he had spent six months there in 1943–4 in the Oxford University naval division), with his twin Norris to resume reading jurisprudence. He graduated in 1948 with a third class in jurisprudence (shortened course) having represented the university in athletics abroad and against Cambridge. In the same year he ran in the Achilles Club team that won the Amateur Athletic Association relay championship.

In 1951 Ross and Norris McWhirter established an agency in London to provide facts, figures, and features to the press, publishers, and advertisers. The business immediately prospered and Ross McWhirter was appointed the lawn tennis and rugby football correspondent of the London evening *Star*. The twins, who always worked as a team, published in 1951 their first book *Get To Your Marks* on the history of athletics. It was later quoted as being 'distinguished by a degree of precision and thoroughness which no athletics historian had achieved before'.

The first of Ross McWhirter's many law cases was in 1954 against the National Union of Journalism of which he was an involuntary 'closed shop' member. A union officer had defamed his twin brother and when the editor of the *Star* declined to give evidence against the union, McWhirter insisted on a subpoena and the case went against the union along with damages and costs. In the same year the brothers became the only company directors in the country to insist on their names being placed on the local government electoral register after the County Court accepted that the words 'does not entitle' have a different meaning from 'disentitle'.

Ross McWhirter's next foray, in 1967, brought four High Court actions in forty-three days to challenge the conversion of Enfield grammar and secondary modern schools into an entirely 'comprehensive' scheme. After partial success by the defending parents represented by (Sir) Geoffrey Howe QC, McWhirter personally intervened to win injunctions against the Enfield Council and the secretary of state who was forced to go back to Parliament for new powers. The *Daily Mirror* carried a leader which rejoiced: 'Liberty still has its vigilant defenders.'

In November 1968 McWhirter fought the Home Office lone-handed to challenge the miscounting of votes in the Enfield local government elections the previous May. Having lost in the Crown Court he appeared in person before the High Court and defeated the Home Office to win an order signed by the lord chief justice requiring a unique recount of votes which confirmed his suspicions of massive mathematical discrepancies between the ballot papers issued and the votes declared.

In 1969 he took James Callaghan, the home secretary, to court for not giving effect to the recommendations of the boundary commissions to redistribute parliamentary seats. Since the statutory time limit of fifteen years had been exceeded, he moved the court for an order of mandamus. The attorney-general compromised the action by assuring the court that the boundary commissions' orders would be laid forthwith. The home secretary circumvented his undertaking by forcing through the Commons an affirmative motion ending with the words 'be not approved', although the Act spoke only of 'a motion to approve'. No appeal was possible because proceedings in Parliament are non-justiciable. The press however denounced this manoeuvre which McWhirter always referred to as the 'boundary fiddle'.

McWhirter's attention now turned to the Independent Broadcasting Authority. A High Court judge refused on grounds of *locus standi* to give him a declaration that the IBA had acted unlawfully in transmitting messages by subliminal flashes (expressly forbidden by statute), during a Labour Party political broadcast on 8 May 1970. In the Appeal Court Lord Denning accepted his plea that having a television licence gave him the maximum possible *locus* and the IBA took the unusual step of giving McWhirter a written undertaking that no further subliminal messages would be transmitted. The IBA were again defendants in the Andy Warhol case in 1973 when McWhirter succeeded uniquely, without the fiat of the attorney-general, in getting the transmission of a television programme stopped by court injunction, until members of the

Authority had discharged their statutory duty 'to satisfy themselves' that the programme was not 'offensive to public feeling'.

Between the two IBA cases Ross McWhirter was again before Lord Denning questioning the legality of the prime minister's action in signing the Treaty of Accession to the EEC. He contended that this use of the prerogative power by Edward Heath, the prime minister, put the monarch in breach of her coronation oath to govern her peoples 'according to *their* laws and customs'. The judges exercised their discretion not to make a declaration, but accepted McWhirter's view against Treasury counsel that the scope of the exercise of prerogative power is justiciable.

The last case he personally fought was against Eagle Ferry and the National Union of Seamen which had impounded the cars of some forty passengers at Southampton as a bargaining lever in a dispute over redundancy notices. McWhirter revived the tort of detinue and got a rare ex-parte mandatory injunction in nine minutes.

His most important case was concluded posthumously almost six years after his death when the European Court of Human Rights concurred with his view that article ii of the convention on freedom of association protected citizens against the coercion of compulsory unionism. At a cost above £100,000 and after ten governmental delays the British Rail closed shop case of *Young, James and Webster v. United Kingdom* was successfully sustained by Viscount De l'Isle VC, and by his twin brother through the agency of the Freedom Association whose charter had been drafted by Ross McWhirter. The judgment was delivered on 13 August 1981 in Strasburg and resulted six months later in a new Employment Bill including a clause to compensate retrospectively some 400 victims who had been dismissed without remedy under the 1974 Act.

Ross McWhirter was for twenty-one years co-editor with Norris McWhirter of the *Guinness Book of Records* which they had started in 1954. Before his death it had already set its own record for any copyright book by selling more than 25 million copies in thirteen languages. He was also the author of the *Centenary History of Oxford University Rugby Football Club* (1969) and the *Centenary History of the Rugby Football Union* (1971). He served for twenty years as the honorary press officer for the Victoria Cross and George Cross Association.

In 1957 he married Rosemary Joy Hamilton, daughter of Leslie Charles Hamilton Grice, who worked for Nestlé. They had two sons. On 27 November 1975 McWhirter was shot by two Irish Republican Army terrorists at the front door of his home in Village Road, Enfield, and died shortly afterwards in hospital. In the previous weeks he had campaigned to raise £50,000 bounties for people who gave information leading to conviction for the IRA terrorist campaign in London which had killed fifty-four people. On the initiative of his friends the Ross McWhirter Foundation was established with £100,000 subscribed by admirers. It sought to advance Ross McWhirter's qualities of 'good citizenship . . . personal initiative and leadership, and personal courage as an example to others'.

[Norris McWhirter, *Ross: The Story of a Shared Life*, 1976; *All England Law Reports*; personal knowledge.] HARRIS OF HIGH CROSS

MADARIAGA, SALVADOR DE (1886–1978), writer, professor, and diplomat, was born 23 July 1886 at La Coruña, Spain, the second child of José de Madariaga, colonel in the Spanish Army, and his wife, Maria de la Ascensión Rojo. After graduating from the Instituto del Cardenal Cisneros, Madrid, he went in 1900 to Paris to study at the Collège Chaptal. Although naturally inclined towards letters, at the instigation of his father he followed a scientific and technical career, entering in 1906 the prestigious École Polytechnique, and two years later the École Nationale Supérieure des Mines. After graduation he returned to Spain in 1911 and joined the Compañía del Ferrocarril del Norte as a mining engineer.

In 1912 he married at Glasgow Constance Helen (died 1970), eldest daughter of Edmund Archibald, a meteorologist, youngest son of Sir Thomas Archibald [q.v.]; they had two daughters, Nieves, writer and poet, and Isabel, reader in Russian studies in the University of London and historian.

While conscientiously following his chosen career, he began writing under a pseudonym for various Madrid newspapers on French and English topics, and establishing contacts with literary and political circles in the capital. In 1916 he finally decided to abandon his technical career to devote himself to writing. He moved to London, from where he reported on World War I for the Spanish press. In 1920 he published his first book of essays in English, *Shelley and Calderón* (1920). He left London for Geneva in 1921 to become a member of the press section, League of Nations secretariat, and in the following year he was appointed director of the disarmament section, a post which he held until the end of 1927. He left the service of the League to occupy the newly created chair of Spanish at Oxford, which he held from 1928 to 1931. During this time he published *Disarmament* (1929), and essays in collective psychology, *Englishmen, Frenchmen, Spaniards* (1928), his first historical work *Spain* (1930), as well as various other books, thus initiating an outstanding and prolific literary career uninterrupted until his death at the age of ninety-two.

While on a lecture tour in Mexico and Cuba in 1931 the Spanish Republic was proclaimed, and his academic career ended when the republican government appointed him ambassador in Washington, a post which he held briefly, for in January of the following year he was transferred to the embassy in Paris, and was also nominated permanent Spanish delegate at the League of Nations. There he took an active and influential part in League affairs, particularly in the Manchurian and Abyssinian debates. He presided over the committee of five and the committee of thirteen, set up to negotiate a solution.

When in July 1936 the Spanish civil war broke out he took up residence in London, where he devoted himself to historical research. On the outbreak of World War II he moved to Oxford, where he continued his research. There followed the biographies of *Christopher Columbus* (1939), *Hernán Cortes* (1941), and *Bolívar* (1952), *The Rise of the Spanish American Empire* (1947), and *The Fall of the Spanish American Empire* (1947). He profited from the historical material accumulated to write one of the most successful of his novels, *The Heart of Jade* (1944). He wrote all these works also in Spanish; they were translated into many languages. From this fertile period dates the essay *On Hamlet* (1948). He also wrote poetry, plays, and innumerable articles for the world press.

During World War II and for a period of nine years he broadcast weekly from the BBC to Spanish America. After the war he became prominent in European affairs and was a fervent promoter of European unity. He founded and presided over the European College of Bruges (1949–64). He was a founder member, president, and honorary president of Liberal International, as well as president of its cultural commission. He was honorary president of the Congress for the Liberty of Culture (Paris, 1950). Numerous honours, which reflect the world-wide respect in which he was held, were bestowed on him: gold medals of the universities of Yale and Berne; honorary doctorates of the universities of Arequipa, Liège, Lille, Lima, Oxford, Poitiers, and Princeton; honorary fellowship of Exeter College, Oxford; the grand cross of the orders of the Spanish Republic, the Legion of Honour (France), Jade in Gold (China), Aztec Eagle (Mexico), White Lion (Czechoslovakia), and Alfonso el Sabio (Spain), among others. In 1967 he received the Hanseatic Goethe prize of the University of Hamburg and in 1973 the Charlemagne prize of the city of Aachen.

On 18 November 1970, at Oxford, he married, secondly, Mrs Emilia Rauman, daughter of Dr Lajos Szekely, a barrister and head of the Hungarian bar for many years. Mrs Rauman had been his constant collaborator since 1938, and was responsible for translating his books and lectures into German, Italian, and Hungarian. Soon afterwards, and mainly for reasons of health, he left Oxford to take up residence in Locarno. In April 1976 he visited Spain after an absence of forty years; he was then able to deliver his inaugural address—delayed because of the civil war and Franco—to the Real Academia Española, to which he had been elected in 1936.

Madariaga, who considered himself a citizen of the world, was a man of diverse talents. Always a scintillating conversationalist and lecturer, in three languages, he had an intellect of rare brilliance which never deserted him. He died in Locarno 14 December 1978.

[S. de Madariaga, *Morning Without Noon, Memoirs*, 1974; private information; personal knowledge.] J. L. Gili

MAKARIOS III (MOUSKOS, MICHAEL) (1913–1977), archbishop and first president of Cyprus, was born 13 August 1913 at Ano Panayia near Paphos, Cyprus, the eldest child of Christodoulos Mouskos, a peasant farmer, and his wife Eleni. He was educated at the village school, the monastery of Kykko, and the Pan-Cypriot high school in Nicosia. After ordination as a deacon on 7 August 1938, taking the name of Makarios, he went to Athens to study theology and law at the university. On 13 January 1946 he was ordained priest. In the same year he won a scholarship to study at Massachusetts University. While there, he learned unexpectedly in 1948 that he had been elected bishop of Kition.

Upon installation, he became a member of the Cypriot Ethnarchy (national leadership) and began to promote the campaign for *enosis* (union with Greece). In January 1950 he organized a plebiscite among Greek Cypriots, who voted overwhelmingly for *enosis*. While the results were being carried to the United Nations, he succeeded as archbishop on 18 October 1950.

He was a devout churchman, but he also used his sermons to preach *enosis*. In 1951 he urged the Greek government to raise the issue at the UN. Next year he met Colonel George Grivas to discuss more active measures. Since the British government refused to discuss *enosis*, in 1954 the Greek government agreed to appeal to the UN. Early in 1955 Makarios sanctioned a campaign of sabotage (excluding bloodshed) by Grivas's National Organization of Cypriot Fighters (EOKA). The first explosions took place on 1 April 1955. In the same month Makarios attended the first conference of non-aligned nations at Bandung.

During the next four years Makarios lost control of the violence. EOKA fought the Turkish Cypriots as well as the British. Although negotiations were opened, Makarios spurned every

British offer of self-government as insufficient. The British lost patience and deported him on 9 March 1956 to the Seychelles. During his exile things went from bad to worse.

In March 1957 Makarios was released, but not being allowed to return to Cyprus he settled in Athens. When the British government decided in 1958 to impose a new constitution, giving the Turks a formal status in Cyprus and hinting at partition, Makarios decided to accept independence in place of *enosis*.

Early in 1959 the crisis was resolved by the Zurich and London agreements, establishing an independent republic. Both *enosis* and partition were excluded, and Britain retained two sovereign bases. Having reluctantly acquiesced, Makarios was elected president on 13 December 1959, with a Turkish vice-president. The republic was inaugurated on 16 August 1960, and joined the Commonwealth in 1961. Makarios still hoped to achieve *enosis* eventually but he made a visit of reconciliation to Turkey in November 1962.

The complex constitution soon broke down. When Makarios proposed to amend it in December 1963, communal fighting began again. The UN intervened with a peace-keeping force (UNFICYP) in March 1964. Makarios allowed his National Guard, commanded by Grivas, to be reinforced illegally from Greece. He rebuffed proposals by UN mediators, appealed to the Soviet Union for help, and toured the Third World seeking support.

In April 1967 the threat to his position was aggravated by a military *coup* in Athens. The Greek junta and Grivas between them almost provoked war with Turkey over Cyprus in November. Grivas and most of the Greek forces were then forced to withdraw. Mutual attempts at assassination followed: an attack on the Greek dictator, Colonel Papadopoulos, instigated from Cyprus in August 1968; an attack on Makarios on 8 March 1970, and on other occasions.

Makarios was now under pressure from many quarters: the communists, the ultra-nationalists, the Greek junta, Grivas (who returned clandestinely in August 1971), and dissident bishops (who criticized his combination of political and ecclesiastical offices). But his popularity was confirmed by re-election to the presidency in 1968 and 1973.

He faced a supreme crisis in 1974, when the Greek junta plotted to destroy him, using Greek officers in the National Guard and a revived terrorist organization (EOKA-B). Makarios exposed the plot in a letter to the new Greek president on 2 July. On 15 July an attack was made on his residence, but he escaped first to Paphos, then to a British base and to London. The belief that he was politically finished was dispelled when he arrived in New York and addressed the UN on 19 July. Next day the Turks invaded Cyprus, ostensibly exercising their treaty right to restore the status quo. On 23 July the Greek dictatorship fell.

Makarios returned to Cyprus in triumph on 7 December 1974, but the status quo could not be restored. The Turks occupied two-fifths of the island, which they proclaimed a 'Turkish Federated State' in 1975. Discussions at the UN and between the parties concerned failed to produce any improvement during Makarios's remaining years. He died in Nicosia 3 August 1977, and was buried near the monastery of Kykko, within sight of his native village. He had failed to achieve his life's ambition, but he had established himself as a national hero to the Greeks—too large-scale a hero for his small island to accommodate.

[*The Times*, 4 August 1977; Stanley Mayes, *Makarios: a Biography*, 1981.]

C. M. Woodhouse

MALLABY, Sir (HOWARD) GEORGE (CHARLES) (1902–1978), public servant and teacher, was born 17 February 1902 at Worthing, the younger son and the youngest of the three children of William Calthorpe Mallaby, an actor, and his wife, Katharine Mary Frances Miller. He was educated at Radley College and Merton College, Oxford, where he was an open exhibitioner and obtained a third class in classical honour moderations in 1922. A sound classic, his tastes in English literature were strongly influenced by H. W. Garrod [q.v.], who confirmed him in the admiration for Wordsworth he had already acquired.

After a year as assistant master at Clifton College, he held the same post at St. Edward's School, Oxford, 1924–6. A temporary breakdown in health led in 1926 to a short recuperative visit to South Africa, where he taught at the Diocesan College, Rondebosch. He returned to St. Edward's where he remained as assistant master and housemaster (1931) from 1927 to 1935. He was an exceptional schoolmaster. His impressive presence gave him complete authority, in which his gentle idiosyncratic wit provided a relaxed atmosphere. Teaching literature as well as classics, he had a generous understanding of adolescent writing. He had a sure eye for deficiencies, yet his criticism was always tactful. This talent for inspiring confidence also marked his coaching of Rugby football, in which game he was himself a fine player. In personal problems his mature judgement was valued not only by pupils, but by colleagues, some of whom he commemorated appreciatively in his own reminiscences. In later years, as a governor of St. Edward's, chairman of the council of Radley College, and vice-chairman of Bedford College,

University of London, he drew profitably on his own practical experience as a teacher.

From 1935 to 1938 he was headmaster of St. Bees School, Cumberland. Outside the educational world, his powers of organization and wise negotiation became recognized. In 1938–9 he was district commissioner for the Special Area of West Cumberland, where he was successful in attracting industrial concerns needed to alleviate unemployment.

World War II gave him scope to develop these administrative talents. He remained briefly in the north-west as deputy regional transport commissioner for North Western Region. After working as a General Staff officer in the Directorate of Military Operations at the War Office from December 1940, he was posted to the Joint Planning Staff in mid-1942, and remained there until the end of the war, having been secretary of it from mid-1943. The Joint Planning Staff was a key part of the central machine for the higher direction of the war, and in this capacity he attended the great conferences at Cairo, Quebec, and finally Potsdam. His efficiency and ease, under exacting conditions, were notable. For his work, he was appointed OBE in 1945, and was awarded the US Legion of Merit in January 1946. With peace, after a short spell as secretary of the National Trust (1945–6), he became an assistant secretary in the Ministry of Defence (1946–8), and then secretary-general of the Brussels Treaty Defence Organization (1948–50). This was a task for which there was no precedent. Of all his appointments, it provided him with the greatest interest and satisfaction, involving the principles of international co-operation, on which NATO became based. His charm, authority, and persuasive powers were used to weld together an international staff of great complexity, and of interests which often threatened to diverge. Historically, it was his greatest achievement.

As a direct result, he became from 1950 to 1954 an under-secretary in the Cabinet Office, and a key figure in foreign and defence policy. His appreciation of diverse personalities in government made his contribution, though unobtrusive, far more than merely secretarial. He was known as someone who could always be trusted to resolve an urgent difficulty. In some ways this was a slight disservice to his personal career, since he was apt to be seconded to help in a crisis wherever and whenever it might occur. For instance, he was transferred at short notice in 1954 to undertake some delicate negotiations in Kenya, at the time of the Mau Mau rising, as secretary of the war council and council of ministers; Sir Winston Churchill himself is said to have made noises of protest at this switch.

From 1955 to 1957 he found congenial work as deputy secretary of the University Grants Committee, in which his academic interests and administrative flair were happily joined. There followed another overseas appointment as high commissioner for the United Kingdom in New Zealand (1957–9). He had married, in 1955, Elizabeth Greenwood Locker, daughter of Hubert Edward Brooke, private banker. Her high spirits and his quiet sense of fun—perfect foils for one another—made a delightful impact on society there, and aroused goodwill wherever they went. He had one stepson and two stepdaughters.

Appointed in 1959 as first Civil Service commissioner in charge of recruitment to the Civil and Diplomatic Services, he exercised fruitfully his gifts of humanity, humour, and judgement. His decisions were the result of high standards, allied with sympathetic encouragement toward the men and women whose claims he examined; the unseen effect on public life was immeasurable, and later made him sought after as a private recruitment consultant in many organizations. He also did a considerable amount of work for the Overseas Service Resettlement Bureau.

He retired in 1964 to live in East Anglia. His scholarly interests had been maintained throughout his life, and this was recognized by his election in that year to an extraordinary fellowship at Churchill College, Cambridge; he received a Cambridge MA in the year following. His first book had been for the Cambridge University Press, when, as early as 1932, he produced a selection of Wordsworth's poems, original in that it included 2,000 lines of 'The Prelude'. On the centenary of Wordsworth's death, he wrote in 1950 an admirable short critical life, *Wordsworth: a Tribute*, which forms a lucid and balanced introduction to the poet. In 1970 he selected and edited with an introduction *Poems by William Wordsworth* for the Folio Society. He also published two books of reminiscences, *From my Level* (1965) and *Each in his Office* (1972). These portray, with wit and affection, his many acquaintances, from statesmen to schoolmasters. To this Dictionary he contributed the notice of H. W. Garrod.

His activities continued to be varied. In 1967 he was chairman of the committee on the staffing of local government, which culminated in the Mallaby report, and in 1971 he headed the Hong Kong government salaries commission. In 1972–3 he was chairman of the special committee on the structure of the Rugby Football Union. Though not all the committee's recommendations were adopted, a by-product was the important alteration in the rules for kicking to touch, which revivified the game. His final work was a small booklet, *Local Government Councillors—their Motives and Manners* (1976), for which he chose the tongue-in-cheek title, and which contrived to quote Charles Lamb and Samuel Johnson in a far-sighted and inspiring little study.

He was appointed CMG in 1953 and KCMG in 1958. He died at his home in Chevington, Suffolk, 8 December 1978, having devoted his life to 'human beings, sometimes tenacious, sometimes frail', as he himself understandingly wrote.

[George Mallaby, *From my Level*, 1965, and *Each in his Office*, 1972; private information; personal knowledge.] ROBERT GITTINGS

MALLOWAN, SIR MAX EDGAR LUCIEN (1904–1978), archaeologist, was born 6 May 1904 in London, the eldest of the three sons (there were no daughters) of Frederick Mallowan, former officer in the Austrian Horse Artillery and in Britain quality-arbitrator, and his wife, Marguerite Duvivier, of Paris, poetess. He records in *Mallowan's Memoirs* (1977) that at little more than four years of age he excavated Victorian china sherds from deep in 'a jet black soil' in Bedford Gardens, Kensington. Their photograph he kept all his life. He was educated at Lancing, where he was a contemporary of Tom Driberg (later Lord Bradwell, q.v.), (Sir) Roger Fulford, Hugh (later Lord) Molson, Humphrey (later Lord) Trevelyan, and Evelyn Waugh [q.v.], and at New College, Oxford. He obtained a fourth class in classical honour moderations in 1923 and a third in *literae humaniores* in 1925. Thanks to a chance meeting just after his final examinations when he said he feared he might 'be condemned to the Indian Civil Service' he was with the recommendation of the warden, H. A. L. Fisher [q.v.], accepted by (Sir) C. Leonard Woolley [q.v.] as an assistant at Ur of the Chaldees. He later wrote the notice of Woolley for this Dictionary, as well as that of Margaret Murray. It was while working for Woolley at Ur that he met (Dame) Agatha Christie [q.v.] whom he married in 1930, a marriage of true minds that continued until her death in 1976.

Except for the years 1940–5, when he served in the RAFVR as a liaison officer with Allied forces and a civilian affairs officer in North Africa, the rest of his life was devoted to 'filling in the blank pages of history', to quote his own words, firstly as an assistant, soon as a leader of expeditions, finally in writing and academic and administrative posts. He came to rank with Woolley and Seton Lloyd as a pioneer whose work formed the frame on which all subsequent Mesopotamian archaeology hung, and was himself very conscious of his place in a long tradition, delighting for instance that the British School of Archaeology in Iraq, which he was largely responsible for reactivating after the war of 1939–45, could resume at Nimrud 'the work which Austen Layard was obliged to abandon at the outbreak of the Crimean War'.

After five years as assistant to Woolley and a spell with Reginald Campbell Thompson [q.v.], under whom he made a markedly determined twenty-one-metre deep shaft to virgin soil through the Quyunjik mound at Nineveh, he became field director in a long series of expeditions jointly sponsored by the British Museum and the British School of Archaeology in Iraq, then recently founded with a legacy from Gertrude Bell [q.v.]. At the age of twenty-eight, at Arpachiyah, his discoveries showed the prehistoric villager to have been artistic, ingenious, and energetic and, too, a user of cream-bowls, in Mallowan's words, 'exactly similar to the metal milk cans used in the village of Arpachiyah today'. His writing constantly reflected this interest in the humanity revealed by the artefacts he unearthed.

From Arpachiyah he moved to north Syria, first to Chagar Bazar, then in 1937 to Tell Brak, selected for excavation after a particularly methodical survey, where he discovered the third millenium shrines called the Eye Temple and the Palace of Naram-Sin.

In 1947 he returned to Iraq as director of the British School and soon began his major work at Nimrud, a task that was to be carried on for twelve years. The accumulated art treasures, inscribed texts, and architectural remains discovered in this period formed a prodigious addition to knowledge of the past and his account, *Nimrud and its Remains* (2 vols., 1966), was hailed as a monumental work 'rivalling the great classics of its nineteenth-century predecessors' (Seton Lloyd).

Nimrud was the crown of his work in the field. In 1962 while writing the book he was elected a fellow of All Souls College, Oxford (he became an emeritus fellow in 1976), and gave up the chair in western Asiatic archaeology at London University which he had accepted in 1947. This latter period of his life was busy in the extreme, and thick with honours. He was FSA and became FBA in 1954. He was, among other things, president of the British Institute of Persian Studies (1961), vice-president of the British Academy (1961–2), and membre de l'Académie Française des Inscriptions et Belle-Lettres (1964). He was appointed CBE in 1960 and knighted in 1968. He was a trustee of the British Museum (1973–8), editor of *Iraq* (1948–71), advisory editor of *Antiquity*, and editor of the Penguin books Near Eastern and Western Asiatic series (1948–65). He was noted, too, for never failing to answer requests for assistance from students or colleagues. The busy tenor of those days can be appreciated in Professor Glyn Daniel's recollection of him after a London meeting hailing a taxi and saying simply 'Wallingford'.

In 1977 he married, secondly, Barbara,

daughter of Captain R. F. Parker, RN; she had been his assistant in Iraq. He died 19 August 1978 at Greenway House, Churston Ferrars, Devon, the home he had bought with his first wife in 1939 whose trees and rare garden were an abiding interest.

[Max Mallowan, *Mallowan's Memoirs*, 1977, and *Twenty-five Years of Mesopotamian Discovery, 1932–1956*, 1956; Seton Lloyd, *Foundations in the Dust* (1980 edn.); private information.] H. R. F. KEATING

MALTBY, SIR PAUL COPELAND (1892–1971), air vice-marshal, was born 5 August 1892 at Allippey, India, the younger son and fourth in the family of five children of Christopher James Maltby, tea-planter, and his wife Jessie, daughter of an eminent Indian civil servant, William Copeland Capper. He was educated at Bedford School and at the Royal Military College, Sandhurst, of which an uncle, Colonel W. B. Capper, was commandant. Commissioned in the Royal Welch Fusiliers, he served from 1911 to 1914 with his regiment in India and France.

Perhaps inspired by the knowledge that another uncle, Colonel J. E. Capper, had taken part in the first flight over London by a British military airship, Maltby joined the Royal Flying Corps on secondment in 1915. Commanding a squadron from 1916, he ended the war a substantive major and temporary lieutenant-colonel. A daring reconnaissance in 1916 earned him appointment to the DSO in 1917.

In 1919 Maltby accepted a permanent commission in the Royal Air Force in the belief that he would not be called upon to make a formal renunciation of his commission in the army. He commanded a squadron at Quetta from 1920 to 1924, attended courses at the RAF Staff College in 1926–7 and the Imperial Defence College in 1931, and from 1932 to 1934 was commandant of the Central Flying School. At the height of the Abyssinian crisis he commanded the Royal Air Force in the Mediterranean and served as a nominated member of the council of Malta. He was promoted wing commander in 1925, group captain in 1932, air commodore in 1936, and air vice-marshal in 1938.

During the next three years Maltby commanded in turn a training group and two army co-operation groups, and served briefly as senior air staff officer at GHQ Home Forces. He was posted on 5 November 1941 to command the Royal Air Force in Northern Ireland, but eight days later was ordered to Singapore for special duties at GHQ Far East.

He arrived almost on the eve of the Japanese onslaught. The commander-in-chief, Air Chief Marshal Sir H. R. M. Brooke-Popham [q.v.], had been told to rely in the absence of a strong fleet on air power, but he had no air striking force apart from a few light bombers and obsolete torpedo-bombers. About half his aircraft in Malaya were lost on the first day. British North Borneo was almost defenceless. Hong Kong, where Maltby's brother had recently assumed command of the land forces, was not expected to hold out for more than a few weeks.

When, early in 1942, GHQ Far East was abolished and the western Allies set up a unified command for the purpose of defending a line from Singapore through the Indonesian archipelago to Darwin, Maltby became deputy to the air commander in Malaya, Air Vice-Marshal C. W. H. Pulford. He took a leading part in the preparation of plans for a staged withdrawal to the Dutch East Indies and the formation of two groups into which an air force augmented by new arrivals was to be divided. The result of a disagreement between Pulford and his superior formation about the timing of the withdrawal was that Pulford twice refused to embark in aircraft sent to fetch him. Ultimately he obeyed orders to leave Singapore in a launch which was attacked by Japanese aircraft. With other survivors, he was marooned on a desolate island where he died. Maltby was flown to Java, where he did his best to weld depleted squadrons into a coherent air force, and set up an early-warning and fighter-control system staffed largely by local volunteers. But the fate of Java was sealed when the Dutch Admiral Doorman, with no maritime reconnaissance aircraft to help him, lost the naval battle of the Java Sea. Maltby was captured in April 1942.

On his return from a Japanese prisoner-of-war camp in 1945, Maltby took charge of the compilation of reports on operations in Malaya. From 1946 to 1962 he filled the more congenial role of sergeant-at-arms (Black Rod) at the House of Lords. His honours and awards, apart from his DSO and a World War I mention in dispatches, included the AFC (1919), CB (1941), KBE (1946), and KCVO (1962). He was appointed by Queen Wilhelmina of the Netherlands a grand officer of the Order of Orange Nassau, and from 1956 was a deputy lieutenant for the county of Southampton. He married at Bombay in 1921 Winifred Russell, daughter of James Harper Paterson, business man, of Edinburgh; they had two sons (the elder of whom was killed in action in 1945) and a daughter.

Addicted in youth to pranks which sometimes landed him in trouble, Maltby was better known in later years as an enthusiastic gardener and remaker of gardens. Tall and slim, he both looked and always was at heart a soldier. Fashionable theories of air power did not shake his conviction that air forces ought to help land forces. The courage, energy, and sense of dedication to a cause which were part of the Capper inheritance were tempered in him by a sensibility which might have precluded the ruthlessness sometimes demanded of commanders-in-chief in war. The matter was not put to the test, but what he was given to do he did well. His exertions in the closing stages of the campaign in Malaya saved many lives. That Pulford's was not one of them was a sword in his heart. Maltby died at Rotherwick 2 July 1971.

[Air and Army Historical Branches, Ministry of Defence; Royal Military Academy, Sandhurst; private information.] BASIL COLLIER

MALVERN, first VISCOUNT (1883–1971), Rhodesian statesman. [See HUGGINS, GODFREY MARTIN.]

MANN, ARTHUR HENRY (1876–1972), journalist, was born at Warwick 7 July 1876, the eldest of thirteen children of James Wight Mann, merchant, mayor, and freeman of Warwick, and his wife, Annie Elizabeth, daughter of William Lake, of Warwick. He was educated at Warwick School and captained the cricket XI. At seventeen he was apprenticed as a reporter on the *Western Mail* in Cardiff where he played cricket for Glamorgan.

After three years as a reporter Mann became sub-editor of the company's evening paper. In 1900 he moved to Birmingham where he spent five years as sub-editor of the *Birmingham Daily Mail* and seven as editor of the *Birmingham Evening Dispatch*. When the ownership of the latter paper changed hands in 1912 Mann went to work for (Sir) Edward Hulton [q.v.] in London, initially as London editor of the *Manchester Daily Dispatch* and from 1915 onwards as editor of the *Evening Standard* where he started Londoner's Diary.

In December 1919 Mann was offered the editorship of the *Yorkshire Post*, a position he held with unusual distinction for twenty years. With his appointment as managing editor in 1928 he was given broad authority also over the editorial policy and staffing of the two other papers in the group. Mann's editorship was associated with a steady growth in the prestige, if not in the circulation, of the *Post* and will be chiefly remembered for the paper's resolute opposition to Neville Chamberlain's policy of appeasement in 1938–9, as well as for the part it played in precipitating the abdication crisis in 1936 when Mann on his own initiative published a strong leader on the bishop of Bradford's address admonishing the King.

Mann believed that a serious newspaper had a responsibility to inform and educate rather than entertain its readers, and that it needed a directing mind behind it to give it character and to preserve its independence. As editor, he insisted on his right to decide what line the *Yorkshire Post* should take on important issues, and on appeasement he made it clear that he would resign if overruled by his board. The fact that the *Post* was a Conservative newspaper did not in his view require it to lend uncritical support to the party, any more than it had in 1922 when it had distanced itself from the Conservative leadership in advocating the break-up of the coalition. The board chairman, Rupert Beckett, constantly urged him to moderate his criticism of Chamberlain, but Mann stuck to his guns, and when an attempt was made at a shareholders' meeting to have the paper's policy changed, Beckett stood by him.

Mann's effectiveness as an editor rested on a flair for news, shrewd judgement of people, great strength and simplicity of character, and deep concern for the national interest as he saw it. A staunch, but not a diehard Conservative, he was twice offered—and twice declined—a knighthood in the 1920s, writing that 'a journalist who receives a title, particularly if that title be regarded as a recognition of political services, may lessen his power to aid the causes he has at heart'.

Mann wrote little himself for publication. He was not an erudite person and spent only a few weeks of his life outside Britain, but he was well informed on foreign affairs and personally acquainted with many of the leading figures in the governments of his day. In his assessment of Hitler's intentions he relied heavily on his chief leader writer, Charles Tower, who knew Germany well and had studied *Mein Kampf.* Any lingering doubts that Mann may have had about Hitler's character were finally dispelled by the 'Night of the Long Knives' on 30 June 1934.

Declining circulation and deteriorating finances in 1936 brought Mann into conflict with the business managers of the *Yorkshire Post* who wanted to cut editorial costs and seek increased readership by reducing the price of the paper. The issue was temporarily decided in Mann's favour, but it came up again at the beginning of the war when the board decided to merge the *Post* and the *Leeds Mercury* and to sell the combined paper for 1d. This led to Mann's resignation in November 1939.

Mann was appointed CH in the 1941 New Year honours list. Previously, in 1934, he had received an honorary LL D from Leeds University. He served as a governor of the BBC from 1941 to 1946 and as a trustee of the *Observer* from 1945 to 1956 when he resigned because he disagreed with the paper's criticism of government policy over Suez. He was chairman of the Press Association 1937–8 and became a director of the Argus Press in 1946.

Mann was greatly respected by his staff, although some were a little overawed by his imposing figure and seemingly aloof manner. In private he displayed a warm and outgoing personality, had a keen sense of humour, and was a generous host. Always an optimist, he indulged a lifelong passion for racing; golf and bridge were his other favourite diversions. Active and alert almost to the end, he died at Folkestone 23 July 1972, aged ninety-six.

Mann was twice married, first in 1898 to Aida, daughter of Louis Maggi, ship chandler, of Cardiff (died 1948), and secondly in 1948 to Alice Mabel (died 1968), daughter of Frank Wright, manufacturer of buttons, town councillor, and magistrate, of Birmingham. His relationship with his second wife, which extended over more than fifty years, was a singularly happy one; they had one son.

[*The Times*, 28 July 1972; private information; personal knowledge.] E. P. WRIGHT

MANNHEIM, HERMANN (1889–1974), criminologist, was born in Berlin 26 October 1889, the only child of Wilhelm Mannheim and his wife, Clara Marcuse. He came from a well-to-do background: his father represented a German firm in the Baltic seaport of Libau, where he was also vice-president of the chamber of commerce. After tuition at home and at a classical *Gymnasium*, Mannheim took up, at the age of eighteen, the study of law and political science at the universities of Munich, Freiburg, Strasburg, and Königsberg. By 1913 he had obtained the degree of Doctor of Laws. In World War I he served in the German artillery in Russia and in France; towards the end he was appointed judge of a court martial. By 1932 he had become a judge of the Kammergericht in Berlin (the highest court for the whole of Prussia) as well as Professor extraordinarius of the prestigious law faculty of the University of Berlin. He had to his credit many publications and was held in high esteem in governmental, judicial, and academic circles. He was barely forty-five years old.

The advent of the Nazi regime shattered this honourable and substantial achievement. He was forced to relinquish his professorship. Aware where all this would end he also retired from the bench, and in January 1934 this proud man moved to London to start life afresh. He became a naturalized British subject in 1940. Inevitably, the process of readjustment could not but be painful and tortuous. Yet, his capacity to face this new challenge was truly impressive. In this his wife, Mona Mark, whom he married in 1919, proved a gallant companion: they had no children. He switched the focus of his interest from criminal law and procedure to criminology and penal policy, and considerably improved his command of English. The London School of Economics, with its rich and adventurous tradition in social sciences, was the natural intellectual home for him. In 1935 he was appointed an honorary part-time lecturer in criminology. A year later he received the award of the Leon fellowship. In 1944 he became a permanent full-time lecturer and two years later the reader in criminology—the first post of its kind in Great Britain. He retired in 1955. He was a dedicated and enthusiastic teacher.

Between 1939 and 1965 he produced eight publications either as the sole author, co-author, or editor. In addition he wrote many articles, notes, and reviews: in the *British Journal of Criminology* alone there were seventy pieces. His most thought-provoking, original, and enduring books are: *The Dilemma of Penal Reform* (1939), in which he traced the implications of Bentham's famous principle of 'lesser eligibility' throughout the penological spectrum; *Criminal Justice and Social Reconstruction* (1946; 2nd impr. 1949), which is rightly recognized as his most influential and widely read work; and *Prediction Methods in Relation to Borstal Training* (with Leslie T. Wilkins, 1955), the first authoritative study of this kind in England. *Social Aspects of Crime in England Between the Wars* (1940) was too ambitious and turned out to be rather uneven but it contained many useful hints for future researches into the environmental contents of crime. *Group Problems in Crime and Punishment* (1955) was largely a collection of his major articles, which in spite of the passage of time still repay rereading. But his three other books (*War and Crime*, 1941; *Young Offenders*, with A. M. Carr-Saunders and E. C. Rhodes, 1942; and *Juvenile Delinquency in an English Middletown*, 1948), though informative at the time of their appearance, were rather mechanical and pedestrian. *Pioneers in Criminology*, which he edited (1st edn. 1960; 2nd and enlarged edn. 1972), was a splendid pedagogical tool. *Comparative Criminology* (2 vols., 1965) failed to become the *magnum opus*, although it was well received, especially on the continent of Europe. An Italian translation appeared in 1972, a German in 1974. The treatise was confined to the strictly criminological aspect of the subject. It appeared at a time when criminological theory was changing direction and seemed in England and the United States already old-fashioned.

Mannheim's intellectual vitality was remarkable: as late as 1975 there appeared (posthumously) his massive comparative study of recidivism 'Rückfall and Prognose' in the new edition of the *Handwörterbuch der Kriminologie*, Berlin, 1975, pp. 38–93). He helped greatly the Institute for the Study and Treatment of Delinquency; he was the founding editor of the *British Journal of Delinquency* (later *British Journal of Criminology*); he helped launch the International Library of Criminology and the British Society of Criminology. For twenty-five years he was closely associated with the Howard League for

Penal Reform. He played a fruitful part in the work of the International Society of Criminology.

It is to the credit of the Federal Republic of Germany that he was appointed in 1952 to the rank of retired president of the division of Court of Appeal and in 1962 he received the Grosses Verdienstkreuz der Bundesrepublik Deutschland. In the same year he was awarded the Golden Beccaria medal of the German Society of Criminology. A volume of the German Encyclopaedia of Criminology (2nd edn. 1975) was dedicated to his memory. He was awarded the Coronation medal in 1953 and appointed OBE in 1959. He received honorary doctorates from the universities of Utrecht (1957) and Wales (1970) and was made an honorary fellow of the London School of Economics (1965). In 1965 he was presented with a Festschrift edited by three of his former students (*Criminology in Transition*).

There were many up and down the country as well as abroad who were taught by him and in their turn taught others. He was short in stature but robust, mild mannered but determined, sensitive but with a bite of his own. He maintained a formality characteristic of a German professor. He was disappointed that after so rich a contribution he was not made a professor by London University. It also grieved him that the first chair and Institute of Criminology found a home not in London but in Cambridge. Yet his reputation as a scholar–criminologist stands high and will remain high. Compelled to leave his country of birth he became a pioneer in the country which received him.

He died in London 20 January 1974.

[Private information; personal knowledge.]

LEON RADZINOWICZ

MANNING, OLIVIA MARY (1908–1980), novelist, was born in Portsmouth, 2 March 1908, the elder child and only daughter of Lieutenant-Commander Oliver Manning of the Royal Navy, and his wife, Olivia, daughter of David Morrow from Bangor, county Down. It was an unhappy domestic situation: the father, married before, was over forty when he remarried, and, having retired early from the navy, had little money apart from his service pension. A handsome womanizer, he was adored by his two children (the younger, Oliver, was killed in action in 1943) and nagged by his wife who came of Irish peasant stock with American roots. Olivia Manning's maternal grandfather was a slave-owner on the banks of the Missouri river. It was a fraught and mortifying childhood which Olivia Manning used so trenchantly in her short stories and early novels. This childhood insecurity and unhappiness was to shadow her personality and work. Childhood and adolescence described in her books are screams of pain and wounds remembered.

She was educated at Portsmouth Grammar School, and later studied art. Her ambition was to be a painter, and, although this was superseded by her writing, it contributed to the intensely visual descriptions of landscape in her work. *Artist Among the Missing* (1949)—a much underrated novel—testifies to her understanding of the medium she abandoned. Forced by poverty to earn her livelihood in her teens, she worked first in an architect's office in Portsmouth. Determined to get to London she left home and worked as a typist in a department store. Yet, using the pseudonym Jacob Morrow, she launched herself as a novelist, selling the copyright of three novels for £20 each. She was extremely poor, had insufficient money for food, and yet worked far into the night at her writing after a full day's office work.

Encouraged by Hamish Miles, an editor at Jonathan Cape, she finished her first literary novel, *The Wind Changes* (1937). It was autobiographical, depicting the struggles of an aspiring writer in London, a theme which eighteen years later she returned to, with greater maturity, in *The Doves of Venus* (1955). A silence of twelve years between her first and second novel she explained as the 'emotional upset' resulting from her brother's death. She drew attention to the fact that such a work gap was also the experience of Katherine Mansfield and Virginia Woolf [qq.v.], thereby firmly placing herself in the literary establishment.

This gap in fact provided her with material for her greatest and best-known works, the Balkan trilogy and the Levant trilogy. These consist of six interlinking novels based on her experience, starting in August 1939, immediately prior to World War II, when she married Reginald Donald Smith (died 1985), then a lecturer with the British Council and later a BBC drama producer and professor at the new university of Ulster. She travelled with him to Romania where she witnessed King Carol's abdication, the rise of Fascism, and the tyranny of a totalitarian regime. From Romania they escaped to Greece, then occupied by British troops who retreated at the advance of the German Army. In 1942 Olivia Manning was a press officer at the US embassy in Cairo; in 1943–4 she was press assistant at the Public Information Office in Jerusalem and in 1944–5 held the same position at the British Council in Jerusalem. In the novels the young watchful Harriet, newly wed, critical and sharp-tongued, is a self-portrait, and the ebullient, feckless, popular husband, Guy, is a study of her own husband. The books are in effect a ruthless and illuminating analysis of Olivia Manning's marriage.

The Great Fortune (1960), *The Spoilt City*

(1962), and *Friends and Heroes* (1965) comprise the Balkan trilogy which relates the progressive story of Harriet and Guy's relationship, while simultaneously (with a reporter's skill) it records the political and social scene and presents English non-combatants abroad during the early war years, viewing the majority of them as corrupt, mean, and self-centred. Olivia Manning's pitiless clarity about human frailty is directed at the greedy, ambitious, and pretentious. Her compassion—which goes deep—is given to the poor, the persecuted, and animals. Her historical touches are unobtrusively inserted into the tapestry of her overall design, authenticated with a sureness of touch and a sense of place. Her understanding of men dealing with other men, politically and socially, is remarkable. Her humour—dark though its implication often is—reaches a peak in her affectionate portrayal of a great comic character (Prince Yakimov), a tarnished yet innocent-at-heart anachronistic time-server.

Although there were twelve years between the completion of the Balkan trilogy and the Levant trilogy (with the publication of two further novels, *The Play Room*, 1969, and *The Rain Forest*, 1974, and one volume of stories, *A Romantic Hero*, 1967), it was with her last trilogy that Olivia Manning firmly established herself as one of Britain's most outstanding novelists, one who in maturity widened her canvas almost historically, as she juxtaposed her story of Harriet and Guy and important world events. In the Balkan trilogy war is a shadow from which Olivia Manning's protagonists are forever fleeing: in the Levant trilogy a war in the Middle East is the centrepiece of her canvas. Egypt, Jerusalem, and Syria are the landscape of the latter's three parts, *The Danger Tree* (1977), *The Battle Lost and Won* (1978), and *The Sum of Things*, published posthumously in the year of her death (1980). The Battle of Alamein is described with a near-Tolstoyan passion for detail, and Olivia Manning's ability to relate to a young man's first experience of battle is remarkable, for it is an area few women have so authenticated. Great sympathy is expressed for the fighting soldier, contempt for the establishment civilians and GHQ, and compassion for the poor and peasants. Death is the all-pervasive element, and love found to be an illusion. Her final coda reflects on 'the pernicious peace' to come, with which the survivors will have to cope.

In youth Olivia Manning was rather beautiful, in later years 'striking' was the adjective most applied to her physical presence. Slender and seemingly frail, her features were sharp but redeemed by the luminosity of her eyes which mostly looked at human beings to mock and at animals kindly. Between books she knew 'black despair', felt that she was not prolific enough, suffered from 'intellectual paralysis', and worried herself with literary reputations. A reputation for malice and gossip was probably the result of her abnormal honesty in that she would never truckle with any opinion she did not hold. She was devoted to the welfare of animals and increasingly concerned with environmental matters. She was very anxious about money, although she did fairly well and invested in property. She was loyal to her friends though she sorely tried their patience. At her best she was a delightful companion and full of quirky humour. She had an innate sense of elegance and surrounded herself with beautiful objects, paintings, and books. Physically she was not strong, and frequently suffered from illness. In 1976 she was appointed CBE.

She died suddenly, of a stroke, at Ryde in the Isle of Wight when on holiday, 23 July 1980. The Isle of Wight was a place where she had been most happy in childhood with her brother. She once said that her aim as a writer was 'to express the inexpressible'. She was happy, she said, only when writing. She had no children.

[Kay Dick, *Friends and Friendship*, 1974; private information; personal knowledge.]

KAY DICK

MANNINGHAM-BULLER, REGINALD EDWARD, fourth baronet, and first VISCOUNT DILHORNE (1905–1980), lord chancellor, was born at Amersham 1 August 1905, the eldest of the five children and only son of (Lieutenant-Colonel) Mervyn Edward Manningham-Buller, later third baronet, a former MP for Kettering and Northampton, and his wife, Lilah Constance, daughter of Charles Compton William Cavendish, third Baron Chesham. Sir Mervyn was tenth in descent from Sir Edward Coke (1552–1634, q.v.), lord chief justice, and fifth in descent from Sir Francis Buller (1746–1800, q.v.), the youngest man ever to be made a judge in England. After Eton, Manningham-Buller went up to Magdalen College, Oxford. He was placed in the third class of the honour school of jurisprudence in 1926, and just missed his blue for rowing.

Manningham-Buller was called to the bar (Inner Temple) in 1927, and practised on the common law side with chambers at 2 Harcourt Buildings. His practice as a junior was steady rather than sensational, but in 1946, after war service in the judge advocate-general's department, he was able to take silk. Meanwhile he had been returned unopposed in 1943 as Conservative MP for Daventry. In 1950 the constituency was reorganized as the southern division of Northamptonshire, and Manningham-Buller held it until 1962, increasing his majority at each election.

In 1951 (Sir) Winston Churchill, in whose brief caretaker government in 1945 he had been parliamentary secretary to the minister of works, appointed him solicitor-general. In 1954 he was sworn of the Privy Council in June and succeeded Sir Lionel Heald as attorney-general in October. As he held this post until 1962, he was a law officer of the Crown continuously for ten years and nine months—a period five months longer than that achieved by the first Viscount Finlay [q.v.] but four years shorter than that of the first Earl of Mansfield [q.v.].

He took some time to obtain the respect of the bar, whose members found it hard to believe that someone from such a background could have the industry and ability necessary to discharge the responsibilities of his position. The government departments, in particular the Inland Revenue, and the judges were quicker to discern the massive talents hidden under that formidable exterior. 'During his term of office first as Solicitor-General and then as Attorney-General it was not unusual to find him, when all had gone home, working in the small hours in his room just off the central lobby, a pipe firmly in his mouth, alone, and unmoved by the hour of the night or the fatigues of the day, in court and in the House, that would have exhausted a less robust man' (*The Times*, 10 September 1980). Parliamentary criticism of his handling of the prosecution for murder of an alleged poisoner, Dr Bodkin Adams, was decisively beaten off, but may have had some effect on the decision to ignore his claims to succeed Lord Goddard [q.v.] as lord chief justice in 1958.

In July 1962 Manningham-Buller was appointed lord chancellor in place of the Earl of Kilmuir [q.v.] in the drastic Cabinet reconstruction undertaken by Harold Macmillan (later the Earl of Stockton). Of the sixteen attorneys-general since 1901 who have reached the woolsack, only three have been promoted direct from the position of first law officer—Westbury, Birkenhead [qq.v.], and Dilhorne, as Manningham-Buller now became, taking the title of his barony from a Buller property on the Cheadle side of Stoke-on-Trent. (The inhabitants of the area now call it Dill-horne: but the lord chancellor insisted on the traditional pronunciation Dil-urne.) He was a few weeks short of his fifty-seventh birthday in a Cabinet of which the average age was fifty-one. So Dilhorne was amongst the seniors to whom the prime minister turned for help in a succession of government crises in 1963—Nyasaland, William Vassall, and John Profumo. When strain and ill health drove Macmillan into retirement in the autumn of that eventful year, Dilhorne was asked to sound the Cabinet as to the succession. This he did, in the words of R. A. Butler (later Lord Butler of Saffron Walden), 'like a large Clumber spaniel sniffing the bottoms of the hedgerows', and duly reported a clear majority for the Earl of Home (later Lord Home of the Hirsel), who continued Dilhorne in his position until he was replaced by Lord Gardiner in October 1964. In the dissolution and resignation honours list of that year he was promoted viscount. (But the fellows of Magdalen did not then feel able to elect either him or Lord Gardiner to an honorary fellowship.) In 1967 he became a deputy lieutenant of Northamptonshire, a distinction which in that county of squires and spires he valued as much as any which he had achieved. (He had succeeded his father as fourth baronet in 1956.)

His time on the woolsack was too short for Dilhorne to make any permanent mark on the statute book or the law reports. But as an ex-lord chancellor he threw himself with such vigour into the judicial and parliamentary work available to him, in particular sitting constantly on the Privy Council, that there was general welcome in 1969 for the unusual step of appointing him a lord of appeal in ordinary. (The rules of precedence had previously been altered so as to deprive an ex-lord chancellor of his automatic right to preside.) Over the next decade a series of weighty judgements fully justified the appointment. He was especially good in the areas of constitutional and revenue law.

Dilhorne disdained the arts by which a lawyer–politician often seeks popularity. He evoked respect rather than affection: even some of his Cabinet colleagues were a little frightened of him. But the respect was given to qualities which were once thought to be characteristic of his class and his profession—integrity, loyalty, and a desire to do the state some service. In an age when the characters and capacities of public men were probed more mercilessly than at any time since the late seventeenth century, this was an important achievement.

During a lecture tour in Canada and the United States in 1956 honorary degrees were conferred on him at McGill University, Montreal, and the Southern Methodist University, Dallas, Texas.

In 1930 he married Lady Mary Lilian Lindsay, fourth of the six daughters of David Alexander Edward Lindsay, the twenty-seventh Earl of Crawford and Balcarres [q.v.], and sister of the twenty-eighth Earl [q.v.]. They had one son and three daughters. Dilhorne died suddenly at Knoydart in Inverness-shire 7 September 1980, and it was characteristic of him that he had prepared for delivery in October a judgement in a major appeal. He was buried at Deene in Northamptonshire, his estate being sworn for probate at £111,754. He was succeeded in the viscountcy by his son, John Mervyn (born 1932).

There is a portrait of Dilhorne in the hall of the Inner Temple.

[*The Times*, 10 September 1980; private information; personal knowledge.]

R. F. V. Heuston

MANTON, SIDNIE MILANA (1902–1979), zoologist, was born 4 May 1902 in London, the elder daughter and second of three children (the son died in infancy) of George Sidney Frederick Manton, dental surgeon, of London, and his wife, Milana Angele Terese d'Humy. She was educated at the school of the Froebel Educational Institute, Kensington, and St. Paul's Girls' School, Hammersmith, from where she obtained a leaving exhibition and proceeded to Girton College, Cambridge. There she won the Montefiore prize and obtained first classes in both parts of the natural sciences tripos (1923 and 1925), topping the list in zoology in the latter examination. After a year as Alfred Yarrow student at Imperial College, London, she returned to Cambridge, becoming university demonstrator in comparative anatomy in 1927, and served variously as supervisor in zoology, director of studies (1935–42), a staff fellow (1928–35 and 1942–5), and research fellow (1945–8) of Girton College. She was awarded her Ph.D. in 1928 and her Sc.D. in 1934.

In 1928 she visited Tasmania to study the primitive freshwater syncarid crustaceans, *Anaspides* and *Paranaspides*, and then joined the Great Barrier Reef expedition for the last four months of its stay at Low Isles—a never-to-be-forgotten experience.

From 1949 to 1960 she was reader in zoology at King's College, London (she had been visiting lecturer there, 1943–6) and subsequently honorary fellow at Queen Mary College, London, and honorary associate of the British Museum (Natural History).

An all-round zoologist, Sidnie Manton's particular eminence lay in the fields of arthropod embryology and functional morphology and in her ability to bring her findings to bear on the problems of evolution. Her embryological work on the crustaceans *Hemimysis lamornae* and *Nebalia bipes* elucidated many of the complex processes that take place during their development and set new standards in this field. Much interested in the enigmatic Onychophora, she discovered how, in *Peripatopsis*, spermatozoa reach the ovary from spermatophores deposited on the surface of the body and she studied the development of certain viviparous non-placental species of that genus. Later, with Donald T. Anderson, she studied the relationship between the embryo and the oviduct in two viviparous placental species.

Her work on functional morphology, which began with studies on crustacean feeding mechanisms, some of it in collaboration with H. Graham Cannon [q.v.], extended to a wide-ranging study of arthropod mandibles, and culminated in a long series of investigations on arthropod locomotory mechanisms. The latter embraced a diversity of organisms and, beginning in 1950, the published results appeared at intervals over a period of more than twenty years. These studies broke new ground in elucidating the means whereby many-legged arthropods—onychophorans, centipedes, and millipedes—organize and co-ordinate the movements of their limbs and showed how the many differences revealed in this diverse assemblage were related to different ways of life. This work, which also produced much new morphological information, led to the development of new concepts of arthropod relationships, one outcome being the erection of a new phylum, the Uniramia, to embrace the Onychophora, Tardigrada, Hexapoda, and Myriapoda. Much of it was summarized and synthesized in a book, *The Arthropoda. Habits, Functional Morphology and Evolution* (1977), in which she was able to draw out its evolutionary implications.

As well as other contributions to invertebrate zoology, and to meet the needs of students in a different field, she produced, with J. T. Saunders, *A Manual of Practical Vertebrate Morphology (1931)* which went through four editions. An interest in the breeding of colourpoint cats, at which, by virtue of her understanding of the genetic principles involved she was very successful, led to a book, *Colourpoint, Himalayan and Longhair Cats* (1971) of which a second edition appeared in 1979.

She was honoured by election as a fellow of the Royal Society in 1948. Her sister, Irene, professor of botany at Leeds University, later achieved this distinction, the only case involving two sisters in the history of the society. She was awarded the gold medal for zoology of the Linnean Society (1963) and the Frink medal of the Zoological Society (1977), as well as an honorary doctorate of the University of Lund, Sweden.

Spare of frame and always interested in sport, she was the Cambridge swimming captain in 1923, a hockey blue in 1924, and played tennis until well into her sixties. Forthright in manner, her criticism of loose thinking could be scathing, but she devoted much time to helping students and those less gifted than herself with their work.

In 1937 she married Dr John Philip Harding, son of Philip William Harding, a bank official. Her husband eventually became keeper of zoology at the British Museum (Natural History). They had one daughter and an adopted son. She died in London, 2 January 1979.

[G. Fryer in *Biographical Memoirs of Fellows of the Royal Society*, vol. xxvi, 1980; *The Times*, 16

November, 1979; private information; personal knowledge.] GEOFFREY FRYER

MARPLES, ALFRED ERNEST, first BARON MARPLES (1907–1978), politician, was born in Levenshulme in Manchester 9 December 1907, the only child of Alfred Ernest Marples, foreman engineer, and his wife, Mary Hammon. After attending the neighbourhood council school he took his place as one of the first pupils at the new grammar school established at the end of World War I in the growing Manchester suburb of Stretford. He left school early in order to become an incorporated accountant. After qualifying as a chartered accountant in 1928 he moved to London in 1929 and left accounting for the building industry, converting Victorian houses into flats and letting them.

He became friendly with Jack Huntington, a civil servant, who lent him £20 on which, together with his savings, he established Marples, Ridgway, and Partners, a contracting business which was later to build motorways, dry docks, and power stations both in Britain and abroad. Huntington, a scholar and traditionalist, filled in many gaps in Marples's education by conversation and proposing courses of study.

Before war broke out Marples had joined the London Scottish Territorials as a private. During World War II he served in the Royal Artillery, rising to the rank of captain in 1941. He became Conservative MP for Wallasey in 1945. He frequently spoke on housing matters between 1945 and 1950 and when, at the Conservative Party conference in 1950, Lord Woolton [q.v.] accepted 300,000 houses a year as the Conservative target, it was Marples who was chosen to implement the promise. As parliamentary secretary to the Ministry of Housing and Local Government from 1951 to 1954 he masterminded and supervised the campaign, which achieved the set target. He was joint parliamentary secretary to the Ministry of Pensions and National Insurance in 1954–5 but reverted to business and the back-benches when Anthony Eden (later the Earl of Avon) became prime minister.

Harold Macmillan (later the Earl of Stockton) appointed Marples postmaster-general in 1957. His period in that office until 1959 was marked by a series of striking events and developments. Letter-sorting automation took its first decisive strides. The Post Office, not always the most prestigious of state departments, began to find itself in the glare of publicity led by a political head who understood and valued its morale-boosting possibilities. It supported his efforts to maintain good relations with the Post Office unions. Subscriber trunk dialling and a new Atlantic cable came into use. Marples was also identified with the newly introduced premium bonds when he switched on the electronic random number indicating equipment and he and Ernie were one.

In 1959 Marples entered the Cabinet as minister of transport—a post which he held until the Conservative defeat of 1964. At a time when road traffic was growing rapidly and transport patterns changing as a consequence, it was inevitable that the Cabinet minister holding the transport portfolio should find himself at the centre of public controversy. Within weeks Marples was putting forward solutions for some of central London's worst problems. From 1959 to 1964 motorways, seat belts, yellow lines, parking meters with ticketed fines, and much else figured constantly in the news.

The problems of the urban motorist had been set out in a comprehensive report prepared by (Sir) Colin Buchanan—'Traffic in Towns'. Marples firmly supported the demands of the road user for more and better roads and insisted on the best design for bridges, flyovers, and embankments. The railways, suffering from a loss of traffic to the roads, were subject to a searching enquiry similar to Buchanan's. It was conducted by Richard (later Lord) Beeching, a high ICI executive brought in by Marples specially for the purpose. The appointment was controversial, the eventual proposals to cut many lines doubly so. But Marples, determined to modernize the railways to be a competitive industry, faced the controversy head on and pushed his legislation through Parliament. He also took up successfully the challenge to British shipping interests which had grown as a result of American discrimination in favour of their state-protected lines and he introduced important improvements in the credit facilities available for British shipbuilders and operators. His was an exacting, exciting, and strenuous time at the Transport Ministry. 'Marples Must Go' campaigns were frequently followed by outbreaks of car stickers proclaiming 'Come Back, Marples —All is Forgiven'.

With the socialists in office in 1964 Marples took over the shadow technology brief. Typically he produced thoroughly prepared forward-looking policy statements for the party. His 'No choice but change' speech in 1967 was highly acclaimed and its theme echoed years later.

Marples was an intelligent dissenter and purposeful innovator. He was always convinced of his high destiny and pursued his chosen path with great energy and enthusiasm. Those who worked with him were occasionally irritated by the certainty which appeared to sustain him in moments of crisis or surrounding confusion. Some also felt that he went too far in his use of publicity. He was accused of finding a frivolous delight in seeing his name and picture in print; it was said that the greatest hurt that could be inflicted on him was to come between him and the camera. But he collected the originals of the most barbed cartoons with no less glee. Marples never forgot his humble origins and savoured the comparison between his own background and the public schools, Oxbridge, and country mansions of those with whom he competed so successfully.

He never smoked, he ate well but with discernment, and he so enjoyed a good wine that, as the years passed and he became increasingly discriminating, he became recognized as a wine expert. After he left the ranks of government he found both pride and satisfaction in owning his own vineyard in a favoured French district, and in enjoying its products. As he grew older he came to regard physical fitness as a cardinal precept. He walked endlessly, cycled everywhere, climbed mountains, and trained with professional footballers.

Marples was admitted to the Privy Council in 1957, became a freeman of Wallasey in 1970, and was created a life peer in 1974.

He was twice married, first in 1937 to Edna Harwood. This marriage was dissolved in 1945 and in 1956 he married Ruth, daughter of Frederic William Dobson, FSA, a business man in the Nottingham lace trade. She had worked as his secretary and they were ideally suited. Marples died in the Princess Grace Hospital in Monte Carlo 6 July 1978.

[*The Times*, 7 July 1978; private information; personal knowledge.]

KENNETH P. THOMPSON

MARQUAND, HILARY ADAIR (1901–1972), economist and politician, was born 24 December 1901 at Cardiff, the elder son of Alfred Marquand, a clerk in a coal-exporting firm, and his wife, Mary Adair. His father had come from Guernsey though his grandfather and an uncle were shipowners in Cardiff. His mother was Scottish. Marquand was educated at Cardiff High School and the University College, Cardiff, where he went with a state scholarship. He graduated with first class honours in history (1923) and economics (1924) and obtained the Gladstone and Cobden prizes. There followed two years in the United States on a Laura Spelman Rockefeller Foundation fellowship spent mainly at the University of Wisconsin, and from 1926 to 1930 a lectureship in economics at the University of Birmingham. He married in 1929 Rachel Eluned, a teacher, daughter of David James Rees, owner of the *Llais Llafur* (*Voice of Labour*), the first labour newspaper in Wales, founded by his father and later to become the *South Wales Voice*.

In 1930 he returned to his old university in Cardiff as professor of industrial relations. He was then twenty-nine years old and the youngest university professor in Britain. From that time until the outbreak of the war Marquand continued his academic work of teaching and research, including a year in 1932–3 studying industrial relations in the USA and a further year in 1938–9 as visiting professor at the University of Wisconsin. His period as professor at Cardiff was particularly productive. In 1931 he published his first book, *The Dynamics of Industrial Combination*. This, based in part on American experience, was a major contribution to a subject relatively new in British economic literature. In 1934 he published a study on *Industrial Relations in the United States of America* and in 1939 he was editor and co-author of *Organized Labour in Four Continents*. But his main preoccupation during the decade preceding the war was the study of the industrial and economic conditions in south Wales. He made a survey for the Board of Trade, *Industrial Survey of South Wales*, published in 1931, and a second one for the commissioner for special areas in 1937. In the meantime, in 1936, he wrote a book, *South Wales Needs a Plan*, which established him with a wider audience as an important contributor to pressing problems of economic policy. During the war he was a temporary civil servant, first in the Board of Trade, later in the Ministry of Labour and in the Ministry of Production.

Marquand had been a member of the Labour Party since 1920, having broken away from a family tradition which, unlike that of his wife's, was thoroughly Conservative, and, believing that post-war problems were not going to be either in the field of economic theory or administration but in politics, he took the earliest opportunity to stand for Parliament. In 1945 he was elected for Cardiff East of which he remained the member until 1950; then, from 1950 to 1961, he was member for Middlesbrough East, a seat held with big majorities until he resigned in 1961. The initial momentum of his political career was striking. He achieved office immediately on election, becoming secretary for overseas trade, a post, subsequently held by Harold Wilson (later Lord Wilson of Rievaulx), in which he travelled widely. He led the British delegation to the Havana conference on trade and employment which set up the General Agreement on Tariffs and Trade (GATT). Between 1947 and 1948 Marquand was paymaster-general. He had no specific departmental responsibilities but again travelled widely in Africa on trade promotion missions. From 1948 to 1951 he was minister of pensions (becoming a privy councillor in 1949) and then succeeded Aneurin Bevan [q.v.] as minister of health, a post, however, with reduced scope and no longer in the Cabinet.

After the 1951 election, in which Marquand maintained a large majority, he became an active member of the opposition front bench, from 1959 as chief spokesman on Commonwealth affairs. The prospect of long years in opposition and possibly some disillusion with the new tendencies in his party led him to abandon active politics. In 1961 he resigned his seat to take up the post of director of the newly created Institute of Labour Studies at the International Labour Office in Geneva, a post in which his large circle of international friendships served him well. He returned to England in 1965 and for three years served as deputy chairman of the Prices and Incomes Board. His last years were spent in relative inactivity and this, together with failing health, contributed to a sense of frustration, relieved, however, by a happy family life. He had two sons and a daughter. The eldest, David Ian Marquand, born in 1934, showed the same academic and political inclinations as his father, holding various university teaching posts and being at one time Labour MP for Ashfield (1966–77). He later became professor of contemporary history and politics at Salford University.

Hilary Marquand, a gentle and kindly man, was not without ambition, but a strong, at times passionate, concern with the welfare of the underprivileged of society probably militated against his energetically pursuing the highest academic laurels, while a deeply-founded respect for the criteria of scholarship made him less than wholly comfortable in the turmoil of politics. In a period in which political economy was increasingly forsaken for the more austere and mathematical forms of economics, his researches into the practical problems of modern industry gained less notice in professional circles than they otherwise might have done. On the other hand, his lack of skill in, indeed distaste for, the small change of trafficking in day-to-day politics probably prevented him from reaching the higher offices of state to which his intellectual equipment and scholarly background entitled him.

In a small circle he could be witty, entertaining, and eloquent; and his consistently high polls in elections are evidence of a somewhat surprising talent for the requirements of the hustings. In the House of Commons, though his style lacked the stirring quality of many of his contemporaries, his quiet, scholarly manner and obvious mastery of intricate subjects always commanded respectful recognition. His life and work were characteristic of a new generation of scholars who emerged in public affairs on the early post-war British political scene. He died at Hellingly Hospital, East Sussex, 6 November 1972.

[Personal knowledge.] ERIC ROLL

MARTIN, SIR DAVID CHRISTIE (1914–1976), scientist and administrator, was born 7 October 1914 at Kirkcaldy, Fife, Scotland, the youngest of the three sons (there were no daughters) of David Christie Martin, who worked in a local factory, and his wife, Helen Linton. He attended the local primary school and Kirkcaldy High School where he was school captain. At the early age of twelve Martin showed his gift for organization by forming a football team of boys from different schools. He entered Edinburgh University in 1933 and graduated B.Sc. with first class honours in chemistry in 1937; research on some properties of deuterium compounds, under Dr J. A. V. Butler, led to a Ph.D. in June 1939. He was active in student affairs, including the students representative council.

In 1939 Martin was awarded a Carnegie Trust research scholarship but resigned two months later to become assistant secretary of the Royal Society of Arts in London. He retained that post until 1945, but was seconded almost immediately to the department of research and development in the Ministry of Supply. There he worked under H. J. Gough [q.v.] and met many of Britain's leading scientists.

When the war ended, instead of going back to the Royal Society of Arts, Martin became the general secretary of the Chemical Society, but in January 1947 was appointed, at the early age of thirty-two, assistant secretary (later changed to executive secretary) of the Royal Society, a post he held with great distinction until the day of his death. The Society's activities and responsibilities increased very considerably during Martin's secretaryship. Much of this expansion was related to international activities to which Martin personally contributed a great deal. During the 1950s the Royal Society, with Martin at the centre, played a leading role in organizing the International Geophysical Year that took place in 1957. Two major parts of this programme and the work that led to and followed it were the beginning of space research in Britain and the establishment of a British scientific laboratory at Halley Bay in the Antarctic. Both projects received much expert and enthusiastic support from David Martin. In recognition of his contributions to Antarctic research, the Martin Ice Rise in the George VI Shelf was named after him.

Soon after the IGY, Martin became deeply involved in arrangements for the Royal Society's tercentenary in 1960 and then, under the presidency of Sir Howard (later Lord) Florey [q.v.], in negotiations and the raising of a million pounds to create a new home for the Society in 6–9 Carlton House Terrace. The Society moved there in 1967 and the Martins occupied a flat above the library, thus re-establishing an earlier tradition of a resident secretary. The international activities of the Society continued to flourish both in the framework of the International Council of Scientific Unions and in bilateral arrangements which started with the Soviet Union in 1956. In particular Martin played a crucial role in starting the Society's European exchange programme.

During his thirty years with the Royal Society he served seven presidents and more than twenty other honorary officers, all of whom came to respect and rely greatly on his experience and wisdom. A dark and stockily built man, he had an equable temperament and a keen sense of duty. He was not a fellow of the Royal Society, indeed the statutes stipulated that the executive secretary should not be a fellow, but he contributed very notably to all its activities. In addition he made important contributions to the work of the British Association for the Advancement of Science and took a special interest in its activities for young scientists. An annual British Association Young Scientists lecture has since 1977 been named the David Martin lecture. He worked hard to improve the public understanding of science, giving much encouragement to science writers and serving as a member and later chairman of the BBC Science Consultative Group.

He was appointed CBE in 1960 and knighted in 1970. He was a fellow of the Royal Society of Edinburgh (1956) and received honorary degrees from the universities of Edinburgh (1968) and Newcastle upon Tyne (1973).

In 1943 he married a fellow Edinburgh graduate, Jean MacGaradh, daughter of Thomas Hay Wilson, a timber merchant, of Edinburgh; she worked for many years with the International Social Service of Great Britain. They had no children. Martin died in his flat at the Royal Society's premises, London, 16 December 1976.

[Sir Harrie Massey and Sir Harold Thompson in *Biographical Memoirs of Fellows of the Royal Society*, vol. xxiv, 1978; Lord Todd, address at the memorial service, in *Notes and Records of the Royal Society*, vol. xxxii, 1977.]

RONALD W. J. KEAY

MARTIN, SIR DOUGLAS ERIC (DERIC) HOLLAND- (1906–1977), admiral. [See HOLLAND-MARTIN.]

MASTERMAN, SIR JOHN CECIL (1891–1977), academic and intelligence officer, was born 12 January 1891 at Kingston upon Thames, the younger of the two sons who were the only children of Commander (later Captain) John Masterman, RN, and his wife, Edith Margaret, daughter of the Revd (James) Roydon Hughes.

He was educated at Evelyns and, as a naval cadet, at Osborne and Dartmouth. Naval discipline and the moral effort required to leave the navy, contrary to parental hopes in 1908, confirmed a strong character. In 1909 he was elected to a scholarship in modern history at Worcester College, Oxford, which thereafter had his assured loyalty. His appearance in the first class in the final honour school of modern history (1913) was followed immediately by appointment to a lectureship at Christ Church, Oxford.

He was caught in Germany in August 1914 and spent the war interned at Ruhleben, where he played a significant part in the self-organized life of the prisoners. In 1919 he was elected a Student of Christ Church. There he was soon appointed to major offices: he was junior censor 1921–4, senior censor 1925–6. As a tutor he had a lasting effect on his pupils many of whom rose to academic or other eminence. Excelling in several games he represented England at lawn tennis in 1920 and in 1925 and 1927 at hockey. He was a member of the MCC team which toured Canada in 1937. Although he published no academic work he was on the way to a minor literary reputation with the publication of a detective story, a novel, and a play (1933, 1935, 1937).

His powerful and attractive character and diverse talents ensured that he was increasingly known and respected. (The contacts which came through games meshed with and extended those which came through academic life and Christ Church.) He could almost certainly have become headmaster of Eton in 1933; and in the same year he was offered the post of output controller (effectively second-in-command) at the BBC.

He joined the army in 1940 and from January 1941 to 1945 acted, on behalf of MI5, as chairman of a committee (known as XX) which was responsible for the employment of spies who had been unmasked and were being used to send false information to Germany. The use of such double agents was very difficult and delicate, and of great importance, above all in the scheme of deception which in 1944 gave the enemy the impression that the main Allied landings were to be in the Pas de Calais. Here Masterman rendered a major national service.

In 1946 he was elected provost of Worcester College. The regime of his predecessor Lys's later years had not been in all respects forward-looking. (Lys had retired at the age of eighty-three.) Masterman brought energetic devotion, clear aims, and a willingness to take great pains, not least in helping undergraduates. His qualities, his fame—enhanced by a popular work on Oxford, *To Teach the Senators Wisdom* (1952)—and his wide contacts (for example, in 1947 he was on the governing bodies of five public schools) did much for the college. The most important achievements of his vice-chancellorship (1957–8) were the raising of the Oxford Historic Buildings Fund of £1,750,000 and the transformation of St. Catherine's Society into St. Catherine's College.

In 1947–8 he was chairman of a committee to examine the restrictions on the political activities of civil servants. Its report recommended that the existing freedom of most 'industrial' civil servants to engage in party politics should be extended to most in the 'minor and manipulative' grades, but to no others. It was criticized as too restrictive and the policy ultimately adopted was somewhat more generous. From 1952 to 1956 he was chairman of the Army Education Advisory Board and from 1952 to 1959 a member of the BBC general advisory council.

On his retirement from Worcester in 1961 he became adviser on personnel matters to the Birfield Group, an important group of engineering companies, and took an active interest in the fields of industrial relations, appointments and training, which were new to him. At the same time (1961–7) he served on the educational advisory committee for Associated Television.

These appointments ended in 1967. Masterman then had time to fulfil his determination to publish the account which he had written in 1945 (for very restricted official circulation) of the work of the XX committee. So convinced was he that this story should be told that he was prepared to defy prosecution under the Official Secrets Act. In 1970 he reached an accommodation with the government, largely arrived at by a meeting with the home secretary to which the prelude was Masterman's being entertained to lunch by his former pupil, the then foreign secretary. *The Double-Cross System in the War of 1939 to 1945* was published in 1972.

His last years were largely devoted to his autobiography. He died in Oxford 6 June 1977. His will was proved at only £16,241; he was notably unmercenary.

Masterman cannot be simply summed up in a description of the phases of a distinguished public career. He was often regarded as an *éminence grise*, not without some justice. Few can have had wider connections within the upper-class establishment, and the scenes behind which he exerted influence were fairly numerous. Such influence depended on his personality. His will was strong, his presence weighty. His papers were always in order, his day and his year well planned. Humane, humorous, and loyal he was wonderful company and a very good friend. Though conventional, he was far from ordinary, and not least in his concentrated dedication to whatever game, ploy, or major task was in hand, and in his power to influence others. He was unmarried.

He was appointed OBE in 1944 and knighted in 1959. He received honorary degrees from Toronto (LL D, 1958), King's College, Halifax (DCL, 1958), and Heriot Watt University (D.Litt., 1966). He was an honorary fellow of Worcester College (1961) and of St. Catharine's College, Cambridge (1957), and an honorary Student of Christ Church (1952).

[J. C. Masterman, *On the Chariot Wheel; an Autobiography*, 1975; *The Times*, 7 June 1977; private information.] J. CAMPBELL

MATHEW, DAVID JAMES (1902–1975), archbishop of Apamea in Bithynia, was born at Lyme Regis, Dorset, 15 January 1902, the elder son of Francis James Mathew, barrister-at-law and novelist, and his wife, Agnes Elizabeth Anna, daughter of James Tisdall Woodroffe, advocate-general of Bengal from 1899 to 1904, who was a son of the rector of Glanmire, county Cork. His father was a nephew of Sir James Mathew [q.v.] and a great-nephew of Father Theobald Mathew [q.v.], and thus belonged to a prominent family in county Tipperary.

Mathew was educated at Osborne and Dartmouth, serving as a midshipman in the last year of World War I. In 1920 he went to Balliol College, Oxford. Awarded a second class in modern history (1923), he received a War Memorial scholarship and then the Amy Mary Preston Read scholarship, which enabled him to spend two more years in Oxford. His research, which was to bear fruit partly in *The Reformation and the Contemplative Life* (1934), written with his younger brother Gervase (see below), attracted him to the Carthusian life. He put aside the intention of entering for a fellowship at All Souls and went to the Beda College in Rome to prepare to go as a priest to the Charterhouse in Sussex. He was ordained under his own patrimony in 1929, but ten months as a novice at Parkminster proved that he was not to be a monk—the chief obstacle apparently being his inability to master plainchant. He used to say that, for the Carthusian life, one needed to have no imagination—it was 'suitable for the products of provincial grammar schools who were good at games'—but how much he wished that he was one of them!

Mathew now offered hmself to the diocese of Cardiff. He spent four happy years as a curate at St. David's Cathedral, enjoying the pastoral work in the dock district. In 1933 he was awarded the Litt.D. by Trinity College, Dublin, for *The Celtic Peoples and Renaissance Europe*, his first book: it was, at five hundred pages, to be his most substantial, and deals, in a series of impressionistic studies, with the effects on Roman Catholics on the Celtic fringe of the Elizabethan settlement and the counter-reformation. In 1934, since he had a small private income, he was able to become chaplain to Roman Catholics in the University of London, a post which he held until 1944. He divided his days between the British Museum and his widely spread flock, some of whom found his elliptical humour baffling but many became lifelong friends. To this Dictionary he contributed the notice of Cardinal Louis Bégin.

In 1936 he published *Catholicism in England 1535–1935*, subtitled *Portrait of a Minority: its Culture and Tradition*. Crisp, intuitive, and witty, this represents David Mathew at his best. It provided English Roman Catholics with a fresh sense of their identity and helped thereby to articulate the confidence of a whole generation, many of whom also had Oxford connections. Mathew's characteristically toneless and dead-pan epigrams extended even to judgements on the recently deceased Cardinal F. A. Bourne [q.v.]: 'In such a character, with its strength and mastering sense of duty, it is almost inevitable that a desire for centralization should have been found and a tendency to concentrate authority. Monarchical institutions appealed to him.'

In 1938, at the age of thirty-six, Mathew became bishop auxiliary of Westminster. Bourne's successor, Arthur Hinsley [q.v.], evidently taking advice from Mathew's circle of friends, may well have been surprised by his own decision. As the war came, he clearly placed more and more trust in his young auxiliary. An intrepid pastor in the blitz, Mathew was also at the centre of the Catholic laity in London who sought greater participation in national life, particularly through the movement known as 'the Sword of the Spirit'.

Hinsley was thought by some to have wanted Mathew to succeed him, but at his death in 1943 Bernard Griffin [q.v.] was appointed. Though loyally accepted, it is impossible to exaggerate the blow that Griffin's preferment was to Mathew. At that time, auxiliary bishops had to be reappointed by the new ordinary: Griffin reappointed Mathew, after some delay, but made no difficulties when the Vatican chose him as apostolic visitor to Ethiopia in 1945 (his cousin had been judicial adviser to the emperor throughout the war). This was obviously a trial run for the Vatican diplomatic service. Mathew's report to the Holy See was hailed as brilliant; it included an unprecedented account of Ethiopian flora and fauna. In 1945–6 he delivered the Ford lectures in Oxford, published as *The Social Structure in Caroline England* (1948). But Griffin, on his visit to Rome late in 1945, had persuaded the authorities to choose Mathew as apostolic delegate to the British colonies in Africa, East and West, and so, with the dignity of archbishop of Apamea, he moved to Mombasa in 1946.

His seven years as a diplomat in Africa were undoubtedly successful, although to him they felt like exile. He carried out the Vatican's policy of preparing the way for native bishops. His greatest triumph was the appointment of Rugambwa as the first African cardinal in 1953. In that year he also published the last volume of his trilogy of novels—*In Vallombrosa* (1950–3)—and signified that he had served in Africa long enough. The Vatican offered him the important nunciature at Berne. His refusal displeased Pope Pius XII and seemed incomprehensible to the then Monsignor Montini. But Mathew, having apparently demonstrated his qualities as a pastor and an administrator, dearly wanted a diocese in England; the prospect of a career which would no doubt lead to high office in some Vatican dicastery did not attract. He returned home in 1953, at the age of fifty-one and at the height of his powers, apparently not knowing, or anyway unwilling to believe, that 'lack of the common touch' and 'impaired health' had already become the accepted reasons that excluded him from consideration. His cryptic manner in conversation and increasingly eccentric appearance no doubt worked against him, but in 1954 he was appointed bishop-in-ordinary (RC) to HM Forces: his early connection with the Royal Navy served as a pretext. The bishops were thus able to accommodate him, while many senior officers learned to dread entertaining him in the mess. His curial office was in Stanhope Lines, Aldershot, but his quarters were, for most of this period, in the ladies' annexe of the Athenaeum.

In 1960 the Vatican called upon him to become secretary to the preparatory commission on missions for the forthcoming general council of the church, a demanding task which excited him, although he found living in Rome wearisome. A great deal had happened in the few years since he left Africa; forces which he had himself helped to release made him something of an anachronism. When the council opened in 1962 he was not even elected a member of the commission, let alone reinstated as secretary. He attended the first session of the council and was horrified, when he cast his vote against substantial changes in the Roman liturgy, to find what sort of bigoted theological company he was keeping. In March 1963 he resigned as bishop to the forces and went into retirement.

He spent the next ten years with Lord and Lady Camoys at Stonor, near Henley, publishing several books in that genre of light biography which he had perfected—*James I* (1967), *Lord Acton and his Times* (1968), *The Courtiers of Henry VIII* (1970), and *Lady Jane Grey* (1972). He could now make frequent visits to Oxford to stay with his brother at Blackfriars or to take him travelling in England or the Mediterranean. The two brothers, always in correct clerical dress though otherwise distressingly dishevelled and unkempt, were often to be seen in the streets of Oxford, sometimes arm in arm, as they made their way somewhat ponderously to a small French restaurant for a special celebration (at which the sweet trolley was always their great delight), or pottering over to Blackwell's to leaf through the latest book by one of their many friends. The enigmatic silences, the sudden hilarity which ended with the disconcerting abruptness with which it began, and the oracular manner, which the brothers shared, alarmed many people; but many others found in their love for one another, and in the absolute simplicity of their religion, a touchstone of fidelity.

To save it from demolition in 1938 David Mathew bought the ruins of Thomastown Castle, county Tipperary, the mansion where Father Theobald Mathew was born. He was proud to have inherited his chalice, but pictures also show a strong family likeness between David Mathew and the apostle of temperance—'a broad, solid-looking man, with grey hair, mild, intelligent eyes, massive rather aquiline nose and countenance', as Thomas Carlyle described him when he saw him in Liverpool in 1843.

As his strength failed Mathew moved to the Hospital of St. John and St. Elizabeth in London, where he was able to receive his friends to the last. He died 12 December 1975, a few weeks after the death of Cardinal Heenan [q.v.], whose catafalque he visited on his last outing. There was thus no archbishop of Westminster to preside at Mathew's funeral in Westminster Cathedral. He was buried at Downside Abbey in Somerset.

His younger brother ANTHONY (1905–1976), scholar, who received the name of GERVASE when he entered the Dominican Order, was born in Chelsea, 14 March 1905. He was educated privately, partly by his father, with whom he also travelled a good deal in the Mediterranean immediately after the war of 1914–18. He went to Balliol College, Oxford, in Hilary term 1925 and read modern history, in which he received a third class in 1927. In 1928 he joined the Dominican friars and was ordained priest in 1934 at Blackfriars, Oxford, where he spent the rest of his life. He began to lecture on the Greek fathers in 1937. His published work ranges over many fields—classical antiquity, Byzantine art, historical theology and patristics, fourteenth century English literature and society. He deserves to be remembered as a main creator of Byzantine studies at Oxford. In 1947 he was appointed university lecturer in Byzantine studies, a post which he held until 1971 and for which he never drew a salary. During this period he took part in archaeological investigations in East Africa and southern Arabia and offered advice on medieval art in Cyprus and Malta. In 1963, with Roland Oliver, he edited the first volume of a *History of East Africa* sponsored by the Colonial Office. In the same year he published *Byzantine Aesthetics*, no doubt his most important book. In nearly forty years of teaching in Oxford he drew on his polymathy to illuminate hundreds of students in various disciplines. He conducted many retreats, particularly for nuns, and had great gifts of insight as a confessor. His collaboration in most of his brother's writing was always generously acknowledged. He suffered from emphysema for many years and survived his brother by four months, almost to the day, dying in Oxford, 4 April 1976.

[*The Times*, 13 and 18 December 1975, 6 and 20 April and 11 May 1976; private information; personal knowledge.] FERGUS KERR

MATTHEW, SIR ROBERT HOGG (1906–1975), architect, was born 12 December 1906 in Edinburgh, second son in the family of four sons (the first of whom died in infancy) and one daughter of John Fraser Matthew, architect and partner of (Sir) Robert Lorimer [q.v.], the most celebrated Scots architect of his day, and his wife, Annie B. Hogg. From Melville College he passed into Edinburgh University, but after a year moved across to the School of Architecture. It was while they were both students that he met, and in 1931 married, Lorna Louise, daughter of Robert Stuart Pilcher, general manager of the Manchester Corporation transport department; they had a son and two daughters.

Matthew's professional career falls into three parts, the first and last centred in Edinburgh. With Lorimer's death in 1929, followed by the world slump, his father's practice could not support him, and for two years he lived on a college studentship which enabled him to study slum housing and to confirm his interest in the social role of architecture. On the advice of a family friend, Professor L. B. Budden of Liverpool, in 1936 he took employment in the department of health for Scotland, which gave him an insight into the present limitations and future potential of a public office, and it was through Budden that he came to the notice of (Sir) L. Patrick Abercrombie [q.v.], with whom he worked on the wartime Clyde Valley regional plan. He made the first sketches for the new towns of East Kilbride and Glenrothes, and on a visit to Sweden to buy timber cottages he was much taken by the attractive co-operative housing, in particular the modestly-scaled 'point blocks' of flats going up in the wooded fringes of Stockholm. In 1945 he became chief architect and planning officer to the health department for Scotland and a member of RIBA's reconstruction committee. At its first meeting in London Sir Charles Reilly [q.v.], Budden's successor, urged him to apply for the vacant post of chief architect to the London County Council.

This second period of his career lasted only seven years (1946–53) but it was of permanent significance for London and for architecture. Convinced that city planning, housing, and architecture were inseparable, and that only in this unison could quality be combined with quantity, he was able to persuade the council to reunite the three under his charge. But he rejected the traditional hierarchical structure in favour of group working with fully delegated responsibility, which made his office, despite its being now the largest in the world, specially attractive to the young. He and his chief housing architect, Whitfield Lewis, proceeded to scrap all existing designs and to substitute, under Scandinavian influence, the 'mixed development' of little towers and terraces whose prototype was the delightful Ackroyden estate on Putney Heath. Simultaneously, with his chosen deputy (and successor), (Sir) J. Leslie Martin, he initiated the LCC's permanent contributions to the 1951 Festival of Britain—the charming Lansbury neighbourhood in the East End and the Royal Festival Hall.

But local government, even at this level, could not long satisfy his acute and speculative mind, and in 1953, in the belief that education had not kept pace with the vast power for good or evil that the architect and planner now wielded, he accepted the Forbes chair of architecture at Edinburgh. His enlargement of the role of his school now went hand in hand with the creation of a private practice which became internationally known as RMJM when he invited (Sir) Stirrat Johnson-Marshall, whose work at the Ministry of Education he admired, to take charge of its London end. His own first significant job was Turnhouse airport, whose human scale and unaffected use of timber again showed Scandinavian influence. Cockenzie power station, Stirling University, and the international pool at the foot of Arthur's Seat were the work of his office, and he was influential in Scotland as a member of its Historic Buildings Council and Royal Fine Art Commission.

In 1962 he succeeded Sir William (later Lord) Holford [q.v.] as president of RIBA, and had much to do with the expansion of its work and influence. His shrewd judgement and quiet authority had by now made him a father figure at international conferences, as president of the International Union of Architects (1961–5) and creator of the Commonwealth Association of Architects (president 1965–8). He was an honorary fellow of the American Institute of Architects (1951) and of the Canadian (1964) and New Zealand (1959) institutes, and an honorary LL D of the University of Sheffield (1963). In 1970 he received architecture's highest award—RIBA's Royal gold medal. He was appointed CBE in 1952 and knighted in 1962.

Like many a private man, not given to self-exposure in word or print, Matthew was eminently sociable and able to endure international bonhomie without a sign of strain. Partly this stemmed from a profound sense of obligation to, and affection for, the Third World. But behind his distinguished looks, his charm of manner, and his soft lowland voice lay an iron determination to get his way—the way he thought right for a liberal and caring society. He was the most conspicuous of the new kind of architect that emerged in Britain after 1945, who believed that if we could get the system right, the rest would follow.

He died at his country house near Edinburgh 21 June 1975.

[Personal knowledge.] ESHER

MATTHEWS, WALTER ROBERT (1881–1973), dean of St. Paul's and theologian, was born 22 September 1881 in Camberwell, London, the eldest of four children (three boys and a girl) of Philip Walter Matthews, banker, and his wife, Sophia Alice Self. After being educated in Wilson's Grammar School, Camberwell, he spent five years as a clerk in the Westminster Bank. He then became a student at King's College, London, where he graduated in 1907. He was ordained in the same year. From 1908 to 1918 he was a lecturer in philosophy at King's College, London. From 1918 to 1932 he was dean of the college and professor of the philosophy of religion. He was appointed chaplain to Gray's Inn in 1920 and preacher in 1929. He later became an honorary bencher. He was chaplain to the King in 1923–31. In 1931 he became dean of Exeter, and in 1934 he succeeded W. R. Inge [q.v.] as dean of St. Paul's where he remained until his retirement in 1967. Later he wrote for this Dictionary the notice of Inge, as also that of J. K. Mozley. Among the public questions on which he spoke during his time in St. Paul's he became known chiefly for (and was sometimes unfairly criticized for) his opposition to unilateral disarmament.

Matthews was a prolific writer. He poured out a constant stream of books, articles, reviews, and published sermons. Among the more important of his books are *Studies in Christian Philosophy* (1921), *God in Christian Thought and Experience* (1930), and *The Problem of Christ in the Twentieth Century* (1950) which consisted of the Maurice lectures of 1949 which he delivered at King's College, London. The second of these books was widely read and was, in its day, one of the most significant contributions to the study of theism. Matthews's main interest was in philosophical theology. His work in this area bears comparison with similar work produced by such distinguished philosophical theologians of his period as William Temple [q.v.] and John Baillie. But he also wrote perceptively on both the theoretical and the practical aspects of ethics. His thought was governed by a determination to give due weight to all the elements in Christian faith and so to establish the right relation between them. This led him to avoid extremes and to achieve a new synthesis at many major points. Thus while he held that Christian revelation is a supernatural reality that can be discerned only by spiritual experience he also insisted that all religious truth-claims must satisfy the appropriate rational criteria. A theological 'label' cannot be applied to him. His belief in natural theology distinguished him from the disciples of Karl Barth. Also, although he spoke of medieval theology with respect he did not belong to the movement known as 'Neo-Thomism' or, indeed, use scholastic modes of thought. He was sometimes called, with his consent, a Modernist. Certainly he shared the Modernists' conviction that the theologian must take full account of modern knowledge; but he never attenuated traditional Christianity for the sake of accommodating it to non-Christian presuppositions; and he remained unwavering in his adherence to the Christian doctrines of Creation, the Incarnation, and the Trinity in their traditional forms. Thus although he used psychological categories in order to interpret the person of Christ he admitted that the metaphysical terminology adopted by the Fathers was ultimately required in order to affirm belief in the Incarnation.

Matthews was capable of writing with equal effectiveness at different levels for different audiences. In the books cited, as well as in other books and in many articles, he wrote in a manner suited to meet the technical requirements of professional philosophers and theologians. Yet (as his Saturday sermons contributed to the *Daily Telegraph* over a period of twenty-four years show) he could also put profound truths simply and with a lucidity that characterized everything he wrote. The approach he adopted in his published work was nearly always objective. He rarely referred to his own religious experience even in his autobiography. Yet such references as there are confirm the impression, indirectly given by all his writings, of a sincerely and deeply held personal faith which, though instilled in childhood, developed through a continuing process of rational re-examination. Among his personal qualities those that especially impressed people who knew him well were his modesty and his combination of firmness with gentleness. He also possessed a distinctive sense of humour. There is a lively photograph of him at the beginning of his autobiography.

He was appointed KCVO in 1935 and CH in 1962. He was honoured with the degree of DD by the universities of Cambridge, St. Andrews, Glasgow, Trinity College (Dublin), and Trinity College (Toronto).

In 1912 Matthews married Margaret Bryan (died 1963), the daughter of a school inspector. They had two sons and one daughter. One of the sons was killed in action in 1940. The other son, (Walter) Bryan, became professor of clinical neurology in the University of Oxford. Matthews died in London 4 December 1973.

[*The Times*, 5 December 1973; W. R. Matthews, *Memories and Meanings* (autobiography), 1969; H. P. Owen, *W. R. Matthews: Philosopher and Theologian*, 1976; private information.] H. P. OWEN

MAUDLING, REGINALD (1917–1979), politician, was born in North Finchley 7 March 1917, the only child of Reginald George Maudling, actuary, of Hastings Court, Worthing, and his wife, Elizabeth Emilie Pearson. Educated at Merchant Taylors' School, he gained a scholarship to Merton College, Oxford, where he obtained a first in *literae humaniores* in 1938, and was *proxime accessit* for the John Locke scholarship in philosophy. G. R. G. Mure (later warden), a lifelong friend, regarded Maudling as among the three ablest pupils he ever taught. As an undergraduate Maudling developed a lifelong habit of travelling widely.

Maudling was called to the bar, Middle Temple, in 1940. The previous year he had married Beryl, daughter of Eli Laverick, naval architect. They had three sons and one daughter. At the outbreak of World War II he volunteered for active service but, owing to defective eyesight, was commissioned in RAF intelligence and subsequently became private secretary to Sir Archibald Sinclair (later Viscount Thurso, q.v.), secretary of state for air. The belief that relations between government and industry would present the most urgent post-war problems caused Maudling to take the decision to enter politics he had first contemplated in 1939. By temperament a Conservative, he had been convinced by Mure that political progress depended more on the clarification of relevant questions than on strongly partisan commitment to conflicting answers.

Maudling unsuccessfully contested Heston and Isleworth at the 1945 general election, after which he became the first recruit to the Conservative Parliamentary Secretariat (amalgamated with the Research Department in 1948). Maudling not only serviced the party finance committee, but also gave assistance to (Sir) Winston Churchill and Anthony Eden (later the Earl of Avon), both on economic and broader issues. He was an assistant secretary to the group headed by R. A. Butler (later Lord Butler of Saffron Walden) which produced the industrial charter, and successfully moved an amendment committing the 1947 Conservative Party conference to its acceptance.

In February 1950 Maudling won the constituency of Barnet, which he represented until his death. He became parliamentary secretary to the Ministry of Civil Aviation in April 1952, and economic secretary to the Treasury the following November. In his *Memoirs* (1978) he has described this post, which he held until April 1955, as 'on the whole the most exciting and most satisfying time of my political career'. This was the most successful period of post-war Conservative economic policy, and Maudling's personal relations both with the chancellor of the Exchequer, R. A. Butler, and with leading Treasury civil servants, were excellent. He deputized for Butler at the annual meeting of the World Bank and International Monetary Fund in 1953, at a time when Britain was still the second world power in monetary terms. The quality of Maudling's mind, together with his ease and speed of working, already impressed those who were closest to him. Once policy was agreed he did not require detailed briefing, nor full drafts for speeches which he practically extemporized. His style in debate, sometimes slipshod, lacked the lucid force of his letters to the press.

When Eden succeeded Churchill in 1955 he appointed Maudling minister of supply, his first full ministerial post, and a member of the Privy Council. Maudling was never convinced by the argument for a Ministry which interposed a third party between customer and supplier, and he recommended its abolition. He had a realistic appreciation of the problem caused by the competition of the American air industry, and was possibly the first minister explicitly to recognize, in a memorandum written in January 1956, that Britain must henceforward regard herself as 'at the top of the second league' of world powers. Nevertheless Maudling strongly defended the Suez episode as 'a morally correct action'.

In the government of Harold Macmillan (later the Earl of Stockton) of January 1957, Maudling became paymaster-general, deputizing in the Commons for Lord Mills [q.v.], minister of fuel and power, and within three months displayed a typically rapid mastery of British energy policy. In August Maudling was invited to lead the British delegation at the discussions designed to negotiate a European free trade area, with the members of the common market who had recently signed the treaty of Rome. Maudling was promoted to the Cabinet in September, and a successful Commons speech in November caused him to be described as 'the best chancellor of the Exchequer we could have'. The period 1957 to 1965 can be regarded as the most significant of his career.

It is doubtful whether, due to French opposition, the negotiations for a free trade area, which finally broke down in November 1958, could ever have succeeded. But Maudling's own position was handicapped by the reiterated pledge to British farmers that agriculture would be excluded, and by doubts as to the wholeheartedness, as yet, of Britain's desire to enter Europe. In a debate in February 1959 Maudling forcefully argued the case against common market membership in a speech which was to be remembered (and quoted against him) by 'anti-marketeers' in later years. Maudling believed that freedom of trade in industrial products should at least be expanded as widely as possible, and the personal reputation he had built up in the Paris negotiations played a notable part in bringing about a European Free Trade Association in November 1959 between Britain, the Scandinavian countries, Portugal, and Switzerland. When in 1961 the Macmillan government made formal application to see if a satisfactory basis existed for joining the EEC, Maudling changed his mind, mainly on the grounds of the advantage for Britain in participating in a large single market. He never became a European 'supra-nationalist', and in one of his last speeches in the Commons (1978) opposed Britain's joining the European monetary system, arguing that the achievement of a common currency should constitute the last stage of the natural development of economic unity rather than be a means of achieving it.

After the election of 1959, Maudling went to the Board of Trade where he administered effectively the Local Employment Act which improved distribution of industry policy and, against some departmental advice, he insisted that the new Rootes factory should be located at Linwood. He also took much interest in export promotion, recognizing the centrality of rising exports to the future of the British economy. There followed the economic crisis of 1961, and Maudling now had his gaze fixed firmly on his own prospects for a spell at the Treasury. But before he could fulfil this ambition, he spent nine months (October 1961 to July 1962), among the most fruitful of his career, as colonial secretary. He pushed through, against strong right-wing resistance within his own Cabinet (and a threat of resignation), the independence constitution for Zambia; and he devised an African land settlement scheme for Kenya, which by its provision for fair compensation for European farmers virtually ended their monopoly of the White Highlands and thereby contributed to lasting stability.

The appointment of Butler in March 1962, with overall responsibility for Central African affairs, helped to bring Maudling's promotion closer. The 'pay pause' of J. S. B. Lloyd (later Lord Selwyn-Lloyd, q.v.) had raised a number of unprecedented problems and Maudling, while not a member of the Cabinet economic policy committee, was invited to attend ministerial meetings on this subject. In June Maudling published an 'open letter' to his constituents, stressing that 'freedom ... does not include the right to undermine the economy', which was widely admired. His choice as Lloyd's successor as chancellor of the Exchequer in July was generally welcomed and had the leadership of the party fallen vacant at this time, Maudling would have been better placed to 'emerge', under the old system, than any rival.

Maudling's period as chancellor remains controversial. The approval in February 1963 by the recently-established National Economic Development Council of a 4 per cent growth target not only committed Maudling (himself chairman of NEDC) to endorsing this figure, but also influenced the shape of his 1963 budget which distributed £250 million so as to maximize union support for the incomes policy he regarded as indispensable to the achievement of sustained growth. Maudling's 1963 budget speech did, however, acknowledge the need for adequate borrowing facilities within the International Monetary Fund, at whose meetings he consistently advocated measures to increase international liquidity during a period of industrial recovery. In October 1963 the enforced resignation of Macmillan left Maudling a potential successor, though it is doubtful whether he now stood so high with the parliamentary party as in 1962, and a disappointing performance at the party conference (an audience with whom he was never at his best) further damaged his chances.

Those who had regarded Maudling's 1963 budget as overcautious made the opposite criticism of his 1964 budget, which increased indirect taxation by £100 million. But the boom in manufacturing output, down to midsummer, appeared to be moderating. Maudling was much hampered by the decision to postpone the impending general election to October which made it impossible to achieve agreement on incomes policy with the Trades Union Congress. As the election approached it became clear that the balance of payments constituted the most urgent problem, mainly because exports were still holding back. But there was as yet no sign of lack of confidence in sterling, and as Maudling told the Commons after the Conservative defeat 'no figure (of the prospective 1964 deficit) larger than £600 million was ever given to the previous government'. Whatever the outcome of the 1964 election, some immediate action would no doubt have become imperative. But Labour's repeated claim that they had inherited an '£800 million deficit' damaged confidence unnecessarily, and the prospects for consistent growth might have remained brighter had Maudling remained chancellor; certainly he would have avoided the series of often contradictory decisions taken during the years that immediately followed.

Nevertheless Maudling's reputation had become tarnished by the charge that he had misled the electorate, nor did he retrieve his position as his friends had hoped, and in February 1965 he permanently lost his position as principal party spokesman on economic affairs. When Sir A. Douglas-Home (later Lord Home of the Hirsel) resigned in July, the feeling that Edward Heath would provide a new style of opposition may have accounted for his (albeit narrow) victory over Maudling in the first leadership election in the party's history. Maudling felt this rejection intensely (as those who saw him in the Commons that afternoon will vividly remember) and his political determination became permanently weakened. He became Heath's deputy, but played little part in the rethinking of policy, finding himself out of sympathy with the growing party support for an economic policy based solely on market forces and monetary controls.

When in 1970 Maudling became home secretary, his innate reasonableness and liberal instincts enabled him to bring an exceptional range of qualities to the exercise of his powers. For instance his handling of the Immigration Bill meant that never again could it be claimed that repatriation was a significant part of Conservative immigration policy. It was Maudling's misfortune that so much of his period at the Home Office was dominated by Northern Ireland, and by passions and irrationality of a kind particularly abhorrent to him. Maudling began by believing that the co-operation of Stormont was essential, and for this reason, and with many misgivings, he was prepared to concede the policy of internment; but eventually he became convinced that the slide towards civil war in Northern Ireland could only be averted by a complete political break with the past including a secretary of state who would take over from the home secretary responsibility for the province.

In July 1972 Maudling felt compelled to resign when it was decided that there were issues arising out of the bankruptcy case of John Poulson, with whose export business Maudling had been associated in the later 1960s, which required criminal investigation by the Metropolitan Police for whom Maudling bore ministerial responsibility. Maudling's business judgement had never been good and even fifteen years earlier civil servants had been concerned at his tendency to be careless about protecting himself from possible criticism. Indeed, a more serious error on Maudling's part had been his brief acceptance of the presidency of the Real Estate Fund of America, a Bermuda-based investment company run by an American whose activities eventually landed him in prison for fraud. But the Poulson affair pursued Maudling unrelentingly. One of Poulson's companies which Maudling had joined had obtained the contract for a hospital on the island of Gozo which resulted in a heavy loss for the taxpayer; and in July 1977 a select committee of the Commons reported that Maudling should have declared his interest to the House when aid to Malta had been debated ten years earlier since, while Maudling himself received no salary, Poulson had contributed generously to a trust to which Maudling's wife was devoted. A motion to approve the report of the select committee was defeated, but innuendoes persisted, and during his last illness he was unwilling to undergo treatment that might have interfered with his plans for a costly libel action in which he would be the principal witness and which, he firmly believed, would finally clear his own name and that of his family. Maudling, at Heath's advice, had not left public life when he resigned in 1972. He returned to the shadow cabinet when Margaret Thatcher succeeded Heath in 1975, but was dropped in November of the following year. He now had little political following in the Commons but his Conservative colleagues, practically without exception, rallied to him when the crisis came.

Maudling had one of the quickest and best analytic brains in recent British politics. Frequently accused of laziness he could certainly appear casual, yet he had also a capacity for intense concentration when he chose. Nor was it true that he lacked convictions; in his later years he cared a great deal about what he regarded as the growth of ugliness in our society. But there was perhaps more justice in the suggestion that his political outlook was not founded in an ultimate sense of purpose. While eager to be chancellor he was never sure he would succeed, and he knew very well the limitations of economic forecasts. The events of 1964 left him jaded, and his crucial rejection in the following year not only sapped his determination but left him more vulnerable than ever to his inherent weakness of business judgement. Yet whether the consequences of victory in 1965 would have made him happier may be doubted. He would surely have been most suited as prime minister to that era of 'Butskellism' and 'consensus' to which he seems so clearly in retrospect to belong. What can be claimed with confidence is that his easy-going and affable temperament, with its dispassionate rationality, more interested in solving problems than in the rhetoric that moves party conferences, represents one aspect both of politics and of Conservatism that can too easily be underrated in harassing times. Maudling died at the Royal Free Hospital, London, 14 February 1979.

[Reginald Maudling, *Memoirs*, 1978; personal knowledge.] EDWARD BOYLE

MAUFE, SIR EDWARD BRANTWOOD (1883–1974), architect, was born at Ilkley, Yorkshire, 12 December 1883, the second of three children and younger son of Henry Muff, a member of Lloyd's and of the firm Brown, Muff & Company Limited, and his wife, Maude Alice Smithies, who was the niece of Sir Titus Salt [q.v.], the founder of Saltaire. He was educated at Wharfedale School, Ilkley, but was sent in 1899, at the age of fifteen, to serve a five-year pupillage with the London architect William A. Pite. His family had moved south to live in the former home of William Morris [q.v.], Red House, Bexley Heath, designed by Philip Webb [q.v.], which Maufe acknowledged as an early architectural influence; his father also corresponded with John Ruskin [q.v.] and was an amateur watercolourist. In 1904 Maufe took an unusual step, for a student in the midst of his training, and went up to Oxford, to St. John's College, where he learned Greek for the first time, obtaining a BA (pass degree) in 1908 (MA 1919). In August 1909 he changed his surname by deed poll from 'Muff' to 'Maufe'. When he went down Maufe worked hard for his final examination, attending the design class at the Architectural Association school. He became an associate member of RIBA in 1910.

He immediately set up in practice on his own and in 1912 received his first large commission—Kelling Hall in Norfolk for (Sir) Henri Deterding. This is a building which shows Maufe's early links with the Arts and Crafts Movement; it has a butterfly plan, knapped flint walls, and a grey tiled and gabled roof. His other chief prewar work was the decoration of St. Martin-in-the-Fields and chapels and alterations at All Saints, Southampton, and St. John, Hackney, which first brought him into notice in church circles and obtained for him his well-known Acton church later.

During World War I Maufe served as staff lieutenant in the Royal Artillery in Salonika. He did very useful work in camouflage and was subsequently made aide-de-camp to GOC, RA XII Corps.

After the war he became a fellow of RIBA in 1920, and first came into prominence in 1924 with his design for the palace of industry at the Wembley Exhibition. He was a silver medallist at the Paris Exhibition of 1925 and began to secure a wide variety of commissions. Two buildings, particularly, made his name amongst architects: the church of St. Bede for the Royal Association in Aid of the Deaf and Dumb at Clapham (1922–3) and St. Saviour's, Acton, also for RADD (1924–6). The latter was particularly admired for its simplification of form and for its affinities with contemporary Swedish architecture, for example Ivar Tengbom's Hogelin church in Stockholm, which Maufe said was 'the most completely satisfying modern Swedish building' he had seen. At this period Maufe was a constant champion of modern Swedish architecture, often writing on this theme in the architectural press, and his own buildings, with their reticent and simplified elevations, painted ceilings, and applied sculpture, show this influence. Maufe felt that Swedish architecture 'combined freshness *without* obviously breaking with tradition'.

Maufe's domestic work had a stylish modernity in direct contrast with the new functionalism. In the architectural language of the time it was called 'modernity with manners' and very much reflected the established taste of the inter-war period. Maufe wrote and lectured a good deal—on 'furnishing and decorating the home', on furniture and present-day architecture. His interiors were very stylish, with built-in fitments and pastel colour schemes, particularly pink, mauve, and cream, contrasted with silver-lacquered furniture and mirrors. One of his best houses was Yaffle Hill, Broadstone, Dorset, built in 1929 for Cyril Carter of Poole Potteries; other schemes included an extension to Baylins, Beaconsfield, for (Sir) Ambrose Heal [q.v.] (1927), Miss Gluck's studio in Bolton Hill, Hampstead (1932), and the studio for religious services at Broadcasting House (1931). He also designed several branch banks for Lloyds, one of the best being No. 50 Notting Hill Gate (1930).

In 1932 Maufe won the competition for the new Guildford Cathedral, his design being placed first from among 200 entries. When the building was dedicated in 1961, taste had moved away from its neo-Gothic exterior but the splendid proportions of the nave and aisles and, in particular, Maufe's masterly use of space won general admiration. His design carried the simplification of Gothic still further than the Liverpool Cathedral of Sir Giles Gilbert Scott [q.v.] and his own earlier work. Maufe has been called 'a designer of churches by conviction': he attempted to produce buildings of austere simplicity aiming directly at the creation of a religious atmosphere. At Guildford he also wanted 'to produce a design definitely of our time, yet in the line of the great English cathedrals, to build anew on tradition'.

Later works by Maufe include buildings for Trinity and St. John's colleges, Cambridge, and Balliol and St. John's colleges, Oxford (of which he was made an honorary fellow in 1943), the Festival Theatre at Cambridge, the Playhouse at Oxford, and the rebuilding, in the late 1940s and 1950s, in a scholarly neo-Georgian style, of the war-damaged Middle Temple and of Gray's Inn, who made him an honorary master of the bench in 1951.

From 1943 until 1969 Maufe was first principal architect UK and then chief architect and artistic adviser to the Imperial (later Commonwealth) War Graves Commission. Among his many designs for memorials are those at Tower Hill (an extension to the Mercantile Marine memorial by Sir Edwin Lutyens, q.v.), the RAF record cloister and Canadian record building, Brookwood military cemetery (1947), and the RAF memorial at Cooper's Hill at Runnymede (1950–3).

He was much honoured. He was elected ARA in 1938, RA in 1947, and served as treasurer from 1954 to 1959. From 1946 to 1953 he was a member of the Royal Fine Art Commission. In 1944 he received the Royal gold medal for architecture and he was knighted in 1954 for his services to the War Graves Commission.

Although Maufe was a traditionalist and admired Lutyens above all his contemporaries, he was always open-minded, being for example one of the assessors who chose the design for Coventry Cathedral by (Sir) Basil Spence [q.v.]. His own work, particularly before World War II, took a middle course of well-mannered modernity without the grammar of classicism.

In 1910 he married Gladys Evelyn Prudence, daughter of Edward Stutchbury of the Geological Survey of India. She was a designer and interior decorator who joined Heal's during World War I and became a director. They had one son who died in 1968. Maufe was tall and handsome while his wife was beautiful and always romantically dressed; together they were much admired. Maufe died 12 December 1974, his ninety-first birthday, in the farmhouse he had restored in the late 1920s at Shepherd's Hill, Buxted, Sussex. The contents of the house including works of sculpture and artefacts by the Maufes and their associates—Eric A. R. Gill [q.v.], Vernon Hill, Gluck, and Carl Milles—were sadly dispersed by sale on 2 and 3 February 1977, after Lady Maufe's death in 1976. Maufe's architectural drawings and correspondence were deposited at the RIBA.

[C. H. Reilly in *Building*, May 1931; *The Times*, 14 and 28 December 1974; *Building*, vol. 227, 1974; *Architect's Journal*, vol. 161, 1975; John Cornforth, 'Shepherd's Hill' in *Country Life*, 9 October 1975; Maufe correspondence, writings, and press cuttings, MSS collection, British architectural library, RIBA; private information.] MARGARET RICHARDSON

MELCHETT, third BARON (1925–1973), merchant banker and first chairman of the British Steel Corporation. [See MOND, JULIAN EDWARD ALFRED.]

MENON, VENGALIL KRISHNAN KUNJIKRISHNA (1896–1974), Indian politician, was born 3 May 1896 at Calicut, the third of the eight children of Komathu Krishna Kurup Menon, lawyer, and his wife, Lakshmi Kutty Amma, both members of the matriarchal Nayar caste and the Malabar aristocracy. He graduated from the Madras Presidency College in 1918 and, under the influence of the Theosophical Society of Annie Besant [q.v.], became an active worker for the home rule movement. He went to England in 1924, and took his B.Sc. with first class honours in 1927 and later M.Sc. in political science from the London School of Economics (of which he later became an honorary fellow) and an MA in psychology from University College, London, in 1930. He was called to the bar at the Middle Temple in 1934.

Menon settled in London, earning a meagre living from casual journalistic and editorial work. As an editor for Bodley Head, he sponsored the 'Twentieth Century Library'. In 1935, he and (Sir) Allen Lane [q.v.] started the Penguin and Pelican Books. His chief activity, however, was propaganda for Indian nationalism through the India League which he founded. Living in a garret in St. Pancras on a starvation diet, he used every means available to propagate the cause of India's freedom. He lobbied MPs and worked through the Labour Party and thus came into close contact with leaders like Harold Laski, Sir Stafford Cripps, and Aneurin Bevan [qq.v.]. In 1932 he acted as secretary to the Labour Fact Finding Mission on the civil disobedience movement in India. He was elected as a Labour member to the St. Pancras Borough Council in 1934 and held the seat for fourteen years. He resigned from the party in 1940 when his nomination as parliamentary candidate for Dundee was withdrawn on grounds of his primary loyalty to India, but rejoined in 1944 when the party adopted a resolution demanding freedom for India, partly through his influence. He developed a close friendship with Jawaharlal Nehru [q.v.] whom he first met in 1927. At Nehru's instance, he acted as representative of the Indian National Congress on international forums and played a crucial role as his aide in the negotiations leading to transfer of power. Their shared political beliefs emphasized a distinction between the British people and imperialism, global perspectives on colonialism, and egalitarian as well as anti-totalitarian values.

As the first high commissioner for independent India in London from 1947 to 1952—an appointment not favoured by the Labour government—he helped foster good relations between the two countries. India's decision to stay in the Commonwealth and the formula reconciling a republican constitution to Commonwealth membership owed much to his influence. His tenure was terminated in unhappy circumstances in 1952, but he was soon appointed deputy leader and then leader of the Indian delegation to the UN, where he championed the cause of non-alignment, fought hard to assert the importance of Afro-Asian nations, and developed a style of personal diplomacy to resolve international crises. His contribution towards solving the deadlock over the issue of US prisoners of war in Korea and the crises in Indo-China and Cyprus were widely recognized. But his radical image and abrasive personality earned him many powerful enemies in India. On the other hand his spirited defence of India's stand on Kashmir and Goa in the UN made him immensely popular with the Indian public. His attack on western powers on these questions and the issue of colonialism, especially during the Suez crisis of 1956, in contrast to his refusal to condemn outright the Soviet intervention in Hungary, provoked intense hostility in the conservative western press, especially in the US. India's non-aligned stance which he represented and which the western leaders like Dulles considered a camouflage for pro-Soviet policies, as well as his aggressive style, explain this hostility. The ambivalence in Indian policy and Menon's personal attitudes both derived from a deep-rooted suspicion of western colonialism. Menon's anti-colonial concerns contributed to India's brief entente with China and the Bandung conference of Afro-Asian nations in 1955.

Despite strong opposition from conservative lobbies, Nehru appointed Menon a minister without portfolio in 1956 and defence minister in his Cabinet (1957–62). It was in the latter capacity that he was held responsible for the débâcle in India's war with China in 1962. His career never recovered from the set-back though he was re-elected to the Indian parliament as a left-sponsored independent member in 1969 after two earlier defeats. He died in New Delhi 5 October 1974. He was unmarried.

[T. J. A. George, *Krishna Menon, a Biography*, 1964; M. Brecher, *India and World Politics, Krishna Menon's View of the World*, 1967; *Link*, 13 October 1974.] T. RAYCHAUDHURI

MENZIES, SIR ROBERT GORDON (1894–1978), prime minister of Australia, was born at Jeparit, Australia, 20 December 1894, the third of the four sons and fourth of the five children of James Menzies, who came from a line of Scottish farming folk, and his wife, Kate, daughter of James Sampson, a former miner whose roots were in Cornwall. James and Kate Menzies kept a general store in Jeparit, a small rural community 250 miles north-west of Melbourne. Menzies was educated at the local primary school until he was twelve, then at the Humffray Street State School in Ballarat, and subsequently, with a state scholarship, at a Ballarat private school, Grenville College. At fifteen an exhibition took him to a second private school, Wesley College at Melbourne. His parents went to live in Melbourne when his father had been elected to the Legislative Assembly, the lower house of the Victorian Parliament. At eighteen he won an exhibition at Melbourne University, where he read law.

After the outbreak of World War I, with two older sons in France with the Australian Imperial Forces and the youngest still at school, the family decided that Robert Menzies should stay in Melbourne to finish his course. This brought upon Menzies wounding imputations against his conduct and courage. But he always maintained that this was a family and private affair which did not need defence. In 1916 he obtained first class honours in law, winning the Supreme Court Judges prize and other awards. He was called to the Victorian bar in 1918. He then practised as a barrister, his reputation grew, especially as a constitutional lawyer, and within ten years he was earning £10,000 a year.

In 1928 he won a seat in the Upper House of the Victorian Parliament as a Nationalist and was soon appointed an honorary minister. The following year he resigned to contest a seat in the Victorian Legislative Assembly and won. In 1929 he took silk. After Labour's defeat in 1932, the new premier of Victoria, Sir Stanley Argyle, made Menzies his deputy premier as well as attorney-general and minister for railways. In 1934 the Australian prime minister, Joseph Lyons [q.v.], invited Menzies to contest in the Commonwealth House of Representatives the Melbourne seat of Kooyong for the United Australian Party and indicated that the attorney-generalship could be his. Although reluctant to go to Canberra, which meant frequent separation from his wife and young children, Menzies won the seat (which he held until his retirement in 1966) and accepted office. His parliamentary skill was quickly recognized and he was soon appointed deputy leader of his party. Menzies was attorney-general and minister for industry from October 1934 until November 1938. Lyons won the next election with a much reduced majority and shelved a National Insurance Act which had been passed. Menzies, who had pledged himself to its implementation, resigned his offices in March 1939. In April that year Lyons died. After a contested election Menzies succeeded to the leadership of the UAP. Sir Earle Page, leader of the Country Party, which had been in coalition with the UAP, became prime minister and attacked Menzies sharply, criticizing his wartime record. Menzies made a dignified reply. After nineteen days Page, whose virulence had alienated some of his own party members, resigned and Menzies formed a government without the Country Party on 26 April 1939.

After the outbreak of war between Britain and Germany Menzies led Australia into the war on the evening of 3 September 1939. There followed an uncomfortable period for the government. After the general election in September 1940 its majority in the House of Representatives sank to one. Australia became increasingly anxious about Japan's intentions. Through his high commissioner in London, Stanley Bruce (later Viscount Bruce of Melbourne, q.v.) Menzies constantly reminded (Sir) Winston Churchill of the Japanese menace. Despite his precarious parliamentary position he flew to London early in 1941, visiting *en route* the Australian forces in the Middle East. In London, which he had previously visited as attorney-general, Menzies attended meetings of the War Cabinet. Impressed by the courage of the people and inspired by Churchill's defiant leadership he found little satisfaction in Whitehall's lack of interest in Far Eastern defence. Realizing how little Britain could do he refrained from public disagreement. This London visit was later to guide his policy in the Pacific.

Back home again, Menzies found the feuding between the parties exacerbated by the divided opinions within the UAP. He offered to resign and serve in a national government under Labour's leader, John Curtin [q.v.], but his offer was declined. He finally resigned in August 1941. (Sir) Arthur Fadden, the elected leader of the government parties, formed a new ministry with Menzies as minister for the co-ordination of defence.

The Fadden government was defeated, two Independents voting with the opposition. The Labour Party, under John Curtin, won the election of October 1941 and remained in power for eight years.

Menzies's first experience of office had ended in bitterness. After the election he retired to the back-benches. He could have left politics and returned to the bar to earn a large income but towards the end of 1943 he accepted the leadership of the opposition on his own terms. He saw that his first task must be to create a broadly based but united anti-socialist party, an organized party of the right such as had never existed in Australia. He drew together all the disunited elements supporting the UAP, creating a new Liberal Party, supported by the Country Party. The alliance gained a few seats in the first post-war election in 1946 and in the election of December 1949 Menzies led it to victory. J. B. Chifley, by his Banking Act to nationalize the private banks which was rejected as unconstitutional by the High Court, had given his rival an effective challenge on grounds of his own choosing. Menzies was now at the head of a coherent anti-socialist coalition with a working majority in the House of Representatives though not yet in the Senate.

A plank of Menzies's election platform had been the Communist Party Dissolution Bill. With other government measures this was delayed, amended by the Labour majority in the Senate, and eventually passed. Chifley's successor, Herbert Evatt [q.v.], then chose to appear for the Communist Party when it sought a declaration from the High Court that this was unconstitutional. The appeal succeeded. Then Menzies's proposal to amend the constitution to admit the Act failed at a specially held referendum. Though this was a serious blow to the new government Evatt was exposed to the imputation of sympathizing with communism.

The Labour Party favoured the development of a Commonwealth Bank enjoying a highly centralized control of banking and finance, as an instrument for the eventual advancement of socialism. Menzies saw that the introduction of a Bill to modify the central banking system might give him grounds for seeking a double dissolution of parliament as provided by the constitution. The prolonged and unresolved differences between the House and the Senate over this Bill moved the governor-general, (Sir) William McKell, to agree, much to Labour's discontent, to grant such a dissolution. Menzies won the subsequent election which was held in April 1951. Then early in 1952 he imposed measures to curb the boom which resulted from the Korean war. These measures were highly unpopular not least with the supporters of the Country Party. Labour, not unjustly, accused Menzies of concealing his intentions until after the election.

In April 1954 another election fell due. The opinion polls were forecasting a Labour victory when a third secretary at the Soviet embassy, Vladimir Petrov, defected, revealing his own spying activities and other parallel practices by the Soviet government in the international field. In announcing this in the House Menzies moved for a royal commission of inquiry in order to place the matter immediately *sub judice*. Although the opposition agreed, the Petrov affair was detrimental to the Labour Party. The government was returned with a much reduced majority. The 1954 election proved a climacteric in Menzies's political fortunes. Evatt felt cheated of victory. His egregious conduct before the commission and in the House proved divisive. Many Roman Catholics loyal to Labour were repelled by his leftward style of leadership. The Labour Party split and a Democratic Labour Party with strong church support was formed. The DLP voters' second preferences were thereafter deliberately directed to the government parties, thus giving them an advantage in several elections.

In 1950 Menzies had agreed to send Australian forces to the Korean theatre. In 1951 he had successfully pressed in Washington for a treaty of mutual defence between Australia, the USA, and New Zealand—the Anzus treaty, from which Britain was excluded, despite Churchill's objections. Against Labour's opposition a 'soft' Japanese peace treaty had been signed immediately after the Anzus treaty. In 1956 Australia negotiated a comprehensive trade treaty with Japan which became her principal market for minerals and wool. Pursuing a policy of 'forward defence' of Australia, in 1954 Menzies took his country into the South-East Asia Defence Treaty, to which the USA also acceded. Meanwhile Australia had maintained with New Zealand a joint military contingent in support of the British forces fighting communist insurgency in Malaya. In 1955 Menzies agreed to contribute to the Commonwealth strategic reserve in the South-East Asia area. Only when it became clear that the USA would not support Australia against Indonesia over Dutch New Guinea did Menzies abandon his own support for the Dutch administration. Later he sent an Australian contingent to help in the defence of Sarawak against threatening Indonesian forces.

At Commonwealth conferences in London Menzies was a regular contributor. He saw communism as the main threat to peace in the South Pacific region. He felt little sympathy with the policies of non-alignment and anti-colonialism propounded by Jawaharlal Nehru [q.v.]. His objections to external interference in another country's internal affairs were felt the more forcibly when Canada proposed the exclusion of South Africa from the Commonwealth for its policy of apartheid. He was dismayed by the result. Menzies also contemplated with anxiety the negotiations for Britain's entry into the European Economic Community. But since he maintained that the political stability of western Europe and Britain's influence there were a major Australian interest he declined to organize opposition.

In May 1956 Menzies attended the prime ministers' conference in London. He was on his way home when the Suez crisis developed and he returned to London. He accepted the invitation of Sir Anthony Eden (later the Earl of Avon) to lead a delegation to Egypt with a plan approved by seventeen nations for international control of the canal. The talks ended in stalemate. He suffered domestic criticism for heading the mission to Cairo, but despite its failure he continued to justify on principle Anglo-French military action.

In economic policy Menzies began early to mitigate Labour's stance of financial self-sufficiency. He persuaded the World Bank in Washington to provide a large dollar loan to be used principally to supply American construction equipment. He continued to tap both the Washington and London money markets from time to time. He wished to sustain the large immigration programme inherited from Labour and realized that his government must in the process encourage private as well as public international investment. When, as in the early 1950s, credit expanded too rapidly Menzies had, from time to time, to impose government controls to restrain it. He was reluctant however to revive old controversies over tariffs and wage arbitration in a search for lasting solutions to these recurring problems. At the same time he displayed his willingness to take unpopular measures. Though listening to advice from professional bankers and economists, he followed his own judgement over the timing of his moves. His timing helped him to win the 1955 and 1958 elections. However the 1961 election left him with a majority of only one. Thereafter he moved quickly to reflate the economy. Arthur Calwell, the leader of the ALP, pointed out that Menzies was adopting some of the very measures recommended by the Labour Party at the election. Nevertheless in 1962 the popular tide ran again for the government and brought the coalition to victory with a record majority.

The Constitution Act of 1900 limits the federal government's powers to those specifically vested in it. But after the war the financial agreement of 1944, whereby the States had ceded to the Australian Commonwealth the right to impose direct taxes, continued. With this power under his control Menzies could encourage many development schemes, through grants or loans to the States from the Commonwealth Exchequer. He kept himself constantly before the public eye through well-publicized association with such projects. Without formally amending the constitution he was able to extend the power of the Commonwealth government in areas formally reserved to the States. Menzies himself remained by conviction on the side of the 'State Righters'.

World War II stimulated in Australia a demand for tertiary education. The Australian National University in Canberra, founded under Chifley, was generously funded under Menzies. Menzies also argued, successfully, that federal monies be available to State universities, despite the constitutional reservation that education was reserved to the States. Primary and secondary schools benefited under his similar arguments.

Under Menzies's inspiration Canberra, the capital city, was developed with a purpose and vigour hitherto lacking. Unified supervision was achieved by the creation in 1957 of the national capital development commission. Menzies did much to improve the level of competence and raise the status of the public service.

Although Menzies remained very much in charge after the election in 1962 speculation about his retirement increased. In December 1964 he reached the age of seventy. He was becoming less tolerant of criticism and more contemptuous of opposition. Yet a year later he won another election, a victory which allowed him a deliberate choice. After a month's deep and private reflection he tendered his resignation and announced his retirement on Australia Day, 26 January 1966. He bought a house in Melbourne, 2 Haverbrack Avenue, Malvern, where he spent his retirement. During 1966 and 1967 he spent some months at the University of Virginia as visiting professor.

Menzies never kept a political diary. In his books *Afternoon Light* (1967) and *The Measure of the Years* (1970) he considered in retrospect a number of events in which he had been concerned. In 1971 he suffered a severe stroke which incapacitated him physically though not mentally. Thereafter his public appearances were few.

By temperament and conviction a traditionalist, he insisted that the monarchy, responsible government within the parliamentary system, and an independent judicature were the true foundations of Australian democracy. He expressed his views forthrightly and was dismissive of populist opinions. He maintained that his country's interests were best served by close relations with Britain and the 'old' Commonwealth as well as with America. By his alliance with the USA he obtained a high degree of protection for his country with limited defence expenditure. In line with this policy in the 1960s he supported America in Vietnam with an infantry battalion and naval forces. His long domination of Australian national politics generated impatience as well as criticism. His successes were ascribed by his opponents to tactics both ruthless and less than scrupulous.

There are deeper explanations for his ascendancy. A former governor-general, Sir Paul Hasluck, wrote that 'Menzies had a better mind than anyone else in and around Australia' and again that 'he was a statesman singularly free from over-confidence, petty vanity and vexation of spirit'. To this judgement must be added mention of his courage and unswerving devotion to the service of his country to the neglect of any private interest.

In private life he was a generous friend, a genial companion, and a witty conversationalist. He was kind and encouraging to the young. He specially enjoyed legal stories and recollections of the bar. In build he was large. He had a fine head and his features were expressive. In later life his well-marked dark eyebrows contrasted with his white hair. When delivering an occasional address such as he made at his institution as lord warden of the Cinque Ports at Dover in July 1966 his tone of voice and delivery commanded attention.

Among Menzies's many honorary degrees were those from Melbourne, Oxford, and Cambridge. His other honours were numerous and included CH (1951) and FRS (1965). He was admitted to the Privy Council in 1937, became a knight of the Thistle (1963) and a knight of the Order of Australia (1976).

He married in 1920 (Dame) Pattie Maie, daughter of Senator J. W. Leckie, of Melbourne. They had two sons and a daughter. His younger son died in 1974. His family life was singularly happy. His wife, by her firm character and devotion, gave him the domestic security and support throughout his career which he needed. She cared for her husband untiringly during the years of declining health. He died at his home in Melbourne 15 May 1978.

[Sir Robert Menzies, *Afternoon Light*, 1967, and *The Measure of the Years*, 1970; Sir Frederick White in *Biographical Memoirs of Fellows of the Royal Society*, vol. xxv, 1979; personal knowledge.] DE L'ISLE

MESSEL, OLIVER HILARY SAMBOURNE (1904–1978), artist and stage designer, was born 13 January 1904 at 28 Gloucester Terrace, Hyde Park, London, the younger son (there was also a daughter) of Lieutenant-Colonel Leonard Charles Rudolph Messel, OBE, member of the London Stock Exchange, of Cuckfield, Sussex, and his wife, Maud Frances, daughter of Edward Linley Sambourne [q.v.], artist. Between 1917 and 1921 he was at Eton, leaving early to join his contemporary Rex Whistler [q.v.] at the Slade School of Art under Henry Tonks [q.v.], where he impressed his director and fellow pupils by the head masks, worn at student parties, which he modelled from wax by ingenious contrivances. This was a light-hearted affair which was soon to burgeon into the revival of an ancient but long forgotten art. In 1925 Messel held an exhibition of his masks at the Claridge Galleries in London which awakened considerable interest and led to his first professional commission—to decorate with masks a scene from the ballet, *Zephyr and Flora*, directed by Georges Braque at the London Coliseum.

(Sir) C. B. Cochran [q.v.], alert as ever to encourage young talent, engaged Messel to design masks for his 1926 *Cochran's Revue* at the London Pavilion. They revealed an early proof of their creator's flair for depicting—or rather suggesting—diverse periods and nationalities which in the ensuing years he was to develop further in designs for opera, ballet, and (eventually) cinematic screen.

Throughout the 1920s Messel contributed designs for costume and scenery to a succession of Cochran revues, of which perhaps the most enduringly remembered is the *mise-en-scène* he devised for the song by (Sir) Noël Coward [q.v.], 'Dance, Dance, Little Lady'. Each figure (including the singer) was masked to exhibit a vapid and fundamentally unhappy and unfulfilled visage, reflecting at any rate one facet of society at that period (*This Year of Grace*, 1928).

In 1932 Cochran forsook revues and embarked on two theatrically more ambitious ventures, for both of which Messel made designs regarded by many as among the most distinguished of his career. For the revival of *Helen* (Adelphi Theatre), directed by Max Reinhardt, with a new translation and interpretation, Messel contrived a witty and imaginative décor, draping the famous bedroom and bathroom scenes almost wholly in white, and clothing Helen herself (Miss Evelyn Laye) entirely in white for the final scene. (Messel's predilection for white in his designs for costume and scenery may well have influenced interior decorators in a similar direction and to an extent which induced W. Somerset Maugham [q.v.] mischievously to describe as 'the white-slave traffic'.) For *The Miracle*, in the same year at the Lyceum Theatre, Messel was responsible for the costumes. Although necessarily restricted in this version of a medieval mystery play, fantasy was certainly a welcome feature—for example, in the forest scene, with its macabre 'personalized' trees, and in the diverse costumes for the banquet scene, diverse but always kept within their medieval patterns.

By the end of 1932 Messel was established as one of the foremost stage designers in Britain, and his name attached to a production had become as great a draw as that of any 'star' actor or actress. His talents in later years were stimulated by the rise of a new poetical drama, as in his designs for the production, in 1950, of Christopher Fry's *Ring Round the Moon* which ran at the Globe Theatre for eighteen months. In opera, too, his designs for *The Magic Flute* (Covent Garden, 1947), *Queen of Spades* (Covent Garden, 1950), and *Der Rosenkavalier* (Glyndebourne, 1959) gave his imaginative fantasy full scope. His designs for ballet had the rare quality of aiding, as well as decorating, the dramatic action, an asset which was particularly noticeable in his scenery for *Francesca da Rimini* (Covent Garden and New York, 1937), an adaptation of early Renaissance paintings which provided an entirely appropriate background. His scenery, too, for the revival in 1946 of *Sleeping Beauty* in London and New York was a major contribution to its success.

Between 1934 and 1959 he contributed designs for costumes and backgrounds to films, notably *Romeo and Juliet* (1936), *Caesar and Cleopatra* (1945), and *Suddenly Last Summer* (1959).

Further examples of his diverse talents were the Oliver Messel Suite in the Dorchester Hotel, London; and his plans and designs for public and private buildings locally during his last residence abroad. In 1956 he became a fellow of University College, London, and in 1958 he was appointed CBE.

At the beginning of their careers in the early 1920s Messel and Rex Whistler were confronted in the theatre—to a less extent in opera and ballet—with a general standard of décor which might not unfairly be described as competent but unimaginative. Realism—or naturalism, as it was called—was at a premium with manager and director alike; and theatre design—in London's West End as well as in the provinces—had passed almost entirely into the hands of the interior decorator and house-furnisher reproducing the 'upper-class' late-Victorian and Edwardian domestic background. It is largely due to the influence of Messel and Whistler, working independently and in a different style—Messel's decoration suggested the baroque, Whistler's rococo—that in this country the standard of décor for stage and opera was raised and transformed into an eclectic and well appreciated art. In 1982 the Earl of Snowdon, Messel's nephew, lent for an indefinite period to the theatre museum at the Victoria and Albert Museum the Oliver Messel Collection, comprising masks, head-dresses and costumes, models and moquettes, and designs and drawings for virtually every production Messel had undertaken during the course of his career.

Messel was unmarried. After service as a captain in the army during World War II, and a long spell of ill health, his last years were spent in Barbados where, at his home in St. James, he died 13 July 1978.

[*The Times*, 15 and 21 July 1978; Oliver Messel, *Stage Designs and Costumes*, 1933; James Laver, *Between the Wars*, 1961, and *Costume in the Theatre*, 1964; Charles Castle, *Oliver Messel*, 1986; private information.]

D. Pepys-Whiteley

MESSERVY, Sir FRANK WALTER (1893–1973), general, was born 9 December 1893 in Trinidad, the elder son and eldest of three children of Walter John Messervy, a bank manager of Trinidad, and later England, and his wife, Myra Naida de Boissiere. He was educated at Eton and the Royal Military College, Sandhurst. He was commissioned into the Indian Army in 1913, serving in World War I in Hodson's Horse in France, Palestine, Syria, and Kurdistan. He became a distinctive and high-spirited cavalry officer, with a high handicap at polo.

In 1925–6 he attended the Staff College, Camberley, and then served on regimental duties in India and as brigade-major at Risalpur on the North-West Frontier of India. He then went as instructor at the Staff College in Quetta (where a fellow instructor was a Colonel Bernard Montgomery, later Viscount Montgomery of Alamein, q.v.). From Quetta he went to command the 13th Duke of Connaught's Own Lancers (1938–9) and saw them through mechanization. From 1939 to 1940 he was general staff officer, 1st grade, in the 5th Indian Infantry division, with which he went to the Sudan after the outbreak of World War II. He was given command of a small raiding force, the Gazelle Force, which hunted Italians. When the British advanced into Ethiopia he commanded the 9th Infantry brigade which captured the fort at the battle of Keren (1941). He was then given command of the 4th Indian division in the Western Desert, distinguishing himself in the battle of Sidi Omar (November 1941).

He was an extraordinary figure. He was tall and athletic looking, with a facial expression that clearly showed his strong sense of purpose. In battle, sometimes in somewhat irregular head gear, his spare figure moving amongst his troops in his own fearless fashion, was well known to them and a source of constant inspiration. His religious faith was resolute. He said repeatedly of the way to pronounce his name: 'The accent is not on the Mess, but on the Serve.' He took part in Sir Claude Auchinleck's advance to Benghazi (winter, 1941) and the subsequent retreat. When Major-General J. C. Campbell [q.v.], the commander of the 7th Armoured division, was killed, Messervy succeeded him in the command of the Desert Rats. One of Rommel's battle groups overran his headquarters and he was captured. Removing his badges of rank, he pretended to be a batman and escaped back to the British lines within twenty-four hours.

Messervy was posted to India in 1943, with the rank of major-general. In command of the 7th Indian division, he took part in the battle of Arakan (1944), causing the Japanese force to disintegrate. He then fought in the battles at Kohima and Imphal, leaving in October 1944 to command IV Corps. General W. J. (later Viscount) Slim [q.v.], who promoted him to this post, wrote that he 'had the temperament, sanguine, inspiring, and not too calculating of odds'. He was also heard to say: 'I want a man who will throw his hat over the Chindwin and lead his troops after it—and Messervy's that man.' Messervy did precisely that. The daring thrust of IV Corps on Rangoon played a decisive part in the defeat of the Japanese Army in Burma.

After the Japanese surrender Messervy was appointed general officer commanding-in-chief, Malaya, where he took the surrender of 100,000 Japanese. In 1946 he returned to India as GOC-in-C Northern Command and, on the creation of Pakistan, became that government's first commander-in-chief in 1947. He retired in 1948 with the honorary rank of general. He was colonel of the 16th Light Cavalry (1946–9) and of the Jat Regiment (1947–55).

Messervy was appointed to the DSO (1941), to which a bar was added in 1944. He was created CB (1942), KBE (1945), and KCSI (1947). He was also a commander of the US Legion of Merit.

In 1927 he married Patricia, daughter of Lt.-Col. Edward Arthur Waldegrave Courtney. They had a daughter and two sons, the younger of whom died in a car accident in 1965. Messervy died 2 February 1974 at his home in Heyshott, near Midhurst.

[Henry Maule, *Spearhead General*, 1961; personal knowledge.] R. G. SATTERTHWAITE

METHVEN, SIR (MALCOLM) JOHN (1926–1980), director-general of the Confederation of British Industry, was born 14 February 1926 at Southampton, the younger son and younger child of Lieutenant-Colonel Malcolm David Methven OBE, of Ledbury, and his wife, Helen Marion Watson. He was educated at Mill Hill School and at Gonville and Caius College, Cambridge, where he was a Tapp exhibitioner in law and a Tapp postgraduate law scholar. He gained a first class in part ii of the law tripos in 1949 and was admitted solicitor in 1952.

In 1952 he joined Birmingham Corporation as a solicitor but left local government service in 1957 to move to the metals division of ICI where he worked in the legal department in Birmingham, later moving to Millbank. He became head of the central purchasing department in 1968 and in 1970 was made deputy chairman of Mond division.

In 1973 he left ICI to become the first director-general of the newly-created Office of Fair Trading. As the first consumer watch-dog he strove to maintain a balance of interest between consumers on the one hand and trade and industry on the other—a feat which he performed with considerable skill aided by his knowledge of the law, his experience as a former member of the Monopolies Commission, and a genuine interest in the needs of consumers.

Although previously unaccustomed to working in the public eye he took in his stride the speaking engagements and media interviews necessary to ensure that the aims and activities of the OFT were known to a wide and diverse audience and came to regard publicity as a major tool in attaining his objectives. He developed a close working relationship with journalists who appreciated his accessibility and his straightforward and disarming manner. An early interviewer described him as '... a mild man; mild steel'. As the consumer's champion he brought about changes in standards, safety, and consumer information, and encouraged trade associations to adopt voluntary codes of practice as an alternative to legislation. In particular, he stimulated the advertising industry to improve their self-regulatory procedures.

In 1976 Methven became director-general of the Confederation of British Industry. He wanted it to be an organization with teeth which would provide an alternative voice to the TUC. He determined to broaden its base by attracting trade and commerce into membership in addition to the large manufacturing industries, to develop sound well-argued policies and to publicize them widely in order to ensure that the case for private enterprise did not go by default.

Methven was quickly recognized by the government, trade-union leaders, and Whitehall officials as a tough opponent and a lucid and persistent advocate for industry. CBI members saw in him the ability, tenacity, and vigour to weld together a diverse organization and to provide leadership at a time of political and economic difficulty. Led by him they reacted vigorously against the Bullock report on industrial democracy and, in answer to his rallying call, 1,300 delegates turned up at the first national CBI conference held in Brighton in 1977 to argue the case for British business. One CBI member was heard to say as he waited nervously to speak on this first national occasion: 'I worked my way to the top, I didn't talk my way there'; but, under Methven's leadership, talk they did. In order to ensure the conference's success in media terms Methven walked Fleet Street, bearding editors in their offices, chivvying them to ensure that their papers were well represented in Brighton. As one editor commented, 'Whatever Methven does, he means it'.

Methven was knighted in 1978. A hard task-master, he drove no one harder than himself; and even at times of great personal achievement was driven to self-examination and to moments of self-doubt. He was always quick to seek, and listen to, the advice of others. Tall, lean, and somewhat lugubrious in appearance he was a lively and challenging colleague whose warm, whimsical, and engaging manner won him friends in every walk of life. Music, particularly opera, was one of his greatest pleasures. With his second wife, Karen, he developed a love of sailing and found time to be one of the chief fund raisers for the British entry *Lionheart* in the America's Cup.

In 1952 he married Margaret Field, daughter of Air Commodore Charles Henry Nicholas; they had three daughters. This marriage was dissolved in 1977, and in that year he married Karen Jane, daughter of Walter Anderson Caldwell, research chemist. Methven died in King Edward VII Hospital, London, 23 April 1980 at the age of fifty-four following a cartilage operation. A sculpture of his head in bronze by Franta Belsky is to be seen at the entrance to the Methven room at the CBI headquarters, Centre Point, London.

[*The Times*, 24 and 26 April and 20 May 1980; personal knowledge.] DOROTHY DRAKE

MEYNELL, SIR FRANCIS MEREDITH WILFRID (1891–1975), typographer, publisher, and poet, was born 12 May 1891 at 47 Palace Court, Bayswater, London, the youngest of seven children (three sons and four daughters) of Wilfrid Meynell, manager of the publishing firm Burns & Oates, and his wife, Alice

Christiana Gertrude Meynell [q.v.], poet, the daughter of Thomas James Thompson. He was educated at St. Anthony's School, Eastbourne, and from the age of fourteen at Downside. In 1909 he entered Trinity College, Dublin, but he left early in his third year without taking a degree.

He returned to his father's firm, and shortly afterwards took charge of design and production. Much of the firm's printing was then done by Bernard Newdigate of the Arden Press, Letchworth, but besides Newdigate Meynell also made the acquaintance of Stanley Morison [q.v.], who joined Burns & Oates in 1913 with no previous experience of book production. Meynell and Morison found that they shared a sympathy for left-wing politics and interests in the seventeenth-century Fell types at Oxford University Press, in arabesque ornament in typography, and in good book design generally. They remained friends until Morison's death in 1967, and in typographical matters each owed a great deal to the other, though Meynell's gradual disillusionment with the Roman Catholic faith in the early 1920s, and both men's different marital difficulties, helped to make the friendship less close in later years than it had been.

In 1913 Meynell was also appointed manager of the *Herald*. A socialist in politics, he supported the women's suffrage movement, while in World War I he was a conscientious objector, helping in 1916 to found the Guild of the Pope's Peace. He openly admired the Russian revolution, and at the *Herald* (from 31 March 1919 the *Daily Herald*), where he became assistant editor to George Lansbury [q.v.] and the associate editor Gerald Gould, he waged a campaign of support for the communist cause. The full story of his early political career is recorded in his autobiography *My Lives* (1971). He resigned from the *Daily Herald* in September 1920, and from January to June 1921 was editor of the *Communist*.

In 1916 Meynell founded the Pelican Press, which initially was closely connected with the *Herald*, and set himself 'to do good printing for the daily, not the exceptional, purpose', as he phrased it. Much of Meynell's design was influenced by the American typographer Bruce Rogers, but he also began to install some of the typefaces issued by the Lanston Monotype Corporation, sometimes adding modifications of his own. With the publication of the *Herald* as a daily paper in 1919, Meynell relinquished the management of the Pelican Press to Stanley Morison, but in 1921 he returned to it after the end of his association with the *Communist*. The press quickly gained a reputation not only for the quality of its book printing, but also for the imagination of its advertisement setting. Some of its most characteristic work is to be seen in the publicity book *Typography*, compiled by Meynell and first issued in 1923.

Meynell was however from 1921 no longer in charge of the Pelican Press, and in 1923 he founded the Nonesuch Press with the help of Vera Mendel (shortly afterwards his wife) and David Garnett, in the cellar of whose bookshop Birrell & Garnett in Gerrard Street, Soho, the press began. The Nonesuch Press was unlike the great private presses with which it has sometimes been confused. It possessed only a modicum of type, used chiefly for setting specimen pages. Instead it relied for its type on the best modern ones available commercially, chiefly from among the revivals of classic faces being issued under Morison's auspices by Monotype in the 1920s, and on the best of the new continental designs from Germany, Holland, and France. The press issued both limited and 'unlimited' editions. Its first production, John Donne's *Love Poems* (issued on 3 May 1923), appeared in an edition of 1,250 copies; and although one of its earliest publications *The Book of Ruth* was published in an edition of only 250 copies, many of the volumes in the 'Compendious Series', beginning with (Sir) Geoffrey Keynes's edition of William Blake's *Poetry and Prose* (1927), were reprinted many times over. *The Week-end Book*, an anthology edited by Meynell and his wife Vera and first published in 1924, caught the mood of the times and by December 1932 sales had reached over 120,000 copies according to the press's advertisements. In a different way, besides the compendious edition of Blake, the press also played a major part in the development of modern literary taste. Keynes had already edited Blake for the press in 1925, and among the more notable Nonesuch books were two selections of Blake's drawings (1927 and 1956) and the first facsimile of Blake's so-called Rossetti notebook (1935). Montague Summers's edition of William Congreve was published in 1923, and it was followed by editions of Wycherley (1924), Rochester (1926), Otway (1927), Vanbrugh (1928), Farquhar (1930), and Dryden (1931). The press published two of John Evelyn's works for the first time, while the edition by John Hayward [q.v.] of John Donne's *Complete Poetry and Selected Prose* (1929) scored an immediate and lasting success. Nor did Meynell neglect illustrated books. Among those published by the press the *Anacreon* (1923) of Stephen Gooden [q.v.], the *Genesis* (1924) of Paul Nash [q.v.], and E. McKnight Kauffer's pictures for Burton's *Anatomy of Melancholy* (1925) may be accounted some of the best books of their kind in the period.

Meynell published a full account of the press to date in *The Nonesuch Century*, written with A. J. A. Symons and Desmond Flower, in 1936; but although the Nonesuch Press survived the depression it did so finally only with the help of George Macy, who had founded the Limited Editions Club in America in 1929. After lengthy negotiations Macy took over the press in 1936, with Meynell remaining as designer. Several of the books issued by Macy in the following years however bore little resemblance to the old Nonesuch style, and much to Meynell's pleasure Macy returned the press to him in 1951. Meynell thereupon resumed publication in association with Max Reinhardt and thus later with The Bodley Head. In 1953 he published a coronation Shakespeare, and he continued to wage his campaign for better book production by turning in 1963 to a new series of children's classics, the Nonesuch Cygnets. In 1961 he published his own *Poems & Pieces 1911 to 1961*, where he brought together his poems in a more satisfactory format than he had been able to in the wartime *Fifteen Poems* (1944). The last book to be published by the press in Meynell's lifetime was a collection of poems by Tennyson, illustrated by Aubrey Beardsley [q.v.], in 1968.

Although the Nonesuch Press took up much of his time, the depression in the book trade in the 1930s forced him to turn also for a living elsewhere. In 1929 he had written *The Typography of Newspaper Advertisements*, which immediately became required reading in publicity circles, and in 1930 he joined Charles W. Hobson's advertising agency for four years. He then returned briefly to journalism in the *News Chronicle*, before being employed successively by United Artists and the Gaumont–British Picture Corporation and the advertising agency Mather & Crowther. In 1940 he became an adviser on consumer needs to the Board of Trade, and in 1946 he was appointed to the Cement and Concrete Association where he became director and remained until 1958.

Meynell was knighted in 1946, and appointed Royal Designer for Industry in 1945. He was a member of the Royal Mint advisory committee from 1954 to 1970, and as honorary typographic adviser to HM Stationery Office from 1945 to 1966 was responsible for much of the official printing for the Festival of Britain in 1951 and the coronation in 1953. He was vice-president of the Poetry Society in 1960–5, and the University of Reading gave him the honorary degree of D.Litt. in 1964.

A portrait of Meynell drawn by Eric Gill in 1933 was reproduced as an engraving in the *Nonesuch Century*. He was married three times, first in August 1914 to Hilda Peppercorn, better known as the concert pianist Hilda Saxe, who bore their daughter Cynthia in 1915; secondly, in 1925, to Vera Mendel, who bore their son Benedict in 1930; and thirdly, in 1946, to Alix Hester Marie ('Bay'), daughter of Surgeon Commander L. Kilroy, RN. She was under-secretary of the Board of Trade from 1946 to 1955, and was appointed DBE in 1949. Meynell died at his home in Lavenham, Suffolk, 9 July 1975.

[Francis Meynell, *My Lives*, 1971; J. G. Dreyfus, D. McKitterick, and S. Rendall, *The Nonesuch Press*, 1981; personal knowledge.]

DAVID MCKITTERICK

MICKLEM, NATHANIEL (1888–1976), theologian and church leader, was born at Brondesbury 10 April 1888, the eldest of the four sons of Nathaniel Micklem, QC, of Brondesbury and Boxmoor, and his wife, Ellen Ruth Curwen. From Rugby he went to New College, Oxford, to read classics, and obtained a second class in both honour moderations (1909) and *literae humaniores* (1911). He spent a further three years at Mansfield College, Oxford, in the study of theology. During his years in Oxford he showed as an outstanding president of the Union in 1912 the clarity and wit which were always to characterize his speech. He wondered about a career in politics (his father being a noted Liberal MP), but not for long. Ordained a Congregational minister in 1914, he was assistant in Bristol to the Revd Dr Arnold Thomas, holding the sole pastorate of Withington, Manchester, from 1916 to 1918, before working with the YMCA near Dieppe. He returned as chaplain to Mansfield College (1918–21), where he developed a lifelong friendship with C. H. Dodd [q.v.]. He left to become professor of Old Testament at Birmingham in Selly Oak, whence he turned to New Testament as professor at Queen's Theological College, Kingston, Ontario, from 1927 to 1931. His return to England came with the invitation to be professor of dogmatic theology at Mansfield College. In the following year he was appointed principal of Mansfield. This office he combined with the responsibility for the teaching of systematic theology until his retirement in 1953.

As a theologian Micklem wrote with directness and grace, not disappointed in the hope of reaching the minds of intelligent people not educated in theological disciplines, as well as striking fire in the thoughts of those who were. His grounding in biblical studies remained vital alongside the philosophical enthusiasms which had gripped him since his New College days and earlier. He claimed the insights of the Puritan tradition and brought new understanding in *A Book of Personal Religion* (1938), while probing delicately into Platonism and the medieval church, not least into the works of Aquinas. The purity of his meditation is not corroded by the practical and passionate intention of his work. He spoke to those of his own churchmanship of the need for clearly held, defensible tenets of faith, in place of the vagueness, if not inanity, he found in much contemporary expression. *What is the Faith?* (1936) and *The Creed of a Christian* (1940) open out questions for informed Christian minds. Always there is apparent an intensity of concern all the more telling for the subdued refinement of its form. Integrated in Micklem's mind with theology was its embodiment in worship. In *Prayers and Praises* (1941) there is evidence of a delicate ear for cadences and the control of language which marked his conduct of public worship and which stood as an example to Free Churchmen of true liberty in devotion.

While emerging as a, if not the, foremost Free Church leader, Micklem was to extend far beyond his own tradition. As a young man visiting India in 1912 he had caught a feeling for the world-wide church and as a theologian he was to range freely and effortlessly over many varieties of belief and practice. In Canada he was impressed by the United Church and in England a sensitive awareness allowed him to penetrate the thinking of other denominations. He was to experience the perils of his convictions, as not a few of his own order chose to see disloyalty in his discovery of the treasures of others. He was attacked with asperity, a quality not always absent in his elegant replies. He worked for the union of Congregationalists and Presbyterians in England and to the end of his life hoped for ever extending bounds of unity. He evinced surprise, but was none the less recognized by his own church when elected chairman in 1944–5. As an emissary of co-operation he went beyond his own country in one outstanding direction, identifying himself with the struggle of German Christians under the Nazis and visiting Germany as long as it was possible. Throughout World War II and beyond he remained in close touch with their leaders.

Micklem's early glance towards politics was not ephemeral. He wrote on many aspects of Christian responsibility, consistently maintaining the place of individual liberty against any form of power-state. In *The Idea of Liberal Democracy* (1957) he stressed the primary duty of Christian thinkers for its maintenance. Being more than a theorist, he was active in the Liberal Party in Oxford for many years and was its president in 1957–8. The son of a distinguished Chancery lawyer, he developed interests in law, as is evident in *Law and the Laws* (1952), based upon his Wilde lectures, in which he attempted to relate theology and legal theory by tethering jurisprudence firmly to moral law. To this Dictionary he contributed the notices of W. B. Selbie and William Paton.

Achievement and mastery continued into a retirement which saw mature reflective writing. Micklem was a man held in affection as well as awe. His candour, perspicacity, *esprit*, and warmth drew the friendship of scholars, but no less of people who would have followed only a little way the intricacy and subtlety of 'Nat's' mind. A man of strong family feeling, he shared with his wife Agatha Frances, daughter of the architect Thomas Ball Silcock, of Bath, from their marriage in 1916 to her death in 1961, as with his three sons, a life rich in literary and musical interest. He wrote about much of that life in *The Box and the Puppets (1888–1953)*, published in 1957, but held that his most revealing autobiography was his verse, particularly *The Labyrinth* of 1945, a sequence of accomplished poems which were nevertheless unfashionable in content, form, and diction.

Queen's University, Ontario, awarded Micklem the honorary degrees of LL D and DD and Glasgow the honorary DD. He was an honorary fellow of Mansfield College from 1972. In 1974 he was created CH.

Micklem died at his home in Abingdon 26 December 1976. He is recalled by Archie Utin's portrait in Mansfield College hall, catching perhaps the seriousness rather than the grace of the sitter, and by the epitaph in the college chapel: 'Salem caritate condiens, fide sapientiam'.

[Nathaniel Micklem, *The Box and the Puppets 1888–1953* (autobiography), 1957; Mansfield College *Magazine* and *Reports*; N. Goodall in *Journal of the United Reformed Church History Society*, vol. i, No. 10, 1977, pp. 286–295; *The Times*, 29 December 1976; personal knowledge.]

D. A. SYKES

MILVERTON, first BARON (1885–1978), colonial governor. [See RICHARDS, ARTHUR FREDERICK.]

MITFORD, NANCY FREEMAN- (1904–1973), novelist and biographer, was born at 1 Graham Street (now Terrace), Chelsea, 28 November 1904, the eldest child in the family of six daughters and one son of David Bertram Ogilvy Freeman-Mitford, the second Baron Redesdale, and his wife, Sydney, daughter of Thomas Gibson Bowles, MP [q.v.]. In different ways her grandfathers were remarkable men: the first Baron Redesdale [q.v.] being a diplomat, oriental traveller (author of *Tales of Old Japan*, 1871), horticulturist, and intimate friend of King Edward VII, whereas Gibson Bowles, the creator of *Vanity Fair*, was a brilliant *enfant terrible* backbencher. Through her Redesdale grandmother, Lady Clementine Ogilvy, Nancy had the blood of the Stanleys in her veins. She was to edit two volumes of their correspondence, *The Ladies of Alderley* (1938), of whom one was her great-grandmother, and *The Stanleys of Alderley* (1939). She was also directly descended from William Mitford the historian [q.v.]. With these antecedents it is hardly surprising that, in spite of a conventional upbringing, the six sisters and one brother Thomas David (killed in action in Burma, 1945), all endowed with striking good looks and gifts, have emerged in different degrees of fame and notoriety as a legendary family.

After her father succeeded to the Redesdale title and estates in 1916 Nancy Mitford's childhood was spent in the Cotswolds—at Batsford Park (sold in 1919), Asthall Manor (sold 1927), and Swinbrook Manor, a rather cumbersome house designed by her father. Her education was sketchy. Her father would not hear of her being sent to an ordinary boarding-school, deeming education of his daughters quite unnecessary, if not reprehensible. All her life Nancy Mitford deplored her lack of academic education, which she held against her parents. Yet she became an early and avid reader of biographies, memoirs, and letters which she found in the library her father had inherited but never himself looked at. For he was, in spite of natural intelligence and humour, a professed low-brow,whom Nancy Mitford caricatured mercilessly but affectionately as the blustering 'Uncle Matthew' of her novels. Indeed he was the source of most of her family jokes.

After a short spell at a finishing school at Hatherop Castle, Gloucestershire, and then as an art student at the Slade School under Henry Tonks [q.v.] (where she did not excel) she was sent, heavily chaperoned, to Paris. The French way of life immediately captivated her. After a first taste she was obliged to return to England in order to 'come out'. For three seasons she flung herself into London balls and country house parties where she was extremely popular. She soon met a group of Bohemian contemporaries—Evelyn Waugh, Robert Byron [qq.v.], Brian Howard, Mark Ogilvie-Grant, John Sutro, Christopher Sykes, and (Sir) Harold Acton, to name a few. They were fascinated by her intelligence, vivacity, wit, and beauty. On the fringe of these clever, sophisticated, provocative, and bright young people was James Alexander (Hamish) St. Clair-Erskine, a beguiling younger son of Lord Rosslyn, but improvident, impecunious, and five years her junior. For five unsatisfactory years they were engaged.

Not until she was twenty-four was Nancy Mitford able to break away from her family. In 1928 she took a room in the London flat of Evelyn Waugh and his first wife (Evelyn Gardner), then a close friend. But when the Waughs' marriage collapsed Nancy's sympathies were transferred to the 'he-Evelyn'. She soon took to writing, precariously supporting herself by articles for *Vogue* and *Harper's Magazine*. In 1931 her first novel, *Highland Fling*, was published. *Christmas Pudding* (1932), in which Hamish Erskine and (Sir) John Betjeman were thinly disguised, and *Wigs on the Green* (1935) followed.

In 1933 she married Peter Murray Rennell Rodd (died 1968), a younger son of the first Baron Rennell [q.v.]; he was handsome and intelligent, with a certain panache. But he was impecunious, with no regular job. Moreover he was from the start unfaithful and neglectful. The marriage was not happy although his wife would never brook any criticism of him by her friends. When she could no longer tolerate his escapades she left him and at his request agreed to a divorce in 1958. There were no children. In 1939 she followed him to Perpignan where he was working in a camp for Spanish refugee victims of Franco's regime. The experience made her violently anti-fascist and turned her into a socialist.

On the outbreak of war in 1939 she became an ARP driver. Then once again she worked for evacuees, this time from Nazi-invaded countries. In 1940 her fourth novel, *Pigeon Pie*, a skit about the phoney war, was published. In March 1942 she became employed as an assistant in Heywood Hill's Curzon Street Bookshop. She helped make this shop into a favourite wartime rendezvous of intellectuals who were drawn by her astonishing knowledge of the books she sold, her cheerfulness and vaunted enjoyment of the war. On her retirement in 1946 she was made a partner of the firm.

Almost overnight her state of poverty and insecurity was turned to affluence by the publication of her fifth novel, *The Pursuit of Love* (1945). It was a wild success and sold over a million copies. The theme was a consequence and the reflection of the most important crisis of her life, namely her meeting and falling deeply in love with Gaston Palewski, a member of the Free French forces, a gallant and cultivated follower of General de Gaulle, who was to become one of his closest advisers and future ministers. The 'Colonel', as he was known to her friends, aroused in Nancy a latent capacity for hero-worship and a total dedication to France and all things French. Henceforth the 'Colonel' was transmuted into the idealized characters of her future books, whether the Duc de Sauveterre in *The Pursuit of Love*, or Louis XV in *Madame de Pompadour* (1954). When the war was over Nancy went straight to Paris. In 1947 she rented the ground floor of an old 'hotel' in the rue Monsieur where she lived with her faithful maid, Marie, until obliged to move to a house in the rue d'Artois, Versailles, in 1967.

Until she was forty Nancy Mitford was not a public figure. Her excitement and pleasure in her sudden popularity and comparative riches were endearing. With *Love in a Cold Climate* (1949) and *The Blessing* (1951), the most accomplished of her novels having for theme fashionable French society, she had changed from amateur to professional status. Her writing was now compact, terse, and simple. Her plots were subtle, satirical, and humorous. In Parisian circles she was in great demand because of her renown, elegance (beautiful clothes from Dior), sparkling wit, and mischievous fun. Yet for all her extolling of France and the French and her disparagement (occasionally tiresome) of England and the English, her most intimate friends were her own countrymen.

In the 1950s she turned to biography, of which *Madame de Pompadour* was her first and most lively. She was an industrious researcher who soaked herself in the court life of Louis XV's reign. In spite of an air of self-confidence she went in much anxiety and fear of reviewers. However, their reception of the book was generally rapturous. It was followed by *Voltaire in Love* (1957), the profusely illustrated *The Sun King* (1966), a life of Louis XIV on whom and whose satellites she also became a specialist, and *Frederick the Great* (1970), whose battles she revelled in. During her biographical phase she wrote one more novel, *Don't Tell Alfred* (1960), a story centred on the British embassy, which she frequented during the ambassadorships of her friends the Duff Coopers and Gladwyn Jebbs.

Her one attempt at drama was a translation of André Roussin's farce, *The Little Hut*. In 1950 it appeared in the provinces and London where it was highly acclaimed. Her contribution, more serious than comical, to *Noblesse Oblige* (1956) on correct upper-class usage of words brought her prominently into the limelight as arbiter of social conduct. Of all her books *The Water Beetle* (1962), a collection of fourteen short essays, perhaps shows her to greatest advantage as a writer. In these succinct, perceptive, evocative, and extremely funny stories and anecdotes she shared her private jokes and prejudices with her readers. They are the nearest approach to the as yet unpublished correspondence with her family and friends. She took her writing extremely seriously and mastered an unmistakably individual style, which at first was marred by too frequent lapses into the exclusive jargon of her class and generation. For she was essentially a child of the twenties. Yet with all her sophistication she remained fastidious, abstemious, and seemingly spinsterish. She was a marvellous guest, staying for weeks on end with friends, whom she entertained during the intervals of her reading and writing.

She was much photographed by (Sir) Cecil Beaton [q.v.]. She was painted as a young woman by William Acton and in middle age by Mogens Tvede (1947), seated at her writing-table in the rue Monsieur. She was slim and vivacious. She had dark brown hair and delicately moulded features. Her dancing blue-green eyes and downward-sloping brows were vibrantly expressive of her moods which alternated from insatiable curiosity to mockery and merriment.

In January 1969 she was stricken with agonizing pains which persisted, with intermittent periods of relief, until her death 30 June 1973 at no. 4 rue d'Artois, Versailles. She bore these cruel sufferings with almost superhuman courage and cheerfulness. In 1972 she was awarded the Légion d'Honneur, which gave her inordinate pleasure, and appointed CBE, of which she remarked, 'I've never heard of the CBE but of course I'm delighted to have it . . . I hear it ranks above a knight's widow, oh, good.'

[Harold Acton, *Nancy Mitford, a Memoir*, 1975; Selina Hastings, *Nancy Mitford*, 1985; private information; personal knowledge.]

JAMES LEES-MILNE

MOBERLY, SIR WALTER HAMILTON (1881–1974), philosopher and vice-chancellor, was born at Budworth in Cheshire 20 October 1881, the eldest of four sons (there was also a daughter who died in the influenza epidemic of 1919) of Robert Campbell Moberly [q.v.], vicar of Great Budworth and later canon of Christ Church, Oxford, and his wife, Alice Sidney, daughter of Walter Kerr Hamilton [q.v.], bishop of Salisbury. Following schooldays at Winchester, he entered New College, Oxford, as a scholar and in 1903 was awarded a first class in *literae humaniores*. Elected a fellow of Merton in 1904, a year later he was appointed to a lectureship in political science at Aberdeen. He returned to Oxford in 1906 as a fellow of Lincoln and lecturer in philosophy. During World War I he served in France and Belgium with the Oxford and Buckinghamshire Light Infantry. He was appointed to the DSO in 1917 and was twice mentioned in dispatches.

After returning to Oxford for a brief spell following the war, Moberly was appointed professor of philosophy at the University of Birmingham in 1921. Three years later he was persuaded to become principal of the University College in Exeter. There his success as an administrator was such that in 1926 he was chosen to succeed Sir Henry Miers [q.v.] as vice-chancellor of the University of Manchester. For the next eight years Moberly strove to integrate the university into the industrial and business life of the city, for he was profoundly convinced that learning and the common life were inextricably bound up together.

In 1935 Moberly became chairman of the University Grants Committee, a position he held for fourteen years. In allocating government funds an instrument was required which would respect the autonomy of the universities in settling their own priorities and at the same time safeguard public accountability. Such an instrument was fashioned under Moberly's skilled leadership. By the time he retired from office in 1949 the University Grants Committee had gained the confidence of all concerned. For the next six years (1949–65), as principal of St. Catherine's, Cumberland Lodge, Moberly once again took up his teaching and pastoral role with the students and staff who came there for a variety of courses.

Like William Temple [q.v.], whose friendship he enjoyed, Moberly was always concerned to bring philosophy to bear upon Christian thought. His father had been the author of an influential work on *Atonement and Personality* (1901), and, while still a young don at Oxford, Moberly was instrumental in the publication in 1912 of *Foundations*, a symposium, edited by B. H. Streeter [q.v.], to which he contributed two essays—on 'The Atonement' and 'God and the Absolute'. But for him philosophy and theology were not to be confined to the academic ivory tower. As a leading churchman, he played an important part in the Oxford conference on 'Church, Community, and State' in 1937 and became a lay member of its successor body, the Council on the Christian Faith and the Common Life. When in 1942 it divided to form the British Council of Churches and the Christian Frontier Council, Moberly became chairman of the latter. One of its many projects was the Universities Teachers Group which led to the publication in 1949 of *The Crisis in the University* in which Moberly critically examined the presuppositions and aims of higher education. He was also an influential member of 'the Moot', inspired by J. H. Oldham [q.v.], where his companions in debate included T. S. Eliot, Michael Polanyi [qq.v.], and Karl Mannheim. Out of these discussions he wrote a penetrating critique of the Nuremberg trials in the *Christian News Letter*, the organ of the Frontier Council. This led, after years of reflection, to the publication of *Responsibility*, 1956 (his Riddell memorial lectures at Durham, 1951) and of his major work, *The Ethics of Punishment* (1968).

Moberly was awarded an honorary LL D at Belfast, and an honorary D.Litt. at Manchester, Nottingham, and Keele. He was an honorary fellow of three Oxford colleges—Lincoln (1930), Merton (1937), and New College (1942). He was knighted in 1934, and appointed KCB in 1944 and GCB in 1949.

To those who met him only on official business he could be a highly respected, but slightly forbidding figure: tall, almost military in bearing, old fashioned in courtesy. But in any more intimate group of friends his warmth and wit, his loud laugh and fund of stories, showed what humanity lay behind his customary reserve.

Moberly was married in 1921 to Gwendolen, daughter of Walter Myers Gardner, a chemist. They had four sons. He died at Oxford 31 January 1974.

[*The Times*, 2 February 1974; information from Kathleen Bliss and public records.]

PAUL ROWNTREE CLIFFORD

MOCKLER-FERRYMAN, ERIC EDWARD (1896–1978), soldier, was born 27 June 1896 at Thornhills, Maidstone, the younger son (there were no daughters) of Augustus Ferryman Mockler-Ferryman, major—later lieutenant-colonel—in the 43rd Light Infantry, and his wife, Evelyn Letitia, daughter of Sir Charles Whitehead, agriculturist. He went from Wellington to the Royal Military Academy, Woolwich, was commissioned into the Royal Artillery in 1915, and spent three years fighting in France and Flanders with medium batteries, emerging as a captain with an MC (1919) for gallantry under fire. His brother was killed in the war.

He had a short disagreeable spell of duty in Dublin in the winter of 1921–2, and then settled to peacetime soldiering. He was a tall, burly man, nicknamed The Moke. He passed the Staff College in 1928, returned there as an instructor in 1933–5, and spent 1937–9 in Australia as chief staff officer to the 4th Australian division. Early in World War II he served in the military intelligence directorate of the War Office, and was promoted brigadier in August 1940 to head the intelligence branch of GHQ Home Forces. As such he was privy to ultra-secret material obtained by decipher at Bletchley Park.

In the same rank, still knowing the secrets, he headed the intelligence branch of General Eisenhower's Anglo-American army which invaded north-west Africa in November 1942, and worked in Algiers. After the American defeat at Kasserine in February 1943 Eisenhower dismissed the American corps commander concerned, and felt that to preserve Anglo-American amity he should dismiss a British general also; the lot fell on Mockler-Ferryman, who had not been to blame but could most easily be spared. He returned to London in apparent disgrace to work in the Boy Scout movement.

He was at once snapped up by his friend (Sir) Colin Gubbins [q.v.] for the Special Operations Executive (SOE). He became its director of operations into north-west Europe. For over two years he sat on SOE's directing council and helped to form its policies. In particular, he took responsibility for clearing up a disaster and for two outstanding victories. It was he who supervised the extrication of the Netherlands section from an all too deep entanglement with the Gestapo; he who secured the completion by SOE of harassing heavy water production at Rjukan, west of Oslo—this stymied German attempts to produce an atomic bomb. It was he who received Eisenhower's order that a maximum sabotage effort was to be launched all over France and Belgium on the night of 5/6 June 1944, a resistance outburst that lost the Germans the control of their own rear areas during the Normandy invasion, which then began. He was appointed CBE in 1941 and CB in 1945, and held high American, Belgian, French, and Dutch orders, as well as the French and Belgian croix de guerre. He had an honorary MA from London University.

After the war he had a brief, uncomfortable spell with the Allied Control Commission in Hungary in 1945–6. He wrote a lengthy history, never published, of British wartime intelligence organization. His secret activities during the war had put him behind in the race for regimental promotion, and no place was found for his talents in the cold war. He retired to Eastbourne and became an expert botanist, identifying and photographing wild flowers on the South Downs. He died, unmarried, at Eastbourne 19 November 1978.

[*The Times*, 28 November 1978; M. R. D. Foot, *SOE in France*, 1966; F. H. Hinsley *et al.*, *British Intelligence in the Second World War*, 1981, vol. ii, chapters 24 and 27 and appendix 18; private information.] M. R. D. FOOT

MOND, JULIAN EDWARD ALFRED, third BARON MELCHETT (1925–1973), merchant banker and first chairman of the British Steel Corporation, was born in London 9 January 1925, the second of three children and younger son of Henry Ludwig Mond, later second Baron Melchett, MP and financier, and his wife, (Amy) Gwen, daughter of Edward John Wilson, of Parktown, Johannesburg. Mond's grandfather, Alfred Mond [q.v.] was managing director of ICI, the chemical company founded by his father, Ludwig Mond [q.v.]. Julian Mond's elder brother, Derek, was killed during the last month of the war while serving in the Royal Navy, and so he succeeded to the barony when his father died in 1949.

He was educated at Eton and passed into Oxford, but he decided to go straight into the Fleet Air Arm (RNVR) in 1942, serving first on the lower deck. He was commissioned and became a senior pilot in his squadron. After training in Canada and South Africa he served in the Atlantic and on the Russian convoys, flying Seafires. During his time with the Royal Navy he took a correspondence course in farming. In 1947 he joined the merchant bankers M. Samuel & Co.

In 1947 he married Sonia Elizabeth, the daughter of Lieutenant-Colonel Roland Harris Graham, a doctor in the Royal Army Medical Corps. They had a son and two daughters. They lived between a mews house in London and a farm in Norfolk where Mond was chairman of British Field Products Ltd., a farming company he had founded which specialized in grass-drying and animal feeding stuffs.

By the time he was thirty-four he had become a recognized member of the exclusive banking establishment. He was an adviser to the government's Export Credits Guarantee Department and the British Transport Docks Board and he was on the council of administration of the Malta dockyard. He also became a director of the Guardian Assurance Company and of the Bermuda-based Anglo-American Shipping Co. Ltd. In 1965 M. Samuel & Co. merged with Philip Hill, Higginson & Erlanger Ltd. and after a boardroom battle Melchett became the director in charge of the banking and overseas departments. At the age of forty-one he held more than a dozen directorships and was on the council of the Confederation of British Industry and the National Economic Development Council.

In the meantime British Field Products was becoming a rapidly expanding enterprise whose activities extended to selling seed and corn, grass-drying, and renting land to grow lucerne for the grass-drying scheme. Melchett persuaded the Guardian Assurance to become a major shareholder and in 1964 the company acquired Weasenham Farm Ltd. with more than 14,000 Norfolk acres. They introduced the most up-to-date methods, becoming one of the largest companies of the kind in the country, run by Melchett from his farm Courtyard, Ringstead, near Hunstanton. There he relaxed from his many business and social activities, and enjoyed leading a quiet informal family life. He owned a single-engine Cessna plane and never lost his passion for flying, taking a night-flying course to enable him to fly from London after office hours and land on a grass runway a few yards from the house. His other recreational activities were riding and sailing. In the summer he took his wife and children to Majorca where they had built a villa at Formentor.

In April 1966 Harold Wilson (later Lord Wilson of Rievaulx), the prime minister, invited Melchett to be the chairman of the organizing committee for the nationalization of the British steel industry and from 1967 until his death he was chairman of what became the British Steel Corporation. He had some misgivings about taking on a nationalized industry—one being the fear of government intervention—but the challenge was something he could not refuse. However, before accepting the invitation to mastermind the biggest amalgamation ever conceived in British industry, he consulted the heads of the fourteen major iron and steel companies, each with its own traditions and loyalties and together involving 270,000 people. It was his task to weld them into one financially viable corporation. Possessing a disarming gift for bridging the class barriers and free from class prejudice, he set himself the task of modernizing an ailing industry, making it more competitive with overseas companies and international in operation. A progressive employer, one of his first decisions was to establish a two-year notice of any major plant closure so that workers could be retrained for other jobs. He introduced worker-directorships, whereby members of the trade unions were appointed to both main and divisional boards.

Despite the critics' scepticism the unique innovation worked. The climax came in 1972 when he was asked by the prime minister, Edward Heath, to explain to a full Cabinet his long-term development plan for the corporation. Afterwards the government agreed to a large modernization and expansion programme involving an investment of three thousand million pounds over the next ten years. In 1973 Melchett triumphantly announced a profit of £26,000,000. As president-elect of the International Iron and Steel Institute he had also established himself as a world figure. His reputation as an unpompous tycoon with a dynamic personality was spreading. He was immensely hard-working with a charm of manner and sense of humour which could beguile the fiercest opponents. He accepted the appointment of non-executive director of Orion Bank in 1972 and it was thought that he might possibly not choose to renew his contract with the BSC.

On Friday 11 June 1973 he flew with his wife to their villa in Majorca where he died of a heart attack on the 15th. He was succeeded in the barony by his son, Peter Robert Henry (born 1948).

[Private information; personal knowledge.]

SHACKLETON

MONNINGTON, SIR (WALTER) THOMAS (1902–1976), artist, was born in Westminster 2 October 1902, the younger son of Walter Monnington, barrister, and his wife, Catherine Brown. He grew up in Sussex, where he attended preparatory school, but developed heart trouble at the age of twelve. Invalided for a year, he set himself to draw and paint. Later he spent eighteen months at a farm school near Ross-on-Wye, a period congenial to his fundamentally practical turn of mind. In January 1918 he entered the Slade School.

At the Slade Henry Tonks [q.v.] had a decisive influence on Monnington's development, particularly through his insistence that artists should be as objective as possible—like Ingres, 'who always drew as nearly as possible what he saw in front of him'. Encouraged by Tonks, Monnington specialized in decorative painting, and in 1922 won the scholarship in decorative painting offered by the British School at Rome.

Monnington spent most of the years 1922–5 in Italy. Artists of the quattrocento deeply influenced him, particularly Piero della Francesca, to whose mathematical principles and muted colours he instinctively responded. A reproduction of a single authoritative figure from one of the Arezzo frescoes was to hang in Monnington's house all his life.

In 1924 Monnington married the artist Winifred Margaret, daughter of Walter Henry Knights, sugar merchant. She had preceded Monnington at the Slade and the British School at Rome; her meticulous style influenced his work for the next decade. Monnington's chief work in Italy was a large tempera 'Allegory', purchased by the Contemporary Art Society and presented to the Tate Gallery. This picture made his early reputation.

From 1925 to 1937 the Monningtons lived in London, first in Putney and then in a studio flat in Tonks's house in The Vale, Chelsea. Monnington taught part-time at the Royal College of Art and later in the Royal Academy Schools. He was involved between 1926 and 1937 with other artists, including Sir David Cameron, Sir George Clausen, A. K. Lawrence, Sir William Rothenstein [qq.v.], and Colin Gill, in two major decorative schemes, for St. Stephen's Hall, Westminster, and for the new Bank of England designed by Sir Herbert Baker [q.v.]. Monnington's contributions are distinguished by their austere linear style. Meanwhile he completed (1931) a 'Supper at Emmaus' for a reredos in Bolton parish church.

In the early 1930s Monnington received commissions for portraits of eminent contemporaries, including Sir James Barrie, Sir Joseph Thomson, Stanley Baldwin (later Earl Baldwin of Bewdley), and Earl Jellicoe [qq.v.]. As a portraitist Monnington was objective, accurate and, since he was incapable of an ingratiating line, often devastatingly candid.

In 1931 Monnington was elected ARA. After Tonks's death in 1937, the Monningtons moved to Groombridge, Sussex, Monnington's home for the rest of his life; but his work now faltered, and he envied other professions. Despite his lack of training, physics and higher mathematics deeply interested him. He liked to gaze on pylons, radio transmitters, and television masts; he loved cars and fast, accurate driving, and took flying lessons. His election as RA in 1938 seemed to Monnington himself an unreal event; as his diploma work he deposited 'Piediluco', an Umbrian landscape painted fifteen years earlier.

In May 1939 Monnington joined the Ministry of Defence's camouflage team, and for the next four years was chiefly responsible for designing camouflage for aircraft production airfields. He threw himself into this with energy, indeed with relief. From 1943 he flew as an official war artist with a Yorkshire training squadron and later with light Mitchell bombers over Germany. He spent winter 1944–5 in Holland with the 2nd Tactical Air Force, drawing pioneer mobile radar equipment.

After the war, Monnington found it impossible to return to his former representational work. He taught at Camberwell School of Art until 1949, then at the Slade until 1967. Winifred Knights died 7 February 1947. Later that year Monnington married Evelyn Janet, daughter of Bernard Hunt, mining engineer and silver prospector. Monnington had one son by each marriage. His second marriage proved very happy; but for a while he produced little work. Contemporaries, observing his sparse Royal Academy exhibits between 1946 and 1953, believed he had 'dried up'; in fact he was essaying new directions.

Monnington's early work and the very different geometric paintings of his last twenty-five years are linked by his consistent interest in Piero della Francesca's mathematical principles. The metamorphosis was slow, and accompanied by periods of waning self-confidence. A commission in 1953 to paint the ceiling of the conference hall in Bristol's new Council House provided just the stimulus he needed. A suggestion by the Bristol city fathers that he should do 'something connected with the Merchant Adventurers' fell on deaf ears. Monnington's design instead symbolizes twentieth-century progress in nuclear physics, electronics, aeronautics, and biochemistry. The Bristol ceiling (over 4,000 square feet) is one of the largest painted ceilings in Britain, and one of the few painted in true fresco technique; it was completed in 1956. In 1959 he began fourteen 'Stations of the Cross' for Brede parish church.

In the 1960s most of Monnington's works were geometric designs. He had become a fellow of University College, London, in 1957; in 1964 he completed two murals, painted in polyvinyl acetate, for the University of London Students' Union. 'Square Design' (1966) was purchased for the Tate Gallery under the terms of the Chantrey Bequest. All Monnington's geometric paintings were based on drawings as exact and fastidious as his earlier representational studies.

Monnington was elected president of the Royal Academy on 6 December 1966; he was knighted the following year, and in 1968 presided over the Academy's bicentenary celebrations. He proved himself a popular president, and was annually re-elected. He was chiefly responsible for opening the treasures of the Academy's private rooms to the public; but exhibitions such as 'Big Paintings for Public Places', 1969, and 'British Sculptors '72' demonstrated equal concern for living artists. He continued his lively interest in the Academy Schools, and contributed to this Dictionary the notice of Sir Walter Russell, under whom he himself had first taught there. He was a warm-hearted man, and a shrewd and perceptive teacher, who well understood what Tonks called 'the difficulties of doing'. It was characteristic of Monnington that on Christmas Eve he should telephone the Academy night watchman to make sure he was not lonely.

The presidency added to his long commitments to the British School at Rome (1926–72) and the National Art Collections Fund (1941–76), left Monnington little time for painting, though he himself remarked in 1972 that its complexities were 'in some ways less difficult than trying to paint'. Monnington died in office in London 7 January 1976.

[*The Times*, 8 January 1976; *Drawings and Paintings by Sir Thomas Monnington PRA*, Royal Academy exhibition, 1977 (the catalogue includes an essay on 'Monnington, the Teacher and the Man' by Lawrence Gowing); Imperial War Museum archives; private information.] JUDY EGERTON

MONSARRAT, NICHOLAS JOHN TURNEY (1910–1979), writer, was born in Liverpool 22 March 1910, the second son and fourth child of Keith Waldegrave Monsarrat, FRCS, who was of French descent, and his wife, Ada Marguerite, daughter of Sir John Turney, a wealthy leather merchant who was mayor of Nottingham in 1889. His mother preferred the spelling 'Montserrat', which she recorded on Nicholas's birth certificate. His elder brother was killed in a cliff fall near their holiday home at Treardurr Bay, Anglesey, in 1908, to be replaced by another brother, born in 1914, who died in World War II. His early childhood and youth were spent in well-to-do circumstances in Liverpool; and it was at the family country home in Anglesey that over the years he developed his mastery of sailing and his love of the sea.

He was educated at Winchester and at Trinity College, Cambridge, where he obtained a third class in law in 1931. He was articled to a firm of Nottingham solicitors, but was determined to live by his pen. He then had extreme left-wing views: at one time he sold the *Daily Worker* on the streets of London and took part in a number of pacifist marches. He published three novels of no consequence (*Think of To-morrow*, 1934; *At First Sight*, 1935; *The Whipping Boy*, 1937). In 1938 he wrote his first novel to make an impact: *This is the Schoolroom*. It had the misfortune to appear days before the declaration of war, but it received considerable critical acclaim and (although the sales figures may later have appeared small) sold out its comparatively large edition.

With war begun, his conscience directed him to the St. John Ambulance Brigade. But the disasters of 1940 changed his mind and when he saw an advertisement advising 'gentlemen with yachting experience' to apply for commissions in the Royal Naval Volunteer Reserve, he put his name forward and was accepted. Within a few weeks he was at sea as temporary probationary sub-lieutenant on a corvette in the Atlantic. He remained in the western approaches for the rest of the war, commanding corvettes and, at the end, captaining a frigate as lieutenant-commander; he was mentioned in dispatches. In 1953 he received the Coronation medal. During his service he wrote three small books about his ships which were brought together in one volume, *Three Corvettes* (1945).

On his release in 1946 Monsarrat went into government service and was appointed director to open the UK Information Office in Johannesburg, where he remained until 1953. Towards the end of this time he was required to answer questions about Mau Mau atrocities in Kenya. Revolted by what he had seen, he refused to answer ghoulish questions from the world press and despised those journalists who pressed him: in return they considered him uncooperative and there developed a bad relationship which took some years to heal.

He wrote two more books before his life was to change radically: *Depends what you mean by Love* (1947) and *My Brother Denys* (1948). In 1951 the novel on which he had spent three years appeared: *The Cruel Sea*. It was an overwhelming success throughout the world, one of the greatest triumphs of fiction in the English language. By 1981 his English publishers alone had sold over 1,330,000 copies in hard-back—there having been no cheap edition. Sales figures were similar around the world. Monsarrat was immediately a wealthy man, enjoying an affluence greater than that in which he had been brought up as a child, and he unashamedly set out to enjoy every moment of it.

In 1953 he was transferred to Ottawa as British Information Officer, where he remained until 1956, when he resigned to devote the rest of his life to writing. Before he retired from public service he occupied various offices: a councillor of Kensington Borough Council, 1946; chairman of the National War Memorial Health Foundation (South Africa), 1951–3; a governor of the Stratford Festival of Canada, 1956; and a director of the board of the Ottawa Philharmonic Orchestra, 1956.

Although always in demand for public appearances, the rest of Monsarrat's life was private and is really told by the tally of his books: *The Story of Esther Costello*, 1953; *Canada Coast to Coast*, 1955; *The Tribe that lost its Head*, 1956; *The Ship that died of Shame*, 1959; *The Nylon Pirates*, 1960; *The White Rajah*, 1961; *The Time before This*, 1962; *Smith and Jones*, 1963; *To Stratford with Love*, 1963; *A Fair Day's Work*, 1964; *The Pillow Fight*, 1965; *Something to Hide*, 1965; *Richer than all his Tribe*, 1968; *The Kapillan of Malta*, 1973; *The Master Mariner*, vol. i, 1978, and vol. ii, 1980. He also wrote his autobiography, *Life is a Four-Letter Word*, 2 vols., 1966 and 1970. Three films were made of his major works.

After 1946 Monsarrat wrote one trivial book and one bad one; otherwise his work retained his own remarkably high standard. He was a narrator, a teller of tales, like the writer whom he admired so much—Thackeray. He had no 'style'; he had a story to tell and he told it. There were no tricks, no wanderings; nothing could ever distract him from the task which he saw before him. As a result, his prose had great clarity. Sometimes, if he was deeply moved by his subject, he could purify it to the point at which it became almost lyric poetry (for example, 'H.M.S. Marlborough will enter Harbour'—one of the three tales in *Depends what you mean by Love*, 1947). It seems probable that three of his novels will rank in the canon of English fiction: *The Cruel Sea*, *The Kapillan of Malta*, and *The Master Mariner*. The last he had planned for many years, but left its accomplishment too late and so died before he could complete the second volume.

Monsarrat was a handsome man of medium height, dark with blue eyes. He was quiet—even the barbs of his uproariously sardonic sense of humour reached their target in a low tone. Nevertheless he was a strong character and it was virtually impossible to make him change his mind once he had made it up. Next to writing, his deepest love was music. Publicly, when he had brushes with the media, he could be abrasive. But privately he was gentle, sensitive, with an enormous love of and faith in humanity. He was a romantic who always believed that the best in the world was possible. Often it was not and he was hurt, but he never changed his views or his beliefs.

In 1951 Monsarrat won the Heinemann Foundation prize for literature and in 1961 Liverpool mounted in the City Library a one-man exhibition of his work: the first time it had so honoured one of its sons; happily his father, at ninety the doyen of the city's surgeons, was able to be present. Monsarrat was also a fellow of the Royal Society of Literature.

Monsarrat was thrice married. In 1939 he married Eileen Rowland, daughter of an industrialist; they had one son. The marriage was dissolved in 1952 and in the same year he married Philippa Crosby, a South African journalist; they had two sons. The marriage was dissolved in 1961 and in that year he married Ann Griffiths, journalist, the daughter of a chartered accountant.

Monsarrat went to Gozo in Malta in the late 1960s to research for *The Kapillan of Malta*. He found the island so agreeable that he decided to linger for a while, writing and gardening. But eventually his health declined and his wife brought him back to die of cancer in King Edward VII Hospital for Officers, London, 8

August 1979. His ashes were scattered at sea by the Royal Navy.

[Nicholas Monsarrat, *Life is a Four-Letter Word*, 2 vols., 1966 and 1970, and *The Master Mariner*, vol. ii, 1980, with an introduction by Ann Monsarrat; private information; personal knowledge.] DESMOND FLOWER

MONTGOMERY, BERNARD LAW, first VISCOUNT MONTGOMERY OF ALAMEIN (1887–1976), field marshal, was born in St. Mark's vicarage, Kennington Oval, 17 November 1887, the third of the six sons and fourth of the nine children of the Revd Henry Hutchinson Montgomery, son of Sir Robert Montgomery [q.v.], lieutenant-governor of the Punjab, and his wife, Maud, third daughter of Canon (later Dean) Frederic William Farrar [q.v.], author of *Eric, or Little by Little* (1858). Their family was to grow up in Tasmania where Henry Montgomery became bishop in 1889.

A self-willed larrikin of fourteen, at odds with a mother as determined as he was, Bernard went with a brother as a day-boy to St. Paul's School, when the Montgomerys finally returned from Hobart in 1902, to live frugally in Chiswick; but high-spirited family holidays—there were eight children by now (a daughter died young and a son later died as a schoolboy)—were spent at New Park, the property at Moville, Donegal, which the bishop had inherited from his father.

Good at games and eager to lead, Bernard was 'very happy' at St. Paul's and at nineteen (and 5ft. 7ins.) 'the Monkey' eventually managed to pass, not very impressively (seventy-second out of 177), into Sandhurst. Lucky to be allowed to continue there after a cruel jape, he failed to pass out high enough (he was thirty-sixth) to make the coveted Indian Army; instead, he was commissioned, 19 September 1908, into the Royal Warwickshire Regiment with which he had no previous connection. Entirely dependent upon his pay and never having tasted alcohol, he was posted in December to the 1st battalion, then on the North-West Frontier at Peshawar. He rode hard at everything, his chosen profession and the study of Urdu and Pushtu. He always wanted to win, whether an argument or a steeplechase. Wilful and opinionated, he was continually straining at the leash.

Returning to England by 1913 in time to play hockey for the army and to pass out top of the musketry course at Hythe, Lieutenant B. L. Montgomery was acting adjutant when the 1st Warwickshire Regiment was mobilized at Shorncliffe in August 1914, and he crossed to Boulogne 23 August with the 10th brigade in the 4th division. Scarcely twenty-four hours after disembarkation they were under fire at Le Cateau. A notably fearless young officer, Montgomery was reported missing, gravely wounded and left for dead at Meteren, but survived in hospital at Woolwich to learn that he had been appointed, 13 October 1914, as a temporary captain of twenty-seven, to the DSO—the Military Cross was not instituted until December—for his bearing at the first battle of Ypres.

There followed early in the New Year a formative posting to Lancashire as brigade-major, 112th (later 104th) brigade, which enabled him not only to survive (which his return to a battalion would have rendered most improbable) but to begin to take on responsibilities and to uncover that flair for training which characterized his whole career. He pierced impatiently into the heart of matters to discover the most straightforward tactical solution to be used by the new armies which Lord Kitchener [q.v.] was raising to succeed the original British Expeditionary Force. Montgomery's written orders tingled with clarity; he was becoming highly professional.

His dedication soon inspired trust; he was brigade-major, 104th brigade on the Somme, January 1916; GSO 2, 33rd division (at Arras again), 1917; then, from July 1917, GSO 2 of IX Corps at Passchendaele; thereafter, from 16 July 1918, until the war ended, GSO 1, 47th (London) division. Then, at Cologne, with the connivance of Sir William Robertson [q.v.], he contrived to get himself selected for the Staff College at Camberley for January 1920. A brevet-major (3 June 1918), he had been mentioned in dispatches six times, wounded thrice, and awarded the French croix de guerre.

He came to ponder his experiences deeply only after he had left Camberley. In 1921 he was posted to Cork as brigade-major, 17th (the largest) Infantry brigade, in a war to him 'far worse' than the one he had survived. During the next few years in England, under sympathetic leadership, he became determined that costly mistakes should not be perpetrated again: there should be no more 'useless' carnage under remote generals and their cosy staffs; future battles were to be fought with decent economy and orchestrated artillery—metal saving flesh. Hence it was important to have accurate information, good communication and wireless, and the use of aircraft; there was also a need for sound understanding between effectively trained officers and an informed soldiery. All these considerations underlined the importance of training to which Montgomery now devoted his single-minded bachelor career. He was brigade-major, 8th Infantry brigade at Devonport, then GSO 2, 49th West Riding Territorial division at York where he lived in the same friendly mess as (Sir) F. W. de Guingand [q.v.], his future chief of staff. In March 1925 he went back to his regiment at Shorncliffe, but the turning point, Montgomery himself believed, was his posting in January 1926 to the Staff College, this time as an instructor, alongside Alan Brooke (later Viscount Alanbrooke), (Sir) Bernard Paget [qq.v.], and (Sir) Richard O'Connor. Their pupils included Harold Alexander (later Earl Alexander of Tunis), (Sir) Miles Dempsey, (Sir) Oliver Leese, (Sir) Richard McCreery, (Sir) Archibald Nye, Brian Robertson (later Lord Robertson of Oakridge, (Sir) Gerald Templer [qq.v.], and A. F. ('John') Harding (later Lord Harding of Petherton). Montgomery was an inspired teacher, unforgettably clear-headed.

To everybody's surprise he married, 27 July 1927, Elizabeth, widow of Captain Oswald Armitage Carver, a sapper officer killed at Gallipoli, the sister of P. B. S. Hobart [q.v.], and the daughter of Robert Thompson Hobart, Indian Civil Service, of Tunbridge Wells. She had two sons at preparatory school. They had met on successive skiing holidays in Switzerland. The marriage, which opened new horizons to the monastic, dogmatic soldier, was intensely happy.

Contentment did not attenuate a marked independence of spirit and not infrequent clashes with authority. Set to revise, as secretary of a War Office committee, the manual of *Infantry Training* in 1929, Montgomery, by his own account, published his personal version ignoring amendments; 'exploitation' was a significant omission. Three years followed while he fulfilled a natural ambition, the command of his own first regiment, in Jerusalem, Alexandria, and Poona. His seniors noted 'a certain high-handedness' as a possible handicap to future advancement.

In 1934 he succeeded Paget as chief instructor at Quetta, where he remained until 1937, experiencing the earthquake in May 1935. Then, at the instigation of A. P. (later Earl) Wavell [q.v.], he was posted May 1937 to Portsmouth to command 9th brigade. Tragedy struck. After ten enjoyable years of their marriage, 'Betty' Montgomery died of septicaemia (19 October 1937) after an insect bite on the beach at Burnham-on-Sea. Montgomery, left a widower with a young son, was utterly desolate. He hid himself in the army and was never the same man again: he had lost his firm base.

Lonely wilfulness could land him in trouble. War Department land at Southsea was let without reference to authority for an August fairground, the rent being spent on garrison amenities. The solitary brigadier found himself for a while 'dicky on the perch', but Wavell (at Southern Command) was never a man to waste eccentric talent, and a successful career was resumed in October 1938 with Montgomery's promotion to Palestine to command the 8th Infantry division from Haifa. O'Connor's 7th division was stationed to his south. Their grip was soon felt: terrorism was dealt with rigorously and the civilian administration regained confidence. By now evidently a most promising major-general, Montgomery was told that, should war break out in Europe, he might expect to command the 3rd division in the proposed expeditionary force. At this moment he was suddenly struck by a feverish illness affecting the lung which had been penetrated in 1914. Taken on board at Port Said on a stretcher, he forced himself to walk confidently ashore at Tilbury and proceeded to badger the military secretary until on 28 August 1939 he received the command he had been promised.

With Brooke, his Corps commander in II Corps, and with Alexander, he was one of the few to emerge from the inglorious campaign in Belgium with an enhanced reputation. However, before the fighting began Brooke had to protect him—not for the last time—from the consequences of acting off his own bat. In this instance, he had issued a tactless ordinance about brothels, which had started an outcry.

Highly trained and diligently rehearsed, Montgomery's 'Third Division worked like clockwork', the Corps commander noted, from the Dyle and Louvain back to Dunkirk where he and Alexander were responsible for the rear-guard. Montgomery was appointed CB (1940).

The 3rd division was the first to be re-equipped in England but in July 1940 Montgomery left it to succeed Sir Claude Auchinleck (promoted to Southern Command) as commander, V Corps. Cheerfully disobedient, he held that the way to repel the expected invasion was not on the beaches but by counter-attack after the enemy had landed; yet the army still lacked mobility and he himself had had to beg the prime minister at Brighton that summer for buses for his own division. Brooke, the only soldier Montgomery genuinely respected, and who was to become his surrogate conscience, besought him (3 August 1940) not to let him down 'by doing anything silly'.

In April, having lost all his worldly goods in an enemy bombing raid on Portsmouth in January, Montgomery moved from V Corps to XII Corps, and thence to command South-Eastern Army (17 November 1941). It was from this spell in England that, by his own reckoning, his 'real influence on the training of the army began' and with it the growth of the legend (which reached the Middle East) of the abstemious, dedicated widower, the ruthless oddity who made physical fitness a fetish and declared war on 'dead wood', wives, and complacency. Once the threat of invasion abated (and Montgomery spotted this sooner than most) the army in England had to be made ready for aggressive warfare in all weathers overseas, and this he set about achieving in a series of formidable exercises.

In mid-1942 planning for a Canadian raid on Dieppe was put in train and Montgomery was involved (although in later years he was inclined to be reticent on this score). He felt that since secrecy had been forfeited, another venue should be sought. The raid took place on 19 August 1942; Montgomery had left the United Kingdom nine days earlier.

He had been told to be ready to succeed Alexander (who had been sent to Cairo to succeed Auchinleck as C-in-C Middle East) in command of First Army, which was to invade French North Africa (Operation Torch) under General Eisenhower's overall command. Then, when W. H. E. Gott [q.v.] was killed, Montgomery was dispatched to take his place at El Alamein, in command of Eighth Army. Placing his son David in the care of his friends the Reynolds, he reached Cairo on 12 August. He knew in his bones that he was stepping into history.

Disregarding instructions, he took over in the Western Desert two days early and at once set about imposing his strong will. He was unprepossessing in appearance, skinny, sharp-faced 'like a Parson Jack Russell terrier', and his English knees were still white, but he knew exactly what he wanted: an abrupt change of 'atmosphere', the end of 'bellyaching' (the discussion of orders rather than their execution) and of looking over one's shoulder. There was to be no withdrawal. Eighth Army would fight and die at the Alamein position where the enemy had been halted by Auchinleck's resolution in July. De Guingand was promoted from brigadier general staff to chief of staff, to free the army commander from detail. New corps commanders and a new brigadier Royal Artillery were summoned from England, the 44th division was ordered up imperiously from the delta, and the army headquarters was set down by the sea alongside the desert air force. The armour was rehearsed in its defensive role, dug in or hull down.

Montgomery quickly imposed his personal authority as he quickened the pulse of his new command. In a crisis of confidence among men far from home he provided reassurance and certainty. His army (or enough of it) soon became convinced, as they saw him darting about in unexpected headgear, that, despite his sartorial eccentricity, he knew what he was up to, talked sense (in an odd but readily quotable vocabulary), would deliver the goods, and, above all, not waste their lives. It was a new and exciting technique of command. The model defensive battle (from 31 August) at Alam Halfa, in which the air force played a substantial role, furnished Montgomery with the mastery and Eighth Army with the morale demanded in the major offensive battle to follow. Although he himself came to exaggerate the uniqueness and novelty of his own contribution and to maintain that everything went according to preconceived plan, the unfamiliar sight of Rommel's forces on their way back (3 September) through the minefields they had penetrated with such difficulty heartened Eighth Army enormously and hardened belief in 'Monty' and his self-assurance.

There was political pressure on him to resume battle, partly because the Martuba airfields in the North African bulge had to be regained by mid-November to allow for air cover for the last convoy leaving Alexandria to replenish Malta's almost exhausted aviation fuel, and partly because the departure of 'Torch' in early November would have been hazarded had news reached England of any apathy. With Alexander's imperturbable backing, Montgomery took his own time to mount his offensive. He had to learn to master the new American Sherman tanks and anti-tank guns, to improve the training (especially in dealing with minefields), and to institute deception measures for what was inevitably frontal attack on the strong enemy defences at El Alamein between the sea and the virtually impassable Qattara depression. These requirements, together with the state of the moon and of the Eighth Army's readiness, set the date for 23 October. By then, of course, the enemy defences were deeper and stronger.

His design (Operation Lightfoot) was to feint in the south whilst cutting corridors through the northern Axis positions in a moonlit operation with massed artillery support, to hold off the German armour during the 'crumbling' operations which would ensue, and in this 'dogfight', lasting perhaps twelve days, to hold the initiative so as to deprive the enemy armour of firm bases from which to manoeuvre or within which to refurbish.

By 23 October the desert air force had conclusively won the air battle and thereafter successfully devoted its full attention to the close support of the land forces, which had already been so effective at Alam Halfa. By 25 October Eighth Army had gained a bridgehead in the northern Axis positions, which was slowly developed into a salient increasingly menacing the coastal road. With controlled flexibility Montgomery alternated the direction of his thrusts—until, fearful of his ultimate line of advance, the main German forces were congregated, not without severe losses, in the northern sector about Sidi Abd al Rahman. Maintaining his apparent thrust line, Montgomery, who, by shrewd regrouping since 26 October had been accumulating reserves as steadily as the returning Rommel had been forced to commit his, early on 2 November cut through south of the main German concentrations into the preponderantly Italian positions (Operation Supercharge). A quickly improvised Axis anti-tank screen prevented immediate breakthrough but on 4 November this was forced back and the over-extended Axis defences crumpled. Those with vehicles could attempt retreat; for the rest, mainly Italian, surrender was the only option. Eighth Army's casualties were 13,500.

It was a considerable victory. With air supremacy and, on the ground, unparalleled numerical superiority in armour and artillery, Montgomery could call on resources denied to his predecessors. But he used them (and a remarkable flow of intelligence) in a unique revelation of determination and skill to enforce the attrition. It was 'a killing match'.

He could be criticized—there were willing critics of, for example, the way he used his armour and the cumbersome arrangements of corps commands with which he began. This was strange indeed in a general who made tidiness a shibboleth. Yet Montgomery retained throughout those twelve days in that chaotic man-made dust storm a clinical control of the mine-filled battlefield, a serenity and balance in his own deployments, and, above all, an intense unswerving determination which dominated the situation and compelled both his own troops and their adversary to submit to his unremitting will. By insisting when it was all over that it had all gone according to plan, he did not do justice (a curious sacrifice) to his own generalship, his trained skill, and his power to improvise in an emergency.

A compulsive student of the military art, he could pierce with fierce concentration into the essence of a battlefield. This talent for simplification could be pressed to excess, as the nuances or rougher edges became subsumed in an overriding certainty. Personal vanity nourished in him a deliberate (and infectious) self-assurance. Within a self-compelled taut serenity lay genuine physical bravery: he made himself ignore danger. There was always too a didactic note: lessons must be drawn from all that was happening. To this educational concern was added a capacity to inspire, an unexpectedly Messianic quality. He had the gift of seeing into the hearts of men, of sensing what was worrying them; they must be convinced (despite a spinsterly voice) that what he and they were going to do together was the best recipe, and it must be readily, memorably explicable. Therefore every battle must be seen to go according to plan, in order to persuade and inspire men to undertake it and sustain their morale for future campaigns.

A caustic critic of others, he was far too intelligent not to know that matters do not go according to plan, but he was often too vain to admit this publicly, too much wrapped up in what he was doing to unravel the problems fully afterwards. In convincing others (or some of them), he came to convince himself too.

He became a full general and was appointed KCB (11 November 1942). The tight control of the battlefield was momentarily relaxed. Montgomery would argue that the sluggish pursuit was ensuring that the Rommel bogey laid at Alamein should never return—to disturb the assiduously nourished morale which had made the victory possible. Eighth Army did not think itself as slow as the outside world found it: it throve on carefully planned success, the build-up which avoided the unnecessary casualty, the assured maintenance before the next hammer-blow by orchestrated artillery, air, infantry, and armour. The brilliant improvisation which cut off the retreating Italians at Beda Fomm in February 1941 was not in Montgomery's repertoire: he wanted Rommel finally expelled from El Agheila, his original springboard. In the event he was unable to cut Rommel off at Benghazi, El Agheila, or Buerat. He personally superintended from his 'Tac HQ' the drive on Tripoli (Eighth Army's perennial target) which he reached on 23 January 1943 because storms in Benghazi had made his maintenance more tenuous than he liked. On the way he prepared a training pamphlet on *High Command in War* which could scarcely have enhanced his popularity outside Eighth Army; neither did the 'teach-in' in Tripoli and the parades there for Churchill's benefit.

Knowing that Rommel, having savaged the Americans at Kasserine in mid-February, would turn on Eighth Army before it was fully ready to tackle the Mareth Line, Montgomery hastened up his tanks by transporter and gave himself time to arrange his anti-tank guns for another model defensive battle at Medenine (6 March). At Mareth an uncharacteristic attack on the coastal flank was repulsed (20 March), but Montgomery cut his losses, swiftly reinforced his attacking forces on his left, and forced the Axis switch-line (27 March) west of the hills before El Hamma. The Akarit position remained to be stormed (6–7 April). A day or so later Eighth Army's armoured cars made contact with tanks of US II Corps on the Gabes–Gafsa road, and Eighth Army's private war was over.

When he arrived in Sfax (10 April 1943) Montgomery tactlessly insisted that as payment of a bet made in Tripoli with General Walter Bedell Smith, Eisenhower's chief of staff, he should receive a Flying Fortress aircraft with its American crew, for his personal use: an early sign that he was to be a difficult ally to work with. Despite his quite remarkable understanding of his own soldiers and his staff, he made no attempt to comprehend American sensibilities.

He was now anxious for the speedy termination of the North African campaign to release his troops and staff to prepare for the invasion of Sicily. He overestimated the ease of the problem and was rebuffed at Enfidaville: even Eighth Army could not move mountains; but he swiftly recognized that, by switching some of his troops and commanders to First Army, Tunis might rapidly be captured.

Meanwhile he had emphatically rejected the plans proposed for the capture of Sicily, and insisted that his army and the Americans (under General George S. Patton) should invade the south-east corner, side by side, a proposal eventually adopted although not without argument and friction. He became increasingly offhand with Alexander, his old pupil, whose headquarters was to co-ordinate the invasion, and, although in the event the campaign took only thirty-eight days, his selfishness in insisting upon Eighth Army's priorities led to further wrangling. But, as at Enfidaville, he could make himself realize better ways of accomplishing military purposes, and to Patton's surprise he deliberately yielded the capture of Messina to him.

Before Sicily was invaded (10 July 1943) he had taken some leave in London where he found himself a popular hero, an enjoyable discovery which made him less and less amenable to subordination or advice. He had come to regard himself as the greatest fighting commander alive. He was ready to lay down the military law and he had no hesitation in criticizing anyone. His hold on his soldiers remained secure and he took great trouble about them, but senior officers of other services and nations became increasingly critical of his unbridled self-importance.

He was thus disconcerted to learn at Taormina in August that in the invasion of Italy his was to be a minor role, since Eisenhower planned to employ forces at Salerno under General Mark Clark quite separately from Eighth Army, which was allocated the secondary task of getting across the straits of Messina and then switching from Reggio to the heel of Italy, to secure the Foggia airfields and the ports of Taranto and Brindisi. The task was over-elaborately performed (3 September 1943) and did little to take pressure off the Allied forces at Salerno.

When it became evident that the Germans (with more than twenty divisions) proposed to hold a line as far south in Italy as they were able, Montgomery was faced with a slow slog up the Adriatic coast until checked at the end of 1943, after an expensive battle, at the Sangro. From the start he was highly critical of the campaign: no master plan; no operational grip; and administratively, 'a dog's breakfast'.

He was therefore overjoyed at Christmas in Vasto to be posted to England to command 21st Army Group in the cross-Channel invasion of France.

As with the Sicilian campaign, his decisive contribution to the Normandy invasion was his insistence upon the invasion plan he himself had proposed. On his way back to the United Kingdom Churchill at Marrakesh showed him the draft plans, which Montgomery sulkily criticized. He was authorized by Eisenhower, the new supreme commander for Operation Overlord, to undertake the initial role of C-in-C of the ground forces, and he insisted upon a widening of the frontage, an increase in the invading forces, two armies to go in side by side, and the consequent postponement of the proposed D-Day until early June to allow additional landing craft to become available. From the first, the British on the left were to go for Caen and the airfield country beyond, the Americans for the Cotentin peninsula to gain the port of Cherbourg. To decisiveness he added inspiration. Having secured the major decisions he required from the navy and air forces and General Omar Bradley, the American army commander, he set about enthusing not only those who would actually take part in the invasion, the troops on the ground, but also the populace who would sustain them. Detailed planning, once the major decisions had been agreed (in a surprisingly short time considering their importance), was left to the staff to get on with: they were more grateful for what they inherited than Montgomery would show himself to be. Instead, he occupied himself in an astonishing revivalist campaign in which he toured the country addressing not only troops but railwaymen, dockers, factory workers, and the City. Since the darker days of 1940 there can scarcely have been a more enthusiastically united nation as the weeks before D-Day lessened: people came to believe that the invasion would happen, and were convinced of victory at last. The whistle-stop tour was interrupted for Montgomery to give a quite remarkable exposition of his assault plans on 15 May at St. Paul's School, Hammersmith (his temporary headquarters before moving close to Portsmouth to be ready for D-Day) to a spellbound senior audience which included the King, the prime minister, J. C. Smuts [q.v.], Sir Alan Brooke, and Eisenhower, the supreme commander.

With complete air supremacy, the landings of 6 June, though fiercely opposed, were very successful and a firm bridgehead was established fairly rapidly. The danger was stalemate, and Montgomery, whilst the deception plan was still holding enemy reinforcements in the Pas de Calais, managed to sustain the initiative in Normandy by forcing Rommel to commit more and more of his Panzer divisions to plugging holes against expensive British thrusts in the Caen sector until such time as the Americans, having secured Cherbourg, could turn south, then wheel to drive the enemy against the Seine. He was criticized for the slowness of his progress by an impatient supreme commander awaiting more rapid results, by the air marshals anxious to secure their promised airfields, and by the prime minister and the press, especially the American press. From the serenity of his 'Tac HQ' at

Creuilly, or later at Bray, with his young liaison officers keeping him well informed of the battlefield (as Ultra did of his enemy), Montgomery's confidence never wavered and he carried with him that of his troops. He was supported by the sturdy loyalty of Dempsey at British Second Army and Bradley at American First Army who both well understood his overall purpose and saw him daily. It was an anxious period, more anxious the further removed one was from Normandy, and there were cries for Montgomery's head. The American break out which he had patiently awaited eventually started on 25 July, the British and Canadian forces having successfully tied down enough of the German Panzers on the further flank; Montgomery's balanced arrangements paid off when, through Hitler's intervention, the enemy launched a desperate counter-offensive on 7 August at Mortain directed towards the coast at Avranches, to cut the Americans in two. But Bradley kept his nerve: the American right was ordered to wheel north whilst the Canadians thrust south to create 'the Falaise pocket'. Fighting was intense and casualties very heavy indeed, and though the enemy left many dead, many escaped to cross the Seine to fight again. However, Montgomery's determination and sustained initiative, together with the punishment meted out by the air forces, resulted in Allied victory and German losses of 400,000—half of them prisoners.

It had always been the intention as Montgomery himself well knew, that around 1 September, once Eisenhower's headquarters were established in France and there were two Army Groups each of two armies under his overall command, the supreme commander would assume direct control of the ground forces himself. Montgomery however was so sure that he had the military answer, just proven by substantial success, that in his heart of hearts he never genuinely accepted the simple political fact: had the Americans considered him the best available commander of ground forces (they did not), it was still impossible, once the restricting emergencies of Normandy had been successfully surmounted, for a British general, however distinguished, to continue in overall command when, through manpower shortages, the British contribution—at first roughly equal—was shrinking and the American effort becoming daily more preponderant.

Normandy was followed by an unseemly period of patronizing, querulous, and insubordinate disagreement about how the campaign should develop and whose ideas should prevail, until eventually a long-suffering Eisenhower was girding himself to demand Montgomery's dismissal when de Guingand intervened and prevailed upon the supreme commander to hold his hand and Montgomery his tongue.

Meanwhile Montgomery had become a field marshal (30 August 1944) and 21st Army Group had reached Brussels and Antwerp. He wanted the Allied advance to be concentrated in a powerful thrust of some forty divisions (which he hoped to command) north-east to cut off the Ruhr. Eisenhower however preferred to advance to the Rhine on a broader front and refused to give Montgomery priority in fuel supply by rationing American advances further south.

As the Allied front broadened, so distance widened the difference of opinion. Whereas it appeared to Montgomery's staff that the first priority was to get the Schelde river open to nourish further advances (especially after the uncovenanted capture of Antwerp on 4 September), Montgomery himself persuaded Eisenhower that this might be delayed (or conducted *pari passu*) whilst an operation was mounted to advance into Germany by vaulting the great Dutch rivers with airborne troops. Eisenhower released his strategic reserve to Montgomery. The subsequent operation (Arnhem, 17 September) was neither well planned nor well conducted. Communications were erratic, the intelligence was untuned, and Montgomery paid the penalty for acting impulsively and out of character in the first and only defeat of his military career. He hoped (it may be supposed) that had he succeeded, the whole Allied *Schwerpunkt* would be dragged north-east, but in his desire to have his own way, the war over, and the sites of the missiles assailing London cut off from their supply, he underestimated both the extent of German recovery and the marked reluctance of American generals to return under his governance. Defeat at Arnhem cost him his bargaining arm and thereafter the northern flank ceased to figure importantly in SHAEF's priorities.

Montgomery bounced back into the forefront when, on 16 December 1944, a surprise German offensive in the Ardennes drove a wedge between the strung-out American divisions. He was called upon to command those north of the new German salient. He rose to the opportunity, and sorted out the front with his former clarity and verve, but the manner of his coming (as if 'to cleanse the temple') and the cocksureness of his subsequent press conference (7 January) left much bitterness, and once the campaign was successfully resumed he was kept increasingly out on a limb. American speed in crossing the Rhine at Remagen (First Army) and Oppenheim (Third Army) was in sharp contrast to the deliberation with which Montgomery prepared to cross at Wesel. Having forfeited his infallibility at Arnhem, he reverted to his proven ways, over-insurance which might lose pace but made for certainty.

The argument about having a ground forces

commander (as distinct from Eisenhower's direct command from SHAEF in Versailles) was inextricably entangled with the personality—and nationality—of Montgomery himself. Montgomery even volunteered, how genuinely it is difficult to guess, to serve under Bradley. But this was difficult to envisage, and Churchill's clumsy intervention was too late in the day to bring back Alexander from Italy in the role Montgomery himself objected to. The dispute spilled over into contention over control of US Ninth Army and whether it should be comprised within Bradley's left or Montgomery's right wing. Montgomery's trouble was that he could not achieve his aims without considerable American support; his own forces were by now inadequate for a 'master plan' finishing in Berlin. He was not therefore brought back into the middle of matters but left with the limited role of closing off the entrances to Scandinavia before the Russians reached them. His troops reached Wismar on 2 May 1945 and two days later the German forces in north-west Germany, Holland, and Denmark were surrendered to him on Lüneberg heath.

All his life Montgomery's methods and personality provoked controversy and animosities. By cutting himself off from SHAEF which he visited but once and maintaining, instead, a running correspondence with the War Office, from his sanctuary in 'Tac HQ', he was encouraged by the chief of the imperial general staff and P. J. Grigg [q.v.], the secretary of state, in an anti-American bias which hindered his getting on with the job. His was not the only way to win the war, and he paid all too little recognition to American resourcefulness, Bradley's dour professionalism, or Patton's outstanding talent for exploitation.

Montgomery—perhaps uniquely—knew how to handle large amounts of military equipment without becoming overwhelmed by them and to inspire large bodies of men (and not just his own fellow countrymen) for military purposes. It was easy to deride his strut, his preoccupation with personal publicity, his two-badged beret, his evangelical messages to his troops; but, whatever one's distaste for 'Montification', he was not 'just a PR general'. He was a very professional soldier, and citizen soldiers at the sharp end felt 'safe' in his hands, a belief their families came to share. It was not just a prolonged stunt: his care for his men was deep-seated. He might rile military clubland by the frankness of his 'ungentlemanly' self-aggrandizement; yet there is not much room for 'nice' men in war. In the dread trade, to which his life was dedicated, of killing considerable numbers of enemy in the most economical way possible, he exhibited a clinical concentration on the essential with morals taking a major share in the calculations. His talents and his behaviour were evidently best fitted to circumscribed command in which he got his own way—he was at his best in the Western Desert commanding Eighth Army in whom he instilled his own especial arrogance, the army of the film *Desert Victory*. As an army group commander, which eventually entailed working loyally alongside allies, he was less well placed. One is tempted to conclude that he had got beyond his ceiling—it was his own view that each officer has his ceiling—yet any account of his command in Normandy would go a long way to challenge that evaluation.

Most awkward to serve alongside, impossible to serve over, he was an excellent man to serve under, especially on his staff. The staff he had mostly inherited from Auchinleck he retained until the war ended. He was indulgent to the young aides-de-camp and liaison officers whom he picked, trusted, and trained.

His sense of fairness and especially of truth were not as other men's. In his convictions he was ruthless, even baleful, yet his insensitively arrogant self-confidence was combined with an indiscreet, mischievous, schoolboyish sense of humour which buoyed up the spirits of those far from home. Above all, he trusted those who worked with him to get on with the job, treating them as experienced professionals. His competence as a general, his economy in the use of his troops, the clarity of his commands, and, quintessentially, his decisiveness made a profound impression. One felt that he would get the war over, so that 'we could all pack up and go home again'. Until that happened, he won ready allegiance.

Montgomery became C-in-C of the British forces of occupation and the British member of the Allied Control Council in Berlin. Having secured what he believed mattered most—the establishment of order, the restoration of communications, the demobilization of the German armed forces, the reopening of the mines, and the sowing of the harvest—he left the fuller implementation to able subordinates: Sir Ronald (later Lord) Weeks [q.v.] and then Brian Robertson in Berlin, and Gerald Templer in the British zone.

In 1945 he was advanced to GCB. Honours were now showered upon him by nations, cities, and universities. He was granted a peerage in the New Year honours of 1946. He took the title Viscount Montgomery of Alamein, of Hindhead, in the county of Surrey. In December 1946 he was installed as a Knight of the Garter. All these were accolades which he enjoyed to the full.

Accounts of his campaigns (ghost-written in the main by 'David' Belchem and issued ostensibly as training manuals for the Rhine Army) were soon published generally: *El Alamein to the River Sangro* (1948) and *Normandy to the Baltic* (1947). Bedell Smith remarked that he now knew that Montgomery's battles had always gone according to plan 'from end to beginning'.

In June 1946 Montgomery, discarding de Guingand like yesterday's shirt, succeeded Alanbrooke ('Brookie'), the only man he recognized as a better soldier, as chief of the imperial general staff. It was a virtually unavoidable succession but the appointment brought out some of his less admirable qualities. He was too set in his ways. He clashed again with Lord Tedder [q.v.], who was now chief of the air staff: a lack of rapport dating from Alamein. He got on well with C. R. (later Earl) Attlee and Ernest Bevin [q.v.], and in the War Office itself was soon on nickname terms with Emanuel ('Manny') (later Lord) Shinwell, but he became increasingly at odds with the less convincing A. V. Alexander (later Earl Alexander of Hillsborough, q.v.) at the Ministry of Defence. After two uncomfortable years for everybody, Montgomery was eased out of Whitehall to become chairman of the Western Union commanders-in-chief, a stop-gap appointment until he became, in March 1951, deputy supreme commander to Eisenhower, commanding the Allied forces of NATO in Europe. He continued to serve as a sort of inspector-general under three other successive supreme commanders until he retired in September 1958. He took the task seriously and, given his limitations, was thought to have performed it well. He had adjusted to the anti-climax with surprising willingness.

The first drafts of his *Memoirs* were in his own clear pencilled handwriting: they were published with too few changes in 1958 and were so much in character that no opinions were altered by them. Publication ended an uneasy friendship with Eisenhower, by then president of the United States. Hackles were also raised in Italy. The book sold well everywhere.

Montgomery lived in active retirement, amidst mementoes and portraits, in a reconstructed mill at Isington on the river Wey near Alton in Hampshire. Tidiness and punctuality were the order of the day. He was a thoughtful and generous host, himself as abstemious as ever. He remained very fit and was to travel widely (though rarely without raising controversy). He wrote in the press about his visits to the USSR (1959), China, and South Africa and published an account of them in *Three Continents* (1962). He was an occasional broadcaster and lecturer and sometimes spoke in the House of Lords, with all his old vigour and habitual reiteration; but he was not well enough to act as pallbearer at Churchill's funeral in 1965. Four years later, however, he performed that office for Field Marshal Alexander and later in the year carried the Sword of State at the opening of Parliament (although in the following year he had to yield it to another). He also had to abandon going to the annual Alamein reunions in London. He used to spend Christmas with the Griggs at the mill and he also enjoyed his seaside arguments with Basil Liddell Hart [q.v.]. His own *History of Warfare* (1968) was mostly by other hands and he recommended his surviving friends to read only those sections he specified as written by himself, but the preface made it clear that his interests were well maintained and was revealing about the commentaries which had impressed him. He continued to be a good correspondent and remained the eager listener he had always been, and he brooded, as he always had, on what he had heard or read. He had come to believe his own legend and to wrap himself in memories which excluded the inconvenient. He died full of years on 25 March 1976 and was succeeded as viscount by his son David Bernard (born 1928). The funeral service was in St. George's chapel, Windsor, and he was buried in a country churchyard at Binstead, Hampshire, a mile from his home.

A statue by Oscar Nemon outside the Ministry of Defence in Whitehall was unveiled by the Queen Mother on 6 June 1980, the anniversary of D-Day.

Montgomery's formidable military skills were best exhibited in the defensive battle, yet it fell to him to mastermind and infuse the two great frontal assaults which heralded the Axis defeats in North Africa and in western Europe, two victories most needed in this country, which forced him, warts and all, into the company of the great captains: the best British field commander, it has been held, since Wellington himself.

[*The Times*, 25 and 26 March 1976; Nigel Hamilton, *Monty, the Making of a General, 1887–1942*, 1981, *Monty, the Master of the Battlefield, 1942–1944*, 1983, and *Monty, the Field Marshal, 1944–1976*, 1986; Ronald Lewin, *Montgomery as Military Commander*, 1971; C. J. C. Malony, *The Mediterranean and the Middle East* (vol. v of the official war history), 1973, pp. 510–13; Michael Howard, *The Causes of Wars*, 1983, pp. 208–23; Corelli Barnett, *The Desert Generals*, 2nd edn., 1983; Max Hastings, *Overlord*, 1984; Stephen Russell F. Weigley, *Eisenhower's Lieutenants*, 1981; Brian Montgomery, *A Field Marshal in the Family*, 1973; Goronwy Rees, *A Bundle of Sensations*, 1960, pp. 113–51; T. E. B. Howarth (ed.), *Monty at Close Quarters*, 1985; private information; personal knowledge.]

E. T. WILLIAMS

MONTGOMERY, (ROBERT) BRUCE (1921–1978), detective novelist under the pseudonym of EDMUND CRISPIN, and composer in his own name, was born 2 October 1921 at Chesham Bois, Buckinghamshire, the fourth child and only son of Robert Ernest Montgomery, sometime secretary to the high commissioner for India, of Chesham Bois, and his wife, Marion Blackwood Jarvie. He was educated at

Merchant Taylors' School and at St. John's College, Oxford, where he obtained a second class in French and German in 1943.

Of his two careers, that of writer of crime fiction, though it occupied him less—he wrote only nine novels—brought him the greater renown. In both he began early, producing his first novel, *The Case of the Gilded Fly* (1944), while still an undergraduate and performing as pianist, organist, and conductor while still a schoolboy.

His earliest published music was a choral *Ode on the Resurrection of Christ* (1947) written in memory of Charles W. S. Williams [q.v.]. Other works, mostly for voices, followed in a fairly regular procession until the early 1950s when until the mid 1960s he devoted almost all his energies to film music, an art no less demanding for being at times used in the service of such lightweight productions as *Carry on Nurse* (1959). His major composition was *An Oxford Requiem* for chorus and orchestra (1951). He composed, he said of himself, in 'a relatively traditional idiom tinged with romanticism', and it was to (Sir) William Walton that he owed especial allegiance, having been electrified as a boy by a radio performance of the Symphony No. 1 which, on holiday without a wireless, he cajoled an unwilling garage proprietor into letting him hear.

As a writer, he acknowledged the influence of John Dickson Carr, producing himself locked-room and other puzzles every bit as ingenious as Carr's, as well as Gladys Mitchell and Michael Innes from whose *Hamlet, Revenge!* (1937) his pen-name was derived and in whose mould of the donnish detective story he largely wrote. He has, too, admitted in his work 'a dash of Evelyn Waugh' while the American critic, Anthony Boucher, has added to Carr and Innes as being blended in his books the Marx Brothers and M. R. James [q.v.]. There is, certainly, an occasional touch of the macabre and he had a considerable gift for the farcical set-piece such as the irruption of a party of clue-seekers into a sedate choral society rehearsal in what is perhaps his most successful work, *The Moving Toyshop* (1946).

To classical ingenuity of plot he added a dazzling sense of fun. 'I believe', he once wrote, 'that crime stories in general and detective stories in particular should be essentially imaginative and artificial to make their best effect.' In pursuit of this aim he could produce such pleasant touches as having his hero, Gervase Fen, professor of English language and literature at the University of Oxford, pause during a case to spend some moments 'making up titles for Crispin' and he employed to the full the resources of a well-stocked mind and a gift for splendidly inappropriate metaphor as well as the pointed literary dig and a taste for the bizarre. He was a stylist in a tradition going back through P. G. Wodehouse, through a major strain in Charles Dickens, through Laurence Sterne to Sir Thomas Urquhart's Rabelais translation.

Until he found time for little else than film music—he was dogged by ill health and never fit for war service—he had produced only eight novels, and on these till the ninth, *The Glimpses of the Moon* (1977), followed near the end of his life his reputation had to rest. But it rested high. He did, however, write as well a number of short stories, some of conjuror's ingenuity ('Baker Dies'), others gigglingly hilarious ('We Know You're Busy Writing...'). He also reviewed crime literature with acumen and edited a number of anthologies, his annual choices of science fiction over some seven years doing much to raise the status of that genre in Britain.

In person, particularly in his latter years, he appeared unusually deliberate, and indeed he cited as one of his recreations 'sleeping'. After Oxford and three years' teaching at Shrewsbury he retired to Devon where for the rest of his life he led, in his own words, a 'hermit-like' existence. His outward demeanour, however, did not tell the whole story. Philip Larkin, the poet, a friend from undergraduate days, speaks of 'unsuspected depths of frivolity' and recalls time spent together 'swaying about with laughter on bar-stools'.

In 1976 he married Barbara Clements, daughter of Charles Camille Dornat Youings, mineral water manufacturer. He died in hospital at Plymouth 15 September 1978.

[*The Times*, 18 September 1978; C. Steinbrunner and O. Penzler (eds.), *Encyclopedia of Mystery and Detection*, 1976; J. M. Reilly (ed.), *Twentieth Century Crime and Mystery Writers*, 1980; Erik Routley, *The Puritan Pleasures of the Detective Story* (1972); Philip Larkin, *Jill* (1964 edn.); private information; personal knowledge.]

H. R. F. KEATING

MORAN, first BARON (1882–1977), physician and writer. [See WILSON, CHARLES MCMORAN.]

MORDELL, LOUIS JOEL (1888–1972), mathematician, was born 28 January 1888 in Philadelphia, Pennsylvania, the third in the family of eight children (four sons and four daughters) of the Hebrew scholar Phineas Mordell and his wife, Annie, who were both immigrants from Lithuania. When at the age of fourteen he entered the Central High School of Philadelphia he was already fascinated by mathematics and had read widely. In 1906 he scraped together the single fare to Cambridge to compete in the scholarship examination. Top of the list, he was awarded a scholarship at St. John's College. In 1909, the last year of the 'order of merit', he sat part i of the mathematical tripos and was third wrangler. The following year he was put in the middle of the three divisions of the first class in part ii.

Mordell's reading had already attracted him to the theory of numbers, which in its various aspects was to become his life's work. There was little interest in the subject at that time in England, and he regarded himself as self-taught. Now he started to investigate the integral solutions of the equation $y^2 = x^3 + k$, a theme to which he continually recurred. This work won him a Smith's prize, but not a college fellowship.

In 1913 he left Cambridge for a lectureship at Birkbeck College, London, where he remained, apart from two years as a statistician at the Ministry of Munitions, until 1920. This was a very productive period, his main interest being in modular functions and their application to number theory. He proved the multiplicativity of Ramanujan's celebrated tau-function. This was later shown by E. Hecke to be a special case of a general phenomenon but, typically, having solved the problem he was not interested in generalizations. One argument was rediscovered by Hecke and is central in the theory of modular forms (the 'Hecke operator'). Mordell also used modular forms to study the number of representations of an integer as the sum of a given number of squares. The connection with modular forms was well known, but Mordell was the first to use the finite-dimensionality of spaces of modular forms to establish identities. This powerful approach was later used by Hecke and others in more general contexts.

From 1920 to 1922 Mordell was lecturer at the Manchester College of Technology. This period saw his most important single discovery, his 'finite basis theorem'. This states that the rational points on a non-singular plane cubic can all be obtained from a finite number of them by a definite process. This had already been conjectured by Poincaré, who had shown that it implies the corresponding result for all curves of genus one. Later André Weil gave a generalization to abelian varieties of any dimension with any algebraic number field as ground field ('the Mordell–Weil theorem') and this is central in much of modern number theory. It seems not unlikely that Mordell failed to realize the full significance of his work: in any case he had no part in later developments.

In 1922 he moved to the University of Manchester where, after a year as reader, he was appointed to the Fielden chair of pure mathematics, which he occupied until 1945. He was now a leading figure in the mathematical world and was elected FRS in 1924. By a certificate of naturalization dated 10 December 1929 he became a British citizen.

Mordell was an enlightened head of department and very concerned with the quality of the teaching. He built up an extremely strong school of mathematics, particularly in the 1930s when almost any young mathematician of note seems to have passed through the department either on the staff or as a visitor. He was very active in assisting refugee mathematicians from Germany or Italy. A topic which occupied him at this time was the estimation of the number of points on algebraic varieties over finite fields. The ideas are ingenious but the results were later completely superseded by the 'Riemann hypothesis for function fields' of Hasse and Weil. In the early 1940s Mordell became interested in the geometry of numbers and initiated a period of great advance by himself and others.

In 1945 Mordell succeeded G. H. Hardy [q.v.] in the Sadleirian chair in Cambridge and was elected to a fellowship of St. John's. He rapidly built up a powerful research school. After his retirement in 1953 he retained his fellowship and his house in Cambridge, though he travelled extensively. His enthusiasm for the theory of numbers never left him: he was working and publishing right to the end. He was a problem solver of great ingenuity and resource: it gave him particular pleasure to obtain or extend by elementary means results that had first been found by sophisticated ones. He had the gift of imparting his enthusiasm and was in great demand as a lecturer. He enjoyed travelling. To foreign or international audiences he normally used English, but made a special point of speaking slowly and clearly. He enjoyed robust health until the end, which came after a brief illness.

Mordell was awarded the Sylvester medal of the Royal Society in 1949. He was president of the London Mathematical Society (1943–5) and received both its De Morgan medal (1941) and its senior Berwick prize (1946). He was a foreign member of the academies of Norway, Uppsala, and Bologna and an honorary doctor of the universities of Glasgow (1956), Mount Allison (1959), and Waterloo (1970).

In May 1916 Mordell married Mabel Elizabeth (died 1971), the only daughter of Rosa and Joseph Cambridge, a small farmer in the town of the same name. They had a son and a daughter. He died 12 March 1972 in Cambridge.

[L. J. Mordell, *American Mathematical Monthly*, vol. lxxviii, 1971, pp. 1952–61; H. Davenport, *Acta Arithmetica*, vol. ix, 1964, pp. 1–22; J. W. S. Cassels in *Biographical Memoirs of Fellows of the Royal Society*, vol. xix, 1973, reprinted in *Bulletin of the London Mathematical Society*, vol. vi, 1974, pp. 69–96; personal knowledge.]

J. W. S. Cassels

MORGAN, Sir MORIEN BEDFORD (1912–1978), aeronautical engineer, was born 20 December 1912 at Bridgend, Glamorgan, the elder son (there were no surviving daughters) of John Bedford Morgan, draper, and his wife, Edith Mary Thomas, teacher. He was educated at Bridgend elementary school; Magdalen College School, Oxford; Aberdare Boys County School; Canton secondary school, Cardiff; and finally Rutlish School, Merton, London. His family was very musical and he became a skilled pianist and organist as well as having a good tenor voice.

Morgan entered St. Catharine's College, Cambridge, in 1931 and obtained a second class in part i of the mathematical tripos (1932) and a first class in the mechanical sciences tripos (aeronautics, 1934). In 1934 he was awarded the John Bernard Seely prize in aeronautics. During a long vacation he had spent some time at Vickers Aviation and was keen to make a career in aeronautics, but jobs were scarce and he spent an unhappy nine months as an apprentice with Mather & Platt Ltd. in Manchester before being recruited in 1935 as a junior scientific officer at the Royal Aircraft Establishment, Farnborough.

He spent his first thirteen years at RAE doing research with Aero Flight (a division of the establishment concerned with all the flying qualities of an aircraft), leaving as its head in 1948 to become head of the new guided weapons department, where he remained until 1953. In 1954 he became deputy director (A) of the establishment, in charge of its 'aircraft' as distinct from its 'equipment' half. In 1959 he was moved from RAE to spend one year as scientific adviser to the Air Ministry, followed by nine years in the Ministry of Aviation headquarters, first as deputy controller of aircraft (research and development) until 1963, then as controller of aircraft until 1966, when he became controller of guided weapons and electronics before his final government posting as director RAE from 1969 to 1972.

By 1939 rearmament prior to war meant that there were more than a dozen major aircraft firms each designing and building one or more prototype aircraft. Before these were off the drawing board others would be started and twelve months could see an aircraft through from first concept to first flight. The man to whom each firm took its aerodynamic problems was Morgan, and his unique blend of knowledge, research experience, scientific judgement, energy, and enthusiasm often led to successful solutions being quickly found. In addition, his infectious good humour inspired the whole of Aero Flight, and created a talented team. In his Cambridge days Morgan learnt much from (Sir) B. Melvill Jones [q.v.] and (Sir) W. S. Farren, whose notice he later wrote for this Dictionary, and at Farnborough he worked closely with S. B. Gates. At Aero Flight he was particularly concerned with aircraft control and stability, and especially with making these as congenial as possible for the pilot, thus improving both safety and handling characteristics. Moreover, he felt strongly that practical experience was important, and held a pilot's A licence himself from 1944. Many if not all of Britain's wartime aircraft were improved in their fighting qualities by application of Morgan's ideas and suggestions.

After leaving Aero Flight, Morgan contributed greatly to the growth of Britain's guided weapons industry, but the years from 1948 to 1959 will probably be chiefly remembered for two undertakings while he was deputy director. The first of these was the public inquiry into the Comet accidents, in which he directed the scientific investigation that demonstrated in the astonishingly short time of three months that metal fatigue of the pressure cabin was to blame. The second was the programme of research he directed into the feasibility of a supersonic civil aircraft that culminated in Concorde. Once again he welded together a talented team and the remarkable technical success of Concorde owes much to him, whatever view is taken of its commercial significance.

During Morgan's time in higher management at headquarters many far-reaching decisions were taken, including a few much-publicized cancellations of aircraft projects, sometimes against his advice. He showed much humanity and understanding in persuading so many diverse groups of people to work together and also great courage in refusing to be browbeaten into taking decisions that were against his better judgement.

In 1972 Morgan became master of Downing College, Cambridge, where his enthusiasm and good humour together with his Welsh charm, eloquence, and love of music made sure that he was well received. He got on well with both young and old, and was happy to chat (or to have a serious argument) with anyone; he was completely unaffected and had a knack of getting to know and understand all kinds of people. At home he enjoyed a happy and relaxed family life until the day of his death.

Morgan was appointed CB in 1958 and knighted in 1969. He was president of the Royal Aeronautical Society in 1967–8 and was awarded the society's silver medal in 1957, the gold medal in 1971, and an honorary fellowship in 1976. He was elected to an honorary fellowship at St. Catharine's College, Cambridge, in 1972, became FRS in 1972, and was a founder fellow of the Fellowship of Engineering in 1976. He was also awarded honorary doctorates at Cranfield and Southampton in 1976. He was a governor of the College of Aeronautics and later (1971) a council member of the Cranfield Institute of Technology. In 1973 he became a member of the Airworthiness Requirements Board and chairman of its research committee, and in 1975 he was appointed chairman of the Air Traffic Control Board and a member of the Post Office Board. His chief publications were his lectures to the Royal Aeronautical Society, published in its *Journal*, and various reports and memoranda for the Aeronautical Research Council.

In 1941 he married Sylvia, the daughter of George Frederick Axford, instrument maker, of Farnborough. They had three daughters. Morgan died suddenly at the master's lodge, Downing College, Cambridge, 4 April 1978.

[*The Times*, 6 April 1978; E. G. Broadbent in *Biographical Memoirs of Fellows of the Royal Society*, vol. xxvi, 1980; personal knowledge.]

E. G. BROADBENT

MORRAH, DERMOT MICHAEL MACGREGOR (1896–1974), journalist, historian, and herald, was born in Ryde, Isle of Wight, 26 April 1896, the eldest in the family of two sons and two daughters of Herbert Arthur Morrah, a novelist and poet whose career reached its peak early with his election to the presidency of the Oxford Union, and his wife, Alice Elise, daughter of Major Cortlandt Alexander Macgregor, of the Royal Engineers, who was of mixed Scottish and Polish descent. Morrah sometimes claimed, though not entirely seriously since historical evidence was lacking, descent from the Dermot MacMurrough of Leinster who invited Strongbow to Ireland. The second Christian name, Michael, was given to him not at his baptism but at his reception into the Roman Catholic Church. At Winchester, which awarded him an exhibition in classics, he was almost equally distinguished as a classicist and mathematician and it was as a mathematical scholar that he entered New College, Oxford. He played against Cambridge in the Oxford chess team. In 1915, to his disappointment, he obtained only second class honours in mathematical moderations and promptly joined the Royal Engineers, where his mathematical learning could be put to practical use.

In 1916–18 he served in Palestine and Egypt, being wounded at Gaza, but one of his commanding officers is said to have described him, with exasperated affection, as the 'most unsoldierly soldier I've ever known'. On demobilization he returned to New College, deserted mathematics for history and in 1921 after two years' study obtained first class honours in modern history. In the same year he was elected to a prize fellowship at All Souls College which was to play an important role in his life. In the immediately succeeding years, however, there occurred two events of even greater importance to him: his reception in 1922 into the Roman Catholic Church and in 1923 his marriage to Gertrude Ruth, daughter of Wilmott Houselander, a bank manager. His wife, by whom he had two daughters, subsequently had a distinguished career as a magistrate, becoming for twenty years a chairman of the metropolitan juvenile courts.

At All Souls his fellowship expired after seven years, as then invariably happened in the case of married non-academic fellows, but he remained a permanent member of common room and was invited to all college gaudies, which are held three times a year. At these feasts Morrah was the most regular of attenders and he became the omniscient collector and recorder of college customs and conventions, however recondite or trivial. In the 1920s the fellows included two groups who were to be of particular importance to him. One consisted of two editors of *The Times*, G. E. Buckle (by then a quondam fellow) and G. Geoffrey Dawson [qq.v.], and the other included Lionel Curtis, R. H. (later Lord) Brand, L. C. M. S. Amery [qq.v.], and, as a frequent visitor though not as a fellow, Philip Kerr, later Marquess of Lothian [q.v.]. All of these had been members of 'Milner's kindergarten' and had been associated with Baron (later Viscount) Milner [q.v.] in his work in South Africa after the Boer War. Kerr for some years edited *Round Table*, a journal which reflected the group's political philosophy and which, despite its small circulation, exercised considerable influence. This editorship was a post which Morrah himself was to fill some years later.

In 1922 Morrah entered the Civil Service and until 1928 worked in the Mines Department, an occupation which was to him profoundly boring. When G. E. Buckle, who was then at work on the great history of *The Times*, invited him to become his assistant, Morrah accepted without hesitation. At the suggestion of Dawson, who had earmarked him as a future *Times* leader writer, he joined the *Daily Mail* in effect to serve an apprenticeship in journalism; in 1931 this period of training came to an end and he became in 1932 a full member of *The Times* staff which he remained for twenty-nine years.

During this period he began to publish. In his *Daily Mail* days there was an entertaining *jeu d'esprit*, *If it Had Happened Yesterday* (1931), a retelling of various important events in English history in the style of popular journalism, and shortly afterwards *The Mummy Case* (1932), a detective story with an Oxford setting; in collaboration with G. Campbell Dixon he wrote a play *Caesar's Friend* (1933), about the events of the first Good Friday, which ran for only a week in the West End. He also wrote a nativity play for children, *Chorus Angelorum*, originally for the convent where his two daughters were at school but rejected by the nuns as too frivolous. It was eventually performed successfully in London with music specially written for it by Sir H.

Walford Davies [q.v.]. More importantly, Morrah embarked after World War II on a series of studies of the royal family which included books on Queen Elizabeth II both before and after her accession and on Charles, Prince of Wales. Respectful but unsycophantic, lively but serious, based on a Bagehotian view of the monarchy's role in modern constitutional politics, these were widely admired and earned for him in 1953 not the knighthood which some had expected—at the time the convention still prevailed at *The Times* that members of its staff did not accept honours—but something which gave him infinitely more pleasure: the position of Arundel herald extraordinary, which was specially revived for him. It enabled him to take part in the coronation ceremony, in full heraldic splendour.

In 1961 he retired from *The Times* at the age of sixty-five and was invited to join the *Daily Telegraph* as a leader writer. He continued to edit *Round Table*, a task which he first took up in 1944, and continued to make occasional contributions to journals as various as *West Indian Cultural Circular*, *Farmers' Weekly*, and *Policewoman's Gazette*. A prominent member of the Commonwealth Press Union, he sat as a member of its council and from 1956 to 1971 was chairman of its press freedom committee. Wine was among his chief outside interests and in 1959–63 he was chairman of the Wine Society and for two years (1964–6) chairman of the Circle of Wine Writers.

In 1972, at a requiem mass at Westminster Cathedral for his friend Charles Curran, he suffered a severe stroke and from then until his death in the Westminster Hospital, London, 30 September 1974, he never fully recovered his faculties.

Dermot Morrah possessed a very individual and richly flavoured personality. In 1938 at the Oxford Encaenia garden party one of his vocal cords was suddenly paralysed and afterwards he always spoke in a hoarse, penetrating croak as distinctive as his herald's tabard. A polymath traditionalist, he was deeply attached to the Roman Catholic Church, the tridentine mass, the constitution, common law, all ritual both sacred and secular, heraldry, the medieval concepts of feudalism and status, such pleasures as wine, chess, and the ancient card-game of ombre (which he firmly pronounced 'umber'). Driven neither by worldly ambition nor by the desire for wealth he pursued a varied life at a pace not unduly hurried. In later years his appearance—erect, with luxuriant grey hair and moustache, alert, friendly eyes, quick movements—recalled that of an elderly but active and distinguished bird. In heraldic plumage he was particularly impressive. Until his stroke his conversation was lively, wide-ranging, informative but never boring. Unsurprisingly, he had a wide and very varied circle of friends.

[Private information; personal knowledge.]

CHARLES MONTEITH

MORRIS, (ALFRED) EDWIN (1894–1971), fifth archbishop of Wales, was born at Lye, near Stourbridge, Worcestershire, 8 May 1894, the eldest of four sons (a daughter died in infancy) of Alfred Morris, jeweller, of 42 Stourbridge Road, and his wife, Maria Beatrice Lickert. His first school was at Stambermill, Worcestershire, and he later went to St. David's College School, Lampeter.

In World War I he joined the RAMC, returning to Lampeter in 1919 with a senior scholarship. He took his initial degree (BA) there in 1922, gaining a first class in theology in 1924. He won the junior Septuagint prize at Oxford in 1923, and the junior Greek Testament prize in 1924. Appointed to the chair of Hebrew and theology at Lampeter in 1924, he was made deacon that year, being priested the following year, both ordinations taking place at St. David's Cathedral.

From 1925 to 1928 he was an examining chaplain to the bishop of Bangor, and from 1931 to 1934 to the bishop of Llandaff. From 1931 to 1945 he was Lloyd Williams fellow of St. David's College, Lampeter, taking his Lampeter BD in 1932. In 1945 he was elected to the bishopric of Monmouth on the death of A. E. Monahan. There appeared in quick succession his *The Church in Wales and Nonconformity* (1949), *The Problem of Life and Death* (1950), and *The Catholicity of the Book of Common Prayer* (1952). He became a DD (Lambeth) in 1950 and an honorary DD of the University of Wales in 1971. In 1957, on the death of Archbishop John Morgan of Llandaff, he was elected to the archbishopric of Wales, though remaining bishop of Monmouth with his residence at Newport, Monmouthshire. In 1958 he became an honorary fellow of St. John's College, Oxford. After his retirement he commented wryly: 'I was the first Englishman to become archbishop of Wales and probably I shall also be the last.'

Morris was a controversial figure and rather enjoyed being such. There were controversies during his time at Lampeter, where he clashed with others on the staff there. One colleague insinuated that Morris, an Englishman by birth, was learning Welsh with a view to promotion in the Church in Wales. When he began to learn Welsh in 1924 he was put off by those who should have encouraged him. One ardent Welshman commented that he supposed that Morris was aiming to become a Welsh bishop. This wounded him so deeply that he resolved that he would never lend any colour to such an innuendo and at once dropped his attempt to learn Welsh. Perhaps he was over-sensitive, but the thought of being suspected of scheming to use the Welsh language to aid an ambition which seemed to him to be wrong in itself, was most distasteful to him.

Later in his life, Bishop W. Glyn H. Simon of Llandaff was critical of the electoral college of the Church in Wales for electing Morris as the fifth archbishop of Wales. Simon regarded Morris as an Englishman through and through and, at a time when the Welsh language movement was gaining strength, not prepared to bow to the 'winds of change', a phrase whose inventor was half English and half Celtic.

Nevertheless Simon acknowledged that Morris was a good theologian who argued his proposals and statements from firm theological bases. As one who felt tempted to pay little attention to the piles of documents that reached the episcopal desks, Simon acknowledged that he could rely on Morris for a well balanced and theologically informed summary of these.

Other controversies in which Morris became involved were the papal utterances about the choice between mother and unborn child where it was a case of saving one or the other. He always saw to it that the press received advance copy of what he intended to say at his diocesan conference, or at the governing body of the Church in Wales, or wherever else he chose to make his platform. One such occasion caused much publicity, for Morris had been invited to preach in Westminster Abbey on the Sunday before the coronation of Queen Elizabeth II. His exposition of the so-called 'Protestant oath' in the coronation service provoked a battle of words that raged for many weeks, first in the columns of *The Times*, then in the *Spectator*, with the result that the Dixie professor of ecclesiastical history at Cambridge entered the arena with some considerable force and achieved a superiority which Morris refused to acknowledge.

In 1925 Morris married Emily Louisa (died 1968), daughter of William Charles Davis, gardener at Prestcot House, Stourbridge. They had four sons and a daughter.

Morris has been described as probably the last archbishop who spurned the typewriter and wrote his own letters in longhand. He was a considerable correspondent, taking infinite pains in answering those who sought his advice on a variety of subjects.

Among his recreations were gardening, painting (in oils), swimming, and writing letters to newspapers. A portrait by Colin Jones hangs in the study at Bishopstow, Newport. Morris retired in 1967 to Llanfair Clydogan, near Lampeter, retaining his holiday bungalow at St. David's. He died at Hafdir, Lampeter, 19 October 1971.

[Owain W. Jones, *Glyn Simon*, 1981; John S. Peart-Binns, *The Life and Letters of Alfred Edwin Morris, Archbishop of Wales*, 1983; *The Times*, 20 October 1971; private information; personal knowledge.] C. WITTON-DAVIES

MORRIS, JOHN WILLIAM, BARON MORRIS OF BORTH-Y-GEST (1896–1979), lawyer, public servant, and ardent Welshman, was born at 189 Faulkner St., Liverpool, 11 September 1896, the only son and younger child of Daniel Morris, a bank manager in that city, and his wife, Ellen, daughter of John Edwards, of Liverpool. He was educated at the Liverpool Institute, which he left in 1914 to join the Royal Welch Fusiliers at the outbreak of war. He saw service in France, reaching the rank of captain, and was awarded the MC. On demobilization he went to Trinity Hall, Cambridge, that breeding ground of eminent lawyers, of which he subsequently (1951) became an honorary fellow. In 1919 he was elected president of the Cambridge Union. He gained second classes in both parts i (1919) and ii (1920) of the law tripos and gained his LL B in 1920. In the same year he was awarded a Joseph Hodges Choate fellowship at Harvard University, where he remained for a year.

In 1921 Morris was called to the bar at the Inner Temple, of which in 1943 he became a bencher and in 1967 treasurer. A Liverpool man, he localized there and naturally joined the Northern circuit, quickly acquiring a large junior practice. In 1923 and 1924 he unsuccessfully contested the Ilford division in the Liberal interest. On taking silk in 1935 he moved to London and in a short time became an established and busy leader. In 1945 he was appointed a judge of the King's Bench division and in 1951 he became a lord justice of appeal. From 1960 to 1975 he sat as a lord of appeal in ordinary, having assumed on elevation in 1960 the title of Baron Morris of Borth-y-Gest, the charming seaside village near Porthmadog which he had loved from childhood. Although not obliged to do so, he retired from his judicial appointment in 1975, and he was created CH in the same year. He had been appointed CBE and knighted in 1945 and admitted to the Privy Council in 1951.

Morris was a tall, handsome man possessed of great charm, a prodigious worker and a golden-voiced orator. His chief personal characteristics were unfailing courtesy, instinctive kindness, devotion to duty, and unsparing readiness to serve the public interest. His life was by no means restricted to the law, for he was called upon to preside over many wide-ranging committees, of which probably the most important was the Home Office committee on jury service (1963–4). He was a deeply impressive speaker on formal occasions and a delightful one at social events.

Throughout his long tenure of judicial office, Morris was the soul of consideration to all who appeared before him. Some would say that at times he was over-patient and could with advantage have speeded the hearing of a case. But in his determination to ensure that a just conclusion was arrived at, he saw to it that every point raised was carefully and, indeed, exhaustively examined. Above all, he was vigilant in protecting the freedom of the individual when threatened by the Executive, and he exhibited judicial valour consistently and in full measure.

His judgments were most learned, admirably lucid, and of high literary quality. These virtues were recognized by the conferment upon him of honorary doctorates in law by the universities of Wales (1946), British Columbia (1952), Liverpool (1966), and Cambridge (1967). He was an honorary member of both the Canadian and the American Bar Associations, and a member of the Pilgrims' Society, of the University Grants Committee (1955–69), and of the Charing Cross Hospital council of management (1941–8, chairman of the board of governors, 1948–68).

Probably due to his Liverpool upbringing, Morris was not fully fluent in Welsh. He was nevertheless devoted to Wales and he served her splendidly. While in practice at the bar he was honorary standing counsel to the University of Wales from 1938 to 1945, and he was its pro-chancellor from 1956 to 1974. A member of the Gorsedd of Bards, he regularly robed and processed at the annual Royal National Eisteddfod, he was a vice-president and life member of the Honourable Society of Cymmrodorion, and he presided over the London Welsh Association (1951–3). For over a quarter of a century he sat as chairman of Caernarfonshire quarter-sessions. When in London he worshipped regularly at the Welsh Congregational chapel in King's Cross. After retirement from judicial office he took particular interest in Welsh political affairs, and during the 1977 parliamentary debates over the ill-fated Wales Bill he spoke most eloquently in favour of devolution. To this Dictionary he contributed the notice of Sir Harold Morris.

Morris never married, and he died 9 June 1979 at Porthmadog.

[Personal knowledge.] EDMUND-DAVIES

MORRIS, SIR PHILIP ROBERT (1901–1979), educationist, was born 6 July 1901, the younger son of Meshach Charles Morris, HM inspector of schools, of Sutton Valence, Kent, and his wife, Jane, daughter of James Brasier, of St. Cross, Winchester, Hampshire. He was educated at Tonbridge School, St. Peter's School, York, and Trinity College, Oxford, where he obtained a second class in philosophy, politics, and economics in 1923. He then gained a teacher's diploma at London University (1924) and became a lecturer in history and classics at Westminster Training College (1923–5).

Morris's career fell into three main parts; service in local government administration; war service as the head of army education; and in higher education, as vice-chancellor of Bristol University (1946–66). The record overall shows him to have been one of the two or three ablest administrators of his time in English education.

Morris graduated at a critical time for English education, which faced new responsibilities under the 1918 Education Act of H. A. L. Fisher [q.v.]. Morris joined the Kent education authority and was soon picked out by Salter Davies, a remarkable director of education under whom Kent education was forging ahead. Both before and after 1938, the year in which he succeeded Salter Davies as director, Morris was especially concerned with the new relationship that was called for between administrators, teachers, and governing bodies of all the schools of the county, whether grammar schools or village schools. He was given credit for somehow managing to build this personal relationship between the director, the teachers, and the laymen. His was a new style and he thought it the style of the future.

In the second phase, he was appointed to a newly created post as director-general of army education (1944–6). His single-minded aim was to build a bridge between the experiences of war and the return of the servicemen to peacetime occupations: and the measure of his success was the confidence he won for the programme from soldiers and civilians alike. Whether, as some have thought, it affected the politics of the time, the essential achievement was undoubtedly an educational one.

The third stage began in 1946 when he was appointed vice-chancellor of Bristol, undoubtedly because the university felt the need for first-rate administration in the post-war years. Although some doubted the wisdom of a transplant to a university from the world of local government, Morris quickly showed that he combined in himself the necessary ingredients: administrative skills, familiarity with the world of affairs, and sympathy with the special aspirations of academic workers. As in Kent, his personal influence on individuals under his authority was strongly felt. One who worked closely with him wrote: 'He asked a lot from those under him . . . and encouraged everyone to give more than they thought they had to give; they were rewarded by the satisfaction of having contributed to the whole. Above all, he communicated to individuals his confidence in them.' He took pride in the distinction of the university's scholarship; building on it, he consolidated the support of the great manufacturing and mercantile interests that had been the mark of Bristol through centuries of enterprise, as well as that of the elected governments of the city and the region.

Morris's contribution to the well-being of the

universities was not confined to Bristol; it was most widely evident during his chairmanship (1955–8) of the vice-chancellors' committee. He succeeded his brother, C. R. Morris (later Lord Morris of Grasmere), who was then vice-chancellor of Leeds, in that office, and the six years of their tenure wrote a notable chapter in the history of the growth of collaboration between universities during the critical post-war decade of the 1950s. Among other things, Morris clearly foresaw that the universities would have to submit to a degree of social audit and accountability, and that they would be wise to see that they themselves should be the main architects of the new structures. He pointed to methods and practices where his experience of public affairs suggested that changes were needed; in particular, he ensured the establishment of the central council for admissions; and he played a decisive part in the discussions with the Treasury which resulted in a radical provision of supplementary pensions for university teachers from public funds. To the end of his career he believed that by active discussion and negotiation in all matters affecting the universities and government the essential interests of the universities could be made secure.

Beyond these major elements in his career, he contributed with seemingly tireless effectiveness to the work of many public bodies and causes. Three need special mention, because they illustrate the range of his interest and the issues he regarded as of primary importance. He served on the committee on the supply and training of teachers (1943–4), chaired by Sir Arnold (later Lord) McNair, and on the committee on higher education (1961–4), chaired by Lord Robbins—two committees which laid down the pattern for teachers' colleges and for universities in Great Britain for ensuing years. Both reports gave inspiration for a period of lively development.

Morris was long a member (latterly as chairman) of the Secondary Schools Examination Council. Here he revealed his stance on a major social and educational issue of his time. Morris believed that the grammar schools were on their way to success in their task of providing centres of excellence in the state system to match the best of the private schools. But he felt a deep concern for the seventy per cent or so of boys and girls outside the range of these schools. He would have no part with those who saw only a downward adjustment of the grammar schools as appropriate for this great majority of young people. On the contrary, he took the view that a fundamental re-thinking was needed to provide positively the education that suited their needs.

Many individuals and groups turned to Morris for help because of his exceptional skill in administration and also because they recognized a characteristic he brought from his parental home. Both his parents had been committed teachers in village schools. Thus the family background was one in which teaching as a vocation was of the very essence. To the end of his life there was a natural rapport between him and those who in a great variety of forms shared such a commitment; in the medical, nursing, and other social services; in the BBC (as governor from 1952 to 1960 and vice-chairman from 1954 to 1960); in the fine arts and the Bristol Old Vic Trust, of which he was chairman from 1946 to 1971.

Morris was a man who stood out in his time for his skill in getting things done. He believed that almost anything could be done by good administration. And his personal mark was to use his administrative skills to release the abilities and enthusiasms of his fellow men.

Morris was appointed CBE in 1941, knighted in 1946, and created KCMG in 1960. He had honorary degrees from many universities and was FRSA (1961) and honorary FRCS (1966). In 1926 he married Florence Redvers Davis, daughter of Walford Davis Green, barrister. They had two sons and two daughters. Morris died at Bryncoedifor, near Dolgellau, 21 November 1979. There is a portrait by George Sweet (1966) at the University of Bristol.

[Kent Education Authority; War Office; Bristol University; private information; personal knowledge.] JOHN FULTON

MORTIMER, (CHARLES) RAYMOND (BELL) (1895–1980), literary and art critic and editor, was born at 62 Albert Gate Mansions, Knightsbridge, London, 25 April 1895, the only child of Charles Edward Mortimer, a prosperous solicitor of Devon stock, and his wife, (Marion) Josephine Cantrell. His mother dying young, Mortimer was brought up in Redhill, Surrey, by an aunt and uncle—and two educated Swiss girls, who taught him French. Though the household, he reported, was neither intellectual nor aesthetic, he 'relished pleasant old pictures, furniture and, above all, quite a lot of books'. He gave a charming glimpse of this phase in a sketch, 'First Disobedience and the Fruit', contributed to a collection of childhood reminiscences edited by Alan Pryce-Jones (*Little Innocents*, 1932). He was also often taken to France for holidays; the foundations of a lifelong affinity were laid early.

He was sent away at nine to 'an over-large, harsh preparatory school' at Eastbourne, moving in 1909 as a minor scholar to Malvern College, which he was later to describe as 'one of the most philistine and brutal public schools of the period'. Going up to Balliol to study history in 1913, he read under, among others, the inevitable F. F. ('Sligger') Urquhart; but in 1915, medically rejected for active service, he worked at a hospital for French soldiers in the South of France. In 1918, again medically rejected, he returned to England as a cipher clerk in the Foreign Office. After the war he did not return to Oxford but was given a 'war BA'. He also briefly joined the Roman Catholic Church; this voyage of spiritual exploration proved fruitless, his subsequent interest in any church being almost entirely confined to a lively relish, expressed with humane acerbity, for the intellectual and personal oddities of Anglican bishops. A self-proclaimed hedonist, he combined enjoyment with irreverence and unflagging curiosity. Reading, looking at pictures, and party-going were, with the help of a private income, diversified by swimming, skating, skiing, and later bridge and croquet, which he played with stern intensity. He was in fact regarded as rather frivolous by the literary and artistic circle known as 'Bloomsbury'. Others often found his mixture of mischief and dismissiveness alarming: 'a frightening person to those who do not know him, and even more frightening to those who do' (Violet Trefusis—an opinion ruefully echoed by, among others, the novelist L. P. Hartley, q.v.). He readily indulged a lifelong appetite for travel, and in Paris almost established a second home, rapidly becoming friendly with such leaders of contemporary art and letters as Jean Cocteau, Tristan Tzara, and Louis Aragon.

In 1922, in collaboration with Hamish Miles (J. E. Miles, a Balliol friend), he published a light-hearted novel, *The Oxford Circus*, a lark some distance in the wake of Oscar Wilde, H. H. Munro ('Saki'), (Sir) H. M. Beerbohm [qq.v.], and A. A. Ronald Firbank. A Jamesian pastiche, 'The Lion's Den', originally published in the *London Mercury*, achieved inclusion in *The Best British Short Stories of 1924*. His lively and provocative style soon won him a readership in *Vogue*, the *Nation*, and the *New Statesman* (precariously congenial with his own liberal opinions). He took over from T. S. Eliot [q.v.] the London Letter to the influential New York periodical the *Dial* for some years; but it was ultimately in the *New Statesman*, under the gratefully acknowledged tutelage of (Sir) C. O. Desmond MacCarthy [q.v.], that he made his mark as an outstanding critic and reviewer of both literature and the visual arts. The latter interest was marked in 1929 by the publication of *The New Interior Decoration* in association with Dorothy Todd. Mortimer's hand is evident in a coruscating text, both picturesque and polemical. In 1932 Mortimer published *The French Pictures, a Letter to Harriet* in the Hogarth Letters series: a genial exposition, addressed to an intelligent married woman, of how to look at pictures, in the light of a current Royal Academy exhibition. In 1944 he published an introduction to Edouard Manet's *Un Bar aux Folies-Bergère* and a small monograph, *Duncan Grant* (the artist who had painted murals in Mortimer's Bloomsbury flat). He was for some years a member of the Royal Fine Art Commission.

He became literary editor of the *New Statesman* in 1935, retaining the post until 1947, with an interlude in 1940–1, when he went to the Ministry of Information, playing a large part in liaison with the BBC and the setting up of the Free French Service. His contributions to his own *New Statesman* pages, under the heading '*Books in General*', fully established his reputation. His editorship of the 'back half' of the weekly in no way reflected the political pressures of the front half—the editor, B. Kingsley Martin [q.v.], treated Mortimer with unwonted respect—but greatly enhanced the already high standing of its arts and book reviews. He was assiduous, like MacCarthy before him, in supervising his contributors and their use of English, and even more so in searching out and encouraging new talent, as tributes from, among others, Sir V. S. Pritchett testify. In 1948, however, he went to the *Sunday Times* as running mate to his former mentor, MacCarthy, whom he succeeded as chief reviewer after the latter's death in 1952. He was soon to be joined by another MacCarthy-trained critic, Cyril Connolly [q.v.]—whom he outlived, continuing to write for the paper until his own death in 1980.

His qualities as a critic are fully displayed in two collections: *Channel Packet* (1942) and *Try Anything Once* (1976). These seventy or so selected pieces hardly at all reflect his interest in painting, except in occasional cross-reference, and a third of them are not specifically concerned with literature, being mostly travel sketches. Nevertheless the best writing in the books is to be found in his response to literature—but to literature as an enhancement of life. Unrelentingly hostile to and derisive of any approach which placed evaluation before delight, all the same he saw the art of reading as requiring a pleasurable concentration of the faculties. His own concentration upon nineteenth-century England and France may be seen as a limitation: but his response was in no sense antiquarian or nostalgic, always that of a man alertly alive in a real, twentieth-century world. At its best it was illuminated by a vigorous lyricism of phrase, effectively mingling mandarin and vernacular, shot through with ironic humour. It is significant that, although Proust and Gide ranked high for him, his ultimate preference was for Balzac—and it is no wonder that he should have been instrumental in introducing the works of Simenon to Britain. It was not so much literature itself which enthralled him, for all the acuteness of his ear and sense of form, but rather the power of fiction or biography to make apprehensible the splendours and miseries, and not least the inherent absurdities, of human nature.

He greatly valued and was valued by the London Library, and was for many years a most effective member of its committee. In 1955 he was appointed CBE and an officer of the French Legion of Honour. In 1977 he was awarded the prix de l'Académie Française.

Unmarried, he shared the Bloomsbury flat, and after 1952 a handsome house in Canonbury, Islington, with the architect Geddes Hyslop; in Dorset he enjoyed a delightful country house with his fellow-critics Edward Sackville-West, fifth Baron Sackville [q.v.], and Desmond Shawe-Taylor. Portraits were painted by Derek Hill and Edward le Bas, the latter notably characteristic, showing him, as relaxed as he ever was, on the sofa in the dining-room of the Bloomsbury flat, his much-loved pictures lining the wall behind him. A life-mask was made by an unknown German artist. Mortimer died 9 January 1980 at his home in Canonbury, Islington.

[Mortimer's own writings; Frances Partridge, *A Pacifist's War*, 1978, and *Memories*, 1981; Marie-Jacqueline Lancaster, *Brian Howard, Portrait of a Failure*, 1968; Violet Trefusis, *Don't Look Round*, 1952; Edward Hyams, *The New Statesman*, 1963; Kingsley Martin, *Father Figures*, 1966; recollections of various friends, including Geddes Hyslop, Desmond Shawe-Taylor, and Sir Victor Pritchett; personal knowledge.] J. W. LAMBERT

MORTIMER, ROBERT CECIL (1902–1976), bishop of Exeter, was born at Bishopston, Bristol, 6 December 1902, the youngest but one in the family of three sons and three daughters of Edward Mortimer, vicar of the parish of Bishopston, and his wife, Ellen Merrick. In 1916 he won an entrance scholarship to St. Edward's School, Oxford, an Anglo-Catholic foundation where the worship of the chapel was a major influence in determining Mortimer's religious outlook throughout his life. Here he also acquired his lifelong interest in a wide variety of sporting activities.

In 1921 he entered Keble College, Oxford, as a classical exhibitioner. His moral tutor was K. E. Kirk [q.v.], who became a close personal friend and later directed his interests to the study of moral theology. He gained firsts in classical honour moderations (1923) and *literae humaniores* (1925). In 1925 he proceeded to Wells Theological College, and in 1926 he was ordained deacon to a title at the important parish of St. Mary Redcliffe, Bristol.

A turning-point in Mortimer's life came with his appointment as lecturer in theology at Christ Church, Oxford, in 1929, and as a Student the next year. He devoted himself to the specialist study of canon law, an area hitherto somewhat neglected in Anglican scholarship, and was made university lecturer in this subject in 1935. His researches bore fruit in his first important book, *The Origins of Private Penance in the Western Church* (1939). In the same year he became a member of the archbishops' commission for the complete revision of the canon law of the Church of England. This work was to occupy him for some thirty years but perhaps his most important contribution was to the commission's report of 1947, which owed much to his scholarship and literary skill.

In 1933 Mortimer had married Mary Hope, daughter of James Ronald Walker, a barrister, of Kensington. They had two sons and two daughters. Mortimer's reputation in Oxford continued to grow and it was no surprise when in 1944 he was appointed regius professor of moral and pastoral theology in succession to Leonard Hodgson. The year 1947 saw the publication of his best-known work, *The Elements of Moral Theology*, as a result of which he was awarded the DD. He had been elected proctor in convocation for Oxford University in 1943, beginning a membership of convocation and church assembly which continued until 1973, and in 1948 his eminence as a canonist received singular recognition when he was appointed chancellor of the diocese of Blackburn.

By this time, he was clearly marked out for high preferment and in 1949 he was appointed to the see of Exeter. The diocese was still suffering from the effects of the war and his first years were occupied with the work of reconstruction. He made no spectacular innovations, for his temperament was essentially conservative and pragmatic, and he never allowed himself to be overwhelmed by administration. Rather, he devoted himself to the steady improvement of church life and worship and to laying a foundation for future growth. Tall, handsome, and dignified, he was an impressive figure, although he could sometimes appear remote: he had little small talk, tended to find ordinary parochial occasions something of a bore, and was at his best in a small group of like-minded friends. But his diocese respected his intellectual gifts and soon came to be aware of his deep pastoral concern, especially for the clergy and their families, whom he knew well. His learning was worn lightly and he could appear indolent—his letters of two or three lines, in reply to correspondence, were renowned—but he was a hard worker who never neglected essential business. He was an excellent, and very succinct, preacher and his addresses to his diocesan conference and his monthly contributions to the *Exeter Diocesan Leaflet* were models of clear, yet profound, exposition of complicated issues affecting Church and State. The affection in which he was held found expression in the celebrations, which deeply moved him, of the twenty-first anniversary of his episcopate in 1970.

Mortimer's episcopal responsibilities prevented him from writing the major scholarly contributions which many hoped for, but he found time to publish during his time at Exeter a number of short popular books in his particular field, *Christian Ethics* (1950), *The Duties of a Churchman* (1951), and *Western Canon Law* (1953). Much of his most significant thinking went anonymously into a series of important reports of convocation and church assembly commissions, of which he was a member or chairman. As time went by, he became one of the elder statesmen of the church and, as one of the few members of the bench with an academic background, his speeches in debate were impressive and influential. Although he was always recognized as a leader of the Anglo-Catholic wing of the church, his views grew increasingly independent of any narrow party line: he was, for example, a strong supporter both of the church of South India and of the Anglican–Methodist unity scheme.

In 1955 Mortimer was introduced into the House of Lords and was soon recognized as one of the church's leading spokesmen on moral and social questions: probably no other bishop made more expert contributions in these areas during his seventeen years in the upper house. He was a member of a number of government committees on the treatment of prisoners and other offenders, but perhaps his most significant achievement was in connection with the reform of the divorce laws. He was the chairman of the archbishop of Canterbury's group that in 1966 produced the report *Putting Asunder*, which became the basis of the Divorce Reform Bill of 1969. It was largely Mortimer who negotiated with the Law Commission the compromise which made marital breakdown the sole ground for divorce, as proposed by *Putting Asunder*, but without its further proposal for a preceding enquiry into the state of the marriage. The eventual outcome was little to Mortimer's liking, although he felt bound to support the Bill in Parliament, since he feared it would open the door to divorce by consent. He always insisted that the reform was concerned with secular law and society and remained resolutely opposed to any suggestion that divorced parties should be allowed to remarry in church.

As he neared the age of seventy, Mortimer found the strain of a large diocese, involving a great deal of travelling, increasingly tiring and his health seems to have begun to deteriorate. He announced his resignation in 1973 and retired with his wife to Newton Reigny in Cumbria. There he lived quietly until his sudden death at home 11 September 1976. He was an honorary fellow of Keble (1951) and an honorary Student of Christ Church (1968).

[B. G. Skinner, *Robert Exon*, 1979; *The Times*, 13 September 1976; private information; personal knowledge.] J. R. Porter

MORTON, Sir DESMOND JOHN FALKINER (1891–1971), soldier, intelligence officer, and public servant, was born 13 November 1891, the only son of Colonel Charles Falkiner Morton, Royal Dragoons, and his wife Edith Harriet, daughter of John Towlerton Leather, of Middleton Hall, Bedford, Northumberland. Educated at Eton and the Royal Military Academy, Woolwich, he joined the Royal Horse and Royal Field Artillery in 1911 and served throughout World War I. While he was commanding a forward battery at Arras a bullet lodged in his heart, but with characteristic resilience he survived to be awarded the MC and become an aide-de-camp to Field-Marshal Douglas (later Earl) Haig [q.v.]. The appointment profoundly affected his future career. He had to conduct round the front line the minister of munitions, (Sir) Winston Churchill, who formed what in his memoirs he called 'a great regard and friendship for this brilliant and gallant officer'. In 1919 the influence of Churchill, Lloyd George, and Sir Eyre Crowe [qq.v.] drew Morton into the Foreign Office as an intelligence officer.

His work was at its peak in the thirties. From 1929 to September 1939 he was head of the Committee of Imperial Defence's Industrial Intelligence Centre, concentrating for his masters on the rearmament of Germany but also using his private sources to keep Churchill, then in the political wilderness, fully briefed. He did so—it has been claimed—by a unique authority granted to him by Ramsay MacDonald and endorsed by Stanley Baldwin and Neville Chamberlain, though Churchill's official biographer, Martin Gilbert, has stated that 'no evidence has been found for any of these assertions'. In any case the relationship was eased by the fact that Morton lived only a mile from Churchill's home at Chartwell where, apart from regular meetings to share his secret information, he assisted Churchill in his literary work—notably during the composition of *The World Crisis* (5 vols., 1923–31). In 1947 Churchill wrote to Morton: 'When I read all these letters and papers you wrote for me and think of our prolonged conversations I feel how very great is my debt to you, and I know that no other thought ever crossed your mind but that of the public interest.' The private papers of Sir Maurice (later Lord) Hankey [q.v.], the pivot of the Cabinet and the Committee of Imperial Defence, also disclose an intimate collaboration with Morton during this decade.

On the outbreak of war he was made a principal assistant secretary, Ministry of Economic Warfare, but when Churchill became prime minister in May 1940 he placed Morton in his private office as his personal assistant. Here, for a time, Morton's position was central and strong. Initially he was the filter through which Churchill received the Ultra intelligence obtained at Bletchley Park from breaking the German Enigma cipher, and he was active in liaison with the foreign 'governments in exile'. But as the war ran on Churchill depended increasingly on the chiefs of staff and their highly integrated network of subsidiary committees, whilst the voluminous flow of Ultra and other intelligence required a systematic handling. Inevitably, therefore, Morton's role was reduced. In contemporary documents and in photographs of the major wartime conferences his name and his face often appear, but as an *éminence grise* his authority waned.

He was apointed CMG in 1937, CB in 1941, and KCB in 1945. In addition he was awarded the croix de guerre *avec palmes*, the officership of the Legion of Honour, and the Knight's Grand Cross of Orange-Nassau. In 1949 he served on the economic survey mission, Middle East, and from 1950 to 1953 he was seconded to the Ministry of Civil Aviation.

In spite of an ebullient style he was a man of inner sensitivities, and obsessive about preserving his anonymity in respect of secret matters. Before World War I he became a Roman Catholic, and he relished theological discussion. His post-war home at Kew, though small, was distinctively elegant. After his retirement in 1953 he committed himself wholeheartedly to the governorship of the Hammersmith group of hospitals. Yet the extensive correspondence between Morton and the military commentator R. W. Thompson (which was published posthumously) reveals him as a man diminished by disappointment. His criticisms of Churchill, though sometimes just, at other times have almost a vengeful character. The letters are an unhappy footnote to the story of one who had done the state much service.

Morton died at Hammersmith Postgraduate Hospital, London, 31 July 1971. He was unmarried.

[Martin Gilbert, *Winston S. Churchill*, vol. v (1922–1939), 1976; R. W. Thompson, *Churchill and Morton*, 1976; Sir John Colville, *The Churchillians*, 1981; Ronald Lewin, *Ultra Goes to War*, 1978; private information.]

RONALD LEWIN

MORTON, FERGUS DUNLOP, BARON MORTON OF HENRYTON (1887–1973), lord of appeal in ordinary, was born at Wilmore, Kelvinside, Glasgow, 17 October 1887, the youngest of the four children (three boys and a girl) of George Morton, of Troon, Ayrshire, a Glasgow stockbroker, and his wife, Janet, daughter of William Wilson, of Richmond House, Dowanhill, Glasgow. His father came of long-established Ayrshire farming stock and amassed a considerable fortune before his death in 1927. In 1897 Morton was (in his own words) 'at last allowed to go to school' at Kelvinside Academy, where he continued until 1906, becoming head boy on the classical side. In 1906 he obtained an open exhibition in classics at St. John's College, Cambridge. In 1908 he was awarded a foundation scholarship. He missed a first class in part i of the classical tripos in 1909 'by a few marks', as an examiner told him, having had to take the examination in bed on account of an attack of influenza. He went on to obtain the first place in the first class of part ii of the law tripos in 1910.

After spending a year in a solicitor's office, Morton was called to the English bar by the Inner Temple in November 1912. In 1914 he also joined Lincoln's Inn. He chose to practise at the Chancery bar and was a pupil first of A. L. Ellis, a distinguished conveyancer, and then of Dighton Pollock, who enjoyed a large junior practice at the Chancery bar.

Morton's legal career was then interrupted by military service in the Highland Light Infantry. He saw active service in German East Africa, attained the rank of captain (1915), and was awarded the MC. From 1918 until February 1919 he served in the War Office. In September 1919 he returned to practise at the bar, devilling for George Northcote. Northcote died in January 1921 and Morton inherited some of his clients. This was his real start at the bar. His practice grew rapidly, and when he took silk in 1929 he was one of the busiest Chancery juniors.

Morton was knighted and appointed High Court judge (Chancery division) in 1938. In 1944 he was promoted to the Court of Appeal and sworn of the Privy Council. In 1947 he became a life peer and a lord of appeal in ordinary, a position which he held until his retirement in 1959.

In 1939 he was appointed deputy chairman of the contraband committee at the Ministry of Economic Warfare and from 1941 to 1946 he was chairman of the black list committee at that ministry. From 1949 to 1953 he was chairman of the Council of Legal Education. In 1950 he was appointed chairman of the committee on the law of intestate succession and in 1951 he became chairman of the royal commission on marriage and divorce, which reported in 1955.

He was tall, slim, and lithe in appearance: his expression was mild but lively: he possessed a ready and impish sense of humour which won him general friendship and affection: and, as might be expected of one who never set foot outside his native Scotland before he first went to Cambridge and who continued throughout his life to pay regular visits to Scotland, his conversation and his advocacy were graced by a gentle and melodious Scottish accent. His advocacy was consistently careful, constructive, concise, and cogent, and in his judicial judgements he never seemed to find any difficulty in reaching a clear and convincing conclusion lucidly expressed. He was a delightful judge to whom to present an argument but a testing one.

All his life Morton was an enthusiastic player of ball games, of which golf undoubtedly held pride of place. At this he excelled at Kelvinside. In his early years at Cambridge devotion to cricket interfered with his golf, but in 1907–8 he played golf in three matches for the university and in his final year (1908–9) he played for the university in every match except that against Oxford, winning ten matches and losing only two. He played on very many occasions for the Oxford and Cambridge Golfing Society, and succeeded Bernard Darwin [q.v.] as its president in 1953. Darwin wrote in *The Times* of the Society's 1951 match against Oxford; 'Never before in the history of golf has the issue of a match depended on a lord of appeal getting a two at the last hole and this is what happened.'

He received honorary LL Ds from the universities of Cambridge (1951), Glasgow (1951), St. Andrews (1956), and Sydney (1957). He became an honorary fellow of St. John's (1940) and was deputy high steward of Cambridge University. From 1932 he was an elder at St. Columba's church, Pont Street, London. In 1953 he received the unusual honour of election as an honorary member of the Faculty of Advocates, which had thitherto been conferred only on reigning sovereigns. In the same year he served as treasurer of Lincoln's Inn, of which he had been elected a bencher in 1932. He received the Grand Cross of the Order of Orange Nassau (Netherlands) and the US Medal of Freedom (with silver palms).

He married in 1914 Margaret Greenlees, elder daughter of James Begg, grain merchant. Morton died 18 July 1973 at his country house Grey Thatch, Cookham, Berkshire. His wife survived him, as also did their only child, a daughter.

[Private information; personal knowledge.]

DENYS B. BUCKLEY

MORTON, JOHN CAMERON ANDRIEU BINGHAM MICHAEL (1893–1975), humorous journalist who wrote under the pseudonym of BEACHCOMBER, was born 7 June 1893 in London, the only child of Edward Arthur Morton, journalist and dramatist, and his wife, Rosamond, daughter of Captain Devereux Bingham, of Wartnaby Hall, Leicestershire. His father began his career as a journalist in Paris and later became the dramatic critic of the *Sunday Referee*. He wrote the 'book' of the long running musical *San Toy* and also adapted the libretto of *The Merry Widow* for the English stage. J. B. Morton was educated at Park House Preparatory School, Southborough, and went to Harrow in 1907 but made no particular mark there. (It is fair to assume that Harrow inspired his later fictional creation, Narkover.) Morton spent a year at Worcester College, Oxford, but left on account of his father's illness.

Morton was a romantic young man whose first ambition was to be a poet. He was writing revue material for the theatre when war broke out in 1914. He enlisted in the Royal Fusiliers and was eventually commissioned in the Suffolk Regiment and sent out to the trenches. He was wounded on the Somme, returned to England suffering from shell shock and spent the rest of the war in a branch of intelligence known as MI7b. When the war ended Morton published a novel *The Barber of Putney* (1919) based on his experiences in the trenches.

In 1919 he was taken on the staff of the *Sunday Express* as a columnist and was for a short time a reporter on the *Daily Express*, a job at which, he said, he was 'a howling failure'. He took over the Beachcomber column from D. B. Wyndham Lewis in 1924 and wrote it continuously until he was retired in 1975, surviving a number of attempts by Lord Beaverbrook to dismiss him. Over the years he built up a cast of comic characters who became classics of nonsense writing—Mr Justice Cocklecarrot, Dr Smart-Allick, headmaster of Narkover, Captain Foulenough, and the mad scientist Dr Strabismus (Whom God Preserve) of Utrecht. Morton chronicled their activities in short paragraphs parodying the newspaper style. His humour was based on a strong dislike of the twentieth century which he thought of as Godless, noisy, and unpleasant. (Personally he would have no truck with it and refused to use a typewriter or even ride a bicycle). Nevertheless his funniest work was pure nonsense which had little or no reference to the real world: for example the saga of the Filthistan Trio, a group of see-sawing Persian acrobats, the List of Huntingdonshire Cabmen, and the Trial of the Seven Red-Bearded Dwarves, one of many legal marathons. ('Justice', he once said, 'must not only be done; it must be seen to be believed.') The character Prodnose, a pedantic interrupter, passed into the parlance of newspapers while others of Morton's sayings—for example, 'Wagner is the Puccini of music'—found their way to the quotation books.

Morton wrote the Beachcomber column daily, until the last years when he was limited to once a week. His output was colossal, running to millions of words. He wrote effortlessly in small neat handwriting on ordinary notepaper, in which form it was sent to the *Daily Express*. Only a small fraction was reprinted in Beachcomber collections of which there were about twenty in all, many of them illustrated by Nicolas Bentley [q.v.]. Evelyn Waugh [q.v.] said of him that he showed 'the greatest comic fertility of any Englishman'.

Morton was a stocky thickset man who wore his hair in a crew cut like his mentor Hilaire Belloc [q.v.]. In his early days as a journalist he was a familiar figure in the pubs of Fleet Street with his loud laugh, muddy boots, and blackthorn walking stick. He was well known for his practical jokes and once assembled a large and indignant crowd round a pillar box on the pretext that a small boy had been trapped inside. Morton belonged to the circle of Sir John Squire [q.v.] and there are fictional portraits of him as Mr Huggins in *England their England* by A. G. Macdonell (1933) and as Rowley Meek in *The Innocent Moon* (1961) by Henry Williamson [q.v.].

Morton was a disciple of Hilaire Belloc of whom he wrote an affectionate memoir (*Hilaire Belloc*, 1955). He became a Roman Catholic in 1922 and accompanied Belloc on several walking tours. Along with Belloc he championed the French and wrote a number of historical books on French themes such as *The Bastille Falls* (1936) and *The Dauphin* (1937). These he regarded as his serious work, though they did not enjoy any great success. He also wrote *St Therese of Lisieux, the Making of a Saint* (1954) in which he outlined his strong religious beliefs.

Morton married in 1927 Dr Mary O'Leary of Cappoquin, county Wexford. There were no children. She died in 1974. Morton died in Worthing 10 May 1979 and was buried at Bagshot.

[*The Best of Beachcomber*, selected and introduced by Michael Frayn, 1963.]

RICHARD INGRAMS

MORTON, RICHARD ALAN (1899–1977), biochemist, was born 22 September 1899 in Liverpool, the younger child and only son of John Morton, engine driver, of Wrexham, and his wife Ann Humphreys, maidservant, of Nantgwynant. He was named Richard Alun and later changed the spelling of his second forename. He received his secondary education at Oulton School, Liverpool, after winning a junior city scholarship at the age of ten. After leaving school he spent the time before joining the army working for Watson Gray, a consultant chemist. This shows that he had early decided on a career in science. After nine months in the army he contracted Spanish influenza and was demobilized just in time to enter the 1919 session at the University of Liverpool. He graduated with first class honours in chemistry (1922) and proceeded to a Ph.D. under Professor E. C. C. Baly, a pioneer in chemical spectroscopy.

In 1924 he was appointed to a special lectureship in spectroscopy and remained in that post until 1944 when he was appointed to the Johnston chair of biochemistry in the university. During these twenty years he was awarded the Meldola medal (1930) at the Institute of Chemistry (later amalgamated with the Chemical Society into the Royal Society of Chemistry) and gradually turned away from pure chemical spectroscopy to become a pioneer in the application of this powerful technique to biological problems, particularly those associated with fat-soluble vitamins. He played a large part in perfecting two methods of assay of vitamin A and in 1937 discovered that the liver oil industry was throwing as much vitamin A back into the sea as was present in the fish livers, mainly halibut and cod, it was retaining. The reason was that fish intestines and particularly the pyloric caeca were extremely rich in vitamin A. Morton took out a provisional patent on this discovery and handed it to the Medical Research Council which was supporting his research. The council, however, did not pursue the matter further because they did not wish to protect a source or a method of extraction. Morton was disconsolate because he could point to the magnificent science campus at the University of Wisconsin at Madison, built to a great extent on the proceeds of a patent granted to Professor Steenbock, who produced vitamin D activity in yeasts by irradiating them with ultraviolet light.

During the war of 1939–45 Sir Jack Drummond [q.v.], then scientific adviser to the Ministry of Food, utilized Morton's expertise to monitor the programme initiated to fortify the British diet, particularly margarine, with fish liver concentrates rich in vitamin A and D. It soon became clear that the human daily requirement for vitamin A was not accurately known and the accessory food factors committee of the Medical Research Council arranged that conscientious objectors, who had volunteered to act as experimental animals, were housed at Sheffield and provided with a controlled diet as nearly as possible devoid of vitamin A activity. Morton was a protagonist in this investigation which lasted over two years. The resulting report (MRC Special Report Series No. 264), 'Vitamin A requirements of human adults', was a model of its kind and the reported findings still stand.

Morton's appointment to the Johnston chair of biochemistry at Liverpool (the senior chair of biochemistry in the country) in 1944 was not without controversy but after much discussion and the strong advocacy of Sir Jack Drummond, he was chosen in the face of considerable opposition from more conventionally trained biochemists. The appointment was outstandingly successful and for twenty-two years he guided the department through the difficulties of the post-war years to reach a position of international eminence in the sixties. This eminence was the result of a combination of his personal research, his encouragement of colleagues, and his kind and friendly attitude to overseas research students who were attracted to his department in large numbers. The position achieved by Morton's department was clearly acknowledged when the university agreed to build the fine building in which the department is now housed.

The research fields which Morton developed after the war included the biochemistry of vision, in which the elucidation of the structure of retinene, the prosthetic group of the visual pigment rhodopsin, as vitamin A aldehyde (retinal), was outstanding; the discovery of ubiquinone, a lipid component of the respiratory chain; the discovery of polyprenols, compounds concerned with glycoprotein biosynthesis and studies of tocopherols (vitamin E). He was elected a fellow of the Royal Society in 1950.

In spite of his impressive research activities Morton always found time to serve on numerous university committees and was keenly interested in university affairs. He also served on many committees of the DSIR (later SERC) and was chairman of the food additives and contaminants committee from 1963 to 1968. He was twice a member of the council of the Royal Society and chairman of its publications board in 1961–2. He was also chairman of the Biochemical Society from 1959 to 1961, a crucial period in the society's development, and an editor of the *Biochemical Journal* from 1947 to 1953. He was elected an honorary member of the Society in 1966 when he retired from his university chair. The American Institute of Nutrition elected him an honorary member in 1969. In 1978 a biennial Morton lectureship was established and administered by the Biochemical Society.

In his retirement he continued to be professionally active and in 1969 spent one year in Malta as Royal Society visiting professor in the department of physiology and biochemistry in the university. He acted as adviser to the Egg Marketing Board and was chairman of a working party on marine biochemistry. He received honorary degrees from the University of Wales (1966), Trinity College Dublin (1967), and the University of Coimbra (Portugal) (1964) where his first research student (A. J. A. de Gouveia) eventually became rector. His interest in biochemistry never flagged and shortly before his final illness he had taken a major part in a conference in India and had undertaken the task of editing the proceedings.

In 1926 Morton married (Myfanwy) Heulwen, only daughter of Elizabeth and Hugh Roberts, clerk in a wholesale grocery firm in Liverpool. They had one daughter, Gillian [Lewis], who became a tutorial fellow at St. Anne's College, Oxford. Outside his professional activities he lived a quiet, happy family life in which he never forgot his Welsh roots. He died at his Liverpool home 21 January 1977. A portrait by Stanley Reed is in the Life Science Building at the University of Liverpool.

[*The Times*, 26 January 1977; *Nature*, vol. cclxvi, 1977, p. 394; J. Glover and others in *Biographical Memoirs of Fellows of the Royal Society*, vol. xxiv, 1978; private information; personal knowledge.] T. W. Goodwin

MOSLEY, Sir OSWALD ERNALD, sixth baronet (1896–1980), politician and Fascist leader, was born at 47 Hill St., Mayfair, London, 16 November 1896, the grandson of Sir Oswald Mosley, fourth baronet, of Rolleston Hall, Burton-on-Trent, and the eldest of the three sons of Oswald Mosley (who succeeded to the baronetcy in 1915) and his wife, Katharine Maud, the second child of Captain Justinian Edwards-Heathcote, of Longton Hall, Stoke-on-Trent, and Betton Hall, Market Drayton, Shropshire. The Mosleys were an old landed Staffordshire family, who had also, until 1846, been lords of the manor of Manchester.

When Mosley was five years old, his mother obtained a judicial separation from her husband, and took her three young children to live near her father's Shropshire house. Mosley's paternal grandfather, Sir Oswald, took a great interest in him, and encouraged him to spend a good deal of his time at Rolleston. His close relationship with his grandfather and his mother, who both adulated him, was to remain a strong influence in his life.

After three years at the private school West Down, Mosley went in 1909 to Winchester, where he developed considerable skill at boxing and fencing, achieving his first of many distinctions in the latter sport when, aged fifteen, he won the public schools championship at sabre and foil. He left Winchester at the end of 1912. In January 1914 he entered Sandhurst, but, after an incident the details of which still remain obscure, was rusticated in June of that year.

Recalled to Sandhurst at the outbreak of war, Mosley was commissioned into the 16th Lancers that October. He immediately applied to join the Royal Flying Corps, and was in the 6th Squadron near Poperinghe, as an observer, from December 1914 to April 1915. He returned to Shoreham-by-sea to take his pilot's licence; but in a foolish escapade he crashed his plane while performing a risky manoeuvre to impress his mother, and broke his ankle. He returned to the trenches with the 16th Lancers, but his injured ankle seriously worsened, and in March 1916 he was invalided out with a severe and permanent limp.

Part of the rest of the war was spent in the Ministry of Munitions and in the Foreign Office.

In London, Mosley swiftly became a well-known figure in the salons of the great hostesses, and came into contact with many leading politicians. Encouraged by F. E. Smith (later Earl of Birkenhead) and Sir George Younger (later Viscount Younger of Leckie) [qq.v.], Mosley became Conservative candidate for the Harrow Division of Middlesex, and won the seat in December 1918 by a very large majority. On 11 May 1920 he married Lady Cynthia Blanche, second daughter of the formidable Conservative politician Lord Curzon of Kedleston [q.v.].

Mosley appeared to live, at this stage, an almost 'double life'. On the one hand, 'Tom' Mosley (as he was known to his intimates) and his wife led a brilliant social life. To Mosley's own considerable income Cynthia had brought the fortune bequeathed by her grandfather Levi Leiter, the Chicago millionaire. The gilded and handsome young couple became the smartest of the smart set. On the other hand, Mosley was showing a serious concern with politics. He saw himself as a representative of the 'younger generation', for whom the war had sown doubts about the traditional political creeds and line-ups. Under the influence of Lord Robert Cecil (later Viscount Cecil of Chelwood, q.v.) he became an enthusiastic backer of the League of Nations. He strongly attacked military expenditure and foreign involvements, which were preventing spending on home needs. Far more devastating, however, was his opposition to the government's Irish policy, and in particular to the alleged reprisals operated by the Black and Tans. A series of critical speeches and questions, in late 1920, culminated in his crossing the House to sit on the opposition benches. He became the secretary of the newly-formed Peace with Ireland Council. On this occasion his local party gave him a unanimous vote of confidence; but, by 1922, in view of his independent line on a variety of issues, it felt constrained to ask for an assurance of his party loyalty. This Mosley loftily declined to give, claiming complete freedom of action. A new Conservative candidate was adopted, and Mosley stood as an Independent in the election that followed the collapse of the coalition in 1922. He was returned with a large majority.

It has been suggested that Mosley's career consisted of a series of mistimed opportunities, of which the first was a revolt against the coalition only months before its end. It is clear, however, that Mosley would have broken with his party, or indeed with any party, at this stage, and that his confidence in his own views and abilities made him scorn the constraints of party discipline. The same pattern was to follow him through the rest of his career.

In the 1923 election Mosley held Harrow with a reduced majority. It was already obvious that, if his political career was to continue, he needed some party affiliation. He had developed contacts with the Liberals, but, given the situation in 1923–4, his eventual choice could hardly be in doubt. In March 1924, two months after Ramsay MacDonald formed the first Labour government, Mosley joined the Labour Party, becoming a member of the ILP.

In the 1924 election he stood against Neville Chamberlain at Birmingham Ladywood, and was narrowly defeated, returning to Parliament in December 1926, after winning the Smethwick by-election with a large majority. The intervening period had been put to good use; together with (Evelyn) John St. Loe Strachey [q.v.] he had developed a series of economic policies which challenged the conventional wisdom of the time, and owed much to J. M. (later Lord) Keynes [q.v.]; and by his active work on behalf of the miners' strike he had built up support on the Left.

He was already being regarded as a possible future leader of the Labour Party, despite the arrogance and self-confidence which repelled so many of his colleagues, and the apparent frivolity of his social life. In 1928 he succeeded to the baronetcy. In the 1929 election he was returned for Smethwick, and his wife Cynthia became the Labour MP for Stoke-on-Trent. Mosley became chancellor of the Duchy of Lancaster in the new government.

J. H. Thomas [q.v.], lord privy seal, had been given special responsibility for the unemployment problem, helped by Mosley, George Lansbury [q.v.], and George Johnston. Friction was great between Mosley and Thomas, who stood, as did the chancellor of the Exchequer, Philip (later Viscount) Snowden [q.v.], for orthodox solutions. Things came to a head with the Mosley memorandum of 1930 which made radical recommendations for economic recovery, involving state intervention and a public works programme. When it was rejected by the Cabinet, Mosley resigned on 20 May 1930.

He was already considering leaving the party. The experiences of Harrow, of Smethwick, and of innumerable miners' galas had convinced him that he had a popular appeal which could transcend the conventional party system. When his proposals were defeated at the party conference in October, he set about planning the New Party, which was launched on 1 March 1931. At first this party was conceived entirely in parliamentary terms. Mosley and four other MPs (including his wife) remained in Parliament under the new banner. Discussions about alliances took place. Mosley hoped for at least a dozen seats in the October elections; but the election results were disastrous, all twenty-four candidates being defeated.

In early 1932 Mosley visited Italy, and on his return set about creating a British Fascist movement. He was impatient with the parliamentary system which had rejected him, and, in the 1932 situation, when so many people were predicting the demise of democracy, saw the future as lying with a dictatorial system which, alone, could solve the problems of the modern economy. On 1 October the British Union of Fascists was launched.

The first two years of the new movement were successful and comparatively respectable. Mosley's outstanding oratory and charisma proved capable of swaying mass meetings. The main influence was Mussolini's Italy, which still mustered considerable respect in Britain; and, despite the rough tactics of some of the party's members at ground level, a great effort was made to convince the traditional Right of the movement's respectable credentials. Many Conservatives saw it as a kind of 'Tory ginger group'. But in 1934 the picture changed. The violence at the great Olympia meeting in June estranged a good number of supporters of this type, and during the year many people became aware of the violence, extremism, and anti-Semitism which underlay the surface, and shied away.

Mosley's response was to stress, as central policies of the movement, the very aspects which had caused this rejection. From late 1934, anti-Semitism became a major plank in the BUF's platform. Deprived of much of his middle-class support, Mosley turned to the streets. There he appears to have hoped to gain that popular acclaim which would be the basis for the new regime to be built on the ruins of democracy.

The calculation was mistaken. Membership fell rapidly. Within a year the movement had ceased to be of any political importance. Its activities got considerable press coverage, of course, but it never came near to possessing any political power, even in areas like the East End, where its anti-Semitic policies had their greatest effect. The movement now became much more influenced by Nazism, and in 1936 its name was changed to the 'British Union of Fascists and National Socialists'. Mosley's Keynesian policies of 1930 had been replaced by a heady and over-simplified mixture of corporatism, totalitarianism, patriotism, and racialism.

Mosley's personal life changed considerably in this period. Lady Cynthia Mosley died of peritonitis on 16 May 1933. In October 1936, in Berlin, Mosley privately married, in Hitler's presence, the Hon. Mrs Diana Guinness, third daughter of the second Baron Redesdale, and sister of Nancy Mitford [q.v.], Jessica, and Unity.

From 1936 onwards the BUF mounted a peace campaign, denouncing the coming war as a conspiracy organized by the Jews. The campaign was of much less importance nationally than the widespread acceptance of Nazi Germany in far more respectable circles. It continued, however, into the first year of the war, and in May 1940 Mosley and his wife were arrested and detained under Regulation 18B. In November 1943 they were released, on humanitarian grounds, on account of Mosley's physical condition.

After the war Mosley concerned himself with justification of his pre-war attitudes, as in *My Answer* (1946) and *My Life* (1968), and also with the leadership, from 1948 to 1966, of the Union Movement, whose theme was European unity, based on racial criteria. After a short stay in Ireland, he lived mainly in France, in a house at Orsay, outside Paris; but he made forays into Britain. He stood for Parliament at North Kensington in 1959, in the aftermath of the Notting Hill race riots, and to his amazement lost his deposit. A similar result met him at Shoreditch in 1966. To his death he was convinced that in the event of a European crisis he still had a contribution to make. He died at his house at Orsay 3 December 1980.

Some have called Mosley one of the most intelligent politicians of this century. He was, however, singularly lacking in judgement. His were simple, uncomplicated enthusiasms. Even where the policies were subtle, and correct, as with the Strachey-inspired Keynesian theories of his Labour period, his commitment was simple, demanding, and obdurate; in the case of later 'conspiracy theories' this was even more so. In each case he had unbounded confidence in his own judgement and capabilities, and scorn for those around him. Behind all this lay almost a caricature of traditional public school values; patriotism, the belief in the 'manly' virtues, dislike of outsiders, and rejection of those whom he believed to be opposed to this pattern—whether Black and Tans terrorizing a civilian population, or Jewish capitalists undermining traditional English virtues. Personal ambition played a great part, too; but his decisions, at every point, achieved the opposite of what he desired. He continually gave the impression of a 'coming man', but his impatience defeated him.

By his first wife Cynthia he had two sons and a daughter, and by his second wife Diana two sons. His eldest son is Nicholas Mosley (born 1923), the author, who in 1966 became the third Baron Ravensdale in succession to his aunt, Irene Curzon, and who succeeded to the baronetcy on his father's death.

[Sir Oswald Mosley, *My Life*, 1968; Robert Skidelsky, *Oswald Mosley*, 1975; Maurice Cowling, *The Impact of Labour 1920–1924*, 1971; Kenneth Lunn and Richard Thurlow (eds.), *British Fascism*, 1980; Robert Benewick, *The Fascist Movement in Britain*, 1972; contemporary diaries and journals; numbers of *Action*, *Blackshirt*, and *Fascist Week*; Nicholas Mosley, *Rules of the Game: Sir Oswald and Lady*

Cynthia Mosley 1896–1933, 1982, and *Beyond the Pale, Sir Oswald Mosley 1933–80*, 1983.]

RICHARD GRIFFITHS

MOTTRAM, RALPH HALE (1883–1971), writer, was born 30 October 1883 in Gurney's bank house, Norwich, the elder son of James Mottram, who, like his father and grandfather, was resident chief clerk, and his second wife, Fanny Ann Hale, an attractive and capable young woman, full of sensible ideas on the new position of women in the world. Their second son, Hugh, became an architect, practised in Edinburgh, and illustrated some of his brother's books. The boys were educated at a private school in Norwich.

When Ralph left school his mother decided that, before entering the bank, he must spend a year in France (she had been educated in Versailles). He therefore spent 1899 at M. Rosselet's school in Lausanne. On 3 December 1899 Mottram entered the bank, where he stayed, with the exception of the war years, until 1927. He described his years there as his period of servitude for he was longing all the time to write and was getting up at five or six in the morning to practise his craft. His father was trustee of the marriage settlement of Mrs John Galsworthy. She became interested in Mottram's poetry and she and her husband encouraged him to continue writing. In 1907 and 1909 two slim volumes of Mottram's verse were published under the pen-name of J. Marjoram.

At the outbreak of war in 1914 Mottram joined a territorial battalion of the Norfolk Regiment. The next year he was commissioned and sent to Flanders. There he was quickly withdrawn from the trenches when it was found 'I was the only person who could make myself understood in the sort of French spoken by the inhabitants of the Franco-Belgian border.' It was his task to collect and investigate the complaints of damage done to crops and property by the British troops and present them to the complaints commission. It was these experiences recorded in his diary, which after the war, with the strong encouragement of the Galsworthys, enabled him to write *The Spanish Farm*. Galsworthy himself took the script to all the publishers, but in vain, until at last Chatto and Windus accepted it, on condition that Galsworthy wrote a preface to it—without a fee. So this outstanding war book was published in 1924. There is no anger or hatred in it but compassion and admiration for the independent people of Flanders, typified in the sturdy character of Madeleine, which Galsworthy described as one of the finest studies of a Frenchwoman by an Englishman.

At first the book hung fire but when it was awarded the Hawthornden prize it became a bestseller. It was filmed under the title of *Roses of Picardy* (1927) and televised in 1968. The sale of the film rights enabled Mottram to retire from the bank and at forty-four to start life again as a professional writer. Two other war books, *Sixty-four, Ninety-four* and *The Crime at Vanderlynden's* were published in 1925 and 1926. The three parts were reissued together in 1927 as *The Spanish Farm Trilogy*. In this new life he continued to write before breakfast (often 1,000 words) and on through the morning. The afternoon was kept free for recreation (gardening whenever possible) and the evening for revision of the morning's work and further writing.

In addition to *The Spanish Farm Trilogy* and many other novels including *Our Mr. Dormer* (1927), Mottram wrote numerous books on banking, on East Anglia, the Broads, and Norwich, and biographies of Norfolk worthies such as *John Crome of Norwich* (1931), the founder of the Norwich school of painters; he also continued to write and publish poetry.

Writing was constantly interrupted by committee meetings and visits to London and elsewere, for Mottram was no literary recluse. He was in great demand as a lecturer. Like his forbears he was a staunch supporter of the Octagon chapel (Unitarian) in Norwich and its many activities, especially in the war of 1939–45. For twenty years he was a trustee of Manchester College, the Unitarian foundation at Oxford. He was a founder member of the Norwich Society and its secretary for twenty years. He was a member of the Norwich public libraries committee from 1929 to 1963 and of the council of the Norfolk and Norwich Archaeological Society for thirty-one years. His many services did not go unacknowledged. In 1932 he became a fellow of the Royal Society of Literature. In coronation year, 1953, Norwich City Council elected him lord mayor, an honour well deserved and worthily maintained. He had been an active promoter of the new University of East Anglia, which in 1966 conferred on him an honorary D.Litt.

In 1918 he married Margaret ('Madge'), daughter of John Gray Allan, the schoolmaster of Longniddry, East Lothian, whose seven children all became graduates of Edinburgh. The Mottrams had two sons and a daughter.

Mottram was of average height and sturdy build and fond of walking and swimming. His erect figure striding along with head held high suggested a man of confidence and resolution. He greatly respected ceremony and tradition and was proud of being a hereditary freeman of Norwich. On all civic occasions he was correctly, almost dapperly, dressed but he was essentially a family man, enjoying conversation and delighting to entertain his friends and visitors, whether distinguished or unknown, in his modest and comfortable home designed by his brother Hugh.

In his eighties his health began to fail and he became increasingly deaf. In 1970 the death of his wife, his close 'participator' for fifty-two years, was a severe blow. Mottram went to live with his widowed daughter in King's Lynn, where he died 15 April 1971.

There is a memorial to Mottram, erected on the highest point of Mousehold heath, overlooking the city of Norwich which he loved so dearly.

[R. H. Mottram, *Autobiography with a Difference*, 1938; and *The Window Seat*, 1954, *Another Window Seat*, 1957, and *Vanities and Verities*, 1958 (3 vols. of autobiography).]

A. STEPHENSON

MOTTRAM, VERNON HENRY (1882–1976), physiologist and nutritionist, was born at Tewkesbury 14 March 1882, one of six children and the youngest of three sons of William Mottram, a Congregational minister, and his wife, Elizabeth Fruen, a schoolmistress. He was educated at Caterham School and St. Olave's Grammar School, London, winning a scholarship of Trinity College, Cambridge, where he took a first in both parts of the natural sciences tripos (1903 and 1905). He wrote his thesis on fat metabolism, and was elected to a fellowship in 1907. He worked with (Sir) Frederick Gowland Hopkins [q.v.] as a physiology demonstrator at Cambridge (1907–9), with F. G. Benedict and Graham Lusk in the USA and with Carl Voigt in Munich (1910–11), and in 1911–14 as senior demonstrator at Liverpool University with (Sir) C. S. Sherrington [q.v.]. He was lecturer at McGill University, Montreal, and at Toronto (1914–15), was senior science master at Caterham School, and then he engaged in biological research for Lever Bros. (1918–20).

In 1921 he succeeded (Sir) Edward Mellanby [q.v.] as professor of physiology at King's College of Household and Social Science, London (KCHSS), supervising a pioneer degree course where a high standard of physiology, chemistry, biology, and economics was integrated with dietetics and food preparation and applied to family and community health and welfare.

Mottram was the author of many books, both for students and for the general public. These include *A Manual of Histology* (1923), *Food and the Family* (1925), which showed how nutrition research can help to feed people both healthily and economically, *The Functions of the Body* (1926), and (with Jessie Lindsay) *Manual of Modern Cookery* (1927), which applied the sciences of nutrition, physiology, and chemistry to the choice and preparation of food and the designing of meals. In 1929, with W. M. Clifford, he published *Properties of Food*. He revised several editions of the classic *Food and the Principles of Dietetics*, first with (Sir) Robert Hutchinson [q.v.] and later with George Graham. Between 1927 and 1955 he also produced many popular talks and articles on diet and health for the press and the BBC. In 1933, as a member of the British Medical Association nutrition committee, he was involved in a clash with the government on the minimum cost of an adequate diet for 'health and working capacity'. The BMA's figures of 19s. 5½d. per week for a family of five with three children under six years, and 5s. 7d. for a single adult, were disputed by the Ministry of Health as 'too high'.

In 1936 Mottram organized a postgraduate dietetics diploma course at KCHSS. His strong concern for social welfare inspired his students, producing nutritionists and dietitians of national and international repute. In 1937, with E. M. Radloff, he published *Food Tables*. During World War II he brought out in 1942 a Red Cross booklet, *Our Food Today* (with A. E. Rowlett), and in 1940 contributed 'Food and the Housewife' to a series of popular lectures by leading nutritionists at the Royal Institution, published as *The Nation's Larder in Wartime*. In 1941 the Nutrition Society was founded, and Mottram chaired its third meeting, in May 1942.

Mottram retired in 1944, and was succeeded as professor by John Yudkin in 1945. By 1954 nutrition studies and research at the college—started by Mellanby and then developed by Mottram and Yudkin—had grown so much in scope and status that a separate Nutrition Department was formed. Yudkin became the first professor of nutrition in Great Britain.

Mottram's social concern, his scholarship, and his interest in the arts and in religion and mysticism came together in a remarkable book, *The Physical Basis of Personality*, published in 1944. His last book, *Human Nutrition*, appeared in 1948. It has been reprinted many times, and was revised by his son, R. F. Mottram, in 1979. In the preface Mottram suggests that civilization is based on agriculture, which must provide the right sort of food for human nutrition. While specialists are required, the public also needed an elementary knowledge of which foods to choose and how to store and prepare them. Mottram was keenly interested in the enjoyment and preparation of food. With foresight he 'owns to a prejudice that food should be produced for consumption, not for profit, that it should be planned on a national and global scale. Malnutrition in Asia, Africa, and South America has its repercussions in Great Britain.'

Mottram is remembered for his social concern and for his skill as a communicator. His students remember him for his brilliant lectures and beautiful physiological blackboard drawings. He was kind but also critical, expecting a high standard of work. He was the first president of the Cambridge Fabian Society, and later became a member of the Society of Friends. Elected to the Physiology Society in 1909, he was its longest serving member in 1976.

In 1921 Mottram married Elsie Charlotte Bulley (died 1970), daughter of Harry Samson King, entrepreneur, of St. Albans; she shared his interest in social nutrition. They had three sons. Mottram died 11 March 1976 at 'Waterhouse', Limpley Stoke.

[Private information; personal knowledge.]

PATTY FISHER

MOUNTBATTEN, LOUIS FRANCIS ALBERT VICTOR NICHOLAS, first EARL MOUNTBATTEN OF BURMA (1900–1979), admiral of the fleet, was born at Frogmore House, Windsor, 25 June 1900 as Prince Louis of Battenberg, the younger son and youngest of the four children of Prince Louis Alexander of Battenberg (later Louis Mountbatten, Marquess of Milford Haven, admiral of the fleet, q.v.), and his wife, Princess Victoria Alberta Elizabeth Marie Irene, daughter of Louis IV of Hesse-Darmstadt. Prince Louis Alexander, himself head of a cadet branch of the house of Hesse-Darmstadt, was brother-in-law to Queen Victoria's daughter, Princess Beatrice; his wife was Victoria's granddaughter. By both father and mother, therefore, Prince Louis was closely connected with the British royal family. One of his sisters married King Gustav VI of Sweden and the other Prince Andrew of Greece.

Prince Louis, 'Dickie' as he was known from childhood, was educated as befitted the son of a senior naval officer—a conventional upbringing varied by holidays with his German relations or with his aunt, the tsarina, in Russia. At Locker's Park School in Hertfordshire he was praised for his industry, enthusiasm, sense of humour, and modesty—the first two at least being characteristics conspicuous throughout his life. From there in May 1913 he entered the naval training college of Osborne as fifteenth out of eighty-three, a respectable if unglamorous position which he more or less maintained during his eighteen months there. Towards the end of his stay his father, now first sea lord, was hounded from office because of his German ancestry. This affected young Prince Louis deeply, though a contemporary recalls him remarking nonchalantly: 'It doesn't really matter very much. Of course I shall take his place.' Certainly his passionate ambition owed something to his desire to avenge his father's disgrace.

In November 1914 Prince Louis moved on to Dartmouth. Though he never shone athletically, nor impressed himself markedly on his contemporaries, his last years of education showed increasing confidence and ability, and at Keyham, the Royal Naval College at Devonport where he did his final course, he came first out of seventy-two. In July 1916 he was assigned as a midshipman to the *Lion*, the flagship of Admiral Sir David (later Earl) Beatty [q.v.]. His flag captain, (Sir) Roger Backhouse [q.v.], described him as 'a very promising young officer' but his immediate superior felt he lacked the brilliance of his elder brother George—a judgement which Prince Louis himself frequently echoed. The *Lion* saw action in the eight months Prince Louis was aboard but suffered no damage, and by the time he transferred to the *Queen Elizabeth* in February 1917 the prospects of a major naval battle seemed remote. Prince Louis served briefly aboard the submarine K6—'the happiest month I've ever spent in the service'—and visited the western front, but his time on the *Queen Elizabeth* was uneventful and he was delighted to be posted in July 1918 as first lieutenant on one of the P-boats, small torpedo boats designed primarily for anti-submarine warfare. It was while he was on the *Queen Elizabeth* that his father, in common with other members of the royal family, abandoned his German title and was created Marquess of Milford Haven, with the family name of Mountbatten. His younger son was known henceforth as Lord Louis Mountbatten.

At the end of 1919 Mountbatten was one of a group of naval officers sent to widen their intellectual horizons at Cambridge. During his year at Christ's College (of which he became an honorary fellow in 1946) he acquired a taste for public affairs, regularly attending the Union and achieving the distinction, remarkable for someone in his position, of being elected to the committee. Through his close friend Peter Murphy, he also opened his mind to radical opinions—'We all thought him rather left-wing', said the then president of the Union, (Sir) Geoffrey Shakespeare.

While still at Cambridge, Mountbatten was invited by his cousin, the Prince of Wales, to attend him on the forthcoming tour of Australasia in the *Renown*. Mountbatten's roles were those of unofficial diarist, dogsbody, and, above all, companion to his sometimes moody and disobliging cousin. These he performed admirably—'you will never know', wrote the Prince to Lord Milford Haven, 'what very great friends we have become, what he has meant and been to me on this trip.' His reward was to be invited to join the next royal tour to India and Japan in the winter of 1921–2; a journey that doubly marked his life in that in India he learnt to play polo and became engaged to Edwina Cynthia Annette [q.v.] (died 1960), daughter of Wilfrid William Ashley (later Baron Mount Temple, q.v.).

Edwina Ashley was descended from the third Viscount Palmerston and the Earls of Shaftesbury, while her maternal grandfather was the immensely rich Sir Ernest Cassel [q.v.], friend and financial adviser to King Edward VII. At Cassel's death in 1921 his granddaughter inherited some £2.3 million, and eventually also a palace on Park Lane, Classiebawn Castle in Ireland, and the Broadlands estate at Romsey in Hampshire. The marriage of two powerful and fiercely competitive characters was never wholly harmonious and sometimes caused unhappiness to both partners. On the whole, however, it worked well and they established a formidable partnership at several stages of their lives. They had two daughters.

Early in 1923 Mountbatten joined the *Revenge*. For the next fifteen years his popular image was that of a playboy. Fast cars, speedboats, polo, were his delights; above all the last, about which he wrote the classic *Introduction to Polo* (1931) by 'Marco'. Yet nobody who knew his work could doubt his essential seriousness. 'This officer's heart and soul is in the Navy', reported the captain of the *Revenge*, 'No outside interests are ever allowed to interfere with his duties.' His professionalism was proved beyond doubt when he selected signals as his speciality and passed out top of the course in July 1925. As assistant fleet wireless officer (1927–8) and fleet wireless officer (1931–3) in the Mediterranean, and at the signals school at Portsmouth in between, he won a reputation for energy, efficiency, and inventiveness. He raised the standard of signalling in the Mediterranean Fleet to new heights and was known, respected, and almost always liked by everyone under his command.

In 1932 Mountbatten was promoted commander and in April 1934 took over the *Daring*, a new destroyer of 1,375 tons. After only a few months, however, he had to exchange her for an older and markedly inferior destroyer, the *Wishart*. Undiscomfited, he set to work to make his ship the most efficient in the Mediterranean Fleet. He succeeded and *Wishart* was Cock of the Fleet in the regatta of 1935. It was at this time that he perfected the 'Mountbatten station-keeping gear', an ingenious device which was adopted by the Admiralty for use in destroyers but which never really proved itself in wartime.

Enthusiastically recommended for promotion, Mountbatten returned to the Naval Air Division of the Admiralty. He was prominent in the campaign to recapture the Fleet Air Arm from the Royal Air Force, lobbying (Sir) Winston Churchill, Sir Samuel Hoare (later Viscount Templewood), and A. Duff Cooper (later Viscount Norwich) [qq.v.] with a freedom unusual among junior officers. He vigorously applauded the latter's resignation over the Munich agreement and maintained a working relationship with Anthony Eden (later the Earl of Avon) and the fourth Marquess of Salisbury [qq.v.] in their opposition to appeasement. More practically he was instrumental in drawing the Admiralty's attention to the merits of the Oerlikon gun, the adoption of which he urged vigorously for more than two years. It was during this period that he also succeeded in launching the Royal Naval Film Corporation, an organization designed to secure the latest films for British sailors at sea.

The abdication crisis caused him much distress but left him personally unscathed. Some time earlier he had hopefully prepared for the Prince of Wales a list of eligible Protestant princesses, but by the time of the accession he had little influence left. He had been King Edward VIII's personal naval aide-de-camp and in February 1937 King George VI appointed him to the same position, simultaneously appointing him to the GCVO.

Since the autumn of 1938 Mountbatten had been contributing ideas to the construction at Newcastle of a new destroyer, the *Kelly*. In June 1939 he took over as captain and *Kelly* was commissioned by the outbreak of war. On 20 September she was joined by her sister ship *Kingston*, and Mountbatten became captain (D) of the fifth destroyer flotilla.

Mountbatten was not markedly successful as a wartime destroyer captain. In surprisingly few months at sea he almost capsized in a high sea, collided with another destroyer, and was mined once, torpedoed twice, and finally sunk by enemy aircraft. In most of these incidents he could plead circumstances beyond his control, but the consensus of professional opinion is that he lacked 'sea-sense', the quality that ensures a ship is doing the right thing in the right place at the right time. Nevertheless he acted with immense panache and courage, and displayed such qualities of leadership that when *Kelly* was recommissioned after several months refitting, an embarrassingly large number of her former crew clamoured to rejoin. When he took his flotilla into Namsos in March 1940 to evacuate (Sir) Adrian Carton de Wiart [q.v.] and several thousand Allied troops, he conducted the operation with cool determination. The return of *Kelly* to port in May, after ninety-one hours in tow under almost constant bombardment and with a fifty-foot hole in the port side, was an epic of fortitude and seamanship. It was feats like this that caught Churchill's imagination and thus altered the course of Mountbatten's career.

In the spring of 1941 the *Kelly* was dispatched to the Mediterranean. Placed in an impossible position, Admiral Sir A. B. Cunningham (later Viscount Cunningham of Hyndhope, q.v.) in May decided to support the army in Crete even though there was no possibility of air cover. The *Kashmir* and the *Kelly* were attacked by dive-bombers on 23 May and soon sunk. More than half the crew of *Kelly* was lost and Mountbatten only escaped by swimming from under the ship as it turned turtle. The survivors were machine-gunned in the water but were picked up by the

Kipling. The *Kelly* lived on in *In Which We Serve*, a skilful propaganda film by (Sir) Noël Coward [q.v.], which was based in detail on the achievements of Lord Louis Mountbatten and his ship. Mountbatten was now appointed to command the aircraft-carrier *Illustrious*, which had been severely damaged and sent for repair to the United States. In October he flew to America to take over his ship and pay a round of visits. He established many useful contacts and made a considerable impression on the American leadership: '. . . he has been a great help to all of us, and I mean literally ALL', wrote Admiral Starke to Sir A. Dudley Pound [q.v.]. Before the *Illustrious* was ready, however, Mountbatten was called home by Churchill to take charge of Combined Operations. His predecessor, Sir Roger (later Lord) Keyes [q.v.], had fallen foul of the chiefs of staff and Mountbatten was initially appointed only as 'chief adviser'. In April 1942, however, he became chief of Combined Operations with the acting rank of vice-admiral, lieutenant-general, and air marshal and with *de facto* membership of the chiefs of staff committee. This phenomenally rapid promotion earned him some unpopularity, but on the whole the chiefs of staff gave him full support.

'You are to give no thought for the defensive. Your whole attention is to be concentrated on the offensive', Churchill told him. Mountbatten's duties fell into two main parts: to organize raids against the European coast designed to raise morale, harass the Germans, and achieve limited military objectives; and to prepare for an eventual invasion. The first responsibility, more dramatic though less important, gave rise to a multitude of raids involving only a handful of men and a few more complex operations such as the costly but successful attack on the dry dock at St. Nazaire. Combined Operations were responsible for planning such forays, but their execution was handed over to the designated force commander, a system which led sometimes to confusion.

The ill results of divided responsibilities were particularly apparent in the Dieppe operation of August 1942. Dieppe taught the Allies valuable lessons for the eventual invasion and misled the Germans about their intentions, but the price paid in lives and material was exceedingly, probably disproportionately, high. For this Mountbatten, ultimately responsible for planning the operation, must accept some responsibility. Nevertheless the errors which both British and German analysts subsequently condemned—the adoption of frontal rather than flank assault, the selection of relatively inexperienced Canadian troops for the assault, the abandonment of any previous air bombardment, and the failure to provide the support of capital ships—were all taken against his advice or over his head. Certainly he was not guilty of the blunders which Lord Beaverbrook [q.v.] and some later commentators attributed to him.

When it came to preparation for invasion, Mountbatten's energy, enthusiasm, and receptivity to new ideas showed to great advantage. His principal contribution was to see clearly what is now obvious but was then not generally recognized, that successful landings on a fortified enemy coast called for an immense range of specialized equipment and skills. To secure an armada of landing craft of different shapes and sizes, and to train the crews to operate them, involved a diversion of resources, both British and American, which was vigorously opposed in many quarters. The genesis of such devices as Mulberry (the floating port) and Pluto (pipe line under the ocean) is often hard to establish, but the zeal with which Mountbatten and his staff supported their development was a major factor in their success. Mountbatten surrounded himself with a team of talented if sometimes maverick advisers—Professor J. D. Bernal [q.v.], Geoffrey Pyke, Solly (later Lord) Zuckerman—and was ready to listen to anything they suggested. Sometimes this led him into wasteful extravagances—as in his championship of the iceberg/aircraft carrier Habbakuk—but there were more good ideas than bad. His contribution to D-Day was recognized in the tribute paid him by the Allied leaders shortly after the invasion: '. . . we realize that much of . . . the success of this venture has its origins in developments effected by you and your staff.'

His contribution to the higher strategy is less easy to establish. He himself always claimed responsibility for the selection of Normandy as the invasion site rather than the Pas de Calais. Certainly when Operation Sledgehammer, the plan for a limited re-entry into the Continent in 1942, was debated by the chiefs of staff, Mountbatten was alone in arguing for the Cherbourg peninsula. His consistent support of Normandy may have contributed to the change of heart when the venue of the invasion proper was decided. In general, however, Sir Alan Brooke (later Viscount Alanbrooke, q.v.) and the other chiefs of staff resented Mountbatten's ventures outside the field of his immediate interests and he usually confined himself to matters directly concerned with Combined Operations.

His headquarters, COHQ, indeed the whole of his command, was sometimes criticized for its lavishness in personnel and encouragement of extravagant ideas. Mountbatten was never economical, and waste there undoubtedly was. Nevertheless he built up at great speed an organization of remarkable complexity and effectiveness. By April 1943 Combined Operations Command included 2,600 landing-craft and over 50,000 men. He almost killed himself in the process for in July 1942 he was told by his doctors that he would die unless he worked less intensely. A man with less imagination who played safe could never have done as much. It was Alan Brooke, initially unenthusiastic about his elevation, who concluded: 'His appointment as Chief of Combined Operations . . . was excellent, and he played a remarkable part as the driving force and main-spring of this organization. Without his energy and drive it would never have reached the high standard it achieved.'

Mountbatten arrived at the Quebec conference in August 1943 as chief of Combined Operations; he left as acting admiral and supreme commander designate, South East Asia. 'He is young, enthusiastic and triphibious', Churchill telegraphed C. R. (later Earl) Attlee, but though the Americans welcomed the appointment enthusiastically, he was only selected after half a dozen candidates had been eliminated for various reasons.

He took over a command where everything had gone wrong. The British and Indian army, ravaged by disease and soundly beaten by the Japanese, had been chased out of Burma. A feeble attempt at counter-attack in the Arakan peninsula had ended in disaster. Morale was low, air support inadequate, communications within India slow and uncertain. There seemed little to oppose the Japanese if they decided to resume their assault. Yet before Mountbatten could concentrate on his official adversaries he had to resolve the anomalies within his own Command.

Most conspicuous of these was General Stilwell. As well as being deputy supreme commander, Stilwell was chief of staff to Chiang Kai-shek and his twin roles inevitably involved conflicts of interest and loyalty. A superb leader of troops in the field but cantankerous, anglophobe, and narrow-minded, Stilwell would have been a difficult colleague in any circumstances. In South East Asia, where his preoccupation was to reopen the road through north Burma to China, he proved almost impossible to work with. But Mountbatten also found his relationship difficult with his own, British, commanders-in-chief, in particular the naval commander, Sir James Somerville [q.v.]. Partly this arose from differences of temperament; more important it demonstrated a fundamental difference of opinion about the supreme commander's role. Mountbatten, encouraged by Churchill and members of his own entourage, believed that he should operate on the MacArthur model, with his own planning staff, consulting his commanders-in-chief but ultimately instructing them on future operations. Somerville, General Sir G. J. Giffard [q.v.], and Air Marshal Sir R. E. C. Peirse, on the other hand, envisaged him as a chairman of committee, operating like Eisenhower and working through the planning staffs of the commanders-in-chief. The chiefs of staff in London proved reluctant to rule categorically on the issue but Mountbatten eventually abandoned his central planning staff and the situation was further eased when Somerville was replaced by Admiral Sir Bruce Fraser (later Lord Fraser of North Cape).

Mountbatten defined the three principal problems facing him as being those of monsoon, malaria, and morale. His determination that Allied troops must fight through the monsoon, though of greater psychological than military significance, undoubtedly assisted the eventual victories of the Fourteenth Army. In 1943, for every casualty evacuated because of wounds, there were 120 sick, and Mountbatten, by his emphasis on hygiene and improved medical techniques, can claim much credit for the vast improvement over the next year. But it was in the transformation of the soldiers' morale that he made his greatest contribution. By publicity, propaganda, and the impact of his personality, he restored their pride in themselves and gave them confidence that they could defeat the Japanese.

Deciding what campaign they were to fight proved difficult. Mountbatten, with Churchill's enthusiastic backing, envisaged a bold amphibious strategy which would bypass the Burmese jungles and strike through the Andaman Islands to Rangoon or, more ambitious still, through northern Sumatra towards Singapore. The Americans, however, who would have provided the material resources for such adventures, nicknamed South East Asia Command (SEAC) 'Save England's Asiatic Colonies' and were suspicious of any operation which seemed designed to this end. They felt that the solitary justification for the Burma campaign was to restore land communications with China. The ambitious projects with which Mountbatten had left London withered as his few landing-craft were withdrawn. A mission he dispatched to London and Washington returned empty-handed. 'You might send out the waxwork which I hear Madame Tussauds has made', wrote Mountbatten bitterly to his friend (Sir) Charles Lambe [q.v.], 'it could have my Admiral's uniform and sit at my desk . . . as well as I could.'

It was the Japanese who saved him from so ignoble a role. In spring 1944 they attacked in Arakan and across the Imphal plain into India. The Allied capacity to supply troops by air and their new-found determination to stand firm, even when cut off, turned potential disaster into almost total victory. Mountbatten himself played a major role, being personally responsible at a crucial moment for the switch of two divisions by air from Arakan to Imphal and the diversion of the necessary American aircraft from the supply routes to China. Imphal confirmed Mountbatten's faith in the commander of the Fourteenth

Army, General W. J. (later Viscount) Slim [q.v.] and led to his final loss of confidence in the commander-in-chief, General Giffard, whom he now dismissed. The battle cost the Japanese 7,000 dead; much hard fighting lay ahead but the Fourteenth Army was on the march that would end at Rangoon.

Mountbatten still hoped to avoid the re-conquest of Burma by land. In April 1944 he transferred his headquarters from Delhi to Kandy in Ceylon, reaffirming his faith in a maritime strategy. He himself believed the next move should be a powerful sea and air strike against Rangoon; Churchill still hankered after the more ambitious attack on northern Sumatra; the chiefs of staff felt the British effort should be switched to support the American offensive in the Pacific. In the end shortage of resources dictated the course of events. Mountbatten was able to launch a small seaborne invasion to support the Fourteenth Army's advance, but it was Slim's men who bore the brunt of the fighting and reached Rangoon just before the monsoon broke in April 1945.

Giffard had been replaced as supreme commander by Sir Oliver Leese [q.v.]. Mountbatten's original enthusiasm for Leese did not endure; the latter soon fell out with his supreme commander and proved unpopular with the other commanders-in-chief. A climax came in May 1945 when Leese informed Slim that he was to be relieved from command of the Fourteenth Army because he was tired out and anyway had no experience in maritime operations. Mountbatten's role in this curious transaction remains slightly obscure; Leese definitely went too far, but there may have been some ambiguity about his instructions. In the event Leese's action was disavowed in London and he himself was dismissed and Slim appointed in his place.

The next phase of the campaign—an invasion by sea of the Malay peninsula—should have been the apotheosis of Mountbatten's command. When he went to the Potsdam conference in July 1945, however, he was told of the existence of the atom bomb. He realized at once that this was likely to rob him of his victory and, sure enough, the Japanese surrender reduced Operation Zipper to an unopposed landing. This was perhaps just as well; faulty intelligence meant that one of the two landings was made on unsuitable beaches and was quickly bogged down. The invasion would have succeeded but the cost might have been high.

On 12 September 1945, Mountbatten received the formal surrender of the Japanese at Singapore. Not long afterwards he was created a viscount. The honour was deserved. His role had been crucial. 'We did it together', Slim said to him on his deathbed, and the two men, in many ways so different, had indeed complemented each other admirably and proved the joint architects of victory in South East Asia.

Mountbatten's work in SEAC did not end with the Japanese surrender; indeed in some ways it grew still more onerous. His Command was now extended to include South Vietnam and the Netherlands East Indies: 1½ million square miles containing 128 million inhabitants, ¾ million armed and potentially truculent Japanese, and 123,000 Allied prisoners, many in urgent need of medical attention. Mountbatten had to rescue the prisoners, disarm the Japanese, and restore the various territories to stability so that civil government could resume. This last function proved most difficult, since the Japanese had swept away the old colonial regimes and new nationalist movements had grown up to fill the vacuum. Mountbatten's instincts told him that such movements were inevitable and even desirable. Every effort, he felt, should be made to take account of their justified aspirations. His disposition to sympathize with the radical nationalists sometimes led him into naïvely optimistic assessment of their readiness to compromise with the former colonialist regimes—as proved to be the case with the communist Chinese in Malaya—but the course of subsequent history suggests that he often saw the situation more clearly than the so-called 'realists' who criticized him.

Even before the end of the war he had had a foretaste of the problems that lay ahead. Aung San, head of the pro-Japanese Burmese National Army, defected with all his troops. Mountbatten was anxious to accept his co-operation and cajoled the somewhat reluctant chiefs of staff into agreeing on military grounds. Inevitably, this gave Aung San a stronger position than the traditionalists thought desirable when the time came to form Burma's post-war government. Mountbatten felt that, though left wing and fiercely nationalistic, Aung San was honourable, basically reasonable, and ready to accept the concept of an independent Burma within the British Commonwealth; '... with proper treatment', judged Slim, 'Aung San would have proved a Burmese Smuts'. The governor, Sir Reginald Dorman-Smith, conceded Aung San was the most popular man in Burma but considered him a dangerous Marxist revolutionary. When Aung San was accused of war crimes committed during the Japanese occupation, Dorman-Smith wished to arrest and try him. This Mountbatten forestalled; but the hand-over to civil government in April 1946 and the murder of Aung San the following year meant that the supreme commander's view of his character was never properly tested.

In Malaya the problem was more immediately one of law and order. Confronted by the threat of a politically-motivated general strike, the authorities proposed to arrest all the leaders.

'Naturally I ordered them to cancel these orders', wrote Mountbatten, 'as I could not imagine anything more disastrous than to make martyrs of these men.' Reluctantly he agreed that in certain circumstances Chinese trouble-makers might be deported, but rescinded that approval when it was proposed to deport certain detainees who had not had time to profit by his warnings. His critics maintained that sterner action in 1945–6 could have prevented, or at least mitigated the future troubles in Malaya, but Mountbatten was convinced that the prosperity of Malaya and Singapore depended on the co-operation of Malay and Chinese, and was determined to countenance nothing that might divide the two communities.

In Vietnam and Indonesia Mountbatten's problem was to balance nationalist aspirations against the demands of Britain's Allies for support in the recovery of their colonies. He was better disposed to the French than the Dutch, and though he complained when General (Sir) Douglas Gracey exceeded his instructions and suppressed the Viet Minh—'General Gracey has saved French Indo-China', Leclerc told him—the reproof was more formal than real. In Indonesia Mountbatten believed that Dutch intransigence was the principal factor preventing a peaceful settlement. Misled by Dutch intelligence, he had no suspicion of the force of nationalist sentiment until Lady Mounbatten returned from her brave foray to rescue Allied prisoners of war. His forces could not avoid conflict with the Indonesian nationalists but Mountbatten sought to limit their commitment, with the result that both Dutch and Indonesians believed the British were favouring the other side. He did, however, contrive to keep open the possibility of political settlement; only after the departure of the British forces did full-scale civil war become inevitable.

Mountbatten left South East Asia in mid-1946 with the reputation of a liberal committed to decolonization. Though he had no thought beyond his return to the navy, with the now substantive rank of rear-admiral, his reputation influenced the Labour government when they were looking for a successor to Viscount (later Earl) Wavell [q.v.] who could resuscitate the faltering negotiations for Indian independence. On 18 December 1946 he was invited to become India's last viceroy. That year he had been created first Viscount Mountbatten of Burma.

Mountbatten longed to go to sea again, but this was a challenge no man of ambition and public spirit could reject. His reluctance enabled him to extract favourable terms from the government, and though the plenipotentiary powers to which he was often to refer are not specifically set out in any document, he enjoyed far greater freedom of action than his immediate predecessors. His original insistence that he would go only on the invitation of the Indian leaders was soon abandoned but it was on his initiative that a terminal date of June 1948 was fixed, by which time the British would definitely have left India.

Mountbatten's directive was that he should strive to implement the recommendations of the Cabinet mission of 1946, led by Sir R. Stafford Cripps [q.v.] which maintained the principle of a united India. By the time he arrived, however, this objective had been tacitly abandoned by every major politician of the sub-continent with the important exception of M. K. Gandhi [q.v.]. The viceroy dutifully tried to persuade all concerned of the benefits of unity but his efforts foundered on the intransigence of the Muslim leader Mahomed Ali Jinnah [q.v.]. His problem thereafter was to find some formula which would reconcile the desire of the Hindus for a central India from which a few peripheral and wholly Muslim areas would secede, with Jinnah's aspiration to secure a greater Pakistan including all the Punjab and as much as possible of Bengal. In this task he was supported by Wavell's staff from the Indian Civil Service, reinforced by General H. L. (later Lord) Ismay [q.v.] and Sir Eric Miéville. He himself contributed immense energy, charm and persuasiveness, negotiating skills, agility of mind, and endless optimism.

He quickly concluded that not only was time not on his side but that the urgency was desperate. The run-down of the British military and civil presence, coupled with swelling intercommunal hatred, were intensely dangerous. 'The situation is everywhere electric, and I get the feeling that the mine may go up at any moment', wrote Ismay to his wife on 25 March 1947, the day after Mountbatten was sworn in as viceroy. This conviction that every moment counted dictated Mountbatten's activities over the next five months. He threw himself into a hectic series of interviews with the various political leaders. With Jawaharlal Nehru [q.v.] he established an immediate and lasting rapport which was to assume great importance in the future. With V. J. Patel [q.v.], in whom he identified a major power in Indian politics, his initial relationship was less easy, but they soon enjoyed mutual confidence. Gandhi fascinated and delighted him, but he shrewdly concluded that he was likely to be pushed to one side in the forthcoming negotiations. With Jinnah alone did he fail; the full blast of his charm did not thaw or even moderate the chill intractability of the Muslim leader.

Nevertheless negotiations advanced so rapidly that by 2 May Ismay was taking to London a plan which Mountbatten believed all the principal parties would accept. Only when the British Cabinet had already approved the plan did he realize that he had gravely underestimated

Nehru's objections to any proposal that left room for the 'Balkanization' of India. With extraordinary speed a new draft was produced, which provided for India's membership of the Commonwealth, and put less emphasis on the right of the individual components of British India to reject India or Pakistan and opt for independence. After what Mountbatten described as 'the worst 24 hours of my life', the plan was accepted by all parties on 3 June. He was convinced that any relaxation of the feverish pace would risk destroying the fragile basis of understanding. Independence, he announced, was to be granted in only ten weeks, on 15 August 1947.

Before this date the institutions of British India had to be carved in two. Mountbatten initially hoped to retain a unified army but quickly realized this would be impossible and concentrated instead on ensuring rough justice in the division of the assets. To have given satisfaction to everyone would have been impossible, but at the time few people accused him of partiality. He tackled the problems, wrote Michael Edwardes in a book not generally sympathetic to the last viceroy, 'with a speed and brilliance which it is difficult to believe would have been exercised by any other man'.

The princely states posed a particularly complex problem, since with the end of British rule paramountcy lapsed and there was in theory nothing to stop the princes opting for self-rule. This would have made a geographical nonsense of India and, to a lesser extent, Pakistan; as well as creating a plethora of independent states, many incapable of sustaining such a role. Mountbatten at first attached little importance to the question, but once he was fully aware of it, used every trick to get the rulers to accept accession. Some indeed felt that he was using improper influence on loyal subjects of the Crown, but it is hard to see that any other course would in the long run have contributed to their prosperity. Indeed the two states which Mountbatten failed to shepherd into the fold of India or Pakistan—Hyderabad and Kashmir—were those which were subsequently to cause most trouble.

Most provinces, like the princely states, clearly belonged either to India or to Pakistan. In the Punjab and Bengal, however, partition was necessary. This posed horrifying problems, since millions of Hindus and Muslims would find themselves on the wrong side of whatever frontier was established. The Punjab was likely to prove most troublesome, because 14 per cent of its population consisted of Sikhs, who were warlike, fanatically anti-Muslim, and determined that their homelands should remain inviolate. Partition was not Mountbatten's direct responsibility, since Sir Cyril (later Viscount) Radcliffe [q.v.] was appointed to divide the two provinces. Popular opinion, however, found it hard to accept that he was not involved, and even today it is sometimes suggested he may have helped shape Radcliffe's final conclusions.

Mountbatten had hoped that independence day would see him installed as governor-general of both new dominions; able to act, in Churchill's phrase, as 'moderator' during their inevitable differences. Nehru was ready for such a transmogrification but Jinnah, after some months of apparent indecision, concluded that he himself must be Pakistan's first head of state. Mountbatten was uncertain whether the last viceroy of a united India should now reappear as governor-general of a part of it, but the Indian government pressed him to accept and in London both Attlee and George VI felt the appointment was desirable. With some misgivings, Mountbatten gave way. Independence day in both Pakistan and India was a triumph; tumultuous millions applauding his progress and demonstrating that, for the moment at least, he enjoyed a place in the pantheon with their national leaders. 'No other living man could have got the thing through', wrote Lord Killearn [q.v.] to Ismay; '. . . it has been a job supremely well done.'

The euphoria quickly faded. Though Bengal remained calm, thanks largely to Gandhi's personal intervention, the Punjab exploded. Vast movements of population across the new frontier exacerbated the already inflamed communal hatred, and massacres on an appalling scale developed. The largely British-officered Boundary Force was taxed far beyond its powers and Delhi itself was engulfed in the violence. Mountbatten was called back from holiday to help master the mergency, and brought desperately needed energy and organizational skills to the despondent government. 'I've never been through such a time in my life', he wrote on 28 September, 'The War, the Viceroyalty were jokes, for we have been dealing with life and death in our own city.' Gradually order was restored and by November 1947 Mountbatten felt the situation was stable enough to permit him to attend the wedding of Princess Elizabeth and his nephew Philip Mountbatten in London. He was created first Earl Mountbatten of Burma, with special remainder to his daughter Patricia.

Estimates vary widely, but the best-documented assessments agree that between 200,000 and 250,000 people lost their lives in the communal riots. Those who criticize Mountbatten's viceroyalty do so most often on the grounds that these massacres could have been averted, or at least mitigated, if partition had not been hurried through. Mountbatten's champions maintain that delay would only have made things worse and allowed the disorders to spread further. It is impossible to state conclusively what *might* have happened if independence had been postponed by a few months, or even years, but it is noteworthy that the closer people were to the problem, the more they support Mountbatten's policy. Almost every senior member of the British administration in India and of the Indian government has recorded his conviction that security was deteriorating so fast and the maintenance of non-communal forces of law and order proving so difficult, that a far greater catastrophe would have ensued if there had been further delay.

Mountbatten as governor-general was a servant of the Indian government and, as Ismay put it, 'it is only natural that they . . . should regard themselves as having proprietary rights over you'. Mountbatten accepted this role and fought doughtily for India's interests. He did not wholly abandon impartiality, however. When in January 1948 the Indian government withheld from Pakistan the 55 million crores of rupees owing after the division of assets, the governor-general argued that such conduct was dishonourable as well as unwise. He recruited Gandhi as his ally, and together they forced a change of policy on the reluctant Indian ministers. It was one of Gandhi's final contributions to Indian history. On 30 January he was assassinated by a Hindu extremist. Mountbatten mourned him sincerely. 'What a remarkable old boy he was', he wrote to a friend, 'I think history will link him with Buddha and Mahomet.'

His stand over the division of assets did the governor-general little good in Pakistan where he was believed to be an inveterate enemy and, by persuading Radcliffe to award Gurdaspur to India, to have secured that country access to Kashmir. When, in October 1947, Pathan tribesmen invaded the Vale of Kashmir, Mountbatten approved and helped organize military intervention by India. He insisted, however, that the state must first accede and that, as soon as possible, a plebiscite should establish the wishes of the Kashmiri people. When war between India and Pakistan seemed imminent he was instrumental in persuading Nehru that the matter should be referred to the United Nations.

The other problem that bedevilled Mountbatten was that of Hyderabad. He constituted himself, in effect, chief negotiator for the Indian government and almost brought off a deal that would have secured reasonably generous terms for the Nizam. Muslim extremists in Hyderabad, however, defeated his efforts, and the dispute grumbled on. Mountbatten protested when he found contingency plans existed for the invasion of Hyderabad and his presence was undoubtedly a main factor in inhibiting the Indian take-over that quickly followed his departure.

On 21 June 1948 the Mountbattens left India. In his final address, Nehru referred to the vast crowds that had attended their last appearances and 'wondered how it was that an Englishman and Englishwoman could become so popular in India during this brief period'. Even his harshest critics could not deny that Mountbatten had won the love and trust of the people and got the relationship between India and her former ruler off to a far better start than had seemed possible fifteen months before.

At last Mountbatten was free to return to sea. Reverting to his substantive rank of rear-admiral he took command of the first cruiser squadron in the Mediterranean. To assume this relatively lowly position after the splendours of supreme command and viceroyalty could not have been easy, but with goodwill all round it was achieved successfully. He was 'as great a subordinate as he is a leader', reported the commander-in-chief, Admiral Sir Arthur Power [q.v.]. He brought his squadron up to a high level of efficiency, though not concealing the fact that he felt obsolescent material and undermanning diminished its real effectiveness. After his previous jobs, this command was something of a holiday, and he revelled in the opportunities to play his beloved polo and take up skin-diving. In Malta he stuck to his inconspicuous role, but abroad he was fêted by the rulers of the countries his squadron visited. 'I suppose I oughtn't to get a kick out of being treated like a Viceroy', he confessed after one particularly successful visit, 'but I'd have been less than human if I hadn't been affected by the treatment I received at Trieste.' He was never less, nor more than human.

Mountbatten was promoted vice-admiral in 1949 and in June 1950 returned to the Admiralty as fourth sea lord. He was at first disappointed, since he had set his heart on being second sea lord, responsible for personnel, and found himself instead concerned with supplies and transport. In fact the post proved excellent for his career. He flung himself into the work with characteristic zeal, cleared up many anomalies and outdated practices, and acquired a range of information which was to stand him in good stead when he became first sea lord. On the whole he confined himself to the duties of his department, but when the Persians nationalized Anglo-Iranian Oil in 1951, he could not resist making his opinions known. He felt that it was futile to oppose strong nationalist movements of this kind and that Britain would do better to work with them. He converted the first lord to his point of view but conspicuously failed to impress the bellicose foreign secretary, Herbert Morrison (later Lord Morrison of Lambeth, q.v.).

The next step was command of a major fleet and in June 1952 he was appointed to the Mediterranean, being promoted to admiral the following year. St. Vincent remarked that naval command in the Mediterranean 'required an officer of splendour', and this Mountbatten certainly provided. He was not a great operational commander like Andrew Cunningham, but he knew his ships and personnel, maintained the fleet at the highest level of peacetime efficiency, and was immensely popular with the men. When 'Cassandra' of the *Daily Mirror* arrived to report on Mountbatten's position, he kept aloof for four days, then came to the flagship with the news that the commander-in-chief was 'O.K. with the sailors'. But it was on the representational side that Mountbatten excelled. He loved showing the flag and, given half a chance, would act as honorary ambassador into the bargain. Sometimes he overdid it, and in September 1952 the first lord, at the instance of the prime minister, wrote to urge him 'to take the greatest care to keep out of political discussions'.

His diplomatic as well as administrative skills were taxed when in January 1953 he was appointed supreme Allied commander of a new NATO Mediterranean Command (SACMED). Under him were the Mediterranean fleets of Britain, France, Italy, Greece, and Turkey, but not the most powerful single unit in the area, the American Sixth Fleet. He was required to set up an integrated international naval/air headquarters in Malta and managed this formidable organizational task with great efficiency. The smoothing over of national susceptibilities and the reconciliation of his British with his NATO role proved taxing, but his worst difficulty lay with the other NATO headquarters in the Mediterranean, CINCSOUTH, at Naples under the American Admiral R. B. Carney. There were real problems of demarcation, but as had happened with Somerville in South East Asia, these were made far worse by a clash of personalities. When Carney was replaced in the autumn of 1953, the differences melted away and the two commands began to co-operate.

In October 1954, when he became first sea lord, Mountbatten achieved what he had always held to be his ultimate ambition. It did not come easily. A formidable body of senior naval opinion distrusted him and was at first opposed to his appointment, and it was not until the conviction hardened that the navy was losing the Whitehall battle against the other services that opinion rallied behind him. 'The Navy wants badly a man and a leader', wrote Andrew Cunningham, who had formerly been Mountbatten's opponent. 'You have the ability and the drive and it is you that the Navy wants.' Churchill, still unreconciled to Mountbatten's role in India, held out longer, but in the end he too gave way.

Since the war the navy had become the Cinderella of the fighting Services, and morale was low. Under Mountbatten's leadership, the Admiralty's voice in Whitehall became louder and more articulate. By setting up the 'Way Ahead' committee, he initiated an overdue rethinking of the shore establishments which were absorbing an undue proportion of the navy's resources. He scrapped plans for the construction of a heavy missile-carrying cruiser and instead concentrated on destroyers carrying the Sea Slug missile: 'Once we can obtain Government agreement to the fact that we are the mobile large scale rocket carriers of the future then everything else will fall into place.' The Reserve Fleet was cut severely and expenditure diverted from the already excellent communications system to relatively underdeveloped fields such as radar. Probably his most important single contribution, however, was to establish an excellent relationship with the notoriously prickly Admiral Rickover, which was to lead to Britain acquiring US technology for its nuclear submarines and, eventually, to the adoption of the Polaris missile as the core of its nuclear deterrent.

In July 1956 Nasser nationalized the Suez canal. Mountbatten was asked what military steps could be taken to restore the situation. He said that the Mediterranean Fleet with the Royal Marine commandos aboard could be at Port Said within three days and take the port and its hinterland. Eden rejected the proposal since he wished to reoccupy the whole canal zone, and it is unlikely anyway that the other chiefs of staff would have approved a plan that might have left lightly armed British forces exposed to tank attack and with inadequate air cover. As plans for full-scale invasion were prepared, Mountbatten became more and more uneasy about the contemplated action. To the chiefs of staff he consistently said that political implications should be considered and more thought given to the long-term future of the Middle East. His views were reflected in the chiefs' recommendations to the government, a point that caused considerable irritation to Anthony Eden, who insisted that politics should be left to the politicians. In August Mountbatten drafted a letter of resignation to the prime minister but, without too much difficulty, was dissuaded from sending it by the first lord, Viscount Cilcennin [q.v.]. He was, however, instrumental in substituting the invasion plan of General Sir Charles Keightley [q.v.] for that previously approved by the Cabinet, a move that saved the lives of many hundreds of civilians. On 2 November, when the invasion fleet had already sailed, Mountbatten made a written appeal to Eden to accept the United Nations resolution and 'turn back the assault convoy before it is too late'. His appeal was ignored. Mountbatten again offered his resignation to the first lord and again was told that it was his duty to stay on. He was promoted admiral of the fleet in October 1956.

With Harold Macmillan (later the Earl of Stockton) succeeding Eden as prime minister in January 1957, Duncan Sandys (later Lord Duncan-Sandys) was appointed minister of defence with a mandate to rationalize the armed services and impose sweeping economies. There were many embittered battles before Sandys's first defence white paper appeared in the summer of 1957. The thirteenth and final draft contained the ominous words: 'the role of the Navy in Global War is somewhat uncertain'. In the event, however, the navy suffered relatively lightly, losing only one-sixth of its personnel over the next five years, as opposed to the army's 45 per cent and the air force's 35 per cent. The role of the navy east of Suez was enshrined as an accepted dogma of defence policy.

In July 1959 Mountbatten took over as chief of defence staff (CDS). He was the second incumbent, Sir William Dickson having been appointed in 1958, with Mountbatten's support but against the fierce opposition of Field-Marshal Sir Gerald Templer [q.v.]. Dickson's role was little more than that of permanent chairman of the chiefs of staff committee but Sandys tried to increase the CDS's powers. He was defeated, and the defence white paper of 1958 made only modest changes to the existing system. Mountbatten made the principal objective of his time as CDS the integration of the three Services, not to the extent achieved by the Canadians of one homogenized fighting force, but abolishing the independent ministries and setting up a common list for all senior officers. During his first two years, however, he had to remain content with the creation of a director of defence plans to unify the work of the three planning departments and the acceptance of the principle of unified command in the Far and Middle East. Then, at the end of 1962, Macmillan agreed that another attempt should be made to impose unification on the reluctant Services. 'Pray take no notice of any obstructions', he told the minister of defence, 'You should approach this . . . with dashing, slashing methods. Anyone who raises any objection can go.'

At Mountbatten's suggestion Lord Ismay and Sir E. Ian Jacob were asked to report. While not accepting all Mountbatten's recommendations—which involved a sweeping increase in the powers of the CDS—their report went a long way towards realizing the concept of a unified Ministry of Defence. The reforms, which were finally promulgated in 1964, acknowledged the supreme authority of the secretary of state for defence and strengthened the central role of the CDS. To Mountbatten this was an important first step, but only a step. He believed that so long as separate departments survived, with differing interests and loyalties, it would be impossible to use limited resources to the best advantage. Admiralty, War Office, Air Ministry—not to mention Ministry of Aviation—should be abolished. Ministers should be responsible, not for the navy or the air force, but for communications or supplies. 'We cannot, in my opinion, afford to stand pat', he wrote to Harold Wilson (later Lord Wilson of Rievaulx) when the latter became prime minister in October 1964, 'and must move on to, or at least towards the ultimate aim of a functional, closely knit, smoothly working machine.' 'Functionalization' was the objective which he repeatedly pressed on the new minister of defence, Denis Healey. Healey was well disposed in principle, but felt that other reforms enjoyed higher priority. Though Mountbatten appealed to Wilson he got little satisfaction, and the machinery which he left behind him at his retirement was in his eyes only an unsatisfactory half-way house.

Even for this he paid a high price in popularity. His ideas were for the most part repugnant to the chiefs of staff, who suspected him of seeking personal aggrandizement and doubted the propriety of his methods. Relations tended to be worst with the chiefs of air staff. The latter believed that Mountbatten, though ostensibly above inter-Service rivalries, in fact remained devoted to the interests of the navy. It is hard entirely to slough off a lifetime's loyalties, but Mountbatten *tried* to be impartial. He did not always succeed. On the long-drawn-out battle over the merits of aircraft-carriers and island bases, he espoused the former. When he urged the first sea lord to work out some compromise which would accommodate both points of view, Sir Caspar John retorted that only a month before Mountbatten had advised him: 'Don't compromise—fight him to the death!' Similarly in the conflict between the TSR 2, sponsored by the air force, and the navy's Buccaneer, Mountbatten believed strongly that the former, though potentially the better plane, was too expensive to be practicable and would take too long to develop. He lobbied the minister of defence and urged his right-hand man, Solly Zuckerman, to argue the case against the TSR 2—'You know why I can't help you in Public. It is *not* moral cowardice but fear that my usefulness as Chairman would be seriously impaired.'

The question of the British nuclear deterrent also involved inter-Service rivalries. Mountbatten believed that an independent deterrent was essential, arguing to Harold Wilson that it would 'dispel in Russian minds the thought that they will escape scot-free if by any chance the Americans decide to hold back release of a strategic nuclear response to an attack'. He was instrumental in persuading the incoming Labour government not to adopt unilateral nuclear disarmament. In this he had the support of the three chiefs of staff. But there was controversy over what weapon best suited Britain's needs. From long before he became CDS, Mountbatten had privately preferred the submarine-launched Polaris missile to any of the airborne missiles favoured by the air force. Though not himself present at the meeting at Nassau between Macmillan and President John F. Kennedy at which Polaris was offered and accepted in exchange for the cancelled Skybolt missile, he had already urged this solution and had made plans accordingly.

Though he defended the nuclear deterrent, he was wholly opposed to the accumulation of unnecessary stockpiles or the development of new weapons designed to kill more effectively people who would be dead anyway if the existing armouries were employed. At NATO in July 1963 he pleaded that 'it was madness to hold further tests when all men of goodwill were about to try and bring about test-banning'. He conceded that tactical nuclear weapons added to the efficacy of the deterrent, but argued that their numbers should be limited and their use subject to stringent control. To use *any* nuclear weapon, however small or 'clean', would, he insisted, lead to general nuclear war. He opposed the 'mixed manned multilateral force' not just as being military nonsense, but because there were more than enough strategic nuclear weapons already. What were needed, he told the NATO commanders in his valedictory address, were more 'highly mobile, well-equipped, self-supporting and balanced "Fire Brigade" forces, with first-class communications, able to converge quickly on the enemy force'.

Mountbatten's original tenure of office as CDS had been for three years. Macmillan pressed him to lengthen this by a further two years to July 1964. Mountbatten was initially reluctant but changed his mind after the death of his wife in 1960. Subsequently he agreed to a further extension to July 1965, in order to see through the first phase of defence reorganization. Wilson would have happily sanctioned yet another year but Healey established that there would be considerable resentment at such a move on the part of the other Service leaders and felt anyway that he would never be fully master of the Ministry of Defence while this potent relic from the past remained in office. Whether Mountbatten would have stayed on if pressed to do so is in any case doubtful; he was tired and stale, and had a multiplicity of interests to pursue outside.

His last few months as CDS were in fact spent partly abroad leading a mission on Commonwealth immigration. The main purpose of this exercise was to explain British policy and persuade Commonwealth governments to control illegal immigration at source. The mission was a success; indeed Mountbatten found that he was largely preaching to the converted, since only in Jamaica did the policy he was expounding meet with serious opposition. He presented the mission's report on 13 June 1965 and the following month took his formal farewell of the Ministry of Defence.

Retirement did not mean inactivity; indeed he was still officially enjoying his retirement leave when the prime minister invited him to go to Rhodesia as governor to forestall a declaration of independence by the white settler population. Mountbatten had little hesitation in refusing: 'Nothing could be worse for the cause you have at heart than to think that a tired out widower of 65 could recapture the youth, strength and enthusiasm of twenty years ago.' However, he accepted a later suggestion that he should fly briefly to Rhodesia in November 1965 to invest the governor, Sir Humphrey Gibbs, with a decoration on behalf of the Queen and generally to offer moral support. At the last minute the project was deferred and never revived.

The following year the home secretary asked him to undertake an enquiry into prison security, in view of a number of recent sensational escapes. Mountbatten agreed, provided it could be a one-man report prepared with the help of three assessors. The report was complete within two months and most of the recommendations were carried out. The two most important, however—the appointment of an inspector-general responsible to the home secretary to head the prison service and the building of a separate maximum security gaol for prisoners whose escape would be particularly damaging—were never implemented. For the latter proposal Mountbatten was much criticized by liberal reformers who felt the step a retrograde one; this Mountbatten contested, arguing that, isolated within a completely secure outer perimeter, the dangerous criminal could be allowed more freedom than would otherwise be the case.

Mountbatten was associated with 179 organizations, ranging alphabetically from the Admiralty Dramatic Society to the Zoological Society. In some of these his role was formal, in many more it was not. In time and effort the United World Colleges, a network of international schools modelled on the Gordonstoun of Kurt Hahn [q.v.], received the largest share. Mountbatten worked indefatigably to whip up support and raise funds for the schools, lobbying the leaders of every country he visited. The electronics industry, also, engaged his attention and he was an active first chairman of the National Electronic Research Council. In 1965 he was installed as governor of the Isle of Wight and conscientiously visited the island seven or eight times a year, in 1974 becoming the first lord lieutenant when the island was raised to the status of a shire. A role which gave him still greater pleasure was that of colonel of the Life Guards, to which he was also appointed in 1965. He took his duties at Trooping the Colour very seriously and for weeks beforehand would ride around the Hampshire lanes near Broadlands in hacking jacket and Life Guards helmet.

His personal life was equally crowded. The years 1966 and 1967 were much occupied with the filming of the thirteen-part television series *The Life and Times of Lord Mountbatten*, every detail of which absorbed him and whose sale he promoted energetically all over the world. He devoted much time to running the family estates and putting his massive archive in order, involving himself enthusiastically in the opening of Broadlands to the public, which took place in 1978. He never lost his interest in naval affairs or in high strategy. One of his last major speeches was delivered at Strasburg in May 1979, when he pleaded eloquently for arms control: 'As a military man who has given half a century of active service I say in all sincerity that the nuclear arms race has no military purpose. Wars cannot be fought with nuclear weapons. Their existence only adds to our perils because of the illusions which they have generated.'

Some of his happiest hours were spent on tour with the royal family in their official yacht *Britannia*. He derived particular pleasure from his friendship with the Prince of Wales, who treated him as 'honorary grandfather' and attached great value to his counsel. When Princess Anne married, the certificate gave as her surname 'Mountbatten-Windsor'. This was the culmination of a long battle Mountbatten had waged to ensure that his family name, adopted by Prince Philip, should be preserved among his nephew's descendants. He took an intense interest in all the royal houses of Europe, and was a source of advice on every subject. Harold Wilson once called him 'the shop-steward of royalty' and Mountbatten rejoiced in the description.

Every summer he enjoyed a family holiday at his Irish home in county Sligo, Classiebawn Castle. Over the years the size of his police escort increased but the Irish authorities were insistent that the cancellation of his holiday would be a victory for the Irish Republican Army. On 27 August 1979 a family party went out in a fishing boat, to collect lobster-pots set the previous day. A bomb exploded when the boat was half a mile from Mullaghmoor harbour. Mountbatten was killed instantly, as was his grandson Nicholas and a local Irish boy. His daughter's mother-in-law, Doreen Lady Brabourne, died shortly afterwards. His funeral took place in Westminster Abbey and he was buried in Romsey Abbey. He had begun his preparations for the ceremony more than ten years before and was responsible for planning every detail, down to the lunch to be eaten by the mourners on the train from Waterloo to Romsey.

Mountbatten was a giant of a man, and his weaknesses were appropriately gigantic. His vanity was monstrous, his ambition unbridled. The truth, in his hands, was swiftly converted from what it was to what it should have been. But such frailties were far outweighed by his qualities. His energy was prodigious, as was his moral and physical courage. He was endlessly resilient in the face of disaster. No intellectual, he possessed a powerfully analytical intelligence; he could rapidly master a complex brief, spot the essential and argue it persuasively. His flexibility of mind was extraordinary, as was his tolerance—he accepted all comers for what they were, not measured against some scale of predetermined values. He had style and panache, commanding the loyal devotion of those who served him. To his opponents in Whitehall he was 'tricky Dickie', devious and unscrupulous. To his family and close friends he was a man of wisdom and generosity. He adored his two daughters, Patricia and Pamela, and his ten grandchildren. However pressing his preoccupations he would make time to comfort, encourage, or advise them. Almost always the advice was good.

Among Mountbatten's honours were MVO (1920), KCVO (1922), GCVO (1937), DSO (1941), CB (1943), KCB (1945), KG (1946), PC (1947), GCSI (1947), GCIE (1947), GCB (1955), OM (1965), and FRS (1966). He had an honorary DCL from Oxford (1946), and honorary LL Ds from Cambridge (1946), Leeds (1950), Edinburgh (1954), Southampton (1955), London (1960), and Sussex (1963). He was honorary D.Sc. of Delhi and Patna (1948).

Mountbatten was much painted. His head, by John Ulbricht, is held by the National Portrait Gallery, while portraits by Philip de László, Brenda Bury, Derek Hill, and Carlos Sancha are in the possession of the family. His state portrait by Edward Halliday hangs in the former viceroy's house, New Delhi, and by Da Cruz in the Victoria Memorial Building, Calcutta. A memorial statue by Franta Belsky was erected in 1983 on Foreign Office Green in London.

On Mountbatten's death the title passed to his elder daughter, Patricia Edwina Victoria Knatchbull (born 1924), who became Countess Mountbatten of Burma.

[Philip Ziegler, *Mountbatten*, 1985; family papers.] PHILIP ZIEGLER

MOUSKOS, MICHAEL (1913–1977), archbishop and first president of Cyprus. [See MAKARIOS III.]

MUNBY, ALAN NOEL LATIMER (1913–1974), bibliographical historian, librarian, and book collector, was born in Hampstead 25 December 1913, the elder child and only son of Alan Edward Munby, architect, and his wife, Ethel Annie Greenhill. He was educated at Clifton and King's College, Cambridge, where he obtained second classes in part i of both the classical (1934) and English (1935) triposes. His keen interest in old books, first aroused by schoolboy visits to the dozen or so booksellers in Bristol, blossomed under the stimulus of Cambridge. There he formed his earliest, and remarkably ambitious, collection, of eighteenth-century English verse, largely through purchases at Gustave David's shop. On leaving Cambridge in 1935 he obtained a post, through the good offices of his parents' friend, Mrs Quaritch Wrentmore, as a cataloguer in the antiquarian bookshop of Bernard Quaritch [q.v.]. Two years later he moved to Sotheby's, again as a book cataloguer.

In 1936 Munby had joined the Territorial Army as an officer in Queen Victoria's Rifles and at the outbreak of war he was posted to the first battalion in Kent. On 22 May 1940 they landed at Calais as part of a small and hastily assembled garrison to defend the town against three Panzer divisions. They had to surrender and five years in German prisoner-of-war camps followed, at Laufen, Warburg, and Eichstätt. Munby consoled himself by producing a camp guide in the style of Baedeker, by lecturing on the English novelists, and by writing Betjemanesque verse and ghost stories in the style of M. R. James [q.v.]. He even managed to have a limited and signed edition of one story printed on the private press of the bishop of Eichstätt. When the war ended he was posted to London and after demobilization returned to Sotheby's.

In 1947 he was invited to return to King's as librarian and a year later was elected to a fellowship. The college had already received the bequest of the library of Lord Keynes [q.v.] and Munby was outstandingly successful in attracting other gifts and deposits: an early tenth-century Juvenal given by J. W. Hely-Hutchinson, the T. S. Eliot collection of John Hayward [q.v.], and the papers of Rupert Brooke, E. M. Forster, Maynard Keynes, Roger Fry, Clive and Vanessa Bell [qq.v.], and many others. He did not confine his enthusiasm for bibliographical pursuits to King's. One of his earliest initiatives after returning to Cambridge was to organize a weekend for visiting bibliophiles, marked by exhibitions in colleges and at the Fitzwilliam Museum. He was president of a society of undergraduate book collectors which met in his rooms, co-founder (in 1949) of the Cambridge Bibliographical Society, and author of a valuable short guide, *Cambridge College Libraries* (1960).

Before returning to Cambridge Munby had already collaborated with Desmond Flower in writing *English Poetical Autographs* (1938). Some of his wartime verse was issued in a rigorously limited edition (*Lyra Catenata*, 1948) and his ghost stories appeared under the title *The Alabaster Hand* (1949). Meanwhile, in 1946, he had been invited to write the life of Sir Thomas Phillipps [q.v.]. It was a subject which gave full range to Munby's scholarly gifts and wide bibliographical knowledge, and to his feeling for human eccentricity and sense of the absurd. *Phillipps Studies*, published in five volumes betweeen 1951 and 1960, provided the first comprehensive account of the bibliophiles and book dealers of the nineteenth century, besides evoking so vivid a portrait of the baronet himself that Phillipps has since become of interest to collectors in his own right. The book was written with a rare sense of style, somewhat influenced by Macaulay, of whose works Munby formed the pre-eminent collection.

Munby served his college as praelector from 1951 to 1960 and as domus bursar from 1964 to 1967, when his duties involved supervising a major programme of building. He was a learned and witty lecturer with a felicitous sense of timing, much in demand in both England and America. His appointments included the Lyell readership in bibliography at Oxford in 1962–3 and the Sandars readership at Cambridge in 1969–70, the latter lectures being published under the title of *Connoisseurs and Medieval Miniatures 1750–1850* (1972). *The Cult of the Autograph Letter in England* (1962) was based on lectures given at King's College, London. He was made Litt.D. (Cambridge) in 1962, honorary fellow of the Pierpont Morgan Library, trustee of the British Museum in 1969, a member of the British Library board in 1973, and was serving as president of the Bibliographical Society at the time of his death.

Besides illuminating the most spectacular age of English book collecting Munby's writings broke new ground in drawing attention to the importance of booksellers' and auction catalogues as historical sources. He was general editor of the series of reprints, *Sale Catalogues of Libraries of Eminent Persons*, and joint author, with Lenore Coral, of the posthumously published *British Book Sale Catalogues 1676–1800* (1977). His own collection consisted of 7,000 to 8,000 volumes of early bibliography, sale catalogues, and material relating to libraries, the book trade, and connoisseurship, and included many notable rarities. Part was acquired after his death by Cambridge University Library, the remainder forming two sales at Sotheby's. The Macaulay collection had been given during his lifetime to Trinity College, Cambridge.

Munby (always known as 'Tim' from the second syllable of his third name) was married twice. His first wife, Joan Edelsten, whom he married in 1939, died before his return from captivity. In 1945 he married Sheila Rachel, daughter of Vivian Francis Crowther-Smith, solicitor, of London. They had one son. Munby died in Cambridge 26 December 1974. A Munby fellowship in the University Library was established in his memory with money subscribed by his friends.

Generosity was the outstanding trait of his character, expressed in gifts, in help and advice to friends and acquaintances, in hospitality liberally offered by his wife and himself at their successive Cambridge homes. Although a dedicated collector he could hardly be prevented from giving his books away to those he considered better qualified to own them, and he was never happier than when discovering volumes bearing on the history of their collections to present to his fellow members of the Roxburghe Club. He took particular pleasure in matching a friend's qualifications to an appropriate appointment. His sense of fun added a special delight to time spent in his company. He was a keen shot, often combining a day's shooting with a visit to his host's library, and a skilful carpenter.

[Airey Neave, *The Flames of Calais*, 1972; *Times Literary Supplement*, 11 May 1973; Patrick WIlkinson, *Alan Noel Latimer Munby*, privately printed for King's College, Cambridge, 1975; *Book Collector*, summer 1975; *Modern Literary Manuscripts from King's College, Cambridge*, Fitzwilliam Museum, Cambridge, 1976; Nicolas Barker (ed.), introduction to A. N. L. Munby, *Essays and Papers*, 1977; private information; personal knowledge.]

A. R. A. HOBSON

MUNROW, DAVID JOHN (1942–1976), early woodwind instrumentalist, was born in Birmingham 12 August 1942, the only child of Albert David Munrow, director of physical education in Birmingham University, and his wife, Hilda Ivy Norman. He was educated at King Edward VI School, Birmingham, where he became proficient on the bassoon and recorder, and after a period of teaching and travelling in South America (which laid the foundations of his considerable collection of exotic and folk instruments) he read English at Pembroke College, Cambridge (1961–4), obtaining a second class in both parts of the tripos (1963 and 1964). His enthusiasm and organizational energy quickly brought him to the forefront of university musical life (he was elected president of the University Music Club in 1964), and a partiality for early music (especially Purcell and the English baroque) was encouraged by Thurston Dart [q.v.] and bore fruit in a recorder consort, several chamber ensembles, and many large-scale concerts, including the first modern performance of William Boyce's *Cambridge Ode*. His lecture–recitals demonstrating many species of woodwind instrument (given first with Christopher Hogwood and later with his wife Gillian Reid) marked the start of a career of evangelistic communication with all levels of music-lover.

In 1964 he enrolled at Birmingham University for an MA on a study of D'Urfey's *Pills to Purge Melancholy*, and from 1966 to 1968 he was a member of the wind band of the Royal Shakespeare Company, providing incidental music in Stratford and London, during which time he founded the ensemble with which he was associated for the remainder of his life, the Early Music Consort of London. This made its début in Louvain in 1967 and first appeared in London in 1968. With a variety of well constructed and strikingly presented programmes this ensemble (James Bowman, Oliver Brookes, Christopher Hogwood, and, later, James Tyler) conveyed his enthusiastic and colourful ideas on music ranging from early medieval to late baroque to a worldwide audience, with frequent international tours (the Middle East in 1973, Italy in 1973 and 1975, Australia in 1974, USA in 1974 and 1976), an annual series of London concerts, and regular recordings for Decca (Argo) and later EMI, which attracted major awards, such as the Grammy award in 1975 and the Edison award in 1976. He became honorary ARAM in 1970.

Between 1967 and 1974 he was a part-time lecturer in the music department of Leicester University, and in 1968 became professor of recorder at the Royal Academy of Music, London, a post he held until 1975. During this period he was in demand as a virtuoso exponent of the repertoire for the baroque recorder (he recorded Bach's Brandenburg Concertos several times under conductors including Sir Adrian Boult and Neville Marriner) and made several recordings which displayed and documented the full range of the recorder family (particularly *The Art of the Recorder*, EMI, 1975).

Munrow was constantly willing to experiment; in addition to the wide range of little known repertoire which he researched for the consort's programmes and recordings (Dufay, Mouton, Landini, Binchois, Josquin), he co-operated with folk musicians such as Dolly Collins and The Young Tradition in studio recordings, and arranged (occasionally composed) music for television and cinema where he felt it could increase the public awareness of early instruments and their repertoire (*The Six Wives of Henry VIII*, *Elizabeth R.*, *A Man for All Seasons*, *The Devils*—with Peter Maxwell-Davies—*Zardoz*, *La Course en Tête* etc.). First performances given by the consort and Munrow include *Translations* (1971) and *Recorder Music for Recorder Player and Tape* (1973) by Peter Dickenson, and Elisabeth Lutyens's *The Tears of Night* (1972). Almost all his published writings were associated with recordings, in particular *Instruments of the Middle Ages and Renaissance* (1976), a popular and well illustrated book that incorporated and assessed current thinking on organology, combining musicological tenacity with a player's insight.

Such a venture he held to be meaningless without the accompaniment of a series of recordings to bring the instrumental sounds to life.

He devised and presented radio and television programmes with vitality and wit, the most influential being a BBC Radio 3 series, *Pied Piper*, which ran from 1971 to 1976 with four programmes a week, and attracted an audience far wider than the younger listeners for whom it was designed. The same impetuous enthusiasm, restrained by a very conscious self-discipline, informed all his music-making; he abhorred the idea of remoteness, and as a keen (though diminutive) athlete and sailor (once an Outward Bound instructor), a lover of literature and paintings, an informed historian, a good linguist, and an animated mimic and raconteur he was the antitheses of an academic specialist. While at the start of his public career showmanship sometimes got the better of discretion and a certain brashness was criticized in his performances, he later developed a strong feeling for the liturgical repertoire of the late medieval and Renaissance periods; shortly before he died he was planning a reformed consort to explore this territory. His last recordings (*Music of the Gothic Era*) reflect this maturity.

In 1966 he married Gillian Veronica, daughter of William Robert Reid, principal officer in the Ministry of Home Affairs in Northern Ireland. There were no children. Munrow died by his own hand, at Chesham Bois, Buckinghamshire, 15 May 1976.

[David Scott, 'David (John) Munrow', *The New Grove Dictionary of Music and Musicians*, vol. xii, 1980; *Early Music*, vol. iv, 1976; *The Times*, 17 and 18 May 1976; *Musical Times*, vol. cxvii, 1976; personal knowledge.]

CHRISTOPHER HOGWOOD

MURPHY, ALFRED JOHN (1901–1980), metallurgist and first vice-chancellor of Cranfield Institute of Technology, was born at Altrincham, Cheshire, 26 February 1901, the son of William Murphy, journeyman iron turner, and his wife, Martha Ann Goodier. He was educated at Altrincham High School. Later he went on to Manchester University, where he graduated in chemistry in 1920 with first class honours.

After leaving he soon became involved in metallurgical research, first at University College, Swansea, in 1920–3, and later at the National Physical Laboratory from 1923 to 1931. It was while he was working at the latter that he met, and in 1927 married, Helen Eulalie Blanche (died 1974), daughter of the Revd Herbert Findlay Millar, of Ulster Spring, Jamaica. They had two sons.

In 1931 he went into industry as chief metallurgist of J. Stone & Co. Ltd., continuing in this post until 1949. He was appointed a director of J. Stone & Co. Light Metal Forgings Ltd., and chairman of Stone–Fry Magnesium Ltd., in 1946. By this time his interests in industrial metallurgy, and particularly in the structure of engineering applications of non-ferrous metals and alloys, were well established. He retained strong research interests throughout his life.

In 1950 he returned to academic life on his appointment to the newly established chair of industrial metallurgy at the University of Birmingham, and he became director of the departments of metallurgy at that university in 1953.

On 1 October 1955 Murphy was appointed principal of the College of Aeronautics at Cranfield, Bedfordshire. By the time of his appointment the college was in its tenth year, and it had already established its role in the expanding aerospace industry in Britain, as a centre for aerospace education, with a growing international reputation. Murphy quickly recognized the potential of the college and that its structure could be applied to serve the needs of a wider range of industry. This potential was also recognized in the 1963 report of the committee on higher education chaired by Lord Robbins (Cmnd. 2154). In referring to the College of Aeronautics the report recommended that higher degrees be made available to its students. However, it also opened up the question as to whether the college should be substantially enlarged and play a more ambitious role in the total pattern of higher education, or whether it should retain its relatively small size and form links with a university.

Following investigations by the college's academic advisory committee, Murphy announced in August 1965 that proposals had been made to the secretary of state for education and science, seeking degree-awarding status for Cranfield. He conducted a long, hard, and finally successful campaign, backed fully by the board of governors, towards this goal. Finally, at the end of his fifteen-year stay, the College of Aeronautics became, by royal charter, Cranfield Institute of Technology. Murphy enjoyed the privilege of being its first vice-chancellor for a short period before his retirement in early 1970.

Beyond the work of Cranfield itself Murphy pursued his interests in metallurgy in many organizations and committees. He was president of the Institution of Metallurgists; president of the Institute of Metals (he was awarded their platinum medal in 1971); president of the British Cast Iron Research Association in 1968–70; and vice-president of the British Non-Ferrous Metals Research Association. From 1949 to 1955 he was chairman of the Inter-Service Metallurgical Research Council, in 1962–5 a member of that council, and in 1961–4 an independent member of the Aeronautical

Research Council. He was a fellow of the Royal Aeronautical Society. He was appointed CBE in 1964.

He edited an authoritative monograph, *Non-Ferrous Foundry Metallurgy* (1954). He also contributed articles and papers to the journals of his professional societies.

Murphy was respected by his friends and colleagues for his sound judgement and knowledge, for his interest in people, and for his sense of humour. Above all, he was admired for the determination with which he succesfully pursued the goal of degree-awarding status for Cranfield and the objective of making Cranfield a centre of excellence in higher education and research. He died at his home in Bedford 25 September 1980.

[*The Times*, 1 October 1980; personal knowledge.] HENRY CHILVER

N

NABARRO, Sir GERALD DAVID NUNES (1913–1973), politician, was born in London 29 June 1913, the second child in the family of two sons and two daughters of Solomon Nunes Nabarro and his wife, Lena Drucquer. The family were Sephardic Jews by origin, with several members well established in the medical and legal professions: but Nabarro's father was a retail tobacconist who went bankrupt in 1921. In the same year his mother died and the children were dispersed to various relations until their father remarried. Nabarro received little formal education, leaving elementary school at the age of fourteen. After a few months as an office boy he ran away to sea. In 1930 he joined the King's Royal Rifle Corps (60th Rifles) and rose to be staff sergeant instructor. After years of self-education, in 1937 he applied successfully for officer training but decided that he would be unable to support a commission financially. He left the army for industry and was later proud of having worked in every grade from labourer to managing director. He returned to the army as an officer on the outbreak of World War II.

Nabarro's fascination with the personality of (Sir) Winston Churchill led him into politics. He joined the Conservative Party in 1945 and was soon adopted to contest the safe Labour seat of West Bromwich in the general election that year. In 1950 he won Kidderminster from Labour and retained it until obliged to retire because of ill health in 1964, returning as member for the neighbouring constituency of South Worcestershire in 1966. He was knighted in 1963.

Nabarro did not aspire to political office. He always described himself as an 'amateur' politician. By the late 1950s he had established a place for himself in public life to which ministerial preferment had little relevance. He was an exemplary constituency member. As a self-made man he never lost the common touch, nor his sympathy with and understanding of the fears and aspirations of very ordinary people. His frequent appearances on radio and television gave him a national following. On many issues of his time he adopted positions of which the official leaders of his party were wary but which often coincided with the views of the majority of the people. He opposed Britain's entry into the European Economic Community; supported Enoch Powell in his fears about immigration; supported Rhodesia in its stand against black majority rule; campaigned against the relaxation of censorship, especially that governing pornography. In the social revolution of the early 1960s Nabarro upheld the values of the previous decade which to many came to look like a golden age. To them, oblivious of his origins, Nabarro personified the independent-minded Tory squire whose eccentricities were endearing and who was a welcome contrast to the middle-class, professional politicians who accompanied Edward Heath into the front rank of the party establishment after 1964.

Within Parliament Nabarro made sedulous use of question time, especially in the field of taxation. A question from Nabarro caused much stir in the Treasury. Many ministers went in fear of his devastating supplementaries. Successive chancellors of the Exchequer were confronted with three questions every Tuesday and Thursday on purchase tax in a four-year campaign which achieved the rationalization of the tax.

Nabarro promoted seven private members' bills, four of which became law. The most notable led to the Clean Air Act of 1956, which was instrumental in the eradication of smog.

In 1958 Nabarro sought to introduce an amendment to the Life Peerages Bill to enable hereditary peers to renounce their peerages and seek election to the Commons. He was unsuccessful; but action was precipitated in November 1960, when the Labour member for Bristol South-East (Anthony Wedgwood Benn) succeeded to the viscountcy of Stansgate and began a long battle to secure the reform. Nabarro was Benn's principal Conservative supporter in the Commons. Their alliance led to the Peerage Act of 1963, which became law just in time for the fourteenth Earl of Home (Sir Alec Douglas-Home, later Lord Home of the Hirsel) to renounce his peerage and return to the Commons as prime minister in October 1963.

Nabarro had announced his intention to retire again from the Commons for health reasons when he died, aged sixty, 18 November 1973, at The Orchard House, Broadway, Worcestershire, which had been his home since 1950. Nabarro married in 1943 Joan Maud Violet, eldest daughter of Lieutenant-Colonel Bernhardt Basil von Brumsey im Thurn, DSO, MC, of Dawn House, Winchester; they had two sons and two daughters.

Nabarro was below middle height. A large head and small feet gave him a top-heavy appearance. His huge handle-bar moustache made him instantly recognizable and with his constantly newsworthy activities made him a favourite of the cartoonists. There are portraits by Edward Halliday (1964), Michael Noakes (1968), and John Bratby (1969) in private hands.

[R. J. Goldman (ed.), *Breakthrough*, 1968; Sir Gerald Nabarro, *NAB 1, Portrait of a Politician*, 1969, and *Exploits of a Politician*, 1973; *The*

Times, 19 November 1973; private information; personal knowledge.]

TIMOTHY O'SULLIVAN

NASH, JOHN NORTHCOTE (1893–1977), artist, was born in Kensington, London, 11 April 1893, the younger son and second of the three children of William Harry Nash, barrister and recorder of Abingdon, and his first wife, Caroline Maude, daughter of Captain John Milbourne Jackson, RN. He was the brother of the artist Paul Nash [q.v.] and of Barbara Nash, a gifted horticulturist. The family returned to live in Buckinghamshire, which had been its home for centuries, in 1901. Among Nash's earliest influences here were the Chilterns landscape, the nurse who taught him botany, and the long illness of his mother, who died when he was seventeen. He was educated at Langley Place, Slough, and Wellington College. His emergence fully fledged, as it were, without any formal training, at a joint exhibition with Paul in November 1913 was one of the chief artistic events of that year. The brothers had simply hired a lampshade shop in Pelham Street, hung their pictures round its walls, and drawn their own poster. The directness and simplicity of John's work was seen as something new and advanced by (Sir) William Rothenstein, Walter Sickert [qq.v.], Robert Bevan, and others.

John Nash's decision to become an artist had been taken the year before during a walking tour in Norfolk with the artist Claughton Pellew. Previous to this he had thought about becoming a journalist and had already begun an unpaid apprenticeship on the *Middlesex and Berks Gazette.* Paul, who was a student at the Slade, and not very happy there, advised his brother against art schools, and so he continued his own self-training and development. Eventually he was to do this, not only with painting, but with music and horticulture, and as an art teacher, and all of it to the highest professional degree.

Before joining the Artists' Rifles in September 1916 Nash lived for some months in London, helping to make tents at the White City and also becoming friends with members of the Cumberland Market Group, especially Harold Gilman. The most significant of the landscapes completed by Nash before he left for the western front is 'The Viaduct' (Leeds City Art Gallery). He had also become engaged to a German-Scottish student at the Slade, introduced to him by his friend Dora Carrington. She was (Dorothy) Christine, daughter of Wilhelm Kühlenthal, a merchant chemist living at Gerrard's Cross, and his wife Ada. They were married in May 1918 and his wife was for nearly sixty years to provide the rather exacting regime and cheerfulness which Nash, a more complex personality than most people supposed, demanded. There was one child of the marriage, a son William born in 1930 and killed in a car accident in 1935.

Although 'Over the Top' (1918–19) gradually became recognized as the greatest of the paintings made by World War I artists, Nash scarcely made so much as a sketch while in the trenches. As a sergeant involved in the preparations for Passchendaele and who fought at Cambrai, his experience of the war was much more analogous to that of its poets than its painters. His and Paul's war pictures were in fact created in a seed-shed in Chalfont St. Peter, Buckinghamshire, and John's most famous work, 'The Cornfield' (1918, Tate Gallery) was, he said, his way of celebrating his release from all the toil and emotion of the war and its art.

From now until 1944 he made his home at Meadle, near Princes Risborough, although with annual long painting holidays in the Stour valley, where he was to settle after World War II. He worked with extreme regularity and energy. Making a living and expressing his own vision of the landscape were two compulsions which had to come to terms with each other. He was as down to earth with the landscape as a countryman usually is, but also profoundly involved with it as pattern, and as poetry. Regarded as a modern and an English Post-Impressionist in his youth, he very soon went his own way, with an indifference to movements.

In 1919 he began to illustrate books. His range was enormous, from comic drawings originally inspired by Edward Lear [q.v.] in the possession of his Aunt Augusta, to his finest achievement, the botanical illustrations in such works as his own *Poisonous Plants* (ed. A. W. Hill, 1927) and the lithographs in *The Natural History of Selborne* (1951 and 1972), by Gilbert White [q.v.]. In so many ways 'literary' himself, he had an intuitive understanding of the relationship between pictures and words which placed him among the finest book illustrators of his time.

Nash taught nearly all his life, first at the Ruskin School, Oxford (1922–7), then at the Royal College of Art (1934–57) and later at Colchester, and he especially delighted in the flower-drawing classes he held at the Flatford Mill Field Studies Centre near his home. His first one-man show was held at the Goupil Gallery (1921) and he exhibited regularly. His method was to take a working holiday in Cornwall, Skye, Dorset, Wales, Norfolk, or elsewhere—he was a great in-Britain traveller—and bring back full sketch-books to his Stour valley studio and translate them into oils and water-colours. In 1940 he was elected ARA and also once more made an official war artist, this time for the Admiralty, but he resigned the latter appointment the following year and became a captain in the Royal Marines. His brother Paul's death in 1946 coincided with the start of the long last stage of John Nash's life at Wormingford on the Suffolk–Essex border, which he was to make so much his own 'country'. He was elected RA in 1951 and appointed CBE in 1964. In 1967 the University of Essex gave him an honorary degree and in the same year the Royal Academy honoured him with the first retrospective exhibition they had mounted for a living artist.

Nash was a passionate 'artist plantsman', as he liked to style himself, and a celebrated gardener. Almost equal passions were music and fishing. His nature combined wit, charm, solitude, and gregariousness with a deep underlying melancholy—'the Nash blackness', as he called it. He was extremely demanding, much like a child, yet capable all his life of sustaining profoundly loyal friendships. He suffered from severe arthritis during his last years but continued to paint to within a few months of his death, which occurred in hospital in Colchester 23 September 1977.

[John Rothenstein, *Modern British Painters*, 1950; Sidney Schiff, 'John Nash, *Fleuron*, 1925; John Lewis, *John Nash, the Painter as Illustrator*, 1978; John Rothenstein, *John Nash*, 1983; *A Painter in the Country*, BBC2 film, 1969, written by Ronald Blythe, directed by John Read; private information; personal knowledge.] RONALD BLYTHE

NEALE, SIR JOHN ERNEST (1890–1975), historian, was born at Liverpool 7 December 1890, the son of Arthur Neale, a joiner and master builder, and his wife, Mary Emily Latham, who supported herself and her son by turning seamstress when her husband died in 1895. He attended the Bluecoat Hospital School at Liverpool, leaving school at fourteen and working for his matriculation at night school. He went on to Liverpool University, from which he graduated with a second class degree in history (1914). In 1914 he began research in London under A. F. Pollard [q.v.], in 1915 obtained a Liverpool MA, and in 1919 became assistant at University College, London.

After two years spent as professor of modern history at Manchester (1925–7) he returned to University College, London, to succeed Pollard in the Astor chair of English history which he held to his retirement (1927–56). At University College he built up, and dominated, an excellent department, and during his long tenure of the Astor chair he became in effect ruler of the London school of history. In his well-known research seminar he encountered large numbers of budding scholars from both sides of the Atlantic, and although only a few of his immediate pupils made academic careers his influence extended to a wide circle. He was a severe, if intermittent, taskmaster who demanded from his students his own sort of dedication to the sources.

Neale built his successful academic career with singular consistency around one specific concern which resulted in four highly regarded books: *Queen Elizabeth* (1934), which won the James Tait Black memorial prize, *The Elizabethan House of Commons* (1949), and *Elizabeth I and her Parliaments* (2 vols., 1953, 1957). Neale was a painstaking research scholar who, having discovered an ability to write readable (though sometimes rather lush) prose, believed himself to be called to bring serious history to a wide readership. The startling success of his first book induced him to design also the later ones for agreeable reading, with the result that his writings created an influential orthodoxy but often made it quite difficult to discover the basis on which the argument rested. From the start of his career he had set himself the task of finding every bit of evidence that bore on the thirteen parliamentary sessions of the reign, and in this area, where he made a number of striking discoveries, his scholarship was profound and solid. At the same time, as his early papers (1916–34) show, he had formulated the essentials of his interpretation from the first, so that increasing knowledge tended to be subordinated to a scheme framed on insufficient knowledge.

Throughout Neale held to two convictions: the supreme statesmanship of the queen, and the growing independence and political assertiveness of the House of Commons. In addition he wished to write a coherent story. Thus when he completed the history of those Parliaments, he discarded all he knew about the day-to-day work of the institution and concentrated on occasions of dispute and conflict which in actual fact were quite rare. Convinced of the primacy of conflict, he misread some of the evidence, overlooked the pervasive control of the queen, privy council, and House of Lords, and discerned a formed Puritan opposition which did not really exist. Neale was always liable to allow personal experience to shape his view of the past: he several times, in print, likened Elizabethan Puritanism to modern Communism, and he was fond of explaining that he understood the Elizabethan Parliament from the many hours spent on academic committees.

However, Neale's learning saved him from the worst consequences of such quirks. It was displayed at its best in the book on the House of Commons which revealed the local roots of parliamentary participation and analysed the social composition of the House. For this last task he borrowed the prosopographical techniques popularized in modern history by Sir Lewis Namier [q.v.]; the work rested on a detailed study of knights and burgesses, Parliament by Parliament, undertaken partly by himself and partly by his students. This approach to history was to occupy him even more in his retirement, in his contribution (which remained uncompleted at his death) to the History of Parliament on whose editorial board he served from 1951 to 1971. Despite such additions to his armoury, Neale remained in essence a scholar of the Pollard school—a constitutional historian and historical biographer, and in politics a Liberal to whom the rise of Parliament was the most important feature of English history.

Neale received seven honorary degrees: from Wales (1948), Birmingham (1954), Liverpool (1956), Amherst (1958), London (1960), Leeds (1960), and Cambridge (1960). In 1949 he became a fellow of the British Academy and in 1955 he was knighted. He was Ford's lecturer at Oxford in 1941–2, and gave the Raleigh lecture of the British Academy in 1948. In 1970, on his eightieth birthday, an annual Neale lecture in English history was instituted at University College, London.

Neale's relations with the world were much shaped by a Nonconformist background and the stern example of Pollard. His friendships were few but very close, and he knew little in the way of relaxation. In appearance he resembled, as was often remarked, Mr Pickwick: short, stockily solid, round-faced and rubicund. In times of stress a ruthless streak emerged which gave a Torquemadan cast to his normally smiling features.

In 1932 he married Elfreda, daughter of William Skelton, of Harrogate; they had one daughter. Neale died at his home in Beaconsfield 2 September 1975.

[Joel Hurstfield in *Proceedings* of the British Academy, vol. lxiii, 1977; personal knowledge.] G. R. ELTON

NEAVE, AIREY MIDDLETON SHEFFIELD (1916–1979), intelligence officer and politician, was born in London 23 January 1916, the elder son in the family of two sons and three daughters of Sheffield Airey Neave, well-known entomologist and honorary secretary of the Zoological Society, of Mill Green Park, Ingatestone, Essex, and his wife, Dorothy, daughter of Lt.-Col. Arthur Thomson Middleton, JP, of Ayshe Court, Horsham. He was educated at Eton and Merton College, Oxford, where he obtained a third class in jurisprudence in 1938.

He joined the Territorial Army Royal Artillery in 1939. As a lone subaltern in the chaos of the retreat of May 1940 he took part in the battle of Calais. He later described this in *The Flames of Calais* (1972). He was wounded at Calais and taken prisoner. From then on his thoughts were on escape, which he achieved from the camp at Torun, only to be recaptured in Poland. His admiration for the Poles and his later fight for a memorial for the Katyn massacre stem from that time. His interrogation then by the Gestapo, which he never forgot, made him a devotee of freedom under the laws of any country. Later this was to lead to his view that, if action had been taken outside the law by police or soldiers in Northern Ireland, the culprits should be brought to justice.

Neave was then sent to the maximum security prison at Colditz. His first attempt to escape was hindered by his colour-blindness, but ultimately in 1942 he succeeded, reached Switzerland, and then went through Vichy France to Gibraltar and back to London. His, possibly best, book, *They Have Their Exits* (1953), gives a moving account of both escapes.

He had brought back valuable intelligence information, and was soon operating at MI9 helping underground movements and training air-crews to escape. He described this period in *Saturday at MI9* (1969).

In 1942 Neave married Diana Josceline Barbara, daughter of Thomas Arthur Walter Giffard, landowner and county councillor, of Chillington Hall, Wolverhampton. After Neave's murder in 1979 she was created Baroness Airey of Abingdon. They had two sons and one daughter.

By the end of the war Neave had been honoured many times. In 1942 he was awarded the MC, and in 1945 the DSO and TD with clasp, the croix de guerre, the US bronze star, and the order of Orange Nassau. In 1947 he was appointed OBE.

Neave was called to the bar at the Middle Temple in 1943, and at the end of the war became assistant secretary to the International Military Tribunal, and thus, as a lieutenant-colonel, served the charges on the main Nazi war criminals. His last book, *Nuremberg* (1978), dealt with each one.

After the war while establishing a practice at the bar, he was from 1949 to 1951 officer commanding Intelligence School No. 9 (TA), which later became 23 SAS Regiment. But his thoughts were turning to politics. Having contested Thurrock (1950), and Ealing North (1951), he was elected Conservative MP for the Abingdon division of Berkshire in July 1953. He became parliamentary private secretary to the colonial secretary, Alan Lennox-Boyd (later Viscount Boyd of Merton), and to the minister of transport, H. A. (later Viscount) Watkinson, before becoming parliamentary under-secretary at the Air Ministry in 1959. Then came a heart attack which Edward Heath, as chief whip, thought might end Neave's parliamentary career.

But his greatest influence on events was to come. He specialized in science and technology (Harwell was in his constituency). He was a governor of Imperial College from 1963 to 1971; and a member from 1965 and subsequent chairman (1970–5) of the House of Commons select committee on science and technology. He fought a long and successful battle against the Foreign Office for compensation to former prisoners at Sachsenhausen, but in another battle he failed to get Hess released. He campaigned successfully for pensions for those over eighty. He was chairman of the British Standing Conference on Refugees (1972–4) and delegate to the United Nations High Commissioner for Refugees (1970–5).

He also played a predominant part in ousting Edward Heath as leader of the Conservative Party in 1975. Though at one time he considered among others Edward du Cann as a possible successor, he soon came to prefer Margaret Thatcher, and thereafter gave her undivided support and loyalty. When Margaret Thatcher became leader, Neave was made head of her private office, and shadow secretary of state for Northern Ireland. Although he had directorships connected largely with his energy, engineering, and scientific interests, politics and writing were his real loves.

Neave quietly, and often alone, planned, worked, and even intrigued for what he thought was right for his country. Patient, even slow, efficient, methodical, 'he thought before he fired'. Smiling often, laughing seldom, speaking in a low voice, he was almost self-sufficient. He had a cold calculating courage. Yet he had no personal ambition. He would have been amazed at the number of people at his memorial service overflowing St. Martin's-in-the-Fields, at the sums raised for his memorial trusts. He was essentially a private man. He appeared shy, almost reticent, but to friends he had a charming sense of humour, though his friendship was not given easily. He expected his friends to live up to his own high standard of integrity. He would always say when he did not know.

Neave had no ordinary recreations. He enjoyed most perfecting his own writing, and being with his wife and family. He was a good observer and listener, but would then make up his own mind. He loathed tyranny. He believed in freedom under the law. He thought that though power-sharing in Northern Ireland was not politically feasible, there should be more local government, and that if British troops were withdrawn the Catholic minority would suffer most. But to the Irish Republican Army and the Irish National Liberation Army he was a detested politician. It was by an Irish terrorist bomb hidden in his car that he was assassinated 30 March 1979 on the ramp of the House of Commons car park.

[Private information; personal knowledge.]

JOHN TILNEY

NEILL, ALEXANDER SUTHERLAND (1883–1973), founder of Summerhill School, was born in Forfar in Scotland 17 October 1883, the third son and third of the thirteen children (one of them stillborn) of George Neill, schoolmaster, and his wife Mary, daughter of Neil Sutherland, who worked in the docks at Leith. Both his parents were teachers and he attended his father's school at Kingsmuir. He left school at fourteen to become (for a short while) first a clerk and then a draper's apprentice. His upbringing was within a rigid pattern of order, and the strongest personal influence upon him was that of his sister, Clunes.

Unimpressed by his life in Edinburgh, he returned to his father's school as a pupil-teacher, although he failed to win a place at teachers' training college. He worked harder to pass the matriculation requirements of Edinburgh University in 1908, rapidly deserting the study of agriculture for that of English. More significantly, he was a lively editor of the student magazine and went to London to find work on the fringes of publishing and journalism. A leg injury kept him (temporarily) out of the army in 1914, and he accepted an appointment as temporary headmaster in Gretna Green school. His work as teacher and as publicist now merged, and in 1916 appeared the first of many books, *A Dominie's Log*. Significantly, too, the *Weekly Dispatch* discovered him and he was never thereafter to be short of publicity. His distrust of the conventional curriculum, his belief in freedom rather than orthodox discipline, his capacity to provoke criticism were already evident. 'I send my Tommie to school to learn, not to dig in the garden', objected one parent.

In 1917 he joined the army and was commissioned as an artillery officer. He became a friend of educationist Homer Lane, whom Neill was to acknowledge as the strongest influence upon his whole life and through whom, albeit unsystematically, he encountered the ideas and practices of Sigmund Freud. His first book had already brought him some fame, and he taught for a short while at the King Alfred School in Hampstead. His advanced views on self-government by pupils offended the restrained liberal customs of the well-known progressive school, and he was obliged to resign.

Neill became in 1920 the joint editor with Beatrice Ensor of *Education for the New Era* and so joined that loosely articulated, and often disputatious, group of educational reformers that had emerged in the last decade. Beatrice Ensor was a founder member of the 'Ideals in Education Group' which had grown up around Edmond G. A. Holmes after his retirement from His Majesty's Inspectorate schools and the publication in 1911 of his deeply influential *What Is and What Might Be*. Bertrand (Earl) Russell [q.v.] and his wife Dora opened Beacon Hill School in 1927, and Dartington Hall began its life in 1925. Rousseau, Pestalozzi, Froebel, Dewey, and

Freud were the ill-assorted intellectual patrons of these educational novelties.

The New Education Fellowship—'new' was the keynote of these hopeful years after the war—was part of these loosely related developments although Neill himself was contemptuous of attempts to induct the young into a 'higher life' or the cultivation of 'good taste'. For him, the important task was to free children from fear, to replace an emphasis upon intellect with one upon emotion, rather than to teach or instruct. 'No man is good enough to tell another how to live. No man is wise enough to guide another's footsteps.'

Under the auspices of the Fellowship Neill went in 1921 to the international section of a new school at Hellerau, near Salzburg, where he developed more confidently his theories or intuitions on the ways in which the young should be reared. The new school, trapped within a bureaucratic system, collapsed in 1924, and Neill moved with five pupils and his partner's wife (whom he was later to marry) to start a tiny school at Lyme Regis in Dorset, in a rented house called Summerhill. Three years later, with some thirty pupils, they moved to Leiston in Suffolk. By 1934 there were seventy pupils: Neill and Summerhill had become, and for the rest of his life remained, synonymous. The school attracted a steady stream of comment, criticism, and visitors. During World War II it was removed to Ffestiniog in north Wales, which Neill hated. It was formally inspected and Neill himself commented on the liberalism of an educational system which allowed his own creation to flourish. Nevertheless, it remained in difficulties after the war, and by 1960 numbers declined to twenty-five.

Neill's American publisher, Harold Hart, produced an edition of his book on Summerhill and opened the last and most public chapter of Neill at Summerhill. A. S. Neill became even better known in the United States than at home and, to his indignation, an American Summerhill Society was founded. He rejected the notion that anything so particular as Summerhill could be organized and generalized.

His influence as a propagandist was great, while many of the notions—which he shared with others—on the necessary child-centredness of education became commonplace in his own lifetime. He preferred to be described as 'author and child psychologist'. 'I do not want to be remembered as a great educator, for I am not, but because I tried to abolish fear in schools.' Nor was his thinking systematic: for him, Summerhill was a demonstration and not an experiment. The influence of Freud was largely mediated through his intense relationship with Homer Lane. After 1937, the influence of Wilhelm Reich was similarly potent. His underlying principles and prejudices remained clear: 'Let us think of a bad school. I mean a school where children sit at desks and speak when they are spoken to.'

Neill could not afford to retire, even if he had wished to, and died at the age of eighty-nine at Aldeburgh 23 September 1973. He was twice married: in 1927 to Ada Lilian Lindesay-Neustätter, an Australian, a matron at his school and the former wife of Dr Otto Neustätter. She died in 1944, and in 1945 he married Ena May Wood, née Wooff, who survived him and by whom he had one daughter. Unimpressed by honours, he nevertheless accepted the honorary degrees of M.Ed. from Newcastle in 1967, LL D from Exeter in 1968, and D.Univ. from Essex in 1971.

[*The Times*, 25 September 1973; Neill's own writings, notably *Summerhill: A Radical Approach to Education*, 1962, and *Neill! Neill! Orange Peel*, 1973; R. E. Hemmings, *Fifty Years of Freedom: A Study of the Development of the Ideas of A. S. Neill*, 1972; Jonathan Croall, *Neill of Summerhill*, 1983.]
HARRY JUDGE

NEWITT, DUDLEY MAURICE (1894–1980), chemical engineer, was born 28 April 1894 in London, the second son in the family of four sons and three daughters of Edward James Dunn Newitt, a ballistics engineer, and his wife, Alice Gertrude Lewis, daughter of a craftsman in Windsor. After secondary school at Wandsworth, in 1910 he was appointed assistant chemist at the Nobel's explosives factory, Ardeer, which enabled him to attend evening classes at the Royal Technical College, Glasgow, to study for the London University external B.Sc. in chemistry. He passed his intermediate B.Sc. in 1912, and planned to continue studies for higher degrees whilst being paid as an elementary schoolteacher. The advent of World War I changed this programme drastically.

Newitt joined up with the East Surrey Regiment, and was drafted to the Indian Army Officer Reserve in November 1914. After some service on the North-West Frontier with the 54th Sikhs, he was transferred to the 53rd Sikhs in Mesopotamia, where he shared in the capture of Kut and of Baghdad, battles with heavy losses. For a time he was second-in-command of his battalion, and he was mentioned in dispatches. He was appointed adjutant in 1917, and shared in the memorable entries into Damascus and Jerusalem. In 1918 he received the MC for his participation in the capture of Samaria, and was promoted major. He continued as administrator of the Beryck area in Syria up to his demobilization in 1919.

After his five stirring war years, Newitt returned to pursue his career in chemical research with tenacity, but under less strenuous conditions. He now enrolled as an undergraduate in chemistry in the Royal College of Science in South Kensington, and passed his B.Sc., with first class honours and a Governor's medal for skills in chemistry, in 1921. He went on to postgraduate studies in chemical engineering with Professor J. W. Hinchley and research in fuel technology with Professor W. A. Bone [q.v.] at Imperial College. Newitt became one of Bone's leading research colleagues. Together with Bone and with another colleague, D. T. A. Townend, he published numerous researches and a monograph, *Gaseous Combustion at High Pressures* (1929). Newitt obtained higher external degrees at London University (Ph.D. 1924, D.Sc. 1930).

At that time established university posts were few. Newitt's first senior teaching appointment at Imperial College was in 1936. Its title, reader in high pressure technology, marked an abiding feature of his interest in researches at high pressures. In 1940 he published a weighty monograph, *The Design of High Pressure Plant and the Properties of Fluids at High Pressures*.

World War II stopped any further sheltered academic growth for Newitt, who was appointed scientific director of Special Operations Executive in 1941. In this post he had to supervise the invention, manufacture, and supply of every kind of gadget to secret agents in enemy-occupied country, to further their operations of sabotage. He did not return to university affairs until 31 May 1945, as the first Courtaulds professor of chemical engineering at Imperial College. This highlighted his many commitments in the development of chemical engineering science as a distinctive academic discipline in Britain, including his office as president of the British Institution of Chemical Engineers (1949–51). Eight of his former students later became university professors.

In 1952 Newitt became head of department, and had much to do with the planning and building (from 1954 to 1967) of a large modern home for chemical engineering and chemical technology at Imperial College. He was skilful at delegating and the leader of what he liked to term 'a mettlesome team'. In 1956 he was appointed pro-rector of Imperial College, a post held until his retirement in 1961. He gave untiring services to the student community. To this Dictionary he contributed the notice of Sir A. C. G. Egerton.

His many human qualities made him much sought after for numerous public professional duties, such as council member of the Royal Society (1957–9), chairman of the Water Pollution Board (1950 onwards), member of the scientific advisory committee of the TUC, and member of the Federation of British Industry committee to set up a college of technology at Delhi. For several years Newitt gave powerful support to international collaboration on thermodynamic reference standards, and, in particular, steam tables.

Newitt was elected FRS in 1942. His many honours included the Rumford medal of the Royal Society (1962), and the Osborne Reynolds, Moulton, and Hawksley medals of the engineering institutions. He was appointed a fellow of Imperial College, and honorary D.Sc. of the universities of Toulouse (1961) and Bradford (1969).

Newitt was a clubbable man who astonished his friends with his zest for 'travelling rough' by sea and by land over enormous distances, but whose hospitality in his own home at Runfold in Surrey made up for this. In 1919 he married Alix, daughter of Angele Schaeffer, hotel owner, of Rouen; she had been a friend of the family for a long time. She died in 1923 at Nice, giving birth to their first child, which was stillborn. In 1933 he married his second wife, Dorothy Wallis Arthur (died 1953) daughter of George William Arthur Garrod ('Wallis Arthur'), concert party agent. They had a son and a daughter. Newitt died 14 March 1980 at home in Runfold, Farnham, Surrey.

[A. R. Ubbelohde in *Biographical Memoirs of Fellows of the Royal Society*, vol. xxvii, 1981; personal knowledge.] A. R. UBBELOHDE

NEWSOM, SIR JOHN HUBERT (1910–1971), educationist, was born in Glasgow 8 June 1910, the elder son (there were no daughters) of Hubert Nash Newsom and his wife Dorothy Elliott. His brother died young. His father, having served as an army officer in South Africa, held various administrative jobs in India, Britain, and Ireland. John Newsom, after attending schools in England, Scotland, and Ireland, went to the Imperial Service College from 1924 to 1928 from where he won a scholarship to The Queen's College, Oxford.

He went down in 1931 with a second in philosophy, politics, and economics. The same year he married Barbara Joan, daughter of Louis Day, who worked in the building industry; they had one son and one daughter.

Between 1931 and 1938 he was engaged in social work in the London area, the midlands, and the north-east. His interest in social service began while at Oxford; he had no income but his scholarship and he supported himself by unskilled work in the East End of London during vacations, living in lodging-houses and rented rooms. This pre-Orwellian experience gave rise to a remarkable book, written when he was only nineteen and published in 1930 by his old friend (Sir) Basil Blackwell, under the title *On the Other Side*.

His main work in education began in 1939 when he was appointed deputy county education officer for Hertfordshire, having arrived in the county in 1938 in connection with Home Office plans for civil defence and evacuation. In 1940, still only twenty-nine, he became county education officer, a post he held till 1957.

During this time Hertfordshire became a leading education authority with, in particular, a national and international reputation for school building. Newsom had little administrative and no school-teaching experience but he had flair and enthusiasm and an individual style which permeated his administration. He was a skilled manipulator inside County Hall: his close relationship with R. S. McDougall, county treasurer, helped forward the rapid and costly expansion of the education service. Between them they devised a way of decentralizing control of much day-to-day spending—each head had a budget, cheque-book, and bank account. Critics disputed how much real difference this made: heads welcomed it and the vote of confidence it signified.

With a large influx of population to LCC housing estates and three new towns, Hertfordshire's school building needs were great. The secret of Hertfordshire's success in this field was the close co-operation between C. H. Aslin [q.v.], the county architect, and (Sir) Stirrat Johnson-Marshall, his deputy, and Newsom and his deputy, Sidney Broad. The moving spirit was Johnson-Marshall, who overcame the shortage of building materials and labour by prefabricated methods, and (more important) insisted on a new and creative relationship between the architects and the educators. Newsom instinctively responded and encouraged his staff to do so too. Newsom had early come to the belief that good education deserved the best physical environment. He wanted children to encounter original works of art and persuaded Hertfordshire to build up a collection, which included work by (Dame) Barbara Hepworth [q.v.], Henry Moore, and Ben Nicholson, among many others. For many years the contract for each new school included provision for a mural or a piece of sculpture. But before Newsom departed the philistines had whittled away at the budget and the policy was abandoned. In 1954 he was appointed CBE.

In 1957 Newsom resigned on health grounds and joined the board of Longmans, Green and Co. Ltd., the educational publishers. It was intended to reduce his work-load but in the event the respite was brief. On the death of a colleague he found himself in the managing director's chair. Newsom never became an expert publisher, but he knew a lot about running a big organization and he cheerfully applied to Longmans the arts he had learnt in local government.

In 1961 he joined the central advisory council for education (England) as deputy chairman to Viscount Amory—who was promptly sent to Canada as governor-general—and it fell to Newsom to conduct the inquiry into the education of children of average and below average ability which resulted in *Half Our Future* (the Newsom report) in 1963.

The report was compassionate and practical. It showed Newsom's concern for social disadvantage, and it located education's opportunities and limitations within the complex of social and economic forces at work in English cities. The concerted policies it advocated were taken up again by the central advisory committee in Lady Plowden's report on primary education (1967), when Newsom served as deputy chairman, and in the community development policies subsequently adopted by the Department of the Environment, but the large resources needed to make a reality of educational priority areas were never forthcoming. In 1964 Newsom's services were recognized by the award of a knighthood.

From 1966 to 1968 he was chairman of the public schools commission set up by the first administration of Harold Wilson (later Lord Wilson of Rievaulx). The commission's task was unsatisfactory from the start: it was to serve as a substitute for action; to keep an election promise, not to formulate policy. Its suggested ways of integrating the public schools with the maintained sector were never seriously considered and its useful study of 'boarding need' was largely ignored. Newsom took it philosophically but he was aware that he had been used and did not enjoy the experience.

Among his many other interests were various committees and institutions connected with the arts. He was a member of the Arts Council from 1953 to 1957. He was a vice-chairman of the National Youth Orchestra, a governor of the Royal College of Art, the British Film Institute, Haileybury and the Imperial Service College, and St. Edmund's, Ware, an honorary fellow of The Queen's College, Oxford (1969), and an honorary FRIBA. He received an honorary LL D from the University of Pennsylvania. In 1964 he became the first chairman of the Independent Television Authority's education advisory council. He served on government committees on colonial education, public libraries, and charitable trusts. From 1966 to the time of his death he was chairman of the Harlow Development Corporation. He was made an officer of the Legion of Honour in recognition of a brief period of secret service in Europe on secondment from Hertfordshire at the end of the war.

A fluent and combative writer and broadcaster, his best known book was *The Education of Girls* (1948) in which he argued the unfashionable case for more emphasis on home-making and the domestic arts.

Newsom's inner seriousness was combined with a cheerful and amusing manner. Brought up an Anglican, he became an agnostic for a time, before joining the Roman Catholic Church in 1946. His deep humanitarian ideals never dimmed the mischievous sense of humour which made him excellent company. He was a good cook; given to hospitality, interested in all around him, especially young people with their way to make. Even his little weaknesses had charm. He clearly loved being an establishment figure, knowing the top people and being in the know, while retaining somewhere at the back of it all a radical commitment to those social and religious values which had once made him throw in his lot with those *On the Other Side*.

He died at Sawbridgeworth, Hertfordshire, 23 May 1971.

[*The Times* 24 May 1971; private information; personal knowledge.] STUART MACLURE

NICHOLLS, FREDERICK WILLIAM (1889–1974), signals expert, was born 27 May 1889 at 21 Holdenhurst Road, Bournemouth, the eldest of three children and only son of Thomas Arthur Nicholls, a master photographic printer, and his wife, Sabina Mapstone. He volunteered as an infantry private in 1914, and by the end of World War I was a lieutenant in the Royal Corps of Signals, having served in Mesopotamia in 1916–18. He obtained a regular commission, and worked in the army Y service (wireless interception) in Russia in 1919, and thereafter in Afghanistan, Burma, Iraq, Persia, Palestine, India, and—in 1939–40—France.

He was thus *persona grata* to all sorts of secret authorities; this made him useful when in November 1942 he was posted as a lieutenant-colonel to be GSO 1 (signals) to the Special Operations Executive. SOE had suffered much from rivalry with MI6, which Nicholls was able in part to appease. From 1 May 1943 he was SOE's director of signals and sat on its governing council. He was promoted brigadier in July 1944. He supervised both the design and development of clandestine equipment for wireless telegraphy, and codes and ciphers, and a world-wide range of wireless communication which at peak periods handled two million groups a week. Without these wireless links, SOE would have been helpless; with them, it exercised an influence on the war out of all proportion to its size, which was about that of a single division.

Nicholls's subordinates found him a just and generous chief, and his equals admired his judgement. So did (Sir) Colin Gubbins [q.v.], his chief, who had long known him. At the war's end, his networks were summarily closed down, on the orders of C. R. (later Earl) Attlee. Nicholls devoted himself for four months to finding new work for his juniors, and retired in mid-January 1946 to settle in Wiltshire.

After the death in 1952 of his first wife, Jessie Jane Lindsay, who was American, he married in March 1955 Marjorie Emilie ('Marianne'), daughter of Arthur West Tindall, miller; she had served under his command in SOE's signals section, and outlived him. He had no children.

He was appointed MBE in 1918, OBE in 1929, and CBE in 1946. He also held American, Danish, Dutch, and French orders. He died, at a doctor's house near his home at Coombe Bissett outside Salisbury, 18 December 1974.

[M. R. D. Foot, *SOE in France*, 1966, and *SOE*, 1984; Pierre Lorain (adapted by David Kahn), *Secret Warfare*, 1984; private information.] M. R. D. FOOT

NICOLL, (JOHN RAMSAY) ALLARDYCE (1894–1976), university teacher and administrator, and scholar and historian of the drama, was born 28 June 1894 at Partick, Lanarkshire, the younger child and only son of David Binny Nicoll, law clerk of Partick, and his wife, Elsie Jane Allardyce. He was educated at Stirling High School and the University of Glasgow, where he was G. A. Clark scholar in English; he graduated in 1915.

After holding appointments as lecturer in English at Loughborough College and, from 1920, King's College, London, he was professor of English language and literature at the East London (later Queen Mary) College from 1924 to 1933, when he moved to Yale University as professor of the history of drama and dramatic criticism and chairman of the department of drama. He was active in the presentation as well as the study of plays. From 1942 he was attached to the British embassy in Washington, returning to England to become professor of English language and literature in the University of Birmingham in 1945.

In 1951 he founded and became director of the Shakespeare Institute, a centre for graduate studies in the dramatic and other literature of the Elizabethan and Jacobean periods. The initial impetus to establish the Institute in Stratford-upon-Avon was the appointment in 1946 of Nicoll's friend, Sir Barry Jackson [q.v.], as director of the Shakespeare Memorial Theatre. Nicoll hoped to lower the barriers between academic study of drama and its practice, but Jackson resigned in 1948, and later administrators of the Theatre did not share their ideals. Nicoll retired in 1961; he became emeritus professor in the University of Birmingham, and was Andrew Mellon professor of English in the University of Pittsburgh in 1963–4, 1965, 1967, and 1969.

Nicoll's first book (1922) was a study of William Blake [q.v.]; he prepared a detailed edition of the translation of Homer by George Chapman [q.v.] (2 vols., 1957), and lectured over wide areas of English literature; but he had a passion for the theatre and dedicated most of his extraordinarily disciplined energies to the study of drama. *An Introduction to Dramatic Theory* and *Dryden and his Poetry* both appeared in 1923, as did his *A History of Restoration Drama, 1600–1700*. This volume, a historical and critical survey followed by a list of all known plays arranged under their authors, formed the pattern for a sequence of related studies which appeared over half a century. *A History of Late Eighteenth Century Drama* (1927), *A History of Early Nineteenth Century Drama* (1930), and *A History of Late Nineteenth Century Drama* (1946) were revised as *A History of English Drama, 1660–1900* (6 vols., 1952–9). *English Drama 1900–1930*, on the same plan, appeared in 1973.

The publication of these books was interspersed with and followed by many other writings including such authoritative and deeply studied volumes as *British Drama* (1925, etc.), *The Development of the Theatre* (1927), *Masks, Mimes and Miracles* (1931), *Stuart Masques and the Renaissance Stage* (1937), *World Drama* (1949, substantially revised in 1976), *The Elizabethans* (1957), and *The World of Harlequin: A Study of the Commedia dell' Arte* (1963). *The Garrick Stage*, originally conceived as a text to accompany a comprehensive series of illustrations, appeared posthumously in 1980. Nicoll wrote one of the early studies of film (*Film and Theatre*, 1936), and his willingness to take note of all aspects of theatre, whatever their literary quality, demonstrated his interest in its social function. He founded the annual *Shakespeare Survey* in 1948 and edited it till 1965. At the time of his death he was working on a study of Greek and Roman theatres.

Nicoll was a humanely efficient, fair-minded administrator, a distinguished lecturer, and a generous stimulator of talent in his colleagues and pupils. He inculcated high standards of scholarship and encouraged originality of research. His achievement in his unfailingly lucid writings is primarily that of an analytical chronicler, a learned enthusiast who perceived relationships and charted previously uninvestigated territory, who cared for detail but was not afraid to work on a broad canvas. His remarkable range of ability as a linguist and (to a lesser degree) his talent as a photographer contributed to his work. At Yale he instituted a collection of photographs of theatres of the world. His essential modesty is reflected in the self-effacement with which he pursued his ideals of collaboration in scholarship, best realized in his founding of the Shakespeare Institute, with its biennial international Shakespeare conference, and in his conduct of the Institute as an international community and true fellowship of senior and junior scholars. A tall, slim, elegant figure, with a twinkle in his eye and a shy but ready smile, he moved among people of all kinds with a courteous, slightly diffident grace. But he was perhaps happiest in the peace and seclusion of his home at Colwall, close to British Camp, and in his walks in the neighbouring Malvern Hills. A drawing by Dame Laura Knight portrays him amid his favourite countryside.

Nicoll's honours included a life trusteeship of the Shakespeare Birthplace Trust (1961–76), honorary membership of the Modern Language Association of America and of the Accademia Ligure di Scienze a Lettere, the presidency of the Society for Theatre Research (1958–76), and honorary doctorates of the universities of Toulouse (1949), Montpellier (1952), Durham (1964), Glasgow (1964), and Brandeis (1965).

In 1919 he married Josephine Calina, a Polish refugee four years his senior. After her death in 1962 he married Maria Dubno, librarian of the Shakespeare Institute, in 1963. There were no children of either marriage. Nicoll died at Malvern 17 April 1976.

[*Who's Who in the Theatre*, 1972; *Theatre Notebook*, vol. xxx, 2, 1976; private information; personal knowledge.] STANLEY WELLS

NICOLSON, (LIONEL) BENEDICT (1914–1978), art historian, was born 6 August 1914 in his grandfather's house, Knole in Kent, the elder son and elder child of (Sir) Harold George Nicolson, the diplomat author, and MP, and his wife, Victoria Mary ('Vita') Sackville-West, the poet, novelist, biographer, and gardener [qq.v.]. He was educated at Eton and Balliol College, Oxford, where he made lifelong friends like (Sir) Isaiah Berlin, (Sir) John Pope-Hennessy, and Philip Toynbee. With his deep interest in the arts, acquired during school holidays on visits to Italy, he helped to found the Florentine Club, an undergraduate society which enticed to Oxford speakers of the calibre of Kenneth (later Lord) Clark, Duncan Grant [q.v.], and Clive Bell, whose notice Nicolson later wrote for this Dictionary.

Nicolson had no formal education in art history, but on leaving Oxford in 1936 with a second class degree in modern history he travelled widely, visiting the art galleries and private collections of Europe and America, and spent several months at I Tatti, Florence, as the pupil of Bernard Berenson. In 1937 he was invited by Kenneth Clark (then director) to fill an unpaid post in the National Gallery, and worked there for some months before pursuing his studies at the Fogg Museum, Boston. On his return to London, Clark appointed him deputy surveyor of the King's pictures (Clark himself was surveyor till 1944) and he helped to catalogue the royal collection and find wartime refuges for its major works of art until he was called up. After serving in an anti-aircraft battery at Chatham, he obtained a commission in the Intelligence Corps.

Posted as an interpreter to camps for Italian prisoners of war, he was found to be too sympathetic to the young Italians to make a good gaoler, and was transferred to the Middle East in 1942 as an instructor in the interpretation of military air photographs. He was invalided home from Italy in March 1945 after a road accident which broke two bones in his spine.

He resumed his work as deputy surveyor, now under Anthony Blunt, organizing at Burlington House an exhibition of the paintings of Sir Thomas Lawrence [q.v.], and began to publish articles and introductions on a wide variety of artists like Modigliani, Vermeer, Cézanne, Seurat, and the painters of Ferrara. Never a natural courtier, he was perhaps relieved to resign his official functions in 1947 when he was invited, largely at the instigation of (Sir) Herbert Read [q.v.] and (Sir) Ellis Waterhouse, to edit the *Burlington Magazine*, which from then onwards became the central interest of his life. He remained editor until his death thirty-one years later.

The *Burlington* already had an international reputation as a scholarly journal of the history of the fine arts, but during the war years it had suffered in quality, esteem, financial viability, and bulk, and having no full-time editor, lacked an editorial policy. Nicolson soon changed all that. He was not a man who imposed his authority, being more diffident and slower witted than many of the formidable scholars whom he attracted to write for him or the museum administrators whose decisions he often challenged in his editorials. His strength lay in his gentleness. He was totally without guile. In a profession reputed to be malevolent, he appeared an innocent, and looked increasingly like an El Greco. His integrity was unquestioned. As an editor he was meticulous, setting a standard of accuracy by his own frequent contributions, and he attracted writers of distinction by his own distinction. Slowly he developed qualities of tact, humour, and self-confidence. He made the *Burlington* something entirely his own, in defiance of advice and sometimes of instruction from his editorial board, even cooking its minutes, it was said, to get his own way. Under his long editorship the *Burlington* became the most respected art journal in the English language, and probably in the world.

His interests ranged over the whole field of western painting except the most modern, for he preferred realism to abstract, but he did not pretend to an equivalent knowledge of other visual arts like architecture and furniture, which were allowed only a subordinate place in the magazine and on which he took careful advice. His major books indicate a sustained interest in paintings which made dramatic use of light, particularly candle-light, in the Caravaggesque tradition. The first (1958) was on the Dutch painter Hendrick Terbrugghen, the second (1968) on Joseph Wright of Derby, and the third (1974) on Georges de La Tour, which he wrote in collaboration with Christopher Wright. In between, he wrote two minor books, *The Treasures of the Foundling Hospital* (1972), and *Courbet: The Studio of the Painter* (1973). For many years before his death he had been working on lists of paintings by followers of Caravaggio, and the book was published posthumously (1979) under the title *The International Caravaggesque Movement*, with an introduction by Anthony Blunt.

Nicolson's style of writing, in which one could trace the influence of both his parents, was elegant and clear, and his research profound, but what distinguished his books and articles was his gift for evoking the social and historical background of the artists whom he admired, for example the early Industrial Revolution in *Joseph Wright of Derby*. 'The enemies of scholarship', he wrote in the foreword to his *Terbrugghen*, 'are tact and urbanity', and the gentleness of his nature was stiffened, when his professional talents were engaged, by a steely determination to discover and express the truth. His friends would often be startled by the candour with which he would expose a fake, whether a painting or a person. But seldom can a scholar who knew so much have confessed his ignorance so often.

His death on 22 May 1978 was very sudden. He collapsed with a massive stroke in a London underground station as he was returning from dining at his club. He was sixty-three.

He was appointed MVO in 1947 and CBE in 1971, and in 1977 was elected a fellow of the British Academy. In 1955 he married Luisa, daughter of Professor Giacomo Vertova of Florence, herself a distinguished art historian and a previous assistant to Berenson. There was a daughter of the marriage, which was dissolved in 1962.

A portrait of Nicolson by Rodrigo Moynihan is in the National Portrait Gallery, and the best photograph of him in later years, by Bern Schwarz, was published in the *Burlington Magazine* of July 1978.

[*Burlington Magazine* (particularly articles about Nicolson by Frances Haskell in the issues of April 1977 and July 1978); James Lees-Milne, *Harold Nicolson*, 2 vols., 1980 and 1981; Victoria Glendinning, *Vita Sackville-West*, 1983; Giles Roberton in *Proceedings* of the British Academy, vol. lxviii, 1982; private information; personal knowledge.]

NIGEL NICOLSON

NIEMEYER, SIR OTTO ERNST (1883–1971), civil servant and banker, was born in

Streatham, London, 23 November 1883, the eldest of three children and only son (another had died in infancy) of Ernst August Wilhelm Niemeyer, merchant of Hanover, who emigrated to Liverpool in England in 1870, moved to London in 1882, became a naturalized British subject, and married Ethel, the daughter of Roderick Rayner of J. H. Rayner & Co., Liverpool, West African merchants. He had a distinguished academic career at St. Paul's School and Balliol College, Oxford, and he remained a keen classicist throughout his life. He obtained first classes in both classical honour moderations (1904) and *literae humaniores* (1906). In 1906 he won first place in the Civil Service examination, beating J. M. (later Lord) Keynes [q.v.] into second and being immediately posted to the Treasury.

His progress was rapid. In 1922, at the age of thirty-nine, he was appointed controller of finance. The Treasury at that time was split into three departments, of which finance was one: the controller was directly responsible, as his principal adviser on all financial matters, to the chancellor of the Exchequer. The most important and controversial episode during Niemeyer's controllership was the return of sterling in 1925 to the gold standard, at the pre-war parity. The influence of Niemeyer and Montagu (later Lord) Norman [q.v.] in this matter was vital. (Sir) Winston Churchill, as chancellor, was no financial expert and on such matters relied heavily on Niemeyer: but, as a politician, he was far more sensitive than Niemeyer to the social effects of what was bound to be a deflationary policy. He was naturally inclined to favour Keynes's opposition to the majority view, which Niemeyer supported whole-heartedly, that a return to the gold standard was essential. Churchill reluctantly acquiesced in the decision and defended it brilliantly in Parliament; but, as the results became clearer, he resented what Norman and Niemeyer had persuaded him to do.

In 1927 Niemeyer resigned from the Treasury and joined the Bank of England, first as an adviser and then in 1938 as an executive director, one of the first two holders of this newly created position, which he held until he retired in 1952. His resignation at the age of forty-four, and nearly at the top of the official tree, caused surprise, but there were good reasons for it. Niemeyer had worked very closely with Norman, particularly on the international side of the Bank's business. When Norman asked him to come to the Bank and help to develop this side, he probably found the offer irresistible. Moreover, he may well have felt himself at a dead end in the Treasury. Sir N. F. Warren Fisher [q.v.], the permanent secretary, was only four years older and Niemeyer could not hope to succeed him. Fisher disliked the system of semi-independent controllers: if Niemeyer remained his wings were likely to be clipped. It was no coincidence that the premature resignations of Niemeyer and of Sir George Barstow [q.v.], the other remaining independent controller, were announced on the same day.

Niemeyer's work while at the Bank of England fell broadly into four categories. First, there was his work in the Bank itself, where his advice was greatly valued by Montagu Norman and the governors who succeeded him. On the outbreak of war he took an active part in dealing with the many new problems facing the Bank, and in the dark days of June 1940 he went to Ottawa to be ready in the event of a breakdown in communications.

Secondly he did much on behalf of the Bank for outside bodies in Britain. He took an active part in the 1930s in the Bank's efforts to assist various depressed industries, notably in forming the Agricultural Mortgage Corporation and the Lancashire Cotton Corporation. He also sat for many years on the capital issues committee, advising the Treasury on control of borrowing. Thirdly, a number of overseas countries invited him to make reports on their financial and economic problems. These included Australia in 1930 and India in 1936. In both cases his controversial proposals suggesting major cuts in public expenditure were largely accepted. Other less taxing missions during the 1930s to Brazil, Greece, Egypt, and Argentina were also successful. In 1941 he went to China at the request of General Chiang Kai-Shek to advise on the state of the economy and the use of foreign aid. Into the fourth category fell his work on two important international bodies, the financial committee of the League of Nations and the Bank for International Settlements. Many observers would rate his contribution to these as the outstanding achievement of his life.

In 1922 Niemeyer joined the financial committee of the League of Nations which played an important role in the economic reconstruction of the Central European, Baltic, and Balkan powers after World War I. On arrival at the Bank, Niemeyer became chairman of this committee and was deeply involved for ten years in the economic welfare of its client states, and also of their unfortunate bondholders. All the League loans defaulted after the crisis of 1931. As a member and later president of the council of foreign bondholders, Niemeyer was for many years an astute and effective protector of their interests. He became a director of the Bank for International Settlements in 1932, soon after its formation. He was chairman from 1937 until the beginning of the war and vice-chairman until 1964. Throughout this long period he went regularly with the governor to the monthly board meetings in Basle. He provided continuity at top level, enjoying the confidence of successive managements and supporting the Bank in waters which were sometimes rough, especially when the existence of the BIS was threatened during the Bretton Woods discussions.

Niemeyer combined to an unusual degree a first-class intellect with practical common sense and judgement. He had complete integrity, held strong views, particularly about sound money, and was not easily shaken. He could be an outspoken critic, but his criticisms were always softened by personal charm and an innate simplicity. His rare compliments were the more appreciated for their rarity. Montagu Norman, himself fastidious in dress and appearance, and a great admirer of Niemeyer, always teased him about his untidiness and unwillingness to 'smarten himself up'.

Niemeyer also took a lively interest in the worlds of education and mental health and, after retirement from the Bank, held several important directorships. He was appointed CB in 1921, KCB in 1924, and GBE in 1927. He became a fellow of the London School of Economics, of which he was chairman of governors (1941–57) and governor (1958–65).

He married in 1910 a distant cousin, Sophie Charlotte Benedicte, daughter of Landgerichtsrat Dr Theodor Niemeyer, of Hildesheim. They had three sons and one daughter. The second son was killed on active service in 1943. Niemeyer died 6 February 1971 at his home, Nash House, Lindfield, Sussex.

[*The Times*, 8 February 1971; private information; personal knowledge.] COBBOLD

NIMPTSCH, ULI (1897–1977), sculptor, was born in Berlin 22 May 1897, the younger son and second of four children of Siegfried Nimptsch, a broker on the Berlin stock exchange. He was a descendant of the distinguished German poet Nikolaus Nimptsch von Lenau. He studied sculpture at the Berlin Academy and was awarded a Rome prize in 1928. Rome was his base throughout the 1930s, although he visited Paris and returned to Germany in 1936–7. He lived in Bavaria but left Germany for the sake of his Jewish wife. He went to Paris and Rome again before settling in London in 1939. He arrived with no knowledge of English, but took British nationality after the war.

In Italy he had worked privately and there is no record of public exhibition. He is reported to have said that he studied his 'masters the Greeks and Romans'. He was always a modeller and not a carver, and several studies of the female nude survive from this period. The life model—usually young—was his preferred subject, and, despite working in Rome, it was the naturalistic style of Jules Dalou and Charles Despiau that was his example. His masterpiece from the 1930s was 'Marietta' (1936–8), a full-length standing nude with her hands over her head, a cast of which was acquired by the City Art Gallery, Leeds, in 1944 at the time of the exhibition arranged by (Sir) Philip Hendy [q.v.]. This life study of a young girl, in a restrained and self-contained pose, is typical of his work, except that it is life-size and not a small-scale study.

His wartime sculptures made in London were different, being small-scale high reliefs in bronze or lead, of narratives from the Bible or classical mythology. He returned, however, to life studies, and was not influenced by British sculpture. He exhibited comparatively rarely, with one-man exhibitions at the Redfern Gallery (1942) and at Leeds (1944), then at the Walker Art Gallery, Liverpool (1957), the Stone Gallery, Newcastle upon Tyne (1965), and finally at the Diploma Gallery of the Royal Academy (1973). Work was included in some of the Arts Council's outdoor sculpture exhibitions in the 1950s and 1960s. In 1951 'Girl Sitting on a Stone Plinth' was acquired for the Arts Council's collection and his best-known work, 'Olympia' (1956), a reclining nude lying full length, supported on an elbow and an arm, was acquired by the Tate Gallery (Chantrey Bequest) in the year that it was finished.

Portrait busts were commissioned of Paul Oppé (1949, British Museum Print Room), Sir Mortimer Wheeler (1969, British Academy), and Brendan (Viscount) Bracken (Bracken House) [qq.v.]. The over life-size Lloyd George (1961–3) for the House of Commons had been originally commissioned from Sir Jacob Epstein [q.v.], but after his death in 1959 it was awarded to Nimptsch. A group, 'The Good Samaritan' (1961), was commissioned by Selly Oak Hospital, Birmingham, and 'Neighbourly Encounter' (1961) by the London County Council for Silwood housing estate.

Nimptsch exhibited at the Royal Academy almost annually from 1957, and was elected ARA in 1958 and RA in 1967. He bequeathed ten of his sculptures to the Academy, along with the portrait of himself by Oskar Kokoschka [q.v.], who had been a friend in London. In Britain after the war his work as a life sculptor was unfashionable, but he persevered with the subject he most admired in work that is consistent over forty years. His best nude studies possess an admirable sense of the conflict between liveliness and restraint, and few other sculptors in Britain took on this subject with such seriousness or such a sense of decorum.

In 1925 he married Ruth Berthe (died 1974), the daughter of Max Steinthal, of Berlin, a director of the Deutsches Bank; there was one son. Nimptsch died 2 January 1977 in London.

[Exhibition catalogues of Walker Art Gallery, Liverpool, 1957, and Royal Academy of Arts, 1973; *The Times*, 6 January 1977; private information.] A. D. FRASER JENKINS

NKRUMAH, KWAME (1909–1972), first president of Ghana, was born in the village of Nkroful in the extreme south-west of the country. He believed that the most likely date of his birth was 18 September 1909. Being a male child born into the Akan tribe on a Saturday, he was called Kwame although baptized Francis Nwia Kofie, the priest recording the date of birth as 21 September, which is the date used officially. His mother, Nyaniban, a petty trader, whose only child he was, gave him a claim to two minor chieftaincies, those of Nsaeum and of Dadieo. His father was a goldsmith at Half Assini. At the age of six he went to the Roman Catholic school at Half Assini, where he later taught for a year before proceeding in 1926 to the Government Training College at Accra, moving in 1928 to Achimota when the colleges merged. In 1930 he became a teacher at the RC junior school at Elmina, moving in 1931 to become head teacher at the RC junior school, Axim. In 1933 he became first indigenous teacher at the RC seminary at Amissano.

In August 1935 he left the Gold Coast for the USA where he enrolled at Lincoln University, taking a BA in economics and sociology in 1939 and a B.Theology in 1942. He took masters degrees in education and philosophy at the University of Pennsylvania. For a while he lectured at Lincoln which conferred its honorary LL D degree on him in 1951. There he began to write his pamphlet *Towards Colonial Freedom* with its Marxist interpretation of colonialism. In later years he described himself as a non-denominational Christian and scientific Marxist, finding no conflict. While in America he realized the importance of organization and determined to master the technique. This he was able to exercise in London (May 1945–November 1947) as joint secretary of the organizing committee for the fifth Pan-African Congress, which was held in Manchester in October 1945, and as secretary of the West African National Secretariat, which aimed at the unification of all colonies in West Africa.

In August 1947 the inaugural meeting was held at Saltpond in the Gold Coast of a nationalist movement, the United Gold Coast Convention (UGCC), which needed to reconcile its leadership by the local intelligentsia with the mass of people. Nkrumah was invited to become general secretary on the basis of his political activities in the USA and Britain. He accepted, determined to turn the UGCC into a popular movement. Within six months of his return in December 1947 some 500 branches were established. He was fortunate in the time of his return as a whole array of discontents had accumulated. The final annoyance came when the government declined to act over the dispute with traders about the high prices of imported goods, which led to an organized boycott in January–February 1948, and ended with disturbances on 28 February. The Watson commission of inquiry into the disturbances was impressed by the need to give Africans a greater share in the formation and execution of policy and made recommendations with that object. In his evidence to the commission, Nkrumah agreed that he had adopted communist views, though he denied ever being a party member. He was already a star speaker of the UGCC, having charisma and qualities of leadership, and was obviously a man with a mission. He established an anti-chief committee on youth organization (CYO) composed of thoroughgoing opponents of the existing social order, which, on 12 June 1949, formed the Convention People's Party (CPP) with the motto 'We prefer self-government with danger to servitude in tranquillity' and its policy 'Seek ye first the political kingdom and all things shall be added unto you'. The motto turned out to be as apt as the policy hope was naïve. Nkrumah resigned from the UGCC, leaving a party of chiefs, merchants, and professional men which, in the movement to universal suffrage, was doomed.

In January 1950 the CPP called a general strike in order to coerce the government on constitutional reform. A state of emergency was declared and seven CPP leaders who had openly instigated the strike were imprisoned for calling an illegal strike, Nkrumah and one other being also found guilty of sedition. All were released after the general election of February 1950 when Nkrumah received 22,780 votes out of a possible 23,122 in Accra Central. The CPP won 33 out of the 38 seats elected by direct franchise. So it continued: in the 1954 election on the basis of universal adult suffrage and the abolition of the three ex-officio ministers, the CPP won 72 of the 104 seats while at the 1956 general election which had to precede the grant of independence, the CPP won 71 seats. There was never a viable alternative government. Nkrumah's rise to power was swift: in 1951 he was leader of government business, in 1952 prime minister, in 1957 prime minister of Ghana, and in 1960 president of the republic, when he assumed the title Osagyefo (redeemer). He had found the political kingdom, albeit with the help of the Watson commission and the more flexible policy of the British government after the Suez crisis.

When he had achieved his first mission, the independence of Ghana, he turned immediately to his second, the unity of Africa, which became an *idée fixe* with him. In April 1958 he convened a conference of eight independent African states and toured them in May and June. Already there was disappointment in his party, especially among ex-servicemen, and also among the Ga people of Accra, who formed the Ga Shifimo Kpee (Ga Standfast Organization) against the influx of other tribal people into their area. As a tribal organization, it was unlawful. It operated conspiratorially, threatening violence, including indiscriminate murder by bomb-throwing in Accra. The police were reluctant to prosecute as they wished to conceal their sources of information. Nkrumah allowed those suspected to be detained under the Preventive Detention Act of 1958 which was intended to be used only in an emergency and was not expected to be used against members of opposition parties. By the end of 1960 318 detention orders had been made, although 255 of them were made in 1960 after the Act had been extended at the request of the police to detain the new kind of gangster that had emerged. Of the 788 persons released after the *coup* of January 1966, approximately half were political and the rest criminal detainees. None was executed for a political offence. On his side, it was argued that with two attempted assassinations and the bomb-throwing, Nkrumah was justified in detaining suspects. Nevertheless, he received general condemnation in the world's press, which in turn made him frustrated and withdrawn. Much of the political unrest was due to the complete dominance of the CPP and its increasing corruption.

Nkrumah tried to call a halt to the corruption and high living of ministers and party officials by making a broadcast at dawn, the hour when a chief made an important pronouncement, on 18 April 1961. After the subsequent investigations, six ministers, including some of Nkrumah's oldest colleagues, were asked to resign and six others had to surrender specified properties. Nkrumah made enemies but did little to suppress corruption because it arose largely as a by-product of his economic policy. At independence, Ghana had a viable economy, a good balance of payments and strong foreign exchange reserves. It was heavily dependent on the price and quantity of its exports of cocoa for its foreign exchange receipts and Nkrumah determined to reduce this dependence by diversifying the economy despite the obvious shortages of skilled manpower both within and outside the Civil Service. His haste was not balanced by the good luck which had helped him when he sought the political kingdom. The world price of cocoa declined catastrophically while the introduction of the cedi unattached to any international currency led to the large-scale smuggling of cocoa, foodstuffs, and manufactures across the border by those intent on holding hard currency.

By 1965 it was clear that Ghana would be unable to repay its international short-term debts of some £155 million. Apparently unaware of the disillusionment with him, Nkrumah went to North Vietnam to seek a peaceful solution to the conflict there. On 24 February 1966 he was deposed by the army in a coup which had been planned long before. It had been felt that he was leaning too far towards the East, that the deprivation of liberties had gone too far, and that the economy was crumbling. Nkrumah went into exile in Conakry, Guinea, where he was welcomed as co-president by President Sekou Touré. He died 27 April 1972, in Bucharest, Rumania, while being treated for cancer of the skin. The government of General I. K. Acheampong persuaded Sekou Touré to allow his body to be buried at Nkroful. His widow, formerly Fathia Halen Ritz, of Egypt, whom he married in 1957, their son, and two daughters were invited to reside in Ghana at the government's expense. It was felt by 1972 that the mania of denigration had gone too far. It was thought that, had he permitted a fair and open general election in 1964 and avoided many of the excesses, he might well have survived. As it was, his positive legacy was considerable: he was the chief protagonist of Pan-Africanism, playing a leading role in the formation of the Organization for African Unity (OAU); he introduced free elementary education for the first time in Africa and a free basic medical service; he built a network of roads and constructed the Tema harbour; he brought the massive Volta river hydro-electric project to completion, and did much besides. However, all was not well with Ghana politically, socially, and economically after 1960 and the Osagyefo had to pay the price of disillusion and failure.

Nkrumah was admitted to the Privy Council in 1959 and won the Lenin peace prize in 1962. He also received honorary doctorates.

[*The Autobiography of Kwame Nkrumah*, 1957; Geoffrey Bing, *Reap the Whirlwind*, 1968; D. J. Morgan, *The Official History of Colonial Development* (5 vols.), 1980; private information.] D. J. MORGAN

NORFOLK, DUKE OF (1908–1975), Earl Marshal and Hereditary Marshal of England. [See HOWARD, BERNARD MARMADUKE FITZALAN-.]

NORRISH, RONALD GEORGE WREYFORD (1897–1978), physical chemist and Nobel prize-winner, was born at Cambridge 9 November 1897, the elder son (there were no daughters) of Herbert Norrish, pharmacist, and his wife, Amy Norris, from the Isle of Wight. After periods of residence in the Isle of Wight and Oxford, Herbert Norrish settled in Cambridge. His wife died in 1905 and in 1908 he married Susan Duff. In 1908 Ronald Norrish won a scholarship to the Perse School, Cambridge, where he was encouraged successively by two able chemistry teachers to develop his natural inclination to that subject. His father, recognizing his son's talent for experimental chemistry, allowed him to set up a small laboratory in the garden shed of the family home in Panton Street. The apparatus can be seen in the Science Museum at South Kensington.

In 1915 Norrish was awarded a foundation scholarship to Emmanuel College, Cambridge, but did not begin his studies until four years later after war service in the Royal Field Artillery and six months as a prisoner of war. His undergraduate studies, from which he gained a first class in both parts of the natural sciences tripos (1920 and 1921) were compressed into two years, after which he began research under the supervision of (Sir) E. K. Rideal [q.v.]. Apart from brief visits overseas, all Norrish's life was spent in Cambridge and its university and Emmanuel College shared pride of place in his loyalty and affection. In 1924 he obtained his Ph.D. degree and was elected a research fellow of his college. In 1926 he became university demonstrator in the physical chemistry department. Two years later he was promoted to H. O. Jones lecturer. In 1936 he was elected FRS and awarded the Sc.D. degree. The following year he was appointed professor and head of department and elected by his college to a professorial fellowship, a post he held until his retirement in 1965.

When he secured his first university post he felt financially justified in marrying in 1921 Anne, daughter of Albert E. Smith, of Heaton Mersey, near Manchester, departmental manager in a cotton mill in Stockport. Then a lecturer in child psychology at University College, Cardiff, she never lost her Mancunian common sense and was not in the least overawed by her distinguished and argumentative husband. Shortly after the birth of their twin daughters, the Norrishes moved from 48 Kimberley Road to a handsome semi-detached house at 7 Park Terrace, the back garden of which abutted on to Emmanuel College. Both house and garden were big enough to accommodate the large parties Norrish delighted to give to colleagues and visitors.

Norrish was one of the founders of modern photochemistry and also made significant advances in the field of chain reactions, especially those exemplified by combustion and addition polymerization processes. His forte was not in theory, where his understanding was often rudimentary, but in his quite remarkable, almost intuitive, flair and 'feel' for the way molecules might react and then for devising and executing, with great precision and reliability, experiments the results of which would conclusively establish (or demolish) the reaction mechanisms under consideration. His first work in classical photochemistry, which attracted international attention, was his demonstration that the decomposition of nitrogen dioxide did not begin until the wavelength of the incident light reached a value at which fluorescence ceased which was also the point at which the absorption spectrum ceased to show fine structure. This was followed by equally important work on the photodecomposition of compounds containing the carbonyl group (e.g., aldehydes, ketones, esters, ketenes, and amides) and on the photocombination of hydrogen with chlorine. The main conclusions of this work have not been falsified by later investigations. His major innovation, with (Sir) George Porter, for which he won a share of the Nobel prize for chemistry in 1967 (announced two days before his seventieth birthday) was flash photolysis. In this method a very brief flash of intense light is used to cause photochemical change and immediately after the flash the absorption spectrum of the unstable, short-lived, intermediate species (excited states or free radicals) thereby formed can be measured and used to identify the intermediates and the reactions they subsequently and very quickly undergo. Without doubt this technique has proved to be the most powerful in discerning the nature of the primary photochemical act in fluid systems. The last two decades of Norrish's scientific life was spent in exploiting this new method.

Norrish was of medium height and strong physique, always neatly dressed and with a carefully trimmed military moustache. In sport and in work he was combative and competitive, being much more impressed by a good experimental result than by closely reasoned argument. He was a doer rather than a thinker. He had fierce loyalties to his town, university, and college. He worked hard and drove his students equally hard. In later years when he had given up tennis and squash his major pleasure was in post-prandial conversation in college or the Savage Club. He had little sympathy with administrators and was not a good one himself.

He received honorary doctorates from the Sorbonne (1958), and Lancaster (1968), Leeds (1965), Liverpool (1968), Sheffield (1965), and British Columbia (1969) universities. He received the Meldola medal of the Institute of Chemistry (1928), the Davy medal of the Royal Society (1958), the Liversidge medal of the Chemical Society (1958), the Lewis gold medal of the Combustion Institute (1964), and the

Faraday (1965) and Longstaff (1969) medals of the Chemical Society. He was the Bakerian lecturer of the Royal Society (1966). He was elected honorary FRSE, honorary member of the Polish Chemical Society, the Polish Academy of Sciences, the Göttingen Academy of Science, the Royal Society of Science of Liège, the Royal Society of Sciences in Uppsala, the New York Academy of Science, the Bulgarian Academy of Sciences, the Belgian Academy of Sciences, and the Société de Chimie Physique. In 1974 he was awarded the Knight's Cross of the Order of Polonia Restituta and the Order of Cyril and Methodius of Bulgaria. He died in Cambridge 7 June 1978.

[Sir Frederick Dainton and B. A. Thrush in *Biographical Memoirs of Fellows of the Royal Society*, vol. xxvii, 1981; personal knowledge.

FREDERICK DAINTON

NYHOLM, SIR RONALD SYDNEY (1917–1971), professor of chemistry, was born 29 January 1917 in Broken Hill, New South Wales, Australia, the fourth child in the family of four sons and two daughters of Eric Edward Nyholm, railwayman, of Adelaide, and his wife, Gertrude Mary Woods. After Broken Hill High School, he entered the University of Sydney, graduating in 1938 with first class honours in science. He then joined the Ever Ready Battery Company as a research chemist.

In 1940 he was appointed to his first academic post, in Sydney Technical College. There he spent the war years until, in 1947, he sailed from Sydney to join (Sir) C. K. Ingold [q.v.] at University College London, in the department of chemistry. Nyholm was first an Imperial Chemical Industries fellow, and was later appointed to a lectureship. He gained a London Ph.D. in 1950 and D.Sc. in 1953 (he had received a Sydney M.Sc. in 1942). He left the college in 1951 to become associate professor in inorganic chemistry in the University of New South Wales in 1952. In 1955 he returned to a chair of inorganic chemistry at University College, a post which he occupied with distinction until his death. From 1963 he was head of the department of chemistry.

Nyholm's contributions to inorganic chemistry were in the stabilization of new or unusual valence states, in stereochemistry, and in magnetochemistry. With Francis P. J. Dwyer (1900–1952) he prepared the first properly characterized complex of the metal rhodium in its quadrivalent state and later made complexes of trivalent nickel and of quadrivalent nickel and iron. In his inaugural address at University College entitled *The Renaissance of Inorganic Chemistry* (H. K. Lewis & Co., London, 1956), he spoke of inorganic chemistry growing from 'a collection of largely unconnected facts' into 'the integrated study of the formation, composition, structure and reactions of the chemical elements and their compounds, excepting most of those of carbon'. In his work on stereochemistry, especially with Professor Ronald Gillespie, he aimed to systematize understanding of the spatial arrangement of inorganic molecules. Many see their work as a lasting advance. His studies of the complexes of the transition metals, particularly nickel and iron, were notable for his use of physical methods, especially magnetic susceptibility, in investigating molecular structure and bond type.

New thinking in the 1950s and 1960s about chemical education in schools and universities roused Nyholm's enthusiasm. He was the first chairman of the Nuffield Foundation chemistry consultative committee, and oversaw the creation of the Nuffield O-level chemistry materials. His sympathy with teachers, personal warmth, and ability to convince were a powerful combination. The establishment of a new British journal, *Education in Chemistry*, owed much to his persuasive skills.

Nyholm was a member of the chemistry committee of the Department of Scientific and Industrial Research in 1961–4, its chairman in 1964–7, and a member of the Science Research Council from 1967 to 1971. He was Corday-Morgan medallist (1950), Tilden lecturer (1960), and Liversidge lecturer (1967)—all of the Chemical Society, and president in 1968–70. In that office he saw to completion the amalgamation, long in the making, of the Chemical Society, Faraday Society, Royal Institute of Chemistry, and the Society for Analytical Chemistry. He was elected FRS in 1958, and corresponding member of the Finnish Chemical Society (1959). The Italian Chemical Society (1968) and the University of Bologna (1969) bestowed honours on him. He held honorary doctorates of the University of East Anglia (1968), the City University (1968), and the University of New South Wales (1969). He was knighted in 1967.

Nyholm's success both in scientific research and in public science reflected high qualities of personality coupled to technical flair. In his address at Nyholm's memorial service Lord Annan, provost of University College, said: 'Ron Nyholm was a life enhancer. There are great scientists, and I do not think the worse of them, who are silent, retiring, cool and judicious. Nyholm was not one of them. Wherever he was, he raised the temperature. But he raised it, not with pugnacious self-assertiveness but with bonhomie, good sense, and enthusiasm.'

Nyholm was a cricket devotee, with precise

recall of score-cards and events, especially from the era of Sir Donald Bradman. He was himself a competent and spirited performer on the field. In 1948 he married Maureen, daughter of Norman Richard Richardson, merchant, of Sydney. There were one son and two daughters. Nyholm died in a motor-car accident on the outskirts of Cambridge 4 December 1971.

[D. P. Craig in *Biographical Memoirs of Fellows of the Royal Society*, vol. xviii, 1972; family information; personal knowledge.]

DAVID CRAIG

O

O'BRIEN, KATE (1897–1974), novelist, playwright, and critic, was born 3 December 1897 in Limerick, Ireland, the fourth daughter and sixth of the nine children of Thomas O'Brien, horse dealer, of Boru House, Limerick, county Limerick, and his wife, Catherine Thornhill. Her mother died when she was five and a half and she was sent to Laurel Hill Convent, Limerick, where her three elder sisters were boarders. Here she spent twelve happy years as a serious and hard-working schoolgirl, enjoying her school holidays as a member of a large and lively family. In 1916 she went to University College, Dublin, and after getting her degree went to England and worked for a time in the foreign languages department of the *Manchester Guardian*. She then went to London, and taught for a short time at a convent school in Hampstead. After a visit to the USA as secretary to Stephen O'Mara, her brother-in-law, she spent a year in Bilbao, Spain, as a governess. This was her first introduction to Spain, a country she was to love and revisit for the rest of her life. In 1923 she returned to England and married a Dutch journalist, Gustaaf Renier. The marriage only lasted a few months and they separated.

Living in Bloomsbury and writing in her spare time (she was working as a secretary) she had a remarkable success with her first play, *Distinguished Villa*, in 1926. From then on she contributed articles and stories to various periodicals, and in 1931 her first novel *Without My Cloak* was published on her thirty-fourth birthday. This was a chronicle of Irish bourgeois life, set in Mellick (her native city Limerick). It was awarded the Hawthornden prize and the James Tait Black memorial prize (1931). Her second book, *The Ante-Room* (1934) was again set in the same milieu, but was on a much smaller scale, and in this sombre and tragic novel she wrote of the conflict between the Catholic conscience and the demands of love, a theme which recurs in many of her novels.

From this time on she distinguished herself as a novelist, writing one book about every two years, and as a critic. Her fine novel of convent life, *The Land of Spices* (1941), was banned in Ireland by the censorship board. In 1946 *That Lady* was published. This novel, set in the Spain of Philip II, was immediately recognized as a major work. The critic Naomi Royde-Smith wrote of it: 'The whole book with its passion, its humour, its sense of history and its remarkable piece of special pleading for the lost soul of Philip II, is not only the finest novel its author has so far given us, it is one of the finest historical novels in any European language.'

At intervals during the years she wrote plays, sometimes dramatizations of her novels, and in 1949 visited New York as the guest of Katharine Cornell and Guthrie McClintic to dramatize *That Lady*. The play was not a success, and on the whole her dramatic work never received recognition.

She was an individual and enthusiastic traveller in Spain throughout the years, and in the 1960s visited Russia and Italy as representative of Irish letters on the council of Comes, the Comunita Europea degli Scrittori. In 1947 she was elected fellow of the Royal Society of Literature, and to the Irish Academy of Letters.

After the war she decided she would like to 'die in Ireland', and bought a house in the beautiful village of Roundstone in county Galway. The years there were very happy, but finally she felt she was too far away from many of her friends, and she returned to England. For the last ten years of her life she lived in a charming little house in the village of Boughton in Kent. She had always loved English village life and had written her first novel in a village in Kent.

As a young woman she was very beautiful—thin and ethereal. In later life she became heavier and her appearance took on a noble classic look. As she matured she became more extrovert and dynamic, most entertaining and lively. She had a very strong critical faculty and was aware of, and admired, much of the work produced by younger authors.

After her death F. S. L. Lyons wrote in the *Irish Times*, 'Outwardly she could be rather gruff and mannish—she often wore the suits and severe white blouse which were her generation's gesture against male chauvinist pigs—but underneath she was all perception, delicacy, compassion.' Kate O'Brien died in Canterbury 13 August 1974.

['Half Forgotten' (unpublished fragment of autobiography by Kate O'Brien); *The Times* and *Irish Times*, 14 August 1974; private information; personal knowledge.] MARY O'NEILL

OGG, SIR WILLIAM GAMMIE (1891–1979), soil scientist and farmer, was born 2 November 1891 at Craigbank Farm, Cults, Peterculter in the county of Aberdeen, the only child of James Ogg and his wife, Janet Gammie, whose families had farmed in Aberdeenshire for generations. Ogg's father died within a few months of his birth, leaving his widowed mother and her sister to continue running Craigbank Farm and to bring up the young Ogg. He was educated at Robert Gordon's College, Aberdeen, and at the University of Aberdeen where he was awarded the degrees of MA, B.Sc.(Agr.), and B.Sc. in 1912, 1913, and 1914 respectively.

After graduating Ogg was appointed a research assistant in soil science in the agricultural chemistry department of Aberdeen University by Professor James Hendrick, but was almost immediately recruited for war service in explosives factories, at Oldbury and at Greetland, Yorkshire. At the end of the war, he accepted a research fellowship from the Board of Agriculture for Scotland which enabled him to travel to the United States and Canada in 1919–20, where he became interested in soil classification and the techniques of soil survey propounded by the Russian soil scientist Glinka. He returned briefly to Aberdeen to work on a survey of Scottish soils in 1920, but soon moved to Cambridge where he spent four years as a postgraduate student at Christ's College.

Ogg returned to Scotland in 1924 to an appointment as government advisory officer in soils based on the Edinburgh and East of Scotland College of Agriculture. He was awarded his Cambridge Ph.D. (1925) for research on pectins. In 1930 he was offered the post of founding director of the newly established Macaulay Institute of Soil Research at Craigiebuckler, Aberdeen, and immediately set about recruiting promising young research staff and shaping the scientific programme of the Institute. The soil analysis and interpretation services of the North of Scotland College were transferred there, and research on soil fertility, soil survey, pedology, mineralogy, organic soils, soil acidity, and the reclamation of peat moorland was quickly set in train. In 1935 Ogg established a spectrochemistry department, having correctly perceived that the novel spectrographic methods for analysing soils and plants would greatly improve the scientist's knowledge of the chemical properties and composition of these materials, and also aid in advisory work on fertilizing and manuring. The Macaulay Institute soon achieved, and continued to enjoy, an international reputation for its analytical facilities and its research on trace elements and the molecular structure of soil minerals.

When Sir E. John Russell [q.v.] retired as director of the prestigious Rothamsted Experimental Station in 1943, Ogg was invited to succeed him. He accepted, apparently with some reluctance, but remained honorary director of the Macaulay until 1945, whereupon he became a member of its council of management and remained so until his death. At Rothamsted there were many new challenges to meet at a time when British agriculture was struggling to come to terms with the upheavals of the war years and the attendant food shortages. During Ogg's directorship (1943–58) the number of staff increased from 140 to 471 and three new departments—biochemistry, nematology, and pedology—were formed. In 1946 the headquarters of the Soil Survey of England and Wales were transferred to Rothamsted and Ogg served as chairman of the Agricultural Research Council's Soil Survey Research Board from 1950 to 1965. His other responsibilities included those of director of Woburn Experimental Station, consultant director of the Imperial Bureau of Soil Science (subsequently the Commonwealth Bureau of Soils), and secretary of the Lawes Agricultural Trust committee. He served as president of the Society of Chemical Industry for two years (1953–5) and participated in many overseas visits and tours as a lecturer.

In 1925 Ogg was elected to the Royal Society of Edinburgh and became one of its senior fellows. He was knighted for his services to agriculture in 1949 and awarded an honorary LL D by the University of Aberdeen in 1951. He received many other honours and awards during his career. He was chairman of the governors of the North of Scotland College of Agriculture from 1958 to 1968 and in 1975 was elected one of the first honorary fellows of the Macaulay Institute.

Following his retirement in 1958, Ogg returned to Scotland where he farmed in partnership with his son Douglas at Arnhall near Edzell, Angus. Ogg is remembered as a self-reliant man, of strong character, who was not only a perceptive judge of people but also a scientist and administrator with a sound sense of practicalities. These attributes stood him in good stead in the important tasks he had of founding an international centre for soil research in Scotland, and of expanding agricultural research at Rothamsted during a crucial stage in its history.

In 1922 he married Helen, younger daughter of Henry Hilbert, of Halifax. One son and one daughter were born of the marriage. Ogg died at Arnhall, near Edgell, 25 September 1979, after a fall in the garden of his home.

[R. L. Mitchell in *Year Book* of the Royal Society of Edinburgh, 1980; *Chemistry and Industry*, 18 July 1953; *Profile 39*, Macaulay Institute for Soil Research, 1979; reports of Rothamsted Experimental Station; private information.]
ROBERT E. WHITE

OLIVER, SIR GEOFFREY NIGEL (1898–1980), admiral, was born in London 22 January 1898, the eldest of the two sons and three children of Francis Wall Oliver (1864–1951, q.v.), a distinguished palaeobotanist and ecologist who held the Quain chair in botany at London University in succession to his father and was a fellow of the Royal Society, and his wife, Mildred Alice, daughter of Charles Robert Thompson, a surgeon who advanced the technique of the trepanning operation.

Oliver was educated at a preparatory school in Dorset and at Rugby School, from which he entered the navy as a 'special entry' cadet in 1915. His first ships were the famous but then elderly battleship *Dreadnought* and the new battle cruiser *Renown*, both of which took part in World War I but in which Oliver saw no actual fighting.

After that war Oliver, in common with all officers whose education had been cut short, went to Cambridge University for two terms but did not take a degree. Courses for the rank of lieutenant followed, in which he obtained first class certificates in all five subjects and won the Goodenough medal for the best results in the gunnery examination. In 1921 he was selected to specialize in that subject and did brilliantly in both the technical and theoretical sections of the course. He was placed first of his class and awarded the Commander Egerton prize. In 1924 he joined the experimental department of HMS *Excellent*, the navy's premier gunnery school at Portsmouth.

In 1925–7 Oliver served as gunnery officer of the light cruiser *Carlisle* on the China station, after which he was reappointed to the *Excellent*'s experimental department in a higher capacity. His next ship (1930) was the fairly new battleship *Rodney* in which he attracted the attention of Captain A. B. Cunningham (later Viscount Cunningham of Hyndhope, q.v.). He received money awards from the Admiralty for improvements to the ship's armaments, and was promoted commander in January 1932. In that rank he returned to the *Excellent* as head of the experimental department for two years, after which he was selected for command of destroyers and from 1934 to 1936 served in ships of that class on the China and Mediterranean stations. He was next appointed to the *Excellent* for the fourth time but as the executive officer and second-in-command of the establishment. In June 1937 he was promoted captain at the early age of thirty-nine, and for the first year of World War II he served on the naval staff's tactical and training and staff duties divisions.

Late in 1940 Oliver took command of the new light cruiser *Hermione*, in which he took part in the *Bismarck* operation (May 1941) and in Malta convoys. The latter brought him the first of his three gazettes as companion of the DSO. He then took his ship round the Cape of Good Hope to join the Mediterranean Fleet, playing a part in the capture of Madagascar (May 1942) on the way. On 16 June the *Hermione*, which had just taken part in the last and abortive attempt to supply Malta from the east, was torpedoed and sunk off Tobruk by U-205; but Oliver was among the survivors and stayed on the station, initially for liaison duties with the army.

Oliver was next selected for the important but shore-based post of director of naval ordnance; but Admiral Cunningham, who was to be allied naval commander-in-chief for the invasion of North Africa, got the appointment cancelled and put him in charge of the enormous number of small craft then assembling at Gibraltar for the attacks on Algiers and Oran (November 1942). After the initial assaults had succeeded Oliver played an important part in the naval side of the operations for the clearance of the Germans from North Africa by developing an advanced base at Bône and in the capture of the key port of Bizerta in Tunisia (7 May 1943). For these services he received a bar to his DSO and the American Legion of Merit. He then took command of the inshore squadron which was to support the army's invasion of Sicily (10 July 1943). The next major operation was the invasion of the Italian mainland, and for the landings at Salerno (September 1943) Oliver was appointed naval commander of the British assault force in the rank of commodore 1st class. In that capacity he was instrumental in getting cancelled the plan proposed by the American General Mark Clark, the commander of the whole Fifth Army, to withdraw the American assault force, which had run into serious difficulties, and re-land it in the British sector or to transfer the British force to the American sector—which Oliver realized would be a recipe for disaster. For his part in this critical operation Oliver was appointed CB (1944).

For the invasion of Normandy (June 1944) Oliver was given command of one of the three British naval assault forces, and the success he achieved brought him a third bar to his DSO. He was next given command of a squadron of escort carriers which took part in the liberation and relief of Greece and then transferred to the Eastern Fleet in time to join in the recapture of Rangoon (May 1945). He was promoted rear-admiral in the following July.

In 1946 Oliver was appointed admiral (air) and hoisted his flag at the naval air station of Lee-on-Solent. Later that year he returned to the Admiralty as assistant chief of naval staff, which then carried membership of the board. In 1948 he became president of the Royal Naval College, Greenwich, where he was promoted vice-admiral in 1949. In 1950–2 he was commander-in-chief, East Indies. He was created KCB in 1951 and was promoted admiral in the following year. He had not expected further employment but an unexpected vacancy for the important post of commander-in-chief, the Nore, brought him his final appointment in 1953–5. On retiring in 1955 he was created GBE and took up farming in Sussex.

Oliver was not only a man of outstanding integrity and inviolable modesty but that very rare officer in any fighting service, having not only a first-class technical brain but also great gifts of leadership in war. In 1933 he married Barbara, daughter of Sir Francis Adolphus Jones, KBE, legal adviser to the Board of Agriculture. They had two sons and a daughter; but the younger son died while a child and the daughter was lost in a bathing accident while on holiday on the east coast. Oliver died at Henfield, Sussex, 26 May 1980.

[Stephen W. Roskill, *The War at Sea 1939–1945*, 4 vols., 1954–61; Andrew B. Cunningham, *A Sailor's Odyssey*, 1951; memoir in the *Naval Review*, vol. lxix, No. 1, January 1981; *The Times* 28 and 31 May 1980; personal knowledge and correspondence.]

STEPHEN W. ROSKILL

OLIVIER, GIORGIO BORG (GEORGE) (1911–1980), prime minister of Malta, was born 5 July 1911 in Valletta, the youngest of seven sons (there was subsequently one daughter) of Oliviero Borg Olivier, architect and civil engineer, and his wife Rosa Amato, both of Malta. He was educated at the Lyceum and at the Royal University of Malta, gaining his LL D in 1937 and establishing himself as a notary public in 1938.

As a student leader and staunch nationalist he could not fail to be interested in the dramatic developments of the 1930s. The 1921 constitution was suspended in 1930, the year Borg Olivier entered the university, restored in 1932, suspended in 1933, and revoked altogether in 1936—the broad issue being whether Maltese internal politics should be dominated at the time of Mussolini's rise to power by a pro-Italian (Nationalist) or a pro-British (Constitutional) party. It was not surprising then that barely two years after graduating Borg Olivier should be elected in 1939 to the newly formed Council of Government. With the internment of the most prominent Nationalists on account of their Italian sympathies, leadership of the remaining group fell on Borg Olivier's shoulders. After the war at first he became deputy leader (from 1947 with a seat in the new Legislative Assembly) and in 1950 he became minister of works and reconstruction as well as minister of education. On the death of Enrico Mizzi in December 1950 he entered on his first period as prime minister of a coalition government.

He fought elections in 1951 and 1953 and headed coalition governments until he was defeated by Dominic Mintoff in 1955. During this period he proposed dominion status for Malta. This was unacceptable at the time to the British government because of Malta's strategic importance and its financial dependence. He subsequently opposed Mintoff's concept of integration with Britain which was the subject of the Round Table conference of 1955 and of the ensuing referendum which was boycotted by the Nationalist Party. Of those voting, 76 per cent (but only 44 per cent of the electorate) approved integration. In the event implementation of Mintoff's proposal broke down over financial issues and both Borg Olivier and Mintoff called separately for independence. In 1958 Mintoff resigned, Borg Olivier refused to take over, disturbances broke out, and the constitution was suspended for the third time in 1959.

On the restoration of ministerial government in 1962 Borg Olivier's return to power was indirectly due, or so said his opponents, to the dispute between the Malta Labour Party and the Catholic Church. On 20 August he again pressed for independence. Following the inconclusive Malta independence conference and further talks in London he eventually produced a constitution which was approved by 54.5 per cent of the electorate voting in a referendum of February 1964, although it was still opposed by Mintoff and the Malta Labour Party. On 21 July 1964 the British House of Commons was told that negotiations had been finally completed and Malta's constitution settled for the time at least.

On 21 September 1964 Malta became independent within the Commonwealth and Borg Olivier at the peak of his career received the constitutional documents from the Duke of Edinburgh at the traditional midnight ceremony. At the same time he signed a defence agreement providing for British and NATO forces to remain in Malta for a period of ten years and a finance agreement providing £50 million for diversification of the economy against the eventual withdrawal of British forces and £1 million for restoration of historic buildings.

In the general election of 1966, while the church was still involved in a politico-religious dispute with the Malta Labour Party, he was again successful at the polls and held power until the narrow defeat of the Nationalists in 1971. In 1974 when Malta was declared a republic Borg Olivier was one of the few to vote against it in parliament because he insisted that the constitutional changes should be endorsed by the electorate. He remained leader of the opposition until 1976 when in failing health he relinquished the leadership of the party but retained his seat in Parliament. He had been an active member of the Council of Government or of Parliament for over forty years and had held every important ministerial portfolio.

Brought up in a strongly pro-Italian tradition and culture, he yet became a consistent Commonwealth supporter and an admirer of Britain and of the monarchy. These two disparate influences came into harmony when he sought a place for Malta in the European Community—an ambition which he never saw realized. He was a European through and through and saw no future for Malta in the Arab world.

He was said to be indecisive but he was patient in resolving difficulties. He was criticized for his lack of dynamic ability but during his period in office the economy was transformed by the development of a tourist industry and by the introduction of light industry to offset the run-down of the dockyard and of British forces. He was a shrewd political operator but he was always consistent and showed considerable moral courage. He was a tough, patient, and at times exasperating opponent in negotiation, refusing to compromise on issues of importance to his people or his party whether these were political, economic, or financial. Broadminded, cultured, courteous to his opponents and loyal to his colleagues, he was a devout Catholic and a family man.

In 1943 he married Alexandra, daughter of Alfred Mattei, business administrator. They had two sons and a daughter. He died at his home in Sliema 29 October 1980.

[Personal knowledge.] MAURICE DORMAN

ONSLOW, SIR RICHARD GEORGE (1904–1975), admiral, was born at Garmston, Shropshire, 15 April 1904, the second child and eldest son in the family of four sons and four daughters of Major George Arthur Onslow, farmer, and his first wife, Charlotte Riou, daughter of the Revd Riou George Benson. He came of a family which had provided the Royal Navy with many distinguished officers since the late eighteenth century. Destroyers which took part in both world wars bore his family's name. He joined the navy as a cadet in 1918 and was educated at the Royal Naval Colleges of Osborne and Dartmouth.

After two years as midshipman in the battleship *Warspite* he underwent the usual courses for the rank of lieutenant, in which he obtained first-class certificates in all five subjects; but contrary to the practice of most officers who achieved that distinction he declined to specialize in a technical branch and decided to make his career in destroyers. After serving a successful apprenticeship in a number of ships of that class he obtained his first command at an early age and quickly proved a fine leader and a superb ship handler. He was promoted commander when in command of the destroyer *Gypsy* in 1938 and then served two years in the plans division of the naval staff—punctuated by an adventurous but unsuccessful journey to Bordeaux on the fall of France in 1940 to try and rescue the Belgian government and its gold reserves, a trip in which Onslow narrowly escaped being taken prisoner by the Germans.

In May 1941 Onslow took command of the Tribal class destroyer *Ashanti*, in which he took part in some of the most arduous Arctic and Malta convoys. His service in the former brought him appointment as a companion of the DSO (1942) as well as the Soviet Order of the Red Banner; while the part he played in later convoy operations in the same theatres, including the 'Pedestal' convoy to Malta which saved the besieged island (August 1942), brought him two bars to his DSO. Perhaps his most famous exploit was his attempt to tow a very badly damaged sister ship 700 miles to safety through stormy Arctic waters.

In 1944 Onslow was promoted captain (D) and given command of a destroyer flotilla which joined the Eastern Fleet as part of the reinforcements being sent out to take the offensive against Japan. For his part in the attack on Sabang, Sumatra (25 July 1944), he received a third bar to his DSO. He then took his flotilla to join the British Pacific Fleet and played a distinguished part in all that fleet's operations during the final stage of the war against Japan.

After the war Onslow first took the Imperial Defence College course in 1946 and the following year became naval officer in charge, Londonderry, and director of the Joint Anti-Submarine School, after which he returned to 1947 to the naval staff as director of the tactics and staff duties division. His next sea appointment (1951) was in command of the cadet training cruiser *Devonshire*—in which one of his sons was undergoing training. He was promoted rear-admiral in July 1952 and became naval secretary to the first lord of the Admiralty J. P. L. Thomas (later Viscount Cilcennin, q.v.), after which he hoisted his flag afloat as flag officer (flotillas) and second-in-command of the Home Fleet (1955–6). He was promoted vice-admiral while holding that appointment and at the end of the usual term he was given command of the Reserve Fleet (1956–7). In 1958 he was promoted admiral and hoisted his flag as commander-in-chief, Plymouth. While holding that appointment an unexpected vacancy occurred in the command of the Mediterranean Fleet and it was offered to Onslow. Despite the fact that to hold that key appointment might have led to him becoming first sea lord he tactfully declined it—possibly because the rigours of his war service had begun to take toll of his health. In 1958 he was appointed KCB (having been created CB in 1954) and retired two years later, returning to the county where his family's roots spread so deeply. He was appointed deputy lieutenant of Shropshire in 1960 and gave much time to local and naval charitable organizations.

The outstanding feature of Onslow's career was the profound respect and affection which he inspired in the officers and men of all the ships which he commanded. Under the most taxing circumstances he invariably showed the greatest gift of leadership, as well as a sense of humour which made him one of the best-loved officers of his generation. In 1932 he married Kathleen Meriel, daughter of Edmund Coston Taylor, cotton merchant, of Longnor Bank House, Shrewsbury. They had two sons. Onslow died at Dorrington, Shropshire, 16 December 1975.

[Stephen W. Roskill, *The War at Sea 1939–1945*, 4 vols., 1954–61; memoir in the *Naval Review*, vol. lxviii, No. 2, April 1980; Admiralty records; *The Times*, 18 December 1975; personal knowledge and correspondence.]

STEPHEN W. ROSKILL

ORR, JOHN BOYD, BARON BOYD ORR (1880–1971), nutritional physiologist and Nobel peace prize-winner, was born 23 September 1880 at Kilmaurs, Ayrshire, the middle child in the family of seven (a sister and two brothers were older and two brothers and a sister younger) of Robert Clark Orr, a quarry owner, and his wife, Annie Boyd, daughter of a quarry master. He was educated first at the local school in West Kilbride and, after winning a bursary, at Kilmarnock Academy. He returned to West Kilbride as a pupil teacher and in 1899 won a Queen's scholarship to enable him to train in Glasgow as a teacher, graduating MA in 1902. After teaching for three years he had saved sufficient to enable him to re-enter Glasgow University where he graduated B.Sc. in 1910 and MB, Ch.B. in 1912. He then received a Carnegie research fellowship to enable him to work with E. P. Cathcart [q.v.], head of physiological chemistry in the Institute of Physiology at Glasgow University. He graduated MD with honours in 1914, being awarded the Bellahouston gold medal for his thesis.

With funds from the development commissioners, a joint committee of the University of Aberdeen and the North of Scotland College of Agriculture planned to establish an 'Institute of Nutrition' at Aberdeen and invited Cathcart to direct it. Cathcart, who wished Orr to accompany him, did not accept the invitation for he was appointed to a chair of physiology in London. Orr was appointed by the joint committee in his place. Orr began work in Aberdeen in 1913 and commenced building new laboratories on a limited scale before war broke out.

During World War I Orr was first attached to the Royal Army Medical Corps and was later medical officer to the 1st battalion, Sherwood Foresters. He was at the battle of the Somme in 1916 where he won the MC and at the battle of Passchendaele where he was appointed to the DSO. He resigned his army commission in 1918 to join the navy, serving at Chatham Naval Hospital and on HMS *Furious*. In 1918 he was seconded to the army at the request of the Royal Society to study food resource allocation, and having completed this returned to Aberdeen in 1919.

Orr did not regard the laboratory building he had started in 1914 as sufficient for the new institute, and obtained funds from both John Quiller Rowett and the government which enabled him to build the Rowett Institute, opened in 1923. The Reid Library, the Duthie Farm, and Strathcona House also owed much to his perseverance and advocacy in fund-raising.

Orr's scientific work at Glasgow had been concerned with human physiology. At the Rowett Institute he turned his attention to the nutrition of farm animals and to the study of the nutritional status of populations in Africa. In 1927 he showed by experiments the value of milk in the health and growth of British children. This led Orr's lifelong friend, Walter Elliot [q.v.], then under-secretary of state for Scotland, to introduce legislation to provide milk for children in Scottish schools. Orr continued to draw attention to the poor state of health and nutrition of the British people and advocated a national food policy linked to an agricultural policy and one which had concern for human need. Elliot, by then minister of agriculture, asked Orr to bring together all the relevant information. This he did, but the political implications of his findings were such that they were not published by the government. Orr published them himself in 1936 under the title *Food, Health and Income*, and continued to advocate national action. He indeed enlarged his concepts to include an international dimension. His contribution to scientific thought was recognized when he was elected FRS in 1932 and knighted in 1935.

Orr's views were at the base of national food policy in the war of 1939–45. He advised Lord Woolton [q.v.], then minister of food, and was asked to attend meetings of the relevant Cabinet committee.

In 1942 he visited the USA to describe to Henry Wallace, vice-president, and Dean Acheson, under-secretary of state, his ideas for a World Food Plan. He was not, however, a UK delegate to the Hot Springs conference of 1943 where it was agreed that an international Food and Agriculture Organization (FAO) should be established. Nor did the British government include him as a representative at the Quebec conference of 1945, but he was asked to attend as an unofficial adviser. He addressed this conference and pleaded that the new agency should be granted executive power, to enable it to deal with the serious problems of human undernutrition. He was then asked to become its first director-general. At this time Orr had retired from directing the Rowett Institute and was farming in Angus. He was professor of agriculture in the university of Aberdeen from 1942 to 1945. He had also been elected to parliament as the independent member for the Scottish universities (1945–6) and to be rector of the University of Glasgow in 1945 (he became its chancellor in 1946). He nevertheless accepted the invitation and thus became the first director-general of FAO, a post he held from 1945 to 1948. Initial work commenced to provide the statistical information on population, agricultural production, and trade, necessary for large-scale monitoring and planning. Orr also continued planning for a world food board, a supra-national body with powers to buy and hold food stocks, provide funds for technical development of agriculture, and finance the supply of food to needy countries. This proposal was debated at a meeting of member countries of the UN in Copenhagen in 1946, and a preparatory commission on world food proposals was established, but the supra-national body proposed by Orr was not supported by the major world powers, and his World Food Plan was rejected in September 1947.

Orr was bitterly disappointed and resigned from FAO a few months later. He took an active part in world peace organizations and travelled widely. Within the developing countries he advised on food and agricultural problems. He was created Baron Boyd Orr in 1949. In the same year he also received the Nobel peace prize and was made a commander of the Legion of Honour. He was appointed CH in 1968.

Orr received honorary degrees from twelve universities in Britain and abroad, and honorary memberships of the New York Academy of Sciences and of the American Public Health Association. He never lost his strong west of Scotland accent, and while he spoke well, convinced people by his sincerity and his own conviction rather than by oratory. He had eyebrows like eaves (under which it was said that suffering nations had only to take shelter for all to be well), penetrating blue eyes, and a spare figure.

In 1915 he married Elizabeth Pearson, daughter of John Callum, business man, of West Kilbride. They had two daughters and a son, who was killed on active service in 1942. Orr died 25 June 1971 at his home at Brechin. His barony became extinct.

[*The Times*, 26 June 1971; H. D. Kay in *Biographical Memoirs of Fellows of the Royal Society*, vol. xviii, 1972; John Boyd Orr, *As I Recall*, 1966; *British Journal of Nutrition*, vol. xxvii, 1972, pp. 1–5; personal knowledge.]

K. L. Blaxter

OSBORN, Sir FREDERIC JAMES (1885–1978), town planner and writer, was born 26 May 1885 in Kennington, London, the eldest in the family of the two sons and one daughter of Thomas Frederick Osborn, mercantile clerk of Kennington, and his wife Edith Paull. He was educated at dame and council schools, leaving Hackford Road board school, Brixton, at fifteen for an office boy's job with a firm of City importers, the first of several clerking jobs over the next twelve years which, although demanding little of him, allowed plenty of time to read and lay the foundations of his lifelong enthusiasm for literature. His free time was largely devoted to the Fabian Society and the Independent Labour Party, to evening classes, and to numerous amateur literary, dramatic, debating, and cricket clubs in the south London area. With G. B. Shaw and H. G. Wells [qq.v.] his idols, he became a typical self-educated, lower middle class, metropolitan intellectual, developed an enthusiasm for socialism, and discovered in himself an above-average talent as writer and behind-the-scenes organizer.

In 1912, almost fortuitously and knowing nothing of Sir Ebenezer Howard [q.v.] and his proposals for garden cities, he successfully applied for the post of secretary to the Howard Cottage Society in Letchworth garden city, Hertfordshire. Letchworth, then nine years old and with 8,000 inhabitants, was a revelation. Overnight he found himself in a gracious, planned town which combined healthy housing with town and countryside, which embodied a radical form of land ownership and control, which offered a rich, do-it-yourself culture, and which had been founded as a model for the reconstruction of urban society. Letchworth and Howard's ideals provided a focus, a practical outlet, for Osborn's reforming enthusiasms: he became an ardent convert to the garden city movement and discovered in the ideal of planned towns the cause to which he would devote the rest of his life.

As Howard's disciple and friend, Osborn became an accomplished, nationally known exponent of the garden city case and an influential figure in Letchworth life. With Howard, C. B. Purdom, and W. G. Taylor he founded the New Townsmen to rescue garden city principles from garden suburb deviations, and under whose auspices he published *New Towns after the War* (1918), an argument for 100 government-sponsored new towns, which he wrote in the British Museum while declining military service on political grounds. When Howard purchased land for a second garden city in 1919, it was no surprise that Osborn moved with him to become company secretary and later estate manager of Welwyn Garden City Limited.

At Welwyn, one of a brilliant team working in difficult circumstances, Osborn learned the skills and experienced the problems of town-building, contributing to most aspects of the town's planning and development and playing a full part in its social and political life. He held Parish and Urban District Council offices from 1921 to 1931, was a founder of the local Labour Party and Fabian Society, founded the Welwyn Drama Festival with (Dame) Flora Robson in 1929, and was a prominent figure in business and cultural life. It was, therefore, something of a bombshell when he was abruptly dismissed from his job in

1936, when the Welwyn Company was restructured. Within the year, however, he was appointed financial director to the local Murphy Radio Limited and became honorary secretary to the Garden Cities and Town Planning Association, subsequently the Town and Country Planning Association.

For the next forty years, variously as honorary secretary, chairman of the executive committee, editor of *Town and Country Planning*, chairman of the Association, president or *éminence grise*, Osborn worked with astonishing energy, single-mindedness, and political acumen to further the Association's policies for limiting the size of cities, industrial relocation, low-density housing, green belts, and planned decentralization to new towns. The 1940 report of the royal commission on the geographical distribution of the industrial population, for which he had prepared and argued evidence and whose findings were something of a triumph for him, marked the beginning of seven intense years which would prove his most active and effective. He sat on the government's panel of physical reconstruction, was a member of the Labour Party post-war reconstruction committee (while advising the Conservative and Liberal Party equivalents), advised (Sir) L. P. Abercrombie [q.v.] over the County of London and Greater London plans, and as member or lobbyist was involved with innumerable committees and organizations concerned with planning or the environment. He became particularly identified as an advocate of low-density housing—one who, on the basis of his first-hand knowledge of ordinary people's housing preferences, vigorously contested prevailing architectural fashions for urbanity and multi-storey flats. His labours were crowned by membership of the 1946 new towns committee, chaired by Lord Reith [q.v.], which in nine arduous months produced the blueprints for establishing and administering new towns which Lewis (later Lord) Silkin [q.v.] embodied in his historic New Towns Act (1946) and Town and Country Planning Act (1947).

During these years, in his 'free time', he revised *New Towns after the War* (1942), produced a new edition of Howard's *Garden Cities of To-Morrow* (1946), wrote *Green-belt Cities* (1946, 1969), edited and contributed to the Rebuilding of Britain series, and through journalism, pamphlets, correspondence, lectures, and broadcasts, incessantly bombarded politicians, planners, and public with propaganda for dispersal and new town policies.

The war years had offered Osborn a unique opportunity to affect future events and were undoubtedly the period of his greatest influence. The new towns committee marked the high point of these endeavours, for to his regret he was not to play an official part in developing the new towns, although he was offered the chairmanship of Bracknell. He continued to be active as writer and propagandist, becoming the conscience of the movement against the vicissitudes and fashions of governments, planners, and architects, and remained a force within the Association into his eighties. With Arnold Whittick he wrote *The New Towns: The Answer to Megalopolis* (1963, 1969, 1977), the standard work on the British experience, while his *Can Man Plan?* (1959) recorded his lifelong devotion to writing light verse. *The Letters of Lewis Mumford and Frederic J. Osborn, 1939–70* (1971) give a rounded picture of a literate 'specialist on things in general', a man for whom new towns were but one of many interests. To this Dictionary Osborn contributed the notice of Sir George Pepler.

He received many honours and was knighted in 1956. He was particularly proud of receiving the Ebenezer Howard memorial medal (1968) and the gold medal of the Royal Town Planning Institute (1963), and took mischievous delight, as scourge of architectural fashions, in his honorary fellowship of RIBA. His election as vice-president and honorary member of the International Federation for Housing and Planning recognized his world-wide influence.

In 1916 he married Margaret Paterson (died 1970), daughter of Andrew Robb, commercial traveller, of Glasgow; her wisdom and strength were an essential part of his achievements. They had a son and a daughter. In 1974 he married Shirley Catherine, daughter of Brinley Stephens, musician. Osborn died in Welwyn Garden City 1 November 1978.

[Osborn papers; private information; personal knowledge.] MICHAEL HUGHES

OWEN, (HUMPHREY) FRANK (1905–1979), journalist, author, editor, and Liberal MP, was born 4 November 1905 at 10 Widemarsh Street, Hereford, the only son of Thomas Humphrey Owen and his wife, Cicely Hannah Green. Marjorie Elizabeth was the only daughter; Frank retained a close friendship with her to his dying day. His father was the innkeeper of the Black Swan, and Frank never ceased to honour his father's trade. He was sent first to Monmouth School, and from that Haberdashers' foundation to Sidney Sussex College, Cambridge. He obtained a second class (division I) of part i (1926) and a first class (division II) of part ii (1927) of the history tripos, a rugby blue, and a glowing reputation as a scholar, athlete, and drinking companion. During his studies he had made himself an expert on the American civil war, and his interest in military history had become a passion. Reading in general had become a passion too.

After a sharp apprenticeship as a journalist in

Geneva, in 1928 he joined the staff of the *South Wales Argus*, published in Newport. A few months later he was nominated as prospective Liberal candidate for his native city of Hereford and at the general election of 1929, was elected, with a majority of 1,121, as the youngest member in the new Parliament. He immediately attached himself to the Lloyd George section of the Liberal Party, and thereafter never wavered, for the rest of his life, in his allegiance to Lloyd George's special brand of vibrant radicalism (apart from a comparable and excusable hero-worship of Leon Trotsky in the years when Stalinism was supposedly a respectable creed). Mostly, in that 1929 Parliament, he voted to sustain the Labour government and found his most congenial associates on the left of the Labour Party, among the spokesmen of the Independent Labour Party, or with a fellow Welshman, Aneurin Bevan [q.v.], the young MP for neighbouring Ebbw Vale, with whom he formed an immediate and lasting friendship. His voting record and his insistence in 1931 on following Lloyd George in rejecting the national government appeal together ensured his defeat by a thumping 6,953 votes. 'In 1929', he would later recite, 'the wise, far-seeing, independent electors of my native Hereford sent me to Westminster, and two years later, in 1931, the lousy bastards kicked me out.'

For all his potential gifts as a speaker after the Lloyd George pattern, journalism suited him better, and after a brief spell on the *News Chronicle* he found his real home on the Beaverbrook newspapers and with Lord Beaverbrook [q.v.] himself. The two men approached the task of producing the next morning's newspaper with the same relish and tingling excitement. Owen worked first as reporter and leader writer for the *Daily Express* (1931–7). He also turned his hand, partly on Beaverbrook's prompting, to pamphleteering. *His was the Kingdom* (1937) offered an anti-Baldwinite, pro-Beaverbrookish account of King Edward's abdication.

However, it was as editor of Beaverbrook's *Evening Standard*, from 1938 to 1941, that he showed himself an editor of genius. He had had two years' practice to get his hand in before the actual outbreak of war. He was the first popular journalist to discover how Hitler's awful name sold newspapers; in the wretched years of appeasement, and in the same Beaverbrook press which carried the headlines 'no war this year or next', be it not forgotten, he made a special feature of rewriting *Mein Kampf* week after week to sound the alarm and raise sales by the same stroke of his dashing pen.

When the war actually came in September 1939, he led the deputation of Beaverbrook editors who privately told their proprietor that he must change his mind. Then, in the months of 1939 of the phoney war, when Beaverbrook himself was still sulking in his appeaser's tent, Owen started to fashion the paper into what it truly became, a combined sword and shield for the people of London. By the time Hitler was pushing through the Ardennes, and Lloyd George was overthrowing Neville Chamberlain in the House of Commons, and Beaverbrook was re-establishing his beneficent alliance with Churchill in the War Cabinet, and the people of London were roused to save themselves and the world, the *Evening Standard* had been transformed from the West End house journal which it was in the mid-1930s into the flaming herald of the embattled city.

Even the wartime *Evening Standard*, in the liberal and inspired hands of Frank Owen, could not say everything he wanted to say—after all, his still ever-vigilant proprietor was a member of the War Cabinet. Something more was needed to touch the ferment of the times. So, after the retreat from Dunkirk, Owen joined with two of his fellow Beaverbrook journalists, Peter Howard and Michael Foot, to write, under the pseudonym of Cato, the pamphlet *Guilty Men* (1940). The declared purpose of the project was to drive the Chamberlainites from Churchill's Cabinet. The pseudonym was designed to deceive Beaverbrook among others, and for a while it succeeded. However, exposure when it came was not fatal, since Beaverbrook and, more still, Churchill were not included on the guilty list. *Guilty Men* was a runaway success story, even though the agent who sold the manuscript to (Sir) Victor Gollancz [q.v.] did in fact literally run away with part of the royalties.

Owen sought some other outlets too. When Hitler's armies invaded the Soviet Union in the summer of 1941 he joined the campaign for demanding British and American support for the Soviet forces and later a demand for the opening of a second front. Again, in 1941 and 1942, under another pseudonym of Thomas Rainboro', the Leveller captain in Cromwell's army, he contributed a series on the conduct of the war to *Tribune*, then being edited by his old ally of the 1931 Parliament, Aneurin Bevan. No such criticism of Churchill himself, no comparable condemnation of the general war strategy, had been published anywhere in any wartime newspaper before. Owen drew upon his own military knowledge but also upon the special relationship he had with such figures as General Sir A. P. (later Earl) Wavell, Major-General J. F. C. Fuller, (Sir) B. H. Liddell Hart, Orde Wingate, Lord Louis Mountbatten (later Earl Mountbatten of Burma) [qq.v.], and several more. Owen was a journalist of the first order, but it was his special touch as a military correspondent which found the chinks in the Churchillian armour.

Owen himself had always wanted to serve in the Services; journalism, even in bomb-battered

London, was no tolerable substitute. Even before his Rainboro' exploits were complete, he was taken off to train in the Royal Armoured Corps. He quickly became a tank enthusiast, like one of his mentors, J. F. C. Fuller. Lord Louis Mountbatten requested his services for *SEAC*, the paper which served the army in Burma. Once again, as with Beaverbrook, the kinship with Mountbatten became explosive and decisive. The two men together helped to shape the Burma campaign. Owen was rewarded with the rank of lieutenant-colonel, and appointed to the OBE (1946), and at the end of hostilities he wrote an excellent official document, *The Campaign in Burma* (1946). Mountbatten would swear by him, as all who ever served nearby him in any cause would.

He returned to Fleet Street after the war, first as a contributor for the *Daily Mail*, and later, from 1947 to 1950, as its editor. The relationship with the second Viscount Rothermere [q.v.] could never be compared with his Beaverbrook association, and when the relationship collapsed, he renewed his work with Beaverbrook who was looking for someone to use the extensive Lloyd George papers which he had acquired. Owen seemed to be the ideal biographer. He knew Lloyd George more intimately than any other Fleet Street observer; he held Lloyd George's trust, an uneasy hold at any time, thanks to his conduct in 1931. The result was *Tempestuous Journey*, published in 1954; not by any reckoning the definitive Lloyd George biography but one which still offers flashes of perception, not to be seen elsewhere, by one Welshman on another.

The remaining years of his life were sad; the shining talents, the glittering insights, the sparkle lost their power. He still wrote for the newspapers; he stood again as an unsuccessful Liberal candidate on two occasions for Hereford (1955 and 1956). He wrote several books, but none of the same substance as his biography of Lloyd George: *The Eddie Chapman Story* in 1953; *Peron, his Rise and Fall* in 1957; *The Fall of Singapore* in 1960. All these were themes which stirred his sympathies but, especially after the death of his wife, Grace Stewart McGillivray, whom he had married in 1939, and who died in 1968, he lost his self-confidence. She was from Boston, USA, the daughter of Daniel Augustine McGillivray, decorative artist. They had no children.

He was an outstanding journalist; for a short period, and a great period in British history and especially London's history, the very best of his time. In the late 1930s and the early 1940s he understood the military and political requirements of the age better than anyone else in any editorial chair in Fleet Street during a period when Fleet Street truly helped to shape Britain's history. He died 23 January 1979 at Worthing. He was a freeman of the City of London.

[Private information; personal knowledge.]

MICHAEL FOOT

OWEN, SIR (WILLIAM) LEONARD (1897–1971), engineer, was born at Walton, Liverpool, 3 May 1897, the only child of Thomas John Owen, mariner, and his wife, Levina Elizabeth Victoria Isabella Smith. He was educated at the Liverpool Collegiate School. By the time he left school, in 1915, World War I had broken out and he joined the 6th King's Liverpool Regiment, serving as a private in the trenches. At the end of the war he returned to Liverpool as an undergraduate student in the faculty of engineering at the university. He graduated with honours in 1922 and was awarded the degree of Master of Engineering in 1924.

His first professional work as an engineer was at Northwich in Cheshire with Brunner, Mond & Company. This later became one of the founding companies of Imperial Chemical Industries as ICI (Alkali) Limited. The factory was concerned with the production of bulk chemicals on a large scale and Owen's responsibilities in the engineering department were concerned with the design of additions to the plant and with the development of new plant. Shortly after the outbreak of World War II he was 'loaned' to the Ministry of Supply as director of the Royal Filling Factories, a post that he held between 1940 and 1945.

The end of the war marked a watershed in Owen's career for it was in 1946 that he began his work on the industrial development of nuclear energy in the United Kingdom—on appointment as director of engineering on the production side of the Ministry of Supply. In the following year the Atomic Energy Division was formed with Owen as assistant controller.

For the next decade he worked closely with Christopher Hinton (later Lord Hinton of Bankside), with headquarters at Risley near to Warrington, in taking responsibility for the design and construction of the atomic energy factories in the north of England. Hinton held the senior post but it is not easy to separate the contributions of the two men. Their qualities were in some measure complementary though both combined incisive engineering judgement with driving purposefulness. They set themselves clear objectives and approached them with determination and expert professionalism. One outstanding achievement of the partnership was the construction of the atomic power station at Calder Hall on the Cumbrian coast—the first in the world to generate electrical power on a commercial scale.

Hinton has been recognized as an engineer of world stature but throughout their association Owen maintained his influence by quiet advice, often given in private and seldom assertive, but highly regarded for its basis in shrewd judgement and long experience. However, the two men were never warm friends and when, in 1957, their work took them in different directions they separated in an atmosphere which was cool. The cool relationship persisted though it was clear, on later occasions when they met, that they understood and respected each other.

The United Kingdom Atomic Energy Authority had been formed in 1954, Owen taking the title of director of engineering and deputy managing director. In 1957 he was appointed managing director, Industrial Group, and he was knighted in the same year, having been appointed CBE in 1950. He became member for production of the Atomic Energy Authority in 1959 and continued to serve in different capacities until his retirement from the Authority in 1964.

Owen was an outstanding project engineer. He was a great believer in programme planning and the immutability of target dates. He believed in taking firm decisions and he vigorously resisted changes which could not be proved to be essential. His earlier life had given him a clear insight into the complexities of human relations and he won the respect and friendship of most of the staff working under him, whether relatively academic in outlook or down-to-earth site engineers engaged in heavy construction. He had great strength of character and a gift for swift detection of the weaknesses of any new proposals or design changes which were submitted for his comment or approval. Most of the ideas and features of the early atomic energy engineering programme were subjected to his critical analysis and were usually modified accordingly before adoption.

When he left the Atomic Energy Authority Owen continued to exercise his profession in a variety of posts. For example, he was for two years (1968–9) chairman of Cammell Laird Shipbuilders Limited. His engineering experience was an invaluable asset during a period in which three nuclear-powered submarines were under construction.

In 1960 the University of Manchester conferred on him the honorary degree of D.Sc.

By way of relaxation Owen took a great pride in his garden and he was for many years an enthusiastic member of the Liverpool Rugby Football Club.

In 1923 he married Phyllis, daughter of Martin Condliff. They had two sons. Owen died 25 March 1971 at his home in Beaumaris, Anglesey.

[*The Times*, 26 and 29 March 1971; *Atom*, May 1971; private information; personal knowledge.] J. F. NORBURY

P

PAGE, Sir DENYS LIONEL (1908–1978), classical scholar, was born in Reading 11 May 1908, the third in the family of five children (three boys and two girls) of Frederick Harold Dunn Page, a chartered civil engineer in the Great Western Railway, and his wife, Elsie Daniels. He was educated at Newbury Grammar School, and in 1926 won a scholarship to Christ Church, Oxford. He benefited much from the teaching of G. Gilbert A. Murray [q.v.], and received special coaching from J. D. Denniston, who became a close friend and whose notice Page subsequently wrote for this Dictionary. In 1928 Page was Craven and De Paravicini scholar, and won the Chancellor's prize for Latin verse and the Gaisford prize for Greek verse. He obtained first classes both in classical moderations (1928) and *literae humaniores* (1930). One of his closest Christ Church friends was Quintin Hogg, later Lord Hailsham of St. Marylebone. Page did not confine himself only to the classics but earned his place in the Christ Church cricket team as a terrifying fast bowler. Next he went as Derby scholar to Vienna, where he spent a year working under Ludwig Radermacher. In 1931 he became a lecturer at Christ Church, and the next year student and tutor of the House. He quickly made his mark as tutor and lecturer, and was highly congenial to his pupils and his colleagues. In 1937 he became junior censor, but a year later resigned the office to marry Katharine Elizabeth, daughter of Joseph Michael Dohan, of Philadelphia, Pennsylvania. Their married life was singularly happy, and they had four daughters.

In 1934 Page published a study of *Actors' Interpolations in Greek Tragedy, with special reference to Euripides' Iphigeneia in Aulis*. His close acquaintance with the texts and keen critical intelligence were immediately apparent, and the book received high praise. In 1938 he brought out a text of Euripides' *Medea* with introduction and commentary, which made a striking contribution to the understanding of the play, not seriously marred by youthful dogmatism. At this time Page was making a close study of the early Greek lyric poets, whose remains had been notably increased by new papyrus discoveries. Most current texts of them were disfigured by rash supplements and conjectures, but Edgar Lobel in his editions of Sappho (1925) and Alcaeus (1927) had set new standards of accuracy and learning, and Page followed in his tracks. The Loeb Classical Library asked him to edit and translate all the fragments of Greek poetry on papyrus not included in the volumes devoted to individual authors, and the resulting volume of *Greek Literary Papyri* (1942) was a masterly performance which proved Page to be a scholar of the first order.

During World War II Page served in the Government Code and Cipher School located at Bletchley Park which dealt with the branch of intelligence known as Ultra. He was assigned to the section which under the direction of Oliver Strachey dealt with the various hand ciphers used by Britain's enemies, and was so successful that when Strachey retired in 1942 he was chosen to succeed him. After the war he headed for a year a special command mission to the headquarters of Viscount (later Earl) Mountbatten of Burma [q.v.], first at Kandy and then at Singapore.

Page resumed his teaching and research with all his usual vigour, serving as senior proctor in 1948–9. But in 1950 he was elected to the regius chair of Greek in Cambridge, and to a professorial fellowship at Trinity College. Classical studies in Cambridge at that time were by no means as lively as in Oxford, where the presence of learned refugees from Germany, the work of Sir J. D. Beazley [q.v.] and other distinguished scholars, and the publication of the papyri were having an exhilarating effect. But Page by his outstanding lecturing and his influence upon colleagues and pupils had from the first a powerful effect. He was also highly congenial to his Trinity colleagues, and was soon elected to the college council.

His long and intensive study of early Greek lyric now bore fruit in a series of important publications. In 1951 appeared a book on Alcman's Louvre Partheneion, in 1953 an edition of Corinna, with commentary, and in 1955 *Lesbiorum Poetarum Fragmenta*, in which Page added the texts published since Lobel's editions of the twenties to Lobel's work, and a book called *Sappho and Alcaeus*, which included commentaries on the more substantial fragments and discussions of various problems which the poems raised. Page took over from Lobel a somewhat austere editorial technique, but the texts are edited in masterly fashion; the commentaries are no less admirable, though the treatment of purely literary questions leaves something to be desired.

Page's book *The Homeric Odyssey* (1955) was based on Flexner lectures given at Bryn Mawr (1954) and his *History and the Homeric Iliad* (1959) on Sather lectures given at Berkeley (1957–8). Both books show mastery of the relevant material, including archaeological data, the newly deciphered Linear B tablets and oriental evidence thought to be relevant to the poems, and both are written with great clarity and elegance. But they are marked by a displeasing dogmatism, accentuated by the rhetorical manner in which the argument is presented, and the assumption of multiple authorship is too readily used to account for features of the poems which might be explained by other considerations.

Denniston had prepared a small-scale edition of the *Agamemnon* of Aeschylus, with commentary, which he had intended to revise in the light of the long-awaited *Agamemnon* of Eduard Fraenkel [q.v.]. But he died in 1949, a year before Fraenkel's edition appeared, and it was left to Page to prepare the work for publication. Perhaps Page was too eager to differ from Fraenkel, but the work has great value and did good service in showing that the vastly learned editor was not infallible. The weakest part was the introduction, whose confident assumption that the poet's outlook and technique were crude and primitive has not gone unchallenged.

During the late fifties Page's life was complicated by his wife's serious illness; but in 1959 his domestic difficulties were alleviated by his election to be master of Jesus College, Cambridge. His wife's health improved, and his great energy enabled him to discharge the duties of his new office without reducing his production of learned work. In 1962 he published *Poetae Melici Graeci*, a critical edition of the Greek lyric poets other than the Lesbians, in 1968 a minor edition of these poets called *Lyrica Graeca Selecta*, and in 1974 a supplement including newly published material with the title *Supplementum Lyricis Graecis*. All these works are of a high order.

In 1965 Page contributed the edition of Meleager to the two-volume work *The Greek Anthology: Hellenistic Epigrams* which was otherwise the work of his Trinity colleague A. S. F. Gow, and when in 1968 the same two editors brought out the two volumes of *The Greek Anthology: the Garland of Philip, and Some Contemporary Epigrams* Gow was responsible for Antipater of Thessalonica, but Page for all the other poets; in 1975 Page published a minor edition of many of the poems contained in these collections with the title *Epigrammata Graeca*. His last book, *The Epigrams of Rufinus*, appeared in 1978, just before his death, and a further volume containing all epigrams not included in the other volumes down to the year AD 50 was published posthumously. These books constitute a major contribution to the study of Hellenistic poetry.

In 1972 Page published a new Oxford Text of Aeschylus, using and supplementing the work on the manuscripts of his former pupil R. D. Dawe; it is undoubtedly an improvement on all previous editions of this author. A full bibliography of his writings may be found in the volume *Dionysiaca: Nine Studies in Greek Poetry by Former Pupils, presented to Sir Denys Page on his Seventieth Birthday* (1978).

Many people regretted that Page was denied, almost certainly on grounds of his political conservatism, the office of vice-chancellor, which he would certainly have filled with great distinction; he was an effective president of the British Academy from 1971 to 1974. In 1973 his wife's ill health obliged him to resign the offices of master and professor and to retire to his house at Tarset near Hexham in Northumberland, where he continued to work without remission. He died at home 6 July 1978, and his wife survived him only by a few weeks.

In the work of editing and explaining the Greek poets Page's achievement is very great; he combined intimate knowledge of the texts, mastery of grammar, syntax and metre, and much skill in the reading of papyri with keen critical acumen. He was weaker in literary appreciation, and his tendency to see things and people in strong black and white made it hard for him to do justice to the complexity of life. He was for several years not on speaking terms with E. R. Dodds [q.v.] of whose appointment to the regius chair in Oxford he deeply disapproved, and, after early friendship, he parted company with Sir C. M. Bowra [q.v.], for whose scholarship he had little regard. But he was always ready to help pupils or colleagues, and his charm and gaiety delighted most of those who met him. His place in the history of Greek scholarship is assured.

Page was knighted in 1971. He was elected fellow of the British Academy in 1952, and received its Kenyon medal in 1969; he was a corresponding member of the Academy of Athens, the American Academy of Arts and Sciences, the American Philosophical Society, and the Greek Humanistic Society. He was a Doctor of Letters of Cambridge (1960), and held honorary doctorates from Oxford (1972), Trinity College, Dublin, and the universities of Newcastle, Hull, and Bristol. He was an honorary fellow of Trinity and Jesus colleges and an honorary Student of Christ Church.

[H. Lloyd-Jones in *Proceedings* of the British Academy, vol. lxv, 1979, reprinted in *Blood for the Ghosts*, 1981; private information; personal knowledge.] HUGH LLOYD-JONES

PAGET, EDWARD FRANCIS (1886–1971), archbishop of Central Africa, was born 8 July 1886 at the Canon's House, Christ Church, Oxford, the third child and second son in the family of four sons and two daughters of Francis Paget [q.v.], canon of Christ Church, of which he became dean in 1892, and bishop of Oxford from 1901, and his wife, Beatrice, daughter of Richard William Church, dean of St. Paul's. One of his brothers was (Sir) Bernard Paget [q.v.]. Paget was educated at Shrewsbury and at Christ Church, Oxford, where he obtained in 1908 a pass degree. He then decided to follow in his father's footsteps, and went to Cuddesdon in 1910 for his theological training. He made no mark at school or college, but was noted for his humour and his friendliness. His hearty manner did not conceal his deeply religious nature. While still at Oxford he became a lay worker at the Christ Church mission in Poplar, a son after his father's heart. In 1911 he was ordained by his father, and then returned for three years to Poplar.

In 1914 Bishop Michael Furse of Pretoria invited him to go to South Africa, where he became vicar of Benoni. This period of his ministry was interrupted by World War I. He became a chaplain to the forces, served with the 3rd brigade of the South African Infantry, and was awarded the MC. Under his leadership the parish of Benoni was very much alive. Paget, still in his early thirties, had developed great gifts of personality. He was a tall commanding figure, a man who spoke with authority, free of vanity, with a personal warmth and strong sense of humour. He was an unconventional preacher who held his congregation's rapt attention. He was not an intellectual. He was not at home in philosophical and theological discussions, but on moral questions, particularly those that concerned justice and the social order, his judgements were swift and authoritative. During the 1922 rebellion on the Reef he played a valuable part as a go-between and both sides could meet in his house and put their points of view to each other.

It was not surprising that in 1925 he was elected bishop of Southern Rhodesia, and went to live in Salisbury. He was not yet forty, full of courage and vigour, and his presence was felt everywhere in the diocese. The missionary work of the church, and the welfare of its African people, were very near to his heart. He made enemies, particularly among those whites who upheld the colour bar, and those who held the view that the rich should pay for the rich and the poor for the poor. He was, however, highly respected by the white rulers of the country, and could speak to them with authority on matters of right and justice.

Paget had always held firm views, for himself at least, on the importance of celibacy in the priesthood, but now he met Rosemary, daughter of Auriol Sealy Allin, a civil engineer. He found that circumstances alter cases, and married her on 20 October 1932. There were no children. Their home became a haven for many people, for tired priests and tired wives, for the black clergy, and for anyone who was lonely.

Paget's priests were by no means uncritical of him, but most of them felt for him a strong affection. There is one story which better than any captures his relationship with his younger priests. Ronald Tyndale-Biscoe wrote: 'Playing tennis against him was a frightening experience, for his drives came over like cannon-balls. I for one always ducked, and he roared out to me, "Stand up to it, man!"'

When World War II broke out in 1939 Paget was appointed chaplain-general to the forces, and he allowed as many priests as he could to become chaplains to the army. He himself was tireless, and in return for his labours he was appointed CBE in 1950. King Paul of Greece conferred on him the Cross of a Commander of the Order of the Phoenix, for his 'great kindness' to members of the Royal Hellenic Air Force who trained in Rhodesia. Geoffrey Fisher, archbishop of Canterbury (later Lord Fisher of Lambeth, q.v.), made him a DD in recognition of his devoted service to the Anglican communion.

In 1955 the new province of Central Africa was created, and he became its first archbishop. He was now almost seventy, and two years later he retired, to go to live with his wife in Everton Road, Gillitts, in the parish of Kloof, Natal, where they became faithful worshippers in the church of St. Agnes. He was still active as a priest, and in 1960 acted as vicar-general of the diocese of Johannesburg after Bishop Ambrose Reeves had been deported. Paget and his wife visited Rhodesia often, and the defeat of the liberal Sir Edgar Whitehead [q.v.] in 1962 greatly distressed him.

In his last years he was much troubled by arthritis, mainly in the knees. He called it an occupational hazard, but he would always kneel to pray and to communicate. He had to give up his beloved golf and took to the croquet lawn. His attitude towards his opponents was simple—it was to 'smash 'em up'.

He died 21 April 1971, in St. Mary's Hospital at Mariannhill. The immediate cause was a flight in an unpressurized plane from the Cape to Knysna. His ashes were placed in the cathedral at Salisbury.

[Private information; personal knowledge.]

ALAN PATON

PALMER, ROUNDELL CECIL, third EARL OF SELBORNE (1887–1971), was born 15 April 1887 at his mother's parents' house, 20 Arlington Street, Mayfair, London. He was the eldest of three sons (one of whom was killed in action in World War I) and second of four children of William Waldegrave Palmer [q.v.], the future second Earl of Selborne, statesman, and his wife, Lady (Beatrix) Maud Cecil, elder daughter of Robert Arthur Talbot Gascoyne-Cecil [q.v.], third Marquess of Salisbury, then prime minister. After the first Earl's death in 1895 he was styled Viscount Wolmer. He was educated at Winchester College, of which he later became a fellow, and at University College, Oxford, where he founded and ran a vigorous New Tory Club and took a third class in modern history (1909). His friends called him 'Top'.

His Liberal–Conservative ancestry settled his career. He contested the Newton division of south-west Lancashire in January 1910, and narrowly carried it, in the Conservative interest, in the following December. He sat in the Commons for all but thirty years, representing the safer seat of Aldershot from December 1918 until in October 1940 he was called up to the House of Lords in his father's subsidiary title, Baron Selborne. He left Winchester in July 1905 and in 1906 was commissioned into the 3rd (Militia) battalion of the Hampshire Regiment, of which his father was honorary colonel. He was promoted captain on 19 September 1914, early in World War I, and served with this training unit in the Isle of Wight and at Gosport for nearly two years. In 1916 his brother-in-law Lord Robert Cecil (later Viscount Cecil of Chelwood, q.v.), who was organizing blockade, made him his parliamentary private secretary, and when David Lloyd George (later Earl Lloyd-George of Dwyfor) formed his government that December Wolmer became assistant director of the war trade department, under Lord Emmott [q.v.]. He was still in constant official touch with Lord Robert Cecil, now minister of blockade.

Wolmer returned to the back-benches at the end of the war, and resigned from the army with the rank of major in 1922. That October he again took minor office, and served for fourteen months as parliamentary secretary to the Board of Trade. From 1924 to 1929, as assistant postmaster-general, he developed technical ideas rather ahead of his time. He was sworn of the Privy Council 5 July 1929, just after he resigned. That autumn he wrote several articles, in *The Times* and elsewhere, which he developed into his only book, on *Post Office Reform* (1932). He also wrote a pamphlet on church affairs, noticed below, and an article for this Dictionary on another brother-in-law, the fourth Marquess of Salisbury.

He became known as the embodiment in the House of the Conservative Party's conscience. There was no room for him in the coalition governments of 1931–40, though he sat on the Sea-Fish Commission in 1934–6. He aligned himself with his friend (Sir) Winston Churchill in the struggle against the India Act of 1935. He was a shrewd and capable administrator, and began to develop some business interests, which led him to the chairmanship of the Cement Makers' Federation (1934–42, 1945–51) and to a directorship of Boots drug company (from 1936, deputy chairman from 1951 to 1963). Under Churchill's wartime coalition he served in 1940–2 as director of cement in the Ministry of Works: anti-invasion pillboxes in concrete, still scattered all over southern England, thus provide mementoes of him.

On 23 February 1942, three days before his father's death, he succeeded E. H. J. N. (later Lord) Dalton [q.v.] as minister of economic warfare. The title was little more than a cover: economic war took up, in his own estimate, about a fifth of his time. The rest went on managing the Special Operations Executive (SOE), the secret service devoted to fostering subversion in enemy-occupied territory, of which he now became the politically responsible head.

Under-informed men thought that his slight and stooping figure indicated an insignificant character: they were soon undeceived. He early showed himself a minister of principle. Within a week of taking office he had written a commentary on a Cabinet paper on the Indian question by Sir R. Stafford Cripps [q.v.] so sharp that his staff supposed it would cost him his new post. He dealt resolutely with those in the high command of SOE whom he thought unfit for their tasks, sending them briskly into retirement or back to the departments that had seconded them to his. In 1942 he replaced Sir Frank Nelson with Sir Charles Hambro [qq.v.] as SOE's executive head; even Hambro, within eighteen months, had to bow before the storm of Selborne's displeasure. With Hambro and his successor (Sir) Colin Gubbins [q.v.] Selborne had a daily meeting at noon, whenever both were in London. This enabled him to keep his finger on the pulse of SOE's principal activities; he never wished nor sought to interfere in technical detail. In spite of all the work that Dalton and Nelson had already done, Selborne had to fight incessantly to maintain for SOE the position that he was sure it deserved to hold in the British strategic machine, and was several times able to appeal to his friendship with Churchill to rescue SOE from its worst domestic enemies.

He bore ultimate responsibility for numerous important clandestine coups and, much more, for helping to restore their self-respect to the populations of the Axis-occupied countries. In recognition of his wartime work he was appointed CH on the conclusion of the war in Europe in 1945. A proposal of his to use SOE's world-wide friendships and signals facilities as a base for a permanent peacetime intelligence network was brusquely rejected by C. R. (later Earl) Attlee.

Selborne then gave his main attention to his significant parallel career in the Church of England. He strove ardently for self-government in it. His pamphlet on *The Freedom of the Kirk* (1928) argued that the Church of England would do well to cut itself off, as the Scots Kirk had done by the Act of 1921 (11 & 12 Geo. V, c.29), from any doctrinal interference by the state. He was president of the Church Army, 1949–61, and chairman of the house of laity of the church assembly from 1955 till increasing deafness compelled him to resign in 1959. He also did much to improve the church's financial position; as chairman of the National Provincial Bank, 1951–4, he could speak with authority.

On the family estates, something under 2,000 acres round Blackmoor on the Hampshire–Surrey border, he diversified from hops as a main crop into dairy farming and fruit growing; he initiated the use of concrete posts for training soft fruit bushes. Even during the war he tried to visit Blackmoor once a week at least, to advise and supervise, and he greatly increased productivity over the years.

He married in 1910 Grace (died 1959), youngest daughter of Sir Matthew White Ridley, first Viscount Ridley [q.v.]; they had four sons (one of whom died in infancy) and three daughters. His eldest son was killed on active service in the Hampshire Regiment in 1942. He married, secondly, in 1966 Mrs Valerie Irene Josephine Margaret de Thomka Bevan (died 1968), daughter of J. A. N. de Thomka de Tomkahaza, secretary of state for Hungary. He died at Blackmoor 3 September 1971 and was succeeded in the earldom by his grandson John Roundell Palmer (born 1940), the eldest son of his deceased eldest son.

There is a full-length oil portrait of him (*c.*1945) by Clarence White in the Special Forces Club.

[*The Times*, 6, 9, and 11 September 1971; private information.] M. R. D. FOOT

PARK, SIR KEITH RODNEY (1892–1975), air chief marshal, was born in Thames, New Zealand, 15 June 1892, the youngest son in the family of three sons and seven daughters of James Park, director of the Thames School of Mines and later professor of mining at the University of Otago, Dunedin, and his first wife, Frances, daughter of Captain W. Rogers, of Surrey. He was educated at King's College, Auckland, Selwyn Collegiate School, the Otago Boys' High School in Dunedin, and Otago University where he studied mining. After a shore job as a clerk in Dunedin with the Union Steamship Company, he managed to get to sea as a purser but the outbreak of war in 1914 gave his adventurous spirit its first great opportunity. In December of that year he volunteered as a gunner and he fought with the New Zealand Expeditionary Force at Gallipoli where distinguished conduct in the field gained him a commission (1915) in the NZ Artillery and he decided to become a regular soldier. He next saw service in France and was so severely wounded (for the second time) on the Somme that he was relegated to Woolwich as artillery officer instructor.

Vigorous and energetic by temperament, he decided it would be better to be airborne than chairbound and so volunteered for the Royal Flying Corps where, between 1917 and 1919, he served with Nos. 8 and 38 (Reserve) Squadrons and ended in command of No. 48 Squadron. When the Royal Air Force replaced the RFC in 1918 he was promoted captain. He gained the MC and bar in 1917, the croix de guerre in 1918, and the DFC in 1919.

Between the wars he was chief instructor in the Oxford University Air Squadron and commanded Northolt and Hornchurch fighter stations, organized flying pageants at Hendon, served as air attaché at Buenos Aires, became an ADC to the King at his coronation in 1937, passed the Imperial Defence College course that year, became officer commanding at Tangmere in 1938, and, as an air commodore later that year, was senior staff officer at HQ, RAF Fighter Command.

In April 1940 he was appointed air officer commanding No. 11 Fighter Group and in July was promoted air vice-marshal. As such he was responsible for much of the protective fighter patrolling during the operations preceding and accompanying the withdrawal from Dunkirk. Here he regularly flew his own Hurricane to get a direct view of the operation and himself took part in the final patrol. He later described Dunkirk as 'a most exciting time' and was convinced that the evacuation could not have succeeded without the fighter protection given by his Group over Calais, Boulogne, and Cherbourg as well as Dunkirk itself. And he believed that the air-fighting over France and Dunkirk gave British fighter squadrons their first real experience of battle, an experience to prove invaluable very soon afterwards.

In his view the Battle of Britain lasted from July till October 1940 and divided into two main phases, the first—the fight for the airfields—ending on 7 September. His own Group had the most extensive and vital area to protect, from Southampton to Norwich, and virtually had to defend London against attack by all the nearest approaches. Although his working day began at 0730 hours in the operations room at Northolt, deep underground, where he was able to see plotted the incoming waves of German aircraft and to order relevant counter-measures, he was no remote figure to his men: at 1730 hours he would set off in his own Hurricane and visit all his fighter stations to see how his pilots, ground-service staff, and squadrons were faring. In general, he found that their morale resembled his own and they all believed, rightly, that they had to defeat the *Luftwaffe* if invasion by sea was not to be inevitable.

Park's strategy, approved by Air Marshal Sir Hugh (later Lord) Dowding [q.v.], was to place his squadrons where radar helped to predict enemy attack, and to have them intercept and break up the enemy formations before they could reach and bomb their objectives. At no stage did he have at his disposal more than twenty-five squadrons along the south coast and they often had to be serviced by men who had almost no time to eat and were working on the frontiers of exhaustion. Park appreciated their dedication as he did that of his pilots, and of the indispensable WAAF he said: 'Those girls—by God, they were stout-hearted girls.'

Unfortunately, (Sir) Trafford Leigh-Mallory [q.v.], air officer commanding No. 12 Fighter Group in the midlands, believed in a different strategy: he preferred to concentrate larger 'wing' formations (groups of five to seven squadrons) against the bombing assaults. Eventually the Air Council transferred both Dowding and Park to other posts, in order to resolve the dispute. By that time, however, in Park's view the Battle of Britain had already been won by 7 September when the Germans gave up trying to eliminate the fighter stations and switched to the mass bombing of London. The old dispute was scarcely relevant any more and Park, if at all given to regret (which is unlikely), could have consoled himself that the main battle had been fought and won while he commanded the largest and most important fighter group—in the same period he had flown about 100 hours, mostly in his own fighter, an example as well as an inspiring leader.

Meanwhile, after a brief interlude as air officer commanding No. 23 Group Training Command, he was appointed in January 1942 air officer commanding Egypt, and in the following July moved to become air officer commanding Malta. According to Park himself, the Malta operations were a smaller version of the Battle of Britain itself, except that he found the island's defences in a bad way to begin with, he had a much smaller force to manœuvre, and food and fuel supplies were so sparse that often the pilots had to trust to luck that their engines had been serviced, engine tests being impossible because of fuel shortage. Under Park, however, drive and improvisation were always inspired. He resorted unrepentantly to his earlier strategy of leaving the ground as quickly as possible, swift interception, and early attack. During his time, Malta endured the impact of just under 1,300 tons of bombs but he made sure the island was no 'bomb-sponge' but a fortress which tied up superior enemy forces and made a vital contribution to the campaigns of Eisenhower in Tunisia and of Sir Bernard Montgomery (later Viscount Montgomery of Alamein, q.v.) in the Western Desert and at Alamein. Simultaneously he conducted a private war with the *Luftwaffe* in Sicily and Sardinia. Having crippled the Germans over Malta, he attacked their massed force of 700 fighters and bombers in Sicily. And when the fighters ceased to come up against him in the air he defied the experts by equipping his Spitfires and Beaufighters with a pair each of 250-pound bombs to deal with them on the ground.

He also set about sinking Rommel's supply convoys to Benghazi, as soon as they set out from Brindisi and Taranto; and he bombed Benghazi itself, Sfax, Tunis, Bizerta, and Tripoli. He also introduced the use of intruder Mosquitoes by day and by night to disrupt and destroy the convoys on land behind Rommel's forward positions. Here his ability to inspire and communicate a fiery zeal at all levels paid off: his men sometimes did two raids in a single night on airfields and installations in Sardinia where the Germans tried to build up a torpedo-bomber force against the Allied armada for the invasion of Tunisia, and he thus eliminated in advance what could have been a serious danger.

After a similar energetic and invaluable contribution to the invasion of Sicily he became, in January 1944, air officer commander in chief in the RAF, Middle East. But the main weight of the German war had now moved to Europe and so he was sent as acting air chief marshal, to become Allied air commander, South-East Asia, in February 1945. Here he made an essential contribution to the reconquest of Burma and to the successful conclusion of the war in the Far East.

Tall and lean of stature, he combined stamina, personal courage, power to organize and improvise, personal modesty, and a natural easy command over men, all these in a rare degree.

He retired in 1946, with the rank of air chief marshal, and in 1947 Oxford University conferred on him an honorary DCL. He was appointed CB in 1940, KCB in 1945, and GCB in 1946. In 1942 he was appointed CBE.

In 1918 he married Dorothy Margarita, daughter of Lt.-Col. Woodbine Parish, CMG, CBE, director of Buenos Aires Great Southern Railway. She died in 1971. There were two sons of the marriage, of whom one was killed on active service in 1951. His retired years were spent in Remuera, Auckland, New Zealand, where, so long as he was able, he indulged in his favourite recreation, sailing. He died in hospital in Auckland, New Zealand, 5 February 1975.

[Alan W. Mitchell, *New Zealanders in the Air War*, 1945; Field-Marshal Michael Carver (ed.), *The War Lords*, 1976; Sir Basil Liddell-Hart, *Short History of the Second World War*, 1970; *The Times*, 7 February 1975.]

D. M. Davin

PARKER, HUBERT LISTER, Baron Parker of Waddington (1900–1972), lord chief justice, was born 28 May 1900 at Thursley, Surrey, the youngest in the family of three sons and two daughters of Robert John Parker, later Baron Parker of Waddington [q.v.], a lord of appeal in ordinary, and his wife, Constance, daughter of John Trevor Barkley, civil engineer. He was educated at Rugby School and at Trinity College, Cambridge. He obtained first classes in both parts i (1921) and ii (1922) of the natural sciences tripos. His special subject was geology and he intended to pursue a career in oil but, being advised by a careers officer that there was 'no future in oil' he decided to read for the bar instead. He joined Lincoln's Inn, was called to the bar in 1924, and entered the chambers of Donald Somervell (later Lord Somervell of Harrow, q.v.).

He built up a substantial practice in civil cases, mostly those of a commercial kind. His advocacy was marked by fairness, clarity, and good temper—passionate rhetoric was not for him. In 1945 he succeeded (Sir) Valentine Holmes [q.v.] as junior counsel in common law to the Treasury (his father had held the corresponding post on the Chancery side). Such an appointment usually leads to a High Court judgeship and in 1950 he was made a judge of the King's Bench division and was knighted.

The work of a King's Bench judge entailed his entering fields in which he had had little or no experience at the bar. He had to sit as an assize judge, spending much of his time presiding over criminal trials. He said that the first summing-up in a criminal case that he heard was one he delivered himself. He was, however, an excellent judge, whatever type of case he was trying, being always fair, patient, and courteous.

In 1954 he became a lord justice of appeal and was sworn of the Privy Council. His gifts and temperament were well suited to the work of the Court of Appeal. He was a sound lawyer who had a great capacity for identifying the essentials of a case, stating the problem and his answer to it in the fewest possible words—and usually getting the answer right. In 1957 he presided most successfully over a tribunal which inquired into alleged malpractices in connection with the Bank rate.

In 1958 Lord Goddard [q.v.] retired from the office of lord chief justice of England. Parker was appointed in his place. He was the first chief justice to come from the ranks of stuff gownsmen (i.e. those who had never taken silk) since Chief Justice Charles Abbot [q.v.] in 1818. He was made a life peer and took the same title as his father.

As chief justice he was an admirable leader of his team of judges, always approachable and ready to help them with their problems. The courts in which he mainly presided were the Divisional Court and the Court of Criminal Appeal (from 1966 the latter was replaced by the Criminal division of the Court of Appeal). It may be that in the Divisional Court the years he had spent as 'Treasury devil' had caused him to have a greater tendency to support the actions of the Executive than had been the case with some of his predecessors but there was never any doubt of his particular aptitude for the work of that court or of his willingness to listen to both sides before reaching a decision. In criminal appeals he often displayed what was regarded as an extreme degree of leniency—not infrequently his court would substitute a probation order for a long term of imprisonment imposed at the trial. But when he thought it necessary he could be severe indeed, as when he sentenced George Blake, a spy, to forty-two years' imprisonment. In a newspaper interview given shortly after his retirement he expressed in strong terms the view that violent crimes committed by hardened criminals should meet with stern punishment.

An innovation which he made in connection with the sentencing of criminals was the organizing of conferences to which he invited judges, police, probation officers, psychiatrists, and others, to exchange views of the appropriate sentences for typical imaginary cases.

Chief justices had always had considerable extra-judicial work to do in organizing the work of the division and in particular with assizes. The work-load had much expanded as the number of judges increased and the crime rate grew. Parker was a first-class administrator. He had always been a prodigiously hard worker—with a preference for working very early in the morning rather than at night. As chief justice he was usually at work in his private room in his shirt sleeves hours before his court was due to sit.

In 1971 a report made by Lord Beeching led to legislation which, among other fundamental changes for the courts and the judiciary, set up a new system of circuit administration, greatly lightening the chief justice's load of work. It was at least partly because he thought it would be best for a younger man to see the new arrangements into operation that Parker decided to resign. He did so on 7 April 1971, being succeeded by Lord Justice Widgery.

He was greatly attached to his old school, Rugby, and was for some years chairman of its governors. A new science building there was named after him. He enjoyed, among other activities, collecting books and antiques, shooting, fishing, watching birds, and building garden walls. He was a quiet, unassuming man, never well known to the public but greatly admired and liked by all who knew him.

He married in 1924 Loryn, daughter of Oscar Tilton-Bowser, of Covington, Kentucky, USA. They had no children. During most of the time of his marriage (which was an exceedingly happy one and lasted for forty-eight years) he and his wife ran a farm, first in Sussex and later in Essex, specializing in cattle breeding. The two of them took a very active part in initiating and carrying through the rebuilding after war damage of St.

John's Church, Smith Square, London SW1. Parker died 15 September 1972 at Donhead St. Andrew, Wiltshire.

[*The Times*, 8 April 1971 and 16 September 1972; private information; personal knowledge.] D. A. S. CAIRNS

PARRY, SIR DAVID HUGHES (1893–1973), university administrator, was born 3 January 1893 at Llanaelhaearn, Caernarfonshire, the eldest of three sons and of four children of John Parry JP, a farmer, and his wife Anne Hughes, great-great-niece of Griffith Davies [q.v.]. Childhood on a hill farm from which a living could be wrested only by unremitting labour left an indelible mark on him. The family and community in which he grew up were both Welsh-speaking and deeply religious; Parry started to learn English only when he went to school and he became a full member of his local chapel at an early age and a lay preacher.

Educated at Pwllheli County School, he won a scholarship to the University College of Wales, Aberystwyth, in 1910, graduating four years later with first class honours in economics. He was commissioned in the Royal Welch Fusiliers in 1915 and, after active service on the western front, was invalided out of the army in 1919. After demobilization he went to Peterhouse, Cambridge, of which he became an honorary fellow in 1956, and was placed in the first class of part ii of the law tripos in 1920. In that year he became a lecturer in law at Aberystwyth. He was called to the bar in 1922 by the Inner Temple, of which he later became a bencher (1952), and took silk in 1955.

From 1924 to 1928 Hughes Parry was lecturer in law at the London School of Economics and Political Science, and from 1928 to 1930 reader. He was appointed professor of English law in 1930 in succession to Edward Jenks [q.v.]. He built up a law department which, by the time he retired in 1959, was second to none in the country. His other outstanding academic achievement was to create in the University of London the Institute of Advanced Legal Studies which became an international centre for legal research. He was its part-time director from 1947 to 1959.

He combined academic work with part-time practice in chambers at the Chancery bar from 1924 to 1946, being the joint editor of important works of reference such as the eleventh (1927) and the twelfth (1932) editions of *Wolstenholme and Cherry's Conveyancing Statutes*. His skill in the drafting and construction of documents was of great value to the many organizations with which he was connected. He was no stranger to the criminal law and was deputy chairman of Caernarfonshire quarter-sessions from 1950 to 1966.

At the University of London Hughes Parry had a unique career, holding practically every important elective office open to him, including the vice-chancellorship (1945–8) and the chairmanship of the court (1962–70). He played a leading part in the provision of adequate social and athletic facilities for students on a university, as opposed to a college, basis and a university hall of residence fittingly bears his name.

Hughes Parry remained devoted to Aberystwyth in spite of being passed over twice for the principalship (which affected him more deeply than he cared to admit) and was its president from 1954 to 1964. His early years in that office were clouded by a controversy within the college connected with the principal, Goronwy Rees [q.v.], but, after Rees resigned in 1957, under Hughes Parry's guidance there was a remarkable growth in facilities and student numbers. He was also very influential on the court and council of the University of Wales and successfully championed retention of its federal structure.

He was deputy chairman of the National Council for Social Service from 1948 to 1962. From 1953 to 1963 he was a member of the lord chancellor's committee on legal reform, on which he did invaluable service for he was not only careful and scholarly but also had a genuine legal imagination. He was also a member of departmental committees on subjects as diverse as war damage, the remuneration of doctors and dentists, colonial universities, and post-war reconstruction in Wales. Indeed his non-legal and non-academic activities were centred on Wales with which he never lost touch; he and his wife retained their Welsh house at Llanuwchllyn while they lived in London and returned to it after retirement. From 1963 to 1965 Hughes Parry chaired the committee on the legal status of the Welsh language which reached a common-sense compromise (later given statutory force) that Welsh should have equal validity with English. He was also closely connected with the Welsh League of Youth (founded by his brother-in-law) for over a quarter of a century and for even longer with the Eisteddfod, of which he was chairman for the last three years of his life. He was an elder of the Presbyterian Church of Wales in 1927, moderator of the North Wales Association in 1963–4, and moderator of the general assembly in 1964–5, an honour previously accorded to only one layman.

Though a devout Christian he found it hard to obey the injunction in the Lord's Prayer to forgive, particularly those who did not live up to his own high standards—or Welshmen who could but would not speak their native tongue. His generosity to others and to the institutions with which he was connected was in sharp contrast to the frugality of his own way of life which sometimes bordered on parsimony, and yet in his later years he took great pleasure in driving expensive motor cars. A puritan by nature, he had a distaste for the pleasures of the table. He was an imposing figure—tall, spare, and in his later years with a shock of white, wavy hair which marked him out in any company.

In London he was greatly liked and admired, not least for the skill with which he mediated between opposing groups and encouraged compromise solutions often of his own devising. In Wales the reaction to him was mixed and he had his critics to whom he appeared vain and obstinate. Perhaps he allowed his justified pride in his many achievements to come a little too often to the surface while his passionate devotion to Wales tended to blunt his judgement in the controversies, often denominational, in which he became involved.

Hughes Parry was the recipient of many honorary degrees, of which he prized most highly those of Wales (1947), Western Ontario (1948), Cambridge (1953), and London (1963). He was knighted in 1951.

In 1923 he married Haf (died 1965), only daughter of (Sir) Owen Morgan Edwards [q.v.], man of letters and inspector of education for Wales. They had no children. In a sense Hughes Parry lived in his father-in-law's shadow. His wife inherited her father's house at Llanuwchllyn, which remained their Welsh home from 1923 onwards. She herself was uncompromisingly Welsh. Hughes Parry died at his home in Llanuwchllyn 8 January 1973.

[Sir David Hughes Parry, *O Bentref Llanaelhaearn i Ddinas Llundain* (*From the Village of Llanaelhaearn to the City of London*) (unfinished autobiography), 1973 (privately published); D. M. Clitheroe, *Impressions of David Hughes Parry*, 1974 (privately published); private information; personal knowledge.]

D. W. Logan

PARRY, Sir (WILLIAM) EDWARD (1893–1972), admiral, was born in London 8 April 1893, the elder child and only son of (Sir) (Frederick) Sydney Parry KBE, CB, (1861–1941), civil servant, and his wife, Anna Mary, daughter of William Henry Fremantle, DD, a canon of Canterbury and fellow of All Souls and Balliol Colleges, Oxford, and later dean of Ripon. His paternal grandfather Edward Parry (1830–1890, q.v.) was archdeacon of Canterbury and later suffragan bishop of Dover. Parry came of a family with a long and distinguished naval tradition, going back almost 200 years. His great-grandfather Admiral Sir (William) Edward Parry (1790–1855, q.v.) was the well-known Arctic explorer, and Admiral Sir Thomas Francis Fremantle (1765–1819, q.v.), one of Nelson's captains at Trafalgar, was a great-great-grandfather.

Parry entered Osborne College as a naval cadet in September 1905 and quickly showed great intellectual ability. He passed out of Dartmouth College top of his term four years later and gained five prizes. As a lieutenant Parry specialized in the torpedo branch which then included responsibility for all the navy's electrical equipment. In World War I he served as torpedo officer of the cruiser *Birmingham* in the Grand Fleet. He was promoted commander in 1927 and in 1934, after a very successful commission as executive officer and second-in-command of the aircraft carrier *Eagle* on the China station, he was promoted captain. His first command was the anti-submarine school at Portland 1936–7, after which he took the Imperial Defence College course. In 1938 he was lent to the Royal New Zealand Navy for command of the cruiser *Achilles*, and in that appointment he took part in the battle of the river Plate (13 December 1939), in which he was wounded but continued in command. The battle resulted in the self-destruction of the formidable German 'pocket battleship' *Admiral Graf Spee* off Montevideo four days later. Parry was appointed CB (1939) for his part in that action, and in 1940–2 served as commodore commanding the New Zealand squadron and first naval member of the New Zealand Naval Board.

After returning home Parry took command of the recently modernized battle cruiser *Renown*, which among other duties carried (Sir) Winston Churchill and his staff to Canada and Egypt for the second Quebec and Cairo conferences. In 1944 he was promoted rear-admiral and for the invasion of Normandy (June 1944) he was in command of one of the two 'follow-up' forces. After a period as deputy head of the naval division of the Control Commission for Germany, in 1946 he was appointed director of naval intelligence, an important post which he held for two difficult years. In 1948 he was promoted vice-admiral and was lent to India as commander-in-chief of the Royal Indian Navy. His task was a very taxing one as not only had the RIN recently been riven by mutinies but 'Indianization' of the service was rapidly being carried out and the British withdrawal from the sub-continent was imminent. In 1950 Parry was advanced to KCB and he was promoted admiral in the following year. He retired in 1952 and took up fruit farming in Kent.

In 1922 Parry married Maude Mary Douglas-Hamilton (died 1971), whose first marriage had been annulled, daughter of Dr Arthur Charles de Beauvoir Phillips. They had a son and a daughter who were twins. His daughter wrote biographies of her Parry and Fremantle ancestors. His wife was of great help to him both in New Zealand, where they won the confidence of the Labour politicians then in power and of the naval personnel, and in India where they were equally successful with the Congress leaders and became friends of Jawaharlal Nehru [q.v.]. Parry died in London 21 August 1972.

[Stephen W. Roskill, *The War at Sea 1939–1945*, 4 vols., 1954–61; S. D. Waters, *The Royal New Zealand Navy* (Wellington, 1956); Sir Eugen Millington-Drake, *The Drama of Graf Spee and Battle of the Plate*, 1967; personal knowledge and correspondence.]

STEPHEN W. ROSKILL

PARTRIDGE, ERIC HONEYWOOD (1894–1979), lexicographer and etymologist, was born 6 February 1894 in the Waimata Valley, a farming district near Gisborne in New Zealand, the son of John Thomas Partridge, grazier, and his wife, Ethel Annabella Norris. About 1907 his family emigrated to Australia and he attended Toowoomba Grammar School before entering the University of Queensland in 1914. His studies were interrupted by the war and he served with the Australian Imperial Forces at Gallipoli and on the western front. He completed his BA at the University of Queensland in 1921.

A travelling scholarship took him to Oxford, where, as a non-collegiate student, he wrote a thesis on Romantic poetry of the eighteenth century before the Lyrical Ballads as the requirement for his University of Queensland MA. In 1923 he completed a B.Litt. thesis for the University of Oxford on English and French literature of the Romantic period. Both were published as books in Paris in 1924.

He was a lecturer in English literature at the universities of Manchester, 1925–6, and London, 1926–7. In 1927 he left the academic world in order to become a writer and a publisher. He founded the Scholartis Press with a capital of £100, and it published a number of works, including some of his own, before it went out of business in the economic depression of the early 1930s. Using the pseudonym 'Corrie Denison' he wrote three novels, but they went unregarded.

Other works that he wrote or edited at about this time pointed the way to his later obsessional interest in popular vocabulary: *Songs and Slang of the British Soldier (1914–1918)* with John Brophy (1930); *American Tramp and Underworld Slang*, with G. Irwin (1931); and *Francis Grose's Classical Dictionary of the Vulgar Tongue* (1931), reprinted from the third edition of 1796.

His most celebrated work, *A Dictionary of Slang and Unconventional English*, was published in 1937. He revised it at regular intervals rather in the informal way in which a child extends a hastily constructed sand-castle.

In the war of 1939–45 he served first in the Army Education Corps (1940–1) and later in a propaganda department of the RAF (1942–5) with H. E. Bates [q.v.] and other writers. These duties appear not to have greatly impeded his own writing and he produced an astonishing number of books in the 1940s. The best known of these were *A Dictionary of Clichés* (1940), *Usage and Abusage* (1942), *A Dictionary of RAF Slang* (1945), *Shakespeare's Bawdy* (1947), and *A Dictionary of Forces' Slang, 1939–45* (with W. Granville and F. Roberts, 1948).

By the end of the 1940s Partridge had established his reputation partly by using a technique well known to eighteenth-century lexicographers—the taking over, more or less verbatim, of material published at an earlier date, and wrapping it in a cloak of evidence he had gathered himself. In 1949 some of the contents of his *Dictionary of the Underworld British and American* was found to be closely related to work published by an American scholar, David W. Maurer. The matter was settled out of court in Maurer's favour.

Much of his primary lexicographical evidence came from a kind of proletariat army of devoted correspondents. Thousands of scholars and laymen throughout the world accepted his invitation to submit details of local usage. For Partridge—the great word peasant—these other peasants were the equivalent of staff, as he continued to work, otherwise without assistance, at the same desk, K1, in the British Museum. He rewarded the more productive of them with autographed copies of his books and with his autobiographical Christmas cards.

The pattern remained the same for the rest of his life. He compiled new editions of his dictionaries and wrote many books about English usage. Two works of more enduring value stand out from the rest: *Origins: a Short Etymological Dictionary of Modern English* (1958); and *A Dictionary of Catch Phrases: British and American from the Sixteenth Century to the Present Day* (1977).

Amateur enthusiasts of words who knew him through his books spoke of him with unqualified admiration and sympathy. Edmund Wilson called him 'the word king', and Benny Green 'the Middleweight Champion of the Word'. Others caught from him 'a sense of passionate and infectious curiosity about words'. This may have been his greatest contribution, for his professional contemporaries judged his work as partially flawed by its derivative nature and by a quirky mode of presentation.

In appearance a cheerful, rather shambling, and self-effacing figure, he was obsessively interested in tennis and cricket. He played tennis himself and for many years forecast the Wimbledon results in *Time and Tide*. He was a member of the Surrey and Middlesex cricket clubs and often went to The Oval and Lord's on working days. His other main obsession, apart from his work, was an incurable belief in his own impecuniosity, though in the end his estate was, by any normal standard, substantial.

In 1964 the University of Queensland awarded him the honorary degree of Doctor of Letters.

In 1925 he married Agnes Dora (died 1978), daughter of Arthur James Vye-Parminter, an architect. They had one daughter. Partridge died 1 June 1979 at Moretonhampstead, Devon.

[David Crystal (ed.), *Eric Partridge in his Own Words*, 1980; private information; personal knowledge.] ROBERT BURCHFIELD

PATCH, SIR EDMUND LEO HALL- (1896–1975), civil servant. [See HALL-PATCH.]

PAYNE, BEN IDEN (1881–1976), director and actor, was born at Newcastle upon Tyne 5 September 1881, the youngest in the family of two sons and two daughters of the Revd Alfred Payne, a Unitarian minister, and his wife, Sarah Glover. He was educated privately and at Manchester Grammar School. He went into the theatre, making a début in November 1899 with the company of (Sir) F. R. (Frank) Benson [q.v.]—regarded then as the university of the theatre—at Worcester as Diggory in *She Stoops to Conquer.* During the following spring he had a few small parts with Benson in a London season at the Lyceum. He acted in various minor tours; and while he was at Waterford, in his mid-twenties, he met somebody he would describe later as 'a tall, dark man who looked, in his coal black suit and the dim light behind the scenery, so like a priest that for a moment I thought he was one'. This personage was the poet W. B. Yeats [q.v.]; it appeared that the actor-director A. Granville-Barker [q.v.], impressed by Payne after one short talk in an ABC teashop, had recommended the thoughtful and intelligent young man to Yeats as stage director of the Abbey Theatre, Dublin. Payne was out of key there; but presently he met the wealthy theatre-minded philanthropist, Miss A. E. F. Horniman [q.v.], who was dissatisfied with events in Dublin where, a critic said, she had been 'acting as fairy godmother to the singularly ungrateful Cinderella' of the Abbey; she and Lady Gregory [q.v.] had been antipathetic. Liking Iden Payne, she engaged him to advise on her further theatrical activities; he told her that Manchester, civilized in the arts, should be her centre, and when he was twenty-six, wise beyond his years, he inaugurated the English repertory movement—at first, during the autumn of 1907, in an oblong ballroom known as the Midland Hotel Theatre.

Soon, at Easter 1908, the company moved to the old Gaiety Theatre, before long to be reconstructed without any concession to more flamboyant tastes: no gilt, no flock wallpaper, neither brass nor drums in the orchestra. Payne's tastes, which matched those of Miss Horniman, were for a quiet, gentle austerity that he would not lose during the rest of his long career. The first Gaiety production was *Measure for Measure*, directed by a single-minded puritan zealot, William Poel [q.v.], whose work for Shakespeare, with its insistence on fluidity of action, influenced Payne all his life. The Gaiety company was remarkable; it would include, at various times, (Dame) Sybil Thorndike [q.v.], (Sir) Lewis Casson, Mona Limerick, Herbert Lomas, Ada King, and the young Basil Dean [q.v.]. After four years of tireless, unassuming endeavour during which he encouraged a regional school of dramatists and gave to Manchester an uncommon run of major plays, he left to tour and to originate seasons elsewhere, with his first wife, the actress Mona Limerick, a much more forceful figure than the calm idealist Payne, though he did have an idealist's persistence. In the autumn of 1913 he went to America where he directed at Chicago and Philadelphia and where most of his later life would be spent.

As general producer to Charles Frohman's company in New York (1917–22), he directed a wide variety of plays; with his experience he was able to take on anything and face the frustrations of the commercial Broadway stage, but his heart was always with the intellectual drama and particularly with Shakespeare. Later he held a number of academic appointments and acted two or three times (Henry Straker in *Man and Superman* by G. B. Shaw [q.v.] in Newport, Rhode Island, 1932, was the last); he still thought of himself as primarily an actor. His special reputation was as visiting professor (1919–28) at the Carnegie Institute of Technology in Pittsburgh (the 'Carnegie Tech'), which had the first American university drama department.

Payne was particularly delighted when Sir Archibald Flower invited him to succeed W. Bridges-Adams [q.v.] as director of what was then the new Shakespeare Memorial Theatre in Stratford-upon-Avon, opened only three years before. He was there for eight years from 1935 (when he began with *Antony and Cleopatra*), a disappointing period in a theatre unkind to his methods and to his use of modified Elizabethan staging, with its penthouse, various acting areas, and 'curtain-boys'. Relinquishing his post in 1942, in 1943 he gratefully returned to the United States. He became head of drama at several American universities; his work, now largely Shakespearian, was almost entirely so from 1946. He was appointed guest professor of drama at the University of Texas; a new 500-seat theatre there was named after him in 1976, only a month before his death. One production, *Hobson's Choice* (1953) would be a wistful memory of the 'Manchester school'.

As innovator and teacher (his great gift) he was always warmly respected, though his name—for he believed modesty to be the best policy—was never as potent as it should have been in the wider world of the theatre. E. Martin Browne, the English director, who for some time in the late 1920s was his assistant at the 'Carnegie Tech', called him a professional to the bone, 'slight and smallish, very agile, with a mobile face of great charm'. He was 'quite without the grand manner that his record in the theatre would have justified'. He had many theatrical awards and was honorary LL D of the University of Alberta, Canada (1963).

Payne's first marriage in 1906, to Mary Charlotte Louise Gadney ('Mona Limerick') was dissolved in 1950. They had one son and two daughters, one of whom married (Sir) Donald Wolfit [q.v.]. In 1950 he married, secondly, Barbara Rankin Chiaroni who survived him. He died in Austin, Texas, 6 April 1976, at the age of ninety-four.

[Ben Iden Payne, *A Life in a Wooden O*, 1977; E. Martin Browne, with Henzie Browne, *Two in One*, 1981; Sally Beauman, *The Royal Shakespeare Company: a History of Ten Decades*, 1982; *The Times*, 8 April 1976, 9 May 1977, and 2 April 1978; personal knowledge.]

J. C. Trewin

PEARSON, COLIN HARGREAVES, Baron Pearson (1899–1980), lord of appeal in ordinary, was born in Minnedosa, Manitoba, Canada, 28 July 1899, the youngest of three children and the younger son of Ernest William Pearson, a lawyer, and his wife, Jessie Borland. The family moved to London when Pearson was seven. He was educated at St. Paul's School. His sister died in childbirth and his brother was killed in World War I. After military service in 1918 in the 5th Guards Machine Gun Regiment he went to Balliol College, Oxford, where he was a classical scholar and a Jenkyns exhibitioner. He obtained a first class in classical honour moderations (1920) and a second in *literae humaniores* (1922). He then turned to law. He was called to the bar in 1924 by the Inner Temple and held a Yarborough Anderson exhibition.

Pearson built up a sizeable common law practice. In 1930 he was appointed junior counsel to the Office of Works, and in 1937 recorder of Hythe. During World War II he worked in the Treasury solicitor's office. He returned to the bar in 1945 and took silk in 1949. Only two years later, in 1951, although not well known as an advocate, he was appointed a judge of the King's Bench division of the High Court. It proved to be an inspired choice. It soon became apparent that he had now found his true role.

In 1960 Pearson briefly became president of the Restrictive Practices Court, but in the following January he was promoted to be lord justice of appeal. In 1965 he was further promoted to the House of Lords and sat as a lord of appeal in ordinary until 1974. After 1974 he occasionally spoke in debates.

Pearson never thought of himself as a great judicial intellectual. But he had a clear mind, profound legal knowledge, and unfailing courtesy. His judgements in some leading cases, if not couched in scintillating terms, have stood up well.

Pearson was a valuable committee man. He chaired a committee in 1958–9 about managing funds paid into court for widows and infants; served on the Supreme Court rule committee (1957–65); and chaired the Law Reform Committee (1963–73). But he did not restrict himself to the law. His name was increasingly brought before a wider public as he conducted inquiries into a whole series of industrial disputes—electricity supply (1964), shipping (1966–7), civil air transport (1967–8), steel (1968), and docks (1970). In 1971–2 he chaired the arbitral body on teachers' pay.

In 1973 Pearson was asked to head the royal commission on civil liability and compensation for personal injury. He regarded this assignment as the culmination of his career. The existing compensation arrangements, especially over the operation of tort in regard to work and road accidents, had been much criticized, and the review which he now undertook, lasting five years and involving the taking of much evidence at home and abroad, was the most thorough survey of its kind ever conducted. The commission had a widely drawn membership, but Pearson achieved a report which, on essentials, was unanimous. It concluded that social security and tort had developed as though they had little to do with each other, and proposed a new relationship, with tort having a junior topping-up role. Detailed recommendations included a 'no fault' scheme for road accidents and a regime of strict liability for defective products, including drugs, a proposal especially relevant to the thalidomide tragedy.

Pearson was greatly disappointed that there was so little response by government, and in his own profession, to the ideas so carefully argued in his monumental report. He admitted that he had underrated the strength of the forces opposed to change.

Pearson always took a close interest in education. He did much to help St. Paul's School and Bedford College, London. He took particular pleasure in his appointment as visitor to Balliol College (1965–74). He was appointed CBE in 1946, knighted in 1951, and sworn of the Privy Council in 1961. He became a bencher of his Inn in 1951, and was treasurer in 1974.

Pearson was a gentle, courteous, and patient man who inspired great affection. To the end, he remained remarkably receptive to new ideas. He made a notable contribution, not just to the law, but also to wider concerns of society.

In 1931 Pearson married Sophie Grace, eldest daughter of Arthur Hermann Thomas, an antiquarian and deputy keeper of records at Guildhall. There was one son and one daughter. Pearson died in London 31 January 1980.

[*The Times*, 1 and 7 February 1980; private information; personal knowledge.]

ALLEN OF ABBEYDALE

PEARSON, EGON SHARPE (1895–1980), statistician, was born 11 August 1895 at Hampstead, London, the only son and second of the three children of Karl Pearson [q.v.], biometrician, of Hampstead, and his wife Maria, fifth daughter and sixth child of William Sharpe, solicitor, of Islington. He was educated at the Dragon School, Oxford, and Winchester College, and was then accepted in June 1914 as an entrance scholar to Trinity College, Cambridge. Following the outbreak of war, he went to Trinity somewhat reluctantly, where, in spite of ill health, he obtained at the end of one year a first class in part i of the mathematical tripos. After a period of war service at the Admiralty and Ministry of Shipping, he was able to return to Cambridge and qualify for a BA in 1920 (and MA in 1924) after a further approved course of study.

After leaving Cambridge Pearson joined his father's department at University College, London, as a statistics lecturer. He obtained his London D.Sc. in 1926. He helped with the editing of the journal *Biometrika*, founded in 1901 by Karl Pearson and W. F. R. Weldon [q.v.] with the support of (Sir) Francis Galton [q.v.], who had also on his death endowed the chair held by Karl Pearson at University College from 1911. By 1924 E. S. Pearson was appointed assistant editor of *Biometrika*, becoming managing editor in 1936 after his father's death. Three years earlier Karl Pearson had retired from the Galton chair, and his department was split into two, the eugenics (later renamed human genetics) department with which the Galton chair was associated, and a statistics department, of which E. S. Pearson was made head with promotion to reader, becoming a professor in 1935.

An animosity between Karl Pearson and the new Galton professor, (Sir) R. A. Fisher [q.v.], both of whom had not approved the separation of the statistics department, did not augur well for its development. Moreover, E. S. Pearson was to have an important professional collaboration with Jerzy Neyman, a Polish mathematician whose interest in mathematical statistics had been stimulated both by his friendly association with E. S. Pearson while studying at University College, and indirectly by the work of R. A. Fisher, but whose theoretical approach appeared to Fisher of little relevance. Nevertheless, the Neyman–Pearson theory of testing statistical hypotheses, resulting from a collaboration extending over eight or nine years, secured a recognized place in textbooks on statistical inference, introducing such new and useful concepts as the 'power' of statistical tests against alternative hypotheses.

A less controversial development was E. S. Pearson's encouragement of statistical methods in industry in the United Kingdom, arising from a contact established with W. H. Shewhart of the Bell Telephone Laboratories during a visit to North America in 1931. This utilitarian approach to statistical methodology contributed also after 1939 to Pearson's war work, when he, with some of his staff, was seconded to the Ordnance Board, where they were involved in such problems as assessing the effectiveness of patterns of fragmentation of anti-aircraft shells.

After the war Pearson returned to University College where he retained an office even after his retirement in 1960 from his chair, in order to continue with his editorial work for *Biometrika*. In 1934 he had married (Dorothy) Eileen, younger daughter of Russell Jolly, solicitor, and they had two daughters. It was a great personal loss when his wife died from pneumonia in 1949, though he kept on their Hampstead house with the aid of a housekeeper, until 1967 when he moved to Cambridge after marrying Margaret Theodosia, widow of Laurence Beddome Turner, reader emeritus in engineering, Cambridge, and second daughter of George Frederick Ebenezer Scott, architect, and Mrs Bernard Turner, of Godstowe School, High Wycombe. In 1975, after her death, he finally severed his remaining links with *Biometrika*, and moved to West Lavington, near Midhurst in Sussex, where he lived until his death at Midhurst 12 June 1980.

Pearson had a quiet disposition, but his shy and rather diffident manner hid an independent and pertinacious spirit which had enabled him to surmount both the controversies surrounding his father Karl and contemporaries like Fisher and Neyman, and some health problems, such as his delicate health when an undergraduate, a heart condition of long standing, and occasional back trouble due to his considerable height. To this Dictionary he contributed the notice of W. S. Gosset ('Student').

Honours and awards included the Weldon prize and medal in 1935, appointment as CBE in 1946, and in 1955 the gold medal of the Royal Statistical Society, of which he was president in 1955–6. He was elected FRS in 1966.

[M. S. Bartlett in *Biographical Memoirs of Fellows of the Royal Society*, vol. xxvii, 1981; private information; personal knowledge.]

M. S. Bartlett

PEARSON, LESTER BOWLES (1897–1972), prime minister of Canada, was born 23 April 1897 in Newtonbrook, Ontario, the second of the three sons (there were no daughters) of the Revd Edwin Arthur Pearson, a Methodist minister, and his wife, Annie Sarah, daughter of Thomas Bowles, a well-known figure in local business and politics. The origins of the family were predominantly Irish. He was educated at high schools in Peterborough and Hamilton and entered the University of Toronto in 1913. In 1915 he enlisted in the Canadian Army Medical Corps as a private; after two years at a hospital camp at Salonika he was sent to England on an officers' training course; but he was injured in a traffic accident in London and returned to Canada in April 1918. He went back to Toronto University and graduated in 1919 with honours in history. After two false starts, in law and business, he decided on an academic career; in 1921 he secured a scholarship which enabled him to spend two years at St. John's College, Oxford. In 1923 he was appointed a lecturer in modern history at Toronto University, and in 1926 assistant professor. He enjoyed teaching and appeared settled in university life.

In 1928, however, he was persuaded to sit the entrance examination for the Department of External Affairs; he passed first and entered the Department as a first secretary. He served in Ottawa until 1935, when he went to the High Commission in London as first secretary, and was promoted to counsellor in 1939. In 1941 he returned to Ottawa and in 1942 was posted to Washington, where he remained until 1946, first as minister-counsellor and then, from 1945, as ambassador. While in Washington, in addition to his representational duties, he was closely involved in the planning of the United Nations and other post-war international organizations.

In 1946 he returned to Ottawa as deputy minister (namely, permanent secretary) to Louis St. Laurent [q.v.], who had recently been appointed secretary of state for external affairs in the Liberal government of W. L. Mackenzie King [q.v.]. The two were much attached, and when in 1948 King retired and St. Laurent succeeded him as prime minister, Pearson was offered, and accepted, the vacant portfolio of external affairs. He obtained a seat in the House of Commons in October 1948, at a by-election in the riding of Algoma East, in northern Ontario.

Pearson was not enthusiastic about entering upon a political career; but the next nine years, handling foreign affairs with the authority of ministerial status and the confidence of a congenial prime minister, were the most satisfying and fruitful of his life. In the post-war decade, the influence of Canada as a 'middle power' was at its height, and Pearson won an unrivalled reputation on the international scene: he played a part in the creation of the North Atlantic Treaty Organization (NATO), in the evolution of the Commonwealth into its modern shape, in the negotiations over the future of Palestine, and in the ending of the war in Korea. His most notable exploit was in the Suez crisis of October 1956. He was deeply shocked by the Anglo–French invasion of Egypt; but his immediate reaction was to speed to New York and strive, through the United Nations, to contain the damage. By a prodigious display of energy and patience, he succeeded in securing agreement on a cease-fire, the withdrawal of the invading forces, and the dispatch to the area of a United Nations peace-keeping force. His efforts were recognized by the award of the Nobel peace prize in 1957.

Meanwhile at home the Liberal government was running into trouble, and in the election of 1957 the Conservatives were returned as the largest party in the House of Commons. John Diefenbaker [q.v.] formed his first administration in June 1957, and St. Laurent, aged seventy-five, resigned the Liberal leadership in September. At the subsequent party convention Pearson was elected to succeed him. He had allowed his name to be put forward with hesitation, more from a sense of public duty than from personal inclination. His training for political leadership was, as he himself put it, 'unusual': he had entered politics at the age of fifty, he had no back-bench experience, and his only ministerial portfolio had been that of external affairs.

His début in the House of Commons as leader of the opposition was disastrous. He was persuaded by colleagues to move a foolish no-confidence motion calling for the resignation of the government, which gave Diefenbaker an opening for a devastating attack on Pearson personally and on the Liberal record, and also a pretext for seeking a renewed mandate from the electorate. The election, in March 1958, was a landslide for the Conservatives, and the Liberals were in opposition for the next five years. While in opposition, Pearson devoted much time to a thorough overhaul of the Liberal party, which had become somewhat ossified in its twenty-two years in office; he and his friends brought in new blood and a new momentum.

The federal election of 1962 was a disaster for the Conservatives (they lost ninety-two seats), chiefly because of their own errors and internal dissensions, and in a further election in April 1963 the Liberals were returned as the largest party, though in a minority in the House of Commons. When Pearson called another election in 1965 the result was not very different, and throughout his period as prime minister the Liberals never had an outright majority to rely on. Nevertheless, his government's record, in his five years of office, was a creditable one. They stimulated business activity and reduced unemployment, and they implemented many of the plans they had evolved in opposition, especially in the field of social legislation.

Above all, Pearson tackled the Quebec problem. French-speaking Canadians were demanding a more equal partnership with their English-speaking compatriots. Quebec was emerging as a modern, progressive society, jealous of its full rights as a province. Pearson understood the strength of the feelings of the Québecois and saw the need for giving them reasonable satisfaction within the federal structure. He set up a strong royal commission on bilingualism and biculturalism, which recommended linguistic equality. Against a barrage of opposition he established a new national flag, which did not feature the Union Jack. The most difficult problems were presented by Quebec's demand for full control of every aspect of provincial jurisdiction, involving a greater share of national revenue than existing arrangements provided. The interests of the other provinces were affected, and in the complicated negotiations Pearson deployed his incomparable talent for finding constructive compromises. He regarded his contribution to improving the balance between English and French Canada as his most important achievement.

Pearson's two administrations were bedevilled by a series of incidents involving accusations against ministers, ranging from minor irregularities to corruption; some were serious, some trivial, but the opposition and the press made the most of them, and the government's reputation suffered. In the handling of these painful cases and in some other matters Pearson's lack of practical political experience showed itself; it did not help that he was, for almost the whole of his time as prime minister, face to face with Diefenbaker, who outclassed him in the rough-and-tumble of a very unruly House.

He had intended to retire at seventy, in April 1967, but felt that he had to see through the celebrations in that year of the centenary of Canadian confederation. He played his part with good-humoured grace in the innumerable ceremonies, including a highly successful visit by the Queen. But when General de Gaulle, in a speech at Montreal on his way to Ottawa, had the effrontery not only to utter a slogan of the Quebec separatists but to compare his progress through Quebec with the liberation of Paris in 1944, he reacted with fury and the rest of de Gaulle's visit was cancelled.

In April 1968 Pearson resigned from the office of prime minister and from the leadership of the Liberal Party, and he did not stand at the election later that year. In retirement, he returned with gusto to the international scene: he gave lectures, including the BBC's Reith lectures in 1968 ('Peace in the Family of Man'); in 1968–9 he was chairman of a World Bank commission on development problems; and he was chairman of the International Institute for Strategic Studies from 1968. He finished the first of three volumes of memoirs and left enough material for the other two to be completed by others after his death.

As a man, 'Mike' Pearson (as he was universally named) had great personal charm: he was warm, friendly, easy, with a ready turn of wit, often self-deprecating; he had no trace of pomposity or conceit. He was happiest in small gatherings, and unfortunately he did not succeed in conveying his charm to the public; he was not impressive on the platform or on television. He had a slight lisp, and his speaking manner was that of the lecturer rather than the orator. He was no match for Diefenbaker as a campaigner.

He had a consuming passion for sport: he had half blues for lacrosse and ice hockey at Oxford, he was a baseball coach at Toronto University, and an addicted spectator of all games in later life.

He married Maryon Elspeth, daughter of Dr A. W. Moody, of Winnipeg, in 1925; they had a son, who entered the Canadian foreign service, and a daughter.

Pearson was appointed OBE in 1935 and CC (Canada) in 1968. He was admitted to the Privy Council (Canada) in 1948 and the Privy Council in 1963. He was admitted to the Order of Merit in 1971, and awarded numerous honorary degrees including an Oxford DCL (1951). He died in Ottawa 27 December 1972.

[*The Times*, 29 December 1972; L. B. Pearson, *Memoirs*, 3 vols., 1973–5; private information; personal knowledge.]

H. Lintott

PENROSE, LIONEL SHARPLES (1898–1972), physician, was born in London 11 June 1898 of Quaker stock, the second of the four sons (there were no daughters) of James Doyle Penrose, portrait painter, and his wife, Elizabeth Josephine, daughter of Alexander (later Lord) Peckover FSA, banker and collector. He was educated at the Downs School, Colwall, and Leighton Park School, Reading. On leaving school in 1916 he served in the Friends' Ambulance Train of the British Red Cross in France until the end of World War I, when he went up to St. John's College, Cambridge. His main interests were in mathematics and psychology. He eventually chose the moral sciences tripos, in which he gained a first in part ii in 1921; he was also awarded the Newcombe prize. After a year's postgraduate work in psychology at Cambridge he repaired to Vienna, then a centre of psychiatric research, where he stayed for two years and became deeply interested in mental illness. He decided that for this work a medical qualification was desirable. He did his clinical work at St. Thomas's Hospital, London, where he qualified MRCS, LRCP in 1928 and gained the Bristowe medal (1929).

His first post was at the City Mental Hospital, Cardiff, where his study of schizophrenia formed the basis of a successful MD thesis (1930). In 1931 he moved to the Royal Eastern Counties Institution at Colchester, a mental hospital with a large number of mentally defective patients. He at once became interested in this hitherto neglected branch of medicine, not only because of the human aspects, but also because the 300,000 patients in the general population posed a serious social problem, and little thought had been given to the possibilities of the prevention of mental illness. Over seven years he made a detailed study of 1,280 mentally defective patients and their 6,629 sibs, plus their parents and other relatives. This was published in a Medical Research Council special report and later expanded in two books, *Mental Defect* (1933) and *The Biology of Mental Defect* (1949, 4th edn., revised by J. M. Berg and H. Lang-Brown, 1972). This work not only shaped Penrose's own research career in mental defect and human genetics, but had a profound effect on the whole future of these subjects.

From 1939 to 1945 he was director of psychiatric research in Ontario, Canada, where he made an important study on the efficacy of shock therapy. He was then appointed to the Galton chair of eugenics at University College, London. He reorganized the department and in 1963 had the name of the chair changed to the Galton chair of human genetics. He continued his work on mental defect, in particular on mongolism, which he renamed Down's anomaly (later Down's syndrome), and he wrote a notable monograph on the subject in 1966, the centenary of J. Langdon Down's first description of the condition.

In the 1950s methods were developed for isolating, counting, classifying, and examining chromosomes. His use of these methods made striking advances in the knowledge of human genetics. His *Outline of Human Genetics* (1960) had a third edition in 1973. He was apt at suggesting new and original lines of research. He was an authority on dermatoglyphs—the finger, palm, and sole prints which are of diagnostic value in mental disease. He made contributions to the diagnosis and treatment of phenylketonuria, an inherited metabolic anomaly, which if not diagnosed and treated early in life causes mental defect. He was one of the first to determine the mutation rate of harmful genes in man. He followed clues with unusual tenacity. One example was his reconstruction of the Lambert pedigree, dating from 1732. This family suffered from a peculiar skin disease, with an even more peculiar mode of inheritance, and was cited in most books on human genetics. With the aid of his wife, who was also a doctor of medicine, Penrose examined diocesan and parish records in Suffolk and showed that the pedigree abounded in errors and that the mode of inheritance was quite different from what had been claimed. When he retired from the Galton chair in 1965 he continued his work at the Kennedy–Galton Centre at Harperbury Hospital, near St. Albans.

His work gained international recognition. He was awarded honorary degrees by McGill (1958), Edinburgh (1970), Newcastle (1968), and Göteborg (1966), the Weldon medal from Oxford (1950), the Albert Lasker award (1960), the International award of the Joseph P. Kennedy Foundation (1964), and the James Calvert Spence medal in paediatrics (1964). He was president of the Genetical Society of Great Britain (1955–8) and of the Third International Congress of Human Genetics in Chicago in 1966. He was elected to fellowship of the Royal Society in 1953, of the Royal College of Physicians of London in 1962, and of the Royal College of Psychiatrists in 1971.

Apart from his scientific work, an enduring interest was his opposition to war, both on moral and practical grounds. He was one of the founders and for over ten years president of the Medical Association for the Prevention of War. He had many other interests, including music, painting, chess, and making ingenious puzzles both for children and adults, some of which were of scientific value in illustrating the biological principle of replication, as seen in the copying of genetic material. The combination of high intelligence, modesty, and a sense of humour made him an agreeable companion.

In 1928 he married Margaret, daughter of John Beresford Leathes, FRS, professor of physiology at Leeds. They had three sons and one daughter—Oliver became professor of mathematics at the Open University, Roger became Rouse Ball professor of mathematics at Oxford and FRS, Jonathan was British chess champion on ten occasions, and Shirley became a consultant paediatrician.

[Harry Harris in *Biographical Memoirs of Fellows of the Royal Society*, vol. xix, 1973; *Munk's Roll of the Royal College of Physicians of London*, vol. vi, 1982; private information; personal knowledge.] A. M. COOKE

PETERS, AUGUST DETLOF ('AUGUSTUS DUDLEY') (1892–1973), literary agent, was born in Schleswig-Holstein, 25 August 1892, the fourth of the seven children of George Peters, farmer and, later, civil servant. His father was born Danish, but, due to Prussia's annexation of Schleswig-Holstein, Peters was born German. When he was three his father went bankrupt as a farmer and four aunts took charge of the young children until their father's fortunes improved. In Peters's words 'they never did. He was persuaded to sign the pledge and that broke his spirit.' His aunt Lisette, his father's sister, adopted Peters. She ran a girls' school in Brighton, so he began life in England as an alien and the only boy in a girls' school. In about 1900 his aunt moved to a boarding-house in Hampstead, and in due course Peters went to the Haberdashers' Aske's School, Hampstead. In 1911 he went up to St. John's College, Cambridge. He obtained a second class in medieval and modern languages in 1913 and a third in part ii of the economics tripos in 1914.

He had developed a passion for cricket and in the summer of 1914, while he was with the college cricket team on tour in Kent, the war broke out. He and two friends left to join the Artists' Rifles. But it was discovered that Peters had been born in Schleswig-Holstein and was thus technically German. As an enemy alien he was handed over to the police but was told that he could do anything he liked except join the armed forces. This incident left him with a deep resentment of Germany and Germans. He worked for a Manchester cotton merchant and a lead mine in north Wales until 1917, when the shortage of troops brought a change in the rules whereby aliens could join up. But he was only allowed into a labour battalion, and served in Belgium from 1917 until June 1919, when he became first assistant editor of the *World* and then editor of this and other magazines at Odhams Press until 1923.

But he was already more interested in the theatre and in the early 1920s was a regular contributor to the drama page of the *Daily Telegraph*. He heard from James Agate [q.v.] that the *Daily Chronicle* was looking for a new dramatic critic. He got the job in 1923, but was bored by it and disillusioned about the future. In the following year, at the age of thirty-two, partly due to pressure from writer friends who were unprotected against their publishers, he found his true vocation and started a literary agency. He realized, or perhaps imagined, that he did not have the makings of a first-class writer, and throughout his life maintained that in order to be a good agent you first had to be a writer *manqué*. The kind of insight which, in Arthur Koestler's words, 'turns many a bitter young man into a jaundiced literary critic, had the opposite effect on Peters. He gave up his job as a critic and became a catalyst.'

In 1924 there were few literary agencies, and even fewer with good reputations. Peters prospered in this role from the start. W. N. Roughead, a Scottish rugby international, joined the firm in 1927. In 1929 he bought the Andrew Dakers agency, and Dakers's secretary Margaret Stephens agreed to stay with him. She was to become his right hand and a pillar of the agency. Already his list of authors included (Sir) J. C. Squire, Hilaire Belloc, Edmund Blunden [qq.v.], Alec Waugh, J. B. Priestley, Gerald Bullett, Martin Armstrong, (Dame) Rebecca West, and Sheila Kaye-Smith. In the early 1930s these were joined by (Sir) Terence Rattigan, James Agate, Eric Linklater, C. S. Forester, A. E. Coppard, Evelyn Waugh, C. Day Lewis [qq.v.], Margaret Irwin, John Moore, Frank O'Connor, Margery Sharp, J. L. Hodson, Norman Collins, and others who joined as clients and became friends.

Throughout his career Peters probably did more than anyone else to secure and defend the rights and standing of authors, having started as an agent at a time when publishers were notorious for the harshness of their contracts and the arrogance of their business dealings. In so doing, in the words of Arthur Koestler at his eightieth birthday dinner, 'he conferred upon the profession of literary agent an aura of integrity, humanity and dignity which it had not possessed before'. His work was his hobby and because his love of good writing, or the germ of good writing, never left him, his enjoyment in his work never diminished. He was easy to like, yet difficult to know, and his reserve was legendary. The steady growth and success of the agency was of course based in the main on his talent for furthering and enhancing his authors' careers financially. But he always had time for young authors and for sane encouragement, never believing in raising false hopes or in telling an author his work was better than he thought it was. In fact he was never happier than when encouraging and guiding young authors, on whom he would lavish great pains, sometimes of course for little material return. His professional ethic was based on the view that an agent is an advocate, his loyalty first and last to his author. The abundant evidence of the value of this was the extraordinary extent to which his professional relationships almost invariably became close personal ties.

At the same time his work dovetailed with a wide variety of interests. Cricket was a great passion. Throughout the 1920s and 1930s he played with Alec Waugh, J. C. Squire, and Clifford Bax in a team known as the Invalids, and a fictional version of Peters may be found in the pages of *England, Their England.* He retained a lifelong passion for the theatre, in and around which he worked effectively for a time. He launched Terence Rattigan after *French Without Tears* had been repeatedly rejected and in the

1930s was responsible for the series of J. B. Priestley plays at the Duchess Theatre. He also produced a number of films, notably *An Inspector Calls* (1953). He was a great lover of the arts and a discerning collector of pictures, sculpture, and furniture. He was an undercover philanthropist, who gave time and money to various causes, such as the abolition of the death penalty, a fund-raising campaign for refugee writers, and towards the end of his life the Arthur Koestler award for prisoners, for which he was for seven years chairman of the board of trustees.

During World War II he worked in various capacities for the Ministry of Information, the Board of Trade, and the Ministry of Food, while at the same time keeping his business going. During the 1950s he was associated with Norman Collins and Lew (later Lord) Grade in forming the company which was as Associated Television (ATV) successful in the first round of bids for commercial television franchises.

He worked with undiminished enthusiasm until only six weeks before his death, having made over his by now very successful and profitable business to his junior partners without profit to himself. His mellow private life was reflected in a quite unusual style of enjoyment without ostentation, or, as Sir V. S. Pritchett put it, 'satisfaction without exhaustion'.

Peters married first in 1921 Helen MacGregor, by whom he had one son Richard and one daughter Catherine. Richard was killed on active service in Burma in 1945. Catherine married the psychiatrist and writer Anthony Storr. He married secondly in 1933 Margaret Lucy Mayne, by whom he had one daughter Hilary. He shared the last twenty-five years of his life with Margot Grahame, the actress and film star. He literary, she theatrical, they complemented each other well. He died a contented and much-loved man, at his London flat, 26 Barrie House, Lancaster Gate, 3 February 1973.

[Peters's autobiographical note and obituaries in the *Bookseller*, 10 February 1973; *The Times*, 5 February 1973; private information; personal knowledge.] MICHAEL SISSONS

PHILLIPSON, ANDREW TINDAL (1910–1977), professor of veterinary clinical studies, was born at Finchley, London, 19 August 1910, the second son and youngest of four children of John Tindal Phillipson and his wife, Cicely Gough Paterson. He was educated at Christ's College, Finchley, where his father was headmaster, and from 1928 to 1931 at St. Catharine's College, Cambridge, where he read agriculture. He gained a second class BA in 1931. After a year at University College, London, to study physiology he entered the Royal Veterinary College, London, from which he qualified in 1936. He then remained as a house surgeon for another year.

Phillipson returned to Cambridge in 1937 as a research student at the (then) Institute of Animal Pathology with the support of a number of awards and scholarships. This allowed him to work on ruminant digestion which was to be the primary research interest throughout his life. In 1941, the year before he gained his Ph.D., he transferred to the Unit of Animal Physiology when it was formed by Sir Joseph Barcroft and W. W. C. Topley (then secretary of the Agricultural Research Council) [qq.v.], at the Physiological Laboratory, Cambridge. In 1947, before the unexpected death of Barcroft, Phillipson was attracted to the Rowett Research Institute at Aberdeen by its new director, (Sir) David Cuthbertson. He remained there as head of the department of physiology, and from 1952 as deputy director until his election in 1963 as professor of veterinary clinical studies at Cambridge with a fellowship at Churchill College.

Of the four periods of research in Phillipson's life there is no doubt that the comparatively short time at the physiological laboratory in Cambridge was by far the most productive and exciting. Although it later attracted a galaxy of talented individuals the Unit at the start was essentially a small group that concentrated on studies of the foetal sheep (which was Barcroft's great interest) and on ruminant digestion (which was Phillipson's). In a comparatively short period Phillipson with Rachel McAnally (later Mrs Marshall) showed that the hitherto neglected volatile fatty acids were the end products of microbial digestion within the rumen and that after their absorption through the heavily keratinized epithelium of that organ, provided a significant proportion of the energy requirements of the host. The results solved the conundrum left unanswered by Kellner who, forty years earlier, had shown that purified cellulose had the same capacity as starch to lay down fat in the ruminant. This summary, however, barely conveys the excitement and empathy of that short period of six to seven years when fresh results seemed to open new fields with invigorating rapidity. Perhaps part of the attraction was the simple and elegant experiments on which the conclusions were based; indeed when the general principle was applied to other dietary components, such as proteins, it completely changed the possibly pedestrian concepts of ruminant nutrition and formed the basis of much of the subsequent work on the ruminant throughout the next two decades.

The period at Aberdeen was one of consolidation and development of the previous advances. But again Phillipson created an atmosphere that encouraged research and clear thinking. He also began to appreciate the pleasures of travel and of lecturing in other countries, including the antipodes which was appropriate, for Australia and New Zealand contributed several research workers to the later developments in Cambridge. After he returned to Cambridge Phillipson's tenure was perhaps marred by the problems of the veterinary school and his energy may have been sapped by the condition that ultimately led to his death. Yet he was chairman of the organizing committee of the successful symposium on the physiology of the digestion and metabolism in the ruminant in 1969 and continued to advance his subject and write lucid reviews.

Phillipson received honorary degrees from the universities of Edinburgh (1970), Copenhagen (1958), and Ghent (1968) and many major prizes in agricultural and veterinary fields. He was elected as FRSE in 1953 but whether he received the credit for his original work in a wider sphere is a matter of opinion. Few who knew him will fail to remember the charm and flair for research especially in the early days, when the interest kindled during his course of agriculture and subsequently during his periods as a research student, came to fruition and caused such a revolutionary change in our concepts of ruminant physiology.

Phillipson had a charming and gentle manner; outside his work and family he found his greatest pleasure in music. In 1936 he married Rachel Margaret, daughter of Philip Young, engineer. They had three sons. He died 10 January 1977 on a train between Audley End and Cambridge stations when returning to Cambridge from a meeting in London.

[St. Catharine's College records; private information; personal knowledge.]

R. S. Comline

PICKERING, Sir GEORGE WHITE (1904–1980), medical scientist and professor of medicine, was born 26 June 1904 in the Mansion House at Whalton, Northumberland, the only son and younger child of George Pickering, a schoolmaster in Elsdon, and his wife, Ann Hall. Both his parents came from families which had farmed in Northumberland for centuries.

Pickering entered the Royal Grammar School in Newcastle upon Tyne at the age of nine and at fourteen became the youngest member of the Newcastle Literary and Philosophical Society. From Newcastle he transferred to Dulwich College. There he won a scholarship to Pembroke College, Cambridge, where he obtained a first in both parts of the natural sciences tripos (1925 and 1926), coming top of the whole university in his first year. While at Cambridge he met (Mary) Carola, the daughter of (Sir) Albert Seward [q.v.], the distinguished palaeobotanist who was master of Downing College and vice-chancellor of the university. They were married in 1930.

Pickering obtained an entrance scholarship to St. Thomas's Hospital in 1926 and during his first year was elected a fellow of Pembroke College. After much thought, he declined to take up the offer because of his growing interest in clinical medicine. He qualified MRCS, LRCP in October 1928 and obtained the MRCP two years later in 1930.

Pickering's subsequent career falls into three parts: first in London at University College Hospital with Sir Thomas Lewis [q.v.]; then, from 1939, as professor of medicine at St. Mary's Hospital Medical School, and finally in Oxford from 1956 to 1968 as regius professor of medicine and Student of Christ Church and later, from 1968 until he retired in 1974, as master of Pembroke College, Oxford. Throughout his life he loved to accept a challenge, and this perhaps explains why he moved from St. Mary's, where he was very happy, to the regius chair at Oxford and later relinquished this to become master of Pembroke College.

Pickering would have thought of himself as a medical scientist, but, although he did make significant contributions to our understanding of the control of blood flow and the cause of raised blood pressure, it was his influence on education that was his most important contribution to the medicine of his day. He served on the University Grants Committee from 1944 until 1954 and later became chairman of the planning committee which set up the new medical school at Nottingham and contributed much to the plans for the medical school at Southampton. As regius professor he played a vital part in the development of medical teaching at Oxford. Largely as a result of his foresight and determination, the independent departments of postgraduate medicine that had been set up under the Nuffield benefaction were brought together to become the central focus of the rapidly expanding clinical school.

His interests in education extended far beyond medicine itself and in 1947 and in 1950 he wrote of the need to establish schools of business studies and to encourage technology. Among his books were *The Challenge to Education* (1967) and *Quest for Excellence in Medical Education* (1978).

He combined a scientific approach with a humanity and an interest in his patients' problems that made him an outstanding bedside teacher of clinical medicine. An enthusiast himself, he responded to the eagerness and enterprise of young people, and he lived up to his conviction that the main duty of a professor was to create the conditions where his young men and women could do their best work.

A fluent and compelling writer of English, he was insistent that the technology of medicine should not extinguish the art of writing. He was also concerned that the curriculum should not become overcrowded to the exclusion of general cultural interests and study.

At a time when the great teaching hospitals had the monopoly of funds for research and teaching, Pickering realized that if the National Health Service was to flourish, the need to spread the spirit of enquiry throughout every major hospital was paramount. In 1964, with the encouragement of the Nuffield Provincial Hospitals Trust, he called a meeting at Christ Church, Oxford, as a result of which the establishment of centres for postgraduate education in large regional hospitals, each under its own tutor, was accepted as national policy. The effect on the general standard of medical practice was immediate and the continuing improvement was a tribute to his vision. He wrote for this Dictionary the articles on Lord Brain and W. N. Pickles.

Pickering was made FRCP in 1938, knighted in 1957, and elected FRS in 1960. He received many academic honours from universities at home and abroad. He was president of the British Medical Association in 1963–4. Pickering had a robust personality and was vigorous for his years, with piercing blue eyes and a most interesting congenital tremor which became more noticeable when his enthusiasm was aroused, but which, none the less, did not prevent him from using his hands to carry out delicate and meticulous scientific experiments.

Pickering and his wife Carola had one son and three daughters. The son and two of the daughters became members of the medical profession. Pickering died in the John Radcliffe Hospital, Oxford, 3 September 1980. A portrait of him by John Ward hangs in Pembroke College, Oxford.

[Sir John McMichael in *Biographical Memoirs of Fellows of the Royal Society*, vol. xxviii, 1982; private information; personal knowledge.]

John Badenoch

PICKTHORN, Sir KENNETH WILLIAM MURRAY, first baronet (1892–1975), historian and parliamentarian, was born in London 23 April 1892, the elder son of Charles Wright Pickthorn and his wife, Edith Maud Berkeley Murray. He had two sisters. His father (as he would recall with pride) was a master mariner, whose home when ashore was at Ilford. He went to Aldenham School, and from there proceeded to Trinity College, Cambridge, as a scholar, where he took a first class in both parts of the history tripos (1912 and 1913). During World War I he served with the 15th London Regiment and the RFC in France and Macedonia, and, after being wounded, in the War Office.

Pickthorn returned after the war to Cambridge, where he had already in 1914 been elected to a fellowship at Corpus Christi College. He was successively dean (1919–29), tutor (1927–35), and president (1937–44) of the college, which was enjoying a post-war revival under the mastership of (Sir) Will Spens [q.v.]. He found its Tory outlook congenial and contributed much to it, with his sharp criticism of the liberalism fashionable in so many Cambridge circles. His twin passions were history and politics, and in 1935 he became one of the burgesses of the university as a Conservative. He nursed his university constituency with care, but in 1950 university representation in Parliament was abolished, and, rather to the surprise of many who knew him, in that year he won the seat for the Carlton division of Nottinghamshire for the Conservatives. He had a directness of approach and an occasional luridness of expression which appealed to his midlands constituents, many of them miners, and held the seat until he retired in 1966.

From 1951 to 1954 he was parliamentary secretary to the Ministry of Education. But office was not his forte; he was by nature a critic and disliked bureaucratic procedures, and despite his freedom from doctrinaire prejudice, his knowledge of teaching, and his sympathy with the working teacher, his tenure of office was not one of his happier periods. His real genius and his contribution to the politics of his day was as a parliamentarian. He was devoted to parliamentary practice and tradition, a devotion which owed much to his historical studies and which was recognized by the conferment of a baronetcy in 1959 and a privy councillorship in 1964. He was always ready to express and defend an unpopular position, and indeed was at his best when cutting down fashionably accepted opinions to size. He was unsparing in his criticism of any kind of muddled thinking—'clear your mind of cant', he would say, quoting Dr Johnson—and was particularly merciless in exposing what he regarded as the collectivist errors and illusions of his contemporaries. During the period of Churchill's wartime ascendancy he was one of the few who kept alive the spirit of criticism of the executive. Such criticism at the time often sounded ungrateful, but he cared more for the truth as he saw it than for popularity, and a contemporary of his in the House wrote, 'All credit to him that he kept up the pressure upon the muddled thinking of friend and foe.' No doubt he did not always win gratitude, but he had a sovereign wit and a saving humanity and humour which won him many friends and admirers both in the House and in the smaller world of Cambridge.

Pickthorn had taken his Litt.D. in 1936 and continued after his election to lecture and teach at weekends, remaining a devoted member of Corpus. His lectures were pungent and well attended; as someone remarked, he really *cared* about the Tudors, and as he himself wrote, 'The belief that history is a tendency, especially when combined with the delusion that its destination is known, is a bar to the understanding of a constitution in which much depends on practice.' His politics were rooted in history. His teaching of individuals (the Cambridge 'supervision') was invigorating though occasionally hampered by a reluctance to suffer fools (yet he was endlessly patient with pupils in difficulties or in any way disadvantaged). From his lecturing and teaching sprang his most noteworthy published works, *Some Historical Principles of the Constitution* (1925) and *Early Tudor Government* (2 vols., 1934). As a colleague and conversationalist he was at his best. His conversation was in itself a lesson in clear thinking and was studded with quotable phrases. It was he who originated the quip about the leader of the Gadarene swine claiming to be 'in the van of progress'.

He married in 1924 Nancy Catherine, daughter of Lewis Matthew Richards, barrister-at-law, and granddaughter of Sir William Grantham [q.v.]. They had two sons and a daughter. His retired to Orford in Suffolk, where he had long had a holiday house. His mind and critical faculties remained clear and sharp to the end. He died in Orford 12 November 1975.

[*The Times*, 13 November 1975; obituary notices in *Letter* of the Corpus Association; *Cambridge Review*, 30 January 1976; private information; personal knowledge.]

DESMOND LEE

PILE, SIR FREDERICK ALFRED, second baronet (1884–1976), general, was born in Dublin 14 September 1884, the second of four children and eldest of three sons (the youngest of whom was killed in action in 1917) of Sir Thomas Devereux Pile, first baronet, lord mayor of Dublin in 1900, and his wife, Caroline Maude, daughter of John Mann Nicholson, JP, of Rathgar. From the first he was an enthusiast—be it for the rather inadequate mixed school at which he was educated, horse riding, polo, or tennis. But the insufficiency of his initial education all but robbed him of the opportunity to indulge in what proved to be his greatest enthusiasm—the business of soldiering as a member, to begin with, of the Royal Artillery. Only by desperate cramming was he able to enter, bottom of his term, the Royal Military Academy, Woolwich, in 1902. Yet by hard work he passed out twenty-sixth, endowed with the foundations of knowledge which were to stand him in good stead throughout a career rich in managerial and technical experience.

As a battery commander in the Royal Horse Artillery, he took part in the retreat from Mons; and in the four years of war to come later performed the duties of brigade-major and general staff officer, 2nd grade, Royal Artillery, in France, where artillery dominated the battlefield and field gunnery underwent a revolution. New ideas stimulated Pile but were not necessarily greeted with acclaim by the instructors at the Staff College, which he attended from 1922 to 1923. At the suggestion of Colonel J. F. C. Fuller [q.v.] he transferred to the Royal Tank Corps in 1923 'because they liked bright ideas there', and he at once embarked upon development work at the heart of the mechanization and modernization of the army. During World War I he had won the MC and been appointed to the DSO (1918), as well as being mentioned in dispatches.

Two years with the RAF/Army Co-operation School and a short spell with the 5th battalion RTC before taking command in 1927, as lieutenant-colonel, of the 3rd battalion were good grounding for his work in command of the fast group of the experimental mechanized force which, in 1927, established, on Salisbury Plain, the kind of armoured warfare which lay at the heart of *Blitzkrieg* as practised by the Germans in 1939. With a reputation as a 'dangerous' commander who would 'chance his arm' and pull things off in battle, he was sent in 1928 to work for four years as assistant director of mechanization at the War Office, where he was immersed in the effort to design and produce the war machines of the future—medium and light tanks, self-propelled and lorry-towed artillery, swimming tanks, and the wide variety of prototypes which were, within a decade, the operational paraphernalia of the British Army.

Pile, who had succeeded his father in the baronetcy in 1931, was not to lead these new forces he helped create. Instead in 1932 he was sent to Egypt to command the Canal Infantry brigade (in which one of his battalion commanders was Bernard Montgomery, later Viscount Montgomery of Alamein, q.v.). There he demonstrated his prowess as a trainer until returning to Britain in 1936. In 1937 he re-entered the world of artillery as major-general in command of the 1st Anti-Aircraft division (TA) guarding London.

With war imminent and air raids certain, Pile found himself in command of a part-time force, equipped for the most part with obsolete weapons and employing antiquated methods which had little hope of deterring enemy bomber pilots. His responsibility became all the heavier when on 28 July 1939 he assumed command of Anti-Aircraft Command, a post he was to hold until 15 April 1945 (he was promoted general in 1941), as the only commander to retain the same high position throughout World War II. He was to tell the story after the war, in his official dispatch and in his book, *Ack-Ack* (1949). It was a tale of expansion to meet dire threat with resources which were tardily provided and several times whittled down to the bone, an unremitting struggle to obtain modern guns, improved searchlights, and radar to replace sound locating while the battle was in progress and to use them effectively while constantly under pressure to reduce manpower. He filled the gaps by the voluntary recruitment of 70,000 young women. Eventually 74,000 members of the ATS took their place on the gun sites, joined later by part-time members of the Home Guard.

It was a measure of his success that he kept the prime minister's confidence in all the crises of the Battle of Britain, the night blitz, and the concluding attack by pilotless aircraft and rockets in 1944–5. One reason for that success was openness of mind when tackling a new problem, a willingness to work closely with scientists and operational researchers, and a keen sympathy with subordinates. It was no accident that, in Anti-Aircraft Command, courts martial and absence without leave were less than 50 per cent of other commands. And it was Pile who managed the incredible large-scale redeployment of guns and ammunition to meet each change of enemy tactics and he, incidentally, who pressed hard for permission to fire shells in the direction of enemy rockets as the first attempt at an anti-missile—in 1945.

After the war he became director-general of housing in the Ministry of Works, but soon entered private industry on the board of Fothergill & Harvey and, later, as chairman of Cementation Ltd. He was colonel commandant of the Royal Artillery in 1945–52.

Pile was appointed CB (1938), KCB (1941), and GCB (1945). In 1946 he received an honorary LL D from Leeds University.

Pile married firstly, in 1915, Vera Millicent, daughter of Brigadier-General Frederick Charles Lloyd; they had two sons. This marriage was dissolved in 1929 and in 1932 Pile married, secondly, Hester Mary Melba, daughter of George Grenville Phillimore, barrister, of Shedfield, Hampshire. She died in 1949 and he married thirdly, in 1951, Molly Eveline Louise Mary, widow of Brigadier Francis Wyville Home, of the Royal Marines, and daughter of Ralph Smyth, gentleman, of Newtown, Drogheda. She had been chief commander of the ATS. Pile died 14 November 1976 in the Lister Hospital, Stevenage. He was succeeded in the baronetcy by his elder son, Frederick Devereux Pile (born 1915).

[Sir Frederick Pile, *Ack-Ack*, 1949; personal knowledge.] KENNETH MACKSEY

PLAMENATZ, JOHN PETROV (1912–1975), social and political theorist, one of the four children of Petar Plamenatz and his wife Liubitza Matanovitch, was born 16 May 1912, in Cetinje, capital of (the then independent Kingdom of) Montenegro. His father was descended from a family of peasant warriors who had fought against the Turks, and appears to be the first member of his family to have obtained a western education or died elsewhere than on the field of battle. His mother was the daughter of one of the king's aristocratic advisers and the god-daughter of Queen Elena of Italy. Petar Plamenatz, who had at one time been foreign minister of Montenegro, was forced to leave his country in 1917. The family went first to France, then to Austria, and returned to Montenegro in the mid-thirties. John Plamenatz was sent to England to be educated at Clayesmore School (then in Northolt Park, now in Dorset), with the headmaster of which his father had come to be on friendly terms. He stayed at Clayesmore from 1919 to 1930, when he entered Oriel College, Oxford, as a scholar, and took the school of philosophy, politics, and economics. In 1933 he fell ill, and was awarded an *aegrotat* degree in the final examination. In 1934 he took the history school, in which he obtained a first class.

In 1936 he was elected to a research fellowship at All Souls College on the strength of a doctoral thesis (failed by the Oxford examiners) soon afterwards published under the title of *Consent, Freedom and Political Obligation* (1938). Three years later, when World War II broke out, he enrolled in an anti-aircraft battery and later became a member of the War Cabinet of King Peter of Yugoslavia, then in exile in England. He was naturalized in 1941. He married Marjorie, daughter of Captain Thomas Morison Hunter of Scotland and New Zealand, in 1943. They had no children. When the war ended, he returned to All Souls College, and his life thereafter was spent in Oxford. In 1951 he left All Souls to become a research fellow of Nuffield College. He was elected to a fellowship of the British Academy in 1962. In 1967 he returned to All Souls as Chichele professor of social and political theory.

Plamenatz was one of the most respected (and prolific) writers on political theory in the English-speaking world. He developed no theoretical system of his own, sought no unifying historical or metaphysical pattern, and neither belonged to, nor created a school of political thought. For forty years he was engaged in the exposition and criticism of the classical political texts of the West, seeking to sift the true from the false, the profound from the shallow, substance from rhetoric, in a lifelong effort to examine the relations of the individual to society. He made little use of secondary sources, but addressed himself directly to some of the central topics discussed by the major political philosophers—the nature of political obligation, of rights, interests, law, the state, justice, liberty, equality, democracy, self-fulfilment and the like, and developed his own views by means of confrontation with the doctrines and arguments of thinkers who seemed to him to have said profound or important things about the social and political life of men. The philosophical movement dominant in Oxford during his undergraduate days was that of British realism; he was trained in the use of the methods of such British thinkers as G. E. Moore, Bertrand Russell, G. A. Prichard, C. D. Broad [qq.v.], and W. D. Ross which dominated the Oxford scene in the 1920s and early 1930s. His tutor in philosophy, W. G. Maclagan, was a follower of this movement and had a considerable influence on the intellectual formation of his pupils.

Plamenatz believed in, and rigorously practised, careful, rational analysis: he examined the meaning, implications, presuppositions, internal consistency, and validity of each and every view he discussed, and did so in exceptionally clear language, free from rhetoric or the use beyond absolute necessity of technical terms—the prose of a rational man intending to be understood by other equally rational, critically minded readers. This was in the tradition of British political thought before and after its late nineteenth-century Hegelian phase, and Plamenatz fitted into it perfectly. His major works—the expanded doctoral thesis, rejected in 1935 and published with much critical acclaim in 1938, the examination eleven years later of the English Utilitarians, the remarkable studies of Marxism in 1953 and 1954, above all, his fullest and most important work, *Man and Society*, of 1963, a series of essays on the major political thinkers since the Renaissance, and, posthumously published in 1975, *Karl Marx's Philosophy of Man*—were all cast in this mould.

Though by nature somewhat withdrawn, addressing himself mainly to an academic audience, detached from day-to-day politics, his views were not conceived in a political vacuum. The communist revolution in Yugoslavia affected him deeply: during the war, when he was on the staff of King Peter of Yugoslavia, he wrote a pamphlet, privately printed, in defence of General Mihailovitch against his detractors; but his attitude to the east European regimes remained temperate. His critiques of Marxism are among the most fair-minded analyses of its strengths and weaknesses, lucid, detailed and singularly free from bias or failure of understanding. Plamenatz did not expound his own political views explicitly, but his writings reveal their essence: he was a freedom-loving liberal with sympathy for western social democracy; his sharpest arguments were directed at totalitarian ideologists, both of the right and of the left; his last book, on Marx's theory of human nature, reveals no less about his own. Although a master of elucidation and of quietly effective, apparently naïve, deflation of vast, air-filled philosophical and ideological balloons, he rejected the view that the sole business of philosophers was, by means of linguistic analysis, to clear up confusions, but not defend or attack or seek to establish the truth or validity of any given doctrine. So, for example, when (in 1949 and again in 1963) he wrote on the Utilitarians, he gave his reasons for rejecting their central doctrine. Nor do his chapters on Hegel (one of the clearest expositions in English) or on Marx (the value of whose ideas he did not underestimate) leave any doubt about his own position. Unlike those who argue that ideas, especially where value judgements are involved, cannot be correctly interpreted without the fullest possible understanding of motives, purposes, social, historical and personal circumstances (and, indeed, the changing use of words) of those who hold them, Plamenatz did not believe that this was necessary, although it might be of some help. For this mainly analytical approach he has been much criticized by historically and sociologically minded writers on political theory.

The thinkers whose outlook and style Plamenatz found most sympathetic were those who spoke most clearly: Machiavelli, Hobbes, the writers of the French Enlightenment and those whom they influenced. At the same time, he remained an independent, somewhat solitary thinker, neither a follower nor disciple of others, to some degree drawn to other inward-looking, self-absorbed thinkers who stood aside from their societies—particularly Pascal and Rousseau. He seemed to move in a timeless world of great thinkers who spoke directly to him; to them he addressed his questions, and from them, like Machiavelli, he obtained answers which he discussed in a uniquely fresh and first-hand fashion.

He was profoundly affected by British empiricism, yet his origins exercised an equally important influence on his outlook: when he wrote about equality, or the bonds of society, his feeling for the pre-feudal, semi-pastoral society from which he sprang came through clearly; so it did in his essay of 1967 on 'Alien Rule and Self-Government', and in his occasional writings on Serbian history. The interplay between the objective, rational method which he had learned in Oxford and made his own, and a knowledge of the very different life of the country of his birth, provided him with a vantage point from which to contemplate and criticize the industrial West in which he lived. His writings express a highly personal and direct moral and political vision, an ability to see issues unmediated by the spectacles provided by generations of western commentators; his style and tone are not found among other political theorists of his time. His upbringing had been partly French, and this, too, left a deep imprint upon his mind: he paid great attention to the writings of Hobbes or Hume, but he took almost physical pleasure in reading Montaigne, Montesquieu, Pascal, the plays of Racine, Molière, Marivaux, and J.-B. Rousseau: the quality of their feeling and civilized and delicate imagination appealed to him more deeply than the plainer, less fine-grained British or German ways of thinking.

John Plamenatz was a proud and dignified man, sensitive, acute and courteous in argument, learned and unswervingly dedicated to the pursuit of truth. He was not a dominant thinker; he lacked the intellectual force and originality of an innovator or a destroyer of previous orthodoxies, but his combination of critical power, scrupulous honesty, psychological insight, skill in unravelling, and impeccable sense of justice in assessing the arguments for and against the central social and political doctrines of the West, earned him great and continuing admiration in his profession.

His methods and personal character greatly influenced his pupils, some of whom became respected teachers of politics. The number of first-rate British writers and teachers in the field of social and political theory in the twentieth century has not been great: he was outstanding among them. He died of a heart attack at his home in Hook Norton, near Banbury, 19 February 1975, precisely fifty-six years to the day after he had landed at Dover.

[Geoffrey Marshall in *Proceedings* of the British Academy, vol. lxii, 1976; private information; personal knowledge.] ISAIAH BERLIN

PLASKETT, HARRY HEMLEY (1893–1980), astronomer, was born at Toronto, Canada, 5 July 1893, the elder son and elder child of Dr John Stanley Plaskett [q.v.], the eminent Canadian astronomer, and his wife, Rebecca Hope, daughter of Alexander Hemley. The bond between father and son was always very close; and both received the highest award, the gold medal, of the Royal Astronomical Society of London. In 1984 a minor planet was named Plaskett in their honour, jointly.

Plaskett was educated at Ottawa Collegiate School and the University of Toronto (1912–16). Immediately after completing his BA degree he joined the Canadian Field Artillery and served in Flanders 1917–18. While awaiting demobilization he was seconded to Imperial College, London, where he studied under Alfred Fowler [q.v.]. From 1919 to 1927 he held an appointment at the Dominion Astrophysical Observatory, Victoria, British Columbia, of which his father was director. In 1928 he was appointed as lecturer to Harvard College Observatory by its director, Harlow Shapley, and assigned the task of establishing a graduate programme in astronomy, the first of such courses to be set up. He was appointed professor of astrophysics at Harvard in 1930, and in 1932 he was chosen to succeed H. H. Turner [q.v.], who had died in 1930, as Savilian professor of astronomy at Oxford, and became a fellow of New College. Thus both Harvard and Oxford in their turn felt that Plaskett was an outstanding leader in the field of modern observational astrophysics. His tenure of office was interrupted by a second period of war service from 1939 to 1944, for the first year as an anti-aircraft officer and then in the Ministry of Aircraft Production, where he made distinguished contributions to solving problems of aircraft navigation. Although he reached retiring age in 1960 and was made professor emeritus, the generosity of his successor, D. E. Blackwell, enabled him to continue his work in solar physics almost to the end of his life.

Although Plaskett had a penetrating insight into almost all branches of astronomy his name is especially associated with solar physics, to which he made contributions over sixty-three years. His first paper, written as an undergraduate, was on solar rotation. Through his own work and that of the school of solar physics he established in Oxford, 'solar rotation' developed into 'motions in the sun at the photospheric level'. Solar oscillations and surface flow patterns became leading topics in solar physics, and Plaskett's work was the precursor of much that was done later. He was always quick to apply the new insights of physics to astronomy and he made important contributions, both observational and theoretical, to the problems of line formation in the solar spectrum, solar limb darkening, and solar granulation. His observations were meticulously planned and the measurements were carried through with the greatest objectivity and care and subjected to sophisticated mathematical analysis.

As observatory director, and supervisor to a long line of research students (many of whom became eminent and influential in their respective spheres), Plaskett exacted high standards of industry and concentration. He was generosity itself in suggesting and assisting in research problems for both colleagues and students. These problems included the theory and observation of line contours, solar wavelengths and red-shifts, material motions and magnetic fields in sunspots, and the development of new observational techniques. Instrument design was another of Plaskett's keen interests. He was responsible for the erection of two solar telescopes at Oxford, each associated with its powerful spectroscope. He was tireless in the testing and maintenance of these instruments and the ancillary equipment, which were the foundation of the Oxford work. It was he who first (1946) suggested the Isaac Newton 100-inch telescope for Britain, which was finally completed in 1967.

In the university Plaskett's influence extended well outside his own department. He was for a period a member of the hebdomadal council and was often consulted on university matters. He always gave his opinions firmly, but in all his dealings his force and strength of character was coupled with a modesty and charm that endeared him to colleagues and students alike.

Plaskett was elected FRAS in 1919, and from his return to England in 1932 he was devoted to the interests of the Society. He served as a secretary, 1937–40, and as president, 1945–7, and was a gold medallist in 1963. He was elected FRS in 1936 and awarded an honorary LL D by the University of St. Andrews in 1961.

Home and family were the great joy of Plaskett's life. He was married in 1921 to Edith Alice (died 1981), elder daughter of John James Smith, a barrister in Ottawa. She supported and encouraged her husband through a lifetime of astronomical research. There were two children of the marriage, a daughter Barbara Rochester, wife of Arthur L. Pidgeon (formerly of the Canadian Broadcasting Corporation), and a son, John Stanley, formerly lecturer in mathematical physics at the University of Sussex. Plaskett died 26 January 1980 in hospital at Oxford.

[W. H. McCrea in *Biographical Memoirs of Fellows of the Royal Society*, vol. xxvii, 1981; personal knowledge.] M. G. ADAM

PLATT, ROBERT, first baronet, and BARON PLATT (1900–1978), physician, was born in St. Marylebone, London, 16 April 1900, the younger son and younger child of William Platt, who worked in the family wholesale woollen business and was later a schoolmaster, of Hampstead, and his wife, Susan Jane, schoolmistress and later inspector of schools, eldest daughter of William Willis, seafarer and later hotelier of Loughgall, county Armagh, and later of Forfar. He was educated at King Alfred's School, Hampstead, and at the Home School, Grindleford, Derbyshire, which was kept by his parents after 1910; his medical training at Sheffield University began in 1917, but was interrupted by a short period of commissioned service in 1918. In spite of this he qualified MB, Ch.B. (Sheffield) in 1921, and proceeded to the MD degree in 1923. He proceeded to MRCP (1925) and FRCP (1935).

Platt's early medical career was spent in Sheffield, where he built up a busy consulting practice as a physician to the Royal Infirmary, and also became generally known for his work on nephritis and other renal diseases. This conventional mould, which can never have fitted him too closely, was broken in 1941 by military service in the Royal Army Medical Corps in Britain, North Africa, and India, where he was consultant physician to Southern Command, with the rank of brigadier in the Army Medical Service.

At the end of the war, his career again changed course sharply with his appointment in 1945 as the first full-time professor of medicine in the University of Manchester, becoming at the same time a physician to the Manchester Royal Infirmary. With his reputation already established as a general physician with a special interest in renal disease and in hypertension, he was readily accepted by senior clinical colleagues; but he also took special pains to encourage young doctors, to stimulate the growth of research in his unit, and to play a part in general university affairs. He was an enthusiastic supporter of the National Health Service from its inception, even though he seemed occasionally to regret, not the rewards of private practice, but the greater amount of time which it had allowed him to spend with individual patients. He developed a strong interest in clinical genetics, and he developed views on the inheritance of high blood pressure which seemed to him to be reasonable, but which sparked off a public exchange with (Sir) George Pickering [q.v.] that lasted for years and became known as 'the battle of the knights'—a battle in which the enthusiasm of the contestants outran and outlasted that of most spectators. Platt also developed a theory of the function of the failing kidney known as 'the intact nephron hypothesis', which has remained of influence. However, his greatest contribution at Manchester was as a quite outstanding physician, kind, painstaking, and knowledgeable, and consequently an inspiration to staff and students. An amateur violoncellist, he was active in the musical life of the city, and was chairman of the Manchester Chamber Concerts Society from 1952 until 1965, the year in which he retired from his chair, which he had held on a part-time basis from 1962.

While serving as professor at Manchester he became well known on the national medical scene, as a member of the Medical Research Council, and chairman of its clinical research board from 1964 to 1967; on the royal commission on medical education (1965); on the first of many working parties on medical staffing in hospitals; and later as chairman of the distinction awards committee, an office of some delicacy. As Rock Carling fellow, he published in 1963 a monograph *Doctor and Patient: Ethics, Morale, Government.* He reached the apogee of his medical career with his election as president of the Royal College of Physicians, and with the quite remarkable achievements of his presidency (1957–62), in which he combined personal resolution with quiet skill in carrying potentially reluctant colleagues along with him. He was the chief architect of the translation of the College from restricted quarters in Pall Mall to the new building in St. Andrew's Place, which provided the material base for the burgeoning of postgraduate activity which he equally inspired. He also encouraged the College to take greater interest in matters of public health, such as the dangers of smoking.

In 1959 he was created first baronet. In 1967 he was made a life peer and found yet another scene of congenial and effective activity in the House of Lords, where he dispensed medical advice both privately and publicly, and also spoke on wider issues such as divorce, pornography, and voluntary euthanasia, although he opposed the compulsory wearing of seat belts. In these later years he became more aware of his own distinction, but he never quite lost the common touch.

Platt was a man of small physical stature, of deep feeling, of many interests, a good companion but with periods of private sadness. He has given us a remarkably clear and candid view of himself in his informal autobiography, *Private and Controversial* (1972). The book reveals much of its author, with its frank and penetrating views on medicine and music (his two great loves), his interesting family background, his experiences in wartime, medical ethics, religion—which he approached negatively—statistics, and euthanasia. One chapter is headed 'Modern medicine and how to avoid it' and has the subheading 'How to be an expert patient'.

The chief beneficiaries of Platt's dedication and talents were the Manchester Medical School and the Royal College of Physicians. His incursions into wider public life were perhaps based on less experience, and may have been less sure and happy than the conviction with which his views were expressed. He had many honorary degrees and honorary fellowships of learned societies. Among the many distinguished lectures he delivered was the Harveian oration of 1967. To this Dictionary he contributed the article on Sir A. J. Hall.

In 1922 Platt married Margaret Irene, psychiatrist, the daughter of Arthur Charles Cannon, a schoolmaster, of Sheffield. They had a son, Peter Platt (born 1924), professor of music at the University of Sydney, and two daughters. After the dissolution of this marriage in 1974, Platt married in the same year a musician, Sylvia Jean, formerly wife of John Alfred Haggard, and daughter of Sydney Charles Caveley. Platt died in University College Hospital, London, 30 June 1978 and his son succeeded to the baronetcy. A tape, 'Talking with Robert', is preserved in the library of the Royal College of Physicians.

[*British Medical Journal*, vol. ii, 1978, p. 211; *Lancet*, vol. ii, 1978, p. 114; *The Times*, 1 July 1978; Lord Platt, *Private and Controversial*, 1972.] DOUGLAS BLACK

PLATT, SIR WILLIAM (1885–1975), general, was born 14 June 1885, at Brooklands, Cheshire, the only son and elder child of John Platt, engineer, of Carnforth, and his wife, Margaret Oudney Graham. He was educated at Marlborough and the Royal Military College, Sandhurst, and was commissioned in the 4th battalion the Northumberland Fusiliers in 1905. Two years later he was transferred to the 1st battalion, then serving in India. Within a few months he saw active service with the Mohmand expedition on the North-West Frontier. For gallant and distinguished conduct at the engagement of Matta he was mentioned in dispatches and appointed to the DSO (1908), a remarkable achievement for a second lieutenant aged twenty-four. He continued serving in India until 1913 when his battalion returned to England, but not before Platt's adventurous and enquiring nature had taken him, on leave, to Japan, Korea, Manchuria, and the battlefields of the Russo-Japanese war.

Platt went to France in August 1914 and, although severely wounded in October while acting adjutant, was soon back on the western front where, for the remainder of the war, he held various staff appointments ending up as general staff officer, 1st grade, 37th division. He was mentioned in dispatches four times and given the brevets of major and lieutenant-colonel.

He attended the Staff College in 1919, and for the next six years saw further service in India, and also in Egypt. He was a deputy assistant adjutant-general at the War Office from 1927 to 1930. In 1930 he was given accelerated promotion out of his regiment to command the 2nd battalion the Wiltshire Regiment. Here he showed his outstanding ability as a trainer of troops and within three years he was in command of an experimental brigade—the 7th Infantry brigade—at Tidworth.

In 1938 Platt was promoted major-general and appointed commandant of the Sudan Defence Force and in command of British forces in the Sudan, with the Arabic title of 'Al-Qā'id al-'Āmm'. The entry of Italy into the war, with 300,000 ground troops and 200 aircraft stationed in Abyssinia, faced him with the greatest challenge of his career. He responded to it with outstanding imagination and drive. By the skill with which, between June 1940 and January 1941, he deceived the Italians into believing that his force, consisting initially of no more than 7,000 troops and seven aircraft, was infinitely greater, he held a frontier of 1,200 miles intact save for the loss of a few minor positions.

The strategy of Sir A. P. (later Earl) Wavell [q.v.] for the 1941 East African campaign became feasible with the arrival in the Sudan of the 4th and 5th Indian divisions and six air squadrons. It consisted of two vast pincer movements, one, the southern arm, led by General Sir Alan Cunningham, advanced through Somaliland, while the northern arm, under Platt, moved into Eritrea. As the two arms of the pincer began to operate the exiled emperor, supported by patriot forces, entered Abyssinia from the Sudan. Platt achieved early success in driving the Italians back from Kassala but at the almost impregnable mountain stronghold of Keren the Italians stood, and it took from 3 February until 27 March 1941, and heavy casualties on both sides, before they were dislodged. His advance towards the southern arm of the pincer was pressed, Addis Ababa fell, and Platt's and Cunningham's forces came together at Amba Alagi. Here the Italian commander, the Duke of Aosta, surrendered with the honours of war on 19 May 1941.

Platt was then appointed general officer commanding-in-chief East Africa, an assignment that led to his taking command in September 1942 of operations to complete the occupation of Madagascar. His duties from now on were mainly confined to the organization and training of African troops required for the Burma campaign. It was due to him that they achieved a remarkably high standard of efficiency and morale, for one of Platt's great gifts was his understanding of and sympathy for African soldiers and his faith in their quality and capability.

In 1945 Platt reached the age of sixty and retired from the army, having been promoted lieutenant-general in 1941 and general two years later. He went to live in the Lake District and the interests that he thereafter followed were both varied and demanding. He became a member of the board of the family engineering firm of Mather & Platt, and a member of the management committee of the Outward Bound Mountain School at Eskdale. He pursued a long-standing interest in the theatre by serving for more than eight years as an active and popular member of the drama panel of the Arts Council. He was a freeman of the Fruiterers' Company.

Resolute, resilient, and resourceful Platt was above all a man of immense activity, drive, and enthusiasm. He was lean and athletic, and of average height. At times he could be an intimidating and even an explosive figure to those who served under him, and his relations with civil administrations were not always entirely harmonious. But whatever the rebuff or the disagreement the warmth of his nature and his quick sense of humour swiftly emerged, leaving not only respect but also a great deal of affection.

Platt was appointed CB (1939), KCB (1941), and GBE (1943). He was ADC to the King in 1937–8, and colonel of the Wiltshire Regiment from 1942 to 1954. He was a commander of the Legion of Honour, and a grand officer of the Star of Ethiopia, of the Order of the Nile, and of the Belgian Orders of both Leopold I and the Crown. He held the Belgian croix de guerre.

He married in 1921 Mollie Dendy, daughter of Dendy Watney, architect and surveyor, of Addlestone. They had two sons. He died 28 September 1975 in London.

[Military records; private information.]

GAWAIN BELL

PLOMER, WILLIAM CHARLES FRANKLYN (1903–1973), writer, was born 10 December 1903 at Pietersburg, Transvaal, the eldest of the three sons, the second of whom died in 1908 (there were no daughters), of Charles Campbell Plomer, then an official in the Department of Native Affairs, and his wife Edythe Mary, daughter of Edward Waite-Browne, farmer. William Plomer's English ancestry was a source of pride and research throughout a life to which a start in South Africa had imparted a feeling of rootlessness, which he balanced with the keen social and literary observation of an outsider. He was educated first at St. John's College, Johannesburg, then spent three disagreeable years at a preparatory school in Kent before a brief but very happy period at Rugby (1917–18) which was brought to an end by rapidly deteriorating eyesight. His vision stabilized soon after his return to South Africa, where he worked as an apprentice farmer on the Basutoland border and later with his parents at a native trading station in Zululand.

Plomer's keen aesthetic response to the scenery and native people encountered on his return to South Africa was combined with an increasing awareness of the injustices of colour prejudice there. His literary reading was intense, and his writing (encouraged by correspondence with Harold Monro [q.v.] of the Poetry Bookshop) developed remarkably in the isolation of his lonely country postings. His literary solitude was ended by his encounter with the unpredictable but still liberal-minded Roy Campbell [q.v.], with whom and (Sir) Laurens van der Post he edited the short-lived but influential English magazine *Voorslag*, which rapidly proved to be the mental 'whiplash' of its Afrikaans title. Plomer's novel *Turbott Wolfe*, published in 1926, gave even greater offence; ferocious and passionate, dealing with love and marriage between black and white, it was well calculated to provoke South African racial sensitivities. More measured in tone is Plomer's 'Ula Masondo', a long story from the same fertile period, in which an African confronts industrial society.

Local outrage was predictable enough. Plomer soon took the opportunity to travel, initially as a journalist, to Japan. He was not to return to Africa for thirty years, a visit in 1956 proving a tense and depressing experience for him. The three years he spent in Japan, mainly in teaching work, were aesthetically stimulating and productive of several close friendships; Plomer's sympathetic responses showed themselves in poetry and short stories, and in the novel *Sado* (1931) with its quietly voiced homosexual overtones.

In 1929 he moved to London to pursue a literary career, characteristically choosing the transience and anonymity of lodgings in Bayswater; too diffident and independent to belong to a group, he was nevertheless on the fringes of 'Bloomsbury' and friendly individually with Virginia Woolf and E. M. Forster [qq.v.]. His friendships remained compartmentalized but each mattered much to him; closest among them between the wars was that with Anthony Butts, with whom he collaborated in the whimsical *Curious Relations* (by 'William D'Arfey', 1945).

In addition to productive work in poetry and fiction, and as a reviewer, Plomer succeeded Edward Garnett as literary consultant to the firm of Jonathan Cape, proving a discerning and discreet adviser. Amongst his particular successes was the recognition of the quality of the unpublished diaries of (Robert) Francis Kilvert (1840–79), of which he produced a three-volume edition (1938–40) which established their obscure clerical author as a noteworthy Victorian writer. The 'James Bond' novels of Ian Fleming [q.v.] were another valuable property he brought to the firm.

Plomer had encountered Fleming during war service in the Admiralty, as a temporary civilian officer (1940–5) in the Naval Intelligence Division, providing current affairs briefings for naval staff. During the war he contributed (as 'Robert Pagan') a series of topical essays to *Penguin New Writing*. Although he published little fiction after 1934, his poetical output continued, wartime conditions stimulating his wryly humorous ballads with violent themes, and he wrote much other verse in which the muted emotional force secures a penetration that poignant observation and metrical skill might otherwise have concealed. His *Collected Poems*, incorporating several smaller volumes, appeared in 1960, and was amplified in 1973.

His post-war work included a collaboration with Benjamin (later Lord) Britten [q.v.], as librettist first of *Gloriana* (1953), the coronation-tide opera, and then more fruitfully in using his oriental experience to introduce Britten to the Noh plays, resulting in the fusion of Japanese theatre and European music in the three 'church operas' (1964–8). His autobiography *At Home* (1958) continued *Double Lives* published fifteen years before; neither volume is deeply self-revealing; he was working on a revision at the time of his death.

Latterly he lived quietly at Rustington (1953–66) and from 1966 at Hassocks, in Sussex. Although decorously reticent about sexual matters, he was of definite homosexual disposition, and shared the last thirty years of his life with a devoted friend, a German refugee, Charles Erdman. Plomer died at Hassocks, 21 September 1973.

His extensive correspondence and papers were presented by his literary executor to the library of Durham University, of which he was an honorary D.Litt. (1959). He was awarded the Queen's gold medal for poetry in 1963, and was appointed CBE in 1968.

[*The Times*, 22 and 28 September and 8 November 1973; *London Magazine*, December 1973; William Plomer, *Autobiography* (with postscript by Simon Nowell-Smith), 1975; Michael Herbert, 'William Plomer', B.Litt. thesis, Oxford, 1976, with full bibliography.]

ALAN BELL

PLURENDEN, BARON (1917–1978), business man, farmer, and livestock breeder. [See STERNBERG, RUDY.]

POLANYI, MICHAEL (1891–1976), physical chemist and philosopher, was born in Budapest in March 1891, the fifth of six children and third son of Mihály Polacsek, a railway entrepreneur and civil engineer of Jewish extraction, and his wife, Cecília Wohl, who was at the centre of a lively intellectual circle in Budapest. Due to carelessness in registering his birth its exact date is unknown. His family celebrated his birthday on 11 March. He was educated at the Minta Gymnasium and at the University of Budapest where he qualified in medicine. He also studied physical chemistry under Professor G. Bredig at the Karlsruhe Technical High School, Germany.

Polanyi's early studies on the third law of thermodynamics led to a stimulating contact with Albert Einstein. During World War I he served as a medical officer in the Austro-Hungarian army and then took his doctoral degree in chemistry at Budapest University. He returned to Karlsruhe where he met his future wife, Magda Kemeny, who was also a chemist. In 1920 he moved to the Kaiser Wilhelm Institute of Fibre Chemistry in Berlin. Here he met many inspiring colleagues and developed the technique of using X-ray analysis for studying fibrous and metallic structures. Here too he wrote more than half of his many papers on this and other topics—topics which were to continue to engross him for twenty years. They concerned, particularly, the rates of chemical reactions—the precise study of gases meeting each other in a tube for example—and, second, some highly original studies of the adsorption of gas molecules on to solids. In 1923 he moved to the Institute of Physical Chemistry as head of department. His professorial title, received in 1926, and his life membership of the Max Planck Institute were the result of his work on reaction kinetics and his stimulating influence on many collaborators. Notable among these were H. Eyring, H. Mark, and E. P. Wigner.

Even before Hitler came to power, Polanyi, Erwin Schrödinger and others in the Institute began to organize resistance to the pressures which were being put on Jewish scholars; the danger signals were becoming clear. In 1933

Polanyi resigned and accepted the chair of physical chemistry at Manchester University. He was naturalized in 1939.

Polanyi's researches continued in the new setting. Perhaps the major methodological and conceptual innovations to come out of his laboratory were, first, the exact method of investigating the properties of gaseous diffusion and, second, the development of transition state theory of chemical reactions generally. These continued to be valuable elements in research and discussion half a century later.

During the 1930s Polanyi's attention turned to a quite different theme—the growing threat to science and to all human culture from totalitarianism. Unlike most intellectuals at that time he understood the danger from the left as well as from the right. He and a few others, such as J. R. Baker, challenged J. D. Bernal and J. B. S. Haldane [qq.v.] for their advocacy of centrally planned science. Polanyi's first philosophical–political book, *The Contempt of Freedom*, appeared in 1940. He was elected FRS in 1944 but his interest was beginning to settle, beyond scientific research, on wider cultural and philosophical issues. He also built up a fine research school and was a highly successful teacher of undergraduates.

Polanyi, like his near contemporaries, F. A. Hayek and Sir Karl Popper, was trying to understand the relationship between freedom and orderliness, not only in the depths of nature but in the dynamic processes of human action and knowledge. In 1948 he gave up his chair of chemistry and accepted a personal chair at Manchester in what was termed 'social studies', which he held until 1958. But it was the vision of a new kind of philosophy, one that would relate science harmoniously to other modes of human knowing, which drew him on. In 1951 Polanyi published *The Logic of Liberty* which, with the Gifford lectures (1951, 1952), were forerunners of his great work on these themes, *Personal Knowledge* (1958).

The subtitle of *Personal Knowledge* was *Towards a Post-critical Philosophy.* Though Polanyi made full use of critical, empirical, and analytical methods, he never gave them priority. He knew that the roots of science lay deeper and he claimed that the commitment of an explorer, or of a group of explorers, to the discovery of hidden order in the universe and of faith in that order were prior requirements for all acts of discovery. Empirical search and critical analysis follow. This reversal was the linch-pin of his thought. It grew out of what he would have called his own 'tacit knowledge' for he knew it in his bones, from having done thirty years of successful, co-operative scientific research. He saw it supremely illustrated not only by Einstein's theories of relativity but also by the way in which these had been discovered. Yet when Polanyi came to set all these insights down in black and white many people did not like it. He was challenging the conventional wisdom: that scientists are cool and detached and that their judgements are value free. Polanyi's further writings, *The Tacit Dimension* (1967) and *Knowing and Being* (1969), consolidated and further developed the new approach. Many of his insights were taken up by others: by T. H. Kuhn, for example, in the philosophy of science and by T. F. Torrance in theology.

In 1959 Polanyi moved to Merton College, Oxford, as senior research fellow. He retired in 1961. During the fifteen years after leaving Manchester he travelled widely and published papers on philosophical, political, and aesthetic subjects. In a somewhat wry epigram, which suggests something of his humility, his deep commitment, and his openness to truth, he states his purpose: 'to achieve a frame of mind in which I firmly hold what I believe to be true, even though I know it might conceivably be false' (1958). He was a member or fellow of many learned societies and received honorary degrees from Princeton (1946), Leeds (1947), Manchester (1966), Cambridge (1969), Aberdeen (1959), Notre Dame (1965), Wesleyan (1965), and Toronto (1967).

In 1921 he married Magda Elizabeth Kemeny, daughter of a miller and mill owner. They had two sons, George (died 1975), an economist, and John, who became professor of chemistry in Toronto University and a fellow of the Royal Society. Polanyi died 22 February 1976 in a nursing home at Northampton.

[E. P. Wigner and R. A. Hodgkin in *Biographical Memoirs of Fellows of the Royal Society*, vol. xxiii, 1977; memoir by Paul Ignotus in Polanyi's Festschrift, *The Logic of Personal Knowledge*, 1961; W. T. Scott, unpublished biographical material; personal knowledge.]

R. A. Hodgkin

POPE-HENNESSY, (RICHARD) JAMES (ARTHUR) (1916–1974), writer, was born in London 20 November 1916, the younger son (there were no daughters) of Major-General Ladislaus Herbert Richard Pope-Hennessy and his wife, (Dame) Una Constance, daughter of Sir Arthur Birch, lieutenant-governor of Ceylon. With his elder brother (Sir) John, James was brought up in an exclusively intellectual, closely knit Catholic family. The father was a tolerant, cultivated soldier, the mother a highly educated writer and woman of formidable personality. She exercised a strong hold upon her sons and inculcated in both the desire to work. Pope-Hennessy was educated at Downside School and Balliol College, Oxford, but at neither of these institutions was he wholly happy. He did not take a degree. He had no respect for organized games or the accepted diversions of youth. While remaining devoted to his family he developed a questing, questioning spirit which induced him never to take for granted the shibboleths of his class and upbringing. A natural rebelliousness was accentuated by his unremitting homosexuality. By mixing with people of every sort he became totally un-class conscious. Indeed he detested all forms of injustice and snobbishness. His strong compassion for the underdog sometimes induced him to express intemperate opinions. Although physically attracted to his own sex he loved the companionship of women to whom most of his enchanting correspondence was addressed. They were fascinated by his understanding and sensitivity. All his life he was much sought after by hostesses for his sparkling conversation.

Thanks to his mother's influence Pope-Hennessy knew from an early age that he was destined to be a writer; and writing always had first call upon his time and energies. In consequence by relentless discipline he developed a natural gift into a fluent, witty, beautifully descriptive, and often poetic prose style. His parents were never well off and Pope-Hennessy had to earn a living. On leaving Oxford he worked in 1937–8 as an editorial assistant for Sheed & Ward, the Catholic publishers in Paternoster Row. There he got to know intimately the churches and Dickensian alleys of the City of London. They were lovingly described in his first book, *London Fabric* (1939), for which he was awarded the Hawthornden prize. The publishing of religious books, however, bored him and just before the war broke out his mother got him a job as private secretary to Sir Hubert Young [q.v.], governor of Trinidad. He hated the flag-waving formality of Government House protocol, making his views plain in *West Indian Summer* (1943), an account of the experiences of nine English visitors to the West Indies. On the outbreak of war he returned to England and enlisted as a private in an aircraft battery. Commissioned in 1940 to military intelligence he was sent in 1943 as a member of the British army staff to Washington. When the war was over he returned to London.

On demobilization Pope-Hennessy lived on his writings, if that is an accurate account of an author so profligate of his earnings that he underwent recurrent financial crises, from which he was constantly relieved by the bounty of friends. From 1947 to 1949 only did he have regular employment as literary editor of the *Spectator.* He continued to produce books between bouts of travelling. *America is an Atmosphere* (1947) was an engaging travel book inspired by affection for Washington, just as *Aspects of Provence* (1952) echoed his delight in the song and sunburnt mirth of the warm south. But the two books which established his reputation as an outstanding biographer were parts i and ii of *Monckton Milnes* (1949), namely *The Years of Promise* and *The Flight of Youth.* These volumes epitomized the Victorian patrician, political, and literary milieu. They were followed by the less inspired *Lord Crewe, the Likeness of a Liberal* (1955). After an interval came *Queen Mary* (1959), for which he was appointed CVO (1960). With the possible exception of *George V* (1952) by his friend (Sir) Harold Nicolson [q.v.] no other royal biography of the century has so successfully combined sympathetic character-study with social history in such brilliant narrative form.

After preparatory visits to Ireland, Malaysia, Hong Kong, Africa, and Mauritius appeared what may be his best book, *Verandah* (1964), about scenes in the life of his grandfather, Sir John Pope-Hennessy [q.v.], an impulsive and provocative colonial governor who hailed from county Kerry and was immortalized by Anthony Trollope [q.v.] as Phineas Finn. The portrait Pope-Hennessy drew of his Irish progenitor's character bears no small resemblance to his own. There can be little doubt that he inherited many of the qualities of this fascinating but disturbing reformer, who sided with the Negro labourers against the planters and was repeatedly at loggerheads with the home government.

As a break in the catalogue of his biographies *Sins of the Fathers* (1967) was an angry indictment of the Atlantic slave traffickers. *Anthony Trollope* (1971) and the posthumous *Robert Louis Stevenson* (1974) marked a resumption of his literary biographies. These books were written mostly in Banagher, county Offaly, where in 1970 he had gone to live, quixotically adopting Irish citizenship. Trollope's was a character to which Pope-Hennessy had long been attached although so staid and unlike his own. With Stevenson's he was not in total sympathy. Besides he did not live to correct the proofs. The book is the least convincing of his literary studies and suggests too hasty composition. Pope-Hennessy was in truth in a hurry to embark upon the life of Sir Noël Coward [q.v.], for which he received a handsome advance. Alas, it was owing to indiscreet mentions of this welcome fortune that he met his death in his maisonette, no. 9 Ladbroke Grove, London. On 25 January 1974 he was brutally murdered by some ruffianly associates of the unscrupulous youths with whom he chose to consort. For during his last years an addiction to alcohol and what Peter Quennell has called the 'denizens of back-street bars and pubs' led him to take appalling risks of blackmail and violence. Sad though these habits were they did not intrude upon his writings or forfeit him the affection of his friends, even though they curtailed some old relationships. That charm, which in his youth was so irresistible, never entirely deserted him. To the last he remained the brilliant raconteur with a mischievous sense of humour and a sense of the ludicrous.

His good looks were striking. Slender and well built he carried his head proudly. He had a pale alabaster complexion, strangely hooded eyes, and thick raven-black hair, features which he liked to attribute to the Malaysian blood of his grandmother, Lady Pope-Hennessy. All his movements, like his mind, were rapid and darting. In walking he would outpace a companion in a sort of bounding gait. He was painted by Lucian Freud and photographed by (Sir) Cecil Beaton.

[Peter Quennell (ed.), *A Lonely Business, A Self-Portrait of James Pope-Hennessy*, 1981, comprising a selection of his letters, intermittent diary 1950–2, and royal portraits; personal knowledge.] JAMES LEES-MILNE

PORTAL, CHARLES FREDERICK ALGERNON, VISCOUNT PORTAL OF HUNGERFORD (1893–1971), marshal of the Royal Air Force, was born 21 May 1893 at Eddington House, near Hungerford, Berkshire, the first child of Edward Robert Portal, country gentleman and former barrister, and his second wife, Ellinor Kate Hill, daughter of Captain Charles West Hill, governor of Winchester prison. There were already two young sons from E. R. Portal's earlier marriage, and later he had four more sons by his second wife. There were no daughters.

The Portals were of Huguenot descent. Their long line of ancestors in southern France had flourished until Louis XIV's persecution, to avoid which two young Portal brothers fled abroad. Apparently they were shipped from Bordeaux in empty wine casks. In England the elder later established a family whose most distinguished member, until Portal of Hungerford, was the eighteenth-century silversmith and dramatist Abraham Portal [q.v.]. The younger founded a family which grew rich on the manufacture of banknote-paper; its most distinguished member in recent times was Viscount Portal [q.v.], chairman of Portal's Ltd. and the initiator of prefabricated houses.

Charles Portal was reared in a leisured but unluxurious household. E. R. Portal had inherited enough from a family wine business in Northampton to give up the law at thirty and devote himself to country life. The Eddington House estate comprised 400 acres, half of which he himself farmed; but most of his time was given to shooting, fishing, riding, hunting (as master of the Craven Hounds), and to his duties as landlord, JP, and major in the Berkshire Yeomanry. The world in which his seven sons grew up was one of manly sport and strict attention to duty. They were taught above all to be honourable, brave, active, well mannered, and considerate. Friendly competitiveness was encouraged, any trace of boasting or ostentation abhorred. Virility and patriotism were family hallmarks, and of the six sons who reached manhood, five opted from youth for a Service career. (Of these the most distinguished was Admiral Sir Reginald Portal, who died in 1983.) Only Charles Portal had no intention of entering the armed forces.

As a boy Portal (who was always known to his relatives and friends by his nickname Peter) soon excelled at shooting, fishing, ferreting, and ball games. At fourteen he took up hawking, which long remained an enthusiasm. By sixteen he was an acknowledged expert on this, writing paid articles for *The Field*.

Portal's education was that of his class: governess, preparatory school, public school. The public school was Winchester, where despite the hours he spent with the hawks he kept there he did well in both work and games. In October 1912 he went up to Christ Church, Oxford, as his father had done, to take a pass degree and subsequently qualify as a barrister of the Inner Temple. Though he spent most of his time hawking, beagling, and motor-cycle racing—he rode victoriously for Oxford against Cambridge in May 1914—he also passed his examinations. Had he gone into the law he would undoubtedly have made a great judge; but August 1914 dictated other courses.

On 6 August, hearing of a call for dispatch-riders, Portal enlisted in the motor-cyclist section of the Royal Engineers. Eight days later he was a corporal in France, about to begin almost incessant riding as the British Expeditionary Force advanced to Mons and retreated to the Marne. His tiredness became such that he once fell asleep on his machine and crashed into the back of the staff car carrying Sir Douglas (later Earl) Haig [q.v.]. But his courage and devotion to duty were quickly recognized. On 26 September he was commissioned, on 8 October he was mentioned in a dispatch of Sir John French (later Earl of Ypres, q.v.), by late November he was commanding all the riders in HQ Signals Company, 1st Corps.

Staff duties and a stable front made dispatch-riding less appealing, and Portal soon applied for secondment to the Royal Flying Corps as an air observer. In July 1915 he joined No. 3 Squadron, a reconnaissance and artillery observation unit. He had two days' ground training, and on his third day—never having been in the air before—flew on reconnaissance over the enemy lines.

In August 1915 Portal nearly killed himself on home leave when the front fork of his motor cycle broke; his lingual artery was severed, but a passing doctor saved his life. He was back in France within six weeks. At the end of 1915 he left No. 3 Squadron to train as a pilot, graduated flying officer RFC in April 1916, and joined No. 60

Squadron (fighter-reconnaissance) in time for the Somme offensive. In mid-July, less than three months after he had qualified as a pilot, he was promoted temporary captain and returned to No. 3 Squadron as a flight commander. Back on tactical reconnaissance and artillery observation, he made 326 operational flights in the next eleven months. His outstanding service during the five months of the Somme offensive resulted in a recommendation for an immediate award of the MC 'for conspicuous skill and gallantry' (gazetted 19 January 1917).

On 14 June 1917 Portal was promoted temporary major and given command of No. 16 Squadron (reconnaissance and artillery observation). A month later he was appointed to the DSO, also given for his earlier work on the Somme. During the autumn his squadron was required to bomb by night behind the battle front. Its RE 8s, far from easy to fly, had not been designed to carry bombs, and there was apprehension when the order came through. Portal quenched all doubts by personal example. He took off by night alone, with a 112 lb. bomb slung under each wing, and then landed with the bombs still on. He paused, repeated the flight—and then repeated it again. Very soon No. 16 Squadron was skilled in night bombing, with Portal continuing to set an example. One night in January 1918 he made five raids beyond the enemy lines; later, during the German spring offensive, when his squadron was working for the Canadian Corps of the First Army, he flew over the enemy lines for three and a quarter hours one day, sending down calls for action against hostile batteries, and then during the ensuing night flew a bombing mission in driving snow.

Promotion to temporary lieutenant-colonel followed on 17 June 1918 when Portal was sent home to command No. 24 (Training) Wing at Grantham. A few weeks later he was awarded a bar to his DSO. The recommendation, emanating from the Canadian Corps, stated that 'whenever difficult or dangerous work has had to be carried out, this officer has done it himself'.

Portal's fighting war was now over. He had flown over 900 operational sorties and successfully registered more than 250 artillery shoots. A lieutenant-colonel with three decorations and twice mentioned in dispatches, he was still only twenty-five. Such a man was not to be lost to the new Royal Air Force, and Sir Hugh (later Viscount) Trenchard [q.v.], who had marked him out in France, made sure that he was not. At the end of July 1919 he was appointed to a permanent commission in the rank of major (shortly, squadron leader).

For the next three and a half years Portal was an outstanding chief flying instructor at the newly established RAF Cadet College, Cranwell. He left in April 1922 to attend the first course at the new RAF Staff College, Andover. Posted next to operations and intelligence in the Air Ministry, he came into close contact with Trenchard, by then chief of the air staff, who initiated him into many aspects of RAF work and policy. Trenchard's high opinion of him was seen in Portal's promotion to wing commander in July 1925 and his nomination to attend the senior officers' war course at the Royal Naval College, Greenwich, where the other students were mostly admirals.

After Greenwich came command in March 1927 of No. 7 Squadron. It had experienced troubles before Portal took over, but his efficiency and enthusiasm soon had their effect. That summer, while based at Worthy Down, the squadron won the long-distance bomber event, entitling it to lead the bomber fly-past at the Hendon display; and in September 1927, and again in 1928, an aircraft of No. 7 Squadron won the annual competition for bombing accuracy. The bomb-aimer—lying on his stomach—was in both years the squadron commander, Portal. Another impressive feat at this time was Portal's disproof of an army assertion during manœuvres that tanks moving by night could not be spotted from the air. Patrolling during an evening of blinding rain and poor visibility, he picked out an armoured force with the aid of an Aldis lamp, and was still over it when dawn came nine hours later.

In 1929 Portal was chosen to attend the recently founded Imperial Defence College, after which he toured the RAF stations in India. On his return in 1931 he was promoted group captain and again appointed to the air staff. This time he was deputy director of plans, a post which brought him into close contact with the other Services. His main concerns were with Singapore (where he pleaded for aircraft as opposed to more heavy guns), with the 'air versus gun' controversy as it also related to other bases and the home ports, with questions of future RAF equipment, and with briefs for the British representatives at the disarmament conference. In this work he made a reputation for the speed at which he could produce a concise and convincing paper, and for his skill and fair-mindedness as a negotiator.

In February 1934 Portal received his first big command—over the British forces in Aden. There he brilliantly justified the decision to make the Air Ministry responsible for the defence of the settlement and the tribal protectorate. Soon after he arrived Quteibi tribesmen in the protectorate plundered some passing caravans, and order had to be restored. When the tribe refused to pay a fine and hand over the culprits Portal took action, not by punitive bombing, but by instituting an air blockade which, by threatening attack, kept the Quteibis from their fields and villages. After two months' incessant patrolling by his aircraft the tribesmen gave in, agreed to terms, and returned to good behaviour. This classic, and almost bloodless, demonstration of 'air control' over unadministered territory brought Portal further prestige and, on 1 January 1935, promotion to air commodore.

In the quieter months which then preceded the Abyssinian crisis Portal took up one of the Aden pastimes—sailing. Characteristically he won his first race and headed the table of successes in his first season. On one occasion he beat a naval commander first in his own yacht, and then, when they changed boats, in the commander's.

By the later summer of 1935 Mussolini's designs on Abyssinia were clear, and Portal was at full stretch preparing to repel any attack on Aden and receive reinforcements. With the arrival of these the post of commander, British forces in Aden, was upgraded, and Portal returned home—to a place on the directing staff of the Imperial Defence College. There he preached inter-Service collaboration rather than any purely 'air' doctrine, and made friendships in the other Services which stood him in good stead later.

Portal left the IDC in July 1937 on promotion to air vice-marshal and appointment as director of organization in the Air Ministry. The RAF was then in the midst of expansion schemes to counter the danger from Hitler's Germany. To determine and meet the Service's rapidly shifting requirements for organization, accommodation, equipment, and trained manpower was a vast and vital task to which Portal now sacrificed all leisure interests. Among the developments which owed much to his work were the creation of Maintenance Command, the organization of the London balloon barrage and Balloon Command, progress with camouflage, the provision of high octane fuel, and the framing of mobilization procedures and administrative plans to support operational projects. The development of the reserve forces and the creation of special units for operational flying training (previously done in the squadrons) were other achievements. The most difficult task of all was finding and developing, with the airfields board and the directorate of works, all the airfields and depot sites needed under the successive expansion schemes. During Portal's eighteen months at organization over thirty new main airfield stations were in fact begun or completed and many satellite sites acquired—work without which victory in the Battle of Britain would hardly have been possible. It was recognized by his appointment as CB in the New Year's honours of 1939.

On 1 February 1939 Portal became air member for personnel. This gave him a seat on the Air Council and responsibility for providing the RAF with its totals of skilled officers and men. To match requirements exactly when these were constantly changing was a formidable task, and when war came in September the RAF still had grave deficiencies in many trades. Had it not been for Portal, however, these would have been much worse. He insisted, for instance, that problems of manning should be considered before expansion schemes were adopted, not afterwards; he recruited air gunners, instead of wastefully using volunteer ground tradesmen in this role; he helped to create a new technical branch of officers; to make women more readily available for work on operational stations, he helped to free the women's RAF companies from the Auxiliary Territorial Service and create instead the Women's Auxiliary Air Force. Above all he played a major part, when war came, in initiating two vital elements in the expansion of aircrew training. The first was a big new initial training organization to deal solely with aircrew training which could be done on the ground. The second, in which he was concerned from the earlier prewar proposals, was the Commonwealth air training scheme approved in December 1939, and subsequently augmented. This scheme ensured, throughout the rest of the war, aircrew training facilities in safe areas and a wonderful flow of well-trained crews.

Portal was promoted temporary air marshal at the outbreak of war and remained at personnel. But a summons to a major operational post was bound to come and on 4 April 1940 he was appointed to Bomber Command. He had been there less than a week when the Germans invaded Norway. Once the enemy was established there it became Portal's task to attack German ships and German-occupied Norwegian airfields. But attack on warships only confirmed that the British bombers of the time could not operate safely by day without fighter escort; and not much could be achieved by trying to attack airfields at night or under cloud cover across the width of the North Sea—as Portal vainly pointed out to the air staff. His bombers obtained successes by laying mines on the German sea routes, but in general his force of some 240 aircraft was far too small, and too distant, to have any effect on the campaign.

On 10 May 1940 Portal's tasks changed abruptly when the Germans invaded France and the Low Countries. He was now required to use his 'medium' bombers—the Blenheims—against the advancing columns and their communications. This was at once revealed as suicidal work, and only Portal's rapid insistence on fighter cover saved the Blenheims from annihilation. Any delays imposed on the invaders were of the slightest—though in the Dunkirk period even slight delays had value. Little more success was achieved by Portal's 'heavy' bombers—the Wellingtons, Whitleys, and Hampdens. These were required to operate by night against the invaders' communications and—after much Anglo-

French controversy—against oil plants, marshalling yards, and aircraft factories in Germany. Attack on German industrial targets was an extension of the war strongly urged by Portal. His small forces, inadequately equipped for accurate navigation and bombing on moonless nights, did little damage—much less than was thought at the time—but at least they suffered few losses, and they carried the war to the enemy's homeland.

Portal's reputation in no way suffered from the Allied failures in Norway and France, and his firm leadership was recognized by his appointment in July 1940 as KCB. In the weeks which followed, Sir Charles Portal—as he now became known—commended himself greatly to the prime minister by the energy he put into preparations to resist a German invasion and by the effective use of his force against enemy invasion ports and barge concentrations. His desire for offensive action against objectives in Germany, and his stimulation of research into better methods of navigation, also appealed to (Sir) Winston Churchill, as did his readiness to attack targets in Berlin immediately after the first German bombs fell on London. These attacks on Berlin in fact did negligible damage, but they had a profound effect on the Battle of Britain then raging. They caused Hitler to direct the *Luftwaffe* prematurely against London, and so took the weight of its attack from Fighter Command's vital sector stations.

While stimulating technical improvements to make the British night bombing more effective, Portal now also began to press for the selection of targets which would be easier to find and hit. Thus far the targets had been precise ones, for both military and humanitarian reasons. Portal urged that German industrial areas, rather than particular plants or factories, should be his prime objective. This was not yet the official policy; but on 4 October 1940 Portal left Bomber Command to succeed, three weeks later, Sir Cyril (later Lord) Newall [q.v.] as chief of the air staff. In a matter of weeks 'area bombing' was initiated, and Bomber Command began its long assault on the German industrial towns.

Promoted acting air chief marshal on his new appointment, Portal had now risen to be head of his Service. The 'accepted star of the Royal Air Force' (in Churchill's words), he drove himself relentlessly throughout the rest of the war. His leadership was never remotely challenged; and he survived strains in dealing with the prime minister which seriously impaired the health or temper of more than one of his colleagues.

As CAS Portal fought his war almost entirely in Whitehall and at the great Anglo-American conferences. He concerned himself not with the day-to-day supervision of the RAF but, in essence, with the settling of strategic plans, priorities, and allocations. This he did both on the RAF level and, in conjunction with the prime minister and his fellow chiefs of staff, on the inter-Service and later inter-Allied levels. The work of determining first British, and then Anglo-American, higher strategy and military policy was particularly arduous. At the end of the war Portal reckoned that he had attended nearly 2,000 chiefs of staff meetings, 'each taking 1½ to 2 hours or more, and needing perhaps 3 or 4 hours of reading beforehand'.

Portal's first battle as CAS was for the retention of Coastal Command. In the autumn of 1940 A. V. Alexander (later Earl Alexander of Hillsborough) and Lord Beaverbrook [qq.v.] led a campaign for its transfer to the Admiralty. In Portal's view the shipping protection problem of that time arose not from faulty organization but from the general shortage of aircraft, and he worked out a compromise with the chief of naval staff, Sir A. Dudley Pound [q.v.] by which Coastal Command would be strengthened and formally placed under the Admiralty's 'operational control'. (It already was so in practice, but the phrase was a guarantee.) Thanks to this, Alexander and Beaverbrook were worsted. Later, in 1942, Portal had to fight a similar battle against Sir Alan Brooke (later Viscount Alanbrooke, q.v.), who was demanding a very large and virtually separate air force for army support. Together with naval demands at the time, it would have absorbed almost the entire British output of operational aircraft. Again Portal succeeded in satisfying the demand in another way—by demonstrating, through the forces of Sir Arthur (later Lord) Tedder [q.v.] in North Africa, that where the army was actively engaged it could by that time rely on a powerful RAF presence and constantly improving techniques of air support. In resisting such demands Portal preserved both his own Service and the principle of centralized higher control of air power to avoid waste of resources and give maximum flexibility of application. This in itself was a notable contribution to victory.

Portal's other internal battles included several with the prime minister, none of which diminished their mutual liking and respect. Apart from those on strategic issues, the most serious was that over the position of Tedder in the Middle East in the autumn of 1941. Churchill had had little confidence in Tedder's appointment, and was moving towards dismissing him. Portal, convinced of Tedder's outstanding abilities, skilfully averted this by sending out his able and devoted vice-chief of air staff, Sir Wilfrid Freeman [q.v.], who was also an admirer of Tedder, on a mission of enquiry, and by concerting with the secretary of state for air, Sir Archibald Sinclair (later Viscount Thurso, q.v.), a joint resignation should the prime minister insist on having his way.

Portal's contributions to the higher strategy and direction of the war were mostly made within the framework of written exchanges with the prime minister (two or three times a week) and meetings with his fellow chiefs of staff, American as well as British. On a few detailed issues his views did not prevail, but in general they did. They were extremely consistent. He steadfastly upheld the basic strategy which he had agreed with his fellow British chiefs of staff, and which he later helped to persuade the Americans to accept—the strategy which brought victory. The essentials of this were the primacy of the war in Europe and North Africa over the war in the Far East; the building up of US armaments and forces and the maintenance of sea communications; and the waging of a bombing offensive against Germany to the point where her capacity to resist invasion by the Allied armies would be fatally weakened. This strategy Portal helped to defend successfully against all attempts to change it, or weaken it by diversions. He overcame Churchill's periodic waverings about the bombing offensive and, in conjunction with Brooke, frustrated the prime minister's proposals for invasions of Norway and Sumatra. He firmly resisted the American Admiral King's inclination in 1942–3 to switch the greater effort to the Pacific. He and Brooke also played a major part in convincing the Americans that the return to France would have to wait until 1944.

It was naturally, however, in the bombing offensive against Germany that Portal's most distinctive contribution lay. After the fall of France the War Cabinet and the chiefs of staff, knowing that years must elapse before the British army could return to the Continent, pinned their faith on a bombing offensive as the only immediate means, with a blockade, of putting direct pressure on the Germans. On becoming chief of the air staff in October 1940 Portal had to make this strategy work; and his first contribution, as indicated above, was for reasons of practicality to introduce night attack on industrial areas instead of precise targets. During 1941, however, it became apparent that much of the British bombing was still ineffective. This crisis Portal met by stimulating the efforts to produce new night navigational and bombing aids and more powerful bombs, and by advocating incendiary attack by selected crews before the arrival of the main bomber stream. He also appointed to Bomber Command a man whose experience, abilities, and character fitted him exceptionally well for the task in hand—Sir Arthur Harris.

The entry of the Americans into the war gave Portal the chance to concert, with General Arnold, the Anglo-American day and night air offensive which ultimately brought decisive results. During 1942, however, the USAAF bombers, purely a daylight force, were unable successfully to penetrate Germany, and voices were raised—especially Churchill's—urging them to go over to attack by night. But Portal, who after the early operations himself felt uneasy, was more aware than Churchill of the difficulties of conversion, and threw all his weight behind the American air leaders in their desire to persist with daylight operations. He helped to still Churchill's criticisms; and eventually long-range fighters, especially the Mustangs backed by Portal, supplied the cover which enabled the Americans to win their daylight battle over Germany. Throughout it was obvious to Portal that a day and night offensive, if it could be achieved, would be vastly more effective than one solely by night: the strain on the defences, the choice of targets, the moral and material effects would be immeasurably greater.

Until the immediate bombing campaign in preparation for the Allied landings in Normandy, Portal was the designated agent of the combined chiefs of staff for the superior control of the strategic air forces of both countries. With the approach of the invasion, 'direction' of these was vested in General Eisenhower—an arrangement which Portal accepted because in practice it would be exercised by Tedder, Eisenhower's deputy. With the establishment and advance of the Allied armies, control reverted in November 1944 to Portal in conjunction with Arnold—working in practice through their deputies.

During the winter months of 1944–5 the primary target systems chosen met strong opposition from Harris. With the development of night navigation and bombing aids Portal was convinced that Bomber Command could now operate effectively against precise targets, notably oil plants, which became the first priority. Harris, distrustful from past experience of 'panacea' targets, would have preferred, for reasons both of effect and operational safety, to complete as his primary task the destruction of his listed German industrial towns. Portal's patience in dealing with Harris was criticized in the British official history, but he was convinced that Harris, while arguing against his orders, had no intention of disobeying them. In point of fact area attacks continued until almost the last month of the war, but attack on more precise targets took precedence when operational conditions permitted.

The strategic air offensive has come under strong criticism since the war, particularly from humanitarians and naval historians. There is no doubt, however, that though its course was long, arduous, and bloody, it finally worked. The Germans were forced to put an enormous effort into defending their homeland; their production suffered and their communications were disrupted; their air force became almost purely defensive and was finally withering away for lack of fuel. Exactly as the chiefs of staff had hoped, Germany's capacity to resist an armed invasion was fatally weakened. Once the possibility of a return to the Continent dawned in 1942, this was always Portal's main intention. In promoting the bombing offensive he did not, like Harris, believe that it could virtually win the war without a serious invasion. If the Germans surrendered before the invasion so much the better; but essentially his concept was first to make the invasion possible, and then to speed, by both tactical and strategic operations, the advance of the Allied armies.

The close involvement of Portal with the strategic air offensive did not mean that he ignored the needs of the army and the navy for direct air support. As supplies of aircraft increased and technical developments were pressed forward, the U-boats were duly mastered and the Allied armies fought under an overwhelming Allied air superiority. Portal was essentially a co-operator: he was determined that the ground and maritime forces should have adequate air support, but equally determined not to sacrifice to this end the embryonic strategic air offensive with all its wide potentialities. It is not only as a proponent of that offensive but also as a great all-round airman and clear-brained strategist co-operating in the closest way with his colleagues at the head of the other British and American Services that Portal qualifies as one of the prime architects of the Allied victory.

The opinions entertained of Portal's ability by his wartime colleagues were extraordinarily high. Harris summed up his lifelong admiration in the words 'anything you could do, Peter Portal could do better'. Churchill remarked to Lord Moran [q.v.] 'Portal has everything'. Eisenhower, while president, told Lord Plowden that he regarded Portal as the greatest British war leader, 'greater even than Churchill'. Lord Ismay [q.v.] told an enquirer that in his opinion Portal was the best of the wartime military leaders 'quite easily'.

During the war Portal had received several honours in addition to his knighthood. They were the Order of Polonia Restituta (1st class), the GCB (June 1942), the Order of St. Olaf (Grand Cross), and the Czechoslovakian Order of the White Lion. On January 1944 he was promoted marshal of the Royal Air Force. At the end of the war a spate of further honours descended upon him. In August 1945, on the recommendation of the departing prime minister, he received a barony, under the title of Baron Portal of Hungerford; and in the New Year's honours of 1946 he became first Viscount Portal of Hungerford and was at the same time admitted to the Order of Merit. Later in 1946 he was awarded the French Legion of Honour (Grand Cross) and croix de guerre with palm, the Distinguished Service Medal (by the president of the USA), and the Grand Cross of the Order of George I (by the King of the Hellenes); and in December King George VI appointed him a Knight of the Garter. In 1947 he was made Knight Grand Cross of the Order of the Netherlands Lion and in 1948 Belgium honoured him with the Order of Crown with palm and croix de guerre 1940. In 1941 Portal had been made an honorary Student of Christ Church, Oxford, and in 1945-7 further honours came in the form of the freedom of the City of London and honorary doctorates from eight universities. In 1951 he was also appointed deputy lieutenant in the county of Sussex.

Once the war was over Portal determined to lay down his office, and he did so at the end of 1945. His intention was to relax, to establish a family home, and to take up a City directorship or two. But he had retired only a few days when the prime minister, C. R. (later Earl) Attlee, pressed him to accept another important post. The government had decided to develop the uses of atomic energy, and Attlee wanted Portal to head the organization to be responsible for producing fissile material.

Portal had no wish at all to do this, but he was one of the few leading figures in the country conversant with the broader aspects of the wartime atomic energy developments. Moreover, almost his last action on the chiefs of staff committee had been to recommend the creation of a British nuclear deterrent force and the building of two atomic piles for the production of plutonium. In these circumstances his patriotism overcame his longing for a rest, and in March 1946 he became controller of production in the highly secret atomic energy directorate of the Ministry of Supply. This was an untidy assignment, for the production organization had yet to be created, and its purposes were still undefined, but the necessary research would mostly have to emanate from the Ministry's Atomic Energy Research Establishment at Harwell, which was functioning separately under (Sir) John Cockcroft [q.v.], and was not to be within Portal's province. Fortunately Portal and Cockcroft got on well; and in January 1950 the organizational structure was tidied up when Portal was appointed controller of atomic energy and given superior direction over all branches of the atomic energy organization, including Harwell.

The official history of British atomic energy takes the view that Portal was not a very effective head of the atomic energy project except in preserving priorities at the government level and in dealing with the chiefs of staff. Undoubtedly the main work lay in the research achievements of Cockcroft's teams at Harwell; the creation of a production organization by Christopher Hinton (later Lord Hinton of Bankside) and his teams (resulting in the uranium factory at Risley, the graphite piles at Windscale, and the diffusion plant at Copenhurst); and the development under W. G. (later Lord) Penney of the weapons establishments at Fort Halstead and Aldermaston, culminating in the fabrication of the British atomic bomb. These were astonishing achievements in the short space of six years, and though they emanated mainly from the genius of his subordinates it would seem only logical to accord Portal, as co-ordinator generalissimo, some share of the credit. It was Portal, too, who precipitated the government's decision that the bomb should actually be made. When he was appointed the decision went only as far as producing fissile material; but in January 1947 Portal, knowing his views coincided with those of the chiefs of staff, asked for a definite decision that the appropriate research should be undertaken and atomic weapons developed. He got it by showing how this could be done economically, and in the utmost secrecy, by a small specially created organization within the Ministry of Supply headed by Penney and responsible to himself.

With the production of the bomb a certainty Portal felt free to resign in August 1951. Firmly declining Churchill's invitation to become minister of defence if the Conservatives won the forthcoming general election, he added instead to his directorates. He was already on the board of Barclays Bank DCO, Barclays Bank Ltd., Commercial Union Assurance, and the Ford Motor Company Ltd., and was later to take on directorships of Portals Ltd. and the Whitbread Investment Trust. In October 1951 he became a director of the British Aluminium Co. Ltd., and in 1953 its chairman. This involved him in 1958 in a battle—one of the few in his life which he did not win—to resist a take-over bid from the American-backed Tube Investments Ltd. Much greater success attended his subsequent work as director and for a time (1959–64) chairman of the British Match Corporation, and as chairman, from its inception in 1960 until 1968, of the British Aircraft Corporation.

BAC was a difficult assignment undertaken, like atomic energy, only from patriotic motives. The Corporation involved the association, but not amalgamation, of three of the largest manufacturers of airframes. The marriage was virtually dictated by the government, which promised a rational division of orders for new enterprises. A national figure was needed as impartial non-executive chairman, and Portal reluctantly agreed to serve. In the event, he much enjoyed the work and his happy relationship with the deputy chairman and managing director, Sir George Edwards. He and Edwards lost two or three battles to retain projects which governments decided to cancel—notably the TSR 2—but Concorde was preserved and several successful aircraft including the Jaguar strike/trainer developed. Portal was able to retain the goodwill of the various components of the Corporation, to achieve an increasing degree of integration, and to report satisfactory profits—no mean feat for the aircraft industry.

Otherwise, Portal's main interests after the war were in voluntary work and in reconstructing an elegant house at West Ashling, near Chichester, and tending its gardens. The charitable causes with which he was closely associated were the RAF Benevolent Fund, the RAF Escaping Society, the King Edward VII Hospital at Midhurst, the Nuffield Trust for the forces of the Crown, and the Dominion Students Hall Trust (providing accommodation in London for overseas students). He remained an active sportsman—fishing, shooting, and deerstalking in particular—and was president of the MCC in 1958–9. He spoke very infrequently in the House of Lords, where he sat on the cross-benches.

In appearance, Portal was tall and dark, with a large beaked nose and deep facial lines. In his sixties he lost much of his hair and his angular look. His main characteristics were intelligence, integrity, self-control, courage, great powers of endurance, a strong sense of discipline and duty, modesty, a quiet charm of manner, fundamental simplicity, and a deep inner reserve. This last quality was sometimes misunderstood, or resented, by subordinates who expected to be on more intimate terms with their chief. Portal's charm, wit, and sense of fun were not always displayed. They emerged most readily when he had people to convince or entertain, speeches to make, or a few hours to spend with genuine friends.

In 1919 he married Joan Margaret, daughter of a leading Norfolk landowner, Sir Charles Glynne Earle Welby, fifth baronet, CB, and of Lady Welby, a sister of the Marquess of Bristol. Their only son died at birth in 1921. They subsequently had two daughters. After some months' illness from cancer, stoically borne, Portal died at West Ashling House 22 April 1971. As a special privilege in 1945 a remainder of the barony had been granted through the daughters, and that title was inherited by the elder, Rosemary Ann (born 1923).

A statue of Portal by Oscar Nemon was erected in 1975 on the lawns of the Ministry of Defence, facing the Thames Embankment. There are portraits by Sir Oswald Birley (Christ Church, Oxford), Augustus John (National Museum of Wales), Eric Kennington (Imperial War Museum), and F. Egerton Cooper (RAF Museum).

[Air Ministry and Cabinet papers in the Public Record Office; the Portal papers at Christ Church, Oxford; family papers at West Ashling House; Denis Richards, *Portal of Hungerford*, 1977 (for March 1978); M. M. Gowing, *Independence and Deterrence: Britain and Atomic*

Energy, 1945–52, 2 vols., 1974; private information; personal knowledge.]

DENIS RICHARDS

POSTGATE, RAYMOND WILLIAM (1896–1971), journalist, social historian, and gastronome, was born in Cambridge 6 November 1896, the eldest of four sons and second of the six children of John Percival Postgate, classical scholar and fellow of Trinity College, Cambridge, and his wife, Edith Allen. His paternal grandfather was John Postgate FRCS [q.v.], a campaigner against the adulteration of food substances. His mother had attended Miss Buss's North London Collegiate School before entering Girton College, Cambridge.

Postgate was a pupil at the Perse School, Cambridge, but transferred to Liverpool College when his father became professor of Latin at Liverpool University. With his sister, (Dame) Margaret (who married G. D. H. Cole, q.v.), Postgate received a classical education and in 1915 he went up to Oxford with a scholarship tenable at St. John's College. He obtained a first class in classical honour moderations in 1917, but he did not complete his studies. He had seen the industrial strife in Liverpool during the 1911 dock strikes, and had read Cole's first book, *The World of Labour* (1913). In 1915 he joined the Edge Hill branch of the Independent Labour Party and he entered Oxford a convinced believer in the class struggle. He refused military service in 1916 and was sent to gaol, although he was soon released on medical grounds. When called up again he became a conscientious objector on the run and as repudiated by his father and forbidden to return home.

To earn a living, Postgate wrote occasional articles for the *Weekly Herald* and, in 1918, just prior to the armistice, he married Daisy, daughter of the *Herald*'s editor, George Lansbury [q.v.], whom he much admired and whose biography he published in 1951. In 1919 the *Herald* reverted to a daily paper and Postgate was employed as a foreign news sub-editor. His first book, *The International (Socialist Bureau) during the War* (1918), was followed in 1920 by *The Bolshevik Theory, Revolution from 1789 to 1906: documents selected and edited with notes* and *The Workers' International.* A regular supporter of the Plebs League, a left-wing educational organization, he wrote for its journal *Plebs.* In 1920 he was among the founder members of the Communist Party of Great Britain and in July 1921 became editor of its journal, the *Communist.* But, in May 1922, he resigned his editorship and soon left the British Communist Party, returning to the *Daily Herald.* At this time the Communist Party was attempting to bring the Plebs League under its control and Postgate was influential in the transfer of the League's work to the National Council of Labour Colleges.

His literary work continued with the publication in 1923 of *The Builders' History*, but when Lansbury retired from the *Daily Herald* in 1925, Postgate lost his full-time employment. Together they then produced *Lansbury's Labour Weekly* but this ceased publication about a year after the 1926 general strike. Postgate had, however, published in 1924 the first of two classical works—a translation, edited with a commentary, of *Pervigilium Veneris* and this may have been influential in his subsequent appointment, by J. L. Garvin [q.v.], as departmental editor of the ancient history and classics section of the fourteenth edition of *Encyclopaedia Britannica.* It was through this work that he met the American publisher, Alfred A. Knopf, and he became his European representative from 1930 to 1949.

Postgate's reputation as a writer of labour and radical history was extended in the 1930s with biographies of John Wilkes [q.v.] (*That Devil Wilkes*, 1930) and Robert Emmet [q.v.] (*Robert Emmet*, 1931) and in 1938, by the most successful of his historical works, *The Common People*, written with G. D. H. Cole. But he had no permanent appointment and welcomed the chance in 1937 to edit *Fact*, a monthly sponsored by Rudolph Messel. This survived for two years and early in 1940 he was invited to edit the weekly, *Tribune*, which, much to the concern of George (later Lord) Strauss and Aneurin Bevan [q.v.], was then taking a pro-Soviet line. In the same year appeared the first, and very successful, of his three detective stories: *Verdict of Twelve.*

He left *Tribune* in late 1941 and, from 1942 until 1950, was employed as a temporary civil servant in the Board of Trade. Before he left the service he had embarked on the enterprise which brought him fame on an international scale: *Good Food Guide.* He conceived the idea of improving Britain's poor reputation for public food by pioneering a British hotel and restaurant guide. He assembled a volunteer team, and their reports, edited by him and including suggestions for reforms needed in the catering trade, were first published in 1951. His wife helped, and the annual volumes were published from their home until 1962 when the organization was handed over to the Consumers' Association. Postgate continued to edit the series until 1968. He always had a particular interest in wine and his books, *The Plain Man's Guide to Wine* (1951, revised edn., 1970), and *The Home Wine Cellar* (1960) were popular; articles on the same subject appeared in the *New Statesman*, *Spectator*, and other journals. In the 1950s the vintners of St. Emilion in the Bordeaux country conferred on him the status of honorary bourgeois, rising to that of grand chancelier d'ambassade pour la

Grande Bretagne. He was appointed OBE in 1966.

His early interest in classical studies was maintained and in 1969 he published an edited edition of *The Agamemnon of Aeschylus*; and although he was not very active in political affairs after World War II, he remained a socialist. He died 29 March 1971 at the Kent and Canterbury Hospital, three weeks before his wife, and they were survived by their two sons, John Raymond who became professor of microbiology at Sussex University and Richard Oliver, independent script writer and cartoonist in children's television.

[*Dictionary of Labour Biography*, vol. ii, ed. Joyce M. Bellamy and John Saville, 1974, for biographies of Daisy and Raymond Postgate by Dame Margaret Cole (with bibliography); *Guardian* and *The Times*, 30 March 1971; autobiographical articles posthumously published in the *New Statesman*, 9, 16, and 23 April 1971.] JOYCE M. BELLAMY

POWELL, OLAVE ST. CLAIR BADEN-, LADY (1889–1977), leader of the world Guide movement. [See BADEN-POWELL.]

PRIESTLEY, SIR RAYMOND EDWARD (1886–1974), Antarctic scientist and educationist, was born in Tewkesbury, Gloucestershire, 20 July 1886, the second son and second of eight children of Joseph Edward Priestley, headmaster of Tewkesbury Grammar School, and his wife, Henrietta Rice. Priestley was educated in his father's school and taught there for a year before reading geology at Bristol University College (1905–7) where he was captain of hockey and in the cricket XI. At the end of his second year in the university a chance contact led to him joining the British Antarctic expedition of 1907–9 led by Sir E. H. Shackleton [q.v.].

Although from a staunch Methodist background, Priestley adapted well to expedition life with sailors, adventurers, and two outstanding university geologists—(Sir) T. W. Edgeworth David and (Sir) Douglas Mawson [qq.v.]. Because of a knee injury, Priestley spent more time caring for ponies and less on geological field-work than expected. The achievements of Shackleton, who reached a position ninety-seven miles from the South Pole, and David, who attained the South Magnetic Pole, brought fame to the expedition on its return. Priestley spent four months in England and contributed to the geological sections of Shackleton's classic book, *The Heart of the Antarctic* (1909), before returning to Sydney, Australia, in October to work with Edgeworth David on volume i of the geological report which was published in 1914.

Captain R. F. Scott [q.v.] recruited Priestley when passing through Sydney to the Antarctic in 1910. He joined the northern party under Victor Campbell. After spending 1911 at Cape Adare the six-man party was landed 200 miles further south for summer field-work with provisions for eight weeks. The ship was stopped by pack-ice from returning and the epic story of how the party survived and then sledged 250 miles to the main party early in the following summer is told in Priestley's book *Antarctic Adventure* (1914, reprinted 1974). They survived the fierce winds by digging a cave in a snow-drift. A line across the middle of the twelve feet by nine feet floor separated the wardroom from the mess deck of three petty officers. By agreement, nothing said on one side of the line could be 'heard' or answered by those on the other side. Priestley considered this splendid training for dealing with unreasonable, irascible professors in later life without loss of temper. His responsibility for the commissariat in the ice cave in these circumstances shows an early reputation for fairness and reliability.

On return, Priestley matriculated as a pensioner in Christ's College, Cambridge, for a course of research study. World War I intervened and he served as adjutant at the Wireless Training Centre (1914–17), and then with the 46th divisional Signal company in France. He won the MC. After the armistice he wrote the official *The Work of the Royal Engineers 1914–19. The Signal Service* (1921) and *Breaking the Hindenburg Line* (1919). After return to Cambridge he completed sections of *British (Terra Nova) Antarctic Expedition 1910–13*: *Glaciology* (1922), written jointly with (Sir) Charles S. Wright), a classic of early glaciological literature. A thesis on this subject brought him a BA in 1920 after which he studied agriculture (diploma, 1922) before becoming a fellow of Clare College, Cambridge (1923–34; honorary fellow, 1956).

Priestley's career then turned to academic administration. He was secretary to the board of research studies as assistant registrary (1924–7), first assistant registrary and secretary to the general board (1927–34), and secretary general of the faculties (1934–5). His keen interest in the British Commonwealth led him to become first vice-chancellor of Melbourne University (1935–8) before returning as vice-chancellor of Birmingham University (1938–52). In these posts he took a deep interest in students, their sport, and student unions. Although he felt a lack of support from industry and government in Melbourne he left a fine Student's Union building. In Birmingham, thanks to public support and despite World War II, the university doubled in size, started new departments, and recruited some outstanding professors. In the wider field, Priestley helped found the University College of the West Indies and was chairman of the Imperial College of Tropical Agriculture, Trinidad (1949–53).

After his retirement to Bredons Norton near Tewkesbury in 1952, he continued his public service, first as chairman of the royal commission on the Civil Service (1953–5). The Priestley commission accepted the principle and set out guide-lines to link pay throughout the Civil Service with equivalent posts in industry—a concept which helped maintain the flow of first-class people to the Civil Service, possibly to the detriment of industry.

Priestley never lost his love of the Antarctic and often lectured on his experiences to undergraduates in Cambridge, to servicemen in World War II, and to many others. He helped his expedition colleague, Frank Debenham [q.v.], to found the Scott Polar Research Institute in the University of Cambridge in 1920, but his academic activities gave him little time for polar affairs until retirement. From 1955 to 1958 he deputized as acting director, London headquarters of the Falkland Islands Dependencies Survey (later the British Antarctic Survey) for (Sir) Vivian Fuchs during his absence on the Trans Antarctic expedition. His presidential address to the British Association for the Advancement of Science in 1956 was titled 'Twentieth Century Man against the Antarctic'. He twice visited the Antarctic again, with the Duke of Edinburgh to the Falkland Islands Dependencies in 1956 and to Victoria Land with the US navy in 1959, when he visited his early expedition area. During the former trip on the *Britannia*, his fondness for talking about polar subjects led the ornithologists and the Duke to call him the 'Lesser Polar Backchat' but this was soon upgraded to 'Greater Polar Backchat'. *Antarctic Research* (1964), edited by Priestley, R. J. Adie, and G. de Q. Robin, reflected the recognition and consolidation of British research activities in the Antarctic following the International Geophysical Year (1957–8), Fuchs's success, and Priestley's influence as acting director. Priestley contributed to this Dictionary the notice of G. M. Levick.

Priestley's last considerable public office was as president of the Royal Geographical Society (1961–3), after which the effects of old war injuries kept him increasingly in Bredons Norton, where he enjoyed family life and visitors while remaining mentally alert and active to the end. He was a patient man of modest tastes and a sense of humour whose sympathetic and realistic judgements left their mark on twentieth-century education and research. He was knighted in 1949, and held the Polar medal and bar and the Founder's medal of the Royal Geographical Society. He held honorary doctorates from Melbourne, New Zealand, St. Andrews, Natal, Dalhousie, Birmingham, Malaya, Sheffield, and the West Indies.

In 1915 he married Phyllis Mary (died 1961), daughter of William Boyle Boyd, from Dunedin, New Zealand, the master of a barquentine; they had two daughters. Priestley died in the Nuffield Nursing Home, Cheltenham, 24 June 1974.

[Autobiographical notes of his early years; private information from Mrs Margaret Hubert (daughter); obituaries for NZ *Antarctic* and the Central Office of Information; archives of University of Cambridge; personal knowledge.] G. DE Q. ROBIN

PRIMROSE, (ALBERT EDWARD) HARRY (MAYER ARCHIBALD), sixth EARL OF ROSEBERY (1882–1974), landowner and racehorse breeder, was born at Dalmeny in Scotland 8 January 1882, the elder son (there were also two daughters) of Archibald Philip Primrose, fifth Earl and former Liberal prime minister [q.v.]. His mother was Hannah, only daughter of Baron Meyer Amschel de Rothschild [q.v.], of Mentmore, Buckinghamshire. The Prince of Wales, later King Edward VII, was one of his godfathers. Harry, Lord Dalmeny—his courtesy title as heir to the earldom—was educated at Eton from where he passed top into the Royal Military Academy (Sandhurst) and was commissioned in the Grenadier Guards.

At the age of twenty-one, at the insistence of his father Lord Rosebery, he very reluctantly resigned his commission to stand as Liberal candidate for the county of Edinburgh, which he represented from 1906 to 1910. At twenty-four he thus became the youngest MP. The prime minister, Campbell-Bannerman, in an attempt to heal an old feud with Dalmeny's father, invited the former to second the motion for the royal address in the Commons. He told his father of the proffered honour, but his father replied: 'If you accept Campbell-Bannerman's invitation you are no son of mine.' It was, said Harry Rosebery many years later, 'very embarrassing'. It effectively quenched whatever political ambitions he had.

His maiden speech in March 1906 was on army expenditure and reorganization, but after that he spoke very little and confined his interventions to local issues. This was regrettable for Dalmeny was a loss to English politics because he had both political ambition and political interest. He also possessed political skill as was shown many years later, in 1941, when he became regional commissioner for Scotland. He combined his father's intelligence with common sense and an ability to get on with very different sorts of people, which his father never had.

Meanwhile, Dalmeny was making a name for himself as a cricketer. While still at school he had distinguished himself in the Eton v. Harrow match at Lord's in 1900. He played for Buckinghamshire in 1901, twice for Middlesex in 1902, and finally in 1905 became captain of Surrey, the youngest captain the county had ever had. In 1906 he played for Scotland v. the Australians.

In 1907 he resigned the captaincy because of conflicting duties in the House of Commons. But in December 1908 he wrote to his constituency agent: 'It is with great regret that I write to inform you that I do not propose to stand for Parliament at the next General Election. It is being forced upon me more and more that my politics are not far enough advanced to meet the views of the Liberal Party as at present constituted.'

Dalmeny insisted to the end of his life that he was a Liberal; in fact, he was a Conservative, or perhaps a Liberal of so old a vintage as to merit the designation Whig. Later, in the stress of a major economic crisis, he became a National Liberal, ultimately becoming the party's president. But he never took the final step of joining the Conservatives.

In 1914, shortly after the outbreak of war on 4 August, Dalmeny rejoined the Grenadier Guards and, after a short spell at GHQ in France, became an aide-de-camp to General E. H. H. Allenby (later Viscount Allenby of Megiddo, q.v.). In June 1917 he joined Allenby in Palestine as assistant military secretary. This was a remarkable and happy relationship. Each had the reputation of being difficult to get on with; each was outspoken, did not suffer fools gladly, and possessed great common sense. He was mentioned in dispatches, was awarded the MC (1916) and French Legion of Honour (1917), and was appointed to the DSO (1918).

His younger brother, Neil Primrose, MP for Wisbech, was also in Palestine serving with the Buckinghamshire Yeomanry. On 18 November 1917 he was killed in the last shot of a battle with the Turks at Gaza. Their father, Lord Rosebery, never got over this blow and in 1919 suffered a severe stroke from which he did not recover. Thus Dalmeny became in fact head of the family although his father did not die until 1929. Then he entered the House of Lords as second Earl of Midlothian, a title bestowed on his father in 1911 but never used. Nevertheless, he continued to be known as the sixth Earl of Rosebery.

In 1909 Dalmeny married Dorothy Alice Margaret Augusta, daughter of Lord Henry George Grosvenor and sister of the third Duke of Westminster. The marriage was brief and unhappy, but produced a son and daughter to whom he was devoted. In 1919 the marriage was dissolved and in 1924 Dalmeny married Eva Isabel Marian (DBE, 1955), daughter of Henry Campbell Bruce, second Baron Aberdare, and former wife of Algernon Henry Strutt, third Baron Belper. They had a son, and a daughter who died at birth.

In 1931 his son and heir by his first marriage, Archibald Ronald, Lord Dalmeny, died suddenly at the age of twenty-one from blood poisoning contracted during a dental operation at Oxford. By all accounts a golden boy, modest, charming, and intelligent, he was, to his father's delight, an excellent cricketer and it had been prophesied that he would have a glittering future as a batsman and bowler.

Between the wars, apart from managing his great estates, Rosebery established himself as a racehorse breeder and owner and won most of the famous races. Perhaps his best-known horse was Blue Peter, foaled at Mentmore, which won not only the Two Thousand Guineas, the Blue Riband at Epsom, the Eclipse Stakes, and—Rosebery's proudest racing moment—the Derby in 1939. Ocean Swell, sired by Blue Peter, later won the Derby (1944) and the Ascot Gold Cup. Rosebery was elected to the Jockey Club in 1924. He became president of the Thoroughbred Breeders Association and remained so until 1955.

From 1941 until the beginning of 1945 Rosebery was regional commissioner for Scotland. Like his father, he had a passionate love for Scotland and he worked indefatigably at his difficult task. He never courted popularity; but this did him no harm in the long run, both with the prime minister and the Scottish people. In 1945 he became secretary of state for Scotland in the brief caretaker government and, after its defeat, he led the National Liberals in the Lords. In 1947 he was created a Knight of the Order of the Thistle. He was sworn of the Privy Council in 1945.

Henceforth his public interests were varied but non-political. He was chairman of the Royal Fine Art Commission for Scotland (1952–7) and president of the Royal Scottish Corporation. He was president of the Surrey Cricket Club (1947–50) and of the MCC (1953–4). He was a member of the royal commission on justices of the peace (1946–8) and was himself a JP for many years. He was lord lieutenant for Midlothian (1929–64). In 1949 the Labour government asked him to preside over a committee of enquiry into the export and slaughter of horses and from 1955 to 1965 he was chairman of the Scottish Tourist Board. He was one of the original supporters of the Edinburgh Festival in which his wife, Eva, played a notable part.

Rosebery had fantastic energy and was interested in and curious about everything, down to the minutest detail. These characteristics, combined with a marvellous memory, enabled him to sift, analyse, and digest information at a speed which made his opinions seem intuitive. He was an excellent judge of character. This was coupled with the ability to form personal relationships equally well with soldiers, stockmen, the young and the very young, financiers, policemen, and politicians.

He died at Mentmore 30 May 1974, aged ninety-two. Having handed his Dalmeny estates to his son and heir, Neil Archibald Primrose (who was born in 1929 and succeeded to the earldom on his father's death), he was delighted that the birth of a grandson in 1967 ensured the continuation of the family name.

[Charles Kenneth Young, *Harry, Lord Rosebery*, 1974; personal knowledge.]

ROTHSCHILD

PRITCHARD, Sir EDWARD EVAN EVANS- (1902–1973), social anthropologist. [See Evans-Pritchard.]

PRITT, DENIS NOWELL (1887–1972), lawyer, was born at Willesden, Hendon, 22 September 1887, the younger son and younger child of Harry Walter Pritt, metal merchant, and his wife, Mary Owen Wilson. His parents came from Lancashire and 'Johnny', as he was always known to his friends, regarded himself as a Lancashire man. He was educated at Winchester where he won a scholarship but left after four years to study French at Geneva, having then the intention of joining his father's business. He early showed a gift for foreign languages and, after Geneva, he mastered Spanish when an unpaid employee at a bank at Corunna. His father was anxious that he should be called to the bar and in 1906 he joined the Middle Temple and started to study law. He continued to widen his knowledge of foreign languages, adding German while in Berlin after he had been called to the bar in November 1909. In 1910 he obtained a pass degree in law at the University of London.

In the Middle Temple Pritt was a pupil of R. F. Colam to whose guidance he frequently paid tribute. After his year of pupillage he entered the chambers of a specialist in workmen's compensation cases. He continued in practice until 1917, building up a substantial body of small work and learning from practical experience the niceties of legal procedure and the art of advocacy. In 1917 he joined the postal censorship department in the War Office where he was helped by his knowledge of languages. He returned to the bar after the war and in 1923 joined the chambers of R. A. (later Lord) Wright [q.v.], then the outstanding leader in commercial work and subsequently a lord of appeal and master of the Rolls. Pritt soon acquired a large junior practice, including substantial work before the judicial committee of the Privy Council, particularly in Canadian appeals when his knowledge of French was useful. Contrary to views sometimes expressed, at the height of his practice both as a junior and after he took silk (in 1927) his practice was large and varied and included many cases in the commercial field.

Pritt enjoyed inexhaustible mental energy and a phenomenally retentive memory. He was capable of working twenty-four hours at a stretch without sleep. His capacity for rapid and accurate work was remarkable. As a lawyer he was largely self-taught and claimed to have studied every case mentioned in *The Principles of the English Law of Contract* (1879) by Sir William Anson [q.v.]. As a 'pleader' in the technical sense of the term his work was outstanding. A fearless advocate, he was at his best in the appellate courts where his quick wits were pitted against those of judges of the calibre of Viscounts Haldane and Dunedin [qq.v.], both of whom held him in high regard. At courts of first instance, particularly when political issues arose, his urbanity could be impaired by insufficient control of his temper.

His reputation was such that, in 1924 and again in 1928, he was approached about the possibility of accepting in a future Labour administration the position of a law officer, but his answer was ambivalent. He may have felt that he would find it difficult to work harmoniously with those then in positions of influence in the Labour Party, and indeed he never took any step with a view to advancing his own political or professional career.

On the political scene, Pritt in his youth worked for the Conservatives in Bromley but was fairly soon disillusioned and shortly before the outbreak of war in 1914 he joined the Liberal Party. He later joined the Labour Party and was for some years prospective candidate for Sunderland. In 1935 he was elected Labour member for Hammersmith North. Five years later he was expelled from the Labour Party after writing a book which defended the Soviet attack on Finland in the winter of 1939; in spite of considerable support he was never readmitted. In 1945 he stood as Labour independent for Hammersmith North and was returned by a large majority. In 1950 he lost the seat and never again sat in the House of Commons. In the year of his death he was made an honorary freeman of Hammersmith.

As a member of Parliament he made full use of his right to question ministers, to obtain interviews with them or their advisers, and to put down parliamentary questions. In 1936–7 he was a member of the party executive. After his expulsion he redoubled his efforts to remedy individual grievances, for his natural sympathies were with the underdog. He was never in the mainstream of political life, had no lasting influence on policy, and was something of a political gadfly. He was among the first to recognize the growing menace of Nazism in Germany. After the Reichstag fire in February 1933 he and six other lawyers of varying nationalities formed a commission (over which Pritt presided) which came to be known as the 'Reichstag Fire Enquiry'. It provoked criticism in official circles but its conclusion that the fire had been engineered for political reasons by the Nazi authorities was ultimately generally accepted as accurate.

From about 1940 Pritt faced with equanimity the loss of a practice in about as many months as it had taken years to build. His political views had by that time developed into a virtually uncritical acceptance of the Marxist–Leninist approach. The boycott of his professional employment by those who had been among his best clients developed remorsely as his practice became increasingly concentrated on what he called 'political cases'. An early example of these had been his successful defence in 1934 of Tom Mann who, with Harry Pollitt [qq.v.], then the general secretary of the Communist Party, was charged with sedition. Among the most notable of Pritt's 'political cases' was his defence in 1952 of Jomo Kenyatta [q.v.] and other Africans on charges connected with Mau Mau activities. He was charged with contempt of court during the hearing but successfully defended himself. In his three-volume autobiography Pritt deals at length with the many 'political cases' in which he appeared. In his own words 'the primary object of a good political defence . . . is . . . to defend and propagate one's political point of view'. It was therefore inevitable that some tribunals before which he appeared regarded him as using a court of law for political propaganda. He was awarded a Lenin peace prize in 1954 and received several honorary doctorates from communist countries.

Pritt was elected to the bench of the Middle Temple but he declined the office of treasurer. In 1960 he retired from the bar and thereafter was less active politically. In 1965 he was appointed presidential professor of law in the University of Ghana and held the post until Kwame Nkrumah [q.v.] was deposed the following year.

Pritt was of medium height, very short-sighted, flat-footed, and had an increasing tendency to corpulence. He took little physical exercise and his principal social pleasures were good food and drink and good conversation. His face, in repose, bore an expression of warm-hearted benevolence and his practical generosity was outstanding and often rendered anonymously. He married in July 1914 Marie Frances ('Molly'), daughter of Walter Maurice Gough, accountant. There was an adopted son who died in his early teens and a daughter. Pritt died at his house at Pamber Heath, near Silchester, 23 May 1972.

[D. N. Pritt, *From Right to Left*, 1965, *Brasshats and Bureaucrats*, 1966, and *The Defence Accuses*, 1966 (three volumes of autobiography); *The Times*, 24, 27, and 31 May, and 3 June 1972; private information; personal knowledge.]

ASHTON ROSKILL

PROUDMAN, JOSEPH (1888–1975), mathematician and oceanographer, was born 30 December 1888 at Unsworth near Bury in Lancashire, the elder son and elder child of John Proudman, farm bailiff and later tenant farmer at Bold, near Widnes, Lancashire, and his wife, Nancy Blease. He attended primary schools at Unsworth and Bold. From 1902 to 1907 he was a pupil-teacher at Farnworth Primary School. During the winters of 1902–4 he attended evening classes at the Widnes Technical School; from 1903 to 1907 he only taught for half of each week, and during the other half he attended classes at the Widnes Secondary School. In 1907 he was awarded the Tate technical science entrance scholarship at Liverpool University, where in 1910 he received a B.Sc. (first class) with honours in mathematics. He was also awarded the Derby scholarship for mathematics and an entrance exhibition to Trinity College, Cambridge, where he became a senior scholar in 1911. In 1912 he received a first class in schedule A and a distinction in schedule B of part ii of the mathematical tripos. Following a suggestion by Professor (Sir) Horace Lamb [q.v.] of Manchester, he started research on a problem in the theory of ocean tides which set the course for his entire subsequent career.

In 1913 he became a lecturer in mathematics at Liverpool University. During the first year he had no time for research except during vacations, but he did find time to direct the postgraduate work of A. T. Doodson [q.v.] for the M.Sc. degree and thus began a collaboration which continued until Doodson's death. His salary was £150 a year for six years but in 1915 he became a fellow of Trinity College, Cambridge, and thus received an additional £350 for six years without any prescribed duties. He always said that this was of the greatest help to him. When World War I broke out Proudman was placed in a low medical category and did not serve in the armed forces. He spent the war years in Liverpool, and for the second half of 1918 when he worked in the research department of Woolwich Arsenal. In 1919 he was instrumental in obtaining funds from two shipowners for the foundation of a Tidal Institute which was later amalgamated with the Liverpool Observatory, and he was its director until 1945. Also in 1919 he was appointed professor of applied mathematics in the University of Liverpool, a post which was created for him. In 1933 he was transferred at his own request to the chair of oceanography from which he retired in 1954, when he was made professor emeritus.

Proudman took a full share in the administration of the university, serving as pro-vice-chancellor and deputy chairman of senate from 1940 to 1946 during the difficult war and post-war years.

Proudman's scientific work was concerned mainly with tidal theory, almost every aspect of which was treated by him during his scientific career, including large-scale oceanic tides, a great variety of problems relating to smaller seas, and the tidal elastic yielding of the Earth's crust. In collaboration with Doodson he made significant improvements in tidal predictions for British ports and in charts for tidal streams and elevations in British waters. When he became professor of oceanography he widened his range of marine studies, studied surface temperatures and salinities in the Irish sea, and deduced from them the main patterns of circulation. His membership of the Waverley committee, set up to report on the disastrous floods of 1953, led to his important work on storm surge equations. He worked on the interaction of storm surges and tides in an estuary. He was the author of an influential textbook on *Dynamical Oceanography* (1953) which for many years had few rivals. Undoubtedly though, tides were his prime interest throughout his long career. He solved practically all the remaining tidal problems which are soluble within the framework of classical hydrodynamics and analytical mathematics. His significant scientific contributions were not, however, confined to oceanography.

In 1923 he was awarded the Adams prize in mathematics by the University of Cambridge. He was elected a fellow of the Royal Society in 1925. He was appointed CBE in 1952 and was made an honorary LL D of Liverpool University in 1956. He became chairman of the British National Committee for Geodesy and Geophysics in 1943 and in this capacity he took a leading part in the negotiations leading to the foundation of the National Institute of Oceanography. His work also received recognition from the international scientific community. In 1951–6 he was president of the International Association of Physical Oceanography, after serving as its vice-president from 1948 to 1951 and its general secretary for the preceding fifteen years. In 1944 he was the George Darwin lecturer of the Royal Astronomical Society, in 1946 he received the Alexander Agassiz medal for oceanography of the National Academy of Sciences of the United States, and he was also elected a foreign member of the Norwegian Academy of Science and Letters. He received the Hughes medal of the Royal Society in 1957.

Proudman married in 1916 at Manchester Rubina (died 1958), daughter of Thomas Ormrod, insurance company manager. In 1961 he married at Poole Mrs Beryl Gladys Waugh Gould who survived him. Her maiden name was Barker. He had two sons and one daughter from his first marriage. One of his sons, Ian, became professor of applied mathematics at Essex University. Proudman died 26 June 1975 at a nursing home in Fordingbridge, Hampshire.

[D. E. Cartwright and F. Ursell in *Biographical Memoirs of Fellows of the Royal Society*, vol. xxii, 1976; personal knowledge.] F. URSELL

PUDNEY, JOHN SLEIGH (1909–1977), poet and journalist, was born 19 January 1909 at Homewood Farm, Langley, Buckinghamshire, the only child of Henry William Pudney, a tenant farmer, and his wife, Mabel Elizabeth, daughter of H. C. Sleigh, who had spent her early life nursing in Dublin and Australia. His father abandoned farming in 1907, but continued to live a rural life at Langley, and there John grew up. He was sent to boarding-school at Westerham Hill, and later even further away, to Gresham's School, Holt. Soon after he went there, his mother died, and thus much of Pudney's holidays were spent as a solitary boy in the countryside. Later in life he looked back to a happy childhood and stimulating schooldays—among his friends at Gresham's were W. H. Auden, Benjamin (later Lord) Britten [qq.v.], and Humphrey Spender—but already he was aware of being something of a loner, a countryman at heart, with an inner withdrawal which needed to find expression in poetry.

His father persuaded him to leave school at sixteen, and to go to work for an estate agent in London. For several years he worked towards a surveyor's qualification, but meanwhile was also writing—short stories, articles, verse—frequenting David Archer's bookshop, and soon achieving publication. In 1933 his first volume of verse, *Spring Encounter*, was published by Methuen, and this swiftly brought Pudney into the literary circle of Lady Ottoline Morrell [q.v.]. The following year he married Crystal, eldest child of (Sir) A. P. Herbert [q.v.], and, supported by these connections, decided to give up the property business for the more precarious trade of writing.

Spring Encounter contained some lines that already struck a distinctive note which the author would maintain in all his verse—incisive rhythm, simple diction, and a courageous, if occasionally mawkish, effort to celebrate man's place in nature and the importance of nature's influence on man's imagination:

> Here avenues, ways begin,
> April to June, river to tidal basin,
> This summer's crop and new stock on the farm.
> This is where I, abashed to hesitate,
> In eagerness must pause, and O my love,
> Certain that I must gather strength, with you
> Tidal become, the traffic way for ships.

In those early years of married life, Pudney took jobs on the *Listener*, and as a writer-producer in the BBC (1934–7), incidentally becoming concerned with the first broadcasting of music by Britten. He was able to move back into the country, first near Thaxted, and later at Chipstead in Kent. In 1937 he became a journalist with the *News Chronicle*, and the following year his first novel, *Jacobson's Ladder*, appeared. In August 1940 he was commissioned into the RAF as an intelligence officer, and later, with H. E. Bates [q.v.] and Patrick Balfour (third Baron Kinross) joined the Air Ministry's 'Creative Writers Unit', formed by Hilary St. George Saunders, and for it wrote the anonymously published *The Air Battle of Malta*, 1944, and *Atlantic Bridge*, 1945 (about RAF Transport Command).

After flying over the beaches during the invasion of France, Pudney accompanied General Leclerc's victorious troops into Paris, and was the first member of Allied forces to visit Pablo Picasso in his studio. He had never fired a gun during his brief training, but an involvement in street-fighting at Billancourt, and some hazardous scrapes during the many flying sorties which he accompanied, gave rise to his claim to have been the only wartime officer who 'never fired a shot except in anger'.

It was while he was serving as squadron intelligence officer at St. Eval in Cornwall that Pudney wrote one of the best-known poems of the war. First published over initials by the *News Chronicle* in 1941, it was broadcast on radio by Laurence (later Lord) Olivier, and spoken by (Sir) Michael Redgrave in *The Way to the Stars* (1945), a film directed by Anthony Asquith [q.v.]. After that it almost attained the status of a ballad, and was often quoted without permission or attribution.

Do not despair
For Johnny-head-in-air;
He sleeps as sound
As Johnny underground.

Fetch out no shroud
For Johnny-in-the-cloud;
And keep your tears
For him in after years.

Better by far
For Johnny-the-bright-star,
To keep your head,
And see his children fed.

Pudney wrote more considerable war poems, and more deeply felt ones—for example, 'Elegy for Tom Roding', or 'Missing'—but 'For Johnny' became the most renowned.

After the war he returned to free-lance journalism and book reviewing, and to fight (unsuccessfully) the 1945 general election for Labour at Sevenoaks. During the next few years he published a novel and a children's book (the *Fred and I* adventure stories) every year, as well as regular features in *Illustrated* and *News Review*, short stories, television and radio plays, and his first volume of collected verse in 1957. Of Pudney's ten published novels, probably the most successful was *The Net* (Michael Joseph, 1952) a romantic thriller about an aeronautical research station. He also worked as a resourceful 'literary adviser' first to Evans Bros. and then to Putnam & Co. This versatile energy, and his talent for turning out effective prose to order, may have tended to discourage critical appreciation of his more serious work.

In those years, like many others in the London literary world, he was often rather drunk. His first marriage had been dissolved in 1955, and he had unhappily moved out of the country into the town. He had been used to create around himself a vigorous social life at home with his family and friends, enlivened by music, acting, dancing (like many plump men, he was very light on his feet), singing—and, naturally, a cheering flow of good drink. This enthusiastic conviviality started to turn into 'overdrinking' (as he later described it) and then led to an alcoholic addiction which began to wreck his work, his relationships, and himself.

In 1965 he made up his own mind to tackle his 'problem' by therapy, and then described his successful cure in periodicals and a later book. This public confession was deliberately made, for Pudney believed that medical efforts to treat alcoholism were being handicapped by the general reluctance to discuss it as a normal medical problem. Unlike many converts to abstinence, he lost neither his creative energy nor his sociability—drink still flowed for his thirstier guests. Instead of being a jolly, boozy, curly-haired, fat man, he became a jolly, abstemious, white-haired, thin man.

By 1967 he had made a complete recovery from addiction, with the tireless support of his second wife, Monica Forbes Curtis. She was the daughter of J. Grant Forbes and they had married in 1955. He became enthusiastically involved in a new activity, poetry-reading, for which he wrote prolifically—verses often to be accompanied by jazz music.

In 1976 he developed cancer of the throat, and after a year of pain and fearsome surgery, he died in his London home 10 November 1977. Author to the last, he wrote of this final agonizing phase of his life in a courageous and remarkable book, *Thank Goodness for Cake*, published posthumously by Michael Joseph (1978). His two last poems appeared in the *Times Literary Supplement* a few days after his death.

By his first marriage John Pudney had two daughters and a son.

[John Pudney, 'For Johnny' and extract from 'Source' from *Collected Poems*, 1957 (Putnam), reprinted by permission of David Higham Associates Ltd., *Home and Away*, 1960, and *Thank Goodness for Cake*, 1978; personal knowledge.] ROGER LUBBOCK

PYM, BARBARA MARY CRAMPTON (1913–1980), novelist, was born 2 June 1913 at Oswestry in Shropshire, the elder daughter of Frederick Crampton Pym, solicitor, of Oswestry, and his wife, Irena Spenser Thomas. She was educated at Liverpool College, Huyton (later Huyton College, Liverpool) and St. Hilda's College, Oxford (1931–4), gaining second class honours in English language and literature. After leaving Oxford she lived mostly at home until war began in 1939; in 1938 she went to Poland to teach English to a family in Katowice, but returned owing to the international situation. When hostilities broke out, she undertook voluntary work in the Oswestry area, then in October 1941 became a postal censor in Bristol. From 1943 to 1946 she served with the Women's Royal Naval Service, attaining the rank of third officer and being posted to Naples. On demobilization she joined the International African Institute in London, first as a research assistant, then from 1958 until she retired in 1974 as editorial secretary and assistant editor of *Africa*, under the director, Daryll Forde.

Barbara Pym started writing at school, and it is remarkable that her first novel *Some Tame Gazelle* (1950), an amused vision of herself and her sister as fiftyish spinsters, was begun on leaving Oxford in 1934 and rejected by Jonathan Cape, who were to publish it fourteen years later. It was quickly followed by *Excellent Women* (1952), *Jane and Prudence* (1953), *Less Than Angels* (1955), *A Glass of Blessings* (1958), and *No Fond Return of Love* (1961). They were warmly received by discerning critics, and enjoyed by a faithful band of readers, but their unsensational subject matter and deceptively mild irony did not match the spirit of the times, and her publisher saw fit to refuse subsequent submissions. Although she continued to write, a depressing period of rejection followed, and when she retired her career as a novelist seemed long over. In 1977, however, the *Times Literary Supplement* published a symposium on the most over- and underrated writers of the century, and two contributors nominated Barbara Pym in the latter category. As she was the only living writer to be named twice, strong interest in her work was aroused, and a new novel, *Quartet in Autumn*, was published that year by Macmillan, the firm it had reached at the time. *The Sweet Dove Died* (in fact written earlier) followed in 1978, and *A Few Green Leaves* and *Crampton Hodnet* appeared posthumously in 1980 and 1985 respectively. While retaining many characteristics of her earlier work, her later themes were more sombre, and reflected changed fashions of society.

In her last three years Barbara Pym enjoyed many of the rewards of successful authorship: her novels were reprinted in Britain and America, and paperback editions planned; she was interviewed by press and radio, and a BBC television programme 'Tea with Miss Pym' charmingly evoked her life in the Finstock cottage (near Oxford) to which she had retired with her sister and their cats. She would probably have accepted her own description of 'most Englishwomen' ('not pretty but quite a pleasant face'), but the programme suggested the gracefulness she retained through life (she was rather tall) and the gentle watchfulness of her conversation. She frequently holidayed abroad, but took great pleasure in domesticities such as gardening and jam-making, and was always an active churchwoman. *Quartet in Autumn* was short-listed for the Booker prize in 1977, and she was elected a fellow of the Royal Society of Literature in 1979. She sustained her celebrity with unassuming pleasure, but occasionally showed that she had not ceased to regret her fifteen years of unjustified neglect.

In 1971 she had been operated on for cancer; in early 1979 a recurrence of this malady did not respond to treatment, a fact she reported unemotionally to her friends. In the constant care of her sister she completed her final novel, but did not live to see the proofs, dying in the Churchill Hospital in Oxford 11 January 1980. She was buried at Holy Trinity, Finstock, where T. S. Eliot [q.v.] had been baptized into the Church of England in 1927. Reviewing her last book, a younger novelist, A. N. Wilson, wrote, 'Why have all her novels survived so well, when others, more daring, or more recent, already seem jaded or unrealistic?' The answer lies not only in their alertness of eye and ear and unsleeping sense of the ridiculous, but in their continual awareness of life's small poignancies and the need for courage in meeting them, expressed in a style exactly suited to her material and for which she never had to strive.

[Barbara Pym, *A Very Private Eye, an Autobiography in Letters and Diaries*, 1984; private information; personal knowledge.] PHILIP LARKIN

R

RADCLIFFE, CYRIL JOHN, VISCOUNT RADCLIFFE (1899–1977), lawyer and public servant, was born in Llanychan, Denbighshire, 30 March 1899, the third of the four children (all sons) of Captain Alfred Ernest Radcliffe, of the Royal Lancashire Regiment, and his wife, Sybil Harriet, daughter of Robert Cunliffe, a London solicitor, who was president of the Law Society in 1890–1.

Radcliffe was at school at Haileybury. After service in the Labour Corps—because of his poor eyesight the only form of war service open to him—he entered New College, Oxford, as a scholar in 1919, and took first class honours in *literae humaniores* in 1921. He was a fellow of All Souls from 1922 to 1937. In 1923 he became Eldon law scholar and was called to the bar by the Inner Temple in 1924. He went into the chambers of Wilfrid (later Lord) Greene [q.v.]. He took silk in 1935, and by 1938, after Greene and Sir Gavin (later Viscount Simonds) [q.v.] were appointed to the bench, he had become the outstanding figure at the Chancery bar.

This meteoric legal career was interrupted by World War II. Radcliffe joined the Ministry of Information, and by 1941 had become its director-general. His gifts and skills complemented those of his minister, Brendan (later Viscount) Bracken [q.v.], in an unlikely but effective partnership.

In May 1945 he resumed his practice at the bar; and in 1949 he was appointed a lord of appeal in ordinary, the first man (other than ex-law officers) for over sixty years to be appointed to the House of Lords direct from the bar.

In 1947 he was appointed chairman of the two boundary commissions set up with the passing of the Indian Independence Act of that year. The time he spent in India, and his eldest brother's death there while serving in the army, left him with a lifelong feeling for the country, and an intense admiration for the achievements, courage, and dedication of the early generations of British administrators there.

Over the next thirty years Radcliffe was the chairman of a series of public inquiries, including the royal commission on taxation of profits and income (1951–5); the constitutional commission for Cyprus (1956); committees on the working of the monetary system (1957–9) and on security procedures and practices in the public service (1961); the tribunal of inquiry into the Vassall case (1962); and committees of privy councillors on the *Daily Express* and D notices (1967) and on ministerial memoirs (1975–6). Though he continued to carry out judicial duties when he was not fully engaged on an inquiry, the law was no longer enough to satisfy his intellectual appetite; he enjoyed the succession of challenges provided by these public inquiries, whose reports reflected his own thoroughness, lucidity, and wisdom of judgement. The frequency with which his skill as a chairman was pressed into service led Sir A. P. Herbert [q.v.] to comment on 'Government by Radcliffery', but it is perhaps the fact that his achievements covered so diverse a range of activities that partly accounts for a sense that his outstanding gifts were never really put to full use.

He retired from judicial work in 1964. He became a trustee of the British Museum in 1957, and was chairman of the trustees from 1963 to 1968. He was chairman of the governors of the School of Oriental and African Studies from 1960 to 1975. He became the first chancellor of the University of Warwick in 1966. In his last ten years he withdrew increasingly into private life, partly in order to care for his wife but also because of his increasing disenchantment with the quality of public life.

Radcliffe was much in demand as a speaker and lecturer. He spoke, as he wrote, with exceptional lucidity and power, and with a sense of style well characterized as intellectual eloquence. He had an abiding interest in the arts, and assembled—but eventually disposed of—a small but distinguished collection of Impressionist paintings. For many years a trusted friend of Calouste Gulbenkian, he was disappointed not to be able to fulfil Gulbenkian's and indeed his own hope that he might become the first chairman of the Gulbenkian trustees.

Radcliffe was by common consent one of the outstanding intelligences of his generation. He had a capacious and powerful mind, disciplined by his academic and legal training, and nurtured by extensive reading, particularly in English history and literature. He cherished freedom and the liberal values, and order and the rule of law as the condition of freedom. He believed in the power of reason as a determinant of human conduct, and measured the foibles and follies of men with a detached and unsparing perceptiveness. He was a reserved and fastidious man. All this made him for some people unapproachable, and he had relatively few close friends; but their devotion was rewarded by the discovery of a keen sense of humour, a dry wit, and a warm and steadfast affection.

He was a man of middle height, with a large, square head: a high forehead, with crinkly brown—later silvery grey—hair brushed tight back from his forehead; a blunt mouth and a firm chin; and blue-grey eyes behind thick spectacles.

Radcliffe's principal publications were *The Problem of Power* (1951 Reith lectures, 1952, reissued with new preface, 1958), *The Law and its*

Compass (1960 Rosenthal lectures, 1961), *Mountstuart Elphinstone* (Romanes lecture, 1962), *Government by Contempt: Whitehall's Way with Parliament and People* (1968), and *Not in Feather Beds* (a collection of speeches, lectures, and articles, 1968).

Radcliffe was appointed KBE in 1944 and GBE in 1948. As a law lord, he became a life peer and a privy councillor in 1949; and he was created viscount in 1962. He was elected FBA in 1968 and had many honorary degrees, including an Oxford DCL (1961).

Radcliffe married in 1939 Antonia Mary Roby (died 1982), the daughter of Godfrey Rathbone Benson, first Baron Charnwood [q.v.], politician and man of letters. She was the former wife of John Tennant. There were no children of the marriage. Radcliffe died at his home in Hampton Lucy, Warwickshire, 1 April 1977. The viscountcy became extinct.

[*The Times*, 4 April 1977; Robert Stevens, 'Four interpretations' in *Law and Politics*, 1979; private information; personal knowledge.] ROBERT ARMSTRONG

RADHAKRISHNAN, SIR SARVEPALLI (1888–1975), philosopher and president of India, was born 5 September 1888, in the pilgrimage-centre village of Tiruttani, in the then undivided presidency of Madras. He was the second son of middle-class but poor parents, Sarvepalli Veeraswamiah, a *tahsildar*, a minor revenue official, and his wife, Sitamma. The father was orthodox and would have preferred his son not to learn English and to become a priest. But scholarships were to take Radhakrishnan from the age of nine into Christian missionary institutions, his secondary education at Lutheran Mission High School at Tirupati, 1896–1900, and Voorhees College, Vellore, 1900–4, his university education at Madras Christian College, 1904–8, and into a quite different career. It was an education which bred a defensive reaction in favour of Hindu religious culture and significantly his choice of subject for his MA dissertation was on an area always derided by Christian missionaries, the Ethics of the Vedanta. His later philosophical work, however, was to be largely on metaphysics rather than ethics. But his study of European philosophy (absurdly he could not study Indian philosophy at the University of Madras at that time) had also bred scepticism and prompted his lifelong search for a synthesis between the European scientific and humanist tradition and that of eastern religions.

He began his academic career at Madras Presidency College, 1909–16, and thence went to Rajamundry and Mysore, till Sir Asutosh Mookerjee, vice-chancellor of the University of Calcutta, invited him in 1921 to succeed (Sir) Brajendranath Seal to India's most distinguished post in philosophy, the King George V chair of mental and moral philosophy. His twenty years in Calcutta were to lay the foundations of his Indian and international reputation. Professor J. H. Muirhead [q.v.] had in 1917 invited him to write an account of Indian philosophy and the first volume of his astonishing work of synthesis, *Indian Philosophy*, appeared in 1923, the second in 1927. Higher academic honours within India followed; the vice-chancellorships of Andhra University, Waltair, 1931–6, and of Benares Hindu University, 1939–48. Now began Radhakrishnan's ambassadorship to the West, a series of invitations to lecture in England and America: the Upton lectures at Manchester College, Oxford, in 1926, which led to a more speculative if tentative work, *The Hindu View of Life* (1927), to Chicago also in 1926, and the Hibbert lectures at the University of London in 1929, which led to a more forceful assertion of Hindu values, *An Idealist View of Life* (1932). The generosity of a North Oxford philanthropist allowed Radhakrishnan to take up (1936–52) the Spalding professorship of eastern religions and ethics at All Souls College, very much to be his second home from now on, and his Spalding lectures were published in 1939 as *Eastern Religions and Western Thought*, more a work of comparative religion than of philosophy. His achievements as a philosopher had led to his appointment between 1931 and 1939 as the Indian delegate to the international committee on intellectual co-operation of the League of Nations, the viceroy Lord Irwin (later Earl of Halifax, q.v.) gracing a somewhat embarrassed Radhakrishnan with a knighthood for the role, and thus Radhakrishnan was launched on a second and political career.

If always a patriot, Radhakrishnan did not join the Congress Party, but his foreign contacts, above all through All Souls, with such members of the English establishment as Sir John (later Viscount) Simon [q.v.] and Halifax, made him a useful contact man for Congress. He had met M. K. Gandhi [q.v.] as early as 1915 but did not meet Jawaharlal Nehru [q.v.] till the Calcutta Congress of 1928. Radhakrishnan's international reputation as an exponent of Indian culture was bound to make him attractive to Congress, but it was his resistance to the attempt by the Marquess of Linlithgow [q.v.] to close down the Benares Hindu University as a centre for the freedom fighters of 1942 which finally gave him the seal of approval as a nationalist, and led to his election to the constituent assembly of 1947–8, when he sat on the backward classes committee. The real breakthrough in his political career came, however, with his appointment as ambassador to the Soviet Union, 1949–52. His achievement there was not those famous friendly interviews with Stalin but his role in persuading the Russian government that Nehru was sincere in his policy of non-alignment. In 1952 he was elected vice-president, and, ex officio, chairman of the Rajya Sabha. These were to be years of much foreign travel. If disappointed at not becoming president in 1957, he was persuaded to run for a second term as vice-president. In 1960, during Prasad's illness, he was acting president, and 12 May 1962 he was elected president of India. A man above parties, Radhakrishnan had always worked well with Nehru, believing that Nehru's were consensus politics and sharing much of his social idealism, but their relationship was to falter after the Indo-China border crisis of 1962, Nehru's seemingly perverse favouritism of Krishna Menon [q.v.] a large part of the cause. As president, Radhakrishnan was to play an invaluable stabilizing role, steadying Indian nerve during two wars, with China in 1962 and Pakistan in 1965, and facilitating twice a peaceful succession to the prime ministership, Shastri in 1964, Indira Gandhi in 1966. He became, however, increasingly disaffected with the standards and performance of government and after his retirement in January 1967 he became a virtual recluse.

His political career had been combined with a continuing academic involvement, most noticeably a lecture tour to China in 1944, the chairmanship of the university education commission in 1948, and the chancellorship of the University of Delhi, 1953–62. He also made a valuable contribution to Unesco as India's delegate, 1946–54, and as chairman of its executive board, 1948–9.

Radhakrishnan's philosophy was the most eloquent reformulation in recent times of India's Vedantic tradition and an impressive contribution to comparative philosophy and religion. His Idealism had been learnt as much from his Christian missionary teachers, Hegelianism being very much then in vogue, as from India's own Idealist tradition. His was a non-dualist position, an acceptance of the world as itself a part of an absolute reality, an intellectual stance which made possible his dialogue with western science, his passionate concern for social justice, and his marriage of the contemplative and the active in his dual career as philosopher and statesman. Some have doubted his Sanskritic learning but his prolonged contact with pundits in Mysore, Calcutta, and Benares gives the lie to this charge. Some have doubted his originality. More serious is the criticism that his Vedantism continued to saddle India with a reactionary philosophy. Radhakrishnan saw himself as offering some new transcendental philosophy which would steer mankind away from the muddle and confusion engendered by the twentieth-century ideologies of fascism and communism, by the destitution of wars and the threat of nuclear destruction. Yet his ultimate vision was mystical, a very Indian belief in the power of intuition to achieve beatitude, curiously optimistic and democratic, believing that history had meaning and that all could become liberated souls.

Numerous honours came the way of Radhakrishnan, amongst them the honorary DCL (Oxford, 1952), honorary Litt.D. (Cambridge, 1943), LL D (London, 1948), the Bharat Ratna (1954), and honorary membership of the Order of Merit (1963). He was knighted in 1931 and became FBA in 1939 and honorary FBA in 1962.

In 1903 he married Sivakamamma (died 1956), daughter of Talpuru Chenchurammiah, a railway station-master, by whom he had five daughters and one son, the distinguished historian, Sarvepalli Gopal. He was a man of simple tastes, delighting in the company of friends, and a brilliant conversationalist. He was a discriminating but voracious reader. A fluent lecturer, he was, maybe, above all, a teacher. In Derek Hill's 1967 portrait, in the hall of All Souls, Radhakrishnan looks out, quizzical, searching, with a would-be mystic's face, a touch of dourness—hardly the fun-loving extrovert personality many believed him to be. He died at his home in Madras 16 April 1975.

[*The Hindu*, 17 April 1975; K. Iswara Dutt (ed.), *Sarvepalli Radhakrishnan, a Study of the President of India*, 1966; P. A. Schilpp (ed.), *The Philosophy of Sarvepalli Radhakrishnan*, 1952; private information.] ANTONY R. H. COPLEY

RAISTRICK, HAROLD (1890–1971), organic chemist and biochemist, was born 26 November 1890 at Pudsey in the west riding of Yorkshire, the second of four children (the eldest of whom, a son, died in infancy) of Mark Walker Raistrick, described as an engineer but with no formal qualifications, who was employed in the local woollen mill to keep some of the machinery in good working order. Nowadays he might be described as a tradesman service engineer. He married a local elementary school teacher, Bertha Anne Galloway. Harold's younger sister graduated in chemistry at Leeds University and her younger brother became director of a firm of gas engineers in Halifax.

During Raistrick's childhood every penny had to be watched. Social intercourse centred on the local Primitive Methodist chapel, attendance at the morning and evening services, and afternoon Sunday school which occupied most of Sunday. Indulgence in smoking and alcohol was prohibited as much from religious conviction as from financial necessity. Education was regarded as a high priority both as a means of improving status and financial prospects and for its own sake as assisting personal growth. Harold Raistrick went to the local elementary school where his diligent study secured for him a scholarship at the age of eleven which enabled him to enter Leeds Central High School, which had a strong science tradition. A trusted and able pupil, he augmented his meagre resources by acting as a 'lab boy' for a payment of one shilling per day and, provided he discharged his duties satisfactorily, he was permitted to experiment as he wished during and sometimes after school hours. At seventeen he secured a county major scholarship and progressed to Leeds University chemistry department, then strongly led by Professors Arthur Smithells [q.v.] and Julius B. Cohen. Cohen inspired him to become an organic chemist concerned with the unravelling of the structures of organic molecules of special biological significance.

Having secured in 1912 a first class B.Sc. and in 1913 an M.Sc., Raistrick decided to work with the well-known German sugar chemist, Emil Fischer. The war prevented this and instead Raistrick, debarred from active military service by ill health, went to Cambridge, working first in the agriculture department and transferring in 1915 to work under the supervision of (Sir) Frederick Gowland Hopkins [q.v.], the 'father' of British biochemistry. This experience confirmed Raistrick's earlier decision and in 1920 he gladly became head of the biochemical department of Nobel's Explosives Company in Stevenston, Ayrshire (which later became part of ICI's explosives and Nobel division research department). In the same year he obtained his Leeds D.Sc. He left in 1929 to become professor of biochemistry at the London School of Hygiene and Tropical Medicine, a post he held until retirement in 1956.

Raistrick's approach to his scientific work was meticulous, painstaking, and persevering, reflecting the values inculcated in his youth. Consequently, undeterred by long laborious bench procedures, by keen observation he got more out of applying existing methods of research than many of his contemporaries though having less human and material resources. His output of high-quality scientific work was outstanding.

In his early work on the breakdown of amino acids by bacteria he was the first to show that they could be converted to unsaturated acids. His speculations on the mechanism of bacterial breakdown of simple organic acids later seemed unusually prescient, containing elements of the famous citric acid cycle for which (Sir) Hans Krebs received the Nobel prize thirty years later. There followed a long series of useful researches on the metabolic products of micro-organisms from pure strains of lower fungi grown in various media, some of which were antibiotics. His achievement in the isolation, structure identification, and synthesis of many of these important and often labile substances is remarkable. They included the mould tropolones, the tetronic acids, griseofulvin, and the fungal polyhydroxy benzoquinones and anthraquinones. His high reputation for skill and reliability commanded the respect of both the biochemical fraternity and of redoubtable organic chemists such as A. R. (later Lord) Todd and (Sir) Robert Robinson [q.v.], who showed no reluctance to profit from collaboration and publication with him.

Despite the evident high esteem of his colleagues, his early election as FRS, and his major responsibilities such as that of scientific adviser on penicillin production during World War II, to the Ministry of Supply, Raistrick remained to the end the dark-haired, bushy-eyebrowed, firm-lipped, unaffected, quiet Yorkshireman who drew refreshment from solitary walking and fishing in the fells and mountains.

Raistrick was elected FRS in 1934. He was Bakerian lecturer of the Royal Society in 1949 and Flintoff medallist of the Chemical Society in 1963.

In 1917 he married Martha Louisa (died 1945), daughter of Jonathan Coates, of Pudsey. They had two daughters, both of whom became doctors of medicine. In 1947 he married Betty Helen, daughter of Edward Young, of London. Raistrick died 8 March 1971 at Felpham in Sussex.

[J. H. Birkinshaw in *Biographical Memoirs of Fellows of the Royal Society*, vol. xviii, 1972; personal knowledge.] FREDERICK DAINTON

RAJAGOPALACHARI, CHAKRAVARTI (1878–1972), Indian politician, was born 8 December 1878, the third child of Chakravarti Venkatarya Iyengar and his wife, Singaramma, in the village of Thorapalli, near Hosur, then in the princely state of Mysore. His father was a moderately well-off landowner, *munsiff* (revenue official) of Hosur, and a recognized Sanskrit scholar. A natural conservative, C.R., as he was familiarly known, found himself invariably the dissident, a rebel against his father's strict Vaishnavite beliefs, against caste Hindu traditionalism, above all its oppression of the untouchables, and against the political authority of the Raj, suffering frequent periods of imprisonment at its hand. This led to inner tension and may explain his chronic asthma, which only left him when he moved to his ashram at Tiruchengode in 1925. His secondary education was at Bangalore Central College. He graduated in law from Presidency College, Madras, in 1897, and went on to enjoy great success, above all as a criminal lawyer, at the Salem bar. In 1897 he married Alarmelu Mangammal, daughter of an itinerant preacher; four of their children were to survive (two sons and two daughters), and her early death in 1916 was one factor which drew Rajagopalachari, then only thirty-seven, to make a deeper commitment to politics. In 1918 he became chairman of the Salem Municipal Council. In 1919 he moved to Madras and an almost chance encounter with M. K. Gandhi [q.v.] led to his being drawn into the new politics of civil disobedience.

His was to be an extraordinary political career, straddling an enormous time-span, invariably in the front rank of national life. His power-base in the presidency of Madras was never strong and he relied heavily on personal influence over the Congress triumvirate of Gandhi, Jawaharlal Nehru, and V. J. Patel [qq.v.] to outwit his southern adversaries and sustain a role as an all-Indian political figure. His exceptional talent for administration was given but brief opportunities for expression, in two periods as head of the Madras provincial government, 1937–9 and 1952–4, and at the centre, as successor to Earl Mountbatten of Burma [q.v.] as governor-general from 1948 to 1950, and to Patel, as home minister, in 1951. Most of his political career was in opposition, as a leading defendant of non-co-operation with the Raj from 1919 to 1937 and, after 1954, as a critic of Congress rule, culminating in his founding in 1959 of an opposition conservative party, Swatantra. The contradictions in Rajagopalachari's political temperament were never more apparent than during World War II, when his statesmanlike search for some *modus vivendi* between Congress and the Raj against the common enemy of Japan led to his advocacy of some concession to M. A. Jinnah [q.v.] and the Muslim League over a future state of Pakistan and to his resignation from Congress over its quit India movement of August 1942. Only Nehru's generosity was to rescue Rajagopalachari from political oblivion and give him a second chance as a Congress politician after 1946.

As a Tamil and a Brahmin he was peculiarly exposed in another dimension of his political career, his resistance to the forces of linguistic nationalism, in particular Andhra, and non-Brahmin casteism. Here he had to accept defeat, with the setting up in 1953 of a new state of Andhradesa, breaking up the old presidency of Madras, and the coming to power in Tamilnadu in 1967 of the non-Brahmin party, the DMK.

His was a highly distinctive contribution, in theory and practice, to India's continuing debate between the claims of tradition and modernization. He sought attitudinal rather than structural change in society, reflected in his endeavours to ease the burden of debt on the Madras peasantry in his Agricultural Debt Relief Act of March 1938 and to lessen the oppression of the untouchables by his Temple Entry Act of July 1939. Strikingly modern was his insistence on a clean administration, his fierce contempt for corruption and nepotism, but in later years, under Nehru's quasi-socialist administration, he came to distrust the excessive control by the state of the economy, Licence-Raj as he called it, and turned back to the caste system as an alternative source of authority to the modern state. He was much criticized for his seeming defence of caste in his craft-centred education scheme of 1953. His continuing preference lay in the simpler and more moral life, as he saw it, of village India. He was an ardent champion of prohibition and his first act as head of the Madras administration was to introduce the Prohibition Act of October 1937.

His was an immensely cultured intelligence, astonishingly widely versed in both Indian and western culture. He was a superb craftsman of English prose. Amongst his many writings one might single out his Tamil versions, translated into English, of the Mahabharata and the Ramayana. He was not an easy political colleague, so unsparing were the moral demands he made both on himself and others. He was a man of slight build, always immaculately dressed. In later years he mellowed and his natural, aristocratic charm and simplicity of manner shone through. His was a far more Indian-based career than those of Gandhi or Nehru. His education was entirely home-based. His first journey outside India was, amazingly, as late as 1962, to visit President Kennedy. Maybe his was the most immediate and concrete involvement with the great debates within India on economic and social modernization and political change. He died in Madras 25 December 1972.

[*The Hindu*, 26 December 1972; *Rajmohan Gandhi. The Rajaji Story*, vol. i: *A Warrior from the Truth*, 1978; A. R. H. Copley, *The Political Career of C. Rajagopalachari, 1937–1954, a Moralist in Politics*, 1978; personal knowledge.]

ANTONY R. H. COPLEY

RAMSAY, LADY (VICTORIA) PATRICIA (HELENA ELIZABETH) (1886–1974), princess of Great Britain and Ireland, was born in London at Buckingham Palace on St. Patrick's Day, 17 March 1886. She was the third and youngest child and younger daughter of Prince Arthur William Patrick Albert, Duke of Connaught and Strathearn [q.v.], the third son of Queen Victoria, and his wife, Princess Louise Margaret Alexandra Victoria Agnes, third daughter of Prince Frederick Charles Nicholas of Prussia. The Duchess of Connaught, the dominant partner in the marriage, who had herself spent an unhappy childhood, was an undemonstrative and sometimes neglectful parent. The young princess, 'Patsy', as she was called in the family, had to wear her elder sister's cast-off clothing, and to the end of her life suffered from painful feet, the result of her mother's refusal to buy her well-fitting shoes.

Although Princess Patricia of Connaught grew up to be tall, handsome, and intelligent, she was handicapped by an inculcated lack of self-confidence that made her feel unwanted and helped delay her acceptance of a suitor in marriage until she was thirty-three. King Alfonso XIII of Spain, who in 1906 married her cousin Princess Victoria Eugénie, was among those who sought her hand in vain.

Meanwhile, she travelled the world in the wake of her father, who held a succession of military appointments in India, the Mediterranean, Canada, and Ireland. During the Duke's years as governor-general of Canada, 1911–16, his wife was in declining health (she died in 1917) and Princess Patricia acted as his hostess. The Canadians appreciated her beauty, her charm, and her devotion to war work. She was persuaded to sign innumerable miniature portraits of herself to be sold in aid of the Red Cross, and embroidered the original colour of Princess Patricia's Canadian Light Infantry which was carried into battle on the western front. Immensely proud at being appointed their colonel-in-chief, she visited her regiment many times over the years, even after her retirement from public duties. Canada also paid the princess the compliment of naming after her an extension to Ontario's boundaries and a bay in British Columbia.

On 27 February 1919 she was married in Westminster Abbey to Captain the Honourable (Sir) Alexander Robert Maule Ramsay, a younger son of John William Ramsay, the thirteenth Earl of Dalhousie and a serving naval officer. It was a love match born of a friendship that had begun even before Ramsay's attachment to the Duke of Connaught's staff in Canada; impossible during her mother's lifetime, it also marked the more relaxed post-war attitude of the royal family towards marriage with a commoner, and was to bring the princess the first real happiness she knew. There was one child of the marriage, Alexander Arthur Alfonso David, born 21 December 1919, who fought in the Grenadier Guards during World War II and was severely wounded. Admiral Ramsay died in 1972. Two days before the wedding King George V gave his permission for the bride to relinquish, at her own wish, her royal title, style, and rank and to assume the style of Lady Patricia Ramsay, with precedence immediately before the marchionesses of England.

Thereafter Lady Patricia scarcely ever emerged from the seclusion of her private life except to attend an exhibition of her own paintings; even then she would not submit her work to the Royal Academy, although willing to become patron of the less publicized Royal West of England Academy. She found much fulfilment in her art, insisting always that it be judged only by exacting professional standards. The earliest of her 600 paintings were of flowers. During travels abroad, her imagination was caught by marine life and tropical vegetation, and in later years she turned to abstracts. Lady Patricia experimented boldly with bright colours and bold contrasts that owed something to the influence of Gauguin and Van Gogh. She was equally deft in oils, watercolours, pen-and-ink, and gouache. Most of her works are in the possession of her son.

As the wife of a naval officer, Lady Patricia had no house of her own until 1942, when she took possession of Ribsden Holt, Windlesham, bequeathed to her by her aunt Princess Louise, Duchess of Argyll [q.v.]. It was there that she died 12 January 1974 in her eighty-eighth year. The funeral took place in St. George's chapel, Windsor, and the burial at Frogmore.

The most striking portraits of Lady Patricia Ramsay are by Ambrose McEvoy (1926), in the possession of her son, and A. S. Hartrick (*c.* 1920), of whom she was a pupil, in the possession of the artist's niece. There are more formal portraits by Charles Sims at Bagshot Park, Surrey, on loan to the Royal Army chaplains department; and by Charles Shannon in Currie Barracks, Edmonton, Alberta.

[*The Times*, 14 January 1974; private information.] KENNETH ROSE

RAMSBOTTOM, JOHN (1885–1974), mycologist, was born in Manchester, 25 October 1885, the second of the five children and eldest of four sons of Stephen Ramsbottom, letter-carrier in the leather trade, and his wife, Hannah Crosdale. After elementary schooling and four years as a pupil-teacher in Manchester he entered Emmanuel College, Cambridge, in 1905, obtaining a first class in part i of the natural science tripos (1908) and a second class in part ii (botany, 1909). He then returned to Manchester to take up the Robert Platt scholarship in botany and zoology at the university under Professor F. E. Weiss. In 1910 he entered the Civil Service as assistant in the cryptogamic section of the British Museum (Natural History), South Kensington, where—apart from war service as a protozoologist with the army in Salonika (1917–19), during which he became a captain attached to the Royal Army Medical Corps, was thrice mentioned in dispatches, and was appointed MBE (1918) and OBE (1919)—he worked until his retirement in 1950, having become a deputy keeper in 1928 and keeper of botany in 1930.

Under his keepership the department of botany began a collaboration with Portuguese botanists, and as a result Ramsbottom was awarded an honorary doctorate by Coimbra University in 1938. Later, a major preoccupation was salvaging the collections and organizing the rebuilding of the department after the disastrous fire at the Museum caused by incendiary bombs in September 1940. It was, however, through his activities outside the Museum that Ramsbottom exerted his greatest influence.

Ramsbottom was sociable, and joined many and diverse societies and organizations which he served in various ways—frequently as president—and was in turn honoured by. The Royal Horticultural Society elected him an honorary fellow in 1912 and awarded him the Veitch memorial gold medal in 1944 and the Victoria medal of honour in 1950, and also in 1950 he received the Dean Hole medal from the (Royal) National Rose Society. Other societies which he supported included the Quekett Microscopical Club, the Essex Field Club, the Society for the Bibliography of Natural History (president, 1942–72), the British Society for Mycopathology, and the Société Mycologique de France. He was also associated with the South London Botanical Institute (president, 1938–68) and the Haslemere Educational Museum and presided over Section K of the British Association for the Advancement of Science, 1936, and Section X, 1947. He was in demand at international congresses of botany and microbiology and by working parties on international botanical nomenclature. It was, however, to the Linnean Society and the British Mycological Society that Ramsbottom was most loyal, being an active member of both for more than sixty years and holding office in each for a quarter of a century. In 1957 Uppsala University conferred on him an honorary doctorate for his interest in Linnaeus.

Ramsbottom will be remembered as a mycologist. As he said of himself, 'I have been closely connected with mycology for more years than most, more generally than most'; and his personal propaganda for mycology was indefatigable. He wrote scholarly reviews. During the first years at the Museum he surveyed developments in the cytology of fungus reproduction and made summaries of the British discomycetes, Uredinales, and phycomycetes. He rewrote W. G. Smith's guide to the models of British fungi by James Sowerby [q.v.] as *A Handbook of the Larger British Fungi* (1923), which stayed popular for the next fifty years. His *Fungi, an Introduction to Mycology* (Benn's Sixpenny Library, 1929) was a model of lucid popularization. One of Ramsbottom's long-standing interests was the history of mycology and many of his addresses were variants on this theme; notably his presidential address to the Linnean Society, 'The Expanding Knowledge of Mycology since Linnaeus', which set a standard for mycological historians. Other interests included orchid mycorrhiza and medical mycology. Finally, Ramsbottom distilled his wide knowledge of fungi into *Mushrooms and Toadstools* (1953), a unique mycological contribution which will serve as his memorial. To this Dictionary he contributed the notice of A. B. Rendle.

Ramsbottom was a complex, erudite, and cultured man. He seemed to have read everything mycological, met every living mycologist of note, and forgotten nothing. His manner was genial. He liked teaching and was as willing to offer advice to the merest tyro as to the expert. On the other hand, to exasperate people by procrastination was an integral part of his character. Whenever he attended a meeting he spoke and he had a fund of stories, both proper and improper. Much anecdote (some self-generated) became associated with his name and for long he was a familiar figure at fungus 'forays' in conventional dark city clothes as though he had just stepped from the Museum into the woods.

In 1917 Ramsbottom married Beatrice (died 1957), daughter of Henry Westwood Broome, of Cambridge. They had a daughter. He died 14 December 1974 in a nursing home at Richmond, Surrey.

[*The Times*, 1 June 1938, 17 and 28 December 1974; *Transactions of the British Mycological Society*, vol. xlix, 1966; P. H. Gregory, ibid., vol. lxv, 1975; private information; personal knowledge.] G. C. AINSWORTH

RAMSEY, IAN THOMAS (1915–1972), bishop of Durham, was born 31 January 1915 in Kearsley, Lancashire, the only child of Arthur Ramsey, who worked in the Post Office and ended up as postmaster of Norwich, and his wife, May Cornthwaite. He won a scholarship to Farnworth Grammar School at the age of ten and another to Christ's College, Cambridge, at the age of eighteen. He was placed in the first class in the mathematical tripos, part i (1936), and in moral sciences (philosophy), part iia (1938), and to the end of his life maintained a keen interest in mathematics and science. But during his first year as an undergraduate he contracted tuberculosis. During eight months in hospital, followed by long restrictions on his activity, he pondered the use to which he ought to put the life which had been spared, formed close friendships with other young men with Christian convictions, and began to read widely.

He emerged from his ordeal with the desire to be ordained and the third 'first' which he gained (in 1939) was in the philosophical section of the theological tripos, part ii. He won the Burney prize in 1938 and became Burney student in 1939. He prepared for ordination in 1940 at Ripon Hall, choosing a modernist college in an Oxford environment because he recognized the challenge of the anti-metaphysical philosophy then flourishing in the university. It was already his ambition 'to try to build a bridge between theology and philosophy'. He was always, however, more devout than most modernists and avoided disputes about the Bible.

After a curacy in Headington Quarry near Oxford, he returned to Christ's College in 1943. He quietly shared the pacifism of the master, Charles Raven [q.v.], but had a more eirenic personality and quickly became a popular figure, first as the chaplain and then as a tutor. He was soon appointed a university lecturer and began the attempt to rescue what seemed valid in the insights of Christian metaphysical philosophers while recognizing the validity in the demand of most of the academic philosophers of his own age for logical analysis and linguistic rigour. Behind this academic discussion lay the tension between the religious and scientific values which he had absorbed in his Lancashire boyhood. His rare equipment for a difficult debate was recognized by his election as Nolloth professor of the philosophy of the Christian religion at Oxford in 1951.

The chair carried with it a fellowship of Oriel College and he again played an active role in college life. He was also now busy in wider administration, in the divinity faculty, and as chairman of the Warneford and Park Hospitals management committee (1954–66). He became fascinated by contemporary ethical dilemmas, particularly on the frontiers between religion, medicine, and law, and was prominent in groups which on behalf of the Church of England's board for social responsibility studied problems such as suicide, sterilization, punishment, doctors' decisions about life and death, and abortion. Above all he developed as an energetic and stimulating teacher, in lectures and seminars which attracted a growing number of students, and as director (1964–7) of the Lambeth diploma in theology for part-time students outside Oxford.

A stream of publications began to appear, mostly arising out of lectures. The most important were *Religious Language* (1957) and *Freedom and Immortality* (1960). He admitted that all religious language was 'odd' and consisted largely of the use of 'models', all of which needed 'qualifiers' since no one model could fully describe the ineffable God or his actions in time or eternity. Such admissions about the fallibility of traditional dogmas often alarmed Ramsey's fellow Christians, while non-Christian philosophers tended to rate him as prejudiced if not amateurish; they were astonished that in 1963 he could entitle a book *On Being Sure in Religion.* Thus despite his personal popularity with colleagues and his appeal to students in America as well as the United Kingdom, his intellectual position was not widely shared.

However, he felt compelled to argue for the importance of religious worship and belief, and of the demand of the conscience acknowledged in ethics, because on the basis of his own experience he maintained that human life included certain situations which constituted 'disclosures' of a more than everyday reality and which led to 'commitments' to beliefs and to devout and moral actions. To him, religion's 'characteristic claim is that there are situations which are spatio-temporal and more'.

He admired the philosophical theology of past Anglicans such as Bishop George Berkeley (to whom the world was essentially persons perceiving) and Bishop Joseph Butler [qq.v.] (to whom the person's most important perception was of duty), while also insisting on the empiricism enshrined in Butler's phrase: 'Everything is what it is, and not another thing.' He was encouraged when Oxford philosophers paid an attention subtler than in earlier periods to the significance of personality and duty, and between 1961 and 1971 he edited five symposia designed to encourage such developments and a wider awareness of them. Many of his own essays were collected posthumously under the title *Christian Empiricism* (1974).

But the question whether Ramsey could have constructed a convincing system of modern metaphysics, given leisure, cannot be answered, for in 1966 he accepted a call to be bishop of Durham.

As such he had a seat in the House of Lords and there he fulfilled the hope that he would take the lead in expressing the Church of England's reactions to moral problems of the day. He criticized the Conservative government, pleading for a new recognition of the multiracial world and for a new spirit in industry. His episcopal activities were, however, far wider. He threw himself enthusiastically into his mainly industrial diocese, making up for his lack of experience of the church's ordinary life by the warmth of his affection and the energy of his calls for modernization. In his enthronement sermon he declared that 'words, persons, institutions, possess genuine authority as and when they are vehicles of a vision'; and his strongly personal episcopate in the north-east was such a vehicle.

One of his many assets was that he was totally unprelatical. He was short and stocky in appearance, his accent retained traces of his Lancashire boyhood, and his friendliness was outgoing. The Durham miners invited him to speak on their gala day; when he was criticized for one of his many controversial comments, Durham students demonstrated in his favour; the clergy knew that their bishop was a man of prayer who was able to relate prayer to the age of science and industry; and in the Church of England at large he was soon being talked about as the inevitable successor to Archbishop Michael Ramsey at Canterbury.

He was chairman of the doctrine commission appointed in 1967 (producing *Subscription and Assent to the 39 Articles*), of a national commission on religious education in schools (producing *The*

Fourth R, 1970), of the Institute of Religion and Medicine, of William Temple College, and of the central religious advisory council relating to the BBC and the Independent Broadcasting Authority. He was in demand as a bishop able to talk sense about modern problems and as a chairman whose sunny temperament was combined with a tireless attention to detail and a total honesty in wrestling with problems which were often slippery and dark. And he had a vision of a 'new culture' where science and religion, industrial technology and humane ethics, were reconciled. He was able to create an atmosphere of excitement and hope.

Because his life was poured out in the service of his pupils, his diocese, and the church and nation in a time of widespread perplexity, his best legacy lay in thousands of memories of the quality of his mind and character, rather than in any substantial literary or administrative achievement. It is absurdly inadequate to identify him with the relaxation of the terms of the clergy's assent to the historic Anglican formularies, or with the decrease in the hostility of secular humanists to religious education in state schools, or with any other one point that he made, since once he had helped to vindicate a place for metaphysics in the English academic world many looked to him for leadership of a spiritual movement which might have halted the splitting asunder of English theology into radicalism and conservatism and the secularization of English life and schools.

It is by no means certain that had he lived he would have been chosen as archbishop of Canterbury, since, balancing his appeal to the Labour movement (and Labour was in power when the vacancy occurred in 1974), there was disquiet both about his theological and political outspokenness and about his eagerness to speak whenever the opportunity arose, dissipating his energies and diluting his wisdom. Perhaps the highest office would have been wrong for him. But the Church of England had not been given a leader marked by his combination of intellectual power with a cheerful populism since the death of Archbishop William Temple [q.v.] in 1944—and, unlike Temple, he shared the interests of scientists and technologists. The gap which he left was not filled.

He was an honorary fellow of Oriel (1967) and Christ's (1967) and had honorary doctorates at the universities of Oxford (1966), Durham (1967), and Glasgow (1968). In 1943 he married Margretta (Margaret), daughter of John McKay, from Coleraine near Londonderry. She and their two sons survived him when he died after a heart attack in Broadcasting House, London, 6 October 1972. He had worn himself out because, in Archbishop Ramsey's words, 'it had become a deep and inseparable part of his character never to say "no"'. Although he always tried to be accessible to troubled individuals, his willingness to lecture to, or take the chair at, meetings outside his own diocese consumed much of his time. There is no good portrait of him.

[David L. Edwards, *Ian Ramsey, Bishop of Durham: A Memoir*, 1973; Jerry H. Gill, *Ian Ramsey: To Speak Responsibly of God*, 1976; personal knowledge.] DAVID L. EDWARDS

RANK, (JOSEPH) ARTHUR, first BARON RANK (1888–1972), business man, was born in Hull, Yorkshire, 22 December 1888, the youngest of the seven children (three of them boys) of Joseph Rank, miller, and his wife, Emily Voase. Educated at the Leys School, Cambridge, at the age of seventeen he was sent straight into apprenticeship in his father's flour-milling business. Shortly afterwards he was taken south by his father to work in London. During World War I he served in France as a captain in the Royal Field Artillery.

On 18 October 1917 he married Laura Ellen (died 1971), the elder daughter of Sir Horace Brooks Marshall (later Baron Marshall of Chipstead), publisher. They were to have two daughters.

The first important contribution he made to the expansion of Joseph Rank Ltd. was in the 1930s and involved the production and sale of branded animal feeds. This followed from the acquisition and merger of small mills in London, whose flour-milling by-products were provender and animal feed. At this time Rank lived quietly in Reigate.

Following the death of his father (1943) and of his elder brother Rank took control of the business in 1952, becoming in turn executive chairman (1952–69) and life president (from 1969). Under his chairmanship Ranks Ltd. bought bakeries to protect against imports its outlets for flour, expanded into agricultural merchandising and, in its final integrated form, extended its interests beyond animal feed into cereals, seed grain trading, and farm products. In 1962 the company acquired Hovis McDougall and in 1968 Cerebos Ltd., both of which provided the nucleus of the grocery division and the building point for overseas interests.

Rank's chairmanship saw twenty years of unprecedented growth, expansion, and diversification. He had the vision to take Joseph Rank Ltd. from a milling business to a multi-faceted food-processing concern, opening up unlimited opportunities at home and abroad.

Rank was a devout Christian. It was his interest in showing religious films to children in his local Methodist church's Sunday school (in which he taught) which first brought him into the world of the cinema. He realized that films made especially for this purpose would have a powerful impact for good if they were of equal quality to those shown in the commercial cinema. In 1933 he founded the Religious Film Society.

He discovered that the structure of the film industry was more complicated than he had anticipated. Frustrated by his inability to obtain general distribution for the first production he sponsored, a prize-winning religious film entitled *The Turn of the Tide* (1935), Rank's answer was to set up a new film distribution company and buy a West End cinema as a show-case. In 1934 he agreed to join the board of a new film production company, British National, and in 1936 he became one of the founders of Pinewood Studios.

As his interest and knowledge of the commercial cinema grew, he became increasingly motivated by an ambition to reinvigorate Britain's film production industry so that it could present the British point of view to the world in order to balance the dominant position of Hollywood, whose films so effectively portrayed the American way of life.

In 1941 Rank acquired control of Gaumont British Picture Corporation Limited and its subsidiary companies, and, early in 1942, of Odeon Theatres Limited. At that time (Sir) John Davis was secretary of the company; from then onwards the two became close colleagues, working together to build what was to become the Rank Organization.

Rank was by now a leading force in film production, distribution, and exhibition in Britain, controlling over 600 cinemas and studios at Pinewood, Shepherd's Bush, Islington, Denham, and later Highbury. The operation, which changed its name to the Rank Organization in 1955, also acquired and subsequently developed important interests in the technical side of the film industry.

Throughout World War II Rank was encouraged by the government to regard the making and showing of films as a highly important contribution to national morale and the war effort. In 1944 he and his colleague Davis began the task of building up a world-wide distribution organization to market British films overseas. However, in 1947 the Rank Organization ran into financial difficulty. This was caused by abrupt changes in government policy about the importation of films, the imposition of an *ad valorem* duty, and an over-ambitious production programme on which Rank had embarked for patriotic motives. A period of retrenchment and diversification of interests followed.

In 1953 Arthur and Ellen Rank made over their controlling interests in the Rank Organization to a company limited by guarantee, created to ensure that its control remained in British hands. At the same time a charitable trust was formed to receive the dividends from shares held in the Rank Organization. The trustees were to apply the proceeds to charitable purposes. Rank retired from the chairmanship of the Rank Organization in October 1962, accepting the title of life president.

Rank was a tall and well-built man, with a merry twinkle in his eye. He had a zest for life and led it to the full. He was a good family man, humane, and with great compassion for others. He was profoundly loyal to all those with whom he was associated.

Rank and his wife were joint founders of the Rank Foundation. He was chairman of the Animal Health Trust, president of the Royal Agricultural Society of England in 1969, founder and president of the Southern and Western Counties Field Trial Society and also of the International Gun Dog League (one of his recreations was shooting), and joint treasurer (with Viscount Mackintosh of Halifax) of the Methodist Church.

Rank was lieutenant of the City of London (1927), JP for Surrey (1923), and commander of the Order of St. John of Jerusalem. He received an honorary LL D from Southampton University in 1967. In 1957 he was created first Baron Bank, of Sutton Scotney.

Rank died 29 March 1972 at Sutton Manor, Sutton Scotney, Hampshire. The barony became extinct.

[Private information; personal knowledge.]

JOHN DAVIS

RATTIGAN, SIR TERENCE MERVYN (1911–1977), playwright, was born in Cornwall Gardens, Kensington, 10 June 1911, the second of two children, both sons, born to (William) Frank (Arthur) Rattigan and his wife, Vera Houston. His father, Frank, was the son of Sir William Rattigan [q.v.], at one time chief justice of the Punjab and, later, MP for North-East Lanark. Frank's career was less distinguished than his father's had been. He resigned from the Diplomatic Service in 1922 after a disagreement with the foreign secretary, the Marquess Curzon of Kedleston [q.v.], over the best approach to the Chanak crisis. (Frank, who was assistant high commissioner at Constantinople, favoured intervention on behalf of Greece.) Thereafter the finances of the family were never soundly based.

Vera was seventeen when she married. She outlived her husband who, by all accounts, had a lifelong attachment to 'fluffy blondes' (his second son's expression) which may have steered that impressionable boy, not only into the arms of his mother but also, in true Freudian style, down less conventional emotional paths in later life. One of his mother's Houston relatives had, in 1863, given a public lecture, later published (Arthur Houston, 'The English Drama. Its Past History and Probable Future' in *The Afternoon Lectures on*

English Literature, 1863), in which may be read the following prophetic passage: 'The highest type of dramatic composition is that which supplies us with studies of character, skilfully worked out, in a plot not deficient in probability, and by means of incidents not wanting in interest.' No truer definition of the future products of his relative, as yet unborn, is ever likely to be penned.

In 1920 Rattigan went to Sandroyd, a preparatory school near Cobham in Surrey. For one summer holiday his mother took a cottage, in which the bookshelves held nothing but plays, from a drama critic, Hugh Griffiths. Rattigan read them all and, as he said in later years, that holiday determined his career. In 1925 he won a scholarship to Harrow, thus relieving his now hard-up father from the onus of financing him. He wrote a one-act play in French, which the French master marked two out of ten, conceding that the 'theatre sense was first class'. He also wrote an article, in the *Harrovian*, on modern drama, in which he discussed 'the ceaseless conflict between Entertainment and Instruction'. Broadly speaking, the position he adopted in that article foreshadowed the stance he took, forty years on, in his battle with the New Guard drama critics, during which, in his own words, 'I had no chance with anything. They didn't give me reasons for it. They just said, "It must be bad".'

At Harrow he played cricket for the school and took the Bourchier history prize. In 1930, having won a minor scholarship to Trinity College, he went up to Oxford. By now he was a fair-haired, charming youth, with one foot on the playing-fields, the other firmly planted in the Oxford University Dramatic Society. His father, whose ambition was that he should be a diplomat, sent him to France in his first long vacation. Rattigan came home with the idea for his first successful play already in his mind.

In 1932 he and a friend, Philip Heimann, collaborated in the writing of *First Episode*, produced in 1933 at the Q Theatre and transferred to the Comedy in 1934. This play, though adolescent in conception and, indeed, in plot—the scene was set in Oxford—earned mild praise from the reviewers (not excluding James Agate [q.v.], of the *Sunday Times*). At once, the fledgling dramatist left Oxford with his father's grudging blessing and a small allowance from the same source.

In November 1936 the play he had conceived in France, *French Without Tears*, came on at the Criterion. From curtain-fall until the day of his death, forty-one years later, in the same month, Rattigan was famous and his name a household word. Unhappily, the path Rattigan trod, as an outstanding British dramatist, was not invariably strewn with roses. None the less, for more than twenty years in London and New York, his touch was golden. Audiences felt not only confidence but also fulfilment in his company.

French Without Tears, his greatest comedy success (in spite of Agate's strong aversion to it) was succeeded by another triumph. With *Flare Path* (1942), based on his RAF experience, he proved himself to be a good all-rounder, capable of writing with uncanny skill on any theme that took his fancy. He reverted to light comedy, in 1943, with *While the Sun Shines*; then—his war service concluded—he again took up more serious themes—*The Winslow Boy* (1946), *The Browning Version* (1948), *The Deep Blue Sea* (1952), and *Separate Tables* (1954). His screen-plays, too, were equally successful. Many of them were produced by Anatole de Grunwald and directed by Anthony Asquith [q.v.], with both of whom he worked in total harmony.

In later life the quality of Rattigan's plays fell somewhat short of what it had been at its zenith. It was never less than adequate, however, and did not merit the hostile criticism it received. His obituary in *The Times* (1 December 1977) states: 'Rattigan's opponents, at an hour of theatrical rebellion, took every chance to belittle a probing storyteller.' Kenneth Tynan [q.v.] called him 'the Formosa of the British Theatre', asserting that he had betrayed the revolution (the New Wave) by staying with the Old Guard. None the less, although the argument around which this sad controversy raged was sterile from the start, it needled Rattigan beyond endurance and—unwisely—to the point of fighting back, thus provoking the New Wave with his constant references to his middle-class 'Aunt Edna'—a fictitious figure he invented—whose tastes, so he said, deserved as much attention as the avant-garde.

Rattigan was a homosexual and never married. He received a knighthood in 1971, having been appointed CBE in 1958. He came to England from Bermuda, for his last play *Cause Célèbre* (1977), aware that he was dying. '*Cause Célèbre*', wrote Bernard Levin, in the *Sunday Times*, 'betrays no sign of failing powers.' Its author died, back in Bermuda, 30 November 1977. *The Times* described him as an 'enduring influence in the English theatre'. Sir Harold Hobson, in the *Sunday Times*, wrote that 'he had the greatest natural talent for the stage of any man in this century'.

In a memoir for the *Sunday Telegraph* William Douglas-Home said: 'Consider *Separate Tables*. Here, most notably, in all the goings-on concerning an unhappy army officer, the many gifts bestowed on Rattigan by providence are on parade, his humour, his integrity—above all, his compassion. There is not one character who does not speak true. There is not one sentiment expressed which is not grounded in humanity, not one line that, in any way, diminishes the dignity of man. And, as for the compassion, that most Christian of all Christian virtues, it is there in such full measure that no member of the audience, unless his heart be made of stone, will go into the street at curtain-fall, without a lift in spirit and a fuller understanding of mankind as his companion. That is Rattigan's achievement and his triumph. That, so long as theatres exist and players strut their hour upon the stage and speak the dialogue he wrote for them, is his eternal monument.'

[Michael Darlow and Gillian Hodson, *Terence Rattigan. The Man and his Work*, 1979; personal knowledge.] WILLIAM DOUGLAS-HOME

RAWCLIFFE, GORDON HINDLE (1910–1979), electrical engineer and academic, was born 2 June 1910 at Sunny Bank, Sheffield, the elder son and first of three children of the Revd James Hindle Rawcliffe (1874–1920), of St. Matthias Church, Sheffield, the son of a Burnley grocer, and his wife, Mary Jane (1883–1940), the daughter of a Lytham hotelier named Thompson. The family moved to Gloucester when Rawcliffe was two; his father died there eight years later. Rawcliffe was educated at King's School, Gloucester (1921–3), Hereford Cathedral School (1923–4), and St. Edmund's School, Canterbury (1924–9). He then went, as an exhibitioner, to Keble College, Oxford; he first read mathematics, obtaining class ii in mathematical moderations (1930); then, under (Sir) Richard V. Southwell [q.v.], he read engineering science, achieving first class honours in 1932.

His first professional appointment was with Metropolitan-Vickers Electrical Co. Ltd. of Manchester, where he spent two years as a college apprentice and upwards of three as a design engineer. This comparatively short period in industry made him thoroughly familiar with electrical machinery, and gave him opportunities for writing and debate; not least, it brought him into contact with men like E. S. Booth, Willis Jackson (later Lord Jackson of Burnley, q.v.) and (Sir) Frederic C. Williams. However, Rawcliffe was more interested in the science of engineering than in production processes; and in 1937 he accepted appointment as lecturer in electrical engineering in the University of Liverpool, whence in 1941 he moved to Aberdeen to take up the joint post of lecturer in charge of electrical engineering in the university and head of department in Robert Gordon's Technical College. Three years later the university awarded him the degree of D.Sc. In the same year he moved again, having been appointed at the early age of thirty-four to the chair of electrical engineering in the University of Bristol, where he was to remain until his retirement in 1975.

Rawcliffe began the major work for which he is remembered in 1955, when he started a systematic reconsideration of the polyphase winding of alternating current machinery: a reconsideration which involved questioning and ultimately changing some of the established dogma of the electrical world. Initially he concentrated on the induction motor, the simple, reliable machine which drives most of the world's industry, but which then had one unfortunate characteristic: it would run at only one speed. From Rawcliffe's studies emerged what he called the principle of pole amplitude modulation—PAM—which showed how by simple means current could be reversed in parts of motor windings, so changing the pole distribution and number, and with it the speed of rotation. The ramifications of this simple idea were many; Rawcliffe devoted to its development years of intense single-minded concentration and by the time of his death he and his collaborators (in particular W. Fong and A. R. W. Broadway) had filed some sixty patents worldwide and published numerous scientific papers, while the large-scale manufacture of PAM motors had already become common throughout the world.

Rawcliffe was the recipient of many honours. The Royal Society elected him FRS (1972) and Clifford Paterson lecturer (1977); to his MA (Oxon., 1937) and D.Sc. (Aberdeen, 1944) were added honorary D.Tech. (Loughborough, 1974) and honorary D.Sc. (Bath, 1976). Keble College elected him to an honorary fellowship (1976). He became vice-president (1972–5) and honorary fellow (1978) of the Institution of Electrical Engineers. The Fellowship of Engineering elected him F.Eng. (1976).

Rawcliffe was a vital character, with an apparently inexhaustible store of restless energy; this was despite chronic ill health, especially bronchial asthma, which dogged him throughout his life and which was at times totally disabling. Because of his intense devotion to PAM, his scientific interests were perhaps narrow. His general interests ranged widely. Education, languages (especially English, for he loved poetry), law, and music were all important to him. A former president and life member of the Oxford University Archaeological Society, he had a wide knowledge of church and cathedral origins and architecture. He was a most positive man: he liked bright colours and loud music, and saw most problems in black and white. He would make a rapid assessment and decision, giving his views bluntly and without equivocation.

Rawcliffe married first (1940) Stella Mary, daughter of Arthur Eustace Morgan, principal of McGill University, Canada, and later of the Ministry of Labour, London; they had two daughters. Separation and divorce ended the marriage in 1952. In the same year he married

Sheila Mary, daughter of Charles William Wicks, schoolmaster; they also had two daughters. Rawcliffe died of a heart attack following a bout of asthma 3 September 1979 at his home in Clifton, Bristol.

[A. R. Collar and A. R. W. Broadway in *Biographical Memoirs of Fellows of the Royal Society*, vol. xxvii, 1981; private information; personal knowledge.] RODERICK COLLAR

RAWSTHORNE, ALAN (1905–1971), composer, was born in Haslingden, Lancashire, 2 May 1905, the younger child and only son of Hubert Rawsthorne, medical practitioner, of Haslingden and Southport, Lancashire, and his wife, Janet Bridge. He was educated, after preparatory school, at Sandringham School, Southport, for two years, then continued his education with a private tutor, also in Southport. His parents were initially opposed to his following the profession of music and consequently he briefly and abortively studied dentistry and architecture. He did not begin serious musical training until, at the age of twenty, he entered the Royal Manchester College of Music. Here he studied piano under Frank Merrick and cello under Carl Fuchs, gaining diplomas in teaching and performance and becoming a gold medallist and later (1943) an honorary fellow of the college. He continued his piano studies abroad, notably under Egon Petri in Berlin. In 1932–4 he taught, played the piano, and was generally responsible for the music in the School of Dance Mime at Dartington Hall.

It was not until the mid-1930s that he settled in London, married in 1934 as his first wife the orchestral violinist, Jessie, daughter of Herbert Hinchcliffe, schoolmaster, and began to devote himself solely to composition.

In the few years before World War II he began to make his mark, notably with his Theme and Variations for Two Violins (1938) and Symphonic Studies for Orchestra (1939). Both were performed in the annual festivals of the International Society for Contemporary Music (London, 1938, and Warsaw, 1939, respectively). With the dislocation of war—Rawsthorne served in the army from 1941 onwards—his career was hampered but not at a standstill. Both his First Piano Concerto (1942) and the *Street Corner Overture* (1944) were successes. After the war, he was to have a working life of only twenty-five years. They were productive but not prolific. Major post-war works included three symphonies, a Second Piano Concerto written for the 1951 Festival of Britain; Concertos for Violin, Cello, Oboe, and Orchestra; a Concerto for String Orchestra; chamber music including three String Quartets and an outstanding Sonata for Violin and Piano; works for piano solo, few in number unfortunately, since he wrote beautifully for the instrument; and some extended cycles or cantatas both for solo voice and for chorus, with orchestra: these did not perhaps display his gifts as fully as his purely orchestral and instrumental work did.

Much of this output was written after he left London and moved to a fairly remote village in Essex in the 1950s. He was divorced in 1954 and in the following year married the painter Isabel Delmer Lambert, daughter of Philip Owen Nicholas, master mariner. She was the former wife of D. Sefton Delmer [q.v.] and the widow of Constant Lambert [q.v.], who died in 1951 and who was one of Rawsthorne's closest friends and musical associates. There were no children by either marriage. Isabel Lambert was responsible for the décor of Rawsthorne's ballet, *Madame Chrysanthème* (Covent Garden, 1955). This was his only stage work, though he was planning at the end of his life to write a full-length opera, and earlier in his career he had composed music for numerous films.

'A musicians' composer' is a phrase commonly applied to Alan Rawsthorne and with some justice. Certainly the meticulously clean writing, the polish and refinement which inform his work appeal to professional musicians and to the more knowledgeable listeners, rather than to a wider public. Yet there is much to enjoy in his best work: the clarity of thought and expression, at times witty, more often introspective, with a gentle melancholy yet not without occasional bursts of power and intensity. His style was remarkably consistent throughout his career though it lost some of its precise texture in his last years. It was a style that was as remote from the traditional twentieth-century English school as it was from the European avant-garde. In the crucial period of Rawsthorne's post-war development, fashion and taste in England tended to follow one or other of these two opposed movements and thus his music, not conforming to either, probably suffered in public esteem. But in any historical assessment of mid-twentieth-century English music, his place is assured. Influences on his writing are to be found, in composers such as Hindemith, Roussel, and Prokofiev. But Rawsthorne was always very recognizably himself, certain of his 'trade marks' (such as his liking for rapidly shifting tonalities) sometimes becoming near to mannerisms.

As a man he displayed several of the characteristics to be found in his music. Quiet, unhurried, and courteous in manner, his conversation nevertheless had a sharp cutting edge: he chose his words with the same precision as he did his black-and-white notes. At heart an intensely serious man, there was yet an urbanity about him and a stylish elegance which is reflected in the immaculate manuscript of his scores. He was well versed in literature and the pictorial arts, and, though not generally gregarious, he had many friends among painters, sculptors, actors, and poets. By his fellow musicians he was held in unusually warm regard.

Rawsthorne was appointed CBE in 1961 and received three honorary doctorates (University of Belfast, 1969; Liverpool, 1969; Essex, 1971). He became an honorary fellow of Downing College, Cambridge, in 1969. He died in Cambridge 24 July 1971.

[*The Times*, 26 July 1971; Peter Evans, 'Alan Rawsthorne', *The New Grove Dictionary of Music and Musicians*, ed. Stanley Sadie, vol. xv, 1980; private information; personal knowledge.] ALAN FRANK

READING, MARCHIONESS OF, and BARONESS SWANBOROUGH (1894–1971), chairman and founder, Women's Royal Voluntary Service. [See ISAACS, STELLA.]

RECKITT, MAURICE BENINGTON (1888–1980), writer and Christian sociologist, was born in Beverley, east Yorkshire, 19 June 1888, the eldest of the three children and elder son of Arthur Benington Reckitt and his wife, Helen Annie Thomas. His parents' influence on his character was both creditable and corrosive. Arthur Reckitt, a director of Reckitt's ('Blue') of Hull ensured there was always an income (and later a fortune) without his son having to work for it. But his suicide in 1927 bequeathed to Maurice Reckitt a deep emotional fear of himself. His mother, nurtured in the Catholic tradition of the Church of England, gave her son the foundation of a firm faith. The too-distant father was more than complemented by an over-protective and possessive mother. Her doting fondness fostered her son's vanity which later sometimes led to a morbid egotism.

Delicate health in boyhood deprived Reckitt of formal education and prevented him serving in World War I, but a procession of private tutors enabled him to reach St. John's College, Oxford, in 1907. He gained a second class in modern history in 1911. (Sir) Ernest Barker [q.v.] kindled in him an abiding interest in the nature and significance of medieval order. Other educators at this and later stages of his life were H. A. L. Fisher, G. K. Chesterton, A. R. Orage [qq.v.], J. N. Figgis, P. E. T. Widdrington, and V. A. Demant.

For two years only Reckitt earned his living as a schoolmaster at Ipswich Grammar School. 'A meteor flashed across our sky', was the headmaster's comment. Returning to Oxford in 1913 Reckitt intended writing a thesis but he was diverted by other claims and interests. An unlikely friendship developed between Reckitt and G. D. H. Cole [q.v.]. Cole, the unapproachable cold atheist, and at root an anarchist, joined forces with Reckitt, the clubbable, romantic medievalist, archetypal bourgeois, and unswerving Anglican with a dogmatic faith, to found the National Guilds League in 1915. Its aim was to promote the abolition of the wage system and the establishment of self-government in industry through a system of national guilds working in conjunction with the state. Reckitt's interest in the restoration of medieval guilds waned when the guild movement began to split in 1920. He became a prominent member of the Church Socialist League and editor of its journal, *Church Socialist* (1915–19) and in 1923 chairman of the new League of the Kingdom of God. This developed as a reaction against the politicization of the church's social teaching and the adulation of communism by some of his friends. If Reckitt hated anything it was Soviet communism, which he saw as atheist, autocratic, ruthless, and materialist. This caused many strains in his relationships, not least with his sister Eva Collet Reckitt (the founder of Collet's bookshop—known as the 'Bomb Shop'). If Reckitt's conviction was always socialist his commitment was to 'earth and altar', to *church* social action rather than political action.

Reckitt's vocation was to be available. He spent a lifetime co-ordinating and leavening the thinking of small groups together with such people as T. S. Eliot, Dorothy L. Sayers [qq.v.], T. M. Heron, Philip Mairet, and many priests. He spoke at most of the major church conferences of his time. He was a good organizer. Though voluble and loquacious he always expressed an independent judgement. The dullest committee was enlivened and shaken by the friendly lash of his tongue. He was a member of the church assembly, the British Council of Churches, and many other bodies. He chaired committees, some of which produced significant reports such as *Gambling, an Ethical Discussion* (1950).

Above all Reckitt was a writer and Christian sociologist. His literary output was prodigious. Books, pamphlets, essays, articles, and reviews flowed from his pen. He was a contributor and reviewer for Orage's *New Age*, a member of the editorial board of *G.K.'s Weekly*, and an editorial writer for the *New English Weekly*. Among his books *Faith and Society* (1932) was a seminal work and his Scott Holland memorial lectures of 1946 *Maurice to Temple* (1947), describing a century of the social movement in the Church of England, are of permanent value. He most enjoyed collaborating with others in producing books, the most notable being *Prospect for Christendom* (1945), which he edited.

Perhaps his abiding legacy is *Christendom*, a quarterly journal of Christian sociology which he edited from 1931 to 1950. Together with the annual summer school of sociology at Oxford they shone like beacons for those churchmen who felt despondent, disillusioned, and discontented. Spirited thinkers and debaters wrote in *Christendom* and spoke at the summer schools. The Christendom Group stood for autochthonous thought and activity and was once denounced as 'the rudest group in the Church of England'. Reckitt himself eschewed social scientists and scientific economics and bypassed sociological evidence. Reckitt was one of the best-known names in the church, which he maintained had three functions: to worship God, to bind up the wounds of the world, and to prophesy. He endeavoured to live according to the spirit of a phrase of G. K. Chesterton's which he often quoted: 'One must somehow learn to love the world without trusting it.'

He had some irritating quirks of character. He was fastidious about what he ate and when he ate it. His handwriting was notoriously illegible. Towards the end of his life he was much given to introspection and anxiety about whether he would get through the needle's eye. His recreations were pursued with verve and vigour. He was a ballroom dancer of distinction, a writer of revues and ballades, and a patron of the theatre. Chiefly he played 'the noble game' of croquet and was president of the Croquet Association from 1967 until 1975. He played in every Brighton August tournament for sixty years and represented Surrey on forty occasions. The Christendom Trust was established in 1968 and there is an M. B. Reckitt research fellowship at the University of Sussex.

In 1920 he married Evelyn Aimée (died 1968), daughter of Arthur Douglas Peppercorn, artist. She was a professional violinist (Aimée Carvel). She shared many of her husband's recreational pursuits but not his faith. They had no children. Reckitt died 11 January 1980 at Roehampton.

Two portraits were painted by Michael Noakes.

[Maurice Reckitt, *As it Happened* (autobiography), 1941; V. A. Demant, *Maurice B. Reckitt—a Record of Vocation and Versatility*, 1978; private papers and information.]

JOHN S. PEART-BINNS

REED, SIR CAROL (1906–1976), film director, was born 30 December 1906 in Wandsworth, London, the fourth son (there were subsequently another son and a daughter) of (Sir) Herbert Beerbohm Tree [q.v.], actor-manager, and his friend, (Beatrice) May Pinney, who took the name of Reed by deed poll in 1904. She named Herbert Reed, of independent means, as the father on the birth certificate, but in 1911 she altered the birth certificate by statutory declaration, leaving the father's name a blank. Tree shared his time between his wife and three daughters and his family by May Pinney. Carol Reed was educated at King's School, Canterbury. After a brief spell of farming in America he returned to London to become an actor. In 1924 he walked on in *St. Joan* by G. B. Shaw [q.v.], starring (Dame) Sybil Thorndike [q.v.], at the New Theatre but his first credited appearance was later that year in *Heraclius* at the Empire Theatre, Leicester Square. There followed three years of touring before he returned to the West End as understudy and assistant stage manager at the Lyceum in 1927. The play was *The Terror* whose author, R. H. Edgar Wallace [q.v.], became an important influence in Reed's life. Reed produced and performed in Wallace's plays and gained his first film experience with Wallace's company at Beaconsfield Studios. After Wallace's death in 1932 he joined Basil Dean [q.v.] at Ealing Studios as a dialogue director and it was there, in 1935, that he directed his first film, *Midshipman Easy*, a vigorous and amusing version of the book by Captain Frederick Marryat [q.v.].

During the next seven years Reed's many films included an adapted play, *Laburnum Grove* (1936); a backstage comedy, *A Girl Must Live* (1939); a mining drama, *The Stars Look Down* (1939); two entertaining thrillers, *Night Train to Munich* (1940) and *The Girl in the News* (1940); and a pair of costume pieces, *Kipps* (1941) and *The Young Mr Pitt* (1942). All showed a flair for story-telling in cinematic terms and a sympathetic interest in the lives of ordinary people. Now Reed was beginning to tackle weightier and more expensive projects, often as his own producer, but his real maturity as a film-maker came with work he did for the army, which he joined in 1941. He made a training film showing raw recruits being turned into efficient fighting men, *The New Lot* (1943), and the military authorities asked for an expanded version to be shown to the public. The result was *The Way Ahead* (1944), one of Britain's best war films. Reed went on to collaborate with the Americans on an actuality film about the European campaign, *The True Glory* (1945), which won the American Academy award (Oscar) for the best documentary.

Reed was now Britain's leading director. His next film, *Odd Man Out* (1947), an account of the dying hours of an Irish gunman, was hailed as a masterpiece. He followed with two collaborations with Graham Greene, *The Fallen Idol* (1948) and *The Third Man* (1949), both studies in disillusion, which confirmed his status as an international figure. These three films and the next, *Outcast of the Islands* (1952), a version of the book by Joseph Conrad [q.v.], share a dark view of the world; their visual style, using sharp black and white photography and unusual camera angles, is deliberately disturbing. They reflect what one critic has described as 'a humane pessimism'.

They form a body of work unsurpassed in the British cinema, a peak of achievement that Reed never quite scaled again. In 1952 he was knighted for his services to the cinema.

There was a further successful collaboration with Graham Greene, this time in a lighter vein, with *Our Man in Havana* (1960) but Reed's return to international acclaim came with his first musical, *Oliver* (1968), adapted from Lionel Bart's version of *Oliver Twist.* It was visually splendid, making full use of colour and the wide screen, and had a truly Dickensian gusto. It won an Oscar for the best film of the year and another for Reed as the best director, as well as four more for technical qualities.

Carol Reed was a meticulous craftsman and a brilliant technician who had a special sympathy with actors. He worked closely with scriptwriters and editors but he saw himself as an interpreter rather than an initiator of ideas. His most characteristic films were made in Britain and he never seemed entirely at ease in Hollywood. Indeed, he was temperamentally averse to much of the Hollywood ethic. A quiet, gentle man, he shunned publicity, gave few interviews, and protected his private life. He was very tall but his commanding presence belied a likeable modesty.

In 1943 Reed married the actress Diana Wynyard (died 1964, q.v.), daughter of Edward Thomas Cox, master printer. The marriage was dissolved in 1947 and there were no children. In 1948 he married Penelope (died 1982), also an actress, daughter of William Dudley Ward, MP for Southampton, and former wife of Harry Anthony Compton Pelissier, son of H. G. Pelissier and Fay Compton [q.v.]. They had one son. Reed died in London, 25 April 1976.

[Madeleine Bingham, *The Great Lover. The life and Art of Herbert Beerbohm Tree*, 1978; Oliver Reed, *Reed All About Me* (autobiography), 1979; Brenda Davies (ed.), *Carol Reed*, British Film Institute, 1978.] BRENDA DAVIES

REES, (MORGAN) GORONWY (1909–1979), author, journalist, man of business, and university administrator, was born 29 November 1909 at Aberystwyth, the younger son and youngest of the four children of the Revd Richard Jenkyn Rees, a Calvinist minister, and his wife, Apphia Mary James, the daughter of a small tenant farmer, of Cardiganshire. He was educated at Cardiff High School for Boys, and, as a scholar, at New College, Oxford. He took first class honours in philosophy, politics, and economics in 1931 and in the same year was elected to a fellowship at All Souls. He wrote his first novel, *The Summer Flood*, while still an undergraduate, and it was published in 1932.

After a brief interlude in Berlin, where he did some abortive research on Ferdinand Lassalle and played a minor role, impersonating a Highland officer, in a German film, he returned to England to become a leader writer for the *Manchester Guardian.* He held this position from 1932 to 1936 when he became assistant editor of the *Spectator.* His second novel, *A Bridge to Divide Them*, was published in 1937.

At the outbreak of war, Rees, who had already joined the Territorials, was mobilized as a gunner in the 90th Field Regiment of the Royal Artillery. After taking a short course at Sandhurst as an officer cadet he was commissioned in 1940 in the Royal Welch Fusiliers. He took part in the raid on Dieppe, served in Europe on the staff of Sir Bernard Montgomery (later Viscount Montgomery of Alamein, q.v.), and ended the war as a colonel in the British military government in Germany.

In 1940, when he was stationed in Liverpool, he met and married Margaret Ewing, daughter of Thomas Tuckness Morris, underwriter, of Liverpool. The marriage was a very happy one, and his wife a strong and stabilizing influence in his life. They had five children, two girls and three boys.

After the war Rees became a director of Pontifex, general engineers and coppersmiths, the family firm of his friend Henry Yorke [q.v.], the novelist 'Henry Green'. His duties allowed him leisure to write and in 1950 he published his third and best novel, *Where No Wounds Were.* In 1951 he returned to All Souls as estates bursar and succeeded in increasing that college's already considerable wealth.

In 1953 Rees accepted an invitation to become principal of the University College of Wales at Aberystwyth. He was too much of a hedonist and too little of a Welsh nationalist to be suited to the position, but he made light of its drawbacks and earned the esteem of the students and the younger members of the staff. He came to grief in 1957 through his publication of a series of articles, sensationalized in a Sunday newspaper, about his former friendship with the defector Guy Burgess. Though the articles were far from condoning Burgess's conduct and showed no sympathy with communism, their tone was sufficiently shocking for Rees's enemies in Aberystwyth to contrive to set up a commission of enquiry which reported adversely on the conduct of the principal. A majority of the college council voted that no further action be taken but the opposition was strong enough to force Rees's resignation.

Bad luck pursued him. A rash venture into the building trade left him with next to no money and he suffered a motor accident which nearly cost him his life. His experiences in hospital are brilliantly recounted in his most impressive book, *A Bundle of Sensations*, which appeared in 1960.

The title, which refers to Hume's theory of the self, expresses Rees's view of his own personality.

In the following year Rees published *The Multi-Millionaires*, an amusing study of six contemporary men of wealth. A long period of research on behalf of the firm of Marks & Spencer led to the publication in 1969 of *St. Michael*, a history of the firm. In 1969 also he published a historical guidebook to *The Rhine* and in 1970 a study of *The Great Slump*. His outstanding gift for autobiography was displayed in *A Chapter of Accidents*, which appeared in 1972. For some years he had been writing an incisive monthly column for *Encounter*, and a collection of these pieces was published in 1974 under the title of *Brief Encounters*.

Rees's last years were clouded by the death of his wife, after a long and painful illness, but he never lost his courage, his gaiety, and his zest for experience. He himself died in a London hospital 12 December 1979.

[Goronwy Rees, *A Chapter of Accidents*, 1972; personal knowledge.] A. J. Ayer

REID, JAMES SCOTT CUMBERLAND, Baron Reid (1890–1975), lord of appeal in ordinary, was born 30 July 1890 at Drem in the county of Haddington, the eldest of the three children (all boys) of James Reid, writer to the Signet, of Drem House, who also farmed in East Lothian, and his wife, Kate, daughter of William Scott, merchant, of Calcutta. From the Edinburgh Academy Reid went as a scholar to Jesus College, Cambridge, where he graduated BA, LL B, with first class honours in part i of both the natural sciences (1910) and law (1911) triposes. His legal studies, which he found arid and remote from the living law practised in London, were his only direct contact with English law until he was appointed lord of appeal. After Cambridge he attended Scots law classes at Edinburgh University, to qualify himself for admission to the Faculty of Advocates. Having by then joined the 8th battalion of the Royal Scots, in November 1914 he was the first advocate to be admitted to the Faculty wearing uniform. He transferred to the Machine Gun Corps, and had an active war in several theatres. Demobilized with the rank of major he began practice in Parliament House in 1919.

At the outset progress was slow, and he found time for legal writing, including a book on the Agricultural Holdings (Scotland) Act of 1923 which established his reputation as an authority on agricultural law. In time he came to be recognized as an exceptionally competent counsel in handling complex cases which gave scope for his quick analytical mind—his arguments in court being presented in a somewhat didactic manner. His practice was distinguished rather than extensive. Partly because of commitment to politics and partly because of prolonged service as law officer, Reid never became a great forensic figure in Scotland. Nevertheless in 1932, the year after his election to Parliament, he took silk, and in 1945 the Faculty of Advocates elected him dean. A shy man, tall and lean, he had seemed a somewhat aloof and Olympian figure in Parliament House. However, as dean until 1948, he did all he could to be helpful, friendly, and hospitable at the difficult time he held office, but his commitments in London prevented him from giving the guidance and support normally expected of the elected leader of the Scottish bar. Reid's professional career illustrates in striking fashion that eminence at the Scottish bar and a political career cannot be satisfactorily combined.

Long active in Conservative politics, in 1931 Reid was elected member for Stirling and Falkirk Burghs, and soon became recognized as a formidable debater and able politician. He lost his seat narrowly in 1935, but in 1937 he was elected for the Hillhead division of Glasgow, which he represented until appointed lord of appeal. In 1936 he became solicitor-general for Scotland and in 1941 lord advocate, holding office until the Labour Party formed a government in 1945. Thereafter he assumed a prominent role in opposition—subjecting to penetrating and devastating criticism much proposed government legislation. He was viewed by certain Labour politicians with hostility, but C. R. (later Earl) Attlee's offer to Reid of a vacancy as lord of appeal was probably prompted more by appreciation of his potential contribution than to remove a powerful critic from the Commons. In fact Reid did not accept until he had consulted the Conservative hierarchy regarding his political prospects and received no adequate encouragement.

Appointed lord of appeal and a life peer in 1948, he held office for twenty-six years—a longer period than any before him—and retired in January 1975 at the age of eighty-four with his judicial faculties unimpaired. From 1962 he had been the senior member of the Judicial Committee, presiding in the absence of the lord chancellor, and responsible for the management of its business. This was an astonishing achievement, since in 1958 he had been operated on for cancer of the stomach and a colostomy had been performed.

Scots lawyers acquiesce unenthusiastically in the curious constitutional fiction which imputes to English lords of appeal on appointment judicial knowledge of Scots law. What was unique about Reid's contribution in the Lords was that, though a Scots lawyer exclusively by professional training, he was accepted by his English colleagues and by the whole legal profession in England as the 'helmsman of the [English] common law'. Since his conception of the judicial function accorded with the older Scottish tradition, his exercise of it in Scottish appeals, though widely respected, was not considered remarkable. Not having been formed in both Scots and English law, he assumed somewhat readily their identity on certain matters where there were latent distinctions. When Reid spoke in House of Lords debates, on matters of Scots law he was accepted as an infallible oracle.

However, the great majority of appeals on which he sat—well over 500—concerned English law. In most he wrote a full speech, seldom dissenting since his views usually persuaded his brethren. Presiding in the Lords after Reid's death, Lord Wilberforce observed that the qualities which made him so outstanding a judge were accuracy of thought and precision of reasoning, broad common sense, generous humanity, simple and elegant use of language: '[He] has guided us with the influence of an equal in status, of a superior in wisdom, common sense, and where appropriate imagination.'

Reid's 'inside feeling' for English law he attributed to his long and close association with Gray's Inn of which he was made an honorary bencher (1948). He prescribed criteria for applying creatively but cautiously the Practice Statement of July 1966 regarding House of Lords precedents, and considered that judges as lawmakers should apply common sense, principle rather than narrow precedent, and regard for an evolving public policy. Some reforms were for Parliament alone. His conduct of appeals, probing arguments closely to test principle, was a major contribution. If he kept the law moving in the right direction at the right speed, he was content to influence the present rather than preempt the future.

His friends were few but close, his refreshment gardening, and, especially in his later years, he was very agreeable and encouraging company to his juniors. Among other contributions, Reid was chairman of the Malaya constitutional commission (1956–7) and of the committee on registration of title to land in Scotland (Reid report Cmnd. 2032/63).

Reid was sworn of the Privy Council in 1941 and appointed CH in 1967. He held honorary degrees from Edinburgh (LL D, 1945) and Oxford (DCL, 1971). He was FRSE, and an honorary fellow of Jesus College, Cambridge (1948).

In 1933 Reid married Esther May (died 1980), widow of Gerald Frank Brierley and daughter of Charles Banks Nelson, advocate, solicitor, and attorney at the Manx bar. They had no children. Reid died 29 March 1975 in London.

[L. Blom-Cooper and G. Drewry, *Final Appeal*, 1972; A. Paterson, *The Law Lords*, 1982; R. B. Stevens, *Law and Politics*, 1979; *The Times*, 14 January, 31 March, 3, 5, 6 April, and 17 June 1975.] T. B. Smith

REITH, JOHN CHARLES WALSHAM, first Baron Reith (1889–1971), creator of the BBC, wartime minister and peacetime administrator, was born 20 July 1889 at Stonehaven, Kincardineshire, the fifth son and the last of the seven children of the Revd George Reith, a Glasgow minister of the Free Church, and his wife, Adah Mary, daughter of Edward Weston, a London stockbroker. He was educated at Glasgow Academy, at Gresham's School in Norfolk, and at the Royal Technical College, Glasgow. He was apprenticed in 1908 to the Hyde Park works of the North British Locomotive Company, Glasgow. In February 1914 he obtained employment with S. Pearson & Son Ltd. at the Royal Albert Dock extension in London.

He had been keen on military activities from his youth, joining various Cadet and Officers' Training Corps. He went to France in November 1914 with the 5th Scottish Rifles, and despite quarrels with his colonel and adjutant he had, as he noted in his diary, 'a thoroughly happy war'. Early evidence of one of his major characteristics is a 1915 entry. After seeing Sir John French (later Earl of Ypres, q.v.), the commander-in-chief, and 'crowds of brass-hatted Olympians', he thought he 'could do their jobs—some of them anyhow—as well as they'. When turning these war diaries into his book *Wearing Spurs* twenty-two years later (but not published till 1966) he added 'I am sure of it now'. During the battle of Loos in October 1915 a sniper's bullet gashed his face and ended his fighting.

Back in Britain he first had a post in the Ministry of Munitions, then a rewarding eighteen months (1916–17) in America, controlling contracts for munitions. He got on well with Americans all his life. America's entry into the war in April 1917 brought him home again, to work on an Admiralty construction project. He ended his World War I service in the Ministry of Munitions.

The war gave him the greatest boon of his life. In 1918 he fell in love with the driver of his colonel's car. She was Muriel Katharine, younger daughter of John Lynch Odhams, head of the publishing firm of that name. They were married in 1921. Through the fifty years of Reith's public life, which were increasingly unhappy in spite of all the successes and honours that they brought him, his wife was, in the last resort, a powerful stabilizer, a calm companion in the midst of every storm.

In 1920 Reith joined William Beardmore & Co. as general manager at Coatbridge. Seeing no path there for his growing ambition, he resigned and moved to London. Ever since youth he had envisaged a political career. In 1914, 'awfully keen to go into Parliament', he had approached the Liberals. In March 1920 he sounded J. R. Clynes [q.v.] of the Labour Party. In October 1922 he worked for Sir William Bull, Conservative MP for Hammersmith, in the preparations for the general election following Lloyd George's fall. An advertisement offering the post of general manager of the British Broadcasting Company, then being formed, caught his eye. He applied and was appointed in December 1922. Not only was he on the threshold of his greatest achievement; he had been saved from inevitable disaster. Reith's strengths and weaknesses prohibited his ever becoming a successful politician. He could be neither subtle nor supple. He spurned compromise.

Reith's accomplishment in creating the BBC must be measured by the void that confronted him. He had no precedents, no rules, no standards, no established purpose to guide him. There was doubt whether the new device would last. Even the prophetic H. G. Wells [q.v.] saw little future for it. Disregarding all doubts Reith was determined from the beginning to give broadcasting status and purpose. The high proportion of his staff recruits from Oxford and Cambridge became a matter of criticism in later years. He battled ceaselessly to get radio's importance accepted. He persuaded Robert Bridges [q.v.] to include some lines on broadcasting in *The Testament of Beauty*. C. F. Garbett [q.v.], later archbishop of York, told how Reith had formed a religious broadcasting advisory committee in the earliest days. When its members failed to attend meetings he would upbraid them individually for their lack of vision. He restricted broadcasting on Sundays. He insisted his staff should be chaste.

When, after four years, the manufacturers-owned British Broadcasting Company was replaced under royal charter by the British Broadcasting Corporation, he was its architect as a public service. His claim to have originated the idea has been disputed. Whatever the exact sequence of events, it was what he wanted and built. He had outlined the ideals and policy of the company in *Broadcast Over Britain* (1924). As first director-general of the Corporation he made no change in his policies. Education, religion, and culture were to have their places alongside information and entertainment. The most eminent speakers and musicians were invited to broadcast. Anyone going to the microphone at Savoy Hill or Broadcasting House was given a sense of occasion. Development of regional broadcasting must not weaken the BBC as a national unifying force. Reith's engineering background determined him to have the finest and most efficient system in the world.

While the BBC's charter had settled its status for a quarter of a century, it had given Reith new problems. The governors who replaced the former directors could not be so easily handled. The Earl of Clarendon [q.v.], the corporation's first chairman, became one of Reith's *bêtes noires*. Viscountess Snowden, a member of the Board of Governors, was an even greater one. When ex-Speaker J. H. Whitley [q.v.] replaced Clarendon in 1930 there came not only peace but mutual affection.

More important was the opposition to Reith growing outside the BBC. The general strike of 1926 had willy-nilly taken the company into politics. The corporation was a fair target for critics in Parliament. Reith was accused of being dictatorial, of poor staff relations (in fact the staff's loyalty to 'Sir John'—he was knighted in 1927—was great), and of bias. He was not deterred. He had the satisfaction of seeing what he had created copied in other parts of the Commonwealth. In 1936 he inaugurated British television.

By 1938 all was going too well for his peace of mind. The BBC was stretching him (a favourite term) no longer. He became bored. He let it be known he would welcome a call to some new national challenge. The government responded. The prime minister, Neville Chamberlain, told him he should leave the BBC to become chairman of Imperial Airways. He went.

The 1938 move soured the rest of his life. 'Stupendous folly', he was to call it in his autobiography *Into the Wind* (1949). Immediately he quarrelled with the BBC governors because they would not give him a major role in choosing his successor. Many and outstanding as were his subsequent achievements, they could not kill his sense of loss. If he had held on for just another year, the problems of broadcasting in wartime, the vast extension and ramifying of the BBC's activities, the establishing of television throughout the kingdom on the standards he had set for radio, all would have given him in war and in peace the new challenge he had been seeking. But patience was never one of Reith's virtues. For the rest of his life the BBC remained a lost Shangri-La.

The imminence of war has been given as the reason for Reith's achieving little in his new post. He did become in 1939 the first chairman of the new British Overseas Airways Corporation, but his heart was not in the job. In January 1940 Chamberlain made him minister of information and on 1 February he became National MP for Southampton. In May (Sir) Winston Churchill, having become prime minister, made him minister of transport, and within five months of that minister of works and a peer (he became first Baron Reith). Early in 1942 Planning was added to his Ministry. The combined posts seemed to promise Reith the scope he craved. In fact he was never at ease with politicians. In a government reshuffle ten days after the last announcement Churchill dismissed him. After the war, on 1 January 1946, Reith wrote a remarkable rebuke to Churchill for never having tested his full powers. Churchill's reasoned soft answer did not mollify him. Reith's hatred of Churchill stayed virulent for his remaining twenty-five years.

Out of office and unemployed Reith turned to the Royal Navy. As a lieutenant-commander RNVR he rationalized coastal forces, and in 1943–4, as a captain and director of Combined Operations, Material Department, Admiralty, planned the movements of all supplies, materials, and transport for the D-day landings. Tributes from those qualified to assess what he had done declared the work to have been wellnigh perfect. Reith valued the CB (military) he was awarded for this in 1945 above almost all of his many other honours.

Meanwhile, Reith had begun to diversify into other work. In 1943 he joined the board of Cable and Wireless. After leaving the navy he made in 1945 a world flight of 45,000 miles to study future Commonwealth communications. He was chairman of the Commonwealth Telecommunications Board in 1946–50. In 1945–6 he was chairman of the New Towns Committee, and from 1947 to 1950 was chairman of the board of the Hemel Hempstead development corporation. In 1949–50 he chaired the National Film Finance Corporation. His last major achievement was to rescue, revivify, and make viable the ailing Colonial Development Corporation (1950–9). But here his scant respect for his political masters led to bitterness. Commercial appointments were to the boards of Tube Investments, Phoenix Assurance, and British Oxygen, of which he became vice-chairman, characteristically chafing because he was not the chairman. His administrative drive was felt wherever he went. His only fault was sometimes to take his logic beyond what was practical.

His closing years were sad. Not until almost the very end of a long life would he give up hope of being called upon for one last great national effort. When such posts became vacant he would ask friends to mention his name to the prime minister. He would sit by his telephone for hours, waiting for the call that never came. A solitary solace was his appointment to be lord high commissioner of the General Assembly of the Church of Scotland in 1967 and 1968, leading to his being appointed Knight of the Thistle in 1969. He was a member of the Queen's Body Guard for Scotland and of the Royal Company of Archers.

Reith was outsize physically as well as in character. Six feet six inches in height, the scar of his war wound added to his gauntness. He was a man of fierce hates, unrelenting and unforgiving. At the same time he won deep affections. His personal kindness could be overpowering. To ask of him a small service was to switch on a dynamo of energy. He had no wit, but a sense of fun. Some of his quirks, such as misnaming people of whom he did not approve, could become tiresome. But to be with him was to be taken on to a higher and more exciting level.

He accepted no limits to his capabilities. He believed his gifts fitted him for posts for which he had the wrong qualifications. Both as viceroy of India and British ambassador in Washington—two posts he openly confessed to have coveted—he would have been miscast. Even his lord rectorship of Glasgow University (1965–8) was not altogether happy. He was a man of fixed principles. An instinctive leader, he showed when in the navy that he could work happily under authority he could respect. While he justly regarded all he did after he left the BBC as anticlimax, a number of his successes would singly have made the reputation of less extraordinary men.

Reith's honours in addition to those already mentioned included the GBE (1934), GCVO (1939), PC (1940). He had LLDs from Aberdeen and Manchester (1933), DCL Oxford (1935), and LLD Glasgow (1951). Worcester College, Oxford, made him an honorary fellow in 1962. Reith died in Edinburgh 16 June 1971. His only son Christopher (born 1928) disclaimed the peerage in 1972. The heir to the barony became the Hon. James Harry John Reith (born 1972). Lady Reith, who unveiled a memorial to her husband in Westminster Abbey in 1972, died in 1977. Their only daughter, Marista, married the Revd Dr Murray Leishman.

The BBC has portraits of Reith by (Sir) Oswald Birley (*c.* 1934), by Sir Gerald Kelly (1967), a drawing by (Sir) Max Beerbohm (1938), and a bust (1929) by Lady Scott (later Lady Kennet, q.v.). There is a chalk drawing by Sir William Rothenstein in the National Portrait Gallery. The portrayal of the inmost man will remain Charles Stuart's fine volume of *The Reith Diaries* (1975).

[*The Times*, 17 June 1971; works above mentioned; personal knowledge.] WILLIAM HALEY

RENNELL OF RODD, second BARON (1895–1978), merchant banker and explorer. [See RODD, FRANCIS JAMES RENNELL.]

RHODES, WILFRED (1877–1973), cricketer, was born at Kirkheaton, Yorkshire, 29 October 1877, the son (another son died in a railway accident) of Alfred Rhodes, coal miner, keen cricketer, and enthusiastic captain of Kirkheaton 2nd XI, and his wife, Elizabeth Holliday. Rhodes attended the Spring Grove school in Huddersfield, left at the age of sixteen, and took a job on the Lancashire and Yorkshire Railway. But this interfered with what was already the inescapable passion of his life, cricket, and Yorkshire cricket in particular. From his own village the great George Hirst [q.v.], six years older than himself, had already distinguished himself in the Yorkshire XI; Rhodes was determined to follow, but for the time being he had a season with Kirkheaton 1st XI before being appointed professional to the Scottish side of Galashiels, with which he had two successful seasons.

By 1898 there was a vacancy in the Yorkshire side for a slow left-arm bowler, and Rhodes was chosen to fill it. In this season he took 154 wickets and began on the career which over the next thirty-two years made him a record holder of records. No bowler has approached his total of 4,187 wickets, few batsmen have exceeded his aggregate of 39,802 runs. Only his partner George Hirst came near to his record number of sixteen 'doubles', 100 wickets and 1,000 runs in a season, and nobody else has taken 100 wickets in a season on twenty-three occasions. In October 1899, at the end of his second season, Rhodes felt secure enough to marry Sarah Elizabeth Stancliffe, of Kirkheaton; they had one daughter.

The first of his fifty-eight appearances for England was in the first test against Australia in 1899, the last in which W. G. Grace [q.v.] played. On the next Australian tour in 1902 Rhodes and Hirst had the satisfaction of bowling the opposition out in the first test for 36, Rhodes 7 for 17 off 11 overs. The fifth test was the cliff-hanger when G. L. Jessop [q.v.] scored 100 in forty-three minutes to make victory possible; 15 runs were still needed, however, when Rhodes, last man in, joined Hirst in a legendary last wicket partnership. 'Don't worry, Wilf, we'll get 'em in ones', Hirst is alleged to have said, but it seems more likely that no words passed between the two Yorkshiremen and that unlike the spectators Rhodes remained entirely calm. He never knew 'nerves'. And they got the runs.

Rhodes turned his attention to batting, working his way up the order from No. 11 to opener. At Sydney on the 1903–4 tour he shared a record last wicket partnership of 130 with R. E. Foster; at Melbourne in 1911–12 he shared a record opening partnership with Sir Jack Hobbs [q.v.] of 323 in four and a half hours. This record stood for thirty-five years. Throughout this prolific period with the bat before World War I Rhodes never neglected his bowling. He has frequently been described as the greatest all-rounder after Grace.

As a batsman Rhodes may have been pedestrian compared with some of his dashing contemporaries, but he had unlimited patience and a sufficiency of strokes to keep the score moving. Although some of his youthful slimness had gone by his mid-twenties, and he was becoming the ruddy-faced stocky figure, blue-eyed and phlegmatic, who appeared to be a permanent part of the cricketing scene, his opening partnerships with Hobbs were remarkable for the running between wickets, which was brilliantly opportunist, both men equally nimble and swift.

His bowling depended on flight and spin, and deadly nagging accuracy. Off a short economical run, which allowed him to bowl for very long spells, often unchanged throughout an innings, he could tease, tempt, or worry the best batsmen out. His sturdy physique never let him down; the only vulnerable spot was the spinning finger on his left hand.

In 1914 Rhodes did not join up: he was thirty-eight and chose to work in a weapons factory in Huddersfield. When the game was resumed in 1919 he reverted to bowling as his primary function and headed the national bowling averages in 1919, 1920, 1922, and 1923. At the end of the 1921 season it was generally thought that Rhodes had played in his last test match. But when the Australians returned in 1926, Rhodes was recalled for the final test at the Oval when the Ashes were at stake. He was forty-eight. (Sir) Neville Cardus [q.v.] recorded that 'Rhodes at deep third-man did not make a quite decent spectacle'. In the second innings he took 4 for 44 and won the match and the rubber. In consequence England won the Ashes after fourteen years.

In 1929 he toured the West Indies—becoming the oldest test cricketer at fifty-two—but already in his last few seasons as a player his eyesight was failing. He won fifty-eight caps for England, forty-one of them against Australia. On retirement he became coach at Harrow (Hirst had gone to Eton), introducing to the young gentlemen the pungent philosophy of the North—'In Yorkshire we don't play cricket for foon'. When the war came the world was steadily darkening for Rhodes, but he still played golf, gardened, and relaxed at the local Conservative Club. In 1945 glaucoma was diagnosed, and in 1952 he was totally blind after an unsuccessful operation. His wife too was old and infirm: after her death in 1952 he lived with his daughter. He still went to the cricket as a matter of course, 'watching' the game by sound, and generally a group of admirers or old colleagues would gather about him. A reserved, reticent man for most of his life, he now became almost garrulous, ready to entertain anybody prepared to listen to him. He died 8 July 1973 in Broadstone, Dorset, at the age of ninety-five.

[Sidney Rogerson, *Wilfred Rhodes—Professional and Gentleman*, 1960; *The Times*, 9 July 1973; *Wisden Cricketers' Almanack*, 1974.]

PETER SUTCLIFFE

RHYS, JEAN (1890?–1979), writer. [See WILLIAMS, ELLA GWENDOLEN REES.]

RICARDO, SIR HARRY RALPH (1885–1974), mechanical engineer, was born 26 January 1885 at 13 Bedford Square, London, the eldest of three children and only son of Halsey Ralph Ricardo, architect, a descendant of the brother of David Ricardo, economist [q.v.], and his wife, Catherine Jane, daughter of Sir Alexander Meadows Rendel [q.v.], civil engineer. He was educated at Rugby School (1898–1903) and Trinity College, Cambridge. From the age of ten he was using tools and building engines and in his first two terms at Cambridge he built a single-cylinder motor-cycle engine with which he covered forty miles on a quart of petrol, thereby both winning a fuel economy race and bringing himself to the notice of Bertram Hopkinson [q.v.], professor of mechanism and applied mechanics. Hopkinson persuaded Ricardo to spend his four years at Cambridge helping him with some research on the factors limiting the performance of the petrol engine even though it meant reading for an ordinary rather than an honours degree. While at Cambridge Ricardo also designed a two-stroke cycle engine to study the flow of air and gas through the cylinder. A version of this engine named the Dolphin and yielding 15 hp was produced for fishing boats and motor cars by a company started by a cousin.

He obtained his ordinary degree in 1906 and spent a further year researching at Cambridge. In 1907 he joined his grandfather's firm, Rendel & Robertson (later Rendel, Palmer, & Tritton), first as an inspector of machinery, then as head of a department for designing the specialized mechanical equipment needed for large civil engineering projects. At the outbreak of war he was classified in a reserved occupation but military work was slow in coming, although he designed aero-engines made in 1915 by Brotherhood & Beardmore.

His big opportunity came in 1916 with the development of the tank and his appointment as consulting engineer to the Mechanical Warfare Department. He was asked first to explore the willingness of some manufacturers to make a new and more powerful engine and, when they agreed, to undertake its design. The successful design and production of the 150 hp engine and two larger engines giving 225 hp and 300 hp incorporating features for improving combustion turned Ricardo into a professional and gave him the confidence to start his own company. By April 1917 one hundred of his engines were being produced per week, and the two larger engines were developed. In 1918 he became consulting engineer in aero-engines to the Air Ministry.

In July 1917 after the death of his grandfather Ricardo chose to launch his own company with the help of a three-year contract from the Asiatic Petroleum Company for research on fuels and detonation. Apart from this research Ricardo & Company undertook the design of any form of internal combustion or related engine and also offered consulting services. A laboratory designed by his father was built at Shoreham by Sea, Sussex, in 1919 and, except during 1940–5 when they moved to Oxford for security reasons, the company remained at Shoreham. Ricardo communicated his results on the effect of fuel properties to Sir Robert Waley Cohen [q.v.] whose company sponsored the extensive research on fuels and detonation at Shoreham (1918–21). During this contract Ricardo and his team which consisted of (Sir) H. T. Tizard, (Sir) D. R. Pye [qq.v.], and Oliver Thorneycroft, developed the single-cylinder variable compression engine and the concept of the toluene (later octane) number for rating fuels. In 1922 and 1923 Ricardo's *The Internal Combustion Engine* (2 vols.) was published. In later editions the title was *The High-Speed Internal Combustion Engine.*

Ricardo's lifelong contributions to the development of the internal combustion petrol and diesel engine were based on skilful research and outstanding design. His diffident and polite manner concealed great determination and tenacity in the pursuit of technical achievement. Many notable designs were produced over the years including a side-valve engine giving as good performance as the more expensive overhead-valve design, two-stroke and four-stroke cycle diesel engines for automotive and aircraft usage, and sleeve-valve designs for advanced aircraft engines. Most of the world's engine manufacturers used Ricardo's designs at some stage of their history and, after a successful patent case in 1932, paid royalties or consulting fees to the company. In 1939–46 Ricardo was very active in government research and particularly on the sleeve-valve aero-engine. He was a member of the War Cabinet engineering advisory committee (1941–5). He also undertook the design of a governor and fuel control for the first Whittle jet engine. Ricardo published extensively in professional journals and long after he retired (in 1964) kept in touch with engineers, young and old, in the company. *Memories and Machines, the Pattern of my Life* was published in 1968. To this Dictionary he contributed the notice of F. W. Lanchester.

In 1929 he was elected FRS. He was president of the Institution of Mechanical Engineers, 1944–5, and was knighted in 1948. He received honorary degrees from Birmingham (1943), Turin Polytechnic (1960), and Sussex (1970), and an honorary fellowship of Trinity College, Cambridge (1967). He was an honorary member of the British, Dutch, and American mechanical engineering institutions, Manchester College of Technology (1935), and the Deutsche Akademie der Luftfahrtvorschung (1938). He was awarded the Rumford medal of the Royal Society (1944), the Clayton and James Watt (1953) medals of the Institution of Mechanical Engineers, the Lanchester and Crompton medals of the Institution of Automobile Engineers, and medals from the Royal Aeronautical Society, the Institute of Fuel, the Society of Automotive Engineers, USA, and others.

He married in 1911 Beatrice Bertha (died 1975), daughter of Charles Bowdich Hale, their family doctor; she was an art student at the Slade School. They had three daughters. They lived for most of their happy family life near Shoreham, where his hobby was boating, and after 1945 at Woodside, Graffham, in Sussex, where in his ninetieth year Ricardo broke his leg in a fall and died six weeks later, 18 May 1974, at King Edward VII hospital, Midhurst, Sussex.

[Sir Harry Ricardo, *Memories and Machines, the Pattern of my Life*, 1968; Sir William Hawthorne in *Biographical Memoirs of Fellows of the Royal Society*, vol. xxii, 1976; personal knowledge.]

WILLIAM HAWTHORNE

RICHARDS, ARTHUR FREDERICK, first BARON MILVERTON (1885–1978), colonial governor, was born in Bristol 21 February 1885, the second of the four children (all boys) of William Richards, timber merchant, of Bristol, and his wife, Amelia Sophie Elizabeth Orchard. He was educated at Clifton College, winning an open classical scholarship to Christ Church, Oxford, in 1904. A serious illness restricted him to taking a pass degree. He sat the eastern cadetship examination and entered the Malayan Civil Service in 1908. Quickly making his mark as an administrator of conspicuous efficiency, in both field and secretariat posts, he rose steadily and in 1926 became under-secretary to the government of the Federated Malay States. After acting as adviser to the government of Johore in 1929, he was seconded in 1930 as governor of North Borneo, then administered by the Chartered Company.

By now Richards had been singled out by the Colonial Office, and his appointment to his first governorship came in 1933, to The Gambia. Further recognition followed in quick succession (Richards had been given to understand that he need not remain long at Bathurst), with a spell as governor of Fiji and high commissioner for the Western Pacific from 1936 being interrupted, in 1938, by a crisis transfer to the first-class governorship of Jamaica, where the incumbent had died suddenly. The West Indies were then in a state of unrest, and Richards saw his task as that of restoring order to the island. It had been expected that after Fiji he would succeed Sir T. Shenton Thomas [q.v.] in Singapore, a posting dear to his hopes, but the war meant fewer inter-territorial transfers. By the time he concluded his term in Jamaica, not only was Malaya under enemy occupation but Richards was nearing the conventional retiring age. However, his innate talents, added to the political experience gained from the characteristic rough-and-tumble of a grooming Caribbean governorship, persuaded the Colonial Office that it could not afford to let Richards go. He was offered one of the plums of the Service, and in 1943 returned to West Africa as governor of Nigeria.

Exactly why Richards, with his reputation for firm leadership linked to a trenchant tongue and a name for no-nonsense administration, as his decisive government of Jamaica had shown, was selected for the sensitive Nigerian post is still not totally clear. Many (Richards among them) thought he was the right man to rebuild Malaya, shattered by the Japanese occupation, but the Colonial Office felt the task might impose too much strain on an older man. With neither Ceylon nor Kenya vacant, it had, for a governor of Richards's seniority and stature, to be Nigeria or nothing.

Nigeria, whose size and complexity led Richards to describe it as more of an empire than a colony, was already beginning to point its positive way towards post-war evolution. With his usual thoroughness, Richards at once set his own stamp on the level of political advance that he thought best. His dispatches home on what became known as the Richards constitution are typical of the man and his mind, mastering the problems as he saw them and devising incisive solutions to what he believed the shape of politics in Nigeria should be. Whether he gave enough credit to the spadework undertaken by his predecessor, Sir Bernard Bourdillon [q.v.], is a moot point; Richards himself found those ideas too imprecise to accept them as plans. Once again, he saw his role as one of action, not of more minutes on more files. He was never loath to make up his own mind. This brought him into conflict with the emergent political class in Nigeria, who protested against what they called his 'obnoxious ordinances' as well as his refusal to consult Nigerians (Richards later answered that in a country as divided as Nigeria, consultation would only have led to confusion).

On the initiative of its leader, Nnamdi Azikiwe, the nascent National Council for Nigeria and the Cameroons (NCNC) sent a protest delegation to London, but the secretary of state paid them little attention. In the event, the new constitution, envisaged to last nine years, was quickly replaced by Richards's successor, Sir John Macpherson. In retrospect, it is arguable how far Richards's plan to emphasize the essential unity of the country by fully involving the reluctant northern emirs in the constitutional process for the first time, while providing for its underlying diversity through the device of elected regional assemblies in addition to a strong central legislature (originally envisaged on a peripatetic basis, sitting in each regional capital), represented the limit of Nigeria's fragile unitary potential or the irrevocable first step in its subsequent history of creeping federalism.

Richards left Nigeria in 1947. In the same year his outstanding proconsular career was recognized by his elevation to a peerage. Unlike Lords Lugard and Hailey but like Lord Twining [qq.v.], Richards incorporated the name of 'his' African capital into the title of his barony, Lord Milverton, of Lagos and of Clifton in the City of Bristol. His was not the nature to equate retirement from public service with withdrawal from public life. He at once threw himself into political affairs. In the House of Lords his attachment to the Labour Party did not survive its views on nationalization or its handling of the Indonesian question, and in June 1949 he resigned. His association with the Liberals lasted no longer, and within eighteen months he declared for the Conservative Party. Outside Parliament, Milverton showed himself the indefatigable administrator he had ever been. At various times he became a part-time director of the Colonial Development Corporation; director of the Bank of West Africa, the Perak Rubber and Tin Co., and the West Indian Sugar Company; member of the board of governors of Clifton College; chairman of the council of the London School of Hygiene and Tropical Medicine, the Empire Day Movement, the British Leprosy Association, and the Royal African Society; vice-president of the Royal Empire Society; and president of the Association of British Malaya. During the tragic years of the Nigerian civil war, he restored some of the shine to his reputation in Nigeria by speaking out forcefully against secession.

Milverton published only a few, short articles. He excelled as a raconteur and had an enviable memory for quotations. He did not find accessibility easy to practise, preferring to live up to his image of one who spoke his mind, often in sharp epigrams or with a wit tinged with irony. Unwilling to suffer fools gladly, he never disguised his contempt for the glib or hasty and was prouder of being right than popular or fashionable in his views. Sarcasm he knew, but never cynicism. Golf, sailing, snooker, and tennis were among his hobbies, and, to the consternation of his Government House aides, late nights and dawn rising. Appointed CMG in 1933, he was advanced to KCMG in 1935 and GCMG in 1942. In 1927 he married Noelle Benda, daughter of Charles Basil Whitehead, of Torquay, and chief police officer of Province Wellesley, Straits Settlements. They had two sons and one daughter, the barony passing to the elder son, the Revd Fraser Arthur Richard Richards (born 1930) when Milverton died 27 October 1978, at his home in Cox Green, Maidenhead.

[*Colonial Office List*; A. H. M. Kirk-Greene, *Biographical Dictionary of the British Colonial Governor*, 1980; *The Times*, 28 October 1978; interview (tape), Oxford Colonial Records Project, 22 February 1969; *West Africa*, 1948, p. 997, and 1978, p. 2182; memorial service address, 21 February 1979; unpublished biography by R. L. Peel; private information; personal knowledge.] A. H. M. KIRK-GREENE

RICHARDS, CERI GIRALDUS (1903–1971), artist, was born 6 June 1903 at Dunvant near Swansea, the eldest of three children and elder son of Thomas Coslette Richards, tinplate worker, of Preswylfa, Dunvant, and his wife, Sarah Jones. He was educated at Dunvant Council School and Gowerton Intermediate School, and followed an interest in mechanical drawing by a brief apprenticeship to an electrical firm in Morriston. From 1920 to 1924 he studied at Swansea School of Art, and from there won a scholarship to the Royal College of Art (1924–7).

He continued to live in London until 1939, where he became a leading contributor amongst the small group of artists interested in the international modern movement. At the Royal College his skill in drawing had been remarked, and his best works of the early 1930s are rhythmical and confident life and figure drawings. In March 1934 he showed two paintings at the one and only 'Objective Abstractions' exhibition (neither of them abstract), which indicated his distance from the more purely abstract artists gathered around Ben Nicholson. Also in 1934 he began to make pictorial relief constructions assembled from pieces of wood, which were associated at first with a number of drawings of an artist contemplating a piece of abstract sculpture. The abstraction of the figures in the reliefs is comparable to contemporary work by Picasso and Arp which he had seen in reproduction, and which were then also influencing others in London. His early relief constructions were never totally abstract, and the extraordinary variety of material he used implied uniquely ironic references to their figure subjects. He first exhibited these with the 'Surrealist Objects' exhibition at the London Gallery in 1937. He joined the staff of Chelsea College of Art the same year.

In 1939 he moved to Cardiff where he remained during the war, teaching graphic art at Cardiff School of Art. He was commissioned by the Ministry of Information to record tinplate workers in south Wales, and the series of black and white ink drawings that he made both referred to his father's occupation and became a means of developing the rhythms of the relief constructions into a popular and realistic subject.

His response to the poetry of Dylan Thomas [q.v.]—whom he met only once, in 1953—which was in the first place a print commission for *Poetry London* (1947), became the major theme of his post-war work. 'The Cycle of Nature' (of which there are several oil paintings, from 1944) was inspired by Thomas's poem 'The force that through the green fuse' and extends the allusive subjects of the later constructions into an active display of human and botanical sexuality. It led on to associated subjects, notably 'The Rape of the Sabines' and a number of interiors with a woman at a piano, which exploit bright colours and rapid application reminiscent of Matisse, although the decorative surface rhythms are typical of Richards. Following his own illness, and after the death of Dylan Thomas in 1953, another group of works deal with these subjects, including two church commissions, 'The Deposition' (St. Mary's, Swansea, 1958) and 'The Supper at Emmaus' (St. Edmund Hall, Oxford, 1958–9).

Retrospective exhibitions were held at the Whitechapel Art Gallery in 1960, the Venice Biennale in 1962–3, Fischer Fine Art Ltd. in 1972, and, after his death, at the Tate Gallery in 1981. In 1985 there was an exhibition of his work, entitled 'The Lyrical Vision' at the Gillian Jason Gallery in Camden Town, London. During the 1960s he returned to more abstract paintings, and also constructions, often based on Debussy's 'La Cathédrale Engloutie', which he himself played on the piano. Some of these paintings were large, with a technique variously geometrical or painterly, but also with, most importantly, intense and unusual colour harmonies. From the 1950s he continued to work on many of his subjects as lithographs and screen-prints, often working with the Curwen Press. In 1964–5 he designed stained glass for Derby Cathedral and in 1965 was commissioned to design the Blessed Sacrament Chapel at Liverpool Roman Catholic Cathedral, for which he made stained glass, the painted reredos, the tabernacle, and the altar frontal.

Ceri Richards married Frances (died 1985), daughter of John Clayton, kiln fireman at Stoke-on-Trent, in 1929, and had two daughters. They had been contemporaries at the Royal College, and she also became a distinguished painter and graphic artist. Richards was a trustee of the Tate Gallery from 1958 to 1965. He was appointed CBE in 1960 and received an honorary D.Litt. from the University of Wales in 1961. He won the gold medal, Royal National Eisteddfod of Wales, in 1961 and the Einaudi prize for painting at the Venice Biennale of 1962–3. He died in London 9 November 1971.

[David Thompson, *Ceri Richards*, 1963; Roberto Sanesi, *The Graphic Work of Ceri Richards*, 1973, and *Ceri Richards, Rilievi, disegni e dipinti, 1931/1940*, 1976; John Ormond in *Catalogue* of memorial exhibition, National Museum of Wales, 1973; Mel Gooding, *Ceri Richards Graphics*, 1979; Bryan Robertson, introduction in Tate Gallery *Catalogue*, 1981; private information.] A. D. FRASER JENKINS

RICHARDS, IVOR ARMSTRONG (1893–1979), literary critic and writer, was born at Sandbach, Cheshire, 26 February 1893, the third son and third and youngest child of William Armstrong Richards, engineer, and his wife, Mary Ann, daughter of George Haigh, wool manufacturer. He was educated at Clifton College and at Magdalene College, Cambridge, where he read moral sciences. He graduated with a second class in part i in 1915, having lost a year to tuberculosis; the disease recurred in 1916, and he spent a long period of recuperation in north Wales before returning to Cambridge in 1917. His intention was to read medicine as a preparation for training in psychoanalysis, but the Cambridge philosophy of the day, and especially that of G. E. Moore [q.v.], continued to fascinate him; later he was to describe his relationship with Moore as an example of the Complementarity Principle: 'Where there's a hole in him there's a bulge in me'.

Richards was already at this time a mountaineer of great accomplishment, and he even contemplated a career as a professional guide. Later, with his wife, he made several Alpine first ascents, including the north ridge of the Dent Blanche. Another first ascent, of the Picion Epicoun in 1923, was followed by a dangerous night descent of the glacier, memorably recorded in his wife's *Climbing Days* (1935) and in one of Richards's finest poems, 'Hope—to D.E.P. [Mrs. Richards] in hospital . . .'. Richards climbed and walked strenuously, almost until the end of his life, and his reputation among mountaineers always stood very high, especially as an inventor of new routes; he was made an honorary member of the Alpine Club. But his plan to turn professional was forestalled by an invitation to teach for the new Cambridge English tripos, established in 1919.

He published his first book, *The Foundations of Aesthetics*, written in collaboration with D. K. Ogden [q.v.] and James Wood, in 1922; but a more important work, the true foundation of his own career, was *The Meaning of Meaning* (1923), in which he again collaborated with Ogden in a stimulating partnership. This was a remarkable book, extravagant and irreverent but intensely curious, scanning very wide horizons, and terminologically most inventive.

Richards, who offered two courses, one on the theory of criticism and one on the modern novel, soon acquired fame as a teacher. The lectures on criticism led to his first non-collaborative book, *Principles of Literary Criticism* (1925), which inaugurated the modern critical movement. He saw the need, at a time of crisis, for a kind of poetry and a kind of reading that might do the work which formerly fell to religion. He gave more popular expression to his beliefs in a brief book *Science and Poetry* (1926, 2nd edn. revised, 1935), which had a much broader audience, and established him as a potent influence on the young poets of the day.

In 1926 he was elected to a fellowship at Magdalene. As a teacher he showed in the classroom, as on the rocks, a measured audacity; and in the Cambridge of the twenties he developed methods of teaching advanced reading, which he made generally available in *Practical Criticism* (1929). At each meeting of a class he distributed an unfamiliar poem; the students commented in writing; and he subsequently used their remarks to categorize common faults of reading. This may have been the origin of his lifelong passion for cleansing the channels of communication, and removing impediments to the understanding of language at all levels from the highest to the lowest.

The language of poetry, in Richards's view, is always 'overdetermined'; and so it offers the reader his greatest challenge. Ambiguity, he said, was 'the indispensable means of our most important utterances'; if we learned how to deal with it in poetry, that most complex form of communication, we might be on the way to mastering the human world, as science was mastering the physical world. In the 1930s Richards continued to meditate on the language of poetry, notably in *Coleridge on Imagination* (1934) and *The Philosophy of Rhetoric* (1936), which displayed his usual terminological resourcefulness—the description of metaphor in terms of 'tenor' and 'vehicle' has passed into critical currency at least as securely as the 'stock response' of *Principles of Literary Criticism*.

But Richards was already enlarging his pedagogic and corrective programmes. He first visited China in 1927, and in 1929–30 he served as visiting professor at the Tsing Hua University in Peking. A consequence of this visit was the bold and speculative *Mencius on the Mind* (1932), which studied the difficulties of translating Chinese, a language 'not governed by explicit logic', into English. In 1931 Richards returned to Cambridge, where he remained till 1936; but a visit in 1931 had already begun his long association with Harvard. From 1936 to 1938 he was again in China, working for Basic English at the Orthological Institute in Peking. He had now, in his own phrase, 'crossed the railway tracks' into 'elementary education'. *Interpretation in Teaching* (1937) develops methods for teaching the reading of prose, and, though it prospered less, Richards thought it a much more important book than *Practical Criticism*, which was meant for a much smaller and much more privileged audience. As 'the beginning of a vast collective *clinical* study of the aberrations of average intelligence', *Interpretation in Teaching* was an attempt, to be followed by many more, at remedying the almost universal 'incompetence' he saw to be threatening 'the human prospect'.

In 1939, being assured that it was the way in which he could best help the war effort, he exchanged the English Cambridge for the American, becoming a Harvard University professor in 1944, and he remained in that office until he retired in 1963. At Harvard, too, his lectures were renowned though unorthodox. He continued to lecture on poetry, but to 'save the planet' it was necessary to provide the world with an international language; and much of his great energy was henceforth devoted to Basic English. *How to Read a Page* (1943) is a study of a hundred 'great words' (all Basic). He also published a translation into an expanded version of Basic of Plato's *Republic* (1942); *Basic English and its Uses* (1943); and many other books, including *Speculative Instruments* (1955), *Poetries and Sciences*, an extensively revised version of *Science and Poetry* (1970), and *Complementarities* (1973). Richards also experimented with the use of radio and television for mass education in communication, and edited many language-learning booklets.

His lifelong preoccupation with language and poetry had one unexpected and welcome consequence: in his sixty-fifth year he commenced poet, with *Goodbye Earth, and Other Poems* (1958). *The Screens* followed in 1960, and a collected poems (with plays), *Internal Colloquies*, in 1972. The verse is very distinctive, owing little to any recent school but much to Richards's own lifelong thinking about poetry. It is often gnarled and tortuous: 'around every phrase—behind, on all sides, and ahead—there are other phrases: ready to complete or support, or recklessly bent on having their own way', he remarked. Another interest of his later years was drama; his first play, *A Leak in the Universe*, was presented by the Poet's Theatre in 1956, and he followed it with *Tomorrow Morning, Faustus!* (1962) and *Why so, Socrates?*, a dramatization of Plato, in 1964.

An honorary LL D of Cambridge (1977) and Litt.D. of Harvard (1944), Richards was made an honorary fellow of Magdalene and CH in 1964. He received the Loines award for poetry in 1962, and the Emerson–Thoreau medal of the American Academy of Arts and Sciences in 1970.

In 1926 Richards married Dorothy Eleanor, daughter of John J. Pilley, science master at Alleyn's School, Dulwich. There were no children. In 1974 Richards and his wife returned to live in Cambridge, though they spent some months of each year in Cambridge, Massachusetts. In 1979 Richards accepted an invitation to revisit China, where he taught in the universities and continued the struggle for Basic. He fell ill there; the Chinese government flew him to England, and he died at Cambridge 7 September 1979.

[*The Times*, 23 November 1979; *Cambridge Review*, 14 December 1979; John Paul Russo in *Critical Inquiry*, summer 1979; Reuben Brower, Helen Vendler, and John Hollander (eds.), *I. A. Richards: Essays in his Honor*, 1973; private information; personal knowledge.]

FRANK KERMODE

RICHARDSON, ALAN (1905–1975), dean of York, was born in Highfield, Wigan, 17 October 1905, the younger son of William Richardson, company director, and his wife, Anne Moss. He was educated at Ashfield High School, Wigan, and Liverpool University, where he took first class honours in philosophy in 1927. After preparing at Ridley Hall, Cambridge, for ordination (1927–8), he became inter-collegiate secretary of the Student Christian Movement in Liverpool (1928–31), and in 1931 chaplain of Ripon Hall, Oxford, also taking a first in theology at Oxford in 1933.

From 1934 to 1938 he was vicar of Cambo, a sparsely populated rural parish in Northumberland. In 1938 he returned to the staff of the SCM as study secretary and editor, before becoming a canon residentiary of Durham in 1943. Ten years later he succeeded to the chair of Christian theology at Nottingham University. These were to be some of his happiest days. The department grew in range and influence. Richardson was noted for his accessibility and lack of pomp. He played a large part in university life, and was dean of arts in 1962–4. His home was a centre of hospitality for staff, students, and distinguished visitors. He demonstrated that the place of theology in the university went far beyond the training of ordinands; it was a central, humanistic intellectual discipline in its own right, and the basis of a sound general education.

In 1964 he became dean of York, but almost immediately suffered the first of what were to be a number of heart attacks, which were to slow him, but the effects of which he bore with courage, taking care but making no fuss. It was soon discovered that York Minster was in imminent danger of collapse owing to the fall in the level of the water table because of the growth of York. The Minster had literally to be re-founded. The engineering works needed required the raising of over £2 million. Richardson had the wisdom to seek the best advice and secure the best people for each job, and with their combined efforts that money was raised and the Minster saved and improved. Richardson's establishment of the York Glaziers' Trust made it a leading European centre of stained glass restoration and conservation. His achievements were recognized when he was appointed KBE in 1973. In the midst of this work, as at Nottingham, he was noted for the calmness and peaceableness he exemplified and created around him.

Throughout his life academic work continued. His many books and writings reflect the range of his scholarship, from biblical studies, the history of ideas, and the philosophy of history, to contemporary theology and apologetics. He was an extremely lucid lecturer and writer both at a scholarly and a popular level. Several of his books were reprinted many times, and translated into up to ten languages. Among the best known were *Christian Apologetics* (1947), *An Introduction to the Theology of the New Testament* (1958), and *History Sacred and Profane* (1964). All but two were published by the SCM Press, of which he was chairman from 1957 to 1973 and to which he gave a great deal of care.

His connection with the SCM led him to have a large number of friends in different confessional traditions from an early age, and made the ecumenical movement his constant concern. He was a frequent participator in ecumenical meetings before and after the formation of the World Council of Churches in 1948. After the second Vatican Council Roman Catholic links developed, particularly with Ampleforth Abbey. Richardson lectured and preached all over the world, and was one of the two or three best-known Anglican theologians of his day. His aim was to expound the Christian faith as a convincing understanding of human life amid the intellectual heterogeneity of the twentieth century. He moved from a position akin to that of Anglican Modernism of the 1930s to what was known as 'Biblical Theology', with which he came too neatly to be associated, for he was never the kind of 'neo-orthodox' to whom the term 'liberal' was merely one of condemnation, and he maintained the traditional Anglican position of seeking to understand and maintain the use of 'right reason' in theology. However, in spite of his philosophical training he distanced himself from the current positivist and analytical preoccupations of Anglo-Saxon philosophy, whilst the problems of York did not give him the opportunity to come to terms with the collapse of Biblical Theology by the 1960s. He gained the DD of Oxford in 1947, and the honorary degrees of DD (Glasgow) in 1952 and D.Univ. (York) in 1973.

In 1933 he married Phyllis Mary, third child of William Alfred Parkhouse, company director of Blundellsands, who identified himself with his work in every way and made notable contributions to it, particularly at York. There were no children. Richardson died after the end of evensong, 23 February 1975, in the Minster from which he had intended to retire later in the year. There is no portrait, only a very large photograph in the Castle Museum, York.

[*The Times*, 24 February and 3 March 1975; R. H. Preston (ed.), *Theology and Change*, 1975 (with memoir and bibliography); *Ampleforth Journal*, summer 1975; private information; personal knowledge.] RONALD PRESTON

RIDEAL, SIR ERIC KEIGHTLEY (1890–1974), physical chemist and colloid scientist, was born 11 April 1890 at Sydenham, Kent, the eldest in the family of four children (three sons and a daughter) of Samuel Rideal, public analyst, remembered for the Rideal–Walker test for disinfectants, and his wife, Elizabeth ('Lilla'), daughter of Samuel Keightley, JP, of Bangor, county Down. He was educated at Farnham Grammar School and Oundle. In 1907 he entered Trinity Hall, Cambridge, with an open scholarship in natural sciences. He graduated with first class honours in both parts of the tripos (1910 and 1911). It was a lecturer in physiology, (Sir) William Bate Hardy [q.v.], who kindled his interest in surface chemistry. For research he went to Aachen, transferring to Bonn to complete his Ph.D. thesis on the electrochemistry of uranium in 1912, for which he received the gold medal of the Bonn Society of Engineers (1913). He returned to England to enter his father's Westminster consulting practice and the outbreak of war in 1914 found him dealing with water supply problems in Ecuador.

Returning to England Rideal joined the Artists' Rifles and, after a spell of work on respirators, was transferred to the Royal Engineers as a captain, to supervise water supplies to Australian troops on the Somme. Invalided out in 1916, he joined the nitrogen research laboratory at University College, London, where a team under J. A. Harker was working on the Haber process. Here he collaborated with (Sir) H. S. Taylor on catalyst development, and in their spare time the two scientists wrote *Catalysis in Theory and Practice* (1919). Rideal's war work earned him appointment as MBE (1918).

In 1919 he was appointed visiting professor at the University of Illinois where he made contact with the leading American physical chemists and developed a lifelong interest in the USA. While returning by ship in 1920 he met Margaret ('Peggy') Atlee (died 1964), daughter of Philip Nye Jackson, financier, of Princeton, New Jersey, and widow of William Agnew Paton, a Princeton professor. They married in 1921 and had one daughter, Mary, who married Lord Justice Oliver. The Rideals settled in Cambridge, at Thorndyke on the Huntingdon Road, where Rideal could indulge his interest in gardening.

In 1920 Rideal had been appointed H. O. Jones lecturer in physical chemistry and a fellow of Trinity Hall in Cambridge. Here in the department of T. M. Lowry [q.v.] he built up a large, broadly based research group, covering electrochemistry, heterogeneous catalysis, colloid and surface chemistry, and kinetics spectroscopy. The first of his many research students, R. G. W. Norrish [q.v.] (joint Nobel prize-winner in 1967), described Rideal as 'bubbling with ideas, good and bad, but not strong on experimental detail, leaving the working out of his ideas to the (hopeful) ingenuity of his students, by whom he was much loved'. So it continued throughout a long life.

In 1930 Rideal was elected FRS and made professor of colloid science, with his own laboratory of some 9,000 square feet in Free School Lane. Here in the years up to 1939 much progress was made in studying gas adsorption and catalysis, insoluble monolayers on water, and polymerization kinetics. During the war of 1939–45 the laboratory was largely devoted to classified work, on explosives, fuels, polymers, and other topics, and was a hive of industry.

In 1946 Rideal left Cambridge (with an honorary fellowship at Trinity Hall), on accepting the Fullerian professorship and directorship of the Davy–Faraday laboratory at the Royal Institution in London. Here he built up another thriving research laboratory, but finding the social duties onerous, he resigned in 1949. In 1950 he was appointed professor of physical chemistry at King's College, London, where in somewhat cramped conditions he assembled for the third time a large and active group of surface chemists. In 1955 came retirement, and he transferred to the chemistry department at Imperial College as senior research fellow. He continued active research and writing until 1974.

Rideal was knighted in 1951, and in the same year gave the Bakerian lecture to the Royal Society and received its Davy medal. He was elected a fellow of King's College, London, in 1963. He had honorary degrees from Dublin (1951), Birmingham (1955), Belfast (1960), Turin (1962), Bonn (1963), and Brunel (1967). During 1953–8 he was chairman of the advisory council on scientific research and technical development of the Ministry of Supply. He served terms as president of the Faraday Society, Society of Chemical Industry, and the Chemical Society. He published some 300 papers and eight books. He died 25 September 1974 in a nursing home at 20 Fitzjames Avenue, London W14.

[D. D. Eley in *Biographical Memoirs of Fellows of the Royal Society*, vol. xxii, 1976; *The Times*, 27 September 1974; private information; personal knowledge.] D. D. ELEY

RIEU, EMILE VICTOR (1887–1972), editor and translator, was born in London 10 February 1887, the seventh and youngest child and fifth son of Charles Pierre Henri Rieu, of Geneva, keeper of oriental MSS at the British Museum and later professor of Arabic at Cambridge, and of his wife, Agnes, daughter of Julius Heinrich Hisgen, of Utrecht. He held scholarships at St. Paul's School and Balliol College, Oxford, and took a first in classical honour moderations (1908). After a year's travel abroad for health reasons he left Oxford. He joined the Oxford University Press in 1910 and in 1912 was appointed manager in India to open a branch in Bombay. In 1914 he married Nelly, daughter of Henry Thomas Lewis, business man, of Pembrokeshire; they had two sons and two daughters.

He was commissioned in the 105th Mahratta Light Infantry in 1918, but returned to his work in Bombay in 1919 and left India the same year after repeated attacks of malaria. In 1923 he became educational manager of Methuen & Co. and held the post with distinction until he was made managing director in 1933. There he was less happy, resigning in 1936, though he remained an academic and literary adviser to the firm, and returned to full-time work in 1940. He also served as a major in the Home Guard from 1944.

Only after 1936 could he truly fulfil his promise as a classical scholar, though he had edited a well-chosen anthology (*A Book of Latin Poetry*) for Methuens in 1925. He formed the habit of translating aloud to his wife, and her interest in the Odyssey encouraged him to start polishing and writing his version. After the interruptions of the war years he offered it to (Sir) Allen Lane [q.v.], who published it in 1946 (early copies misdated 1945) as the first of a new series, Penguin Classics in translation, which Rieu edited until his retirement in 1964. By then the translations numbered two hundred, and *The Odyssey* had sold over two million copies.

Rieu went on to translate Virgil's *The Pastoral Poems* (1949), *The Iliad* (1950), *The Four Gospels* (1952), and Apollonius Rhodius, *The Voyage of Argo* (1959). All exemplified his firm belief that translation should be into contemporary but not too topical prose, readily intelligible to all, not only to scholars of the original. His *Odyssey* won greatest fame, but he continued to receive letters from readers of *The Four Gospels* after publication of *The New English Bible*, on the committee for which he served.

He also wrote light verse in the best English tradition: *Cuckoo Calling* was published in 1933 and reissued with additional poems in 1962 as *The Flattered Flying Fish, and Other Poems*; a selection was included in *A Puffin Quartet of Poets* in 1958. His output was modest but his craftsmanship was meticulous, providing the right medium for his fanciful humour and imaginative sympathy for children and small animals.

Rieu took unaffected pleasure in the public honours of his later years, perhaps as the result of his early academic disappointment. He was made an honorary Litt.D. (Leeds) in 1949, and appointed CBE in 1953, and was happy in his recognition by the Royal Society of Literature of which he was a fellow from 1951, vice-president in 1958, and recipient of the Benson silver medal in 1968. He was also president of the Virgil Society in 1951 and was awarded the Golden Jubilee medal of the Institute of Linguists in 1971.

He had sometimes appeared stiff and uneasy in business relations, but became more relaxed and genial as the Penguin Classics enabled him to realize his gift for independent editing. He was sure of his purpose, and won his translators' affection for his personal encouragement and their appreciation of his sound critical judgement. 'Write English' was his advice on how to translate, and 'Read it aloud' as a test whether the written English was free from obscurity, translationese, outdated phrasing, and current slang. He had a sensitive ear for a well-turned sentence (Jane Austen was a favourite author), and anyone who supposed that plain prose was easily written was soon disillusioned, though always with courtesy and understanding.

Rieu had been a runner and a rugby footballer at school and college, and listed his recreations as carpentry, mountains, and petrology. His delight in verbal wit and paradox was matched by his relish for a schoolboyish pun or joke, but beneath a lightly humorous manner lay his basically serious views. He could seem very much an Englishman of his generation in his affection for British institutions and in some of his prejudices, though the Rieu family, French in origin, was settled in Protestant Switzerland; he was proud to be both a British subject and a citizen of Geneva, and liked to recall that his grandfather had fought in Napoleon's army.

Rieu died in his London home 11 May 1972.

[*The Times*, 13 May 1972; private information; personal knowledge.] BETTY RADICE

RITCHIE, SIR JOHN NEISH (1904–1977), veterinarian, was born 19 January 1904 in Turriff, Aberdeenshire, the youngest of three sons in a family of five children of John Neish Ritchie, a general merchant of Schoolhill, Turriff, and his wife, Annie Watson, who was for some time a governess in Australia. He was educated at Turriff Higher Grade School and in 1921 went to study at the Royal (Dick) Veterinary College and Edinburgh University. He graduated as a veterinary surgeon in 1925, obtained the Diploma of Veterinary State Medicine in 1926, and graduated with a B.Sc. from the university in 1927.

He became interested in veterinary public health and joined the veterinary department of the city of Edinburgh in 1927. There he remained until 1929 when he became the chief veterinary officer of the county of Midlothian (1929–35). In 1935 he served as senior veterinary officer with the Scottish Office in the Department of Agriculture advising on animal health and played an important part in promoting a scheme to eradicate tuberculosis in dairy cattle (1935–8).

In 1938 he joined the staff of the animal health division of the Ministry of Agriculture and worked in many areas in the United Kingdom. He was promoted to be chief veterinary officer (CVO) in London in 1952 and retired in 1965.

During this period he had ample opportunity to apply schemes of disease eradication in domestic animals. His epizootic interests widened and he became involved in planning the control of the infectious diseases of domestic animals on a global scale and particularly in Europe. He took a great interest in veterinary education and served on the council of the Royal College of Veterinary Surgeons (the body responsible for education and discipline in the profession) from 1951 to 1970 and was president from 1959 to 1961. He advised the University Grants Committee on the development of veterinary disciplines within the universities. He played a major part in organizing the eradication of tuberculosis from the national herd and the entire country was virtually free of this scourge before he retired. He served on the governing bodies of a number of academic and research institutes including Houghton Poultry Research Station, the Pirbright Animal Virus Disease Institute, and Wye Agricultural College of the University of London. He chaired the veterinary advisory committee of the Horse Race Betting Levy Board in 1961–73. He also served as a member of the Agricultural Research Council from 1954 to 1973, and played a prominent part in its animals committee.

During his time as CVO his interests in veterinary epizootology became global; he was chairman of the European Commission for the Control of Foot and Mouth Disease and chaired an expert panel on veterinary education for the Food and Agriculture Organization/World Health Organization at a time when the developing countries were beginning to train their own veterinarians. During this time he visited many of these countries to advise on programmes on disease control, preventive medicine, and technical and higher education.

In 1965 he accepted an offer to become dean and principal of the Royal Veterinary College in the University of London and continued there until he retired in 1970. He was interested in promoting postgraduate studies in the college, particularly in veterinary public health and preventive medicine. He also continued his overseas interests in disease control and education in many parts of the world and his work was recognized in Britain and abroad: he was appointed CB in 1955 and knighted in 1961. He received three honorary degrees: D.V.Sc. (Liverpool, 1961), LL D (Toronto, 1962), and LL D (Edinburgh, 1965). He became an honorary fellow of the RCVS (1955). He was elected a fellow of the Royal Society of Edinburgh in 1957.

He numbered among his wide circle of friends people from many parts of the world and from all walks of life. He had a talent for friendship and a pawky sense of humour characteristic of his birthplace. He was very much a family man and enjoyed his return to country life. He and his wife never lost their love of the north-east and he retired to St. Brandons in the High Street in Banff. He became an honorary sheriff of the county of Banff (1973), was active in the church, and became an elder in Trinity and Alvah church in Banff. He was treasurer of Banff Preservation Society. He continued his interest in painting and antiques.

In 1930 he married Florina Margaret Drummond (died 1975), a private nurse, daughter of William Drummond, farmer in Aberdeenshire. They had two sons and two daughters. Ritchie died 28 September 1977 in Forresterhill Hospital, Aberdeen.

[Private information; personal knowledge.]

WILLIAM L. WEIPERS

ROBERTS, THOMAS D'ESTERRE (1893–1976), Roman Catholic archbishop of Bombay, was born in Le Havre 7 March 1893, the second son and seventh of nine children of William d'Esterre Roberts, who had moved to France after ill health had caused his early retirement from the Consular Service, and his wife (who was also his cousin), Clara Louise Roberts. William Roberts, of Huguenot stock, became a Catholic in 1900, shortly before his death in 1901. At the semi-nautical Dominican boarding-school of St. Elme, near Bordeaux, Thomas Roberts began to develop his lifelong love of the sea. After his father's death the family settled in Liverpool. In 1909, a year after moving, at his own request, from Parkfield School to St. Francis Xavier's College, Thomas entered the Jesuit novitiate at Manresa House, Roehampton.

Ordained priest in 1925, Roberts taught at Preston Catholic College and Beaumont College, returning to Liverpool in 1935 as rector of St. Francis Xavier's. There, on 3 August 1937, he received a telephone call from the *Liverpool Post* which provoked him to cable the Vatican: 'Newspapers appoint me Archbishop of Bombay.

Kindly comment'. He held the post from 1937 to 1950.

The controversial style of his later years has obscured the significance of his work in Bombay. The *padroado* system (giving Portugal rights of episcopal appointment) had for generations caused divisions between Goan and British-Indian Catholics. Roberts's first step towards reconciliation was to visit Lisbon and talk to the Portuguese. In his diocese, his down-to-earth solution to the problem of how to influence entrenched attitudes without arousing antagonism was to appeal to adults through children: he bought two tiny crocodiles which, as Jickey and Joe, became the focus of wise and humorous 'Letters to Children' in the diocesan newspaper.

In Bombay, Roberts established centres where seamen could stay while in port; organized a range of social services for the poor, orphans, and prostitutes; and established (against stiff opposition) a university hall for women. During World War II he was appointed bishop for the armed forces in India.

But it is for the way he relinquished his ministry that Roberts especially deserves a place in the history of the church in India. Becoming convinced that his successor, in an independent India, must be Indian, he persuaded Pope Pius XII to break with the custom of alternating English and Portuguese archbishops of Bombay. In 1946, granted leave of absence while his Indian auxiliary gained experience, he began to travel, give retreats, even sign on as a crew member in an oil-tanker. On 18 July 1950 the concordat was terminated, the *padroado* became a dead letter, and Roberts returned to Bombay to hand over full control to Archbishop (later Cardinal) Valerian Gracias.

In retirement in England, as titular Archbishop of Sygdea, he settled into the life of an ordinary Jesuit. The simplicity, forthrightness, and humanity with which, as in India, he responded to pastoral questions soon gave him a reputation for 'dangerous' outspokenness. The publication in 1954 of *Black Popes: Authority, its Use and Abuse* reinforced this reputation, as did his association with the Campaign for Nuclear Disarmament (CND). His consequent sense of isolation was exacerbated when, in 1960, the apostolic delegate formally complained to Rome of his 'indiscretions'. No inquiry followed but Roberts felt institutionally (rather than personally) betrayed upon hearing from a Vatican official, two years later, that inactivity signified acquittal.

He attended the second Vatican Council (1962–5) and, although not called to speak, he influenced its statement on conscientious objection.

It was, however, for opening up the debate on contraception that he acquired greatest notoriety. In an article published in 1964 he said that the position taken by the Lambeth conference could not be refuted by reason alone. This drew a statement from the English hierarchy which Roberts countered, in the *Evening Standard*, with 'My Answer to Doctor Heenan'. The vigorous debate that ensued within the Catholic community did much to destroy stereotyped perceptions of lay passivity and uniform clerical paternalism.

Roberts was a strong man. Thickset and careless of his appearance, his humour and warmth were reflected in numerous anecdotes. Unswervingly loyal to his church, he never confused fidelity with conformity. The contraception debate was but a symptom of his overriding concern, which, coming from a bishop, unsettled some but encouraged others, that authority be set at the service of conscience. His was the radicalism not of innovative speculation but of sturdy common sense. He died in London 28 February 1976. Eleven bishops, including the apostolic delegate, were among the large congregation at his requiem at Farm Street on 8 March. B. C. Butler, auxiliary bishop to the archbishop of Westminster, who was closely associated with Roberts at the second Vatican Council, gave the address.

[David Abner Hurn, *Archbishop Roberts S.J.*, 1966; private information; personal knowledge.] NICHOLAS LASH

ROBERTS, WILLIAM PATRICK (1895–1980), painter, was born in London 5 June 1895, the third of four children (a daughter and three sons) of Edward Roberts, carpenter, and his wife, Emma Collins. Roberts left school at the age of fourteen and became apprenticed to the commercial art firm of Sir Joseph Causton Ltd., also attending evening classes at St. Martin's School of Art. After a year he won an LCC scholarship to the Slade School where he studied from 1910 to 1913 and where his fellow pupils included E. A. Wadsworth, C. R. W. Nevinson, Mark Gertler, D. G. Bomberg, (Sir) Stanley Spencer, and Paul Nash [qq.v.], who like him were to play a major role in establishing Post-Impressionism in Britain. By the end of 1913, soon after leaving the Slade, he had begun to paint in a Cubist style, with stylized, angular figures and a shallow picture space. After working for several months in 1913–14 in the Omega Workshops of Roger Fry [q.v.], decorating table tops, lampshades, and the like, he joined the rebel group of P. Wyndham Lewis [q.v.], Wadsworth, and Frederick Etchells who had earlier left the workshops in protest against Fry's management. This group became soon afterwards the nucleus of the Vorticist movement: Roberts was among the artists represented in the Vorticist exhibition at the Doré Galleries in June-July 1915. His principal works of this period have unfortunately disappeared, but it is clear from photographs and surviving studies that his Vorticist style was sometimes almost abstract.

Enrolled as a gunner in the Royal Field Artillery in March 1916 he saw active service in France, then was recalled in April 1918 as an official war artist to paint a large picture of 'The First German Gas Attack at Ypres' for the Canadian War Records Office. While still working on this, he also began another large painting of 'A Shell Dump, France' for the Ministry of Information. These works, which required a more realistic treatment, led him to move away from Cubism. By the early 1920s, he had evolved his characteristic style based on the human figure and, above all, on groups of people engaged in some specific activity such as playing chess, sunbathing, or riding bicycles; the kind of scene which is an everyday sight in the parts of London where he lived (particularly in the region of Camden Town and Regent's Park). There is a strong element of humorous observation and the grotesque, for instance in the grimacing faces and gesticulating hands, but this is combined with a classical concern with design and structure, so that every form has a firm outline and the design spreads right out to the edges of the picture. From time to time he also made a few works on traditional religious or classical themes, or inspired by T. E. Lawrence [q.v.] and the Arabs: he had met Lawrence and was one of those who contributed illustrations to the first edition of his *Seven Pillars of Wisdom* published in 1926.

In 1925 he became a visiting teacher at the Central School, where he continued to teach, apart from the war years, until 1960. Shortly after the outbreak of war in 1939, he moved to Oxford, where he remained until 1945, living mainly at Marston on the outskirts of the city (which inspired a few paintings and water-colours of rural scenes). Then in 1948 he began to exhibit at the Royal Academy, where he showed regularly each year from then on; a practice which led him to produce a series of large figure compositions, elaborate set pieces, such as 'Trooping the Colour' and 'The Vorticists at the Restaurant de la Tour Eiffel: Spring 1915'. He was elected ARA in 1958 and RA in 1966. There was a large retrospective exhibition of his work in 1965 at the Tate Gallery, which owns fourteen oils by him and six drawings.

In 1956, incensed by the exhibition *Wyndham Lewis and Vorticism* at the Tate Gallery and Lewis's claim to have influenced the other Vorticists, he published the first of a series of polemical pamphlets, later known as *The Vortex Pamphlets*, in which he revealed a lively pen and an ironic sense of humour; these were later followed by several further booklets, also published by himself, with photographs of his own works and introductory texts.

A short, ruddy-complexioned man, he often gave the impression to outsiders of being exceptionally withdrawn and silent. In 1922 he married Sarah, daughter of Max Kramer, painter, and a sister of the Leeds painter Jacob Kramer. She provided him with a very understanding and supportive home life and also served as model for most of his portraits. They had one son. Roberts died in London 20 January 1980.

[William Roberts, *The Vortex Pamphlets 1956–8*, 1958; William Roberts, *Early Years* (privately published, 1982); *Daily Telegraph*, 31 January 1980; personal knowledge.]

RONALD ALLEY

ROBERTSON, ANDREW (1883–1977), engineer and educationist, was born 30 January 1883 at Fleetwood, Lancashire, the youngest in the family of five sons and one daughter of James Robertson, marine engineer, of Fleetwood, and his wife Elizabeth, daughter of another Robertson family. Andrew Robertson was apprenticed, at the age of fourteen, in his father's engineering works, where he remained for five years. He was admitted to Owens College, Manchester, in 1902 to read engineering. He obtained his degree in 1905 with first class honours, a Fairbairn engineering prize, and a graduate scholarship. He became a demonstrator and a resident tutor at Dalton Hall, taking his M.Sc. degree in 1909 and winning a Vulcan research fellowship in 1913. At this time Robertson began, with Gilbert Cook, who was to become a lifelong friend, the first of his two major investigations, the behaviour of mild steel as it was strained from the elastic to the plastic state; for this he received the D.Sc. degree in 1915.

World War I took Robertson to the Royal Aircraft Establishment, Farnborough, where he became chief assistant in the newly established materials testing department. One of Robertson's responsibilities was the determination of the strength of struts and in 1925 he published an important paper on this subject. His results, in which the imperfections of the member are represented by an initial curvature, were soon adopted by the structural steel industry and became part of standard practice. He rose to the rank of major.

In 1919 he was appointed to the chair of mechanical and mining engineering in the University of Bristol. The organization there was unusual. The university faculty had been set up in the Merchant Venturers' Technical College, the principal of which, Julius Vertheimer, had been made a professor in the university and permanent dean of the faculty.

In 1924 Vertheimer died suddenly and Robertson, the youngest of his professors, was, surprisingly, elected dean and principal. Many must have hoped that the union between the university and the college would have been broken at this juncture but this did not happen. Perhaps the support of the influential Society of Merchant Venturers was so valuable that the university preferred to let the arrangement stand. The new dean almost certainly enjoyed the power that had so unexpectedly come to him, but he used it fairly in the interests of both the organizations for which he had become responsible. Though a somewhat stern and forbidding exterior gave a different impression, he was far too kind and wise a man to allow his unsought power to turn him into a dictator.

His service to the university down the years was immense. He was most successful in filling the chairs of engineering with able men. He it was who persuaded the university to build in the period of recession between the wars. Two magnificent halls of residence, Wills Hall and Manor Hall, were his particular pride but he advised and supported the vice-chancellor in every department of administration. His last major work was the design of Queen's Building into which he moved the university faculty of engineering. He retired from his chair in 1946 and from the headship of the Merchant Venturers' College in 1949.

Robertson was active in industry as a designer of machines and as a consultant. He became a member of the Clifton Suspension Bridge Trust in 1935 and, having become deputy chairman and chairman of the technical committee, served until 1970, being responsible for organizing the strengthening of the bridge chain anchorages—but no detail was too small to receive his attention. He was elected a fellow of the Royal Society in 1940 and was president of the Institution of Mechanical Engineers in 1945–6. The University of Bristol gave him the rare distinction of an honorary fellowship in 1949 and an honorary LL D in 1959. He was honorary D.Sc. of the University of Bath (1969).

Though Robertson published his last scientific paper in 1928 and was responsible for only two major researches, they continue to be basic to all designs of steel structures and machines. He was a great engineer, alert and active to the last.

Before leaving Manchester, Robertson married Mabel Bailey (died 1960). She supported him in all his activities including his fell walking. They had no children of their own but many godchildren whose progress in life they followed with interest and to whom they were most generous. Robertson died in Bristol 22 October 1977.

[Sir Alfred Pugsley in *Biographical Memoirs of Fellows of the Royal Society*, vol. xxiv, 1978; personal knowledge.] BAKER

ROBERTSON, BRIAN HUBERT, first BARON ROBERTSON OF OAKRIDGE (1896–1974), general, was born at Simla, India, 22 July 1896, the eldest of the four children (there were subsequently two daughters and a son who died at the age of eighteen) of (Sir) William Robert Robertson [q.v.], later first baronet and field-marshal, and his wife, Mildred Adelaide, daughter of Lt.-Gen. Charles Thomas Palin, of the Indian Army. A scholar of Charterhouse, he passed through the Royal Military Academy, Woolwich, and was commissioned in the Royal Engineers in 1914. He served in France (1914–19), winning the MC and three mentions in dispatches and being appointed to the DSO, and then joined King George's Own Bengal Sappers and Miners at Peshawar. He took part in the Waziristan expedition (1922–3) and was again mentioned in dispatches. As a brevet-major, he attended the Staff College, Camberley, in 1926–7 and then joined the staff of the disarmament conference in Geneva.

In 1935 he was offered the appointment of managing director of Dunlop, South Africa. Judging that this might provide a greater challenge and more rapid promotion, with employment to the age of sixty-five rather than an earlier retirement 'perhaps as a major-general', he accepted, commenting to a friend that if a war broke out he would return to the army. This first step in widening his experience was to lead to an outstanding career of great versatility as an administrator, diplomat, and general.

As an industrialist from 1935 to 1940 he was successful in management and external relations, and he became friendly with J. C. Smuts [q.v.]. In 1940 he was recalled as a reserve officer in the South African forces. A year later his talents as an administrator became apparent; in organizing the difficult logistic support of the forces in Italian Somaliland, Abyssinia, and Eritrea he won high praise. Then in North Africa he became brigadier in charge of administration, Eighth Army. There he met the exacting requirements of General Bernard Montgomery (later Viscount Montgomery of Alamein, q.v.) over an immensely long line of communication. His rapid improvisation when, unexpectedly, the port of Benghazi was seriously blocked, demonstrated his quick, determined reaction to an emergency.

In 1944, after the capture of Sicily, he became chief administrative officer (lieutenant-general) to Field-Marshal Sir H. R. L. G. Alexander (later Earl Alexander of Tunis, q.v.), C-in-C Allied forces in Italy. There the more complex problems of an international force were managed smoothly and successfully. His firm but courteous handling of Americans was masterly; on all sides he was recognized as an outstanding military administrator.

In 1945, though invited back to Dunlop Ltd., he became deputy military governor to Field-Marshal Montgomery, and later to Marshal of the Royal Air Force Sir W. S. Douglas (later Lord Douglas of Kirtleside, q.v.), in the British zone of Germany. Thereby he was restored to the active list of the British Army. In 1947 he became C-in-C and military governor (as his father had been in 1918), and in 1949–50 he was seconded to become UK commissioner in the Allied High Commission. Thus for five years he was the military administrator responsible for restoring the economic, social, and political life of the heartland of Western Germany.

He was a forceful interpreter of British policy and a trusted guardian of British interests, dominating from the start the diplomatic proceedings of the Allied Commission, where his colleagues, including the Russians, recognized his lucid intellect, negotiating skill, and manifest integrity. He made a profound impression on Ernest Bevin [q.v.], who invited from him a personal letter every week. Robertson's cool judgement and skilled diplomacy helped the western powers through many dangers created by the cold war tactics of the Soviet Union, notably their attempt to blockade Berlin which, with his American colleagues, he countered successfully by the Berlin airlift.

His relations with the Germans evolved with the development of British policy, on which he exerted a powerful influence. Firm but compassionate in the initial phase as the representative of the occupying power, he moved later to the role of a liberal and sympathetic 'viceroy' intent on guiding the social and democratic advancement of a future ally. He gained the respect of German politicians and trade unions and, eventually, he won the admiration and lasting friendship of Konrad Adenauer, who spoke of him as a great British 'soldier statesman'. For the remainder of his life, Robertson worked devotedly to foster Anglo–German relations.

In 1950 he became C-in-C Middle East land forces. Anglo–Egyptian relations were difficult, but the military problems including the emergence of Mau Mau were comparatively simple. Though successful, Robertson never became a well-known, popular military commander. Having followed in his father's footsteps in the Rhine Army, he aspired with some encouragement to become chief of the imperial general staff, but that door was closed to him. Though selected to become adjutant-general, he retired from the army in 1953 to become chairman of the British Transport Commission.

For over seven years, controlling an immense and run-down industrial undertaking, he was under insistent but diverse political pressures. Although a modernization plan was promulgated in 1955, consistent long-term ministerial policy was lacking. Despite this, he coped with unceasing criticism, much of it unfair, while struggling to implement the directives of successive masters. Nevertheless, he won the deep respect of railwaymen and trade-union leaders. In 1961 he was created Baron Robertson of Oakridge.

In 1933 he had succeeded his father in the baronetcy. In addition to his DSO and MC, he was appointed CBE (1942), CB (1943), KCVO (1944), KCMG (1947), GBE (1949), and GCB (1952). He was ADC general to King George VI 1949–52 and then to Queen Elizabeth II. He was a colonel commandant of the Royal Engineers and of the Royal Electrical and Mechanical Engineers, and honorary colonel, Engineer and Railway Staff Corps. He was DL (Gloucestershire, 1965) and honorary LL D (Cambridge, 1950), honorary FI Mech. E (1971), and a Commander of St. John, the Legion of Honour, and the US Legion of Merit.

In 1965 he was elected master of the Salters' Company. He remained a director of Dunlop Ltd. until 1969 and of International Sleeping Cars Ltd. until 1973. He was a member of the general advisory council of the Independent Television Authority 1965–8. In all these roles his wise and constructive counsel was much valued. He gave active support to many charities, particularly the National Association of Boys' Clubs.

Robertson, who inherited much of the impressive presence of his father, was always strongly influenced by his memory. To some he seemed reserved and austere, yet many colleagues and subordinates found him particularly approachable. He did not suffer fools gladly and he could be daunting; but those who penetrated this carapace found affection, kindness, and a sense of fun, particularly apparent with the young, with whom he liked to relax in strenuous outdoor sports. He was a natural leader, and an able linguist and public speaker, endowed with a brilliant analytical brain backed by industriousness and sustained by a determination to pursue what was morally right, be the problem military, political, industrial, or commercial. Much loved by his family, he retained inward humility despite his brilliant record of versatile success as a soldier, administrator, and diplomat. He had a strong Christian faith, and a deep sense of loyalty to his country and its traditions.

In 1926 he married Edith Christine, daughter of James Black Macindoe, company director, of Glasgow. She died in 1982 from injuries after being attacked and robbed in London. They had one son (William) Ronald (born 1930), who inherited the barony, and two daughters. Robertson died 29 April 1974 at Far Oakridge, Gloucestershire.

[Private information; personal knowledge.]

CHARLES RICHARDSON

ROBINSON, SIR ROBERT (1886–1975), chemist and Nobel prize-winner, was born at

Rufford Farm near Chesterfield 13 September 1886, the eldest of the five children (three daughters and two sons) of William Bradbury Robinson, developer of the family firm of Robinson and Sons Ltd., manufacturers of surgical dressings, which had been established in Chesterfield since 1794, and his second wife, Jane Davenport. Since there were eight surviving children of the first marriage (the first wife, Elizabeth Lowe, died in 1871) Robert's early days were spent in a large and boisterous family circle. His father was a man of great energy and something of an inventor as well as a good business man. Robert's early education was obtained in Chesterfield first at Mrs Wilkes's kindergarten and then at Chesterfield Grammar School from which at the age of twelve he moved to Fulneck School at Pudsey Greenside. Fulneck School was run by the Moravian Church in Britain and had a high scholastic reputation which explains why the Robinsons—all prominent Congregationalists—sent both Robert and his younger brother Victor to it. No attempt seems to have been made to convert non-Moravian pupils at the school but the extreme Congregationalist fervour of the family circle engendered in Robert a marked revulsion to all forms of organized religion in later life.

From Fulneck School he proceeded to the University of Manchester where he matriculated in 1902 to read chemistry. Robinson had wished to study mathematics but his father insisted that he should read chemistry which he reckoned would be of more practical use in the family business to which he hoped his son would succeed. As it turned out, the choice was a good one for, although Robinson never entered the family business, he was in due course to make outstanding contributions to science and in particular to organic chemistry.

In 1902 the Manchester department of chemistry occupied a dominant position in organic chemistry in Britain and, under its young Professor W. H. Perkin Jr. (whose notice Robinson later wrote for this Dictionary), rivalled the famous organic schools of Germany. It was Perkin who not only was quick to recognize the potential of Robinson but who also awoke in him a lifelong passion for organic chemistry. Robinson graduated with first class honours in 1905 and at once proceeded to do research under Perkin on natural colouring matters and alkaloids, topics which remained major interests throughout his long career in chemistry. In the course of his postgraduate work he acquired in 1903 the Ph.D. degree and took his D.Sc. in 1910, by which time he was an established worker in his own right. In 1909 he became assistant lecturer and struck up a close and enduring friendship with Arthur Lapworth (1872–1941) who came to Manchester in that year as senior lecturer in organic and physical chemistry. Robinson even at that time had shown interest in the mechanism of some of the reactions used in his research and Lapworth, with his theories of reaction involving alternate polarities, had a profound influence on the development of the theoretical views of the younger man.

In 1913 Robinson became the first professor of organic chemistry in the University of Sydney, only to be recalled to the newly created Heath Harrison chair of organic chemistry in the University of Liverpool in 1915. His career continued at a breathless pace—from Liverpool in 1920 to be director of research at Huddersfield for the newly created British Dyestuffs Corporation, then in 1920 to St. Andrews University as professor of organic chemistry, on to the chair of organic chemistry in Manchester in 1922, to the organic chemistry chair at University College, London, in 1928, and finally to the Waynflete chair of chemistry in Oxford in 1930 following the death of its previous occupant, his former teacher W. H. Perkin Jr. There he remained as professor and fellow of Magdalen College until his retirement in 1955, when he became a consultant to Shell Research Ltd., a position which he occupied until his death in 1975. During World War II he made contributions to the national effort, notably concerning chemical warfare, explosives, and medicinals.

Robinson's published research spans a period of some seventy years and is prodigious in volume and in scope, embracing 750 publications, many of outstanding importance to the development of organic chemistry, both theoretical and practical, during the twentieth century. Among his most important contributions were those on natural colouring matters, alkaloids, steroids, and synthetic oestrogens, as well as his work on theoretical chemistry and his biogenetic theories and speculations on biosynthesis. In addition he made many important contributions to chemical synthesis in the study of antimalarials, penicillin, aliphatic acids, and, in his later days, to theories of the origin of petroleum. His immense appetite for work was maintained to the end of his life; despite rapidly failing eyesight in his later years he completed (in collaboration with E. D. Morgan) a textbook entitled *An Introduction to Organic Chemistry* published posthumously in 1975 as well as a book on chess. Up to the day of his death he was working on his memoirs, one volume of which has been published (*Memoirs of a Minor Prophet*, 1976). In addition to his piece on Perkin, Robinson also wrote the notices of Maurice Copisarow and Sir John Simonsen for this Dictionary.

Robinson was a man of great mental and physical toughness with a brilliant and restless mind; he could also be a charming companion with an astonishing memory and interests spreading far beyond his science. Within his science he displayed a penetrating insight which seemed capable of going to the heart of any chemical problem almost instantaneously. His first response to events was usually emotional and he was often impatient of those holding views contrary to his own; these characteristics find a reflection in his scientific work and help to explain its tremendous scope and variety and how it came about that Robinson's name is associated much more with new reactions and theories than with extended syntheses of individual substances. Robinson's interests were not wholly confined to his chemical studies. He was a keen and accomplished chess player, his introduction to the game being, according to him, the only thing he ever acquired from the regular visits of the Congregationalist ministers to his boyhood home in Chesterfield. He did indeed become quite a noted amateur chess player and in later life wrote, in collaboration with R. Edwards, *The Art and Science of Chess* (1973). Fond of music, he played the piano with more than average skill but his real passion was for hill climbing and mountaineering. He became a well-known Alpinist and climbed in Europe, America, Africa, Australia, and New Zealand.

As befitted his status as the leading organic chemist of his generation Robinson received many honours in his lifetime. He was awarded the Nobel prize for chemistry in 1947 and was president of the Royal Society (1945–50). He had been elected FRS in 1920. Knighted in 1939 he was admitted to the Order of Merit in 1949. Overseas honours included membership of the Order of the Rising Sun (Japan) and the Legion of Honour (France). He received a large number of medals for his scientific work, was an honorary or foreign member of more than forty scientific societies and academies world-wide and received a total of twenty-four honorary degrees. Robinson also served as president of the Chemical Society (1939–41), the Society of Chemical Industry (1958–9), and the British Association for the Advancement of Science (1955). He was president of the British Chess Federation from 1950 to 1953.

In 1912 Robinson married, first, Gertrude Maud (died 1954), daughter of Thomas Makinson Walsh, coal buyer, of Winsford, Cheshire. She was a fellow student of chemistry in Manchester. They had a son and a daughter. In 1957 he married Mrs Stearn Sylvia Hillstrom (née Hershey), of New York. Robinson died in London 8 February 1975. There is a portrait by A. K. Lawrence in the rooms of the Royal Society.

[Lord Todd and J. W. Cornforth in *Biographical Memoirs of Fellows of the Royal Society*, vol. xxii, 1976; Sir Robert Robinson, *Memoirs of a Minor Prophet*, 1976; private information; personal knowledge.] A. R. TODD

ROBSON, WILLIAM ALEXANDER (1895–1980), scholar and editor, was born 14 July 1895 at Finchley, London, the first son and last of the three children of Jack Robson, pearl merchant of Hampstead, and his wife, Esther Afriat. He was educated at Peterborough Lodge School, but left school at fifteen on the death of his father to work as a clerk in an aviation company. Subsequently (1915–19) he saw active service in World War I as a lieutenant in the Royal Flying Corps and a flying officer in the Royal Air Force. He wrote a book, *Aircraft in War and Peace* (1916) which attracted the attention of G. Bernard Shaw [q.v.], and through the offices of Sidney and Beatrice Webb [qq.v.] he entered the London School of Economics and Political Science in 1919, passing the B.Sc. Econ. (first class honours) in 1922, Ph.D. (1924), and LL M (1928), while also becoming a barrister-at-law of Lincoln's Inn (1922). From 1926 to 1980, except for an interval in World War II, he taught at the London School of Economics, first (1926–33) as lecturer in industrial and administrative law, then (1933–47) as reader in administrative law, and from 1947 to 1962 as the first professor of public administration in the University of London, continuing thereafter to teach and conduct research as an emeritus professor until just before his death.

Robson was a pioneer of the academic study of public administration in Britain, and a founder and editor of an influential journal, the *Political Quarterly*. His first major work, and his most original one, *Justice and Administrative Law* (1928) contained a penetrating criticism of the theory of A. V. Dicey [q.v.] that in Britain acts of government were safely and effectively controlled by the ordinary courts of law. Robson showed that civil servants possessed substantial discretionary powers which were only erratically and sporadically controlled by the courts; and he argued that a systematic set of administrative tribunals, such as the French *droit administratif* provided, would not be (as Dicey supposed) a danger, but an advantage for individual liberty. He gave evidence along these lines to the committee on ministers' powers (1929–32) and wrote *Civilization and the Growth of Law* (1935). His correction of Dicey became widely accepted, but his plan for the systematization of administrative law was only very partially realized in his lifetime. His status as a pioneer in administrative law was recognized by the special lecture at the University of London which he gave on the fiftieth anniversary of his book (1978), and by honorary degrees from three French universities (Lille, 1953, Grenoble, 1955, and Paris, 1955).

Influenced by the Webbs and the Fabian Society (of which he was an active member),

Robson also became strongly and increasingly interested in the study of local government, especially the government and planning of big cities. His first publication in this field, *The Town Councillor* (1925), was written jointly with the future premier Clement Attlee, then a colleague at the LSE. Subsequent works included *The Development of Local Government* (1931), *The Government and Misgovernment of London* (1939), *Great Cities of the World* (1954), and *Local Government in Crisis* (1966). Robson had a reformer's wish to strengthen and adapt the local government system to modern requirements. His book on London, after a historical survey, urged the case for a single elective authority to perform certain functions for the whole conurbation, and his chance to realize this aim came with the appointment of the royal commission on local government in Greater London (1957–60). Robson formed the Greater London group at LSE whose evidence to the commission proved a critical factor in their recommendations which led to the creation of the Greater London Council (1963).

Robson played a leading part in the foundation of the *Political Quarterly*, of which he was joint editor for forty-five years (1930–75). He had the support among others of Kingsley Martin, Bernard Shaw, and Leonard Woolf [qq.v.], his co-editor from 1931 to 1959. Robson's aim was to produce a serious political review in which progressive ideas could be discussed at adequate length, and which would appeal to a limited élite of opinion-formers. To a considerable extent he succeeded, and developed a journal with a limited but influential readership, and with serious but readable coverage of policy issues.

In World War II Robson worked in the Mines Department, Ministry of Fuel and Power, Air Ministry, and Ministry of Civil Aviation. This experience, and his membership of several government committees, gave him practical insight into administrative issues, and was also reflected in his much-translated textbook about public corporations, *Nationalized Industry and Public Ownership* (1960).

Although he taught throughout his life at the same institution Robson's interests and connections (like his publications) were very varied. He was a leading member of professional bodies such as the Royal Institute of Public Administration, the Town and Country Planning Association, the Political Studies Association, and the International Political Science Association, of which he was president (1950–3). He was a visiting professor at several American universities and an adviser to Middle East governments on public corporations as well as to Tokyo on local government where he acquired a considerable reputation. He had honorary degrees from Dunelm (1963), Manchester (1964), and Birmingham (1970), besides the three from France, and he was an honorary fellow of the London School of Economics.

Robson was a critic of legal institutions, but his own work showed a powerful barristerial ability to marshal facts and to present a well-documented and reasoned argument. He was an ardent reformer of administrative institutions, and his writings on administrative law and local government were particularly influential. He shared the Utilitarian and Fabian distaste for administrative waste or inefficiency, but he was also a strong believer in representative institutions, especially local self-government, and a humanist who watched with concern the evolution of the post-1945 Welfare State in Britain. This concern emerged in his last book, *Welfare State and Welfare Society* (1976), which took a broad view of the desirable scope of welfare measures but stressed their dependence upon a strong social ethic. To this Dictionary he contributed the notice of Sir Ivor Jennings.

He was a very earnest and well-disciplined person, who showed great persistence and determination in achieving his many objectives. He did all his writing and editing by hand in green ink, green being his favourite colour. He was a very hard worker, but he was also fond of walking, tennis, and music. He could seem rather austere and forbidding at work, but he could be a relaxed and kindly companion. He was never put off his course by criticism or lack of recognition, although his single-minded approach to reform inevitably made political enemies.

In 1929 he married Juliette, daughter of Henri Alvin, a civil engineer. She was a pioneer of music therapy. They had two sons and one daughter. Robson died 12 May 1980 in a London nursing home.

[*The Times*, 15 May 1980; personal knowledge.] PETER SELF

RODD, FRANCIS JAMES RENNELL, second BARON RENNELL OF RODD (1895–1978), merchant banker and explorer, was born in London 25 October 1895, the eldest in the family of four sons and two daughters of James Rennell Rodd, first Baron Rennell [q.v.], diplomat and scholar, and his wife, Lilias Georgina, daughter of James Alexander Guthrie, of Craigie, Forfar. One of his brothers married Nancy Mitford [q.v.] and one of his sisters married Simon Elwes [q.v.]. His other sister became Baroness Emmet of Amberley. Because of his father's profession, during his childhood he spent much time abroad and acquired fluency in Italian, French, and German. He was educated at Eton and, from 1913, at Balliol College, Oxford. In September 1914 he left Oxford to join the Royal Field Artillery. After serving in France he became an intelligence officer in Italy (1916) and also served on the staff in the Middle East. He was mentioned in dispatches and awarded the Italian Order of St. Maurice and St. Lazarus.

In 1919 Rodd joined the Diplomatic Service. He held posts in Rome and Sofia, where he was chargé d'affaires, but he resigned in 1924. From 1924 to 1928 he was at the Stock Exchange, and from 1929 to 1932 at the Bank of England. In 1933 he joined the bank Morgan Grenfell, as a partner.

The spirit of exploration was strong within Rodd—he was the great-great-grandson of Major James Rennell (1742–1830, q.v.), one of the leading British geographers of his time. In 1922 he had taken leave to travel with others in the southern Sahara and enjoyed 'the happiest year I have ever spent'. His studies of the Tuareg, assisted by further journeys in 1927, gained him the Royal Geographical Society's Cuthbert Peek award (1927) and the Founder's medal (1929). He published *People of the Veil* in 1926. He was particularly interested in Libya; his book on *General William Eaton*, recording a singular episode in the diplomatic history of the USA, appeared in 1933.

With such experience Rennell (he succeeded his father in 1941) was ideally suited to the tasks of civil affairs administration in the Middle East, West and East Africa, Madagascar, and Italy during World War II. He became a major-general (1942): he was created CB in 1943 and KBE in 1944. His account of *British Military Administration of Occupied Territories in Africa* appeared in 1948. When the war was over he continued his career in banking as a director and, until 1961, managing director of Morgan Grenfell & Co.

In 1945 the Royal Geographical Society, which had been working under severe difficulties during the war, elected him president. He devoted himself until 1948, with great success, to re-establishing its activities and fortunes. After his presidency he continued to work actively for the society, which accorded him the rare honour of honorary membership in 1971.

Rennell was active in the House of Lords first as a Liberal and after 1951 on the Conservative benches. He served as deputy lieutenant (1948) and vice-lieutenant (1957–73) of Herefordshire. From 1954 to 1965 he was a member of the BOAC board and for a time served as a vice-chairman.

With a strong sense of family and love of home, he was delighted to acquire The Rodd house and farm near Presteigne in Herefordshire. He could thus reinstate his family in the home of its ancestors. His love of the Herefordshire countryside led him to investigate the historical geography of the Lugg valley. He published a number of papers and in 1958 *Valley on the March*, a study of the 'local history written especially in relation to geography' of the Hindwell valley.

After 1950 he developed a great affection for Australia, partly because he was a director in England of the National Bank of Australasia and partly for family reasons. He continued his visits long after his business interests ceased. He was a keen observer of Australian agriculture, experimenting at The Rodd farm with breeding sheep to improve fleece weight, and publishing his results.

Rennell was a scholarly man, at home in his splendid library at The Rodd. He left some 450 books to the Royal Geographical Society which now form its Rennell Collection. He gave his energy to many academic organizations, notably the British School at Rome and the British Association for the Advancement of Science, on whose councils he served. He watched, with sometimes critical interest, the post-war flowering of geography as an academic discipline. The University of Manchester awarded him an honorary LL D in 1962. He was a visiting fellow of Nuffield College, Oxford, 1947–59.

Rennell was thoughtful yet decisive in action. His force of personality and innate strength made him readily acceptable as a leader. Highly successful though he was, he was never the complete, conventional banker or administrator. Many differing interests attracted the attention of his lively and unusual mind and the enthusiasm with which he attacked each one of these was one of his most attractive qualities.

In 1928 he married Mary Constance Vivian, daughter of Vivian Hugh Smith, first Baron Bicester, banker, whose notice he later wrote for this Dictionary. She achieved distinction as a painter: they had four daughters. Rennell died at The Rodd 15 March 1978 and was buried in Presteigne. He was succeeded in the barony by his nephew, (John Adrian) Tremayne Rodd (born 1935).

[*The Times*, 16 March 1948; *Geographical Journal*, vols. cxliv, 1978, and cxlviii, 1982; Rennell of Rodd papers; private information; personal knowledge.] M. J. WISE

ROGERS, CLAUDE MAURICE (1907–1979), painter and teacher, was born 24 January 1907 in London, the eldest of three children and elder son of David de Sola Cohen Rogers, dental surgeon (LDS, RCS) of 28 Sutherland Avenue, Maida Vale, and his wife, Rebecca Ida, fifth daughter of Bernard Rubinstein, of Maida Vale. He was educated at St. Paul's School (1920–5) and at the Slade School of Fine Art, University College, London (1925–9) where he was awarded a certificate in drawing (1926), the first prize for figure drawing (1927), prizes for landscape painting (1928) and figure composition (1929), a Slade scholarship in 1926 and 1927, and the Robert Ross leaving scholarship in 1929. For a while in 1927 he worked in Paris.

His work was exhibited for the first time with the London Group in 1930, and he was elected to the London Artists' Association in 1932, having his first one-man exhibition there in 1933. In 1935 he obtained the University of London diploma in fine art and became a part-time art master at Raynes Park County School for Boys, Wimbledon. In 1936 his work was shown at the Carnegie International Exhibition.

On 11 January 1937 he married Elsie Evelyn, elder daughter of Jethro Few, general merchant, of Kingston, Jamaica. They had one child, a son.

In that same year he went to the International Exhibition in Paris, exhibited at the Storran Gallery and, with (Sir) William Coldstream and E. J. Victor Pasmore, was a founder member of the School of Drawing and Painting at 12 Fitzroy Street, which later moved to 314/316 Euston Road, WC1. In 1938 his work was included in an exhibition '15 Paintings of London', and A. Clive H. Bell [q.v.], reviewing it on 15 November was the first to refer to the Euston Road Group.

In 1939 he visited Aix en Provence, and in 1940 had a one-man exhibition at the Leicester Galleries, when his 'Mrs. Richard Chilver' was bought through the Chantry Bequest for the Tate Gallery. He joined the Royal Engineers in 1941, becoming a corporal before being invalided out of the army in 1943. He then taught painting part-time at Hammersmith and St. Martin's Schools of Art in 1944–5, and at Camberwell School of Art and Crafts for four years from 1945. After showing work in 1946 at the Unesco Exhibition in Paris, he had another one-man exhibition in 1947 at the Leicester Galleries. His work was included in many Arts Council exhibitions, including 'The Euston Road School and others', shown at the Wakefield Art Gallery and elsewhere in 1948; and in British Council exhibitions, over many years, in America, Canada, Italy, South Africa, Sweden, and elsewhere. In 1949 he became a part-time teacher at the Slade. In 1950 he exhibited again at the Carnegie International Exhibition, and in 1951 his 'Miss Lynn' gained an Arts Council Festival of Britain purchase prize.

He had further one-man exhibitions at the Leicester Galleries in 1954 and 1960, and a retrospective exhibition at Bristol, Leicester, Manchester, and Newcastle in 1955. He was president of the London Group 1952–65, a member of the UK executive committee of the International Association of Plastic Arts (Unesco) and of the Guggenheim committee, 1954, of the art panel of the Arts Council, 1955–63, of the Gulbenkian Foundation's advisory committee on art, 1960, and of the National Council for Diplomas in Art and Design and chairman of the Fine Arts Panel, 1961–8. In 1959 he was appointed OBE. In 1963 he became professor of fine art, University of Reading, retiring in 1972 as professor emeritus. He was elected fellow of University College, London, in 1965.

His retrospective exhibition at Whitechapel Art Gallery, in 1973, toured Birmingham, Bradford, Newcastle, Reading, Sheffield, and Southampton. He exhibited in London with Fischer Fine Art in 1975 and 1978, at Gainsborough's House, Sudbury, in 1976, at Bury St. Edmunds, King's Lynn, and Ipswich in 1978 and, in the month of his death, at Harlow in 1979.

As a teacher and examiner he was much in demand: visitor at the West of England College of Art and the Royal College of Art, teacher and lecturer at the Slade for fourteen years, and assessor at Chelsea School of Art, Birmingham College of Art, the Royal College of Art, the universities of Birmingham and Durham, and the Confederation of Scottish Art Institutions. He was also a governor of Trent Park Training College.

He was an important figurative artist, whose imagination, memory, perception, and sensibility, combined with his passionate visual energy and enquiry, produced work of remarkable richness and emotion, which is widely represented in collections and galleries throughout the world.

A stocky, bespectacled, bearded, warmly ebullient but gentle man, with a delightful sense of humour, lively mind, and sensitive nature, he died 18 February 1979, at his home in London, 36 Southwood Lane, Highgate.

[Slade School archives; exhibition catalogues (especially Whitechapel, 1973, Sudbury, 1976, and Fischer Fine Art, 1978); private information; personal knowledge.]

IAN TREGARTHEN JENKIN

ROSE, JOHN DONALD (1911–1976), industrial chemist, was born 2 January 1911 at Greasbrough near Rotherham, the elder son and the second of the three children of Rimington Wilson Rose, schoolmaster (the son of John Rose, colliery engineer), and his wife, Martha Ellen Minnie, daughter of John Dawson, representative for a Rotherham foundry. His forebears thus all came from south Yorkshire. He went to Rotherham Grammar School with the aid of a county scholarship. Despite the strong appeal of art, chemistry became his favourite study and in 1929 he went up to read chemistry at Jesus College, Oxford, with a county scholarship. He graduated BA (first class) in 1932 and spent his fourth year, leading to a B.Sc. degree (first class, 1933), with (Sir) Robert Robinson [q.v.], probably the greatest organic chemist of his day. The award of a two-year Salters' fellowship enabled him to continue research with Robinson but a characteristic urge to gain wider experience led him to spend the second year at the Eidgenössische Technische Hochschule in Zürich. There he worked with Leopold Ruzicka who, like Robinson, was destined for a Nobel prize.

Robinson had a long connection with Imperial Chemical Industries as a consultant and in 1935 Rose joined their Dyestuffs Division in Blackley, Manchester, as a research chemist. The research was very different in kind and quality from what he had done before, but it appealed strongly to his practical nature. Among his early assignments was an evaluation of the new textile polymer, nylon, which had been sent from the USA under the terms of an agreement with Dupont.

In 1939 the Dyestuffs Division's resources had to be concentrated on the urgent demands of the war, but much thought was given to research that might generate new business in the post-war era. Rose was seconded to the exploratory research group set up for this purpose. One task of this think-tank was to investigate the possible use of acetylene as an intermediary for making organic chemicals. In the interest of self-sufficiency the German chemical industry had developed this intensively but a post-war mission to Germany, to which Rose was attached, confirmed that acetylene was quite inappropriate to the chemical industry in Britain, which in fact switched increasingly to petroleum.

It was apparent that Rose needed wider challenges than the bench could offer and in 1949 he became associate research manager and, in 1951, director of research. During this time the division was associated with two major innovations—the highly reactive Procion dyes and the important new artificial fibre Terylene, developed with the Calico Printers Association. In 1958 he gained new experience as production director. A year later he was appointed to a very different part of ICI, as joint managing director, later chairman, of its Paints Division. Here the emphasis was on sales, whereas at Dyestuffs it was on research.

This equipped him for his final move: in 1966 he was appointed ICI research and development director. He was thus responsible within the company for ensuring that its wide range of business ventures was firmly supported by its scientific expertise. Briefly (1968–9) he was chairman of Ilford Ltd., which had been acquired jointly by ICI and the Swiss chemical company Ciba, who were both interested in the photographic industry as an outlet for dyes. Unfortunately, the views of the two companies proved incompatible; Ciba bought ICI's share, and Rose resigned.

Rose was keenly interested in both pure and applied chemistry. It was, therefore, appropriate that the Royal Society elected him to fellowship in 1971 and the Society of Chemical Industry to its vice-presidency in 1968.

On retiring from ICI in March 1972, Rose found his knowledge and experience much in demand. He became a director of Laporte Industries (1972–6) and chairman of the Fulmer Research Institute (1974). In 1972 the University of Salford, of which he was a governor, awarded him an honorary D.Sc. degree and in 1973 he was elected master of the Salters' Company. Sadly, illness put a sudden end to these constructive activities in 1976 and he died at his home in Chalfont St. Peter on 14 October in that year.

In 1941 Rose married Yvonne Valerie, daughter of Evan Meredith Evans, schoolmaster. She, and their son and daughter, were always at the centre of his life. At home he enjoyed his large garden and the bird life he encouraged in it. He never lost his interest in art: he drew well himself, especially caricatures of friends and colleagues. In dealings with others he had the typical bluntness of a Yorkshireman but this was combined with such personal charm and modesty, and a keen sense of humour, that none could take offence. Professionally, his strength lay in the fact that he knew his own business thoroughly and had a great gift of listening patiently to the views of others and then very quickly evaluating the essential facts.

[*The Times*, 19 October 1976; *ICI Magazine*, March 1972 and November 1976; A. W. Johnson in *Biographical Memoirs of Fellows of the Royal Society*, vol. xxiii, 1977; personal knowledge.] TREVOR I. WILLIAMS

ROSE, REGINALD LESLIE SMITH- (1894–1980), physicist. [See SMITH-ROSE.]

ROSEBERY, sixth EARL OF (1882–1974), landowner and racehorse breeder. [See PRIMROSE, (ALBERT EDWARD) HARRY (MAYER ARCHIBALD).]

ROSENHEIM, MAX LEONARD, BARON ROSENHEIM (1908–1972), physician, was born 15 March 1908 in Hampstead, London, the elder son and second of the three children of Ludwig Rosenheim, who left Würzburg in Germany as a young man to become a naturalized British subject and member of the Stock Exchange, and his wife, Martha, the daughter of Carl Reichenbach, a genial, forceful general medical practitioner of St. Gall, Switzerland, where he became Stadtrat and later Kantonsrat. Max's paternal uncle was the biochemist S. O. Rosenheim [q.v.].

His early schooling at The Hall in Hampstead was clouded by the death of his father from cerebrospinal fever in 1915 and interrupted by recurrent illness, which, however, did not prevent him from winning scholarships to Shrewsbury School in 1922 and to St. John's College, Cambridge, in 1926. He obtained a first class in part i of the natural sciences tripos in 1929. He graduated from University College Hospital Medical School in 1932 and, after a brief spell at Westminster Hospital, returned to UCH as medical registrar in 1936. He became B.Chir. in 1932, MB in 1933, MRCP in 1934, and MD in 1938. In 1939 he was awarded the Bilton Pollard travelling fellowship which took him to work with Fuller Albright at the Massachusetts General Hospital, where he laid the foundations of the international network of friendships which later became such an important part of his life. The outbreak of war curtailed this visit to North America, he returned to UCH again, took charge of the first-year clinical students evacuated to Cardiff, and, after a short subsequent stay in London at the height of the blitz, during which he evolved Rosenheim's law of sleep (which states that you sleep more soundly if you believe that there is nowhere you might sleep more safely), joined the Royal Army Medical Corps in 1941, in which year he was elected FRCP.

He became officer in charge, medical division, in various hospitals in the Middle East, North Africa, and Europe, ending his army service as consulting physician to the Allied Land Forces, South-East Asia. He developed a lasting interest in tropical diseases and a deep concern for the health problems of the third world, for which he was later to do so much. He visited Indonesia with a World Health Organization team in 1953, India under the Colombo plan in 1955, and Pakistan, Australia, and New Zealand as Sir Arthur Sims Commonwealth travelling professor in 1958. He was external examiner in many universities overseas and never failed, in the course of his travels, to keep his friends and colleagues all over the world in touch by means of a profusion of postcards.

Back at UCH in 1946, he succeeded (Sir) Harold Himsworth as professor of medicine in 1950. His research contributions had previously been on the therapy of infections of the urinary tract, for which he had pioneered the use of mandelic acid. When this was overtaken by the advent of sulphonamides he turned his attention to hypertension and launched the era of treatment of high blood pressure by hexamethonium and related drugs which had been developed, with Eleanor Zaimis, by (Sir) William Paton working in his department. Later still, he and his radiologist colleagues did much to elucidate the nature and optimal control of chronic pyelonephritis.

This notable clinical work was yet outshone by his administrative achievements. He had great gifts as a leader and was able to bring together men of diverse interests and get them to cooperate. His benign and humorous chairmanship, massive common sense, wide knowledge, and sound judgement were combined with an indomitable sense of purpose. These qualities were valued by the World Health Organization, Medical Research Council, British Council, Ministry of Health, and various foundations but were most productive during his six years as president of the Royal College of Physicians, which began in 1966. The fusion of the postgraduate medical examinations of the Royal Colleges of Edinburgh, Glasgow, and London into one MRCP, the setting up of part i of this examination in many developing countries overseas, and, giving expression to his view that the basis of medical education needed broadening, the establishment of the faculty of community medicine, were three of his major successes.

The honours of CBE in 1955, KBE in 1967, and a life peerage in 1970 did not alter the unpretentious style of his life, in which good fellowship, good food and wine, books, talk, music, fishing, and sailing played a substantial part. He became an honorary fellow of many colleges of physicians and of University College, London (1967), and St. John's College, Cambridge (1969). He was awarded five honorary degrees. He never married and lived in Hampstead with his mother until she died in 1971. His brother had been killed in action in 1945. In the last year of his life, 1972, he was elected FRS and in December 1971 he became chairman of the Medicines Commission. His death, after a short illness, in London 2 December 1972 deprived the House of Lords of a warm-hearted and enlightened elder statesman.

[*The Times*, 4, 8, and 9 December 1972; *British Medical Journal*, 16 December 1972; *Hansard*, 4 December 1972; Sir George Pickering in *Biographical Memoirs of Fellows of the Royal Society*, vol. xx, 1974; personal knowledge.]

JOHN F. STOKES

ROSS, SIR (WILLIAM) DAVID (1877–1971), scholar and philosopher, was born 15 April 1877 at Thurso, the third of the four sons (four other children died in infancy) of John Ross and his wife, Julia Keith. His father, who had been a schoolmaster in Caithness, was then principal of the Maharajah's College, Travancore, and Ross's home was there for the first six years of his life. He was educated at the Royal High School in Edinburgh and at Edinburgh University, where he graduated with first class honours in classics in 1895. In the same year he entered Balliol College, Oxford, as an exhibitioner, where he again obtained first class honours both in classical honour moderations (1898) and *literae humaniores* (1900).

His first academic appointment, in 1900, was as a lecturer at Oriel College, Oxford, but almost immediately he was elected to a fellowship by examination at Merton, which he held until, in

1902, he was elected fellow and tutor in philosophy at Oriel. For five years from 1923 he acted as deputy White's professor of moral philosophy (because of the illness of the professor), but in 1928 he was not a candidate for the chair, judging that H. A. Prichard [q.v.], who was elected, had stronger claims. In 1929, on the resignation of the provost of Oriel, L. R. Phelps [q.v.], Ross was elected as provost, and held that office until 1947. He was vice-chancellor of the university from 1941 to 1944, and a delegate of the Oxford University Press from 1922 to 1952.

His enduring academic concern was with the works of Aristotle, on whom he was the leading authority of his time in Britain. He edited—for the first few years with J. A. Smith [q.v.]—a major series of translations, himself undertaking the *Metaphysics* (1908) and *Nicomachean Ethics* (1925). He edited six of the works for the series Oxford Classical Texts, and five with revised texts and full introduction and commentary, the last appearing in 1961. His book *Aristotle* (1923), which offers, in his own words, 'an account of the main features of Aristotle's philosophy as it stands before us in his work', remains valuable and was several times reissued and revised. By contrast his work in moral philosophy, though highly regarded in its time, looks somewhat dated. *The Right and the Good* (1930) and his Gifford lectures (1935–6) *Foundations of Ethics* (1939), though admirably careful and clear, lack (as perhaps he recognized) the argumentative incisiveness and independence of H. A. Prichard, by whom they were much influenced, and are little read today. Ross later wrote the notice of Prichard for this Dictionary, to which he made four other contributions—on Shadworth Hodgson, J. A. Smith, Dawes Hicks, and L. R. Phelps.

Another aspect of Ross's career began in 1915, with his war service. Until 1919 he worked in Whitehall in a succession of posts concerned with the supply of munitions. He left with the OBE (1918) and the rank of major, but for the next thirty years his gifts of industry, clarity, and fair-minded good sense were constantly in demand on many public bodies, for his contributions to which he was appointed KBE in 1938. These included, in World War II, chairmanship of the National Arbitration Tribunal (1941–52) and the Civil Service Arbitration Tribunal (1942–52), and his last such appointment, from 1947 to 1949, was as chairman of a royal commission on the press, in whose recommendations the present Press Council had its origin.

Ross was elected a fellow of the British Academy in 1927, and was its president from 1936 to 1940, in which period he was much involved, both officially and personally, with the problems of scholars seeking refuge from Europe. In 1947 he was president of the Union Académique Internationale.

In carrying on over so many years so many diverse activities, Ross wasted neither words nor sentiment nor time. He was a somewhat taciturn and impersonal tutor; and while he took pleasure in golf, tennis, and (more surprisingly) charades, he much disliked aimless talk and detested gossip. His great talent, in both academic and practical matters, was for hard work, clarity, the simplification of tangled issues, and rapid decision; and it was perhaps because he brought these same qualities of mind to all his undertakings that he could move so easily and tirelessly from one to another. A naturally modest, reserved disposition was unaffected by his accumulation of honours: besides those already mentioned, he was a commander, first class, of the Order of St. Olaf, a grand officer of the Order of Polonia Restituta, and he held honorary degrees of Edinburgh, Manchester, Dublin, London, Paris, Oslo, and Columbia. He was an honorary fellow of Merton, Balliol, and Oriel colleges, and of Trinity College, Dublin.

He married in 1906 Edith Helen (died 1953), daughter of John Ogden, of Manchester, a solicitor. There were four daughters of the marriage. He died in Oxford 5 May 1971.

[G. N. Clark in *Proceedings* of the British Academy, vol. lvii; notes by R. W. B. Burton, R. Robinson, and R. Walzer in *Oriel Record*, 1971; *The Times*, 6 May 1971; private information.] G. J. WARNOCK

ROTHERMERE, second VISCOUNT (1898–1978), newspaper proprietor. [See HARMSWORTH, ESMOND CECIL.]

ROUGHTON, FRANCIS JOHN WORSLEY (1899–1972), physiologist, was born at Kettering 6 June 1899, the only child of John Paul Roughton MD, surgeon, and his wife, Caroline Margaret, daughter of Charles Fortescue Worsley, of the Indian Civil Service. His father was the fifth consecutive Roughton to practise medicine at Kettering, and it was expected that he would follow this profession. After Winchester he was a scholar of Trinity College, Cambridge, but because of repeated attacks of paroxysmal tachycardia, was unable to sit part ii of the natural sciences tripos (he obtained a first class in part i in 1919), and medicine was set aside in favour of a presumably less taxing academic career. His distinction was such that he was awarded a research fellowship at Trinity, and was appointed lecturer in biochemistry in 1923. He held the position of lecturer in physiology from 1927 until 1947, when he succeeded (Sir) Eric Rideal [q.v.] as professor of colloid science. He was a fellow of Trinity from 1923 until his death.

He married in 1925 Dr Alice Isabella Hopkinson, one of the seven daughters of Bertram

Hopkinson [q.v.], formerly professor of mechanism and applied mechanics at Cambridge, and his wife, Mariana Siemens. They had a son and daughter. Until World War II the family lived in a conventional middle-class manner. During the war their large house at 9 Adams Road was used to billet the Ballets Jooss, and this contact with another world may have brought about the post-war transformation in their lives. The house was split into apartments which were rented out to young visitors to the university. The kitchen became a general meeting place where the residents and their friends met to share from a common pot, eat home-baked bread, and drink cider. Roughton, already troubled by hypertension, was in, but not of, much of this activity. Trinity and his laboratory became the centre of a quietly regulated life which included an afternoon rest, the *Daily Telegraph* crossword, and a gentle constitutional, but no formal recreations. He believed whole-heartedly in what he was doing, and his scientific work filled the greater part of his day.

This scientific work began under (Sir) Joseph Barcroft (whose notice Roughton later wrote for this Dictionary), in close association with Hamilton Hartridge. In the first fifteen years of the century Barcroft and his associates had established the basic facts about the binding of oxygen to haemoglobin, the protein which takes up oxygen in the lungs and releases it in the tissues, but all of this work was on the equilibrium between oxygen and haemoglobin and time did not enter into the experiments. In the body, however, the time available to haemoglobin to take up or release oxygen in the capillaries is about a second, and Barcroft wondered if this were enough to allow equilibrium to be approached closely. To attack the problem the rate of reaction between haemoglobin and oxygen had to be measured but, in 1921, the fastest way of doing this was by mixing liquids in a beaker, stirring them up, and removing samples at intervals for analysis. The fastest reaction which could be followed would have to take minutes.

Hartridge and Roughton conceived and constructed an apparatus in which solutions containing haemoglobin and oxygen were intimately mixed in 1/10,000th of a second, and in which a reaction half complete in 1/1,000th of a second could be followed. This was all done with common household and laboratory equipment, and before photocells and cathode ray oscilloscopes had emerged from physics laboratories. The jump in time resolution was perhaps 100,000-fold, a gain of a size rarely seen in science. Their apparatus, developed almost in a single step, did not undergo evolution, however, and stands in relation to later work much as Daguerre's process does to silver bromide photography. Much of Roughton's later work continued to involve the element of time, and he laid the foundations of later knowledge of the transport of oxygen and of carbon monoxide in the blood.

Roughton was co-editor of the *Biochemical Journal* (1935–41) until he became visiting research fellow in war science and medicine at Harvard and Columbia universities, where he worked on problems of war medicine. He held the Cambridge chair of colloid science from 1947 until his retirement in 1966, after which he divided his time between Milan and California.

He obtained his Cambridge BA in 1920, MA in 1924, and Ph.D. in 1925. He became FRS in 1936 and was an honorary member of many foreign societies. He died in Cambridge, following a stroke, 29 April 1972.

[Q. H. Gibson in *Biographical Memoirs of Fellows of the Royal Society*, vol. xix, 1973; family information; personal knowledge.]

QUENTIN H. GIBSON

ROWALLAN, second BARON (1895–1977), chief scout. [See CORBETT, THOMAS GODFREY POLSON.]

ROWAN, SIR (THOMAS) LESLIE (1908–1972), civil servant and industrialist, was born in Dunlavin, county Wicklow, Ireland, 22 February 1908, the younger son and child of the Revd Thomas Rowan of Dromore, county Sligo, clerk in holy orders, Church of England missionary, and headmaster of Panchgani School for Boys in India, and his wife, Hannah Josephine Birrel, of Halifax, Yorkshire. He was educated at Panchgani High School, won a scholarship to Tonbridge School, and went from there to Queens' College, Cambridge, on scholarships both from Tonbridge and from Queens'. He graduated with a first class in part ii of the modern and medieval languages tripos in 1929, and was made an honorary fellow of Queens' College in 1954. At school and at Cambridge he excelled at games, particularly hockey. He loved the spirit of working together as a team and this principle continued throughout his life. He captained Cambridge at hockey in 1929 and 1930 and England in 1937 and 1938 and again, remarkably, in 1947 despite the rigours of World War II. Later he captained the Civil Service at hockey and was also their sports and tennis champion.

After leaving Cambridge Rowan entered the Colonial Office in 1930. Quickly making his mark as a young civil servant, he was transferred to the Treasury in 1933, becoming assistant private secretary to the chancellor of the Exchequer, Neville Chamberlain, shortly after. His ability in this role undoubtedly influenced his transfer from the Treasury in 1941 to the private office of the wartime prime minister, (Sir) Winston Churchill, first as private secretary and then as principal private secretary in 1945. His service with Churchill began the close friendship with him and his family which continued in later years; he gained, as he richly deserved, the affection of the Churchill family for whose interests he was always concerned. This did not prevent him, in the best tradition of the Civil Service, from serving with equal loyalty another prime minister, Clement Attlee, when the change of government came.

In 1947 Rowan became permanent secretary and head of the newly formed office of the minister for economic affairs, Sir R. Stafford Cripps [q.v.], and later went with him to the Treasury as second secretary when Cripps became chancellor of the Exchequer. Rowan was principally concerned with the international work of trade and payments and economic co-operation in Europe growing out of the Marshall Plan. His reliability, wise judgement, and complete honesty in stating his view earned him the trust both of his own minister and of other Whitehall departments. But the work, coming after the strain of the war years, had made demands on his health. The idea that he should go to Washington as economic minister at the British embassy to strengthen the liaison between the two governments, following the tripartite economic agreement between the United States, Britain, and Canada in 1949, came at an opportune time. His two years in America were an outstanding success. He and his wife were immensely popular, entertained with warmth and skill, and left behind them many enduring friendships.

On his return to the Treasury in 1951 as head of the overseas finance division, there followed seven challenging years when Britain's economy was under constant strain. Balance of payments difficulties were accentuated by international disputes, first over Abadan and then Suez. There were sharp divisions in Whitehall, but Rowan's advice was always frank and courageous. He was a person of immense authority who could, to those who did not know him, be a little alarming. But behind this authority lay a humour and humanity which could not be repressed, and he had a delightful gift for irony. While defence of Britain's interests was paramount—and he was a skilled negotiator—Leslie Rowan worked to be fair to everybody and wasted no time on grievances. Standards to him were the important thing, and he hated to see these fall, either in public or in private life. He brought to his whole life a quality of leadership and integrity which encouraged those working with him to aim for the same high standards, and he and his team contributed significantly to the achievements of Britain's post-war economic effort at a time when success was not always easy to come by.

But after the taxing post-war years, Rowan was ready for a change, and in 1958 accepted the invitation of the second Viscount Knollys [q.v.] to join the board of Vickers as finance director. Progress once again was swift. He became managing director in 1962, deputy chairman in 1966, and chairman a year later. He brought to industry the same talents he had exercised in the public service, and the problems to be faced as head of a great industrial company were no less formidable than those of a great government department. He tackled them with his customary intelligence and resolution. His knowledge of Whitehall and a long-held belief in closer liaison between government and industry undoubtedly helped. He was one of the founders at this time of a dining club drawing its members from Whitehall and the City with the purpose of serious discussion of national and international affairs.

In 1971, after thirteen years at Vickers, Rowan became chairman of the British Council, an appointment emphasizing once again the versatility of his interests and ideals. The Council had not been having an easy time and he brought his clarity of mind and good sense to bear on a number of immediate problems. He died quite suddenly only a year later 29 April 1972 at his country home in Langford, Somerset.

It was while accompanying Churchill to the first Quebec conference in 1943 that Rowan met the Wren officer, one of the delegation's cipher team, who later became his wife. She was Catherine Patricia (Judy), third daughter of Brigadier R. H. A. D. Love, and this romantic courtship is forever recorded in Winston Churchill's *The Second World War* (vol. v, chapter 8, 1952). They were married on 19 January 1944, and had two sons and two daughters. Rowan was an excellent father and children loved him, at the same time being absolutely aware of his high standards and respecting them. He was a committed Christian and churchwarden of Chelsea Old Church. In all this he combined most serious purpose with unfailing gaiety, proving that unselfishness and dedication to what is right to not demand a puritan drabness. His medium height and friendly countenance belied the toughness of mind and body which gave his character and physical prowess its persistence and fortitude.

Rowan was appointed CB in 1946, CVO in 1947, and KCB in 1949. A portrait by Will Evans hangs in Vickers House, Millbank Tower, London.

Rowan wrote the final chapter of *Action This Day: Working with Churchill* (1968), *Arms and Economics, the Changing Challenge* (Lees Knowles lectures, 1960), and the introduction to *Investment and Development* (Overseas Development Institute, 1965).

[*The Times*, 1 May 1972; Sir John Colville's memorial address; private information; personal knowledge.] PAUL GORE-BOOTH

RUCK, AMY ROBERTA (BERTA) (1878–1978), romantic novelist, was born 2 August 1878 at Murree, India, the eldest child of Arthur Ashley Ruck, a lieutenant in the Isle of Man Regiment (8th Foot), and his wife, Elizabeth Eleanor, the daughter of Robert West D'Arcy, a colonel in the Bombay Grenadiers. They had seven further children: three sons and four daughters. Arthur Ruck's sister Amy married (Sir) Francis Darwin [q.v.] and died giving birth to their son Bernard [q.v.].

Berta Ruck, as she came to be known, was brought to Britain at the age of two and lived for a while at Panlludw, near Machynlleth, Merionethshire, the home of her paternal grandmother, Mary Anne Ruck (née Mathews), and both the place and the person were to make a deep impression on her. Before long, however, her father also returned from India to an adjutancy of the Liverpool Volunteers, and the family spent some five years at residences in Fleetwood and Formby. In 1886 her father retired with the honorary rank of lieutenant-colonel and in 1888 he was appointed chief constable of Caernarvonshire. The rest of Berta Ruck's childhood was spent at Caernarvon, where she was educated at home, and at Bangor, where she was a boarder at St. Winifred's School.

In the summer of 1892 she spent some time with a family at Halberstadt, Germany, and, as well as prompting what was to be a permanent liking for travel, this trip caused her to develop her latent talent for drawing. On leaving school she became a student at the Lambeth School of Art, with some thought of becoming a book illustrator, and on being awarded a London County Council scholarship in 1901, she moved to the Slade, where she studied under Henry Tonks [q.v.]. An extension of her scholarship in 1904 enabled her to spend a year at Calorossi's in Paris, and it was there that she befriended Iris Bland, whose mother, E. Nesbit [q.v.], was an influential mentor when Berta Ruck turned to writing.

Berta Ruck's earliest published work was in the form of illustrations for magazines (two illustrations and a headpiece appeared in volume xxiii of the *Idler*, 1903). She also drew for the short-lived periodical the *Jabberwock*, whose editor, Brenda Girvin, encouraged her to write. From 1905 onwards she began to contribute short stories and serials to magazines, much of her work appearing in *Home Chat*.

While Berta Ruck was at the Slade she had been introduced to Oliver Onions (died 1961), then a draughtsman for the Harmsworth Press, and a friendship developed from this meeting. In 1909 she married him; they had two sons. Out of a desire to protect them from possible ridicule their father, in 1918, changed his name to George Oliver, and Oliver has remained the family name.

In 1912 a *Home Chat* serial by Berta Ruck, 'His Official Fiancée', attracted the interest of a book publisher, who asked her to expand it to a full-length novel. This she did, with advice from her husband, and the book was published in 1913 under the same title as the serial. It had an immediate success in Britain and the United States and marked the start of Berta Ruck's long career as a popular novelist. In 1915 she produced *The Courtship of Rosamond Fayre*, based on a *Home Chat* serial, *The Lad with Wings*, which showed her interest in flying, and in 1916 *Khaki and Kisses* (short stories). She continued to publish one, two, or sometimes three books a year up to the early 1960s. Her last novel was *Shopping for a Husband* (1967).

Most of these books had what *Home Chat* termed 'a strong love interest' and they followed a similar pattern, whereby, after many vicissitudes, a neglected or impoverished heroine gained a rich and loving husband. It is likely that her readers' satisfaction with these books stemmed from the ingenuity with which she was able to withhold the inevitable denouement, a technique whose inherent artificiality was partly cloaked by the attention which she gave to contemporary detail, and partly by the intrusion of her own narrative voice. Her place as one of the leading popular romantic novelists of her day is attested, diversely, by the appearance in 1920 of a *Berta Ruck Birthday Book*, and in her inclusion, in 1930, among those best-selling authors approached by Mrs Q. D. Leavis during her work on *Fiction and the Reading Public* (1932). (This led to Miss Ruck taking tea with Mrs Leavis at Girton College on what must have been a memorable occasion.)

Between the wars Berta Ruck's steady life of writing was conducted in the family home, first at Henley, later at Hampstead—interspersed with periods of travel in Europe and the United States, where her books continued to be popular. After 1939 she moved back to Merioneth and, co-opted as a lecturer in adult education for the forces, discovered a talent for public speaking. This she continued after the war, eventually giving broadcasts on Welsh regional programmes of the BBC and appearing in BBC television's 'Yesterday's Witness' series in 1970.

After her husband's death she continued to live a busy life—vigour and longevity stemming, she believed, from plenty of open-air bathing, summer and winter alike. She celebrated her one hundredth birthday 2 August 1978 and died shortly afterwards on 11 August at home in Aberdovey.

A drawn self-portrait and a portrait drawing by Oliver Onions are in the possession of the family.

[Berta Ruck, *A Story-teller Tells the Truth* (1935, parts of which were incorporated in *A Smile for the Past*, 1959), *A Trickle of Welsh Blood*, 1967, *An Asset to Wales*, 1970, and *Ancestral Voices*, 1972; private information.]

BRIAN ALDERSON

RUSHTON, WILLIAM ALBERT HUGH (1901–1980), neurophysiologist, was born in London 8 December 1901, the eldest of the three children and elder son of William Rushton, a dentist from Liverpool, and his wife, Alice Louise Jane Amsler, granddaughter of the Swiss engraver Samuel Amsler, and also related to Jacob Amsler, the inventor of the planimeter in common use until the 1970s. Alice Amsler was a good pianist and Rushton thought he acquired his love of music from her.

Rushton was educated at Gresham's School, Holt, Emmanuel College, Cambridge (1921–8), and University College, London (1932–5). He gained a college scholarship in 1923, a second in part i of the natural sciences tripos in 1924, and a first class in part ii of the same tripos in 1925 (physiology). He was awarded the George Henry Lewes studentship in 1926, and obtained his Ph.D. under E. D. (later Lord) Adrian [q.v.] in 1928. His research at this time was on the electrical excitability of peripheral nerves. His major contribution was to analyse the spatial spread of excitability, and he did the groundwork upon which (Sir) Alan Hodgkin and (Sir) Andrew Huxley built the ionic theory of nervous conduction a few years later. He continued this line of work until about 1950, and it was upon the strength of it that he was elected FRS in 1948.

His academic progress was not, however, entirely smooth: he only succeeded in getting medically qualified (MRCS, Eng., LRCP, Lond.) in 1937 after numerous attempts, and he expressed dissatisfaction with his own research achievements. Nevertheless, he was awarded a visiting fellowship with Detlev Bronk at the Johnson Foundation, Philadelphia (1929–31), was elected research fellow of Emmanuel for two years in 1932 and again in 1935, and was appointed to a university lectureship at Cambridge in the latter year. In 1938 he became staff fellow and director of medical studies at Trinity College, where he remained a fellow for the rest of his life. He spent the years 1942–7 under psychoanalysis with Susan Isaacs, and said afterwards that the process had 'renewed' him. It is certainly remarkable that at the age of fifty he should turn to a new subject and achieve even greater success in it than he had in his earlier years of research.

Rushton started his renewed career as a visual physiologist with R. Granit in Stockholm on a sabbatical year, 1948–9. He ultimately chose to measure the photosensitive visual pigments in the living human eye, analysing how visual sensitivity depended upon the amounts that were bleached by bright adapting lights. He also succeeded in providing the first direct confirmation that colour blindness was caused by lack of photosensitive pigments. But perhaps his revitalization of the psychophysical side of vision research was even more important. Many prominent contemporaries were content to sort out the facts in their own speciality—and noteworthy advances were being made in the photochemistry and neurophysiology of vision—yet Rushton sought for explanations of the whole process, from incident photon to effective vision, and his ingenious psychophysical experiments set an example that the world attempted to follow.

Rushton's basic character was introspective and thoughtful, but at the same time he was intensely interested in other people, and responded with great personal warmth to anyone who displayed intelligence or originality on the topics he was interested in. He sometimes cut a flamboyant figure, both to the undergraduates he taught and at scientific meetings, yet the purpose behind his outrageous questions and witty comments was clear, for he constantly championed the reasoning power of the intellect against the mere dull amassing of facts.

He gained numerous honours for his work on vision, including foreign honorary membership of the American Academy of Arts and Sciences and the Prentice medal of the American Academy of Optometry in 1963, the Feldberg prize in 1967, membership of the Royal Swedish Academy of Sciences in 1968, the Royal medal of the Royal Society (London) in 1970, and the Proctor medal in 1971. He was appointed professor of visual physiology at Cambridge in 1966 (he had become reader in physiology in 1953), and after retirement in 1968 spent eight more very active years as distinguished research professor in psychobiology in Tallahassee. The major scientific periodical in his subject, *Vision Research*, published a memorial issue in 1982 in which more appreciations of his life and work can be found.

Rushton married Marjorie Glasson, daughter of Norman Kendrick, of Cardiff, in 1930. They had five children, of whom one died in infancy. He took great pride in his family, who shared his musical accomplishment, Marjorie playing piano and oboe, and his children (two sons and two daughters) cello, horn, clarinet, and flute, while Rushton himself played the bassoon, viola, and violin. The youngest son, Julian, later became professor of music at Leeds. Rushton died 21 June 1980 at Cambridge.

[W. A. H. Rushton, 'From nerves to eyes' in *The Neurosciences: Paths of Discovery* (ed. F. G.

Worden *et al.*), 1975; *The Times*, 23 June 1980; H. B. Barlow in *Biographical Memoirs of Fellows of the Royal Society*, vol xxxii, 1986; *Vision Research*, vol. xxii, 1975; private information; personal knowledge.] HORACE BARLOW

RUSSELL, SIR GUY HERBRAND EDWARD (1898–1977), admiral, was born in London 14 April 1898, the second son in the family of four sons and one daughter of Arthur Oliver Villiers Russell, second Baron Ampthill [q.v.], later governor of Madras, and his wife, Lady (later Dame) Margaret Lygon, CI, GCVO, GBE, daughter of Frederick Lygon, sixth Earl Beauchamp [q.v.]. A notice of his elder brother appears below. Entering the navy in 1911 from Stonehouse School, he went to the Royal Naval Colleges of Osborne and Dartmouth. On the outbreak of war in 1914 he went to sea as a midshipman aged sixteen in the *Implacable*. He was present at the Dardanelles campaign and escorted the Royal Fusiliers to 'X' beach on the day of the assault. Later he served on the *Royal Oak* at the Battle of Jutland. He was mentioned in dispatches for his services during the war.

Russell had a more varied career than falls to the lot of most naval officers. Eschewing technical specialization which he contended restricted service experience, he remained a 'salt horse'. Up to the time of his comparatively early promotion to commander in 1931, he had seen service in destroyers, training establishments, cruisers, and battleships, and on the staff of the commander-in-chief, Mediterranean, at a time of recurring crises. He proved himself both adaptable and imaginative in all these posts. In 1931 he completed the naval staff course at Greenwich and returned to the Mediterranean as the executive officer of the *Queen Elizabeth*, the fleet flagship of Admiral Sir William Fisher [q.v.]. He soon made a reputation as an outstanding executive officer, and was universally admired, being promoted to captain in 1936 at the early age of thirty-eight. After promotion he returned to England for a course at the Imperial Defence College which was followed by a number of staff appointments.

After the outbreak of war in 1939 he held two sea appointments; firstly as commanding officer of the *Protector*, a net layer, and then of the *Cumberland*, a cruiser employed in the North Atlantic on trade protection. At the end of 1941 he joined Viscount Gort [q.v.], governor of Gibraltar, as naval liaison officer, and transferred with him to Malta as his chief of staff during the time of the siege of Malta. Few more competent and resolute characters than Gort and Russell could have been chosen to command Malta during this crucial period of the war in the Mediterranean.

After Malta was relieved, Russell became captain of the battleship *Nelson*, then of the *Duke of York*, fleet flagship of the Home Fleet in the action off the North Cape in December 1943, when she sank the German battle cruiser *Scharnhorst*. For this he was appointed to the DSO for great gallantry, determination, and skill, having already been mentioned in dispatches twice since the start of the war. Returning to the Admiralty a year after the action he was appointed naval assistant to the chief of personnel, a post for which he was admirably suited. Promoted to rear-admiral in 1945 he soon made his way to the top of the admirals list. Back again at the Imperial Defence College (1946–8), then commanding the second cruiser squadron (1948–9), he earned the lasting admiration of the C-in-C of the Home Fleet, Admiral Sir Rhoderick McGrigor [q.v.].

After a period with the Reserves (1949–51) Russell was appointed C-in-C Far East Station (1951–3) where he did outstandingly well during the Korean war and troubles in Malaysia. He became an admiral in 1952. After this he served as second sea lord and chief of naval personnel (1953–5) at a time of much change during which his wide experience and sympathies for officers and ratings alike had full scope. In 1956–8 he was commandant of the Imperial Defence College where he was able to give students of all services the benefit of his wide experience.

He retired in 1958 and devoted himself wholeheartedly to training young people and running schools. He soon made an impact with his width of vision and strength of character. He was chairman of the National Association of Boys' Clubs (1958–63) and of the Missions to Seamen (1960–5). He served on the governing bodies of Wellington College, Cranleigh College, and Gordon Boys' School, and was chairman of Radley College for six years.

He was an imposing and handsome figure who at first sight perhaps awed an onlooker, unless he detected the twinkle in his eye. Behind a bluff exterior he had an acute intelligence, which soon saw through any pretensions. He was gifted with great common sense and brought to bear a splendid sense of the ridiculous on unwise propositions. His sense of humour delighted his friends and confounded his opponents. In Admiralty Board meetings he could always be relied upon to deflate plausible but unwise suggestions, to the delight of his supporters. He was a modest and kind-hearted man. A magnificent oarsman, which delighted his father, who was also a great oarsman, he was in addition a very good shot and an enthusiastic golfer.

Russell was appointed CBE (1943), CB (1948), KCB (1951), and GBE (1953). In 1939 he married the Hon. (Helen) Elizabeth, daughter of (George) Rowland Blades, first Baron Ebbisham, GBE, MP for Epsom (1918–28) and lord mayor of London (1926–7); they had two sons and one daughter. Russell died 25 September 1977 at his home at Wisborough Green, Sussex.

[*The Times*, 27 September 1977; Stephen W. Roskill, *The War at Sea 1939–1945*, 4 vols., 1954–61; personal knowledge.]

WILLIAM DAVIS

RUSSELL, JOHN HUGO, third BARON AMPTHILL (1896–1973), naval officer and company director, was born at his father's London house, 109 Park Street, Mayfair, 4 October 1896, the eldest in the family of four sons and one daughter of Arthur Oliver Villiers Russell, second Baron Ampthill [q.v.], later governor of Madras, and his wife, Lady (later Dame) Margaret Lygon, CI, GCVO, GBE, daughter of Frederick Lygon, sixth Earl Beauchamp [q.v.]. His childhood was spent in India where his father was governor of Madras and interim acting viceroy. After going through the Royal Naval Colleges at Osborne and Dartmouth as a cadet, Russell joined the navy as a midshipman in 1912. Nicknamed 'Stilts' on account of his height (six feet two), he was from the outset a dedicated sailor and popular with superiors and subordinates alike. He served throughout World War I, initially in HMS *Defence*, which was sunk at Jutland with no survivors a week after he had left her to join a sloop in the Mediterranean on promotion to sub-lieutenant. Later in the war he qualified as a submarine officer and took part in numerous underwater patrols in the North Sea. Soon after the war he retired from the service for domestic reasons. Most of the inter-war years he spent with Carrier Engineering and Gallaher Limited, the tobacco manufacturing company in Belfast, of which he became a director in 1937, particularly interesting himself in the welfare of its employees. He succeeded his father in 1935.

Recalled to the navy with the rank of commander on the outbreak of war in 1939, Ampthill served throughout, first in the torpedo and mining department of the Admiralty and then on the staff of Admiral Sir Bertram Ramsay [q.v.], Allied naval commander-in-chief of the Expeditionary Force under General Eisenhower. As senior administrative officer with the rank of captain, Ampthill played an important part behind the scenes in the planning and execution of the naval aspects of the Allied landings in North Africa and Europe. For his services in these campaigns he was created CBE (1945) and chevalier of the Legion of Honour, besides being awarded the croix de guerre with palms and the US Order of the Legion of Merit.

Immediately after the war Ampthill returned to Gallaher's as an executive director and he remained on the board of the company until his retirement in 1966. From 1949 until his death he was also a member of the council of the Industrial Welfare Society, later the Industrial Society, and from 1964 to 1969 he was its chairman. Meanwhile, he continued to take a keen part in defence debates in the House of Lords as a staunch supporter of the Royal Navy and also in debates on industrial welfare.

Ampthill married first, in 1918, Christabel Hulme, second daughter of Lieutenant-Colonel John Hart, Leinster Regiment, and his wife Blanche Anstruther Erskine, of Broadhurst, Heathfield, Sussex. By her he had one son Geoffrey Denis Erskine, who was born on 15 October 1921. A year later he petitioned for a divorce on the grounds of his wife's adultery, denying that he was Geoffrey's father. The jury disagreed, but at the re-hearing of the case in 1923 the petitioner was granted a decree *nisi*. After Christabel Russell's appeal had been dismissed by the Court of Appeal, she appealed to the House of Lords, who by a majority of three to two in May 1924 allowed her appeal on the ground that her husband's evidence in the court below was inadmissible. Having thus established her son's legitimacy, judicially confirmed in 1926, Christabel Lady Ampthill's marriage was dissolved by divorce on her petition in 1937.

In the same year Ampthill married, secondly, Sibell Faithfull, daughter of Thomas Wilkinson Lumley, chief constable of Leicestershire. She died in 1947 without issue. In 1948, he married, thirdly, Adeline Mary Constance, eldest daughter of Canon Henry Evelyn Hone, vicar and rural dean of Godalming, Surrey. They had a son and a daughter. After a successful business career in London, Ampthill's first wife Christabel, who was noted for her good looks, high spirits, and prowess in the hunting field, spent her later years in Ireland where she died 16 February 1976, in Galway, aged eighty.

The House of Lords judgement in the so-called Russell baby case in 1924 was of considerable social as well as legal importance. It established the principle (reversed by Parliament in 1949) that no evidence can be given by a husband and wife in any legal proceedings, if the effect of such evidence would be to bastardize a child born in wedlock. It also led to the passing two years later of the Act of Parliament restricting the reporting of divorce proceedings in England and Wales to the identity of the parties, the grounds for the petition, the judge's summing up, and the verdict.

Ampthill died 3 June 1973 at his London home in St. John's Wood. His elder son Geoffrey's claim to succeed him in title and sit in the Upper House as fourth Baron was contested by his younger son John. The matter came before the House of Lords committee of privileges which after hearing legal argument upheld the elder son's claim.

[*The Times*, 4 June 1973 and 18 February 1976; *Law Reports* (1924) AC 687; Eileen Hunter, *Christabel: The Russell Case and After*, 1973; private information.]

H. MONTGOMERY HYDE

RUSSELL, SIR (SYDNEY) GORDON (1892–1980), designer and craftsman, was born in Elm Grove, Cricklewood, 20 May 1892, the eldest of three sons (there were no daughters) of Sydney Bolton Russell, a banker's clerk, who later became a hotel keeper, and his wife, Elizabeth Shefford. By the time Gordon Russell was of school age his father was owner of the Lygon Arms Hotel in Broadway and thus began Russell's lifelong association with the Cotswolds. He went to the grammar school in Chipping Camden, where he came under the influence of C. R. Ashbee [q.v.] and his Camden Guild of Handicraft, for at that time the Cotswolds were, in the wake of William Morris [q.v.], still the centre for much creative activity by many distinguished artist craftsmen. It was inevitable that the young Russell should have been stirred by their invention just as he was impressed by his father's love of traditional stone building and of old furniture. Indeed while still at school he began working in his father's furniture repair shop behind the Lygon Arms, so it was natural that, after four years in the trenches with the Worcester Regiment from which he emerged commissioned, wounded, and decorated (MC), he should return there, but full of ideas for creating something new with traditions that were old.

His earliest designs were much influenced by the English Arts and Crafts Movement, being primarily meant for hand production, but gradually he became more interested in larger contracts and eventually in selling to a wider public, first through his own showrooms in Broadway and London and then through selected retailers—the Good Furnishing Group of the late 1930s. By this time had had gained much experience of quantity production through working for Frank Murphy and E. J. Power, the pioneer manufacturers of well-designed radio sets, whose cabinets were made by Gordon Russell in a factory at Park Royal to designs by his younger brother R. D. Russell, RDI.

The 1920s and 1930s were years of expansion for Gordon Russell Ltd., but Russell's great contribution was that in an industry which was continuously lowering its standards in search of mass markets he maintained at a reasonable price only that level of quality and design that could satisfy his own conscience. In those years too he learned some of the problems of retailing, while, as a director with his brother, Don Russell, of a thriving and enlarged Lygon Arms, something of the power to be exerted on suppliers by the bulk buyer. At the same time through his interest in the Design and Industries Association he began taking on more and more speaking and writing in the cause of good design, all of which was admirably preparing him for his future directorship of the as yet unthought-of Council of Industrial Design.

But first he had to survive another war and the closing of his London showrooms, the fire-bombing of his Broadway ones, the selling of his Park Royal factory, and the turning of his Broadway one over to the manufacture of ammunition boxes and parts of RAF Mosquitoes. He joined the committee at the Board of Trade under the chairmanship of Sir Charles Tennyson that led to the production of the excellent but ill-named 'utility furniture', with which from 1943 to 1947 Russell was closely associated as chairman of the Board of Trade design panel. He became a powerful, if controversial, educational force in the British furniture industry, which made him a natural choice for membership of the Council of Industrial Design, formed in 1944, and for its directorship three years later from which he retired in 1959 having successfully launched the Design Centre for British Industries in Haymarket. It would be hard to underestimate the impact of his directorship, for, although himself a craftsman and a profound believer in handwork, he was the most articulate champion of designing for the machine in the age of the machine. He wrote: 'There is a job for the hand and a job for the machine', but no one could be more scathing when manufacturers deliberately or through ignorance confused the two and tried to reproduce by machine things originally designed to be made by hand. 'Are we to admire things', he asked, 'because they are beautiful or because they are old? The doctrine that nothing is beautiful unless it is old has created an army of swindlers, whose artful work may in time even bring discredit on the lovely craftsmanship which they attempt to imitate.' And elsewhere he wrote: 'There is no reason why things made by machine should be ugly or shoddy; it is only apathy, greed, ignorance and prejudice which make them so.'

Fortunately, with his large frame and cheerful nature, he lived long enough to see his early battles largely won; to find himself, who had so long been the target for misunderstanding and even abuse in commercial circles, honoured and emulated far beyond his own industry; to see his place in the history of design fully secure and recorded; and to watch the Council of Industrial Design, which he had so imaginatively directed for twelve of his late middle years (1947–59), grow into a national institution with an international reputation.

He was appointed CBE in 1947 and knighted in 1955. He received the Albert medal of the Royal Society of Arts in 1962 and honorary doctorates of the universities of Birmingham

(1960), York (1969), and of the Royal College of Art. He was master of the Faculty of Royal Designers for Industry, master of the Art Workers Guild, president of the Design and Industries Association, first fellow of the Society of Industrial Artists and Designers, and first chairman of the Crafts Council of Great Britain. He was also RDI. He modestly but fundamentally changed the outlook of his contemporaries on what should be demanded of things in everyday use. He wrote many popular books on design and furniture and in 1968 published his autobiography, *Designer's Trade.* He contributed the notice of Sir Thomas Barlow to this Dictionary.

In 1921 he married Constance Elizabeth Jane Vere ('Toni'), daughter of Frederick Arthur Vere Denning, surgeon, of Sligo; they had three sons and one daughter. His portrait was painted by Carel Weight, RA. He died at Kingcombe, Chipping Camden, 7 October 1980.

[Gordon Russell, *Designer's Trade*, 1968; *The Times*, 8 October 1980; the Design Council; Ken and Kate Baynes, *Gordon Russell*, 1981; personal knowledge.] PAUL REILLY

RUSSELL, (WILLIAM) RITCHIE (1903–1980), neurologist, was born in Edinburgh 7 February 1903, the eldest of three sons and fourth of the six children of William Russell, professor of medicine at Edinburgh University, and his wife, Beatrice, daughter of James Ritchie, civil engineer. She was a graduate in medicine of the University of Brussels. Of his three older sisters, two were also doctors, as was one of his younger brothers, Scott Russell, who became professor of obstetrics and gynaecology at Sheffield University. He was educated at Edinburgh Academy and later at Edinburgh University, graduating MB, Ch.B. in 1926. After holding resident appointments at the Royal Infirmary, Edinburgh, and, in 1928–30, at the National Hospital for Nervous Diseases at Queen Square in London, he was appointed as assistant physician at the Royal Infirmary, Edinburgh, in 1934, working in internal medicine with an interest in neurology. He was awarded the gold medal for his MD thesis in 1932.

In 1938 he was appointed lecturer in neurology at Edinburgh University and began to confine his practice largely to neurological medicine. In 1940 he joined the Royal Army Medical Corps as a specialist neurologist, ultimately attaining the rank of brigadier. For much of the war he was closely associated with the Military Hospital for Head Injuries established in Oxford at St. Hugh's College and at Wheatley but for a time in 1943 he served as consultant in neurology to the Middle East Forces. It was during this time that he developed his major interest in head injury and in the effects of wounds upon the brain. After demobilization, he was appointed in 1945 as consultant neurologist to the United Oxford Hospitals and in 1949 became lecturer in clinical neurology in the University of Oxford. In 1948 he was appointed honorary consultant in neurology to the army. In Oxford, in collaboration with Sir Hugh Cairns (whose notice he later wrote for this Dictionary), he studied in detail the thousand or more British war pensioners suffering from focal brain wounds. Some of this work was carried out at the Ministry of Pensions Hospital at Stoke Mandeville and at Headington Hill Hall Rehabilitation Centre (established by the Red Cross and Order of St. John).

In 1966 he became the first holder of the chair of clinical neurology in Oxford, a chair which was endowed by the National Fund for Research into Poliomyelitis and Other Crippling Diseases. His stay in Oxford was marked by the building up of a strong academic department of neurology, by the establishment of an increasingly effective regional neurological service, and by an administrative ability and a doggedness which secured for neurology its due place, if not in the sun, at least in the teaching hospital. Besides inspiring and teaching others, he continued research not only into the effects of closed head injury and multiple sclerosis, but also into poliomyelitis. It was largely his work which drew the profession's attention to the deleterious effects of injections and of tonsillectomy in the preparalytic stage of poliomyelitis, and his book on this topic (*Poliomyelitis*, 2nd edn., 1956) clearly analysed the effects of exercise and trauma upon the extent and distribution of paralysis in this disease.

He was also one of those who initiated the scientific investigation of methods of assisted respiration and of their value in neurological disease, and in his later years he did important work on speech and memory, editing with M. L. E. Espir *Traumatic Aphasia* (1961). He also wrote *The Traumatic Amnesias* (1971) and *Explaining the Brain* (1975). For many years a member of the Association of British Neurologists, he was its president from 1970 to 1972, and also edited the *Journal of Neurology, Neurosurgery and Psychiatry* from 1948 to 1969, making this specialist journal one that was to be reckoned with in the field of neurology.

As a clinician he was also outstanding; in conclave with his peers, his words on diagnosis, treatment, or prognosis, though never the loudest, were often the last. Those who got to know him well, and not least his patients, appreciated that his activities were suffused with deep kindliness, generosity, and a quick humour that emerged with unexpected sparkle from behind a solemn countenance. In his later years, and even after retirement, his work on behalf of the neurologically disabled won increasing international renown.

He became FRCP in 1943. He was appointed CBE in 1952 and his publications won him an Oxford D.Sc. in 1955. In 1953 he was president of the section of neurology at the British Medical Association annual meeting and in 1963 was elected an honorary member of the American Neurological Association. He retired in 1970.

He married in 1932 Jean, daughter of Robert Stuart Low, an engineer. They had one son, later a general medical practitioner in Wimborne, Dorset, and a daughter. He died by his own hand at his home in Oxford 8 December 1980.

[*British Medical Journal*, 20 December 1980; *Lancet*, 20 December 1980; private information; personal knowledge.] JOHN WALTON

RUTHERFORD, DAME MARGARET (1892–1972), actress, was born in Balham 11 May 1892, the only child of William Rutherford, a traveller in silks in India, and his wife, Florence Nicholson. William Rutherford had been born a Benn, the brother of Sir Joshua Benn, but decided to change his name to Rutherford, as being more suitable for a writer. Margaret Rutherford was taken to India as a baby, but was returned to England, to live with an aunt, Bessie Nicholson, when her mother died when the child was three. The father died shortly afterwards. Margaret Rutherford was educated at Wimbledon High School and Raven's Croft School in Seaford. She qualified as a licentiate of the Royal Academy of Music and became a music teacher, doing nothing to further her wish to act professionally until, at the age of thirty-three, she inherited a small income when her aunt died. A letter of introduction from John Drinkwater [q.v.] enabled her to join the Old Vic Company as a student in 1925, the year in which (Dame) Edith Evans [q.v.] played the leading parts there, but this led to no further work in the theatre, and she returned to teaching at Wimbledon, where she spent two more years before being engaged to understudy at the Lyric, Hammersmith, by (Sir) Nigel Playfair [q.v.].

From Hammersmith she went to Croydon, Epsom, and Oxford, playing in weekly repertory, and at Oxford she made the acquaintance of (Sir) Tyrone Guthrie [q.v.], who immediately recognized her unique personality and talent. He directed her soon afterwards at His Majesty's in London (where in 1935 she played for him in an ill-fated but star-studded drama called *Hervey House*, with Fay Compton, Gertrude Lawrence [qq.v.], and Nicholas Hannen) and later in *Short Story*, a comedy by Robert Morley. On this occasion she won a spirited battle against the redoubtable (Dame) Marie Tempest [q.v.], who was attempting to thwart her by distracting the attention of the audience during their scenes together, but finally capitulated good humouredly when she found her rival had the courage to stand up to her. In 1938, under the direction of (Sir) John Gielgud, she achieved a big personal success as a comic aunt, betting secretly on horses with the butler, in an Irish comedy, *Spring Meeting*. But the director had considerable difficulty in persuading her to undertake the part, since she saw little humour in the play when it was first given her to read. 'Don't you think that as we are living in such gloomy times', she wrote, 'that people want to laugh?'

Her seriousness was, of course, an invaluable asset in her solemn acting of farce. With an unfailing instinct for execution and timing, there was always a hint of sadness, as in many of the greatest comedians, behind the comicality of her performances.

In 1939 (a year before she somewhat improbably created the part of Mrs Danvers, the baleful housekeeper in (Dame) Daphne du Maurier's *Rebecca*) she appeared as Miss Prism in John Gielgud's production of *The Importance of Being Earnest* for some special matinées. For the run of the play which followed she accepted the offer to repeat her performance, but only on condition that she might also understudy Edith Evans—an unheard of stipulation for an important actress. When, some years later, the production was taken to America, Edith Evans did not wish to go and Margaret Rutherford was asked to replace her, which she did with notable success. But even then she begged to be allowed to wear similar costumes to those that Edith Evans had worn in London, and despite her own markedly different personality, she played the part on exactly similar lines, though without appearing to imitate Edith Evans, whose work she so greatly admired.

Her successes in films did not perhaps give her very great satisfaction, though she was always touchingly appreciative of praise and popularity. As the spiritualist Madame Arcati in *Blithe Spirit* (1941) by (Sir) Noël Coward [q.v.]—another of her great successes in the theatre—she suffered great agonies in fearing to make mock of a cult which she knew to be taken very seriously by its devotees, and at the end of the long run she suffered a nervous breakdown as a result.

Not long before Margaret Rutherford's death, her friends were approached by a lady journalist who was endeavouring to help her complete her autobiography, for which she had already accepted an advance fee. Dame Margaret had been incapacitated by illness, and neither she herself, nor her husband, J. B. Stringer Davis, an actor whom she had married in 1945, were able to complete the assignment, and the ghost-writer was at a loss how to gain the further material which she needed and was trying to fill the gaps with tributes from some of her friends and colleagues. But it appeared that in the course of detailed researches, a certain amount of information had come to light about Margaret Rutherford's earlier life involving an unhappy family background and recurrences of mental disturbance which would be pointless and painful to bring to light, and the book was finally cobbled together as well as possible under these unhappy circumstances.

Margaret Rutherford was a most modest and dedicated actress. She adored her husband, was infinitely kind, unassuming, and intensely professional, but increasingly disturbed. She insisted on continuing to fulfil commitments after she was already seriously ill, and failed to complete a film, from which she retired, after some humiliation at the hands of the impatient director, with the greatest dignity. And her last appearance at the Haymarket with Sir Ralph Richardson in *The Rivals*, an engagement which she was finally obliged to give up after a few weeks, was a most poignant struggle against her obviously failing powers.

Though never slender, or good-looking, she had extraordinary grace and charm. Light on her feet, she moved with grace and distinction, taking the stage with confidence and apparent ease. She wore costume to perfection, and her phrasing and diction, whether in William Congreve, R. B. Sheridan, or Oscar Wilde [qq.v.], were equally impeccable. On the night she left the cast of *The School for Scandal* (1962), in which she was a memorable Mrs Candour, she gave a party on the stage after the performance, and there is a last happy memory of her dancing joyously up and down the stage hand in hand with the stage carpenter.

Among the awards she won was an Oscar for best supporting actress for the film *The VIPs* in 1964. She was appointed OBE in 1961 and DBE in 1967. She died at Chalfont and Gerrard's Cross Hospital 22 May 1972.

[*Margaret Rutherford*, an autobiography as told to Gwen Robyns, 1972; Eric Keown, *Margaret Rutherford*, 1956; personal knowledge.]

JOHN GIELGUD

RYAN, ELIZABETH MONTAGUE (1892–1979), tennis champion, was born at Anaheim, a suburb of Los Angeles, 5 February 1892, the younger daughter and younger child of Francis George Ryan, who had emigrated from London to California and invested shrewdly in land (on a census form he described himself as 'a capitalist'), and his wife, Matilda Brooks, of San Francisco. Her father died in 1898 after the family had moved to Santa Monica. She and her sister Alice, born in 1890, learned to play tennis there and soon established themselves as determined match players, meeting the strongest Californians of the day and even travelling to tournaments in Canada.

They made their most important journey, however, in 1912. After Mrs Ryan's second marriage had ended in disappointment, she decided to take her daughters to England. Elizabeth Ryan was to live there for most of the rest of her life. The trip began as a holiday but soon they were competing enthusiastically in British tournaments. Disconcerted at first by the difference in pace and bounce of Californian cement courts and English grass, the younger Miss Ryan adapted her game with sufficient success to play at Wimbledon. She was only the sixth overseas player—and the third American—to enter the women's singles and may have been regarded as brash and over confident but she reached the fourth round and held two match points against Mrs Hillyard, six times the champion, before losing 3–6, 8–6, 6–3.

If she came to England as a stranger, she learnt its geography from the map of the tournament circuit. In that first year she won prizes at Liverpool, Malton, Warwick, Winchester, Edgbaston, Lincoln, Tunbridge Wells, Saxmundham, Felixstowe, Chichester, Eastbourne, and Hythe. Partnered by many of the best players of the day and invariably playing singles, doubles, and mixed at each tournament, she had begun to amass her huge collection of trophies and titles. An American journalist, who interviewed her soon after she turned professional in 1935, estimated that during her years of play she won or was runner-up in 1,500 events. London was her base. She returned only occasionally to the United States but she competed frequently in the major European tournaments.

It seemed that she played whenever she could and her performances were remarkable for dedication, skill, and strength, for endurance and sheer appetite for competition. Her range of shots was formidable. If Hazel Wightman was the first woman to use the volley at a time when players generally felt safer at the back of the court, Elizabeth Ryan took matters further by showing that the volley could be a central part of a woman's technique by playing at the net consistently and forcefully. Alice Marble, speaking for the next generation, called her the greatest woman volleyer of all time: 'I never saw her make a really defensive volley. Hugging the net, hitting high volleys like rifle shots, she had every angle known to the game at her command.'

She had been forced to learn to volley, she told Ted Tinling, during a final against her sister at Vancouver when she was fifteen. Alice was making the ball bounce awkwardly from a rough patch and she decided that the only way to stop this was to meet the ball before it bounced. She possessed a most effective drop shot and a chop, which was notoriously difficult to take on wet grass. As for her smash, Fred Perry said that of all the women who played mixed doubles in the 1930s only Elizabeth Ryan could kill an overhead against a man waiting behind the baseline.

She played in two Wimbledon singles finals but, unable to overcome either Suzanne Lenglen or Helen Wills and injured in 1931, a year when the field was weaker than usual, she was generally regarded as 'unlucky' in singles. In doubles, however, she was dominating. 'Miss Ryan, in my humble opinion, is the best player in ladies' doubles since lawn tennis was invented', said Commander G. W. Hillyard in 1924, writing from long experience as a player and an observer of the championships.

She won the first of her nineteen Wimbledon doubles titles—twelve women's and seven mixed—with Agatha Morton in 1914. She and Suzanne Lenglen, whom she partnered for the first time on the Riviera in 1913 when Miss Lenglen, at thirteen, was just about to be recognized as the prodigy of the circuit, held the title from 1919 to 1923, losing only one set in five years. Then, after a year when Miss Lenglen withdrew through illness, they regained it in 1925. Elizabeth Ryan was also champion with Mary K. Browne (1926), Helen Wills Moody (1927 and 1930), and Simone Mathieu (1933 and 1934). In mixed doubles she won the title with Randolph Lycett (1919, 1921, and 1923), Francis Hunter (1927), Patrick Spence (1928), Jack Crawford (1930), and Enrique Maier (1932). She won the French doubles title four times and the US doubles and mixed in 1926 and the US doubles title again in 1933.

'Of late years it had become almost a certainty that the ladies doubles would go to Miss Ryan and her partner, whoever that partner might be', wrote F. R. Burrow, the Wimbledon referee, after her last appearance in the championships. 'It was unfortunate that the years when she was at her best as a singles player were just the years when Miss Lenglen was dominating the courts. But for the French girl, it is fairly certain that Miss Ryan would have had a couple of wins in the singles to add to her successes in the doubles.' She returned to the centre court during Wimbledon's centenary celebrations in 1977 when she and Toto Brugnon were invited to represent Wimbledon's doubles winners at the champions' parade.

There was a final irony. For more than forty years her nineteen titles stood as the highest total gained by any player at Wimbledon but every year she was more and more conscious of the fact that Billie Jean King, another remarkable Californian, was approaching her record. On 8 July 1979, the penultimate day of the championships and the day before Mrs King gained her twentieth title, Elizabeth Ryan collapsed and died at the All England Club, at Wimbledon. Some time before she had told friends that she hoped she would take her record to the grave. She died as she had played, determined not to be beaten. She was unmarried.

[*Ayres Lawn Tennis Almanack*; *Lowe's Lawn Tennis Annual*; Ted Tinling, *Love and Faults*, 1979; F. G. Lowe, *Gordon Lowe on Lawn Tennis*, 1924; F. R. Burrow, *The Centre Court, and Others*, 1937; G. W. Hillyard, *Forty Years of First-Class Lawn Tennis*, 1924; personal knowledge.] DAVID GRAY

RYLE, GILBERT (1900–1976), philosopher, was born in his family's home in Brighton 19 August 1900. His twin sister, Mary, and he were the eighth and ninth of the ten children of Reginald John Ryle MD, general practitioner, and his wife, Catherine Scott. His grandfather, John Charles Ryle [q.v.], was the first bishop of Liverpool. Both his parents had shed the strict evangelicalism of their upbringing and Ryle himself was without religious beliefs. He was educated at Brighton College and at the Queen's College, Oxford, to which he won a classical scholarship (1919) and where he gained first class honours in, successively, classical honour moderations (1921) and the honour schools of *literae humaniores* (1923) and philosophy, politics, and economics (1924). He was invited to sit the final examination in this latter, new school in order to set a standard for first class performance in it. Joining athletic to academic achievement, he was captain of the Queen's College Boat Club in 1923 and rowed in the university trial eights in that year. In 1924 he was appointed lecturer in philosophy at Christ Church, Oxford, and in 1925 was elected a Student and tutor in philosophy in that college. He served the college both as junior and as senior censor and was junior proctor of the university, 1937–8. In 1940 he was commissioned in the Welsh Guards and was employed on intelligence work until demobilized in 1945 with the rank of major. From 1945 until his retirement in 1968 he was Waynflete professor of metaphysical philosophy and fellow of Magdalen College. He edited *Mind*, in succession to G. E. Moore [q.v.], from 1947 to 1971.

As he says in the autobiographical introduction to a collection of critical essays on his work (1971), Ryle was, from the start of his Oxford career, 'philosophically eager'. Finding the local philosophical atmosphere, in the early and middle 1920s, distinctly tepid, he turned to the work of Bertrand Russell [q.v.], at that time an object of disapproval or neglect in Oxford, taught himself German and read Frege, Husserl, Brentano, Bolzano, and Meinong. Towards the end of the decade he made the acquaintance of the Cambridge philosophers, Moore and Ludwig Wittgenstein [q.v.], and became a friend of the latter. During this period, in which he helped to start an informal discussion group of the younger Oxford philosophers, he formed the conviction, which remained with him, that philosophical questions were essentially questions about the meaning or 'logical grammar' of expressions. Above all, he thought it was important to establish the distinction, and the rationale of the distinction, between what collocations of expressions made sense and what made, perhaps unobviously, nonsense. Philosophical error and perplexity typically arose from treating expressions belonging to one logical type or category as if they belonged to another. Such confusions, often encouraged by superficial grammar, could be exposed by pressing them to the limit of obvious absurdity.

The most influential of Ryle's pre-war papers on these logical and meta-philosophical themes were 'Systematically Misleading Expressions' (1932) and 'Categories (1938). In this latter essay and in his inaugural lecture as Waynflete professor ('Philosophical Arguments', 1945) he appeared to be aiming at a precise and general theoretical account of the notion of a logical type or category. This attempt, if it was one, was imperfectly successful and he later (*Dilemmas*, 1954) disavowed the belief that his notion of a logical category was capable of a precise and general explication; an admission that disturbed him little, if at all, since he remained convinced of the philosophical utility of the notion and became increasingly concerned with the practice, rather than the theory, of his method.

Ryle found a major field for the application of that method in what he described as the 'official', or Cartesian, theory of the mind, which formed the target of attack in his principal work, *The Concept of Mind* (1949). Calling it, 'with deliberate abusiveness', the myth of 'the ghost in the machine', he described the official theory as embodying one big category-mistake, ramifying into a family of related category-mistakes: the mind was conceived of as a ghostly analogue of the body and mental operations as private and immaterial counterparts of public and physical operations. Ryle saw his task as a twofold one: destructively, he was to exhibit the absurdities which followed from the official doctrine; constructively, he was to establish the true logical character of 'mental-conduct concepts', i.e. of the words we use when we speak of mental faculties, qualities, and performances. In successive chapters he dealt with intelligence, the will, emotion, self-knowledge, sensation, imagination, and intellect. He repeatedly succeeded in showing that many expressions which, on the official view, were taken to refer exclusively to private inner episodes or processes are in fact dispositional or semi-dispositional in character, where the dispositions in question are dispositions to overt and observable behaviour. Not all his analyses were equally successful; his treatment of some topics, notably sensation, imagination, and thinking, gave some ground for the suspicion that he really wished, quite implausibly, to deny the existence of private, subjective experiences altogether. (His chapter on the intellect elicited from J. L. Austin [q.v.], who reviewed the work in the *Times Literary Supplement* of 7 April 1950, the comment: '"Ponderings", once firmly distinguished from what they are not, are thenceforward left in the air, where they are surely not more happily located than "in the mind".')

Ryle's next book, *Dilemmas*, was a slightly modified version of the Tarner lectures which he delivered in Trinity College, Cambridge, in the previous year. In it he demonstrated, in a number of diverse cases, how specialist and non-specialist accounts of what is in some sense the same subject-matter may generate apparent conflicts in the speculative mind if the concepts concerned are allowed to become detached from the background of their working employment. The resolution of such conflicts then calls for the reimposition of 'category-disciplines' by the critical philosopher. In this way, for example, we are delivered from the threat of being forced by classical logic into fatalism, or by simple mathematics into Zeno's paradox of Achilles and the tortoise, or by the discoveries of natural science into the repudiation of our common-sense picture of the world.

Throughout his philosophical career Ryle produced a steady stream of articles and reviews. Many were concerned with the philosophy of language, the theory of meaning, or the nature of philosophy itself; some reflected his early interest in phenomenology; others were devoted to his great predecessors or contemporaries, Locke, Moore, and Wittgenstein; yet others to questions in the philosophy of mind, particularly, in his later years, to the topic of thinking. Most of those which were published in his lifetime were assembled in two large volumes of *Collected Papers* (1971). Plato, whose *Parmenides* he made the subject of an important and original study published in 1939, continued to fascinate Ryle throughout his life; it was to him that he devoted his last unitary book, *Plato's Progress* (1966), a piece of ingenious detective work on the life of the philosopher. Novel and brilliant as Ryle's theories were, they were received with scepticism by classical scholars, whose general view was that adequate materials for a life of Plato did not exist.

A posthumously published collection of papers, *On Thinking* (ed. K. Kolenda, 1979), reflected the preoccupation of Ryle's later years and his own dissatisfaction with his earlier treatment of the topic. He described his 'long-range objective' as that of finding out 'how to talk sense about the thinking that *Le Penseur* is occupied in doing' without falling into the category-errors of Behaviourism on the one hand or Cartesianism on the other. He approached the question by considering what it is that distinguishes thoughtful from thoughtless performances of ordinary overt activities like climbing, driving or dissecting; found the distinction in a variety of adverbial qualifications such as 'vigilantly', 'carefully', 'noticingly', 'experimentally' etc.; and concluded that there is no one specific type of *content* essential to *Le Penseur*'s doing (it may, but need not, consist in experimental inner speech or in imagining modifications of a studied situation), but that, whatever the specific content may be, it is essentially *qualified* in the same way as thoughtfully conducted overt activities.

In these last essays, as in all his work, the distinction and originality of Ryle's thought and style were abundantly manifest. The dominant characteristics of that style were: verve and brilliance; concreteness and wit; and an utter freedom from pretentiousness or jargon. Striking epigram, balanced antithesis, and memorable phrase were combined with homely illustration and analogy to illuminate each recalcitrant topic in turn. His *oeuvre* as a whole remains a brilliant and lasting contribution both to philosophy and to English letters.

During the years which followed World War II Oxford University emerged once more as a distinguished centre of philosophy in the western world. Ryle, at the centre of this centre, played a greater part in this development than any other single individual. He contributed to it not only by his writings, lectures, and classes, influential as these were. He was also primarily responsible for the introduction, by a statute of 1946, of the new postgraduate degree of bachelor of philosophy, which was first examined in 1948. This innovation led to an expansion and flourishing of graduate philosophical study in Oxford, attracting students from outside as well as inside the United Kingdom, particularly from Australia and the United States, and greatly stimulating the philosophical activity of Oxford tutors. In contrast with the degree of doctor of philosophy, which required the student to produce a dissertation on a single subject, the new degree demanded that he show competence, in written papers, over a relatively wide area of problems, besides submitting a shorter thesis on a topic of his choice. Ryle held, correctly, that the fulfilment of these requirements formed a better preparation for the aspirant teacher of the subject that the premature concentration on a single issue which was demanded of the man who proceeded directly from undergraduate studies to reading for a doctorate. In the decades which followed, and as the British university system expanded, new and already established philosophy departments were increasingly staffed by holders of the Oxford B.Phil.

Always impatient of pretentiousness, fashion, or mere orthodoxy, always ready with sharp and pertinent criticism both of style and of content, Ryle was at the same time untiring in his encouragement of young, and thus far unknown, philosophers. As editor of *Mind*, he tended to prefer the offerings of philosophers with unfamiliar names, often from unfamiliar places, to those of the well established, who could easily find outlets for their writings elsewhere. This tendency was not without its critics; but the journal flourished. The number of members of the Mind Association more than trebled during his editorship. The brisk unfussiness of his conduct of the periodical was exemplary.

Ryle was little interested in the arts, except the literary arts – more specifically the writing of prose. The exception is important. Though the relatively abstract problems of philosophy and the furtherance of philosophical studies were, throughout his life, his dominant concern, he was a man of great literary and moral sensitivity. The former kind of sensitivity was amply evidenced in his own writing and in the criticism which he privately offered of the drafts of others; but the union of both kinds is admirably displayed in his fine essay, 'Jane Austen and the Moralists' (1966). Of the works of that author, indeed, he was a devoted admirer. (Once, when asked whether he ever read novels, he is said to have replied: 'Oh yes, all six of them, every year.')

His most strongly marked personal characteristics were directness, friendliness, candour, and a strong sense of justice. He was uncompromising in his judgements and could be brusque. He had no use for gossip. He was tall, slim, and soldierly in appearance. A painting of him, in uniform, hangs in the summer common room in Magdalen College.

He received many academic honours: he was a foreign honorary member of the American Academy of Arts and Sciences (1968), an honorary Student of Christ Church, and an honorary fellow of Queen's and Magdalen colleges; he was awarded honorary doctorates by the universities of Birmingham, Warwick, Sussex, Hull, Keele, Trent (Ontario), and Trinity College, Dublin.

On retirement from the Waynflete chair Ryle lived in Islip, near Oxford, with his twin sister, who survived him. He suffered a stroke and died 6 October 1976 while on holiday in Yorkshire. He was unmarried. In his will he left a considerable sum of money to Hertford College, chosen, as being less well endowed than those colleges with which he was more closely connected.

[O. P. Wood and G. Pitcher (eds.), *Ryle: a Collection of Critical Essays*, 1971; preface by G. J. Warnock to G. Ryle, *On Thinking* (ed. K. Kolenda), 1979; G. J. Warnock, 'Gilbert Ryle's Editorship', *Mind*, 1976; private information; personal knowledge.]

P. F. STRAWSON

S

SACHS, SIR ERIC LEOPOLD OTHO (1898–1979), judge, was born in London 23 July 1898, the only child of Edwin Otho Sachs FRSE, an architect and expert on fire prevention, and his wife, Flora Jacoby. His grandfather, a banker, had come to Britain from Germany. Sachs was educated at Charterhouse. He then joined the Royal Artillery with whom he served as a gunner officer from 1917 to 1919. He was seriously wounded in his left hand which remained partially disabled throughout his life. Upon demobilization early in 1919 he at once went to Christ Church, Oxford, where he read law. (He was to become an honorary student of Christ Church in 1971.) He passed the shortened honours course in jurisprudence in 1920 after only five terms' residence.

He was called to the bar by the Middle Temple in 1921. He became a pupil of (Sir) Wilfrid Lewis [q.v.], later junior counsel to the Treasury, and subsequently a High Court judge. Sachs joined the Oxford circuit and in due course acquired a first-class junior practice both in London and on circuit which well justified his taking silk in 1938. At the same time he was appointed recorder of Dudley, his first judicial appointment. Characteristically in 1939 he at once rejoined the army and served, at first as a very junior officer, in various departments of the War Office under the control of the adjutant-general. Sachs's fierce courage in dealing with his military and civil superiors—they in their turn were somewhat frightened of a KC—did much to mitigate the mindless meanness over pay and allowances which did so much to damage service morale in the early stages of the war. He was appointed MBE in 1941.

In 1942 Sachs moved into the world of intelligence in the Political Warfare Department and was promoted to brigadier. To that body and to Sachs in particular was assigned the task of producing 'basic handbooks'. These were instructions for those to be responsible for the administration of territories still to be reoccupied. In due course Sachs presented a complete set of these volumes to the Middle Temple library.

Upon demobilization in 1945 Sachs returned to the bar. He had still to build a practice as a silk and it was not easy to start again. Stress of work during the war had not improved his health. In the ensuing years he was twice employed as a commissioner of assize and in 1946 he was appointed special commissioner to inquire into allegations of serious corruption in the Gold Coast. From 1943 to 1954 he was recorder of Stoke-on-Trent and for the last two of those years leader of the Oxford circuit. All these tasks he discharged admirably and at the same time acquired a substantial practice. Amidst his many services was his leadership of the bar team which in conjunction with the Law Society team headed by (Sir) Sydney Littlewood (whose notice Sachs was to write for this Dictionary), was responsible for the Legal Aid scheme which later was established by the Legal Aid and Advice Act of 1949. Sachs was in truth one of the principal architects of that great social reform. He did much to ensure the independence of both branches of the profession from its new paymasters.

In 1954 Sachs was appointed a judge of the High Court and knighted. He served in the Probate, Divorce, and Admiralty division of that court until 1960 when he was transferred to the Queen's Bench division. After six further years he was appointed a lord justice of appeal in 1966, an office which he held until retirement in 1973. On appointment he was also sworn of the Privy Council. He never claimed profound knowledge of the law. His judicial qualities were great industry and an intense zeal to find the right answer and to prevent injustice wherever it might be found. His weakness was undue attention to detail which occasionally led to overcomplication of a simple case by concentration on inessentials. But the faults were in part due to his qualities.

His second great service was to his Inn, the Middle Temple. He became a bencher in 1947 and treasurer in 1967. He transformed the government of that Inn from an inefficient oligarchical system to one suitable to the post-war era. The treasurership, which had too often been regarded as a post of honour rather than of obligation, thenceforth became an office to be held only by the active. He devised the committee system which not only made the burden of that office tolerable but also ensured proper financial control of the Inn's limited resources. He also brought younger members of the Inn into the machinery of its government. The subsequent strength of the Middle Temple, both financial and intellectual, is perhaps his best memorial.

Increasing deafness and a sense of duty requiring him not to remain too long on the bench combined to dictate retirement in 1973. He moved from his flat in the Temple to live entirely in East Sussex, but until afflicted by ill health he remained in contact with his many friends in London and his lifelong interest in the law continued. But he never fully recovered from a serious operation and he died 1 September 1979 at his home in Wadhurst.

In 1934 he married Margaret, the second daughter of the future lord chief justice of England, Rayner (later Lord) Goddard [q.v.]. They had a son and daughter. His married and family life was one of great personal happiness. There is an indifferent portrait of him in the Middle Temple.

[Private information; personal knowledge.]

ROSKILL

SACKVILLE, HERBRAND EDWARD DUNDONALD BRASSEY, ninth EARL DE LA WARR (1900–1976), government minister, was born 20 June 1900 at the Manor House, Bexhill-on-Sea, Sussex, the only son and youngest of the three children of Gilbert George Reginald Sackville, eighth Earl De La Warr, and his wife, Muriel Agnes, daughter of Thomas, the first Baron (later first Earl) Brassey [q.v.]. His parents were divorced in 1902. 'Buck', as he was universally known, was educated at Eton (1913–17), where he founded and became president of the Eton Political Society, and, briefly, at Magdalen College, Oxford. In 1918 he joined the Royal Naval Reserve (trawler section), as he was a conscientious objector at the time. He had succeeded to the earldom in 1915 at the age of fifteen and was, perhaps, the only able seaman who sat, of right, on the steps of the throne in the House of Lords—the place reserved for peers who have succeeded as minors and so cannot take their place in the chamber until they are twenty-one.

After coming of age he actively supported the Labour Party in the House of Lords and was appointed lord-in-waiting in Ramsay MacDonald's government in 1924. In MacDonald's second Labour administration he was parliamentary under-secretary at the War Office, 1929–30, and at the Ministry of Agriculture, 1930–1. He followed MacDonald into the national government in August 1931 and served successively as parliamentary secretary to the Ministry of Agriculture and deputy minister to the Department of Fisheries, 1931–5, and parliamentary secretary to the Board of Education, 1935–6. He was admitted to the Privy Council in 1936. He was appointed parliamentary under-secretary of state for the colonies, 1936–7. Under Neville Chamberlain he entered the Cabinet as lord privy seal, May 1937–October 1938. At this critical period he said in Cabinet that he would face war to free the world from the constant threat of ultimatums. This may explain his demotion to the less prestigious offices of president of the Board of Education, 1938–April 1940, and first commissioner of works (not in the Cabinet), April–May 1940. He was chairman of the National Labour Party, 1931–43.

He did not find a place in (Sir) Winston Churchill's government in May 1940, probably because National Labour was not acceptable to the Labour Party. He served in the Ministry of Supply as director of home flax production during much of the war.

In the autumn of 1951 he was appointed postmaster-general by Churchill, and held the post until Churchill resigned in April 1955. During his term of office there was trouble in Scotland with Post Office property which carried the royal emblem EIIR. On the positive side, several important developments were introduced, the most notable of which were the starting of the international telex service, the development of letter-sorting machines, the planning of the national telephone numbering scheme, and the laying of the trans-Atlantic cable from Scotland to Newfoundland. The public benefit of these only became apparent after he had left office. De La Warr, assisted by his wife, also took a personal interest in selecting the new high-value definitive stamps. His period of office is best remembered, however, by the introduction of commercial television, which met with virulent opposition firmly expressed in the House of Lords. It was only the calm, polite, and clear exposition of De La Warr which persuaded the House to accept the proposals.

He had thus served in the governments of four prime ministers—Labour, National, and Conservative. He was never a keen party politician, but was deeply and sincerely interested in the realities of politics; he had no love for dogmatic theories. He maintained a close interest in the welfare of the Commonwealth; besides holding the office of under-secretary of state for the colonies, he was a member of the Empire Marketing Board from 1930, chairman of the Royal Commonwealth Society (1960), and chairman of the Joint East and Central Africa Board from 1955 to 1958. He visited Africa most years.

His constant and abiding affection lay in agriculture and land in general. He ran his farm with ability and enthusiasm and was a pioneer in new agricultural ideas and practice. It was from these interests that he was appointed a member of the council of the Duchy of Lancaster from 1931, chairman of the Agricultural Research Council from 1944 to 1949, and chairman of the National Trust estates committee (1950–1). He served in government, off and on, over a period of thirty years and was an active member of the House of Lords for fifty years. His humility and simplicity of bearing tended to conceal his shrewd political judgement. He combined a warm heart and much personal charm. He was appointed GBE in 1956.

In 1920 he married (Helen) Diana (died 1966), daughter of Captain Henry Gerard Leigh, 1st Life Guards, of Luton Hoo. They had two sons and a daughter, who married F. T. R. Giles. Their second son was missing, presumed killed, on active service in 1943. In 1968 he married Sylvia Margaret, Countess of Kilmuir, DBE, widow of the Earl of Kilmuir [q.v.], daughter of William Reginald Harrison, of Liverpool, and sister of Rex Harrison, actor.

He died on the pavement outside St. James's Palace while walking to the theatre 28 January 1976. He was succeeded in the earldom by his son, William Herbrand Sackville (born 1921).

[Private information; personal knowledge.]

SELKIRK

ST. LAURENT, LOUIS STEPHEN (1882–1973), Canadian prime minister, was born 1 February 1882 at Compton, Quebec Province, the eldest of the seven children of Jean Baptiste Moise St. Laurent, a storekeeper, and his wife, Mary Ann, the schoolteacher daughter of Stephen and Bridget Broderick, immigrants to Canada from Ireland.

Perfectly bilingual from his earliest years, St. Laurent was educated first by his mother, and then successively at a Roman Catholic primary school in Compton; St. Charles Seminary, Sherbrooke; and Laval University, Quebec City, from whose law school he graduated with highest honours in 1905. He was called to the bar of Quebec in the same year and took silk in 1915.

As a professional lawyer he built up an important practice and a national reputation in corporation and constitutional law, becoming professor of law at Laval University in 1914, and president of the Canadian Bar Association in 1930–2. But he remained wedded to family life in Quebec with the five children of his marriage in 1908 to Jeanne (died 1966), daughter of P. F. Renault, a storekeeper in Beauceville, and twice refused appointment to the Supreme Court in Ottawa.

In 1941, the death in office of Ernest Lapointe deprived the prime minister, W. L. Mackenzie King [q.v.], of his invaluable French-Canadian lieutenant, and he asked St. Laurent to take his place as minister of justice. Reluctantly, and from a sense of wartime duty, St. Laurent agreed, but for the duration of the war only. He was elected MP for Quebec East in 1942. It was not long before Mackenzie King was referring to him as 'the ablest man in the Cabinet' and increasingly sharing with him the management of external affairs and the general burdens of government.

By the end of the war St. Laurent had become, after Mackenzie King, the dominant political figure in Canada, and despite his desire to return to private life found it impossible to disengage with honour from his political responsibilities. He was admitted to the Privy Council in 1946. In the same year he became secretary of state for external affairs and with Lester Pearson [q.v.], his under-secretary (and eventual successor), began to construct a distinctive and more positive Canadian foreign policy. On Mackenzie King's retirement he was overwhelmingly elected as leader of the Liberal Party, and was sworn in as prime minister in November 1948.

He won the 1949 general election by the largest majority until then attained, and by the end of his first administration in 1953 could look back on a period of solid achievement. His manifest integrity and unfailing courtesy had made him 'Uncle Louis' to the whole country. To its sense of nationality he had contributed the completion of confederation by the union with Newfoundland; the appointment of the first Canadian governor-general; the abolition of appeals to the Privy Council; and the transfer to Canada of the power to amend the constitution in matters of federal competence. Externally, Canada had been firmly committed to the multiracial development of the Commonwealth, to membership of NATO, and to strong support for the UN. Canadian troops had been stationed in Europe and supplied to the UN force in Korea. Joint defence arrangements had been concluded with the United States. At home, inflation was under control, and both the national debt and the level of taxation had been reduced. Projects for a trans-Canada highway, and for the development of nuclear power, had been launched. In the general election of 1953 St. Laurent was again massively victorious.

His second administration (1953–7) lacked the programme and drive of his first, though it comprehended his crowning achievement in federal–provincial relations, the successful negotiation of a new method of tax-sharing and revenue equalization between the federal and provincial governments. Administratively and financially the country was ably governed, but prolonged and bitter political controversy over proposals for a trans-Canada gas pipeline left the government discredited. St. Laurent himself had periods of ill health and depression which contributed to the government's loss of ascendancy in Parliament. But the Suez crisis of 1956 gave Lester Pearson and St. Laurent an opportunity to apply themselves to the tasks of peacemaking and conciliation which they had sought to make the hallmark of Canadian foreign policy. They were instrumental in achieving the UN resolution establishing a UN emergency force, to which Canada duly contributed.

St. Laurent was defeated in the 1957 general election, and handed over the leadership of the Liberal Party to Lester Pearson in January 1958. He was at last free to return to Quebec City, his family, and his practice, in which he continued until his death there 25 July 1973.

St. Laurent had many honorary degrees, including an Oxford DCL (1953). In 1967 he was appointed CC (Canada).

[Dale C. Thomson, *Louis St. Laurent, Canadian*, 1967; J. W. Pickersgill, *My Years with Louis St. Laurent*, 1975; Lester B. Pearson, *Memoirs 1897–1948*, 1973.]

J. B. JOHNSTON

SALISBURY, fifth MARQUESS OF (1893–1972). [See CECIL, ROBERT ARTHUR JAMES GASCOYNE-.]

SALISBURY, SIR EDWARD JAMES (1886–1978), ecologist, professor of botany and director of the Royal Botanic Gardens, Kew, was born at Limbrick Hall, Harpenden, Hertfordshire, 16 April 1886, the youngest of the nine children (six boys and three girls) of James Wright Salisbury, a business man and company director, and his wife, Elizabeth Stimpson. Artistically the most distinguished of his family was a cousin, the portrait painter Frank O. Salisbury [q.v.], but Edward and his sister Ethel both had skill in drawing for botanical illustration. Very early he acquired a strong interest in living plants maintained during his schooldays at University College School. He entered University College, London, in 1905 and, after graduating with second class honours in botany became a research student under the botanical professor F. W. Oliver, whose notice Salisbury later wrote for this Dictionary (he also wrote that of H. N. Ridley). Salisbury's participation in Oliver's ecological work had a lasting effect on his thought.

Salisbury gained his D.Sc. in 1913 with a thesis on a fossil seed. In 1914 he moved to East London College (now Queen Mary College) as senior lecturer in botany. He returned to University College in 1918 and was appointed senior lecturer in 1919, reader in plant ecology in 1924, and finally Quain professor of botany in 1929, resigning in 1943 to become director of the Royal Botanic Gardens, Kew. From 1908 onwards the woodlands of his native Hertfordshire increasingly engaged his attention leading to a series of important papers on woodland ecology, listed in the Royal Society memoir mentioned below, and also to a King Penguin booklet, *Flowers of the Woods* (1946). He made numerous observations on light intensity in woods at different times of the year and studied the effect of this, together with coppicing and soil leaching, on the ground flora, thus revealing the importance of these hitherto somewhat neglected factors in woodland ecology. They led him to investigate the number of stomata on a square millimetre of leaf surface of different species and of the same species growing under different conditions and to establish a stomatal index for comparison. Studies involving laborious counting always fascinated Salisbury.

Of wider significance and of much financial gain was the publication of textbooks jointly prepared by F. E. Fritsch [q.v.] and Salisbury: *An Introduction to the Study of Plants* (1914, 9th edn. 1928), *Elementary Studies in Plant Life* (1915, 8th edn. 1926), *An Introduction to the Structure and Reproduction of Plants* (1920, 2nd edn. 1927), and *Botany for Students of Medicine and Pharmacy* (1921, 3rd edn. 1928), followed by *Plant Form and Function* (1938) which combined the two *Introduction* volumes. Clearly written and well illustrated, adequate in coverage and presenting information not readily available elsewhere, they were immediately appreciated. The title of the first chapter of the 1914 *Introduction*, 'The plant as a whole', epitomizes their approach. Salisbury himself was much interested in the quantity of seeds produced by individual plants of many species, notably weeds, which he rightly viewed as of great significance in relation to their spread and establishment. He painstakingly counted and weighed seeds belonging to over 240 species, his examination extending to hundreds of thousands of individual plants. His calculation that individuals of some weedy species produced on average 35,000 seeds indicates the labour involved. He embodied most of these observations in his *The Reproductive Capacity of Plants* (1942) but others occur in *Downs and Dunes* (1952), *Weeds and Aliens* (1961), and later publications in journals. Chapters 10, 12, and 13 of his *The Living Garden or the How and Why of Garden Life* (1935, 2nd edn. 1942) manifest the same interest.

Salisbury was a keen and successful gardener all his life but little known before 1935 in horticultural circles. On the publication of *The Living Garden* members of the council of the Royal Horticultural Society received presentation copies. It was an astute well-timed publicity act. Attractively illustrated and, by its scientific approach, refreshingly different from most horticultural literature, *The Living Garden* so impressed the Society's council members that they awarded Salisbury the Veitch memorial medal in 1936 and invited him to deliver the Masters memorial lecture in 1937; later, in 1953, he received the Society's highest honour, the Victoria medal of honour. This association, together with fellowship of the Royal Society, to which he was elected in 1933, served him well in 1943 when the post of director of the Royal Botanic Gardens, Kew, became vacant. Hitherto the director had always been a distinguished taxonomic botanist; owing to wartime conditions none was available and Salisbury was appointed. He received the then customary knighthood in 1946 (he had been appointed CBE in 1939). He retired in 1956.

His tenure of office began at a very difficult time, with Kew still subject to bombing, the garden and scientific staff depleted, the herbarium and library evacuated. The restoration of the war-damaged garden and the return to Kew of its collections and of staff members from the armed forces, together with inadequate funding, presented many problems. Salisbury's service on a diversity of boards and committees inevitably occupied much time which some thought he should have devoted to Kew exclusively; frustrated staff members, unaware perhaps of the long hours he worked in the Kew office and his dedication to the institution as a whole, tended to blame him for deficiencies over which he had little control; inevitably there was much friction and discontent. The Australian House built in 1952 still stands but his other horticultural innovations, the Chalk Garden and the Clematis Wall, have been demolished. More important was post-war restoration, notably of the Palm House, which he succeeded in getting the government to undertake.

He was a founder member and from 1917 to 1932 honorary secretary of the British Ecological Society and the president in 1923, a vice-president of the Royal Society for 1943 and 1948–55 and the biological secretary from 1945 to 1955, vice-chairman of the Agricultural Improvement Council from 1945 to 1956, honorary secretary of the Hertfordshire Natural History Society from 1912 to 1922 and president from 1922 to 1925, president of the Norfolk and Norwich Naturalists Society for 1931, his *The East Anglian Flora* (1932) being based on his presidential address, and a member of other councils, boards, and committees. On all these bodies his geniality, self-confidence, vitality, breadth of interest, and grasp of essentials made him a valuable member; he was, moreover, a popular lecturer. The Royal Society awarded him the Royal medal in 1945 and he had honorary doctorates from Edinburgh (1950) and Glasgow (1956).

Salisbury married in 1917 Mabel, daughter of John Elwin-Coles; they had no children. She suffered much ill health at Kew; on Salisbury's retirement in 1956 they moved to a seaside house at Felpham, Bognor Regis, West Sussex, for the sake of her health. Tragically she died that year, but Salisbury lived at Felpham until his death at his home there 10 November 1978. He returned to the investigation of fruit and seed production and published a further eighteen articles and notes, the last in 1978.

[*New Scientist*, 11 June 1959; *The Times*, 14 November 1978; Alison Ross in *West Sussex Gazette*, 23 November 1978; A. R. Clapham in *Nature*, 24 May 1979; P. Richards in *British Ecological Society Bulletin*, vol. x, pp. 30–1, 1979; J. P. M. Brenan in *Journal of Horticultural Science*, vol. liv, pp. 165–6, 1979; A. R. Clapham in *Biographical Memoirs of Fellows of the Royal Society*, vol. xxvi, 1980; personal knowledge.] WILLIAM T. STEARN

SALT, DAME BARBARA (1904–1975), diplomat, was born at Oreville, California, 30 September 1904, the second of the three children (all girls) of Reginald John Salt, banker, and his wife, Maud Fanny, daughter of Robert Wigram, of Broomfield, Weybridge, Surrey. The family returned to England shortly after her birth and settled at The Close, North Place, Headington, Oxford. After matriculation her education was desultory. Her German, polished at the universities of Munich and Cologne, was fluent.

From 1933 to 1938 she worked as a secretary in England. In 1940, still as a secretary, she joined the Special Operations Executive (SOE), where her ability was recognized. From 1942 to 1946 she served in the SOE office in Tangier, first as assistant head and from 1944 as head.

In November 1946 the Foreign Office, alerted to the excellence of her work for SOE, secured her services and assigned her to the United Nations (Economic and Social) Department. There her critical and analytical mind, her quickness, her practical common sense, and her mature judgement earned her a sterling reputation.

In 1949 she passed second in the open competition for principals in the Home Civil Service. There was talk of her moving to the Treasury; but at her request she was established in the Foreign Service. She had a brief spell in Moscow in 1950 as first secretary (commercial). In July 1951 she was posted to Washington. Her ambassador regarded her as a debunker by nature, but he enjoyed her lively, ironic sense of humour and thought that with her acuteness and self-possession she was a match for anyone. She was promoted counsellor *sur place* in 1955.

In 1956 she was offered, but thought she could not afford to accept, the post of head of the United Nations Department in the Foreign Office.

The following year she was transferred to the British embassy in Israel and was in charge there when the Iraq crisis broke in 1958. It was decided to send British troops to Jordan. On 17 July she was instructed to obtain immediate permission for the RAF to overfly Israel. Her handling of this delicate negotiation earned her a message of thanks and congratulation from Harold Macmillan (later the Earl of Stockton).

On promotion to minister in 1960 she was appointed deputy head of the United Kingdom combined disarmament and nuclear tests delegation. This involved work in Geneva and New York. A year later, against her will, she was appointed United Kingdom representative to the Economic and Social Council of the United Nations. In these two posts she suffered severely from migraine but coped with the work admirably.

It was decided in April 1962 that she should be appointed ambassador to Israel. In October she developed thromboses which did not respond to treatment. In 1963, in successive operations, both her legs were amputated. Her appointment to Israel was cancelled.

She bore pain, disablement, and disappointment with fortitude. She resumed work as soon as she had made herself mobile. She served on Civil Service selection boards. She updated the handbook on etiquette for young diplomatists. Her talks to new entrants to the Diplomatic Service were witty and merry. Between 1963 and 1966 she led United Kingdom delegations in financial negotiations with Israel, the USSR, and Romania. Thereafter until she retired at the beginning of 1973 she was engaged on historical research covering the period of World War II.

In the Diplomatic Service she had been the first woman to become counsellor, minister, and ambassador-designate.

She was elegant in her appearance and way of life. She had been a good dancer. She liked gardening and music. In negotiation she had few equals. Her perfectionism had made her mistress of the art; and her alertness, grasp, directness, strength of will, and obstinacy could make her formidable. Conscious of her worth, she would remonstrate with the administration when she thought her talents were not being used to advantage. In adversity her spirit was indomitable. But it was not for that spirit that she wished to be remembered. For preservation in her personal file she chose a passport photograph of herself as a young woman—a sensitive, thoughtful face, winsome and full of grace.

She died at home in Montagu Square, London, 28 December 1975.

She was appointed MBE in 1946, CBE in 1959, and DBE in 1963.

[*The Times*, 31 December 1975; Foreign and Commonwealth Office records; private information; personal knowledge.]

THOMAS BRIMELOW

SALTER, (JAMES) ARTHUR, first BARON SALTER (1881–1975), politician and academic, was born 15 March 1881 at Oxford, the eldest of the four sons of James Edward Salter, a member of a well-known Oxford firm of boat builders, who served as a member of the City Council for many years, becoming mayor of the city, and his wife, Julia Maria Millin, the daughter of an Oxford draper. Salter was educated at the Oxford City High School and at Brasenose College, Oxford, where he won a scholarship in classics. He gained a first class both in classical honour moderations (1901) and in *literae humaniores* (1903). His college elected him after graduation to a senior scholarship, enabling him to spend a further year reading widely in history, law, and economics.

In 1904 he entered the Civil Service spending at first seven frustrating years in the transport department of the Admiralty. Then came a great opportunity. In 1911 he was transferred to the staff set up first to plan and later to administer the national insurance scheme introduced by Lloyd George. He found himself a member of a *corps d'élite*, including such men as (Sir) N. F. Warren Fisher, J. S. (later Lord) Bradbury, and John Anderson (later Viscount Waverley) [qq.v.], all destined to reach the highest positions in the public service. Within a year he was appointed private secretary to C. F. G. Masterman [q.v.], the minister in charge of health insurance, and in 1913 he was promoted to be assistant secretary of the Insurance Commission.

Then came the war. Salter found himself recalled to the transport department of the Admiralty where he soon achieved a key position. As director of ship requisitioning, at first in the Admiralty and subsequently in the Ministry of Shipping, he was in charge of the allocation of all merchant shipping, and as losses mounted and demands both civil and military increased, shipping became the vital central point in the supply system both of this country and of its allies.

The entry of America into the war brought new demands for shipping and inevitably increased the pressure on Britain's dwindling resources. Salter was sent to Washington to urge upon the Americans the vital need to build ships on the largest practicable scale. In this he was successful and the American programme of new construction soon exceeded the most optimistic estimates. At the same time losses were reduced through the convoy system; and the system of allocation and programming which had been so successfully built up in Britain was extended to cover the needs of all the Allied powers. To achieve this Salter with John Anderson and with Jean Monnet, then a young man in his twenties, drew up a plan for an Allied maritime transport council which was adopted at an Allied conference in Paris. The council was served by an Allied maritime transport executive of which Salter became the chairman in 1918, retaining at the same time his position in the ministry in London.

The ending of the war brought new problems such as the repatriation of demobilized forces and the sending of relief supplies to starving and disorganized countries in Europe. Salter played a prominent part in the handling of these, serving in 1919 as one of the secretaries of the supreme economic council in Paris. It was natural therefore that when the League of Nations was set up Salter should have been chosen to head (June 1919–January 1920) the economic and financial section of the secretariat. For two years he was diverted to a position much higher in status though not, as it turned out, in importance, as general secretary of the reparations commission. But in 1922 he was glad to return to his position in the League secretariat in Geneva.

The next nine years were spent in stimulating and constructive work in which much progress was made in the financial and economic reconstruction of Europe, notably in the stabilization of the currencies of Austria and Hungary, and the resettlement of refugees in Greece and Bulgaria. In all this work Salter added greatly to his already high reputation and other governments, including those of India and China, sought his advice in framing their policies.

In 1930 he left the League secretariat and returned to London. There followed years of varied activity as a journalist and author, as a member of the economic advisory council and as chairman of the road and rail conference whose unanimous recommendations were passed into law in 1933. In 1934 he was appointed to the Gladstone professorship of political theory and institutions at Oxford, a chair which carried with it a fellowship of All Souls. He made many friends there and the college continued to be his academic home until almost the end of his life.

In 1937 he was elected with support from all three parties as MP for Oxford University. He continued to hold this position until the university seats were abolished in 1950. In the years before the war Salter was active both in and out of Parliament in pressing upon the government a more vigorous policy of defence preparations, particularly in the building up of reserve stocks of food and raw materials about which from his experience of shipping control in the first war he could speak with special authority.

After the outbreak of war he was appointed in November 1939 as parliamentary secretary to the Ministry of Shipping set up by Neville Chamberlain's government, and he held a similar position in (Sir) Winston Churchill's coalition government. In the earlier months of the war he worked closely with his old friend Jean Monnet, becoming vice-chairman of the Anglo-French co-ordination committee of which Monnet was chairman. Together they did important work in placing contracts for war supplies in North America. In March 1941 he was summoned to Chequers by Churchill and invited to head a British shipping mission to Washington. Once more as in the first war shortage of shipping had become a growing threat to Britain's survival. Again Salter had to press upon the US administration the urgent need for a vast programme of new construction, in a country where shipbuilding had virtually ceased between the wars. In his work in Washington Salter was greatly helped by his wife whom he had married in June 1940. She was Ethel Mather, daughter of John Sherman Bagg, doctor, and widow of Arthur Bullard, who had been one of Salter's colleagues in Geneva. American by birth but cosmopolitan in education and experience she had a house in Washington and knew well many of the leading figures in the administration. She died in 1969. There were no children.

The crisis in shipping was at its most acute not only in the spring of 1941 but also in 1942 after the entry of the United States into the war. But by the middle of 1943 Salter had the satisfaction of seeing this danger overcome thanks to a shipbuilding programme in the USA which reached the staggering total of 20 million tons a year, all of which was made available for the war effort of the Allies as a whole.

With his work in Washington successfully accomplished Salter returned to London, and after a brief and unsatisfactory period of service in 1944 as deputy director-general of Unrra he joined Churchill's caretaker government as chancellor of the Duchy of Lancaster 'with special responsibility for questions affecting European relief'. In February 1951, after a year without a seat in Parliament, he was invited to stand for Ormskirk at a by-election as a Conservative. He was re-elected at the general election in October and appointed to be minister of state for economic affairs in the Treasury. He served there for a year during which he found himself in strong disagreement with the policy of making sterling convertible at a floating rate of exchange advocated by the Treasury and the Bank of England. The proposal was rejected by the Cabinet and the prime minister subsequently acknowledged to Salter, as he himself recounts, the importance of the part he had played in opposing it. He was appointed in November 1952 to be minister of materials, with responsibility for supervising the orderly winding up of the department. In 1953 he left the government and was elevated to the peerage, as first Baron Salter, of Kidlington.

Many other honours had been conferred upon him in his long career. He was appointed CB in 1918, KCB in 1922, PC in 1941, and GBE in 1944. By foreign governments he was appointed officier de la Couronne Belgique in 1919, commandeur de la Légion d'Honneur in 1920, and commendatore of the Crown of Italy in 1922, and he received the Chinese decoration of the Brilliant Jade in 1937. He was made an honorary fellow of his old college BNC and after relinquishing his professorial fellowship at All Souls was re-elected as a 'distinguished person'. He received honorary doctorates from Oxford, Manchester, Vienna, Harvard, Columbia, McGill, California, and Amherst.

Among his books were *Allied Shipping Control* (1921) and *Recovery* (1932). He contributed to this Dictionary the notices of Sir Hubert Llewellyn Smith, Viscount Waverley, the sixteenth Earl of Perth, the first Baron Maclay, and Sir Alfred Zimmern.

Salter died at his home in Chelsea 27 June 1975, and the peerage became extinct.

[Arthur Salter, *Memoirs of a Public Servant*, 1961, and *Slave of the Lamp*, 1967; *The Times*, 30 June and 5 and 22 July 1975; personal knowledge.] DENIS RICKETT

SALZMAN, LOUIS FRANCIS (1878–1971), originally Salzmann, antiquary and historian, was born 26 March 1878 at Brighton, the younger son and child of Frederick William Salzmann, a physician, and his wife, Clara Sinnock. He was educated at Haileybury School and Pembroke College, Cambridge, where he read, though ingloriously, the natural sciences tripos. Inheriting a small private income while still young, he lived awhile in Hailsham, Sussex, and there exchanged medicine for history, publishing *The History of the Parish of Hailsham* in 1901, the first of some twenty books that he wrote or edited.

Through indifferent health he escaped military service in World War I and instead taught at St. George's School, Harpenden, Hertfordshire. In 1918 he moved to Cambridge and coached and supervised history students. In 1904 he had married Maud Elizabeth, daughter of George Monro Russell, then vicar of Upper Dicker, Sussex; they had three sons, the youngest of whom died in 1943, and two daughters. The marriage was dissolved in 1934 and Salzman thereupon left Cambridge for London.

When Salzman's literary career began, English economic history was still comparatively unexplored. Some of Salzman's earliest essays were in that field, for he contributed the articles on all the Sussex industries then identified to *Sussex* II (1907) in the *Victoria History of the Counties of England*, which had been founded at the turn of the century and itself pioneered economic history. Those articles were complemented by *English Industries in the Middle Ages* (1913), and *English Trade in the Middle Ages* (1931), learned textbooks which were indispensable to students at a time when little of the kind was readily available. The first had originally excluded building but the enlarged edition of 1923 supplied the lack. That in turn was replaced in 1952 by *Building in England down to 1540* (2nd edn. 1967), which deals with the early organization of the trade, technique, and materials, and prints many documents, notably contracts. This will be Salzman's permanent contribution to scholarship. An outcome was the Vernacular Architecture Group, of which Salzman was a founder and whose meetings he still attended in his eighties.

The *Victoria County History*, after wartime discontinuance and painful resuscitation, was eventually acquired by William Page [q.v.], its editor, who in 1932 presented it, though unendowed, to the University of London. The university entrusted it to its Institute of Historical Research. In 1934 Page died and Salzman became editor. The moment was inauspicious, for the *History* was doubtfully popular and the university had little money for its support. Nevertheless, Salzman resumed the Oxfordshire and Warwickshire series and started Cambridgeshire, without halting Sussex. Before retiring in 1949 he had brought out fifteen volumes, of eleven of which he was the sole editor. Some of the general chapters that he commissioned were attractively original but the volumes of parish histories continued the Page convention. Given contemporary calamities, that conservatism was prudent, for extravagant innovations could have killed the *History* or hampered its later evolution. As an editor Salzman justifiably condemned both verbosity and procrastination, and, if always fair, could express his displeasure forcefully.

Sussex was a leading beneficiary of Salzman's industry. Joining the council of its Archaeological Society in 1903 he became president in 1954 and 1955. He edited forty-five volumes of its transactions, 1909–59, and published its history in 1946. He helped to excavate Pevensey castle and Alfriston's Saxon cemetery in youth, and Robertsbridge abbey in 1935. He was a founder of the Sussex Record Society and its joint or sole literary director from 1905, himself preparing for it ten texts. For these and other services to learning he was appointed CBE in 1955 and made an Hon. D.Litt. of the University of Sussex in 1965.

His knowledge of antiquities was deep, versatile, and generously shared. He had widely explored the public records, as his books called *Medieval Byways* (1913) and two others descriptive of English social life (medieval and Tudor, both 1926) reveal. He also wrote biographies of Henry II (1917) and, less successfully, Edward I (1968). His prose was clear and easy and he seldom altered his first drafts. He thought out many of his serious works on long walks. Latterly his personality seemed somewhat forbidding and he could be devastatingly outspoken, but there was a far lighter touch: he wrote plays and verses for children and he commemorated in verse occurrences in the Institute of Historical Research. He was sparely built and to the last retained his abundant locks and eyebrows. From about 1938 he lived at Lewes and died there 4 April 1971. A photograph, taken in 1970, was published in *Sussex Archaeological Collections*, vol. cix (1971).

[*The Times*, 6 and 15 April 1971; *Victoria History of the Counties of England, General Introduction*, 1970; *West Sussex Gazette*, 11 March 1954; *Sussex Archaeological Collections*, vol. cix, 1971; personal and family information.] RALPH B. PUGH

SANSOM, WILLIAM NORMAN TREVOR (1912–1976), short-story writer and novelist, was born 18 January 1912 at Camberwell, London, the third son of Ernest Brooks Sansom, naval architect, and his wife, Mabel Clark, of Barrow. He was named Norman Trevor and at some later date added the name William. Educated at Uppingham School, he saw much of Europe when quite young, travelling with his father. Though he enjoyed writing he did not settle immediately to a writing career. He worked in a bank, as an advertising copy-writer—employment which taught him not to waste words—and played a piano in a night club. World War II was a watershed in his life; he joined the National Fire Service and saw the bombing of London at very close quarters. Later, he made the acquaintance of Cyril Connolly [q.v.] and John Lehmann and this led to the appearance of some of his stories in *New Writing* and *Horizon*. It was soon seen that here was a highly original writer with a keen and unflinching eye for the human condition, able to encompass with equal ease the whimsical, the macabre, and the exotic. His experiences during the blitz in London undoubtedly influenced his work.

His first volume, *Fireman Flower, and Other Stories*, appeared in 1944 and two years later his promise was rewarded by a literary bursary of £200 a year under an arrangement between Hodder & Stoughton and the Society of Authors. Further tales, some with Kafkaesque undertones (Kafka had a marked influence on his early work) were published in 1946 under the title of *Three, Stories*. In 1947 Sansom brought out *Westminster in War* for which he was allowed access to official records.

By now he was a full-time writer enhancing his reputation with *Something Terrible, Something Lovely* and *South*. Both were published in 1948. One showed his mastery of the bizarre and the other, a series of brilliant Mediterranean sketches, his gift for travel writing. But he was no writer for the eager tourist; he wished to evoke the spirit of place; he was unlikely to be found perched on a camel. The year 1949 saw the publication of arguably his best novel, *The Body*, a study in jealousy which showed his ability to transcend the bounds of the short story.

None the less he continued to practise in the genre which had made his name. He was always versatile; he could as well convey the rivalries of a beauty contest as the sadness of the solitary life.

In 1963 a collection of his stories was published with a perceptive introduction by Elizabeth Bowen [q.v.]. Among others, the collection contained the chilling 'The Vertical Ladder' in which a youth is dared to climb a gasometer, and hauls himself, sweating, upwards to find that the rungs of the ladder end before the summit.

In 1954 he married and later moved to Hamilton Terrace, London. It was at this period of his life that he turned his attention to ballads, revue sketches and songs, and a script for one of his novels *The Loving Eye*, published in 1956. In later years his health deteriorated but he continued to write with professional regularity. If no masterpiece appeared he showed repeatedly that he could produce tales that were unmistakably Sansomian, taut, brilliant in description (he was never without his notebook), and displaying that unerring eye for the London landscape that always fascinated him and characterized throughout his career his best tales. He did not abandon books of travel; if *Grand Tour Today*, published in 1968, and *Away to it All*, published four years earlier, did not perhaps equal *South* or *The Passionate North* (1950) this may have been because he now travelled with rather less zest than formerly. Even so, his keen eye missed little and his humour and his curiosity never deserted him. Sansom is widely recognized as being among the best short-story writers of his time, a time when some said the short story was in decline.

Sansom was of medium height, in later life stoutish and neatly bearded affecting Edwardian clothes. Like many another he was not greatly at ease with those whom he did not know well but to his circle of friends he was charming, hospitable, and excellent company, revealing at times an imaginatively comical side to his nature. As a close friend remarked, he had grace of manner—as indeed, as a writer, he had grace of style. He was made a fellow of the Royal Society of Literature.

He married in 1954 Ruth Evelyn Blake (Ruth Grundy, the actress), the daughter of Norman Denis Grundy, chartered accountant. They had one son, and there was also a stepson by Ruth's previous marriage. He died 20 April 1976 in St. Mary's Hospital, Paddington.

[*The Times*, 21 April 1976; private information.] COLIN WATSON

SAVILL, SIR ERIC HUMPHREY (1895–1980), estate administrator and plantsman, was born in Chelsea, London, 20 October 1895, the second son in a family of three sons and a daughter of (Sir) Edwin Savill, partner in the firm of Alfred Savill & Sons, chartered surveyors, of Lincoln's Inn Fields, and his wife, Helen Webster, a woman of strong character and conviction who vigorously espoused the campaign for women's rights and was at times an orator for that cause at Speaker's Corner, Hyde Park. She also practised as a horticulturist. To Savill's distress his parents became estranged. He never married and cared devotedly for his mother until her death on 10 April 1956.

He was educated at Malvern College, where he was a pupil from 1909 to 1913, and at Magdalene College, Cambridge. At the outbreak of World War I Savill broke off his studies at Cambridge and enlisted in the ranks of the Officers' Training Corps. In December 1914 he was commissioned in the 8th Devonshire Regiment. Next year he went with his regiment to France and during the battle of the Somme in July 1916 he was awarded the MC. Later he was severely wounded in the chest and left leg.

After the war he returned to Cambridge, graduating BA in 1920 (MA, 1930). In 1920 he joined his father's firm and was elected a professional associate of the Royal Institution of Chartered Surveyors in 1920 (he advanced to the fellowship in 1930). In 1926 he became a partner in the family firm where he remained until in 1930 he was offered the post of deputy surveyor at Windsor which he readily accepted. This involved the management of a vast estate extending from Virginia Water to Bagshot with farmland, forests, and mature woodland. During the thirty years he held the post he knew four monarchs and their consorts and this made possible the creation of the Savill Gardens and Valley Gardens at Windsor as an enduring living memorial. Indeed it was by command of George VI in 1951 that the woodland and bog gardens at Windsor were to be designated the Savill Gardens. In 1937 he was promoted to deputy ranger, in 1958 he became director of forestry to the Crown Estate, and in 1959 he was made director of the gardens, Windsor Great Park. He retired in 1970.

Savill was an inspired yet highly controversial gardening genius. The Gardens which he created at Windsor are a testimony to his instinctive flair. Clever use was made of the natural features of Windsor Park, its woodlands, heaths, hillsides, streams, and lakes and it is generally acknowledged that he was responsible for making the most outstanding garden of the twentieth century in England. In 1954 Savill became a founder member of the Ministry of Transport's landscape advisory committee and from 1962 to 1969 he was its chairman.

Savill held office on two hospital boards—those of King Edward VII Hospital, Windsor, and the Hospital for Sick Children in Great Ormond Street, London. He was generous and unassuming, softly spoken and with a natural dignity. Yet he could be sharply critical and forthright in expressing his views. He was of medium build, physically tough though his activities were plainly restricted by his war injuries which he bore uncomplainingly and which with frequent bronchial attacks remained painful. Nevertheless, he actively engaged in tennis, athletics, and golf though latterly fishing became his principal joy.

He was appointed MVO (1938), CVO (1950), KCVO (1955), and CBE (1946). He was prominent in the affairs of the Royal Horticultural Society on whose council he served (1952–68) and whose vice-president he was. In 1955 he received the Society's highest accolade, the Victoria medal of honour, and in 1963 a gold Veitch memorial medal. He died 15 April 1980 at Windsor.

[Private information; personal knowledge.]

GEORGE TAYLOR

SCAMP, SIR (ATHELSTAN) JACK (1913–1977), company director and industrial conciliator, was born 22 May 1913 in Handsworth, Birmingham, the second son of a house decorator, Edward Henry Scamp, and his wife, Jane Lamb. There was also one daughter. The family was very active locally in the Church of England, where Jack became a choirboy. From childhood he was a keen sportsman; he was particularly successful at association football and played as an amateur for West Bromwich Albion. After leaving a local school at fourteen, he spent about ten years on the clerical staff of the Great Western Railway in Birmingham. He married Jane, the daughter of John Kendall, a builder, in 1939; they were a close family, with one daughter and one son.

Following brief periods of insurance work, war service in the Royal Artillery, and with his father-in-law's business, Scamp began the career which led in only twenty years to a position unique in British industrial relations. He held successive personnel management appointments in the Rover Car Company, Butlers of Birmingham, Rugby Portland Cement, the Plessey Company, and Massey-Ferguson (UK), before joining the General Electric Company as personnel director in 1962. He had developed an unusually direct and friendly way of working with trade unionists, and his sense of humour was a great tension reliever. In GEC these characteristics proved particularly valuable in helping to resolve the labour relations problems which inevitably accompanied the reorganization of the British electrical engineering industry, in the late 1960s and early 1970s.

In the middle of the 1960s, when the Labour Party returned to government, there was great national concern about the effects of increasing industrial unrest. The government wished to improve labour relations, but without further legislation. In 1964 a committee was appointed under the chairmanship of Lord Devlin, to inquire into pay and methods of working in the docks, and Scamp became a member. In 1965 he chaired a court of inquiry into the industrial relations problems of British Railways footplate staff. A busy and varied period of public conciliation and arbitration work followed, conducted in a very distinctive way—such inquiries usually having been chaired in the past by academics or lawyers, in a more detached and formal style. His work covered the shipyards and airlines, as well as the railways, docks, and motor-car manufacturing. From 1964 he was a member of the Industrial Court, subsequently the Industrial Arbitration Board. During 1965 he began a year's secondment from GEC, as one of the team of industrial advisers to the government's new Department of Economic Affairs, and he took on the chairmanship of the newly formed Motor Industries Joint Labour Council, for which he was knighted in 1968.

The MIJLC, described by some as a 'great national experiment' and by others as a temporary expedient, was intended to bring order to labour relations in a particularly strike-prone industry. By the end of Scamp's period of office in 1969, many believed the task was impossible, but by then he had resolved dozens of labour disputes with remarkable success. For five or six years he was called upon over and over again as peacemaker in many different industries.

His calm manner, presence, and clean-cut physical appearance became well known. He was popular and inspired extraordinarily widespread trust, respect, and affection in a sphere better known for active antagonism. Although he often blamed management and unions publicly, he kept their support, as well as that of the government and the press. In 1967–8, during an experimental period of public ownership, he was a non-executive director of the shipbuilders Fairfields (Glasgow) Limited. In 1970 the new Conservative government decided not to intervene in a serious dispute involving dustmen and other local authority manual workers, the so-called 'dirty jobs strike'. A three-man committee was appointed jointly by the parties, under Scamp's chairmanship. The pay award was criticized in public by Edward Heath, the prime minister—unfairly, many thought—as being detrimental to the rate of inflation and the national interest.

This criticism hurt. Thereafter his talents as a conciliator were rarely used by the government, much to his regret, although he was asked for advice on incomes policy in 1972. An unusual figure in public life, he had caught the imagination of the nation with his warmth and his straightforward manner. He suffered badly from heart trouble for the last five years of his life, but that did not stop him helping to settle disputes.

In 1970 Scamp became associate professor of industrial relations at Warwick University. He resigned from executive responsibility at GEC in 1972 due to ill health, while remaining a director of the company and becoming chairman of the management consultancy firm Urwick, Orr & Partners.

He was Companion of the Institute of Electrical Engineers, served on several committees of the Engineering Employers' Federation, and was made a fellow of both the Institute of Personnel Management and the British Institute of Management. He was active in several charitable, Christian, and community organizations, and his chairmanship of Coventry City Football Club gave him particular joy. Scamp sat regularly as a magistrate for many years, and was deputy lieutenant of Warwickshire. He had far fewer faults than most of us. He died at Moretonhampstead in Devon 31 October 1977.

[*The Times*, 1 November 1977.]

G. H. TROLLOPE

SCHONLAND, SIR BASIL FERDINAND JAMIESON (1896–1972), physicist, was born in Grahamstown, Cape Colony, 5 February 1896, the eldest of three sons (there were no daughters) of (Professor) Selmar Schönland, a botanist who had taken a Ph.D. in Kiel University before being appointed curator of the Albany Museum of Grahamstown, and his wife, Flora, daughter of Professor MacOwan, rector of Gill College, Somerset East, South Africa.

Schonland attended St. Andrew's College School and then in 1914 took a BA degree in mathematics at Rhodes University College, Grahamstown. He entered Gonville and Caius College, Cambridge, in 1914, gained a first class in part i of the mathematical tripos (1915), and was elected to an exhibition. Immediately after the examination he enlisted in the Royal Engineers, and as a second lieutenant was placed in charge of a team learning to lay communication cables. Early in 1916 he went to France with his team as officer in charge of the RE's 43rd Airline Section, and for two years without a break he endured the gunfire and mud of Flanders, receiving severe concussion at Arras. He was twice mentioned in dispatches for bravery, appointed OBE (military), and finished the war with the rank of captain and chief instructor, wireless communications.

He was demobilized in March 1919 and completed part ii of the natural sciences tripos (physics, first class, 1920), winning the Francis Schuldham plate of the college and a George Green studentship for research. He then worked for two years in the Cavendish Laboratory, on the scattering of β-particles. He also discussed atmospheric electricity and thunderstorms with C. T. R. Wilson [q.v.], a world authority on the subject.

In 1922 Schonland returned to South Africa as senior lecturer in physics at Cape Town and after completing experiments he had started in Cambridge he switched over to atmospheric electricity, measuring electric fields under thunder-clouds. He returned to Cambridge with an 1851 Exhibition in 1928 and met (Sir) C. V. Boys [q.v.], who had made a special camera with which to photograph lightning; this Schonland borrowed, and chased storms as they developed over the Rand. From many photographs taken with his small team of collaborators the complex sequence of events in the flash were unravelled and were correlated with the measurements of electric field changes at ground level as the storm approached and receded. All this pioneering work has stood the test of time and is of great benefit to the electrical engineer concerned with overhead transmission lines.

Schonland used to spend summer months at his wife's parents' home, 2,500 feet above sea-level, a site well placed to observe storm clouds approaching from the west. In addition to measuring thunderstorm fields he planted a medium-sized tree in a pot isolated from the ground and measured the electric current flowing up from its branches as the thunder-cloud passed overhead. This was the first of many attempts to estimate the total current flowing in the lower atmosphere. In 1932 he equipped a small mobile laboratory to follow storm clouds. He showed for the first time that a flash consists of several strokes and measured the time intervals between them. The most important information was related to the way the air broke down from cloud to earth; he found that the first discharge, having relatively weak illumination, travelled from the cloud in a jerky fashion, step by step, branching as it travelled. He called this the 'leader stroke'. When it reached the earth the 'main stroke' of high luminosity travelled back to the cloud.

As a result of this excellent beginning, financial support for a permanent laboratory was forthcoming from Bernard Price, chairman of the Victoria Falls and Transvaal Power Company, and from the Carnegie Institute. By 1937 the Bernard Price Institute for Geophysical Research had been built at Witwatersrand University, with Schonland as its director; his work won him election as FRS in 1938.

With the coming of war Schonland was invited by General J. C. Smuts [q.v.] to establish a unit in the South African Corps of Signals to develop radio direction finding (RDF) and his group moved with the forces up Africa, joining Sir A. P. (later Earl) Wavell [q.v.] before the great desert offensive of December 1940. His army experience was invaluable in persuading army and airforce chiefs to accept new ideas; his personality was right, for he was a good listener, a kindly persuasive speaker, and an obvious authority. He went to England to gather information from Sir John Cockcroft [q.v.] at the Air Defence Research and Development Establishment and was asked to remain as his deputy, but after a short time he joined Anti-Aircraft Command where he planned the very successful Bruneval raid to capture the latest German radio apparatus. In 1941 he moved on to the Army Operational Research Group, as a brigadier, and later accompanied the army of liberation as scientific adviser to General B. L. Montgomery (later Viscount Montgomery of Alamein, q.v.).

In 1945 Smuts called him home to establish the South African Council for Scientific and Industrial Research while still remaining in charge of the Bernard Price Institute. In 1951 he became the first chancellor of Rhodes University, and in 1952, president of the South African Association for the Advancement of Science; he received the gold medal of the Franklin Institute (1950).

In 1954 Schonland moved to the Atomic Energy Research Establishment at Harwell as deputy to Cockcroft. He became director in 1958, and was knighted in 1960. He retired in 1961, but remained chancellor of Rhodes and addressed the university with many fine speeches, although he was greatly worried by some of the changes he saw coming in South Africa. He was appointed CBE in 1945, and had honorary degrees from the universities of Cambridge, Cape Town, Rhodes, Southampton, and Natal. In 1959 he became an honorary fellow of Gonville and Caius College.

Schonland's great achievement was his immense contribution to our knowledge of lightning. He remained truly modest, a scientist in the pursuit of truth. In 1923 he married Isabel Marian ('Ismay'), daughter of James Craib, teacher of mathematics and later inspector of schools, Cape Province, of Somerset East. They had one son and two daughters; their family life was extremely happy.

Schonland's last years were clouded by illness, and he died in a nursing home in Shawford, Hampshire, 24 November 1972 after a long period of suffering in silence.

[T. E. Allibone in *Biographical Memoirs of Fellows of the Royal Society*, vol. xix, 1973; information from several military heads; personal knowledge.] T. E. Allibone

SCHUMACHER, ERNST FRIEDRICH (1911–1977), economist, conservationist, and writer, was born at Bonn, Germany, 16 August 1911, the third of the five children (three sons and two daughters) of Hermann Albert Schumacher (1868–1952), professor of economics at Bonn and Berlin universities, and his wife, Edith Zitelmann (1884–1975). His early education was at Arndt Gymnasium, Berlin, followed by Berlin and Bonn universities. After a spell learning English he proceeded on a Rhodes scholarship to New College, Oxford, where he spent two years reading philosophy, politics, and economics, taking a diploma in economics at the end of the first year. The third year of his scholarship was spent at the school of banking, Columbia University, USA, and during his studies in a second year at Columbia he gave a number of lectures.

At the end of this time he returned to Germany but found difficulty in securing satisfying employment there as he was out of sympathy with the Nazi government. To the deep disappointment of his mother and father, he therefore returned to Britain in 1937.

After war with Germany began in 1939 the British authorities were anxious to make full use of Schumacher's substantial gifts. Consequently he was not interned in 1940 but spent the next five years working as 'Fritz, the agricultural labourer' in Oxfordshire, and attending frequent conferences in Whitehall with economic and financial experts. These were unusual years for him, switching from cabbages to ministers in Whitehall, constantly reporting to the police as an alien, and burying himself in Karl Marx when he had spare moments for study.

From 1946 to 1950 Schumacher was in Western Germany as a member of the British section of the Control Commission. In order to take up this post he had to apply for naturalization as a British subject (1946), which he had hitherto felt reluctant to do because of his attachment to the German people. While he served on the commission his special qualities were recognized by Sir R. Stafford Cripps, Lord Keynes [qq.v.], and other influential persons. As a result, in 1950 he was appointed economic adviser to the National Coal Board. There he remained for the next twenty years, emerging with the same number of staff as he had when he entered—one assistant and a secretary. He was very proud of this example of restraint in the face of an opportunity to build an empire. Under-utilized in his job, Schumacher was tempted to respond to an invitation by J. P. Narayan to set up and lead an Indian Institute of Economics. However, the situation was radically altered on the appointment in 1961 of Lord Robens of Woldingham as chairman of the National Coal Board. Robens quickly established a very close working relationship with Schumacher. This, together with substantial domestic changes, persuaded Schumacher to stay with the NCB and not follow up Narayan's invitation. From 1963 to 1970 he was also the NCB's director of statistics.

In 1936 Schumacher married Anna Maria, daughter of Rudolf Petersen, a business man dealing in import and export; they had two sons and two daughters. In 1960, after a short illness, she died of cancer. It was then that Schumacher began to develop the particular ideas which he refined and put into practice over the next fifteen years. He started questioning not only his ready acceptance of current economic practices and theories but also his personal philosophy of life. As a result of his studies of mysticism, Buddhism, and other eastern religions he accepted the appointment of economic adviser to the Burmese government, a position which might provide the opportunity to sit at the feet of Buddhist teachers. He said: 'I went to Burma a thirsty wanderer and there I found living water.' Although he never rejected the basic tenets of Buddhist teaching, he eventually decided that Buddhism was alien to the mainstream of western civilization, the teachings of the Christian religion being the more fitting for him. Later he, his second wife Verena (daughter of Johann Rosenberger, a worker in the gas industry), whom he had married in 1962, and one of his daughters, Barbara, were accepted into the Catholic faith. There were also two sons and two daughters of his second marriage.

Schumacher's period of critical thought coincided with substantial changes in the world scene—the leaders of many newly independent but under-developed and poverty-ridden African and Asian countries took as models for their development plans the labour-saving, capital-intensive technologies of the rich industrialized countries. Schumacher, however, pointed in a different direction, emphasizing that the source and centre of world poverty and under-development lay primarily in the rural areas of poor countries where unemployment would continue to grow unless self-help technology was made available to them and their inhabitants were encouraged and assisted in its application.

In the 1960s and 1970s Schumacher was the main propagandist of intermediate or appropriate technology, set out in the first instance in the report he prepared for the Indian Planning Commission in 1963. In 1966 the Intermediate Technology Development Group, a company limited by guarantee and registered as a charity, was set up with Schumacher as the founder-chairman—an office he held until his death.

Small is Beautiful, a collection of Schumacher's essays published in 1973, with its arresting subtitle—'Economics as if People Mattered'—struck the right note at the right time. It became a bestseller and was translated into at least fifteen languages. After retiring from the National Coal Board in 1970 Schumacher lectured widely and gave himself without restraint to consultations and conferences. He was appointed CBE in 1974. He was prepared to meet and discuss with all kinds of groups, of whatever size, provided they were action-oriented and anxious to follow up his ideas. Perhaps this excessive travel hastened his death—he was taken ill when travelling by train through Switzerland to attend a conference and died on the train 4 September 1977.

'Fritz' Schumacher was a prophet whose diagnosis and recommendations appealed to those people young and old, of the left or right, black, brown and white, who found the current consumer-based, materialistic society unattractive and disenchanting. His economic expertise, combined with religious commitment, a charismatic presence, and personal magnetism, made him something of a cult figure, particularly in the USA. This very attractive, fascinating, and dedicated personality made a lasting impact on his time. 'To very few people', wrote Barbara Ward, 'it is given to begin to change, drastically and creatively, the direction of human thought. Dr Schumacher belongs to this intensely creative minority.'

[*The Times*, 6, 9, and 10 September 1977; Barbara Wood (daughter), *Alias Papa* (biography), 1984; private information; personal knowledge.] LESLIE KIRKLEY

SCOTT, PAUL MARK (1920–1978), writer, was born in Palmer's Green, London, 25 March 1920, the younger son (there were no daughters) of Thomas Scott, a commercial artist, and his wife Frances Mark. He was educated at Winchmore Hill Collegiate School and entered accountancy training. He joined the army in 1940, serving in intelligence until he was posted to India where he was commissioned in 1943. He travelled extensively in India, Burma, and Malaya before returning to Britain at the end of the war with the rank of captain.

Demobilized in 1946, Scott joined the Falcon Press, a new publishing house founded by Captain Peter Baker MC (later Conservative MP for South Norfolk), in whose wartime Resurgam Younger Poets series Scott's poem 'I, Gerontius' had appeared in 1941. Associated with the Falcon Press was the Grey Walls Press, founded and directed by the writer Charles Wrey Gardiner (1901–81), who was also editor of *Poetry Quarterly*. Scott was company secretary of these two firms and during his four years there among his colleagues were the writers Muriel Spark, Seán Jennett, and Roland Gant. In 1950 Scott joined the literary agency Pearn, Pollinger & Higham and later became a director of David Higham Associates.

After having been rejected by seventeen publishers, Scott's first novel *Johnnie Sahib* was published in 1952 by Eyre & Spottiswoode who awarded it their Literary Fellowship prize. In it Scott made use of his experiences as an air supply officer in India to examine the questions of command and loyalty in a small military unit. His second novel, *The Alien Sky* (1953), was also set in India and is to some extent an exercise in the study of India at independence that was a major part of the theme of his principal work completed twenty years later. *A Male Child* (1956) was a novel set in London but *The Mark of the Warrior* (1958) saw a return to the jungle warfare of 1942 Burma and the interplay of action and emotion among soldiers at war.

After ten years as a literary agent Scott left David Higham Associates in 1960, the year in which *The Chinese Love Pavilion* was published, a novel in which India exerts its fascination on both those who have served the British interest there for generations and on new wartime visitors in uniform. *The Birds of Paradise* (1962) continued Scott's progress towards *The Raj Quartet* and here the birds of the novel's title are dead and stuffed, hanging in a large cage in an Indian prince's gardens and haunting the memory of a man since he first saw them in childhood and returns to see them again in middle age when he and his friends, the British in India, and the princely states have like them become tattered and decayed by time.

In both *The Bender* (1963) and *The Corrída at San Felíu* (1964) Scott temporarily abandoned India as a background and seemed to take a deep creative breath to embark on his greatest work. He also experimented with some of his preoccupations as an artist—setting down a complicated choreography in a series of time levels, initiating the search for identity and meaning in society and the interplay between life's reality and artistic creation. *The Bender* is set in London in the early 1960s and while humorous and satirical it exudes a never specific unease. *The Corrída* is a kind of Chinese puzzle of fragments, about a writer who is killed in a car crash and leaves his efforts to release himself from a writing block in the form of short stories, two openings of a novel, and a novella. Yet both these novels, pauses in the margin of his main work though they seem to be, contain or simply statements that were to recur in his later work.

In 1964 Scott returned to India to revisit wartime friends and, in his own words, to 'recharge batteries'. The revival of memories and his experience of post-partition India inspired the conception of *The Jewel in the Crown* (1966) which Scott said might be the first novel of a trilogy but which, in fact, was the beginning of what came to be known as *The Raj Quartet* with the subsequent publication of *The Day of the Scorpion* (1968), *The Towers of Silence* (1971), and *A Division of the Spoils* (1975), the four novels being gathered into one volume called *The Raj Quartet* in 1976.

Apart from two further visits to India, in 1969 and 1972, Paul Scott, during the decade he was writing his *Quartet*, led an almost cloistered life, working in an upstairs room overlooking his garden and some Hampstead Garden Suburb woodland. Apart from working on his novels he wrote book reviews for *Country Life*, *The Times*, and the *Times Literary Supplement*. Although he was a most amusing companion, with a gift for mimicry, he kept away from cliques and what he considered to be the 'literary establishment'. On one of his rare excursions into the London literary scene he gave a talk entitled 'India: a post-Forsterian View' to the Royal Society of Literature of which he was a fellow. It was published in *Essays by Divers Hands* (Royal Society of Literature, 1970).

Recognition of Scott as a major novelist came slowly. Reviewers noted the imaginative inventiveness and the mastery of technique but were cautious about forecasting 'where it would all end'. In fact the rape of the English girl Daphne Manners in the Bibighar Gardens with which *The Jewel in the Crown* begins symbolizes, but never portentously, the relationship between India and the British: love and hate, the duality of emotion, inter-racial tension and mutual attraction, the pull of disparate loyalties, national pride, and aspirations in individuals and nations—this is what Paul Scott wrote about with such persuasive skill.

In 1976 and 1977 Paul Scott was visiting professor at the University of Tulsa, Oklahoma. Just before his second visit his last novel, *Staying On* (1977), was published. Taking two minor characters from his *Raj Quartet* who chose to stay on in India rather than to return to England Scott wrote both a pendant to the *Quartet* and a valedictory masterpiece about the relationship between a retired colonel, his wife, and their Indian landlords and servants. While recovering from surgery for cancer in Tulsa he was awarded the Booker prize for fiction in November 1977. Scott returned to England in the following month and died of cancer in the Middlesex Hospital, London, 1 March 1978.

The Granada television film of *Staying On*, starring Celia Johnson and Trevor Howard, had its first showing in December 1980 and Granada went on to film *The Raj Quartet* (under the title of *The Jewel in the Crown*) in 1982. These television plays were not Scott's first excursion into drama. He had a play, *Pillars of Salt*, published in 1948, his first novel *Johnnie Sahib* was adapted for BBC radio and television as *Lines of Communication* in 1953, and in 1955 his play *Sahibs and Memsahibs* was produced by the BBC.

In 1941 Scott married Nancy Edith, daughter of Francis Percival Avery, a Conservative political agent. She is the author of novels under the name Elizabeth Avery. There were two daughters of the marriage, one of whom illustrated Scott's story *After the Funeral*, which was produced in a limited edition of 200 copies, with a personal view of the author by Roland Gant (Whittington Press, 1979).

[Patrick Swinden, *Paul Scott—Images of India*, 1980; K. Bhaskara Rao, *Paul Scott* (Twayne English Authors No. 285), 1980; personal knowledge.]

ROLAND GANT

SEAGO, EDWARD BRIAN (1910–1974), landscape artist, was born in Norwich, 31 March 1910, the younger son (there were no daughters) of Francis Brian Seago, a coal merchant, and his wife, Mabel Reeve Woodroffe, from Beccles. A severe heart complaint prevented him from receiving any formal education after the age of fourteen; but he was determined to become a painter and although his parents did not greatly encourage him, he studied under Bertram Priestman RA.

Seago imposed a ruthless discipline upon himself (for example by following a cow for hours, sketching as he walked) and during periods of convalescence he would spend days making studies of the skies he could see from his bed. He absorbed the work of John Crome and J. S. Cotman [qq.v.], aiming to emulate their portrayal of the East Anglian landscape.

Seago first supported himself by making equestrian portraits and in 1929 he had his first exhibition in London. Like (Sir) Alfred Munnings [q.v.], whose work he admired, Seago was attracted to the circus, and he wrote of his experiences touring with circuses in *Circus Company* (1933), *Sons of Sawdust* (1934), and *Caravan* (1937), all illustrated with sketches and paintings. He made good friends with the poet laureate John Masefield [q.v.], and together they produced *The Country Scene* (1937), a book of forty-two poems, each with a reproduction of a painting. This led to two further collaborations, *Tribute to Ballet* (1938) and *A Generation Risen* (1942). Seago's paintings of this time included studies of actors and dancers, circus pictures, equestrian commissions, and scenes of rural life.

During the war Seago was a camouflage officer under Sir C. J. E. Auchinleck, and then Sir H. R. L. G. Alexander (later Earl Alexander of Tunis, q.v.), both keen amateur painters. He learned to fly, fulfilling an ambition 'to see the other side of the clouds' and he designed the insignia for the airborne forces. He wrote *Peace in War* (1943) and *High Endeavour* (1944). In 1944 he was invalided out of the army but was invited by Alexander to paint scenes of the Italian campaign. In *With the Allied Armies in Italy* (1945) Seago wrote how he tried to reconcile his love of light and atmosphere with the confused emotions that he felt as a spectator of war. The paintings of the campaign were shown with considerable success in London in 1945—the exhibition was opened by Alexander, who became a close friend.

After the war, Seago settled in Norfolk to paint the landscape that he knew and loved. He bought a boat in which he made painting expeditions to Holland and France, and although he travelled widely, painting a variety of subjects, it was the marshes, rivers, and coasts of East Anglia that inspired him most. He built on the achievements of English and French artists such as John Constable, P. Wilson Steer [qq.v.], and Camille Pissaro, excelling in his interpretation of the qualities of light and the wide skies of his native county. He was a subtle water-colourist, for the medium was perfectly suited to his desire to 'get air into the picture'. In later years he did not paint outdoors, but sketched rapidly relying on his photographic memory to make the complete picture in his studio. Seago's philosophy was expressed in his books *A Canvas to Cover* (1947), *Tideline* (1948), and *With Capricorn to Paris* (1956).

Testimony to Seago's success was the fact that nearly every annual exhibition was sold out on the first day, and successful shows were held regularly in Canada, the USA, and South Africa. In 1956 he was invited by the Duke of Edinburgh to join the royal yacht *Britannia* on a round-the-world trip. Many of Seago's paintings are in royal collections, and he made portraits of King George VI and Elizabeth II. Seago was elected RBA in 1946, ARWS in 1957, and RWS in 1959.

Seago received little critical attention. He himself had scant sympathy for major art 'movements' but he felt that he followed a living tradition and was hurt by the critics' neglect. He found support in his wide circle of friends, who included Sir Noël Coward, Sir Benjamin (later Lord) Britten, Henry Williamson [qq.v.], and Sir Laurens van der Post. Seago's portraits of his friends are particularly fine.

Seago was direct and unpretentious with strong opinions on a wide range of subjects. He enjoyed the theatre, music, and sailing. His deep feeling for nature was derived from years of patient observation, and his achievement was to paint pictures that calmly invite the observer to share the artist's joy.

Seago did not marry. After a visit to Hong Kong in 1962, he adopted Edward Tsui, whom he brought to England to be educated. He died in London 19 January 1974.

[Horace Shipp, *Edward Seago—Painter in the English Tradition*, 1952; Francis W. Hawcroft, *Edward Seago—a Review of the Years 1953–1964*, 1965; Jean Goodman, *Edward Seago: the Other Side of the Canvas*, 1978; *The Times*, 21 January 1974; private information; personal knowledge.] JEREMY CUNNINGHAM

SELBORNE, third EARL OF (1887–1971), government minister and manager of Special Operations Executive. [See PALMER, ROUNDELL CECIL.]

SELLERS, RICHARD HENRY ('PETER') (1925–1980), comedian, was born in Portsmouth 8 September 1925, the only child of William Sellers, a pianist of modest ability, and his wife, Agnes ('Peg') Marks, who was one of the Ray Sisters entertainers, and the great-grand-daughter of Daniel Mendoza [q.v.], the pugilist. Although his mother was Jewish, he was primarily educated at St. Aloysius College in Hornsey Lane, Highgate, a Roman Catholic school run by the Brothers of Our Lady of Mercy. He left school at fourteen and entered the theatre world, doing most backstage jobs. He then developed a desire to play drums in a dance band. At this he became very proficient and, but for his ability at mimicry, might well have stayed a jazz drummer.

Called up into the RAF during the war despite his mother's desperate efforts to have him disqualified on medical grounds, he finally ended up in its Entertainment Section in India, Ceylon, and Burma with Ralph Reader's Gang Show. Within a short time of leaving the Services in 1947, such was his confidence and his ability as an impressionist, that he duped a BBC producer, Roy Speer, by using the voice of Kenneth Horne. The producer was duly impressed, and gave him a small part in a comedy show.

In a short space of time he had appeared in the following series: 'Petticoat Lane', 'Ray's a Laugh', 'Variety Bandbox', 'Workers' Playtime', 'Third Division' (the first comedy show to come on the erudite Third Programme), finally reaching the highest acclaim in the revolutionary *The Goon Show*, which began in 1951 and ran for nine years. During this period he also appeared in Variety, including the Royal Command Performance. There were a few second-rate films: *Penny Points to Paradise* (1951), *Orders are Orders* (1954), *John and Julie* (1955), and *The Smallest Show on Earth* (1957). Then came a strangely original short film written and directed by Spike Milligan, entitled *The Running Jumping Standing Still Film* (1957–8), which won numerous awards because of its innovatory ideas. Sellers's big commercial break came with *The Ladykillers* (1955), but he received world acclaim for his outstanding performance in *I'm All Right Jack* (1959).

There followed a series of quality films, some successful and some not, including *The Millionairess* (1960), where he played opposite Sophia Loren, and *Waltz of the Toreadors* (1962), and one produced and directed by himself, *Mr. Topaze* (1961). He soared to new heights in his multi-character *Dr. Strangelove.* He did some black comedy films, one being *What's New Pussycat?* (1965), with Peter O'Toole and Woody Allen. But the watershed in his career was his portrayal of Inspector Clouseau, in *The Pink Panther* (1963). There followed a period of indifference, and it would appear at one time that his career might have come to a conclusion. However, there followed *The Return of the Pink Panther* (1974) and *The Pink Panther Strikes Again* (1976), which renovated his career and made him a millionaire.

To summarize him, one would say that he had one of the most glittering comic talents of our age, but what few people knew was that he never reached or was allowed to perform the levels of comedy that he delighted in most: the nonsense school. To his dying day he said his happiest days were performing in the Goon Shows. He made a desperate attempt to recreate *The Goon Show* atmosphere by making the film *The Fiendish Plot of Dr. Fu Manchu* (1980), which he co-wrote. But the fact that he never was a writer, or ever would be, and the collaboration with Americans, who had no like sense of humour, made the film a failure. However, most extraordinarily, he gave his finest performance in his last but one film, *Being There* (1979). This showed his incredible ability to recreate a character, in which Peter Sellers himself seemed to be totally excluded. His last wry contribution to comedy was having Glen Miller's 'In the Mood' played at his cremation.

Sellers was appointed CBE in 1966. He won many awards: Best Actor for 1959 (British Film Academy award); the Golden Gate award, 1959; the San Sebastian film award for the best British actor, 1962; Best Actor award, Tehran Film Festival, 1973; and the *Evening News* best actor of the year award, 1975.

Sellers suffered from a heart condition for his last fifteen years which made life difficult for him and had a debilitating effect on his personality. None of his marriages lasted long. His first one, in 1951, to Anne Howe produced two children, Michael and Sarah, but was terminated in 1964. In the same year, after a whirlwind romance, he married the starlet, Britt Ekland. There was one daughter of this marriage, Victoria, but the marriage was dissolved in 1969. In 1970 he married Miranda, daughter of Richard St. John Quarry and Lady Mancroft; the marriage was dissolved in 1974; there were no children. His last marriage, in 1977, to Lynne Frederick, also underwent emotional undulations, and all the signs point to a marriage that had failed; they had no children.

Sellers died in the Middlesex Hospital, London, 24 July 1980. Among the many who attended a later service of thanksgiving in London were Spike Milligan, Harry Secombe, and Michael Bentine, his former colleagues on *The Goon Show*.

[Peter Evans, *The Mask Behind the Mask, a Life of Peter Sellers*, 1968 and 1969; Alexander Walker, *Peter Sellers*, 1981; Michael Sellers with Sarah and Victoria Sellers, *P.S. I Love You*, 1981; personal knowledge.]

SPIKE MILLIGAN

SELWYN-LLOYD, BARON (1904–1978), Speaker of the House of Commons and politician. [See LLOYD, JOHN SELWYN BROOKE.]

SHARP, THOMAS WILFRED (1901–1978), town planner and writer, was born 12 April 1901 at Bishop Auckland, County Durham, the only son and second of three children of Francis Sharp, insurance agent, and his wife, Margaret Ann Beresford, of Salatyn, Shropshire. On both sides of the family most of the menfolk were miners. Sharp was educated at the grammar school, Bishop Auckland, which he left in 1918 to become a trainee surveyor with the town's borough surveyor. Four years later he moved to Margate to help prepare a development plan. From there he went to Canterbury and thence to London, to the offices of town planning consultants Thomas Adams and Longstreth Thompson. Following this, an important post as regional planning assistant to the South West Lancashire Regional Advisory Group should have promised much for Sharp's career. But when credit for his mammoth report on the area in 1930 was given, as tradition demanded, to the honorary surveyor, he resigned in anger, setting a precedent he was to follow more than once. He was unable to find a job for two years.

Turning misfortune to good purpose, he wrote his first book, *Town and Countryside* (1932), an angry polemic which established his reputation as an eloquent writer who was not afraid to be controversial. His argument rested on the separate, individual qualities of town and countryside and challenged the popular garden city movement which sought to unite them, and which had been bastardized in the suburb. He finished the book at the family home in County Durham. The area's squalid mining inheritance and its magnificent cathedral were to provide inspiration for much of Sharp's writing. He spent years as a consultant protecting Durham city from adverse development.

Sharp regarded the man-made English landscape as one of the most beautiful in the world, and the English village as the perfection of the village idea. He loved the beauty of formal street architecture as expressed in Renaissance towns, though over the years he came to prefer the less predictable richness of medieval streets. These ideas were expressed in *English Panorama* (1936), written after an unplanned move took him into the academic world, as a lecturer (from 1937) and later as reader, in Durham University's architecture department at Newcastle. Here he wrote *Town Planning* (1940), a Pelican paperback which popularized his ideas amongst a war-torn populace. It sold a quarter of a million copies.

Sharp spent part of the war in London, as a senior research officer from 1941 to 1943 in the planning section of the Ministry of Works and

Planning set up by Lord Reith [q.v.]. He contributed substantially to the influential Scott report on land utilization in rural areas, which laid the foundations for post-war legislation to protect the countryside. He also produced *The Anatomy of the Village* (1946), which became a classic on the subject of village design, despite almost being suppressed by the Ministry. In it Sharp for the first time consciously developed the concept of townscape, then almost unknown and still widely misunderstood, as a counterpart to landscape. It was a dramatic vision of the quality of urban space which he perfected, in outstanding analyses of historic towns, in his post-war plans—notably those for Durham, Oxford, Exeter, Salisbury, and Chichester, between 1943 and 1949. This work followed a brief return to Durham University in 1941. He devised the first undergraduate planning course in the country before leaving to concentrate on his own planning consultancy in Oxford, after it was made clear that there would be no immediate opportunity of a chair in the new subject. Soon after he left, however, a chair in town planning was created, leaving Sharp extremely bitter.

He was made D.Litt. of Durham in 1948 (he had obtained his Durham MA in 1940) and held office as president of the Town Planning Institute in 1945–6 and of the Institute of Landscape Architects in 1949–51. In 1951 he was appointed CBE, and he became FRIBA in 1961. But after his decade of achievement in the 1940s, the remaining years were ones of frustration and disillusionment as changes in the profession and his own inability to compromise made work hard to find. Post-war legislation created more local authority planning departments, and even when consultants came briefly back into the limelight in the 1960s building boom, Sharp chose to remain an offstage critic of his profession. He took occasional commissions, fought for a road across Christ Church meadow as the only way of saving Oxford's peerless High Street from traffic, and wrote poems and novels which, to his disappointment, remained largely unpublished. His last planning book was *Town and Townscape* (1968).

These years were brightened by Sharp's marriage in 1963 to Rachel Dorothy Morrison whom he had known for many years. She was the daughter of Cameron Morrison, principal of Newington College, Madras, and later a lecturer at St. Andrews University, whom he had known for many years. They had no children. Their home, 1 Farndon Road, Oxford, was constantly visited by friends and admirers, and Sharp's refuge was his study, lined with his collection of books, in which he took great delight until his death in hospital at Oxford 27 January 1978.

[Chapter by K. M. Stansfield in *Pioneers in British Planning*, ed. Gordon E. Cherry, 1981; K. M. Stansfield, 'The Poetry of Planning' (unpubl. MA thesis for Manchester University), 1974; private information.]

K. M. STANSFIELD

SHEPARD, ERNEST HOWARD (1879–1976), painter and illustrator, was born in St. John's Wood, London, 10 December 1879, the second son and youngest of the three children of Henry Donkin Shepard, architect, and his wife, Jessie Harriet, daughter of William Lee [q.v.], water-colour painter. Ernest's parents encouraged his talent for drawing and some of his sketches drawn when he was only seven are remarkable for the lively accuracy of observation which became such a feature of his later work. His mother died when he was ten, after which his aunts helped to bring him up.

He was educated at St. Paul's School, Hammersmith, where his uncle was a senior master. At sixteen he went to Heatherleys Art School from where, a year later, he gained a five-year studentship to the Royal Academy Schools. While at Heatherleys he received the nickname 'Kipper' by which he was known to his friends for the rest of his life. At the RA Schools he was taught by such academicians as John Singer Sargent [q.v.] who, he said, 'inspired us all'. (Sir) Frank Dicksee [q.v.], who was later president of the Royal Academy, was a family friend and a very early influence.

In 1899 he won both the Landseer and British Institution scholarships and in the following year he was awarded a silver medal for figure painting and the third prize for figure drawing. Shepard was, while still studying, supplementing his meagre finances by selling drawings to magazines.

He first exhibited at the Royal Academy in 1901 and continued to do so fairly regularly till 1924 after which he only exhibited three times. He took his work very seriously, and though light-hearted, was also most thorough and industrious. Gradually his illustrative work took over more or less completely and he only painted in oils as a recreation. His early commissions were for book illustrations. Among the books he illustrated before World War I were *David Copperfield*, *Tom Brown's Schooldays*, *Aesop's Fables*, and *Henry Esmond*.

While at the Royal Academy Schools Shepard had met another gifted student, Florence Eleanor Chaplin. She was the second daughter of James Hopper Chaplin, a gem expert and member of Lloyd's, and granddaughter of Ebenezer Landells [q.v.], one of the founders of *Punch*. In 1904 they married; in 1907 their son Graham was born and in 1909 their daughter Mary, who was to marry E. V. Knox [q.v.]. Graham was to die in 1943.

It was an ambition of his to become a '*Punch* artist' as the magazine was famous for the quality of the artists on its staff. It was not until 1906 that his first drawings were accepted and it was not until 1914 that he was having drawings regularly accepted. In 1915 he applied for a commission in the Royal Artillery. He always said he was fascinated by guns. He was in the battles of the Somme, Arras, and Ypres and ended the war serving in Italy as Major Shepard, MC. Somehow he managed to do a surprising amount of work during that period, but suffered another blow when his beloved elder brother was killed. In 1921 he was invited to become a member of the staff of *Punch* which meant that he had to produce at least one drawing a week and which provided him with the blessing of a regular income.

A. A. Milne [q.v.] had written a series of children's verses for *Punch* and Shepard was asked to illustrate them. This was a wonderful marriage of verse and vision. His delicately precise and fresh drawings had an instant appeal and were published as the book *When We Were Very Young* in 1924. The success of this led to a series of books: *Winnie the Pooh* (1926), *Now We Are Six* (1927), *The House at Pooh Corner* (1928), and a number of others. It established both Milne and Shepard, though it was Christopher Robin and Pooh who became household names for generations of children and adults.

By now Shepard had all the work he could cope with. G. Bell & Sons commissioned him to do sixty full-page drawings for *Everybody's Pepys* (1926), followed by *Everybody's Boswell* (1930), and *Everybody's Lamb* (1933). But at home tragedy struck, for Florence died very suddenly in 1927 and Shepard lost not only a wife but a valued critic.

During the 1930s he buried himself in work. He did drawings for the 1931 edition of *The Wind in the Willows* by Kenneth Grahame [q.v.], the 1932 edition of *Bevis* by Richard Jefferies, and *Victoria Regina* (1934) by Laurence Housman [q.v.]. In 1935 he was appointed second cartoonist on the editorial staff of *Punch*, another landmark of success in his career. He carried on this responsible job through the war to 1949, and finally left in 1953 when editorial changes were made. During the war, in 1944, he married again, Norah, eldest daughter of J. C. Carroll, of Australia. She was a nurse working at St. Mary's Hospital, Paddington.

After Shepard's dismissal from *Punch* he illustrated more books than ever and began to lecture and broadcast. In 1957 he wrote *Drawn from Memory* which is full of endearingly clear memories of his family and of himself as a little boy of eight. In 1961 *Drawn from Life* followed taking the reader through his school and art student days to the time of his marriage. His writing has the same observant and sympathetic charm that characterizes his drawings.

He was fairly tall with penetrating light blue eyes. His personality was warm and friendly and was allied to a shrewd mind and an immense capacity for work. 'A man for all men' was how fellow *Punch* cartoonist, Leslie Illingworth, described him. The enormous popularity of Winnie the Pooh which grew through the years meant that towards the end of his very long life Shepard was constantly involved with new projects concerned with the A. A. Milne books, and particularly with coloured editions. In 1972 he was appointed OBE. He managed to celebrate his ninety-sixth birthday and died at Midhurst, Sussex, 24 March 1976.

[E. H. Shepard, *Drawn from Memory*, 1957, and *Drawn from Life*, 1961; Rawle Knox (ed.), *The Work of E. H. Shepard*, 1979; Royal Academy records; personal knowledge.]

CONSTANCE ANNE PARKER

SHEPPARD, PHILIP MACDONALD (1921–1976), geneticist, was born at Marlborough 27 July 1921, the only child of George Sheppard, mathematics master at Bradfield College, and his wife, Alison, daughter of William Henry Macdonald, who was related to the Cornfords and consequently, by marriage, to the Darwins. He was educated at Marlborough College. In 1939 he joined the Royal Air Force Volunteer Reserve, trained as an air crew member, and was posted to Bomber Command. He took part in the first 1,000-bomber raid on Cologne in July 1942 but on the way home his plane was damaged and over the North Sea it was shot down by a German minesweeper. The crew were rescued by the Germans and Sheppard remained a prisoner for the rest of the war.

In 1946 Sheppard entered Worcester College, Oxford, to read honours zoology. He was an excellent shot and captain of the Oxford University Rifle Club in 1948. He was also a keen fisherman. Attracted to the genetical theory of natural selection propounded by (Sir) R. A. Fisher [q.v.] he came under the influence of E. B. Ford, who interested him in the genetics of the scarlet tiger moth *Panaxia dominula* and the snail *Cepaea nemoralis*. These formed the basis of his doctoral research during the time he held the Christopher Welch scholarship in genetics. He had obtained second class honours in zoology in 1948.

From 1951 (when he gained his D.Phil.) to 1956 he was junior research officer in zoology in Oxford, during which time he spent a year (1954–5) with Professor T. Dobzhansky at Columbia University, New York, on a Rockefeller fellowship, working on *Drosophila melanogaster*. In 1956 he went to Liverpool University as senior lecturer in genetics at the department of zoology.

He became reader in the new sub-department of genetics in 1959 and the first professor in 1963.

The first of the four editions of his *Natural Selection and Heredity* appeared in 1958. Its main purpose was to explain genetic principles and 'to avoid giving the impression that most problems concerned with natural selection are solved and that controversy no longer exists, an idea which elementary books often impart to their readers'.

Shortly after Sheppard's arrival at Liverpool the Nuffield Unit of Medical Genetics was set up in the medical school, financed by a grant of £350,000 from the Nuffield Foundation to the university—one of the biggest ever given by the foundation. The director was (Sir) Cyril A. Clarke, who had previously worked with Sheppard for some years. The unit's medical work stemmed from that on the Lepidoptera. After the tiger moth and snails it studied the evolution of mimicry in butterflies and for twenty-five years worked on the three classical mimics, *Papilio dardanus* from Africa and *Papilio polytes* and *Papilio memnon* from South-East Asia. It was shown that a combination of only a few characters controlled the various wing patterns, which suggested that an apparent multiple allelomorphic series was really a supergene composed of alleles at several closely linked loci. Thus crossing over could occur within the supergene and this could explain some of the rarer forms.

It was directly because of this, and the genetic interactions in swallow-tails, that Clarke and Sheppard looked for a corresponding situation in man. This was found in the rhesus blood groups and led to a method of preventing rhesus haemolytic disease of the newborn by giving an injection of anti-rhesus antibody (anti-D) to Rh-negative mothers after they had been delivered of an Rh-positive baby. The preliminary work which took about ten years was carried out first on Rh-negative male volunteers and, when success was achieved, on mothers. Sheppard strongly advised that women should be used in whom there had been a considerable feto-maternal haemorrhage, i.e. a high risk group. The trial was very successful and in 1970 the treatment was adopted by the National Health Service and became standard practice, leading to a great reduction of the disease.

In 1962 Sheppard went to Trinidad and Surinam to study the genetics of the mimetic Heliconius butterflies and in 1971 he went as a Royal Society Leverhulme visiting professor to the Museum of Zoology, University of Sao Paulo, and elsewhere in Brazil for lecturing and research. While there he collected living *Heliconius melpomene* and *H. erato*, and because of a Royal Society grant returned via Panama and Trinidad to obtain more material.

Living near Liverpool, on the edge of one of Britain's worst industrial polluted areas, he and Clarke were stimulated by H. B. D. Kettlewell to carry out a detailed local survey of the classical melanic moth *Biston betularia.* Perhaps the most interesting of the findings over twenty-five years was the large decrease in the frequencies of the melanic form in smokeless zones and the beginning of the possible reversal of this extraordinary piece of evolution.

With the help of the Liverpool Tropical School Sheppard played a major part in studying population changes in mosquitoes in Bangkok. He also worked on neural tube defects in man and served on the Royal College of Physicians committee which reported in 1976 on the value of fluoridation of water supplies to prevent dental caries.

He became FRS in 1965. In 1974 he was awarded the Darwin medal of the Royal Society and in 1975 the gold medal of the Linnean Society. In 1975 he was made an honorary fellow of the Royal College of Physicians of London.

In 1948 he married Patricia Beatrice who accompanied him on many expeditions. She was the daughter of Reginald Harold Lee, master chef. They had three sons. Though doctors at first maddened Sheppard, he was so fascinated by medical problems that he threw himself into medical research and showed its practitioners how to design experiments which would give an early answer, with the minimum of risk to volunteers. In his last illness, although still critical of doctors as pure scientists, he secretly admired the way he was looked after and the Hippocratic tradition in action. He died of leukaemia 17 October 1976 at Liverpool Royal Infirmary.

[Sir Cyril Clarke in *Biographical Memoirs of Fellows of the Royal Society*, vol. xxiii, 1977; *The Times*, 19 October 1976; personal knowledge.]

CYRIL A. CLARKE

SHERRIFF, ROBERT CEDRIC (1896–1975), dramatist and novelist, was born 6 June 1896 at Hampton-Wick, Surrey, the only child of Herbert Hankin Sherriff, insurance clerk, and his wife, Constance, daughter of Charles Winder, of Iver, Buckinghamshire. Educated at Kingston Grammar School, he was on the London staff of the Sun Insurance Office from 1914, and served from 1917 as a captain in the East Surrey Regiment. He was severely wounded at Ypres in 1917. After the war, back as an insurance official, he began to write plays for his Thames-side rowing club.

Suddenly and remarkably, in the New Year of 1929, he became one of the most discussed English dramatists when *Journey's End*, which various managements had turned down but which had had an applauded production by the Stage Society at the Apollo Theatre in December 1928, began a long London run at the Savoy. James Agate [q.v.], then drama critic for the

BBC, had been largely responsible for the transference when he called the play, in a broadcast, 'a work of extraordinary quality and interest'. It is set throughout in a claustrophobic dug-out before St. Quentin on the eve of the March offensive of 1918. Sherriff, always a man of the naturalistic theatre, had sought to give no more than a straight, simple impression of the terrors of the western front in a play written with so much honesty—no heroics, no pretence—that its people stamped themselves upon the English theatre of their time: Osborne, the gentle schoolmaster; Raleigh, straight from school to the front line; Trotter, the ranker subaltern without imagination; Stanhope, the captain with too much; Hibbert, his nerve gone. *Journey's End* was translated and performed in every European language; it toured extensively in the United States (where it had 485 performances in New York) and throughout the world; and it has been twice revived in London.

It was usual, at the time of *Journey's End*, to suggest that Sherriff was a one-play man, likely to do nothing else. Actually, through a career during which he kept the quietness and modesty that never left him, he wrote another nine stage plays, the scripts for many distinguished films, and half a dozen novels. His second West End piece was a mild cricketing comedy, *Badger's Green* (1930), the tale of a speculative builder who turned from public enemy to hero at the twelfth hour. It did not last; neither did Sherriff's next comedy, *Windfall* (1933). But *St. Helena* (1935), written in partnership with the actress Jeanne de Casalis, acted first at the Old Vic and then running briefly at Daly's, was an affecting and persuasive portrait of Napoleon at his journey's end, an eagle caged in the gloom of Longwood. Before this, Sherriff, at the age of thirty-five, had fulfilled a boyhood longing by going up to Oxford in 1931 to spend two years as a 'special student' reading history at New College. In 1937 he founded a scholarship at the college.

It was thirteen years before his name appeared again on a West End programme, this time with an ironic comedy, *Miss Mabel* (1948), a likeable confidence trick but less good than its successor, *Home at Seven* (1950). With Sir Ralph Richardson as a City bank clerk of regular habits who inexplicably fails to return home for twenty-four hours (during which anything might have happened), the piece was a sustained exercise in suspense, helped by Sherriff's ear for dialogue which never failed him. He wrote four more plays, *The White Carnation* (1953), an implausible story of a ghost, an intermittently haunting little piece composed in a chain of duologues; *The Long Sunset* (1955), *The Telescope* (1957), and *A Shred of Evidence* (1960). Of these, *The Long Sunset*, originally a radio play, was the most durable; it did not reach London, at the Mermaid Theatre, until 1961, six years after its production at the Birmingham Repertory. Another journey's end, it takes place at the close of the Roman occupation of Britain early in the fifth century, Professor Wheeler's 'age of *crépuscule* and quicksand', a sudden chaos in the ordered realm between Vectis and the Wall. On three levels, the Rome that was, the Roman province that is ceasing to be, and the Britain that will emerge, *The Long Sunset* is proof of Sherriff's sustained interest in archaeology which came to be his principal hobby.

He wrote several screen-plays in Britain and Hollywood, of which some of the most familiar, retrospectively, were *Goodbye Mr. Chips* (from the book by James Hilton, q.v.), *The Four Feathers* (from A. E. W. Mason, q.v.), and *Lady Hamilton*. Among his novels—in which, as in his other work, he seldom raises his voice—the best is the first, *The Fortnight in September* (1931), a sympathetic, detailed picture of a London suburban family's holiday at the seaside.

Sherriff, who never married, was devoted to his mother. Lacking self-confidence, he preferred the company of people younger than himself. He was an endearingly kind and gentle man, qualities evident in his memoir, *No Leading Lady* (1968). He spent much of his life, after his early success, in a house at Esher, later adding to this a Dorset farm. He was elected FSA and FRSL. He died in Kingston Hospital, Kingston upon Thames, 13 November 1975.

[R. C. Sherriff, *No Leading Lady*, 1968; personal knowledge.] J. C. Trewin

SHIPTON, ERIC EARLE (1907–1977), explorer and mountaineer, was born 1 August 1907 in Ceylon, the younger child and only son of Cecil Shipton, a tea planter, and his wife, Alice Lilian Earle. His father died before he was three and his upbringing, in his mother's hands, was characterized by constant travelling between Ceylon and Europe. Suffering from dyslexia he failed to pass common entrance and at eighteen had no enthusiasm for university or for any conventional career.

Following holidays in France and Norway his interest in travel had become focused on mountaineering; he did a number of climbs in the Alps. But climbing did not offer a career and in 1928 he went off to Kenya to work on a coffee plantation. He expected to spend the rest of his life there but three things conspired to make this otherwise. Shipton's plantation was only twenty miles from the twin peaks of Mt. Kenya, of which Batian had been climbed but once while Nelion remained virgin. As climbing companion he found first (Sir) Percy Wyn-Harris [q.v.], a notable Cambridge athlete and mountaineer with whom he made the second ascent of Batian and the first of Nelion. Shortly after this he found another companion who was to play an even bigger part in his life, H. W. Tilman [q.v.], with whom he made the first complete traverse of the twin peaks.

In 1931 some neighbours found a rich gold deposit close at hand and invited Shipton to join in exploiting it, but this opportunity he declined in order to join the expedition led by F. S. Smythe [q.v.] to Kamet in Garhwal Himalaya. It was to be the first of a whole series of Himalayan ventures occupying the rest of the thirties, and shortly after Kamet, with prospects depressed by the world slump, he abandoned his Kenya interests altogether.

After the success of Kamet, Shipton was a natural choice for the Mt. Everest expedition of 1933 on which he reached 8,500 m. but the experience of those two lavishly organized undertakings convinced him that this was the wrong way to travel in the Himalayas and his next venture was in stark contrast. In company with H. W. Tilman and three Sherpas he spent three months in Garhwal Himalaya living largely off the country and at a total cost of £286. Instead of travelling as sahibs and retainers they went as companions sharing the same food and privations. In this remarkable journey they forced an entry, for the first time, up the formidable Rishi gorge and into the Nanda Devi sanctuary which, with its satellite peaks, they surveyed.

In the years that followed there were further expeditions to the north side of Everest (1935, 1936, and 1938), and two journeys of exploration to the remote areas of the Karakoram bordering on Tibet and Sinkiang (1937 and 1938). In 1938 Shipton was awarded the Patron's medal of the Royal Geographical Society and his reputation and style were well established. He was not really a professional but had no other career and made do with modest earnings from books and lectures.

When war came in the middle of his second Karakoram expedition the government of India offered him the post of consul-general at Kashgar which he accepted with enthusiasm as an opportunity to see yet another region of Central Asia. It was, however, to prove a difficult assignment, his freedom of action being curbed by Chinese hostility combined with Russian suspicion. He was, in fact, to have a second tour of duty here in easier political circumstances from 1946 to 1948 by which time he was married. This, in turn, was to be followed by two years as consul-general at Kunming in Yunnan (1949–51), an unhappy experience due to increasing pressure from the communist authorities which concluded with his expulsion from the country and an agonizing journey, with wife and children, to the coast.

Although the reassertion in 1950 of Chinese authority in Tibet had put an end to any early prospect of using the northern approach to Everest, Nepal was gradually becoming accessible and in 1951 a reconnaissance of the south side of the mountain was being planned. On Shipton's return from China the leadership of this undertaking was immediately offered to him. The task was successfully completed, thus demonstrating that despite a dangerous ice-fall there was indeed a feasible route. By then, however, the British monopoly of access to Everest was over and for 1952 the Swiss had permission from the Nepalese government to attempt to climb the mountain. Britain had to await its turn in 1953.

The years that followed brought great disappointments and unhappiness to Shipton. The 1952 expedition to Cho Oyu, which he led, failed in its main object. While his experience made him the chief contender for the leadership on Everest in 1953 his dislike of large expeditions and national rivalries and his aversion to elaborate planning were strong and, in the end, decisive arguments against his appointment. The initial offer of the leadership was later so circumscribed that he felt bound to refuse. At a loss for what to do he took an unsuitable job as warden of the Outward Bound School in Eskdale. This came to a disastrous end when his marriage broke up at the end of 1954. In disgust he retired into the obscurity of a forester's job in Shropshire.

But by the end of the decade he emerged from the shadows and started with a fresh group of friends on a series of exploratory journeys (1958–64) in Patagonia and Tierra del Fuego, at that time virtually unknown country. This period culminated in his appointment by the Chilean government as their adviser in the boundary dispute with Argentina. He was appointed CBE in 1955 and was president of the Alpine Club in 1965–7.

Shipton was a good-looking man with intense blue deep-set eyes. He was gregarious and interested in people, ready to talk on any subject, with friends of both sexes and various nationalities. His travels are well recorded in his books: *Nanda Devi* (1936), *Blank on the Map* (1938), *Upon That Mountain* (1948), *Mountains of Tartary* (1951), *Mount Everest Reconnaissance Expedition* (1951), *Land of Tempest* (1963), and the autobiography, *That Untravelled World* (1969). He also wrote the notice of Tom Longstaff for this Dictionary.

He married in 1942 Diana Kendall, younger daughter of Frederick Francis Ralph Channer, of the Indian Forest Service. They had two sons. The marriage was dissolved in 1955. He died 28 March 1977 at Anstey in Wiltshire.

[Eric Shipton, *That Untravelled World*, 1969; private information; personal knowledge.]

PETER LLOYD

SIEFF, ISRAEL MOSES, BARON SIEFF (1889–1972), industrialist and merchant, was born in

Manchester 4 May 1889, the eldest in the family of three sons and two daughters of Ephraim Sieff and his wife, Sarah Saffer, who had arrived in Britain, penniless immigrants from Lithuania. Beginning with a handcart, his father built up a textile scrap business in Manchester which enabled him later to purchase Beaumont and Company, well-established dealers in the trade. This subsequently became Sieff and Beaumont, and Sieff became a wealthy man.

Israel Sieff was brought up in the same street as Simon Marks (later Lord Marks of Broughton, whose notice he subsequently wrote for this Dictionary), the son of the founder of Marks and Spencer Ltd. The boys became close friends, passed through Manchester Grammar School in the same class, and each married the other's sister. In 1909 Sieff took a degree in economics at Manchester University, and then joined his father's firm. In 1915, to help Simon Marks, who was about to become chairman of Marks and Spencer, to ward off a take-over bid, Sieff joined him on the board, helping him with a substantial loan.

In 1913, already a Zionist, Sieff encountered Chaim Weizmann [q.v.], then a lecturer at Manchester University, and 'fell under his spell'. With Simon Marks's ardent support, he became Weizmann's unpaid personal assistant. In 1918, as secretary to the Zionist Commission, which was to report on how the Balfour Declaration of 1917 was to be implemented, he accompanied Weizmann to the peace conference at Versailles, and in 1920 to the conference of San Remo. Throughout the 1920s he spent many months in Palestine with his wife as Weizmann's 'eyes and ears'.

When in 1926 Simon Marks made Marks and Spencer a public company and embarked upon an ambitious programme of expansion, he asked Sieff to move his home to London and become a full-time member of the board, as vice-chairman and joint managing director. These posts Sieff held until Marks's death in 1964, when he became chairman. The partnership brought Marks and Spencer great commercial success and high repute, based on high-quality goods representing good value for the customer, and good wages and working conditions for the employees. Marks was a merchandiser of genius and a brilliant business man, but preferred to work at his desk or visit his own stores. It was Sieff who roved the country seeking manufacturing firms willing to bypass the wholesalers and manufacture goods at lower cost to Marks and Spencer's specifications, and it was Sieff, with Marks's whole-hearted backing, who developed their models for human relations in industry. Between them they made Marks and Spencer into a national institution, the household term, 'Marks and Sparks', indicating the affection with which the public came to regard it.

In 1931, to try and deal with the problems of a declining economy and mounting unemployment, a number of politicians of all parties, economists, and publicists founded Political and Economic Planning, a discussion group to collate current knowledge in the economic, industrial, and social field and publish it for the benefit of policy-makers in government, the Civil Service, and the business world. Sieff was invited to become chairman of PEP's industry group. With his practical knowledge and personal energy, he soon corrected its bias to the theoretical. He produced PEP's first report, known as A1, on Britain's industrial problems, and it became the model for valuable practical publications on iron and steel, coal, cotton, and housing, and then for publications in other fields. He was consequently asked to become chairman of PEP and remained in that position from 1931 to 1939. He was vice-chairman from 1939 to 1964.

Sieff had wide interests. For academic studies, he particularly favoured the Royal Anthropological Society, of which he was a fellow. He bred prize-winning cattle on his estate in Berkshire, developed strawberry cultivation, and was an expert grower of orchids. His love of music was deep and well informed. A good-looking man, elegantly though quietly dressed, he was an excellent host, a master of anecdote, his mild, wise words disarming critics and quietening trouble-makers. He loved the company of men and women, enjoyed good food, and was a connoisseur of claret. At the age of eighty-one he published his memoirs, only, he said, to record his gratitude to the two families and his friends who had enriched his life, 'giving thanks in the words of the prophet Isaiah for "a joy of many generations"'.

He was created a life peer in 1966. He was FRGS, and was made honorary FRCS (1968) and LL D (Manchester, 1969).

In 1910 Sieff married Rebecca Doro (died 1966), daughter of Michael Marks, of Manchester, founder of Marks and Spencer Ltd. She was one of the six co-founders of WIZO, the Women's International Zionist Organization, and she was appointed OBE in 1960. They had three sons, one of whom died in 1933, and a daughter. The younger surviving son, Marcus Joseph (born 1913), was created a life peer, Baron Sieff of Brimpton, in 1980. Sieff died in London 14 February 1972.

[*The Times*, 15 February 1972; Lord Sieff, *Memoirs*, 1970; personal knowledge.]

KENNETH HARRIS

SIEVEKING, LANCELOT DE GIBERNE (1896–1972), author and radio and television producer, was born in Harrow 19 March 1896, the third son and third child (there was also a daughter) of Edward Gustavus Sieveking, timber merchant, and his wife, Isabel Giberne, writer and suffragist and cousin of Gerard Manley Hopkins. His godfather was G. K. Chesterton [q.v.], described by Lancelot as 'the first great friend I ever had', and he was the great-nephew of Sir Edward Sieveking [q.v.], physician. He was removed from prep school when the family doctor said he had 'outgrown his strength'. He was tutored at home from the age of thirteen to eighteen. Writing later, he much regretted the absence of childhood friends. But this at least enabled him early to indulge his literary bent. His first novel, *Stampede!*, begun at the age of thirteen, was published in 1924. His first book, *Dressing Gowns and Glue*, a slim volume of nonsense verse published in 1920, ran through four editions.

When war was declared in 1914 he joined the Artists' Rifles but soon transferred to the Royal Naval Air Service. On active service, first in East Africa, later in France, he went on night bombing raids, was promoted captain, and was awarded the DSC. But on 28 October 1917 he was shot down behind the German lines and imprisoned until war's end.

In 1919 he went to St. Catharine's College, Cambridge. Here, for the first time (apart from the abnormal war years) he was able to make friends with his contemporaries as well as many of the leading literary figures of the day. A major influence and lifelong friend was the eccentric genius, C. K. Ogden [q.v.], who, Sieveking claimed, 'managed everything I did for the next seven years'. It was Ogden who encouraged him to buy and edit the *New Cambridge*. After failing to qualify for the English tripos, he went down and for a while drifted from job to job, toured as an actor (1919–22), took the unlikely post of assistant inspector of taxes in Sussex (1922), and then rejoined the air force in which from 1923 to 1924 he was stationed in India.

In April 1925 his life first took on shape and direction. He applied and was accepted for a job at the British Broadcasting Company, then four years old. Sieveking was six feet six inches tall, handsome, and elegant. Anyone less like an assistant to the director of education (for such was his title), whether in appearance or professional experience, would be hard to imagine. But then seldom had the term education been applied to so grotesque a miscellany of duties. Sieveking's main tasks combined public relations (wining and dining distinguished public figures to win their goodwill for a fledgling and not yet respected institution), editing news bulletins, and organizing topical talks and the first outside broadcasts to be put on the air.

Despite the rampant amateurism of these early days at the BBC, Sieveking soon found his proper niche and, with a small band of fellow workers, lent his imagination to creating a new, distinctive art—radio drama. His output over the next fifteen years was prolific (he produced over 200 plays and wrote several books) and original. In 1926 he produced *The Wheel of Time*, the first 'feature programme' to be broadcast, and this was followed in 1928 by *Kaleidoscope*, the first multi-studio production. This, like everything else he did, provoked both favourable and hostile opinions.

After 1938 he ceased to be a dominant influence in broadcasting. Though he produced the first television play (in 1930), he never achieved comparable success in this new medium. 'In three-quarters of a century', he wistfully wrote, 'no one in any field of activity has been anything but friendly and co-operative—except in the field of television. Why?'

In 1938–9 he was seconded to the Canadian Broadcasting Corporation, and in 1939 he was transferred to BBC Bristol as a producer in the feature and drama department. From 1942 to 1944 he was the BBC's west regional programme director. But administration bored him and in 1944 he accepted the job of drama script editor, a post he held until he was retired in 1956.

In 1924 Sieveking married April, daughter of Harry Quilter, writer; they had one son. The marriage was dissolved in 1928 and in 1929 he married Natalie, daughter of Court Denny, business man; they had two daughters. The marriage was dissolved in 1939 and in 1949 he married Maisie, daughter of Max John Christian Meiklejohn, writer and publisher; they had one son. He lived his last years at the White House, Snape, Suffolk, entertaining and delighting his friends with lively conversation and a fund of anecdotes. He died 6 January 1972 in Ipswich, Suffolk.

[Lance Sieveking, unpublished autobiography, and other records in BBC Written Archives Centre; private information.]

C. A. SIEPMANN

SILKIN, LEWIS, first BARON SILKIN (1889–1972), solicitor and government minister, was born in London 14 November 1889, shortly after his parents, Abraham Silkin and his wife Fanny Sopher, had sailed across the Baltic from Lithuania and settled in the East End of London, where his father ran a shop and taught Hebrew. Lewis was the eldest of seven children of the marriage. At eleven he won a scholarship to the Central Foundation School, City Road, London. He gained a mathematical scholarship to Worcester College, Oxford. Since his headmaster, oddly, thought Silkin 'would not benefit from university education', and his parents were too poor to send him, he worked for a while in the East India docks. He did manage a year at

London University and then became a managing clerk to a solicitor. After himself qualifying as a solicitor he early started his own legal firm.

In 1915 he married Rosa Neft (died 1947), whom he used to take to listen to William Crooks MP [q.v.] eloquently preaching socialism at the dock gates, for Silkin was now, like many of his contemporaries, absorbing a socialist philosophy, largely inspired by the *Merrie England* of Robert Blatchford [q.v.]. Silkin and his wife went to live at Balham in a large house, increasingly filled with relatives and children—noisy, intelligent, questioning, impoverished in the tradition of a close-knit Jewish family. There perhaps he acquired the ability to concentrate on his papers, shut off his mind to what went on around him, and yet join in the family noise when he wanted. There were three sons of his marriage, the younger two of whom also became MPs. Though city-born Silkin acquired a passionate love of the English countryside, which informed his later work. After books, music was his second love. As a young man rambling through England he sang as he walked.

In 1925 he was elected to the London County Council, soon becoming leader of the opposition. Later Labour was in a majority and he and Herbert Morrison (later Lord Morrison of Lambeth, q.v.) worked together to build anew the London they loved. Silkin became chairman of the Council's housing and public health committee in 1934 and headed the building drive. He did not much approve of modern architecture. He appreciated the necessity to preserve the community life of the East End into which he was born and which he understood. Though many years later he had a measure of responsibility for the planning of them, he was not fond of the tower blocks which the blitz and post-war economy forced upon London. He became convinced that industry and housing must diminish in urban areas and that this could only be achieved if planning legislation were strengthened and the profit motive regulated. He objected to the fortunes made, as he saw it, by enhanced land values created by the community but turned into cash for individuals. He wanted to hive off the ownership of development rights in land into the possession of the community.

In May 1936, in a by-election, he became Labour MP for the Peckham division of Camberwell. As World War II neared its end, the government became increasingly concerned with post-war reconstruction. Nothing was more urgent than to re-plan bombed-out London. By the beginning of 1943 there was a minister of town and country planning. In 1945 the new Labour government enhanced the powers of the Ministry and appointed Lewis Silkin to it, with Cabinet rank. He was now a master in this field with great experience of London's politics. Here was the opportunity to put into legal form the principles on which he had long been brooding. He had the advantage of operating in an esoteric field. Few MPs understood the implications of Silkin's 1947 Town and Country Planning Act, which finally removed all development rights from landlords, urban and rural, and gave new and substantial powers to local planning authorities. It was preceded by the New Towns Act of 1946. Silkin then translated his love of the countryside into the National Parks and Access to the Countryside Act of 1949, which completed his 'trilogy'. There were amendments later, particularly in the financial field, but the grand design survived the test of time.

He was skilled in his relationships with his staff and a master of negotiation. In 1950, when at the height of his powers, he lost his seat in the Commons. Unwillingly, in that year he went to the Lords, as first Baron Silkin. He could argue a case with impeccable logic and a ready smile, but his voice was low and he was not, and did not seek to be, an orator. For nine years (1955–64) he was deputy leader of the opposition in the House of Lords, but his talent was creative, rather than party political. He was sworn of the Privy Council in 1945 and appointed CH in 1965. The gold medal of the Royal Town Planning Institute was conferred on him.

Silkin married secondly, in 1948, Frieda M. (died 1963), widow of J. F. F. Johnson, and daughter of the Revd Canon Pilling, of Norwich. He married thirdly, in 1964, Marguerite Schlageter. He died in London 11 May 1972, and was succeeded in the barony by his eldest son, Arthur (born 1916).

[*The Times*, 12 and 16 May 1972; personal knowledge.] EVELYN KING

SILVESTER, VICTOR MARLBOROUGH (1900–1978), dance instructor and bandleader, was born 25 February 1900 at the vicarage of St. John's church, Wembley, the younger son and second of the six children of the Revd John William Potts Silvester and his wife, Katherine Hudson. Victor was so named because a victory in the Boer war was reported on the day he was born; his second name was in honour of the bishop of Marlborough. His father was a stern disciplinarian but his mother was more understanding and approachable.

He ran away from each of the schools he was sent to: Ardingly College in Sussex; St. John's, Leatherhead, Surrey; and John Lyons' School at Harrow in Middlesex. In November 1914 he joined the army by lying about his age. He spent six months in France, in the front line near Arras, until he was discovered to be under age, when he joined the 1st British Ambulance Unit in Italy, where he was wounded in 1917 by shrapnel in the leg and won the Italian bronze medal for military valour. Returning to England in December 1917, he was given a commission but demobbed immediately the war ended.

He applied to go to Sandhurst but meanwhile he was noticed at a tea dance by Belle Harding, who employed him to partner dancers at her headquarters in Kensington. He soon became one of her team of instructors and, although he went to Sandhurst in September 1919, he left there after three weeks and returned to London to work as a dancing partner and teacher.

On 17 December 1922 he married Dorothy Frances (died 1981), daughter of Frank Newton, a schoolmaster. Five days later he won the world ballroom dancing championship at Queen's Hall in London, partnered by Phyllis Clarke. When Phyllis Clarke married, his wife became his dancing partner. In 1923 the Silvesters opened a dancing school at Rector's Club in London. Their only child, a son—Victor Newton—was born in 1924. In that year the Imperial Society of Teachers of Dancing invited Silvester on to the committee of their newly formed ballroom branch, which codified the standard steps of ballroom dancing. He became chairman of the society in 1945; during the 1960s he was made its first life president.

The dancing school moved to 19 Maddox Street, off Regent Street, and then—in 1927—to 20 New Bond Street. In 1927 Silvester published *Modern Ballroom Dancing* of which more than a million copies were sold, the book reaching its fifty-seventh edition in 1974. His later books included *Theory and Technique of Ballroom Dancing* (1932), *Sequence Dancing* (1950), and *Dancing for the Millions* (1952).

In August 1935, dissatisfied with the lack of strict-tempo recordings for dancers, Silvester formed his Ballroom Orchestra. His first recording—'You're Dancing on my Heart'—sold 17,000 copies and became his signature tune. Eventually over 75 million copies of his records were sold: more than any other dance orchestra in the world. His orchestra produced a unique sound, keeping closely to the melody but decorating it with the twinkling sound of two pianos. It began broadcasting for the BBC in April 1937. By 1939 it was more successful than the dancing school, which Silvester closed on the outbreak of war to concentrate on broadcasting. In 1941 he started 'BBC Dancing Club', in which he became famous for his spoken instructions for dances ('Slow, slow, quick, quick, slow'). In 1949 he started 'Television Dancing Club' on BBC television, which continued until 1964. In 1953, 1954, 1956, and (posthumously) 1978, he won the Carl-Alan award for services to ballroom dancing.

In 1957 he opened the first of twenty-three 'Victor Silvester Dancing Studios' in collaboration with the Rank Organization. His orchestra appeared at the royal command performance in 1958, the year he published his autobiography, *Dancing is My Life*. In 1961 he was appointed OBE for his services to ballroom dancing. Although his son took over the running of the orchestra in September 1971, he continued to take an active interest in it. In 1972 he was president of the Lord's Taverners. For twenty-eight years up to 1975, he had a weekly request programme on the BBC's World Service. In 1977 he was presented with a golden microphone by the BBC for forty years of broadcasting.

He died 14 August 1978 of a heart attack after going for a swim on holiday at Aiguebelle, near Le Lavandou in the South of France. A tall, athletic man, he was an enthusiast for physical culture and trained regularly in a gymnasium. More than anybody else, he popularized ballroom dancing in Britain and symbolized that popularity.

[Victor Silvester, *Dancing is My Life*, 1958; *The Times*, 15 August 1978; *Guardian*, 15 August 1978; information from Victor Silvester (son).]

TONY AUGARDE

SIM, ALASTAIR GEORGE BELL (1900–1976), actor and director, was born 9 October 1900 at Lothian Road, Edinburgh, the youngest in the family of two sons and two daughters of Alexander Sim, tailor and clothier, and his wife, Isabella McIntyre. He was educated at the James Gillespie School at Edinburgh which he left at the age of fourteen, taking successive jobs as a delivery boy, a clerk with Gieves the outfitters, and, later, a post in the borough assessor's office. He had ideas, at this time, of becoming an analytical chemist and was studying at Edinburgh University, leaving it to join the Officers' Training Corps. The war ended before he had any opportunity of putting his military training to the test.

His first connection with the stage was from 1925 to 1930 when he was Fulton lecturer in elocution at New College, Edinburgh, a post which he obtained as a result of his work in the Edinburgh Provincial Training Centre. While holding this post he had established his own School of Drama and Speech Training. It was here that he first met Naomi Merlith, daughter of Hugh Plaskitt, solicitor. She was herself a promising actress, who gained a scholarship at RADA. They were married in 1932 and she was able to help him, professionally and enthusiastically, throughout his subsequent career. They had one daughter.

At the comparatively late age of thirty he played his first part on the professional stage, doubling the roles of messenger and sentry in the production of *Othello* (1930) in which Paul Robeson and (Dame) Peggy Ashcroft played the principal parts. This was followed by two years at the Old

Vic. He was then out of action for a year with a slipped disc which was put right by an osteopath, and in the mid-thirties his face and personality became increasingly familiar to audiences in a series of film comedies and comedy-thrillers; the Inspector Hornleigh series, Edgar Wallace's *The Squeaker* (1937), *Alf's Button Afloat* (1938), and *Wedding Group* (1936), in which Sim played the Scottish minister and his wife the maid-of-all-work.

A return to the stage and to more serious work was signalled by the last of the pre-war Malvern drama festivals where he took one of the leading parts in *What Say They?* (1940) by James Bridie (O. H. Mavor, q.v.). It was the beginning of a valuable, though not always peaceful, association as Bridie wrote and Sim both acted in and directed plays of the calibre of *Mr. Bolfry* (1943), *Dr Angelus* (1947), *The Forrigan Reel* (1945), and *Mr Gillie* (1950).

It was in *Mr Bolfry* that he introduced one of his best-remembered directorial touches. The play dealt with a confrontation between a Scots minister and the Devil. As written by Bridie (who, said James Agate, q.v., could never construct a satisfactory third act) the Devil turned out to be an escaped lunatic. Sim reacted strongly against the feebleness of this. He insisted 'the Devil must be the Devil'. The difficulty was how to get him off the stage at the end of the play and back where he belonged. Sim's solution was a *coup de théâtre.* The Devil, off stage at that point, had left his umbrella propped in a corner. The door opened. No one appeared. The umbrella picked itself up and walked slowly out by the far door.

The death of Bridie in 1951 put an end to this fruitful association and in some ways Sim never achieved the same magical alchemy which results when the separate talents of author, actor, and director are fused into a single whole. He gave many notable performances on stage and screen. On the screen he played in *Scrooge* (1951) and (fondest memory for many) *The Happiest Days of Your Life* (1950) with (Dame) Margaret Rutherford [q.v.]. On the stage there were William Golding's *The Brass Butterfly* (1958), annual appearances as the sardonic old Etonian, Captain Hook, and towards the end of his career two notable successes at the Chichester Festival, both of which came subsequently to the West End, *The Magistrate* (1969) and *Dandy Dick* (1973) by Sir A. W. Pinero [q.v.].

In 1948 Sim achieved a remarkable feat, being elected rector of Edinburgh University by a majority greater than that achieved by any of the prime ministers and field marshals who had preceded him. His address ('the only one of eight that I have actually been able to hear', said Bridie) was delivered to that most critical of audiences, with all his professional skill. As one reads it one can hear it being spoken, in the inimitable Sim manner; the clipped words, the sardonic intonation, the crocodile smile. His own character appears in every line: 'I admit that even to this day I enjoy being called an artiste, and if anyone likes to qualify it with some such adjective as "great", "incomparable", "superb", then you can rely on me to finish the ritual by reacting with becoming modesty. But I shall know it is all nonsense.'

He was as devastating at the pricking of pomposity in others as in himself.

He was made an honorary LL D of Edinburgh University in 1951 on his retirement as rector, appointed CBE in 1953, and refused the knighthood offered to him by Edward Heath on the grounds that it would be ridiculous to be addressed as Sir Alastair. He died in London 19 August 1976. There is a portrait of him by Edward Seago in the Garrick Club of which he was a long and enthusiastic member and from which he regularly threatened to resign.

[Private information; personal knowledge.]

MICHAEL GILBERT

SIMONDS, GAVIN TURNBULL, VISCOUNT SIMONDS (1881–1971), lord chancellor, was born at Reading 28 November 1881, the second of the three sons and four children of Louis de Luze Simonds, of the family of brewers long established in Berkshire, and his wife, Mary Elizabeth, daughter of Surgeon-General Gavin Ainslie Turnbull. His ancestry included Border and Bordeaux families and some thought that his tall stature, ruddy countenance, and remarkably bushy eyebrows reflected his descent. Simonds went to Winchester as a scholar in 1894 and in 1900 won an exhibition to New College, Oxford. There he displayed his all-round abilities by playing football and tennis for the university (but without getting blues) and by gaining first classes in classical honour moderations in 1902 and in *literae humaniores* in 1904.

Choosing the Chancery bar as a career he was called by Lincoln's Inn in 1906 and entered the chambers of James Austen-Cartmell, a busy Chancery junior. In 1914 he joined the Royal Berkshire Regiment (Territorial Army) but was invalided out of the army in 1916 after a serious illness. In 1921 Cartmell died and Simonds succeeded to much of his practice. He attracted much business and in 1924 he took silk. As a leader Simonds soon acquired a big practice in the Chancery courts and particularly in the appellate courts, finding the serener and more intellectual atmosphere of the Lords and Privy Council much to his taste. With such talents as Sir John (later Viscount) Simon and Wilfred (later Lord) Greene [qq.v.] at full flood, the competition in the front row was fierce, and it involved prodigious effort on his part. Nevertheless, he found time in those years to fulfil public duties: from 1929 to 1932 he was an active member of the committee on ministers' powers chaired by the Earl of Donoughmore [q.v.], and in 1936 he was one of the three members of the tribunal of inquiry about unauthorized disclosure of information relating to the budget, which led to the resignation of J. H. Thomas [q.v.], the colonial secretary.

In 1937 Simonds was appointed a Chancery judge (with the customary knighthood) in succession to Sir Harry Eve [q.v.] who had resigned. Though not always apparent except to close friends, his nature was essentially sensitive and compassionate and he felt keenly the isolation and responsibility of judicial office. On the bench his thorough knowledge of equity principles, and the clarity and speed of his decisions were soon recognized. In 1940 the minister of labour, Ernest Bevin [q.v.], appointed Simonds to be chairman of the national arbitration tribunal set up to settle industrial disputes during the war. It was a heavy assignment and left him little time for judicial sittings, but he had already made his mark on the bench. There was no surprise when in 1944 he was appointed as a life peer to succeed Lord Romer [q.v.] as a lord of appeal in ordinary, although his promotion from the Chancery division straight to the House of Lords, while not unprecedented, was exceptional. At the same time he was sworn of the Privy Council.

In the Lords Simonds's intellectual abilities had full scope, and the quality of his judgements was ranked high, particularly in Chancery cases. The cast of his mind was conservative and traditional. Unlike Lord Denning, who went up to the Lords after him, Simonds's notion of justice (equally passionately sought) did not extend to the overthrow of long-established principles of law by judicial decision: he preferred the Baconian doctrine that the law should, so far as possible, be certain of ascertainment, and that radical changes were a matter for Parliament, not for the judiciary.

When (Sir) Winston Churchill formed his government in October 1951 he appointed Simonds to be lord chancellor. (His barony was made hereditary in 1952.) Simonds was mystified by his appointment: he was politically inexperienced and he was not one of Churchill's cronies. Conservative politicians regarded it as a stop-gap appointment as they had expected that Sir David Maxwell Fyfe (later the Earl of Kilmuir, q.v.) would get it. The public received the news with mild surprise, but the legal profession were delighted that a great judge was to sit on the woolsack. Aided by his experienced friends and Cabinet colleagues Lord Salisbury and Lord Swinton [qq.v.], Simonds applied himself diligently to promoting the government's business in the Lords, where he presided with distinction, if occasionally with barely concealed impatience. He resolutely declined to stump the country making political speeches outside the House, holding that it is not the function of a lord chancellor to do so. Doubtful of the value of any scheme of institutionalized law reform (though no enemy of reform as such) perhaps his most significant achievement as lord chancellor was in carrying through the first major reform in judicial salaries for 120 years, the second reading of the Judges' Remuneration Bill being moved by Churchill himself in March 1954. With his fine voice, dignified bearing, and lucid and authoritative delivery Simonds was also well suited to the part which the lord chancellor traditionally plays on great occasions of State.

In October 1954 Simonds was succeeded by Kilmuir and was reappointed a lord of appeal, his services as lord chancellor being acknowledged by the conferment of a viscountcy. Although disenchanted by the manner of his dismissal, he resumed his judicial sittings with relief. He was then seventy-three: a countryman, a lover of birds, a fine fisherman, and a good shot, he felt 'mewed up' at Westminster where he both lived and worked. Henceforth, until his retirement in March 1962, Simonds presided regularly over the courts in the Lords and Privy Council, adding to his reputation as a great judge, delivering judgements remarkable for their classic simplicity of style, always alert to avoid delay in the dispatch of judicial business. To this Dictionary Simonds contributed the notice of Viscount Maugham who likewise reached the woolsack without previous political experience.

He received many honours. Winchester, to which he was devotedly attached throughout his life, elected him a fellow in 1933 and warden in 1946. He was an honorary fellow of New College (1944). He was Oxford's high steward from 1954 to 1967, and the university conferred on him an honorary DCL (1954). He was a bencher of Lincoln's Inn (1929) and treasurer in 1951. He was an honorary D.Litt. of Reading University (1947), an honorary FRCOG (1954), the professor of law at the Royal Academy of Arts (1951), and a Docteur en Droit, Laval University, Toronto (1953).

In 1912 Simonds married Mary Hope (died 1973), daughter of Francis Hamilton Mellor, judge. They had three sons: one died in infancy, another was killed in action at Arnhem in 1944 and the third died in 1951. Simonds died in London 28 June 1971 and the title became extinct. There is a portrait by Sir Gerald Kelly at Lincoln's Inn.

[The Earl of Kilmuir, *Political Adventure*, 1964; Harold Macmillan, *Tides of Fortune*, 1969; *The Times*, 29 June 1971; private information; personal knowledge.]

George Coldstream

SIMPSON, FREDERICK ARTHUR (1883-1974), historian, preacher, and eccentric, was born at Caldbeck in Cumberland, 22 November 1883, the second son in the family of two sons and one daughter of William Frederick Simpson, rector of the parish, and his wife, Frances, daughter of Edward Fidler, JP, of Standing Stone, Wigton, Cumberland. He was educated at Rossall and at Queen's College, Oxford, where he obtained a third class in classical honour moderations in 1904 and a first in modern history in 1906. He gained the award of a research studentship, something which was then a rarity.

When he followed in his father's footsteps as a cleric in Cumberland, becoming curate of Ambleside from 1909 to 1911, he busied himself writing up his research. It was to yield a four-volume work on Louis Napoleon, sometime emperor of the French. The first volume came out in 1909 as *The Rise of Louis Napoleon* and was extremely well received, for its judicious judgements, fresh information, extracted with extraordinary ingenuity and persistence from the archives, and what was frequently referred to as its lapidary style. The book attracted the attention of a scholar on the way to becoming the best-known historian in the country, G. M. Trevelyan [q.v.] of Trinity College, Cambridge. Simpson himself became a fellow of Trinity in 1911, and remained so until his death sixty-three years later at the age of eighty-nine. From 1915 to 1918 he was a chaplain in the forces.

One further volume of his promised series appeared after a dozen years, *Louis Napoleon and the Recovery of France* (1923). This is, however, the only title Simpson had to show for half a century and more of a scholar's life. The reason was believed to have been a hostile review of his second book, in fact two reviews, the one in the *Times Literary Supplement* being anonymous, both of them by the historian and journalist Philip Guedalla [q.v.]. Work was certainly done towards the later volumes, for a chapter was published in 1962 (*Historical Journal*, vol. v, part 2). To all intents and purposes, nevertheless, Simpson's career as a historical writer was over in his fortieth year.

There was an exception, if a five-page article could be said to qualify, in a commentary which he published as a note to the 1943 Rede lecture on G. Lytton Strachey by Sir H. Max Beerbohm [qq.v.]. Simpson caught Strachey cheating in his account of Cardinal H. E. Manning [q.v.] in *Eminent Victorians* (1918). Apart from this, the intellectual activity of this quintessentially donnish, unmarried college figure, who scarcely stirred out of Cambridge, seems to have consisted in the chiselling out of a few sermons. Each of those he did compose he delivered, with electric effect, on many occasions. He was twice select preacher at Oxford, and three times at Cambridge. There were also his required university lectures, and his college supervision attended by generation upon generation of Trinity undergraduates.

Nearly all the rest of his time, for the remainder of his life, was given over to his eccentricities. These developed themselves as he inhabited his college: at the common table in hall, in his rooms in the Great Court, and above all as a walker through Trinity and its neighbours, snipping, clipping, pruning, lopping the leaves, the twigs, and the branches of the trees and bushes. He seemed omnipresent and could be pointed out with satisfaction to the wondering visitor as Snipper Simpson, the college eccentric. His rooms finally contained a glittering array of pruning instruments, from scissors to pole secateurs. You could often follow his track round the courts and walks by the litter of vegetation which he left behind him.

In his earlier years he had made rather bolder excursions into oddity: he owned and had flown for him his own aeroplane of what he would have called a Heath Robinsonian kind. This was piloted by a series of persons who became distinguished aviators, and stories of his flying adventures proliferated. For all the narrowness of his ambit, Simpson was well informed, if sometimes inaccurate in his statements, and could argue with considerable skill even with the most distinguished college guest. He made important and often surprising friends amongst the hierarchy of the Church of England in spite of the fact that in his later years his belief in the divinity of Jesus seems to have become uncertain. He was undoubtedly popular with undergraduates, to whom he made a number of little benefactions, and showed considerable skill in reconciling the society of fellows to his vagaries, though the long-suffering college servants were naturally the least amenable.

He had the capacity to sustain an attitude and a way of living which were almost entirely anachronistic in his own time, and to attain a degree of eminence in spite of that fact, even because of it. By the end of his long life—and his reputation was due in no small degree to his longevity—he acted as if he were the last representative of an otherwise extinct race of bachelor don, of Christian priest whose vocation was pulpit eloquence, and of conscious, deliberate eccentric, able to behave in ways which successive cohorts of colleagues and students delighted to make good stories out of.

Nevertheless, Simpson was a man of real gifts as a writer, and as a historian of the early twentieth-century type. If ever a tradition of the haunting of the Great Court at Trinity College, Cambridge, should arise, it must inevitably be the shade of F. A. Simpson which walks in it: a tall, dark, stooped, craggy-faced man in a cloth cap and a dangling grey scarf, in his hand the ghostly glitter of a pair of pruning shears. He died 8 February 1974 at Cambridge.

[Eric James, 'A Last Eccentric', *Listener*, 30 October 1980; *Mr. Simpson Portrayed*, an undated pamphlet, reprinted from a Trinity College publication; 'F. A. Simpson, a Fragment of Autobiography', *Trinity Review*, 1964, reprinted separately 1972; private information; personal knowledge.] PETER LASLETT

SIMS, SIR ALFRED JOHN (1907–1977), naval architect, was born 11 October 1907 in Revelstoke, near Plymouth, the fourth son and youngest of five children of John Thomas Sims, maintenance engineer on the estate of Lord Revelstoke, and his wife, Jessie Finch. He attended Regent Street higher elementary school in Plymouth, from which he entered HM Dockyard Devonport, as an apprentice in 1923. The royal dockyards in those days had excellent schools for the brighter apprentices, from which it was possible to win cadetships to study naval architecture at the Royal Naval College at Greenwich as probationary members of the Royal Corps of Naval Constructors (RCNC), a civilian body whose students by tradition train in naval uniform. Sims, from his early days in Devonport Dockyard School, demonstrated high academic ability combined with great capacity for hard work, and duly won a cadetship and in 1928 entered the Royal Naval College. In 1931 he graduated with an outstanding first-class professional certificate, and embarked on a career in the RCNC that was to bring him eminence in the Corps, in the naval architecture profession, and in society at large.

In the eight years between leaving college and the outbreak of World War II he gained wide experience of different types of warship in service with the Mediterranean Fleet; at Chatham dockyard, where he did pioneering work on the application of welding to warship construction; at the Admiralty, where he worked on submarine design; and then on the staff of rear-admiral submarines at HMS *Dolphin*. In the first four war years he worked on submarine design and operation as a constructor commander closely alongside Admiral Sir Max Horton [q.v.], and won respect for his dedication to duty in those difficult days. In 1943 he was appointed OBE and was sent to the Admiralty at Bath to become, in 1944, a very young chief constructor in charge of submarine design and building—a post he retained for the rest of the war.

In 1947 his career took a new turn as he was appointed professor of naval architecture at the Royal Naval College at Greenwich, a position he occupied for five years. This appointment restored an RCNC tradition, which had been interrupted by the war, of having serving officers of high potential with up-to-date design experience to teach RCNC probationers. To this academic role Sims brought not only experience of the lessons learned in the recent war but also a determination to restore the Greenwich course to its pre-war pre-eminence amongst schools of naval architecture in Britain.

Two years after his return to the Admiralty at Bath in 1952, Sims was promoted to the post of assistant director of naval construction in charge of both aircraft-carrier and submarine design and in-service support, which he occupied until 1958 when, in a drastic reorganization of the Admiralty, he was selected at the relatively early age of fifty to be the first director-general ships, the most senior technical officer responsible to the Admiralty Board for all vessels of the Royal Navy. At the same time he became head of the Royal Corps of Naval Constructors. In both roles he was the leader of an élite group of professional engineers at the start of a decade in which there were to be profound changes in the surface ships and submarines of the Royal Navy. He was appointed KCB in 1960.

The navy's first nuclear submarine, *Dreadnought*, entered service in 1962, having been designed in the ship department at Bath under Sims's overall direction. This development led to the even more momentous introduction of the Royal Navy's ballistic missile (Polaris) submarines. At the end of the decade, following the cancellation of the navy's last traditional aircraft-carrier design, CVA01, in 1966, a very ambitious design and construction programme was embarked on with a large helicopter-carrying cruiser, a compact guided missile destroyer, a new anti-submarine frigate, and a new mine-countermeasure vessel. The ships were highly innovative with extensive use of electronics, with gas turbine propulsion, and with new weapon systems. It was probably the most intensive period of change the navy had known and Sims presided over the upheaval with calm good humour and considerable industry, harnessing the efforts of a unique group of highly original but sometimes unruly naval constructors. He retired in 1968.

From 1971 to 1975 he was the first professional president of the Royal Institution of Naval Architects. In 1975–6 he was prime warden of the Worshipful Company of Shipwrights. He was a member of council of Bath University, which in 1974 conferred on him an honorary D.Sc. His other interests were wide: from 1969 to 1977 he was president of the Bath Choral and Orchestral Society; he was a Savoyard; a churchwarden of Bath Abbey parochial church council; president of the Bath branch of the YMCA; in 1967–71 the first chairman of the western branch of the Royal Society of Arts.

His work and social activities were characterized by great energy and drive, boundless enthusiasm, much ambition, and an enormous and rather ruthless capacity for hard work, all coupled with a benign personality, which matched well his rather Pickwickian proportions.

He married in 1933 Barbara Mary Hunking, daughter of John Lewis Paul, cabinet maker of Plymouth, and they had a son and a daughter. Sims died at Bath 27 August 1977.

[*Naval Architect*, September 1977; private information; personal knowledge.]

L. J. Rydill

SINCLAIR, Sir JOHN ALEXANDER (1897–1977), sailor, soldier, and intelligence director, was born 29 May 1897 in Fulham, the younger son and second of the four children of John Stewart Sinclair, later archdeacon of Cirencester (who was the grandson of Sir John Sinclair, first baronet, q.v.), and his wife, Clara Sophia, daughter of John Dearman Birchall JP, of Bowden Hall, Gloucestershire. He was educated at Osborne and Dartmouth, finishing his education just in time to serve as a midshipman RN for the first two years of World War I. During that time he was almost continuously at sea, mainly in submarines, but scarcely ever free from seasickness. Soon after he had taken part in the landing of the Lancashire Fusiliers on the west beach at Gallipolli his health broke down completely and he had to be invalided out of the navy after only six years' service. During his long convalescence he was able to do some teaching at the Downs School, Winchester, where he had been a pupil formerly, until well enough to apply for a new career in the army. In 1918 he entered the Royal Military Academy, Woolwich, where he proved himself an outstanding cadet winning the sword of honour and other Academy prizes. Commissioned in the Royal Field Artillery in 1919, he served first with the Murmansk force in northern Russia and then in India. Returning to duty at Aldershot, he married in 1927 Esme Beatrice (died 1983), daughter of Thomas Kark Sopwith, of Maidstone, who was later archdeacon of Canterbury. There were two sons and two daughters.

After serving as adjutant in the Honourable Artillery Company (1929–31) he went on to the Staff College, Camberley (1932–3), and from 1938 to 1939 he was an instructor at the Senior Staff College at Minley. By the opening of World War II his reputation in the army was that of a studious and thoughtful soldier and a fine all-round sportsman. He began the war as an operational planner with the BEF. Although the British were always sceptical of one of its basic concepts, namely the impassability of the Ardennes to German armour, the British plans had to be fitted into the overall Gamelin plan. It was Alec Sinclair who drafted the operational order for the advance of the BEF to the river Kyle but having done so was himself almost immediately recalled to London to become GSO 1 in Military Operations 4 close to the highest levels of command, and at a time when the planners had to take simultaneous account of the calls for reinforcement and the possibility of evacuation. When this phase was over he had become brigadier and deputy director of operations. In 1941 he was appointed brigadier general staff South-Eastern Command and in 1942 deputy chief of the general staff Home Forces.

Promoted major-general he concentrated on training and planning for the Normandy invasion, though his hopes of himself joining the invasion forces were later dashed by the split up of Home Forces Command and the formation of the 21st Army Group of Sir B. L. Montgomery (later Viscount Montgomery of Alamein, q.v.). Instead he was appointed director of military intelligence at the War Office in 1944 and thus found himself entering at the highest level a field that was new to him. Intelligence played a great part in the war and was at that time needed more than ever. He quickly showed that he had the qualities for the job; a capacity for detail, good judgement, and a ready acceptance of responsibility. 'Sinbad' Sinclair, as he was called by his colleagues, became a much-respected DMI and held the post until the end of the war.

Then, near the expected end of his military career, a new prospect opened for him. It was to become in 1951, after first serving as deputy director until 1950, the director of MI6, the civilian intelligence service responsible to the foreign secretary and the prime minister. The choice of a successful DMI, admired for his strong character and organizational skills, was particularly appropriate for the transitional period that lay ahead of the service. A large wartime organization had to be scaled down, new methods and standards of recruitment for permanent staff agreed, and old international alliances renegotiated for new peacetime tasks. He achieved these things in ways that lasted well, while at the same time directing current operations in his usual practical and responsible way. It was therefore unfair to his reputation that the only time he came to public notice was in connection with the intelligence operation of 19 April 1956 in which the diver Commander Lionel Crabb was lost when making an underwater inspection of a Russian ship awaiting in Portsmouth harbour the return of Khrushchev and Bulganin, who were on a goodwill visit to Britain. The intelligence urgencies of those times had led to a hastily planned operation for which he had to accept responsibility without having been able to supervise its details.

He retired in 1956 leaving behind him the reputation of a notable reformer and much-trusted chief. He was now free to enjoy twenty-one years of a happy and united family life at his home at East Ashling, Sussex, where he died 22 March 1977.

He was appointed OBE in 1940, CB in 1945, and KCMG in 1953. He was also a commander of the US Legion of Merit (1945).

[Personal knowledge.] DICK WHITE

SLESSOR, SIR JOHN COTESWORTH (1897–1979), marshal of the Royal Air Force, was born at Ranikhet in India 3 June 1897, the eldest in the family of three sons and one daughter of Major Arthur Kerr Slessor, of the Sherwood Foresters, and his wife, Adelaide Cotesworth. He was educated at Haileybury, where he later claimed to have been 'rather an idle boy with a capacity for making friends and getting a good deal of fun out of life, but with a marked distaste for hard work'. An attack of poliomyelitis as a child left him lame in both legs, and an army medical board in 1914 rejected him as 'totally unfit for any form of military service'. But a family friend responsible for selecting officers for the Royal Flying Corps enabled him to circumvent regulations. He was commissioned on his eighteenth birthday, and four months later was seeking vainly to engage a Zeppelin night raider over central London.

Posted to No. 17 Squadron in the Middle East, Slessor spent some months bombing and strafing Turks in the Sinai and rebels in the Sudan until in the spring of 1916 he was sent home to England with a wound in the thigh and the MC. After a tour as an instructor at Northolt, he went to France in May 1917 as a flight commander in No. 5 Squadron, with whom he served until June 1918. He returned to England to lead a squadron at the Central Flying School, Upavon, of which he briefly took command in September. The armistice reduced him to his substantive rank of flight-lieutenant in the new Royal Air Force. Following a bitter quarrel with a senior officer, Slessor became sufficiently disenchanted with Service life to request demobilization. But after just two months as a civilian, he accepted a short-service commission early in 1920, and in the spring of 1921 went to India as a flight commander in No. 20 Squadron, flying Bristol fighters. He then served briefly on the air headquarters staff before attending the third course at the new RAF Staff College at Andover. From 1925 to 1928 he commanded No. 4 (Army Co-operation) Squadron at Farnborough. In 1928 he was posted to the plans branch of the Air Ministry's Directorate of Operations and Intelligence, where he remained until 1931.

This was the decisive period in Slessor's formative years. He was already marked as an officer of exceptional ability, charm, and force of personality. But his thinking and most of his experience had centred upon the role of aircraft in direct support of ground forces. In his years at the Air Ministry, he now became one of the most passionate disciples of Lord Trenchard [q.v.] and his theories of strategic air power as a war-winning weapon. Slessor was one of that select group of officers which included C. F. A. Portal (later Viscount Portal of Hungerford) and (Sir) Ralph Cochrane [qq.v.], who were clearly destined for the highest ranks of the air force. In the years that followed, he served a second tour of duty in India where he almost died in the Quetta earthquake and won a DSO commanding a wing in the Waziristan operations. But he achieved greater distinction for his lecturing as an instructor at the Army Staff College, Camberley, for his authorship of the RAF manual on army co-operation, and for his book *Air Power and Armies*, published in 1936. The book reflected the belief not only of Slessor, but of his generation of senior airmen, in the moral impact of air attack upon civilian populations. He wrote: 'In air operations against production, the weight of attack will inevitably fall upon a vitally important, and not by nature very amenable, section of the community—the industrial workers, whose morale and sticking power cannot be expected to equal that of the disciplined soldier. And we should remember that if the moral effect of air bombardment was serious seventeen years ago, it will be immensely more so under modern conditions.' Here was the core of the strategic theory which would lie at the heart of the British bomber offensive against Germany, and of which Slessor was among the most articulate proponents.

From 1937 to 1940 Slessor held the critical post of director of plans at the Air Ministry. It must be said that in this role he shared his colleagues' delusions about the power of bombers to influence the course of the war even when these were few in number, and were wholly inadequately trained and equipped to carry out the tasks to which the RAF war plans committed them. In a memorandum to the chief of air staff four days after the outbreak of war, Slessor urged an all-out bomber attack on the Germans: 'Although our numerical inferiority in the air is a most important factor, it should not be allowed to obscure other potent considerations. We are now at war with a nation which possesses an impressive façade of armed might, but which, behind that façade, is politically rotten, weak in financial and economic resources, and already heavily engaged on another front [Poland]. The lessons of history prove that victory does not always go to the big battalions. At present we have the initiative. If we seize it now we may gain important results; if we lose it by waiting we shall probably lose more than we gain.' In the two years that followed, the RAF painfully discovered that the difficulties of implementing Trenchard's doctrine were caused not merely by the limits on resources imposed by pre-war politicians, but also by the failure of the Service to match its skills and training to the ends it sought to achieve. Slessor must share responsibility with his generation of airmen for the lamentable shortcomings of the RAF in close support of ground and naval forces and low-level bombing techniques. It is impossible to escape the conclusion that their failure to address themselves to these problems in the same fashion as the pre-war Luftwaffe was influenced by the RAF's determination to find a role in war both more decisive than that of mere flying eyes and artillery for the two older Services, and independent of them.

At the end of 1940, Slessor went to the United States to take part in the 'ABC' staff conversations. In April 1941 he returned to take command of No. 5 Group of Bomber Command at perhaps the most frustrating period of the air offensive, when this was the sole means of carrying the war directly to Germany, and yet it had become evident that its impact upon the enemy was very small. In April 1942 he became assistant chief of air staff (policy), and played an important role in the development, alongside the American airmen, of the plans for Operation Pointblank (a combined air offensive against Germany, designed specifically to pave the way for the invasion of north-west Europe, which was approved at the Casablanca conference).

In February 1943 Slessor took on the role for which he is best remembered in World War II, as C-in-C of Coastal Command. He arrived at Northwood at an exceptionally difficult period in the battle of the Atlantic, when sinkings were running at an alarming level. He controlled some sixty squadrons of which thirty-four (430 aircraft) were committed to the anti-submarine war. Even with the vital assistance of Ultra decrypts of U-boat wireless traffic, which contributed decisively to the Atlantic victory, Slessor faced immense problems in extending air cover into the mid-ocean gap where convoy losses had been so heavy. He possessed only two squadrons of very long-range Liberators with the ability to operate at these distances, and the business of co-ordinating operations not only with the Admiralty but with the American and Canadian navies and air forces taxed Slessor to the utmost. He proved himself both an able administrator of large forces, and a sensitive leader and motivator of his Command.

In January 1944, a little to his own disappointment, he was taken from Coastal Command to succeed Sir Arthur (later Lord) Tedder [q.v.] commanding the RAF in the Mediterranean and Middle East, and acting as deputy to General Ira Eaker of the USAAF, who was C-in-C Allied Air Forces in that theatre. Slessor shared with Eaker the disappointments and frustrations of the Italian campaign, the complexities of support for Yugoslavia, the vain efforts to supply the Warsaw insurgents. In March 1945 he was brought back to London to serve as air member for personnel, a job in which over the next three years he bore responsibility for the demobilization of the huge wartime air force. He served as commandant of the Imperial Defence College until in January 1950 he succeeded Tedder as chief of air staff. The coming of the atomic bomb had provided an entirely new dimension to air power. Both in office and after his retirement in 1953, Slessor was an impassioned advocate of the need for powerful air forces as a deterrent against war. In his retirement, from his home in Somerset he continued to produce a succession of essays, lectures, broadcast talks, and articles, and he also wrote a lively autobiography. He served as a director of Blackburn Aircraft and of the English and Scottish Investment Trust, and also as a governor of Haileybury, Sherborne, and Wellington schools.

Slessor stood foremost among the second rank of airmen of World War II, behind Portal, Tedder, and Sir Arthur Harris. Sir Maurice Dean [q.v.], among the most prominent civil servants of Slessor's generation at the Air Ministry, wrote of his 'warmth, knowledge, experience and adaptability'. A devoted countryman, he maintained a lifelong devotion to fishing and shooting. His charm and force of personality won him great affection and respect among his contemporaries, although he never achieved the wider celebrity of the top airmen of the war. He shared with his generation the passionate determination to win a place for the air force alongside the two older services in the councils of national defence. His strategic vision, like theirs, was perhaps narrowed by the years of struggle to bring this about. He was appointed air commodore in 1939, air vice-marshal in 1941, air marshal in 1943, air chief marshal in 1946, and marshal of the Royal Air Force in 1950.

For his services during the war of 1914–18 he was awarded the MC (1916), the Belgian Order of Leopold (chevalier), and the Belgian croix de guerre. He was appointed to the DSO in 1937, and was created CB (1942), KCB (1943), and GCB (1948). He was a member of the French Legion of Honour, the Greek Order of Phoenix, the Norwegian Order of St. Olaf, and the Swedish Order of the Sword; he also held the American Legion of Merit and the Yugoslav Partisan Star. He received the gold medal of the Royal United Services Institute in 1936, and the Chesney memorial award in 1965.

In 1923 he married Hermione Grace, daughter of Gerald Seymour Guinness, merchant banker, and widow of Lt.-Col. Herbert Francis George Carter. They had one son and one daughter. She died in 1970. He married in

1971 Marcella Florence, widow of Brigadier Robert Thomas Priest of the Royal Artillery, and daughter of Christopher Edward Spurgeon, engineer.

There is a portrait of Slessor by Cuthbert Orde in the possession of the Imperial War Museum, on loan to the Royal College of Defence Studies, and another in the possession of Haileybury School.

Slessor died 12 July 1979 at the Princess Alexandra Hospital, Wroughton.

[Sir John Slessor, *The Central Blue*, 1956, *Air Power and Armies*, 1936, *Strategy For The West*, 1954, and *The Great Deterrent*, 1957; Air files of the Public Record Office; private information.]

MAX HASTINGS

SMITH, (ARTHUR) LIONEL (FORSTER) (1880–1972), adviser in education in Iraq and rector of the Edinburgh Academy, was born 19 August 1880 at Villa Marx, Baden Baden, the eldest in the family of two sons and seven daughters of Arthur Lionel Smith, fellow and tutor (later master) of Balliol College, Oxford, and his wife, Mary Florence, eldest daughter of John Forster Baird, a landowner in Northumberland. From the Dragon School he became a scholar of Rugby School, where he shared a study with William Temple [q.v.], later archbishop of Canterbury. He won a classical scholarship at Balliol, and took seconds in classical honour moderations (1901) and *literae humaniores* (1903) and a first in history (1904).

He was elected a fellow of All Souls in 1904, and in 1908 a fellow of Magdalen where he had become a lecturer in 1906. He was dean of Magdalen from 1910 to 1913. He was a good teacher, careful and sympathetic, though his pupils, who included the Prince of Wales, were not always rewarding for someone from the golden age of a Balliol which had prepared many fine minds for public service; the system at Magdalen encouraged passmen to retain knowledge rather than scholars to develop understanding, and when war came Smith was already dissatisfied.

Soon after the outbreak of war he joined the 9th battalion of the Hampshire Regiment, serving in India until he was posted to Basra in 1917. He became involved in the administration of the conquered territory of Mesopotamia, principally in the Education Department. After an unsatisfying return to Magdalen during 1919, he spent from February 1920 to August 1921 in Baghdad, being appointed director of education in August 1920. He was, however, in England on sick leave for two years, and taught at Harrow for the first two terms of 1923.

From August 1923 to May 1931, under the British mandate, he was in Iraq as adviser and sometimes inspector-general, mediating between largely Shi'ite ministers and their directors-general, principally the Arab nationalist Sati Bey al-Husri. King Faisal admired him and called him a friend. Sati Bey, who respected him and worked well with him, wrote of him in a complimentary manner in his memoir of Iraq. Though it became almost treasonable for Iraqis to speak well of the mandate, Smith's memory was cherished long after he had left the country. And yet it was a losing battle he fought, because there was never any money—law and order mattered far more than education to the British government, and the Iraqis were not ready to accept the widespread and liberalizing education he so desired. Personally, he was loved and respected for his integrity, his sportsmanship, his mind, his friendship, and his devotion to the Iraqis; but professionally when he resigned he had to present to his superiors a masterly paper which is a damning indictment of the whole system of education—background, policy, examinations, teacher training, and political control—despite what had undoubtedly been achieved.

The directors of the Edinburgh Academy chose Smith as rector in 1931 for his personality and his record, preferring him to another man nearly twenty years younger. Two years later Smith refused the headmastership of Eton. At the Academy his wide learning, ready sympathy, athletic gifts, and fine presence, combined with a genuine shyness and humility, earned him the respect and loyalty of masters and boys alike. He loved teaching, and the company of boys, and found the rectorship wholly absorbing. He could talk on equal terms with anyone, high or low, hating 'humbug' and 'snobs'. He spoke in public unwillingly but well. There was little development in his time, but he held a reduced and scattered school together during the war years. His ideal of education was as something to transform understanding, not to prepare for a function, and boys remembered working under him as a marvellous experience. He brought out the best in other people. He went unwillingly in 1945, which he thought a bad year for changing rectors.

Smith was appointed MVO in 1914 and CBE in 1927. The universities of Edinburgh and St. Andrews gave him honorary LL Ds in 1945 and 1947. He was one of the best amateur athletes of his day; in the Rugby cricket XI; captain of the Balliol Boat Club and member of Leander and of a winning Visitors Cup IV at Henley; captain of the Oxford University hockey XI; an English international hockey player from 1903 to 1913; a squash player, skater, and walker of legendary endurance and skill in Baghdad and Edinburgh; modest about his achievements. These gifts, and his exceptional good looks, predisposed people to accept him; but his greatness was in his spirit. He had from childhood a simple faith which he lived by naturally. His sternest judgements were tempered by a smile of self-deprecation.

On 9 August 1932, at St. Peter's church, Bywell, Northumberland, he married Mary Fletcher, daughter of Henry Lloyd Wilson, chemical manufacturer, mother of three, and widow of his connection George Lloyd Hodgkin, who died in 1918. They had no children, but her affectionate companionship warmed the rest of his long life. He undertook no further duties after the rectorship, but his many large private charities and his love of gardening, walking, birds, and painting continued through his twenty-seven years of retirement in Edinburgh, where he died 3 June 1972.

[A. L. F. Smith, 'The Present State of Education in Iraq, 1931, reprinted in *Middle Eastern Studies*, April 1983; E. C. Hodgkin, *A. L. F. Smith* (privately printed), 1979; Peter Sluglett, *Britain in Iraq, 1914–1932*, 1976; Magnus Magnusson, *The Clacken and the Slate, the Story of the Edinburgh Academy 1824–1974*, 1974; *Edinburgh Academy Chronicle*; *The Times*, 5 June 1972 and 4 June 1977; private information.]

L. E. Ellis

SMITH, CECIL BLANCHE WOODHAM- (1896–1977), biographer and historian. [See Woodham-Smith.]

SMITH, FLORENCE MARGARET ('STEVIE') (1902–1971), poet and novelist, was born in Hull, 20 September 1902, the younger daughter of Charles Ward Smith, shipping agent, and his wife, Ethel Rahel Spear. There was a naval tradition in the family: Charles Ward Smith's father was a consultant engineer to the Admiralty. The family business having failed, following Stevie Smith's birth her father joined the merchant navy (his two elder brothers had drowned while serving, which had prohibited his joining earlier). Her parents' marriage was described by Stevie Smith as 'unsuitable'. She was brought up by her mother and her aunt, whom she immortalized in her work as 'the lion aunt'. When she was three, her mother and aunt moved to Palmers Green, in London, which was then a small hamlet surrounded by countryside. As a child she was sickly: at the age of five she spent three years in a sanatorium recovering from tuberculosis.

She was educated at Palmers Green High School and at the North London Collegiate School for Girls. When she was sixteen her mother died. Although her father continued to visit her when ashore, he soon remarried and thenceforth all her emotional life was concentrated on her aunt, who provided the basic security for her personal and working life, and who acted as a lodestar of all that was rational, ordinary, and common-sensical. Thus she countered the volatility of her fantastical imagination and safeguarded herself against the depressive, suicidal streak in her nature.

After leaving school she took a secretarial course. Her first, and only, job was with the publishing house of Newnes where she worked as personal secretary to Sir Neville Pearson, Bt.; over the thirty years she spent there she acquired privileges in the manner of a court jester, writing her first novel on the firm's yellow copying paper.

Novel on Yellow Paper was published in 1936, and was an immediate success because of its extraordinary originality. Autobiographical in content, its rambling, seemingly naïve, idiom annotates daily happenings in the life of female Pompey (clearly Stevie Smith herself), living in an outer London suburb with a 'lion' aunt, going to work for Sir Phoebus, enduring an unsatisfactory attachment to one Freddy, and meeting her friends, most of them literary. Stevie Smith wrote two later autobiographical fictions—*Over the Frontier* (1938) and *The Holiday* (1949). These are variations on the same theme, introducing us to her world with wit and a heightened sense of overall absurdity, and describing a very English person, a Protestant, much concerned with the finer points of theology, amusingly insular, and given to considering foreigners and travel abroad as rather nasty, if interesting, experiences. Evident throughout is a devotion to the 'lion' aunt and a deep love for England, its establishment, and its constitution; there are simultaneous expressions of doubt from a well-read mind viewing the frailties of human communication with affection and solid common sense.

Whereas Stevie Smith's talent flourished in her novels, her creative genius perfected itself in her poetry, because in the seven volumes (gathered together in *The Collected Poems of Stevie Smith*, 1975) she transformed autobiographical material into pure art. Whether short or long, the poems are classical in concept, contemporaneous in idiom, sharp in vivid imagery, free-running, and have strong rhymes. They are further commentaries about the world of personal relationships, social manners, loneliness, the flight and despair of love, and the beatitude of death. Behind the wittiest line often lies a grim truth. In her later years her poetry brought her fame and her readings and recordings (chanted in her inimitable voice) were extraordinarily popular. The line drawings (reminiscent of those of Edward Lear [q.v.] and James Thurber), with which she frequently illustrated her poems, were as remarkable as the text.

She did not marry, having once considered the possibility and decided against it. Not only could she not desert her aunt, but sexually she rebelled against the intimacy of marriage. Her friendships, with both sexes, were deep and often fraught. Although she had an intense social life, she was basically a loner. Physically she was frail and slender, yet she gave an impression of boundless energy. Dark in features, with remarkable eyes, she had a childlike quality about her, and, as with an over-active child, her ebullience was followed by periods of great fatigue. Her personal appeal went beyond age and sex; to the young she appeared as one of them. She enjoyed being made much of; in fact she demanded constant attention from her friends. Intense depression frequently assailed her, and often her dark despairs neared suicide. What she loved best was the company of one friend, country walks, and seashore meanderings. When the 'lion' aunt died in 1966 she confronted her aloneness with courage, and enjoyed her later fame and her retirement from the publishing firm. She never retired from writing poetry.

In 1966 she received the Cholmondeley award, and in 1969 the Queen's gold medal for poetry, an occasion which she described with verve. She died 7 March 1971 at Ashburton Cottage Hospital in Devon, after suffering a brain tumour. Death was to her an angel of mercy to be welcomed. She once said: 'Being alive is like being in enemy territory.' Her legend was perpetrated after her death by the production of a play, *Stevie*, by Hugh Whitemore, which was based on her work, letters, and interviews.

[Kay Dick, *Ivy & Stevie*, 1971; Jack Barbera and William McBrien (eds.), *Me Again: Uncollected Writings of Stevie Smith*, 1981, and *Stevie*, 1985; personal knowledge.] KAY DICK

SMITH, FRANCES (1924–1978), golfer, better known as BUNTY STEPHENS, was born at Old Swan, Liverpool, 26 July 1924, the only child of Frederick Wade Stephens, a professional golfer, and his wife, Frances Elsie Clark. As her father was a professional and designed the course at Bootle in Liverpool, golf was the central part of her life from childhood. She owed much to the teaching of her father who worked hard to create a swing which, as far as possible, would withstand all pressures. Her list of achievements is proof of his success although she might well have won more had she been blessed with a stronger physique. She was educated at Bootle Grammar School.

Her first national title was the English Women's Championship in 1948, a victory she repeated in 1954 and 1955 when her opponent in the final on both occasions was Elizabeth Price. In 1954, at Woodhall Spa, Frances Smith covered the first nine holes in 30 including a hole-in-one at the fifth but she only won at the thirty-seventh.

She was Ladies British Open amateur champion in 1949 from a field which included several good Americans, and she won again in 1954. She was runner-up in 1951 and 1952 and in the English in 1959 but her finest contribution came in the Curtis Cup against the United States. In five matches between 1950 and 1958 she was undefeated in singles; she won three of her foursomes and, with Elizabeth Price, was largely responsible for the British victories in 1952 and 1956, and for the halved match in 1958—easily the most successful era from the British point of view.

Twice she was the heroine, twice finding herself in the deciding match with Polly Riley, and twice defeating her on the thirty-sixth green. Nobody else had faced such an ordeal in the long history of competition between Britain and America and never was Frances Smith's composure and control of nerve under acute pressure more vividly illustrated.

At Prince's, Sandwich, in 1956 she ended by winning the last hole after being 2 up on the thirty-first tee but at Brae Burn near Boston, two years later, she came to the thirty-fourth 1 up and played the last three holes superbly.

She did not have an elegant swing, a pronounced pause at the top prohibiting the rhythmic flow, but she had confidence in her method and never allowed it to speed up whatever the situation. She was also a perfectionist, which explained the hours of practice she put in to make it work. None of her contemporaries hit the ball as consistently straight as she did and none showed the same stern, competitive determination. Her outlook was always positive and, in a golfing sense, aggressive, but she was the kindest and most modest of women and, like Joyce Wethered (Lady Heathcoat-Amory), a most courteous opponent.

She never harboured thoughts of failure and a wonderfully calm exterior enabled her to sustain a high level of concentration in moments when only a perfect shot would do. In the afterglow of one of her most memorable triumphs in 1958, Herbert Warren Wind, the eminent American writer on golf, paid this tribute: 'She holds on to her timing in the most nerve-racking situations because she has superb concentration. She holds on to her concentration because she has a purposefulness that never wavers and a wondrous heart.'

With such a wealth of experience, she later became a fountain of help to the young, particularly in Lancashire, and an invaluable administrator, captaining the Curtis Cup in a non-playing capacity in 1962 and 1972. She also captained England in the Home Internationals in 1962 and the victorious team in the European Women's Championship in Belgium in 1973. She was appointed OBE in 1977 for her services to the game and was president of the English Ladies Golf Association and an honorary member of her own club, Royal Birkdale, at the time of her premature death from cancer, which she fought with the same quiet, brave spirit that characterized her golf. As a mark of the affection in which she was held all over the golfing world, a fund was set up which raised £20,000 for the Clatterbridge Hospital in the Wirral where she received treatment.

In 1955 she married Roy Smith, a test pilot for Scottish Aviation, and they had one daughter, Caroline. Her husband was killed in a flying accident in December 1957 while the child was a baby. Frances Smith died in Southport 23 July 1978.

[*The Times* and *Guardian*, 24 July 1978.]

DONALD STEEL

SMITH, STEVIE (1902–1971), poet and novelist. [See SMITH, FLORENCE MARGARET.]

SMITH-ROSE, REGINALD LESLIE (1894–1980), physicist, was born 2 April 1894 at 7 Westbourne Gardens, Paddington, London, the younger son and youngest of four children of William Smith, church clerk, and his wife, Louisa Copp. He was educated at Latymer Upper School, Hammersmith, from which he obtained a Board of Education Royal scholarship to Imperial College in 1912. In 1914 he was awarded the Imperial College Governors' prize for physics and graduated at London University with a first class honours degree in physics. He was awarded the Ph.D. degree in 1923 and the D.Sc. in 1926. Before 1919 he changed his name to Smith-Rose.

Immediately after graduation he carried out postgraduate work at Imperial College for a short period, before going to Siemens Bros. of Woolwich, where he was employed as an assistant engineer in 1915–19. In 1919 he joined the National Physical Laboratory (NPL). He was superintendent of the radio department (1937–47) and director of the Radio Research Station, Ditton Park (1948–60). For two short periods he was acting director of the NPL. He retired in 1960.

When Smith-Rose joined the NPL, knowledge of the transmission of radio waves through the atmosphere was in an unsatisfactory state. It was not clear why the waves apparently followed the curvature of the earth, allowing communication over much greater distances than theory predicted: nor why the signal strength at the receiver varied greatly with the time of day or night. Both anomalies could be explained by postulating a conducting layer in the upper atmosphere, which would reflect radio waves, but there was no direct evidence that such a layer existed. Smith-Rose and R. H. Barfield set out to obtain such evidence by making measurements on the direction and polarization of waves arriving at the receiver. Their first results, published in 1925, were inconclusive, but later experiments on a shorter wavelength were successful. However, by the time these later results were published, the existence of the conducting layer had already been demonstrated by other methods.

Smith-Rose's work on radio direction-finding began in 1920 when he was given responsibility for organizing a long-term study of the magnitudes and directions of signals received at a number of sites in the United Kingdom. From the analysis of some quarter of a million observations, coupled with measurements of the electrical characteristics of the ground, he was able to elucidate the causes of errors in direction-finding and to make improvements in equipment to eliminate some of these errors. As higher and higher radio frequencies came into use, so his investigations were extended to provide new data. In this field he was a world leader.

Smith-Rose was a very active member of the Institution of Electrical Engineers, which he joined in 1915 as a student. He became a member (later termed fellow) in 1936. He was a member of the wireless (later radio) section committee for four separate periods and was chairman in 1942–3. He served on numerous other committees, was a member of the council of the Institution in 1953–6 and 1960–1, and became a vice-president in 1961–4. Much of his scientific work was published in the *Proceedings* of the Institution. He was a fellow of the United States Institute of Electrical and Electronic Engineers.

For many years Smith-Rose was a British representative on two important committees which foster world-wide collaboration on radio matters—the International Union of Radio Science (URSI) and the International Radio Consultative Committee (CCIR). He was president of URSI in 1960–3 and remained an honorary president until his death. In CCIR he was chairman of the study group concerned with ground-wave propagation 1949–70 and, in 1978, when CCIR celebrated the fiftieth anniversary of its foundation, he was one of those selected for special awards for distinguished contributions to the work of the committee. It was on these and other similar committees that Smith-Rose did some of his most valuable work. It involved travel throughout the world and gained him a host of friends. He was awarded the United States medal of freedom with silver palm in 1947, for his effective collaboration with organizations in that country. He was appointed CBE in 1952.

Smith-Rose was a man of great integrity, but of rather reserved personality. He was keen on swimming and walking and, in his earlier days, on camping. After his retirement from the NPL he remained on national and international committees and travelled a great deal on their business. His leisure was devoted to his hobbies of photography and stamp-collecting and to reading. For several years he was church warden at his local church.

In 1919 he married Elsie, daughter of Sydney John Masters, restaurant proprietor; they had two daughters. He died 19 March 1980 in hospital at Banstead, Surrey.

[Private information; personal knowledge.]

C. W. OATLEY

SNOW, CHARLES PERCY, BARON SNOW (1905–1980), author and publicist, was born in Leicester 15 October 1905, the second of four sons of William Edward Snow and his wife, Ada Sophia Robinson. His father was a clerk in a shoe factory and a church organist, an FRCO. From a local elementary school Snow entered Alderman Newton's grammar school, Leicester, with a scholarship, and then studied science at the local university college (later Leicester University). He gained a first class degree in chemistry, followed by an M.Sc. (1928) in physics there, both London University external degrees, and proceeded, again by scholarship, to do postgraduate research at the Cavendish Laboratory in Cambridge. He became a fellow of Christ's College in 1930, the same year in which he gained a Ph.D. He was tutor of the college from 1935 to 1945 and was later a frequent visitor and honorary fellow. He had been a fairly good cricketer at school, and, at Cambridge, he enjoyed watching cricket at Fenner's with other bachelor dons such as G. H. Hardy [q.v.] to whom he dedicated *The Masters*; later, he became a member of the MCC.

Snow's research in infra-red spectroscopy failed, since it was built upon an intuition that careful experimental results did not confirm; in consequence he was not subsequently taken entirely seriously as a scientist. But he remained dedicated to science, with both a reasoned sympathy and a boyish enthusiasm for great scientists. His years at Cambridge coincided with a golden age of Cambridge physics, and he was starry-eyed about the achievements of the brilliant men whom he knew, and whom he thought (correctly) that the world in general and cultivated society in particular neither understood nor appreciated. It became his mission to explain their achievement. He read widely, increasingly in the body of European literature, and in the Cambridge English studies of Sir Arthur Quiller-Couch [q.v.] and Basil Willey: he adopted a posture of a cultured (and left-wing) serious interest in literature and the arts, which was deeply opposed as dilettantism by the growing body of professional scholars of English literature, especially the school represented by F. R. Leavis [q.v.], university reader in English, with whom he later had a celebrated controversy. Snow published *Death under Sail* in 1932 and a second novel, *The Search*, in 1934, and in 1940 began what was to be a series, taking its title from the first book, *Strangers and Brothers*. It was this series that made his name.

Snow had three careers. He was a scientific administrator. He was a novelist and critic. He was a public man, much in demand to lecture, broadcast, and pontificate. Each career fed on the others. Though the *Strangers and Brothers* sequence was not directly autobiographical, each novel drew upon Snow's own experience, in *The Masters* (1951) of a Cambridge combination room, in *The Corridors of Power* (1964) of the relation between senior civil servants and politicians, in *The New Men* (1954) of the early attempts to develop a nuclear weapon. In form the novels harked back to the Victorian writers. Like Trollope, with well-described characters, scenes firmly set, and a strong plot, he deliberately avoided the lessons of Henry James and even more of James Joyce [qq.v.]. The hero, Lewis Eliot, an academic lawyer, was an idealized version of the author himself made more sensitive, given to more suffering, and more respected.

In 1939 Snow joined a group organized by the Royal Society to deploy British scientific manpower; by 1942 he was director of technical personnel at the Ministry of Labour, under Ernest Bevin [q.v.]; and from 1945 until his retirement in 1960 he was a Civil Service commissioner in charge of recruiting scientists to government service. He was also a director of English Electric, a company designing and building nuclear power stations. He was appointed CBE in 1943, knighted in 1957, and became a life peer in 1964, joining (Sir) Harold Wilson's first government as parliamentary secretary of the newly created Ministry of Technology, which was intended to bring the benefit of technological revolution to a backward nation. Both the Ministry and Snow failed, and he left the government in 1966. As a back-bencher Snow became a popular member of the House of Lords, with his ungainly figure and heavy jowled features, frequently seen in its bar and dining-room, exchanging gossip with other heavyweights.

It was this full public life, and his own chequered emotional life till his marriage, that provided the scenes and personalities of his novels. He married, on 15 October 1950, the novelist Pamela Hansford Johnson (died 1981), by whom he had a much-loved son, Philip, who to Snow's joy became a scholar of Eton. She was the daughter of R. Kenneth Johnson and had been married previously to Gordon Stewart, by whom she had a son and a daughter. Snow's novels deal much with the unhappy private and inner lives of his characters, in dissonance with their active and often successful public lives; he was an acute observer both of public and private stress. The books are most gripping when dealing with Snow's own lived experience, they have narrative strength, and are useful documentary sources about life in the Civil Service, politics, and the universities. He rejoiced in the diverse social origins of the British élite. His own ascent from the working class to the peerage was a source of delight to him, and social mobility was a theme of his novels. They lack high art, the characterization is often shallow, and the prose pedestrian, showing little gift for wit, style, or literary craftsmanship. Yet, though he was dismissed like W. Somerset Maugham [q.v.] as a mere story-teller, his novels were widely read, discussed, and enjoyed, and seen as a genuine insight into these important parts of national life. He was a perceptive and generous critic, revealing especially in his weekly article for the *Financial Times* a wide and deep knowledge of European literature, especially of the French and Russian masters, as well as an encyclopaedic knowledge of science, history, and current affairs.

Some of Snow's novels were produced as plays, notably *The Affair* (Strand theatre, 1961–2), and *The Masters* (Savoy and Piccadilly theatres, 1963–4), both adapted by Ronald Millar.

Snow was a generous and affable host, a kind friend, and a supporter of young writers, notably his Leicester friend Harry Hoff (William Cooper), who emulated his career as a scientific administrator and novelist. Snow's generous and broad sympathies led him to see the strengths rather than the weaknesses of people, and similarly of countries like the United States and the Soviet Union, in both of which as well as in Britain, he was honoured with numerous academic awards. He sought to be a sympathetic interpreter of different styles of life, and thus to extend mutual understanding. This was the origin of his Rede lectures at Cambridge in 1959, *The Two Cultures and the Scientific Revolution*, in which his theme was that ignorance by humanists of modern science was as barbaric as ignorance of the arts by scientists. This doctrine endorsed a fashionable view and was part of a feeling, widespread at the time, that Britain's relatively poor economic performance was due to the lack of scientific and technological knowledge in the ruling group. F. R. Leavis attacked the thesis with passion, asserting that his own interpretation of culture, based upon that of T. S. Eliot [q.v.], as a knowledge of what great artists said of life, was in direct conflict with Snow's more pedestrian view of culture as knowledge. This controversy to some degree proved Snow's point, since he held that the imaginative insights formerly the monopoly of artists and religious thinkers had now become the prerogative of those who (like Newton) voyaged through strange seas of thought alone.

It was this enthusiasm for science, its intellectual excitement and its potentiality for good which, like H. G. Wells [q.v.], he communicated. It also led him into further controversy such as that aroused by *Science and Government* (1961) and its *Postscript* (1962), covering his Godkin lectures at Harvard in 1960, in which he denounced as highly dangerous the influence in scientific matters during the 1939–45 war exercised by F. A. Lindemann (Viscount Cherwell, q.v.) over (Sir) Winston Churchill, using as his argument the disagreements between the 'Prof' and Sir Henry Tizard [q.v.] on the development of radar and the effectiveness of the strategic bombing of German towns. Snow's sympathies were clearly with Tizard.

His later years, again like Wells, showed disillusion with the government's attempts to sponsor the technological revolution, and disappointment at the senseless violence abroad and in the streets of London. He always showed in his writing an inner pessimism of despair and death, faced with stoic determination by the men in his novels who were professionally successful.

Snow died in London 1 July 1980.

[*The Times*, 2 July 1980; R. Greacen (ed.), *The World of Snow*, 1962; S. Weintraub (ed.), *C. P. Snow—a Spectrum: Science, Criticism, Fiction*, 1963; David Shusterman, *C. P. Snow*, 1975; William Cooper, *C. P. Snow*, 1959; personal knowledge.]
VAIZEY

SNOW, SIR FREDERICK SYDNEY (1899–1976), civil engineer, was born in Lambeth, London, 14 February 1899, the third son of a family of five, of whom two were girls, of William Snow, a printer, of Blackfriars, London, and his wife, Sarah Byron Holmes. He was educated at Brownhill School, Catford, which he left at the age of fourteen to work manually on stone dressing at a pepper mill. In 1914 he joined the Royal Horse Artillery, and served in France in both the Artillery and the Royal Engineers before demobilization in 1919. He was twice seriously wounded. On returning to civilian life he began his lifelong career in engineering by five years of training in Ipswich. In 1924 he was employed by the large contracting firm Holland Hannen & Cubitts, in which he achieved ever-increasing responsibility and self-confidence. He was sent to classes in reinforced concrete design at Regent Street Polytechnic.

During his eighteen years in contracting Snow became an acknowledged expert, first on the timbering of deep excavations, and then on foundations in general, especially those in London. In 1936 he published *Foundations of London Structures*, a proof that it was not only on building sites and in contractors' offices that this bluff, forceful young man could express his views and command respect.

During the 1930s many social barriers from past ages still exerted a strong influence on relations in the construction industries between workmen, craftsmen, and managers in the contracting industry on the one hand, and the clients, consulting engineers, and academics on the other. Good humour generally prevailed among the participants but, with rare exceptions, it was supposed that analysis and conceptual thinking would be contributed to the professional bodies of engineering from the latter group, while the former confined themselves to strictly practical applications, and commercial implications, of actual projects. In September 1942 Snow, by that time a member of the Institution of Civil Engineers, and of the Institution of Structural Engineers, contributed a remarkable paper entitled 'Human Needs and the Engineer', based on his experience in contracting on a number of important works. This covered with great penetration and wide vision the historical background and current realities of the motivations of labour and of management in the implementation of large construction projects. Forty years later it is still possible to read this work with pleasure and profit, and to understand from it the qualities in Snow which subsequently made him a great and well-loved figure spanning uniquely both the practical and commercial world where trade unions, bonus payments, and the techniques of man-management are all-important, and the professional engineering establishment with its respect for detachment and the widest public interest.

In 1942 Snow took the bold step of setting up his own firm of consulting engineers; by 1944 he was engaged in the design of the de Havilland airfield, Hatfield. He gave details of this task, with a wealth of theoretical and practical detail, in a paper to the Institution of Civil Engineers in 1949. The firm he founded grew and prospered, attracting such well-known partners as G. F. Brian Scruby (who succeeded him as senior partner) and Sir Norman Payne (subsequently chairman of the British Airports Authority). The firm became responsible for the design and supervision of construction of many airports throughout the world, including Gatwick, Jerusalem, Amman, and Kuwait.

Snow achieved full recognition in the world of technology, becoming president of the Institution of Structural Engineers in 1948, of the British section of the Société des Ingénieurs Civils de France in 1955, of the Reinforced Concrete Association in 1956, and of the newly formed Concrete Society in 1966. He won the Istiqlal medal of Jordan (1968), was a chevalier of the Legion of Honour (1969), and was master of the Worshipful Company of Glaziers and Painters of Glass (1972). He was made an honorary LL D (Leeds) in 1974, appointed OBE in 1954 and CBE in 1958, and knighted in 1965.

His outstanding qualities, which made him irresistible as a leader and as a colleague, were courage, warmth, and indomitable common sense. He would bring beer with his own hands for labourers to induce them to work overtime, but he would equally enjoy entertaining social celebrities in St. James's Street.

In 1924 he married (Rosetta) Elizabeth, daughter of Edmund William Brown, a customs officer, of Colchester; they had two sons, and a daughter who died in infancy. Snow died 5 June 1976 at his home in Eastbourne.

[Private information; personal knowledge.]

F. A. SHARMAN

SOMERVELL, (THEODORE) HOWARD (1890–1975), medical missionary and mountaineer, was born 16 April 1890, the eldest of three children and elder son of William Henry Somervell, of Brantfield, Kendal, Cumbria, and his wife, Florence Howard. W. H. Somervell was then directing the affairs of Somervell Brothers of Kendal, later more widely known as 'K Shoes'. But a business career was not attractive to Howard Somervell, although he was fully grateful to his father for giving him an income and the key of the house at seventeen. At Rugby School (1904–9) he was unhappy, leaving school labelled 'unbusinesslike and forgetful'. But his mother's comfort and their common solace in music gave him the kind of courage fit for the great mountains. By twenty he knew the Beethoven symphonies by heart, and would cycle 150 miles to hear a promenade concert. When he was eighteen he became a member of the Keswick-based Fell and Rock Climbing Club and thus started a lifetime's devotion to the mountains of the English Lake District.

He went on to Caius College, Cambridge, where he obtained first classes in both parts of the natural sciences tripos (1911 and 1913) and where he developed his essentially personal approach to the Christian faith. He then served with the British Expeditionary Force in France (1915–18) as a captain in the Royal Army Medical Corps. He was mentioned in dispatches. After the war he graduated from London's University College Hospital (MB, B.Ch., 1921) and became FRCS in 1920.

Somervell's Everest ambitions were stimulated during 1921 by much mountaineering in Britain and Europe. He was a tough physical product of the Cumbrian heights, and of the Alps, but he realized that the Himalayan region called for constant movement above 20,000 feet. Everest was to be his physical test in 1922 and 1924, but his colleagues commented too on his mental endurance. 'When one shares', Somervell wrote about George Leigh Mallory [q.v.], 'a tent for days on end throughout the better part of six months with a man one gets an insight into his character such as is vouchsafed to few other men. These many days of companionship with a man whose outlook on life was lofty and choice, human and loving and in a measure divine still remain for me a priceless memory.' Even when in 1924 Somervell threatened to choke, E. F. Norton [q.v.] wrote: 'Somervell very nearly choked, and was handicapped for three days. Only saved by coughing up the obstructing matter with a lot of blood. That he achieved what he did in this condition was a remarkable performance.'

After the 1922 Everest expedition and with £60 in his pocket Somervell set out to see India from the northern frontier to Cape Comorin and what he saw changed his life. He saw a continent ill-equipped medically and poorly provided for in those skills which he possessed, something more powerful than the Himalayas and more compelling than the 'call of the mountains'. He described it as the 'unrelieved suffering of India'. When he visited the main hospital of the south Travancore medical mission and its group of outstations centred on Neyyoor he found only one qualified surgeon, Stephen Pugh, struggling with a queue of waiting patients which would take ten days to reduce. There and then Somervell offered to perform those overdue operations, and then within a fortnight he was back in London telling his friends in London hospitals of his decision to devote his life to India after another attempt on Everest. He joined the 1924 expedition on which Mallory died and Somervell and E. F. Norton climbed to within a thousand feet of the summit.

From 1924 to 1949 Somervell was deep in the affairs of the south Travancore medical mission which, with its branch hospitals, could claim to be the largest of its kind in the world. He attracted young surgeons to work with him, especially in the surgery of the stomach. He established a confidence between surgeon and patient by building a gallery in the operating theatre where visitors and relations could watch what was going on. 'Many thousands have seen us at work', he wrote, 'and know that a surgical operation is a careful and intelligent procedure. They have been shown the disease inside and been given an explanation of how the operation cures it. Thus not only have we spread a little knowledge among the people around, but they have learned to come to us for treatment far earlier than was their custom in the past.' In 1934 out of 2,000 major operations performed at Neyyoor 590 of them were for cancer.

Somervell also pioneered the modern treatment of leprosy. He practised the modern belief that leprosy can be cured. His home for leprosy patients had four big dormitories for eighty patients, and a leprosy settlement for permanent residents. By 1936 several scores of patients had been sent home 'cured and free from all symptoms of the disease which was once considered incurable'. Describing a day's visit to a branch hospital Somervell wrote: 'The amount of work one has to do here is appalling. Yesterday and the day before over 150 patients who had come five miles and more to the hospital had to go home without seeing me. From 7 a.m. to 8.30 p.m. I saw 153 sick folk continuously.' In 1938 he was awarded the Kaisar-i-Hind gold medal and he was appointed OBE in 1953.

India continued to tug at Somervell's heart and he accepted the post of associate professor of surgery at the Vellore Christian Medical College (1949–61), then at a crucial stage of its development as a teaching hospital. It was a fitting climax to his forty years' service in India. From 1961 to 1964 Somervell was president of the Alpine Club. When the news of his death at Ambleside, 23 January 1975, reached Neyyoor the whole community broke into a spontaneous public procession of thanksgiving, while in London the Geographical Society showed some of Somervell's magnificent Everest paintings, as did his own Lake District friends, thus fulfilling the description of him given by Sir Francis Younghusband [q.v.] as 'a man of science, a man of art, a man of warm humanity and of strong religious feeling'.

In 1925 Somervell married Margaret, daughter of Sir James Hope Simpson, director of the Bank of Liverpool; they had three sons.

[London Missionary Society archives; Howard Somervell, *After Everest*, 1936, and *Knife and Life in India*, 1940; Sir Francis Younghusband, *The Epic of Mount Everest*, 1926; *Alpine Journal*, 1921–46; *Fell and Rock Journal*, 1924; *Geographical Journal*, 1922; *Indian Medical Journal*, 1938; personal knowledge.] CECIL NORTHCOTT

SORLEY, SIR RALPH SQUIRE (1898–1974), air marshal, was born in Hornsey, London, 9 January 1898, the son of James Graham Sorley, soft goods manufacturer, of Stroud Green, and his wife, Ellen Merson. He was educated at the University School, Hastings, and by a private tutor. He joined the Royal Naval Air Service on 4 December 1914, rising to the rank of flight commander before transferring to the Royal Air force as captain (air) on its formation in 1918. He was awarded the DSC in 1918 and the DFC while commanding No. 6 Squadron in Mesopotamia in 1920.

Sorley's extended and invaluable connections with future aircraft and weapons began with his posting as a test pilot to Felixstowe in 1924 and then to No. 22 Squadron at Martlesham Heath in 1925. These stations were the centres of development of seaplanes and land-planes. In 1927 he went to the Air Ministry in the directorate of technical development before going to the Staff College in 1929. He then was posted to Aden to command No. 8 Squadron for two years before returning to the Air Ministry in 1933.

Sorley's crusading dedication and drive ensured that the eight-gun fighter was a reality when World War II began. His calculations had showed that a mere two seconds would be available to destroy a high-speed monoplane fighter and that eight guns would be necessary to achieve a lethal burst in that time. Sorley, only thirty-five years old and a wing commander, against immense opposition persuaded the Air Ministry and the designers, (Sir) Sydney Camm and R. J. Mitchell [qq.v.], of the importance of the 'two-second squirt', which was possibly the biggest single factor of the many which contributed to Britain's victory in the Battle of Britain.

At the outbreak of war Sorley was posted to command Royal Air Force, Upwood, but very soon went to command the Aeroplane and Armament Experimental Establishment for which all his experience had trained him. From 1943 to 1945 he worked in the Ministry of Aircraft Production, becoming controller of research and development and a member of the Air Council. When peace came he was promoted to air marshal and given command of Technical Training Command of the Royal Air Force until he retired at his own request in 1948.

In 1948 Sorley became managing director of De Havilland Propellers Ltd., Hatfield. The advent of the jet engine made the future look bleak and the possibility of entering the helicopter field was studied and rejected. Instead it was decided to concentrate on guided weapons. Sorley formed the nucleus of a design team to study the new technology and seek research and development contracts from the Air Ministry, the first of which was obtained in 1951—for an infrared homing head which became the guidance system for the Firestreak air-to-air weapon, the RAF's first airborne missile. Sorley played a large part in the initial discussions with the RAF which formulated its operational requirements and specifications.

The respect in which he was held caused Sorley to be appointed head of the industrial team for a new project in 1955—a British independent deterrent consisting of a ballistic missile, code-named Blue Streak, with a range of 2,000 miles and carrying a thermo-nuclear warhead. Sorley formed a separate design team with design offices in London, assembly facilities at Stevenage, and test sites at Hatfield, Spadeadam (Cumbria), and Woomera (Australia). In 1960, however, a government decision was made to cancel Blue Streak and in the same year Sorley retired.

Sorley was FRAeS and FRSA. He was appointed OBE (1936), CB (1942), and KCB (1944). In 1925 he married Mary Eileen (died 1977), daughter of Ernest Robert Gayford, of Hadleigh, Suffolk, and sister of Wing Commander Oswald Robert Gayford, DFC, AFC, who held the world long-distance flying record (1930) and then commanded the long-range development which regained the record for Great Britain. There were two daughters of the marriage. Sorley died 17 November 1974 at the RAF Hospital, Wroughton.

[Private information; personal knowledge.]

GEOFFREY TUTTLE

SOSKICE, FRANK, BARON STOW HILL (1902–1979), politician and lawyer, was born in Geneva 23 July 1902, the eldest of three sons (there were no daughters) of the second marriage of David Vladimir Soskice, Doctor of Law of Kiev University, who was Russian Jewish by birth but not by faith. There was also a son of a previous marriage. His father joined the revolutionary movement in Russia after witnessing an anti-Jewish pogrom in Kiev in 1881. While a student he was in prison several times and went abroad in 1893 to escape arrest. He settled in England in 1893 and married Juliet, daughter of Francis Hueffer [q.v.], music critic of *The Times*. Her brother was Ford Madox Ford [q.v.] and her grandfather the painter Ford Madox Brown [q.v.]; the family's links with the pre-Raphaelites were strong. The Rossettis [qq.v.] were relatives. David Soskice became foreign correspondent of the *Manchester Guardian* and other papers, living in Geneva. He was naturalized later when the family lived in Brook Green, London. He also became the St. Petersburg (Petrograd) correspondent of the *Tribune*. Some of Frank's earliest memories were of living there on two occasions between 1906 and 1909 and riding in a horse-drawn tram on rails laid on the ice of the Neva. He wrote: 'I have a curious memory of men on horseback in black uniforms—the Black Hundreds?—beating up the crowds on a bridge crossing the Neva.'

In 1917 his father became special correspondent of the *Manchester Guardian* in St. Petersburg and a member of Kerensky's secretariat, witnessing at first hand the Kornilov mutiny and Kerensky's last days in the Winter Palace. Frank became a considerable linguist—he read widely, in the original, French, German, Russian, Spanish, Italian, Greek, and Latin literature. After being a foundation scholar at St. Paul's, he went to Balliol College, Oxford, on a classics scholarship. He obtained a first class in classical honour moderations in 1922 and a third in philosophy, politics, and economics in 1924. He was naturalized in 1924.

Soskice was called to the bar by the Inner Temple in 1926. He already had a busy practice prior to the outbreak of war in 1939 when he joined the Oxfordshire and Buckinghamshire Light Infantry, serving in East Africa and in Cairo in Political Warfare Executive and later in Special Operations Executive in London. As an advocate he pressed his client's case with vigour and persistence. His greatest strength in private practice lay in the sound and far-sighted advice which he gave to his clients. He had a strong sense of the practical. Despite his gentleness and modesty he was also a man of the world. He inspired by his probity instant and complete trust in his clients. This was reflected in the number of foreign governments which instructed him at the International Court of Justice at The Hague. He acted for the government of India against Portugal, for Greece against the United Kingdom in the Ambatielos dispute, and for Thailand against Cambodia in the Pra Viharn temples case.

Soskice entered Parliament in 1945 as Labour MP for East Birkenhead. His constituency was abolished in boundary changes but he secured the Neepsend division of Sheffield seat and represented it from 1950 to 1955 when it too was abolished. He returned to Parliament in a by-election in 1956 as member for Newport (Monmouthshire) which he represented until 1966.

C. R. (later Earl) Attlee appointed him solicitor-general in 1945 and he took silk in the same year. His legal expertise strengthened the first post-war Labour government. As a law officer he advised on a wide range of matters domestic and international, and appeared for the Crown in many cases, particularly in the specialist revenue field. His parliamentary skill, natural courtesy, and wit enabled him to steer controversial legislation through the Commons sometimes through stormy all-night sessions. There can be few public figures who inspired so much friendship and so little antipathy. He became attorney-general for a few months in 1951 when he appeared for the United Kingdom at The Hague in the Norwegian fisheries dispute. He was knighted in 1945, made a privy councillor in 1948, and became UK delegate to the United Nations General Assembly in 1950. Many of his colleagues on both sides of the House would have liked him to become Speaker in 1959 but he preferred to continue in the law and politics.

In opposition from 1951 to 1964, he was a member of the shadow cabinet aligning himself with Hugh Gaitskell [q.v.] on economic and defence issues. Harold Wilson (later Lord Wilson of Rievaulx) appointed him to the Home Office in the 1964 Labour Cabinet. As home secretary he had both strengths and weaknesses. He had a good lively mind and a quite exceptional measure of integrity and fairmindedness. His weakness was a degree of indecisiveness. One civil servant has said of him: 'I sometimes felt that he enjoyed acting as counsel for both sides and presenting the arguments to himself as judge.' But there were many questions of policy about which he had no doubt. The death penalty was one. He was against it and before the Labour government abolished it he reprieved everyone sentenced to death. He dealt humanely with parole applications and made a point of visiting prisons. He introduced useful measures of penal reform particularly in regard to the treatment of adult offenders and procedures in juvenile courts.

While he was as anxious as anyone to improve race relations he doubted the value of legislation in this field, although it fell to him to present the 1965 Race Relations Bill, which was strengthened in a further Bill in 1968. On immigration he favoured much more severe restrictions than either his Cabinet or parliamentary colleagues would have found acceptable.

He was appointed lord privy seal in 1965 and chaired the Cabinet committee on winter emergency powers. After the 1966 general election which he did not contest he was made a life peer. Despite illness he played an effective part in the proceedings of the Lords, particularly in promoting bills produced by the law commissions. He was treasurer of the Inner Temple in 1968. He contributed to this Dictionary the notice of W. G. G. Hall.

He married in 1940 Susan Isabella Cloudesley, daughter of William Auchterlony Hunter, of Spean Bridge, Inverness-shire, a member of the London Stock Exchange. They had two sons. His wife was his constant support and companion and the marriage was a very happy one. He was an entertaining host and loved dancing in the company of friends. He died at his home in Hampstead 1 January 1979.

[Private information; personal knowledge.]

ELWYN-JONES

SPEAIGHT, ROBERT WILLIAM (1904–1976), actor and literary scholar, was born 14 January 1904 at the Corner Cottage, St. Margaret's Bay, Kent, the eldest of three sons of Frederick William Speaight and his wife, Emily Isabella, daughter of Frederick Elliott. His father ran a Bond Street photographer's, but had varied artistic interests, designing the decorations for Edward VII's funeral, the Marble Arch Improvement Scheme of 1905, and restoring old houses, including a Georgian mansion at Hatfield to which he moved his family in 1910.

Speaight's first contact with the stage was at the age of nine when he saw Sir H. Beerbohm Tree [q.v.] play Henry VIII. He went to school at The Wick, Hove, and then to Haileybury, where he played Mark Antony, audaciously writing to

(Dame) Sybil Thorndike [q.v.] for advice. She replied: 'Acting is one of the greatest studies in the world: whether it is your living or not, the study of it helps you in every walk in life', a truth which proved exceedingly apt for Speaight's career.

It was the great age of the country-house theatre, and when Bobby, as he was known, played Macbeth at Hatfield, aged seventeen, his father persuaded Charles Morgan [q.v.] of *The Times* and W. A. Darlington [q.v.] of the *Daily Telegraph* to review the performance. At Oxford, where he won a scholarship to Lincoln College, his Falstaff (1926) reduced James Agate [q.v.] to tears: the great critic told him, 'You are the best Falstaff I have seen since Louis Calvert', and gave him a glowing notice in the *Sunday Times*.

After that there was no doubt about a theatrical career. Having taken a third class in English in 1926, Speaight spent a year with the Liverpool Repertory, followed by a tour of Egypt (1927) with Ernest Milton, whom he regarded as one of the finest actors of his day. In 1928 the scholar-director William Poel [q.v.] (whose biography Speaight published in 1954) invited him to play Arruntius in the *Sejanus* of Ben Jonson [q.v.], and that autumn he created Smerdyakov in the dramatization of *The Brothers Karamazov* by Theodore Komisarjevsky [q.v.].

Speaight's first West End success was in the all-male trench drama, *Journey's End*, by R. C. Sherriff [q.v.], in which he played the coward Hibbert, first with Laurence (later Lord) Olivier in the lead, later with Colin Clive in an eighteen-month run (1929–30). He recalled: 'We gave one performance to an audience exclusively of VCs. We almost came to believe that we had been through the war ourselves.' Then followed a clutch of Shakespearian roles: first player in the *Hamlet* of Henry Ainley [q.v.], Edmund in (Sir) John Gielgud's *King Lear* (1931), and in the 1931–2 Old Vic season he shared leads (and a dressing-room) with (Sir) Ralph Richardson, playing Hamlet, King John, Cassius ('I won the best notice I have ever received from an English critic in a Shakespearian part') and Fluellen, which remained his favourite minor part.

By this time his interests had broadened with the publication of a novel, *Mutinous Wind* (1932), the first of four, and deepened with his religious conversion. Speaight's parents had been fervent Protestants, and both his godfathers were Anglican clergymen, but after a visit to Bavaria and the Oberammergau passion play, 'I suddenly felt with quite overwhelming force that I wanted to become a Catholic.' In October 1930 he was received into the Church at Farm Street, following instruction by Fr Martin d'Arcy and Fr C. C. Martindale [qq.v.]. His new faith, and his growing interest in writing, brought him into contact with a wide circle of Catholic intellectuals: Hilaire Belloc and G. K. Chesterton [qq.v.], Douglas Woodruff and Tom Burns (in turn editors of the *Tablet*, to which Speaight contributed for nearly forty years), (Sir) Compton Mackenzie and Christopher Hollis [qq.v.]. In 1935 Michael de la Bedoyere [q.v.] sent him to Rome to report the canonization of Sir Thomas More and John Fisher [qq.v.] for the *Catholic Herald*, and on his return he seemed a natural choice to create the part of Thomas à Becket in *Murder in the Cathedral*, which T. S. Eliot [q.v.] had written for the Canterbury Festival.

Thus Speaight entered what he later wryly called 'the crypt of St. Eliot's'. His acting career had already reached a plateau. Short and stocky, he lacked the ideal physique for what he called the *optique du théâtre*, and he had, as *The Times* put it, 'an interesting and mobile but not handsome face'. On the other hand, his voice had operatic power, stamina, and control, so that he adjusted easily to the acoustics of a cathedral or concert hall. He spoke verse with great intuitive skill, perfected by much study. He liked to quote Jean Cocteau's dictum: 'There are actors who think what they are saying, and actors who think about what they are saying', and Speaight was certainly among the latter. He was the first to discover how to recite Gerard Manley Hopkins's poems in such a way as to bring out both their full meaning and their sprung rhythm, though as Eliot said 'he would have made a laundry-list sound like great poetry'. In short he was the ideal festival actor.

Thanks to Speaight, *Murder in the Cathedral* was a surprising popular success, and he played it over 1,000 times throughout the British Isles and North America. His performance evoked a characteristic 'compliment' from W. B. Yeats [q.v.]: 'Long before I saw you act I divined that you were important—because your acting was derided by all the people I most dislike.' In 1941 it won him the coveted role of Christ in the twelve-part adaption of the Gospels for the BBC by Dorothy L. Sayers [q.v.]. In those days representation of Christ in a place of public entertainment was forbidden, but broadcasting was not covered by the law. Though each episode was vetted by C. F. Garbett [q.v.], the bishop of Winchester, *The Man Born to be King* (1942) was a sensational success. Unfortunately it typecast Speaight for good: thereafter he found it hard to get parts which were not saints or clerics. He played Christian in *The Pilgrim's Progress* at Covent Garden (1948), Gerontius in Newman's *The Dream of Gerontius* (1951), St. Peter at Westminster Abbey (1953) and, the same year, Cardinal Pole at Canterbury. Oddly enough, the most enviable post-war role, for which he was ideally suited, Thomas More in Robert Bolt's *A Man for All Seasons*, eluded him in the West End, though he played it with distinction in Australia (1962–3).

Speaight did not regret the etiolation of his acting career. He directed plays, adjudicated drama festivals, and published many books about the theatre, especially on Shakespeare. As J. C. Trewin said, 'No one wrote as he did about the plays in performance.' His *Nature in Shakespearian Tragedy* (1955) struck many as the best study of its kind since that of A. C. Bradley [q.v.]; he put all his practical knowledge of Elizabethan stagecraft into *Shakespeare on the Stage* (1973), and his delightful *Shakespeare: the Man and his Achievement* (1977), published posthumously, has been well described as 'the actor-scholar's legacy to his friends'. But though he called his autobiography *The Property Basket* (1970), he noted in it: 'Stage doors no longer have the slightest magic for me. . . . My roots and my freedom are elsewhere.'

They were indeed. Speaight was a Catholic intellectual in the great European tradition. Among his mentors the man he most admired was Maurice Baring because he was 'the most spontaneously international person I have ever known'. For this Dictionary he wrote the notice of Baring (as of several others). He could not emulate Baring's astonishing command of languages, but no other actor of his day was capable, as he was, of performing in German or of directing a French version of *Antony and Cleopatra*. It was typical of Speaight that his novel *The Unbroken Heart* (1939) was 'inspired by a gnomic saying of Leon Bloy . . . and by a sculpture . . . on the outside of Chartres Cathedral', and who else would have described Jaques at the end of *As You Like It* 'wandering off like Proust returning to a monastery'?

Like Belloc, whose official life he wrote in 1957, Speaight enjoyed tramping through the French countryside, exploring the vineyards, and his *The Companion Guide to Burgundy* (1975) is a model of its kind. But his chief interest was in French literature, especially the neo-Thomism of Jacques Maritain, of whom he wrote 'his philosophy . . . is as hard and clear as a diamond . . . But his heart is a mine of charity.' Thomism led him to join with Christopher Dawson in 'The Sword of the Spirit', a thirties ecumenical movement which adumbrated Pope John XXIII's *aggiornamento*. After the war he became a familiar figure in the Maritain circle at Meudon and the Paris salons, where he got to know Valéry, Claudel, Malraux, Mauriac, and Bernanos. In 1967 he published a study of *Teilhard de Chardin*, whom he admired, though not as a philosophical guide, and in 1973 and 1976 rather more weighty books on *Georges Bernanos* and *François Mauriac*. Bernanos he revered as the finest novelist of his generation, but Mauriac he loved as a friend. Speaight was thus a close observer of the last great phase of European Christian culture, which gave joy to his life and meaning to his religion, and whose strength and pathos he captured in his best critical writing.

In 1935 he married Esther Evelyn Bowen; they had one son. In 1951 he married Bridget Laura Bramwell, a painter and musician. She was the daughter of Nevil Digby Bosworth-Smith, under-secretary in the Ministry of Education. They had one adopted son. They shared a passion for Joseph Conrad, Henry James [qq.v.], and Proust, and a delight in the engaging Tudor house they found and adorned near Benenden in the Kentish weald. He died there 4 November 1976. There are recordings of Speaight's voice in the BBC sound archives, and some fine photographic studies, notably by Karsh of Ottawa and Anthony Buckley; but a portrait of him by Marie Laurencin has been lost.

[*The Times*, 6 November 1976; Robert Speaight, *The Property Basket*, 1970; private information; personal knowledge.]

PAUL JOHNSON

SPEARS, SIR EDWARD LOUIS, baronet (1886–1974), major-general, was born in Paris 7 August 1886, the only son and elder child of Charles McCarthy Spiers and his wife, Marguerite Melicent, daughter of Edward Louis Hack, railway engineer. C. M. Spiers was one of the five sons of Alexander Spiers [q.v.], lexicographer. E. L. Spiers was brought up in France, largely by his Irish grandmother, sister of Sir Gerald Aylmer, ninth baronet. He was educated privately on the Continent, joined the Kildare Militia in 1903, and was gazetted into the 8th Hussars in 1906. As the result of severe head injuries sustained in a polo accident, he had a long spell on the sick list and was not passed fit to accompany the 8th Hussars to India. He transferred to the 11th Hussars in 1910.

Being completely bilingual in French and English (it was often said that his French accent was purer than his English), he was sent to the French War Office in Paris shortly before the outbreak of World War I in August 1914, to help to compile a military cipher book, in which the groups were interchangeable in both languages. When this task was less than half complete, war broke out and, having unsuccessfully tried to rejoin his regiment, he was ordered to serve as a liaison officer between General Lanrezac at French Fifth Army headquarters and Sir John French (later the Earl of Ypres, q.v.), the British commander-in-chief. Spiers must be almost the only soldier who saw with his own eyes both the battle of Mons fought by British troops and the battle of Charleroi fought by the French. Extraordinarily successful as a liaison officer, he was wounded four times and rose from subaltern to bridgadier by 1917, when he was appointed head of the military mission in Paris. Among other awards, he won the MC and the croix de guerre with three palms, became commander of the Legion of Honour, and was appointed CBE (1919) and CB (1921).

When he married in 1918 he changed the spelling of his name from Spiers to Spears because it was frequently mispronounced. After the war he entered Parliament first as a National Liberal for the Loughborough division of Leicestershire (1922–4), and later, as a Conservative, he sat for Carlisle from 1931 to 1945. He acquired extensive business interests, was on the boards of a number of companies, and was chairman of Ashanti Goldfields. A devoted admirer of (Sir) Winston Churchill, with whom he had been in close contact in France during World War I, Spears was his close companion in political exile in the 1930s. Churchill greatly admired Spear's two books about World War I, *Liaison, 1914* (1930) and *Prelude to Victory* (1939). In 1940 when Churchill became prime minister, he sent Spears, appointed major-general that year, to Paris as his personal representative with the French prime minister. The events that led up to the collapse of France are brilliantly described in Spears's next book, *Assignment to Catastrophe* (2 vols., 1954). Selecting General de Gaulle as the most likely senior French officer to be able to reform French units overseas, Spears travelled with him in the same aircraft to England, introduced him to Churchill, and launched him into government circles at a crucial period in Anglo-French relations.

Early in 1941 Spears was sent to the Middle East as head of the military mission to the Free French forces in Africa, and as the prime minister's representative with General de Gaulle. Here his troubles soon began, when it became clear that de Gaulle was singularly unwilling to implement the terms of the Catroux–Lampson declaration, made when the Allied forces crossed into Syria in June 1941. This declaration, signed jointly by General Catroux on behalf of the French Free forces, and by Sir Miles Lampson (later Lord Killearn, q.v.) on behalf of the British government, promised Syria and the Lebanon (French mandated territories) independence forthwith. Spears was under constant pressure from London to correct de Gaulle's dangerous procrastination in a country where the Syrian and Lebanese dislike of the French administration was intense.

By this time de Gaulle was no longer the child of Spears's own creation and was developing policies of his own increasingly at variance with the policies of the British government. Spears's relationship with him entered a new phase. A clash of personalities unhappily coincided with the clash of policies, and Spears was the mouthpiece of Churchill's policies.

In 1942 Spears was made the first British minister to the Syrian and Lebanese republics, and a member of the Middle East War Council. He was appointed KBE the same year. These events he described in his book, *Fulfilment of a Mission*, published in 1977. In 1966 he had also published *Two Men Who Saved France: Pétain and de Gaulle*, followed by *The Picnic Basket* (1967), a vignette chiefly of his youth in Ireland and France. Spears was much criticized, particularly in Algiers, where Eisenhower and Harold Macmillan (later the Earl of Stockton) under totally different circumstances were doing everything possible to get on to good terms with de Gaulle's administration in North Africa, for his forcible handling of the French in Syria and the Lebanon during his period as minister from 1942 to 1944. He was certainly urged on by the Syrians and Lebanese, both deeply suspicious of Free French intentions, when they realized that he was the protagonist of their independence. But Spears's instructions from Britain were perfectly clear. He was not to allow de Gaulle to harass the embryo independence of Syria and Lebanon. He became violently anti-French and pro-Arab. It was as though a lifelong love affair with France had turned to hatred.

After World War II Spears concentrated on his writing and business interests, becoming president of Ashanti Goldfields in 1971. He was chairman of council of the Institute of Directors until 1965. In 1953 he was created first baronet.

Spears was a fascinating conversationalist and a delightful host. His memory was extremely clear right to the end and his reminiscences about World War I were superb. He enjoyed being a controversial character, displaying violent likes and dislikes, and ruthlessly pursuing vendettas. To his friends he was loyal, warm-hearted, and generous. He married first, in 1918, the well-known novelist Mary Borden, daughter of William Borden, of Borden's Milk (Chicago), and former wife of George Douglas Turner. She had three daughters by her previous marriage. She equipped and ran a highly efficient hospital and ambulance unit for the Free French forces, which she accompanied throughout the whole of the campaigns in North Africa, the Levant, and later in France. She died in 1968, and he married secondly, in 1969, Nancy, daughter of Major-General Sir Frederick Barton Maurice [q.v.]. She died in 1975. There was one son of his first marriage, who died in 1969. The baronetcy became extinct when Spears died 27 January 1974 at a nursing home in Windsor.

[Sir Edward Spears, *The Picnic Basket*, 1967; personal knowledge.]

CHARLES MOTT-RADCLYFFE

SPENCE, SIR BASIL URWIN (1907–1976), architect, was born 13 August 1907 in Bombay, the elder son (there were no daughters) of Urwin Spence, an analytical chemist serving in the

Indian Civil Service, and his wife, Daisy Crisp. The Spences were an Orcadian family. Basil Spence was educated first in India and then at George Watson's College, Edinburgh. From there he went to Edinburgh College of Art to study architecture, continuing his studies at the Bartlett School of Architecture, University College, London. He was an outstanding student, winning the RIBA Recognized Schools silver medal in 1931, the Arthur Cates prize in 1932, and the Pugin studentship in 1933.

After qualifying as an architect in 1933 Spence worked for a year in London in the office of Sir Edwin Lutyens [q.v.], engaged principally on the drawings for the viceroy's house, New Delhi. He then moved back to Edinburgh where he set up in practice and built several country houses. At the outbreak of World War II he joined the Royal Artillery; he rose to the rank of major and was twice mentioned in dispatches. After the war he began to make his mark as a display and exhibition designer. He was successively chief architect for the 'Britain Can Make It' exhibition of 1947 and for the Scottish Industries exhibition of 1949 and designer of the Sea and Ships pavilion at the South Bank exhibition of the 1951 Festival of Britain. In fact he was in danger of becoming labelled as a designer only of such ephemeral affairs as exhibitions when, in 1951, he won first prize in the competition for a new cathedral at Coventry.

This brought him immediate celebrity. Coventry Cathedral was widely regarded as a symbol of the reconstruction of Britain after the war and therefore received a vast amount of public attention. Spence showed his flair for public relations and threw himself enthusiastically into many activities indirectly arising from the building of the cathedral. He made for example a lecture tour of Canada to raise money for the project and worked hard at arousing the interest of artists and craftsmen whose collaboration he sought. The cathedral as built was orthodox in conception compared with some of the adventurous structures entered for the competition and was thought by some critics to be too frankly theatrical, but it was admired as a skilfully planned repository for the works of art that Spence commissioned to embellish it, which included a tapestry by Graham Sutherland [q.v.], stained glass by John Piper, and sculpture by Sir Jacob Epstein [q.v.]. His design in addition showed one masterly stroke of imagination: the notion of preserving the burnt-out shell of the medieval cathedral as an approach to the new one, thus emphasizing the latter's symbolic role.

Although Spence complained that for three years after winning the Coventry competition he had no new commissions, the fame it brought made him in due course one of the most sought-after architects in Britain. He built up large offices in London and Edinburgh, with partners in each who for the most part remained in the background but controlled an ever-increasing flow of work. This included housing, schools, and churches (three of the last also in Coventry), undergraduate residences for Queens' College, Cambridge (completed in 1960), teaching buildings for Liverpool and Southampton universities (1960 onwards), the layout and initial phase of the new Sussex University (1962–72), a civic centre for Hampstead (1964), Abbotsinch airport, Glasgow (1966), Edinburgh University library (1967)—these two Scottish buildings being among his most successful—Knightsbridge Barracks, London (1970), a new chancery for the British embassy at Rome (1971)—not one of his happiest designs—and Kensington Town Hall, London, completed after his death.

In spite of the prominence he achieved, Spence's position in the profession remained somewhat isolated. He never became involved with the movements and groups seeking new images and ideals that characterized the 1950s and 1960s. This was perhaps due to his being, by instinct and in many of his attitudes, a man of the eighteenth rather than of the twentieth century. He placed emphasis on an initial pictorial conception rather than on architectural character emerging gradually from the design process. His usual method was to produce rough but vivid sketches—he was a more skilful draughtsman than most architects of his day—which were then worked up in detail in one of his offices. Among his best qualities were his ability to solve difficult problems quickly and to handle the relation of buildings to landscape. His design, for example, for the first buildings of Sussex University, which determined the layout and character of the whole subsequent development, showed a sensitive exploitation of their beautiful downland setting.

He was an indefatigable worker, with confidence in the validity of his own ideas with which he became emotionally involved with the result that he felt persecuted when subjected to criticism of a kind that most artists and architects accept as all in the day's work. On several occasions in his career his buildings were the subject of public controversy, and when his design for Knightsbridge Barracks was criticized because its tower would intrude on the leafy skyline of Hyde Park it was typical of him that he chose passionately to defend it and used his considerable persuasive powers to carry the design past all objections.

Apart from his buildings, Spence's contributions to the architectural profession were notable. In 1958 he was chosen president of the Royal Institute of British Architects at a time when the institute's influence had been declining under a succession of mediocre figures. Spence, with his engaging personality and his flair for public appearances, did much to revitalize it. He played an energetic part in all its activities, taking trouble especially to encourage the young. In 1955–6 he was Hoffman professor of architecture at Leeds University and, after being elected ARA in 1953 and RA in 1960, he became a conscientious member of the Royal Academy, serving as treasurer in 1962–4 and professor of architecture 1961–8. He was also an associate of the Royal Scottish Academy (1952), a Royal Designer for Industry (1960), and for fourteen years (1956–70) a member of the Royal Fine Art Commission. He was an honorary fellow of the American Institute of Architects and had honorary degrees from Leicester (1963), Manitoba (1963), and Southampton (1965). He was appointed OBE in 1948, knighted in 1960, and two years later, in the wake of all the attention Coventry Cathedral had aroused, he was admitted to the Order of Merit.

In 1934 Spence married Mary Joan, daughter of John Ferris, a butcher and farmer. They had one son and one daughter. Spence died at his home at Eye, Suffolk, 19 November 1976. A bronze bust by Sir Jacob Epstein is in the RIBA headquarters in Portland Place, London.

[Private information; personal knowledge.]

J. M. Richards

SPENCER, GILBERT (1892–1979), painter, was born at Cookham, Berkshire, 4 August 1892, the eighth son and youngest of the twelve children of William Spencer, organist and music teacher, and his wife, Anna Caroline Slack. His brother Stanley [q.v.] was thirteen months older. There was little money and their formal education was of the sketchiest, but what they lacked in schooling was made up for by the talk they heard between their elders at meal times. Gilbert followed Stanley to the Slade in 1913, having previously attended the Camberwell School of Art and a school of wood carving in Thurlow Place.

At the Slade Gilbert Spencer came under the powerful influence of Henry Tonks [q.v.], which stayed with him to the end of his life. He won the coveted life drawing prize in 1914 and was runner-up for the summer competition prize with a huge mural, 'The Seven Ages of Man' (Hamilton Art Gallery, Canada).

The outbreak of war in August 1914 interrupted his career. He left unfinished the picture he was working on, 'Sashes Meadow' (later acquired by the Tate), enlisted in the Royal Army Medical Corps, and was drafted out to Macedonia. After the war, in 1919 Spencer returned to the Slade with a scholarship for another year.

By the early 1920s he was producing some of his best pictures, at first much under the influence of Stanley, such as 'Crucifixion' (Tate Gallery) and 'Shepherds Amazed' (Leeds Art Gallery). Family links between the brothers remained strong for the rest of their lives, yet in the course of time the fact that they followed the same vocation inevitably caused a certain tension in their relationship. In time Gilbert was to mark out a special place for himself, chiefly as a very English landscape painter.

While at the Slade in 1919 Spencer met Hilda Carline, later to become the wife of Stanley, and her brother Sydney, Ruskin master of drawing at Oxford, who invited Gilbert to join his staff there in 1922. This provided him with a happy *modus vivendi* until he could put on his first one-man show at the Goupil Gallery in 1923. There he met Lady Ottoline Morrell [q.v.] who solved his domestic problem by arranging a room for him in the village of Garsington and giving him what he called 'tap and enter' rights at the manor. Thus he came into contact with many notable artists and members of the 'Bloomsbury set'. His paintings of this time, such as 'Trees at Garsington' (Ashmolean), 'Garsington Roofs', and 'The Sheep Fold at Upper Farm' have a characteristic directness of line and clarity of colour.

When the Morrells gave up Garsington, Spencer moved with Sydney Carline from lodgings in Oxfordshire and Berkshire to Hampstead where he painted a remarkable portrait of Mrs Carline and started an eight-foot canvas which was to prove his best-known painting, 'A Cotswold Farm' (Tate Gallery), first exhibited at his highly successful one-man show at the Goupil Gallery in 1932. In 1930 he was appointed to the staff of the Royal College of Art by Sir William Rothenstein [q.v.], and on the strength of it married (Margaret) Ursula, daughter of John Gerald Bradshaw, headmaster of Packwood Haugh preparatory school for boys, Warwickshire. They had one daughter.

In 1934 Spencer was commissioned by Balliol College to paint murals for its new building at Holywell Manor, Oxford. On completion of the work in 1936 the Spencers left Oxford with their only daughter and made their home at Tree Cottage, Upper Basildon, near Reading, spending the long holidays from the College of Art in a much-loved Dorset farmhouse. The college was evacuated to Ambleside in 1941, which gave Spencer yet another landscape to paint. Also, to escape from the restrictions of the time, he made a series of water-colour paintings of semi-imaginary comic episodes in the Home Guard.

In 1948, with the advent of (Sir) Robin Darwin [q.v.], Spencer was peremptorily dismissed from his post at the Royal College, but happily he was immediately appointed head of the department of painting and drawing at the Glasgow School of Art, where he spent two rewarding years. In 1950 he was elected ARA on the strength of a small picture, 'Culcrenth'. That year, for his wife's sake, he came south and became head of the department of painting at the Camberwell School of Arts and Crafts for the next six years. This proved to be a less happy appointment, but while still at Camberwell his frustrations were relieved by a commission from the Abbey Trust for a mural in the students' union of University College, London, for which he chose the subject of 'The Scholar Gypsy'. He greatly enjoyed the work, but his fee was so small that, to make up, the president of the Royal Academy commissioned him to paint a mural, which he called 'An Artist's Progress' (Royal Academy restaurant). He was elected RA in 1959; like his brother he was a somewhat stormy member of that body, resigning from time to time, but always glad to return.

In 1959 both his wife and brother died, a double blow which resulted in his writing and illustrating a book *Stanley Spencer* (1961). In 1964 he held a retrospective exhibition at Reading of his life's work, and ten years later a further retrospective was arranged by the Fine Art Society in London. He left his beloved Berkshire in 1970 for a farm cottage in Walsham le Willows, Suffolk, and, though he could no longer paint, he wrote his *Memoirs of a Painter* (1974) and entered ardently into family and village life to the end. He died there 14 January 1979.

[Gilbert Spencer, *Stanley Spencer*, 1961, and *Memoirs of a Painter*, 1974; personal knowledge.] CATHERINE MARTINEAU

SPENCER-CHURCHILL, BARONESS (1885–1977). [See CHURCHILL, CLEMENTINE OGILVY SPENCER-.]

SPENS, (WILLIAM) PATRICK, first BARON SPENS (1885–1973), lawyer and politician, was born 9 August 1885 at Frimley Park, Surrey, the first child of Nathaniel Spens, chartered accountant, and his wife, Emily Jessie Connal: both were of Scots descent. Spens had two brothers and three sisters. He was educated at Rugby School and New College, Oxford, which he entered as a commoner in 1904. He obtained second classes in both classical honour moderations (1905) and *literae humaniores* (1907). He was called to the bar by the Inner Temple in January 1910 and was commissioned in a Surrey territorial unit, the 5th battalion of the Queen's Royal Regiment, in 1911: he served with them as adjutant throughout World War I, first in India, then in Mesopotamia, then in India again. He was thrice mentioned in dispatches and appointed OBE (1918).

On his return in 1919 he appeared before the 'Chancery Bar', specializing in company work. He took silk in 1925. In May 1929 he stood as Conservative candidate in a by-election for St. Pancras South-West but was unsuccessful. He was chosen as National candidate in a by-election for the Ashford division of Kent in March 1933. He held the seat with 48 per cent of the vote against a strong Liberal challenge. At the general election of 1935 he increased his majority (against the national trend), obtaining 59 per cent of the vote. As an MP he was popular though not prominent in the House. L. C. M. S. Amery [q.v.] observed: 'Spens is not in any sense an active party politician. . . . He hasn't spoken often and though universally liked and respected has never been a conspicuous figure in the cut-and-thrust of parliamentary debate.'

Unexpectedly, at the age of fifty-eight, Spens attained high office. The chief justice of India, Sir Maurice Gwyer [q.v.], was due to retire in 1943. Three eminent counsel were invited to succeed—Sir Walter Monckton (later Viscount Monkton of Brenchley), Sir Cyril (later Viscount) Radcliffe, and Sir William (later Earl) Jowitt [qq.v.]—but none felt able to leave his current position. An offer was then made to Spens. When the outgoing chief justice was informed he bitterly opposed the selection, insisting that under the agreed procedure he ought to have been invited to suggest names first. He objected to Spens on three main grounds: an Indian should have been considered initially; a party political appointee would not be deemed impartial; and, finally, Spens's professional qualifications were inadequate. Gwyer observed testily that no lord chancellor had thought to consider him for a High Court judgeship. The viceroy, the second Marquess of Linlithgow [q.v.], acknowledged that there had been 'a serious error in procedure', but he was not disposed to make this an issue. Spens took up the appointment in June 1943.

His personal relations with successive viceroys were good: Linlithgow described Spens as 'quick, sensible' and Viscount (later Earl) Wavell [q.v.] called him 'sensible and helpful . . . practical'. However, his judicial experiences proved frustrating. The federal provisions of the 1935 Government of India Act had not been implemented and the Court had no explicit role. Between 1937 and 1943 only forty-six cases were decided, and on his arrival Spens reported a 'lack of confidence' in the Court throughout India. He proposed to amend this by enlarging its sphere so as to include appeals from the Indian high courts which had gone up to the Privy Council. Legislation was drafted, but opposition was soon expressed. The newspaper *Dawn* described the Federal Court as 'a queer bottleneck in the political system' and advised Spens to 'curb his missionary zeal'. Wavell concluded that the proposals had aroused an 'adverse verdict by organized opinion in India', and the initiative lapsed. Spens also produced elaborate proposals for the reform of the system of high courts but these too did not find favour: Wavell observed that 'his knowledge of India is inadequate' and nothing further was done.

After the return of peace the political tempo in India became urgent with increasing rivalry between Congress and Muslim League. Communal tensions exploded in 'the Great Calcutta Killing' of August 1946. Wavell asked Spens to head a judicial inquiry into its causes. Spens informed the viceroy privately that 'there was Hindu incitement and a sudden and concerted attack without provocation on the Muslims', but in the deteriorating political situation any agreed report became impossible. The commission of inquiry was adjourned *sine die* and then dissolved. When partition between India and Pakistan was agreed in June 1947 it appeared probable that disputes would arise between the two new states over the division of assets. It was decided to appoint an arbitral tribunal. Once again, Radcliffe was approached and this time agreed to serve: but he was reserved for the more vexing task of determining the boundary between the two new states. Jawaharlal Nehru [q.v.] proposed that the Federal Court should constitute the tribunal but M. A. Jinnah [q.v.] was adamant in opposing this, saying of the Federal Court judges 'the present lot were particularly poor'. As a compromise, Spens was asked to be chairman of the tribunal, with India and Pakistan each nominating their own assessors. The tribunal considered fifty-eight references: its last award was made on 25 April 1948. Thereafter, Spens returned to London and by March 1949 was again in practice in King's Bench Walk.

For the general election of February 1950 he was adopted as candidate for the safe Conservative seat of South Kensington. In a three-cornered contest he obtained 75 per cent of the vote. At subsequent elections in 1951 and 1955, in straight fights with Labour he increased his share of the poll to 79.5 per cent and then to an astonishing 82.5 per cent. He decided not to contest the next general election and in August 1959 he moved to the House of Lords, receiving one of the last hereditary peerages.

Spens was knighted in 1943, appointed KBE in 1948, admitted to the Privy Council in 1953, and made treasurer of the Inner Temple in 1958.

In 1913 Spens married Hilda Mary, daughter of Lieutenant-Colonel Wentworth Grenville Bowyer. They had two sons, the younger of whom was killed in 1942 during World War II, and two daughters. His wife died in 1962 and he married Kathleen Annie Fedden, daughter of Roger Dodds, of Northumberland and Bath. In retirement he lived in Kent. He died at his home, Beacon Cottage, Benenden, Kent, 15 November 1973, and was succeeded in the title by his elder son, William George Michael (born 1914).

[India Office Records; *Burke's Peerage*, 1970; *The Times*, 16 November 1973; private information.]
HUGH TINKER

STABLE, SIR WINTRINGHAM NORTON (1888–1977), judge, was born at Holly Lodge, Wanstead, Essex, 19 March 1888, the youngest of the three children, all sons, of Daniel Wintringham Stable, a solicitor employed by the Prudential Assurance Company, and his wife, Gertrude Mary Law. The eldest son died in infancy and the second son was killed in action in 1914. His mother's family came from Montgomeryshire where they had a house and an estate at Plas Llwyn Owen, Llanbrynmair. This property became vested in his mother and was later occupied by Wintringham Stable and his wife.

He was educated at Winchester and Christ Church, Oxford, where he obtained a second class in modern history in 1910 and of which he later became an honorary student (1960). He was called to the bar by the Middle Temple in 1913. He served during the whole of the war of 1914–18, at first with the Montgomeryshire Yeomanry and later with the 25th battalion of the Royal Welch Fusiliers. He saw service in Egypt, Palestine, and France, and was awarded the MC and mentioned in dispatches. In 1916 he married Lucie Haden (died 1976), widow of Richard Bayley Murphy, a barrister who had died in 1912, and daughter of Francis Ford Freeman, of Tavistock, Devon. They had two sons, both of whom were appointed QCs during their father's lifetime. One became a circuit judge.

On starting practice at the bar after the end of the war Stable entered a set of chambers which specialized in bankruptcy and company insolvency work. By the beginning of the 1930s he was the leading junior doing this kind of work. It requires a sound knowledge of the relevant branches of the law and can provide a comfortable, but not a substantial, income for its practitioners; but it seldom attracts the attention of the general public or leads to high judicial office. Stable was to be an exception. Being a sensitive practitioner he learned to distinguish those who had got into financial trouble through bad luck from those who sought to live at other people's expense. This ability stayed with him all his working life. He had a sensitive nose for fraudulent villains. In 1935 he took silk. Thereafter the area of his legal work broadened. He became chancellor of the diocese of Portsmouth in 1937. In 1938, to the pleasure of the legal profession, who had come to know his likeable personal qualities, he was made a judge of the High Court, with the customary knighthood, and appointed to the King's Bench division. He served as such till 30 September 1968 when he retired. His long and distinguished service as a puisne judge was acknowledged and rewarded by his admission to the Privy Council in 1965. To this Dictionary he contributed the notice of Sir Wilfrid Lewis.

He will long be remembered by the legal profession as a lovable, somewhat eccentric character, wholly lacking in pomposity and showing in his dealings with everyone a deep and compassionate understanding of human virtues and frailties. He was known to all his friends and to the bar as 'Owlie'. This nickname could have been derived from his appearance. He was of medium height and wiry build: he had a long face, high forehead, dark eyes, a sallow complexion, and a beaky nose. He himself said that the name had been given him by a nursemaid when he was a baby because of his propensity to cry.

Towards the end of his judicial career he normally chose to go out on circuit. The bar were always pleased to hear that he was coming. They knew that cases would be dealt with expeditiously and sensibly but with humour and compassion. He liked to pose as a judge who was more concerned with justice than the law. He had little use for legalism; but the justice he administered was nearly always justice according to law. His weakness as a judge came from his virtues. He loathed bureaucratic stupidity, oppression of the weak, and all kinds of cruelty. When he thought he saw any of these (and sometimes he was mistaken) his feelings could get the better of his judgement. It was said of him by his junior brethren on the bench that not to have travelled with him on circuit was to have had an inadequate judicial training.

He was a countryman who put on judicial robes for as short a time as possible to do a job which he knew had to be done but which he did not consider set him apart from other men. Indeed on occasions his country footwear and trousers showed beneath his robes.

He liked all field sports and was a fine horseman who loved hunting. In 1913 he won the bar heavyweight race at the Pegasus Club point to point meeting and the lightweight race in 1938. When the Pegasus Club restarted after World War II a young barrister proposed that he should never be allowed in a Pegasus Club race again because if he won, another world war would probably start the next year. He accepted the proposition but went on riding to hounds. He did so for the last time in 1950 when he was sixty-two.

His end became him. He had a long terminal illness which he bore cheerfully. The esteem in which he was held is evidenced by the fact that in the last months of his life he was visited at Plas Llwyn Owen by many of his friends who travelled long distances to hear for the last time his racy comments on the world and those in it and to hear the short chuckle with which he showed his pleasure and contentment. He died there 23 November 1977.

[Private information; personal knowledge.]

FREDERICK LAWTON

STALLARD, HYLA BRISTOW (1901-1973), ophthalmologist, was born in Leeds 28 April 1901, the eldest of three sons (there were no daughters) of Hyla Holden Stallard, bank manager, and his wife, Eveline Bessie Walsh. He was educated at Sherborne School, entered Gonville and Caius College, Cambridge, in 1919 and graduated BA in 1922. He won the Shuter scholarship to St. Bartholomew's Hospital and qualified B.Chir. in 1925, MB in 1928, MD in 1933, and M.Chir. in 1967. Always known as 'Henry', his student career was distinguished by academic achievement and athletic prowess. In the years 1923-5 he was the Amateur Athletics Association champion for the mile, half mile, and quarter mile and was a member of the world-record-breaking two-mile relay team in Pennsylvania in 1920. He won the mile for Cambridge against Oxford in 1920, 1921, and 1922 and also in the famous match with Harvard, Yale, Princeton, and Cornell in 1921. He represented Great Britain in the 800 and 1,500 metres at the Olympic Games in Paris in 1924, coming fourth in the former and badly injuring his foot, and, heavily bandaged, winning the bronze medal in the latter.

In 1926 he became MRCS (Eng.) and LRCP (Lond.) and was appointed house surgeon to Professor G. E. Gask [q.v.] at St. Bartholomew's (Barts) and was awarded the Bentley prize as the outstanding houseman of the year. Initially, he intended to specialize in orthopaedic surgery but his great manual dexterity and application to detail soon led him to ophthalmic surgery and he became house surgeon and subsequently clinical assistant to Robert Foster Moore at Barts. In 1928 he became FRCS and pathologist to Moorfields Eye Hospital. In 1933 he was appointed ophthalmic surgeon to Moorfields and Barts. His international reputation as an ophthalmic surgeon was soon established but his career in London was interrupted by World War II. As a Territorial reservist he was in uniform in the Royal Army Medical Corps shortly after the outbreak of war and served in the Middle East campaign and with advance units in Normandy; he was appointed MBE (1942) and mentioned in dispatches. He refused promotion beyond the rank of major since this would have divorced him from active ophthalmic surgery. His experience in treating war injuries led to major contributions in traumatic and reconstructive surgery, an interest he retained when he returned to civilian life. During active service, he found time to write the first draft of his *Eye Surgery* which subsequently ran to five editions (1946, 1950, 1958, 1965, and

1972) and was acknowledged as an outstanding contribution to ophthalmology. At the end of the war he returned to Moorfields and Barts and re-established his private practice. He retired from his hospital appointments in 1965 but continued the practice of ophthalmic surgery until a few weeks before his death.

Stallard was one of the great innovative surgeons of the twentieth century and he played a major role in laying the foundations of modern ophthalmic surgery. His meticulous technique and attention to detail, his enquiring and questioning attitude to surgery, and the high standards he set for himself profoundly influenced those who learned from him. Notable among his other achievements was his work on the treatment by irradiation of retinoblastoma, a malignant tumour of children's eyes, which resulted in the saving of both the sight and the life of many patients.

A cultured and artistic man of humility and courtesy, he abhored ostentation; he was spartan in his self-discipline and a model of physical fitness. He devoted himself to the care of his patients and resented time spent on committees or administrative duties.

His academic honours and awards included Hon. LL D (St. Andrews), three Hunterian professorships at the Royal College of Surgeons of England (1954, 1960, and 1967), the Gifford Edmonds prize (1932), the Nettleship medal (1936), the Charles H. May memorial lectureship (1953), the Doyne memorial lectureship (1962), the Middlemore lectureship (1963), and the Craig lectureship (1965). He was president of the section of ophthalmology of the Royal Society of Medicine (1967–9) and president of the Ophthalmological Society of the United Kingdom (1972–3). In 1964 the Order of the Southern Cross was conferred on him by the president of Brazil.

In 1932 he married Gwynneth Constance, daughter of Canon Frederick Gosnell Jameson Page. They had no children. Stallard died at his home in Sussex 21 October 1973.

[Private information; personal knowledge.]

N. S. C. Rice

STARR, GEORGE REGINALD (1904–1980), British agent whose code name was Hilaire, was born 6 April 1904 in Holland Park, London, the elder son (there were no daughters) of Alfred Demarest Starr, bookkeeper, a US subject who became naturalized British, whose own father was bookkeeper–secretary with the Barnum and Bailey Circus, and his wife, Ethel Semina Renshaw. For a spell Alfred Starr worked in France and his sons learned French at the local school. When the family returned to England George Starr pursued his studies at Ardingley School in Sussex and entered the Royal School of Mines, at the Imperial College of Science and Technology in London, to read mining engineering and related subjects. He left before the end of his course and joined Mavor & Coulson Ltd., of Glasgow, manufacturers of mining equipment, who sent him to French and Belgian coal mines.

Starr's first wife was French. After a divorce he married by proxy, in 1935, at the consulate in Barcelona, Pilar Canudas, the daughter of a Spanish casino manager; her mother's maiden name was Ristol. They had a daughter and a son. At the outbreak of World War II he sent his wife and two children to Spain and himself returned to England to join the army. After a time of initial army postings he was attached to Special Operations Executive (F Section); submitted to rigorous training to become a leader of a group; then was sent to France by troopship to Gibraltar, then by a Free Polish felucca, disembarking on the south coast of France near Cassis. After hearing news about events in the south-east, he felt it unwise to proceed there as directed, as it would be too dangerous. In November 1942 he somehow reached the town of Agen on the river Garonne, where he met Albert Rendier, a Belgian who had started to form a small cell. Between them they expanded the cell which first consisted of a few Resistance members and later became the 'Wheelwright' circuit covering many departments in the south-west of France from the Gironde down to the Pyrenees. In 1943 Rendier came to England for training and subsequently returned to another district of France.

Starr's mission was to form cells of resisters, recruiting, on the recommendation of those he trusted, local farmers, doctors, printers, and tradesmen. Much admired by those who joined him, he was a born leader who was able to concentrate on both work and the well-being of his circuit members. Later he was to arm and train his men.

He was fortunate in many ways. For instance, Philippe de Gunzbourg, a well-known Frenchman who had previously worked for some months with Eugène, another British agent in Toulouse, who had been arrested, came and offered his services. Hilaire gladly accepted him, appointing him chief organizer of his own region covering the Dordogne and Lot-et-Garonne, within the Wheelwright circuit. Philibert, as de Gunzbourg was known, was much admired and respected by his men.

In 1943 'Hilaire' met Larribeau, the mayor of a hamlet in the Gers, who made him a deputy mayor; they liked and trusted each other and set to work enlarging and consolidating the circuit, planning the jobs to be done by the resisters. Despite the danger of having a British agent in his home, Larribeau offered Hilaire accommodation but Hilaire preferred living in the countryside. Since tobacco was grown over a wide area in the

Gers, early in 1943 he made himself 'inspector of tobacco', an appointment duly confirmed by the necessary documents (obtained like identity cards) from Larribeau's colleagues. This enabled him to roam far on his bike, meeting people, discussing matters which certainly did not appertain to tobacco, though, as he was a heavy smoker, his nicotine-stained fingers gave credence to his cover story. His group specialized in attacks on communications. The headquarters of the German Army Group G near Toulouse was sometimes cut off from the rest of France and frequently main telephone lines and power stations were put out of action for days at a time.

His contacts with London were through a courier service via Switzerland or Spain where a French 'député', Louis Dubosc, took messages for him. As this was a slow procedure Hilaire asked London for a radio operator. After her arrival communications rapidly improved and arrangements were made for the dropping of supplies on certain chosen grounds, instructions were given for disrupting road and rail traffic or demolishing bridges, and preparations were made for D-Day. When D-Day finally arrived Resistance members came out of hiding, set to work, and, in the south-west, freed their own part of France because Allied troops were not sent to the region. On the day after D-Day Wheelwright and eleven other circuits imposed a seventeen-day delay on the SS armoured division summoned from Toulouse to take part in the Normandy battle. Starr's 'groupe' still speak of him with great admiration, some with awe, saying his eyes willed them to succeed. He was appointed to the DSO, and was awarded the MC, the American medal of freedom, and the French Legion of Honour and croix de guerre.

After Remagen, Starr went to Essen in Germany's Ruhr district, where he directed the reopening of the coal mines. He finally returned to Mavor & Coulson as their managing director in Brussels. He died 2 September 1980 in hospital at Chantilly, France.

[Private information; personal knowledge.]

YVONNE CORMEAU ('ANNETTE')

STEELE, SIR JAMES STUART (1894–1975), adjutant-general, was born 26 October 1894 at Ballycarry, county Antrim, the only son and younger child of Samuel Steele, farmer, of Leefield, Ballycarry, and his wife, Rachael Stuart. He was educated at the Royal Belfast Academical Institution and the Queen's University, Belfast. He did not finish his university course because of the outbreak of World War I, whereupon he was gazetted temporary second lieutenant (26 September 1914) in the Royal Irish Rifles and posted to the 7th battalion.

He went to France in 1915 and served in the trenches at the battles of Messines and the Somme, and at the third battle of Ypres. In June 1916 he was given a regular commission. He was mentioned in dispatches in April 1917 and in August was awarded the MC. On the amalgamation of his battalion he was seconded to the Indian Army and spent the rest of the war in India, being again mentioned in dispatches for gallantry on the North-West Frontier. After the war he rejoined his regiment, now the Royal Ulster Rifles, in Mesopotamia and served with them in Egypt and India.

After attending the Staff College in Quetta in 1926 he returned to Britain in 1928. He was made brevet lieutenant-colonel and in 1937 given accelerated promotion to the command of the 1st battalion the Sherwood Foresters in Jamaica. Under his command they did well during the riots there and then under trying conditions in Palestine.

In July 1939 he was posted to the mobilization branch of the War Office staff; it was he who signed the executive signal for the mobilization of the army. In November he was given command of the 132nd Infantry (Surrey and Kent) brigade, which he took to France and Belgium. In the operations before Dunkirk in May 1940 he was given an immediate appointment to the DSO for his part in the engagement on the river Escaut and the subsequent withdrawal. Back in Britain he was given command of the 59th Staffordshire division in 1941. This was a largely Territorial Army formation, but he set to work to make it truly professional. He identified himself with it so much that to many he 'was' the division. He gained the affection of all ranks and they called him 'Dad'. For a short time in 1942 he commanded II Corps with the rank of acting lieutenant-general.

In October 1942 he was appointed deputy chief of staff Middle East Command. Here he was concerned with the planning and assembly for the battle of Alamein, whilst having to balance the claims of the other active operations in the Middle East. His success in this appointment led to his return to Britain to take up the appointment of director of staff duties at the War Office in 1943. In this key post he considered that he did the hardest work of his life in the army. He became responsible for the mounting of the Normandy landings in 1944 and for dealing with the allocation of resources and the conflicting claims of other major operations in Italy and Burma. He was also chairman of a committee to plan the post-war shape of the army and the demobilization that would be required. He had a special flair as chairman of a committee, always thinking about the subject carefully in advance and then, however different the members' opinions and difficult the solution, ensuring a tight and relevant discussion which steered the members to a wise conclusion.

In 1946 he was appointed commander-in-chief and high commissioner in Austria. As such he was a member of the Allied Quadrilateral Mission in Vienna. His last appointment was in 1947 when he became adjutant-general to the forces. The army was in the process of run-down from a wartime to a peacetime footing, with many acute problems on the personnel side. Steele was in his element and worked well with Labour politicians, especially Emanuel (later Lord) Shinwell, the secretary of state for war, who greatly appreciated his experience, kindness, and wise advice.

After retirement in 1950 Steele became ADC general to the King. He was colonel of the Royal Ulster Rifles from 1945 to 1957, colonel commandant of the Army Educational Corps 1950–9, and honorary colonel of the Queen's University OTC 1954–62. He was also chairman of the Northern Ireland legal aid committee 1958–60. A continuous thread in all his service was his concern for the soldiers and in particular his beloved riflemen with whom he had served in 1914. In 1966 he became chairman of the Northern Ireland government Somme committee and led the pilgrimage to Thiepval on the fiftieth anniversary of the battle. He was also a keen supporter of the Dunkirk Veterans' Association.

The same concern caused him to promote the Army Benevolent Fund which had been set up when he was adjutant-general, and which was to operate for twenty-five years only. When he became its president in 1955 he was at once concerned with its limited life, as he clearly saw a continuing need for a central army fund. He was able to get the Army Board to back an appeal organization throughout Britain and the two schemes provided the income necessary to prevent the run-down of the initial capital and to continue and increase the benefits paid.

Known throughout his regiment as 'Jas' he was known widely in the army as 'Daddy', perhaps because of his habit of addressing senior officers as 'Sonny' or 'Boy', much to the delight of their juniors. He worked hard and demanded high standards. He got results by his wise guidance, kindness, and sense of humour. He was a master of detail and planning—it was typical of him to leave instructions for his funeral. There was to be no gloom, only thanksgiving for his life. He died 24 July 1975, after a short illness and before his mind became inactive, at his home, Churchills, Stourpaine, Blandford. There had not been many wasted minutes in his life.

He married in 1923 at the Citadel in Cairo, Janet Gibson Gordon, of Melbourne, the third daughter of David Ferguson Gordon, farmer, who had been born in county Armagh in 1861. They had two daughters.

Steele was appointed CB (1943), KBE (1946), KCB (1949), and GCB (1950). In 1947 he received an honorary LL D from the Queen's University, Belfast.

[Private information; personal knowledge.]

R. H. Hewetson

STEIN, LEONARD JACQUES (1887–1973), scholar, lawyer, politician, and leading Zionist personality, was born in London 12 December 1887, the only son (he had one sister) of Philip David Stein, a merchant, and his wife, Matilda Esther, daughter of Louis Beaver, jeweller in Manchester. His parents were of German-Jewish origin; the family had come to England in 1821. Stein was educated at St. Paul's School and Balliol College, Oxford, where he had a distinguished career; he was a classical scholar, took a first in *literae humaniores* (1910) and gained the Craven scholarship (1907), the first professing Jew to hold office. In 1910 he was elected president of the Oxford Union. In 1912, specializing in tax law, he was called to the bar by the Inner Temple. He joined the army on the outbreak of World War I in 1914 and rose to the rank of captain; he served in France and Egypt. During the years 1918–20 he was attached to the British military administration in Palestine—a country he first visited in 1908.

On being demobilized from the army Stein took on the key office of political secretary of the World Zionist Organization (1920–9); he became one of Chaim Weizmann's principal lieutenants, and accompanied him and Albert Einstein on a visit to the United States. He was later to write the notice of Weizmann for this Dictionary. He was the author of numerous documents—written with great lucidity—dealing with matters affecting the Jewish national home in Palestine. In 1929 he retired from his position but became honorary counsel to the Jewish Agency (1929–39) and an unofficial adviser to Weizmann, who admired his legal training, drafting abilities, and knowledge of political affairs. In 1937 he gave evidence before the royal commission on Palestine.

Since his student days Stein had been associated with the cause of Liberalism in British politics. He was parliamentary candidate in the Dover area (1922), North Kensington (1923), and West Bermondsey (1929). In spite of his brilliant mind, eloquence, and keen desire to be a member of the House of Commons, he was unsuccessful. In 1930 he joined the Liberal National Party, was vice-chairman of the London organization, and chairman of its international affairs committee. He was also active in the League of Nations Union and a founder-member of the Council of Christians and Jews.

For many years Stein was closely associated with the Anglo-Jewish Association, being its president during the years 1939–49. At times he was out of step with official Zionist leadership because he believed in the progress of a Jewish national home in an undivided Palestine. But he warmly greeted the establishment of the state of Israel which he visited several times. In 1953 he was appointed OBE for political and public services.

He was president of the Jewish Historical Society (1964–5), and a member of the council of the Jewish Colonization Association (1941–8) and the Weizmann Institute Foundation. For thirty-six years he was a director of the *Jewish Chronicle*; to mark his eightieth birthday, the paper founded a lectureship in medieval Hebrew in his name at Oxford.

He was the author of an authoritative study of the origin of the Balfour declaration (1961). He was joint editor of volume i of the *Letters and Papers of Chaim Weizmann* (1968); at his death he had just completed volume vii which dealt with the years 1914–17. His other publications include: an edition of *The Vicar of Wakefield*, 1912; *Zionism*, 1925 (republished in a new edition, 1932); *Syria*, 1926; (with H. H. Marks) *Tax Avoidance* (1936), *The National Defence Contribution* (1937) and *The Excess Profits Tax*, (1940).

An Englishman by upbringing and temperament, Stein was religiously committed to Judaism; while outspoken in public affairs, he was—as a private person—a warm, witty, and compassionate individual, who cared deeply about social issues and the future of the Jewish people. In his own circle of friends he was deeply respected as a man of total integrity and deep loyalties and as a true aristocrat. He went to the bar as a gateway to politics where his ambitions were not fulfilled, but he made an important contribution to research work, scholarship, and many Jewish causes. Physically tall and distinguished looking, he was no sportsman, but loved cricket.

In 1928 he married Sarah, daughter of Herman Benjamin Kitey, orthodox Jew, merchant, and prominent philanthropist, of Paterson, New Jersey, USA; they had two sons. Stein died in London 23 April 1973.

[Bill Williams, *The Making of Manchester Jewry*, 1976; *The Times*, 25 April 1973; *Jewish Chronicle*, 27 April 1973; *Common Ground*, summer 1973; family papers in the Mocatta Library; private information; personal knowledge.] S. I. LEVENBERG

STENTON, DORIS MARY (1894–1971), historian, was born 27 August 1894, the only child of Joseph Parsons, cabinet maker of Reading, Berkshire, and his wife, Amelia Wadhams. From the Abbey School, Reading, she entered in 1912 the University College at Reading where (Sir) Frank Merry Stenton [q.v.] had just been appointed to the first chair of history. In 1916 she took a first class London degree and even before the end of her undergraduate days had been given small pieces of research by her professor. In 1917 a research grant was obtained for her and she was appointed to an assistant lectureship. In 1919 she married Stenton and for the next forty-eight years, as she says in her memoir of him, 'we did everything together'. She became a senior lecturer in 1952 and a reader in 1955 in the department of which she was a member until her retirement.

Before her marriage she went to share the transcription of the charters of the dean and chapter of Lincoln which Canon C. W. Foster had been urged by Stenton to publish. Her sojourn at Timberland, near Lincoln, for this purpose gave her valuable experience in a countryside very different from Berkshire and led also to the starting of her first piece of editing: *The Earliest Lincolnshire Assize Rolls A.D. 1202–1209* (1926).

But while legal records were to absorb half her academic interest, a conversation in 1922 in Lincoln between the Stentons, Canon Foster, and Professor L. V. D. Owen led to the resuscitation of the moribund Pipe Roll Society. Discussions with Sir Henry Maxwell Lyte [q.v.], deputy keeper of the public records, followed and in 1923 she was appointed organizing secretary. From this time, through her remarkable work in securing members, editing, and later securing editors among her pupils, colleagues, and friends, she transformed a nearly extinct body into one of the most important learned societies for medievalists at the present time. The close connection which the society from its foundation in 1883 had had with the Public Record Office, has continued and it was appropriate that the presentation of *A Medieval Miscellany for Doris Mary Stenton* (1962) was made at a gathering of her friends there to celebrate her seventieth birthday.

Her next edition of legal records appeared as the fifty-third volume of the Selden Society in 1934—*Rolls of the Justices in Eyre for Lincolnshire, 1218–19 and Worcestershire 1221*. This was followed in 1937 by *Rolls of the Justices in Eyre for Yorkshire in 3 Henry III* and in 1940 by *Rolls of the Justices in Eyre for Gloucestershire, Warwickshire and Staffordshire (recte Shropshire) 1221, 1222*. Between 1952 and 1968 *Pleas before the King or his Justices 1198–1202* came out in four volumes and when she was asked by the American Philosophical Society of Philadelphia to give the Jayne lectures in 1963 she considered this 'a propitious moment to look at the litigation of the 12th century', a subject of equal interest for American and English scholars. She was then nearing the completion of her Selden Society volumes and was able to survey the preceding century and a half, appropriately concluding the volume with a reprint of her Raleigh lecture to the British

Academy, 1958: 'King John and the Courts of Justice'. In 1950 with Lewis C. Loyd she had edited as a presentation for her husband's seventieth birthday *Sir Christopher Hatton's Book of Seals* and the following year produced *English Society in the Early Middle Ages* (1066–1307) as volume iii of the Pelican History of England. The latter was written most successfully for the general reader bringing alive from her great knowledge of the original sources the ordinary people of the time as well as the notables. Six years later came *The English Woman in History* (1957).

In 1948 she took the degree of Doctor of Letters at Reading; in 1953 she was elected a fellow of the British Academy; in 1958 she received an honorary LL D at Glasgow and in 1968 an honorary D.Litt. at Oxford. She was also elected an honorary fellow of St. Hilda's College that year.

Her splendid editions will serve historians of many generations and her training of research students ensures the continuance of her standards of excellence. Her interests were centred in history to which she and her husband were dedicated and her life until his death in 1967 was singularly happy. As long ago as 1935 (Sir) Maurice Powicke [q.v.] summed up her qualities in a review of one of her volumes: 'She is a true historian as well as a fine editor and palaeographer and her insight like a good lamp burns with a clear and steady flame.' After her husband's death her concern was to record his life and complete the edition of his collected papers as well as the third edition of *Anglo-Saxon England* (1971). This done, she had no interest in life and it was perhaps fortunate for her, with the disability of increasing deafness, that her final illness lasted only one week. She died at Reading 29 December 1971 and was buried in the same grave as her husband at Halloughton, Nottinghamshire, 5 January 1972.

[Pipe Roll Society, new series, vol. xxxvi, *A Medieval Miscellany for Doris Mary Stenton* with photograph and bibliography to 1962; Pipe Roll Society, new series, vol. xli, *Liber Memorialis* with photograph, memoir by C. F. Slade, and bibliography 1963–1976; D. M. Stenton, 'Frank Merry Stenton 1880–1967' in *Proceedings* of the British Academy, vol. liv, 1968; K. Major, 'Doris Mary Stenton 1894–1971' in *Proceedings* of the British Academy vol. lviii, 1972; J. C. Holt, 'Doris Mary Stenton 1894–1971', *American History Review*, vol. lxxix, 1974; personal knowledge.]

KATHLEEN MAJOR

STEPHENS, BUNTY (1924–1978), golfer. [See SMITH, FRANCES.]

STEPHENSON, SIR GILBERT OWEN (1878–1972), vice-admiral, was born in London 13 February 1878, the third of four sons (there were no daughters) of Rowland Macdonald Stephenson, merchant in India and company secretary, and his wife, Henrietta Gilbert Owen-Smith. Nicknamed 'Puggy' by his contemporaries and 'Monkey' by later generations of sailors, Stephenson became a legend in his lifetime and the subject of innumerable anecdotes, thanks to a disconcertingly, though deceptively, fierce manner which was relished even by his victims. After entering the training ship *Britannia* at Dartmouth in 1892, Stephenson served as midshipman in the cruisers *Endymion* and *Forte*. As sub-lieutenant, he was appointed to the first destroyer flotilla and in 1900 to the Mediterranean Fleet flaghip *Ramillies*. A year later, as commanding officer of the torpedo boat TB 90, he took full advantage of his right of direct access to the C-in-C Mediterranean, Admiral Sir John (later Lord) Fisher [q.v.], whose originality greatly influenced the young man. Fisher, reciprocally impressed, gave Stephenson command of the destroyer *Scourge* at the age of twenty-three. After taking the Greenwich torpedo course, and spending a period on the staff of the torpedo school at the *Vernon*, Stephenson was appointed torpedo officer of the cruisers *Monmouth* (1904–6) and *Black Prince* (1906–8). As a lieutenant-commander, he served at the Royal Naval College and as first and torpedo lieutenant of the battleship *Duncan*. In 1912 he was promoted commander.

Stephenson was serving in the intelligence division of the Admiralty at the outbreak of World War I but soon managed to secure a sea appointment. He took part in the Dardanelles operation and subsequently, as commander Crete patrols, carried out a series of exploits with a flotilla of trawlers which earned him acknowledgement as 'uncrowned king' of the island. Appointed acting captain in 1916, he conducted pioneering experiments using hydrophones to detect enemy submarines and set up the 'Otranto barrage' with a force of some 200 ships which restricted the movement of submarines in the Adriatic. This work led to Stephenson's first post-war appointment, as director of the anti-submarine division of the Admiralty. Here he felt frustrated by official resistance to new ideas and in 1921, greatly to his relief, he was appointed in command of the light cruiser *Dauntless*. In 1923 he assumed command of the battleship *Revenge*, with the young lieutenant Lord Louis Mountbatten (later Earl Mountbatten of Burma, q.v.) as one of his divisional officers. Two shore appointments completed Stephenson's first active career in the Royal Navy: as chief of staff to the C-in-C Portsmouth (1924–6), and as commodore of the Royal Naval Barracks in Portsmouth (1926–8), where he introduced community singing and other unprecedented activities to promote good morale. In 1929, with a reputation which was perhaps a touch too unconventional for the highest promotion, he was placed on the retired list with the rank of rear-admiral.

It was not to be expected that so active a character would subside quietly into civilian life. From 1932 to 1935 he was a notable secretary of the Navy League, and in his spare time ran a flourishing boys' club in Hampshire. Here he acquired the nickname 'Monkey Brand', because his bewhiskered face resembled that of the monkey on a well-known brand of household cleanser.

In 1939 Stephenson was recalled to the navy in the rank of commodore Royal Naval Reserve and served briefly as commodore of convoys. In 1940, after a characteristically fearless episode in charge of a section of beach at the Dunkirk evacuation, he set up HMS *Western Isles*, a working-up base for convoy escort ships in Tobermory Bay on the Isle of Mull, a task for which his anti-submarine experience was an ideal qualification; it was to prove his finest achievement.

Realizing that he would have to deal largely with raw recruits to the wartime navy, he established the following order of priorities in his training: first, spirit—the determination to win; second, discipline; third, administration; and, a surprising fourth and last, technique—how to use the weapons and equipment. Stephenson considered skill in this regard would be useless if the essential spirit were lacking. In the course of the next four and a half years 911 different ships were put through a total of 1,132 courses at Western Isles. Stephenson's Tobermory work had a lasting influence on the Royal Navy's methods of training a ship's company.

Stephenson retired for the second time in 1945, with the rank of vice-admiral, and his second retirement was no less active than the first. From 1949 to 1958 he was honorary commodore of the Sea Cadet Corps, an appointment from which he felt it necessary to retire at the age of eighty. He maintained a very close association with the RNR and RNVR, having formed a high opinion of the non-professional sailors who had served under him in two world wars. For many years he was an indispensable guest at the annual Western Approaches reunion dinner and at the battle of the Atlantic service at Liverpool Cathedral. He also played an extremely vigorous part in local affairs in and around Saffron Walden in Essex where he made his home in the later part of his life.

Stephenson made an indelible impression on all who met him. Small, florid of countenance, fiercely energetic, interested in everything to the point of inquisition, he was a challenging man who expected others to accept his own peremptory standards of moral behaviour. Many of his well-known conversational ploys were the product of an extremely mischievous sense of humour. Any victim pressed into a confession who was unwise enough to begin with the words: 'To tell the truth . . .' could expect the roared reply: 'To tell the *truth*? Don't you *always* tell the truth?' Another favourite trick was to buttonhole some highly respected figure, a bishop perhaps, in a roomful of people, and bellow at him: 'There you are, you rogue . . . Still married to the *same wife*?' The most frequently told of many anecdotes of the Tobermory days concerns the commodore's visit to a certain ship whose sleepy quartermaster at the head of the gangway seemed to need a sharp awakening to the realities of war. Flinging his gold-braided cap on the deck, Stephenson shouted 'That's an unexploded enemy bomb! What are you going to do about it, eh?' After a moment's thought, the sailor kicked the cap over the side of the ship. 'Well done, my boy', said the commodore, apparently full of approval. 'Now . . . [change of tone] that's a man overboard! What are you going to do about *that*, eh?' And the poor lad was forced to dive over the side fully clothed to retrieve the cap. Some were indeed nonplussed by such behaviour, but most enjoyed—at least after the event—the eccentricities which guaranteed Stephenson a lasting place among the great characters of the Royal Navy. Behind the alarming façade was a gentleman of infinite courtesy with a Socratic passion for truth. He was appointed CMG (1919), CB (1930), and KBE (1943). He also held several foreign decorations.

Stephenson attached great importance to his happy family life. In 1903 he married Helen Chesney (died 1954), daughter of Colonel Robert Frederic Williamson, CB, of the Royal Welch Fusiliers. They had a daughter and two sons. Sephenson died 27 May 1972 at Saffron Walden.

[Richard Baker, *The Terror of Tobermory*, 1972; personal knowledge.] RICHARD BAKER

STERNBERG, RUDY, BARON PLURENDEN (1917–1978), business man, farmer, and livestock breeder, was born at Thorn, Austria, 17 April 1917, the youngest of four sons (there were no daughters) of George Sternberg, miller and corn merchant, and his wife, Paula Michel. Sternberg was educated at Johanns Gymnasium in Germany and came to England in 1937 to study chemical engineering at London University. He remained when war broke out as a refugee from Hitler's persecution of the Jews in which many of his family suffered. His early days in Britain were inevitably shrouded in obscurity but he joined the army in 1939 as a non-combatant because of his foreign status and became a naturalized British subject in 1945. He was demobilized on health grounds in 1943 and began his business life as a messenger delivering goods.

It was a time of acute material shortages and he saw a market for old buttons which he purchased and dyed for the fashion trade, using his knowledge of chemical processes. In 1948 he bought a disused mill at Stalybridge, Lancashire, to manufacture raw materials for the rapidly developing plastics industry and within a decade owned the fourth largest petrochemical company in Europe, the Sterling Group, and an international trading company, Dominion Exports Limited.

By 1950 he was wealthy enough to be able to buy a farm and develop an interest in livestock breeding. His rapid rise to fortune reflected the entrepreneurial skills and energy characteristic of so many central European immigrants in Britain. But his early release from the army had enabled him to start while his contemporaries were still under arms.

He concentrated on developing trade with the east European communist bloc countries, particularly East Germany whose oppressive regime under Ulbricht was not officially recognized by the western nations. There was nothing illegal in such trade but at a time of East–West tension it was inevitably charged with politics. Sternberg obtained a contract for the export of potash from East Germany to Britain which gave him partial control over exports from Britain. He believed the trade should be expanded in spite of the political difficulties and appointed two Conservative MPs as directors of his company to campaign for it. They formed an all-party committee of MPs and peers who visited the Leipzig Trade Fair in 1961.

This was the regime's propaganda show-place and the committee was effusively welcomed by Ulbricht as an official parliamentary delegation with Sternberg as its leader. It was a role he clearly relished and he drove around Leipzig in a Rolls-Royce flying the Union Jack. Whether or not he intended it, the delegation's presence provided a valuable propaganda coup for a regime craving international recognition and acutely embarrassed the British government.

The well-founded suspicion that some of the MPs were being paid commission on orders Sternberg obtained angered legitimate traders and also the House of Commons where they were accused of exploiting their position as MPs for personal gain.

Sternberg thus became the centre of a political storm as, allegedly, a rich and mysterious manipulator while his close associations with leaders of the communist countries inevitably led to suspicions that he had communist sympathies. He emphatically denied this, insisting that his interests were purely commercial, and he appeared to observers at the Leipzig Fair genuinely bewildered by the controversy his activities created; a man probably more politically naïve than sinister.

Like many Jewish immigrants at that time, Sternberg found himself in sympathy more with the Labour Party than the Conservative which, although the business party, seemed less welcoming to the newcomers. He got to know Harold Wilson (later Lord Wilson of Rievaulx) before he became prime minister and became one of the group of wealthy self-made entrepreneurs, frequently *emigrés*, whose qualities particularly appealed to Wilson but whose business careers were often controversial.

Sternberg was among a group of wealthy business men who financed Wilson's political office as leader of the opposition from 1970 to 1974 and whose existence was bitterly criticized by Labour MPs when it became known, particularly as Wilson bestowed honours on some of them including Sternberg who received a life peerage in 1975.

He had been knighted in 1970, also on Wilson's recommendation, for his work as president of the British Agricultural Export Council. He became a freeman of the City of London in 1960 and liveryman of the Worshipful Company of Farmers in 1963.

He married in 1951 Dorothée Monica, daughter of Major Robert Bateman Prust, OBE, of Vancouver. They had two daughters. Sternberg collapsed and died at Tenerife airport 5 January 1978 while returning from holiday.

[Personal knowledge.] Ian Waller

STOCKS, MARY DANVERS, Baroness Stocks (1891–1975), principal of Westfield College and broadcaster, was born in Kensington 25 July 1891, the daughter of Roland Danvers Brinton MD, MRCP, of Queen's Gate Terrace, and his wife, Helen Constance Rendel. She was educated at St. Paul's School and the London School of Economics, where she obtained a B.Sc. Econ. She was an assistant lecturer at LSE from 1916 to 1919. She also became a lecturer in economics at King's College for Women from 1918 to 1919. Before she completed her degree course at the London School of Economics she became engaged to John Leofric Stocks [q.v.], then fellow and tutor at St. John's College, Oxford. They married on 14 December 1913. John Stocks was the sixth son of the Revd Canon John Edward Stocks. They had one son and two daughters.

In 1924 she and her husband left Oxford on his election to the chair of philosophy in Manchester University, and from then until 1937 she was an extension lecturer and extra-mural tutor in the university. During this time she was a magistrate for the city and as a partner with her husband she found great opportunities in the development of the work of the University Settlement and of the Wilbraham community associations. It was for members of these associations that she wrote a number of plays which were performed by them.

In 1936 her husband was appointed vice-chancellor of Liverpool University, and for her this move meant a new role. However, her husband died suddenly in 1937 and from 1938 to 1939 she was the general secretary of the London Council of Social Service. In 1939 she was appointed principal of Westfield College, London, where she stayed until her retirement in 1951.

Professor Rosalind Hill, writing in *The Times* on 15 July 1975, remembers Mary Stocks's influence upon her colleagues and her students during her years as principal of Westfield and in particular during the difficult war years when the college was uprooted from London: 'Gallant, gay and extremely witty, she carried us through our troubles by the sheer force of her infectious courage. In the cold and blacked-out chapel, before our exiguous breakfast, she read to us from the Bible with a depth of knowledge and an appropriateness of choice which I have never heard equalled by a professional theologian .... She was a delight to us. She was also an inspiration. She made it impossible for the community to sink into that sorry self-regard which is the fate of so many institutions in difficult times. "Don't be a volcanic mole-hill" she once warned us. She had an unusual and most perceptive understanding of her students, and helped them far more than anyone knew. Always she stood clearly for the right as she saw it, brave, uncomprising and completely sincere.' During her time as principal of Westfield, the college gained a new public recognition by her fame, although within the university she was criticized for views tenaciously held and within the college for somewhat unorthodox conceptions of her office.

Mary Stocks was from time to time a member of various government committees including, in particular, the Unemployment Insurance Statutory Committee. She was a strong advocate of euthanasia. It was her participation in radio programmes, in particular 'Any Questions' and 'Petticoat Line', that made Mary Stocks a public figure. Those who shared panels and platforms with her were left in no doubt as to her keenness of mind, and the muscular language in which she expressed that keenness, and if they were daunted by her ability, they, like her radio audiences, were warmed by the genuine humanity of her approach to the variety of questions to which she contributed.

She maintained her lively interest in the Workers' Educational Association, with which she had worked closely in Manchester, and was for several years its deputy president. Her *The Workers' Educational Association, the First Fifty Years* was published in 1953. Her publications showed her preoccupation with social and educational questions, as exemplified in her lives of *Eleanor Rathbone* (1949) and *Ernest Simon of Manchester* (1963), and in 1960 her *A Hundred Years of District Nursing*. Her autobiography *My Commonplace Book* was published in 1970 and was followed by *Still More Commonplace* in 1973. To this Dictionary she contributed the notices of Eleanor Rathbone, Lord Simon of Wythenshawe, and the Duchess of Atholl.

Her public services were recognized by honorary degrees conferred upon her, among which were an LL D from Manchester (1955) and a Litt.D. from Liverpool (1956). She was appointed a member of both the Observer and Cassel Trusts. Raised to the peerage in 1966, she brought to the House of Lords the same qualities of robust common sense and trenchant argument which had characterized her activities in so many spheres. Accepting the Labour whip she displayed her customary independence of spirit which latterly led her to the cross benches but her contributions were invariably received with respect from all sides of the House. Mary Stocks died in London 6 July 1975.

[Mary Stocks, *My Commonplace Book*, 1970, and *Still More Commonplace*, 1973; personal knowledge.] DONALD SOPER

STOKES, ADRIAN DURHAM (1902–1972), writer and painter, was born at 18 Radnor Place, Bayswater, London, 27 October 1902, the third son and youngest of the three children of Durham Stokes, a business man of independent views, and his wife, (Alice) Ethel, daughter of Philip Leon and his wife, Alice Montefiore. In *Inside Out* (1947) he described a conventional and less than happy childhood through the fantasies with which the child invested it. He was educated at Rugby School and at Magdalen College, Oxford, where in 1923 he obtained a second class in philosophy, politics, and economics. On his return from a visit to India he produced two works of general reflections on culture, which he later dismissed as juvenilia: *The Thread of Ariadne* (1925) and *Sunrise in the West* (1927).

Meanwhile what was to prove one of the two momentous events in his life had occurred in the winter of 1921–2: his first visit to Italy. Over the next ten years he returned many times, once staying several months in Venice. Though mostly alone he made two important friendships: in 1924 with (Sir) Osbert Sitwell [q.v.]—the Sitwells, he said, were 'the first to open my eyes'—and in autumn 1926, on the tennis-court at Rapallo, with Ezra Pound. Stokes and Pound shared a passion for the then neglected Tempio

Malatestiano Rimini, and Pound commended the young writer to his friend T. S. Eliot [q.v.] at Faber & Faber.

The specific visual value which drew Stokes so powerfully to Italy was something he found in some great works of art—in addition to the Tempio, the Palazzo Ducale Urbino, certain sculpture of Verocchio and Donatello but not all, and Venice in its entirety. But he also found it in old farm-buildings in Tuscany and the Veneto, and in the man-made landscape of olive terraces and vineyards. In *The Quattro Cento* (1932) he articulated this value into several aspects—in his words, the 'love of stone' and 'stone-blossom', the cultivation of 'mass-effect' or visual immediacy, the 'love of perspective' which employs perspective to unify the surface rather than just to represent depth, and the pursuit of the 'emblematic'—and he then used this value to define one tradition of art. He named this tradition '*the Quattro Cento*' or the 'carving' tradition, though in *Colour and Form* (1937) he demonstrated that it is restricted neither to a single period nor to a single art. Piero, Breughel, Giorgione, Cézanne were also carvers. The carving tradition is contrasted—at this stage, wholly to its advantage—with the modelling tradition, which exhibits traits which are disparate—flourish, fragmentation, finish—but which have the common aim of absorbing the spectator into the work. Carving and modelling are complex concepts but Stokes applied them to deep effect.

The other momentous event in Stokes's life was his psychoanalysis with Melanie Klein [q.v.], which began in January 1930 and with an interruption in 1936 lasted for seven years: it was briefly resumed in 1946–7. One immediate consequence was that the Italian journeys were curtailed, and Stokes who began painting in the mid 1930s—for the avowed reason that no one else seemed ready to paint the kind of painting he thought should be painted—became friendly with a group of artists to whom carving values seemed important: (Dame) Barbara Hepworth [q.v.], Ben Nicholson, Henry Moore, and the Lanyons. In the late 1930s he painted from life in the studio organized by (Sir) William Coldstream, later known as the Euston Road school.

Another consequence of analysis was an enrichment of the aesthetic theory. However, this happened only after the war, which Stokes spent in Cornwall, running Little Park Owles, Carbis Bay, as a market garden. Central to Melanie Klein's theory was the identification of two 'positions' or phases of infantile life, crucial for later psycho-sexual development. These were the (earlier) paranoid-schizoid position, in which the infant's world is peopled with part-objects, which inspire alternately fear and delusional triumph, and the (later) manic-depressive position, when the infant, now aware of whole objects, experiences towards them love, gratitude, and the yearning to make reparation. Stokes's insight was to associate these two persisting attitudes with, respectively, the modelling and the carving traditions, to recognize that they do not come separately, and so to provide an overall view of visual art as polarized between the two ideals of envelopment and free-standing self-sufficiency. The modelling tradition, to which Stokes assigned Michelangelo and J. M. Turner [q.v.], had now come into its own. In six thin volumes—*Michelangelo* (1955), *Greek Culture and the Ego* (1958), *Three Essays on the Painting of our Time* (1961), *Painting and the Inner World* (1963), *The Invitation in Art* (1965), and *Reflections on the Nude* (1967)—Stokes coaxed these very difficult ideas into a prose that was abstruse, vivid, and highly personal. No book sold more than 500 copies, but Stokes had a significant following. On the completion of this series Stokes wrote poetry—collected posthumously as *With All the Views* (1981)—and occasional lectures.

Stokes painted right up to his death. His 'fuzzy' paintings (as he called them) of bottles, landscapes, and occasionally nudes aimed at stillness, they rejected gesture, and they not infrequently achieved a modest and elegiac perfection. From 1960 to 1967 he served as a trustee of the Tate Gallery and displayed unsparing devotion to the work. His artistic taste was catholic, excluding only surrealism. On his retirement he declined a knighthood.

As a young man Stokes was remarkably beautiful with a crest of fair to reddish hair, an aquiline nose, and dark blue eyes, and his looks won him admirers of both sexes, to the intensification of his natural shyness. In later life, his delicate skin now criss-crossed with lines, his hair still thick, he remained immediately and deeply impressive. Never gregarious, he could be boyishly high-spirited with friends, and he laughed till he cried. A meeting would often be followed up next day by a letter, expressing gratitude or continuing the conversation.

In July 1938 Stokes married Margaret Nairne Mellis, a young painter, the elder daughter of the Revd David Barclay Mellis, of Edinburgh, a minister of the Church of Scotland. A son Telfer was born in 1940. The marriage broke up in 1947, and in Switzerland in the same year Stokes married Ann Mellis, Margaret's sister. A son Philip was born in 1948 and a daughter Ariadne in 1951. The family returned to England in 1950, lived first in Berkshire, then at Hurtwood, Surrey, and in 1956 moved to 20 Church Row, Hampstead, London. Stokes had a serious operation in 1971. He gave a farewell party to his friends and died at home 15 December 1972.

[Private information; personal knowledge.]

RICHARD WOLLHEIM

STOKOWSKI, LEOPOLD ANTHONY (1882–1977), orchestral conductor, was born 18 April 1882, in London, the eldest child (a sister was born in 1884 and a brother in 1890) of Kopernik Joseph Boleslaw Stokowski, cabinet maker, of London, and his wife, Annie Marion Moore, of Irish parentage. He was a student at the Royal College of Music, London, first from January 1896 to December 1899, specializing in piano- and organ-playing for which his teacher was (Sir) H. Walford Davies [q.v.], and also studying composition with (Sir) C. V. Stanford [q.v.]; he later re-entered the college in November 1903, finishing in July 1904. He also made several visits to France and Germany. He became Bachelor of Music of Oxford University in 1903, taking his degree through Queen's College, a procedure followed by many RCM students at about this time; the manuscript of his exercise for the degree, 'The Redeemer', for mezzo-soprano soloist, chorus, and string orchestra, is preserved in the Bodleian Library. He became an American citizen in 1915.

Stokowski's professional career began with various posts as organist and choirmaster. From 1900 to 1901 he was at St. Mary's, Charing Cross Road, and was appointed to St. James's, Piccadilly, in March 1902. In 1905, after an approach by the rector of St. Bartholomew's, New York, he accepted the organist's appointment at this wealthy and fashionable church, holding the post for three years. Here he was introduced to Olga Samaroff (born Lucie Hickenlooper, from San Antonio, Texas), a concert pianist who had studied in Paris and Berlin, and it was she who engineered his first appointment as a conductor, of the Cincinnati Symphony Orchestra, which he held from 1909 to 1912. Immediately on resigning from the Cincinnati conductorship, Stokowski was appointed conductor of the Philadelphia Orchestra, to begin at the start of the 1913–14 season. In fact he took over at once, from the autumn of 1912, remaining with the orchestra until 1936. From then on, Stokowski seldom had a regular orchestra for more than a short time, but embraced more varied musical activity. From 1937 he conducted music for Hollywood films (among them *One Hundred Men and a Girl*, 1937, and Walt Disney's *Fantasia*, 1940), appearing in some of them himself. In 1940 he formed the All-American Youth Orchestra (later the All-American Orchestra, 1941) and was co-conductor, with Toscanini, of the NBC Orchestra from 1941 to 1944. He was with the New York City Symphony Orchestra (1944–5), and was musical director of the Hollywood Bowl (1945–6), the New York Philharmonic (1947–50), the Houston Symphony Orchestra (1955–60), and the American Symphony Orchestra (1962–72).

Stokowski was possibly the greatest celebrity among twentieth-century conductors, a magician of the orchestra although a controversial interpreter. His first appointment, in Cincinnati, was achieved despite an almost complete lack of previous conducting experience, but he immediately showed such ability as an orchestral trainer combined with a showman's flair that the standard of the orchestra rose dramatically in a very short time. A comparable transformation occurred in Philadelphia and by 1916, with the performances of Mahler's *Symphony of a Thousand* in Philadelphia and New York, both orchestra and conductor were considered unequalled in the USA. Stokowski was indebted to Edward Bok, publisher and member of the Philadelphia Orchestra board, for the provision of adequate rehearsal facilities and assistance in the endowment of the orchestra. In 1924 Mrs Mary Curtis Bok formed the Curtis Institute in Philadelphia for the training of musicians; Stokowski became the teaching conductor for the first three years, continuing his direct association with the school until 1930. Many of the Philadelphia Orchestra members were active as teachers in the school, which in turn provided a very high proportion of recruits for the orchestra. Stokowski throughout his life showed great enthusiasm for performing new works, and is said to have given about two thousand first performances, most of the works being by American composers. His policies frequently brought him into conflict with the orchestra board and with concert managers, his last years in Philadelphia being particularly acrimonious in this respect.

Noteworthy among his American premières were: several works of Schönberg, including *Pelléas et Mélisande* and *Five Pieces for Orchestra*, during the 1920s; Stravinsky's *Les Noces* (at the Metropolitan Opera, 1929); Stravinsky's *Le Sacre du Printemps* (the first American production of the ballet, also at the Metropolitan Opera, 1929–30 season); Mussorgsky's *Boris Godunov*, in the original version (1929–30 season); Berg's *Wozzeck* (March 1931), which is said to have involved eighty-eight preliminary rehearsals and sixty on-stage rehearsals, all directed by Stokowski; and Charles Ives's Symphony no. 4 (a first performance in the American Symphony Orchestra's 1965–6 season). Several works by Rachmaninov were first performed during the Philadelphia years, among them the Symphony no. 3 and, with the composer as soloist, Piano Concerto no. 4 and *Rhapsody on a Theme of Paganini*.

Although Stokowski made some notable contributions to opera and ballet performances, his unyielding and overbearing nature made collaboration with choreographers and producers practically impossible, and he remained primarily a concert conductor, albeit a highly spectacular one. He was tall, striking looking, in his later years sporting a mane of white hair and, for most of his career, dispensed with a baton, carving out elegant designs of the greatest clarity with his arms and hands. He was keenly interested in recording and left a large legacy of records made over a period of more than fifty years; several of these date from the 1970s when he was living in England and recorded with a specially chosen orchestra in London. His preferred composers are, not surprisingly, late Romantic and Slavonic, while classical composers such as Haydn and Mozart appear scarcely at all, and Bach exclusively in his symphonic transcriptions. The unconventional orchestral layouts which he devised were aimed at achieving the most effective balance in particular acoustical conditions; the tendency was to place the strings on the left and wind instruments on the right, with sometimes a surrounding arc of double basses at the rear.

He was tireless in striving to enable living composers to have their works performed, as he was to encourage young people to play in orchestras and to listen to concerts. The founding of the Curtis Institute enabled him to fill many of the places in the Philadelphia Orchestra with American-born and -trained musicians, in contrast to the state prevailing previously, where a high proportion of players in American orchestras came from Europe. His view was basically one of not discriminating against the American, and he extended it over the contentious areas of sex and race, refusing to countenance discrimination against women and negroes, if they were the best candidates for the positions to be filled. He did not conduct in England between 1912 and 1951, but thereafter was a regular summer visitor, and in 1972 at the age of ninety performed the same programme (with the London Symphony Orchestra) which he had given sixty years earlier.

Stokowski was married three times: first, to Olga Samaroff, on 24 April 1911; there was one daughter, born in 1921. The marriage was dissolved in 1923 and he married, secondly, in 1926, Evangeline Brewster Johnson, daughter of the chemist who established the pharmaceutical company. There were two daughters of this marriage, which was dissolved in 1937. Thirdly, he married Gloria Vanderbilt di Cicco, in April 1945. There were two sons of this marriage, which was dissolved in 1955. Stokowski died 13 September 1977 at his home in Nether Wallop, Hampshire, England.

He was elected FRCM and an honorary fellow of Queen's College, Oxford (1951), and was awarded a D.Mus. by the University of Pennsylvania and LL D by the University of California.

[H. C. Shonberg, *The Great Conductors*, 1967; H. Kupferberg, *Those Fabulous Philadelphians*, 1969; D. Wooldridge, *Conductor's World*, 1970; E. Johnson (ed.), *Stokowski: Essays in Analysis of his Art*, 1973; A. Chasins, *Leopold Stokowski: a Profile*, 1979; H. Stoddard, *Symphony Conductors of the USA*, 1957; *New Grove Dictionary of Music and Musicians* (article on Stokowski), 1980; personal knowledge.]

JAMES DALTON

STONE, (ALAN) REYNOLDS (1909–1979), engraver, letter cutter, and painter, was born at Eton College, Windsor, 13 March 1909, the eldest of the three children and only son of Edward Wellington Stone, Eton housemaster, and his wife, Laura Neville, daughter of J. E. Bovill, corn merchant, of Dorking. Laura Stone had studied drawing under Henry Tonks [q.v.]. Edward Wellington Stone's sister married (Sir) Compton Mackenzie [q.v.]. Stone was educated at Eton and Magdalene College, Cambridge, where he read history, in which he obtained second classes (second division) in both parts i and ii of the historical tripos (1929 and 1930).

He began work at the Cambridge University Press under a scheme inaugurated by Walter Lewis, the university printer, for the training of graduate apprentices. It was here that he began his first experiments as an engraver, first on pieces of type-metal but later on boxwood. Two great influences of this period were F. G. Nobbs, the press overseer, and the work of Stanley Morison [q.v.], at that time typographical adviser to the Cambridge University Press. Morison was in part responsible for the revival of interest in classical letter forms and had edited three volumes of *Fleuron*, a typographical periodical, which Stone read at Cambridge. In 1932 he spent a very formative fortnight at Pigotts, the home and workplace of A. Eric R. Gill [q.v.], the master craftsman and engraver, who had such a profound effect on modern typography and design. Stone found the atmosphere of worship and work at Eric Gill's too powerful; he felt a need to make his own way.

In 1932 he moved to Taunton to work for the printers Barnicott & Pearce. It was there that he produced some of his first engraved designs including his first book-plate for Armide Oppé. Then in 1934 he left to pursue his own career as a free-lance engraver and designer. This was the year in which he exhibited book-plates at the *Sunday Times* Book Exhibition and first attracted critical attention.

Until World War II he worked on numerous book-plate designs, armorial devices, and illustrations. Notable books he illustrated include *The Shakespeare Anthology* (Nonesuch Press, 1935), *The Praise and Happinesse of the Countrie*

Life (Gregynog Press, 1938), and *The Confessions of J. J. Rousseau* (Nonesuch Press, 1938).

In 1938 he married Janet, daughter of Edward Sydney Woods, bishop of Lichfield, and they moved to Bracken Cottage, Bucklebury, Berkshire. In 1939 he taught himself to cut letters in stone; his mastery of this form led to various important commissions such as the memorials to Alfred Duff Cooper, Viscount Norwich (1955), Sir Winston Churchill (Westminster Abbey, 1965), T. S. Eliot (Westminster Abbey, 1966), and Lord Britten (Aldeburgh, 1977) [qq.v.].

During the war he worked with the RAF, in photo interpretation, but still produced designs. The post-war period saw some of his finest work including illustrations for Adrian Bell's *The Open Air* (1936 and 1949) and designs for *Breviarium Romanum* (1946), commissioned by Stanley Morison. He also engraved devices for *The Times* including the famous mast-head, 1951.

He moved with his family to Dorset in 1953 to the Old Rectory, Litton Cheney, where he was to live for the rest of his life. In 1955 he designed the coat of arms for HMSO and in 1963–4 the five and ten pound notes for the Bank of England. To this Dictionary he contributed the notice of Gwendolen Raverat.

He always painted, often using his water-colours as starting points for engravings. The wilderness of his large wooded garden with its stream and ponds was a constant source of inspiration. He had one-man exhibitions at the Aldeburgh Festival (1958), the Arts Council (1959), Agnews (1965 and 1969), and the New Grafton Gallery (1972, 1975, and 1978). Stylistically he is a descendant of Thomas Bewick (1753–1828, q.v.), and in lettering of the Renaissance calligraphic masters. He achieved near perfection with his engraved alphabets and roman capitals on wood and stone. In 1953 he was appointed CBE, in 1956 RDI, and in 1964 FRSA.

Stone was a man of quiet charm and humour, whose friendship was greatly valued. He died 23 June 1979 in Dorchester, Dorset, being survived by his wife and four children: Edward, painter; Humphrey, typographer; Phillida, illustrator and writer of children's books; and Emma, art historian and researcher.

[*Reynolds Stone—Early Development as an Engraver*, Cambridge University Press Christmas book, 1947; Myfanwy Piper, *Reynolds Stone*, 1951; *Reynolds Stone Engravings*, with an appreciation by Kenneth Clark and an autobiographical introduction, 1977; personal knowledge.]

DAVID WOLFERS

STOPFORD, ROBERT WRIGHT (1901–1976), bishop of London, was born 20 February 1901, at Garston, Liverpool, the only son of John William Stopford, timber merchant, and his wife, Mary Ethel, daughter of Robert Wright, a schoolmaster. Educated at Garston Church of England School and Liverpool College, he won a scholarship to Hertford College, Oxford, and gained first classes in classical honour moderations (1922) and modern history (1924). After a year as a history master at Highgate School, in 1925 he became senior history master at Oundle, then a housemaster and assistant chaplain (having been ordained in 1932, after preparation at Cuddesdon Theological College). Judged an inspiring teacher, he was also versatile in school dramatics.

From 1935 to 1941, as principal of Trinity College, Kandy, Stopford's quiet but firm leadership, administrative efficiency, and ready perception of educational needs raised standards, widened the curriculum, and reformed the organization. He became prominent in Ceylon through the commission on education and in the councils of the church. In 1941 he moved to the principalship of Achimota College in the Gold Coast (founded 1927). With characteristic vigour he applied principles proven in Ceylon—rooting education in the culture and languages of the country and introducing practical and scientific courses, notably in agriculture and crafts. His views were influential in the important report of the education committee (1937–41), where he promoted wider extension of educational opportunity and improved teacher training, and prepared the way for a university college. ('Stopfordization' signified the removal of the lazy.)

He resigned for health reasons and, after a short time as rector of Chipping Barnet in 1946, he was asked in 1947 by Archbishop G. F. Fisher (later Lord Fisher of Lambeth, q.v.) to be moderator of the Church Training Colleges. In 1952 he added the general secretaryship of the National Society (for Religious Education) and the schools council of the church assembly. The colleges were expanding and the schools reorganizing following the 1944 Education Act, and Stopford provided the skills of the negotiator, the professionalism and imagination of the good educator, and the mastery of the able administrator. He was deeply involved with Christian educational bodies, and was also from 1945 to 1955 a valued member of the advisory committee for education in the colonies, and chairman of its Africa sub-committee.

Already chaplain to the Queen (1952–5) and honorary canon of Canterbury (1951–6), Stopford was nominated suffragan bishop of Fulham in 1955, and applied his customary vigour to the jurisdiction of north and central Europe, undertaking extensive journeys and encouraging appropriate training for continental chaplains, while perceiving the need for a diocese of Europe (which eventually emerged). As bishop of Peterborough from 1956 to 1961 he again proved his administrative efficiency, realistically assessed diocesan church life, and initiated pastoral provision for the growth areas. In 1958 he was invited by Archbishop Fisher to be episcopal secretary of the Lambeth conference, which required hard concentration, diplomatic tact, a cool temper, and dexterity in drafting. His highly successful work was a useful background to his chairmanship of the Lambeth steering committee in 1968.

Translated to London in 1961, he fulfilled his multifarious responsibilities with customary zest. He delegated episcopal functions to four suffragans, retaining direct responsibility for the City and Westminster, and reorganized area and deanery boundaries to match more closely the London boroughs. He secured acceptance of the view that his successor should abandon Fulham for a house in Westminster. He was consulted by the Crown on senior ecclesiastical appointments, and was the trusted adviser of Archbishop A. M. Ramsey (later Lord Ramsey of Canterbury). As chairman of the Church of England Board of Education (1958–73) he was the church's spokesman and principal negotiator on all educational matters, and, through his ecumenical relationships, spoke for all the churches. In the Lords his speeches also touched on other subjects, Africa, race relations, and London issues among them. He had always tried to work ecumenically, and was disappointed, as co-chairman with Dr Harold Roberts of the Anglican–Methodist unity commission (1965–8), when the Church of England rejected the scheme, though he refrained from vigorous advocacy of its acceptance. One of his major interests was the ethics of defence and disarmament, a subject on which he arranged seminars.

He retired in 1973 and in 1974 was appointed by Archbishop Ramsey vicar-general in Jerusalem and the Middle East (Stopford had been chairman of the Jerusalem and East Mission), and by January 1976 he had successfully devised a scheme for the reorganization of the dioceses and the transfer of the archbishop's authority to a central synod, a formidable task given the racial and ecclesiastical complications. He returned to accept from Bermuda (with Archbishop Donald Coggan's support) an invitation to be bishop there, and to create a constitution for the recently disestablished church. Within a few months he fell ill and returned to England.

Stopford was appointed CBE in 1949 and KCVO in 1973. He was sworn of the Privy Council in 1961 and was a freeman of the City of London (1965) and honorary fellow of the Grocers' Company. Among his academic distinctions, English and American, were DCL Durham (1951), DD Lambeth (1957), and DD London (1965), an honorary fellowship of Hertford College (1956) (he was president of the Hertford Society), and a fellowship of King's College, London. He took special pleasure in being chairman in 1972 of the D'Oyly Carte Trust. He was an inveterate traveller, and frequently visited the USA. He had an inexhaustible capacity for work and was an indefatigable correspondent. He avoided controversy, dextrously handled debate, and characteristically achieved agreement by private consultation. Witty in personal converse and after-dinner speeches, he was less interesting in his addresses and sermons: however assiduously prepared, their presentation often lacked colour. That he was a good listener with shrewd judgement contributed to his being an effective pastoral counsellor. A central churchman, he was much more widely read in theology than was often supposed. He had many friends, if few intimates, for his bonhomie could not entirely conceal some shyness. That he was much favoured by Archbishop Fisher and deeply trusted by Archbishop Ramsey was a testimony to his abilities and stature: he was a bishop of wide but discreet influence.

In 1935 he married Winifred Sophia, a teacher in Ceylon, the daughter of William Morton, governor of Derry gaol. She was drowned in 1942 when their ship was torpedoed. They had two sons. In 1945 he married, secondly, Kathleen Mary (died 1973), daughter of Harold Holt, a brass founder, of Bury. They had one daughter. He died in the Royal Berkshire Hospital 13 August 1976.

There are portraits by Edward Halliday in Liverpool College and London House.

[Stopford papers; proceedings of the church assembly and general synod; *Hansard*; National Society and Church of England Board of Education minutes; Kingsley Williams, *Achimota*, 1962; ms. autobiography; private information; personal knowledge.]

ROBERT T. HOLTBY

STOW HILL, BARON (1902–1979), politician and lawyer. [See SOSKICE, FRANK.]

STRACHEY, CHRISTOPHER (1916–1975), professor of computer science, was born 16 November 1916 at Hampstead, London, the only son and the youngest of the three children of Oliver Strachey CBE, cryptographer, of London, and his second wife, Rachel ('Ray') Conn, the daughter of B. Frank C. Costelloe and Mary Pearsall Smith of the United States. His father was the sixth of the ten children of Sir Richard Strachey FRS [q.v.], whose other children included (Giles) Lytton Strachey [q.v.] and several others prominent in public life. His mother was educated as a mathematician and engineer, and was, as Ray Costelloe, a notable suffragist. From his parents Christopher Strachey inherited mathematical gifts and a talent for puzzle-solving. Like his father, he took great pleasure in music and was an accomplished pianist.

Strachey was educated at Gresham's School, Norfolk, where he showed some promise in science and mathematics. He won an exhibition to King's College, Cambridge, where he began to read for the mathematical tripos in 1935. After making rather uneven academic progress, he transferred from mathematics (in which he gained a second class in 1936) to physics, graduating with a lower second in the natural sciences tripos in the summer of 1939.

After graduating Strachey became a physicist in the valve development laboratories of Standard Telephones and Cables Ltd., London, in August 1939, shortly before the outbreak of World War II. Evacuated to Ilminster, Somerset, he worked on the theoretical design of radar valves, returning to London in July 1944 to work in the radio division of the company. During his period with the company he obtained some experience in practical computing methods using a differential analyser.

Strachey had a strong vocation to be a schoolmaster. As the war drew to its close, he obtained release from his STC work to become, in October 1945, a teacher of physics and mathematics at St. Edmund's School, Canterbury. In September 1949 he advanced to a similar post at Harrow School. While at Harrow, Strachey's interest in computing was reawakened. Early in 1951 he became acquainted with the Pilot ACE computer, one of only three practical electronic computers in the country, which was then under construction at the National Physical Laboratory. Returning to Harrow, he began to write a program to make the machine play the game of draughts—a very novel and difficult task. Later in 1951 he began to use the Mark I computer at Manchester University. His status was purely that of an amateur, but his remarkable programming ability soon came to the attention of the Earl of Halsbury, managing director of the National Research and Development Corporation (NRDC).

In June 1952, as a result of an offer from Halsbury, Strachey became a technical officer in the NRDC. During his period with the corporation he was responsible for a number of important computer projects: these included undertaking calculations for the construction of the St. Lawrence Seaway in Canada, and most notably the logical design of the Ferranti Pegasus computer. During the late 1950s, Strachey was one of the most influential voices in the development of the 'multiprogramming' and 'time-sharing' use of computers.

In June 1959, having resigned from the NRDC, Strachey set up in practice as a private consultant, working from his home in Bedford Gardens, London. During his years as a consultant, he worked on a wide range of projects that included computer design, programming, and applications. During the early 1960s Strachey was very active in the new field of 'automatic programming'. In June 1962 he joined the University Mathematical Laboratory at Cambridge on a half-time basis, to lead the development of a new computer language, CPL. Although the language itself was never satisfactorily implemented, its design and the people associated with the project were an important influence in the development of the subject. In the same year he became a fellow of Churchill College, Cambridge.

In the summer of 1965, attracted by the academic life, Strachey wound up his consultancy. After a brief period at the Massachusetts Institute of Technology, he became leader of the Programming Research Group at Oxford University, taking up residence in April 1966. Under his guidance, during the next few years the group gained an outstanding international reputation in theoretical computer science. He was appointed to a personal chair in April 1971. At Oxford Strachey developed the foundations of 'denotational semantics', probably his most important contribution to the development of computing; in this work he collaborated closely with the American logician Dana S. Scott. This work had reached a well-developed stage when he died 18 May 1975 at Oxford. He was unmarried.

Strachey showed a notorious reluctance to publish throughout his life, and consequently his work is not well represented by his own publications; it is, however, well represented in the work and writings of his collaborators and students.

A tall, good-looking man, he inherited many of his family's intellectual and physical traits. He was an inveterate talker—witty and sarcastic by turn—in the highly modulated voice characteristic of the Strachey family.

[M. Campbell-Kelly, 'Christopher Strachey (1916–1975): a Biographical Note', *Annals of the History of Computing*, vol. vii, No. 1, January 1985.] MARTIN CAMPBELL-KELLY

STRAIGHT, WHITNEY WILLARD (1912–1979), racing motorist, aviator, and industrialist, was born at Old Westbury, Long Island, New York, 6 November 1912, the elder son and eldest of the three children of the wealthy Major Willard Dickerman Straight (1880–1918), American diplomat and financier, and his wife, Dorothy Payne (1887–1968), daughter of William Collins Whitney, lawyer, politician, and millionaire business man, of Cleveland, Ohio. After the death of his father of pneumonia on US war service in Paris on 1 December 1918, Whitney Straight first went to Lincoln School in New York City. On his mother's marriage to Leonard Knight Elmhirst [q.v.] he came to live in England in 1926 in the experimental community founded by his mother and stepfather at Dartington Hall, Totnes, Devon. He attended the school there which they set up as part of the community. His mother was to have another son and daughter. Straight gained a private pilot's licence in 1929, having flown solo at the age of sixteen.

In 1931 he acquired a 1,100-cc Riley with which he entered races at Brooklands and competed in motor trials at Shelsley Walsh and Southport, thus beginning a short but brilliant motor-racing career.

In October 1931 Straight went up to Trinity College, Cambridge, to read moral sciences. However, motor racing remained his chief interest. Since first-year undergraduates were not allowed to drive in Cambridge he kept a De Havilland Puss Moth at Marshall's aerodrome to which he would bicycle before flying to race at Brooklands, where he set up a lap record in 1934. In 1933 Straight left Cambridge to establish a professional racing-car stable with H. C. Hamilton, R. E. L. Featherstonhaugh, and Dick Seamen as drivers. Led by Straight the team achieved international success but suffered a severe loss when H. C. Hamilton was killed in a race at Berne.

Straight gave up motor racing for aviation in 1935 and formed the Straight Corporation on 17 April. By September 1938 it had a staff of 160, owned forty aircraft, and operated eight aerodromes, some flying schools, and a number of internal air routes. In 1936 the Miles Whitney Straight two-seat light monoplane appeared and sixty were sold. In the same year Straight took British citizenship.

As a pilot officer in No. 601 (County of London) Squadron, Royal Auxiliary Air Force, Straight was seriously wounded during the Norwegian campaign in 1940. He was awarded the MC and the Norwegian war cross. During his convalescence he was for a short while personal assistant to the Duke of Kent. Back in No. 601 Squadron, flying Hawker Hurricanes, he was officially credited with four confirmed victories in air combat during the Battle of Britain.

In August 1941, while commanding No. 242 Fighter Squadron, RAF, Straight was shot down over the Channel and crash-landed in France. He made for the Spanish frontier, was captured, escaped from a prison camp, reached Gibraltar, and returned to active service. Promoted group captain, he was posted to Egypt to form No. 216 Group, RAF Transport Command. When the war ended he was an air commodore commanding No. 46 Group, RAF Transport Command in the United Kingdom. In 1944 he was appointed air ADC to King George VI. During the war he was also awarded the DFC (1942) and the US Legion of Merit (1941), and was mentioned in dispatches. He was appointed CBE in 1944.

When British European Airways was formed in 1946 Straight became its first deputy chairman and managing director. At the same time he chaired a government advisory committee on private flying (1947). In 1947 he moved to the British Overseas Airways Corporation as deputy chairman; he was its executive vice-chairman from 1949 to 1957. He took a leading part in introducing the first commercial jet services with the De Havilland Comet. From 1946 to 1951 he was chairman of the Royal Aero Club of the United Kingdom. From BOAC Straight became executive vice-chairman of Rolls–Royce Ltd. in November 1955, a director of the Midland Bank in 1956, and deputy chairman of the new Post Office Corporation from 1969 to 1974.

An enthusiast in everything he did, Straight had a wide circle of friends and interests and he was financially able to indulge his desire for the best in architecture, in motor cars, and in his house and garden. His recreations included underwater swimming, skiing, squash rackets, ornithology, industrial design, music, and art.

On 17 July 1935 Straight married Lady Daphne Margarita, the elder daughter of Guy Montagu George Finch-Hatton, fourteenth Earl of Winchilsea and Nottingham. They had two daughters. Straight died in London 5 April 1979.

[*The Times*, 23 November 1979; *Motor Sport*, May 1979; information from Michael Straight (brother) and Phillip Gordon-Marshall; Michael Straight, *After Long Silence*, 1983; personal knowledge.] PETER G. MASEFIELD

STRANG, WILLIAM, first BARON STRANG (1893–1978), diplomat, was born at Rainham, Essex, 2 January 1893, the eldest of the seven sons (there were no daughters) of James Strang, farmer, of Englefield, Berkshire, and his wife, Margaret, daughter of James Steven, farmer. He was educated at Palmer's School and at University College, London, where he obtained an honours degree in English language and literature in 1912, and at the Sorbonne.

After military service in World War I at the front and in brigade and divisional headquarters (he was appointed MBE, military, in 1918), he joined the Foreign Office and Diplomatic Service in 1919, serving in Belgrade until 1922, the Foreign Office 1922–30, Moscow 1930–3, and the Foreign Office 1933–45 as head of the League of Nations section until 1937 and of Central Department until 1939. He was assistant under-secretary for Europe until 1943 and

British representative on the European advisory commission with the rank of ambassador until 1945. He was political adviser to the C-in-C Germany (Field-Marshal B. L. Montgomery, q.v.) from 1945 to 1947, returning to the Foreign Office as permanent under-secretary in the German section throughout 1948 and as permanent under-secretary of the Foreign Office 1949–53.

Strang came of Scottish lowland farming stock. He had an academic bent and developed a strong taste for English and French literature, which he never lost. In 1919 he had provisionally accepted a post as lecturer in English at Hong Kong University before passing into the Diplomatic Service. His appointment showed that a distinguished career was then open to those without family influence, private means, or even an Oxbridge education.

Although he first made his name abroad by his handling of the Metro-Vickers engineers trial in Moscow in the early thirties, his career lay mainly in the Foreign Office (twenty-five out of thirty-four years) and he preferred it this way. He soon acquired a reputation for hard work, competence, reliability, and good judgement. These qualities, with a strong sense of public duty, made him an outstanding civil servant and a valued adviser to ministers of very different characters and political persuasions, and more especially to the greatest foreign secretaries of his time, for each of whom he had a high regard, Anthony Eden (later Earl of Avon) and Ernest Bevin [qq.v.]. As permanent under-secretary he told new entrants to remember that diplomats were also civil servants, who would be well advised to cultivate good relations with their colleagues in other departments as well as with the general public, to be truthful and so maintain the confidence of their own and other governments, to preserve a calm, clear judgement without espousing causes or being carried away by enthusiasms or antipathies, and finally to regard accuracy as second nature, which should not however impair drive, rapidity, or self-confidence.

Although sometimes criticized for undue caution and even for accepting too readily the role of an official carrying out with every professional skill even policies where Foreign Office advice had been overruled, he was highly regarded in the Diplomatic Service not only for his efficiency but also for his humanity and personal consideration, enlivened by a pawky wit and a keen sense of humour. Behind the reserve of a loyal civil servant, he had strong, if always disciplined, feelings of his own about right and wrong courses of action. He became increasingly unhappy over the development and execution of Britain's 'Munich' policies under Neville Chamberlain in the late 1930s, but his sense of duty did not allow him to follow the path of Sir Robert (later Lord) Vansittart [q.v.] and some others in working outside the Foreign Office to oppose or modify them. Indeed, whatever his personal feelings, he worked most loyally with the prime minister, Neville Chamberlain, and the foreign secretary, Viscount (later Earl of) Halifax [q.v.], to produce the best results possible.

During his six years as permanent under-secretary the major achievements of British diplomacy, working together with the USA and France, were the European recovery programme through the Marshall Plan and what later became the OECD, the breaking of the Berlin blockade, the creation of the Atlantic alliance, NATO and western European union, and the restoration of Western Germany as a fully independent and democratic state. These policies have been summarized as keeping America in (western Europe) and the Soviet Union out. They were a fitting climax to a career which had been mainly concerned with European and Atlantic affairs and to a great extent with the different dangers coming from Hitler's Germany and Stalin's Soviet Union.

Other highlights in his career, apart from the Metro-Vickers trial in Moscow, already mentioned, and his role as adviser at major international meetings between 1934 and 1937, where he first came in contact with Hitler, Mussolini, and Stalin, at Chamberlain's meetings with Hitler in 1938 at Berchtesgaden, Godesberg, and Munich and at the wartime and post-war conferences with Stalin and the American leaders, were his mission to Moscow in 1939 and his contribution to the European advisory commission after 1943.

The first was a failure and the second a considerable success. Strang, with his knowledge of Russia and of the political realities at home, could not be held personally responsible for the failure; indeed critics attacked not him but the government for not having sent a senior minister to conduct these vital negotiations. It later became clear, however, that Britain could not have persuaded the Poles to accept Soviet conditions for military assistance nor indeed have then given the Russians what amounted to a free hand in the Baltic states. Britain could not outbid the Germans who offered the Russians peace and pickings in Poland and elsewhere instead of the prospect, as Stalin saw it, of pulling western chestnuts out of the fire in a war which would then have directly involved the Soviet Union from the outset.

The European advisory commission, on which Strang's colleagues were the American and Soviet ambassadors, Winant and Gusev, achieved the almost impossible task of laying down agreed conditions for the occupation and control of a conquered Germany by the three victorious powers, USA, the Soviet Union, and

Britain. The eventual breakdown of the wartime alliance, most obvious in the division of Germany, does not invalidate the success of the highly complicated arrangements made in 1945.

Strang was appointed CB (1939), KCB (1953), CMG (1932), KCMG (1943), and GCMG (1950). After his retirement from the Foreign Office at the end of 1953, marked by a peerage in 1954, Strang devoted himself to writing and resuming his reading (French and English), to his garden in Oxfordshire, and to a wide range of activities, to which he brought his sense of public duty and wide-ranging interests. They included such diverse roles as chairman of the National Parks Commission (1954–66), member of the Nature Conservancy Council (1954–66), chairman of the Food Hygiene Advisory Council (1955–71), chairman of the council of the Royal Institute of International Affairs (1958–65), and chairman of the college committee of University College, London (1963–71). He was made a fellow of University College, London, in 1946 and an honorary LL D of London University in 1954. He showed characteristic zest, good judgement, and a sense of enjoyment in all these functions, but he enjoyed even more his duties in the House of Lords, especially as deputy speaker and chairman of committees after 1962. He published *The Foreign Office* (1955), *Home and Abroad* (1956), *Britain in World Affairs* (1961), and *The Diplomatic Career* (1962).

In 1920 he married Elsie Wynne (died 1974), daughter of Josiah E. Jones, of Addiscombe, Welsh district manager of the Joint City and Midland Bank Ltd. They had a daughter and a son, Colin (born 1922), who succeeded his father in the peerage, and who became professor of philosophy at the University of Newcastle upon Tyne. Strang died in hospital in Newcastle 27 May 1978.

[Lord Strang, *Home and Abroad* (autobiography), 1956; personal knowledge.]

FRANK K. ROBERTS

STRAUSS, HENRY GEORGE, first BARON CONESFORD (1892–1974), lawyer and politician, was born in Kensington, London, 24 June 1892, the only son of Alphonse Henry Strauss, general merchant, of 19 Pembridge Gardens, London, and his wife, Hedwig Aschrott. He won scholarships both to Rugby School and to Christ Church, Oxford; was junior treasurer of the Oxford Union in 1914; and obtained first classes in both classical honour moderations (1913) and *literae humaniores* (1915). He enlisted in 1914, but was discharged on medical grounds, and served in the Ministry of Munitions, the Board of Trade, and the Ministry of Food until he was called to the bar by the Inner Temple in 1919.

Although he never enjoyed a substantial practice at the bar, he had the good fortune to be in chambers headed by Walter Monckton (later Viscount Monckton of Brenchley, q.v.), which also contained several of the most talented young members of the bar, several of them destined for high judicial preferment. This experience gave him a deep reverence for the law and a passionate devotion to the rights of the citizen under the law. He also became friends with and was much influenced by (Sir) A. P. Herbert [q.v.]. One of the results of this was a lifelong enthusiasm for the purity of the English language, and a dislike of those who misused it.

He entered the House of Commons at the general election of 1935 as Conservative member for Norwich. He had little sympathy with the appeasement policy then prevailing, but as a very junior member was in no position to influence it. He performed efficiently, and likeably, the duties of parliamentary private secretary to the attorney-general, Sir Thomas Inskip (later Viscount Caldecote, q.v.). But in 1942 (Sir) Winston Churchill appointed him joint parliamentary secretary at the Ministry of Works and Buildings, under Sir Wyndham (later Viscount) Portal [q.v.]. In 1943 he was transferred to the new Ministry of Town and Country Planning, and played a large part in seeing through the Commons the controversial, and in the event unfortunate, Town and Country Planning Act.

In 1945 he performed the most characteristically courageous and honourable action of his life. Although his departmental duties involved no concern with foreign affairs, he felt so strongly about the Yalta agreement, and what he regarded as its betrayal of the Poles, that he resigned his office and left the government. He lost his seat at Norwich in the Labour landslide election of 1945, but returned to the House of Commons in March 1946 as the result of a by-election in the Combined English Universities seat. He also took silk in 1946 and in the same year published *Trade Unions and the Law*. When the Attlee government abolished the university seats Strauss returned to Norwich and was re-elected as member for Norwich South at the 1950 election. He held this seat until he was created a peer in 1955.

In October 1951, on the return of the Conservatives to power, Churchill, who characteristically did not hold Strauss's Yalta resignation against him, appointed him parliamentary secretary to the Board of Trade. He was seventeen years older than Peter (later Lord) Thorneycroft, the president of the Board of Trade, and had no experience of business life or of an economic department. He did not fit in well in the department, although he did his full share of work for it in the House of Commons and at the innumerable functions of a social character which trade associations organize and are the bane of ministers in this type of Ministry. Indeed Strauss, only half humorously, used to accuse Thorneycroft of having had made a special stamp embossed 'Refer to Parliamentary Secretary' which he used to apply remorselessly to invitations to trade lunches. And the trade associations got good value, for Strauss was a witty and polished speaker. Sometimes however his wit was not wholly understood or appreciated by those attending functions organized by the less sophisticated trades. In the House of Commons, though handicapped by a somewhat high-pitched voice, he could argue the departmental case with precision and elegance. He retained even in the utilitarian milieu of the Board of Trade his passion for the right use of the English language. His colleagues appreciated this, and sometimes exploited it. On one occasion a hard-pressed financial secretary to the Treasury beside whom Strauss was sitting on the Treasury bench used a clumsy cliché, and by way of recovery added 'if I may quote my honourable and learned friend the parliamentary secretary to the Board of Trade'. A high-pitched 'Good God' echoed through the chamber, and an amused House of Commons was distracted from an awkward point.

In 1955 Strauss was one of a number of able men whose qualities did not appeal to the incoming prime minister, Sir Anthony Eden (later the Earl of Avon, q.v.). He went to the House of Lords as first Baron Conesford. The atmosphere of the upper House, courteous, civilized, tolerant of eccentricity, suited him from the start. He attained a standing and popularity there greater than he had had in the Commons. In April 1964 he was elected chairman of the Association of Independent Unionist peers, the body which includes all back-bench Conservative peers, and is broadly the equivalent of the 1922 Committee in the House of Commons. He retained this office until July 1970, and made a considerable mark on the evolving character of the House of Lords.

Strauss married in 1927 Anne Sadelbia Mary, the daughter of John Bowyer Nichols FSA, of Lawford Hall, Manningtree. She was artistically talented, and her calm personality provided an ideal foil for Harry's excitable liveliness. Their life in their lovely house in Cheyne Walk was peaceful and happy. They had, however, no children. They adopted, when very young, a boy and a girl whom they brought up as their own, the boy following Strauss to Rugby School.

Conesford died at home in London 28 August 1974, and the barony became extinct. Although his health had been clearly failing for some time, the fact that he was eighty-two came as a surprise to many friends. For, as one of them wrote at the time, 'he did not grow old gracefully; he simply didn't grow old at all'. He retained to the end his gift for friendship, his wit, and his enjoyment of social life among congenial friends. He was a much valued member of many dining clubs, able to enliven any gathering. This he combined with integrity and lack of malice. He was president of the Architecture Club and in 1965 became honorary FRIBA. In 1969 he became honorary bencher.

[*The Times*, 30 August and 6 September 1974; private information; personal knowledge.]

BOYD-CARPENTER

STUART, SIR CAMPBELL ARTHUR (1885–1972), director of *The Times*, was born in Montreal, 5 July 1885, the youngest son of Ernest Henry Stuart, stockbroker, and his wife (Letitia) Mary S. Brydges, daughter of Charles John Brydges, head of the Grand Trunk Railway. He was educated at private schools. Throughout his life Canada, England, and America formed a triangle of allegiances. He was proud to trace his ancestry back to emigrants from Buckinghamshire to New York in 1715; proud that others had, as United Empire Loyalists, emigrated to Canada as a result of the war of independence; and proud that in Canada they had filled posts of distinction. Three of his forebears had been chief justices. No matter what other interests he had at various times of his life, these associations were chords he struck time and again.

He was a director of *The Times* from 1919 to 1960. He filled a succession of roles in imperial and Commonwealth communications from 1923 to 1945. He was deputy director of propaganda in enemy countries at the end of World War I and, briefly (1939–40), director at the beginning of World War II. All these activities were overshadowed by the many projects he helped bring to fruition. The King George's Jubilee Trust (treasurer 1935–47); the Hudson's Bay Record Society (chairman 1938–59); the Wolfe memorial at Greenwich (committee member 1930); the statue of President Franklin Roosevelt in Grosvenor Square, London (treasurer 1946–8); the Canadian History Society, and its French counterpart to do justice to Quebec; the Pilgrims (chairman 1948–58)—he had a hand in them all.

In 1915–16 he raised in Quebec Province an Irish–Canadian battalion, half Protestant and half Roman Catholic, to fight in France. He then marched it through Protestant and Roman Catholic cities in Ireland, falsifying forebodings of trouble. His description in his autobiography, *Opportunity Knocks Once* (1952), of how he went about getting ecclesiastical approval for this, is revealing of his pertinacity. It led Sir Robert Borden [q.v.], then prime minister of Canada, to send the thirty-one-years-old Stuart to see Pope Benedict XV and interest him in French Canada's part in the war. The speed with which he obtained his audience with the pontiff astonished Vatican officials.

A short spell in 1917 as an assistant military attaché at the British embassy in Washington was not a success. He was happier as military secretary to Lord Northcliffe's British war mission in New York. From there he moved with Northcliffe [q.v.] to the propaganda post in London. His *Secrets of Crewe House*, dealing with this work, was a pioneer book when it was published in 1920. He ended the war as a lieutenant-colonel in the Canadian Army, having been mentioned in dispatches.

Northcliffe claimed Campbell Stuart was his find, and that he had 'made' him. This was not so. Stuart was assured of an influential future in Canada before he met Northcliffe. A choice of careers was open to him. Lord Atholstan [q.v.], who owned the *Montreal Star*, had asked Stuart to join him, with the promise he would own the paper on Atholstan's death. He could have entered Canadian politics.

What Northcliffe did was to move Stuart's life from Canada to England. When Stuart was about to return to Canada to be demobilized in 1920, Northcliffe offered him the managing-directorship of *The Times*, including supervision of the editorial staff and the news services. Northcliffe also made him managing editor of the *Daily Mail* (1921). Stuart accepted. As Northcliffe became increasingly irresponsible, Stuart protected both papers with courage. He played a leading part in the battle for the ownership of *The Times* that followed Northcliffe's death, favouring J. J. Astor (later Lord Astor of Hever, q.v.). It was not Stuart, however, who first thought of Astor as the ideal proprietor of the paper. The credit for that must go to (Sir) Bruce Richmond [q.v.]. Stuart's active role in the paper ceased in 1923 with the reinstatement of G. Geoffrey Dawson [q.v.] as editor of *The Times* by the new owners; but he retained his directorship for thirty-seven years thereafter. To this Dictionary he contributed the notice of Sir William McLintock.

Stuart was said to be a snob. Rather he was a latter-day patrician. He cultivated the company of the titled and the eminent. He always went straight to the top to enlist help in each of his undertakings. He was an assiduous host. Princes, prime ministers, ambassadors, bankers, and others—he gained access to them all. He did things in style. When he gave a lunch to form the French Canadian History Society, he held it at Versailles, and insured at Lloyd's the palace and all its contents for twenty-four hours to make this possible. He died in his seventeenth-century home in Highgate, London, 14 September 1972. He never married.

Stuart was appointed KBE in 1918 and GCMG in 1939, and he held honorary LL Ds from Melbourne University (1942) and William and Mary College, Virginia (1938). A portrait of him in robes was painted by Maurice Codner in 1955.

[*The History of 'The Times'*, 4 vols., 1935–52; Sir Campbell Stuart, *Opportunity Knocks Once* (autobiography), 1952; personal knowledge.]

WILLIAM HALEY

STUART, JAMES GRAY, first VISCOUNT STUART OF FINDHORN (1897–1971), chief whip, was born at 2 Bedford Park, Edinburgh, 9 February 1897, the third son and third of the four children of Morton Gray Stuart, seventeenth Earl of Moray, and his wife, Edith Douglas, daughter of Rear-Admiral George Palmer. He was educated at Eton and intended to go to Cambridge, but when war broke out in 1914 he joined the army. He was commissioned in the 3rd (Special Reserve) battalion of the Royal Scots and was at the front in January 1915. He was invalided home, returned to France in 1916, gained the MC and bar, and ended the war with the 15th Infantry brigade, as a brigade-major. He then read law for a year at the Scottish bar in Edinburgh, but found it uncongenial and in 1920 became first equerry to Prince Albert, the future King George VI. He served for eighteen months, leaving in 1921, having been appointed MVO.

Stuart decided on a business career and spent over a year in the USA learning about oil production. When he returned home in 1923 he was invited to stand as Conservative candidate for Moray and Nairn and was elected MP the same year. He represented the constituency until 1959. In 1935 he was appointed a lord commissioner of the Treasury and Scottish whip. He retained the former position until 1941; in 1937 he became deputy to the government chief whip, H. D. R. (later Viscount) Margesson [q.v.]. When Margesson became secretary of state for war on 22 December 1940, Stuart succeeded him as joint chief whip in the coalition government, working in harness with Sir Charles Edwards, chief Labour whip, until 1942, and then with Edwards's successor, William Whiteley [q.v.]. When the caretaker government was formed in 1945 Stuart became sole chief whip, and then opposition chief whip from 1945 until 1948, when he resigned because of ill health.

Stuart was an excellent chief whip, his character perfectly suiting the job. He did not fuss but rather assumed a casual air of indifference or carelessness. Although fastidious in his choice of intimate friends, he had a gregarious side to his personality and was at ease with all and sundry in palace or public house or Parliament. These qualities, allied to a perceptive mind and down-to-earth common sense, made him popular with prime minister and humble politician alike. Firm and fair, he was acknowledged by all sides in

Parliament as a good manager of the business of the House. Beneath the apparently lackadaisical veneer he had a strong will which it was unwise to test too often. Reluctant to be dominated by anyone, whatever his reputation, he could express himself strongly and in pungent language. Yet he was no orator, and used silence as his most powerful weapon. Enigmatic and laconic, he would bide his time and then strike with a few words of devastating authority.

After an improvement in Stuart's health, in 1950 he assumed the duties for which the Scottish Unionist whip had hitherto been responsible. When the Conservatives returned to power in 1951, he was appointed secretary of state for Scotland, a post he held until 1957. His years in office coincided with the decline of the old industries of coal, shipbuilding, and steel, and the need for diversification with a variety of more modern factories. During his term of office a good start was made with this process. Stuart was adept at handling matters of local government, which loom large in the life of every Scottish secretary of state. He was closely attentive not only to the problems faced by Scotland's hill farmers but also to the needs of local authorities, in particular those of Glasgow and some others whose councils were of a different political complexion to his own. Early in his term of office a royal commission was appointed; its recommendation that responsibility for Scottish highways and other matters be transferred to the secretary of state was accepted by the government. He was also given responsibility for the generation of electricity. While Stuart was secretary of state the trend towards Scottish nationalism declined.

However, Stuart's health continued to be troublesome and when a new government was formed in January 1957 he resigned. In 1959 he was raised to the peerage and took the title of Viscount Stuart of Findhorn. He had been admitted to the Privy Council in 1939 and appointed CH in 1957.

In 1923 Stuart married Rachel (died 1977), daughter of Victor Christian William Cavendish, ninth Duke of Devonshire [q.v.]. They had two sons and a daughter. Remarkably handsome, with good reason Stuart was a somewhat vain man. He died in the Salisbury Infirmary 20 February 1971 and was succeeded in the title by his elder son, David Randolph Moray Stuart (born 1924).

[Stuart of Findhorn, *Within the Fringe* (autobiography), 1967; personal knowledge.]

HOME OF THE HIRSEL

SUMMERSKILL, EDITH CLARA, BARONESS SUMMERSKILL (1901–1980), politician, was born 19 April 1901 at Doughty Street, London, the youngest of three children and younger daughter of Dr William Summerskill, MRCS LRCP, and his wife, Edith West. Her father held radical views and favoured the emancipation of women. He was not active politically but he was once provoked to contest a local government election 'to do battle with the plague of fleas and the smells'. Edith Summerskill claimed that she was 'a boisterous, noisy, talkative girl' at school. When she was seventeen she left Eltham Hill Grammar School for King's College and later Charing Cross Hospital, where she qualified MRCS LRCP in 1924.

In the following year she married Dr (Edward) Jeffrey Samuel MB BS (died 1983), a fellow student, from Llanelly. For many years they practised together as doctors. There were two children, a son and a daughter, and, for a long time, the family included Nana, who looked after the children. Edith Summerskill was always most proud of her family. Her husband accompanied her and was well known at Labour Party conferences and functions. Nothing pleased her more than that her daughter Shirley became a doctor, an MP, and a minister. Like her mother, Shirley kept the name Summerskill.

In 1928 Edith Summerskill accepted an invitation to become a co-opted member of the maternity and child welfare committee in Wood Green, where she practised. This was an incentive. Soon she became a member of the Socialist Medical Association and an active propagandist for the local Labour Party. In 1934 she won a by-election for the Middlesex County Council, a dramatic Labour gain. Then she was chosen as candidate in a parliamentary by-election at Putney, after the previously selected candidate had been rejected by the party's national executive committee. A vigorous campaign greatly reduced the Conservative majority. In the 1935 general election she was a hopeful Labour candidate at Bury, but she was unsuccessful in an unhappy election. However, she was soon chosen as prospective candidate for West Fulham and, when the Conservative member died in 1938, she made a significant gain against the government of Neville Chamberlain. Edith Summerskill remained in Parliament for the rest of her life. When her constituency was changed in 1955, she left Fulham and became MP for Warrington until she went to the House of Lords as a life peer in 1961.

Edith Summerskill was an active constituency member and she was attracted to many causes. This did not prejudice her influence nationally in the Labour Party. First elected in 1944, for a long time she was a member of the national executive committee and chairman of the party in 1954–5. After the defeat of the government of C. R. (later Earl) Attlee she was elected to the parliamentary committee and, with the exception of one session, held her place until 1959. Although her views were essentially radical, she was regarded as being on the right of the party hierarchy.

Always a combative feminist, during the war Edith Summerskill was one of the founders of the Women's Home Defence and took rifle practice. In 1945 Attlee appointed her parliamentary secretary to the Ministry of Food. With rationing and food shortages she had a rough time, particularly from the Housewives League, but, as a vigorous campaigner against tuberculosis, she felt the legislation in 1949 on the pasteurization of milk was her 'finest hour'. After the 1950 election she was promoted and became minister of national insurance and industrial injuries. The government had an inadequate majority and Edith Summerskill had little opportunity to demonstrate ministerial ability. The fall of the Labour government in 1951 prevented her from completing the Pneumoconiosis Bill.

She continued to be active in the House of Commons and later in the Lords. Her main interests were clean food, abortion, medicine, boxing, which she fiercely criticized, and married women's rights. She was imposingly tall and good looking. She could have a sharp tongue but more important she had a pervasive smile which embraced nearly everyone. She was one of the most successful feminists of her generation and wrote *Babies without Tears* (1941), *The Ignoble Art* (1956), *Letters to my Daughter* (1957), and *A Woman's World* (1967). She was admitted to the Privy Council in 1949 and appointed CH in 1966. She died at her home in Highgate, London, 4 February 1980.

[*The Times*, 5 February 1980; personal knowledge.] FRED T. WILLEY

SUTCLIFFE, HERBERT WILLIAM (1894–1978), Yorkshire and England cricketer, was born at Summerbridge, near Hartwith, Yorkshire, 24 November 1894, the second of three sons (there were no daughters) of William Sutcliffe, bobbin turner, journeyman, and later hotel proprietor, of Pateley Bridge, and his wife Jane Elizabeth Bell. He was educated at Pudsey School in Pudsey, a town also associated with two other great Yorkshire cricketers, Sir Leonard Hutton and Raymond Illingworth.

Sutcliffe's appearance in first-class cricket was delayed by World War I, during which he was commissioned in the Green Howards. At the age of twenty-four he was an immediate success as an opening batsman for Yorkshire in 1919 when he scored five centuries. He first played for England in 1924, and was at once a success against South Africa putting on 136 and 268 with (Sir) Jack Hobbs [q.v.] in his first two test matches. The following winter in Australia he had a triumphant series, making 734 runs at an average of 81 including two hundreds in the second test at Melbourne (176 and 127), despite which England were beaten. He was always at his best when the challenge was greatest, for England against Australia, or for Yorkshire against Lancashire, and his supreme skill was most famously demonstrated at the Oval in 1926 and at Melbourne in 1929 when he scored hundreds on pitches made treacherous by rain.

In his prime, from 1925 to 1932, Sutcliffe averaged over 50 in eight consecutive seasons and on four overseas tours, and from May 1931 to May 1933 he scored 7,687 runs. On 15 and 16 June 1932 he and Percy Holmes broke the world record for an opening partnership, putting on 555 against Essex at Leyton, a record in first-class cricket which stood until 1977. Having attained the record, Sutcliffe deliberately threw away his wicket after making 313. He seldom showed such charity to bowlers.

The only cricketer to play through every season between the wars, scoring more than 1,000 runs in each of those twenty-one seasons, Sutcliffe made 3,336 runs in 1932 alone, at an average of 74, hitting 14 centuries in a wet season. By the time he retired from first-class cricket (effectively in 1939, although he played one more match in 1945) he had scored 50,135 runs at an average of 52, with 149 hundreds, 16 of them in tests.

The partner in two famous opening pairs, with Percy Holmes for Yorkshire and Jack Hobbs for England, Sutcliffe's cricketing hallmarks were courage, calmness—even against the trickiest or fiercest bowling—concentration, and an exemplary technique. Everything about him, from his smoothed-down, carefully-parted hair, to his perfectly white boots, was immaculate. Nothing worried him, or if it did he never showed it. If a ball beat his bat, he would show no reaction, whatever the provocation from the unfortunate bowler; if a spectator moved behind the sight-screen, Sutcliffe would stop the bowler in the middle of his run-up and with an imperious gesture wave the culprit, as (Sir) Neville Cardus [q.v.] remarked, 'out of all decent society'.

Sutcliffe's right-handed batting method was strictly functional and simple, lacking the easy grace of Hobbs, yet not without its own artistic flourish. His attacking shots would finish with a late curve of the bat, like a writer adding the last touch to his signature. Moreover, though contemporaries rated Hobbs the greatest English batsman of his time, it was Sutcliffe who finished with the higher test batting average, a remarkable one of 60.73, the highest attained by any England player of any era who has scored more than 1,500 test runs. With Hobbs he had a perfect understanding, each batsman entirely confident of the other's ability and judgement and each a speedy runner between the wickets. They shared 26 century opening partnerships and Sutcliffe shared 74 more with Holmes.

Jack Hobbs wrote of Sutcliffe: 'What I admired in Herbert was his thoroughness. Evidently his motto is "what is worth doing is worth doing well". As an illustration, he was, a few years ago, quite an ordinary speaker, but recently I heard him make a speech on a big occasion, and it was a wonderful bit of oratory. I felt very envious of him.' If Sutcliffe himself ever felt envy, he never showed it. Always assured, he was the sort, as R. C. Robertson-Glasgow remarked, who would rather miss a train than be seen to hurry. When Sutcliffe finally lost his place in the England side, during the series against South Africa in 1935, he was replaced by Denis Smith of Derbyshire. On being told of his replacement Sutcliffe remarked without expression: 'Who is Smith?' The story may be apocryphal, but it is indicative of the man's unshakeable poise.

As organized and determined in his private and business life as he was on the cricket field, Sutcliffe built up a very successful sports outfitting business in Yorkshire and during World War II rose to the rank of major in the Royal Army Ordnance Corps, having spoken frequently before hostilities began in the cause of wider recruitment. He also spoke in aid of the Red Cross and organized cricket matches to raise money for them. He was an England cricket selector and also served on the Yorkshire CCC committee, on the royal commission on betting, and on the Rugby League disciplinary committee. He was a high-ranking official in the London Lodge of the Masons. Deliberately turning his Yorkshire accent into one more associated with Oxford, he sent his children to private schools. Dogged by arthritis in later years he made a final appearance on the field at Headingley in a wheelchair, in 1977, when he was honoured by a large crowd during the test match in which Geoffrey Boycott followed Sutcliffe and Len Hutton as the third Yorkshireman to score 100 first-class centuries. Hutton said of Sutcliffe: 'He was correct in all he did, on and off the field, but never so ambitious as to forget that he was playing in a team game.'

Sutcliffe married Emily (died 1974), who had lived in the same street in Pudsey (Robin Lane), the daughter of William Pease, farmer, in the parish church of Pudsey on 21 September 1921; they had two sons and one daughter. One of his sons, W. H. H. ('Billy') Sutcliffe, born in 1926, played for Yorkshire as an amateur and captained them in 1956 and 1957: Herbert Sutcliffe had himself been offered the honour but, as a professional, refused it. Sutcliffe died at Beanlands Nursing Home, Crosshills, near Skipton, 22 January 1978.

[Herbert Sutcliffe, *For England and Yorkshire*, 1935; J. B. Hobbs, *My Life Story*, 1935; E. W. Swanton and Michael Melford (eds.), *The World of Cricket*, 1966; Christopher Martin-Jenkins, *The Complete Who's Who of Test Cricketers*, 1980; R. C. Robertson-Glasgow, *Cricket Prints*, 1943; Neville Cardus, *Days in the Sun*, 1924; private information.]

CHRISTOPHER MARTIN-JENKINS

SUTHERLAND, SIR GORDON BRIMS BLACK McIVOR (1907–1980), physicist, was born 8 April 1907 at Watten, Caithness, the youngest of seven children (of whom five survived) of Peter Sutherland, a teacher, of Dundee, and his wife, Eliza Hope, also a teacher, daughter of Alexander Morrison, grocer, of Dufftown, Banffshire. Sutherland attended Morgan Academy, Dundee, where he excelled in mathematics and science. He entered St. Andrews University in 1924 and spent five years there, obtaining two first class honours degrees, the MA in mathematics (1928), and the B.Sc. in physics (1929). He was attracted by the possibility of a university career, and moved with the aid of scholarships to Trinity College, Cambridge, where he worked with (Sir) Ralph H. Fowler [q.v.]. As part of his introduction to research, he was to draft a chapter on the specific heats of gases for the second edition of Fowler's well-known book, *Statistical Mechanics*.

At Cambridge Sutherland met Professor David M. Dennison, who was on leave from the University of Michigan. Dennison was a leading theorist on the vibrations and rotations of molecules, topics very close to those which Sutherland was reviewing in his chapter for Fowler. Sutherland decided that he would try to work with Dennison and applied for a Commonwealth fellowship to take him to America. His application was successful and he spent two rewarding years at Ann Arbor. He went there a promising young research student; he returned to Cambridge an experienced research scientist.

At Cambridge again, Sutherland resumed work on some of the molecules he had studied earlier, and collaborated with W. G. (later Lord) Penney who was working theoretically on similar molecules. The positions of the atoms in the molecules of hydrogen peroxide, hydrazine, ozone, and nitrogen tetroxide were all determined by a combined study of their electronic structures, their vibrational motions, and their Raman spectra. While this work was in progress, Sutherland was appointed in 1934 to the Stokes studentship of Pembroke College, Cambridge.

Sutherland was elected a fellow of Pembroke College in 1935 and soon assembled a research group, well equipped in infra-red and Raman spectroscopy. The outbreak of war in 1939 caused the research to be suspended and Sutherland worked in London on bomb disposal. In

1941 a military need arose to determine rapidly the sources of the fuel mixtures being used by enemy aircraft. The group was reassembled at Cambridge and, in collaboration with others, analysed fuel recovered from destroyed enemy aircraft, and identified the main sources.

The return of British science to peacetime conditions was slow and difficult. Sutherland did well at Cambridge, becoming reader in spectroscopy in 1947, and when he received in 1949 an offer of a full professorship (of physics) at Ann Arbor he was uncertain what to do. He accepted but hoped he might some day return to Britain if a suitable opportunity arose. His work at Michigan was notable for some papers on crystalline polymers. The offer from Britain came in 1956, the directorship of the National Physical Laboratory.

The time Sutherland spent at NPL (1956–64) was a period of rapidly increasing prosperity in the western world. Growth rates and ever-increasing wealth were said to depend on science. Sutherland agreed with this view and under his energetic leadership the NPL grew in numbers and facilities. Particular emphasis was laid on the new Basic Physics Division. However, by the 1960s the total cost of science to the Exchequer was growing so rapidly that constraints began to be imposed. Basic research was now to be conducted mainly in the universities or in specialist institutes. Sutherland was disappointed, and, as at this moment he was offered the mastership of Emmanuel College, Cambridge, he accepted.

Many improvements were made to the college during Sutherland's period as master (1964–77). New rooms were added and the library was completed. The master and his wife were noted for their hospitality. Sutherland presided easily and with dignity, showing his natural Scots courtesy, caution, and wit, qualities which were especially important during the student troubles of the late 1960s.

Sutherland contributed to national and university science policy. He was mainly responsible for the first authoritative collection of statistics showing the large number of scientists emigrating from Britain to the United States, the so-called brain drain.

In appearance, Sutherland was a little over average height, strong but not heavy, with dark hair and wearing glasses. He enjoyed mountaineering, hockey, and golf: he had a keen sense of humour and relished stories about the careful Scot.

He received many academic honours (including an honorary LL D at St. Andrews in 1958 and an honorary D.Sc. at Strathclyde in 1966) and many other awards and marks of distinction. He was elected FRS in 1949, knighted in 1960, and was a vice-president of the Royal Society in 1961–3.

In 1936 Sutherland married Gunborg Elisabeth, elder daughter of (Konstnar) Filip Wahlström, artist, of Göteborg, Sweden. The marriage was a happy one, and they had three daughters. Sutherland died at Cambridge 27 June 1980.

[N. Sheppard in *Biographical Memoirs of Fellows of the Royal Society*, vol. xxviii, 1982; personal knowledge.] PENNEY

SUTHERLAND, GRAHAM VIVIAN (1903–1980), painter and print-maker, was born in Streatham, London, 24 August 1903, the elder son and first of the three children of George Humphreys Vivian Sutherland, barrister and civil servant (a principal in the then Board of Education), and his wife Elsie Foster. His younger brother, Humphrey, became a distinguished numismatist. The Sutherlands lived in south London, successively in Streatham, Merton Park, and Sutton, building a small house for holiday use in Rustington, Sussex, in about 1913. Graham Sutherland was educated in Sutton at Epsom College, 1918–19. In 1919 he was sent as an engineering apprentice to the Midland Railway Works, Derby, where his uncle was a senior engineer; ill-equipped mathematically for this profession, and devoted since a lonely childhood to studying and drawing nature, he persuaded his father to let him give up engineering and entered the Goldsmiths' College school of art in 1921.

There, after a sound general art education, he specialized in etching, studying first under Malcolm Osborne and then under Stanley Anderson [q.v.]; his closest friends, Paul Drury, Edward Bouverie Hoyton, and William Larkins, were all to distinguish themselves in this field. Drawn to a 'strongly romantic' view of nature, he came deeply under the spell of Samuel Palmer [q.v.], then recently rediscovered, and was befriended by F. L. M. Griggs, the most accomplished print-maker of the day and a devotee of Palmer. He had his first exhibition, at the Twenty-One Gallery, in October 1924, and in the following year was elected an associate of the Royal Society of Painter–Etchers and Engravers. After leaving Goldsmiths' in the summer of 1926 he was appointed (in December) to teach engraving at the Chelsea School of Art. But Sutherland's successful, and to some extent remunerative, career as a print-maker was brought to an abrupt end by the collapse of the market, chiefly American, in 1929. In 1932 he switched to the teaching of composition and book illustration at Chelsea and, during the 1930s, helped by his friend, Milner Gray, later founder of the Society of Industrial Artists and Designers, with whom he had shared 'digs' in 1925–7, engaged more seriously than hitherto in commercial work: glassware, ceramics, and, most notably, poster design for companies with such artistically enlightened direction as Shell–Mex and the London Transport Board. He also turned, for the first time, to painting.

In the spring of 1934 Sutherland visited Pembrokeshire. 'From the first moment I set foot in Wales I was obsessed.' He spent each summer there until the war, was able to revisit it during the war years, and returned every year from 1967 onwards, his imagination rekindled by a television retrospective in which he took part. The increasingly bold imagery and rich colour harmonies of his semi-abstract Welsh landscapes—paraphrases, painted in the studio, derived from his sketches of minuscule organic forms, roots and the like, and 'bringing out the anonymous personality of these things'—won critical acclaim at the first one-man show of his paintings, which had been arranged for him by his patron, Sir Kenneth (later Lord) Clark, at the Rosenberg and Helft Gallery in September 1938. As an official war artist in 1940–5, again at the invitation of Clark, with whom he had stayed in Gloucestershire during the first year of the war, Sutherland produced equally evocative work derived from his studies of air-raid devastation in Swansea and the East End of London, and of such subjects as the Cornish tin mines, iron foundries, limestone quarries, and (in 1944) the flying-bomb sites in Normandy. It was these works which made the deepest impression on his contemporaries. In 1944 Sutherland was commissioned to paint a large-scale 'Crucifixion' (completed in 1946) for St. Matthew's, Northampton. His studies of thorns (some transformed into thorn heads, symbols of cruelty) date from this period.

Following his long and regular post-war visits to the Riviera, prompted at first by a search for new subjects and his love of the sun, Sutherland bought a villa in the hills above Menton in 1955, thenceforward alternating between there and his home in Trottiscliffe, Kent. In the decade after the war his style lightened and broadened, he met and came under the influence of Picasso and Matisse, remained in close touch with Francis Bacon, and was accepted as a leader of the avant-garde; a series of shows in London and New York culminated in retrospectives at the Venice Biennale and at the Musée d'Art Moderne, Paris (both 1952)—'perhaps', wrote Clark, 'no other English painter since Constable has been received with so much respect in the critical atmosphere of Paris'—and at the Tate Gallery in coronation year (1953), where the critics were less favourable. He painted 'The Origins of the Land', a large-scale work for the Festival of Britain, 1951, and in 1952 was commissioned to design the huge tapestry of 'Christ in Glory' (completed in 1962) for the new Coventry Cathedral. His growing reputation was then at its height.

In 1949 Sutherland painted his first portrait, a startling, expressionist full-length of W. Somerset Maugham [q.v.] which (when it was first seen at the Tate Gallery in 1951) shocked a public accustomed to the time-honoured conventions of British portraiture. This remarkable picture led to the commission in 1951 to paint Lord Beaverbrook [q.v.], Maugham's neighbour at Cap d'Ail, and this in turn to the ill-fated request by the all-party committee of both houses of Parliament to paint Sir Winston Churchill as a celebration of his eightieth birthday. This portrait, presented in 1954, was hated by Churchill—he disliked its realism and the truncated feet and said it 'makes me look half-witted'—and it was destroyed secretly on Lady Churchill's orders only a year or two after its completion. Among Sutherland's best portraits are those of Paul Sacher (1956), Helena Rubinstein (1957), Prince von Fürstenberg (1959), Konrad Adenauer (1965), and Lord Goodman (1973); his masterpieces are probably the 'Maugham' and the searching characterization of his friend, Edward Sackville-West (1954, q.v.). A portrait of Queen Elizabeth the Queen Mother did not come to fruition. Sutherland was not a naturally gifted draughtsman, and certain weaknesses, of which he was fully conscious, are perhaps most apparent in his portraiture.

Sutherland spent ten years, working at intervals between portraits and other work, on the Coventry tapestry, producing three distinct designs and supervising the weaving (by Pinton Frères, at the Aubusson factory at Felletin) in detail. He was embittered by the authorities' refusal, owing to the exigencies of the final timetable, to allow him to see the tapestry hung before its dispatch to Coventry (Malraux had offered him the Sainte Chapelle), aware that 'with an area that size every tonality has got to be *dead* right or it doesn't tell at a distance'.

In 1959 Marlborough Fine Art became Sutherland's dealers; he had his first exhibition there in 1962. He formed a Swiss company to handle his affairs in the mid-1960s, and in the last ten years of his life became a tax exile. His chief patrons in these years were Italian, following a successful retrospective in Turin in 1965. None the less the inspiration for his work in the last twelve years of his life was Wales, to which he returned each year: 'I thought I had exhausted what the countryside had to offer both as a "vocabulary" & as inspiration. I was sadly mistaken.' In 1976 the Graham Sutherland Gallery, which he had endowed, was opened at Picton Castle. He was also devoting more of his time to print-making, producing a 'Bestiary', composed of twenty-six colour lithographs, in 1968, and developing a refined process of aquatint in 'Bees' (1977), perhaps his most accomplished late work, and in a further 'Bestiary' based on poems by Apollinaire (1979). His equally prodigious later output of paintings included the moving 'The Thicket' (1978), a tangle of mysterious natural forms in front of which he depicted himself sketching.

Sutherland's life was his work: 'I am, I have to admit, a tireless worker—with regular hours.' He tended to take on too many commitments. Thus he disliked travel, or staying with people. In 1927 he had married Kathleen ('Katharine') Frances, daughter of John Barry, who worked at Woolwich Arsenal. She was a fellow student at Goldsmiths', who then gave up her own career in fashion to further his. They lived in Kent, first at Farningham, then at Eynsford (1931), Sutton-at-Hone (1933) and, finally, Trottiscliffe: the White House was leased in 1937 and purchased in 1945. They were a devoted and inseparable couple until the day of his death. There was one child of the marriage, John Vivian, who died when he was barely three months old.

Sutherland, neat in appearance and always elegantly dressed, possessed striking good looks and immense charm; he had perfect manners, was naturally courteous and considerate of other people, generous and trusting, in some ways naïve. He had a soft but clear and attractive voice, with an engaging smile as he talked, was fastidious in his choice and use of words, and articulate about his work, which conscientiously he discussed with numerous interviewers. His writing was involved, but fresh and elegant, at times poetic. By upbringing and disposition solitary, he loved the company of close friends, enjoyed good food and wine, and had a whimsical sense of fun. A perfectionist in everything he did, which sometimes led to ruffled professional relationships, he was self-analytical but emotional and deeply impressionable, which occasionally led him into difficulties, too, as in the case of the so-called 'Tate affair' (appointed a trustee in 1948, he became deeply involved with the attack on the administration of the Gallery and, influenced by friends but out of touch with his fellow trustees, felt obliged to resign in 1954). 'Graham', one of his friends remarked, 'was born to complicate things.' His biographer suggested that 'he positively needed an element of tension and drama in his life'. He always loved fast cars (as a young man it was motor cycles), and was for a time an addict of the casino at Monte Carlo. Otherwise, he had few leisure pursuits. His musical predilections were almost exclusively for Bach: 'I am conscious that to such great tight knit architecture I owe more than I can ever realise.' From 1952 he went every year to Venice for summer holidays.

Sutherland once called himself 'tough *and* vulnerable'. The opposites in his complex character were reflected in his work. His style was governed by the realization, learnt early from Samuel Palmer, and reinforced later by Picasso's 'Guernica', that the force of emotion can change and revitalize appearances; the method he employed to express his feeling was metaphor. Sutherland described his creative process well. On his daily walks in search of material he reacted to 'certain things only, as if in response to some internal need of the nerves. . . . In the studio, I remember; it may be an hour ago or years, and I react afresh. The images dissolve; objects may lose their normal environment and relationship. Then things seem to be drawn together and redefined in the mind's eye in a new life and a new mould—there has been a substitution, a change. But I feel this to be valid only in so far as the process of digestion has preserved in the substance of my material—paint and canvas—the sensation of the original presence, in its new and permanent form'. He was not a Surrealist, and he hated being called one. It was his consciousness that his motifs had a kind of presence that led to his impulse 'to make landscape more figurative than in fact it is, and more within the four walls of a possible canvas'; he was especially moved by enclosed landscape, never interested in projecting more than a shallow space. He was obsessed by correspondences, 'between machines and organic forms, between organic forms and people, and of people with stones'. The head of his 'Somerset Maugham' has often been compared with rock forms. Though he believed that Picassoesque metamorphosis was 'the highest form of portraiture', in this genre he himself sought for likeness, 'likeness which is the result of an attempt to fuse all the characteristic directions, movements, and tension of the head and body into terms of paint'. Not every commission fired his imagination. 'The last state of man holds for me the greatest interest. He has faced the responsibilities and temptations of life.'

Tension was inherent in much of Sutherland's work. In Wales he was possessed by 'an emotional feeling of being on the brink of some drama'. He was fascinated by the opposition of forms, by combat, by 'the struggle of a tree to remain standing and grow, against all odds', by duality resolved in a 'precarious balanced moment', in art by Grünewald above all. There was nothing superficial about his attitude to nature, which was broadly pantheistic: 'Through the closest scrutiny and observation we may work parallel to the invisible order & perhaps catch a reflection of it.' Sutherland had been a convert to Roman Catholicism in 1926. Though never devout, and always questioning, religion remained a support to him.

Modest about his work, Sutherland was in constant need of reassurance and thus especially vulnerable to criticism. In the last twenty years of his career he was a celebrity but, understandably in the heyday of abstract painting, his reputation suffered an eclipse and he had few advocates among English critics. His work continued, however, to be admired abroad, and it is symptomatic that the memorial exhibition held in 1982 was warmly received in Darmstadt but less so at the Tate. He was admitted to the Order of Merit in 1960, became honorary D.Litt. at Oxford in 1962, and was the first artist to be awarded the Shakespeare prize in Hamburg in 1974. He was elected honorary fellow of the American Academy of Arts and Letters in 1972, and Commandeur des Arts et Lettres, France, and honorary fellow of the Accademia di San Luca, Rome, in 1973.

Sutherland had a sound, if not a robust, constitution. He never spared himself, though in the latter part of his life the regular routine of his day included an afternoon siesta. Hard at work until the last month or two of his life, he died at the Royal Free Hospital, Hampstead, 17 February 1980. He was buried in Trottiscliffe, Kent.

A self-portrait executed in 1977 is in the National Portrait Gallery; a slightly larger version, painted in the following year, is in a private collection in Turin.

[Douglas Cooper, *The Work of Graham Sutherland*, 1961; John Hayes, *The Art of Graham Sutherland*, 1980 (with full bibliography updating Cooper); Roger Berthoud, *Graham Sutherland*, 1982; Graham Sutherland, *Correspondences: Selected Writings on Art*, ed. Julian Andrews, 1982; personal knowledge.]

JOHN HAYES

SUTHERLAND, DAME LUCY STUART (1903–1980), historian and administrator, was born in Geelong, Australia, 21 June 1903, the only daughter (she had one brother who died young) of Alexander Charles Sutherland (1870–1941) and his wife, Margaret Mabel Goddard (1871–1950). Both her parents, Australians by birth, were graduates of the University of Melbourne, her father, a mining engineer, being descended from Scottish Highland stock, and her mother (whose father had emigrated in 1865) from a family with City of London affiliations. She was brought up in South Africa, and educated at Roedean School, Johannesburg, and the University of Witwatersrand, where she won a scholarship which enabled her to go to Oxford. After a first class in the honour school of modern history (1927), her college, Somerville, appointed her a tutor, and later elected her to a tutorial fellowship (1928–45). In 1926 she had been the first woman to speak at the Oxford Union, winning applause for her opposition to the motion 'That the women's colleges . . . should be levelled to the ground'.

Three scholars, very different in their interests and approach, were to form her as a historian. At Witwatersrand she enjoyed much encouragement from Professor William N. Macmillan. The distinguished medievalist, Maude Clarke [q.v.], her tutor at Somerville, instilled into her the most rigorous scholarly standards. *The Structure of Politics at the Accession of George III* (1929) by (Sir) Lewis Namier [q.v.] gave her the conceptual framework upon which rested her output of eighteenth-century history. During the 1930s she built up a growing reputation as a scholar, while her ability was increasingly recognized in her college and in the university.

When war came she felt herself increasingly restless in Oxford, and in 1941 accepted the offer of a principalship in the Board of Trade. She immediately proved a talented civil servant, rising by 1945 to the rank of assistant secretary. But though she found it hard to live without any time for her research, these years were of crucial significance in turning her from a somewhat shy Oxford don, who had not yet shed her 'colonial' accent, into a sophisticated woman of the world.

In 1945 both Somerville and Lady Margaret Hall were looking for a new principal; she was a forerunner in both elections, withdrawing from that at Somerville when she perceived that her candidature was likely to split the college. Her appointment as principal of Lady Margaret Hall was to bring her great happiness. Brought up a Presbyterian, she had been confirmed into the Church of England in 1931, and found the Anglican ambience of the Hall a congenial one. Her administrative talents were fully stretched by the problems of post-war Oxford, but she was soon recalled to outside responsibilities, including the chairmanship of the Board of Trade working party on the lace industry (1946), and membership of the committee of inquiry into the distribution and exhibition of cinematographic films (1949), the royal commission on taxation of profits and income (1951), the committee into grants for students (1958), and, later, the University Grants Committee (1964–9). She was actively engaged, in addition, with the administration of many educational bodies.

But her commitments outside Oxford never displaced her central interest in her college and university. During her time, Lady Margaret Hall doubled in size; she took an intense interest in the new buildings. Its intellectual standing was her major concern, but she also enjoyed it greatly as a human community. In the university she became increasingly prominent; it gave her great pleasure to act as pro-vice-chancellor between 1961 and 1969, the first woman to do so. In these and many other spheres, she showed the same businesslike and financial capacity, always tempered by humanity and common sense. Her services to the university were marked by an honorary DCL (1972) after her retirement in 1971, when her college made her an honorary fellow. She had been awarded an Oxford D.Litt. in 1955; her other honorary degrees included those from Cambridge (1963), Glasgow (1966), Kent (1967), Keele (1968), and Belfast (1970).

Lucy Sutherland's notable contribution to eighteenth-century studies was recognized by her election in 1954 to a fellowship of the British Academy, in the affairs of which she played a characteristically wise and active part. Three years later she was approached by the then prime minister, Harold Macmillan (later the Earl of Stockton), to see whether, if offered to her, she would accept the regius chair of modern history. Since at Oxford the tenure of a college headship and a professorial chair is not compatible, she was faced with an acutely difficult choice, but decided eventually to remain at Lady Margaret Hall. Her interest in the East India Company remained constant all her life; her book on its part in eighteenth-century politics was published in 1952 and later reprinted. She also became an expert on the eighteenth-century City of London. Co-operation with other scholars came easily to her, as in the edition of volume ii of *The Correspondence of Edmund Burke* (1960), and in the *History of Parliament*.

In the last decade of her life, when her sphere of interest became the history of the University of Oxford in the eighteenth century, she found a perfect subject in which to exercise her intellectual energy and her ability to organize a team of willing contributors, besides making a noteworthy contribution to the understanding of the university in that period. Although primarily a historian of institutions, she always had regard to the importance of ideas; her judgements were based on an exceptionally thorough examination of a mass of evidence, but she never lacked the courage to come to a conclusion about its import. She was an admirable tutor and supervisor of young historians.

Lucy Sutherland made and kept friends easily; among historians of her time she much enjoyed discussions with Lewis Namier and Richard Pares. She was a splendid conversationalist, and excellent company, as well as compassionate and generous. Of medium height, she was a dynamic personality, quick in her movements and often disconcertingly rapid in her speech and her response to situations. One of the outstanding women of her generation, she did a great deal, though always unobtrusively and wisely, to show how effectively women could take their part in academic and public life. She was appointed CBE in 1947 and DBE in 1969.

Lucy Sutherland died at Oxford, at her home in Park Town, 20 August 1980. She was unmarried.

[Anne Whiteman in *Proceedings* of the British Academy, vol. lxix, 1983; private papers; personal knowledge.] ANNE WHITEMAN

SUTTON, SIR (OLIVER) GRAHAM (1903–1977), meteorologist and mathematician, was born 4 February 1903 at Cwmcarn, Gwent, the second child in the family of three sons and one daughter of Oliver Sutton, headmaster of the local elementary school, and his wife, Rachel, daughter of William Rhydderch, haulage contractor, of Blaenau, Gwent. He was educated at the local elementary school, Pontywaun Grammar School (1914–20), the University College of Wales, Aberystwyth (1920–3), and Jesus College, Oxford (1923–5). His brothers Leslie and Jack also graduated in mathematics, the elder at Oxford, the younger at Aberystwyth, and his sister Margaret graduated in history at Aberystwyth. The early mathematical training of the three boys was initially guided by their headmaster father and was later continued at the grammar school, which had an established reputation in science and mathematics. At Aberystwyth where, in 1923, he graduated with first class honours in pure mathematics, Sutton's teachers included W. H. Young [q.v.] and G. A. Schott, and his postgraduate work at Oxford (for which he obtained a B.Sc. in 1925) was supervised by G. H. Hardy [q.v.]. In 1926–8 he was a lecturer at his former college in Aberystwyth.

His interest in meteorology was stimulated by (Sir) David Brunt [q.v.], himself a graduate of Aberystwyth, and in 1928 Sutton joined the Meteorological Office as a professional assistant. Seconded by the office in 1929 to the Chemical Defence Experimental Station at Porton, for the next twelve years he worked on problems in atmospheric turbulence and diffusion. Security requirements restricted freedom of publication from Porton and it was not until the conclusion of World War II that open recognition of Sutton's major contributions became possible. His gift for lucid explanation, which stemmed naturally from his deep physical and mathematical understanding of complex problems, was widely recognized and in addition to his scientific papers he wrote many specialist and general books on meteorological and mathematical topics, a task which gave him great satisfaction. To this Dictionary he contributed the notice of Sir Nelson Johnson.

Throughout his career Sutton displayed considerable ability in the organization of research and development, a quality which was well recognized by the various posts to which he was appointed during World War II. At Porton he was, in turn, head of the meteorological section, superintendent of research (1942–3), and head of tank armament research (1943–5). When the war ended he was for a time chief superintendent of the Radar Research and Development Establishment at Malvern (1945–7).

During 1947–53 Sutton was Bashforth professor of mathematical physics at the Royal Military College of Science at Shrivenham. He greatly enjoyed this temporary return to academic life where, in addition to his teaching duties, he maintained his research activity and it was in these years that he published the key papers which established his reputation.

Sutton's second period at the Meteorological Office extended from 1953 to 1965, during which time he was director-general. It was a period which saw a complete reorganization of the Office with a greatly enhanced emphasis on research and the centralization of the organization in a new headquarters building at Bracknell. Sutton vigorously pressed forward with this reorganization and also with the development of mathematical methods and the use of electronic computers in weather forecasting. As part of the expansion on the research side he also established a section for high atmosphere research using the latest space research techniques. At the same time the public service aspects of the Meteorological Office were greatly extended. These included the establishment of weather centres open to the public, the provision of automatic telephone weather forecasts, and the extended use of television broadcasts of weather information.

For the last three years of his career in government scientific administration (1965–8) Sutton was chairman of the newly established Research Council for the Natural Environment (NERC), in the establishment of which he had played a leading part.

Sutton received many honours and awards, both national and international. He was president of the Royal Meteorological Society (1953–5), was awarded the society's Symons memorial gold medal in 1959, and was elected honorary fellow in 1976. He was also an honorary fellow of the American Meteorological Society and a gold medallist and fellow of the Society of Engineers. He was elected a fellow of the Royal Society in 1949, appointed CBE in 1950, and knighted in 1955. He received honorary degrees from the universities of Leeds (1956) and Wales (1961) and was an honorary fellow of Jesus College, Oxford (1958). For many years he was a leading figure in the World Meteorological Organization and received the WMO international medal and prize in 1968.

In his last years Sutton returned to Wales, to Swansea, and an interesting glimpse of his continued concern with organization is provided by the fact that the house he built for his retirement at Swansea was of identical design to the one he had earlier built at Bracknell—'in this way all the furniture fitted perfectly and the upheaval of moving house was reduced to a minimum'. He served as a JP at both Bracknell and Swansea. He also became a member of the council (and later vice-president) of his old college at Aberystwyth.

In 1931 he married Doris, daughter of Thomas Oswald Morgan, boot and shoe merchant with a business at Pontycymmer, Glamorgan. They had two sons. Sutton died at his home at Sketty Green, near Swansea, 26 May 1977.

[F. Pasquill, P. A. Sheppard, and R. C. Sutcliffe in *Biographical Memoirs of Fellows of the Royal Society*, vol. xxiv, 1978; private information; personal knowledge.]

W. J. Granville Beynon

SWANBOROUGH, Baroness, and Marchioness of Reading (1894–1971), chairman and founder, Women's Royal Voluntary Service. [See Isaacs, Stella.]

SWINTON, first Earl of (1884–1972), politician. [See Cunliffe-Lister, Philip.]

SYFRET, Sir (EDWARD) NEVILLE (1889–1972), admiral, was born in Cape Town, South Africa, 20 June 1889, the second child of five of Edward Ridge Syfret, a surgeon in Cape Town, and his wife, whose family name was Jones. His one brother was killed in World War I. His early education was at the Diocesan College in South Africa and he passed into HMS *Britannia* at Dartmouth in 1904, becoming a chief cadet captain during his final year. In 1909, as a lieutenant, he specialized in gunnery and during World War I was gunnery officer of the cruisers *Aurora*, *Centaur*, and *Curaçoa*, all of which served for varying periods as flagship of (Sir) Reginald Tyrwhitt [q.v.] commanding the Harwich Force.

He was promoted commander in 1922 and captain in 1929 and on the outbreak of World War II in 1939 was commanding the *Rodney* in the Home Fleet. Near the top of the captains' list and recognized in the navy as an 'intellectual', he was selected in November 1939 as naval secretary to the first lord, serving both (Sir) Winston Churchill until he became prime minister in May 1940 and his successor A. V. Alexander (later Earl Alexander of Hillsborough, q.v.). He was promoted rear-admiral in 1940 and was appointed to command one of the Home Fleet cruiser squadrons, flying his flag in the *Edinburgh*. His first chance of showing his quality in command came a month later when his squadron was ordered to the Mediterranean as a temporary reinforcement for Force H, based on Gibraltar, for an operation to pass a convoy of reinforcements and stores to Malta. Syfret was in charge of the last stages of the operation after the heavy ships of Force H had turned back on reaching the Sicilian narrows, and, by taking the bold course of steering directly towards the enemy bases in Sicily, the attacking Italian aircraft were thrown off the scent. The success of the operation was complete, the convoy reaching Malta without the loss of a single ship. Syfret was appointed CB (1941) for his skill and daring in getting the convoy through.

In January 1942 he succeeded Vice-Admiral Sir James Somerville [q.v.] in command of Force H. His first major operation in this new command was the capture of Diego Suarez harbour in Madagascar to deny its use to Japanese naval forces in the Indian Ocean. With Force H, temporarily renamed Force F and reinforced with units of the Home Fleet, an amphibious assault was planned on the harbour defences resolutely held by pro-Vichy French troops. To avoid the inevitable difficulties and casualties of a frontal attack on the harbour installations, Syfret directed his attack across the narrow isthmus at the rear of the harbour in spite of the navigational difficulties of approaching a rock-bound coast at night through narrow channels which had been mined. Complete surprise was achieved and the harbour was captured intact after only a few hours of hard fighting.

His next major operation was the passage of another convoy to Malta in August 1942. Known as Operation Pedestal, it was probably the best remembered and hardest fought of all the great convoy battles in the Mediterranean. For over two days the convoy and its escorting force were repeatedly attacked by day and night by heavy concentrations of German and Italian submarines and aircraft and by Italian motor-torpedo boats, and though several ships were sunk or damaged, five merchant ships were successfully brought to Malta with sufficient stores to maintain the island until its siege was lifted with the Allied invasion of North Africa. Syfret was promoted KCB (1942) 'for bravery and dauntless resolution in fighting an important convoy through to Malta'.

In November 1942 an enlarged Force H played a crucial part in covering the Allied landings in North Africa from possible attacks by the Italian fleet, and later dominated the central Mediterranean to enable convoys to resupply and reinforce Malta without loss in preparation for the next offensives against Sicily and Italy. A serious illness forced Syfret to relinquish his command of Force H in January 1943 but he was sufficiently recovered by June of that year to be appointed vice-chief of naval staff, having been promoted vice-admiral in the meantime.

Syfret's undoubted qualities of quick decision and intellectual approach to problems made him an ideal choice as VCNS and he proved an admirable partner for Admiral of the Fleet Sir Andrew Cunningham (later Viscount Cunningham of Hyndhope, q.v.) in the top direction of the war when Cunningham became first sea lord in October 1943. To Syfret as VCNS fell much of the overall direction of the Allied landings in Normandy and the succeeding naval capture and clearance of French, Belgian, and Dutch ports as the armies advanced in Europe. To him also fell the organization and implementation of the British decision to send a major fleet into the Pacific to assist the United States in the naval war against Japan. At the end of his two years as VCNS in 1945 he was appointed KBE. He became admiral in 1946.

Shortly after the end of the war he received his last appointment as commander-in-chief of the Home Fleet, a post he held for three difficult years. The run-down of the navy from a war to a peace establishment, accompanied by the problems of the demobilization of personnel, presented considerable difficulties in the maintenance of efficiency in the fleet, but throughout his three years of command he kept the Home Fleet in a state of high morale and readiness for any duty with which it might be faced. He was promoted GCB (1948) at the end of his tenure of this command and was placed on the retired list.

In 1913 Syfret married Hildegarde (died 1976), daughter of Herbert Warner, of Hyères, France. They had one son and one daughter. He died at his home in Highgate Village, London, 10 December 1972.

[Admiralty records; *The Times*, 11 December 1972; Stephen W. Roskill, *The War at Sea 1939–1945*, 4 vols., 1954–61; private information.]
P. K. Kemp

SYMONDS, Sir CHARLES PUTNAM (1890–1978), neurologist, was born in London 11 April 1890, the elder son (there were no daughters) of Sir Charters James Symonds [q.v.], surgeon to Guy's Hospital, and his wife, Fanny Marie, the daughter of David Shaw, lieutenant-general in the Madras Army. He was educated at Rugby School and won a classics scholarship to New College, Oxford. At Oxford he changed to medicine and in 1912 obtained a second class in physiology and entered Guy's Hospital with a scholarship.

When war broke out he enlisted as a dispatch rider, served with the 1st division through the retreat from Mons and the battles of the Marne and Aisne, and was awarded the Médaille Militaire. He was wounded in September 1914 and returned to Guy's Hospital to complete his clinical studies, qualifying MRCS (Eng.), LRCP (Lond.) early the following year. He was then commissioned in the RAMC and posted as medical officer to the Royal Flying Corps squadron at Farnborough. The post included duties at the Connaught Hospital, Aldershot, where E. D. (later Lord) Adrian [q.v.] was among his colleagues. It was at this point that Symonds decided to make his career in clinical neurology.

Symonds took his MRCP in 1916 and returned to France to serve with 101 Field Ambulance and as medical officer of the 1st Middlesex Regiment. After demobilization he qualified BM, B.Ch. in 1919 and proceeded to the MA and DM (Oxon.) in the same year. In 1919 he was resident medical officer at the National Hospital, Queen Square, and in 1920 was appointed assistant physician for nervous diseases at Guy's Hospital. He was awarded a Radcliffe travelling fellowship at Oxford in 1920 and, at the insistence of (Sir) Arthur Hurst [q.v.], spent his time in the United States learning the elements of psychiatry and neurosurgery, working under Adolf Meyer at the Johns Hopkins Hospital and under Harvey Cushing at Boston. At Boston he made his first important contribution to neurology when he diagnosed a cerebral aneurysm in a patient.

When Symonds returned to London he applied successfully (in 1926) to join the staff of the National Hospital, Queen Square, and was also appointed consultant in neurology to the Throat, Nose and Ear Hospital in Gray's Inn Road. He had been elected FRCP in 1924.

From his experience at these hospitals Symonds came to recognize a group of patients he described as suffering from Otitic Hydrocephalus. This proved to be a misnomer, but his clinical observations were accurate and his work resulted in an increased interest in cerebral venous thrombosis.

In 1934 Symonds became civilian consultant in neurology to the RAF and at the outbreak of World War II he was commissioned with the rank of group captain as a consultant in neurology and posted to the Central Medical Establishment at Halton to serve on medical boards. At first he spent much of his time in Oxford, organizing the military hospital for head injuries at St. Hugh's College, with (Sir) Hugh Cairns [q.v.].

As part of his duties with the RAF Symonds had the difficult task of dealing with the condition known as 'flying stress'. With Denis Williams he analysed nearly 3,000 cases of psychological disorder for a report entitled *Clinical and Statistical Study of Neurosis Precipitated by Flying Duties*, for which he received the Raymond Longacre award for scientific contribution to aviation medicine in 1949.

In 1944 Symonds was appointed CB. Early in 1945 he was promoted from air commodore to air vice-marshal, and retired later the same year. In 1946 he was appointed KBE.

Symonds returned to his hospital and private practice and continued to publish important papers and to teach. He was a magnificent teacher and with his intellectual ability and clinical acumen was able to impart information clearly and concisely. By the time he retired from hospital practice in 1955 he was regarded as the greatest clinical neurologist of his time, following in the footsteps of John Hughlings Jackson and Sir William Gowers [qq.v.] and having assumed the mantle of Sir Gordon Holmes [q.v.], whom he looked on as his teacher.

In 1953 Symonds visited Canada, Australia, and New Zealand as Sims travelling professor. Later he was visiting professor at San Francisco and at the Montreal Neurological Institute. He was visiting neurologist at the Johns Hopkins Hospital, an honorary member of the American Neurological Association and of the New York Neurological Association, and membre correspondant de la Société de Neurologie de Paris. He was also an honorary FRCP of Edinburgh.

Symonds delivered many named lectures, including the Harveian oration in 1954. In 1956 he became president of the Association of British Neurologists. He had earlier been president of both the section of neurology and the section of psychiatry of the Royal Society of Medicine and in 1964 he was elected an honorary fellow.

In 1963 Symonds retired from practice to a house he had built in Ham, Wiltshire. Here he pursued his interests of bird-watching and fly-fishing. He had contributed the neurological section in Sir Frederick Taylor's *Practice of Medicine* (12th edn., 1922), and in 1970 he published a selection of his own papers as *Studies in Neurology*.

In 1915 Symonds married Janet Palmer, daughter of (Sir) Edward Bagnall Poulton [q.v.], Hope professor of zoology at Oxford. They had two sons. She died in 1919, and in 1920, in Baltimore, he married Edythe Eva, daughter of Frank Dorton, a tea planter, of Simla; they also had two sons. Symonds died in London 7 December 1978.

There are three drawings made by Andrew Freeth in 1963. One is in the possession of Symonds's family, another in the department of neurology at Guy's Hospital, and the third in the National Hospital, Queen Square.

[Private information; personal knowledge.]

IAN MACKENZIE

SZAMUELY, TIBOR (1925–1972), historian and polemicist, was born in Moscow 14 May 1925, the eldest of three children and elder son of Gyorgy Szamuely and his wife Elsa Szanto. Both Szamuely's parents came from Hungarian Jewish mercantile stock, his grandfather on his father's side being a corn merchant. In the Hungarian revolution of 1919 his uncle Tibor, as commissar for war, was held to have been responsible for the repression under the regime, and subsequently killed himself on being apprehended by Admiral Horthy's police while trying to flee across the Austrian border.

Gyorgy Szamuely, who had worked as a journalist and had also taken part in the revolutionary government, secured passage to Moscow where he obtained employment in the Soviet trade commissariat. In this capacity he came to London in 1932 with his family though he was also secretly working for the Comintern. The young Tibor Szamuely went to Beacon Hill School, near Petersfield, which was run by Bertrand (Lord) Russell [q.v.] and his wife which he enjoyed and where he acquired an excellent knowledge of English. He also was sent briefly to the school at Summerhill near Leiston in Suffolk run by A. S. Neill [q.v.], of which he thought less highly. In 1934 the Szamuelys returned to Moscow. Three years later Gyorgy Szamuely was arrested and condemned to ten years of jail 'without the right of correspondence'. He was never seen again.

The Szamuely family were evacuated to Tomsk in World War II, along with other Hungarians living in Moscow. Tibor Szamuely was eventually called up. In 1945 he found himself a member of the Allied Control Commission in Hungary, perhaps working for the NKVD, the Soviet secret service. He returned to Russia after a dispute in Budapest and attended the University of Moscow to study history. Szamuely next worked as a contributor to encyclopaedias. He also had imprudent connections with the United States embassy. On 2 December 1950 at dawn, he was arrested on a charge of being an American spy, for planning a terroristic attack on Georgi Malenkov, and for uttering anti-Soviet opinions. He denied the first two of these charges but admitted the third. He was sentenced to eight years' imprisonment. He discharged eighteen months of this sentence, at a lumber camp in a marshy region, but was released on the request of Mátyás Rákosi, then the secretary-general of the Hungarian Communist Party, still a family friend.

Szamuely then returned to Budapest as a lecturer in history at the university. He formed part of the so-called 'Petöfi Circle' but, though already disillusioned about communism, played little part in the revolution of 1956 due to his family connections with the old regime. As a result of this inactivity he was named vice-rector of the University of Budapest in 1957. He was, however, dismissed from this post, and from his teaching position, for refusing to lead an attack on the philosopher George Lukács.

After this he worked in the Hungarian Academy of Sciences. At that time, he produced most of his written work such as *Modern History 1849–1945* (with György Ránki) (1959), *The Foundation of the Hungarian Communist Party* (1963), and *National Socialism* (1963). He afterwards accepted a teaching post offered to him at the Kwame Nkrumah Ideological Institute at Winneba in Ghana. He obtained this post through Kodwo Addison, whom he himself had taught in Hungary in the 1950s and who was at the time head of the Institute. He profited from a holiday in Ghana to go to England in 1964 where he remained, being in 1965 appointed lecturer in politics at the University of Reading, then expanding its activities. He became a British subject in 1969.

He swiftly established a reputation in Britain as a brilliant critic of the Soviet regime. He often wrote for the *Spectator*. His lectures at Reading were successful, though he lived in London, finally establishing himself at 17 Sutherland Place, Bayswater. He never, however, completed his long-planned history of the Soviet Union though his introduction to that work—a sparkling analysis of Soviet history—was published posthumously as *The Russian Tradition* (edited, with an introduction by Robert Conquest—Secker & Warburg, 1974).

Tibor Szamuely was a warm-hearted conversationalist, always ready to recall his tragic experiences for those who cared to interest themselves. He died 10 December 1972 of cancer in a London hospital. He was married in 1948 in Moscow to Nina Orlova, daughter of an expert in pestilence married to a doctor. Her grandfather, a merchant in old Russia, had been tortured and exiled in the first years of the Soviet regime. During the Szamuelys' London years, she taught Russian at St. Paul's Girls' School, and worked as a contributor to the *Concise Oxford English–Russian Dictionary*. She died in 1974. There were two children of the marriage, a son George, and a daughter Helen.

[Private information; personal knowledge.]

THOMAS OF SWYNNERTON

T

TANGLEY, BARON (1899–1973), solicitor, company director, and public servant. [See HERBERT, EDWIN SAVORY.]

TAYLOR, SIR GEOFFREY INGRAM (1886–1975), physicist, mathematician, and engineer, was born 7 March 1886 at St. John's Wood, London, the elder son (there were no daughters) of Edward Ingram Taylor, artist, of St. John's Wood, and his wife, Margaret, daughter of George Boole [q.v.], professor of mathematics at Queen's College, Cork. He was educated at University College School (1899–1905) where already he was strongly attracted to physical science. At Trinity College, Cambridge, he read first mathematics (part i, 1907, twenty-second wrangler) and then natural sciences, in which he obtained first class honours in part ii (1908). The award of a major scholarship by Trinity College in 1908, followed by a prize fellowship two years later, enabled him to stay on in the Cavendish Laboratory.

Taylor's first research project, suggested to him by Sir J. J. Thomson [q.v.], was a simple test of the compatibility of the new idea of quantization of energy with the wave character of light when the intensity of the light is extremely small. But tangible macroscopic physics had a greater appeal for Taylor, and virtually all his subsequent investigations were concerned with the mechanics of fluid and solid materials and their applications in geophysics and engineering. He was actively engaged in research from the time of his graduation in 1908 to 1972 when he suffered a severe stroke, during which time he wrote over 200 scientific papers and articles, nearly all of which were later republished by Cambridge University Press in four volumes. His research was profoundly original. In his ability to combine incisive mathematical analysis and simple imaginative experiments to illuminate a fundamental mechanical process or phenomenon, he has had few equals. For all the acuteness and brilliance of his mind, he was modest, unassuming, gentle, and boyish in manner, and much loved by those who knew him.

Taylor's first major investigation concerned the turbulent transfer processes in the friction layer of the earth's atmosphere, and was undertaken on his appointment in 1911 to the Schuster readership in dynamical meteorology at Cambridge. A year or so later he was invited to serve as the meteorologist on an expedition to observe the path of icebergs in the north Atlantic following the sinking of the *Titanic*, and this gave him an opportunity of observing the distributions of mean wind velocity, temperature, and water-vapour content at different heights above the sea. This early work was the beginning of a preoccupation with the nature of turbulent motion of fluids and led to a remarkable series of pioneering papers which extended over twenty-seven years and transformed the understanding of turbulence.

Early in World War I Taylor was recruited to the Royal Aircraft Factory at Farnborough with several other able young scientists to help put the design and military operation of aeroplanes on a scientific basis, a task for which Taylor's adventurous curiosity made him ideally suitable. This experience led directly to some useful investigations in aerodynamics and in the strength of materials, and it was also the origin of a continuing interest in aeronautics and many important research developments in later years, for example in supersonic flow. He also gained a pilot's certificate in 1915.

Taylor returned to Cambridge in 1919 as a fellow and lecturer in mathematics at Trinity College and was given the use of experimental facilities in the Cavendish Laboratory by the newly appointed Cavendish professor, Sir E. Rutherford (later Lord Rutherford of Nelson, q.v.). He was elected FRS in 1919, and then in 1923 was appointed to the Royal Society Yarrow research professorship. This appointment, which he chose to hold at the Cavendish Laboratory, made possible a pattern of life to which his character and inclination were perfectly adapted, and he took full advantage of it. There followed a tremendously productive period, up to the outbreak of World War II, during which he pursued and brought to fruition two great research themes, one on the deformation of crystalline materials and dislocation theory and the other on the statistical theory of turbulence, as well as a host of other novel investigations in fluid and solid mechanics.

During World War II Taylor was much in demand as a consultant and adviser to civil and military authorities faced with new technical problems. The detonation of high explosives, propagation of blast waves, effects of blast waves on structures, and undersea explosions represented the main areas of his work. In 1944–5 he visited Los Alamos, New Mexico, and worked with the group making the first nuclear explosion. Many of these wartime problems suggested basic research investigations in new areas of mechanics to which Taylor turned later.

In 1952 he retired formally from his research professorship, but he continued working in the Cavendish Laboratory with undiminished enthusiasm and fertility and for twenty years explored a remarkable range of novel and unconventional problems in fluid mechanics. In this last phase of his research life he was the international great man of mechanics, welcome at every conference, and he enjoyed the opportunities for travel and the honours that came to him.

Taylor was knighted in 1944 and admitted to the Order of Merit in 1969. He was awarded many honorary degrees by universities at home and abroad (including Oxford, 1938, and Cambridge, 1957), was elected to honorary membership of a large number of learned societies, and received many prizes and medals, among which were the Copley medal of the Royal Society in 1944 and the US medal for merit in 1946.

In 1925 Taylor married (Grace) Stephanie (Frances) (died 1967), a schoolmistress who was daughter of Thomas Holmes Ravenhill, a medical general practitioner in Birmingham. There were no children. Sailing was one of their common interests, and they made a number of notable voyages together, in one case to the Lofoten Islands. These voyages provided part of the stimulus for Taylor to produce a startlingly original design of anchor which had a much better holding power than conventional designs and became popular with owners of small boats. Taylor died 27 June 1975 at his home in Cambridge soon after a second stroke.

[G. K. Batchelor in *Biographical Memoirs of Fellows of the Royal Society*, vol. xxii, 1976; personal knowledge.] G. K. BATCHELOR

TEMPLER, SIR GERALD WALTER ROBERT (1898–1979), field-marshal, was born at Colchester, Essex, 11 September 1898, the only child of (Lt.-Col.) Walter Francis Templer, CBE, DL, of the Royal Irish Fusiliers and later of the army pay department, and his wife, Mabel Eileen, daughter of (Major) Robert Johnston, from county Antrim, of the army pay department in India.

After attending private schools in Edinburgh and Weymouth, Templer went to Wellington College, where, as a small boy who was not good at games, his life was made unhappy by bullying. In December 1915 he entered the Royal Military College, Sandhurst, leaving in July 1916 with no distinction. Being then under the age of nineteen, he was not allowed to join a battalion on active service and had to spend a year in Ireland before he joined the 1st battalion Royal Irish Fusiliers in France in November 1917. He accompanied them to Persia, Iraq, and Egypt after the war, returning to Dover in 1922. There he became a noted athlete, gaining his army colours as a hurdler and being chosen as a reserve for the 1924 Olympics team.

Still a platoon commander, he went to Egypt again in 1925, returning on leave that summer to become engaged to Ethel Margery ('Peggie'), daughter of Charles Davie, a retired solicitor. Married in 1926, they were to have a daughter and a son. In 1927 Templer was finally successful in gaining entry to the Staff College. While a student there, he transferred to the Loyal Regiment, on so-called accelerated promotion to captain, joining them in Aldershot in 1930 for a few months before he was posted as general staff officer, 3rd grade, to the 3rd division on Salisbury Plain. There he fell foul of his GSO 1, who wrote an adverse report, recommending his removal from the army. Templer refused to accept it. The general, (Sir) Harry Knox, tore it up and wrote a favourable one. His next appointment was as GSO 2 at Northern Command at York, where his relations with his GSO 1, H. R. L. G. Alexander (later Earl Alexander of Tunis, q.v.) were cordial.

The year 1935 saw Templer, still a captain, commanding a company, first in the 2nd battalion the Loyals on Salisbury Plain and then, as a brevet major, with the 1st battalion in Palestine, where the Arab population was causing trouble. There were only two battalions in Palestine at that stage and Templer's company was charged with supporting the police in a large area of the north. He revelled in the independence and responsibility this gave him. In retrospect he regarded it as the best job he ever had. His performance gained him both a mention in dispatches and appointment to the DSO (1936), an exceptional award for a company commander.

In 1936 he returned to a staff appointment in England, becoming a Royal Irish Fusilier again when their 2nd battalion was resuscitated in 1937, but never serving with them at regimental duty. In 1938, at last a substantive major and now a brevet lieutenant-colonel, he became a GSO 2 in the military intelligence directorate in the War Office, responsible for preparing plans for intelligence in wartime, including the formation of an Intelligence Corps and for the organization of clandestine operations. His imagination and the thoroughness of his staff work made a major contribution in these fields. When war broke out, he went to GHQ in France as a GSO 1 under the head of intelligence, Major-General (Sir) F. N. Mason-Macfarlane [q.v.], and acted as his chief of staff when the latter was ordered by Viscount Gort [q.v.] on 16 May 1940 to take command of an *ad hoc* force to link up with the French on the western flank of the British Expeditionary Force. Returning from France on 27 May, he was charged with raising the 9th battalion of the Royal Sussex Regiment, in November being promoted to command 210th Infantry brigade at Weymouth under the 3rd division of B. L. Montgomery (later Viscount Montgomery of Alamein, q.v.). In May 1941 he went as brigadier general staff to V Corps and in April 1942 was promoted to major-general to command 47th (London) division at Winchester. Five months later he was promoted again to command II Corps district at

Newmarket, at forty-four the youngest lieutenant-general in the army, but very short of experience in active service command. When it appeared that his corps was never going to engage in active fighting, he asked to be allowed to go down in rank to major-general and be given command of a division in an active theatre of war.

His request was granted, and on 31 July 1943 he took over command of the 1st division, resting in North Africa. His chance to see action at last came in October, when he was transferred to the command of 56th division in the British X Corps in the US Fifth Army in Italy. It had just crossed the Volturno near Capua and was struggling through the rain-soaked hills on the far side. In the first week of November the division had closed up to the German positions south of the river Garigliano and was ordered to throw them off Monte Camino. Conditions of weather and terrain were severe, and the attack failed, 201st Guards brigade, which had borne the brunt and suffered heavy casualties, justifiably feeling that the higher command had underestimated the force needed. Templer was not popular with the Guards for some time after that. A month later the assault was renewed in greater strength, notably in artillery support, and was successful, as was the division's crossing of the Garigliano in mid-January. Attempts to expand the bridgehead did not however get far and were called off, just as the need to reinforce the landing at Anzio became urgent. One of Templer's brigades was sent there on 30 January and he followed with the rest of the division on 12 February 1944. He was heavily involved in beating off German counter-attacks, at one time also assuming command of 1st division, whose commander was wounded. After four weeks in the bridgehead, in which it had suffered heavy casualties, 56th division was relieved and sailed for Egypt to rest and refit, returning to Italy in July. On the 26th of that month Templer was transferred to the command of 6th Armoured division, which was leading the advance as the Germans withdrew to Florence. Two weeks later, as he was driving up to the front, a lorry, in which was a looted piano, pulled off the road to let him pass and blew up on a mine. Debris struck his back, crushing one vertebra and damaging two others. In great pain he was removed to hospital, and returned to England in plaster in September. His short active war service was at an end.

When he had recovered, he was employed for a time by Special Operations Executive before, in March 1945, being appointed to the staff of his erstwhile instructor at the Staff College, Field-Marshal Montgomery, at 21st Army Group as director of civil affairs and military government in Germany. As the war drew to an end, and when it ended in May, with a staff of only fifty officers he controlled and directed a population, whose economic and social structure had collapsed. He flung himself into the task with all his accustomed energy and directness, one incident becoming notorious. Exasperated by the failure of the mayor of Cologne, Dr Konrad Adenauer, to take practical steps to improve the physical conditions of his city, while he concentrated on political matters, Templer ordered his dismissal. Adenauer bore him no grudge, and, although when he became chancellor he would never meet Templer socially, he would send him a case of the best hock whenever he visited London.

In March 1946 Templer moved to join Montgomery at the War Office, first as director of military intelligence and, in 1948, as vice-chief of the imperial general staff, remaining in that post with Montgomery's successor, Sir W. J. (later Viscount) Slim [q.v.], until June 1950, when, promoted general at the age of fifty-two, he took over Eastern Command. He had expected this to be his last post, and it might well have been, had not Sir Henry Gurney [q.v.], high commissioner in Malaya, been ambushed and killed by communist terrorists in October 1951. The suggestion had already been made that a soldier should be appointed to bring both military operations and civil government under one head. The colonial secretary, Oliver Lyttelton (later Viscount Chandos, q.v.), accepted Slim's recommendation of Templer for the post, having first tried to obtain the services of General Sir Brian Robertson (later Lord Robertson of Oakridge, q.v.) and then Slim himself.

Templer's success in Malaya, where he arrived in February 1952, was to compensate for all his previous disappointments. The basis of it was the Briggs plan, proposed and initiated by Lieutenant-General Sir Harold Briggs, brought in from retirement as director of operations in April 1950. He had not however been able to obtain the authority and full co-operation from all branches of the administration, including the police, to implement it effectively. Briggs had left in December 1951, and Templer provided all the authority, drive, and imagination that had been lacking. His arrival was not greeted with universal enthusiasm, many fearing that he would concentrate on security to the neglect of political development. But perhaps his greatest contribution to the success of the long struggle against the communists in Malaya was his insistence on rapid progress to independence and the assumption of political responsibility, including that for security, by the Malay, Chinese, and Indian inhabitants of the Federation.

By the summer of 1954 such progress had been made that Templer could recommend that his place be taken by his civilian deputy, Sir Donald MacGillivray [q.v.], and this was effected in October. The chief of the imperial general staff, Field-Marshal Sir A. F. Harding (later

Lord Harding of Petherton), had recommended Templer as his successor, and wished him to spend a year as commander-in-chief of the British Army of the Rhine in order to gain some first-hand experience of NATO before doing so; but this was blocked by the foreign secretary, Sir R. A. Eden (later the Earl of Avon), who objected to such a short tenure at a crucial period of German rearmament, not, as some suggested, because of Templer's brush with Adenauer.

In September 1955 he became the army's professional head as CIGS. At that time the situation in the Middle East was of major concern to the chiefs of staff and to Eden's Conservative administration. In December Templer was sent to try and persuade the young King Hussain that Jordan should join the Baghdad Pact. The pro-Egyptian faction, supported by the Palestinian element, strongly opposed this, forcing a series of political crises, starting while Templer was in Amman, which culminated in March 1956 with the dismissal of the British General (Sir) John Glubb from the Jordanian Arab Legion.

Templer's whole period as CIGS was an unhappy one for him, including, as it did, the fiasco of Suez and the reductions in the size of the army resulting from the decision of Harold Macmillan (later the Earl of Stockton) to work towards the ending of conscription. At heart an imperialist and a dedicated infantryman, Templer regarded with extreme distaste the abandonment of imperial responsibilities and the reductions in infantry which flowed from them. He was never much interested in the defence problems of Europe and had an instinctive dislike of alliances. He was above all a man dedicated to his duty, and he faced the unpleasant task of cutting down the army, reinforced by the knowledge that his subordinates knew that he would be as fair and just in his decisions as he would be relentless and vigorous in seeing that they were executed promptly and obediently. Exacting in his demands on himself, he demanded high standards in others. A martinet in appearance and manner, his displeasure—even his presence—was intimidating.

He became a field-marshal in 1956. He was appointed OBE (1940), CB (1944), CMG (1946), KBE (1949), KCB (1951), GCMG (1953), GCB (1955), and KG (1963). He had honorary doctorates from Oxford and St. Andrews. His other honours were numerous. His principal activity after leaving active duty in 1958 was the foundation and support of the National Army Museum. He was tireless in raising the money and in badgering government departments and other authorities to lend their support to the project, which owed its success mainly to him. He died at his home in Chelsea, London, 25 October 1979.

[John Cloake, *Templer, Tiger of Malaya*, 1985; private information; personal knowledge.]

MICHAEL CARVER

TERTIS, LIONEL (1876–1975), viola player, was born in West Hartlepool 29 December 1876, the elder son and eldest of three children of Polish immigrants Alexander Tertis, a Jewish minister, and his wife, Phoebe Hermann. Three months later the family moved to Spitalfields where he went to the board school. His first instrument was the piano and he gave a concert when he was six. At thirteen he left home to earn a living as a pianist, and saved enough to enter Trinity College of Music in 1892, where he had violin lessons under B. M. Carrodus, continuing the piano under R. W. Lewis for three intermittent terms.

In 1895, after six months at Leipzig Conservatorium, he entered the Royal Academy of Music and studied the violin under Hans Wessely, changing to the viola in 1897. He had to teach himself, fell in love with the instrument, and dedicated his life to raising the neglected viola to full recognition as a solo instrument. Two of his friends were so inspired by his playing that they composed works for him; E. York Bowen wrote a concerto and two sonatas, and Benjamin Dale a suite.

In 1897 Tertis joined the Queen's Hall Orchestra under (Sir) Henry Wood [q.v.], who promoted him to principal viola. He returned to the RAM as a sub-professor in 1899 and was appointed full professor of the viola in 1901. He left the orchestra in 1904 to concentrate on solo work, and by 1908 had made such a reputation that the Royal Philharmonic Society engaged him to play Bowen's Concerto, and in 1911 the orchestrated version of Dale's Suite under Artur Nikisch; it was in 1911 too that he gave his first performance of Bach's Chaconne, and his monumental interpretation became unsurpassed by any violinist.

In World War I he became involved with many distinguished Belgian refugee musicians, including the violinist Eugène Ysaÿe, who invited him to play Mozart's *Sinfonia Concertante* with him under Henry Wood. He played informal chamber music at Muriel Draper's house in Chelsea with many great artists, including Pau Casals, Alfred Cortot, Jacques Thibaud, Artur Rubinstein, and Harold Bauer. He later toured America with the Bauer Piano Quartet and played the first performance of Ernest Bloch's Suite in Washington.

Meanwhile the era of 'recording' had opened, and, accepted as the greatest exponent of the viola, he made countless recordings between 1920 and 1933, from which a selection was reissued by EMI on long-playing records in 1966 and 1974, and others by the Pearl Company in

1981. One of the highest moments in his career was in 1924 at the Albert Hall, when he performed Mozart's *Sinfonia Concertante* with Fritz Kreisler, whom he admired beyond any other violinist. He had triumphed in his task, the viola had come into its own, and none had helped him more than the composers. After Bowen and Dale came Sir Arnold Bax, Ralph Vaughan Williams, Gustav Holst, Sir Arthur Bliss [qq.v.], and Sir William Walton. John Ireland, Sir Edward Elgar, and Frederick Delius [qq.v.] all sanctioned his arrangements of their works. He returned to the RAM from 1924 to 1929 to teach the viola and direct the chamber music. During this time he trained the Griller Quartet.

In 1937 fibrositis compelled him to give up playing in public, and he then directed his unabated energies (with the co-operation of the outstanding lutenist, Arthur Richardson) to the creation of the ideal viola. The first was completed in 1938, and Richardson made over a hundred himself. By 1965 there were over 600 Tertis models in existence, and in 1973 makers were producing them in seventeen countries.

In 1940 Tertis returned to the concert platform, giving charity concerts and demonstration recitals on the TM viola. He published numerous arrangements for the viola and also wrote an autobiography, *Cinderella No More* (1953), which he revised and enlarged as *My Viola and I* (1974). In 1956 he went to America to demonstrate the new viola, and two years later to South Africa. He finally retired in 1964. He succeeded in his mission because of his amazing virtuosity on the large viola, hitherto unused, and for the magnetism that seemed to flow out of that immensely strong figure, rooted to the platform like an oak tree. One became inevitably drawn into the very heart of the music he was performing.

Tertis was appointed CBE in 1950. He was also FRAM and an honorary fellow of Trinity College, London (1966). He won the Kreisler award of merit (1950), the gold medal of the Royal Philharmonic Society (1964) and of the Worshipful Company of Musicians, and the Eugène Ysayë medal and diploma of honour of the Ysayë Foundation, Brussels (1968).

In 1913 Tertis married Ada Bell (died 1951), daughter of the Revd Hugh Gawthrop. In 1959 he married the cellist Lillian Florence Margaret Warmington, daughter of Harold Henry Warmington, solicitor. He died in his Wimbledon home 22 February 1975.

[Lionel Tertis, *My Viola and I*, 1974 (autobiography); *Times Educational Supplement*, 14 December 1974; personal knowledge.]

BERNARD SHORE

TEYTE, DAME MARGARET (MAGGIE) (1888–1976), soprano, was born 17 April 1888 at Wolverhampton, the seventh of eight children (five boys and three girls) of Jacob James Tate, and his second wife, Maria Doughty. There were also two sons of a previous marriage. Jacob Tate was a prosperous wine merchant and a keen amateur musician who had once journeyed to Leipzig in order to take piano lessons with Theodor Leschetizky. Maria Tate was also musical, and sang. When the family moved to London in 1898, Maggie began to have some music lessons, at first in piano and theory at the Royal College of Music. She was invited to sing, as an amateur, at a church charity concert in 1903, and aroused the interest of her accompanist, a young man of social as well as musical background named Walter Rubens, the brother of Paul Rubens who composed musical comedies. She was in effect adopted by the Rubens family, who divined her promise and introduced her to Lady Ripon, the musical hostess and friend of Jean de Reszke.

In 1904 she was sent by her English patrons to study with de Reszke in Paris for two years, and at once impressed him with what seems to have been from the first a pure timbre and easy emission of tone. She quickly absorbed both the vocal training of de Reszke and the general artistic atmosphere of Paris. In 1906, when not yet eighteen, she made her first public appearances in a Mozart festival organized by Reynaldo Hahn and Lilli Lehmann, at which she sang in scenes from *Le Nozze di Figaro* (as Cherubino) and *Don Giovanni* (as Zerlina), still using the original spelling of her surname, which she was soon to change in order to preserve its correct pronunciation in France. On 7 February 1907 she made her stage début at Monte Carlo as Tyrcis in Offenbach's *Myriame et Daphné* (a new version of the first act of *Les Bergers*), as Zerlina, and as Rosa in Saint-Saëns's *Le Timbre d'argent*. On her twentieth birthday she made her first appearance at the Paris Opéra-Comique, as Glycère in *Circé* by the brothers Hillemacher, appearing there also in other roles, including that of Mignon.

Her chance came when she was chosen to succeed Mary Garden in the role of Mélisande in Debussy's *Pelléas et Mélisande*, and coached for the part by the composer himself (her first performance was on 13 June 1908). Debussy also accompanied her, both at the piano and as conductor, in performances of his own songs; and from that time French song in general, and the music of Debussy in particular, became the centre of her artistic career, at least in its more serious aspect. On her return to England in 1910 she sang Mélisande and her Mozart roles (adding to them Blonde in *Die Entführung aus dem Serail*), besides such leading parts as Madam Butterfly, Gounod's Marguerite (in *Faust*), and Offenbach's Antonia (in *The Tales of Hoffmann*), with the Beecham Opera Company and later with its successor, the British National Opera Company

(BNOC), both at Covent Garden and on provincial tours.

For three consecutive seasons (1911–14) Maggie Teyte sang with the Chicago Opera Company, both in Chicago itself and on tour in Philadelphia and New York; among her parts with this company was the title-role in Massenet's *Cendrillon*, which was the sole occasion that she sang in the same production as Mary Garden, the Prince Charming. At Boston, where she was a member of the Opera Company from 1914 to 1917, her Mimi and Nedda were specially admired; but America was not to see her Mélisande until as late as 1948. In England, after World War I, she continued her appearances as Mimi, Butterfly, Hansel, and the Princess in the BNOC's first performances of *The Perfect Fool*, a satirical opera by Gustav Holst [q.v.]; but for a while she also made frequent sallies into operetta and musical comedy (*Monsieur Beaucaire*, *A Little Dutch Girl*, *Tantivy Towers*), and was at one time in some danger of being regarded as a lightweight artist.

It was therefore fortunate that in the mid-thirties her career should have received a fresh impetus from an unexpected source. Joe Brogan, a great admirer of her art who was the founder of the Gramophone Shop in New York, had been campaigning for some authentic Debussy recordings from her, and in 1936 succeeded in persuading HMV to make an album. Maggie Teyte, accompanied by Alfred Cortot, made a recording that became famous. Thenceforward, her status as an interpreter of French song was indisputable; and during the next decade she made many further records of Fauré, Hahn, and other French composers with Gerald Moore as accompanist, as well as a few orchestrally accompanied songs by Berlioz, Duparc, and Ravel. Her London and New York recitals became notable events; and in 1948 her Mélisande was at last seen, at the New York City Center, some forty years after her first appearance in the part. In 1951 she sang Belinda in *Dido and Aeneas* by Purcell [q.v.], to the Dido of Kirsten Flagstad, at the Mermaid Theatre (then located in Acacia Road, St. John's Wood); and on 17 April 1955 (her sixty-seventh birthday) she gave what proved to be her farewell concert at the Royal Festival Hall, still in remarkably good voice.

Maggie Teyte was small and slight, with a personality that was often charming, always downright, and sometimes abrasive. Throughout her long career, the quality of voice remained inimitable and unmistakable: it was a very pure sound, always under perfect control, with softly floated head-notes devoid of shrillness, and with an uncommonly free and fearless use of the chest register which gave strong character and humour to such renowned performances of hers as that of 'Tu n'es pas beau' from Offenbach's *La Périchole*. She could still sound fresh and youthful even in Ravel's taxing 'Shéhérazade' at the age of sixty. Although her French accent was not flawless (containing certain exotic intonations that were said to have charmed Debussy), she showed an acute sensibility to the colour and meaning of the phrase, and in such songs as Debussy's 'Chansons de Bilitis' she has hardly been surpassed. A slightly excessive use of the downward portamento occasionally introduced a sentimental touch into otherwise immaculate interpretations; but her combination of natural gifts, spontaneity, and musical taste secured for her a unique position in her chosen field which was eventually, if belatedly, recognized in official circles. In 1943, at a dinner given in her honour in London, she received the Croix de Lorraine accompanied by a letter from General de Gaulle; she was made a chevalier of the Legion of Honour in 1957, and appointed DBE in 1958.

In 1909 Maggie Teyte married Eugène de Plumon, a French lawyer. They were divorced in 1915 and in 1921 she married Walter Sherwin Cottingham, son of Walter Horace Cottingham, a Canadian–American millionaire; they were divorced in 1931. There were no children of either marriage. Maggie Teyte died in a London nursing home, after a long illness, 26 May 1976.

[Maggie Teyte, *Star on the Door*, 1958; Garry O'Connor, *The Pursuit of Perfection: A Life of Maggie Teyte*, 1979; personal knowledge.]

DESMOND SHAWE-TAYLOR

THOMAS, SIR GEORGE ALAN, seventh baronet (1881–1972), player of chess and badminton, was born in the British consulate in Constantinople 14 June 1881, the son (an elder son died in infancy and there were two younger sisters) of Sir George Sidney Meade Thomas, sixth baronet, and his wife, Edith Margaret, daughter of Morgan Hugh Foster, CB, of Brickhill, Bedfordshire. He succeeded his father in the baronetcy (created 1766) in 1918. He learned chess at the age of four from his mother who was one of the best English lady players and who won the first ladies tournament which was held during the great international tournament at Hastings in 1895, in which her son acted as a wall-board demonstration boy. He was educated at Westminster School, where he soon excelled at a number of sports as well as at chess. He played hockey for Hampshire, was a good enough lawn tennis player to figure in the last eight at Wimbledon, and became an excellent badminton player. In chess he won some small tournaments before World War I and played twice with success for England against the USA in the Newnes Cup in 1910 and 1911.

During World War I Thomas was a lieutenant in the 6th battalion of the Hampshire Regiment and took part in the Mesopotamian campaign, during which he gave up his place in a vehicle to a wounded soldier and walked in the retreat from Kut. After the war Thomas played fine chess for two decades. He won the British championship in 1923 and 1934 and had a long run of successes in the championship tournaments of the City of London Club, the strongest British club of the time. He played for England in the Olympiads from their start in 1927, when he tied with the Danish player K. Norman Hansen for the best score. He played in the subsequent Olympiads of 1930, 1931, 1933, 1935, 1937, and 1939, having the fine score of 12½ points in the Prague team tournament of 1931. His best results in international tournaments were: joint first with Sämisch at Spa in 1926, second at Nice in 1930, second again at Sopron in 1934, and, most outstanding of all, joint first with Euwe and Flohr, ahead of Capablanca and Botwinnik, at Hastings in 1934–5.

After World War II Thomas played for a few more years, but gave up competing in tournaments after 1950. He then became a keen spectator who was especially interested in the play of juniors. He excelled at most phases of the game, having a good eye for a combination and a fine grasp of positional play. That he failed to attain supreme heights was due to his lifelong status as an amateur and to a certain lack of originality in his play. He was noted for his fine sportsmanship. Never acting dictatorially, he possessed a certain quiet strength of purpose that made him a good captain. He was for some time the games editor of the *British Chess Magazine*.

Thomas was awarded the first brilliancy prize for the following game which was played in the London international tournament of1927.

White Sir George Thomas Black F. D. Yates
Q.P. King's Indian Defence
1 P–Q4 N–KB3. 2 N–KB3 P–KN3. 3 P–KN3 B–N2. 4 B–N2 o–o. 5 o–o P–Q3. 6 P–B4 QN–Q2. 7 N–B3 P–B4. 8 P–Q5 N–N5. 9 Q–B2 QN–K4. 10 N–Q2 P–KR4. 11 P–KR3 N–R3. 12 P–B4 N–Q2. 13 N–B3 N–B4. 14 K–R2 N–N3. 15 Q–Q3 P–K4. 16 PxP PxP. 17 N–K4 N–Q3. 18 B–N5 Q–B2. 19 N–B6 ch BxN. 20 BxB P–K5. 21 Q–K3 N–B4. 22 Q–N5 N–Q2. 23 N–K5 NxB. 24 QxN(B6) R–K1. 25 P–Q6 NxQP. 26 NxNP PxN. 27 QxP ch K–R1. 28 R–B6 B–B4. 29 QxP ch B–R2. 30 R–Q1 Q–N2. 31 R(Q1)xN P–N3. 32 R–R6 R–K2. 33 RxB ch, resigns.

Thomas also excelled at badminton. He was all-England badminton singles champion from 1920 to 1923 and he was nine times doubles champion. He wrote two books on the subject: *The Art of Badminton* (1923) and *Badminton* (1936). However, his health suffered from his World War I experiences. He developed insomnia in the 1930s—he once remarked that he was lucky if he had three hours sleep in the night. In his later years Thomas's sight began to fail, eventually forcing him to give up attending chess events. He died in a London nursing home 23 July 1972. As he was unmarried and had no heir the baronetcy became extinct.

[*British Chess Magazine*, 1895–1972; Harry Golombek, *The Encyclopedia of Chess*, 1977; Adriano Chicco and Giorgio Porreca, *Dizionario Enciclopedico degli Scacchi*; private information; personal knowledge.]

HARRY GOLOMBEK

THOMAS, MEIRION (1894–1977), plant physiologist, was born in Bangor, north Wales, 28 December 1894, the only son and youngest of the three children of John Thomas, vice-principal of Bangor Normal College, and his wife, Catherine Anne, daughter of John Roberts, quarryman, of Llandegai, Caernarvonshire. John Thomas died when Meirion was six. Thomas was educated at the Friars' School, Bangor (1906–12), the University College of North Wales (1912–14), and Trinity Hall, Cambridge (1919–1924). He obtained a second class in part i of the natural sciences tripos in 1921. At Cambridge he was inspired by F. F. Blackman [q.v.], reader in plant physiology, and (Sir) F. Gowland Hopkins [q.v.], head of the school of biochemistry. A lifelong sportsman, Thomas played association football and cricket for his college and he obtained his blue in 1922 in the football match against Oxford at the Crystal Palace.

In 1914 Thomas enlisted in the Royal Welch Fusiliers, was commissioned into the South Wales Borderers, and transferred to one of the newly formed gas warfare companies in 1915 with which he was engaged in front-line operations in France until his promotion to captain and a staff position in 1917. From 1939 to 1944 he held a Territorial Army commission for service with the Durham University Officers' Training Corps.

Thomas commenced research, at Cambridge, on respiratory problems in stored apples but after a year he declined an offer for the renewal of the grant and in due course was appointed lecturer in botany at Armstrong College, Newcastle upon Tyne (1924), the larger of the two divisions of the University of Durham and subsequently King's College and then the University of Newcastle upon Tyne. He was successively lecturer, senior lecturer, reader in plant physiology, and professor and head of department (1946) until he became professor emeritus on retirement in 1961.

In a department with four staff he carried a heavy teaching load and throughout his academic career gave many lectures. Even when relieved of the day-to-day running of practical classes in plant physiology he usually managed to spend some time in the teaching laboratories talking to students. The main substance of his teaching, in which plant biochemistry was an essential part of plant physiology, can be seen in his textbook *Plant Physiology* (1935). The outstanding reception of the third edition (1947) led Thomas to observe that 'it was unbelievable that there could be that many plant physiologists in the world'. Subsequently the book was revised and expanded twice with the co-authorship of his colleagues S. L. Ranson and J. A. Richardson (fourth and fifth editions appeared in 1956 and 1973).

Above all Thomas was a true scholar whose probing mind illuminated his subject. His most noteworthy achievement arose from his evaluation of the literature during the preparation of the third edition of his book. On the basis of the discovery, by H. G. Wood and C. H. Werkman, of β-carboxylation in propionic acid bacteria Thomas explained the previously incomprehensible gaseous exchange data of Crassulacean plants by the occurrence of their spectacular accumulation of malic acid in the dark through the fixation of CO_2 by β-carboxylation. Novel experiments conducted by his student H. Beevers confirmed the hypothesis which was reported to the Society for Experimental Biology in 1945, first published in the 1947 edition of his book, and for which the definitive papers, which surveyed literature going back to the eighteenth century, were published in the *New Phytologist* in 1949. The comprehensive understanding of Crassulacean acid metabolism developed by Thomas in collaboration with S. L. Ranson and several postgraduate students has provided the basis for world-wide research on this important phenomenon which is one of the three main strategies for carbon assimilation found in green plants.

Although he had a number of other research interests his continuing research activity was in plant respiration and he was one of a small number of pioneers who established the scientific basis for fruit transport and storage technology. His publications were comparatively few (one book, twelve research papers, and thirteen reviews) but excellent.

Amongst the honours he received, the most noteworthy were fellowships of the Royal Society of Edinburgh (1946) and the Royal Society (1949), the Charles Reid Barnes life membership of the American Society of Plant Physiologists (1963), and an honorary D.Sc. (Wales, 1964).

Thomas was a bachelor and a rather shy man between whom and his colleagues and students there always seemed to be something of a gap. However there was always a twinkle in his eye and he was well liked and admired. After retirement he returned to Wales where he blended into the small community of Bryn Crug, near Tywyn, from whence he sallied at intervals to maintain contact with his family, friends, and subject. He died there 5 April 1977.

[Helen K. Porter and S. L. Ranson in *Biographical Memoirs of Fellows of the Royal Society*, vol. xxiv, 1978; private information; personal knowledge.] J. W. Bradbeer

THOMPSON, Sir (JOHN) ERIC (SIDNEY) (1898–1975), archaeologist, was born 31 December 1898 in London, the younger son and third child of George William Thompson, surgeon (FRCS), and his wife, Mary, daughter of William Cullen. He was educated at Winchester College, which he entered in 1912, leaving it a few years later to join the British Army, in which he served with distinction, emerging as second lieutenant in the Coldstream Guards. After a brief period during which he worked as a rancher on a family estate in Argentina, he matriculated at Cambridge University (Fitzwilliam House) in 1924, studying anthropology under A. C. Haddon [q.v.] in 1924–5. He obtained a diploma in anthropology in 1925 and in 1926 joined a Maya archaeological field expedition to Central America, and from that time forward he was devoted to Mayan archaeological, ethnological, and historical studies during a long and distinguished career.

He was affiliated, first, with the Carnegie Institution of Washington, then launching its long-term programme of Maya research under S. G. Morley. In 1926, however, he became an assistant curator in the Field Museum of Natural History, in Chicago; and from this base he collaborated with Thomas A. Joyce, of the British Museum, in Maya field research in British Honduras between 1927 and 1929. From 1929 to 1935 he conducted various expeditions of his own into British Honduras, engaging in both archaeological and ethnological research. In 1935 he returned to the Carnegie Institution staff, carrying out further Central American field-work in Mexico, British Honduras, and Guatemala, although from 1940 until 1958, the year of his retirement, he was mainly engaged in library research and writing, with special emphasis on Maya hieroglyphics and Maya religion. These same interests held his attention after his formal retirement and his return to England, where he settled at Ashdon, near Saffron Walden, Essex. Indeed, as a scholar, the term 'retirement' had little meaning to Thompson who continued his research and writing until the time of his death.

Thompson's career in Maya archaeology, spanning as it did the decades from the mid-1920s, paralleled the transformation of that discipline from one of *belles lettres* romanticism to one of scientific academicism; and Thompson was an influential figure in this transformation. At the time of his death he was, without question, the recognized 'dean' of Maya archaeological studies, and he had established himself in this position through mastery of many aspects of investigation. In his early British Honduras explorations his two monographs, *Archaeological Investigations in the Southern Cayo District, British Honduras* (1931) and *Excavations at San José, British Honduras* (1939), set new high standards for careful field excavation reporting, helped to establish relative chronology for the region through pottery stylistic seriations and stratigraphy, and broached the complex problems of the organization of ancient Maya settlement. In the 1930s and 1940s a series of outstanding articles gave proof of his mastery of such subjects as the Maya–Christian calendrical correlation, lowland–highland Maya relationships, and various aspects of Maya mythology and religion as revealed from combined studies of both archaeology and ethnohistory. In this same period he also published two important articles of synthesis, drawing together culture-historical data for the entire Maya area and foreshadowing his well-known text and popular book, *The Rise and Fall of Maya Civilization* (1955). His scholarship and achievements in hieroglyphic studies were drawn together in two major works, *Maya Hieroglyphic Writing: Introduction* (1950) and *A Catalog of Maya Hieroglyphs* (1962). His last major book, *Maya History and Religion* (1970), draws together the several strands of archaeology, ethnology, and history in an attempt to understand the belief systems of the ancient Maya. It was a subject close to Thompson's heart. While his contributions toward 'scientific' Maya archaeology were extensive he was also committed to a deeply humanistic pursuit of knowledge.

Thompson received many honours. These included the Rivers memorial medal (1945), the Viking Fund medal (1955), the Drexel medal (1962), the Huxley memorial medal (1966), and honorary degrees from the universities of Yucatan (1959), Pennsylvania (1962), Tulane (1972), and Cambridge (1973). He became FBA in 1959 and in 1975 was appointed KBE. He became an honorary fellow of Fitzwilliam College in 1973.

In 1930 Thompson married Florence Lucy (died 1981), daughter of Herbert Edward Keens. They had one son, Donald E. Thompson, also an archaeologist, who became a professor at the University of Wisconsin. Thompson died in Cambridge 9 September 1975.

[*The Times*, 11 September 1975; personal knowledge.] GORDON R. WILLEY

THOMSON, SIR (ARTHUR) LANDSBOROUGH (1890–1977), ornithologist and administrator, was born in Edinburgh 8 October 1890, the oldest of a family of three boys and a girl born to Sir (John) Arthur Thomson and his wife, Margaret Stewart. Sir Arthur was later regius professor of natural history in the University of Aberdeen (1899–1930), and belonged to a group of scholars, among whom T. H. Huxley [q.v.] was the most prominent, who made it their business to inform the reading public about the revolution in biological thought that had been engendered by the Darwinian concept of evolution. The Thomson family had close intellectual ties with that of Sir George Adam Smith [q.v.], the principal of Aberdeen University.

Landsborough, the great-grandparental name by which he became known, was educated first at the Royal High School, Edinburgh, and then at Aberdeen Grammar School. Doubtless inspired by parental example, his own first publication, a note in *British Birds*, appeared when he was only seventeen. His first book, *Britain's Birds and Their Nests*, appeared in 1910 when he was twenty. He went to Aberdeen University, from which he graduated MA in 1911. He continued his studies first at Heidelberg and then in Vienna, from which he returned at the outbreak of World War I in August 1914. He immediately joined the Argyll and Sutherland Highlanders, with whom he served in France for the whole of the war. A flair for administration having revealed itself, he was transferred to staff duties, his service career ending as assistant quartermaster-general at General Headquarters with the rank of lieutenant-colonel. After demobilization he was appointed to a post in the Treasury before being transferred as chief administrative officer to the newly-fledged Medical Research Council, with which he remained some forty years, advancing gradually to the post of second secretary.

Thomson's professional life was made up of three intertwined strands of interest: the advancement of ornithology and zoology, the conservation of nature, and the organization of medical research. While concerned with all aspects of ornithology, his overriding interest was in the problem of bird migration. When an undergraduate, he organized the first British bird-ringing scheme, which on his return from the war was combined with the British Birds scheme inspired by H. F. Witherby. In 1926 he published his first major work, *Problems of Bird Migration*. In addition to several papers on the same subject, he published a second book, entitled *Bird Migration: a Short Account*, in 1936. In 1964 he edited a comprehensive work of reference entitled *A New Dictionary of Birds*, to which he contributed some forty of the main sections. His services to ornithology included the chairmanship of the British Ornithologists Club (1938–43), and of the British Trust for Ornithology (1941–7). He was president of the

British Ornithologists' Union from 1948 to 1955, of the eleventh International Ornithological Congress at Basle in 1954, and of the Zoological Society of London from 1954 to 1960.

Thomson's contribution to the cause of conservation was no less outstanding than it was to ornithology. In 1957 he was a member of the committee of enquiry into the Serengeti National Park, and from 1954 to 1969 chairman of the Home Office advisory committee on the protection of birds. He also chaired the scientific advisory committee of the Wildfowl Trust from 1953 to 1966, and the Council for Nature from 1964 to 1969. From 1967 to 1969 he was chairman of the trustees of the British Museum (Natural History).

When Thomson joined the Medical Research Council in 1919 it had only recently been established by the government as a successor body to a Medical Research Committee, and it had a staff of six. When he reached retiring age in 1957 the figure had grown to 130. The fields of medical research which the Council encouraged in almost all the universities and teaching hospitals of the United Kingdom had grown commensurately, with Thomson in charge of all the administrative duties that were entailed. When World War II broke out, he played a major part in establishing the Public Health Laboratory, first as an offshoot of the Medical Research Council, and then as a service with a network of laboratories under the aegis of the National Health Service. Thomson remained chairman of the advisory board which then oversaw the work of the service. After his formal retirement, Thomson wrote on behalf of the Council a record of its work, which was published in two volumes under the title, *Half a Century of Medical Research* (1973 and 1975).

Thomson had an immense capacity for work, and conscientiously discharged the responsibilities of every office which he was persuaded to accept, both within and outside the ambit of the Medical Research Council. Because so many were interrelated, he was able to bring to all an unequalled wealth of knowledge, as well as the modesty and patience which only a highly experienced chairman could exercise. He was appointed military OBE on his demobilization in 1919, and CB in 1933. In 1953 he was knighted. Thomson received the Buchanan medal of the Royal Society in 1962, and was the recipient of numerous honours from ornithological societies. He received honorary LL Ds from the universities of Aberdeen (1956) and Birmingham (1974).

In 1920 Thomson married Mary Moir (died 1969), second daughter of James William Helenus Trail, regius professor of botany in Aberdeen University. They had no children. Thomson died 9 June 1977 in Queen Mary's Hospital, Roehampton.

[E. M. Nicholson, *British Birds*, vol. lxx, 1977, pp. 384–7; Hugh Elliott, *Ibis*, vol. cxx, 1978, pp. 68–72; K. W., *Bird Study*, vol. xxiv, 1977, pp. 202–3; Harold Himsworth, *Nature*, vol. cclxviii, 1977, pp. 471–2; S. Zuckerman, *Journal of Zoology*, vol. clxxxviii, 1979, pp. 1–4; personal knowledge.] S. ZUCKERMAN

THOMSON, SIR GEORGE PAGET (1892–1975), physicist and Nobel prize-winner, was born in Cambridge, 3 May 1892, the elder child and only son of (Sir) Joseph John Thomson FRS [q.v.], later Cavendish professor of experimental physics and master of Trinity College, Cambridge, and his wife Rose Elizabeth, daughter of Sir George Edward Paget [q.v.], regius professor of physic at Cambridge. As his sister was some eleven years younger, he had virtually a full-time teacher in his mother and great encouragement, particularly in practical things, from his father. His early hobbies were model soldiery, ships, and armament, largely home-made; these led to a lifelong love of sailing and a highly professional interest in aircraft.

From Perse School, Cambridge, Thomson entered Trinity College, Cambridge, in 1910 as a scholar. He gained first class honours in both parts of the mathematical tripos (1911 and 1912) and in part ii of the natural sciences tripos (physics) in 1913, and was elected fellow and lecturer of Corpus Christi College, Cambridge, in 1914.

Thomson was on war service from late 1914 until 1919, first with the Queen's Regiment in France, then on secondment to the Royal Flying Corps and based at what later became the Royal Aircraft Establishment at Farnborough. He worked, in the air as at the desk, on navigational problems and on general aerodynamics, with particular attention to stability and performance of aircraft. His first book, *Applied Aerodynamics* (1919), remains a valuable record of the contemporary state of that science.

In 1922, after three years of college and university teaching and of research into the physics of electrical discharges in gases, including the discovery (simultaneously with F. W. Aston, q.v.) that lithium has two isotopes, Thomson left Cambridge for Aberdeen. As professor of natural philosophy, he was now in full charge of a small department in which his gas-discharge research included equipment for applying comparatively high voltages (around 50 kilovolts) to positive ions. In 1926, following discussions at the Oxford meeting of the British Association about de Broglie's suggestion that all particles had wavelike properties, of which Thomson knew the most characteristic would be diffraction of a beam passing through a crystalline foil, he simply modified his equipment, reversing the voltage to give a beam of electrons, and obtained diffraction haloes first with a film of celluloid, later with foils of gold and other metals. He had shown in a few weeks that electrons, discovered thirty years earlier by his father as particles, had also exactly the wave properties predicted by de Broglie. At almost the same time C. J. Davisson and L. H. Germer in New York reached the same conclusion from lengthy experiments of much greater technical sophistication. Davisson and Thomson shared the 1937 Nobel prize for physics.

Appointed in 1930 as professor of physics at Imperial College, London, Thomson used the more extensive resources to exploit electron diffraction as a tool for the study of metal surfaces, as well as for investigating details of the diffraction process itself. He also introduced nuclear physics on a small scale, which became significant when the discovery that neutrons could cause nuclear fission in uranium raised the possibility of a chain reaction. Members of his laboratory had shown that neutrons losing speed by passage through matter could reach equilibrium with the thermal motions of the molecules of the material, and he had rapidly organized equipment for directly measuring their velocities. In 1938, with war imminent, he obtained a ton of uranium oxide, used paraffin wax and water as slowing-down materials, and by the end of 1939 had satisfied himself that no simple assembly of these materials would work. (The first successful reactor, in the USA in 1942, used graphite.)

Having already organized a semi-official 'uranium committee', Thomson was well placed when in March 1940 O. R. Frisch [q.v.] and (Sir) R. E. Peierls realized that a chain reaction using *fast* neutrons was feasible if uranium-235 could be separated from the much more abundant isotope uranium-238, to produce not merely heat but an explosion of unprecedented power. Their memorandum was quickly passed to the highest government circles, Thomson's committee (known by the code-name 'Maud') was strengthened, and a British organization looking to isotope-separation for nuclear weapons was set up. The vast cost, and the growing links with America, led to the abandonment of this project and the transfer of staff to the USA. By this time, Thomson had withdrawn from organizational prominence in favour of specialist nuclear physicists, notably (Sir) James Chadwick and (Sir) John Cockcroft [qq.v.]. He became UK scientific liaison officer in Ottawa until 1942 when he returned to England as scientific adviser to the Air Ministry. He was knighted in 1943, and was already resuming some contact with Imperial College.

In 1945–6, Thomson conceived and partly developed the idea that an electrodeless ring discharge in deuterium might release energy by nuclear fusion; experiments, first started at Imperial College, were moved by several stages and on an increasing scale to the government's laboratory at Aldermaston where their descendant became part of a major European project.

In 1952 Thomson returned to Cambridge as master of Corpus. His decisive approach to practical matters had full scope here, for there was much college development in the ten years of his mastership. He combined great charm as a host with a certain pugnacity in conversation. His voice was powerful, his philosophy generally conservative but occasionally iconoclastic, and his sizing-up of a conversational situation very rapid. So formidable an equipment naturally tended to overwhelm; but, as one of his sons wrote, he did not press for unconditional surrender but left open a line of retreat. He read widely and critically, with more attention to content than to craftsmanship; his pleasure in pictures was concentrated on nautical subjects, while of music he said, 'I judge it by its mean square amplitude'. He was essentially a practical man, and his distinction both in physics and in service to the nation rested much upon catching the tide of events. Of medium build, with an oddly springy step, he remained physically active even after his retirement, which began in 1962 and which was spent quietly in Cambridge.

In 1924 Thomson married Kathleen Buchanan (died 1941), daughter of the Very Revd Sir George Adam Smith [q.v.], principal of the University of Aberdeen. They had two sons and two daughters; one son, John Adam, became British ambassador to the UN.

In the University of Cambridge, Thomson was Smith's prizeman, 1916; five other universities conferred honorary degrees upon him and in later years he was an honorary fellow of Trinity and Corpus Christi Colleges, Cambridge, and Imperial College, London. Elected FRS in 1930, he received the Royal Society's Hughes medal in 1939 and Royal medal in 1949; he was also a medallist of the Institution of Electrical Engineers and of the Franklin Institute of Philadelphia, USA.

Thomson died in Cambridge 10 September 1975. He is commemorated by the George Thomson building in Leckhampton.

[P. B. Moon in *Biographical Memoirs of Fellows of the Royal Society*, vol. xxiii, 1977; private information; personal knowledge.]

P. B. Moon

THOMSON, ROY HERBERT, first Baron Thomson of Fleet (1894–1976), newspaper proprietor, was born 5 June 1894 in Toronto, Canada, the elder son and elder child of Herbert Thomson, a barber, and his wife, Alice Maud, a hotel maid, the daughter of William Coombs, of Dunkerton, Somerset. His great-great-grandfather, who came from Dumfriesshire, had emigrated to Canada in 1773. He was educated at Jarvis Collegiate school, Toronto, which he left at the age of fourteen. After learning bookkeeping for a year he was a clerk and salesman for ten years. In 1920 he failed as a farmer in Saskatchewan; in 1925 as a dealer in motor supplies in Toronto; in 1928 as a salesman of radio sets in Ottawa. He then moved to the northern part of Ontario; and there, in 1931, at the depth of the depression, he founded a radio station at North Bay. In 1933 he founded a second station yet further north at Timmins, and bought an ailing weekly paper on the floor below.

All these transactions were made largely on credit. It was not until 1944 that his little empire was financially secure. By then he owned eight radio stations, and in that year he bought four more newspapers. He was guided, then and later, by a simple but powerful philosophy which made legitimate profit-making into an ideal. As a multiple newspaper owner he now added to this his great discovery: that, on grounds of both practicality and principle, editors were best left alone to do their job.

His acquisitions continued; but it was when he was in his sixtieth year that his life changed—indeed, he titled his biography *After I Was Sixty* (1975). He had married, in 1916, Edna Alice, daughter of John Irvine, of Drayton, Ontario; they had two daughters (the younger of whom died in 1966) and a son. Edna Thomson died in 1951 and at about the same time Jack Kent Cooke, one of Thomson's colleagues, left him to run a rival company. Thomson simultaneously failed in an attempt to enter Canadian federal politics. As a result of these three blows he decided to embark on a new career in Britain. By then wealthy, he bought from the reluctant Findlay family a majority interest in the Edinburgh daily paper the *Scotsman*. Thus, with one trusted colleague, James Coltart, he ousted the family interests, horrified the entrenched Edinburgh establishment, and gained the foothold he needed for other and larger conquests. The editor left and he appointed in his place Alastair Dunnett. From then on Thomson became a remarkably consistent and successful newspaper proprietor.

Although he moved for a while to Edinburgh, he continued to regard Canada as his home country and its mores as the basis of his outlook. In 1954 he took a stake in two Canadian television stations. Thus stimulated, and against the advice of his fellow Canadian, Lord Beaverbrook [q.v.], he saw an opportunity to enter the new world of commercial television in Britain. Against the odds, and with very modest backing, he was awarded the franchise for Scotland (which, with his characteristic frankness, and in a phrase which became famous, he later described as 'a licence to print money').

He had been twice rebuffed in his attempt to buy an Aberdeen paper belonging to J. G. Berry, Viscount Kemsley [q.v.]. But in July 1959 it was to Thomson that Kemsley turned when he decided to sell his whole newspaper group, which was the largest in Britain; and Thomson's television holding was important in the convoluted deal which enabled him to take it over. The jewel of the group was the *Sunday Times*, but in addition there were two other national Sunday papers, two provincial Sundays, thirteen provincial dailies, and several weeklies. Thomson closed some, exchanged others, and introduced new budgetary disciplines into all. At the *Sunday Times* he put in new presses and in 1962 launched—in face of scepticism—the first newspaper colour magazine in the country. Its success was later to lead to other Sunday papers following suit.

In 1964 Thomson became first Baron Thomson of Fleet. In January 1967, after long negotiation, he acquired *The Times*, which was making heavy losses. Part of Thomson's promise to the owners (the Astor family) and the Monopolies Commission was that he and his son would be prepared to put all their large personal fortune in the United Kingdom at the disposal of the paper in order to keep it going. This pledge, honoured when necessary, gave *The Times* fifteen years of financial stability. Thomson was a model newspaper proprietor. 'The attitude of Lord Thomson to *The Times*', wrote that paper in its first leader on the morning after his death, 'was utterly generous and utterly reassuring . . . He never complained to us about the very heavy losses that he was bearing in the worst years of the 1960s, or the smaller losses of the 1970s. He made us know that he loved and respected *The Times*, and his attitude towards the newspaper was totally unselfish. He was determined that the standards and authority of the paper should be maintained.'

In addition to newspapers and periodicals—he was still buying in America, and ventured briefly into Africa—he acquired a number of publishing houses, including Nelson, Hamish Hamilton, and Michael Joseph. He rationalized his extensive holdings in provincial newspapers into Thomson Regional Newspapers, expanded into publishing Yellow Pages directories, and saw the successful launch of Thomson Travel. A last coup was the most financially rewarding of all—with Armand Hammer, J. Paul Getty, and others he invested in drilling for oil in the North Sea, acquiring a 20 per cent interest in the Piper and Claymore fields.

Thomson was a thickset figure with pebble glasses and a flat, North American style; a good mixer, he moved immediately to forenames and enjoyed bantering conversations, appraising new people for intelligence and acumen, with a shrewd eye on future business dealings. He was in many ways a simple man. He had a Victorian belief in the virtues of work and thrift, and a New World faith in technical progress. If he lacked elegance, he also lacked megalomania. He was notable for common sense and candour; and he ruled his staffs through encouragement not fear. He was a self-taught genius with a balance sheet, who could discern trends, strengths, and potential weaknesses within seconds. In the good years of the 1960s and early 1970s his touch was a golden one. First, he imposed financial order on the newspaper industry, inculcating the importance of revenue, chiefly from advertising (and especially classified advertising). Second, and even more vital, he was scrupulously non-interventionist. His editors were genuinely independent. Lobbyists were told that they must communicate with the editors themselves, since he would not. More than any newspaper owner of the century, he justified the principle of a privately owned press.

He is commemorated in a portrait by Sir William Coldstream (owned by the Thomson family), and in a plaque in the crypt of St. Paul's Cathedral in London, unveiled in 1979 by the former prime minister, Harold Macmillan (later the Earl of Stockton), which reads: 'He gave a new direction to the British newspaper industry. A strange and adventurous man from nowhere, ennobled by the great virtues of courage and integrity and faithfulness'.

Thomson was appointed GBE in 1970. He died 4 August 1976 in the Wellington Hospital, St. John's Wood, London, and was succeeded in the barony by his son Kenneth Roy (born 1923).

[Russell Braddon, *Roy Thomson of Fleet Street*, 1965; Lord Thomson of Fleet, *After I Was Sixty, a Chapter of Autobiography*, 1975; *The Times*, 5, 6, 11, 13 August, and 27 October 1976, 11 December 1979; personal knowledge.]

R. A. DENNISTON
DENIS HAMILTON

THORNDIKE, DAME (AGNES) SYBIL (1882–1976), actress, was born 24 October 1882 at Gainsborough in Lincolnshire, the elder daughter and eldest of the four children of the Revd Arthur John Webster Thorndike and his wife, Agnes Macdonald, daughter of John Bowers, shipping merchant. The other children—Russell, Eileen, and Frank—all went into the theatre for some time as, later, did all four of Sybil Thorndike's own children and many of her grandchildren. When she was two her father was appointed a minor canon of Rochester Cathedral and the family moved to Kent where they stayed throughout the rest of her childhood.

Sybil Thorndike made her parlour début at the age of four and within three years was regularly performing, for family and cathedral friends in Rochester, a melodrama called 'The Dentist's Cure' and subtitled 'Saw Their Silly Heads Off' (after *Sweeney Todd*), which she and Russell had written and produced—the beginnings, perhaps, of a fascination with Grand Guignol which was to lead to her celebrated seasons at the Little Theatre in the 1920s.

Around the time of her tenth birthday, her father was offered the living of the nearby St. Margaret's parish and the family moved from Minor Canon Row (immortalized by Charles Dickens in *Edwin Drood*) to more spacious vicarage quarters. By now there was little doubt that Sybil Thorndike would be going into public performance of one kind or another, although it might well have been musical rather than dramatic since her mother was an excellent pianist. Educated at Rochester High School, she also made weekly visits to London for lessons at the Guildhall, which were coupled with occasional visits to Her Majesty's when (Sir) Herbert Beerbohm Tree [q.v.] was performing Mark Antony.

On 13 May 1899 Sybil Thorndike gave a recital of Bach, Schumann, and Chopin at the Corn Exchange in Rochester. Very soon afterwards however, she began to feel pain in her right wrist which made it impossible to span an octave; piano cramp was diagnosed, and although she persevered for a while with the dogged tenacity which was already a hallmark of her personality, it was soon clear that she would be in need of another career.

She auditioned for (Sir) P. B. Ben Greet [q.v.] who agreed that she should join his company on 24 August 1904 as they set off to tour America; in the preceding weeks she was to walk on with the company during a summer season at Cambridge where she made her professional début in the grounds of Downing College on 14 June, as Palmis in *The Palace of Truth*.

The following two years were spent largely with Greet in America, touring the length and breadth of the country in often rough conditions, playing a clutch of lesser roles (including Lucianus, nephew to the king, in the play scene of *Hamlet* and Ceres in the masque of *The Tempest*) as well as frequently stepping into the breach for more important actresses afflicted by the rigours of primitive touring schedules and appalling transport. Thus by 1907 Sybil Thorndike had played 112 parts in all for Greet on the road, ranging from Viola, Helena, Gertrude, and Rosalind to Ophelia, Nerissa, 'Noises Off' and (in Kansas City, 1905) Everyman. It was a baptism of fire, but on those American tours Sybil Thorndike, still in her twenties, learnt the elements of her trade, of which the most important remained sheer survival.

On her final return to London in 1907 she landed a Sunday-night job with the Play Actors' Society as an American girl in a farce called *The Marquis*; G. B. Shaw [q.v.] was present for the play's sole performance and next morning asked her if she would be willing to understudy Ellen O'Malley in a revival of *Candida* for the company of Miss A. E. F. Horniman [q.v.]. They were to play a split week in Belfast, the first three evenings being taken up with Shaw's *Widowers' Houses* in which Sybil Thorndike noticed, playing Trench, 'a young man called Lewis Casson'. Lewis Thomas Casson, who was knighted in 1945, was born in Birkenhead 26 October 1875, the son of Major Thomas Casson, of Festiniog and Port Madoc.

That one Belfast week in the spring of 1908 was to condition the remaining seventy years of Sybil Thorndike's public and private life; it established an alliance with Shaw (who in 1923 was to write *St. Joan* for her) and with Casson whom she married the Christmas after that first meeting. They had two sons and two daughters and celebrated their diamond wedding anniversary in 1968 by which time she was over eighty and he over ninety. He died the following year.

At the time of her wedding Sybil Thorndike was a permanent member of Miss Horniman's pioneering repertory company at the Gaiety, Manchester; the following year she joined the Charles Frohman company at the Duke of York's in London, before returning briefly to America to tour and appear on Broadway as Emily Chapman in *Smith* by W. Somerset Maugham [q.v.]. Then, in June 1912, she returned to the Gaiety, Manchester, to play Beatrice in *Hindle Wakes* by W. Stanley Houghton [q.v.], a major play of the 'northern' school of semi-documentary dramas. Until the outbreak of World War I she remained a leading player for Miss Horniman's company in Manchester and on their occasional London visits with productions of which Lewis Casson was, increasingly, the director.

Three children were born to Sybil Thorndike during short breaks from repertory work at the Gaiety; when war was declared Lewis Casson at once joined the army and his wife moved the rest of the family down to London where she had been offered a season at the Old Vic by Lilian Baylis [q.v.]. In the event she was to stay at the Vic for four years playing Rosalind, Lady Macbeth, Portia, Beatrice, Imogen, Ophelia, the Fool in *King Lear* (male actors being hard to come by in wartime), Kate Hardcastle, Lydia Languish, and Lady Teazle among a vast range of other and sometimes lesser roles: 'Miss Thorndike will be a great actress', wrote a *Sunday Times* critic, 'so long as she learns to keep her hands beneath her shoulders'. But those wartime seasons at the Vic, some of them played during the earliest air raids, forged and fired and confirmed for London audiences the talent that was soon to hallmark her St. Joan.

But first came the Greek plays: she played Hecuba in the translation by G. Gilbert Murray [q.v.] of Euripides' *The Trojan Women* for a series of special matinées at the Vic in October 1919; by March 1920 she was at the Holborn Empire (though again for matinées only) as Hecuba and Medea, performances to which she would also add Candida for good measure. Then came a two-year run at the Little Theatre in a series of Grand Guignol melodramas which was something of a family concern: Sybil Thorndike and her brother Russell co-starred with Casson (who also directed) in plays like *The Hand of Death*, *The Kill*, and *Fear* in which they were gainfully employed terrifying theatre-goers, never more so than in *The Old Women* where Sybil Thorndike had her eyes gouged out by the knitting needles of the crazed fellow inmates of an asylum.

But as the vogue for horror drew to a close, the Cassons themselves set up in management of the New Theatre, with (Sir) Bronson Albery and Lady Wyndham [qq.v.]; they opened with *The Cenci* in 1922, and at one of its matinées Sybil Thorndike was seen again by Bernard Shaw. *St. Joan*, which he then wrote for her, opened at the New Theatre in March 1924, and marked the early but unchallenged climax of her career. It ran initially for 244 performances, and was to be revived at regular intervals at home and abroad until Sybil Thorndike's final performance of the role in March 1941. Throughout the late 1920s and 1930s she also did a great deal of other classical and modern work, often under her husband's direction, ranging from Jane Clegg in the play of that name to Emilia in *Othello* in 1930, playing with Paul Robeson, to Miss Moffat in *The Corn is Green* (1938) by Emlyn Williams. In 1931 she was appointed DBE, the sixth actress to be so honoured.

As World War II started the Cassons toured the Welsh mining villages and towns, bringing *Macbeth*, *Medea*, and *Candida* to audiences who had often never seen them before. In 1944 Sybil Thorndike joined the legendary (Lord) Olivier–(Sir) Ralph Richardson Old Vic season at the New, playing, among many other roles, Margaret to Olivier's Richard III and Aase to Richardson's Peer Gynt as well as the Nurse in *Uncle Vanya* and, in 1946, Jocasta in *Oedipus Rex*.

Then began a gentle post-war decline; the great years of Shaw and the Greeks and Miss Horniman all belonged to a lost pre-war world. Sybil Thorndike was already in her early sixties and, though still indefatigable, having now to spend her time in minor West End comedies or guest-starring in films. The 1950s brought her considerable successes (*Waters of the Moon*, *A Day by the Sea*) in London but it was on long and gruelling tours of Australia and South Africa only that the Cassons were now to be seen in their more classical work.

But in 1962, when Olivier was forming at Chichester the company he would take with him to open the National Theatre at the Old Vic, both Cassons were in his *Uncle Vanya* again, Sybil Thorndike now playing the old nurse Marina. From that, as if to prove her now septuagenarian versatility and vitality, she went into a short-lived musical of *Vanity Fair* (1962). The stage roles now were fewer and further between, and in 1966 the Cassons made their farewell appearance in London with a revival of *Arsenic and Old Lace*. Then came the opening of the Thorndike Theatre in Leatherhead where she was to make her final appearance in October 1969, six months after the death of her husband. In 1970 she was made a Companion of Honour; she also had several honorary degrees, including an Oxford D.Litt. (1966). After two heart attacks within four days, Sybil Thorndike died at her flat in Swan Court, Chelsea, 9 June 1976.

[J. C. Trewin, *Sybil Thorndike*, 1955; Russell Thorndike, *Sybil Thorndike*, 1950; Sheridan Morley, *Sybil Thorndike*, 1977; E. Sprigge, *Sybil Thorndike Casson*, 1971; John Casson, *Lewis and Sybil*, 1972; personal knowledge.]

SHERIDAN MORLEY

TILLEY, CECIL EDGAR (1894–1973), mineralogist and petrologist, was born 14 May 1894 at Adelaide, South Australia, the son of John Thomas Edward Tilley, civil engineer, and his wife, Catherine Jane Nicholas. After attending schools in the city he proceeded to the University of Adelaide and in 1914 graduated with first class honours in geology. The following year he completed the final year B.Sc. course at the University of Sydney, and was awarded medals in chemistry and geology. Both departments offered him the post of junior demonstrator. He chose geology but in late 1916 went to the UK to an appointment as chemist in the department of explosives supply at Queensferry, Edinburgh. He returned to Australia in 1918 to resume his post as demonstrator in geology at Adelaide. An award of an 1851 Exhibition a year later enabled him to go in 1920 to Cambridge to work under Alfred Harker [q.v.], university reader in petrology. In 1923 Tilley was appointed to a university demonstratorship in geology and in 1928 to a lectureship in petrology in the Sedgwick Museum of Geology.

Rapid changes in mineralogy and petrology, consequent on the application of X-ray diffraction techniques to mineral structure determination and the increasing use of analytical and physical chemistry in the investigation of igneous and metamorphic rocks occurred during the 1920s. The opportunity to reorganize these subjects with the natural science tripos came in 1931 on the retirement of Harker and Arthur Hutchinson [q.v.], professor of mineralogy. A new department of mineralogy and petrology was established. Tilley was appointed its first head, and a new building, largely designed by him, was ready for occupation in 1933. Tilley's reputation for hard work was now legendary and he made it clear by his example that nothing less than an outstanding teaching and research laboratory would be acceptable.

Tilley ranged very widely across the span of his science. His work divides roughly into two periods. The first, covering the field of metamorphism, was initiated in 1920 by his investigation of the Precambrian dolomites of the Southern Eyre Peninsula, South Australia, and continued to 1950. During this period he published a succession of outstanding papers which included the classical account of the contact metamorphism in the Comrie area, Perthshire (1924), and the major innovating investigation of the dolerite–chalk contact of Scawt Hill, Larne, county Antrim (1931). No less important were his studies of the anthophyllite–cordierite hornfelses of the Kenidjack and Lizard areas, Cornwall, the Green Schists of the Start area, Devon, and the eulysites of the Glenelg inlier, Argyllshire. This period was also marked by the discovery of the new minerals, larnite, scawtite, portlandite, hydro-calumite, rankinite, and harkerite. This list is illustrative of Tilley's skill with the petrological microscope, and his flair for discovering new minerals. In addition to these specialized studies Tilley published a number of papers dealing with more general aspects of metamorphism. Usually quite short, each was an outstanding contribution to subjects that included the paragenesis of kyanite eclogites and kyanite amphibolites, the paragenesis of anthophyllite, the kanite–gedrite association, contact assemblages in the system $CaO–MgO–Al_2O_3–SiO_2$, the facies classification of metamorphic rocks, and the genesis of rhombic and aluminus pyroxenes.

Tilley was now internationally recognized as the outstanding figure in metamorphic petrology. It was thus not strange that the switch to problems of the igneous rocks, marked by his presidential address to the Geological Society of London in 1950, evoked surprise. A forerunner of the move had, however, appeared as early as 1933 with the publication of the phase relations in the system $Na_2O–Al_2O_3–SiO_2$ undertaken at the Geophysical Laboratory, Washington. His interest in the genesis of alkaline rocks was stimulated during the course of this work and between 1952 and 1961 was expressed in eleven papers. His study of the nepheline–feldspar association of the nepheline syenites and their relation to the $NaAlSiO_4–KAlSiO_4–SiO_2$ system was instrumental in stimulating the experimental studies that provided the basis of our understanding of the crystallization processes of the undersaturated rocks. Prior to these studies Tilley's interests had concentrated on the diversity of basalt magma types on which subject his presidential address provided an authoritative and comprehensive survey. It was a decade later that Tilley, in collaboration with H. S. Yoder, the American experimental petrologist, again turned to basalt. Their classic paper on the origin of basalt magma was published in 1962. Problems of the genesis of primary and derived basic and intermediate magmas continued as Tilley's main interest and, in collaboration with Yoder, I. D. Muir, and others, he wrote a succession of papers that ended only shortly before his death.

Tilley's contributions to mineralogy and petrology were widely recognized. The Geological Society of London awarded him the Bigsby medal in 1937 and the Wollaston medal, their highest award, in 1960. He was president of the Society in 1949 and their William Smith lecturer in 1957. That he had two spells, 1948–51 and 1957–60, as president of the Mineralogical Society, is unique in the annals of the Society as was their publication of a special volume of the *Mineralogical Magazine* on the occasion of his seventieth birthday. Tilley was elected a fellow of the Royal Society in 1938 and awarded a Royal medal in 1967. Abroad his reputation was acknowledged by his presidency, 1964–70, of the International Mineralogical Association, an honorary D.Sc. of Sydney University, honorary fellowships of many foreign academies and societies, and in 1954 by the award of the Roebling medal of the Mineralogical Society of America. He also received an honorary D.Sc. from Manchester University.

In 1928 Tilley married Irene Doris Marshall. They had one daughter. Tilley died quietly by his fireside at his home in Cambridge 24 January 1973.

[W. A. Deer and S. R. Nockolds in *Biographical Memoirs of Fellows of the Royal Society*, vol. xx, 1974; personal knowledge.] W. A. Deer

TILMAN, HAROLD WILLIAM (1898–?1977), mountaineer and sailor, was born in Wallasey, Cheshire, 14 February 1898, the youngest of three children and younger son of John Hinkes Tilman, Liverpool sugar broker residing in Wallasey, and his wife, Adeline Rees, who came from a long line of Cumberland hill farmers. He went to Berkhamsted School in 1909, and then to the Royal Military Academy, Woolwich, in 1915. He was commissioned 28 July 1915 into the Royal Field Artillery, and began active service on the western front in January 1916, taking part in the battles of the Somme, Nieuport, Ypres, and Passchendaele. He was twice wounded, and was awarded the MC and bar. He was promoted lieutenant in 1917 and transferred to the Royal Horse Artillery, leaving the army in 1919.

'Bill' Tilman, as he was always known, moved out to Kenya that same year to become a coffee planter, at Kericho and Sotik. For the next twelve years he concentrated on building up the farm he had cleared from the bush, but in 1930 he met Eric Shipton [q.v.], another young planter, and they started their long and successful climbing partnership with ascents of the two peaks of Kilimanjaro (Kibo and Mawenzi) and of Mt. Kenya and the Ruwenzori range (the Mountains of the Moon).

In 1932 Tilman returned to England and damaged his back in a serious fall while climbing on Dow Crag in the Lake District; he was told he would never climb again. As soon as he was out of hospital he went to the Alps to prove the doctors wrong. In 1933 he prospected for gold in Kenya and bicycled across Africa from Uganda to the west coast.

He visited the Himalayas for the first time in 1934, making a reconnaissance of Nanda Devi with Eric Shipton. They found their way through the Rishi gorge, the formidable barrier blocking the route to the foot of the mountain. In 1935 he took part in the reconnaissance expedition to Mt. Everest and then in 1936 climbed Nanda Devi, which, at 7,817 metres, was the highest peak hitherto climbed. This record, which established Tilman as one of the most distinguished mountaineers in the world and earned him the leadership of the 1938 Mt. Everest expedition, was to remain unbroken until 1950. In 1937 Tilman explored and mapped a little-known area of the Karakoram. The small and lightly-equipped Mt. Everest expedition which he led the following year reached a height of 8,290 metres before being driven back by bad weather.

Tilman's mountaineering activities were halted by the outbreak of World War II. He immediately returned to Britain to rejoin the Royal Artillery with his former rank of lieutenant. He served in France in 1940, was mentioned in dispatches, and took part in the evacuation at Dunkirk. After a short spell in India and Iraq he joined the Eighth Army in the Western Desert in 1942. In 1943 he volunteered for parachute training and special service behind the lines in the SOE, fighting with the partisans in Albania in 1943 and in Italy during 1944 and 1945, when he was appointed to the DSO and awarded the freedom of Belluno. He reached the rank of major.

After the war he returned to mountaineering, attempting Rakaposhi (7,788 m.) in the Karakoram and Muztagh Ata (7,546 m.) in the Chinese Pamirs in 1947. In 1948 he travelled across China to the Chitral, attempting with Eric

Shipton ascents of Bogdo Ola (5,445 m.) in the Tien Shan range of mountains and also Chakar Aghil (6,727 m.) in the Chinese Pamirs. In 1949 he explored in Nepal, which had just opened its frontiers to foreigners and in 1950 he undertook his last Himalayan expedition to Annapurna IV in Nepal and accompanied Charles Houston on the first ever approach to Everest from the south up the Khumbu glacier.

Tilman now felt that he was getting too old for high altitude mountaineering, and so, after a spell in 1952 as British consul at Maymyo in Burma, he returned to Britain, making his home at Bod Owen near Barmouth, north Wales, with his sister Adeline. He took up sailing and commenced a series of unique voyages in *Mischief*, an old Bristol channel pilot cutter. He was particularly interested in sailing in the far north and south, making his first voyage to Patagonia from 1955 to 1956, crossing the Patagonian ice-cap, and circumnavigating South America. From 1957 to 1958 he circumnavigated Africa and in 1959–60 sailed to the Crozet Islands and Kerguelen in the southern Indian Ocean.

From 1961 to 1964 he made a series of voyages to East Greenland, and in 1964–5 navigated the schooner *Patanela* for Warwick Deacock's Heard Island expedition. From 1966 to 1967 he sailed *Mischief* to the south Shetlands and South Georgia in the south Atlantic but in 1968 the boat foundered off Jan Mayen island off the east coast of Greenland. Though deeply distressed by its loss he was not deterred from sailing and purchased another cutter, *Sea Breeze*, in which he made four further voyages to Greenland before it was shipwrecked off East Greenland in 1972. He then bought the cutter *Baroque* in which he made three further voyages to Greenland and in 1974 circumnavigated Spitsbergen.

In 1977 he set sail in the converted tugboat *En Avant* with an expedition led by Simon Richardson to Smith Island in the south Shetlands. On 1 November *En Avant* left Rio bound for the Falklands and was never seen again. Tilman was presumed dead in April 1979.

Tilman was one of Britain's most distinguished mountain explorers and long-distance voyagers. He was renowned for his modesty, his sharp wit, and his austerity while in the mountains or at sea. He always avoided all forms of publicity and was more interested in mountain exploration than the attainment of height records or ascents of extreme technical difficulty. He was ascetic in his ways and a staunch believer in small expeditions that lived off the land and made the minimum impact on the local environment. He was unmarried.

He was awarded the Founder's medal of the Royal Geographical Society in 1952 and an honorary LL D by the University of St. Andrews in 1954. In 1973 he was appointed CBE. He wrote fifteen books describing his various expeditions and voyages.

[J. R. L. Anderson, *High Mountains and Cold Seas* (biography), 1980.] CHRIS BONINGTON

TITMUSS, RICHARD MORRIS (1907–1973), social historian, was born 16 October 1907 at Stopsley, near Luton in Bedfordshire, the second child of an unsuccessful small farmer, Morris Titmuss, whose wife, Maud Louise Farr, of rather less modest farming origins, bore him four children. The family lived an isolated and impecunious life in Bedfordshire and, from the early 1920s, in Hendon where, as a haulage contractor, Morris was no more successful than as a farmer. He died in 1926, leaving Richard to support the family, and particularly to accommodate his mother's emotional and financial needs until her death in 1972.

Titmuss's education was not untypical of the son of a petty proprietor in his day. He began at St. Gregory's, a small preparatory school at Luton, and was 'finished' at Clark's Commercial College to which he went at the age of fourteen for a six-months course in bookkeeping. He was then employed as an office-boy in Standard Telephones until aged eighteen when he was engaged as a clerk by the County Fire Insurance Office, and there he served for sixteen years.

He never sat an examination or secured a formal credential. Nor did he regret his uncertified career, preferring instead to applaud the public library as among the most precious of British social services, and to hold the Ph.D. in sceptical suspicion. Yet in 1950 he was elected to the chair of social administration at the London School of Economics. In the years between, and indeed as a child often absent from school with poor health, he had been an indefatigable and imaginative autodidact. Afterwards, when fellowship of the British Academy (1972) and honorary degrees from the University of Wales (1959), Edinburgh (1962), Toronto (1964), Chicago (1970), and Brunel (1971) were conferred on him, he remained a devotee of the spirit rather than the conventions of academic institutions. He was also appointed CBE in 1966.

The first step out of obscurity was made in 1934 in a Welsh Youth Hostel where Titmuss met Kathleen Caston ('Kay') Miller who became his wife in 1937, and his encouraging companion for the rest of his life. His first unpublished writing in 1936 was under his wife's middle name. Her father, Thomas Miller, was a sales representative for a cutlery firm. They set up house at St. George's Drive near Victoria Station, Titmuss still working for the County Fire Insurance Office, his wife supporting his efforts to write in the evenings and stimulating his social and political interests.

Titmuss's first book, *Poverty and Population* (1938), reflected both his wife's influence in its social concern, and his insurance work in its mastery of vital statistics and statistical technique. It was noticed enthusiastically by Lord Horder the physician, Eleanor Rathbone [qq.v.], Harold Macmillan (later the Earl of Stockton), and the liberal intellectuals of the day, including the Laytons, the Rowntrees, and the Cadburys. It established his place in the distinctive English tradition of political arithmetic which runs from Sir Thomas More to R. H. Tawney [qq.v.], and bears a literature down the centuries of responsible social criticism based on private numerical enquiry into public issues. Titmuss became the main inheritor and exponent of this tradition of humanistic social accounting.

The second step towards distinction eventually yielded a book which made him nationally and internationally well known, the official history *Problems of Social Policy* (1950). Titmuss had been invited by (Sir) W. Keith Hancock to join the group of historians commissioned to write the official civil histories of World War II and to cover the work of the Ministry of Health. So Titmuss entered Whitehall, became industriously familiar with the social services, and was recognized by Hancock as possessed of 'really creative insight into human problems' and 'the most unusual gift for asking the right questions'.

The answers led Titmuss from his pre-war allegiance to the Liberal Party, through active interest in the short-lived Commonwealth Party, to the Fabian wing of the Labour Party. Not that his passions for social justice and equality ever made him a strident politician, for he was always essentially a private citizen and scholar, a teacher and adviser, rather than a political leader, though he was strenuously dutiful in public service, whether as a member of the fire-watching squad at St. Paul's during the war, or as deputy chairman of the Supplementary Benefits Commission from 1968. His socialism was as English as his patriotism, ethical and non-Marxist, insisting that capitalism was not only economically but socially wasteful, in failing to harness individual altruism to the common good. The most startling and impassioned statement of his conviction was in his book, *The Gift Relationship: From Human Blood to Social Policy* (1970), in which, on the basis of characteristically meticulous statistical enquiry, he expounded the theory of a Gresham's law of selfishness such that commercialized blood markets undermine social integration.

This book, and many others, were the product of over twenty years as the incumbent of the LSE chair. From that position he established the academic respectability of social administration, and taught it to a generation of university teachers, administrators, and social workers from New York and Toronto to Mauritius and Tanganyika, until he died in the Central Middlesex Hospital 6 April 1973.

He was indeed a remarkable figure. Indefatigable in his obligation to his colleagues and students, unsparing in his loyalty to his college and his country, a bench-mark of integrity and virtue for the vast majority of those who knew him, whether at work in Houghton Street or at his modest house in Acton with his wife and their daughter, who was born in 1944. In another age he might have been an ascetic divine, painted by El Greco, with his long, thin body and large, round compelling eyes. In fact, he was no saint, but a secular agnostic—in Sir Edmund Leach's phrase, 'the high priest of the welfare state'.

[*The Times*, 9, 12, 15, and 16 April 1973; Margaret Gowing in *Proceedings* of the British Academy, vol. lix, 1975; personal knowledge.]

A. H. Halsey

TIZARD, JACK (1919–1979), psychologist, was born in Stratford, New Zealand, 25 February 1919, the only son and eldest of three children of John Marsh Tizard, policeman, and his wife, Leonelle Washington Ward. He was educated at Timaru Boys High School and after 1936 at Canterbury University College, Christchurch. He graduated from the University of New Zealand in psychology in 1940 with first class honours. Between 1940 and 1945 he served with the New Zealand Expeditionary Force in the Middle East as a member of the Medical Corps.

In 1945 he was made assistant lecturer in educational psychology at the University of New Zealand and in 1946 accepted an ex-servicemen's study grant to go to Oxford where he studied industrial history under G. D. H. Cole [q.v.] and was awarded a B.Litt. (1948). In 1947 he became a lecturer in psychology at the University of St. Andrews but resigned in 1948 to join the newly established Medical Research Council unit for research in occupational adaptation, later the Social Psychiatry Unit, headed by Sir Aubrey Lewis [q.v.]. He began work on 1 April 1948 and stayed in this post until 1964.

The work initiated at this time was concerned with the suitability of the mildly mentally handicapped for industrial employment and social independence. Social aspects of this investigation were developed subsequently by Tizard to include surveys of prevalence (with N. Goodman, 1962), demonstrations of 'model' improvements in services (1964), and critical evaluation of existing services. By using social psychological techniques Tizard attempted to influence social policy. There is little doubt that work carried out in this way by him and by others at this time had considerable effects on the deliberations of the royal commission on the law relating to mental illness and mental deficiency (1954–7) and on the Mental Health Act (1959).

Tizard was awarded a London Ph.D. in 1951. In 1964 he became professor of child development at London University Institute of Education, a post he held until 1971. Among other distinctions awarded him during this period and subsequently, Tizard was the winner of a Kennedy international scientific award, 1968. He was president of the British Psychological Society, 1975–6. A member of the Social Science Research Council, he was chairman of its educational research board in 1969–71. He was consultant adviser in mental subnormality to the Department of Health and Social Security (1965–75); consultant to the Home Office Research Unit (1975–8); member of the secretary of state's advisory committee on handicapped children (1970–3); member of the chief scientists' research committee, DHSS (1973–7); and consultant on mental subnormality to the World Health Organization. He was an honorary member of the British Paediatric Association, a fellow of the British Psychological Society, a fellow of the Royal Society of Medicine, and the recipient of a research award from the American Association on Mental Deficiency. In 1973 he was appointed CBE and also the Thomas Coram Research Unit was set up under his direction.

Tizard's research philosophy was set out in detail in his presidential address to the BPS of 1976. There he cautioned against the preoccupation of academic psychology with 'causes' and recommended instead the exploration of the effects of remedial intervention and favourable environmental conditions in minimizing handicap. He advised at one point: 'Devote less time to the study of supposedly general laws governing the behaviour of a species and more to the rules governing the behaviours of individuals in different environments.' His approach to psychology was not that of the experimental method which he consciously rejected, but an attempt to provide demonstrations of the feasibility of fulfilling patently desirable human needs. Always an egalitarian, Tizard was in many senses a crusader for the underprivileged and used social psychology in the service of the handicapped. After 1964 his studies were concerned with general childhood disorders such as malnutrition and its consequences and with services for the under-fives.

His personality was characterized by attractive qualities of humour, sympathy, and generosity of spirit which inspired both loyalty and regard in many friends and colleagues. His interests outside his profession and his family were predominantly political, but whether in his work or outside it, his sharp wit and healthy iconoclasm made him both an amusing and agreeable colleague.

In 1947 Tizard married Barbara Patricia, daughter of Herbert Parker, journalist. She was a psychologist. There were three children, two boys (one of whom died in 1983) and a girl, and two adopted children, one boy, who died in 1975, and one girl. Tizard died in the Royal Free Hospital in London 2 August 1979.

[Private information; personal knowledge.]

NEIL O'CONNOR

TOLANSKY, SAMUEL (1907–1973), physicist, was born at Newcastle upon Tyne 17 November 1907, the second child in the family of two boys and two girls of Barnet Turlausky (the name was changed to Tolansky some time before 1912), a tailor, and his wife, Moise Chaiet. His parents, of Lithuanian Jewish origin, had recently migrated from Odessa. For the first ten years of Tolansky's life the family was very poor, and although there was some amelioration later, his progress beyond primary education depended on winning scholarships. He attended Rutherford College (secondary school) from 1919 to 1925, when college scholarships enabled him to enter Armstrong College, then part of Durham University. He obtained a first class degree in 1928 and then spent a year in the education department. He received a prize as the best student of the year (one of eight awards which he won at Armstrong College) but decided to undertake research work rather than become a teacher.

Tolansky was a research student under W. E. Curtis [q.v.] at Newcastle from 1929 to 1931. He gained a travelling scholarship to study at Berlin under L. C. H. F. Paschen (the leading spectroscopist of that time) and an 1851 Exhibition gave him two years under Alfred Fowler [q.v.] at Imperial College, London. Between 1929 and 1934 he published twenty-one papers, a substantial contribution to high-resolution spectroscopy.

In 1934 Tolansky was appointed assistant lecturer at Manchester University under (Sir) W. L. Bragg [q.v.]. He was subsequently promoted lecturer (1937), senior lecturer (1945), and reader (1946). In 1947, at the age of thirty-nine, he became professor of physics at Royal Holloway College, London, and held this post until his death.

Tolansky's researches were in spectroscopy, in surface microtopography by multiple-beam interferometry, and in diamond physics. He also made a contribution to the examination of moon dust where his prediction of the presence of tektites (small glassy spheres) was abundantly justified. Although the work on moon dust was a very small part of his total contribution to science, it made him widely known to the general public.

Surface topography studied by optical interference began with Newton's rings. Irregularities in the rings revealed surface defects of 200 nm in depth (1nm = 10^{-9} metre). This limit did not change much until in 1943 Tolansky evaporated metal on to the surfaces, producing highly reflecting films which gave multiple-beam interference. He obtained very sharp fringes, and steps on a surface of only 1.5 nm were observed. This was the main work of his life. In spectroscopy he had used, albeit with special skill and with improvements of his own, methods previously known. In the new microtopography of surfaces he was the leader and many others followed. The most important part of his work on diamonds was the discovery of many small but important features on the surfaces of natural diamonds, synthetic diamond, and diamonds which had been etched or cleaved, though he made contributions to other aspects of diamond physics.

Tolansky was a kindly man, never known to speak ill of anyone. He was witty but without malice and he could enjoy a joke against himself. He was a man of many qualities beside his scientific ability, and always retained a deep feeling for the Jewish religion. He had wide interests in history, music, and art, and it must have given him much happiness that his wife was recognized as a distinguished artist and his son became a professional musician. Apart from his interest in music generally, Tolansky gave much time to the study of Jewish music in a historical context, and had original ideas on the interpretation of musical instructions in the Psalms. It was no accident that many of the photographs chosen for reproduction in his scientific papers were of considerable artistic merit. His book on the *History and Use of Diamond* (1962) was finely illustrated with well-chosen portraits of historical people wearing diamonds, and of diamonds in settings of great beauty. His capacity for prolonged work was profound. He examined tens of thousands of small diamonds under a microscope, looking for rare shapes. He published over 250 papers and sixteen books.

Tolansky was elected FRS in 1952, a fellow of the Royal Astronomical Society in 1947, an honorary member of the American Association for the Advancement of Science in 1966, and honorary fellow of the Royal Microscopical Society in 1970.

In 1935 Tolansky married Ottilie ('Ethel') Pinkasovich (died 1977), whose father Salomo was Obercantor at the Alte Synagogue in Berlin and a singer of international repute. They had a son and a daughter.

Tolansky died in London 4 March 1973.

[R. W. Ditchburn and G. D. Rochester in *Biographical Memoirs of Fellows of the Royal Society*, vol. xx, 1974; private information; personal knowledge.] R. W. Ditchburn

TOLKIEN, JOHN RONALD REUEL (1892–1973), author and philologist, was born in Bloemfontein, Orange Free State, 3 January 1892, the elder son of Arthur Reuel Tolkien and his wife, Mabel, daughter of John Suffield, formerly the owner of a drapery business in Birmingham; his father, whose family had emigrated from Saxony some generations earlier, was at the time of his son's birth a branch manager with the Bank of Africa. When J. R. R. Tolkien was three, he and his younger brother were taken back to England by their mother for a holiday. While they were there, his father, who had remained in South Africa, died of rheumatic fever in February 1896, leaving only a few hundred pounds in shares. Tolkien's mother set up home with her boys in the hamlet of Sarehole, to the south of Birmingham. Here Tolkien experienced a few years of contentment, playing with his brother in the Warwickshire lanes and fields, and receiving an elementary education from his mother. Many years later he identified Sarehole with the peaceful village of 'Hobbiton' in *The Lord of the Rings*.

At the age of eight he entered King Edward VI's School, Birmingham. He was very happy there; he made close friendships, and became noted for precocity at languages. A form-master introduced him to Anglo-Saxon and Chaucerian English, and he also began to read the Norse sagas.

When he was twelve his mother died of diabetes. A few years earlier she had been received into the Roman Catholic Church, and by the terms of her will her sons were made wards of Father Francis Morgan of the Birmingham Oratory, who brought them up to be deeply attached to the Catholic faith. J. R. R. Tolkien's Catholicism was one of the most important strands in his intellect; he once described *The Lord of the Rings* as 'a fundamentally religious and Catholic work'.

At the age of sixteen Tolkien fell in love with Edith Bratt, three years his senior, the orphaned daughter of Frances Bratt of Wolverhampton. She had a room in the Birmingham lodging-house where Tolkien and his brother were living, and she and Tolkien began a romance. They were separated when his guardian discovered this; Edith was sent away, and Tolkien unwillingly agreed not to communicate with her until he came of age.

In 1911 he went up to Exeter College, Oxford, as an exhibitioner, reading for classical honour moderations. He achieved only a second class in 1913, largely because he spent much of his time studying Germanic languages. He was also occupying himself by building private linguistic systems; the eventual result was the two invented languages which he came to call 'Quenya' and 'Sindarin'. A concern to provide what he called 'a history and a habitation' for these languages led him to begin to imagine a world in which they could have a living existence. The earliest results of this were poems and prose, fragmentary in character, but already hinting at the work that would become *The Silmarillion*.

In his second year as an Oxford undergraduate, Tolkien was allowed to join the still comparatively new honour school of English language and literature. His tutor was Kenneth Sisam, later of the Oxford University Press, but Tolkien's real academic mentor was the philologist Joseph Wright [q.v.], editor of *The English Dialect Dictionary* (1896–1905). In 1915 Tolkien achieved a first class in his finals. He was immediately commissioned in the Lancashire Fusiliers, and during his period of military training he married in 1916 Edith Bratt, to whom he had become engaged shortly after his twenty-first birthday. Three sons and one daughter were born of the marriage.

During 1916 Tolkien took part in the battle of the Somme, as battalion signalling officer to the 11th Lancashire Fusiliers. He was uninjured, but was deeply shaken by the loss of two close friends in the battle. After some months he was taken ill with trench fever and returned to England. During a period in hospital he began work on the tales which make up *The Silmarillion*.

He continued in poor health for the rest of the war, and was not sent back to France. After the armistice he returned to Oxford and worked for some months on the staff of the *New English Dictionary*, under Henry Bradley [q.v.]. In 1920 he was appointed reader in English language at the University of Leeds. During the next four years, partly due to the encouragement of his head of department, George S. Gordon [q.v.], Tolkien built up the 'language' side of English studies at Leeds until it rivalled 'literature' in popularity with undergraduates. With a junior colleague, E. V. Gordon, he produced an edition of *Sir Gawain and the Green Knight* (1925).

In 1925 he was elected Rawlinson and Bosworth professor of Anglo-Saxon at Oxford. On his return to that university, he soon made his mark on the English faculty, allying himself with C. S. Lewis [q.v.] of Magdalen to improve the 'language' side of the undergraduate syllabus. Though not a born lecturer (his speech was hasty and indistinct), he gave a course on *Beowulf* which made a great impression on many undergraduates, including W. H. Auden [q.v.]. In 1929, in *Essays and Studies*, volume xiv, he published an essay on the Middle English *Ancrene Wisse*; this article typified his qualities as a philologist: a brilliant, detective-like, ability to unravel a problem, together with the skill to make linguistic matters accessible and even exciting to the layman. However, the major scholarly works which were expected from him by many of his colleagues did not materialize. Although in 1936 he delivered the remarkable British Academy lecture 'Beowulf: the Monsters and the Critics', which revolutionized studies of that poem, his various projected editions of works in Old and Middle English failed to appear. Tolkien's energies were now, in fact, largely absorbed in the writing of fiction.

Most of the stories in *The Silmarillion* had been drafted by the mid 1920s, though in a very different form from that in which they eventually appeared. Tolkien also amused himself by making up stories for his children. One product can be seen in *The Father Christmas Letters*, published posthumously in 1976, but composed during the 1920s and 1930s. The most notable result, however, was *The Hobbit*, begun as a small *jeu d'esprit*, but soon drawn into the already existing mythological world of *The Silmarillion*. It was almost complete by the end of 1931, but did not come to the notice of a publisher until 1936, and then almost by accident. When it appeared in print the following year it was immediately recognized as one of the best children's books of all times.

Tolkien's publisher, (Sir) Stanley Unwin [q.v.] of George Allen & Unwin Ltd., pressed him for a sequel. Tolkien quickly obliged, without much idea of what he was going to write; he was speedily absorbed in the new story, which grew and grew, and which by the end of 1938 had been given the title *The Lord of the Rings*. It enriched itself, just as *The Hobbit* had done, from the myths and legends of Tolkien's 'Middle-Earth' writings in *The Silmarillion*. These provide a backdrop to the adventures of Frodo Baggins the hobbit, as he journeys with his companions towards the Land of Mordor, where the One Ruling Ring must be cast into the Cracks of Doom to free Middle-Earth from the domination of Sauron, the Dark Lord.

The book progressed by fits and starts, and would probably never have been finished without the encouragement of C. S. Lewis. Tolkien read it aloud, chapter by chapter, to Lewis and to the group that called itself 'The Inklings', which met in Lewis's college rooms and in various Oxford pubs. Even with this ready-made audience, he did not finish *The Lord of the Rings* until 1949. His publishers would probably have accepted it immediately, but the issue was confused by Tolkien's wish to publish *The Silmarillion* simultaneously with the new book, and the first volume of *The Lord of the Rings* did not appear in print until 1954. The second volume followed a few months later, and the third was published in 1955.

Critical reaction to such an unusual work was, inevitably, mixed, and there were attacks on the book's supposed 'escapism'. (Tolkien had effectively countered these in his essay 'On Fairy-Stories', first printed in 1947 and reissued in 1964 in *Tree and Leaf*.) But many critics, including W. H. Auden, praised it as an extraordinary achievement. The book sold well from the outset, and in 1965 its sales began to soar to almost unprecedented heights for fiction as a result of a 'campus cult' in American colleges. The resulting fame and publicity disconcerted Tolkien as much as it pleased him. After his retirement from university teaching in 1959 (since 1945 he had held the Merton professorship of English language and literature at Oxford) he found himself increasingly besieged by fan mail and callers, and in 1968 he and his wife retreated to a house in a Bournemouth suburb whose address was kept secret outside his family and close friends. Meanwhile he struggled to complete *The Silmarillion*, which had never been finished or organized for publication. When his wife died in 1971 he returned to Oxford, occupying rooms provided by Merton College, of which he was made an honorary fellow in 1973. (Other honours conferred during his later years included appointment as CBE in 1972, honorary doctorates from Liège, Dublin, Nottingham, and Oxford, and an honorary fellowship at Exeter College, Oxford.) He continued to work at *The Silmarillion*, but when he died in Bournemouth 2 September 1973 at the age of eighty-one he left it in disarray. It was subsequently edited by his third son, Christopher, then a fellow of New College, Oxford, and it was published in 1977.

Tolkien's academic work represents the highest achievement of the philological methods developed in Germany and England during the nineteenth century. Though he is chiefly remembered for *The Lord of the Rings*, a book never seriously rivalled by the many imitations which have appeared since its publication, his fiction is enriched by his extraordinary abilities as a philologist and a student of ancient Germanic literature.

[Humphrey Carpenter, *J. R. R. Tolkien: a Biography*, 1977; *The Letters of J. R. R. Tolkien*, ed. H. Carpenter, 1981.]

HUMPHREY CARPENTER

TOLLEY, CYRIL JAMES HASTINGS (1895–1978), golfer, was born at Deptford, London, 14 September 1895, the only child (there was previously a son who was stillborn) of James Thomas Tolley, a coffee merchant's clerk, and his wife, Christiana Mary Pascall. His delicate health as a boy of nine prompted his parents to move to Eastbourne, where he learned his golf and attended St. George's Preparatory School. As he was still supposed to be in frail health, his schooling was continued privately but he was fit enough to join up in World War I. He obtained the rank of major in the Royal Tank Corps, was awarded the MC for leading his tank on foot in the early mist of the battle of Cambrai, and was taken prisoner in November 1917. At twenty-six, therefore, he was older than the average freshman when he went up to University College, Oxford, in 1919.

It was during his years in the university side that he became known as one of the best and most famous players in the history of amateur golf, first notice of his ability coming when he went to Muirfield in 1920 during his first summer term at Oxford, and, despite being almost completely out of practice, won the Amateur Championship. This established him as a leading figure who quickly became an automatic choice for any international team at a time when international golf was just becoming fashionable. He played in the first Walker Cup match against the United States in 1922, continuing to do so, with the exception of 1928 and 1932, until 1934. On three occasions, his foursomes partner was Roger Wethered, a contemporary at Oxford and a great friend, whose name was invariably linked with Tolley's.

Although he never finished higher than equal eighteenth in the Open Championship, Tolley showed how considerable his powers could be by winning the French Open on two occasions (1924 and 1928) against a field of strong professionals, including some of the best of the Americans. He won the Amateur Championship for a second time in 1929 at Sandwich but his championship successes scarcely do him justice. On his best days, he reached magnificent proportions. There seemed no reason why a swing of rhythmic beauty should ever hit the ball anything but straight; and it rarely did. His demeanour and general game had an unmistakably majestic air and he possessed the capacity for holing long putts, an act made more impressive by his habit, as Bernard Darwin [q.v.] wrote, 'of walking after the still moving ball with a view to picking it out. Occasionally, the ball disobeyed this imperious behest but very often it submitted'.

On the other hand, his sturdy build, given an impression of even greater imperturbability by his pipe smoking, concealed the fact that he was a highly strung person, who, like Bobby Jones, could suffer agonies. He could be temperamental, not always giving of his best and not always trying to. He lacked the competitive instinct of many champions who regarded every opponent as one to be beaten. Wethered wrote in a tribute after his death (*The Times*, 26 May 1978): 'The unpredictable aspects of Cyril's character ... sprang from a peculiar sensitivity and at the same time a dramatic element in his temperament. ... He was a better player against a redoubtable opponent than against a poorer golfer.' As an example of this dramatic element, he cited the time Tolley paid his caddie the winner's tip before holing his winning putt in the 1920 Amateur Championship but he added: 'It was, I am sure, the unexpected and contradictory sides of his nature, combined with his benevolence and kindness, that made him such a lovable and enjoyable companion as well as such an entertaining partner at golf.'

One of Tolley's greatest matches ended in defeat. Defending his title in the Amateur Championship of 1930, Tolley met Bobby Jones in a renowned match in the fourth round at St. Andrews, Tolley eventually stymying himself and losing at the nineteenth. Having cleared his greatest hurdle, Jones went on to complete the coveted 'grand slam'. But whereas Jones, a good six years' Tolley's junior, retired from competitive golf later that same year, Tolley reached the semi-final again in 1950 at the age of fifty-four, thus demonstrating his natural genius for the game. Nearly all the honours of golfing office befell him. He was captain of the Oxford and Cambridge Golfing Society (1946–8) and of the Royal and Ancient Golf Club in 1948.

He worked periodically as a stockbroker but after World War II became active in politics, standing as a Liberal at Hendon South in 1950. He was not elected but, unlike many of his party, saved his deposit. He was treasurer of the London Liberal Party for one year and served from 1958 to 1962 as a Conservative councillor at Eastbourne, where he died 18 May 1978.

In 1924 he wrote *The Modern Golfer*. In addition to golf he played bowls and croquet and was also a keen apiarist and philatelist. He was not married.

[Bernard Darwin, *Golf Between Two Wars*, 1944; Donald Steel and Peter Ryde (eds.), *The Shell International Encyclopaedia of Golf*, 1975; *The Times*, 20 May 1978.] DONALD STEEL

TOVEY, JOHN CRONYN, first BARON TOVEY (1885–1971), admiral of the fleet, was born 7 March 1885 at Borley Hill, Rochester, Kent, the youngest of the eleven children (four girls and seven boys, one of whom was killed in World War I) of Colonel Hamilton Tovey, Royal Engineers, and his wife, Maria Elizabeth Goodhue of London, Ontario. Tovey was educated at Durnford House School at Langton Matravers in Dorset, from where in January 1900 he joined the Royal Navy as a cadet in the training ship *Britannia*.

Tovey's first sea appointment was as a midshipman for a year in the battleship *Majestic*, flagship of the Channel Squadron. This was followed by three years in the cruiser *Ariadne*, flagship of the North America and West Indies station under Vice-Admiral Sir A. L. Douglas. In 1905–6 he undertook sub-lieutenant's courses in gunnery, torpedo, navigation, and pilotage. There followed various appointments, mainly sea-going, during the years leading to the outbreak of war in 1914.

Tovey received his first command on 13 January 1915 when appointed to the 750-ton oil-fired destroyer *Jackal*. He was already a dedicated destroyer man, being described in a report by his flotilla captain as 'entirely to my satisfaction. A good destroyer officer. Keen and zealous'. Tovey was given another destroyer command on 7 May 1916 when appointed to the new destroyer *Onslow* in which he was soon to make his name at the Battle of Jutland on 31 May 1916. Tovey was accaimed for his great courage. In addition to his being appointed to the DSO (1919), he was given special promotion to commander 'for the persistent and determined manner in which he attacked enemy ships'. Although only thirty-one he had established a reputation of star quality, particularly as a destroyer man.

Tovey remained in command of the *Onslow* until October 1917 when he was given *Ursa*, a new destroyer of 1,000 to 1,200 tons. His subsequent command of *Wolfhound* gave him still more experience until May 1919 when he joined the Royal Naval Staff College, Greenwich, for a year.

A spell of duty for Tovey in the Admiralty operations division from June 1920 until June 1922, as a young commander, showed that he was already marked as an officer of promise. Tovey's promotion to captain came in December 1923 at the early age of thirty-eight at a time when the number of promotions was tending to diminish because of disarmament. Then followed a number of shore appointments, interspersed with further destroyer work as captain (D). In 1925 his flotilla was based on Port Edgar in the Firth of Forth, where another promising officer, Andrew Cunningham (later Viscount Cunningham of Hyndhope, q.v.), was captain in charge. Cunningham and Tovey between them developed a scheme which increased exercises at sea and rectified lapses in training.

A year at the Imperial Defence College in 1927 was followed by the senior officers technical course, and then by a testing two years as naval assistant to the second sea lord at the Admiralty. In April 1932 he was given command of the 35,000 ton 16-inch battleship *Rodney*. A responsible appointment, this marked him as a candidate for flag rank, at a time when the navy was recovering from the shock of mutiny at Invergordon. From the *Rodney* Tovey was appointed commodore of the Royal Naval Barracks, Chatham, at the beginning of 1935, and seven months later was promoted rear-admiral.

After other courses, in March 1938 Tovey received his first sea-going flag appointment, becoming rear-admiral (destroyers) in the Mediterranean, and flying his flag in the cruiser *Galatea*. He was promoted vice-admiral in May 1939.

From the outbreak of war with Germany in 1939 there was great mutual admiration between Cunningham, C-in-C Mediterranean Fleet, and Tovey. Both were destroyer men and had highly developed qualities of leadership. With the fall of France and the entry of Italy into the war it was necessary at once to adopt the offensive. Gradually the fleet was increased, in support of the policy of retaining the Mediterranean and control of the sea routes at all costs. In late June 1940 Cunningham gave Tovey command of all the Allied light forces in the Mediterranean and made him second-in-command of the fleet.

Protracted discussion ensued between the French and the British as to the policy to be adopted concerning those French ships at Alexandria. It was imperative that they should not fall into enemy hands. But French co-operation seemed unlikely until Cunningham obtained an agreement that the ships should be immobilized for the duration. Widespread gloom changed to relief. The situation was briefly summarized by a smiling Tovey who, when calling on Cunningham, said: 'Now I know we shall win the war, sir. We have no more allies.'

Tovey had established a great fighting reputation for the destroyer flotillas in the Mediterranean, and was now to do the same for his light forces of five cruisers and seventeen destroyers, which he handled magnificently in action against the Italians off Calabria on 9 July 1940. The main action between rival fleets was brief and indeterminate, each side being much concerned about the safety of its own convoy. Although the Italians sustained only minor damage at Calabria, it was to be the beginning of a British campaign in which the British fleet maintained an ascendancy in the Mediterranean that lasted through years of both triumph and adversity. Ten days after Calabria, Tovey's force sank the Italian cruiser *Bartolomeo Colleoni*.

Tovey's distinguished service in the Mediterranean in command of the light forces came to an abrupt end late in 1940 when he was given the acting rank of admiral and transferred to the Home Fleet as C-in-C, in succession to Admiral Sir Charles Forbes [q.v.]. Tovey, though not yet fifty-five, was approaching the peak of his active service career.

Tovey faced a very difficult situation in the first part of 1941. Britain was still alone, and the possibility of a German invasion remained, though no longer imminent. More serious, however, was the threat to Britain's Atlantic lifeline, and also the increasing production of German submarines and aircraft. In spite of Britain's blockade of the northern passages, German warships were able to break out from the Baltic and roam the high seas, largely sustained by the supply bases acquired in western France. The new battle cruisers *Scharnhorst* and *Gneisenau* were both at large. Admiral (Sir) Richard Onslow [q.v.] recorded that in those long hard days of 1941 Tovey's leadership was of the finest: it stemmed from strength of character and fearlessness.

The German Admiral Raeder planned for a rendezvous in April 1941, whereby the 'unsinkable' battleship *Bismarck* and the heavy cruiser *Prinz Eugen* should escape unseen from the Baltic, and join forces in the Atlantic with the battle cruisers *Scharnhorst* and *Gneisenau* from Brest. Such a force could cope with almost any likely situation, and would pose a powerful threat to Britain's lifeline. Tovey was aware of the plan and disposed his fleet accordingly, ordering his cruisers to keep a particularly close watch on the Denmark Strait. He had received a great accretion of strength in the new aircraft carrier *Victorious* which joined him at Scapa Flow. Bomb damage prevented the sailing of those German ships at Brest, but the *Bismarck* and *Prinz Eugen* were reported on 22 May 1941 as having left Bergen, indicating that a break out was imminent. Tovey had already sailed the battle cruiser *Hood* and the battleship *Prince of Wales* for the Denmark Strait, and at 7.45 p.m. on 22 May with his flag in the battleship *King George V*, sailed the rest of the Home Fleet, including *Victorious* and the battle cruiser *Repulse*, from Scapa Flow. In view of the vast distances to be covered, due care had to be taken over fuel supply.

At 7.22 p.m. on 23 May, in spite of sleet and snow that impaired the visibility, the cruiser *Suffolk* sighted and reported the *Bismarck* and the *Prinz Eugen* as seven miles ahead of her in the Denmark Strait, steering a south-westerly course. Action was joined at 5.53 a.m. on 24 May. All four ships opened fire. Within seconds the *Hood* was straddled by the *Bismarck* and blew up with a huge explosion. There were only three survivors. With her own fighting capacity drastically reduced by breakdowns and accurate enemy fire, the *Prince of Wales* withdrew under cover of smoke. The German ships continued to steer a south-westerly course. But the *Prince of Wales* had obtained two hits on the *Bismarck*, one of which caused a leak of oil fuel and was to have dire consequences. Reduction of endurance might compel the *Bismarck* to make for a French port.

Tovey, with the *King George V*, *Repulse*, and *Victorious*, was still 300 miles away steaming westward, intent on intercepting the *Bismarck*. Meanwhile the Admiralty diverted various ships to come under Tovey's command so as to be in areas where a renewal of action appeared likely. These included the aircraft carrier *Ark Royal* (from Force H), and the *Rodney* and *Ramillies* with various cruisers and destroyers. Late on 24

May, torpedo reconnaissance bombers from the *Victorious* found the *Bismarck* and delivered with great gallantry, in squally weather, an attack which scored a hit. *Bismarck* escaped yet again.

Tovey had great anxiety at the prospect of fuel shortage in so many of his ships, in an area favourable both for German aircraft and submarines. He decided that if the *Bismarck* had not been slowed down before midnight on 26 May he would be compelled to break off the chase. His margin of success was slender, for at 8.47 p.m. on 26 May, *Ark Royal*'s striking force scored a hit which damaged *Bismarck*'s propellers, jammed her rudder, and effectively stopped her. On the morning of 27 May she faced the combined fire of *King George V* and *Rodney* and sustained overwhelming damage, though gallantly returning fire to the end. Tovey ordered that she should be finished off by torpedoes.

Tovey remarked favourably on the speed and accuracy of the information signalled by the Admiralty. He was however soon to come into conflict with the Admiralty, and with (Sir) Winston Churchill too. He was much concerned at the lack of air support, and never hesitated to stress the point, thereby earning Churchill's description of him as 'stubborn and obstinate'. Interference by the Admiralty reached a climax in July 1942 when a valuable British convoy, PQ 17 in the Barents Sea, was ordered by the Admiralty (without Tovey's concurrence) to scatter. It resulted in disastrous losses. However, Tovey's forthright opinions, and his utter integrity and courage inspired confidence throughout the fleet. In July 1943, after two and a half years in command, he relinquished the Home Fleet to become C-in-C the Nore. Preparations were already in hand, not only for the 1943 Allied invasion of Sicily, but also for the 1944 entry into Europe.

Tovey was appointed KBE in 1941 after sinking the *Bismarck*. Also in 1941 he was promoted KCB, having been appointed CB in 1937. In 1943 he was further advanced to GCB and also promoted to the highest rank, admiral of the fleet, having been confirmed full admiral in 1942. He was raised to the peerage in 1946.

Tovey was for four years (1948–52) third church estates commissioner, an appointment made by the archbishop of Canterbury, and one which Tovey enjoyed to the full, and carried out with efficiency.

On 28 March 1916 Tovey married Aida (died 1970), daughter of John Rowe, an independent gentleman, of Plymouth, Devon. There were no children of the marriage. Tovey died at Funchal, Madeira, 12 January 1971, and the barony became extinct.

[*The Times*, 13 and 18 January 1971; family and private information.]

S. W. C. Pack
C. S. Nicholls

TOYNBEE, ARNOLD JOSEPH (1889–1975) author, scholar, and historian, was born in London, 14 April 1889, the only son and eldest of the three children of Harry Valpy Toynbee, worker for the Charity Organization Society, and his wife, Sarah Edith Marshall. He gained a scholarship to Winchester College and another from there to Balliol College, Oxford, in 1907. He acquired a remarkable knowledge of Latin and Greek, obtaining first classes in both classical honour moderations (1909) and *literae humaniores* (1911). He then became a tutor in ancient Greek and Roman history at Balliol; his scholarship was renewed and he was encouraged to travel. In 1911 and 1912 he explored Greece and Italy alone and on foot. For a year he became a student at the British School of Archaeology at Athens. He contracted dysentery which rendered him unfit for the army (the death on active service of many contemporaries haunted him all his life) and he spent most of the war years in government work, notably in the Political Intelligence Department of the Foreign Office. He was a member of the British delegation to the Paris peace conference of 1919, after which he was appointed to the Koraes chair of Byzantine and Modern Greek language, literature, and history at London University. He resigned in 1924.

Toynbee had married in 1913 Rosalind, daughter of G. Gilbert Murray [q.v.], scholar, poet, and author. There were three sons, of whom the eldest died in 1939. (Theodore) Philip (died 1981) was a distinguished novelist and journalist, and Lawrence is a gifted artist. The marriage was dissolved in 1946 and in the same year Toynbee married Veronica Marjorie (died 1980), daughter of the Revd Sidney Boulter. This marriage, a very happy one, continued a working partnership which had begun in 1925, when Toynbee went to Chatham House (the Royal Institute of International Affairs), as director of studies. Miss Boulter, already on the Chatham House staff, soon became his collaborator, sharing with him until 1946 the writing of the annual *Survey of International Affairs*. Simultaneously he was research professor of international history in the University of London. During World War II Toynbee was director of the Foreign Office Research Department (called the Foreign Research and Press Service before 1943). He retired from Chatham House and his chair in 1955.

When still a very young man he had made a programme of what he wished to accomplish in his writing, and he carried it through, with the aid of a large number of small notebooks, filled with ideas and references to be used, sometimes years later, in fulfilment of the plan. It was in about 1914 that it struck him that, with the outbreak of World War I, our world had entered on an experience that the Greek world had been through in the Peloponnesian war. That flash of perception gave him the idea of making comparisons between civilizations. As a result, *A Study of History* in twelve volumes was published by the Oxford University Press between 1934 and 1961, and it is largely on this great work that Toynbee's fame rests. His theory of 'challenge and response' in relation to civilizations brought him many critics, two of the most vociferous being Pieter Geyl and Hugh Trevor-Roper (later Lord Dacre of Glanton). Toynbee was untroubled by their views, since he had every confidence in his own. A venture which made the *Study* accessible to a vast new public was the abridgement prepared, on his own initiative, by David C. Somervell, and to the publication of which Toynbee gave his reluctant approval. Volumes i–vi appeared in 1946; volumes vii–x in 1957; the complete edition, in one volume, in 1960. Much later (1972) the illustrated version, in which Toynbee had the collaboration of Jane Caplan, reached another new public.

He was a writer of prodigious output and many of his books became bestsellers, though they often attracted controversy. Mention should be made here of *Hannibal's Legacy* (1965) and *Constantine Porphyrogenitus and his World* (1973) for their profound scholarship. His two 'personal' books, *Acquaintances* (1967) and *Experiences* (1969), reveal a great deal about their author, and the few short travel books show another facet of this many-faceted man. He was a regular contributor to the *Manchester Guardian* and the *Observer* and wrote a weekly column in the *Economist* between 1930 and 1939. His lectures, notably the Reith lectures of 1952 and the Gifford series of 1953 and 1954, were published in book form. His last major published works, both of which appeared posthumously, were *Mankind and Mother Earth* (1976) in which his aim was 'to give a comprehensive bird's-eye view of mankind's history in narrational form' and *The Greeks and their Heritages* (1981). To this Dictionary he contributed the notice of Sir Edwin Pears.

His main publishers, the Oxford University Press, found him a co-operative and appreciative author. He was genuinely interested in the minutiae involved in book production. In 1972 the Press, in conjunction with the National Book League, mounted an exhibition of his work at the League's premises. Called 'A Study of Toynbee', and consisting mainly of photographs, manuscripts, and copies of his books (including translations into twenty-five languages), it attracted a large number of visitors.

Toynbee's preoccupation with religion is well documented. He became an agnostic early in life, but was convinced that Man was not the highest form of creation; he believed in an 'ultimate spiritual reality', but he could not conceive of a god who was both all-loving and all-powerful. He was, in fact, a deeply religious agnostic, and his writings on, or touching on, religious subjects indicate that perhaps his agnosticism was nearer belief than the belief of some practitioners of conventional religion.

Toynbee was a quiet, charming, courteous, and kindly man. A generous host, he had a personal life-style that was simple to the point of austerity. His regular (and early) hours enabled him to produce the maximum amount of work every day. He wasted nothing, least of all, time. He admitted that his need to work was obsessional and was able to produce reasons for the obsession.

He had a deep feeling for the countryside, and a historical vision of landscape. He loved travel, and visited many countries of the world, sometimes on his own, but often with his wife, Veronica. (It was in a ship between Panama and Auckland, in 1956, that he learned of the offer of his appointment as a Companion of Honour, which he accepted.) A holiday 'for pleasure', though, he would have seen as a waste of time. Not for him the superficial sightseeing trip or the 'beach' holiday. All that he saw and did was transmuted into books or articles or lectures.

Toynbee received many honours apart from his CH. He was elected FBA in 1937, made an honorary fellow of Balliol in 1957, and presented with honorary degrees from many universities including Oxford, Cambridge, and Princeton. It delighted him when, in 1968, he was made a *membre associé de l'Institut de France*, taking the place of Sir Winston Churchill. But what was perhaps the crowning honour came in 1974, when he was received *ad portas* at his old school, Winchester College. His reply, in Latin, written in his minute, beautiful handwriting, was in his pocket, but his memory did not falter: he had no need to refer to it.

In the same year he suffered a severe stroke. From then on he had little power to communicate, and none to work. He longed for death and died in Purey Cust nursing home in York fourteen months later, 22 October 1975. His ashes lie in the burial ground at Terrington, near his Yorkshire home.

[S. Fiona Morton, *A Bibliography of Arnold J. Toynbee*, 1981; family papers; personal knowledge.]

LOUISE ORR

TRAVERS, BENJAMIN (1886–1980), dramatist, was born 12 November 1886 in Hendon, Middlesex, the elder son and the second of the three children of Walter Francis Travers, clerk and later merchant, of London, and his wife, Margaret Travers Burges. He was a great-grandson of Benjamin Travers [q.v.], pioneer in eye surgery and serjeant-surgeon to Queen Victoria. Always called Ben by his family and friends, he was educated at the Abbey School, Beckenham, and Charterhouse, where his first form master in the lower school was Leonard Huxley, father of Aldous and (Sir) Julian [qq.v.]. He was an unusually small boy for his age. 'And that was a terrible handicap to me', he later recalled, adding 'I was a complete failure at school'. The only thing he enjoyed there was cricket, having become an enthusiast for the sport when he saw England's legendary batsman W. G. Grace [q.v.] make a century.

On leaving Charterhouse, in 1904, his parents sent him to Dresden for a few months to learn German. The performances of Sarah Bernhardt and Lucien Guitry which he saw there gave him a taste for the theatre, so that on his return he informed his parents that he wished to become an actor. This request was promptly vetoed, and instead he was put into the family business, Messrs Joseph Travers and Sons Ltd., one of the oldest wholesale grocery firms in the City dating from 1666. He found the work of 'tea-clearing' which he was set to do uncongenial, and after six months he was transferred to the Malayan branch in Singapore. Here the local manager took an instant dislike to him with the result that he was then consigned to the branch in Malacca where he had practically no work to do but was able to find a complete set of plays of Sir A. W. Pinero [q.v.] in the local library. This further stimulated his interest in the theatre, since he found them an excellent guide to the technique of stagecraft. In 1908 his mother died, and as his sister Mabel was already married and his younger brother Frank was still at school, he felt he should return home to keep his father company. This he did, but at the same time he unwillingly went back to the family business in the City, which he found as distasteful as before. However he endured it until 1911 when a literary friend introduced him to the *avant-garde* publisher John Lane [q.v.] of the Bodley Head. He spent the next three years in Lane's office and Lane took him with him on business visits to the United States and Canada.

In 1914 Travers joined the Royal Naval Air Service, in which he served throughout the war, much of the time as a flying instructor, in the rank of flight lieutenant and later as a major when the RNAS was amalgamated with the Royal Flying Corps. For his wartime exploits, which ended with a brief spell of duty in Russia during the allied intervention, he was awarded the Air Force Cross (1920).

During the war he had got married, and his wife had an income of £1,000 a year, a useful sum in those days, which was a help when he returned to civilian life and decided to become a writer, settling with her in Somerset. He began as a novelist, returning as an author to the Bodley Head, where Lane published his first novel *The Dippers* (1922). He then turned the novel into a farce and sent it to the actor-manager Sir Charles Hawtrey [q.v.] who produced it, after a try-out in the provinces, at the Criterion Theatre in August 1922 with Cyril Maude in the lead. It had a fair success, running for 173 performances. *The Dippers* was followed by another novel, *A Cuckoo in the Nest* (1925), which he also dramatized after the reviewers praised its humour. Then Travers had a stroke of luck. Tom Walls [q.v.], ex-policeman, actor-manager, and future Derby winner, needed a new play to succeed his current success *It Pays to Advertise* at the Aldwych. In the result he produced *A Cuckoo in the Nest* there in July 1925, with Yvonne Arnaud, Mary Brough, Ralph Lynn, J. Robertson Hare [q.v.], and himself in the principal parts. It was an immediate success and notched up 376 performances.

During the next seven years Travers wrote eight more farces for the Aldwych: *Rookery Nook* (1926), *Thark* (1927), *Plunder* (1928), *A Cup of Kindness* (1929), *A Night Like This* (1930), *Turkey Time* (1931), *Dirty Work* (1932), and *A Bit of a Test* (1933). Between 1926 and 1932 the Aldwych box office grossed £1,500,000 in receipts, while the aggregate number of performances of the nine farces totalled nearly 2,700.

Travers continued to write plays, but with one exception he never repeated the success of the Aldwych farces. His later most successful pre-World War II play was *Banana Ridge* (1938). The scene was laid in Malaya, and the author himself played the part of a Chinese servant, whose colloquial Malay, which Travers remembered from his Malacca days, was most convincing. However, he was disappointed by the failure of his only serious play, *Chastity My Brother* (1936), based on the life of St. Paul, which suffered when the author's anonymous identity became known. During World War II he was commissioned in RAF intelligence, becoming a squadron leader and being attached to the Ministry of Information as air adviser on censorship. He wrote several more plays, and also some film scripts and short stories. Then, in 1951, his wife died of cancer. Grief-stricken, he lost most of his old zest for writing, and spent more and more time in travelling and staying with friends in Malaya.

Then the removal of the lord chamberlain's censorship of the theatre in 1968 encouraged Travers to write a comedy extolling the joys of sex, which was in some ways his greatest theatrical triumph. This was *The Bed Before Yesterday* which was produced at the Lyric in 1975 with Joan Plowright in the lead. Its public acclaim owed much to the fact that the author treated the subject with urbanity and sophistication, never, as he put it, 'dragging in dirt for dirt's sake'.

He also wrote two autobiographies, *Vale of Laughter* (1957) and *A-sitting on a Gate* (1978), and a volume of cricket reminiscences *94 Declared* (1981) published posthumously.

Travers was a most amusing companion, full of fun, and greatly loved in the theatre and in the Garrick Club, with his eager eye for a pretty woman and a similar ear for a good story. His hobby was watching cricket and he used to visit Australia regularly to do so. He was vice-president of the Somerset County Cricket Club and belonged to the MCC. He was also an entertaining after-dinner speaker and in 1946 served as prime warden of the Fishmongers' Company, an office which gave full scope to his characteristic wit. In 1976, when he was in his ninetieth year, he was appointed CBE, a somewhat belated honour for the country's greatest living master of theatrical farce. In the same year he received the *Evening Standard* special award for services to the theatre.

In 1916 he married (Dorothy Ethel) Violet, daughter of Daniel Burton William Mouncey, a captain in the Leicester Regiment. They had two sons and a daughter. Ben Travers died in London 18 December 1980. Shortly before his death he told an interviewer that he would like his last words, engraved on his tombstone, to be 'This is where the real fun starts'.

His portrait, painted for the Garrick Club by his friend and fellow member Edward Halliday, hangs in the club.

[Ben Travers, *Vale of Laughter*, 1957, and *A-sitting on a Gate*, 1978 (autobiographies); *The Times*, 9 December 1980; J. W. Lambert, 'Ben Travers', *Listener*, 31 December 1981; personal knowledge.] H. MONTGOMERY HYDE

TREDGOLD, SIR ROBERT CLARKSON (1899–1977), first chief justice of the Federation of Rhodesia and Nyasaland, was born in Bulawayo 2 June 1899, the second son and third of the five children of (Sir) Clarkson Henry Tredgold, KC, later attorney-general and senior judge of Southern Rhodesia, and his wife, (Emily) Ruth, second daughter of John Smith Moffat, missionary of Inyati Mission and later colonial official.

Tredgold was proud of his family's humanitarian traditions and association for four generations with Central Africa: his great-grandfather was Robert Moffat [q.v.], explorer, missionary, and father-in-law of David Livingstone [q.v.]; his mother, aunt, and uncle were the first three white children born in the country; his father had liberalized legal administration under the Chartered Company; and his paternal great-great-grandfather had striven with Thomas Clarkson [q.v.] for the abolition of slavery (generations of Tredgolds bore the forename Clarkson). Tredgold's younger sister Barbara, founder of Harari Mission in Salisbury, continued the humanitarian tradition.

Tredgold's autobiography, *The Rhodesia that was My Life* (1968), describes himself as growing up with a country and tells of childhood in early Salisbury, life in a warm closely-knit community, friendships with servants, learning African folklore around the camp-fire, and exploration of the veld leading to his love of wild flowers, animals, especially dogs, and the remote 'bundu' (bush). From Prince Edward School, Salisbury, and Rondebosch Boys High, Cape Town, Tredgold arrived in England in spring 1918 to join the Royal Scots, in which his elder brother John Tredgold MC had died at Arras. Before completion of his training war had ended. On demobilization he became a Rhodes scholar and a member of Hertford College, Oxford, of which he became an honorary fellow in 1961 and where the chapel contains a memorial to him. He obtained a second class in jurisprudence in 1922.

After being called to the bar (Inner Temple) in 1923, Tredgold set up practice in Bulawayo. In 1925 he married Lorna Doris, daughter of John Danby Downing Keilor, Anglican clergyman, of Wallingford, Berkshire. She had been the lord chancellor's Richmond Palace gardener, and their common interest in plants contributed to their happy marriage, which ended in July 1972 with her death. They had no children.

At the small Bulawayo bar work came quickly, briefs coming also from Northern Rhodesia, where in 1931 Tredgold became an acting judge. Specialization was impossible, and Tredgold took civil and criminal work. One case, involving the British South Africa Company's mining rights, ultimately purchased by the government, was a factor in a major realignment in Rhodesian politics and the 1933 election victory of Godfrey Huggins (later Viscount Malvern, q.v.) on a policy of racial segregation. Huggins, finding his Reform Party unreliable, formed a national government, and under a new United Party banner won an election in November 1934, with Tredgold being returned for rural Insiza, which he represented until 1943.

Tredgold had always held liberal views. In 1936 he opposed a Native Preachers Bill giving government control over African religious activity. In the same year he took silk and became minister of justice and internal affairs. He influenced Huggins away from segregationist policies towards economic advancement of Africans, persuaded him not to close the voters' rolls to Africans, and mitigated the application of the Land Apportionment Act, particularly between 1941 and 1943, when he was also minister of native affairs. Unhappy about racial policies, Tredgold escaped his dilemma in 1943 by accepting a High Court judgeship. In the same year he was appointed CMG.

Tredgold's other significant contributions were to imperial defence. As first minister of defence in 1939 he was unwilling to employ the small group of white Rhodesians as cannon fodder, thereby destroying the country's élite. He formulated the policy of seconding them as officers and NCOs to the regiments of other colonial territories. Tredgold's intervention secured reinforcements from South Africa which greatly assisted General (Sir) Alan Cunningham's Abyssinian campaign. Tredgold was probably progenitor of the Empire Training Scheme. In 1936 he had invited the RAF to train pilots in Rhodesia. After war started he sent Air Vice-Marshal (Sir) C. W. Meredith to persuade the RAF. The idea expanded into the Empire Scheme, and, after London negotiations by Tredgold, the first air school opened in 1940 in Salisbury. He also established the Rhodesian African Rifles, despite pre-war opposition 'to the arming of natives'.

Tredgold's judicial advancement was rapid. In 1950 he became Southern Rhodesian chief justice and in 1951 ex-officio president of the Rhodesia and Nyasaland Court of Appeal. Knighted in 1951 and appointed KCMG in 1955, he became chief justice of the new Federation of Rhodesia and Nyasaland, inaugurating Lord Llewellin [q.v.] as first governor-general on 4 September 1953. Ironically, Tredgold had warned the secretary of state, Patrick Gordon Walker (later Lord Gordon-Walker) that federation could not succeed because divergent territorial policies towards Africans would lead to dissolution. He was admitted to the Privy Council in 1957.

Tredgold's liberalism found extra-judicial scope. Following an African railway workers' strike, he chaired a commission urging better wages, housing, and negotiating machinery. His 1946 report stimulated United Kingdom insistence on legislation for Native Labour Boards, which became significant in enabling African industrial organization. His 1957 report on the franchise sought to balance just representation and the retention of government in responsible hands. In the Rhodesian context these were enlightened proposals, giving Africans substantial voting power. However, as enacted, many of the generous aspects were discarded.

In 1957 Tredgold gave fateful advice to R. S. Garfield Todd, the Southern Rhodesian prime minister. Todd, facing a party revolt because of his liberal image, was advised that a dissolution would be refused unless he first called a congress. Todd took the advice and was replaced at congress. An election might have altered Rhodesian history.

In Southern Rhodesia a succession of emergency laws, publicly criticized by Tredgold in 1959, was enacted to counter African nationalism. In November 1960, on the introduction of the Law and Order Maintenance Bill, Tredgold resigned as federal chief justice, because, in his words, the Bill 'outraged almost every basic human right and is an unwarranted invasion by the Executive of the sphere of the courts'.

Tredgold now sought to form a broad national front of all races. He had no success, being regarded as a visionary, and suffered the agonies of a prophet. In July 1964 he warned that it was the duty of the army and police to suppress UDI. Had he not resigned, he would have been able to give the governor, Sir Humphrey Gibbs, the unequivocal official support he so lacked in November 1965, and the crucial order to Crown servants to co-operate with the regime of Ian Smith would not have been given.

Despite Tredgold's sadness at Rhodesian events he could treat these with humour, and gave consolation and advice to a stream of visitors and friends. Throughout life, he obtained contentment from interests as a naturalist, from poetry, music, the telling of tales, precision carpentry, and an inexhaustible passion for Rhodesian history. He received an honorary LL D from Witwatersrand in 1953.

He was a man of lean and ascetic appearance and upright carriage. From his sunburnt face piercing blue eyes, under a broad forehead, looked out with an apparent seriousness that disappeared with a shy but ready smile. He was a great walker, even in his seventies leaving others far behind. In 1956 he had revised a guide to *The Matopos*. These were his beloved hills, a place from which to view the world, think of all humanity, and commune with the elemental powers of the universe. Even during the guerrilla war he returned. In 1973 he published *Xhosa, Tales of Life from the African Veld*. This was illustrated by Margaret Helen Phear, who became the second Lady Tredgold in 1974. She was the daughter of Colin Cuthbert Baines, South African police commandant. In a final joint project Tredgold and his wife contributed plants and information for *Rhodesian Wild Flowers* (1979).

[*The Times*, 12 April 1977; Sir R. C. Tredgold, *The Rhodesia that was My Life*, 1968; L. H. Gann and M. Gelfand, *Huggins of Rhodesia*, 1964; Robert Blake, *A History of Rhodesia*, 1977; private information; personal knowledge.] CLAIRE PALLEY

TRENCH, ANTHONY CHENEVIX- (1919–1979), headmaster. [See CHENEVIX-TRENCH.]

TRUETA, JOSEP ANTHONY (1897–1977), orthopaedic surgeon, was born in Barcelona 27 October 1897, the elder son and second of three children of Rafel Trueta, physician, and his wife, Mercè Raspall, daughter of a haberdasher. He attended the Barcelona Institute of Secondary Education until 1916 and then began the study of medicine at the University of Barcelona, graduating in 1921.

From 1922 he held junior surgical posts at the Hospital de la Santa Creu until his appointment as assistant surgeon to Manuel Corachan, professor of surgery at the hospital. In 1929 he became chief surgeon to the Caja de Provision y Socorro which treated 40,000 accident cases a year and in 1933 was appointed assistant professor of surgical pathology at the University of Barcelona. He reached the rank of professor of surgery as chief surgeon to the Hospital de la Santa Creu i de Sant Pau in Barcelona in 1935, just before the outbreak of the Spanish civil war. Trueta was faced with the mammoth problem of treating casualties from the continuous air raids on the civilian population of Barcelona by Nationalist forces. It was from these and the treatment of battlefield casualties that he perfected the 'closed-plaster' technique, previously pioneered by Winnett Orr but forgotten, of treating severe compound war wounds, particularly those involving damage to bones. The usual practice had previously been amputation. Trueta was convinced that this should be unnecessary. By the end of the civil war he had personally treated over one thousand casualties, with only six deaths. This experience and the techniques which he had developed were to prove invaluable during World War II, particularly in the early days of the blitz.

A man of fervent liberal convictions, Trueta realized that it would be impossible for him to work with the victorious Nationalist forces and early in 1939 he emigrated to England with his young family. He was much in demand as a lecturer on air-raid surgery and practical air-raid precautions because of his immense first-hand experience, and he became an adviser to the Ministry of Health.

In September 1939 G. R. Girdlestone [q.v.], the founder Nuffield professor of orthopaedic surgery, heard Trueta lecture on bombing casualties and invited him to Oxford. This was the start of a long and close friendship which led to the establishment of the Oxford school of orthopaedics.

From 1942 to the end of the war, Trueta was surgeon in charge of the busy accident department at the Radcliffe Infirmary, Oxford. In spite of this heavy clinical load, his research became more experimental, particularly in the field of kidney neurovascular physiology, and he wrote with one of his assistants, M. Agerholm, one of the first papers on the use of penicillin in bone infection (1946).

In 1949 Trueta was elected Nuffield professor of orthopaedic surgery in the University of Oxford and professorial fellow of Worcester College, Oxford. From this position and with remarkable vision he reorganized the Wingfield-Morris Orthopaedic Hospital as the Nuffield Orthopaedic Centre to become the leading centre in the country for treatment, study, and research in orthopaedic surgery. He continued to produce a continuous flow of publications on almost every aspect of orthopaedics. The essence of his scientific philosophy and experimental attack was the primary position of vascularity in health and disease. This concept he researched extensively and with marked originality in renal circulation, in osteogenesis and epiphyseal growth, in the pathology of osteoarthritis and in the treatment of osteomyelitis, to name but a few examples. Many young assistants from Britain and Europe, particularly from the Iberian peninsula, joined him in these studies and were fired by his enthusiasm and lively imagination, to become scientists as well as surgeons. He retired in 1966, and returned to Barcelona.

The most widely known of Trueta's works are *Treatment of War Wounds and Fractures* (1939) and *The Principles and Practice of War Surgery* (1943). His world-wide reputation as an experimental clinician was established by the publication with colleagues in 1947 of *Studies of the Renal Circulation. The Spirit of Catalonia* (1946) is a work of filial piety containing a unique collection of biographies of Catalan medical men and philosophers and examining their contribution to western civilization. In 1956, with other colleagues, he published a *Handbook on Poliomyelitis* and he gathered together much of his lifetime's work and philosophy in *Studies of the Development and Decay of the Human Frame* (1968).

Trueta's many honours included an honorary D.Sc. from Oxford (1943), appointment as chevalier of the French Legion of Honour, and honorary fellowships of many orthopaedic associations around the world. He was also honoured by the universities of Buenos Aires and of Brazil. He was FRCS (1954). In New York he served in 1960 as president of the Société Internationale de Chirurgie Orthopédique et de Traumatologie, and was made an honorary fellow of the American College of Surgeons (1960).

Trueta was a handsome, athletic, vivacious man, friendly, particularly to the young, who recognized the colour, warmth, and indeed drama behind this Catalan. He adored the society of Oxford, and indeed 'the establishment'.

In 1923 Trueta married Amelia (died 1975), daughter of Jaume Llacuna, business man. They had three daughters and a son (who died at the age of four). Theirs was a very close and religious family and when Trueta retired to Barcelona in 1967 to continue his surgical and scientific work, the three daughters with their own families were already living permanently in Spain.

After a courageous battle against cancer

Trueta died 19 January 1977 in Barcelona. A few days before his death King Juan Carlos I bestowed upon him the Gran Cruz de Carlos III, the most prestigious award of Spain.

[*The Times*, 21 and 27 January 1977; Meli and Michael Strubell (translators), *Trueta: Surgeon in War and Peace, Memoirs*, 1980; *Journal of Bone and Joint Surgery*, vol. 59B, No. 2, May 1977; private information; personal knowledge.] ROBERT B. DUTHIE

TUCKER, (FREDERICK) JAMES, BARON TUCKER (1888–1975), lord of appeal in ordinary, was born at Pietermaritzburg, Natal, 22 May 1888, the only child of Frederick Nugent Tucker, member of the Legislative Assembly, Natal, South Africa, and later of the Grey House, Epsom, and his wife, (Eliza) Alice (Sophia), daughter of the Very Revd James Green DD, of Pietermaritzburg, Natal. His mother died in childbirth fifteen months after he was born. He was educated at Winchester and at New College, Oxford, where he obtained a third class in classical honour moderations in 1909 and a second in jurisprudence in 1911. He was called to the bar by the Inner Temple in 1914, but he thereafter immediately joined the army on the outbreak of World War I, becoming a lieutenant (General List) in 1917.

After the armistice Tucker returned to the Temple to commence his career as a barrister and he became the pupil of Rayner (later Lord) Goddard [q.v.] with whom he formed a lifelong friendship, remaining in Goddard's chambers after completing his pupillage. He also joined Goddard's circuit, the Western, where he soon acquired a busy criminal practice at the Wiltshire sessions, as well as some civil work in London. His physical presence and his ease of manner attracted clients and tribunals alike, and he was early marked for distinction in his profession. He was always a 'clubbable' man. He enjoyed circuit life, and he had a fund of good stories. He was excellent company in the bar messes at the circuit towns. Although success came early and easily, he was wholly free from side or conceit, while he won immediate pre-eminence among his contemporaries. When Goddard took silk in 1923 Tucker inherited some of the former's junior banking work so that he thereafter graduated into a substantial civil practice in London. From 1930 to 1937 he was a member of the Bar Council. He took silk in 1933 and subsequently was a leading barrister in London, although on occasions and in important cases he still went on circuit. In 1936 he was appointed recorder of Southampton. The following year Viscount Hailsham [q.v.] nominated him, at the early age of forty-nine, as a judge of the High Court attached to the King's Bench division, an appointment which proved as successful as it was popular. At the same time he received the customary knighthood. In 1945 he presided over the trial at the Central Criminal Court of William Joyce (Lord 'Haw Haw') for treason. Later in 1945 he was promoted to the Court of Appeal and sworn of the Privy Council.

It was at this time that he was an obvious candidate for appointment as lord chief justice on the retirement of Chief Justice Inskip, Viscount Caldecote [q.v.]. But Goddard was preferred, and Tucker remained in the Court of Appeal until he went to the House of Lords in 1950 as a life peer and lord of appeal in ordinary.

On the bench he reflected the qualities which he had shown at the bar. He was civil, courteous, and humane, doing his judicial work with skill and celerity although he was never brusque and always appeared open to argument and attentive to pleas in mitigation.

In June 1954, as chairman of a departmental committee on new trials in criminal cases, he recommended that the Court of Criminal Appeal and the House of Lords should be empowered to order a new trial where the appeal was based upon the ground of fresh evidence but (by a majority of five to three) not in other cases. It was not, however, until 1964 (three years after he had retired at the age of seventy-three) that power was given under the Criminal Appeal Act to order a new trial in certain cases.

Wykehamist, with the legendary manners; Oxonian, with the legendary graces; barrister, with the legendary style; judge, with the legendary 'gravitas', Tucker followed and enhanced the tradition of the English barrister and judge. His career at the bar and on the bench exhibited high standards of courteous and attractive address and of fair and reasonable judgement. A fine Latin scholar, a sound common lawyer, and above all a man of sense and personal grace, he was only unfortunate in the sense that when the time came in 1945 for the selection of a new lord chief justice there was already in the lists his former pupil-master, the formidable Rayner Goddard. Tucker's talents lay in the cultivated and lucid exposition of the law, delivered always with style and polish, often with wit, and without the trenchant and sometime abrasive language of his rival. It is improbable, however, that Tucker regretted (as most certainly he never resented) the preferment of his friend. He went on to serve as a distinguished member of the Judicial Committee, retaining the high regard and affection of his colleagues and of the bar which accompanied his whole progress through his career. He was made an honorary fellow of New College in 1946. He became a bencher of his Inn in 1937 and treasurer in 1960.

In 1918 he married (Elisabeth) Benedicta (Palmer), daughter of the Revd Charles Powell

Berryman, vicar of Camberley, Surrey. In 1973 she predeceased him. There were no children of the marriage. Tucker passed fourteen years in retirement in Great Bookham, in Surrey, where he died at home 17 November 1975.

[Personal knowledge.] RAWLINSON OF EWELL

TUNNICLIFFE, CHARLES FREDERICK (1901–1979), painter, engraver, and illustrator, was born 1 December 1901 at Langley, East Cheshire, the only son of the family of five children of William Tunnicliffe, shoemaker, of Langley, and Margaret, daughter of George Mitchell, a farmer. Tunnicliffe was raised on a twenty-acre farm in the nearby village of Sutton, whither his father had moved in 1902, and was educated at the local St. James church school.

In 1915 he entered Macclesfield School of Art and soon afterwards Manchester School of Art. In 1921 he was awarded a Royal Exhibition scholarship to the Royal College of Art in London and he stayed there, perfecting his skill as an engraver, until he left in 1925 to join the staff of Woolwich Polytechnic.

Tunnicliffe's prodigious industry and rapidly developing skill as an etcher soon became known to the public and he found that there was a market for his work. He first exhibited in the Royal Academy in 1934 and from that date his work was to be seen in every summer exhibition until 1978. The same year he was elected a fellow of the Royal Society of Painters, Etchers and Engravers.

In 1929 Tunnicliffe had married Winifred, daughter of Frederick Wonnacott, a sewing machine salesman in Belfast. She had been a fellow student at the Royal College of Art and shared her husband's passion for natural history. After their marriage the Tunnicliffes settled in Macclesfield where the artist began his record of the birds of Britain. These drawings, accurate to within one millimetre, were made from dead specimens and carried out in water-colour, gouache, and ink, together with informative hand-written notes. His sketch books date from this period.

As Tunnicliffe had become a master craftsman as well as an artist he was able to carry out commissions covering a very wide field. Commercial firms became aware that his work was accurate and well executed; furthermore they knew that the artist was reliable.

In 1932 he illustrated *Tarka the Otter*, by Henry Williamson [q.v.], and consequently Tunnicliffe was seldom without work as an illustrator. He held his first one-man show in 1938 in the Arthur Greatorex Galleries in London.

From 1939 to 1945 he worked as an assistant art master at Manchester Grammar School and in 1942 his first book, *My Country Book*, was published. Tunnicliffe was an able writer and his best known book was *Shorelands Summer Diary*, published in 1952, in which he described and illustrated the land and life around his home in Anglesey.

In 1944 the artist was elected an associate of the Royal Academy as an engraver and in 1947, with the security of an established reputation, he bought Shorelands, a house on the Cefni estuary at Malltraeth in Anglesey. This was to be the Tunnicliffes' home for the rest of their lives.

In 1954 Tunnicliffe was elected RA and a vice-president of the Royal Society for the Protection of Birds. In 1968 he was made a vice-president of the Society of Wild Life Artists. In 1974 the Royal Academy mounted a major exhibition of the measured drawings and sketch-books and for the first time the art world and the public were able to see the importance of Tunnicliffe's work. In 1975 Tunnicliffe was awarded the gold medal of the Royal Society for the Protection of Birds and in 1978 he was appointed OBE.

As a man Tunnicliffe seemed to be more at ease in the countryside than with people, for to a certain extent he retained the suspicions of his peasant background. Consequently he avoided society in general, contenting himself with a few good friends who benefited from his generosity and cheerful company. Physically he was a large ruddy-faced man with a ready laugh, but this compensated for a natural reticence that allowed the development of the dedication and obsession that resulted in his extraordinary output.

Tunnicliffe was admired internationally for his water-colours of birds and animals and nationally for his wood engravings and etchings. Nevertheless it became apparent in the last decade of his life that his greatest contribution to art lay in his measured drawings and sketch-books. He never truly mastered the handling of oil-paint.

Tunnicliffe died in his home at Malltraeth 7 February 1979. In May 1981 his measured drawings and sketch-books were purchased by Anglesey Borough Council. Winifred Tunnicliffe died in May 1969; there were no children of the marriage.

[Private information; personal knowledge.]

KYFFIN WILLIAMS

TYNAN, KENNETH PEACOCK (1927–1980), theatre critic, was born 2 April 1927 in Birmingham, the only son (a daughter had previously died in infancy) of Sir Peter Peacock, merchant and former mayor of Warrington, and Letitia Rose Tynan, a union kept quite separate from Peacock's accepted household and family in Lancashire. Tynan never met his much older half-brothers and half-sisters. From King Edward's School, Birmingham, he won a demyship to Magdalen College, Oxford, where he obtained a second class in English in 1948. At Oxford he embarked upon a systematic campaign to outshine or outrage all contemporaries as undergraduate journalist, actor, impresario, party-giver, and (despite a stammer) debater. If you were going to be a show-off in the midst of colonels, fighter pilots, and other heroes back from the war, he said later, you had to be a professional show-off. At the same time he was amassing enough serious and enthusiastic consideration of the theatre to provide him with his first book, *He that Plays the King* (1950), and a wider reputation.

After a spell as a repertory theatre director he seized the chance to become a professional theatre critic. Invited by (Sir) Alec Guinness to take the part of the Player King in Guinness's luckless production of *Hamlet* for the Festival of Britain, Tynan became the target of especially scornful remarks from the *Evening Standard*'s reviewer (Sir) A. Beverley Baxter. He replied with a letter to the editor so droll that according to legend he was immediately hired in Baxter's place. In fact some weeks elapsed, and he had in any case been writing about the theatre in the *Spectator*, but no doubt his flair for attracting attention played its part. With the *Evening Standard* (1952–3) and to a lesser extent with the *Daily Sketch* (1953–4) Tynan established himself as a funny and scathing writer on the theatre, if still one who wanted from it heroics and illusions. It was only after he was invited to join the *Observer* in 1954 that he started to apply to drama the political convictions which he was in the process of acquiring, with characteristic intemperance, about this time. 'I doubt that I could love anyone who did not wish to see it', he affirmed in a review of John Osborne's *Look Back in Anger* inspired as much by the play's tirades against respectability and authority as by its theatrical virtues. He went on to embrace socialism, nuclear disarmament, and the didactic drama of Bertolt Brecht.

His new-found beliefs did not prevent him from remaining a socializer as well as a socialist. He had married in 1951 Elaine, daughter of Samuel M. Brimberg, office equipment manufacturer, of New York. As Elaine Dundy she published two sparkling novels of the decade, *The Dud Avocado* (1958) in which a barely-disguised Kenneth Tynan appears, and *The Old Man and Me* (1964). Their Mayfair flat became a salon for celebrities passing through London, particularly from the United States. Tynan was fascinated by the outsize stars of Hollywood and Broadway. It was inevitable that he would be lured to America himself, as theatre critic of the *New Yorker*, though without severing his *Observer* connection. In the end he stayed only two years before returning to London in 1960.

Tynan was never averse to trying his hand in some production capacity as an adjunct to his criticism. He was story editor for Ealing Films in its last years (1955–7); produced two television programmes for ATV on the Stanislavskian method (1958) and dissent in America (1960), and edited the arts magazine *Tempo* for ABC Television (England) (1961–2). In 1963 came the invitation which was to tempt him away from his critic's seat altogether. Sir Laurence (later Lord) Olivier asked him to be literary manager of the National Theatre which was finally being set up in the temporary home of the Old Vic Theatre. Tynan threw himself into the task with energy and confidence. He disinterred forgotten classics, edited texts, and directly inspired such new works as Tom Stoppard's *Rosencrantz and Guildenstern are Dead* and Peter Shaffer's *Black Comedy*. These first seasons are generally regarded as having given the National's repertoire its stamp, but among the hits were one or two misfires, including a Brecht, which Tynan's critics could cite when in 1968 he clashed with the governors of the theatre over his determination to introduce *Soldiers*, by the German dramatist Rolf Hochhuth. The play alleged *inter alia* that Sir Winston Churchill had ordered the death of the wartime Polish leader General Sikorski. As a former colleague of Churchill's, the National's chairman Viscount Chandos [q.v.] was adamant that the production should not go ahead. Tynan responded by mounting the play himself in the commercial theatre and the following year resigned his post, though he remained a consultant until 1973.

There followed the exploit which prompts the most mixed feelings among Tynan's friends and admirers, the revue *Oh! Calcutta!* which he devised and produced first in New York, in 1969, and then in London. He had embraced the sexual 'liberation' of the era with the same enthusiasm he brought to its political concomitant, listing his recreations in *Who's Who* as sex and eating and in 1965 earning himself a footnote in the annals as the first Briton to say the word 'fuck' on television. *Oh! Calcutta!*'s mix of rather attractive nudity and distinctly seedy humour might have been designed to shock the bourgeoisie; ironically (if inevitably) it was a commercial success everywhere, and made Tynan well off.

He also ventured into film production with the 1971 version of *Macbeth* directed by Roman Polanski, but as the seventies wore on journalism reclaimed his energies, sadly beginning to dwindle as his health deteriorated. Mainly for American magazines he wrote a series of lengthy reflective profiles of actors and entertainers which, published in book form as *Show People* (1979), confirm Tynan's talent as a writer, his ability to conjure up time and place, people and performances, whether he is defining the extraordinary allure of Louise Brooks or conveying exactly what it was like to experience (Sir) Donald Wolfit and Frederick Valk (two of his heroes) in a barnstorming wartime production of *Othello*. He became FRSL in 1956.

He also published two collections of theatre reviews but disappointingly few original books. A long-planned memoir of his Oxford days materialized only in the form of his contribution to the television series *One Pair of Eyes* in 1968. Towards the end of his life he was planning an autobiography, but it was not to be realized. To lessen the ravages of the emphysema from which he suffered he was now living in Santa Monica, California. He died there 26 July 1980.

His first marriage had ended in divorce in 1964. There was one daughter. In 1967 Tynan married Kathleen, daughter of Matthew Halton, journalist and writer, herself a novelist and screenwriter; they had a son and daughter. Tynan was tall, slender, always elegant. In youth his habit of baring his teeth as he strove to overcome the stammer, coupled with flaring nostrils and a rather skull-like head, gave him the look of a startled rocking-horse. He matured into a relaxed and attractive human being, full of unexpected subsidiary enthusiasms (cricket, word games, bullfighting). His conversation, as Tom Stoppard put it, always had the jingle of loose change about it. When he died it was apparent that he had inspired quite exceptional affection in many who knew him. Whatever his enduring influence on the theatre may prove to be, he brought excitement, authority, and glamour to the business of writing about it.

[Godfrey Smith in *Sunday Times* (magazine section), 25 August 1963; Laurence Olivier, *Confessions of an Actor*, 1982; personal knowledge.] PHILIP PURSER

U

UNDERWOOD, (GEORGE CLAUDE) LEON (1890–1975), sculptor, painter, print maker, and writer, was born in Askew Road, Shepherd's Bush, London, 25 December 1890, the eldest of three sons (there were no daughters) of Theodore George Black Underwood and his wife, Rose Vesey. The previous three generations of his family had all been antiquarians and numismatists, and Leon was first inspired to draw by prints he saw when working in his father's shop. He was educated at Hampden Gurney School. At seventeen he won a scholarship to the Royal College of Art where he was awarded prizes but began a lifelong struggle with officialdom. He left to paint landscapes and portraits at Vilna, Poland, escaping via Finland and Sweden at the outbreak of war to enlist. He saw service in France in 1916, and ended the war as a captain in the camouflage section of the Royal Engineers. During this time he submitted designs for a repeating trench mortar to the War Office, sent home drawings for the *Illustrated London News*, and painted a commissioned picture on the subject of camouflage for the Imperial War Museum. He began carving on leave in 1917.

After the war he spent a year at the Slade in the life-drawing class of Henry Tonks [q.v.]. He was awarded a premium in the Prix de Rome, but persuaded the prize committee to let him visit Iceland to study primitive culture instead of going to Italy. He became a founder member of the Seven and Five Society. He joined the staff of the RCA in 1920 but resigned after a disagreement with (Sir) William Rothenstein [q.v.] in 1923 and opened his own school of drawing, the Brook Green School, at Girdlers Road, Hammersmith, where his early students included Eileen Agar, Gertrude Hermes, and Henry Moore.

From the mid 1920s Underwood's fiercely independent nature and his sheer diversity made critics uneasy. He was quickly interested in primitive art, and was led by studies he made at Altamira in 1923 and during a journey through Mexico in 1926–7 to develop a theory of the Cycle of Styles in which he linked the highest art of successive cultures to its function and meaning and to technological change.

His etchings and wood engravings, at first on rural themes and then showing an apocalyptic approach to mythological and biblical subject matter, were widely influential. He published his verse and woodcut illustrations *Animalia* while living in the United States in 1926, and illustrated a book about his Mexican travels, *The Red Tiger* (by Phillips Russell, 1929), which extended into a long sequence of lively colour prints on Mexican themes. He illustrated his own novel *The Siamese Cat* (1928) and founded and published a magazine, *The Island*, in 1931, and later executed commissioned stained glass and murals.

As a painter he began in a strong Slade tradition with figure paintings full of mass and volume, best exemplified by his extraordinary 'Venus in Kensington Gardens' (1921). His palette became richer and hotter, and the forms more voluptuous, as he developed Icelandic themes and pictures on the subject of Cortez and Montezuma, with a short-lived burst of Surrealism in 1930. He was also capable of very beautiful landscape water-colours, but it was his figure paintings' insistence on three-dimensional form and his dependence on dazzling life drawings that led him to make his crucial contribution as a sculptor.

This began with small carvings in a primitive style, gathered pace in marble and wood torsos and figures—'The Cathedral' (poplar, 1932), and 'Mindslave' (Carrara marble, 1934)—and developed into bronzes with a flickering rhythm and apparent weightlessness—'The New Spirit' (1932) and 'Violin Rhythm' (1934). On many sculptures he used chasing and inlaid lines. His figures dance, sow, pipe, and stretch. Many, like 'Lark' (1934), in which he first pierced a form to link front and back, threaten to leave their bases altogether. At this time he carved totems in acacia and lime: 'Serpent and Birds' is an acacia totem inlaid with fragments of light bulbs. After visiting West Africa in 1944 for the British Council and studying Ife and Benin bronzes, he wrote three books on African art and largely abandoned carving and painting in favour of increasingly exuberant bronze sculpture which he cast himself, slitting and folding back the skin of the sculptures to emphasize their volume, as in 'Joy as it Flies' (1961).

He believed passionately in subject and spiritual content. He had a low opinion of his own period but was volatile and optimistic by nature. He worked often in isolation, and was invariably at odds with the art establishment, but he is seen increasingly as an important figure in the development of sculpture.

In 1917 he married Mary Louise, daughter of John Coleman, upholsterer at the London Midland and Scottish Railway coach works. They had met at the Royal College in 1911 and she gave him vital support throughout a difficult career. They had two sons (one of whom predeceased Underwood) and a daughter. Underwood died in the Hostel of God, Clapham, London, 9 October 1975.

[Christopher Neve, *Leon Underwood*, 1974; *The Times*, 11 October 1975; private information; personal knowledge.]

CHRISTOPHER NEVE

UPJOHN, GERALD RITCHIE, BARON UPJOHN (1903–1971), lord of appeal in ordinary, was born in Wimbledon 25 February 1903, the younger son and youngest of five children of William Henry Upjohn KC, of Annersley, Lyndhurst, Hampshire, and his wife, Lucy, daughter of Rees Williams, small landowner, of independent means, of Aberdare. Upjohn's father was a well-known leading counsel with a large practice, whose considerable reputation as lawyer and advocate was somewhat marred by an irascibility which he notably failed to control. He was fifty-one when his youngest child was born and was still in practice when that child was called to the bar. The choler for which the father was noted in public did not characterize his relations with his younger son. These were warm and Upjohn owed much to his father's solicitous attention to his training for a legal career. There is little doubt that Upjohn owed part of his imperturbable courtesy to his affectionate but shrewd assessment of his father's temperament.

Upjohn was educated at Eton and (as an exhibitioner) at Trinity College, Cambridge, where he gained a first class in the mechanical sciences tripos in 1925 and a first class in part ii of the law tripos the following year. Thereafter his preparation for the bar was thorough, even by the standards of his time. He worked successively in solicitors' and accountants' offices and also in the mining industry, and he served pupillages in common law and Chancery chambers.

On being called to the bar (Lincoln's Inn) in 1929, Upjohn quickly acquired a large and varied practice. He had good looks, a distinguished presence, fine manners, a beautifully modulated voice, a first class and penetrating brain, and a capacity for hard work. He rapidly became a persuasive and lucid advocate and his reputation in the early days of his career can perhaps be illustrated by a comment by his clerk who like many barristers' clerks was a worldly and percipient judge of form. To a student arriving as a pupil in Upjohn's chambers in 1933 (but with a different pupil master) the clerk said: 'Learn what you can from Mr X but model yourself on Mr Upjohn. He is bound to reach the House of Lords.'

Upjohn's journey to the House of Lords was interrupted by the outbreak of war in September 1939. He immediately joined the Welsh Guards and served from 1941, to 1943 as technical adjutant, in the rank of captain, of the 2nd (Armoured) battalion. In 1943 he was appointed, in the rank of colonel, chief legal adviser of the Allied Control Commission, Italy, and in the same year he was one of the rare wartime recipients of a silk gown. In 1944 he was promoted to brigadier on appointment as vice-president of the Allied Control Commission. He was mentioned in dispatches.

For his services to the Control Commission, Upjohn was appointed CBE (1945) and an officer of the US Legion of Merit (1946). Those who served with him on the Commission remember his capacity for work, his tact, his fine judgement, and his kindness and approachability.

In 1945 Upjohn returned to practise at the bar. Success as leading counsel was immediate. His presence, his legal scholarship, at once comprehensive and distinguished, and his ability to master a complicated brief impressed judges and solicitors alike. In addition to a busy practice he undertook a remarkably wide variety of duties. He was an ideal committee man, always master of his subject, courteous and patient when dealing with less acute minds, and with an enviable capacity for well-timed interventions destructive of irrelevance and leading to sensible decisions. He served as treasurer of the Bar Council from 1946 to 1951 and was a member of the committee on the practice and procedure of the Supreme Court (1947–53). He also served as attorney-general of the Duchy of Lancaster (1947–51) and on a number of quasi-judicial bodies. He was one of three members, appointed in circumstances of great publicity in 1948, to enquire, under the chairmanship of Sir George Lynskey [q.v.], into allegations of irregularities on the part of certain ministers of the Crown and public servants. The report threw a clear but steadying light on the squalid activities of certain minor officials.

Upjohn's life until he was appointed a judge was extremely arduous. Its burdens were eased and sweetened by his very happy marriage in 1947 to Marjorie Dorothy Bertha ('Bubbles'), daughter of Major Ernest Murray Lucas, who survived him. There were no children.

When Upjohn was appointed a Chancery judge and knighted in 1951 he defined courtesy and silence as two of the greatest judicial attributes. These he displayed throughout his career. He was an admirable judge at first instance, patient, courteous, and attentive. One who frequently appeared before him, and who subsequently became lord chancellor, has written: 'Despite his Chancery background (which is not normally associated with this particular excellence) Gerald Upjohn was almost the best, if not quite the best, judge of fact that I have ever appeared before ... his qualities as a judge of law were also of the first order.'

In 1956 Upjohn was appointed as a judge of the Restrictive Practices Court on its inception, and to the Court of Appeal in 1960, being then sworn of the Privy Council. In 1963 unusually rapid promotion took him to the House of Lords.

His views carried weight with his colleagues in the Court of Appeal and the House of Lords. His judgements were carefully reasoned and lucid, his judicial approach being based on acceptance of orthodox law, which he sought to expound.

Upjohn was a devoted member of Lincoln's Inn. He was elected a bencher in 1948 and served as treasurer in 1965. For eleven years from 1954 he was chairman of the general purposes committee which effectively ran the Inn's activities.

He served as fellow on the governing body of Eton College from 1963 until his death. He enjoyed work and gave pleasure and comfort to his colleagues. His wisdom, common sense, and capacity to master administrative detail were always evident; so were his understanding of and acceptance by the young. The provost of Eton, at his memorial service, told how when his death became known, a boy who had only met him as a fellow telephoned his parents to say, 'Something dreadful has happened; Lord Upjohn has died.' Upjohn was also a valued governor of Felsted School.

Upjohn was a prominent Freemason, the Order giving scope both to his conviviality and to his public spirit. He gave much time and thought to Masonic charities. He was also, from 1954 to 1964, chairman of the St. George's Hospital Medical School. His recreations were fishing, sailing, and gardening. He had notably green fingers. He died 27 January 1971 at the London Clinic.

There is a pastel portrait of him by Juliet Pannett in the possession of his family.

[*The Times*, 28, 29, and 30 January and 4 February 1971; private information; personal knowledge.] HILARY MAGNUS

UTTLEY, ALICE JANE (1884–1976), author, known as ALISON UTTLEY, was born 17 December 1884 at Castle Top Farm, Cromford, Derbyshire, the elder child of Henry Taylor, farmer, and his wife, Hannah Dickens. A son, William Henry, was born to them a year later.

Alice Taylor was first educated at home and at the Lea School in the village of Holloway, where, unusually for the time, she was encouraged to take an interest in geology and the scientific examination of natural phenomena. At the age of thirteen she gained a scholarship to the Lady Manners School, Bakewell, and here her enthusiasm for science was directed into more formal channels. She won several school prizes (for sport as well as for academic subjects) and in 1903 she gained a county major scholarship to Manchester University to read physics, taking her B.Sc. in 1906 as only the second woman honours graduate of the university. She greatly enjoyed these years as a student, during which she lived in the residential Ashburne Hall, and the university in its turn was to recognize her achievements by awarding her an honorary Litt.D. in 1970.

Having decided to become a teacher, Alice Taylor moved on to the Training College at Cambridge (later Hughes Hall), and in 1908 she took up the post of physics teacher at the Fulham Secondary School for Girls. In 1911 she married James Arthur Uttley, a civil engineer working in Cheshire, and she moved with him to Knutsford where her only child, John Corin Taylor, was born in 1915 (he died in 1978). During World War I her husband served with the Royal Engineers and suffered illness which permanently impaired his health, and in 1930 he died, leaving his wife with the need to earn a living for herself and her son, who was a scholar at Sedbergh School. At this time of crisis she received great support through her friendship with the former professor of philosophy at Manchester, Samuel Alexander [q.v.], and he encouraged her to develop her latent talent for writing.

This had first manifested itself before her husband's death in articles written for magazines and in a little children's book published in 1929: *The Squirrel, the Hare and the Little Grey Rabbit*. Based on a story which she had invented to amuse her son, it exploited the popular device of recreating a rural society largely peopled by animals. Charmingly illustrated with muted water-colours by Margaret Tempest it was to have over thirty successors (the last five accompanied by rather more heavy-handed pictures by Katherine Wigglesworth) and the series formed a reliable foundation upon which, in the second half of her long life, Alison Uttley was able to extend her reputation as a professional writer.

The nature of this reputation can clearly be gauged from her first publication for an adult readership: *The Country Child* of 1931. As she was later to say of her Little Grey Rabbit books, 'the country ways ... were the country ways known to the author' and in this lightly fictionalized autobiography she set out to explore the rich experiences of her Derbyshire childhood. In simple but evocative prose she celebrated the life of a Victorian farming community, steeped in its own traditions, and although she was to go on to write more than a hundred books, almost all of them drew upon this powerful perception of a rural life still only marginally affected by the Industrial Revolution.

Her many books include several series of stories like the Sam Pig books or the Tim Rabbit books, where a family of animals stands substitute for, and thus generalizes the experience of, a human family, and to these must be added numerous tales of magic for children and children's plays, most notably the full length play on the life of Hans Christian Andersen, *The Washerwoman's Child* (1946). There were also successors to *The Country Child* in *Ambush of Young Days* (1937) and *The Farm on the Hill* (1941), and the novels *High Meadows* (1938) and *When All is Done* (1945), and there were numerous essay collections on country themes, beginning with *Country Hoard* (1943) and often made distinctive by the black and white illustrations of C. F. Tunnicliffe [q.v.].

Her most original, and perhaps her most deeply-felt, work is the fantasy story *A Traveller in Time* (1939) in which there came together in near-perfect conjunction her childhood experiences at Castle Top Farm and her fascination with a plot that had been put under way by Anthony Babington [q.v.] in 1569 to rescue Mary Queen of Scots from imprisonment in nearby Wingfield Manor. Careful research underlies the fabric of the romance, but the book draws too on Alison Uttley's lifelong interest in dreams, aspects of which she discussed in her annotated essay *The Stuff of Dreams* (1953).

Although she moved house several times after her husband's death Alison Uttley soon came to make her home near Beaconsfield (at a house which she called Thackers after the farm-house in *A Traveller in Time*) and it was here that she spent the rest of her life. She had a fairly strict working regime recognizing the need for writers constantly to exercise their skills, and she proved to be a shrewd woman of business. Her time was not so full though as to exclude her enthusiasm for gardening, music and cricket. She also had a keen interest in art and assembled a small, but well-chosen collection of Flemish paintings.

Notwithstanding her intense feeling for the place of her childhood, and her affection for Manchester (not least Old Trafford) Alison Uttley developed strong ties with her adoptive county, which she was able to express in her lovingly detailed study *Buckinghamshire* (1950). Only after illness and a fall was she persuaded to leave Thackers and she died in hospital at High Wycombe 7 May 1976. In her will she left many of her books and papers, together with an unsigned head portrait, to Manchester University. The portrait is now on permanent loan to Ashburne Hall, where it has been joined by a second seated portrait, probably by the same hand.

[*The Times*, 8 May 1976; E. Saintsbury, *The World of Alison Uttley*, 1980; private information.] BRIAN ALDERSON

UWINS, CYRIL FRANK (1896–1972), test pilot, was born at 2 Carmichael Road, South Norwood, Croydon, 2 August 1896, the elder son (there were no daughters) of Frank Uwins, wood broker, and his wife, Annie Henton. He was educated at the Whitgift School, Croydon, where he developed a schoolboy interest in kites—an appropriate introduction to an aeronautical career. When World War I broke out in 1914 Uwins joined a London regiment and in 1916 managed to achieve a transfer to the Royal Flying Corps. The following year, on a ferry flight from Hounslow aerodrome to St. Omer in France, the engine failed in the Morane–Parasol monoplane he was flying and in the ensuing crash Uwins broke his neck—but survived. He suffered from a stiff neck for the rest of his life.

Out of hospital, Uwins was judged medically unfit for active service and on 25 October 1918 was posted to the Bristol Aeroplane Company's works at Filton to succeed Captain Joseph Hammond of the RFC, Bristol's test pilot from 19 January 1917, who had been killed flying an American-built Bristol Fighter.

Uwins's first test flight—on 26 October 1918, the day after he joined Bristol—was in a Bristol Scout F (B 3991). Six months later, on 1 May 1919, he was demobilized from the Royal Air Force and formally joined the Bristol Aeroplane Company. On that same day, still in uniform, he made the first post-war commercial air flight in Britain when he flew the Bristol Company's general manager, Herbert Thomas, from Filton to Hounslow aerodrome in a Bristol Tourer Coupé (M 1460)—a civil variant of the wartime Bristol Fighter.

During the next thirty years Uwins made the first flights of every new Bristol aeroplane, ranging from the heavy twin-engine Bristol Braemar triplane of February 1918, through the little Bristol Brownie ultra-light monoplane of August 1926 (in which he gained third place in the Lympne light aeroplane trials), to the Bristol Bulldog single-seat biplane fighter of May 1927, and the Bristol Blenheim twin-engine bomber of June 1936 to the Bristol Type 170 Freighter of December 1945.

The fifty-eight prototype aircraft which Uwins flew, and the very large number of production machines, spanned the transformation of aeronautical design from the simple wooden fabric-covered biplane of the World War I to the all-metal stressed-skin monoplane with retractable undercarriage and variable-pitch propellers. Uwins coped with them all in a steady, careful, self-possessed, and taciturn manner and, through skill—and a measure of good luck—survived and, indeed, had no serious accident though many close calls. Eventually he headed a team of eight assistant test pilots, none of whom ever made the first flight of a new aeroplane while Uwins was in charge.

In the course of his work, on 16 September 1932—almost exactly half way through his test-flying career—Uwins regained for Britain the world's aeroplane height record by climbing to 43,976 feet (nearly 8½ miles), flying an open cockpit Vickers Vespa biplane with a specially tuned Bristol Pegasus engine. The climb took a hundred minutes, the descent twenty minutes. On the way down he ran out of fuel and made a successful forced landing in a field near Chippenham. For this feat he was awarded the Britannia trophy.

Uwin's phlegmatic and somewhat austere nature went to the extent that, when intercom arrangements were developed between pilot and flight observer in two-seat aircraft he insisted that he could speak to the flight observer but the flight observer could never answer back. In any discussion he habitually ended the briefest of conversations with 'We won't say anything more about that'. Tall, quiet, with aquiline features and—from middle age—plentiful white hair, Uwins was absorbed in his work, never smoked, and drank sparingly, allowing himself one major holiday each year in the South of France.

Uwins retired as deputy chairman of the Bristol Aeroplane Company in 1964 following its merger with Vickers and the English Electric Company to form the British Aircraft Corporation.

He was awarded the silver medal for aeronautics of the Royal Aeronautical Society, of which he became a fellow, and he was made an honorary M.Sc. of Bristol University in 1964. He was president of the Society of British Aircraft Constructors from 1956 to 1958 and a member of the Air Registration Board from 1959 to 1964. He won the AFC in 1937 and was appointed OBE in 1943.

Uwins was twice married: first in 1919 to Joyce Marguerite, daughter of Charles Ernest Boucher, a director of a local company. They had two daughters. Joyce Uwins was killed in a motor-car accident in 1950. He married, secondly, in 1955, Naomi Scott Short, widow of Captain E. D. Short of the King's Regiment and daughter of Henry Augustus Scott-Barrett. Uwins died 11 September 1972 at the Lansdown Nursing Home, Bath.

[C. F. Barnes, *Bristol Aircraft*, 1964; personal knowledge.]

PETER G. MASEFIELD

V

VAUGHAN, (JOHN) KEITH (1912–1977), painter and book illustrator, was born at Selsey, Sussex, 23 August 1912, the elder son (there were no daughters) of Eric George Story Vaughan, a civil engineer, and his wife, Gladys Regina Marion Mackintosh. The parents separated in 1922. On the paternal side his grandfather and great-grandfather were successful London cabinet-makers and came of a long line of craftsmen. From 1921 to 1930 he was an unhappy boarder at Christ's Hospital but the art master of the time, H. A. Rigby, stimulated his interest in the visual arts, especially in landscape drawing. On leaving school however a vocation was not clear to him, and in 1931 he took employment with Lintas, a Unilever advertising agency, an occupation which, fortunately, left him energy to develop skills in painting and photography and to study the work of the masters, Cézanne, Matisse, and Picasso in particular. On a visit to Paris in 1937 he was greatly impressed by Gauguin. During this period he also frequented the ballet, an experience which was seminal to his later work.

Vaughan was a slow developer, and he was lucky that when he left Lintas in 1939 he was able to spend a year painting in the country. On the outbreak of war he was a conscientious objector. He joined the Pioneer Corps in 1941 and for most of his time in the service worked as a clerk and German interpreter at the POW camp at Malton, Yorkshire, where he found time to draw and to work in gouache and also to write. The journal which he began in 1939 and continued throughout his life was published in extracts selected and illustrated by himself in 1966. His introvert and reticent nature inhibited professional progress in this field, but he was a natural writer and during the war he graduated into the company of John Lehmann and his friends, and contributed to Penguin *New Writing* in 1944–6; and in 1949 he made lithograph illustrations for Norman Cameron's translation of Rimbaud's *Une Saison en Enfer* which Lehmann published.

His first exhibition of drawings was held in 1942 at Reid and Lefèvre where in 1946 he also exhibited paintings. He had never received a formal art training but at the same time as he was slowly making his name as an artist he established himself as a teacher, at Camberwell 1946–8, at the Central School 1948–57, and from 1954 as a visiting teacher at the Slade. He was visiting resident artist at Iowa State University in 1959.

The subject-matter of Vaughan's painting is confined almost entirely to landscape and the male nude. The patterned grey-green and ochreous spaces of the Sussex Downs had impressed their images on him in his schooldays, and experiments in photographing groups of bathers at Pagham in 1939 developed his interest and experience in figure-group composition. The many variations on this latter theme (which he liked to call an 'assembly'), which occupied him over decades, owed much to Cézanne, whereas his landscapes are often in the spirit, if not the vocabulary, of Graham Sutherland [q.v.]. Study of Cézanne's late bathing groups stiffened his intellectual approach to painting at the right moment. It would have been all too easy for him to have developed an idiom of more facile appeal. As it was he pushed himself almost to the clumsy in such experimental works as 'Leaping Figure' (1951) in the Tate Gallery. His rich palette of ochre, corn-yellow, olive-green, deep blues, and white was intensely personal, growing more Mediterranean in its verve when he began to respond with some passion to the painting of Nicolas de Stael. There were many influences on him, John Minton (with whom he once shared a house) and John Craxton notably among his contemporaries; but his work always had a character apart. His reduction of the human figure to near impersonality and his spreading of colour into wide and formal patterning are symptomatic of this somewhat withdrawn attitude. He was essentially a private artist and received few public commissions, the best-known being the Theseus mural for the Dome of Discovery at the Festival of Britain in 1951, and in 1955 a tile-mural for a bus shelter in Corby New Town whose abstract design so baffled the local authority that it was bricked up.

Having signified assent Vaughan was elected ARA in 1960 but resigned within a month. In 1964 he was elected an honorary fellow of the Royal College of Art, and in 1965 was appointed CBE. He held a number of exhibitions in this country, was given one-man shows in New York, Los Angeles, Buenos Aires, and San Paolo, and was accorded a retrospective exhibition at the Whitechapel Art Gallery in 1962. He never married. Threatened by cancer, he committed suicide at his Hampstead home 4 November 1977.

A self-portrait drawing was reproduced in *Art News and Review*, 8 April 1950. Photographs by Felix H. Maw, probably c.1950, and J. S. Lewinski, 1968, are in the National Portrait Gallery archives.

[*The Times*, 8 and 14 November 1977; Keith Vaughan, *Journal and Drawings 1939–1965*, 1966; catalogue, *Keith Vaughan, Images of Man*, Geffrye Museum, London, 1981; Tate Gallery archives; private information.]

K. J. GARLICK

VEALE, SIR DOUGLAS (1891–1973), university registrar, was born in Bristol 2 April 1891, the third and youngest son (there were no daughters) of Edward Woodhouse Veale, solicitor, and his wife, Maud Mary Rootham. He was educated at Bristol Grammar School which he left in 1910 with a classical scholarship to Corpus Christi College, Oxford, where he was placed in the first class in classical honour moderations in 1912 and in the second class in *literae humaniores* in 1914.

Veale was called up as a Territorial to serve in the 4th battalion of the Gloucestershire Regiment. He took the Civil Service examinations, was appointed a second class clerk, under the Local Government Board, married in 1914 Evelyn Annie (died 1970), daughter of James Alexander Henderson, surveyor, of Westbury on Trym, Bristol, and rejoined his battalion to see service as a captain in France and Belgium in 1915 during which he never caught sight of a staff officer. He was invalided home to become adjutant to the Reserve battalion but in 1917 was released to take up his clerkship.

Veale was soon marked out as the Board itself burgeoned into the Ministry of Health. By 1920 he was private secretary to the permanent secretary and from 1921 to 1928 private secretary to successive ministers of health from Christopher (later Viscount) Addison [q.v.] onwards. It was Veale who supplied Sir Alfred Mond (later Lord Melchett, q.v.)—and thereby the Cabinet—with the formula 'the British Commonwealth of Nations' during the negotiations over the Irish treaty of 1921. In 1926 he became a principal. As Neville Chamberlain's private secretary he played a major role, with his friend and colleague Sir Maurice Gwyer (whose notice he later wrote for this Dictionary) in implementing the complicated Local Government Act of 1929; he was appointed CBE that year.

It was evident in Whitehall that he was striding to the top, but Oxford's pull proved stronger. A royal commission had recommended in 1922 that the post of registrar there should become an appointment of far greater significance. In 1930 Veale was appointed registrar from a strong field. His exiguous Civil Service pension was frozen and with accustomed quiet vigour he grasped his destiny.

Oxford colleges have never sought central guidance, and Veale was the object of early suspicion, as a young man in a hurry (and he remained both young and in a hurry all his life). But his tirelessness, accessibility, knowledge, and supple draftsmanship soon made him indispensable. As a fellow (1930) of his old college, the smallest in Oxford, he was sensitive to college susceptibilities and his own particular experience of Whitehall made him sensitive also to town–gown relations. He was patient, impartial (but not so impartial as to lose impetus), energetic, and imperturbable. He worked his small staff hard but took personal responsibility for any error, never forgetting how Maurice (later Lord) Hankey [q.v.] had once saved his own face by letting Veale be blamed for one of Hankey's rare omissions. He always went to a meeting knowing what he expected to be the result and wrote the minutes of hebdomadal council in advance, leaving narrow spaces for the dissenting view. He was never a 'mere administrator' but he liked clear decisions and yielded no sympathy to the self-indulgent who rejoiced in making university politics the art of the impossible. He had the rapid knack of harnessing the soaring imagination of others to the longer haul without developing tunnel vision.

It was significant that his favourite vice-chancellor, amongst the many he served so strenuously, should be A. D. Lindsay (later Lord Lindsay of Birker, q.v.), the master of Balliol, the least effective in Veale's view Sir Richard Livingstone [q.v.], the president of Veale's own college.

Veale's integrity was combined with ingenuity: blocked at the front entrance, he was having a cup of tea at the back door while the slam of the front one was still echoing down the street. As time went on his contemporaries in Whitehall became very important men and Whitehall itself became increasingly important to Oxford as the Treasury and the University Grants Committee came to play a more significant part in its future. Veale did not scruple to use them and all his own widespread friendships to the hilt. His hospitality was at once generous and purposeful.

He was the principal architect of the modern Oxford University. Inevitably the Clarendon Building, in those days the abode of the university offices, was known as the Hotel de Veale. The various Nuffield benefactions were in part the result of his skill in steering vision into practicality. He was keenly interested in the Commonwealth, and was a forceful ally to the Colonial Office and its Oxford connections, to Sir Ralph Furse [q.v.], Sir Charles Jeffries, and Dame Margery Perham. He was active in many good causes in Oxford too numerous to mention. The medical world of city and university owe him a particular debt; likewise the Oxford Society, the Historic Buildings Appeal, Dorset House, the Casson Trust, St. Antony's College, and St. Edmund Hall of which he became an honorary fellow in 1958 (the same year as that in which he was made an honorary fellow of his own college). Outside Oxford his favourite charity was the Abbey School at Malvern of which he was chairman and where his two daughters were educated. Retiring as registrar (1958) he remained as energetic as ever. He was also remarkably fit—a great walker and a keen tennis player who at the age of eighty-one complained that doubles in the

University Parks did not give him enough exercise. He became secretary at the Oxford Preservation Trust and displayed a vigour which caused primmer members to murmur that what was needed was not preservation by but from Douglas Veale. He worked hard to get his genial way and usually did; but he never repined at defeat: he was a strong swimmer. Knowing his own worth, he was cheerful but serious minded, a stout Anglican, staunch to the Arnoldian values of a generation too few of whom survived Flanders. Silent at the major bodies which he serviced, for he always briefed his chairman so well that words by him were unnecessary, he would in compensation read aloud to his wife of an evening the book of *his* choice. Lady Veale (he was knighted in 1954) was a person of quiet strength and whimsical humour. It was a most happy marriage. They were survived by three children: John, musician and film critic; (Evelyn) Margaret, widow of R. B. McCallum [q.v.], master of Pembroke College, Oxford; and Janet.

Veale died in Oxford 27 September 1973 at the Acland Hospital, the extension of which owed much to his efforts long before. Veale was an honorary DCL of Oxford (1958) and honorary LL D of Melbourne (1948). He is commemorated in Oxford by a carving of his head in the archway leading from the Bodleian quadrangle to the Clarendon Building and by sheltered housing in Headington named after him.

[*The Times*, 29 September 1973; *Oxford Times*, 5 October 1973; Sir Kenneth Wheare in *Oxford*, vol. xxvi, No. 1, 1974; Robert Heussler, *Yesterday's Rulers*, 1963; Sir Ralph Furse, *Aucuparius*, 1962; *The Lyttelton–Hart-Davis Letters*, vol. iv, 1982; David Dilks, *Neville Chamberlain*, vol. i, 1984; private information; personal knowledge.] E. T. WILLIAMS

VENABLES, SIR PERCY FREDERICK RONALD ('PETER') (1904–1979), educationist and vice-chancellor, was born 5 August 1904 at Birkenhead, the second of the seven children of Percy Venables, a post office clerk, and his wife, Ethel Kate Paull. He was educated at Birkenhead Secondary School and the Birkenhead Institute and, subsequently, from 1922, at Liverpool University where he was to spend eight years. In 1925 he obtained a first class honours B.Sc. in chemistry. He also represented the university at rugby in which, as his chunky figure dictated, he was a front row forward.

His first intention was to enter school-teaching and with this in mind he spent a further year taking the education diploma in 1926. He was diverted, however, into chemical research and spent two years as a research student working on the photosynthesis of nitrogen compounds. His thesis on this subject earned him a Ph.D. in 1928 and a research fellowship which he held until 1930.

In 1930 he was appointed to a lectureship in chemistry at the Leicester College of Technology. Here he threw himself into the challenges of teaching during the dark days of the depression and he left himself little time for further research. He published several papers on chemical analysis and also, as co-author, a slim volume entitled *A Chemistry Course for Painters and Decorators* (1933), a title which was perhaps the first indication of his lasting commitment to the technical education of the underprivileged. In 1936 he moved from Leicester to become head of the chemistry department at the South-East Essex Technical College, and in 1941 he was appointed principal of the Municipal College in Southend-on-Sea. Thus by the age of thirty-seven he had already established himself as an academic administrator. It was a wise move for his great gifts as an administrator were called on continuously thereafter and he cannot have regretted that he abandoned a career in chemical research.

It was while he was a lecturer in Leicester that he married in 1932 Ethel Craig, daughter of Alfred Howell, a wharfinger of Middlesbrough. This was a match of intellectual equals; she, too, was a graduate in chemistry but, as Venables himself put it, they were both 'lapsed chemists'—he into administration, she into educational psychology in which she gained a Ph.D. in 1956. In later years she became an authority on marriage guidance. They were a devoted couple sharing for forty-seven years not only intellectual but social and cultural interests, and establishing close links with the worlds of music, theatre, and art. They had two sons and two daughters; their younger daughter, Clare, who made a career in the theatre, succeeded Joan Littlewood as director of the Stratford Theatre.

In 1947 Venables was appointed principal of the Royal Technical College, Salford. For nine years he was intimately involved in the process of creation of the eight CATs (Colleges of Advanced Technology), of which his institution was one. This was the first attempt to upgrade technical education in Britain which still tended to classify engineers as artisans rather than professionals. In 1955 Venables published his first major work *Technical Education* and, in the same year, moved from Salford to the Birmingham CAT where he was to remain until his retirement in 1969. He was again involved in the process of upgrading for his new institution became Aston University and he himself became a vice-chancellor in 1966. Throughout all this period of stress and change Venables clung to his visions of expanded opportunities for vocational training for all who could benefit, and of vocational training that was in no sense narrow but was instead an education for a full and rewarding life. In articles and speeches he pressed for close links between education and industry and was a tireless advocate of the sandwich course as a means to this end. His second major work, *Higher Education Developments: the Technological Universities 1956–76*, was published in 1978.

Despite the pressures of his appointments Venables found time to undertake a very large range of services of many kinds. He was president of the Association of Principals of Technical Institutions (1953–4) and president of the Manchester Literary and Philosophical Society (1954–6). His government appointments included membership of the central advisory council for education (England) (1956–60), of the advisory council on scientific policy (1962–4), of the Northern Ireland committee on university and higher technical education (1963–4), and of the committee on manpower resources (1965–8). With a fine impartiality he was concurrently chairman (1965–9) both of the ITA adult education advisory committee and of the BBC further education advisory council. In 1969–73 he was vice-president of BACIE and in 1971–7 president of the National Institute of Adult Education. In addition to all this he was a member of the West Midlands economic planning council (1965–8) and of the Midlands Electricity Board (1967–73).

In 1967, having been elected vice-chairman of the committee of vice-chancellors and principals of the United Kingdom, he was asked by Jennie Lee (later Baroness Lee of Asheridge), the minister of state at the Department of Education and Science, to become chairman of the planning committee of the Open University. To the astonishment of his vice-chancellorial colleagues he accepted. The planning committee was dissolved in 1969 when the Open University received its royal charter which named Venables first pro-chancellor and chairman of council, a position he held for five years.

He was punctilious as chairman, never encroaching on the job of the vice-chancellor. He saw his role as that of ensuring that the policies of the university were in harmony with the spirit of the charter, with the views of the lay members of the governing body, and with the motivation and commitment of the staff. This he accomplished with a lightness of touch and a firmness of purpose. He was a wonderful chairman, always totally prepared, willing to listen patiently to all who wished to speak, however foolishly, summarizing with unerring insight any consensus that he perceived, and able to give a lead when there was no consensus by offering his own well-thought-out suggestion.

It was a measure of the trust in his total integrity which he inspired that he was recalled from retirement to be chairman of the university's committee on continuing education. By 1975 the first objective of the university, namely the provision of courses leading to a first degree, had been largely accomplished. But another objective, 'to provide for the educational well-being of the community generally', was still to be tackled. This phrase, almost certainly drafted by Venables himself, covers all the egalitarian and humanitarian ideas that had inspired him throughout his life. It could be implemented through the provision of continuing education. The report of the committee was published in 1977.

This was the last formal contribution that Venables made to the Open University, of which he had been, as it were, the consultant architect, while others erected the buildings. Venables was knighted in 1963 and received honorary degrees from Aston (1969), Sussex (1971), and the Open University (1973). He was made an honorary fellow of the University of Manchester Institute of Science and Technology (1970) and of Chelsea College (1973). He became FRIC in 1938.

Despite his many commitments, about which he was conscientious in the extreme, Venables was a warm and friendly man with an impish sense of humour, making his wisecracks with a completely dead-pan face. He had endless patience, sympathy, and goodwill towards those who worked with him. He died, after a short illness, at his home in Birmingham 17 June 1979.

A portrait by David Poole (1974) hangs on the main staircase of Walton Hall, at the Open University.

[*The Times*, 23 November 1979; *Chemistry in Britain*, vol. xvi, 1980, p. 555; private information; personal knowledge.] WALTER PERRY

VOYCE, (ANTHONY) THOMAS (1897–1980), England international rugby footballer, was born 18 May 1897 at Gloucester, the only son and the sixth of seven children of Thomas Voyce, stevedore, of Gloucester, whose family came from the village of Ashleworth, and his wife, Anne Hackney, also of Gloucester. He was educated at the National School, Gloucester, and while he was there he was capped for England in 1911 as a schoolboy international rugby player. He was also a chorister at Gloucester Cathedral.

Even though under age he joined the army as a private at the outbreak of war in 1914 and served in the Gloucestershire Regiment in France. While there he contracted peritonitis and was repatriated for an operation. He thus missed the first battle of the Somme. Subsequently, he went to Sandhurst at the same time as Prince Henry of Gloucester and was commissioned into the Royal West Kent Regiment. He was severely wounded in his right eye by a shell-burst in France in 1917.

The wound left him with permanently impaired vision, but despite the handicap he took up rugby football again and played for the army and Blackheath. After the war he returned to captain Gloucester and Gloucestershire and also played for Cheltenham, Richmond, the Barbarians, England, and the British Lions. He won 27 consecutive caps for England between 1920 and 1926, and under the captaincy of W. Wavell Wakefield (later Lord Wakefield of Kendal) contributed a great deal to one of the most successful periods in England's Rugby Union history. Before the days of Wakefield and Voyce forward specialization was almost unheard of, but Voyce, at wing forward, and Wakefield, at number eight, pioneered the basis of the loose forward game as it was later played.

Voyce toured South Africa with the British Lions in 1924, and represented Gloucestershire on the Rugby Football Union from 1931 until he became its president in 1960–1. He was appointed OBE in 1962 for his services to the National Playing Fields Association, to various hospital authorities in Gloucestershire, to the National Savings movement, and to the St. John Ambulance Brigade. He was also chairman of the Ministry of Pensions in Gloucestershire.

Voyce was a man of rich character: a hard man who played, as one of his contemporaries put it, 'like a pirate coming over the side of a ship with a knife in his mouth. The only difference was that Tom didn't need a black patch over one eye. He couldn't see out of it in any case'. His interests were wide-ranging. Apart from his public work, he played golf to a single-figure handicap and was an ardent salmon and trout fisherman. He also collected antique clocks and at one stage had seven grandfather clocks in his house in Gloucester.

In 1926, his last year of international rugby, Voyce married Hilda ('Pat'), daughter of Joseph Weekes King, farmer, of Berkeley, Gloucestershire; they had a son and a daughter. Voyce died at his home in Tewkesbury Road, Gloucester, 22 January 1980.

[Private information; personal knowledge.]

John Reason

W

WADDINGTON, CONRAD HAL (1905–1975), geneticist, was born in Evesham 8 November 1905, the only son and elder child of Hal Waddington and his wife, Mary Ellen Warner, who came from long-established Quaker families. Not only were they first cousins but so also were Mary Ellen's parents. Waddington spent his early years in India where his father was a tea planter in Madras. He returned to England at the age of four to live first with an aunt and uncle in the shadow of Bredon Hill, and then with his grandmother in Evesham. She and an elderly member of the Quaker meeting in Evesham, a Dr Doeg, were the main influences on him as a child. He describes the latter as 'almost the last surviving real . . . scientist. By that I mean that he reckoned to deal with the whole of science'.

From his preparatory school, Aymestrey House, Waddington won a scholarship to Clifton, followed by another to Sidney Sussex in Cambridge where he took first classes in both parts of the natural sciences tripos (1925 and 1927), specializing in geology in part ii. He chose geology 'because it seemed that becoming an oil geologist would be a good way of earning a living'. But his interests were many-sided. He held at the same time an 1851 studentship in palaeontology and an Arnold Gerstenberg studentship in philosophy (1927). Gradually his interests moved towards evolutionary biology. He worked for two years on the systematics of fossil ammonites (though this was never completed) and he published on the genetics of germination in *Matthiola*.

In 1930 he approached (Dame) Honor B. Fell, the director of the Strangeways Laboratory, Cambridge, for help in applying to chick embryos the techniques which Spemann had used in Germany on developing amphibians. Success in this was perhaps the decisive turn in his career. He was a lecturer in zoology there from 1933 and a fellow of Christ's College, Cambridge, from 1934 to 1945 (and an honorary fellow from 1966).

For the next few years Waddington was concerned in the understanding of the early stages of chick and amphibian development which came to focus on evocation and in particular on the chemical nature of the 'evocator'. This interest eventually petered out, partly at the coming of World War II and partly because it was discovered that many substances had the necessary properties. He summarized his views in his book *Organisers and Genes* (1940).

In 1940 he joined a scientific dining club in London which included P. M. S. (later Lord) Blackett, J. D. Bernal, Lancelot Hogben [qq.v.], N. W. Pirie, and Solly (later Lord) Zuckerman. The publisher (Sir) Allen Lane [q.v.], having attended a meeting at which it transpired that less than one half the scientists present were involved in war work, suggested that here was the basis of a book. The members wrote *Science at War* in eleven days and had it published in a month. At the time, Blackett was director of the operational research section at RAF Coastal Command. Waddington joined him there in 1942 and became director from 1944 to 1946. His monograph on operational research against the U-boat was not published until 1973.

As the war ended he was offered the position of chief geneticist in the proposed National Breeding and Genetics Research Organization. As his position in Cambridge teaching had not been secure, he accepted, to receive an unexpected second offer—the chair of animal genetics at Edinburgh. After some thought, he refused the latter but was then offered a compromise—that he accept both, with the new organization going to Edinburgh.

He found there in 1947 an almost empty laboratory and an atmosphere of expansion in which he created one of the largest genetics departments in the world. In addition to the animal breeding group, there were units with diverse financial support devoted to mutagenesis, protozoan genetics, and radiation mutagenesis in small animals. Waddington himself returned to his main interest in evolution and development but with many diversions. He played a major role in the organization of the International Biological Programme. He wrote several stimulating books on genetics and development and his main contribution to biology was to bring together the two disciplines (and to provide words for many of the new concepts), culminating in the four meetings held in Bellagio which, supported by the International Union of Biological Sciences, led to four volumes with the general title *Towards a Theoretical Biology* (1968, 1969, 1971, 1972). Waddington was president of IUBS in 1961–7.

He remained interested in the arts and in philosophy—among his publications in 1969 was *Behind Appearance*, a study of modern art, and then in 1972 he contributed to the Gifford lectures on *The Nature of Mind*. In his last years he was much interested in the future of human society and was a founder member of the Club of Rome. He was heavily built but very light on his feet and a nimble dancer. He became bald at the age of twenty-one and this, coupled with his erudition, caused many people to think that he was much older than he actually was.

He was elected a fellow of the Royal Society in 1947 and of the Royal Society of Edinburgh in

1948. He was appointed CBE in 1958. He held honorary degrees from Montreal (1958), Trinity College, Dublin (1965), Prague (1966), Aberdeen (1966), Geneva (1968), and Cincinnati (1971).

In 1926 he married Cecil Elizabeth ('Lass') daughter of Cecil Henry Lascelles, son of the sixth son of the fourth Earl of Harewood. They had one son (a physicist). This marriage was dissolved in 1936 and in the same year he married an architect, Margaret Justin, daughter of George Rivers Blanco White, recorder of Croydon; they had two daughters, one an anthropologist and one a mathematician. Waddington died 26 September 1975 outside his Edinburgh home.

[Alan Robertson in *Biographical Memoirs of Fellows of the Royal Society*, vol. xxiii, 1977; personal knowledge.] ALAN ROBERTSON

WALCAN-BRIGHT, GERALD (1904–1974), dance-band leader and musician who used the name GERALDO, was born in Islington, north London, 10 August 1904, the twin son (there were also three daughters) of Isaac Walcan-Bright, master tailor, and his wife, Frances Feldman. Like his brother, Sidney, he was musical from an early age. He started to learn the piano when he was five and he continued his training at the Royal Academy of Music, after attending the Hugh Middleton Central School at Islington. His first professional engagement was as a relief pianist accompanying silent films at a cinema in the Old Kent Road. His first band was formed in 1924 to play at the Metropole in Blackpool, but recognition came for him during the five years he spent as musical director at the Hotel Majestic, St. Anne's on Sea. His band broadcast from the hotel three times a week and became the most popular dance orchestra in the north of England.

In 1929 he disbanded the orchestra and went to South America, where he spent some time in Argentina and Brazil studying Latin-American rhythms. Returning to London, he formed his Gaucho Tango orchestra, which started playing at the Savoy Hotel in August 1930. He remained there for ten successful years. During this time, he changed his stage name from Gerald Bright to Geraldo. He made his first recordings in 1930 with the orchestra, which gave more than 2,000 broadcasts from the Savoy. In 1933 they appeared at the royal command performance. In September that year he formed a new orchestra for the Savoy, widening his repertoire to include dance music and changing his signature tune from 'Lady of Spain' to 'I Bring You Sweet Music' (it later became 'Hello Again'). This orchestra made brief appearances in the films *Lilies of the Field* and *Ten-Minute Alibi* and played the whole score for *Brewster's Millions*. At one time during the 1930s, Geraldo was leading four bands and employing more than 200 musicians.

At the outbreak of World War II, he was appointed supervisor of the bands division of ENSA (Entertainments National Service Association) and director of bands for the BBC. Broadcasting several times a week in such programmes as 'Tip-Top Tunes', 'Over to You', and 'Dancing Through', Geraldo's orchestra became the most popular in Britain. His wartime band was more oriented towards jazz and swing than his groups of the 1930s—it included such men as trombonist Ted Heath, trumpeter Leslie 'Jiver' Hutchinson, and clarinettist Nat Temple, who all led their own orchestras later. Geraldo took the orchestra to entertain the troops in the Middle East, North Africa, and Europe, covering nearly 20,000 miles and twice crash-landing (in Italy and Gibraltar).

After the war he ran several orchestras, the largest comprising seventy-five musicians, but he became more interested in the business side of music, supplying orchestras for liners (including the Cunard Line), dance halls, theatres, and restaurants. His own orchestra continued to broadcast, and he was the first bandleader to appear on British television when it reopened after the war. He was a founder-director of Harlech Television and, for a while, musical director of Scottish Television. In the early days of ITV, he appeared in a long-running television series called 'Gerry's Inn'.

Although his public appearances diminished, he returned for a series of nostalgic concerts at the Royal Festival Hall from 1969, which led to a television series recalling the era of swing music. He was still recording in the 1970s. His last public appearance was at a concert in Eastbourne a few weeks before his death.

Geraldo was of medium height, sturdily built, with dark brown hair and brown eyes. He was always immaculately dressed and his voice had a slight cockney accent. He loved classical music but firmly believed in the value of dance music. When (Sir) Malcolm Sargent [q.v.] criticized dance music in 1942, Geraldo said that he would conduct Sargent's orchestra in any piece of classical music if Sargent would conduct Geraldo's orchestra in a piece of swing music. Sargent refused the challenge.

He married Alice Plumb in 1948 and they were divorced in 1965, when he married Marya, daughter of Leopold Detsinyi, a Hungarian textile-manufacturer. He died 4 May 1974 of a heart attack while on holiday with his wife in Vevey, Switzerland.

[*The Times*, 6 and 20 May 1974; *Guardian*, 6 May 1974; Julien Vedey, *Band Leaders*, 1950; Albert McCarthy, *The Dance Band Era*, 1971; private information.] TONY AUGARDE

WALKER, PATRICK CHRESTIEN GORDON, BARON GORDON-WALKER (1907–1980), politician, don, author, and broadcaster. [See GORDON WALKER.]

WALLACE, PHILIP ADRIAN HOPE- (1911–1979), music and theatre critic. [See HOPE-WALLACE.]

WALLIS, SIR BARNES NEVILLE (1887–1979), engineer, was born at Ripley, Derbyshire, 26 September 1887, the second child and second son in the family of three sons and one daughter of Charles George Wallis, general practitioner, and his wife, Edith Eyre, daughter of the Revd John Ashby. He was educated at Haberdashers' Aske's School at Hatcham and at Christ's Hospital in London.

Early in Wallis's childhood, his father, who had moved to London, became handicapped by poliomyelitis and although he struggled to maintain his practice, his family felt the need for rigid economy and his wife Edith had to shoulder the family responsibilities. It was due to her encouragement that Wallis, at the age of twelve, entered Christ's Hospital by way of a competitive examination. In spite of frequent illness and some attacks of migraine, he did well, particularly in English, science, and mathematics. He was afterwards always grateful to the school, especially to his science master, and to his mother for the sacrifices she made to keep him there.

Seeking to earn his living as early as possible, he chose to become an engineer and left school at the age of seventeen to become an apprentice in the Thames Engineering Works at Blackheath. Later he moved his indentures to J. S. White's shipyard at Cowes. There he did well, and after attending local evening classes, passed the London matriculation examination. Throughout, he kept in touch with his mother, under whose leadership he had become, and remained throughout his life, a devout Anglo-Catholic.

Two events now occurred that were to have much influence on his life: first, his mother died in 1911, leaving him with a permanent sense of loss and a determination to do his best for his family; and second, a new recruit to Cowes, H. B. Pratt, came to work alongside him.

Pratt had worked for Vickers at Barrow when the first British rigid airship, the R 1, was built there, and in 1913 he was recalled by Vickers to start on the design of a new airship, the R 9. He persuaded Wallis to join him, and it was not long before both, caught by the romance of these great ships of the air, were working long hours every day of the week. Under Pratt, who had already appreciated Wallis's design flair, Wallis became chief designer, and J. E. Temple, another Vickers engineer, was placed alongside him as chief calculator. The R 9 was completed in 1916. It closely followed Zeppelin practice and became popular in the navy for the training of officers and men for subsequent airships. The same team later produced the R 23 and the R 26, which entered naval service too late to contribute much to the 1914–18 war effort. Meanwhile Wallis served in the Artists' Rifles and RNVR in 1915.

After the war Pratt and Temple moved out of airship work and Wallis started upon the design of his favourite airship, the R 80. It was intended for Atlantic convoy work and was to be faster and more manoeuvrable than previous airships. Wallis, impressed by the results of aerodynamic tests on some airship models at the National Physical Laboratory, boldly stepped away from the cigar shape of the wartime Zeppelins and adopted a streamline form for the R 80. It first flew in 1920 and, after some minor troubles and modifications, was soon acclaimed as the best rigid airship of its day. However, government airship work ceased in 1921 after the R 38 disaster, and Vickers closed their airship department.

Wallis, in despair, and suffering increasingly from migraine, sought without success an airship appointment in the USA. He turned to studying for an external degree in engineering of London University, which he gained in 1922, and then went to Switzerland to teach in a school there. He proved a good teacher and discovered the ability to lecture with clarity and charm for which he was well known for the rest of his life.

Meanwhile, largely due to the advocacy of (Sir) C. Dennistoun Burney [q.v.] of Vickers, ideas for large airships for commercial purposes were astir in England and the government was considering an airship service to India. The Zeppelin Company had started upon the design and construction of the Graf Zeppelin, the most successful of all commercial airships. Wallis, full of enthusiasm, returned to Vickers and at Howden was put in charge, under Burney, of the design of the R 100, one of the two great airships finally authorized by the government in 1924. The other, the R 101, was to be built at the Royal Airship Works at Cardington. Both ships were to be much larger, even, than the Graf Zeppelin and were to be capable of carrying a hundred passengers to India with a single stop in Egypt, using diesel engines to reduce fire risks in the tropics.

For the R 100 Wallis again adopted a streamline form, this time adjusted to enable the ship to be handled in and out of the large shed provided for it at Cardington. Its structure, as in the R 80, followed in layout the best Zeppelin practice and was built mainly of duralumin. However, the great increase in size introduced new problems. The structure of a rigid airship consists primarily of longitudinal girders arranged around a number of transverse frames.

The gasbags fit between these frames and the whole structure is covered by fabric supported by the longitudinals. Wallis had difficulties—as did the designers of the R 101—with all of these components and solved them in his own way.

To try to save weight, Wallis spaced his longitudinals more widely than ever before, and so had to use a stronger fabric covering and fit internal wiring to pull it taut to prevent flapping. This gave the R 100 a rather 'hungry horse' appearance and did not leave it entirely free from outer cover troubles. Moreover, for the booms of the widely spaced longitudinals Wallis found he needed four-inch diameter tubes, a size beyond available manufacturing equipment. He met this in characteristic fashion by inventing a new process for manufacturing large duralumin tubes from strip, a fine example of his skill as a mechanical engineer. The wire bracing of the ship's structure followed Zeppelin practice, but the wiring to contain the gasbags and transmit their lift to the frames was novel. For this he developed a system of intersecting helical wires to which he gave the name 'geodetics', an arrangement later to influence his aeroplane structures.

Meanwhile, development of suitable diesel engines for the R 100 and R 101 was proving difficult, and in view of their excessive weight Wallis pleaded to forgo diesel power (and hence the ability to travel safely to India) and revert to well-tried petrol engines. It was this that led to the successful demonstration flight of the R 100 across the Atlantic instead of to the east.

All this was not done without hard work and nervous stress. Burney, who had retained Temple as a personal assistant, sometimes sought to influence Wallis on technical matters; and while Wallis usually managed to reject such interventions, he did so only with great nervous strain. Migraine troubles and a strike by fitters brought matters to a head and in 1928, beset by insomnia, Wallis had a nervous breakdown and went away to Menton with his wife. When he returned, he had made up his mind to move to aeroplane design. He stayed at Howden to see the R 100 off on its first flight to Cardington, and then went to Weybridge to start a new life as chief designer (structures) alongside R. K. Pierson, chief designer at Vickers Aviation there. Pierson welcomed Wallis as a leader in duralumin construction and as a colleague with a common interest in long-range aircraft.

It was not long before Wallis began to experiment with a geodetic structure for a biplane fuselage. His intersecting spiral structure surrounded four main longerons both to brace them and to support the fabric covering. Following the success of this arrangement, Wallis applied the method to a monoplane wing by wrapping his geodetics around a single spar to form the basis of the wing profile. For long range, Pierson had planned for wings of unusually high span to chord ratio, which called for high wing stiffness in torsion to prevent flutter and related troubles. This stiffness Wallis achieved and the Wellesley bomber was born. At first the geodetics were made by hand, but the ingenuity of Wallis and the production team at Vickers soon mechanized the process. In 1938 a Wellesley flew to Australia to establish a record range of 7,158 miles non-stop, a triumph for both Pierson and Wallis. Nearly 180 of these bombers were built, a large number for pre-war aeroplanes.

With the approach of the war of 1939–45, larger bombers were called for, and Pierson and Wallis started upon the design of a twin-engine bomber with a shape and structure based on the Wellesley. The resulting bomber—the Wellington—came into production before the war started, and remained in service throughout. In all, nearly 12,000 Wellingtons were built. The Wellington proved popular with the RAF, particularly when it was found to fly well when its fabric covering or some of its geodetics had been damaged by gunfire. But its speed was high for a fabric-covered aeroplane and Wallis had often to deal with flapping and tearing troubles. Towards the end of the war a more fundamental trouble emerged. Most bombers had very short flying lives, but some Wellingtons survived an unusual 1,500 flying hours and began to develop fatigue cracks in the wing spar booms at their joints. It was a knowledge of this metal fatigue problem—the first of its kind in aeroplane structures—that led N. S. Norway [q.v.], who had worked under Wallis on the R 100, to write, as Nevil Shute, his famous novel *No Highway* (1948).

The Wellington had its rivals among English bombers and was finally outclassed by the Lancaster, a metal-covered four-engine bomber designed by Roy Chadwick [q.v.] of Avro, Manchester. Wallis strangely failed to recognize the merits of metal covering which, unlike fabric, contributed substantially to the strength and stiffness of aeroplane structures; so he made further efforts to produce a new larger geodetic aeroplane. This never went into production and he came to accept, with the generous co-operation of Chadwick, variants of the Lancaster for the delivery of the great bombs to which he began to devote his energies.

By 1941 he had become convinced of the need to attack German industry at its roots—its sources of power—and persuaded Sir Henry T. Tizard [q.v.], then scientific adviser to the Ministry of Aircraft Production, to support him in the development of a mode of attacking the great Möhne dam in the Ruhr. He first thought of using a large bomb which, if it could be delivered nearby, would set up shock waves in the ground at the base of the dam sufficient to crack it. However, experiments conducted with the help of (Sir) W. H. Glanville [q.v.] of the Road Research Laboratory quickly showed that, to be effective, impracticably large bombs would be needed unless they could be made to explode very close to the dam face. It was this impasse that led Wallis to think of a spherical bomb to be sent on a ricochet path over the water with a spin to ensure that when it struck the dam face it would roll down it and explode at a depth predetermined by a pressure fuse. As a result of many experiments in government research establishments and in Wales, he was able to convince Bomber Command of the feasibility of his scheme. The attack on the Möhne and Eder dams, using spinning bombs in cylindrical form, took place in May 1943, with complete success. Soon afterwards Wallis produced much bigger deep penetration bombs for dropping from high altitude on vital targets such as the launching sites for German flying bombs, and submarine pens. With the improved aiming methods by then available in the RAF, Wallis's great bombs were often dramatically successful; in the words of Sir Henry Tizard, he had made the 'finest individual technical achievement of the war'.

The war over, (Sir) George R. Edwards, who had been at Weybridge since 1935, had become interested with Pierson in metal-covered aeroplanes. Vickers Aviation was reorganized and while Edwards went on to design the successful Viscount civil aeroplane, Wallis was moved to head a special research department. Encouraged by Tizard, Wallis now sought to develop a new type of aeroplane, one with variable geometry wings and no tailplane, as the basis for a high-speed, high-altitude bomber. The scheme was beset with difficulties, many of which Wallis overcame, but changes in government and air staff views rendered his work abortive.

His mind turned to other fields. Waterloo bridge had just been replaced and a scheme for another road bridge over the Thames, near Charing Cross, was mooted. Wallis enjoyed advancing the idea of spanning the Thames there with a glorious single duralumin arch, incorporating an ingenious automatic control over its deflections. But collapse of the backing for the proposed bridge led to the scheme being abandoned.

Reverting to his early interest in marine engineering, he made, without success, a somewhat similar invasion into submarine design, advancing the idea of a large submarine as a cargo ship, less vulnerable to enemy action than surface ships.

Wallis's last major engineering activity was more successful. The astronomer royal, at the instance of Tizard, invited him to attend a committee considering the design of the new Isaac Newton telescope, for which a specially rigid frame was required. His suggestions proved too unconventional for the British astronomers, but caught the interest of those concerned in Australia with the design of a large radio telescope comparable with that at Jodrell Bank. The construction of the disc and the control of its movement interested Wallis, and he made valuable contributions in both respects to its final design by Freeman, Fox, & Partners. Wallis, thus active, did not finally retire from Vickers until 1971, when he was eighty-four.

At the end of the war of 1939–45 Wallis became an almoner at Christ's Hospital. Thus started a new association with his old school, for which he worked with devotion for the rest of his life. It led also to his establishment of a foundation for the education at the school of children of RAF personnel, an expression of his deepest loyalties. Later, when Wallis had become school treasurer, he led an appeal for funds that resulted in the collection of nearly £1,000,000.

Wallis had a deep spiritual approach to life that was manifested not only by formal religious observances but also by his generous help to others, typified by his foundation. He was intensely patriotic as well as very loyal to his school and to Vickers. Professionally, however, he was a severe master, demanding hard work and high standards from all under him. He was always willing to seek advice from specialists, but when his mind was made up he was intolerant of the ideas or criticisms of others. He could, nevertheless, be very persuasive and charming, characteristics that led many to support his work.

His achievements were honoured in 1943 by appointment as CBE, in 1945 by election as FRS, by honorary doctorates from six British universities (Bristol, Cambridge, Heriot-Watt, London, Loughborough, and Oxford), and by a knighthood in 1968. He was an honorary fellow of the Royal Aeronautical Society (1967) and became an RDI in 1943. He was awarded the James Alfred Ewing medal in 1945, the Albert gold medal in 1968, and the Royal medal in 1975. He was an honorary fellow of Churchill College, Cambridge, from 1965 and a freeman of the city of London.

In 1925 Wallis married Mary ('Molly') Frances (died 1986), his step-cousin, daughter of Arthur George Bloxam, managing director of the firm of Abel & Imray, patent agents, of Hampstead. They had two sons and two daughters, and also adopted Molly's sister's two sons (aged ten and eight), who were orphaned in 1940. Wallis died in Leatherhead Hospital 30 October 1979.

[J. E. Morpurgo, *Barnes Wallis, a Biography*, 1972; Sir Alfred Pugsley and N. E. Rowe in *Biographical Memoirs of Fellows of the Royal Society*, vol. xxvii, 1981; personal knowledge.]

A. G. Pugsley

WALSHE, SIR FRANCIS MARTIN ROUSE (1885–1973), neurologist, was born in London 19 September 1885, the elder child and only son (a first son had died as a baby) of Michael Charles Walshe, a pioneer of agency nursing, originally from county Mayo in Ireland, and his wife Rose, daughter of Samuel Light, a yeoman farmer from Brixham. He was educated at Prior Park College, Bath (1898–1901) and University College School, London (1901–3). The celebrated physicians John Hughlings Jackson and Sir William Gowers [qq.v.] were both familiar figures of his youth. Walshe took first class honours in the London B.Sc. (1908) and in the MB, BS (1910) at University College Hospital. During training at the National Hospital, Queen Square, he added the MD (Lond.) in 1912 and MRCP in 1913.

In 1915 Walshe joined the Royal Army Medical Corps and became consulting neurologist to the British forces in Egypt and the Middle East where he worked with Sir Victor Horsley [q.v.]. He was appointed OBE (1919) and mentioned in dispatches. He was elected FRCP (Lond.) in 1920, and appointed to the staff of the National Hospital in 1921. In 1924 the department of neurology was founded for him at University College Hospital and in the same year he obtained the London D.Sc. Between 1920 and 1930 he produced 'work of the first importance as the pioneering description and analysis of human reflexes in physiological terms'. In 1931 and 1932 he was associated, with (Sir) Gordon Holmes [q.v.] and James Taylor, in the publication of *Selected Writings of John Hughlings Jackson*, a part of his lifelong championship of Jacksonian principles. Between 1940 and 1960 he published, mainly in the journal *Brain*, an important series of critical papers on the function of the cerebral cortex in relation to movements, and on neural physiology in relation to the awareness of pain. He wrote *Critical Studies in Neurology* (1948) and *Further Critical Studies in Neurology* (1965). He advised caution about some 'miraculous' cures at Lourdes (*Catholic Medical Guardian*, 1938 and 1939).

From 1937 to 1953 Walshe was editor of *Brain*, a post which provided lasting satisfaction and on his eightieth birthday, in a special issue of the journal, he provided a summary of his own thoughts and experience during fifty years as a neurologist.

Walshe established a reputation in medical education both as a teacher of clinical neurology and as a prolific author. He was responsible for the neurological sections of Conybeare's (1936) and Price's (1937) *Textbook of Medicine*, and in 1940 produced his highly individual *Diseases of the Nervous System*, which reached its eleventh edition in 1970 and was translated into many languages. Between 1910 and 1973 he amassed 181 publications.

From 1953 onwards Walshe became more and more absorbed in the philosophical problems of the mind–brain relationship, and his last paper (1972) was on the neurophysiological approach to consciousness. He was critical of those who maintained that psychology and biology are 'nothing but' physics and chemistry, and his criticisms could be wounding. Though his work had been based on Sherringtonian physiology, later in life he came to believe that patients with nervous disease must benefit more from advances in biochemistry and pharmacology than from physiological elaborations. He maintained an extensive correspondence with those in his own field and in allied subjects, and his critical writings did not impair many friendships at home and abroad.

Walshe continued in consulting practice until his late seventies. He disapproved of the National Health Service and never accepted any salary for his extensive hospital work. He disliked a merit award system based on secret negotiations. He needed 'a freedom of life and action that are essential to me. I was born to be a free-lance and not a power-seeker.' He realized that his way of life was passing, but his example caused many colleagues and students to attempt to imitate him. To this Dictionary he contributed the article on W. B. L. Trotter.

Walshe was elected FRS in 1946 and knighted in 1953. He was widely honoured, being a fellow of University College, London, and holding honorary doctorates of the National University of Ireland (1941) and of Cincinnati (1959). He was an honorary member of the neurological societies of America, Canada, Denmark, France, Germany, Spain, and Uruguay, and of the New York and American Academies of Neurology. He particularly enjoyed his presidency of the Association of British Neurologists (1950–1) and of the Royal Society of Medicine (1952–4). He was president of the Royal Institute of Public Health and Hygiene (1962–4). He delivered the Oliver Sharpey lecture (1929) and the Harveian oration (1948) at the Royal College of Physicians of London; the Ferrier lecture (1953) at the Royal Society; and the Hughlings Jackson, Gowers, and Victor Horsley lectures among many other named lectures; and he received five gold medals.

In 1916 Walshe married Bertha Marie (died 1950), daughter of Charles Dennehy, surgeon, of St. Lucia, West Indies, and Lismore, county Cork. They had two sons, the elder of whom became a solicitor, and the younger a physician and an international authority on the nervous disease named after S. A. Kinnier Wilson [q.v.], with whom Walshe had written his first paper in *Brain* in 1914. Walshe died at Brampton, near Huntingdon, 21 February 1973.

There are portraits at the National Hospital, Queen Square, and at the Royal Society of Medicine, London.

[C. G. Phillips in *Biographical Memoirs of Fellows of the Royal Society*, vol. xx, 1974; private information; personal knowledge.]

WILLIAM GOODDY

WAND, (JOHN) WILLIAM (CHARLES) (1885–1977), bishop, was born in Grantham 25 January 1885, the eldest of the family of three sons of Arthur James Henry Wand, a shopkeeper, at first a butcher and later a grocer, and his wife, Elizabeth Ann Ovelin Turner. His parents had both been confirmed in the Church of England, but on Sunday mornings the father played the harmonium at the Calvinist chapel, taking his sons with him. The future bishop was always to remember that he had known undiluted Calvinism from the inside. He was educated at King's School, Grantham, during which period he was himself confirmed; and, with a scholarship, at St. Edmund Hall, Oxford, where he graduated with a first class in theology in 1907. After a further year as a theological student at Bishop Jacob Hostel, Newcastle upon Tyne, he was ordained in 1908, and served curacies at Benwell (1908–11) and Lancaster (1911–14).

Wand's scholarly interests were part of the attraction which led to his appointment in 1914 as a vicar choral of Salisbury Cathedral, a post which also opened to him the opportunity of lecturing at the local theological college; but the outbreak of World War I came soon after his arrival, and in 1915 he became an army chaplain, serving first in Gallipoli and then in France. His post at Salisbury had been kept open, but on his return in 1919 he was appointed vicar of St. Mark's, Salisbury, and also resumed his lecturing at the theological college.

In 1925 he became fellow, dean, and tutor of Oriel College, Oxford, a post for which his capacity for business and his approachability were an ideal combination, and which had for him the great attraction of bringing him into touch with a wider world of scholarship. He published his first scholarly books at this time, notably his commentary on the Epistles of Peter and Jude (1934).

In 1934, through the recommendation of St. Clair G. A. Donaldson (whose notice Wand later wrote for this Dictionary), bishop of Salisbury, who had held the same office, he was elected archbishop of Brisbane. His arrival there was almost immediately clouded by a personal tragedy, the death when mountaineering in the Alps of his undergraduate son, for whom he had the deepest affection. To the diocese of Brisbane, and to the Province of Queensland of which he was metropolitan, he brought outstanding qualities of leadership and administration, and he did much to raise the standard of the clergy. He made full use of the opportunities provided by broadcasting and journalism to address the widest possible public. When after the fall of France in World War II there was widespread anxiety in Australia about British policy, Wand tried to allay this by publishing a pamphlet entitled *Has Britain Let us Down?* It was to have a wide sale, and incidentally, through the approval it received in British government circles, to influence the decision to recall him in 1943 to be bishop of Bath and Wells.

His period of office there was marked by fresh energy for the reorganization which the war had made necessary, and, as a new Education Act was passed in 1944, by vigorous support for church schools. Their maintenance was dear to Wand's heart, for he had started life in one himself. His stay in the diocese was however to be short; in 1945 he was nominated by (Sir) Winston Churchill to succeed G. F. Fisher (later Lord Fisher of Lambeth, q.v.) as bishop of London.

Wand saw it as his task in London to achieve recovery from the effects of war. Many churches and schools had been damaged or destroyed, the clergy were fewer and beset by many problems. The diocese, with the largest population of any in England, needed considerable reorganization. Wand set out to achieve this. Some Protestant groups were at first hostile to him as an acknowledged Anglo-Catholic, but his tolerance and understanding soon brought this hostility to an end.

The new bishop began with the organization of a teaching mission throughout the diocese, and followed this up with a more directly evangelistic mission to London. As he realized, this was to be more effective in the encouragement of church people than in bringing in new members, but this was a necessary stage in the process of recovery. In the City of London, with its many redundant parish churches, a scheme for guild churches, with specialized tasks, set a new pattern. And by greater delegation of responsibility to suffragan bishops, Wand began a process that was to develop further after his episcopate. In the wider affairs of the church he took a full part, notably in the ecumenical movement, and he was chairman of commissions on artificial insemination and on nullity.

As he had planned, he retired from his bishopric at the age of seventy, but to his delight he was appointed as a canon of St. Paul's, where he became cathedral treasurer. He was appointed KCVO in the same year (1955). His canonry gave him sufficient leisure for reading and writing, and an opportunity, which he valued highly, to preach and take part in the services of the cathedral.

Sturdy in appearance and genial in manner, Wand always combined friendliness with dignity. He was a man of wide, rather than specialized, scholarship. He spoke of reading and writing as his 'favourite hobbies', and published a number of books, these often being based on courses of lectures he had given, especially in Lent. His wide-ranging theological and historical interests made him a suitable appointment as editor, from 1956 to 1968, of the *Church Quarterly Review*.

He was admitted to the Privy Council in 1945. He had travelled widely, and received doctorates on both sides of the Atlantic: from Oxford (1934); Columbia (STP 1947); Toronto (STD 1947); Ripon, USA (D.Litt. 1949); King's College, London (DD and honorary fellow 1955, fellow 1956); Western Ontario (DD 1957). He was also an honorary fellow of St. Edmund Hall and Oriel College. He was dean of the Chapels Royal (1945–55); prelate of the Order of the British Empire (1946–55) and prelate emeritus from 1957 to his death.

He married in 1911 Amy Agnes (died 1966), the youngest daughter of William Wiggins, JP, a farmer at Watlington. There was one son and one daughter. In 1969 he retired to a cottage at Maplehurst, Sussex; he died at the College of St. Barnabas, Lingfield, 16 August 1977.

[*The Times*, 17 August 1977; William Wand, *Changeful Page* (autobiography), 1955; personal knowledge.] HAROLD RILEY

WARNER, SYLVIA TOWNSEND (1893–1978), novelist and poet, was born at Harrow, Middlesex, 6 December 1893, the only child of George Townsend Warner, assistant master and later head of the modern side at Harrow School, and his wife, Nora Hudleston. She was, briefly, privately educated. After a short time working in a munitions factory in World War I she was from 1918 to 1928 a member of the editorial board of *Tudor Church Music* (Oxford University Press, 1923–9). During this period she began to write. Her first book of verse, *The Espalier*, appeared in 1925. In 1926 she published the novel *Lolly Willowes*. This deft and fanciful elaboration on the theme of witchcraft won her a loyal following in the United States as well as in Britain. In 1927 she became guest critic of the *New York Herald-Tribune*: in the next four decades the *New Yorker* would publish more than 140 of her short stories.

Warner's first literary connections in England were with David Garnett and other writers associated with Bloomsbury. A more important influence was T. F. Powys, who appreciated the strength of her individuality and introduced her to her lifelong companion Valentine Ackland (died 1969). With Ms Ackland she issued a book of verse *Whether a Dove or a Seagull* (1934), in which the separate authors of the poems were not identified. Her own second book of poetry, *Time Importuned* (1928) had found only a small, though discriminating, audience. The poems' formal sense, their assimilation of both Emily Dickinson and English seventeenth-century verse, were remarkable; but Sylvia Townsend Warner remains best known for her fiction. She published in all seven novels and eight collections of short stories. *Mr. Fortune's Maggot* (1927) is a bizarre tale in an imaginary island. It was followed in 1929 by *The True Heart*, a historical fiction with a background in rural Victorian Essex. Her most substantial novel, *Summer will Show* (1936), was once more historical, for its characters are caught up in the Paris revolution of 1848.

This is also a political book. From about 1933 Sylvia Townsend Warner was a committed though never narrowly partisan writer of the Left. Her association with *Left Review* led to a friendship with the writer John Edgell Rickword. In 1936 she visited Spain, returning there the following year to attend the congress of anti-Fascist writers. She also became a member of the Association of Writers for Intellectual Liberty. She felt *After the Death of Don Juan* (1938), a satirical political fable, to be one of the most personal of her books. But this novella, like other of her writings, was too easily regarded as 'miscellaneous' to be recognized as the product of a distinct literary imagination. *Opus 7* (1931), a short novel in verse, was overlooked: her short stories were collected but too seldom found a place in anthologies.

After World War II she published a further historical novel, *The Corner that Held Them* (1948), memorable for its depiction of a fourteenth-century nunnery and in part inspired by her study of early music, while a more acid social observation (so much part of her short stories) was found in *The Flint Anchor* (1954). This was her last novel. She had undertaken, but never brought to completion, a biography of her friend T. F. Powys. A love of her adopted county of Dorset led to an account of its neighbour *Somerset* (1949), and her literary and rural interests were reflected in selections from the writings of Gilbert White (1946) and in *Jane Austen* (1951). At the prompting of mutual friends she wrote a biography (1967) of T. H. White, a writer younger than herself whom she had never met. This unusual assignment called forth a subtle power of empathy surely nurtured by her fiction. She was also, in her late years, a distinguished translator, as is shown by her version of Proust's *Contre Sainte-Beuve* (1958). Her last complete work was both a new departure and a return to the folklore themes found in *Lolly Willowes* and much of her poetry: the stories of *Kingdoms of Elfin* (1977) are obstinately of fairyland. She resisted the suggestion that she write her autobiography, 'because I'm too imaginative', but a selection of her letters was published in 1982. She was a fellow of the Royal Society of

Literature and an honorary member of the American Academy of Arts and Letters. She won the prix Menton in 1969.

She was unmarried. She died at home at Maldon Newton, Dorset, 1 May 1978.

[*Guardian*, 5 January 1977; *New York Times*, 27 March 1977; *The Times*, 2 May 1978; *P.N. Review*, vol. viii, No. 3, 1981; *Letters of Sylvia Townsend Warner*, ed. William Maxwell, 1982.]

ALEXANDRA PRINGLE

WARREN, MAX ALEXANDER CUNNINGHAM (1904–1977), clergyman, writer, and missionary statesman, was born in Dun Laoghaire, Ireland, 13 August 1904, the youngest of three sons and four children of the Revd John Alexander Faris Warren, a clergyman of the Church of Ireland, and his wife, Mary Kathleen East. After spending his first eight years in India, where his parents were missionaries of the Church Missionary Society, he was educated at Marlborough and Jesus College, Cambridge, where he was a scholar, gaining firsts in part i of the history tripos (1925) and part ii of the theology tripos (1926). While still an undergraduate he showed remarkable gifts of intellect and leadership, organizing a group of friends, the Hausa Band, to serve as missionaries in Northern Nigeria. After studying for a year at Ridley Hall, Cambridge, he sailed to Nigeria in 1927 but was invalided home ten months later with tuberculosis. During three years of illness in bed he read widely and prodigiously, a practice he continued throughout his life. He also learned about darkness and the depths, but later he described it as one of his most worthwhile experiences.

In 1932 he married Mary, daughter of the Revd Thomas Collett, and was ordained to a curacy at St. John's, Boscombe, by C. F. Garbett [q.v.], then bishop of Winchester, who also appointed him joint secretary to the Winchester diocesan council of youth. In 1936 he became vicar of Holy Trinity, Cambridge, which from the days of Charles Simeon [q.v.], who died exactly a hundred years earlier, had been one of the most famous evangelical churches in the land and a place of great influence on successive generations of undergraduates. He soon established himself as a thoughtful preacher with marked gifts of leadership in public worship and pastoral counselling. As many fled from Nazi Germany, he welcomed to his church the Lutheran congregation of Pastor Franz Hildebrandt, giving an early example of the ecumenical spirit which characterized his whole life. Despite the coming of war in 1939 and the responsibilities of a busy parish he continued his contacts with the Church Missionary Society and in 1942 was chosen to succeed W. Wilson Cash, who had become bishop of Worcester, as its general secretary.

For the next twenty-one years Warren was one of the most influential and best known men in the Church of England and in the Anglican communion. Bishops and archbishops, scholars and students, from all six continents read what he wrote and turned to him for advice and help. He covered a vast range of subjects in his monthly *CMS News-Letter* which gave a Christian interpretation to current affairs and particularly to the rapid changes occurring in Africa and Asia, which he visited frequently. More than anyone else he prepared the churches for the consequences of the rise of nationalism in these two continents and the resurgence of the old ethnic religions which followed the war. He was in great demand as a speaker at international conferences, particularly those of the International Missionary Council (Whitby, Canada, 1947; Willingen, Germany, 1952; Accra, Ghana, 1959), and gave one of the most notable and oft-quoted addresses at the Anglican congress at Toronto in 1963. Although a supporter of the World Council of Churches he was also one of its critics, being opposed always to mammoth organizations and therefore to the integration of the International Missionary Council with the World Council of Churches which took place at New Delhi in 1961. He was a staunch defender of the voluntary principle, disliking and distrusting centralization and bureaucracy in church as well as state.

For over thirty years his was the leading evangelical voice in Britain but he was always liberal and forward looking, enjoying the friendship and confidence of many from whom he differed. His lifelong support of the Church of South India and of movements towards intercommunion in Britain was based on his insistence on a theology of difference. The revival of scholarship and theological research and writing among Anglican evangelicals owed much to his initiative in founding with others the Evangelical Fellowship of Theological Literature which had annual conferences from 1942 to 1971. He also encouraged the formation of religious communities outside the catholic tradition, the most notable of these being St. Julian's near Horsham. He himself wrote a large number of books, mainly on missionary subjects and related themes, always scholarly and often original. He made substantial contributions to the preparatory documents for the 1958 Lambeth conference, and he chaired the group which produced what was regarded as its most significant contribution, *The Family in Contemporary Society*.

In 1963 he resigned from CMS and became a canon of Westminster and later sub-dean. He took a leading part in the 900th anniversary of the Abbey and was a prophetic preacher in its pulpit, bringing together his world vision and his devotion to the Bible. In 1973 he retired to Sussex where he died 23 August 1977.

During these last years he pursued his long-standing concern with the relationship between Christianity and other world religions, particularly the implications of inter-faith dialogue. He had refused more than one bishopric but he became an honorary fellow of Jesus College, Cambridge (1967), and was awarded five honorary doctorates. He had a winning smile, a keen sense of humour, and a well-stocked mind: he was an indefatigable letter writer. He and his wife extended hospitality almost daily to people of many races. They had two daughters. His portrait by Brenda Bury is in the CMS headquarters, London.

[*The Times*, 25 August 1977; Max Warren, *Crowded Canvas, Some Experiences of a Lifetime*, 1974; F. W. Dillistone, *Into All the World: a Biography of Max Warren*, 1980; personal knowledge.] DOUGLAS WEBSTER

WATSON, DAVID MEREDITH SEARES (1886–1973), palaeontologist, zoologist, and geologist, was born 18 June 1886 at Higher Broughton, near Salford, Lancashire, the only son of the two children of David Watson, chemist, metallurgist, and pioneer of the electrolytic refining of copper, and his wife, Mary Louise, daughter of Samuel Seares, a London stockbroker. His father was of Scottish descent; the Watsons included a number of men of some distinction. The Seares claimed descent from a former governor of Rhode Island and his Red Indian wife; the Sears of Sears, Roebuck were collaterals. His sister took a first in classics at Manchester, went on to Somerville College, Oxford, where she won the Chancellor's prize for Greek prose, and died tragically in her second year there.

Watson entered Manchester Grammar School in 1899; he began in classics but turned to science. His father died in 1900, his mother a year later. His guardian was his uncle, Henry Seares, a cotton exporter. By the time he left school, he was a capable photographer and worker in wood and metal, and worked during vacations in the laboratories of the county analyst at Salford.

He entered the University of Manchester (1904), intending a career in chemistry and industry, but turned to geology, having already been introduced to fossils and minerals by his father. He graduated with a first in geology in 1907, becoming Beyer fellow (1908) and demonstrator (1909). While still an undergraduate he began to study the remarkably well-preserved plants from coal balls and other Coal Measures deposits, and worked with Marie Stopes [q.v.], the palaeobotanist who later became widely known in other fields. The seminal paper on coal balls, with its integration of geological, chemical, and botanical evidence, by Stopes and Watson (*Philosophical Transactions*, 1907, vol. 200B), and some other papers on fossil plants of 1907 and 1908, must have been written while Watson was still an undergraduate. It is clear that he could have become a leading palaeobotanist.

Mr Sutcliffe, a cotton manufacturer and amateur geologist, who had reopened a coal mine to obtain coal balls, had also collected a plesiosaur from the Whitby Upper Lias, and the two men collected another. Watson became committed to working on fossil reptiles and other vertebrates. He visited many fossil localities in Britain, and worked intensively in the British Museum (Natural History) in 1908–11. In 1911 James P. Hill invited Watson to be an honorary lecturer in vertebrate palaeontology at University College London; Watson was to succeed him as Jodrell professor of zoology and comparative anatomy in 1921.

Watson became deeply interested in the BMNH collection of fossil reptiles from the Karroo 'System' of South Africa, well known particularly through the work of Robert Brook, whose notice Watson subsequently wrote for this Dictionary. To further his knowledge of these fossils he collected extensively in South Africa in 1911, among other things setting up a subdivision of the Beaufort Series into biostratigraphical zones—work that is still fundamental. In 1914 he went to Australia with a similar purpose, and wrote a fine account of the embryological development of the skull of the platypus. He returned through North America, making useful collections in Texas. Back in Britain he took a technical commission in the Royal Naval Volunteer Reserve, then became a captain in the Royal Air Force, working on airship and balloon fabrics.

From 1921 to 1965 he was at University College London, building up a new department. In 1939, as acting secretary of the Agricultural Research Council he was in the USA, and returned to supervise the evacuation of the department to Bangor. In 1940 he became secretary of the scientific subcommittee of the food policy committee of the War Cabinet, and he left an account of his work, deposited with the Royal Society. He rejoined University College first 'in exile', then back in London, where the war-damaged department was made habitable. He was again able to travel abroad (including the USSR, South Africa, and Ceylon) but became ill and had a lung removed. His recovery was remarkable, and after his retirement from his chair in 1951 he had the use of a room at University College, where with his secretary and illustrator since 1928, Joyce Townend, he continued writing papers until his full retirement in 1965. He was Alexander Agassiz visiting professor at Harvard (1952–3) and worked with A. S. Romer. The Watsons moved from Frognal Lane to Harrow, and then to Godalming.

Watson's scientific papers, apart from his early and significant work on fossil plants, deal almost exclusively with vertebrates. Concerning fishes, he will be remembered in particular for his monograph on Acanthodii; his papers on the structure of palaeoniscoids and Carboniferous lungfishes; and his recognition of the crossopterygians as likely tetrapod ancestors. His works on the Carboniferous amphibians and their descendants was fundamental to further advance. But fossil reptiles, especially the 'mammal-like' reptiles, received even more attention, based largely on his own collections from South Africa, Texas, and elsewhere. Watson wrote one book, *Paleontology and Modern Biology* (1951). A Festschrift, *Studies on Fossil Vertebrates presented to David Meredith Seares Watson* (ed. T. Stanley Westoll), appeared in 1958.

He had already in 1914, with E. H. Hankin, applied aerodynamic concepts to deduce the flying potential of pterodactyls. An unpublished lecture on this problem was subsequently rediscovered, and he anticipated later results by forty years. He was involved in the design of the Pterodactyl aircraft, which actually flew. He was also an excellent teacher, informal but stimulating.

Among Watson's medals were the Lyell (1935), Darwin (1942), Linnean (1949), and Wollaston (1965). He was elected a fellow of the Royal Society in 1922, and gave the Croonian lecture (1924) and the Romanes lecture at Oxford (1928). He was a member or fellow of many foreign learned societies and became an honorary fellow of University College London (1948). He had honorary degrees from Cape Town (1929), Manchester (1943), Aberdeen (1943), Reading (1948), Wales (1948), and Witwatersrand (1948).

He married in 1917 Katharine Margarite (died 1969), daughter of the Revd I. Parker. She was an embryologist (D.Sc., Lond.). They had two daughters: Katharine Mary (Mrs P. A. J. Powell) and Janet Vida (died 1983), FRS, a geologist, who married Professor John Sutton, FRS. After his wife's death, Watson's superb memory began to fail, and he died 23 July 1973 in a convalescent home at Midhurst.

[*The Times*, 27 July 1973; F. R. Parrington and T. S. Westoll in *Biographical Memoirs of Fellows of the Royal Society*, vol. xx, 1974; Watson's personal record deposited in the Royal Society; information from Miss Joyce Townend; personal knowledge.]

T. Stanley Westoll

WATSON-WATT, Sir ROBERT ALEXANDER (1892–1973), radar pioneer, was born in Brechin, Angus, 13 April 1892, the fifth son and youngest of seven children of Patrick Watson Watt, a carpenter and joiner, and his wife, Mary Small Matthew. Both the Watsons and the Watts were Aberdeenshire families, the most illustrious scion of the latter being James Watt [q.v.], the inventor of the condensing steam engine. Watson Watt first attended Damacre School in Brechin. After winning a local bursary, he went on to Brechin High School, and thence with a further bursary to University College, Dundee, then part of the University of St. Andrews. He graduated B.Sc. (engineering) in 1912, having won medals in applied mathematics and electrical engineering as well as the class prize in natural philosophy. The last led the professor of natural philosophy, William Peddie, to offer him an assistantship after graduation, and it was Peddie who excited his interest in radio waves.

On the outbreak of war in 1914 Watson Watt volunteered his services in any capacity that would make use of his training, and in September 1915 started as a meteorologist at the Royal Aircraft Factory at Farnborough, where he proposed to apply his knowledge of radio to locate thunderstorms by the 'atmospherics' which they emit, so as to provide warnings to airmen. Experiences with the newly created Admiralty network of radio direction-finding stations convinced him that some extremely rapid method of recording and display would be essential, and in 1916 he proposed the use of cathode ray oscilloscopes for this purpose. These, however, did not become available until 1923, when he quickly showed that the method was feasible: by 1927 cathode ray direction finders (CRDF) were installed at Slough and Cupar. The system could be used to locate the sources of other radio signals besides atmospherics and became one of Watson Watt's 'three steps to victory' in World War II; he described this phase of his work in *Applications of the Cathode Ray Oscillograph in Radio Research* (1933). Also to this phase belongs his proposal (1926) of the term 'ionosphere' for the ionized upper layers of the Earth's atmosphere (see *Nature*, vol. 224, p. 1096, 1969).

In 1924 Watson Watt's work had been moved from the Aldershot area to Slough, where the Radio Research Station had been formed under the auspices of the Meteorological Office and the Department of Scientific and Industrial Research; in December 1927 the work at Slough was amalgamated with that of the radio section of the National Physical Laboratory into an expanded Radio Research Station, with Watson Watt as superintendent at Slough, an outstation of NPL. In 1933, with a further reorganization, he became superintendent of a new radio department at NPL in Teddington.

With the growing menace to Britain from the German air force after 1933, the Air Ministry began to seek scientific help to counter the doctrine that 'the bomber will always get through'. One of the wildest proposals was to direct beams of high frequency radio energy at the bomber so that its metal components would be heated, if not to destruction, at least so as to set off explosions in its bombs, or make conditions intolerable for the crew by heating their body tissue. H. E. Wimperis [q.v.], then director of scientific research at the Air Ministry, asked Watson Watt to look at the feasibility of the proposal, a task which Watson Watt handed on to his assistant, A. F. Wilkins, presenting it as a request to calculate the amount of radio energy that would have to be radiated to raise the temperature of eight pints of water five kilometres distant from 98°F to 105°F. Wilkins's calculations quickly showed that the idea was quite impracticable: but in reply to Watson Watt's question of whether anything could be done for air defence, he recalled some earlier work on VHF communications by the General Post Office, whose engineers had noticed that the signals 'fluttered' when an aircraft flew nearby. Wilkins then calculated the amount of energy that could be reflected by an aircraft from a transmitter of feasible strength, and showed that there should be enough for detection at useful distances.

Watson Watt reported this conclusion qualitatively to Wimperis, and his report was laid before the first meeting of the newly-formed committee for the scientific survey of air defence under (Sir) H. T. Tizard [q.v.]. On 12 February 1935 Watson Watt submitted a draft giving detailed proposals and estimates; this draft was finalized by 27 February 1935, under the title 'The Detection of Aircraft by Radio Methods'. A trial took place on 26 February 1935, using the BBC's short-wave (about 50 metres wavelength) transmitter at Daventry against a Heyford bomber with a mobile receiver a few miles away. The trial was immediately successful and on 1 September 1936 Watson Watt became superintendent of a new establishment, Bawdsey Research Station, under the Air Ministry and based at Bawdsey Manor near Felixstowe. Its objective was to exploit for air defence the principles of radar under the cover of RDF (radio direction finding, to camouflage its *modus operandi* which involved range finding in addition to direction finding).

Despite many difficulties, and sometimes failures, the achievements of Watson Watt's team of physicists and engineers were such that by 1938 the first chain of CH (chain, home) radar stations was working on the east coast, using wavelengths between 7 and 14 metres. A second chain (CHL) to provide low cover on 1.5 metres wavelength for aircraft flying below the detection zones of the CH stations was planned; and trials had shown it feasible to provide airborne radar sets (also on 1.5 metre wavelength) which would enable a fighter to close with a bomber at night (AI) and a maritime reconnaissance aircraft to locate ships at sea (ASV). A 1.5 metre radar set for controlling anti-aircraft fire (GL) was also being made, an identification device (IFF) which would enable friendly targets to identify themselves was being developed, and a method of radio-navigation for aircraft using pulses (GEE) had been proposed. Co-operation between scientists and serving officers was exemplary: Tizard described it as 'the great lesson of the last war'. The transition from the flickering and truant radio echoes of 1936 into the reliable defence system of 1940 was one of the greatest combined feats of science, engineering, and organization in the annals of human achievement.

Watson Watt's part in all this had been that of the leader who had recruited the original team, who foresaw both the possibilities and the problems, and who fought the team's administrative battles with overwhelming enthusiasm and energy. By the time he left Bawdsey in the summer of 1938, the organization that fought the Battle of Britain two years later was safely in being.

Watson Watt moved from Bawdsey to the Air Ministry as director of communications development, with general responsibilities for radar, radio, and other aspects of detection and communication. By 1940 he had become scientific adviser on telecommunications, with footings both in the Air Ministry and (from May 1940) in the newly formed Ministry of Aircraft Production. This work in the administrative centre of the war effort probably called for a greater aptitude in personal relations than his qualities would allow: and his proposal, for example, that he should become responsible for all scientific activities in the Air Ministry and the RAF came to nothing, despite his great contributions in the nascent stages of radar and of operational research.

In 1941 Watson Watt was appointed CB and elected FRS; in 1942 he was knighted, and at this stage he hyphenated his surname to Watson-Watt. At the end of the war he set up the private firm of Sir Robert Watson-Watt and Partners, as consultants to a range of industrial enterprises, including the Rank Organization, which sought advice as to the most suitable material from which to construct God's throne for a film, and received the answer 'Perspex'. The royal commission on awards to inventors gave a tax-free sum of £87,950 to the Bawdsey team, Watson-Watt's share being £52,000. He moved for some years to Canada, but later returned to Britain.

In the meantime he had led the UK delegations in 1946 and 1947 to the international meetings on radio aids to marine navigation and to a meeting of the International Civil Aviation

Organization in Montreal. He had been president of the Royal Meteorological Society, of the Institute of Navigation, and of the Institute of Professional Civil Servants (in which he had been very active in the 1920s), and a vice-president of the Institute of Radio Engineers in New York. His civil honours included the US medal for merit (1946)—a direct award from the president—the Hughes medal of the Royal Society (1948), and the Elliott Cresson medal of the Franklin Institute (1957), as well as honorary degrees from St. Andrews, Toronto, and Laval. From 1958 to 1960 he took part in the Pugwash conferences, writing up his ideas elaborately in *Man's Means to his End* (1961). Previously he had written his autobiography up to the mid-1950s in *Three Steps to Victory* (1957). To this Dictionary he contributed the notice of H. R. Mill.

In 1916 Watt married Margaret, daughter of David Robertson, of Perth. He was divorced from her in 1952, and in the same year married Jean Wilkinson, a Canadian, the widow of a historian, Professor George M. Smith. She died in 1964, and two years later he married Air Chief Commandant Dame Katherine Jane Trefusis Forbes (died 1971), the wartime head of the WAAF, and daughter of Edmund Batten Forbes, MICE. There were no children of any of the marriages.

Watson-Watt described himself in a broadcast talk of 1948: 'Now I am fifty-six, five foot six, an unlucky thirteen stone, tubby if you want to be unkind, chubby if you want to be a little kind, fresh complexioned, organically sound and functionally fortunate, if fat, after a thirty-years' war of resistance to taking exercise . . . I smile a lot . . . Thirty years a civil servant, now a socialist in private enterprise.' Both in speech and in writing his style was usually elaborate, sometimes to the point of ornateness, which led one colleague to comment 'He never said in one word what could be said in a thousand'; but by contrast the most vital thing he ever wrote, his report to the Tizard committee on the feasibility of radar in February 1935, was a model of brevity and clarity. Without the crucial step that it represented, and without the drive that he put into its realization, the Battle of Britain would have been much more difficult to win, and could have been lost.

Watt died at Inverness 5 December 1973.

[Basil Collier, *The Defence of the United Kingdom*, HMSO 1957; J. A. Ratcliffe in *Biographical Memoirs of Fellows of the Royal Society*, vol. xxi, 1975; R. A. Watson-Watt, 'The Evolution of Radio Location', *Journal of the Institution of Electrical Engineers*, vol. 93, IIIA, pp. 11–19; A. F. Wilkins, 'The Early Days of Radar in Britain', Churchill College archives.]

R. V. JONES

WATT, SIR ROBERT ALEXANDER WATSON- (1892–1973), radar pioneer. [See WATSON-WATT.]

WEATHERHEAD, LESLIE DIXON (1893–1976), Methodist minister, was born 14 October 1893 at Harlesden, London, the youngest of the three children and only son of Andrew Weatherhead, a factory manager from Moffat, and his wife, Elizabeth Mary Dixon, of London. Both his parents were Methodists. He was educated at Alderman Newton's Secondary School, Leicester, and Richmond Theological College, and obtained an MA in English literature from Manchester University (1926).

His ministry began in 1915 at Farnham, but in 1917 he joined the Indian Army as second lieutenant, and later served as chaplain to the Devonshire Regiment in Mesopotamia. In 1919 he became minister of the English Methodist Church in Madras. On his return to England in 1922 he joined the Manchester (Oxford Road) circuit until 1925, when he became minister of Brunswick church, Leeds. In 1936 he was called to the City Temple, where he remained until his retirement in 1960. Although more than half his career was spent in a Congregational church, he remained a Methodist throughout, and in 1955–6 and 1966–7 was elected president of the Methodist conference.

In every church he served Weatherhead's preaching drew large congregations. His eloquence was not achieved without careful preparation. He took delight in the apt use of words, and he preached with a passionate simplicity, ample illustration, sympathy with the needs of ordinary people, and a conviction of the day-to-day relevance of the gospel. The centre of his own faith was expressed in the title of his best known book, *The Transforming Friendship* (1928), and he had a lifelong impatience with any orthodoxy which robbed the humanity of Jesus of its power by converting it into a dogma in a creed.

Weatherhead's desire to help people in their daily problems and frustrations led him early in his ministry to the study of psychology, and he became a pioneer in establishing a partnership between religion and psychiatry. His experience in counselling, both in clinics and by correspondence, convinced him that much physical and mental illness was caused by the loss of true religion. He was particularly outspoken on matters of sex, even at a time when the subject was still taboo, particularly in religious circles. His book *Psychology, Religion and Healing* (1951) was an original contribution to the subject, for which he received the degree of Ph.D. from London University. He believed in working in close co-operation with medical specialists, and in 1966–7 became president of the Institute of Religion and Medicine.

He was a prolific writer of books on popular and pastoral theology, and the world-wide reputation he earned by preaching, counselling, and writing led to many invitations to lecture. When on 16 April 1941 the City Temple was destroyed by a bomb, he not only kept his congregation together in a variety of temporary homes, but never wavered in his confidence that the church would be rebuilt; and it was largely his fame in the United States that made the appeal for funds successful.

Weatherhead had his critics, who could point to his concentration on personal problems and piety to the neglect of matters of public concern, his disregard for traditional forms of theology and churchmanship, his appeal more to the emotions than to the intellect and particularly his emphasis on sex, and to the personality cult which he never intended or courted but could not prevent. But no criticism could detract from the gratitude of the thousands he had helped to live a fuller life, or from the public recognition which came in the award of the honorary degree of DD by the universities of Edinburgh and California and an honorary D.Litt. from Puget Sound, and in his appointment as CBE in 1959. He was also a freeman of the City of London.

He liked people, especially the young, and even in old age he never lost his faith in the idealism of youth. But his love of people was balanced by a love of solitude, and he was never happier or more relaxed than when he could return to the hills of his boyhood round his grandfather's home. He had a boyish sense of humour, often mischievous, sometimes macabre, regularly evoked by false solemnity, never held in restraint for fear of causing embarrassment.

In spite of his devotion to the cause of healing, he himself never enjoyed robust health. One reason why he was able to help others was that he himself was sensitive and vulnerable, and his immense labours took their toll of his strength.

In 1920 he married Evelyn (died 1970), daughter of Arthur Triggs, a Wesleyan minister from the Isle of Wight. She was at the time vice-principal of a girls' boarding-school in Madras. They had two sons and one daughter. After retirement he lived at Bexhill, his public activity increasingly restricted by ill health; and there he died 3 January 1976.

[Kingsley Weatherhead, *Leslie Weatherhead, a Personal Portrait*, 1975; *The Times*, 5 January 1976; minutes of the Methodist conference, 1976; private information.] G. B. Caird

WEBSTER, Sir DAVID LUMSDEN (1903–1971), theatre administrator, was born in Dundee 3 July 1903, the only child of Robert Lumsden Webster, advertising agent, and his wife, Mary Ann Alice, née Webster. In 1913 the family moved to Liverpool where he was educated at the Holt School. In 1921 he won a scholarship to Liverpool University where he read economics and became deeply involved in university life as secretary of the University Guild and chairman of the Dramatic Society. Such was his interest in the theatre that many believed that it was there that he would find a career.

Following postgraduate studies in education at Oxford and Liverpool, Webster joined the retail store organization run by F. J. Marquis (later Earl of Woolton, q.v.). He quickly made his mark and in 1932 was appointed general manager of the Bon Marché in Liverpool. On the outbreak of World War II he became general manager of Lewis's. Meanwhile he maintained his interest in opera and in the theatre, becoming in 1940 chairman of the Liverpool Philharmonic Society. During his tenure of office (which lasted until 1945), he made the Liverpool Philharmonic Orchestra into a permanent body.

In 1942, on the recommendation of Lord Woolton, Webster was seconded from Lewis's to the Ministry of Supply with the brief to improve productivity and quality at ordnance factories. This mission was successfully completed and at its conclusion in 1944 Webster was offered and accepted a post with Metal Box.

Boosey & Hawkes, the music publishers, who had acquired a lease on the Royal Opera House, Covent Garden, intended (contrary to the practice of the inter-war years) to present opera and ballet throughout the year and began to search for a person to organize this inspired venture. Their choice fell upon David Webster, who was released from his Metal Box commitment and took up his Covent Garden post, as administrator of its preliminary committee, in August 1944. In 1946 he was appointed general administrator of the Royal Opera House. For many it was an unlikely choice and for years Webster was the subject of harsh criticism which he bore silently, but not painlessly. Few understood the formidable task of setting up permanent opera and ballet companies at Covent Garden and this hostility and lack of understanding drove Webster, a shy man, into an obsessive secretiveness and desire for procrastination, which was not always for his good, but which he could use to good effect on occasions.

For ballet, there was a relatively simple solution. The Sadler's Wells Ballet, founded by (Dame) Ninette de Valois in 1931, was again at its theatre in Rosebery Avenue and was beginning to look for bigger challenges. Covent Garden offered these and eventually the Sadler's Wells governors agreed to release the company to the Covent Garden Trust, which had been created in February 1946, under the chairmanship of Lord Keynes [q.v.], to supervise the running of the opera house. It became known as the Royal Ballet.

For opera, there was no simple answer, for nothing of permanence had been created in the inter-war years. It was thus a matter of starting from scratch and after the appointment of Karl Rankl as music director, work on the formation of a company (known as the Royal Opera) began with the selection of soloists, choristers, and orchestral musicians.

A lesser man than Webster would not have survived these early and chequered years, but such was his faith in Covent Garden and in those who performed and worked there, and such were his patience and skill, that the enterprise prospered through many financial crises, through various changes of policy in relation to language and presentation of performances, and through changes of music director (Karl Rankl 1946–51, Rafael Kubelik 1955–8, and Sir George Solti 1961–71). In many ways the years of interregnum between music directors were the happiest for Webster. He enjoyed the freedom of choice of repertory and of artists just as he sometimes felt that he would like to run Covent Garden without a board of directors, although inwardly he knew the value of that and the depth of support which he could expect from it. Webster also had a flair for discovering singers and furthering their careers at home and abroad—for example, (Dame) Joan Sutherland, Jon Vickers, and (Sir) Geraint Evans.

Webster also developed his interests in other directions. From 1948 he was chairman of the Orchestral Employers' Association. He became governor and treasurer of the Royal Ballet School in 1955 and governor and general administrator of the Royal Ballet Company in 1957. In 1962 he became general administrator of the London Opera Centre. From 1957 he was a director of Southern Television Ltd. and from 1965 chairman of the London Concerts Board. He held visiting lectureships at the universities of Bristol (1955–6) and Liverpool (1958). He became president of the Wagner Society in 1957 and worked hard to raise the reputation of Wagner's work in Britain.

The strain of the vast tasks which Webster had undertaken since the mid-1940s and the burden of maintaining and improving standards of performance at Covent Garden in the face of general under-finance, and the early days of fierce criticism, eventually took their toll. The last few years at Covent Garden were not happy for him. He was unwell and he became prey to doubts and fears about himself and his ability to carry on. In July 1970 he retired and was appointed KCVO (he had been knighted in 1960). He also became honorary FRCM and RAM, was an officer of the French Legion of Honour, and had Swedish, Portuguese, and Italian honours.

Webster enjoyed food and wine and giving parties, which he frequently did with great style at his house in Weymouth Street. From 1931 his companion was James Cleveland Belle. Webster died at his London home 11 May 1971.

[Montague Haltrecht, *The Quiet Showman: Sir David Webster and the Royal Opera House*, 1975; *The Times*, 12 May 1971; personal knowledge.]

JOHN TOOLEY

WEIR, SIR JOHN (1879-1971), homeopathic physician, was born in Glasgow 19 October 1879, the second of three sons (there were no daughters) of James Weir, joiner, of East Kilbride, and his wife, Agnes Baird. He was educated at the Allan Glen School and worked as an engineer before entering Glasgow University Medical School. His interest in homeopathy began before his decision to embark on a medical career. As a teenager he suffered severely from boils, and, after traditional medicine had failed, was cured by a homeopathic doctor in Glasgow, Dr Dishington.

Weir graduated MB, B.Ch. in 1906 and held several resident appointments at the Glasgow Western Infirmary. He was then awarded a Tyler scholarship to study homeopathy at the clinic of Dr James Tyler Kent in Chicago. Weir returned with the firm conviction that Kent was the greatest exponent in the world of Samuel Hahnemann's homeopathic philosophy and determined to put his materia medica into practice, in spite of criticism from some of his senior colleagues in England. He set up in practice at 47b Welbeck Street in London, and soon acquired a reputation that led to his appointment in 1910 to the staff of the London Homeopathic Hospital. In later years he acted as a consultant to homeopathic hospitals in Bristol, Birmingham, Bromley, and Eastbourne. However, he never allowed his success in private practice to interfere with his academic responsibilities for teaching, lecturing, and initiating clinical research at his hospitals.

In 1911 Weir acted as assistant secretary to the eighth international homeopathic congress in London and in the same year was appointed Compton Burnett professor of materia medica by the Homeopathic Society. In 1916 he was appointed secretary of the Society. In the following years he devoted much time and energy to promoting the Society's growth and influence, and when in 1943 it became a faculty with responsibilities for teaching, training, and examining candidates for its fellowship (F.F.Hom.) he served two terms as its first president. Five years later the royal charter was granted to the Homeopathic Hospital. During the important post-war changes that led to the establishment of the National Health Service Weir fought hard to ensure that, although the hospital was transferred to the Ministry of Health, the practice of homeopathy and postgraduate courses in that subject should continue as before. His long association with the Royal Homeopathic Hospital was recognized when one of its wards was named after him. When the Homeopathic Research and Educational Trust was founded, Weir became a trustee and played a leading part in the drafting of the Faculty of Homeopathy Act (1950).

Weir's connection with the royal family, whose interest in homeopathy was well known, began in 1923, when he was appointed physician in ordinary to the Prince of Wales. The royal connection continued until his retirement in 1968. From 1929 to 1938 he was physician to Queen Maud of Norway and from 1936 onwards to Queen Mary, the Duke and Duchess of York (later King George VI and Queen Elizabeth), and to Princess Elizabeth (later Queen Elizabeth II). Many royal honours were conferred upon him: CVO (1926), KCVO (1932), Knight Grand Cross of the Order of St. Olaf of Norway (1938), and GCVO (1939). In 1949 he was awarded a unique accolade by the King, the Royal Victorian Chain, a 'pre-eminent mark by the Sovereign of esteem and affection towards such persons as His Majesty especially desired to honour'.

Weir was a bachelor, a traditionalist with firm religious convictions. His conservatism spilled over into his personal life-style. His annual golfing holiday at Gullane in Scotland took him to the same bedroom in the same hotel year after year. For all that he was a superb mixer, joining in the many activities of the medical societies and clubs to which he belonged in Glasgow, Ayrshire, and London. He was a great raconteur and delighted to accost his friends with the question 'Have you heard this one?' He always carried a little notebook as an *aide-mémoire* for his stories. His patients were very fond of him, for although he was strict about the details of any treatment he prescribed, he always showed a great understanding and kindness. He is reported to have told the Prince of Wales on one occasion, 'No cigars, four cigarettes a day, and not more than two small slices of beef for lunch'. He was punctilious to a degree and delighted to spend endless time making sure that any bulletins issued by his colleagues and himself concerning any of his royal patients were absolutely correct in wording and allowed of no misunderstanding.

Weir contributed many papers to academic journals and was in great demand as a lecturer. He occupied a pre-eminent place in the history of homeopathic medicine in Britain. For those who knew him personally he was the epitome of the traditional compassionate physician. Weir died 17 April 1971 at St. George's Nursing Home, St. George's Square, London.

There is a portrait by Sir James Gunn in the boardroom of the Royal Homeopathic Hospital.

[*British Medical Journal*, 1 May 1971, p. 282; *The Times*, 19 April 1971; private information; personal knowledge.] JOHN PEEL

WELLESZ, EGON JOSEPH (1885–1974), composer, music scholar, and teacher, was born in Vienna 21 October 1885, the only child of (Solomon) Josef Wellesz, textile manufacturer, and his wife, Ilona Lövenyi. He was educated at Vienna Hegel-gymnasium and studied musicology at the Vienna University under Guido Adler. He started composing at the age of thirteen and six years later became a private composition-pupil of Arnold Schönberg. The greatest musical influence in his early life was that of Gustav Mahler, whose musical personality and methods he was able to study by frequently attending his rehearsals at the Opera. This double interest in the remoter past of music, as research student, and in the modern development of the art, as composer, was to mark the whole of his long life and to impart a quite unusual breadth of interest and vision to his work not only as composer but also as teacher.

Wellesz's first researches were into the music, and particularly the opera, of the baroque period in Venice and in Vienna itself. But the subject that was to be his life-work was the history of Byzantine ecclesiastical chant and its relationship to the Gregorian chant of the western church. His earliest publications on the subject date from 1914, and his successful deciphering of Middle Byzantine musical notation (1918) gave him a unique authority, of which the non-specialist musician can appreciate something in his *A History of Byzantine Music and Hymnography* (1949, 2nd edn. 1961). On the other hand his earliest published book (1921) was a study of Schönberg's music, which had a marked though by no means exclusive influence on the five operas and four ballets that Wellesz wrote between 1918 and 1930. If Richard Strauss was a strong influence in these works, their subject-matter and character owed even more to Strauss's librettist, Hugo von Hofmannsthal, a close friend who provided Wellesz himself with librettos for the ballet *Achilles auf Skyros* (1926) and the opera *Alkestis* (1924).

Ballet particularly interested Wellesz at this time, both as an avenue of escape from the Wagnerian conception of opera and also as a form related to the Bzyantine liturgy, conceived as a terrestrial reflection of the court of the Divine Pantokrator. This establishment of widely drawn parallels was an essential characteristic of Wellesz's mentality and explains his instinctive sense of the essential similarity between the new movements in all the arts of the day. His song-texts included poems by Stefan George and Francis Jammes and his friends included the writer Jacob Wassermann and the painter Oskar

Kokoschka [q.v.], whose portrait of Wellesz dates from 1911. The ballets and operas of these years were successful on German stages but, despite Wellesz's deep sense of belonging to a native Viennese tradition—both baroque and classical—he assiduously cultivated links with both France and England (which he visited for the first time in 1906, attending lectures at Cambridge) and he was active in the foundation and administration of both the International Society of Contemporary Music (1922) and the International Musicological Society. In 1932 he was the first Austrian composer since Haydn to receive an honorary doctorate of music from Oxford University. During these years he was professor of music history at Vienna University (1929–38).

It was therefore not wholly unexpected that when, in 1938, Hitler annexed Austria, it should have been England that offered Wellesz a new home. In that year Bruno Walter had conducted a major orchestral work based by Wellesz on *The Tempest* (*Prosperos Beschwörungen*) but the sudden and violent interruption of his career, and exile from the centre of new musical developments to the still musically insular atmosphere of England, caused a break of years in his development as a composer. During the 1930s he had taken an active interest in a movement aimed at the renewal, enlargement, and *aggiornamento* of the Catholic tradition in Austria; and this, with his Jewish origins and known hostility to National Socialism, would have made him an inevitable victim of persecution had he remained in Vienna. Through Henry Colles [q.v.], the chief music critic of *The Times*, and other friends he was able to settle with his family in Oxford, where in 1939 he was made a fellow of Lincoln College and later university lecturer in the history of music (1944) and university reader in Byzantine music (1948). He was naturalized in 1946. It was now that his career as teacher assumed a primary importance, and it seemed for a time as though this and his Byzantine studies might well occupy the rest of his life. In 1957 appeared volume i, which he edited, of *The New Oxford History of Music*, of which he was one of the four editors.

Instead of this, however, Wellesz entered a new and extremely prolific period of creative activity. This began in 1944 with a chamber work based on Gerard Manley Hopkins's *The Leaden Echo and the Golden Echo*; and during the next thirty years he was to write a large quantity of music of all kinds, bringing the number of his string quartets (the first of which is dated 1911–12) to nine and including, most importantly, nine symphonies, written between 1945 and 1971. In all these works Wellesz, whose attitude to Schönberg's serialism had never been that of a doctrinaire, was clearly concerned to continue and expand the Viennese symphonic tradition, as represented particularly by Schubert, Bruckner, and, above all, Mahler. These works interested and were championed by a number of English musicians and, taken with Wellesz's activities as teacher, lecturer, and writer, played an important part in what may be called the 'de-insulation' of English music. On the Continent, however, and particularly in his native Vienna, enthusiasm for the music of first Schönberg and then Anton von Webern was inextricably associated with hostility to the ideas of defeated National Socialism: so that Wellesz's more traditionally based and basically eclectic 'Austro-European' music found at first little favour. Although he was made a fellow of the Royal Danish Academy of Science and Letters in 1946, became a fellow of the British Academy in 1953, and was appointed CBE in 1957, it was not until 1961 that he received the Austrian Great State prize. In the same year he was also made a Knight of the Order of Saint Gregory the Great.

He spent the rest of his long life in Oxford, though returning regularly to Austria during the summer months. He remained active until two years before his death, when he had a severe stroke. He died in Oxford 9 November 1974. In 1908 Wellesz married Emmy Franzisca, daughter of Ludwig Stross. There were two daughters of this marriage. If the specialist nature of his Byzantine studies (of which his greatest work was editing the *Monumenta Musicae Byzantinae*) has made it hard for the general musical world to appreciate fully his quality as a scholar, his activities as teacher, writer, and inspirer of a generation of musicians in Britain and his part in bringing British music 'into Europe' will always be remembered; and the profusion, variety, and craftsmanship of his music remain to reflect the warmth and generosity of his personality and the scope of his artistic interests.

[Robert Schollum, *Egon Wellesz*, 1963; Egon and Emmy Wellesz (ed. Franz Endler), *Egon Wellesz—Leben und Werk*, 1981; C. C. Benser, *Egon Wellesz* 1985; Robert Layton, 'Egon Wellesz' in *The New Grove Dictionary of Music and Musicians*, ed. Stanley Sadie, vol. xx, 1980; Walter Oakeshott in *Proceedings* of the British Academy, vol. lix, 1975; personal knowledge.]

MARTIN COOPER

WESTRUP, SIR JACK ALLAN (1904–1975), musician, author, and conductor, was born in Dulwich, London, 26 July 1904, the second of the three sons (there were no daughters) of George Westrup, insurance clerk, of Dulwich, and his wife, Harriet Sophia Allan.

He was educated at Alleyn's School, Dulwich, where he was a scholar, and then gained a Nettleship scholarship in music to Balliol College, Oxford. There was no honours degree in music at that time, so he first read classics in which he gained first class honours in moderations (1924) and second class honours in *literae humaniores* (1926) before proceeding to the B.Mus. degree in 1926. He took an active part in music in the university both as a keyboard and brass player. However, his most important contribution to Oxford music was his part in the foundation of the University Opera Club whilst still an undergraduate to which he returned later as conductor, when he was elected to the Heather professorship in 1947.

In spite of a research grant on going down from Oxford—when he worked on 'Noëls Provençaux' in Avignon—appointments for musical scholars were then so scarce that he went back to his old school and taught classics. Then in 1934 he returned to music as a critic on the *Daily Telegraph* until the war virtually put an end to concerts in London, whereupon he did another short stint as a schoolmaster. His chance to enter academic life came in 1941 when he was offered and accepted a lectureship at King's College, Newcastle upon Tyne, and this was followed by his election to the Peyton and Barber chair of music at Birmingham University in 1944. He flourished at Birmingham, making full use of the excellent facilities offered by the Barber Institute library, and the opportunities for conducting.

Oxford conferred upon him the degree of honorary D.Mus. in 1944, and in 1947 he returned to his old university as Heather professor of music. Much as this pleased him, it was not an easy time for him, as there were some Oxford musicians who did not welcome his election. However, in 1950 the university finally allowed music to become an honours course and Westrup was mainly instrumental in designing a new syllabus which demanded a wider knowledge of musical scholarship than the old B.Mus. This gave him satisfaction and confidence.

His energy was remarkable. Not only did he fulfil meticulously his duties as professor, but during his twenty-four years at Oxford he conducted seventeen operas for the University Opera Club—mostly unfamiliar and including one first performance and one British première—, edited *Music & Letters* from 1959 and was president of the Royal Musical Association (1958–63), the Incorporated Society of Musicians (1963), and the Royal College of Organists (1964–6).

As a man Westrup was a person with complete self-control and with a presence which alarmed those who did not know him well. He did not suffer fools gladly and had no patience with the yes-man. If one disagreed with him his face would light up and his interest immediately would be stimulated. In matters of detail he was most meticulous and expected others to be likewise. But to those who had the fortune to know him well he was a kind and humble man, never too busy to offer help and almost incapable of saying 'no' to the most mundane of requests.

Apart from his university degrees he was a fellow of the British Academy (1954), the Royal College of Organists (1942), Trinity College, London (1946), the Royal College of Music (1961), and the Royal School of Church Music (1963). He was also honorary RAM (1960). For his services to music he was knighted in 1961.

It was to the lasting regret of his friends and colleagues and a serious loss to music that while at Oxford his energies were not directed more towards the writing of books. It was hoped—nay, assumed—that he would follow up his outstanding books on *Purcell* (1937), *Handel* (1939), and *An Introduction to Musical History* (1955) with works of similar stature. Instead he indulged in much editing (in 1947 he became chairman of the editorial board of *The New Oxford History of Music*), writing articles, compiling lexicons, and lecturing abroad which, although of importance, were no substitute for what a man of his talent should have achieved.

His versatility—as a practical musician and as a musicologist—can best be summed up by two quotations from his 1945 Deneke lecture (published in 1946): 'Nothing can better aid our endeavours than performance—performance not merely by amateurs, to whose enthusiasm we so often owe a lively acquaintance with the past, but by expert musicians who unite with their skill an understanding of what they are trying to do.' And: 'Perhaps the virtue that we need most of all is humility—not the crawling acquiescence that accepts great reputations and can find no flaw, but the readiness to believe in lesser men until we can prove them to be charlatans.' The last paragraph of this lecture might well have been written of him rather than by him: 'The great historians of music are those who have carried musical souls about them, who to industry and scholarship have added vision and found the power to share it with their readers.'

In 1938 he married Solweig Maria (died 1984), daughter of Per Johan Gustaf Rösell, musical director of an infantry regiment in Linköping, Sweden; they had one daughter and three sons. Westrup died at his home in Headley, Hampshire, 21 April 1975.

[Gerald Abraham in *Proceedings* of the British Academy, vol. lxiii, 1977, P. Dennison in *The New Grove Dictionary of Music and Musicians* (ed. Stanley Sadie), vol. xx, 1980; J. A. Westrup, *The Meaning of Musical History* (Deneke lecture), 1946; private information; personal knowledge.] BERNARD ROSE

WHEARE, SIR KENNETH CLINTON (1907–1979), constitutional expert, the elder son (the other died in infancy) of Eustace Leonard Wheare, insurance agent, and his wife, Kathleen Frances Kinahan, was born at Warragul, Victoria, Australia, 26 March 1907. He had one sister. He was educated at Scotch College, Melbourne, and at the University of Melbourne. Wheare entered Oriel College, Oxford, as a Rhodes scholar in 1929 and obtained a first class in the honours school of philosophy, politics, and economics in 1932. He rapidly thereafter took a leading place in the university's teaching of colonial history and political institutions as lecturer at Christ Church (1934–9), Beit lecturer in colonial history (1935–44), and fellow of University College (1939–44).

In 1944 Wheare was elected to the Gladstone chair of government and public administration and to a fellowship at All Souls College. He was the first holder of the Gladstone chair to have come to it from academic rather than public life and his tenure witnessed an important extension in the systematic study of his subject in the university. Public service in his case followed upon his appointment. He was constitutional adviser to the National Convention of Newfoundland (1946–7) and to the conferences on Central African Federation (1951, 1952, 1953). He was also chairman of the departmental committee on children and the cinema (1947–50), and a member of the committee on administrative tribunals and inquiries (1955–7) chaired by Sir Oliver (later Lord) Franks.

Wheare's activities in the university itself were extended through his representation of it on the Oxford City Council (1940–57), his fellowship of Nuffield College (1944–58), and his membership of the hebdomadal council (1947–67).

Wheare was elected rector of Exeter College in 1956 and there presided over an important period of expansion and development, physical and academic. While not altogether sympathetic to the social trends which were to culminate later on in the College becoming 'mixed' in common with nearly all the others, his relations with the undergraduates themselves were exceptionally warm and confident, and he and Lady Wheare made the lodgings a centre of hospitality for the whole college and for wider circles in the university at large. He gave himself ungrudgingly to the administrative aspects of the college's affairs and was further burdened during his rectorship by university business culminating in his vice-chancellorship (1964–6) and by the affairs of the Rhodes Trust of which he was trustee from 1948 to 1977 and chairman from 1962 to 1969. It was thus not surprising that he decided to relinquish the rectorship in 1972, five years before attaining the statutory age limit, so as to return to the life of scholarship at All Souls College which elected him to a distinguished fellowship in 1973.

The calls upon Wheare's practical services were not, however, at an end. He had served on the University Grants Committee from 1959 to 1963 and was a Nuffield trustee from 1966 to 1975 and a member of the governing body of the University of London's School of Oriental and African Studies. But it was the University of Liverpool which—a rare honour for an academic—elected him to the high office of chancellor in 1972. He retained the post until forced to resign it through failing health not long before his death in 1979. Wheare much enjoyed his new association with a great provincial city and was punctilious in fulfilling the duties of his office, although he found the hierarchical aspects of redbrick university life and his enforced distance from junior staff and students less congenial than the more democratic ways of Oxford. An honour he appreciated, arising from his new connection with the north-west, was that of honorary admiral of the Isle of Man herring fishery fleet (1973–5).

During the whole of his career Wheare continued to study and publish in his chosen fields: British government, the institutions of the evolving Commonwealth, and comparative institutions, particularly federalism in its various incarnations. His first book, *The Statute of Westminster, 1931* (1933) was superseded by his *The Statute of Westminster and Dominion Status* (1938) and that in turn by *The Constitutional Structure of the Commonwealth* (1960). His other books were *Federal Government* (1946); *Abraham Lincoln and the United States* (1948); *Modern Constitutions* (1951); *Government by Committee* (1955); *Legislatures* (1963); and *Maladministration and its Remedies* (the Hamlyn lectures, 1973). His published lectures included important contributions on the centenary of the Northcote–Trevelyan Report and on Walter Bagehot [qq.v.], a political writer with whom he shared a robust and direct approach to the business of government. He was also a regular contributor to this Dictionary.

Wheare, who was averse to air travel and believed that the place for Oxford professors was Oxford, was never subjected to the total immersion in American political science common among his juniors; nor were its pretensions much to his taste. His own writings combined three principal strands—a respect for the legal and conventional framework of political action in all democratic systems, an understanding of the historical roots of the different Anglo-Saxon polities and institutions, and above all an awareness of how men actually behave in the political and administrative context—an awareness solidly based on his own practical experience in getting things done. It was this combination that enabled him to write the most original of all his books, *Government by Committee*, and to subtitle it, without compunction, 'an essay on the British constitution'.

For Wheare style was inseparable from content. He did not go in for massive compilations nor for discursive treatments of his themes; he valued brevity and elegance and worked hard and successfully to achieve them both. While devoid of ideological fervour and without overt party commitment he was in matters political and academic throughout a reforming conservative. It is not out of character that he was engaged in his last years in studying the life and work of an innovating administrator turned statesman, Sir George Cornewall Lewis [q.v.].

Wheare's contributions to learning were recognized by election to the British Academy in 1952—he was president from 1967 to 1971—and by the award in 1957 of the Oxford degree of D.Litt. Honorary doctorates came his way from Columbia, Cambridge, Exeter, Liverpool, and Manchester, and he was elected to honorary fellowships at Exeter, Nuffield, Oriel, University, and Wolfson colleges. For his public services, he was appointed CMG in 1953, was knighted in 1966, and awarded the Queen's Jubilee medal in 1977. A witty speaker, much in demand, he remained however a private rather than a public person, enjoying the affection of a close-knit family and of many friends. Never strong in health, his exercise was limited to the sociable pastime of walking. Wheare was a regular church-goer and his (Anglican) faith helped him to support uncomplainingly the inroads of sickness in his last years. His university sermon on the annual theme of the 'Sin of Pride' in 1974 will long be remembered by the crowded congregation which attended. In many ways, and not least in some carefully and humorously cultivated foibles, he represented the model of a true Oxford don.

In 1934 he married, first, Helen Mary Allan; they had one son. In 1943 he married, secondly, Joan, daughter of Thomas Jones Randell, solicitor; they had two sons and two daughters. Wheare died in Oxford 7 September 1979.

[Private information; personal knowledge.]

MAX BELOFF

WHEATLEY, DENNIS YATES (1897–1977), writer, was born 8 January 1897 in London, the elder child and only son of Albert David Wheatley, wine merchant, and his wife, Florence Elizabeth Harriet, youngest of the three children of William Yates Baker, ironmaster, of London. After an unhappy year at Dulwich College he became a cadet in HMS Worcester where he acquired much practical knowledge and a sense of discipline. His homes were in Streatham and Brixton where his four grandparents also lived. At seventeen, after a year learning something of the wine trade in Germany, he worked in his father's shop in the West End of London. During the war he was, after determined efforts, commissioned in the Royal Field Artillery and, in spite of ill health, later spent a year on the western front where he was gassed and invalided home. For eight years after the war he played a small part in the family business and in 1923 he married Nancy Madelaine Leslie Robinson, by whom he had a son, Anthony. Throughout this period he read a vast amount of fiction, thus developing a literary taste, and he also acquired a taste for good living which he could then ill afford.

Wheatley's father died in 1927 and, on inheriting the business, he embarked on a scheme of expansion which fell foul of the 1930 slump, forcing him out of business. His first marriage having failed, he married in 1931 Joan Gwendoline, daughter of the Hon. Louis Johnstone; it was she who urged him to take up writing as a rehabilitation and *The Forbidden Territory* (1933) had immediate success, assisted by vigorous promotion on Wheatley's part. Forty years later it had sold a million and a half copies and the quartet of characters he had created, headed by the Duke de Richleau, continued their adventures in ten subsequent books.

Wheatley's course was now set but he determined from the start to extend his range of characters and type of story. *Black August* (1934) introduced Gregory Sallust, who served him for eleven novels over thirty-four years, and in the same year he wrote *The Devil Rides Out* (1935) with a background of 'Black Magic'. This subject proved so popular that eight novels were based on it and Wheatley came to be regarded as something of an expert in a field of which he knew nothing except through reading. This was only one example of the immense care Wheatley took in all his work to provide a factual, often historical, background to the highly imaginative events he was describing, with the result that most of his books ran to 160,000 words or more.

His early success as a writer of adventure stories was reinforced by a diversion in 1936–9 in the form of 'crime dossiers' (with J. G. Links). The novelty of these 'books' (reproduced in facsimile over forty years later) not only sold them by the hundred thousand: they made the name of Dennis Wheatley celebrated in many countries.

During the first two years of World War II Wheatley, now with fourteen novels to his credit, wrote a series of papers on various aspects of the war and current affairs. These were circulated to acquaintances in influential positions and resulted, in 1941, in an invitation to join the planning staff responsible for enemy deception. He was commissioned in the Royal Air Force Volunteer Reserve (his third Service) and for four years his fertile imagination was given full rein. He also became privy to a great deal of secret information of which he could make no direct use when he returned to writing. He therefore began, with *The Launching of Roger Brooke* (1947), a series of twelve novels set in the period 1785–1815 and so free from any restraints. Many years later he was able to tell the story of his war years in *The Deception Planners* (1980), which was published posthumously, following three volumes of memoirs.

Wheatley wrote seventy-five books in his forty-five years as an author, most of which remained in print throughout his life, published under the same imprint. His wide reading had little influence on his own style and if a colloquial or well-worn phrase expressed his meaning he did not halt the action to improve upon it. Despite some thirteen hours of work a day while writing, he led a full life with much travel and enjoyment of the fruits of his success, particularly good food and wine. He aged remarkably little physically, his black hair always parted in the middle as in his youth. It was not until 10 November 1977, at the age of eighty, that he at long last, to use his own words, ran out of steam, his wife surviving him.

[Dennis Wheatley, *The Time Has Come . . .*, 1977, 1978, and 1979 (3 vols. of memoirs); personal knowledge.] J. G. LINKS

WHEELER, SIR CHARLES THOMAS (1892–1974), sculptor, was born in Codsall, Staffordshire, 14 March 1892, the second son and second child in the family of five sons and one daughter of Sam Phipps Wheeler, journalist, and his wife, Annie Florence, third child of Jeremiah Crowther, a works manager. He studied at Wolverhampton School of Art from the age of sixteen, under R. J. Emerson, following his education at St. Luke's, Wolverhampton. He became an exhibitioner at the Royal College of Art in 1912 where he studied under douard Lantéri until 1917. Fellow students were William McMillan, Gilbert Ledward, Alfred Hardiman [qq.v.], and James Woodford. Later Wheeler was to write the notices of Ledward and Hardiman for this Dictionary.

Having gained his diploma, Wheeler found a studio in Justice Walk, Chelsea, and on a recommendation from the architect, (Sir) Herbert Baker [q.v.], he received his first commission: a bronze memorial plaque to the memory of John Kipling, who was killed at Loos at the age of seventeen. On completion this memorial to the son of Rudyard Kipling [q.v.] was placed in Burwash church. Wheeler's first joint commission with Baker was a sculpture of the 'Madonna and Child' (1924) for Winchester College war memorial cloister. This was followed by two tigers at the base of the column of the Indian memorial to the missing at Neuve Chapelle (1928), and then came the great series of sculptures for the Bank of England. In the meanwhile 'Infant Christ' (bronze bust)—a portrait of his son Robin—was purchased for the nation under the terms of the Chantrey Bequest in 1924. Similarly in 1930 a bronze statue entitled 'Spring' was purchased, and both are in the collection of the Tate Gallery.

Wheeler first exhibited at the Royal Academy in 1914 but it was not until 1934 that he was elected an associate, despite the opposition of Sir S. H. William Llewellyn [q.v.], then president and himself at one time regarded as a rebel. While Llewellyn declared that the Academy would be lost if it showed work of such revolutionary character, *The Times* commented that Wheeler's election was a tribute to the advanced school. He chose 'Ariel of the Bank' (gilded bronze, 1932) for his diploma work (Royal Academy collection). His last commission before World War II, when he worked together with Sir Edwin Lutyens [q.v.], as architect and William McMillan as sculptor of the Beatty fountain, was the Triton group for the Jellicoe memorial fountain in Trafalgar Square, London.

Wheeler's best-known commissions were his works for the Bank of England (1930). These were described as the work of a lyric poet commissioned to write narratives or epics, for they were inclined to over-emphasis. The criticism particularly applies to the buttress figures representing the guardians and bearers of wealth which link the old building with the new. The three bronze doors indicate Wheeler's lighter manner. The relief of the old lady of Threadneedle Street on the pediment of the central pavilion, which is his symbolic interpretation of Britannia, derived from a coin, demonstrates his individuality.

Wheeler was elected RA in 1940 and was president from 1956 to 1966, in succession to Sir Albert Richardson [q.v.]. As president, one of the problems which faced him was how to carry on with his many commissions and at the same time manage the affairs of the Academy. He was ably assisted in both these: firstly by William Stafford Chadwick, a friend of the family and a skilled and faithful assistant in the studio, and secondly by Humphrey Brooke, the secretary of the Royal Academy. Brooke supported Wheeler through one of the most difficult periods in the Academy's history, when there was a desperate need to secure its finances. The decision in 1962 to sell a most treasured possession, the Leonardo cartoon 'Virgin and Child with the Infant St. John', provoked extensive public and press obloquy. However, their single-mindedness did secure the finances for almost the next twenty years.

From 1944 to 1949 Wheeler was the president of the Royal Society of British Sculptors (he had become a fellow in 1935), and in 1949 he received the Society's gold medal. He was instrumental in founding the Society of Portrait Sculptors, of which he became the first president in 1953. A trustee of the Tate Gallery (1942–9), he was a member of the Royal Fine Art Commission from 1946 to 1952. He was also honorary FRIBA, RSA, RE, RWS, and RI. Among his honorary degrees was an Oxford DCL (1960). He was appointed CBE in 1948 and KCVO in 1958.

Wheeler's physical stature was lilliputian against his monuments. A dapper little man with a bow tie, his unassuming charm and sensitivity transcended even his monolithic telamons on the Bank of England.

In 1918 he married the sculptress Muriel Bourne (died 1979). She was the daughter of the Revd Arthur Ward Bourne; they had one son and one daughter. There is a bust (lead) of him by his wife in the collection of the National Portrait Gallery. Wheeler died at Mayfield, Sussex, 22 August 1974.

[*The Times*, 9 August 1966, 24 and 29 August 1974; *High Relief, the Autobiography of Sir Charles Wheeler, Sculptor*, 1968; private information.] HANS FLETCHER

WHEELER, SIR (ROBERT ERIC) MORTIMER (1890–1976), archaeologist, author, and broadcaster, was born in Glasgow 10 September 1890, the eldest of the three children and only son of (Robert) Mortimer Wheeler, a journalist, and his wife, Emily Baynes, niece and ward of Thomas Spencer Baynes [q.v.], of St. Andrews University. When he was four the family moved to Bradford, living at Saltaire on the edge of the moors. His father interested him in the arts, in rough shooting, and fishing, which he was always to enjoy. They also studied the local antiquities. At Bradford Grammar School (where he refused to play any games) Wheeler read classics, but had only just (precociously) reached the sixth form when another move took the family to London. There he educated himself by reading and visiting museums and galleries, before entering University College in 1907, winning a classical scholarship in his intermediate arts examination. He stayed to take an MA (1912) and D.Litt. and gave time to classical archaeology, but was not committed to his future career until he won the first Franks studentship in 1913.

The next year he married Tessa Verney who was to share so closely in his work that they were known to the archaeological world as 'the Wheelers'. Their only child (Michael Wheeler, QC) was born in 1915, by which time his father, after a spell with the Royal Commission on Historical Monuments, was in the Royal Field Artillery. Posted to France in 1917, Major Wheeler had one week in the thick of Passchendaele, then went on to Italy, and back for the fighting advance into Germany. He won the MC for a daring exploit and was mentioned in dispatches. The war discovered his powers of leadership and a dashing style that were to develop with the years. He was tall, lean, and handsome with a mop of wavy hair.

On demobilization, he returned briefly to the Commission, but in 1920 was appointed keeper of archaeology in the struggling National Museum of Wales, and was advanced to director in 1924. He soon got the place on its feet, while he and his wife and students from the University of Wales excavated at Roman military sites, developing new techniques as they went. His first book, *Prehistoric and Roman Wales*, original in its day, was published in 1925.

'Rik' Wheeler, as a lucky 'survivor', felt that he had a mission to lead the way to a scientific study of archaeology: if it was to be fulfilled there must be an academically acceptable Institute. It was with this in mind that he left Wales in 1926 for the directorship of the London Museum. He threw himself into transforming the motley collections in Lancaster House, into lecturing, and, with his wife, into fighting to find funds and premises for an Institute of Archaeology. It was opened at last in 1937.

Meanwhile the Wheelers excavated at Lydney, Gloucestershire (1928–9), at Roman and Belgic Verulamium (1930–3), and at the vast Dorset hill fort of Maiden Castle (1934–7), setting new standards in British archaeology and training many of those who were to ensure its future. The results were handsomely published through the Society of Antiquaries of London, of which they were both fellows. In 1936 a great partnership was broken by his wife's death after a minor operation.

Seeking origins for the cultures of Maiden Castle, in 1938–9 Wheeler led flying columns to explore the little known hill forts of Brittany and Normandy. He had been deeply shocked by the surrender of Munich, and in August 1939 dashed home to raise an anti-aircraft battery at Enfield, his extraordinary energy soon leading to its expansion into the 42nd Royal Artillery Regiment. After stern training, its colonel and three batteries joined the Eighth Army and did well at Alamein and in the long advance to Tunis. At Tripoli Wheeler acted swiftly to secure the official protection of ancient monuments threatened by the war. Just before Medenine he was made brigadier in command of the 12th Anti-aircraft brigade and fought with the X Corps at Salerno and during the breakthrough to Naples.

In 1943 he had accepted the director-generalship of archaeology in India. On arrival the next year, again he faced a task of regeneration; the service responsible for the museums, historic monuments, and excavations of a subcontinent was demoralized. Ruthlessly he reformed the administration, wrung money from the Treasury, and launched a journal, *Ancient India*. He ran a training school for staff and students, while his excavations revolutionized thinking on the Indus civilization and established a dating system for much of India. He was appointed CIE in 1947. Though serving as archaeological adviser to the government of Pakistan and later excavating there (Charsada, 1958) he returned to London in 1948, held a part-time professorship at the University of London, and became honorary secretary to the British Academy (1949–68). He raised the Academy, of which he had become a fellow in 1941, from a sleepy backwater to the principal source of state aid to the humanities. Among many offices he was director of the Society of Antiquaries (1940–4 and 1949–54), president (1954–59); trustee of the British Museum (1963–73); president of the Royal Archaeological Institute (1951–3); chairman of the Ancient Monuments Board, England (1964–6); and professor of ancient history to the Royal Academy. He was Rhind (1951) and Hobhouse (1955) lecturer at home and Norton lecturer (1952) for the prestigious Archaeological Institute of America, of which he later became an honorary fellow.

In addition to his distinguished excavation reports, Wheeler published many books, among the best of the more specialized being *The Indus Civilization* (1953, 1960, and 1968) and *Rome Beyond the Imperial Frontiers* (1954). *Still Digging* (1955) was a lively and successful autobiography. To this Dictionary he contributed the notices of Sir John Marshall and Sir Charles Peers.

He had always believed in popularizing his subject, and this he did through attracting the public to his excavations, and above all by his brilliance in the BBC's television game, 'Animal, Vegetable, and Mineral'; he was chosen television personality of the year in 1954.

Honours flowed in: the Society of Antiquaries gold medal (1944), a knighthood in 1952, the CH in 1967, and FRS in 1968. Honorary degrees came from the universities of Bristol, Wales, Oxford, Liverpool, Bradford, and Delhi, and the National University of Ireland.

Women were of importance to Wheeler throughout his life: he was readily attracted to them and they to him. His passion for work, however, made him a difficult husband: his rash marriage in 1939 to Mavis de Vere Cole (died 1970) did not last long, being dissolved in 1942, and his third, in 1945, to Margaret Norfolk, also ended in failure. Though still active, he spent much of his last years lodging with his assistant of the British Academy years, Molly Myers, at the Bothy Downs Lane, Leatherhead, where he died 22 July 1976.

[Sir Mortimer Wheeler, *Still Digging*, 1955 (autobiography); Ronald W. Clark, *Sir Mortimer Wheeler*, 1960; Jacquetta Hawkes in *Proceedings* of the British Academy, vol. lxiii, 1977, and *Mortimer Wheeler*, 1982; S. Piggott in *Biographical Memoirs of Fellows of the Royal Society*, vol. xxiii, 1977; personal knowledge.]

JACQUETTA HAWKES

WHEELER-BENNETT, SIR JOHN WHEELER (1902–1975), historian and authority on international affairs, was born 13 October 1902, at Keston in Kent, the youngest in the family of three sons (the first of whom died in childhood) and one daughter of John Wheeler Wheeler-Bennett, a wealthy merchant in the City of London, and his wife, Christina Hill McNutt, of Truro, Nova Scotia. He went to a preparatory school in Westgate, where, in April 1916, he was shell-shocked in an air raid, an experience which left him with a severe stammer. He only overcame this disability after fifteen years of effort, and with the aid of Lionel Logue who also treated George VI. He completed his education at Malvern College but further ill health prevented him from going as intended to Christ Church, Oxford. Instead he became unpaid personal assistant to General (Sir) Neill Malcolm, who had been head of the British military mission in Berlin immediately after the armistice and who encouraged him to deepen his knowledge of international affairs, in particular to concentrate on the situation in Germany.

Wheeler-Bennett started to work in the publicity department of the League of Nations Union, and in 1924, whilst still a fairly impecunious young man, he established his own information service on international affairs, with a fortnightly *Bulletin of International News*. He also inaugurated a series of authoritative studies on contemporary international problems. The first of these, *Information on the Problem of Security*, was published in 1925. He became closely involved with the Royal Institute of International Affairs (Chatham House) whose chairman was Malcolm, and in 1929 he produced on their behalf the first of a new series of annual *Documents on International Affairs*, which he continued to edit until 1936. It was a major contribution to the subject.

In 1929 Wheeler-Bennett was persuaded by Malcolm to go to Germany and make a special study of conditions there. He rented a small stud at Fallingbostel on the Lüneberg Heath, not far from the training headquarters of the German Army Olympic riding team. He met conspicuous figures like Franz von Papen, who was to become German chancellor in 1932. In Berlin he established himself in the Hotel Kaiserhof, well placed for access to the Foreign Ministry and a social centre for many important people, including the leaders of the Nazi Party. He cultivated the acquaintance of leading Germans of various shades of opinion, including the minister of defence and the president of the Reichsbank. His most valuable friendship was with Heinrich

Brüning, who became Reich chancellor at the end of March 1930. During the crisis which led to his downfall in May 1932 Wheeler-Bennett saw him every night. To the end of his life he retained loyal affection for the ex-chancellor though he may have underestimated the authoritarian, nationalist traits in Brüning's policies. Wheeler-Bennett's many contacts in Berlin gave him a first-hand experience, unrivalled by any other historian, of the collapse of the Weimar Republic. He ran considerable risks in helping Brüning to flee the country. At the end of June 1934, during the so-called 'Röhm purge', his rooms at the Kaiserhof were ransacked. He believed that he would have been killed, had he not been called away to visit Neill Malcolm in Switzerland. He did not return to Germany until 1945.

Wheeler-Bennett saw himself as an 'unofficial channel of communication between leading German politicians (excepting Nazis) and London'. His work in Germany was approved by Sir R. G. (later Lord) Vansittart [q.v.], the head of the British Foreign Office. Many Germans regarded him as a well-connected Englishman whose good opinion might be useful in relations with the British government. He made an open foray into diplomacy in November 1932, when he sent a letter to *The Times* suggesting a scheme for disarmament, to which he believed he had obtained the agreement of the German chancellor, von Papen. The Foreign Office was sceptical about the latter's good faith, and Wheeler-Bennett was reproved for his action.

It was after he left Germany that he really began to write history. His first major work was a biography of Germany's ill-starred president, *Hindenburg, the Wooden Titan*, published in 1936. It combined careful scholarship with unique personal knowledge of the events which had led to the collapse of the Weimar Republic. He then began what some historians regard as his finest book, *Brest–Litovsk, the Forgotten Peace.* The importance of the eastern front in World War I had already impressed him when writing *Hindenburg*, and one of his earliest military acquaintances in Germany had been General Seeckt, the architect of the German victory at Gorlice in 1915. Wheeler-Bennett interviewed the major German participants in the peace negotiations, the former Austrian foreign minister, Count Czernin, and, most remarkable of all, some of the Bolshevik actors in the drama. He travelled to the Soviet Union in 1935 and talked to Bukharin, Kamenev, Radek, and others, most of whom were soon to perish in the purges. Two years later he visited Trotsky in Mexico. The book appeared in 1938. By then war clouds were gathering in Europe and Wheeler-Bennett was greatly exercised by the German threat to Czechoslovakia. He deplored the Munich agreement. It caused him later to write his vivid account *Munich: Prologue to Tragedy*, which appeared in 1948. Soon the German threat came nearer home, and Wheeler-Bennett, physically unfit for military service, threw himself into political warfare. As personal assistant to the British ambassador in Washington he travelled widely in the USA putting the British point of view. He helped to establish the British Information Services in New York, and later was posted to Washington in the Political Warfare Mission, where he worked closely with the US Office of War Information. In May 1944 he was back in London in the Political Intelligence Department, ending as assistant director-general. During these years he was often called to advise on the British attitude towards Hitler's opponents in Germany, many of whom he knew personally. He opposed any bargain, partly because he doubted their capacity to carry out effective resistance, but mainly because he feared that a new 'stab-in-the-back' legend might again give German nationalists an excuse for the failure of their disastrous policies. He attended the Nuremberg war crimes trials as an adviser to the British prosecution team, and he was also appointed British editor-in-chief of the captured archives of the German Foreign Office.

In 1945 he married Ruth Harrison, daughter of Alvin Daniel Risher, inventor and scientist, of Charlottesville, Virginia; they had no children. They settled down near Oxford at Garsington Manor, former abode of Lady Ottoline Morrell [q.v.], which again became a notable centre of hospitality. There he forged close links with Oxford University. He taught at New College and he was elected a member of the Christ Church senior common room. In 1950 he became a founding fellow of St. Antony's College, an international graduate centre for the study of recent history and politics. He returned to the writing of German history, and in 1953 published *Nemesis of Power*, a study of the German Army in politics, from the collapse of the Wilhelmine Reich to Hitler's defeat in 1945. It was a literary and historical *tour de force* which aroused indignation as well as admiration. He honoured the bravery of those who resisted the Nazis, but pointed out the errors of Hitler's conservative opponents and the responsibility which the German Army leaders bore for World War II. The main conclusions of the book have stood the test of time.

Wheeler-Bennett then turned to the task of writing the official biography of King George VI. A staunch monarchist, he enjoyed personal contacts with many royal houses and was able to put these to good use. He had a remarkable facial resemblance to the Kaiser, and would often joke about it. The book appeared in 1958 and in the following year the Queen appointed him KCVO, as well as historical adviser to the Royal Archives. In 1962 he published the authorized biography of Sir John Anderson, Viscount Waverley [q.v.]. At the suggestion of Harold Macmillan (later the Earl of Stockton), his publisher as well as a close friend, he decided to write a history of the political settlement after World War II. Here again, he was able to draw on a wealth of personal knowledge and reminiscences. The result was *The Semblance of Peace* (1972), which he wrote in collaboration with Anthony Nicholls. He contributed to this Dictionary the notices of Alexandra (Princess Arthur of Connaught) and Sir Charles Fergusson. In his final years he devoted himself to writing his autobiography; the first two volumes give a vivid picture of his life in Europe and America. Lord Avon, whom he had always admired, asked him to write his biography but his health, never robust, deteriorated and he died in a London hospital 9 December 1975.

Wheeler-Bennett was an expert on international relations, an adviser and informant to governments, and a pioneer in the art of writing contemporary history. His best works were based on rigorous historical scholarship and top level oral evidence. Despite a certain weakness for purple prose, his books attracted the general reader as well as the specialist. He benefited much from the advice and friendship of Sir Lewis Namier [q.v.] whom he had helped financially at the outset of his career.

Wheeler-Bennett possessed a great personal charm which assisted him to gain access to the mighty, but it also illuminated the lives of many others—numerous young scholars in Britain and America where he taught at the universities of Virginia, New York, and Arizona. For them he was always accessible and unstintingly generous of his time. He was a great 'club man' and universally popular wherever he dined.

He was appointed OBE in 1946, CMG in 1953, and GCVO in 1974. He was also FRSL (1958), FZS (1973), a fellow of the British Academy (1972), and honorary DCL of Oxford University (1960). There is a portrait of Wheeler-Bennett by Juliet Pannett in the possession of his wife, and a bronze head, by Lord Charteris of Amisfield, in St. Antony's College, Oxford.

[Sir John Wheeler-Bennett, *Knaves, Fools and Heroes*, 1974, *Special Relationships*, 1975, and *Friends, Enemies, and Sovereigns*, 1976 (autobiographies); Alan Bullock in *Proceedings* of the British Academy, vol. lxv, 1979; private information; personal knowledge.] A. J. NICHOLLS

WHITEHEAD, SIR EDGAR CUTHBERT FREMANTLE (1905–1971), Rhodesian politician, was born 8 February 1905 in Berlin, the third son in the family of five sons and two daughters of (Sir) (James) Beethom Whitehead, then chancellor at the British embassy in the German capital (later knighted for his diplomatic services), and his wife, Marian Cecilia Broderick, youngest daughter of the eighth Viscount Midleton. He was educated at Shrewsbury and later at University College, Oxford, where he read history, obtaining a second class degree in 1926. Owing to weak health, he emigrated to Southern Rhodesia where he briefly served in the local administration, and then became a farmer in the Vumba district as well as a prominent member of the Umtali District Farmers' Association.

In 1939 Whitehead was elected to the Southern Rhodesia Legislative Assembly as member for Umtali North, a white farming and commercial constituency. When World War II broke out, he went back to England, joined the Royal Army Service Corps, and served in West Africa where in 1944 he was appointed OBE in recognition of his administrative ability. In 1945 he retired from the army with the rank of lieutenant-colonel and subsequently represented Southern Rhodesia in London as acting high commissioner. On his return to Rhodesia in 1946, he was re-elected to the Legislative Assembly and from 1946 to 1953 served under Sir Godfrey Huggins (later Viscount Malvern, q.v.) as minister of finance, and of posts and telegraphs. Whitehead, though an advocate of private enterprise, favoured a considerable degree of government involvement in the economy. He played a major part in purchasing the Rhodesian railway system for the Rhodesian government. Whitehead also took an important part in the creation of the Federation of Rhodesia and Nyasaland (1953). Like Huggins, Whitehead hoped thereby to create a larger market that would benefit Southern Rhodesian manufacturing, mining, and farming industries; he also looked to the formation of a British counterweight to the Union (later the Republic) of South Africa.

In 1953 failing health and deteriorating eyesight forced Whitehead to retire from politics for a time. He was appointed CMG in 1952 and KCMG in 1954. By 1957 he had sufficiently recovered to accept appointment as the Federation's first minister in Washington. In 1958 a special congress of the United Federal Party of Southern Rhodesia elected Whitehead as their leader, a compromise candidate standing about half-way between (Sir) Patrick Fletcher, a conservative, and R. S. Garfield Todd, prime minister of Southern Rhodesia since 1953 and a reputed liberal. In the general election of 1958, Whitehead was elected member for Salisbury North, a white upper-middle-class constituency and Huggins's former seat. From February 1958 to December 1962 he served as prime minister of Southern Rhodesia (as well as minister of native affairs, 1958–60).

Whitehead considered that only rapid industrialization would provide sufficient jobs for a black population that kept doubling every generation. The system of migrant labour would no longer serve the country's needs. The existing system of land apportionment (that had divided the country into 'white' and 'black' areas) should gradually be liquidated. A free land market would contribute to the country's growing agricultural productivity. Traditional systems of land-holding in the African reserves should give way to individual tenure for a technically competent and politically conservative class of African landowners. The landless villagers would move to the towns, get permanent jobs in factories, and become a settled and reasonably contented urban proletariat, enjoying a new range of social services, and capable of buying locally produced manufactures. Whitehead realized that his policy could entail some political as well as economic concessions to the African middle- and lower-middle classes. In 1961 a constitutional conference convened in Salisbury. Under the new constitution, the Rhodesian legislature was enlarged from thirty to sixty-five members. Fifty of these would be elected on the old upper (predominantly white) voters' roll, and fifteen on a lower (predominantly black) voters' roll, thus assuring for the first time an African presence, and providing some representation for the growing class of African 'master farmers', contractors, store keepers, transport operators, craftsmen, and white-collar workers. In addition, Whitehead looked to an expansion of educational services for Africans. (Between 1955 and 1958 he served on the council of the multi-racial University College of Rhodesia and Nyasaland.)

Whitehead's policy, however, failed. He overlooked the hostility that the introduction of individual tenure would arouse among those African villagers and townsmen who continued to look to tribal land-holdings for their security in old age. The African nationalists, represented at the time by the National Democratic Party, repudiated the 1961 constitution to which they had originally agreed. Finally, the British government lost faith in the federal experiment which finally broke down in 1963. Once the Europeans realized that cautious reform would neither conciliate the Africans nor ensure the future of the federal state, they turned against Whitehead. In 1962 the European right, reorganized as the Rhodesian Front, gained a decisive victory at the polls. Whitehead continued in opposition, but failed to prevent Rhodesia's unilateral declaration of independence (UDI) in 1965. Whitehead thereafter returned to England, and died in a nursing home in Newbury, Berkshire, 22 September 1971.

In an intellectual sense, Whitehead was probably the ablest man ever to hold office as prime minister in Salisbury. Not even his most bitter opponents questioned his personal integrity. Africans, under his stewardship, made more progress than at any other time in Rhodesian history. Yet Whitehead was unable to gain any personal popularity. A confirmed bachelor and a recluse, he had a remarkable reputation for personal eccentricity. (Rumour had it, quite wrongly, that he would invite his prize bull from his farm into his parlour.) There was about him an air of quiet and courteous arrogance that went with a streak of shyness and an inability to mix, striking disadvantages in a country where the electorate was as yet small, and where personal contacts played an important part in white politics. In white Rhodesian history, Whitehead stood for the traditional Anglo-Rhodesian establishment, linked to Great Britain by ties of upper middle-class origins, education, and political loyalty. He died as one of its most outstanding representatives.

[Robert Blake, *A History of Rhodesia*, 1977; L. H. Gann and Michael Gelfand, *Huggins of Rhodesia: the Man and His Country*, 1964; Claire Palley, *The Constitutional History and Law of Southern Rhodesia*, 1966; personal knowledge.] L. H. Gann

WIGAN, Baron (1900–1975), connoisseur of the arts. [See Lindsay, David Alexander Robert.]

WILCOX, HERBERT SYDNEY (1890–1977), film producer and director, was born at Norwood, London, 19 April 1890, of Irish parentage, the third of the four sons and the fourth of the five children of Joseph John Wilcox, sculptor and manager of a billiard hall, and his wife Mary Healy. He was educated at a succession of Brighton elementary schools and subsequently embarked on a career as a billiards professional in London. On the outbreak of World War I, he enlisted as a private in the 17th battalion, Royal Fusiliers, and was later commissioned as a second lieutenant in the East Kents. He transferred to the Royal Flying Corps in 1916. At the end of the war he became a film salesman in Leeds and in 1922 entered film production in London.

Wilcox's first production, *The Wonderful Story*, a rural drama, received great critical acclaim but was a box office failure. A second film, the highly coloured melodrama, *Flames of Passion*, was a success with the public. This experience decisively shaped Wilcox's philosophy of film-making for the rest of his career. 'No more stark realism', he wrote later, '... My objective now was escape entertainment of pleasant people in pleasant surroundings doing pleasant things.' He began directing films with *Chu Chin Chow* in 1923 and demonstrated his instinct for showmanship by importing established Hollywood stars and by shooting some of his films in Germany to take advantage of superior technical facilities there.

From 1928 to 1935 he was head of production for the newly formed British and Dominions Film Corporation. Having mastered the new techniques of sound on a trip to Hollywood, he launched an annual production schedule of thirty films. For one of them, *Goodnight Vienna* (1932), he signed the comparatively inexperienced (Dame) Anna Neagle, whom he was later to marry and with whom he formed a partnership unique in British film history, directing her in thirty-two films over the next twenty-seven years. She achieved her first great success in Wilcox's *Nell Gwyn* (1934). Then in 1936 he decided that she should play the title role in a full-scale biographical film about Queen Victoria. Unable to find a backer, Wilcox shot the film with his own money in five weeks. Released in the coronation year of 1937, *Victoria the Great* won both critical and popular acclaim. Wilcox followed it with an even more successful Technicolor sequel, *Sixty Glorious Years*. Released in 1938, the year of Munich, this film answered a popular mood of nostalgia for a more settled age, one of moral and political certainty when Britain successfully policed the world. Hollywood beckoned and there Wilcox directed Anna Neagle in *Nurse Edith Cavell* (1939) and a trio of musicals before they returned to Britain to film the life of Amy Johnson [q.v.], *They Flew Alone* (1941).

With the war over, Wilcox once again implemented his film-making creed by providing glamour, romance, and escapism for a public in the grip of austerity. He teamed Anna Neagle with Michael Wilding in what became the much loved 'London series': *Piccadilly Incident* (1946), *The Courtneys of Curzon Street* (1947), *Spring in Park Lane* (1948), and *Maytime in Mayfair* (1949). These were essentially light-hearted and undemanding pieces. But Anna Neagle's stature as a dramatic actress was confirmed when she played the French Resistance heroine in *Odette* (1950), the film Wilcox said he would most like to be remembered by, and Florence Nightingale in *The Lady with a Lamp* (1951). These years saw the Wilcox–Neagle partnership at its peak critically and financially. For seven consecutive years from 1947 to 1952 Anna Neagle was the top British film actress at the cinema box office and four of the Wilcox–Neagle films won the prestigious *Daily Mail* national film award.

But the 1950s saw the beginning of the lean years. A combination of financial misfortune and changing audience tastes led eventually to the bankruptcy court. The films Wilcox was making in the 1950s still had the look and feel of the 1930s about them. He directed his last film, *The Heart of a Man*, in 1959. Subsequent film projects failed to reach the screen and in 1964 Wilcox was made bankrupt. Revealing that he had had to borrow £341,800 since 1955, he said that 'the so-called realistic vogue was upon us' but he refused to make 'films about unpleasant themes and unpleasant people'. Plans for a come-back were hampered by a coronary thrombosis which he suffered in 1965. He regained his health, was discharged from bankruptcy in 1966, and in 1967 published his autobiography, *Twenty-five Thousand Sunsets*. He was to make no further films.

Wilcox was a Roman Catholic and intensely proud of his Irish background. He liked to believe that he may have been born in Cork and repeated the story so often that it found its way into many of his obituaries. He had many of the qualities traditionally associated with the Irish. He was loyal, sentimental, charming, shrewd, and tenacious. He was fond of telling stories and willing to back his judgement up to the hilt.

As a film-maker he was a showman and an entertainer rather than an artist. As a producer, he was able instinctively to gauge the public's taste in films for thirty years and he proudly provided 'mass entertainment for mass audiences', furnishing escapism in the depression and the period of post-war austerity and inspiration before and during the war. As a director, he was painstaking rather than exciting, visually unadventurous but technically proficient. His entire output over more than thirty years was never less than highly professional and in the best of taste, the two qualities he most prized.

Wilcox was appointed CBE in 1951. He was married three times. In 1916 he married Dorothy, daughter of Ernest Addison Brown, retired captain, of the merchant marine; they had no children. The marriage was dissolved in 1917 and in 1918 he married Mrs Maude Violet Clark, daughter of Ernest David Bower, a dentist. There were three daughters and one son of this marriage, which was dissolved in 1943, the year he married Anna Neagle (Florence Marjorie Robertson), daughter of Captain Herbert William Robertson, RNR. They had no children. Wilcox died in London 15 May 1977.

[Herbert Wilcox, *Twenty-Five Thousand Sunsets*, 1967; Anna Neagle, *There's Always Tomorrow*, 1974; Pamela Wilcox, *Between Hell and Charing Cross*, 1977; private information.]

JEFFREY RICHARDS

WILLIAM HENRY ANDREW FREDERICK (1941–1972), prince of Great Britain. [See under HENRY WILLIAM FREDERICK ALBERT, DUKE OF GLOUCESTER.]

WILLIAMS, ELLA GWENDOLEN REES (1890?–1979), writer under the name of JEAN RHYS, was born 24 August probably in 1890, the second of three daughters and the fourth of five children of William Rees Williams, MD, of Roseau, Dominica, and his wife Minna, the daughter of James Potter Lockhart. According to his daughter, Dr Rees Williams, the son of a Welsh Anglican clergyman, 'accepted a government post' in Dominica 'when he was nearly thirty', after working as a ship's doctor. His wife's family had been established on the island as sugar planters for several generations.

Although the family was not Catholic, Gwen was sent to the island's convent school. All her life she remembered how the magic of words was revealed to her by a particularly spirited and congenial Sister. At the age of sixteen she was sent to England, to the Perse School in Cambridge, where she felt lost and awkward and which she left after one term. She persuaded her father to let her change to 'Tree's School of Dramatic Art', which was later to become the Royal Academy of Dramatic Art. Here, too, she spent only one term. Her father died, leaving her mother unable to afford the fees. Gwen was told to come home to the West Indies but decided instead to find herself a job. She was no actress but she was very pretty, so she was taken into the chorus line of a company which was touring *Our Miss Gibbs*. She changed her name, using a number of pseudonyms before deciding on Jean Rhys.

Almost at once she drifted into her first love affair which lasted for about eighteen months and ended when the man thought better of it and 'paid her off' with a small allowance on which (with occasional theatre work) she managed to live until she married in 1919. She discovered that she could purge her misery by writing a full account of this affair in what she thought of as a diary. This she hid in a suitcase, not touching it again for many years. It finally became *Voyage in the Dark* (1934). For Jean Rhys writing was always to be a way of ordering disorder and mastering pain.

She often described how her novels and stories began as attempts to pin down some experience 'as it really was', and would then take on lives of their own as her instinct for form came into operation. This could mean omitting details, or altering them, so her books are not exact mirrors of her career; but that they are autobiographical she—a person of scrupulous honesty—never denied.

Her life certainly resembled that of the women with West Indian childhoods who drift so precariously through London and Paris in her novels. She never had money and never—until she was an old woman—any possessions apart from a few books and her clothes (both very important to her). She felt acutely that 'respectable' people despised her, retaliating by disliking and distrusting them and preferring outsiders. She did not, however, make a raffish impression. Her manners were delicately formal and her charm was that of a cultivated woman. She underwent dark periods—some of them very dark—in which she drank, but these left no trace. To the end of her life she was able to summon up elegance and charm.

The main difference between her characters and their creator was that they were not artists and she was. She could always fend off disintegration by looking at life with eyes so clear that they might have belonged to another being. In her books the people who represent her own viewpoint and those who fail or exploit those people are shown with equal honesty and understanding. Occasionally Jean Rhys the woman could present herself as the innocent victim of a cruel world; Jean Rhys the writer had too great a sense of truth and style to take sides.

Her marriage in 1919 was to Jean Lenglet, a Dutchman, who was a songwriter and journalist, with whom she went to live in Paris. In 1920 they had a son who died almost at once, and in 1922 a daughter who survived her mother. In 1923 Jean Lenglet was arrested and imprisoned for disobeying an order extraditing him from France (he had offended against currency regulations). His wife, left penniless, was befriended by Ford Madox Ford [q.v.] who encouraged her to write, published her first 'sketches' in the *Transatlantic Review*, and wrote an enthusiastic introduction to them when they were collected as *The Left Bank* (1927). The first novel she published, *Postures* (1928—later it was retitled *Quartet*, 1969) was based on her relationship with Ford.

Divorce from Jean Lenglet followed in 1932, whereupon she married an Englishman, Leslie Tilden Smith, in the same year. In 1945 she awoke one morning to find him lying dead beside her (see her story 'The Sound of the River'). She rarely spoke about the following years, although hints of how bad they were occur in her short stories. Little peace was brought to her by her third marriage, to Max Hamer, because they were desperately poor and in 1952, five years after they were married, Max Hamer was sent to prison for six months, charged by the firm for which he worked with misappropriating funds. After his release they went to live first in Bude, then (1956) in Cheriton Fitzpaine, Devonshire, where Jean Rhys stayed on after Max Hamer's death in 1964.

She cut herself off so completely from her former acquaintance (never extensive and rarely intimate) that she was thought to be dead and her books were forgotten by all but a few enthusiasts. In addition to the three mentioned above there had been *After Leaving Mr Mackenzie* (1931) and *Good Morning, Midnight* (1939). Reviewers had called attention to their quality but they had made little impression on the reading public, possibly because of the very distinction of style which has prevented their becoming dated. Jean Rhys's prose, unerringly true to the ironic clarity of her vision, is spare and sounds as natural as speech. Comparison with much of the writing considered fine in the twenties and thirties suggests that it may have seemed bleak to readers attuned to the mannerisms of the day.

In 1957 Jean Rhys 'reappeared' by answering an advertisement which the BBC had inserted in a weekly review, asking for information about her. The publishing house of André Deutsch then learned that she was working on a new novel and bought an option on it. It turned out to be *Wide Sargasso Sea*, the least obviously autobiographical of her books, although perhaps the closest to her inner life. It was published in 1966 and won the W. H. Smith award for that year, and the Royal Society of Literature's Heinemann award. In the next four years André Deutsch republished all her earlier novels and brought out a volume which contained new stories and also those of her *Left Bank* sketches which she wished to preserve (*Tigers Are Better Looking*, 1968). These publications led to her recognition by a large public, as well as by the critics.

In 1978 Jean Rhys was appointed CBE for her services to literature. This honour, the praise now being bestowed on her work, and the income it had at last started to earn for her all gave her pleasure—but only moderate pleasure. Success had come too late to be greatly enjoyable. She resented age and she was lonely. She played with the idea of moving to London, where she spent much of every winter, but although she insisted that she detested rural life she would always end by deciding that she could work better in the cottage to which she had become accustomed. Perhaps the only real satisfaction of her eighties was that she managed—albeit with great difficulty owing to her physical frailty—to go on writing. In 1976 she published the collection of stories *Sleep it Off, Lady* (the title story is unique in the detachment with which it reports back from the frontier of old age); and before she died in Devonshire 14 May 1979, her struggle to complete an essay in autobiography, *Smile Please*, had produced a manuscript which could stand up to posthumous publication in 1979. Even had it been finished, this would probably have remained the slightest of her books, but it is gallant evidence of her dedication to her gift.

[Jean Rhys, *Smile Please*, 1979; Francis Wyndham and Diana Melly (eds.), *Jean Rhys Letters 1931–1966*, 1984; private information; personal knowledge.] DIANA ATHILL

WILLIAMS, SIR FREDERIC CALLAND (1911–1977), professor of electrical engineering, was born at Romiley, Cheshire, 26 June 1911, the younger child and only son of Frederic Williams, a locomotive draughtsman employed by Beyer Peacock, and his wife, Ethel Alice Smith. He was educated at a private school in the village and at Stockport Grammar School. In 1929 he was awarded the Matthew Kirtley scholarship and entered the school of engineering at the University of Manchester, graduating in 1932 with first class honours and winning the Fairbairn prize. For the next year he worked at the university under the direction of Frank Roberts and was awarded the degree of M.Sc. in 1933. He then joined the Metropolitan-Vickers Electrical Company Ltd., as a 'college apprentice', but did not complete the two-year course. In 1934 the Institution of Electrical Engineers awarded him the Ferranti scholarship and he joined E. B. Moullin [q.v.] at the engineering laboratories in Oxford, to investigate circuit and valve noise. For this work he was awarded a D.Phil. in 1936. He was a commoner at Magdalen and during his residence he twice coxed a college eight in bumping races.

From Oxford he returned to his old department at Manchester as an assistant lecturer; his further researches led to the award of a D.Sc. in 1939.

Williams then left Manchester to join the Experimental Establishment at Bawdsey. During the war he worked on radar at Malvern at the Telecommunications Research Establishment (later called the Royal Signals and Radar Establishment), and it was here that his ability in circuitry became apparent. His ingenuity and his quick mind enabled him to invent extraordinary circuits whose operation he would explain in picturesque language largely of his own devising.

At the end of the war, Williams was appointed in 1946 to the Edward Stocks Massey chair of electro-technics in the University of Manchester. While at TRE he had devised a method of storing binary digits on the screen of a cathode ray tube (c.r.t.). Although digital computers existed before 1946, they lacked any system of digit storage ('memory'). The 'Williams tube' stored digits as a charge pattern on the screen and it was possible to inspect any point of the pattern at random; access time was thus shorter than in such rival systems as acoustic delay lines. The c.r.t. store was developed at Manchester until it became the central part of the first stored program digital computer. A complete prototype was built in the laboratory at Manchester, and a commercial version was produced by Ferranti Ltd., who installed about twenty of these computers in Britain and abroad. Williams gradually assembled a team of computer specialists, and, after the development of a second machine, left the direction of the team to Tom Kilburn, and started work on induction machinery.

The induction motor is essentially a constant-speed machine. Williams set out to make induction motors whose speed could be continuously varied. Several successful designs emerged from his work, the spherical motor, the 'log' motor, and the phase-change motor among them. These machines were based on ingenious ideas, and although the laboratory-produced models behaved satisfactorily, manufacturing difficulties precluded commercial production. There followed several machines with discrete speeds, an induction-excited alternator, a traction scheme, and slow-speed high-torque motors using the direct pull between magnetized surfaces.

Williams's last successful project was an automatic (mechanical) transmission for a motor car; an experimental version of the gadget (his word for it) was installed in a car and for a year or two he drove it daily between his home and the university. The Institution of Mechanical Engineers made the first award of the Clifford Steadman prize to him for a paper describing the system.

In the early days of computer development, Williams had to contend with the conservative element in the university for the right of university staff to patent their inventions; this right was in the end acknowledged, but Williams and his co-inventors, with characteristic selflessness, handed over all patents to the university, giving it absolute discretion in the distribution of benefits. The early computing machine patents were among the first handled by the National Research Development Corporation, which in consequence got off to a good start.

In his department Williams concerned himself almost entirely with his research, leaving administrative work as much as possible to others. His advice, however, was always available and he could usually make a constructive suggestion.

He served a turn as dean of the faculty of science, as dean of the faculty of music, and as pro-vice-chancellor. He was elected FRS in 1950, appointed OBE in 1945 and CBE in 1961, and knighted in 1976. His awards included the Benjamin Franklin medal of the Royal Society of Arts (1957), the John Scott award, City of Philadelphia (1960), the Hughes medal of the Royal Society (1963), and the Faraday medal of the Institution of Electrical Engineers (1972); he also received honorary doctorates from the universities of Durham, Sussex, Wales, and Liverpool.

In 1938 Williams married Gladys, daughter of Thomas Ward, builder, of Romiley. They had a son, who became a professor of civil engineering, and a daughter.

Williams died in hospital in Manchester 11 August 1977.

[T. Kilburn and L. S. Piggott in *Biographical Memoirs of Fellows of the Royal Society*, vol. xxiv, 1978; private information; personal knowledge.] L. S. PIGGOTT

WILLIAMS, (LAURENCE FREDERICK) RUSHBROOK (1890–1978), scholar, historian, and publicist, was born at Wandsworth 10 July 1890, the son of Laurence Ambrose Williams, a company secretary in Shell, and his wife, Edith Eliza Oxenford. Educated privately, he entered University College, Oxford, as a Linton exhibitioner in 1909. His academic career was successful and in 1912 he won both a first class in the final honours school of modern history and the Gladstone prize. He followed this with a B.Litt. in 1913. His academic career was capped by election to a fellowship at All Souls College, Oxford, in 1914, which he held for seven years.

Rushbrook Williams was a man of outstanding and versatile talents who achieved distinction in many fields. Perhaps this very versatility hindered the highest achievement in any one of them. Through his life he bore the mark of his Oxford experience; precise, polished, amply endowed with learning, style, and judgement. The title of professor, earned during his four years at Allahabad University, India, remained with him as a prefix for the rest of his life.

In 1914, after a brief experience as a history lecturer in Canada, and partly, perhaps, through the persuasion of the Bajpai brothers whom he had known at Oxford, he became professor of modern Indian history in the University of Allahabad in north India. Apart from his Indian friendships, the attraction of this post lay in the fact that, with Lord Hardinge of Penshurst [q.v.] as viceroy and the current Morley–Minto reforms, India presented an enticing prospect of further constitutional change. His impact on the study of Indian history was immediate. He formed a school of historians, whose best known member was Sir Shafaat Ahmad Khan, and he provided a model of historical method in his book on Babur, *An Empire Builder of the Sixteenth Century* (1918). Its influence in India was far greater than its modest compass would suggest.

The year of this publication marked the beginning of the second stage of his career as a constitutional expert, publicist, and popularizer. He was called on special duty by the government of India in connection with the planning of the Montagu–Chelmsford reforms. The impression he made was such that in 1920 he became the first director of the Central Bureau of Public Information, and as such charged with popularizing the new reforms. In his six years of office his method was to transform the factual *Moral and Material Progress Reports* of the government of India into vividly written and brilliantly presented annual expositions of governmental policy and achievement. He was appointed OBE in 1919 and CBE in 1923.

There followed the third stage when the publicist became a diplomatist as well. This was his connection with the Indian princes beginning with his appointment as foreign minister to the Maharajah of Patiala, a post he held from 1925 to 1931. He became the confidential adviser to the forward-looking princely group who believed that joining an all-India federation was the best way to safeguard their position in the emerging self-governing India. He was secretary to the chamber of princes and adviser to the states delegation to the Indian constitutional Round Table conference (1930–2). For a time he was a key figure in the Indian political scene.

When hope turned into disillusion with the princely retreat into isolationism he returned to Britain to resume an advisory informative role. He worked with the Colonial Office (1935–8) and Foreign Office (1938–9) and as adviser on Middle Eastern affairs at the Ministry of Information (1939–41). He was director of the BBC Eastern Service (1941–4). After the war he completed his formal career as a specialist writer for eleven years on the editorial staff of *The Times*. He served with three editors and was a power behind the editorial chair.

In later years he lived in Silchester, Hampshire. He soon became a magistrate and was chairman of the local branch for many years. He returned first to Scotland and finally to Great Kimble, Aylesbury. He became again a great traveller: the intellectual became an enthusiast, first for Israel, then for Pakistan. He wrote on both these subjects: *The State of Israel* (1957), *The State of Pakistan* (1962 and 1966), *Pakistan under Challenge* (1975), and *The East Pakistan Tragedy* (1972). He also contributed to local history, first *Marco Sanudo* with J. K. Fotheringham [q.v.], and then studies of St. Albans abbey and of the state of Kutch.

He married in 1923 Freda May, daughter of Frederick Henry Chance, solicitor, of Coward, Hawksley Sons, & Chance; they had two sons and a daughter. His wife was his constant companion and helper, inspiring and sustaining his work. Rushbrook Williams died at Stoke Mandeville Hospital, Buckinghamshire, 1 October 1978.

[*The Times*, 5 and 12 October 1978; private information; personal knowledge.]

PERCIVAL SPEAR

WILLIAMS, (RICHARD) TECWYN (1909–1979), clinical pharmacologist, was born in Abertillery, south Wales, 20 February 1909, the eldest of the four sons and five children of Richard Williams, of Tanygrisiau, Merioneth, coal miner, and his wife, Mary Ellen, a schoolteacher at Blaenau Festiniog at the time of her marriage, and daughter of John Elias Jones, a tailor in Abertillery. It was his mother's influence which persuaded Tecwyn to seek further education and a career as a teacher. Having won a scholarship to Abertillery County School, he went on to University College, Cardiff, to study chemistry and physiology. He gained his B.Sc. degree in 1928. He then trained as a teacher and was awarded a diploma in education. However, in 1930 an opportunity arose of doing research in carbohydrate chemistry in the Physiology Institute in Cardiff with Dr John Pryde, and Williams obtained his Ph.D. degree in 1932 with a thesis dealing with the structure of glycosidic derivatives of borneol and theophylline. This work, which dealt with the metabolism of two substances foreign to the mammalian body, determined the scope and direction of Williams's scientific contribution throughout his life.

Following post-doctoral research work at Cardiff, Williams was appointed in 1934 as a lecturer in biochemistry in the University of Birmingham. He continued his researches on the metabolism of drugs and established a small research group. He gained his D.Sc. in 1939. In 1942 Williams was appointed senior lecturer in biochemistry in the University of Liverpool, and this allowed him to expand considerably his research activities. By that time he had established himself as one of the leading scientists in the field called 'xenobiotics', i.e. the metabolism of compounds foreign to the body. He took up an appointment as professor of biochemistry at St. Mary's Hospital Medical School, part of the University of London, in January 1949 and spent the rest of his scientific career there, until his retirement in 1976.

Williams's work covered a very large field: it involved terpenes, benzene, phenols, sulphonamides, and a great variety of other compounds. During World War II he was asked by the Medical Research Council to investigate the metabolism of the synthetic explosive 2:4:6-trinitrotoluene (TNT), and this led to interesting results. He also showed that the weak analgesic and antipyretic substance, phenacetin, is metabolized to the active paracetamol. Useful work was also done on the metabolism of oestrogens which is of clinical interest. Thus, the work of Williams largely created a new science which could be called 'chemical pharmacology', and this was recognized to be of increasing importance for the general understanding of the action of drugs.

Public interest in the new science was increased remarkably by the thalidomide tragedy in 1961. This clearly indicated the need for having full information on the metabolic handling of substances foreign to the body, whether they are drugs or food additives. An important additional interest in this field was provided by the belief that cancer may be caused by the ingestion of substances present in our environment. The creation of chemical pharmacology or toxicology as a major field of biological investigation in Britain was to a large extent due to the efforts of Williams, together with those of Eric Boyland. In the United States, the main force for the development of this field of investigation was Bernard B. Brodie, with whom Williams developed a close personal and scientific relationship.

Williams was a true scholar, and he was suspicious of trendiness, of the dramatic or spectacular. He preferred to work with the whole animal and used only rarely *in vitro* systems such as cell cultures or pure enzymes. His standards of work were very high, and he was somewhat intolerant of what he considered sloppiness. He was very proud of his Welsh origin.

He much appreciated his honorary doctorate of the University of Paris (1966), as well as the MD of Tübingen (1972). He was also awarded D.Scs. by the universities of Wales (1976), and Ibadan (1974), and was elected a fellow of the Royal Society in 1967. In 1968 he was the recipient of the merit award of the Society of Toxicology, USA. He served on various national committees dealing with toxicology, and he was also involved in international activities with the Food and Agriculture Organization and the World Health Organization.

In 1937 he married Josephine Teresa, apprenticed as a lady's and gentleman's tailor, daughter of William Sullivan, a bricklayer in the Cardiff steelworks. They had two sons and three daughters. Williams died 29 December 1979 in Northwick Park Hospital, Harrow, Middlesex.

[Albert Neuberger in *Biographical Memoirs of Fellows of the Royal Society*, volume xxviii, 1982; private information; personal knowledge.]

ALBERT NEUBERGER

WILLIAMS, SIR WILLIAM EMRYS (1896–1977), educationist and publisher, was born at Capel Issac in Carmarthenshire 5 October 1896, the only son and second of the four children (of whom the two youngest died in childhood) of Thomas Owen Williams, a journeyman joiner, and his wife, Annie Jones, the daughter of a farmer in Llandilo. Living in Wales until his eighth year, he was brought up to speak Welsh and retained marked Welsh characteristics throughout life.

His childhood education was in local primary and secondary schools in Manchester. He then proceeded by scholarship to Manchester University and the study of English literature. In 1919 he married Gertrude, daughter of Israel Rosenblum, shipper; she was also a Manchester graduate. Ultimately professor of social economics at the University of London, she was appointed CBE in 1963. She died in 1983. There were no children of the marriage.

This background of early life and education offers clues to Williams's strong and lasting concern for the educational and cultural well-being of his fellows. He had great and unusual ability in relating practical and political skills to a fertile creative imagination. His formal commitment to adult education began in 1928 with his innovative appointment as a staff tutor in literature, in the Extra-Mural Department of the University of London. Literature was not at that time a staple fare of the tutorial classes offered. The record of his widening and developing influence continued from that date.

From 1934 to 1940 he was secretary of the British Institute of Adult Education; from 1941 to 1945 (technically on secondment from the British Institute) he was director of the Army Bureau of Current Affairs (ABCA) and from 1946 to 1951 director of its civilian extension, the Bureau of Current Affairs, which was supported by the Carnegie Trust; and from 1951 to 1963 he was secretary-general of the Arts Council of Great Britain. He was secretary of the National Art Collection Fund from 1963 to 1970. For thirty years he was closely implicated in the development of that remarkable educational publishing venture, Penguin Books, of which he was editor-in-chief (1935–65). He was also arts adviser to the Institute of Directors for a period.

Throughout his career he was a pungent and distinctive writer with great journalistic and editorial skills. In pre-war days he so vivified the *Highway*, the journal of the Workers' Educational Association, that it achieved a remarkable circulation and a reputation as 'the poor man's *New Statesman*'. In a wider field he was, until 1951, a trenchant television critic for the *Observer* and he wrote the notice of 'Tommy' Handley for this Dictionary. During his tenure of office the annual reports of the Arts Council reflected his pleasure and skill in the use of language and a degree of ironical humour that clothed but never submerged his humane concerns. He had an acute feeling, not only for the content, but also for the appearance and production standards of any publication in which he was involved.

His early working experience, communication skills, and personal charm helped him to enlist essential support for new projects. One example was his instigation of the decisive intervention by Thomas Jones [q.v.] in providing a grant of £25,000 from the Pilgrim Trust towards the establishment in 1941 of the Council for the Encouragement of Music and the Arts, (CEMA), which later developed into the Arts Council. The prototype of CEMA was the 'Arts for the People' Scheme—begun by Williams in 1934—of the Institute of Adult Education. This idea of providing travelling exhibitions for 'galleryless towns' was also strongly supported by Sir Kenneth (later Lord) Clark. It was appropriate that Williams should become a trustee of the National Gallery from 1949 to 1956.

Another and momentous example was the initiation and conduct of ABCA. Controversy was inseparable from his assertion 'that the fighting men and women had a right to basic information, to political curiosity, and to a feeling of partnership in deciding what kind of a country Britain should be after the war had been won' (obituary in *The Times*, 1 April 1977). In the tenor of the time, the promotion of such objectives inevitably had political implications favourable to the left rather than to the right. Distaste in high quarters, extending to the prime minister, could scarcely have been ignored without the unswerving support of the adjutant-general (and subsequent colonel-commandant of the Royal Army Education Corps), Sir Ronald Adam.

His work was recognized by honours at home and abroad: CBE in 1946, a knighthood in 1955, and the American medal of freedom (1946). He received an honorary D.Litt. from the University of Wales (1963) and was an honorary member of the Architectural Association. Greatly gifted he gave of himself widely, wisely, and generously. He died at Stoke Mandeville Hospital 30 March 1977.

[*The Times*, 1 April 1977; private information; personal knowledge.]

EDWARD M. HUTCHINSON

WILLIAMS-ELLIS, SIR (BERTRAM) CLOUGH (1883–1978), architect, was born in his father's rectory at Gayton, Northamptonshire, 28 May 1883, the fourth of the six sons (there were no daughters) of the Revd John Clough Williams Ellis, formerly fellow and tutor of Sidney Sussex College, Cambridge, and his wife, Ellen Mabel (May), daughter of John Whitehead Greves, JP and DL, of Bericote House, Warwickshire. On his father's side he descended from the Ellises of Glasfryn, Caernarfonshire, and from the Williamses of Plâs Brondanw in Merioneth, while his mother's family owned slate quarries at Blaenau Festiniog. In 1887, when he was five, his father gave up his Cambridge University living to move back to Glasfryn on its bleak and boggy plateau in the Lleyn peninsula. Here Clough learnt to build and sail small boats and with his mother's help to draw and dream (for lack of the reality) of architecture. A 'born' architect, as opposed to the 'made' kind of whom he later disapproved, it surprised him that his playful baroque taste should have emerged from this austere environment.

He was sent to Oundle, where the headmaster was F. W. Sanderson [q.v.], whose 'modern' outlook his father admired, and inevitably to Cambridge to read science at Trinity College, which he had selected himself because of its Great Court and blue gowns. Determined to be an architect, he soon abandoned Cambridge and science and to support himself in London took a job in electrical engineering. From this too he soon fled, looked up 'architecture' in the telephone directory, and enrolled as a student at the Architectural Association. In the intervening vacation he worked as an assistant to a country builder and got his first commission (both through 'family jobbery') for a fee of £10. On the strength of this he left the AA within three months and set up in practice, which his family connections and his appetite for dining and dancing rapidly expanded. His most important prewar building was the romantic Tudoresque Llangoed Castle on the upper Wye, but to him the most exciting event was the handing over to him by his father of Plâs Brondanw, then a quarry-workers' tenement. Its classically conceived garden was wholly his creation, and his delight.

Physically tough and ever ingenious, Williams-Ellis had an adventurous war, first in the Welsh Guards and later as an intelligence officer in the Tank Corps in which he won the MC and bar and was mentioned in dispatches, and on the history of which he collaborated with his young wife, (Mary) Amabel (Nassau), daughter of John St. Loe Strachey [q.v.], the owner and editor of the *Spectator*; they had married in 1915. Her influence and the experience of war developed in him a determination to campaign for effective town and country planning in Britain. He had met (Sir) Patrick Geddes [q.v.] in Edinburgh, formed a working alliance with other disciples such as (Sir) Frederic Osborn, (Sir) Charles Reilly, and (Sir) L. P. Abercrombie [qq.v.], and was the most effective, because the wittiest, propagandist of this lively group, with a distinctive writing style. His *Cautionary Guides* to supposedly beautiful cities, illustrating the 'horrors' being perpetrated in them, and his books (mostly written with his wife), such as *England and the Octopus* (1928) and, as editor, *Britain and the Beast* (1937) were both enjoyable and disturbing, and he was among the founders of the councils for the preservation of rural England and of Wales and an enthusiast for the National Trust and for the creation of national parks. *The Pleasures of Architecture* (1924) on which he worked with his wife (by then herself a delightful writer) was reissued in 1954, and he wrote two autobiographies. He contributed the notice of Benno Elkan to this Dictionary.

His practice, mainly domestic in character, flourished between the wars. It included the adaptation of and additions to Stowe, a handsome baroque chapel at Bishop's Stortford (the first building by a living architect to be 'listed'), and neo-Georgian country-house work and cottages at Cornwell (Oxfordshire) and Oare (Wiltshire). Later he designed the Lloyd George memorial at Llanystymdwy. The romantic holiday village of Portmeirion, his most celebrated work, was begun in 1925, mainly for fun, but also as a demonstration of enlightened exploitation. In it he showed an almost Chinese sensitivity to the relation between buildings and landscape. Striding the peninsula in yellow stockings and cravat, he cut a dashing figure, powerful and elegant, his strong features an expression of his zest for life.

He was briefly chairman of the Stevenage New Town Development Corporation, vice-president of the Institute of Landscape Architects, an honorary LL D of the University of Wales (1971), and FRIBA (1929). He was appointed CBE in 1958 and knighted in 1972.

Williams-Ellis had two talented daughters and a son who was killed in 1944. He died at Plâs Brondanw 8 April 1978 at the age of ninety-four, still full of physical and mental energy, having lived to see Modernism (with which he was never at ease) come and go, and to be admired by a new generation for the lightheartedness of his approach to architecture, for the pleasures of his company and his wife's, and for his lifelong battle against the philistines.

[Clough Williams-Ellis, *Architect Errant*, 1971, and *Around the World in Ninety Years*, 1978 (autobiographies); personal knowledge.]

ESHER

WILLIAMSON, HENRY (1895-1977), author and journalist, was born 1 December 1895 in Brockley, near Lewisham, only son of William Williamson, bank clerk, of Parkstone, Dorset, and his wife, Gertrude, daughter of Thomas William Leaver. He was educated at Colfe's School, London.

On the outbreak of war he joined the army. His mind was scarred for life by the Christmas truce in 1914, when men who had been trying to kill each other for months past briefly fraternized, only to revert to war again. The Somme was always in his memory. He would not come to terms with the deadly phenomenon of incited patriotic fervour with its power to drive men into a hell of other men's devising. He felt that the land to which he returned at the age of twenty-three, at the end of the war, was in no way fit for heroes. Like many other young men who survived the test to destruction he could not adjust to the peace. He was emotionally burnt out, deeply depressed, and practically without money. He lived on a £40 a year war pension supplemented by what he could earn from newspapers and periodicals. It was then that he came upon *The Story of my Heart* (1883) by Richard Jefferies, the Wiltshire nature writer, and his spirit was invigorated. He went to Devon and began writing in an Exmoor cottage.

He wrote the four books that make up *The Flax of Dream* between 1918 and 1928 (1921, 1922, 1924, and 1928) but by 1924 had also produced two nature books, *The Lone Swallows* (1922) and *The Peregrine's Saga* (1923). On this theme came *Tarka the Otter* in 1927 which won the Hawthornden prize of 1928. There followed *The Wet Flanders Plain* (1929), *The Patriot's Progress* (1930), *Tales of a Devon Village* (1932), *The Gold Falcon* (1933), *Salar the Salmon* (1935), and then two books concerning Richard Jefferies.

As the years went by his books brought him security but he was deeply troubled by international trends. He saw it all happening again and, knowing how it had been, he clutched at any straw for peace, even the most unlikely. 'I salute the great man across the Rhine whose life symbol is the happy child', he wrote in 1936. Hindsight gives such a remark a sick absurdity but Williamson was far from alone in believing it. To some it seemed that Germany was rising from the ashes, firmly, hopefully, and in full employment, whereas in England the heroes still lived in slums and some men had never worked since before the war.

Such opinions, and his support of Sir Oswald Mosley [q.v.] did Williamson no good. When World War II broke out he was imprisoned briefly under defence regulations before being allowed to return to the Norfolk farm which he had owned for eight years and had 'brought from a state of near-dereliction' to full production. *The Children of Shallowford* came out in 1939, *The Story of a Norfolk Farm* in 1941, and six further books before *The Dark Lantern* in 1951 opened his fifteen-part saga *A Chronicle of Ancient Sunlight* which ended in 1969 with *The Gale of the World*, his last book. The *Chronicle* is a peerless social history and a damning indictment of war and his nature books most perfect of their kind, but his ill-conceived *affaire* with fascism was not forgotten and may have denied him honours.

In his narrative writing Williamson is thorough and painstaking and reveals a microscopic eye for detail; he speaks with authority and is always believable, often shockingly as in his war books. Yet much of his philosophy seems to be founded on original innocence. Here perhaps we may perceive an interaction between two great influences on his thinking; the effect of front line service on a sensitive mind and the subsequent discovery of Richard Jefferies's esoteric testament *The Story of my Heart*.

As a man Williamson was said to be often amusing, with a quick puckish humour, a conversationalist with holding power; at other times he could be perverse and irritating, touchy, unable to conceal boredom. He was a loyal and helpful friend. In his writing he was an obsessive perfectionist who wrote and rewrote, never sparing himself. Yet he remained vigorous until almost the close of his long life, striding across the placid hills and beside the clear rivers of the Devon countryside, to which he returned after leaving his Norfolk farm.

Williamson married first, in 1925, Ida Loetitia, daughter of Charles Calvert Hibbert; they had four sons and two daughters. The marriage was dissolved in 1947 and in 1948 he married Christine Mary, only daughter of Hedley Duffield, of Keswick; there was one son. The marriage was dissolved in 1968. Williamson died in a London hospital 13 August 1977.

[Brocard Sewell (ed.), *Henry Williamson: the Man, the Writings*, 1980; Daniel Farson, *Henry*, 1982; Williamson's autobiographical works; private information.] RICHARD FRERE

WILLINK, SIR HENRY URMSTON, first baronet (1894–1973), lawyer, politician, academic administrator, and public servant, was born at Liverpool 7 March 1894, the elder son of William Edward Willink, architect, and his wife, Florence Macan, daughter of Colonel H. B. Urmston. He was a king's scholar at Eton, winning the Newcastle scholarship and a scholarship to Trinity College, Cambridge. In 1914 war broke out before he could take his degree; he volunteered immediately and was captain and acting major in the Royal Field Artillery, gaining the MC, croix de guerre, and mention in dispatches. He was called to the bar, Inner Temple, in 1920, where he was a pupil of W. A. (later Earl) Jowitt [q.v.], afterwards lord chancellor. Willink took silk in 1935 and became a bencher in 1942.

In 1938 he unsuccessfully contested Ipswich for the Conservatives but won Croydon North at the 1940 by-election. He became special commissioner for the homeless in London in 1940 until appointed minister of health and privy councillor in November 1943. He held his seat in the general election of July 1945 against the swing, but was never happy in opposition. He had to combine his legal work with 'shadowing' Aneurin Bevan [q.v.] on health and housing. This affected his health, but though he was clearly glad to leave politics, his friends were surprised when he abandoned the law also to become master of Magdalene College, Cambridge, from 1 January 1948. Many had forecast a distinguished legal career for him, ending possibly as lord chancellor.

Willink never regretted his decision and it was at Magdalene where he remained master until 1966 that he was happiest. He had a well-cultivated mind and a commanding presence. He read widely and was a witty conversationalist. Architecture, music, and travelling were among his many interests, and he was essentially devoted to his family which extended to an unusually large number of cousins. He took a great interest in his undergraduates and had many friends; he excelled as a host with a great gift of making the least important guest feel really at home. But with all his wisdom, wit, charm, and geniality he was in some ways strangely diffident, vulnerable, and never fully confident of his own considerable abilities.

He was a popular master and resisted unnecesary change, taking pride in preserving Magdalene's special character. This had its reward when he presided over a very successful appeal to raise funds for what was the least well endowed of the ancient Cambridge colleges: this brought him into contact with many old members of the college by whom he was well loved, and it gave him great pleasure. It was a special joy to him when the fellows prolonged his tenure of the mastership for two years beyond the normal retiring age of seventy. Towards the end of this period he had a severe coronary thrombosis, from which he recovered; but in retirement, though for some years as busy as ever, his health was never good. He became an honorary fellow of Magdalene in 1966. 'History will place him alongside the best of our masters' was part of the tribute paid to him at his memorial service in Westminster Abbey by Archbishop Michael Ramsey (later Lord Ramsey of Canterbury), himself an honorary fellow of the college.

Willink served the university on the council of the senate (1951–60) and was vice-chancellor (1953–5). He chaired various university and local committees but found time for and greatly enjoyed a variety of interests outside Cambridge. He was high bailiff of Westminster (1942–67), fellow of Eton (1946–56), and held many important ecclesiastical offices in addition to being dean of the Court of Arches (1955–69).

He took a great interest in the mentally ill and was chairman of the hospital management committee at Fulbourn (1962–9). He found time also to give distinguished public service as chairman of the royal commission on betting, lotteries, and gaming (1949–51), a subsequently controversial committee on medical manpower (1955), a commission on minorities in Nigeria (1957), and the royal commission on the police, which reported in stages (1961 and 1962). At an earlier date he had chaired a steering committee out of which the Royal College of General Practitioners was established. He had honorary degrees from Liverpool and Melbourne and was also honorary FRIBA.

In 1923 he married Cynthia Frances (died 1959), daughter of Herbert Morley Fletcher, physician; they had two sons and two daughters. He married, secondly, in 1964, Mrs Doris Campbell Preston, daughter of William Campbell Sharman. His second wife survived him.

Willink died in Cambridge 1 January 1973. He was succeeded in the baronetcy, which he accepted in 1957, by his elder son, Charles William Willink (born 1929).

There is a portrait by Middleton Todd at Magdalene College.

[Private information; personal knowledge.]

J. F. BURNET

WILLIS, SIR ALGERNON USBORNE (1889–1976), admiral of the fleet, was born in Hampstead 17 May 1889, the younger son and youngest of three children of Herbert Bourdillon Willis, a company director, and his wife, Edith Florence Moore. From Eastbourne College he entered the *Britannia* as a naval cadet, and became midshipman in September 1905 and sub-lieutenant three years later. He gained early promotion to lieutenant in November 1909. After a commission in the *Good Hope* in the Mediterranean he qualified as a torpedo specialist in the *Vernon* and went on to an advanced course at Greenwich.

On the outbreak of war in 1914 he spent six months in the battleship *Magnificent* before recall to special duties in the *Vernon*. After service in the cruiser *Donegal* in the Atlantic and the *Defiance*, the torpedo school at Devonport, he joined the flotilla leader *Fearless* which was attached to the battle cruiser squadron in the Grand Fleet at the Battle of Jutland in 1916. Willis then rejoined the *Vernon* until September 1918, when he returned to destroyers in the flotilla leaders *Saumarez* and *Wallace*. Here his efficiency in maintaining his weapons in Arctic conditions in the Baltic earned him appointment to the DSO in 1920.

In 1920 he joined the battle cruiser *Renown* taking the Prince of Wales, with (Admiral Sir) Dudley North [q.v.] in attendance, to Australia and New Zealand. Further service in the *Vernon* brought promotion to commander (1922) and appointment to the staff course. Returning to sea Willis spent two years as squadron torpedo officer in the *Coventry*, the destroyer flagship, followed by two more on the staff of the senior officers' tactical course in Portsmouth. Rejoining destroyers in the *Warwick* he was promoted to captain in 1929. After two years on the staff of the Royal Naval War College (1930–2), he became flag captain in the *Kent* on the China station (1933–4) and again in the Home Fleet flagship *Nelson* (1934–5). In September 1935 his return to the *Vernon* in command until April 1938 had a notably good effect in maintaining efficiency at a time when gunnery seemed to be in the ascendancy.

Thence he went to the *Barham* in the Mediterranean as flag captain and chief staff officer, transferring in February 1939 as a commodore and chief of staff to the C-in-C, initially Sir Dudley Pound and then Admiral Sir Andrew Cunningham (later Viscount Cunningham of Hyndhope, q.v.). Here he was promoted to rear-admiral and appointed CB (1940) for services against the Italian navy. In 1941 as an acting vice-admiral he was briefly C-in-C South Atlantic but when Japan entered the war he was transferred to the Eastern Fleet (under Sir James Somerville, q.v.) which suffered losses during an attack on Ceylon but regained control of the western Indian Ocean when the Americans struck further east. He was confirmed in the rank of vice-admiral (1942) and given command of Force H in the western Mediterranean in April 1943, for the operations in North Africa and the landings in Sicily, Salerno, and Anzio which forced Italy to seek peace. His actions earned him promotion to KCB (1943). After a brief spell as C-in-C Levant (1943) he became second sea lord and chief of naval personnel (1944–6). He was promoted to admiral in October 1945 and appointed KBE. He handled the difficulties of transition from war to an uncertain peace with great ability.

In April 1946 he returned to the Mediterranean for two years as C-in-C. Problems in Palestine, war-damaged Malta, and the restless Balkans disrupted normal peacetime routine. He was promoted to GCB in 1947. His last appointment was as C-in-C Portsmouth from 1948 to 1950, during which he was promoted to admiral of the fleet (1949).

His remarkable succession of service with outstanding officers of strongly independent and varied outlook showed great adaptability, but without concession to anything he thought wrong; and behind his austere appearance was an unexpected sense of quiet dry humour. As a young man he played hockey for the navy and he enjoyed tennis for many years. Golf and carpentry were among his later hobbies. He declined nomination as lieutenant-governor of Tasmania and became a deputy lieutenant of Hampshire in 1951. His post-war activities included work for the Royal Naval Benevolent Trust and the Soldiers, Sailors and Airmen's Institute, and chairmanship of the trustees of the Imperial War Museum.

He married in 1916 Olive Christine, daughter of Henry Edward Millar, company director, of Hampstead, and twin sister of Violet Helen, who married the Labour prime minister, C. R. (later Earl) Attlee. Lady Willis was actively interested in naval charities and was appointed CBE in 1951. They had two daughters. Willis died in the Haslar Royal Naval Hospital, Gosport, 12 April 1976.

[Private information; personal knowledge.]

P. W. BROCK

WILLS, LEONARD JOHNSTON (1884–1979), geologist, was born 27 February 1884 at the Gables, Barnt Green, Birmingham, the eldest in the family of two sons and two daughters of William Leonard Wills (partner in his own father's firm of A. W. Wills, edge tool manufacturers, of Nechells) and his wife, Gertrude Annie

Johnston. His great-uncle was Sir Alfred Wills, a mountaineer who was a co-founder of the Alpine Club. He went to Uppingham School, winning an exhibition to King's College, Cambridge, where he was awarded the Walsingham medal and the Harkness research scholarship. He obtained first classes in both parts of the natural sciences tripos (1906 and 1907), specializing in geology. Despite his academic prowess he denigrated his educational opportunities in later life, regarding his subsequent self-education as more effective and more relevant.

While holding the Harkness scholarship (1907–9) Wills began research on the building stones of the Bromsgrove district, a Triassic horizon which he made notable for fossil plants, mollusca, and arthropods. He later extended the investigations of the arthropods to the eurypterids, ostracoderm fish, and other denizens of the Devonian and Coal Measures, developing unique methods of dissecting these fossils to reveal previously unknown anatomical details.

He joined the Geological Survey in 1909 and worked in the Llangollen district. He left the Survey in 1913 on appointment as lecturer in geology at Birmingham University. In 1932 he became professor of geology at Birmingham. There he developed his strong interest in the geology of the Midlands, initially in the Pleistocene and the glacial history. Later he studied the long-term evolution of the Midlands basins and their deep geology. In this work he was well ahead of his time. He produced successively his books on *The Physiographical Evolution of Britain* (1929), *The Palaeogeography of the Midlands* (1948), *A Palaeogeographical Atlas of the British Isles* (1951), and *Concealed Coalfields* (1956). These books showed a rare grasp of three-dimensional problems in stratigraphy and structure together, and the *Palaeogeographical Atlas* in particular provided most valuable background for the burgeoning oil industry which followed the early North Sea discoveries.

For these and other works he was awarded by Cambridge an Sc.D. (1928), by the Geological Society its Wollaston Fund (1922), Lyell medal (1936), in 1954 the Wollaston medal (its highest honour rarely given in Britain), and the unique distinction (for a Briton) of an honorary fellowship (1976). He was made an honorary member of the Yorkshire Geological Society, the East Midlands Geological Society, and the Petroleum Exploration Society of Great Britain.

Willis left his academic post in 1949, to retirement at Romsley, initially to a small estate which he equipped with water-powered electricity, and which he later handed over to the National Trust. He then embarked upon publishing much of his earlier work and also undertook compilation of data on the deep geology of England and Wales. He produced a palaeogeological map of the Pre-Permian formations (1973), a map of the Lower Palaeozoic floor beneath the Upper Devonian and Carboniferous (1975), and later still—at the age of ninety-two—published 'A conjectural Palaeogeological Map of Wales and England as in end-Silurian Times'.

These unique maps, which were published by the Geological Society with financial support from the Petroleum Exploration Society, were compiled with the assistance of many consultants, and in the face of the most severe physical difficulties, including near-blindness and a heart condition. Wills was a man deeply respected for his diligence and originality.

In 1910 he married Maud Janet, daughter of Sir J. Alfred Ewing [q.v.], a distinguished scientist. His son, Leonard, born in 1911, predeceased him in 1976, a blow from which he never really recovered. His other child, his daughter Penissa, born in 1913, sustained him (after a happy marriage which ended with his wife's death in 1952) through his later years of infirmity, and made possible the superlative compilatory work of his retirement. Wills died 12 December 1979 at home in Romsley.

[Personal knowledge.] PETER KENT

WILSON, CHARLES McMORAN, first BARON MORAN (1882–1977), physician and writer, was born at Skipton in Craven, Yorkshire, 10 November 1882, the younger son and youngest of three children of John Forsythe Wilson MD, general practitioner, and his wife, Mary Jane, daughter of the Revd John Julius Hannah, Presbyterian minister, of Clogher, and granddaughter of Dr John McMorran MD. The family had roots in Northern Ireland, and William Hazlitt [q.v.], the literary critic and essayist, was one of Wilson's forebears.

Wilson was educated at Pocklington Grammar School and in 1902 entered St. Mary's Hospital Medical School. He qualified MB, BS (Lond.) in 1908, and after his resident appointments he spent a year travelling in Italy and Egypt before returning to take his MRCP and MD (Lond., 1913), for which he won the gold medal. In 1913 he was appointed medical registrar at St. Mary's Hospital.

When war broke out in 1914 he enlisted in the Royal Army Medical Corps and was posted as medical officer to the 1st battalion of the Royal Fusiliers. He spent two years in the front line where the horrors and heroism of trench warfare made a lasting impression on his mind. He was awarded the MC (1916) for bravery during the battle of the Somme, the Italian silver medal for valour, and was twice mentioned in dispatches. He ended the war as a major.

His deep interest in soldiers under the stress of war led him to keep a diary and later to write *The Anatomy of Courage* (1945), a work which described how courage may be strengthened or spent. For many years he lectured on courage to the Staff College at Camberley.

In 1919 he was appointed assistant physician at St. Mary's Hospital and, in 1920, dean of the Medical School at the early age of thirty-eight. The School was then in a poor state, and its future was in jeopardy, but Wilson was determined that it should become one of the finest in the country, and campaigned successfully for better students, better staff, new buildings, and a bigger budget. The premises were rebuilt with the help of generous donations from Lord Beaverbrook [q.v.] and the second Baron Revelstoke, professorial clinical units were established, and teaching was extended to nearby Paddington Infirmary. Wilson loved games and acquired for the School a splendid sports ground at Teddington. He also served as chairman of the committee which planned the medical services of London to receive casualties during the war of 1939–45.

He devoted his professional life to three great causes: to medical education as expressed through St. Mary's Medical School; to the reshaping of medical practice to the needs of modern society through the influence of the Royal College of Physicians; and to (Sir) Winston Churchill, as his personal physician. He published his ideas on medical education in a trenchant but sympathetic article entitled 'The Student in Irons' (*British Medical Journal*, 3 March 1933) which pointed out the woeful inadequacies of medical education in failing properly to train the student's mind, cramming it instead with facts of doubtful validity.

He foresaw that the growing discontent which later expressed itself in the Beveridge report would ultimately require a new approach in medical affairs. After a great struggle with Lord Horder [q.v.] who was the conservatives' choice, he was elected president of the Royal College of Physicians in 1941 and served for nine years. He set out to provide in the College an independent source of expert information and advice to which the government of the day could refer. In this way the College played an important role in setting up the National Health Service. Also in 1941 Wilson became consultant adviser to the Ministry of Health. As a member of the House of Lords from 1943, Moran broached the question of doctors' and dentists' remuneration, and this led to the formation of the Spens committee, which recommended merit awards solely for the quality of service to patients. He was appointed a member of the General Medical Council in 1945. By taking infinite pains, Moran became an excellent orator, expressing his ideas with clarity, succinctly, and without a note.

Wilson became Churchill's physician, and confidant, shortly after the outbreak of war in 1939. He accompanied Churchill on most of his journeys during the war. The two men were attracted to each other by a common interest in literature, people, and military adventures. Wilson was convinced that Churchill would be regarded by posterity as one of the greatest Englishmen of all time and therefore kept a detailed diary of his clinical observations of his unique patient. While Churchill was alive his medical bulletins were wholly discreet but, after Churchill's death, encouraged some years earlier by the historian G. M. Trevelyan [q.v.], he published his controversial book *Winston Churchill: The Struggle for Survival* (1966), which gave an informed account of Churchill's illnesses and behaviour in relation to events. The book raised a storm of protest, but Moran was careless of popularity and never lacked the courage to do what he believed to be right. He felt that his contribution to history was more important than any indiscretion he might have been committing after the death of the patient he had cared for so discreetly, and so well, when alive.

Moran was knighted in 1938, and raised to the peerage as first Baron in 1943. He was elected an honorary fellow of the Royal Colleges of Physicians of Edinburgh, Glasgow, and Australia. He was Harveian orator in 1952 (*Lancet*, 23 January 1954).

In 1919 Moran married Dorothy (died 1983), a research physiologist, the daughter of Samuel Felix Dufton, inspector of schools for Yorkshire. In 1918 she was appointed MBE for her work in the Ministry of Munitions. The marriage was extremely happy. They had two sons, (Richard) John (McMoran) (born 1924) who became high commissioner to Canada and succeeded his father in the barony, and Geoffrey Hazlitt, chairman of Delta Group. Moran died at Newton Valence, Hampshire, 12 April 1977.

There is a portrait by Pietro Annigoni in the Royal College of Physicians. At St. Mary's Moran is remembered by Wilson House, the students' hostel, and the Moran scholarship, but the whole School is really his memorial.

[Private information; personal knowledge.]

T. A. Kemp

WILSON, ELEANORA MARY CARUS- (1897–1977), English medieval economic historian. [See Carus-Wilson.]

WILSON, Sir HORACE JOHN (1882–1972), civil servant, was born 23 August 1882, the sixth of the seven children and the youngest of the three sons of Harry Wilson, a furniture dealer, of Bournemouth, and his wife, Elizabeth Ann Smith. He was educated at Kurnella School, Bournemouth. He entered the Patent Office as a boy clerk in 1898, and passed into the second division of the Civil Service in 1900. In 1904 he enrolled as a 'night school' student at the London School of Economics, where he took a B.Sc. (Econ.) in 1908. He served in the labour department of the Board of Trade when the chief industrial commissioner was Sir George (later Lord) Askwith [q.v.], and in 1915 he was made secretary of the committee on production and of the government arbitration committee under the Munitions of War Acts, of both of which Askwith was chairman. Wilson used later to say that it was on Askwith's techniques as an arbitrator and conciliator that he modelled his own.

The labour department of the Board of Trade became the nucleus of the Ministry of Labour which was created when David Lloyd George became prime minister in 1916. Wilson went to the new ministry, and by 1919 had become the principal assistant secretary in charge of the industrial relations and conciliation department. In this post he helped to implement the reports of the committee chaired by J. H. Whitley [q.v.], as a result of which joint industrial councils were set up in a wide variety of industries and services which had hitherto had no formal negotiating machinery. In 1921, still under forty, he became the permanent secretary of the Ministry of Labour. With the extended powers of the new ministry he was able to play a more positive part in the settlement of industrial disputes at national level. He thus acquired considerable experience of industrial conciliation and an extensive knowledge of the personalities, organizations, and forces at work on both sides of industry; and he earned the respect and confidence not only of employers' and union leaders but also of his political masters. He was at the heart of the discussions and negotiations in which the government was involved at the time of the general strike in 1926.

When the Labour government took office in 1929, a team of officials was set up under the direction of the lord privy seal (J. H. Thomas, q.v.) to deal with the problem of unemployment and to foster more active co-operation by the government in the reorganization and development of industry. Wilson was put at the head of this team, first as permanent secretary at the Ministry of Labour and then, from 1930, in a new appointment as chief industrial adviser to the government which enabled him to concentrate all his attention on the problems of industry and employment. He continued as chief industrial adviser under the national government of 1931. In July 1932 he accompanied the British delegation (which included Stanley Baldwin and Neville Chamberlain) to the imperial economic conference at Ottawa. He virtually took over the spadework of the British delegation, and was one of the main architects of the agreement, although his influence did not commend itself to those observers who would have favoured a larger commitment to imperial preference than the British government was prepared to make. This phase of his career culminated in his contribution to the reorganization of the cotton industry in 1935.

In 1935 Wilson was asked by the new prime minister (Stanley Baldwin) to join his staff as a personal adviser. Although conscious of the risk that this might arouse the jealousy and antagonism of his departmental colleagues, he accepted it as his duty to do so. Accordingly, while retaining his position and title as chief industrial adviser to the government, he was seconded to the Treasury for service with the prime minister: an unusual appointment which brought him to the prime minister's right hand, and to an office next door to the Cabinet Room in 10 Downing Street. He was involved as the prime minister's adviser over the whole range of business, including the crisis that led to the abdication of King Edward VIII.

Wilson expected this personal appointment to come to an end when Baldwin retired in 1937, but Neville Chamberlain asked him to 'stay around for a bit'; so he did, and made himself even more indispensable to the new prime minister than to his predecessor. In the deepening international crisis caused by the expanding ambitions of Hitler's Germany and Mussolini's Italy, Chamberlain was determined to prevent, if he could, or at least to defer for as long as possible, the outbreak of another European war. He disagreed with the policies and distrusted the attitudes of the Foreign Office, and reposed great confidence in Wilson as his principal adviser, on international as well as domestic affairs.

In this difficult and exposed position Wilson sought to work very closely with the permanent under-secretary of state at the Foreign Office, Sir Alexander Cadogan [q.v.]. But others in the Foreign Office, itself divided, distrusted him. They were suspicious of his inexperience of diplomacy, and resentful of his influence with the prime minister. They believed that he encouraged the prime minister in the view that other foreign policy objectives, and in particular co-ordination with French policy (and stiffening of French resolve where necessary), should be subordinated to the attempt to develop better understandings with Germany and with Italy; and they thought that he helped to foster in the prime minister's mind the illusion that the conduct of foreign relations resembled the handling of industrial disputes.

Wilson was the senior member of the small party of official advisers who accompanied Chamberlain on his visits to Berchtesgaden, Bad Godesberg, and Munich in September 1938, and Chamberlain sent him as an emissary to Hitler in Berlin between the visits to Bad Godesberg and

Munich. Both before and after this time he had direct contact with various representatives of the German government, in the hope of discovering a basis for settling areas of dispute and reaching an Anglo-German agreement which would prevent war.

Early in 1939 Wilson was appointed to succeed Sir N. F. Warren Fisher [q.v.] as permanent secretary to the Treasury and official head of the Civil Service. He combined his new duties with his position with the prime minister until Chamberlain's resignation in May 1940. As permanent secretary to the Treasury he was concerned for the problems of war finance, but he concentrated mainly on directing the adaptation of the machinery of government to its wartime functions. He retired from the public service on reaching his sixtieth birthday in 1942.

Wilson's association in the public mind with 'the men of Munich' no doubt prevented him from being offered the further public appointments which might have been expected (particularly in wartime) to come the way of a retiring permanent secretary to the Treasury. From 1944 to 1951 he served as independent chairman of the National Joint Council for Local Authorities' Administrative, Professional, Technical, and Clerical Services. In 1956, when Nigel Nicolson (the Conservative member of Parliament for the Bournemouth constituency in which Wilson lived) publicly dissociated himself from the Eden government on the Suez affair, Wilson emerged briefly as one of Nicolson's strongest supporters in the disagreement which he had with his constituency association. Apart from that, his retirement from public affairs was complete.

Wilson had in the highest degree many of the attributes of a great public servant; intelligence, clarity of mind and expression, skill in conciliation, impartiality, and integrity. The attribute which made him especially valuable to ministers was his ability to see issues plain and clear, and then to present them plainly and clearly to his political chiefs. His experience as a negotiator led him to believe that, given a modicum of good will, there was no problem or dispute which could not be resolved by the use of an appropriate form of words; and his skill in devising such formulae was one of the qualities which most commended him to the ministers with whom he was associated, though it was sometimes felt that he was not always sufficiently mindful of the longer-term implications of the formulae which he produced. His qualities were valued equally by the ministers whom he served from both of the main political parties—J. H. Thomas, for instance, described him as 'a ruddy wonder'—and by the employers' and union leaders with whom he dealt. His industry and devotion to duty, to the exclusion of every other interest save that of family life, were tireless. He was at or near the centre of government for over twenty years. But his achievements in the rest of his career were eclipsed by the two pre-war years with Chamberlain. Close observers thought that in a difficult position he conducted himself with complete official propriety; but his association with the policy of appeasement attracted considerable obloquy, both at the time and subsequently, and it is arguable that to his misfortune and not primarily by his own fault he was thrust into a role at 10 Downing Street which ought never to have been allowed to take the form it did.

Wilson was not, as some said, the chief architect of the policy of appeasement: Chamberlain was nobody's puppet. But there can be no doubt of the loyalty and conviction with which he supported and helped the prime minister in carrying it out. It was not just a matter of professional loyalty to his minister, though that consideration would certainly have weighed with any civil servant with Wilson's sense of public duty. There was a high degree of intellectual and personal sympathy, even affinity, between the two men; and Wilson was convinced of the rightness of Chamberlain's policies. He believed that there was no need or cause for a war between Britain and Germany; that Germany's legitimate grievances and aspirations could be satisfied; that if they were satisfied Hitler would either not need or (for lack of support at home) not be able to go to war; and that a strong and non-communist Germany could be a bastion against what he saw as the supreme menace of Soviet communism. The aim of the policy of appeasement was thus, as he saw it, to avert war, not just to defer it. Even after the policy had failed to achieve that aim, however, Wilson continued to believe not only that it had been right in conception and intention but also that it had been advantageous and even necessary as a means of gaining time in which to demonstrate the inevitability of war beyond a peradventure, to rally the support of public opinion at home and in the Empire, and to bring the country's preparations to a point where, if war at last became inescapable, at least it could be faced with some hope of avoiding defeat.

Wilson was a slim figure of medium height, with a considerable presence: reserved, rather solitary, and of a grave mien and disposition; not given to laughter but with a ready smile. He was a very gentle and self-controlled man, virtually never moved to anger or even to raising his voice; and a man of great charm and unfailing courtesy, widely respected, and held in affection by many of his colleagues.

Wilson was appointed CBE in 1918, CB in 1920, KCB in 1924, and GCB in 1937. He was appointed GCMG in 1933, after the imperial economic conference in Ottawa. He was an honorary LL D at Aberdeen (1934) and Liverpool (1939); and became an honorary fellow of the London School of Economics in 1960.

Wilson married in 1908 Emily, daughter of John Sheather, a farmer of Beckley in Sussex; she died eighteen months after her husband, in October 1973. They had one son and two daughters. He died in Bournemouth, the town where he was born, 19 May 1972, nearly ninety years old.

[*The Times*, 26 May 1978, and other obituaries; biographies, diaries, and memoirs of contemporaries; personal recollections; private information.] ROBERT ARMSTRONG

WINDSOR, DUKE OF (1894–1972), King of Great Britain. [See EDWARD VIII.]

WINN, SIR (CHARLES) RODGER (NOEL) (1903–1972), lord justice of appeal, was born 22 December 1903 in Barnt Green, Worcestershire, the elder son and elder child of Ernest Burton Winn, manufacturer, and his wife, Joan Bristow who was later divorced and married Edward Blunden Martino. His younger brother Godfrey became a popular author and journalist. When eleven years old Winn was crippled by poliomyelitis but with great will-power forced himself to walk again, although he was left with a twisted back and a pronounced limp. Educated at Oundle School and Trinity College, Cambridge, he took first classes in part i of the classical tripos (1924), part ii of the law tripos (1926), and the LL B. He was Davison scholar at Yale (1925) and Choate fellow at Harvard (1927). Called to the bar by the Inner Temple in 1928, he entered the chambers of Sir Patrick Hastings [q.v.] and rapidly began to make a name for himself.

In 1939, despite his physical disabilities, he offered his services to the Admiralty and was appointed a civilian assistant to the head of the recently re-formed Submarine Tracking Room, Paymaster Captain E. W. C. Thring, who had filled the same post in World War I. In January 1941 Winn was chosen to succeed Thring and was commissioned as a temporary commander RNVR (special branch). Notwithstanding the great advantages accruing to British naval intelligence from the work of the code breakers at Bletchley Park, it is difficult to overemphasize the personal contribution made by Winn to the Allied victory in the battle of the Atlantic.

Working from often contradictory or inconclusive evidence and sometimes from inspired intuition, he repeatedly anticipated Admiral Doenitz's moves, thereby saving hundreds of lives and thousands of tons of shipping. He gained the complete confidence of the naval and air staffs and came to exercise a remarkable influence over anti-U-boat operations, a feat all the more extraordinary for an intelligence officer and one without any naval training.

In April 1942, when shipping losses on the US eastern seaboard had reached truly alarming proportions, he was sent to Washington. After overcoming initial distrust and scepticism he persuaded the US Navy to set up its own submarine tracking room which thereafter worked in the most intimate co-operation with Winn's department. He was equally successful in Canada. Winn's standards were extremely high and he drove both himself and his small staff to the limit, but he gained their unstinted admiration and affection. The strain was great and at the end of 1942 he collapsed and was forbidden by his doctor ever to return to duty. Characteristically he was back at his post in four weeks. His great achievements were recognized by his appointment as OBE (1943), his promotion to acting captain (1944), and his creation as CB (1947) and officer of the US Legion of Merit (1946).

Returning to the bar in 1946 he established himself as a leading junior. After a period as counsel to the General Post Office, he was appointed junior counsel to the Treasury (1954) and then, five years later, a judge of the Queen's Bench division, with the customary knighthood (he had become a bencher in 1953). His best-known judgement was that made in 1961 declaring the election of the secretary of the Electrical Trade Union to be void. In 1965 he was appointed to be a lord justice of appeal and was admitted to the Privy Council. He was a member of the committee of personal injury litigation (1966–8) and chairman of the security commission investigating defects in the security of the country (1964–71). Both at the bar and on the bench he was outstanding for his quickness of perception, his clarity of thought, and the incisiveness of his presentation, qualities already displayed in the Admiralty. As a judge he was courteous and firm. He rarely interrupted counsel, but when he did it was always to the point. He was not a profound case lawyer but he had a sound grasp of principle, fortified by wide experience and great common sense. He made a notable contribution to the Court of Appeal.

Winn also somehow made time to serve as a governor of St. Thomas's Hospital and as chairman of the council of its medical school, both with great success. He had married in 1930 Helen Joyce (died 1979), daughter of Colonel E. V. Sydenham DSO; they had one daughter. His wife was a great source of strength to him, particularly when, at the end of 1970, he suffered a severe stroke which left him unable to speak or write. He faced this ordeal with his usual courage, but died in London 4 June 1972.

[*The Times*, 5 June 1972; Patrick Beesly, *Very Special Intelligence*, 1977; Donald McLachlan,

Room 39, 1968; private information; personal knowledge.] PATRICK BEESLY

WISKEMANN, ELIZABETH META (1899–1971), historian and journalist, was born 13 August 1899 at Sidcup, Kent, the youngest child of (Heinrich Odomar) Hugo Wiskemann, a merchant who had emigrated from Germany, and his wife, Emily Myra Burton. She was educated at Notting Hill High School and Newnham College, Cambridge, obtaining a first class in part ii of the history tripos in 1921. She worked for a Ph.D. and was bitterly disappointed when in 1927 her dissertation on Napoleon III and the Roman Question only gained her an M.Litt. She was convinced that this was due to the prejudice of one of her examiners and remained somewhat suspicious of professional academics all her life.

After this set-back she went in the autumn of 1930 to Berlin where she spent much of the next five years, although she continued to do some teaching in Cambridge till 1937. She rapidly made friends with a large number of Germans and especially with the leading British journalists in Berlin and she developed a passionate interest in German politics. She was quick to understand the nature of National Socialism and was soon writing articles on German affairs for the *New Statesman* and other English periodicals and warning her friends and acquaintances in England of the extent of the Nazi danger. By 1935 she had acquired a considerable reputation—not least with the Nazis who realized what an effective reporter she was and began to watch her movements. In July 1936 she was expelled from Germany by the Gestapo but continued her reports on the political situation from other parts of central Europe. In 1937 she was commissioned by the Royal Institute of International Affairs to do a study of the problem of the Germans in Czechoslovakia, which appeared as her first book, *Czechs and Germans*, in June 1938. This was a remarkable historical and political analysis written against time, as the crisis she foresaw was rapidly developing. Her second book, *Undeclared War*, appeared in the autumn of 1939 and was an account of the situation in central and eastern Europe and of the methods of German penetration there. By now her urgent warnings had turned out to be true and her reputation as a journalist and political analyst was enhanced accordingly.

At the end of 1939 she went to Switzerland where she was to spend the war years except for a short visit to Lisbon and London in 1941; from September 1941 she was officially attached to the British legation in Berne as assistant press attaché and was in fact responsible for the collection of non-military intelligence from Germany and the occupied countries. After the war she returned to journalism, turning her attention especially to Italy, a country which she had always loved and with which she had new ties because of her contacts from Switzerland with the Italian Resistance. In 1947 she published a short book *Italy* as well as acting for a time as the Rome correspondent of *The Economist*. However, while continuing to contribute occasional articles to periodicals, she was now becoming a serious academic historian. Her study of the relations between Hitler and Mussolini, *The Rome–Berlin Axis* (1949), was a pioneering work and the basis for later studies by other scholars. It was followed by *Germany's Eastern Neighbours* (1956), a lucid and balanced analysis of the problem of Germany's eastern frontiers. By the late 1950s she was winning academic recognition: she was Montague Burton professor of international relations at Edinburgh University—a visiting post—from 1958 to 1961 and a tutor in modern European history at the University of Sussex from 1961 to 1964. In 1965 the University of Oxford conferred an honorary doctorate on her.

In 1959 she paid a tribute to the importance in her life of her experiences in Switzerland with her *A Great Swiss Newspaper, the Story of the Neue Zürcher Zeitung*, with which she had retained close contact and to which she was an occasional contributor. In 1966 came a general account of Europe between the wars, *Europe of the Dictators*, followed by a volume of memoirs *The Europe I Saw* (1968)—a book which, though full of interest, disappointed some of her friends because her account of the eminent people she had known seemed somewhat bland in comparison with the pungent comments she would pass on them in conversation. At the end of her life she published a study of *Fascism in Italy* (1969) while a book on *Italy since 1945* was published posthumously in 1971. To this Dictionary she contributed the notice of F. A. Voigt.

During the years after World War II she was living in London renewing and extending her remarkably wide circle of friends from the world of the arts and literature as well as the universities, politics, and journalism. Her last years were made increasingly difficult by failing sight; and, rather than give up her independence and live a life in which she would be unable to read, she took her life in her home in London 5 July 1971. She was unmarried.

Elizabeth Wiskemann was a small, vivacious woman of great charm and independence, always outspoken in defence of her strongly held opinions, sensitive and quick to reply to criticism, and justly proud of her record as, to quote the public orator at Oxford who presented her for her D.Litt., 'a Cassandra who had lived to record the war she had foretold', though modest about her achievement as, again in the public orator's words, 'a historian who had obtained international recognition'.

[*The Times*, 6, 9, 12, and 15 July 1971; Elizabeth Wiskemann, *The Europe I Saw*, 1968; private information; personal knowledge.] JAMES JOLL

WITTKOWER, RUDOLF (1901–1971), art historian, was born in Berlin, Germany, 22 June 1901, the second of four children and elder son of Henry Wittkower, a German financier born in England, and his wife, Gertrude Ansbach. Wittkower studied at the University of Munich and then at Berlin under the medievalist Adolph Goldschmidt; his Ph.D. thesis (1923) was on Renaissance painting in Verona. In 1923 Wittkower became assistant and in 1928 research fellow at the Bibliotheca Hertziana in Rome, where he remained until 1933. He first collaborated with the director, E. Steinmann, on an annotated bibliography of Michelangelo (1927).

Independently, Wittkower worked on a neglected subject, baroque sculpture, and collaborated with H. Brauer on a masterly catalogue of Bernini's drawings (1931) in preparation for a definitive monograph on the central figure of Roman seventeenth-century art. European events interrupted this research, but Wittkower finally published a catalogue of Bernini's sculpture in 1955 (3rd edn. 1981). While working on Bernini, Wittkower also began to study architecture, which ultimately became his chief contribution. Following a controversy with C. de Tolnay, he published a major article on Michelangelo's dome of St. Peter's (1933; revised as a monograph, 1964). He then turned to Michelangelo's earlier architecture in an influential article, his first published in English, on the Laurentian Library (1934, reprinted 1978). Its combination of careful archaeological study with close scrutiny of the drawings and documents led to a visual analysis of great probity that concluded with a study of 'The Vestibule and the Problem of Mannerism', an early attempt to adapt the concept of mannerism to the history of architecture.

By 1934 Wittkower, a British citizen, was in London with his family. In 1923 he had married Margot, daughter of Max Holzmann, a Berlin physician. She collaborated in his work; a son Mario was born in 1925. These were difficult years, for his first position, with the newly transferred Warburg Library, was unpaid. Always a prodigious worker, Wittkower became co-editor of the new Warburg *Journal* (1937–56) and published a number of essays in it that can be called Warburgian—notably 'Eagle and Serpent' (1939), in which he traced the migration and transformation of two widespread symbols, a study on the representation of monsters (1942), and an article on illustrations to the manuscripts of Marco Polo (all reprinted 1977).

In 1937 Wittkower published a major study of the architecture of Carlo Rainaldi, which included an epoch-making consideration of the centralized churches of the Roman baroque (reprinted 1975). He then turned to earlier Italian architecture with seminal articles on Alberti (1941) and Palladio (1944). These were incorporated into an influential and popular book, *Architectural Principles in the Age of Humanism* (1949; 4th edn. 1971). In it he examined the centrally planned churches of the Renaissance, showing that their antique forms had Christian significance. In 'The Problem of Harmonic Proportion in Architecture' he tried to show that Palladio planned his buildings according to proportional ratios based on musical theory. The idea had a surprising vogue with practising architects, some of whom tried to adapt its principles to modular design.

Wittkower made his way in the rather closed world of English art history through force of personality, intelligence, and unfailing good humour. In 1949 he became Durning Lawrence professor in the history of art in the University of London, teaching students at the Slade School. These were productive years: the catalogue of Carracci drawings at Windsor Castle (1952); the Bernini catalogue; and in 1958 his monumental and original synthesis of Italian baroque art and architecture for the Pelican History of Art (3rd edn. 1973). In the early 1940s Wittkower also began to study English architecture, particularly Palladianism. Other eighteenth-century studies appeared in later years—he was fascinated by Piranesi (a result of his purchase of old books) and was a propagandist for the architecture of Piedmont.

In 1955 Wittkower took up an invitation to become visiting professor at Columbia University in New York, where the remainder of his career unfolded, chiefly as chairman of the department of art history and archaeology from 1956 to 1969. At Columbia he rejuvenated and expanded a moribund department; he himself taught hundreds of graduate students and supervised dozens of doctoral dissertations. He was also a familiar, gregarious figure at post-war exhibitions and congresses, often a chairman or chief speaker.

Wittkower was huge in physical stature, possessed of great energy and an ambition that transcended mere personal achievement. He fostered the careers of countless scholars in many countries, inspiring devoted friendship everywhere. To the end he returned annually to England and Italy, and in 1970–1 he was Slade professor of fine art at Cambridge University. He was a member or fellow of many honorary societies and academies, among them the British Academy (1958), and the Accademia dei Lincei (1960). A Festschrift in two volumes (1967) printed his imposing bibliography to 1966. He retired from Columbia as Avalon Foundation professor in the humanities in 1969 but continued research, lecturing, and teaching until his sudden death in New York 11 October 1971.

[*Burlington Magazine*, vol. cxiv, 1972, pp. 173–7; *Journal of the Society of Architectural Historians*, vol. xxxi, 1972, pp. 83–91; private information; personal knowledge.]

HOWARD HIBBARD

WODEHOUSE, SIR PELHAM GRENVILLE (1881–1975), writer, was born 15 October 1881 at 1 Vale Place, Epsom Road, Guildford, the third son of Henry Ernest Wodehouse, a magistrate in Hong Kong, and his wife, Eleanor, daughter of the Revd John Bathurst Deane. She was in England only for the birth of her child and quickly returned to Hong Kong taking him with her. Henry Ernest Wodehouse belonged to a collateral branch of the family of the Earls of Kimberley, being the son of the second son of Sir Armine Wodehouse (fifth baronet), whose descendants were created first Baron Wodehouse in 1797 and first Earl of Kimberley [q.v.] in 1866. His wife belonged to the equally ancient and extremely widespread family of Deane or Adeane.

When their eldest son was six the Wodehouse parents followed the custom of the time in sending him home to England to be educated. For reasons, which are not obvious and which have never been explained, they also sent his younger brothers with him (Pelham then aged two), taking a house in Bath and engaging a Miss Roper to look after them. This regime lasted for three years and then the boys were moved to a dame school in Croydon. Later they were sent to a small public school in Guernsey and finally Armine, the second son, and then Pelham (whose name had been shortened to 'Plum') went to Dulwich College. There were a large number of uncles and aunts on both sides of the family and they were sent to one or other of these in their holidays. Apart from a short period when he was fifteen, and when his parents returned to England and at first took a house near the school (later moving to Shropshire), Armine and Plum boarded at Dulwich.

Deprived so early, not merely of maternal love, but of home life and even a stable background, Wodehouse consoled himself from the youngest age in an imaginary world of his own. He said later in life that he never remembered the time when he did not intend to write and one small story, written when he was seven, remains to prove the skill with which he already handled language. When he went to Dulwich he achieved for the first time in his life some continuity and a stable and ordered life, and, because of the multiplicity of shared interests, he was able to communicate easily with his fellows without any great demands being made upon him. He repaid the happiness he felt there by a lifetime's devotion to the school which sometimes seemed almost obsessive. 'To me', he said in late life, 'the years between 1894 and 1900 were like heaven.'

He was in the school teams for cricket and rugby football and he had the good fortune to be at Dulwich with A. H. Gilkes, a distinguished headmaster and a renowned classicist, whose teaching must have been an important influence. His report for the year 1899 contained the following remarks: 'He has the most distorted ideas about wit and humour; he draws over his books and examination papers in the most distressing way and writes foolish rhymes in other people's books. Notwithstanding he has a genuine interest in literature and can often talk with enthusiasm and good sense about it.'

At first he worked for a scholarship at Oxford, but, when his brother, Armine, succeeded in this ambition (later winning the Newdigate prize), his father told him he could not afford to send them both. When he left school, he therefore went into the Hong Kong and Shanghai Bank. Here he was both unhappy and inefficient and he lived for the end of the day when, in 'horrible lodgings', he could spend his evenings writing. He left the Bank when (Sir) William Beach Thomas [q.v.], lately a master at Dulwich, offered him a job (at first temporary but later becoming permanent) to write the 'By the Way' column on the *Globe* newspaper. From that time he supported himself by writing and his enormous output (written anonymously, under his own, other people's, and assumed names) included light verse, articles (some of which appeared in *Punch*), and short stories. Chiefly, however, this was the period of the school stories run as serials in the *Public School Magazine* or its rival, *The Captain*. In 1902 his first book, *The Pothunters*, was published by A. & C. Black and this was followed by six other volumes of school stories. *Mike* (1909), the last of these, was distinguished by the entrance of a character called Psmith, an event which Evelyn Waugh [q.v.] said marked the date exactly when Wodehouse was touched by the sacred flame: 'Psmith appears and the light was kindled which has burned with growing brilliance for half a century.'

In 1904 he went for the first time to America, the country which would become his second home, and after that he often travelled backwards and forwards across the Atlantic. He soon began to set some of his novels in the American scene and to use the dialect of the New York gangs. He was in America in 1914 and he stayed there for the duration of the war. He had exceedingly bad eyesight and, although he attempted to register when America came into the war, he was rejected. He could not have served England in any military capacity but, more by his attitudes than by any action, he showed, as he would in the second war, how slight were his hold on reality and his ability to respond to abstractions such as country or tragedy on an impersonal scale.

In 1914 he married Ethel Newton (died 1984), the young widow of Leonard Rowley, of Dee Bank, Cheshire. She had one daughter, Leonora, whom he adopted and to whom he became as devoted as if she had been his own. Leonora later married Peter Cazalet [q.v.]. The Wodehouses were to have no children of their own. From the start Ethel Wodehouse was the dominant partner and she managed all their affairs, leaving him free to write. He had by now begun the extremely successful partnership in musical comedies with Guy Bolton and Jerome Kern, which led to a career in the theatre which seemed at the time as important as his career as a novelist and even more lucrative.

After the war he returned to England, but, although he had a house in London for some years, he still spent much time in America. In 1930 he made the first of two visits to Hollywood, causing a national sensation in 1931 by explaining in an interview that, although he had been paid enormous sums to write films, he had never been asked to do any real work. Finally, in 1934 he and his wife settled in Le Touquet.

In 1939 the Wodehouses remained in Le Touquet, and, when the Germans captured northern France, the writer was interned in Upper Silesia. On being released in 1941, he made five broadcasts to America from Berlin, and, although these were the equivalent of comic articles in his personal vein, and were made with the motive of reassuring all those people who had written to him or sent parcels, this was not understood at the time, particularly as the British propaganda machine was put to work to present him as a man who had served the enemy in return for his release from internment. Although this was proved to be quite untrue, it was held that he might, nevertheless, have committed a technical offence by speaking in wartime on an enemy wavelength, no matter what the content of his speech, and for many years he could not be guaranteed immunity from prosecution if he entered the jurisdiction of his own country. He accordingly went to America and, after settling down there, became an American citizen in 1955.

Because he wrote under other names and often turned novels into plays or plays into novels, it is difficult to be sure of his total output. He published under his own name ninety-seven books (including twenty-one collections of short stories), he wrote the lyrics or some of the lyrics for twenty-eight musical plays, and wrote or collaborated in the writing of sixteen plays. He wrote the scenario for six films and much light verse and innumerable articles. His work was translated into all the major languages of the world and his sales, which ran into many millions, cannot be estimated.

It seems likely that he achieved a permanent place in English literature. He was unique in that, although he wrote primarily for the general public, he had an inspired humour, and a prose style of so much freshness, suppleness, simplicity, and exactitude that, from such early admirers as Asquith, Hilaire Belloc and M. R. James [qq.v.], he has been the delight of generation after generation of writers and intellectuals, his name standing ever higher.

His most famous books are the Jeeves and the Blandings Castle series, and he achieved the ambition of every novelist in that at least two of his characters, Jeeves and Bertie Wooster, and possibly two others, Lord Emsworth and Psmith, have entered what Belloc called 'that long gallery of living figures which make up the glory of English fiction'. He also wrote more amusingly on golf than anyone before or since, *The Clicking of Cuthbert* (1922) and *The Heart of a Goof* (1926) being his masterpieces in this field.

In 1939 the University of Oxford made him an honorary D.Litt. and in 1975 he was created KBE. He died in a Long Island Hospital 14 February 1975, at the age of ninety-three, one of the most admired and probably the most loved of all the writers of his time.

[P. G. Wodehouse, *Performing Flea*, 1953 (autobiography); Richard Usborne, *Wodehouse at Work to the End*, 1977; Benny Green, *P. G. Wodehouse*, 1981; Iain Sproat, *Wodehouse at War*, 1981; James H. Heineman and Donald R. Bensen (eds.), *P. G. Wodehouse, a Centenary Celebration*, 1982; Frances Donaldson, *P. G. Wodehouse*, 1982; David A. Jasen, *P. G. Wodehouse*, 1982; personal knowledge.]

FRANCES DONALDSON

WOLFF, MICHAEL (1930–1976), journalist, author, and political adviser, was born 24 October 1930. He was adopted as a baby by Dr Max Wolff, a German Jewish barrister, who settled in Cheltenham, and his second wife. He was educated at Oakley Hall preparatory school, Cirencester, at Cheltenham College (1943–8), and at Wadham College, Oxford (1948–50). During his National Service he served with the Greenjackets, was commissioned into the Royal Fusiliers, and fought in Korea, attaining the rank of captain.

On his return to civilian life he became a journalist, working for a succession of newspapers—the *Sphere*, *John Bull*, *Truth*, of which he was deputy editor, the *Sunday Telegraph*, and the *Daily Express*, first as leader writer, then as its chief American correspondent. Of these, undoubtedly the *Express* and its owner, Lord Beaverbrook [q.v.], made the deepest mark, impressing upon him that the basic purpose of journalism is to communicate effectively to the reader speedily and accurately what is topical. He enjoyed the atmosphere of excitement and achievement which accompanied it. Yet he always concentrated on the substance of the matter and especially on any new aspect of it but never on the sensational for its own sake.

An opportunity for a closer connection between writing and politics came when he was appointed to organize and lead the research team for the official biography of Sir Winston Churchill, a task he undertook from 1961 to 1966. Here his ability to handle people stood him in good stead, especially with so volatile a person as its author, Randolph Churchill. On his death Michael Wolff might have expected to succeed him in completing this major historical work but this he was denied. During this time the London Bow Group provided the outlet he required for his political activities. The Group then represented by its attitude and policies the centre and centre-left of the Conservative Party with which Wolff was entirely in sympathy. From 1964 to 1966 he edited its journal *Crossbow*.

In 1966 he turned his full attention to practical politics, first as a member of the Conservative Research Department with special responsibilities to the leader in opposition, in 1970 as a special adviser to the lord president of the Council in the Conservative government, and in 1974, after the defeat of that government at the general election, as director-general of the Conservative Central Office. In all these positions he worked closely with Edward Heath both when leader of the opposition and as prime minister.

These activities did not prevent him from maintaining his compassionate though realistic interest in the penal system and its reform. He became a JP for inner London in 1967, and later deputy chairman of the west London bench and a member of the lord chancellor's advisory committee on JPs for inner London. He was meticulous in carrying out these responsibilities and seldom missed his turn to sit on the bench. The most important of his books, *Prison* (1967), is a comprehensive and detailed description of the prison system at that time together with recommendations for its reform.

At the Conservative Research Department he concentrated on organizing the research, briefing, and preparation of speeches for Edward Heath whom he accompanied on his numerous tours inside Britain, including the party conferences and the general election campaigns of both 1966 and 1970. As special adviser to the government he assisted the lord president of the Council in handling the government's public relations and also continued his work for the prime minister, especially during the 1974 general election campaign. He was well equipped for these responsibilities with qualities which he used to the full. His knowledge of political history gave him an admirable background as well as a sense of perspective. He had a remarkable ability to extract the kernel of a complicated argument and express it in phrases which made an immediate impact on an audience or a reader. His stamina allowed him to work long hours, often throughout the night, a special asset during party conferences when the leader's speeches were set against a deadline and yet had to deal with matters occurring up to the last moment. He was calm, patient, and seldom ruffled. His relations with the members of the press were close and understanding. The contribution he made to the Conservative Party behind the scenes for eight years was substantial.

With the knowledge he had acquired of the party organization and its officials, both voluntary and paid, throughout the country, the administrative capabilities he had displayed throughout the life of the Conservative government, his happy relationship with the media, and his natural gift of handling people it was not surprising that after the election of February 1974 Lord Carrington, chairman of the Conservative Party, appointed him director-general of the Conservative Party Organization with a remit to unify its various sections. He began this work with his customary energy and tact. When Margaret Thatcher succeeded Heath as leader of the party in March 1975, Wolff was peremptorily sacked. He was badly hit by this blow because his loyalty to the party and its leaders, whoever they may be, could never be doubted. Throughout this ordeal he retained his characteristic equanimity.

Wolff enjoyed life to the full. Books, music, pictures, wine and food, and sport were all his delight. He was an excellent host and head of the family. In 1956 he had married Rosemary Langley, daughter of Arthur Charles Victor Clarkson, advertising manager. They had two daughters. Wolff died suddenly from a heart attack near Liphook, Hampshire, 13 May 1976.

[Personal knowledge.] EDWARD HEATH

WOLMER, VISCOUNT, later third EARL OF SELBORNE (1887–1971), government minister and manager of Special Operations Executive. [See PALMER, ROUNDELL CECIL.]

WOODCOCK, GEORGE (1904–1979), general secretary of the Trades Union Congress, was born 20 October 1904, at Walton le Dale, Lancashire, the second of the four sons and of the five children of Peter Woodcock, cotton weaver (and later tackler), and his wife, Ann Baxendale. Woodcock went to Brownedge Roman Catholic Elementary School until he left for full-time employment as a cotton weaver when he was thirteen. At twelve, he had become a half-timer: one week he worked in the mill from 6 a.m. till 1 p.m. and attended school in the afternoon, the next week he went to school in the morning and worked in the mill till 5.30 p.m. At thirteen, he had two looms, and then three, and at fourteen he had four looms, as high as a weaver in those days could go.

His ambition was to become a professional footballer; his father and three uncles had played for Blackburn Rovers. Woodcock himself played for Brownedge in the Catholic League. He spent all his free time training, and later believed he had overdone it, for he suffered a long illness which ended his career as a weaver and a footballer.

He was a minor official of the Bamber Bridge and District Weavers' Union, and was active in the Independent Labour Party and the Labour Party. He was an election agent for Labour during the 1929 election, and at the same time worked for a TUC scholarship to Ruskin College, Oxford, which he won in 1929. In 1930 he won the Club and Institute Union scholarship, and in 1931 an extra-mural scholarship, being accepted by New College, Oxford. He took a first in philosophy, politics, and economics in 1933, and won the Jessie Theresa Rowden senior scholarship. He was later (1963) to be an honorary fellow of New College.

After two years (1934–6) in the Civil Service, Woodcock joined the TUC as head of the research and economic department. He remained in that post, working closely with Walter (later Lord) Citrine, the general secretary, until 1946; from the following year until 1960 he was assistant general secretary under Sir H. Vincent Tewson; and he was general secretary from 1960 until 1969. In 1969 he was appointed chairman of the Commission on Industrial Relations by Harold Wilson (later Lord Wilson of Rievaulx) but resigned two years later when Edward Heath tried to give the CIR legal functions under his Industrial Relations Act.

When he joined the TUC as its first young university-trained intellectual, the depression and unemployment were the dominant problems. Woodcock was captivated by the ideas of J. M. (later Lord) Keynes [q.v.]. He was proud of his part in the discussions which led to the 1944 white paper on employment policy, the charter of Britain's post-war economic consensus. There was one sentence he cherished, and he thought his career would have been worthwhile for it alone: 'The Government accept as one of their primary aims and responsibilities the maintenance of a high and stable level of employment after the war.' It was a sentence which was to dominate the thinking of all governments for thirty-five years, and to run like a silver thread through Woodcock's own life. For he foresaw—with an insight denied to most people in politics, Whitehall, industry, and the unions—that there was a price to be paid for full employment. From the era of Keynes, Ernest Bevin, and Sir R. Stafford Cripps [qq.v.] to that of Harold Macmillan (later the Earl of Stockton) and Harold Wilson, Woodcock was wrestling with the unresolved problems of all western societies: how to combine free trade unionism with reasonable freedom from inflation.

For Woodcock realized that the commitment of governments to full employment had shifted the balance of power in industry, so that unions now were often more powerful than employers. He rejected the attempts by various politicians to reverse this process by legislation, arguing that this 'peremptory' method of reform, while it might appeal to ministers working within the time-span of a single Parliament, led inevitably into short cuts that would prove to be culs-de-sac. This, Woodcock believed, was true of legislation on both industrial relations and on incomes policy: they might have some temporary effect, but so long as free trade unions existed they would leave no permanent system. His own life was devoted to bringing about reform by voluntary methods. His obsession was with the relationship between trade unions and government. Woodcock maintained that since unions drew their new authority from full employment, rather than from better organization or greater militancy, it was in their interests to see that governments adopted—or continued to adopt—economic and financial policies which would maintain full employment. And only trade-union co-operation, particularly in wage fixing, could allow governments to persist with such policies.

Consequently Woodcock's later life, particularly during those nine years when he led the TUC, was devoted to the education of both politicians and his own colleagues who headed the major unions and served on the TUC general council, about the subtlety and fragility of this relationship. On the one hand, he would say to ministers that unions were by nature organizations which could only respond to governments, and that therefore governments must put them under pressure by challenging them to undertake difficult tasks. Simultaneously he would be arguing against those in the TUC who saw their role—particularly during Conservative governments—as being a protest movement. 'We have left Trafalgar Square', he would say, maintaining that the TUC's primary task was not protest, but to work with ministers and civil servants in the corridors of Whitehall, so that benign economic policies would add to their members' prosperity, and make it secure.

One of Woodcock's great achievements was to persuade the TUC in 1962 to take part in the National Economic Development Council, created by a Conservative chancellor of the Exchequer, J. S. B. Selwyn Lloyd (later Lord Selwyn-Lloyd, q.v.). He hoped that it would ultimately develop into a major instrument of national planning, where the social partners—government, industry, and the unions—would commit themselves to policies of economic co-operation for the prosperity of all. When a Labour government was elected in 1964 Woodcock persuaded the TUC to accept a prices and incomes policy and individual unions to submit wage claims to the TUC before pursuing them. He agreed with the government's proposal to establish a royal commission on trade unions and employers' associations and was himself a member of it from 1965 to 1968.

In a paper Woodcock delivered to the British Association a few years before his death, he looked bleakly, and prophetically, at the alternatives: 'Neither the employers nor the trade unions could or would be willing to hand over their responsibilities or their powers to the State, and compulsion has been shown to be impracticable. The most likely alternative to co-operation is that governments will have to modify their commitment to maintain a high level of employment, and their consequential responsibilities for economic growth, stable prices and good industrial relations. If this country were to return to the industrial instability and the heavy unemployment of pre-war days, that would certainly not improve the ability of the trade unions collectively to secure greater social justice and fairness for their members.' Within three years of Woodcock's death, co-operation between government and unions had almost completely broken down, and there were three million unemployed in Britain.

Woodcock was also a member of the British Guiana constitutional commission in 1954, of the royal commission on the taxation of profits and incomes, 1952–5, and of the Radcliffe committee on the working of the monetary system, 1957–9. He was vice-chairman of the National Savings Committee (1952–75) and a member of the BBC advisory council.

George Woodcock delighted in conversation. He was a marvellous raconteur, particularly about his early life in Lancashire and at Oxford. An emotional man, he was an impassioned debater, by turns analytical and persuasive, his large and bushy eyebrows raised in protest at the irrationality of humankind. There was no more patient, and determined, exponent of the causes he believed in, but he retained a down-to-earth view that both politics and industrial relations were arts of the possible. This sometimes produced a Hamlet-like quality of philosophical introspection that those who knew how right his ideas were occasionally found irritating. Yet Woodcock throughout his career kept facing the unions with the fundamental question: 'What are we here for?' Although he knew his own answer, he could never persuade the trade-union leadership as a whole to think deeply enough about its response.

Woodcock had honorary degrees from Oxford (1964), Sussex (1963), Manchester (1968), Kent (1968), Aston in Birmingham (1967), Lancaster (1970), and London (1970). He became a freeman of the City of London in 1965. He was appointed CBE in 1953 and admitted to the Privy Council in 1967.

In 1933, while still a student, Woodcock married Laura Mary, also a devout Roman Catholic, daughter of Francis McKernan, an engine fitter, of Horwich in Lancashire. During his TUC years, they lived in Epsom, Surrey, where Mrs Woodcock was a magistrate and, successively, councillor, alderman, and mayor of the town. She was the first woman to be made a freeman of Epsom. They had a son and a daughter, both of whom went to Oxford. Woodcock died at Epsom District Hospital 30 October 1979.

[Personal knowledge.] JOHN COLE

WOODHAM-SMITH, CECIL BLANCHE (1896–1977), biographer and historian, was born 29 April 1896 at Tenby in Wales. Though her mother, Blanche Elizabeth Philipps, was Welsh, she felt Irish, since her father, Colonel James FitzGerald, an Indian Army officer who served in the Mutiny, belonged to the family of Lord Edward FitzGerald [q.v.], hero of the 1798 rising. Educated at the Royal School for Officers' Daughters, Bath, until expelled for rebelliously taking French leave to visit the National Gallery, she finished her schooling at a convent in France. At St. Hilda's College, Oxford, she took a second class in English in 1917, despite a term's rustication for joining Irish demonstrators in the streets. She then learnt typing and copywriting with an advertising firm.

In 1928 she married a distinguished London solicitor, George Ivon Woodham-Smith, her mainstay as woman and writer. But, like so many women of her period, she waited until her son and daughter were at boarding-school before beginning her literary career. Meanwhile she wrote pot-boilers under a pen-name. Her gift for fast narrative and human detail, she would say, was learnt at the feet of 'Janet Gordon'. To aspiring biographers her advice was: 'Keep the story moving'.

After nine years' research, writing, and rewriting, her first biography, *Florence Nightingale* (1950), won the James Tait Black memorial prize and carried her straight to the top. Wit, empathy, and finely sifted information showed what could be done with a Victorian subject conceived on the grand scale. Lytton Strachey [q.v.] had left

Florence Nightingale deftly debunked. (The Stracheys were good friends of the Woodham-Smiths, especially Lytton's brother Oliver.) Cecil Woodham-Smith built her up again into more than a legend; into a living complex woman. Those who afterwards had occasion to use the Nightingale papers in the British Library found that Cecil Woodham-Smith had missed nothing.

The Reason Why (1953) was no less dashing than the charge of the Light Brigade which it described, and became perhaps the most popular of her four masterpieces. It emerged organically from its predecessor, as did all her books; but whereas her *Florence Nightingale* involved much administrative detail, lucidly presented, *The Reason Why* hardly ever touched ground, except to expose low-down intrigues with the most beguiling irony. On television she explained how she wrote the charge itself, working at a gallop through thirty-six hours non-stop without food or other break until the last gun was fired, when she poured a stiff drink and slept for two days.

In *The Great Hunger* (1962), her Irish ancestry caused her to see the potato famine with the savage anger of Jonathan Swift [q.v.]. Her meticulously handled source material produced pictures of the potato disease and coffin-ships at once macabre and memorable. Some of her readers might have preferred to forget them. Historians had wondered whether she had not this time bitten off more than she could chew. But the general verdict was, 'She did not put a foot wrong'. In a review Conor Cruise O'Brien wrote that the book was 'One of the great works not only of Irish nineteenth-century history but of nineteenth-century history in general'. Later a younger school of Irish-born historians argued that Cecil Woodham-Smith was less than fair to the English home secretary, George Trevelyan. However, what she told her English readers about the horrors of the Irish famine was what they needed to hear.

The death of her husband in 1968 took some of the elasticity from her writing and great happiness from her life. Nevertheless *Queen Victoria: Her Life and Times*, volume i (1972), showed remarkable feats of research in the Windsor archives, for which she learnt old German script. A superlatively readable panorama resulted, studded with original case histories of characters like Sir John Conroy, Princess Victoria's bogeyman, and Sir George Anson, Prince Albert's private secretary. Her account of the Prince's death was the fullest and most moving ever written. The last sentence of this first volume showed her skill as the composer of biography, for it was both a conclusion and a looking forward. 'What is going to happen now', she quoted, 'to the poor Queen?' Sadly, Cecil Woodham-Smith did not live to answer that query. She died in London 16 March 1977.

Noel Blakiston, one of her close literary friends, recalled her aristocratic appearance, high-spirited entertaining, and long hours at the Public Record Office, her arrivals and departures made in a chauffeur-driven car. Another friend asked her, near her end, which of Queen Victoria's children she put next to the Queen herself. Raising her head, she said with the old flash of her bright blue eyes, 'None!'

She was appointed CBE in 1960, received honorary doctorates from the National University of Ireland, 1964, and St. Andrews, 1965, and became an honorary fellow of St. Hilda's, 1967.

[Private information; personal knowledge.]

ELIZABETH LONGFORD

WOODRUFF, (JOHN) DOUGLAS (1897–1978), Catholic journalist, scholar, and wit, was born at Wimbledon 8 May 1897, the second of three children and the younger son of Cumberland Woodruff, a barrister employed in the Public Record Office, and his wife, Emily Louisa, daughter of William Hewett, of Norton Fitzwarren Manor, Somerset. Although Cumberland Woodruff earned his living as keeper of the Chancery master's documents, his chief interest was in archaeology, which hobby earned him a fellowship of the Royal Society of Antiquaries and may have accounted in part for Douglas Woodruff's early absorption in history.

Both parents were of staunchly Protestant stock, but Emily Woodruff became a Catholic five years after her marriage and Douglas followed his widowed mother into the same church at the age of thirteen, being influenced, as he later said, by the writings of Robert Hugh Benson [q.v.]—among them *Come Rack, Come Rope* (1912). If so, it must be counted a signal achievement on the part of Benson (himself the son of an archbishop of Canterbury) although later influences—G. K. Chesterton [q.v.], whose works Woodruff collected long before Chesterton's conversion, and Hilaire Belloc [q.v.], who became a friend—may have been stronger on the grown man.

After education at St. Augustine's, Ramsgate, and, for a year, at Downside, Woodruff found himself, in 1916, rejected for military service on grounds of a weak heart. Instead he joined the Foreign Service, acting as vice-consul in Amsterdam in 1917–19, chiefly concerned with the repatriation of wounded soldiers and, later, prisoners of war.

It was not until 1920, at the age of twenty-three, that he took up his exhibition in modern history at New College, Oxford, where his qualities were soon recognized. Lothian prizeman in 1921, president of the Union in 1922, the year in which he completed the shortened course in *literae humaniores*, he won a first in modern history in 1923. Among fellow undergraduates, who included such distinguished Catholic converts as Evelyn Waugh, M. Christopher Hollis [qq.v.], and (Sir) Harold Acton, he was already seen as a venerable figure, as much for his age and slow, portly carriage, as for his enormous erudition and wit.

After Oxford he undertook a debating tour of the English-speaking world, in the company of Malcolm MacDonald and Christopher Hollis. This produced his first written work, *Plato's American Republic* (1926) which, despite its gentle humour, was thought to have given much offence in the United States. The experience may have reinforced a disinclination to give unnecessary offence which already existed in his gentle nature, and which stood him in good stead in the choppy waters of Catholic journalism.

At about this time he lost a part of what little fortune he possessed in a scheme to reinstate mead as the national drink of England. It did not prosper. After a short spell in academic life at Sheffield University, Woodruff turned to journalism and in 1926 became colonial editor of *The Times* under the editorship of G. Geoffrey Dawson [q.v.]. He held the post for ten years and was chiefly remembered as the inventor of the humorous fourth leader, although Dawson later claimed credit for this. A collection of his fourth leaders, called *Light and Leading*, was later published anonymously by *The Times*.

In 1936 he accepted editorship of the *Tablet*, then a moribund Roman Catholic weekly. There, for the next thirty years, his talents found their fullest expression until, on his resignation in 1967, he could boast that the *Tablet* was required reading for any student of foreign affairs, being received in every British embassy abroad and most foreign embassies in London.

His secret, apart from a formidable intellect and prodigious memory, was his unfailing interest in everything that happened. Nothing bored him. For thirty years readers of the *Tablet* were treated to a three-page unsigned weekly leading article which, in Woodruff's rolling English sentences, took them on a *tour d'horizon* of the whole domestic and foreign scene. His source of information was the entire Catholic Church, which, in its more sophisticated manifestations, beat a path to his door in Evelyn Mansions, Victoria.

He interpreted the world to English Roman Catholics at the same time as he interpreted Roman Catholicism to the outside world. A close friend of Pope Paul VI before his elevation to the papacy, Woodruff knew every bishop, cardinal, and foreign prelate of the slightest intellectual eminence. His own politics inclined towards conservatism—he was an early supporter of the rebel cause in Spain—and he found much to distress him in the post-Conciliar church. A further sorrow in his last years was to see the *Tablet*, now edited by another hand, embrace all the liberal Catholic causes which he found least congenial. He was deputy chairman of the publishers Burns & Oates (1948–62), director of Hollis & Carter (1948–62), chairman of Allied Circle (1947–62), and chairman of Associated Catholic Newspapers (1953–70).

He left no great work of scholarship by which he might be remembered, apart from the corpus of his weekly journalism, although his study of a famous Victorian court case, *The Tichborne Claimant* (1957), is noteworthy. Four selections from his signed notebook in the *Tablet*, 'Talking at Random', are unmistakable offspring of his learned and witty fourth leaders in *The Times*.

In 1933 he married Marie Immaculée Antoinette ('Mia') Acton, eldest daughter of Richard Maximilian, the second Baron Acton, of the Foreign Service. Although there were no children by the marriage, she filled his life with nephews and nieces so that, like Chesterton, he was constantly surrounded by younger people. She also dispensed the generous hospitality which was such a feature of his life at their large flat near Westminster Cathedral, and later at his country retreat, Marcham Priory, near Abingdon. When failing eyesight removed his greatest pleasure, she read to him, often through the night, so that he was still contributing witty articles to the *Tablet* until a short time before his death, which occurred at Marcham Priory 9 March 1978.

Among his published works were *Plato's American Republic* (1926), *The British Empire* (1929), *Plato's Britannia* (1930), *Charlemagne* (1934), *Great Tudors* (1935), *European Civilization: The Grand Tour* (1935), *The Story of the British Colonial Empire* (1939), *Talking at Random* (1941), *More Talking at Random* (1944), *Still Talking at Random* (1948), *Walrus Talk* (1954), *The Tichborne Claimant* (1957), *Church and State in History* (1962), *The Popes* (1964), and *The Life and Times of Alfred the Great* (1974). He also wrote several notices for this Dictionary. A study of Milton may yet be published posthumously. There is a portrait by Simon Elwes (1949) in the possession of his widow. He was appointed CBE in 1962. In 1968 he was awarded the Grand Cross of the Order of St. Gregory the Great.

[*The Times*, 11 March 1978; Mary Craig (ed.), *Woodruff at Random*, 1978; Evelyn Waugh, *Diaries*, 1976, and private papers; *Tablet*, 15 March 1978 and *passim*; personal knowledge.]

AUBERON WAUGH

WOODWARD, SIR (ERNEST) LLEWELLYN (1890–1971), historian, was born in Ealing 14 May 1890, the only son of George Ernest Woodward, admiralty civil servant, and his wife, Helen Thwaites. He had one sister. From the old Merchant Taylors' school he won a scholarship to Corpus Christi College, Oxford. He obtained a second class in *literae humaniores* (1911), followed by a first class in modern history (1913). In 1913–14, with a senior scholarship from St. John's College, he studied in Paris. During the war of 1914–18 he served with the artillery in France and then on the staff at Salonika. While on sick leave from France he completed his first book, *Christianity and Nationalism in the Later Roman Empire* (1916). On 19 September 1917 he married Florence Marie, youngest daughter of the Very Revd Robert Stuart O'Loughlin, dean of Dromore. In 1918 he was invalided home from Salonika and employed by the Foreign Office to write a short handbook on the 1878 Congress of Berlin in preparation for the Versailles peace conference.

After the war he was for three months a history master at Eton before returning to Oxford as lecturer at Keble College. In 1919 he was elected to a fellowship at All Souls. This he held until 1944, combining it from 1922 until 1939 with a lecturership at New College. He was domestic bursar of All Souls from 1925 and university senior proctor in 1927–8. In these years he published three volumes of essays upon nineteenth-century topics and two notable books. In *Great Britain and the German Navy* (1935), a primarily diplomatic study, he was one of the first English historians to make critical comparative use of the various nations' official publications of pre-war documents and to cast doubts upon the impartiality of the German series *Die grosse Politik der europäischen Kabinette*. In *The Age of Reform 1815–70* (Oxford History of England, vol. xiii, 1938, 2nd edn. 1962), while emphasizing the primacy 'of English politics centred in Westminster', he showed a remarkable range of knowledge and sympathy and fine mastery of his material. Believing that 'history does not repeat itself but historical situations recur', he was one of the first, in a letter to *The Times* on 27 March 1933, to warn against 'appeasing' Hitler's Germany. When war came in 1939 he was called back to the Foreign Office and became responsible for launching the *Documents on British Foreign Policy 1919–39*, of which for a decade from 1944 he was founding editor. He also wrote the official history of *British Foreign Policy in the Second World War* (1970–6). This was policy as seen from the Foreign Office, but based upon an impressive documentation. It was originally written 'for official reference' only and Woodward lived to see only one of its five volumes in print, although in 1962 he published a much condensed single volume version. The *Documents* came in for some criticism over their arrangement and their exclusion of most Foreign Office minutes, but remain a monument to Woodward's skill, judgement, and industry as an editor. He also published in 1942 his autobiographical *Short Journey* and in 1947 a very brief *History of England*. To this Dictionary he contributed the notice of W. H. Hudson.

In 1944 he returned to Oxford as professor of international relations, with a fellowship at Balliol College. He exchanged this in 1947 for a new chair of modern history, with the fellowship at Worcester College. But although he found Worcester most congenial, post-war Oxford and indeed the post-war world were less so. He felt that the university was somewhat too parochial, that the world was entering upon 'a phase of popular materialism and intellectual anarchy', and the atom bomb (as he wrote in a letter in August 1945), sounded to him 'like the turning up of the Last Trump'.

In 1951 he moved to the United States as research professor at the Princeton Institute for Advanced Study. He returned to Oxford in 1961, eventually to a house which he built in the grounds of Worcester and left to the college on his death. In 1967 he published *Great Britain and the War of 1914–1918*, but he spent these last years mainly upon his *British Foreign Policy in the Second World War*, four volumes of which he had revised before his death. Knighted in 1952, he was elected to honorary fellowships at Worcester, Corpus Christi, and All Souls colleges. As a historian Woodward did not, and would not have wished to, found a school or create a fashion, for he had a strong sense of what his favourite novelist Thomas Hardy called 'the mournful manysidedness of things' and he also believed strongly that 'a tutor ought to take the greatest care not to try to "convert" his pupils'. He was a man of broad interests and complex character, who enjoyed life but set no great store by material possessions; a good talker and lively letter writer; easier to get to know than to know well. In his youth he had thought of taking holy orders (some later nicknamed him 'the Abbé'), but the war of 1914–18 finally turned him to 'a sceptical but confident deism'.

Woodward's wife died in 1961. They had had no children. He himself died in Oxford 11 March 1971.

[*The Times*, 13 March 1971; Rohan Butler in *Proceedings* of the British Academy, vol. lvii, 1971; Llewellyn Woodward, *Short Journey*, 1942; letters in Worcester College, Oxford, archives; personal knowledge.]

R. B. WERNHAM

WOOLLEY, FRANK EDWARD (1887–1978), cricketer, was born 27 May 1887 at Tonbridge, the fourth and youngest son (there were no daughters) of Charles William Woolley, a motor engineer, of Tonbridge, and his wife, Louise Lewis, of Ashford.

At his birthplace young Kentish cricketers were schooled in the Tonbridge nursery on the

Angel ground and here Woolley, like most of his pre-World War I professional contemporaries, was coached to admirable effect by Captain William McCanlis. When his first chance came for Kent at Old Trafford in May 1906 he began by scoring 0, missing a catch, and taking one for 103. However, in the second innings he made 64, and, despite the wealth of talent available, by the end of the season had secured his place in the side which for the first time won the championship for Kent. Woolley was tall, spare, and upright of stature, and he batted left-handed with a power of stroke and uninhibited freedom which over a playing career of thirty-three seasons (less the four years of war) won him a unique place in the annals of the game. There was no batsman of whom bowlers stood more in awe. He seemingly disdained them all, as an estimated rate of scoring throughout his career of 55 runs an hour (based on his longer innings) bears ample testimony. Yet when he did opt for defence his bat was rigidly straight and his head unerringly behind the line of the ball.

After the middle 1920s Kent asked less of him as a bowler. Before the war however he was rated the best all-rounder in England, and on turning pitches his slow left-arm bowling delivered from his full height and with sharp finger-spin was often rated even more difficult than that of his friend with Kent and England, Colin ('Charlie') Blythe.

Only Sir Jack Hobbs [q.v.] has exceeded his aggregate of 58,969 runs. He shares with W. G. Grace [q.v.] the record of having made 1,000 runs twenty-eight times, in his case in successive seasons. Twelve of these times he reached 2,000, and, in 1928, 3,352. Only twenty-four bowlers have bettered his tally of 2,068 wickets, and only Wilfred Rhodes [q.v.] can match his all-round record. No one approaches his 1,017 catches, most of them taken at slip where his exceptional reach made them look, like everything else he did, deceptively easy. In his younger days he was adept anywhere, and he never lost the ability to throw flat, fast, and straight to the top of the stumps.

Massive though these figures are—and possible only in a strong, fit man dedicated to his profession—they are no adequate evidence of the measure of the enjoyment his cricket afforded. He was truly labelled the Pride of Kent, but in his last summer, 1938, at the age of fifty-one, the crowds rose to him all over England, and his reception at Lord's when, as captain of the Players, he came in to bat was as memorable to those present as Woolley's dignified acknowledgement. Standing at the crease with his bat in the 'order arms' position he raised his cap to left and right, before taking guard. He then, in scoring 41, gave an object-lesson in playing the fastest bowling against Kenneth Farnes, whose great speed earned him an analysis of eight for 43 in this match.

The first of Woolley's 145 hundreds was made in his first match at his native Tonbridge in 1906, according to Wisden 'in about an hour and a half'. In his last match there thirty-two years later he took a hundred off Worcestershire before lunch. He made no fetish of three figures however, and in fact was got out thirty-five times in the 90s.

As it happens, the two innings Woolley himself rated his best were those of 95 and 93 against Warwick Armstrong's victorious Australians at Lord's in 1921 when J. M. Gregory and E. A. McDonald, the fast bowlers, were at their peak. Since it is sometimes adduced from his test batting average of 36 that he was unduly vulnerable against the best bowling it is worth mentioning that, such was the strength of English batting, coupled with the value of his bowling, he never batted higher than No. 5 until he had played in eighteen of his sixty-four test matches. Before that he had been put in more often at No. 6, 7, or even 8. No opponent ever doubted his supreme quality, from Sir Donald Bradman downwards.

He married first in 1914 Sibyl Fordham, of Ashford, Kent; they had one son, Richard, killed in action at sea in 1940, and two daughters; she died in 1962; secondly in 1971 Martha Morse (née Wilson), of Akron, Ohio, widow of Major Sydney J. Morse, of the Royal Tank Corps. Woolley died 18 October 1978 at Chester, Nova Scotia.

[Frank Woolley, *The King of Games*, 1936; *Early Memoirs of Frank Woolley as told to Martha Woolley*, 1976; Ian Peebles, *Woolley, the Pride of Kent*, 1969; Oliver Warner, *Frank Woolley*, 1952; personal knowledge.] E. W. SWANTON

WYNDHAM, JOHN EDWARD REGINALD, first BARON EGREMONT and sixth BARON LECONFIELD (1920–1972), civil servant and author, was born at Windsor 5 June 1920, the third child in the family of one daughter and three sons of Edward Scawen Wyndham and his wife, Gladys Mary, daughter of FitzRoy James Wilberforce Farquhar. His father, fifth son of the second Baron Leconfield, was a professional soldier in the Life Guards and commanded his regiment before leaving the army in 1923 to live at Edmonthorpe in Leicestershire where Wyndham spent his childhood. Wyndham was educated at Eton, where he edited the Eton College *Chronicle*, and went up to Trinity College, Cambridge, in 1939 to read history. The war interrupted his university career and he left after a year to try to join the armed forces but was turned down on grounds of defective eyesight. He then applied to go into the Civil Service and was accepted by the Ministry of Supply. Here, after working in the purchasing and requisitioning department, he was appointed private secretary to the parliamentary under-secretary, Harold Macmillan (later the Earl of Stockton). Thus began a remarkable working relationship, which was to last until Macmillan's retirement from active politics some twenty-four years later, and a personal friendship which endured to the end of Wyndham's life.

For the rest of the war Macmillan and Wyndham were together. In 1942 Wyndham went to the Colonial Office where Macmillan had been moved as parliamentary under-secretary of state in charge of the economic section; and in 1943 he left for north Africa to work under Macmillan whom Churchill made minister resident (with Cabinet rank) at Allied Force Headquarters in Algiers. From here his work took him to Italy in 1944 at the time of the Allied invasion and to Greece during the revolution. Wyndham was appointed MBE in 1945.

After the end of the war in Europe, he went back to London to the Air Ministry, under Harold Macmillan who had been made secretary of state for air in Churchill's caretaker government. In 1945, on the fall of the caretaker government, Wyndham was transferred for a year to Washington as private secretary to R. H. (later Lord) Brand [q.v.], head of the British Treasury delegation and chairman of the British Supply Council in North America. Here he became involved in the negotiations for the celebrated American loan to Britain. On his return to England, Wyndham was offered a Treasury post in Egypt. But he left the Civil Service and made a journey with Macmillan (then in opposition) to Persia and India at the start of 1947. In this same year Wyndham joined the Conservative Research Department. Here he worked for five years alongside the brilliant band of young men—many of whom were later to make their mark in politics—assembled by the department's chairman, R. A. Butler (later Lord Butler of Saffron Walden). In 1952, however, he had to leave after the death of his uncle, the third Lord Leconfield, whose heir Wyndham was, to devote himself to the problems of his inheritance of the Wyndham family estates.

Family matters occupied the next few years. These included the negotiations with the Treasury over the large death duties and the principle, established for the first time, of the acceptance by the nation of works of art to help pay these. Wyndham moved to Petworth, and became a member of the West Sussex County Council and a magistrate. Then in 1955 Macmillan, by now foreign secretary, suggested that Wyndham might rejoin him as his private secretary. For a year the old relationship was renewed but in 1956 Wyndham had to return to Petworth again on his master becoming chancellor of the Exchequer; he was still negotiating with the Treasury over death duties and therefore could not work in that department. In this way Wyndham was absent from Whitehall throughout the Suez crisis and the succession of Macmillan to the prime ministership in January 1957. However in May 1957 the new prime minister wrote to ask if they might resume their old connection and later that year Wyndham joined the private office at 10 Downing Street. Here he remained until Macmillan's resignation in 1963, occupying a unique position of personal friend and professional adviser.

In 1963 Wyndham was created first Baron Egremont in recognition of his services during these years, and thus revived an extinct family title. He was introduced into the House of Lords on the same day as his father, who had recently succeeded as the fifth Baron Leconfield: the first time that father and son have taken their seats together.

Wyndham occupied the rest of his life with writing and the management of his estates. He contributed a column to the *Spectator*, and reviews and articles to other newspapers and periodicals; but the culmination of his literary work was his autobiography *Wyndham and Children First*, published in 1968, which enjoyed considerable commercial and critical success.

Wyndham had a remarkable, almost unique, effect upon the people he met during his short life. In the social world he was loved by a mass of friends, young and old, men and women. His wit, his charm, his originality and sometimes almost eccentricity, delighted all who knew him. In the political world it is difficult to find a parallel for the part he played. He brought to Whitehall all his humour, with its whimsical and often unexpected turns. Yet he was very discreet and very devoted to the interests of what he used to call his 'master'. Perhaps the only similar case was that of Montagu Corry (later Lord Rowton, q.v.). Both served prime ministers with complete devotion; both were young, charming, and commanded not merely the affection but the respect of their chiefs. Both were recommended for peerages on their masters' resignation, the first by Lord Beaconsfield, the second by Harold Macmillan.

In 1947 Wyndham married Pamela, youngest daughter of Captain Valentine Maurice Wyndham-Quin, RN, younger son of the fifth Earl of Dunraven. They had two sons and one daughter. Egremont died at Petworth House, Sussex, 6 June 1972 and was succeeded by his elder son, (John) Max (Henry Scawen) Wyndham (born 1948). A drawing by Augustus John and a bust by Fiore de Henriques are in the possession of the family.

[Personal knowledge.] HAROLD MACMILLAN

WYN-HARRIS, SIR PERCY (1903–1979), colonial governor, mountaineer, and yachtsman, was born at Acton, London, 24 August 1903, the eldest of the three sons and the second of the five children of Percy Martin Harris, company director, and his wife, Catherine Mary Davies. He was educated at Gresham's School and at Gonville and Caius College, Cambridge, where he obtained a second class in part i of the natural sciences tripos in 1925. At Cambridge he gained a half-blue for cross-country running and was secretary of the Mountaineering Club, which pioneered the guideless climbs then frowned on by the Alpine establishment. He aspired to a career in business, but having found vacation work in a cement works and, on going down, employment as a moulder in the family iron foundry far too dull, he applied for the Sudan Service and for the Colonial Service.

Posted to Kenya in 1926, Harris (he added the hyphen in 1953, having been named Wynne on his birth certificate), was to spend the next twenty years in district administration, rising steadily from district officer to settlement officer for Kikuyu land claims (1939–40) arising from the Carter commission of 1932, to district commissioner among nomadic Turkana, in crowded Kakamega, urban Nairobi, and in Kitui and Nyeri. In 1944–6 he was labour commissioner (his department's memorandum was one of the administration's earliest proposals to solve the squatter problem), and from 1947 to 1949 he was chief native commissioner and member for African affairs on the governor's executive council. His appointment as governor of The Gambia in 1949 was to result in its longest governorship since the turn of the century. He quickly galvanized the place, for he was, as Elspeth Huxley once said, 'not the sort to paddle backwards'.

On retirement to Suffolk in 1958, it was not long before his profound and sympathetic experience of African administration was invoked. In 1959 he was appointed to the commission of inquiry led by Sir P. A. (later Lord) Devlin into the disturbances which had rocked Nyasaland and resulted in the arrest of the nationalist leader Hastings Banda. No sooner was this difficult task completed than Wyn-Harris was again called upon, to take on the unique post, in decolonizing Africa, of Britain's administrator of the Northern Cameroons during the interim period of plebiscite about the future of the trust territory areas of Northern Nigeria (October 1960–June 1961). His relationships with the administrators of Nigeria, by then an independent country, required all Wyn-Harris's gifted combination of correctness, courage, and courtesy.

But if Wyn-Harris made his mark as a notable colonial administrator, he also made his name as a distinguished mountaineer. Taking advantage of his posting to Kenya, he profited from his local leaves and in 1929, along with Eric Shipton [q.v.], at that time a young settler, he made a successful ascent of the Batian peak of Mt. Kenya, only the second such climb since (Sir) Halford Mackinder [q.v.] reached the summit in the 1890s; they also became the first mountaineers to scale its other peak, Nelion. Two years later another first came Wyn-Harris's way, his visit to North Island on Lake Rudolf. Then, despite the routine of district life in Kenya, he earned a place among the fourteen picked for the 1933 assault on Mt. Everest led by Hugh Ruttledge [q.v.]. With the blessing of the colonial government but without pay, he and L. R. Wager [q.v.], another newcomer to the Himalayas, participated in the first ascent, reaching an altitude of 8,500 metres. It was Wyn-Harris who retrieved the ice-axe, probably that of G. L. Mallory [q.v.], from the site of the 1924 disaster. When the 1936 Everest expedition was assembled, again led by Hugh Ruttledge, Wyn-Harris's reputation at once ensured his nomination. On both expeditions he narrowly missed death on the slopes. Subsequently Lord Hunt, who led the triumphant 1952–3 Everest expedition, was to number him among the 'stout spirits' of the Everest saga.

If Wyn-Harris's transfer from mountainous Kenya to sea-level Gambia spelled finis to one recreation, it was not to end his prominence as a sportsman. In the Atlantic-swept estuary off Bathurst he took up sailing, long a second string to his recreational bow (in Nairobi, he had built his own boat in his garden). He spent his leaves in the discomfort of a four-ton yawl, sailed single-handed to Accra to attend Ghana's independence celebrations, and in his retirement was to fill several years unhurriedly circumnavigating the world in nothing more solid than a twelve-ton sloop, the *Spurwing*. As chief commissioner, he had already exploited his ability to fly solo by making sudden safaris to outlying bomas. Determined and adventurous rather than a master of do-it-yourself (he was, in fact, all fingers and thumbs in his construction work), and an amateur photographer who had filmed the 1933 Everest expedition, Wyn-Harris was an obvious choice to tour the dominions as the special representative of the Duke of Edinburgh's award in 1962–3.

Quick of speech and friendy, yet with a positive sense of authority in his build (that of the ideal mountaineer) and manner, P. Wyn, as he was widely known, was tough, stocky, and 'packed with Welsh pugnacity and vigour' (Huxley). A glutton for work, he was intolerant of slovenly standards and disloyalty to the Service.

Wyn-Harris was appointed MBE in 1941 and CMG in 1949, being advanced to KCMG in 1952. He was twice married. In 1932 he married Mary Moata ('Mo'), daughter of Ranald Macintosh Macdonald, CBE, civil engineer, of Christchurch, New Zealand. She died in 1976, and later that year he married Julie Gunning-Scheltem, widow of Maximiliaan Frederik Gunning, a Dutch naval architect. From the first marriage there was one son, Timothy, born in 1934. Wyn-Harris died at Petersfield, Hampshire, 25 February 1979.

[*The Times*, 23 November and 17 December 1979; *West Africa*, 19 November 1949; *Colonial Office List*; A. H. M. Kirk-Greene (ed.), *Biographical Dictionary of the British Colonial Governor*, 1980; W. H. Murray, *The Story of Everest*, 1953; Elspeth Huxley, *Four Guineas*, 1954; Hugh Ruttledge, *Everest*, 1933; unpublished autobiography; private information.]

A. H. M. Kirk-Greene

WYNNE-EDWARDS, Sir ROBERT MEREDYDD (1897–1974), civil engineer, was born 1 May 1897 at Cheltenham, the eldest in the family of four sons and two daughters of the Revd John Rosindale Wynne-Edwards, schoolmaster and later headmaster of Leeds Grammar School and canon of Ripon Cathedral, and his wife, Lilian Agnes Streatfield, daughter of Champion Welbank. Educated at Giggleswick and Leeds Grammar School, at the outbreak of war in 1914 he joined the Royal Army Medical Corps and on reaching the age of eighteen obtained a commission in the Royal Welch Fusiliers in October 1914. He served in France from December 1915, being mentioned in dispatches, awarded the MC, appointed to the DSO (1919), and promoted temporary major.

On demobilization in January 1919 he went to Christ Church, Oxford, and obtained second class honours in engineering science (1921). In July 1921 his adventurous spirit took him to Canada where he accumulated a mass of varied experience with consulting engineers and contractors both in design and construction of harbour works, dams, bridges, deep foundations, earth moving, piling, caisson sinking, and tunnelling in rock and in compressed air in soft ground, notably on the Detroit–Windsor tunnel. At the early age of twenty-eight he was awarded a Telford prize by the Institution of Civil Engineers of which he had become a member for his paper on unusual concrete piling in Vancouver harbour. There he often inspected work under water as a trained full-suit diver. He also joined the American Society of Civil Engineers and studied Karl Terzaghi's vital work on his new science of soil mechanics.

When in 1934 Canadian engineering collapsed in the slump he brought his family back to England. In 1935 he joined John Mowlem & Co., with the task of building an earth-bank reservoir for the Metropolitan Water Board at Chingford, using the first fleet of newly-developed American earth-moving equipment to reach Britain. In 1937 a length of newly-compacted bank collapsed and the fall was studied by some young engineers in the Building Research Station who were studying soil mechanics. They proved that the slip had occurred through a bed of soft clay for the removal of which Wynne-Edwards had pressed unsuccessfully. When elderly consultants derided this idea Wynne-Edwards traced Terzaghi to Paris, flew over, and persuaded him to represent the firm. Terzaghi emphatically supported the BRS solution and was asked to redesign the bank to suit tests on the site. He then delivered the James Forrest lecture to the Institution of Civil Engineers with the title 'Soil Mechanics—a New Chapter in Engineering Science', and was also asked to lecture in universities. These events, of which Wynne-Edwards was the catalyst, led to the rapid spread of the science of soil mechanics in Britain.

From the start of World War II in 1939 Wynne-Edwards's work in building a shell-filling factory at Swynnerton so impressed the Ministry of Works that it asked his firm to lend him as their director of plant for the rest of the war. His wide experience was invaluable, especially as chairman of joint Anglo-American committees. He was appointed OBE in 1944.

After the war he became a director of Richard Costain Ltd. and in 1948 became managing director of a new consortium—Costain John Brown (CJB), later to become the wholly-owned Constructors John Brown. This was formed to break the American monopoly in combined design and construction of oil refineries and chemical works at home and abroad. He pioneered British pipe laying, especially on the Abadan–Tehran pipe line, laying up to three miles in a day. When he reached the age of sixty-five he continued as a director of CJB, spending even more of his time in serving his profession. A keen supporter of the Institution of Civil Engineers, he won awards for several papers and was elected to its council in 1950, becoming the hundredth president in 1963–4 and the first serving contractor so to be. He also undertook to be the founder-chairman of the newly formed Council of Engineering Institutions for 1964–5.

He served from 1960 to 1965 as chairman both of the Building Research Board and of the Road Research Board for which he was appointed CBE in 1962. He was knighted in 1965. He was an honorary member of the Institution of Structural Engineers and the American Society of Civil Engineers, an honorary fellow of Manchester Institute of Science and Technology (1965), and in 1969 president of the Manchester Technology Association. He was also an honorary D.Sc. of Salford University (1966).

Wynne-Edwards was witty, modest, and a restful and entertaining companion, who also took care of his staff. He was a keen naturalist and read widely. After the war while professionally busy he found time to keep bees, develop gardens, and keep horses for light-hearted hunting with the Old Surrey and Burstow.

In 1924 he married Hope Elizabeth Day, daughter of Francis Fletcher, surveyor, of Nelson, British Columbia. They had one son and three daughters. He retired to Blandford but died in Southport General Hospital 22 June 1974 after an accident while on a visit to a daughter.

[Institution of Civil Engineers; private information; personal knowledge.]

HAROLD HARDING

Y

YORKE, HENRY VINCENT (1905–1973), writer under the name of HENRY GREEN, was born 29 October 1905 at Forthampton Court, near Tewkesbury, Gloucestershire, the third son and youngest of three children (the eldest died at the age of sixteen) of Vincent Wodehouse Yorke, who had manufacturing interests in the midlands, and his wife, Maud Evelyn, daughter of Henry Wyndham, second Baron Leconfield. He was educated at Eton and at Magdalen College, Oxford. After leaving Oxford early, under family pressure, he spent an apprenticeship in one of the firm's factories, and he thereafter looked after the firm's affairs from its London office.

Henry Green was one of the most original prose writers of his generation. He was the author of nine novels, one autobiographical book (*Pack My Bag*, 1940), and a number of shorter pieces which were published in various periodicals. The first of his novels, *Blindness*, was begun while he was still at Eton and published in 1926. He followed this in 1929 with *Living*, already remarkable for his prose style. After a ten-year interval came *Party Going* (1939). At the outbreak of war he joined the Auxiliary Fire Service, and his next novel, *Caught* (1943), was based on his experiences in the Fire Service during the London blitz. All his subsequent books also had one-word titles, *Loving* (1945), *Back* (1946), *Concluding* (1948), *Nothing* (1950), and *Doting* (1952). After the publication of the last-named he fell silent for the remainder of his life.

His novels show above all an extraordinarily acute ear for the way people talk in the most various walks of life; from the factory hands in *Living*, the domestic servants in *Loving*, the state bureaucrats in *Concluding*, and the upper-class rich in *Party Going*. His last two novels were deliberately created almost entirely out of dialogue. His prose style was distinctly his own and consisted mainly of very simple words and an idiosyncratic syntax, which might make the unwary reader embarking on one of his novels for the first time imagine he was dealing with a novice writer with little experience of language—until he gradually became aware of the extreme sophistication of the artifice, which concealed a hilarious sense of comedy and a capacity to rise to passages of pure poetic description, as in the extended dreamy metaphors which illuminate the scene of the overcrowded fog-bound railway terminus in *Party Going* and the glimpses the reader is given of the romantic flower-filled park surroundings of the State Institution (formerly a private estate) in the futuristic fantasy of *Concluding*.

His peak scenes of comedy nearly always arise from confusion and misunderstanding, as in *Loving* when Mrs Tennant confronts Mrs Welch, her drunken cook, about her mislaid sapphire ring, and, in *Concluding*, when there are muddled rumours about the disappearance of the student Mary and her doll. Henry Green revels in such confusions, and extracts the maximum of humour from them, while never giving the reader satisfactory explanations. Mary's disappearance remains a mystery, though it is hinted that some of the other young girls know the real answer. Henry Green seems in such scenes to suggest that there are puzzles in life which one can never solve however hard one enlists the aid of reason.

His use of symbolism is often closely connected with his sense of the irrational in human life. There seems no reason why Miss Fellowes's discovery of and concern for the dead pigeon should play such an important part in *Party Going* until one sees, or rather feels intuitively, what an effective foil it is to the behaviour of the stranded upper-class passengers locked in the hotel while the fog stops all trains. Birds appear again and again as his obsessive symbols: for instance, the peacocks in *Loving*, the starlings that gather in the trees of the park at sunset in *Concluding*, and Mr Rock's goose. There are other symbols, too, which he delights to introduce: he uses the word 'rose' in *Back* to create a maximum of both confusion and poetic suggestion; and throughout his work roses and other flowers appear, to give the hint of another dimension to the foreground action.

Henry Green's novels, in fact, move us not only by their cunning mixture of comedy and poetry, their subtle strokes of characterization, and the bravura dramatic descriptions of human crisis, as in *Caught* and some of the shorter fire-fighting pieces, but also by their sense of the mystery and strangeness of life, which lingers like a haunting melody long after we have come to the last page.

Henry Green was an extremely lively conversationalist, and delighted in not always unmalicious gossip about his Eton and Oxford contemporaries who had become part of the literary world. He also told very amusing stories about his meetings with business delegates from abroad, particularly—during the war—from the Soviet Union. He seldom spoke about his work as a writer, and almost never about politics. In fact he gave the impression that he thought of politicians as rather inferior beings. He had a lasting dislike of being photographed full-face, with the result that nearly all the pictures that have survived are of the back of his head.

In 1929 he married Adelaide Mary, daughter of John Michael Gordon Biddulph, second

Baron Biddulph. They had one son. Green was a bedridden invalid during his last years. He died in London 13 December 1973.

[Henry Green, *Pack my Bag*, 1940; personal knowledge.] JOHN LEHMANN

YOUNGER, SIR KENNETH GILMOUR (1908–1976), politician and reformer, was born 15 December 1908 at Colton, Dunfermline, Fife, the second child and younger son (there were also two daughters) of James Younger (later second Viscount Younger of Leckie), the son of the first Viscount [q.v.], who was chairman of the Conservative Party. His mother was Maud, daughter of Sir John Gilmour, baronet, and sister of Sir John Gilmour [q.v.], a Conservative secretary of state for Scotland. Such parentage did not prevent Younger from joining the Labour Party which he did as a young man after leaving New College, Oxford, which he had entered from Winchester. In 1930 he obtained a third class degree in philosophy, politics, and economics.

In 1932 Younger was called to the bar (Inner Temple) and practised up to 1939. During the war he served in the Intelligence Corps, finishing as a temporary major on the staff of Field Marshal Montgomery (later Viscount Montgomery of Alamein, q.v.).

After the general election of 1945, at which he was returned as Labour member for Grimsby, he seemed set on a political career destined to take him to the highest office. Almost at once he was attached as parliamentary private secretary to the minister of state at the Foreign Office. Thus he put down the root of one of the interests he was to follow all his life, the promotion of international goodwill and the development of supra-national institutions.

In December 1945 he was sent as a British alternate delegate to the UN and in 1946 was appointed chairman of the European committee of the United Nations Relief and Rehabilitation Administration. In 1947 he moved to the Home Office after a brief spell in the Ministry of Civil Aviation and there put down the root of his other interest, individual rights and penal reform.

In the Parliament of 1950–1 he was minister of state at the Foreign Office under Ernest Bevin [q.v.]. Owing to Bevin's ill health a great deal of the work fell to Younger in the difficult and shifting world of post-war international relations. These two, looking, as someone remarked, like an old polar bear attended by a lively cub, became a familiar and welcome sight in the House of Commons. Younger was an outstandingly efficient departmental minister who inspired trust and affection in those with whom he dealt, and some of the acclaim which has rightly been accorded to Bevin as foreign secretary should be shared by his minister of state. In 1951 he was made a privy councillor.

Though Younger joined the shadow cabinet after 1951 when Labour went into opposition his heart was not in the often negative and wearisome battles which an opposition must wage. He was essentially constructive. Nor could he pretend to an indignation he did not feel which is a faculty considered essential to the ambitious. He was in politics not for the glittering prizes but to achieve results in his chosen fields. When he felt this could be done better by service elsewhere he felt no great compulsion to stay in Parliament. So in 1959 he left the House of Commons and shortly afterwards became director of Chatham House—the Royal Institute of International Affairs.

Here he was able to return to one of his main interests—foreign policy. Younger realized sooner than most people that Britain was no longer an imperial power nor a superpower but that her role lay through the UN and world and regional co-operation. To such co-operation Younger believed Britain could bring particular talents through her long experience and through her position on the Atlantic seaboard of Europe and in the Commonwealth.

In the meantime he maintained his interest in legal and penal matters. From 1966 he was chairman of the advisory council on the penal system. In 1970 he was appointed chairman of the committee of inquiry into privacy. In 1972 he was a member of the committee on Northern Ireland chaired by Lord Diplock and for thirteen years from 1960 to 1973 chairman of the Howard League for Penal Reform. He served on many other bodies and was a governor of St. George's Hospital. In 1968 he was given an honorary doctorate by St. John's University, New York, and in 1972 appointed KBE.

He published and edited various Fabian and other essays connected with his public work. He contributed the notice of Hector McNeil to this Dictionary. *A Study in International Affairs* (ed. Roger P. Morgan, 1972) was compiled in his honour.

His premature death deprived the country of an able and unselfish public servant and his friends of a delightful and incisive companion. His modesty, his innocent appearance, and his courtesy could mislead casual acquaintances. They would be brought up short by his precise and often radical opinions caustically expressed. He was no tolerator of slovenliness. Indeed at Chatham House he ruthlessly weeded out those whom he felt had nothing to contribute however venerable and respected they might be. His own contributions whether in formal meetings or private conversation were invariably to the point. He was in the tradition of practical reformers. He had no great interest in fashionable dogma but to the end developed his opinions from a firm belief in the possibility of improving the human lot by firm guidance of the institutions at our command. In 1934 he married Elizabeth Kirsteen, daughter of William Duncan Stewart JP, of Achara, Duror, Argyll, a wife who matched his abilities and his temperament. They had one son and two daughters. Younger died at his London home 19 May 1976.

[Personal knowledge.] J. GRIMOND

CUMULATIVE INDEX

TO THE BIOGRAPHIES CONTAINED IN THE SUPPLEMENTS OF THE DICTIONARY OF NATIONAL BIOGRAPHY

1901–1980

Backhouse, Sir Edmund Trelawny 1873–1944
Backhouse, Sir Roger Roland Charles 1878–1939
Bacon, John Mackenzie 1846–1904
Bacon, Sir Reginald Hugh Spencer 1863–1947
Badcock, Sir Alexander Robert 1844–1907
Baddeley, Mountford John Byrde 1843–1906
Badeley, Henry John Fanshawe, Baron 1874–1951
Baden-Powell, Olave St. Clair, Lady 1889–1977
Baden-Powell, Robert Stephenson Smyth, Baron 1857–1941
Bagrit, Sir Leon 1902–1979
Bailey, Sir Abe 1864–1940
Bailey, Cyril 1871–1957
Bailey, Sir Edward Battersby 1881–1965
Bailey, Frederick Marshman 1882–1967
Bailey, Sir George Edwin 1879–1965
Bailey, John Cann 1864–1931
Bailey, Kenneth 1909–1963
Bailey, Mary, Lady 1890–1960
Bailey, Philip James 1816–1902
Bailhache, Sir Clement Meacher 1856–1924
Baillie, Charles Wallace Alexander Napier Ross Cochrane-, Baron Lamington 1860–1940
Baillie, Sir James Black 1872–1940
Bain, Alexander 1818–1903
Bain, Francis William 1863–1940
Bain, Sir Frederick William 1889–1950
Bain, Robert Nisbet 1854–1909
Bainbridge, Francis Arthur 1874–1921
Baines, Frederick Ebenezer 1832–1911
Baird, Andrew Wilson 1842–1908
Baird, John Logie 1888–1946
Bairnsfather, Charles Bruce 1888–1959
Bairstow, Sir Edward Cuthbert 1874–1946
Bairstow, Sir Leonard 1880–1963
Bajpai, Sir Girja Shankar 1891–1954
Baker, Sir Benjamin 1840–1907
Baker, Sir Geoffrey Harding 1912–1980
Baker, Henry Frederick 1866–1956
Baker, Sir Herbert 1862–1946
Baker, Herbert Brereton 1862–1935
Baker, James Franklin Bethune-. See Bethune-Baker 1861–1951
Baker, Shirley Waldemar 1835–1903
Balcarres, Earl of. See Lindsay, David Alexander Robert 1900–1975
Balcon, Sir Michael Elias 1896–1977
Baldwin, Stanley, Earl Baldwin of Bewdley 1867–1947
Baldwin Brown, Gerard. See Brown 1849–1932
Balewa, Alhaji Sir Abu Bakar Tafawa. See Tafawa Balewa 1912–1966
Balfour, Sir Andrew 1873–1931
Balfour, Arthur, Baron Riverdale 1873–1957
Balfour, Arthur James, Earl of Balfour 1848–1930
Balfour, Lady Frances 1858–1931
Balfour, George William 1823–1903
Balfour, Gerald William, Earl of Balfour 1853–1945
Balfour, Henry 1863–1939
Balfour, Sir Isaac Bayley 1853–1922
Balfour, John Blair, Baron Kinross 1837–1905
Balfour, Sir Thomas Graham 1858–1929
Balfour of Burleigh, Baron. See Bruce, Alexander Hugh 1849–1921
Balfour-Browne, William Alexander Francis 1874–1967
Ball, Albert 1896–1917
Ball, Francis Elrington 1863–1928
Ball, Sir (George) Joseph 1885–1961
Ball, John 1861–1940
Ball, Sir Robert Stawell 1840–1913
Ballance, Sir Charles Alfred 1856–1936
Ballantrae, Baron. See Fergusson, Bernard Edward 1911–1980
Balniel, Lord. See Lindsay, David Alexander Robert 1900–1975
Banbury, Frederick George, Baron Banbury of Southam 1850–1936
Bancroft, Marie Effie (formerly Wilton), Lady (1839–1921). See under Bancroft, Sir Squire Bancroft
Bancroft, Sir Squire Bancroft 1841–1926
Bandaranaike, Solomon West Ridgeway Dias 1899–1959
Bandon, Earl of. See Bernard, Percy Ronald Gardner 1904–1979
Bankes, Sir John Eldon 1854–1946
Banks, Sir John Thomas 1815?–1908
Banks, Leslie James 1890–1952
Banks, Sir William Mitchell 1842–1904
Bannerman, Sir Henry Campbell-. See Campbell-Bannerman 1836–1908
Banting, Sir Frederick Grant 1891–1941
Bantock, Sir Granville Ransome 1868–1946
Barbellion, W. N. P., *pseudonym*. See Cummings, Bruce Frederick 1889–1919
Barbirolli, Sir John (Giovanni Battista) 1899–1970
Barbour, Sir David Miller 1841–1928
Barcroft, Sir Joseph 1872–1947
Bardsley, John Wareing 1835–1904
Barger, George 1878–1939
Baring, (Charles) Evelyn, Baron Howick of Glendale 1903–1973
Baring, Evelyn, Earl of Cromer 1841–1917
Baring, Maurice 1874–1945
Baring, Rowland Thomas, Earl of Cromer 1877–1953
Baring, Thomas George, Earl of Northbrook 1826–1904
Baring-Gould, Sabine 1834–1924
Barker, Sir Ernest 1874–1960
Barker, Harley Granville Granville-. See Granville-Barker 1877–1946
Barker, Sir Herbert Atkinson 1869–1950
Barker, Dame Lilian Charlotte 1874–1955

Boot, Jesse, Baron Trent	1850–**1931**
Booth, Charles	1840–**1916**
Booth, Hubert Cecil	1871–**1955**
Booth, William ('General' Booth)	1829–**1912**
Booth, William Bramwell	1856–**1929**
Boothby, Guy Newell	1867–**1905**
Boothman, Sir John Nelson	1901–**1957**
Borden, Sir Robert Laird	1854–**1937**
Borg Olivier, Giorgio (George). See Olivier	1911–**1980**
Borthwick, Algernon, Baron Glenesk	1830–**1908**
Bosanquet, Bernard	1848–**1923**
Bosanquet, Sir Frederick Albert	1837–**1923**
Bosanquet, Robert Carr	1871–**1935**
Bose, Satyendranath	1894–**1974**
Boswell, John James	1835–**1908**
Boswell, Percy George Hamnall	1886–**1960**
Bosworth Smith, Reginald. See Smith	1839–**1908**
Botha, Louis	1862–**1919**
Bottomley, Gordon	1874–**1948**
Bottomley, Horatio William	1860–**1933**
Boucherett, Emilia Jessie	1825–**1905**
Boucicault, Dion, the younger	1859–**1929**
Boughton, George Henry	1833–**1905**
Boughton, Rutland	1878–**1960**
Bourchier, Arthur	1863–**1927**
Bourchier, James David	1850–**1920**
Bourdillon, Sir Bernard Henry	1883–**1948**
Bourinot, Sir John George	1837–**1902**
Bourke, Robert, Baron Connemara	1827–**1902**
Bourne, Francis Alphonsus	1861–**1935**
Bourne, Gilbert Charles	1861–**1933**
Bourne, Henry Richard Fox	1837–**1909**
Bourne, Robert Croft	1888–**1938**
Bousfield, Henry Brougham	1832–**1902**
Bovenschen, Sir Frederick Carl	1884–**1977**
Bowater, Sir Eric Vansittart	1895–**1962**
Bowden, Frank Philip	1903–**1968**
Bowen, Edmund John	1898–**1980**
Bowen, Edward Ernest	1836–**1901**
Bowen, Elizabeth Dorothea Cole	1899–**1973**
Bower, Frederick Orpen	1855–**1948**
Bowes, Robert	1835–**1919**
Bowes-Lyon, Claude George, Earl of Strathmore and Kinghorne	1855–**1944**
Bowhill, Sir Frederick William	1880–**1960**
Bowlby, Sir Anthony Alfred	1855–**1929**
Bowler, Henry Alexander	1824–**1903**
Bowles, Thomas Gibson	1842–**1922**
Bowley, Sir Arthur Lyon	1869–**1957**
Bowman, Sir James	1898–**1978**
Bowra, Sir (Cecil) Maurice	1898–**1971**
Boyce, Sir Rubert William	1863–**1911**
Boycott, Arthur Edwin	1877–**1938**
Boyd, Henry	1831–**1922**
Boyd, Sir Thomas Jamieson	1818–**1902**
Boyd Carpenter, William. See Carpenter	1841–**1918**
Boyd Orr, John, Baron. See Orr, John Boyd	1880–**1971**
Boyle, Sir Courtenay Edmund	1845–**1901**
Boyle, Sir Edward	1848–**1909**
Boyle, George David	1828–**1901**
Boyle, Richard Vicars	1822–**1908**
Boyle, William Henry Dudley, Earl of Cork and Orrery	1873–**1967**
Boys, Sir Charles Vernon	1855–**1944**
Brabazon, Hercules Brabazon	1821–**1906**
Brabazon, John Theodore Cuthbert Moore-, Baron Brabazon of Tara	1884–**1964**
Brabazon, Reginald, Earl of Meath	1841–**1929**
Bracken, Brendan Rendall, Viscount	1901–**1958**
Brackenbury, Sir Henry	1837–**1914**
Brackley, Herbert George	1894–**1948**
Bradbury, John Swanwick, Baron	1872–**1950**
Braddon, Sir Edward Nicholas Coventry	1829–**1904**
Braddon, Mary Elizabeth. See Maxwell	1837–**1915**
Bradford, Sir Edward Ridley Colborne	1836–**1911**
Bradford, Sir John Rose	1863–**1935**
Bradley, Andrew Cecil	1851–**1935**
Bradley, Francis Herbert	1846–**1924**
Bradley, George Granville	1821–**1903**
Bradley, Henry	1845–**1923**
Bradwell, Baron. See Driberg, Thomas Edward Neil	1905–**1976**
Bragg, Sir William Henry	1862–**1942**
Bragg, Sir (William) Lawrence	1890–**1971**
Braid, James	1870–**1950**
Brailsford, Henry Noel	1873–**1958**
Brain, Dennis	1921–**1957**
Brain, Walter Russell, Baron	1895–**1966**
Braithwaite, Dame (Florence) Lilian	1873–**1948**
Braithwaite, Sir Walter Pipon	1865–**1945**
Brambell, Francis William Rogers	1901–**1970**
Brampton, Baron. See Hawkins, Henry	1817–**1907**
Bramwell, Sir Byrom	1847–**1931**
Bramwell, Sir Frederick Joseph	1818–**1903**
Brancker, Sir William Sefton	1877–**1930**
Brand, Henry Robert, Viscount Hampden	1841–**1906**
Brand, Herbert Charles Alexander	1839–**1901**
Brand, Robert Henry, Baron	1878–**1963**
Brandis, Sir Dietrich	1824–**1907**
Brangwyn, Sir Frank (François Guillaume)	1867–**1956**
Brassey, Thomas, Earl	1836–**1918**
Bray, Caroline	1814–**1905**
Bray, Sir Reginald More	1842–**1923**
Brayley, (John) Desmond, Baron	1917–**1977**
Brazil, Angela	1868–**1947**
Brennan, Louis	1852–**1932**
Brentford, Viscount. See Hicks, William Joynson-	1865–**1932**
Brereton, Joseph Lloyd	1822–**1901**
Bressey, Sir Charles Herbert	1874–**1951**

Cardew, Philip 1851–**1910**
Cardus, Sir (John Frederick) Neville 1889–**1975**
Carey, Rosa Nouchette 1840–**1909**
Carlile, Wilson 1847–**1942**
Carline, Richard Cotton 1896–**1980**
Carling, Sir Ernest Rock 1877–**1960**
Carlisle, Earl of. See Howard, George James 1843–**1911**
Carlisle, Countess of. See Howard, Rosalind Frances 1845–**1921**
Carlyle, Alexander James 1861–**1943**
Carlyle, Benjamin Fearnley (Dom Aelred) 1874–**1955**
Carlyle, Sir Robert Warrand 1859–**1934**
Carman, William Bliss 1861–**1929**
Carmichael, Sir Thomas David Gibson-, Baron 1859–**1926**
Carnarvon, Earl of. See Herbert, George Edward Stanhope Molyneux 1866–**1923**
Carnegie, Andrew 1835–**1919**
Carnegie, James, Earl of Southesk 1827–**1905**
Carnell, Edward John 1912–**1972**
Carnock, Baron. See Nicolson, Sir Arthur 1849–**1928**
Caröe, William Douglas 1857–**1938**
Carpenter, Alfred Francis Blakeney 1881–**1955**
Carpenter, Edward 1844–**1929**
Carpenter, George Alfred 1859–**1910**
Carpenter, Sir (Henry Cort) Harold 1875–**1940**
Carpenter, Joseph Estlin 1844–**1927**
Carpenter, Robert 1830–**1901**
Carpenter, William Boyd 1841–**1918**
Carr, Sir Cecil Thomas 1878–**1966**
Carrington, Sir Frederick 1844–**1913**
Carr-Saunders, Sir Alexander Morris 1886–**1966**
Carruthers, (Alexander) Douglas (Mitchell) 1882–**1962**
Carson, Edward Henry, Baron 1854–**1935**
Carte, Richard D'Oyly 1844–**1901**
Carter, Sir Edgar Bonham-. See Bonham-Carter 1870–**1956**
Carter, (Helen) Violet Bonham, Baroness Asquith of Yarnbury. See Bonham Carter 1887–**1969**
Carter, Howard 1874–**1939**
Carter, Hugh 1837–**1903**
Carter, John Waynflete 1905–**1975**
Carter, Thomas Thellusson 1808–**1901**
Carton, Richard Claude 1856–**1928**
Carton de Wiart, Sir Adrian 1880–**1963**
Carus-Wilson, Eleanora Mary 1897–**1977**
Carver, Alfred James 1826–**1909**
Cary, Arthur Joyce Lunel 1888–**1957**
Cary, Sir (Arthur Lucius) Michael 1917–**1976**
Case, Thomas 1844–**1925**
Casement, Roger David 1864–**1916**
Casey, Richard Gardiner, Baron 1890–**1976**
Casey, William Francis 1884–**1957**
Cash, John Theodore 1854–**1936**
Cassel, Sir Ernest Joseph 1852–**1921**
Cassels, Sir Robert Archibald 1876–**1959**
Cassels, Walter Richard 1826–**1907**
Cates, Arthur 1829–**1901**
Cathcart, Edward Provan 1877–**1954**
Catto, Thomas Sivewright, Baron 1879–**1959**
Cavan, Earl of. See Lambart, Frederick Rudolph 1865–**1946**
Cave, George, Viscount 1856–**1928**
Cavell, Edith 1865–**1915**
Cavendish, Spencer Compton, Marquess of Hartington, afterwards Duke of Devonshire 1833–**1908**
Cavendish, Victor Christian William, Duke of Devonshire 1868–**1938**
Cawdor, Earl. See Campbell, Frederick Archibald Vaughan 1847–**1911**
Cawood, Sir Walter 1907–**1967**
Cawthorne, Sir Terence Edward 1902–**1970**
Cazalet, Peter Victor Ferdinand 1907–**1973**
Cecil, Edgar Algernon Robert Gascoyne-, Viscount Cecil of Chelwood 1864–**1958**
Cecil, Lord Edward Herbert Gascoyne- 1867–**1918**
Cecil, Henry, *pseudonym*. See Leon, Henry Cecil 1902–**1976**
Cecil, Hugh Richard Heathcote Gascoyne-, Baron Quickswood 1869–**1956**
Cecil, James Edward Hubert Gascoyne-, Marquess of Salisbury 1861–**1947**
Cecil, Robert Arthur James Gascoyne-, Marquess of Salisbury 1893–**1972**
Cecil, Robert Arthur Talbot Gascoyne-, Marquess of Salisbury 1830–**1903**
Centlivres, Albert van de Sandt 1887–**1966**
Chads, Sir Henry 1819–**1906**
Chadwick, Hector Munro 1870–**1947**
Chadwick, Sir James 1891–**1974**
Chadwick, Roy 1893–**1947**
Chain, Sir Ernst Boris 1906–**1979**
Chalmers, James 1841–**1901**
Chalmers, Sir Mackenzie Dalzell 1847–**1927**
Chalmers, Robert, Baron 1858–**1938**
Chamberlain, (Arthur) Neville 1869–**1940**
Chamberlain, Sir Crawford Trotter 1821–**1902**
Chamberlain, Houston Stewart 1855–**1927**
Chamberlain, Joseph 1836–**1914**
Chamberlain, Sir (Joseph) Austen 1863–**1937**
Chamberlain, Sir Neville Bowles 1820–**1902**
Chamberlin, Peter Hugh Girard 1919–**1978**
Chambers, Dorothea Katharine 1878–**1960**
Chambers, Sir Edmund Kerchever 1866–**1954**
Chambers, Raymond Wilson 1874–**1942**
Chamier, Stephen Henry Edward 1834–**1910**
Champneys, Basil 1842–**1935**
Champneys, Sir Francis Henry 1848–**1930**
Chance, Sir James Timmins 1814–**1902**

Davenport, Harold 1907–**1969**
Davenport-Hill, Rosamond. See Hill 1825–**1902**
Davey, Horace, Baron 1833–**1907**
David, Albert Augustus 1867–**1950**
David, Sir (Tannatt William) Edgeworth 1858–**1934**
Davids, Thomas William Rhys 1843–**1922**
Davidson, Andrew Bruce 1831–**1902**
Davidson, Charles 1824–**1902**
Davidson, James Leigh Strachan-. See Strachan-Davidson 1843–**1916**
Davidson, (James) Norman 1911–**1972**
Davidson, John 1857–**1909**
Davidson, John Colin Campbell, Viscount 1889–**1970**
Davidson, Sir John Humphrey 1876–**1954**
Davidson, John Thain 1833–**1904**
Davidson, Randall Thomas, Baron Davidson of Lambeth 1848–**1930**
Davie, Thomas Benjamin 1895–**1955**
Davies, Charles Maurice 1828–**1910**
Davies, Clement Edward 1884–**1962**
Davies, David, Baron 1880–**1944**
Davies, Sir (Henry) Walford 1869–**1941**
Davies, John Emerson Harding 1916–**1979**
Davies, John Llewelyn 1826–**1916**
Davies, Sir Martin 1908–**1975**
Davies, Rhys 1901–**1978**
Davies, Robert 1816–**1905**
Davies, (Sarah) Emily 1830–**1921**
Davies, William Henry 1871–**1940**
Davies, William John Abbott 1890–**1967**
Davies, Sir William (Llewelyn) 1887–**1952**
D'Avigdor-Goldsmid, Sir Henry Joseph 1909–**1976**
Davis, Charles Edward 1827–**1902**
Davis, Henry William Carless 1874–**1928**
Davis, Joseph 1901–**1978**
Davitt, Michael 1846–**1906**
Dawber, Sir (Edward) Guy 1861–**1938**
Dawkins, Richard McGillivray 1871–**1955**
Dawkins, Sir William Boyd 1837–**1929**
Dawson, Bertrand Edward, Viscount Dawson of Penn 1864–**1945**
Dawson, (George) Geoffrey 1874–**1944**
Dawson, George Mercer 1849–**1901**
Dawson, John 1827–**1903**
Dawtry, Frank Dalmeny 1902–**1968**
Day, Sir John Charles Frederic Sigismund 1826–**1908**
Day, Lewis Foreman 1845–**1910**
Day, William Henry 1823–**1908**
Day-Lewis, Cecil 1904–**1972**
Deacon, George Frederick 1843–**1909**
Deakin, Alfred 1856–**1919**
Deakin, Arthur 1890–**1955**
Dean, Basil Herbert 1888–**1978**
Dean, Sir Maurice Joseph 1906–**1978**
Dean, William Ralph ('Dixie') 1907–**1980**
Deane, Sir James Parker 1812–**1902**
Dearmer, Percy 1867–**1936**
De Baissac, (Marc) Claude (de Boucherville) 1907–**1974**
De Beer, Sir Gavin Rylands 1899–**1972**
Debenham, Frank 1883–**1965**
De Bunsen, Sir Maurice William Ernest 1852–**1932**
De Burgh, William George 1866–**1943**
De Burgh Canning, Hubert George, Marquess of Clanricarde. See Burgh Canning 1832–**1916**
De Chair, Sir Dudley Rawson Stratford 1864–**1958**
Deedes, Sir Wyndham Henry 1883–**1956**
De Ferranti, Sebastian Ziani. See Ferranti 1864–**1930**
De Guingand, Sir Francis Wilfred 1900–**1979**
De Havilland, Sir Geoffrey 1882–**1965**
De Havilland, Geoffrey Raoul 1910–**1946**
De la Bedoyere, Count Michael Anthony Maurice Huchet 1900–**1973**
Delafield, E. M., *pseudonym*. See Dashwood, Edmée Elizabeth Monica 1890–**1943**
De la Mare, Walter John 1873–**1956**
Delamere, Baron. See Cholmondeley, Hugh 1870–**1931**
De la Ramée, Marie Louise, 'Ouida' 1839–**1908**
De la Rue, Sir Thomas Andros 1849–**1911**
De László, Philip Alexius. See László de Lombos 1869–**1937**
De La Warr, Earl. See Sackville, Herbrand Edward Dundonald Brassey 1900–**1976**
Delevingne, Sir Malcolm 1868–**1950**
Delius, Frederick 1862–**1934**
Dell, Ethel Mary. See Savage 1881–**1939**
Deller, Sir Edwin 1883–**1936**
Delmer, (Denis) Sefton 1904–**1979**
De Madariaga, Salvador. See Madariaga 1886–**1978**
De Montmorency, James Edward Geoffrey 1866–**1934**
De Montmorency, Raymond Harvey, Viscount Frankfort de Montmorency 1835–**1902**
De Morgan, William Frend 1839–**1917**
Dempsey, Sir Miles Christopher 1896–**1969**
Denman, Gertrude Mary, Lady 1884–**1954**
Denney, James 1856–**1917**
Denning, Sir Norman Egbert 1904–**1979**
Denniston, Alexander Guthrie (Alastair) 1881–**1961**
Denniston, John Dewar 1887–**1949**
Denny, Sir Archibald 1860–**1936**
Denny, Sir Maurice Edward 1886–**1955**
Denny, Sir Michael Maynard 1896–**1972**
Dent, Charles Enrique 1911–**1976**
Dent, Edward Joseph 1876–**1957**
Dent, Joseph Malaby 1849–**1926**

Doubleday, Herbert Arthur 1867–**1941**
Doughty, Charles Montagu 1843–**1926**
Doughty-Wylie, Charles Hotham Montagu 1868–**1915**
Douglas, Sir Adye 1815–**1906**
Douglas, Lord Alfred Bruce 1870–**1945**
Douglas, Sir Charles Whittingham Horsley 1850–**1914**
Douglas, Claude Gordon 1882–**1963**
Douglas, Clifford (Hugh) 1879–**1952**
Douglas, George, *pseudonym*. See Brown, George Douglas 1869–**1902**
Douglas, George Cunninghame Monteath 1826–**1904**
Douglas, (George) Norman 1868–**1952**
Douglas, Sir (Henry) Percy 1876–**1939**
Douglas, William Sholto, Baron Douglas of Kirtleside 1893–**1969**
Douglas, Sir William Scott 1890–**1953**
Douglas-Pennant, George Sholto Gordon, Baron Penrhyn 1836–**1907**
Douglas-Scott-Montagu, John Walter Edward, Baron Montagu of Beaulieu 1866–**1929**
Dove, Dame (Jane) Frances 1847–**1942**
Dove, John 1872–**1934**
Dover Wilson, John. See Wilson 1881–**1969**
Dowden, Edward 1843–**1913**
Dowden, John 1840–**1910**
Dowding, Hugh Caswall Tremenheere, Baron 1882–**1970**
Dowie, John Alexander 1847–**1907**
Downey, Richard Joseph 1881–**1953**
Dowty, Sir George Herbert 1901–**1975**
Doyle, Sir Arthur Conan 1859–**1930**
Doyle, John Andrew 1844–**1907**
Drax, Sir Reginald Aylmer Ranfurly Plunkett-Ernle-Erle-. See Plunkett 1880–**1967**
Drayton, Harold Charles Gilbert (Harley) 1901–**1966**
Dredge, James 1840–**1906**
Dreschfeld, Julius 1846–**1907**
Drew, Sir Thomas 1838–**1910**
Dreyer, Sir Frederic Charles 1878–**1956**
Dreyer, Georges 1873–**1934**
Dreyer, John Louis Emil 1852–**1926**
Driberg, Thomas Edward Neil, Baron Bradwell 1905–**1976**
Drinkwater, John 1882–**1937**
Driver, Sir Godfrey Rolles 1892–**1975**
Driver, Samuel Rolles 1846–**1914**
Druce, George Claridge 1850–**1932**
Drummond, Sir George Alexander 1829–**1910**
Drummond, Sir Jack Cecil 1891–**1952**
Drummond, James 1835–**1918**
Drummond, James Eric, Earl of Perth 1876–**1951**
Drummond, Sir Peter Roy Maxwell 1894–**1945**
Drummond, William Henry 1854–**1907**
Drury, Sir Alan Nigel 1889–**1980**
Drury, (Edward) Alfred (Briscoe) 1856–**1944**
Drury-Lowe, Sir Drury Curzon 1830–**1908**
Dryland, Alfred 1865–**1946**
Drysdale, Charles Vickery 1874–**1961**
Drysdale, Learmont 1866–**1909**
Du Cane, Sir Edmund Frederick 1830–**1903**
Duckett, Sir George Floyd 1811–**1902**
Duckworth, Sir Dyce 1840–**1928**
Duckworth, Wynfrid Laurence Henry 1870–**1956**
Du Cros, Sir Arthur Philip 1871–**1955**
Dudgeon, Leonard Stanley 1876–**1938**
Dudgeon, Robert Ellis 1820–**1904**
Dudley, Earl of. See Ward, William Humble 1867–**1932**
Duff, Sir Alexander Ludovic 1862–**1933**
Duff, Sir Beauchamp 1855–**1918**
Duff, Sir James Fitzjames 1898–**1970**
Duff, Sir Lyman Poore 1865–**1955**
Duff, Sir Mountstuart Elphinstone Grant. See Grant Duff 1829–**1906**
Dufferin and Ava, Marquess of. See Blackwood, Frederick Temple Hamilton-Temple 1826–**1902**
Duffy, Sir Charles Gavan 1816–**1903**
Duffy, Sir Frank Gavan 1852–**1936**
Duffy, Patrick Vincent 1836–**1909**
Dugdale, William Lionel, Baron Crathorne 1897–**1977**
Duke, Sir Frederick William 1863–**1924**
Duke, Henry Edward, Baron Merrivale 1855–**1939**
Duke-Elder, Sir (William) Stewart 1898–**1978**
Dukes, Ashley 1885–**1959**
Dulac, Edmund 1882–**1953**
Du Maurier, Sir Gerald Hubert Edward Busson 1873–**1934**
Duncan, Sir Andrew Rae 1884–**1952**
Duncan, George Simpson 1884–**1965**
Duncan, Sir John Norman Valette (Val) 1913–**1975**
Duncan, Sir Patrick 1870–**1943**
Dundas, Lawrence John Lumley, Marquess of Zetland 1876–**1961**
Dundonald, Earl of. See Cochrane, Douglas Mackinnon Baillie Hamilton 1852–**1935**
Dunedin, Viscount. See Murray, Andrew Graham 1849–**1942**
Dunhill, Thomas Frederick 1877–**1946**
Dunhill, Sir Thomas Peel 1876–**1957**
Dunlop, Sir Derrick Melville 1902–**1980**
Dunlop, John Boyd 1840–**1921**
Dunmore, Earl of. See Murray, Charles Adolphus 1841–**1907**
Dunne, Sir Laurence Rivers 1893–**1970**
Dunphie, Charles James 1820–**1908**
Dunraven and Mount-Earl, Earl of. See Quin, Windham Thomas Wyndham- 1841–**1926**

Ellis, Sir William Henry 1860–**1945**
Elmhirst, Leonard Knight 1893–**1974**
Elphinstone, Sir (George) Keith (Buller) 1865–**1941**
Elsie, Lily 1886–**1962**
Elsmie, George Robert 1838–**1909**
Elton, Sir Arthur Hallam Rice 1906–**1973**
Elton, Godfrey, Baron 1892–**1973**
Elton, Oliver 1861–**1945**
Elvin, Sir (James) Arthur 1899–**1957**
Elwes, Gervase Henry Cary- 1866–**1921**
Elwes, Henry John 1846–**1922**
Elwes, Simon Edmund Vincent Paul 1902–**1975**
Elworthy, Frederick Thomas 1830–**1907**
Embry, Sir Basil Edward 1902–**1977**
Emery, (Walter) Bryan 1903–**1971**
Emery, William 1825–**1910**
Emmott, Alfred, Baron 1858–**1926**
Ensor, Sir Robert Charles Kirkwood 1877–**1958**
Entwistle, William James 1895–**1952**
Epstein, Sir Jacob 1880–**1959**
Erdélyi, Arthur 1908–**1977**
Erith, Raymond Charles 1904–**1973**
Ernle, Baron. See Prothero, Rowland Edmund 1851–**1937**
Ervine, (John) St. John (Greer) 1883–**1971**
Esdaile, Katharine Ada 1881–**1950**
Esher, Viscount. See Brett, Reginald Baliol 1852–**1930**
Esmond, Henry Vernon 1869–**1922**
Etheridge, Robert 1819–**1903**
Euan-Smith, Sir Charles Bean 1842–**1910**
Eumorfopoulos, George 1863–**1939**
Eva, *pseudonym*. See under O'Doherty, Kevin Izod 1823–**1905**
Evan-Thomas, Sir Hugh 1862–**1928**
Evans, Sir Arthur John 1851–**1941**
Evans, Sir Charles Arthur Lovatt 1884–**1968**
Evans, Daniel Silvan 1818–**1903**
Evans, Dame Edith Mary 1888–**1976**
Evans, Edmund 1826–**1905**
Evans, Edward Ratcliffe Garth Russell, Baron Mountevans 1880–**1957**
Evans, Sir (Evan) Vincent 1851–**1934**
8[Evans, George Essex 1863–**1909**
Evans, Sir Guildhaume Myrddin-. See Myrddin-Evans 1894–**1964**
Evans, Horace, Baron 1903–**1963**
Evans, Sir John 1823–**1908**
Evans, John Gwenogvryn 1852–**1930**
Evans, Meredith Gwynne 1904–**1952**
Evans, Sir Samuel Thomas 1859–**1918**
Evans, Sebastian 1830–**1909**
Evans, Sir (Worthington) Laming Worthington- 1868–**1931**
Evans-Pritchard, Sir Edward Evan 1902–**1973**
Evatt, Herbert Vere 1894–**1965**
Eve, Sir Harry Trelawney 1856–**1940**
Everard, Harry Stirling Crawfurd 1848–**1909**
Everett, Joseph David 1831–**1904**
Everett, Sir William 1844–**1908**
Evershed, (Francis) Raymond, Baron 1899–**1966**
Evershed, John 1864–**1956**
Eversley, Baron. See Shaw-Lefevre, George John 1831–**1928**
Eves, Reginald Grenville 1876–**1941**
Evill, Sir Douglas Claude Strathern 1892–**1971**
Ewart, Alfred James 1872–**1937**
Ewart, Charles Brisbane 1827–**1903**
Ewart, Sir John Alexander 1821–**1904**
Ewart, Sir John Spencer 1861–**1930**
Ewer, William Norman 1885–**1977**
Ewing, Sir (James) Alfred 1855–**1935**
Ewins, Arthur James 1882–**1957**
Eyre, Edward John 1815–**1901**
Eyston, George Edward Thomas 1897–**1979**

Faber, Sir Geoffrey Cust 1889–**1961**
Faber, Oscar 1886–**1956**
Fachiri, Adila Adrienne Adalbertina Maria 1886–**1962**
Faed, John 1819–**1902**
Fagan, James Bernard 1873–**1933**
Fagan, Louis Alexander 1845–**1903**
Fairbairn, Andrew Martin 1838–**1912**
Fairbairn, Stephen 1862–**1938**
Fairbridge, Kingsley Ogilvie 1885–**1924**
Fairey, Sir (Charles) Richard 1887–**1956**
Fairfield, Baron. See Greer, (Frederick) Arthur 1863–**1945**
Fairley, Sir Neil Hamilton 1891–**1966**
Falcke, Isaac 1819–**1909**
Falconer, Lanoe, *pseudonym*. See Hawker, Mary Elizabeth 1848–**1908**
Falconer, Sir Robert Alexander 1867–**1943**
Falkiner, Caesar Litton 1863–**1908**
Falkiner, Sir Frederick Richard 1831–**1908**
Falkner, John Meade 1858–**1932**
Falls, Cyril Bentham 1888–**1971**
Fane, Violet, *pseudonym*. See Currie, Mary Montgomerie, Lady 1843–**1905**
Fanshawe, Sir Edward Gennys 1814–**1906**
Faringdon, Baron. See Henderson, (Alexander) Gavin 1902–**1977**
Farjeon, Benjamin Leopold 1838–**1903**
Farjeon, Eleanor 1881–**1965**
Farmer, Emily 1826–**1905**
Farmer, John 1835–**1901**
Farmer, Sir John Bretland 1865–**1944**
Farnell, Lewis Richard 1856–**1934**
Farningham, Marianne, *pseudonym*. See Hearn, Mary Anne 1834–**1909**
Farnol, (John) Jeffery 1878–**1952**
Farquhar, John Nicol 1861–**1929**
Farquharson, David 1840–**1907**
Farrar, Adam Storey 1826–**1905**
Farrar, Frederic William 1831–**1903**
Farrell, James Gordon 1935–**1979**
Farren (afterwards Soutar), Ellen (Nellie) 1848–**1904**

Gowrie, Earl of. See Hore-Ruthven, Alexander Gore Arkwright 1872–**1955**
Grace, Edward Mills 1841–**1911**
Grace, William Gilbert 1848–**1915**
Graham, Henry Grey 1842–**1906**
Graham, Hugh, Baron Atholstan 1848–**1938**
Graham, John Anderson 1861–**1942**
Graham, Robert Bontine Cunninghame 1852–**1936**
Graham, Sir Ronald William 1870–**1949**
Graham, Thomas Alexander Ferguson 1840–**1906**
Graham, William 1839–**1911**
Graham, William 1887–**1932**
Graham Brown, Thomas. See Brown 1882–**1965**
Graham-Harrison, Sir William Montagu 1871–**1949**
Graham-Little, Sir Ernest Gordon Graham 1867–**1950**
Grahame, Kenneth 1859–**1932**
Grahame-White, Claude 1879–**1959**
Granet, Sir (William) Guy 1867–**1943**
Grant, Sir (Alfred) Hamilton 1872–**1937**
Grant, Sir Charles (1836–1903). See under Grant, Sir Robert
Grant, Duncan James Corrowr 1885–**1978**
Grant, George Monro 1835–**1902**
Grant, Sir Robert 1837–**1904**
Grant Duff, Sir Mountstuart Elphinstone 1829–**1906**
Grantham, Sir William 1835–**1911**
Granville-Barker, Harley Granville 1877–**1946**
Graves, Alfred Perceval 1846–**1931**
Graves, George Windsor 1873?–**1949**
Gray, Sir Alexander 1882–**1968**
Gray, Sir Archibald Montague Henry 1880–**1967**
Gray, Benjamin Kirkman 1862–**1907**
Gray, George Buchanan 1865–**1922**
Gray, George Edward Kruger 1880–**1943**
Gray, Herbert Branston 1851–**1929**
Gray, Sir James 1891–**1975**
Gray, (Kathleen) Eileen (Moray) 1879–**1976**
Gray, Louis Harold 1905–**1965**
Greame, Philip Lloyd-, Earl of Swinton. See Cunliffe-Lister 1884–**1972**
Greaves, Walter 1846–**1930**
Green, Alice Sophia Amelia (Mrs Stopford Green) 1847–**1929**
Green, Charles Alfred Howell 1864–**1944**
Green, Frederick William Edridge-. See Edridge-Green 1863–**1953**
Green, Gustavus 1865–**1964**
Green, Henry, *pseudonym*. See Yorke, Henry Vincent 1905–**1973**
Green, Samuel Gosnell 1822–**1905**
Green, William Curtis 1875–**1960**
Greenaway, Catherine (Kate) 1846–**1901**
Greene, Harry Plunket 1865–**1936**
Greene, Wilfrid Arthur, Baron 1883–**1952**
Greene, William Friese- 1855–**1921**
Greene, Sir (William) Graham 1857–**1950**
Greenidge, Abel Hendy Jones 1865–**1906**
Greenwell, William 1820–**1918**
Greenwood, Arthur 1880–**1954**
Greenwood, Frederick 1830–**1909**
Greenwood, Hamar, Viscount 1870–**1948**
Greenwood, Thomas 1851–**1908**
Greenwood, Walter 1903–**1974**
Greer, (Frederick) Arthur, Baron Fairfield 1863–**1945**
Greer, William Derrick Lindsay 1902–**1972**
Greet, Sir Philip Barling Ben 1857–**1936**
Greg, Sir Walter Wilson 1875–**1959**
Grego, Joseph 1843–**1908**
Gregory, Sir Augustus Charles 1819–**1905**
Gregory, Edward John 1850–**1909**
Gregory, Frederick Gugenheim 1893–**1961**
Gregory, Isabella Augusta, Lady 1852–**1932**
Gregory, John Walter 1864–**1932**
Gregory, Sir Richard Arman 1864–**1952**
Gregory, Robert 1819–**1911**
Greiffenhagen, Maurice William 1862–**1931**
Grenfell, Bernard Pyne 1869–**1926**
Grenfell, Edward Charles, Baron St. Just 1870–**1941**
Grenfell, Francis Wallace, Baron 1841–**1925**
Grenfell, George 1849–**1906**
Grenfell, Hubert Henry 1845–**1906**
Grenfell, Joyce Irene 1910–**1979**
Grenfell, Julian Henry Francis 1888–**1915**
Grenfell, Sir Wilfred Thomason 1865–**1940**
Grenfell, William Henry, Baron Desborough 1855–**1945**
Greville, Frances Evelyn, Countess of Warwick 1861–**1938**
Grey, Albert Henry George, Earl 1851–**1917**
Grey, Charles Grey 1875–**1953**
Grey, Sir Edward, Viscount Grey of Fallodon 1862–**1933**
Grey (formerly Shirreff), Maria Georgina 1816–**1906**
Grierson, Sir George Abraham 1851–**1941**
Grierson, Sir Herbert John Clifford 1866–**1960**
Grierson, Sir James Moncrieff 1859–**1914**
Grierson, John 1898–**1972**
Grieve, Christopher Murray, 'Hugh MacDiarmid' 1892–**1978**
Griffin, Bernard William 1899–**1956**
Griffin, Sir Lepel Henry 1838–**1908**
Griffith, Alan Arnold 1893–**1963**
Griffith, Arthur 1872–**1922**
Griffith, Francis Llewellyn 1862–**1934**
Griffith, Ralph Thomas Hotchkin 1826–**1906**
Griffiths, Arthur George Frederick 1838–**1908**
Griffiths, Ernest Howard 1851–**1932**
Griffiths, Ezer 1888–**1962**
Griffiths, James 1890–**1975**
Griffiths, Sir John Norton-. See Norton-Griffiths 1871–**1930**

Hope, James Fitzalan, Baron Rankeillour 1870–**1949**
Hope, John Adrian Louis, Earl of Hopetoun and Marquess of Linlithgow 1860–**1908**
Hope, Laurence, *pseudonym*. See Nicolson, Adela Florence 1865–**1904**
Hope, Victor Alexander John, Marquess of Linlithgow 1887–**1952**
Hope, Sir William Henry St. John 1854–**1919**
Hope-Wallace, Philip Adrian 1911–**1979**
Hopetoun, Earl of. See Hope, John Adrian Louis 1860–**1908**
Hopkins, Edward John 1818–**1901**
Hopkins, Sir Frederick Gowland 1861–**1947**
Hopkins, Jane Ellice 1836–**1904**
Hopkins, Sir Richard Valentine Nind 1880–**1955**
Hopkinson, Sir Alfred 1851–**1939**
Hopkinson, Bertram 1874–**1918**
Hopwood, Charles Henry 1829–**1904**
Hopwood, Francis John Stephens, Baron Southborough 1860–**1947**
Horder, Percy (Richard) Morley 1870–**1944**
Horder, Thomas Jeeves, Baron 1871–**1955**
Hore-Belisha, (Isaac) Leslie, Baron 1893–**1957**
Hore-Ruthven, Alexander Gore Arkwright, Earl of Gowrie 1872–**1955**
Hornby, Charles Harry St. John 1867–**1946**
Hornby, James John 1826–**1909**
Horne, Henry Sinclair, Baron 1861–**1929**
Horne, Robert Stevenson, Viscount Horne of Slamannan 1871–**1940**
Horner, Arthur Lewis 1894–**1968**
Horniman, Annie Elizabeth Fredericka 1860–**1937**
Horniman, Frederick John 1835–**1906**
Horrabin, James Francis 1884–**1962**
Horridge, Sir Thomas Gardner 1857–**1938**
Horsbrugh, Florence Gertrude, Baroness 1889–**1969**
Horsley, John Callcott 1817–**1903**
Horsley, John William 1845–**1921**
Horsley, Sir Victor Alexander Haden 1857–**1916**
Horton, Sir Max Kennedy 1883–**1951**
Horton, Percy Frederick 1897–**1970**
Horton, Robert Forman 1855–**1934**
Hose, Charles 1863–**1929**
Hosie, Sir Alexander 1853–**1925**
Hosier, Arthur Julius 1877–**1963**
Hoskins, Sir Anthony Hiley 1828–**1901**
Hoskyns, Sir Edwyn Clement 1884–**1937**
Hotine, Martin 1898–**1968**
Houghton, William Stanley 1881–**1913**
Houldsworth, Sir Hubert Stanley 1889–**1956**
House, (Arthur) Humphry 1908–**1955**
Housman, Alfred Edward 1859–**1936**
Housman, Laurence 1865–**1959**
Houston, Dame Fanny Lucy 1857–**1936**
Howard, Bernard Marmaduke FitzAlan-, sixteenth Duke of Norfolk 1908–**1975**
Howard, Sir Ebenezer 1850–**1928**
Howard, Edmund Bernard FitzAlan-, Viscount FitzAlan of Derwent 1855–**1947**
Howard, Esme William, Baron Howard of Penrith 1863–**1939**
Howard, George James, Earl of Carlisle 1843–**1911**
Howard, Henry FitzAlan-, Duke of Norfolk 1847–**1917**
Howard, Leslie 1893–**1943**
Howard, Rosalind Frances, Countess of Carlisle 1845–**1921**
Howard de Walden, Baron. See Scott-Ellis, Thomas Evelyn 1880–**1946**
Howe, Clarence Decatur 1886–**1960**
Howell, David 1831–**1903**
Howell, George 1833–**1910**
Howell, William Gough 1922–**1974**
Howes, Frank Stewart 1891–**1974**
Howes, Thomas George Bond 1853–**1905**
Howick of Glendale, Baron. See Baring, (Charles) Evelyn 1903–**1973**
Howitt, Alfred William 1830–**1908**
Howitt, Sir Harold Gibson 1886–**1969**
Howland, Sir William Pearce 1811–**1907**
Hubbard, Louisa Maria 1836–**1906**
Huddart, James 1847–**1901**
Huddleston, Sir Hubert Jervoise 1880–**1950**
Hudleston (formerly Simpson), Wilfred Hudleston 1828–**1909**
Hudson, Charles Thomas 1828–**1903**
Hudson, Sir Robert Arundell 1864–**1927**
Hudson, Robert George Spencer 1895–**1965**
Hudson, Robert Spear, Viscount 1886–**1957**
Hudson, William Henry 1841–**1922**
Hueffer, Ford Hermann. See Ford, Ford Madox 1873–**1939**
Hügel, Friedrich von, Baron of the Holy Roman Empire. See Von Hügel 1852–**1925**
Hugessen, Sir Hughe Montgomery Knatchbull-. See Knatchbull-Hugessen 1886–**1971**
Huggins, Godfrey Martin, Viscount Malvern 1883–**1971**
Huggins, Sir William 1824–**1910**
Hughes, Arthur 1832–**1915**
Hughes, Edward 1832–**1908**
Hughes, Edward David 1906–**1963**
Hughes, Hugh Price 1847–**1902**
Hughes, John 1842–**1902**
Hughes, Richard Arthur Warren 1900–**1976**
Hughes, Sir Sam 1853–**1921**
Hughes, William Morris 1862–**1952**
Hughes-Hallett, John 1901–**1972**
Hulbert, John Norman (Jack) 1892–**1978**
Hulme, Frederick Edward 1841–**1909**

Loch, Sir Charles Stewart 1849–1923
Lock, Walter 1846–1933
Locke, William John 1863–1930
Lockey, Charles 1820–1901
Lockhart, Sir Robert Hamilton Bruce 1887–1970
Lockwood, Amelius Mark Richard, Baron Lambourne 1847–1928
Lockwood, Sir John Francis 1903–1965
Lockyer, Sir (Joseph) Norman 1836–1920
Lodge, Eleanor Constance 1869–1936
Lodge, Sir Oliver Joseph 1851–1940
Lodge, Sir Richard 1855–1936
Loftie, William John 1839–1911
Loftus, Lord Augustus William Frederick Spencer 1817–1904
Logue, Michael 1840–1924
Lohmann, George Alfred 1865–1901
Lombard, Adrian Albert 1915–1967
London, Heinz 1907–1970
Londonderry, Marquess of. See Vane-Tempest-Stewart, Charles Stewart 1852–1915
Londonderry, Marquess of. See Vane-Tempest-Stewart, Charles Stewart Henry 1878–1949
Long, Walter Hume, Viscount Long of Wraxall 1854–1924
Longhurst, Henry Carpenter 1909–1979
Longhurst, William Henry 1819–1904
Longmore, Sir Arthur Murray 1885–1970
Longstaff, Tom George 1875–1964
Lonsdale, Earl of. See Lowther, Hugh Cecil 1857–1944
Lonsdale, Frederick 1881–1954
Lonsdale, Dame Kathleen 1903–1971
Lopes, Sir Lopes Massey 1818–1908
Loraine, Sir Percy Lyham 1880–1961
Loraine, Violet Mary 1886–1956
Lord, Thomas 1808–1908
Loreburn, Earl. See Reid, Robert Threshie 1846–1923
Lorimer, Sir Robert Stodart 1864–1929
Lotbinière, Sir Henry Gustave Joly de. See Joly de Lotbinière 1829–1908
Lothian, Marquess of. See Kerr, Philip Henry 1882–1940
Louise Caroline Alberta, princess of Great Britain 1848–1939
Louise Victoria Alexandra Dagmar, Princess Royal of Great Britain 1867–1931
Lovat, Baron. See Fraser, Simon Joseph 1871–1933
Lovatt Evans, Sir Charles Arthur. See Evans 1884–1968
Love, Augustus Edward Hough 1863–1940
Lovelace, Earl of. See Milbanke, Ralph Gordon Noel King 1839–1906
Lovett, Richard 1851–1904
Low, Alexander, Lord 1845–1910
Low, Sir David Alexander Cecil 1891–1963
Low, Sir Robert Cunliffe 1838–1911
Low, Sir Sidney James Mark 1857–1932
Lowe, Sir Drury Curzon Drury-. See Drury-Lowe 1830–1908
Lowe, Eveline Mary 1869–1956
Lowke, Wenman Joseph Bassett-. See Bassett-Lowke 1877–1953
Lowry, Clarence Malcolm 1909–1957
Lowry, Henry Dawson 1869–1906
Lowry, Laurence Stephen 1887–1976
Lowry, Thomas Martin 1874–1936
Lowson, Sir Denys Colquhoun Flowerdew 1906–1975
Lowther, Hugh Cecil, Earl of Lonsdale 1857–1944
Lowther, James 1840–1904
Lowther, James William, Viscount Ullswater 1855–1949
Löwy, Albert or Abraham 1816–1908
Loyd-Lindsay, Robert James, Baron Wantage. See Lindsay 1832–1901
Luard, Sir William Garnham 1820–1910
Lubbock, Sir John, Baron Avebury 1834–1913
Lubbock, Percy 1879–1965
Luby, Thomas Clarke 1821–1901
Lucas, Baron. See Herbert, Auberon Thomas 1876–1916
Lucas, Sir Charles Prestwood 1853–1931
Lucas, Edward Verrall 1868–1938
Lucas, Frank Laurence 1894–1967
Lucas, Keith 1879–1916
Luckock, Herbert Mortimer 1833–1909
Lucy, Sir Henry William 1843–1924
Ludlow, John Malcolm Forbes 1821–1911
Ludlow-Hewitt, Sir Edgar Rainey 1886–1973
Lugard, Frederick John Dealtry, Baron 1858–1945
Luke, Baron. See Johnston, George Lawson 1873–1943
Luke, Sir Harry Charles 1884–1969
Luke, Jemima 1813–1906
Lukin, Sir Henry Timson 1860–1925
Lumley, Lawrence Roger, Earl of Scarbrough 1896–1969
Lunn, Sir Arnold Henry Moore 1888–1974
Lunn, Sir Henry Simpson 1859–1939
Lupton, Joseph Hirst 1836–1905
Lush, Sir Charles Montague 1853–1930
Lusk, Sir Andrew 1810–1909
Luthuli, Albert John 1898?–1967
Lutyens, Sir Edwin Landseer 1869–1944
Lutz, (Wilhelm) Meyer 1829–1903
Luxmoore, Sir (Arthur) Fairfax (Charles Coryndon) 1876–1944
Lyall, Sir Alfred Comyn 1835–1911
Lyall, Sir Charles James 1845–1920
Lyall, Edna, *pseudonym*. See Bayly, Ada Ellen 1857–1903
Lygon, William, Earl Beauchamp 1872–1938
Lyle, Charles Ernest Leonard, Baron Lyle of Westbourne 1882–1954

Mackay, James Lyle, Earl of Inchcape 1852–**1932**
Mackay, Mary, 'Marie Corelli' 1855–**1924**
McKechnie, William Sharp 1863–**1930**
McKenna, Reginald 1863–**1943**
Mackennal, Alexander 1835–**1904**
Mackennal, Sir (Edgar) Bertram 1863–**1931**
Mackenzie, Sir Alexander 1842–**1902**
McKenzie, Alexander 1869–**1951**
Mackenzie, Sir Alexander Campbell 1847–**1935**
Mackenzie, Sir (Edward Montague) Compton 1883–**1972**
Mackenzie, Sir George Sutherland 1844–**1910**
Mackenzie, Sir James 1853–**1925**
M'Kenzie, Sir John 1836–**1901**
MacKenzie, John Stuart 1860–**1935**
McKenzie, (Robert) Tait 1867–**1938**
Mackenzie, Sir Stephen 1844–**1909**
Mackenzie, Sir William 1849–**1923**
Mackenzie, William Warrender, Baron Amulree 1860–**1942**
Mackenzie King, William Lyon. See King 1874–**1950**
McKerrow, Ronald Brunlees 1872–**1940**
McKie, Douglas 1896–**1967**
Mackinder, Sir Halford John 1861–**1947**
MacKinlay, Antoinette. See Sterling 1843–**1904**
Mackinnon, Sir Frank Douglas 1871–**1946**
Mackinnon, Sir William Henry 1852–**1929**
Mackintosh, Sir Alexander 1858–**1948**
Mackintosh, Charles Rennie 1868–**1928**
Mackintosh, Harold Vincent, Viscount Mackintosh of Halifax 1891–**1964**
Mackintosh, Hugh Ross 1870–**1936**
Mackintosh, James Macalister 1891–**1966**
Mackintosh, John 1833–**1907**
Mackintosh, John Pitcairn 1929–**1978**
Mackworth-Young, Gerard 1884–**1965**
McLachlan, Robert 1837–**1904**
Maclagan, Christian 1811–**1901**
Maclagan, Sir Eric Robert Dalrymple 1879–**1951**
Maclagan, William Dalrymple 1826–**1910**
Maclaren, Alexander 1826–**1910**
MacLaren, Archibald Campbell 1871–**1944**
McLaren, Charles Benjamin Bright, Baron Aberconway 1850–**1934**
McLaren, Henry Duncan, Baron Aberconway 1879–**1953**
Maclaren, Ian, *pseudonym*. See Watson, John 1850–**1907**
McLaren, John, Lord 1831–**1910**
Maclay, Joseph Paton, Baron 1857–**1951**
Maclean, Sir Donald 1864–**1932**
Maclean, Sir Harry Aubrey de Vere 1848–**1920**
Maclean, James Mackenzie 1835–**1906**
McLean, Norman 1865–**1947**
Maclear, George Frederick 1833–**1902**
Maclear, John Fiot Lee Pearse 1838–**1907**
McLennan, Sir John Cunningham 1867–**1935**
Macleod, Fiona, *pseudonym*. See Sharp, William 1855–**1905**
Macleod, Henry Dunning 1821–**1902**
Macleod, Iain Norman 1913–**1970**
McLeod, (James) Walter 1887–**1978**
Macleod, John James Rickard 1876–**1935**
McLintock, Sir William 1873–**1947**
McLintock, William Francis Porter 1887–**1960**
Maclure, Edward Craig 1833–**1906**
Maclure, Sir John William (1835–1901). See under Maclure, Edward Craig
McMahon, Sir (Arthur) Henry 1862–**1949**
McMahon, Charles Alexander 1830–**1904**
MacMahon, Percy Alexander 1854–**1929**
MacMichael, Sir Harold Alfred 1882–**1969**
Macmillan, Sir Frederick Orridge 1851–**1936**
Macmillan, Hugh 1833–**1903**
Macmillan, Hugh Pattison, Baron 1873–**1952**
McMillan, Margaret 1860–**1931**
McMillan, William 1887–**1977**
McMurrich, James Playfair 1859–**1939**
Macnaghten, Sir Edward, Baron 1830–**1913**
McNair, Arnold Duncan, Baron 1885–**1975**
McNair, John Frederick Adolphus 1828–**1910**
MacNalty, Sir Arthur Salusbury 1880–**1969**
Macnamara, Thomas James 1861–**1931**
McNaughton, Andrew George Latta 1887–**1966**
MacNeice, (Frederick) Louis 1907–**1963**
McNeil, Hector 1907–**1955**
McNeile, (Herman) Cyril, 'Sapper' 1888–**1937**
McNeill, James 1869–**1938**
McNeill, Sir James McFadyen 1892–**1964**
MacNeill, John (otherwise Eoin) 1867–**1945**
McNeill, Sir John Carstairs 1831–**1904**
MacNeill, John Gordon Swift 1849–**1926**
McNeill, Ronald John, Baron Cushendun 1861–**1934**
Macphail, Sir (John) Andrew 1864–**1938**
Macpherson, (James) Ian, Baron Strathcarron 1880–**1937**
Macpherson, Sir John Molesworth 1853–**1914**
McQueen, Sir John Withers 1836–**1909**
Macqueen-Pope, Walter James 1888–**1960**
Macready, Sir (Cecil Frederick) Nevil 1862–**1946**
Macrorie, William Kenneth 1831–**1905**
M'Taggart, John M'Taggart Ellis 1866–**1925**
McTaggart, William 1835–**1910**
McWhirter, (Alan) Ross 1925–**1975**
MacWhirter, John 1839–**1911**
Madariaga, Salvador de 1886–**1978**
Madden, Sir Charles Edward 1862–**1935**
Madden, Frederic William 1839–**1904**
Madden, Katherine Cecil. See Thurston 1875–**1911**
Madden, Thomas More 1844–**1902**
Maffey, John Loader, Baron Rugby 1877–**1969**
Magrath, John Richard 1839–**1930**
Maguire, James Rochfort 1855–**1925**
Mahaffy, Sir John Pentland 1839–**1919**

Pinero, Sir Arthur Wing	1855–**1934**
Pinsent, Dame Ellen Frances	1866–**1949**
Pippard, (Alfred John) Sutton	1891–**1969**
Pirbright, Baron. See De Worms, Henry	1840–**1903**
Pirow, Oswald	1890–**1959**
Pirrie, William James, Viscount	1847–**1924**
Pissarro, Lucien	1863–**1944**
Pitman, Sir Henry Alfred	1808–**1908**
Plamenatz, John Petrov	1912–**1975**
Plaskett, Harry Hemley	1893–**1980**
Plaskett, John Stanley	1865–**1941**
Plater, Charles Dominic	1875–**1921**
Platt, Robert, Baron	1900–**1978**
Platt, Sir William	1885–**1975**
Platts, John Thompson	1830–**1904**
Playfair, Sir Nigel Ross	1874–**1934**
Playfair, William Smoult	1835–**1903**
Plender, William, Baron	1861–**1946**
Pleydell, John Clavell Mansel-. See Mansel-Pleydell	1817–**1902**
Plimmer, Robert Henry Aders	1877–**1955**
Plomer, William Charles Franklyn	1903–**1973**
Plucknett, Theodore Frank Thomas	1897–**1965**
Plumer, Herbert Charles Onslow, Viscount	1857–**1932**
Plummer, Henry Crozier Keating	1875–**1946**
Plunkett, Edward John Moreton Drax, Baron of Dunsany	1878–**1957**
Plunkett, Sir Francis Richard	1835–**1907**
Plunkett, Sir Horace Curzon	1854–**1932**
Plunkett-Ernle-Erle-Drax, Sir Reginald Aylmer Ranfurly	1880–**1967**
Plurenden, Baron. See Sternberg, Rudy	1917–**1978**
Pode, Sir (Edward) Julian	1902–**1968**
Podmore, Frank	1855–**1910**
Poel, William	1852–**1934**
Poland, Sir Harry Bodkin	1829–**1928**
Polanyi, Michael	1891–**1976**
Pole, Sir Felix John Clewett	1877–**1956**
Pollard, Albert Frederick	1869–**1948**
Pollard, Alfred William	1859–**1944**
Pollen, John Hungerford	1820–**1902**
Pollitt, George Paton	1878–**1964**
Pollitt, Harry	1890–**1960**
Pollock, Bertram	1863–**1943**
Pollock, Ernest Murray, Viscount Hanworth	1861–**1936**
Pollock, Sir Frederick	1845–**1937**
Pollock, Hugh McDowell	1852–**1937**
Pollock, Sir (John) Donald	1868–**1962**
Ponsonby, Arthur Augustus William Harry, Baron Ponsonby of Shulbrede	1871–**1946**
Ponsonby, Vere Brabazon, Earl of Bessborough	1880–**1956**
Poole, Reginald Lane	1857–**1939**
Poole, Stanley Edward Lane-	1854–**1931**
Pooley, Sir Ernest Henry	1876–**1966**
Poore, George Vivian	1843–**1904**
Pope, George Uglow	1820–**1908**
Pope, Samuel	1826–**1901**
Pope, Walter James Macqueen-. See Macqueen-Pope	1888–**1960**
Pope, William Burt	1822–**1903**
Pope, Sir William Jackson	1870–**1939**
Pope-Hennessy, (Richard) James (Arthur)	1916–**1974**
Popham, Arthur Ewart	1889–**1970**
Popham, Sir (Henry) Robert (Moore) Brooke-. See Brooke-Popham	1878–**1953**
Portal, Charles Frederick Algernon, Viscount Portal of Hungerford	1893–**1971**
Portal, Melville	1819–**1904**
Portal, Sir Wyndham Raymond, Viscount	1885–**1949**
Porter, Sir Andrew Marshall	1837–**1919**
Porter, Samuel Lowry, Baron	1877–**1956**
Postan (formerly Power), Eileen Edna le Poer	1889–**1940**
Postgate, John Percival	1853–**1926**
Postgate, Raymond William	1896–**1971**
Pott, Alfred	1822–**1908**
Potter, (Helen), Beatrix (Mrs Heelis)	1866–**1943**
Potter, Stephen Meredith	1900–**1969**
Poulton, Sir Edward Bagnall	1856–**1943**
Pound, Sir (Alfred) Dudley (Pickman Rogers)	1877–**1943**
Powell, Cecil Frank	1903–**1969**
Powell, Frederick York	1850–**1904**
Powell, Sir (George) Allan	1876–**1948**
Powell, Olave St. Clair Baden-, Lady Baden-Powell. See Baden-Powell	1889–**1977**
Powell, Sir Richard Douglas	1842–**1925**
Powell, Robert Stephenson Smyth Baden-, Baron Baden-Powell. See Baden-Powell	1857–**1941**
Power, Sir Arthur John	1889–**1960**
Power, Sir D'Arcy	1855–**1941**
Power, Eileen Edna le Poer. See Postan	1889–**1940**
Power, Sir John Cecil	1870–**1950**
Power, Sir William Henry	1842–**1916**
Powicke, Sir (Frederick) Maurice	1879–**1963**
Pownall, Sir Henry Royds	1887–**1961**
Powys, John Cowper	1872–**1963**
Poynder, Sir John Poynder Dickson-, Baron Islington	1866–**1936**
Poynter, Sir Edward John	1836–**1919**
Poynting, John Henry	1852–**1914**
Prain, Sir David	1857–**1944**
Pratt, Hodgson	1824–**1907**
Pratt, Joseph Bishop	1854–**1910**
Preece, Sir William Henry	1834–**1913**
Prendergast, Sir Harry North Dalrymple	1834–**1913**
Prestage, Edgar	1869–**1951**
Previté-Orton, Charles William	1877–**1947**

Rattigan, Sir Terence Mervyn 1911–**1977**
Rattigan, Sir William Henry 1842–**1904**
Rau, Sir Benegal Narsing 1887–**1953**
Raven, Charles Earle 1885–**1964**
Raven, John James 1833–**1906**
Raven-Hill, Leonard 1867–**1942**
Raverat, Gwendolen Mary 1885–**1957**
Raverty, Henry George 1825–**1906**
Ravilious, Eric William 1903–**1942**
Rawcliffe, Gordon Hindle 1910–**1979**
Rawling, Cecil Godfrey 1870–**1917**
Rawlinson, George 1812–**1902**
Rawlinson, Sir Henry Seymour, Baron 1864–**1925**
Rawlinson, William George 1840–**1928**
Rawson, Sir Harry Holdsworth 1843–**1910**
Rawsthorne, Alan 1905–**1971**
Rayleigh, Baron. See Strutt, John William 1842–**1919**
Rayleigh, Baron. See Strutt, Robert John 1875–**1947**
Read, Sir Charles Hercules 1857–**1929**
Read, Clare Sewell 1826–**1905**
Read, Grantly Dick-. See Dick-Read 1890–**1959**
Read, Sir Herbert Edward 1893–**1968**
Read, Herbert Harold 1889–**1970**
Read, Sir Herbert James 1863–**1949**
Read, John 1884–**1963**
Read, Walter William 1855–**1907**
Reade, Thomas Mellard 1832–**1909**
Reading, Marchioness of. See Isaacs, Stella 1894–**1971**
Reading, Marquess of. See Isaacs, Rufus Daniel 1860–**1935**
Reay, Baron. See Mackay, Donald James 1839–**1921**
Reckitt, Maurice Benington 1888–**1980**
Redesdale, Baron. See Mitford, Algernon Bertram Freeman- 1837–**1916**
Redmayne, Sir Richard Augustine Studdert 1865–**1955**
Redmond, John Edward 1856–**1918**
Redmond, William Hoey Kearney 1861–**1917**
Redpath, Anne 1895–**1965**
Redpath, Henry Adeney 1848–**1908**
Reed, Austin Leonard 1873–**1954**
Reed, Sir Carol 1906–**1976**
Reed, Sir Edward James 1830–**1906**
Reed, Edward Tennyson 1860–**1933**
Reed, Sir (Herbert) Stanley 1872–**1969**
Rees, (Morgan) Goronwy 1909–**1979**
Reeves, Sir William Conrad 1821–**1902**
Regan, Charles Tate 1878–**1943**
Reich, Emil 1854–**1910**
Reid, Archibald David 1844–**1908**
Reid, Forrest 1875–**1947**
Reid, Sir George Houstoun 1845–**1918**
Reid, James Scott Cumberland, Baron 1890–**1975**
Reid, James Smith 1846–**1926**
Reid, Sir John Watt 1823–**1909**
Reid, Sir Robert Gillespie 1842–**1908**
Reid, Robert Threshie, Earl Loreburn 1846–**1923**
Reid, Sir Thomas Wemyss 1842–**1905**
Reid Dick, Sir William. See Dick 1878–**1961**
Reilly, Sir Charles Herbert 1874–**1948**
Reith, John Charles Walsham, Baron 1889–**1971**
Reitz, Deneys 1882–**1944**
Relf, Ernest Frederick 1888–**1970**
Rendall, Montague John 1862–**1950**
Rendel, Sir Alexander Meadows 1829–**1918**
Rendel, George Wightwick 1833–**1902**
Rendel, Harry Stuart Goodhart-. See Goodhart-Rendel 1887–**1959**
Rendle, Alfred Barton 1865–**1938**
Rennell of Rodd, Baron. See Rodd, Francis James Rennell 1895–**1978**
Rennell, Baron. See Rodd, James Rennell 1858–**1941**
Repington, Charles à Court 1858–**1925**
Reynolds, James Emerson 1844–**1920**
Reynolds, Osborne 1842–**1912**
Rhodes, Cecil John 1853–**1902**
Rhodes, Francis William 1851–**1905**
Rhodes, Wilfred 1877–**1973**
Rhondda, Viscount. See Thomas, David Alfred 1856–**1918**
Rhondda, Viscountess. See Thomas, Margaret Haig 1883–**1958**
Rhys, Ernest Percival 1859–**1946**
Rhys, Jean. See Williams, Ella Gwendolen Rees 1890?–**1979**
Rhys, Sir John 1840–**1915**
Ricardo, Sir Harry Ralph 1885–**1974**
Richards, Arthur Frederick, Baron Milverton 1885–**1978**
Richards, Ceri Giraldus 1903–**1971**
Richards, Francis John 1901–**1965**
Richards, Frank, *pseudonym*. See Hamilton, Charles Harold St. John 1876–**1961**
Richards, Sir Frederick William 1833–**1912**
Richards, Ivor Armstrong 1893–**1979**
Richardson, Alan 1905–**1975**
Richardson, Sir Albert Edward 1880–**1964**
Richardson, Ethel Florence Lindesay, 'Henry Handel Richardson' 1870–**1946**
Richardson, Henry Handel. See Richardson, Ethel Florence Lindesay 1870–**1946**
Richardson, Lewis Fry 1881–**1953**
Richardson, Sir Owen Willans 1879–**1959**
Richey, James Ernest 1886–**1968**
Richmond, Sir Bruce Lyttelton 1871–**1964**
Richmond, Sir Herbert William 1871–**1946**
Richmond, Sir Ian Archibald 1902–**1965**
Richmond, Sir William Blake 1842–**1921**

Satow, Sir Ernest Mason 1843–**1929**
Saumarez, Thomas 1827–**1903**
Saunders, Sir Alexander Morris Carr-. See Carr-Saunders 1886–**1966**
Saunders, Edward 1848–**1910**
Saunders, Sir Edwin 1814–**1901**
Saunders, Howard 1835–**1907**
Saunderson, Edward James 1837–**1906**
Savage (formerly Dell), Ethel Mary 1881–**1939**
Savage-Armstrong, George Francis 1845–**1906**
Savill, Sir Eric Humphrey 1895–**1980**
Savill, Thomas Dixon 1855–**1910**
Saxe-Weimar, Prince Edward of. See Edward of Saxe-Weimar 1823–**1902**
Saxl, Friedrich ('Fritz') 1890–**1948**
Sayce, Archibald 1845–**1933**
Sayers, Dorothy Leigh 1893–**1957**
Scamp, Sir (Athelstan) Jack 1913–**1977**
Scarbrough, Earl of. See Lumley, Lawrence Roger 1896–**1969**
Schafer, Sir Edward Albert Sharpey- 1850–**1935**
Scharlieb, Dame Mary Ann Dacomb 1845–**1930**
Schiller, Ferdinand Canning Scott 1864–**1937**
Schlich, Sir William 1840–**1925**
Scholes, Percy Alfred 1877–**1958**
Schonland, Sir Basil Ferdinand Jamieson 1896–**1972**
Schreiner, Olive Emilie Albertina (1855–1920). See under Schreiner, William Philip
Schreiner, William Philip 1857–**1919**
Schumacher, Ernst Friedrich 1911–**1977**
Schunck, Henry Edward 1820–**1903**
Schuster, Sir Arthur 1851–**1934**
Schuster, Claud, Baron 1869–**1956**
Schuster, Sir Felix Otto 1854–**1936**
Schwabe, Randolph 1885–**1948**
Scott, Archibald 1837–**1909**
Scott, Charles Prestwich 1846–**1932**
Scott, Lord Charles Thomas Montagu-Douglas- 1839–**1911**
Scott, Clement William 1841–**1904**
Scott, Cyril Meir 1879–**1970**
Scott, Dukinfield Henry 1854–**1934**
Scott, Lord Francis George Montagu-Douglas- 1879–**1952**
Scott, George Herbert 1888–**1930**
Scott, Sir Giles Gilbert 1880–**1960**
Scott, Hugh Stowell, 'Henry Seton Merriman' 1862–**1903**
Scott, Sir (James) George 1851–**1935**
Scott, John 1830–**1903**
Scott, Sir John 1841–**1904**
Scott, John William Robertson. See Robertson Scott 1866–**1962**
Scott, Kathleen. See Kennet, (Edith Agnes) Kathleen, Lady 1878–**1947**
Scott, Leader, *pseudonym*. See Baxter, Lucy 1837–**1902**
Scott, Sir Leslie Frederic 1869–**1950**
Scott, Paul Mark 1920–**1978**
Scott, Sir Percy Moreton 1853–**1924**
Scott, Robert Falcon 1868–**1912**
Scott-Ellis, Thomas Evelyn, Baron Howard de Walden 1880–**1946**
Scott-James, Rolfe Arnold 1878–**1959**
Scott-Paine, Charles Hubert 1891–**1954**
Scrutton, Sir Thomas Edward 1856–**1934**
Seago, Edward Brian 1910–**1974**
Seale-Hayne, Charles Hayne 1833–**1903**
Seaman, Sir Owen 1861–**1936**
Seccombe, Thomas 1866–**1923**
Seddon, Richard John 1845–**1906**
Sedgwick, Adam 1854–**1913**
See, Sir John 1844–**1907**
Seebohm, Frederic 1833–**1912**
Seeley, Harry Govier 1839–**1909**
Seely, John Edward Bernard, Baron Mottistone 1868–**1947**
Selbie, William Boothby 1862–**1944**
Selborne, Earl of. See Palmer, Roundell Cecil 1887–**1971**
Selborne, Earl of. See Palmer, William Waldegrave 1859–**1942**
Selby, Viscount. See Gully, William Court 1835–**1909**
Selby, Thomas Gunn 1846–**1910**
Selfridge, Harry Gordon 1858–**1947**
Seligman, Charles Gabriel 1873–**1940**
Selincourt, Ernest de 1870–**1943**
Sellers, Richard Henry ('Peter') 1925–**1980**
Selous, Frederick Courteney 1851–**1917**
Selwin-Ibbetson, Henry John, Baron Rookwood 1826–**1902**
Selwyn, Alfred Richard Cecil 1824–**1902**
Selwyn-Lloyd, Baron. See Lloyd, John Selwyn Brooke 1904–**1978**
Semon, Sir Felix 1849–**1921**
Sempill, Baron. See Forbes-Sempill, William Francis 1893–**1965**
Senanayake, Don Stephen 1884–**1952**
Sendall, Sir Walter Joseph 1832–**1904**
Sequeira, James Harry 1865–**1948**
Sergeant, (Emily Frances) Adeline 1851–**1904**
Sergeant, Lewis 1841–**1902**
Service, Robert William 1874–**1958**
Seth, Andrew. See Pattison, Andrew Seth Pringle- 1856–**1931**
Seton, George 1822–**1908**
Seton-Watson, Robert William 1879–**1951**
Severn, Walter 1830–**1904**
Seward, Sir Albert Charles 1863–**1941**
Sewell, Elizabeth Missing 1815–**1906**
Sewell, James Edwards 1810–**1903**
Sewell, Robert Beresford Seymour 1880–**1964**
Sexton, Sir James 1856–**1938**
Sexton, Thomas 1848–**1932**
Seymour, Sir Edward Hobart 1840–**1929**
Shackleton, Sir David James 1863–**1938**
Shackleton, Sir Ernest Henry 1874–**1922**

Taylor, James Haward 1909–1968
Taylor, Sir John 1833–1912
Taylor, John Edward 1830–1905
Taylor, John Henry 1871–1963
Taylor, Louisa. See Parr *d.*1903
Taylor, Sir Thomas Murray 1897–1962
Taylor, Sir Thomas Weston Johns 1895–1953
Taylor, Walter Ross 1838–1907
Taylor, William 1865–1937
Teale, Thomas Pridgin 1831–1923
Teall, Sir Jethro Justinian Harris 1849–1924
Tearle, (George) Osmond 1852–1901
Tearle, Sir Godfrey Seymour 1884–1953
Tedder, Arthur William, Baron 1890–1967
Tegart, Sir Charles Augustus 1881–1946
Teichman, Sir Eric 1884–1944
Temperley, Harold William Vazeille 1879–1939
Tempest, Dame Marie 1864–1942
Temple, Frederick 1821–1902
Temple, Sir Richard 1826–1902
Temple, Sir Richard Carnac 1850–1931
Temple, William 1881–1944
Templer, Sir Gerald Walter Robert 1898–1979
Templewood, Viscount. See Hoare, Sir Samuel John Gurney 1880–1959
Tenby, Viscount. See Lloyd-George, Gwilym 1894–1967
Tennant, Sir Charles 1823–1906
Tennant, Sir David 1829–1905
Tennant, Margaret Mary Edith (May) 1869–1946
Tenniel, Sir John 1820–1914
Tennyson-d'Eyncourt, Sir Eustace Henry William 1868–1951
Terry, Dame (Alice) Ellen 1847–1928
Terry, Charles Sanford 1864–1936
Terry, Fred 1863–1933
Terry, Sir Richard Runciman 1865–1938
Tertis, Lionel 1876–1975
Teyte, Dame Margaret (Maggie) 1888–1976
Thankerton, Baron. See Watson, William 1873–1948
Thesiger, Frederic Augustus, Baron Chelmsford 1827–1905
Thesiger, Frederic John Napier, Viscount Chelmsford 1868–1933
Thirkell, Angela Margaret 1890–1961
Thiselton-Dyer, Sir William Turner 1843–1928
Thoday, David 1883–1964
Thomas, Bertram Sidney 1892–1950
Thomas, David Alfred, Viscount Rhondda 1856–1918
Thomas, Dylan Marlais 1914–1953
Thomas, Forest Frederic Edward Yeo-. See Yeo-Thomas 1902–1964
Thomas, Frederick William 1867–1956
Thomas, Freeman Freeman-, Marquess of Willingdon. See Freeman-Thomas 1866–1941
Thomas, Sir George Alan 1881–1972
Thomas, George Holt 1869–1929
Thomas, Sir Henry 1878–1952
Thomas, Herbert Henry 1876–1935
Thomas, Sir Hugh Evan-. See Evan-Thomas 1862–1928
Thomas, Hugh Hamshaw 1885–1962
Thomas, James Henry 1874–1949
Thomas, James Purdon Lewes, Viscount Cilcennin 1903–1960
Thomas, Margaret Haig, Viscountess Rhondda 1883–1958
Thomas, Meirion 1894–1977
Thomas, (Philip) Edward 1878–1917
Thomas, Sir (Thomas) Shenton (Whitelegge) 1879–1962
Thomas, Sir William Beach 1868–1957
Thomas, William Moy 1828–1910
Thompson, Alexander Hamilton 1873–1952
Thompson, D'Arcy Wentworth 1829–1902
Thompson, Sir D'Arcy Wentworth 1860–1948
Thompson, Edmund Symes-. See Symes-Thompson 1837–1906
Thompson, Edward John 1886–1946
Thompson, Sir Edward Maunde 1840–1929
Thompson, Francis 1859–1907
Thompson, Sir Henry 1820–1904
Thompson, Sir (Henry Francis) Herbert 1859–1944
Thompson, Henry Yates 1838–1928
Thompson, James Matthew 1878–1956
Thompson, Sir John Eric Sidney 1898–1975
Thompson, Lydia 1836–1908
Thompson, Reginald Campbell 1876–1941
Thompson, Silvanus Phillips 1851–1916
Thompson, William Marcus 1857–1907
Thomson, Arthur 1858–1935
Thomson, Sir (Arthur) Landsborough 1890–1977
Thomson, Sir Basil Home 1861–1939
Thomson, Christopher Birdwood, Baron 1875–1930
Thomson, Sir George Paget 1892–1975
Thomson, Sir George Pirie 1887–1965
Thomson, George Reid, Lord 1893–1962
Thomson, Hugh 1860–1920
Thomson, Jocelyn Home 1859–1908
Thomson, John 1856–1926
Thomson, Sir Joseph John 1856–1940
Thomson, Roy Herbert, Baron Thomson of Fleet 1894–1976
Thomson, William, Baron Kelvin 1824–1907
Thomson, Sir William 1843–1909
Thorndike, Dame (Agnes) Sybil 1882–1976
Thorne, William James (Will) 1857–1946
Thornton, Alfred Henry Robinson 1863–1939
Thornton, Sir Edward 1817–1906
Thornycroft, Sir John Isaac 1843–1928
Thornycroft, Sir (William) Hamo 1850–1925
Thorpe, Sir Thomas Edward 1845–1925
Threlfall, Sir Richard 1861–1932
Thring, Godfrey 1823–1903
Thring, Henry, Baron 1818–1907